ALGEBRA

Exponents and Radicals

$$x^a x^b = x^{a+b} \qquad \frac{x^a}{x^b} = x^{a-b} \qquad x^{-a} = \frac{1}{x^a} \qquad (x^a)^b = x^{ab} \qquad \left(\frac{x}{y}\right)^a = \frac{x^a}{y^a}$$

$$x^{1/n} = \sqrt[n]{x} \qquad x^{m/n} = \sqrt[n]{x^m} = (\sqrt[n]{x})^m \qquad \sqrt[n]{xy} = \sqrt[n]{x}\sqrt[n]{y} \qquad \sqrt[n]{x/y} = \sqrt[n]{x}/\sqrt[n]{y}$$

Factoring Formulas

$$a^2 - b^2 = (a - b)(a + b) \qquad\qquad a^2 + b^2 \text{ does not factor over real numbers}$$
$$a^3 - b^3 = (a - b)(a^2 + ab + b^2) \qquad a^3 + b^3 = (a + b)(a^2 - ab + b^2)$$
$$a^n - b^n = (a - b)(a^{n-1} + a^{n-2}b + a^{n-3}b^2 + \cdots + ab^{n-2} + b^{n-1})$$

Binomials

$$(a \pm b)^2 = a^2 \pm 2ab + b^2$$
$$(a \pm b)^3 = a^3 \pm 3a^2b + 3ab^2 \pm b^3$$

Binomial Theorem

$$(a + b)^n = a^n + \binom{n}{1}a^{n-1}b + \binom{n}{2}a^{n-2}b^2 + \cdots + \binom{n}{n-1}ab^{n-1} + b^n,$$

$$\text{where } \binom{n}{k} = \frac{n(n - 1)(n - 2) \cdots (n - k + 1)}{k(k - 1)(k - 2) \cdots 3 \cdot 2 \cdot 1} = \frac{n!}{k!(n - k)!}$$

Quadratic Formula

The solutions of $ax^2 + bx + c = 0$ are

$$x = \frac{-b \pm \sqrt{b^2 - 4ac}}{2a}$$

GEOMETRY

Parallelogram

$$A = bh$$

Triangle

$$A = \frac{1}{2}bh$$

Trapezoid

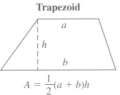

$$A = \frac{1}{2}(a + b)h$$

Circle

$$A = \pi r^2$$
$$C = 2\pi r$$

Sector

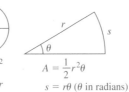

$$A = \frac{1}{2}r^2\theta$$
$$s = r\theta \ (\theta \text{ in radians})$$

Cylinder

$$V = \pi r^2 h$$
$$S = 2\pi rh$$
(lateral surface area)

Cone

$$V = \frac{1}{3}\pi r^2 h$$
$$S = \pi r \ell$$
(lateral surface area)

Sphere

$$V = \frac{4}{3}\pi r^3$$
$$S = 4\pi r^2$$

Equations of Lines and Circles

$$m = \frac{y_2 - y_1}{x_2 - x_1} \qquad \text{slope of line through } (x_1, y_1) \text{ and } (x_2, y_2)$$

$$y - y_1 = m(x - x_1) \qquad \text{point-slope form of line through } (x_1, y_1) \text{ with slope } m$$

$$y = mx + b \qquad \text{slope-intercept form of line with slope } m \text{ and } y\text{-intercept } (0, b)$$

$$(x - h)^2 + (y - k)^2 = r^2 \qquad \text{circle of radius } r \text{ with center } (h, k)$$

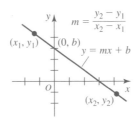

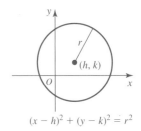

TRIGONOMETRY

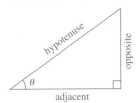

$$\cos \theta = \frac{\text{adj}}{\text{hyp}} \qquad \sin \theta = \frac{\text{opp}}{\text{hyp}} \qquad \tan \theta = \frac{\text{opp}}{\text{adj}}$$

$$\sec \theta = \frac{\text{hyp}}{\text{adj}} \qquad \csc \theta = \frac{\text{hyp}}{\text{opp}} \qquad \cot \theta = \frac{\text{adj}}{\text{opp}}$$

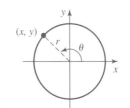

$$\cos \theta = \frac{x}{r} \qquad \sec \theta = \frac{r}{x}$$
$$\sin \theta = \frac{y}{r} \qquad \csc \theta = \frac{r}{y}$$
$$\tan \theta = \frac{y}{x} \qquad \cot \theta = \frac{x}{y}$$

(Continued)

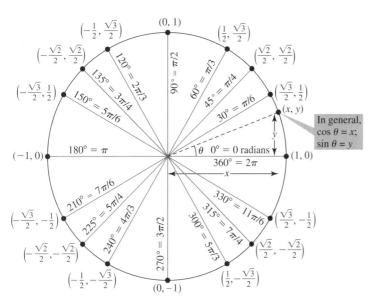

Reciprocal Identities

$$\tan \theta = \frac{\sin \theta}{\cos \theta} \quad \cot \theta = \frac{\cos \theta}{\sin \theta} \quad \sec \theta = \frac{1}{\cos \theta} \quad \csc \theta = \frac{1}{\sin \theta}$$

Pythagorean Identities

$$\sin^2 \theta + \cos^2 \theta = 1 \quad \tan^2 \theta + 1 = \sec^2 \theta \quad 1 + \cot^2 \theta = \csc^2 \theta$$

Sign Identities

$$\sin(-\theta) = -\sin \theta \quad \cos(-\theta) = \cos \theta \quad \tan(-\theta) = -\tan \theta$$
$$\csc(-\theta) = -\csc \theta \quad \sec(-\theta) = \sec \theta \quad \cot(-\theta) = -\cot \theta$$

Double-Angle Identities

$$\sin 2\theta = 2 \sin \theta \cos \theta \qquad \cos 2\theta = \cos^2 \theta - \sin^2 \theta$$
$$= 2 \cos^2 \theta - 1$$
$$\tan 2\theta = \frac{2 \tan \theta}{1 - \tan^2 \theta} \qquad = 1 - 2 \sin^2 \theta$$

Half-Angle Formulas

$$\cos^2 \theta = \frac{1 + \cos 2\theta}{2} \qquad \sin^2 \theta = \frac{1 - \cos 2\theta}{2}$$

Addition Formulas

$$\sin(\alpha + \beta) = \sin \alpha \cos \beta + \cos \alpha \sin \beta \qquad \sin(\alpha - \beta) = \sin \alpha \cos \beta - \cos \alpha \sin \beta$$
$$\cos(\alpha + \beta) = \cos \alpha \cos \beta - \sin \alpha \sin \beta \qquad \cos(\alpha - \beta) = \cos \alpha \cos \beta + \sin \alpha \sin \beta$$
$$\tan(\alpha + \beta) = \frac{\tan \alpha + \tan \beta}{1 - \tan \alpha \tan \beta} \qquad \tan(\alpha - \beta) = \frac{\tan \alpha - \tan \beta}{1 + \tan \alpha \tan \beta}$$

Law of Sines

$$\frac{\sin \alpha}{a} = \frac{\sin \beta}{b} = \frac{\sin \gamma}{c}$$

Law of Cosines

$$a^2 = b^2 + c^2 - 2bc \cos \alpha$$

Graphs of Trigonometric Functions and Their Inverses

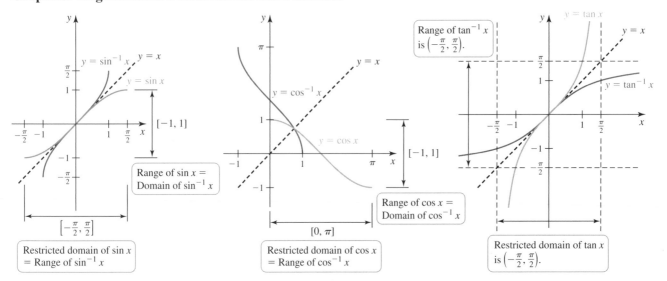

Calculus

AP® Edition

Calculus
AP® Edition

WILLIAM BRIGGS
University of Colorado, Denver

LYLE COCHRAN
Whitworth University

BERNARD GILLETT
University of Colorado, Boulder

with the assistance of
ERIC SCHULZ
Walla Walla Community College

PEARSON

Boston Columbus Indianapolis New York San Francisco Upper Saddle River
Amsterdam Cape Town Dubai London Madrid Milan Munich Paris Montréal Toronto
Delhi Mexico City São Paulo Sydney Hong Kong Seoul Singapore Taipei Tokyo

Editor in Chief:	Deirdre Lynch
Senior Acquisitions Editor:	William Hoffman
Senior Content Editor:	Rachel S. Reeve
Senior Managing Editor:	Karen Wernholm
Senior Production Project Manager:	Kathleen A. Manley
Digital Assets Manager:	Marianne Groth
Associate Media Producer:	Stephanie Green
Software Development:	Kristina Evans (Math XL) and Marty Wright (TestGen)
Executive Market Development Manager:	Dona Kenly
Marketing Manager:	Jackie Flynn
Senior Author Support/Technology Specialist:	Joe Vetere
Procurement Specialist:	Carol Melville
Production Coordination and Composition:	PreMediaGlobal
Illustrations:	Network Graphics and Scientific Illustrators
Associate Director of Design:	Andrea Nix
Senior Design Specialist:	Heather Scott
Cover Design:	Heather Scott
Cover Photo:	Paul Silverman/ Fundamental Photographs

For permission to use copyrighted material, grateful acknowledgment has been made to the copyright holders listed on p. xxvii, which is hereby made part of the copyright page.

Many of the designations used by manufacturers and sellers to distinguish their products are claimed as trademarks. Where those designations appear in this book, and Pearson, Inc. was aware of a trademark claim, the designations have been printed in initial caps or all caps.

AP® is a trademark registered and/or owned by the College Board, which was not involved in the production of, and does not endorse, this product.

5 6 7 8 9 10—V011—16 15

www.PearsonSchool.com/Advanced

ISBN-13 978-0-13-347571-5 (High School Binding)
ISBN-10   0-13-347571-9 (High School Binding)

For Julie, Susan, Sally, Sue,
Katie, Jeremy, Elise, Mary, Claire, Katie, Chris, and Annie
whose support, patience, and encouragement made this book possible.

Table of Contents

Preface

This book was specifically designed and written for teachers and students of Advanced Placement® Calculus. Our approach is based on many years of teaching calculus at diverse institutions using the best teaching practices we know. We collaborated with over 90 academic experts and classroom practitioners to develop the correct blend of rigorous content, accessible support, flexible resources, and engaging instruction to help students master the essential mathematical and communication skills they need to achieve their AP goals.

Although the book was written with the most recent AP syllabi in mind, it also contains several topics that do not appear on those syllabi, but are often covered in the first two semesters of a standard college-level calculus sequence. For this reason, the book not only provides preparation for the AP Exam, but also serves as a foundation for additional mathematical course work at the college level.

Throughout this book, a concise and lively narrative motivates the ideas of calculus. All topics are introduced through concrete examples, applications, and analogies rather than through abstract arguments. We appeal to students' intuition and geometric instincts to make calculus natural and believable. Once this intuitive foundation is established, generalizations and abstractions follow.

Pedagogical Features

Exercises

The exercises at the end of each section are one of the strongest features of the text. They are graded, varied, and original. In addition, they are labeled and carefully organized into groups.

- Each exercise set begins with *Review Questions* that check students' conceptual understanding of the essential ideas from the section.

- *Basic Skills* exercises are confidence-building problems that provide a solid foundation for the more challenging exercises to follow. Each example in the narrative is linked directly to a block of *Basic Skills* exercises via *Related Exercises* references at the end of the example solution.

- *Further Explorations* exercises expand on the *Basic Skills* exercises by challenging students to think creatively and to generalize newly acquired skills.

- *Applications* exercises connect skills developed in previous exercises to applications and modeling problems that demonstrate the power and utility of calculus.

- *Additional Exercises* are generally the most difficult and challenging problems; they include proofs of results cited in the narrative.

- *Technology Exercises* provide additional exercises that emphasize the use of graphing calculators or mathematical software.

Each chapter concludes with a comprehensive set of *Review Exercises* and a set of *AP Practice Questions*. Although these practice questions are not taken from actual AP Exams, they are designed to help students prepare for the AP Exam.

Figures

Given the power of graphics software and the ease with which many students assimilate visual images, we devoted considerable time and deliberation to the figures in this book. Whenever possible, we let the figures communicate essential ideas using annotations reminiscent of a teacher's voice at the board. Readers will quickly find that the figures facilitate learning in new ways.

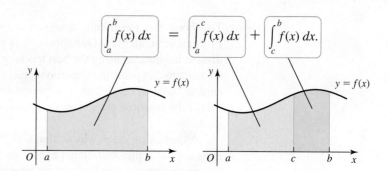

FIGURE 5.35

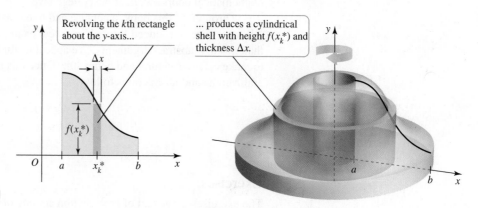

FIGURE 6.41

Quick Check and *Margin Notes*

The narrative is interspersed with *Quick Check* questions that encourage students to read with pencil in hand. These questions resemble the kinds of questions teachers pose in class. Answers to the *Quick Check* questions are found at the end of the section in which they occur. *Margin Notes* offer reminders, provide insight, and clarify technical points.

Guided Projects

The *Teacher's Resource Guide* contains 59 *Guided Projects*. These projects allow students to work in a directed, step-by-step fashion, with various objectives: to carry out extended calculations, to derive physical models, to explore related theoretical topics, or to investigate new applications of calculus. The *Guided Projects* vividly demonstrate the breadth of calculus and provide a wealth of mathematical excursions that go beyond the typical classroom experience. A list of suggested *Guided Projects* is included at the end of each chapter.

Technology

We believe that a calculus text should help students strengthen their analytical skills and demonstrate how technology can extend (not replace) those skills. The exercises and examples in this text emphasize this balance. Calculators and graphing utilities are additional tools in the kit, and students must learn when and when not to use them. Our goal is to accommodate the different policies about technology that various teachers may use.

Throughout the book, exercises marked with ▯ indicate that the use of technology—ranging from plotting a function with a graphing calculator to carrying out a calculation using a computer algebra system—may be needed.

eBook with Interactive Figures (optional, available for purchase)

The textbook is supported by a groundbreaking and award-winning electronic book, created by Eric Schulz of Walla Walla Community College. This "live book" contains the complete text of the print book in addition to interactive versions of approximately 400 figures. Teachers can use these interactive figures in the classroom to illustrate the important ideas of calculus, and students can explore them while they are reading the textbook. Our experience confirms that the interactive figures help build students' geometric intuition of calculus. The authors have written Interactive Figure Exercises that can be assigned via MyMathLab for School so that students can study the figures outside of class in a directed way. In addition, the authors have created short videos, accessed through the eBook, that tell the story of key Interactive Figures. Available only within MyMathLab for School, the eBook provides teachers with powerful new teaching tools that expand and enrich the learning experience for students.

Accuracy Assurance

One of the challenges we face with a first edition is ensuring the book meets the high standards of accuracy that teachers expect. In developing the higher education versions of this book, more than 200 mathematicians reviewed the manuscript for accuracy, level of difficulty, and effective pedagogy. In addition, nearly 1000 students participated in class-testing this book before publication. A team of mathematicians carefully examined each example, exercise, and figure in multiple rounds of editing, proofreading, and accuracy checking. We have incorporated improvements recommended by professors using the higher education version of this book at colleges and universities across the country. The new material here underwent rigorous editing, proofing, and accuracy checking as well. From the beginning and throughout development, our goal has been to craft a textbook that is mathematically precise and pedagogically sound.

Supplements and Resources

Most of the teacher supplements and resources for this text are available electronically to qualified adopters through the Instructor Resource Center (IRC). Upon adoption or to preview, please go to www.PearsonSchool.com/Access_Request and select Instructor Resource Center. You will be required to complete a brief one-time registration subject to verification of educator status. Upon verification, access information and instructions will be sent to you via e-mail. Once logged into the IRC, enter ISBN 0-13-347571-9 in the **Search our Catalog** box to locate your resources.

Annotated Teacher's Edition

- *Teacher Notes* on the page give an overview of the material being taught, helpful tips, and warnings, as well as suggested assignments.
- Answers are included on the same page as the problem for most exercises. All answers are included in the back of the book.

Pearson Education Test Prep Series for AP® Calculus

- AP® AB and BC Calculus Practice Exams
- Answers

Graphing Calculator Manual

- An introduction to Texas Instruments graphing calculators, as they are used for calculus
- Discussion of the TI-84 Plus Silver Edition featuring MathPrint, the TI-83 Plus Silver Edition, and the TI-89 Titanium.
- The keystrokes, menus, and screens for the TI-84 Plus are similar to those of the TI-84 Plus Silver Edition. Those for the TI-83 Plus are similar to the TI-83 Plus Silver Edition. The TI-89, TI-92 Plus, and Voyage™ 200 are similar to the TI-89 Titanium.

Teacher's Resource Guide

- Fifty-nine *Guided Projects*, correlated to specific chapters of the text, can be assigned to students for individual or group work. The *Guided Projects* vividly demonstrate the breadth of calculus and provide a wealth of mathematical excursions that go beyond the typical classroom experience.
- An annotated Table of Contents gives teacher's insight into overall content and organization of the text.
- *Learning Objectives Lists* and an *Index of Applications* are tools to help teachers gear the text to their course goals and students' interests.

Teacher's Solutions Manual

The *Teacher Solutions Manual* contains complete solutions to all the exercises in the text.

TestGen®

TestGen® enables teachers to build, edit, print, and administer tests using a computerized bank of questions developed to cover all the objectives of the text. TestGen is algorithmically based, allowing teachers to create multiple but equivalent versions of the same question or test with the click of a button. Teachers can also modify test bank questions or add new questions.

PowerPoint® Lecture Slides

These PowerPoint slides contain key concepts, definitions, figures, and tables from the textbook. Available only through MyMathLab for School.

MathXL® for School (optional, for purchase only), access code required, www.mathxlforschool.com

MathXL for School is a powerful online homework, tutorial, and assessment supplement that aligns to Pearson Education's textbooks in mathematics or statistics. MathXL for

School is the homework and assessment engine that runs MyMathLab for School. With MathXL for School, teachers can do the following:

- Create, edit, and assign auto-graded online homework and tests correlated at the objective level to the textbook.
- Utilize automatic grading to rapidly assess student understanding.
- Track both student and group performance in an online gradebook.
- Prepare students for high-stakes testing, including aligning assignments to state and Common Core State Standards, where available.
- Deliver quality, effective instruction regardless of experience level.

With MathXL for School, students can do the following:

- Complete their homework and receive immediate feedback.
- Get self-paced assistance on problems in a variety of ways (guided solutions, step-by-step examples, video clips, and animations).
- Choose from a large number of practice problems, helping them master a topic.
- Receive personalized study plans and homework based on test results.

For more information and to purchase student access codes after the first year, visit our website at www.mathxlforschool.com or contact your Pearson School Account Executive.

MyMathLab® for School Online Course (optional, for purchase only)—access code required www.mymathlabforschool.com

MyMathLab for School delivers **proven results** in helping individual students succeed. It provides **engaging experiences** that personalize, stimulate, and measure learning for each student. And it comes from a **trusted partner** with educational expertise and an eye on the future. To learn more about how MyMathLab combines proven learning applications with powerful assessment, visit **www.mymathlabforschool.com** or contact your Pearson School Account Executive. In this **MyMathLab® for School** course, you have access to the most cutting-edge, innovative study solutions proven to increase student success. Noteworthy features include the following:

eBook featuring over 400 Interactive Figures that can be manipulated to illuminate difficult-to-convey concepts. Teachers can use these interactive figures in the classroom to illustrate the important ideas of calculus, and students can manipulate the interactive figures while they are using MyMathLab. In each case, these interactive figures help build geometric intuition of calculus. Exercises for the Interactive Figures can be assigned as homework to encourage students to explore the concepts presented.

Video Resources

The Video Lectures With Optional Captioning feature an engaging team of mathematics teachers who present comprehensive coverage of topics in the text. The lecturers' presentations include illustrative examples and exercises and support an approach that emphasizes visualization and problem solving. Available only through MyMathLab for School and MathXL for School.

Acknowledgments

We would like to express our thanks to the people who made many valuable contributions to this edition as it evolved through its many stages:

Development Editor

Elaine Page

Accuracy Checkers

Jennifer A. Blue

Blaise DeSesa

Patricia Espinoza-Toro

Greg Friedman

David Grinstein

Ebony Harvey

Michele Jean-Louis

Nickolas Mavrikidis

Renato Mirollo

Patricia Nelson

Robert Pierce

Thomas Polaski

John Sammons

Joan Saniuk

Marie Vanisko

Diana Watson

Thomas Wegleitner

Gary Williams

Roman Zadov

Reviewers, Class Testers, Focus Group Participants

Storie L. Atkins, Columbus High School

Chantal A. Ayotte, Cathedral High School

Matthew Barlin, McCann Technical School

James Bartuska, Ralston Valley High School

Thomas Becvar, St. Louis University High School

Gerald E. Bilodeau, Boston Latin School

Sean Bird, Covenant Christian High School

Corey Boby, Lakeside High School

Elisa Bolotin, Saint Stephen's Episcopal School

Judith Broadwin, Baruch College

Melissa Brown, Riverton High School

T. Michael Brown, The Prairie School

Robert Butterfield, Pittsburg High School

Melissa Churchill, Temple High School

William Compton, Montgomery Bell Academy

Virginia Cornelius, Lafayette High School

Deborah Costello, Trinity Preparatory School

Alison Crowley, Lafayette High School

Michelle B. de los Reyes, George Washington High School

Mary Lee DeBelina, Saint Viator High School

Thomas DeHart, Antioch High School

Cynthia Depoe, Saint Ursula Academy

Scott DeRuiter, Monta Vista High School

Lyubomir Detchkov, Hunter College High School

Thomas P. Dick, Oregon State University

Allen Dimacali, Teachers College, Columbia University

Doug Dougherty, Bishop O'Dowd High School

Ruth Dover, Illinois Mathematics and Science Academy

Marian Ferrara, Drew School

Carrie Fraher, Dwight Township High School

Mitchell Francis, Horace Mann School

Scott Gaddis, Grove City High School

Benjamin Goldstein, Thayer Academy

Lana Golembeski, Minnetonka High School

Sugen S. Grano, Thousand Oaks High School

Gregory Guayante, El Camino High School

Chris Harrow, The Westminster Schools

Michael Houston, Riverside High School

Mark Howell, Gonzaga College High School

Judith Isaac, Central High School

David Johnston, Neuqua Valley High School

Jessica J. Kachur, Whitnall High School

Michael H. Koehler, Blue Valley North High School

Stephen Kokoska, Bloomsburg University

James Krzeminski, Niles West High School

Jennifer Lamb, Marian Catholic High School

Vic Levine, Madison Area Technical College—West Campus

Sandra Lowell, Brandeis High School

Kirk McCall, Big Valley Christian School

Ruth Miller, Roland Park County School

Rebecca Minton, Mercy Academy

Debora Misanin, Dominion High School

Brendan Murphy, John Bapst Memorial High School

Stephanie B. Ogden, L&N STEM Academy

Larry J. Peterson, Northridge High School

Dixie Ross, Pflugerville High School

Daniel Rusk, Niles West High School

David Sabol, Saint Ignatius High School

Jill Saphir, Metea Valley High School

James Schierer, King City High School

Sameen Ahmad Shoenhair, Prospect High School

Daniel Spradley, Joliet West High School

Sergio Stadler, Marist School

Howard A. Stern, DeWitt Clinton High School

Emily J. Sturman, Park Tudor School

Miriam Symonds, Convent of the Sacred Hearts High School

Katarzyna Szczurek, Kenwood Academy

Greg Timm, Roland Park Country School

Sarada Toomey, Bishop Gorman High School

George Watson, Bishop O'Dowd High School

Mina Wender, McDonogh School

Robert Wilder, Middletown High School

Aimee Witulski, Thomas Jefferson High School

Allen Wolmer, Yeshiva Atlanta High School

Alicia Womick, Oakbrook Preparatory School

Ismael Zamora, Hinsdale South High School

Guide to AP Calculus

AB Exam Topics (AP College Board Description)	BC Exam Topics (AP College Board Description)	Calculus: AP Edition
I. Functions, Graphs and Limits **Analysis of Graphs** With the aid of technology, graphs of functions are often easy to produce. The emphasis is on the interplay between geometric and analytical information and on the use of calculus both to predict and to explain the observed local and global behavior of a function.		Sections 4.1– 4.3
Limits of Functions (including one-sided limits) Intuitive understanding of limiting process Calculating limits using algebra Estimating limits from graphs or tables of data		Sections 2.1, 2.2 Section 2.3 Section 2.2
Asymptotic and Unbounded Behavior Understanding asymptotes in terms of graphical behavior Describing asymptotic behavior in terms of limits involving infinity Comparing relative magnitudes of functions and their rates of change (e.g., contrasting exp growth, polynomial growth, and log growth)		Sections 2.4, 2.5 Sections 2.4, 2.5 Sections 2.5, 4.7, 9.2
Continuity as a Property of Functions An intuitive understanding of continuity. (The function can be made as close as desired by taking sufficiently close values of the domain.) Understanding continuity in terms of limits Geometric understanding of graphs of continuous functions (Intermediate Value Theorem and Extreme Value Theorem)		Section 2.6 Section 2.6 Section 2.6, 4.1
	Parametric, Polar and Vector Functions The analysis of planar curves includes those given in parametric form, polar form, and vector form.	Sections 11.1–11.6

AB Exam Topics (AP College Board Description)	BC Exam Topics (AP College Board Description)	Calculus: AP Edition
II. Derivatives		
Concept of the Derivative		
Derivative presented graphically, numerically and analytically		Sections 3.1, 3.2
Derivative interpreted as an instantaneous rate of change		Sections 2.1, 3.1, 3.6, 3.11
Derivative defined as the limit of the difference quotient		Section 3.1
Relationship between differentiability and continuity		Section 3.2
Derivative at a Point		
Slope of a curve at a point. Examples are emphasized, including points at which there are vertical tangents and points at which there are no tangents.		Section 3.1
Tangent line to a curve at a point and local linear approximation		Sections 3.1, 4.5
Instantaneous rate of change as the limit of average rate of change		Sections 2.1, 3.6
Approximate rate of change from graphs and tables of values		Sections 2.1, 3.1
Derivative as a Function		
Corresponding characteristics of graphs of f and f'		Section 3.2
Relationship between the increasing and decreasing behavior of f and the sign of f'		Section 4.2
The Mean Value Theorem and its geometric interpretation		Section 4.6
Equations involving derivatives. Verbal descriptions are translated into equations involving derivatives and vice versa.		Sections 3.6, 3.11
Second Derivatives		
Corresponding characteristics of the graphs of f, f', and f''		Section 4.2
Relationship between the concavity of f and the sign of f''		Sections 4.2, 4.3
Points of inflection as places where concavity changes		Section 4.2
Applications of Derivatives		
Analysis of curves, including the notions of monotonicity and concavity		Sections 4.1–4.3
	Analysis of planar curves given in parametric form, polar form, and vector form, including velocity and acceleration	Sections 11.1–11.7
Optimization, both absolute (global) and relative (local) extrema		Sections 4.1–4.4
Modeling rates of change, including related rates problems		Sections 3.6, 3.11
Use of implicit differentiation to find the derivative of an inverse function		Sections 3.8–3.10
Interpretation of the derivative as a rate of change in varied applied contexts, including velocity, speed, and acceleration		Sections 3.6, 3.11
Geometric interpretation of differential equations via slope fields and the relationship between slope fields and solution curves for differential equations		Section 8.2
	Numerical solutions of differential equations using Euler's method	Section 8.2
	L'Hôpital's Rule, including its use in determining limits and convergence of improper integrals and sequences	Sections 4.7, 7.4, 9.2

AB Exam Topics (AP College Board Description)	BC Exam Topics (AP College Board Description)	Calculus: AP Edition
Computation of Derivatives		
Knowledge of derivatives of basic functions, including power, exponential, logarithmic, trigonometric and inverse trigonometric functions		Sections 3.3, 3.5, 3.4, 3.10
Derivative rules for sums, products, and quotients of functions		Sections 3.3, 3.4
Chain rule and implicit differentiation		Sections 3.7, 3.8
	Derivatives of parametric, polar, and vector functions	Sections 11.2, 11.4, 11.6
III. Integrals		
Interpretations and Properties of Definite Integrals		
Definite integral as a limit of Riemann sums		Section 5.3
Definite integral of the rate of change of a quantity over an interval interpreted as the change of the quantity over the interval: $$\int_a^b f'(x)\,dx = f(b) - f(a)$$		Sections 5.4, 6.1
Basic properties of definite integrals (examples of additivity and linearity)		Section 5.5
Applications of Integrals		
Appropriate integrals are used in a variety of applications to model physical, biological, or economic situations. Although only a sampling of applications can be included in any specific course, students should be able to adapt their knowledge and techniques to solve other similar application problems.		Section 5.5, Chapter 6
Whatever applications are chosen, the emphasis is on using the method of setting up an approximating Riemann sum and representing its limit as a definite integral. To provide a common foundation, specific applications should include finding the area of a region, the volume of a solid with known cross sections, the average value of a function, the distance traveled by a particle along a line, and accumulated change from a rate of change.		
Fundamental Theorem of Calculus (FTC)		
Use of the FTC to evaluate definite integrals		Section 5.4
Use of the FTC to represent a particular antiderivative, and the analytical and graphical analysis of functions so defined.		Sections 5.4, 6.1
Techniques of Antidifferentiation		
Antiderivatives following directly from derivatives of basic functions		Section 5.1
Antiderivatives by substitution of variables (including change of limits for definite integrals)		Section 5.6
	Integration by parts	Section 7.2
	Simple partial fractions (nonrepeating linear factors only)	Section 7.3
Applications of Antidifferentiation		
Finding specific antiderivatives using initial conditions, including applications to motion along a line		Sections 5.1, 6.1, 8.1
Solving separable differential equations and using them in modeling (including the study of the equation $y' = ky$ and exponential growth)		Sections 8.3, 8.4
	Solving logistic differential equations and using them in modeling	Sections 8.1–8.3

AB Exam Topics (AP College Board Description)	BC Exam Topics (AP College Board Description)	Calculus: AP Edition
Numerical approximations to Definite Integrals Use of Riemann sums (using left, right, and midpoint evaluation points) and trapezoidal sums to approximate definite integrals of functions represented algebraically, graphically and by tables of values		Sections 5.1, 5.2, 5.7
	IV. Polynomial Approximations and Series **Concept of Series**	
	A series is defined as a sequence of partial sums, and convergence is defined in terms of the limit of the sequence of partial sums. Technology can be used to explore convergence and divergence.	Sections 9.1, 9.3
	Series of Constants	
	Motivating examples, including decimal expansion	Sections 9.1, 9.3
	Geometric series with applications	Section 9.3
	Harmonic series	Section 9.4
	Alternating series with error bound	Section 9.6
	Terms of series as areas of rectangles and their relationship to improper integrals, including the integral test and its use in testing the convergence of p-series	Section 9.4
	The ratio test for convergence and divergence	Section 9.5
	Comparing series to test for convergence or divergence	Section 9.5
	Taylor Series	
	Taylor polynomial approximation with graphical demonstration of convergence (i.e. viewing graphs of various Taylor polynomials for the sine function approximating the sine curve)	Section 10.1
	Maclaurin series and the general Taylor series centered at $x = a$	Section 10.3
	Maclaurin series for the functions e^x, $\sin x$, $\cos x$, and $1/(1-x)$	Sections 10.2, 10.3
	Formal manipulation of Taylor series and shortcuts to computing Taylor series, including substitution, differentiation, antidifferentiation, and the formation of new series from known series	Sections 10.2–10.4
	Functions defined by power series	Sections 10.2–10.4
	Radius and interval of convergence of power series	Section 10.2
	Lagrange error bound for Taylor polynomials	Section 10.3

AP Calculus Pacing Guide

		AB	BC
Chapter 1 Functions		**7 days**	**0 day**
1.1	Review of Functions	2	0
1.2	Representing Functions	1	0
1.3	Inverse, Exponential, and Logarithmic Functions	1	0
1.4	Trigonometric Functions and Their Inverses	1	0
Review Exercises		2	0
AP Practice Questions			
Chapter 2 Limits		**19 days**	**10 days**
2.1	The Idea of Limits	2	1
2.2	Definitions of Limits	3	2
2.3	Techniques for Computing Limits	3	1
2.4	Infinite Limits	1	1
2.5	Limits at Infinity	2	1
2.6	Continuity	2	1
2.7	Precise Definitions of Limits	3	1
Review Exercises		3	2
AP Practice Questions			
Chapter 3 Derivatives		**37 days**	**25 days**
3.1	Introducing the Derivative	2	1
3.2	Working with Derivatives	3	2
3.3	Rules of Differentiation	3	2
3.4	The Product and Quotient Rules	3	2
3.5	Derivatives of Trigonometric Functions	3	2
3.6	Derivatives as Rates of Change	3	2
3.7	The Chain Rule	3	2
3.8	Implicit Differentiation	3	2
3.9	Derivatives of Logarithmic and Exponential Functions	3	2
3.10	Derivatives of Inverse Trigonometric Functions	3	2
3.11	Related Rates	5	4
Review Exercises		3	2
AP Practice Questions			

	AB	BC
Chapter 8 Differential Equations	**16 days**	**11 days**
8.1 Basic Ideas	4	2
8.2 Slope Fields and Euler's Method	2	2
8.3 Separable Differential Equations	4	3
8.4 Exponential Models	3	2
Review Exercises	3	2
AP Practice Questions		

	AB	BC
Chapter 9 Sequences and Infinite Series	**0 day**	**15 days**
9.1 An Overview	0	2
9.2 Sequences	0	2
9.3 Infinite Series	0	2
9.4 The Divergence and Integral Tests	0	2
9.5 The Ratio, Root, and Comparison Tests	0	2
9.6 Alternating Series	0	3
Review Exercises	0	2
AP Practice Questions		

	AB	BC
Chapter 10 Power Series	**0 day**	**18 days**
10.1 Approximating Functions with Polynomials	0	4
10.2 Properties of Power Series	0	4
10.3 Taylor Series	0	4
10.4 Working with Taylor Series	0	4
Review Exercises	0	2
AP Practice Questions		

	AB	BC
Chapter 11 Polar, Parametric, and Vector Curves	**0 day**	**12 days**
11.1 Parametric Equations	0	1
11.2 Calculus with Parametric Equations	0	1
11.3 Polar Coordinates	0	1
11.4 Calculus in Polar Coordinates	0	2
11.5 Vectors in The Plane	0	1
11.6 Calculus of Vector-Valued Functions	0	2
11.7 Two-Dimensional Motion	0	2
Review Exercises	0	2
AP Practice Questions		

Total: 146 Teaching Days

Note: This timeline is based on a school year starting after Labor Day, with approximately 160 teaching days before the Advanced Placement® exam. This timeline gives approximately 14 days to review the course before the exam. This review time is essential, and 3 weeks is a minimum time to set aside for this purpose.

Credits

THE COLLEGE MATHEMATICS JOURNAL, Vol. 34, No.6. Copyright © 2003 Mathematical Association of America. Reprinted by permission. All rights reserved. **Page 291,** "Energetic Savings and The Body Size Distributions of Gliding Mammals," Evolutionary Ecology Research 5 (2003): 1151–1162. **Page 291,** Calculus, Vol. 1, Tom M. Apostol, John Wiley & Sons, 1967.

Chapter 5

Page 336, "World Money," Rafael Ben-Ari/Fotolia. **Page 400,** Mathematics Magazine 78, No. 5 (December 2005).

Chapter 6

Page 430, "pump jack oil field," Edelweiss/Fotolia. **Page 439,** Collecte Localisation Satellites/Centre National d' études Apatiales/Legos. **Page 442,** National Snow and Ice Data Center. **Page 442,** National Oceanic and Atmospheric Administration. **Page 448,** THOMAS' CALCULUS, EARLY TRANSCENDENTALS, MEDIA UPGRADE, 11th edition, by George B. Thomas, Maurice D. Weir, Joel Hass, and Frank R. Giordano. Copyright © 2008 Pearson Education, Inc. Printed and Electronically reproduced by permission of Pearson Education, Inc., Upper Saddle River, New Jersey. **Page 453,** Mathematics Magazine 81, No. 2, April 2008. **Page 455,** THOMAS' CALCULUS, EARLY TRANSCENDENTALS, MEDIA UPGRADE, 11th edition, by George B. Thomas, Maurice D. Weir, Joel Hass, and Frank R. Giordano. Copyright © 2008 Pearson Education, Inc. Printed and Electronically reproduced by permission of Pearson Education, Inc., Upper Saddle River, New Jersey. **Page 459,** THOMAS' CALCULUS, EARLY TRANSCENDENTALS, MEDIA UPGRADE, 11th edition, by George B. Thomas, Maurice D. Weir, Joel Hass, and Frank R. Giordano. Copyright © 2008 Pearson Education, Inc. Printed and Electronically reproduced by permission of Pearson Education, Inc., Upper Saddle River, New Jersey. **Page 459,** THOMAS' CALCULUS, EARLY TRANSCENDENTALS, MEDIA UPGRADE, 11th edition, by George B. Thomas, Maurice D. Weir, Joel Hass, and Frank R. Giordano. Copyright © 2008 Pearson Education, Inc. Printed and Electronically reproduced by permission of Pearson Education, Inc., Upper Saddle River, New Jersey. **Page 460,** THOMAS' CALCULUS, EARLY TRANSCENDENTALS, MEDIA UPGRADE, 11th edition, by George B. Thomas, Maurice D. Weir, Joel Hass, and Frank R. Giordano. Copyright © 2008 Pearson Education, Inc. Printed and Electronically reproduced by permission of Pearson Education, Inc., Upper Saddle River, New Jersey. **Page 468,** THOMAS' CALCULUS, EARLY TRANSCENDENTALS, MEDIA UPGRADE, 11th edition, by George B. Thomas, Maurice D. Weir, Joel Hass, and Frank R. Giordano. Copyright © 2008 Pearson Education, Inc. Printed and Electronically reproduced by permission of Pearson Education, Inc., Upper Saddle River, New Jersey. **Page 469,** THOMAS' CALCULUS, EARLY TRANSCENDENTALS, MEDIA UPGRADE, 11th edition, by George B. Thomas, Maurice D. Weir, Joel Hass, and Frank R. Giordano. Copyright © 2008 Pearson Education, Inc. Printed and Electronically reproduced by permission of Pearson Education, Inc., Upper Saddle River, New Jersey.

Chapter 7

Page 505, "Boy In Hospital Gown About To Get An Injection," Jaimie Duplass/Fotolia. **Page 509,** The College Mathematics Journal 32, No. 5, November 2001. **Page 523,** The College Mathematics Journal 32, No. 5, Nov. 2001. **Page 536,** P. Weidman, I. Pinelis, Comptes Rendu, Mechanique 332 (2004). **Page 537,** Mathematics Magazine 59, No. 1 (Feb. 1986).

Chapter 8

Page 548, "King penguin colony," Andreanita/Fotolia. **Page 590,** 2nd Putnam Exam, 1939. **Page 590,** "A Theory of Competitive Running," Physics Today 26 (Sept. 1973).

Chapter 9

Page 598, "Child taking medicine," Photophonie/Fotolia. **Page 643,** The College Mathematics Journal 30, No. 1 (Jan. 1999).

Chapter 10

Page 666, "Green leaves with water drop above water," Maksim Kostenko/Fotolia.

Chapter 11

Page 715, "music performer on scene; singer with guitar," 26kot/Shutterstock. **Page 723,** Wagon, Stan; Mathematica in Action, 3e. **Page 725,** THE SUN, THE MOON, AND CONVEXITY, by Noah Samuel Brannen, The College Mathematics Journal 32 (Sept. 2001). **Page 741,** The butterfly curve is due to T.H. Fay, AMERICAN MATHEMATICAL MONTHLY 96 (1989) revived in Wagon and Packel, ANIMATING CALCULUS, Freeman, 1994. **Page 746,** S. Wagon and E. Packel, ANIMATING CALCULUS, Freeman, New York, 1994. **Page 768,** CALCULUS by Gilbert Strang. Copyright © 1991 Wellesley-Cambridge Press. Reprinted by permission of the author.

Appendix B

Pages 803 and 811, THOMAS' CALCULUS, EARLY TRANSCENDENTALS, MEDIA UPGRADE, 11th edition, by George B. Thomas, Maurice D. Weir, Joel Hass, and Frank R. Giordano. Copyright © 2008 Pearson Education, Inc. Printed and Electronically reproduced by permission of Pearson Education, Inc., Upper Saddle River, New Jersey.

Calculus
AP® Edition

1 Functions

Among the challenges facing climbers of the world's highest mountains is the decrease in atmospheric pressure, which in turn causes a life-threatening decrease in oxygen. The relationship between altitude and atmospheric pressure can be described accurately using a *function*. The graph of this function is shown below.

Functions express relationships among quantities, or *variables*, that depend on each other. For example, the *consumer price index* (a variable that measures the cost of living) changes with respect to the variable *time*, and the *temperature* of the Pacific Ocean changes with *latitude*. Calculus is the study of functions and how they change; and because functions are used to describe the world around us, calculus is a universal language for human inquiry.

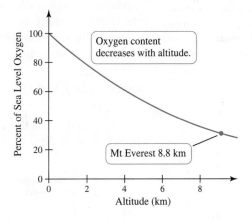

Chapter Preview   Before beginning your calculus journey, you should be equipped with the necessary tools. Among these tools are basic algebra skills; the notation and terminology for various sets of real numbers; and the descriptions of lines, circles, and other basic sets in the coordinate plane. A review of this material can be found in Appendix A. This chapter begins with the fundamental concept of a function, and then presents the entire cast of functions needed for calculus: polynomials, rational functions, algebraic functions, exponential and logarithmic functions, and the trigonometric functions, along with their inverses. Before you begin studying calculus, it is important that you work hard to master the ideas in this chapter.

1.1 Review of Functions

Mathematics is a language with an alphabet, a vocabulary, and many rules. If you are unfamiliar with set notation, intervals on the real number line, absolute value, the Cartesian coordinate system, or equations of lines and circles, please refer to Appendix A. We begin with functions.

DEFINITION Function

A **function** f is a rule that assigns to each value x in a set D a *unique* value denoted $f(x)$. The set D is the **domain** of the function. The **range** is the set of all values of $f(x)$ produced as x varies over the domain (Figure 1.1).

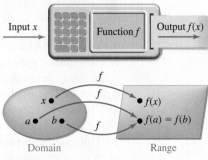

FIGURE 1.1

> If the domain is not specified, we take it to be the set of all values of x for which f is defined. We will see shortly that the domain and range of a function may be restricted by the context of the problem.

The **independent variable** is the variable associated with the domain; the **dependent variable** belongs to the range. The **graph** of a function f is the set of all points (x, y) in the xy-plane that satisfy the equation $y = f(x)$. The **argument** of a function is the expression on which the function works. For example, x is the argument when we write $f(x)$. Similarly, 2 is the argument in $f(2)$ and $x^2 + 4$ is the argument in $f(x^2 + 4)$.

QUICK CHECK 1 If $f(x) = x^2 - 2x$, find $f(-1)$, $f(x^2)$, $f(t)$, and $f(p - 1)$. ◄

The requirement that a function must assign a *unique* value of the dependent variable to each value in the domain is expressed in the vertical line test (Figure 1.2).

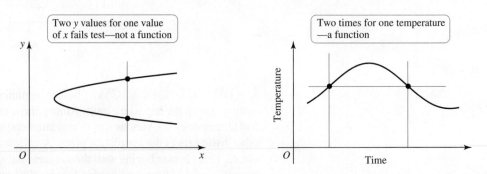

FIGURE 1.2

> A set of points or a graph that does *not* correspond to a function represents a **relation** between the variables. All functions are relations, but not all relations are functions.

Vertical Line Test

A graph represents a function if and only if it passes the **vertical line test**: Every vertical line intersects the graph at most once. A graph that fails this test does not represent a function.

EXAMPLE 1   Identifying functions State whether each graph in Figure 1.3 represents a function.

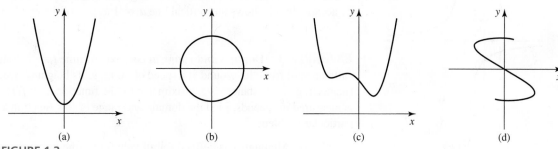

(a)   (b)   (c)   (d)

FIGURE 1.3

SOLUTION The vertical line test indicates that only graphs (a) and (c) represent functions. In graphs (b) and (d), it is possible to draw vertical lines that intersect the graph more than once. Equivalently, it is possible to find values of x that correspond to more than one value of y. Therefore, graphs (b) and (d) do not pass the vertical line test and do not represent functions.

Related Exercises 11–12 ◄

EXAMPLE 2   Domain and range Graph each function with a graphing utility using the given window. Then state the domain and range of the function.

a. $y = f(x) = x^2 + 1$; $[-3, 3] \times [-1, 5]$
b. $z = g(t) = \sqrt{4 - t^2}$; $[-3, 3] \times [-1, 3]$
c. $w = h(u) = \dfrac{1}{u - 1}$; $[-3, 5] \times [-4, 4]$

> A window of $[a, b] \times [c, d]$ means $a \le x \le b$ and $c \le y \le d$.

SOLUTION

a. Figure 1.4 shows the graph of $f(x) = x^2 + 1$. Because f is defined for all values of x, its domain is the set of all real numbers, or $(-\infty, \infty)$. Because $x^2 \ge 0$ for all x, it follows that $x^2 + 1 \ge 1$ and the range of f is $[1, \infty)$.

b. When n is even, functions involving nth roots are defined provided the quantity under the root is nonnegative (or in some cases positive). In this case, the function g is defined provided $4 - t^2 \ge 0$, which means $t^2 \le 4$, or $-2 \le t \le 2$. Therefore, the domain of g is $[-2, 2]$. By the definition of the square root, the range consists only of nonnegative numbers. When $t = 0$, z reaches its maximum value of $g(0) = \sqrt{4} = 2$, and when $t = \pm 2$, z attains its minimum value of $g(\pm 2) = 0$. Therefore, the range of g is $[0, 2]$ (Figure 1.5).

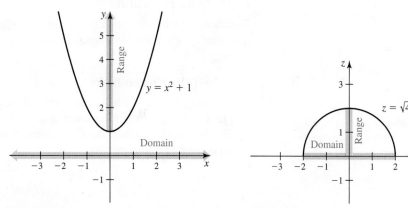

FIGURE 1.4   **FIGURE 1.5**

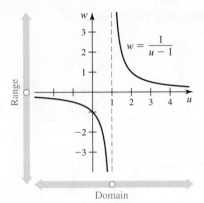

FIGURE 1.6

> The dashed vertical line $u = 1$ in Figure 1.6 indicates that the graph of $w = h(u)$ approaches a *vertical asymptote* as u approaches 1 and that w becomes large in magnitude for u near 1. Vertical and horizontal asymptotes are discussed in detail in Chapter 2.

c. The function h is undefined at $u = 1$, so its domain is $\{u : u \neq 1\}$ and the graph does not have a point corresponding to $u = 1$. We see that w takes on all values except 0; therefore, the range is $\{w : w \neq 0\}$. A graphing utility does *not* represent this function accurately if it shows the vertical line $u = 1$ as part of the graph (Figure 1.6).

Related Exercises 13–20 ◄

EXAMPLE 3   Domain and range in context At time $t = 0$, a stone is thrown vertically upward from the ground at a speed of 30 m/s. Its height above the ground in meters (neglecting air resistance) is approximated by the function $h = f(t) = 30t - 5t^2$, where t is measured in seconds. Find the domain and range of this function as they apply to this particular problem.

SOLUTION Although f is defined for all values of t, the only relevant times are between the time the stone is thrown ($t = 0$) and the time it strikes the ground, when $h = f(t) = 0$. Solving the equation $h = 30t - 5t^2 = 0$, we find that

$$30t - 5t^2 = 0$$
$$5t(6 - t) = 0 \qquad \text{Factor.}$$
$$5t = 0 \quad \text{or} \quad 6 - t = 0 \quad \text{Set each factor equal to 0.}$$
$$t = 0 \quad \text{or} \quad t = 6. \qquad \text{Solve.}$$

Therefore, the stone leaves the ground at $t = 0$ and returns to the ground at $t = 6$. An appropriate domain that fits the context of this problem is the interval $[0, 6]$. The range consists of all values of $h = 30t - 5t^2$ as t varies over $[0, 6]$. The largest value of h occurs when the stone reaches its highest point at $t = 3$, which is $h = f(3) = 45$. Therefore, the range is $[0, 45]$. These observations are confirmed by the graph of the height function (Figure 1.7). Note that this graph is *not* the trajectory of the stone; the stone moves vertically.

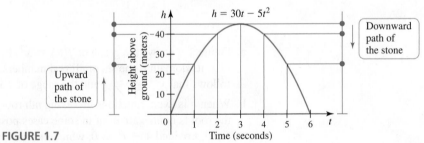

FIGURE 1.7

Related Exercises 21–24 ◄

QUICK CHECK 2 What are the domain and range of $f(x) = (x^2 + 1)^{-1}$? ◄

Composite Functions

Functions may be combined using sums $(f + g)$, differences $(f - g)$, products (fg), or quotients (f/g). The process called *composition* also produces new functions.

> In the composition $y = f(g(x))$, f is called the *outer function* and g is the *inner function*.

DEFINITION Composite Functions

Given two functions f and g, the composite function $f \circ g$ is defined by $(f \circ g)(x) = f(g(x))$. It is evaluated in two steps: $y = f(u)$, where $u = g(x)$. The domain of $f \circ g$ consists of all x in the domain of g such that $u = g(x)$ is in the domain of f (Figure 1.8).

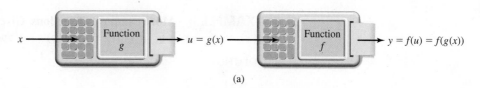

(a)

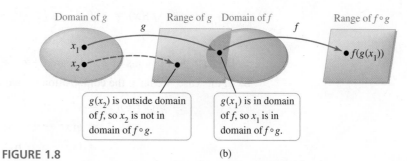

$g(x_2)$ is outside domain of f, so x_2 is not in domain of $f \circ g$.

$g(x_1)$ is in domain of f, so x_1 is in domain of $f \circ g$.

FIGURE 1.8

(b)

EXAMPLE 4 **Composite functions and notation** Let $f(x) = 3x^2 - x$ and $g(x) = 1/x$. Simplify the following expressions.

a. $f(5p + 1)$ **b.** $g(1/x)$ **c.** $f(g(x))$ **d.** $g(f(x))$

SOLUTION In each case, the functions work on their arguments.

a. The argument of f is $5p + 1$, so

$$f(5p + 1) = 3(5p + 1)^2 - (5p + 1) = 75p^2 + 25p + 2.$$

b. Because g requires taking the reciprocal of the argument, we take the reciprocal of $1/x$ and find that $g(1/x) = 1/(1/x) = x$.

c. The argument of f is $g(x)$, so

> Examples 4c and 4d demonstrate that, in general,
>
> $$f(g(x)) \neq g(f(x)).$$

$$f(g(x)) = f\left(\frac{1}{x}\right) = 3\left(\frac{1}{x}\right)^2 - \left(\frac{1}{x}\right) = \frac{3 - x}{x^2}.$$

d. The argument of g is $f(x)$, so

$$g(f(x)) = g(3x^2 - x) = \frac{1}{3x^2 - x}.$$

Related Exercises 25–36 ◄

EXAMPLE 5 **Working with composite functions** Identify possible choices for the inner and outer functions in the following composite functions. Give the domain of the composite function.

a. $h(x) = \sqrt{9x - x^2}$ **b.** $h(x) = \frac{2}{(x^2 - 1)^3}$

SOLUTION

> You have now seen three different notations for intervals on the real number line, all of which will be used throughout the book:
> • interval notation; for example, $[-2, 3)$,
> • inequality notation; for example, $-2 \leq x < 3$, and
> • set notation; for example, $\{x: -2 \leq x < 3\}$.

a. An obvious outer function is $f(x) = \sqrt{x}$, which works on the inner function $g(x) = 9x - x^2$. Therefore, h can be expressed as $h = f \circ g$ or $h(x) = f(g(x))$. The domain of $f \circ g$ consists of all values of x such that $9x - x^2 \geq 0$. Solving this inequality gives the interval $[0, 9]$ as the domain of $f \circ g$.

b. A good choice for an outer function is $f(x) = 2/x^3 = 2x^{-3}$, which works on the inner function $g(x) = x^2 - 1$. Therefore, h can be expressed as $h = f \circ g$ or $h(x) = f(g(x))$. The domain of $f \circ g$ consists of all values of $g(x)$ such that $g(x) \neq 0$, which is $\{x: x \neq \pm 1\}$.

Related Exercises 37–40 ◄

EXAMPLE 6   More composite functions Given $f(x) = \sqrt[3]{x}$ and $g(x) = x^2 - x - 6$, find (a) $g \circ f$ and (b) $g \circ g$, and their domains.

SOLUTION

a. We have

$$(g \circ f)(x) = g(f(x)) = (\underbrace{\sqrt[3]{x}}_{f(x)})^2 - \underbrace{\sqrt[3]{x}}_{f(x)} - 6 = x^{2/3} - x^{1/3} - 6.$$

Because the domains of f and g are $(-\infty, \infty)$, the domain of $f \circ g$ is also $(-\infty, \infty)$.

b. In this case, we have the composition of two polynomials:

$$(g \circ g)(x) = g(g(x))$$
$$= g(x^2 - x - 6)$$
$$= (\underbrace{x^2 - x - 6}_{g(x)})^2 - (\underbrace{x^2 - x - 6}_{g(x)}) - 6$$
$$= x^4 - 2x^3 - 12x^2 + 13x + 36.$$

The domain of the composition of two polynomials is $(-\infty, \infty)$.

Related Exercises 41–54◄

QUICK CHECK 3 If $f(x) = x^2 + 1$ and $g(x) = x^2$, find $f \circ g$ and $g \circ f$. ◄

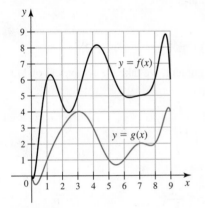

FIGURE 1.9

EXAMPLE 7   Using graphs to evaluate composite functions Use the graphs of f and g in Figure 1.9 to find the following values.

a. $f(g(5))$ **b.** $f(g(3))$ **c.** $g(f(3))$ **d.** $f(f(4))$

SOLUTION

a. According to the graphs, $g(5) = 1$ and $f(1) = 6$; it follows that $f(g(5)) = f(1) = 6$.
b. The graphs indicate that $g(3) = 4$ and $f(4) = 8$, so $f(g(3)) = f(4) = 8$.
c. We see that $g(f(3)) = g(5) = 1$. Observe that $f(g(3)) \neq g(f(3))$.
d. In this case, $f(f(4)) = f(\underbrace{8}) = 6$.

Related Exercises 55–56◄

EXAMPLE 8   Using a table to evaluate composite functions Use the function values in Table 1.1 to evaluate the following composite functions.

a. $f(g(0))$ **b.** $g(f(-1))$ **c.** $f(g(g(-1)))$

Table 1.1

x	−2	−1	0	1	2
$f(x)$	0	1	3	4	2
$g(x)$	−1	0	−2	−3	−4

SOLUTION

a. Using the table, we see that $g(0) = -2$ and $f(-2) = 0$. Therefore, $f(g(0)) = 0$.
b. Because $f(-1) = 1$ and $g(1) = -3$, it follows that $g(f(-1)) = -3$.
c. Note that $g(-1) = 0$, $g(0) = -2$, and $f(-2) = 0$. Therefore, $f(g(g(-1))) = 0$.

Related Exercises 55–56◄

Secant Lines and the Difference Quotient

Figure 1.10 shows two points $P(x, f(x))$ and $Q(x + h, f(x + h))$ on the graph of $y = f(x)$, in the case that $h > 0$. A line through any two points on a curve is called a **secant line**, and it plays an important role in calculus. The slope of the secant line through P and Q, denoted m_{sec}, is given by

$$m_{sec} = \frac{\text{change in } y}{\text{change in } x} = \frac{f(x + h) - f(x)}{(x + h) - x} = \frac{f(x + h) - f(x)}{h}.$$

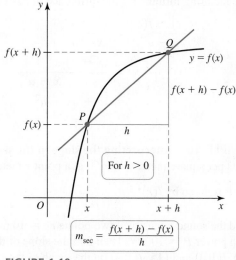

$$m_{\text{sec}} = \frac{f(x + h) - f(x)}{h}$$

FIGURE 1.10

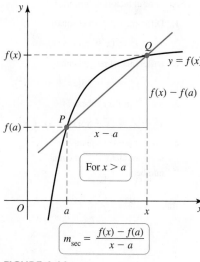

$$m_{\text{sec}} = \frac{f(x) - f(a)}{x - a}$$

FIGURE 1.11

The slope formula $\dfrac{f(x + h) - f(x)}{h}$ is also known as a **difference quotient**, and it can be expressed in several ways depending on how the coordinates of P and Q are labeled. For example, given the coordinates $P(a, f(a))$ and $Q(x, f(x))$ (Figure 1.11), the difference quotient is

$$m_{\text{sec}} = \frac{f(x) - f(a)}{x - a}.$$

We interpret the slope of the secant line in this form as the **average rate of change** of f over the interval $[a, x]$.

EXAMPLE 9 Working with the difference quotient

a. Simplify the difference quotient $\dfrac{f(x + h) - f(x)}{h}$, for $f(x) = 3x^2 - x$.

b. Simplify the difference quotient $\dfrac{f(x) - f(a)}{x - a}$, for $f(x) = x^3$.

SOLUTION

a. First note that $f(x + h) = 3(x + h)^2 - (x + h)$. We substitute this expression into the difference quotient and simplify:

$$\frac{f(x + h) - f(x)}{h} = \frac{\overbrace{3(x + h)^2 - (x + h)}^{f(x+h)} - \overbrace{(3x^2 - x)}^{f(x)}}{h}$$

$$= \frac{3(x^2 + 2xh + h^2) - (x + h) - (3x^2 - x)}{h} \quad \text{Expand } (x + h)^2.$$

$$= \frac{3x^2 + 6xh + 3h^2 - x - h - 3x^2 + x}{h} \quad \text{Distribute.}$$

$$= \frac{6xh + 3h^2 - h}{h} \quad \text{Simplify.}$$

$$= \frac{h(6x + 3h - 1)}{h} = 6x + 3h - 1. \quad \text{Factor and simplify.}$$

▶ Treat $f(x + h)$ like the composition $f(g(x))$, where $x + h$ plays the role of $g(x)$. It may help to establish a pattern in your mind before evaluating $f(x + h)$. For instance, using the function in Example 9a, we have

$$f(x) = 3x^2 - x;$$
$$f(12) = 3 \cdot 12^2 - 12;$$
$$f(b) = 3b^2 - b;$$

$f(\text{math}) = 3 \cdot \text{math}^2 - \text{math};$
therefore,

$$f(x + h) = 3(x + h)^2 - (x + h).$$

> Some useful factoring formulas:

1. Difference of perfect squares:
   $x^2 - y^2 = (x - y)(x + y)$.

2. Difference of perfect cubes:
   $x^3 - y^3 = (x - y)(x^2 + xy + y^2)$.

3. Sum of perfect cubes:
   $x^3 + y^3 = (x + y)(x^2 - xy + y^2)$.

4. Sum of perfect squares: $x^2 + y^2$
   does not factor over the real
   numbers.

b. The factoring formula for the difference of perfect cubes is needed:

$$\frac{f(x) - f(a)}{x - a} = \frac{x^3 - a^3}{x - a}$$

$$= \frac{(x - a)(x^2 + ax + a^2)}{x - a} \quad \text{Factoring formula.}$$

$$= x^2 + ax + a^2. \quad \text{Simplify.}$$

Related Exercises 57–66◄

EXAMPLE 10   Interpreting the slope of the secant line Sound intensity I, measured in watts per square meter (W/m^2), at a point r meters from a sound source with acoustic power P is given by $I(r) = \dfrac{P}{4\pi r^2}$.

a. Find the sound intensity at two points $r_1 = 10$ m and $r_2 = 15$ m from a sound source with power $P = 100$ W. Then find the slope of the secant line through the points $(10, I(10))$ and $(15, I(15))$ on the graph of the intensity function and interpret the result.

b. Find the slope of the secant line through any two points $(r_1, I(r_1))$ and $(r_2, I(r_2))$ on the graph of the intensity function with acoustic power P.

SOLUTION

a. The sound intensity 10 m from the source is $I(10) = \dfrac{100 \text{ W}}{4\pi(10 \text{ m})^2} = \dfrac{1}{4\pi} \text{ W/m}^2$. At

15 m, the intensity is $I(15) = \dfrac{100 \text{ W}}{4\pi(15 \text{ m})^2} = \dfrac{1}{9\pi} \text{ W/m}^2$. To find the slope of the

secant line (Figure 1.12), we compute the change in intensity divided by the change in distance:

$$m_{\text{sec}} = \frac{I(15) - I(10)}{15 - 10} = \frac{\dfrac{1}{9\pi} - \dfrac{1}{4\pi}}{5} = -\frac{1}{36\pi} \text{ W/m}^2 \text{ per meter.}$$

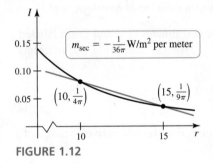

$m_{\text{sec}} = -\frac{1}{36\pi} \text{W/m}^2$ per meter

$\left(10, \frac{1}{4\pi}\right)$ $\left(15, \frac{1}{9\pi}\right)$

FIGURE 1.12

The units provide a clue to the physical meaning of the slope: It measures the average rate at which the intensity changes as one moves from 10 m to 15 m away from the sound source. In this case, because the slope of the secant line is negative, the intensity *decreases* at an average rate of $1/(36\pi)$ W/m^2 per meter.

b.

$$m_{\text{sec}} = \frac{I(r_2) - I(r_1)}{r_2 - r_1} = \frac{\dfrac{P}{4\pi r_2^2} - \dfrac{P}{4\pi r_1^2}}{r_2 - r_1} \quad \text{Evaluate } I(r_2) \text{ and } I(r_1).$$

$$= \frac{\dfrac{P}{4\pi}\left(\dfrac{1}{r_2^2} - \dfrac{1}{r_1^2}\right)}{r_2 - r_1} \quad \text{Factor.}$$

$$= \frac{P}{4\pi} \cdot \frac{r_1^2 - r_2^2}{r_1^2 r_2^2} \cdot \frac{1}{r_2 - r_1} \quad \text{Simplify.}$$

$$= \frac{P}{4\pi} \cdot \frac{(r_1 - r_2)(r_1 + r_2)}{r_1^2 r_2^2} \cdot \frac{1}{-(r_1 - r_2)} \quad \text{Factor.}$$

$$= -\frac{P(r_1 + r_2)}{4\pi r_1^2 r_2^2} \quad \text{Cancel and simplify.}$$

The result represents the average rate at which the sound intensity changes over an interval $[r_1, r_2]$. Because $r_1 > 0$ and $r_2 > 0$, we see that m_{sec} is always negative. Therefore, the sound intensity $I(r)$ decreases as r increases, for $r > 0$.

Related Exercises 67–70◄

Symmetry

The word *symmetry* has many meanings in mathematics. Here we consider symmetries of graphs and the relations they represent. Taking advantage of symmetry often saves time and leads to insights.

> **DEFINITION** **Symmetry in Graphs**
>
> A graph is **symmetric with respect to the *y*-axis** if whenever the point (x, y) is on the graph, the point $(-x, y)$ is also on the graph. This property means that the graph is unchanged when reflected across the *y*-axis (Figure 1.13a).
>
> A graph is **symmetric with respect to the *x*-axis** if whenever the point (x, y) is on the graph, the point $(x, -y)$ is also on the graph. This property means that the graph is unchanged when reflected across the *x*-axis (Figure 1.13b).
>
> A graph is **symmetric with respect to the origin** if whenever the point (x, y) is on the graph, the point $(-x, -y)$ is also on the graph (Figure 1.13c). Symmetry about both the *x*- and *y*-axes implies symmetry about the origin, but not vice versa.

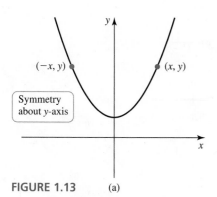

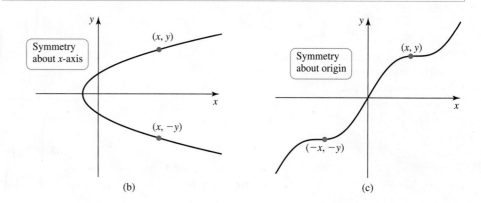

FIGURE 1.13   (a)   (b)   (c)

> **DEFINITION** **Symmetry in Functions**
>
> An **even function** f has the property that $f(-x) = f(x)$, for all x in the domain. The graph of an even function is symmetric about the *y*-axis. Polynomials consisting of only even powers of the variable (of the form x^{2n}, where n is a nonnegative integer) are even functions.
>
> An **odd function** f has the property that $f(-x) = -f(x)$, for all x in the domain. The graph of an odd function is symmetric about the origin. Polynomials consisting of only odd powers of the variable (of the form x^{2n+1}, where n is a nonnegative integer) are odd functions.

QUICK CHECK 4 Explain why the graph of a nonzero function cannot be symmetric with respect to the *x*-axis. ◄

EXAMPLE 11   **Identifying symmetry in functions**   Identify the symmetry, if any, in the following functions.

a. $f(x) = x^4 - 2x^2 - 20$ **b.** $g(x) = x^3 - 3x + 1$ **c.** $h(x) = \dfrac{1}{x^3 - x}$

SOLUTION

a. The function f consists of only even powers of x (where $20 = 20 \cdot 1 = 20x^0$ and x^0 is considered an even power). Therefore, f is an even function (Figure 1.14). This fact is verified by showing that $f(-x) = f(x)$:

$$f(-x) = (-x)^4 - 2(-x)^2 - 20 = x^4 - 2x^2 - 20 = f(x).$$

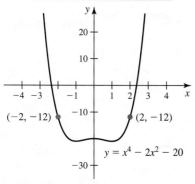

Even function: if (x, y) is on the graph, then $(-x, y)$ is on the graph.

$y = x^4 - 2x^2 - 20$

$(-2, -12)$ $(2, -12)$

FIGURE 1.14

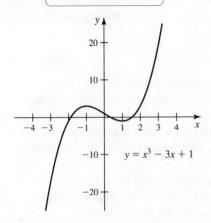

No symmetry: neither an
even nor odd function.

$y = x^3 - 3x + 1$

FIGURE 1.15

▷ The symmetry of compositions of even
and odd functions is considered in
Exercises 95–101.

b. The function g consists of two odd powers and one even power (again, $1 = x^0$ is considered an even power). Therefore, we expect that the function has no symmetry about the y-axis or the origin (Figure 1.15). Note that

$$g(-x) = (-x)^3 - 3(-x) + 1 = -x^3 + 3x + 1,$$

so $g(-x)$ equals neither $g(x)$ nor $-g(x)$, and the function has no symmetry.

c. In this case, h is a composition of an odd function $f(x) = 1/x$ with an odd function $g(x) = x^3 - x$. Note that

$$h(-x) = \frac{1}{(-x)^3 - (-x)} = -\frac{1}{x^3 - x} = -h(x).$$

Because $h(-x) = -h(x)$, h is an odd function (Figure 1.16).

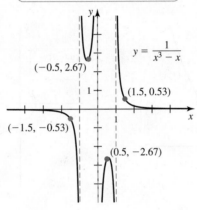

Odd function: if (x, y) is on the
graph, then $(-x, -y)$ is on the graph.

$y = \dfrac{1}{x^3 - x}$

$(-0.5, 2.67)$

$(1.5, 0.53)$

$(-1.5, -0.53)$

$(0.5, -2.67)$

FIGURE 1.16

Related Exercises 71–80 ◀

SECTION 1.1 EXERCISES

Review Questions

1. Use the terms *domain, range, independent variable*, and *dependent variable* to explain how a function relates one variable to another variable.

2. Does the independent variable of a function belong to the domain or range? Does the dependent variable belong to the domain or range?

3. Explain how the vertical line test is used to detect functions.

4. If $f(x) = 1/(x^3 + 1)$, what is $f(2)$? What is $f(y^2)$?

5. Which statement about a function is true? (i) For each value of x in the domain, there corresponds one unique value of y in the range; (ii) for each value of y in the range, there corresponds one value of x in the domain. Explain.

6. If $f(x) = \sqrt{x}$ and $g(x) = x^3 - 2$, find the compositions $f \circ g, g \circ f, f \circ f$, and $g \circ g$.

7. Suppose f and g are even functions with $f(2) = 2$ and $g(2) = -2$. Evaluate $f(g(2))$ and $g(f(-2))$.

8. Explain how to find the domain of $f \circ g$ if you know the domain and range of f and g.

9. Sketch a graph of an even function f and state how $f(x)$ and $f(-x)$ are related.

10. Sketch a graph of an odd function f and state how $f(x)$ and $f(-x)$ are related.

Basic Skills

11–12. Vertical line test *Decide whether graphs A, B, or both represent functions.*

11.

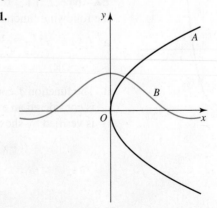

12.

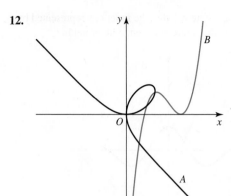

13–20. Domain and range *Graph each function with a graphing utility using the given window. Then state the domain and range of the function.*

13. $f(x) = 3x^4 - 10$; $[-2, 2] \times [-10, 15]$

14. $g(y) = \dfrac{y + 1}{(y + 2)(y - 3)}$; $[-4, 6] \times [-3, 3]$

15. $f(x) = \sqrt{4 - x^2}$; $[-4, 4] \times [-4, 4]$

16. $F(w) = \sqrt[4]{2 - w}$; $[-3, 2] \times [0, 2]$

17. $h(u) = \sqrt[3]{u - 1}$; $[-7, 9] \times [-2, 2]$

18. $g(x) = (x^2 - 4)\sqrt{x + 5}$; $[-5, 5] \times [-10, 50]$

19. $f(x) = (9 - x^2)^{3/2}$; $[-4, 4] \times [0, 30]$

20. $g(t) = \dfrac{1}{1 + t^2}$; $[-7, 7] \times [0, 1.5]$

21–24. Domain in context *Determine an appropriate domain of each function. Identify the independent and dependent variables.*

21. A stone is thrown vertically upward from the ground at a speed of 40 m/s at time $t = 0$. Its distance d (in meters) above the ground (neglecting air resistance) is approximated by the function $f(t) = 40t - 5t^2$.

22. A stone is dropped off a bridge from a height of 20 m above a river. If t represents the elapsed time (in seconds) after the stone is released, then its distance d (in meters) above the river is approximated by the function $f(t) = 20 - 5t^2$.

23. A cylindrical water tower with a radius of 10 m and a height of 50 m is filled to a height of h. The volume V of water (in cubic meters) is given by the function $g(h) = 100\pi h$.

24. The volume V of a balloon of radius r (in meters) filled with helium is given by the function $f(r) = \frac{4}{3}\pi r^3$. Assume the balloon can hold up to 1 m³ of helium.

25–36. Composite functions and notation *Let $f(x) = x^2 - 4$, $g(x) = x^3$, and $F(x) = 1/(x - 3)$. Simplify or evaluate the following expressions.*

25. $f(10)$

26. $f(p^2)$

27. $g(1/z)$

28. $F(y^4)$

29. $F(g(y))$

30. $f(g(w))$

31. $g(f(u))$

32. $\dfrac{f(2 + h) - f(2)}{h}$

33. $F(F(x))$

34. $g(F(f(x)))$

35. $f(\sqrt{x + 4})$

36. $F\left(\dfrac{3x + 1}{x}\right)$

37–40. Working with composite functions *Find possible choices for outer and inner functions f and g such that the given function h equals $f \circ g$. Give the domain of h.*

37. $h(x) = (x^3 - 5)^{10}$

38. $h(x) = \dfrac{2}{(x^6 + x^2 + 1)^2}$

39. $h(x) = \sqrt{x^4 + 2}$

40. $h(x) = \dfrac{1}{\sqrt{x^3 - 1}}$

41–48. More composite functions *Let $f(x) = |x|$, $g(x) = x^2 - 4$, $F(x) = \sqrt{x}$, and $G(x) = 1/(x - 2)$. Determine the following composite functions and give their domains.*

41. $f \circ g$

42. $g \circ f$

43. $f \circ G$

44. $f \circ g \circ G$

45. $G \circ g \circ f$

46. $F \circ g \circ g$

47. $g \circ g$

48. $G \circ G$

49–54. Missing piece *Let $g(x) = x^2 + 3$. Find a function f that produces the given composition.*

49. $(f \circ g)(x) = x^2$

50. $(f \circ g)(x) = \dfrac{1}{x^2 + 3}$

51. $(f \circ g)(x) = x^4 + 6x^2 + 9$

52. $(f \circ g)(x) = x^4 + 6x^2 + 20$

53. $(g \circ f)(x) = x^4 + 3$

54. $(g \circ f)(x) = x^{2/3} + 3$

55. Composite functions from graphs Use the graphs of f and g in the figure to determine the following function values.

 a. $f(g(2))$ **b.** $g(f(2))$ **c.** $f(g(4))$
 d. $g(f(5))$ **e.** $f(g(7))$ **f.** $f(f(8))$

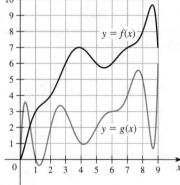

56. Composite functions from tables Use the table to evaluate the given compositions.

x	-1	0	1	2	3	4
$f(x)$	3	1	0	-1	-3	-1
$g(x)$	-1	0	2	3	4	5
$h(x)$	0	-1	0	3	0	4

 a. $h(g(0))$ **b.** $g(f(4))$ **c.** $h(h(0))$
 d. $g(h(f(4)))$ **e.** $f(f(f(1)))$ **f.** $h(h(h(0)))$
 g. $f(h(g(2)))$ **h.** $g(f(h(4)))$ **i.** $g(g(g(1)))$
 j. $f(f(h(3)))$

57–66. Working with difference quotients *Simplify the difference*

quotients $\dfrac{f(x+h)-f(x)}{h}$ *and* $\dfrac{f(x)-f(a)}{x-a}$ *for the following functions.*

57. $f(x) = x^2$

58. $f(x) = 4x - 3$

59. $f(x) = 2/x$

60. $f(x) = 2x^2 - 3x + 1$

61. $f(x) = \dfrac{x}{x+1}$

62. $f(x) = x^4$

63. $f(x) = x^3 - 2x$

64. $f(x) = 4 - 4x - x^2$

65. $f(x) = -\dfrac{4}{x^2}$

66. $f(x) = \dfrac{1}{x} - x^2$

67–70. Interpreting the slope of secant lines *In each exercise, a function and an interval of its independent variable are given. The endpoints of the interval are associated with the points P and Q on the graph of the function.*

a. Sketch a graph of the function and the secant line through P and Q.
b. Find the slope of the secant line in part (a), and interpret your answer in terms of an average rate of change over the interval. Include units in your answer.

67. After t seconds, an object dropped from rest falls a distance $d = 16t^2$, where d is measured in feet and $2 \le t \le 5$.

68. After t seconds, the second hand on a clock moves through an angle $D = 6t$, where D is measured in degrees and $5 \le t \le 20$.

69. The volume V of an ideal gas in cubic centimeters is given by $V = 2/p$, where p is the pressure in atmospheres and $0.5 \le p \le 2$.

70. The speed of a car prior to hard braking can be estimated by the length of the skid mark. One model claims that the speed S in mi/hr is $S = \sqrt{30\ell}$, where ℓ is the length of the skid mark in feet and $50 \le \ell \le 150$.

71–78. Symmetry *Determine whether the graphs of the following equations and functions have symmetry about the x-axis, the y-axis, or the origin. Check your work by graphing.*

71. $f(x) = x^4 + 5x^2 - 12$

72. $f(x) = 3x^5 + 2x^3 - x$

73. $f(x) = x^5 - x^3 - 2$

74. $f(x) = 2|x|$

75. $x^{2/3} + y^{2/3} = 1$

76. $x^3 - y^5 = 0$

77. $f(x) = x|x|$

78. $|x| + |y| = 1$

79. Symmetry in graphs State whether the functions represented by graphs A, B, and C in the figure are even, odd, or neither.

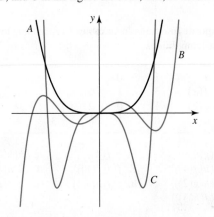

80. Symmetry in graphs State whether the functions represented by graphs A, B, and C in the figure are even, odd, or neither.

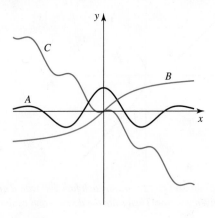

Further Explorations

81. Explain why or why not Determine whether the following statements are true and give an explanation or counterexample.

a. The range of $f(x) = 2x - 38$ is all real numbers.
b. The relation $f(x) = x^6 + 1$ is *not* a function because $f(1) = f(-1) = 2$.
c. If $f(x) = x^{-1}$, then $f(1/x) = 1/f(x)$.
d. In general, $f(f(x)) = (f(x))^2$.
e. In general, $f(g(x)) = g(f(x))$.
f. In general, $f(g(x)) = (f \circ g)(x)$.
g. If $f(x)$ is an even function, then $cf(ax)$ is an even function, where a and c are nonzero real numbers.
h. If $f(x)$ is an odd function, then $f(x) + d$ is an odd function, where d is a real number.
i. If f is both even *and* odd, then $f(x) = 0$ for all x.

82. Range of power functions Using words and figures, explain why the range of $f(x) = x^n$, where n is a positive odd integer, is all real numbers. Explain why the range of $g(x) = x^n$, where n is a positive even integer, is all nonnegative real numbers.

83. Absolute value graph Use the definition of absolute value to graph the equation $|x| - |y| = 1$. Use a graphing utility only to check your work.

84. Even and odd at the origin

a. If $f(0)$ is defined and f is an even function, is it necessarily true that $f(0) = 0$? Explain.
b. If $f(0)$ is defined and f is an odd function, is it necessarily true that $f(0) = 0$? Explain.

85–88. Polynomial calculations *Find polynomials f that satisfy the following properties. (Hint: Determine the degree of f; then substitute a polynomial of that degree and solve for its coefficients.)*

85. $f(f(x)) = 9x - 8$

86. $(f(x))^2 = 9x^2 - 12x + 4$

87. $f(f(x)) = x^4 - 12x^2 + 30$

88. $(f(x))^2 = x^4 - 12x^2 + 36$

89–92. Difference quotients *Simplify the difference quotients*
$$\frac{f(x+h)-f(x)}{h} \text{ and } \frac{f(x)-f(a)}{x-a} \text{ by rationalizing the numerator.}$$

89. $f(x) = \sqrt{x}$

90. $f(x) = \sqrt{1-2x}$

91. $f(x) = -\dfrac{3}{\sqrt{x}}$

92. $f(x) = \sqrt{x^2+1}$

Applications

93. Launching a rocket A small rocket is launched vertically upward from the edge of a cliff 80 ft off the ground at a speed of 96 ft/s. Its height in feet above the ground is given by $h(t) = -16t^2 + 96t + 80$, where t represents time measured in seconds.

  a. Assuming the rocket is launched at $t = 0$, what is an appropriate domain for h?

  b. Graph h and determine the time at which the rocket reaches its highest point. What is the height at that time?

94. Draining a tank (Torricelli's law) A cylindrical tank with a cross-sectional area of 100 cm² is filled to a depth of 100 cm with water. At $t = 0$, a drain in the bottom of the tank with an area of 10 cm² is opened, allowing water to flow out of the tank. The depth of water in the tank at time $t \geq 0$ is $d(t) = (10 - 2.2t)^2$.

  a. Check that $d(0) = 100$, as specified.

  b. At what time is the tank empty?

  c. What is an appropriate domain for d?

Additional Exercises

95–101. Combining even and odd functions *Let E be an even function and O be an odd function. Determine the symmetry, if any, of the following functions.*

95. $E + O$ **96.** $E \cdot O$ **97.** E/O **98.** $E \circ O$

99. $E \circ E$ **100.** $O \circ O$ **101.** $O \circ E$

102. Composite even and odd functions from tables Assume f is an even function and g is an odd function. Use the table to evaluate the given compositions.

x	1	2	3	4
$f(x)$	2	−1	3	−4
$g(x)$	−3	−1	−4	−2

  a. $f(g(-1))$ **b.** $g(f(-4))$ **c.** $f(g(-3))$
  d. $f(g(-2))$ **e.** $g(g(-1))$ **f.** $f(g(0)) - 1$
  g. $f(g(g(-2)))$ **h.** $g(f(f(-4)))$ **i.** $g(g(g(-1)))$

103. Composite even and odd functions from graphs Assume f is an even function and g is an odd function. Use the (incomplete) graphs of f and g in the figure to determine the following function values.

  a. $f(g(-2))$ **b.** $g(f(-2))$ **c.** $f(g(-4))$
  d. $g(f(5) - 8)$ **e.** $g(g(-7))$ **f.** $f(1 - f(8))$

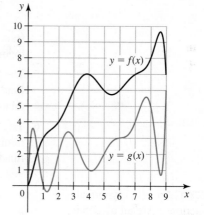

QUICK CHECK ANSWERS

1. $3, x^4 - 2x^2, t^2 - 2t, p^2 - 4p + 3$ **2.** Domain is all real numbers; range is $\{y: 0 < y \leq 1\}$. **3.** $(f \circ g)(x) = x^4 + 1$ and $(g \circ f)(x) = (x^2 + 1)^2$. **4.** If the graph were symmetric with respect to the x-axis, it would not pass the vertical line test. ◄

1.2 Representing Functions

We consider four different approaches to defining and representing functions: formulas, graphs, tables, and words.

Using Formulas

The following list is a brief catalog of the families of functions that are introduced in this chapter and studied systematically throughout this book; they are all defined by *formulas*.

> One version of the Fundamental Theorem of Algebra states that a nonconstant polynomial of degree n has exactly n (possibly complex) roots, counting each root up to its multiplicity.

1. Polynomials are functions of the form
$$f(x) = a_n x^n + a_{n-1} x^{n-1} + \cdots + a_1 x + a_0,$$

where the **coefficients** $a_0, a_1, \ldots, a_n$ are real numbers with $a_n \neq 0$ and the nonnegative integer n is the **degree** of the polynomial. The domain of any polynomial is the set of all real numbers. An nth-degree polynomial can have as many as n real

zeros or **roots**—values of x at which $f(x) = 0$; the zeros are points at which the graph of f intersects the x-axis.

2. **Rational functions** are ratios of the form $f(x) = p(x)/q(x)$, where p and q are polynomials. Because division by zero is prohibited, the domain of a rational function is the set of all real numbers except those for which the denominator is zero.

3. **Algebraic functions** are constructed using the operations of algebra: addition, subtraction, multiplication, division, and roots. Examples of algebraic functions are $f(x) = \sqrt{2x^3 + 4}$ and $f(x) = x^{1/4}(x^3 + 2)$. In general, if an even root (square root, fourth root, and so forth) appears, then the domain does not contain points at which the quantity under the root is negative (and perhaps other points).

4. **Exponential functions** have the form $f(x) = b^x$, where the base $b \neq 1$ is a positive real number. Closely associated with exponential functions are **logarithmic functions** of the form $f(x) = \log_b x$, where $b > 0$ and $b \neq 1$. An exponential function has a domain consisting of all real numbers. Logarithmic functions are defined for positive real numbers.

   The most important exponential function is the **natural exponential function** $f(x) = e^x$, with base $b = e$, where $e \approx 2.71828\ldots$ is one of the fundamental constants of mathematics. Associated with the natural exponential function is the **natural logarithm function** $f(x) = \ln x$, which also has the base $b = e$.

5. The **trigonometric functions** are $\sin x$, $\cos x$, $\tan x$, $\cot x$, $\sec x$, and $\csc x$; they are fundamental to mathematics and many areas of application. Also important are their relatives, the **inverse trigonometric functions**.

6. Trigonometric, exponential, and logarithmic functions are a few examples of a large family called **transcendental functions**. Figure 1.17 shows the organization of these functions, all of which are explored in detail in upcoming chapters.

QUICK CHECK 1 Are all polynomials rational functions? Are all algebraic functions polynomials? ◄

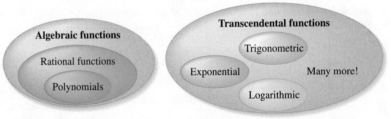

FIGURE 1.17

Using Graphs

Although formulas are the most compact way to represent many functions, graphs often provide the most illuminating representations. Two of many examples of functions and their graphs are shown in Figure 1.18. Much of this book is devoted to creating and analyzing graphs of functions.

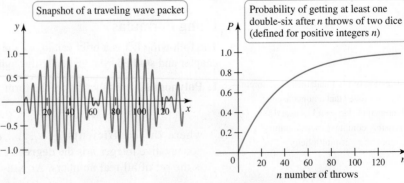

FIGURE 1.18

There are two approaches to graphing functions.

• Graphing calculators and software are easy to use and powerful. Such **technology** produces graphs of most functions encountered in this book. We assume you know how to use a graphing utility.

• Graphing calculators, however, are not infallible. Therefore, you should also strive to master **analytical methods** (pencil-and-paper methods) in order to analyze functions and make accurate graphs by hand. Analytical methods rely heavily on calculus and are presented throughout this book.

The important message is this: Both technology and analytical methods are essential and must be used together in an integrated way to produce accurate graphs.

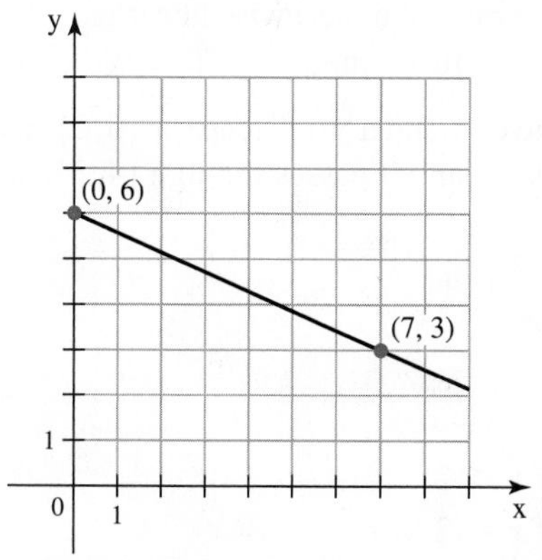

Linear Functions   One form of the equation of a line (see Appendix A) is $y = mx + b$, where m and b are constants. Therefore, the function $f(x) = mx + b$ has a straight-line graph and is called a **linear function**.

EXAMPLE 1   Linear functions and their graphs   Determine the function represented by the line in Figure 1.19.

SOLUTION From the graph, we see that the y-intercept is $(0, 6)$. Using the points $(0, 6)$ and $(7, 3)$, the slope of the line is

$$m = \frac{3 - 6}{7 - 0} = -\frac{3}{7}.$$

Therefore, the line is described by the function $f(x) = -3x/7 + 6$.

Related Exercises 11–14 ◄

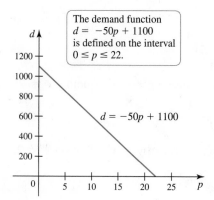

FIGURE 1.20

▷ The units of the slope have meaning:
For every dollar that the price is reduced,
50 more CDs can be sold.

EXAMPLE 2   Demand function for CDs   After studying sales for several months, the owner of a large CD retail outlet knows that the number of new CDs sold in a day (called the *demand*) decreases as the retail price increases. Specifically, her data indicate that at a price of $14 per CD an average of 400 CDs are sold per day, while at a price of $17 per CD an average of 250 CDs are sold per day. Assume that the demand d is a *linear* function of the price p.

a. Find and graph the demand function $d = f(p) = mp + b$.

b. According to this model, how many CDs (on average) are sold at a price of $20?

SOLUTION

a. Two points on the graph of the demand function are given: $(p, d) = (14, 400)$ and $(17, 250)$. Therefore, the slope of the demand line is

$$m = \frac{400 - 250}{14 - 17} = -50 \text{ CDs per dollar.}$$

It follows that the equation of the linear demand function is

$$d - 250 = -50(p - 17).$$

Expressing d as a function of p, we have $d = f(p) = -50p + 1100$ (Figure 1.20).

b. Using the demand function with a price of $20, the average number of CDs that could be sold per day is $f(20) = 100$.

Related Exercises 15–18 ◄

FIGURE 1.19

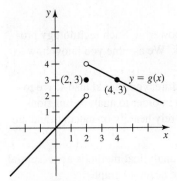

FIGURE 1.21

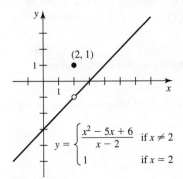

FIGURE 1.22

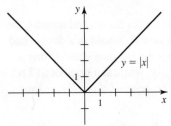

FIGURE 1.23

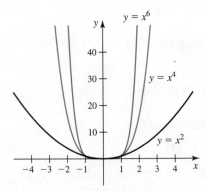

FIGURE 1.24

Piecewise Functions   A function may have different definitions on different parts of its domain. For example, income tax is levied in tax brackets that have different tax rates. Functions that have different definitions on different parts of the domain are called **piecewise functions**. If all the pieces are linear, the function is **piecewise linear**. Here are some examples.

EXAMPLE 3   **Defining a piecewise function**   The graph of a piecewise linear function g is shown in Figure 1.21. Find a formula for the function.

SOLUTION   For $x < 2$, the graph is linear with a slope of 1 and a y-intercept of $(0, 0)$; its equation is $y = x$. For $x > 2$, the slope of the line is $-\frac{1}{2}$ and it passes through $(4, 3)$, so an equation of this piece of the function is

$$y - 3 = -\frac{1}{2}(x - 4) \quad \text{or} \quad y = -\frac{1}{2}x + 5.$$

For $x = 2$, we have $g(2) = 3$. Therefore,

$$g(x) = \begin{cases} x & \text{if } x < 2 \\ 3 & \text{if } x = 2 \\ -\frac{1}{2}x + 5 & \text{if } x > 2. \end{cases}$$

Related Exercises 19–22 ◄

EXAMPLE 4   **Graphing piecewise functions**   Graph the following functions.

a. $f(x) = \begin{cases} \dfrac{x^2 - 5x + 6}{x - 2} & \text{if } x \neq 2 \\ 1 & \text{if } x = 2 \end{cases}$

b. $f(x) = |x|$, the absolute value function

SOLUTION

a. The function f is simplified by factoring and then canceling $x - 2$, assuming $x \neq 2$:

$$\frac{x^2 - 5x + 6}{x - 2} = \frac{(x - 2)(x - 3)}{x - 2} = x - 3.$$

Therefore, the graph of f is identical to the graph of the line $y = x - 3$ when $x \neq 2$. We are given that $f(2) = 1$ (Figure 1.22).

b. The absolute value of a real number is defined as

$$f(x) = |x| = \begin{cases} x & \text{if } x \geq 0 \\ -x & \text{if } x < 0. \end{cases}$$

Graphing $y = -x$, for $x < 0$, and $y = x$, for $x \geq 0$, produces the graph in Figure 1.23.

Related Exercises 23–28 ◄

Power Functions   Power functions are a special case of polynomials; they have the form $f(x) = x^n$, where n is a positive integer. When n is an even integer, the function values are nonnegative and the graph passes through the origin, opening upward (Figure 1.24). For odd integers, the power function $f(x) = x^n$ has values that are positive when x is positive and negative when x is negative (Figure 1.25).

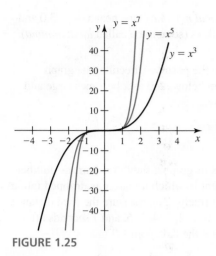

FIGURE 1.25

QUICK CHECK 2 What is the range of $f(x) = x^7$? What is the range of $f(x) = x^8$? ◄

Root Functions   Root functions are a special case of algebraic functions; they have the form $f(x) = x^{1/n}$, where $n > 1$ is a positive integer. Notice that when n is even (square roots, fourth roots, and so forth), the domain and range consist of nonnegative numbers. Their graphs begin steeply at the origin and then flatten out as x increases (Figure 1.26).

By contrast, the odd root functions (cube roots, fifth roots, and so forth) are defined for all real values of x; their range also consists of all real numbers. Their graphs pass through the origin, open upward for $x < 0$ and downward for $x > 0$, and flatten out as x increases in magnitude (Figure 1.27).

► Recall that if n is a positive integer, then $x^{1/n}$ is the nth root of x; that is, $f(x) = x^{1/n} = \sqrt[n]{x}$.

QUICK CHECK 3 What are the domain and range of $f(x) = x^{1/7}$? What are the domain and range of $f(x) = x^{1/10}$? ◄

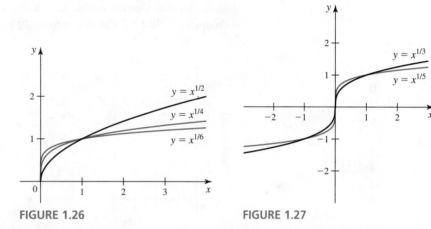

FIGURE 1.26   FIGURE 1.27

Rational Functions   Rational functions figure prominently in this book, and much is said later about graphing rational functions. The following example illustrates how analysis and technology work together.

EXAMPLE 5   **Technology and analysis**   Consider the rational function

$$f(x) = \frac{3x^3 - x - 1}{x^3 + 2x^2 - 6}.$$

a. What is the domain of f?

b. Find the roots (zeros) of f.

c. Graph the function using a graphing utility.

d. At what points does the function have peaks and valleys?

e. How does f behave as x grows large in magnitude?

SOLUTION

a. The domain consists of all real numbers except those at which the denominator is zero. A graphing utility shows that the denominator has one real zero at $x \approx 1.340$.

b. The roots of a rational function are the roots of the numerator, provided they are not also roots of the denominator. Using a graphing utility, the only real root of the numerator is $x \approx 0.851$.

c. After experimenting with the graphing window, a reasonable graph of f is obtained (Figure 1.28). At the point where the denominator is zero, $x \approx 1.340$, the function becomes large in magnitude and f has a *vertical asymptote*.

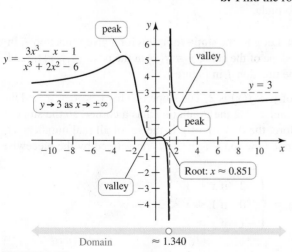

FIGURE 1.28

d. The function has two peaks (soon to be called *local maxima*), one near $x = -3.0$ and one near $x = 0.4$. The function also has two valleys (soon to be called *local minima*), one near $x = -0.3$ and one near $x = 2.6$.

e. By zooming out, it appears that as x increases in the positive direction, the graph approaches the *horizontal asymptote* $y = 3$ from below, and as x becomes large and negative, the graph approaches $y = 3$ from above.

Related Exercises 29–34 ◄

Using Tables

Sometimes functions do not originate as formulas or graphs; they may start as numbers or data. For example, suppose you do an experiment in which a marble is dropped into a cylinder filled with heavy oil and is allowed to fall freely. You measure the total distance d, in centimeters, that the marble falls at times $t = 0, 1, 2, 3, 4, 5, 6,$ and 7 seconds after it is dropped (Table 1.2). The first step might be to plot the data points (Figure 1.29).

Table 1.2

t (s)	d (cm)
0	0
1	2
2	6
3	14
4	24
5	34
6	44
7	54

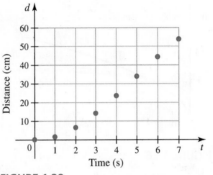

FIGURE 1.29

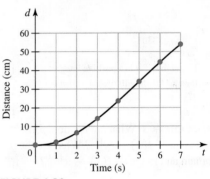

FIGURE 1.30

The data points suggest that there is a function $d = f(t)$ that gives the distance that the marble falls at *all* times of interest. Because the marble falls through the oil without abrupt changes, a smooth graph passing through the data points (Figure 1.30) is reasonable. Finding the best function that fits the data is a more difficult problem, which we discuss later in the text.

Using Words

Using words may be the least mathematical way to define functions, but it is often the way in which functions originate. Once a function is defined in words, it can often be tabulated, graphed, or expressed as a formula.

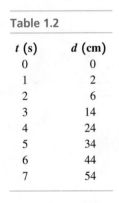

FIGURE 1.31

EXAMPLE 6 A slope function Let g be the **slope function** for a given function f. In words, this means that $g(x)$ is the slope of the curve $y = f(x)$ at the point $(x, f(x))$. Find and graph the slope function for the function f in Figure 1.31.

SOLUTION For $x < 1$, the slope of $y = f(x)$ is 2. The slope is 0 for $1 < x < 2$, and the slope is -1 for $x > 2$. At $x = 1$ and $x = 2$ the graph of f has a corner, so the slope is undefined at these points. Therefore, the domain of g is the set of all real numbers except $x = 1$ and $x = 2$, and the slope function (Figure 1.32) is defined by the piecewise function

$$g(x) = \begin{cases} 2 & \text{if } x < 1 \\ 0 & \text{if } 1 < x < 2 \\ -1 & \text{if } x > 2. \end{cases}$$

Related Exercises 35–38 ◄

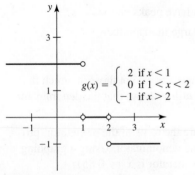

FIGURE 1.32

$$g(x) = \begin{cases} 2 & \text{if } x < 1 \\ 0 & \text{if } 1 < x < 2 \\ -1 & \text{if } x > 2 \end{cases}$$

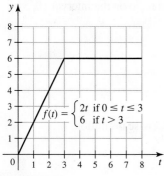

FIGURE 1.33

EXAMPLE 7   An area function Let A be an **area function** for a positive function f. In words, this means that $A(x)$ is the area of the region between the graph of f and the t-axis from $t = 0$ to $t = x$. Consider the function (Figure 1.33)

$$f(t) = \begin{cases} 2t & \text{if } 0 \le t \le 3 \\ 6 & \text{if } t > 3. \end{cases}$$

a. Find $A(2)$ and $A(5)$.

b. Find a piecewise formula for the area function for f.

SOLUTION

a. The value of $A(2)$ is the area of the shaded region between the graph of f and the t-axis from $t = 0$ to $t = 2$ (Figure 1.34a). Using the formula for the area of a triangle,

$$A(2) = \frac{1}{2}(2)(4) = 4.$$

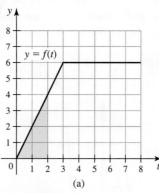
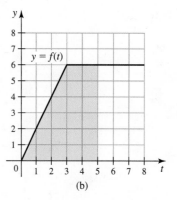

FIGURE 1.34

The value of $A(5)$ is the area of the shaded region between the graph of f and the t-axis on the interval $[0, 5]$ (Figure 1.34b). This area equals the area of the triangle whose base is the interval $[0, 3]$ plus the area of the rectangle whose base is the interval $[3, 5]$:

$$A(5) = \underbrace{\frac{1}{2}(3)(6)}_{\substack{\text{area of the} \\ \text{triangle}}} + \underbrace{(2)(6)}_{\substack{\text{area of the} \\ \text{rectangle}}} = 21.$$

b. For $0 \le x \le 3$ (Figure 1.35a), $A(x)$ is the area of the triangle whose base is the interval $[0, x]$. Because the height of the triangle at $t = x$ is $f(x)$,

$$A(x) = \frac{1}{2}xf(x) = \frac{1}{2}x\underbrace{(2x)}_{f(x)} = x^2.$$

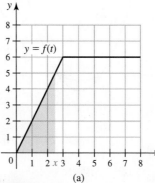
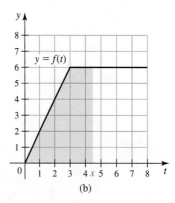

FIGURE 1.35

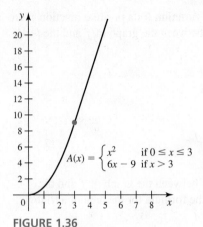

FIGURE 1.36

For $x > 3$ (Figure 1.35b), $A(x)$ is the area of the triangle on the interval $[0, 3]$ plus the area of the rectangle on the interval $[3, x]$:

$$A(x) = \underbrace{\frac{1}{2}(3)(6)}_{\text{area of the triangle}} + \overbrace{(x - 3)(6)}^{\text{area of the rectangle}} = 6x - 9.$$

Therefore, the area function A (Figure 1.36) has the piecewise definition

$$y = A(x) = \begin{cases} x^2 & \text{if } 0 \le x \le 3 \\ 6x - 9 & \text{if } x > 3. \end{cases}$$

Related Exercises 39–42 ◄

Transformations of Functions and Graphs

There are several ways to transform the graph of a function to produce graphs of new functions. Four transformations are common: *shifts* in the x- and y-directions and *scalings* in the x- and y-directions. These transformations, summarized in Figures 1.37–1.42, can save time in graphing and visualizing functions.

The graph of $y = f(x) + d$ is the graph of $y = f(x)$ shifted vertically by d units (up if $d > 0$ and down if $d < 0$).

The graph of $y = f(x - b)$ is the graph of $y = f(x)$ shifted horizontally by b units (right if $b > 0$ and left if $b < 0$).

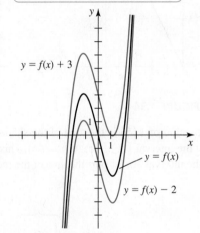

FIGURE 1.37

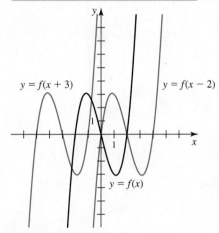

FIGURE 1.38

For $c > 0$, the graph of $y = cf(x)$ is the graph of $y = f(x)$ scaled vertically by a factor of c (broadened if $0 < c < 1$ and steepened if $c > 1$).

For $c < 0$, the graph of $y = cf(x)$ is the graph of $y = f(x)$ scaled vertically by a factor of $|c|$ and reflected across the x-axis (broadened if $-1 < c < 0$ and steepened if $c < -1$).

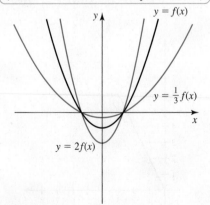

FIGURE 1.39

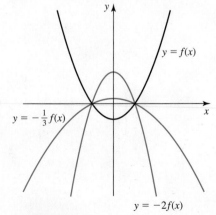

FIGURE 1.40

For $a > 0$, the graph of $y = f(ax)$ is the graph of $y = f(x)$ scaled horizontally by a factor of a (broadened if $0 < a < 1$ and steepened if $a > 1$).

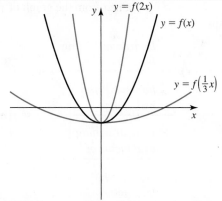

FIGURE 1.41

For $a < 0$, the graph of $y = f(ax)$ is the graph of $y = f(x)$ scaled horizontally by a factor of $|a|$ and reflected across the y-axis (broadened if $-1 < a < 0$ and steepened if $a < -1$).

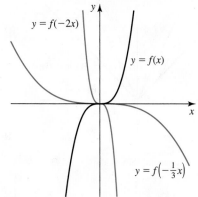

FIGURE 1.42

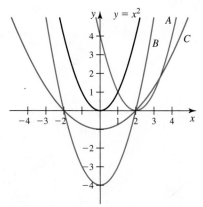

FIGURE 1.43

▷ You should verify that graph C also corresponds to a horizontal scaling and a vertical shift. It has the equation $y = f(ax) - 1$, where $a = \frac{1}{2}$.

EXAMPLE 8 **Shifting parabolas** The graphs A, B, and C in Figure 1.43 are obtained from the graph of $f(x) = x^2$ using shifts and scalings. Find the function that describes each graph.

SOLUTION

a. Graph A is the graph of f shifted to the right by 2 units. It represents the function

$$f(x - 2) = (x - 2)^2 = x^2 - 4x + 4.$$

b. Graph B is the graph of f shifted down by 4 units. It represents the function

$$f(x) - 4 = x^2 - 4.$$

c. Graph C is a broadened version of the graph of f shifted down by 1 unit. Therefore, it represents $cf(x) - 1 = cx^2 - 1$, for some value of c, with $0 < c < 1$ (because the graph is broadened). Using the fact that graph C passes through the points $(\pm 2, 0)$, we find that $c = \frac{1}{4}$. Therefore, the graph represents

$$y = \frac{1}{4}f(x) - 1 = \frac{1}{4}x^2 - 1.$$

Related Exercises 43–54 ◀

QUICK CHECK 4 How do you modify the graph of $f(x) = 1/x$ to produce the graph of $g(x) = 1/(x + 4)$? ◀

▷ Note that we can also write $g(x) = 2\left|x + \frac{1}{2}\right|$, which means the graph of g may also be obtained by a vertical scaling and a horizontal shift.

EXAMPLE 9 **Scaling and shifting** Graph $g(x) = |2x + 1|$.

SOLUTION We write the function as $g(x) = \left|2\left(x + \frac{1}{2}\right)\right|$. Letting $f(x) = |x|$, we have $g(x) = f\left(2\left(x + \frac{1}{2}\right)\right)$. Thus, the graph of g is obtained by scaling (steepening) the graph of f horizontally and shifting it $\frac{1}{2}$-unit to the left (Figure 1.44).

Related Exercises 43–54 ◀

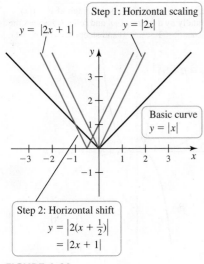

FIGURE 1.44

SUMMARY   **Transformations**

Given the real numbers a, b, c, and d and the function f, the graph of $y = cf(a(x - b)) + d$ is obtained from the graph of $y = f(x)$ in the following steps.

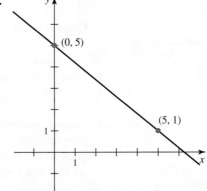

SECTION 1.2 EXERCISES

Review Questions

1. Give four ways that functions may be defined and represented.

2. What is the domain of a polynomial?

3. What is the domain of a rational function?

4. Describe what is meant by a piecewise linear function.

5. Sketch a graph of $y = x^5$.

6. Sketch a graph of $y = x^{1/5}$.

7. If you have the graph of $y = f(x)$, how do you obtain the graph of $y = f(x + 2)$?

8. If you have the graph of $y = f(x)$, how do you obtain the graph of $y = -3f(x)$?

9. If you have the graph of $y = f(x)$, how do you obtain the graph of $y = f(3x)$?

10. Given the graph of $y = x^2$, how do you obtain the graph of $y = 4(x + 3)^2 + 6$?

Basic Skills

11–12. Graphs of functions *Find the linear functions that correspond to the following graphs.*

11.

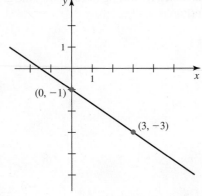

12.

13. **Graph of a linear function** Find and graph the linear function that passes through the points $(1, 3)$ and $(2, 5)$.

14. **Graph of a linear function** Find and graph the linear function that passes through the points $(2, -3)$ and $(5, 0)$.

15. **Demand function** Sales records indicate that if DVD players are priced at \$250, then a large store sells an average of 12 units per day. If they are priced at \$200, then the store sells an average of 15 units per day. Find and graph the linear demand function for DVD sales. For what prices is the demand function defined?

16. **Fund raiser** The Biology Club plans to have a fundraiser for which \$8 tickets will be sold. The cost of room rental and refreshments is \$175. Find and graph the function $p = f(n)$ that gives the profit from the fundraiser when n tickets are sold. Notice that $f(0) = -\$175$; that is, the cost of room rental and refreshments must be paid regardless of how many tickets are sold. How many tickets must be sold to break even (zero profit)?

17. **Population function** The population of a small town was 500 in 2010 and is growing at a rate of 24 people per year. Find and graph the linear population function $p(t)$ that gives the population of the town t years after 2010. Then use this model to predict the population in 2025.

18. Taxicab fees A taxicab ride costs $3.50 plus $2.50 per mile. Let m be the distance (in miles) from the airport to a hotel. Find and graph the function $c(m)$ that represents the cost of taking a taxi from the airport to the hotel. Also determine how much it costs if the hotel is 9 miles from the airport.

19–20. Graphs of piecewise functions *Write a definition of the functions whose graphs are given.*

19.

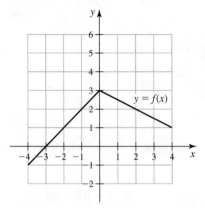

20.

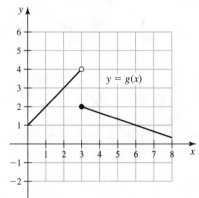

21. Parking fees Suppose that it costs 5¢ per minute to park at the airport with the rate dropping to 3¢ per minute after 9 P.M. Find and graph the cost function $c(t)$ for values of t satisfying $0 \le t \le 120$. Assume that t is the number of minutes after 8:00 P.M.

22. Taxicab fees A taxicab ride costs $3.50 plus $2.50 per mile for the first 5 miles, with the rate dropping to $1.50 per mile after the fifth mile. Let m be the distance (in miles) from the airport to a hotel. Find and graph the piecewise linear function $c(m)$ that represents the cost of taking a taxi from the airport to a hotel m miles away.

23–28. Piecewise linear functions *Graph the following functions.*

23. $f(x) = \begin{cases} \dfrac{x^2 - x}{x - 1} & \text{if } x \ne 1 \\ 2 & \text{if } x = 1 \end{cases}$

24. $f(x) = \begin{cases} \dfrac{x^2 - x - 2}{x - 2} & \text{if } x \ne 2 \\ 4 & \text{if } x = 2 \end{cases}$

25. $f(x) = \begin{cases} 3x - 1 & \text{if } x \le 0 \\ -2x + 1 & \text{if } x > 0 \end{cases}$

26. $f(x) = \begin{cases} 3x - 1 & \text{if } x < 1 \\ x + 1 & \text{if } x \ge 1 \end{cases}$

27. $f(x) = \begin{cases} -2x - 1 & \text{if } x < -1 \\ 1 & \text{if } -1 \le x \le 1 \\ 2x - 1 & \text{if } x > 1 \end{cases}$

28. $f(x) = \begin{cases} 2x + 2 & \text{if } x < 0 \\ x + 2 & \text{if } 0 \le x \le 2 \\ 3 - x/2 & \text{if } x > 2 \end{cases}$

29–34. Graphs of functions

a. Use a graphing utility to produce a graph of the given function. Experiment with different windows to see how the graph changes on different scales.

b. Give the domain of the function.

c. Discuss the interesting features of the function such as peaks, valleys, and intercepts (as in Example 5).

29. $f(x) = x^3 - 2x^2 + 6$

30. $f(x) = \sqrt[3]{2x^2 - 8}$

31. $g(x) = \left| \dfrac{x^2 - 4}{x + 3} \right|$

32. $f(x) = \dfrac{\sqrt{3x^2 - 12}}{x + 1}$

33. $f(x) = 3 - |2x - 1|$

34. $f(x) = \begin{cases} \dfrac{|x - 1|}{x - 1} & \text{if } x \ne 1 \\ 0 & \text{if } x = 1 \end{cases}$

(*Hint:* Sketch a more accurate graph by hand after first using a graphing utility.)

35–38. Slope functions *Determine the slope function for the following functions.*

35. $f(x) = 2x + 1$

36. $f(x) = |x|$

37. Use the figure for Exercise 19.

38. Use the figure for Exercise 20.

39–42. Area functions *Let $A(x)$ be the area of the region bounded by the t-axis and the graph of $y = f(t)$ from $t = 0$ to $t = x$. Consider the following functions and graphs.*

a. Find $A(2)$.   **b.** Find $A(6)$.   **c.** Find a formula for $A(x)$.

39. $f(t) = 6$

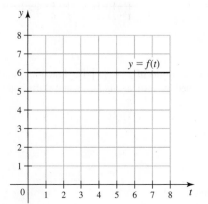

40. $f(t) = \dfrac{t}{2}$

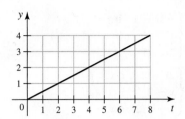

41. $f(t) = \begin{cases} -2t + 8 & \text{if } t \le 3 \\ 2 & \text{if } t > 3 \end{cases}$

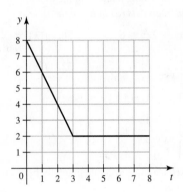

42. $f(t) = |t - 2| + 1$

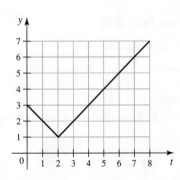

43. Transformations of $y = |x|$ The functions f and g in the figure are obtained by vertical and horizontal shifts and scalings of $y = |x|$. Find formulas for f and g. Verify your answers with a graphing utility.

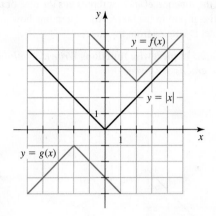

44. Transformations Use the graph of f in the figure to plot the following functions.

   a. $y = -f(x)$ **b.** $y = f(x + 2)$
   c. $y = f(x - 2)$ **d.** $y = f(2x)$
   e. $y = f(x - 1) + 2$ **f.** $y = 2f(x)$

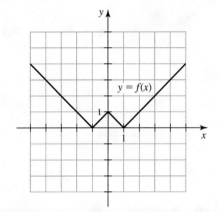

45. Transformations of $f(x) = x^2$ Use shifts and scalings to transform the graph of $f(x) = x^2$ into the graph of g. Use a graphing utility only to check your work.

   a. $g(x) = f(x - 3)$ **b.** $g(x) = f(2x - 4)$

   c. $g(x) = -3f(x - 2) + 4$ **d.** $g(x) = 6f\left(\dfrac{x - 2}{3}\right) + 1$

46. Transformations of $f(x) = \sqrt{x}$ Use shifts and scalings to transform the graph of $f(x) = \sqrt{x}$ into the graph of g. Use a graphing utility only to check your work.

   a. $g(x) = f(x + 4)$ **b.** $g(x) = 2f(2x - 1)$
   c. $g(x) = \sqrt{x - 1}$ **d.** $g(x) = 3\sqrt{x - 1} - 5$

47–54. Shifting and scaling *Use shifts and scalings to graph the given functions. Then check your work with a graphing utility. Be sure to identify an original function on which the shifts and scalings are performed.*

47. $f(x) = (x - 2)^2 + 1$

48. $f(x) = x^2 - 2x + 3$ (*Hint:* Complete the square first.)

49. $g(x) = -3x^2$

50. $g(x) = 2x^3 - 1$

51. $g(x) = 2(x + 3)^2$

52. $p(x) = x^2 + 3x - 5$

53. $h(x) = -4x^2 - 4x + 12$

54. $h(x) = |3x - 6| + 1$

Further Explorations

55. Explain why or why not Determine whether the following statements are true and give an explanation or counterexample.

  a. All polynomials are rational functions, but not all rational functions are polynomials.

  b. If f is a linear polynomial, then $f \circ f$ is a quadratic polynomial.

  c. If f and g are polynomials, then the degrees of $f \circ g$ and $g \circ f$ are equal.

  d. To graph $g(x) = f(x + 2)$, shift the graph of f two units to the right.

56–57. Intersection problems *Use analytical methods to find the following points of intersection. Use a graphing utility only to check your work.*

56. Find the point(s) of intersection of the parabola $y = x^2 + 2$ and the line $y = x + 4$.

57. Find the point(s) of intersection of the parabolas $y = x^2$ and $y = -x^2 + 8x$.

58–59. Functions from tables *Find a simple function that fits the data in the tables.*

58.

x	y
−1	0
0	1
1	2
2	3
3	4

59.

x	y
0	−1
1	0
4	1
9	2
16	3

60–63. Functions from words *Find a formula for a function describing the given situation. Graph the function and give a domain that makes sense for the problem. Recall that with constant speed, distance = speed · time elapsed or d = vt.*

60. A function $y = f(x)$ such that y is 1 less than the cube of x

61. A function $y = f(x)$ such that if you run at a constant rate of 5 mi/hr for x hours, then you run y miles

62. A function $y = f(x)$ such that if you ride a bike for 50 mi at x miles per hour, you arrive at your destination in y hours

63. A function $y = f(x)$ such that if your car gets 32 mi/gal and gasoline costs x/gallon, then $100 is the cost of taking a y-mile trip

64. Floor function The floor function, or greatest integer function, $f(x) = \lfloor x \rfloor$, gives the greatest integer less than or equal to x. Graph the floor function, for $-3 \le x \le 3$.

65. Ceiling function The ceiling function, or smallest integer function, $f(x) = \lceil x \rceil$, gives the smallest integer greater than or equal to x. Graph the ceiling function, for $-3 \le x \le 3$.

66. Sawtooth wave Graph the sawtooth wave defined by

$$f(x) = \begin{cases} \ \ \vdots \\ x + 1 & \text{if } -1 \le x < 0 \\ x & \text{if } 0 \le x < 1 \\ x - 1 & \text{if } 1 \le x < 2 \\ x - 2 & \text{if } 2 \le x < 3 \\ \ \ \vdots \end{cases}$$

67. Square wave Graph the square wave defined by

$$f(x) = \begin{cases} 0 & \text{if } x < 0 \\ 1 & \text{if } 0 \le x < 1 \\ 0 & \text{if } 1 \le x < 2 \\ 1 & \text{if } 2 \le x < 3 \\ \ \ \vdots \end{cases}$$

68–70. Roots and powers *Make a sketch of the given pairs of functions. Be sure to draw the graphs accurately relative to each other.*

68. $y = x^4$ and $y = x^6$

69. $y = x^3$ and $y = x^7$

70. $y = x^{1/3}$ and $y = x^{1/5}$

71. Features of a graph Consider the graph of the function f shown in the figure. Answer the following questions by referring to the points A–I.

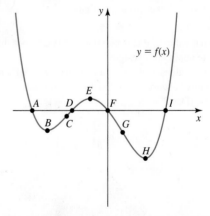

  a. Which points correspond to the roots (zeros) of f?

  b. Which points on the graph correspond to high points of peaks (soon to be called *local maximum* values of f)?

  c. Which points on the graph correspond to low points of valleys (soon to be called *local minimum* values of f)?

  d. As you move along the curve in the positive x-direction, at which point is the graph rising most rapidly?

  e. As you move along the curve in the positive x-direction, at which point is the graph falling most rapidly?

72. Features of a graph Consider the graph of the function g shown in the figure.

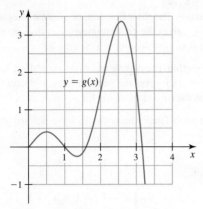

a. Give the approximate roots (zeros) of g.

b. Give the approximate coordinates of the high points of peaks (soon to be called *local maximum* values of f).

c. Give the approximate coordinates of the low points of valleys (soon to be called *local minimum* values of f).

d. Imagine moving along the curve in the positive x-direction on the interval $[0, 3]$. Give the approximate coordinates of the point at which the graph is rising most rapidly.

e. Imagine moving along the curve in the positive x-direction on the interval $[0, 3]$. Give the approximate coordinates of the point at which the graph is falling most rapidly.

Applications

73. Relative acuity of the human eye The **fovea centralis** (or **fovea**) is responsible for the sharp central vision that humans use for reading and other detail-oriented eyesight. The relative acuity of a human eye, which measures the sharpness of vision, is modeled by the function

$$R(\theta) = \frac{0.568}{0.331|\theta| + 0.568},$$

where θ (in degrees) is the angular deviation of the line of sight from the center of the fovea (see figure).

a. Graph R, for $-15 \le \theta \le 15$.

b. For what value of θ is R maximized? What does this fact indicate about our eyesight?

c. For what values of θ do we maintain at least 90% of our relative acuity? (*Source: The Journal of Experimental Biology*, 203, 24, (Dec 2000))

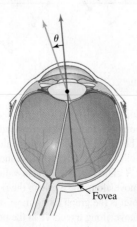

Fovea

74. Tennis probabilities Suppose the probability of a server winning any given point in a tennis match is a constant p, with $0 \le p \le 1$. Then the probability of the server winning a game when serving from deuce is

$$f(p) = \frac{p^2}{1 - 2p(1 - p)}.$$

a. Evaluate $f(0.75)$ and interpret the result.

b. Evaluate $f(0.25)$ and interpret the result.

(*Source: The College Mathematics Journal* 38, 1, (Jan 2000)).

75. Bald eagle population Since DDT was banned and the Endangered Species Act was passed in 1973, the number of bald eagles in the United States has increased dramatically (see figure). In the lower 48 states, the number of breeding pairs of bald eagles increased at a nearly linear rate from 1875 pairs in 1986 to 6471 pairs in 2000.

a. Find a linear function $p(t)$ that models the number of breeding pairs from 1986 to 2000 ($0 \le t \le 14$).

b. Using the function in part (a), approximately how many breeding pairs were in the lower 48 states in 1995?

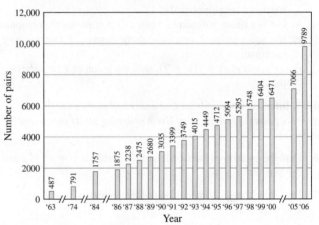

Source: U.S. Fish and Wildlife Service.

76. Temperature scales

a. Find the linear function $C = f(F)$ that gives the reading on the Celsius temperature scale corresponding to a reading on the Fahrenheit scale. Use the facts that $C = 0$ when $F = 32$ (freezing point) and $C = 100$ when $F = 212$ (boiling point).

b. At what temperature are the Celsius and Fahrenheit readings equal?

77. Automobile lease vs. purchase A car dealer offers a purchase option and a lease option on all new cars. Suppose you are interested in a car that can be bought outright for $25,000 or leased for a start-up fee of $1200 plus monthly payments of $350.

a. Find the linear function $y = f(m)$ that gives the total amount you have paid on the lease option after m months.

b. With the lease option, after a 48-month (4-year) term, the car has a residual value of $10,000, which is the amount that you could pay to purchase the car. Assuming no other costs, should you lease or buy?

78. Surface area of a sphere The surface area of a sphere of radius r is $S = 4\pi r^2$. Solve for r in terms of S and graph the radius function for $S \geq 0$.

79. Volume of a spherical cap A single slice through a sphere of radius r produces a *cap* of the sphere. If the thickness of the cap is h, then its volume is $V = \frac{1}{3}\pi h^2 (3r - h)$. Graph the volume as a function of h for a sphere of radius 1. For what values of h does this function make sense?

80. Walking and rowing Kelly has finished a picnic on an island that is 200 m off shore (see figure). She wants to return to a beach house that is 600 m from the point P on the shore closest to the island. She plans to row a boat to a point on shore x meters from P and then jog along the (straight) shore to the house.

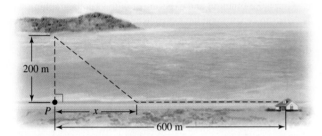

a. Let $d(x)$ be the total length of her trip as a function of x. Graph this function.

b. Suppose that Kelly can row at 2 m/s and jog at 4 m/s. Let $T(x)$ be the total time for her trip as a function of x. Find and graph $y = T(x)$.

c. Based on your graph in part (b), estimate the point on the shore at which Kelly should land in order to minimize the total time of her trip. What is that minimum time?

81. Optimal boxes Imagine a lidless box with height h and a square base whose sides have length x. The box must have a volume of 125 ft³.

a. Find and graph the function $S(x)$ that gives the surface area of the box, for all values of $x > 0$.

b. Based on your graph in part (a), estimate the value of x that produces the box with a minimum surface area.

Additional Exercises

82. Composition of polynomials Let f be an nth-degree polynomial and let g be an mth-degree polynomial. What is the degree of the following polynomials?

a. $f \cdot f$ **b.** $f \circ f$ **c.** $f \cdot g$ **d.** $f \circ g$

83. Parabola vertex property Prove that if a parabola crosses the x-axis twice, the x-coordinate of the vertex of the parabola is halfway between the x-intercepts.

84. Parabola properties Consider the general quadratic function $f(x) = ax^2 + bx + c$, with $a \neq 0$.

a. Find the coordinates of the vertex in terms of a, b, and c.

b. Find the conditions on a, b, and c that guarantee that the graph of f crosses the x-axis twice.

85. Factorial function The factorial function is defined for positive integers as $n! = n(n-1)(n-2) \cdots 3 \cdot 2 \cdot 1$.

a. Make a table of the factorial function, for $n = 1, 2, 3, 4, 5$.

b. Graph these data points and then connect them with a smooth curve.

c. What is the least value of n for which $n! > 10^6$?

86. Sum of integers Let $S(n) = 1 + 2 + \cdots + n$, where n is a positive integer. It can be shown that $S(n) = n(n+1)/2$.

a. Make a table of $S(n)$, for $n = 1, 2, \ldots, 10$.

b. How would you describe the domain of this function?

c. What is the least value of n for which $S(n) > 1000$?

87. Sum of squared integers Let $T(n) = 1^2 + 2^2 + \cdots + n^2$, where n is a positive integer. It can be shown that $T(n) = n(n+1)(2n+1)/6$.

a. Make a table of $T(n)$, for $n = 1, 2, \ldots, 10$.

b. How would you describe the domain of this function?

c. What is the least value of n for which $T(n) > 1000$?

Technology Exercises

88. Analyzing a cubic function Consider the function $f(x) = x^3 - 3x^2 - 144x - 140$.

a. What is the domain of f?

b. Does the graph have symmetry with respect to the origin or y-axis?

c. Graph the function and experiment with various graphing windows to be sure you have displayed all the interesting features of the graph.

d. Using the graph of part (c), find the roots (zeros) of f.

e. Using the graph of part (c), find the y-intercept of the graph of f.

f. Suppose a graph has a high point (the top of a hill) at $x = c$. As explained in Chapter 4, we say that f has a *local maximum* value of $f(c)$ at c. Similarly, if a graph has a low point (the bottom of a valley) at $x = c$, we say that f has a *local minimum* value of $f(c)$ at c. Find the points at which f has a local maximum or a local minimum value. Give the function value at these points.

g. Imagine moving along the curve in the positive x-direction on the interval $[-5, 5]$. Estimate the coordinates of the point at which the curve is falling most rapidly.

89. Analyzing a rational function Consider the function
$$f(x) = \frac{x^3}{x^2 - 9}.$$

a. What is the domain of f?

b. Does the graph have symmetry with respect to the origin or y-axis?

c. Graph the function and experiment with various graphing windows to be sure you have displayed all the interesting features of the graph.

d. Find the roots (zeros) of f.

e. Approximate the points at which f has a local maximum or a local minimum value. Give the function value at these points (see Exercise 88f for definitions).

f. Describe the behavior of f as x approaches $x = 3$ through values with $x < 3$. Describe the behavior of f as x approaches $x = 3$ through values with $x > 3$.

g. Describe the behavior of f as x becomes increasingly large and positive. Describe the behavior of f as x becomes increasingly large in magnitude and negative.

90. Analyzing an algebraic function Consider the function
$$f(x) = \frac{x^2 - x + 1}{\sqrt{x^4 + 2}}.$$

a. What is the domain of f?

b. Does the graph have symmetry with respect to the origin or y-axis?

c. Graph the function and experiment with various graphing windows to be sure you have displayed all the interesting features of the graph.

d. Find the roots (zeros) of f (approximately).

e. Using the graph of part (c), find the y-intercept of the graph of f.

f. Find the points (approximately) at which f has a local maximum or a local minimum value. Give the function value at these points (see Exercise 88f for definitions).

g. Imagine moving along the curve in the positive x-direction. Estimate the coordinates of the point at which the curve is falling most rapidly. Estimate the coordinates of the point at which the curve is rising most rapidly.

h. Describe the behavior of f as x becomes increasingly large and positive. Describe the behavior of f as x becomes increasingly large in magnitude and negative.

91. Peaks, valleys, and cusps Consider the function
$$f(x) = \frac{x\sqrt{|x^2 - 1|}}{x^4 + 1}.$$

a. What is the domain of f?

b. Does the graph have symmetry with respect to the origin or y-axis?

c. Graph the function and experiment with various graphing windows to be sure you have displayed all the interesting features of the graph.

d. Find the roots (zeros) of f.

e. At what point does the graph cross the y-axis?

f. A sharp point on a graph is called a *cusp*. At what points does the graph of f have a cusp?

g. Approximate the points at which f has a local maximum or a local minimum value. Give the function value at these points. Be sure to include cusps (see Exercise 88f for definitions).

h. Describe the behavior of f as x becomes increasingly large and positive. Describe the behavior of f as x becomes increasingly large in magnitude and negative.

92. Analyzing an algebraic function Consider the function
$$f(x) = \frac{6\sqrt{x^2 - x - 12}}{x^2 + 10}.$$

a. What is the domain of f?

b. Does the graph have symmetry with respect to the origin or y-axis?

c. Graph the function and experiment with various graphing windows to be sure you have displayed all the interesting features of the graph.

d. Find the roots (zeros) of f.

e. Approximate the points at which f has a local maximum or a local minimum value. Give the function value at these points (see Exercise 88f for definitions).

f. Describe the behavior of f as x becomes increasingly large and positive. Describe the behavior of f as x becomes increasingly large in magnitude and negative.

QUICK CHECK ANSWERS

1. Yes; no **2.** $(-\infty, \infty)$, $[0, \infty)$ **3.** Domain and range are $(-\infty, \infty)$. Domain and range are $[0, \infty)$. **4.** Shift the graph of f horizontally 4 units to the left. ◄

1.3 Inverse, Exponential, and Logarithmic Functions

Exponential functions are fundamental to all of mathematics. Many processes in the world around us are modeled by *exponential functions*—they appear in finance, medicine, ecology, biology, economics, anthropology, and physics (among other disciplines). Every exponential function has an inverse function, which is a member of the family of *logarithmic functions*, also discussed in this section.

Exponential Functions

Exponential functions have the form $f(x) = b^x$, where the base $b \neq 1$ is a positive real number. An important question arises immediately: For what values of x can b^x be evaluated? We certainly know how to compute b^x when x is an integer. For example, $2^3 = 8$ and $2^{-4} = 1/2^4 = 1/16$. When x is rational, the numerator and denominator are interpreted as a power and root, respectively:

$$16^{3/4} = 16^{3/4} = \left(\sqrt[4]{16}\right)^3 = 8.$$

power
root

But what happens when x is irrational? How should 2^π be understood? Your calculator provides an approximation to 2^π, but where does the approximation come from? For now, we assume that b^x can be defined for all real numbers x and that it can be approximated as closely as desired by using rational numbers as close to x as needed.

> **Exponent Rules**
>
> For any base $b > 0$ and real numbers x and y, the following relations hold:
>
> **E1.** $b^x b^y = b^{x+y}$
>
> **E2.** $\dfrac{b^x}{b^y} = b^{x-y}$
>
> $\left(\text{which includes } \dfrac{1}{b^y} = b^{-y}\right)$
>
> **E3.** $(b^x)^y = b^{xy}$
>
> **E4.** $b^x > 0$, for all x

QUICK CHECK 1 Is it possible to raise a positive number b to a power and obtain a negative number? Is it possible to obtain zero?◄

Properties of Exponential Functions $f(x) = b^x$

1. Because b^x is defined for all real numbers, the domain of f is $\{x: -\infty < x < \infty\}$. Because $b^x > 0$ for all values of x, the range of f is $\{y: 0 < y < \infty\}$.

2. For all $b > 0$, $b^0 = 1$, and thus $f(0) = 1$.

3. If $b > 1$, then f is an increasing function of x (Figure 1.45). For example, if $b = 2$, then $2^x > 2^y$ whenever $x > y$.

4. If $0 < b < 1$, then f is a decreasing function of x. For example, if $b = \frac{1}{2}$,

$$f(x) = \left(\frac{1}{2}\right)^x = \frac{1}{2^x} = 2^{-x},$$

and because 2^x increases with x, 2^{-x} decreases with x (Figure 1.46).

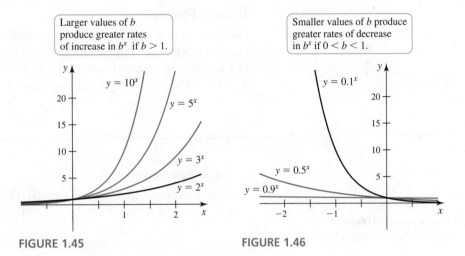

FIGURE 1.45　　　　FIGURE 1.46

QUICK CHECK 2 Explain why $f(x) = (1/3)^x$ is a decreasing function. ◄

> The notation e was proposed by the Swiss mathematician Leonhard Euler (pronounced *oiler*) (1707–1783).

The Natural Exponential Function One of the bases used for exponential functions is special. For reasons that will become evident in upcoming chapters, the special base is e, one of the fundamental constants of mathematics. It is an irrational number with a value of $e = 2.718281828459\ldots$.

DEFINITION The Natural Exponential Function

The **natural exponential function** is $f(x) = e^x$, which has the base $e = 2.718281828459\ldots$.

The base e gives an exponential function that has the following valuable property. As shown in Figure 1.47a, the graph of $y = e^x$ lies between the graphs of $y = 2^x$ and $y = 3^x$ (because $2 < e < 3$). At every point on the graph of $y = e^x$, it is possible to draw a *tangent line* (discussed in Chapters 2 and 3) that touches the graph only at that point. The natural exponential function is the only exponential function with the property that the slope of the tangent line at $x = 0$ is 1 (Figure 1.47b); thus, e^x has both value and slope equal to 1 at $x = 0$. This property—minor as it may seem—leads to many simplifications when we do calculus with exponential functions.

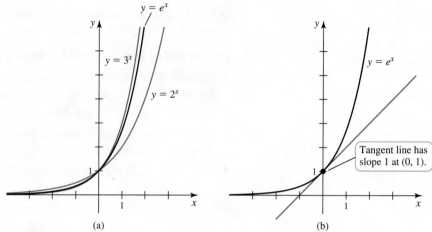

(a)   (b)

FIGURE 1.47

Inverse Functions

Consider the linear function $f(x) = 2x$, which takes any value of x and doubles it. The function that reverses this process by taking any value of $f(x) = 2x$ and mapping it back to x is called the *inverse function* of f, denoted f^{-1}. In this case, the inverse function is $f^{-1}(x) = x/2$. The effect of applying these two functions in succession looks like this:

$$x \xrightarrow{f} 2x \xrightarrow{f^{-1}} x$$

We now generalize this idea.

DEFINITION Inverse Function

Given a function f, its inverse (if it exists) is a function f^{-1} such that whenever $y = f(x)$, then $f^{-1}(y) = x$ (Figure 1.48).

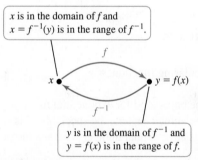

x is in the domain of *f* and $x = f^{-1}(y)$ is in the range of f^{-1}.

y is in the domain of f^{-1} and $y = f(x)$ is in the range of *f*.

FIGURE 1.48

➤ The notation f^{-1} for the inverse can be confusing. The inverse is not the reciprocal; that is, $f^{-1}(x)$ is not $1/f(x) = (f(x))^{-1}$. We adopt the common convention of using simply *inverse* to mean *inverse function*.

QUICK CHECK 3 What is the inverse of $f(x) = \frac{1}{3}x$? What is the inverse of $f(x) = x - 7$? ◄

Because the inverse "undoes" the original function, if we start with a value of x, apply f to it, and then apply f^{-1} to the result, we recover the original value of x; that is,

$$f^{-1}(f(x)) = x$$

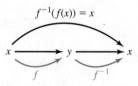

Similarly, if we apply f^{-1} to a value of y and then apply f to the result, we recover the original value of y; that is,

$$f(f^{-1}(y)) = y$$

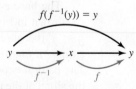

One-to-One Functions   We have defined the inverse of a function, but said nothing about when it exists. To ensure that f has an inverse on a domain, f must be *one-to-one* on that domain. This property means that every output of the function f must correspond to exactly one input. The one-to-one property is checked graphically by using the *horizontal line test*.

DEFINITION   One-to-One Functions and the Horizontal Line Test

A function f is **one-to-one** on a domain D if each value of $f(x)$ corresponds to exactly one value of x in D. More precisely, f is one-to-one on D if $f(x_1) \neq f(x_2)$ whenever $x_1 \neq x_2$, for x_1 and x_2 in D. The **horizontal line test** says that every horizontal line intersects the graph of a one-to-one function at most once (Figure 1.49).

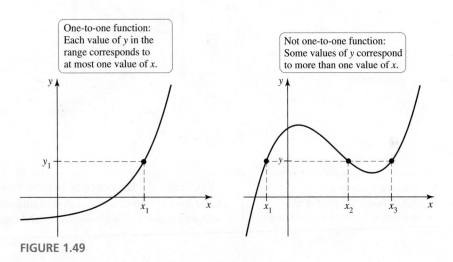

One-to-one function:
Each value of y in the range corresponds to at most one value of x.

Not one-to-one function:
Some values of y correspond to more than one value of x.

FIGURE 1.49

For example, in Figure 1.50, some horizontal lines intersect the graph of $f(x) = x^2$ twice. Therefore, f does not have an inverse function on the interval $(-\infty, \infty)$. However, if f is restricted to the interval $(-\infty, 0]$ or $[0, \infty)$, then it does pass the horizontal line test and it is one-to-one on these intervals.

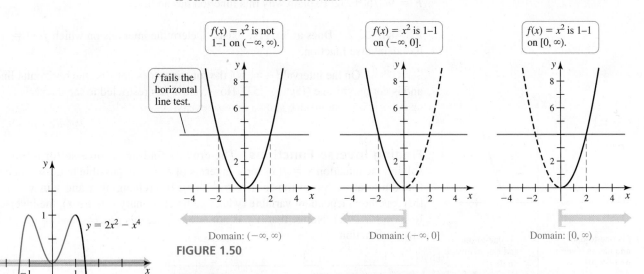

$f(x) = x^2$ is not 1–1 on $(-\infty, \infty)$.

$f(x) = x^2$ is 1–1 on $(-\infty, 0]$.

$f(x) = x^2$ is 1–1 on $[0, \infty)$.

f fails the horizontal line test.

Domain: $(-\infty, \infty)$ Domain: $(-\infty, 0]$ Domain: $[0, \infty)$

FIGURE 1.50

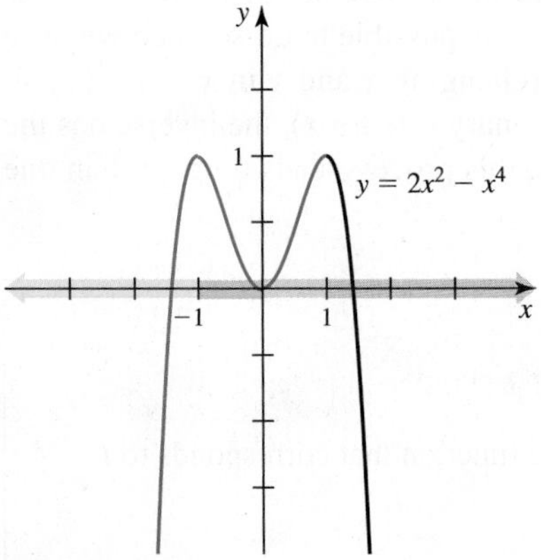

EXAMPLE 1   One-to-one functions Determine the (largest possible) intervals on which the function $f(x) = 2x^2 - x^4$ (Figure 1.51) is one-to-one.

SOLUTION The function is not one-to-one on the entire real line because it fails the horizontal line test. However, on the intervals $(-\infty, -1]$, $[-1, 0]$, $[0, 1]$, and $[1, \infty)$, f is one-to-one. The function is also one-to-one on any subinterval of these four intervals.

Related Exercises 11–14 ◄

$y = 2x^2 - x^4$

FIGURE 1.51

Existence of Inverse Functions   Figure 1.52a illustrates the actions of a one-to-one function f and its inverse f^{-1}. We see that f maps a value of x to a unique value of y. In turn, f^{-1} maps that value of y back to the original value of x. When f is *not* one-to-one, this procedure cannot be carried out (Figure 1.52b).

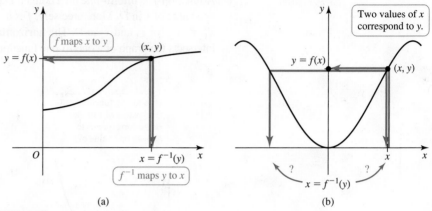

(a)   (b)

FIGURE 1.52

▷ The statement that a one-to-one function has an inverse is plausible based on its graph. However, the proof of this theorem is fairly technical and is omitted.

THEOREM 1.1   Existence of Inverse Functions

Let f be a one-to-one function on a domain D with a range R. Then f has a unique inverse f^{-1} with domain R and range D such that

$$f^{-1}(f(x)) = x \quad \text{and} \quad f(f^{-1}(y)) = y,$$

where x is in D and y is in R.

QUICK CHECK 4 The function that gives degrees Fahrenheit in terms of degrees Celsius is $F = 9C/5 + 32$. Explain why this function has an inverse. ◁

EXAMPLE 2   Does an inverse exist? Determine intervals on which $f(x) = x^2 - 1$ has an inverse function.

SOLUTION On the interval $(-\infty, \infty)$ the function does not pass the horizontal line test and is not one-to-one (Figure 1.53). However, if f is restricted to the intervals $(-\infty, 0]$ or $[0, \infty)$, it is one-to-one and an inverse exists.

Related Exercises 15–20◀

Finding Inverse Functions   The crux of finding an inverse for a function f is solving the equation $y = f(x)$ for x in terms of y. If it is possible to do so, then we have found a relationship of the form $x = f^{-1}(y)$. Interchanging x and y in $x = f^{-1}(y)$ so that x is the independent variable (which is the customary role for x), the inverse has the form $y = f^{-1}(x)$. Notice that if f is not one-to-one, this process leads to more than one inverse function.

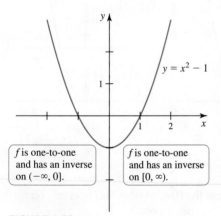

FIGURE 1.53

▷ Once you find a formula for f^{-1}, you can check your work by verifying that $f^{-1}(f(x)) = x$ and $f(f^{-1}(x)) = x$.

PROCEDURE   Finding an Inverse Function

Suppose f is one-to-one on an interval I. To find f^{-1}:

1. Solve $y = f(x)$ for x. If necessary, choose the function that corresponds to I.

2. Interchange x and y and write $y = f^{-1}(x)$.

EXAMPLE 3   Finding inverse functions Find the inverse(s) of the following functions. Restrict the domain of f if necessary.

a. $f(x) = 2x + 6$ **b.** $f(x) = x^2 - 1$

SOLUTION

▷ A constant function (whose graph is a horizontal line) fails the horizontal line test and does not have an inverse.

a. Linear functions (except constant linear functions) are one-to-one on the entire real line. Therefore, an inverse function for f exists for all values of x.

Step 1: Solve $y = f(x)$ for x: We see that $y = 2x + 6$ implies that $2x = y - 6$, or $x = (y - 6)/2$.

Step 2: Interchange x and y and write $y = f^{-1}(x)$:

$$y = f^{-1}(x) = \frac{x - 6}{2}.$$

It is instructive to verify that the inverse relations $f(f^{-1}(x)) = x$ and $f^{-1}(f(x)) = x$ are satisfied:

$$f(f^{-1}(x)) = f\left(\frac{x - 6}{2}\right) = 2\underbrace{\left(\frac{x - 6}{2}\right) + 6}_{f(x) = 2x + 6} = x - 6 + 6 = x,$$

$$f^{-1}(f(x)) = f^{-1}(2x + 6) = \underbrace{\frac{(2x + 6) - 6}{2}}_{f^{-1}(x) = (x - 6)/2} = x.$$

b. As shown in Example 2, the function $f(x) = x^2 - 1$ is not one-to-one on the entire real line; however, it is one-to-one on $(-\infty, 0]$ and on $[0, \infty)$. If we restrict our attention to either of these intervals, then an inverse function can be found.

Step 1: Solve $y = f(x)$ for x:

$$y = x^2 - 1$$
$$x^2 = y + 1$$
$$x = \begin{cases} \sqrt{y + 1} \\ -\sqrt{y + 1}. \end{cases}$$

Each branch of the square root corresponds to an inverse function.

Step 2: Interchange x and y and write $y = f^{-1}(x)$:

$$y = f^{-1}(x) = \sqrt{x + 1} \quad \text{or} \quad y = f^{-1}(x) = -\sqrt{x + 1}.$$

The interpretation of this result is important. Taking the positive branch of the square root, the inverse function $y = f^{-1}(x) = \sqrt{x + 1}$ gives positive values of y; it corresponds to the branch of $f(x) = x^2 - 1$ on the interval $[0, \infty)$ (Figure 1.54). The negative branch of the square root, $y = f^{-1}(x) = -\sqrt{x + 1}$, is another inverse function that gives negative values of y; it corresponds to the branch of $f(x) = x^2 - 1$ on the interval $(-\infty, 0]$.

Related Exercises 21–30◀

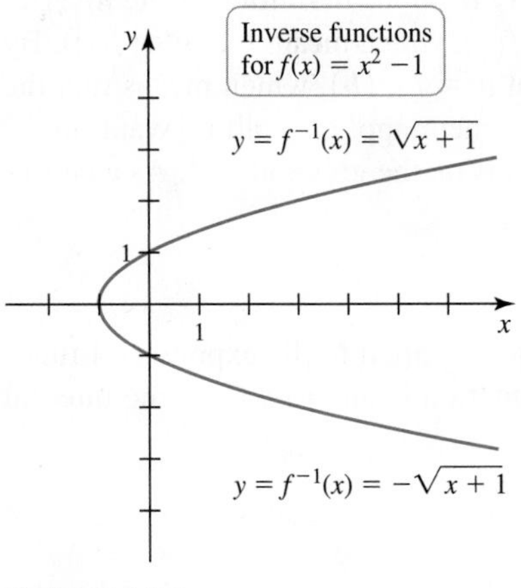

FIGURE 1.54

Inverse functions for $f(x) = x^2 - 1$

$y = f^{-1}(x) = \sqrt{x + 1}$

$y = f^{-1}(x) = -\sqrt{x + 1}$

QUICK CHECK 5 On what interval(s) does the function $f(x) = x^3$ have an inverse?◀

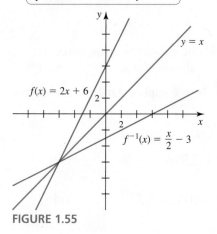

The function $f(x) = 2x + 6$ and its inverse $f^{-1}(x) = \frac{x}{2} - 3$ are symmetric about the line $y = x$.

FIGURE 1.55

Graphing Inverse Functions

The graphs of a function and its inverse have a special relationship, which is illustrated in the following example.

EXAMPLE 4   **Graphing inverse functions** Plot f and f^{-1} on the same coordinate axes.

a. $f(x) = 2x + 6$ **b.** $f(x) = \sqrt{x - 1}$

SOLUTION

a. The inverse of $f(x) = 2x + 6$, found in Example 3, is

$$y = f^{-1}(x) = \frac{x - 6}{2} = \frac{x}{2} - 3.$$

The graphs of f and f^{-1} are shown in Figure 1.55. Notice that both f and f^{-1} are increasing linear functions and they intersect at $(-6, -6)$.

b. The domain of $f(x) = \sqrt{x - 1}$ is $[1, \infty)$ and its range is $[0, \infty)$. On this domain f is one-to-one and has an inverse. It can be found in two steps:

Step 1: Solve $y = \sqrt{x - 1}$ for x:

$$y^2 = x - 1 \quad \text{or} \quad x = y^2 + 1.$$

Step 2: Interchange x and y and write $y = f^{-1}(x)$:

$$y = f^{-1}(x) = x^2 + 1.$$

The graphs of f and f^{-1} are shown in Figure 1.56; notice that the domain of f^{-1} $(x \geq 0)$ corresponds to the range of f $(y \geq 0)$.   *Related Exercises 31–40* ◄

Looking closely at the graphs in Figure 1.55 and Figure 1.56, you see a symmetry that always occurs when a function and its inverse are plotted on the same set of axes. In each figure, one curve is the reflection of the other curve across the line $y = x$. These curves have *symmetry about the line $y = x$*, which means that the point (a, b) is on one curve whenever the point (b, a) is on the other curve (Figure 1.57).

The explanation for the symmetry comes directly from the definition of the inverse. Suppose that the point (a, b) is on the graph of $y = f(x)$, which means that $b = f(a)$. By the definition of the inverse function, we know that $a = f^{-1}(b)$, which means that the point (b, a) is on the graph of $y = f^{-1}(x)$. This argument applies to all relevant points (a, b), so whenever (a, b) is on the graph of f, (b, a) is on the graph of f^{-1}. As a consequence, the graphs are symmetric about the line $y = x$.

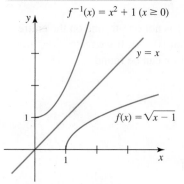

The function $f(x) = \sqrt{x - 1}$ $(x \geq 1)$ and its inverse $f^{-1}(x) = x^2 + 1$ $(x \geq 0)$ are symmetric about $y = x$.

FIGURE 1.56

Logarithmic Functions

Everything we learned about inverse functions is now applied to the exponential function $f(x) = b^x$. For any $b > 0$, with $b \neq 1$, this function is one-to-one on the interval $(-\infty, \infty)$. Therefore, it has an inverse.

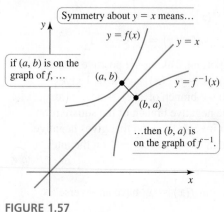

Symmetry about $y = x$ means...

if (a, b) is on the graph of f, ...

...then (b, a) is on the graph of f^{-1}.

FIGURE 1.57

DEFINITION **Logarithmic Function Base b**

For any base $b > 0$, with $b \neq 1$, the **logarithmic function base b**, denoted $y = \log_b x$, is the inverse of the exponential function $y = b^x$. The inverse of the natural exponential function with base $b = e$ is the **natural logarithm function**, denoted $y = \ln x$.

The inverse relationship between logarithmic and exponential functions may be stated concisely in several ways. First, we have

$$y = \log_b x \quad \text{if and only if} \quad b^y = x.$$

Logarithms were invented around 1600 for calculating purposes by the Scotsman John Napier and the Englishman Henry Briggs. Unfortunately, the word *logarithm*, derived from the Greek for reasoning (*logos*) with numbers (*arithmos*), doesn't help with the meaning of the word. **When you see *logarithm*, you should think *exponent*.**

> **Logarithm Rules**

For any base $b > 0$ ($b \neq 1$), positive real numbers x and y, and real numbers z, the following relations hold:

L1. $\log_b (xy) = \log_b x + \log_b y$

L2. $\log_b \left(\dfrac{x}{y} \right) = \log_b x - \log_b y$

$\left(\text{includes } \log_b \dfrac{1}{y} = -\log_b y \right)$

L3. $\log_b (x^z) = z \log_b x$

L4. $\log_b b = 1$

Combining these two conditions results in two important relations.

> **Inverse Relations for Exponential and Logarithmic Functions**
>
> For any base $b > 0$, with $b \neq 1$, the following inverse relations hold.
>
> **I1.** $b^{\log_b x} = x$, for $x > 0$
>
> **I2.** $\log_b b^x = x$, for real values of x

Properties of Logarithmic Functions   The graph of the logarithmic function is generated using the symmetry of the graphs of a function and its inverse. Figure 1.58 shows how the graph of $y = b^x$, for $b > 1$, is reflected across the line $y = x$ to obtain the graph of $y = \log_b x$.

The graphs of $y = \log_b x$ are shown (Figure 1.59) for several bases $b > 1$. Logarithms with bases $0 < b < 1$, although well defined, are generally not used (and they can be expressed in terms of bases with $b > 1$).

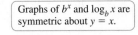

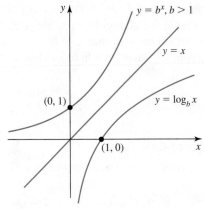

FIGURE 1.58

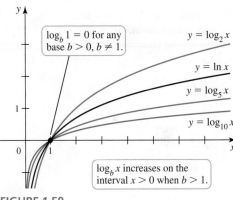

FIGURE 1.59

Logarithmic functions with base $b > 0$ satisfy properties that parallel the properties of the exponential functions given earlier.

1. Because the range of b^x is $\{y: 0 < y < \infty\}$, the domain of $\log_b x$ is $\{x: 0 < x < \infty\}$.

2. The domain of b^x is all real numbers, which implies that the range of $\log_b x$ is all real numbers.

3. Because $b^0 = 1$, it follows that $\log_b 1 = 0$.

4. If $b > 1$, then $\log_b x$ is an increasing function of x. For example, if $b = e$, then $\ln x > \ln y$ whenever $x > y$ (Figure 1.59).

QUICK CHECK 6 What is the domain of $f(x) = \log_b (x^2)$? What is the range of $f(x) = \log_b (x^2)$? ◄

EXAMPLE 5   **Using inverse relations**   One thousand grams of a particular radioactive substance decays according to the function $m(t) = 1000e^{-t/850}$, where $t \geq 0$ measures time in years. When does the mass of the substance reach the safe level deemed to be 1 g?

SOLUTION Setting $m(t) = 1$, we solve $1000e^{-t/850} = 1$ by dividing both sides by 1000 and taking the natural logarithm of both sides:

$$\ln (e^{-t/850}) = \ln \left(\frac{1}{1000} \right).$$

> Provided the arguments are positive, we can take the $\log_b$ of both sides of an equation and produce an equivalent equation.

This equation is simplified by calculating $\ln{(1/1000)} \approx -6.908$ and observing that $\ln{(e^{-t/850})} = -\dfrac{t}{850}$ (inverse property I2). Therefore,

$$-\frac{t}{850} \approx -6.908.$$

Solving for t, we find that $t \approx (-850)(-6.908) \approx 5872$ years.

Related Exercises 41–58 ◀

Change of Base

When working with logarithms and exponentials, it doesn't matter *in principle* which base is used. However, there are practical reasons for switching between bases. For example, most calculators have built-in logarithmic functions in just one or two bases. If you need to use a different base, then the change-of-base rules are essential.

Consider changing bases with exponential functions. Specifically, suppose you wish to express b^x (base b) in the form e^y (base e), where y must be determined. Taking the natural logarithm of both sides of $e^y = b^x$, we have

$$\underbrace{\ln{e^y}}_{y} = \underbrace{\ln{b^x}}_{x \ln b} \quad \text{which implies that } y = x \ln b.$$

It follows that $b^x = e^y = e^{x \ln b}$. For example, $4^x = e^{x \ln 4}$.

> A similar argument is used to derive more general formulas for changing from base b to any other positive base c.

The formula for changing from $\log_b x$ to $\ln x$ is derived in a similar way. We let $y = \log_b x$, which implies that $x = b^y$. Taking the natural logarithm of both sides of $x = b^y$ gives $\ln x = \ln b^y = y \ln b$. Solving for $y = \log_b x$ gives the required formula:

$$y = \log_b x = \frac{\ln x}{\ln b}.$$

Change-of-Base Rules

Let b be a positive real number with $b \neq 1$. Then

$$b^x = e^{x \ln b}, \text{ for all } x \quad \text{and} \quad \log_b x = \frac{\ln x}{\ln b}, \text{ for } x > 0.$$

More generally, if c is a positive real number with $c \neq 1$, then

$$b^x = c^{x \log_c b}, \text{ for all } x \quad \text{and} \quad \log_b x = \frac{\log_c x}{\log_c b}, \text{ for } x > 0.$$

EXAMPLE 6   Changing bases

a. Express 2^{x+4} as an exponential with base e.

b. Express $\log_2 x$ using base e and base 32.

SOLUTION

a. Using the change-of-base rule for exponentials, we have

$$2^{x+4} = e^{(x+4)\ln 2}.$$

b. Using the change-of-base rule for logarithms, we have

$$\log_2 x = \frac{\ln x}{\ln 2} \approx 1.44 \ln x.$$

To change from base 2 to base 32, we use the general change-of-base formula:

$$\log_2 x = \frac{\log_{32} x}{\log_{32} 2} = \frac{\log_{32} x}{1/5} = 5 \log_{32} x.$$

The middle step follows from the fact that $2 = 32^{1/5}$, so $\log_{32} 2 = \frac{1}{5}$.

Related Exercises 59–68◄

SECTION 1.3 EXERCISES

Review Questions

1. For $b > 0$, what are the domain and range of $f(x) = b^x$?

2. Give an example of a function that is one-to-one on the entire real number line.

3. Explain why a function that is not one-to-one on an interval I cannot have an inverse function on I.

4. Explain with pictures why (a, b) is on the graph of f whenever (b, a) is on the graph of f^{-1}.

5. Sketch a function that is one-to-one and positive for $x \geq 0$. Make a rough sketch of its inverse.

6. Express the inverse of $f(x) = 3x - 4$ in the form $y = f^{-1}(x)$.

7. Explain the meaning of $\log_b x$.

8. How is the property $b^{x+y} = b^x b^y$ related to the property $\log_b (xy) = \log_b x + \log_b y$?

9. For $b > 0$ with $b \neq 1$, what are the domain and range of $f(x) = \log_b x$ and why?

10. Express 2^5 using base e.

Basic Skills

11–14. One-to-one functions

11. Find three intervals on which f is one-to-one, making each interval as large as possible.

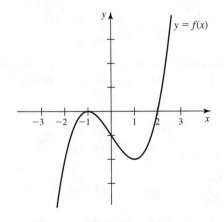

12. Find four intervals on which f is one-to-one, making each interval as large as possible.

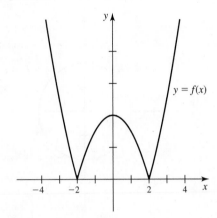

13. Sketch a graph of a function that is one-to-one on the interval $(-\infty, 0)$, but is not one-to-one on $(-\infty, \infty)$.

14. Sketch a graph of a function that is one-to-one on the intervals $(-\infty, -2)$, and $(-2, \infty)$ but is not one-to-one on $(-\infty, \infty)$.

15–20. Where do inverses exist? *Use analytical and/or graphical methods to determine the largest possible set of points on which the following functions have an inverse.*

15. $f(x) = 3x + 4$

16. $f(x) = |2x + 1|$

17. $f(x) = 1/(x - 5)$

18. $f(x) = -(6 - x)^2$

19. $f(x) = 1/x^2$

20. $f(x) = x^2 - 2x + 8$ (*Hint:* Complete the square.)

21–28. Finding inverse functions

a. *Find the inverse of each function (on the given interval, if specified) and write it in the form $y = f^{-1}(x)$.*
b. *Verify the relationships $f(f^{-1}(x)) = x$ and $f^{-1}(f(x)) = x$.*

21. $f(x) = 2x$

22. $f(x) = x/4 + 1$

23. $f(x) = 6 - 4x$

24. $f(x) = 3x^3$

25. $f(x) = 3x + 5$

26. $f(x) = x^2 + 4$, for $x \geq 0$

27. $f(x) = \sqrt{x + 2}$, for $x \geq -2$

28. $f(x) = 2/(x^2 + 1)$, for $x \geq 0$

29. Splitting up curves The unit circle $x^2 + y^2 = 1$ consists of four one-to-one functions, $f_1(x)$, $f_2(x)$, $f_3(x)$, and $f_4(x)$ (see figure).

   a. Find the domain and a formula for each function.
   b. Find the inverse of each function and write it as $y = f^{-1}(x)$.

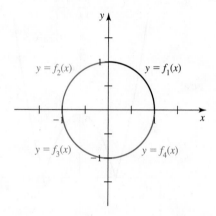

30. Splitting up curves The equation $y^4 = 4x^2$ is associated with four one-to-one functions $f_1(x)$, $f_2(x)$, $f_3(x)$, and $f_4(x)$ (see figure).

   a. Find the domain and a formula for each function.
   b. Find the inverse of each function and write it as $y = f^{-1}(x)$.

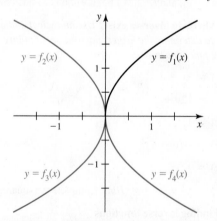

31–38. Graphing inverse functions *Find the inverse function (on the given interval, if specified) and graph both f and f^{-1} on the same set of axes. Check your work by looking for the required symmetry in the graphs.*

31. $f(x) = 8 - 4x$

32. $f(x) = 4x - 12$

33. $f(x) = \sqrt{x}$, for $x \geq 0$

34. $f(x) = \sqrt{3 - x}$, for $x \leq 3$

35. $f(x) = x^4 + 4$, for $x \geq 0$

36. $f(x) = 6/(x^2 - 9)$, for $x > 3$

37. $f(x) = x^2 - 2x + 6$, for $x \geq 1$ (*Hint:* Complete the square.)

38. $f(x) = -x^2 - 4x - 3$, for $x \leq -2$ (*Hint:* Complete the square.)

39–40. Graphs of inverses *Sketch the graph of the inverse function.*

39.

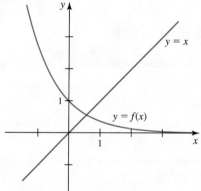

40.

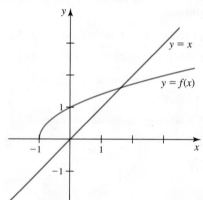

41–46. Solving logarithmic equations *Solve the following equations.*

41. $\log_{10} x = 3$

42. $\log_5 x = -1$

43. $\log_8 x = \frac{1}{3}$

44. $\log_b 125 = 3$

45. $\ln x = -1$

46. $\ln y = 3$

47–52. Properties of logarithms *Assume $\log_b x = 0.36$, $\log_b y = 0.56$, and $\log_b z = 0.83$. Evaluate the following expressions.*

47. $\log_b \dfrac{x}{y}$

48. $\log_b x^2$

49. $\log_b xz$

50. $\log_b \dfrac{\sqrt{xy}}{z}$

51. $\log_b \dfrac{\sqrt{x}}{\sqrt[3]{z}}$

52. $\log_b \dfrac{b^2 x^{5/2}}{\sqrt{y}}$

53–56. Solving equations *Solve the following equations.*

53. $7^x = 21$

54. $2^x = 55$

55. $3^{3x-4} = 15$

56. $5^{3x} = 29$

57. Using inverse relations One hundred grams of a particular radioactive substance decays according to the function $m(t) = 100\,e^{-t/650}$, where $t > 0$ measures time in years. When does the mass reach 50 grams?

58. Using inverse relations The population P of a small town is growing according to the function $P(t) = 100\,e^{t/50}$, where t measures the number of years after 2010. How long does it take the population to double?

59–62. Calculator base change *Write the following logarithms in terms of the natural logarithm. Then use a calculator to find the value of the logarithm, rounding your result to three decimal places.*

59. $\log_2 15$ **60.** $\log_3 30$ **61.** $\log_4 40$ **62.** $\log_6 60$

63–68. Changing bases *Convert the following expressions to the indicated base.*

63. 2^x using base e

64. $3^{\sin x}$ using base e

65. $\ln |x|$ using base 5

66. $\log_2 (x^2 + 1)$ using base e

67. $a^{1/\ln a}$ using base e, for $a > 0$ and $a \neq 1$

68. $a^{1/\log_{10} a}$ using base 10, for $a > 0$ and $a \neq 1$

Further Explorations

69. Explain why or why not Determine whether the following statements are true and give an explanation or counterexample.

   a. If $y = 3^x$, then $x = \sqrt[3]{y}$.

   b. $\dfrac{\log_b x}{\log_b y} = \log_b x - \log_b y$

   c. $\log_5 4^6 = 4 \log_5 6$

   d. $2 = 10^{\log_{10} 2}$

   e. $2 = \ln 2^e$

   f. If $f(x) = x^2 + 1$, then $f^{-1}(x) = 1/(x^2 + 1)$.

   g. If $f(x) = 1/x$, then $f^{-1}(x) = 1/x$.

70. Graphs of exponential functions The following figure shows the graphs of $y = 2^x$, $y = 3^x$, $y = 2^{-x}$, and $y = 3^{-x}$. Match each curve with the correct function.

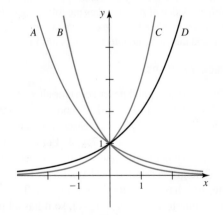

71. Graphs of logarithmic functions The following figure shows the graphs of $y = \log_2 x$, $y = \log_4 x$, and $y = \log_{10} x$. Match each curve with the correct function.

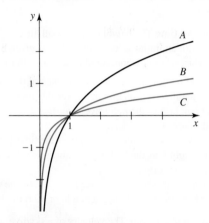

72. Graphs of modified exponential functions Without using a graphing utility, sketch the graph of $y = 2^x$. Then, on the same set of axes, sketch the graphs of $y = 2^{-x}$, $y = 2^{x-1}$, $y = 2^x + 1$, and $y = 2^{2x}$.

73. Graphs of modified logarithmic functions Without using a graphing utility, sketch the graph of $y = \log_2 x$. Then, on the same set of axes, sketch the graphs of $y = \log_2 (x - 1)$, $y = \log_2 x^2$, $y = (\log_2 x)^2$, and $y = \log_2 x + 1$.

74. Large intersection point Use any means to approximate the intersection point(s) of the graphs of $f(x) = e^x$ and $g(x) = x^{123}$. (*Hint:* Consider using logarithms.)

75–78. Finding all inverses *Find all the inverses associated with the following functions and state their domains.*

75. $f(x) = (x + 1)^3$ **76.** $f(x) = (x - 4)^2$

77. $f(x) = 2/(x^2 + 2)$ **78.** $f(x) = 2x/(x + 2)$

Applications

79. Population model A culture of bacteria has a population of 150 cells when it is first observed. The population doubles every 12 hr, which means its population is governed by the function $p(t) = 150 \times 2^{t/12}$, where t is the number of hours after the first observation.

   a. Verify that $p(0) = 150$, as claimed.

   b. Show that the population doubles every 12 hr, as claimed.

   c. What is the population 4 days after the first observation?

   d. How long does it take the population to triple in size?

   e. How long does it take the population to reach 10,000?

80. Charging a capacitor A capacitor is a device that stores electrical charge. The charge on a capacitor accumulates according to the function $Q(t) = a(1 - e^{-t/c})$, where t is measured in seconds, and a and $c > 0$ are physical constants. The *steady-state charge* is the value that $Q(t)$ approaches as t becomes large.

   a. Graph the charge function for $t \geq 0$ using $a = 1$ and $c = 10$. Find a graphing window that shows the full range of the function.

   b. Vary the value of a holding c fixed. Describe the effect on the curve. How does the steady-state charge vary with a?

c. Vary the value of c holding a fixed. Describe the effect on the curve. How does the steady-state charge vary with c?

d. Find a formula that gives the steady-state charge in terms of a and c.

81. Height and time The height of a baseball hit straight up from the ground with an initial velocity of 64 ft/s is given by $h = f(t) = 64t - 16t^2$, where t is measured in seconds after the hit.

a. Is this function one-to-one on the interval $0 \le t \le 4$?

b. Find the inverse function that gives the time t at which the ball is at height h as the ball travels *upward*. Express your answer in the form $t = f^{-1}(h)$.

c. Find the inverse function that gives the time t at which the ball is at height h as the ball travels *downward*. Express your answer in the form $t = f^{-1}(h)$.

d. At what time is the ball at a height of 30 ft on the way up?

e. At what time is the ball at a height of 10 ft on the way down?

82. Velocity of a skydiver The velocity of a skydiver (in m/s) t seconds after jumping from the plane is $v(t) = 600(1 - e^{-kt/60})/k$, where $k > 0$ is a constant. The *terminal velocity* of the skydiver is the value that $v(t)$ approaches as t becomes large. Graph v with $k = 11$ and estimate the terminal velocity.

Additional Exercises

83. Reciprocal bases Assume that $b > 0$ and $b \ne 1$. Show that $\log_{1/b} x = -\log_b x$.

84. Proof of rule L1 Use the following steps to prove that $\log_b(xy) = \log_b x + \log_b y$.

a. Let $x = b^p$ and $y = b^q$. Solve these expressions for p and q, respectively.

b. Use property E1 for exponents to express xy in terms of b, p, and q.

c. Compute $\log_b(xy)$ and simplify.

85. Proof of rule L2 Modify Exercise 84 and use property E2 for exponents to prove that $\log_b(x/y) = \log_b x - \log_b y$.

86. Proof of rule L3 Use the following steps to prove that $\log_b(x^z) = z \log_b x$.

a. Let $x = b^p$. Solve this expression for p.

b. Use property E3 for exponents to express x^z in terms of b and p.

c. Compute $\log_b x^z$ and simplify.

87. Inverses of a quartic Consider the quartic polynomial $y = f(x) = x^4 - x^2$.

a. Graph f and estimate the largest intervals on which it is one-to-one. The goal is to find the inverse function on each of these intervals.

b. Make the substitution $u = x^2$ to solve the equation $y = f(x)$ for x in terms of y. Be sure you have included all possible solutions.

c. Write each inverse function in the form $y = f^{-1}(x)$ for each of the intervals found in part (a).

88. Inverse of composite functions

a. Let $g(x) = 2x + 3$ and $h(x) = x^3$. Consider the composite function $f(x) = g(h(x))$. Find f^{-1} directly and then express it in terms of g^{-1} and h^{-1}.

b. Let $g(x) = x^2 + 1$ and $h(x) = \sqrt{x}$. Consider the composite function $f(x) = g(h(x))$. Find f^{-1} directly and then express it in terms of g^{-1} and h^{-1}.

c. Explain why if g and h are one-to-one, the inverse of $f(x) = g(h(x))$ exists.

89–90. Inverses of (some) cubics *Finding the inverse of a cubic polynomial is equivalent to solving a cubic equation. A special case that is simpler than the general case is the cubic $y = f(x) = x^3 + ax$. Find the inverse of the following cubics using the substitution (known as Vieta's substitution) $x = z - a/(3z)$. Be sure to determine where the function is one-to-one.*

89. $f(x) = x^3 + 2x$ **90.** $f(x) = x^3 - 2x$

91. Nice property Prove that $(\log_b c)(\log_c b) = 1$, for $b > 0$, $c > 0$, $b \ne 1$, and $c \ne 1$.

Technology Exercises

92. Finding roots Consider the function $f(x) = \ln x - x^2 - 2x + 4$.

a. What is the domain of f?

b. Graph f with a graphing window that shows all the interesting features of the graph.

c. Use the graph of part (b) to estimate the roots of f.

93. Points of intersection

a. Graph the curves $y = \ln x$ and $y = 0.3x$, and approximate the coordinates of their intersection points.

b. Graph the curves $y = \ln x$ and $y = 0.4x$ and approximate the coordinates of their intersection points.

c. Estimate the value of a such that the curves $y = \ln x$ and $y = ax$ intersect exactly once. What are the coordinates of the intersection point?

94. Points of intersection

a. Graph the curves $y = e^{x/2}$ and $y = 2x$, and approximate the coordinates of their intersection points.

b. Graph the curves $y = e^{x/2}$ and $y = x$ and approximate the coordinates of their intersection points.

c. Estimate the value of a such that the curves $y = e^{x/2}$ and $y = ax$ intersect exactly once. What are the coordinates of the intersection point?

95. Threshold point Use any means to approximate as closely as possible the value of A that makes the following statement true. The curves $y = e^x$ and $y = \ln ax$ have two intersection points for $a > A$, and they have no intersection points for $a < A$.

QUICK CHECK ANSWERS

1. b^x is always positive (and never zero) for all x and for positive bases b.   **2.** Because $(1/3)^x = 1/3^x$ and 3^x increases as x increases, it follows that $(1/3)^x$ decreases as x increases. **3.** $f^{-1}(x) = 3x; f^{-1}(x) = x + 7$.   **4.** For every Fahrenheit temperature, there is exactly one Celsius temperature, and vice versa. The given relation is also a linear function. It is one-to-one, so it has an inverse function.   **5.** The function $f(x) = x^3$ is one-to-one on $(-\infty, \infty)$, so it has an inverse for all values of x.   **6.** The domain of $\log_b(x^2)$ is all real numbers except zero (because x^2 is positive for $x \ne 0$). The range of $\log_b(x^2)$ is all real numbers. ◂

1.4 Trigonometric Functions and Their Inverses

This section is a review of what you need to know in order to study the calculus of trigonometric functions. Once the trigonometric functions are on stage, it makes sense to present the inverse trigonometric functions and their basic properties.

Radian Measure

Calculus typically requires that angles be measured in **radians** (rad). Working with a circle of radius r, the radian measure of an angle θ is the length of the arc associated with θ, denoted s, divided by the radius of the circle r (Figure 1.60a). Working on a unit circle ($r = 1$), the radian measure of an angle is simply the length of the arc associated with θ (Figure 1.60b). For example, the length of a full unit circle is 2π; therefore, an angle with a radian measure of π corresponds to a half circle ($\theta = 180°$) and an angle with a radian measure of $\pi/2$ corresponds to a quarter circle ($\theta = 90°$).

Degrees	Radians
0	0
30	$\pi/6$
45	$\pi/4$
60	$\pi/3$
90	$\pi/2$
120	$2\pi/3$
135	$3\pi/4$
150	$5\pi/6$
180	π

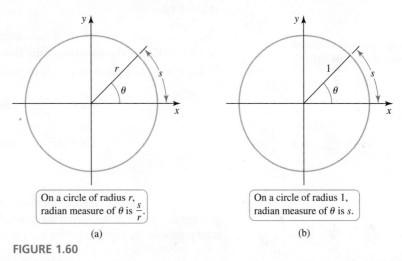

On a circle of radius r, radian measure of θ is $\dfrac{s}{r}$.

(a)

On a circle of radius 1, radian measure of θ is s.

(b)

FIGURE 1.60

Why is it important to use radians? If we divide a full circle into 360 equal parts, we get *degrees*. If we divide a full circle into 400 equal parts, we get *gradians*. In fact, we could choose any fraction of a full circle as a basis for angle measurement, but the resulting unit would be arbitrary. Said differently, there is no geometrical reason that 90 (degrees) should be associated with a right angle.

We use the radian because it is the natural unit for measuring angles. It is the ratio of two lengths that can be measured: the radius of a circle and the length of the arc associated with the angle. Another less obvious advantage of using radians is that if we work on a unit circle (radius equal to 1), then the radian measure of the angle equals the length of the corresponding arc. The fact that *angle equals arc length* on a unit circle is important in upcoming topics.

QUICK CHECK 1 What is the radian measure of a 270° angle? What is the degree measure of a $5\pi/4$-rad angle? ◄

Trigonometric Functions

For acute angles, the trigonometric functions are defined as ratios of the sides of a right triangle (Figure 1.61). To extend these definitions to include all angles, we work in an xy-coordinate system with a circle of radius r centered at the origin. Suppose that $P(x, y)$ is a point on the circle. An angle θ is in **standard position** if its initial side is on the positive x-axis and its terminal side is the line segment OP between the origin and P. An angle is positive if it is obtained by a counterclockwise rotation from the positive x-axis (Figure 1.62). When the right-triangle definitions of Figure 1.61 are used with the right triangle in Figure 1.62, the trigonometric functions may be expressed in terms of x, y, and the radius of the circle, $r = \sqrt{x^2 + y^2}$.

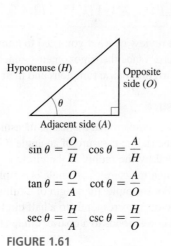

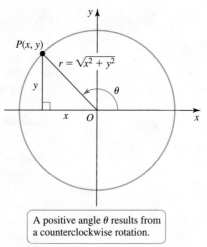

A positive angle θ results from a counterclockwise rotation.

$$\sin \theta = \frac{O}{H} \quad \cos \theta = \frac{A}{H}$$

$$\tan \theta = \frac{O}{A} \quad \cot \theta = \frac{A}{O}$$

$$\sec \theta = \frac{H}{A} \quad \csc \theta = \frac{H}{O}$$

FIGURE 1.61   **FIGURE 1.62**

➤ When working on a unit circle ($r = 1$), these definitions become

$$\sin \theta = y \qquad \cos \theta = x$$

$$\tan \theta = \frac{y}{x} \qquad \cot \theta = \frac{x}{y}$$

$$\sec \theta = \frac{1}{x} \qquad \csc \theta = \frac{1}{y}$$

DEFINITION Trigonometric Functions

Let $P(x, y)$ be a point on a circle of radius r associated with the angle θ. Then

$$\sin \theta = \frac{y}{r}, \qquad \cos \theta = \frac{x}{r}, \qquad \tan \theta = \frac{y}{x},$$

$$\cot \theta = \frac{x}{y}, \qquad \sec \theta = \frac{r}{x}, \qquad \csc \theta = \frac{r}{y}.$$

To find the trigonometric functions of the standard angles (multiples of 30° and 45°), it is helpful to know the radian measure of those angles and the coordinates of the associated points on the unit circle (Figure 1.63).

➤ Standard triangles

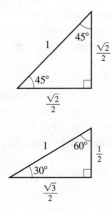

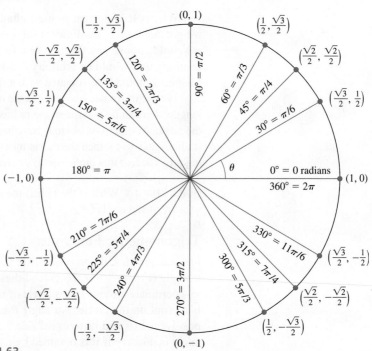

FIGURE 1.63

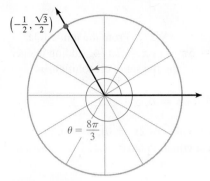

$\left(-\frac{1}{2}, \frac{\sqrt{3}}{2}\right)$

$\theta = \frac{8\pi}{3}$

FIGURE 1.64

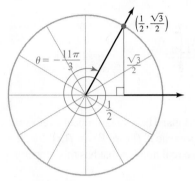

$\left(\frac{1}{2}, \frac{\sqrt{3}}{2}\right)$

$\theta = -\frac{11\pi}{3}$

$\frac{\sqrt{3}}{2}$

$\frac{1}{2}$

FIGURE 1.65

Combining the definitions of the trigonometric functions with the coordinates shown in Figure 1.63, we may evaluate these functions at any standard angle. For example,

$$\sin \frac{2\pi}{3} = \frac{\sqrt{3}}{2}, \qquad \cos \frac{5\pi}{6} = -\frac{\sqrt{3}}{2}, \qquad \tan \frac{7\pi}{6} = \frac{1}{\sqrt{3}}, \qquad \tan \frac{3\pi}{2} \text{ is undefined,}$$

$$\cot \frac{5\pi}{3} = -\frac{1}{\sqrt{3}}, \qquad \sec \frac{7\pi}{4} = \sqrt{2}, \qquad \csc \frac{3\pi}{2} = -1, \qquad \sec \frac{\pi}{2} \text{ is undefined.}$$

EXAMPLE 1   Evaluating trigonometric functions Evaluate the following expressions.

a. $\sin (8\pi/3)$ **b.** $\csc (-11\pi/3)$

SOLUTION

a. The angle $8\pi/3 = 2\pi + 2\pi/3$ corresponds to a *counterclockwise* revolution of one full circle (2π rad) plus an additional $2\pi/3$ rad (Figure 1.64). Therefore, this angle has the same terminal side as the angle $2\pi/3$, and the corresponding point on the unit circle is $(-1/2, \sqrt{3}/2)$. It follows that $\sin (8\pi/3) = y = \sqrt{3}/2$.

b. The angle $\theta = -11\pi/3 = -2\pi - 5\pi/3$ corresponds to a *clockwise* revolution of one full circle (2π rad) plus an additional $5\pi/3$ rad (Figure 1.65). Therefore, this angle has the same terminal side as the angle $\pi/3$. The coordinates of the corresponding point on the unit circle are $(1/2, \sqrt{3}/2)$, so $\csc (-11\pi/3) = 1/y = 2/\sqrt{3}$.

Related Exercises 15–28◄

QUICK CHECK 2 Evaluate $\cos (11\pi/6)$ and $\sin (5\pi/4)$. ◄

Trigonometric Identities

Trigonometric functions have a variety of properties, called identities, that are true for all angles in the domain. Here is a list of some commonly used identities.

Trigonometric Identities

Reciprocal Identities

$$\tan \theta = \frac{\sin \theta}{\cos \theta} \qquad \cot \theta = \frac{1}{\tan \theta} = \frac{\cos \theta}{\sin \theta}$$

$$\csc \theta = \frac{1}{\sin \theta} \qquad \sec \theta = \frac{1}{\cos \theta}$$

Pythagorean Identities

$$\sin^2 \theta + \cos^2 \theta = 1 \qquad 1 + \cot^2 \theta = \csc^2 \theta \qquad \tan^2 \theta + 1 = \sec^2 \theta$$

Double- and Half-Angle Formulas

$$\sin 2\theta = 2 \sin \theta \cos \theta \qquad \cos 2\theta = \cos^2 \theta - \sin^2 \theta$$

$$\cos^2 \theta = \frac{1 + \cos 2\theta}{2} \qquad \sin^2 \theta = \frac{1 - \cos 2\theta}{2}$$

QUICK CHECK 3 Use $\sin^2 \theta + \cos^2 \theta = 1$ to prove that $1 + \cot^2 \theta = \csc^2 \theta$. ◄

EXAMPLE 2   Solving trigonometric equations Solve the following equations.

a. $\sqrt{2} \sin x + 1 = 0$ **b.** $\cos 2x = \sin 2x$, where $0 \le x < 2\pi$.

> By rationalizing the denominator, observe that $\dfrac{1}{\sqrt{2}} = \dfrac{1}{\sqrt{2}} \cdot \dfrac{\sqrt{2}}{\sqrt{2}} = \dfrac{\sqrt{2}}{2}$.

SOLUTION

a. First, we solve for $\sin x$ to obtain $\sin x = -1/\sqrt{2} = -\sqrt{2}/2$. From the unit circle (Figure 1.63), we find that $\sin x = -\sqrt{2}/2$ if $x = 5\pi/4$ or $x = 7\pi/4$. Adding integer multiples of 2π produces additional solutions. Therefore, the set of all solutions is

$$x = \frac{5\pi}{4} + 2n\pi \quad \text{and} \quad x = \frac{7\pi}{4} + 2n\pi, \quad \text{for } n = 0, \pm 1, \pm 2, \pm 3, \ldots.$$

> Notice that the assumption $\cos 2x \neq 0$ is valid for these values of x.

b. Dividing both sides of the equation by $\cos 2x$ (assuming $\cos 2x \neq 0$), we obtain $\tan 2x = 1$. Letting $\theta = 2x$ gives us the equivalent equation $\tan \theta = 1$. This equation is satisfied by

$$\theta = \frac{\pi}{4}, \frac{5\pi}{4}, \frac{9\pi}{4}, \frac{13\pi}{4}, \frac{17\pi}{4}, \ldots.$$

Dividing by two and using the restriction $0 \le x < 2\pi$ gives the solutions

$$x = \frac{\theta}{2} = \frac{\pi}{8}, \frac{5\pi}{8}, \frac{9\pi}{8}, \text{ and } \frac{13\pi}{8}.$$

Related Exercises 29–46 ◀

Graphs of the Trigonometric Functions

Trigonometric functions are examples of **periodic functions**: Their values repeat over every interval of some fixed length. A function f is said to be periodic if $f(x + P) = f(x)$, for all x in the domain, where the **period** P is the smallest positive real number that has this property.

Period of Trigonometric Functions

The functions $\sin \theta$, $\cos \theta$, $\sec \theta$, and $\csc \theta$ have a period of 2π:

$$\sin (\theta + 2\pi) = \sin \theta \qquad \cos (\theta + 2\pi) = \cos \theta$$
$$\sec (\theta + 2\pi) = \sec \theta \qquad \csc (\theta + 2\pi) = \csc \theta,$$

for all θ in the domain.

The functions $\tan \theta$ and $\cot \theta$ have a period of π:

$$\tan (\theta + \pi) = \tan \theta \qquad \cot (\theta + \pi) = \cot \theta,$$

for all θ in the domain.

The graph of $y = \sin \theta$ is shown in Figure 1.66a. Because $\csc \theta = 1/\sin \theta$, these two functions have the same sign, but $y = \csc \theta$ is undefined with vertical asymptotes at $\theta = 0, \pm \pi, \pm 2\pi, \ldots$. The functions $\cos \theta$ and $\sec \theta$ have a similar relationship (Figure 1.66b).

The graphs of $y = \sin \theta$ and its reciprocal, $y = \csc \theta$

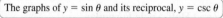
The graphs of $y = \cos \theta$ and its reciprocal, $y = \sec \theta$

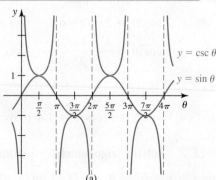

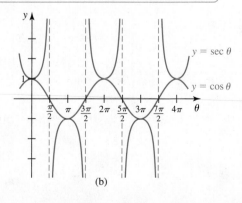

FIGURE 1.66   (a)   (b)

The graphs of $\tan \theta$ and $\cot \theta$ are shown in Figure 1.67. Each function has points, separated by π units, at which it is undefined.

The graph of $y = \tan \theta$ has period π.

The graph of $y = \cot \theta$ has period π.

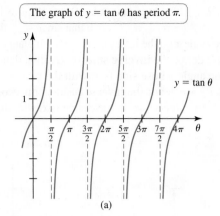

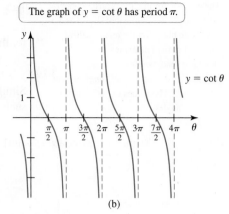

FIGURE 1.67

(a)

(b)

$y = A \sin(B(\theta - C)) + D$

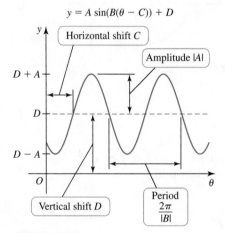

FIGURE 1.68

Transforming Graphs

Many physical phenomena, such as the motion of waves or the rising and setting of the sun, can be modeled using trigonometric functions; the sine and cosine functions are especially useful. With the transformation methods introduced in Section 1.2, we can show that the functions

$$y = A \sin (B(\theta - C)) + D \quad \text{and} \quad y = A \cos (B(\theta - C)) + D,$$

when compared to the graphs of $y = \sin \theta$ and $y = \cos \theta$, have a vertical stretch (or **amplitude**) of $|A|$, a **period** of $2\pi / |B|$, a horizontal shift (or **phase shift**) of C, and a **vertical shift** of D (Figure 1.68).

For example, at latitude 40° north (Beijing, Madrid, Philadelphia) there are 12 hours of daylight on the equinoxes (approximately March 21 and September 21), with a maximum of 14.8 hours of daylight on the summer solstice (approximately June 21) and a minimum of 9.2 hours of daylight on the winter solstice (approximately December 21). Using this information, it can be shown that the function

$$D(t) = 2.8 \sin\left(\frac{2\pi}{365}(t - 81)\right) + 12$$

models the number of daylight hours t days after January 1 (Figure 1.69; Exercise 100). The graph of this function is obtained from the graph of $y = \sin t$ by (1) a horizontal scaling by a factor of $2\pi / 365$, (2) a horizontal shift of 81, (3) a vertical scaling by a factor of 2.8, and (4) a vertical shift of 12.

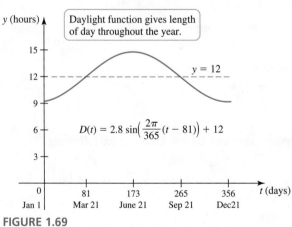

FIGURE 1.69

Inverse Trigonometric Functions

The notion of inverse functions led from exponential functions to logarithmic functions (Section 1.3). We now carry out a similar procedure—this time with trigonometric functions.

Inverse Sine and Cosine Our goal is to develop the inverses of the sine and cosine in detail. The inverses of the other four trigonometric functions then follow in an analogous way. So far, we have asked this question: Given an angle x, what is $\sin x$ or $\cos x$? Now we ask the opposite question: Given a number y, what is the angle x such that $\sin x = y$? Or, what is the angle x such that $\cos x = y$? These are inverse questions.

There are a few things to notice right away. First, these questions don't make sense if $|y| > 1$, because $-1 \le \sin x \le 1$ and $-1 \le \cos x \le 1$. Next, let's select an acceptable value of y, say $y = \frac{1}{2}$, and find the angle x that satisfies $\sin x = y = \frac{1}{2}$. It is apparent that infinitely many angles satisfy $\sin x = \frac{1}{2}$; all angles of the form $\pi/6 \pm 2n\pi$ and $5\pi/6 \pm 2n\pi$, where n is an integer, answer the inverse question (Figure 1.70). A similar situation occurs with the cosine function.

These inverse questions do not have unique answers because $\sin x$ and $\cos x$ are not one-to-one on their domains. To define their inverses, these functions must be restricted to intervals on which they are one-to-one. For the sine function, the standard choice is

Infinitely many values of x satisfy $\sin x = \frac{1}{2}$.

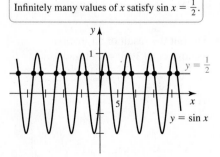

FIGURE 1.70

▷ The notation for the inverse trigonometric functions invites confusion: $\sin^{-1} x$ and $\cos^{-1} x$ do not mean the reciprocals of $\sin x$ and $\cos x$. The expression $\sin^{-1} x$ should be read "*angle whose sine is x,*" and $\cos^{-1} x$ should be read "*angle whose cosine is x.*" The values of $\sin^{-1}$ and $\cos^{-1}$ are angles.

$[-\pi/2, \pi/2]$; for cosine, it is $[0, \pi]$ (Figure 1.71). Now when we ask for the angle x on the interval $[-\pi/2, \pi/2]$ such that $\sin x = \frac{1}{2}$, there is one answer: $x = \pi/6$. When we ask for the angle x on the interval $[0, \pi]$ such that $\cos x = -\frac{1}{2}$, there is one answer: $x = 2\pi/3$.

We define the **inverse sine**, or **arcsine**, denoted $y = \sin^{-1} x$ or $y = \arcsin x$, such that y is the angle whose sine is x, with the provision that y lies in the interval $[-\pi/2, \pi/2]$. Similarly, we define the **inverse cosine**, or **arccosine**, denoted $y = \cos^{-1} x$ or $y = \arccos x$, such that y is the angle whose cosine is x, with the provision that y lies in the interval $[0, \pi]$.

Restrict the domain of $y = \sin x$ to $\left[-\frac{\pi}{2}, \frac{\pi}{2}\right]$.

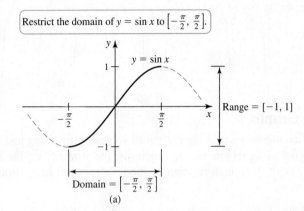

Restrict the domain of $y = \cos x$ to $[0, \pi]$.

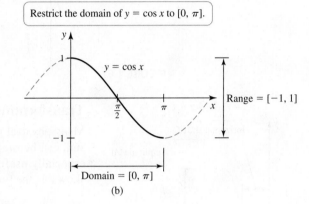

FIGURE 1.71   (a)   (b)

DEFINITION   Inverse Sine and Cosine

$y = \sin^{-1} x$ is the value of y such that $x = \sin y$, where $-\pi/2 \le y \le \pi/2$.
$y = \cos^{-1} x$ is the value of y such that $x = \cos y$, where $0 \le y \le \pi$.
The domain of both $\sin^{-1} x$ and $\cos^{-1} x$ is $\{x: -1 \le x \le 1\}$.

Any invertible function and its inverse satisfy the properties

$$f(f^{-1}(y)) = y \quad \text{and} \quad f^{-1}(f(x)) = x.$$

These properties apply to the inverse sine and cosine, as long as we observe the restrictions on the domains. Here is what we can say:

• $\sin(\sin^{-1} x) = x$ and $\cos(\cos^{-1} x) = x$, for $-1 \le x \le 1$.
• $\sin^{-1}(\sin y) = y$, for $-\pi/2 \le y \le \pi/2$.
• $\cos^{-1}(\cos y) = y$, for $0 \le y \le \pi$.

QUICK CHECK 4 Explain why $\sin^{-1}(\sin 0) = 0$, but $\sin^{-1}(\sin 2\pi) \ne 2\pi$. ◁

EXAMPLE 3   Working with inverse sine and cosine Evaluate the following expressions.

a. $\sin^{-1}(\sqrt{3}/2)$ **b.** $\cos^{-1}(-\sqrt{3}/2)$ **c.** $\cos^{-1}(\cos 3\pi)$ **d.** $\sin\left(\sin^{-1}\frac{1}{2}\right)$

SOLUTION

a. $\sin^{-1}(\sqrt{3}/2) = \pi/3$ because $\sin(\pi/3) = \sqrt{3}/2$ and $\pi/3$ is in the interval $[-\pi/2, \pi/2]$.

b. $\cos^{-1}(-\sqrt{3}/2) = 5\pi/6$ because $\cos(5\pi/6) = -\sqrt{3}/2$ and $5\pi/6$ is in the interval $[0, \pi]$.

c. It's tempting to conclude that $\cos^{-1}(\cos 3\pi) = 3\pi$, but the result of an inverse cosine operation must lie in the interval $[0, \pi]$. Because $\cos(3\pi) = -1$ and $\cos^{-1}(-1) = \pi$, we have

$$\cos^{-1}(\underbrace{\cos 3\pi}_{-1}) = \cos^{-1}(-1) = \pi.$$

d. $\sin\left(\underbrace{\sin^{-1}\frac{1}{2}}_{\pi/6}\right) = \sin\frac{\pi}{6} = \frac{1}{2}$

Graphs and Properties Recall from Section 1.3 that the graph of f^{-1} is obtained by reflecting the graph of f about the identity line $y = x$. This operation produces the graphs of the inverse sine (Figure 1.72) and inverse cosine (Figure 1.73). The graphs make it easy to compare the domain and range of each function and its inverse.

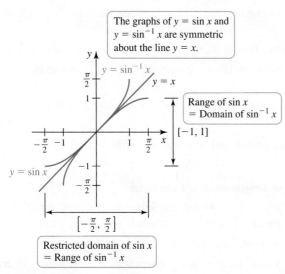

FIGURE 1.72

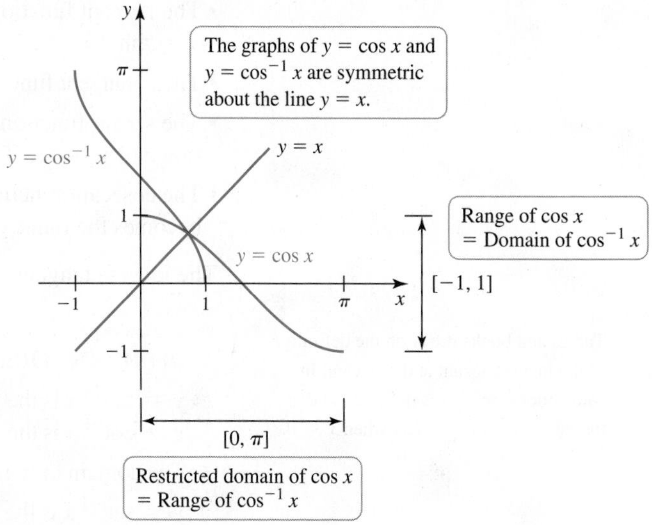

FIGURE 1.73

EXAMPLE 4 Right-triangle relationships

a. Suppose $\theta = \sin^{-1}(2/5)$. Find $\cos \theta$ and $\tan \theta$.

b. Find an alternative form for $\cot(\cos^{-1}(x/4))$ in terms of x.

SOLUTION

a. Relationships between the trigonometric functions and their inverses can often be simplified using a right-triangle sketch. The right triangle in Figure 1.74 satisfies the relationship $\sin \theta = \frac{2}{5}$, or, equivalently, $\theta = \sin^{-1}\frac{2}{5}$. We label the angle θ and the lengths of two sides; then the length of the third side is $\sqrt{21}$ (by the Pythagorean theorem). Now it is easy to read directly from the triangle:

$$\cos \theta = \frac{\sqrt{21}}{5} \quad \text{and} \quad \tan \theta = \frac{2}{\sqrt{21}}.$$

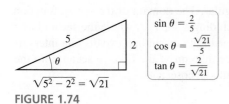

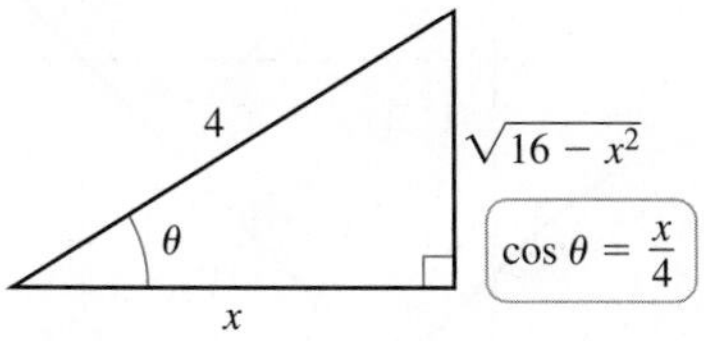

FIGURE 1.74

b. We draw a right triangle with an angle θ satisfying $\cos \theta = x/4$, or, equivalently, $\theta = \cos^{-1}(x/4)$ (Figure 1.75). The length of the third side of the triangle is $\sqrt{16 - x^2}$. It now follows that

$$\cot\left(\underbrace{\cos^{-1}\frac{x}{4}}_{\theta}\right) = \frac{x}{\sqrt{16 - x^2}}.$$

FIGURE 1.75

Related Exercises 57–62 ◄

EXAMPLE 5 A useful identity Use right triangles to explain why $\cos^{-1} x + \sin^{-1} x = \pi/2$.

SOLUTION We draw a right triangle in a unit circle and label the acute angles θ and φ (Figure 1.76). These angles satisfy $\cos \theta = x$, or $\theta = \cos^{-1} x$, and $\sin \varphi = x$, or $\varphi = \sin^{-1} x$. Because θ and φ are complementary angles, we have

$$\frac{\pi}{2} = \theta + \varphi = \cos^{-1} x + \sin^{-1} x.$$

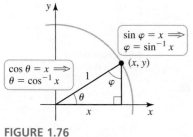

FIGURE 1.76

This result holds for $0 \le x \le 1$. An analogous argument extends the property to $-1 \le x \le 1$.

Related Exercises 63–66 ◄

Other Inverse Trigonometric Functions

The procedures that led to the inverse sine and inverse cosine functions can be used to obtain the other four inverse trigonometric functions. Each of these functions carries a restriction that must be imposed to ensure that an inverse exists:

- The tangent function is one-to-one on $(-\pi/2, \pi/2)$, which becomes the range of $y = \tan^{-1} x$.
- The cotangent function is one-to-one on $(0, \pi)$, which becomes the range of $y = \cot^{-1} x$.
- The secant function is one-to-one on $[0, \pi]$, excluding $x = \pi/2$; this set becomes the range of $y = \sec^{-1} x$.
- The cosecant function is one-to-one on $[-\pi/2, \pi/2]$, excluding $x = 0$; this set becomes the range of $y = \csc^{-1} x$.

The inverse tangent, cotangent, secant, and cosecant are defined as follows.

> ▶ Tables and books differ on the definition of the inverse secant and cosecant. In some books, $\sec^{-1} x$ is defined to lie in the interval $[-\pi, -\pi/2)$ when $x < 0$.

DEFINITION Other Inverse Trigonometric Functions

$y = \tan^{-1} x$ is the value of y such that $x = \tan y$, where $-\pi/2 < y < \pi/2$.
$y = \cot^{-1} x$ is the value of y such that $x = \cot y$, where $0 < y < \pi$.
The domain of both $\tan^{-1} x$ and $\cot^{-1} x$ is $\{x: -\infty < x < \infty\}$.

$y = \sec^{-1} x$ is the value of y such that $x = \sec y$, where $0 \le y \le \pi$, with $y \ne \pi/2$.
$y = \csc^{-1} x$ is the value of y such that $x = \csc y$, where $-\pi/2 \le y \le \pi/2$, with $y \ne 0$.
The domain of both $\sec^{-1} x$ and $\csc^{-1} x$ is $\{x: |x| \ge 1\}$.

The graphs of these inverse functions are obtained by reflecting the graphs of the original trigonometric functions about the line $y = x$ (Figures 1.77–1.80). The inverse secant and cosecant are somewhat irregular. The domain of the secant function (Figure 1.79) is restricted to the set $[0, \pi]$, excluding $x = \pi/2$, where the secant has a vertical asymptote. This asymptote splits the range of the secant into two disjoint intervals $(-\infty, -1]$ and $[1, \infty)$, which, in turn, splits the domain of the inverse secant into the same two intervals. A similar situation occurs with the cosecant.

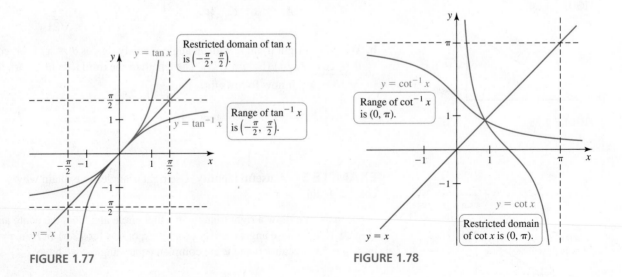

Restricted domain of $\tan x$ is $\left(-\frac{\pi}{2}, \frac{\pi}{2}\right)$.

Range of $\tan^{-1} x$ is $\left(-\frac{\pi}{2}, \frac{\pi}{2}\right)$.

FIGURE 1.77

Range of $\cot^{-1} x$ is $(0, \pi)$.

Restricted domain of $\cot x$ is $(0, \pi)$.

FIGURE 1.78

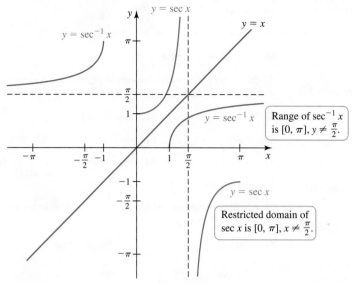

FIGURE 1.79

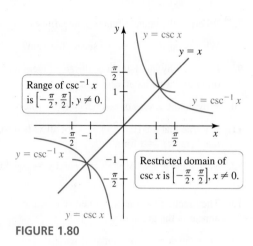

FIGURE 1.80

EXAMPLE 6 **Working with inverse trigonometric functions** Evaluate or simplify the following expressions.

a. $\tan^{-1}\left(-1/\sqrt{3}\right)$ **b.** $\sec^{-1}(-2)$ **c.** $\sin\left(\tan^{-1}x\right)$

SOLUTION

a. The result of an inverse tangent operation must lie in the interval $(-\pi/2, \pi/2)$. Therefore,

$$\tan^{-1}\left(-\frac{1}{\sqrt{3}}\right) = -\frac{\pi}{6} \quad \text{because} \quad \tan\left(-\frac{\pi}{6}\right) = -\frac{1}{\sqrt{3}}.$$

b. The result of an inverse secant operation when $x \le -1$ must lie in the interval $(\pi/2, \pi]$. Therefore,

$$\sec^{-1}(-2) = \frac{2\pi}{3} \quad \text{because} \quad \sec\frac{2\pi}{3} = -2.$$

c. Figure 1.81 shows a right triangle with the relationship $x = \tan\theta$ or $\theta = \tan^{-1}x$, in the case that $0 \le \theta < \pi/2$. We see that

$$\sin\underbrace{\left(\tan^{-1}x\right)}_{\theta} = \frac{x}{\sqrt{1 + x^2}}.$$

The same result follows if $-\pi/2 < \theta < 0$, in which case $x < 0$ and $\sin\theta < 0$.

Related Exercises 67–82 ◄

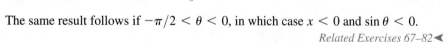

$\tan\theta = x \implies$
$\theta = \tan^{-1}x$

FIGURE 1.81

QUICK CHECK 5 Evaluate $\sec^{-1}1$ and $\tan^{-1}1$. ◄

SECTION 1.4 EXERCISES

Review Questions

1. Define the six trigonometric functions in terms of the sides of a right triangle.

2. Explain how a point $P(x, y)$ on a circle of radius r determines an angle θ and the values of the six trigonometric functions at θ.

3. How is the radian measure of an angle determined?

4. Explain what is meant by the period of a trigonometric function. What are the periods of the six trigonometric functions?

5. What are the three Pythagorean identities for the trigonometric functions?

6. How are the sine and cosine functions related to the other four trigonometric functions?

7. Where is the tangent function undefined?

8. What is the domain of the secant function?

9. Explain why the domain of the sine function must be restricted in order to define its inverse function.

10. Why do the values of $\cos^{-1} x$ lie in the interval $[0, \pi]$?

11. Is it true that $\tan(\tan^{-1} x) = x$ for all x? Is it true that $\tan^{-1}(\tan x) = x$ for all x?

12. Sketch the graphs of $y = \cos x$ and $y = \cos^{-1} x$ on the same set of axes.

13. The function $\tan x$ is undefined at $x = \pm \pi/2$. How does this fact appear in the graph of $y = \tan^{-1} x$?

14. State the domain and range of $\sec^{-1} x$.

Basic Skills

15–22. Evaluating trigonometric functions *Evaluate the following expressions by drawing the unit circle and the appropriate right triangle. Use a calculator only to check your work. All angles are in radians.*

15. $\cos(2\pi/3)$ **16.** $\sin(2\pi/3)$ **17.** $\tan(-3\pi/4)$

18. $\tan(15\pi/4)$ **19.** $\cot(-13\pi/3)$ **20.** $\sec(7\pi/6)$

21. $\cot(-17\pi/3)$ **22.** $\sin(16\pi/3)$

23–28. Evaluating trigonometric functions *Evaluate the following expressions or state that the quantity is undefined. Use a calculator only to check your work.*

23. $\cos 0$ **24.** $\sin(-\pi/2)$ **25.** $\cos(-\pi)$

26. $\tan 3\pi$ **27.** $\sec(5\pi/2)$ **28.** $\cot \pi$

29–36. Trigonometric identities

29. Prove that $\sec \theta = \dfrac{1}{\cos \theta}$.

30. Prove that $\tan \theta = \dfrac{\sin \theta}{\cos \theta}$.

31. Prove that $\tan^2 \theta + 1 = \sec^2 \theta$.

32. Prove that $\dfrac{\sin \theta}{\csc \theta} + \dfrac{\cos \theta}{\sec \theta} = 1$.

33. Prove that $\sec(\pi/2 - \theta) = \csc \theta$.

34. Prove that $\sec(x + \pi) = -\sec x$.

35. Find the exact value of $\cos(\pi/12)$.

36. Find the exact value of $\tan(3\pi/8)$.

37–46. Solving trigonometric equations *Solve the following equations.*

37. $\tan x = 1$ **38.** $2\theta \cos \theta + \theta = 0$

39. $\sin^2 \theta = \frac{1}{4}, 0 \le \theta < 2\pi$ **40.** $\cos^2 \theta = \frac{1}{2}, 0 \le \theta < 2\pi$

41. $\sqrt{2} \sin x - 1 = 0$ **42.** $\sin 3x = \frac{\sqrt{2}}{2}, 0 \le x < 2\pi$

43. $\cos 3x = \sin 3x, 0 \le x < 2\pi$

44. $\sin^2 \theta - 1 = 0$

45. $\sin \theta \cos \theta = 0, 0 \le \theta < 2\pi$

46. $\tan^2 2\theta = 1, 0 \le \theta < \pi$

47–56. Inverse sines and cosines *Without using a calculator, evaluate, if possible, the following expressions.*

47. $\sin^{-1} 1$ **48.** $\cos^{-1}(-1)$ **49.** $\tan^{-1} 1$

50. $\cos^{-1}\left(-\frac{\sqrt{2}}{2}\right)$ **51.** $\sin^{-1} \frac{\sqrt{3}}{2}$ **52.** $\cos^{-1} 2$

53. $\cos^{-1}\left(-\frac{1}{2}\right)$ **54.** $\sin^{-1}(-1)$ **55.** $\cos(\cos^{-1}(-1))$

56. $\cos^{-1}(\cos 7\pi/6)$

57–62. Right-triangle relationships *Draw a right triangle to simplify the given expressions.*

57. $\cos(\sin^{-1} x)$ **58.** $\cos(\sin^{-1}(x/3))$

59. $\sin(\cos^{-1}(x/2))$ **60.** $\sin^{-1}(\cos \theta)$, for $0 \le \theta \le \dfrac{\pi}{2}$

61. $\sin(2 \cos^{-1} x)$ (*Hint:* Use $\sin 2\theta = 2 \sin \theta \cos \theta$.)

62. $\cos(2 \sin^{-1} x)$ (*Hint:* Use $\cos 2\theta = \cos^2 \theta - \sin^2 \theta$.)

63–64. Identities *Prove the following identities.*

63. $\cos^{-1} x + \cos^{-1}(-x) = \pi$ **64.** $\sin^{-1} y + \sin^{-1}(-y) = 0$

65–66. Verifying identities *Sketch a graph of the given pair of functions to conjecture a relationship between the two functions. Then verify the conjecture.*

65. $\sin^{-1} x; \dfrac{\pi}{2} - \cos^{-1} x$ **66.** $\tan^{-1} x; \dfrac{\pi}{2} - \cot^{-1} x$

67–74. Evaluating inverse trigonometric functions *Without using a calculator, evaluate or simplify the following expressions.*

67. $\tan^{-1} \sqrt{3}$ **68.** $\cot^{-1}(-1/\sqrt{3})$

69. $\sec^{-1} 2$ **70.** $\csc^{-1}(-1)$

71. $\tan^{-1}(\tan \pi/4)$ **72.** $\tan^{-1}(\tan 3\pi/4)$

73. $\csc^{-1}(\sec 2)$ **74.** $\tan(\tan^{-1} 1)$

75–80. Right-triangle relationships *Draw a right triangle to simplify the given expressions.*

75. $\cos(\tan^{-1} x)$ **76.** $\tan(\cos^{-1} x)$

77. $\cos(\sec^{-1} x)$ **78.** $\cot(\tan^{-1} 2x)$

79. $\sin\left(\sec^{-1}\left(\dfrac{\sqrt{x^2 + 16}}{4}\right)\right)$ **80.** $\cos\left(\tan^{-1}\left(\dfrac{x}{\sqrt{9 - x^2}}\right)\right)$

81–82. Right-triangle pictures *Express θ in terms of x using the inverse sine, inverse tangent, and inverse secant functions.*

81.   **82.**

Further Explorations

83. Explain why or why not Determine whether the following statements are true and give an explanation or counterexample.

   a. $\sin(a + b) = \sin a + \sin b$.

   b. The equation $\cos\theta = 2$ has multiple real solutions.

   c. The equation $\sin\theta = \frac{1}{2}$ has exactly one solution.

   d. The function $\sin(\pi x/12)$ has a period of 12.

   e. Of the six basic trigonometric functions, only tangent and cotangent have a range of $(-\infty, \infty)$.

   f. $\dfrac{\sin^{-1}x}{\cos^{-1}x} = \tan^{-1}x$.

   g. $\cos^{-1}(\cos(15\pi/16)) = 15\pi/16$.

   h. $\sin^{-1}x = 1/\sin x$.

84–87. One function gives all six *Given the following information about one trigonometric function, evaluate the other five functions.*

84. $\sin\theta = -\dfrac{4}{5}$ and $\pi < \theta < 3\pi/2$ (Find $\cos\theta$, $\tan\theta$, $\cot\theta$, $\sec\theta$, and $\csc\theta$.)

85. $\cos\theta = \dfrac{5}{13}$ and $0 < \theta < \pi/2$

86. $\sec\theta = \dfrac{5}{3}$ and $3\pi/2 < \theta < 2\pi$

87. $\csc\theta = \dfrac{13}{12}$ and $0 < \theta < \pi/2$

88–91. Amplitude and period *Identify the amplitude and period of the following functions.*

88. $f(\theta) = 2\sin 2\theta$

89. $g(\theta) = 3\cos(\theta/3)$

90. $p(t) = 2.5\sin\left(\frac{1}{2}(t - 3)\right)$

91. $q(x) = 3.6\cos(\pi x/24)$

92–95. Graphing sine and cosine functions *Beginning with the graphs of $y = \sin x$ or $y = \cos x$, use shifting and scaling transformations to sketch the graph of the following functions. Use a graphing utility only to check your work.*

92. $f(x) = 3\sin 2x$

93. $g(x) = -2\cos(x/3)$

94. $p(x) = 3\sin(2x - \pi/3) + 1$

95. $q(x) = 3.6\cos(\pi x/24) + 2$

96–97. Designer functions *Design a sine function with the given properties.*

96. It has a period of 12 hr with a minimum value of -4 at $t = 0$ hr and a maximum value of 4 at $t = 6$ hr.

97. It has a period of 24 hr with a minimum value of 10 at $t = 3$ hr and a maximum value of 16 at $t = 15$ hr.

98. Field goal attempt Near the end of the 1950 Rose Bowl football game between the University of California and Ohio State University, Ohio State was preparing to attempt a field goal from a distance of 23 yd from the endline at point A on the edge of the kicking region (see figure). But before the kick, Ohio State committed a penalty and

the ball was backed up 5 yd to point B on the edge of the kicking region. After the game, the Ohio State coach claimed that his team deliberately committed a penalty to improve the kicking angle. Given that a successful kick must go between the uprights of the goal posts G_1 and G_2, is $\angle G_1BG_2$ greater than $\angle G_1AG_2$? (In 1950, the uprights were 23 ft, 4 in apart, equidistant from the origin on the end line. The boundaries of the kicking region are 53 ft, 4 in apart and are equidistant from the y-axis.) (*Source: The College Mathematics Journal, 27,* 4 (Sep 1996))

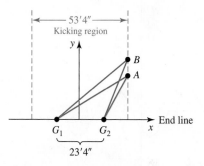

99. A surprising result The Earth is approximately circular in cross section, with a circumference at the equator of 24,882 miles. Suppose we use two ropes to create two concentric circles; one by wrapping a rope around the equator and another using a rope 38 ft longer (see figure). How much space is between the ropes?

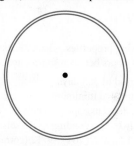

100–103. Graphs to trigonometric functions *Use shifts and scalings of either $y = \sin x$ or $y = \cos x$ to find a function that describes each of the following curves. Answers are unique up to trigonometric identities.*

100.

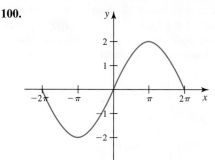

101.

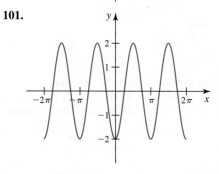

102.

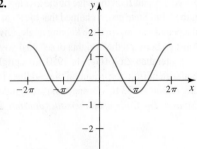

103.

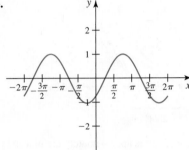

Applications

104. Daylight function for 40° N Verify that the function

$$D(t) = 2.8 \sin\left(\frac{2\pi}{365}(t - 81)\right) + 12$$

has the following properties, where t is measured in days and D is the number of hours between sunrise and sunset.

a. It has a period of 365 days.

b. Its maximum and minimum values are 14.8 and 9.2, respectively, which occur approximately at $t = 172$ and $t = 355$, respectively (corresponding to the solstices).

c. $D(81) = 12$ and $D(264) \approx 12$ (corresponding to the equinoxes).

105. Block on a spring A light block hangs at rest from the end of a spring when it is pulled down 10 cm and released. Assume the block oscillates with an amplitude of 10 cm on either side of its rest position with a period of 1.5 s. Find a function $d(t)$ that gives the displacement of the block t seconds after it is released, where $d(t) > 0$ represents downward displacement.

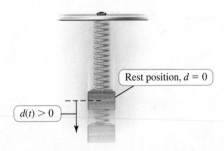

106. Approaching a lighthouse A boat approaches a 50-ft-high lighthouse whose base is at sea level. Let d be the distance between the boat and the base of the lighthouse. Let L be the distance between the boat and the top of the lighthouse. Let θ be the angle of elevation between the boat and the top of the lighthouse.

a. Express d as a function of θ.

b. Express L as a function of θ.

107. Ladders Two ladders of length a lean against opposite walls of an alley with their feet touching (see figure). One ladder extends h feet up the wall and makes a 75° angle with the ground. The other ladder extends k feet up the opposite wall and makes a 45° angle with the ground. Find the width of the alley in terms of h. Assume the ground is horizontal and perpendicular to both walls.

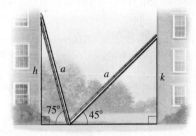

108. Pole in a corner A pole of length L is carried horizontally around a corner where a 3-ft-wide hallway meets a 4-ft-wide hallway. For $0 < \theta < \pi/2$, find the relationship between L and θ at the moment when the pole simultaneously touches both walls and the corner P. Estimate θ when $L = 10$ ft.

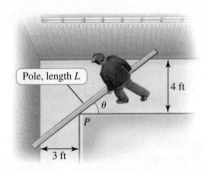

109. Little-known fact The shortest day of the year occurs on the winter solstice (near December 21) and the longest day of the year occurs on the summer solstice (near June 21). However, the latest sunrise and the earliest sunset do not occur on the winter solstice, and the earliest sunrise and the latest sunset do not occur on the summer solstice. At latitude 40° north, the latest sunrise occurs on January 4 at 7:25 A.M. (14 days after the solstice), and the earliest sunset occurs on December 7 at 4:37 P.M. (14 days before the solstice). Similarly, the earliest sunrise occurs on July 2 at 4:30 A.M. (14 days after the solstice) and the latest sunset occurs on June 7 at 7:32 P.M. (14 days before the solstice). Using sine functions, devise a function $s(t)$ that gives the time of sunrise t days after January 1 and a function $S(t)$ that gives the time of sunset t days after January 1. Assume that s and S are measured in minutes and $s = 0$ and $S = 0$ correspond to 4:00 A.M. (all times are standard times). Graph the functions. Then graph the length of the day function $D(t) = S(t) - s(t)$ and show that the longest and shortest days occur on the solstices.

110. Viewing angles An auditorium with a flat floor has a large flat-panel television on one wall. The lower edge of the television is 3 ft above the floor, and the upper edge is 10 ft above the floor (see figure). Express θ in terms of x.

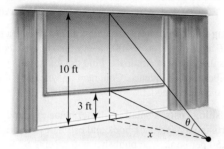

Additional Exercises

111. Area of a circular sector Prove that the area of a sector of a circle of radius r associated with a central angle θ (measured in radians) is $A = \frac{1}{2} r^2 \theta$.

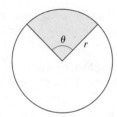

112. Law of cosines Use the figure to prove the law of cosines (which is a generalization of the Pythagorean theorem):
$$c^2 = a^2 + b^2 - 2ab \cos \theta.$$

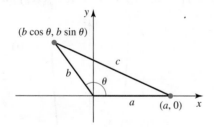

113. Law of sines Use the figure to prove the law of sines:
$$\frac{\sin A}{a} = \frac{\sin B}{b} = \frac{\sin C}{c}.$$

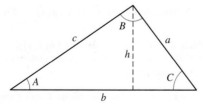

Technology Exercises

114. Intersection points Consider the curves $y = \cos x$ and $y = \dfrac{x}{a}$, where $a > 0$ and $x \geq 0$.

a. At how many points do the curves intersect in the first quadrant when $a = 2$? Find the (approximate) coordinates of the intersection point(s).

b. At how many points do the curves intersect in the first quadrant when $a = 8$? Find the (approximate) coordinates of the intersection point(s).

c. Estimate the value of a such that $y = \cos x$ and $y = \dfrac{x}{a}$ intersect exactly twice in the first quadrant. Find the (approximate) coordinates of the intersection points.

115. The sinc function The sinc (pronounced *sink*) function
$$\text{sinc } x = \begin{cases} \dfrac{\sin x}{x} & \text{if } x \neq 0 \\ 1 & \text{if } x = 0 \end{cases}$$

is used in applications such as digital signal processing.

a. What is the domain of the function $f(x) = \dfrac{\sin x}{x}$?

b. Graph sinc x on the interval $\left[-3\pi, 3\pi \right]$.

c. In the definition of sinc x, why must a value be specified at $x = 0$? Based on the graph in part (b), why is the value sinc $0 = 1$ given?

d. What is the range of sinc x?

e. Describe the roots of sinc x.

f. Describe the behavior of sinc x as $|x|$ increases, with x both positive and negative.

116. Hidden oscillations Consider the function $f(x) = \dfrac{1 - \sin^3 x}{x^2 + 1}$ on $[0, 10]$.

a. Graph the function using a graphing window that reveals all the interesting features of the graph.

b. Using the graph of part (a), find the range of f.

c. Using the graph of part (a), find the roots of f on $[0, 10]$. You may need to use different graphing windows to locate all the roots.

d. Find the points (approximately) at which f has a peak (a local maximum value) or a valley (a local minimum value). Give the function values at these points. Again, different graphing windows or a zoom feature may be needed.

117. A Fourier series Working on the interval $\left[-\pi, \pi \right]$, consider the sum
$$\frac{1}{2} + \frac{4}{\pi^2} \left(\cos x + \frac{\cos 3x}{9} + \frac{\cos 5x}{25} + \frac{\cos 7x}{49} + \cdots \right),$$

where the dots mean that the pattern in the sum continues indefinitely.

a. Graph the first two terms of the sum $\left(\dfrac{1}{2} + \dfrac{4}{\pi^2} \cos x \right)$ on the interval $\left[-\pi, \pi \right]$.

b. Now successively add new terms to the sum and plot the sum with three, four, and five terms. Comment on how the graph changes as you add new terms to the sum.

c. Graph the sum with six, seven, and eight terms. Do the graphs appear to approach a specific function? Describe that function.

QUICK CHECK ANSWERS

1. $3\pi/2$; $225°$ **2.** $\sqrt{3}/2$; $-\sqrt{2}/2$ **3.** Divide both sides of $\sin^2 \theta + \cos^2 \theta = 1$ by $\sin^2 \theta$.   **4.** $\sin^{-1}(\sin 0) = \sin^{-1} 0 = 0$ and $\sin^{-1}(\sin(2\pi)) = \sin^{-1} 0 = 0$ **5.** $0, \pi/4$ ◄

CHAPTER 1   REVIEW EXERCISES

1. **Explain why or why not** Determine whether the following statements are true and give an explanation or counterexample.

a. A function could have the property that $f(-x) = f(x)$, for all x.

b. $\cos(a + b) = \cos a + \cos b$, for all a and b in $[0, 2\pi]$.

c. If f is a linear function of the form $f(x) = mx + b$, then $f(u + v) = f(u) + f(v)$, for all u and v.

d. The function $f(x) = 1 - x$ has the property that $f(f(x)) = x$.

e. The set $\{x : |x + 3| > 4\}$ can be drawn on the number line without lifting your pencil.

f. $\log_{10}(xy) = (\log_{10} x)(\log_{10} y)$.

g. $\sin^{-1}(\sin(2\pi)) = 0$.

2. **Domain and range** Find the domain and range of the following functions.

a. $f(x) = x^5 + \sqrt{x}$ **b.** $g(y) = \dfrac{1}{y - 2}$

c. $h(z) = \sqrt{z^2 - 2z - 3}$

3. **Equations of lines** Find an equation of the lines with the following properties (three different lines). Graph the lines.

a. The line passing through the points $(2, -3)$ and $(4, 2)$

b. The line with slope $\frac{3}{4}$ and x-intercept $(-4, 0)$

c. The line with intercepts $(4, 0)$ and $(0, -2)$

4. **Piecewise linear functions** The parking costs in a city garage are $2.00 for the first half hour and $1.00 for each additional half hour. Graph the function $C = f(t)$ that gives the cost of parking for t hours, where $0 \le t \le 3$.

⊤ 5. **Graphing absolute value** Consider the function $f(x) = 2(x - |x|)$. Express the function in two pieces without using the absolute value. Then graph the function by hand. Use a graphing utility only to check your work.

6. **Function from words** Suppose you plan to take a 500-mile trip in a car that gets 35 mi/gal. Find the function $C = f(p)$ that gives the cost of gasoline for the trip when gasoline costs $p per gallon.

⊤ 7. **Graphing equations** Graph the following equations. Use a graphing utility only to check your work.

a. $2x - 3y + 10 = 0$

b. $y = x^2 + 2x - 3$

c. $x^2 + 2x + y^2 + 4y + 1 = 0$

d. $x^2 - 2x + y^2 - 8y + 5 = 0$

8. **Root functions** Graph the functions $f(x) = x^{1/3}$ and $g(x) = x^{1/4}$. Find all points where the two graphs intersect. For $x > 1$, is $f(x) > g(x)$ or is $g(x) > f(x)$?

9. **Root functions** Find the domain and range of the functions $f(x) = x^{1/7}$ and $g(x) = x^{1/4}$.

10. **Intersection points** Graph the equations $y = x^2$ and $x^2 + y^2 - 7y + 8 = 0$. At what point(s) do the curves intersect?

11. **Boiling-point function** Water boils at $212°$ F at sea level and at $200°$ F at an elevation of 6000 ft. Assume that the boiling point B varies linearly with altitude a. Find the function $B = f(a)$ that describes the dependence. Comment on whether a linear function gives a realistic model.

12. **Publishing costs** A small publisher plans to spend $1000 for advertising a paperback book and estimates the printing cost is $2.50 per book. The publisher will receive $7 for each book sold.

a. Find the function $C = f(x)$ that gives the cost of producing x books.

b. Find the function $R = g(x)$ that gives the revenue from selling x books.

c. Graph the cost and revenue functions, and find the number of books that must be sold for the publisher to break even.

⊤ 13. **Shifting and scaling** Starting with the graph of $f(x) = x^2$, plot the following functions. Use a graphing calculator only to check your work.

a. $f(x + 3)$ **b.** $2f(x - 4)$ **c.** $-f(3x)$ **d.** $f(2(x - 3))$

14. **Shifting and scaling** The graph of f is shown in the figure. Graph the following functions.

a. $f(x + 1)$ **b.** $2f(x - 1)$ **c.** $-f(x/2)$ **d.** $f(2(x - 1))$

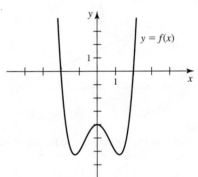

15. **Composite functions** Let $f(x) = x^3$, $g(x) = \sin x$, and $h(x) = \sqrt{x}$.

a. Evaluate $h(g(\pi/2))$.   **b.** Find $h(f(x))$.

c. Find $f(g(h(x)))$.   **d.** Find the domain of $g \circ f$.

e. Find the range of $f \circ g$.

16. **Composite functions** Find functions f and g such that $h = f \circ g$.

a. $h(x) = \sin(x^2 + 1)$ **b.** $h(x) = (x^2 - 4)^{-3}$

c. $h(x) = e^{\cos 2x}$

17–20. Simplifying difference quotients *Evaluate and simplify the difference quotients* $\dfrac{f(x+h)-f(x)}{h}$ *and* $\dfrac{f(x)-f(a)}{x-a}$ *for each function.*

17. $f(x) = x^2 - 2x$

18. $f(x) = 4 - 5x$

19. $f(x) = x^3 + 2$

20. $f(x) = \dfrac{7}{x+3}$

21. Symmetry Identify the symmetry (if any) in the graphs of the following equations.

a. $y = \cos 3x$ **b.** $y = 3x^4 - 3x^2 + 1$
c. $y^2 - 4x^2 = 4$

22–23. Properties of logarithms and exponentials *Use properties of logarithms and exponentials, not a calculator, for the following exercises.*

22. Solve the equation $48 = 6e^{4k}$ for k.

23. Solve the equation $\log_{10} x^2 + 3 \log_{10} x = \log_{10} 32$ for x. Does the answer depend on the base of the log in the equation?

24. Graphs of logarithmic and exponential functions The figure shows the graphs of $y = 2^x$, $y = 3^{-x}$, and $y = -\ln x$. Match each curve with the correct function.

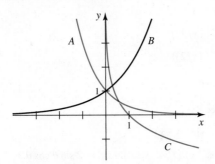

25–26. Existence of inverses *Use analytical methods and/or graphing to determine the intervals on which the following functions have an inverse.*

25. $f(x) = x^3 - 3x^2$ **26.** $g(t) = 2 \sin (t/3)$

27–28. Finding inverses *Find the inverse on the specified interval and express it in the form $y = f^{-1}(x)$. Then graph f and f^{-1}.*

27. $f(x) = x^2 - 4x + 5$, for $x > 2$

28. $f(x) = 1/x^2$, for $x > 0$

29. Degrees and radians

a. Convert $135°$ to radian measure.
b. Convert $4\pi/5$ to degree measure.
c. What is the length of the arc on a circle of radius 10 associated with an angle of $4\pi/3$ (radians)?

30. Graphing sine and cosine functions Use shifts and scalings to graph the following functions, and identify the amplitude and period.

a. $f(x) = 4 \cos (x/2)$ **b.** $g(\theta) = 2 \sin (2\pi\theta/3)$
c. $h(\theta) = -\cos (2(\theta - \pi/4))$

31. Designing functions Find a trigonometric function f that satisfies each set of properties. Answers are not unique.

a. It has a period of 6 with a minimum value of -2 at $t = 0$ and a maximum value of 2 at $t = 3$.
b. It has a period of 24 with a maximum value of 20 at $t = 6$ and a minimum value of 10 at $t = 18$.

32. Graph to function Find a trigonometric function f represented by the graph in the figure.

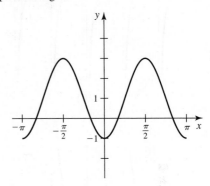

33. Matching Match each function a–f with the corresponding graphs A–F.

a. $f(x) = -\sin x$ **b.** $f(x) = \cos 2x$
c. $f(x) = \tan (x/2)$ **d.** $f(x) = -\sec x$
e. $f(x) = \cot 2x$ **f.** $f(x) = \sin^2 x$

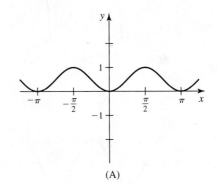

(A)

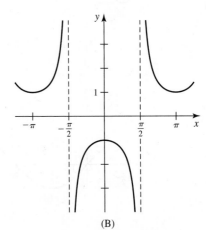

(B)

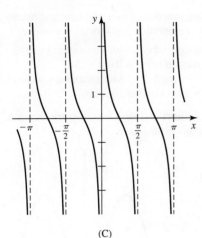

(C)

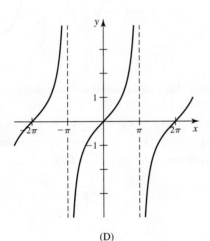

(D)

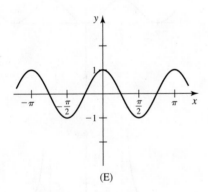

(E)

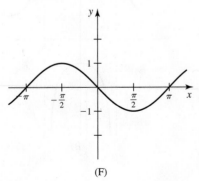

(F)

34–35. Intersection points *Find the points at which the curves intersect on the given interval.*

34. $y = \sec x$ and $y = 2$ on $(-\pi/2, \pi/2)$

35. $y = \sin x$ and $y = -\frac{1}{2}$ on $(0, 2\pi)$

36–42. Inverse sines and cosines *Without using a calculator, evaluate or simplify the following expressions.*

36. $\sin^{-1} \frac{\sqrt{3}}{2}$

37. $\cos^{-1} \frac{\sqrt{3}}{2}$

38. $\cos^{-1}\left(-\frac{1}{2}\right)$

39. $\sin^{-1}(-1)$

40. $\cos\left(\cos^{-1}(-1)\right)$

41. $\sin\left(\sin^{-1} x\right)$

42. $\cos^{-1}(\sin 3\pi)$

43. Right triangles Given that $\theta = \sin^{-1}\left(\frac{12}{13}\right)$, evaluate $\cos\theta$, $\tan\theta$, $\cot\theta$, $\sec\theta$, and $\csc\theta$.

44–51. Right-triangle relationships *Draw a right triangle to simplify the given expression. Assume $x > 0$ and $0 \le \theta \le \pi/2$.*

44. $\cos\left(\tan^{-1} x\right)$

45. $\sin\left(\cos^{-1}(x/2)\right)$

46. $\tan\left(\sec^{-1}(x/2)\right)$

47. $\cot^{-1}(\tan\theta)$

48. $\csc^{-1}(\sec\theta)$

49. $\sin^{-1} x + \sin^{-1}(-x)$

50. $\sin\left(2\cos^{-1} x\right)$ (*Hint:* Use $\sin 2\theta = 2\sin\theta\cos\theta$.)

51. $\cos\left(2\sin^{-1} x\right)$ (*Hint:* Use $\cos 2\theta = \cos^2\theta - \sin^2\theta$.)

52. Stereographic projections A common way of displaying a sphere (such as Earth) on a plane (such as a map) is to use a *stereographic projection*. Here is the two-dimensional version of the method, which maps a circle to a line. Let P be a point on the right half of a circle of radius R identified by the angle φ. Find the function $x = F(\varphi)$ that gives the x-coordinate ($x \ge 0$) corresponding to φ for $0 < \varphi \le \pi$.

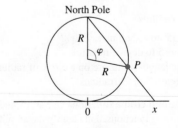

AP®   PRACTICE QUESTIONS

The following questions are intended to help you prepare for the AP exam. They are not questions from actual AP exams.

Section 1 Part A, Multiple Choice, No Technology

1. The domain of the function $f(x) = \sqrt{4 - x^2}$ is
   (A) $|x| \geq 2.$ (B) $-2 < x < 2.$
   (C) $|x| > 2.$ (D) $-2 \leq x \leq 2.$
   (E) $-2 < x \leq 2.$

2. If $f(x) = x^2$, then which of the following graphs corresponds to $-f(x - 2) + 1$?

   (A)
   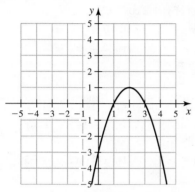

   (B)
   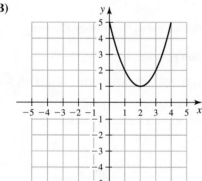

   (C)
   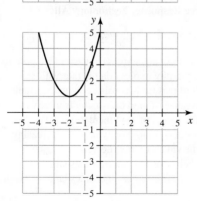

   (D)
   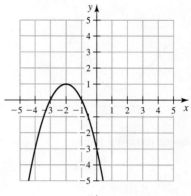

   (E)
   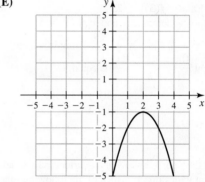

3. Which of the following functions has the range $0 < y < \infty$?
   (A) $y = 3x^2$ (B) $y = e^{-2x}$ (C) $y = \ln 2x$
   (D) $y = \tan x$ (E) $y = x^2 + 1$

4. Which of the following functions has a graph that is symmetric about the origin?
   I. $f(x) = x \sin x$ II. $f(x) = x^5 + 3x + 1$ III. $f(x) = x^3 - 4x$
   (A) I only   (B) II only   (C) III only
   (D) I and II only   (E) I and III only

5. Which function describes the following graph?

   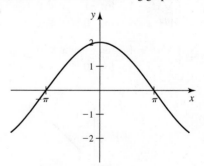

   (A) $f(x) = 2 \sin \dfrac{x}{2}$ (B) $f(x) = 2 \sin 2x$ (C) $f(x) = \cos 2x$

   (D) $f(x) = \cos \dfrac{x}{2}$ (E) $f(x) = 2 \cos \dfrac{x}{2}$

6. Consider the graphs of the functions f and g shown below.

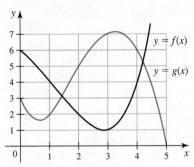

Which of the following statements is true?

(A) $f(g(1)) = 2$ and $g(f(1)) = 6$.
(B) $f(g(0)) = 1$ and $g(f(0)) = 6$.
(C) $f(g(2)) = 7$ and $g(f(2)) = 5$.
(D) $f(g(3)) = 1$ and $g(f(3)) = 2$.
(E) $f(g(4))$ cannot be determined and $g(f(4)) = 5$.

7. Suppose $f(x) = x^2 - 3$ and $x = 4$. When simplified, the difference quotient $\dfrac{f(x + h) - f(x)}{h}$ is equal to

(A) 1.
(B) $f(h)/h$.
(C) $8 + h - 6$.
(D) $8 + h$.
(E) $\dfrac{h^2 + 8h - 6}{h}$.

8. The graph of f in the figure consists of a quarter circle of radius 1 and a line segment with slope 1. Which of the following functions is a correct definition of f on the interval $[-1, 1]$?

(A) $f(x) = \begin{cases} 1 + x & \text{for } -1 \le x \le 0 \\ \sqrt{1 - x^2} & \text{for } 0 < x \le 1 \end{cases}$

(B) $f(x) = \begin{cases} \sqrt{1 - x^2} & \text{for } -1 \le x \le 0 \\ 1 - x & \text{for } 0 < x \le 1 \end{cases}$

(C) $f(x) = \begin{cases} \sqrt{1 - x^2} & \text{for } -1 \le x \le 0 \\ 1 + x & \text{for } 0 < x \le 1 \end{cases}$

(D) $f(x) = \begin{cases} \sqrt{x^2 - 1} & \text{for } -1 \le x \le 0 \\ 1 + x & \text{for } 0 < x \le 1 \end{cases}$

(E) $f(x) = \begin{cases} \sqrt{x^2 + 1} & \text{for } -1 \le x \le 0 \\ 1 + x & \text{for } 0 < x \le 1 \end{cases}$

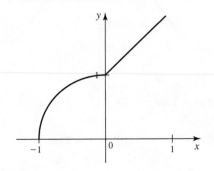

9. The functions f and g have values shown in the table. For which values of x does $f(g(x)) = g(f(x))$?

x	1	2	3	4	5
$f(x)$	3	4	5	1	2
$g(x)$	2	1	4	5	3

(A) 1, 2, 3, 4, and 5   **(B)** 1, 3, and 4 only   **(C)** 1, 4, and 5 only
(D) 1 and 4 only   **(E)** 4 and 5 only

10. Simplify the expression $6e^{2 \ln 4 + 3}$.
(A) $96e^3$ **(B)** $24e^2$ **(C)** $48e^2$ **(D)** $12e^4$ **(E)** $48e^3$

11. What is the range of $y = 2 \cos^{-1} x$?
(A) $0 \le y \le \pi$ **(B)** $0 < y < \pi$
(C) $0 \le y \le 2\pi$ **(D)** $-\pi \le y \le \pi$
(E) $-\dfrac{\pi}{2} \le y \le \dfrac{\pi}{2}$

12. Where does the curve $y = e^{-x} - 2$ intersect the x- and y-axes?

(A) $x = \ln\dfrac{1}{2}, y = -2$ **(B)** $x = \ln 2, y = -1$

(C) $x = \ln\dfrac{1}{2}, y = -1$ **(D)** $x = \ln 2, y = -2$

(E) $x = 1, y = -1$

Section 1 Part B, Multiple Choice, Technology Allowed

13. Estimate the smallest positive root of $f(x) = x^2 e^{-x} - \dfrac{1}{5}$.

(A) -0.371 **(B)** 0.605   **(C)** 4.708   **(D)** 3.816   **(E)** -4.708

14. Find the slope of the secant line on the graph of $y = 2 \tan^{-1} x$ connecting the points whose x-coordinates are 0 and 1.

(A) $\dfrac{\pi}{2}$ **(B)** $\dfrac{4}{\pi}$ **(C)** $\dfrac{2}{\pi}$ **(D)** $-\dfrac{4}{\pi}$ **(E)** $\dfrac{\pi}{4}$

Section 2 Part A, Free Response, Technology Allowed

1. Consider the function $f(x) = \dfrac{e^x + 3e^{-x}}{2e^x - e^{-x}}$.

a. Find the domain of f and express any excluded points exactly.
b. Use a graphing utility to plot f on the interval $[-3, 3]$. Be sure that the result of part (a) is consistent with the graph.
c. Give the interval(s) (if any) on which f is increasing; that is, as x increases, the values of $f(x)$ increases.
d. Give the interval(s) (if any) on which f is decreasing; that is, as x increases, the values of $f(x)$ decreases.
e. Describe the behavior of f as x becomes large and positive.
f. Describe the behavior of f as x becomes large in magnitude and negative.

Section 2 Part B, Free Response, No Technology

2. Consider the function $f(x) = \sqrt{9 - x^2}$.

a. What is the domain of f?
b. What is the range of f?
c. Find the zeros of f.

d. Evaluate $f(0)$.

e. As x increases from $x = -3$ to $x = 0$, do the values of $f(x)$ increase or decrease?

f. As x increases from $x = 0$ to $x = 3$, do the values of $f(x)$ increase or decrease?

g. Based only on the results of parts (a)–(f), sketch a plausible graph of f.

3. Use the following steps to graph the function

$$f(x) = 2 \sin\left(2x - \frac{\pi}{2}\right).$$

a. Find constants a, b, and c such that $f(x) = c \sin(a(x - b))$.

b. Graph $y = \sin x$ on the interval $[-2\pi, 2\pi]$.

c. Using parts (a)–(b), graph $y = \sin ax$.

d. Using parts (a)–(c), graph $y = \sin a(x - b)$.

e. Using parts (a)–(d), graph $y = c \sin a(x - b)$.

4. When an object falls from rest in a vacuum, the time in seconds required for the object to fall a distance of d feet is given by the function $f(d) = \dfrac{\sqrt{d}}{4}$.

a. Sketch a graph of the function with the points $(16, f(16))$ and $(64, f(64))$ plotted on the graph. Choose an appropriate scale for each axis of your graph. What are the units on the horizontal axis? What are the units on the vertical axis?

b. Find an equation of the secant line that passes though the points $(16, f(16))$ and $(64, f(64))$. State the units associated with the slope of the secant line.

c. Compute and simplify the difference quotient $\dfrac{f(d) - f(a)}{d - a}$ by rationalizing the numerator. What does this difference quotient measure in physical terms?

Chapter 1 Guided Projects

Applications of the material in this chapter and related topics can be found in the following Guided Projects. For additional information, see the Preface.

- Problem-solving skills
- Constant-rate problems
- Functions in action I
- Functions in action II

- Supply and demand
- Phase and amplitude
- Atmospheric CO_2
- Acid, noise, and earthquakes

2 Limits

Biologists often use mathematical models to describe communities of organisms—anything from a culture of cells to a herd of zebras. These models result in functions that approximate the population of the community as it changes in time. An important question concerns the long-term behavior of these population functions. Does the population approach a steady-state level, which corresponds to a stable community (as in the first figure)? Does the population oscillate continually without settling at some fixed level (as in the second figure)? Or does the population decrease to zero, indicating that the organism becomes extinct (as in the third figure)? Such questions about the behavior of functions are answered using the powerful idea of a *limit*.

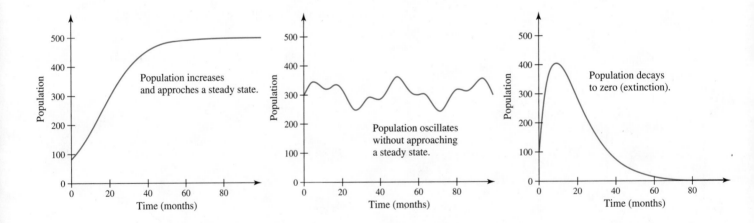

Population increases and approches a steady state.

Population oscillates without approaching a steady state.

Population decays to zero (extinction).

Chapter Preview   All of calculus is based on the idea of a *limit*. Not only are limits important in their own right, but they underlie the two fundamental operations of calculus: differentiation (calculating derivatives) and integration (evaluating integrals). Derivatives enable us to talk about the instantaneous rate of change of a function, which, in turn, leads to concepts such as velocity and acceleration, population growth rates, marginal cost, and flow rates. Integrals enable us to compute areas under curves, surface areas, and volumes. Because of the incredible reach of this single idea, it is essential to develop a solid understanding of limits. We first present limits intuitively by showing how they arise in computing instantaneous velocities and finding slopes of tangent lines. As the chapter progresses, we build more rigor into the definition of the limit, and we examine the different ways in which limits exist or fail to exist. The chapter concludes by introducing the important property called *continuity* and by giving the formal definition of a limit.

2.1 The Idea of Limits

This brief opening section illustrates how limits arise in two seemingly unrelated problems: finding the instantaneous velocity of a moving object and finding the slope of a line tangent to a curve. These two problems provide important insights into limits, and they reappear in various forms throughout the book.

Average Velocity

Suppose you want to calculate your average velocity as you travel along a straight highway. If you pass milepost 100 at noon and milepost 130 at 12:30 P.M., you travel 30 miles in a half-hour, so your **average velocity** over this time interval is $(30 \text{ mi})/(0.5 \text{ hr}) = 60 \text{ mi/hr}$. By contrast, even though your average velocity may be 60 mi/hr, it's almost certain that your **instantaneous velocity**, the speed indicated by the speedometer, varies from one moment to the next.

EXAMPLE 1   Average velocity A rock is launched vertically upward from the ground with a speed of 96 ft/s. Neglecting air resistance, a well-known formula from physics states that the position of the rock after t seconds is given by the function

$$s(t) = -16t^2 + 96t.$$

The position s is measured in feet with $s = 0$ corresponding to the ground. Find the average velocity of the rock between each pair of times.

a. $t = 1$ s and $t = 3$ s   **b.** $t = 1$ s and $t = 2$ s

SOLUTION Figure 2.1 shows the position of the rock on the time interval $0 \le t \le 3$.

a. The average velocity of the rock over any time interval $[t_0, t_1]$ is the change in position divided by the elapsed time:

$$v_{av} = \frac{s(t_1) - s(t_0)}{t_1 - t_0}$$

Therefore, the average velocity over the interval $[1, 3]$ is

$$v_{av} = \frac{s(3) - s(1)}{3 - 1} = \frac{144 \text{ ft} - 80 \text{ ft}}{3 \text{ s} - 1 \text{ s}} = \frac{64 \text{ ft}}{2 \text{ s}} = 32 \text{ ft/s}.$$

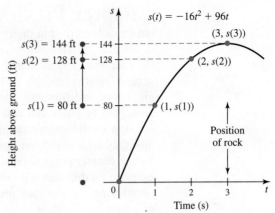

FIGURE 2.1

Here is an important observation: As shown in Figure 2.2a, the average velocity is simply the slope of the line joining the points $(1, s(1))$ and $(3, s(3))$ on the graph of the position function.

b. The average velocity of the rock over the interval $[1, 2]$ is

$$v_{av} = \frac{s(2) - s(1)}{2 - 1} = \frac{128 \text{ ft} - 80 \text{ ft}}{2 \text{ s} - 1 \text{ s}} = \frac{48 \text{ ft}}{1 \text{ s}} = 48 \text{ ft/s}.$$

Again, the average velocity is the slope of the line joining the points $(1, s(1))$ and $(2, s(2))$ on the graph of the position function (Figure 2.2b).

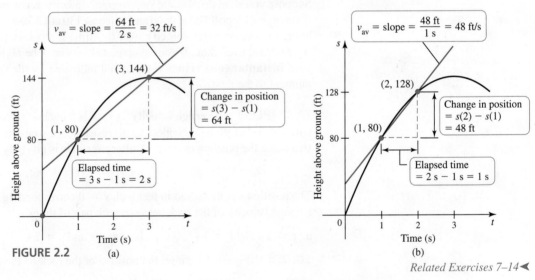

FIGURE 2.2   (a)   (b)

Related Exercises 7–14 ◄

> **QUICK CHECK 1** In Example 1, what is the average velocity between $t = 2$ and $t = 3$? ◄

> ▷ See Section 1.1 for a discussion of secant lines.

In Example 1, we computed slopes of lines passing through two points on a curve. Any such line joining two points on a curve is called a **secant line**. The slope of the secant line, denoted m_{sec}, for the position function in Example 1 on the interval $[t_0, t_1]$ is

$$m_{sec} = \frac{s(t_1) - s(t_0)}{t_1 - t_0}$$

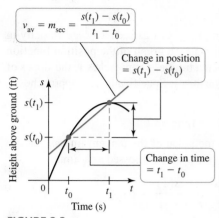

$$v_{av} = m_{sec} = \frac{s(t_1) - s(t_0)}{t_1 - t_0}$$

Change in position $= s(t_1) - s(t_0)$

Change in time $= t_1 - t_0$

Height above ground (ft)

$s(t_1)$

$s(t_0)$

$0 \quad t_0 \quad t_1 \quad t$

Time (s)

FIGURE 2.3

Example 1 demonstrates that the average velocity is the slope of a secant line on the graph of the position function; that is, $v_{av} = m_{sec}$ (Figure 2.3).

Instantaneous Velocity

To compute the average velocity, we use the position of the object at *two* distinct points in time. How do we compute the instantaneous velocity at a *single* point in time? As illustrated in Example 2, the instantaneous velocity at a point $t = t_0$ is determined by computing average velocities over intervals $[t_0, t_1]$ that decrease in length. As t_1 approaches t_0, the average velocities typically approach a unique number, which is the instantaneous velocity. This single number is called a **limit**.

QUICK CHECK 2 Explain the difference between average velocity and instantaneous velocity. ◄

EXAMPLE 2 **Instantaneous velocity** Estimate the *instantaneous velocity* of the rock in Example 1 at the *single* point $t = 1$.

SOLUTION We are interested in the instantaneous velocity at $t = 1$, so we compute the average velocity over smaller and smaller time intervals $[1, t]$ using the formula

$$v_{av} = \frac{s(t) - s(1)}{t - 1}.$$

Notice that these average velocities are also slopes of secant lines, several of which are shown in Table 2.1. We see that as t approaches 1, the average velocities appear to approach 64 ft/s. In fact, we could make the average velocity as close to 64 ft/s as we like by taking t sufficiently close to 1. Therefore, 64 ft/s is a reasonable estimate of the instantaneous velocity at $t = 1$.

Related Exercises 15–20 ◄

In language to be introduced in Section 2.2, we say that the limit of v_{av} as t approaches 1 equals the instantaneous velocity v_{inst}, which is 64 ft/s. This statement is written compactly as

$$v_{inst} = \lim_{t \to 1} v_{av} = \lim_{t \to 1} \frac{s(t) - s(1)}{t - 1} = 64 \text{ ft/s}.$$

Figure 2.4 gives a graphical illustration of this limit.

Table 2.1

Time interval	Average velocity
$[1, 2]$	48 ft/s
$[1, 1.5]$	56 ft/s
$[1, 1.1]$	62.4 ft/s
$[1, 1.01]$	63.84 ft/s
$[1, 1.001]$	63.984 ft/s
$[1, 1.0001]$	63.998 ft/s

➤ The same instantaneous velocity is obtained as t approaches 1 from the left (with $t < 1$) and as t approaches 1 from the right (with $t > 1$).

$0 \qquad t \quad 1 \quad t \qquad 2 \qquad t$

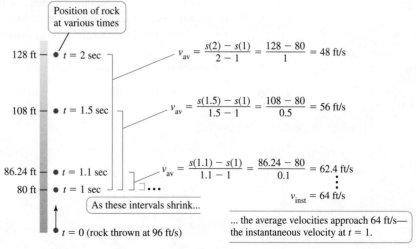

Position of rock at various times

128 ft — ● $t = 2$ sec

108 ft — ● $t = 1.5$ sec

86.24 ft — ● $t = 1.1$ sec
80 ft — ● $t = 1$ sec

As these intervals shrink...

↑
● $t = 0$ (rock thrown at 96 ft/s)

$v_{av} = \dfrac{s(2) - s(1)}{2 - 1} = \dfrac{128 - 80}{1} = 48$ ft/s

$v_{av} = \dfrac{s(1.5) - s(1)}{1.5 - 1} = \dfrac{108 - 80}{0.5} = 56$ ft/s

$v_{av} = \dfrac{s(1.1) - s(1)}{1.1 - 1} = \dfrac{86.24 - 80}{0.1} = 62.4$ ft/s
⋮

$v_{inst} = 64$ ft/s

... the average velocities approach 64 ft/s— the instantaneous velocity at $t = 1$.

FIGURE 2.4

▷ We define tangent lines carefully in Section 3.1. For the moment, imagine zooming in on a point P on a smooth curve. As you zoom in, the curve appears more and more like a line passing through P. This line is the *tangent line* at P. Because a smooth curve approaches a line as we zoom in on a point, a smooth curve is said to be *locally linear* at any given point.

Slope of the Tangent Line

Several important conclusions follow from Examples 1 and 2. Each average velocity in Table 2.1 corresponds to the slope of a secant line on the graph of the position function (Figure 2.5). Just as the average velocities approach a limit as t approaches 1, the slopes of the secant lines approach the same limit as t approaches 1. Specifically, as t approaches 1, two things happen:

1. The secant lines approach a unique line called the **tangent line**.

2. The slopes of the secant lines m_{sec} approach the slope of the tangent line m_{tan} at the point $(1, s(1))$. Thus, the slope of the tangent line is also expressed as a limit:

$$m_{tan} = \lim_{t \to 1} m_{sec} = \lim_{t \to 1} \frac{s(t) - s(1)}{t - 1} = 64.$$

This limit is the same limit that defines the instantaneous velocity. Therefore, the instantaneous velocity at $t = 1$ is the slope of the line tangent to the position curve at $t = 1$.

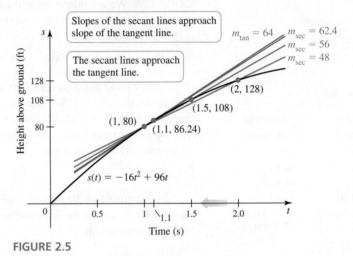

FIGURE 2.5

QUICK CHECK 3 In Figure 2.5, is m_{tan} at $t = 2$ greater than or less than m_{tan} at $t = 1$? ◁

The parallels between average and instantaneous velocities, on one hand, and between slopes of secant lines and tangent lines, on the other, illuminate the power behind the idea of a limit. As $t \to 1$, slopes of secant lines approach the slope of a tangent line. And as $t \to 1$, average velocities approach an instantaneous velocity. Figure 2.6 summarizes these two parallel limit processes. These ideas lie at the foundation of what follows in the coming chapters.

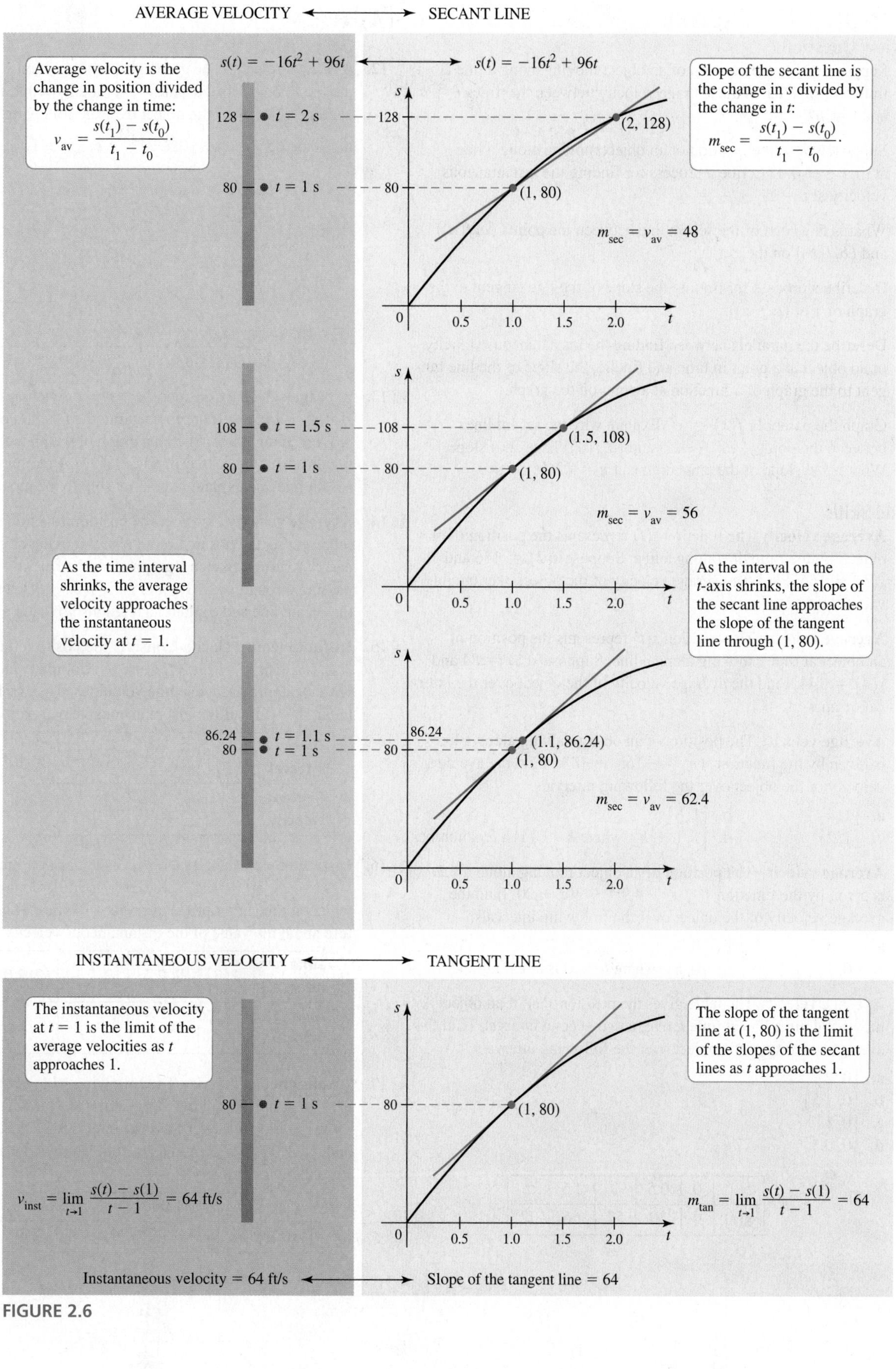

AVERAGE VELOCITY ⟷ SECANT LINE

Average velocity is the change in position divided by the change in time:
$$v_{av} = \frac{s(t_1) - s(t_0)}{t_1 - t_0}.$$

$s(t) = -16t^2 + 96t$ ⟷ $s(t) = -16t^2 + 96t$

Slope of the secant line is the change in s divided by the change in t:
$$m_{sec} = \frac{s(t_1) - s(t_0)}{t_1 - t_0}.$$

128 $\bullet$ $t = 2$ s

80 $\bullet$ $t = 1$ s

(2, 128)

(1, 80)

$m_{sec} = v_{av} = 48$

108 $\bullet$ $t = 1.5$ s

80 $\bullet$ $t = 1$ s

(1.5, 108)

(1, 80)

$m_{sec} = v_{av} = 56$

As the time interval shrinks, the average velocity approaches the instantaneous velocity at $t = 1$.

As the interval on the t-axis shrinks, the slope of the secant line approaches the slope of the tangent line through (1, 80).

86.24 $\bullet$ $t = 1.1$ s
80 $\bullet$ $t = 1$ s

(1.1, 86.24)
(1, 80)

$m_{sec} = v_{av} = 62.4$

INSTANTANEOUS VELOCITY ⟷ TANGENT LINE

The instantaneous velocity at $t = 1$ is the limit of the average velocities as t approaches 1.

The slope of the tangent line at (1, 80) is the limit of the slopes of the secant lines as t approaches 1.

80 $\bullet$ $t = 1$ s

(1, 80)

$v_{inst} = \lim_{t \to 1} \frac{s(t) - s(1)}{t - 1} = 64$ ft/s

$m_{tan} = \lim_{t \to 1} \frac{s(t) - s(1)}{t - 1} = 64$

Instantaneous velocity = 64 ft/s ⟷ Slope of the tangent line = 64

FIGURE 2.6

SECTION 2.1 EXERCISES

Review Questions

1. Suppose $s(t)$ is the position of an object moving along a line at time $t \geq 0$. What is the average velocity between the times $t = a$ and $t = b$?

2. Suppose $s(t)$ is the position of an object moving along a line at time $t \geq 0$. Describe a process for finding the instantaneous velocity at $t = a$.

3. What is the slope of the secant line between the points $(a, f(a))$ and $(b, f(b))$ on the graph of f?

4. Describe a process for finding the slope of the line tangent to the graph of f at $(a, f(a))$.

5. Describe the parallels between finding the instantaneous velocity of an object at a point in time and finding the slope of the line tangent to the graph of a function at a point on the graph.

6. Graph the parabola $f(x) = x^2$. Explain why the secant lines between the points $(-a, f(-a))$ and $(a, f(a))$ have zero slope. What is the slope of the tangent line at $x = 0$?

Basic Skills

7. **Average velocity** The function $s(t)$ represents the position of an object at time t moving along a line. Suppose $s(2) = 136$ and $s(3) = 156$. Find the average velocity of the object over the interval of time $[2, 3]$.

8. **Average velocity** The function $s(t)$ represents the position of an object at time t moving along a line. Suppose $s(1) = 84$ and $s(4) = 144$. Find the average velocity of the object over the interval of time $[1, 4]$.

9. **Average velocity** The position of an object moving along a line is given by the function $s(t) = -16t^2 + 128t$. Find the average velocity of the object over the following intervals.

   a. $[1, 4]$ b. $[1, 3]$
   c. $[1, 2]$ d. $[1, 1 + h]$, where $h > 0$ is a real number

10. **Average velocity** The position of an object moving along a line is given by the function $s(t) = -4.9t^2 + 30t + 20$. Find the average velocity of the object over the following intervals.

    a. $[0, 3]$ b. $[0, 2]$
    c. $[0, 1]$ d. $[0, h]$, where $h > 0$ is a real number

11. **Average velocity** The table gives the position $s(t)$ of an object moving along a line at time t, over a two-second interval. Find the average velocity of the object over the following intervals.

    a. $[0, 2]$
    b. $[0, 1.5]$
    c. $[0, 1]$
    d. $[0, 0.5]$

t	0	0.5	1	1.5	2
$s(t)$	0	30	52	66	72

12. **Average velocity** The graph gives the position $s(t)$ of an object moving along a line at time t, over a 2.5-second interval. Find the average velocity of the object over the following intervals.

    a. $[0.5, 2.5]$ b. $[0.5, 2]$ c. $[0.5, 1.5]$ d. $[0.5, 1]$

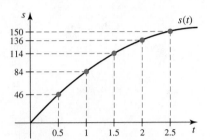

13. **Average velocity** Consider the position function $s(t) = -16t^2 + 100t$ representing the position of an object moving along a line. Sketch a graph of s with the secant line passing through $(0.5, s(0.5))$ and $(2, s(2))$. Determine the slope of the secant line and explain its relationship to the moving object.

14. **Average velocity** Consider the position function $s(t) = \sin \pi t$ representing the position of an object moving along a line on the end of a spring. Sketch a graph of s together with a secant line passing through $(0, s(0))$ and $(0.5, s(0.5))$. Determine the slope of the secant line and explain its relationship to the moving object.

15. **Instantaneous velocity** Consider the position function $s(t) = -16t^2 + 128t$ (Exercise 9). Complete the following table with the appropriate average velocities. Then make a conjecture about the value of the instantaneous velocity at $t = 1$.

Time interval	$[1, 2]$	$[1, 1.5]$	$[1, 1.1]$	$[1, 1.01]$	$[1, 1.001]$
Average velocity					

16. **Instantaneous velocity** Consider the position function $s(t) = -4.9t^2 + 30t + 20$ (Exercise 10). Complete the following table with the appropriate average velocities. Then make a conjecture about the value of the instantaneous velocity at $t = 2$.

Time interval	$[2, 3]$	$[2, 2.5]$	$[2, 2.1]$	$[2, 2.01]$	$[2, 2.001]$
Average velocity					

17. **Instantaneous velocity** The following table gives the position $s(t)$ of an object moving along a line at time t. Determine the average velocities over the time intervals $[1, 1.01]$, $[1, 1.001]$, and $[1, 1.0001]$. Then make a conjecture about the value of the instantaneous velocity at $t = 1$.

t	1	1.0001	1.001	1.01
$s(t)$	64	64.00479984	64.047984	64.4784

18. Instantaneous velocity The following table gives the position $s(t)$ of an object moving along a line at time t. Determine the average velocities over the time intervals $[2, 2.01]$, $[2, 2.001]$, and $[2, 2.0001]$. Then make a conjecture about the value of the instantaneous velocity at $t = 2$.

t	2	2.0001	2.001	2.01
$s(t)$	56	55.99959984	55.995984	55.9584

19. Instantaneous velocity Consider the position function $s(t) = -16t^2 + 100t$. Complete the following table with the appropriate average velocities. Then make a conjecture about the value of the instantaneous velocity at $t = 3$.

Time interval	Average velocity
$[2, 3]$	
$[2.9, 3]$	
$[2.99, 3]$	
$[2.999, 3]$	
$[2.9999, 3]$	

20. Instantaneous velocity Consider the position function $s(t) = 3 \sin t$ that describes a block bouncing vertically on a spring. Complete the following table with the appropriate average velocities. Then make a conjecture about the value of the instantaneous velocity at $t = \pi/2$.

Time interval	Average velocity
$[\pi/2, \pi]$	
$[\pi/2, \pi/2 + 0.1]$	
$[\pi/2, \pi/2 + 0.01]$	
$[\pi/2, \pi/2 + 0.001]$	
$[\pi/2, \pi/2 + 0.0001]$	

Further Explorations

21–24. Instantaneous velocity *For the following position functions, make a table of average velocities similar to those in Exercises 19 and 20 and make a conjecture about the instantaneous velocity at the indicated time.*

21. $s(t) = -16t^2 + 80t + 60$ at $t = 3$

22. $s(t) = 20 \cos t$ at $t = \pi/2$

23. $s(t) = 40 \sin 2t$ at $t = 0$

24. $s(t) = 20/(t + 1)$ at $t = 0$

25–28. Slopes of tangent lines *For the following functions, make a table of slopes of secant lines and make a conjecture about the slope of the tangent line at the indicated point.*

25. $f(x) = 2x^2$ at $x = 2$ **26.** $f(x) = 3 \cos x$ at $x = \pi/2$

27. $f(x) = e^x$ at $x = 0$ **28.** $f(x) = x^3 - x$ at $x = 1$

29. Tangent lines with zero slope

a. Graph the function $f(x) = x^2 - 4x + 3$.
b. Identify the point $(a, f(a))$ at which the function has a tangent line with zero slope.
c. Confirm your answer to part (b) by making a table of slopes of secant lines to approximate the slope of the tangent line at this point.

30. Tangent lines with zero slope

a. Graph the function $f(x) = 4 - x^2$.
b. Identify the point $(a, f(a))$ at which the function has a tangent line with zero slope.
c. Consider the point $(a, f(a))$ found in part (b). Is it true that the secant line between $(a - h, f(a - h))$ and $(a + h, f(a + h))$ has slope zero for any value of $h \neq 0$?

31. Zero velocity A projectile is fired vertically upward and has a position given by $s(t) = -16t^2 + 128t + 192$, for $0 \leq t \leq 9$.

a. Graph the position function, for $0 \leq t \leq 9$.
b. From the graph of the position function, identify the time at which the projectile has an instantaneous velocity of zero; call this time $t = a$.
c. Confirm your answer to part (b) by making a table of average velocities to approximate the instantaneous velocity at $t = a$.
d. For what values of t on the interval $[0, 9]$ is the instantaneous velocity positive (the projectile moves upward)?
e. For what values of t on the interval $[0, 9]$ is the instantaneous velocity negative (the projectile moves downward)?

32. Impact speed A rock is dropped off the edge of a cliff, and its distance s (in feet) from the top of the cliff after t seconds is $s(t) = 16t^2$. Assume the distance from the top of the cliff to the ground is 96 ft.

a. When will the rock strike the ground?
b. Make a table of average velocities and approximate the velocity at which the rock strikes the ground.

33. Slope of tangent line Given the function $f(x) = 1 - \cos x$ and the points $A(\pi/2, f(\pi/2))$, $B(\pi/2 + 0.05, f(\pi/2 + 0.05))$, $C(\pi/2 + 0.5, f(\pi/2 + 0.5))$, and $D(\pi, f(\pi))$ (see figure), find the slopes of the secant lines through A and D, A and C, and A and B. Then use your calculations to make a conjecture about the slope of the line tangent to the graph of f at $x = \pi/2$.

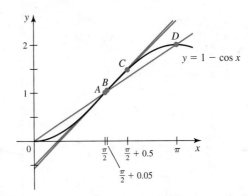

QUICK CHECK ANSWERS

1. 16 ft/s   **2.** Average velocity is the velocity over an interval of time. Instantaneous velocity is the velocity at one point of time.   **3.** Less than ◄

2.2 Definitions of Limits

Computing slopes of tangent lines and instantaneous velocities (Section 2.1) are just two of many important calculus problems that rely on limits. We now put these two problems aside until Chapter 3 and begin with a preliminary definition of the limit of a function.

> The terms *arbitrarily close* and *sufficiently close* will be made precise when rigorous definitions of limits are given in Section 2.7.

DEFINITION Limit of a Function (Preliminary)

Suppose the function f is defined for all x near a except possibly at a. If $f(x)$ is arbitrarily close to L (as close to L as we like) for all x sufficiently close (but not equal) to a, we write

$$\lim_{x \to a} f(x) = L$$

and say the limit of $f(x)$ as x approaches a equals L.

Informally, we say that $\lim_{x \to a} f(x) = L$ if $f(x)$ gets closer and closer to L as x gets closer and closer to a from both sides of a. The value of $\lim_{x \to a} f(x)$ (if it exists) depends upon the values of f near a, but it does not depend on the value of $f(a)$. In some cases, the limit $\lim_{x \to a} f(x)$ equals $f(a)$. In other instances, $\lim_{x \to a} f(x)$ and $f(a)$ differ, or $f(a)$ may not even be defined.

EXAMPLE 1 Finding limits from a graph Use the graph of f (Figure 2.7) to determine the following values, if possible.

a. $f(1)$ and $\lim_{x \to 1} f(x)$ **b.** $f(2)$ and $\lim_{x \to 2} f(x)$ **c.** $f(3)$ and $\lim_{x \to 3} f(x)$

SOLUTION

a. We see that $f(1) = 2$. As x approaches 1 from either side, the values of $f(x)$ approach 2 (Figure 2.8). Therefore, $\lim_{x \to 1} f(x) = 2$.

b. We see that $f(2) = 5$. However, as x approaches 2 from either side, $f(x)$ approaches 3 because the points on the graph of f approach the open circle at $(2, 3)$ (Figure 2.9). Therefore, $\lim_{x \to 2} f(x) = 3$ even though $f(2) = 5$.

c. In this case, $f(3)$ is undefined. We see that $f(x)$ approaches 4 as x approaches 3 from either side (Figure 2.10). Therefore, $\lim_{x \to 3} f(x) = 4$ even though $f(3)$ does not exist.

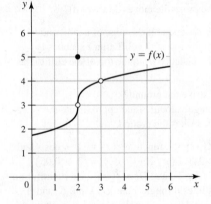

FIGURE 2.7

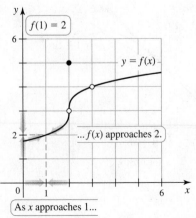

FIGURE 2.8

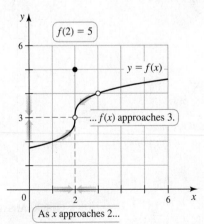

FIGURE 2.9

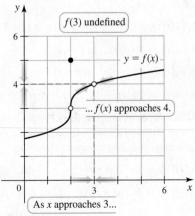

FIGURE 2.10

Related Exercises 7–10 ◄

QUICK CHECK 1 In Example 1, suppose we redefine the function at one point so that $f(1) = 1$. Does this change the value of $\lim\limits_{x \to 1} f(x)$? ◄

In Example 1, we worked with the graph of a function. Let's now work with tabulated values of a function.

EXAMPLE 2 **Finding limits from a table** Create a table of values of $f(x) = \dfrac{\sqrt{x} - 1}{x - 1}$ corresponding to values of x near 1. Then make a conjecture about the value of $\lim\limits_{x \to 1} f(x)$.

> In Example 2, we have not stated with certainty that $\lim\limits_{x \to 1} f(x) = 0.5$. But this is our best guess based upon the numerical evidence. Methods for calculating limits precisely are introduced in Section 2.3.

SOLUTION Table 2.2 lists values of f corresponding to values of x approaching 1 from both sides. The numerical evidence suggests that $f(x)$ approaches 0.5 as x approaches 1. Therefore, we make the conjecture that $\lim\limits_{x \to 1} f(x) = 0.5$.

Table 2.2   ⟶ 1 ⟵

x	0.9	0.99	0.999	0.9999	1.0001	1.001	1.01	1.1
$f(x) = \dfrac{\sqrt{x} - 1}{x - 1}$	0.5131670	0.5012563	0.5001251	0.5000125	0.4999875	0.4998751	0.4987562	0.4880885

Related Exercises 11–14 ◄

One-Sided Limits

The limit $\lim\limits_{x \to a} f(x) = L$ is referred to as a *two-sided* limit because $f(x)$ approaches L as x approaches a for values of x less than a *and* for values of x greater than a. For some functions, it makes sense to examine *one-sided* limits called *left-sided* and *right-sided* limits.

> As with two-sided limits, the value of a one-sided limit (if it exists) depends on the values of $f(x)$ near a but not on the value of $f(a)$.

DEFINITION **One-Sided Limits**

1. **Right-sided limit** Suppose f is defined for all x near a with $x > a$. If $f(x)$ is arbitrarily close to L for all x sufficiently close to a with $x > a$, we write

$$\lim_{x \to a^+} f(x) = L$$

and say the limit of $f(x)$ as x approaches a from the right equals L.

2. **Left-sided limit** Suppose f is defined for all x near a with $x < a$. If $f(x)$ is arbitrarily close to L for all x sufficiently close to a with $x < a$, we write

$$\lim_{x \to a^-} f(x) = L$$

and say the limit of $f(x)$ as x approaches a from the left equals L.

EXAMPLE 3 **Examining limits graphically and numerically** Let $f(x) = \dfrac{x^3 - 8}{4(x - 2)}$. Use tables and graphs to make a conjecture about the values of $\lim\limits_{x \to 2^+} f(x)$, $\lim\limits_{x \to 2^-} f(x)$, and $\lim\limits_{x \to 2} f(x)$, if they exist.

> Computer-generated graphs and tables help us understand the idea of a limit. Keep in mind, however, that computers are not infallible and they may produce incorrect results, even for simple functions (see Example 5).

SOLUTION Figure 2.11a shows the graph of f obtained with a graphing utility. The graph is misleading because $f(2)$ is undefined, which means there should be a hole in the graph at $(2, 3)$ (Figure 2.11b).

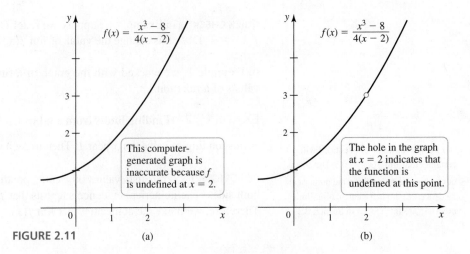

FIGURE 2.11   (a)   (b)

The graph in Figure 2.12a and the function values in Table 2.3 suggest that $f(x)$ approaches 3 as x approaches 2 from the right. Therefore, we write

$$\lim_{x \to 2^+} f(x) = 3,$$

which says the limit of $f(x)$ as x approaches 2 from the right equals 3.

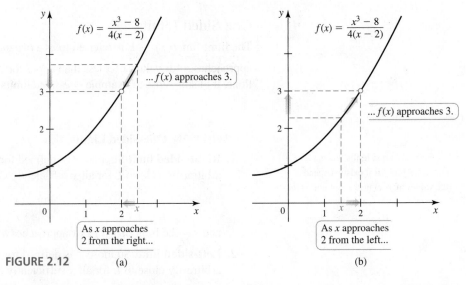

FIGURE 2.12   (a)   (b)

▷ Remember that the value of the limit does not depend upon the value of $f(2)$. In this case, $\lim_{x \to 2} f(x) = 3$ despite the fact that $f(2)$ is undefined.

Similarly, Figure 2.12b and Table 2.3 suggest that as x approaches 2 from the left, $f(x)$ approaches 3. So, we write

$$\lim_{x \to 2^-} f(x) = 3,$$

which says the limit of $f(x)$ as x approaches 2 from the left equals 3. Because $f(x)$ approaches 3 as x approaches 2 from either side, we write $\lim_{x \to 2} f(x) = 3$.

Table 2.3   ⟶ 2 ⟵

x	1.9	1.99	1.999	1.9999	2.0001	2.001	2.01	2.1
$f(x) = \dfrac{x^3 - 8}{4(x - 2)}$	2.8525	2.985025	2.99850025	2.99985000	3.00015000	3.00150025	3.015025	3.1525

Related Exercises 15–18 ◄

Based upon the previous example, you might wonder whether the limits $\lim_{x \to a^-} f(x)$, $\lim_{x \to a^+} f(x)$, and $\lim_{x \to a} f(x)$ always exist and are equal. The remaining examples demonstrate that these limits may have different values, and in other cases, some or all of these limits may not exist. The following theorem is useful when comparing one-sided and two-sided limits.

> If P and Q are statements, we write P if and only if Q when P implies Q and Q implies P.

THEOREM 2.1   Relationship Between One-Sided and Two-Sided Limits
Assume f is defined for all x near a except possibly at a. Then $\lim_{x \to a} f(x) = L$ if and only if $\lim_{x \to a^+} f(x) = L$ and $\lim_{x \to a^-} f(x) = L$.

A proof of Theorem 2.1 is outlined in Exercise 44 of Section 2.7. Using this theorem, it follows that $\lim_{x \to a} f(x) \neq L$ if either $\lim_{x \to a^+} f(x) \neq L$ or $\lim_{x \to a^-} f(x) \neq L$ (or both). Furthermore, if either $\lim_{x \to a^+} f(x)$ or $\lim_{x \to a^-} f(x)$ does not exist, then $\lim_{x \to a} f(x)$ does not exist. We put these ideas to work in the next two examples.

EXAMPLE 4   A function with a jump Given the graph of g in Figure 2.13, find the following limits, if they exist.

a. $\lim_{x \to 2^-} g(x)$ **b.** $\lim_{x \to 2^+} g(x)$ **c.** $\lim_{x \to 2} g(x)$

SOLUTION

a. As x approaches 2 from the left, $g(x)$ approaches 4. Therefore, $\lim_{x \to 2^-} g(x) = 4$.

b. Because $g(x) = 1$, for all $x \geq 2$, $\lim_{x \to 2^+} g(x) = 1$.

c. By Theorem 2.1, $\lim_{x \to 2} g(x)$ does not exist because $\lim_{x \to 2^-} g(x) \neq \lim_{x \to 2^+} g(x)$.

Related Exercises 19–24 ◄

FIGURE 2.13

EXAMPLE 5   Some strange behavior Examine $\lim_{x \to 0} \cos(1/x)$.

SOLUTION From the first three values of $\cos(1/x)$ in Table 2.4, it is tempting to conclude that $\lim_{x \to 0^+} \cos(1/x) = -1$. But this conclusion is not confirmed when we evaluate $\cos(1/x)$ for values of x closer to 0.

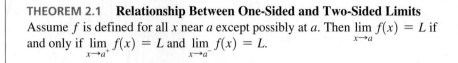

Table 2.4	
x	$\cos(1/x)$
0.001	0.56238
0.0001	−0.95216
0.00001	−0.99936
0.000001	0.93675
0.0000001	−0.90727
0.00000001	−0.36338

We might *incorrectly* conclude that $\cos(1/x)$ approaches -1 as x approaches 0 from the right.

The behavior of $\cos(1/x)$ near 0 is better understood by letting $x = 1/(n\pi)$, where n is a positive integer. By making this substitution, we can sample the function at discrete points that approach zero. In this case

$$\cos \frac{1}{x} = \cos n\pi = \begin{cases} 1 & \text{if } n \text{ is even} \\ -1 & \text{if } n \text{ is odd.} \end{cases}$$

QUICK CHECK 2 Why is the graph of $y = \cos(1/x)$ difficult to plot near $x = 0$, as suggested by Figure 2.14? ◄

As n increases, the values of $x = 1/(n\pi)$ approach zero, while the values of $\cos(1/x)$ oscillate between -1 and 1 (Figure 2.14). Therefore, $\cos(1/x)$ does not approach a single number as x approaches 0 from the right. We conclude that $\lim_{x \to 0^+} \cos(1/x)$ does *not* exist, which implies that $\lim_{x \to 0} \cos(1/x)$ does not exist.

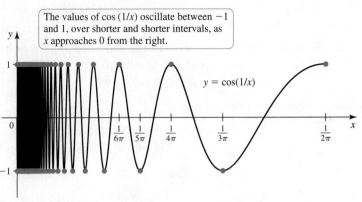

The values of cos $(1/x)$ oscillate between -1 and 1, over shorter and shorter intervals, as x approaches 0 from the right.

$y = \cos(1/x)$

FIGURE 2.14

Related Exercises 25–26◄

Using tables and graphs to make conjectures for the values of limits worked well until Example 5. The limitation of technology in this example is not an isolated incident. For this reason, analytical techniques (paper-and-pencil methods) for finding limits are developed in the next section.

SECTION 2.2 EXERCISES

Review Questions

1. Explain the meaning of $\lim_{x \to a} f(x) = L$.

2. True or false: When $\lim_{x \to a} f(x)$ exists, it always equals $f(a)$. Explain.

3. Explain the meaning of $\lim_{x \to a^+} f(x) = L$.

4. Explain the meaning of $\lim_{x \to a^-} f(x) = L$.

5. If $\lim_{x \to a^-} f(x) = L$ and $\lim_{x \to a^+} f(x) = M$, where L and M are finite real numbers, then how are L and M related if $\lim_{x \to a} f(x)$ exists?

6. What are the potential problems of using a graphing utility to estimate $\lim_{x \to a} f(x)$?

Basic Skills

7. **Finding limits from a graph** Use the graph of h in the figure to find the following values, if they exist.

   a. $h(2)$ **b.** $\lim_{x \to 2} h(x)$ **c.** $h(4)$ **d.** $\lim_{x \to 4} h(x)$ **e.** $\lim_{x \to 5} h(x)$

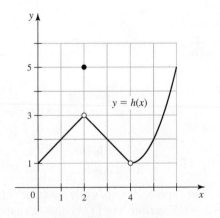

8. **Finding limits from a graph** Use the graph of g in the figure to find the following values, if they exist.

   a. $g(0)$ **b.** $\lim_{x \to 0} g(x)$ **c.** $g(1)$ **d.** $\lim_{x \to 1} g(x)$

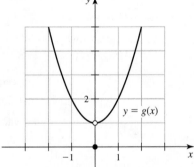

9. **Finding limits from a graph** Use the graph of f in the figure to find the following values, if they exist.

   a. $f(1)$ **b.** $\lim_{x \to 1} f(x)$ **c.** $f(0)$ **d.** $\lim_{x \to 0} f(x)$

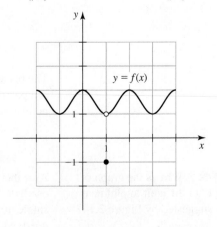

10. Finding limits from a graph Use the graph of f in the figure to find the following values, if they exist.

    a. $f(2)$ **b.** $\lim_{x \to 2} f(x)$ **c.** $\lim_{x \to 4} f(x)$ **d.** $\lim_{x \to 5} f(x)$

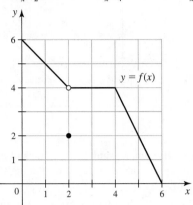

11. Estimating a limit from tables Let $f(x) = \dfrac{x^2 - 4}{x - 2}$.

    a. Calculate $f(x)$ for each value of x in the following table.

    b. Make a conjecture about the value of $\lim\limits_{x \to 2} \dfrac{x^2 - 4}{x - 2}$.

x	1.9	1.99	1.999	1.9999
$f(x) = \dfrac{x^2 - 4}{x - 2}$				
x	2.1	2.01	2.001	2.0001
$f(x) = \dfrac{x^2 - 4}{x - 2}$				

12. Estimating a limit from tables Let $f(x) = \dfrac{x^3 - 1}{x - 1}$.

    a. Calculate $f(x)$ for each value of x in the following table.

    b. Make a conjecture about the value of $\lim\limits_{x \to 1} \dfrac{x^3 - 1}{x - 1}$.

x	0.9	0.99	0.999	0.9999
$f(x) = \dfrac{x^3 - 1}{x - 1}$				
x	1.1	1.01	1.001	1.0001
$f(x) = \dfrac{x^3 - 1}{x - 1}$				

13. Estimating a limit of a function Let $g(t) = \dfrac{t - 9}{\sqrt{t} - 3}$.

    a. Make two tables, one showing the values of g for $t = 8.9, 8.99,$ and 8.999 and one showing values of g for $t = 9.1, 9.01,$ and 9.001.

    b. Make a conjecture about the value of $\lim\limits_{t \to 9} \dfrac{t - 9}{\sqrt{t} - 3}$.

14. Estimating a limit of a function Let $f(x) = (1 + x)^{1/x}$.

    a. Make two tables, one showing the values of f for $x = 0.01$, $0.001, 0.0001,$ and 0.00001 and one showing values of f for $x = -0.01, -0.001, -0.0001,$ and -0.00001. Round your answers to five digits.

    b. Estimate the value of $\lim\limits_{x \to 0} (1 + x)^{1/x}$.

    c. What mathematical constant does $\lim\limits_{x \to 0} (1 + x)^{1/x}$ appear to equal?

15. Estimating a limit graphically and numerically

    Let $f(x) = \dfrac{x - 2}{\ln |x - 2|}$.

    a. Plot a graph of f to estimate $\lim\limits_{x \to 2} f(x)$.

    b. Evaluate $f(x)$ for values of x near 2 to support your conjecture in part (a).

16. Estimating a limit graphically and numerically

    Let $g(x) = \dfrac{e^{2x} - 2x - 1}{x^2}$.

    a. Plot a graph of g to estimate $\lim\limits_{x \to 0} g(x)$.

    b. Evaluate $g(x)$ for values of x near 0 to support your conjecture in part (a).

17. Estimating a limit graphically and numerically

    Let $f(x) = \dfrac{1 - \cos(2x - 2)}{(x - 1)^2}$.

    a. Plot a graph of f to estimate $\lim\limits_{x \to 1} f(x)$.

    b. Evaluate $f(x)$ for values of x near 1 to support your conjecture in part (a).

18. Estimating a limit graphically and numerically

    Let $g(x) = \dfrac{3 \sin x - 2 \cos x + 2}{x}$.

    a. Plot a graph of g to estimate $\lim\limits_{x \to 0} g(x)$.

    b. Evaluate $g(x)$ for values of x near 0 to support your conjecture in part (a).

19. One-sided and two-sided limits Let $f(x) = \dfrac{x^2 - 25}{x - 5}$. Use tables and graphs to make a conjecture about the values of $\lim\limits_{x \to 5^+} f(x)$, $\lim\limits_{x \to 5^-} f(x)$, and $\lim\limits_{x \to 5} f(x)$, if they exist.

20. One-sided and two-sided limits Let $g(x) = \dfrac{x - 100}{\sqrt{x} - 10}$. Use tables and graphs to make a conjecture about the values of $\lim\limits_{x \to 100^+} g(x)$, $\lim\limits_{x \to 100^-} g(x)$, and $\lim\limits_{x \to 100} g(x)$, if they exist.

21. One-sided and two-sided limits Use the graph of f in the figure to find the following values, if they exist. If a limit does not exist, explain why.

  a. $f(1)$ **b.** $\lim\limits_{x \to 1^-} f(x)$ **c.** $\lim\limits_{x \to 1^+} f(x)$ **d.** $\lim\limits_{x \to 1} f(x)$

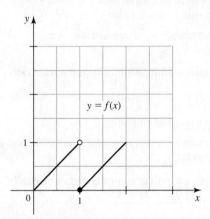

22. One-sided and two-sided limits Use the graph of g in the figure to find the following values, if they exist. If a limit does not exist, explain why.

  a. $g(2)$ **b.** $\lim\limits_{x \to 2^-} g(x)$ **c.** $\lim\limits_{x \to 2^+} g(x)$

  d. $\lim\limits_{x \to 2} g(x)$ **e.** $g(3)$ **f.** $\lim\limits_{x \to 3^-} g(x)$

  g. $\lim\limits_{x \to 3^+} g(x)$ **h.** $g(4)$ **i.** $\lim\limits_{x \to 4} g(x)$

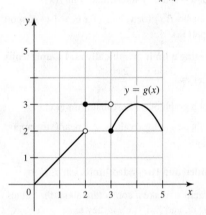

23. Finding limits from a graph Use the graph of f in the figure to find the following values, if they exist. If a limit does not exist, explain why.

  a. $f(1)$ **b.** $\lim\limits_{x \to 1^-} f(x)$ **c.** $\lim\limits_{x \to 1^+} f(x)$

  d. $\lim\limits_{x \to 1} f(x)$ **e.** $f(3)$ **f.** $\lim\limits_{x \to 3^-} f(x)$

  g. $\lim\limits_{x \to 3^+} f(x)$ **h.** $\lim\limits_{x \to 3} f(x)$ **i.** $f(2)$

  j. $\lim\limits_{x \to 2^-} f(x)$ **k.** $\lim\limits_{x \to 2^+} f(x)$ **l.** $\lim\limits_{x \to 2} f(x)$

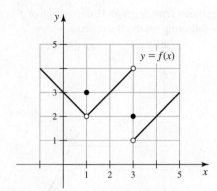

24. Finding limits from a graph Use the graph of g in the figure to find the following values, if they exist. If a limit does not exist, explain why.

  a. $g(-1)$ **b.** $\lim\limits_{x \to -1^-} g(x)$ **c.** $\lim\limits_{x \to -1^+} g(x)$

  d. $\lim\limits_{x \to -1} g(x)$ **e.** $g(1)$ **f.** $\lim\limits_{x \to 1} g(x)$

  g. $\lim\limits_{x \to 3} g(x)$ **h.** $g(5)$ **i.** $\lim\limits_{x \to 5^-} g(x)$

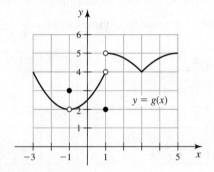

25. Strange behavior near $x = 0$

  a. Create a table of values of $\sin\left(1/x\right)$, for $x = \dfrac{2}{\pi}, \dfrac{2}{3\pi}, \dfrac{2}{5\pi}$, $\dfrac{2}{7\pi}, \dfrac{2}{9\pi}$, and $\dfrac{2}{11\pi}$. Describe the pattern of values you observe.

  b. Why does a graphing utility have difficulty plotting the graph of $y = \sin\left(1/x\right)$ near $x = 0$ (see figure)?

  c. What do you conclude about $\lim\limits_{x \to 0} \sin\left(1/x\right)$?

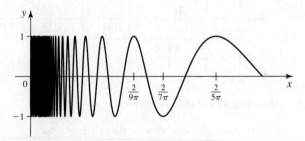

26. Strange behavior near $x = 0$

  a. Create a table of values of $\tan\left(3/x\right)$ for $x = 12/\pi, 12/(3\pi)$, $12/(5\pi), \ldots, 12/(11\pi)$. Describe the general pattern in the values you observe.

  b. Use a graphing utility to graph $y = \tan\left(3/x\right)$. Why does a graphing utility have difficulty plotting the graph near $x = 0$?

  c. What do you conclude about $\lim\limits_{x \to 0} \tan\left(3/x\right)$?

Further Explorations

27. Explain why or why not Determine whether the following statements are true and give an explanation or counterexample.

a. The value of $\lim\limits_{x \to 3} \dfrac{x^2 - 9}{x - 3}$ does not exist.

b. The value of $\lim\limits_{x \to a} f(x)$ is always found by computing $f(a)$.

c. The value of $\lim\limits_{x \to a} f(x)$ does not exist if $f(a)$ is undefined.

d. $\lim\limits_{x \to 0} \sqrt{x} = 0$

e. $\lim\limits_{x \to \pi/2} \cot x = 0$

28–29. Sketching graphs of functions *Sketch the graph of a function with the given properties. You do not need to find a formula for the function.*

28. $f(1) = 0, f(2) = 4, f(3) = 6, \lim\limits_{x \to 2^-} f(x) = -3, \lim\limits_{x \to 2^+} f(x) = 5$

29. $g(1) = 0, g(2) = 1, g(3) = -2, \lim\limits_{x \to 2} g(x) = 0,$

$\lim\limits_{x \to 3^-} g(x) = -1, \lim\limits_{x \to 3^+} g(x) = -2$

30. $h(-1) = 2, \lim\limits_{x \to -1^-} h(x) = 0, \lim\limits_{x \to -1^+} h(x) = 3,$

$h(1) = \lim\limits_{x \to 1^-} h(x) = 1, \lim\limits_{x \to 1^+} h(x) = 4$

31. $p(0) = 2, \lim\limits_{x \to 0} p(x) = 0, \lim\limits_{x \to 2} p(x)$ does not exist,

$p(2) = \lim\limits_{x \to 2^+} p(x) = 1$

▣ 32–35. Calculator limits *Estimate the value of the following limits by creating a table of function values for $h = 0.01, 0.001,$ and $0.0001,$ and $h = -0.01, -0.001,$ and $-0.0001.$*

32. $\lim\limits_{h \to 0} (1 + 2h)^{1/h}$

33. $\lim\limits_{h \to 0} (1 + 3h)^{2/h}$

34. $\lim\limits_{h \to 0} \dfrac{2^h - 1}{h}$

35. $\lim\limits_{h \to 0} \dfrac{\ln (1 + h)}{h}$

36. A step function Let $f(x) = \dfrac{|x|}{x}$, for $x \neq 0$.

a. Sketch a graph of f on the interval $[-2, 2]$.

b. Does $\lim\limits_{x \to 0} f(x)$ exist? Explain your reasoning after first examining $\lim\limits_{x \to 0^-} f(x)$ and $\lim\limits_{x \to 0^+} f(x)$.

37. The floor function For any real number x, the *floor function* (or *greatest integer function*) $\lfloor x \rfloor$ is the greatest integer less than or equal to x (see figure).

a. Compute $\lim\limits_{x \to -1^-} \lfloor x \rfloor, \lim\limits_{x \to -1^+} \lfloor x \rfloor, \lim\limits_{x \to 2^-} \lfloor x \rfloor,$ and $\lim\limits_{x \to 2^+} \lfloor x \rfloor$.

b. Compute $\lim\limits_{x \to 2.3^-} \lfloor x \rfloor, \lim\limits_{x \to 2.3^+} \lfloor x \rfloor,$ and $\lim\limits_{x \to 2.3} \lfloor x \rfloor$.

c. For a given integer a, state the values of $\lim\limits_{x \to a^-} \lfloor x \rfloor$ and $\lim\limits_{x \to a^+} \lfloor x \rfloor$.

d. In general, if a is not an integer, state the values of $\lim\limits_{x \to a^-} \lfloor x \rfloor$ and $\lim\limits_{x \to a^+} \lfloor x \rfloor$.

e. For what values of a does $\lim\limits_{x \to a} \lfloor x \rfloor$ exist? Explain.

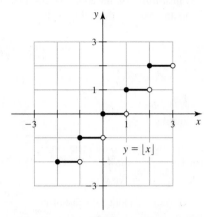

$y = \lfloor x \rfloor$

38. The ceiling function For any real number x, the *ceiling function* $\lceil x \rceil$ is the least integer greater than or equal to x.

a. Graph the ceiling function $y = \lceil x \rceil$, for $-2 \leq x \leq 3$.

b. Evaluate $\lim\limits_{x \to 2^-} \lceil x \rceil, \lim\limits_{x \to 1^+} \lceil x \rceil,$ and $\lim\limits_{x \to 1.5} \lceil x \rceil$.

c. For what values of a does $\lim\limits_{x \to a} \lceil x \rceil$ exist? Explain.

Applications

39. Postage rates Assume that postage for sending a first-class letter in the United States is \$0.44 for the first ounce (up to and including 1 oz) plus \$0.17 for each additional ounce (up to and including each additional ounce).

a. Graph the function $p = f(w)$ that gives the postage p for sending a letter that weighs w ounces, for $0 < w \leq 5$.

b. Evaluate $\lim\limits_{w \to 3.3} f(w)$.

c. Interpret the limits $\lim\limits_{w \to 1^+} f(w)$ and $\lim\limits_{w \to 1^-} f(w)$.

d. Does $\lim\limits_{w \to 4} f(w)$ exist? Explain.

40. The Heaviside function The Heaviside function is used in engineering applications to model flipping a switch. It is defined as

$$H(x) = \begin{cases} 0 & \text{if } x < 0 \\ 1 & \text{if } x \geq 0. \end{cases}$$

a. Sketch a graph of H on the interval $[-1, 2]$.

b. Does $\lim\limits_{x \to 0} H(x)$ exist? Explain your reasoning after first examining $\lim\limits_{x \to 0^-} H(x)$ and $\lim\limits_{x \to 0^+} H(x)$.

Additional Exercises

41. Limits of even functions A function f is even if $f(-x) = f(x)$, for all x in the domain of f. If f is even, with $\lim\limits_{x \to 2^+} f(x) = 5$ and $\lim\limits_{x \to 2^-} f(x) = 8$, find the following limits.

a. $\lim\limits_{x \to -2^+} f(x)$

b. $\lim\limits_{x \to -2^-} f(x)$

42. Limits of odd functions A function g is odd if $g(-x) = -g(x)$, for all x in the domain of g. If g is odd, with $\lim\limits_{x \to 2^+} g(x) = 5$ and $\lim\limits_{x \to 2^-} g(x) = 8$, find the following limits.

a. $\lim\limits_{x \to -2^+} g(x)$

b. $\lim\limits_{x \to -2^-} g(x)$

Technology Exercises

43–46. Limit by graphing Use the zoom and trace features of a graphing utility to approximate the following limits.

43. $\displaystyle\lim_{x\to 0} x \sin\frac{1}{x}$

44. $\displaystyle\lim_{x\to 1} \frac{18(\sqrt[3]{x} - 1)}{x^3 - 1}$

45. $\displaystyle\lim_{x\to 1} \frac{9\left(\sqrt{2x - x^4} - \sqrt[3]{x}\right)}{1 - x^{3/4}}$

46. $\displaystyle\lim_{x\to 0} \frac{6^x - 3^x}{x \ln 2}$

47. Limits by graphs

a. Use a graphing utility to estimate $\displaystyle\lim_{x\to 0} \frac{\tan 2x}{\sin x}$, $\displaystyle\lim_{x\to 0} \frac{\tan 3x}{\sin x}$, and $\displaystyle\lim_{x\to 0} \frac{\tan 4x}{\sin x}$.

b. Make a conjecture about the value of $\displaystyle\lim_{x\to 0} \frac{\tan px}{\sin x}$, for any real constant p.

48. Limits by graphs Graph $f(x) = \dfrac{\sin nx}{x}$, for $n = 1, 2, 3,$ and 4 (four graphs). Use the window $[-1, 1] \times [0, 5]$.

a. Estimate $\displaystyle\lim_{x\to 0} \frac{\sin x}{x}$, $\displaystyle\lim_{x\to 0} \frac{\sin 2x}{x}$, $\displaystyle\lim_{x\to 0} \frac{\sin 3x}{x}$, and $\displaystyle\lim_{x\to 0} \frac{\sin 4x}{x}$.

b. Make a conjecture about the value of $\displaystyle\lim_{x\to 0} \frac{\sin px}{x}$, for any real constant p.

49. Limits by graphs Use a graphing utility to plot $y = \dfrac{\sin px}{\sin qx}$ for at least three different pairs of nonzero constants p and q of your choice. Estimate $\displaystyle\lim_{x\to 0} \frac{\sin px}{\sin qx}$ in each case. Then use your work to make a conjecture about the value of $\displaystyle\lim_{x\to 0} \frac{\sin px}{\sin qx}$ for any nonzero values of p and q.

QUICK CHECK ANSWERS

1. The value of $\displaystyle\lim_{x\to 1} f(x)$ depends on the value of f only *near* 1, not at 1. Therefore, changing the value of $f(1)$ will not change the value of $\displaystyle\lim_{x\to 1} f(x)$.   **2.** A graphing device has difficulty plotting $y = \cos(1/x)$ near 0 because values of the function vary between -1 and 1 over shorter and shorter intervals as x approaches 0. ◄

2.3 Techniques for Computing Limits

Graphical and numerical techniques for estimating limits, like those presented in the previous section, provide intuition about limits. These techniques, however, occasionally lead to incorrect results. Therefore, we turn our attention to analytical methods for evaluating limits precisely.

Limits of Linear Functions

The graph of $f(x) = mx + b$ is a line with slope m and y-intercept b. From Figure 2.15, we see that $f(x)$ approaches $f(a)$ as x approaches a. Therefore, if f is a linear function we have $\displaystyle\lim_{x\to a} f(x) = f(a)$. It follows that for linear functions, $\displaystyle\lim_{x\to a} f(x)$ is found by direct substitution of $x = a$ into $f(x)$. This observation leads to the following theorem, which is proved in Exercise 28 of Section 2.7.

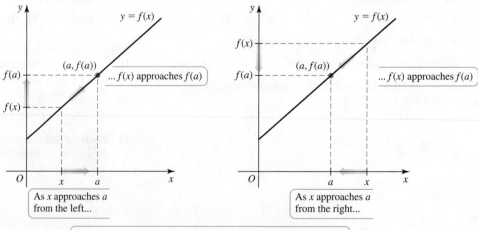

FIGURE 2.15

THEOREM 2.2   Limits of Linear Functions
Let a, b, and m be real numbers. For linear functions $f(x) = mx + b$,

$$\lim_{x \to a} f(x) = f(a) = ma + b.$$

EXAMPLE 1   Limits of linear functions Evaluate the following limits.

a. $\lim_{x \to 3} f(x)$, where $f(x) = \frac{1}{2}x - 7$ **b.** $\lim_{x \to 2} g(x)$, where $g(x) = 6$

SOLUTION

a. $\lim_{x \to 3} f(x) = \lim_{x \to 3} \left(\frac{1}{2}x - 7 \right) = f(3) = -\frac{11}{2}.$ **b.** $\lim_{x \to 2} g(x) = \lim_{x \to 2} 6 = g(2) = 6.$

Related Exercises 11–16 ◄

Limit Laws

The following limit laws greatly simplify the evaluation of many limits.

THEOREM 2.3   Limit Laws
Assume $\lim_{x \to a} f(x)$ and $\lim_{x \to a} g(x)$ exist. The following properties hold, where c is a real number, and $m > 0$ and $n > 0$ are integers.

1. **Sum** $\lim_{x \to a} [f(x) + g(x)] = \lim_{x \to a} f(x) + \lim_{x \to a} g(x)$

2. **Difference** $\lim_{x \to a} [f(x) - g(x)] = \lim_{x \to a} f(x) - \lim_{x \to a} g(x)$

3. **Constant multiple** $\lim_{x \to a} [cf(x)] = c \lim_{x \to a} f(x)$

4. **Product** $\lim_{x \to a} [f(x)g(x)] = \left[\lim_{x \to a} f(x) \right] \left[\lim_{x \to a} g(x) \right]$

5. **Quotient** $\lim_{x \to a} \left[\dfrac{f(x)}{g(x)} \right] = \dfrac{\lim_{x \to a} f(x)}{\lim_{x \to a} g(x)}$, provided $\lim_{x \to a} g(x) \neq 0$

6. **Power** $\lim_{x \to a} [f(x)]^n = \left[\lim_{x \to a} f(x) \right]^n$

7. **Fractional power** $\lim_{x \to a} [f(x)]^{n/m} = \left[\lim_{x \to a} f(x) \right]^{n/m}$, provided $f(x) \geq 0$, for x near a, if m is even and n/m is reduced to lowest terms

---

► Law 6 is a special case of Law 7. Letting $m = 1$ in Law 7 gives Law 6.

A proof of Law 1 is outlined in Section 2.7. Laws 2–5 are proved in Appendix B. Law 6 is proved from Law 4 as follows. For a positive integer n, if $\lim_{x \to a} f(x)$ exists, we have

$$\lim_{x \to a} [f(x)]^n = \lim_{x \to a} \underbrace{[f(x) f(x) \cdots f(x)]}_{n \text{ factors of } f(x)}$$

$$= \underbrace{\left[\lim_{x \to a} f(x) \right] \left[\lim_{x \to a} f(x) \right] \cdots \left[\lim_{x \to a} f(x) \right]}_{n \text{ factors of } \lim_{x \to a} f(x)} \quad \text{Repeated use of Law 4}$$

$$= \left[\lim_{x \to a} f(x) \right]^n.$$

> Recall that to take even roots of a number (for example, square roots or fourth roots), the number must be nonnegative if the result is to be real.

In Law 7, the limit of $[f(x)]^{n/m}$ involves the mth root of $f(x)$ when x is near a. If the fraction n/m is in lowest terms and m is even, this root is undefined unless $f(x)$ is nonnegative for all x near a, which explains the restrictions shown.

EXAMPLE 2   Evaluating limits Suppose $\lim_{x \to 2} f(x) = 4$, $\lim_{x \to 2} g(x) = 5$, and $\lim_{x \to 2} h(x) = 8$. Use the limit laws in Theorem 2.3 to compute each limit.

a. $\lim_{x \to 2} \dfrac{f(x) - g(x)}{h(x)}$ **b.** $\lim_{x \to 2} [6f(x)g(x) + h(x)]$ **c.** $\lim_{x \to 2} [g(x)]^3$

SOLUTION

a. $\displaystyle \lim_{x \to 2} \frac{f(x) - g(x)}{h(x)} = \frac{\displaystyle \lim_{x \to 2} [f(x) - g(x)]}{\displaystyle \lim_{x \to 2} h(x)}$ Law 5

$\displaystyle = \frac{\displaystyle \lim_{x \to 2} f(x) - \lim_{x \to 2} g(x)}{\displaystyle \lim_{x \to 2} h(x)}$ Law 2

$\displaystyle = \frac{4 - 5}{8} = -\frac{1}{8}.$

b. $\displaystyle \lim_{x \to 2} [6f(x)g(x) + h(x)] = \lim_{x \to 2} [6f(x)g(x)] + \lim_{x \to 2} h(x)$ Law 1

$\displaystyle = 6 \cdot \lim_{x \to 2} [f(x)g(x)] + \lim_{x \to 2} h(x)$ Law 3

$\displaystyle = 6 \cdot \left[\lim_{x \to 2} f(x)\right] \cdot \left[\lim_{x \to 2} g(x)\right] + \lim_{x \to 2} h(x)$ Law 4

$\displaystyle = 6 \cdot 4 \cdot 5 + 8 = 128.$

c. $\displaystyle \lim_{x \to 2} [g(x)]^3 = \left[\lim_{x \to 2} g(x)\right]^3 = 5^3 = 125.$ Law 6

Related Exercises 17–24 ◄

Limits of Polynomial and Rational Functions

The limit laws are now used to find the limits of polynomial and rational functions. For example, to evaluate the limit of the polynomial $p(x) = 7x^3 + 3x^2 + 4x + 2$ at an arbitrary point a, we proceed as follows:

$\displaystyle \lim_{x \to a} p(x) = \lim_{x \to a} (7x^3 + 3x^2 + 4x + 2)$

$\displaystyle = \lim_{x \to a} (7x^3) + \lim_{x \to a} (3x^2) + \lim_{x \to a} (4x + 2)$ Law 1

$\displaystyle = 7 \lim_{x \to a} (x^3) + 3 \lim_{x \to a} (x^2) + \lim_{x \to a} (4x + 2)$ Law 3

$\displaystyle = 7 \underbrace{\left(\lim_{x \to a} x\right)^3}_{a} + 3 \underbrace{\left(\lim_{x \to a} x\right)^2}_{a} + \underbrace{\lim_{x \to a} (4x + 2)}_{4a + 2}$ Law 6

$\displaystyle = 7a^3 + 3a^2 + 4a + 2 = p(a).$ Theorem 2.2

As in the case of linear functions, the limit of a polynomial is found by direct substitution; that is, $\lim_{x \to a} p(x) = p(a)$ (Exercise 91).

It is now a short step to evaluating limits of rational functions of the form $f(x) = p(x)/q(x)$, where p and q are polynomials. Applying Law 5, we have

$$\lim_{x \to a} \frac{p(x)}{q(x)} = \frac{\displaystyle \lim_{x \to a} p(x)}{\displaystyle \lim_{x \to a} q(x)} = \frac{p(a)}{q(a)}, \quad \text{provided } q(a) \neq 0,$$

which shows that limits of rational functions are also evaluated by direct substitution.

> The conditions under which direct substitution $\left(\lim_{x \to a} f(x) = f(a)\right)$ can be used to evaluate a limit become clear in Section 2.6, when the important property of *continuity* is discussed.

THEOREM 2.4   Limits of Polynomial and Rational Functions
Assume p and q are polynomials and a is a constant.

a. Polynomial functions: $\lim_{x \to a} p(x) = p(a)$

b. Rational functions: $\lim_{x \to a} \dfrac{p(x)}{q(x)} = \dfrac{p(a)}{q(a)}$, provided $q(a) \neq 0$

QUICK CHECK 1 Evaluate $\lim_{x \to 2} (2x^4 - 8x - 16)$ and $\lim_{x \to -1} \dfrac{x - 1}{x}$. ◄

EXAMPLE 3   Limit of a rational function Evaluate $\lim_{x \to 2} \dfrac{3x^2 - 4x}{5x^3 - 36}$.

SOLUTION Notice that the denominator of this function is nonzero at $x = 2$. Using Theorem 2.4b,

$$\lim_{x \to 2} \frac{3x^2 - 4x}{5x^3 - 36} = \frac{3(2^2) - 4(2)}{5(2^3) - 36} = 1.$$

Related Exercises 25–27 ◄

QUICK CHECK 2 Use Theorem 2.4b to compute $\lim_{x \to 1} \dfrac{5x^4 - 3x^2 + 8x - 6}{x + 1}$. ◄

EXAMPLE 4   An algebraic function Evaluate $\lim_{x \to 2} \dfrac{\sqrt{2x^3 + 9} + 3x - 1}{4x + 1}$.

SOLUTION Using Theorems 2.3 and 2.4, we have

$$\lim_{x \to 2} \frac{\sqrt{2x^3 + 9} + 3x - 1}{4x + 1} = \frac{\lim_{x \to 2} \left(\sqrt{2x^3 + 9} + 3x - 1 \right)}{\lim_{x \to 2} (4x + 1)} \qquad \text{Law 5}$$

$$= \frac{\sqrt{\lim_{x \to 2} (2x^3 + 9)} + \lim_{x \to 2} (3x - 1)}{\lim_{x \to 2} (4x + 1)} \qquad \text{Laws 1 and 7}$$

$$= \frac{\sqrt{(2(2)^3 + 9)} + (3(2) - 1)}{(4(2) + 1)} \qquad \text{Theorem 2.4}$$

$$= \frac{\sqrt{25} + 5}{9} = \frac{10}{9}.$$

Notice that the limit at $x = 2$ equals the value of the function at $x = 2$.

Related Exercises 28–32 ◄

One-Sided Limits

Theorem 2.2, Limit Laws 1–6, and Theorem 2.4 also hold for left-sided and right-sided limits. In other words, these laws remain valid if we replace $\lim_{x \to a}$ with $\lim_{x \to a^+}$ or $\lim_{x \to a^-}$. Law 7 must be modified slightly for one-sided limits, as shown in the next theorem.

> **THEOREM 2.3 (CONTINUED)   Limit Laws for One-Sided Limits**
> Laws 1–6 hold with $\lim\limits_{x \to a}$ replaced by $\lim\limits_{x \to a^+}$ or $\lim\limits_{x \to a^-}$. Law 7 is modified as follows. Assume $m > 0$ and $n > 0$ are integers.
>
> **7. Fractional power**
>
> **a.** $\lim\limits_{x \to a^+} [f(x)]^{n/m} = \left[\lim\limits_{x \to a^+} f(x) \right]^{n/m}$, provided $f(x) \geq 0$, for x near a with $x > a$, if m is even and n/m is reduced to lowest terms.
>
> **b.** $\lim\limits_{x \to a^-} [f(x)]^{n/m} = \left[\lim\limits_{x \to a^-} f(x) \right]^{n/m}$, provided $f(x) \geq 0$, for x near a with $x < a$, if m is even and n/m is reduced to lowest terms.

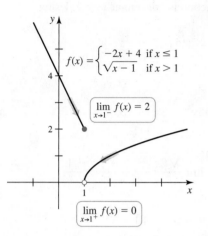

$$f(x) = \begin{cases} -2x + 4 & \text{if } x \leq 1 \\ \sqrt{x - 1} & \text{if } x > 1 \end{cases}$$

$$\lim_{x \to 1^-} f(x) = 2$$

$$\lim_{x \to 1^+} f(x) = 0$$

FIGURE 2.16

EXAMPLE 5   Calculating left- and right-sided limits Let

$$f(x) = \begin{cases} -2x + 4 & \text{if } x \leq 1 \\ \sqrt{x - 1} & \text{if } x > 1. \end{cases}$$

Find the values of $\lim\limits_{x \to 1^-} f(x)$, $\lim\limits_{x \to 1^+} f(x)$, and $\lim\limits_{x \to 1} f(x)$, or state that they do not exist.

SOLUTION The graph of f (Figure 2.16) suggests that $\lim\limits_{x \to 1^-} f(x) = 2$ and $\lim\limits_{x \to 1^+} f(x) = 0$. We verify this observation analytically by applying the limit laws. For $x \leq 1$, $f(x) = -2x + 4$; therefore,

$$\lim_{x \to 1^-} f(x) = \lim_{x \to 1^-} (-2x + 4) = 2. \quad \text{Theorem 2.2}$$

For $x > 1$, note that $x - 1 > 0$; it follows that

$$\lim_{x \to 1^+} f(x) = \lim_{x \to 1^+} \sqrt{x - 1} = 0. \quad \text{Law 7}$$

Because $\lim\limits_{x \to 1^-} f(x) = 2$ and $\lim\limits_{x \to 1^+} f(x) = 0$, $\lim\limits_{x \to 1} f(x)$ does not exist by Theorem 2.1.

Related Exercises 33–38 ◄

Other Techniques

So far, we have evaluated limits by direct substitution. A more challenging problem is finding $\lim\limits_{x \to a} f(x)$ when the limit exists, but $\lim\limits_{x \to a} f(x) \neq f(a)$. Two typical cases are shown in Figure 2.17. In the first case, $f(a)$ is defined, but it is not equal to $\lim\limits_{x \to a} f(x)$; in the second case, $f(a)$ is not defined at all.

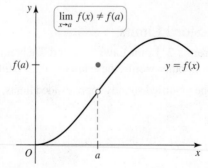

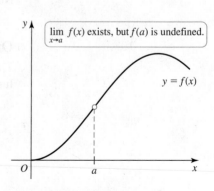

FIGURE 2.17

EXAMPLE 6 **Other techniques** Evaluate the following limits.

a. $\lim\limits_{x \to 2} \dfrac{x^2 - 6x + 8}{x^2 - 4}$

b. $\lim\limits_{x \to 1} \dfrac{\sqrt{x} - 1}{x - 1}$

SOLUTION

> The argument used in this example is common. In the limit process, x approaches 2, but $x \neq 2$. Therefore, we may cancel like factors.

a. Factor and Cancel This limit cannot be found by direct substitution because the denominator is zero when $x = 2$. Instead, the numerator and denominator are factored; then, assuming $x \neq 2$, we cancel like factors:

$$\frac{x^2 - 6x + 8}{x^2 - 4} = \frac{(x - 2)(x - 4)}{(x - 2)(x + 2)} = \frac{x - 4}{x + 2}.$$

Because $\dfrac{x^2 - 6x + 8}{x^2 - 4} = \dfrac{x - 4}{x + 2}$ whenever $x \neq 2$, the two functions have the same limit as x approaches 2 (Figure 2.18). Therefore,

$$\lim_{x \to 2} \frac{x^2 - 6x + 8}{x^2 - 4} = \lim_{x \to 2} \frac{x - 4}{x + 2} = \frac{2 - 4}{2 + 2} = -\frac{1}{2}.$$

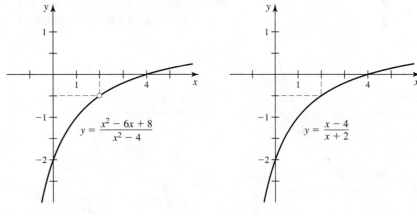

$$\lim_{x \to 2} \frac{x^2 - 6x + 8}{x^2 - 4} = \lim_{x \to 2} \frac{x - 4}{x + 2} = -\frac{1}{2}$$

FIGURE 2.18

b. Use Conjugates This limit was approximated numerically in Example 2 of Section 2.2; we conjectured that the value of the limit is $\frac{1}{2}$. Direct substitution fails in this case because the denominator is zero at $x = 1$. Instead, we first simplify the function by multiplying the numerator and denominator by the *algebraic conjugate* of the numerator. The conjugate of $\sqrt{x} - 1$ is $\sqrt{x} + 1$; therefore,

> We multiply the given function by
> $$1 = \frac{\sqrt{x} + 1}{\sqrt{x} + 1}.$$

$$\frac{\sqrt{x} - 1}{x - 1} = \frac{(\sqrt{x} - 1)(\sqrt{x} + 1)}{(x - 1)(\sqrt{x} + 1)} \qquad \text{Rationalize the numerator; multiply by 1.}$$

$$= \frac{x + \sqrt{x} - \sqrt{x} - 1}{(x - 1)(\sqrt{x} + 1)} \qquad \text{Expand the numerator.}$$

$$= \frac{x - 1}{(x - 1)(\sqrt{x} + 1)} \qquad \text{Simplify.}$$

$$= \frac{1}{\sqrt{x} + 1}. \qquad \text{Cancel like factors when } x \neq 1.$$

The limit can now be evaluated:

$$\lim_{x \to 1} \frac{\sqrt{x} - 1}{x - 1} = \lim_{x \to 1} \frac{1}{\sqrt{x} + 1} = \frac{1}{1 + 1} = \frac{1}{2}.$$

Related Exercises 39–52 ◄

QUICK CHECK 3 Evaluate
$$\lim_{x \to 5} \frac{x^2 - 7x + 10}{x - 5}.$$ ◄

An Important Limit

Despite our success in evaluating limits using direct substitution, algebraic manipulation, and the limit laws, there are important limits for which these techniques do not work. One such limit arises when investigating the slope of a line tangent to the graph of an exponential function.

EXAMPLE 7 Slope of a line tangent to $f(x) = 2^x$ Estimate the slope of the line tangent to the graph of $f(x) = 2^x$ at the point $P(0, 1)$.

SOLUTION In Section 2.1, the slope of a tangent line was obtained by finding the limit of slopes of secant lines; the same strategy is employed here. We begin by selecting a point Q near P on the graph of f with coordinates $(x, 2^x)$. The secant line joining the points $P(0, 1)$ and $Q(x, 2^x)$ is an approximation to the tangent line. To compute the slope of the tangent line (denoted by m_{tan}) at $x = 0$, we look at the slope of the secant line $m_{sec} = (2^x - 1)/x$ and take the limit as x approaches 0.

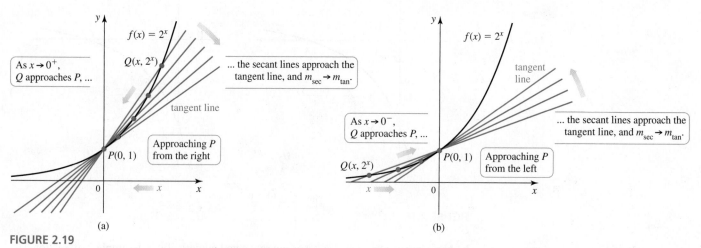

FIGURE 2.19

The limit $\lim_{x \to 0} \dfrac{2^x - 1}{x}$ exists only if it has the same value as $x \to 0^+$ (Figure 2.19a) and as $x \to 0^-$ (Figure 2.19b). Because it is not an elementary limit, it cannot be evaluated using the limit laws of this section. Instead, we investigate the limit using numerical evidence. Choosing positive values of x near 0 results in Table 2.5.

Table 2.5

x	1.0	0.1	0.01	0.001	0.0001	0.00001
$m_{sec} = \dfrac{2^x - 1}{x}$	1.000000	0.7177	0.6956	0.6934	0.6932	0.6931

> Example 7 shows that
> $$\lim_{x\to 0}\frac{2^x - 1}{x} \approx 0.693,\text{ which is}$$
> approximately ln 2. The connection
> between the natural logarithm and slopes
> of lines tangent to exponential curves is
> made clear in Chapters 3 and 6.

We see that as x approaches 0 from the right, the slopes of the secant lines approach the slope of the tangent line, which is approximately 0.693. A similar calculation (Exercise 53) gives the same approximation for the limit as x approaches 0 from the left.

Because the left-sided and right-sided limits are the same, we conclude that $\lim_{x\to 0}(2^x - 1)/x \approx 0.693$ (Theorem 2.1). Therefore, the slope of the line tangent to $f(x) = 2^x$ at $x = 0$ is approximately 0.693.

Related Exercises 53–54 ◄

The Squeeze Theorem

> The Squeeze Theorem is also called
> the Pinching Theorem or the Sandwich
> Theorem.

The *Squeeze Theorem* provides another useful method for calculating limits. Suppose the functions f and h have the same limit L at a and assume the function g is trapped between f and h (Figure 2.20). The Squeeze Theorem says that g must also have the limit L at a. A proof of this theorem is outlined in Exercise 54 of Section 2.7.

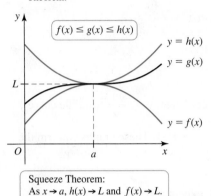

Squeeze Theorem:
As $x \to a$, $h(x) \to L$ and $f(x) \to L$.
Therefore, $g(x) \to L$.

FIGURE 2.20

THEOREM 2.5   The Squeeze Theorem
Assume the functions f, g, and h satisfy $f(x) \le g(x) \le h(x)$ for all values of x near a, except possibly at a. If $\lim_{x\to a} f(x) = \lim_{x\to a} h(x) = L$, then $\lim_{x\to a} g(x) = L$.

EXAMPLE 8   Sine and cosine limits   A geometric argument (Exercise 90) may be used to show that for $-\pi/2 < x < \pi/2$,

$$-|x| \le \sin x \le |x| \quad \text{and} \quad 0 \le 1 - \cos x \le |x|.$$

Use the Squeeze Theorem to confirm the following limits.

a. $\lim_{x\to 0} \sin x = 0$ **b.** $\lim_{x\to 0} \cos x = 1$

SOLUTION

a. Letting $f(x) = -|x|$, $g(x) = \sin x$, and $h(x) = |x|$, we see that g is trapped between f and h on $-\pi/2 < x < \pi/2$ (Figure 2.21a). Because $\lim_{x\to 0} f(x) = \lim_{x\to 0} h(x) = 0$ (Exercise 37), the Squeeze Theorem implies that $\lim_{x\to 0} g(x) = \lim_{x\to 0} \sin x = 0$.

> The two limits in Example 8 play a
> crucial role in establishing fundamental
> properties of the trigonometric functions.
> The limits reappear in Section 2.6.

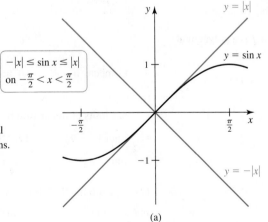

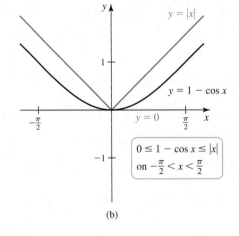

FIGURE 2.21

b. In this case, we let $f(x) = 0$, $g(x) = 1 - \cos x$, and $h(x) = |x|$ (Figure 2.21b). Because $\lim_{x\to 0} f(x) = \lim_{x\to 0} h(x) = 0$, the Squeeze Theorem implies that $\lim_{x\to 0} g(x) = \lim_{x\to 0} (1 - \cos x) = 0$. By the limit laws, it follows that $\lim_{x\to 0} 1 - \lim_{x\to 0} \cos x = 0$, or $\lim_{x\to 0} \cos x = 1$.   *Related Exercises 55–58* ◄

EXAMPLE 9   Squeeze Theorem for an important limit

a. Use a graphing utility to confirm that

$$\cos x \le \frac{\sin x}{x} \le \frac{1}{\cos x}, \text{ for } 0 < |x| \le 1.$$

b. Use part (a) and the Squeeze Theorem to prove that

$$\lim_{x\to 0} \frac{\sin x}{x} = 1.$$

SOLUTION

a. Figure 2.22 shows the graphs of $y = \cos x$ (lower curve), $y = \dfrac{\sin x}{x}$ (middle curve), and $y = \dfrac{1}{\cos x}$ (upper curve) on the interval $-1 \le x \le 1$. These graphs confirm the given inequalities.

b. By part (a), $\cos x \le \dfrac{\sin x}{x} \le \dfrac{1}{\cos x}$, for x near 0, except at 0. Furthermore,

$$\lim_{x\to 0} \cos x = \lim_{x\to 0} \frac{1}{\cos x} = 1.$$ The conditions of the Squeeze Theorem are satisfied and we conclude that

$$\lim_{x\to 0} \frac{\sin x}{x} = 1.$$

This important limit is used in Chapter 3 to discover derivative rules for trigonometric functions.   *Related Exercises 55–58* ◄

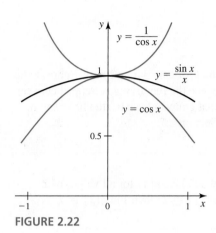

FIGURE 2.22

> **QUICK CHECK 4** Suppose f satisfies $1 \le f(x) \le 1 + \dfrac{x^2}{6}$ for all values of x near zero. Find $\lim_{x\to 0} f(x)$, if possible. ◄

SECTION 2.3 EXERCISES

Review Questions

1. How is $\lim_{x\to a} f(x)$ calculated if f is a polynomial function?

2. How are $\lim_{x\to a^-} f(x)$ and $\lim_{x\to a^+} f(x)$ calculated if f is a polynomial function?

3. For what values of a does $\lim_{x\to a} r(x) = r(a)$ if r is a rational function?

4. Assume $\lim_{x\to 3} g(x) = 4$ and $f(x) = g(x)$ whenever $x \ne 3$. Evaluate $\lim_{x\to 3} f(x)$, if possible.

5. Explain why $\lim_{x\to 3} \dfrac{x^2 - 7x + 12}{x - 3} = \lim_{x\to 3} (x - 4)$.

6. If $\lim_{x\to 2} f(x) = -8$, find $\lim_{x\to 2} [f(x)]^{2/3}$.

7. Suppose p and q are polynomials. If $\lim_{x\to 0} \dfrac{p(x)}{q(x)} = 10$ and $q(0) = 2$, find $p(0)$.

8. Suppose $\lim_{x\to 2} f(x) = \lim_{x\to 2} h(x) = 5$. Find $\lim_{x\to 2} g(x)$, where $f(x) \le g(x) \le h(x)$, for all x.

9. Evaluate $\lim_{x\to 5} \sqrt{x^2 - 9}$.

10. Suppose

$$f(x) = \begin{cases} 4 & \text{if } x \le 3 \\ x + 2 & \text{if } x > 3. \end{cases}$$

Compute $\lim_{x\to 3^-} f(x)$ and $\lim_{x\to 3^+} f(x)$.

Basic Skills

11–16. Limits of linear functions *Evaluate the following limits.*

11. $\lim_{x\to 4} (3x - 7)$

12. $\lim_{x\to 1} (-2x + 5)$

13. $\lim_{x\to -9} 5x$

14. $\lim_{x\to 2} (-3x)$

15. $\lim_{x\to 6} 4$

16. $\lim_{x\to -5} \pi$

17–24. Applying limit laws *Assume $\lim_{x\to 1} f(x) = 8$, $\lim_{x\to 1} g(x) = 3$, and $\lim_{x\to 1} h(x) = 2$. Compute the following limits and state the limit laws used to justify your computations.*

17. $\lim_{x\to 1} [4f(x)]$

18. $\lim_{x\to 1} \left[\dfrac{f(x)}{h(x)} \right]$

19. $\lim_{x\to 1} [f(x) - g(x)]$

20. $\lim_{x\to 1} [f(x)h(x)]$

21. $\lim_{x\to 1} \left[\dfrac{f(x)g(x)}{h(x)} \right]$

22. $\lim_{x\to 1} \left[\dfrac{f(x)}{g(x) - h(x)} \right]$

23. $\lim_{x\to 1} [h(x)]^5$

24. $\lim_{x\to 1} \sqrt[3]{f(x)g(x) + 3}$

25–32. Evaluating limits *Evaluate the following limits.*

25. $\lim\limits_{x \to 1} (2x^3 - 3x^2 + 4x + 5)$

26. $\lim\limits_{t \to -2} (t^2 + 5t + 7)$

27. $\lim\limits_{x \to 1} \dfrac{5x^2 + 6x + 1}{8x - 4}$

28. $\lim\limits_{t \to 3} \sqrt[3]{t^2 - 10}$

29. $\lim\limits_{b \to 2} \dfrac{3b}{\sqrt{4b + 1} - 1}$

30. $\lim\limits_{x \to 2} (x^2 - x)^5$

31. $\lim\limits_{x \to 3} \dfrac{-5x}{\sqrt{4x - 3}}$

32. $\lim\limits_{h \to 0} \dfrac{3}{\sqrt{16 + 3h} + 4}$

33. One-sided limits Let

$$f(x) = \begin{cases} x^2 + 1 & \text{if } x < -1 \\ \sqrt{x + 1} & \text{if } x \geq -1. \end{cases}$$

Compute the following limits or state that they do not exist.

a. $\lim\limits_{x \to -1^-} f(x)$
b. $\lim\limits_{x \to -1^+} f(x)$
c. $\lim\limits_{x \to -1} f(x)$

34. One-sided limits Let

$$f(x) = \begin{cases} 0 & \text{if } x \leq -5 \\ \sqrt{25 - x^2} & \text{if } -5 < x < 5 \\ 3x & \text{if } x \geq 5. \end{cases}$$

Compute the following limits, or state that they do not exist.

a. $\lim\limits_{x \to -5^-} f(x)$
b. $\lim\limits_{x \to -5^+} f(x)$
c. $\lim\limits_{x \to -5} f(x)$
d. $\lim\limits_{x \to 5^-} f(x)$
e. $\lim\limits_{x \to 5^+} f(x)$
f. $\lim\limits_{x \to 5} f(x)$

35. One-sided limits

a. Evaluate $\lim\limits_{x \to 2^+} \sqrt{x - 2}$.
b. Explain why $\lim\limits_{x \to 2^-} \sqrt{x - 2}$ does not exist.

36. One-sided limits

a. Evaluate $\lim\limits_{x \to 3^-} \sqrt{\dfrac{x - 3}{2 - x}}$.

b. Explain why $\lim\limits_{x \to 3^+} \sqrt{\dfrac{x - 3}{2 - x}}$ does not exist.

37. Absolute value limit Show that $\lim\limits_{x \to 0} |x| = 0$ by first evaluating $\lim\limits_{x \to 0^-} |x|$ and $\lim\limits_{x \to 0^+} |x|$. Recall that

$$|x| = \begin{cases} x & \text{if } x \geq 0 \\ -x & \text{if } x < 0. \end{cases}$$

38. Absolute value limit Show that $\lim\limits_{x \to a} |x| = |a|$, for any real number. (*Hint:* Consider the cases $a < 0$ and $a \geq 0$.)

39–52. Other techniques *Evaluate the following limits, where a and b are fixed real numbers.*

39. $\lim\limits_{x \to 1} \dfrac{x^2 - 1}{x - 1}$

40. $\lim\limits_{x \to 3} \dfrac{x^2 - 2x - 3}{x - 3}$

41. $\lim\limits_{x \to 4} \dfrac{x^2 - 16}{4 - x}$

42. $\lim\limits_{t \to 2} \dfrac{3t^2 - 7t + 2}{2 - t}$

43. $\lim\limits_{x \to b} \dfrac{(x - b)^{50} - x + b}{x - b}$

44. $\lim\limits_{x \to -b} \dfrac{(x + b)^7 + (x + b)^{10}}{4(x + b)}$

45. $\lim\limits_{x \to -1} \dfrac{(2x - 1)^2 - 9}{x + 1}$

46. $\lim\limits_{h \to 0} \dfrac{\frac{1}{5 + h} - \frac{1}{5}}{h}$

47. $\lim\limits_{x \to 9} \dfrac{\sqrt{x} - 3}{x - 9}$

48. $\lim\limits_{t \to 3} \left(4t - \dfrac{2}{t - 3}\right)(6 + t - t^2)$

49. $\lim\limits_{x \to a} \dfrac{x - a}{\sqrt{x} - \sqrt{a}}, a > 0$

50. $\lim\limits_{x \to a} \dfrac{x^2 - a^2}{\sqrt{x} - \sqrt{a}}, a > 0$

51. $\lim\limits_{h \to 0} \dfrac{\sqrt{16 + h} - 4}{h}$

52. $\lim\limits_{x \to a} \dfrac{x^3 - a}{x - a}$

T 53. Slope of a tangent line

a. Sketch a graph of $y = 2^x$ and carefully draw three secant lines connecting the points $P(0, 1)$ and $Q(x, 2^x)$, for $x = -3, -2,$ and -1.

b. Find the slope of the line that joins $P(0, 1)$ and $Q(x, 2^x)$, for $x \neq 0$.

c. Complete the table and make a conjecture about the value of $\lim\limits_{x \to 0^-} \dfrac{2^x - 1}{x}$.

x	-1	-0.1	-0.01	-0.001	-0.0001	-0.00001
$\dfrac{2^x - 1}{x}$						

T 54. Slope of a tangent line

a. Sketch a graph of $y = 3^x$ and carefully draw four secant lines connecting the points $P(0, 1)$ and $Q(x, 3^x)$, for $x = -2, -1, 1,$ and 2.

b. Find the slope of the line that joins $P(0, 1)$ and $Q(x, 3^x)$, for $x \neq 0$.

c. Complete the table and make a conjecture about the value of $\lim\limits_{x \to 0} \dfrac{3^x - 1}{x}$.

x	-0.1	-0.01	-0.001	-0.0001	0.0001	0.001	0.01	0.1
$\dfrac{3^x - 1}{x}$								

T 55. Applying the Squeeze Theorem

a. Show that $-|x| \leq x \sin \dfrac{1}{x} \leq |x|$, for $x \neq 0$.

b. Illustrate the inequalities in part (a) with a graph.

c. Use the Squeeze Theorem to show that $\lim\limits_{x \to 0} x \sin \dfrac{1}{x} = 0$.

T 56. A cosine limit by the Squeeze Theorem It can be shown that $1 - \dfrac{x^2}{2} \leq \cos x \leq 1$, for x near 0.

a. Illustrate these inequalities with a graph.

b. Use these inequalities to find $\lim\limits_{x \to 0} \cos x$.

T 57. A sine limit by the Squeeze Theorem It can be shown that $1 - \dfrac{x^2}{6} \leq \dfrac{\sin x}{x} \leq 1$, for x near 0.

a. Illustrate these inequalities with a graph.

b. Use these inequalities to find $\lim\limits_{x \to 0} \dfrac{\sin x}{x}$.

58. A logarithm limit by the Squeeze Theorem

   a. Draw a graph to verify that $-|x| \leq x^2 \ln x^2 \leq |x|$, for $-1 \leq x \leq 1$, where $x \neq 0$.

   b. Use the Squeeze Theorem to determine $\lim\limits_{x \to 0} x^2 \ln x^2$.

Further Explorations

59. Explain why or why not Determine whether the following statements are true and give an explanation or counterexample. Assume a and L are finite numbers.

   a. If $\lim\limits_{x \to a} f(x) = L$, then $f(a) = L$.

   b. If $\lim\limits_{x \to a^-} f(x) = L$, then $\lim\limits_{x \to a^+} f(x) = L$.

   c. If $\lim\limits_{x \to a} f(x) = L$ and $\lim\limits_{x \to a} g(x) = L$, then $f(a) = g(a)$.

   d. The limit $\lim\limits_{x \to a} \dfrac{f(x)}{g(x)}$ does not exist if $g(a) = 0$.

   e. If $\lim\limits_{x \to 1^+} \sqrt{f(x)} = \sqrt{\lim\limits_{x \to 1^+} f(x)}$, it follows that $\lim\limits_{x \to 1} \sqrt{f(x)} = \sqrt{\lim\limits_{x \to 1} f(x)}$.

60–67. Evaluating limits *Evaluate the following limits, where c and k are constants.*

60. $\lim\limits_{h \to 0} \dfrac{100}{(10h - 1)^{11} + 2}$

61. $\lim\limits_{x \to 2} (5x - 6)^{3/2}$

62. $\lim\limits_{x \to 3} \dfrac{\dfrac{1}{x^2 + 2x} - \dfrac{1}{15}}{x - 3}$

63. $\lim\limits_{x \to 1} \dfrac{\sqrt{10x - 9} - 1}{x - 1}$

64. $\lim\limits_{x \to 2} \left(\dfrac{1}{x - 2} - \dfrac{2}{x^2 - 2x} \right)$

65. $\lim\limits_{h \to 0} \dfrac{(5 + h)^2 - 25}{h}$

66. $\lim\limits_{x \to c} \dfrac{x^2 - 2cx + c^2}{x - c}$

67. $\lim\limits_{w \to -k} \dfrac{w^2 + 5kw + 4k^2}{w^2 + kw}$, for $k \neq 0$

68. Finding a constant Suppose

$$f(x) = \begin{cases} 3x + b & \text{if } x \leq 2 \\ x - 2 & \text{if } x > 2. \end{cases}$$

Determine a value of the constant b for which $\lim\limits_{x \to 2} f(x)$ exists and state the value of the limit, if possible.

69. Finding a constant Suppose

$$g(x) = \begin{cases} x^2 - 5x & \text{if } x \leq -1 \\ ax^3 - 7 & \text{if } x > -1. \end{cases}$$

Determine a value of the constant a for which $\lim\limits_{x \to -1} g(x)$ exists and state the value of the limit, if possible.

70–76. Useful factorization formula *Calculate the following limits using the factorization formula*

$$x^n - a^n = (x - a)(x^{n-1} + x^{n-2}a + x^{n-3}a^2 + \cdots + xa^{n-2} + a^{n-1}),$$

where n is a positive integer and a is a real number.

70. $\lim\limits_{x \to 2} \dfrac{x^5 - 32}{x - 2}$

71. $\lim\limits_{x \to 1} \dfrac{x^6 - 1}{x - 1}$

72. $\lim\limits_{x \to -1} \dfrac{x^7 + 1}{x + 1}$ (*Hint:* Use the formula for $x^7 - a^7$ with $a = -1$.)

73. $\lim\limits_{x \to a} \dfrac{x^5 - a^5}{x - a}$

74. $\lim\limits_{x \to a} \dfrac{x^n - a^n}{x - a}$, for any positive integer n

75. $\lim\limits_{x \to 1} \dfrac{\sqrt[3]{x} - 1}{x - 1}$ (*Hint:* $x - 1 = \left(\sqrt[3]{x} \right)^3 - (1)^3$)

76. $\lim\limits_{x \to 16} \dfrac{\sqrt[4]{x} - 2}{x - 16}$

77–80. Limits involving conjugates *Evaluate the following limits.*

77. $\lim\limits_{x \to 1} \dfrac{x - 1}{\sqrt{x} - 1}$

78. $\lim\limits_{x \to 1} \dfrac{x - 1}{\sqrt{4x + 5} - 3}$

79. $\lim\limits_{x \to 4} \dfrac{3(x - 4)\sqrt{x + 5}}{3 - \sqrt{x + 5}}$

80. $\lim\limits_{x \to 0} \dfrac{x}{\sqrt{cx + 1} - 1}$, where c is a nonzero constant

81. Creating functions satisfying given limit conditions Find functions f and g such that $\lim\limits_{x \to 1} f(x) = 0$ and $\lim\limits_{x \to 1} (f(x) \, g(x)) = 5$.

82. Creating functions satisfying given limit conditions Find a function f satisfying $\lim\limits_{x \to 1} \left(\dfrac{f(x)}{x - 1} \right) = 2$.

83. Finding constants Find constants b and c in the polynomial $p(x) = x^2 + bx + c$ such that $\lim\limits_{x \to 2} \dfrac{p(x)}{x - 2} = 6$. Are the constants unique?

Applications

84. A problem from relativity theory Suppose a spaceship of length L_0 is traveling at a high speed v relative to an observer. To the observer, the ship appears to have a smaller length given by the *Lorentz contraction formula*

$$L = L_0 \sqrt{1 - \dfrac{v^2}{c^2}},$$

where c is the speed of light.

   a. What is the observed length L of the ship if it is traveling at 50% of the speed of light?

   b. What is the observed length L of the ship if it is traveling at 75% of the speed of light?

   c. In parts (a) and (b), what happens to L as the speed of the ship increases?

   d. Find $\lim\limits_{v \to c^-} L_0 \sqrt{1 - \dfrac{v^2}{c^2}}$ and explain the significance of this limit.

85. Limit of the radius of a cylinder A right circular cylinder with a height of 10 cm and a surface area of S cm^2 has a radius given by

$$r(S) = \dfrac{1}{2} \left(\sqrt{100 + \dfrac{2S}{\pi}} - 10 \right).$$

Find $\lim\limits_{S \to 0^+} r(S)$ and interpret your result.

86. Torricelli's Law A cylindrical tank is filled with water to a depth of 9 meters. At $t = 0$, a drain in the bottom of the tank is opened and water flows out of the tank. The depth of water in the tank (measured from the bottom of the tank) t seconds after the drain is opened is approximated by $d(t) = (3 - 0.015t)^2$, for $0 \le t \le 200$. Evaluate and interpret $\lim_{t \to 200^-} d(t)$.

87. Electric field The magnitude of the electric field at a point x meters from the midpoint of a 0.1m line of charge is given by

$$E(x) = \frac{4.35}{x\sqrt{x^2 + 0.01}} \text{ (in units of newtons per coulomb, N/C).}$$

Evaluate $\lim_{x \to 10} E(x)$.

Additional Exercises

88–89. Limits of composite functions

88. If $\lim_{x \to 1} f(x) = 4$, find $\lim_{x \to -1} f(x^2)$.

89. Suppose $g(x) = f(1 - x)$, for all x, $\lim_{x \to 1^+} f(x) = 4$, and $\lim_{x \to 1^-} f(x) = 6$. Find $\lim_{x \to 0^+} g(x)$ and $\lim_{x \to 0^-} g(x)$.

90. Two trigonometric inequalities Consider the angle θ in standard position in a unit circle, where $0 \le \theta < \pi/2$ or $-\pi/2 < \theta < 0$ (use both figures).

   a. Show that $|AC| = |\sin \theta|$, for $-\pi/2 < \theta < \pi/2$. (*Hint:* Consider the cases $0 \le \theta < \pi/2$ and $-\pi/2 < \theta < 0$ separately.)

   b. Show that $|\sin \theta| < |\theta|$, for $-\pi/2 < \theta < \pi/2$. (*Hint:* The length of arc AB is θ, if $0 \le \theta < \pi/2$, and $-\theta$, if $-\pi/2 < \theta < 0$.)

   c. Conclude that $-|\theta| \le \sin \theta \le |\theta|$, for $-\pi/2 < \theta < \pi/2$.

   d. Show that $0 \le 1 - \cos \theta \le |\theta|$, for $-\pi/2 < \theta < \pi/2$.

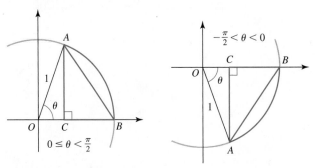

91. Theorem 2.4a Given the polynomial

$$p(x) = b_n x^n + b_{n-1} x^{n-1} + \cdots + b_1 x + b_0,$$

prove that $\lim_{x \to a} p(x) = p(a)$ for any value of a.

QUICK CHECK ANSWERS

1. $0, 2$ **2.** 2 **3.** 3 **4.** 1 ◄

2.4 Infinite Limits

Two more limit scenarios are frequently encountered in calculus and are discussed in this and the following section. An *infinite limit* occurs when function values increase or decrease without bound near a point. The other type of limit, known as a *limit at infinity*, occurs when the independent variable x increases or decreases without bound. The ideas behind infinite limits and limits at infinity are quite different. Therefore, it is important to distinguish these limits and the methods used to calculate them.

An Overview

To illustrate the differences between infinite limits and limits at infinity, consider the values of $f(x) = 1/x^2$ in Table 2.6. As x approaches 0 from either side, $f(x)$ grows larger and larger. Because $f(x)$ does not approach a finite number as x approaches 0, $\lim_{x \to 0} f(x)$ does not exist. Nevertheless, we use limit notation and write $\lim_{x \to 0} f(x) = \infty$. The infinity symbol indicates that $f(x)$ grows arbitrarily large as x approaches 0. This is an example of an *infinite limit*; in general, the *dependent variable* becomes arbitrarily large in magnitude as the *independent variable* approaches a finite number.

Table 2.6

x	$f(x) = 1/x^2$
± 0.1	100
± 0.01	10,000
± 0.001	1,000,000
$\downarrow$	$\downarrow$
0	∞

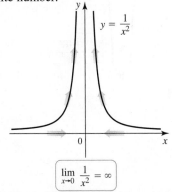

With *limits at infinity*, the opposite occurs: The *dependent variable* approaches a finite number as the *independent variable* becomes arbitrarily large in magnitude. In Table 2.7, we see that $f(x) = 1/x^2$ approaches 0 as x increases. In this case, we write $\lim_{x \to \infty} f(x) = 0$.

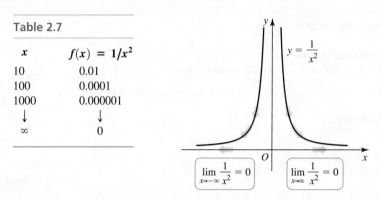

Table 2.7

x	$f(x) = 1/x^2$
10	0.01
100	0.0001
1000	0.000001
$\downarrow$	$\downarrow$
∞	0

$$y = \frac{1}{x^2}$$

$$\lim_{x \to -\infty} \frac{1}{x^2} = 0 \qquad \lim_{x \to \infty} \frac{1}{x^2} = 0$$

A general picture of these two limit scenarios is shown in Figure 2.23.

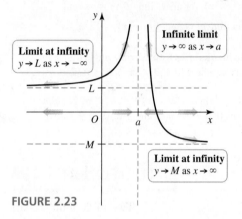

Limit at infinity
$y \to L$ as $x \to -\infty$

Infinite limit
$y \to \infty$ as $x \to a$

Limit at infinity
$y \to M$ as $x \to \infty$

FIGURE 2.23

Infinite Limits

The following definition of infinite limits is informal, but it is adequate for most functions encountered in this book. A precise definition is given in Section 2.7.

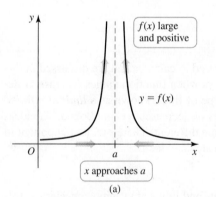

$f(x)$ large and positive

$y = f(x)$

x approaches a

(a)

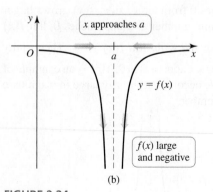

x approaches a

$y = f(x)$

$f(x)$ large and negative

(b)

FIGURE 2.24

DEFINITION Infinite Limits

Suppose f is defined for all x near a. If $f(x)$ grows arbitrarily large for all x sufficiently close (but not equal) to a (Figure 2.24a), we write

$$\lim_{x \to a} f(x) = \infty.$$

We say the limit of $f(x)$ as x approaches a is infinity.

If $f(x)$ is negative and grows arbitrarily large in magnitude for all x sufficiently close (but not equal) to a (Figure 2.24b), we write

$$\lim_{x \to a} f(x) = -\infty.$$

In this case, we say the limit of $f(x)$ as x approaches a is negative infinity. In both cases, the limit does not exist.

EXAMPLE 1   Infinite limits Evaluate $\lim\limits_{x \to 1} \dfrac{x}{(x^2 - 1)^2}$ and $\lim\limits_{x \to -1} \dfrac{x}{(x^2 - 1)^2}$ using the

graph of the function.

SOLUTION The graph of $f(x) = \dfrac{x}{(x^2 - 1)^2}$ (Figure 2.25) shows that as x approaches 1 (from either side), the values of f grow arbitrarily large. Therefore, the limit does not exist and we write

$$\lim_{x \to 1} \frac{x}{(x^2 - 1)^2} = \infty.$$

As x approaches -1, the values of f are negative and grow arbitrarily large in magnitude; therefore,

$$\lim_{x \to -1} \frac{x}{(x^2 - 1)^2} = -\infty.$$

Related Exercises 7–8 ◄

Example 1 illustrates *two-sided* infinite limits. As with finite limits, we also need to work with right-sided and left-sided infinite limits.

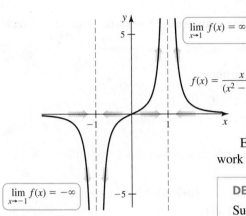

$\lim\limits_{x \to 1} f(x) = \infty$

$f(x) = \dfrac{x}{(x^2 - 1)^2}$

$\lim\limits_{x \to -1} f(x) = -\infty$

FIGURE 2.25

> **DEFINITION One-Sided Infinite Limits**
>
> Suppose f is defined for all x near a with $x > a$. If $f(x)$ becomes arbitrarily large for all x sufficiently close to a with $x > a$, we write $\lim\limits_{x \to a^+} f(x) = \infty$ (Figure 2.26a). The one-sided infinite limits $\lim\limits_{x \to a^+} f(x) = -\infty$ (Figure 2.26b), $\lim\limits_{x \to a^-} f(x) = \infty$ (Figure 2.26c), and $\lim\limits_{x \to a^-} f(x) = -\infty$ (Figure 2.26d) are defined analogously.

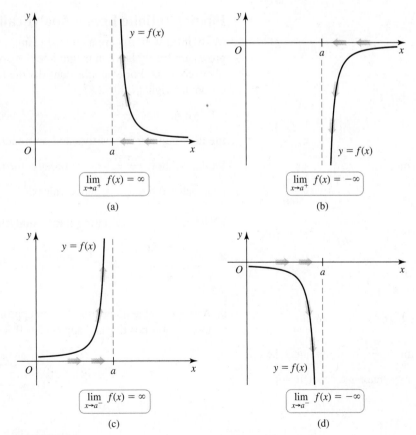

FIGURE 2.26

QUICK CHECK 1 Sketch the graph of a function and its vertical asymptote that satisfies the conditions $\lim\limits_{x \to 2^+} f(x) = -\infty$ and $\lim\limits_{x \to 2^-} f(x) = \infty$.◄

In all the infinite limits illustrated in Figure 2.26, the line $x = a$ is called a *vertical asymptote*; it is a vertical line that is approached by the graph of f as x approaches a.

> **DEFINITION Vertical Asymptote**
>
> If $\lim\limits_{x \to a} f(x) = \pm\infty$, $\lim\limits_{x \to a^+} f(x) = \pm\infty$, or $\lim\limits_{x \to a^-} f(x) = \pm\infty$, the line $x = a$ is called a **vertical asymptote** of f.

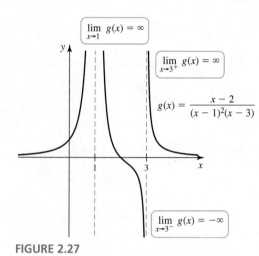

FIGURE 2.27

EXAMPLE 2 Determining limits graphically The vertical lines $x = 1$ and $x = 3$ are vertical asymptotes of the function $g(x) = \dfrac{x - 2}{(x - 1)^2 (x - 3)}$. Use Figure 2.27 to analyze the following limits.

a. $\lim\limits_{x \to 1} g(x)$ **b.** $\lim\limits_{x \to 3^-} g(x)$ **c.** $\lim\limits_{x \to 3} g(x)$

SOLUTION

a. The values of g grow arbitrarily large as x approaches 1 from either side. Therefore, $\lim\limits_{x \to 1} g(x) = \infty$.

b. The values of g are negative and grow arbitrarily large in magnitude as x approaches 3 from the left, so $\lim\limits_{x \to 3^-} g(x) = -\infty$.

c. Note that $\lim\limits_{x \to 3^+} g(x) = \infty$ and $\lim\limits_{x \to 3^-} g(x) = -\infty$. Therefore, $\lim\limits_{x \to 3} g(x)$ does not exist. Because g behaves differently as $x \to 3^-$ and as $x \to 3^+$, we do not write $\lim\limits_{x \to 3} g(x) = \infty$. We simply say that the limit does not exist.

Related Exercises 9–16◄

Finding Infinite Limits Analytically

Many infinite limits are analyzed using a simple arithmetic property: The fraction a/b grows arbitrarily large in magnitude if b approaches 0 while a remains nonzero and relatively constant. For example, consider the fraction $(5 + x)/x$ for values of x approaching 0 from the right (Table 2.8).

We see that $\dfrac{5 + x}{x} \to \infty$ as $x \to 0^+$ because the numerator $5 + x$ approaches 5 while the denominator is positive and approaches 0. Therefore, we write $\lim\limits_{x \to 0^+} \dfrac{5 + x}{x} = \infty$. Similarly, $\lim\limits_{x \to 0^-} \dfrac{5 + x}{x} = -\infty$ because the numerator approaches 5 while the denominator approaches 0 through negative values.

Table 2.8

x	$\dfrac{5 + x}{x}$
0.01	$\dfrac{5.01}{0.01} = 501$
0.001	$\dfrac{5.001}{0.001} = 5001$
0.0001	$\dfrac{5.0001}{0.0001} = 50{,}001$
$\downarrow$	$\downarrow$
0^+	∞

QUICK CHECK 2 Evaluate $\lim\limits_{x \to 0^+} \dfrac{x - 5}{x}$ and $\lim\limits_{x \to 0^-} \dfrac{x - 5}{x}$ by determining the sign of the numerator and denominator.◄

EXAMPLE 3 Evaluating limits analytically Evaluate the following limits.

a. $\lim\limits_{x \to 3^+} \dfrac{2 - 5x}{x - 3}$ **b.** $\lim\limits_{x \to 3^-} \dfrac{2 - 5x}{x - 3}$

SOLUTION

a. As $x \to 3^+$, the numerator $2 - 5x$ approaches $2 - 5(3) = -13$ while the denominator $x - 3$ is positive and approaches 0. Therefore,

$$\lim\limits_{x \to 3^+} \underbrace{\overbrace{2 - 5x}^{\text{approaches } -13}}_{\substack{\text{positive and} \\ \text{approaches } 0}} = -\infty.$$

b. As $x \to 3^-$, $2 - 5x$ approaches $2 - 5(3) = -13$ while $x - 3$ is negative and approaches 0. Therefore,

$$\lim_{x \to 3^-} \overbrace{\underbrace{\frac{2 - 5x}{x - 3}}_{\substack{\text{negative and} \\ \text{approaches } 0}}}^{\text{approaches } -13} = \infty.$$

These limits imply that the given function has a vertical asymptote at $x = 3$.

Related Exercises 17–28 ◄

EXAMPLE 4 **Evaluating limits analytically** Evaluate $\displaystyle\lim_{x \to -4^+} \frac{-x^3 + 5x^2 - 6x}{-x^3 - 4x^2}$.

> We can assume that $x \neq 0$ because we are considering function values near $x = -4$.

SOLUTION First we factor and simplify, assuming $x \neq 0$:

$$\frac{-x^3 + 5x^2 - 6x}{-x^3 - 4x^2} = \frac{-x(x - 2)(x - 3)}{-x^2(x + 4)} = \frac{(x - 2)(x - 3)}{x(x + 4)}.$$

As $x \to -4^+$, we find that

$$\lim_{x \to -4^+} \frac{-x^3 + 5x^2 - 6x}{-x^3 - 4x^2} = \lim_{x \to -4^+} \frac{\overbrace{(x - 2)(x - 3)}^{\text{approaches } 42}}{\underbrace{x(x + 4)}_{\substack{\text{negative and} \\ \text{approaches } 0}}} = -\infty.$$

QUICK CHECK 3 Verify that $x(x + 4) \to 0$ through negative values as $x \to -4^+$. ◄

This limit implies that the given function has a vertical asymptote at $x = -4$.

Related Exercises 17–28 ◄

> Example 5 illustrates that $f(x)/g(x)$ might not grow arbitrarily large in magnitude if *both* $f(x)$ and $g(x)$ approach 0. Such limits are called *indeterminate forms* and are examined in detail in Section 4.7.

EXAMPLE 5 **Location of vertical asymptotes** Let $f(x) = \dfrac{x^2 - 4x + 3}{x^2 - 1}$. Evaluate the following limits and find the vertical asymptotes of f. Verify your work with a graphing utility.

a. $\displaystyle\lim_{x \to 1} f(x)$ **b.** $\displaystyle\lim_{x \to -1^-} f(x)$ **c.** $\displaystyle\lim_{x \to -1^+} f(x)$

SOLUTION

a. Notice that as $x \to 1$, both the numerator and denominator of f approach 0, and the function is undefined at $x = 1$. To compute $\displaystyle\lim_{x \to 1} f(x)$, we first factor:

> It is permissible to cancel the $x - 1$ factors in $\displaystyle\lim_{x \to 1} \frac{(x - 1)(x - 3)}{(x - 1)(x + 1)}$ because x approaches 1 but is not equal to 1. Therefore, $x - 1 \neq 0$.

$$\begin{aligned}
\lim_{x \to 1} f(x) &= \lim_{x \to 1} \frac{x^2 - 4x + 3}{x^2 - 1} \\[2mm]
&= \lim_{x \to 1} \frac{(x - 1)(x - 3)}{(x - 1)(x + 1)} &&\text{Factor.} \\[2mm]
&= \lim_{x \to 1} \frac{(x - 3)}{(x + 1)} &&\text{Cancel like factors, } x \neq 1. \\[2mm]
&= \frac{1 - 3}{1 + 1} = -1. &&\text{Substitute } x = 1.
\end{aligned}$$

Therefore, $\displaystyle\lim_{x \to 1} f(x) = -1$ (even though $f(1)$ is undefined). The line $x = 1$ is *not* a vertical asymptote of f.

b. In part (a), we showed that

$$f(x) = \frac{x^2 - 4x + 3}{x^2 - 1} = \frac{x - 3}{x + 1}, \quad \text{provided } x \neq 1.$$

We use this fact again. As x approaches -1 from the left, the one-sided limit is

$$\lim_{x \to -1^-} f(x) = \lim_{x \to -1^-} \frac{\overbrace{x - 3}^{\text{approaches } -4}}{\underbrace{x + 1}_{\substack{\text{negative and} \\ \text{approaches } 0}}} = \infty.$$

c. As x approaches -1 from the right, the one-sided limit is

$$\lim_{x \to -1^+} f(x) = \lim_{x \to -1^+} \frac{\overbrace{x - 3}^{\text{approaches } -4}}{\underbrace{x + 1}_{\substack{\text{positive and} \\ \text{approaches } 0}}} = -\infty.$$

The infinite limits $\lim_{x \to -1^+} f(x) = -\infty$ and $\lim_{x \to -1^-} f(x) = \infty$ each imply that the line $x = -1$ is a vertical asymptote of f. The graph of f generated by a graphing utility *may* appear as shown in Figure 2.28a. If so, two corrections must be made. A hole should appear in the graph at $(1, -1)$ because $\lim_{x \to 1} f(x) = -1$, but $f(1)$ is undefined. It is also a good idea to replace the solid vertical line with a dashed line to emphasize that the vertical asymptote is not a part of the graph of f (Figure 2.28b).

> Graphing utilities vary in how they display vertical asymptotes. The errors shown in Figure 2.28a do not occur on all graphing utilities.

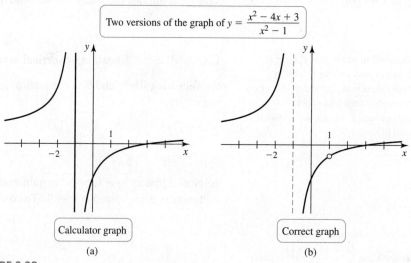

Two versions of the graph of $y = \dfrac{x^2 - 4x + 3}{x^2 - 1}$

Calculator graph
(a)

Correct graph
(b)

FIGURE 2.28

Related Exercises 29–34 ◀

QUICK CHECK 4 The line $x = 2$ is not a vertical asymptote of $y = \dfrac{(x - 1)(x - 2)}{x - 2}$. Why not? ◀

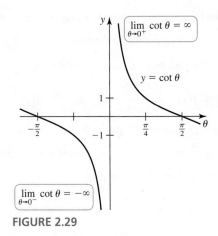

FIGURE 2.29

EXAMPLE 6 **Limits of trigonometric functions** Evaluate the following limits.

a. $\lim\limits_{\theta \to 0^+} \cot \theta$　　　**b.** $\lim\limits_{\theta \to 0^-} \cot \theta$

SOLUTION

a. Recall that $\cot \theta = \cos \theta / \sin \theta$. Furthermore (Example 8, Section 2.3), $\lim\limits_{\theta \to 0^+} \cos \theta = 1$ and $\sin \theta$ is positive and approaches 0 as $\theta \to 0^+$. Therefore, as $\theta \to 0^+$, $\cot \theta$ becomes arbitrarily large and positive, which means $\lim\limits_{\theta \to 0^+} \cot \theta = \infty$. This limit is confirmed by the graph of $\cot \theta$ (Figure 2.29), which has a vertical asymptote at $\theta = 0$.

b. In this case, $\lim\limits_{\theta \to 0^-} \cos \theta = 1$ and as $\theta \to 0^-$, $\sin \theta \to 0$ with $\sin \theta < 0$. Therefore, as $\theta \to 0^-$, $\cot \theta$ is negative and becomes arbitrarily large in magnitude. It follows that $\lim\limits_{\theta \to 0^-} \cot \theta = -\infty$, as confirmed by the graph of $\cot \theta$.

Related Exercises 35–40◄

SECTION 2.4 EXERCISES

Review Questions

1. Use a graph to explain the meaning of $\lim\limits_{x \to a^+} f(x) = -\infty$.

2. Use a graph to explain the meaning of $\lim\limits_{x \to a} f(x) = \infty$.

3. What is a vertical asymptote?

4. Consider the function $F(x) = f(x)/g(x)$ with $g(a) = 0$. Does F necessarily have a vertical asymptote at $x = a$? Explain your reasoning.

5. Suppose $f(x) \to 100$ and $g(x) \to 0$, with $g(x) < 0$, as $x \to 2$. Determine $\lim\limits_{x \to 2} \dfrac{f(x)}{g(x)}$.

6. Evaluate $\lim\limits_{x \to 3^-} \dfrac{1}{x - 3}$ and $\lim\limits_{x \to 3^+} \dfrac{1}{x - 3}$.

Basic Skills

T 7. **Analyzing infinite limits numerically** Compute the values of $f(x) = \dfrac{x + 1}{(x - 1)^2}$ in the following table and use them to discuss $\lim\limits_{x \to 1} f(x)$.

x	$\dfrac{x + 1}{(x - 1)^2}$	x	$\dfrac{x + 1}{(x - 1)^2}$
1.1		0.9	
1.01		0.99	
1.001		0.999	
1.0001		0.9999	

8. **Analyzing infinite limits graphically** Use the graph of $f(x) = \dfrac{x}{(x^2 - 2x - 3)^2}$ to discuss $\lim\limits_{x \to -1} f(x)$ and $\lim\limits_{x \to 3} f(x)$.

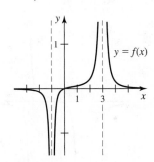

9. **Analyzing infinite limits graphically** The graph of f in the figure has vertical asymptotes at $x = 1$ and $x = 2$. Analyze the following limits.

a. $\lim\limits_{x \to 1^-} f(x)$　　**b.** $\lim\limits_{x \to 1^+} f(x)$　　**c.** $\lim\limits_{x \to 1} f(x)$

d. $\lim\limits_{x \to 2^-} f(x)$　　**e.** $\lim\limits_{x \to 2^+} f(x)$　　**f.** $\lim\limits_{x \to 2} f(x)$

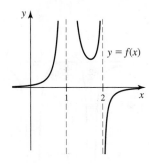

10. Analyzing infinite limits graphically The graph of g in the figure has vertical asymptotes at $x = 2$ and $x = 4$. Analyze the following limits.

a. $\displaystyle\lim_{x\to2^-} g(x)$ **b.** $\displaystyle\lim_{x\to2^+} g(x)$ **c.** $\displaystyle\lim_{x\to2} g(x)$

d. $\displaystyle\lim_{x\to4^-} g(x)$ **e.** $\displaystyle\lim_{x\to4^+} g(x)$ **f.** $\displaystyle\lim_{x\to4} g(x)$

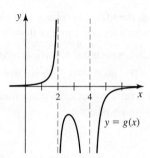

$y = g(x)$

11. Analyzing infinite limits graphically The graph of h in the figure has vertical asymptotes at $x = -2$ and $x = 3$. Investigate the following limits.

a. $\displaystyle\lim_{x\to-2^-} h(x)$ **b.** $\displaystyle\lim_{x\to-2^+} h(x)$ **c.** $\displaystyle\lim_{x\to-2} h(x)$

d. $\displaystyle\lim_{x\to3^-} h(x)$ **e.** $\displaystyle\lim_{x\to3^+} h(x)$ **f.** $\displaystyle\lim_{x\to3} h(x)$

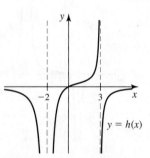

$y = h(x)$

12. Analyzing infinite limits graphically The graph of p in the figure has vertical asymptotes at $x = -2$ and $x = 3$. Investigate the following limits.

a. $\displaystyle\lim_{x\to-2^-} p(x)$ **b.** $\displaystyle\lim_{x\to-2^+} p(x)$ **c.** $\displaystyle\lim_{x\to-2} p(x)$

d. $\displaystyle\lim_{x\to3^-} p(x)$ **e.** $\displaystyle\lim_{x\to3^+} p(x)$ **f.** $\displaystyle\lim_{x\to3} p(x)$

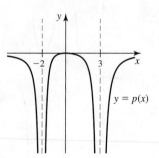

$y = p(x)$

13. Analyzing infinite limits graphically Graph the function
$$f(x) = \frac{1}{x^2 - x}$$ using a graphing utility with the window $[-1, 2] \times [-10, 10]$. Use your graph to discuss the following limits.

a. $\displaystyle\lim_{x\to0^-} f(x)$ **b.** $\displaystyle\lim_{x\to0^+} f(x)$ **c.** $\displaystyle\lim_{x\to1^-} f(x)$ **d.** $\displaystyle\lim_{x\to1^+} f(x)$

14. Analyzing infinite limits graphically Graph the function
$$f(x) = \frac{e^{-x}}{x(x+2)^2}$$ using a graphing utility. (Experiment with your choice of a graphing window.) Use your graph to discuss the following limits.

a. $\displaystyle\lim_{x\to-2^+} f(x)$ **b.** $\displaystyle\lim_{x\to-2} f(x)$ **c.** $\displaystyle\lim_{x\to0^-} f(x)$ **d.** $\displaystyle\lim_{x\to0^+} f(x)$

15. Sketching graphs Sketch a possible graph of a function f, together with vertical asymptotes, satisfying all the following conditions on $[0, 4]$.

$$f(1) = 0, \quad f(3) \text{ is undefined}, \quad \lim_{x\to3} f(x) = 1,$$
$$\lim_{x\to0^+} f(x) = -\infty, \quad \lim_{x\to2} f(x) = \infty, \quad \lim_{x\to4^-} f(x) = \infty$$

16. Sketching graphs Sketch a possible graph of a function g, together with vertical asymptotes, satisfying all the following conditions.

$$g(2) = 1, \quad g(5) = -1, \quad \lim_{x\to4} g(x) = -\infty,$$
$$\lim_{x\to7^-} g(x) = \infty, \quad \lim_{x\to7^+} g(x) = -\infty$$

17–28. Evaluating limits analytically *Evaluate the following limits or state that they do not exist.*

17. a. $\displaystyle\lim_{x\to2^+} \frac{1}{x-2}$ **b.** $\displaystyle\lim_{x\to2^-} \frac{1}{x-2}$ **c.** $\displaystyle\lim_{x\to2} \frac{1}{x-2}$

18. a. $\displaystyle\lim_{x\to3^+} \frac{2}{(x-3)^3}$ **b.** $\displaystyle\lim_{x\to3^-} \frac{2}{(x-3)^3}$ **c.** $\displaystyle\lim_{x\to3} \frac{2}{(x-3)^3}$

19. a. $\displaystyle\lim_{x\to4^+} \frac{x-5}{(x-4)^2}$ **b.** $\displaystyle\lim_{x\to4^-} \frac{x-5}{(x-4)^2}$ **c.** $\displaystyle\lim_{x\to4} \frac{x-5}{(x-4)^2}$

20. a. $\displaystyle\lim_{x\to1^+} \frac{x-2}{(x-1)^3}$ **b.** $\displaystyle\lim_{x\to1^-} \frac{x-2}{(x-1)^3}$ **c.** $\displaystyle\lim_{x\to1} \frac{x-2}{(x-1)^3}$

21. a. $\displaystyle\lim_{x\to3^+} \frac{(x-1)(x-2)}{(x-3)}$ **b.** $\displaystyle\lim_{x\to3^-} \frac{(x-1)(x-2)}{(x-3)}$

 c. $\displaystyle\lim_{x\to3} \frac{(x-1)(x-2)}{(x-3)}$

22. a. $\displaystyle\lim_{x\to-2^+} \frac{(x-4)}{x(x+2)}$ **b.** $\displaystyle\lim_{x\to-2^-} \frac{(x-4)}{x(x+2)}$ **c.** $\displaystyle\lim_{x\to-2} \frac{(x-4)}{x(x+2)}$

23. $\displaystyle\lim_{x\to0} \frac{x^3 - 5x^2}{x^2}$ **24.** $\displaystyle\lim_{t\to5} \frac{4t^2 - 100}{t - 5}$

25. $\displaystyle\lim_{x\to1^+} \frac{x^2 - 5x + 6}{x - 1}$ **26.** $\displaystyle\lim_{z\to4} \frac{z - 5}{(z^2 - 10z + 24)^2}$

27. a. $\lim\limits_{x \to 2^+} \dfrac{x^2 - 4x + 3}{(x - 2)^2}$ **b.** $\lim\limits_{x \to 2^-} \dfrac{x^2 - 4x + 3}{(x - 2)^2}$

c. $\lim\limits_{x \to 2} \dfrac{x^2 - 4x + 3}{(x - 2)^2}$

28. a. $\lim\limits_{x \to -2^+} \dfrac{x^3 - 5x^2 + 6x}{x^4 - 4x^2}$ **b.** $\lim\limits_{x \to -2^-} \dfrac{x^3 - 5x^2 + 6x}{x^4 - 4x^2}$

c. $\lim\limits_{x \to -2} \dfrac{x^3 - 5x^2 + 6x}{x^4 - 4x^2}$ **d.** $\lim\limits_{x \to 2} \dfrac{x^3 - 5x^2 + 6x}{x^4 - 4x^2}$

29. Location of vertical asymptotes Analyze the following limits and find the vertical asymptotes of $f(x) = \dfrac{x - 5}{x^2 - 25}$.

a. $\lim\limits_{x \to 5} f(x)$ **b.** $\lim\limits_{x \to -5^-} f(x)$ **c.** $\lim\limits_{x \to -5^+} f(x)$

30. Location of vertical asymptotes Analyze the following limits and find the vertical asymptotes of $f(x) = \dfrac{x + 7}{x^4 - 49x^2}$.

a. $\lim\limits_{x \to 7^-} f(x)$ **b.** $\lim\limits_{x \to 7^+} f(x)$ **c.** $\lim\limits_{x \to -7} f(x)$ **d.** $\lim\limits_{x \to 0} f(x)$

31–34. Finding vertical asymptotes *Find all vertical asymptotes $x = a$ of the following functions. For each value of a, discuss* $\lim\limits_{x \to a^+} f(x),\ \lim\limits_{x \to a^-} f(x),\ \text{and}\ \lim\limits_{x \to a} f(x)$.

31. $f(x) = \dfrac{x^2 - 9x + 14}{x^2 - 5x + 6}$ **32.** $f(x) = \dfrac{\cos x}{x^2 + 2x}$

33. $f(x) = \dfrac{x + 1}{x^3 - 4x^2 + 4x}$ **34.** $f(x) = \dfrac{x^3 - 10x^2 + 16x}{x^2 - 8x}$

35–38. Trigonometric limits *Investigate the following limits.*

35. $\lim\limits_{\theta \to 0^+} \csc \theta$ **36.** $\lim\limits_{x \to 0^-} \csc x$

37. $\lim\limits_{x \to 0^+} (-10 \cot x)$ **38.** $\lim\limits_{\theta \to \pi/2^+} \dfrac{1}{3} \tan \theta$

⊤ 39. Analyzing infinite limits graphically Graph the function $y = \tan x$ with the window $[-\pi, \pi] \times [-10, 10]$. Use the graph to analyze the following limits.

a. $\lim\limits_{x \to \pi/2^+} \tan x$ **b.** $\lim\limits_{x \to \pi/2^-} \tan x$
c. $\lim\limits_{x \to -\pi/2^+} \tan x$ **d.** $\lim\limits_{x \to -\pi/2^-} \tan x$

⊤ 40. Analyzing infinite limits graphically Graph the function $y = \sec x \tan x$ with the window $[-\pi, \pi] \times [-10, 10]$. Use the graph to analyze the following limits.

a. $\lim\limits_{x \to \pi/2^+} \sec x \tan x$ **b.** $\lim\limits_{x \to \pi/2^-} \sec x \tan x$
c. $\lim\limits_{x \to -\pi/2^+} \sec x \tan x$ **d.** $\lim\limits_{x \to -\pi/2^-} \sec x \tan x$

Further Explorations

41. Explain why or why not Determine whether the following statements are true and give an explanation or counterexample.

a. The line $x = 1$ is a vertical asymptote of the function $f(x) = \dfrac{x^2 - 7x + 6}{x^2 - 1}$.

b. The line $x = -1$ is a vertical asymptote of the function $f(x) = \dfrac{x^2 - 7x + 6}{x^2 - 1}$.

c. If g has a vertical asymptote at $x = 1$ and $\lim\limits_{x \to 1^+} g(x) = \infty$, then $\lim\limits_{x \to 1^-} g(x) = \infty$.

42. Finding a function with vertical asymptotes Find polynomials p and q such that $f = p/q$ is undefined at 1 and 2, but p/q has a vertical asymptote only at 2. Sketch a graph of your function.

43. Finding a function with infinite limits Give a formula for a function f that satisfies $\lim\limits_{x \to 6^+} f(x) = \infty$ and $\lim\limits_{x \to 6^-} f(x) = -\infty$.

44. Matching Match functions a–f with graphs A–F in the figure without using a graphing utility.

a. $f(x) = \dfrac{x}{x^2 + 1}$ **b.** $f(x) = \dfrac{x}{x^2 - 1}$

c. $f(x) = \dfrac{1}{x^2 - 1}$ **d.** $f(x) = \dfrac{x}{(x - 1)^2}$

e. $f(x) = \dfrac{1}{(x - 1)^2}$ **f.** $f(x) = \dfrac{x}{x + 1}$

A.
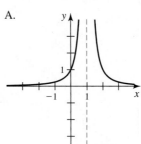

B.
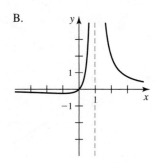

C.
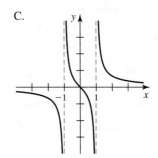

D.
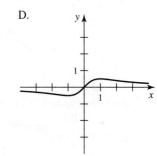

E.
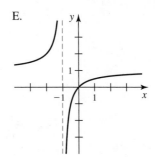

F.
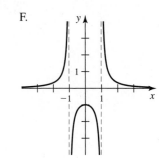

Additional Exercises

45. Limits with a parameter Let $f(x) = \dfrac{x^2 - 7x + 12}{x - a}$.

a. For what values of a, if any, does $\lim\limits_{x \to a^+} f(x)$ equal a finite number?

b. For what values of a, if any, does $\lim\limits_{x \to a^+} f(x) = \infty$?

c. For what values of a, if any, does $\lim\limits_{x \to a^+} f(x) = -\infty$?

46–47. Steep secant lines

a. *Given the graph of f in the following figures, find the slope of the secant line that passes through $(0, 0)$ and $(h, f(h))$ in terms of h, for $h > 0$ and $h < 0$.*

b. *Evaluate the limit of the slope of the secant line found in part (a) as $h \to 0^+$ and $h \to 0^-$. What does this tell you about the line tangent to the curve at $(0, 0)$?*

46. $f(x) = x^{1/3}$

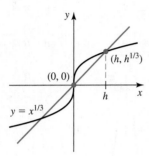

47. $f(x) = x^{2/3}$

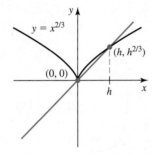

48. Care with graphing The figure shows the graph of the function $f(x) = \dfrac{2000}{50 + 100x^2}$ graphed in the window $[-4, 4] \times [0, 20]$.

a. Evaluate $\lim\limits_{x \to 0^+} f(x)$, $\lim\limits_{x \to 0^-} f(x)$, and $\lim\limits_{x \to 0} f(x)$.

b. Create a graph that gives a more complete representation of f.

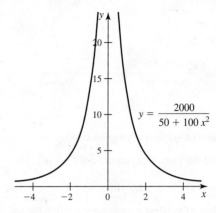

$$y = \frac{2000}{50 + 100\, x^2}$$

Technology Exercises

49–56. Asymptotes *Use analytical methods and/or a graphing utility to identify the vertical asymptotes (if any) of the following functions.*

49. $f(x) = \dfrac{x^2 - 3x + 2}{x^{10} - x^9}$ **50.** $g(x) = 2 - \ln x^2$

51. $h(x) = \dfrac{e^x}{(x + 1)^3}$ **52.** $p(x) = \sec\left(\dfrac{\pi x}{2}\right)$, for $|x| < 2$

53. $g(\theta) = \tan\left(\dfrac{\pi\theta}{10}\right)$ **54.** $q(s) = \dfrac{\pi}{s - \sin s}$

55. $f(x) = \dfrac{1}{\sqrt{x}\,\sec x}$ **56.** $g(x) = e^{1/x}$

57. Can a graph intersect a vertical asymptote? A common misconception is that the graph of a function never intersects its vertical asymptotes. Let

$$f(x) = \begin{cases} \dfrac{4}{x - 1} & \text{if } x < 1 \\[2mm] x^2 & \text{if } x \geq 1. \end{cases}$$

Explain why $x = 1$ is a vertical asymptote of the graph of f and show that the graph of f intersects the line $x = 1$.

QUICK CHECK   ANSWERS

1. Answers will vary, but all graphs should have a vertical asymptote at $x = 2$.   **2.** $-\infty$; ∞ **3.** As $x \to -4^+$, $x < 0$ and $(x + 4) > 0$, so $x(x + 4) \to 0$ through negative values.

4. $\lim\limits_{x \to 2} \dfrac{(x - 1)(x - 2)}{x - 2} = \lim\limits_{x \to 2} (x - 1) = 1$, which is not an infinite limit, so $x = 2$ is not a vertical asymptote. ◄

2.5 Limits at Infinity

Limits at infinity—as opposed to infinite limits—occur when the independent variable becomes large in magnitude. For this reason, limits at infinity determine what is called the *end behavior* of a function. An application of these limits is to determine whether a system (such as an ecosystem or a large oscillating structure) reaches a steady state as time increases.

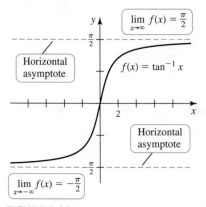

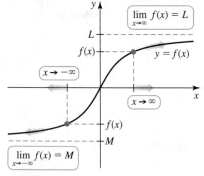

FIGURE 2.30

FIGURE 2.31

Limits at Infinity and Horizontal Asymptotes

Consider the function $f(x) = \tan^{-1} x$, whose domain is $(-\infty, \infty)$ (Figure 2.30). As x becomes arbitrarily large (denoted $x \to \infty$), $f(x)$ approaches $\pi/2$, and as x becomes arbitrarily large in magnitude and negative (denoted $x \to -\infty$), $f(x)$ approaches $-\pi/2$. These limits are expressed as

$$\lim_{x \to \infty} \tan^{-1} x = \frac{\pi}{2} \quad \text{and} \quad \lim_{x \to -\infty} \tan^{-1} x = -\frac{\pi}{2}.$$

The graph of f approaches the horizontal line $y = \pi/2$ as $x \to \infty$, and it approaches the horizontal line $y = -\pi/2$ as $x \to -\infty$. These lines are called *horizontal asymptotes*.

DEFINITION Limits at Infinity and Horizontal Asymptotes

If $f(x)$ becomes arbitrarily close to a finite number L for all sufficiently large and positive x, then we write

$$\lim_{x \to \infty} f(x) = L.$$

We say the limit of $f(x)$ as x approaches infinity is L. In this case, the line $y = L$ is a **horizontal asymptote** of f (Figure 2.31). The limit at negative infinity, $\lim_{x \to -\infty} f(x) = M$, is defined analogously. When the limit exists, the horizontal asymptote is $y = M$.

> The limit laws of Theorem 2.3 and the Squeeze Theorem apply if $x \to a$ is replaced with $x \to \infty$ or $x \to -\infty$.

QUICK CHECK 1 Evaluate $x/(x + 1)$ for $x = 10$, 100, and 1000. What is $\displaystyle\lim_{x \to \infty} \frac{x}{x + 1}$?

EXAMPLE 1   Limits at infinity Evaluate the following limits.

a. $\displaystyle\lim_{x \to -\infty} \left(2 + \frac{10}{x^2}\right)$ **b.** $\displaystyle\lim_{x \to \infty} \left(3 + \frac{3 \sin x}{\sqrt{x}}\right)$

SOLUTION

a. As x becomes large and negative, x^2 becomes large and positive; in turn, $10/x^2$ approaches 0. By the limit laws of Theorem 2.3,

$$\lim_{x \to -\infty} \left(2 + \frac{10}{x^2}\right) = \underbrace{\lim_{x \to -\infty} 2}_{\text{equals 2}} + \underbrace{\lim_{x \to -\infty} \left(\frac{10}{x^2}\right)}_{\text{equals 0}} = 2 + 0 = 2.$$

Notice that $\displaystyle\lim_{x \to \infty} \left(2 + \frac{10}{x^2}\right)$ is also equal to 2. Therefore, the graph of $y = 2 + 10/x^2$ approaches the horizontal asymptote $y = 2$ as $x \to \infty$ and as $x \to -\infty$ (Figure 2.32).

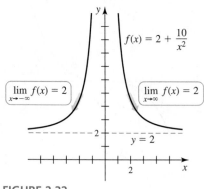

FIGURE 2.32

b. The numerator of $\sin x/\sqrt{x}$ is bounded between -1 and 1; therefore, for $x > 0$,

$$-\frac{1}{\sqrt{x}} \le \frac{\sin x}{\sqrt{x}} \le \frac{1}{\sqrt{x}}.$$

As $x \to \infty$, $\sqrt{x}$ becomes arbitrarily large, which means that

$$\lim_{x \to \infty} \frac{-1}{\sqrt{x}} = \lim_{x \to \infty} \frac{1}{\sqrt{x}} = 0.$$

It follows by the Squeeze Theorem (Theorem 2.5) that $\displaystyle\lim_{x \to \infty} \frac{\sin x}{\sqrt{x}} = 0$.

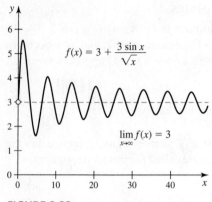

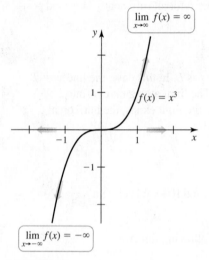

FIGURE 2.33

FIGURE 2.34

Using the limit laws of Theorem 2.3,

$$\lim_{x \to \infty} \left(3 + \frac{3 \sin x}{\sqrt{x}} \right) = \underbrace{\lim_{x \to \infty} 3}_{\text{equals 3}} + 3 \underbrace{\lim_{x \to \infty} \left(\frac{\sin x}{\sqrt{x}} \right)}_{\text{equals 0}} = 3.$$

The graph of $y = 3 + \dfrac{3 \sin x}{\sqrt{x}}$ approaches the horizontal asymptote $y = 3$ as x becomes large (Figure 2.33). Note that the curve intersects its asymptote infinitely many times.   *Related Exercises 9–14* ◄

Infinite Limits at Infinity

It is possible for a limit to be *both* an infinite limit and a limit at infinity. This type of limit occurs if $f(x)$ becomes arbitrarily large in magnitude as x becomes arbitrarily large in magnitude. Such a limit is called an *infinite limit at infinity* and is illustrated by the function $f(x) = x^3$ (Figure 2.34).

DEFINITION Infinite Limits at Infinity

If $f(x)$ becomes arbitrarily large as x becomes arbitrarily large, then we write

$$\lim_{x \to \infty} f(x) = \infty.$$

The limits $\lim_{x \to \infty} f(x) = -\infty$, $\lim_{x \to -\infty} f(x) = \infty$, and $\lim_{x \to -\infty} f(x) = -\infty$ are defined similarly.

Infinite limits at infinity tell us about the behavior of polynomials for large-magnitude values of x. First, consider power functions $f(x) = x^n$, where n is a positive integer. Figure 2.35 shows that when n is even, $\lim_{x \to \pm\infty} x^n = \infty$, and when n is odd, $\lim_{x \to \infty} x^n = \infty$ and $\lim_{x \to -\infty} x^n = -\infty$.

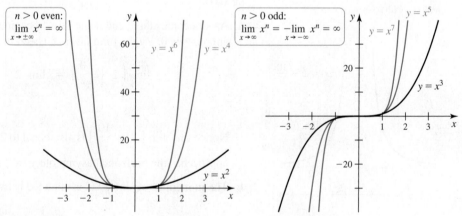

FIGURE 2.35

It follows that reciprocals of power functions $f(x) = 1/x^n = x^{-n}$, where n is a positive integer, behave as follows:

$$\lim_{x \to \infty} \frac{1}{x^n} = \lim_{x \to \infty} x^{-n} = 0 \quad \text{and} \quad \lim_{x \to -\infty} \frac{1}{x^n} = \lim_{x \to -\infty} x^{-n} = 0.$$

QUICK CHECK 2 Describe the behavior of $p(x) = -3x^3$ as $x \to \infty$ and as $x \to -\infty$. ◄

From here, it is a short step to finding the behavior of any polynomial as $x \to \pm\infty$. Let $p(x) = a_n x^n + a_{n-1} x^{n-1} + \cdots + a_2 x^2 + a_1 x + a_0$. We now write p in the equivalent form

$$p(x) = x^n \left(a_n + \underbrace{\frac{a_{n-1}}{x}}_{\to 0} + \underbrace{\frac{a_{n-2}}{x^2}}_{\to 0} + \cdots + \underbrace{\frac{a_0}{x^n}}_{\to 0} \right).$$

Notice that as x becomes large in magnitude, all the terms in p except the first term approach zero. Therefore, as $x \to \pm\infty$, we see that $p(x) \approx a_n x^n$. This means that as $x \to \pm\infty$, the behavior of p is determined by the term $a_n x^n$ with the highest power of x.

THEOREM 2.6   Limits at Infinity of Powers and Polynomials
Let n be a positive integer and let p be the polynomial
$p(x) = a_n x^n + a_{n-1} x^{n-1} + \cdots + a_2 x^2 + a_1 x + a_0$, where $a_n \neq 0$.

1. $\displaystyle\lim_{x \to \pm\infty} x^n = \infty$ when n is even.

2. $\displaystyle\lim_{x \to \infty} x^n = \infty$ and $\displaystyle\lim_{x \to -\infty} x^n = -\infty$ when n is odd.

3. $\displaystyle\lim_{x \to \pm\infty} \frac{1}{x^n} = \lim_{x \to \pm\infty} x^{-n} = 0.$

4. $\displaystyle\lim_{x \to \pm\infty} p(x) = \lim_{x \to \pm\infty} a_n x^n = \infty$ or $-\infty$, depending on the degree of the polynomial and the sign of the leading coefficient a_n.

EXAMPLE 2   Limits at infinity Evaluate the limits as $x \to \pm\infty$ of the following functions.

a. $p(x) = 3x^4 - 6x^2 + x - 10$ **b.** $q(x) = -2x^3 + 3x^2 - 12$

SOLUTION

a. We use the fact that the limit is determined by the behavior of the leading term:

$$\lim_{x \to \infty} (3x^4 - 6x^2 + x - 10) = \lim_{x \to \infty} \underbrace{3x^4}_{\to \infty} = \infty.$$

Similarly,

$$\lim_{x \to -\infty} (3x^4 - 6x^2 + x - 10) = \lim_{x \to -\infty} \underbrace{3x^4}_{\to \infty} = \infty.$$

b. Noting that the leading coefficient is negative, we have

$$\lim_{x \to \infty} (-2x^3 + 3x^2 - 12) = \lim_{x \to \infty} (\underbrace{-2x^3}_{\to \infty}) = -\infty$$

$$\lim_{x \to -\infty} (-2x^3 + 3x^2 - 12) = \lim_{x \to -\infty} (\underbrace{-2x^3}_{\to -\infty}) = \infty.$$

Related Exercises 15–24 ◄

End Behavior

The behavior of polynomials as $x \to \pm\infty$ is an example of what is often called *end behavior*. Having treated polynomials, we now turn to the end behavior of rational, algebraic, and transcendental functions.

EXAMPLE 3   End behavior of rational functions Determine the end behavior for the following rational functions.

a. $f(x) = \dfrac{3x + 2}{x^2 - 1}$ **b.** $g(x) = \dfrac{40x^4 + 4x^2 - 1}{10x^4 + 8x^2 + 1}$ **c.** $h(x) = \dfrac{x^3 - 2x + 1}{2x + 4}$

SOLUTION

a. An effective approach for evaluating limits of rational functions at infinity is to divide both the numerator and denominator by x^n, where n is the largest power appearing in the denominator. This strategy forces the terms corresponding to lower powers of x to approach 0 in the limit. In this case, we divide by x^2:

$$\lim_{x \to \infty} \frac{3x + 2}{x^2 - 1} = \lim_{x \to \infty} \frac{\dfrac{3x + 2}{x^2}}{\dfrac{x^2 - 1}{x^2}} = \lim_{x \to \infty} \frac{\overbrace{\dfrac{3}{x} + \dfrac{2}{x^2}}^{\text{approaches } 0}}{\underbrace{1 - \dfrac{1}{x^2}}_{\text{approaches } 0}} = \frac{0}{1} = 0.$$

> Recall that the *degree* of a polynomial is the highest power of x that appears.

A similar calculation gives $\lim\limits_{x \to -\infty} \dfrac{3x + 2}{x^2 - 1} = 0$, and thus the graph of f has the horizontal asymptote $y = 0$. You should confirm that the zeros of the denominator are -1 and 1, which correspond to vertical asymptotes (Figure 2.36). In this example, the degree of the polynomial in the numerator is *less than* the degree of the polynomial in the denominator.

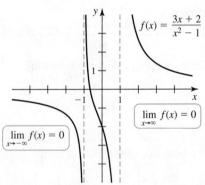

$$f(x) = \frac{3x + 2}{x^2 - 1}$$

$$\lim_{x \to \infty} f(x) = 0$$

$$\lim_{x \to -\infty} f(x) = 0$$

FIGURE 2.36

b. Again we divide both the numerator and denominator by the largest power appearing in the denominator, which is x^4:

$$\lim_{x \to \infty} \frac{40x^4 + 4x^2 - 1}{10x^4 + 8x^2 + 1} = \lim_{x \to \infty} \frac{\dfrac{40x^4}{x^4} + \dfrac{4x^2}{x^4} - \dfrac{1}{x^4}}{\dfrac{10x^4}{x^4} + \dfrac{8x^2}{x^4} + \dfrac{1}{x^4}} \qquad \text{Divide the numerator and denominator by } x^4.$$

$$= \lim_{x \to \infty} \frac{40 + \overbrace{\dfrac{4}{x^2}}^{\text{approaches } 0} - \overbrace{\dfrac{1}{x^4}}^{\text{approaches } 0}}{10 + \underbrace{\dfrac{8}{x^2}}_{\text{approaches } 0} + \underbrace{\dfrac{1}{x^4}}_{\text{approaches } 0}} \qquad \text{Simplify.}$$

$$= \frac{40 + 0 + 0}{10 + 0 + 0} = 4. \qquad \text{Evaluate limits.}$$

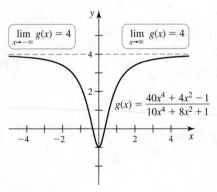

$$\lim_{x \to -\infty} g(x) = 4$$

$$\lim_{x \to \infty} g(x) = 4$$

$$g(x) = \frac{40x^4 + 4x^2 - 1}{10x^4 + 8x^2 + 1}$$

FIGURE 2.37

Using the same steps (dividing each term by x^4), it can be shown that $\lim\limits_{x \to -\infty} \dfrac{40x^4 + 4x^2 - 1}{10x^4 + 8x^2 + 1} = 4$. This function has the horizontal asymptote $y = 4$ (Figure 2.37). Notice that the degree of the polynomial in the numerator *equals* the degree of the polynomial in the denominator.

c. We divide the numerator and denominator by the largest power of x appearing in the denominator, which is x, and then take the limit:

$$\lim_{x \to \infty} \frac{x^3 - 2x + 1}{2x + 4} = \lim_{x \to \infty} \frac{\dfrac{x^3}{x} - \dfrac{2x}{x} + \dfrac{1}{x}}{\dfrac{2x}{x} + \dfrac{4}{x}}$$ Divide numerator and denominator by x.

$$= \lim_{x \to \infty} \frac{\overset{\text{arbitrarily large}}{\overbrace{x^2}} - \overset{\text{constant}}{\overbrace{2}} + \overset{\text{approaches 0}}{\overbrace{\dfrac{1}{x}}}}{\underset{\text{constant}}{\underbrace{2}} + \underset{\text{approaches 0}}{\underbrace{\dfrac{4}{x}}}}$$ Simplify.

$$= \infty.$$ Take limits.

As $x \to \infty$, all the terms in this function either approach zero or are constant—except the x^2-term in the numerator, which becomes arbitrarily large. Therefore, the limit of the function does not exist. Using a similar analysis, we find that $\displaystyle \lim_{x \to -\infty} \frac{x^3 - 2x + 1}{2x + 4} = \infty$.

These limits are not finite, and so the graph of the function has no horizontal asymptote. In this case, the degree of the polynomial in the numerator is *greater than* the degree of the polynomial in the denominator.

Related Exercises 25–34 ◄

The conclusions reached in Example 3 can be generalized for all rational functions. These results are summarized in Theorem 2.7 (Exercise 74).

THEOREM 2.7   End Behavior and Asymptotes of Rational Functions

Suppose $f(x) = \dfrac{p(x)}{q(x)}$ is a rational function, where

$$p(x) = a_m x^m + a_{m-1} x^{m-1} + \cdots + a_2 x^2 + a_1 x + a_0 \quad \text{and}$$
$$q(x) = b_n x^n + b_{n-1} x^{n-1} + \cdots + b_2 x^2 + b_1 x + b_0,$$

with $a_m \neq 0$ and $b_n \neq 0$.

a. **Degree of numerator less than degree of denominator** If $m < n$, then $\displaystyle \lim_{x \to \pm\infty} f(x) = 0$, and $y = 0$ is a horizontal asymptote of f.

b. **Degree of numerator equals degree of denominator** If $m = n$, then $\displaystyle \lim_{x \to \pm\infty} f(x) = a_m/b_n$, and $y = a_m/b_n$ is a horizontal asymptote of f.

c. **Degree of numerator greater than degree of denominator** If $m > n$, then $\displaystyle \lim_{x \to \pm\infty} f(x) = \infty$ or $-\infty$, and f has no horizontal asymptote.

d. Assuming that $f(x)$ is in reduced form (p and q share no common factors), vertical asymptotes occur at the zeros of q.

QUICK CHECK 3 Use Theorem 2.7 to find the vertical and horizontal asymptotes of $y = \dfrac{10x}{3x - 1}$. ◄

Although it isn't stated explicitly, Theorem 2.7 implies that a rational function can have at most one horizontal asymptote, and whenever there is a horizontal asymptote, $\lim\limits_{x \to \infty} \dfrac{p(x)}{q(x)} = \lim\limits_{x \to -\infty} \dfrac{p(x)}{q(x)}$. The same cannot be said of other functions, as the next examples show.

EXAMPLE 4   End behavior of an algebraic function Examine the end behavior of
$$f(x) = \frac{10x^3 - 3x^2 + 8}{\sqrt{25x^6 + x^4 + 2}}.$$

SOLUTION The square root in the denominator forces us to revise the strategy used with rational functions. First, consider the limit as $x \to \infty$. The highest power of the polynomial in the denominator is 6. However, the polynomial is under a square root, so effectively, the highest power in the denominator is $\sqrt{x^6} = x^3$. Dividing the numerator and denominator by x^3, for $x > 0$, the limit is evaluated as follows:

$$\lim_{x \to \infty} \frac{10x^3 - 3x^2 + 8}{\sqrt{25x^6 + x^4 + 2}} = \lim_{x \to \infty} \frac{\dfrac{10x^3}{x^3} - \dfrac{3x^2}{x^3} + \dfrac{8}{x^3}}{\sqrt{\dfrac{25x^6}{x^6} + \dfrac{x^4}{x^6} + \dfrac{2}{x^6}}}$$ Divide by $\sqrt{x^6} = x^3$.

$$= \lim_{x \to \infty} \frac{10 - \overbrace{\dfrac{3}{x}}^{\text{approaches } 0} + \overbrace{\dfrac{8}{x^3}}^{\text{approaches } 0}}{\sqrt{25 + \underbrace{\dfrac{1}{x^2}}_{\text{approaches } 0} + \underbrace{\dfrac{2}{x^6}}_{\text{approaches } 0}}}$$ Simplify.

$$= \frac{10}{\sqrt{25}} = 2.$$ Evaluate limits.

> Recall that
> $$\sqrt{x^2} = |x| = \begin{cases} x & \text{if } x \geq 0 \\ -x & \text{if } x < 0. \end{cases}$$
> Therefore,
> $$\sqrt{x^6} = |x^3| = \begin{cases} x^3 & \text{if } x \geq 0 \\ -x^3 & \text{if } x < 0. \end{cases}$$
> Because x is negative as $x \to -\infty$, we have $\sqrt{x^6} = -x^3$.

As $x \to -\infty$, x^3 is negative, so we divide numerator and denominator by $\sqrt{x^6} = -x^3$ (which is positive):

$$\lim_{x \to -\infty} \frac{10x^3 - 3x^2 + 8}{\sqrt{25x^6 + x^4 + 2}} = \lim_{x \to -\infty} \frac{\dfrac{10x^3}{-x^3} - \dfrac{3x^2}{-x^3} + \dfrac{8}{-x^3}}{\sqrt{\dfrac{25x^6}{x^6} + \dfrac{x^4}{x^6} + \dfrac{2}{x^6}}}$$ Divide by $\sqrt{x^6} = -x^3 > 0$.

$$= \lim_{x \to -\infty} \frac{-10 + \overbrace{\dfrac{3}{x}}^{\text{approaches } 0} - \overbrace{\dfrac{8}{x^3}}^{\text{approaches } 0}}{\sqrt{25 + \underbrace{\dfrac{1}{x^2}}_{\text{approaches } 0} + \underbrace{\dfrac{2}{x^6}}_{\text{approaches } 0}}}$$ Simplify.

$$= -\frac{10}{\sqrt{25}} = -2.$$ Evaluate limits.

The limits reveal two asymptotes, $y = 2$ and $y = -2$. Observe that the graph crosses both horizontal asymptotes (Figure 2.38).

Related Exercises 35–38 ◄

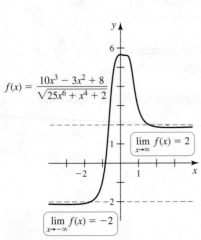

$$f(x) = \frac{10x^3 - 3x^2 + 8}{\sqrt{25x^6 + x^4 + 2}}$$

$\lim\limits_{x \to \infty} f(x) = 2$

$\lim\limits_{x \to -\infty} f(x) = -2$

FIGURE 2.38

EXAMPLE 5   End behavior of transcendental functions Determine the end behavior of the following transcendental functions.

a. $f(x) = e^x$ and $g(x) = e^{-x}$ **b.** $h(x) = \ln x$ **c.** $f(x) = \cos x$

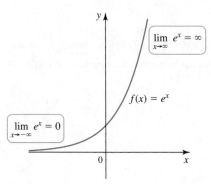

FIGURE 2.39

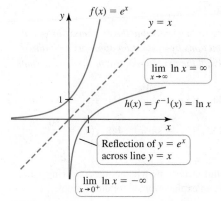

FIGURE 2.40

Table 2.9

x	$\ln x$
10	2.303
10^5	11.513
10^{10}	23.026
10^{50}	115.129
10^{99}	227.956
↓	↓
∞	???

QUICK CHECK 4 How do the functions e^{10x} and e^{-10x} behave as $x \to \infty$ and as $x \to -\infty$? ◄

SOLUTION

a. The graph of $f(x) = e^x$ (Figure 2.39) makes it clear that as $x \to \infty$, e^x increases without bound. All exponential functions b^x with $b > 1$ behave this way, because raising a number greater than 1 to ever-larger powers produces numbers that increase without bound. The figure also suggests that as $x \to -\infty$, the graph of e^x approaches the horizontal asymptote $y = 0$. This claim is confirmed analytically by recognizing that

$$\lim_{x \to -\infty} e^x = \lim_{x \to \infty} e^{-x} = \lim_{x \to \infty} \frac{1}{e^x} = 0.$$

Therefore, $\lim_{x \to \infty} e^x = \infty$ and $\lim_{x \to -\infty} e^x = 0$. Because $e^{-x} = 1/e^x$, it follows that $\lim_{x \to \infty} e^{-x} = 0$ and $\lim_{x \to -\infty} e^{-x} = \infty$.

b. The domain of $\ln x$ is $\{x: x > 0\}$, so we evaluate $\lim_{x \to 0^+} \ln x$ and $\lim_{x \to \infty} \ln x$ to determine end behavior. For the first limit, recall that $\ln x$ is the inverse of e^x (Figure 2.40), and the graph of $\ln x$ is a reflection of the graph of e^x across the line $y = x$. The horizontal asymptote ($y = 0$) of e^x is also reflected across $y = x$, becoming a vertical asymptote ($x = 0$) for $\ln x$. These observations imply that $\lim_{x \to 0^+} \ln x = -\infty$.

It is not obvious whether the graph of $\ln x$ approaches a horizontal asymptote or whether the function grows without bound as $x \to \infty$. Furthermore, the numerical evidence (Table 2.9) is inconclusive because $\ln x$ increases very slowly. The inverse relation between e^x and $\ln x$ is again useful. The fact that the *domain* of e^x is $(-\infty, \infty)$ implies that the *range* of $\ln x$ is also $(-\infty, \infty)$. Therefore, the values of $\ln x$ lie in the interval $(-\infty, \infty)$, and it follows that $\lim_{x \to \infty} \ln x = \infty$.

c. The cosine function oscillates between -1 and 1 as x approaches infinity (Figure 2.41). Therefore, $\lim_{x \to \infty} \cos x$ does not exist. For the same reason, $\lim_{x \to -\infty} \cos x$ does not exist.

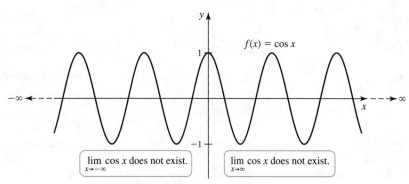

FIGURE 2.41

Related Exercises 39–44 ◄

The end behavior of exponential and logarithmic functions are important in upcoming work. We summarize these results in the following theorem.

THEOREM 2.8   End Behavior of e^x, e^{-x}, and $\ln x$

The end behavior for e^x and e^{-x} on $(-\infty, \infty)$ and $\ln x$ on $(0, \infty)$ is given by the following limits:

$$\lim_{x \to \infty} e^x = \infty \qquad \text{and} \qquad \lim_{x \to -\infty} e^x = 0,$$

$$\lim_{x \to \infty} e^{-x} = 0 \qquad \text{and} \qquad \lim_{x \to -\infty} e^{-x} = \infty,$$

$$\lim_{x \to 0^+} \ln x = -\infty \qquad \text{and} \qquad \lim_{x \to \infty} \ln x = \infty.$$

SECTION 2.5 EXERCISES

Review Questions

1. Explain the meaning of $\lim\limits_{x \to -\infty} f(x) = 10$.

2. What is a horizontal asymptote?

3. Determine $\lim\limits_{x \to \infty} \dfrac{f(x)}{g(x)}$ if $f(x) \to 100{,}000$ and $g(x) \to \infty$ as $x \to \infty$.

4. Describe the end behavior of $g(x) = e^{-2x}$.

5. Describe the end behavior of $f(x) = -2x^3$.

6. The text describes three cases that arise when examining the end behavior of a rational function $f(x) = p(x)/q(x)$. Describe the end behavior associated with each case.

7. Evaluate $\lim\limits_{x \to \infty} e^x$, $\lim\limits_{x \to -\infty} e^x$, and $\lim\limits_{x \to \infty} e^{-x}$.

8. Use a sketch to find the end behavior of $f(x) = \ln x$.

Basic Skills

9–14. Limits at infinity *Evaluate the following limits.*

9. $\lim\limits_{x \to \infty} \left(3 + \dfrac{10}{x^2} \right)$

10. $\lim\limits_{x \to \infty} \left(5 + \dfrac{1}{x} + \dfrac{10}{x^2} \right)$

11. $\lim\limits_{\theta \to \infty} \dfrac{\cos \theta}{\theta^2}$

12. $\lim\limits_{x \to \infty} \dfrac{3 + 2x + 4x^2}{x^2}$

13. $\lim\limits_{x \to \infty} \dfrac{\cos x^5}{\sqrt{x}}$

14. $\lim\limits_{x \to -\infty} \left(5 + \dfrac{100}{x} + \dfrac{\sin^4 x^3}{x^2} \right)$

15–24. Infinite limits at infinity *Determine the following limits.*

15. $\lim\limits_{x \to \infty} x^{12}$

16. $\lim\limits_{x \to -\infty} 3\,x^{11}$

17. $\lim\limits_{x \to \infty} x^{-6}$

18. $\lim\limits_{x \to -\infty} x^{-11}$

19. $\lim\limits_{x \to \infty} (3x^{12} - 9x^7)$

20. $\lim\limits_{x \to -\infty} (3x^7 + x^2)$

21. $\lim\limits_{x \to -\infty} (-3x^{16} + 2)$

22. $\lim\limits_{x \to -\infty} 2x^{-8}$

23. $\lim\limits_{x \to \infty} (-12x^{-5})$

24. $\lim\limits_{x \to -\infty} (2x^{-8} + 4x^3)$

25–34. Rational functions *Evaluate $\lim\limits_{x \to \infty} f(x)$ and $\lim\limits_{x \to -\infty} f(x)$ for the following rational functions. Then give the horizontal asymptote of f (if any).*

25. $f(x) = \dfrac{4x}{20x + 1}$

26. $f(x) = \dfrac{3x^2 - 7}{x^2 + 5x}$

27. $f(x) = \dfrac{6x^2 - 9x + 8}{3x^2 + 2}$

28. $f(x) = \dfrac{4x^2 - 7}{8x^2 + 5x + 2}$

29. $f(x) = \dfrac{3x^3 - 7}{x^4 + 5x^2}$

30. $f(x) = \dfrac{x^4 + 7}{x^5 + x^2 - x}$

31. $f(x) = \dfrac{2x + 1}{3x^4 - 2}$

32. $f(x) = \dfrac{12x^8 - 3}{3x^8 - 2x^7}$

33. $f(x) = \dfrac{40x^5 + x^2}{16x^4 - 2x}$

34. $f(x) = \dfrac{-x^3 + 1}{2x + 8}$

35–38. Algebraic functions *Evaluate $\lim\limits_{x \to \infty} f(x)$ and $\lim\limits_{x \to -\infty} f(x)$ for the following functions. Then give the horizontal asymptote(s) of f (if any).*

35. $f(x) = \dfrac{4x^3 + 1}{2x^3 + \sqrt{16x^6 + 1}}$

36. $f(x) = \dfrac{\sqrt{x^2 + 1}}{2x + 1}$

37. $f(x) = \dfrac{\sqrt[3]{x^6 + 8}}{4x^2 + \sqrt{3x^4 + 1}}$

38. $f(x) = 4x\left(3x - \sqrt{9x^2 + 1} \right)$

39–44. Transcendental functions *Determine the end behavior of the following transcendental functions by evaluating appropriate limits. Then provide a simple sketch of the associated graph, showing asymptotes if they exist.*

39. $f(x) = -3e^{-x}$

40. $f(x) = 2^x$

41. $f(x) = 1 - \ln x$

42. $f(x) = |\ln x|$

43. $f(x) = \sin x$

44. $f(x) = \dfrac{50}{e^{2x}}$

Further Explorations

45. **Explain why or why not** Determine whether the following statements are true and give an explanation or counterexample.

    a. The graph of a function can never cross one of its horizontal asymptotes.

    b. A rational function f can have both $\lim\limits_{x \to \infty} f(x) = L$ and $\lim\limits_{x \to -\infty} f(x) = \infty$.

    c. The graph of any function can have at most two horizontal asymptotes.

46–55. Horizontal and vertical asymptotes

a. *Evaluate $\lim\limits_{x \to \infty} f(x)$ and $\lim\limits_{x \to -\infty} f(x)$, and then identify any horizontal asymptotes.*

b. *Find the vertical asymptotes. For each vertical asymptote $x = a$, evaluate $\lim\limits_{x \to a^-} f(x)$ and $\lim\limits_{x \to a^+} f(x)$.*

46. $f(x) = \dfrac{x^2 - 4x + 3}{x - 1}$

47. $f(x) = \dfrac{2x^3 + 10x^2 + 12x}{x^3 + 2x^2}$

48. $f(x) = \dfrac{\sqrt{16x^4 + 64x^2} + x^2}{2x^2 - 4}$

49. $f(x) = \dfrac{3x^4 + 3x^3 - 36x^2}{x^4 - 25x^2 + 144}$

50. $f(x) = 16x^2\left(4x^2 - \sqrt{16x^4 + 1} \right)$

51. $f(x) = \dfrac{x^2 - 9}{x(x - 3)}$

52. $f(x) = \dfrac{x - 1}{x^{2/3} - 1}$

53. $f(x) = \dfrac{\sqrt{x^2 + 2x + 6} - 3}{x - 1}$

54. $f(x) = \dfrac{|1 - x^2|}{x(x + 1)}$

55. $f(x) = \sqrt{|x|} - \sqrt{|x - 1|}$

56–59. End behavior for transcendental functions

56. The central branch of $f(x) = \tan x$ is shown in the figure.

    a. Evaluate $\lim\limits_{x \to \pi/2^-} \tan x$ and $\lim\limits_{x \to -\pi/2^+} \tan x$. Are these infinite limits or limits at infinity?

    b. Sketch a graph of $g(x) = \tan^{-1} x$ by reflecting the graph of f over the line $y = x$, and use it to evaluate $\lim\limits_{x \to \infty} \tan^{-1} x$ and $\lim\limits_{x \to -\infty} \tan^{-1} x$.

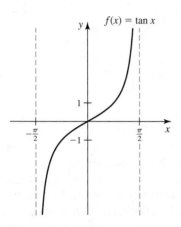

57. Graph $y = \sec^{-1} x$ and evaluate the following limits using the graph. Assume the domain is $\{x : |x| \geq 1\}$.

    a. $\lim\limits_{x \to \infty} \sec^{-1} x$ **b.** $\lim\limits_{x \to -\infty} \sec^{-1} x$

58. The **hyperbolic cosine function**, denoted $\cosh x$, is used to model the shape of a hanging cable (a telephone wire, for example). It is defined as $\cosh x = \dfrac{e^x + e^{-x}}{2}$.

    a. Determine its end behavior by evaluating $\lim\limits_{x \to \infty} \cosh x$ and $\lim\limits_{x \to -\infty} \cosh x$.

    b. Evaluate $\cosh 0$. Use symmetry and part (a) to sketch a plausible graph for $y = \cosh x$.

59. The **hyperbolic sine function** is defined as $\sinh x = \dfrac{e^x - e^{-x}}{2}$.

    a. Determine its end behavior by evaluating $\lim\limits_{x \to \infty} \sinh x$ and $\lim\limits_{x \to -\infty} \sinh x$.

    b. Evaluate $\sinh 0$. Use symmetry and part (a) to sketch a plausible graph for $y = \sinh x$.

60–61. Sketching graphs *Sketch a possible graph of a function f that satisfies all the given conditions. Be sure to identify all vertical and horizontal asymptotes.*

60. $f(-1) = -2$, $f(1) = 2$, $f(0) = 0$, $\lim\limits_{x \to \infty} f(x) = 1$, $\lim\limits_{x \to -\infty} f(x) = -1$

61. $\lim\limits_{x \to 0^+} f(x) = \infty$, $\lim\limits_{x \to 0^-} f(x) = -\infty$, $\lim\limits_{x \to \infty} f(x) = 1$, $\lim\limits_{x \to -\infty} f(x) = -2$

62. Asymptotes Find the vertical and horizontal asymptotes of $f(x) = e^{1/x}$.

63. Asymptotes Find the vertical and horizontal asymptotes of $f(x) = \dfrac{\cos x + 2\sqrt{x}}{\sqrt{x}}$.

Applications

64–69. Steady states *If a function f represents a system that varies in time, the existence of $\lim\limits_{t \to \infty} f(t)$ means that the system reaches a steady state (or equilibrium). For the following systems, determine if a steady state exists and give the steady-state value.*

64. The population of a bacteria culture is given by $p(t) = \dfrac{2500}{t + 1}$.

65. The population of a culture of tumor cells is given by $p(t) = \dfrac{3500t}{t + 1}$.

66. The amount of drug (in milligrams) in the blood after an IV tube is inserted is $m(t) = 200(1 - 2^{-t})$.

67. The value of an investment in dollars is given by $v(t) = 1000e^{0.065t}$.

68. The population of a colony of squirrels is given by $p(t) = \dfrac{1500}{3 + 2e^{-0.1t}}$.

69. The amplitude of an oscillator is given by $a(t) = 2\left(\dfrac{t + \sin t}{t}\right)$.

70–73. Looking ahead to sequences *A sequence is an infinite, ordered list of numbers that is often defined by a function. For example, the sequence $\{2, 4, 6, 8, \ldots\}$ is specified by the function $f(n) = 2n$, where $n = 1, 2, 3, \ldots$. The limit of such a sequence is $\lim\limits_{n \to \infty} f(n)$, provided the limit exists. All the limit laws for limits at infinity may be applied to limits of sequences. Find the limit of the following sequences, or state that the limit does not exist.*

70. $\left\{4, 2, \dfrac{4}{3}, 1, \dfrac{4}{5}, \dfrac{2}{3}, \ldots\right\}$, which is defined by $f(n) = \dfrac{4}{n}$, for $n = 1, 2, 3, \ldots$

71. $\left\{0, \dfrac{1}{2}, \dfrac{2}{3}, \dfrac{3}{4}, \ldots\right\}$, which is defined by $f(n) = \dfrac{n - 1}{n}$, for $n = 1, 2, 3, \ldots$

72. $\left\{\dfrac{1}{2}, \dfrac{4}{3}, \dfrac{9}{4}, \dfrac{16}{5}, \ldots\right\}$, which is defined by $f(n) = \dfrac{n^2}{n + 1}$, for $n = 1, 2, 3, \ldots$

73. $\left\{2, \dfrac{3}{4}, \dfrac{4}{9}, \dfrac{5}{16}, \ldots\right\}$, which is defined by $f(n) = \dfrac{n + 1}{n^2}$, for $n = 1, 2, 3, \ldots$

Additional Exercises

74. End behavior of a rational function Suppose $f(x) = \dfrac{p(x)}{q(x)}$
is a rational function, where

$p(x) = a_m x^m + a_{m-1} x^{m-1} + \cdots + a_2 x^2 + a_1 x + a_0,$
$q(x) = b_n x^n + b_{n-1} x^{n-1} + \cdots + b_2 x^2 + b_1 x + b_0, a_m \neq 0,$
and $b_n \neq 0$.

a. Prove that if $m = n$, then $\displaystyle\lim_{x \to \pm\infty} f(x) = \dfrac{a_m}{b_n}$.

b. Prove that if $m < n$, then $\displaystyle\lim_{x \to \pm\infty} f(x) = 0$.

75–76. Limits of exponentials *Evaluate* $\displaystyle\lim_{x \to \infty} f(x)$ *and* $\displaystyle\lim_{x \to -\infty} f(x)$.
Then state the horizontal asymptote(s) of f. Confirm your findings by plotting f.

75. $f(x) = \dfrac{2e^x + 3e^{2x}}{e^{2x} + e^{3x}}$

76. $f(x) = \dfrac{3e^x + e^{-x}}{e^x + e^{-x}}$

77. Subtle asymptotes Use analytical methods to identify all the
asymptotes of $f(x) = \dfrac{\ln(9 - x^2)}{2e^x - e^{-x}}$. Then confirm your results by
locating the asymptotes using a graphing calculator.

QUICK CHECK ANSWERS

1. $10/11, 100/101, 1000/1001, 1$ **2.** $p(x) \to -\infty$ as
$x \to \infty$ and $p(x) \to \infty$ as $x \to -\infty$ **3.** Horizontal
asymptote is $y = \frac{10}{3}$; vertical asymptote is $x = \frac{1}{3}$.
4. $\displaystyle\lim_{x \to \infty} e^{10x} = \infty$, $\displaystyle\lim_{x \to -\infty} e^{10x} = 0$, $\displaystyle\lim_{x \to \infty} e^{-10x} = 0$,
$\displaystyle\lim_{x \to -\infty} e^{-10x} = \infty$ ◄

2.6 Continuity

The graphs of many functions encountered in this text contain no holes, jumps, or breaks.
For example, if $L = f(t)$ represents the length of a fish t years after it is hatched, then the
length of the fish changes gradually as t increases. Consequently, the graph of $L = f(t)$
contains no breaks (Figure 2.42a). Some functions, however, do contain abrupt changes
in their values. Consider a parking meter that accepts only quarters and each quarter buys
15 minutes of parking. Letting $c(t)$ be the cost (in dollars) of parking for t minutes, the
graph of c has breaks at integer multiples of 15 minutes (Figure 2.42b).

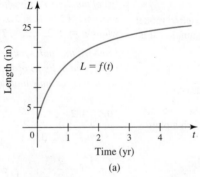

(a)

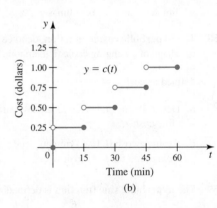

(b)

FIGURE 2.42

QUICK CHECK 1 For what values of t in
$(0, 60)$ does the graph of $y = c(t)$ in
Figure 2.42b have a discontinuity? ◄

Informally, we say that a function f is *continuous* at a if the graph of f contains no
holes or breaks at a (that is, if the graph near a can be drawn without lifting the pencil). If
a function is not continuous at a, then a is a point of discontinuity.

Continuity at a Point

This informal description of continuity is sufficient for determining the continuity of simple functions, but it is not precise enough to deal with more complicated functions such as

$$h(x) = \begin{cases} x \sin \dfrac{1}{x} & \text{if } x \neq 0 \\ 0 & \text{if } x = 0. \end{cases}$$

It is difficult to determine whether the graph of h has a break at 0 because it oscillates rapidly as x approaches 0 (Figure 2.43). We need a better definition.

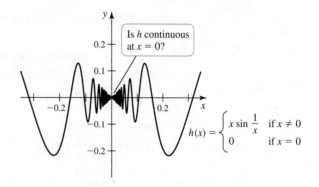

$$h(x) = \begin{cases} x \sin \dfrac{1}{x} & \text{if } x \neq 0 \\ 0 & \text{if } x = 0 \end{cases}$$

FIGURE 2.43

DEFINITION Continuity at a Point

A function f is **continuous** at a if $\lim\limits_{x \to a} f(x) = f(a)$. If f is not continuous at a, then a is a point of discontinuity.

There is more to this definition than first appears. If $\lim\limits_{x \to a} f(x) = f(a)$, then $f(a)$ and $\lim\limits_{x \to a} f(x)$ must both exist, and they must be equal. The following checklist is helpful in determining whether a function is continuous at a.

Continuity Checklist

In order for f to be continuous at a, the following three conditions must hold.

1. $f(a)$ is defined (a is in the domain of f).

2. $\lim\limits_{x \to a} f(x)$ exists.

3. $\lim\limits_{x \to a} f(x) = f(a)$ (the value of f equals the limit of f at a).

If *any* item in the continuity checklist fails to hold, the function fails to be continuous at a. From this definition, we see that continuity has an important practical consequence:

If f is continuous at a, then $\lim\limits_{x \to a} f(x) = f(a)$, and direct substitution may be used to evaluate $\lim\limits_{x \to a} f(x)$.

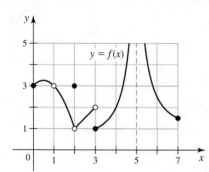

FIGURE 2.44

➤ In Example 1, the discontinuities at $x = 1$ and $x = 2$ are called **removable discontinuities** because they can be removed by redefining the function at these points (in this case $f(1) = 3$ and $f(2) = 1$). The discontinuity at $x = 3$ is called a **jump discontinuity**. The discontinuity at $x = 5$ is called an **infinite discontinuity**. These terms are discussed in Exercises 95–101.

EXAMPLE 1 Points of discontinuity Use the graph of f in Figure 2.44 to identify values of x on the interval $(0, 7)$ at which f has a discontinuity.

SOLUTION The function f has discontinuities at $x = 1, 2, 3$, and 5 because the graph contains holes or breaks at each of these locations. These claims are verified using the continuity checklist.

• $f(1)$ is not defined.

• $f(2) = 3$ and $\lim\limits_{x \to 2} f(x) = 1$. Therefore, $f(2)$ and $\lim\limits_{x \to 2} f(x)$ exist but are not equal.

- $\lim\limits_{x\to3} f(x)$ does not exist because the left-sided limit $\lim\limits_{x\to3^-} f(x) = 2$ differs from the right-sided limit $\lim\limits_{x\to3^+} f(x) = 1$.

- Neither $\lim\limits_{x\to5} f(x)$ nor $f(5)$ exists.   *Related Exercises 9–12*◄

EXAMPLE 2 **Identifying discontinuities** Determine whether the following functions are continuous at a. Justify each answer using the continuity checklist.

a. $f(x) = \dfrac{3x^2 + 2x + 1}{x - 1}$; $a = 1$

b. $g(x) = \dfrac{3x^2 + 2x + 1}{x - 1}$; $a = 2$

c. $h(x) = \begin{cases} x \sin \dfrac{1}{x} & \text{if } x \neq 0 \\ 0 & \text{if } x = 0 \end{cases}$; $a = 0$

SOLUTION

a. The function f is not continuous at 1 because $f(1)$ is undefined.

b. Because g is a rational function and the denominator is nonzero at 2, it follows by Theorem 2.3 that $\lim\limits_{x\to2} g(x) = g(2) = 17$. Therefore, g is continuous at 2.

c. By definition, $h(0) = 0$. In Exercise 55 of Section 2.3, we used the Squeeze Theorem to show that $\lim\limits_{x\to0} x \sin \dfrac{1}{x} = 0$. Therefore, $\lim\limits_{x\to0} h(x) = h(0)$, which implies that h is continuous at 0.   *Related Exercises 13–20*◄

The following theorems make it easier to test various combinations of functions for continuity at a point.

THEOREM 2.9 **Continuity Rules**

If f and g are continuous at a, then the following functions are also continuous at a. Assume c is a constant and $n > 0$ is an integer.

a. $f + g$ **b.** $f - g$

c. cf **d.** fg

e. f/g, provided $g(a) \neq 0$ **f.** $(f(x))^n$

To prove the first result, note that if f and g are continuous at a, then $\lim\limits_{x\to a} f(x) = f(a)$ and $\lim\limits_{x\to a} g(x) = g(a)$. From the limit laws of Theorem 2.3, it follows that

$$\lim_{x\to a} (f(x) + g(x)) = f(a) + g(a).$$

Therefore, $f + g$ is continuous at a. Similar arguments lead to the continuity of differences, products, quotients, and powers of continuous functions. The next theorem is a direct consequence of Theorem 2.9.

> **THEOREM 2.10   Polynomial and Rational Functions**
>
> **a.** A polynomial function is continuous for all x.
>
> **b.** A rational function (a function of the form $\dfrac{p}{q}$, where p and q are polynomials) is continuous for all x for which $q(x) \neq 0$.

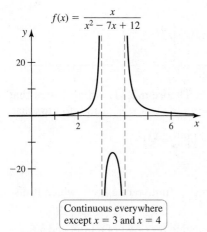

$$f(x) = \frac{x}{x^2 - 7x + 12}$$

Continuous everywhere except $x = 3$ and $x = 4$

FIGURE 2.45

EXAMPLE 3   Applying the continuity theorems For what values of x is the function

$$f(x) = \frac{x}{x^2 - 7x + 12} \text{ continuous?}$$

SOLUTION

a. Because f is rational, Theorem 2.10b implies it is continuous for all x at which the denominator is nonzero. The denominator factors as $(x - 3)(x - 4)$, so it is zero at $x = 3$ and $x = 4$. Therefore, f is continuous for all x except $x = 3$ and $x = 4$ (Figure 2.45).
Related Exercises 21–26 ◄

The following theorem allows us to determine when a composition of two functions is continuous at a point. Its proof is informative and is outlined in Exercise 102.

> **THEOREM 2.11   Continuity of Composite Functions at a Point**
> If g is continuous at a and f is continuous at $g(a)$, then the composite function $f \circ g$ is continuous at a.

QUICK CHECK 2 Evaluate $\lim\limits_{x \to 4} \sqrt{x^2 + 9}$ and $\sqrt{\lim\limits_{x \to 4} (x^2 + 9)}$. How do these results illustrate that the order of a function evaluation and a limit may be switched for continuous functions? ◄

Theorem 2.11 is useful because it allows us to conclude that the composition of two continuous functions is continuous at a point. For example, the composite function $\left(\dfrac{x}{x - 1}\right)^3$ is continuous for all $x \neq 1$. The theorem also says that under the stated conditions on f and g, the limit of their composition is evaluated by direct substitution; that is,

$$\lim_{x \to a} f(g(x)) = f(g(a)).$$

EXAMPLE 4   Limit of a composition Evaluate $\lim\limits_{x \to 0} \left(\dfrac{x^4 - 2x + 2}{x^6 + 2x^4 + 1}\right)^{10}$.

SOLUTION The rational function $\dfrac{x^4 - 2x + 2}{x^6 + 2x^4 + 1}$ is continuous for all x because its denominator is always positive (Theorem 2.10b). Therefore, $\left(\dfrac{x^4 - 2x + 2}{x^6 + 2x^4 + 1}\right)^{10}$, which is the composition of the continuous function $f(x) = x^{10}$ and a continuous rational function, is continuous for all x by Theorem 2.11. By direct substitution,

$$\lim_{x \to 0} \left(\frac{x^4 - 2x + 2}{x^6 + 2x^4 + 1}\right)^{10} = \left(\frac{0^4 - 2 \cdot 0 + 2}{0^6 + 2 \cdot 0^4 + 1}\right)^{10} = 2^{10} = 1024.$$

Related Exercises 27–30 ◄

Closely related to Theorem 2.11 are two results dealing with limits of composite functions; they are used frequently in upcoming chapters. We present these two results—one a more general version of the other—in a single theorem.

THEOREM 2.12   Limits of Composite Functions

1. If g is continuous at a and f is continuous at $g(a)$, then

$$\lim_{x \to a} f(g(x)) = f\left(\lim_{x \to a} g(x)\right).$$

2. If $\lim_{x \to a} g(x) = L$ and f is continuous at L, then

$$\lim_{x \to a} f(g(x)) = f\left(\lim_{x \to a} g(x)\right).$$

Proof: The first statement follows directly from Theorem 2.11, which states that $\lim_{x \to a} f(g(x)) = f(g(a))$. If g is continuous at a, then $\lim_{x \to a} g(x) = g(a)$, and it follows that

$$\lim_{x \to a} f(g(x)) = f(g(a)) = f\left(\underbrace{\lim_{x \to a} g(x)}_{\lim_{x \to a} g(x)}\right).$$

The proof of the second statement relies on the formal definition of a limit, which is discussed in Section 2.7.   ◄

Both statements of Theorem 2.12 justify interchanging the order of a limit and a function evaluation. By the second statement, the inner function of the composition needn't be continuous at the point of interest, but it must have a limit at that point.

EXAMPLE 5   Limits of composite functions Evaluate the following limits.

a. $\displaystyle\lim_{x \to -1} \sqrt{2x^2 - 1}$ **b.** $\displaystyle\lim_{x \to 2} \cos\left(\dfrac{x^2 - 4}{x - 2}\right)$

SOLUTION

a. We show later in this section that $\sqrt{x}$ is continuous for $x \geq 0$. The inner function of the composite function $\sqrt{2x^2 - 1}$ is $2x^2 - 1$ and it is continuous and positive at -1. By the first statement of Theorem 2.12,

$$\lim_{x \to -1} \sqrt{2x^2 - 1} = \sqrt{\underbrace{\lim_{x \to -1} 2x^2 - 1}_{1}} = \sqrt{1} = 1.$$

b. We show later in this section that $\cos x$ is continuous at all points of its domain. The inner function of the composite function $\cos\left(\dfrac{x^2 - 4}{x - 2}\right)$ is $\dfrac{x^2 - 4}{x - 2}$, which is not continuous at 2. However,

$$\lim_{x \to 2}\left(\frac{x^2 - 4}{x - 2}\right) = \lim_{x \to 2} \frac{(x - 2)(x + 2)}{x - 2} = \lim_{x \to 2}(x + 2) = 4.$$

Therefore, by the second statement of Theorem 2.12,

$$\lim_{x \to 2} \cos\left(\frac{x^2 - 4}{x - 2}\right) = \cos\left(\underbrace{\lim_{x \to 2}\left(\frac{x^2 - 4}{x - 2}\right)}_{4}\right) = \cos 4 \approx -0.654.$$

Related Exercises 31–34 ◄

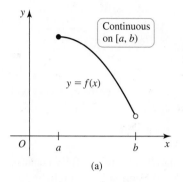

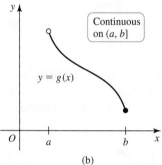

FIGURE 2.46

Continuity on an Interval

A function is *continuous on an interval* if it is continuous at every point in that interval. Consider the functions f and g whose graphs are shown in Figure 2.46. Both these functions are continuous for all x in (a, b), but what about the endpoints? To answer this question, we introduce the ideas of *left-continuity* and *right-continuity*.

DEFINITION Continuity at Endpoints

A function f is **continuous from the left** (or **left-continuous**) at a if $\lim\limits_{x \to a^-} f(x) = f(a)$ and f is **continuous from the right** (or **right-continuous**) at a if $\lim\limits_{x \to a^+} f(x) = f(a)$.

Combining the definitions of left-continuous and right-continuous with the definition of continuity at a point, we define what it means for a function to be continuous on an interval.

DEFINITION Continuity on an Interval

A function f is **continuous on an interval I** if it is continuous at all points of I. If I contains its endpoints, continuity on I means continuous from the right or left at the endpoints.

To illustrate these definitions, consider again the functions in Figure 2.46. In Figure 2.46a, f is continuous from the right at a because $\lim\limits_{x \to a^+} f(x) = f(a)$; but it is not continuous from the left at b because $f(b)$ is not defined. Therefore, f is continuous on the interval $[a, b)$. The behavior of the function g in Figure 2.46b is the opposite: It is continuous from the left at b, but it is not continuous from the right at a. Therefore, g is continuous on $(a, b]$.

QUICK CHECK 3 Modify the graphs of the functions f and g in Figure 2.46 to obtain functions that are continuous on $[a, b]$. ◄

EXAMPLE 6 Intervals of continuity Determine the intervals of continuity for

$$f(x) = \begin{cases} x^2 + 1 & \text{if } x \le 0 \\ 3x + 5 & \text{if } x > 0. \end{cases}$$

SOLUTION This piecewise function consists of two polynomials that describe a parabola and a line (Figure 2.47). By Theorem 2.10, f is continuous for all $x \ne 0$. From its graph, it appears that f is left-continuous at 0. This observation is verified by noting that

$$\lim_{x \to 0^-} f(x) = \lim_{x \to 0^-} (x^2 + 1) = 1,$$

which means that $\lim\limits_{x \to 0^-} f(x) = f(0)$. However, because

$$\lim_{x \to 0^+} f(x) = \lim_{x \to 0^+} (3x + 5) = 5 \ne f(0),$$

we see that f is not right-continuous at 0. Therefore, we can also say that f is continuous on $(-\infty, 0]$ and on $(0, \infty)$.

Related Exercises 35–40 ◄

FIGURE 2.47

Functions Involving Roots

Recall that Limit Law 7 of Theorem 2.3 states

$$\lim_{x \to a} [f(x)]^{n/m} = \left[\lim_{x \to a} f(x) \right]^{n/m},$$

provided $f(x) \geq 0$, for x near a, if m is even and n/m is reduced. Therefore, if m is odd and f is continuous at a, then $[f(x)]^{n/m}$ is continuous at a, because

$$\lim_{x \to a} [f(x)]^{n/m} = \left[\lim_{x \to a} f(x) \right]^{n/m} = [f(a)]^{n/m}.$$

When m is even, the continuity of $[f(x)]^{n/m}$ must be handled more carefully because this function is defined only when $f(x) \geq 0$. Exercise 59 of Section 2.7 establishes an important fact:

> If f is continuous at a and $f(a) > 0$, then f is positive for all values of x in the domain sufficiently close to a.

Combining this fact with Theorem 2.11 (the continuity of composite functions), it follows that $[f(x)]^{n/m}$ is continuous at a provided $f(a) > 0$. At points where $f(a) = 0$, the behavior of $[f(x)]^{n/m}$ varies. Often we find that $[f(x)]^{n/m}$ is left- or right-continuous at that point, or it may be continuous from both sides.

THEOREM 2.13   Continuity of Functions with Roots
Assume that m and n are positive integers with no common factors. If m is an odd integer, then $[f(x)]^{n/m}$ is continuous at all points at which f is continuous. If m is even, then $[f(x)]^{n/m}$ is continuous at all points a at which f is continuous and $f(a) > 0$.

EXAMPLE 7   Continuity with roots For what values of x are the following functions continuous?

a. $g(x) = \sqrt{9 - x^2}$ **b.** $f(x) = (x^2 - 2x + 4)^{2/3}$

SOLUTION

a. The graph of g is the upper half of the circle $x^2 + y^2 = 9$ (which can be verified by solving $x^2 + y^2 = 9$ for y). From Figure 2.48, it appears that g is continuous on $[-3, 3]$. To verify this fact, note that g involves an even root ($m = 2, n = 1$ in Theorem 2.13). If $-3 < x < 3$, then $9 - x^2 > 0$ and by Theorem 2.13, g is continuous for all x on $(-3, 3)$.
  At the right endpoint, $\lim_{x \to 3^-} \sqrt{9 - x^2} = 0 = g(3)$ by Limit Law 7, which implies that g is left-continuous at 3. Similarly, g is right-continuous at -3 because $\lim_{x \to -3^+} \sqrt{9 - x^2} = 0 = g(-3)$. Therefore, g is continuous on $[-3, 3]$.

b. The polynomial $x^2 - 2x + 4$ is continuous for all x by Theorem 2.10a. Because f involves an odd root ($m = 3, n = 2$ in Theorem 2.13), f is continuous for all x.

Related Exercises 41–50 ◄

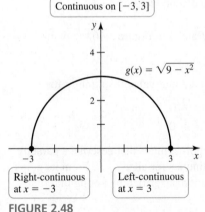

$\boxed{\text{Continuous on } [-3, 3]}$

$g(x) = \sqrt{9 - x^2}$

$\boxed{\begin{array}{l}\text{Right-continuous} \\ \text{at } x = -3\end{array}}$ $\boxed{\begin{array}{l}\text{Left-continuous} \\ \text{at } x = 3\end{array}}$

FIGURE 2.48

QUICK CHECK 4 On what interval is $f(x) = x^{1/4}$ continuous? On what interval is $f(x) = x^{2/5}$ continuous? ◄

Continuity of Transcendental Functions

The understanding of continuity that we have developed with algebraic functions may now be applied to transcendental functions.

Trigonometric Functions   In Example 8 of Section 2.3, we used the Squeeze Theorem to show that $\lim_{x \to 0} \sin x = 0$ and $\lim_{x \to 0} \cos x = 1$. Because $\sin 0 = 0$ and $\cos 0 = 1$, these limits imply that sin x and cos x are continuous at 0. The graph of $y = \sin x$ (Figure 2.49) suggests that $\lim_{x \to a} \sin x = \sin a$ for any value of a, which means that sin x is continuous everywhere. The graph of $y = \cos x$ also indicates that cos x is continuous for all x. Exercise 105 outlines a proof of these results.

With these facts in hand, we appeal to Theorem 2.9e to discover that the remaining trigonometric functions are continuous on their domains. For example, because $\sec x = 1/\cos x$, the secant function is continuous for all x for which $\cos x \neq 0$ (for all x except odd multiples of $\pi/2$) (Figure 2.50). Likewise, the tangent, cotangent, and cosecant functions are continuous at all points of their domains.

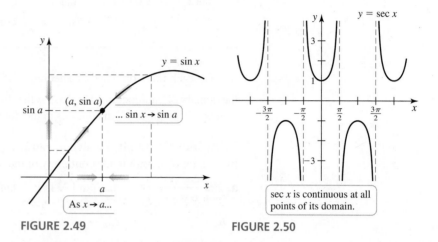

FIGURE 2.49

sec x is continuous at all points of its domain.

FIGURE 2.50

Exponential Functions The continuity of exponential functions of the form $f(x) = b^x$, with $0 < b < 1$ or $b > 1$, raises an important question. Consider the function $f(x) = 4^x$ (Figure 2.51). Evaluating f is routine if x is rational:

$$4^3 = 4 \cdot 4 \cdot 4 = 64; \quad 4^{-2} = \frac{1}{4^2} = \frac{1}{16}; \quad 4^{3/2} = \sqrt{4^3} = 8; \quad \text{and} \quad 4^{-1/3} = \frac{1}{\sqrt[3]{4}}.$$

But what is meant by 4^x when x is an irrational number, such as $\sqrt{2}$? In order for $f(x) = 4^x$ to be continuous for all real numbers, it must also be defined when x is an irrational number. Providing a working definition for an expression such as $4^{\sqrt{2}}$ requires mathematical results that don't appear until Chapter 6. Until then, we assume without proof that the domain of $f(x) = b^x$ is the set of all real numbers and that f is continuous at all points of its domain.

Inverse Functions Suppose a function f is continuous and one-to-one on an interval I. Reflecting the graph of f through the line $y = x$ generates the graph of f^{-1}. The reflection process introduces no discontinuities in the graph of f^{-1}, so it is plausible (and indeed, true) that f^{-1} is continuous on the interval corresponding to I. We state this fact without a formal proof.

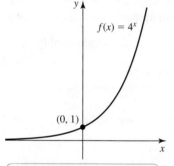

Exponential functions are defined for all real numbers and are continuous on $(-\infty, \infty)$, as shown in Chapter 6

FIGURE 2.51

THEOREM 2.14   Continuity of Inverse Functions
If a continuous function f has an inverse on an interval I, then its inverse f^{-1} is also continuous (on the interval consisting of the points $f(x)$, where x is in I).

Because all the trigonometric functions are continuous on their domains, they are also continuous when their domains are restricted for the purpose of defining inverse functions. Therefore, by Theorem 2.14, the inverse trigonometric functions are continuous at all points of their domains.

Logarithmic functions of the form $f(x) = \log_b x$ are continuous at all points of their domains for the same reason: They are inverses of exponential functions, which are one-to-one and continuous. Collecting all these facts together, we have the following theorem.

THEOREM 2.15   Continuity of Transcendental Functions
The following functions are continuous at all points of their domains.

Trigonometric		**Inverse Trigonometric**		**Exponential**	
$\sin x$	$\cos x$	$\sin^{-1} x$	$\cos^{-1} x$	b^x	e^x
$\tan x$	$\cot x$	$\tan^{-1} x$	$\cot^{-1} x$	**Logarithmic**	
$\sec x$	$\csc x$	$\sec^{-1} x$	$\csc^{-1} x$	$\log_b x$	$\ln x$

For each function listed in Theorem 2.15, we have $\lim_{x \to a} f(x) = f(a)$, provided a is in the domain of the function. This means that limits involving these functions may be evaluated by direct substitution at points in the domain.

EXAMPLE 8   Limits involving transcendental functions Evaluate the following limits after determining the continuity of the functions involved.

a. $\displaystyle\lim_{x \to 0} \frac{\cos^2 x - 1}{\cos x - 1}$ **b.** $\displaystyle\lim_{x \to 1} \left(\sqrt[4]{\ln x} + \tan^{-1} x \right)$

SOLUTION

> Limits like the one in Example 8a are denoted 0/0 and are known as *indeterminate forms*, to be studied further in Section 4.7.

a. Both $\cos^2 x - 1$ and $\cos x - 1$ are continuous for all x by Theorems 2.9 and 2.15. However, the ratio of these functions is continuous only when $\cos x - 1 \neq 0$, which occurs when x is not an integer multiple of 2π. Note that both the numerator and denominator of $\dfrac{\cos^2 x - 1}{\cos x - 1}$ approach 0 as $x \to 0$. To evaluate the limit, we factor and simplify:

$$\lim_{x \to 0} \frac{\cos^2 x - 1}{\cos x - 1} = \lim_{x \to 0} \frac{(\cos x - 1)(\cos x + 1)}{\cos x - 1} = \lim_{x \to 0} (\cos x + 1)$$

(where $\cos x - 1$ may be canceled because it is nonzero as x approaches 0). The limit on the right is now evaluated using direct substitution:

$$\lim_{x \to 0} (\cos x + 1) = \cos 0 + 1 = 2.$$

QUICK CHECK 5 Show that $f(x) = \sqrt[4]{\ln x}$ is right-continuous at $x = 1$. ◄

b. By Theorem 2.15, $\ln x$ is continuous on its domain $(0, \infty)$. However, $\ln x > 0$ only when $x > 1$, so Theorem 2.13 implies $\sqrt[4]{\ln x}$ is continuous on $(1, \infty)$. At $x = 1$, $\sqrt[4]{\ln x}$ is right-continuous (Quick Check 5). The domain of $\tan^{-1} x$ is all real numbers, and it is continuous on $(-\infty, \infty)$. Therefore, $f(x) = \sqrt[4]{\ln x} + \tan^{-1} x$ is continuous on $[1, \infty)$. Because the domain of f does not include points with $x < 1$, $\lim_{x \to 1^-} \left(\sqrt[4]{\ln x} + \tan^{-1} x \right)$ does not exist, which implies that $\lim_{x \to 1} \left(\sqrt[4]{\ln x} + \tan^{-1} x \right)$ does not exist.
Related Exercises 51–56 ◄

We close this section with an important theorem that has both practical and theoretical uses.

The Intermediate Value Theorem

A common problem in mathematics is finding solutions to equations of the form $f(x) = L$. Before attempting to find values of x satisfying this equation, it is worthwhile to determine whether a solution exists.

The existence of solutions is often established using a result known as the *Intermediate Value Theorem*. Given a function f and a constant L, we assume L lies between $f(a)$ and $f(b)$. The Intermediate Value Theorem says that if f is continuous on $[a, b]$, then the graph of f must cross the horizontal line $y = L$ at least once (Figure 2.52). Although this theorem is easily illustrated, its proof goes beyond the scope of this text.

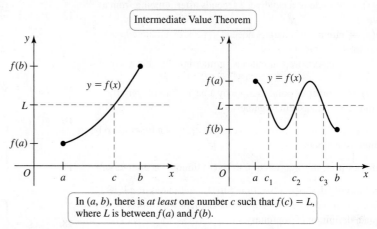

Intermediate Value Theorem

In (a, b), there is *at least* one number c such that $f(c) = L$, where L is between $f(a)$ and $f(b)$.

FIGURE 2.52

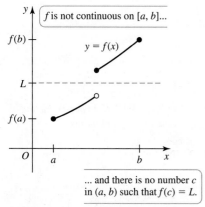

f is not continuous on $[a, b]$...

$y = f(x)$

... and there is no number c in (a, b) such that $f(c) = L$.

FIGURE 2.53

QUICK CHECK 6 Does the equation $f(x) = x^3 + x + 1 = 0$ have a solution on the interval $[-1, 1]$? Explain. ◄

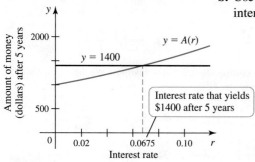

Amount of money (dollars) after 5 years

$y = A(r)$

$y = 1400$

Interest rate that yields $1400 after 5 years

Interest rate

FIGURE 2.54

> **THEOREM 2.16   The Intermediate Value Theorem**
> Suppose f is continuous on the interval $[a, b]$ and L is a number strictly between $f(a)$ and $f(b)$. Then there exists at least one number c in (a, b) satisfying $f(c) = L$.

The importance of continuity in Theorem 2.16 is illustrated in Figure 2.53, where we see a function f that is not continuous on $[a, b]$. For the value of L shown in the figure, there is no value of c in (a, b) satisfying $f(c) = L$. The next example illustrates a practical application of the Intermediate Value Theorem.

EXAMPLE 9   Finding an interest rate Suppose you invest $1000 in a special 5-year savings account with a fixed annual interest rate r, with monthly compounding. The amount of money A in the account after 5 years (60 months) is $A(r) = 1000\left(1 + \dfrac{r}{12}\right)^{60}$.

Your goal is to have $1400 in the account after 5 years.

a. Use the Intermediate Value Theorem to show there is a value of r in $(0, 0.08)$—that is, an interest rate between 0% and 8%—for which $A(r) = 1400$.

b. Use a graphing utility to illustrate your explanation in part (a), and then estimate the interest rate required to reach your goal.

SOLUTION

a. As a polynomial in r (of degree 60), $A(r) = 1000\left(1 + \dfrac{r}{12}\right)^{60}$ is continuous for all r.
Evaluating $A(r)$ at the endpoints of the interval $[0, 0.08]$, we have $A(0) = 1000$ and $A(0.08) \approx 1489.85$. Therefore,

$$A(0) < 1400 < A(0.08),$$

and it follows, by the Intermediate Value Theorem, that there is a value of r in $(0, 0.08)$ for which $A(r) = 1400$.

b. The graphs of $y = A(r)$ and the horizontal line $y = 1400$ are shown in Figure 2.54; it is evident that they intersect between $r = 0$ and $r = 0.08$. Solving $A(r) = 1400$ algebraically or using a root finder reveals that the curve and line intersect at $r \approx 0.0675$. Therefore, an interest rate of approximately 6.75% is required for the investment to be worth $1400 after 5 years.

Related Exercises 57–64 ◄

SECTION 2.6 EXERCISES

Review Questions

1. Which of the following functions are continuous for all values in their domain? Justify your answers.

    a. $a(t)$ = altitude of a skydiver t seconds after jumping from a plane

    b. $n(t)$ = number of quarters needed to park in a metered parking space for t minutes

    c. $T(t)$ = temperature t minutes after midnight in Chicago on January 1

    d. $p(t)$ = number of points scored by a basketball player after t minutes of a basketball game

2. Give the three conditions that must be satisfied by a function to be continuous at a point.

3. What does it mean for a function to be continuous on an interval?

4. We informally describe a function f to be continuous at a if its graph contains no holes or breaks at a. Explain why this is not an adequate definition of continuity.

5. Complete the following sentences.

    a. A function is continuous from the left at a if _____.

    b. A function is continuous from the right at a if _____.

6. Describe the points (if any) at which a rational function fails to be continuous.

7. What is the domain of $f(x) = e^x/x$ and where is f continuous?

8. Explain in words and pictures what the Intermediate Value Theorem says.

Basic Skills

9–12. Discontinuities from a graph *Determine the points at which the following functions f have discontinuities. For each point, state the conditions in the continuity checklist that are violated.*

9.
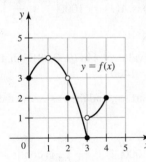

10.
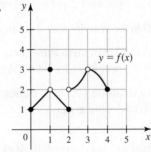

11.
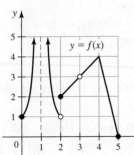

12.
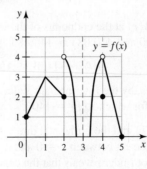

13–20. Continuity at a point *Determine whether the following functions are continuous at a. Use the continuity checklist to justify your answer.*

13. $f(x) = \dfrac{2x^2 + 3x + 1}{x^2 + 5x}$; $a = 5$

14. $f(x) = \dfrac{2x^2 + 3x + 1}{x^2 + 5x}$; $a = -5$

15. $f(x) = \sqrt{x - 2}$; $a = 1$

16. $g(x) = \dfrac{1}{x - 3}$; $a = 3$

17. $f(x) = \begin{cases} \dfrac{x^2 - 1}{x - 1} & \text{if } x \neq 1 \\ 3 & \text{if } x = 1 \end{cases}$; $a = 1$

18. $f(x) = \begin{cases} \dfrac{x^2 - 4x + 3}{x - 3} & \text{if } x \neq 3 \\ 2 & \text{if } x = 3 \end{cases}$; $a = 3$

19. $f(x) = \dfrac{5x - 2}{x^2 - 9x + 20}$; $a = 4$

20. $f(x) = \begin{cases} \dfrac{x^2 + x}{x + 1} & \text{if } x \neq -1 \\ 2 & \text{if } x = -1 \end{cases}$; $a = -1$

21–26. Continuity on intervals *Use Theorem 2.10 to determine the intervals on which the following functions are continuous.*

21. $p(x) = 4x^5 - 3x^2 + 1$

22. $g(x) = \dfrac{3x^2 - 6x + 7}{x^2 + x + 1}$

23. $f(x) = \dfrac{x^5 + 6x + 17}{x^2 - 9}$

24. $s(x) = \dfrac{x^2 - 4x + 3}{x^2 - 1}$

25. $f(x) = \dfrac{1}{x^2 - 4}$

26. $f(t) = \dfrac{t + 2}{t^2 - 4}$

27–30. Limits of compositions *Evaluate the following limits and justify your answer.*

27. $\lim\limits_{x \to 0} (x^8 - 3x^6 - 1)^{40}$

28. $\lim\limits_{x \to 2} \left(\dfrac{3}{2x^5 - 4x^2 - 50} \right)^4$

29. $\lim\limits_{x \to 1} \left(\dfrac{x + 5}{x + 2} \right)^4$

30. $\lim\limits_{x \to \infty} \left(\dfrac{2x + 1}{x} \right)^3$

31–34. Limits of composite functions *Evaluate the following limits and justify your answer.*

31. $\lim\limits_{x \to 4} \sqrt{\dfrac{x^3 - 2x^2 - 8x}{x - 4}}$

32. $\lim\limits_{t \to 4} \tan \dfrac{t - 4}{\sqrt{t} - 2}$

33. $\lim\limits_{x \to 0} \ln \left(2 \dfrac{\sin x}{x} \right)$

34. $\lim\limits_{x \to 0} \left(\dfrac{x}{\sqrt{16x + 1} - 1} \right)^{1/3}$

35–38. Intervals of continuity *Determine the intervals of continuity for the following functions.*

35. The graph of Exercise 9

36. The graph of Exercise 10

37. The graph of Exercise 11   **38.** The graph of Exercise 12

39. Intervals of continuity Let

$$f(x) = \begin{cases} 2x & \text{if } x < 1 \\ x^2 + 3x & \text{if } x \geq 1. \end{cases}$$

   a. Use the continuity checklist to show that f is not continuous at 1.
   b. Is f continuous from the left or right at 1?
   c. State the interval(s) of continuity.

40. Intervals of continuity Let

$$f(x) = \begin{cases} x^3 + 4x + 1 & \text{if } x \leq 0 \\ 2x^3 & \text{if } x > 0. \end{cases}$$

   a. Use the continuity checklist to show that f is not continuous at 0.
   b. Is f continuous from the left or right at 0?
   c. State the interval(s) of continuity.

41–46. Functions with roots *Determine the interval(s) on which the following functions are continuous. Be sure to consider right- and left-continuity at the endpoints.*

41. $f(x) = \sqrt{2x^2 - 16}$ **42.** $g(x) = \sqrt{x^4 - 1}$

43. $f(x) = \sqrt[3]{x^2 - 2x - 3}$ **44.** $f(t) = (t^2 - 1)^{3/2}$

45. $f(x) = (2x - 3)^{2/3}$ **46.** $f(z) = (z - 1)^{3/4}$

47–50. Limits with roots *Determine the following limits and justify your answers.*

47. $\lim_{x \to 2} \sqrt{\dfrac{4x + 10}{2x - 2}}$ **48.** $\lim_{x \to -1} \left(x^2 - 4 + \sqrt[3]{x^2 - 9}\right)$

49. $\lim_{x \to 3} \left(\sqrt{x^2 + 7}\right)$ **50.** $\lim_{t \to 2} \dfrac{t^2 + 5}{1 + \sqrt{t^2 + 5}}$

51–56. Continuity and limits with transcendental functions *Determine the interval(s) on which the following functions are continuous; then evaluate the given limits.*

51. $f(x) = \csc x;\quad \lim_{x \to \pi/4} f(x);\quad \lim_{x \to 2\pi^-} f(x)$

52. $f(x) = e^{\sqrt{x}};\quad \lim_{x \to 4} f(x);\quad \lim_{x \to 0^+} f(x)$

53. $f(x) = \dfrac{1 + \sin x}{\cos x};\quad \lim_{x \to \pi/2^-} f(x);\quad \lim_{x \to 4\pi/3} f(x)$

54. $f(x) = \dfrac{\ln x}{\sin^{-1} x};\quad \lim_{x \to 1^-} f(x)$

55. $f(x) = \dfrac{e^x}{1 - e^x};\quad \lim_{x \to 0^-} f(x);\quad \lim_{x \to 0^+} f(x)$

56. $f(x) = \dfrac{e^{2x} - 1}{e^x - 1};\quad \lim_{x \to 0} f(x)$

57. Intermediate Value Theorem and interest rates Suppose $5000 is invested in a savings account for 10 years (120 months), with an annual interest rate of r, compounded monthly. The amount of money in the account after 10 years is $A(r) = 5000(1 + r/12)^{120}$.

   a. Use the Intermediate Value Theorem to show there is a value of r in $(0, 0.08)$—an interest rate between 0% and 8%—that allows you to reach your savings goal of $7000 in 10 years.

   b. Use a graph to illustrate your explanation in part (a); then approximate the interest rate required to reach your goal.

58. Intermediate Value Theorem and mortgage payments You are shopping for a $150,000, 30-year (360-month) loan to buy a house. The monthly payment is

$$m(r) = \frac{150,000(r/12)}{1 - (1 + r/12)^{-360}},$$

where r is the annual interest rate. Suppose banks are currently offering interest rates between 6% and 8%.

   a. Use the Intermediate Value Theorem to show there is a value of r in $(0.06, 0.08)$—an interest rate between 6% and 8%—that allows you to make monthly payments of $1000 per month.

   b. Use a graph to illustrate your explanation to part (a). Then determine the interest rate you need for monthly payments of $1000.

59–64. Applying the Intermediate Value Theorem
   a. *Use the Intermediate Value Theorem to show that the following equations have a solution on the given interval.*
   b. *Use a graphing utility to find all the solutions to the equation on the given interval.*
   c. *Illustrate your answers with an appropriate graph.*

59. $2x^3 + x - 2 = 0;\ (-1, 1)$

60. $\sqrt{x^4 + 25x^3 + 10} = 5;\ (0, 1)$

61. $x^3 - 5x^2 + 2x = -1;\ (-1, 5)$

62. $-x^5 - 4x^2 + 2\sqrt{x} + 5 = 0;\ (0, 3)$

63. $x + e^x = 0;\ (-1, 0)$

64. $x \ln x - 1 = 0;\ (1, e)$

Further Explorations

65. Explain why or why not Determine whether the following statements are true and give an explanation or counterexample.

   a. If a function is left-continuous and right-continuous at a, then it is continuous at a.
   b. If a function is continuous at a, then it is left-continuous and right-continuous at a.
   c. If $a < b$ and $f(a) \leq L \leq f(b)$, then there is some value of c in (a, b) for which $f(c) = L$.
   d. Suppose f is continuous on $[a, b]$. Then there is a point c in (a, b) such that $f(c) = (f(a) + f(b))/2$.

66. Continuity of the absolute value function Prove that the absolute value function $|x|$ is continuous for all values of x. (*Hint:* Using the definition of the absolute value function, compute $\lim_{x \to 0^-} |x|$ and $\lim_{x \to 0^+} |x|$.)

67–70. Continuity of functions with absolute values *Use the continuity of the absolute value function (Exercise 66) to determine the interval(s) on which the following functions are continuous.*

67. $f(x) = |x^2 + 3x - 18|$ **68.** $g(x) = \left|\dfrac{x + 4}{x^2 - 4}\right|$

69. $h(x) = \left|\dfrac{1}{\sqrt{x} - 4}\right|$ **70.** $h(x) = |x^2 + 2x + 5| + \sqrt{x}$

71–80. Miscellaneous limits *Evaluate the following limits.*

71. $\displaystyle\lim_{x\to\pi}\frac{\cos^2 x + 3\cos x + 2}{\cos x + 1}$

72. $\displaystyle\lim_{x\to 3\pi/2}\frac{\sin^2 x + 6\sin x + 5}{\sin^2 x - 1}$

73. $\displaystyle\lim_{x\to\pi/2}\frac{\sin x - 1}{\sqrt{\sin x} - 1}$

74. $\displaystyle\lim_{\theta\to 0}\frac{\dfrac{1}{2 + \sin\theta} - \dfrac{1}{2}}{\sin\theta}$

75. $\displaystyle\lim_{x\to 0}\frac{\cos x - 1}{\sin^2 x}$

76. $\displaystyle\lim_{x\to 0^+}\frac{1 - \cos^2 x}{\sin x}$

77. $\displaystyle\lim_{x\to\infty}\frac{\tan^{-1} x}{x}$

78. $\displaystyle\lim_{t\to\infty}\frac{\cos t}{e^{3t}}$

79. $\displaystyle\lim_{x\to 1^-}\frac{x}{\ln x}$

80. $\displaystyle\lim_{x\to 0^+}\frac{x}{\ln x}$

81. Pitfalls using technology The graph of the *sawtooth function* $y = x - \lfloor x \rfloor$, where $\lfloor x \rfloor$ is the greatest integer function or floor function (Exercise 37, Section 2.2), was obtained using a graphing utility (see figure). Identify any inaccuracies appearing in the graph and then plot an accurate graph by hand.

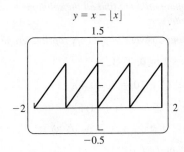

$$y = x - \lfloor x \rfloor$$

82. Pitfalls using technology Graph the function $f(x) = \dfrac{\sin x}{x}$ using a graphing window of $[-\pi, \pi] \times [0, 2]$.

a. Sketch a copy of the graph obtained with your graphing device and describe any inaccuracies appearing in the graph.

b. Sketch an accurate graph of the function. Is f continuous at 0?

c. What is the value of $\displaystyle\lim_{x\to 0}\frac{\sin x}{x}$.

83. Sketching functions

a. Sketch the graph of a function that is not continuous at 1, but is defined at 1.

b. Sketch the graph of a function that is not continuous at 1, but has a limit at 1.

84. An unknown constant Determine the value of the constant a for which the function

$$f(x) = \begin{cases} \dfrac{x^2 + 3x + 2}{x + 1} & \text{if } x \neq -1 \\ a & \text{if } x = -1 \end{cases}$$

is continuous at -1.

85. An unknown constant Let

$$g(x) = \begin{cases} x^2 + x & \text{if } x < 1 \\ a & \text{if } x = 1 \\ 3x + 5 & \text{if } x > 1. \end{cases}$$

a. Determine the value of a for which g is continuous from the left at 1.

b. Determine the value of a for which g is continuous from the right at 1.

c. Is there a value of a for which g is continuous at 1? Explain.

86. Asymptotes of a function containing exponentials Let $f(x) = \dfrac{2e^x + 5e^{3x}}{e^{2x} - e^{3x}}$. Evaluate $\displaystyle\lim_{x\to 0^-} f(x)$, $\displaystyle\lim_{x\to 0^+} f(x)$, $\displaystyle\lim_{x\to -\infty} f(x)$, and $\displaystyle\lim_{x\to\infty} f(x)$. Then give the horizontal and vertical asymptotes of f. Plot f to verify your results.

87. Asymptotes of a function containing exponentials Let $f(x) = \dfrac{2e^x + 10e^{-x}}{e^x + e^{-x}}$. Evaluate $\displaystyle\lim_{x\to 0} f(x)$, $\displaystyle\lim_{x\to -\infty} f(x)$, and $\displaystyle\lim_{x\to\infty} f(x)$. Then give the horizontal and vertical asymptotes of f. Plot f to verify your results.

88–89. Applying the Intermediate Value Theorem *Use the Intermediate Value Theorem to verify that the following equations have three solutions on the given interval. Use a graphing utility to find the approximate roots.*

88. $x^3 + 10x^2 - 100x + 50 = 0; \ (-20, 10)$

89. $70x^3 - 87x^2 + 32x - 3 = 0; \ (0, 1)$

Applications

90. Parking costs Determine the intervals of continuity for the parking cost function c introduced at the outset of this section (see figure). Consider $0 \le t \le 60$.

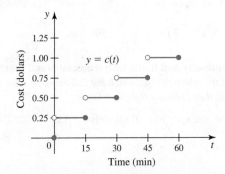

91. Investment problem Assume you invest $250 at the end of each year for 10 years at an annual interest rate of r. The amount of money in your account after 10 years is $A = \dfrac{250((1 + r)^{10} - 1)}{r}$.

Assume your goal is to have $3500 in your account after 10 years.

a. Use the Intermediate Value Theorem to show that there is an interest rate r in the interval $(0.01, 0.10)$—between 1% and 10%—that allows you to reach your financial goal.

b. Use a calculator to estimate the interest rate required to reach your financial goal.

92. Applying the Intermediate Value Theorem Suppose you park your car at a trailhead in a national park and begin a 2-hr hike to a lake at 7 A.M. on a Friday morning. On Sunday morning, you leave the lake at 7 A.M. and start the 2-hr hike back to your car. Assume the lake is 3 mi from your car. Let $f(t)$ be your distance from the car t hours after 7 A.M. on Friday morning and let $g(t)$ be your distance from the car t hours after 7 A.M. on Sunday morning.

a. Evaluate $f(0), f(2), g(0),$ and $g(2)$.

b. Let $h(t) = f(t) - g(t)$. Find $h(0)$ and $h(2)$.

c. Use the Intermediate Value Theorem to show that there is some point along the trail that you will pass at exactly the same time of morning on both days.

93. The monk and the mountain A monk set out from a monastery in the valley at dawn. He walked all day up a winding path, stopping for lunch and taking a nap along the way. At dusk, he arrived at a temple on the mountaintop. The next day, the monk made the return walk to the valley, leaving the temple at dawn, walking the same path for the entire day, and arriving at the monastery in the evening. Must there be one point along the path that the monk occupied at the same time of day on both the ascent and descent? (*Hint:* The question can be answered without the Intermediate Value Theorem.) (*Source:* Arthur Koestler, *The Act of Creation.*)

Additional Exercises

94. Does continuity of $|f|$ imply continuity of f? Let

$$g(x) = \begin{cases} 1 & \text{if } x \geq 0 \\ -1 & \text{if } x < 0. \end{cases}$$

a. Write a formula for $|g(x)|$.

b. Is g continuous at $x = 0$? Explain.

c. Is $|g|$ continuous at $x = 0$? Explain.

d. For any function f, if $|f|$ is continuous at a, does it necessarily follow that f is continuous at a? Explain.

95–96. Classifying discontinuities *The discontinuities in graphs (a) and (b) are* removable discontinuities *because they disappear if we define or redefine f at a so that $f(a) = \lim\limits_{x \to a} f(x)$. The function in graph (c) has a* jump discontinuity *because left and right limits exist at a but are unequal. The discontinuity in graph (d) is an* infinite discontinuity *because the function has a vertical asymptote at a.*

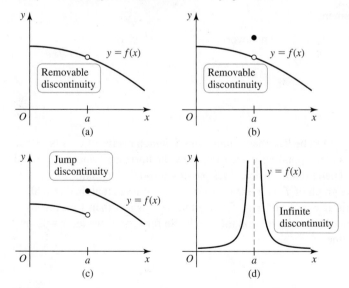

(a)

(b)

(c)

(d)

95. Is the discontinuity at a in graph (c) removable? Explain.

96. Is the discontinuity at a in graph (d) removable? Explain.

97–98. Removable discontinuities *Show that the following functions have a removable discontinuity at the given point. See Exercises 95–96.*

97. $f(x) = \dfrac{x^2 - 7x + 10}{x - 2};\ x = 2$

98. $g(x) = \begin{cases} \dfrac{x^2 - 1}{1 - x} & \text{if } x \neq 1 \\ 3 & \text{if } x = 1 \end{cases};\ x = 1$

99. Do removable discontinuities exist? Refer to Exercises 95–96.

a. Does the function $f(x) = x \sin(1/x)$ have a removable discontinuity at $x = 0$?

b. Does the function $g(x) = \sin(1/x)$ have a removable discontinuity at $x = 0$?

100–101. Classifying discontinuities *Classify the discontinuities in the following functions at the given points. See Exercises 95–96.*

100. $f(x) = \dfrac{|x - 2|}{x - 2};\ x = 2$

101. $h(x) = \dfrac{x^3 - 4x^2 + 4x}{x(x - 1)};\ x = 0 \text{ and } x = 1$

102. Continuity of composite functions Prove Theorem 2.11: If g is continuous at a and f is continuous at $g(a)$, then the composition $f \circ g$ is continuous at a. (*Hint:* Write the definition of continuity for f and g separately; then combine them to form the definition of continuity for $f \circ g$.)

103. Continuity of compositions

a. Find functions f and g such that each function is continuous at 0, but $f \circ g$ is not continuous at 0.

b. Explain why examples satisfying part (a) do not contradict Theorem 2.11.

104. Violation of the Intermediate Value Theorem? Let $f(x) = \dfrac{|x|}{x}$. Then $f(-2) = -1$ and $f(2) = 1$. Therefore, $f(-2) < 0 < f(2)$, but there is no value of c between -2 and 2 for which $f(c) = 0$. Does this fact violate the Intermediate Value Theorem? Explain.

105. Continuity of $\sin x$ and $\cos x$

a. Use the identity $\sin(a + h) = \sin a \cos h + \cos a \sin h$ with the fact that $\lim\limits_{x \to 0} \sin x = 0$ to prove that $\lim\limits_{x \to a} \sin x = \sin a$, thereby establishing that $\sin x$ is continuous for all x. (*Hint:* Let $h = x - a$ so that $x = a + h$ and note that $h \to 0$ as $x \to a$.)

b. Use the identity $\cos(a + h) = \cos a \cos h - \sin a \sin h$ with the fact that $\lim\limits_{x \to 0} \cos x = 1$ to prove that $\lim\limits_{x \to a} \cos x = \cos a$.

QUICK CHECK ANSWERS

1. $t = 15, 30, 45$ **2.** Both expressions have a value of 5, showing that $\lim\limits_{x \to a} f(g(x)) = f(\lim\limits_{x \to a} g(x))$.   **3.** Fill in the endpoints.   **4.** $[0, \infty); (-\infty, \infty)$ **5.** Note that $\lim\limits_{x \to 1^+} \sqrt[4]{\ln x} = \sqrt[4]{\lim\limits_{x \to 1^+} \ln x} = 0$ and $f(1) = \sqrt[4]{\ln 1} = 0$. Because the limit from the right and the value of the function at $x = 1$ are equal, the function is right-continuous at $x = 1$.   **6.** The equation has a solution on the interval $[-1, 1]$ because f is continuous on $[-1, 1]$ and $f(-1) < 0 < f(1)$. ◄

2.7 Precise Definitions of Limits

The limit definitions already encountered in this chapter are adequate for most elementary limits. However, some of the terminology used, such as *sufficiently close* and *arbitrarily large*, needs clarification. The goal of this section is to give limits a solid mathematical foundation by transforming the previous limit definitions into precise mathematical statements.

Moving Toward a Precise Definition

Assume the function f is defined for all x near a, except possibly at a. Recall that $\lim_{x \to a} f(x) = L$ means that $f(x)$ is arbitrarily close to L for all x sufficiently close (but not equal) to a. This limit definition is made precise by observing that the distance between $f(x)$ and L is $|f(x) - L|$ and that the distance between x and a is $|x - a|$. Therefore, we write $\lim_{x \to a} f(x) = L$ if we can make $|f(x) - L|$ arbitrarily small for any x, distinct from a, with $|x - a|$ sufficiently small. For instance, if we want $|f(x) - L|$ to be less than 0.1, then we must find a number $\delta > 0$ such that

$$|f(x) - L| < 0.1 \quad \text{whenever} \quad |x - a| < \delta \quad \text{and} \quad x \neq a.$$

If, instead, we want $|f(x) - L|$ to be less than 0.001, then we must find *another* number $\delta > 0$ such that

$$|f(x) - L| < 0.001 \quad \text{whenever} \quad 0 < |x - a| < \delta.$$

For the limit to exist, it must be true that for *any* $\varepsilon > 0$, we can always find a $\delta > 0$ such that

$$|f(x) - L| < \varepsilon \quad \text{whenever} \quad 0 < |x - a| < \delta.$$

> The phrase *for all x near a* means for all x in an open interval containing a.

> The Greek letters δ (delta) and ε (epsilon) represent small positive numbers when discussing limits.

> The two conditions $|x - a| < \delta$ and $x \neq a$ are written concisely as $0 < |x - a| < \delta$.

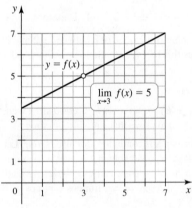

FIGURE 2.55

> The founders of calculus, Isaac Newton (1642–1727) and Gottfried Leibniz (1646–1716), developed the core ideas of calculus without using a precise definition of a limit. It was not until the 19th century that a rigorous definition was introduced by Louis Cauchy (1789–1857) and later refined by Karl Weierstrass (1815–1897).

EXAMPLE 1 Determining values of δ from a graph Figure 2.55 shows the graph of a linear function f with $\lim_{x \to 3} f(x) = 5$. For each value of $\varepsilon > 0$, determine a value of $\delta > 0$ satisfying the statement

$$|f(x) - 5| < \varepsilon \quad \text{whenever} \quad 0 < |x - 3| < \delta.$$

a. $\varepsilon = 1$

b. $\varepsilon = \frac{1}{2}$

SOLUTION

a. With $\varepsilon = 1$, we want $f(x)$ to be less than 1 unit from 5, which means $f(x)$ is between 4 and 6. To determine a corresponding value of δ, draw the horizontal lines $y = 4$ and $y = 6$ (Figure 2.56a). Then sketch vertical lines passing through the points where the horizontal lines and the graph of f intersect (Figure 2.56b). We see that the vertical lines intersect the x-axis at $x = 1$ and $x = 5$. Note that $f(x)$ is less than 1 unit from 5 on the y-axis if x is within 2 units of 3 on the x-axis. So for $\varepsilon = 1$, we let $\delta = 2$ or any smaller positive value.

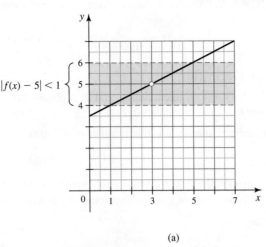

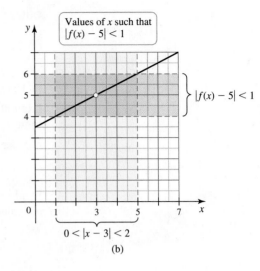

FIGURE 2.56

> Once an acceptable value of δ is found satisfying the statement
>
> $$|f(x) - L| < \varepsilon \quad \text{whenever}$$
> $$0 < |x - a| < \delta,$$
>
> any smaller positive value of δ also works.

b. With $\varepsilon = \frac{1}{2}$, we want $f(x)$ to lie within a half-unit of 5 or, equivalently, $f(x)$ must lie between 4.5 and 5.5. Proceeding as in part (a), we see that $f(x)$ is within a half-unit of 5 on the y-axis (Figure 2.57a) if x is less than 1 unit from 3 (Figure 2.57b). So for $\varepsilon = \frac{1}{2}$, we let $\delta = 1$ or any smaller positive number.

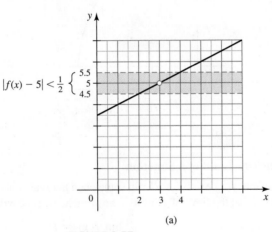

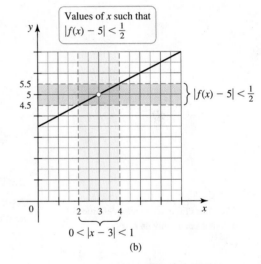

FIGURE 2.57

Related Exercises 9–12 ◄

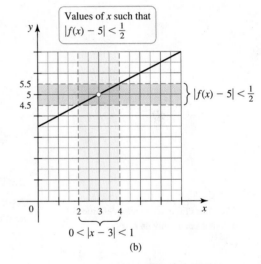

FIGURE 2.58

The idea of a limit, as illustrated in Example 1, may be described in terms of a contest between two people named Epp and Del. First, Epp picks a particular number $\varepsilon > 0$; then he challenges Del to find a corresponding value of $\delta > 0$ such that

$$|f(x) - 5| < \varepsilon \quad \text{whenever} \quad 0 < |x - 3| < \delta. \tag{1}$$

To illustrate, suppose Epp chooses $\varepsilon = 1$. From Example 1, we know that Del will satisfy (1) by choosing $0 < \delta \leq 2$. If Epp chooses $\varepsilon = \frac{1}{2}$, then (by Example 1) Del responds by letting $0 < \delta \leq 1$. If Epp lets $\varepsilon = \frac{1}{8}$, then Del chooses $0 < \delta \leq \frac{1}{4}$ (Figure 2.58). In fact, there is a pattern: For *any* $\varepsilon > 0$ that Epp chooses, no matter how small, Del will satisfy (1) by choosing a positive value of δ satisfying $0 < \delta \leq 2\varepsilon$. Del has discovered a mathematical relationship: If $0 < \delta \leq 2\varepsilon$ and $0 < |x - 3| < \delta$, then $|f(x) - 5| < \varepsilon$, for *any* $\varepsilon > 0$. This conversation illustrates the general procedure for proving that $\lim_{x \to a} f(x) = L$.

In Example 1, find a positive number δ satisfying the statement

$$|f(x) - 5| < \frac{1}{100} \quad \text{whenever} \quad 0 < |x - 3| < \delta. \blacktriangleleft$$

A Precise Definition

Example 1 dealt with a linear function, but it points the way to a precise definition of a limit for any function. As shown in Figure 2.59, $\lim_{x \to a} f(x) = L$ means that for *any* positive number ε, there is another positive number δ such that

$$|f(x) - L| < \varepsilon \quad \text{whenever} \quad 0 < |x - a| < \delta.$$

In all limit proofs, the goal is to find a relationship between ε and δ that gives an admissible value of δ, in terms of ε only. This relationship must work for any positive value of ε.

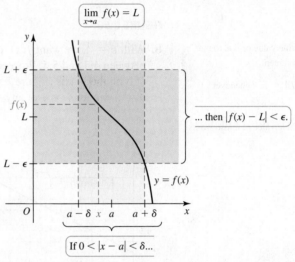

FIGURE 2.59

> The value of δ in the precise definition of a limit depends only on ε.

> Definitions of the one-sided limits $\lim_{x \to a^+} f(x) = L$ and $\lim_{x \to a^-} f(x) = L$ are discussed in Exercises 39–43.

DEFINITION Limit of a Function

Assume that $f(x)$ exists for all x in some open interval containing a, except possibly at a. We say that the **limit of $f(x)$ as x approaches a is L**, written

$$\lim_{x \to a} f(x) = L,$$

if for *any* number $\varepsilon > 0$ there is a corresponding number $\delta > 0$ such that

$$|f(x) - L| < \varepsilon \quad \text{whenever} \quad 0 < |x - a| < \delta.$$

EXAMPLE 2   Finding δ for a given ε using a graphing utility Let $f(x) = x^3 - 6x^2 + 12x - 5$ and demonstrate that $\lim_{x \to 2} f(x) = 3$ as follows. For the given values of ε, use a graphing utility to find a value of $\delta > 0$ such that

$$|f(x) - 3| < \varepsilon \quad \text{whenever} \quad 0 < |x - 2| < \delta.$$

a. $\varepsilon = 1$ **b.** $\varepsilon = \frac{1}{2}$

SOLUTION

a. The condition $|f(x) - 3| < \varepsilon = 1$ implies that $f(x)$ lies between 2 and 4. Using a graphing utility, we graph f and the lines $y = 2$ and $y = 4$ (Figure 2.60). These lines intersect the graph of f at $x = 1$ and at $x = 3$. We now sketch the vertical lines

$x = 1$ and $x = 3$ and observe that $f(x)$ is within 1 unit of 3 whenever x is within 1 unit of 2 on the x-axis (Figure 2.60). Therefore, with $\varepsilon = 1$, we can choose any δ with $0 < \delta \leq 1$.

b. The condition $|f(x) - 3| < \varepsilon = \frac{1}{2}$ implies that $f(x)$ lies between 2.5 and 3.5 on the y-axis. We now find that the lines $y = 2.5$ and $y = 3.5$ intersect the graph of f at $x \approx 1.21$ and $x \approx 2.79$ (Figure 2.61). Observe that if x is less than 0.79 units from 2 on the x-axis, then $f(x)$ is less than a half-unit from 3 on the y-axis. Therefore, with $\varepsilon = \frac{1}{2}$ we can choose any δ with $0 < \delta \leq 0.79$.

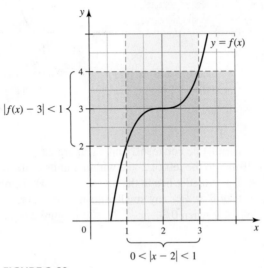

FIGURE 2.60

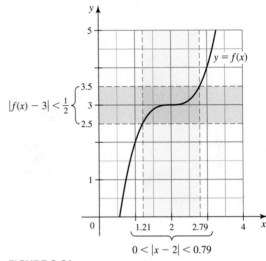

FIGURE 2.61

This procedure could be repeated for smaller and smaller values of $\varepsilon > 0$. For each value of ε, there exists a corresponding value of δ, proving that the limit exists.

Related Exercises 13–14 ◀

QUICK CHECK 2 For the function f given in Example 2, estimate a value of $\delta > 0$ satisfying $|f(x) - 3| < 0.25$ whenever $0 < |x - 2| < \delta$. ◀

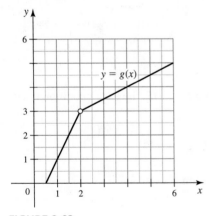

FIGURE 2.62

The inequality $0 < |x - a| < \delta$ means that x lies between $a - \delta$ and $a + \delta$ with $x \neq a$. We say that the interval $(a - \delta, a + \delta)$ is **symmetric about** a because a is the midpoint of the interval. Symmetric intervals are convenient, but Example 3 demonstrates that we don't always get symmetric intervals without a bit of extra work.

EXAMPLE 3   **Finding a symmetric interval** Figure 2.62 shows the graph of g with $\lim\limits_{x \to 2} g(x) = 3$. For each value of ε, find the corresponding values of $\delta > 0$ that satisfy the condition

$$|g(x) - 3| < \varepsilon \quad \text{whenever} \quad 0 < |x - 2| < \delta.$$

a. $\varepsilon = 2$

b. $\varepsilon = 1$

c. For any given value of ε, make a conjecture about the corresponding values of δ that satisfy the limit condition.

SOLUTION

a. With $\varepsilon = 2$, we need a value of $\delta > 0$ such that $g(x)$ is within 2 units of 3, which means between 1 and 5, whenever x is less than δ units from 2. The horizontal lines $y = 1$ and $y = 5$ intersect the graph of g at $x = 1$ and $x = 6$. Therefore, $|g(x) - 3| < 2$ if x lies in the interval $(1, 6)$ with $x \neq 2$ (Figure 2.63a). However, we want x to lie in an interval that is *symmetric* about 2. We can guarantee that $|g(x) - 3| < 2$ only if x is less than 1 unit away from 2, on either side of 2 (Figure 2.63b). Therefore, with $\varepsilon = 2$, we take $\delta = 1$ or any smaller positive number.

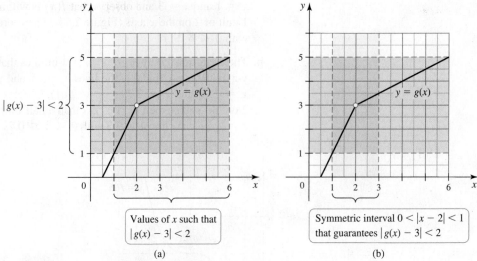

FIGURE 2.63

b. With $\varepsilon = 1$, $g(x)$ must lie between 2 and 4 (Figure 2.64a). This implies that x must be within a half-unit to the left of 2 and within 2 units to the right of 2. Therefore, $|g(x) - 3| < 1$ provided x lies in the interval $(1.5, 4)$. To obtain a symmetric interval about 2, we take $\delta = \frac{1}{2}$ or any smaller positive number. Then we are guaranteed that $|g(x) - 3| < 1$ when $0 < |x - 2| < \frac{1}{2}$ (Figure 2.64b).

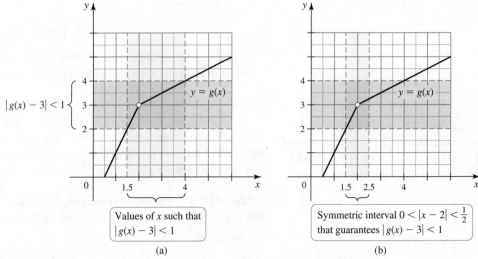

FIGURE 2.64

c. From parts (a) and (b), it appears that if we choose $\delta \le \varepsilon/2$, the limit condition is satisfied for any $\varepsilon > 0$.

Related Exercises 15–18 ◀

Limit Proofs

We use the following two-step process to prove that $\lim\limits_{x \to a} f(x) = L$.

> ▶ The first step of the limit-proving process is the preliminary work of finding a candidate for δ. The second step verifies that the δ found in the first step actually works.

Steps for proving that $\lim\limits_{x \to a} f(x) = L$

1. Find δ. Let ε be an arbitrary positive number. Use the inequality $|f(x) - L| < \varepsilon$ to find a condition of the form $|x - a| < \delta$, where δ depends only on the value of ε.

2. Write a proof. For any $\varepsilon > 0$, assume $0 < |x - a| < \delta$ and use the relationship between ε and δ found in Step 1 to prove that $|f(x) - L| < \varepsilon$.

EXAMPLE 4 **Limit of a linear function** Prove that $\lim\limits_{x \to 4} (4x - 15) = 1$ using the precise definition of a limit.

SOLUTION

Step 1: *Find δ.* In this case, $a = 4$ and $L = 1$. Assuming $\varepsilon > 0$ is given, we use $|(4x - 15) - 1| < \varepsilon$ to find an inequality of the form $|x - 4| < \delta$. If $|(4x - 15) - 1| < \varepsilon$, then

$$|4x - 16| < \varepsilon$$
$$4|x - 4| < \varepsilon \quad \text{Factor } 4x - 16.$$
$$|x - 4| < \frac{\varepsilon}{4}. \quad \text{Divide by 4 and identify } \delta = \varepsilon/4.$$

We have shown that $|(4x - 15) - 1| < \varepsilon$ implies $|x - 4| < \varepsilon/4$. Therefore, a plausible relationship between δ and ε is $\delta = \varepsilon/4$. We now write the actual proof.

Step 2: *Write a proof.* Let $\varepsilon > 0$ be given and assume $0 < |x - 4| < \delta$ where $\delta = \varepsilon/4$. The aim is to show that $|(4x - 15) - 1| < \varepsilon$ for all x such that $0 < |x - 4| < \delta$. We simplify $|(4x - 15) - 1|$ and isolate the $|x - 4|$ term:

$$
\begin{aligned}
|(4x - 15) - 1| &= |4x - 16| \\
&= 4\, \underbrace{|x - 4|}_{\text{less than } \delta\, =\, \varepsilon/4} \\
&< 4\left(\frac{\varepsilon}{4}\right) = \varepsilon.
\end{aligned}
$$

We have shown that for any $\varepsilon > 0$,

$$|f(x) - L| = |(4x - 15) - 1| < \varepsilon \quad \text{whenever} \quad 0 < |x - 4| < \delta,$$

provided $0 < \delta \le \varepsilon/4$. Therefore, $\lim\limits_{x \to 4} (4x - 15) = 1$.

Related Exercises 19–24 ◀

Justifying Limit Laws

The precise definition of a limit is used to prove the limit laws in Theorem 2.3. Essential in several of these proofs is the triangle inequality, which states that

$$|x + y| \le |x| + |y|, \quad \text{for all real numbers } x \text{ and } y.$$

EXAMPLE 5 **Proof of Limit Law 1** Prove that if $\lim\limits_{x \to a} f(x)$ and $\lim\limits_{x \to a} g(x)$ exist, then

$$\lim_{x \to a} [f(x) + g(x)] = \lim_{x \to a} f(x) + \lim_{x \to a} g(x).$$

▶ Because $\lim\limits_{x \to a} f(x)$ exists, if there exists a $\delta > 0$ for any given $\varepsilon > 0$, then there also exists a $\delta > 0$ for any given $\frac{\varepsilon}{2}$.

SOLUTION Assume that $\varepsilon > 0$ is given. Let $\lim\limits_{x \to a} f(x) = L$, which implies that there exists a $\delta_1 > 0$ such that

$$|f(x) - L| < \frac{\varepsilon}{2} \quad \text{whenever} \quad 0 < |x - a| < \delta_1.$$

Similarly, let $\lim\limits_{x \to a} g(x) = M$, which implies there exists a $\delta_2 > 0$ such that

$$|g(x) - M| < \frac{\varepsilon}{2} \quad \text{whenever} \quad 0 < |x - a| < \delta_2.$$

▶ The minimum value of a and b is denoted min $\{a, b\}$. If $x = \min\{a, b\}$, then x is the smaller of a and b. If $a = b$, then x equals the common value of a and b. In either case, $x \leq a$ and $x \leq b$.

Let $\delta = \min\{\delta_1, \delta_2\}$ and suppose $0 < |x - a| < \delta$. Because $\delta \leq \delta_1$, it follows that $0 < |x - a| < \delta_1$ and $|f(x) - L| < \varepsilon/2$. Similarly, because $\delta \leq \delta_2$, it follows that $0 < |x - a| < \delta_2$ and $|g(x) - M| < \varepsilon/2$. Therefore,

$$|(f(x) + g(x)) - (L + M)| = |(f(x) - L) + (g(x) - M)| \quad \text{Rearrange terms.}$$
$$\leq |f(x) - L| + |g(x) - M| \quad \text{Triangle inequality.}$$
$$< \frac{\varepsilon}{2} + \frac{\varepsilon}{2} = \varepsilon.$$

We have shown that given any $\varepsilon > 0$, if $0 < |x - a| < \delta$, then $|(f(x) + g(x)) - (L + M)| < \varepsilon$, which implies that $\lim_{x \to a} [f(x) + g(x)] = L + M = \lim_{x \to a} f(x) + \lim_{x \to a} g(x)$.

▶ Proofs of other limit laws are outlined in Exercises 25 and 26.

Related Exercises 25–28 ◀

Infinite Limits

▶ Notice that for infinite limits, N plays the role that ε plays for regular limits. It sets a tolerance or bound for the function values $f(x)$.

In Section 2.4, we stated that $\lim_{x \to a} f(x) = \infty$ if $f(x)$ grows *arbitrarily large* as x approaches a. More precisely, this means that for any positive number N (no matter how large), $f(x)$ is larger than N if x is sufficiently close to a but not equal to a.

> **DEFINITION Two-Sided Infinite Limit**
>
> The **infinite limit** $\lim_{x \to a} f(x) = \infty$ means that for any positive number N, there exists a corresponding $\delta > 0$ such that
>
> $$f(x) > N \quad \text{whenever} \quad 0 < |x - a| < \delta.$$

As shown in Figure 2.65, to prove that $\lim_{x \to a} f(x) = \infty$, we let N represent *any* positive number. Then we find a value of $\delta > 0$, depending only on N, such that

$$f(x) > N \quad \text{whenever} \quad 0 < |x - a| < \delta.$$

This process is similar to the two-step process for finite limits.

▶ Precise definitions for $\lim_{x \to a} f(x) = -\infty$, $\lim_{x \to a^+} f(x) = -\infty$, $\lim_{x \to a^+} f(x) = \infty$, $\lim_{x \to a^-} f(x) = -\infty$, and $\lim_{x \to a^-} f(x) = \infty$ are given in Exercises 45–49.

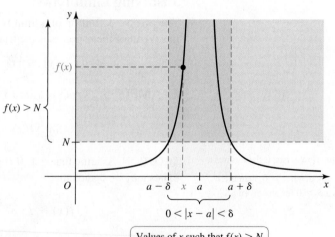

FIGURE 2.65

Steps for proving that $\lim\limits_{x \to a} f(x) = \infty$

1. **Find δ.** Let N be an arbitrary positive number. Use the statement $f(x) > N$ to find an inequality of the form $|x - a| < \delta$, where δ depends only on N.

2. **Write a proof.** For any $N > 0$, assume $0 < |x - a| < \delta$ and use the relationship between N and δ found in Step 1 to prove that $f(x) > N$.

EXAMPLE 6   An Infinite Limit Proof Let $f(x) = \dfrac{1}{(x-2)^2}$. Prove that $\lim\limits_{x \to 2} f(x) = \infty$.

SOLUTION

Step 1:   Find $\delta > 0$. Assuming $N > 0$, we use the inequality $\dfrac{1}{(x-2)^2} > N$ to find δ, where δ depends only on N. Taking reciprocals of this inequality, it follows that

$$(x - 2)^2 < \frac{1}{N}$$

$$|x - 2| < \frac{1}{\sqrt{N}}.   \text{Take the square root of both sides.}$$

> Recall that $\sqrt{x^2} = |x|$.

The inequality $|x - 2| < \dfrac{1}{\sqrt{N}}$ has the form $|x - 2| < \delta$ if we let $\delta = \dfrac{1}{\sqrt{N}}$. We now write a proof based on this relationship between δ and N.

Step 2:   Write a proof. Suppose $N > 0$ is given. Let $\delta = \dfrac{1}{\sqrt{N}}$ and assume $0 < |x - 2| < \delta = \dfrac{1}{\sqrt{N}}$. Squaring both sides of the inequality $|x - 2| < \dfrac{1}{\sqrt{N}}$ and taking reciprocals, we have

$$(x - 2)^2 < \frac{1}{N}   \text{Square both sides.}$$

$$\frac{1}{(x - 2)^2} > N.   \text{Take reciprocals of both sides.}$$

QUICK CHECK 3 In Example 6, if N is increased by a factor of 100, how must δ change? ◄

We see that for any positive N, if $0 < |x - 2| < \delta = \dfrac{1}{\sqrt{N}}$, then

$$f(x) = \frac{1}{(x - 2)^2} > N.\text{ It follows that } \lim_{x \to 2} \frac{1}{(x - 2)^2} = \infty.\text{ Note that}$$

because $\delta = \dfrac{1}{\sqrt{N}}$, δ decreases as N increases.

Related Exercises 29–32 ◄

Limits at Infinity

Precise definitions can also be written for the limits at infinity $\lim\limits_{x \to \infty} f(x) = L$ and $\lim\limits_{x \to -\infty} f(x) = L$. For discussion and examples, see Exercises 50 and 51.

SECTION 2.7 EXERCISES

Review Questions

1. Suppose x lies in the interval $(1, 3)$ with $x \neq 2$. Find the smallest positive value of δ such that the inequality $0 < |x - 2| < \delta$ is true.

2. Suppose $f(x)$ lies in the interval $(2, 6)$. What is the smallest value of ε such that $|f(x) - 4| < \varepsilon$?

3. Which one of the following intervals is not symmetric about $x = 5$?

   a. $(1, 9)$ **b.** $(4, 6)$ **c.** $(3, 8)$ **d.** $(4.5, 5.5)$

4. Does the set $\{x: 0 < |x - a| < \delta\}$ include the point $x = a$? Explain.

5. State the precise definition of $\lim\limits_{x \to a} f(x) = L$.

6. Interpret $|f(x) - L| < \varepsilon$ in words.

7. Suppose $|f(x) - 5| < 0.1$ whenever $0 < x < 5$. Find all values of $\delta > 0$ such that $|f(x) - 5| < 0.1$ whenever $0 < |x - 2| < \delta$.

8. Give the definition of $\lim\limits_{x \to a} f(x) = \infty$ and interpret it using pictures.

Basic Skills

9. **Determining values of δ from a graph** The function f in the figure satisfies $\lim\limits_{x \to 2} f(x) = 5$. Determine the largest value of $\delta > 0$ satisfying each statement.

   a. If $0 < |x - 2| < \delta$, then $|f(x) - 5| < 2$.

   b. If $0 < |x - 2| < \delta$, then $|f(x) - 5| < 1$.

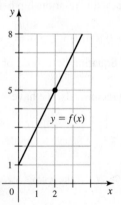

10. **Determining values of δ from a graph** The function f in the figure satisfies $\lim\limits_{x \to 2} f(x) = 4$. Determine the largest value of $\delta > 0$ satisfying each statement.

    a. If $0 < |x - 2| < \delta$, then $|f(x) - 4| < 1$.

    b. If $0 < |x - 2| < \delta$, then $|f(x) - 4| < 1/2$.

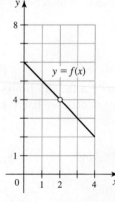

11. **Determining values of δ from a graph** The function f in the figure satisfies $\lim\limits_{x \to 3} f(x) = 6$. Determine the largest value of $\delta > 0$ satisfying each statement.

    a. If $0 < |x - 3| < \delta$, then $|f(x) - 6| < 3$.

    b. If $0 < |x - 3| < \delta$, then $|f(x) - 6| < 1$.

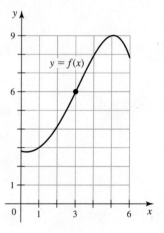

12. **Determining values of δ from a graph** The function f in the figure satisfies $\lim\limits_{x \to 4} f(x) = 5$. Determine the largest value of $\delta > 0$ satisfying each statement.

    a. If $0 < |x - 4| < \delta$, then $|f(x) - 5| < 1$.

    b. If $0 < |x - 4| < \delta$, then $|f(x) - 5| < 0.5$.

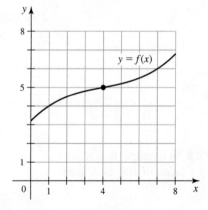

13. **Finding δ for a given ε using a graph** Let $f(x) = x^3 + 3$ and note that $\lim\limits_{x \to 0} f(x) = 3$. For each value of ε, use a graphing utility to find a value of $\delta > 0$ such that $|f(x) - 3| < \varepsilon$ whenever $0 < |x - 0| < \delta$. Sketch graphs illustrating your work.

    a. $\varepsilon = 1$ **b.** $\varepsilon = 0.5$

14. **Finding δ for a given ε using a graph** Let $g(x) = 2x^3 - 12x^2 + 26x + 4$ and note that $\lim\limits_{x \to 2} g(x) = 24$.

    For each value of ε, use a graphing utility to find a value of $\delta > 0$ such that $|g(x) - 24| < \varepsilon$ whenever $0 < |x - 2| < \delta$. Sketch graphs illustrating your work.

    a. $\varepsilon = 1$ **b.** $\varepsilon = 0.5$

15. **Finding a symmetric interval** The function f in the figure satisfies $\lim\limits_{x \to 2} f(x) = 3$. For each value of ε, find a value of $\delta > 0$ such that

$$|f(x) - 3| < \varepsilon \quad \text{whenever} \quad 0 < |x - 2| < \delta. \quad (2)$$

    a. $\varepsilon = 1$ **b.** $\varepsilon = \frac{1}{2}$

c. For any $\varepsilon > 0$, make a conjecture about the corresponding value of δ satisfying (2).

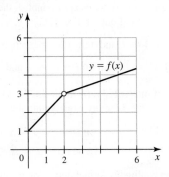

16. **Finding a symmetric interval** The function f in the figure satisfies $\lim_{x \to 4} f(x) = 5$. For each value of ε, find a value of $\delta > 0$ such that

$$|f(x) - 5| < \varepsilon \quad \text{whenever} \quad 0 < |x - 4| < \delta. \qquad (3)$$

a. $\varepsilon = 2$ b. $\varepsilon = 1$
c. For any $\varepsilon > 0$, make a conjecture about the corresponding value of δ satisfying (3).

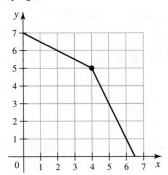

▥ 17. **Finding a symmetric interval** Let $f(x) = \dfrac{2x^2 - 2}{x - 1}$ and note that $\lim_{x \to 1} f(x) = 4$. For each value of ε, use a graphing utility to find a value of $\delta > 0$ such that $|f(x) - 4| < \varepsilon$ whenever $0 < |x - 1| < \delta$.

a. $\varepsilon = 2$ b. $\varepsilon = 1$
c. For any $\varepsilon > 0$, make a conjecture about the value of δ that satisfies the preceding inequality.

▥ 18. **Finding a symmetric interval** Let $f(x) = \begin{cases} \frac{1}{3}x + 1 & \text{if } x \le 3 \\ \frac{1}{2}x + \frac{1}{2} & \text{if } x > 3 \end{cases}$
and note that $\lim_{x \to 3} f(x) = 2$. For each value of ε, use a graphing utility to find a value of $\delta > 0$ such that $|f(x) - 2| < \varepsilon$ whenever $0 < |x - 3| < \delta$.

a. $\varepsilon = \frac{1}{2}$ b. $\varepsilon = \frac{1}{4}$
c. For any $\varepsilon > 0$, make a conjecture about the value of δ that satisfies the preceding inequality.

19–24. Limit proofs *Use the precise definition of a limit to prove the following limits.*

19. $\lim_{x \to 1} (8x + 5) = 13$ 20. $\lim_{x \to 3} (-2x + 8) = 2$

21. $\lim_{x \to 4} \dfrac{x^2 - 16}{x - 4} = 8$ (*Hint:* Factor and simplify.)

22. $\lim_{x \to 3} \dfrac{x^2 - 7x + 12}{x - 3} = -1$

23. $\lim_{x \to 0} x^2 = 0$ (*Hint:* Use the identity $\sqrt{x^2} = |x|$.)

24. $\lim_{x \to 3} (x - 3)^2 = 0$ (*Hint:* Use the identity $\sqrt{x^2} = |x|$.)

25. **Proof of Limit Law 2** Suppose $\lim_{x \to a} f(x) = L$ and $\lim_{x \to a} g(x) = M$. Prove that $\lim_{x \to a} [f(x) - g(x)] = L - M$.

26. **Proof of Limit Law 3** Suppose $\lim_{x \to a} f(x) = L$. Prove that $\lim_{x \to a} [cf(x)] = cL$, where c is a constant.

27. **Limit of a constant function and $f(x) = x$** Give proofs of the following theorems.

a. $\lim_{x \to a} c = c$ for any constant c
b. $\lim_{x \to a} x = a$ for any constant a

28. **Continuity of linear functions** Prove Theorem 2.2: If $f(x) = mx + b$, then $\lim_{x \to a} f(x) = ma + b$ for constants m and b. (*Hint:* For a given $\varepsilon > 0$, let $\delta = \varepsilon / |m|$.) Explain why this result implies that linear functions are continuous.

29–32. Limit proofs for infinite limits *Use the precise definition of infinite limits to prove the following limits.*

29. $\lim_{x \to 4} \dfrac{1}{(x - 4)^2} = \infty$ 30. $\lim_{x \to -1} \dfrac{1}{(x + 1)^4} = \infty$

31. $\lim_{x \to 0} \left(\dfrac{1}{x^2} + 1 \right) = \infty$ 32. $\lim_{x \to 0} \left(\dfrac{1}{x^4} - \sin x \right) = \infty$

Further Explorations

33. **Explain why or why not** Determine whether the following statements are true and give an explanation or counterexample. Assume a and L are finite numbers and assume $\lim_{x \to a} f(x) = L$.

a. For a given $\varepsilon > 0$, there is one value of $\delta > 0$ for which $|f(x) - L| < \varepsilon$ whenever $0 < |x - a| < \delta$.
b. The limit $\lim_{x \to a} f(x) = L$ means that given an arbitrary $\delta > 0$, we can always find an $\varepsilon > 0$ such that $|f(x) - L| < \varepsilon$ whenever $0 < |x - a| < \delta$.
c. The limit $\lim_{x \to a} f(x) = L$ means that for any arbitrary $\varepsilon > 0$, we can always find a $\delta > 0$ such that $|f(x) - L| < \varepsilon$ whenever $0 < |x - a| < \delta$.
d. If $|x - a| < \delta$, then $a - \delta < x < a + \delta$.

34. **Finding δ algebraically** Let $f(x) = x^2 - 2x + 3$.

a. For $\varepsilon = 0.25$, find a corresponding value of $\delta > 0$ satisfying the statement

$$|f(x) - 2| < \varepsilon \quad \text{whenever} \quad 0 < |x - 1| < \delta.$$

b. Verify that $\lim_{x \to 1} f(x) = 2$ as follows. For any $\varepsilon > 0$, find a corresponding value of $\delta > 0$ satisfying the statement

$$|f(x) - 2| < \varepsilon \quad \text{whenever} \quad 0 < |x - 1| < \delta.$$

35–38. Challenging limit proofs *Use the definition of a limit to prove the following results.*

35. $\lim_{x \to 3} \dfrac{1}{x} = \dfrac{1}{3}$ (*Hint:* As $x \to 3$, eventually the distance between x and 3 will be less than 1. Start by assuming $|x - 3| < 1$ and show $\dfrac{1}{|x|} < \dfrac{1}{2}$.)

36. $\lim\limits_{x \to 4} \dfrac{x - 4}{\sqrt{x} - 2} = 4$ (*Hint:* Multiply the numerator and denominator by $\sqrt{x} + 2$.)

37. $\lim\limits_{x \to 1/10} \dfrac{1}{x} = 10$ (*Hint:* To find δ, you will need to bound x away from 0. So let $\left| x - \dfrac{1}{10} \right| < \dfrac{1}{20}$.)

38. $\lim\limits_{x \to 5} \dfrac{1}{x^2} = \dfrac{1}{25}$

39–43. Precise definitions for left- and right-sided limits
Use the following definitions.

Assume f exists for all x near a with $x > a$. We say that the **limit of $f(x)$ as x approaches a from the right of a is L** *and write* $\lim\limits_{x \to a^+} f(x) = L$, *if for any $\varepsilon > 0$ there exists $\delta > 0$ such that*

$$|f(x) - L| < \varepsilon \quad \text{whenever} \quad 0 < x - a < \delta.$$

Assume f exists for all values of x near a with $x < a$. We say that the **limit of $f(x)$ as x approaches a from the left of a is L** *and write* $\lim\limits_{x \to a^-} f(x) = L$, *if for any $\varepsilon > 0$ there exists $\delta > 0$ such that*

$$|f(x) - L| < \varepsilon \quad \text{whenever} \quad 0 < a - x < \delta.$$

39. Comparing definitions Why is the last inequality in the definition of $\lim\limits_{x \to a} f(x) = L$, namely, $0 < |x - a| < \delta$, replaced with $0 < x - a < \delta$ in the definition of $\lim\limits_{x \to a^+} f(x) = L$?

40. Comparing definitions Why is the last inequality in the definition of $\lim\limits_{x \to a} f(x) = L$, namely, $0 < |x - a| < \delta$, replaced with $0 < a - x < \delta$ in the definition of $\lim\limits_{x \to a^-} f(x) = L$?

41. One-sided limit proofs Prove the following limits for

$$f(x) = \begin{cases} 3x - 4 & \text{if } x < 0 \\ 2x - 4 & \text{if } x \geq 0. \end{cases}$$

a. $\lim\limits_{x \to 0^+} f(x) = -4$ **b.** $\lim\limits_{x \to 0^-} f(x) = -4$
c. $\lim\limits_{x \to 0} f(x) = -4$

42. Determining values of δ from a graph The function f in the figure satisfies $\lim\limits_{x \to 2^+} f(x) = 0$ and $\lim\limits_{x \to 2^-} f(x) = 1$. Determine a value of $\delta > 0$ satisfying each statement.

a. $|f(x) - 0| < 2$ whenever $0 < x - 2 < \delta$
b. $|f(x) - 0| < 1$ whenever $0 < x - 2 < \delta$
c. $|f(x) - 1| < 2$ whenever $0 < 2 - x < \delta$
d. $|f(x) - 1| < 1$ whenever $0 < 2 - x < \delta$

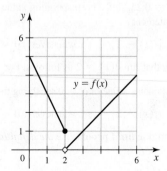

43. One-sided limit proof Prove that $\lim\limits_{x \to 0^+} \sqrt{x} = 0$.

Additional Exercises

44. The relationship between one-sided and two-sided limits
Prove the following statements to establish the fact that $\lim\limits_{x \to a} f(x) = L$ if and only if $\lim\limits_{x \to a^-} f(x) = L$ and $\lim\limits_{x \to a^+} f(x) = L$.

a. If $\lim\limits_{x \to a^-} f(x) = L$ and $\lim\limits_{x \to a^+} f(x) = L$, then $\lim\limits_{x \to a} f(x) = L$.
b. If $\lim\limits_{x \to a} f(x) = L$, then $\lim\limits_{x \to a^-} f(x) = L$ and $\lim\limits_{x \to a^+} f(x) = L$.

45. Definition of one-sided infinite limits We say that $\lim\limits_{x \to a^+} f(x) = -\infty$ if for any negative number N, there exists $\delta > 0$ such that

$$f(x) < N \quad \text{whenever} \quad a < x < a + \delta.$$

a. Write an analogous formal definition for $\lim\limits_{x \to a^+} f(x) = \infty$.
b. Write an analogous formal definition for $\lim\limits_{x \to a^-} f(x) = -\infty$.
c. Write an analogous formal definition for $\lim\limits_{x \to a^-} f(x) = \infty$.

46–47. One-sided infinite limits *Use the definitions given in Exercise 45 to prove the following infinite limits.*

46. $\lim\limits_{x \to 1^+} \dfrac{1}{1 - x} = -\infty$ **47.** $\lim\limits_{x \to 1^-} \dfrac{1}{1 - x} = \infty$

48–49. Definition of an infinite limit *We write $\lim\limits_{x \to a} f(x) = -\infty$ if for any negative number M there exists a $\delta > 0$ such that*

$$f(x) < M \quad \text{whenever} \quad 0 < |x - a| < \delta.$$

Use this definition to prove the following statements.

48. $\lim\limits_{x \to 1} \dfrac{-2}{(x - 1)^2} = -\infty$ **49.** $\lim\limits_{x \to -2} \dfrac{-10}{(x + 2)^4} = -\infty$

50–51. Definition of a limit at infinity *The limit at infinity $\lim\limits_{x \to \infty} f(x) = L$ means that for any $\varepsilon > 0$, there exists $N > 0$ such that*

$$|f(x) - L| < \varepsilon \quad \text{whenever} \quad x > N.$$

Use this definition to prove the following statements.

50. $\lim\limits_{x \to \infty} \dfrac{10}{x} = 0$

51. $\lim\limits_{x \to \infty} \dfrac{2x + 1}{x} = 2$

52–53. Definition of infinite limits at infinity *We say that $\lim\limits_{x \to \infty} f(x) = \infty$ if for any positive number M, there is a corresponding $N > 0$ such that*

$$f(x) > M \quad \text{whenever} \quad x > N.$$

Use this definition to prove the following statements.

52. $\lim\limits_{x \to \infty} \dfrac{x}{100} = \infty$

53. $\lim\limits_{x \to \infty} \dfrac{x^2 + x}{x} = \infty$

54. Proof of the Squeeze Theorem Assume the functions f, g, and h satisfy the inequality $f(x) \leq g(x) \leq h(x)$ for all values of x near a, except possibly at a. Prove that if $\lim\limits_{x \to a} f(x) = \lim\limits_{x \to a} h(x) = L$, then $\lim\limits_{x \to a} g(x) = L$.

55. Limit proof Suppose f is defined for all values of x near a, except possibly at a. Assume for any integer $N > 0$, there is another integer $M > 0$ such that $|f(x) - L| < 1/N$ whenever $|x - a| < 1/M$. Prove that $\lim\limits_{x \to a} f(x) = L$ using the precise definition of a limit.

56–58. Proving that $\lim\limits_{x \to a} f(x) \neq L$ *Use the following definition for the nonexistence of a limit. Assume f is defined for all values of x near a, except possibly at a. We say that $\lim\limits_{x \to a} f(x) \neq L$ if for some $\varepsilon > 0$ there is no value of $\delta > 0$ satisfying the condition*

$$|f(x) - L| < \varepsilon \quad \text{whenever} \quad 0 < |x - a| < \delta.$$

56. For the following function, note that $\lim\limits_{x \to 2} f(x) \neq 3$. Find a value of $\varepsilon > 0$ for which the preceding condition for nonexistence is satisfied.

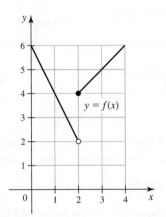

57. Prove that $\lim\limits_{x \to 0} \dfrac{|x|}{x}$ does not exist.

58. Let

$$f(x) = \begin{cases} 0 & \text{if } x \text{ is rational} \\ 1 & \text{if } x \text{ is irrational.} \end{cases}$$

Prove that $\lim\limits_{x \to a} f(x)$ does not exist for any value of a. (*Hint:* Assume $\lim\limits_{x \to a} f(x) = L$ for some values of a and L and let $\varepsilon = \frac{1}{2}$.)

59. A continuity proof Suppose f is continuous at a and assume $f(a) > 0$. Show that there is a positive number $\delta > 0$ for which $f(x) > 0$ for all values of x in $(a - \delta, a + \delta)$. (In other words, f is positive for all values of x in the domain sufficiently close to a.)

QUICK CHECK ANSWERS

1. $\delta = \frac{1}{50}$ or smaller **2.** $\delta = 0.62$ or smaller **3.** δ must decrease by a factor of $\sqrt{100} = 10$ (at least). ◄

CHAPTER 2 REVIEW EXERCISES

1. **Explain why or why not** Determine whether the following statements are true and give an explanation or counterexample.

  a. The rational function $\dfrac{x - 1}{x^2 - 1}$ has vertical asymptotes at $x = -1$ and $x = 1$.

  b. Numerical or graphical methods always produce good estimates of $\lim\limits_{x \to a} f(x)$.

  c. The value of $\lim\limits_{x \to a} f(x)$, if it exists, is found by calculating $f(a)$.

  d. If $\lim\limits_{x \to a} f(x) = \infty$ or $\lim\limits_{x \to a} f(x) = -\infty$, then $\lim\limits_{x \to a} f(x)$ does not exist.

  e. If $\lim\limits_{x \to a} f(x)$ does not exist, then either $\lim\limits_{x \to a} f(x) = \infty$ or $\lim\limits_{x \to a} f(x) = -\infty$.

  f. If a function is continuous on the intervals (a, b) and (b, c), where $a < b < c$, then the function is also continuous on (a, c).

  g. If $\lim\limits_{x \to a} f(x)$ can be calculated by direct substitution, then f is continuous at $x = a$.

2. **Estimating limits graphically** Use the graph of f in the figure to find the following values, if possible.

  a. $f(-1)$ **b.** $\lim\limits_{x \to -1^-} f(x)$ **c.** $\lim\limits_{x \to -1^+} f(x)$ **d.** $\lim\limits_{x \to -1} f(x)$

  e. $f(1)$ **f.** $\lim\limits_{x \to 1} f(x)$ **g.** $\lim\limits_{x \to 2} f(x)$ **h.** $\lim\limits_{x \to 3^-} f(x)$

  i. $\lim\limits_{x \to 3^+} f(x)$ **j.** $\lim\limits_{x \to 3} f(x)$

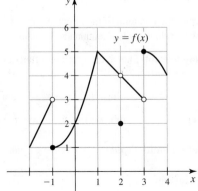

3. Points of discontinuity Use the graph of f in the figure to determine the values of x in the interval $(-3, 5)$ at which f fails to be continuous. Justify your answers using the continuity checklist.

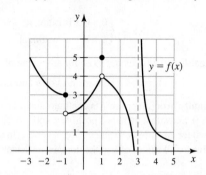

4. Computing a limit graphically and analytically

a. Graph $y = \dfrac{\sin 2\theta}{\sin \theta}$. Comment on any inaccuracies in the graph and then sketch an accurate graph of the function.

b. Estimate $\lim\limits_{\theta \to 0} \dfrac{\sin 2\theta}{\sin \theta}$ using the graph in part (a).

c. Verify your answer to part (b) by finding the value of $\lim\limits_{\theta \to 0} \dfrac{\sin 2\theta}{\sin \theta}$ analytically using the trigonometric identity $\sin 2\theta = 2 \sin \theta \cos \theta$.

5. Computing a limit numerically and analytically

a. Estimate $\lim\limits_{x \to \pi/4} \dfrac{\cos 2x}{\cos x - \sin x}$ by making a table of values of $\dfrac{\cos 2x}{\cos x - \sin x}$ for values of x approaching $\pi/4$. Round your estimate to four digits.

b. Use analytic methods to find the value of $\lim\limits_{x \to \pi/4} \dfrac{\cos 2x}{\cos x - \sin x}$.

6. Long-distance phone calls Suppose a long-distance phone call costs $0.75 for the first minute (or any part of the first minute), plus $0.10 for each additional minute (or any part of a minute).

a. Graph the function $c = f(t)$ that gives the cost for talking on the phone for t minutes, for $0 \le t \le 5$.

b. Evaluate $\lim\limits_{t \to 2.9} f(t)$.

c. Evaluate $\lim\limits_{t \to 3^-} f(t)$ and $\lim\limits_{t \to 3^+} f(t)$.

d. Interpret the meaning of the limits in part (c).

e. For what values of t is f continuous? Explain.

7. Sketching a graph Sketch the graph of a function f with all the following properties.

$$\lim_{x \to -2^-} f(x) = \infty \qquad \lim_{x \to -2^+} f(x) = -\infty \qquad \lim_{x \to 0} f(x) = \infty$$
$$\lim_{x \to 3^-} f(x) = 2 \qquad \lim_{x \to 3^+} f(x) = 4 \qquad f(3) = 1$$

8–21. Evaluating limits *Evaluate the following limits analytically.*

8. $\lim\limits_{x \to 1000} 18\pi^2$

9. $\lim\limits_{x \to 1} \sqrt{5x + 6}$

10. $\lim\limits_{h \to 0} \dfrac{\sqrt{5x + 5h} - \sqrt{5x}}{h}$, where x is constant

11. $\lim\limits_{x \to 1} \dfrac{x^3 - 7x^2 + 12x}{4 - x}$

12. $\lim\limits_{x \to 4} \dfrac{x^3 - 7x^2 + 12x}{4 - x}$

13. $\lim\limits_{x \to 1} \dfrac{1 - x^2}{x^2 - 8x + 7}$

14. $\lim\limits_{x \to 3} \dfrac{\sqrt{3x + 16} - 5}{x - 3}$

15. $\lim\limits_{x \to 3} \dfrac{1}{x - 3}\left(\dfrac{1}{\sqrt{x + 1}} - \dfrac{1}{2}\right)$

16. $\lim\limits_{t \to 1/3} \dfrac{t - 1/3}{(3t - 1)^2}$

17. $\lim\limits_{x \to 3} \dfrac{x^4 - 81}{x - 3}$

18. $\lim\limits_{p \to 1} \dfrac{p^5 - 1}{p - 1}$

19. $\lim\limits_{x \to 81} \dfrac{\sqrt[4]{x} - 3}{x - 81}$

20. $\lim\limits_{\theta \to \pi/4} \dfrac{\sin^2 \theta - \cos^2 \theta}{\sin \theta - \cos \theta}$

21. $\lim\limits_{x \to \pi/2} \dfrac{\dfrac{1}{\sqrt{\sin x}} - 1}{x + \pi/2}$

22. One-sided limits Evaluate $\lim\limits_{x \to 1^+} \sqrt{\dfrac{x - 1}{x - 3}}$ and $\lim\limits_{x \to 1^-} \sqrt{\dfrac{x - 1}{x - 3}}$.

23. Applying the Squeeze Theorem

a. Show that
$$-x^2 \le x^2 \sin \dfrac{1}{x} \le x^2$$
on $[-1, 1]$. Confirm this result with a graphing utility.

b. Use part (a) and the Squeeze Theorem to explain why
$$\lim_{x \to 0} x^2 \sin \dfrac{1}{x} = 0.$$

24. Applying the Squeeze Theorem Assume the function g satisfies the inequality $1 \le g(x) \le \sin^2 x + 1$, for x near 0. Use the Squeeze Theorem to find $\lim\limits_{x \to 0} g(x)$.

25–29. Finding infinite limits *Evaluate the following limits.*

25. $\lim\limits_{x \to 5} \dfrac{x - 7}{x(x - 5)^2}$

26. $\lim\limits_{x \to -5^+} \dfrac{x - 5}{x + 5}$

27. $\lim\limits_{x \to 3^-} \dfrac{x - 4}{x^2 - 3x}$

28. $\lim\limits_{u \to 0^+} \dfrac{u - 1}{\sin u}$

29. $\lim\limits_{x \to 0^-} \dfrac{2}{\tan x}$

30. Finding vertical asymptotes Let $f(x) = \dfrac{x^2 - 5x + 6}{x^2 - 2x}$.

a. Calculate $\lim\limits_{x \to 0^-} f(x)$, $\lim\limits_{x \to 0^+} f(x)$, $\lim\limits_{x \to 2^-} f(x)$, and $\lim\limits_{x \to 2^+} f(x)$.

b. Does the graph of f have any vertical asymptotes? Explain.

c. Graph f and then sketch the graph with paper and pencil, correcting any errors obtained with the graphing utility.

31–36. Limits at infinity *Evaluate the following limits or state that they do not exist.*

31. $\lim\limits_{x \to \infty} \dfrac{2x - 3}{4x + 10}$

32. $\lim\limits_{x \to \infty} \dfrac{x^4 - 1}{x^5 + 2}$

33. $\lim\limits_{x \to -\infty} (-3x^3 + 5)$

34. $\lim\limits_{z \to \infty} \left(e^{-2z} + \dfrac{2}{z}\right)$

35. $\lim\limits_{x \to \infty} (3 \tan^{-1} x + 2)$

36. $\lim\limits_{r \to \infty} \dfrac{1}{\ln r + 1}$

37–40. End behavior *Determine the end behavior of the following functions.*

37. $f(x) = \dfrac{4x^3 + 1}{1 - x^3}$

38. $f(x) = \dfrac{x + 1}{\sqrt{9x^2 + x}}$

39. $f(x) = 1 - e^{-2x}$

40. $f(x) = \dfrac{1}{\ln x^2}$

41–42. Vertical and horizontal asymptotes *Find all vertical and horizontal asymptotes of the following functions.*

41. $f(x) = \dfrac{1}{\tan^{-1} x}$

42. $f(x) = \dfrac{2x^2 + 6}{2x^2 + 3x - 2}$

43–46. Continuity at a point *Determine whether the following functions are continuous at a using the continuity checklist to justify your answers.*

43. $f(x) = \dfrac{1}{x - 5}; \quad a = 5$

44. $g(x) = \begin{cases} \dfrac{x^2 - 16}{x - 4} & \text{if } x \neq 4 \\ 9 & \text{if } x = 4 \end{cases}; \quad a = 4$

45. $h(x) = \sqrt{x^2 - 9}; \quad a = 3$

46. $g(x) = \begin{cases} \dfrac{x^2 - 16}{x - 4} & \text{if } x \neq 4 \\ 8 & \text{if } x = 4 \end{cases}; \quad a = 4$

47–50. Continuity on intervals *Find the intervals on which the following functions are continuous. Specify right- or left-continuity at the endpoints.*

47. $f(x) = \sqrt{x^2 - 5}$

48. $g(x) = e^{\sqrt{x-2}}$

49. $h(x) = \dfrac{2x}{x^3 - 25x}$

50. $g(x) = \cos e^x$

51. Determining unknown constants Let

$$g(x) = \begin{cases} 5x - 2 & \text{if } x < 1 \\ a & \text{if } x = 1 \\ ax^2 + bx & \text{if } x < 1. \end{cases}$$

Determine values of the constants a and b for which g is continuous at $x = 1$.

52. Left- and right-continuity

   a. Is $h(x) = \sqrt{x^2 - 9}$ left-continuous at $x = 3$? Explain.

   b. Is $h(x) = \sqrt{x^2 - 9}$ right-continuous at $x = 3$? Explain.

53. Sketching a graph Sketch the graph of a function that is continuous on $(0, 1)$ and continuous on $(1, 2)$ but is not continuous on $(0, 2)$.

54. Intermediate Value Theorem

   a. Use the Intermediate Value Theorem to show that the equation $x^5 + 7x + 5 = 0$ has a solution in the interval $(-1, 0)$.

   b. Find a solution to $x^5 + 7x + 5 = 0$ in $(-1, 0)$ using a root finder.

55. Antibiotic dosing The amount of an antibiotic (in mg) in the blood t hours after an intravenous line is opened is given by

$$m(t) = 100(e^{-0.1t} - e^{-0.3t}).$$

   a. Use the Intermediate Value Theorem to show the amount of drug is 30 mg at some time in the interval $[0, 5]$ and again at some time in the interval $[5, 15]$.

   b. Estimate the times at which $m = 30$ mg.

   c. Is the amount of drug in the blood ever 50 mg?

56. Limit proof Give a formal proof that $\lim\limits_{x \to 1} (5x - 2) = 3$.

57. Limit proof Give a formal proof that $\lim\limits_{x \to 5} \dfrac{x^2 - 25}{x - 5} = 10$.

58. Limit proofs

   a. Assume $|f(x)| \leq L$ for all x near a and $\lim\limits_{x \to a} g(x) = 0$. Give a formal proof that $\lim\limits_{x \to a} (f(x)g(x)) = 0$.

   b. Find a function f for which $\lim\limits_{x \to 2} (f(x)(x - 2)) \neq 0$. Why doesn't this violate the result stated in (a)?

   c. The Heaviside function is defined as

$$H(x) = \begin{cases} 0 & \text{if } x < 0 \\ 1 & \text{if } x \geq 0. \end{cases}$$

   Explain why $\lim\limits_{x \to 0} [xH(x)] = 0$.

59. Infinite limit proof Give a formal proof that $\lim\limits_{x \to 2} \dfrac{1}{(x - 2)^4} = \infty$.

AP®   **PRACTICE QUESTIONS**   *The following questions are intended to help you prepare for the AP exam. They are not questions from actual AP exams.*

Section 1 Part A, Multiple Choice, No Technology

For Questions 1 and 2, use the graph of the function f shown in the figure below.

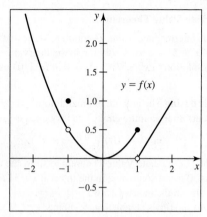

1. Which of the following statements are true?

   I. $f(-1)$ does not exist.

   II. $\lim\limits_{x \to -1} f(x) = \dfrac{1}{2}$

   III. $\lim\limits_{x \to -1} f(x) = f(-1)$

   (A) I and II only
   (B) II and III only
   (C) I only
   (D) II only
   (E) III only

2. Evaluate $\lim\limits_{x \to 1} f(x)$.

   (A) It does not exist.   **(B)** 0   **(C)** $\dfrac{1}{2}$ **(D)** 1   **(E)** -1

3. The average rate of change of the function $f(x) = x^2 - 3x$ on the interval $[2, x]$ is 3. Find x.

   (A) 6   **(B)** 5   **(C)** 4   **(D)** 1   **(E)** 0

4. Given that $\lim\limits_{x \to a} f(x) = A$, which of the following statements must be true?

   (A) $\lim\limits_{x \to a^+} f(x) = \lim\limits_{x \to a^-} f(x)$

   (B) $f(a) = A$

   (C) f is continuous at a.

   (D) $\lim\limits_{x \to a^+} f(x)$ is not necessarily equal to A.

   (E) $f(x) = A$

5. Evaluate $\lim\limits_{x \to 2} \dfrac{\sqrt{3x^2 - x + 6}}{\sin \pi x + \cos 2\pi x}$.

   (A) 2   **(B)** -4 **(C)** 8   **(D)** 4
   (E) The limit does not exist.

6. What are the vertical asymptotes $f(x) = \dfrac{2(x^2 - 1)}{x^2 + x - 2}$?

   (A) $x = 1$ and $x = -2$ **(B)** $x = -2$
   (C) $x = 1$ **(D)** $x = -1$
   (E) $x = -1$ and $x = 2$

7. Evaluate $\lim\limits_{x \to 0} \dfrac{\sin^2 x}{1 - \cos x}$.

   (A) -2 **(B)** 0   **(C)** 2   **(D)** 1
   (E) The limit does not exist.

8. Evaluate $\lim\limits_{x \to \infty} \dfrac{4x^4 - 3x + 2}{3x^4 + x^2 - 1}$.

   (A) $\dfrac{3}{4}$ **(B)** 0   **(C)** $\dfrac{4}{3}$ **(D)** 1
   (E) The limit does not exist.

9. Evaluate $\lim\limits_{x \to -\infty} \dfrac{2e^{2x} - e^{-x}}{3e^{-x} + 4e^{2x}}$.

   (A) $-\dfrac{1}{3}$ **(B)** $\dfrac{1}{2}$ **(C)** 0   **(D)** $\dfrac{1}{3}$ **(E)** $\dfrac{2}{3}$

10. A graph of the function $f(x) = \dfrac{20}{1 + x^2}$ in the standard viewing window $[-10, 10] \times [-10, 10]$ is shown in the figure. Evaluate $\lim\limits_{x \to 0} f(x)$.

    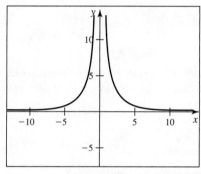

    (A) ∞ **(B)** 20   **(C)** 0   **(D)** 21
    (E) The limit does not exist.

11. For what constant k is the function

    $$f(x) = \begin{cases} \dfrac{x^3 - 6x^2 + 8x}{x - 2} & \text{if } x \neq 2 \\ k & \text{if } x = 2 \end{cases}$$

    continuous at $x = 2$?

    (A) 5   **(B)** -4 **(C)** 4   **(D)** -2
    (E) No value of k will work.

12. Evaluate $\lim\limits_{x \to \infty} \left(\sqrt{x^2 + 8x} - x \right)$.

    (A) 3   **(B)** 0   **(C)** 4   **(D)** 1
    (E) The limit does not exist.

13. Evaluate $\lim\limits_{x \to -\infty} \left(\dfrac{x}{\sqrt{x^2 + 1}} \right)$.

    (A) -1 **(B)** 0   **(C)** $\dfrac{1}{2}$ **(D)** 1
    (E) The limit does not exist.

14. Suppose f and g are continuous functions for all real numbers with values given in the table. Let $h(x) = f(g(x)) + 4$.

x	$f(x)$	$g(x)$
1	8	4
2	12	2
3	15	3
4	20	1

Which of the following statements are true?

I. $h(1) = 24$
II. A number c exists with $3 < c < 4$ such that $h(c) = 13$.
III. $h(2) = 28$

(A) I and II only   **(B)** II and III only   **(C)** I only
(D) II only   **(E)** III only

Section 1 Part B, Multiple Choice, Technology Allowed

15. Based on a graph, what is the value of $\lim\limits_{x \to 0^+} x^{-x}$?

(A) 0   **(B)** 1   **(C)** -1 **(D)** $\dfrac{1}{e}$
(E) The limit does not exist.

16. Based on a graph, what is the value of $\lim\limits_{x \to 0} \dfrac{\sin 3x}{\tan 2x}$?

(A) 0   **(B)** $\dfrac{2}{3}$ **(C)** $\dfrac{3}{2}$ **(D)** 6
(E) The limit does not exist.

17. Describe the behavior of $f(x) = \dfrac{\sqrt{9x^6 - 1}}{2x^3 + 1}$ as x becomes large and positive.

(A) The function values become large and positive.
(B) The function values approach 0.
(C) The function values approach 3/2.
(D) The function values approach 1/3.
(E) The function values approach 9/2.

18. Describe the behavior of $f(x) = e^{-1/x}$ as x approaches 0.

(A) $\lim\limits_{x \to 0} f(x) = 1$

(B) $\lim\limits_{x \to 0^+} f(x) = 1$ and $\lim\limits_{x \to 0^-} f(x) = 0$

(C) $\lim\limits_{x \to 0^+} f(x) = \infty$ and $\lim\limits_{x \to 0^-} f(x) = 0$

(D) $\lim\limits_{x \to 0^+} f(x) = 0$ and $\lim\limits_{x \to 0^-} f(x) = \infty$

(E) $\lim\limits_{x \to 0} f(x) = 0$

19. Suppose that $\lim\limits_{x \to 3} f(x) = \lim\limits_{x \to 3} h(x) = 18$ and $f(x) \le x^2 g(x) \le h(x)$ for all values of x. Which of the following statements are true if $\lim\limits_{x \to 3} g(x)$ exists?

I. $\lim\limits_{x \to 3} x^2 g(x) = 18$ II. $\lim\limits_{x \to 3} g(x) = 2$ III. $\lim\limits_{x \to 3} (x\, g(x)) = 6$

(A) I only   **(B)** II only   **(C)** III only
(D) I and II only   **(E)** I, II, and III

Section 2 Part A, Free Response, Technology Allowed

1. **a.** Determine the value of $\lim\limits_{x \to 0} \dfrac{e^{2x} - e^x}{x}$.

    b. Determine the value of $\lim\limits_{x \to 0} \dfrac{e^{4x} - e^{2x}}{x}$.

    c. Let p and q be real numbers. Based on the results of parts (a) and (b), make a conjecture about the value of $\lim\limits_{x \to 0} \dfrac{e^{px} - e^{qx}}{x}$.

2. Consider the function $f(x) = \dfrac{x + 1}{x^3 + nx}$, where n is an integer.

    a. Give the equation(s) of the horizontal asymptote(s) when $n = 2$ and $n = -2$.

    b. Give equations for the vertical asymptotes of f (if any exist) when $n = 1$ and $n = -1$.

    c. Explain why there is only one vertical asymptote when $n \ge 0$ and why there are three vertical asymptotes when $n \le -2$.

Section 2 Part B, Free Response, No Technology

3. Consider the function $f(x) = \dfrac{5(x^2 - 4)}{x^2 + 2x - 8}$.

    a. What is the domain of f?
    b. Find the roots of f.
    c. Evaluate $\lim\limits_{x \to \infty} f(x)$, and identify all the horizontal asymptotes of f.
    d. Where are the vertical asymptotes of f located?
    e. Explain why the vertical asymptotes are not located at all the excluded points of the domain.

4. For each step, choose an appropriate scale for the x- and y-axes.

    a. Sketch a graph of a function g that has the properties $g(2) = 3$ and $\lim\limits_{x \to 2} g(x) = 2$.

    b. Now sketch a possible graph of a function g that has the properties listed in part (a) and the properties $\lim\limits_{x \to -1^+} g(x) = -\infty$ and $\lim\limits_{x \to -1^-} g(x) = \infty$.

    c. Sketch a possible graph of a function g that has the properties listed in parts (a) and (b) and the properties $\lim\limits_{x \to 0^-} g(x) = g(0) = -1$ and $\lim\limits_{x \to 0^+} g(x) = 1$.

    d. Finally, sketch a graph with all the properties from parts (a)–(c) and the properties $\lim\limits_{x \to \infty} g(x) = \infty$ and $\lim\limits_{x \to -\infty} g(x) = -2$.

Chapter 2 Guided Projects

Applications of the material in this chapter and related topics can be found in the following Guided Projects. For additional information, see the Preface.

- Fixed-point iteration

- Local linearity

3 Derivatives

The world around us is constantly changing. For example, imagine you are at the seashore watching waves roll onto a beach. You see different types of change as the waves move toward the shore. If you focus on one point in time, then you see the water height varying from one location to another. In fact, you can see the *rate* at which the wave height changes: in some places the wave is steep (large rate of change) and in other places the wave is shallow (small rate of change). On the other hand, if you focus on one location, then you see the water height changing in time: sometimes the water surface rises or falls quickly, and at other times the rate of change is small. These two changes—one in time and one in space—combine to give the overall effect of a traveling wave.

You don't have to go to a beach to witness change. Look at the world around you and you will agree with the ancient Greek philosopher Heraclitus, who said, "Only change endures." From the changing volume of air in your lungs to the fluctuations in the stock market, from the variable wind loading on a wind turbine to variations in sea temperature around the Earth, change is everywhere. Calculus gives us tools for describing change. For this reason, calculus is called the language of change.

Chapter Preview Now that you are familiar with limits, the door to calculus stands open. The first task is to introduce the fundamental concept of the *derivative*. Suppose a function f represents a quantity of interest, say the variable cost of manufacturing an item, the population of a country, or the position of an orbiting satellite. The derivative of f is another function, denoted f', which gives the slope of the curve $y = f(x)$ as it changes with respect to x. Equivalently, the derivative of f gives the *instantaneous rate of change* of f with respect to the independent variable. We use limits not only to define the derivative, but also to develop efficient rules for finding derivatives. The applications of the derivative—which we introduce along the way—are endless because almost everything around us is in a state of change, and derivatives describe change.

3.1 Introducing the Derivative

In this section, we return to the problem of finding the slope of a line tangent to a curve, introduced at the beginning of Chapter 2. This concept is important for several reasons.

- We identify the slope of the tangent line with the *instantaneous rate of change* of a function (Figure 3.1).

- The slopes of the tangent lines as they change along a curve are the values of a new function called the *derivative*.

$y = f(x)$

| Slope of tangent line and instantaneous rate of change are negative. | Slope of tangent line and instantaneous rate of change are positive. |

FIGURE 3.1

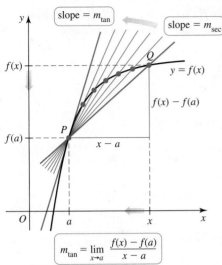

$$m_{\tan} = \lim_{x \to a} \frac{f(x) - f(a)}{x - a}$$

FIGURE 3.3

▷ Figure 3.3 assumes $x > a$. Analogous pictures and arguments apply if $x < a$.

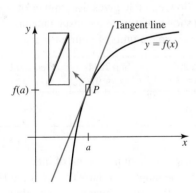

QUICK CHECK 1 Sketch the graph of a function f near a point a. As in Figure 3.3, draw a secant line that passes through $(a, f(a))$ and a neighboring point $(x, f(x))$ with $x < a$. Use arrows to show how the secant lines approach the tangent line as x approaches a. ◀

• If a curve represents the trajectory of a moving object, the line tangent to the curve at a point gives the direction of motion at that point (Figure 3.2).

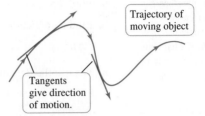

FIGURE 3.2

In Section 2.1, we gave an intuitive definition of a tangent line and used numerical evidence to estimate its slope. We now make these ideas precise.

Tangent Lines and Rates of Change

Consider the curve $y = f(x)$ and a secant line intersecting the curve at the points $P(a, f(a))$ and $Q(x, f(x))$ (Figure 3.3). The difference $f(x) - f(a)$ is the change in the value of f on the interval $[a, x]$, while $x - a$ is the change in x. As discussed in Chapters 1 and 2, the slope of the secant line $\overleftrightarrow{PQ}$ is

$$m_{\sec} = \frac{f(x) - f(a)}{x - a},$$

and it gives the *average rate of change* of f on the interval $[a, x]$.

Figure 3.3 also shows what happens as the variable point x approaches the fixed point a. If the curve is smooth at $P(a, f(a))$—it has no kinks or corners—the secant lines approach a *unique* line that intersects the curve at P; this line is the *tangent line* at P. As x approaches a, the slopes $m_{\sec}$ of the secant lines approach a unique number $m_{\tan}$ that we call the *slope of the tangent line*; that is,

$$m_{\tan} = \lim_{x \to a} \frac{f(x) - f(a)}{x - a}.$$

The slope of the tangent line at P is also called the *instantaneous rate of change* of f at a because it measures how quickly f changes at a.

The tangent line has another geometric interpretation. As discussed in Section 2.1, if the curve $y = f(x)$ is smooth at a point $P(a, f(a))$, then the curve looks more like a line as we zoom in on P (see margin figure). The line that is approached as we zoom in on P is also the tangent line. A smooth curve has the property of *local linearity*, which means that if we look at a point on the curve locally (by zooming in), then the curve appears linear.

DEFINITION **Rate of Change and the Slope of the Tangent Line**

The **average rate of change** in f on the interval $[a, x]$ is the slope of the corresponding secant line:

$$m_{\sec} = \frac{f(x) - f(a)}{x - a}.$$

The **instantaneous rate of change** in f at a is

$$m_{\tan} = \lim_{x \to a} \frac{f(x) - f(a)}{x - a}, \tag{1}$$

which is also the **slope of the tangent line** at $(a, f(a))$, provided this limit exists. The **tangent line** is the unique line through $(a, f(a))$ with slope $m_{\tan}$. Its equation is

$$y - f(a) = m_{\tan}(x - a).$$

> If x and y have physical units, then the average and instantaneous rates of change have units of (units of y)/(units of x). For example, if y has units of meters and x has units of seconds, the units of the rate of change are meters/second (m/s).

EXAMPLE 1   Equation of a tangent line Let $f(x) = -16x^2 + 96x$ (the position function examined in Section 2.1) and consider the point $P(1, 80)$ on the curve.

a. Find the slope of the line tangent to the graph of f at P.

b. Find an equation of the tangent line in part (a).

SOLUTION

a. We use the definition of the slope of the tangent line with $a = 1$:

$$m_{tan} = \lim_{x \to 1} \frac{f(x) - f(1)}{x - 1} \qquad \text{Definition of slope of tangent line}$$

$$= \lim_{x \to 1} \frac{(-16x^2 + 96x) - 80}{x - 1} \qquad f(x) = -16x^2 + 96x; f(1) = 80$$

$$= \lim_{x \to 1} \frac{-16(x - 5)(x - 1)}{x - 1} \qquad \text{Factor the numerator.}$$

$$= -16 \underbrace{\lim_{x \to 1} (x - 5)}_{-4} = 64. \qquad \text{Cancel factors } (x \neq 1) \text{ and evaluate the limit.}$$

We have confirmed the conjecture made in Section 2.1 that the slope of the line tangent to the graph of $f(x) = -16x^2 + 96x$ at $(1, 80)$ is 64.

b. An equation of the line passing through $(1, 80)$ with slope $m_{tan} = 64$ is $y - 80 = 64(x - 1)$ or $y = 64x + 16$. The graph of f and the tangent line at $(1, 80)$ are shown in Figure 3.4.   *Related Exercises 9–14* ◄

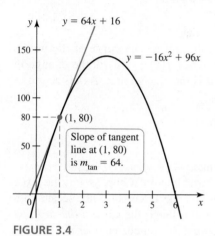

FIGURE 3.4

QUICK CHECK 2 In Example 1, is the slope of the tangent line at $(2, 128)$ greater than or less than the slope at $(1, 80)$? ◄

In the next example, we use a practical problem with real data to show how the rate of change can be approximated by the average rate of change.

EXAMPLE 2   Facebook rate of growth The following table gives the number of daily users of Facebook averaged over each month shown. Estimate the instantaneous rate of growth of Facebook users for June 2011. What are the units of your answer?

Month	Dec 2010 ($t = 0$)	Mar 2011 ($t = 3$)	Jun 2011 ($t = 6$)	Sep 2011 ($t = 9$)	Dec 2011 ($t = 12$)
Daily users (millions)	327	372	417	457	483

Source: Facebook SEC filing.

SOLUTION Letting $t = 0$ represent December 2010, we see that the month of interest, June 2011, corresponds to $t = 6$. We also let $f(t)$ be the number of daily users at time t. The goal is to estimate the rate of change of f at $t = 6$. We use the average rate of change

$$\frac{f(t) - f(6)}{t - 6},$$

which approximates the instantaneous rate of change.

Using the data point at $t = 9$, one approximation to the rate of change is

$$\frac{f(9) - f(6)}{9 - 6} = \frac{457 - 417}{3} = 13.333.$$

Using the data point at $t = 3$, another approximation to the rate of change is

$$\frac{f(3) - f(6)}{3 - 6} = \frac{372 - 417}{-3} = 15.$$

Notice that f has units of *millions of daily users*, while t has units of *months*. Therefore, the rate of change, which is a quotient, has units of *millions of daily users per month*.

An alternative method for approximating the rate of change is to use data points equally spaced on either side of $t = 6$ and form a *centered difference quotient* (see Exercises 43–45 in Section 3.6). The centered difference approximation is

$$\frac{f(9) - f(3)}{9 - 3} = \frac{457 - 372}{6} = 14.167.$$

These three approximations suggest that in June 2011, the number of Facebook users increased at a rate of about 14 million users per month.   *Related Exercises 15–16* ◄

An alternative formula for the slope of the tangent line is helpful for future work. Consider again the curve $y = f(x)$ and the secant line intersecting the curve at the points P and Q. We now let $(a, f(a))$ and $(a + h, f(a + h))$ be the coordinates of P and Q, respectively (Figure 3.5). The difference in the x-coordinates of P and Q is $(a + h) - a = h$. Note that Q is located to the right of P if $h > 0$ and to the left of P if $h < 0$.

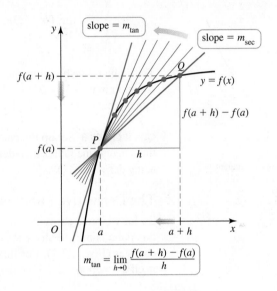

FIGURE 3.5

The slope of the secant line $\overleftrightarrow{PQ}$ using the new notation is $m_{\text{sec}} = \dfrac{f(a + h) - f(a)}{h}$.

As h approaches 0, the variable point Q approaches P and the slopes of the secant lines approach the slope of the tangent line. Therefore, the slope of the tangent line at $(a, f(a))$, which is also the instantaneous rate of change of f at a, is

$$m_{\text{tan}} = \lim_{h \to 0} \frac{f(a + h) - f(a)}{h}.$$

> The definition of m_{sec} involves a *difference quotient*, introduced in Section 1.1.

ALTERNATIVE DEFINITION Rate of Change and the Slope of the Tangent Line

The **average rate of change** in f on the interval $[a, a + h]$ is the slope of the corresponding secant line:

$$m_{\text{sec}} = \frac{f(a + h) - f(a)}{h}.$$

The **instantaneous rate of change** in f at $x = a$ is

$$m_{\text{tan}} = \lim_{h \to 0} \frac{f(a + h) - f(a)}{h}, \qquad (2)$$

which is also the **slope of the tangent line** at $(a, f(a))$, provided this limit exists.

EXAMPLE 3   Equation of a tangent line Find an equation of the line tangent to the graph of $f(x) = x^3 + 4x$ at $(1, 5)$.

SOLUTION We let $a = 1$ in definition (2) and first find $f(1 + h)$. After expanding and collecting terms, we have

$$f(1 + h) = (1 + h)^3 + 4(1 + h) = h^3 + 3h^2 + 7h + 5.$$

Substituting $f(1 + h)$ and $f(1) = 5$, the slope of the tangent line is

> By the definition of the limit as $h \to 0$, notice that h approaches 0 but $h \neq 0$. Therefore, it is permissible to cancel h from the numerator and denominator of $\dfrac{h(h^2 + 3h + 7)}{h}$.

$$
\begin{aligned}
m_{\tan} &= \lim_{h \to 0} \frac{f(1 + h) - f(1)}{h} && \text{Definition of } m_{\tan} \\[2mm]
&= \lim_{h \to 0} \frac{(h^3 + 3h^2 + 7h + 5) - 5}{h} && \text{Substitute } f(1 + h) \text{ and } f(1) = 5. \\[2mm]
&= \lim_{h \to 0} \frac{h(h^2 + 3h + 7)}{h} && \text{Simplify.} \\[2mm]
&= \lim_{h \to 0} (h^2 + 3h + 7) && \text{Cancel } h, \text{ noting } h \neq 0. \\[2mm]
&= 7. && \text{Evaluate the limit.}
\end{aligned}
$$

The tangent line has slope $m_{\tan} = 7$ and passes through the point $(1, 5)$ (Figure 3.6); its equation is $y - 5 = 7(x - 1)$ or $y = 7x - 2$. We could also say that the instantaneous rate of change in f at $x = 1$ is 7.   *Related Exercises 17–26* ◄

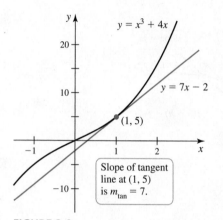

$y = x^3 + 4x$

$y = 7x - 2$

$(1, 5)$

Slope of tangent line at $(1, 5)$ is $m_{\tan} = 7$.

FIGURE 3.6

QUICK CHECK 3 Set up the calculation in Example 3 using definition (1) for the slope of the tangent line rather than definition (2). Does the calculation appear more difficult using definition (1)? ◄

The Derivative Function

So far we have computed the slope of the tangent line at one fixed point on a curve. If this point is moved along the curve, the tangent line also moves, and, in general, its slope changes (Figure 3.7). For this reason, the slope of the tangent line for the function f is itself a function, called the *derivative* of f.

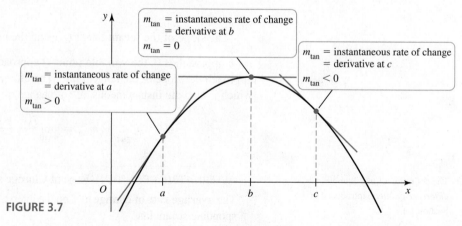

$m_{\tan}$ = instantaneous rate of change = derivative at b

$m_{\tan} = 0$

$m_{\tan}$ = instantaneous rate of change = derivative at c

$m_{\tan} < 0$

$m_{\tan}$ = instantaneous rate of change = derivative at a

$m_{\tan} > 0$

FIGURE 3.7

We let f' (read f *prime*) denote the derivative function for f, which means that $f'(a)$, when it exists, is the slope of the line tangent to the graph of f at $(a, f(a))$. Using definition (2) for the slope of the tangent line, we have

$$f'(a) = m_{\tan} = \lim_{h \to 0} \frac{f(a + h) - f(a)}{h}.$$

We now take an important step. The derivative is a special function, but it works just like any other function. For example, if the graph of f is smooth and 2 is in the domain of f,

> To emphasize an important point, $f'(2)$ or $f'(-2)$ or $f'(a)$, for a real number a, is a real number, whereas f' or $f'(x)$ refers to the derivative *function*.

> The process of finding f' is called *differentiation*, and to *differentiate* f means to find f'.

> Just as we have two definitions for the slope of the tangent line, we may also use the following definition for the derivative of f at a:

$$f'(a) = \lim_{x \to a} \frac{f(x) - f(a)}{x - a}.$$

then $f'(2)$ is the slope of the line tangent to the graph of f at the point $(2, f(2))$. Similarly, if -2 is in the domain of f, then $f'(-2)$ is the slope of the tangent line at the point $(-2, f(-2))$. In fact, if x is *any* point in the domain of f, then $f'(x)$ is the slope of the tangent line at the point $(x, f(x))$. When we introduce a variable point x, the expression $f'(x)$ becomes the *derivative function*.

DEFINITION The Derivative Function

The **derivative** of f is the function

$$f'(x) = \lim_{h \to 0} \frac{f(x + h) - f(x)}{h},$$

provided the limit exists and x is in the domain of f. If $f'(x)$ exists, we say f is **differentiable** at x. If f is differentiable at every point of an open interval I, we say that f is differentiable on I.

Notice that the definition of f' applies only at points in the domain of f. Therefore, the domain of f' is no larger than the domain of f. If the limit in the definition of f' fails to exist at some points, then the domain of f' is smaller than the domain of f. Let's use this definition to compute a derivative function.

EXAMPLE 4   Computing a derivative Consider once again the function $f(x) = -16x^2 + 96x$ of Example 1 and find its derivative.

SOLUTION

> Notice that this argument applies for $h > 0$ and for $h < 0$; that is, the limit as $h \to 0^+$ and the limit as $h \to 0^-$ are equal.

$$f'(x) = \lim_{h \to 0} \frac{f(x + h) - f(x)}{h} \qquad \text{Definition of } f'(x)$$

$$= \lim_{h \to 0} \frac{\overbrace{-16(x + h)^2 + 96(x + h)}^{f(x+h)} - \overbrace{(-16x^2 + 96x)}^{f(x)}}{h} \qquad \text{Substitute.}$$

$$= \lim_{h \to 0} \frac{-16(x^2 + 2xh + h^2) + 96x + 96h + 16x^2 - 96x}{h} \qquad \begin{array}{l}\text{Expand the}\\\text{numerator.}\end{array}$$

$$= \lim_{h \to 0} \frac{h(-32x + 96 - 16h)}{h} \qquad \begin{array}{l}\text{Simplify and}\\\text{factor out } h.\end{array}$$

$$= \lim_{h \to 0} (-32x + 96 - 16h) = -32x + 96 \qquad \begin{array}{l}\text{Cancel } h \text{ and}\\\text{evaluate the limit.}\end{array}$$

The derivative is $f'(x) = -32x + 96$, which gives the slope of the tangent line (equivalently, the instantaneous rate of change) at *any* point on the curve. For example, at the point $(1, 80)$, the slope of the tangent line is $f'(1) = -32(1) + 96 = 64$, confirming the calculation in Example 1. The slope of the tangent line at $(3, 144)$ is $f'(3) = -32(3) + 96 = 0$, which means the tangent line is horizontal at that point (Figure 3.8).

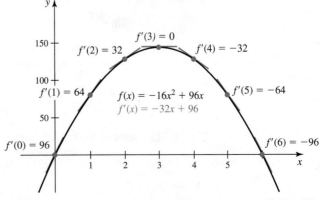

FIGURE 3.8

QUICK CHECK 4 In Example 4, determine the slope of the tangent line at $x = 2$. ◀

Related Exercises 27–40◀

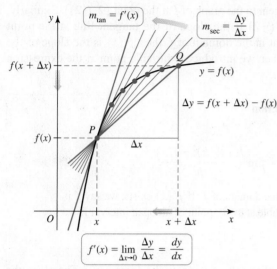

$$f'(x) = \lim_{\Delta x \to 0} \frac{\Delta y}{\Delta x} = \frac{dy}{dx}$$

FIGURE 3.9

> The notation $\dfrac{dy}{dx}$ is read *the derivative of y with respect to x* or *dy dx*. It does not mean dy divided by dx, but it is a reminder of the limit of $\Delta y/\Delta x$.

> The derivative notation dy/dx was introduced by Gottfried Wilhelm von Leibniz (1646–1716), one of the coinventors of calculus. His notation is used today in its original form. The notation used by Sir Isaac Newton (1643–1727), the other coinventor of calculus, is used less frequently.

> Example 5 gives the first of many derivative formulas to be presented in the text:
> $$\frac{d}{dx}\left(\sqrt{x}\right) = \frac{1}{2\sqrt{x}}.$$
> Remember this result. It will be used often.

Derivative Notation

For historical and practical reasons, several notations for the derivative are used. To see the origin of one notation, recall that the slope of the secant line through two points $P(x, f(x))$ and $Q(x + h, f(x + h))$ on the curve $y = f(x)$ is $\dfrac{f(x + h) - f(x)}{h}$. The quantity h is the change in the x-coordinates in moving from P to Q. A standard notation for change is the symbol Δ (uppercase Greek letter delta). So, we replace h with Δx to represent the change in x. Similarly, $f(x + h) - f(x)$ is the change in y, denoted Δy (Figure 3.9). Therefore, the slope of the secant line is

$$m_{\text{sec}} = \frac{f(x + \Delta x) - f(x)}{\Delta x} = \frac{\Delta y}{\Delta x}.$$

By letting $\Delta x \to 0$, the slope of the tangent line at $(x, f(x))$ is

$$f'(x) = \lim_{\Delta x \to 0} \frac{f(x + \Delta x) - f(x)}{\Delta x} = \lim_{\Delta x \to 0} \frac{\Delta y}{\Delta x} = \frac{dy}{dx}.$$

The new notation for the derivative is $\dfrac{dy}{dx}$; it reminds us that $f'(x)$ is the limit of $\dfrac{\Delta y}{\Delta x}$ as $\Delta x \to 0$.

In addition to the notation $f'(x)$ and $\dfrac{dy}{dx}$, other common ways of writing the derivative include

$$\frac{df}{dx}, \qquad \frac{d}{dx}(f(x)), \qquad D_x(f(x)), \quad \text{and} \quad y'(x).$$

Each of the following notations represents the derivative of f evaluated at a.

$$f'(a), \qquad y'(a), \qquad \left.\frac{df}{dx}\right|_{x=a}, \quad \text{and} \quad \left.\frac{dy}{dx}\right|_{x=a}$$

QUICK CHECK 5 What are some other ways to write $f'(3)$, where $y = f(x)$? ◄

EXAMPLE 5   A derivative calculation Let $y = f(x) = \sqrt{x}$.

a. Compute $\dfrac{dy}{dx}$.

b. Find an equation of the line tangent to the graph of f at $(4, 2)$.

SOLUTION

a.
$$\frac{dy}{dx} = \lim_{h \to 0} \frac{f(x + h) - f(x)}{h} \qquad \text{Definition of } \frac{dy}{dx} = f'(x)$$

$$= \lim_{h \to 0} \frac{\sqrt{x + h} - \sqrt{x}}{h} \qquad \text{Substitute } f(x) = \sqrt{x}.$$

$$= \lim_{h \to 0} \frac{\left(\sqrt{x + h} - \sqrt{x}\right)}{h} \frac{\left(\sqrt{x + h} + \sqrt{x}\right)}{\left(\sqrt{x + h} + \sqrt{x}\right)} \qquad \begin{array}{l}\text{Multiply the numerator and} \\ \text{denominator by } \sqrt{x + h} + \sqrt{x}.\end{array}$$

$$= \lim_{h \to 0} \frac{1}{\sqrt{x + h} + \sqrt{x}} = \frac{1}{2\sqrt{x}} \qquad \text{Simplify and evaluate the limit.}$$

b. The slope of the tangent line at $(4, 2)$ is

$$\left.\frac{dy}{dx}\right|_{x=4} = \frac{1}{2\sqrt{4}} = \frac{1}{4}.$$

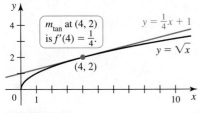

FIGURE 3.10

Therefore, an equation of the tangent line (Figure 3.10) is

$$y - 2 = \frac{1}{4}(x - 4) \text{ or } y = \frac{1}{4}x + 1.$$

Related Exercises 41–42 ◄

QUICK CHECK 6 In Example 5, do the slopes of the tangent lines increase or decrease as x increases? Explain. ◄

If a function is given in terms of variables other than x and y, we make an adjustment to the derivative definition. For example, if $y = g(t)$, we replace f with g and x with t to obtain the *derivative of g with respect to t*:

$$g'(t) = \lim_{h \to 0} \frac{g(t + h) - g(t)}{h}.$$

QUICK CHECK 7 Express the derivative of $p = q(r)$ in three ways. ◄

Other notation for $g'(t)$ includes $\dfrac{dg}{dt}, \dfrac{d}{dt}(g(t)), D_t(g(t))$, and $y'(t)$.

EXAMPLE 6 **Another derivative calculation** Let $g(t) = 1/t^2$ and compute $g'(t)$.

SOLUTION

$$\begin{aligned}
g'(t) &= \lim_{h \to 0} \frac{g(t + h) - g(t)}{h} && \text{Definition of } g' \\[2mm]
&= \lim_{h \to 0} \frac{1}{h}\left[\frac{1}{(t + h)^2} - \frac{1}{t^2}\right] && \text{Substitute } g(t) = 1/t^2. \\[2mm]
&= \lim_{h \to 0} \frac{1}{h}\left[\frac{t^2 - (t + h)^2}{t^2(t + h)^2}\right] && \text{Common denominator} \\[2mm]
&= \lim_{h \to 0} \frac{1}{h}\left[\frac{-2ht - h^2}{t^2(t + h)^2}\right] && \text{Expand the numerator and simplify.} \\[2mm]
&= \lim_{h \to 0} \left[\frac{-2t - h}{t^2(t + h)^2}\right] && h \neq 0; \text{ cancel } h. \\[2mm]
&= -\frac{2}{t^3} && \text{Evaluate the limit.}
\end{aligned}$$

Related Exercises 43–46 ◄

SECTION 3.1 EXERCISES

Review Questions

1. Use definition (1) (p. 137) for the slope of a tangent line to explain how slopes of secant lines approach the slope of the tangent line at a point.

2. Explain why the slope of a secant line can be interpreted as an average rate of change.

3. Explain why the slope of the tangent line can be interpreted as an instantaneous rate of change.

4. For a given function f, what does f' represent?

5. Given a function f and a point a in its domain, what does $f'(a)$ represent?

6. Explain the relationships among the slope of a tangent line, the instantaneous rate of change, and the value of the derivative at a point.

7. Why is the notation $\dfrac{dy}{dx}$ used to represent the derivative?

8. Give three different notations for the derivative of f with respect to x.

Basic Skills

9–14. Equations of tangent lines by definition (1)

a. *Use definition (1) (p. 137) to find the slope of the line tangent to the graph of f at P.*
b. *Determine an equation of the tangent line at P.*
c. *Plot the graph of f and the tangent line at P.*

9. $f(x) = x^2 - 5; \ P(3, 4)$

10. $f(x) = -3x^2 - 5x + 1; \ P(1, -7)$

11. $f(x) = -5x + 1; \ P(1, -4)$ 12. $f(x) = 5; \ P(1, 5)$

13. $f(x) = \dfrac{1}{x}; \ P(-1, -1)$ 14. $f(x) = \dfrac{4}{x^2}; \ P(-1, 4)$

15–16. Approximating rates of change

15. Consider the table in Example 2 showing data for daily Facebook users.

   a. Use three different methods to estimate the rate of change of daily Facebook users in September 2011.

   b. Use three different methods to estimate the rate of change of daily Facebook users in March 2011.

   c. What are the units of your answers in parts (a) and (b)?

   d. Does the rate of change of daily users appear to be increasing or decreasing? Explain.

16. A thermometer outside a kitchen window registers the following temperature readings (in degrees Celsius) during a two-hour interval one morning.

Time	9:00	9:30	10:00	10:30	11:00
Temperature	25	27	30	34	35

   a. Use three different methods to approximate the rate of change of the temperature at 10:00.

   b. What are the units of your answer?

   c. Is the temperature increasing more rapidly at 9:30 or at 10:00?

17–26. Equations of tangent lines by definition (2)

a. *Use definition (2) (p. 139) to find the slope of the line tangent to the graph of f at P.*

b. *Determine an equation of the tangent line at P.*

17. $f(x) = 2x + 1$; $P(0, 1)$ **18.** $f(x) = 3x^2 - 4x$; $P(1, -1)$

19. $f(x) = x^2 - 4$; $P(2, 0)$ **20.** $f(x) = 1/x$; $P(1, 1)$

21. $f(x) = x^3$; $P(1, 1)$ **22.** $f(x) = \dfrac{1}{2x + 1}$; $P(0, 1)$

23. $f(x) = \dfrac{1}{3 - 2x}$; $P\left(-1, \dfrac{1}{5}\right)$ **24.** $f(x) = \sqrt{x - 1}$; $P(2, 1)$

25. $f(x) = \sqrt{x + 3}$; $P(1, 2)$ **26.** $f(x) = \dfrac{x}{x + 1}$; $P(-2, 2)$

27–36. Derivatives and tangent lines

a. *For the following functions and values of a, find f'(a).*

b. *Determine an equation of the line tangent to the graph of f at the point (a, f(a)) for the given value of a.*

27. $f(x) = 8x$; $a = -3$ **28.** $f(x) = x^2$; $a = 3$

29. $f(x) = 4x^2 + 2x$; $a = -2$ **30.** $f(x) = 2x^3$; $a = 10$

31. $f(x) = \dfrac{1}{\sqrt{x}}$; $a = \dfrac{1}{4}$ **32.** $f(x) = \dfrac{1}{x^2}$; $a = 1$

33. $f(x) = \sqrt{2x + 1}$; $a = 4$ **34.** $f(x) = \sqrt{3x}$; $a = 12$

35. $f(x) = \dfrac{1}{x + 5}$; $a = 5$ **36.** $f(x) = \dfrac{1}{3x - 1}$; $a = 2$

37–40. Lines tangent to parabolas

a. *Find the derivative function f' for the following functions f.*

b. *Find an equation of the line tangent to the graph of f at (a, f(a)) for the given value of a.*

c. *Graph f and the tangent line.*

37. $f(x) = 3x^2 + 2x - 10$; $a = 1$

38. $f(x) = 3x^2$; $a = 0$

39. $f(x) = 5x^2 - 6x + 1$; $a = 2$

40. $f(x) = 1 - x^2$; $a = -1$

41. A derivative formula

   a. Use the definition of the derivative to determine $\dfrac{d}{dx}(ax^2 + bx + c)$, where a, b, and c are constants.

   b. Let $f(x) = 4x^2 - 3x + 10$ and use part (a) to find $f'(x)$.

   c. Use part (b) to find $f'(1)$.

42. A derivative formula

   a. Use the definition of the derivative to determine $\dfrac{d}{dx}(\sqrt{ax + b})$, where a and b are constants.

   b. Let $f(x) = \sqrt{5x + 9}$ and use part (a) to find $f'(x)$.

   c. Use part (b) to find $f'(-1)$.

43–46. Derivative calculations *Evaluate the derivative of the following functions at the given point.*

43. $y = 1/(t + 1)$; $t = 1$ **44.** $y = t - t^2$; $t = 2$

45. $c = 2\sqrt{s} - 1$; $s = 25$ **46.** $A = \pi r^2$; $r = 3$

Further Explorations

47. Explain why or why not Determine whether the following statements are true, and give an explanation or a counterexample.

   a. For linear functions, the slope of any secant line always equals the slope of any tangent line.

   b. The slope of the secant line passing through the points P and Q is less than the slope of the tangent line at P.

   c. Consider the graph of the parabola $f(x) = x^2$. For $x > 0$ and $h > 0$, the secant line through $(x, f(x))$ and $(x + h, f(x + h))$ always has a greater slope than the tangent line at $(x, f(x))$.

48. Slope of a line Consider the line $f(x) = mx + b$, where m and b are constants. Show that $f'(x) = m$ for all x. Interpret this result.

49–52. Calculating derivatives

a. *For the following functions, find f' using the definition.*

b. *Determine an equation of the line tangent to the graph of f at (a, f(a)) for the given value of a.*

49. $f(x) = \sqrt{3x + 1}$; $a = 8$ **50.** $f(x) = \sqrt{x + 2}$; $a = 7$

51. $f(x) = \dfrac{2}{3x + 1}$; $a = -1$ **52.** $f(x) = \dfrac{1}{x}$; $a = -5$

53–54. Analyzing slopes *Use the points A, B, C, D, and E in the following graphs to answer these questions.*

a. *At which points is the slope of the curve negative?*
b. *At which points is the slope of the curve positive?*
c. *Using A–E, list the slopes in decreasing order.*

Year	1950	1960	1970	1980	1990	2000	2010
t	0	10	20	30	40	50	60
$p(t)$	59,900	139,126	304,744	528,000	852,737	1,563,282	1,951,269

Source: U.S. Bureau of Census.

53.

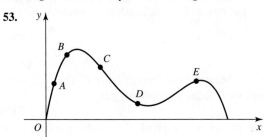

54.

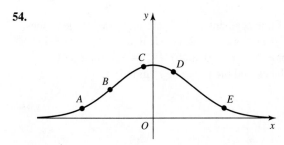

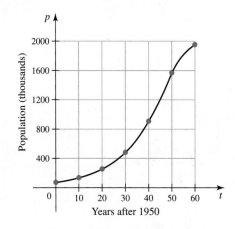

Applications

55. Power and energy Energy is the capacity to do work, and power is the rate at which energy is used or consumed. Therefore, if $E(t)$ is the energy function for a system, then $P(t) = E'(t)$ is the power function. A unit of energy is the kilowatt-hour (1 kWh is the amount of energy needed to light ten 100-W lightbulbs for an hour); the corresponding units for power are kilowatts. The following figure shows the energy consumed by a small community over a 25-hour period.

a. Estimate the power at $t = 10$ and $t = 20$ hr. Be sure to include units in your calculation.
b. At what times on the interval $[0, 25]$ is the power zero?
c. At what times on the interval $[0, 25]$ is the power a maximum?

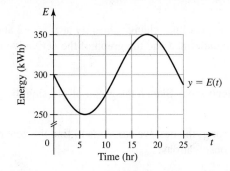

56. Population of Las Vegas Let $p(t)$ represent the population of the Las Vegas metropolitan area t years after 1950, as shown in the table and figure.

a. Compute the average rate of growth of Las Vegas from 1970 to 1980.
b. Explain why the average rate of growth calculated in part (a) is a good estimate of the instantaneous rate of growth of Las Vegas in 1975.
c. Compute the average rate of growth of Las Vegas from 1990 to 2000. Is the average rate of growth an overestimate or underestimate of the instantaneous rate of growth of Las Vegas in 2000? Approximate the growth rate in 2000.

Additional Exercises

57–60. Find the function *The following limits represent the slope of a curve $y = f(x)$ at the point $(a, f(a))$. Determine a possible function f and number a; then calculate the limit.*

57. $\lim\limits_{x \to 2} \dfrac{\frac{1}{x+1} - \frac{1}{3}}{x - 2}$

58. $\lim\limits_{h \to 0} \dfrac{\sqrt{2+h} - \sqrt{2}}{h}$

59. $\lim\limits_{h \to 0} \dfrac{(2+h)^4 - 16}{h}$

60. $\lim\limits_{x \to 1} \dfrac{3x^2 + 4x - 7}{x - 1}$

61. Is it differentiable? Is $f(x) = \dfrac{x^2 - 5x + 6}{x - 2}$ differentiable at $x = 2$? Justify your answer.

62. Looking ahead: Derivative of x^n Use the symbolic capabilities of a calculator to calculate $f'(x)$ using the definition
$$\lim_{h \to 0} \frac{f(x+h) - f(x)}{h}$$ for the following functions.

a. $f(x) = x^2$ **b.** $f(x) = x^3$ **c.** $f(x) = x^4$
d. Based upon your answers to parts (a)–(c), propose a formula for $f'(x)$ if $f(x) = x^n$, where n is a positive integer.

63. Determining the unknown constant Let
$$f(x) = \begin{cases} 2x^2 & \text{if } x \le 1 \\ ax - 2 & \text{if } x > 1. \end{cases}$$

Determine a value of a (if possible) for which f' is continuous at $x = 1$.

QUICK CHECK ANSWERS

2. The slope is less at $x = 2$.   **3.** Definition (1) requires factoring the numerator or long division in order to cancel $(x - 1)$.   **4.** 32   **5.** $\dfrac{df}{dx}\Big|_{x=3}, \dfrac{dy}{dx}\Big|_{x=3}, y'(3)$ **6.** The slopes of tangent lines decrease as x increases. The values of $f'(x) = \dfrac{1}{2\sqrt{x}}$ also decrease as x increases.

7. $\dfrac{dq}{dr}, \dfrac{dp}{dr}, D_r(q(r)), q'(r), p'(r)$ ◄

3.2 Working with Derivatives

Having defined the derivative, we now spend some time becoming acquainted with this new and important function. In this section, we explore how the graphs of a function and its derivative are related, and we explain the important relationship between continuity and differentiability.

Graphs of Derivatives

The function f' is called the derivative of f because it is *derived* from f. The following examples illustrate how to *derive* the graph of f' from the graph of f.

EXAMPLE 1   Graph of the derivative Sketch the graph of f' from the graph of f (Figure 3.11).

SOLUTION The graph of f consists of line segments, which are their own tangent lines. Therefore, the slope of the curve $y = f(x)$, for $x < -2$, is -1; that is, $f'(x) = -1$, for $x < -2$. Similarly, $f'(x) = 1$, for $-2 < x < 0$, and $f'(x) = -\frac{1}{2}$, for $x > 0$ (Figure 3.12 shows the graph of f in black and the graph of f' in red).

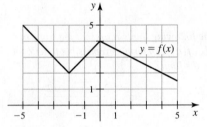

FIGURE 3.11

> In terms of limits at $x = -2$, we can write
> $$\lim_{h \to 0^-} \frac{f(-2 + h) - f(-2)}{h} = -1 \text{ and}$$
> $$\lim_{h \to 0^+} \frac{f(-2 + h) - f(-2)}{h} = 1. \text{ Because}$$
> the one-sided limits are not equal, $f'(-2)$ does not exist. The analogous one-sided limits at $x = 0$ are also unequal.

QUICK CHECK 1 In Example 1, why is f' not continuous at $x = -2$ and at $x = 0$? ◄

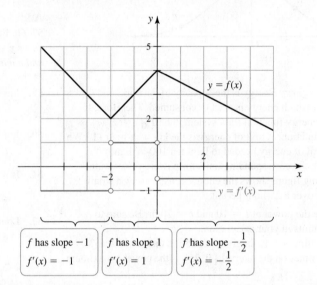

FIGURE 3.12

| f has slope -1 | f has slope 1 | f has slope $-\frac{1}{2}$ |
| $f'(x) = -1$ | $f'(x) = 1$ | $f'(x) = -\frac{1}{2}$ |

Notice that the slopes of the tangent lines change abruptly at $x = -2$ and $x = 0$. As a result, $f'(-2)$ and $f'(0)$ are undefined and the graph of the derivative has a discontinuity at these points.   *Related Exercises 5–12* ◄

EXAMPLE 2   Graph of the derivative Sketch the graph of g' using the graph of g (Figure 3.13).

SOLUTION Without an equation for g, the best we can do is to find the general shape of the graph of g'. Here are the key observations.

1. First note that the lines tangent to the graph of g at $x = -3, -1$, and 1 have a slope of 0. Therefore,

$$g'(-3) = g'(-1) = g'(1) = 0,$$

which means the graph of g' has x-intercepts at these points (Figure 3.14a).

2. For $x < -3$, the slopes of the tangent lines are positive and decrease to 0 as x approaches -3 from the left. Therefore, $g'(x)$ is positive for $x < -3$ and decreases to 0 as x approaches -3.

3. For $-3 < x < -1$, $g'(x)$ is negative; it initially decreases as x increases and then increases to 0 at $x = -1$. For $-1 < x < 1$, $g'(x)$ is positive; it initially increases as x increases and then returns to 0 at $x = 1$.

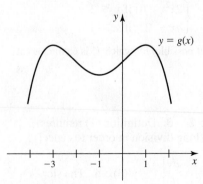

FIGURE 3.13

4. Finally, $g'(x)$ is negative and decreasing for $x > 1$. Because the slope of g changes gradually, the graph of g' is continuous with no jumps or breaks (Figure 3.14b).

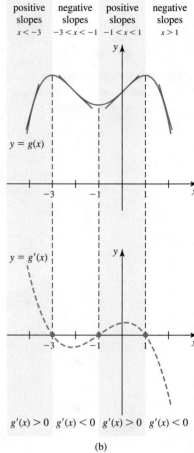

The slope of $y = g(x)$ is zero at $x = -3, -1,$ and 1...

... so $g'(x) = 0$ at $x = -3, -1,$ and 1.

| positive slopes | negative slopes | positive slopes | negative slopes |
| $x < -3$ | $-3 < x < -1$ | $-1 < x < 1$ | $x > 1$ |

$y = g(x)$

$y = g'(x)$

$g'(x) > 0 \quad g'(x) < 0 \quad g'(x) > 0 \quad g'(x) < 0$

(a)   (b)

FIGURE 3.14

QUICK CHECK 2 Is it true that if $f(x) > 0$ at a point, then $f'(x) > 0$ at that point? Is it true that if $f'(x) > 0$ at a point, then $f(x) > 0$ at that point? Explain. ◄

Related Exercises 5–12 ◄

Graphing of the derivative of function with asymptotes presents some additional challenges. Let's consider an example.

EXAMPLE 3   Graphing the derivative with asymptotes The graph of the function f is shown in Figure 3.15. Sketch a graph of its derivative.

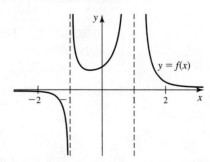

$y = f(x)$

FIGURE 3.15

SOLUTION Identifying intervals on which the slopes of tangent lines are zero, positive, and negative, we make the following observations:

• A horizontal tangent line occurs at approximately $\left(-\frac{1}{3}, f\left(-\frac{1}{3}\right)\right)$. Therefore, $f'\left(-\frac{1}{3}\right) = 0$.

• On the interval $(-\infty, -1)$, slopes of tangent lines are negative and increase in magnitude without bound as we approach -1 from the left.

- On the interval $\left(-1, -\frac{1}{3}\right)$, slopes of tangent lines are negative and increase to zero at $-\frac{1}{3}$.
- On the interval $\left(-\frac{1}{3}, 1\right)$, slopes of tangent lines are positive and increase without bound as we approach 1 from the left.
- On the interval $(1, \infty)$, slopes of tangent lines are negative and increase toward zero.

Assembling all this information, we obtain a graph of f' shown in Figure 3.16. Notice that f and f' have the same vertical asymptotes. However, as we pass through -1, the sign of f changes, while the sign of f' does not. As we pass through 1, the sign of f does not change, while the sign of f' does.

> Although it is the case in Example 3, a function and its derivative do not always share the same vertical asymptotes.

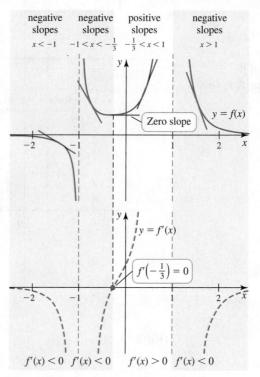

FIGURE 3.16

Related Exercises 13–14 ◄

Continuity

We now return to the discussion of continuity (Section 2.6) and investigate the relationship between continuity and differentiability. Specifically, we show that if a function is differentiable at a point, then it is also continuous at that point.

> **THEOREM 3.1   Differentiable Implies Continuous**
> If f is differentiable at a, then f is continuous at a.

Proof: Because f is differentiable at a, we know that

$$f'(a) = \lim_{x \to a} \frac{f(x) - f(a)}{x - a}$$

exists. To show that f is continuous at a, we must show that $\lim_{x \to a} f(x) = f(a)$. The key is the identity

> Expression (1) is an identity because it holds for all $x \neq a$, which can be seen by canceling $x - a$ and simplifying.

$$f(x) = \frac{f(x) - f(a)}{x - a}(x - a) + f(a), \quad \text{for} \quad x \neq a. \tag{1}$$

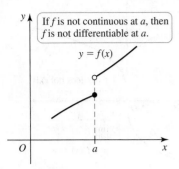

FIGURE 3.17

Taking the limit as x approaches a on both sides of (1) and simplifying, we have

$$\lim_{x \to a} f(x) = \lim_{x \to a} \left[\frac{f(x) - f(a)}{x - a} (x - a) + f(a) \right] \qquad \text{Use identity.}$$

$$= \underbrace{\lim_{x \to a} \left(\frac{f(x) - f(a)}{x - a} \right)}_{f'(a)} \underbrace{\lim_{x \to a} (x - a)}_{0} + \underbrace{\lim_{x \to a} f(x)}_{f(a)} \qquad \text{Theorem 2.3}$$

$$= f'(a) \cdot 0 + f(a) \qquad \text{Evaluate limits.}$$

$$= f(a). \qquad \text{Simplify.}$$

Therefore, $\lim_{x \to a} f(x) = f(a)$, which means that f is continuous at a. ◄

QUICK CHECK 3 Verify that the right-hand side of (1) equals $f(x)$ if $x \neq a$. ◄

> The alternative version of Theorem 3.1 is called the *contrapositive* of the first statement of Theorem 3.1. A statement and its contrapositive are two equivalent ways of expressing the same statement. For example, the statement
>
> If I live in Denver, then I live in Colorado
>
> is logically equivalent to its contrapositive:
>
> If I do not live in Colorado, then I do not live in Denver.

Theorem 3.1 tells us that if f is differentiable at a point, then it is necessarily continuous at that point. Therefore, if f is *not* continuous at a point, then f is *not* differentiable there (Figure 3.17). So, Theorem 3.1 can be stated in another way.

THEOREM 3.1 (ALTERNATIVE VERSION)   Not Continuous Implies Not Differentiable

If f is not continuous at a, then f is not differentiable at a.

It is tempting to read more into Theorem 3.1 than what it actually states. If f is continuous at a point, f is *not* necessarily differentiable at that point. For example, consider the continuous function in Figure 3.18 and note the **corner point** at a. Ignoring the portion of the graph for $x > a$, we might be tempted to conclude that ℓ_1 is the line tangent to the curve at a. Ignoring the part of the graph for $x < a$, we might incorrectly conclude that ℓ_2 is the line tangent to the curve at a. The slopes of ℓ_1 and ℓ_2 are not equal. Because of the abrupt change in the slope of the curve at a, f is not differentiable at a: The limit that defines f' does not exist at a.

> Continuity requires that $\lim_{x \to a} f(x) = f(a)$.
> Differentiability requires more:
> $\lim_{x \to a} \frac{f(x) - f(a)}{x - a}$ must exist.

> To avoid confusion about continuity and differentiability, it helps to think about the function $f(x) = |x|$: It is continuous everywhere but not differentiable at 0.

> See Exercises 27–30 for a formal definition of a vertical tangent line.

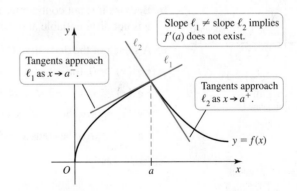

FIGURE 3.18

Another common situation occurs when the graph of a function f has a vertical tangent line at a. In this case, $f'(a)$ is undefined because the slope of a vertical line is undefined. A vertical tangent line may occur at a sharp point on the curve called a **cusp** (for example, the function $f(x) = \sqrt{|x|}$ in Figure 3.19a). In other cases, a vertical tangent line may occur without a cusp (for example, the function $f(x) = \sqrt[3]{x}$ in Figure 3.19b).

vertical
tangent
line

$y = \sqrt{|x|}$

$f'(0)$ does not exist.

O x

$\lim_{x \to 0^+} f'(x) = \infty$

$\lim_{x \to 0^-} f'(x) = -\infty$

FIGURE 3.19   (a)

vertical
tangent
line

$y = \sqrt[3]{x}$

$f'(0)$ does not exist.

O x

$\lim_{x \to 0^+} f'(x) = \infty$

$\lim_{x \to 0^-} f'(x) = \infty$

(b)

> **When Is a Function Not Differentiable at a Point?**
>
> A function f is *not* differentiable at a if at least one of the following conditions holds:
>
> **a.** f is not continuous at a (Figure 3.17).
>
> **b.** f has a corner at a (Figure 3.18).
>
> **c.** f has a vertical tangent at a (Figure 3.19).

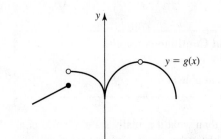

$y = g(x)$

−4 −3 −2 −1   1   2   3   4 x

FIGURE 3.20

EXAMPLE 4   Continuous and differentiable Consider the graph of g in Figure 3.20.

a. Find the values of x in the interval $(-4, 4)$ at which g is not continuous.

b. Find the values of x in the interval $(-4, 4)$ at which g is not differentiable.

c. Sketch a graph of the derivative of g.

SOLUTION

a. The function g fails to be continuous at -2 (where the one-sided limits are not equal) and at 2 (where g is not defined).

b. Because it is not continuous at ± 2, g is not differentiable at those points. Furthermore, g is not differentiable at 0, because the graph has a cusp at that point.

c. A sketch of the derivative (Figure 3.21) has the following features:

- $g'(x) > 0$, for $-4 < x < -2$ and $0 < x < 2$
- $g'(x) < 0$, for $-2 < x < 0$ and $2 < x < 4$
- $g'(x)$ approaches $-\infty$ as $x \to 0^-$ and as $x \to 4^-$; and $g'(x)$ approaches ∞ as $x \to 0^+$
- $g'(x)$ approaches 0 as $x \to 2$ from either side, although $g'(2)$ does not exist.

Related Exercises 15–16 ◄

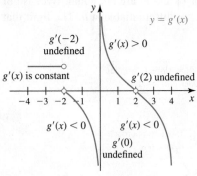

$y = g'(x)$

$g'(-2)$
undefined

$g'(x) > 0$

$g'(x)$ is constant

$g'(2)$ undefined

−4 −3 −2 −1   1   2   3   4 x

$g'(x) < 0$ $g'(x) < 0$

$g'(0)$
undefined

FIGURE 3.21

SECTION 3.2 EXERCISES

Review Questions

1. Explain why $f'(x)$ could be positive or negative at a point at which $f(x) > 0$.

2. Explain why $f(x)$ could be positive or negative at a point at which $f'(x) < 0$.

3. If f is differentiable at a, must f be continuous at a?

4. If f is continuous at a, must f be differentiable at a?

Basic Skills

5–6. Derivatives from graphs *Use the graph of f to sketch a graph of f'.*

5.

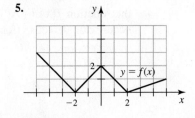

$y = f(x)$

−2   2 x

6.

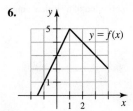

$y = f(x)$

1   2 x

7. **Matching functions with derivatives** Match graphs (a)–(d) of functions with graphs (A)–(C) of their derivatives.

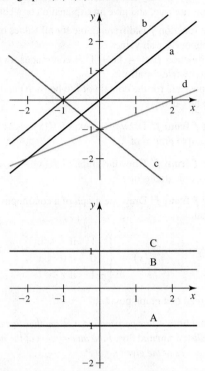

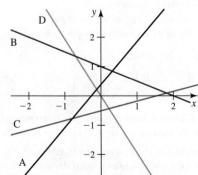

8. **Matching derivatives with functions** Match graphs (a)–(d) of derivative functions with possible graphs (A)–(D) of the corresponding functions.

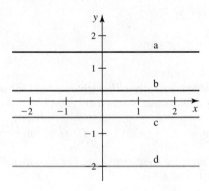

9. **Matching functions with derivatives** Match the functions a–d in the first set of figures with the derivative functions A–D in the next set of figures.

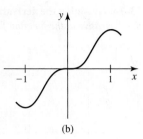

(a)

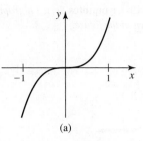

(b)

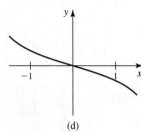

(c)

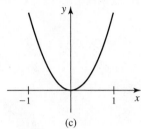

(d)

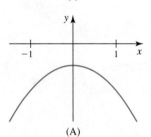

(A)

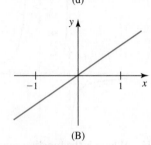

(B)

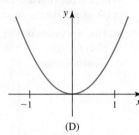

(C)

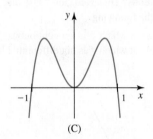

(D)

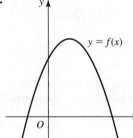

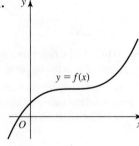

10–12. Sketching derivatives *Reproduce the graph of f and then plot a graph of f′ on the same set of axes.*

10. $y = f(x)$

11. $y = f(x)$

12. $y = f(x)$

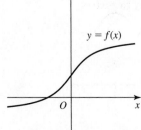

13–14. Graphing the derivative with asymptotes *Sketch a graph of the derivative of the function f shown in the figure.*

13.

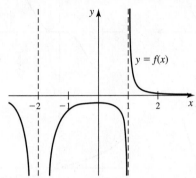

14.

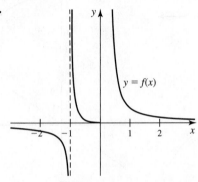

15. **Where is the function continuous? Differentiable?** Use the graph of *f* in the figure to do the following.

   a. Find the values of *x* in $(0, 3)$ at which *f* is not continuous.
   b. Find the values of *x* in $(0, 3)$ at which *f* is not differentiable.
   c. Sketch a graph of *f′*.

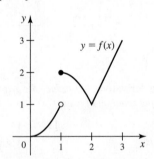

16. **Where is the function continuous? Differentiable?** Use the graph of *g* in the figure to do the following.

   a. Find the values of *x* in $(0, 4)$ at which *g* is not continuous.
   b. Find the values of *x* in $(0, 4)$ at which *g* is not differentiable.
   c. Sketch a graph of *g′*.

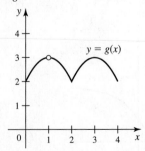

Further Explorations

17. **Explain why or why not** Determine whether the following statements are true, and give an explanation or a counterexample.

   a. If the function *f* is differentiable for all values of *x*, then *f* is continuous for all values of *x*.
   b. The function $f(x) = |x + 1|$ is continuous for all *x*, but not differentiable for all *x*.
   c. It is possible for the domain of *f* to be (a, b) and the domain of *f′* to be $[a, b]$.

18. **Finding f from f′** Draw the graph of $f'(x) = 2$. Then draw three possible graphs of *f*.

19. **Finding f from f′** Draw the graph of $f'(x) = x$. Then draw three possible graphs of *f*.

20. **Finding f from f′** Draw the graph of a continuous function *f* such that

$$f'(x) = \begin{cases} 1 & \text{if } x < 0 \\ 0 & \text{if } 0 < x < 1 \\ -1 & \text{if } x > 1. \end{cases}$$

Is more than one graph possible?

21–24. Normal lines *A line perpendicular to another line or to a tangent line is often called a **normal line**. Find an equation of the normal line for the following curves at the given point P.*

21. $y = 3x - 4; P(1, -1)$

22. $y = \sqrt{x}; P(4, 2)$

23. $y = \dfrac{2}{x}; P(1, 2)$

24. $y = x^2 - 3x; P(3, 0)$

Additional Exercises

25–26. One-sided derivatives *The **right-sided** and **left-sided** derivatives of a function at a point a are given by*

$$f'_+(a) = \lim_{h \to 0^+} \frac{f(a + h) - f(a)}{h} \quad \text{and} \quad f'_-(a) = \lim_{h \to 0^-} \frac{f(a + h) - f(a)}{h},$$

respectively, provided these limits exist. The derivative f′(a) exists if and only if $f'_+(a) = f'_-(a)$.

   a. *Sketch the following functions.*
   b. *Compute $f'_+(a)$ and $f'_-(a)$ at the given point a.*
   c. *Is f continuous at a? Is f differentiable at a?*

25. $f(x) = |x - 2|; \ a = 2$

26. $f(x) = \begin{cases} 4 - x^2 & \text{if } x \leq 1 \\ 2x + 1 & \text{if } x > 1 \end{cases}; \ a = 1$

27–30. Vertical tangent lines *If a function f is continuous at a and $\lim_{x \to a} |f'(x)| = \infty$, then the curve $y = f(x)$ has a vertical tangent line at a and the equation of the tangent line is $x = a$. If a is an endpoint of a domain, then the appropriate one-sided derivative (Exercises 25–26) is used. Use this information to answer the following questions.*

27. Graph the following functions and determine the location of the vertical tangent lines.

   a. $f(x) = (x - 2)^{1/3}$ **b.** $f(x) = \sqrt{|x + 1|}$
   c. $f(x) = (x - 4)^{2/3}$ **d.** $f(x) = x^{5/3} - 2x^{1/3}$

28. The preceding definition of a vertical tangent line includes four cases: $\lim\limits_{x \to a^+} f'(x) = \pm\infty$ combined with $\lim\limits_{x \to a} f'(x) = \pm\infty$ (for example, one case is $\lim\limits_{x \to a^+} f'(x) = -\infty$ and $\lim\limits_{x \to a} f'(x) = \infty$). Sketch a continuous function that has a vertical tangent line at a in each of the four cases.

29. Verify that $f(x) = x^{1/3}$ has a vertical tangent line at $x = 0$.

30. Graph the following curves and determine the location of any vertical tangent lines.

   a. $x^2 + y^2 = 9$ **b.** $x^2 + y^2 + 2x = 0$

31. Continuity is necessary for differentiability

   a. Graph the function

$$f(x) = \begin{cases} x & \text{for } x \le 0 \\ x + 1 & \text{for } x > 0. \end{cases}$$

   b. For $x < 0$, what is $f'(x)$?

   c. For $x > 0$, what is $f'(x)$?

   d. Is f differentiable at 0? Explain.

32. Graph of the derivative of the sine curve

   a. Use the graph of $y = \sin x$ (see figure) to sketch the graph of the derivative of the sine function.

   b. Based upon your graph in part (a), what function appears to equal $\dfrac{d}{dx}(\sin x)$?

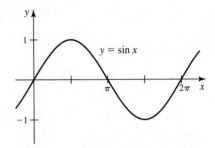

1. The slopes of the tangent lines change abruptly at $x = -2$ and 0. **2.** No. No. ◄

3.3 Rules of Differentiation

If you always had to use limits to evaluate derivatives, as we did in Section 3.1, calculus would be a tedious affair. The goal of this section is to establish rules and formulas for quickly evaluating derivatives—not just for individual functions but for entire families of functions.

The Constant and Power Rules for Derivatives

The graph of the **constant function** $f(x) = c$ is a horizontal line with a slope of 0 at every point (Figure 3.22). It follows that $f'(x) = 0$ or, equivalently, $\dfrac{d}{dx}(c) = 0$ (Exercise 72). This observation leads to the *Constant Rule* for derivatives.

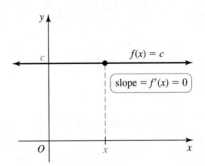

FIGURE 3.22

> We expect the derivative of a constant function to be 0 at every point because the values of a constant function do not change. This means the instantaneous rate of change is 0 at every point.

THEOREM 3.2 Constant Rule

If c is a real number, then $\dfrac{d}{dx}(c) = 0$.

QUICK CHECK 1 Find the values of $\dfrac{d}{dx}(5)$ and $\dfrac{d}{dx}(\pi)$. ◄

Next, consider power functions of the form $f(x) = x^n$, where n is a positive integer. If you completed Exercise 62 in Section 3.1, you found that

$$\frac{d}{dx}(x^2) = 2x, \qquad \frac{d}{dx}(x^3) = 3x^2, \quad \text{and} \quad \frac{d}{dx}(x^4) = 4x^3.$$

In each case, the derivative of x^n appears to be evaluated by placing the exponent n in front of x as a coefficient and decreasing the exponent by 1; in other words, for positive integers n, $\dfrac{d}{dx}(x^n) = nx^{n-1}$. To verify this conjecture, we use the definition of the derivative in the form

$$f'(a) = \lim_{x \to a} \frac{f(x) - f(a)}{x - a}.$$

> Note that if $n = 1$, then factoring is not necessary, and if $n \geq 2$, then this factoring formula agrees with similar factoring formulas for differences of perfect powers:
>
> $x^2 - a^2 = (x - a)(x + a)$
>
> $x^3 - a^3 = (x - a)(x^2 + ax + a^2)$
>
> $x^4 - a^4 = (x - a)$
> $(x^4 + x^3a + x^2a^2 + xa^3 + a^4).$

If $f(x) = x^n$, then $f(x) - f(a) = x^n - a^n$. A factoring formula gives

$$x^n - a^n = (x - a)(x^{n-1} + x^{n-2}a + \cdots + xa^{n-2} + a^{n-1}).$$

Therefore,

$$f'(a) = \lim_{x \to a} \frac{x^n - a^n}{x - a} \qquad \text{Definition of } f'(a)$$

$$= \lim_{x \to a} \frac{(x - a)(x^{n-1} + x^{n-2}a + \cdots + xa^{n-2} + a^{n-1})}{x - a} \qquad \text{Factor } x^n - a^n.$$

$$= \lim_{x \to a} (x^{n-1} + x^{n-2}a + \cdots + xa^{n-2} + a^{n-1}) \qquad \text{Cancel common factors.}$$

$$= \underbrace{a^{n-1} + a^{n-2} \cdot a + \cdots + a \cdot a^{n-2} + a^{n-1}}_{n \text{ terms}} = na^{n-1}. \qquad \text{Evaluate the limit.}$$

> You will see several versions of the Power Rule as we progress. It is extended in exactly the same form, first to negative integer powers, then to rational powers, and finally to real powers.

Replacing a with the variable x in $f'(a) = na^{n-1}$, we obtain the following result, known as the *Power Rule*.

THEOREM 3.3 Power Rule

If n is a positive integer, then $\dfrac{d}{dx}(x^n) = nx^{n-1}$.

EXAMPLE 1 Derivatives of power and constant functions Evaluate the following derivatives.

a. $\dfrac{d}{dx}(x^9)$ **b.** $\dfrac{d}{dx}(x)$ **c.** $\dfrac{d}{dx}(2^8)$

SOLUTION

a. $\dfrac{d}{dx}(x^9) = 9x^{9-1} = 9x^8$ Power Rule

b. $\dfrac{d}{dx}(x) = \dfrac{d}{dx}(x^1) = 1x^0 = 1$ Power Rule

QUICK CHECK 2 Use the graph of $y = x$ to give a geometric explanation of why $\dfrac{d}{dx}(x) = 1$. ◄

c. You might be tempted to use the Power Rule here, but $2^8 = 256$ is a constant. So, by the Constant Rule, $\dfrac{d}{dx}(2^8) = 0.$

Related Exercises 7–12 ◄

Constant Multiple Rule

Consider the problem of finding the derivative of a constant c multiplied by a function f (assuming that f' exists). We apply the definition of the derivative in the form

$$f'(x) = \lim_{h \to 0} \frac{f(x+h) - f(x)}{h}$$

to the function cf:

$$\frac{d}{dx}(cf(x)) = \lim_{h \to 0} \frac{cf(x+h) - cf(x)}{h} \qquad \text{Definition of the derivative of } cf$$

$$= \lim_{h \to 0} \frac{c(f(x+h) - f(x))}{h} \qquad \text{Factor out } c.$$

$$= c \lim_{h \to 0} \frac{f(x+h) - f(x)}{h} \qquad \text{Theorem 2.3}$$

$$= cf'(x). \qquad \text{Definition of } f'(x)$$

This calculation leads to the *Constant Multiple Rule* for derivatives.

> ▷ Theorem 3.4 says that the derivative of a constant multiplied by a function is the constant multiplied by the derivative of the function.

THEOREM 3.4   Constant Multiple Rule

If f is differentiable at x and c is a constant, then

$$\frac{d}{dx}(cf(x)) = cf'(x).$$

EXAMPLE 2   Derivatives of constant multiples of functions Evaluate the following derivatives.

a. $\dfrac{d}{dx}\left(-\dfrac{7x^{11}}{8}\right)$ **b.** $\dfrac{d}{dt}\left(\dfrac{3}{8}\sqrt{t}\right)$

SOLUTION

a.
$$\frac{d}{dx}\left(-\frac{7x^{11}}{8}\right) = -\frac{7}{8} \cdot \frac{d}{dx}(x^{11}) \qquad \text{Constant Multiple Rule}$$

$$= -\frac{7}{8} \cdot 11x^{10} \qquad \text{Power Rule}$$

$$= -\frac{77}{8}x^{10} \qquad \text{Simplify.}$$

> ▷ In Example 5 of Section 3.1, we proved that $\dfrac{d}{dt}(\sqrt{t}) = \dfrac{1}{2\sqrt{t}}$.

b.
$$\frac{d}{dt}\left(\frac{3}{8}\sqrt{t}\right) = \frac{3}{8} \cdot \frac{d}{dt}(\sqrt{t}) \qquad \text{Constant Multiple Rule}$$

$$= \frac{3}{8} \cdot \frac{1}{2\sqrt{t}} \qquad \text{Replace } \frac{d}{dt}(\sqrt{t}) \text{ with } \frac{1}{2\sqrt{t}}.$$

$$= \frac{3}{16\sqrt{t}}$$

Related Exercises 13–18◄

Sum Rule

Many functions are sums of simpler functions. Therefore, it is useful to establish a rule for calculating the derivative of the sum of two or more functions.

> In words, Theorem 3.5 states that the derivative of a sum is the sum of the derivatives. It does not apply to products and quotients of functions.

> **THEOREM 3.5 Sum Rule**
> If f and g are differentiable at x, then
> $$\frac{d}{dx}(f(x) + g(x)) = f'(x) + g'(x).$$

QUICK CHECK 3 If $f(x) = x^2$ and $g(x) = 2x$, what is the derivative of $f(x) + g(x)$? ◄

Proof: Let $F = f + g$, where f and g are differentiable at x, and use the definition of the derivative:

$$\frac{d}{dx}(f(x) + g(x)) = F'(x)$$

$$= \lim_{h \to 0} \frac{F(x + h) - F(x)}{h} \qquad \text{Definition of derivative}$$

$$= \lim_{h \to 0} \frac{(f(x + h) + g(x + h)) - (f(x) + g(x))}{h} \qquad \text{Replace } F \text{ with } f + g.$$

$$= \lim_{h \to 0} \left[\frac{f(x + h) - f(x)}{h} + \frac{g(x + h) - g(x)}{h} \right] \qquad \text{Regroup.}$$

$$= \lim_{h \to 0} \frac{f(x + h) - f(x)}{h} + \lim_{h \to 0} \frac{g(x + h) - g(x)}{h} \qquad \text{Theorem 2.3}$$

$$= f'(x) + g'(x). \qquad \text{Definition of } f' \text{ and } g' \quad ◄$$

The Sum Rule can be extended to three or more differentiable functions, $f_1, f_2, \ldots, f_n$, to obtain the **Generalized Sum Rule**:

$$\frac{d}{dx}(f_1(x) + f_2(x) + \cdots + f_n(x)) = f_1'(x) + f_2'(x) + \cdots + f_n'(x).$$

The difference of two functions $f - g$ can be rewritten as the sum $f + (-g)$. By combining the Sum Rule with the Constant Multiple Rule, the **Difference Rule** is established:

$$\frac{d}{dx}(f(x) - g(x)) = f'(x) - g'(x).$$

Let's put the Sum and Difference Rules to work on one of the most common problems: differentiating polynomials.

EXAMPLE 3 Derivative of a polynomial Determine $\dfrac{d}{dw}(2w^3 + 9w^2 - 6w + 4)$.

SOLUTION

$$\frac{d}{dw}(2w^3 + 9w^2 - 6w + 4)$$

$$= \frac{d}{dw}(2w^3) + \frac{d}{dw}(9w^2) - \frac{d}{dw}(6w) + \frac{d}{dw}(4) \qquad \text{Generalized Sum Rule and Difference Rule}$$

$$= 2\frac{d}{dw}(w^3) + 9\frac{d}{dw}(w^2) - 6\frac{d}{dw}(w) + \frac{d}{dw}(4) \qquad \text{Constant Multiple Rule}$$

$$= 2 \cdot 3w^2 + 9 \cdot 2w - 6 \cdot 1 + 0 \qquad \text{Power Rule and Constant Rule}$$

$$= 6w^2 + 18w - 6 \qquad \text{Simplify.}$$

Related Exercises 19–34 ◄

The technique used to differentiate the polynomial in Example 3 may be used for *any* polynomial. Much of the remainder of this chapter is devoted to discovering differentiation rules for other families of functions: rational, exponential, logarithmic, algebraic, and trigonometric functions.

The Derivative of the Natural Exponential Function

The exponential function $f(x) = b^x$ was introduced in Chapter 1. Let's begin by looking at the graphs of two members of this family, $y = 2^x$ and $y = 3^x$ (Figure 3.23). The slope of the line tangent to the graph of $f(x) = b^x$ at $x = 0$ is given by

$$f'(0) = \lim_{h \to 0} \frac{f(0 + h) - f(0)}{h} = \lim_{h \to 0} \frac{b^h - b^0}{h} = \lim_{h \to 0} \frac{b^h - 1}{h}.$$

We investigate this limit numerically for $b = 2$ and $b = 3$. Table 3.1 shows values of $\dfrac{2^h - 1}{h}$ and $\dfrac{3^h - 1}{h}$ (which are slopes of secant lines) for values of h approaching 0 from the right.

> The limit $\lim\limits_{h \to 0} \dfrac{2^h - 1}{h}$ was explored in Example 7 of Section 2.3.

Table 3.1

h	$\dfrac{2^h - 1}{h}$	$\dfrac{3^h - 1}{h}$
1.0	1.000000	2.000000
0.1	0.717735	1.161232
0.01	0.695555	1.104669
0.001	0.693387	1.099216
0.0001	0.693171	1.098673
0.00001	0.693150	1.098618

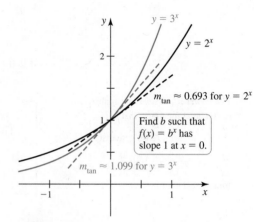

FIGURE 3.23

Exercise 62 gives similar approximations for the limit as h approaches 0 from the left. These numerical values suggest that

$$\lim_{h \to 0} \frac{2^h - 1}{h} \approx 0.693 \quad \text{Less than 1}$$

$$\lim_{h \to 0} \frac{3^h - 1}{h} \approx 1.099. \quad \text{Greater than 1}$$

These two facts, together with the graphs in Figure 3.23, suggest that there is a number b with $2 < b < 3$ such that the graph of $y = b^x$ has a tangent line with slope 1 at $x = 0$. This number b has the property that

$$\lim_{h \to 0} \frac{b^h - 1}{h} = 1.$$

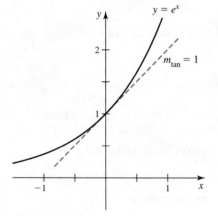

FIGURE 3.24

> The constant e was identified and named by the Swiss mathematician Leonhard Euler (1707–1783) (pronounced "oiler").

It can be shown that, indeed, such a number b exists. In fact, it is the number $e = 2.718281828459 \ldots$ that was introduced in Chapter 1. Therefore, the exponential function whose tangent line has slope 1 at $x = 0$ is the *natural exponential function* $f(x) = e^x$ (Figure 3.24).

DEFINITION The Number e

The number $e = 2.718281828459 \ldots$ satisfies

$$\lim_{h \to 0} \frac{e^h - 1}{h} = 1.$$

It is the base of the natural exponential function $f(x) = e^x$.

With the preceding facts in mind, the derivative of $f(x) = e^x$ is computed as follows:

$$\frac{d}{dx}(e^x) = \lim_{h \to 0} \frac{e^{x+h} - e^x}{h} \qquad \text{Definition of the derivative}$$

$$= \lim_{h \to 0} \frac{e^x \cdot e^h - e^x}{h} \qquad \text{Property of exponents}$$

$$= \lim_{h \to 0} \frac{e^x(e^h - 1)}{h} \qquad \text{Factor out } e^x.$$

$$= e^x \cdot \underbrace{\lim_{h \to 0} \frac{e^h - 1}{h}}_{1} \qquad e^x \text{ is constant as } h \to 0; \text{ definition of } e.$$

$$= e^x \cdot 1 = e^x.$$

We have proved a remarkable fact: The derivative of the exponential function is itself; it is the only function (other than constant multiples of e^x and $f(x) = 0$) with this property.

> The Power Rule *cannot* be applied to exponential functions; that is, $\frac{d}{dx}(e^x) \neq xe^{x-1}$. Also note that $\frac{d}{dx}(e^{10}) \neq e^{10}$. Instead, $\frac{d}{dx}(e^c) = 0$, for any real number c.

THEOREM 3.6   The Derivative of e^x

The function $f(x) = e^x$ is differentiable for all real numbers x, and

$$\frac{d}{dx}(e^x) = e^x.$$

QUICK CHECK 4 Find the derivative of $f(x) = 4e^x - 3x^2$. ◄

Slopes of Tangent Lines

The derivative rules presented in this section allow us to determine slopes of tangent lines and rates of change for many functions.

EXAMPLE 4   Finding tangent lines

a. Write an equation of the line tangent to the graph of $f(x) = 2x - \dfrac{e^x}{2}$ at the point $\left(0, -\tfrac{1}{2}\right)$.

b. Find the point(s) on the graph of f at which the tangent line is horizontal.

SOLUTION

a. To find the slope of the tangent line at $\left(0, -\tfrac{1}{2}\right)$, we first calculate $f'(x)$:

$$f'(x) = \frac{d}{dx}\left(2x - \frac{e^x}{2}\right)$$

$$= \frac{d}{dx}(2x) - \frac{d}{dx}\left(\frac{1}{2}e^x\right) \qquad \text{Difference Rule}$$

$$= 2\underbrace{\frac{d}{dx}(x)}_{1} - \frac{1}{2} \cdot \underbrace{\frac{d}{dx}(e^x)}_{e^x} \qquad \text{Constant Multiple Rule}$$

$$= 2 - \frac{1}{2}e^x. \qquad \text{Evaluate derivatives.}$$

It follows that the slope of the tangent line at $\left(0, -\frac{1}{2}\right)$ is

$$f'(0) = 2 - \frac{1}{2}e^0 = \frac{3}{2}.$$

Figure 3.25 shows the tangent line passing through $\left(0, -\frac{1}{2}\right)$; it has the equation

$$y - \left(-\frac{1}{2}\right) = \frac{3}{2}(x - 0) \quad \text{or} \quad y = \frac{3}{2}x - \frac{1}{2}.$$

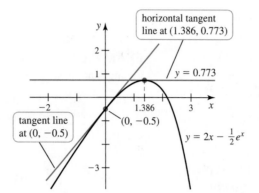

FIGURE 3.25

▷ Observe that the function has a maximum value of approximately 0.773 at the point where the tangent line has a slope of 0. We explore the importance of horizontal tangent lines in Chapter 4.

b. Because the slope of a horizontal tangent line is 0, our goal is to solve $f'(x) = 2 - \frac{1}{2}e^x = 0$. Multiplying both sides of this equation by 2 and rearranging gives the equation $e^x = 4$. Taking the natural logarithm of both sides, we find that $x = \ln 4$. Thus, $f'(x) = 0$ at $x = \ln 4 \approx 1.386$, and f has a horizontal tangent at $(\ln 4, f(\ln 4)) \approx (1.386, 0.773)$ (Figure 3.25).

Related Exercises 35–43 ◄

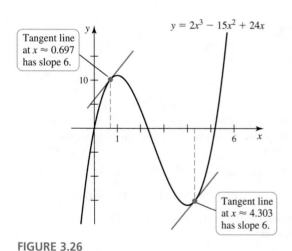

FIGURE 3.26

EXAMPLE 5 Slope of a tangent line Let $f(x) = 2x^3 - 15x^2 + 24x$. For what values of x does the line tangent to the graph of f have a slope of 6?

SOLUTION The tangent line has a slope of 6 when

$$f'(x) = 6x^2 - 30x + 24 = 6.$$

Subtracting 6 from both sides of the equation and factoring, we have

$$6(x^2 - 5x + 3) = 0.$$

Using the quadratic formula, the roots are

$$x = \frac{5 - \sqrt{13}}{2} \approx 0.697 \quad \text{and} \quad x = \frac{5 + \sqrt{13}}{2} \approx 4.303.$$

Therefore, the slope of the curve at these points is 6 (Figure 3.26).

Related Exercises 35–43 ◄

QUICK CHECK 5 Determine the point(s) at which $f(x) = x^3 - 12x$ has a horizontal tangent line. ◄

Higher-Order Derivatives

Because the derivative of a function f is a function in its own right, we can take the derivative of f'. The result is the *second derivative of f*, denoted f'' (read f *double prime*). The derivative of the second derivative is the *third derivative of f*, denoted f''' or $f^{(3)}$. For any positive integer n, $f^{(n)}$ represents the *n*th derivative of f. Other common notations for the *n*th derivative of $y = f(x)$ include $\frac{d^n f}{dx^n}$ and $y^{(n)}$. In general, derivatives of order $n \geq 2$ are called *higher-order derivatives*.

▷ Parentheses are placed around n to distinguish a derivative from a power. Therefore, $f^{(n)}$ is the *n*th derivative of f and f^n is the function f raised to the *n*th power.

▷ The notation $\frac{d^2 f}{dx^2}$ comes from $\frac{d}{dx}\left(\frac{df}{dx}\right)$ and is read *d* 2 *f dx squared*.

▷ The prime notation, f', f'', and f''', is used only for the first, second, and third derivatives.

DEFINITION   **Higher-Order Derivatives**

Assuming f can be differentiated as often as necessary, the **second derivative** of f is

$$f''(x) = f^{(2)}(x) = \frac{d^2f}{dx^2} = \frac{d}{dx}(f'(x)).$$

For integers $n \geq 1$, the **nth derivative** is

$$f^{(n)}(x) = \frac{d^n f}{dx^n} = \frac{d}{dx}(f^{(n-1)}(x)).$$

EXAMPLE 6   Finding higher-order derivatives Find the third derivative of the following functions.

a. $f(x) = 3x^3 - 5x + 12$ **b.** $y = 3t + 2e^t$

SOLUTION

a.

$$f'(x) = 9x^2 - 5$$

$$f''(x) = \frac{d}{dx}(9x^2 - 5) = 18x$$

$$f'''(x) = 18$$

> In Example 6a, note that $f^{(4)}(x) = 0$, which means that all successive derivatives are also 0. In general, the nth derivative of an nth-degree polynomial is a constant, which implies that derivatives of order $k > n$ are 0.

b. Here we use an alternative notation for higher-order derivatives:

$$\frac{dy}{dt} = \frac{d}{dt}(3t + 2e^t) = 3 + 2e^t$$

$$\frac{d^2y}{dt^2} = \frac{d}{dt}(3 + 2e^t) = 2e^t$$

$$\frac{d^3y}{dt^3} = \frac{d}{dt}(2e^t) = 2e^t.$$

QUICK CHECK 6 With $f(x) = x^5$, find $f^{(5)}(x)$ and $f^{(6)}(x)$. With $g(x) = e^x$, find $g^{(100)}(x)$. ◄

In this case, $\dfrac{d^n y}{dt^n} = 2e^t$, for $n \geq 2$.   *Related Exercises 44–48* ◄

SECTION 3.3 EXERCISES

Review Questions

Assume the derivatives of f and g exist in Exercises 1–6.

1.   If the limit definition of a derivative can be used to find f', then what is the purpose of using other rules to find f'?

2.   In this section, we showed that the rule $\dfrac{d}{dx}(x^n) = nx^{n-1}$ is valid for what values of n?

3.   Give a nonzero function that is its own derivative.

4.   How do you find the derivative of the sum of two functions $f + g$?

5.   How do you find the derivative of a constant multiplied by a function?

6.   How do you find the fifth derivative of a function?

Basic Skills

7–12. Derivatives of power and constant functions *Find the derivative of the following functions.*

7. $y = x^5$ 8. $f(t) = t^{11}$ 9. $f(x) = 5$

10. $g(x) = e^3$ 11. $h(t) = t$ 12. $f(v) = v^{100}$

13–18. Derivatives of constant multiples of functions *Find the derivative of the following functions. See Example 5 of Section 3.1 for the derivative of $\sqrt{x}$.*

13. $f(x) = 5x^3$ 14. $g(w) = \frac{5}{6}w^{12}$ 15. $p(x) = 8x$

16. $g(t) = 6\sqrt{t}$ 17. $g(t) = 100t^2$ 18. $f(s) = \dfrac{\sqrt{s}}{4}$

19–24. Derivatives of the sum of functions *Find the derivative of the following functions.*

19. $f(x) = 3x^4 + 7x$ 20. $g(x) = 6x^5 - x$

21. $f(x) = 10x^4 - 32x + e^2$ 22. $f(t) = 6\sqrt{t} - 4t^3 + 9$

23. $g(w) = 2w^3 + 3w^2 + 10w$ 24. $s(t) = 4\sqrt{t} - \frac{1}{4}t^4 + t + 1$

25–28. Derivatives of products *Find the derivative of the following functions by first expanding the expression. Simplify your answers.*

25. $f(x) = (2x + 1)(3x^2 + 2)$

26. $g(r) = (5r^3 + 3r + 1)(r^2 + 3)$

27. $h(x) = (x^2 + 1)^2$

28. $h(x) = \sqrt{x}(\sqrt{x} - 1)$

29–34. Derivatives of quotients *Find the derivative of the following functions by first simplifying the expression.*

29. $f(w) = \dfrac{w^3 - w}{w}$

30. $y = \dfrac{12s^3 - 8s^2 + 12s}{4s}$

31. $g(x) = \dfrac{x^2 - 1}{x - 1}$

32. $h(x) = \dfrac{x^3 - 6x^2 + 8x}{x^2 - 2x}$

33. $y = \dfrac{x - a}{\sqrt{x} - \sqrt{a}}$; a is a positive constant.

34. $y = \dfrac{x^2 - 2ax + a^2}{x - a}$; a is a constant.

■ 35–38. Equations of tangent lines

a. *Find an equation of the line tangent to the given curve at a.*
b. *Use a graphing utility to graph the curve and the tangent line on the same set of axes.*

35. $y = -3x^2 + 2$; $a = 1$

36. $y = x^3 - 4x^2 + 2x - 1$; $a = 2$

37. $y = e^x$; $a = \ln 3$

38. $y = \dfrac{e^x}{4} - x$; $a = 0$

39. Finding slope locations Let $f(x) = x^2 - 6x + 5$.

a. Find the values of x for which the slope of the curve $y = f(x)$ is 0.
b. Find the values of x for which the slope of the curve $y = f(x)$ is 2.

40. Finding slope locations Let $f(t) = t^3 - 27t + 5$.

a. Find the values of t for which the slope of the curve $y = f(t)$ is 0.
b. Find the values of t for which the slope of the curve $y = f(t)$ is 21.

41. Finding slope locations Let $f(x) = 2x^3 - 3x^2 - 12x + 4$.

a. Find all points on the graph of f at which the tangent line is horizontal.
b. Find all points on the graph of f at which the tangent line has slope 60.

42. Finding slope locations Let $f(x) = 2e^x - 6x$.

a. Find all points on the graph of f at which the tangent line is horizontal.
b. Find all points on the graph of f at which the tangent line has slope 12.

43. Finding slope locations Let $f(x) = 4\sqrt{x} - x$.

a. Find all points on the graph of f at which the tangent line is horizontal.
b. Find all points on the graph of f at which the tangent line has slope $-\frac{1}{2}$.

44–48. Higher-order derivatives *Find $f'(x)$, $f''(x)$, and $f^{(3)}(x)$ for the following functions.*

44. $f(x) = 3x^3 + 5x^2 + 6x$

45. $f(x) = 5x^4 + 10x^3 + 3x + 6$

46. $f(x) = 3x^2 + 5e^x$

47. $f(x) = \dfrac{x^2 - 7x - 8}{x + 1}$

48. $f(x) = 10e^x$

Further Explorations

49. Explain why or why not Determine whether the following statements are true, and give an explanation or a counterexample.

a. $\dfrac{d}{dx}(10^5) = 5 \cdot 10^4$

b. The slope of a line tangent to $f(x) = e^x$ is never 0.

c. $\dfrac{d}{dx}(e^3) = e^3$

d. $\dfrac{d}{dx}(e^x) = xe^{x-1}$

e. The nth derivative $\dfrac{d^n}{dx^n}(5x^3 + 2x + 5)$ equals 0, for any integer $n \geq 3$.

50. Tangent lines Suppose $f(3) = 1$ and $f'(3) = 4$. Let $g(x) = x^2 + f(x)$ and $h(x) = 3f(x)$.

a. Find an equation of the line tangent to $y = g(x)$ at $x = 3$.
b. Find an equation of the line tangent to $y = h(x)$ at $x = 3$.

51. Derivatives from tangent lines Suppose the line tangent to the graph of f at $x = 2$ is $y = 4x + 1$ and suppose the line tangent to the graph of g at $x = 2$ has slope 3 and passes through $(0, -2)$. Find an equation of the line tangent to the following curves at $x = 2$.

a. $y = f(x) + g(x)$ **b.** $y = f(x) - 2g(x)$ **c.** $y = 4f(x)$

52–55. Derivatives from a graph *Let $F = f + g$ and $G = 3f - g$, where the graphs of f and g are shown in the figure. Find the following derivatives.*

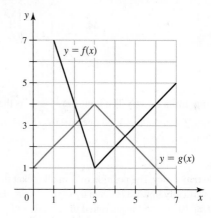

52. $F'(2)$ **53.** $G'(2)$ **54.** $F'(5)$ **55.** $G'(5)$

56–58. Derivatives from a table *Use the table to find the following derivatives.*

x	1	2	3	4	5
$f'(x)$	3	5	2	1	4
$g'(x)$	2	4	3	1	5

56. $\dfrac{d}{dx}(f(x) + g(x))\Big|_{x=1}$

57. $\dfrac{d}{dx}(1.5 f(x))\Big|_{x=2}$

58. $\dfrac{d}{dx}(2x - 3g(x))\Big|_{x=4}$

59–61. Derivatives from limits *The following limits represent $f'(a)$ for some function f and some real number a.*

a. *Find a possible function f and number a.*
b. *Find $f'(a)$ by evaluating the limit.*

59. $\lim\limits_{h \to 0} \dfrac{\sqrt{9+h} - \sqrt{9}}{h}$

60. $\lim\limits_{h \to 0} \dfrac{(1+h)^8 + (1+h)^3 - 2}{h}$

61. $\lim\limits_{x \to 1} \dfrac{x^{100} - 1}{x - 1}$

⊞ 62. Important limits Complete the following table and give approximations for $\lim\limits_{h \to 0^-} \dfrac{2^h - 1}{h}$ and $\lim\limits_{h \to 0^-} \dfrac{3^h - 1}{h}$.

h	$\dfrac{2^h - 1}{h}$	$\dfrac{3^h - 1}{h}$
-1.0		
-0.1		
-0.01		
-0.001		
-0.0001		
-0.00001		

⊞ 63–66. Calculator limits Use a calculator to approximate the following limits.

63. $\lim\limits_{x \to 0} \dfrac{e^{3x} - 1}{x}$

64. $\lim\limits_{n \to \infty} \left(1 + \dfrac{1}{n}\right)^n$

65. $\lim\limits_{x \to 0^+} x^x$

66. $\lim\limits_{x \to 0^+} \left(\dfrac{1}{x}\right)^x$

67. Calculating limits exactly The limit $\lim\limits_{x \to 0} \dfrac{e^x - 1}{x}$ is the derivative of a function f at a point a. Find one possible f and a, and evaluate the limit.

Applications

⊞ 68. Projectile trajectory The position of a small rocket that is launched vertically upward is given by $s(t) = -5t^2 + 40t + 100$, for $0 \le t \le 10$, where t is measured in seconds and s is measured in meters above the ground.

a. Find the rate of change in the position (instantaneous velocity) of the rocket, for $0 \le t \le 10$.
b. At what time is the instantaneous velocity zero?
c. At what time does the instantaneous velocity have the greatest magnitude, for $0 \le t \le 10$?
d. Graph the position and instantaneous velocity, for $0 \le t \le 10$.

69. Height estimate The distance an object falls (when released from rest, under the influence of Earth's gravity, and with no air resistance) is given by $d(t) = 16t^2$, where d is measured in feet and t is measured in seconds. A rock climber sits on a ledge on a vertical wall and carefully observes the time it takes for a small stone to fall from the ledge to the ground.

a. Compute $d'(t)$. What units are associated with the derivative, and what does it measure? Interpret the derivative.
b. If it takes 6 s for a stone to fall to the ground, how high is the ledge? How fast is the stone moving when it strikes the ground (in mi/hr)?

70. Cell growth When observations begin at $t = 0$, a cell culture has 1200 cells and continues to grow according to the function $p(t) = 1200\,e^t$, where p is the number of cells and t is measured in days.

a. Compute $p'(t)$. What units are associated with the derivative, and what does it measure?
b. On the interval $[0, 4]$, when is the growth rate $p'(t)$ the least? When is it the greatest?

71. Gas mileage The distance traveled by a particular car on a full tank of gas (the range of the car), is $D(g) = 0.05g^2 + 35g$, where D is measured in miles and g is the capacity of the tank in gallons.

a. Compute dD/dg. What units are associated with the derivative, and what does it measure?
b. Find dD/dg for $g = 0, 5$, and 10 gal (include units). Interpret dD/dg.
c. What is the range of this car if it has a 12-gal tank?

Additional Exercises

72. Constant Rule proof For the constant function $f(x) = c$, use the definition of the derivative to show that $f'(x) = 0$.

73. Alternative proof of the Power Rule The Binomial Theorem states that for any positive integer n,

$$(a + b)^n = a^n + na^{n-1}b + \frac{n(n-1)}{2 \cdot 1} a^{n-2}b^2$$

$$+ \frac{n(n-1)(n-2)}{3 \cdot 2 \cdot 1} a^{n-3}b^3 + \cdots + nab^{n-1} + b^n.$$

Use this formula and the definition $f'(x) = \lim\limits_{h \to 0} \dfrac{f(x+h) - f(x)}{h}$ to show that $\dfrac{d}{dx}(x^n) = nx^{n-1}$, for any positive integer n.

74. Looking ahead: Power Rule for negative integers Suppose n is a negative integer and $f(x) = x^n$. Use the following steps to prove that $f'(a) = na^{n-1}$, which means the Power Rule for positive integers extends to all integers. This result is proved in Section 3.4 by a different method.

a. Assume that $m = -n$, so that $m > 0$. Use the definition
$$f'(a) = \lim\limits_{x \to a} \frac{x^n - a^n}{x - a} = \lim\limits_{x \to a} \frac{x^{-m} - a^{-m}}{x - a}.$$
Simplify using the factoring rule (which is valid for $n > 0$)
$$x^n - a^n = (x - a)(x^{n-1} + x^{n-2}a + \cdots + xa^{n-2} + a^{n-1})$$
until it is possible to take the limit.

b. Use this result to find $\dfrac{d}{dx}(x^{-7})$ and $\dfrac{d}{dx}\left(\dfrac{1}{x^{10}}\right)$.

75. Extending the Power Rule to $n = \dfrac{1}{2}, \dfrac{3}{2}$, and $\dfrac{5}{2}$ With Theorem 3.3 and Exercise 74, we have shown that the Power Rule,

$\frac{d}{dx}(x^n) = nx^{n-1}$, applies to any integer n. Later in the chapter, we extend this rule so that it applies to any rational number n.

a. Explain why the Power Rule is consistent with the formula $\frac{d}{dx}(\sqrt{x}) = \frac{1}{2\sqrt{x}}$.

b. Prove that the Power Rule holds for $n = \frac{3}{2}$. (*Hint:* Use the definition of the derivative: $\frac{d}{dx}(x^{3/2}) = \lim_{h \to 0} \frac{(x+h)^{3/2} - x^{3/2}}{h}$.)

c. Prove that the Power Rule holds for $n = \frac{5}{2}$.

d. Propose a formula for $\frac{d}{dx}(x^{n/2})$, for any positive integer n.

76. Computing the derivative of $f(x) = e^{-x}$

a. Use the definition of the derivative to show that $\frac{d}{dx}(e^{-x}) = e^{-x} \cdot \lim_{h \to 0} \frac{e^{-h} - 1}{h}$.

b. Show that the limit in part (a) is equal to –1. (*Hint:* Use the facts that $\lim_{h \to 0} \frac{e^h - 1}{h} = 1$ and e^x is continuous for all x.)

c. Use parts (a) and (b) to find the derivative of $f(x) = e^{-x}$.

77. Computing the derivative of $f(x) = e^{2x}$

a. Use the definition of the derivative to show that $\frac{d}{dx}(e^{2x}) = e^{2x} \cdot \lim_{h \to 0} \frac{e^{2h} - 1}{h}$.

b. Show that the limit in part (a) is equal to 2. (*Hint:* Factor $e^{2h} - 1$.)

c. Use parts (a) and (b) to find the derivative of $f(x) = e^{2x}$.

78. Computing the derivative of $f(x) = x^2 e^x$

a. Use the definition of the derivative to show that $\frac{d}{dx}(x^2 e^x) = e^x \cdot \lim_{h \to 0} \frac{(x^2 + 2xh + h^2)e^h - x^2}{h}$.

b. Manipulate the limit in part (a) to arrive at $f'(x) = e^x(x^2 + 2x)$. (*Hint:* Use the fact that $\lim_{h \to 0} \frac{e^h - 1}{h} = 1$.)

Technology Exercises

79–81. Difference quotients *Suppose f is a differentiable function and consider the function*

$$D(x) = \frac{f(x + 0.01) - f(x)}{0.01},$$

where x is in the domain of f. For the following functions, carry out these steps.

a. *Before graphing D, describe the graph you expect to see.*
b. *Graph D on the given interval.*
c. *Change 0.01 to 0.001 and describe the change you see in the graph of D. Explain what you observe.*

79. $f(x) = \frac{x}{2}$ on $[-2, 2]$ **80.** $f(x) = x^2$ on $[-2, 2]$

81. $f(x) = \sqrt{x}$ on $[0, 4]$

QUICK CHECK ANSWERS

1. $\frac{d}{dx}(5) = 0$ and $\frac{d}{dx}(\pi) = 0$ because 5 and π are constants.

2. The slope of the curve $y = x$ is 1 at any point; therefore, $\frac{d}{dx}(x) = 1$.   **3.** $2x + 2$ **4.** $f'(x) = 4e^x - 6x$

5. $x = 2$ and $x = -2$ **6.** $f^{(5)}(x) = 120, f^{(6)}(x) = 0$, $g^{(100)}(x) = e^x$ ◄

3.4 The Product and Quotient Rules

The derivative of a sum of functions is the sum of the derivatives. So you might assume that the derivative of a product of functions is the product of the derivatives. Consider, however, the functions $f(x) = x^3$ and $g(x) = x^4$. In this case, $\frac{d}{dx}(f(x)g(x)) = \frac{d}{dx}(x^7) = 7x^6$, but $f'(x)g'(x) = 3x^2 \cdot 4x^3 = 12x^5$. Therefore, $\frac{d}{dx}(f \cdot g) \neq f' \cdot g'$. Similarly, the derivative of a quotient is *not* the quotient of the derivatives. The purpose of this section is to develop rules for differentiating products and quotients of functions.

Product Rule

Here is an anecdote that suggests the formula for the Product Rule. Imagine running along a road at a constant speed. Your speed is determined by two factors: the length of your stride and the number of strides you take each second. Therefore,

$$\text{running speed} = \text{stride length} \cdot \text{stride rate}.$$

If your stride length is 3 ft and you take 2 strides/s, then your speed is 6 ft/s.

Now suppose your stride length increases by 0.5 ft, from 3 to 3.5 ft. Then the change in speed is calculated as follows:

$$change \text{ in speed} = \text{change in stride length} \cdot \text{stride rate}$$
$$= 0.5 \cdot 2 = 1 \text{ ft/s}.$$

Alternatively, suppose your stride length remains constant but your stride rate increases by 0.25 strides/s, from 2 to 2.25 strides/s. Then

$$change \text{ in speed} = \text{stride length} \cdot \text{change in stride rate}$$
$$= 3 \cdot 0.25 = 0.75 \text{ ft/s}.$$

If both your stride rate and stride length change simultaneously, we expect two contributions to the change in your running speed:

$$change \text{ in speed} = (\text{change in stride length} \cdot \text{stride rate})$$
$$+ (\text{stride length} \cdot \text{change in stride rate})$$
$$= 1 \text{ ft/s} + 0.75 \text{ ft/s} = 1.75 \text{ ft/s}.$$

This argument correctly suggests that the derivative (or rate of change) of a product of two functions has *two components*, as shown by the following rule.

> In words, Theorem 3.7 states that the derivative of the product of two functions equals the derivative of the first function multiplied by the second function plus the first function multiplied by the derivative of the second function.

THEOREM 3.7 Product Rule

If f and g are differentiable at x, then

$$\frac{d}{dx}(f(x)g(x)) = f'(x)g(x) + f(x)g'(x).$$

Proof: We apply the definition of the derivative to the function fg:

$$\frac{d}{dx}(f(x)g(x)) = \lim_{h \to 0} \frac{f(x + h)g(x + h) - f(x)g(x)}{h}.$$

A useful tactic is to add $-f(x)g(x + h) + f(x)g(x + h)$ (which equals 0) to the numerator, so that

$$\frac{d}{dx}(f(x)g(x))$$
$$= \lim_{h \to 0} \frac{f(x + h)g(x + h) - f(x)g(x + h) + f(x)g(x + h) - f(x)g(x)}{h}.$$

The fraction is now split and the numerators are factored:

$$\frac{d}{dx}(f(x)g(x))$$
$$= \lim_{h \to 0} \frac{f(x + h)g(x + h) - f(x)g(x + h)}{h} + \lim_{h \to 0} \frac{f(x)g(x + h) - f(x)g(x)}{h}$$

$$= \lim_{h \to 0} \left[\underbrace{\frac{f(x + h) - f(x)}{h}}_{\substack{\text{approaches } f'(x) \text{ as} \\ h \to 0}} \cdot \overbrace{g(x + h)}^{\substack{\text{approaches} \\ g(x) \\ \text{as } h \to 0}} \right] + \lim_{h \to 0} \left[\overbrace{f(x)}^{\substack{\text{equals} \\ f(x) \text{ as} \\ h \to 0}} \cdot \overbrace{\frac{g(x + h) - g(x)}{h}}^{\substack{\text{approaches } g'(x) \\ \text{as } h \to 0}} \right]$$

$$= f'(x) \cdot g(x) + f(x) \cdot g'(x).$$

> As $h \to 0$, $f(x)$ does not change in value; it is independent of h.

The continuity of g is used to conclude that $\lim_{h \to 0} g(x + h) = g(x)$. ◀

EXAMPLE 1   **Using the Product Rule** Find and simplify the following derivatives.

a. $\dfrac{d}{dv}\left(v^2(2\sqrt{v}+1)\right)$ **b.** $\dfrac{d}{dx}(x^2 e^x)$

SOLUTION

> In Example 5 of Section 3.1, we proved that $\dfrac{d}{dv}(\sqrt{v})=\dfrac{1}{2\sqrt{v}}$.

a. $\dfrac{d}{dv}\left(v^2(2\sqrt{v}+1)\right)=\left[\dfrac{d}{dv}(v^2)\right](2\sqrt{v}+1)+v^2\left[\dfrac{d}{dv}(2\sqrt{v}+1)\right]$ Product Rule

$$=2v(2\sqrt{v}+1)+v^2\left(2\cdot\dfrac{1}{2\sqrt{v}}\right)$$ Evaluate the derivatives.

$$=4v^{3/2}+2v+v^{3/2}=5v^{3/2}+2v$$ Simplify.

QUICK CHECK 1 Find the derivative of $f(x)=x^5$. Then find the same derivative using the Product Rule with $f(x)=x^2x^3$. ◄

b. $\dfrac{d}{dx}(x^2 e^x)=\underbrace{2x}_{\frac{d}{dx}(x^2)}\cdot e^x+x^2\cdot\underbrace{e^x}_{\frac{d}{dx}(e^x)}=xe^x(2+x)$

Related Exercises 7–18 ◄

Quotient Rule

Consider the quotient $q(x)=\dfrac{f(x)}{g(x)}$ and note that $f(x)=g(x)q(x)$. By the Product Rule, we have

$$f'(x)=g'(x)q(x)+g(x)q'(x).$$

Solving for $q'(x)$, we find that

$$q'(x)=\dfrac{f'(x)-g'(x)q(x)}{g(x)}.$$

Substituting $q(x)=\dfrac{f(x)}{g(x)}$ produces a rule for finding $q'(x)$:

$$q'(x)=\dfrac{f'(x)-g'(x)\dfrac{f(x)}{g(x)}}{g(x)}$$ Replace $q(x)$ with $\dfrac{f(x)}{g(x)}$.

$$=\dfrac{g(x)\left(f'(x)-g'(x)\dfrac{f(x)}{g(x)}\right)}{g(x)\cdot g(x)}$$ Multiply numerator and denominator by $g(x)$.

$$=\dfrac{g(x)f'(x)-f(x)g'(x)}{(g(x))^2}.$$ Simplify.

This calculation produces the correct result for the derivative of a quotient. However, there is one subtle point: How do we know that the derivative of f/g exists in the first place? A complete proof of the Quotient Rule is outlined in Exercise 86.

> In words, Theorem 3.8 states that the derivative of the quotient of two functions equals the denominator multiplied by the derivative of the numerator minus the numerator multiplied by the derivative of the denominator, all divided by the denominator squared.
>
>   An easy way to remember the Quotient Rule is with
>
> $$\dfrac{LoD(Hi)-HiD(Lo)}{(Lo)^2}.$$

THEOREM 3.8   **The Quotient Rule**

If f and g are differentiable at x and $g(x)\neq 0$, then the derivative of f/g at x exists and

$$\dfrac{d}{dx}\left(\dfrac{f(x)}{g(x)}\right)=\dfrac{g(x)f'(x)-f(x)g'(x)}{(g(x))^2}.$$

EXAMPLE 2 Using the Quotient Rule Find and simplify the following derivatives.

a. $\dfrac{d}{dx}\left(\dfrac{x^2 + 3x + 4}{x^2 - 1}\right)$ **b.** $\dfrac{d}{dx}(e^{-x})$

SOLUTION

> The Product and Quotient Rules are used on a regular basis throughout this text. It is a good idea to memorize these rules (along with the other derivative rules and formulas presented in this chapter) so that you can evaluate derivatives quickly.

a. $\dfrac{d}{dx}\left(\dfrac{x^2 + 3x + 4}{x^2 - 1}\right) = \dfrac{\overbrace{(x^2 - 1)(2x + 3)}^{\substack{(x^2-1)\,\cdot\,\text{the derivative}\\ \text{of }(x^2+3x+4)}} - \overbrace{(x^2 + 3x + 4)2x}^{\substack{(x^2+3x+4)\,\cdot\,\text{the}\\ \text{derivative of }(x^2-1)}}}{\underbrace{(x^2 - 1)^2}_{\substack{\text{the denominator}\\(x^2-1)\text{ squared}}}}$ Quotient Rule

$= \dfrac{2x^3 - 2x + 3x^2 - 3 - 2x^3 - 6x^2 - 8x}{(x^2 - 1)^2}$ Expand.

$= \dfrac{-3x^2 - 10x - 3}{(x^2 - 1)^2}$ Simplify.

b. We rewrite e^{-x} as $\dfrac{1}{e^x}$ and use the Quotient Rule:

$$\frac{d}{dx}\left(\frac{1}{e^x}\right) = \frac{e^x \cdot 0 - 1 \cdot e^x}{(e^x)^2} = -\frac{1}{e^x} = -e^{-x}.$$

Related Exercises 19–32 ◄

QUICK CHECK 2 Find the derivative of $f(x) = x^5$. Then find the same derivative using the Quotient Rule with $f(x) = x^8/x^3$. ◄

EXAMPLE 3 Finding tangent lines Find an equation of the line tangent to the graph of $f(x) = \dfrac{x^2 + 1}{x^2 - 4}$ at the point $(3, 2)$. Plot the curve and tangent line.

SOLUTION To find the slope of the tangent line, we compute f' using the Quotient Rule:

$$f'(x) = \frac{(x^2 - 4)\,2x - (x^2 + 1)\,2x}{(x^2 - 4)^2}$$ Quotient Rule

$$= \frac{2x^3 - 8x - 2x^3 - 2x}{(x^2 - 4)^2} = -\frac{10x}{(x^2 - 4)^2}.$$ Simplify.

The slope of the tangent line at $(3, 2)$ is

$$m_{\tan} = f'(3) = -\frac{10(3)}{(3^2 - 4)^2} = -\frac{6}{5}.$$

Therefore, an equation of the tangent line is

$$y - 2 = -\frac{6}{5}(x - 3), \quad \text{or} \quad y = -\frac{6}{5}x + \frac{28}{5}.$$

The graphs of f and the tangent line are shown in Figure 3.27.

Related Exercises 33–36 ◄

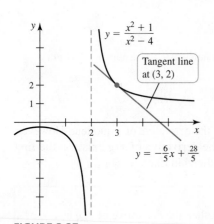

FIGURE 3.27

Extending the Power Rule to Negative Integers

The Power Rule in Section 3.3 says that $\dfrac{d}{dx}(x^n) = nx^{n-1}$, for nonnegative integers n.

Using the Quotient Rule, we show that the Power Rule also holds if n is a negative integer. Assume n is a negative integer and let $m = -n$, so that $m > 0$. Then

$$\frac{d}{dx}(x^n) = \frac{d}{dx}\left(\frac{1}{x^m}\right) \qquad\qquad x^n = \frac{1}{x^{-n}} = \frac{1}{x^m}$$

$$= \frac{\overbrace{x^m\left(\frac{d}{dx}(1)\right)}^{\substack{\text{derivative of a}\\\text{constant is 0}}} - 1\overbrace{\left(\frac{d}{dx}x^m\right)}^{\substack{\text{equals}\\ mx^{m-1}}}}{(x^m)^2} \qquad \text{Quotient Rule}$$

$$= -\frac{mx^{m-1}}{x^{2m}} \qquad\qquad \text{Simplify.}$$

$$= -mx^{-m-1} \qquad\qquad \frac{x^{m-1}}{x^{2m}} = x^{m-1-2m}$$

$$= nx^{n-1}. \qquad\qquad \text{Replace } -m \text{ with } n.$$

This calculation leads to the first extension of the Power Rule. The rule now applies to all integers.

THEOREM 3.9   Extended Power Rule

If n is any integer, then

$$\frac{d}{dx}(x^n) = nx^{n-1}.$$

QUICK CHECK 3 Find the derivative of $f(x) = 1/x^5$ in two different ways: using the Extended Power Rule and using the Quotient Rule. ◄

EXAMPLE 4   Using the Extended Power Rule Find the following derivatives.

a. $\dfrac{d}{dx}\left(\dfrac{9}{x^5}\right)$ **b.** $\dfrac{d}{dt}\left(\dfrac{3t^{16} - 4}{t^6}\right)$

SOLUTION

a. $\dfrac{d}{dx}\left(\dfrac{9}{x^5}\right) = \dfrac{d}{dx}(9x^{-5}) = 9(-5x^{-6}) = -45x^{-6} = -\dfrac{45}{x^6}$

b. The derivative of $\dfrac{3t^{16} - 4}{t^6}$ can be evaluated by the Quotient Rule, but an alternative method is to rewrite the expression using negative powers:

$$\frac{3t^{16} - 4}{t^6} = \frac{3t^{16}}{t^6} - \frac{4}{t^6} = 3t^{10} - 4t^{-6}.$$

We now differentiate using the Extended Power Rule:

$$\frac{d}{dt}\left(\frac{3t^{16} - 4}{t^6}\right) = \frac{d}{dt}(3t^{10} - 4t^{-6}) = 30t^9 + 24t^{-7}.$$

Related Exercises 37–42 ◄

The Derivative of e^{kx}

Consider the composite function $y = e^{2x}$, for which we presently have no differentiation rule. We rewrite the function and apply the Product Rule:

$$\frac{d}{dx}(e^{2x}) = \frac{d}{dx}(e^x \cdot e^x) \qquad\qquad e^{2x} = e^x \cdot e^x$$

$$= \frac{d}{dx}(e^x) \cdot e^x + e^x \cdot \frac{d}{dx}(e^x) \quad \text{Product Rule}$$

$$= e^x \cdot e^x + e^x \cdot e^x = 2e^{2x}. \quad \text{Evaluate derivatives.}$$

In a similar fashion, $y = e^{3x}$ is differentiated by writing it as the product $y = e^x \cdot e^{2x}$. You should verify that $\frac{d}{dx}(e^{3x}) = 3e^{3x}$. Extending this strategy, it can be shown that $\frac{d}{dx}(e^{kx}) = ke^{kx}$, for positive integers k (Exercise 88 illustrates a proof by induction). The Quotient Rule is used to show that the rule holds for negative integers k (Exercise 89). Finally, we prove in Section 3.7 (Exercise 94) that the rule holds for all real numbers k.

THEOREM 3.10   The derivative of e^{kx}
For real numbers k,

$$\frac{d}{dx}(e^{kx}) = ke^{kx}.$$

EXAMPLE 5   Exponential derivatives Compute dy/dx for the following functions.

a. $y = xe^{5x}$ **b.** $y = 1000e^{0.07x}$

SOLUTION

a. We use the Product Rule and the fact that $\frac{d}{dx}(e^{kx}) = ke^{kx}$:

$$\frac{dy}{dx} = \underbrace{1}_{\frac{d}{dx}(x) = 1} \cdot e^{5x} + x \cdot \underbrace{5e^{5x}}_{\frac{d}{dx}(e^{5x}) = 5e^{5x}} = (1 + 5x)e^{5x}.$$

b. Here we use the Constant Multiple Rule:

$$\frac{dy}{dx} = 1000 \cdot \frac{d}{dx}(e^{0.07x}) = 1000 \cdot 0.07e^{0.07x} = 70e^{0.07x}.$$

Related Exercises 43–50 ◄

> **QUICK CHECK 4** Find the derivative of $f(x) = 4e^{0.5x}$. ◄

Rates of Change

Remember that the derivative has multiple uses and interpretations. The following example illustrates the derivative as the rate of change of a population. Specifically, the derivative tells us when the population is growing most rapidly and how the population behaves in the long run.

EXAMPLE 6   Population growth rates The population of a culture of cells increases and approaches a constant level (often called a *steady state* or a *carrying capacity*). The population is modeled by the function $p(t) = \dfrac{400}{1 + 3e^{-0.5t}}$, where $t \geq 0$ is measured in hours (Figure 3.28).

a. Compute and graph the instantaneous growth rate of the population, for any $t \geq 0$.

b. At approximately what time is the instantaneous growth rate the greatest?

c. What is the steady-state population?

SOLUTION

a. The instantaneous growth rate is given by the derivative of the population function:

$$p'(t) = \frac{d}{dt}\left(\frac{400}{1 + 3e^{-0.5t}}\right)$$

$$= \frac{(1 + 3e^{-0.5t}) \cdot \overbrace{\frac{d}{dt}(400)}^{\text{equals } 0} - 400\frac{d}{dt}(1 + 3e^{-0.5t})}{(1 + 3e^{-0.5t})^2} \qquad \text{Quotient Rule}$$

$$= \frac{-400(-1.5e^{-0.5t})}{(1 + 3e^{-0.5t})^2} = \frac{600e^{-0.5t}}{(1 + 3e^{-0.5t})^2}. \qquad \text{Simplify.}$$

> Methods for determining exactly when the growth rate is a maximum are discussed in Chapter 4.

The growth rate has units of cells per hour; its graph is shown in Figure 3.28.

b. The growth rate $p'(t)$ has a maximum at the point at which the population curve is steepest. Using a graphing utility, this point corresponds to $t \approx 2.2$ hr and the growth rate has a value of $p'(2.2) \approx 50$ cells/hr.

c. To determine whether the population approaches a fixed value after a long period of time (the steady-state population), we must investigate the limit of the population function as $t \to \infty$. In this case, the steady-state population exists and is

$$\lim_{t \to \infty} p(t) = \lim_{t \to \infty} \frac{400}{1 + 3\underbrace{e^{-0.5t}}_{\text{approaches } 0}} = 400,$$

which is confirmed by the population curve in Figure 3.28. Notice that as the population approaches its steady state, the growth rate p' approaches zero.

Related Exercises 51–56 ◄

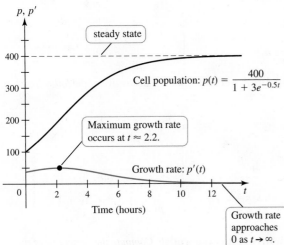

steady state

Cell population: $p(t) = \dfrac{400}{1 + 3e^{-0.5t}}$

Maximum growth rate occurs at $t \approx 2.2$.

Growth rate: $p'(t)$

Time (hours)

Growth rate approaches 0 as $t \to \infty$.

FIGURE 3.28

Combining Derivative Rules

Some situations call for the use of multiple differentiation rules. This section concludes with one such example.

EXAMPLE 7 Combining derivative rules Find the derivative of

$$y = \frac{4xe^x}{x^2 + 1}.$$

SOLUTION In this case, we have the quotient of two functions, with a product $(4x \cdot e^x)$ in the numerator.

$$\frac{dy}{dx} = \frac{(x^2 + 1) \cdot \dfrac{d}{dx}(4xe^x) - (4xe^x) \cdot \dfrac{d}{dx}(x^2 + 1)}{(x^2 + 1)^2} \qquad \text{Quotient Rule}$$

$$= \frac{(x^2 + 1)(4e^x + 4xe^x) - (4xe^x)(2x)}{(x^2 + 1)^2} \qquad \begin{array}{l}\frac{d}{dx}(4xe^x) = 4e^x + 4xe^x \\ \text{by the Product Rule}\end{array}$$

$$= \frac{4e^x(x^3 - x^2 + x + 1)}{(x^2 + 1)^2} \qquad \text{Simplify.}$$

Related Exercises 57–60 ◄

SECTION 3.4 EXERCISES

Review Questions

1. How do you find the derivative of the product of two functions that are differentiable at a point?

2. How do you find the derivative of the quotient of two functions that are differentiable at a point?

3. State the Extended Power Rule for differentiating x^n. For what values of n does the rule apply?

4. Show two ways to differentiate $f(x) = 1/x^{10}$.

5. What is the derivative of $y = e^{kx}$? For what values of k does this rule apply?

6. Show two ways to differentiate $f(x) = (x - 3)(x^2 + 4)$.

Basic Skills

7–14. Derivatives of products *Find the derivative of the following functions.*

7. $f(x) = 3x^4(2x^2 - 1)$ 8. $g(x) = 6x - 2xe^x$

9. $f(t) = t^5 e^t$ 10. $g(w) = e^w(5w^2 + 3w + 1)$

11. $h(x) = (x - 1)(x^3 + x^2 + x + 1)$

12. $f(x) = \left(1 + \dfrac{1}{x^2}\right)(x^2 + 1)$

13. $g(w) = e^w(w^3 - 1)$ 14. $s(t) = 4e^t\sqrt{t}$

15–18. Derivatives by two different methods

a. *Use the Product Rule to find the derivative of the given function. Simplify your result.*

b. *Find the derivative by expanding the product first. Verify that your answer agrees with part (a).*

15. $f(x) = (x - 1)(3x + 4)$

16. $y = (t^2 + 7t)(3t - 4)$

17. $g(y) = (3y^4 - y^2)(y^2 - 4)$

18. $h(z) = (z^3 + 4z^2 + z)(z - 1)$

19–28. Derivatives of quotients *Find the derivative of the following functions.*

19. $f(x) = \dfrac{x}{x + 1}$ 20. $f(x) = \dfrac{x^3 - 4x^2 + x}{x - 2}$

21. $f(x) = \dfrac{e^x}{e^x + 1}$ 22. $f(x) = \dfrac{2e^x - 1}{2e^x + 1}$

23. $f(x) = xe^{-x}$ 24. $f(x) = e^{-x}\sqrt{x}$

25. $y = (3t - 1)(2t - 2)^{-1}$ 26. $h(w) = \dfrac{w^2 - 1}{w^2 + 1}$

27. $g(x) = \dfrac{e^x}{x^2 - 1}$ 28. $y = (2\sqrt{x} - 1)(4x + 1)^{-1}$

29–32. Derivatives by two different methods

a. *Use the Quotient Rule to find the derivative of the given function. Simplify your result.*

b. *Find the derivative by first simplifying the function. Verify that your answer agrees with part (a).*

29. $f(w) = \dfrac{w^3 - w}{w}$ 30. $y = \dfrac{4s^3 - 8s^2 + 4s}{4s}$

31. $y = \dfrac{x^2 - a^2}{x - a}$, where a is a constant.

32. $y = \dfrac{x^2 - 2ax + a^2}{x - a}$, where a is a constant.

▣ 33–36. Equations of tangent lines

a. *Find an equation of the line tangent to the given curve at a.*

b. *Use a graphing utility to graph the curve and the tangent line on the same set of axes.*

33. $y = \dfrac{x + 5}{x - 1}$; $a = 3$ 34. $y = \dfrac{2x^2}{3x - 1}$; $a = 1$

35. $y = 1 + 2x + xe^x$; $a = 0$

36. $y = \dfrac{e^x}{x}$; $a = 1$

37–42. Extended Power Rule *Find the derivative of the following functions.*

37. $f(x) = 3x^{-9}$ 38. $y = \dfrac{4}{p^3}$

39. $g(t) = 3t^2 + \dfrac{6}{t^7}$ 40. $y = \dfrac{w^4 + 5w^2 + w}{w^2}$

41. $g(t) = \dfrac{t^3 + 3t^2 + t}{t^3}$ 42. $p(x) = \dfrac{4x^3 + 3x + 1}{2x^5}$

43–50. Derivatives with exponentials *Compute the derivative of the following functions.*

43. $f(x) = xe^{7x}$ 44. $g(t) = 2te^{t/2}$

45. $f(x) = 15e^{3x}$ 46. $y = 3x^2 - 2x + e^{-2x}$

47. $g(x) = \dfrac{x}{e^{3x}}$ 48. $f(x) = (1 - 2x)e^{-x}$

49. $y = \dfrac{2e^x + 3e^{-x}}{3}$ 50. $A = 2500e^{0.075t}$

▣ 51–52. Population growth *Consider the following population functions.*

a. *Find the instantaneous growth rate of the population, for $t \geq 0$.*

b. *What is the instantaneous growth rate at $t = 5$?*

c. *Estimate the time when the instantaneous growth rate is the greatest.*

d. *Evaluate and interpret $\lim\limits_{t \to \infty} p'(t)$.*

e. *Use a graphing utility to graph the population and its growth rate.*

51. $p(t) = \dfrac{200t}{t + 2}$ 52. $p(t) = \dfrac{800}{1 + 7e^{-0.2t}}$

53. **Antibiotic decay** The half-life of an antibiotic in the bloodstream is 10 hours. If an initial dose of 20 milligrams is administered, the quantity left after t hours is modeled by $Q(t) = 20e^{-0.0693t}$, for $t \geq 0$.

a. Find the instantaneous rate of change of the amount of antibiotic in the bloodstream, for $t \geq 0$.

b. How fast is the amount of antibiotic changing at $t = 0$? At $t = 2$?

c. Evaluate and interpret $\lim_{t \to \infty} Q(t)$ and $\lim_{t \to \infty} Q'(t)$.

54. Bank account A $200 investment in a savings account grows according to $A(t) = 200e^{0.0398t}$, for $t \geq 0$, where t is measured in years.

   a. Find the balance of the account after 10 years.

   b. How fast is the account growing (in dollars/year) at $t = 10$?

   c. Use your answers to parts (a) and (b) to write the equation of the line tangent to the curve $A = 200e^{0.0398t}$ at the point $(10, A(10))$.

55. Finding slope locations Let $f(x) = xe^{2x}$.

   a. Find the values of x for which the slope of the curve $y = f(x)$ is 0.

   b. Explain the meaning of your answer to part (a) in terms of the graph of f.

56. Finding slope locations Let $f(t) = 100e^{-0.05t}$.

   a. Find the values of t for which the slope of the curve $y = f(t)$ is -5.

   b. Does the graph of f have a horizontal tangent line?

57–60. Combining rules *Compute the derivative of the following functions.*

57. $g(x) = \dfrac{(x + 1)e^x}{x - 2}$

58. $h(x) = \dfrac{(x - 1)(2x^2 - 1)}{x^3 - 1}$

59. $h(x) = \dfrac{xe^x}{x + 1}$

60. $h(x) = \dfrac{x + 1}{x^2e^x}$

Further Explorations

61. Explain why or why not Determine whether the following statements are true, and give an explanation or a counterexample.

   a. $\dfrac{d}{dx}(e^5) = 5 \cdot e^4$.

   b. The Quotient Rule must be used to evaluate
   $\dfrac{d}{dx}\left(\dfrac{x^2 + 3x + 2}{x}\right)$.

   c. $\dfrac{d}{dx}\left(\dfrac{1}{x^5}\right) = \dfrac{1}{5x^4}$.

   d. $\dfrac{d^n}{dx^n}(e^{3x}) = 3^n \cdot e^{3x}$, for any integer $n \geq 1$.

62–63. Higher-order derivatives *Find $f'(x)$, $f''(x)$, and $f'''(x)$.*

62. $f(x) = \dfrac{1}{x}$

63. $f(x) = x^2e^{3x}$

64–65. First and second derivatives *Find $f'(x)$ and $f''(x)$.*

64. $f(x) = \dfrac{x}{x + 2}$

65. $f(x) = \dfrac{x^2 - 7x}{x + 1}$

66–71. Choose your method *Use any method to evaluate the derivative of the following functions.*

66. $f(x) = \dfrac{4 - x^2}{x - 2}$

67. $f(x) = 4x^2 - \dfrac{2x}{5x + 1}$

68. $f(z) = z^2(e^{3z} + 4) - \dfrac{2z}{z^2 + 1}$

69. $h(r) = \dfrac{2 - r - \sqrt{r}}{r + 1}$

70. $y = \dfrac{x - a}{\sqrt{x} - \sqrt{a}}$, where a is a positive constant

71. $h(x) = (5x^7 + 5x)(6x^3 + 3x^2 + 3)$

72. Tangent lines Suppose $f(2) = 2$ and $f'(2) = 3$. Let $g(x) = x^2 \cdot f(x)$ and $h(x) = \dfrac{f(x)}{x - 3}$.

   a. Find an equation of the line tangent to $y = g(x)$ at $x = 2$.

   b. Find an equation of the line tangent to $y = h(x)$ at $x = 2$.

73. The Witch of Agnesi The graph of $y = \dfrac{a^3}{x^2 + a^2}$, where a is a constant, is called the *witch of Agnesi* (named after the 18th-century Italian mathematician Maria Agnesi).

   a. Let $a = 3$ and find an equation of the line tangent to $y = \dfrac{27}{x^2 + 9}$ at $x = 2$.

   b. Plot the function and the tangent line found in part (a).

74–79. Derivatives from a table *Use the following table to find the given derivatives.*

x	1	2	3	4
$f(x)$	5	4	3	2
$f'(x)$	3	5	2	1
$g(x)$	4	2	5	3
$g'(x)$	2	4	3	1

74. $\dfrac{d}{dx}(f(x)g(x))\Big|_{x=1}$

75. $\dfrac{d}{dx}\left[\dfrac{f(x)}{g(x)}\right]\Big|_{x=2}$

76. $\dfrac{d}{dx}(xf(x))\Big|_{x=3}$

77. $\dfrac{d}{dx}\left[\dfrac{f(x)}{(x + 2)}\right]\Big|_{x=4}$

78. $\dfrac{d}{dx}\left[\dfrac{xf(x)}{g(x)}\right]\Big|_{x=4}$

79. $\dfrac{d}{dx}\left[\dfrac{f(x)g(x)}{x}\right]\Big|_{x=4}$

80. Derivatives from tangent lines Suppose the line tangent to the graph of f at $x = 2$ is $y = 4x + 1$ and suppose $y = 3x - 2$ is the line tangent to the graph of g at $x = 2$. Find an equation of the line tangent to the following curves at $x = 2$.

   a. $y = f(x)g(x)$

   b. $y = \dfrac{f(x)}{g(x)}$

Applications

81. Electrostatic force The magnitude of the electrostatic force between two point charges Q and q of the same sign is given by $F(x) = \dfrac{kQq}{x^2}$, where x is the distance (measured in meters) between the charges and $k = 9 \times 10^9 \, \text{N} \cdot \text{m}^2/\text{C}^2$ is a physical constant (C stands for coulomb, the unit of charge; N stands for newton, the unit of force).

   a. Find the instantaneous rate of change of the force with respect to the distance between the charges.

b. For two identical charges with $Q = q = 1$ C, what is the instantaneous rate of change of the force at a separation of $x = 0.001$ m?

c. Does the magnitude of the instantaneous rate of change of the force increase or decrease with the separation? Explain.

82. Gravitational force The magnitude of the gravitational force between two objects of mass M and m is given by

$$F(x) = -\frac{GMm}{x^2},$$ where x is the distance between the centers

of mass of the objects and $G = 6.7 \times 10^{-11}$ N·m²/kg² is the gravitational constant (N stands for newton, the unit of force; the negative sign indicates an attractive force).

a. Find the instantaneous rate of change of the force with respect to the distance between the objects.

b. For two identical objects of mass $M = m = 0.1$ kg, what is the instantaneous rate of change of the force at a separation of $x = 0.01$ m?

c. Does the instantaneous rate of change of the force increase or decrease with the separation? Explain.

Additional Exercises

83. Special Product Rule In general, the derivative of a product is not the product of the derivatives. Find nonconstant functions f and g such that the derivative of fg equals $f'g'$.

84. Special Quotient Rule In general, the derivative of a quotient is not the quotient of the derivatives. Find nonconstant functions f and g such that the derivative of f/g equals f'/g'.

85. Means and tangents Suppose f is differentiable on an interval containing a and b, and let $P(a, f(a))$ and $Q(b, f(b))$ be distinct points on the graph of f. Let c be the x-coordinate of the point at which the lines tangent to the curve at P and Q intersect, assuming that the tangent lines are not parallel (see figure).

a. If $f(x) = x^2$, show that $c = (a + b)/2$, the arithmetic mean of a and b, for real numbers a and b.

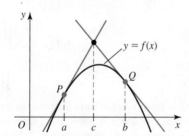

b. If $f(x) = \sqrt{x}$, show that $c = \sqrt{ab}$, the geometric mean of a and b, for $a > 0$ and $b > 0$.

c. If $f(x) = 1/x$, show that $c = 2ab/(a + b)$, the harmonic mean of a and b, for $a > 0$ and $b > 0$.

d. Find an expression for c in terms of a and b for any (differentiable) function f whenever c exists.

86. Proof of the Quotient Rule Let $F = f/g$ be the quotient of two functions that are differentiable at x.

a. Use the definition of F' to show that

$$\frac{d}{dx}\left(\frac{f(x)}{g(x)}\right) = \lim_{h\to 0} \frac{f(x + h)g(x) - f(x)g(x + h)}{hg(x + h)g(x)}.$$

b. Now add $-f(x)g(x) + f(x)g(x)$ (which equals 0) to the numerator in the preceding limit to obtain

$$\lim_{h\to 0} \frac{f(x + h)g(x) - f(x)g(x) + f(x)g(x) - f(x)g(x + h)}{hg(x + h)g(x)}.$$

Use this limit to obtain the Quotient Rule.

c. Explain why $F' = (f/g)'$ exists, whenever $g(x) \neq 0$.

87. Product Rule for the second derivative Assuming the first and second derivatives of f and g exist at x, find a formula for

$$\frac{d^2}{dx^2}(f(x)g(x)).$$

88. Proof by induction: derivative of e^{kx} for positive integers k Proof by induction is a method in which one begins by showing that a statement, which involves positive integers, is true for a particular value (usually $k = 1$). In the second step, the statement is assumed to be true for $k = n$, and the statement is proved for $k = n + 1$, which concludes the proof.

a. Show that $\dfrac{d}{dx}(e^{kx}) = ke^{kx}$, for $k = 1$.

b. Assume the rule is true for $k = n$ (that is, assume $\dfrac{d}{dx}(e^{nx}) = ne^{nx}$), and show this implies that the rule is true for $k = n + 1$. (*Hint:* Write $e^{(n+1)x}$ as the product of two functions, and use the Product Rule.)

89. Derivative of e^{kx} for negative integers k Use the Quotient Rule and Exercise 88 to show that $\dfrac{d}{dx}(e^{kx}) = ke^{kx}$, for negative integers k.

90. Quotient Rule for the second derivative Assuming the first and second derivatives of f and g exist at x, find a formula for

$$\frac{d^2}{dx^2}\left(\frac{f(x)}{g(x)}\right).$$

91. Product Rule for three functions Assume that f, g, and h are differentiable at x.

a. Use the Product Rule (twice) to find a formula for

$$\frac{d}{dx}(f(x)g(x)h(x)).$$

b. Use the formula in (a) to find $\dfrac{d}{dx}(e^{2x}(x - 1)(x + 3))$.

92. One of the Leibniz Rules One of several Leibniz Rules in calculus deals with higher-order derivatives of products. Let $(fg)^{(n)}$ denote the nth derivative of the product fg, for $n \geq 1$.

a. Prove that $(fg)^{(2)} = f''g + 2f'g' + fg''$.

b. Prove that, in general,

$$(fg)^{(n)} = \sum_{k=0}^{n}\binom{n}{k}f^{(k)}g^{(n-k)},$$

where $\dbinom{n}{k} = \dfrac{n!}{k!(n-k)!}$ are the binomial coefficients.

c. Compare the result of (b) to the expansion of $(a + b)^n$.

QUICK CHECK ANSWERS

1. $f'(x) = 5x^4$ by either method   **2.** $f'(x) = 5x^4$ by either method   **3.** $f'(x) = -5x^{-6}$ by either method   **4.** $f'(x) = 2e^{0.5x}$ ◄

3.5 Derivatives of Trigonometric Functions

From variations in market trends and ocean temperatures to daily fluctuations in tides and hormone levels, change is often cyclical or periodic. Trigonometric functions are well suited for describing such cyclical behavior. In this section, we investigate the derivatives of trigonometric functions and their many uses.

> Results stated in this section assume that angles are measured in *radians*.

Two Special Limits

Our principal goal is to determine derivative formulas for $\sin x$ and $\cos x$. In order to do this, we use two special limits.

Table 3.2

x	$\dfrac{\sin x}{x}$
± 0.1	0.9983341665
± 0.01	0.9999833334
± 0.001	0.9999998333

THEOREM 3.11   Trigonometric Limits

$$\lim_{x \to 0} \frac{\sin x}{x} = 1 \qquad \lim_{x \to 0} \frac{\cos x - 1}{x} = 0$$

Note that these limits cannot be evaluated by direct substitution because in both cases, the numerator and denominator approach zero as $x \to 0$. We first examine numerical and graphical evidence supporting Theorem 3.11, and then we offer an analytic proof.

The values of $\dfrac{\sin x}{x}$, rounded to 10 digits, appear in Table 3.2. As x approaches zero from both sides, it appears that $\dfrac{\sin x}{x}$ approaches 1. Figure 3.29 shows a graph of $y = \dfrac{\sin x}{x}$, with a hole at $x = 0$, where the function is undefined. The graphical evidence also strongly suggests (but does not prove) that $\lim\limits_{x \to 0} \dfrac{\sin x}{x} = 1$. Similar evidence also indicates that $\dfrac{\cos x - 1}{x}$ approaches 0 as x approaches 0.

Proof: In Example 9 of Section 2.3, we used graphing to confirm that

$$\cos x \le \frac{\sin x}{x} \le \frac{1}{\cos x},$$

for $0 < |x| < 1$. Taking the limit as $x \to 0$ of each term in these inequalities, we find that

$$\underbrace{\lim_{x \to 0} \cos x}_{1} \le \lim_{x \to 0} \frac{\sin x}{x} \le \underbrace{\lim_{x \to 0} \frac{1}{\cos x}}_{1}.$$

The Squeeze Theorem (Theorem 2.5) now implies that $\lim\limits_{x \to 0} \dfrac{\sin x}{x} = 1$. The proof that $\lim\limits_{x \to 0} \dfrac{\cos x - 1}{x} = 0$ is found in Exercise 73. ◄

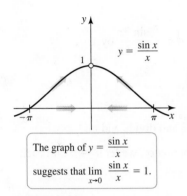

The graph of $y = \dfrac{\sin x}{x}$ suggests that $\lim\limits_{x \to 0} \dfrac{\sin x}{x} = 1$.

FIGURE 3.29

> $\lim\limits_{x \to 0} \dfrac{\sin x}{x} = 1$ implies that if $|x|$ is small, then $\sin x \approx x$.

EXAMPLE 1   **Calculating trigonometric limits** Evaluate the following limits.

a. $\lim\limits_{x \to 0} \dfrac{\sin 4x}{x}$ **b.** $\lim\limits_{x \to 0} \dfrac{\sin 3x}{\sin 5x}$

SOLUTION

a. To use the fact that $\lim\limits_{x \to 0} \dfrac{\sin x}{x} = 1$, the argument of the sine function in the numerator must be the same as the denominator. Multiplying and dividing $\dfrac{\sin 4x}{x}$ by 4, we evaluate the limit as follows:

$$\lim_{x \to 0} \frac{\sin 4x}{x} = \lim_{x \to 0} \frac{4 \sin 4x}{4x} \qquad \text{Multiply and divide by 4.}$$

$$= 4\lim_{t \to 0} \underbrace{\frac{\sin t}{t}}_{1} \qquad \text{Factor out 4 and let } t = 4x; t \to 0 \text{ as } x \to 0.$$

$$= 4(1) = 4. \qquad \text{Theorem 3.11}$$

b. The first step is to divide the numerator and denominator of $\dfrac{\sin 3x}{\sin 5x}$ by x:

$$\frac{\sin 3x}{\sin 5x} = \frac{(\sin 3x)/x}{(\sin 5x)/x}.$$

As in part (a), we now divide and multiply $\dfrac{\sin 3x}{x}$ by 3 and divide and multiply $\dfrac{\sin 5x}{x}$ by 5. In the numerator, we let $t = 3x$, and in the denominator, we let $u = 5x$. In each case, $t \to 0$ and $u \to 0$ as $x \to 0$. Therefore,

$$\lim_{x \to 0} \frac{\sin 3x}{\sin 5x} = \lim_{x \to 0} \frac{\dfrac{3 \sin 3x}{3x}}{\dfrac{5 \sin 5x}{5x}} \qquad \text{Multiply and divide by 3 and 5.}$$

$$= \frac{3}{5} \frac{\lim\limits_{t \to 0} (\sin t)/t}{\lim\limits_{u \to 0} (\sin u)/u} \qquad \text{Let } t = 3x \text{ in numerator and } u = 5x \text{ in denominator.}$$

$$= \frac{3}{5} \cdot \frac{1}{1} = \frac{3}{5}. \qquad \text{Both limits equal 1.}$$

Related Exercises 7–16 ◄

QUICK CHECK 1 Evaluate $\lim\limits_{x \to 0} \dfrac{\tan 2x}{x}$. ◄

We can now use the important limits of Theorem 3.11 to establish the derivatives of $\sin x$ and $\cos x$.

Derivatives of Sine and Cosine Functions

We start with the definition of the derivative,

$$f'(x) = \lim_{h \to 0} \frac{f(x + h) - f(x)}{h},$$

with $f(x) = \sin x$, and then appeal to the sine addition identity

$$\sin(x + h) = \sin x \cos h + \cos x \sin h.$$

The derivative is

$$
\begin{aligned}
f'(x) &= \lim_{h \to 0} \frac{\sin(x + h) - \sin x}{h} && \text{Definition of derivative} \\[2mm]
&= \lim_{h \to 0} \frac{\sin x \cos h + \cos x \sin h - \sin x}{h} && \text{Sine addition identity} \\[2mm]
&= \lim_{h \to 0} \frac{\sin x (\cos h - 1) + \cos x \sin h}{h} && \text{Factor } \sin x. \\[2mm]
&= \lim_{h \to 0} \frac{\sin x (\cos h - 1)}{h} + \lim_{h \to 0} \frac{\cos x \sin h}{h} && \text{Theorem 2.3} \\[2mm]
&= \sin x \underbrace{\left[\lim_{h \to 0} \frac{\cos h - 1}{h} \right]}_{0} + \cos x \underbrace{\left[\lim_{h \to 0} \frac{\sin h}{h} \right]}_{1} && \begin{array}{l}\text{Both } \sin x \text{ and } \cos x \text{ are} \\ \text{independent of } h.\end{array} \\[2mm]
&= (\sin x)(0) + \cos x (1) && \text{Theorem 3.11} \\[2mm]
&= \cos x. && \text{Simplify.}
\end{aligned}
$$

We have proved the important result that $\dfrac{d}{dx}(\sin x) = \cos x$.

The fact that $\dfrac{d}{dx}(\cos x) = -\sin x$ is proved in a similar way using a cosine addition identity (Exercise 75).

THEOREM 3.12   **Derivatives of Sine and Cosine**

$$\frac{d}{dx}(\sin x) = \cos x \qquad \frac{d}{dx}(\cos x) = -\sin x$$

From a geometric point of view, these derivative formulas make sense. Because $f(x) = \sin x$ is a periodic function, we expect its derivative to be periodic. Observe that the horizontal tangent lines on the graph of $f(x) = \sin x$ (Figure 3.30a) occur at the zeros of $f'(x) = \cos x$. Similarly, the horizontal tangent lines on the graph of $f(x) = \cos x$ occur at the zeros of $f'(x) = -\sin x$ (Figure 3.30b).

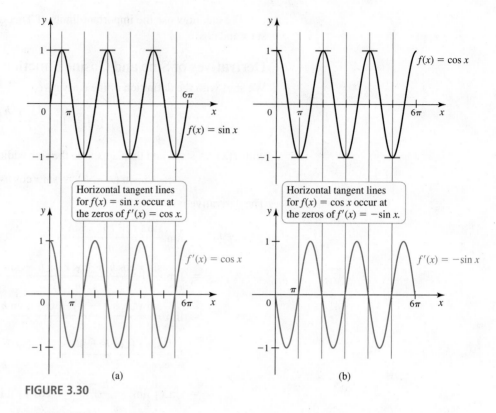

FIGURE 3.30

QUICK CHECK 2 At what points on the interval $[0, 2\pi]$ does the graph of $f(x) = \sin x$ have tangent lines with positive slopes? At what points on the interval $[0, 2\pi]$ is $\cos x > 0$? Explain the connection. ◄

EXAMPLE 2 Derivatives involving trigonometric functions Calculate dy/dx for the following functions.

a. $y = e^{2x} \cos x$ **b.** $y = \sin x - x \cos x$ **c.** $y = \dfrac{1 + \sin x}{1 - \sin x}$

SOLUTION

a. $\dfrac{dy}{dx} = \dfrac{d}{dx}(e^{2x} \cdot \cos x) = \overbrace{2e^{2x} \cos x}^{\substack{\text{derivative of } e^{2x} \\ \cdot \cos x}} + \overbrace{e^{2x}(-\sin x)}^{\substack{e^{2x} \cdot \text{ the} \\ \text{derivative of } \cos x}}$ Product Rule

$\qquad\quad = e^{2x}(2 \cos x - \sin x)$ Simplify.

b. $\dfrac{dy}{dx} = \dfrac{d}{dx}(\sin x) - \dfrac{d}{dx}(x \cos x)$ Difference Rule

$\qquad\quad = \cos x - \big[\underbrace{(1) \cos x}_{\substack{\text{derivative of } x \\ \cdot \cos x}} + \underbrace{x(-\sin x)}_{\substack{x \cdot \text{derivative of} \\ \cos x}}\big]$ Product Rule

$\qquad\quad = x \sin x$ Simplify.

c.
$$\frac{dy}{dx} = \frac{(1 - \sin x)\overbrace{(\cos x)}^{\text{derivative of } 1 + \sin x} - (1 + \sin x)\overbrace{(-\cos x)}^{\text{derivative of } 1 - \sin x}}{(1 - \sin x)^2}$$ Quotient Rule

$$= \frac{\cos x - \cos x \sin x + \cos x + \sin x \cos x}{(1 - \sin x)^2}$$ Expand.

$$= \frac{2 \cos x}{(1 - \sin x)^2}$$ Simplify.

Related Exercises 17–28 ◄

Derivatives of Other Trigonometric Functions

The derivatives of $\tan x$, $\cot x$, $\sec x$, and $\csc x$ are obtained using the derivatives of $\sin x$ and $\cos x$ together with the Quotient Rule and trigonometric identities.

EXAMPLE 3 Derivative of the tangent function Calculate $\dfrac{d}{dx}(\tan x)$.

> Recall that $\tan x = \dfrac{\sin x}{\cos x}$, $\cot x = \dfrac{\cos x}{\sin x}$, $\sec x = \dfrac{1}{\cos x}$, and $\csc x = \dfrac{1}{\sin x}$.

SOLUTION Using the identity $\tan x = \dfrac{\sin x}{\cos x}$ and the Quotient Rule, we have

$$\frac{d}{dx}(\tan x) = \frac{d}{dx}\left(\frac{\sin x}{\cos x}\right)$$

$$= \frac{\cos x \overbrace{\cos x}^{\text{derivative of } \sin x} - \sin x \overbrace{(-\sin x)}^{\text{derivative of } \cos x}}{\cos^2 x}$$ Quotient Rule

$$= \frac{\cos^2 x + \sin^2 x}{\cos^2 x}$$ Simplify numerator.

$$= \frac{1}{\cos^2 x} = \sec^2 x.$$ $\cos^2 x + \sin^2 x = 1$

> One way to remember Theorem 3.13 is to learn the derivatives of the sine, tangent, and secant functions. Then, replace each function by its corresponding **cofunction** and put a negative sign on the right-hand side of the new derivative formula.
>
> $$\frac{d}{dx}(\sin x) = \cos x \quad \leftrightarrow$$
>
> $$\frac{d}{dx}(\cos x) = -\sin x$$
>
> $$\frac{d}{dx}(\tan x) = \sec^2 x \quad \leftrightarrow$$
>
> $$\frac{d}{dx}(\cot x) = -\csc^2 x$$
>
> $$\frac{d}{dx}(\sec x) = \sec x \tan x \quad \leftrightarrow$$
>
> $$\frac{d}{dx}(\csc x) = -\csc x \cot x$$

Therefore, $\dfrac{d}{dx}(\tan x) = \sec^2 x.$ *Related Exercises 29–31* ◄

The derivatives of $\cot x$, $\sec x$, and $\csc x$ are given in Theorem 3.13 (Exercises 29–31).

THEOREM 3.13 Derivatives of the Trigonometric Functions

$$\frac{d}{dx}(\sin x) = \cos x \qquad \frac{d}{dx}(\cos x) = -\sin x$$

$$\frac{d}{dx}(\tan x) = \sec^2 x \qquad \frac{d}{dx}(\cot x) = -\csc^2 x$$

$$\frac{d}{dx}(\sec x) = \sec x \tan x \qquad \frac{d}{dx}(\csc x) = -\csc x \cot x$$

QUICK CHECK 3 The formulas for $\dfrac{d}{dx}(\cot x)$, $\dfrac{d}{dx}(\sec x)$, and $\dfrac{d}{dx}(\csc x)$ can be determined using the Quotient Rule. Why? ◄

EXAMPLE 4   Derivatives involving sec *x* and csc *x*   Find the derivative of $y = \sec x \csc x$.

SOLUTION

$$\frac{dy}{dx} = \frac{d}{dx}\left(\sec x \cdot \csc x\right)$$

$$= \underbrace{\sec x \tan x \csc x}_{\text{derivative of } \sec x} + \sec x \underbrace{\left(-\csc x \cot x\right)}_{\text{derivative of } \csc x} \qquad \text{Product Rule}$$

$$= \underbrace{\frac{1}{\cos x}}_{\sec x} \cdot \underbrace{\frac{\sin x}{\cos x}}_{\tan x} \cdot \underbrace{\frac{1}{\sin x}}_{\csc x} - \underbrace{\frac{1}{\cos x}}_{\sec x} \cdot \underbrace{\frac{1}{\sin x}}_{\csc x} \cdot \underbrace{\frac{\cos x}{\sin x}}_{\cot x} \qquad \begin{array}{l}\text{Write functions in terms of} \\ \sin x \text{ and } \cos x.\end{array}$$

$$= \frac{1}{\cos^2 x} - \frac{1}{\sin^2 x} \qquad\qquad\qquad \text{Cancel and simplify.}$$

$$= \sec^2 x - \csc^2 x \qquad\qquad\qquad \text{Definition of } \sec x \text{ and } \csc x$$

Related Exercises 32–40 ◄

QUICK CHECK 4 Why is the derivative of $\sec x \csc x$ equal to the derivative of $\dfrac{1}{\cos x \sin x}$? ◄

Higher-Order Trigonometric Derivatives

Higher-order derivatives of the sine and cosine functions are important in many applications, particularly in problems that involve oscillations, vibrations, or waves. A few higher-order derivatives of $y = \sin x$ reveal a pattern.

$$\frac{dy}{dx} = \cos x \qquad\qquad \frac{d^2 y}{dx^2} = \frac{d}{dx}(\cos x) = -\sin x$$

$$\frac{d^3 y}{dx^3} = \frac{d}{dx}(-\sin x) = -\cos x \qquad\qquad \frac{d^4 y}{dx^4} = \frac{d}{dx}(-\cos x) = \sin x$$

We see that the higher-order derivatives of $\sin x$ cycle back periodically to $\pm \sin x$. In general, it can be shown that $\dfrac{d^{2n} y}{dx^{2n}} = (-1)^n \sin x$, with a similar result for $\cos x$ (Exercise 80). This cyclic behavior in the derivatives of $\sin x$ and $\cos x$ does not occur with the other trigonometric functions.

QUICK CHECK 5 Find $\dfrac{d^2 y}{dx^2}$ and $\dfrac{d^4 y}{dx^4}$ when $y = \cos x$. Find $\dfrac{d^{40} y}{dx^{40}}$ and $\dfrac{d^{42} y}{dx^{42}}$ when $y = \sin x$. ◄

EXAMPLE 5   Second-order derivatives   Find the second derivative of $y = \csc x$.

SOLUTION   By Theorem 3.13, $\dfrac{dy}{dx} = -\csc x \cot x$.

Applying the Product Rule gives the second derivative:

$$\frac{d^2 y}{dx^2} = \frac{d}{dx}(-\csc x \cot x)$$

$$= \left(\frac{d}{dx}(-\csc x)\right)\cot x - \csc x \frac{d}{dx}(\cot x) \qquad \text{Product Rule}$$

$$= (\csc x \cot x)\cot x - \csc x\left(-\csc^2 x\right) \qquad \text{Calculate derivatives.}$$

$$= \csc x\left(\cot^2 x + \csc^2 x\right). \qquad\qquad\qquad \text{Factor.}$$

Related Exercises 41–48 ◄

SECTION 3.5 EXERCISES

Review Questions

1. Why is it not possible to evaluate $\lim\limits_{x \to 0} \dfrac{\sin x}{x}$ by direct substitution?

2. How is $\lim\limits_{x \to 0} \dfrac{\sin x}{x}$ used in this section?

3. Explain why the Quotient Rule is used to determine the derivative of $\tan x$ and $\cot x$.

4. How can you use the derivatives $\dfrac{d}{dx}(\sin x) = \cos x$, $\dfrac{d}{dx}(\tan x) = \sec^2 x$, and $\dfrac{d}{dx}(\sec x) = \sec x \tan x$ to remember the derivatives of $\cos x$, $\cot x$, and $\csc x$?

5. Let $f(x) = \sin x$. What is the value of $f'(\pi)$?

6. Where does the graph of $\sin x$ have a horizontal tangent line? Where does $\cos x$ have a value of zero? Explain the connection between these two observations.

Basic Skills

7–16. Trigonometric limits *Use Theorem 3.11 to evaluate the following limits.*

7. $\lim\limits_{x \to 0} \dfrac{\sin 3x}{x}$

8. $\lim\limits_{x \to 0} \dfrac{\sin 5x}{3x}$

9. $\lim\limits_{x \to 0} \dfrac{\sin 7x}{\sin 3x}$

10. $\lim\limits_{x \to 0} \dfrac{\sin 3x}{\tan 4x}$

11. $\lim\limits_{x \to 0} \dfrac{\tan 5x}{x}$

12. $\lim\limits_{\theta \to 0} \dfrac{\cos^2 \theta - 1}{\theta}$

13. $\lim\limits_{x \to 0} \dfrac{\tan 7x}{\sin x}$

14. $\lim\limits_{\theta \to 0} \dfrac{\sec \theta - 1}{\theta}$

15. $\lim\limits_{x \to 2} \dfrac{\sin (x - 2)}{x^2 - 4}$

16. $\lim\limits_{x \to -3} \dfrac{\sin (x + 3)}{x^2 + 8x + 15}$

17–28. Calculating derivatives *Find dy/dx for the following functions.*

17. $y = \sin x + \cos x$

18. $y = 5x^2 + \cos x$

19. $y = e^{-x} \sin x$

20. $y = \sin x + 4e^{0.5x}$

21. $y = x \sin x$

22. $y = e^{6x} \sin x$

23. $y = \dfrac{\cos x}{\sin x + 1}$

24. $y = \dfrac{1 - \sin x}{1 + \sin x}$

25. $y = \sin x \cos x$

26. $y = \dfrac{(x^2 - 1) \sin x}{\sin x + 1}$

27. $y = \cos^2 x$

28. $y = \dfrac{x \sin x}{1 + \cos x}$

29–31. Derivatives of other trigonometric functions *Verify the following derivative formulas using the Quotient Rule.*

29. $\dfrac{d}{dx}(\cot x) = -\csc^2 x$

30. $\dfrac{d}{dx}(\sec x) = \sec x \tan x$

31. $\dfrac{d}{dx}(\csc x) = -\csc x \cot x$

32–40. Derivatives involving other trigonometric functions *Find the derivative of the following functions.*

32. $y = \tan x + \cot x$

33. $y = \sec x + \csc x$

34. $y = \sec x \tan x$

35. $y = e^{5x} \csc x$

36. $y = \dfrac{\tan w}{1 + \tan w}$

37. $y = \dfrac{\cot x}{1 + \csc x}$

38. $y = \dfrac{\tan t}{1 + \sec t}$

39. $y = \dfrac{1}{\sec z \csc z}$

40. $y = \csc^2 \theta - 1$

41–48. Second-order derivatives *Find y'' for the following functions.*

41. $y = x \sin x$

42. $y = \cos x$

43. $y = e^x \sin x$

44. $y = \dfrac{1}{2} e^x \cos x$

45. $y = \cot x$

46. $y = \tan x$

47. $y = \sec x \csc x$

48. $y = \cos \theta \sin \theta$

Further Explorations

49. **Explain why or why not** Determine whether the following statements are true, and give an explanation or a counterexample.

    a. $\dfrac{d}{dx}(\sin^2 x) = \cos^2 x$.   b. $\dfrac{d^2}{dx^2}(\sin x) = \sin x$.

    c. $\dfrac{d^4}{dx^4}(\cos x) = \cos x$.

    d. The function $\sec x$ is not differentiable at $x = \pi/2$.

50–55. Trigonometric limits *Evaluate the following limits or state that they do not exist.*

50. $\lim\limits_{x \to 0} \dfrac{\sin ax}{bx}$, where a and b are constants with $b \neq 0$

51. $\lim\limits_{x \to 0} \dfrac{\sin ax}{\sin bx}$, where a and b are constants with $b \neq 0$

52. $\lim\limits_{x \to \pi/2} \dfrac{\cos x}{x - (\pi/2)}$

53. $\lim\limits_{x \to 0} \dfrac{3 \sec^5 x}{x^2 + 4}$

54. $\lim\limits_{x \to \infty} \dfrac{\cos x}{x}$

55. $\lim\limits_{x \to \pi/4} 3 \csc 2x \cot 2x$

56–61. Calculating derivatives *Find dy/dx for the following functions.*

56. $y = \dfrac{\sin x}{1 + \cos x}$

57. $y = x \cos x \sin x$

58. $y = \dfrac{1}{2 + \sin x}$

59. $y = \dfrac{\sin x}{\sin x - \cos x}$

60. $y = \dfrac{x \cos x}{1 + x^3}$

61. $y = \dfrac{1 - \cos x}{1 + \cos x}$

62–65. Equations of tangent lines

a. *Find an equation of the line tangent to the following curves at the given value of x.*

b. *Use a graphing utility to plot the curve and the tangent line.*

62. $y = 4 \sin x \cos x$; $x = \dfrac{\pi}{3}$

63. $y = 1 + 2 \sin x$; $x = \dfrac{\pi}{6}$

64. $y = \csc x$; $x = \dfrac{\pi}{4}$

65. $y = \dfrac{\cos x}{1 - \cos x}$; $x = \dfrac{\pi}{3}$

66. Locations of tangent lines

a. For what values of x does $g(x) = x - \sin x$ have a horizontal tangent line?

b. For what values of x does $g(x) = x - \sin x$ have a slope of 1?

67. Locations of horizontal tangent lines For what values of x does $f(x) = x - 2 \cos x$ have a horizontal tangent line?

68. Matching Match the graphs of the functions in a–d with the graphs of their derivatives in A–D.

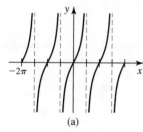

(a)

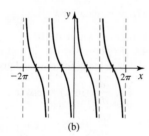

(b)

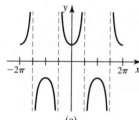

(c)

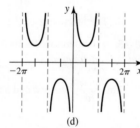

(d)

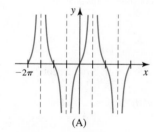

(A)

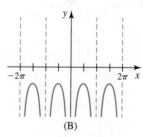

(B)

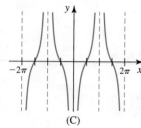

(C)

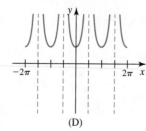

(D)

Applications

69. Velocity of an oscillator An object oscillates along a vertical line, and its position in centimeters is given by $y(t) = 30 (\sin t - 1)$, where $t \geq 0$ is measured in seconds and y is positive in the upward direction.

a. Graph the position function, for $0 \leq t \leq 10$.

b. Find the velocity of the oscillator, $v(t) = y'(t)$.

c. Graph the velocity function, for $0 \leq t \leq 10$.

d. At what times and positions is the velocity zero?

e. At what times and positions is the velocity a maximum?

f. The acceleration of the oscillator is $a(t) = v'(t)$. Find and graph the acceleration function.

70. Damped sine wave The graph of $f(t) = e^{-kt} \sin t$ with $k > 0$ is called a *damped* sine wave; it is used in a variety of applications, such as modeling the vibrations of a shock absorber.

a. Use a graphing utility to graph f for $k = 1, \frac{1}{2}$, and $\frac{1}{10}$ to understand why these curves are called damped sine waves. What effect does k have on the behavior of the graph?

b. Compute $f'(t)$ for $k = 1$, and use it to determine where the graph of f has a horizontal tangent.

c. Evaluate $\lim\limits_{t \to \infty} e^{-t} \sin t$ by using the Squeeze Theorem. What does the result say about the oscillations of a damped sine wave?

71. A differential equation A differential equation is an equation involving an unknown function and its derivatives. Consider the differential equation $y''(t) + y(t) = 0$ (see Chapter 8).

a. Show that $y = A \sin t$ satisfies the equation for any constant A.

b. Show that $y = B \cos t$ satisfies the equation for any constant B.

c. Show that $y = A \sin t + B \cos t$ satisfies the equation for any constants A and B.

Additional Exercises

72. Using identities Use the identity $\sin 2x = 2 \sin x \cos x$ to find $\dfrac{d}{dx} (\sin 2x)$. Then use the identity $\cos 2x = \cos^2 x - \sin^2 x$ to express the derivative of $\sin 2x$ in terms of $\cos 2x$.

73. Proof of $\lim\limits_{x \to 0} \dfrac{\cos x - 1}{x} = 0$ Use the trigonometric identity $\cos^2 x + \sin^2 x = 1$ to prove that $\lim\limits_{x \to 0} \dfrac{\cos x - 1}{x} = 0$. (*Hint:* Begin by multiplying the numerator and denominator by $\cos x + 1$.)

74. Another method for proving $\lim\limits_{x \to 0} \dfrac{\cos x - 1}{x} = 0$

Use the half-angle formula $\sin^2 x = \dfrac{1 - \cos 2x}{2}$ to prove that

$$\lim_{x \to 0} \frac{\cos x - 1}{x} = 0.$$

75. Proof of $\dfrac{d}{dx} (\cos x) = -\sin x$ Use the definition of the derivative and the trigonometric identity

$$\cos (x + h) = \cos x \cos h - \sin x \sin h$$

to prove that $\dfrac{d}{dx} (\cos x) = -\sin x$.

76. Continuity of a piecewise function Let

$$f(x) = \begin{cases} \dfrac{3\sin x}{x} & \text{if } x \neq 0 \\ a & \text{if } x = 0. \end{cases}$$

For what values of a is f continuous?

77. Continuity of a piecewise function Let

$$g(x) = \begin{cases} \dfrac{1 - \cos x}{2x} & \text{if } x \neq 0 \\ a & \text{if } x = 0. \end{cases}$$

For what values of a is g continuous?

78. Computing limits with angles in degrees Suppose your graphing calculator has two functions, one called $\sin x$, which calculates the sine of x when x is in radians, and the other called $s(x)$, which calculates the sine of x when x is in degrees.

a. Explain why $s(x) = \sin\left(\dfrac{\pi}{180}x\right)$.

b. Evaluate $\displaystyle\lim_{x \to 0} \dfrac{s(x)}{x}$. Verify your answer by estimating the limit on your calculator.

79. Derivatives of $\sin^n x$ Calculate the following derivatives using the Product Rule.

a. $\dfrac{d}{dx}(\sin^2 x)$ b. $\dfrac{d}{dx}(\sin^3 x)$ c. $\dfrac{d}{dx}(\sin^4 x)$

d. Based upon your answers to parts (a)–(c), make a conjecture about $\dfrac{d}{dx}(\sin^n x)$, where n is a positive integer. Then prove the result by induction.

80. Higher-order derivatives of $\sin x$ and $\cos x$ Prove that $\dfrac{d^{2n}}{dx^{2n}}(\sin x) = (-1)^n \sin x$ and $\dfrac{d^{2n}}{dx^{2n}}(\cos x) = (-1)^n \cos x$.

81–84. Identifying derivatives from limits *The following limits equal the derivative of a function f at a point a.*

a. *Find one possible f and a.*
b. *Evaluate the limit.*

81. $\displaystyle\lim_{h \to 0} \dfrac{\sin\left(\frac{\pi}{6} + h\right) - \frac{1}{2}}{h}$

82. $\displaystyle\lim_{h \to 0} \dfrac{\cos\left(\frac{\pi}{6} + h\right) - \frac{\sqrt{3}}{2}}{h}$

83. $\displaystyle\lim_{x \to \pi/4} \dfrac{\cot x - 1}{x - \frac{\pi}{4}}$

84. $\displaystyle\lim_{h \to 0} \dfrac{\tan\left(\frac{5\pi}{6} + h\right) + \frac{1}{\sqrt{3}}}{h}$

Technology Exercises

85–88. Difference quotients *Suppose f is a differentiable function and consider the function*

$$D(x) = \dfrac{f(x + 0.01) - f(x)}{0.01},$$

where x is in the domain of f. For the following functions, carry out these steps.

a. *Before graphing D, describe the graph you expect to see.*
b. *Graph D on the given interval.*
c. *Change 0.01 to 0.001 in the definition of D and describe the change you see in the graph of D. Explain what you observe.*

85. $f(x) = \sin x$ on $[-\pi, \pi]$ **86.** $f(x) = \cos x$ on $[0, 2\pi]$

87. $f(x) = \dfrac{x^3}{3} + 1$ on $[-2, 2]$ **88.** $f(x) = \tan x$ on $\left[-\dfrac{\pi}{3}, \dfrac{\pi}{3}\right]$

QUICK CHECK ANSWERS

1. 2 **2.** $0 < x < \frac{\pi}{2}$ and $\frac{3\pi}{2} < x < 2\pi$. The value of $\cos x$ is the slope of the line tangent to the curve $y = \sin x$.

3. The Quotient Rule is used because each function is a quotient when written in terms of the sine and cosine functions.

4. $\dfrac{1}{\cos x \sin x} = \dfrac{1}{\cos x} \cdot \dfrac{1}{\sin x} = \sec x \csc x$

5. $\dfrac{d^2 y}{dx^2} = -\cos x$, $\dfrac{d^4 y}{dx^4} = \cos x$, $\dfrac{d^{40}}{dx^{40}}(\sin x) = \sin x$, $\dfrac{d^{42}}{dx^{42}}(\sin x) = -\sin x$ ◄

3.6 Derivatives as Rates of Change

The theme of this section is the *derivative as a rate of change*. Observing the world around us, we see that almost everything is in a state of change: The size of the Internet is increasing; your blood pressure fluctuates; as supply increases, prices decrease; and the universe is expanding. This section explores a few of the many applications of this idea and demonstrates why calculus is called the mathematics of change.

One-Dimensional Motion

> When describing the motion of objects, it is customary to use t as the independent variable to represent time. Generally, motion is assumed to begin at $t = 0$.

Describing the motion of objects such as projectiles and planets was one of the challenges that led to the development of calculus in the 17th century. We begin by considering the motion of an object confined to one dimension; that is, the object moves along a line. This motion could be horizontal (for example, a car moving along a straight highway) or it could be vertical (such as a projectile launched vertically into the air).

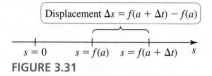

$$\text{Displacement } \Delta s = f(a + \Delta t) - f(a)$$

$s = 0 \quad s = f(a) \quad s = f(a + \Delta t) \quad s$

FIGURE 3.31

Position and Velocity   Suppose an object moves along a straight line and its location at time t is given by the **position function** $s = f(t)$. All positions are measured relative to the reference point $s = 0$. The **displacement** of the object between $t = a$ and $t = a + \Delta t$ is $\Delta s = f(a + \Delta t) - f(a)$, where the elapsed time is Δt units (Figure 3.31).

Recall from Section 2.1 that the *average velocity* of the object over the interval $[a, a + \Delta t]$ is the displacement Δs of the object divided by the elapsed time Δt:

$$v_{av} = \frac{\Delta s}{\Delta t} = \frac{f(a + \Delta t) - f(a)}{\Delta t}.$$

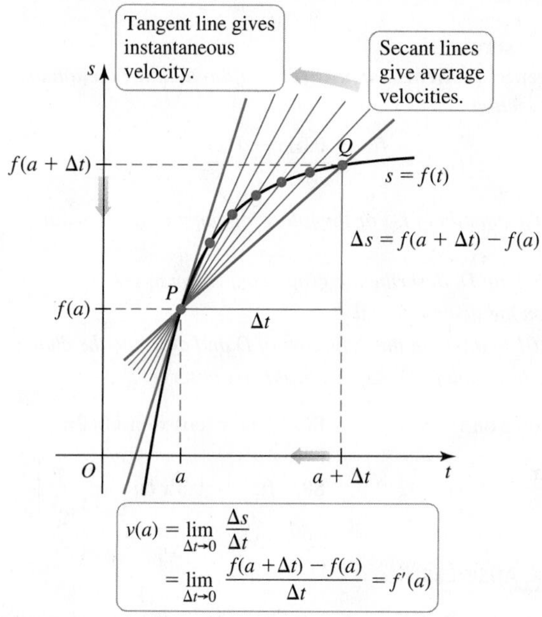

The average velocity is the slope of the secant line passing through the points $P(a, f(a))$ and $Q(a + \Delta t, f(a + \Delta t))$ (Figure 3.32).

As Δt approaches 0, the average velocity is calculated over smaller and smaller time intervals, and the limiting value of these average velocities, when it exists, is the *instantaneous velocity* at a. This is the same argument used to arrive at the derivative. The conclusion is that the instantaneous velocity at time a, denoted $v(a)$, is the derivative of the position function evaluated at a:

$$v(a) = \lim_{\Delta t \to 0} \frac{f(a + \Delta t) - f(a)}{\Delta t} = f'(a).$$

Equivalently, the instantaneous velocity at a is the rate of change of the position function at a; it also equals the slope of the line tangent to the curve $s = f(t)$ at $P(a, f(a))$.

Tangent line gives instantaneous velocity.

Secant lines give average velocities.

$f(a + \Delta t)$

$s = f(t)$

$\Delta s = f(a + \Delta t) - f(a)$

$f(a)$

Δt

$O \quad a \quad a + \Delta t \quad t$

$$v(a) = \lim_{\Delta t \to 0} \frac{\Delta s}{\Delta t}$$
$$= \lim_{\Delta t \to 0} \frac{f(a + \Delta t) - f(a)}{\Delta t} = f'(a)$$

FIGURE 3.32

▷ Using the various derivative notations, the velocity is also written $v(t) = s'(t) = ds/dt$. If *average* or *instantaneous* is not specified, *velocity* is understood to mean instantaneous velocity.

DEFINITION Average and Instantaneous Velocity

Let $s = f(t)$ be the position function of an object moving along a line. The **average velocity** of the object over the time interval $[a, a + \Delta t]$ is the slope of the secant line between $(a, f(a))$ and $(a + \Delta t, f(a + \Delta t))$:

$$v_{av} = \frac{f(a + \Delta t) - f(a)}{\Delta t}.$$

The **instantaneous velocity** at a is the slope of the line tangent to the position curve, which is the derivative of the position function:

$$v(a) = \lim_{\Delta t \to 0} \frac{f(a + \Delta t) - f(a)}{\Delta t} = f'(a).$$

QUICK CHECK 1 Does the speedometer in your car measure average or instantaneous velocity? ◁

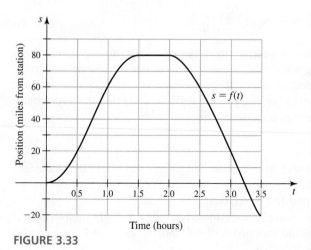

FIGURE 3.33

EXAMPLE 1   Position and velocity of a patrol car   Assume a police station is located along a straight east-west freeway. At noon ($t = 0$), a patrol car leaves the station heading east. The position function of the car $s = f(t)$ gives the location of the car in miles east ($s > 0$) or west ($s < 0$) of the station t hours after noon (Figure 3.33).

a. Describe the location of the patrol car during the first 3.5 hr of the trip.

b. Calculate the average velocity of the car between noon and 2:00 P.M. ($0 \le t \le 2$).

c. Calculate the displacement and average velocity of the car between 2:00 P.M. and 3:30 P.M. ($2 \le t \le 3.5$).

d. At what time(s) is the instantaneous velocity greatest *as the car travels east*?

e. At what time(s) is the patrol car at rest?

SOLUTION

a. The graph of the position function indicates the car travels 80 miles east between $t = 0$ (noon) and $t = 1.5$ (1:30 P.M.). The position of the car does not change from $t = 1.5$ to $t = 2$, and therefore, the car is at rest from 1:30 P.M. to 2:00 P.M. Starting at $t = 2$, the car's distance from the station decreases, which means the car travels west, eventually ending up 20 miles west of the station at $t = 3.5$ (3:30 P.M.) (Figure 3.34).

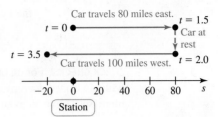

FIGURE 3.34

b. Using Figure 3.33, we find that $f(0) = 0$ and $f(2) = 80$. Therefore, the average velocity during the first 2 hours is

$$v_{av} = \frac{\Delta s}{\Delta t} = \frac{f(2) - f(0)}{2 - 0} = \frac{80 \text{ mi}}{2 \text{ hr}} = 40 \text{ mi/hr.}$$

c. The position of the car at 3:30 P.M. is $f(3.5) = -20$ (the negative sign indicates the car is 20 miles *west* of the station), and the position of the car at 2:00 P.M. is $f(2) = 80$. Therefore, the displacement is

$$\Delta s = f(3.5) - f(2) = -20 \text{ mi} - 80 \text{ mi} = -100 \text{ mi}$$

during an elapsed time of $\Delta t = 3.5 - 2 = 1.5$ hr (the *negative* displacement indicates that the car moved 100 miles *west*). The average velocity is

$$v_{av} = \frac{\Delta s}{\Delta t} = \frac{-100 \text{ mi}}{1.5 \text{ hr}} \approx -66.667 \text{ mi/hr.}$$

d. The greatest eastward instantaneous velocity corresponds to points at which the graph of the position function has the greatest positive slope. The greatest slope appears to occur between $t = 0.5$ and $t = 1$. During this time interval, the car also has a nearly constant velocity because the curve is approximately linear. We conclude that the eastward velocity is largest from 12:30 to 1:00.

e. The car is at rest when the instantaneous velocity is zero. So we look for points at which the slope of the curve is zero. These points occur at times between $t = 1.5$ and $t = 2$.   *Related Exercises 7–8* ◀

Speed and Acceleration   When only the magnitude of the velocity is of interest, we use *speed*, which is the absolute value of the velocity:

$$\text{speed} = |v|.$$

For example, a car with an instantaneous velocity of -30 mi/hr has a speed of 30 mi/hr.

A more complete description of an object moving along a line includes its *acceleration*, which is the rate of change of the velocity; that is, acceleration is the derivative of the velocity function with respect to time t. If the acceleration is positive, the object's velocity increases; if it is negative, the object's velocity decreases. Because velocity is the derivative of the position function, acceleration is the second derivative of the position. Therefore,

> ➤ Newton's First Law of Motion says that in the absence of external forces, a moving object has no acceleration, which means the magnitude and direction of the velocity are constant.

$$a = \frac{dv}{dt} = \frac{d^2 s}{dt^2}.$$

DEFINITION Velocity, Speed, and Acceleration

Suppose an object moves along a line with position $s = f(t)$. Then

$$\text{the velocity at time } t \text{ is} \qquad v = \frac{ds}{dt} = f'(t),$$

$$\text{the speed at time } t \text{ is} \qquad |v| = |f'(t)|, \text{ and}$$

$$\text{the acceleration at time } t \text{ is} \qquad a = \frac{dv}{dt} = \frac{d^2s}{dt^2} = f''(t).$$

QUICK CHECK 2 For an object moving along a line, is it possible for its velocity to increase while its speed decreases? Is it possible for its velocity to decrease while its speed increases? Give an example to support your answers. ◄

> The units of derivatives are consistent with the notation. If s is measured in meters and t is measured in seconds, the units of the velocity $\dfrac{ds}{dt}$ are m/s. The units of the acceleration $\dfrac{d^2s}{dt^2}$ are m/s².

EXAMPLE 2   Velocity and acceleration Suppose the position (in feet) of an object moving horizontally at time t (in seconds) is $s = t^2 - 5t$, for $0 \le t \le 5$ (Figure 3.35). Assume that positive values of s correspond to positions to the right of $s = 0$.

a. Graph the velocity function on the interval $0 \le t \le 5$, and determine when the object is stationary, moving to the left, and moving to the right.

b. Graph the acceleration function on the interval $0 \le t \le 5$.

c. Describe the motion of the object.

SOLUTION

a. The velocity is $v = s'(t) = 2t - 5$. The object is stationary when $v = 2t - 5 = 0$, or at $t = 2.5$. Solving $v = 2t - 5 > 0$, the velocity is positive (motion to the right) for $\frac{5}{2} < t \le 5$. Similarly, the velocity is negative (motion to the left) for $0 \le t < \frac{5}{2}$. Though the velocity of the object is increasing at all times, its speed $|v|$ is decreasing for $0 \le t < \frac{5}{2}$, and then increasing for $\frac{5}{2} < t \le 5$. The graph of the velocity function (Figure 3.36) confirms these observations.

b. The acceleration is the derivative of the velocity or $a = v'(t) = s''(t) = 2$. This means that the acceleration is 2 ft/s², for $0 \le t \le 5$ (Figure 3.37).

c. Starting at an initial position of $s(0) = 0$, the object moves in the negative direction (to the left) with decreasing speed until it comes to rest momentarily at $s\left(\frac{5}{2}\right) = -\frac{25}{4}$. The object then moves in the positive direction (to the right) with increasing speed, reaching its initial position at $t = 5$. During this time interval, the acceleration is constant.

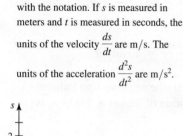

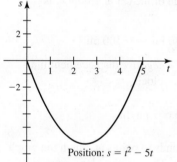

Position: $s = t^2 - 5t$

FIGURE 3.35

> Figure 3.35 gives the graph of the position function, not the path of the object. The motion is along a horizontal line.

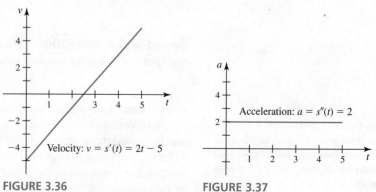

Velocity: $v = s'(t) = 2t - 5$

FIGURE 3.36

Acceleration: $a = s''(t) = 2$

FIGURE 3.37

Related Exercises 9–14 ◄

QUICK CHECK 3 Describe the velocity of an object that has a positive constant acceleration. Could an object have a positive acceleration and a decreasing speed? ◄

> The acceleration due to Earth's gravitational field is denoted g. In metric units $g \approx 9.8$ m/s² on the surface of Earth; in the U.S. Customary System (USCS), $g \approx 32$ ft/s².

Free Fall We now consider a problem in which an object moves vertically in Earth's gravitational field, assuming that no other forces (such as air resistance) are at work.

▷ The position function in Example 3 is derived in Section 6.1. Once again we mention that the graph of the position function is not the path of the stone.

EXAMPLE 3 Motion in a gravitational field Suppose a stone is thrown vertically upward with an initial velocity of 64 ft/s from a bridge 96 ft above a river. By Newton's laws of motion, the position of the stone (measured as the height above the river) after t seconds is

$$s(t) = -16t^2 + 64t + 96,$$

where $s = 0$ is the level of the river (Figure 3.38a).

a. Find the velocity and acceleration functions.

b. What is the highest point above the river reached by the stone?

c. With what velocity will the stone strike the river?

SOLUTION

a. The velocity of the stone is the derivative of the position function, and its acceleration is the derivative of the velocity function. Therefore,

$$v = \frac{ds}{dt} = -32t + 64 \quad \text{and} \quad a = \frac{dv}{dt} = -32.$$

b. When the stone reaches its high point, its velocity is zero (Figure 3.38b). Solving $v(t) = -32t + 64 = 0$ yields $t = 2$, and thus the stone reaches its maximum height 2 seconds after it is thrown. Its height (in feet) at that instant is

$$s(2) = -16(2)^2 + 64(2) + 96 = 160.$$

c. To determine the velocity at which the stone strikes the river, we first determine *when* it reaches the river. The stone strikes the river when $s(t) = -16t^2 + 64t + 96 = 0$. Dividing both sides of the equation by -16, we obtain $t^2 - 4t - 6 = 0$. Using the quadratic formula, the solutions are $t \approx 5.162$ or $t \approx -1.162$. Because the stone is thrown at $t = 0$, only positive values of t are of interest; therefore, the relevant root is $t \approx 5.162$. The velocity of the stone (in ft/s) when it strikes the river is approximately

$$v(5.162) = -32(5.162) + 64 = -101.184.$$

Related Exercises 15–16 ◀

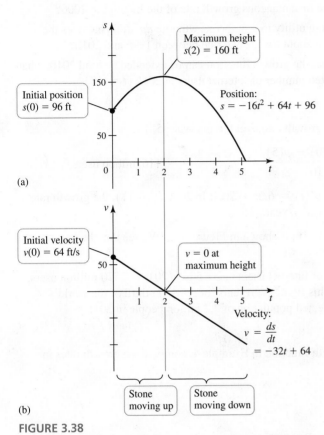

FIGURE 3.38

Maximum height $s(2) = 160$ ft

Initial position $s(0) = 96$ ft

Position: $s = -16t^2 + 64t + 96$

(a)

Initial velocity $v(0) = 64$ ft/s

$v = 0$ at maximum height

Velocity: $v = \dfrac{ds}{dt} = -32t + 64$

Stone moving up

Stone moving down

(b)

QUICK CHECK 4 In Example 3, does the rock have a greater speed at $t = 1$ or $t = 3$? ◀

Growth Models

Much of the change in the world around us can be classified as *growth*: Populations, prices, and computer networks all tend to increase in size. Modeling growth is important because it often leads to an understanding of underlying processes and allows for predictions.

We let $p = f(t)$ be the measure of a quantity of interest (for example, the population of a species or the consumer price index), where $t \geq 0$ represents time. The average growth rate of p between time $t = a$ and a later time $t = a + \Delta t$ is the change Δp divided by elapsed time Δt. Therefore, the **average growth rate** of p on the interval $[a, a + \Delta t]$ is

$$\frac{\Delta p}{\Delta t} = \frac{f(a + \Delta t) - f(a)}{\Delta t}.$$

If we now let $\Delta t \to 0$, then $\dfrac{\Delta p}{\Delta t}$ approaches the derivative $\dfrac{dp}{dt}$, which is the **instantaneous growth rate** (or simply **growth rate**) of p with respect to time:

$$\frac{dp}{dt} = \lim_{\Delta t \to 0} \frac{\Delta p}{\Delta t}.$$

Once again, we see the derivative appearing as an instantaneous rate of change. In the next example, a growth function and its derivative are approximated using real data.

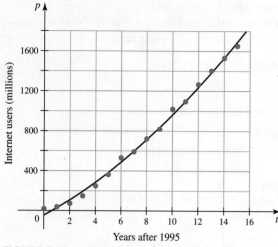

FIGURE 3.39

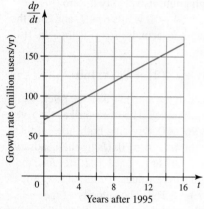

FIGURE 3.40

EXAMPLE 4   Internet growth The number of worldwide Internet users between 1995 and 2010 is shown in Figure 3.39. A reasonable fit to the data is given by the function $p(t) = 3.0t^2 + 70.8t - 45.8$, where t measures years after 1995.

a. Use the function p to approximate the average growth rate of Internet users from 2000 ($t = 5$) to 2005 ($t = 10$).

b. What was the instantaneous growth rate of the Internet in 2006?

c. Use a graphing utility to plot the growth rate dp/dt. What does the graph tell you about the growth rate between 1995 and 2010?

d. Assuming that the growth function can be extended beyond 2010, what is the predicted number of Internet users in 2015 ($t = 20$)?

SOLUTION

a. The average growth rate over the interval $[5, 10]$ is

$$\frac{\Delta p}{\Delta t} = \frac{p(10) - p(5)}{10 - 5} \approx \frac{962 - 383}{5} \approx 116 \text{ million users/year.}$$

b. The growth rate at time t is $p'(t) = 6.0t + 70.8$. In 2006 ($t = 11$), the growth rate was $p'(11) \approx 137$ million users/year.

c. The graph of p', for $0 \leq t \leq 16$, is shown in Figure 3.40. We see that the growth rate is positive and increasing, for $t \geq 0$.

d. A projection of the number of Internet users in 2015 is $p(20) \approx 2570$ million users, or about 2.6 billion users. This figure represents roughly one-third of the world's population, assuming a projected population of 7.2 billion people in 2015.

Related Exercises 17–18 ◄

QUICK CHECK 5 Using the growth function in Example 4, compare the growth rates in 1996 and 2010. ◄

SECTION 3.6 EXERCISES

Review Questions

1. Use a graph to explain the difference between the average rate of change and the instantaneous rate of change of a function f.

2. Complete the following statement. If $\dfrac{dy}{dx}$ is large, then small changes in x will result in relatively _____ changes in the value of y.

3. Complete the following statement: If $\dfrac{dy}{dx}$ is small, then small changes in x will result in relatively _____ changes in the value of y.

4. What is the difference between the *velocity* and *speed* of an object moving in a straight line?

5. Define the acceleration of an object moving in a straight line.

6. An object moving along a line has a constant negative acceleration. Describe the velocity of the object.

Basic Skills

7. **Highway travel** A state patrol station is located on a straight north-south freeway. A patrol car leaves the station at 9:00 A.M. heading north with position function $s = f(t)$ that gives its location in miles t hours after 9:00 A.M. (see figure). Assume s is positive when the car is north of the patrol station.

a. Determine the average velocity of the car during the first 45 minutes of the trip.

b. Find the average velocity of the car over the interval $[0.25, 0.75]$. Is the average velocity a good estimate of the velocity at 9:30 A.M.?

c. Find the average velocity of the car over the interval $[1.75, 2.25]$. Estimate the velocity of the car at 11:00 A.M. and determine the direction in which the patrol car is moving.

d. Describe the motion of the patrol car relative to the patrol station between 9:00 A.M. and noon.

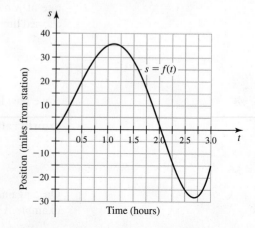

8. **Airline travel** The following figure shows the position function of an airliner on an out-and-back trip from Seattle to Minneapolis, where $s = f(t)$ is the number of ground miles from Seattle t hours after take-off at 6:00 A.M. The plane returns to Seattle 8.5 hours later at 2:30 P.M.

   a. Calculate the average velocity of the airliner during the first 1.5 hours of the trip ($0 \le t \le 1.5$).
   b. Calculate the average velocity of the airliner between 1:30 P.M. and 2:30 P.M. ($7.5 \le t \le 8.5$).
   c. At what time(s) is the velocity 0? Give a plausible explanation.
   d. Determine the velocity of the airliner at noon ($t = 6$) and explain why the velocity is negative.

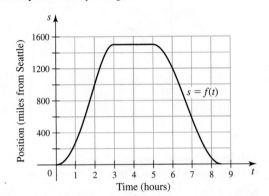

Time (hours)

9–14. Position, velocity, and acceleration *Suppose the position of an object moving horizontally after t seconds is given by the following functions s = f(t), where s is measured in feet, with s > 0 corresponding to positions right of the origin.*

a. *Graph the position function.*
b. *Find and graph the velocity function. When is the object stationary, moving to the right, and moving to the left?*
c. *Determine the velocity and acceleration of the object at t = 1.*
d. *Determine the acceleration of the object when its velocity is zero.*
e. *On what intervals is the speed increasing?*

9. $f(t) = t^2 - 4t; \; 0 \le t \le 5$

10. $f(t) = -t^2 + 4t - 3; \; 0 \le t \le 5$

11. $f(t) = 2t^2 - 9t + 12; \; 0 \le t \le 3$

12. $f(t) = 18t - 3t^2; \; 0 \le t \le 8$

13. $f(t) = 2t^3 - 21t^2 + 60t; \; 0 \le t \le 6$

14. $f(t) = -6t^3 + 36t^2 - 54t; \; 0 \le t \le 4$

15. **A stone thrown vertically** Suppose a stone is thrown vertically upward from the edge of a cliff with an initial velocity of 64 ft/s from a height of 32 ft above the ground. The height s (in ft) of the stone above the ground t seconds after it is thrown is $s = -16t^2 + 64t + 32$.

   a. Determine the velocity v of the stone after t seconds.
   b. When does the stone reach its highest point?
   c. What is the height of the stone at the highest point?
   d. When does the stone strike the ground?
   e. With what velocity does the stone strike the ground?
   f. On what intervals is the speed increasing?

16. **A stone thrown vertically on Mars** Suppose a stone is thrown vertically upward from the edge of a cliff on Mars (where the

acceleration due to gravity is only about 12 ft/s²) with an initial velocity of 64 ft/s from a height of 192 ft above the ground. The height s of the stone above the ground after t seconds is given by $s = -6t^2 + 64t + 192$.

   a. Determine the velocity v of the stone after t seconds.
   b. When does the stone reach its highest point?
   c. What is the height of the stone at the highest point?
   d. When does the stone strike the ground?
   e. With what velocity does the stone strike the ground?

17. **Population growth in Georgia** The population of the state of Georgia (in thousands) from 1995 ($t = 0$) to 2005 ($t = 10$) is modeled by the polynomial $p(t) = -0.27t^2 + 101t + 7055$.

   a. Determine the average growth rate from 1995 to 2005.
   b. What was the growth rate for Georgia in 1997 ($t = 2$) and 2005 ($t = 10$)?
   c. Use a graphing utility to graph p', for $0 \le t \le 10$. What does this graph tell you about population growth in Georgia during the period of time from 1995 to 2005?

18. **Consumer price index** The U.S. consumer price index (CPI) measures the cost of living based on a value of 100 in the years 1982–1984. The CPI for the years 1995–2010 (see figure) is modeled by the function $c(t) = 151e^{0.026t}$, where t represents years after 1995.

   a. Was the average growth rate greater between the years 1995 and 2000, or 2005 and 2010?
   b. Was the growth rate greater in 2000 ($t = 5$) or 2005 ($t = 10$)?
   c. Use a graphing utility to graph the growth rate, for $0 \le t \le 15$. What does the graph tell you about growth in the cost of living during this time period?

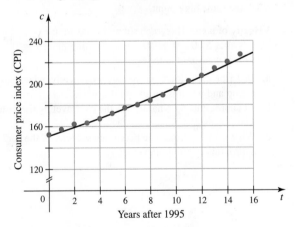

Years after 1995

Further Explorations

19. **Explain why or why not** Determine whether the following statements are true, and give an explanation or a counterexample.

   a. If the acceleration of an object remains constant, then its velocity is constant.
   b. If the acceleration of an object moving along a line is always 0, then its velocity is constant.
   c. It is impossible for the instantaneous velocity at all times $a \le t \le b$ to equal the average velocity over the interval $a \le t \le b$.
   d. A moving object can have negative acceleration and increasing speed.

20. A feather dropped on the moon On the moon, a feather will fall to the ground at the same rate as a heavy stone. Suppose a feather is dropped from a height of 40 m above the surface of the moon. Then, its height s (in meters) above the ground after t seconds is $s = 40 - 0.8t^2$. Determine the velocity and acceleration of the feather the moment it strikes the surface of the moon.

21. Comparing velocities A stone is thrown vertically into the air at an initial velocity of 96 ft/s. On Mars, the height s (in feet) of the stone above the ground after t seconds is $s = 96t - 6t^2$, and on Earth, $s = 96t - 16t^2$. How much higher will the stone travel on Mars than on Earth?

22. Comparing velocities Two stones are thrown vertically upward with matching initial velocities of 48 ft/s at time $t = 0$. One stone is thrown from the edge of a bridge that is 32 ft above the ground and the other stone is thrown from ground level. The height of the stone thrown from the bridge after t seconds is $f(t) = -16t^2 + 48t + 32$, and the height of the stone thrown from the ground after t seconds is $g(t) = -16t^2 + 48t$.

   a. Show that the stones reach their high points at the same time.
   b. How much higher does the stone thrown from the bridge go than the stone thrown from the ground?
   c. When do the stones strike the ground and with what velocities?

23. Matching heights A stone is thrown from the edge of a bridge that is 48 ft above the ground with an initial velocity of 32 ft/s. The height of this stone above the ground t seconds after it is thrown is $f(t) = -16t^2 + 32t + 48$. If a second stone is thrown from the ground, then its height above the ground after t seconds is given by $g(t) = -16t^2 + v_0 t$, where v_0 is the initial velocity of the second stone. Determine the value of v_0 so that both stones reach the same high point.

24. Velocity of a car The graph shows the position $s = f(t)$ of a car t hours after 5:00 P.M. relative to its starting point $s = 0$, where s is measured in miles.

   a. Describe the velocity of the car. Specifically, when is it speeding up and when is it slowing down?
   b. At approximately what time is the car traveling the fastest? The slowest?
   c. What is the approximate maximum velocity of the car? The approximate minimum velocity?

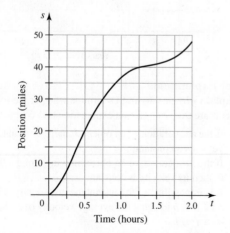

25. Velocity from position The graph of $s = f(t)$ represents the position of an object moving along a line at time $t \geq 0$.

   a. Assume the velocity of the object is 0 when $t = 0$. For what other values of t is the velocity of the object zero?
   b. When is the object moving in the positive direction and when is it moving in the negative direction?
   c. Sketch a graph of the velocity function.
   d. On what intervals is the speed increasing?

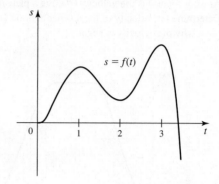

26. Fish length Assume the length L (in cm) of a particular species of fish after t years is modeled by the following graph.

   a. What does dL/dt represent and what happens to this derivative as t increases?
   b. What does the derivative tell you about how this species of fish grows?
   c. Sketch a graph of L' and L''.

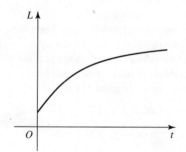

Applications

27. Population growth of the United States Suppose $p(t)$ represents the population of the United States (in millions) t years after the year 1900. The graph of p' is shown in the figure.

   a. Approximately when (in what year) was the U.S. population growing most slowly between 1900 to 1990? Estimate the growth rate in that year.
   b. Approximately when (in what year) was the U.S. population growing most rapidly between 1900 and 1990? Estimate the growth rate in that year.
   c. In what years, if any, was p decreasing?

d. In what years was the population growth rate increasing?

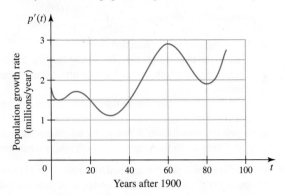

Years after 1900

T 28. Average and marginal production Economists use *production functions* to describe how the output of a system varies with respect to another variable such as labor or capital. For example, the production function $P(L) = 200L + 10L^2 - L^3$ gives the output of a system as a function of the number of laborers L. The *average product* $A(L)$ is the average output per laborer when L laborers are working; that is $A(L) = P(L)/L$. The *marginal product* $M(L)$ is the approximate change in output when one additional laborer is added to L laborers; that is, $M(L) = \dfrac{dP}{dL}$.

a. For the production function given here, compute and graph P, A, and M.

b. Suppose the peak of the average product curve occurs at $L = L_0$, so that $A'(L_0) = 0$. Show that for a general production function, $M(L_0) = A(L_0)$.

T 29. Velocity of a marble The position (in meters) of a marble rolling up a long incline is given by $s = \dfrac{100t}{t + 1}$, where t is measured in seconds and $s = 0$ is the starting point.

a. Graph the position function.

b. Find the velocity function for the marble.

c. Graph the velocity function and give a description of the motion of the marble.

d. At what time is the marble 80 m from its starting point?

e. At what time is the velocity 50 m/s?

T 30. Tree growth Let b represent the base diameter of a conifer tree and let h represent the height of the tree, where b is measured in centimeters and h is measured in meters. Assume the height is related to the base diameter by the function $h = 5.67 + 0.70b + 0.0067b^2$.

a. Graph the height function.

b. Plot and interpret the meaning of $\dfrac{dh}{db}$.

T 31. Revenue function A store manager estimates that the demand for an energy drink decreases with increasing price according to the function $d(p) = \dfrac{100}{p^2 + 1}$, which means that at price p (in dollars), $d(p)$ units can be sold. The revenue generated at price p is $R(p) = p \cdot d(p)$ (price multiplied by number of units).

a. Find and graph the revenue function.

b. Find and graph the marginal revenue $R'(p)$.

c. From the graphs of the R and R', estimate the price that should be charged to maximize the revenue.

T 32. Fuel economy Suppose you own a fuel-efficient hybrid automobile with a monitor on the dashboard that displays the mileage and gas consumption. The number of miles you can drive with g gallons of gas remaining in the tank on a particular stretch of highway is given by $m(g) = 50g - 25.8g^2 + 12.5g^3 - 1.6g^4$, for $0 \le g \le 4$.

a. Graph and interpret the mileage function.

b. Graph and interpret the gas mileage $m(g)/g$.

c. Graph and interpret dm/dg.

T 33. Spring oscillations A spring hangs from the ceiling at equilibrium with a mass attached to its end. Suppose you pull downward on the mass and release it 10 inches below its equilibrium position with an upward push. The distance x (in inches) of the mass from its equilibrium position after t seconds is given by the function $x(t) = 10 \sin t - 10 \cos t$, where x is positive when the mass is above the equilibrium position.

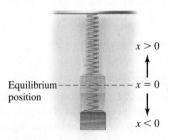

Equilibrium position

$x > 0$

$x = 0$

$x < 0$

a. Graph and interpret this function.

b. Find $\dfrac{dx}{dt}$ and interpret the meaning of this derivative.

c. At what times is the velocity of the mass zero?

d. The function given here is a model for the motion of an object on a spring. In what ways is this model unrealistic?

T 34. Pressure and altitude Earth's atmospheric pressure decreases with altitude from a sea level pressure of 1000 millibars (the unit of pressure used by meteorologists). Letting z be the height above Earth's surface (sea level) in km, the atmospheric pressure is modeled by $p(z) = 1000e^{-z/10}$.

a. Compute the pressure at the summit of Mt. Everest, which has an elevation of roughly 10 km. Compare the pressure on Mt. Everest to the pressure at sea level.

b. Compute the average change in pressure in the first 5 km above Earth's surface.

c. Compute the rate of change of the pressure at an elevation of 5 km.

d. Does $p'(z)$ increase or decrease with z? Explain.

e. What is the meaning of $\lim_{z \to \infty} p(z) = 0$?

35. A race Jean and Juan run a one-lap race on a circular track. Their angular positions on the track during the race are given by the functions $\theta(t)$ and $\varphi(t)$, respectively, where $0 \le t \le 4$ and t is measured in minutes (see figure). These angles are measured in radians, where $\theta = \varphi = 0$ represent the starting position and

$\theta = \varphi = 2\pi$ represent the finish position. The angular velocities of the runners are $\theta'(t)$ and $\varphi'(t)$.

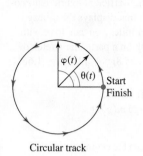

Circular track

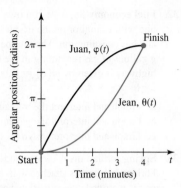

a. Compare in words the angular velocity of the two runners and the progress of the race.
b. Which runner has the greater average angular velocity?
c. Who wins the race?
d. Jean's position is given by $\theta(t) = \pi t^2/8$. What is her angular velocity at $t = 2$ and at what time is her angular velocity the greatest?
e. Juan's position is given by $\varphi(t) = \pi t(8 - t)/8$. What is his angular velocity at $t = 2$ and at what time is his angular velocity the greatest?

36. Power and energy Power and energy are often used interchangeably, but they are quite different. **Energy** is what makes matter move or heat up. It is measured in units of **joules** or **Calories**, where 1 Cal = 4184 J. One hour of walking consumes roughly 10^6 J, or 240 Cal. On the other hand, **power** is the rate at which energy is used, which is measured in **watts**, where 1 W = 1 J/s. Other useful units of power are **kilowatts** (1 kW = 10^3 W) and **megawatts** (1 MW = 10^6 W). If energy is used at a rate of 1 kW for one hour, the total amount of energy used is 1 **kilowatt-hour** (1 kWh = 3.6×10^6 J). Suppose the cumulative energy used in a large building over a 24-hr period is given by

$$E(t) = 100t + 4t^2 - \frac{t^3}{9} \text{ kWh, where } t = 0 \text{ corresponds to}$$

midnight.

a. Graph the energy function.
b. The power is the rate of energy consumption; that is, $P(t) = E'(t)$. Find the power over the interval $0 \le t \le 24$.
c. Graph the power function and interpret the graph. What are the units of power in this case?

37. Flow from a tank A cylindrical tank is full at time $t = 0$ when a valve in the bottom of the tank is opened. By Torricelli's Law, the volume of water in the tank after t hours is $V = 100(200 - t)^2$, measured in cubic meters.

a. Graph the volume function. What is the volume of water in the tank before the valve is opened?
b. How long does it take for the tank to empty?
c. Find the rate at which water flows from the tank and plot the flow rate function.
d. At what time is the magnitude of the flow rate a minimum? A maximum?

38. Cell population The population of a culture of cells after t days is approximated by the function $P(t) = \dfrac{1600}{1 + 7e^{-0.02t}}$, for $t \ge 0$.

a. Graph the population function.
b. What is the average growth rate during the first 10 days?
c. Looking at the graph, when does the growth rate appear to be a maximum?
d. Differentiate the population function to determine the growth rate function $P'(t)$.
e. Graph the growth rate. When is it a maximum and what is the population at the time that the growth rate is a maximum?

39. Bungee jumper A woman attached to a bungee cord jumps from a bridge that is 30 m above a river. Her height in meters above the river t seconds after the jump is $y(t) = 15(1 + e^{-t} \cos t)$, for $t \ge 0$.

a. Determine her velocity at $t = 1$ and $t = 3$.
b. Use a graphing utility to determine when she is moving downward and when she is moving upward during the first 10 s.
c. Use a graphing utility to estimate the maximum upward velocity.

40. Spring runoff The flow of a small stream is monitored for 90 days between May 1 and August 1. The total water that flows past a gauging station is given by

$$V(t) = \begin{cases} \dfrac{4}{5} t^2 & \text{if } 0 \le t < 45 \\[2mm] -\dfrac{4}{5}(t^2 - 180t + 4050) & \text{if } 45 \le t < 90, \end{cases}$$

where V is measured in cubic feet and t is measured in days, with $t = 0$ corresponding to May 1.

a. Graph the volume function.
b. Find the flow rate function $V'(t)$ and graph it. What are the units of the flow rate?
c. Describe the flow of the stream over the 3-month period. Specifically, when is the flow rate a maximum?

41. Temperature distribution A thin copper rod, 4 meters in length, is heated at its midpoint and the ends are held at a constant temperature of 0°. When the temperature reaches equilibrium, the temperature profile is given by $T(x) = 40x(4 - x)$, where $0 \le x \le 4$ is the position along the rod. The **heat flux** at a point on the rod equals $-kT'(x)$, where $k > 0$ is a constant. If the heat flux is positive at a point, heat moves in the positive x-direction at that point, and if the heat flux is negative, heat moves in the negative x-direction.

a. With $k = 1$, what is the heat flux at $x = 1$? At $x = 3$?
b. For what values of x is the heat flux negative? Positive?
c. Explain the statement that heat flows out of the rod at its ends.

Technology Exercises
42–45. Approximating derivatives *Assuming the limit exists, the definition of the derivative $f'(a) = \lim\limits_{h \to 0} \dfrac{f(a + h) - f(a)}{h}$ implies that if h is small, then an approximation to $f'(a)$ is given by*

$$f'(a) \approx \frac{f(a + h) - f(a)}{h}.$$

*If $h > 0$, then this approximation is called a **forward difference quotient**, and if $h < 0$, it is a **backward difference quotient**. As shown in the following exercises, these formulas are used to approximate f' at a point when f is a complicated function or when f is represented by a set of data points.*

42. Let $f(x) = \sqrt{x}$.
  a. Find the exact value of $f'(4)$.
  b. Using the difference quotient, show that
  $$f'(4) \approx \frac{f(4 + h) - f(4)}{h} = \frac{\sqrt{4 + h} - 2}{h}.$$
  c. Complete columns 2 and 5 of the following table and describe how $\dfrac{\sqrt{4 + h} - 2}{h}$ behaves as h approaches 0.

h	$\dfrac{\sqrt{4 + h} - 2}{h}$	Error	h	$\dfrac{\sqrt{4 + h} - 2}{h}$	Error
0.1			−0.1		
0.01			−0.01		
0.001			−0.001		
0.0001			−0.0001		

  d. The accuracy of an approximation is measured by
  $$\text{error} = |\text{exact value} - \text{approximate value}|.$$
  Use the exact value of $f'(4)$ in part (a) to complete columns 3 and 6 in the table. Describe the behavior of the errors as h approaches 0.

43. Another way to approximate derivatives is to use the **centered difference quotient:**
  $$f'(a) \approx \frac{f(a + h) - f(a - h)}{2h}.$$
  Again, consider $f(x) = \sqrt{x}$.
  a. Graph f near the point $(4, 2)$ and let $h = 1/2$ in the centered difference quotient. Draw the line whose slope is computed by the centered difference quotient and explain why the centered difference quotient approximates $f'(4)$.
  b. Use the centered difference quotient to approximate $f'(4)$ by completing the table below.

h	Approximation	Error
0.1		
0.01		
0.001		

  c. Explain why it is not necessary to use negative values of h in the table of part(b).
  d. Compare the accuracy of the derivative estimates in part (b) with those found in Exercise 42.

44. The table provided gives the distance $f(t)$ fallen by a smokejumper t seconds after she opens her chute.
  a. Use the forward difference quotient with $h = 0.5$ to estimate the velocity of the smokejumper at $t = 2$ seconds.

b. Repeat part(a) using the centered difference quotient.

t (seconds)	$f(t)$ (feet)
0	0
0.5	4
1.0	15
1.5	33
2.0	55
2.5	81
3.0	109
3.5	138
4.0	169

45. *The error function* (denoted $\operatorname{erf}(x)$) is an important function in statistics related to the normal distribution. Its graph is shown in the figure, and values at several points are shown in the table.

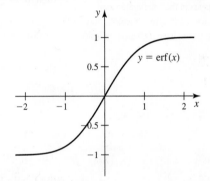

x	$\operatorname{erf}(x)$	x	$\operatorname{erf}(x)$
0.75	0.711156	1.05	0.862436
0.8	0.742101	1.1	0.880205
0.85	0.770668	1.15	0.896124
0.9	0.796908	1.2	0.910314
0.95	0.820891	1.25	0.922900
1.0	0.842701	1.3	0.934008

  a. Use forward and centered difference quotients to find approximations to $\dfrac{d}{dx}(\operatorname{erf}(x))\Big|_{x=1}$.
  b. Given that $\dfrac{d}{dx}(\operatorname{erf}(x))\Big|_{x=1} = \dfrac{2}{e\sqrt{\pi}}$, compute the error in the approximations in part(a).

QUICK CHECK ANSWERS

1. Instantaneous velocity **2.** Yes; yes **3.** If an object has positive acceleration, then its velocity is increasing. If the velocity is negative but increasing, then the acceleration is positive and the speed is decreasing. For example, the velocity may increase from -2 m/s to -1 m/s to 0 m/s.
4. $v(1) = 32$ ft/s and $v(3) = -32$ ft/s, so the speed is 32 ft/s at both times. **5.** The growth rate in 1996 ($t = 1$) is approximately 77 million users/year. It is less than half of the growth rate in 2010 ($t = 15$), which is approximately 161 million users/year. ◄

3.7 The Chain Rule

QUICK CHECK 1 Explain why it is not practical to calculate $\frac{d}{dx}(5x + 4)^{100}$ by first expanding $(5x + 4)^{100}$. ◄

The differentiation rules presented so far allow us to find derivatives of many functions. However, these rules are inadequate for finding the derivatives of most *composite functions*. Here is a typical situation. If $f(x) = x^3$ and $g(x) = 5x + 4$, then their composition is $f(g(x)) = (5x + 4)^3$. One way to find the derivative is by expanding $(5x + 4)^3$ and differentiating the resulting polynomial. Unfortunately, this strategy becomes prohibitive for functions such as $(5x + 4)^{100}$. We need a better approach.

Chain Rule Formulas

An efficient method for differentiating composite functions, called the *Chain Rule*, is motivated by the following example. Suppose Yancey, Uri, and Xan pick apples. Let y, u, and x represent the number of apples picked in some period of time by Yancey, Uri, and Xan, respectively. Yancey picks apples three times faster than Uri, which means the rate at which Yancey picks apples with respect to Uri is $\frac{dy}{du} = 3$. Uri picks apples twice as fast as Xan, so $\frac{du}{dx} = 2$. Therefore, Yancey picks apples at a rate that is $3 \cdot 2 = 6$ times greater than Xan's rate, which means that $\frac{dy}{dx} = 6$ (Figure 3.41). Observe that

$$\frac{dy}{dx} = \frac{dy}{du} \cdot \frac{du}{dx} = 3 \cdot 2 = 6.$$

> Expressions such as dy/dx should not be treated as fractions. Nevertheless, you can check symbolically that you have written the Chain Rule correctly by noting that du appears in the "numerator" and "denominator." If it were "canceled," the Chain Rule would have dy/dx on both sides.

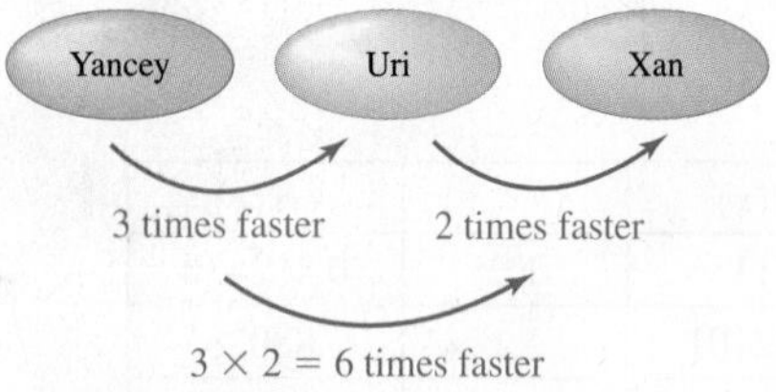

The equation $\frac{dy}{dx} = \frac{dy}{du} \cdot \frac{du}{dx}$ is one form of the Chain Rule. It is referred to as Version 1 of the Chain Rule in this text.

Alternatively, the Chain Rule may be expressed in terms of composite functions. Let $y = f(u)$ and $u = g(x)$, which means y is related to x through the composite function $y = f(u) = f(g(x))$. The derivative $\frac{dy}{dx}$ is now expressed as the product

$$\underbrace{\frac{d}{dx}[f(g(x))]}_{\frac{dy}{dx}} = \underbrace{f'(u)}_{\frac{dy}{du}} \cdot \underbrace{g'(x)}_{\frac{du}{dx}}.$$

Yancey   Uri   Xan

3 times faster   2 times faster

$3 \times 2 = 6$ times faster

FIGURE 3.41

Replacing u with $g(x)$ results in

$$\frac{d}{dx}[f(g(x))] = f'(g(x)) \cdot g'(x),$$

which we refer to as Version 2 of the Chain Rule.

> The two versions of the Chain Rule differ only in notation. Mathematically, they are identical. Version 2 of the Chain Rule states that the derivative of $y = f(g(x))$ is the derivative of f evaluated at $g(x)$ multiplied by the derivative of g evaluated at x.

THEOREM 3.14   The Chain Rule

Suppose $y = f(u)$ is differentiable at $u = g(x)$ and $u = g(x)$ is differentiable at x. The composite function $y = f(g(x))$ is differentiable at x, and its derivative can be expressed in two equivalent ways.

Version 1 $\dfrac{dy}{dx} = \dfrac{dy}{du} \cdot \dfrac{du}{dx}$

Version 2 $\dfrac{d}{dx}[f(g(x))] = f'(g(x)) \cdot g'(x)$

A proof of the Chain Rule is given at the end of this section. For now, it's important to learn how to use it. With the composite function $f(g(x))$, we refer to g as the *inner function* and f as the *outer function* of the composition. The key to using the Chain Rule is identifying the inner and outer functions. The following four steps outline the differentiation process, although you will soon find that the procedure can be streamlined.

> ➤ There may be several ways to choose an inner function $u = g(x)$ and an outer function $y = f(u)$. Nevertheless, we refer to *the* inner and *the* outer function for the most obvious choices.

PROCEDURE   Using the Chain Rule

Assume the differentiable function $y = f(g(x))$ is given.

1. Identify an outer function f and an inner function g, and let $u = g(x)$.

2. Replace $g(x)$ by u to express y in terms of u:
$$y = f(\underbrace{g(x)}_{u}) \Rightarrow y = f(u).$$

3. Calculate the product $\dfrac{dy}{du} \cdot \dfrac{du}{dx}$.

4. Replace u with $g(x)$ in $\dfrac{dy}{du}$ to obtain $\dfrac{dy}{dx}$.

QUICK CHECK 2 Identify an inner function (call it g) of $y = (5x + 4)^3$. Let $u = g(x)$ and express the outer function f in terms of u. ◄

EXAMPLE 1   Version 1 of the Chain Rule For each of the following composite functions, find the inner function $u = g(x)$ and the outer function $y = f(u)$. Use Version 1 of the Chain Rule to find $\dfrac{dy}{dx}$.

a. $y = (5x + 4)^3$ **b.** $y = \sin^3 x$ **c.** $y = \sin x^3$

SOLUTION

a. The inner function of $y = (5x + 4)^3$ is $u = 5x + 4$, and the outer function is $y = u^3$. By Version 1 of the Chain Rule, we have

$$\frac{dy}{dx} = \frac{dy}{du} \cdot \frac{du}{dx}$$

$$= 3u^2 \cdot 5$$

Version 1
$$y = u^3 \Rightarrow \frac{dy}{du} = 3u^2$$
$$u = 5x + 4 \Rightarrow \frac{du}{dx} = 5$$

$$= 3(5x + 4)^2 \cdot 5 \qquad \text{Replace } u \text{ with } 5x + 4.$$

$$= 15(5x + 4)^2.$$

> ➤ When using trigonometric functions, expressions such as $\sin^n x$ always mean $(\sin x)^n$, except when $n = -1$. In Example 1, $\sin^3 x = (\sin x)^3$.

b. Replacing the shorthand form $y = \sin^3 x$ with $y = (\sin x)^3$, we identify the inner function as $u = \sin x$. Letting $y = u^3$, we have

$$\frac{dy}{dx} = \frac{dy}{du} \cdot \frac{du}{dx} = 3u^2 \cdot \cos x = \underbrace{3 \sin^2 x}_{3u^2} \cos x.$$

QUICK CHECK 3 In Example 1a, we showed that
$$\frac{d}{dx}((5x + 4)^3) = 15(5x + 4)^2.$$
Verify this result by expanding $(5x + 4)^3$ and differentiating. ◄

c. Although $y = \sin x^3$ appears to be similar to the function $y = \sin^3 x$ in part (b), the inner function in this case is $u = x^3$ and the outer function is $y = \sin u$. Therefore,

$$\frac{dy}{dx} = \frac{dy}{du} \cdot \frac{du}{dx} = (\cos u) \cdot 3x^2 = 3x^2 \cos x^3.$$

Related Exercises 7–18 ◄

Version 2 of the Chain Rule, $\dfrac{d}{dx}[f(g(x))] = f'(g(x)) \cdot g'(x)$, is equivalent to Version 1; it just uses different derivative notation. With Version 2, we identify the outer function $y = f(u)$ and the inner function $u = g(x)$. Then $\dfrac{d}{dx}[f(g(x))]$ is the product of $f'(u)$ evaluated at $u = g(x)$ and $g'(x)$.

EXAMPLE 2   Version 2 of the Chain Rule Use Version 2 of the Chain Rule to calculate the derivatives of the following functions.

a. $(6x^3 + 3x + 1)^{10}$ **b.** $\sqrt{5x^2 + 1}$ **c.** $\left(\dfrac{5t^2}{3t^2 + 2}\right)^3$

SOLUTION

a. The inner function of $(6x^3 + 3x + 1)^{10}$ is $g(x) = 6x^3 + 3x + 1$, and the outer function is $f(u) = u^{10}$. The derivative of the outer function is $f'(u) = 10u^9$, which, when evaluated at $g(x)$, is $10(6x^3 + 3x + 1)^9$. The derivative of the inner function is $g'(x) = 18x^2 + 3$. Multiplying the derivatives of the outer and inner functions, we have

$$\frac{d}{dx}((6x^3 + 3x + 1)^{10}) = \underbrace{10(6x^3 + 3x + 1)^9}_{f'(u) \text{ evaluated at } g(x)} \cdot \underbrace{(18x^2 + 3)}_{g'(x)}$$

$$= 30(6x^2 + 1)(6x^3 + 3x + 1)^9. \qquad \text{Factor and simplify.}$$

b. The inner function of $\sqrt{5x^2 + 1}$ is $g(x) = 5x^2 + 1$, and the outer function is $f(u) = \sqrt{u}$. The derivatives of these functions are $f'(u) = \dfrac{1}{2\sqrt{u}}$ and $g'(x) = 10x$. Therefore,

$$\frac{d}{dx}\sqrt{5x^2 + 1} = \underbrace{\frac{1}{2\sqrt{5x^2 + 1}}}_{\substack{f'(u) \text{ evaluated} \\ \text{at } g(x)}} \cdot \underbrace{10x}_{g'(x)} = \frac{5x}{\sqrt{5x^2 + 1}}.$$

c. The inner function of $\left(\dfrac{5t^2}{3t^2 + 2}\right)^3$ is $g(t) = \dfrac{5t^2}{3t^2 + 2}$. The outer function is $f(u) = u^3$, whose derivative is $f'(u) = 3u^2$. The derivative of the inner function requires the Quotient Rule. Applying the Chain Rule, we have

$$\frac{d}{dt}\left(\frac{5t^2}{3t^2 + 2}\right)^3 = \underbrace{3\left(\frac{5t^2}{3t^2 + 2}\right)^2}_{\substack{f'(u) \text{ evaluated} \\ \text{at } g(t)}} \cdot \underbrace{\frac{(3t^2 + 2)10t - 5t^2(6t)}{(3t^2 + 2)^2}}_{g'(t) \text{ by the Quotient Rule}} = \frac{1500t^5}{(3t^2 + 2)^4}.$$

Related Exercises 19–36 ◄

The Chain Rule is also used to calculate the derivative of a composite function for a specific value of the variable. If $h(x) = f(g(x))$ and a is a real number, then $h'(a) = f'(g(a))g'(a)$, provided the necessary derivatives exist. Therefore, $h'(a)$ is the derivative of f evaluated at $g(a)$ multiplied by the derivative of g evaluated at a.

Table 3.3

x	$f'(x)$	$g(x)$	$g'(x)$
1	5	2	3
2	7	1	4

EXAMPLE 3   Calculating derivatives at a point Let $h(x) = f(g(x))$. Use the values in Table 3.3 to calculate $h'(1)$ and $h'(2)$.

SOLUTION We use $h'(a) = f'(g(a))g'(a)$ with $a = 1$:

$$h'(1) = f'(g(1))g'(1) = f'(2)g'(1) = 7 \cdot 3 = 21.$$

With $a = 2$, we have

$$h'(2) = f'(g(2))g'(2) = f'(1)g'(2) = 5 \cdot 4 = 20.$$

Related Exercises 37–38 ◄

EXAMPLE 4 **Applying the Chain Rule** A trail runner programs her GPS unit to record her altitude a (in feet) every 10 minutes during a training run in the mountains; the resulting data are shown in Table 3.4. Meanwhile, at a nearby weather station, a weather probe records the atmospheric pressure p (in hectopascals, or hPa) at various altitudes, shown in Table 3.5.

Table 3.4

t (minutes)	0	10	20	30	40	50	60	70	80
$a(t)$ (altitude)	10,000	10,220	10,510	10,980	11,660	12,330	12,710	13,330	13,440

Table 3.5

a (altitude)	5485	7795	10,260	11,330	12,330	13,330	14,330	15,830	16,230
$p(a)$ (pressure)	1000	925	840	821	793	765	738	700	690

a. Use the Chain Rule to estimate the rate of change in pressure per unit time experienced by the trail runner when she is 50 minutes into her run.

b. Plots of the data in Tables 3.4 and 3.5 are shown in Figure 3.42; the functions $a(t) = -0.01t^3 + 1.3t^2 + 3.2t + 10{,}000$ and $p(a) = 1207e^{-0.00003436a}$ provide good fits for the respective data sets. Use these functions to find the rate of change in pressure experienced by the runner 35 minutes into her run.

> The idea of a centered difference quotient was introduced in Example 2 of Section 3.1 and further explored in Exercises 43–45 of Section 3.6. Like all difference quotients, the centered difference quotient is the slope of a secant line joining two points on the graph of a function, as illustrated in the following figure.

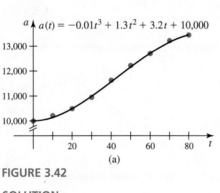

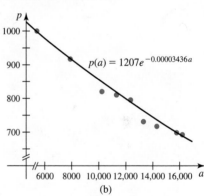

FIGURE 3.42

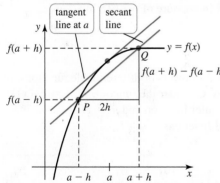

Centered difference quotient: the secant line through P and Q approximates the tangent line, so
$$m_{\tan} = f'(a) \approx \frac{f(a+h) - f(a-h)}{2h}$$

SOLUTION

a. We seek the rate of change in the pressure $\dfrac{dp}{dt}$, which is given by the Chain Rule:

$$\frac{dp}{dt} = \frac{dp}{da}\frac{da}{dt}.$$

The runner is at an altitude of 12,330 feet 50 minutes into her run, so we must compute dp/da when $a = 12{,}330$ and da/dt when $t = 50$. These derivatives can be approximated using the following centered difference quotients:

$$\frac{dp}{da}\bigg|_{a=12{,}330} \approx \frac{p(12{,}330 + 1000) - p(12{,}330 - 1000)}{2 \cdot 1000} \qquad \frac{da}{dt}\bigg|_{t=50} \approx \frac{a(50 + 10) - a(50 - 10)}{2 \cdot 10}$$

$$= \frac{765 - 821}{2000} \qquad\qquad = \frac{12{,}710 - 11{,}660}{20}$$

$$= -0.028 \frac{\text{hPa}}{\text{ft}} \qquad\qquad = 52.5 \frac{\text{ft}}{\text{min}}$$

We now compute the rate of change of the pressure with respect to time:

$$\frac{dp}{dt} = \frac{dp}{da}\frac{da}{dt}$$

$$\approx -0.028\,\frac{\text{hPa}}{\text{ft}} \cdot 52.5\,\frac{\text{ft}}{\text{min}}$$

$$= -1.470\,\frac{\text{hPa}}{\text{min}}.$$

As expected, dp/dt is negative because the pressure decreases with increasing altitude as the runner ascends the trail. Note also that the units are consistent.

b. The function $p(a) = 1207e^{-0.00003436a}$ fits the pressure data in Table 3.5, while $a(t) = -0.01t^3 + 1.3t^2 + 3.2t + 10{,}000$ fits the altitude data in Table 3.4. Therefore, the composition $p(a(t))$ describes the pressure experienced by the runner at various times t.

To find the rate of change in the pressure, we compute $\dfrac{d}{dt}[p(a(t))]$ using the Chain Rule and evaluate it at $t = 35$:

$$\frac{d}{dt}[p(a(t))]\bigg|_{t=35} = p'(a(t)) \cdot a'(t)\big|_{t=35} = p'(a(35)) \cdot a'(35).$$

Now we calculate $p'(a)$, $a'(t)$, and $a(35)$:

$$p'(a) = 1207e^{-0.00003436a} \cdot \underbrace{(-0.00003436)}_{\text{Chain Rule}} \approx -0.0415e^{-0.00003436a}$$

$$a'(t) = -0.03t^2 + 2.6t + 3.2$$
$$a(35) = -0.01(35)^3 + 1.3(35)^2 + 3.2(35) + 10{,}000 = 11{,}275.75.$$

Bringing all the pieces together, we have

$$\frac{d}{dt}[p(a(t))]\bigg|_{t=35} = p'(a(35)) \cdot a'(35)$$

$$= p'(11{,}275.75) \cdot a'(35)$$

$$\approx -0.0282 \cdot 57.45$$

$$\approx -1.618,$$

which means the runner experiences a change in pressure of -1.618 hPa/min.

Related Exercises 39–40 ◄

Chain Rule for Powers

The Chain Rule leads to a general derivative rule for powers of differentiable functions. In fact, we have already used it in several examples. Consider the function $f(x) = (g(x))^n$, where n is an integer. Letting $f(u) = u^n$ be the outer function and $u = g(x)$ be the inner function, we obtain the Chain Rule for powers of functions.

> In Section 3.9, Theorem 3.15 is generalized to all real numbers n.

THEOREM 3.15   Chain Rule for Powers

If g is differentiable for all x in its domain and n is an integer, then

$$\frac{d}{dx}[(g(x))^n] = n(g(x))^{n-1}g'(x).$$

EXAMPLE 5 **Chain Rule for powers** Find $\dfrac{d}{dx}(\tan x + 10)^{21}$.

SOLUTION With $g(x) = \tan x + 10$, the Chain Rule gives

$$\frac{d}{dx}(\tan x + 10)^{21} = 21(\tan x + 10)^{20}\frac{d}{dx}(\tan x + 10)$$

$$= 21(\tan x + 10)^{20}\sec^2 x.$$

Related Exercises 41–44◄

> Before dismissing the function in Example 6 as merely a tool to teach the Chain Rule, consider the graph of a related function, $y = \sin\left(e^{1.3\cos x}\right) + 1$ (Figure 3.43). This periodic function has two peaks per cycle and could be used as a simple model of traffic flow (two rush hours followed by light traffic in the middle of the night), tides (high tide, medium tide, high tide, low tide, . . .), or the presence of certain allergens in the air (peaks in the spring and fall).

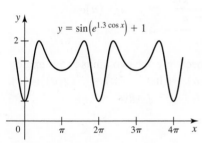

FIGURE 3.43

The Composition of Three or More Functions

We can differentiate the composition of three or more functions by applying the Chain Rule repeatedly, as shown in the following example.

EXAMPLE 6 **Composition of three functions** Calculate the derivative of $\sin\left(e^{\cos x}\right)$.

SOLUTION The inner function of $\sin\left(e^{\cos x}\right)$ is $e^{\cos x}$. Because $e^{\cos x}$ is also a composition of two functions, the Chain Rule is used again to calculate $\dfrac{d}{dx}\left(e^{\cos x}\right)$, where $\cos x$ is the inner function:

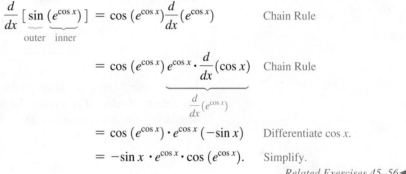

$$\frac{d}{dx}\Big[\sin\underbrace{\left(e^{\cos x}\right)}\Big] = \cos\left(e^{\cos x}\right)\frac{d}{dx}\left(e^{\cos x}\right) \qquad \text{Chain Rule}$$
$$\underset{\text{outer}\quad\text{inner}}{}$$

$$= \cos\left(e^{\cos x}\right)\underbrace{e^{\cos x}\cdot\frac{d}{dx}(\cos x)}_{\frac{d}{dx}\left(e^{\cos x}\right)} \qquad \text{Chain Rule}$$

$$= \cos\left(e^{\cos x}\right)\cdot e^{\cos x}\left(-\sin x\right) \qquad \text{Differentiate } \cos x.$$

$$= -\sin x \cdot e^{\cos x}\cdot\cos\left(e^{\cos x}\right). \qquad \text{Simplify.}$$

Related Exercises 45–56◄

QUICK CHECK 4 Let $y = \tan^{10}\left(x^5\right)$. Find f, g, and h such that $y = f(u)$, where $u = g(v)$ and $v = h(x)$. ◄

The Chain Rule is often used together with other derivative rules. Example 7 illustrates how several differentiation rules are combined.

EXAMPLE 7 **Combining rules** Find $\dfrac{d}{dx}\left(x^2\sqrt{x^2 + 1}\right)$.

SOLUTION The given function is the product of x^2 and $\sqrt{x^2 + 1}$, and $\sqrt{x^2 + 1}$ is a composite function. We apply the Product Rule and then the Chain Rule:

$$\frac{d}{dx}\left(x^2\sqrt{x^2 + 1}\right) = \underbrace{\frac{d}{dx}(x^2)}_{2x}\cdot\sqrt{x^2 + 1} + x^2\cdot\underbrace{\frac{d}{dx}\left(\sqrt{x^2 + 1}\right)}_{\text{Use Chain Rule}} \quad \text{Product Rule}$$

$$= 2x\sqrt{x^2 + 1} + x^2\cdot\frac{1}{2\sqrt{x^2 + 1}}\cdot 2x \qquad \text{Chain Rule}$$

$$= 2x\sqrt{x^2 + 1} + \frac{x^3}{\sqrt{x^2 + 1}} \qquad \text{Simplify.}$$

$$= \frac{3x^3 + 2x}{\sqrt{x^2 + 1}}. \qquad \text{Simplify.}$$

Related Exercises 57–68◄

Proof of the Chain Rule

Suppose f is differentiable at $u = g(a)$, g is differentiable at a, and $h(x) = f(g(x))$. By the definition of the derivative of h,

$$h'(a) = \lim_{x \to a} \frac{h(x) - h(a)}{x - a} = \lim_{x \to a} \frac{f(g(x)) - f(g(a))}{x - a}. \tag{1}$$

We assume that $g(a) \neq g(x)$ for values of x near a but not equal to a. This assumption holds for most, but not all, functions encountered in this text. For a proof of the Chain Rule without this assumption, see Exercise 103.

We multiply the right side of equation (1) by $\dfrac{g(x) - g(a)}{g(x) - g(a)}$, which equals 1, and let $v = g(x)$ and $u = g(a)$. The result is

$$h'(a) = \lim_{x \to a} \frac{f(g(x)) - f(g(a))}{g(x) - g(a)} \cdot \frac{g(x) - g(a)}{x - a}$$

$$= \lim_{x \to a} \frac{f(v) - f(u)}{v - u} \cdot \frac{g(x) - g(a)}{x - a}.$$

By assumption, g is differentiable at a; therefore, it is continuous at a. This means that $\lim_{x \to a} g(x) = g(a)$, so $v \to u$ as $x \to a$. Consequently,

$$h'(a) = \underbrace{\lim_{v \to u} \frac{f(v) - f(u)}{v - u}}_{f'(u)} \cdot \underbrace{\lim_{x \to a} \frac{g(x) - g(a)}{x - a}}_{g'(a)} = f'(u)g'(a).$$

Because f and g are differentiable at u and a, respectively, the two limits in this expression exist; therefore $h'(a)$ exists. Noting that $u = g(a)$, we have $h'(a) = f'(g(a))g'(a)$. Replacing a with the variable x gives the Chain Rule: $h'(x) = f'(g(x))g'(x)$.   ◄

SECTION 3.7 EXERCISES

Review Questions

1. Two equivalent forms of the Chain Rule for calculating the derivative of $y = f(g(x))$ are presented in this section. State both forms.

2. Let $h(x) = f(g(x))$, where f and g are differentiable on their domains. If $g(1) = 3$ and $g'(1) = 5$, what else do you need to know to calculate $h'(1)$?

3. Fill in the blanks. The derivative of $f(g(x))$ equals f' evaluated at _____ multiplied by g' evaluated at _____.

4. Identify the inner and outer functions in the composition $\cos^4 x$.

5. Identify the inner and outer functions in the composition $(x^2 + 10)^{-5}$.

6. Express $Q(x) = \cos^4(x^2 + 1)$ as the composition of three functions; that is, identify f, g, and h so that $Q(x) = f(g(h(x)))$.

Basic Skills

7–18. Version 1 of the Chain Rule *Use Version 1 of the Chain Rule to calculate $\dfrac{dy}{dx}$.*

7. $y = (3x + 7)^{10}$ 8. $y = (5x^2 + 11x)^{20}$ 9. $y = \sin^5 x$

10. $y = \cos^5 x$
11. $y = e^{5x-7}$
12. $y = \sqrt{7x - 1}$

13. $y = \sqrt{x^2 + 1}$
14. $y = e^{\sqrt{x}}$
15. $y = \tan 5x^2$

16. $y = \sin \dfrac{x}{4}$
17. $y = \sec e^x$
18. $y = e^{-x^2}$

19–34. Version 2 of the Chain Rule *Use Version 2 of the Chain Rule to calculate the derivatives of the following composite functions.*

19. $y = (3x^2 + 7x)^{10}$
20. $y = (x^2 + 2x + 7)^8$

21. $y = \sqrt{10x + 1}$
22. $y = \sqrt{x^2 + 9}$

23. $y = 5(7x^3 + 1)^{-3}$
24. $y = \cos(5t + 1)$

25. $y = \sec(3x + 1)$
26. $y = \csc e^x$

27. $y = \tan e^x$
28. $y = e^{\tan t}$

29. $y = \sin(4x^3 + 3x + 1)$
30. $y = \csc(t^2 + t)$

31. $y = \sin(2\sqrt{x})$
32. $y = \cos^4 \theta + \sin^4 \theta$

33. $y = (\sec x + \tan x)^5$
34. $y = \sin(4 \cos z)$

35–36. Similar-looking composite functions *Two composite functions are given that look similar, but in fact are quite different. Identify the inner function $u = g(x)$ and the outer function $y = f(u)$; then evaluate $\dfrac{dy}{dx}$ using the Chain Rule.*

35. a. $y = \cos^3 x$
 b. $y = \cos x^3$

36. a. $y = (e^x)^3$
 b. $y = e^{(x^3)}$

37. Chain Rule using a table Let $h(x) = f(g(x))$ and $p(x) = g(f(x))$. Use the table to compute the following derivatives.

a. $h'(3)$ **b.** $h'(2)$ **c.** $p'(4)$
d. $p'(2)$ **e.** $h'(5)$

x	1	2	3	4	5
$f(x)$	0	3	5	1	0
$f'(x)$	5	2	-5	-8	-10
$g(x)$	4	5	1	3	2
$g'(x)$	2	10	20	15	20

38. Chain Rule using a table Let $h(x) = f(g(x))$ and $k(x) = g(g(x))$. Use the table to compute the following derivatives.

a. $h'(1)$ **b.** $h'(2)$ **c.** $h'(3)$ **d.** $k'(3)$
e. $k'(1)$ **f.** $k'(5)$

x	1	2	3	4	5
$f'(x)$	-6	-3	8	7	2
$g(x)$	4	1	5	2	3
$g'(x)$	9	7	3	-1	-5

39. Applying the Chain Rule Use the data in Tables 3.4 and 3.5 of Example 4 to estimate the rate of change in pressure with respect to time experienced by the runner when she is at an altitude of 13,330 feet. Make use of the centered difference quotient when estimating the required derivatives.

40. Changing temperature The *lapse rate* is the rate at which the temperature in Earth's atmosphere decreases with altitude. For example, a lapse rate of 6.5° Celsius/km means the temperature *decreases* at a rate of 6.5°C per kilometer of altitude. The lapse rate varies with location and with other variables such as humidity. However, at a given time and location, the lapse rate is often nearly constant in the first 10 kilometers of the atmosphere. A radiosonde (weather balloon) is released from Earth's surface, and its altitude (measured in kilometers above sea level) at various times (measured in hours) is given in the table below.

Time (hr)	0	0.5	1	1.5	2	2.5
Altitude (km)	0.5	1.2	1.7	2.1	2.5	2.9

a. Assuming a lapse rate of 6.5°C/km, what is the approximate rate of change of the temperature with respect to time as the balloon rises 1.5 hours into the flight? Specify the units of your result.

b. How does an increase in lapse rate change your answer in part (a)?

c. Is it necessary to know the actual temperature to carry out the calculation in part (a)? Explain why or why not.

41–44. Chain Rule for powers *Use the Chain Rule to find the derivative of the following functions.*

41. $y = (2x^6 - 3x^3 + 3)^{25}$ **42.** $y = (\cos x + 2 \sin x)^8$

43. $y = (1 + 2 \tan x)^{15}$ **44.** $y = (1 - e^x)^4$

45–56. Repeated use of the Chain Rule *Calculate the derivative of the following functions.*

45. $y = \sqrt{1 + \cot^2 x}$ **46.** $y = \sqrt{(3x - 4)^2 + 3x}$

47. $y = \sin(\sin(e^x))$ **48.** $y = \sin^2(e^{3x+1})$

49. $y = \sin^5(\cos 3x)$ **50.** $y = \cos^4(7x^3)$

51. $y = \tan(e^{\sqrt{3x}})$ **52.** $y = (1 - e^{-0.05x})^{-1}$

53. $y = \sqrt{x + \sqrt{x}}$ **54.** $y = \sqrt{x + \sqrt{x + \sqrt{x}}}$

55. $y = f(g(x^2))$, where f and g are differentiable for all real numbers

56. $y = [f(g(x^m))]^n$, where f and g are differentiable for all real numbers, and m and n are integers

57–68. Combining rules *Use the Chain Rule combined with other differentiation rules to find the derivative of the following functions.*

57. $y = \left(\dfrac{x}{x + 1}\right)^5$ **58.** $y = \left(\dfrac{e^x}{x + 1}\right)^8$

59. $y = e^{x^2+1} \sin x^3$ **60.** $y = \tan(x e^x)$

61. $y = \theta^2 \sec 5\theta$ **62.** $y = \left(\dfrac{3x}{4x + 2}\right)^5$

63. $y = ((x + 2)(x^2 + 1))^4$ **64.** $y = e^{2x}(2x - 7)^5$

65. $y = \sqrt{x^4 + \cos 2x}$ **66.** $y = \dfrac{te^t}{t + 1}$

67. $y = (p + \pi)^2 \sin p^2$ **68.** $y = (z + 4)^3 \tan z$

Further Explorations

69. Explain why or why not Determine whether the following statements are true, and give an explanation or a counterexample.

a. The function $x \sin x$ can be differentiated without using the Chain Rule.

b. The function $(x^2 + 10)^{-12}$ should be differentiated using the Chain Rule.

c. The derivative of a product is *not* the product of the derivatives, but the derivative of a composition is a product of derivatives.

d. $\dfrac{d}{dx} P(Q(x)) = P'(x)Q'(x)$

70–73. Second derivatives *Find $\dfrac{d^2y}{dx^2}$ for the following functions.*

70. $y = x \cos x^2$ **71.** $y = \sin x^2$

72. $y = \sqrt{x^2 + 2}$ **73.** $y = e^{-2x^2}$

74. Derivatives by different methods

a. Calculate $\dfrac{d}{dx}(x^2 + x)^2$ using the Chain Rule. Simplify your answer.

b. Expand $(x^2 + x)^2$ first and then calculate the derivative. Verify that your answer agrees with part (a).

75–76. Square root derivatives *Find the derivative of the following functions.*

75. $y = \sqrt{f(x)}$, where f is differentiable and nonnegative at x

76. $y = \sqrt{f(x)g(x)}$, where f and g are differentiable and nonnegative at x

77. Tangent lines Determine an equation of the line tangent to the graph of $y = \dfrac{(x^2 - 1)^2}{x^3 - 6x - 1}$ at the point $(3, 8)$. Graph the function and the tangent line.

78. Tangent lines Determine equations of the lines tangent to the graph of $y = x\sqrt{5 - x^2}$ at the points $(1, 2)$ and $(-2, -2)$. Graph the function and the tangent lines.

79. Tangent lines Assume f and g are differentiable on their domains with $h(x) = f(g(x))$. Suppose the equation of the line tangent to the graph of g at the point $(4, 7)$ is $y = 3x - 5$ and the equation of the line tangent to the graph of f at $(7, 9)$ is $y = -2x + 23$.

   a. Calculate $h(4)$ and $h'(4)$.

   b. Determine an equation of the line tangent to the graph of h at the point on the graph where $x = 4$.

80. Tangent lines Assume f is a differentiable function whose graph passes through the point $(1, 4)$. Suppose $g(x) = f(x^2)$ and the line tangent to the graph of f at $(1, 4)$ is $y = 3x + 1$. Determine each of the following.

   a. $g(1)$ **b.** $g'(x)$ **c.** $g'(1)$

   d. An equation of the line tangent to the graph of g when $x = 1$

81. Tangent lines Find the equation of the line tangent to $y = e^{2x}$ at $x = \frac{1}{2} \ln 3$. Graph the function and the tangent line.

82. Composition containing $\sin x$ Suppose f is differentiable on $[-2, 2]$ with $f'(0) = 3$ and $f'(1) = 5$. Let $g(x) = f(\sin x)$. Evaluate the following expressions.

   a. $g'(0)$ **b.** $g'\left(\dfrac{\pi}{2}\right)$ **c.** $g'(\pi)$

83. Composition containing $\sin x$ Suppose f is differentiable for all real numbers with $f(0) = -3$, $f(1) = 3$, $f'(0) = 3$, and $f'(1) = 5$. Let $g(x) = \sin(\pi f(x))$. Evaluate the following expressions.

   a. $g'(0)$ **b.** $g'(1)$

Applications

84–86. Vibrations of a spring *Suppose an object of mass m is attached to the end of a spring hanging from the ceiling. The mass is at its equilibrium position $y = 0$ when the mass hangs at rest. Suppose you push the mass to a position y_0 units above its equilibrium position and release it. As the mass oscillates up and down (neglecting any friction in the system), the position y of the mass after t seconds is*

$$y = y_0 \cos\left(t\sqrt{\frac{k}{m}}\right), \qquad (2)$$

where $k > 0$ is a constant measuring the stiffness of the spring (the larger the value of k, the stiffer the spring) and y is positive in the upward direction.

84. Use equation (2) to answer the following questions.

   a. Find $\dfrac{dy}{dt}$, the velocity of the mass. Assume k and m are constant.

   b. How would the velocity be affected if the experiment were repeated with four times the mass on the end of the spring?

   c. How would the velocity be affected if the experiment were repeated with a spring having four times the stiffness (k is increased by a factor of 4)?

   d. Assume that y has units of meters, t has units of seconds, m has units of kg, and k has units of kg/s^2. Show that the units of the velocity in part (a) are consistent.

85. Use equation (2) to answer the following questions.

   a. Find the second derivative $\dfrac{d^2y}{dt^2}$.

   b. Verify that $\dfrac{d^2y}{dt^2} = -\dfrac{k}{m}y$.

86. Use equation (2) to answer the following questions.

   a. The *period T* is the time required by the mass to complete one oscillation. Show that $T = 2\pi\sqrt{\dfrac{m}{k}}$.

   b. Assume k is constant and calculate $\dfrac{dT}{dm}$.

   c. Give a physical explanation of why $\dfrac{dT}{dm}$ is positive.

87. A damped oscillator The displacement of a mass on a spring suspended from the ceiling is given by $y = 10e^{-t/2}\cos\left(\dfrac{\pi t}{8}\right)$.

   a. Graph the displacement function.

   b. Compute and graph the velocity of the mass, $v(t) = y'(t)$.

   c. Verify that the velocity is zero when the mass reaches the high and low points of its oscillation.

88. Oscillator equation A mechanical oscillator (such as a mass on a spring or a pendulum) subject to frictional forces satisfies the equation (called a differential equation)

$$y''(t) + 2y'(t) + 5y(t) = 0,$$

where y is the displacement of the oscillator from its equilibrium position. Verify by substitution that the function $y(t) = e^{-t}(\sin 2t - 2\cos 2t)$ satisfies this equation.

89. Hours of daylight The number of hours of daylight at any point on Earth fluctuates throughout the year. In the northern hemisphere, the shortest day is on the winter solstice and the longest day is on the summer solstice. At $40°$ north latitude, the length of a day is approximated by

$$D(t) = 12 - 3\cos\left[\frac{2\pi(t + 10)}{365}\right],$$

where D is measured in hours and $0 \le t \le 365$ is measured in days, with $t = 0$ corresponding to January 1.

   a. Approximately how much daylight is there on March 1 ($t = 59$)?

   b. Find the rate at which the daylight function changes.

c. Find the rate at which the daylight function changes on March 1. Convert your answer to units of min/day and explain what this result means.

d. Graph the function $y = D'(t)$ using a graphing utility.

e. At what times of year is the length of day changing most rapidly? Least rapidly?

90. A mixing tank A 500-liter (L) tank is filled with pure water. At time $t = 0$, a salt solution begins flowing into the tank at a rate of 5 L/min. At the same time, the (fully mixed) solution flows out of the tank at a rate of 5.5 L/min. The mass of salt in grams in the tank at any time $t \geq 0$ is given by

$$M(t) = 250(1000 - t)(1 - 10^{-30}(1000 - t)^{10})$$

and the volume of solution in the tank (in liters) is given by $V(t) = 500 - 0.5t$.

a. Graph the mass function and verify that $M(0) = 0$.

b. Graph the volume function and verify that the tank is empty when $t = 1000$ min.

c. The concentration of the salt solution in the tank (in g/L) is given by $C(t) = M(t)/V(t)$. Graph the concentration function and comment on its properties. Specifically, what are $C(0)$ and $\lim_{t \to 1000^-} C(t)$?

d. Find the rate of change of the mass $M'(t)$, for $0 \leq t \leq 1000$.

e. Find the rate of change of the concentration $C'(t)$, for $0 \leq t \leq 1000$.

f. For what times is the concentration of the solution increasing? Decreasing?

91. Power and energy The total energy in megawatt-hr (MWh) used by a town is given by

$$E(t) = 400t + \frac{2400}{\pi} \sin\left(\frac{\pi t}{12}\right),$$

where $t \geq 0$ is measured in hours, with $t = 0$ corresponding to noon.

a. Find the power, or rate of energy consumption, $P(t) = E'(t)$ in units of megawatts (MW).

b. At what time of day is the rate of energy consumption a maximum? What is the power at that time of day?

c. At what time of day is the rate of energy consumption a minimum? What is the power at that time of day?

d. Sketch a graph of the power function reflecting the times at which energy use is a minimum or maximum.

Additional Exercises

92. Deriving trigonometric identities

a. Recall that $\cos 2t = \cos^2 t - \sin^2 t$. Use differentiation to find a trigonometric identity for $\sin 2t$.

b. Verify that you obtain the same identity for $\sin 2t$ as in part (a) if you use the identity $\cos 2t = 2\cos^2 t - 1$.

c. Verify that you obtain the same identity for $\sin 2t$ as in part (a) if you use the identity $\cos 2t = 1 - 2\sin^2 t$.

93. Proof of $\cos^2 x + \sin^2 x = 1$ Let $f(x) = \cos^2 x + \sin^2 x$.

a. Use the Chain Rule to show that $f'(x) = 0$.

b. Assume that if $f' = 0$, then f is a constant function. Calculate $f(0)$ and use it with part (a) to explain why $\cos^2 x + \sin^2 x = 1$.

94. Using the Chain Rule to prove that $\dfrac{d}{dx}(e^{kx}) = ke^{kx}$

a. Identify the inner function g and the outer function f for the composition $f(g(x)) = e^{kx}$, where k is a real number.

b. Use the Chain Rule to show that $\dfrac{d}{dx}(e^{kx}) = ke^{kx}$.

95. Deriving the Quotient Rule using the Product Rule and Chain Rule Suppose you forgot the Quotient Rule for calculating $\dfrac{d}{dx}\left(\dfrac{f(x)}{g(x)}\right)$. Use the Chain Rule and Product Rule with the identity $\dfrac{f(x)}{g(x)} = f(x)(g(x))^{-1}$ to derive the Quotient Rule.

96. The Chain Rule for second derivatives

a. Derive a formula for the second derivative $\dfrac{d^2}{dx^2}[f(g(x))]$.

b. Use the formula in part (a) to calculate
$$\frac{d^2}{dx^2}(\sin(3x^4 + 5x^2 + 2)).$$

97–100. Calculating limits *The following limits are the derivatives of a composite function h at a point a.*

a. *Find a possible h and a.*

b. *Use the Chain Rule to find each limit. Verify your answer using a calculator.*

97. $\displaystyle\lim_{x \to 2} \frac{(x^2 - 3)^5 - 1}{x - 2}$

98. $\displaystyle\lim_{x \to 0} \frac{\sqrt{4 + \sin x} - 2}{x}$

99. $\displaystyle\lim_{h \to 0} \frac{\sin(\pi/2 + h)^2 - \sin(\pi^2/4)}{h}$

100. $\displaystyle\lim_{h \to 0} \frac{\dfrac{1}{3((1 + h)^5 + 7)^{10}} - \dfrac{1}{3(8)^{10}}}{h}$

101. Limit of a difference quotient Assuming that f is differentiable for all x, simplify $\displaystyle\lim_{x \to 5} \frac{f(x^2) - f(25)}{x - 5}$.

102. Derivatives of even and odd functions Recall that f is even if $f(-x) = f(x)$, for all x in the domain of f, and f is odd if $f(-x) = -f(x)$, for all x in the domain of f.

a. If f is a differentiable, even function on its domain, determine whether f' is even, odd, or neither.

b. If f is a differentiable, odd function on its domain, determine whether f' is even, odd, or neither.

103. A general proof of the Chain Rule Let f and g be differentiable functions with $h(x) = f(g(x))$. For a given constant a, let $u = g(a)$ and $v = g(x)$, and define

$$H(v) = \begin{cases} \dfrac{f(v) - f(u)}{v - u} - f'(u) & \text{if } v \neq u \\[2mm] 0 & \text{if } v = u. \end{cases}$$

a. Show that $\lim\limits_{v \to u} H(v) = 0$.

b. For any value of u show that
$$f(v) - f(u) = (H(v) + f'(u))(v - u).$$

c. Show that
$$h'(a) = \lim_{x \to a}\left[[H(g(x)) + f'(g(a))] \cdot \frac{g(x) - g(a)}{x - a} \right].$$

d. Show that $h'(a) = f'(g(a))g'(a)$.

3.8 Implicit Differentiation

This chapter has been devoted to calculating derivatives of functions of the form $y = f(x)$, where y is defined *explicitly* as a function of x. However, relations between variables are often expressed *implicitly*. For example, the equation of the unit circle $x^2 + y^2 = 1$ does not specify y directly, but rather defines y *implicitly*. This equation does not represent a single function because its graph fails the vertical line test (Figure 3.44a). If, however, the equation $x^2 + y^2 = 1$ is solved for y, then *two* functions, $y = -\sqrt{1 - x^2}$ and $y = \sqrt{1 - x^2}$, emerge (Figure 3.44b). Having identified two explicit functions that describe the circle, their derivatives are found using the Chain Rule.

$$\text{If } y = \sqrt{1 - x^2}, \text{ then } \frac{dy}{dx} = -\frac{x}{\sqrt{1 - x^2}}. \tag{1}$$

$$\text{If } y = -\sqrt{1 - x^2}, \text{ then } \frac{dy}{dx} = \frac{x}{\sqrt{1 - x^2}}. \tag{2}$$

We use equation (1) to find the slope of the curve at any point on the upper half of the unit circle and equation (2) to find the slope of the curve at any point on the lower half of the circle.

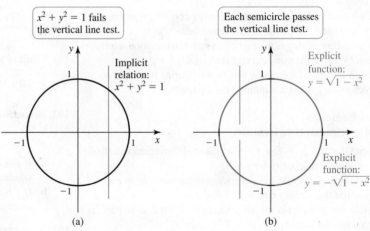

FIGURE 3.44

QUICK CHECK 1 The equation $x - y^2 = 0$ implicitly defines what two functions? ◄

 While it is straightforward to solve some implicit equations for y (such as $x^2 + y^2 = 1$ or $x - y^2 = 0$), it is difficult or impossible to solve other equations for y. For example, the graph of $x + y^3 - xy = 1$ (Figure 3.45a) represents three functions: the upper half of a parabola $y = f_1(x)$, the lower half of a parabola $y = f_2(x)$, and the horizontal line $y = f_3(x)$ (Figure 3.45b). Solving for y to obtain these three functions is challenging (Exercise 59), and even after solving for y, derivatives for each of the three functions must be calculated separately. The goal of this section is to find a *single* expression for the derivative *directly* from an equation without first solving for y. This technique, called **implicit differentiation**, is demonstrated through examples.

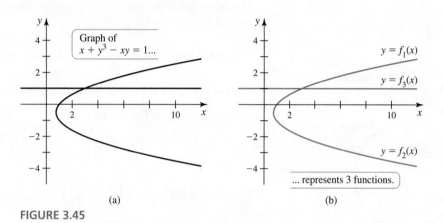

FIGURE 3.45

EXAMPLE 1   Implicit differentiation

a. Calculate $\dfrac{dy}{dx}$ directly from the equation for the unit circle $x^2 + y^2 = 1$.

b. Find the slope of the unit circle at $\left(\dfrac{1}{2}, \dfrac{\sqrt{3}}{2}\right)$ and $\left(\dfrac{1}{2}, -\dfrac{\sqrt{3}}{2}\right)$.

SOLUTION

a. To indicate the choice of x as the independent variable, it is helpful to replace the variable y with $y(x)$:

$$x^2 + (y(x))^2 = 1. \quad \text{Replace } y \text{ with } y(x).$$

We now take the derivative of each term in the equation *with respect to x*:

$$\underbrace{\frac{d}{dx}(x^2)}_{2x} + \underbrace{\frac{d}{dx}(y(x))^2}_{\text{Use the Chain Rule}} = \underbrace{\frac{d}{dx}(1)}_{0}.$$

By the Chain Rule, $\dfrac{d}{dx}(y(x))^2 = 2y(x)y'(x)$, or $\dfrac{d}{dx}(y^2) = 2y\dfrac{dy}{dx}$. Substituting this result, we have

$$2x + 2y\frac{dy}{dx} = 0.$$

The last step is to solve for $\dfrac{dy}{dx}$:

$$2y\frac{dy}{dx} = -2x \qquad \text{Subtract } 2x \text{ from both sides.}$$

$$\frac{dy}{dx} = -\frac{x}{y}. \qquad \text{Divide by } 2y \text{ and simplify.}$$

This result holds provided $y \neq 0$. At the points $(1, 0)$ and $(-1, 0)$, the circle has vertical tangent lines.

b. Notice that the derivative $\dfrac{dy}{dx} = -\dfrac{x}{y}$ depends on *both* x and y. Therefore, to find the slope of the circle at $\left(\dfrac{1}{2}, \dfrac{\sqrt{3}}{2}\right)$, we substitute both $x = 1/2$ and $y = \sqrt{3}/2$ into the derivative formula. The result is

$$\frac{dy}{dx}\bigg|_{\left(\frac{1}{2}, \frac{\sqrt{3}}{2}\right)} = -\frac{1/2}{\sqrt{3}/2} = -\frac{1}{\sqrt{3}}.$$

The slope of the curve at $\left(\dfrac{1}{2}, -\dfrac{\sqrt{3}}{2}\right)$ is

$$\frac{dy}{dx}\bigg|_{\left(\frac{1}{2}, -\frac{\sqrt{3}}{2}\right)} = -\frac{1/2}{-\sqrt{3}/2} = \frac{1}{\sqrt{3}}.$$

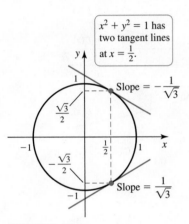

The curve and tangent lines are shown in Figure 3.46.   *Related Exercises 5–12* ◄

FIGURE 3.46

Example 1 illustrates the technique of implicit differentiation. It is done without solving for y, and it produces $\dfrac{dy}{dx}$ in terms of *both* x and y. The derivative obtained in Example 1 is consistent with the derivatives calculated explicitly in equations (1) and (2). For the upper half of the circle, substituting $y = \sqrt{1 - x^2}$ into the implicit derivative $\dfrac{dy}{dx} = -\dfrac{x}{y}$ gives

$$\frac{dy}{dx} = -\frac{x}{y} = -\frac{x}{\sqrt{1 - x^2}},$$

which agrees with equation (1). For the lower half of the circle, substituting $y = -\sqrt{1 - x^2}$ into $\dfrac{dy}{dx} = -\dfrac{x}{y}$ gives

$$\frac{dy}{dx} = -\frac{x}{y} = \frac{x}{\sqrt{1 - x^2}},$$

which is consistent with equation (2). Therefore, implicit differentiation gives a single unified derivative $\dfrac{dy}{dx} = -\dfrac{x}{y}$.

EXAMPLE 2   **Implicit differentiation** Find $y'(x)$ when $\sin xy = x^2 + y$.

SOLUTION It is impossible to solve this equation for y in terms of x, so we differentiate implicitly. Differentiating both sides of the equation with respect to x, using the Chain Rule and the Product Rule on the left side, gives

$$\cos xy(y + xy') = 2x + y'.$$

We now solve for y':

$$xy'\cos xy - y' = 2x - y \cos xy \qquad \text{Rearrange terms.}$$
$$y'(x \cos xy - 1) = 2x - y \cos xy \qquad \text{Factor on left side.}$$
$$y' = \frac{2x - y \cos xy}{x \cos xy - 1}. \qquad \text{Solve for } y'.$$

Notice that the final result gives y' in terms of both x and y.   *Related Exercises 13–24* ◄

QUICK CHECK 2 Use implicit differentiation to find $\dfrac{dy}{dx}$ for $x - y^2 = 3$. ◄

Slopes of Tangent Lines

Derivatives obtained by implicit differentiation typically depend on x *and* y. Therefore, the slope of a curve at a particular point (x, y) requires both the x- and y-coordinates of the point. These coordinates are also needed to find an equation of the tangent line at that point.

QUICK CHECK 3 If a function is defined explicitly in the form $y = f(x)$, which coordinates are needed to find the slope of a tangent line—the x-coordinate, the y-coordinate, or both? ◄

> Because y is a function of x, we have
>
> $$\frac{d}{dx}(x) = 1 \quad \text{and}$$
>
> $$\frac{d}{dx}(y) = y'.$$
>
> To differentiate y^3 with respect to x, we need the Chain Rule.

EXAMPLE 3   **Finding tangent lines with implicit functions** Find an equation of the line tangent to the curve $x^2 + xy - y^3 = 7$ at $(3, 2)$.

SOLUTION We calculate the derivative with respect to x of each term of the equation $x^2 + xy - y^3 = 7$:

$$\frac{d}{dx}(x^2) + \frac{d}{dx}(xy) - \frac{d}{dx}(y^3) = \frac{d}{dx}(7) \qquad \text{Differentiate each term.}$$

$$2x + \underbrace{y + xy'}_{\text{Product Rule}} - \underbrace{3y^2 y'}_{\text{Chain Rule}} = 0 \qquad \text{Calculate the derivatives.}$$

$$3y^2 y' - xy' = 2x + y \qquad \text{Group the terms containing } y'.$$

$$y' = \frac{2x + y}{3y^2 - x}. \qquad \text{Factor and solve for } y'.$$

To find the slope of the tangent line at $(3, 2)$, we substitute $x = 3$ and $y = 2$ into the derivative formula:

$$\left.\frac{dy}{dx}\right|_{(3,2)} = \left.\frac{2x + y}{3y^2 - x}\right|_{(3,2)} = \frac{8}{9}.$$

An equation of the line passing through $(3, 2)$ with slope $\frac{8}{9}$ is

$$y - 2 = \frac{8}{9}(x - 3) \quad \text{or} \quad y = \frac{8}{9}x - \frac{2}{3}.$$

Figure 3.47 shows the graphs of the curve $x^2 + xy - y^3 = 7$ and the tangent line.

Related Exercises 25–30 ◄

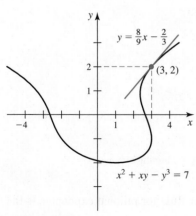

FIGURE 3.47

Higher-Order Derivatives of Implicit Functions

In previous sections of this chapter, we found higher-order derivatives $\dfrac{d^n y}{dx^n}$ by first calculating $\dfrac{dy}{dx}, \dfrac{d^2 y}{dx^2}, \ldots,$ and $\dfrac{d^{n-1} y}{dx^{n-1}}$. The same approach is used with implicit differentiation.

EXAMPLE 4   A second derivative Find $\dfrac{d^2 y}{dx^2}$ if $x^2 + y^2 = 1$.

SOLUTION The first derivative $\dfrac{dy}{dx} = -\dfrac{x}{y}$ was computed in Example 1.

We now calculate the derivative of each side of this equation and simplify the right side:

$$\frac{d}{dx}\left(\frac{dy}{dx}\right) = \frac{d}{dx}\left(-\frac{x}{y}\right) \qquad \text{Take derivatives with respect to } x.$$

$$\frac{d^2 y}{dx^2} = -\frac{y \cdot 1 - x\dfrac{dy}{dx}}{y^2} \qquad \text{Quotient Rule}$$

$$= -\frac{y - x\left(-\dfrac{x}{y}\right)}{y^2} \qquad \text{Substitute for } \dfrac{dy}{dx}.$$

$$= -\frac{x^2 + y^2}{y^3} \qquad \text{Simplify.}$$

$$= -\frac{1}{y^3}. \qquad x^2 + y^2 = 1 \qquad \textit{Related Exercises 31–36} \blacktriangleleft$$

The Power Rule for Rational Exponents

The Extended Power Rule (Section 3.4) states that $\dfrac{d}{dx}(x^n) = nx^{n-1}$, if n is an integer. Using implicit differentiation, this rule can be further extended to rational values of n such as $\frac{1}{2}$ or $-\frac{5}{3}$.

Assume p and q are integers with $q \neq 0$ and let $y = x^{p/q}$, where $x \geq 0$ when q is even. By raising each side of $y = x^{p/q}$ to the power q, we obtain $y^q = x^p$. Assuming that y is a differentiable function of x on its domain, both sides of $y^q = x^p$ are differentiated with respect to x:

$$qy^{q-1}\frac{dy}{dx} = px^{p-1}.$$

We divide both sides by qy^{q-1} and simplify:

$$\frac{dy}{dx} = \frac{p}{q} \cdot \frac{x^{p-1}}{y^{q-1}} = \frac{p}{q} \cdot \frac{x^{p-1}}{(x^{p/q})^{q-1}} \qquad \text{Substitute } x^{p/q} \text{ for } y.$$

$$= \frac{p}{q} \cdot \frac{x^{p-1}}{x^{p-p/q}} \qquad \text{Multiply exponents in the denominator.}$$

$$= \frac{p}{q} \cdot x^{p/q-1}. \qquad \text{Simplify by combining exponents.}$$

If we let $n = \dfrac{p}{q}$, then $\dfrac{d}{dx}(x^n) = nx^{n-1}$. So the Power Rule for rational exponents is the same as the Power Rule for integer exponents.

> The assumption that $y = x^{p/q}$ is differentiable on its domain is proved in Section 3.9, where the Power Rule is proved for all real powers; that is, we prove that $\dfrac{d}{dx}(x^n) = nx^{n-1}$ holds for any real number n.

THEOREM 3.16   Power Rule for Rational Exponents

Assume p and q are integers with $q \neq 0$. Then

$$\frac{d}{dx}(x^{p/q}) = \frac{p}{q}x^{p/q-1},$$

provided $x > 0$ when q is even.

EXAMPLE 5   Rational exponent   Calculate $\dfrac{dy}{dx}$ for the following functions.

a. $y = \sqrt{x}$ **b.** $y = (x^6 + 3x)^{2/3}$

SOLUTION

> The derivative of $\sqrt{x}$ (Example 5a) was determined using the limit definition of the derivative in Example 5 of Section 3.1.

a. $\dfrac{dy}{dx} = \dfrac{d}{dx}(x^{1/2}) = \dfrac{1}{2}x^{-1/2} = \dfrac{1}{2\sqrt{x}}$

b. We apply the Chain Rule, where the outer function is $u^{2/3}$ and the inner function is $x^6 + 3x$:

$$\frac{dy}{dx} = \frac{d}{dx}((x^6 + 3x)^{2/3}) = \underbrace{\frac{2}{3}(x^6 + 3x)^{-1/3}}_{\substack{\text{derivative of}\\\text{outer function}}} \underbrace{(6x^5 + 3)}_{\substack{\text{derivative of}\\\text{inner function}}}$$

$$= \frac{2(2x^5 + 1)}{(x^6 + 3x)^{1/3}}.$$

Related Exercises 37–44 ◄

We now combine several techniques in one problem: implicit differentiation, the Chain Rule, and the Power Rule for rational exponents.

EXAMPLE 6   Implicit differentiation with rational exponents   Find the slope of the curve $2(x + y)^{1/3} = y$ at the point $(4, 4)$.

SOLUTION   We begin by differentiating both sides of the given equation:

$$\frac{2}{3}(x + y)^{-2/3}\left(1 + \frac{dy}{dx}\right) = \frac{dy}{dx} \qquad \begin{array}{l}\text{Implicit differentiation,}\\ \text{Chain Rule, Theorem 3.16}\end{array}$$

$$\frac{2}{3}(x + y)^{-2/3} = \frac{dy}{dx} - \frac{2}{3}(x + y)^{-2/3}\frac{dy}{dx} \qquad \text{Expand and collect like terms.}$$

$$\frac{2}{3}(x + y)^{-2/3} = \frac{dy}{dx}\left(1 - \frac{2}{3}(x + y)^{-2/3}\right). \qquad \text{Factor out } \frac{dy}{dx}.$$

Solving for dy/dx, we find that

$$\frac{dy}{dx} = \frac{\dfrac{2}{3}(x + y)^{-2/3}}{1 - \dfrac{2}{3}(x + y)^{-2/3}} \qquad \text{Divide by } 1 - \frac{2}{3}(x + y)^{-2/3}.$$

$$\frac{dy}{dx} = \frac{2}{3(x + y)^{2/3} - 2} \qquad \text{Multiply by } 3(x + y)^{2/3} \text{ and simplify.}$$

Note that the point $(4, 4)$ *does* lie on the curve (Figure 3.48). The slope of the curve at $(4, 4)$ is found by substituting $x = 4$ and $y = 4$ into the formula for $\dfrac{dy}{dx}$:

$$\left.\frac{dy}{dx}\right|_{(4, 4)} = \frac{2}{3(8)^{2/3} - 2} = \frac{1}{5}.$$

Related Exercises 45–50 ◄

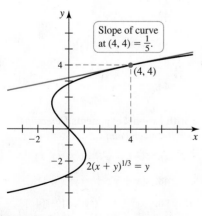

FIGURE 3.48

SECTION 3.8 EXERCISES

Review Questions

1. For some equations, such as $x^2 + y^2 = 1$ or $x - y^2 = 0$, it is possible to solve for y and then calculate $\dfrac{dy}{dx}$. Even in these cases, explain why implicit differentiation is usually a more efficient method for calculating the derivative.

2. Explain the differences between computing the derivatives of functions that are defined implicitly and explicitly.

3. Why are both the x-coordinate and the y-coordinate generally needed to find the slope of the tangent line at a point for an implicitly defined function?

4. In this section, for what values of n did we prove that $\dfrac{d}{dx}(x^n) = nx^{n-1}$?

Basic Skills

5–12. Implicit differentiation *Carry out the following steps.*

a. *Use implicit differentiation to find* $\dfrac{dy}{dx}$.

b. *Find the slope of the curve at the given point.*

5. $x^4 + y^4 = 2$; $(1, -1)$ 6. $x = e^y$; $(2, \ln 2)$

7. $y^2 = 4x$; $(1, 2)$ 8. $y^2 + 3x = 8$; $(1, \sqrt{5})$

9. $\sin y = 5x^4 - 5$; $(1, \pi)$ 10. $\sqrt{x} - 2\sqrt{y} = 0$; $(4, 1)$

11. $\cos y = x$; $\left(0, \dfrac{\pi}{2}\right)$ 12. $\tan xy = x + y$; $(0, 0)$

13–24. Implicit differentiation *Use implicit differentiation to find* $\dfrac{dy}{dx}$.

13. $\sin xy = x + y$ 14. $e^{xy} = 2y$

15. $x + y = \cos y$ 16. $x + 2y = \sqrt{y}$

17. $\cos y^2 + x = e^y$ 18. $y = \dfrac{x + 1}{y - 1}$

19. $x^3 = \dfrac{x + y}{x - y}$ 20. $(xy + 1)^3 = x - y^2 + 8$

21. $6x^3 + 7y^3 = 13xy$ 22. $\sin x \cos y = \sin x + \cos y$

23. $\sqrt{x^4 + y^2} = 5x + 2y^3$ 24. $\sqrt{x + y^2} = \sin y$

25–30. Tangent lines *Carry out the following steps.*

a. *Verify that the given point lies on the curve.*

b. *Determine an equation of the line tangent to the curve at the given point.*

25. $x^2 + xy + y^2 = 7$; $(2, 1)$ 26. $x^4 - x^2y + y^4 = 1$; $(-1, 1)$

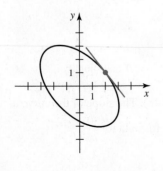
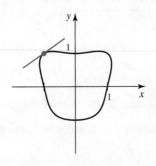

27. $\sin y + 5x = y^2$; $\left(\dfrac{\pi^2}{5}, \pi\right)$ 28. $x^3 + y^3 = 2xy$; $(1, 1)$

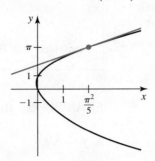
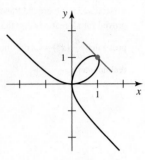

29. $\cos(x - y) + \sin y = \sqrt{2}$; $\left(\dfrac{\pi}{2}, \dfrac{\pi}{4}\right)$

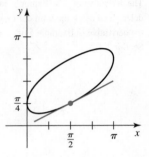

30. $(x^2 + y^2)^2 = \dfrac{25}{4}xy^2$; $(1, 2)$

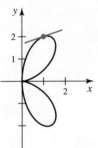

31–36. Second derivatives *Find* $\dfrac{d^2y}{dx^2}$.

31. $x + y^2 = 1$ 32. $2x^2 + y^2 = 4$

33. $x + y = \sin y$ 34. $x^4 + y^4 = 64$

35. $e^{2y} + x = y$ 36. $\sin x + x^2y = 10$

37–44. Derivatives of functions with rational exponents *Find* $\dfrac{dy}{dx}$.

37. $y = x^{5/4}$ 38. $y = \sqrt[3]{x^2 - x + 1}$

39. $y = (5x + 1)^{2/3}$ 40. $y = e^x\sqrt{x^3}$

41. $y = \sqrt[4]{\dfrac{2x}{4x - 3}}$ 42. $y = x(x + 1)^{1/3}$

43. $y = \sqrt[3]{(1 + x^{1/3})^2}$ 44. $y = \dfrac{x}{\sqrt[5]{x} + x}$

45–50. Implicit differentiation with rational exponents *Determine the slope of the following curves at the given point.*

45. $\sqrt[3]{x} + \sqrt[3]{y^4} = 2$; $(1, 1)$ 46. $x^{2/3} + y^{2/3} = 2$; $(1, 1)$

47. $xy^{1/3} + y = 10$; $(1, 8)$ 48. $(x + y)^{2/3} = y$; $(4, 4)$

49. $xy + x^{3/2}y^{-1/2} = 2$; $(1, 1)$ 50. $xy^{5/2} + x^{3/2}y = 12$; $(4, 1)$

Further Explorations

51. Explain why or why not Determine whether the following statements are true, and give an explanation or a counterexample.

a. For any equation containing the variables x and y, the derivative dy/dx can be found by first using algebra to rewrite the equation in the form $y = f(x)$.

b. For the equation of a circle of radius r, $x^2 + y^2 = r^2$, we have $\dfrac{dy}{dx} = -\dfrac{x}{y}$, for $y \neq 0$ and any real number $r > 0$.

c. If $x = 1$, then by implicit differentiation, $1 = 0$.

d. If $xy = 1$, then $y' = 1/x$.

52–54. Multiple tangent lines *Complete the following steps.*

a. *Find equations of all lines tangent to the curve at the given value of x.*

b. *Graph the tangent lines on the given graph.*

52. $x + y^3 - y = 1$; $x = 1$

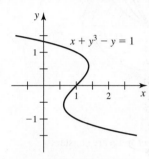

$x + y^3 - y = 1$

53. $x + y^2 - y = 1$; $x = 1$

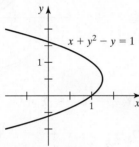

$x + y^2 - y = 1$

54. $4x^3 = y^2(4 - x)$; $x = 2$
(cissoid of Diocles)

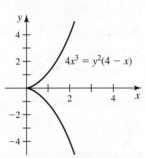

$4x^3 = y^2(4 - x)$

55. Witch of Agnesi Let $y(x^2 + 4) = 8$ (see figure).

a. Use implicit differentiation to find $\dfrac{dy}{dx}$.

b. Find equations of all lines tangent to the curve $y(x^2 + 4) = 8$ when $y = 1$.

c. Solve the equation $y(x^2 + 4) = 8$ for y to find an explicit expression for y and then calculate $\dfrac{dy}{dx}$.

d. Verify that the results of parts (a) and (c) are consistent.

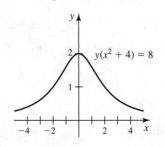

$y(x^2 + 4) = 8$

56. Vertical tangent lines

a. Determine the points at which the curve $x + y^3 - y = 1$ has a vertical tangent line (see Exercise 52).

b. Does the curve have any horizontal tangent lines? Explain.

57. Vertical tangent lines

a. Determine the points at which the curve $x + y^2 - y = 1$ has a vertical tangent line (see Exercise 53).

b. Does the curve have any horizontal tangent lines? Explain.

58–62. Identifying functions from an equation *The following equations implicitly define one or more functions.*

a. *Find $\dfrac{dy}{dx}$ using implicit differentiation.*

b. *Solve the given equation for y to identify the implicitly defined functions $y = f_1(x), y = f_2(x), \ldots$.*

c. *Use the functions found in part (b) to graph the given equation.*

58. $y^3 = ax^2$ (Neile's semicubical parabola)

59. $x + y^3 - xy = 1$ (*Hint:* Rewrite as $y^3 - 1 = xy - x$ and then factor both sides.)

60. $y^2 = \dfrac{x^2(4 - x)}{4 + x}$ (right strophoid)

61. $x^4 = 2(x^2 - y^2)$ (eight curve)

62. $y^2(x + 2) = x^2(6 - x)$ (trisectrix)

63–68. Normal lines A **normal line** *at a point P on a curve passes through P and is perpendicular to the line tangent to the curve at P (see figure). Use the following equations and graphs to determine an equation of the normal line at the given point. Illustrate your work by graphing the curve with the normal line.*

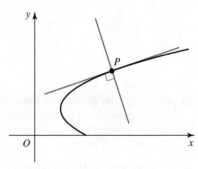

63. Exercise 25	**64.** Exercise 26	**65.** Exercise 27
66. Exercise 28	**67.** Exercise 29	**68.** Exercise 30

69–72. Visualizing tangent and normal lines

a. *Determine an equation of the tangent line and normal line at the given point (x_0, y_0) on the following curves. (See instructions for Exercises 63–68.)*

b. *Graph the tangent and normal lines on the given graph.*

69. $3x^3 + 7y^3 = 10y$; $(x_0, y_0) = (1, 1)$

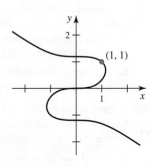

$(1, 1)$

70. $x^4 = 2x^2 + 2y^2$;
$(x_0, y_0) = (2, 2)$
(kampyle of Eudoxus)

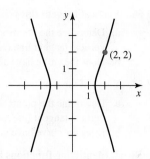

71. $(x^2 + y^2 - 2x)^2 = 2(x^2 + y^2)$;
$(x_0, y_0) = (2, 2)$
(limaçon of Pascal)

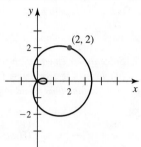

72. $(x^2 + y^2)^2 = \dfrac{25}{3}(x^2 - y^2)$;

$(x_0, y_0) = (2, -1)$
(lemniscate of Bernoulli)

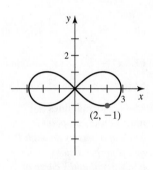

Applications

73. Cobb-Douglas production function The output of an economic system Q, subject to two inputs, such as labor L and capital K, is often modeled by the Cobb-Douglas production function $Q = cL^a K^b$. When $a + b = 1$, the case is called *constant returns to scale*. Suppose $Q = 1280$, $a = \dfrac{1}{3}$, $b = \dfrac{2}{3}$, and $c = 40$.

  a. Find the rate of change of capital with respect to labor, dK/dL.
  b. Evaluate the derivative in part (a) with $L = 8$ and $K = 64$.

74. Surface area of a cone The lateral surface area of a cone of radius r and height h (the surface area excluding the base) is $A = \pi r\sqrt{r^2 + h^2}$.

  a. Find dr/dh for a cone with a lateral surface area of $A = 1500\pi$.
  b. Evaluate this derivative when $r = 30$ and $h = 40$.

75. Volume of a spherical cap Imagine slicing through a sphere with a plane (sheet of paper). The smaller piece produced is called a spherical cap. Its volume is $V = \pi h^2(3r - h)/3$, where r is the radius of the sphere and h is the thickness of the cap.

  a. Find dr/dh for a sphere with a volume of $5\pi/3$.
  b. Evaluate this derivative when $r = 2$ and $h = 1$.

76. Volume of a torus The volume of a torus (doughnut or bagel) with an inner radius of a and an outer radius of b is $V = \pi^2(b + a)(b - a)^2/4$.

  a. Find db/da for a torus with a volume of $64\pi^2$.
  b. Evaluate this derivative when $a = 6$ and $b = 10$.

Additional Exercises

77–79. Orthogonal trajectories *Two curves are* **orthogonal** *to each other if their tangent lines are perpendicular at each point of intersection (recall that two lines are perpendicular to each other if their slopes are negative reciprocals). A family of curves forms* **orthogonal trajectories** *with another family of curves if each curve in one family is orthogonal to each curve in the other family. For example, the parabolas $y = cx^2$ form orthogonal trajectories with the family of ellipses $x^2 + 2y^2 = k$, where c and k are constants (see figure).*

Find dy/dx for each equation of the following pairs. Use the derivatives to explain why the families of curves form orthogonal trajectories.

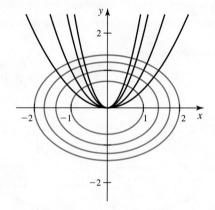

77. $y = mx$; $x^2 + y^2 = a^2$, where m and a are constants

78. $y = cx^2$; $x^2 + 2y^2 = k$, where c and k are constants

79. $xy = a$; $x^2 - y^2 = b$, where a and b are constants

80. Finding slope Find the slope of the curve $5\sqrt{x} - 10\sqrt{y} = \sin x$ at the point $(4\pi, \pi)$.

81. A challenging derivative Find $\dfrac{dy}{dx}$, where
$(x^2 + y^2)(x^2 + y^2 + x) = 8xy^2$.

82. A challenging derivative Find $\dfrac{dy}{dx}$, where
$\sqrt{3x^7 + y^2} = \sin^2 y + 100xy$.

83. A challenging second derivative Find $\dfrac{d^2 y}{dx^2}$, where $\sqrt{y} + xy = 1$.

84–87. Work carefully *Proceed with caution when using implicit differentiation to find points on a curve with a specified slope. For the following curves, find the points on the curve (if they exist) at which the tangent line is horizontal or vertical. Once you have found possible points, be sure that they actually lie on the curve. Confirm your results with a graph.*

84. $y^2 - 3xy = 2$ **85.** $x^2(3y^2 - 2y^3) = 4$

86. $x^2(y - 2) - e^y = 0$ **87.** $x(1 - y^2) + y^3 = 0$

QUICK CHECK ANSWERS

1. $y = \sqrt{x}$ and $y = -\sqrt{x}$ **2.** $\dfrac{dy}{dx} = \dfrac{1}{2y}$ **3.** Only the x-coordinate is needed. ◄

3.9 Derivatives of Logarithmic and Exponential Functions

We return now to the major theme of this chapter: developing rules of differentiation for the standard families of functions. First, we discover how to differentiate the natural logarithmic function. From there, we treat general exponential and logarithmic functions.

The Derivative of $y = \ln x$

Recall from Section 1.3 that the natural exponential function $f(x) = e^x$ is a one-to-one function on the interval $(-\infty, \infty)$. Therefore, it has an inverse, which is the natural logarithmic function $f^{-1}(x) = \ln x$. The domain of f^{-1} is the range of f, which is $(0, \infty)$. The graphs of f and f^{-1} are symmetric about the line $y = x$ (Figure 3.49). This inverse relationship has several important consequences, summarized as follows.

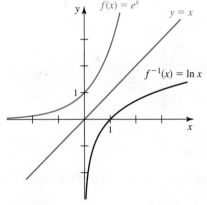

FIGURE 3.49

▷ Figure 3.49 also provides evidence that $\ln x$ is differentiable for $x > 0$: Its graph is smooth with no jumps or cusps.

Inverse Properties for e^x and $\ln x$

1. $e^{\ln x} = x$, for $x > 0$, and $\ln(e^x) = x$, for all x.
2. $y = \ln x$ if and only if $x = e^y$.
3. For real numbers x and $b > 0$, $b^x = e^{\ln b^x} = e^{x \ln b}$.

QUICK CHECK 1 Simplify $e^{2 \ln x}$. Express 5^x using the base e. ◄

With these preliminary observations, we now determine the derivative of $\ln x$. A theorem we prove in Section 3.10 says that because e^x is differentiable on its domain, its inverse $\ln x$ is also differentiable on its domain.

To find the derivative of $y = \ln x$, we begin with inverse property 2 and write $x = e^y$, where $x > 0$. The key step is to compute dy/dx with implicit differentiation. Using the Chain Rule to differentiate both sides of $x = e^y$ with respect to x, we have

$$x = e^y \qquad \text{$y = \ln x$ if and only if $x = e^y$}$$

$$1 = e^y \cdot \frac{dy}{dx} \qquad \text{Differentiate both sides with respect to x.}$$

$$\frac{dy}{dx} = \frac{1}{e^y} = \frac{1}{x}. \qquad \text{Solve for dy/dx and use $x = e^y$.}$$

Therefore,

$$\frac{d}{dx}(\ln x) = \frac{1}{x}.$$

Because the domain of the natural logarithm is $(0, \infty)$, this rule is limited to positive values of x (Figure 3.50a).

An important extension is obtained by considering the function $\ln |x|$, which is defined for all $x \neq 0$. By the definition of the absolute value,

$$\ln |x| = \begin{cases} \ln x & \text{if } x > 0 \\ \ln (-x) & \text{if } x < 0. \end{cases}$$

For $x > 0$, it follows immediately that

$$\frac{d}{dx}(\ln |x|) = \frac{d}{dx}(\ln x) = \frac{1}{x}.$$

▷ Recall that
$$|x| = \begin{cases} x & \text{if } x \geq 0 \\ -x & \text{if } x < 0. \end{cases}$$

When $x < 0$, a similar calculation using the Chain Rule reveals that

$$\frac{d}{dx}(\ln|x|) = \frac{d}{dx}(\ln(-x)) = \frac{1}{(-x)}(-1) = \frac{1}{x}.$$

Therefore, we have the result that the derivative of $\ln|x|$ is $\frac{1}{x}$, for $x \neq 0$ (Figure 3.50b).

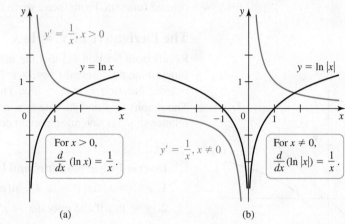

(a)   (b)

FIGURE 3.50

If we take these results one step further and use the Chain Rule to differentiate $\ln|u(x)|$, we obtain the following theorem.

THEOREM 3.17   Derivative of ln x

$$\frac{d}{dx}(\ln x) = \frac{1}{x}, \text{ for } x > 0 \qquad \frac{d}{dx}(\ln|x|) = \frac{1}{x}, \text{ for } x \neq 0$$

If u is differentiable at x and $u(x) \neq 0$, then

$$\frac{d}{dx}(\ln|u(x)|) = \frac{u'(x)}{u(x)}.$$

EXAMPLE 1   Derivatives involving ln x Find $\dfrac{dy}{dx}$ for the following functions.

a. $y = \ln 4x$ **b.** $y = x \ln x$ **c.** $y = \ln|\sec x|$ **d.** $y = \dfrac{\ln x^2}{x^2}$, for $x \neq 0$

SOLUTION

a. Using the Chain Rule,

$$\frac{dy}{dx} = \frac{d}{dx}(\ln 4x) = \frac{1}{4x} \cdot 4 = \frac{1}{x}.$$

> Because $\ln x$ and $\ln 4x$ differ by an additive constant ($\ln 4x = \ln x + \ln 4$), the derivatives of $\ln x$ and $\ln 4x$ are equal.

An alternative method uses a property of logarithms before differentiating:

$$\frac{d}{dx}(\ln 4x) = \frac{d}{dx}(\ln 4 + \ln x) \quad \ln xy = \ln x + \ln y$$

$$= 0 + \frac{1}{x} = \frac{1}{x}. \quad \ln 4 \text{ is a constant.}$$

b. By the Product Rule,

$$\frac{dy}{dx} = \frac{d}{dx}(x \ln x) = 1 \cdot \ln x + x \cdot \frac{1}{x} = \ln x + 1.$$

c. Using the Chain Rule and the second part of Theorem 3.17,

$$\frac{dy}{dx} = \frac{1}{\sec x}\left[\frac{d}{dx}(\sec x)\right] = \frac{1}{\sec x}(\sec x \tan x) = \tan x.$$

> The identity $\ln x^2 = 2\ln x$ was used to simplify the result in Example 1d. It could have been used prior to differentiation to avoid using the Chain Rule.

d. The Quotient Rule and Chain Rule give

$$\frac{dy}{dx} = \frac{x^2\left(\dfrac{1}{x^2}\cdot 2x\right) - (\ln x^2)\, 2x}{(x^2)^2} = \frac{2x - 2x\ln x^2}{x^4} = \frac{2(1 - \ln x^2)}{x^3}.$$

Related Exercises 9–22 ◀

QUICK CHECK 2 Find $\dfrac{d}{dx}(\ln x^p)$, where $x > 0$ and p is a rational number, in two ways: (1) using the Chain Rule and (2) by first using a property of logarithms. ◀

The derivative of b^x

A rule similar to $\dfrac{d}{dx}(e^x) = e^x$ exists for computing the derivative of b^x, where $b > 0$.

Because $b^x = e^{x\ln b}$ by inverse property 3, its derivative is

$$\frac{d}{dx}(b^x) = \frac{d}{dx}(e^{x\ln b}) = \underbrace{e^{x\ln b}}_{b^x}\cdot \ln b. \quad \text{Chain Rule with } \frac{d}{dx}(x\ln b) = \ln b$$

Noting that $e^{x\ln b} = b^x$ results in the following theorem.

> Check that when $b = e$, Theorem 3.18 becomes
> $$\frac{d}{dx}(e^x) = e^x.$$

THEOREM 3.18 Derivative of b^x

If $b > 0$ and $b \neq 1$, then for all x,

$$\frac{d}{dx}(b^x) = b^x \ln b.$$

Notice that when $b > 1$, $\ln b > 0$ and the graph of $y = b^x$ has tangent lines with positive slopes for all x. When $0 < b < 1$, $\ln b < 0$ and the graph of $y = b^x$ has tangent lines with negative slopes for all x. In either case, the tangent line at $(0, 1)$ has slope $\ln b$ (Figure 3.51).

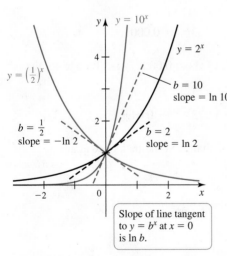

$y = 10^x$
$y = 2^x$
$b = 10$ slope $= \ln 10$
$y = \left(\dfrac{1}{2}\right)^x$
$b = \dfrac{1}{2}$ slope $= -\ln 2$
$b = 2$ slope $= \ln 2$

Slope of line tangent to $y = b^x$ at $x = 0$ is $\ln b$.

FIGURE 3.51

EXAMPLE 2 Derivatives with b^x Find the derivative of the following functions.

a. $f(x) = 3^x$
b. $g(t) = 108 \cdot 2^{t/12}$

SOLUTION

a. Using Theorem 3.18, $f'(x) = 3^x \ln 3$.

b.
$$g'(t) = 108\frac{d}{dt}(2^{t/12}) \qquad \text{Constant Multiple Rule}$$

$$= 108\cdot\ln 2\cdot 2^{t/12}\underbrace{\frac{d}{dt}\left(\frac{t}{12}\right)}_{1/12} \qquad \text{Chain Rule}$$

$$= 9\ln 2\cdot 2^{t/12} \qquad \text{Simplify.}$$

Related Exercises 23–30 ◀

Table 3.6

Mother's Age	Incidence of Down Syndrome	Decimal Equivalent
30	1 in 900	0.00111
35	1 in 400	0.00250
36	1 in 300	0.00333
37	1 in 230	0.00435
38	1 in 180	0.00556
39	1 in 135	0.00741
40	1 in 105	0.00952
42	1 in 60	0.01667
44	1 in 35	0.02875
46	1 in 20	0.05000
48	1 in 16	0.06250
49	1 in 12	0.08333

Source: E.G. Hook and A. Lindsjo, *Down Syndrome in Live Births by Single Year Maternal Age.*

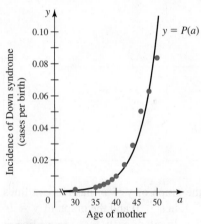

FIGURE 3.52

> The model in Example 3 was created using a method called *exponential regression*. The parameters A and B are chosen so that the function $P(a) = AB^a$ fits the data as closely as possible.

EXAMPLE 3 An exponential model Table 3.6 and Figure 3.52 show how the incidence of Down syndrome in newborn infants increases with the age of the mother. The data can be modeled with the exponential function $P(a) = \dfrac{1}{1,613,000} 1.2733^a$, where a is the age of the mother (in years) and $P(a)$ is the incidence (number of Down syndrome children per total births).

a. According to the model, at what age is the incidence of Down syndrome equal to 0.01 (that is, 1 in 100)?

b. Compute $P'(a)$.

c. Find $P'(35)$ and $P'(46)$, and interpret each.

SOLUTION

a. We let $P(a) = 0.01$ and solve for a:

$$0.01 = \frac{1}{1,613,000} 1.2733^a$$

$$\ln 16{,}130 = \ln(1.2733^a) \qquad \text{Multiply both sides by 1,613,000 and take logarithms of both sides.}$$

$$\ln 16{,}130 = a \ln 1.2733 \qquad \text{Property of logarithms}$$

$$a = \frac{\ln 16{,}130}{\ln 1.2733} \approx 40 \,(\text{years old}). \quad \text{Solve for } a.$$

b.
$$P'(a) = \frac{1}{1,613,000} \frac{d}{da}(1.2733^a)$$

$$= \frac{1}{1,613,000} 1.2733^a \ln 1.2733$$

$$\approx \frac{1}{6,676,000} 1.2733^a$$

c. The derivative measures the rate of change of the incidence with respect to age. For a 35-year-old woman,

$$P'(35) = \frac{1}{6,676,000} 1.2733^{35} \approx 0.0007,$$

which means the incidence increases at a rate of about 0.0007/year. By age 46, the rate of change is

$$P'(46) = \frac{1}{6,676,000} 1.2733^{46} \approx 0.01,$$

which is a significant increase over the rate of change of the incidence at age 35.

Related Exercises 31–33 ◄

QUICK CHECK 3 Suppose $A = 500(1.045)^t$. Compute $\dfrac{dA}{dt}$. ◄

The General Power Rule

As it stands now, the Power Rule for derivatives says that $\dfrac{d}{dx}(x^p) = px^{p-1}$, for rational powers p. The rule is now extended to all real powers.

> **THEOREM 3.19 General Power Rule**
> For real numbers p and for $x > 0$,
>
> $$\frac{d}{dx}(x^p) = px^{p-1}.$$
>
> Furthermore, if u is a positive differentiable function on its domain, then
>
> $$\frac{d}{dx}(u(x)^p) = pu(x)^{p-1} \cdot u'(x).$$

Proof: For $x > 0$ and real numbers p, we have $x^p = e^{p \ln x}$ by inverse property (3). Therefore, the derivative of x^p is computed as follows:

$$\frac{d}{dx}(x^p) = \frac{d}{dx}(e^{p \ln x}) \quad \text{Inverse property (3)}$$

$$= e^{p \ln x} \cdot \frac{p}{x} \quad \text{Chain Rule, } \frac{d}{dx}(p \ln x) = \frac{p}{x}$$

$$= x^p \cdot \frac{p}{x} \quad e^{p \ln x} = x^p$$

$$= px^{p-1}. \quad \text{Simplify.}$$

We see that $\frac{d}{dx}(x^p) = px^{p-1}$ for all real powers p. The second part of the General Power Rule follows from the Chain Rule. ◄

EXAMPLE 4 Computing derivatives Find the derivative of the following functions.

a. $y = x^\pi$ **b.** $y = \pi^x$ **c.** $y = (x^2 + 4)^e$

SOLUTION

> Recall that power functions have the variable in the base, while exponential functions have the variable in the exponent.

a. With $y = x^\pi$, we have a power function with an irrational exponent; by the General Power Rule,

$$\frac{dy}{dx} = \pi x^{\pi-1}, \text{ for } x > 0.$$

b. Here we have an exponential function with base $b = \pi$. By Theorem 3.18,

$$\frac{dy}{dx} = \pi^x \ln \pi.$$

c. The Chain Rule and General Power Rule are required:

$$\frac{dy}{dx} = e(x^2 + 4)^{e-1} \cdot 2x = 2ex(x^2 + 4)^{e-1}.$$

Because $x^2 + 4 > 0$, for all x, the result is valid for all x.   *Related Exercises 34–44* ◄

Functions of the form $f(x) = (g(x))^{h(x)}$, where both g and h are nonconstant functions, are neither exponential functions nor power functions (they are sometimes called *tower functions*). In order to compute their derivatives, we use the identity $b^x = e^{x \ln b}$ to rewrite f with base e:

$$f(x) = (g(x))^{h(x)} = e^{h(x) \ln g(x)}.$$

This function carries the restriction $g(x) > 0$. The derivative of f is then computed using the methods developed in this section. A specific case is illustrated in the following example.

EXAMPLE 5 **General exponential functions** Let $f(x) = x^{\sin x}$, for $x > 0$.

a. Find $f'(x)$.   **b.** Evaluate $f'\left(\dfrac{\pi}{2}\right)$.

SOLUTION

a. The key step is to use $b^x = e^{x \ln b}$ to write f in the form

$$f(x) = x^{\sin x} = e^{\sin x \ln x}.$$

We now differentiate:

$$f'(x) = e^{\sin x \ln x} \frac{d}{dx}(\sin x \ln x) \qquad \text{Chain Rule}$$

$$= \underbrace{e^{\sin x \ln x}}_{x^{\sin x}}\left(\cos x \ln x + \frac{\sin x}{x}\right) \qquad \text{Product Rule}$$

$$= x^{\sin x}\left(\cos x \ln x + \frac{\sin x}{x}\right).$$

b. Letting $x = \dfrac{\pi}{2}$, we find that

$$f'\left(\frac{\pi}{2}\right) = \left(\frac{\pi}{2}\right)^{\sin \pi/2}\left(\underbrace{\cos\frac{\pi}{2}}_{0}\ln\frac{\pi}{2} + \underbrace{\frac{\sin(\pi/2)}{\pi/2}}_{2/\pi}\right) \qquad \text{Substitute } x = \frac{\pi}{2}.$$

$$= \frac{\pi}{2}\left(0 + \frac{2}{\pi}\right) = 1.$$

Related Exercises 45–50 ◀

EXAMPLE 6 **Finding a horizontal tangent line** Determine whether the graph of $f(x) = x^x$, for $x > 0$, has any horizontal tangent lines.

SOLUTION A horizontal tangent occurs when $f'(x) = 0$. In order to find the derivative, we first write $f(x) = x^x = e^{x \ln x}$:

$$\frac{d}{dx}(x^x) = \frac{d}{dx}(e^{x \ln x})$$

$$= \underbrace{e^{x \ln x}}_{x^x}\left(1 \cdot \ln x + x \cdot \frac{1}{x}\right) \qquad \text{Chain Rule; Product Rule}$$

$$= x^x(\ln x + 1). \qquad \text{Simplify; } e^{x \ln x} = x^x.$$

The equation $f'(x) = 0$ implies that $x^x = 0$ or $\ln x + 1 = 0$. The first equation has no solution because $x^x = e^{x \ln x} > 0$, for all $x > 0$. We solve the second equation, $\ln x + 1 = 0$, as follows:

$$\ln x = -1$$

$$e^{\ln x} = e^{-1} \qquad \text{Exponentiate both sides.}$$

$$x = \frac{1}{e}. \qquad e^{\ln x} = x$$

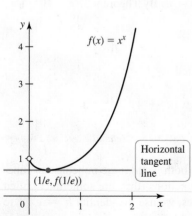

FIGURE 3.53

Therefore, the graph of $f(x) = x^x$ (Figure 3.53) has a single horizontal tangent at $(e^{-1}, f(e^{-1})) \approx (0.368, 0.692)$.

Related Exercises 51–54 ◀

Derivatives of General Logarithmic Functions

The general exponential function $f(x) = b^x$ is one-to-one when $b > 0$ with $b \neq 1$. The inverse function $f^{-1}(x) = \log_b x$ is the logarithmic function with base b. The technique used to differentiate the natural logarithm applies to the general logarithmic function. We begin with the inverse relationship

$$y = \log_b x \Leftrightarrow x = b^y, \text{ where } x > 0.$$

Differentiating both sides of $x = b^y$ with respect to x, we obtain

$$1 = b^y \ln b \cdot \frac{dy}{dx} \quad \text{Implicit differentiation}$$

$$\frac{dy}{dx} = \frac{1}{b^y \ln b} \quad \text{Solve for } \frac{dy}{dx}.$$

$$\frac{dy}{dx} = \frac{1}{x \ln b}. \quad b^y = x.$$

> An alternative proof of Theorem 3.20 uses the change-of-base formula $\log_b x = \dfrac{\ln x}{\ln b}$ (Section 1.3). Differentiating both sides of this equation gives the same result.

THEOREM 3.20   Derivative of $\log_b x$
If $b > 0$ and $b \neq 1$, then

$$\frac{d}{dx}(\log_b x) = \frac{1}{x \ln b}, \text{ for } x > 0 \quad \text{and} \quad \frac{d}{dx}(\log_b |x|) = \frac{1}{x \ln b}, \text{ for } x \neq 0.$$

QUICK CHECK 4 Compute dy/dx for $y = \log_3 x$. ◄

EXAMPLE 7   Derivatives with general logarithms Compute the derivative of the following functions.

a. $f(x) = \log_5(2x + 1)$ **b.** $T(n) = n \log_2 n$

SOLUTION

a. We use Theorem 3.20 with the Chain Rule assuming $2x + 1 > 0$:

$$f'(x) = \frac{1}{(2x + 1)\ln 5} \cdot 2 = \frac{2}{\ln 5} \cdot \frac{1}{2x + 1}.$$

> The function in Example 7b is used in computer science as of estimate of the computing time needed to carry out a *sorting algorithm* on a list of n items.

b.
$$T'(n) = \log_2 n + n \cdot \frac{1}{n \ln 2} = \log_2 n + \frac{1}{\ln 2} \quad \text{Product Rule}$$

We can change bases and write the result in base e:

$$T'(n) = \frac{\ln n}{\ln 2} + \frac{1}{\ln 2} = \frac{\ln n + 1}{\ln 2}.$$

Related Exercises 55–60 ◄

QUICK CHECK 5 Show that the derivative computed in Example 7b can be expressed in base 2 as $T'(n) = \log_2(en)$. ◄

We close with a clever differentiation technique that may in some cases be more efficient than the rules we have discussed so far.

Logarithmic Differentiation

Products, quotients, and powers of functions are usually differentiated using the derivative rules of the same name (perhaps combined with the Chain Rule). There are times, however, when the direct computation of a derivative is very tedious. Consider the function

> The properties of logarithms needed for logarithmic differentiation are:
>
> 1. $\ln xy = \ln x + \ln y$
> 2. $\ln(x/y) = \ln x - \ln y$
> 3. $\ln x^y = y \ln x$
>
> All three properties are used in Example 8.

$$f(x) = \frac{(x^3 - 1)^4 \sqrt{3x - 1}}{x^2 + 4}.$$

We would need the Quotient, Product, and Chain Rules just to compute $f'(x)$, and simplifying the result would require additional work. The properties of logarithms reviewed in Section 1.3 are useful for differentiating such functions.

EXAMPLE 8 **Logarithmic differentiation** Let $f(x) = \dfrac{(x^3 - 1)^4 \sqrt{3x - 1}}{x^2 + 4}$ and compute $f'(x)$.

SOLUTION We begin by taking the natural logarithm of both sides and simplifying the result:

> In the event that $f \leq 0$ for some values of x, $\ln f(x)$ is not defined. In that case, we generally find the derivative of $|y| = |f(x)|$.

$$\ln\left(f(x)\right) = \ln\left[\frac{(x^3 - 1)^4 \sqrt{3x - 1}}{x^2 + 4}\right]$$
$$= \ln(x^3 - 1)^4 + \ln\sqrt{3x - 1} - \ln(x^2 + 4) \qquad \log xy = \log x + \log y$$
$$= 4\ln(x^3 - 1) + \tfrac{1}{2}\ln(3x - 1) - \ln(x^2 + 4). \quad \log x^y = y\log x$$

We now differentiate both sides using the Chain Rule; specifically the derivative of the left side is $\dfrac{d}{dx}(\ln f(x)) = \dfrac{f'(x)}{f(x)}$. Therefore,

$$\frac{f'(x)}{f(x)} = 4 \cdot \frac{1}{x^3 - 1} \cdot 3x^2 + \frac{1}{2} \cdot \frac{1}{3x - 1} \cdot 3 - \frac{1}{x^2 + 4} \cdot 2x.$$

Solving for $f'(x)$, we have

$$f'(x) = f(x)\left[\frac{12x^2}{x^3 - 1} + \frac{3}{2(3x - 1)} - \frac{2x}{x^2 + 4}\right].$$

Finally, we replace $f(x)$ with the original function:

$$f'(x) = \frac{(x^3 - 1)^4 \sqrt{3x - 1}}{x^2 + 4}\left[\frac{12x^2}{x^3 - 1} + \frac{3}{2(3x - 1)} - \frac{2x}{x^2 + 4}\right].$$

Related Exercises 61–68 ◄

Logarithmic differentiation also provides an alternative method for finding derivatives of functions of the form $g(x)^{h(x)}$. The derivative of $f(x) = x^x$ (Example 6) is computed as follows, assuming $x > 0$:

$$f(x) = x^x$$
$$\ln(f(x)) = \ln(x^x) = x\ln x \qquad \text{Take logarithms of both sides; use properties.}$$
$$\frac{1}{f(x)}f'(x) = 1 \cdot \ln x + x \cdot \frac{1}{x} \qquad \text{Differentiate both sides.}$$
$$f'(x) = f(x)(\ln x + 1) \qquad \text{Solve for } f'(x) \text{ and simplify.}$$
$$f'(x) = x^x(\ln x + 1). \qquad \text{Replace } f(x) \text{ with } x^x.$$

This result agrees with Example 6. The decision about which method to use is largely one of preference.

SECTION 3.9 EXERCISES

Review Questions

1. Use $x = e^y$ to explain why $\dfrac{d}{dx}(\ln x) = \dfrac{1}{x}$, for $x > 0$.

2. Sketch the graph of $f(x) = \ln|x|$ and explain how the graph shows that $f'(x) = \dfrac{1}{x}$.

3. Show that $\dfrac{d}{dx}(\ln kx) = \dfrac{d}{dx}(\ln x)$, where $x > 0$ and k is a positive real number.

4. State the derivative rule for the exponential function $f(x) = b^x$. How does it differ from the derivative formula for e^x?

5. State the derivative rule for the logarithmic function $f(x) = \log_b x$. How does it differ from the derivative formula for $\ln x$?

6. Explain why $b^x = e^{x\ln b}$.

7. Express the function $f(x) = g(x)^{h(x)}$ in terms of the natural logarithmic and natural exponential functions (base e).

8. Explain the general procedure of logarithmic differentiation.

Basic Skills

9–22. Derivatives involving ln x *Find the following derivatives.*

9. $\dfrac{d}{dx}(\ln 7x)$ **10.** $\dfrac{d}{dx}(x^2 \ln x)$ **11.** $\dfrac{d}{dx}(\ln x^2)$

12. $\dfrac{d}{dx}(\ln 2x^8)$ **13.** $\dfrac{d}{dx}(\ln |\sin x|)$ **14.** $\dfrac{d}{dx}\left(\dfrac{\ln x^2}{x}\right)$

15. $\dfrac{d}{dx}\left[\ln\left(\dfrac{x+1}{x-1}\right)\right]$ **16.** $\dfrac{d}{dx}(e^x \ln x)$ **17.** $\dfrac{d}{dx}((x^2+1)\ln x)$

18. $\dfrac{d}{dx}(\ln |x^2-1|)$ **19.** $\dfrac{d}{dx}(\ln(\ln x))$ **20.** $\dfrac{d}{dx}(\ln(\cos^2 x))$

21. $\dfrac{d}{dx}\left(\dfrac{\ln x}{\ln x + 1}\right)$ **22.** $\dfrac{d}{dx}(\ln(e^x + e^{-x}))$

23–30. Derivatives of b^x *Find the derivatives of the following functions.*

23. $y = 8^x$ **24.** $y = 5^{3t}$ **25.** $y = 5 \cdot 4^x$

26. $y = 4^{-x} \sin x$ **27.** $y = x^3 \cdot 3^x$ **28.** $P = \dfrac{40}{1 + 2^{-t}}$

29. $A = 250(1.045)^{4t}$ **30.** $y = \ln 10^x$

31. Exponential model The following table shows the *time of useful consciousness* at various altitudes in the situation where a pressurized airplane suddenly loses pressure. The change in pressure drastically reduces available oxygen, and hypoxia sets in. The upper value of each time interval is roughly modeled by $T = 10 \cdot 2^{-0.274a}$, where T measures time in minutes and a is the altitude over 22,000 in thousands of feet ($a = 0$ corresponds to 22,000 ft).

Altitude (in ft)	Time of Useful Consciousness
22,000	5 to 10 min
25,000	3 to 5 min
28,000	2.5 to 3 min
30,000	1 to 2 min
35,000	30 to 60 s
40,000	15 to 20 s
45,000	9 to 15 s

  a. A Learjet flying at 38,000 ft ($a = 16$) suddenly loses pressure when the seal on a window fails. According to this model, how long do the pilot and passengers have to deploy oxygen masks before they become incapacitated?

  b. What is the average rate of change of T with respect to a over the interval from 24,000 to 30,000 ft (include units)?

  c. Find the instantaneous rate of change dT/da, compute it at 30,000 ft, and interpret its meaning.

32. Magnitude of an earthquake The energy (in joules) released by an earthquake of magnitude M is given by the equation $E = 25,000 \cdot 10^{1.5M}$. (This equation can be solved for M to define the magnitude of a given earthquake; it is a refinement of the original Richter scale created by Charles Richter in 1935.)

  a. Compute the energy released by earthquakes of magnitude 1, 2, 3, 4, and 5. Plot the points on a graph and join them with a smooth curve.

  b. Compute dE/dM and evaluate it for $M = 3$. What does this derivative mean? (M has no units, so the units of the derivative are J per change in magnitude.)

33. Diagnostic scanning Iodine-123 is a radioactive isotope used in medicine to test the function of the thyroid gland. If a 350-microcurie (μCi) dose of iodine-123 is administered to a patient, the quantity Q left in the body after t hours is approximately $Q = 350(\tfrac{1}{2})^{t/13.1}$.

  a. How long does it take for the level of iodine-123 to drop to 10 μCi?

  b. Find the rate of change of the quantity of iodine-123 at 12 hr, 1 day, and 2 days. What do your answers say about the rate at which iodine decreases as time increases?

34–44. General Power Rule *Use the General Power Rule where appropriate to find the derivative of the following functions.*

34. $f(x) = x^e$ **35.** $f(x) = 2^x$ **36.** $f(x) = 2x^{\sqrt{2}}$

37. $g(y) = e^y \cdot y^e$ **38.** $s(t) = \cos 2^t$

39. $r = e^{2\theta}$ **40.** $y = \ln(x^3 + 1)^{\pi}$

41. $f(x) = (2x-3)x^{3/2}$ **42.** $y = \tan(x^{0.74})$

43. $f(x) = \dfrac{2^x}{2^x + 1}$ **44.** $f(x) = (2^x + 1)^{\pi}$

45–50. Derivatives of General Exponential Function (or g^h) *Find the derivative of each function and evaluate the derivative at the given value of a.*

45. $f(x) = x^{\cos x}$; $a = \pi/2$ **46.** $g(x) = x^{\ln x}$; $a = e$

47. $h(x) = x^{\sqrt{x}}$; $a = 4$ **48.** $f(x) = (x^2 + 1)^x$; $a = 1$

49. $f(x) = (\sin x)^{\ln x}$; $a = \pi/2$

50. $f(x) = (\tan x)^{x-1}$; $a = \pi/4$

51–54. Tangent lines and general exponential functions

51. Find an equation of the line tangent to $y = x^{\sin x}$ at the point $x = 1$.

52. Determine whether the graph of $y = x^{\sqrt{x}}$ has any horizontal tangent lines.

53. The graph of $y = (x^2)^x$ has two horizontal tangent lines. Find equations for both of them.

54. The graph of $y = x^{\ln x}$ has one horizontal tangent line. Find an equation for it.

55–60. Derivatives of logarithmic functions *Calculate the derivative of the following functions.*

55. $y = 4\log_3(x^2 - 1)$ **56.** $y = \log_{10} x$

57. $y = \cos x \ln(\cos^2 x)$ **58.** $y = \log_8 |\tan x|$

59. $y = \dfrac{1}{\log_4 x}$ **60.** $y = \log_2(\log_2 x)$

61–68. Logarithmic differentiation *Use logarithmic differentiation to evaluate $f'(x)$.*

61. $f(x) = \dfrac{(x+1)^{10}}{(2x-4)^8}$ **62.** $f(x) = x^2 \cos x$

63. $f(x) = x^{\ln x}$ **64.** $f(x) = \dfrac{\tan^{10} x}{(5x+3)^6}$

65. $f(x) = \dfrac{(x+1)^{3/2}(x-4)^{5/2}}{(5x+3)^{2/3}}$

66. $f(x) = \dfrac{x^8 \cos^3 x}{\sqrt{x-1}}$

67. $f(x) = (\sin x)^{\tan x}$

68. $f(x) = \left(1 + \dfrac{1}{x}\right)^{2x}$

Further Explorations

69. Explain why or why not Determine whether the following statements are true, and give an explanation or a counterexample.

  a. The derivative of $\log_2 9 = 1/(9 \ln 2)$.

  b. $\ln(x+1) + \ln(x-1) = \ln(x^2 - 1)$, for all x.

  c. The exponential function 2^{x+1} can be written in base e as $e^{2 \ln(x+1)}$.

  d. $\dfrac{d}{dx}(\sqrt{2}^{\,x}) = x\sqrt{2}^{\,x-1}$

  e. $\dfrac{d}{dx}(x^{\sqrt{2}}) = \sqrt{2}\,x^{\sqrt{2}-1}$

70–73. Higher-order derivatives *Find the following higher-order derivatives.*

70. $\dfrac{d^3}{dx^3}(x^{4.2})\Big|_{x=1}$

71. $\dfrac{d^2}{dx^2}(\log_{10} x)$

72. $\dfrac{d^n}{dx^n}(2^x)$

73. $\dfrac{d^3}{dx^3}(x^2 \ln x)$

74–76. Derivatives by different methods *Calculate the derivative of the following functions (i) using the fact that $b^x = e^{x \ln b}$ and (ii) by using logarithmic differentiation. Verify that both answers are the same.*

74. $y = (x^2 + 1)^x$ **75.** $y = 3^x$ **76.** $y = g(x)^{h(x)}$

77–82. Derivatives of logarithmic functions *Use the properties of logarithms to simplify the following functions before computing $f'(x)$.*

77. $f(x) = \ln(3x + 1)^4$

78. $f(x) = \ln \dfrac{2x}{(x^2 + 1)^3}$

79. $f(x) = \ln \sqrt{10x}$

80. $f(x) = \log_2 \dfrac{8}{\sqrt{x+1}}$

81. $f(x) = \ln \dfrac{(2x-1)(x+2)^3}{(1-4x)^2}$

82. $f(x) = \ln(\sec^4 x \tan^2 x)$

83. Tangent lines Find the equation of the line tangent to $y = 2^{\sin x}$ at $x = \pi/2$. Graph the function and the tangent line.

84. Horizontal tangents The graph of $y = \cos x \cdot \ln \cos^2 x$ has seven horizontal tangent lines on the interval $[0, 2\pi]$. Find the x-coordinates of all points at which these tangent lines occur.

85–92. General logarithmic and exponential derivatives *Compute the following derivatives. Use logarithmic differentiation where appropriate.*

85. $\dfrac{d}{dx}(x^{10x})$

86. $\dfrac{d}{dx}(2x)^{2x}$

87. $\dfrac{d}{dx}(x^{\cos x})$

88. $\dfrac{d}{dx}(x^\pi + \pi^x)$

89. $\dfrac{d}{dx}\left(1 + \dfrac{1}{x}\right)^x$

90. $\dfrac{d}{dx}(1 + x^2)^{\sin x}$

91. $\dfrac{d}{dx}(x^{(x^{10})})$

92. $\dfrac{d}{dx}(\ln x)^{x^2}$

Applications

93–96. Logistic growth *Scientists often use the logistic growth function $P(t) = \dfrac{P_0 K}{P_0 + (K - P_0)e^{-r_0 t}}$ to model population growth, where P_0 is the initial population at time $t = 0$, K is the **carrying capacity**, and r_0 is the base growth rate. The carrying capacity is a theoretical upper bound on the total population that the surrounding environment can support. The figure shows the sigmoid (S-shaped) curve associated with a typical logistic model.*

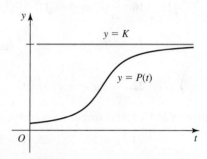

93. Gone fishing When a reservoir is created by a new dam, 50 fish are introduced into the reservoir, which has an estimated carrying capacity of 8000 fish. A logistic model of the fish population is $P(t) = \dfrac{400{,}000}{50 + 7950e^{-0.5t}}$, where t is measured in years.

  a. Graph P using a graphing utility. Experiment with different windows until you produce an S-shaped curve characteristic of the logistic model. What window works well for this function?

  b. How long does it take for the population to reach 5000 fish? How long does it take for the population to reach 90% of the carrying capacity?

  c. How fast (in fish per year) is the population growing at $t = 0$? At $t = 5$?

  d. Graph P' and use the graph to estimate the year in which the population is growing fastest.

94. World population (part 1) The population of the world reached 6 billion in 1999 ($t = 0$). Assume Earth's carrying capacity is 15 billion and the base growth rate is $r_0 = 0.025$ per year.

  a. Write a logistic growth function for the world's population (in billions), and graph your equation on the interval $0 \le t \le 200$ using a graphing utility.

  b. What will the population be in the year 2020? When will it reach 12 billion?

95. World population (part 2) The *relative growth rate r* of a function f measures the rate of change of the function compared to its value at a particular point. It is computed as $r(t) = f'(t)/f(t)$.

  a. Confirm that the relative growth rate in 1999 ($t = 0$) for the logistic model in Exercise 94 is $r(0) = P'(0)/P(0) = 0.015$. This means the world's population was growing at 1.5% per year in 1999.

  b. Compute the relative growth rate of the world's population in 2010 and 2020. What appears to be happening to the relative growth rate as time increases?

  c. Evaluate $\lim\limits_{t \to \infty} r(t) = \lim\limits_{t \to \infty} \dfrac{P'(t)}{P(t)}$, where $P(t)$ is the logistic growth function from Exercise 94. What does your answer say about populations that follow a logistic growth pattern?

96. Population crash The logistic model can be used for situations in which the initial population P_0 is above the carrying capacity K. For example, consider a deer population of 1500 on an island where a large fire has reduced the carrying capacity to 1000 deer.

   a. Assuming a base growth rate of $r_0 = 0.1$ and an initial population of $P(0) = 1500$, write a logistic growth function for the deer population and graph it. Based on the graph, what happens to the deer population in the long run?

   b. How fast (in deer per year) is the population declining immediately after the fire at $t = 0$?

   c. How long does it take for the deer population to decline to 1200 deer?

97. Savings plan Beginning at age 30, a self-employed plumber saves \$250 per month in a retirement account until he reaches age 65. The account offers 6% interest, compounded monthly. The balance in the account after t years is given by $A(t) = 50{,}000(1.005^{12t} - 1)$.

   a. Compute the balance in the account after 5, 15, 25, and 35 years. What is the average rate of change in the value of the account over the intervals $[5, 15]$, $[15, 25]$, and $[25, 35]$?

   b. Suppose the plumber started saving at age 25 instead of age 30. Find the balance at age 65 (after 40 years of investing).

   c. Use the derivative dA/dt to explain the surprising result in part (b) and to explain the advice: Start saving for retirement as early as possible.

Additional Exercises

98. Tangency question It is easily verified that the graphs of $y = x^2$ and $y = e^x$ have no points of intersection (for $x > 0$), while the graphs of $y = x^3$ and $y = e^x$ have two points of intersection. It follows that for some real number $2 < p < 3$, the graphs of $y = x^p$ and $y = e^x$ have exactly one point of intersection (for $x > 0$). Using analytical and/or graphical methods, determine p and the coordinates of the single point of intersection.

99. Tangency question It is easily verified that the graphs of $y = 1.1^x$ and $y = x$ have two points of intersection, while the graphs of $y = 2^x$ and $y = x$ have no points of intersection. It follows that for some real number $1 < p < 2$, the graphs of $y = p^x$ and $y = x$ have exactly one point of intersection. Using analytical and/or graphical methods, determine p and the coordinates of the single point of intersection.

100. Triple intersection Graph the functions $f(x) = x^3$, $g(x) = 3^x$, and $h(x) = x^x$ and find their common intersection point (exactly).

101–104. Calculating limits exactly *Use the definition of the derivative to evaluate the following limits.*

101. $\displaystyle\lim_{x \to e} \frac{\ln x - 1}{x - e}$

102. $\displaystyle\lim_{h \to 0} \frac{\ln(e^8 + h) - 8}{h}$

103. $\displaystyle\lim_{h \to 0} \frac{(3 + h)^{3+h} - 27}{h}$

104. $\displaystyle\lim_{x \to 2} \frac{5^x - 25}{x - 2}$

105. Derivative of $u(x)^{v(x)}$ Use logarithmic differentiation to prove that

$$\frac{d}{dx}\left[u(x)^{v(x)}\right] = u(x)^{v(x)}\left[\frac{v(x)}{u(x)}\frac{du}{dx} + \ln u(x)\frac{dv}{dx}\right].$$

QUICK CHECK ANSWERS

1. $x^2; e^{x \ln 5}$ **2.** Either way, $\dfrac{d}{dx}(\ln x^p) = \dfrac{p}{x}$.

3. $\dfrac{dA}{dt} = 500(1.045)^t \cdot \ln 1.045 \approx 22(1.045)^t$ **4.** $\dfrac{dy}{dx} = \dfrac{1}{x \ln 3}$

5. $T'(n) = \log_2 n + \dfrac{1}{\ln 2} = \log_2 n + \dfrac{1}{\dfrac{\log_2 2}{\log_2 e}} =$

$\log_2 n + \log_2 e = \log_2(en)$ ◄

3.10 Derivatives of Inverse Trigonometric Functions

The inverse trigonometric functions, introduced in Section 1.4, are major players in calculus. In this section, we develop the derivatives of the six inverse trigonometric functions and begin an exploration of their many applications. The method for differentiating the inverses of more general functions is also presented.

Inverse Sine and Its Derivative

Recall from Section 1.4 that $y = \sin^{-1} x$ is the value of y such that $x = \sin y$, where $-\pi/2 \le y \le \pi/2$. The domain of $\sin^{-1} x$ is $\{x: -1 \le x \le 1\}$ (Figure 3.54). The

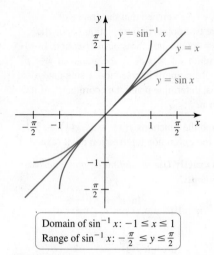

Domain of $\sin^{-1} x$: $-1 \le x \le 1$
Range of $\sin^{-1} x$: $-\frac{\pi}{2} \le y \le \frac{\pi}{2}$

FIGURE 3.54

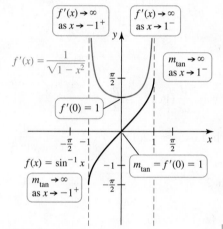

FIGURE 3.55

derivative of $y = \sin^{-1} x$ follows by differentiating both sides of $x = \sin y$ with respect to x, simplifying, and solving for dy/dx:

$$x = \sin y \qquad y = \sin^{-1} x \iff x = \sin y$$

$$\frac{d}{dx}(x) = \frac{d}{dx}(\sin y) \quad \text{Differentiate with respect to } x.$$

$$1 = (\cos y)\frac{dy}{dx} \quad \text{Chain Rule on the right side}$$

$$\frac{dy}{dx} = \frac{1}{\cos y}. \quad \text{Solve for } \frac{dy}{dx}.$$

The identity $\sin^2 y + \cos^2 y = 1$ is used to express this derivative in terms of x. Solving for $\cos y$ yields

$$\cos y = \pm\sqrt{1 - \underbrace{\sin^2 y}_{x^2}} \quad x = \sin y \implies x^2 = \sin^2 y$$

$$= \pm\sqrt{1 - x^2}.$$

Because y is restricted to the interval $-\pi/2 \le y \le \pi/2$, we have $\cos y \ge 0$. Therefore, we choose the positive branch of the square root, and it follows that

$$\frac{dy}{dx} = \frac{d}{dx}(\sin^{-1} x) = \frac{1}{\sqrt{1 - x^2}}.$$

This result is consistent with the graph of $f(x) = \sin^{-1} x$ (Figure 3.55).

THEOREM 3.21   Derivative of Inverse Sine

$$\frac{d}{dx}(\sin^{-1} x) = \frac{1}{\sqrt{1 - x^2}}, \text{ for } -1 < x < 1$$

QUICK CHECK 1 Is $f(x) = \sin^{-1} x$ an even or odd function? Is $f'(x)$ an even or odd function? ◄

EXAMPLE 1   Derivatives involving the inverse sine Compute the following derivatives.

a. $\dfrac{d}{dx}(\sin^{-1}(x^2 - 1))$ **b.** $\dfrac{d}{dx}(\cos(\sin^{-1} x))$

SOLUTION We apply the Chain Rule for both derivatives.

a. $\dfrac{d}{dx}(\sin^{-1}\underbrace{(x^2 - 1)}_{u}) = \underbrace{\dfrac{1}{\sqrt{1 - (x^2 - 1)^2}}}_{\text{derivative of } \sin^{-1} u \text{ evaluated at } u = x^2 - 1} \cdot \underbrace{2x}_{u'(x)} = \dfrac{2x}{\sqrt{2x^2 - x^4}}$

b. $\dfrac{d}{dx}(\cos(\sin^{-1}\underbrace{x}_{u})) = \underbrace{-\sin(\sin^{-1} x)}_{\substack{\text{derivative of the} \\ \text{outer function } \cos u \\ \text{evaluated at } u = \sin^{-1} x}} \cdot \underbrace{\dfrac{1}{\sqrt{1 - x^2}}}_{\substack{\text{derivative of the} \\ \text{inner function } \sin^{-1} x}} = -\dfrac{x}{\sqrt{1 - x^2}}$

> The result in Example 1b could have been obtained by noting that $\cos(\sin^{-1} x) = \sqrt{1 - x^2}$ and differentiating this expression.

This result is valid for $-1 < x < 1$, where $\sin(\sin^{-1} x) = x$.   *Related Exercises 7–12* ◄

Derivatives of Inverse Tangent and Secant

The derivatives of the inverse tangent and inverse secant are derived using a method similar to that used for the inverse sine. Once these three derivative results are known, the derivatives of the inverse cosine, cotangent, and cosecant follow immediately.

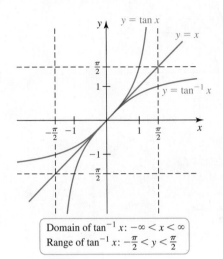

Domain of $\tan^{-1} x$: $-\infty < x < \infty$
Range of $\tan^{-1} x$: $-\frac{\pi}{2} < y < \frac{\pi}{2}$

FIGURE 3.56

Inverse Tangent   Recall from Section 1.4 that $y = \tan^{-1} x$ is the value of y such that $x = \tan y$, where $-\pi/2 < y < \pi/2$. The domain of $y = \tan^{-1} x$ is $\{x: -\infty < x < \infty\}$ (Figure 3.56). To find $\dfrac{dy}{dx}$, we differentiate both sides of $x = \tan y$ with respect to x and simplify:

$$x = \tan y \qquad y = \tan^{-1} x \iff x = \tan y$$

$$\frac{d}{dx}(x) = \frac{d}{dx}(\tan y) \quad \text{Differentiate with respect to } x.$$

$$1 = \sec^2 y \cdot \frac{dy}{dx} \quad \text{Chain Rule}$$

$$\frac{dy}{dx} = \frac{1}{\sec^2 y}. \quad \text{Solve for } \frac{dy}{dx}.$$

To express this derivative in terms of x, we combine the trigonometric identity $\sec^2 y = 1 + \tan^2 y$ with $x = \tan y$ to obtain $\sec^2 y = 1 + x^2$. Substituting this result into the expression for dy/dx, it follows that

$$\frac{dy}{dx} = \frac{d}{dx}(\tan^{-1} x) = \frac{1}{1 + x^2}.$$

The graphs of the inverse tangent and its derivative (Figure 3.57) are informative. Letting $f(x) = \tan^{-1} x$ and $f'(x) = \dfrac{1}{1 + x^2}$, we see that $f'(0) = 1$, which is the maximum value of the derivative; that is, $\tan^{-1} x$ has its maximum slope at $x = 0$. As $x \to \infty$, $f'(x)$ approaches zero; likewise, as $x \to -\infty$, $f'(x)$ approaches zero.

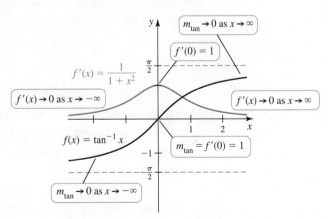

FIGURE 3.57

QUICK CHECK 2 How do the slopes of the lines tangent to the graph of $y = \tan^{-1} x$ behave as $x \to \infty$? ◄

Inverse Secant   Recall from Section 1.4 that $y = \sec^{-1} x$ is the value of y such that $x = \sec y$, where $0 \le y \le \pi$, with $y \ne \pi/2$. The domain of $y = \sec^{-1} x$ is $\{x: |x| \ge 1\}$ (Figure 3.58).

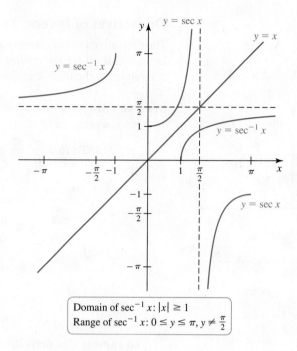

FIGURE 3.58

Domain of $\sec^{-1} x$: $|x| \geq 1$
Range of $\sec^{-1} x$: $0 \leq y \leq \pi, y \neq \frac{\pi}{2}$

The derivative of the inverse secant presents a new twist. Let $y = \sec^{-1} x$, or $x = \sec y$, and then differentiate both sides of $x = \sec y$ with respect to x:

$$1 = \sec y \tan y \frac{dy}{dx}.$$

Solving for $\dfrac{dy}{dx}$ produces

$$\frac{dy}{dx} = \frac{d}{dx}(\sec^{-1} x) = \frac{1}{\sec y \tan y}.$$

The final step is to express $\sec y \tan y$ in terms of x by using the identity $\sec^2 y = 1 + \tan^2 y$. Solving this equation for $\tan y$, we have

$$\tan y = \pm \sqrt{\underbrace{\sec^2 y}_{x^2} - 1} = \pm \sqrt{x^2 - 1}.$$

Two cases must be examined to resolve the sign on the square root:

• By the definition of $y = \sec^{-1} x$, if $x \geq 1$, then $0 \leq y < \pi/2$ and $\tan y > 0$. In this case we choose the positive branch and take $\tan y = \sqrt{x^2 - 1}$.

• However, if $x \leq -1$, then $\pi/2 < y \leq \pi$ and $\tan y < 0$. Now we choose the negative branch.

This argument accounts for the $\tan y$ factor in the derivative. For the $\sec y$ factor, we have $\sec y = x$. Therefore, the derivative of the inverse secant is

$$\frac{d}{dx}(\sec^{-1} x) = \begin{cases} \dfrac{1}{x\sqrt{x^2 - 1}} & \text{if } x > 1 \\[2ex] -\dfrac{1}{x\sqrt{x^2 - 1}} & \text{if } x < -1, \end{cases}$$

which is an awkward result. The absolute value helps here: Recall that $|x| = x$, if $x > 0$, and $|x| = -x$, if $x < 0$. It follows that

$$\frac{d}{dx}(\sec^{-1} x) = \frac{1}{|x|\sqrt{x^2 - 1}}, \text{ for } |x| > 1.$$

We see that the slope of the inverse secant function is always positive, which is consistent with this derivative result (Figure 3.58).

Derivatives of Other Inverse Trigonometric Functions
The hard work is complete. The derivative of the inverse cosine results from the identity

$$\cos^{-1} x + \sin^{-1} x = \frac{\pi}{2}.$$

> This identity was proved in Example 5 of Section 1.4.

Differentiating both sides of this equation with respect to x, we find that

$$\frac{d}{dx}(\cos^{-1} x) + \underbrace{\frac{d}{dx}(\sin^{-1} x)}_{1/\sqrt{1-x^2}} = \underbrace{\frac{d}{dx}\left(\frac{\pi}{2}\right)}_{0}.$$

Solving for $\frac{d}{dx}(\cos^{-1} x)$, the required derivative is

$$\frac{d}{dx}(\cos^{-1} x) = -\frac{1}{\sqrt{1-x^2}}.$$

In a similar manner, the analogous identities

$$\cot^{-1} x + \tan^{-1} x = \frac{\pi}{2} \quad \text{and} \quad \csc^{-1} x + \sec^{-1} x = \frac{\pi}{2}$$

are used to show that the derivatives of $\cot^{-1} x$ and $\csc^{-1} x$ are the negative of the derivatives of $\tan^{-1} x$ and $\sec^{-1} x$, respectively (Exercise 73).

THEOREM 3.22 Derivatives of Inverse Trigonometric Functions

$$\frac{d}{dx}(\sin^{-1} x) = \frac{1}{\sqrt{1-x^2}} \qquad \frac{d}{dx}(\cos^{-1} x) = -\frac{1}{\sqrt{1-x^2}}, \text{ for } -1 < x < 1$$

$$\frac{d}{dx}(\tan^{-1} x) = \frac{1}{1+x^2} \qquad \frac{d}{dx}(\cot^{-1} x) = -\frac{1}{1+x^2}, \text{ for } -\infty < x < \infty$$

$$\frac{d}{dx}(\sec^{-1} x) = \frac{1}{|x|\sqrt{x^2-1}} \qquad \frac{d}{dx}(\csc^{-1} x) = -\frac{1}{|x|\sqrt{x^2-1}}, \text{ for } |x| > 1$$

QUICK CHECK 3 Summarize how the derivatives of inverse trigonometric functions are related to the derivatives of the corresponding inverse cofunctions (for example, inverse tangent and inverse cotangent). ◄

EXAMPLE 2 Derivatives of inverse trigonometric functions

a. Evaluate $f'(2\sqrt{3})$, where $f(x) = x \tan^{-1}(x/2)$.

b. Find an equation of the line tangent to the graph of $g(x) = \sec^{-1} 2x$ at the point $(1, \pi/3)$.

SOLUTION

a. $f'(x) = 1 \cdot \tan^{-1}\dfrac{x}{2} + x \underbrace{\dfrac{1}{1 + (x/2)^2} \cdot \dfrac{1}{2}}_{\frac{d}{dx}(\tan^{-1}(x/2))}$ Product Rule and Chain Rule

$$= \tan^{-1}\frac{x}{2} + \frac{2x}{4 + x^2} \qquad \text{Simplify.}$$

We evaluate f' at $x = 2\sqrt{3}$ and note that $\tan^{-1}\sqrt{3} = \pi/3$:

$$f'(2\sqrt{3}) = \tan^{-1}\sqrt{3} + \frac{2(2\sqrt{3})}{4 + (2\sqrt{3})^2} = \frac{\pi}{3} + \frac{\sqrt{3}}{4}.$$

b. The slope of the tangent line at $(1, \pi/3)$ is $g'(1)$. Using the Chain Rule, we have

$$g'(x) = \frac{d}{dx}(\sec^{-1} 2x) = \frac{2}{|2x|\sqrt{4x^2 - 1}} = \frac{1}{|x|\sqrt{4x^2 - 1}}.$$

It follows that $g'(1) = 1/\sqrt{3}$. An equation of the tangent line is

$$y - \frac{\pi}{3} = \frac{1}{\sqrt{3}}(x - 1) \quad \text{or} \quad y = \frac{1}{\sqrt{3}}x + \frac{\pi}{3} - \frac{1}{\sqrt{3}}.$$

Related Exercises 13–34◀

FIGURE 3.59

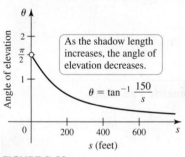

FIGURE 3.60

EXAMPLE 3 Shadows in a ballpark As the sun descends behind the 150-ft grandstand of a baseball stadium, the shadow of the stadium moves across the field (Figure 3.59). Let ℓ be the line segment between the edge of the shadow and the sun, and let θ be the angle of elevation of the sun—the angle between ℓ and the horizontal. The length of the shadow s is the distance between the edge of the shadow and the base of the grandstand.

a. Express θ as a function of the shadow length s.

b. Compute $d\theta/ds$ when $s = 200$ ft and explain what this rate of change measures.

SOLUTION

a. The tangent of θ is

$$\tan \theta = \frac{150}{s},$$

where $s > 0$. Taking the inverse tangent of both sides of this equation, we find that

$$\theta = \tan^{-1} \frac{150}{s}.$$

As shown in Figure 3.60, as the shadow length approaches zero, the sun's angle of elevation θ approaches $\pi/2$ ($\theta = \pi/2$ means the sun is overhead). As the shadow length increases, θ decreases and approaches zero.

b. Using the Chain Rule, we have

$$\frac{d\theta}{ds} = \frac{1}{1 + (150/s)^2} \frac{d}{ds}\left(\frac{150}{s}\right) \qquad \text{Chain Rule; } \frac{d}{du}(\tan^{-1} u) = \frac{1}{1 + u^2}$$

$$= \frac{1}{1 + (150/s)^2}\left(-\frac{150}{s^2}\right) \qquad \text{Evaluate the derivative.}$$

$$= -\frac{150}{s^2 + 22{,}500}. \qquad \text{Simplify.}$$

Notice that $d\theta/ds$ is negative for all values of s, which means longer shadows are associated with smaller angles of elevation (Figure 3.60). At $s = 200$ ft, we have

$$\left.\frac{d\theta}{ds}\right|_{s=200} = -\frac{150}{200^2 + 150^2} = -0.0024 \, \frac{\text{rad}}{\text{ft}}.$$

When the length of the shadow is $s = 200$ ft, the angle of elevation is changing at a rate of -0.0024 rad/ft, or $-0.138°$/ft. *Related Exercises 35–36*◀

QUICK CHECK 4 Example 3 makes the claim that $d\theta/ds = -0.0024$ rad/ft is equivalent to $-0.138°$/ft. Verify this claim. ◀

Derivatives of Inverse Functions in General

We found the derivatives of the inverse trigonometric functions using implicit differentiation. However, this approach does not always work. For example, suppose we know only f and its derivative f' and wish to evaluate the derivative of f^{-1}. The key to finding the derivative of the inverse function lies in the symmetry of the graphs of f and f^{-1}.

EXAMPLE 4 **Linear functions, inverses, and derivatives** Consider the general linear function $y = f(x) = mx + b$, where $m \neq 0$ and b are constants.

a. Write the inverse of f in the form $y = f^{-1}(x)$.

b. Find the derivative of the inverse $\dfrac{d}{dx}\left(f^{-1}(x)\right)$.

c. Consider the specific case $f(x) = 2x - 6$. Graph f and f^{-1}, and find the slope of each line.

SOLUTION

a. Solving $y = mx + b$ for x, we find that $mx = y - b$, or

$$x = \frac{y}{m} - \frac{b}{m}.$$

Writing this function in the form $y = f^{-1}(x)$ (by reversing the roles of x and y), we have

$$y = f^{-1}(x) = \frac{x}{m} - \frac{b}{m},$$

which describes a line with slope $1/m$.

b. The derivative of f^{-1} is

$$\left(f^{-1}\right)'(x) = \frac{1}{m} = \frac{1}{f'(x)}.$$

Notice that $f'(x) = m$, so the derivative of f^{-1} is the reciprocal of f'.

c. In the case that $f(x) = 2x - 6$, we have $f^{-1}(x) = x/2 + 3$. The graphs of these two lines are symmetric about the line $y = x$ (Figure 3.61). Furthermore, the slope of the line $y = f(x)$ is 2 and the slope of $y = f^{-1}(x)$ is $\frac{1}{2}$; that is, the slopes (and, therefore, the derivatives) are reciprocals of each other. *Related Exercises 37–39* ◄

The reciprocal property obeyed by f' and $\left(f^{-1}\right)'$ in Example 4 holds for all functions. Figure 3.62 shows the graphs of a typical one-to-one function and its inverse. It also shows a pair of symmetric points—(x_0, y_0) on the graph of f and (y_0, x_0) on the graph of f^{-1}—along with the tangent lines at these points. Notice that as the lines tangent to the graph of f get steeper (as x increases), the corresponding lines tangent to the graph of f^{-1} get less steep. The next theorem makes this relationship precise.

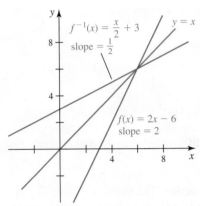

FIGURE 3.61

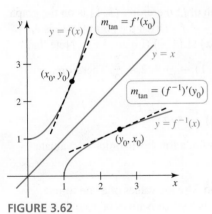

FIGURE 3.62

▷ The result of Theorem 3.23 is also written in the forms

$$\left(f^{-1}\right)'(f(x_0)) = \frac{1}{f'(x_0)}$$

or

$$\left(f^{-1}\right)'(y_0) = \frac{1}{f'(f^{-1}(y_0))}.$$

THEOREM 3.23 **Derivative of the Inverse Function**

Let f be differentiable and have an inverse on an interval I. If x_0 is a point of I at which $f'(x_0) \neq 0$, then f^{-1} is differentiable at $y_0 = f(x_0)$ and

$$\left(f^{-1}\right)'(y_0) = \frac{1}{f'(x_0)}, \quad \text{where} \quad y_0 = f(x_0).$$

To understand this theorem, suppose that (x_0, y_0) is a point on the graph of f, which means that (y_0, x_0) is the corresponding point on the graph of f^{-1}. Then the slope of the line tangent to the graph of f^{-1} at the point (y_0, x_0) is the reciprocal of the slope of the line tangent to the graph of f at the point (x_0, y_0). Importantly, the theorem says that we can evaluate the derivative of the inverse function without finding the inverse function itself.

Proof: Before doing a short calculation, we note two facts:

- At a point x_0 where f is differentiable, $y_0 = f(x_0)$ and $x_0 = f^{-1}(y_0)$.
- As a differentiable function, f is continuous at x_0 (Theorem 3.1), which implies that f^{-1} is continuous at y_0 (Theorem 2.14). Therefore, as $y \to y_0$, $x \to x_0$.

Using the definition of the derivative, we have

$$
\begin{aligned}
(f^{-1})'(y_0) &= \lim_{y \to y_0} \frac{f^{-1}(y) - f^{-1}(y_0)}{y - y_0} \qquad \text{Definition of derivative of } f^{-1} \\
&= \lim_{x \to x_0} \frac{x - x_0}{f(x) - f(x_0)} \qquad y = f(x) \text{ and } x = f^{-1}(y); \ x \to x_0 \text{ as } y \to y_0 \\
&= \lim_{x \to x_0} \frac{1}{\dfrac{f(x) - f(x_0)}{x - x_0}} \qquad \frac{a}{b} = \frac{1}{b/a} \\
&= \frac{1}{f'(x_0)}. \qquad \text{Definition of derivative of } f
\end{aligned}
$$

We have shown that $(f^{-1})'(y_0)$ exists (f^{-1} is differentiable at y_0) and it equals the reciprocal of $f'(x_0)$. ◀

QUICK CHECK 5 Sketch the graphs of $y = \sin x$ and $y = \sin^{-1} x$. Then verify that Theorem 3.23 holds at the point $(0, 0)$. ◀

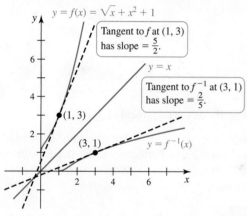

FIGURE 3.63

EXAMPLE 5   Derivative of an inverse function The function $f(x) = \sqrt{x} + x^2 + 1$ is one-to-one, for $x \geq 0$, and has an inverse on that interval. Find the slope of the curve $y = f^{-1}(x)$ at the point $(3, 1)$.

SOLUTION The point $(1, 3)$ is on the graph of f; therefore, $(3, 1)$ is on the graph of f^{-1}. In this case, the slope of the curve $y = f^{-1}(x)$ at the point $(3, 1)$ is the reciprocal of the slope of the curve $y = f(x)$ at $(1, 3)$ (Figure 3.63). Note that $f'(x) = \dfrac{1}{2\sqrt{x}} + 2x$, which means that $f'(1) = \dfrac{1}{2} + 2 = \dfrac{5}{2}$. Therefore,

$$
(f^{-1})'(3) = \frac{1}{f'(1)} = \frac{1}{5/2} = \frac{2}{5}.
$$

Observe that it is not necessary to find a formula for f^{-1} in order to evaluate its derivative at a point.   *Related Exercises 40–50* ◀

EXAMPLE 6   Derivatives of an inverse function Use the values of a one-to-one differentiable function in the table to compute the indicated derivatives or state that the derivative cannot be determined.

x	-1	0	1	2	3
$f(x)$	2	3	5	6	7
$f'(x)$	1/2	2	3/2	1	2/3

a. $(f^{-1})'(5)$ **b.** $(f^{-1})'(2)$ **c.** $(f^{-1})'(1)$

SOLUTION We use the relationship $(f^{-1})'(y_0) = \dfrac{1}{f'(x_0)}$, where $y_0 = f(x_0)$.

a. In this case, $y_0 = f(x_0) = 5$. Using the table, we see that $x_0 = 1$ and $f'(1) = \dfrac{3}{2}$.

Therefore, $(f^{-1})'(5) = \dfrac{1}{f'(1)} = \dfrac{2}{3}$.

b. In this case, $y_0 = f(x_0) = 2$, which implies that $x_0 = -1$ and $f'(-1) = \dfrac{1}{2}$.

Therefore, $(f^{-1})'(2) = \dfrac{1}{f'(-1)} = 2$.

c. With $y_0 = f(x_0) = 1$, the table does not supply a value of x_0. Therefore, $f'(x_0)$ cannot be determined.

Related Exercises 51–52 ◄

SECTION 3.10 EXERCISES

Review Questions

1. State the derivative formulas for $\sin^{-1} x$, $\tan^{-1} x$, and $\sec^{-1} x$.

2. What is the slope of the line tangent to the graph of $y = \sin^{-1} x$ at $x = 0$?

3. What is the slope of the line tangent to the graph of $y = \tan^{-1} x$ at $x = -2$?

4. How are the derivatives of $\sin^{-1} x$ and $\cos^{-1} x$ related?

5. Suppose f is a one-to-one function with $f(2) = 8$ and $f'(2) = 4$. What is the value of $(f^{-1})'(8)$?

6. Explain how to find $(f^{-1})'(y_0)$, given that $y_0 = f(x_0)$.

Basic Skills

7–12. Derivatives of inverse sine *Evaluate the derivatives of the following functions.*

7. $f(x) = \sin^{-1} 2x$

8. $f(x) = x \sin^{-1} x$

9. $f(w) = \cos(\sin^{-1} 2w)$

10. $f(x) = \sin^{-1}(\ln x)$

11. $f(x) = \sin^{-1}(e^{-2x})$

12. $f(x) = \sin^{-1}(e^{\sin x})$

13–30. Derivatives *Evaluate the derivatives of the following functions.*

13. $f(x) = \tan^{-1} 10x$

14. $f(x) = x \cot^{-1}(x/3)$

15. $f(y) = \tan^{-1}(2y^2 - 4)$

16. $g(z) = \tan^{-1}(1/z)$

17. $f(z) = \cot^{-1} \sqrt{z}$

18. $f(x) = \sec^{-1} \sqrt{x}$

19. $f(x) = \cos^{-1}(1/x)$

20. $f(t) = (\cos^{-1} t)^2$

21. $f(u) = \csc^{-1}(2u + 1)$

22. $f(t) = \ln(\tan^{-1} t)$

23. $f(y) = \cot^{-1}(1/(y^2 + 1))$

24. $f(w) = \sin(\sec^{-1} 2w)$

25. $f(x) = \sec^{-1}(\ln x)$

26. $f(x) = \tan^{-1}(e^{4x})$

27. $f(x) = \csc^{-1}(\tan e^x)$

28. $f(x) = \sin(\tan^{-1}(\ln x))$

29. $f(s) = \cot^{-1}(e^s)$

30. $f(x) = 1/\tan^{-1}(x^2 + 4)$

31–34. Tangent lines *Find an equation of the line tangent to the graph of f at the given point.*

31. $f(x) = \tan^{-1} 2x$; $(1/2, \pi/4)$

32. $f(x) = \sin^{-1}(x/4)$; $(2, \pi/6)$

33. $f(x) = \cos^{-1} x^2$; $(1/\sqrt{2}, \pi/3)$

34. $f(x) = \sec^{-1}(e^x)$; $(\ln 2, \pi/3)$

T 35. Angular size A boat sails directly toward a 150-meter skyscraper that stands on the edge of a harbor. The angular size θ of the building is the angle formed by lines from the top and bottom of the building to the observer (see figure).

a. What is the rate of change of the angular size $d\theta/dx$ when the boat is $x = 500$ m from the building?

b. Graph $d\theta/dx$ as a function of x and determine the point at which the angular size changes most rapidly.

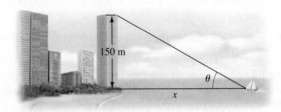

T 36. Angle of elevation A small plane flies horizontally on a line 400 meters directly above an observer with a speed of 70 m/s. Let θ be the angle of elevation of the plane (see figure).

a. What is the rate of change of the angle of elevation $d\theta/dx$ when the plane is $x = 500$ m past the observer?

b. Graph $d\theta/dx$ as a function of x and determine the point at which θ changes most rapidly.

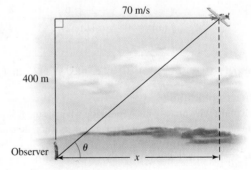

37–42. Derivatives of inverse functions at a point *Find the derivative of the inverse of the following functions at the specified point on the graph of the inverse function. You do not need to find f^{-1}.*

37. $f(x) = 3x + 4$; $(16, 4)$

38. $f(x) = \frac{1}{2}x + 8$; $(10, 4)$

39. $f(x) = -5x + 4$; $(-1, 1)$

40. $f(x) = x^2 + 1$, for $x \geq 0$; $(5, 2)$

41. $f(x) = \tan x$; $(1, \pi/4)$

42. $f(x) = x^2 - 2x - 3$, for $x \le 1$; $(12, -3)$

43–46. Slopes of tangent lines *Given the function f, find the slope of the line tangent to the graph of f^{-1} at the specified point on the graph of f^{-1}.*

43. $f(x) = \sqrt{x}$; $(2, 4)$

44. $f(x) = x^3$; $(8, 2)$

45. $f(x) = (x + 2)^2$; $(36, 4)$

46. $f(x) = -x^2 + 8$; $(7, 1)$

47–50. Derivatives and inverse functions

47. Find $(f^{-1})'(3)$ if $f(x) = x^3 + x + 1$.

48. Find the slope of the curve $y = f^{-1}(x)$ at $(4, 7)$ if the slope of the curve $y = f(x)$ at $(7, 4)$ is $\frac{2}{3}$.

49. Suppose the slope of the curve $y = f^{-1}(x)$ at $(4, 7)$ is $\frac{4}{5}$. Find $f'(7)$.

50. Suppose the slope of the curve $y = f(x)$ at $(4, 7)$ is $\frac{1}{5}$. Find $(f^{-1})'(7)$.

51–52. Derivatives of inverse functions from a table *Use the following tables to determine the indicated derivatives or state that the derivative cannot be determined.*

51.

x	-2	-1	0	1	2
$f(x)$	2	3	4	6	7
$f'(x)$	1	1/2	2	3/2	1

   a. $(f^{-1})'(4)$ **b.** $(f^{-1})'(6)$ **c.** $(f^{-1})'(1)$ **d.** $f'(1)$

52.

x	-4	-2	0	2	4
$f(x)$	0	1	2	3	4
$f'(x)$	5	4	3	2	1

   a. $f'(f(0))$ **b.** $(f^{-1})'(0)$ **c.** $(f^{-1})'(1)$ **d.** $(f^{-1})'(f(4))$

Further Explorations

53. Explain why or why not Determine whether the following statements are true, and give an explanation or a counterexample.

  a. $\dfrac{d}{dx}(\sin^{-1} x + \cos^{-1} x) = 0$

  b. $\dfrac{d}{dx}(\tan^{-1} x) = \sec^2 x$

  c. The lines tangent to the graph of $y = \sin^{-1} x$ on the interval $[-1, 1]$ have a minimum slope of 1.

  d. The lines tangent to the graph of $y = \sin x$ on the interval $[-\pi/2, \pi/2]$ have a maximum slope of 1.

  e. If $f(x) = 1/x$, then $[f^{-1}(x)]' = -1/x^2$

54–57. Graphing f and f'

  a. Graph f with a graphing utility.

  b. Compute and graph f'.

  c. Verify that the zeros of f' correspond to points at which f has a horizontal tangent line.

54. $f(x) = (x - 1) \sin^{-1} x$ on $[-1, 1]$

55. $f(x) = (x^2 - 1) \sin^{-1} x$ on $[-1, 1]$

56. $f(x) = (\sec^{-1} x)/x$ on $[1, \infty)$

57. $f(x) = e^{-x} \tan^{-1} x$ on $[0, \infty)$

58. Graphing with inverse trigonometric functions

  a. Graph the function $f(x) = \dfrac{\tan^{-1} x}{x^2 + 1}$.

  b. Compute and graph f' and determine (perhaps approximately) the points at which $f'(x) = 0$.

  c. Verify that the zeros of f' correspond to points at which f has a horizontal tangent line.

59–66. Derivatives of inverse functions *Consider the following functions (on the given interval, if specified). Find the inverse function, express it as a function of x, and find the derivative of the inverse function.*

59. $f(x) = 3x - 4$

60. $f(x) = |x + 2|$, for $x \le -2$

61. $f(x) = x^2 - 4$, for $x > 0$

62. $f(x) = \dfrac{x}{x + 5}$

63. $f(x) = \sqrt{x + 2}$, for $x \ge -2$

64. $f(x) = x^{2/3}$, for $x > 0$

65. $f(x) = x^{-1/2}$, for $x > 0$

66. $f(x) = x^3 + 3$

Applications

67. Towing a boat A boat is towed toward a dock by a cable attached to a winch that stands 10 feet above the water level (see figure). Let θ be the angle of elevation of the winch and let ℓ be the length of the cable as the boat is towed toward the dock.

  a. Show that the rate of change of θ with respect to ℓ is
$$\frac{d\theta}{d\ell} = \frac{-10}{\ell\sqrt{\ell^2 - 100}}.$$

  b. Compute $\dfrac{d\theta}{d\ell}$ when $\ell = 50, 20$, and 11 ft.

c. Find $\lim\limits_{\ell \to 10^+} \dfrac{d\theta}{d\ell}$, and explain what is happening as the last foot of cable is reeled in (note that the boat is at the dock when $\ell = 10$).

d. It is evident from the figure that θ increases as the boat is towed to the dock. Why, then, is $d\theta/d\ell$ negative?

68. Tracking a dive A biologist standing at the bottom of an 80-foot vertical cliff watches a peregrine falcon dive from the top of the cliff at a 45° angle from the horizontal (see figure).

a. Express the angle of elevation θ from the biologist to the falcon as a function of the height h of the bird above the ground. (*Hint:* The vertical distance between the top of the cliff and the falcon is $80 - h$.)

b. What is the rate of change of θ with respect to the bird's height when it is 60 feet above the ground?

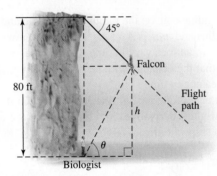

69. Angle to a particle, part I A particle travels clockwise on a circular path of diameter D, monitored by a sensor on the circle at point P; the other endpoint of the diameter on which the sensor lies is Q (see figure). Let θ be the angle between the diameter PQ and the line from the sensor to the particle. Let c be the length of the chord from the particle's position to Q.

a. Calculate $d\theta/dc$.

b. Evaluate $\dfrac{d\theta}{dc}\Big|_{c=0}$.

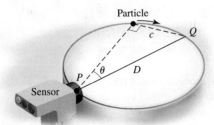

70. Angle to a particle, part II The figure in Exercise 69 shows the particle traveling away from the sensor, which may have influenced your solution (we expect you used the inverse sine function). Suppose instead that the particle approaches the sensor (see figure). How would this change the solution? Explain the differences in the two answers.

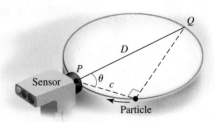

Additional Exercises

71. Derivative of the inverse sine Find the derivative of the inverse sine function using Theorem 3.23.

72. Derivative of the inverse cosine Find the derivative of the inverse cosine function in the following two ways.

a. Using Theorem 3.23
b. Using the identity $\sin^{-1} x + \cos^{-1} x = \pi/2$

73. Derivative of $\cot^{-1} x$ and $\csc^{-1} x$ Use a trigonometric identity to show that the derivatives of the inverse cotangent and inverse cosecant differ from the derivatives of the inverse tangent and inverse secant, respectively, by a multiplicative factor of -1.

74. Tangents and inverses Suppose $y = L(x) = ax + b$ (with $a \neq 0$) is the equation of the line tangent to the graph of a one-to-one function f at (x_0, y_0). Also, suppose that $y = M(x) = cx + d$ is the equation of the line tangent to the graph of f^{-1} at (y_0, x_0).

a. Express a and b in terms of x_0 and y_0.
b. Express c in terms of a, and d in terms of a, x_0, and y_0.
c. Prove that $L^{-1}(x) = M(x)$.

QUICK CHECK **ANSWERS**

1. $f(x) = \sin^{-1} x$ is odd, while $f'(x) = 1/\sqrt{1 - x^2}$ is even.
2. The slopes of the tangent lines approach 0.   **3.** One is the negative of the other.   **4.** Recall that $1° = \pi/180$ rad. So, 0.0024 rad/ft is equivalent to $0.138°$/ft.   **5.** Both curves have a slope of 1 at $(0, 0)$. ◄

3.11 Related Rates

We now return to the theme of derivatives as rates of change in problems in which the variables change with respect to *time*. The essential feature of these problems is that two or more variables, which are related in a known way, are themselves changing in time. Here are two examples illustrating this type of problem.

- An oil rig springs a leak and the oil spreads in a (roughly) circular patch around the rig. If the radius of the oil patch increases at a known rate, how fast is the area of the patch changing (Example 1)?

- Two airliners approach an airport with known speeds, one flying west and one flying north. How fast is the distance between the airliners changing (Example 2)?

In the first problem, the two related variables are the radius and the area of the oil patch. Both are changing in time. The second problem has three related variables: the positions of the two airliners and the distance between them. Again, the three variables change in time. The goal in both problems is to determine the rate of change of one of the variables at a specific moment of time—hence the name *related rates*.

We present a progression of examples in this section. After the first example, a general procedure is given for solving related-rate problems.

EXAMPLE 1   Spreading oil An oil rig springs a leak in calm seas and the oil spreads in a circular patch around the rig. If the radius of the oil patch increases at a rate of 30 m/hr, how fast is the area of the patch increasing when the patch has a radius of 100 meters (Figure 3.64)?

SOLUTION Two variables change simultaneously: the radius of the circle and its area. The key relationship between the radius and area is $A = \pi r^2$. It helps to rewrite the basic relationship showing explicitly which quantities vary in time. In this case, we rewrite A and r as $A(t)$ and $r(t)$ to emphasize that they change with respect to t (time). The general expression relating the radius and area at any time t is $A(t) = \pi r(t)^2$.

The goal is to find the rate of change of the area of the circle, which is $A'(t)$, given that $r'(t) = 30$ m/hr. In order to introduce derivatives into the problem, we differentiate the area relation $A(t) = \pi r(t)^2$ with respect to t:

$$A'(t) = \frac{d}{dt}(\pi r(t)^2)$$

$$= \pi \frac{d}{dt}(r(t)^2)$$

$$= \pi(2r(t))r'(t) \quad \text{Chain Rule}$$

$$= 2\pi r(t)r'(t). \quad \text{Simplify.}$$

Substituting the given values $r(t) = 100$ m and $r'(t) = 30$ m/hr, we have (including units)

$$A'(t) = 2\pi r(t)\, r'(t)$$

$$= 2\pi(100\text{ m})\left(30\,\frac{\text{m}}{\text{hr}}\right)$$

$$= 6000\,\pi\,\frac{\text{m}^2}{\text{hr}}.$$

We see that the area of the oil spill increases at a rate of $6000\pi \approx 18{,}850\text{ m}^2/\text{hr}$. Including units is a simple way to check your work. In this case, we expect an answer with units of area per unit time, so m²/hr makes sense.

Notice that the rate of change of the area depends on the radius of the spill. As the radius increases, the rate of change of the area also increases.

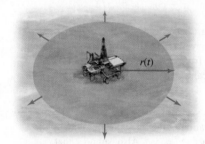

FIGURE 3.64

> It is important to remember that substitution of specific values of the variables occurs *after* differentiating.

QUICK CHECK 1 In Example 1, what is the rate of change of the area when the radius is 200 m? 300 m? ◄

Related Exercises 5–19 ◄

Using Example 1 as a template, we offer a set of guidelines for solving related-rate problems. There are always variations that arise for individual problems, but here is a general procedure.

PROCEDURE Steps for Related-Rate Problems

1. Read the problem carefully, making a sketch to organize the given information. Identify the rates that are given and the rate that is to be determined.

2. Write one or more equations that express the basic relationships among the variables.

3. Introduce rates of change by differentiating the appropriate equation(s) with respect to time t.

4. Substitute known values and solve for the desired quantity.

5. Check that units are consistent and the answer is reasonable. (For example, does it have the correct sign?)

EXAMPLE 2   Converging airplanes Two small planes approach an airport, one flying due west at 120 mi/hr and the other flying due north at 150 mi/hr. Assuming they fly at the same constant elevation, how fast is the distance between the planes changing when the westbound plane is 180 miles from the airport and the northbound plane is 225 miles from the airport?

SOLUTION A sketch such as Figure 3.65 helps us visualize the problem and organize the information. Let $x(t)$ and $y(t)$ denote the distance from the airport to the westbound and northbound planes, respectively. The paths of the two planes form the legs of a right triangle and the distance between them, denoted $z(t)$, is the hypotenuse. By the Pythagorean theorem, $z^2 = x^2 + y^2$.

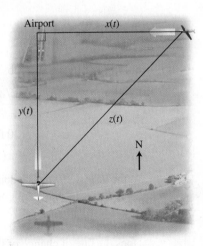

FIGURE 3.65

Our aim is to find dz/dt, the rate of change of the distance between the planes. We first differentiate both sides of $z^2 = x^2 + y^2$ with respect to t:

$$\frac{d}{dt}(z^2) = \frac{d}{dt}(x^2 + y^2) \implies 2z\frac{dz}{dt} = 2x\frac{dx}{dt} + 2y\frac{dy}{dt}.$$

> In Example 1, we replaced A and r with $A(t)$ and $r(t)$, respectively, to remind us of the independent variable. After some practice, this replacement is not necessary.

Notice that the Chain Rule is needed because x, y, and z are functions of t. Solving for dz/dt results in

$$\frac{dz}{dt} = \frac{2x\frac{dx}{dt} + 2y\frac{dy}{dt}}{2z} = \frac{x\frac{dx}{dt} + y\frac{dy}{dt}}{z}.$$

➤ One could solve the equation $z^2 = x^2 + y^2$ for z, with the result

$$z = \sqrt{x^2 + y^2},$$

and then differentiate. However, it is much easier to differentiate implicitly as shown in the example.

This equation relates the unknown rate dz/dt to the known quantities $x, y, z, dx/dt$, and dy/dt. For the westbound plane, $dx/dt = -120$ mi/hr (negative because the distance is decreasing), and for the northbound plane, $dy/dt = -150$ mi/hr. At the moment of interest, when $x = 180$ mi and $y = 225$ mi, the distance between the planes is

$$z = \sqrt{x^2 + y^2} = \sqrt{180^2 + 225^2} \approx 288 \text{ mi}.$$

Substituting these values gives

$$\frac{dz}{dt} = \frac{x\frac{dx}{dt} + y\frac{dy}{dt}}{z} \approx \frac{(180 \text{ mi})(-120 \text{ mi/hr}) + (225 \text{ mi})(-150 \text{ mi/hr})}{288 \text{ mi}}$$

$$\approx -192 \text{ mi/hr}.$$

Notice that $dz/dt < 0$, which means the distance between the planes is *decreasing* at a rate of about 192 mi/hr.   *Related Exercises 20–26*◀

QUICK CHECK 2 Assuming the same plane speeds as in Example 2, how fast is the distance between the planes changing if $x = 60$ mi and $y = 75$ mi? ◀

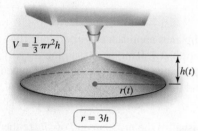

$V = \frac{1}{3}\pi r^2 h$

$h(t)$

$r(t)$

$r = 3h$

FIGURE 3.66

EXAMPLE 3   Sandpile Sand falls from an overhead bin, accumulating in a conical pile with a radius that is always three times its height. If the sand falls from the bin at a rate of 120 ft³/min, how fast is the height of the sandpile changing when the pile is 10 ft high?

SOLUTION A sketch of the problem (Figure 3.66) shows the three relevant variables: the volume V, the radius r, and the height h of the sandpile. The aim is to find the rate of change of the height dh/dt at the instant that $h = 10$ ft, given that $dV/dt = 120$ ft³/min. The basic relationship among the variables is the formula for the volume of a cone, $V = \frac{1}{3}\pi r^2 h$. We now use the given fact that the radius is always three times the height. Substituting $r = 3h$ into the volume relationship gives V in terms of h:

$$V = \frac{1}{3}\pi r^2 h = \frac{1}{3}\pi(3h)^2 h = 3\pi h^3.$$

Rates of change are introduced by differentiating both sides of $V = 3\pi h^3$ with respect to t. Using the Chain Rule, we have

$$\frac{dV}{dt} = 9\pi h^2 \frac{dh}{dt}.$$

Now we find dh/dt at the instant that $h = 10$ ft, given that $dV/dt = 120$ ft³/min. Solving for dh/dt and substituting these values, we have

$$\frac{dh}{dt} = \frac{dV/dt}{9\pi h^2} \qquad \text{Solve for } \frac{dh}{dt}.$$

$$= \frac{120 \text{ ft}^3/\text{min}}{9\pi(10 \text{ ft})^2} \approx 0.042 \frac{\text{ft}}{\text{min}}. \quad \text{Substitute for } \frac{dV}{dt} \text{ and } h.$$

At the instant that the sandpile is 10 ft high, the height is changing at a rate of 0.042 ft/min. Notice how the units work out consistently.   *Related Exercises 27–33*◀

QUICK CHECK 3 In Example 3, what is the rate of change of the height when $h = 2$ ft? Does the rate of change of the height increase or decrease with increasing height? ◀

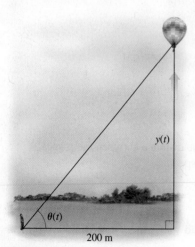

$y(t)$

$\theta(t)$

200 m

FIGURE 3.67

EXAMPLE 4   Observing a launch An observer stands 200 meters from the launch site of a hot-air balloon. The balloon rises vertically at a constant rate of 4 m/s. How fast is the angle of elevation of the balloon increasing 30 seconds after the launch? (The angle of elevation is the angle between the ground and the observer's line of sight to the balloon.)

SOLUTION Figure 3.67 shows the geometry of the launch. As the balloon rises, its distance from the ground y and its angle of elevation θ change simultaneously. An equation expressing the relationship between these variables is $\tan \theta = y/200$.

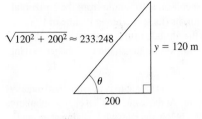

$$\cos \theta \approx \frac{200}{233.248} \approx 0.857$$

FIGURE 3.68

▷ The solution to Example 4 is reported in units of rad/s. Where did radians come from? Because a radian has no physical dimensions (it is the ratio of an arc length and a radius), no unit appears. We write rad/s for clarity because $d\theta/dt$ is the rate of change of an angle.

▷ Recall that to convert radians to degrees, we use

$$\text{degrees} = \frac{180}{\pi}\text{ radians}.$$

In order to find $d\theta/dt$, we differentiate both sides of this relationship using the Chain Rule:

$$\sec^2\theta \frac{d\theta}{dt} = \frac{1}{200}\frac{dy}{dt}.$$

Next we solve for $\dfrac{d\theta}{dt}$:

$$\frac{d\theta}{dt} = \frac{dy/dt}{200\sec^2\theta} = \frac{(dy/dt)\cdot\cos^2\theta}{200}.$$

The rate of change of the angle of elevation depends on the angle of elevation and the speed of the balloon. Thirty seconds after the launch, the balloon has risen $y = (4\text{ m/s})(30\text{ s}) = 120$ m. To complete the problem, we need the value of $\cos\theta$. Note that when $y = 120$ m, the distance between the observer and the balloon is

$$d = \sqrt{120^2 + 200^2} \approx 233.248 \text{ m}.$$

Therefore, $\cos\theta \approx 200/233.248 \approx 0.857$ (Figure 3.68), and the rate of change of the angle of elevation is

$$\frac{d\theta}{dt} = \frac{(dy/dt)\cdot\cos^2\theta}{200} \approx \frac{(4\text{ m/s})(0.857^2)}{200\text{ m}} = 0.0147 \text{ rad/s}.$$

At this instant, the balloon is rising at an angular rate of 0.0147 rad/s, or slightly less than 1°/s, as seen by the observer.   *Related Exercises 34–39* ◀

QUICK CHECK 4 In Example 4, notice that as the balloon rises (as θ increases), the rate of change of the angle of elevation decreases to zero. When does the maximum value of $\theta'(t)$ occur and what is it? ◀

SECTION 3.11 EXERCISES

Review Questions

1. Give an example in which one dimension of a geometric figure changes and produces a corresponding change in the area or volume of the figure.

2. Explain how implicit differentiation can simplify the work in a related-rates problem.

3. If two opposite sides of a rectangle increase in length, how must the other two opposite sides change if the area of the rectangle is to remain constant?

4. Explain why the term *related rates* describes the problems of this section.

Basic Skills

5. **Expanding square** The sides of a square increase in length at a rate of 2 m/s.

   a. At what rate is the area of the square changing when the sides are 10 m long?

   b. At what rate is the area of the square changing when the sides are 20 m long?

   c. Draw a graph of how the rate of change of the area varies with the side length.

6. **Shrinking square** The sides of a square decrease in length at a rate of 1 m/s.

   a. At what rate is the area of the square changing when the sides are 5 m long?

   b. At what rate are the lengths of the diagonals of the square changing?

7. **Expanding isosceles triangle** The legs of an isosceles right triangle increase in length at a rate of 2 m/s.

   a. At what rate is the area of the triangle changing when the legs are 2 m long?

   b. At what rate is the area of the triangle changing when the hypotenuse is 1 m long?

   c. At what rate is the length of the hypotenuse changing?

8. **Shrinking isosceles triangle** The hypotenuse of an isosceles right triangle decreases in length at a rate of 4 m/s.

   a. At what rate is the area of the triangle changing when the legs are 5 m long?

   b. At what rate are the lengths of the legs of the triangle changing?

   c. At what rate is the area of the triangle changing when the area is 4 m²?

9. **Expanding circle** The area of a circle increases at a rate of 1 cm²/s.

   a. How fast is the radius changing when the radius is 2 cm?

   b. How fast is the radius changing when the circumference is 2 cm?

10. **Expanding cube** The edges of a cube increase at a rate of 2 cm/s. How fast is the volume changing when the length of each edge is 50 cm?

11. **Shrinking circle** A circle has an initial radius of 50 ft when the radius begins decreasing at a rate of 2 ft/min. What is the rate of change of the area at the instant the radius is 10 ft?

12. **Shrinking cube** The volume of a cube decreases at a rate of 0.5 ft³/min. What is the rate of change of the side length when the side lengths are 12 ft?

13. **Balloons** A spherical balloon is inflated and its volume increases at a rate of 15 in³/min. What is the rate of change of its radius when the radius is 10 in?

14. **Piston compression** A piston is seated at the top of a cylindrical chamber with radius 5 cm when it starts moving into the chamber at a constant speed of 3 cm/s (see figure). What is the rate of change of the volume of the cylinder when the piston is 2 cm from the base of the chamber?

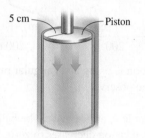

5 cm — Piston

15. **Melting snowball** A spherical snowball melts at a rate proportional to its surface area. Show that the rate of change of the radius is constant. (*Hint:* Surface area = $4\pi r^2$.)

16. **Bug on a parabola** A bug is moving along the right side of the parabola $y = x^2$ at a rate such that its distance from the origin is increasing at 1 cm/min. At what rates are the x- and y-coordinates of the bug increasing when the bug is at the point $(2, 4)$?

17. **Another bug on a parabola** A bug is moving along the parabola $y = x^2$. At what point on the parabola are the x- and y-coordinates changing at the same rate? (*Source: Calculus*, Tom M. Apostol, Vol. 1, John Wiley & Sons, New York, 1967.)

18. **Expanding rectangle** A rectangle initially has dimensions 2 cm by 4 cm. All sides begin increasing in length at a rate of 1 cm/s. At what rate is the area of the rectangle increasing after 20 s?

19. **Filling a pool** A swimming pool is 50 m long and 20 m wide. Its depth decreases linearly along the length from 3 m to 1 m (see figure). It is initially empty and is filled at a rate of 1 m³/min. How fast is the water level rising 250 min after the filling begins? How long will it take to fill the pool?

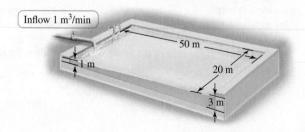

Inflow 1 m³/min

50 m

1 m

20 m

3 m

20. **Altitude of a jet** A jet ascends at a 10° angle from the horizontal with an airspeed of 550 mi/hr (its speed along its line of flight is 550 mi/hr). How fast is the altitude of the jet increasing? If the sun is directly overhead, how fast is the shadow of the jet moving on the ground?

21. **Rate of dive of a submarine** A surface ship is moving (horizontally) in a straight line at 10 km/hr. At the same time, an enemy submarine maintains a position directly below the ship while diving at an angle that is 20° below the horizontal. How fast is the submarine's altitude decreasing?

22. **Divergent paths** Two boats leave a port at the same time, one traveling west at 20 mi/hr and the other traveling south at 15 mi/hr. At what rate is the distance between them changing 30 minutes after they leave the port?

23. **Ladder against the wall** A 13-foot ladder is leaning against a vertical wall (see figure) when Jack begins pulling the foot of the ladder away from the wall at a rate of 0.5 ft/s. How fast is the top of the ladder sliding down the wall when the foot of the ladder is 5 ft from the wall?

13 ft

24. **Ladder against the wall again** A 12-foot ladder is leaning against a vertical wall when Jack begins pulling the foot of the ladder away from the wall at a rate of 0.2 ft/s. What is the configuration of the ladder at the instant that the vertical speed of the top of the ladder equals the horizontal speed of the foot of the ladder?

25. **Moving shadow** A 5-foot-tall woman walks at 8 ft/s toward a street light that is 20 ft above the ground. What is the rate of change of the length of her shadow when she is 15 ft from the street light? At what rate is the tip of her shadow moving?

26. **Baseball runners** Runners stand at first and second base in a baseball game. At the moment a ball is hit, the runner at first base runs to second base at 18 ft/s; simultaneously the runner on second runs to third base at 20 ft/s. How fast is the distance between the runners changing 1 second after the ball is hit (see figure)? (*Hint:* The distance between consecutive bases is 90 ft and the bases lie at the corners of a square.)

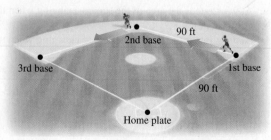

90 ft

2nd base

3rd base

1st base

90 ft

Home plate

27. **Growing sandpile** Sand falls from an overhead bin and accumulates in a conical pile with a radius that is always three times its height. Suppose the height of the pile increases at a rate of 2 cm/s when the pile is 12 cm high. At what rate is the sand leaving the bin at that instant?

28. **Draining a water heater** A water heater that has the shape of a right cylindrical tank with a radius of 1 ft and a height of 4 ft is being drained. How fast is water draining out of the tank (in ft³/min) if the water level is dropping at 6 in/min?

29. **Draining a tank** An inverted conical water tank with a height of 12 ft and a radius of 6 ft is drained through a hole in the vertex at a rate of 2 ft³/s (see figure). What is the rate of change of the water depth when the water depth is 3 ft? (*Hint:* Use similar triangles.)

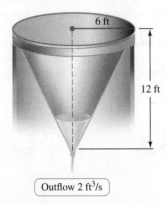

6 ft

12 ft

Outflow 2 ft³/s

30. **Drinking a soda** At what rate is soda being sucked out of a cylindrical glass that is 6 in. tall and has a radius of 2 in.? The depth of the soda decreases at a constant rate of 0.25 in./s.

31. **Draining a cone** Water is drained out of an inverted cone, having the same dimensions as the cone depicted in Exercise 29. If the water level drops at 1 ft/min, at what rate is water (in ft³/min) draining from the tank when the water depth is 6 ft?

32. **Filling a hemispherical tank** A hemispherical tank with a radius of 10 m is filled from an inflow pipe at a rate of 3 m³/min (see figure). How fast is the water level rising when the water level is 5 m from the bottom of the tank? (*Hint:* The volume of a cap of thickness h sliced from a sphere of radius r is $\pi h^2(3r - h)/3$.)

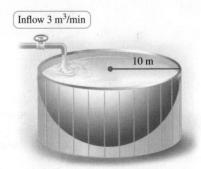

Inflow 3 m³/min

10 m

33. **Surface area of hemispherical tank** For the situation described in Exercise 32, what is the rate of change of the area of the exposed surface of the water when the water is 5 m deep?

34. **Observing a launch** An observer stands 300 ft from the launch site of a hot-air balloon. The balloon is launched vertically and maintains a constant upward velocity of 20 ft/s. What is the rate of change of the angle of elevation of the balloon when it is 400 ft from the ground? The angle of elevation is the angle θ between the observer's line of sight to the balloon and the ground.

35. **Another balloon story** A hot-air balloon is 150 ft above the ground when a motorcycle passes directly beneath it (traveling in a straight line on a horizontal road) going 40 mi/hr (58.67 ft/s). If the balloon is rising vertically at a rate of 10 ft/s, what is the rate of change of the distance between the motorcycle and the balloon 10 seconds later?

36. **Fishing story** An angler hooks a trout and begins turning her circular reel at 1.5 rev/s. If the radius of the reel (and the fishing line on it) is 2 in., then how fast is she reeling in her fishing line?

37. **Another fishing story** An angler hooks a trout and reels in his line at 4 in./s. Assume the tip of the fishing rod is 12 ft above the water and directly above the angler, and the fish is pulled horizontally directly toward the angler (see figure). Find the horizontal speed of the fish when it is 20 ft from the angler.

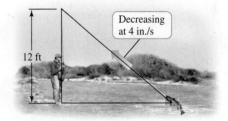

Decreasing at 4 in./s

12 ft

38. **Flying a kite** Once Kate's kite reaches a height of 50 ft (above her hands), it rises no higher but drifts due east in a wind blowing 5 ft/s. How fast is the string running through Kate's hands at the moment that she has released 120 ft of string?

39. **Rope on a boat** A rope passing through a capstan on a dock is attached to a boat offshore. The rope is pulled in at a constant rate of 3 ft/s and the capstan is 5 ft vertically above the water. How fast is the boat traveling when it is 10 ft from the dock?

Further Explorations

40. **Parabolic motion** An arrow is shot into the air and moves along the parabolic path $y = x(50 - x)$ (see figure). The horizontal component of velocity is always 30 ft/s. What is the vertical component of velocity when (i) $x = 10$ and (ii) $x = 40$?

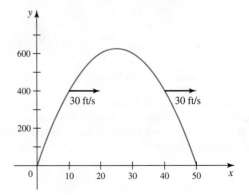

y

600

400

30 ft/s   30 ft/s

200

0   10   20   30   40   50 x

41. Time-lagged flights An airliner passes over an airport at noon traveling 500 mi/hr due west. At 1:00 P.M., another airliner passes over the same airport at the same elevation traveling due north at 550 mi/hr. Assuming both airliners maintain their (equal) elevations, how fast is the distance between them changing at 2:30 P.M.?

42. Disappearing triangle An equilateral triangle initially has sides of length 20 ft when each vertex moves toward the midpoint of the opposite side at a rate of 1.5 ft/min. Assuming the triangle remains equilateral, what is the rate of change of the area of the triangle at the instant the triangle disappears?

43. Clock hands The hands of the clock in the tower of the Houses of Parliament in London are approximately 3 m and 2.5 m in length. How fast is the distance between the tips of the hands changing at 9:00? (*Hint:* Use the Law of Cosines.)

44. Filling two pools Two cylindrical swimming pools are being filled simultaneously at the same rate (in m³/min; see figure). The smaller pool has a radius of 5 m, and the water level rises at a rate of 0.5 m/min. The larger pool has a radius of 8 m. How fast is the water level rising in the larger pool?

45. Filming a race A camera is set up at the starting line of a drag race 50 ft from a dragster at the starting line (camera 1 in the figure). Two seconds after the start of the race, the dragster has traveled 100 ft and the camera is turning at 0.75 rad/s while filming the dragster.

  a. What is the speed of the dragster at this point?

  b. A second camera (camera 2 in the figure) filming the dragster is located on the starting line 100 ft away from the dragster at the start of the race. How fast is this camera turning 2 seconds after the start of the race?

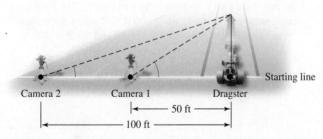

46. Two tanks A conical tank with an upper radius of 4 m and a height of 5 m drains into a cylindrical tank with a radius of 4 m and a height of 5 m (see figure). If the water level in the conical tank drops at a rate of 0.5 m/min, at what rate does the water level

in the cylindrical tank rise when the water level in the conical tank is 3 m? 1 m?

47. Oblique tracking A port and a radar station are 2 mi apart on a straight shore running east and west. A ship leaves the port at noon traveling northeast at a rate of 15 mi/hr. If the ship maintains its speed and course, what is the rate of change of the tracking angle θ between the shore and the line between the radar station and the ship at 12:30 P.M.? (*Hint:* Use the Law of Sines.)

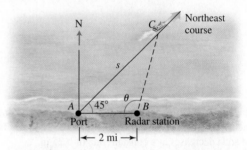

48. Oblique tracking A ship leaves port traveling southwest at a rate of 12 mi/hr. At noon, the ship reaches its closest approach to a radar station, which is on the shore 1.5 mi from the port. If the ship maintains its speed and course, what is the rate of change of the tracking angle θ between the radar station and the ship at 1:30 P.M. (see figure)? (*Hint:* Use the Law of Sines.)

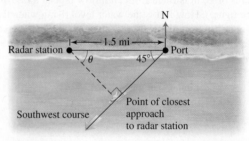

49. Watching an elevator An observer is 20 m above the ground floor of a large hotel atrium looking at a glass-enclosed elevator shaft that is 20 m horizontally from the observer (see figure). The angle of elevation of the elevator is the angle that the observer's line of sight makes with the horizontal (it may be positive or negative). Assuming that the elevator rises at a rate of 5 m/s, what is the rate of change of the angle of elevation when the elevator is 10 m above the ground? When the elevator is 40 m above the ground?

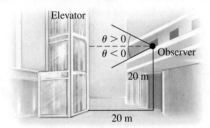

50. A lighthouse problem A lighthouse stands 500 m off of a straight shore, the focused beam of its light revolving four times each minute. As shown in the figure, P is the point on shore closest to the lighthouse and Q is a point on the shore 200 m from P. What is the speed of the beam along the shore when it strikes the point Q? Describe how the speed of the beam along the shore varies with the distance between P and Q. Neglect the height of the lighthouse.

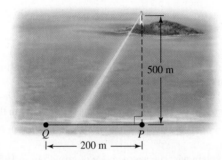

51. Navigation A boat leaves a port traveling due east at 12 mi/hr. At the same time, another boat leaves the same port traveling northeast at 15 mi/hr. The angle θ of the line between the boats is measured relative to due north (see figure). What is the rate of change of this angle 30 min after the boats leave the port? 2 hr after the boats leave the port?

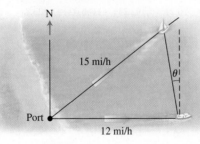

52. Watching a Ferris wheel An observer stands 20 m from the bottom of a 10-m-tall Ferris wheel on a line that is perpendicular to the face of the Ferris wheel. The wheel revolves at a rate of π rad/min and the observer's line of sight with a specific seat on the wheel makes an angle θ with the ground (see figure). Forty seconds after that seat leaves the lowest point on the wheel, what

is the rate of change of θ? Assume the observer's eyes are level with the bottom of the wheel.

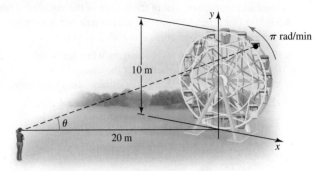

53. Viewing angle The bottom of a large theater screen is 3 ft above your eye level and the top of the screen is 10 ft above your eye level. Assume you walk away from the screen (perpendicular to the screen) at a rate of 3 ft/s while looking at the screen. What is the rate of change of the viewing angle θ when you are 30 ft from the wall on which the screen hangs, assuming the floor is horizontal (see figure)?

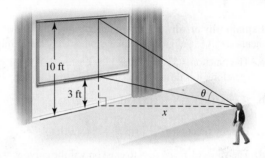

54. Searchlight—wide beam A revolving searchlight, which is 100 m from the nearest point on a straight highway, casts a horizontal beam along a highway (see figure). The beam leaves the spotlight at an angle of $\pi/16$ rad and revolves at a rate of $\pi/6$ rad/s. Let w be the width of the beam as it sweeps along the highway and θ be the angle that the center of the beam makes with the perpendicular to the highway. What is the rate of change of w when $\theta = \pi/3$? Neglect the height of the searchlight.

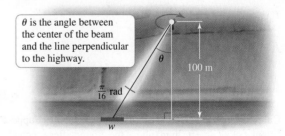

θ is the angle between the center of the beam and the line perpendicular to the highway.

55. Draining a trough A trough is a half cylinder with length 5 m and radius 1 m. The trough is full of water when a valve is opened and water flows out of the bottom of the trough at a rate of 1.5 m³/hr (see figure). (*Hint:* The area of a sector of a circle of a radius r subtended by an angle θ is $r^2\theta/2$.)

a. How fast is the water level changing when the water level is 0.5 m from the bottom of the trough?

b. What is the rate of change of the surface area of the water when the water is 0.5 m deep?

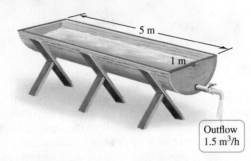

5 m

1 m

Outflow
1.5 m³/h

56. Divergent paths Two boats leave a port at the same time, one traveling west at 20 mi/hr and the other traveling southwest at 15 mi/hr. At what rate is the distance between them changing 30 min after they leave the port?

QUICK CHECK ANSWERS

1. $12{,}000\pi$ m²/hr, $18{,}000\pi$ m²/hr   2. -192 mi/hr
3. 1.1 ft/min; decreases with height   4. $t=0, \theta=0$, $\theta'(0)=0.02$ rad/s ◄

CHAPTER 3 REVIEW EXERCISES

1. Explain why or why not Determine whether the following statements are true, and give an explanation or a counterexample.

a. The function $f(x)=|2x+1|$ is continuous for all x; therefore, it is differentiable for all x.)

b. If $\dfrac{d}{dx}(f(x))=\dfrac{d}{dx}(g(x))$, then $f=g$.

c. For any function f, $\dfrac{d}{dx}|f(x)|=|f'(x)|$.

d. The value of $f'(a)$ fails to exist only if the curve $y=f(x)$ has a vertical tangent line at $x=a$.

e. An object can have negative acceleration and increasing speed.

2–5. Tangent lines

a. *Use either definition of the derivative to determine the slope of the curve $y=f(x)$ at the given point P.*

b. *Find an equation of the line tangent to the curve $y=f(x)$ at P; then graph the curve and the tangent line.*

2. $f(x)=4x^2-7x+5$; $P(2,7)$

3. $f(x)=5x^3+x$; $P(1,6)$

4. $f(x)=\dfrac{x+3}{2x+1}$; $P(0,3)$

5. $f(x)=\dfrac{1}{2\sqrt{3x+1}}$; $P\!\left(0,\dfrac{1}{2}\right)$

6. Calculating average and instantaneous velocities Suppose the height s of an object (in m) above the ground after t seconds is approximated by the function $s=-4.9t^2+25t+1$.

a. Make a table showing the average velocities of the object from time $t=1$ to $t=1+h$, for $h=0.01, 0.001, 0.0001$, and 0.00001.

b. Use the table in part (a) to estimate the instantaneous velocity of the object at $t=1$.

c. Use limits to verify your estimate in part (b).

7. Population of the United States in the 20th century The population of the United States (in millions) by decade is given in the table, where t is the number of years after 1900. These data are plotted and fitted with a smooth curve $y=p(t)$ in the figure.

a. Compute the average rate of population growth from 1950 to 1960.

b. Explain why the average rate of growth from 1950 to 1960 is a good approximation to the (instantaneous) rate of growth in 1955.

c. Estimate the instantaneous rate of growth in 1985.

Year	1900	1910	1920	1930	1940	1950
t	0	10	20	30	40	50
$p(t)$	76.21	92.23	106.02	123.2	132.16	152.32

Year	1960	1970	1980	1990	2000	2010
t	60	70	80	90	100	110
$p(t)$	179.32	203.30	226.54	248.71	281.42	308.94

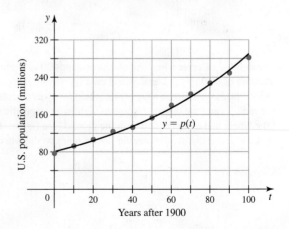

8. Growth rate of bacteria Suppose the following graph represents the number of bacteria in a culture t hours after the start of an experiment.

  a. At approximately what time is the instantaneous growth rate the greatest, for $0 \le t \le 36$? Estimate the growth rate at this time.

  b. At approximately what time in the interval $0 \le t \le 36$ is the instantaneous growth rate the least? Estimate the instantaneous growth rate at this time.

  c. What is the average growth rate over the interval $0 \le t \le 36$?

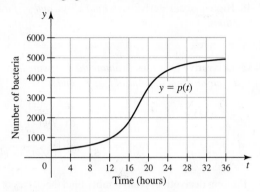

9. Velocity of a skydiver Assume the graph represents the distance (in m) fallen by a skydiver t seconds after jumping out of a plane.

  a. Estimate the velocity of the skydiver at $t = 15$.

  b. Estimate the velocity of the skydiver at $t = 70$.

  c. Estimate the average velocity of the skydiver between $t = 20$ and $t = 90$.

  d. Sketch a graph of the velocity function for, $0 \le t \le 120$.

  e. What significant event do you think occurred at $t = 30$?

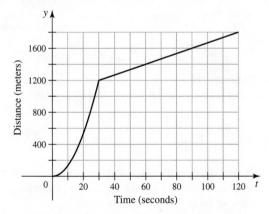

10–11. Using the definition of the derivative *Use the definition of the derivative to do the following.*

10. Verify that $f'(x) = 4x - 3$, where $f(x) = 2x^2 - 3x + 1$.

11. Verify that $g'(x) = \dfrac{1}{\sqrt{2x - 3}}$, where $g(x) = \sqrt{2x - 3}$.

12. Sketching a derivative graph
Sketch a graph of f' for the function f shown in the figure.

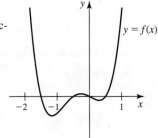

13. Sketching a derivative graph
Sketch a graph of g' for the function g shown in the figure.

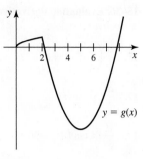

14. Matching functions and derivatives Match the functions in a–d with the derivatives in A–D.

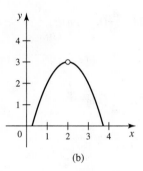

(a)   (b)

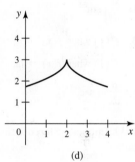

(c)   (d)

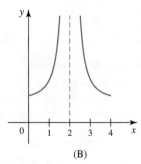

(A)   (B)

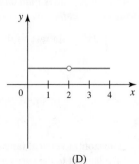

(C)   (D)

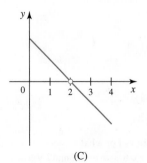

15–36. Evaluating derivatives *Evaluate and simplify the following derivatives.*

15. $\dfrac{d}{dx}\left(\dfrac{2}{3}x^3 + \pi x^2 + 7x + 1\right)$ **16.** $\dfrac{d}{dx}(2x\sqrt{x^2 - 2x + 2})$

17. $\dfrac{d}{dt}(5t^2 \sin t)$ **18.** $\dfrac{d}{dx}(5x + \sin^3 x + \sin x^3)$

19. $\dfrac{d}{d\theta}(4 \tan (\theta^2 + 3\theta + 2))$ **20.** $\dfrac{d}{dx}(\csc^5 3x)$

21. $\dfrac{d}{du}\left(\dfrac{4u^2 + u}{8u + 1}\right)$ **22.** $\dfrac{d}{dt}\left(\dfrac{3t^2 - 1}{3t^2 + 1}\right)^{-3}$

23. $\dfrac{d}{d\theta}(\tan (\sin \theta))$ **24.** $\dfrac{d}{dv}\left(\dfrac{v}{3v^2 + 2v + 1}\right)^{1/3}$

25. $\dfrac{d}{dx}(2x (\sin x)\sqrt{3x - 1})$ **26.** $\dfrac{d}{dx}(xe^{-10x})$

27. $\dfrac{d}{dx}(x \ln^2 x)$ **28.** $\dfrac{d}{dw}(e^{-w} \ln w)$

29. $\dfrac{d}{dx}(2^{x^2 - x})$ **30.** $\dfrac{d}{dx}(\log_3 (x + 8))$

31. $\dfrac{d}{dx}\left[\sin^{-1}\dfrac{1}{x}\right]$ **32.** $\dfrac{d}{dx}(x^{\sin x})$

33. $f'(1)$ when $f(x) = x^{1/x}$

34. $f'(1)$ when $f(x) = \tan^{-1} (4x^2)$

35. $\dfrac{d}{dx}(x \sec^{-1} x)\Big|_{x=2/\sqrt{3}}$ **36.** $\dfrac{d}{dx}(\tan^{-1} e^{-x})\Big|_{x=0}$

37–39. Implicit differentiation *Calculate $y'(x)$ for the following relations.*

37. $y = \dfrac{e^y}{1 + \sin x}$ **38.** $\sin x \cos (y - 1) = \dfrac{1}{2}$

39. $y\sqrt{x^2 + y^2} = 15$

40. Quadratic functions

    a. Show that if $(a, f(a))$ is any point on the graph of $f(x) = x^2$, then the slope of the tangent line at that point is $m = 2a$.

    b. Show that if $(a, f(a))$ is any point on the graph of $f(x) = bx^2 + cx + d$, then the slope of the tangent line at that point is $m = 2ab + c$.

41–44. Tangent lines *Find an equation of the line tangent to the following curves at the given point.*

41. $y = 3x^3 + \sin x;\ x = 0$

42. $y = \dfrac{4x}{x^2 + 3};\ x = 3$

43. $y + \sqrt{xy} = 6;\ (x, y) = (1, 4)$

44. $x^2 y + y^3 = 75;\ (x, y) = (4, 3)$

45. Horizontal/vertical tangent lines For what value(s) of x is the line tangent to the curve $y = x\sqrt{6 - x}$ horizontal? Vertical?

46. A parabola property Let $f(x) = x^2$.

    a. Show that $\dfrac{f(x) - f(y)}{x - y} = f'\left(\dfrac{x + y}{2}\right)$, for all $x \neq y$.

    b. Is this property true for $f(x) = ax^2$, where a is a nonzero real number?

    c. Give a geometrical interpretation of this property.

    d. Is this property true for $f(x) = ax^3$?

47–48. Higher-order derivatives *Find y', y'', and y''' for the following functions.*

47. $y = \sin \sqrt{x}$ **48.** $y = (x-3)\sqrt{x + 2}$

49–52. Derivative formulas *Evaluate the following derivatives. Express your answers in terms of f, g, f', and g'.*

49. $\dfrac{d}{dx}(x^2 f(x))$ **50.** $\dfrac{d}{dx}\sqrt{\dfrac{f(x)}{g(x)}}$

51. $\dfrac{d}{dx}\left(\dfrac{x f(x)}{g(x)}\right)$ **52.** $\dfrac{d}{dx}f(\sqrt{g(x)}),\ g(x) \geq 0$

53. Finding derivatives from a table Find the values of the following derivatives using the table.

x	1	3	5	7	9
$f(x)$	3	1	9	7	5
$f'(x)$	7	9	5	1	3
$g(x)$	9	7	5	3	1
$g'(x)$	5	9	3	1	7

    a. $\dfrac{d}{dx}(f(x) + 2g(x))\Big|_{x=3}$ **b.** $\dfrac{d}{dx}\left[\dfrac{x f(x)}{g(x)}\right]\Big|_{x=1}$

    c. $\dfrac{d}{dx}f(g(x^2))\Big|_{x=3}$ **d.** $\dfrac{d}{dx}(f(x)^3)\Big|_{x=5}$ **e.** $(g^{-1})'(7)$

54–55. Limits *The following limits represent the derivative of a function f at a point a. Find a possible f and a, and then evaluate the limit.*

54. $\displaystyle\lim_{h \to 0} \dfrac{\sin^2\left(\dfrac{\pi}{4} + h\right) - \dfrac{1}{2}}{h}$ **55.** $\displaystyle\lim_{x \to 5} \dfrac{\tan (\pi\sqrt{3x - 11})}{x - 5}$

56–57. Derivative of the inverse at a point *Consider the following functions. In each case, without finding the inverse, evaluate the derivative of the inverse at the given point.*

56. $f(x) = 1/(x + 1)$ at $f(0)$

57. $y = \sqrt{x^3 + x - 1}$ at $y = 3$

58–59. Derivative of the inverse *Find the derivative of the inverse of the following functions. Express the result with x as the independent variable.*

58. $f(x) = 12x - 16$ **59.** $f(x) = x^{-1/3}$

T 60. A function and its inverse function The function $f(x) = \dfrac{x}{x + 1}$ is one-to-one for $x > -1$ and has an inverse on that interval.

    a. Graph f, for $x > -1$.

    b. Find the inverse function f^{-1} corresponding to the function graphed in part (a). Graph f^{-1} on the same set of axes as in part (a).

c. Evaluate the derivative of f^{-1} at the point $\left(\frac{1}{2}, 1\right)$.

d. Sketch the tangent lines on the graphs of f and f^{-1} at $\left(1, \frac{1}{2}\right)$ and $\left(\frac{1}{2}, 1\right)$, respectively.

61. Derivative of the inverse in two ways Let $f(x) = \sin x$, $f^{-1}(x) = \sin^{-1} x$, and $(x_0, y_0) = (\pi/4, 1/\sqrt{2})$.

a. Evaluate $(f^{-1})'(1/\sqrt{2})$ using Theorem 3.23.

b. Evaluate $(f^{-1})'(1/\sqrt{2})$ directly by differentiating f^{-1}. Check for agreement with part (a).

62–63. Derivatives from a graph *Evaluate the following derivatives using the graphs of f and f', if possible.*

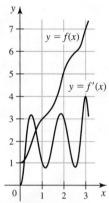

62. a. $\dfrac{d}{dx}[x f(x)]\Big|_{x=2}$

b. $\dfrac{d}{dx} f(x^2)\Big|_{x=1}$

c. $\dfrac{d}{dx} f(f(x))\Big|_{x=1}$

63. a. $(f^{-1})'(7)$

b. $(f^{-1})'(3)$

c. $(f^{-1})'(f(2))$

64. Velocity of a probe A small probe is launched vertically from the ground. When it reaches its high point, a parachute deploys and the probe descends to Earth. The height of the probe above the ground is

$$s(t) = \frac{300t - 50t^2}{t^3 + 2}, \text{ for } 0 \le t \le 6.$$

a. Graph the height function and describe the motion of the probe.

b. Find the velocity of the probe.

c. Graph the velocity function and determine the approximate time at which the velocity is a minimum.

65. Population growth Suppose $p(t) = -1.7t^3 + 72t^2 + 7200t + 80,000$ is the population of a city t years after 1950.

a. Determine the average rate of growth of the city from 1950 to 2000.

b. What was the rate of growth of the city in 1990?

66. Position of a piston The distance between the head of a piston and the end of a cylindrical chamber is given by $x(t) = \dfrac{8t}{t + 1}$ cm, for $t \ge 0$ (measured in seconds). The radius of the cylinder is 4 cm.

a. Find the volume of the chamber, for $t \ge 0$.

b. Find the rate of change of the volume $V'(t)$, for $t \ge 0$.

c. Graph the derivative of the volume function. On what intervals is the volume increasing? Decreasing?

67. Boat rates Two boats leave a dock at the same time. One boat travels south at 30 mi/hr and the other travels east at 40 mi/hr. After half an hour, how fast is the distance between the boats increasing?

68. Rate of inflation of a balloon A spherical balloon is inflated at a rate of 10 cm^3/min. At what rate is the diameter of the balloon increasing when the balloon has a diameter of 5 cm?

69. Rate of descent of a hot-air balloon A rope is attached to the bottom of a hot-air balloon that is floating above a flat field. If the angle of the rope to the ground remains 65° and the rope is pulled in at 5 ft/s, how quickly is the elevation of the balloon changing?

70. Filling a tank Water flows into a conical tank at a rate of 2 ft^3/min. If the radius of the top of the tank is 4 ft and the height is 6 ft, determine how quickly the water level is rising when the water is 2 ft deep in the tank.

71. Angle of elevation A jet flies horizontally 500 ft directly above a spectator at an air show at 450 mi/hr. Determine how quickly the angle of elevation (between the ground and the line from the spectator to the jet) is changing 2 seconds later.

72. Viewing angle A man whose eye level is 6 ft above the ground walks toward a billboard at a rate of 2 ft/s. The bottom of the billboard is 10 ft above the ground and it is 15 ft high. The man's viewing angle is the angle formed by the lines between the man's eyes and the top and bottom of the billboard. At what rate is the viewing angle changing when the man is 30 ft from the billboard?

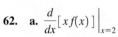 **PRACTICE QUESTIONS**   *The following questions are intended to help you prepare for the AP exam. They are not questions from actual AP exams.*

Section 1 Part A, Multiple Choice, No Technology

1. Find the value of $\lim\limits_{h \to 0} \dfrac{3(2 + h)^2 - 12}{h}$.

(A) 0   (B) 12   (C) -4 (D) 1   (E) The limit does not exit.

2. Find the value of $\lim\limits_{x \to \frac{\pi}{6}} \dfrac{\sin x - \dfrac{1}{2}}{x - \dfrac{\pi}{6}}$.

(A) 0   (B) $\dfrac{1}{2}$ (C) $\dfrac{\sqrt{3}}{2}$ (D) 1   (E) The limit does not exit.

3. Which of the following statements is true about the function $f(x) = |x - 1|$?

(A) It is continuous and differentiable at $x = 1$.

(B) It is not continuous but is differentiable at $x = 1$.

(C) It is continuous but is not differentiable at $x = 1$.

(D) It is neither continuous nor differentiable at $x = 1$.

(E) The derivative of f at 0 is 1.

4. Evaluate $f'(-1)$, where $f(x) = \dfrac{1}{3}(x^3 - x^{-3})$.

(A) undefined   (B) -2 (C) 0   (D) $\dfrac{2}{3}$ (E) 2

5. What is the equation of the line tangent to the graph of $f(x) = 3e^x - 2x + 4$ at the point $(0, 7)$?

(A) $y = 7x$ (B) $y = 3x - 7$ (C) $y = 5x + 7$

(D) $y = 7x - 3$ (E) $y = x + 7$

6. Let $g(x) = x \sin x$ and evaluate $g'\left(\dfrac{\pi}{2}\right)$.

(A) 1 (B) 0 (C) -1 (D) $-\dfrac{\pi}{2}$ (E) $\dfrac{\pi}{2}$

7. Assume $f(x) = 4 \sin x$ and find $f^{(8)}(x)$ (the eighth derivative of f).

(A) $4^8 \sin x$ (B) $4 \sin x$ (C) $4 \cos x$ (D) $-4 \sin x$

(E) $-4 \cos x$

8. $\dfrac{d}{dx}\left(\dfrac{\sin x^2}{x}\right)$ equals

(A) $2 \sin x^2$.

(B) $\dfrac{2 \cos x^2 - \sin x^2}{x^2}$.

(C) $2 \sin x^2 - \dfrac{\cos x^2}{x^2}$.

(D) $2 \cos x^2 - \dfrac{\sin x^2}{x^2}$.

(E) $\cos 2x$.

9. An object moves along a line with a position function $s(t) = 4(t - 3)^2$, for $t \geq 0$. Which of the following statements is true?

(A) The object moves in the positive s direction for $t \geq 0$.

(B) The object initially moves in the positive s direction, stops, and then moves in the negative s direction.

(C) The object initially moves in the negative s direction, stops, and then moves in the positive s direction.

(D) The object moves in the negative s direction for $t \geq 0$.

(E) The path of the object is a parabola.

10. Find the slope of the line tangent to the graph of $y = \dfrac{5}{\sqrt{x^2 + 9}}$ at $x = 4$.

(A) $-\dfrac{4}{25}$ (B) $-\dfrac{1}{50}$ (C) $-\dfrac{4}{125}$ (D) -4 (E) 50

11. Find the slope of the line tangent to the curve $xy^3 - x^3y = 6$ at the point $(1, 2)$.

(A) $-\dfrac{2}{5}$ (B) $-\dfrac{14}{11}$ (C) $-\dfrac{2}{11}$ (D) $\dfrac{4}{5}$ (E) $-\dfrac{5}{2}$

12. If $f(x) = \tan^{-1}(e^{-x})$, then $f'(x)$ equals

(A) $\dfrac{e^x}{1 + e^{2x}}$.   (B) $\dfrac{e^{-x}}{1 + e^{-2x}}$.   (C) $-\dfrac{1}{e^x + e^{-x}}$.

(D) $\dfrac{e^{-x}}{1 - e^{-2x}}$.   (E) $\dfrac{1}{\sqrt{1 - e^{-2x}}}$.

13. The following table gives the values of differentiable functions f and g and their derivatives at $x = 1, 2,$ and 3.

x	1	2	3
$f(x)$	2	1	4
$f'(x)$	−3	3	7
$g(x)$	2	3	1
$g'(x)$	−4	6	5

If $h(x) = f(g(x)) + g(f(x))$, then what is the value of $h'(1)$?

(A) 36 (B) -24 (C) -30 (D) 9 (E) -1

14. Given the following graphs of f and f', what is the value of $(f^{-1})'(5)$?

(A) cannot be determined   (B) 3 (C) $\dfrac{1}{3}$ (D) $\dfrac{1}{5}$ (E) 5

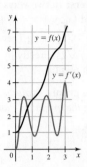

Section 1 Part B, Multiple Choice, Technology Allowed

15. Suppose f is a differentiable function. Consider the following table of function values.

x	$f(x)$
1	−2.800
1.001	−2.805
1.01	−2.806
1.1	−3.308

Based on these values, what is likely to be the best approximation to $f'(1)$?

(A) 5 (B) -3 (C) -1 (D) -5 (E) -0.6

16. Consider the position function $s(t) = 0.5e^{-t/2} \cos(t/2)$ of an oscillator moving along a line, for $0 \leq t \leq 2\pi$. Which of the following statements is true?

(A) The velocity is positive for $0 \leq t < 3\pi/2$ and negative for $3\pi/2 < t \leq 2\pi$.

(B) The velocity is positive for $0 \leq t < \pi$ and negative for $\pi < t \leq 2\pi$.

(C) The velocity is negative for $0 \leq t < 3\pi/2$ and positive for $3\pi/2 < t \leq 2\pi$.

(D) The object is on the positive side of the origin for $0 < t < 3\pi/2$.

(E) The object passes through the origin twice on the interval $0 \leq t \leq 2\pi$.

17. At how many points of the curve $y^4 - 3x^3 = 2$ is there a vertical tangent line?

(A) 0 (B) 1 (C) 2 (D) 3 (E) infinitely many

Section 2 Part A, Free Response, Technology Allowed

1. Use the function $f(x) = |x - 1| + 2|x + 1| - 3$ to complete the following parts.

   a. Graph f on the interval $[-3, 3]$.
   b. Find the zeros of f.
   c. Graph f' on the interval $[-3, 3]$.
   d. For what values of x on $[-3, 3]$ (if any) is f' undefined?

2. The position $x(t)$ of an object moving along the x-axis is given by $x(t) = \sin(\pi e^t)$, for $t \geq 0$.

   a. Find the average velocity of the object on the interval $0 \leq t \leq \ln 2$.
   b. When is the velocity of the object decreasing on the interval $0 \leq t \leq \ln 2$?
   c. When is the speed of the object decreasing on the interval $0 \leq t \leq \ln 2$?
   d. At what time does the object first change directions, for $t > 0$?
   e. When is the object furthest from its starting position on the time interval $0 \leq t \leq \ln 2$?

Section 2 Part B, Free Response, No Technology

3. a. Match the graphs of functions A–D with the graphs of their derivatives a–d.

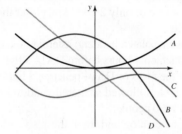

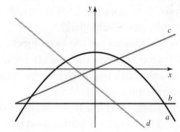

b. Match the functions f, f', and f'' with the graphs A, B, and C.

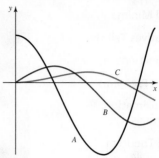

4. Sketch a possible graph of a function g that has the following properties on the interval $[-3, 3]$.

   a. $g'(x) > 0$ for $-3 \leq x < 0$ **b.** $\lim\limits_{x \to 0} g'(x) = \infty$
   c. $g'(x) > 0$ for $0 < x < 2$ **d.** $g'(x) < 0$ for $2 < x \leq 3$
   e. $g'(2) = g(2) = 0$

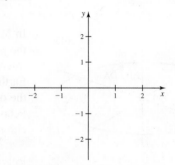

5. The area of a 45-45-90 right triangle is increasing at a rate of $3 \text{ cm}^2/\text{s}$. At what rate is the length of the hypotenuse increasing when the hypotenuse is 10 cm long?

6. Let $f(x) = \begin{cases} e^{-\pi x} & \text{if } x \leq 0 \\ 1 - \sin \pi x & \text{if } x > 0. \end{cases}$

   a. Show that f is continuous at $x = 0$.
   b. Explain why f is differentiable at $x = 0$.
   c. Write $f'(x)$ as a piecewise-defined function and then find the smallest value of x for which $f'(x) = 0$.
   d. Write an equation of the line tangent to f at $x = 0$.

7. Consider the curve given by $x^2 + 4y^2 + 2xy = 12$.

   a. Find $\dfrac{dy}{dx}$.
   b. Find the points on the curve where the tangent lines have a slope of 0.
   c. Find the points on the curve where the tangent lines are vertical.

Chapter 3 Guided Projects

Applications of the material in this chapter and related topics can be found in the following Guided Projects. For additional information, see the Preface.

- Numerical differentiation
- Enzyme kinetics
- Elasticity in economics
- Pharmacokinetics—drug metabolism

4 Applications of the Derivative

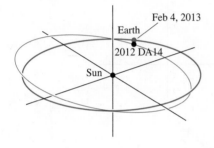

In March 2012, the European Space Agency (ESA) issued a press release informing the public of a recently discovered asteroid named 2012 DA14. At its nearest point, the asteroid passed within 2.7 million km of Earth (roughly seven times the distance from Earth to its moon). With observational data of the asteroid in hand, scientists determined the orbit of 2012 DA14 and made a surprising discovery. The asteroid would return in February 2013, zooming past Earth at a distance of only 24,000 km, closer than the geosynchronous orbit of many commercial satellites.

Asteroid 2012 DA14's near miss is not an isolated incident; asteroids and other space objects pass near Earth on a regular basis. In fact, only hours before DA14's flyby, an unrelated and unexpected rogue meteor roughly 1/14 the mass of DA14 penetrated Earth's atmosphere and exploded over Russia. The shockwave that followed shattered windows throughout the city of Chelyabinsk and injured as many as 1000 people.

Government agencies around the globe catalog and track these so-called *near-Earth objects* to determine whether we can expect a cataclysmic collision. One interesting mathematical question arises with all this analysis: how does the ESA determine the minimum distance between 2012 DA14 and Earth as they pass each other?

It turns out that as long as the orbits (or trajectories) of the two objects are known, we can devise a function that describes the distance between the objects for all points along their trajectories. As you will learn in this chapter, calculus provides the necessary tools to analyze this distance function and determine its minimum value.

The asteroid-Earth proximity scenario just described illustrates only one of a wide range of *optimization problems* that are ideally suited to calculus. Optimization is among the many applications of derivatives you will see in this chapter.

Chapter Preview
Much of the previous chapter was devoted to the basic mechanics of derivatives: evaluating them and interpreting them as rates of change. We now apply derivatives to a variety of mathematical questions, many of which concern the properties of functions and their graphs. One outcome of this work is a set of analytical curve-sketching methods that produce accurate graphs of functions. Equally important, derivatives allow us to formulate and solve a wealth of practical problems. For example, a weather probe dropped from an airplane accelerates until it reaches its terminal velocity: When is the acceleration the greatest? An economist has a mathematical model that relates the demand for a product to its price: What price maximizes the revenue? In this chapter, we develop the tools needed to answer such questions. In addition, we begin an ongoing discussion about approximating functions, we present an important result called the Mean Value Theorem, and we work with a powerful method that enables us to evaluate a new kind of limit. The chapter concludes with a numerical approach to approximating roots of functions called Newton's method.

4.1 Maxima and Minima

With a working understanding of derivatives, we now undertake one of the fundamental tasks of calculus: analyzing the behavior and producing accurate graphs of functions. An important question associated with any function concerns its maximum and minimum values: On a given interval (perhaps the entire domain), where does the function assume its largest and smallest values? Questions about maximum and minimum values take on added significance when a function represents a practical quantity, such as the profits of a company, the surface area of a container, or the speed of a space vehicle.

Absolute Maxima and Minima

Imagine taking a long hike through varying terrain from west to east. Your elevation changes as you walk over hills, through valleys, and across plains; and you reach several high and low points along the journey. Analogously, when we examine a function over an interval on the x-axis, its values increase and decrease, reaching high points and low points (Figure 4.1). You can view our study of functions in this chapter as an exploratory hike along the x-axis.

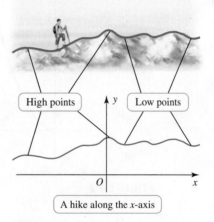

High points | Low points

A hike along the x-axis

FIGURE 4.1

> Absolute maximum and minimum values are also called *global* maximum and minimum values. The plural of maximum is maxima; the plural of minimum is minima.

DEFINITION Absolute Maximum and Minimum

Let f be defined on a set D containing c. If $f(c) \geq f(x)$ for every x in D, then f has an **absolute maximum** value of $f(c)$ on D at c. If $f(c) \leq f(x)$ for every x in D, then f has an **absolute minimum** value of $f(c)$ on D at c. **Absolute extreme value** refers to either absolute maximum or absolute minimum value.

The existence and location of absolute extreme values depend on both the function and the interval of interest. Figure 4.2 shows various cases for the function $f(x) = x^2$. Notice that if the interval of interest is not closed, a function might not attain absolute extreme values (Figure 4.2a, c, and d).

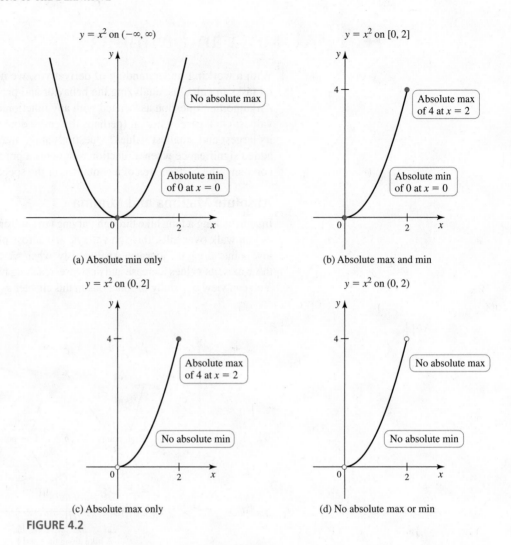

FIGURE 4.2

However, defining a function on a closed interval is not enough to guarantee the existence of absolute extreme values. Both functions in Figure 4.3 are defined at every point of a closed interval, but neither function attains an absolute maximum—the discontinuity in each function prevents it from happening.

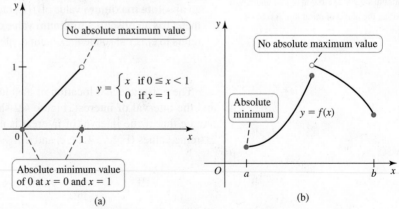

FIGURE 4.3

It turns out that *two* conditions ensure the existence of absolute maximum and minimum values on an interval: The function must be continuous on the interval, and the interval must be closed and bounded.

> The proof of the Extreme Value Theorem relies on properties of the real numbers found in advanced books.

THEOREM 4.1   Extreme Value Theorem
A function that is continuous on a closed interval $[a, b]$ has an absolute maximum value and an absolute minimum value on that interval.

EXAMPLE 1   Locating absolute maximum and minimum values For the functions in Figure 4.4, identify the location of the absolute maximum value and the absolute minimum value on the interval $[a, b]$. Do the functions meet the conditions of the Extreme Value Theorem?

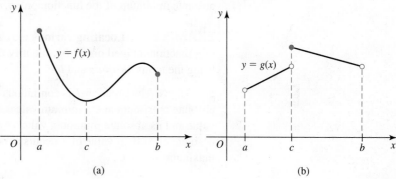

(a)   (b)

FIGURE 4.4

SOLUTION

QUICK CHECK 1 Sketch the graph of a function that is continuous on an interval but does not have an absolute minimum value. Sketch the graph of a function that is defined on a closed interval but does not have an absolute minimum value. ◄

a. The function f is continuous on the closed interval $[a, b]$, so the Extreme Value Theorem guarantees an absolute maximum (which occurs at a) and an absolute minimum (which occurs at c).

b. The function g does not satisfy the conditions of the Extreme Value Theorem because it is not continuous, and it is defined only on the open interval (a, b). It does not have an absolute minimum value. It does, however, have an absolute maximum at c. Therefore, a function may violate the conditions of the Extreme Value Theorem and still have an absolute maximum or minimum (or both). *Related Exercises 11–14* ◄

Local Maxima and Minima

Figure 4.5 shows a function defined on the interval $[a, b]$. It has an absolute minimum at the endpoint a and an absolute maximum at the interior point e. In addition, the function has special behavior at c, where its value is greatest *among nearby points*, and at d, where its value is least *among nearby points*. A point at which a function takes on the maximum or minimum value among nearby points is important.

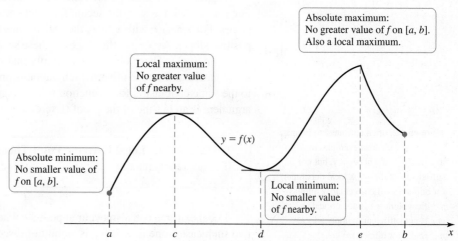

Absolute maximum:
No greater value of f on $[a, b]$.
Also a local maximum.

Local maximum:
No greater value of f nearby.

$y = f(x)$

Absolute minimum:
No smaller value of f on $[a, b]$.

Local minimum:
No smaller value of f nearby.

FIGURE 4.5

▶ Local maximum and minimum values are also called *relative maximum* and *minimum values*. *Local extrema* (plural) and *local extremum* (singular) refer to either local maxima or local minima.

> **DEFINITION Local Maximum and Minimum Values**
>
> Suppose c is an interior point of an interval I on which f is defined. If $f(c) \geq f(x)$ for all x in I, then $f(c)$ is a **local maximum** value of f. If $f(c) \leq f(x)$ for all x in I, then $f(c)$ is a **local minimum** value of f.

In this book, we adopt the convention that local maximum values and local minimum values occur only at interior points of the interval(s) of interest. For example, in Figure 4.5, the minimum value that occurs at the endpoint a is not a local minimum. However, it is the absolute minimum of the function on $[a, b]$.

EXAMPLE 2 Locating various maxima and minima Figure 4.6 shows the graph of a function defined on $[a, b]$. Identify the location of the various maxima and minima using the terms *absolute* and *local*.

SOLUTION The function f is continuous on a closed interval; by Theorem 4.1, it has absolute maximum and minimum values on $[a, b]$. The function has a local minimum value and its absolute minimum value at p. It has another local minimum value at r. The absolute maximum value of f occurs at both q and s (which also correspond to local maximum values).   *Related Exercises 15–22* ◀

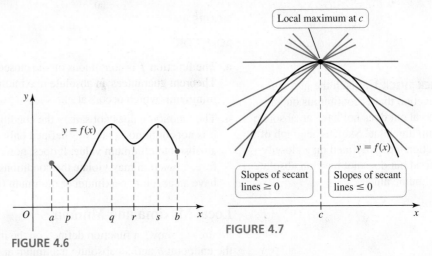

FIGURE 4.6

FIGURE 4.7

Critical Points Another look at Figure 4.6 shows that local maxima and minima occur at points in the open interval (a, b) where the derivative is zero ($x = q, r$, and s) and at points where the derivative fails to exist ($x = p$). We now make this observation precise.

Figure 4.7 illustrates a function that is differentiable at c with a local maximum at c. For x near c with $x < c$, the secant lines between $(x, f(x))$ and $(c, f(c))$ have nonnegative slopes. For x near c with $x > c$, the secant lines between $(x, f(x))$ and $(c, f(c))$ have nonpositive slopes. As $x \to c$, the slopes of these secant lines approach the slope of the tangent line at $(c, f(c))$. These observations imply that the slope of the tangent line must be both nonnegative and nonpositive, which happens only if $f'(c) = 0$. Similar reasoning leads to the same conclusion for a function with a local minimum at c: $f'(c)$ must be zero. This argument is an outline of the proof (Exercise 83) of the following theorem.

▶ Theorem 4.2, often attributed to Fermat, is one of the clearest examples in mathematics of a necessary, but not sufficient, condition. A local maximum (or minimum) at c necessarily implies a critical point at c, but a critical point at c is not sufficient to imply a local maximum (or minimum) there.

> **THEOREM 4.2 Local Extreme Point Theorem**
>
> If f has a local maximum or minimum value at c and $f'(c)$ exists, then $f'(c) = 0$.

Local extrema can also occur at points c where $f'(c)$ does not exist. Figure 4.8 shows two such cases, one in which c is a point of discontinuity and one in which f has a corner

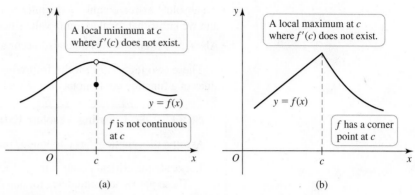

FIGURE 4.8

point at c. Because local extrema may occur at points c where $f'(c) = 0$ *and* where $f'(c)$ does not exist, we make the following definition.

> In this book, we use the convention that a critical point is a value c of the independent variable at which $f'(c)$ is zero or fails to exist. Other books define a critical point to be a point $(c, f(c))$ on the graph of f at which $f'(c)$ is zero or fails to exist. Be sure you know which convention you are expected to use.

DEFINITION Critical Point

An interior point c of the domain of f at which $f'(c) = 0$ or $f'(c)$ fails to exist is called a **critical point** of f.

Note that the converse of the Local Extreme Point Theorem (Theorem 4.2) is not necessarily true. It is possible that $f'(c) = 0$ at a point without a local maximum or local minimum value occurring there (Figure 4.9a). It is also possible that $f'(c)$ fails to exist, with no local extreme value occurring at c (Figure 4.9b). Therefore, critical points are *candidates* for local extreme points, but you must determine whether they actually correspond to local maxima or minima. This procedure is discussed in Section 4.2.

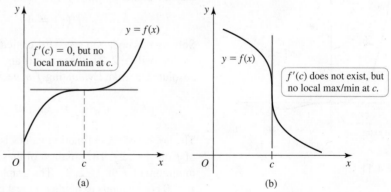

FIGURE 4.9

QUICK CHECK 2 Consider the function $f(x) = x^3$. Where is the critical point of f? Does f have a local maximum or minimum at the critical point? ◄

EXAMPLE 3 Locating critical points Find the critical points of $f(x) = x^2 \ln x$.

SOLUTION Note that f is differentiable on its domain, which is $(0, \infty)$. By the Product Rule,

$$f'(x) = 2x \cdot \ln x + x^2 \cdot \frac{1}{x} = x(2 \ln x + 1).$$

Setting $f'(x) = 0$ gives $x(2 \ln x + 1) = 0$, which has the solution $x = e^{-1/2} = 1/\sqrt{e}$. Because $x = 0$ is not in the domain of f, it is not a critical point. Therefore, the only critical point is $x = 1/\sqrt{e} \approx 0.607$. A graph of f (Figure 4.10) reveals that a local (and, indeed, absolute) minimum value occurs at $(1/\sqrt{e}, -1/(2e))$.

Related Exercises 23–36 ◄

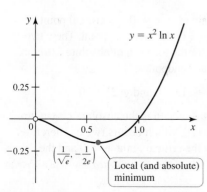

FIGURE 4.10

Locating Absolute Maxima and Minima

Theorem 4.1 guarantees the existence of absolute extreme values of a continuous function on a closed interval $[a, b]$, but it doesn't say where these values are located. Two observations lead to a procedure for locating absolute extreme values.

• An absolute extreme value in the interior of an interval is also a local extreme value, and we know that local extreme values occur at the critical points of f.

• Absolute extreme values may also occur at the endpoints of the interval of interest.

These two facts suggest the following procedure for locating the absolute extreme values of a function continuous on a closed interval.

PROCEDURE   **Locating Absolute Extreme Values on a Closed Interval**

Assume the function f is continuous on the closed interval $[a, b]$.

1. Locate the critical points c in (a, b), where $f'(c) = 0$ or $f'(c)$ does not exist. These points are candidates for absolute maxima and minima.

2. Evaluate f at the critical points and at the endpoints of $[a, b]$.

3. Choose the largest and smallest values of f from Step 2 for the absolute maximum and minimum values, respectively.

If the interval of interest is an open interval, then absolute extreme values—if they exist—occur at interior points.

EXAMPLE 4   **Absolute extreme values**   Find the absolute maximum and minimum values of the following functions.

a. $f(x) = x^4 - 2x^3$ on the interval $[-2, 2]$

b. $g(x) = x^{2/3}(2 - x)$ on the interval $[-1, 2]$

SOLUTION

a. Because f is a polynomial, its derivative exists everywhere. So if f has critical points, they are points at which $f'(x) = 0$. Computing f' and setting it equal to zero, we have

$$f'(x) = 4x^3 - 6x^2 = 2x^2(2x - 3) = 0.$$

Solving this equation gives the critical points $x = 0$ and $x = \frac{3}{2}$, both of which lie in the interval $[-2, 2]$; these points and the endpoints are *candidates* for the location of absolute extrema. Evaluating f at each of these points, we have

$$f(-2) = 32, \, f(0) = 0, \, f\left(\tfrac{3}{2}\right) = \frac{27}{16}, \text{ and } f(2) = 0.$$

The largest of these function values is $f(-2) = 32$, which is the absolute maximum of f on $[-2, 2]$. The smallest of these values is $f\left(\frac{3}{2}\right) = -\frac{27}{16}$, which is the absolute minimum of f on $[-2, 2]$. The graph of f (Figure 4.11) shows that the critical point $x = 0$ corresponds to neither a local maximum nor a local minimum.

b. Differentiating $g(x) = x^{2/3}(2 - x) = 2x^{2/3} - x^{5/3}$, we have

$$g'(x) = \frac{4}{3}x^{-1/3} - \frac{5}{3}x^{2/3} = \frac{4 - 5x}{3x^{1/3}}.$$

Because $g'(0)$ is undefined and 0 is in the domain of g, $x = 0$ is a critical point. In addition, $g'(x) = 0$ when $4 - 5x = 0$, so $x = \frac{4}{5}$ is also a critical point. These two critical points and the endpoints are *candidates* for the location of absolute extrema. The next step is to evaluate g at the critical points and endpoints:

$$g(-1) = 3, \quad g(0) = 0, \quad g\left(\tfrac{4}{5}\right) \approx 1.034, \text{ and } g(2) = 0.$$

The largest of these function values is $g(-1) = 3$, which is the absolute maximum value of g on $[-1, 2]$. The least of these values is 0, which occurs twice. Therefore, g has its absolute minimum value on $[-1, 2]$ at the critical point $x = 0$ and the endpoint $x = 2$ (Figure 4.12).   *Related Exercises 37–50* ◀

We now apply these ideas to a practical situation.

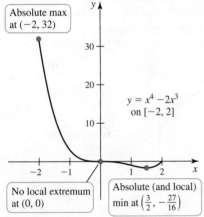

Absolute max at $(-2, 32)$

$y = x^4 - 2x^3$ on $[-2, 2]$

No local extremum at $(0, 0)$

Absolute (and local) min at $\left(\frac{3}{2}, -\frac{27}{16}\right)$

FIGURE 4.11

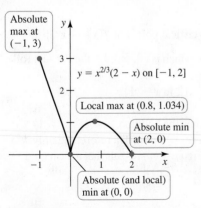

Absolute max at $(-1, 3)$

$y = x^{2/3}(2 - x)$ on $[-1, 2]$

Local max at $(0.8, 1.034)$

Absolute min at $(2, 0)$

Absolute (and local) min at $(0, 0)$

FIGURE 4.12

▷ The derivation of the position function for an object moving in a gravitational field is given in Section 6.1.

EXAMPLE 5   Trajectory high point A stone is launched vertically upward from a bridge 80 ft above the ground at a speed of 64 ft/s. Its height above the ground t seconds after the launch is given by

$$f(t) = -16t^2 + 64t + 80, \quad \text{for } 0 \le t \le 5.$$

When does the stone reach its maximum height?

SOLUTION We must evaluate the height function at the critical points and at the endpoints. The critical points satisfy the equation

$$f'(t) = -32t + 64 = -32(t - 2) = 0,$$

so the only critical point is $t = 2$. We now evaluate f at the endpoints and at the critical point:

$$f(0) = 80, \quad f(2) = 144, \quad \text{and} \quad f(5) = 0.$$

On the interval $[0, 5]$, the absolute maximum occurs at $t = 2$, at which time the stone reaches a height of 144 ft. Because $f'(t)$ is the velocity of the stone, the maximum height occurs at the instant the velocity is zero.   *Related Exercises 51–54*◀

SECTION 4.1 EXERCISES

Review Questions

1. What does it mean for a function to have an absolute extreme value at a point c of an interval $[a, b]$?

2. What are local maximum and minimum values of a function?

3. What conditions must be met to ensure that a function has an absolute maximum value and an absolute minimum value on an interval?

4. Sketch the graph of a function that is continuous on an open interval (a, b) but has neither an absolute maximum nor an absolute minimum value on (a, b).

5. Sketch the graph of a function that has an absolute maximum, a local minimum, but no absolute minimum on $[0, 3]$.

6. What is a critical point of a function?

7. Sketch the graph of a function f that has a local maximum value at a point c where $f'(c) = 0$.

8. Sketch the graph of a function f that has a local minimum value at a point c where $f'(c)$ is undefined.

9. How do you determine the absolute maximum and minimum values of a continuous function on a closed interval?

10. Explain how a function can have an absolute minimum value at an endpoint of an interval.

Basic Skills

11–14. Absolute maximum/minimum values *Use the following graphs to identify the points (if any) on the interval $[a, b]$ at which the function has an absolute maximum value or an absolute minimum value.*

11.   **12.**

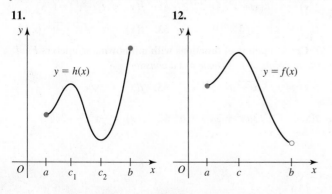

13.   **14.**

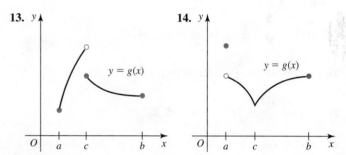

15–18. Local and absolute extreme values *Use the following graphs to identify the points on the interval $[a, b]$ at which local and absolute extreme values occur.*

15.   **16.**

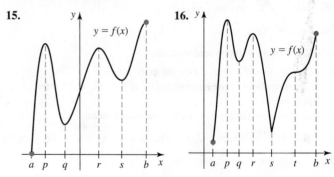

17.   **18.**

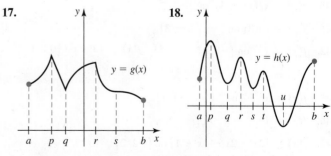

19–22. Designing a function *Sketch the graph of a function f continuous on $[0, 4]$ satisfying the given properties.*

19. $f'(x) = 0$ for $x = 1$ and 2; f has an absolute maximum at $x = 4$; f has an absolute minimum at $x = 0$; and f has a local minimum at $x = 2$.

20. $f'(x) = 0$ for $x = 1, 2$, and 3; f has an absolute minimum at $x = 1$; f has no local extremum at $x = 2$; and f has an absolute maximum at $x = 3$.

21. $f'(1)$ and $f'(3)$ are undefined; $f'(2) = 0$; f has a local maximum at $x = 1$; f has a local minimum at $x = 2$; f has an absolute maximum at $x = 3$; and f has an absolute minimum at $x = 4$.

22. $f'(x) = 0$ at $x = 1$ and 3; $f'(2)$ is undefined; f has an absolute maximum at $x = 2$; f has neither a local maximum nor a local minimum at $x = 1$; and f has an absolute minimum at $x = 3$.

23–36. Locating critical points

a. *Find the critical points of the following functions on the domain or on the given interval.*

b. *Use a graphing utility to determine whether each critical point corresponds to a local maximum, local minimum, or neither.*

23. $f(x) = 3x^2 - 4x + 2$

24. $f(x) = \frac{1}{8}x^3 - \frac{1}{2}x$ on $[-1, 3]$

25. $f(x) = \frac{x^3}{3} - 9x$ on $[-7, 7]$

26. $f(x) = \frac{x^4}{4} - \frac{x^3}{3} - 3x^2 + 10$ on $[-4, 4]$

27. $f(x) = 3x^3 + \frac{3x^2}{2} - 2x$ on $[-1, 1]$

28. $f(x) = \frac{4x^5}{5} - 3x^3 + 5$ on $[-2, 2]$

29. $f(x) = x/(x^2 + 1)$

30. $f(x) = 12x^5 - 20x^3$ on $[-2, 2]$

31. $f(x) = (e^x + e^{-x})/2$

32. $f(x) = \sin x \cos x$ on $[0, 2\pi]$

33. $f(x) = 1/x + \ln x$

34. $f(x) = x - \tan^{-1} x$

35. $f(x) = x^2\sqrt{x + 1}$ on $[-1, 1]$

36. $f(x) = (\sin^{-1} x)(\cos^{-1} x)$ on $[0, 1]$

37–50. Absolute maxima and minima

a. *Find the critical points of f on the given interval.*

b. *Determine the absolute extreme values of f on the given interval when they exist.*

c. *Use a graphing utility to confirm your conclusions.*

37. $f(x) = x^2 - 10$ on $[-2, 3]$ **38.** $f(x) = (x + 1)^{4/3}$ on $[-9, 7]$

39. $f(x) = \cos^2 x$ on $[0, \pi]$

40. $f(x) = x/(x^2 + 3)^2$ on $[-2, 2]$

41. $f(x) = \sin 3x$ on $[-\pi/4, \pi/3]$

42. $f(x) = x^{2/3}$ on $[-8, 8]$ **43.** $f(x) = (2x)^x$ on $[0.1, 1]$

44. $f(x) = xe^{-x/2}$ on $[0, 5]$

45. $f(x) = x^2 + \cos^{-1} x$ on $[-1, 1]$

46. $f(x) = x\sqrt{2 - x^2}$ on $[-\sqrt{2}, \sqrt{2}]$

47. $f(x) = |2x - 2| - |x + 1|$ on $[-2, 2]$

48. $f(x) = |2x - x^2|$ on $[-2, 3]$

49. $f(x) = \frac{4x^3}{3} + 5x^2 - 6x$ on $[-4, 1]$

50. $f(x) = 2x^6 - 15x^4 + 24x^2$ on $[-2, 2]$

51. Trajectory high point A stone is launched vertically upward from a cliff 192 feet above the ground at a speed of 64 ft/s. Its height above the ground t seconds after the launch is given by $s = -16t^2 + 64t + 192$, for $0 \le t \le 6$. When does the stone reach its maximum height?

52. Maximizing revenue A sales analyst determines that the revenue from sales of fruit smoothies is given by $R(x) = -60x^2 + 300x$, where x is the price in dollars charged per item, for $0 \le x \le 5$.

a. Find the critical points of the revenue function.

b. Determine the absolute maximum value of the revenue function and the price that maximizes the revenue.

53. Maximizing profit Suppose a tour guide has a bus that holds a maximum of 100 people. Assume his profit (in dollars) for taking n people on a city tour is $P(n) = n(50 - 0.5n) - 100$. (Although P is defined only for positive integers, treat it as a continuous function.)

a. How many people should the guide take on a tour to maximize the profit?

b. Suppose the bus holds a maximum of 45 people. How many people should be taken on a tour to maximize the profit?

54. Maximizing rectangle perimeters All rectangles with an area of 64 have a perimeter given by $P(x) = 2x + 128/x$, where x is the length of one side of the rectangle. Find the absolute minimum value of the perimeter function. What are the dimensions of the rectangle with minimum perimeter?

Further Explorations

55. Explain why or why not Determine whether the following statements are true and give an explanation or counterexample.

a. The function $f(x) = \sqrt{x}$ has a local maximum on the interval $[0, \infty)$.

b. If a function has an absolute maximum, then the function must be continuous on a closed interval.

c. A function f has the property that $f'(2) = 0$. Therefore, f has a local extreme value at $x = 2$.

d. Absolute extreme values of a function on a closed interval always occur at a critical point or an endpoint of the interval.

56–63. Absolute maxima and minima

a. *Find the critical points of f on the given interval.*

b. *Determine the absolute extreme values of f on the given interval.*

c. *Use a graphing utility to confirm your conclusions.*

56. $f(x) = (x - 2)^{1/2}$; $[2, 6]$ **57.** $f(x) = 2^x \sin x$; $[-2, 6]$

58. $f(x) = x^{1/2}(x^2/5 - 4)$; $[0, 4]$

59. $f(x) = \sec x$; $[-\pi/4, \pi/4]$

60. $f(x) = x^{1/3}(x + 4)$; $[-27, 27]$ **61.** $f(x) = x^3 e^{-x}$; $[-1, 5]$

62. $f(x) = x \ln(x/5)$; $[0.1, 5]$ **63.** $f(x) = x/\sqrt{x - 4}$; $[6, 12]$

64–67. Critical points of functions with unknown parameters *Find the critical points of f. Assume a is a constant.*

64. $f(x) = x/\sqrt{x - a}$ **65.** $f(x) = x\sqrt{x - a}$

66. $f(x) = x^3 - 3ax^2 + 3a^2x - a^3$ **67.** $f(x) = \frac{1}{5}x^5 - a^4x$

68–73. Critical points and extreme values

a. *Find the critical points of the following functions on the given interval.*

b. *Use a graphing utility to determine whether the critical points correspond to local maxima, local minima, or neither.*

c. *Find the absolute maximum and minimum values on the given interval when they exist.*

68. $f(x) = 6x^4 - 16x^3 - 45x^2 + 54x + 23$; $[-5, 5]$

69. $f(\theta) = 2 \sin \theta + \cos \theta$; $[-2\pi, 2\pi]$

70. $f(x) = x^{2/3}(4 - x^2)$; $[-3, 4]$

71. $g(x) = (x - 3)^{5/3}(x + 2)$; $[-4, 4]$

72. $f(t) = 3t/(t^2 + 1)$; $[-2, 2]$

73. $h(x) = (5 - x)/(x^2 + 2x - 3)$; $[-10, 10]$

74–75. Absolute value functions *Graph the following functions, and determine the local and absolute extreme values on the given interval.*

74. $f(x) = |x - 3| + |x + 2|$; $[-4, 4]$

75. $g(x) = |x - 3| - 2|x + 1|$; $[-2, 3]$

Applications

76. Minimum surface area box All boxes with a square base and a volume of 50 ft³ have a surface area given by $S(x) = 2x^2 + 200/x$, where x is the length of the sides of the base. Find the absolute minimum of the surface area function. What are the dimensions of the box with minimum surface area?

77. Every second counts You must get from a point P on the straight shore of a lake to a stranded swimmer who is 50 m from a point Q on the shore that is 50 m from you (see figure). If you can swim at a speed of 2 m/s and run at a speed of 4 m/s, at what point along the shore, x meters from Q, should you stop running and start swimming if you want to reach the swimmer in the minimum time?

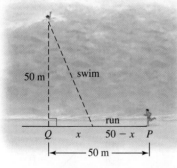

a. Find the function T that gives the travel time as a function of x, where $0 \leq x \leq 50$.

b. Find the critical point of T on $(0, 50)$.

c. Evaluate T at the critical point and the endpoints ($x = 0$ and $x = 50$) to verify that the critical point corresponds to an absolute minimum. What is the minimum travel time?

d. Graph the function T to check your work.

78. Dancing on a parabola Suppose that two people, A and B, walk along the parabola $y = x^2$ in such a way that the line segment L between them is always perpendicular to the line tangent to the parabola at A's position. What are the positions of A and B when L has minimum length?

a. Assume that A's position is (a, a^2), where $a > 0$. Find the slope of the line tangent to the parabola at A and find the slope of the line that is perpendicular to the tangent line at A.

b. Find the equation of the line joining A and B when A is at (a, a^2).

c. Find the position of B on the parabola when A is at (a, a^2).

d. Write the function $F(a)$ that gives the *square* of the distance between A and B as it varies with a. (The square of the distance is minimized at the same point that the distance is minimized; it is easier to work with the square of the distance.)

e. Find the critical point of F on the interval $a > 0$.

f. Evaluate F at the critical point, and verify that it corresponds to an absolute minimum. What are the positions of A and B that minimize the length of L? What is the minimum length?

g. Graph the function F to check your work.

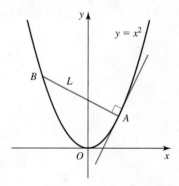

Additional Exercises

79. Values of related functions Suppose f is differentiable on $(-\infty, \infty)$ and assume it has a local extreme value at the point $x = 2$, where $f(2) = 0$. Let $g(x) = xf(x) + 1$ and let $h(x) = xf(x) + x + 1$, for all values of x.

a. Evaluate $g(2)$, $h(2)$, $g'(2)$, and $h'(2)$.

b. Does either g or h have a local extreme value at $x = 2$? Explain.

80. Extreme values of parabolas Consider the function $f(x) = ax^2 + bx + c$, with $a \neq 0$. Explain geometrically why f has exactly one absolute extreme value on $(-\infty, \infty)$. Find the critical point to determine the value of x at which f has an extreme value.

81. Even and odd functions

a. Suppose a nonconstant even function f has a local minimum at c. Does f have a local maximum or minimum at $-c$? Explain. (An even function satisfies $f(-x) = f(x)$.)

b. Suppose a nonconstant odd function f has a local minimum at c. Does f have a local maximum or minimum at $-c$? Explain. (An odd function satisfies $f(-x) = -f(x)$.)

82. A family of double-humped functions Consider the functions $f(x) = x/(x^2 + 1)^n$, where n is a positive integer.

a. Show that these functions are odd for all positive integers n.

b. Show that the critical points of these functions are $x = \pm\dfrac{1}{\sqrt{2n-1}}$, for all positive integers n. (Start with the special cases $n = 1$ and $n = 2$.)

c. Show that as n increases the absolute maximum values of these functions decrease.

d. Use a graphing utility to verify your conclusions.

83. Proof of the Local Extreme Point Theorem Prove Theorem 4.2 for a local maximum: If f has a local maximum at the point c and $f'(c)$ exists, then $f'(c) = 0$. Use the following steps.

a. Suppose f has a local maximum at c. What is the sign of $f(x) - f(c)$ if x is near c and $x > c$? What is the sign of $f(x) - f(c)$ if x is near c and $x < c$?

b. If $f'(c)$ exists, then it is defined by $\displaystyle\lim_{x \to c} \frac{f(x) - f(c)}{x - c}$. Examine this limit as $x \to c^+$ and conclude that $f'(c) \leq 0$.

c. Examine the limit in part (b) as $x \to c^-$ and conclude that $f'(c) \geq 0$.

d. Combine parts (b) and (c) to conclude that $f'(c) = 0$.

QUICK CHECK ANSWERS

1. The continuous function $f(x) = x$ does not have an absolute minimum on the open interval $(0, 1)$. The function $f(x) = -x$ on $\left[0, \frac{1}{2}\right)$ and $f(x) = 0$ on $\left[\frac{1}{2}, 1\right]$ does not have an absolute minimum on $[0, 1]$. **2.** The critical point is $x = 0$. Although $f'(0) = 0$, the function has neither a local maximum nor minimum at $x = 0$. ◄

4.2 What Derivatives Tell Us

In the previous section, we saw that the derivative is a tool for finding critical points, which are related to local maxima and minima. As we show in this section, derivatives (first *and* second derivatives) tell us much more about the behavior of functions.

Increasing and Decreasing Functions

We have used the terms *increasing* and *decreasing* informally in earlier sections to describe a function or its graph. For example, the graph in Figure 4.13a rises as x increases, so the corresponding function is increasing. In Figure 4.13b, the graph falls as x increases, so the corresponding function is decreasing. The following *definition* makes these ideas precise.

> A function is called **monotonic** if it is either increasing or decreasing. Some books make a further distinction by defining **nondecreasing** ($f(x_2) \geq f(x_1)$ whenever $x_2 > x_1$) and **nonincreasing** ($f(x_2) \leq f(x_1)$ whenever $x_2 > x_1$).

> **DEFINITION Increasing and Decreasing Functions**
>
> Suppose a function f is defined on an interval I. We say that f is **increasing** on I if $f(x_2) > f(x_1)$ whenever x_1 and x_2 are in I and $x_2 > x_1$. We say that f is **decreasing** on I if $f(x_2) < f(x_1)$ whenever x_1 and x_2 are in I and $x_2 > x_1$.

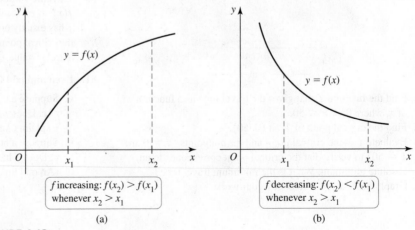

f increasing: $f(x_2) > f(x_1)$ whenever $x_2 > x_1$

(a)

f decreasing: $f(x_2) < f(x_1)$ whenever $x_2 > x_1$

(b)

FIGURE 4.13

Intervals of Increase and Decrease The graph of a function f gives us an idea of the intervals on which f is increasing and decreasing. But how do we determine those intervals precisely? This question is answered by making a connection to the derivative.

Recall that the derivative of a function gives the slopes of tangent lines. If the derivative is positive on an interval, the tangent lines on that interval have positive slopes, and the function is increasing on the interval (Figure 4.14a). Said differently, positive derivatives on an interval imply positive rates of change on the interval, which, in turn, indicate an increase in function values.

Similarly, if the derivative is negative on an interval, the tangent lines on that interval have negative slopes, and the function is decreasing on that interval (Figure 4.14b). These observations are proved in Section 4.6 using a result called the Mean Value Theorem.

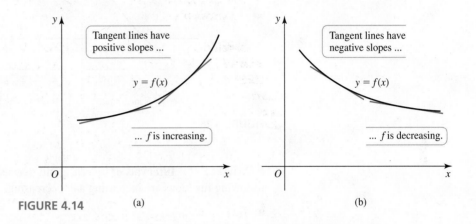

FIGURE 4.14   (a)   (b)

> The converse of Theorem 4.3 may not be true. According to the definition, $f(x) = x^3$ is increasing on $(-\infty, \infty)$, but it is not true that $f'(x) > 0$ on $(-\infty, \infty)$ (because $f'(0) = 0$).

THEOREM 4.3 Test for Intervals of Increase and Decrease
Suppose f is continuous on an interval I and differentiable at all interior points of I. If $f'(x) > 0$ at all interior points of I, then f is increasing on I. If $f'(x) < 0$ at all interior points of I, then f is decreasing on I.

QUICK CHECK 1 Explain why a positive derivative on an interval implies that the function is increasing on the interval. ◀

EXAMPLE 1 Sketching a function Sketch a function f continuous on its domain $(-\infty, \infty)$ satisfying the following conditions.

1. $f' > 0$ on $(-\infty, 0)$, $(4, 6)$, and $(6, \infty)$.
2. $f' < 0$ on $(0, 4)$.
3. $f'(0)$ is undefined.
4. $f'(4) = f'(6) = 0$.

SOLUTION By condition (1), f is increasing on the intervals $(-\infty, 0)$, $(4, 6)$, and $(6, \infty)$. By condition (2), f is decreasing on $(0, 4)$. Condition (3) implies f has a cusp or corner at $x = 0$, and by condition (4), the graph has a horizontal tangent line at $x = 4$ and $x = 6$. It is useful to summarize these results (Figure 4.15) before sketching a graph.

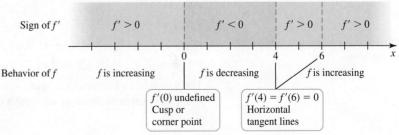

FIGURE 4.15

One possible graph satisfying these conditions is shown in Figure 4.16. Notice that the graph has a cusp at $x = 0$. Furthermore, although $f'(4) = f'(6) = 0$, f has a local minimum at $x = 4$, but has no local extremum at $x = 6$.

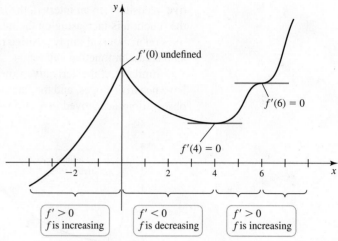

FIGURE 4.16

Related Exercises 11–16 ◄

EXAMPLE 2   Intervals of increase and decrease Find the intervals on which the following functions are increasing and decreasing.

a. $f(x) = xe^{-x}$

b. $f(x) = 2x^3 + 3x^2 + 1$

SOLUTION

a. By the Product Rule, $f'(x) = e^{-x} + x(-e^{-x}) = (1 - x)e^{-x}$. Solving $f'(x) = 0$ and noting that $e^{-x} \neq 0$ for all x, the sole critical point is $x = 1$. Therefore, if f' changes sign, then it does so at $x = 1$ and nowhere else. By evaluating f' at selected points in $(-\infty, 1)$ and $(1, \infty)$, we can determine the sign of f' on the entire interval:

• At $x = 0$, $f'(0) = 1 > 0$. So $f' > 0$ on $(-\infty, 1)$, which means that f is increasing on $(-\infty, 1)$.

• At $x = 2$, $f'(2) = -e^{-2} < 0$. So $f' < 0$ on $(1, \infty)$, which means that f is decreasing on $(1, \infty)$.

Note also that the graph has a horizontal tangent line at $x = 1$. We verify these conclusions by plotting f and f' (Figure 4.17).

b. In this case, $f'(x) = 6x^2 + 6x = 6x(x + 1)$. To find the intervals of increase, we first solve $6x(x + 1) = 0$ and determine that the critical points are $x = 0$ and $x = -1$. If f' changes sign, then it does so at these points and nowhere else; that is, f' has the same sign throughout each of the intervals $(-\infty, -1)$, $(-1, 0)$, and $(0, \infty)$. Evaluating f' at selected points of each interval determines the sign of f' on that interval.

• At $x = -2$, $f'(-2) = 12 > 0$, so $f' > 0$ and f is increasing on $(-\infty, -1)$.

• At $x = -\frac{1}{2}$, $f'\left(-\frac{1}{2}\right) = -\frac{3}{2} < 0$, so $f' < 0$ and f is decreasing on $(-1, 0)$.

• At $x = 1$, $f'(1) = 12 > 0$, so $f' > 0$ and f is increasing on $(0, \infty)$.

The graph has a horizontal tangent line at $x = -1$ and $x = 0$. Figure 4.18 shows the graph of f superimposed on the graph of f', confirming our conclusions.

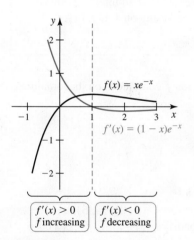

FIGURE 4.17

➤ See Appendix A for solving inequalities using test values.

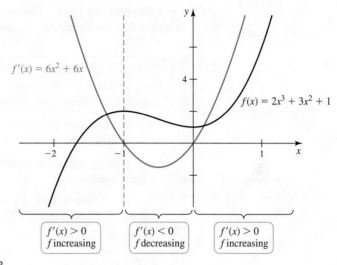

$f'(x) = 6x^2 + 6x$

$f(x) = 2x^3 + 3x^2 + 1$

| $f'(x) > 0$ f increasing | $f'(x) < 0$ f decreasing | $f'(x) > 0$ f increasing |

FIGURE 4.18

Related Exercises 17–38 ◄

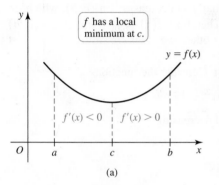

f has a local minimum at c.

$y = f(x)$

$f'(x) < 0$ $f'(x) > 0$

(a)

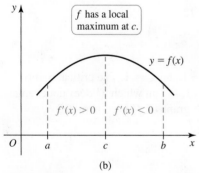

f has a local maximum at c.

$y = f(x)$

$f'(x) > 0$ $f'(x) < 0$

(b)

FIGURE 4.19

Identifying Local Maxima and Minima

Using what we know about increasing and decreasing functions, we can now identify local extrema. Suppose $x = c$ is a critical point of f, where $f'(c) = 0$. Suppose also that f' changes sign at c with $f'(x) < 0$ on an interval (a, c) to the left of c and $f'(x) > 0$ on an interval (c, b) to the right of c. In this case f' is decreasing to the left of c and increasing to the right of c, which means that f has a local minimum at c, as shown in Figure 4.19a.

Similarly, suppose f' changes sign at c with $f'(x) > 0$ on an interval (a, c) to the left of c and $f'(x) < 0$ on an interval (c, b) to the right of c. Then f is increasing to the left of c and decreasing to the right of c, so f has a local maximum at c, as shown in Figure 4.19b.

Figure 4.20 shows typical features of a function on an interval $[a, b]$. At local maxima or minima (c_2, c_3, and c_4), f' changes sign. Although c_1 and c_5 are critical points, f' does not change sign at these points, so there is no local maximum or minimum at these points. As emphasized earlier, *critical points do not always correspond to local extreme values.*

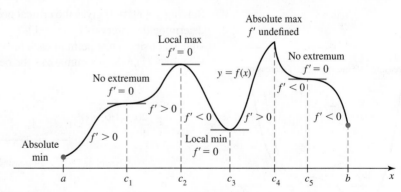

Absolute max
f' undefined

Local max
$f' = 0$

No extremum
$f' = 0$

$y = f(x)$

No extremum
$f' = 0$

$f' > 0$

$f' < 0$

$f' > 0$ $f' < 0$ $f' > 0$ $f' < 0$

Local min
$f' = 0$

Absolute
min

a c_1 c_2 c_3 c_4 c_5 b x

FIGURE 4.20

QUICK CHECK 2 Sketch a function f that is differentiable on $(-\infty, \infty)$ with the following properties: (i) $x = 0$ and $x = 2$ are critical points; (ii) f is increasing on $(-\infty, 2)$; (iii) f is decreasing on $(2, \infty)$. ◄

First Derivative Test   The observations used to interpret Figure 4.20 are summarized in a powerful test for identifying local maxima and minima.

> **THEOREM 4.4   First Derivative Test**
> Suppose that f is continuous on an interval that contains a critical point c and assume f is differentiable on an interval containing c, except perhaps at c itself.
>
> - If f' changes sign from positive to negative as x increases through c, then f has a **local maximum** at c.
> - If f' changes sign from negative to positive as x increases through c, then f has a **local minimum** at c.
> - If f' is positive on both sides near c or is negative on both sides near c, then f has no local extreme value at c.

Proof: Suppose that $f'(x) > 0$ on an interval (a, c), which means that f is increasing on (a, c), which, in turn, implies that $f(x) < f(c)$ for all x in (a, c). Similarly, suppose that $f'(x) < 0$ on an interval (c, b), which means that f is decreasing on (c, b), which, in turn, implies that $f(x) < f(c)$ for all x in (c, b). Therefore, $f(x) \leq f(c)$ for all x in (a, b) and f has a local maximum at c. The proofs of the other two cases are similar.   ◄

EXAMPLE 3   Using the First Derivative Test   Consider the function

$$f(x) = 3x^4 - 4x^3 - 6x^2 + 12x + 1.$$

a. Find the intervals on which f is increasing and decreasing.

b. Identify the local extrema of f.

SOLUTION

a. Differentiating f, we find that

$$
\begin{aligned}
f'(x) &= 12x^3 - 12x^2 - 12x + 12 \\
&= 12(x^3 - x^2 - x + 1) \\
&= 12(x + 1)(x - 1)^2.
\end{aligned}
$$

Solving $f'(x) = 0$ gives the critical points $x = -1$ and $x = 1$. The critical points determine the intervals $(-\infty, -1)$, $(-1, 1)$, and $(1, \infty)$ on which f' does not change sign. Choosing a test point in each interval, a sign graph of f' is constructed (Figure 4.21), which summarizes the behavior of f.

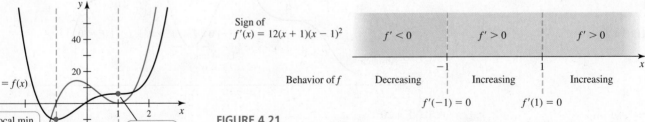

FIGURE 4.21

b. Note that f is a polynomial, so it is continuous on $(-\infty, \infty)$. Because f' changes sign from negative to positive as x passes through the critical point $x = -1$, it follows by the First Derivative Test that f has a local minimum value of $f(-1) = -10$ at $x = -1$. Notice that f' is positive on both sides near $x = 1$, so f does not have a local extreme value at $x = 1$ (Figure 4.22).

Related Exercises 39–48 ◄

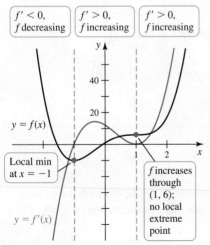

FIGURE 4.22

EXAMPLE 4 **Extreme points** Find the local extrema of the function
$g(x) = x^{2/3}(2 - x)$.

SOLUTION In Example 4b of Section 4.1, we found that

$$g'(x) = \frac{4}{3}x^{-1/3} - \frac{5}{3}x^{2/3} = \frac{4 - 5x}{3x^{1/3}}$$

and that the critical points of g are $x = 0$ and $x = \frac{4}{5}$. These two critical points are *candidates* for local extrema, and Theorem 4.4 is used to classify each as a local maximum, local minimum, or neither.

On the interval $(-\infty, 0)$, the numerator of g' is positive and the denominator is negative (Figure 4.23). Therefore, $g'(x) < 0$ on $(-\infty, 0)$. On the interval $(0, \frac{4}{5})$, the numerator of g' is positive, as is the denominator. Therefore, $g'(x) > 0$ on $(0, \frac{4}{5})$. We see that as x passes through 0, g' changes sign from negative to positive, which means g has a local minimum at 0. A similar argument shows that g' changes sign from positive to negative as x passes through $\frac{4}{5}$, so g has a local maximum at $\frac{4}{5}$. These observations are confirmed by the graphs of g and g' (Figure 4.24).

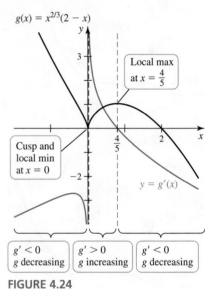

$g(x) = x^{2/3}(2 - x)$

Local max at $x = \frac{4}{5}$

Cusp and local min at $x = 0$

$y = g'(x)$

$g' < 0$ g decreasing

$g' > 0$ g increasing

$g' < 0$ g decreasing

FIGURE 4.24

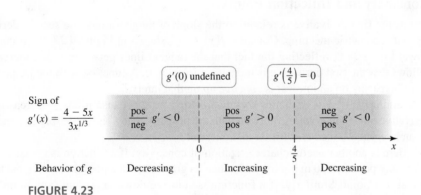

$g'(0)$ undefined

$g'\left(\frac{4}{5}\right) = 0$

Sign of
$g'(x) = \frac{4 - 5x}{3x^{1/3}}$

$\dfrac{\text{pos}}{\text{neg}}$ $g' < 0$

$\dfrac{\text{pos}}{\text{pos}}$ $g' > 0$

$\dfrac{\text{neg}}{\text{pos}}$ $g' < 0$

Behavior of g Decreasing   Increasing   Decreasing

FIGURE 4.23

Related Exercises 39–48◄

QUICK CHECK 3 Explain how the First Derivative Test determines whether $f(x) = x^2$ has a local maximum or local minimum at $x = 0$. ◄

Absolute Extreme Values on Any Interval Theorem 4.1 guarantees the existence of absolute extreme values only on closed intervals. What can be said about absolute extrema on intervals that are not closed? The following theorem provides a valuable test.

THEOREM 4.5   One Local Extremum Implies Absolute Extremum
Suppose f is continuous on an interval I that contains exactly one local extremum at c.

• If a local maximum occurs at c, then $f(c)$ is the absolute maximum of f on I.

• If a local minimum occurs at c, then $f(c)$ is the absolute minimum of f on I.

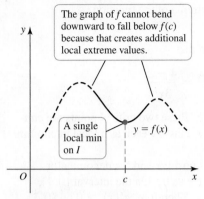

The graph of f cannot bend downward to fall below $f(c)$ because that creates additional local extreme values.

A single local min on I

$y = f(x)$

FIGURE 4.25

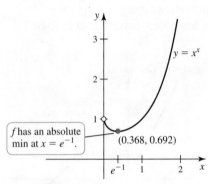

$y = x^x$

f has an absolute min at $x = e^{-1}$.

$(0.368, 0.692)$

FIGURE 4.26

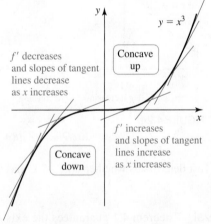

f' decreases and slopes of tangent lines decrease as x increases

Concave up

$y = x^3$

f' increases and slopes of tangent lines increase as x increases

Concave down

FIGURE 4.27

The proof of Theorem 4.5 is beyond the scope of this text, although Figure 4.25 illustrates why the theorem is plausible. Assume f has exactly one local minimum on I at c. Notice that there is no other point on the graph at which f has a value less than $f(c)$. If such a point did exist, the graph would have to bend downward to drop below $f(c)$. Because f is continuous, this cannot happen as it implies additional local extreme values on I. A similar argument applies to a solitary local maximum.

EXAMPLE 5 **Finding an absolute extremum** Verify that $f(x) = x^x$ has an absolute extreme value on its domain.

SOLUTION First note that f is continuous on its domain $(0, \infty)$. Because $f(x) = x^x = e^{x \ln x}$, it follows that

$$f'(x) = e^{x \ln x}(1 + \ln x) = x^x(1 + \ln x).$$

Solving $f'(x) = 0$ gives a single critical point $x = e^{-1}$; there is no point in the domain at which $f'(x)$ does not exist. The critical point splits the domain of f into the intervals $(0, e^{-1})$ and (e^{-1}, ∞). Evaluating the sign of f' on each interval gives $f'(x) < 0$ on $(0, e^{-1})$ and $f'(x) > 0$ on (e^{-1}, ∞); therefore, by Theorem 4.4, a local minimum occurs at $x = e^{-1}$. Because it is the only local extremum on $(0, \infty)$, it follows from Theorem 4.5 that the absolute minimum of f occurs at $x = e^{-1}$ (Figure 4.26). Its value is $f(e^{-1}) \approx 0.692$.

Related Exercises 49–52 ◀

Concavity and Inflection Points

Just as the first derivative is related to the slope of tangent lines, the second derivative also has geometric meaning. Consider $f(x) = x^3$, shown in Figure 4.27. Its graph bends upward for $x > 0$, reflecting the fact that the tangent lines get steeper as x increases. It follows that the first derivative is increasing for $x > 0$. A function with the property that f' is increasing on an interval is *concave up* on that interval.

Similarly, $f(x) = x^3$ bends downward for $x < 0$ because it has a decreasing first derivative on that interval. A function with the property that f' is decreasing as x increases on an interval is *concave down* on that interval.

Here is another useful characterization of concavity. If a function is concave up at a point (any point $x > 0$ in Figure 4.27), then its graph near that point lies *above* the tangent line at that point. Similarly, if a function is concave down at a point (any point $x < 0$ in Figure 4.27), then its graph near that point lies *below* the tangent line at that point (Exercise 104).

Finally, imagine a function that changes concavity (from up to down, or vice versa) at a point c. For example, $f(x) = x^3$ in Figure 4.27 changes from concave down to concave up as x passes through $x = 0$. A point on the graph of f at which f changes concavity is called an *inflection point*.

DEFINITION **Concavity and Inflection Point**

Let f be differentiable on an open interval I. If f' is increasing on I, then f is **concave up** on I. If f' is decreasing on I, then f is **concave down** on I.

If f is continuous at c and f changes concavity at c (from up to down, or vice versa), then f has an **inflection point** at c.

Applying Theorem 4.3 to f' leads to a test for concavity in terms of the second derivative. Specifically, if $f'' > 0$ on an interval I, then f' is increasing on I and f is concave up on I. Similarly, if $f'' < 0$ on I, then f is concave down on I. Additionally, if the values of f'' change sign at a point c (from positive to negative, or vice versa), then the concavity of f changes at c and f has an inflection point at c (Figure 4.28a). We now have a useful interpretation of the second derivative: It measures *concavity*.

> **THEOREM 4.6   Test for Concavity**
> Suppose that f'' exists on an open interval I.
>
> • If $f'' > 0$ on I, then f is concave up on I.
>
> • If $f'' < 0$ on I, then f is concave down on I.
>
> • If c is a point of I at which f'' changes sign at c, then f has an inflection point at c.

There are a few important but subtle points here. The fact that $f''(c) = 0$ does not necessarily imply that f has an inflection point at c. A good example is $f(x) = x^4$. Although $f''(0) = 0$, the concavity does not change at $x = 0$ (a similar function is shown in Figure 4.28b).

Typically, if f has an inflection point at c, then $f''(c) = 0$, reflecting the smooth change in concavity. However, an inflection point may also occur at a point where f'' does not exist. For example, the function $f(x) = x^{1/3}$ has a vertical tangent line and an inflection point at $x = 0$ (a similar function is shown in Figure 4.28c).

Finally, note that the function shown in Figure 4.28d, with behavior similar to that of $f(x) = x^{2/3}$, does not have an inflection point at c despite the fact that $f''(c)$ does not exist. In summary, if $f''(c) = 0$ or $f''(c)$ does not exist, then $(c, f(c))$ is a candidate for an inflection point. To be certain an inflection point occurs at c, we must show that the concavity of f changes at c.

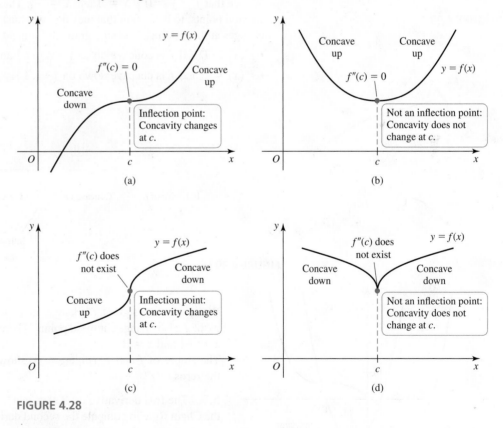

FIGURE 4.28

QUICK CHECK 4 Verify that the function $f(x) = x^4$ is concave up for $x > 0$ and for $x < 0$. Is $x = 0$ an inflection point? Explain. ◄

EXAMPLE 6   Interpreting concavity Sketch a function satisfying each set of conditions on some interval.

a. $f'(t) > 0$ and $f''(t) > 0$ **b.** $g'(t) > 0$ and $g''(t) < 0$

c. Would you rather have f or g as a function representing the market value of a house that you own?

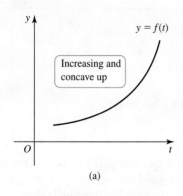

(a)

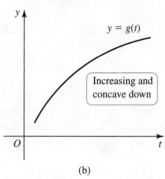

(b)

FIGURE 4.29

SOLUTION

a. Figure 4.29a shows the graph of a function that is increasing ($f'(t) > 0$) and concave up ($f''(t) > 0$).

b. Figure 4.29b shows the graph of a function that is increasing ($g'(t) > 0$) and concave down ($g''(t) < 0$).

c. Because f increases at an *increasing* rate and g increases at a *decreasing* rate, f is a preferable function for the value of your house.

Related Exercises 53–56◄

EXAMPLE 7   Detecting concavity Identify the intervals on which the following functions are concave up or concave down. Then locate the inflection points.

a. $f(x) = 3x^4 - 4x^3 - 6x^2 + 12x + 1$ **b.** $f(x) = \sin^{-1} x$ on $(-1, 1)$

SOLUTION

a. This function was considered in Example 3, where we found that

$$f'(x) = 12(x + 1)(x - 1)^2.$$

It follows that

$$f''(x) = 12(x - 1)(3x + 1).$$

We see that $f''(x) = 0$ at $x = 1$ and $x = -\frac{1}{3}$. These points are *candidates* for inflection points; to be certain that they are, we must determine whether the concavity changes at these points. The sign graph in Figure 4.30 shows the following:

• $f''(x) > 0$ and f is concave up on $\left(-\infty, -\frac{1}{3}\right)$ and $(1, \infty)$.

• $f''(x) < 0$ and f is concave down on $\left(-\frac{1}{3}, 1\right)$.

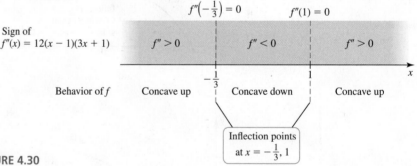

FIGURE 4.30

We see that the sign of f'' changes at $x = -\frac{1}{3}$ and at $x = 1$, so the concavity of f also changes at these points. Therefore, inflection points occur at $x = -\frac{1}{3}$ and $x = 1$.

The graphs of f and f'' (Figure 4.31) show that the concavity of f changes at the zeros of f''.

b.   The first derivative of $f(x) = \sin^{-1} x$ is $f'(x) = 1/\sqrt{1 - x^2}$. We use the Chain Rule to compute the second derivative:

$$f''(x) = -\frac{1}{2}(1 - x^2)^{-3/2} \cdot (-2x) = \frac{x}{(1 - x^2)^{3/2}}.$$

The only zero of f'' is $x = 0$, and because its denominator is positive on $(-1, 1)$, f'' changes sign at $x = 0$ from negative to positive. Therefore, f is concave down on $(-1, 0)$ and concave up on $(0, 1)$, with an inflection point at $x = 0$ (Figure 4.32).

FIGURE 4.31

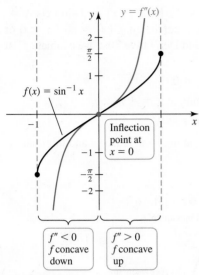

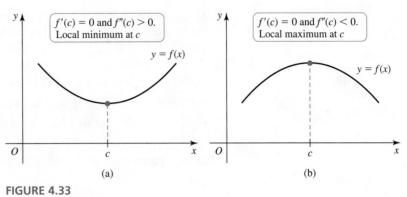

FIGURE 4.33

Related Exercises 57–70 ◄

Second Derivative Test It is now a short step to a test that uses the second derivative to identify local maxima and minima (Figure 4.33).

> In the inconclusive case of Theorem 4.7 in which $f''(c) = 0$, it is usually best to use the First Derivative Test.

THEOREM 4.7   Second Derivative Test for Local Extrema
Suppose that f'' is continuous on an open interval containing c with $f'(c) = 0$.

• If $f''(c) > 0$, then f has a local minimum at c (Figure 4.33a).

• If $f''(c) < 0$, then f has a local maximum at c (Figure 4.33b).

• If $f''(c) = 0$, then the test is inconclusive; f may have a local maximum, local minimum, or neither at c.

Proof: Assume $f''(c) > 0$ (the proofs of the other two parts are similar). Because f'' is continuous on an interval containing c, it follows that $f'' > 0$ on some open interval I containing c, and f' is increasing on I. Because $f'(c) = 0$, it follows that f' changes sign at c from negative to positive, which, by the First Derivative Test, implies that f has a local minimum at c. The proofs of the other two cases are similar. ◄

QUICK CHECK 5 Make a sketch of a function with $f'(x) > 0$ and $f''(x) > 0$ on an interval. Make a sketch of a function with $f'(x) < 0$ and $f''(x) < 0$ on an interval. ◄

EXAMPLE 8   The Second Derivative Test Use the Second Derivative Test to locate the local extrema of the following functions.

a. $f(x) = 3x^4 - 4x^3 - 6x^2 + 12x + 1$ on $[-2, 2]$ **b.** $f(x) = \sin^2 x$

SOLUTION

a. This function was considered in Examples 3 and 7, where we found that

$$f'(x) = 12(x + 1)(x - 1)^2 \quad \text{and} \quad f''(x) = 12(x - 1)(3x + 1).$$

Therefore, the critical points of f are $x = -1$ and $x = 1$. Evaluating f'' at the critical points, we find that $f''(-1) = 48 > 0$. By the Second Derivative Test, f has a local minimum at $x = -1$. At the other critical point, $f''(1) = 0$, so the test is inconclusive. You can check that the first derivative does not change sign at $x = 1$, which means f does not have a local maximum or minimum at $x = 1$ (Figure 4.34).

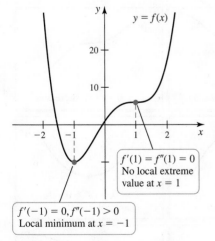

FIGURE 4.34

b. Using the Chain Rule and a trigonometric identity, we have $f'(x) = 2 \sin x \cos x = \sin 2x$ and $f''(x) = 2 \cos 2x$. The critical points occur when $f'(x) = \sin 2x = 0$ or when $x = 0, \pm\pi/2, \pm\pi, \dots$. To apply the Second Derivative Test, we evaluate f'' at the critical points:

- $f''(0) = 2 > 0$, so f has a local minimum at $x = 0$.
- $f''(\pm\pi/2) = -2 < 0$, so f has a local maximum at $x = \pm\pi/2$.
- $f''(\pm\pi) = 2 > 0$, so f has a local minimum at $x = \pm\pi$.

This pattern continues, and we see that f has alternating local maxima and minima, evenly spaced every $\pi/2$ units (Figure 4.35).

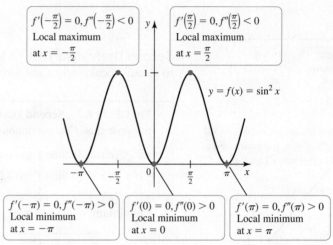

FIGURE 4.35

Related Exercises 71–82◄

Recap of Derivative Properties

This section has demonstrated that the first and second derivatives of a function provide valuable information about its graph. The relationships among a function's derivatives and its extreme points and concavity are summarized in Figure 4.36.

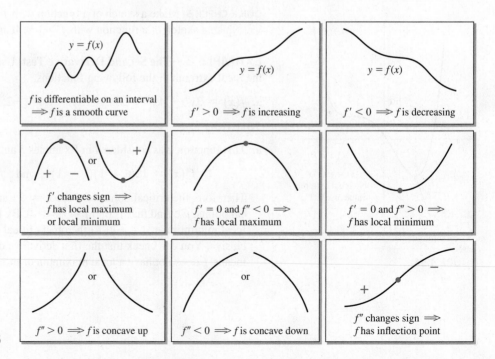

FIGURE 4.36

SECTION 4.2 EXERCISES

Review Questions

1. Explain how the first derivative of a function determines where the function is increasing and decreasing.

2. Explain how to apply the First Derivative Test.

3. Sketch the graph of a function that has neither a local maximum nor a local minimum at a point where $f'(x) = 0$.

4. Explain how to apply the Second Derivative Test.

5. Suppose f'' exists and is positive on an interval I. Describe the relationship between the graph of f and its tangent lines on the interval I.

6. Sketch a function that changes from concave up to concave down as x increases. Describe how the second derivative of this function changes.

7. What is an inflection point?

8. Give a function that does not have an inflection point at a point where $f''(x) = 0$.

9. Is it possible for a function to satisfy $f(x) > 0, f'(x) > 0$, and $f''(x) < 0$ on an interval? Explain.

10. Suppose f is continuous on an interval containing a critical point c and $f''(c) = 0$. How do you determine whether f has a local extreme value at $x = c$?

Basic Skills

11–14. Sketches from properties *Sketch a function that is continuous on $(-\infty, \infty)$ and has the following properties. Use a number line to summarize information about the function.*

11. $f'(x) < 0$ on $(-\infty, 2); f'(x) > 0$ on $(2, 5); f'(x) < 0$ on $(5, \infty)$

12. $f'(-1)$ is undefined; $f'(x) > 0$ on $(-\infty, -1); f'(x) < 0$ on $(-1, \infty)$

13. $f(0) = f(4) = f'(0) = f'(2) = f'(4) = 0; f(x) \geq 0$ on $(-\infty, \infty)$

14. $f'(-2) = f'(2) = f'(6) = 0; f'(x) \geq 0$ on $(-\infty, \infty)$

15–16. Functions from derivatives *The following figures give the graph of the derivative of a continuous function f that passes through the origin. Sketch a possible graph of f on the same set of axes.*

15.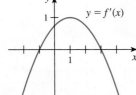

16.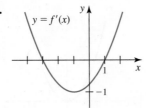

 17–26. Increasing and decreasing functions *Find the intervals on which f is increasing and decreasing. Superimpose the graphs of f and f' to verify your work.*

17. $f(x) = 4 - x^2$

18. $f(x) = x^2 - 16$

19. $f(x) = (x - 1)^2$

20. $f(x) = x^3 + 4x$

21. $f(x) = 12 + x - x^2$

22. $f(x) = x^4 - 4x^3 + 4x^2$

23. $f(x) = -\dfrac{x^4}{4} + x^3 - x^2$

24. $f(x) = 2x^5 - \dfrac{15x^4}{4} + \dfrac{5x^3}{3}$

25. $f(x) = x^2 \ln x^2 + 1$

26. $f(x) = \dfrac{e^x}{e^{2x} + 1}$

27–38. Increasing and decreasing functions *Find the intervals on which f is increasing and decreasing.*

27. $f(x) = 3 \cos 3x$ on $[-\pi, \pi]$

28. $f(x) = \cos^2 x$ on $[-\pi, \pi]$

29. $f(x) = x^{4/3}$

30. $f(x) = x^2 \sqrt{9 - x^2}$ on $(-3, 3)$

31. $f(x) = \tan^{-1} x$

32. $f(x) = \ln |x|$

33. $f(x) = -12x^5 + 75x^4 - 80x^3$

34. $f(x) = x^2 - 2 \ln x$

35. $f(x) = -2x^4 + x^2 + 10$

36. $f(x) = \dfrac{x^4}{4} - \dfrac{8x^3}{3} + \dfrac{15x^2}{2} + 8$

37. $f(x) = xe^{-x^2/2}$

38. $f(x) = \tan^{-1}\left(\dfrac{x}{x^2 + 2}\right)$

39–48. First Derivative Test

a. Locate the critical points of f.

b. Use the First Derivative Test to locate the local maximum and minimum values.

c. Identify the absolute maximum and minimum values of the function on the given interval (when they exist).

39. $f(x) = x^2 + 3; \ [-3, 2]$

40. $f(x) = -x^2 - x + 2; \ [-4, 4]$

41. $f(x) = x\sqrt{9 - x^2}; \ [-3, 3]$

42. $f(x) = 2x^3 + 3x^2 - 12x + 1; \ [-2, 4]$

43. $f(x) = -x^3 + 9x; \ [-4, 3]$

44. $f(x) = 2x^5 - 5x^4 - 10x^3 + 4; \ [-2, 4]$

45. $f(x) = x^{2/3}(x - 5); \ [-5, 5]$

46. $f(x) = \dfrac{x^2}{x^2 - 1}; \ [-4, 4]$

47. $f(x) = \sqrt{x} \ln x; \ (0, \infty)$

48. $f(x) = \tan^{-1} x - x^3; \ [-1, 1]$

49–52. Absolute extreme values *Verify that the following functions satisfy the conditions of Theorem 4.5 on their domains. Then find the location and value of the absolute extremum guaranteed by the theorem.*

49. $f(x) = xe^{-x}$

50. $f(x) = 4x + 1/\sqrt{x}$

51. $A(r) = 24/r + 2\pi r^2, r > 0$

52. $f(x) = x\sqrt{3 - x}$

53–56. Sketching curves *Sketch a graph of a function f that is continuous on $(-\infty, \infty)$ and has the following properties.*

53. $f'(x) > 0, f''(x) > 0$

54. $f'(x) < 0$ and $f''(x) > 0$ on $(-\infty, 0); f'(x) > 0$ and $f''(x) > 0$ on $(0, \infty)$

55. $f'(x) < 0$ and $f''(x) < 0$ on $(-\infty, 0); f'(x) < 0$ and $f''(x) > 0$ on $(0, \infty)$

56. $f'(x) < 0$ and $f''(x) > 0$ on $(-\infty, 0); f'(x) < 0$ and $f''(x) < 0$ on $(0, \infty)$

57–70. Concavity *Determine the intervals on which the following functions are concave up or concave down. Identify any inflection points.*

57. $f(x) = x^4 - 2x^3 + 1$

58. $f(x) = -x^4 - 2x^3 + 12x^2$

59. $f(x) = 5x^4 - 20x^3 + 10$

60. $f(x) = \dfrac{1}{1 + x^2}$

61. $f(x) = e^x(x - 3)$

62. $f(x) = 2x^2 \ln x - 5x^2$

63. $g(t) = \ln(3t^2 + 1)$

64. $g(x) = \sqrt[3]{x - 4}$

65. $f(x) = e^{-x^2/2}$

66. $f(x) = \tan^{-1} x$

67. $f(x) = \sqrt{x} \ln x$

68. $h(t) = 2 + \cos 2t$, for $-\pi \le t \le \pi$

69. $g(t) = 3t^5 - 30t^4 + 80t^3 + 100$

70. $f(x) = 2x^4 + 8x^3 + 12x^2 - x - 2$

71–82. Second Derivative Test *Locate the critical points of the following functions. Then use the Second Derivative Test to determine (if possible) whether they correspond to local maxima or local minima.*

71. $f(x) = x^3 - 3x^2$

72. $f(x) = 6x^2 - x^3$

73. $f(x) = 4 - x^2$

74. $g(x) = x^3 - 6$

75. $f(x) = e^x(x - 7)$

76. $f(x) = e^x(x^2 - 7x - 12)$

77. $f(x) = 2x^3 - 3x^2 + 12$

78. $p(x) = x^4 e^{-x}$

79. $f(x) = x^2 e^{-x}$

80. $g(x) = \dfrac{x^4}{2 - 12x^2}$

81. $f(x) = 2x^2 \ln x - 11x^2$

82. $f(x) = \sqrt{x}\left(\dfrac{12}{7}x^3 - 4x^2\right)$

Further Explorations

83. Explain why or why not Determine whether the following statements are true and give an explanation or counterexample.

a. If $f'(x) > 0$ and $f''(x) < 0$ on an interval, then f is increasing at a decreasing rate on the interval.

b. If $f'(c) > 0$ and $f''(c) = 0$, then f has a local maximum at c.

c. Two functions that differ by an additive constant both increase and decrease on the same intervals.

d. If f and g increase on an interval, then the product fg also increases on that interval.

e. There exists a function f that is continuous on $(-\infty, \infty)$ with exactly three critical points, all of which correspond to local maxima.

84–85. Functions from derivatives *Consider the following graphs of f' and f''. On the same set of axes, sketch the graph of a possible function f. The graphs of f are not unique.*

84.

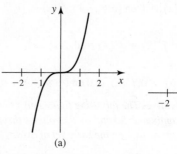

85.

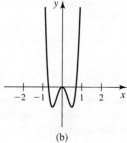

86. Is it possible? Determine whether the following properties can be satisfied by a function that is continuous on $(-\infty, \infty)$. If such a function is possible, provide an example or a sketch of the function. If such a function is not possible, explain why.

a. A function f is concave down and positive everywhere.

b. A function f is increasing and concave down everywhere.

c. A function f has exactly two local extrema and three inflection points.

d. A function f has exactly four zeros and two local extrema.

87. Matching derivatives and functions The following figures show the graphs of three functions (graphs a–c). Match each function with its first derivative (graphs d–f) *and* its second derivative (graphs g–i).

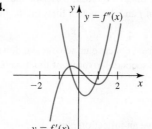

(a)

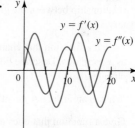

(b)

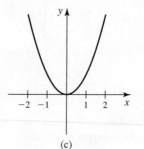

(c)

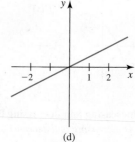

(d)

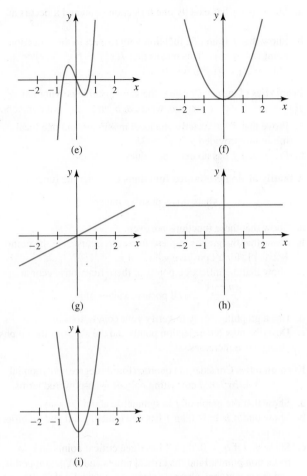

(e)   (f)

(g)   (h)

(i)

88. Graphical analysis The figure shows the graphs of f, f', and f''. Which curve is which?

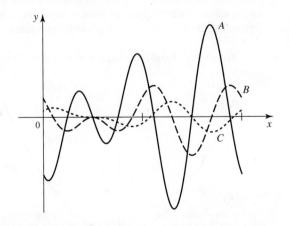

89. Sketching graphs Sketch the graph of a function f continuous on $[a, b]$ such that f, f', and f'' have the signs indicated in the following table on $[a, b]$. There are eight different cases lettered A–H and eight different graphs.

Case	A	B	C	D	E	F	G	H
f	+	+	+	+	−	−	−	−
f'	+	+	−	−	+	+	−	−
f''	+	−	+	−	+	−	+	−

90–93. Designer functions *Sketch the graph of a function that is continuous on* $(-\infty, \infty)$ *and satisfies the following sets of conditions.*

90. $f''(x) > 0$ on $(-\infty, -2)$; $f''(-2) = 0$; $f'(-1) = f'(1) = 0$; $f''(2) = 0$; $f'(3) = 0$; $f''(x) > 0$ on $(4, \infty)$

91. $f(-2) = f''(-1) = 0$; $f'\left(-\frac{3}{2}\right) = 0$; $f(0) = f'(0) = 0$; $f(1) = f'(1) = 0$

92. $f'(x) > 0$, for all x in the domain; $f'(-2)$ and $f'(0)$ do not exist; $f''(0) = 0$

93. $f''(x) > 0$ on $(-\infty, -2)$; $f''(x) < 0$ on $(-2, 1)$; $f''(x) > 0$ on $(1, 3)$; $f''(x) < 0$ on $(3, \infty)$

94. Strength of concavity The functions $f(x) = ax^2$, where $a > 0$, are concave up for all x. Graph these functions for $a = 1, 5$, and 10, and discuss how the concavity varies with a. How does a change the appearance of the graph?

95. Interpreting the derivative The graph of f' on the interval $[-3, 2]$ is shown in the figure.

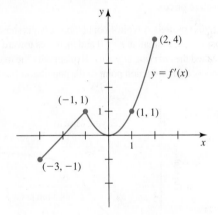

a. On what interval(s) is f increasing? Decreasing?
b. Find the critical points of f. Which critical points correspond to local maxima? Local minima? Neither?
c. At what point(s) does f have an inflection point?
d. On what interval(s) is f concave up? Concave down?
e. Sketch the graph of f''.
f. Sketch one possible graph of f.

96–99. Second Derivative Test *Locate the critical points of the following functions and use the Second Derivative Test to determine (if possible) whether they correspond to local maxima or local minima.*

96. $p(t) = 2t^3 + 3t^2 - 36t$

97. $f(x) = \dfrac{x^4}{4} - \dfrac{5x^3}{3} - 4x^2 + 48x$

98. $h(x) = (x + a)^4$; a constant

99. $f(x) = x^3 + 2x^2 + 4x - 1$

100. Concavity of parabolas Consider the general parabola described by the function $f(x) = ax^2 + bx + c$. For what values of a, b, and c is f concave up? For what values of a, b, and c is f concave down?

Applications

101. Demand functions and elasticity Economists use *demand functions* to describe how much of a commodity can be sold at varying prices. For example, the demand function $D(p) = 500 - 10p$ says that at a price of $p = 10$, a quantity of $D(10) = 400$ units of the commodity can be sold. The elasticity $E = \dfrac{dD}{dp} \dfrac{p}{D}$ of the demand gives the approximate percent change in the demand for every 1% change in the price. (See the Guided Project *Elasticity in Economics* for more on demand functions and elasticity.)

a. Compute the elasticity of the demand function $D(p) = 500 - 10p$.
b. If the price is \$12 and increases by 4.5%, what is the approximate percent change in the demand?
c. Show that for the linear demand function $D(p) = a - bp$, where a and b are positive real numbers, the elasticity is a decreasing function, for $p \geq 0$ and $p \neq a/b$.
d. Show that the demand function $D(p) = a/p^b$, where a and b are positive real numbers, has a constant elasticity for all positive prices.

102. Population models A typical population curve is shown in the figure. The population is small at $t = 0$ and increases toward a steady-state level called the *carrying capacity*. Explain why the maximum growth rate occurs at an inflection point of the population curve.

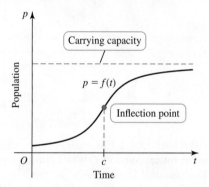

103. Population models The population of a species is given by the function $P(t) = \dfrac{Kt^2}{t^2 + b}$, where $t \geq 0$ is measured in years and K and b are positive real numbers.

a. With $K = 300$ and $b = 30$, what is $\lim\limits_{t \to \infty} P(t)$, the carrying capacity of the population?
b. With $K = 300$ and $b = 30$, when does the maximum growth rate occur?
c. For arbitrary positive values of K and b, when does the maximum growth rate occur (in terms of K and b)?

Additional Exercises

104. Tangent lines and concavity Give an argument to support the claim that if a function is concave up at a point, then the tangent line at that point lies below the curve near that point.

105. Symmetry of cubics Consider the general cubic polynomial $f(x) = x^3 + ax^2 + bx + c$, where a, b, and c are real numbers.

a. Show that f has exactly one inflection point and it occurs at $x^* = -a/3$.
b. Show that f is an odd function with respect to the inflection point $(x^*, f(x^*))$. This means that $f(x^*) - f(x^* + x) = f(x^* - x) - f(x^*)$, for all x.

106. Properties of cubics Consider the general cubic polynomial $f(x) = x^3 + ax^2 + bx + c$, where a, b, and c are real numbers.

a. Prove that f has exactly one local maximum and one local minimum provided that $a^2 > 3b$.
b. Prove that f has no extreme values if $a^2 < 3b$.

107. A family of single-humped functions Consider the functions $f(x) = \dfrac{1}{x^{2n} + 1}$, where n is a positive integer.

a. Show that these functions are even.
b. Show that the graphs of these functions intersect at the points $\left(\pm 1, \frac{1}{2} \right)$, for all positive values of n.
c. Show that the inflection points of these functions occur at $x = \pm \sqrt[2n]{\dfrac{2n - 1}{2n + 1}}$, for all positive values of n.
d. Use a graphing utility to verify your conclusions.
e. Describe how the inflection points and the shape of the graphs change as n increases.

108. Even quartics Consider the quartic (fourth-degree) polynomial $f(x) = x^4 + bx^2 + d$ consisting only of even-powered terms.

a. Show that the graph of f is symmetric about the y-axis.
b. Show that if $b \geq 0$, then f has one critical point and no inflection points.
c. Show that if $b < 0$, then f has three critical points and two inflection points. Find the critical points and inflection points, and show that they alternate along the x-axis. Explain why one critical point is always $x = 0$.
d. Prove that the number of distinct real roots of f depends on the values of the coefficients b and d, as shown in the figure. The curve that divides the plane is the parabola $d = b^2/4$.
e. Find the number of real roots when $b = 0$ or $d = 0$ or $d = b^2/4$.

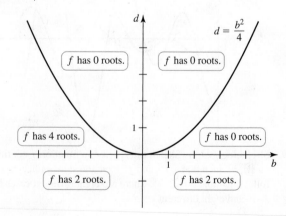

109. General quartic Show that the general quartic (fourth-degree) polynomial $f(x) = x^4 + ax^3 + bx^2 + cx + d$ has either zero or two inflection points, and the latter case occurs provided that $b < 3a^2/8$.

110. First Derivative Test is not exhaustive Propose a (simple) nonconstant function f that has a local maximum at $x = 1$, with $f'(1) = 0$, where the derivative of f does not change sign from positive to negative as x increases through 1.

QUICK CHECK ANSWERS

1. Positive derivatives on an interval mean the curve is rising on the interval, which means the function is increasing on the interval. **2.** The graph of f rises for $x < 0$. At $x = 0$, the graph flattens out momentarily, then continues to rise for $0 < x < 2$. There is a local maximum at $x = 2$ and f is decreasing for $x > 2$.

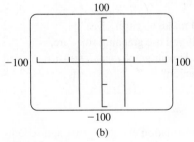

3. $f'(x) < 0$ on $(-\infty, 0)$ and $f'(x) > 0$ on $(0, \infty)$. Therefore, f has a local minimum at $x = 0$ by the First Derivative Test. **4.** $f''(x) = 12x^2$, so $f''(x) > 0$ for $x < 0$ and for $x > 0$. There is no inflection point at $x = 0$ because the second derivative does not change sign. **5.** The first curve should be rising and concave up. The second curve should be falling and concave down.

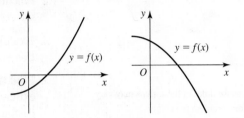

4.3 Graphing Functions

We have now collected the tools required for a comprehensive approach to graphing functions. These *analytical methods* are indispensable, even with the availability of powerful graphing utilities, as illustrated by the following example.

Calculators and Analysis

Suppose you want to graph the harmless-looking function $f(x) = x^3/3 - 400x$. If you plot f using a typical graphing calculator with a default window of $[-10, 10] \times [-10, 10]$, the resulting graph is shown in Figure 4.37a; one vertical line appears on the screen. Zooming out to the window $[-100, 100] \times [-100, 100]$ produces three vertical lines (Figure 4.37b), which is not an accurate graph of the function. Expanding the window even more to $[-1000, 1000] \times [-1000, 1000]$ is no better. So what do we do?

QUICK CHECK 1 Try to graph $f(x) = x^3/3 - 400x$ using various windows on a graphing calculator. Can you find a window that gives a better graph of f than those in Figure 4.37? ◄

The function $f(x) = x^3/3 - 400x$ has a reasonable graph, but it cannot be found automatically by letting technology do all the work. Here is the message of this section: Graphing utilities are valuable for exploring functions, producing preliminary graphs, and checking your work. But they should not be relied on exclusively because they cannot explain *why* a graph has its shape. Rather, graphing utilities should be used in an interactive way with the analytical methods presented in this chapter.

Graphing Guidelines

The following set of guidelines need not be followed exactly for every function, and you will find that several steps can often be done at once. Depending on the specific problem, some of the steps are best done analytically, while other steps can be done with a graphing utility. Experiment with both approaches and try to find a good balance. We

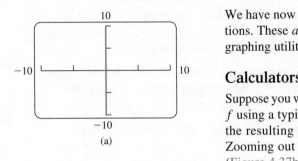

(a)

(b)

FIGURE 4.37

also present a schematic record-keeping procedure to keep track of discoveries as they are made.

> The precise order of these steps may vary from one problem to another.

Graphing Guidelines for $y = f(x)$

1. **Identify the domain or interval of interest.** On what interval should the function be graphed? It may be the domain of the function or some subset of the domain.

2. **Exploit symmetry.** Take advantage of symmetry. For example, is the function *even* $(f(-x) = f(x))$, *odd* $(f(-x) = -f(x))$, or neither?

3. **Find the first and second derivatives.** They are needed to determine extreme values, concavity, inflection points, and intervals of increase and decrease. Computing derivatives—particularly second derivatives—may not be practical, so some functions may need to be graphed without complete derivative information.

4. **Find critical points and possible inflection points.** Determine points at which $f'(x) = 0$ or f' is undefined. Determine points at which $f''(x) = 0$ or f'' is undefined.

5. **Find intervals on which the function is increasing/decreasing and concave up/down.** The first derivative determines the intervals of increase and decrease. The second derivative determines the intervals on which the function is concave up or concave down.

6. **Identify extreme values and inflection points.** Use either the First or the Second Derivative Test to classify the critical points. Both x- and y-coordinates of maxima, minima, and inflection points are needed for graphing.

7. **Locate vertical/horizontal asymptotes and determine end behavior.** Vertical asymptotes often occur at zeros of denominators. Horizontal asymptotes require examining limits as $x \to \pm\infty$; these limits determine end behavior.

8. **Find the intercepts.** The y-intercept of the graph is found by setting $x = 0$. The x-intercepts are found by setting $y = 0$; they are the real zeros (or roots) of f (those values of x that satisfy $f(x) = 0$).

9. **Choose an appropriate graphing window and make a graph.** Use the results of the above steps to graph the function. If you use graphing software, check for consistency with your analytical work. Is your graph *complete*—that is, does it show all the essential details of the function?

EXAMPLE 1 A warm-up Given the following information about the first and second derivatives of a function f that is continuous on $(-\infty, \infty)$, summarize the information using a number line, and then sketch a possible graph of f.

$$f' < 0, f'' > 0 \text{ on } (-\infty, 0) \quad f' > 0, f'' > 0 \text{ on } (0, 1) \quad f' > 0, f'' < 0 \text{ on } (1, 2)$$
$$f' < 0, f'' < 0 \text{ on } (2, 3) \qquad f' < 0, f'' > 0 \text{ on } (3, 4) \quad f' > 0, f'' > 0 \text{ on } (4, \infty)$$

SOLUTION We illustrate the given information on a number line. For example, on the interval $(-\infty, 0)$, f is decreasing and concave up; so we sketch a segment of a curve with these properties on this interval (Figure 4.38). Continuing in this manner, we obtain a useful summary of the properties of f.

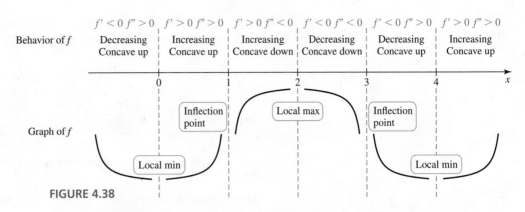

| | $f' < 0\ f'' > 0$ | $f' > 0\ f'' > 0$ | $f' > 0\ f'' < 0$ | $f' < 0\ f'' < 0$ | $f' < 0\ f'' > 0$ | $f' > 0\ f'' > 0$ |

Behavior of f Decreasing   Increasing   Increasing   Decreasing   Decreasing   Increasing
Concave up   Concave up   Concave down   Concave down   Concave up   Concave up

FIGURE 4.38

Assembling the information shown in Figure 4.38, a rough graph of f is produced (Figure 4.39). Notice that derivative information is not sufficient to determine the y-coordinates of points on the curve.

Related Exercises 7–8◄

QUICK CHECK 2 Explain why the function f and $f + C$, where C is a constant, have the same derivative properties. ◄

EXAMPLE 2   A deceptive polynomial Use the graphing guidelines to graph
$$f(x) = \frac{x^3}{3} - 400x \text{ on its domain.}$$

SOLUTION

1. **Domain** The domain of any polynomial is $(-\infty, \infty)$.

2. **Symmetry** Because f consists of odd powers of the variable, it is an odd function. Its graph is symmetric about the origin.

3. **Derivatives** The derivatives of f are
$$f'(x) = x^2 - 400 \quad \text{and} \quad f''(x) = 2x.$$

4. **Critical points and possible inflection points** Solving $f'(x) = 0$, we find that the critical points are $x = \pm 20$. Solving $f''(x) = 0$, we see that a possible inflection point occurs at $x = 0$.

5. **Increasing/decreasing and concavity** Note that
$$f'(x) = x^2 - 400 = (x - 20)(x + 20).$$

Solving the inequality $f'(x) < 0$, we find that f is decreasing on the interval $(-20, 20)$. Solving the inequality $f'(x) > 0$ reveals that f is increasing on the intervals $(-\infty, -20)$ and $(20, \infty)$ (Figure 4.40). By the First Derivative Test, we have enough information to conclude that f has a local maximum at $x = -20$ and a local minimum at $x = 20$.

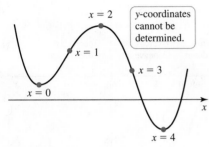

FIGURE 4.39

▷ Notice that the first derivative of an odd polynomial is an even polynomial and the second derivative is an odd polynomial.

▷ See Appendix A for solving inequalities using test values.

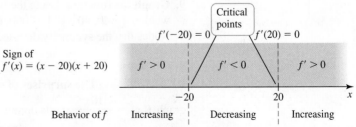

FIGURE 4.40

Furthermore, $f''(x) = 2x < 0$ on $(-\infty, 0)$, so f is concave down on this interval. Also, $f''(x) > 0$ on $(0, \infty)$, so f is concave up on $(0, \infty)$ (Figure 4.41).

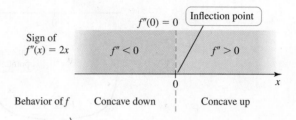

FIGURE 4.41

The evidence obtained so far is summarized in Figure 4.42.

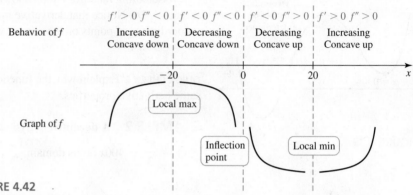

FIGURE 4.42

6. **Extreme values and inflection points** In this case, the Second Derivative Test is easily applied and it confirms what we have already learned. Because $f''(-20) < 0$ and $f''(20) > 0$, f has a local maximum at $x = -20$ and a local minimum at $x = 20$. The corresponding function values are $f(-20) = 16{,}000/3 = 5333\frac{1}{3}$ and $f(20) = -f(-20) = -5333\frac{1}{3}$. Finally, we see that f'' changes sign at $x = 0$, making $(0, 0)$ an inflection point.

7. **Asymptotes and end behavior** Polynomials have neither vertical nor horizontal asymptotes. Because the highest-power term in the polynomial is x^3 (an odd power) and the leading coefficient is positive, we have the end behavior

$$\lim_{x \to \infty} f(x) = \infty \quad \text{and} \quad \lim_{x \to -\infty} f(x) = -\infty.$$

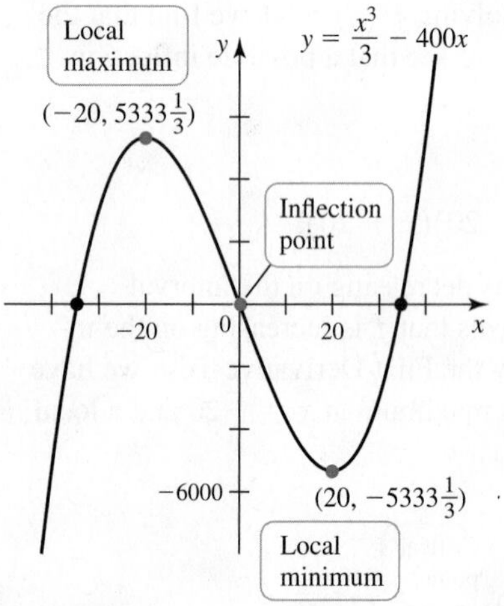

8. **Intercepts** The y-intercept is $(0, 0)$. We solve the equation $f(x) = 0$ to find the x-intercepts:

$$\frac{x^3}{3} - 400x = x\left(\frac{x^2}{3} - 400\right) = 0.$$

The roots of this equation are $x = 0$ and $x = \pm\sqrt{1200} \approx \pm 34.641$.

9. **Graph the function** Using the information found in Steps 1–8, we choose the graphing window $[-40, 40] \times [-6000, 6000]$ and produce the graph shown in Figure 4.43. Notice that the symmetry detected in Step 2 is evident in this graph.

Related Exercises 9–14 ◄

EXAMPLE 3 **The surprises of a rational function** Use the graphing guidelines to graph $f(x) = \dfrac{10x^3}{x^2 - 1}$ on its domain.

Local maximum $(-20, 5333\frac{1}{3})$

Inflection point

$y = \dfrac{x^3}{3} - 400x$

$(20, -5333\frac{1}{3})$

Local minimum

FIGURE 4.43

SOLUTION

1. **Domain** The zeros of the denominator are $x = \pm 1$, so the domain is $\{x: x \neq \pm 1\}$.

2. **Symmetry** This function consists of an odd function divided by an even function. The product or quotient of an even function and an odd function is odd. Therefore, the graph is symmetric about the origin.

3. **Derivatives** The Quotient Rule is used to find the first and second derivatives:

$$f'(x) = \frac{10x^2(x^2 - 3)}{(x^2 - 1)^2} \quad \text{and} \quad f''(x) = \frac{20x(x^2 + 3)}{(x^2 - 1)^3}.$$

4. **Critical points and possible inflection points** The solutions of $f'(x) = 0$ occur where the numerator equals 0, provided the denominator is nonzero at those points. Solving $10x^2(x^2 - 3) = 0$ gives the critical points $x = 0$ and $x = \pm\sqrt{3}$. The solutions of $f''(x) = 0$ are found by solving $20x(x^2 + 3) = 0$; we see that the only possible inflection point occurs at $x = 0$.

5. **Increasing/decreasing and concavity** To find the sign of f', first note that the denominator of f' is nonnegative, as is the factor $10x^2$ in the numerator. So the sign of f' is determined by the sign of the factor $x^2 - 3$, which is negative on $(-\sqrt{3}, \sqrt{3})$ (excluding $x = \pm 1$) and positive on $(-\infty, -\sqrt{3})$ and $(\sqrt{3}, \infty)$. Therefore, f is decreasing on $(-\sqrt{3}, \sqrt{3})$ (excluding $x = \pm 1$) and increasing on $(-\infty, -\sqrt{3})$ and $(\sqrt{3}, \infty)$.

The sign of f'' is a bit trickier. Because $x^2 + 3$ is positive, the sign of f'' is determined by the sign of $20x$ in the numerator and $(x^2 - 1)^3$ in the denominator. When x and $(x^2 - 1)^3$ have the same sign, $f''(x) > 0$; when x and $(x^2 - 1)^3$ have opposite signs, $f''(x) < 0$ (Table 4.1). The results of this analysis are shown in Figure 4.44.

> Care must be used with vertical asymptotes: The sign of f' and f'' may or may not change at an asymptote.

Table 4.1

	$20x$	$x^2 + 3$	$(x^2 - 1)^3$	**Sign of f''**
$(-\infty, -1)$	−	+	+	−
$(-1, 0)$	−	+	−	+
$(0, 1)$	+	+	−	−
$(1, \infty)$	+	+	+	+

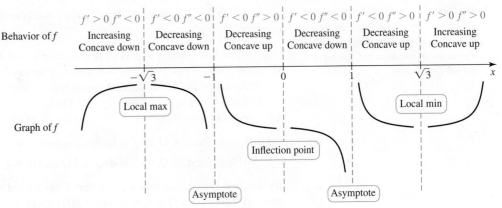

FIGURE 4.44

6. Extreme values and inflection points The First Derivative Test is easily applied by looking at Figure 4.44. The function is increasing on $(-\infty, -\sqrt{3})$ and decreasing on $(-\sqrt{3}, -1)$; therefore, f has a local maximum at $x = -\sqrt{3}$, where $f(-\sqrt{3}) = -15\sqrt{3}$. Similarly, f has a local minimum at $x = \sqrt{3}$, where $f(\sqrt{3}) = 15\sqrt{3}$. (These results could also be obtained with the Second Derivative Test.) There is no local extreme value at the critical point $x = 0$, only a horizontal tangent line.

Using the calculations of Step 5, we see that f'' changes sign at $x = \pm 1$ and at $x = 0$. The points $x = \pm 1$ are not in the domain of f, so they cannot correspond to inflection points. However, there is an inflection point at $(0, 0)$.

7. Asymptotes and end behavior Recall from Section 2.4 that zeros of the denominator, which in this case are $x = \pm 1$, are candidates for vertical asymptotes. Checking the sign of f on either side of $x = \pm 1$, we find

$$\lim_{x \to -1^-} f(x) = -\infty, \qquad \lim_{x \to -1^+} f(x) = \infty.$$

$$\lim_{x \to 1^-} f(x) = -\infty, \qquad \lim_{x \to 1^+} f(x) = \infty.$$

It follows that f has vertical asymptotes at $x = \pm 1$. The degree of the numerator is greater than the degree of the denominator, so there are no horizontal asymptotes.

8. Intercepts The zeros of a rational function coincide with the zeros of the numerator, provided that those points are not also zeros of the denominator. In this case, the zeros of f satisfy $10x^3 = 0$, or $x = 0$ (which is not a zero of the denominator). Therefore, $(0, 0)$ is both the x- and y-intercept.

9. Graphing We now assemble an accurate graph of f, as shown in Figure 4.45. A window of $[-3, 3] \times [-40, 40]$ gives a complete graph of the function. Notice that the symmetry about the origin deduced in Step 2 is apparent in the graph.

Related Exercises 15–20 ◄

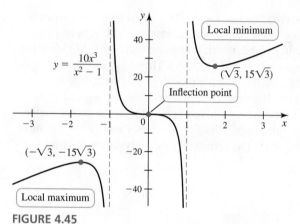

FIGURE 4.45

QUICK CHECK 3 Verify that the function f in Example 3 is symmetric about the origin by showing that $f(-x) = -f(x)$. ◄

In the next two examples, we show how the guidelines may be streamlined to some extent.

> The function $f(x) = e^{-x^2}$ and the family of functions $f(x) = ce^{-ax^2}$ are central to the study of statistics. They have bell-shaped graphs and describe Gaussian or normal distributions.

EXAMPLE 4   The normal distribution Analyze the function $f(x) = e^{-x^2}$ and draw its graph.

SOLUTION The domain of f is all real numbers, and $f(x) > 0$ for all x. Because $f(-x) = f(x)$, f is an even function and its graph is symmetric about the y-axis.

Extreme points and inflection points follow from the derivatives of f. Using the Chain Rule, we have $f'(x) = -2xe^{-x^2}$. The critical points satisfy $f'(x) = 0$, which has the single root $x = 0$ (because $e^{-x^2} > 0$ for all x). It now follows that

• $f'(x) > 0$, for $x < 0$, so f is increasing on $(-\infty, 0)$.

• $f'(x) < 0$, for $x > 0$, so f is decreasing on $(0, \infty)$.

By the First Derivative Test, we see that f has a local maximum (and an absolute maximum by Theorem 4.5) at $x = 0$ where $f(0) = 1$.

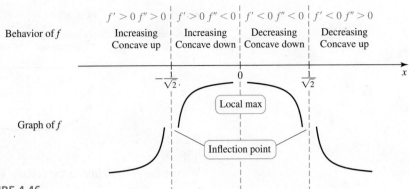

Behavior of f | $f' > 0\ f'' > 0$ | $f' > 0\ f'' < 0$ | $f' < 0\ f'' < 0$ | $f' < 0\ f'' > 0$

Increasing Concave up | Increasing Concave down | Decreasing Concave down | Decreasing Concave up

Graph of f

Local max

Inflection point

FIGURE 4.46

Differentiating $f'(x) = -2xe^{-x^2}$ with the Product Rule yields

$$f''(x) = e^{-x^2}(-2) + (-2x)(-2xe^{-x^2}) \quad \text{Product Rule}$$

$$= 2e^{-x^2}(2x^2 - 1). \quad \text{Simplify.}$$

Again using the fact that $e^{-x^2} > 0$, for all x, we see that $f''(x) = 0$ when $2x^2 - 1 = 0$ or when $x = \pm 1/\sqrt{2}$; these values are candidates for inflection points. Observe that $f''(x) > 0$ and f is concave up on $(-\infty, -1/\sqrt{2})$ and $(1/\sqrt{2}, \infty)$, while $f''(x) < 0$ and f is concave down on $(-1/\sqrt{2}, 1/\sqrt{2})$. Because f'' changes sign at $x = \pm 1/\sqrt{2}$, we have inflection points at $(\pm 1/\sqrt{2}, 1/\sqrt{e})$ (Figure 4.46).

To determine the end behavior, notice that $\lim\limits_{x \to \pm\infty} e^{-x^2} = 0$, so $y = 0$ is a horizontal asymptote of f. Assembling all of these facts, an accurate graph can now be drawn (Figure 4.47). *Related Exercises 21–42*◄

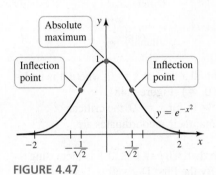

Absolute maximum

Inflection point

Inflection point

$y = e^{-x^2}$

FIGURE 4.47

EXAMPLE 5 **Roots and cusps** Graph $f(x) = \frac{1}{8}x^{2/3}(9x^2 - 8x - 16)$ on its domain.

SOLUTION The domain of f is $(-\infty, \infty)$. The polynomial factor in f consists of both even and odd powers, so f has no special symmetry. Computing the first derivative is straightforward if you first expand f as a sum of three terms:

$$f'(x) = \frac{d}{dx}\left(\frac{9x^{8/3}}{8} - x^{5/3} - 2x^{2/3}\right) \quad \text{Expand } f.$$

$$= 3x^{5/3} - \frac{5}{3}x^{2/3} - \frac{4}{3}x^{-1/3} \quad \text{Differentiate.}$$

$$= \frac{(x - 1)(9x + 4)}{3x^{1/3}}. \quad \text{Simplify.}$$

The critical points are now identified: f' is undefined at $x = 0$ (because $x^{-1/3}$ is undefined there) and $f'(x) = 0$ at $x = 1$ and $x = -\frac{4}{9}$. So we have three critical points to analyze. Table 4.2 tracks the signs of the three factors in f' and shows the sign of f' on the relevant intervals; this information is recorded in Figure 4.48.

Table 4.2

	$\dfrac{x^{-1/3}}{3}$	$9x + 4$	$x - 1$	**Sign of f'**
$\left(-\infty, -\frac{4}{9}\right)$	$-$	$-$	$-$	$-$
$\left(-\frac{4}{9}, 0\right)$	$-$	$+$	$-$	$+$
$(0, 1)$	$+$	$+$	$-$	$-$
$(1, \infty)$	$+$	$+$	$+$	$+$

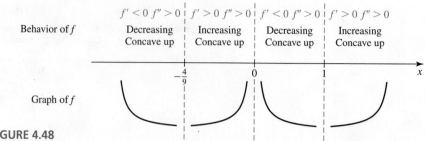

Behavior of f

$f' < 0\ f'' > 0$	$f' > 0\ f'' > 0$	$f' < 0\ f'' > 0$	$f' > 0\ f'' > 0$
Decreasing	Increasing	Decreasing	Increasing
Concave up	Concave up	Concave up	Concave up

Graph of f

FIGURE 4.48

We use the second line in the calculation of f' to compute the second derivative:

$$f''(x) = \frac{d}{dx}\left(3x^{5/3} - \frac{5}{3}x^{2/3} - \frac{4}{3}x^{-1/3}\right)$$

$$= 5x^{2/3} - \frac{10}{9}x^{-1/3} + \frac{4}{9}x^{-4/3} \qquad \text{Differentiate.}$$

$$= \frac{45x^2 - 10x + 4}{9x^{4/3}}. \qquad \text{Simplify.}$$

Solving $f''(x) = 0$, we discover that $f''(x) > 0$, for all x except $x = 0$, where it is undefined. Therefore, f is concave up on $(-\infty, 0)$ and $(0, \infty)$ (Figure 4.48).

By the Second Derivative Test, because $f''(x) > 0$, for $x \neq 0$, the critical points $x = -\frac{4}{9}$ and $x = 1$ correspond to local minima; their y-coordinates are $f\left(-\frac{4}{9}\right) \approx -0.777$ and $f(1) = -\frac{15}{8} = -1.875$.

What about the third critical point $x = 0$? Note that $f(0) = 0$, and f is increasing just to the left of 0 and decreasing just to the right. By the First Derivative Test, f has a local maximum at $x = 0$. Furthermore, $f'(x) \to \infty$ as $x \to 0^-$ and $f'(x) \to -\infty$ as $x \to 0^+$, so the graph of f has a cusp at $x = 0$.

As $x \to \pm\infty$, f is dominated by its highest-power term, which is $9x^{8/3}/8$. This term becomes large and positive as $x \to \pm\infty$; therefore, f has no absolute maximum. Its absolute minimum occurs at $x = 1$ because, comparing the two local minima, $f(1) < f\left(-\frac{4}{9}\right)$.

The roots of f satisfy $\frac{1}{8}x^{2/3}(9x^2 - 8x - 16) = 0$, which gives $x = 0$ and

$$x = \frac{4}{9}(1 \pm \sqrt{10}) \approx -0.961 \quad \text{or} \quad 1.850. \quad \text{Use the quadratic formula.}$$

With the information gathered in this analysis, we obtain the graph shown in Figure 4.49.

Related Exercises 21–42 ◄

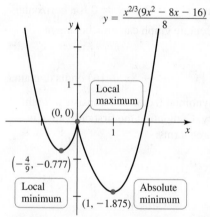

$$y = \frac{x^{2/3}(9x^2 - 8x - 16)}{8}$$

Local maximum

$(0, 0)$

$\left(-\frac{4}{9}, -0.777\right)$

Local minimum

$(1, -1.875)$ Absolute minimum

FIGURE 4.49

SECTION 4.3 EXERCISES

Review Questions

1. Why is it important to determine the domain of f before graphing f?

2. Explain why it is useful to know about symmetry in a function.

3. Can the graph of a polynomial have vertical or horizontal asymptotes? Explain.

4. Where are the vertical asymptotes of a rational function located?

5. How do you find the absolute maximum and minimum values of a function that is continuous on a closed interval?

6. Describe the possible end behavior of a polynomial.

Basic Skills

7–8. Shape of the curve *Sketch a curve with the following properties.*

7. $f' < 0$ and $f'' < 0$, for $x < 3$
   $f' < 0$ and $f'' > 0$, for $x > 3$

8. $f' < 0$ and $f'' < 0$, for $x < -1$
   $f' < 0$ and $f'' > 0$, for $-1 < x < 2$
   $f' > 0$ and $f'' > 0$, for $2 < x < 8$
   $f' > 0$ and $f'' < 0$, for $8 < x < 10$
   $f' > 0$ and $f'' > 0$, for $x > 10$

9–14. Graphing polynomials *Sketch a graph of the following polynomials. Identify local extrema, inflection points, and x- and y-intercepts when they exist.*

9. $f(x) = x^3 - 6x^2 + 9x$

10. $f(x) = 3x - x^3$

11. $f(x) = x^4 - 6x^2$

12. $f(x) = 2x^6 - 3x^4$

13. $f(x) = (x - 6)(x + 6)^2$

14. $f(x) = 27(x - 2)^2(x + 2)$

15–20. Graphing rational functions *Use the guidelines of this section to make a complete graph of f.*

15. $f(x) = \dfrac{x^2}{x - 2}$

16. $f(x) = \dfrac{x^2}{x^2 - 4}$

17. $f(x) = \dfrac{3x}{x^2 - 1}$

18. $f(x) = \dfrac{2x - 3}{2x - 8}$

19. $f(x) = \dfrac{x^2 + 12}{2x + 1}$

20. $f(x) = \dfrac{4x + 4}{x^2 + 3}$

21–36. More graphing *Make a complete graph of the following functions. If an interval is not specified, graph the function on its domain. Use a graphing utility to check your work.*

21. $f(x) = \tan^{-1} x^2$

22. $f(x) = \ln(x^2 + 1)$

23. $f(x) = x + 2\cos x$ on $[-2\pi, 2\pi]$

24. $f(x) = x - 3x^{2/3}$

25. $f(x) = x - 3x^{1/3}$

26. $f(x) = 2 - x^{2/3} + x^{4/3}$

27. $f(x) = \sin x - x$ on $[0, 2\pi]$

28. $f(x) = x\sqrt{x + 3}$

29. $g(t) = e^{-t} \sin t$ on $[-\pi, \pi]$

30. $g(x) = x^2 \ln x$

31. $f(x) = x + \tan x$ on $\left(-\dfrac{3\pi}{2}, \dfrac{3\pi}{2}\right)$

32. $f(x) = (\ln x)/x^2$

33. $f(x) = x \ln x$

34. $g(x) = e^{-x^2/2}$

35. $p(x) = xe^{-x^2}$

36. $g(x) = 1/(e^{-x} - 1)$

37–42. Graphing with technology *Make a complete graph of the following functions. A graphing utility is useful in locating intercepts, local extreme values, and inflection points.*

37. $f(x) = \dfrac{1}{3}x^3 - 2x^2 - 5x + 2$

38. $f(x) = \dfrac{1}{15}x^3 - x + 1$

39. $f(x) = 3x^4 + 4x^3 - 12x^2$

40. $f(x) = x^3 - 33x^2 + 216x - 2$

41. $f(x) = \dfrac{3x - 5}{x^2 - 1}$

42. $f(x) = x^{1/3}(x - 2)^2$

Further Explorations

43. Explain why or why not Determine whether the following statements are true and give an explanation or counterexample.

a. The zeros of f' are -3, 1, and 4, so the local extrema are located at these points.

b. The zeros of f'' are -2 and 4, so the inflection points are located at these points.

c. The zeros of the denominator of f are -3 and 4, so f has vertical asymptotes at these points.

d. If a rational function has a finite limit as $x \to \infty$, it must have a finite limit as $x \to -\infty$.

44–47. Functions from derivatives *Use the derivative f′ to determine the x-coordinates of the local maxima and minima of f, and the intervals of increase and decrease. Sketch a possible graph of f (f is not unique).*

44. $f'(x) = (x - 1)(x + 2)(x + 4)$

45. $f'(x) = 10 \sin 2x$ on $[-2\pi, 2\pi]$

46. $f'(x) = \dfrac{(x + 1)(x - 2)^2(x - 3)}{6}$

47. $f'(x) = x^2(x + 2)(x - 1)$

48–49. Functions from graphs *Use the graphs of f′ and f″ to find the critical points and inflection points of f, the intervals on which f is increasing and decreasing, and the intervals of concavity. Then graph f assuming f(0) = 0.*

48.

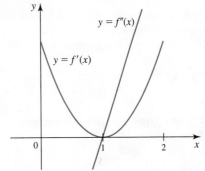

49.

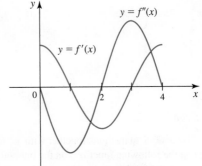

50–53. Nice cubics and quartics *The following third- and fourth-degree polynomials have a property that makes them relatively easy to graph. Make a complete graph and describe the property.*

50. $f(x) = x^4 + 8x^3 - 270x^2 + 1$

51. $f(x) = x^3 - 6x^2 - 135x$

52. $f(x) = x^3 - 147x + 286$

53. $f(x) = x^3 - 3x^2 - 144x - 140$

54. Oscillations Consider the function $f(x) = \cos(\ln x)$, for $x > 0$. Use analytical techniques and a graphing utility.

    a. Locate all local extrema on the interval $(0, 4]$.
    b. Identify the inflection points on the interval $(0, 4]$.
    c. Locate the three smallest zeros of f on the interval $(0.1, \infty)$.
    d. Sketch the graph of f.

55. Local max/min of $x^{1/x}$ Use analytical methods to find all local extreme points of the function $f(x) = x^{1/x}$, for $x > 0$. Verify your work using a graphing utility.

56. Local max/min of x^x Use analytical methods to find all local extreme points of the function $f(x) = x^x$, for $x > 0$. Verify your work using a graphing utility.

57–60. Designer functions *Sketch a continuous function f on some interval that has the properties described.*

57. The function f has one inflection point but no local extrema.

58. The function f has three real zeros and exactly two local minima.

59. The function f satisfies $f'(-2) = 2, f'(0) = 0, f'(1) = -3$, and $f'(4) = 1$.

60. The function f has the same finite limit as $x \to \pm\infty$ and has exactly one absolute minimum and one absolute maximum.

61–68. More graphing *Make a complete graph of the following functions. If an interval is not specified, graph the function on its domain. Use analytical methods and a graphing utility together in a complementary way.*

61. $f(x) = \dfrac{-x\sqrt{x^2 - 4}}{x - 2}$ **62.** $f(x) = 3\sqrt[4]{x} - \sqrt{x} - 2$

63. $f(x) = 3x^4 - 44x^3 + 60x^2$ (*Hint:* Two different graphing windows may be needed.)

64. $f(x) = \dfrac{1}{1 + \cos(\pi x)}$ on $(1, 3)$

65. $f(x) = 10x^6 - 36x^5 - 75x^4 + 300x^3 + 120x^2 - 720x$

66. $f(x) = \dfrac{\sin(\pi x)}{1 + \sin(\pi x)}$ on $[0, 2]$

67. $f(x) = \dfrac{x\sqrt{|x^2 - 1|}}{x^4 + 1}$

68. $f(x) = \sin(3\pi \cos x)$ on $[-\pi/2, \pi/2]$

69. Hidden oscillations Use analytical methods together with a graphing utility to graph the following functions on the interval $[-2\pi, 2\pi]$. Define f at $x = 0$ so that it is continuous there. Be sure to uncover all relevant features of the graph.

    a. $f(x) = \dfrac{1 - \cos^3 x}{x^2}$ **b.** $f(x) = \dfrac{1 - \cos^5 x}{x^2}$

70. Cubic with parameters Locate all local maxima and minima of $f(x) = x^3 - 3bx^2 + 3a^2x + 23$, where a and b are constants, in the following cases.

    a. $|a| < |b|$ **b.** $|a| > |b|$ **c.** $|a| = |b|$

Applications

71. Height functions The figure shows six containers, each of which is filled from the top. Assume that water is poured into the containers at a constant rate and each container is filled in 10 seconds. Assume also that the horizontal cross sections of the containers are always circles. Let $h(t)$ be the depth of water in the container at time t, for $0 \le t \le 10$.

    a. For each container, sketch a graph of the function $y = h(t)$, for $0 \le t \le 10$.
    b. Explain why h is an increasing function.
    c. Describe the concavity of the function. Identify inflection points when they occur.
    d. For each container, where does h' (the derivative of h) have an absolute maximum on $[0, 10]$?

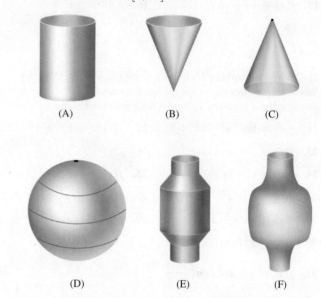

    (A)   (B)   (C)

    (D)   (E)   (F)

72. A pursuit curve Imagine a man standing 1 mi east of a crossroads. At noon, a dog starts walking north from the crossroads at 1 mi/hr (see figure). At the same instant, the man starts walking and at all times walks directly toward the dog at $s > 1$ mi/hr. The path in the xy plane followed by the man as he pursues his dog is given by the function

$$y = f(x) = \frac{s}{2}\left(\frac{x^{(s+1)/s}}{s+1} - \frac{x^{(s-1)/s}}{s-1}\right) + \frac{s}{s^2 - 1}.$$

Select various values of $s > 1$ and graph this pursuit curve. Comment on the changes in the curve as s increases.

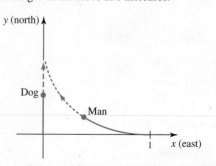

Additional Exercises

73. Derivative information Suppose a continuous function f is concave up on $(-\infty, 0)$ and $(0, \infty)$. Assume f has a local maximum at $x = 0$. What, if anything, do you know about $f'(0)$? Explain with an illustration.

74. $e^{\pi} > \pi^e$ Prove that $e^{\pi} > \pi^e$ by first finding the maximum value of $f(x) = \ln x / x$.

Technology Exercises

75–81. Special curves *The following classical curves have been studied by generations of mathematicians. Use analytical methods (including implicit differentiation) and a graphing utility to graph the curves. Include as much detail as possible.*

75. $x^{2/3} + y^{2/3} = 1$ Astroid or hypocycloid with four cusps

76. $y = \dfrac{8}{x^2 + 4}$ Witch of Agnesi

77. $x^3 + y^3 = 3xy$ Folium of Descartes

78. $y^2 = \dfrac{x^3}{2 - x}$ Cissoid of Diocles

79. $y^4 - x^4 - 4y^2 + 5x^2 = 0$ Devil's curve

80. $y^2 = x^3(1 - x)$ Pear curve

81. $x^4 - x^2 + y^2 = 0$ Figure-8 curve

82. Elliptic curves The equation $y^2 = x^3 - ax + 3$, where a is a parameter, defines a well-known family of *elliptic curves*.

    a. Verify that if $a = 3$, the graph consists of a single curve.
    b. Verify that if $a = 4$, the graph consists of two distinct curves.
    c. By experimentation, determine the value of a ($3 < a < 4$) at which the graph separates into two curves.

83. Lamé curves The equation $|y/a|^n + |x/a|^n = 1$, where n and a are positive real numbers, defines the family of Lamé curves. Make a complete graph of this function with $a = 1$, for $n = \frac{2}{3}, 1, 2, 3$. Describe the progression that you observe as n increases.

84. An exotic curve (Putnam Exam 1942) Find the coordinates of four local maxima of the function $f(x) = \dfrac{x}{1 + x^6 \sin^2 x}$ and graph the function, for $0 \le x \le 10$.

85. A family of superexponential functions Let $f(x) = (a - x)^x$, where $a > 0$.

    a. What is the domain of f (in terms of a)?
    b. Describe the end behavior of f (near the boundary of its domain).
    c. Compute f'. Then graph f and f' for $a = 0.5, 1, 2,$ and 3.
    d. Show that f has a single local maximum at the point z that satisfies $z = (a - z) \ln (a - z)$.
    e. Describe how z (found in part (d)) varies as a increases. Describe how $f(z)$ varies as a increases.

86. x^y **versus** y^x Consider positive real numbers x and y. Notice that $4^3 < 3^4$, while $3^2 > 2^3$ and $4^2 = 2^4$. Describe the regions in the first quadrant of the xy-plane in which $x^y > y^x$ and $x^y < y^x$.

87–90. Combining technology with analytical methods *Use a graphing utility together with analytical methods to create a complete graph of the following functions. Be sure to find and label the intercepts, local extrema, inflection points, asymptotes, intervals where the function is increasing/decreasing, and intervals of concavity.*

87. $f(x) = \dfrac{\tan^{-1} x}{x^2 + 1}$

88. $f(x) = \dfrac{\sqrt{4x^2 + 1}}{x^2 + 1}$

89. $f(x) = \dfrac{x \sin x}{x^2 + 1}$ on $[-2\pi, 2\pi]$

90. $f(x) = x / \ln x$

QUICK CHECK ANSWERS

1. Make the window larger in the y-direction.
2. Notice that f and $f + C$ have the same derivatives.
3. $f(-x) = \dfrac{10(-x)^3}{(-x)^2 - 1} = -\dfrac{10x^3}{x^2 - 1} = -f(x)$ ◄

4.4 Optimization Problems

The theme of this section is *optimization*, a topic arising in many disciplines that rely on mathematics. A structural engineer may seek the dimensions of a beam that maximize strength for a specified cost. A packaging designer may seek the dimensions of a container that maximize the capacity of the container for a given surface area. Airline strategists need to find the best allocation of airliners among several hubs in order to minimize fuel costs and maximize passenger miles. In all these examples, the challenge is to find an *efficient* way to carry out a task, where "efficient" could mean least expensive, most profitable, least time consuming, or, as you will see, many other measures.

To introduce the ideas behind optimization problems, think about pairs of nonnegative real numbers x and y between 0 and 20 with the property that their sum is 20, that is, $x + y = 20$. Of all possible pairs, which has the greatest product?

Table 4.3 displays a few cases showing how the product of two nonnegative numbers varies while their sum remains constant. The condition that $x + y = 20$ is called a **constraint**: It tells us to consider only (nonnegative) values of x and y satisfying this equation.

The quantity that we wish to maximize (or minimize in other cases) is called the **objective function**; in this case, the objective function is the product $P = xy$. From

Table 4.3

x	y	$x + y$	$P = xy$
1	19	20	19
5.5	14.5	20	79.75
9	11	20	99
13	7	20	91
18	2	20	36

Table 4.3, it appears that the product is greatest if both x and y are near the middle of the interval $[0, 20]$.

This simple problem has all the essential features of optimization problems. At their heart, optimization problems take the following form:

What is the maximum (minimum) value of an objective function subject to the given constraint(s)?

For the problem at hand, this question would be stated as, "What pair of nonnegative numbers maximizes $P = xy$ subject to the constraint $x + y = 20$?" The first step is to use the constraint to express the objective function $P = xy$ in terms of a single variable. In this case, the constraint is

$$x + y = 20, \quad \text{or} \quad y = 20 - x.$$

Substituting for y, the objective function becomes

$$P = xy = x(20 - x) = 20x - x^2,$$

which is a function of the single variable x. Notice that the values of x lie in the interval $0 \le x \le 20$ with $P(0) = P(20) = 0$.

To maximize P, we first find the critical points by solving

$$P'(x) = 20 - 2x = 0$$

to obtain the solution $x = 10$. To find the absolute maximum value of P on the interval $[0, 20]$, we check the endpoints and the critical points. Because $P(0) = P(20) = 0$ and $P(10) = 100$, we conclude that P has its absolute maximum value at $x = 10$. By the constraint $x + y = 20$, the numbers with the greatest product are $x = y = 10$, and their product is $P = 100$.

Figure 4.50 summarizes this problem. We see the constraint line $x + y = 20$ in the xy-plane. Above the line is the objective function $P = xy$. As x and y vary along the constraint line, the objective function changes, reaching a maximum value of 100 when $x = y = 10$.

> In this problem, it is just as easy to eliminate x as y. In other problems, eliminating one variable may result in less work than eliminating other variables.

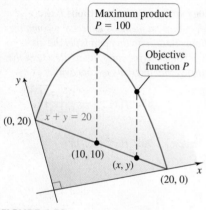

FIGURE 4.50

QUICK CHECK 1 Verify that in the previous example the same result is obtained if the constraint $x + y = 20$ is used to eliminate x rather than y. ◄

Most optimization problems have the same basic structure as the preceding example: There is an objective function, which may involve several variables, and one or more constraints. The methods of calculus (Sections 4.1 and 4.2) are used to find the minimum or maximum values of the objective function.

EXAMPLE 1   Rancher's dilemma A rancher has 400 ft of fence for constructing a rectangular corral. One side of the corral will be formed by a barn and requires no fence. Three exterior fences and two interior fences partition the corral into three rectangular regions as shown in Figure 4.51. What dimensions of the corral maximize the enclosed area? What is the area of that corral?

SOLUTION We first sketch the corral (Figure 4.51), where x is the width and y is the length of the corral. The amount of fence required is $4x + y$, so the constraint is $4x + y = 400$, or $y = 400 - 4x$.

The objective function to be maximized is the area of the corral, $A = xy$. Using $y = 400 - 4x$, we eliminate y and express A as a function of x:

$$A = xy = x(400 - 4x) = 400x - 4x^2.$$

Notice that the width of the corral must be at least $x = 0$, and it cannot exceed $x = 100$ (because 400 ft of fence are available). Therefore, we maximize $A(x) = 400x - 4x^2$, for $0 \le x \le 100$. The critical points of the objective function satisfy

$$A'(x) = 400 - 8x = 0,$$

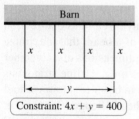

Constraint: $4x + y = 400$

FIGURE 4.51

> Recall from Section 4.1 that the absolute extreme points occur at critical points or endpoints.

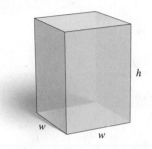

FIGURE 4.52

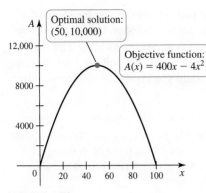

Objective function: $V = w^2h$
Constraint: $2w + h = 64$

FIGURE 4.53

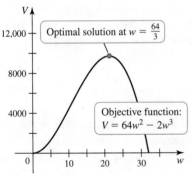

FIGURE 4.54

which has the solution $x = 50$. To find the absolute maximum value of A, we check the endpoints of $[0, 100]$ and the critical point $x = 50$. Because $A(0) = A(100) = 0$ and $A(50) = 10,000$, the absolute maximum value of A occurs when $x = 50$. Using the constraint, the optimal length of the corral is $y = 400 - 4(50) = 200$. Therefore, the maximum area of 10,000 ft^2 is achieved with dimensions $x = 50$ ft and $y = 200$ ft. The objective function A is shown in Figure 4.52. *Related Exercises 5–14*◄

QUICK CHECK 2 Find the objective function in Example 1 (in terms of x) (i) if there is no interior fence and (ii) if there is one interior fence. ◄

EXAMPLE 2 **Airline regulations** Suppose an airline policy states that all baggage must be box-shaped with a sum of length, width, and height not exceeding 64 in. What are the dimensions and volume of a square-based box with the greatest volume under these conditions?

SOLUTION We sketch a square-based box whose length and width are w and whose height is h (Figure 4.53). By the airline policy, the constraint is $2w + h = 64$. The objective function is the volume, $V = w^2h$. Either w or h may be eliminated from the objective function; the constraint $h = 64 - 2w$ implies that the volume is

$$V = w^2h = w^2(64 - 2w) = 64w^2 - 2w^3.$$

The objective function has now been expressed in terms of a single variable. Notice that w is nonnegative and cannot exceed 32, so the domain of V is $0 \leq w \leq 32$. The critical points satisfy

$$V'(w) = 128w - 6w^2 = 2w(64 - 3w) = 0,$$

which has roots $w = 0$ and $w = \frac{64}{3}$. By the First (or Second) Derivative Test, $w = \frac{64}{3}$ corresponds to a local maximum. At the endpoints, $V(0) = V(32) = 0$. Therefore, the volume function has an absolute maximum of $V(64/3) \approx 9709$ in^3. The dimensions of the optimal box are $w = 64/3$ in and $h = 64 - 2w = 64/3$ in, so the optimal box is a cube. A graph of the volume function is shown in Figure 4.54. *Related Exercises 15–17*◄

QUICK CHECK 3 Find the objective function in Example 2 (in terms of w) if the constraint is that the sum of length and width and height cannot exceed 108 in. ◄

Optimization Guidelines With two examples providing some insight, we present a procedure for solving optimization problems. These guidelines provide a general framework, but the details may vary depending upon the problem.

Guidelines for Optimization Problems

1. Read the problem carefully, identify the variables, and organize the given information with a picture.

2. Identify the objective function (the function to be optimized). Write it in terms of the variables of the problem.

3. Identify the constraint(s). Write them in terms of the variables of the problem.

4. Use the constraint(s) to eliminate all but one independent variable of the objective function.

5. With the objective function expressed in terms of a single variable, find the interval of interest for that variable.

6. Use methods of calculus to find the absolute maximum or minimum value of the objective function on the interval of interest. If necessary, check the endpoints.

EXAMPLE 3 Walking and swimming Suppose you are standing on the shore of a circular pond with a radius of 1 mile and you want to get to a point on the shore directly opposite your position (on the other end of a diameter). You plan to swim at 2 mi/hr from your current position to another point P on the shore and then walk at 3 mi/hr along the shore to the terminal point (Figure 4.55). How should you choose P to minimize the total time for the trip?

SOLUTION As shown in Figure 4.55, the initial point is chosen arbitrarily, and the terminal point is at the other end of a diameter. The easiest way to describe the transition point P is to refer to the central angle θ. If $\theta = 0$, then the entire trip is done by walking; if $\theta = \pi$, the entire trip is done by swimming. So the interval of interest is $0 \leq \theta \leq \pi$.

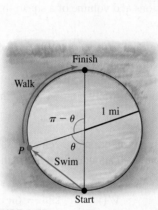

FIGURE 4.55

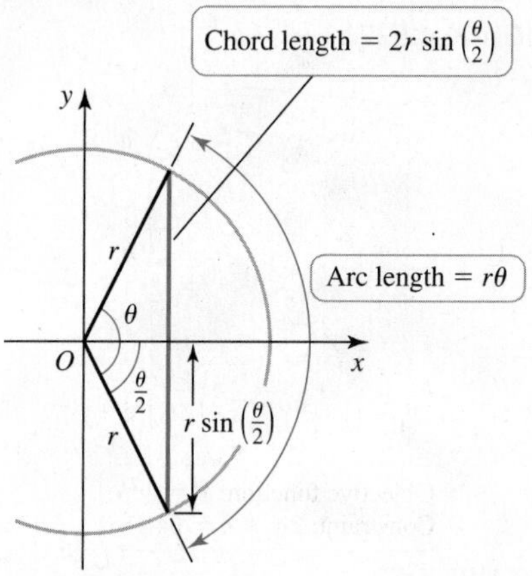

FIGURE 4.56

The objective function is the total travel time as it varies with θ. For each leg of the trip (swim and walk), the travel time is the distance traveled divided by the speed. We need a few facts from circular geometry. The length of the swimming leg is the length of the chord of the circle corresponding to the angle θ. For a circle of radius r, this chord length is given by $2r \sin (\theta/2)$ (Figure 4.56). So the time for the swimming leg (with $r = 1$ and a speed of 2 mi/hr) is

$$\text{time} = \frac{\text{distance}}{\text{rate}} = \frac{2 \sin (\theta/2)}{2} = \sin \frac{\theta}{2}.$$

> To show that the chord length of a circle is $2r \sin (\theta/2)$, draw a line from the center of the circle to the midpoint of the chord. This line bisects the angle θ. Using a right triangle, half the length of the chord is $r \sin (\theta/2)$.

The length of the walking leg is the length of the arc of the circle corresponding to the angle $\pi - \theta$. For a circle of radius r, the arc length corresponding to an angle θ is $r\theta$ (Figure 4.56). Therefore, the time for the walking leg (with an angle $\pi - \theta$, $r = 1$, and a speed of 3 mi/hr) is

$$\text{time} = \frac{\text{distance}}{\text{rate}} = \frac{\pi - \theta}{3}.$$

The total travel time for the trip (in hours) is the objective function

$$T(\theta) = \sin \frac{\theta}{2} + \frac{\pi - \theta}{3}, \quad \text{for} \quad 0 \leq \theta \leq \pi.$$

We now analyze the objective function. The critical points of T satisfy

$$\frac{dT}{d\theta} = \frac{1}{2} \cos \frac{\theta}{2} - \frac{1}{3} = 0 \quad \text{or} \quad \cos \frac{\theta}{2} = \frac{2}{3}.$$

> You can check two special cases: If the entire trip is done walking, the travel time is $(\pi \text{ mi})/(3 \text{ mi/hr}) \approx 1.05$ hr. If the entire trip is done swimming, the travel time is $(2 \text{ mi})/(2 \text{ mi/hr}) = 1$ hr.

Using a calculator, the only solution in the interval $[0, \pi]$ is $\theta = 2 \cos^{-1} \left(\frac{2}{3}\right) \approx 1.682$ rad $\approx 96.379°$, which is the critical point.

Evaluating the objective function at the critical point and at the endpoints, we find that $T(1.682) \approx 1.232$ hr, $T(0) = \pi/3 \approx 1.047$ hr, and $T(\pi) = 1$ hr. We conclude that the minimum travel time is $T(\pi) = 1$ hr when the entire trip is done swimming. The *maximum* travel time, corresponding to $\theta \approx 96.379°$, is $T \approx 1.232$ hr.

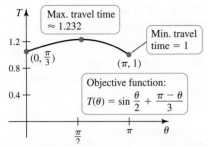

FIGURE 4.57

The objective function is shown in Figure 4.57. In general, the maximum and minimum travel times depend on the walking and swimming speeds (Exercise 18).

Related Exercises 18–21 ◄

EXAMPLE 4   **Ladder over the fence**   An 8-foot-tall fence runs parallel to the side of a house 3 feet away (Figure 4.58a). What is the length of the shortest ladder that clears the fence and reaches the house? Assume that the vertical wall of the house and the horizontal ground have infinite extent (see Exercise 23 for more realistic assumptions).

SOLUTION   Let's first ask why we expect a minimum ladder length. You could put the foot of the ladder far from the fence, making it clear the fence at a shallow angle; but the ladder would be very long. Or you could put the foot of the ladder close to the fence, making it clear the fence at a steep angle; but again, the ladder would be long. Somewhere between these extremes, there is a ladder position that minimizes the ladder length.

The objective function in this problem is the ladder length L. The position of the ladder is specified by x, the distance between the foot of the ladder and the fence (Figure 4.58b). The goal is to express L as a function of x, where $x > 0$.

The Pythagorean theorem gives the relationship

$$L^2 = (x + 3)^2 + b^2,$$

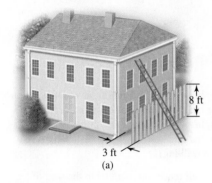

(a)

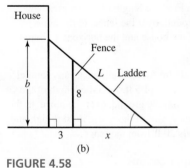

(b)

FIGURE 4.58

where b is the height of the top of the ladder above the ground. Similar triangles give the constraint $8/x = b/(3 + x)$. We now solve the constraint equation for b and substitute to express L^2 in terms of x:

$$L^2 = (x + 3)^2 + \underbrace{\left(\frac{8(x + 3)}{x}\right)^2}_{b} = (x + 3)^2\left(1 + \frac{64}{x^2}\right).$$

At this juncture, we could find the critical points of L by first solving the preceding equation for L, and then solving $L' = 0$. However, the solution is simplified considerably if we note that L is a nonnegative function. Therefore, L and L^2 have local extrema at the same points; so we choose to minimize L^2. The derivative of L^2 is

$$\frac{d}{dx}\left[(x + 3)^2\left(1 + \frac{64}{x^2}\right)\right] = 2(x + 3)\left(1 + \frac{64}{x^2}\right) + (x + 3)^2\left(-\frac{128}{x^3}\right) \quad \text{Chain Rule and Product Rule}$$

$$= \frac{2(x + 3)(x^3 - 192)}{x^3}. \quad \text{Simplify.}$$

Because $x > 0$, we have $x + 3 \neq 0$; therefore, the condition $\dfrac{d}{dx}(L^2) = 0$ becomes $x^3 - 192 = 0$, or $x = 4\sqrt[3]{3} \approx 5.769$. By the First Derivative Test, this critical point corresponds to a local minimum. By Theorem 4.5, this solitary local minimum is also the absolute minimum on the interval $(0, \infty)$. Therefore, the minimum ladder length occurs when the foot of the ladder is approximately 5.769 ft from the fence. We find that $L^2(5.769) \approx 224.765$ and the minimum ladder length is $\sqrt{224.765} \approx 15$ ft.

Related Exercises 22–23 ◄

SECTION 4.4 EXERCISES

Review Questions

1. Fill in the blanks: The goal of an optimization problem is to find the maximum or minimum value of the _____ function subject to the _____ .

2. If the objective function involves more than one independent variable, how are the extra variables eliminated?

3. Suppose the objective function is $Q = x^2y$ and you know that $x + y = 10$. Write the objective function first in terms of x and then in terms of y.

4. Suppose you wish to minimize a continuous objective function on a closed interval, but you find that it has only a single local maximum. Where should you look for the solution to the problem?

Basic Skills

5. **Maximum area rectangles** Of all rectangles with a perimeter of 10, which one has the maximum area? (Give the dimensions.)

6. **Maximum area rectangles** Of all rectangles with a fixed perimeter of P, which one has the maximum area? (Give the dimensions in terms of P.)

7. **Minimum perimeter rectangles** Of all rectangles of area 100, which one has the minimum perimeter?

8. **Minimum perimeter rectangles** Of all rectangles with a fixed area A, which one has the minimum perimeter? (Give the dimensions in terms of A.)

9. **Maximum product** What two nonnegative real numbers with a sum of 23 have the largest possible product?

10. **Sum of squares** What two nonnegative real numbers a and b whose sum is 23 maximize $a^2 + b^2$? Minimize $a^2 + b^2$?

11. **Minimum sum** What two positive real numbers whose product is 50 have the smallest possible sum?

12. **Maximum product** Find numbers x and y satisfying the equation $3x + y = 12$ such that the product of x and y is as large as possible.

13. **Minimum sum** Find positive numbers x and y satisfying the equation $xy = 12$ such that the sum $2x + y$ is as small as possible.

14. **Pen problems**

    a. A rectangular pen is built with one side against a barn. Two hundred meters of fencing are used for the other three sides of the pen. What dimensions maximize the area of the pen?

    b. A rancher plans to make four identical and adjacent rectangular pens against a barn, each with an area of 100 m² (see figure). What are the dimensions of each pen that minimize the amount of fence that must be used?

Barn			
100	100	100	100

15. **Minimum-surface-area box** Of all boxes with a square base and a volume of 100 m³, which one has the minimum surface area? (Give its dimensions.)

16. **Maximum-volume box** Suppose an airline policy states that all baggage must be box-shaped with a sum of length, width, and height not exceeding 108 in. What are the dimensions and volume of a square-based box with the greatest volume under these conditions?

17. **Shipping crates** A square-based, box-shaped shipping crate is designed to have a volume of 16 ft³. The material used to make the base costs twice as much (per square foot) as the material in the sides, and the material used to make the top costs half as much (per square foot) as the material in the sides. What are the dimensions of the crate that minimize the cost of materials?

18. **Walking and swimming** A man wishes to get from an initial point on the shore of a circular lake with radius 1 mi to a point on the shore directly opposite (on the other end of the diameter). He plans to swim from the initial point to another point on the shore and then walk along the shore to the terminal point.

    a. If he swims at 2 mi/hr and walks at 4 mi/hr, what are the minimum and maximum times for the trip?

    b. If he swims at 2 mi/hr and walks at 1.5 mi/hr, what are the minimum and maximum times for the trip?

    c. If he swims at 2 mi/hr, what is the minimum walking speed for which it is quickest to walk the entire distance?

19. **Minimum distance** Find the point P on the line $y = 3x$ that is closest to the point $(50, 0)$. What is the least distance between P and $(50, 0)$?

20. **Minimum distance** Find the point P on the curve $y = x^2$ that is closet to the point $(18, 0)$. What is the least distance between P and $(18, 0)$?

21. **Walking and rowing** A boat on the ocean is 4 mi from the nearest point on a straight shoreline; that point is 6 mi from a restaurant on the shore. A woman plans to row the boat straight to a point on the shore and then walk along the shore to the restaurant.

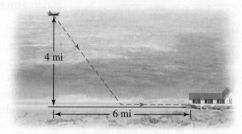

    a. If she walks at 3 mi/hr and rows at 2 mi/hr, at which point on the shore should she land to minimize the total travel time?

    b. If she walks at 3 mi/hr, what is the minimum speed at which she must row so that the quickest way to the restaurant is to row directly (with no walking)?

22. **Shortest ladder** A 10-ft-tall fence runs parallel to the wall of a house at a distance of 4 ft. Find the length of the shortest ladder that extends from the ground, over the fence, to the house. Assume the vertical wall of the house and the horizontal ground have infinite extent.

23. **Shortest ladder—more realistic** An 8-ft-tall fence runs parallel to the wall of a house at a distance of 5 ft. Find the length of the shortest ladder that extends from the ground, over the fence, to the house. Assume that the vertical wall of the house is 20 ft high and the horizontal ground extends 20 ft from the fence.

Further Explorations and Applications

24. **Rectangles beneath a parabola** A rectangle is constructed with its base on the x-axis and two of its vertices on the parabola $y = 16 - x^2$. What are the dimensions of the rectangle with the maximum area? What is that area?

25. **Rectangles beneath a semicircle** A rectangle is constructed with its base on the diameter of a semicircle with radius 5 and with its two other vertices on the semicircle. What are the dimensions of the rectangle with maximum area?

26. **Circle and square** A piece of wire of length 60 is cut, and the resulting two pieces are formed to make a circle and a square. Where should the wire be cut to (a) minimize and (b) maximize the combined area of the circle and the square?

27. **Maximum-volume cone** A cone is constructed by cutting a sector from a circular sheet of metal with radius 20. The cut sheet is then folded up and welded (see figure). Find the radius and height of the cone with maximum volume that can be formed in this way.

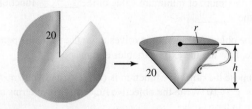

28. Covering a marble Imagine a flat-bottomed cylindrical pot with a circular cross section of radius 4. A marble with radius $0 < r < 4$ is placed in the bottom of the pot. What is the radius of the marble that requires the most water to cover it completely?

29. Optimal garden A rectangular flower garden with an area of 30 m^2 is surrounded by a grass border 1 m wide on two sides and 2 m wide on the other two sides (see figure). What dimensions of the garden minimize the combined area of the garden and borders?

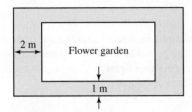

30. Rectangles beneath a line

a. A rectangle is constructed with one side on the positive x-axis, one side on the positive y-axis, and the vertex opposite the origin on the line $y = 10 - 2x$. What dimensions maximize the area of the rectangle? What is the maximum area?

b. Is it possible to construct a rectangle with a greater area than that found in part (a) by placing one side of the rectangle on the line $y = 10 - 2x$ and the two vertices not on that line on the positive x- and y-axes? Find the dimensions of the rectangle of maximum area that can be constructed in this way.

31. Kepler's wine barrel Several mathematical stories originated with the second wedding of the mathematician and astronomer Johannes Kepler. Here is one: While shopping for wine for his wedding, Kepler noticed that the price of a barrel of wine (here assumed to be a cylinder) was determined solely by the length d of a dipstick that was inserted diagonally through a centered hole in the top of the barrel to the edge of the base of the barrel (see figure). Kepler realized that this measurement does not determine the volume of the barrel and that for a fixed value of d, the volume varies with the radius r and height h of the barrel. For a fixed value of d, what is the ratio r/h that maximizes the volume of the barrel?

32. Folded boxes

a. Squares with sides of length x are cut out of each corner of a rectangular piece of cardboard measuring 3 ft by 4 ft. The resulting piece of cardboard is then folded into a box without a lid. Find the volume of the largest box that can be formed in this way.

b. Suppose that in part (a) the original piece of cardboard is a square with sides of length ℓ. Find the volume of the largest box that can be formed in this way.

c. Suppose that in part (a) the original piece of cardboard is a rectangle with sides of length ℓ and L. Holding ℓ fixed, find the size of the corner squares x that maximizes the volume of the box as $L \to \infty$. (*Source: Mathematics Teacher,* Nov 2002)

33. Making silos A grain silo consists of a cylindrical concrete tower surmounted by a metal hemispherical dome. The metal in the dome costs 1.5 times as much as the concrete (per unit of surface area). If the volume of the silo is 750 m^3, what are the dimensions of the silo (radius and height of the cylindrical tower) that minimize the cost of the materials? Assume the silo has no floor and no flat ceiling under the dome.

34. Suspension system A load must be suspended 6 m below a high ceiling using cables attached to two supports that are 2 m apart (see figure). How far below the ceiling (x in the figure) should the cables be joined to minimize the total length of cable used?

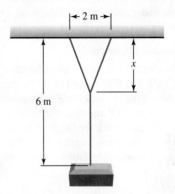

35. Light sources The intensity of a light source at a distance is directly proportional to the strength of the source and inversely proportional to the square of the distance from the source. Two light sources, one twice as strong as the other, are 12 m apart. At what point on the line segment joining the sources is the intensity the weakest?

36. Crease-length problem A rectangular sheet of paper of width a and length b, where $0 < a < b$, is folded by taking one corner of the sheet and placing it at a point P on the opposite long side of the sheet (see figure). The fold is then flattened to form a crease across the sheet. Assuming that the fold is made so that there is no flap extending beyond the original sheet, find the point P that produces the crease of minimum length. What is the length of that crease?

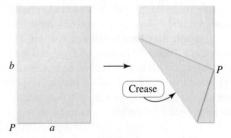

37. Laying cable An island is 3.5 mi from the nearest point on a straight shoreline; that point is 8 mi from a power station (see figure). A utility company plans to lay electrical cable underwater from the island to the shore and then underground along the shore to the power station. Assume that it costs $2400/mi to lay underwater cable and $1200/mi to lay underground cable. At what point should the underwater cable meet the shore in order to minimize the cost of the project?

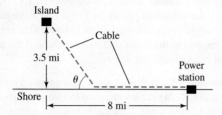

38. Laying cable again Solve the problem in Exercise 37, but this time minimize the cost with respect to the smaller angle θ between the underwater cable and the shore. (You should get the same answer.)

39. Sum of isosceles distances

a. An isosceles triangle has a base of length 4 and two sides of length $2\sqrt{2}$. Let P be a point on the perpendicular bisector of the base. Find the location P that minimizes the sum of the distances between P and the three vertices.

b. Assume in part (a) that the height of the isosceles triangle is $h > 0$ and its base has length 4. Show that the location of P that gives a minimum solution is independent of h for

$$h \geq \frac{2}{\sqrt{3}}.$$

40. Circle in a triangle What are the radius and area of the circle of maximum area that can be inscribed in an isosceles triangle whose two equal sides have length 1?

41. Slant height and cones Among all right circular cones with a slant height of 3, what are the dimensions (radius and height) that maximize the volume of the cone? The slant height of a cone is the distance from the outer edge of the base to the vertex.

⊤ 42. Blood testing Suppose that a blood test for a disease must be given to a population of N people, where N is large. At most, N individual blood tests must be done. The following strategy reduces the number of tests. Suppose 100 people are selected from the population and their blood samples are pooled. One test determines whether any of the 100 people test positive. If the test is positive, those 100 people are tested individually, making 101 tests necessary. However, if the pooled sample tests negative, then 100 people have been tested with one test. This procedure is then repeated. Probability theory shows that if the group size is x (for example, $x = 100$, as described here), then the average number of blood tests required to test N people is $N(1 - q^x + 1/x)$, where q is the probability that any one person tests negative. What group size x minimizes the average number of tests in the case that $N = 10,000$ and $q = 0.95$? Assume that x is a nonnegative real number.

43. Crankshaft A crank of radius r rotates with an angular frequency ω. It is connected to a piston by a connecting rod of length L (see figure). The acceleration of the piston varies with the position of the crank according to the function

$$a(\theta) = \omega^2 r\left(\cos \theta + \frac{r \cos 2\theta}{L}\right).$$

For fixed ω and r, find the values of θ, with $0 \leq \theta \leq 2\pi$, for which the acceleration of the piston is a maximum and minimum.

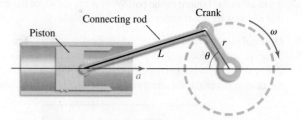

44. Metal rain gutters A rain gutter is made from sheets of metal 9 in wide. The gutters have a 3-in base and two 3-in sides, folded up at an angle θ (see figure). What angle θ maximizes the cross-sectional area of the gutter?

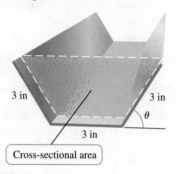

3 in   3 in

3 in

Cross-sectional area

45. Optimal soda can

a. **Classical problem** Find the radius and height of a cylindrical soda can with a volume of 354 cm³ that minimize the surface area.

b. **Real problem** Compare your answer in part (a) to a real soda can, which has a volume of 354 cm³, a radius of 3.1 cm, and a height of 12.0 cm, to conclude that real soda cans do not seem to have an optimal design. Then use the fact that real soda cans have a double thickness in their top and bottom surfaces to find the radius and height that minimizes the surface area of a real can (the surface areas of the top and bottom are now twice their values in part (a)). Are these dimensions closer to the dimensions of a real soda can?

46. Cylinder and cones (Putnam Exam 1938) Right circular cones of height h and radius r are attached to each end of a right circular cylinder of height h and radius r, forming a double-pointed object. For a given surface area A, what are the dimensions r and h that maximize the volume of the object?

47. Viewing angles An auditorium with a flat floor has a large screen on one wall. The lower edge of the screen is 3 ft above eye level, and the upper edge of the screen is 10 ft above eye level (see figure). How far from the screen should you stand to maximize your viewing angle?

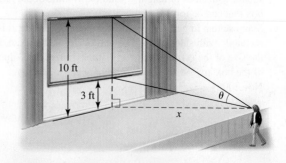

10 ft

3 ft

x

48. Searchlight problem—narrow beam A searchlight is 100 m from the nearest point on a straight highway (see figure). As it rotates, the searchlight casts a horizontal beam that intersects the highway in a point. If the light revolves at a rate of $\pi/6$ rad/s, find the rate at which the beam sweeps along the highway as a function of θ. For what value of θ is this rate maximized?

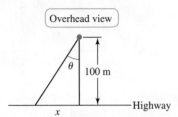

Overhead view

θ 100 m

x Highway

49. Watching a Ferris wheel An observer stands 20 m from the bottom of a Ferris wheel on a line that is perpendicular to the face of the wheel, with her eyes at the level of the bottom of the wheel. The wheel revolves at a rate of π rad/min, and the observer's line of sight with a specific seat on the Ferris wheel makes an angle θ with the horizontal (see figure). At what time during a full revolution is θ changing most rapidly?

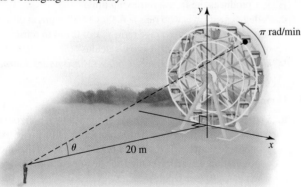

y

π rad/min

θ 20 m x

50. Maximum angle Find the value of x that maximizes θ in the figure.

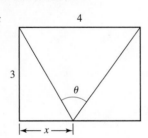

4

3

θ

x

51. Maximum-volume cylinder in a sphere Find the dimensions of the right circular cylinder of maximum volume that can be placed inside of a sphere of radius R.

52. Rectangles in triangles Find the dimensions and area of the rectangle of maximum area that can be inscribed in the following figures.

  a. A right triangle with a given hypotenuse length L
  b. An equilateral triangle with a given side length L
  c. A right triangle with a given area A
  d. An arbitrary triangle with a given area A (The result applies to any triangle, but first consider triangles for which all the angles are less than or equal to 90°.)

53. Cylinder in a cone A right circular cylinder is placed inside a cone of radius R and height H so that the base of the cylinder lies on the base of the cone.

  a. Find the dimensions of the cylinder with maximum volume. Specifically, show that the volume of the maximum-volume cylinder is $\frac{4}{9}$ the volume of the cone.
  b. Find the dimensions of the cylinder with maximum lateral surface area (area of the curved surface).

54. Maximizing profit Suppose you own a tour bus and you book groups of 20 to 70 people for a day tour. The cost per person is $30 minus $0.25 for every ticket sold. If gas and other miscellaneous costs are $200, how many tickets should you sell to maximize your profit? Treat the number of tickets as a nonnegative real number.

55. Cone in a cone A right circular cone is inscribed inside a larger right circular cone with a volume of 150 cm³. The axes of the cones coincide and the vertex of the inner cone touches the center of the base of the outer cone. Find the ratio of the heights of the cones that maximizes the volume of the inner cone.

56. Another pen problem A rancher is building a horse pen on the corner of her property using 1000 ft of fencing. Because of the unusual shape of her property, the pen must be built in the shape of a trapezoid (see figure).

  a. Determine the lengths of the sides that maximize the area of the pen.
  b. Suppose there is already a fence along the side of the property opposite the side of length y. Find the lengths of the sides that maximize the area of the pen, using 1000 ft of fencing.

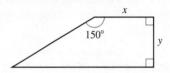

x

150°

y

57. Minimum-length roads A house is located at each corner of a square with side lengths of 1 mi. What is the length of the shortest road system with straight roads that connects all of the houses by roads (that is, a road system that allows one to drive from any house to any other house)? (*Hint:* Place two points inside the square at which roads meet.) (*Source: Problems for Mathematicians Young and Old,* Paul Halmos, MAA, 1991.)

58. Light transmission A window consists of a rectangular pane of clear glass surmounted by a semicircular pane of tinted glass. The clear glass transmits twice as much light per unit of surface area as the tinted glass. Of all such windows with a fixed perimeter P, what are the dimensions of the window that transmits the most light?

59. Slowest shortcut Suppose you are standing in a field near a straight section of railroad tracks just as the locomotive of a train passes the point nearest to you, which is $\frac{1}{4}$ mi away. The train, with length $\frac{1}{3}$ mi, is traveling at 20 mi/hr. If you start running in a straight line across the field, how slowly can you run and still catch the train? In which direction should you run?

60. The arbelos An arbelos is the region enclosed by three mutually tangent semicircles; it is the region inside the larger semicircle and outside the two smaller semicircles (see figure).

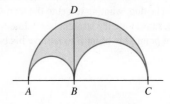

D

A B C

a. Given an arbelos in which the diameter of the largest circle is 1, what positions of point B maximize the area of the arbelos?

b. Show that the area of the arbelos is the area of a circle whose diameter is the distance BD in the figure.

61. Proximity questions

a. What point on the line $y = 3x + 4$ is closest to the origin?

b. What point on the parabola $y = 1 - x^2$ is closest to the point $(1, 1)$?

c. Find the point on the graph of $y = \sqrt{x}$ that is nearest the point $(p, 0)$ if (i) $p > \frac{1}{2}$; and (ii) $0 < p < \frac{1}{2}$. Express the answer in terms of p.

62. Turning a corner with a pole

a. What is the length of the longest pole that can be carried horizontally around a corner at which a 3-ft corridor and a 4-ft corridor meet at right angles?

b. What is the length of the longest pole that can be carried horizontally around a corner at which a corridor that is a feet wide and a corridor that is b feet wide meet at right angles?

c. What is the length of the longest pole that can be carried horizontally around a corner at which a corridor that is $a = 5$ ft wide and a corridor that is $b = 5$ ft wide meet at an angle of 120°?

d. What is the length of the longest pole that can be carried around a corner at which a corridor that is a feet wide and a corridor that is b feet wide meet at right angles, assuming there is an 8-foot ceiling and that you may tilt the pole at any angle?

63. Travel costs A simple model for travel costs involves the cost of gasoline and the cost of a driver. Specifically, assume that gasoline costs $\$\,p$/gallon and the vehicle gets g miles per gallon. Also, assume that the driver earns $\$\,w$/hour.

a. A plausible function to describe how gas mileage (in mi/gal) varies with speed is $g(v) = v(85 - v)/60$. Evaluate $g(0)$, $g(40)$, and $g(60)$, and explain why these values are reasonable.

b. At what speed does the gas mileage function have its maximum?

c. Explain why the cost of a trip of length L miles is $C(v) = Lp/g(v) + Lw/v$.

d. Let $L = 400$ mi, $p = \$4$/gal, and $w = \$20$/hr. At what (constant) speed should the vehicle be driven to minimize the cost of the trip?

e. Should the optimal speed be increased or decreased (compared with part (d)) if L is increased from 400 mi to 500 mi? Explain.

f. Should the optimal speed be increased or decreased (compared with part (d)) if p is increased from $\$4$/gal to $\$4.20$/gal? Explain.

g. Should the optimal speed be increased or decreased (compared with part (d)) if w is decreased from $\$20$/hr to $\$15$/hr? Explain.

64. Do dogs know calculus? A mathematician stands on a beach with his dog at point A. He throws a tennis ball so that it hits the water at point B. The dog, wanting to get to the tennis ball as quickly as possible, runs along the straight beach line to point D and then swims from point D to point B to retrieve his ball. Assume C is the point on the edge of the beach closest to the tennis ball (see figure).

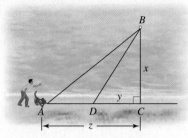

a. Assume the dog runs at speed r and swims at speed s, where $r > s$ and both are measured in meters/second. Also assume the lengths of BC, CD, and AC are x, y, and z, respectively. Find a function $T(y)$ representing the total time it takes for the dog to get to the ball.

b. Verify that the value of y that minimizes the time it takes to retrieve the ball is $y = \dfrac{x}{\sqrt{r/s + 1}\sqrt{r/s - 1}}$.

c. If the dog runs at 8 m/s and swims at 1 m/s, what ratio y/x produces the fastest retrieving time?

d. A dog named Elvis who runs at 6.4 m/s and swims at 0.910 m/s was found to use an average ratio y/x of 0.144 to retrieve his ball. Does Elvis appear to know calculus? (*Source: Do Dogs know Calculus?* T. Pennings, *College Mathematics Journal*, 34, 3, May 2003)

65. Fermat's Principle

a. Two poles of heights m and n are separated by a horizontal distance d. A rope is stretched from the top of one pole to the ground and then to the top of the other pole. Show that the configuration that requires the least amount of rope occurs when $\theta_1 = \theta_2$ (see figure).

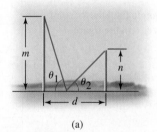

(a)

b. Fermat's Principle states that when light travels between two points in the same medium (at a constant speed), it travels on the path that minimizes the travel time. Show that when light from a source A reflects off of a surface and is received at point B, the angle of incidence equals the angle of reflection, or $\theta_1 = \theta_2$ (see figure).

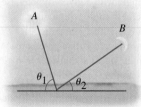

(b)

66. Snell's Law Suppose that a light source at A is in a medium in which light travels at speed v_1 and the point B is in a medium in which light travels at speed v_2 (see figure). Using Fermat's Principle, which states that light travels along the path that requires the minimum travel time (Exercise 65), show that the path taken between points A and B satisfies $(\sin \theta_1)/v_1 = (\sin \theta_2)/v_2$.

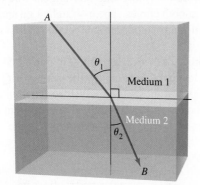

67. Tree notch (Putnam Exam 1938, rephrased) A notch is cut in a cylindrical vertical tree trunk. The notch penetrates to the axis of the cylinder and is bounded by two half-planes that intersect on a diameter D of the tree. The angle between the two half planes is θ. Prove that for a given tree and fixed angle θ, the volume of the notch is minimized by taking the bounding planes at equal angles to the horizontal plane that also passes through D.

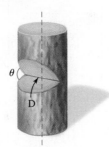

68. Gliding mammals Many species of small mammals (such as flying squirrels and marsupial gliders) have the ability to walk and glide. Recent research suggests that these animals choose the most energy-efficient means of travel. According to one empirical model, the energy required for a glider with body mass m to walk a horizontal distance D is $8.46\ Dm^{2/3}$ (where m is measured in grams, D is measured in meters, and energy is measured in microliters of oxygen consumed in respiration). The energy cost of climbing to a height $D \tan \theta$ and gliding a horizontal distance D at an angle θ is modeled by $1.36\ m D \tan \theta$ (where $\theta = 0$ represents horizontal flight and $\theta > 45°$ represents controlled falling). Therefore, the function

$$S(m, \theta) = 8.46m^{2/3} - 1.36m \tan \theta$$

gives the energy difference per horizontal meter traveled between walking and gliding: If $S > 0$ for given values of m and θ, then it is more costly to walk than glide.

a. For what glide angles is it more efficient for a 200-gram animal to glide rather that walk?

b. Find the threshold function $\theta = g(m)$ that gives the curve along which walking and gliding are equally efficient. Is it an increasing or decreasing function of body mass?

c. In order to make gliding more efficient than walking, do larger gliders have a larger or smaller selection of glide angles than smaller gliders?

d. Let $\theta = 25°$ (a typical glide angle). Graph S as a function of m, for $0 \le m \le 3000$. For what values of m is gliding more efficient?

e. For $\theta = 25°$, what value of m (call it m^*) maximizes S?

f. Does m^*, as defined in part (e), increase or decrease with increasing θ? That is, as a glider reduces its glide angle, does its optimal size become larger or smaller?

g. Assuming Dumbo is a gliding elephant whose weight is 1 metric ton (10^6 g), what glide angle would Dumbo use to be more efficient at gliding than walking?

(*Source: Energetic savings and the body size distribution of gliding mammals*, Roman Dial, *Evolutionary Ecology Research* **5** (2003): 1151–1162)

69. A challenging pen problem Two triangular pens are built against a barn. Two hundred meters of fencing are to be used for the three sides and the diagonal dividing fence (see figure). What dimensions maximize the area of the pen?

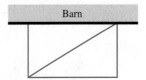

70. Minimizing related functions Find the values of x that minimize each function.

a. $f(x) = (x - 1)^2 + (x - 5)^2$

b. $f(x) = (x - a)^2 + (x - b)^2$, for constants a and b

c. $f(x) = \sum_{k=1}^{n}(x - a_k)^2$, for a positive integer n and constants $a_1, a_2, \ldots, a_n$.

(*Source: Calculus*, Vol. 1, Tom M. Apostol, John Wiley and Sons, 1967)

QUICK CHECK   ANSWERS

2. (i) $A = 400x - 2x^2$, (ii) $A = 400x - 3x^2$
3. $V = 108w^2 - 2w^3$ ◄

4.5 Linear Approximation and Differentials

Imagine plotting a smooth curve with a graphing utility. Now pick a point P on the curve, draw the line tangent to the curve at P, and zoom in on it several times. As you successively enlarge the curve near P, it looks more and more like the tangent line (Figure 4.59a). This fundamental observation—that smooth curves appear straighter on smaller scales—is called *local linearity*; it is the basis of many important mathematical ideas, one of which is *linear approximation*.

Now consider a curve with a corner or cusp at a point Q (Figure 4.59b). No amount of magnification "straightens out" the curve or removes the corner at Q. The different behavior at P and Q is related to the idea of differentiability: The function in Figure 4.59a is differentiable at P, whereas the function in Figure 4.59b is not differentiable at Q. One of the requirements for the techniques presented in this section is that the function be differentiable at the point in question.

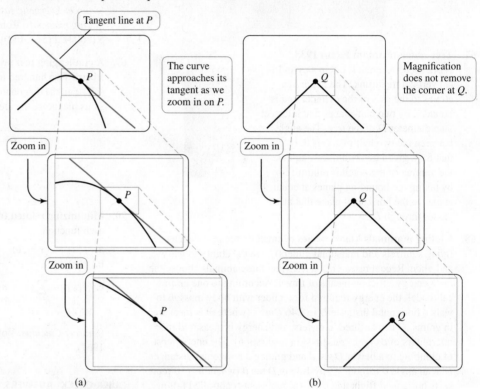

FIGURE 4.59   (a)   (b)

Linear Approximation

Figure 4.59a suggests that when we zoom in on the graph of a smooth function at a point P, the curve approaches its tangent line at P. This fact is the key to understanding linear approximation. The idea is to use the line tangent to the curve at P to approximate the value of the function at points near P. Here's how it works.

Assume f is differentiable on an interval containing the point a. The slope of the line tangent to the curve at the point $(a, f(a))$ is $f'(a)$. Therefore, an equation of the tangent line is

$$y - f(a) = f'(a)(x - a) \quad \text{or} \quad y = \underbrace{f(a) + f'(a)(x - a)}_{L(x)}.$$

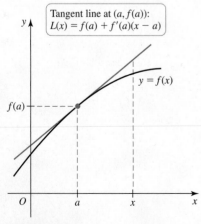

FIGURE 4.60

This tangent line represents a new function L that we call the *linear approximation* to f at the point a (Figure 4.60). If f and f' are easy to evaluate at a, then the value of f at points near a is easily approximated using the linear approximation L. That is,

$$f(x) \approx L(x) = f(a) + f'(a)(x - a).$$

This approximation improves as x approaches a.

> **DEFINITION Linear Approximation to f at a**
>
> Suppose f is differentiable on an interval I containing the point a. The **linear approximation** to f at a is the linear function
> $$L(x) = f(a) + f'(a)(x - a), \quad \text{for } x \text{ in } I.$$

QUICK CHECK 1 Sketch the graph of a function f that is concave up on an interval containing the point a. Sketch the linear approximation to f at a. Is the graph of the linear approximation above or below the graph of f? ◄

EXAMPLE 1   Useful driving math Suppose you are driving along a highway at a nearly constant speed and you record the number of seconds it takes to travel between two consecutive mile markers. If it takes 60 seconds to travel one mile, then your average speed is 1 mi/60 s or 60 mi/hr. Now suppose that you travel one mile in $60 + x$ seconds; for example, if it takes 62 seconds, then $x = 2$, and if it takes 57 seconds, then $x = -3$. The function

$$s(x) = \frac{3600}{60 + x} = 3600(60 + x)^{-1}$$

gives your average speed in mi/hr if you travel one mile in x seconds more or less than 60 seconds (Exercise 59). For example, if you travel one mile in 62 seconds then $x = 2$ and your average speed is $s(2) \approx 58.065$ mi/hr. If you travel one mile in 57 seconds, then $x = -3$ and your average speed is $s(-3) \approx 63.158$ mi/hr. Because you don't want to use a calculator while driving, you need an easy approximation to this function. Use linear approximation to derive such a formula.

SOLUTION The idea is to find the linear approximation to s at the point 0. We first use the Chain Rule to compute

$$s'(x) = -3600(60 + x)^{-2}$$

and then note that $s(0) = 60$ and $s'(0) = -3600 \cdot 60^{-2} = -1$. Using the linear approximation formula, we find that

$$s(x) \approx L(x) = s(0) + s'(0)(x - 0) = 60 - x.$$

For example, if you travel one mile in 62 seconds, then $x = 2$ and your average speed is approximately $L(2) = 58$ mi/hr, which is very close to the exact value given previously. If you travel one mile in 57 seconds, then $x = -3$ and your average speed is approximately $L(-3) = 63$ mi/hr, which again is close to the exact value.

Related Exercises 7–12 ◄

QUICK CHECK 2 In Example 1, suppose you travel one mile in 75 seconds. What is the average speed given by the linear approximation formula? What is the exact average speed? Explain the discrepancy between the two values. ◄

EXAMPLE 2   Linear approximations and errors

a. Find the linear approximation to $f(x) = \sqrt{x}$ at $x = 1$ and use it to approximate $\sqrt{1.1}$.

b. Use linear approximation to estimate the value of $\sqrt{0.1}$.

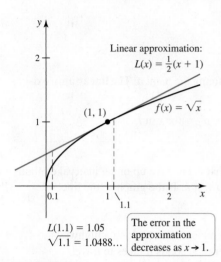

$L(1.1) = 1.05$
$\sqrt{1.1} = 1.0488\ldots$

The error in the approximation decreases as $x \to 1$.

FIGURE 4.61

Table 4.4

x	$L(x)$	Exact $\sqrt{x}$	Error
1.2	1.1	1.0954...	4.6×10^{-3}
1.1	1.05	1.0488...	1.2×10^{-3}
1.01	1.005	1.0049...	1.2×10^{-5}
1.001	1.0005	1.0005...	1.2×10^{-7}

➤ We choose $a = \frac{9}{100}$ because it is close to 0.1 and its square root is easy to evaluate.

SOLUTION

a. We construct the linear approximation

$$L(x) = f(a) + f'(a)(x - a),$$

where $f(x) = \sqrt{x}, f'(x) = 1/(2\sqrt{x})$, and $a = 1$. Noting that $f(a) = f(1) = 1$ and $f'(a) = f'(1) = \frac{1}{2}$, we have

$$L(x) = 1 + \frac{1}{2}(x - 1) = \frac{1}{2}(x + 1),$$

which is an equation of the line tangent to the curve at the point $(1, 1)$ (Figure 4.61). Because $x = 1.1$ is near $x = 1$, we approximate $\sqrt{1.1}$ by $L(1.1)$:

$$\sqrt{1.1} \approx L(1.1) = \frac{1}{2}(1.1 + 1) = 1.05.$$

The exact value is $f(1.1) = \sqrt{1.1} = 1.0488\ldots$; therefore, the linear approximation has an error of about 0.0012. Furthermore, our approximation is an *overestimate* because the tangent line lies above the graph of f. In Table 4.4, we see several approximations to $\sqrt{x}$ for x near 1 and the associated errors $|L(x) - \sqrt{x}|$. Clearly, the errors decrease as x approaches 1.

b. If the linear approximation $L(x) = \frac{1}{2}(x + 1)$ obtained in part (a) is used to approximate $\sqrt{0.1}$, we have

$$\sqrt{0.1} \approx L(0.1) = \frac{1}{2}(0.1 + 1) = 0.55.$$

A calculator gives $\sqrt{0.1} = 0.3162\ldots$, which shows that the approximation is well off the mark. The error arises because the tangent line through $(1, 1)$ is not close to the curve at $x = 0.1$ (Figure 4.61). For this reason, we seek a different value of a, with the requirement that it is near $x = 0.1$, and both $f(a)$ and $f'(a)$ are easily computed. It is tempting to try $a = 0$, but $f'(0)$ is undefined. One choice that works well is $a = \frac{9}{100} = 0.09$. Using the linear approximation $L(x) = f(a) + f'(a)(x - a)$, we have

$$\sqrt{0.1} \approx L(0.1) = \overbrace{\sqrt{\frac{9}{100}}}^{f(a)} + \overbrace{\frac{1}{2\sqrt{9/100}}}^{f'(a)}\overbrace{\left(\frac{1}{10} - \frac{9}{100}\right)}^{(x - a)}$$

$$= \frac{3}{10} + \frac{10}{6}\left(\frac{1}{100}\right)$$

$$= \frac{19}{60} \approx 0.3167.$$

This approximation agrees with the exact value to three decimal places.

Related Exercises 13–20 ◄

QUICK CHECK 3 Suppose you want to use linear approximation to estimate $\sqrt{0.18}$. What is a good choice for a? ◄

EXAMPLE 3   Linear approximation for the sine function   Find the linear approximation to $f(x) = \sin x$ at $x = 0$ and use it to approximate $\sin 2.5°$.

SOLUTION   We first construct a linear approximation $L(x) = f(a) + f'(a)(x - a)$, where $f(x) = \sin x$ and $a = 0$. Noting that $f(0) = 0$ and $f'(0) = \cos(0) = 1$, we have

$$L(x) = 0 + 1(x - 0) = x.$$

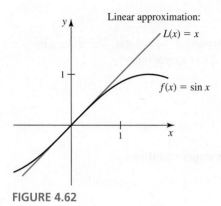

FIGURE 4.62

Again, the linear approximation is the line tangent to the curve at the point $(0, 0)$ (Figure 4.62). Before using $L(x)$ to approximate $\sin 2.5°$, we convert to radian measure (the derivative formulas for trigonometric functions require angles in radians):

$$2.5° = 2.5°\left(\frac{\pi}{180°}\right) = \frac{\pi}{72} \approx 0.0436 \text{ rad.}$$

Therefore, $\sin 2.5° \approx L(0.0436) = 0.0436$. A calculator gives $\sin 2.5° \approx 0.0436$, so the approximation is accurate to four decimal places.

Related Exercises 21–30◄

In Examples 2 and 3, we used a calculator to check the accuracy of our approximations. This begs the question: Why bother with linear approximation when a calculator does a better job? There are some good answers to that question.

Linear approximation is actually just the first step in the process of *polynomial approximation*. While linear approximation does a decent job of estimating function values when x is near a, we can generally do better with higher-degree polynomials. These ideas are explored further in Chapter 10.

Linear approximation also allows us to discover simple approximations to complicated functions. In Example 3, we found the *small-angle approximation to the sine function*: $\sin x \approx x$ for x near 0.

QUICK CHECK 4 Explain why the linear approximation to $f(x) = \cos x$ at $x = 0$ is $L(x) = 1$. ◄

A Variation on Linear Approximation

Linear approximation says that a function f can be approximated as

$$f(x) \approx f(a) + f'(a)(x - a),$$

where a is fixed and x is a nearby point. We first rewrite this expression as

$$\underbrace{f(x) - f(a)}_{\Delta y} \approx f'(a)\underbrace{(x - a)}_{\Delta x}.$$

It is customary to use the notation Δ (capital Greek delta) to denote a change. The factor $x - a$ is the change in the x-coordinate between a and a nearby point x. Similarly, $f(x) - f(a)$ is the corresponding change in the y-coordinate (Figure 4.63). So we write this approximation as

$$\Delta y \approx f'(a)\, \Delta x.$$

In other words, a change in y (the function value) can be approximated by the corresponding change in x magnified or diminished by a factor of $f'(a)$. This interpretation states the familiar fact that $f'(a)$ is the rate of change of y with respect to x.

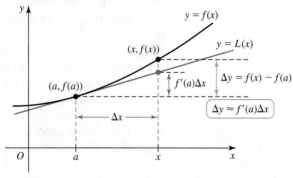

FIGURE 4.63

Relationship Between Δx and Δy

Suppose f is differentiable on an interval I containing the point a. The change in the value of f between two points a and $a + \Delta x$ is approximately

$$\Delta y \approx f'(a)\,\Delta x,$$

where $a + \Delta x$ is in I.

EXAMPLE 4   Estimating changes with linear approximations

a. Approximate the change in $y = f(x) = x^9 - 2x + 1$ when x changes from 1.00 to 1.05.

b. Approximate the change in the surface area of a spherical hot-air balloon when the radius decreases from 4 m to 3.9 m.

SOLUTION

a. The change in y is $\Delta y \approx f'(a)\,\Delta x$, where $a = 1$, $\Delta x = 0.05$, and $f'(x) = 9x^8 - 2$. Substituting these values, we find that

$$\Delta y \approx f'(a)\,\Delta x = f'(1) \cdot 0.05 = 7 \cdot 0.05 = 0.35.$$

If x increases from 1.00 to 1.05, then y increases by approximately 0.35.

> Notice that the units in these calculations are consistent. If r has units of meters (m), S' has units of m²/m = m, so ΔS has units of m², as it should.

b. The surface area of a sphere is $S = 4\pi r^2$, so the change in the surface area when the radius changes by Δr is $\Delta S \approx S'(a)\,\Delta r$. Substituting $S'(r) = 8\pi r$, $a = 4$, and $\Delta r = -0.1$, the approximate change in the surface area is

$$\Delta S \approx S'(a)\,\Delta r = S'(4) \cdot (-0.1) = 32\pi \cdot (-0.1) \approx -10.053.$$

The change in surface area is approximately -10.053 m²; it is negative, reflecting a decrease.

Related Exercises 31–36 ◄

QUICK CHECK 5 Given that the volume of a sphere is $V = 4\pi r^3/3$, find an expression for the approximate change in the volume when the radius changes from a to $a + \Delta r$. ◄

SUMMARY   Uses of Linear Approximation

• To approximate f near $x = a$, use

$$f(x) \approx L(x) = f(a) + f'(a)(x - a).$$

• To approximate the change Δy in the dependent variable when x changes from a to $a + \Delta x$, use

$$\Delta y \approx f'(a)\,\Delta x.$$

Linear Approximation and Concavity

Additional insight into linear approximation is gained by bringing concavity into the picture. Figure 4.64a shows the graph of a function f and its linear approximation (tangent line) at the point $(a, f(a))$. In this particular case, f is concave up on an interval containing a, and the graph of L lies below the graph of f near a. As a result, the linear approximation evaluated at a point near a is less than the exact value of f at that point. In other words, the linear approximation *underestimates* values of f near a.

The contrasting case is shown in Figure 4.64b, where we see graphs of f and L when f is concave down on an interval containing a. Now the graph of L lies above the graph of f, which means the linear approximation *overestimates* values of f near a.

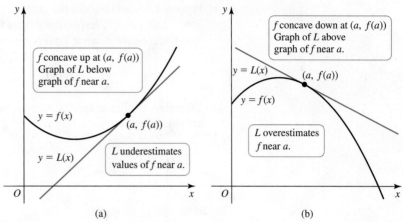

FIGURE 4.64

We can make another observation related to the degree of concavity (also called *curvature*). A large value of $|f''(a)|$ (large curvature) means that near $(a, f(a))$, the slope of the curve changes rapidly and the graph of f separates quickly from the tangent line. A small value of $|f''(a)|$ (small curvature) means that the slope of the curve changes slowly and the curve is relatively flat near $(a, f(a))$; therefore, the curve remains close to the tangent line. As a result, absolute errors in linear approximation are larger when $|f''(a)|$ is large.

EXAMPLE 5   Linear approximation and concavity

a. Find the linear approximation to $f(x) = x^{1/3}$ at $x = 1$ and $x = 27$.

b. Use the linear approximation of part (a) to approximate $\sqrt[3]{2}$ and $\sqrt[3]{26}$.

c. Are the approximations in part (b) overestimates or underestimates?

d. Compute the error in the approximations of part (b). Which error is greater? Explain.

SOLUTION

a. Note that

$$f(1) = 1, \quad f(27) = 3, \quad f'(x) = \frac{1}{3x^{2/3}}, \quad f'(1) = \frac{1}{3}, \quad \text{and } f'(27) = \frac{1}{27}.$$

Therefore, the linear approximation at $x = 1$ is

$$L_1(x) = 1 + \frac{1}{3}(x - 1) = \frac{1}{3}x + \frac{2}{3},$$

and the linear approximation at $x = 27$ is

$$L_2(x) = 3 + \frac{1}{27}(x - 27) = \frac{1}{27}x + 2.$$

b. Using the results of part (a), we find that

$$\sqrt[3]{2} \approx L_1(2) = \frac{1}{3} \cdot 2 + \frac{2}{3} = \frac{4}{3} \approx 1.333$$

and

$$\sqrt[3]{26} \approx L_2(26) = \frac{1}{27} \cdot 26 + 2 \approx 2.963.$$

c. Figures 4.65a and b show the graphs of f and the linear approximations L_1 and L_2 at $x = 1$ and $x = 27$, respectively (note the different scales on the two x-axes). We see that f is concave down at both points, which is confirmed by the fact that

$$f''(x) = -\frac{2}{9}x^{-5/3} < 0, \quad \text{for } x > 0.$$

Therefore, the linear approximations lie above the graph of f and both approximations are overestimates.

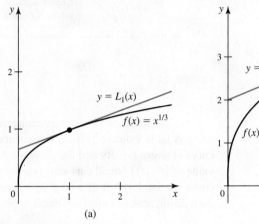

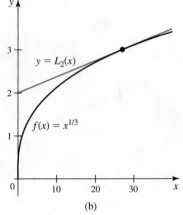

(a)   (b)

FIGURE 4.65

d. The error in the two linear approximations are

$$|L_1(2) - 2^{1/3}| \approx 0.073 \quad \text{and} \quad |L_2(26) - 26^{1/3}| \approx 0.00047$$

Because $|f''(1)| \approx 0.222$ and $|f''(27)| \approx 0.000914$, the curvature of f is much greater at $x = 1$ than at $x = 27$. So the approximation of $\sqrt[3]{26}$ is more accurate than the approximation of $\sqrt[3]{2}$.   *Related Exercises 37–40* ◄

Differentials

We now introduce an important concept that allows us to distinguish two related quantities:

• the change in the function $y = f(x)$ as x changes from a to $a + \Delta x$ (which we call Δy, as before), and

• the change in the linear approximation $y = L(x)$ as x changes from a to $a + \Delta x$ (which we call the *differential dy*).

Consider a function $y = f(x)$ differentiable on an interval containing a. If the x-coordinate changes from a to $a + \Delta x$, the corresponding change in the function is *exactly*

$$\Delta y = f(a + \Delta x) - f(a).$$

Using the linear approximation $L(x) = f(a) + f'(a)(x - a)$, the change in L as x changes from a to $a + \Delta x$ is

$$\Delta L = L(a + \Delta x) - L(a)$$
$$= \underbrace{[f(a) + f'(a)(a + \Delta x - a)]}_{L(a + \Delta x)} - \underbrace{[f(a) + f'(a)(a - a)]}_{L(a)}$$
$$= f'(a)\,\Delta x.$$

In order to distinguish Δy and ΔL, we define two new variables called *differentials*. The differential dx is simply Δx; the differential dy is the change in the linear approximation, which is $\Delta L = f'(a)\,\Delta x$. Using this notation,

$$\Delta L = \underbrace{dy}_{\substack{\text{same} \\ \text{as } \Delta L}} = f'(a)\,\Delta x = f'(a)\,\underbrace{dx}_{\substack{\text{same} \\ \text{as } \Delta x}}.$$

Therefore, at the point a, we have $dy = f'(a)\,dx$. More generally, we replace the fixed point a by a variable point x and write

$$dy = f'(x)\,dx.$$

> DEFINITION **Differentials**
>
> Let f be differentiable on an interval containing x. A small change in x is denoted by the **differential** dx. The corresponding change in f is approximated by the **differential** $dy = f'(x)\,dx$; that is,
>
> $$\Delta y = f(x + dx) - f(x) \approx dy = f'(x)\,dx.$$

Figure 4.66 shows that if $\Delta x = dx$ is small, then the change in f, which is Δy, is well approximated by the change in the linear approximation, which is dy. Furthermore, the approximation $\Delta y \approx dy$ improves as dx approaches 0. The notation for differentials is consistent with the notation for the derivative: If we divide both sides of $dy = f'(x)\,dx$ by dx, we have

$$\frac{dy}{dx} = \frac{f'(x)\,dx}{dx} = f'(x).$$

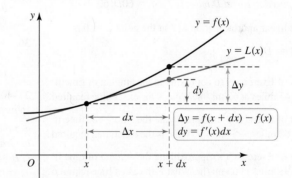

FIGURE 4.66

> Of the two coinventors of calculus, Gottfried Leibniz relied on the idea of differentials in his development of calculus. Leibniz's notation for differentials is essentially the same as the notation we use today. An Irish philosopher of the day, Bishop Berkeley, called differentials "the ghost of departed quantities."

EXAMPLE 6 **Differentials as change** Use the notation of differentials to write the approximate change in $f(x) = 3\cos^2 x$ given a small change dx.

SOLUTION With $f(x) = 3\cos^2 x$, we have $f'(x) = -6\cos x \sin x = -3\sin 2x$. Therefore,

$$dy = f'(x)\,dx = -3\sin 2x\,dx.$$

> Recall that $\sin 2x = 2\sin x \cos x$.

The interpretation is that a small change dx in the independent variable x produces an approximate change in the dependent variable of $dy = -3\sin 2x\,dx$ in y. For example, if x increases from $x = \pi/4$ to $x = \pi/4 + 0.1$, then $dx = 0.1$ and

$$dy = -3\sin(\pi/2)(0.1) = -0.3.$$

The approximate change in the function is -0.3, which means a decrease of approximately 0.3.

Related Exercises 41–50 ◄

SECTION 4.5 EXERCISES

Review Questions

1. Sketch the graph of a smooth function f and label a point $P(a, f(a))$ on the curve. Draw the line that represents the linear approximation to f at P.

2. Suppose you find the linear approximation to a differentiable function at a local maximum of that function. Describe the graph of the linear approximation.

3. How can linear approximation be used to approximate the value of a function f near a point at which f and f' are easily evaluated?

4. How can linear approximation be used to approximate the change in $y = f(x)$ given a change in x?

5. Given a function f differentiable on its domain, write and explain the relationship between the differentials dx and dy.

6. Does the differential dy represent the change in f or the change in the linear approximation to f? Explain.

Basic Skills

7–8. Estimating speed *Use the linear approximation given in Example 1 to answer the following questions.*

7. If you travel one mile in 59 seconds, what is your approximate average speed? What is your exact speed?

8. If you travel one mile in 63 seconds, what is your approximate average speed? What is your exact speed?

9–12. Estimating time *Suppose you want to travel D miles at a constant speed of $(60 + x)$ mi/hr, where x could be positive or negative. The time in minutes required to travel D miles is $T(x) = 60D(60 + x)^{-1}$.*

9. Show that the linear approximation to T at the point $x = 0$ is
$$T(x) \approx L(x) = D\left(1 - \frac{x}{60}\right).$$

10. Use the result of Exercise 9 to approximate the amount of time it takes to drive 45 miles at 62 mi/hr. What is the exact time required?

11. Use the result of Exercise 9 to approximate the amount of time it takes to drive 80 miles at 57 mi/hr. What is the exact time required?

12. Use the result of Exercise 9 to approximate the amount of time it takes to drive 93 miles at 63 mi/hr. What is the exact time required?

13–20. Linear approximation

a. Write the equation of the line that represents the linear approximation to the following functions at the given point a.
b. Graph the function and the linear approximation at a.
c. Use the linear approximation to estimate the given function value.
d. Compute the percent error in your approximation, $100 \cdot |approx - exact|/|exact|$, where the exact value is given by a calculator.

13. $f(x) = 12 - x^2;\ a = 2;\ f(2.1)$

14. $f(x) = \sin x;\ a = \pi/4;\ f(0.75)$

15. $f(x) = \ln(1 + x);\ a = 0;\ f(0.9)$

16. $f(x) = x/(x + 1);\ a = 1;\ f(1.1)$

17. $f(x) = \cos x;\ a = 0;\ f(-0.01)$

18. $f(x) = e^x;\ a = 0;\ f(0.05)$

19. $f(x) = (8 + x)^{-1/3};\ a = 0;\ f(-0.1)$

20. $f(x) = \sqrt[4]{x};\ a = 81;\ f(85)$

21–30. Estimations with linear approximation *Use linear approximations to estimate the following quantities. Choose a value of a to produce a small error.*

21. $1/203$ 22. $\tan 3°$ 23. $\sqrt{146}$ 24. $\sqrt[3]{65}$

25. $\ln(1.05)$ 26. $\sqrt{5/29}$ 27. $e^{0.06}$ 28. $1/\sqrt{119}$

29. $1/\sqrt[3]{510}$ 30. $\cos 31°$

31–36. Approximating changes

31. Approximate the change in the volume of a sphere when its radius changes from $r = 5$ ft to $r = 5.1$ ft $\left(V(r) = \frac{4}{3}\pi r^3\right)$.

32. Approximate the change in the atmospheric pressure when the altitude increases from $z = 2$ km to $z = 2.01$ km $(P(z) = 1000\, e^{-z/10})$.

33. Approximate the change in the volume of a right circular cylinder of fixed radius $r = 20$ cm when its height decreases from $h = 12$ cm to $h = 11.9$ cm $(V(h) = \pi r^2 h)$.

34. Approximate the change in the volume of a right circular cone of fixed height $h = 4$ m when its radius increases from $r = 3$ m to $r = 3.05$ m $(V(r) = \pi r^2 h/3)$.

35. Approximate the change in the lateral surface area (excluding the area of the base) of a right circular cone of fixed height $h = 6$ m when its radius decreases from $r = 10$ m to $r = 9.9$ m $(S = \pi r\sqrt{r^2 + h^2})$.

36. Approximate the change in the magnitude of the electrostatic force between two charges when the distance between them increases from $r = 20$ m to $r = 21$ m $(F(r) = 0.01/r^2)$.

37–40. Linear approximation and concavity *Carry out the following steps for the given functions f and points a.*

a. Find the linear approximation L to the function f at the point a.
b. Graph f and L together.
c. Based on the graphs in part (b), state whether linear approximations to f near a are underestimates or overestimates.
d. Compute $f''(a)$ to confirm your conclusion in part (c).

37. $f(x) = \frac{2}{x}, a = 1$

38. $f(x) = 5 - x^2, a = 2$

39. $f(x) = e^{-x}, a = \ln 2$

40. $f(x) = \sqrt{2}\cos x, a = \frac{\pi}{4}$

41–50. Differentials *Consider the following functions and express the relationship between a small change in x and the corresponding change in y in the form $dy = f'(x)\, dx$.*

41. $f(x) = 2x + 1$ 42. $f(x) = \sin^2 x$

43. $f(x) = 1/x^3$ 44. $f(x) = e^{2x}$

45. $f(x) = 2 - a\cos x, a$ constant

46. $f(x) = (4 + x)/(4 - x)$

47. $f(x) = 3x^3 - 4x$ **48.** $f(x) = \sin^{-1} x$

49. $f(x) = \tan x$ **50.** $f(x) = \ln(1 - x)$

Further Explorations

51. Explain why or why not Determine whether the following statements are true and give an explanation or counterexample.

   a. The linear approximation to $f(x) = x^2$ at $x = 0$ is $L(x) = 0$.
   b. Linear approximation at $x = 0$ provides a good approximation to $f(x) = |x|$.
   c. If $f(x) = mx + b$, then the linear approximation to f at any point is $L(x) = f(x)$.
   d. When linear approximation is used to estimate values of $f(x) = \ln(x)$ near $x = e$, the approximations are overestimates of the true values.

52. Linear approximation Estimate $f(5.1)$ given that $f(5) = 10$ and $f'(5) = -2$.

53. Linear approximation Estimate $f(3.85)$ given that $f(4) = 3$ and $f'(4) = 2$.

54–57. Linear approximation

   a. Write an equation of the line that represents the linear approximation to the following functions at a.
   b. Graph the function and the linear approximation at a.
   c. Use the linear approximation to estimate the given quantity.
   d. Compute the percent error in your approximation.

54. $f(x) = \tan x$; $a = 0$; $\tan 3°$

55. $f(x) = 1/(x + 1)$; $a = 0$; $1/1.1$

56. $f(x) = \cos x$; $a = \pi/4$; $\cos 0.8$

57. $f(x) = e^{-x}$; $a = 0$; $e^{-0.03}$

Applications

58. Ideal Gas Law The pressure P, temperature T, and volume V of an ideal gas are related by $PV = nRT$, where n is the number of moles of the gas and R is the universal gas constant. For the purposes of this exercise, let $nR = 1$; thus, $P = T/V$.

   a. Suppose that the volume is held constant and the temperature increases by $\Delta T = 0.05$. What is the approximate change in the pressure? Does the pressure increase or decrease?
   b. Suppose that the temperature is held constant and the volume increases by $\Delta V = 0.1$. What is the approximate change in the pressure? Does the pressure increase or decrease?
   c. Suppose that the pressure is held constant and the volume increases by $\Delta V = 0.1$. What is the approximate change in the temperature? Does the temperature increase or decrease?

59. Speed function Show that the function $s(x) = 3600(60 + x)^{-1}$ gives your average speed in mi/hr if you travel one mile in x seconds more or less than 60 mi/hr.

60. Time function Show that the function $T(x) = 60 D(60 + x)^{-1}$ gives the time in minutes required to drive D miles at $60 + x$ miles per hour.

61. Errors in approximations Suppose $f(x) = \sqrt[3]{x}$ is to be approximated near $x = 8$. Find the linear approximation to f at 8. Then complete the following table, showing the errors in various

approximations. Use a calculator to obtain the exact values. The percent error is $100 \cdot |\text{approximation} - \text{exact}|/|\text{exact}|$. Comment on the behavior of the errors as x approaches 8.

x	Linear approx.	Exact value	Percent error
8.1			
8.01			
8.001			
8.0001			
7.9999			
7.999			
7.99			
7.9			

62. Errors in approximations Suppose $f(x) = 1/(1 + x)$ is to be approximated near $x = 0$. Find the linear approximation to f at 0. Then complete the following table showing the errors in various approximations. Use a calculator to obtain the exact values. The percent error is $100 \cdot |\text{approximation} - \text{exact}|/|\text{exact}|$. Comment on the behavior of the errors as x approaches 0.

x	Linear approx.	Exact value	Percent error
0.1			
0.01			
0.001			
0.0001			
-0.0001			
-0.001			
-0.01			
-0.1			

Additional Exercises

63. Linear approximation and the second derivative Draw the graph of a function f such that $f(1) = f'(1) = f''(1) = 1$. Draw the linear approximation to the function at the point $(1, 1)$. Now draw the graph of another function g such that $g(1) = g'(1) = 1$ and $g''(1) = 10$. (It is not possible to represent the second derivative exactly, but your graphs should reflect the fact that $f''(1)$ is relatively small and $g''(1)$ is relatively large.) Now suppose that linear approximations are used to approximate $f(1.1)$ and $g(1.1)$.

   a. Which function value has the more accurate linear approximation near $x = 1$ and why?
   b. Explain why the error in the linear approximation to f near a point a is proportional to the magnitude of $f''(a)$.

QUICK CHECK ANSWERS

1. The linear approximation lies below the graph of f for x near a.   **2.** $L(15) = 45$, $s(15) = 48$; $x = 15$ is not close to 0.   **3.** $a = 0.16$ **4.** Note that $f(0) = 1$ and $f'(0) = 0$, so $L(x) = 1$ (this is the line tangent to $y = \cos x$ at $(0, 1)$).
5. $\Delta V \approx 4\pi a^2 \Delta r$ ◄

4.6 Mean Value Theorem

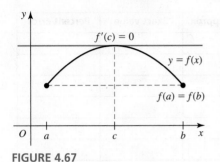

FIGURE 4.67

The *Mean Value Theorem* is a cornerstone in the theoretical framework of calculus. Several critical theorems (some stated in previous sections) rely on the Mean Value Theorem; the theorem also appears in practical applications. We begin with a preliminary result known as Rolle's Theorem.

Rolle's Theorem

Consider a function f that is continuous on a closed interval $[a, b]$ and differentiable on the open interval (a, b). Furthermore, assume f has the special property that $f(a) = f(b)$ (Figure 4.67). The statement of Rolle's Theorem is not surprising: It says that somewhere between a and b, there is at least one point at which f has a horizontal tangent line.

> Michel Rolle (1652–1719) is one of the less celebrated mathematicians whose name is nevertheless attached to a theorem. He worked in Paris most of his life as a scribe and published his theorem in 1691.

THEOREM 4.8 Rolle's Theorem

Let f be continuous on a closed interval $[a, b]$ and differentiable on (a, b) with $f(a) = f(b)$. There is at least one point c in (a, b) such that $f'(c) = 0$.

Proof: The function f satisfies the conditions of Theorem 4.1 (Extreme Value Theorem); therefore, it attains its absolute maximum and minimum values on $[a, b]$. Those values are attained either at an endpoint or at an interior point c.

> The Extreme Value Theorem, discussed in Section 4.1, states that a function that is continuous on a closed bounded interval attains its absolute maximum and minimum values on that interval.

Case 1: First suppose that f attains both its absolute maximum and minimum values at the endpoints. Because $f(a) = f(b)$, the maximum and minimum values are equal, and it follows that f is a constant function on $[a, b]$. Therefore, $f'(x) = 0$ for all x in (a, b), and the conclusion of the theorem holds.

Case 2: Assume at least one of the absolute extreme values of f does not occur at an endpoint. Then f must attain an absolute extreme value at an interior point of $[a, b]$; therefore, f must have either a local maximum or a local minimum at a point c in (a, b). We know from Theorem 4.2 that at a local extremum the derivative is zero. Thus, $f'(c) = 0$ for at least one point c of (a, b), and again the conclusion of the theorem holds. ◄

Why does Rolle's Theorem require continuity? A function that is not continuous on $[a, b]$ may have identical values at both endpoints and still not have a horizontal tangent line at any point on the interval (Figure 4.68a). Similarly, a function that is continuous on $[a, b]$ but not differentiable at a point of (a, b) may also fail to have a horizontal tangent line (Figure 4.68b).

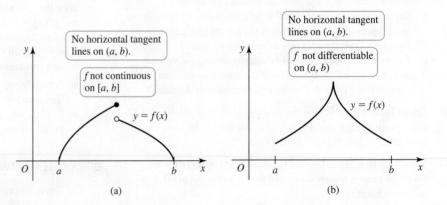

FIGURE 4.68

QUICK CHECK 1 Where on the interval $[0, 4]$ does $f(x) = 4x - x^2$ have a horizontal tangent line? ◄

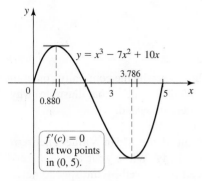

$y = x^3 - 7x^2 + 10x$

3.786

0.880

$f'(c) = 0$
at two points
in $(0, 5)$.

FIGURE 4.69

EXAMPLE 1 **Verifying Rolle's Theorem** Find an interval I on which Rolle's Theorem applies to $f(x) = x^3 - 7x^2 + 10x$. Then find all points c in I at which $f'(c) = 0$.

SOLUTION Because f is a polynomial, it is everywhere continuous and differentiable. We need an interval $[a, b]$ with the property that $f(a) = f(b)$. Noting that $f(x) = x(x - 2)(x - 5)$, we choose the interval $[0, 5]$, because $f(0) = f(5) = 0$ (other intervals are possible). The goal is to find points c in the interval $(0, 5)$ at which $f'(c) = 0$, which amounts to the familiar task of finding the critical points of f. The critical points satisfy

$$f'(x) = 3x^2 - 14x + 10 = 0.$$

Using the quadratic formula, the roots are

$$x = \frac{7 \pm \sqrt{19}}{3}, \quad \text{or} \quad x \approx 0.880 \quad \text{and} \quad x \approx 3.786.$$

As shown in Figure 4.69, the graph of f has two points at which the tangent line is horizontal.   *Related Exercises 7–14* ◀

Mean Value Theorem

The Mean Value Theorem is easily understood with the aid of a picture. Figure 4.70 shows a function f differentiable on (a, b) with a secant line passing through $(a, f(a))$ and $(b, f(b))$; the slope of the secant line is the average rate of change of f over $[a, b]$. The Mean Value Theorem claims that there exists a point c in (a, b) at which the slope of the tangent line at c is equal to the slope of the secant line. In other words, we can find a point on the graph of f where the tangent line is parallel to the secant line.

These lines are parallel and their slopes are equal, that is...

Secant line: slope $= \dfrac{f(b) - f(a)}{b - a}$

Tangent line: slope $= f'(c)$

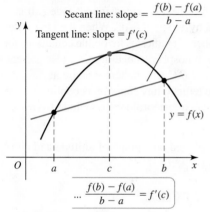

$y = f(x)$

$\ldots \dfrac{f(b) - f(a)}{b - a} = f'(c)$

FIGURE 4.70

THEOREM 4.9   Mean Value Theorem

If f is continuous on the closed interval $[a, b]$ and differentiable on (a, b), then there is at least one point c in (a, b) such that

$$\frac{f(b) - f(a)}{b - a} = f'(c).$$

Proof: The strategy of the proof is to use the function f of the Mean Value Theorem to form a new function g that satisfies Rolle's Theorem. Notice that the continuity and differentiability conditions of Rolle's Theorem and the Mean Value Theorem are the same. We devise g so that it satisfies the conditions $g(a) = g(b) = 0$.

As shown in Figure 4.71, the secant line passing through $(a, f(a))$ and $(b, f(b))$ is described by a function ℓ. We now define a new function g that measures the vertical distance between the given function f and the line ℓ. This function is simply $g(x) = f(x) - \ell(x)$. Because f and ℓ are continuous on $[a, b]$ and differentiable on (a, b), it follows that g is also continuous on $[a, b]$ and differentiable on (a, b). Furthermore, because the graphs of f and ℓ intersect at $x = a$ and $x = b$, we have $g(a) = f(a) - \ell(a) = 0$ and $g(b) = f(b) - \ell(b) = 0$.

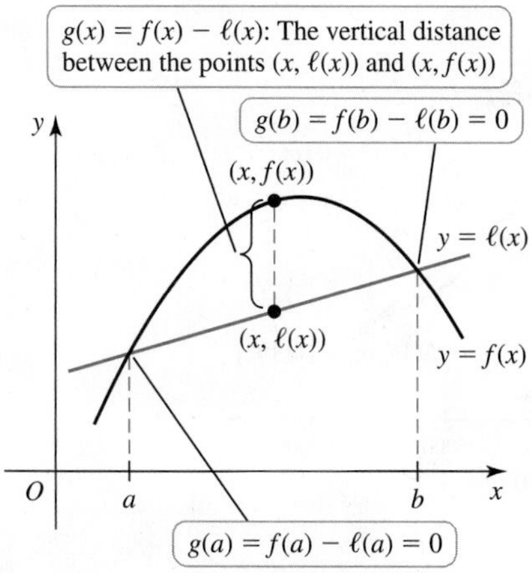

We now have a function g that satisfies the conditions of Rolle's Theorem. By that theorem, we are guaranteed the existence of at least one point c in the interval (a, b) such that $g'(c) = 0$. By the definition of g, this condition implies that $f'(c) - \ell'(c) = 0$, or $f'(c) = \ell'(c)$.

We are almost finished. What is $\ell'(c)$? It is just the slope of the secant line, which is

$$\frac{f(b) - f(a)}{b - a}.$$

$g(x) = f(x) - \ell(x)$: The vertical distance between the points $(x, \ell(x))$ and $(x, f(x))$

$g(b) = f(b) - \ell(b) = 0$

$(x, f(x))$

$y = \ell(x)$

$(x, \ell(x))$

$y = f(x)$

$g(a) = f(a) - \ell(a) = 0$

FIGURE 4.71

> The proofs of Rolle's Theorem and the Mean Value Theorem are nonconstructive: The theorems claim that a certain point exists, but their proofs do not say how to find it.

Therefore, $f'(c) = \ell'(c)$ implies that

$$\frac{f(b) - f(a)}{b - a} = f'(c).$$

◀

QUICK CHECK 2 Sketch the graph of a function that illustrates why the continuity condition of the Mean Value Theorem is needed. Sketch the graph of a function that illustrates why the differentiability condition of the Mean Value Theorem is needed. ◀

The following situation offers an interpretation of the Mean Value Theorem. Imagine taking 2 hours to drive to a town 100 miles away. While your average speed is $100\,\text{mi}/2\,\text{hr} = 50\,\text{mi/hr}$, your instantaneous speed (measured by the speedometer) almost certainly varies. The Mean Value Theorem says that at some point during the trip, your instantaneous speed equals your average speed, which is 50 mi/hr.

EXAMPLE 2   Mean Value Theorem in action The *lapse rate* is the rate at which the temperature T decreases in the atmosphere with respect to increasing altitude z. It is typically reported in units of °C/km and is defined by $\gamma = -dT/dz$. When the lapse rate rises above 7°C/km in a certain layer of the atmosphere, it indicates favorable conditions for thunderstorm and tornado formation, provided other atmospheric conditions are also present.

> Meteorologists look for "steep" lapse rates in the layer of the atmosphere where the pressure is between 700 and 500 hPa (hectopascals). This range of pressure typically corresponds to altitudes between 3 km and 5.5 km. The data in Example 2 were recorded in Denver at nearly the same time a tornado struck 50 mi to the north.

Suppose the temperature at $z = 2.9$ km is $T = 7.6°C$ and the temperature at $z = 5.6$ km is $T = -14.3°C$. Assume also that the temperature function is continuous and differentiable at all altitudes of interest. What can a meteorologist conclude from these data?

SOLUTION Figure 4.72 shows the two data points plotted on a graph of altitude and temperature. The slope of the line joining these points is

$$\frac{-14.3°C - 7.6°C}{5.6\,\text{km} - 2.9\,\text{km}} = -8.1°C/\text{km},$$

which means, on average, the temperature is decreasing at 8.1°C/km in the layer of air between 2.9 km and 5.6 km. With only two data points, we cannot know the entire temperature profile. The Mean Value Theorem, however, guarantees that there is at least one altitude at which $dT/dz = -8.1°C/\text{km}$. At each such altitude, the lapse rate is $\gamma = -dT/dz = 8.1°C/\text{km}$. Because this lapse rate is above the 7°C/km threshold associated with unstable weather, the meteorologist might expect an increased likelihood of severe storms.

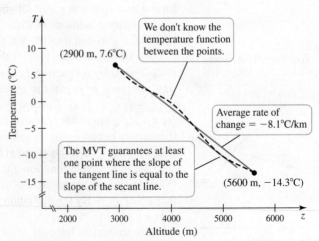

FIGURE 4.72

Related Exercises 15–16 ◀

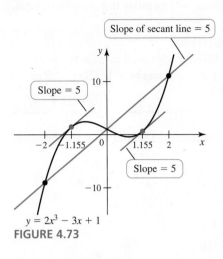

Slope of secant line = 5

Slope = 5

Slope = 5

$y = 2x^3 - 3x + 1$

FIGURE 4.73

EXAMPLE 3 **Verifying the Mean Value Theorem** Determine whether the function $f(x) = 2x^3 - 3x + 1$ satisfies the conditions of the Mean Value Theorem on the interval $[-2, 2]$. If so, find the point(s) guaranteed to exist by the theorem.

SOLUTION The polynomial f is everywhere continuous and differentiable, so it satisfies the conditions of the Mean Value Theorem. The average rate of change of the function on the interval $[-2, 2]$ is

$$\frac{f(2) - f(-2)}{2 - (-2)} = \frac{11 - (-9)}{4} = 5.$$

The goal is to find points in $(-2, 2)$ at which the line tangent to the curve has a slope of 5—that is, to find points at which $f'(x) = 5$. Differentiating f, this condition becomes

$$f'(x) = 6x^2 - 3 = 5 \quad \text{or} \quad x^2 = \frac{4}{3}.$$

Therefore, the points guaranteed to exist by the Mean Value Theorem are $x = \pm 2/\sqrt{3} \approx \pm 1.155$. The tangent lines have slope 5 at the points $(\pm 2/\sqrt{3}, f(\pm 2/\sqrt{3}))$ (Figure 4.73).

Related Exercises 17–24 ◄

Consequences of the Mean Value Theorem

We close with several results—some postponed from previous sections—that follow from the Mean Value Theorem.

We already know that the derivative of a constant function is zero; that is, if $f(x) = C$, then $f'(x) = 0$ (Theorem 3.2). Theorem 4.10 states the converse of this result.

> **THEOREM 4.10** **Zero Derivative Implies Constant Function**
> If f is differentiable and $f'(x) = 0$ at all points of an interval I, then f is a constant function on I.

Proof: Suppose $f'(x) = 0$ on $[a, b]$, where a and b are distinct points of I. By the Mean Value Theorem, there exists a point c in (a, b) such that

$$\frac{f(b) - f(a)}{b - a} = \underbrace{f'(c) = 0}_{\substack{f'(x) = 0 \text{ for} \\ \text{all } x \text{ in } I}}.$$

Multiplying both sides of this equation by $b - a \neq 0$, it follows that $f(b) = f(a)$, and this is true for every pair of points a and b in I. If $f(b) = f(a)$ for every pair of points in an interval, then f is a constant function on that interval. ◄

Theorem 4.11 builds on the conclusion of Theorem 4.10.

> **THEOREM 4.11** **Functions with Equal Derivatives Differ by a Constant**
> If two functions have the property that $f'(x) = g'(x)$, for all x of an interval I, then $f(x) - g(x) = C$ on I, where C is a constant; that is, f and g differ by a constant.

QUICK CHECK 3 Give two linear functions f and g that satisfy $f'(x) = g'(x)$; that is, the lines have equal slopes. Show that f and g differ by a constant. ◄

Proof: The fact that $f'(x) = g'(x)$ on I implies that $f'(x) - g'(x) = 0$ on I. Recall that the derivative of a difference of two functions equals the difference of the derivatives, so we can write

$$f'(x) - g'(x) = (f - g)'(x) = 0.$$

Now we have a function $f - g$ whose derivative is zero on I. By Theorem 4.10, $f(x) - g(x) = C$, for all x in I, where C is a constant; that is, f and g differ by a constant. ◄

In Section 4.2, we stated and gave an argument to support the test for intervals of increase and decrease. With the Mean Value Theorem, we can prove this important result.

THEOREM 4.12   Intervals of Increase and Decrease

Suppose f is continuous on an interval I and differentiable at all interior points of I. If $f'(x) > 0$ at all interior points of I, then f is increasing on I. If $f'(x) < 0$ at all interior points of I, then f is decreasing on I.

Proof: Let a and b be any two distinct points in the interval I with $b > a$. By the Mean Value Theorem,

$$\frac{f(b) - f(a)}{b - a} = f'(c),$$

for some c between a and b. Equivalently,

$$f(b) - f(a) = f'(c)(b - a).$$

Notice that $b - a > 0$ by assumption. So if $f'(c) > 0$, then $f(b) - f(a) > 0$. Therefore, for all a and b in I with $b > a$, we have $f(b) > f(a)$, which implies that f is increasing on I. Similarly, if $f'(c) < 0$, then $f(b) - f(a) < 0$ or $f(b) < f(a)$. It follows that f is decreasing on I.   ◄

SECTION 4.6 EXERCISES

Review Questions

1. Explain Rolle's Theorem with a sketch.

2. Draw the graph of a function for which the conclusion of Rolle's Theorem does not hold.

3. Explain why Rolle's Theorem cannot be applied to the function $f(x) = |x|$ on the interval $[-a, a]$, for any $a > 0$.

4. Explain the Mean Value Theorem with a sketch.

5. Draw the graph of a function for which the conclusion of the Mean Value Theorem does not hold.

6. At what points c does the conclusion of the Mean Value Theorem hold for $f(x) = x^3$ on the interval $[-10, 10]$?

Basic Skills

7–14. Rolle's Theorem *Determine whether Rolle's Theorem applies to the following functions on the given interval. If so, find the point(s) that are guaranteed to exist by Rolle's Theorem.*

7. $f(x) = x(x - 1)^2$; $[0, 1]$ 8. $f(x) = \sin 2x$; $[0, \pi/2]$

9. $f(x) = \cos 4x$; $[\pi/8, 3\pi/8]$ 10. $f(x) = 1 - |x|$; $[-1, 1]$

11. $f(x) = 1 - x^{2/3}$; $[-1, 1]$

12. $f(x) = x^3 - 2x^2 - 8x$; $[-2, 4]$

13. $g(x) = x^3 - x^2 - 5x - 3$; $[-1, 3]$

14. $h(x) = e^{-x^2}$; $[-a, a]$, where $a > 0$

15. **Lapse rates in the atmosphere** Concurrent measurements indicate that at an elevation of 6.1 km, the temperature is $-10.3°C$, and at an elevation of 3.2 km, the temperature is $8.0°C$. Based on the Mean Value Theorem, can you conclude that the lapse rate exceeds the threshold value of $7°C/km$ at some intermediate elevation? Explain.

16. **Drag racer acceleration** The fastest drag racers can reach a speed of 330 mi/hr over a quarter-mile strip in 4.45 seconds (from a standing start). Complete the following sentence about such a drag racer: At some point during the race, the maximum acceleration of the drag racer is at least _____ mi/hr/s.

17–24. Mean Value Theorem

a. *Determine whether the Mean Value Theorem applies to the following functions on the given interval $[a, b]$.*

b. *If so, find or approximate the point(s) that are guaranteed to exist by the Mean Value Theorem.*

c. *Make a sketch of the function and the line that passes through $(a, f(a))$ and $(b, f(b))$. Mark the points P (if they exist) at which the slope of the function equals the slope of the secant line. Then sketch the tangent line at P.*

17. $f(x) = 7 - x^2$; $[-1, 2]$ ▦ 18. $f(x) = 3 \sin 2x$; $[0, \pi/4]$

19. $f(x) = e^x$; $[0, \ln 4]$ 20. $f(x) = \ln 2x$; $[1, e]$

21. $f(x) = \sin^{-1} x$; $[0, 1/2]$ 22. $f(x) = x + 1/x$; $[1, 3]$

23. $f(x) = 2x^{1/3}$; $[-8, 8]$ 24. $f(x) = x/(x + 2)$; $[-1, 2]$

Further Explorations

25. Explain why or why not Determine whether the following statements are true and give an explanation or counterexample.

    a. The continuous function $f(x) = 1 - |x|$ satisfies the conditions of the Mean Value Theorem on the interval $[-1, 1]$.

    b. Two differentiable functions that differ by a constant always have the same derivative.

    c. If $f'(x) = 0$, then $f(x) = 10$.

26–28. Questions about derivatives

26. Without evaluating derivatives, which of the functions $f(x) = \ln x$, $g(x) = \ln 2x$, $h(x) = \ln x^2$, and $p(x) = \ln 10x^2$ have the same derivative?

27. Without evaluating derivatives, which of the functions $g(x) = 2x^{10}$, $h(x) = x^{10} + 2$, and $p(x) = x^{10} - \ln 2$ have the same derivative as $f(x) = x^{10}$?

28. Find all functions f whose derivative is $f'(x) = x + 1$.

29. Mean Value Theorem and graphs By visual inspection, locate all points on the interval $(-4, 4)$ at which the slope of the tangent line equals the average rate of change of the function on the interval $[-4, 4]$.

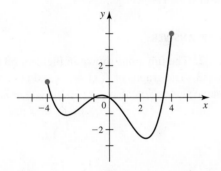

30–31 Mean Value Theorem and graphs Find all points on the interval $(1, 3)$ at which the slope of the tangent line equals the average rate of change of f on $[1, 3]$. Reconcile your results with the Mean Value Theorem.

30.

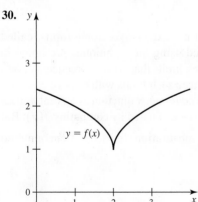

31.

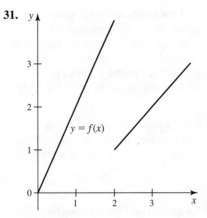

Applications

32. Avalanche forecasting Avalanche forecasters measure the *temperature gradient* dT/dh, which is the rate at which the temperature in a snowpack T changes with respect to its depth h. If the temperature gradient is large, it may lead to a weak layer of snow in the snowpack. When these weak layers collapse, avalanches occur. Avalanche forecasters use the following rule of thumb: If dT/dh exceeds 10°C/m anywhere in the snowpack, conditions are favorable for weak-layer formation, and the risk of avalanche increases. Assume the temperature function is continuous and differentiable.

    a. An avalanche forecaster digs a snow pit and takes two temperature measurements. At the surface $(h = 0)$, the temperature is $-12°C$. At a depth of 1.1 m, the temperature is 2°C. Using the Mean Value Theorem, what can he conclude about the temperature gradient? Is the formation of a weak layer likely?

    b. One mile away, a skier finds that the temperature at a depth of 1.4 m is $-1°C$, and at the surface, it is $-12°C$. What can be concluded about the temperature gradient? Is the formation of a weak layer in her location likely?

    c. Because snow is an excellent insulator, the temperature of snow-covered ground is near 0°C. Furthermore, the surface temperature of snow in a particular area does not vary much from one location to the next. Explain why a weak layer is more likely to form in places where the snowpack is not too deep.

    d. The term *isothermal* is used to describe the situation where all layers of the snowpack are at the same temperature (typically near the freezing point). Is a weak layer likely to form in isothermal snow? Explain.

33. Mean Value Theorem and the police A state patrol officer saw a car start from rest at a highway on-ramp. She radioed ahead to a patrol officer 30 mi along the highway. When the car reached the location of the second officer 28 min later, it was clocked going 60 mi/hr. The driver of the car was given a ticket for exceeding the 60-mi/hr speed limit. Why can the officer conclude that the driver exceeded the speed limit?

34. Mean Value Theorem and the police again Compare carefully to Exercise 33. A state patrol officer saw a car start from rest at a highway on-ramp. She radioed ahead to another officer 30 mi along the highway. When the car reached the location of the second officer 30 min later, it was clocked going 60 mi/hr. Can the patrol officer conclude that the driver exceeded the speed limit?

35. Running pace Explain why if a runner completes a 6.2-mi (10-km) race in 32 min, then he must have been running at exactly 11 mi/hr at least twice in the race. Assume the runner's speed at the finish line is zero.

Additional Exercises

36. Mean Value Theorem for linear functions Interpret the Mean Value Theorem when it is applied to any linear function.

37. Mean Value Theorem for quadratic functions Consider the quadratic function $f(x) = Ax^2 + Bx + C$, where A, B, and C are real numbers with $A \neq 0$. Show that when the Mean Value Theorem is applied to f on the interval $[a, b]$, the number c guaranteed by the theorem is the midpoint of the interval.

38. Means

   a. Show that the point c guaranteed to exist by the Mean Value Theorem for $f(x) = x^2$ on $[a, b]$ is the arithmetic mean of a and b; that is, $c = (a + b)/2$.

   b. Show that the point c guaranteed to exist by the Mean Value Theorem for $f(x) = 1/x$ on $[a, b]$, where $0 < a < b$, is the geometric mean of a and b; that is, $c = \sqrt{ab}$.

39. Equal derivatives Verify that the functions $f(x) = \tan^2 x$ and $g(x) = \sec^2 x$ have the same derivative. What can you say about the difference $f - g$? Explain.

40. Equal derivatives Verify that the functions $f(x) = \sin^2 x$ and $g(x) = -\cos^2 x$ have the same derivative. What can you say about the difference $f - g$? Explain.

41. 100 m speed The Jamaican sprinter Usain Bolt set a world record of 9.58 s in the 100 m dash in the summer of 2009. Did his speed ever exceed 37 km/hr during the race? Explain.

42. Condition for nondifferentiability Suppose $f'(x) < 0 < f''(x)$, for $x < a$, and $f'(x) > 0 > f''(x)$, for $x > a$. Prove that f is not differentiable at a. (*Hint:* Assume f is differentiable at a, and apply the Mean Value Theorem to f'.) More generally, show that if f' and f'' change sign at the same point, then f is not differentiable at that point.

43. Generalized Mean Value Theorem Suppose f and g are functions that are continuous on $[a, b]$ and differentiable on (a, b), where $g(a) \neq g(b)$. Then there is a point c in (a, b) at which

$$\frac{f(b) - f(a)}{g(b) - g(a)} = \frac{f'(c)}{g'(c)}.$$

This result is known as the **Generalized (or Cauchy's) Mean Value Theorem**.

   a. If $g(x) = x$, then show that the Generalized Mean Value Theorem reduces to the Mean Value Theorem.

   b. Suppose $f(x) = x^2 - 1$, $g(x) = 4x + 2$, and $[a, b] = [0, 1]$. Find a value of c satisfying the Generalized Mean Value Theorem.

QUICK CHECK ANSWERS

1. $x = 2$ **2.** The functions shown in Figure 4.68 provide examples.   **3.** The graphs of $f(x) = 3x$ and $g(x) = 3x + 2$ have the same slope. Note that $f(x) - g(x) = -2$, a constant. ◄

4.7 L'Hôpital's Rule

The study of limits in Chapter 2 was thorough but not exhaustive. Some limits, called *indeterminate forms*, cannot generally be evaluated using the techniques presented in Chapter 2. These limits tend to be the more interesting limits that arise in practice. A powerful result called *l'Hôpital's Rule* enables us to evaluate such limits with relative ease.

Here is how indeterminate forms arise. If f is a *continuous* function at a point a, then we know that $\lim_{x \to a} f(x) = f(a)$, allowing the limit to be evaluated by computing $f(a)$. But there are many limits that cannot be evaluated by substitution. In fact, we encountered such a limit in Section 3.4:

$$\lim_{x \to 0} \frac{\sin x}{x} = 1.$$

If we attempt to substitute $x = 0$ into $(\sin x)/x$, we get $0/0$, which has no meaning. Yet we proved that $(\sin x)/x$ has the limit 1 at $x = 0$ (Theorem 3.11). This limit is an example of an *indeterminate form*.

The meaning of an *indeterminate form* is further illustrated by $\lim\limits_{x \to \infty} \dfrac{ax}{x+1}$, where $a \neq 0$ can have any value. This limit has the indeterminate form ∞/∞ (meaning that the numerator and denominator become arbitrarily large in magnitude as $x \to \infty$), but the actual value of the limit is $\lim\limits_{x \to \infty} \dfrac{ax}{x+1} = \lim\limits_{x \to \infty} a = a$. In general, a limit with the form ∞/∞ or $0/0$ can have *any* value—which is why these limits must be handled carefully.

L'Hôpital's Rule for the Form 0/0

Consider a function of the form $f(x)/g(x)$ and assume that $\lim\limits_{x \to a} f(x) = \lim\limits_{x \to a} g(x) = 0$. Then the limit $\lim\limits_{x \to a} \dfrac{f(x)}{g(x)}$ has the indeterminate form $0/0$. We first state l'Hôpital's Rule and then prove a special case.

> The notations $0/0$ and ∞/∞ are merely symbols used to describe various types of indeterminate forms. The notation $0/0$ does not imply division by 0.

> Guillaume François l'Hôpital (lo-pee-tal) (1661–1704) is credited with writing the first calculus textbook. Much of the material in the book, including l'Hôpital's Rule, was provided by the Swiss mathematician Johann Bernoulli (1667–1748).

THEOREM 4.13   L'Hôpital's Rule

Suppose f and g are differentiable on an open interval I containing a with $g'(x) \neq 0$ on I when $x \neq a$. If $\lim\limits_{x \to a} f(x) = \lim\limits_{x \to a} g(x) = 0$, then

$$\lim\limits_{x \to a} \frac{f(x)}{g(x)} = \lim\limits_{x \to a} \frac{f'(x)}{g'(x)},$$

provided the limit on the right exists (or is $\pm\infty$). The rule also applies if $x \to a$ is replaced with $x \to \pm\infty$, $x \to a^+$, or $x \to a^-$.

Proof (special case): The proof of this theorem relies on the Generalized Mean Value Theorem (Exercise 43 of Section 4.6). We prove a special case of the theorem in which we assume that f' and g' are continuous at a, $f(a) = g(a) = 0$, and $g'(a) \neq 0$. We have

$$\lim\limits_{x \to a} \frac{f'(x)}{g'(x)} = \frac{f'(a)}{g'(a)} \qquad \text{Continuity of } f' \text{ and } g'$$

$$= \frac{\lim\limits_{x \to a} \dfrac{f(x) - f(a)}{x - a}}{\lim\limits_{x \to a} \dfrac{g(x) - g(a)}{x - a}} \qquad \text{Definition of } f'(a) \text{ and } g'(a)$$

$$= \lim\limits_{x \to a} \frac{\dfrac{f(x) - f(a)}{x - a}}{\dfrac{g(x) - g(a)}{x - a}} \qquad \text{Limit of a quotient, } g'(a) \neq 0$$

$$= \lim\limits_{x \to a} \frac{f(x) - f(a)}{g(x) - g(a)} \qquad \text{Cancel } x - a.$$

$$= \lim\limits_{x \to a} \frac{f(x)}{g(x)}. \qquad f(a) = g(a) = 0 \qquad \blacktriangleleft$$

> The definition of the derivative provides an example of an indeterminate form:
>
> $$f'(x) = \lim\limits_{h \to 0} \frac{f(x+h) - f(x)}{h}$$
>
> has the form $0/0$.

The geometry of l'Hôpital's Rule offers some insight. First consider two *linear* functions, f and g, whose graphs both pass through the point $(a, 0)$ with slopes 4 and 2, respectively; this means that

$$f(x) = 4(x - a) \quad \text{and} \quad g(x) = 2(x - a).$$

Furthermore, $f(a) = g(a) = 0, f'(x) = 4$, and $g'(x) = 2$ (Figure 4.74).
Looking at the quotient f/g, we see that

$$\frac{f(x)}{g(x)} = \frac{4(x-a)}{2(x-a)} = \frac{4}{2} = \frac{f'(x)}{g'(x)}. \quad \text{Exactly}$$

This argument may be generalized, and we find that for any linear functions f and g with $f(a) = g(a) = 0$,

$$\lim_{x\to a} \frac{f(x)}{g(x)} = \lim_{x\to a} \frac{f'(x)}{g'(x)},$$

provided $g'(a) \neq 0$.

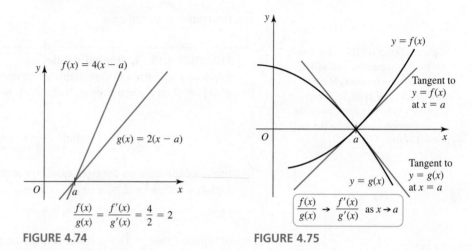

FIGURE 4.74   **FIGURE 4.75**

If f and g are not linear functions, we replace them with their linear approximations at a (Figure 4.75). Zooming in on the point a, the curves are close to their respective tangent lines $y = f'(a)(x - a)$ and $y = g'(a)(x - a)$, which have slopes $f'(a)$ and $g'(a) \neq 0$, respectively. Near $x = a$, we have

$$\frac{f(x)}{g(x)} \approx \frac{f'(a)(x-a)}{g'(a)(x-a)} = \frac{f'(a)}{g'(a)}.$$

Therefore, the ratio of the functions is well approximated by the ratio of the derivatives. In the limit as $x \to a$, we again have

$$\lim_{x\to a} \frac{f(x)}{g(x)} = \lim_{x\to a} \frac{f'(x)}{g'(x)}.$$

QUICK CHECK 1 Which of the following functions lead to an indeterminate form as $x \to 0$: $f(x) = x^2/(x + 2)$, $g(x) = (\tan 3x)/x$, or $h(x) = (1 - \cos x)/x^2$? ◄

EXAMPLE 1 Using l'Hôpital's Rule Evaluate the following limits.

a. $\displaystyle\lim_{x\to 1} \frac{x^3 + x^2 - 2x}{x - 1}$

b. $\displaystyle\lim_{x\to 0} \frac{\sqrt{9 + 3x} - 3}{x}$

SOLUTION

▶ The limit in part (a) can also be evaluated by factoring the numerator and canceling $(x - 1)$:

$$\lim_{x\to 1} \frac{x^3 + x^2 - 2x}{x - 1}$$
$$= \lim_{x\to 1} \frac{x(x - 1)(x + 2)}{x - 1}$$
$$= \lim_{x\to 1} x(x + 2) = 3.$$

a. Direct substitution of $x = 1$ into $\dfrac{x^3 + x^2 - 2x}{x - 1}$ produces the indeterminate form $0/0$.
Applying l'Hôpital's Rule with $f(x) = x^3 + x^2 - 2x$ and $g(x) = x - 1$ gives

$$\lim_{x\to 1} \frac{x^3 + x^2 - 2x}{x - 1} = \lim_{x\to 1} \frac{f'(x)}{g'(x)} = \lim_{x\to 1} \frac{3x^2 + 2x - 2}{1} = 3.$$

b. Substituting $x = 0$ into this function produces the indeterminate form $0/0$. Let $f(x) = \sqrt{9 + 3x} - 3$ and $g(x) = x$, and note that $f'(x) = \dfrac{3}{2\sqrt{9 + 3x}}$ and $g'(x) = 1$. Applying l'Hôpital's Rule, we have

$$\lim_{x \to 0} \underbrace{\frac{\sqrt{9 + 3x} - 3}{x}}_{f/g} = \lim_{x \to 0} \underbrace{\frac{\dfrac{3}{2\sqrt{9 + 3x}}}{1}}_{f'/g'} = \frac{1}{2}.$$

Related Exercises 13–22 ◄

L'Hôpital's Rule requires evaluating $\lim\limits_{x \to a} f'(x)/g'(x)$. It may happen that this second limit is another indeterminate form to which l'Hôpital's Rule may be applied again.

EXAMPLE 2   **L'Hôpital's Rule repeated**   Evaluate the following limits.

a. $\lim\limits_{x \to 0} \dfrac{e^x - x - 1}{x^2}$ **b.** $\lim\limits_{x \to 2} \dfrac{x^3 - 3x^2 + 4}{x^4 - 4x^3 + 7x^2 - 12x + 12}$.

SOLUTION

a. This limit has the indeterminate form $0/0$. Applying l'Hôpital's Rule, we have

$$\lim_{x \to 0} \frac{e^x - x - 1}{x^2} = \lim_{x \to 0} \frac{e^x - 1}{2x},$$

which is another limit of the form $0/0$. Therefore, we apply l'Hôpital's Rule again:

$$\begin{aligned} \lim_{x \to 0} \frac{e^x - x - 1}{x^2} &= \lim_{x \to 0} \frac{e^x - 1}{2x} && \text{L'Hôpital's Rule} \\ &= \lim_{x \to 0} \frac{e^x}{2} && \text{L'Hôpital's Rule again} \\ &= \frac{1}{2}. && \text{Evaluate limit.} \end{aligned}$$

b. Evaluating the numerator and denominator at $x = 2$, we see that this limit has the form $0/0$. Applying l'Hôpital's Rule twice, we have

$$\begin{aligned} \lim_{x \to 2} \frac{x^3 - 3x^2 + 4}{x^4 - 4x^3 + 7x^2 - 12x + 12} &= \lim_{x \to 2} \underbrace{\frac{3x^2 - 6x}{4x^3 - 12x^2 + 14x - 12}}_{\text{limit of the form } 0/0} && \text{L'Hôpital's Rule} \\ &= \lim_{x \to 2} \frac{6x - 6}{12x^2 - 24x + 14} && \text{L'Hôpital's Rule again} \\ &= \frac{3}{7}. && \text{Evaluate limit.} \end{aligned}$$

It is easy to overlook a crucial step in this computation: After applying l'Hôpital's Rule the first time, you *must* establish that the new limit is an indeterminate form before applying l'Hôpital's Rule a second time.

Related Exercises 23–36 ◄

Indeterminate Form ∞ / ∞

L'Hôpital's Rule also applies directly to limits of the form $\lim\limits_{x \to a} f(x)/g(x)$, where $\lim\limits_{x \to a} f(x) = \pm \infty$ and $\lim\limits_{x \to a} g(x) = \pm\infty$; this indeterminate form is denoted ∞ / ∞. The proof of this result is found in advanced books.

THEOREM 4.14   L'Hôpital's Rule (∞ / ∞)

Suppose that f and g are differentiable on an open interval I containing a, with $g'(x) \neq 0$ on I when $x \neq a$. If $\lim\limits_{x \to a} f(x) = \pm \infty$ and $\lim\limits_{x \to a} g(x) = \pm \infty$, then

$$\lim_{x \to a} \frac{f(x)}{g(x)} = \lim_{x \to a} \frac{f'(x)}{g'(x)},$$

provided the limit on the right exists (or is $\pm \infty$). The rule also applies for $x \to \pm \infty$, $x \to a^+$, or $x \to a^-$.

QUICK CHECK 2 Which of the following functions lead to an indeterminate form as $x \to \infty$: $f(x) = \sin x / x$, $g(x) = 2^x / x^2$, or $h(x) = (3x^2 + 4)/x^2$? ◀

EXAMPLE 3   L'Hôpital's Rule for ∞ / ∞ Evaluate the following limits.

a. $\lim\limits_{x \to \infty} \dfrac{4x^3 - 6x^2 + 1}{2x^3 - 10x + 3}$ **b.** $\lim\limits_{x \to \pi/2^-} \dfrac{1 + \tan x}{\sec x}$

SOLUTION

> As shown in Section 2.5, the limit in Example 3a could also be evaluated by first dividing the numerator and denominator by x^3 or by using Theorem 2.7.

a. This limit has the indeterminate form ∞ / ∞ because both the numerator and the denominator approach ∞ as $x \to \infty$. Applying l'Hôpital's Rule three times, we have

$$\underbrace{\lim_{x \to \infty} \frac{4x^3 - 6x^2 + 1}{2x^3 - 10x + 3}}_{\infty / \infty} = \underbrace{\lim_{x \to \infty} \frac{12x^2 - 12x}{6x^2 - 10}}_{\infty / \infty} = \underbrace{\lim_{x \to \infty} \frac{24x - 12}{12x}}_{\infty / \infty} = \lim_{x \to \infty} \frac{24}{12} = 2.$$

b. In this limit, both the numerator and the denominator approach ∞ as $x \to \pi/2^-$. L'Hôpital's Rule gives us

> In Exercise 3b, notice that we simplify $\sec^2 x / (\sec x \tan x)$ before taking the final limit. This step is important.

$$\lim_{x \to \pi/2^-} \frac{1 + \tan x}{\sec x} = \lim_{x \to \pi/2^-} \frac{\sec^2 x}{\sec x \tan x} \quad \text{L'Hôpital's Rule}$$

$$= \lim_{x \to \pi/2^-} \frac{1}{\sin x} \quad \text{Simplify.}$$

$$= 1 \quad \text{Evaluate limit.}$$

Related Exercises 37–44 ◀

Related Indeterminate Forms: $0 \cdot \infty$ and $\infty - \infty$

We now consider limits of the form $\lim\limits_{x \to a} f(x)g(x)$, where $\lim\limits_{x \to a} f(x) = 0$ and $\lim\limits_{x \to a} g(x) = \pm \infty$; such limits are denoted $0 \cdot \infty$. *L'Hôpital's Rule cannot be directly applied to limits of this form.* Furthermore, it's risky to jump to conclusions about such limits.

Suppose $f(x) = x$ and $g(x) = \dfrac{1}{x^2}$, in which case $\lim\limits_{x \to 0} f(x) = 0$, $\lim\limits_{x \to 0} g(x) = \infty$, and

$\lim\limits_{x \to 0} f(x)g(x) = \lim\limits_{x \to 0} \dfrac{1}{x}$ does not exist. On the other hand, if $f(x) = x$ and $g(x) = \dfrac{1}{\sqrt{x}}$, we

have $\lim\limits_{x \to 0} f(x) = 0$, $\lim\limits_{x \to 0^+} g(x) = \infty$, and $\lim\limits_{x \to 0^+} f(x)g(x) = \lim\limits_{x \to 0^+} \sqrt{x} = 0$. So a limit of the form $0 \cdot \infty$, in which the two functions compete with each other, may have any value or may not exist. The following example illustrates how this indeterminate form can be recast in the form $0/0$ or ∞/∞.

EXAMPLE 4 **L'Hôpital's Rule for $0 \cdot \infty$** Evaluate $\displaystyle\lim_{x \to \infty} x^2 \sin\left(\dfrac{1}{4x^2}\right)$.

SOLUTION This limit has the form $0 \cdot \infty$. A common technique that converts this form to either $0/0$ or ∞/∞ is to *divide by the reciprocal*. We rewrite the limit and apply l'Hôpital's Rule:

$$\underbrace{\lim_{x \to \infty} x^2 \sin\left(\frac{1}{4x^2}\right)}_{0 \cdot \infty \text{ form}} = \underbrace{\lim_{x \to \infty} \frac{\sin\left(\dfrac{1}{4x^2}\right)}{\left(\dfrac{1}{x^2}\right)}}_{\text{recast in } 0/0 \text{ form}} \qquad x^2 = \frac{1}{1/x^2}$$

$$= \lim_{x \to \infty} \frac{\cos\left(\dfrac{1}{4x^2}\right)\dfrac{1}{4}(-2x^{-3})}{-2x^{-3}} \qquad \text{L'Hôpital's Rule}$$

$$= \frac{1}{4} \lim_{x \to \infty} \cos\left(\frac{1}{4x^2}\right) \qquad \text{Simplify.}$$

$$= \frac{1}{4}. \qquad \frac{1}{4x^2} \to 0, \cos 0 = 1$$

Related Exercises 45–50 ◄

QUICK CHECK 3 What is the form of the limit $\displaystyle\lim_{x \to \pi/2^-} (x - \pi/2)(\tan x)$? Write it in the form $0/0$. ◄

Limits of the form $\displaystyle\lim_{x \to a} (f(x) - g(x))$, where $\displaystyle\lim_{x \to a} f(x) = \infty$ and $\displaystyle\lim_{x \to a} g(x) = \infty$, are indeterminate forms that we denote $\infty - \infty$. L'Hôpital's Rule cannot be applied directly to an $\infty - \infty$ form. It must first be expressed in the form $0/0$ or ∞/∞. With the $\infty - \infty$ form, it is easy to reach erroneous conclusions. For example, if $f(x) = 3x + 5$ and $g(x) = 3x$, then

$$\lim_{x \to \infty} ((3x + 5) - (3x)) = 5.$$

However, if $f(x) = 3x$ and $g(x) = 2x$, then

$$\lim_{x \to \infty} (3x - 2x) = \lim_{x \to \infty} x = \infty.$$

These examples show again why indeterminate forms are deceptive. Before proceeding, we introduce another useful technique.

Occasionally, it helps to convert a limit as $x \to \infty$ to a limit as $t \to 0^+$ (or vice versa) by a *change of variables*. To evaluate $\displaystyle\lim_{x \to \infty} f(x)$, we define $t = 1/x$ and note that as $x \to \infty$, $t \to 0^+$. Then

$$\lim_{x \to \infty} f(x) = \lim_{t \to 0^+} f\left(\frac{1}{t}\right).$$

This idea is illustrated in the next example.

EXAMPLE 5 **L'Hôpital's Rule for $\infty - \infty$** Evaluate $\lim\limits_{x\to\infty} (x - \sqrt{x^2 - 3x})$.

SOLUTION As $x \to \infty$, both terms in the difference $x - \sqrt{x^2 - 3x}$ approach ∞ and this limit has the form $\infty - \infty$. We first factor x from the expression and form a quotient:

$$\lim_{x\to\infty} (x - \sqrt{x^2 - 3x}) = \lim_{x\to\infty} (x - \sqrt{x^2(1 - 3/x)}) \quad \text{Factor } x^2 \text{ under square root.}$$

$$= \lim_{x\to\infty} x(1 - \sqrt{1 - 3/x}) \quad x > 0, \text{ so } \sqrt{x^2} = x$$

$$= \lim_{x\to\infty} \frac{1 - \sqrt{1 - 3/x}}{1/x}. \quad \begin{array}{l} \text{Write } 0 \cdot \infty \text{ form as } 0/0 \\ \text{form; } x = \dfrac{1}{1/x}. \end{array}$$

This new limit has the form $0/0$, and l'Hôpital's Rule may be applied.

One way to proceed is to use the change of variables $t = 1/x$:

$$\lim_{x\to\infty} \frac{1 - \sqrt{1 - 3/x}}{1/x} = \lim_{t\to 0^+} \frac{1 - \sqrt{1 - 3t}}{t} \quad \text{Let } t = 1/x; \text{ replace } \lim_{x\to\infty} \text{ with } \lim_{t\to 0^+}.$$

$$= \lim_{t\to 0^+} \frac{\dfrac{3}{2\sqrt{1 - 3t}}}{1} \quad \text{L'Hôpital's Rule}$$

$$= \frac{3}{2}. \quad \text{Evaluate limit.}$$

Related Exercises 51–54 ◄

Indeterminate Forms 1^∞, 0^0, and ∞^0

The indeterminate forms 1^∞, 0^0, and ∞^0 all arise in limits of the form $\lim\limits_{x\to a} f(x)^{g(x)}$, where $x \to a$ could be replaced with $x \to a^\pm$ or $x \to \pm\infty$. L'Hôpital's Rule cannot be applied directly to the indeterminate forms 1^∞, 0^0, and ∞^0. They must first be expressed in the form $0/0$ or ∞/∞. Here is how we proceed.

The inverse relationship between $\ln x$ and e^x says that $f^g = e^{g \ln f}$, so we first write

$$\lim_{x\to a} f(x)^{g(x)} = \lim_{x\to a} e^{g(x)\ln f(x)}.$$

By the continuity of the exponential function, we switch the order of the limit and the exponential function (Theorem 2.12); therefore,

$$\lim_{x\to a} f(x)^{g(x)} = \lim_{x\to a} e^{g(x)\ln f(x)} = e^{\lim_{x\to a} g(x)\ln f(x)},$$

provided $\lim\limits_{x\to a} g(x) \ln f(x)$ exists. Therefore, $\lim\limits_{x\to a} f(x)^{g(x)}$ is evaluated using the following two steps.

> Notice the following:
> • For 1^∞, L has the form $\infty \cdot \ln 1 = \infty \cdot 0$.
> • For 0^0, L has the form $0 \cdot \ln 0 = 0 \cdot -\infty$.
> • For ∞^0, L has the form $0 \cdot \ln \infty = 0 \cdot \infty$.

PROCEDURE **Indeterminate forms 1^∞, 0^0, and ∞^0**
Assume $\lim\limits_{x\to a} f(x)^{g(x)}$ has the indeterminate form 1^∞, 0^0, or ∞^0.

1. Analyze $L = \lim\limits_{x\to a} g(x) \ln f(x)$. This limit can be put in the form $0/0$ or ∞/∞, both of which are handled by l'Hôpital's Rule.

2. When L is finite, $\lim\limits_{x\to a} f(x)^{g(x)} = e^L$. If $L = \infty$ or $-\infty$, $\lim\limits_{x\to a} f(x)^{g(x)} = \infty$ or $\lim\limits_{x\to a} f(x)^{g(x)} = 0$, respectively."

QUICK CHECK 4 Explain why a limit of the form 0^∞ is not an indeterminate form. ◄

EXAMPLE 6 **Indeterminate forms 0^0 and 1^∞** Evaluate the following limits.

a. $\displaystyle\lim_{x \to 0^+} x^x$

b. $\displaystyle\lim_{x \to \infty} \left(1 + \frac{1}{x}\right)^x$

SOLUTION

a. This limit has the form 0^0. Using the given two-step procedure, we note that $x^x = e^{x \ln x}$ and first evaluate

$$L = \lim_{x \to 0^+} x \ln x.$$

This limit has the form $0 \cdot \infty$, which may be put in the form ∞/∞ so that l'Hôpital's Rule can be applied:

$$L = \lim_{x \to 0^+} x \ln x = \lim_{x \to 0^+} \frac{\ln x}{1/x} \qquad x = \frac{1}{1/x}$$

$$= \lim_{x \to 0^+} \frac{1/x}{-1/x^2} \qquad \text{L'Hôpital's Rule for } \infty/\infty \text{ form}$$

$$= \lim_{x \to 0^+} (-x) = 0. \qquad \text{Simplify and evaluate the limit.}$$

The second step is to exponentiate the limit:

$$\lim_{x \to 0^+} x^x = e^L = e^0 = 1.$$

We conclude that $\displaystyle\lim_{x \to 0^+} x^x = 1$ (Figure 4.76).

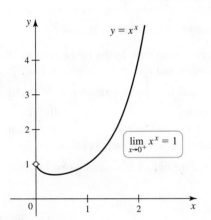

FIGURE 4.76

▷ The limit in Example 6b is often given as a definition of e. It is a special case of the more general limit

$$\lim_{x \to \infty} \left(1 + \frac{a}{x}\right)^x = e^a.$$

See Exercise 113.

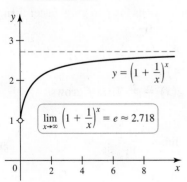

FIGURE 4.77

b. This limit has the form 1^∞. Noting that $(1 + 1/x)^x = e^{x \ln (1+1/x)}$, the first step is to evaluate

$$L = \lim_{x \to \infty} x \ln \left(1 + \frac{1}{x}\right),$$

which has the form $0 \cdot \infty$. Proceeding as in part (a), we have

$$L = \lim_{x \to \infty} x \ln \left(1 + \frac{1}{x}\right) = \lim_{x \to \infty} \frac{\ln (1 + 1/x)}{1/x} \qquad x = \frac{1}{1/x}$$

$$= \lim_{x \to \infty} \frac{\dfrac{1}{1 + 1/x} \cdot \left(-\dfrac{1}{x^2}\right)}{\left(-\dfrac{1}{x^2}\right)} \qquad \text{L'Hôpital's Rule for } 0/0 \text{ form}$$

$$= \lim_{x \to \infty} \frac{1}{1 + 1/x} = 1. \qquad \text{Simplify and evaluate.}$$

The second step is to exponentiate the limit:

$$\lim_{x \to \infty} \left(1 + \frac{1}{x}\right)^x = e^L = e^1 = e.$$

The function $y = (1 + 1/x)^x$ (Figure 4.77) has a horizontal asymptote $y = e \approx 2.71828$.

Related Exercises 55–68 ◄

Growth Rates of Functions

An important use of l'Hôpital's Rule is to compare the growth rates of functions. Here are two questions—one practical and one theoretical—that demonstrate the importance of comparative growth rates of functions.

> Models of epidemics produce more complicated functions than the one given here, but they have the same general features.

• A particular theory for modeling the spread of an epidemic predicts that the number of infected people t days after the start of the epidemic is given by the function

$$N(t) = 2.5t^2 e^{-0.01t} = 2.5 \frac{t^2}{e^{0.01t}}.$$

Question: In the long run (as $t \to \infty$), does the epidemic spread or does it die out?

> The Prime Number Theorem was proved simultaneously (two different proofs) in 1896 by Jacques Hadamard and Charles de la Vallée Poussin, relying on fundamental ideas contributed by Riemann.

• A prime number is an integer $p \geq 2$ that has only two divisors, 1 and itself. The first few prime numbers are 2, 3, 5, 7, and 11. A celebrated theorem states that the number of prime numbers less than x is approximately

$$P(x) = \frac{x}{\ln x}, \quad \text{for large values of } x.$$

Question: According to this theorem, is the number of prime numbers infinite?

These two questions involve a comparison of two functions. In the first question, if t^2 grows faster than $e^{0.01t}$ as $t \to \infty$, then $\lim_{t \to \infty} N(t) = \infty$ and the epidemic grows. If $e^{0.01t}$ grows faster than t^2 as $t \to \infty$, then $\lim_{t \to \infty} N(t) = 0$ and the epidemic dies out. We will explain what is meant by *grows faster than* in a moment.

In the second question, the comparison is between x and $\ln x$. If x grows faster than $\ln x$ as $x \to \infty$, then $\lim_{x \to \infty} P(x) = \infty$ and the number of prime numbers is infinite.

Our goal is to obtain a ranking of the following families of functions based on their growth rates:

> Another function with a large growth rate is the factorial function, defined for integers as $f(n) = n! = n(n-1)\cdots 2 \cdot 1$. See Exercise 110.

• mx, where $m > 0$ (represents linear functions)
• x^p, where $p > 0$ (represents polynomials and algebraic functions)
• x^x (sometimes called a *superexponential* or *tower function*)
• $\ln x$ (represents logarithmic functions)
• $\ln^q x$, where $q > 0$ (represents powers of logarithmic functions)
• $x^p \ln x$, where $p > 0$ (a combination of powers and logarithms)
• e^x (represents exponential functions).

QUICK CHECK 5 Before proceeding, use your intuition and rank these classes of functions in order of their growth rates. ◀

We need to be precise about growth rates and what it means for f to grow faster than g as $x \to \infty$. We work with the following definitions.

DEFINITION Growth Rates of Functions (as $x \to \infty$)

Suppose f and g are functions with $\lim_{x \to \infty} f(x) = \lim_{x \to \infty} g(x) = \infty$. Then f **grows faster than g** as $x \to \infty$ if

$$\lim_{x \to \infty} \frac{g(x)}{f(x)} = 0 \quad \text{or, equivalently, if} \quad \lim_{x \to \infty} \frac{f(x)}{g(x)} = \infty.$$

The functions f and g have **comparable growth rates** if

$$\lim_{x \to \infty} \frac{f(x)}{g(x)} = M,$$

where $0 < M < \infty$ (M is nonzero and finite).

The idea of growth rates is illustrated nicely with graphs. Figure 4.78 shows a family of linear functions of the form $y = mx$, where $m > 0$, and a family of polynomials of the form $y = x^p$, where $p > 1$. We see that the polynomials grow faster (their curves rise at a greater rate) than the linear functions as $x \to \infty$.

Figure 4.79 shows that exponential functions of the form $y = b^x$, where $b > 1$, grow faster than polynomials of the form $y = x^p$, where $p > 0$, as $x \to \infty$ (Example 8).

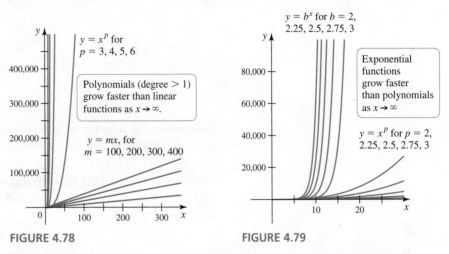

FIGURE 4.78   **FIGURE 4.79**

QUICK CHECK 6 Compare the growth rates of $f(x) = x^2$ and $g(x) = x^3$ as $x \to \infty$. Compare the growth rates of $f(x) = x^2$ and $g(x) = 10x^2$ as $x \to \infty$. ◄

We now begin a systematic comparison of growth rates. Note that a growth rate limit involves an indeterminate form ∞/∞, so l'Hôpital's Rule is always in the picture.

EXAMPLE 7 Powers of x vs. powers of ln x Compare the growth rates as $x \to \infty$ of the following pairs of functions.

a. $f(x) = \ln x$ and $g(x) = x^p$, where $p > 0$

b. $f(x) = \ln^q x$ and $g(x) = x^p$, where $p > 0$ and $q > 0$

SOLUTION

a. The limit of the ratio of the two functions is

$$\lim_{x \to \infty} \frac{\ln x}{x^p} = \lim_{x \to \infty} \frac{1/x}{px^{p-1}} \quad \text{L'Hôpital's Rule}$$

$$= \lim_{x \to \infty} \frac{1}{px^p} \quad \text{Simplify.}$$

$$= 0. \quad \text{Evaluate the limit.}$$

We see that any positive power of x grows faster than $\ln x$.

b. We compare $\ln^q x$ and x^p by observing that

$$\lim_{x \to \infty} \frac{\ln^q x}{x^p} = \lim_{x \to \infty} \left(\frac{\ln x}{x^{p/q}} \right)^q = \left(\underbrace{\lim_{x \to \infty} \frac{\ln x}{x^{p/q}}}_{0} \right)^q.$$

By part (a), $\lim\limits_{x \to \infty} \dfrac{\ln x}{x^{p/q}} = 0$ (because $p/q > 0$). Therefore, $\lim\limits_{x \to \infty} \dfrac{\ln^q x}{x^p} = 0$ (because $q > 0$). We conclude that any positive power of x grows faster than any positive power of $\ln x$.

Related Exercises 69–80 ◄

EXAMPLE 8   Powers of x vs. exponentials Compare the rates of growth of $f(x) = x^p$ and $g(x) = e^x$ as $x \to \infty$, where p is a positive real number.

SOLUTION The goal is to evaluate $\lim\limits_{x \to \infty} \dfrac{x^p}{e^x}$, for $p > 0$. This comparison is most easily done using Example 7 and a change of variables. We let $x = \ln t$ and note that as $x \to \infty$, we also have $t \to \infty$. With this substitution, $x^p = \ln^p t$ and $e^x = e^{\ln t} = t$. Therefore,

$$\lim_{x \to \infty} \frac{x^p}{e^x} = \lim_{t \to \infty} \frac{\ln^p t}{t} = 0. \quad \text{Example 7}$$

We see that increasing exponential functions grow faster than positive powers of x (Figure 4.79).

Related Exercises 69–80 ◀

These examples, together with the comparison of exponential functions b^x and the superexponential x^x (Exercise 114), establish a ranking of growth rates.

THEOREM 4.15   Ranking Growth Rates as $x \to \infty$
Let $f \ll g$ mean that g grows faster than f as $x \to \infty$. With positive real numbers p, q, r, and s and $b > 1$,

$$\ln^q x \ll x^p \ll x^p \ln^r x \ll x^{p+s} \ll b^x \ll x^x.$$

You should try to build these relative growth rates into your intuition. They are useful in future chapters (Chapter 9 on sequences, in particular), and they can be used to evaluate limits at infinity quickly.

Pitfalls in Using l'Hôpital's Rule

We close with a list of common pitfalls when using l'Hôpital's Rule.

1. L'Hôpital's Rule says $\lim\limits_{x \to a} \dfrac{f(x)}{g(x)} = \lim\limits_{x \to a} \dfrac{f'(x)}{g'(x)}$, not

$$\lim_{x \to a} \frac{f(x)}{g(x)} = \lim_{x \to a} \left[\frac{f(x)}{g(x)}\right]' \quad \text{or} \quad \lim_{x \to a} \frac{f(x)}{g(x)} = \lim_{x \to a} \left[\frac{1}{g(x)}\right]' f'(x).$$

In other words, you should evaluate $f'(x)$ and $g'(x)$, form their quotient, and then take the limit. Don't confuse l'Hôpital's Rule with the Quotient Rule.

2. Be sure that the given limit involves the indeterminate form $0/0$ or ∞/∞ before applying l'Hôpital's Rule. For example, consider the following erroneous use of l'Hôpital's Rule:

$$\lim_{x \to 0} \frac{1 - \sin x}{\cos x} = \lim_{x \to 0} \frac{-\cos x}{\sin x},$$

which does not exist. The original limit is not an indeterminate form in the first place. This limit should be evaluated by direct substitution:

$$\lim_{x \to 0} \frac{1 - \sin x}{\cos x} = \frac{1 - \sin 0}{1} = 1.$$

3. When using l'Hôpital's Rule repeatedly, be sure to simplify expressions as much as possible at each step and evaluate the limit as soon as the new limit is no longer an indeterminate form.

4. Repeated use of l'Hôpital's Rule occasionally leads to unending cycles, in which case other methods must be used. For example, limits of the form $\lim\limits_{x \to \infty} \dfrac{\sqrt{ax + 1}}{\sqrt{bx + 1}}$, where a and b are real numbers, lead to such behavior (Exercise 105).

5. Be sure that the final limit exists. Consider $\lim\limits_{x\to\infty} \dfrac{3x + \cos x}{x}$, which has the form ∞/∞. Applying l'Hôpital's Rule, we have

$$\lim_{x\to\infty} \frac{3x + \cos x}{x} = \lim_{x\to\infty} \frac{3 - \sin x}{1}.$$

It is tempting to conclude that because the limit on the right side does not exist, the original limit also does not exist. In fact, the original limit has a value of 3 (divide numerator and denominator by x). In order to reach a conclusion from l'Hôpital's Rule, the final limit in the calculation must exist (or be $\pm\infty$).

SECTION 4.7 EXERCISES

Review Questions

1. Explain with examples what is meant by the indeterminate form $0/0$.

2. Why are special methods, such as l'Hôpital's Rule, needed to evaluate indeterminate forms (as opposed to substitution)?

3. Explain the steps used to apply l'Hôpital's Rule to a limit of the form $0/0$.

4. To which indeterminate forms does l'Hôpital's Rule apply *directly*?

5. Explain how to convert a limit of the form $0 \cdot \infty$ to a limit of the form $0/0$ or ∞/∞.

6. Give an example of a limit of the form ∞/∞ as $x \to 0$.

7. Explain why the form 1^∞ is indeterminate and cannot be evaluated by substitution. Explain how the competing functions behave.

8. Give the two-step method for attacking an indeterminate limit of the form $\lim\limits_{x\to a} f(x)^{g(x)}$.

9. In terms of limits, what does it mean for f to grow faster than g as $x \to \infty$?

10. In terms of limits, what does it mean for the rates of growth of f and g to be comparable as $x \to \infty$?

11. Rank the functions x^3, $\ln x$, x^x, and 2^x in order of increasing growth rates as $x \to \infty$.

12. Rank the functions x^{100}, $\ln x^{10}$, x^x, and 10^x in order of increasing growth rates as $x \to \infty$.

Basic Skills

13–22. 0/0 form *Evaluate the following limits using l'Hôpital's Rule.*

13. $\lim\limits_{x\to 2} \dfrac{x^2 - 2x}{8 - 6x + x^2}$

14. $\lim\limits_{x\to -1} \dfrac{x^4 + x^3 + 2x + 2}{x + 1}$

15. $\lim\limits_{x\to 1} \dfrac{\ln x}{4x - x^2 - 3}$

16. $\lim\limits_{x\to 0} \dfrac{e^x - 1}{x^2 + 3x}$

17. $\lim\limits_{x\to e} \dfrac{\ln x - 1}{x - e}$

18. $\lim\limits_{x\to 1} \dfrac{4 \tan^{-1} x - \pi}{x - 1}$

19. $\lim\limits_{x\to 0} \dfrac{3 \sin 4x}{5x}$

20. $\lim\limits_{x\to 2\pi} \dfrac{x \sin x + x^2 - 4\pi^2}{x - 2\pi}$

21. $\lim\limits_{u\to \pi/4} \dfrac{\tan u - \cot u}{u - \pi/4}$

22. $\lim\limits_{z\to 0} \dfrac{\tan 4z}{\tan 7z}$

23–36. 0/0 form *Evaluate the following limits.*

23. $\lim\limits_{x\to 0} \dfrac{1 - \cos 3x}{8x^2}$

24. $\lim\limits_{x\to 0} \dfrac{\sin^2 3x}{x^2}$

25. $\lim\limits_{x\to \pi} \dfrac{\cos x + 1}{(x - \pi)^2}$

26. $\lim\limits_{x\to 0} \dfrac{e^x - x - 1}{5x^2}$

27. $\lim\limits_{x\to 0} \dfrac{e^x - \sin x - 1}{x^4 + 8x^3 + 12x^2}$

28. $\lim\limits_{x\to 0} \dfrac{\sin x - x}{7x^3}$

29. $\lim\limits_{x\to \infty} \dfrac{e^{1/x} - 1}{1/x}$

30. $\lim\limits_{x\to \infty} \dfrac{\tan^{-1} x - \pi/2}{1/x}$

31. $\lim\limits_{x\to -1} \dfrac{x^3 - x^2 - 5x - 3}{x^4 + 2x^3 - x^2 - 4x - 2}$

32. $\lim\limits_{x\to 1} \dfrac{x^n - 1}{x - 1}$, n is a positive integer

33. $\lim\limits_{v\to 3} \dfrac{v - 1 - \sqrt{v^2 - 5}}{v - 3}$

34. $\lim\limits_{y\to 2} \dfrac{y^2 + y - 6}{\sqrt{8 - y^2} - y}$

35. $\lim\limits_{x\to 2} \dfrac{x^2 - 4x + 4}{\sin^2(\pi x)}$

36. $\lim\limits_{x\to 2} \dfrac{\sqrt[3]{3x + 2} - 2}{x - 2}$

37–44. ∞/∞ form *Evaluate the following limits.*

37. $\lim\limits_{x\to \infty} \dfrac{3x^4 - x^2}{6x^4 + 12}$

38. $\lim\limits_{x\to \infty} \dfrac{4x^3 - 2x^2 + 6}{\pi x^3 + 4}$

39. $\lim\limits_{x\to \pi/2^-} \dfrac{\tan x}{3/(2x - \pi)}$

40. $\lim\limits_{x\to \infty} \dfrac{e^{3x}}{3e^{3x} + 5}$

41. $\lim\limits_{x\to \infty} \dfrac{\ln(3x + 5)}{\ln(7x + 3) + 1}$

42. $\lim\limits_{x\to \infty} \dfrac{\ln(3x + 5e^x)}{\ln(7x + 3e^{2x})}$

43. $\lim\limits_{x\to \infty} \dfrac{x^2 - \ln(2/x)}{3x^2 + 2x}$

44. $\lim\limits_{x\to \pi/2} \dfrac{2 \tan x}{\sec^2 x}$

45–50. 0 · ∞ form *Evaluate the following limits.*

45. $\lim\limits_{x\to 0} x \csc x$

46. $\lim\limits_{x\to 1^-} (1 - x) \tan\left(\dfrac{\pi x}{2}\right)$

47. $\lim\limits_{x\to 0} \csc 6x \sin 7x$

48. $\lim\limits_{x\to \infty} (\csc(1/x)(e^{1/x} - 1))$

49. $\lim\limits_{x \to \pi/2^-} \left(\dfrac{\pi}{2} - x\right) \sec x$

50. $\lim\limits_{x \to 0^+} \sin x \sqrt{\dfrac{1-x}{x}}$

51–54. $\infty - \infty$ form *Evaluate the following limits.*

51. $\lim\limits_{x \to 0^+} \left(\cot x - \dfrac{1}{x}\right)$

52. $\lim\limits_{x \to \infty} \left(x - \sqrt{x^2 + 1}\right)$

53. $\lim\limits_{\theta \to \pi/2^-} (\tan \theta - \sec \theta)$

54. $\lim\limits_{x \to \infty} \left(x - \sqrt{x^2 + 4x}\right)$

55–68. 1^∞, 0^0, ∞^0 forms *Evaluate the following limits or explain why they do not exist. Check your results by graphing.*

55. $\lim\limits_{x \to 0^+} x^{2x}$

56. $\lim\limits_{x \to 0} (1 + 4x)^{3/x}$

57. $\lim\limits_{\theta \to \pi/2^-} (\tan \theta)^{\cos \theta}$

58. $\lim\limits_{\theta \to 0^+} (\sin \theta)^{\tan \theta}$

59. $\lim\limits_{x \to 0^+} (1 + x)^{\cot x}$

60. $\lim\limits_{x \to \infty} \left(1 + \dfrac{1}{x}\right)^{\ln x}$

61. $\lim\limits_{x \to \infty} \left(1 + \dfrac{a}{x}\right)^x$, for a constant a

62. $\lim\limits_{x \to 0} (e^{5x} + x)^{1/x}$

63. $\lim\limits_{x \to 0} (e^{ax} + x)^{1/x}$, for a constant a

64. $\lim\limits_{x \to 0} (2^{ax} + x)^{1/x}$, for a constant a

65. $\lim\limits_{x \to 0^+} (\tan x)^x$

66. $\lim\limits_{z \to \infty} \left(1 + \dfrac{10}{z^2}\right)^{z^2}$

67. $\lim\limits_{x \to 0} (x + \cos x)^{1/x}$

68. $\lim\limits_{x \to 0^+} \left(\dfrac{1}{3} \cdot 3^x + \dfrac{2}{3} \cdot 2^x\right)^{1/x}$

69–80. Comparing growth rates *Use limit methods to determine which of the two given functions grows faster, or state that they have comparable growth rates.*

69. x^{10}; $e^{0.01x}$

70. $x^2 \ln x$; $\ln^2 x$

71. $\ln x^{20}$; $\ln x$

72. $\ln x$; $\ln (\ln x)$

73. 100^x; x^x

74. $x^2 \ln x$; x^3

75. x^{20}; 1.00001^x

76. $x^{10} \ln^{10} x$; x^{11}

77. x^x; $(x/2)^x$

78. $\ln \sqrt{x}$; $\ln^2 x$

79. e^{x^2}; e^{10x}

80. e^{x^2}; $x^{x/10}$

Further Explorations

81. Explain why or why not Determine whether the following statements are true and give an explanation or counterexample.

a. By l'Hôpital's Rule, $\lim\limits_{x \to 2} \dfrac{x-2}{x^2-1} = \lim\limits_{x \to 2} \dfrac{1}{2x} = \dfrac{1}{4}$.

b. $\lim\limits_{x \to 0} (x \sin x) = \lim\limits_{x \to 0} f(x)g(x) = \lim\limits_{x \to 0} f'(x) \lim\limits_{x \to 0} g'(x) = \left(\lim\limits_{x \to 0} 1\right)\left(\lim\limits_{x \to 0} \cos x\right) = 1$

c. $\lim\limits_{x \to 0^+} x^{1/x}$ is an indeterminate form.

d. The number 1 raised to any fixed power is 1. Therefore, because $(1 + x) \to 1$ as $x \to 0$, $(1 + x)^{1/x} \to 1$ as $x \to 0$.

e. The functions $\ln x^{100}$ and $\ln x$ have comparable growth rates as $x \to \infty$.

f. The function e^x grows faster than 2^x as $x \to \infty$.

82–83. Two methods *Evaluate the following limits in two different ways: Use the methods of Chapter 2 and use l'Hôpital's Rule.*

82. $\lim\limits_{x \to \infty} \dfrac{100x^3 - 3}{x^4 - 2}$

83. $\lim\limits_{x \to \infty} \dfrac{2x^3 - x^2 + 1}{5x^3 + 2x}$

84. L'Hôpital's example Evaluate one of the limits l'Hôpital used in his own textbook in about 1700:

$$\lim\limits_{x \to a} \dfrac{\sqrt{2a^3 x - x^4} - a\sqrt[3]{a^2 x}}{a - \sqrt[4]{ax^3}}, \text{ where } a \text{ is a real number.}$$

85–96. Miscellaneous limits by any means *Use analytical methods to evaluate the following limits.*

85. $\lim\limits_{x \to 6} \dfrac{\sqrt[5]{5x + 2} - 2}{1/x - 1/6}$

86. $\lim\limits_{t \to \pi/2^+} \dfrac{\tan 3t}{\sec 5t}$

87. $\lim\limits_{x \to \infty} \left(\sqrt{x - 2} - \sqrt{x - 4}\right)$

88. $\lim\limits_{x \to \pi/2} (\pi - 2x) \tan x$

89. $\lim\limits_{x \to \infty} x^3 \left(\dfrac{1}{x} - \sin \dfrac{1}{x}\right)$

90. $\lim\limits_{x \to \infty} (x^2 e^{1/x} - x^2 - x)$

91. $\lim\limits_{x \to 1^+} \left(\dfrac{1}{x-1} - \dfrac{1}{\sqrt{x-1}}\right)$

92. $\lim\limits_{x \to 0^+} x^{\ln x}$

93. $\lim\limits_{x \to \infty} \dfrac{\log_2 x}{\log_3 x}$

94. $\lim\limits_{x \to \infty} (\log_2 x - \log_3 x)$

95. $\lim\limits_{n \to \infty} \dfrac{1 + 2 + \cdots + n}{n^2}$ (*Hint:* We show in Chapter 5 that

$$1 + 2 + \cdots + n = \dfrac{n(n+1)}{2}.\Big)$$

96. $\lim\limits_{x \to 0} \left(\dfrac{\sin x}{x}\right)^{1/x^2}$

97. It may take time The ranking of growth rates given in the text applies for $x \to \infty$. However, these rates may not be evident for small values of x. For example, an exponential grows faster than any power of x. However, for $1 < x < 19{,}800$, x^2 is greater than $e^{x/1000}$. For the following pairs of functions, estimate the point at which the faster-growing function overtakes the slower-growing function (for the last time).

a. $\ln^3 x$ and $x^{0.3}$
b. $2^{x/100}$ and x^3
c. $x^{x/100}$ and e^x
d. $\ln^{10} x$ and $e^{x/10}$

98–101. Limits with parameters *Evaluate the following limits in terms of the parameters a and b, which are positive real numbers. In each case, graph the function for specific values of the parameters to check your results.*

98. $\lim\limits_{x \to 0} (1 + ax)^{b/x}$

99. $\lim\limits_{x \to 0^+} (a^x - b^x)^x, a > b > 0$

100. $\lim\limits_{x \to 0^+} (a^x - b^x)^{1/x}, a > b > 0$

101. $\lim\limits_{x \to 0} \dfrac{a^x - b^x}{x}$

Applications

102. An optics limit The theory of interference of coherent oscillators requires the limit $\lim\limits_{\delta \to 2m\pi} \dfrac{\sin^2 (N\delta/2)}{\sin^2 (\delta/2)}$, where N is a positive integer and m is any integer. Show that the value of this limit is N^2.

103. Compound interest Suppose you make a deposit of $P into a savings account that earns interest at a rate of 100 r% per year.

  a. Show that if interest is compounded once per year, then the balance after t years is $B(t) = P(1 + r)^t$.

  b. If interest is compounded m times per year, then the balance after t years is $B(t) = P(1 + r/m)^{mt}$. For example, $m = 12$ corresponds to monthly compounding, and the interest rate for each month is $r/12$. In the limit $m \to \infty$, the compounding is said to be *continuous*. Show that with continuous compounding, the balance after t years is $B(t) = Pe^{rt}$.

104. Algorithm complexity The complexity of a computer algorithm is the number of operations or steps the algorithm needs to complete its task assuming there are n pieces of input (for example, the number of steps needed to put n numbers in ascending order). Four algorithms for doing the same task have complexities of A: $n^{3/2}$, B: $n \log_2 n$, C: $n(\log_2 n)^2$, and D: $\sqrt{n} \log_2 n$. Rank the algorithms in order of increasing efficiency for large values of n. Graph the complexities as they vary with n and comment on your observations.

Additional Exercises

105. L'Hôpital loops Consider the limit $\lim\limits_{x \to \infty} \dfrac{\sqrt{ax + b}}{\sqrt{cx + d}}$, where $a, b, c,$ and d are positive real numbers. Show that l'Hôpital's Rule fails for this limit. Find the limit using another method.

106. General $\infty - \infty$ result Let a and b be positive real numbers. Evaluate $\lim\limits_{x \to \infty} (ax - \sqrt{a^2x^2 - bx})$ in terms of a and b.

107. Exponential functions and powers Show that any exponential function b^x, for $b > 1$, grows faster than x^p, for $p > 0$.

108. Exponentials with different bases Show that $f(x) = a^x$ grows faster than $g(x) = b^x$ as $x \to \infty$ if $1 < b < a$.

109. Logs with different bases Show that $f(x) = \log_a x$ and $g(x) = \log_b x$, where $a > 1$ and $b > 1$, grow at a comparable rate as $x \to \infty$.

110. Factorial growth rate The factorial function is defined for positive integers as $n! = n(n - 1)(n - 2) \cdots 3 \cdot 2 \cdot 1$. For example, $5! = 5 \cdot 4 \cdot 3 \cdot 2 \cdot 1 = 120$. A valuable result that gives good approximations to $n!$ for large values of n is *Stirling's formula*, $n! \approx \sqrt{2\pi n}\, n^n e^{-n}$. Use this formula and a calculator to determine where the factorial function appears in the ranking of growth rates given in Theorem 4.15. (See the Guided Project *Stirling's Formula*.)

111. A geometric limit Let $f(\theta)$ be the area of the triangle ABP (see figure) and let $g(\theta)$ be the area of the region between the chord PB and the arc PB. Evaluate $\lim\limits_{\theta \to 0} g(\theta)/f(\theta)$.

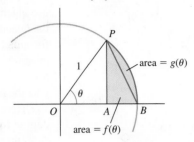

112. A fascinating function Consider the function $f(x) = (ab^x + (1 - a)c^x)^{1/x}$, where $a, b,$ and c are positive real numbers with $0 < a < 1$.

  a. Graph f for several sets of (a, b, c). Verify that in all cases, f is an increasing function with a single inflection point, for all x.

  b. Use analytical methods to determine $\lim\limits_{x \to 0} f(x)$ in terms of $a, b,$ and c.

  c. Show that $\lim\limits_{x \to \infty} f(x) = \max\{b, c\}$ and $\lim\limits_{x \to -\infty} f(x) = \min\{b, c\}$, for any $0 < a < 1$.

  d. Estimate the location of the inflection point of f.

113. Exponential limit Prove that $\lim\limits_{x \to \infty} \left(1 + \dfrac{a}{x}\right)^x = e^a$, for $a \neq 0$.

114. Exponentials vs. super exponentials Show that x^x grows faster than b^x as $x \to \infty$, for $b > 1$.

115. Exponential growth rates

  a. For what values of $b > 0$ does b^x grow faster than e^x as $x \to \infty$?

  b. Compare the growth rates of e^x and e^{ax} as $x \to \infty$, for $a > 0$.

QUICK CHECK   ANSWERS

1. g and h **2.** g and h **3.** $0 \cdot \infty$; $(x - \pi/2)/\cot x$ **4.** The form 0^∞ (for example, $\lim\limits_{x \to 0^+} x^{1/x}$) is not indeterminate, because as the base goes to zero, raising it to larger and larger powers drives the entire function to zero.   **6.** x^3 grows faster than x^2 as $x \to \infty$, whereas x^2 and $10x^2$ have comparable growth rates as $x \to \infty$. ◄

4.8 Newton's Method

> Newton's method is attributed to Sir Isaac Newton, who devised the method in 1669. However, similar methods were known prior to Newton's time. A special case of Newton's method for approximating square roots is called the Babylonian method and was probably invented by Greek mathematicians.

A common problem that arises in mathematics is finding the *roots*, or *zeros*, of a function. The roots of a function are the values of x that satisfy the equation $f(x) = 0$. Equivalently, they correspond to the x-intercepts of the graph of f. You have already seen an important example of a root-finding problem. To find the critical points of a function f, we must solve the equation $f'(x) = 0$; that is, we find the roots of f'. Newton's method, which we discuss in this section, is one of the most effective methods for *approximating* the roots of a function.

Why Approximate?

A little background about roots of functions explains why a method is needed to approximate roots. If you are given a linear function, such as $f(x) = 2x - 9$, you know how to use algebraic methods to solve $f(x) = 0$ and find the single root $x = \frac{9}{2}$. Similarly, given the quadratic function $f(x) = x^2 - 6x - 72$, you know how to factor or use the quadratic formula to discover that the roots are $x = 12$ and $x = -6$. It turns out that formulas also exist for finding the roots of cubic (third-degree) and quartic (fourth-degree) polynomials. Methods such as factoring and algebra are called *analytical methods*; when they work, they give the roots of a function *exactly* in terms of arithmetic operations and radicals.

Here is an important fact: Apart from the functions we have listed—polynomials of degree four or less—analytical methods do not give the roots of most functions. To be sure, there are special cases in which analytical methods work. For example, you should verify that the single root of $f(x) = e^{2x} + 2e^x - 3$ is $x = 0$, and two of the roots of $f(x) = x^{10} - 1$ are $x = 1$ and $x = -1$. But in general, the roots of even relatively simple functions such as $f(x) = e^{-x} - x$ cannot be found exactly using analytical methods.

When analytical methods do not work, which is the majority of cases, we need another approach. That approach is to approximate roots using numerical methods, such as Newton's method.

Deriving Newton's Method

Newton's method is most easily derived geometrically. Assume that r is a root of f that we wish to approximate; this means that $f(r) = 0$. We also assume that f is differentiable on some interval containing r. Suppose x_0 is an initial approximation to r that is generally obtained by some preliminary analysis. A better approximation to r is often obtained by carrying out the following two steps:

• A line tangent to the curve $y = f(x)$ at the point $(x_0, f(x_0))$ is drawn.

• The point $(x_1, 0)$ at which the tangent line intersects the x-axis is found and x_1 becomes the new approximation to r.

For the curve shown in Figure 4.80a, x_1 is a better approximation to the root r than x_0.

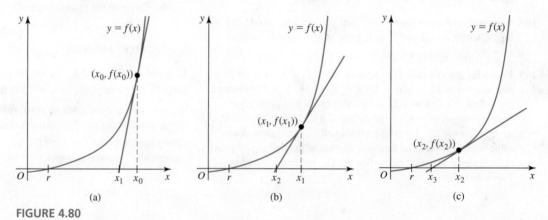

FIGURE 4.80

Sequences are the subject of Chapter 9.
An ordered set of numbers

$$\{x_1, x_2, x_3, \ldots\}$$

is a sequence, and if its values approach a number r, we say that the sequence *converges* to r. If a sequence fails to approach a single number, the sequence *diverges*.

To improve the approximation x_1, we repeat the two-step process, using x_1 to determine the next estimate x_2 (Figure 4.80b). Then x_2 is used to obtain x_3 (Figure 4.80c), and so forth. Continuing in this fashion, we obtain a *sequence* of approximations $\{x_1, x_2, x_3, \ldots\}$ that ideally get closer and closer, or *converge*, to the root r. Several steps of Newton's method and the convergence of the approximations to the root are shown in Figure 4.81.

All that remains is to find a formula that captures the process just described. Assume that we have computed the nth approximation x_n to the root r and we want to obtain the next approximation x_{n+1}. We first draw the line tangent to the curve at the point

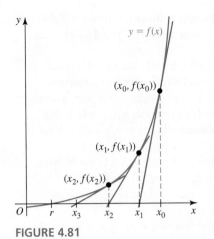

FIGURE 4.81

> ▶ Recall that the point-slope form of the equation of a line with slope m passing through (x_n, y_n) is
>
> $$y - y_n = m(x - x_n).$$

> ▶ Newton's method is an example of a repetitive loop calculation called an *iteration*. The most efficient way to implement the method is with a calculator or computer. The method is also included in many software packages.

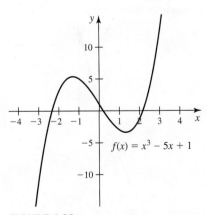

FIGURE 4.82

$(x_n, f(x_n))$; its slope is $m = f'(x_n)$. Using the point-slope form of the equation of a line, an equation of the tangent line at the point $(x_n, f(x_n))$ is

$$y - f(x_n) = \underbrace{f'(x_n)}_{m}(x - x_n).$$

We find the point at which this line intersects the x-axis by setting $y = 0$ in the equation of the line and solving for x. This value of x becomes the new approximation x_{n+1}:

$$\underbrace{0 - f(x_n)}_{\text{set } y \text{ to } 0} = f'(x_n)(\underbrace{x}_{\substack{\text{becomes} \\ x_{n+1}}} - x_n).$$

Solving for x and calling it x_{n+1}, we find that

$$\underbrace{x_{n+1}}_{\substack{\text{new} \\ \text{approximation}}} = \underbrace{x_n}_{\substack{\text{current} \\ \text{approximation}}} - \frac{f(x_n)}{f'(x_n)}, \text{ provided } f'(x_n) \neq 0.$$

We have derived the general step of Newton's method for approximating roots of a function f. This step is repeated for $n = 0, 1, 2, \ldots$, until a termination condition is met (to be discussed).

PROCEDURE   **Newton's Method for Approximating Roots of $f(x) = 0$**

1. Choose an initial approximation x_0 as close to a root as possible.

2. For $n = 0, 1, 2, \ldots$

$$x_{n+1} = x_n - \frac{f(x_n)}{f'(x_n)},$$

provided $f'(x_n) \neq 0$.

3. End the calculations when a termination condition is met.

QUICK CHECK 1 Verify that setting $y = 0$ in the equation $y - f(x_n) = f'(x_n)(x - x_n)$ and solving for x gives the formula for Newton's method. ◀

EXAMPLE 1   **Applying Newton's method** Approximate the roots of $f(x) = x^3 - 5x + 1$ using seven steps of Newton's method. Use $x_0 = -3$, $x_0 = 1$, and $x_0 = 4$ as initial approximations (Figure 4.82).

SOLUTION Noting that $f'(x) = 3x^2 - 5$, Newton's method takes the form

$$x_{n+1} = x_n - \frac{\overbrace{x_n^3 - 5x_n + 1}^{f(x_n)}}{\underbrace{3x_n^2 - 5}_{f'(x_n)}} = \frac{2x_n^3 - 1}{3x_n^2 - 5},$$

where $n = 0, 1, 2, \ldots$, and x_0 is specified. With an initial approximation of $x_0 = -3$, the first approximation is

$$x_1 = \frac{2x_0^3 - 1}{3x_0^2 - 5} = \frac{2(-3)^3 - 1}{3(-3)^2 - 5} = -2.5.$$

The second approximation is

$$x_2 = \frac{2x_1^3 - 1}{3x_1^2 - 5} = \frac{2(-2.5)^3 - 1}{3(-2.5)^2 - 5} \approx -2.345455.$$

Table 4.5

k	x_k	x_k	x_k
0	−3	1	4
1	−2.500000	−0.500000	2.953488
2	−2.345455	0.294118	2.386813
3	−2.330203	0.200215	2.166534
4	−2.330059	0.201639	2.129453
5	−2.330059	0.201640	2.128420
6	−2.330059	0.201640	2.128419
7	−2.330059	0.201640	2.128419

➤ The numbers in Table 4.5 were computed with 16 decimal digits of precision. The results are displayed with 6 digits to the right of the decimal point.

Continuing in this fashion, we generate the first seven approximations shown in Table 4.5. The approximations generated from the initial approximations $x_0 = 1$ and $x_0 = 4$ are also shown in the table.

Notice that with the initial approximation $x_0 = -3$ (second column), the resulting sequence of approximations settles on the value −2.330059 after four iterations, and then there are no further changes in these digits. A similar behavior is seen with the initial approximations $x_0 = 1$ and $x_0 = 4$. Based on this evidence, we conclude that −2.330059, 0.201640, and 2.128419 are approximations to the roots of f with at least six digits (to the right of the decimal point) of accuracy.

A graph of f (Figure 4.83) confirms that f has three real roots and that the Newton approximations to the three roots are reasonable. The figure also shows the first three Newton approximations at each root.   *Related Exercises 5–14* ◄

QUICK CHECK 2 If you applied Newton's method to the function $f(x) = x$, what would the result be?

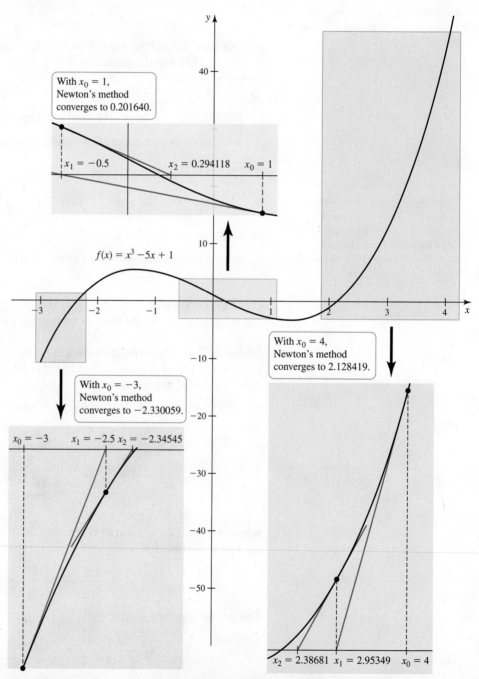

FIGURE 4.83

> If you write a program for Newton's method, it is a good idea to specify a maximum number of iterations as an escape clause in case the method does not converge.

> Small residuals do not always imply small errors: The function represented by this graph has a zero at $x = 0$. An approximation such as 0.5 has a small residual, but a large error.

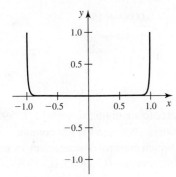

When Do You Stop?

Example 1 raises an important question and gives a practical answer: How many Newton approximations should you compute? Ideally, we would like to compute the **error** in x_n as an approximation to the root r, which is the quantity $|x_n - r|$. Unfortunately, we don't know r in practice; it is the quantity that we are trying to approximate. So we need a practical way to estimate the error.

In the second column of Table 4.5, we see that x_4 and x_5 agree in their seven digits, -2.330059. A general rule of thumb is that if two successive approximations agree to, say, seven digits, then those common digits are accurate (as an approximation to the root). So if you want p digits of accuracy in your approximation, you should compute until either two successive approximations agree to p digits or until some maximum number of iterations is exceeded (in which case Newton's method has failed to find an approximation of the root with the desired accuracy).

There is another practical way to gauge the accuracy of approximations. Because Newton's method generates approximations to a root of f, it follows that as the approximations x_n approach the root, $f(x_n)$ should approach zero. The quantity $f(x_n)$ is called a **residual**, and small residuals usually (but not always) suggest that the approximations have small errors. In Example 1, we find that for the approximations in the second column, $f(x_7) = -1.78 \times 10^{-15}$; for the approximations in the third column, $f(x_7) = 1.11 \times 10^{-16}$; and for the approximations in the fourth column, $f(x_7) = -1.78 \times 10^{-15}$. All these residuals (computed in full precision) are small in magnitude, giving additional confidence that the approximations have small errors.

EXAMPLE 2 **Finding intersection points** Find the points at which the curves $y = \cos x$ and $y = x$ intersect.

SOLUTION The graphs of two functions g and h intersect at points whose x-coordinates satisfy $g(x) = h(x)$, or, equivalently, where

$$f(x) = g(x) - h(x) = 0.$$

We see that finding intersection points is a root-finding problem. In this case, the intersection points of the curves $y = \cos x$ and $y = x$ satisfy

$$f(x) = \cos x - x = 0.$$

A preliminary graph is advisable to determine the number of intersection points and good initial approximations. From Figure 4.84a, we see that the two curves have one intersection point, and its x-coordinate is between 0 and 1. Equivalently, the function f has a zero between 0 and 1 (Figure 4.84b). A reasonable initial approximation is $x_0 = 0.5$.

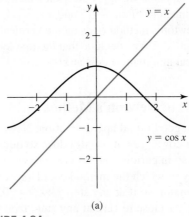

(a)

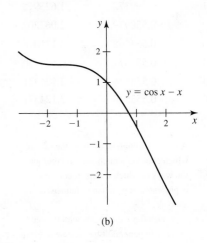

(b)

FIGURE 4.84

Newton's method takes the form

$$x_{n+1} = x_n - \dfrac{\overbrace{\cos x_n - x_n}^{f(x_n)}}{\underbrace{-\sin x_n - 1}_{f'(x_n)}} = \dfrac{x_n \sin x_n + \cos x_n}{\sin x_n + 1}.$$

The results of Newton's method, using an initial approximation of $x_0 = 0.5$, are shown in Table 4.6.

Table 4.6

k	x_k	Residual
0	0.5	0.377583
1	0.755222	−0.0271033
2	0.739142	−0.0000946154
3	0.739085	−1.18098 × 10^{-9}
4	0.739085	0
5	0.739085	0

We see that after four iterations, the approximations agree to six digits; so we take 0.739085 as the approximation to the root. Furthermore, the residuals, shown in the last column and computed with full precision, are essentially zero, which confirms the accuracy of the approximation. Therefore, the intersection point is approximately (0.739085, 0.739085) (because the point lies on the line $y = x$).

Related Exercises 15–20◄

EXAMPLE 3 Finding local extrema Find the x-coordinate of the first local maximum and the first local minimum of the function $f(x) = e^{-x} \sin 2x$ on the interval $(0, \infty)$.

SOLUTION A graph of the function provides some guidance. Figure 4.85 shows that f has an infinite number of local extrema for $x > 0$. The first local maximum occurs on the interval $[0, 1]$, and the first local minimum occurs on the interval $[2, 3]$.

To locate the local extrema, we must find the critical points by solving

$$f'(x) = e^{-x}(2 \cos 2x - \sin 2x) = 0.$$

To this equation we apply Newton's method. The results of the calculations, using initial approximations of $x_0 = 0.2$ and $x_0 = 2.5$, are shown in Table 4.7.

Newton's method finds the two critical points quickly, and they are consistent with the graph of f. We conclude that the first local maximum occurs at $x \approx 0.553574$ and the first local minimum occurs at $x \approx 2.124371$.

Related Exercises 21–24◄

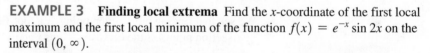

FIGURE 4.85

Table 4.7

k	x_k	x_k
0	0.200000	2.500000
1	0.499372	1.623915
2	0.550979	2.062202
3	0.553568	2.121018
4	0.553574	2.124360
5	0.553574	2.124371
6	0.553574	2.124371

Pitfalls of Newton's Method

Given a good initial approximation, Newton's method usually converges to a root. And when it converges, it usually does so quickly. However, when Newton's method fails, it does so in curious and spectacular ways. The formula for Newton's method suggests one way in which the method could encounter difficulties: The term $f'(x_n)$ appears in a denominator, so if at any step $f'(x_n) = 0$, then the method breaks down. Furthermore, if $f'(x_n)$ is close to zero at any step, then the method may converge slowly or may fail to converge. The following example shows three ways in which Newton's method may go awry.

> A more thorough analysis of the rate at which Newton's method converges and the ways in which it fails to converge is presented in a course in numerical analysis.
>
> Newton's method is widely used because in general, it has a remarkable rate of convergence; the number of digits of accuracy roughly doubles with each iteration.

EXAMPLE 4   Difficulties with Newton's method Find the root of $f(x) = \dfrac{8x^2}{3x^2 + 1}$ using Newton's method with initial approximations of $x_0 = 1$, $x_0 = 0.15$, and $x_0 = 1.1$.

SOLUTION Notice that f has the single root $x = 0$. So the point of the example is not to find the root, but to investigate the performance of Newton's method. Computing f' and doing a few steps of algebra show that the formula for Newton's method is

$$x_{n+1} = x_n - \frac{f(x_n)}{f'(x_n)} = \frac{x_n}{2}\left(1 - 3x_n^2\right).$$

The results of five iterations of Newton's method are displayed in Table 4.8, and they tell three different stories.

Table 4.8

k	x_k	x_k	x_k
0	1	0.15	1.1
1	−1	0.0699375	−1.4465
2	1	0.0344556	3.81665
3	−1	0.0171665	−81.4865
4	1	0.00857564	8.11572×10^5
5	−1	0.00428687	-8.01692×10^{17}

The approximations generated using $x_0 = 1$ (second column) get stuck in a cycle that alternates between $+1$ and -1. The geometry underlying this rare occurrence is illustrated in Figure 4.86.

The approximations generated using $x_0 = 0.15$ (third column) actually converge to the root 0, but they converge slowly (Figure 4.87). Notice that the error is reduced by a factor of approximately 2 with each step. Newton's method usually has a faster rate of error reduction. The slow convergence is due to the fact that both f and f' have zeros at 0. As mentioned earlier, if the approximations x_n approach a zero of f', the rate of convergence is often compromised.

The approximations generated using $x_0 = 1.1$ (fourth column) increase in magnitude quickly and do not converge to a finite value, even though this initial approximation seems reasonable. The geometry of this case is shown in Figure 4.88.

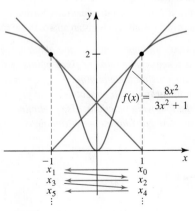

FIGURE 4.86

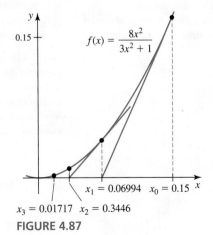

FIGURE 4.87

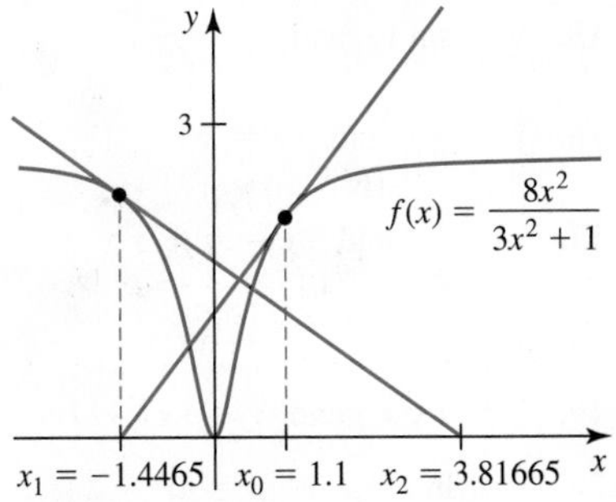

FIGURE 4.88

The three cases in this example illustrate the most common ways that Newton's method may fail to converge at its usual rate: The approximations may cycle or wander, they may converge slowly, or they may diverge (often at a rapid rate).

Related Exercises 25–26 ◄

SECTION 4.8 EXERCISES

Review Questions

1. Give a geometric explanation of Newton's method.

2. Explain how the iteration formula for Newton's method works.

3. How do you decide when to terminate Newton's method?

4. Give the formula for Newton's method for the function $f(x) = x^2 - 5$.

Basic Skills

5–8. Formulating Newton's method *Write the formula for Newton's method and use the given initial approximation to compute the approximations x_1 and x_2.*

5. $f(x) = x^2 - 6;\ x_0 = 3$

6. $f(x) = x^2 - 2x - 3;\ x_0 = 2$

7. $f(x) = e^{-x} - x;\ x_0 = \ln 2$

8. $f(x) = x^3 - 2;\ x_0 = 2$

9–14. Finding roots with Newton's method *Use a calculator or program to compute the first 10 iterations of Newton's method when it is applied to the following functions with the given initial approximation. Make a table similar to that in Example 1.*

9. $f(x) = x^2 - 10;\ x_0 = 4$

10. $f(x) = x^3 + x^2 + 1;\ x_0 = -2$

11. $f(x) = \sin x + x - 1;\ x_0 = 1.5$

12. $f(x) = e^x - 5;\ x_0 = 2$

13. $f(x) = \tan x - 2x;\ x_0 = 1.5$

14. $f(x) = \ln(x + 1) - 1;\ x_0 = 1.7$

15–20. Finding intersection points *Use Newton's method to approximate all the intersection points of the following pairs of curves. Some preliminary graphing or analysis may help in choosing good initial approximations.*

15. $y = \sin x$ and $y = \dfrac{x}{2}$

16. $y = e^x$ and $y = x^3$

17. $y = \dfrac{1}{x}$ and $y = 4 - x^2$

18. $y = x^3$ and $y = x^2 + 1$

19. $y = 4\sqrt{x}$ and $y = x^2 + 1$

20. $y = \ln x$ and $y = x^3 - 2$

21–24. Newton's method and curve sketching *Use Newton's method to find approximate answers to the following questions.*

21. Where is the first local minimum of $f(x) = \dfrac{\cos x}{x}$ on the interval $(0, \infty)$ located?

22. Where are all the local extrema of $f(x) = 3x^4 + 8x^3 + 12x^2 + 48x$ located?

23. Where are the inflection points of $f(x) = \dfrac{9}{5}x^5 - \dfrac{15}{2}x^4 + \dfrac{7}{3}x^3 + 30x^2 + 1$ located?

24. Where is the local extremum of $f(x) = \dfrac{e^x}{x}$ located?

25–26. Slow convergence

25. The functions $f(x) = (x - 1)^2$ and $g(x) = x^2 - 1$ both have a root at $x = 1$. Apply Newton's method to both functions with an initial approximation $x_0 = 2$. Compare the rate at which the method converges in each case and give an explanation.

26. Consider the function $f(x) = x^5 + 4x^4 + x^3 - 10x^2 - 4x + 8$, which has zeros at $x = 1$ and $x = -2$. Apply Newton's method to this function with initial approximations of $x_0 = -1$, $x_0 = -0.2$, $x_0 = 0.2$, and $x_0 = 2$. Discuss and compare the results of the calculations.

Further Explorations

27. **Explain why or why not** Determine whether the following statements are true and give an explanation or counterexample.

   a. Newton's method is an example of a numerical method for approximating the roots of a function.

   b. Newton's method gives a better approximation to the roots of a quadratic equation than the quadratic formula.

   c. Newton's method always finds an approximate root of a function.

28–31. Fixed points *An important question about many functions concerns the existence and location of **fixed points**. A fixed point of f is a value of x that satisfies the equation $f(x) = x$; it corresponds to a point at which the graph of f intersects the line $y = x$. Find all the fixed points of the following functions. Use preliminary analysis and graphing to determine good initial approximations.*

28. $f(x) = 5 - x^2$

29. $f(x) = \dfrac{x^3}{10} + 1$

30. $f(x) = \tan \dfrac{x}{2}$ on $(-\pi, \pi)$

31. $f(x) = 2x \cos x$ on $[0, 2]$

32–38. More root finding *Find all the roots of the following functions. Use preliminary analysis and graphing to determine good initial approximations.*

32. $f(x) = \cos x - \dfrac{x}{7}$

33. $f(x) = \cos 2x - x^2 + 2x$

34. $f(x) = \dfrac{x}{6} - \sec x$ on $[0, 8]$

35. $f(x) = e^{-x} - \dfrac{x+4}{5}$

36. $f(x) = \dfrac{x^5}{5} - \dfrac{x^3}{4} - \dfrac{1}{20}$

37. $f(x) = \ln x - x^2 + 3x - 1$

38. $f(x) = x^2(x - 100) + 1$

39. Residuals and errors Approximate the root of $f(x) = x^{10}$ at $x = 0$ using Newton's method with an initial approximation of $x_0 = 0.5$. Make a table showing the first 10 approximations, the error in these approximations (which is $|x_n - 0| = |x_n|$), and the residual of these approximations (which is $f(x_n)$). Comment on the relative size of the errors and the residuals, and give an explanation.

40. A tangent question Verify by graphing that the graphs of $y = \sin x$ and $y = x/2$ have one point of intersection, for $x > 0$, whereas the graphs of $y = \sin x$ and $y = x/9$ have three points of intersection, for $x > 0$. Approximate the value of a such that the graphs of $y = \sin x$ and $y = x/a$ have exactly two points of intersection, for $x > 0$.

41. A tangent question Verify by graphing that the graphs of $y = e^x$ and $y = x$ have no points of intersection, whereas the graphs of $y = e^{x/3}$ and $y = x$ have two points of intersection. Approximate the value of $a > 0$ such that the graphs of $y = e^{x/a}$ and $y = x$ have exactly one point of intersection.

42. Approximating square roots Let $a > 0$ be given, and suppose we want to approximate $\sqrt{a}$ using Newton's method.

a. Explain why the square root problem is equivalent to finding the positive root of $f(x) = x^2 - a$.

b. Show that Newton's method applied to this function takes the form (sometimes called the Babylonian method)

$$x_{n+1} = \frac{1}{2}\left(x_n + \frac{a}{x_n}\right), \quad \text{for } n = 0, 1, 2, \dots.$$

c. How would you choose initial approximations to approximate $\sqrt{13}$ and $\sqrt{73}$?

d. Approximate $\sqrt{13}$ and $\sqrt{73}$ with at least 10 significant digits.

43. Approximating reciprocals To approximate the reciprocal of a number a without using division, we can apply Newton's method to the function $f(x) = \dfrac{1}{x} - a$.

a. Verify that Newton's method gives the formula $x_{n+1} = (2 - ax_n)x_n$.

b. Apply Newton's method with $a = 7$ using a starting value of your choice. Compute an approximation with eight digits of accuracy. What number does Newton's method approximate in this case?

44. Modified Newton's method The function f has a root of *multiplicity* 2 at r if $f(r) = f'(r) = 0$ and $f''(r) \neq 0$. In this case, a slight modification of Newton's method, known as the *modified* (or *accelerated*) Newton's method, is given by the formula

$$x_{n+1} = x_n - \frac{2f(x_n)}{f'(x_n)}, \quad \text{for } n = 0, 1, 2, \dots.$$

This modified form generally increases the rate of convergence.

a. Verify that 0 is a root of multiplicity 2 of the function $f(x) = e^{2\sin x} - 2x - 1$.

b. Apply Newton's method and the modified Newton's method using $x_0 = 0.1$ to find the value of x_3 in each case. Compare the accuracy of each value of x_3.

c. Consider the function $f(x) = \dfrac{8x^2}{3x^2 + 1}$ given in Example 4. Use the modified Newton's method to find the value of x_3 using $x_0 = 0.15$. Compare this value to the value of x_3 found in Example 4 with $x_0 = 0.15$.

Applications

45. A damped oscillator The displacement of a particular object as it bounces vertically up and down on a spring is given by $y(t) = 2.5e^{-t}\cos 2t$, where the initial displacement is $y(0) = 2.5$ and $y = 0$ corresponds to the rest position (see figure).

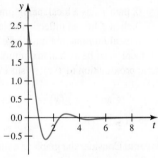

a. Find the time at which the object first passes the rest position, $y = 0$.

b. Find the time and the displacement when the object reaches its lowest point.

c. Find the time at which the object passes the rest position for the second time.

d. Find the time and the displacement when the object reaches its high point for the second time.

46. The sinc function The sinc function $\operatorname{sinc}(x) = \dfrac{\sin x}{x}$ appears frequently in signal-processing applications.

a. Graph the sinc function on $[-2\pi, 2\pi]$.

b. Locate the first local minimum and the first local maximum of $\operatorname{sinc}(x)$, for $x > 0$.

47. An eigenvalue problem A certain kind of differential equation (see Chapter 8) leads to the root-finding problem $\tan \pi\lambda = \lambda$, where the roots λ are called **eigenvalues**. Find the first three positive eigenvalues of this problem.

Additional Exercises

T 48. Fixed points of quadratics and quartics Let $f(x) = ax(1 - x)$, where a is a real number and $0 \leq x \leq 1$. Recall that the fixed point of a function is a value of x such that $f(x) = x$ (Exercises 28–31).

a. Without using a calculator, find the values of a, with $0 < a \leq 4$, such that f has a fixed point. Give the fixed point in terms of a.

b. Consider the polynomial $g(x) = f(f(x))$. Write g in terms of a and powers of x. What is its degree?

c. Graph g for $a = 2, 3,$ and 4.

d. Find the number and location of the fixed points of g for $a = 2, 3,$ and 4 on the interval $0 \leq x \leq 1$.

T 49. Basins of attraction Suppose f has a real root r and Newton's method is used to approximate r with an initial approximation x_0. The **basin of attraction** of r is the set of initial approximations that produce a sequence that converges to r. Points near r are often in the basin of attraction of r—but not always. Sometimes an initial approximation x_0 may produce a sequence that doesn't converge, and sometimes an initial approximation x_0 may produce a sequence that converges to a distant root. Let $f(x) = (x + 2)(x + 1)(x - 3)$, which has roots $x = -2, -1,$ and 3. Use Newton's method with initial approximations on the interval $[-4, 4]$ and determine (approximately) the basin of each root.

QUICK CHECK ANSWERS

1. $0 - f(x_n) = f'(x_n)(x - x_n) \Rightarrow -\dfrac{f(x_n)}{f'(x_n)} = x - x_n \Rightarrow$

$x = x_n - \dfrac{f(x_n)}{f'(x_n)}$ 2. Newton's method will find the root

$x = 0$ exactly in one step. ◄

CHAPTER 4   REVIEW EXERCISES

1. **Explain why or why not** Determine whether the following statements are true and give an explanation or counterexample.

a. If $f'(c) = 0$, then f has a local maximum or minimum at c.

b. If $f''(c) = 0$, then f has an inflection point at c.

c. Between two local minima of a function continuous on $(-\infty, \infty)$, there must be a local maximum.

d. The linear approximation to $f(x) = \sin x$ at $x = 0$ is $L(x) = x$.

e. If $\lim\limits_{x \to \infty} f(x) = \infty$ and $\lim\limits_{x \to \infty} g(x) = \infty$, then $\lim\limits_{x \to \infty} (f(x) - g(x)) = 0$.

2. **Locating extrema** Consider the graph of a function f on the interval $[-3, 3]$.

a. Give the approximate coordinates of the local maxima and minima of f.

b. Give the approximate coordinates of the absolute maximum and minimum of f (if they exist).

c. Give the approximate coordinates of the inflection point(s) of f.

d. Give the approximate coordinates of the zero(s) of f.

e. On what intervals (approximately) is f concave up?

f. On what intervals (approximately) is f concave down?

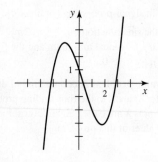

3–4. Designer functions *Sketch the graph of a function continuous on the given interval that satisfies the following conditions.*

3. f is continuous on the interval $[-4, 4]$; $f'(x) = 0$ for $x = -2$, $0,$ and 3; f has an absolute minimum at $x = 3$; f has a local minimum at $x = -2$; f has a local maximum at $x = 0$; f has an absolute maximum at $x = -4$.

4. f is continuous on $(-\infty, \infty)$; $f'(x) < 0$ and $f''(x) < 0$ on $(-\infty, 0)$; $f'(x) > 0$ and $f''(x) > 0$ on $(0, \infty)$.

5. **Functions from derivatives** Given the graphs of f' and f'', sketch a possible graph of f.

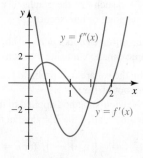

T 6–10. Critical points *Find the critical points of the following functions on the given intervals. Identify the absolute maximum and minimum values (if they exist). Graph the function to confirm your conclusions.*

6. $f(x) = \sin 2x + 3;\ [-\pi, \pi]$

7. $f(x) = 2x^3 - 3x^2 - 36x + 12;\ (-\infty, \infty)$

8. $f(x) = 4x^{1/2} - x^{5/2};\ [0, 4]$

9. $f(x) = 2x \ln x + 10;\ (0, 4)$

10. $g(x) = x^{1/3}(9 - x^2);\ [-4, 4]$

11. Absolute values Consider the function
$f(x) = |x - 2| + |x + 3|$ on $[-4, 4]$. Graph f, identify the critical points, and give the coordinates of the local and absolute extreme values.

12. Inflection points Does $f(x) = 2x^5 - 10x^4 + 20x^3 + x + 1$ have any inflection points? If so, identify them.

13–20. Curve sketching *Use the guidelines given in Section 4.3 to make a complete graph of the following functions on their domains or on the given interval. Use a graphing utility to check your work.*

13. $f(x) = x^4/2 - 3x^2 + 4x + 1$

14. $f(x) = \dfrac{3x}{x^2 + 3}$

15. $f(x) = 4 \cos(\pi(x - 1))$ on $[0, 2]$

16. $f(x) = \dfrac{x^2 + x}{4 - x^2}$

17. $f(x) = \sqrt[3]{x} - \sqrt{x} + 2$

18. $f(x) = \dfrac{\cos \pi x}{1 + x^2}$ on $[-2, 2]$

19. $f(x) = x^{2/3} + (x + 2)^{1/3}$

20. $f(x) = x(x - 1) e^{-x}$

21. Optimization A right triangle has legs of length h and r, and a hypotenuse of length 4 (see figure). It is revolved about the leg of length h to sweep out a right circular cone. What values of h and r maximize the volume of the cone? (Volume of a cone $= \pi r^2 h/3$.)

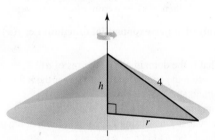

22. Rectangles beneath a curve A rectangle is constructed with one side on the positive x-axis, one side on the positive y-axis, and the vertex opposite the origin on the curve $y = \cos x$, for $0 < x < \pi/2$. Approximate the dimensions of the rectangle that maximize the area of the rectangle. What is the area?

23. Maximum printable area A rectangular page in a textbook (with width x and length y) has an area of 98 in², top and bottom margins set at 1 in, and left and right margins set at $\frac{1}{2}$ in. The printable area of the page is the rectangle that lies within the margins. What are the dimensions of the page that maximize the printable area?

24. Nearest point What point on the graph of $f(x) = \frac{5}{2} - x^2$ is closest to the origin? (*Hint:* You can minimize the square of the distance.)

25. Maximum area A line segment of length 10 joins the points $(0, p)$ and $(q, 0)$ to form a triangle in the first quadrant. Find the values of p and q that maximize the area of the triangle.

26. Minimum painting surface A metal cistern in the shape of a right circular cylinder with volume $V = 50\text{ m}^3$ needs to be painted each year to reduce corrosion. The paint is applied only to surfaces exposed to the elements (the outside cylinder wall and the circular top). Find the dimensions r and h of the cylinder that minimize the area of the painted surfaces.

27–28. Linear approximation

a. *Find the linear approximation to f at the given point a.*
b. *Use your answer from part (a) to estimate the given function value.*

27. $f(x) = x^{2/3}$; $a = 27$; $f(29)$

28. $f(x) = \sin^{-1} x$; $a = 1/2$; $f(0.48)$

29–30. Estimations with linear approximation *Use linear approximation to estimate the following quantities. Choose a value of a to produce a small error.*

29. $1/4.2^2$

30. $\tan^{-1} 1.05$

31. Change in elevation The elevation h (in feet above the ground) of a stone dropped from a height of 1000 ft is modeled by the equation $h(t) = 1000 - 16t^2$, where t is measured in seconds and air resistance is neglected. Approximate the change in elevation over the interval $5 \le t \le 5.7$ (recall that $\Delta h \approx h'(a)\Delta t$).

32. Change in energy The energy E (in joules) released by an earthquake of magnitude M is modeled by the equation $E(M) = 25{,}000 \cdot 10^{1.5 M}$. Approximate the change in energy released when the magnitude changes from 7.0 to 7.5 (recall that $\Delta E \approx E'(a)\Delta M$).

33. Mean Value Theorem The population of a culture of cells grows according to the function $P(t) = \dfrac{100t}{t + 1}$, where $t \ge 0$ is measured in weeks.

a. What is the average rate of change in the population over the interval $[0, 8]$?
b. At what point of the interval $[0, 8]$ is the instantaneous rate of change equal to the average rate of change?

34. Growth rate of bamboo Bamboo belongs to the grass family and is one of the fastest-growing plants in the world.

a. A bamboo shoot was 500 cm tall at 10.00 A.M. and 515 cm at 3:00 P.M. Compute the average growth rate of the bamboo shoot in cm/hr over the period of time from 10:00 A.M. to 3:00 P.M.
b. Based on the Mean Value Theorem, what can you conclude about the instantaneous growth rate of bamboo measured in *millimeters per second* between 10:00 A.M. and 3:00 P.M.?

35. Newton's method Use Newton's method to approximate the roots of $f(x) = 3x^3 - 4x^2 + 1$ to six digits.

36. Newton's method Use Newton's method to approximate the roots of $f(x) = e^{-2x} + 2e^x - 6$ to six digits. Make a table showing the first five approximations for each root using an initial estimate of your choice.

37. Newton's method Use Newton's method to approximate the x-coordinates of the inflection points of $f(x) = 2x^5 - 6x^3 - 4x + 2$ to six digits.

38–51. Limits *Evaluate the following limits. Use l'Hôpital's Rule when needed.*

38. $\displaystyle \lim_{t \to 2} \frac{t^3 - t^2 - 2t}{t^2 - 4}$

39. $\displaystyle \lim_{t \to 0} \frac{1 - \cos 6t}{2t}$

40. $\displaystyle \lim_{x \to \infty} \frac{5x^2 + 2x - 5}{\sqrt{x^4 - 1}}$

41. $\displaystyle \lim_{\theta \to 0} \frac{3 \sin^2 2\theta}{\theta^2}$

42. $\displaystyle \lim_{x \to \infty} \left(\sqrt{x^2 + x + 1} - \sqrt{x^2 - x} \right)$

43. $\displaystyle \lim_{\theta \to 0} 2\theta \cot 3\theta$

44. $\displaystyle \lim_{x \to 0} \frac{e^{-2x} - 1 + 2x}{x^2}$

45. $\displaystyle \lim_{y \to 0^+} \frac{\ln^{10} y}{\sqrt{y}}$

46. $\displaystyle \lim_{\theta \to 0} \frac{3 \sin 8\theta}{8 \sin 3\theta}$

47. $\displaystyle \lim_{x \to 1} \frac{x^4 - x^3 - 3x^2 + 5x - 2}{x^3 + x^2 - 5x + 3}$

48. $\displaystyle \lim_{x \to \infty} \frac{\ln x^{100}}{\sqrt{x}}$

49. $\displaystyle \lim_{x \to 0} \csc x \sin^{-1} x$

50. $\displaystyle \lim_{x \to \infty} \frac{\ln^3 x}{\sqrt{x}}$

51. $\displaystyle \lim_{x \to \infty} \ln \left(\frac{x + 1}{x - 1} \right)$

52–59. $1^\infty, 0^0, \infty^0$ forms *Evaluate the following limits. Check your results by graphing.*

52. $\displaystyle \lim_{x \to 0^+} (1 + x)^{\cot x}$

53. $\displaystyle \lim_{x \to \pi/2^-} (\sin x)^{\tan x}$

54. $\displaystyle \lim_{x \to \infty} (\sqrt{x} + 1)^{1/x}$

55. $\displaystyle \lim_{x \to 0^+} |\ln x|^x$

56. $\displaystyle \lim_{x \to \infty} x^{1/x}$

57. $\displaystyle \lim_{x \to \infty} \left(1 - \frac{3}{x} \right)^x$

58. $\displaystyle \lim_{x \to \infty} \left(\frac{2}{\pi} \tan^{-1} x \right)^x$

59. $\displaystyle \lim_{x \to 1} (x - 1)^{\sin \pi x}$

60–67. Comparing growth rates *Determine which of the two functions grows faster, or state that they have comparable growth rates.*

60. x^{100} and 1.1^x

61. $x^{1/2}$ and $x^{1/3}$

62. $\ln x$ and $\log_{10} x$

63. $\sqrt{x}$ and $\ln^{10} x$

64. $10x$ and $\ln x^2$

65. e^x and 3^x

66. $\sqrt{x^6 + 10}$ and x^3

67. 2^x and $4^{x/2}$

68. Logs of logs Compare the growth rates of $\ln x$, $\ln (\ln x)$, and $\ln (\ln (\ln x))$.

69. Two limits with exponentials Evaluate $\displaystyle \lim_{x \to 0^+} \frac{x}{\sqrt{1 - e^{-x^2}}}$ and $\displaystyle \lim_{x \to 0^+} \frac{x^2}{1 - e^{-x^2}}$ and confirm your result by graphing.

70. Geometric mean Prove that $\displaystyle \lim_{r \to 0} \left(\frac{a^r + b^r + c^r}{3} \right)^{1/r} = \sqrt[3]{abc}$, where a, b, and c are positive real numbers.

71–72. Two methods *Evaluate the following limits in two different ways: Use the methods of Chapter 2 and use l'Hôpital's Rule.*

71. $\displaystyle \lim_{x \to \infty} \frac{2x^5 - x + 1}{5x^6 + x}$

72. $\displaystyle \lim_{x \to \infty} \frac{4x^4 - \sqrt{x}}{2x^4 + x^{-1}}$

73. Towers of exponents The functions $f(x) = (x^x)^x$ and $g(x) = x^{(x^x)}$ are different functions. For example, $f(3) = 19{,}683$ and $g(3) \approx 7.6 \times 10^{12}$. Determine whether $\displaystyle \lim_{x \to 0^+} f(x)$ and $\displaystyle \lim_{x \to 0^+} g(x)$ are indeterminate forms and evaluate the limits.

74. Cosine limits Let n be a positive integer. Use graphical and/or analytical methods to verify the following limits.

a. $\displaystyle \lim_{x \to 0} \frac{1 - \cos x^n}{x^{2n}} = \frac{1}{2}$

b. $\displaystyle \lim_{x \to 0} \frac{1 - \cos^n x}{x^2} = \frac{n}{2}$

75. Limits for e Consider the function $g(x) = (1 + 1/x)^{x+a}$. Show that if $0 \le a < \frac{1}{2}$, then $g(x) \to e$ from *below* as $x \to \infty$; if $\frac{1}{2} \le a < 1$, then $g(x) \to e$ from *above* as $x \to \infty$.

76. A family of super-exponential functions Let $f(x) = (a + x)^x$, where $a > 0$.

a. What is the domain of f (in terms of a)?

b. Describe the end behavior of f (near the left boundary of its domain and as $x \to \infty$).

c. Compute f'. Then graph f and f', for $a = 0.5, 1, 2$, and 3.

d. Show that f has a single local minimum at the point z that satisfies $(z + a) \ln (z + a) + z = 0$.

e. Describe how z (found in part (d)) varies as a increases. Describe how $f(z)$ varies as a increases.

AP® PRACTICE QUESTIONS   *The following questions are intended to help you prepare for the AP exam. They are not questions from actual AP exams.*

Section 1 Part A, Multiple Choice, No Technology

Use the graph of the function *f* shown below for Questions 1–3. Assume that $f'(-1) = f'(0.5) = 0$ and $f''(-1) = f''(-0.25) = 0$.

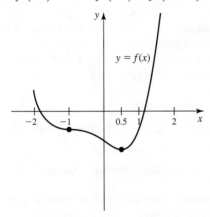

1. Which of the following statements is true?

(A) $x = 0.5$ is the only critical point on the interval $[-2, 1]$.

(B) $x = -1$ is a not a critical point because a local extremum does not occur there.

(C) $x = 0.5$ and $x = -1$ are critical points.

(D) $f(1) = f'(1)$

(E) *f* is decreasing and concave up on the interval $(-1, 0.5)$.

2. Which of the following statements is true on the interval $[-2, 1]$?

(A) The absolute maximum value of *f* occurs at $x = -2$.

(B) The absolute maximum value of *f* occurs at $x = 1$.

(C) A local minimum value of *f* occurs at $x = -1$.

(D) *f* has two local minimum values on the interval.

(E) None of the above is true.

3. How many inflection points does *f* have on the interval $[-2, 1]$?

(A) 0   (B) 1   (C) 2

(D) 3   (E) 4

4. The function $f(x) = xe^{-x}$ is

(A) increasing and concave up for $x > 2$.

(B) increasing and concave down for $x > 2$.

(C) decreasing and concave up for $x > 2$.

(D) decreasing and concave down for $x > 2$.

(E) increasing and concave up for $x < 1$.

5. If $f'(x) = (x - 1)(x - 2)^2(x - 3)$, then which of the following is true?

(A) *f* has one relative minimum and no relative maximum.

(B) *f* has one relative maximum and no relative minimum.

(C) *f* has two relative maximums and one relative minimum.

(D) *f* has two relative minimums and one relative maximum.

(E) *f* has one relative minimum and one relative maximum.

6. Find all the critical points of $f(x) = 2x^3 + 3x^2 - 12x + 10$.

(A) $x = 2$ and $x = 1$ (B) $x = -2$

(C) $x = 1$ (D) $x = -2$ and $x = 1$

(E) $x = -1$ and $x = 2$

7. What is true of the function $f(x) = (x - 1)^3$ at $x = 1$?

(A) It has a zero and a local minimum there.

(B) It has a zero and an inflection point there.

(C) It has a local minimum and an inflection point there.

(D) It has a zero, a local minimum, and an inflection point there.

(E) It has a vertical asymptote there.

8. The linear approximation to $y = \ln x$ at $(1, 0)$ is

(A) $y = x - 1$ (B) $y = x + 1$

(C) $y = 1 - x$ (D) $y = 2x - 2$

(E) $y = \ln x - \dfrac{1}{x}(x - 1)$

9. If the Mean Value Theorem is applied to the function $f(x) = x^2$ on the interval $[-1, 2]$, the point *c* guaranteed to exist by the theorem is

(A) 1   (B) 0   (C) $-\dfrac{1}{2}$

(D) $\dfrac{3}{2}$ (E) $\dfrac{1}{2}$

10. The function $y = \sin x$ has which of the following properties?

(I) Its inflection points are located at its zeros.

(II) It has the same zeros as its derivative.

(III) Its inflection points and local extrema are located at the same points.

(A) I only   (B) III only

(C) I and II only   (D) I and III only

(E) II and III only

11. Evaluate $\displaystyle\lim_{t \to 0} \dfrac{1 - \cos 2t}{3t^2}$.

(A) $\dfrac{3}{2}$ (B) $-\dfrac{1}{3}$ (C) $\dfrac{2}{3}$

(D) $-\dfrac{3}{2}$ (E) 0

12. Evaluate $\displaystyle\lim_{x \to \infty} \dfrac{\ln^3 x}{\sqrt[10]{x}}$.

(A) 1   (B) 0   (C) 2

(D) ∞ (E) 6000

13. Suppose *f* is differentiable on $[1, 5]$ with $f(1) = -2$ and $f(5) = 6$. Which of the following statements is necessarily true?

(I) There exists a number *c* in $(1, 5)$ such that $f'(c) = 0$.

(II) There exists a number *c* in $(1, 5)$ such that $f(c) = 0$.

(III) There exists a number *c* in $(1, 5)$ such that $f'(c) = 2$.

(A) I only   (B) II only

(C) I and II only   (D) I and III only

(E) II and III only

14. The figure shows the graph of the derivative of the function f on the interval $-2 < x < 2$. If f' has exactly five zeros on the interval $-2 < x < 2$, then how many relative minima does f have on $-2 < x < 2$?

(A) 1   (B) 2   (C) 3
(D) 4   (E) 5

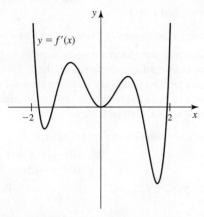

15. The function f is continuous on the interval $[1, 5]$ and differentiable on the interval $(1, 5)$. The following table gives selected values of f on $[1, 5]$.

x	1	2	3	4	5
$f(x)$	6	8	10	7	6

Which of the following statements must be true?

(I)   There exists at least one number c in $(1, 5)$ such that $f'(c) = 0$.
(II) There exist at least two distinct numbers c_1 and c_2 in $(1, 3)$ such that $f'(c_1) = f'(c_2) = 2$.
(III) The maximum value of f on $[1, 5]$ is 10.

(A) I only   (B) II only
(C) III only   (D) I and II only
(E) I, II, and III

Section 1 Part B, Multiple Choice, Technology Allowed

16. The graph of the function whose *derivative* is
$\frac{1}{20}(x - 3)^3(x + 2)^2$ has

(A) one local minimum and one local maxima.
(B) one absolute minimum and two inflection points.
(C) one local extreme value and three inflection points.
(D) two local extreme values and one inflection point.
(E) none of the above.

17. Consider the set of points that lie on the curve $y = 4 - x^3$. What is the maximum product of the x- and y-coordinates of all such points?

(A) 0   (B) 1
(C) $\sqrt[3]{4}$ (D) 3
(E) There is no maximum because the product grows arbitrarily large.

18. Find the linear approximation to $f(x) = \sin^{-1}x$ at the point $\left(\frac{1}{2}, \frac{\pi}{6}\right)$. Then use the linear approximation to estimate the value of $\sin^{-1}0.55$.

(A) 0.524   (B) 0.581
(C) 0.603   (D) 0.568
(E) 0.582

19. Consider the function $f(x) = x \sin x$ on the interval $[0, 6]$. What is the x-coordinate of the point on the graph of f where the line tangent to the graph at that point has a slope equal to 4?

(A) 4.493   (B) 4.913
(C) 5.353   (D) 5.657
(E) There is no such point.

Section 2 Part A, Free Response, Technology Allowed

1. Consider the curve C defined by $y^2 = x^3 - 6x + 6$.

   a. What is the equation of the line tangent to C at the point $(1, 1)$?

   b. Approximate the coordinates of all points on C at which there is a horizontal or vertical tangent line.

   c. How many times does the line $y = \frac{2}{5}x$ intersect C? Justify your answer, and find the coordinates of each intersection point.

2. Consider the function $f(x) = \frac{x^3}{6} + \cos x + 1$.

   a. Approximate the local maximum and local minimum values of f.

   b. Find the linear approximation to f at π.

   c. Use your linear approximation to approximate the value of $f(3)$.

   d. Is your approximation in part (c) an underestimate or an overestimate of the true value? Justify your answer.

Section 2 Part B, Free Response, No Technology

3. Consider the function $f(x) = \frac{e^{4x} - e^{3x}}{2x}$.

   a. What is the domain of f?
   b. Use l'Hôpital's Rule to evaluate $\lim_{x \to 0} f(x)$.
   c. How should $f(0)$ be defined to make f continuous at 0?
   d. Evaluate $\lim_{x \to 0} = \frac{e^{ax} - e^{bx}}{cx}$, where a and b are real numbers, and c is a nonzero real number.

4. The function g is defined by $g(x) = \frac{x^2 - 3x + 4}{x}$.

   a. What is the domain of g?
   b. Determine the location of all local minima and all local maxima.
   c. On what intervals is the graph of g concave up? Concave down?
   d. Locate any vertical asymptotes of g.
   e. Evaluate $\lim_{x \to \infty} g(x)$ and $\lim_{x \to \infty} g(x)$.

5. Consider the function $f(x) = x\sqrt{k - x}$, where k is a real number.

    a. Evaluate and simplify the derivatives $f'(x)$ and $f''(x)$.

    b. For what constant k does $f(x)$ have an absolute maximum at $x = 2$?

    c. For $k = 5$, evaluate $\lim\limits_{x \to -\infty} f(x)$.

    d. For $k = 5$, does $f(x)$ have an absolute minimum value? Justify your answer.

6. Consider the function $f(x) = xe^{1-x}$.

    a. Find all the local extreme values of f.

    b. On what interval(s) is the graph of f concave up and decreasing?

    c. On what interval(s) is the graph of f concave down and increasing?

    d. Evaluate $\lim\limits_{x \to \infty} f(x)$ and $\lim\limits_{x \to -\infty} f(x)$.

    e. Sketch a graph of f.

Chapter 4 Guided Projects

Applications of the material in this chapter and related topics can be found in the following Guided Projects. For additional information, see the Preface.

- Oscillators
- Ice cream, geometry, and calculus
- Newton's method

5 Integration

The distribution of income across a society is an issue that often concerns economists, sociologists, and ordinary citizens. An ingenious device for studying such matters is called a *Lorenz curve* (devised by the American economist Max Lorenz in 1905). This curve gives the fraction of the total income in the society controlled by a given fraction of the households. For example, on the Lorenz curve shown below, one-half of the households control one-fifth of the wealth. If wealth were evenly distributed, the Lorenz curve would be the *line of perfect equality*. The amount that the Lorenz curve departs from that line is a measure of income inequality. One way to quantify income inequality is to measure the area of the region marked A in the figure. How do we find the area of a region bounded by two curves? The answer is *integration*, one of the cornerstones of calculus, and the subject of this chapter.

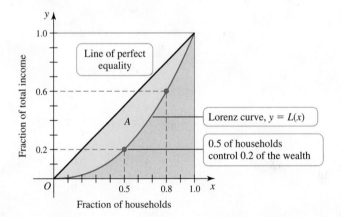

Chapter Preview

We are now at a critical point in the calculus story. Many would argue that this chapter is the cornerstone of calculus because it explains the relationship between the two processes of calculus: differentiation and integration. We begin by investigating antidifferentiation—the process that "undoes" or reverses differentiation. The next step is to explain why finding the area of regions bounded by the graphs of functions is such an important problem in calculus. Then you will see how antiderivatives lead to definite integrals, which are used to solve this area problem. But there is more to the story. You will also see the remarkable connection between derivatives and integrals, which is expressed in the Fundamental Theorem of Calculus. In this chapter, we develop key properties of definite integrals, investigate a few of their many applications, and present the first of several powerful techniques for evaluating definite integrals. The chapter ends with two methods for approximating definite integrals using a calculator or computer.

5.1 Antiderivatives

The goal of differentiation is to find the derivative f' of a given function f. The reverse process, called *antidifferentiation*, is equally important: Given a function f, we look for an *antiderivative* function F whose derivative is f; that is, a function F such that $F' = f$.

> **DEFINITION Antiderivative**
>
> A function F is an **antiderivative** of f on an interval I provided $F'(x) = f(x)$, for all x in I.

In this section, we revisit derivative formulas developed in previous chapters to discover corresponding antiderivative formulas.

Thinking Backward

Consider the derivative formula $\dfrac{d}{dx}(x) = 1$. It implies that an antiderivative of $f(x) = 1$ is $F(x) = x$ because $F'(x) = f(x)$. Using the same logic, we can write

$$\frac{d}{dx}(x^2) = 2x \quad \Rightarrow \quad \text{an antiderivative of } f(x) = 2x \text{ is } F(x) = x^2 \text{ and}$$

$$\frac{d}{dx}(\sin x) = \cos x \quad \Rightarrow \quad \text{an antiderivative of } f(x) = \cos x \text{ is } F(x) = \sin x.$$

QUICK CHECK 1 Verify by differentiation that x^3 is an antiderivative of $3x^2$ and $-\cos x$ is an antiderivative of $\sin x$. ◄

Each of these proposed antiderivative formulas is easily checked by showing that $F' = f$.

An immediate question arises: Does a function have more than one antiderivative? To answer this question, let's focus on $f(x) = 1$ and the antiderivative $F(x) = x$. Because the derivative of a constant C is zero, we see that $F(x) = x + C$ is also an antiderivative of $f(x) = 1$, which is easy to check:

$$F'(x) = \frac{d}{dx}(x + C) = 1 = f(x).$$

Therefore, $f(x) = 1$ actually has an infinite number of antiderivatives. For the same reason, any function of the form $F(x) = x^2 + C$ is an antiderivative of $f(x) = 2x$, and any function of the form $F(x) = \sin x + C$ is an antiderivative of $f(x) = \cos x$, where C is an arbitrary constant.

We might ask whether there are still *more* antiderivatives of a given function. The following theorem provides the answer.

> **THEOREM 5.1 The Family of Antiderivatives**
>
> Let F be any antiderivative of f on an interval I. Then *all* the antiderivatives of f on I have the form $F + C$, where C is an arbitrary constant.

Proof: Suppose that F and G are antiderivatives of f on an interval I. Then $F' = f$ and $G' = f$, which implies that $F' = G'$ on I. From Theorem 4.11, which states that functions with equal derivatives differ by a constant, it follows that $G = F + C$. Therefore, all antiderivatives of f have the form $F + C$, where C is an arbitrary constant.   ◄

Theorem 5.1 says that while there are infinitely many antiderivatives of a function, they are all of one family, namely, those functions of the form $F + C$. Because the antiderivatives of a particular function differ by a constant, the antiderivatives are vertical translations of one another (Figure 5.1).

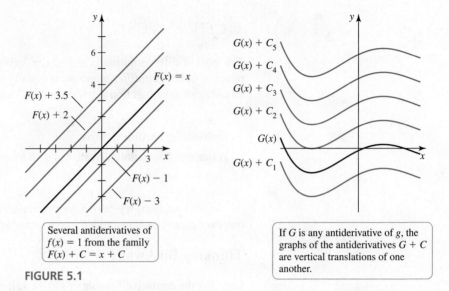

Several antiderivatives of $f(x) = 1$ from the family $F(x) + C = x + C$

If G is any antiderivative of g, the graphs of the antiderivatives $G + C$ are vertical translations of one another.

FIGURE 5.1

EXAMPLE 1 **Finding antiderivatives** Use what you know about derivatives to find all antiderivatives of the following functions.

a. $f(x) = 3x^2$ **b.** $f(x) = \dfrac{1}{1 + x^2}$ **c.** $f(x) = \sin x$

SOLUTION

a. Note that $\dfrac{d}{dx}(x^3) = 3x^2$. Therefore, an antiderivative of $f(x) = 3x^2$ is x^3. By Theorem 5.1, the complete family of antiderivatives is $F(x) = x^3 + C$, where C is an arbitrary constant.

b. Because $\dfrac{d}{dx}(\tan^{-1} x) = \dfrac{1}{1 + x^2}$, all antiderivatives of f are of the form $F(x) = \tan^{-1} x + C$, where C is an arbitrary constant.

c. Recall that $\dfrac{d}{dx}(\cos x) = -\sin x$. We seek a function whose derivative is $\sin x$, not $-\sin x$. Observing that $\dfrac{d}{dx}(-\cos x) = \sin x$, it follows that the antiderivatives of $\sin x$ are $F(x) = -\cos x + C$, where C is an arbitrary constant.

Related Exercises 11–22 ◄

QUICK CHECK 2 Find the family of antiderivatives for each of $f(x) = e^x$, $g(x) = 4x^3$, and $h(x) = \sec^2 x$. ◄

Indefinite Integrals

The notation $\dfrac{d}{dx}(f)$ means *take the derivative of f*. We need analogous notation for antiderivatives. For historical reasons that become apparent in subsequent sections, the notation that means *find the antiderivatives of f* is the **indefinite integral** $\int f(x)\, dx$. Every time an indefinite integral sign $\int$ appears, it is followed by a function called the **integrand**, which in turn is followed by the differential dx. For now, dx simply means that x is the independent variable, or the **variable of integration**. The notation $\int f(x)\, dx$ represents *all* the antiderivatives of f.

Using this new notation, the three results of Example 1 are written

$$\int 3x^2\, dx = x^3 + C, \quad \int \frac{1}{1 + x^2}\, dx = \tan^{-1} x + C, \text{ and } \quad \int \sin x\, dx = -\cos x + C,$$

where C is an arbitrary constant called a **constant of integration**. The derivative formulas presented earlier in the text may be written in terms of indefinite integrals. We begin with the Power Rule.

Notice that if $p = -1$ in Theorem 5.2, then $F(x)$ is undefined. The antiderivative of $f(x) = x^{-1}$ is discussed shortly. The case $p = 0$ says that $\int 1 \, dx = x + C$.

THEOREM 5.2   Power Rule for Indefinite Integrals

$$\int x^p \, dx = \frac{x^{p+1}}{p+1} + C,$$

where $p \neq -1$ is a real number and C is an arbitrary constant.

Proof: The theorem says that the antiderivatives of $f(x) = x^p$ have the form $F(x) = \dfrac{x^{p+1}}{p+1} + C$. Differentiating F, we verify that $F'(x) = f(x)$, provided $p \neq -1$:

$$
\begin{aligned}
F'(x) &= \frac{d}{dx}\left(\frac{x^{p+1}}{p+1} + C \right) \\
&= \frac{d}{dx}\left(\frac{x^{p+1}}{p+1} \right) + \underbrace{\frac{d}{dx}(C)}_{0} \\
&= \frac{(p+1)x^{(p+1)-1}}{p+1} + 0 = x^p.
\end{aligned}
$$

◄

> Any indefinite integral calculation can be checked by differentiation: The derivative of the alleged indefinite integral must equal the integrand.

Theorems 3.4 and 3.5 (Section 3.3) state the Constant Multiple and Sum Rules for derivatives. Here are the corresponding antiderivative rules, which are proved by differentiation.

THEOREM 5.3   Constant Multiple and Sum Rules

Constant Multiple Rule: $\displaystyle\int cf(x) \, dx = c \int f(x) \, dx$, for real numbers c

Sum Rule: $\displaystyle\int (f(x) + g(x)) \, dx = \int f(x) \, dx + \int g(x) \, dx$

The following example shows how this theorem is used.

EXAMPLE 2   Indefinite integrals Determine the following indefinite integrals.

a. $\displaystyle\int (3x^5 + 2 - 5\sqrt{x}) \, dx$ **b.** $\displaystyle\int \left(\frac{4x^{19} - 5x^{-8}}{x^2} \right) dx$ **c.** $\displaystyle\int (x^2 + 1)(2x - 5) \, dx$

SOLUTION

> $\int dx$ means $\int 1 \, dx$, which is the indefinite integral of the constant function $f(x) = 1$, so $\int dx = x + C$.

> Each indefinite integral in Example 2a produces an arbitrary constant, all of which may be combined in one arbitrary constant called C.

a.
$$
\begin{aligned}
\int (3x^5 + 2 - 5\sqrt{x}) \, dx &= \int 3x^5 \, dx + \int 2 \, dx - \int 5x^{1/2} \, dx && \text{Sum Rule} \\
&= 3\int x^5 \, dx + 2\int dx - 5\int x^{1/2} \, dx && \text{Constant Multiple Rule} \\
&= 3 \cdot \frac{x^6}{6} + 2 \cdot x - 5 \cdot \frac{x^{3/2}}{(3/2)} + C && \text{Power Rule} \\
&= \frac{x^6}{2} + 2x - \frac{10}{3}x^{3/2} + C && \text{Simplify.}
\end{aligned}
$$

b. $\int \left(\dfrac{4x^{19} - 5x^{-8}}{x^2} \right) dx = \int (4x^{17} - 5x^{-10})\, dx$ Simplify the integrand.

$$= 4 \int x^{17}\, dx - 5 \int x^{-10}\, dx$$ Sum and Constant Multiple Rules

$$= 4 \cdot \dfrac{x^{18}}{18} - 5 \cdot \dfrac{x^{-9}}{(-9)} + C$$ Power Rule

$$= \dfrac{2x^{18}}{9} + \dfrac{5x^{-9}}{9} + C$$ Simplify.

c. $\int (x^2 + 1)(2x - 5)\,dx = \int (2x^3 - 5x^2 + 2x - 5)\,dx$ Expand integrand.

$$= \dfrac{1}{2}x^4 - \dfrac{5}{3}x^3 + x^2 - 5x + C$$ Integrate each term.

> Examples 2b and 2c show that, in general, the indefinite integral of a product or quotient is not the product or quotient of indefinite integrals.

All these results should be checked by differentiation.

Related Exercises 23–36 ◄

Indefinite Integrals of Trigonometric Functions

In this section, we have two goals that can be accomplished at the same time. The first goal is to write the familiar derivative results for trigonometric functions as indefinite integrals. The second goal is to show how these results can be generalized by bringing the Chain Rule into the picture. The following example illustrates the key ideas.

> Remember the words that go with anti-derivatives and indefinite integrals. The statement $\dfrac{d}{dx}(\tan x) = \sec^2 x$ says that $\tan x$ can be differentiated to get $\sec^2 x$. Therefore,
> $$\int \sec^2 x\, dx = \tan x + C.$$

EXAMPLE 3   Indefinite integrals of trigonometric functions Evaluate the following indefinite integrals.

a. $\int \sec^2 x\, dx$ **b.** $\int \sin 3x\, dx$

c. $\int \sec ax \tan ax\, dx$, where $a \neq 0$ is a real number

SOLUTION

a. The derivative result $\dfrac{d}{dx}(\tan x) = \sec^2 x$ is reversed to produce the indefinite integral

$\int \sec^2 x\, dx = \tan x + C.$

> The statement
> $$\dfrac{d}{dx}(\cos 3x) = -3 \sin 3x$$
> says that $\cos 3x$ can be differentiated to get $-3 \sin 3x$. Therefore,
> $$\int -3 \sin 3x\, dx = \cos 3x + C.$$

b. From Example 1c, we know that $\int \sin x\, dx = -\cos x + C$. The complication in the given integral is the factor of 3 in $\sin 3x$. Here is the thinking that allows us to handle this factor. A derivative result that appears related to the given indefinite integral is $\dfrac{d}{dx}(\cos 3x) = -3 \sin 3x$, which is obtained using the Chain Rule. We write this derivative result as the indefinite integral

$$\int (-3 \sin 3x)\, dx = \cos 3x + C, \quad \text{or} \quad -3 \int \sin 3x\, dx = \cos 3x + C.$$

> If C is an arbitrary constant and a is a real number, then C/a is also an arbitrary constant and we continue to call it C.

Dividing both sides of this equation by -3 gives the desired result:

$$\int \sin 3x\, dx = -\dfrac{1}{3} \cos 3x + C,$$

which can be checked by differentiation. Notice that 3 could be replaced in this example with any constant $a \neq 0$ to produce the more general result

$$\int \sin ax\, dx = -\dfrac{1}{a} \cos ax + C.$$

c. A derivative result that appears related to this indefinite integral is $\dfrac{d}{dx}(\sec x) = \sec x \tan x$, or more generally, using the Chain Rule,

$$\frac{d}{dx}(\sec ax) = a \sec ax \tan ax.$$

Writing this derivative result as an indefinite integral, we have

$$\int a \sec ax \tan ax \, dx = \sec ax + C.$$

After dividing through by a, we have

$$\int \sec ax \tan ax \, dx = \frac{1}{a} \sec ax + C.$$

Related Exercises 37–46◄

The technique used in Example 3 of writing a Chain Rule result as an indefinite integral can be used to obtain the integrals in Table 5.1. We assume that $a \neq 0$ is a real number and C is an arbitrary constant.

> In Section 5.6, we show how to derive the results in Tables 5.1 and 5.2 using the Substitution Rule.

Table 5.1   Indefinite Integrals of Trigonometric Functions

1. $\dfrac{d}{dx}(\sin ax) = a \cos ax \quad \Rightarrow \quad \displaystyle\int \cos ax \, dx = \frac{1}{a} \sin ax + C$

2. $\dfrac{d}{dx}(\cos ax) = -a \sin ax \quad \Rightarrow \quad \displaystyle\int \sin ax \, dx = -\frac{1}{a} \cos ax + C$

3. $\dfrac{d}{dx}(\tan ax) = a \sec^2 ax \quad \Rightarrow \quad \displaystyle\int \sec^2 ax \, dx = \frac{1}{a} \tan ax + C$

4. $\dfrac{d}{dx}(\cot ax) = -a \csc^2 ax \quad \Rightarrow \quad \displaystyle\int \csc^2 ax \, dx = -\frac{1}{a} \cot ax + C$

5. $\dfrac{d}{dx}(\sec ax) = a \sec ax \tan ax \quad \Rightarrow \quad \displaystyle\int \sec ax \tan ax \, dx = \frac{1}{a} \sec ax + C$

6. $\dfrac{d}{dx}(\csc ax) = -a \csc ax \cot ax \quad \Rightarrow \quad \displaystyle\int \csc ax \cot ax \, dx = -\frac{1}{a} \csc ax + C$

QUICK CHECK 3 Use differentiation to verify that $\displaystyle\int \sin 2x \, dx = -\frac{1}{2} \cos 2x + C.$ ◄

The results of Table 5.1 are used throughout the book—and in the next example.

EXAMPLE 4   Indefinite integrals of trigonometric functions Use Table 5.1 to determine the following indefinite integrals.

a. $\displaystyle\int \sec^2 3x \, dx$ **b.** $\displaystyle\int \cos \frac{x}{2} \, dx$

SOLUTION These integrals follow directly from Table 5.1 and can be verified by differentiation.

a. Letting $a = 3$ in result (3) of Table 5.1, we have

$$\int \sec^2 3x \, dx = \frac{\tan 3x}{3} + C.$$

b. We let $a = \frac{1}{2}$ in result (1) of Table 5.1, which says that

$$\int \cos \frac{x}{2} \, dx = \frac{\sin (x/2)}{1/2} + C = 2 \sin \frac{x}{2} + C.$$

Related Exercises 37–46◄

Other Indefinite Integrals

We now continue the process of rewriting familiar derivative results as indefinite integrals. As in Example 3, we generally begin with a derivative based on the Chain Rule, and then express it as an indefinite integral.

EXAMPLE 5 **Additional indefinite integrals** Evaluate the following indefinite integrals. Assume a is a nonzero real number.

a. $\displaystyle\int \frac{dx}{x}$ **b.** $\displaystyle\int e^{ax}\, dx$ **c.** $\displaystyle\int \frac{dx}{a^2 + x^2}$

SOLUTION

a. In this case, we know that $\dfrac{d}{dx}(\ln|x|) = \dfrac{1}{x}$, for $x \neq 0$. The corresponding indefinite integral follows immediately:

$$\int \frac{dx}{x} = \ln|x| + C.$$

This result fills the gap in the Power Rule for the case $p = -1$.

b. By the Chain Rule, we know that $\dfrac{d}{dx}\left(e^{ax}\right) = ae^{ax}$. Written as an indefinite integral, this result is equivalent to $\int ae^{ax}\, dx = e^{ax} + C$. We divide through by a to obtain

$$\int e^{ax}\, dx = \frac{1}{a} e^{ax} + C,$$

which can be verified by differentiation.

c. The integrand $\dfrac{1}{a^2 + x^2}$ looks familiar (see Example 1b); it suggests that we begin with the derivative formula $\dfrac{d}{dx}\left(\tan^{-1} x\right) = \dfrac{1}{1 + x^2}$. As before, we call on the Chain Rule to generalize this result and write

$$\frac{d}{dx}\left(\tan^{-1}\frac{x}{a}\right) = \frac{1/a}{1 + \left(\dfrac{x}{a}\right)^2} = \frac{a}{a^2 + x^2}.$$

> In Example 5c, we could have applied the Chain Rule to $\tan^{-1} ax$ and derived a useful indefinite integral. However, working with $\tan^{-1}\dfrac{x}{a}$ produces the more common form of the integral.

Expressed as an indefinite integral, we find that

$$\int \frac{a}{a^2 + x^2}\, dx = \tan^{-1}\frac{x}{a} + C.$$

Dividing through by a gives

$$\int \frac{dx}{a^2 + x^2} = \frac{1}{a}\tan^{-1}\frac{x}{a} + C.$$

Related Exercises 47–58 ◄

The ideas used in Example 5 lead to the results in Table 5.2, where $a \neq 0$ is a real number and C is an arbitrary constant.

> Tables 5.1 and 5.2 are subsets of the table of integrals at the end of the book.

Table 5.2   Other Indefinite Integrals

7. $\dfrac{d}{dx}(e^{ax}) = ae^{ax} \implies \displaystyle\int e^{ax}\,dx = \dfrac{1}{a}e^{ax} + C$

8. $\dfrac{d}{dx}(b^x) = b^x \ln b \implies \displaystyle\int b^x\,dx = \dfrac{1}{\ln b}b^x + C, b > 0, b \neq 1$

9. $\dfrac{d}{dx}(\ln|x|) = \dfrac{1}{x} \implies \displaystyle\int \dfrac{dx}{x} = \ln|x| + C$

10. $\dfrac{d}{dx}\left(\sin^{-1}\dfrac{x}{a}\right) = \dfrac{1}{\sqrt{a^2 - x^2}} \implies \displaystyle\int \dfrac{dx}{\sqrt{a^2 - x^2}} = \sin^{-1}\dfrac{x}{a} + C$

11. $\dfrac{d}{dx}\left(\tan^{-1}\dfrac{x}{a}\right) = \dfrac{a}{a^2 + x^2} \implies \displaystyle\int \dfrac{dx}{a^2 + x^2} = \dfrac{1}{a}\tan^{-1}\dfrac{x}{a} + C$

12. $\dfrac{d}{dx}\left(\sec^{-1}\left|\dfrac{x}{a}\right|\right) = \dfrac{a}{x\sqrt{x^2 - a^2}} \implies \displaystyle\int \dfrac{dx}{x\sqrt{x^2 - a^2}} = \dfrac{1}{a}\sec^{-1}\left|\dfrac{x}{a}\right| + C, a > 0$

EXAMPLE 6   Indefinite integrals Use Table 5.2 to determine the following indefinite integrals.

a. $\displaystyle\int e^{-10t}\,dt$ **b.** $\displaystyle\int \dfrac{4}{\sqrt{9 - x^2}}\,dx$ **c.** $\displaystyle\int \dfrac{dx}{16x^2 + 1}$

SOLUTION

> The results of Tables 5.1 and 5.2 apply regardless of what we call the variable of integration.

a. Setting $a = -10$ in result (7) of Table 5.2, we find that

$$\int e^{-10t}\,dt = -\dfrac{1}{10}e^{-10t} + C,$$

which should be verified by differentiation.

b. Setting $a = 3$ in result (10) of Table 5.2, we have

$$\int \dfrac{4}{\sqrt{9 - x^2}}\,dx = 4\int \dfrac{dx}{\sqrt{3^2 - x^2}} = 4\sin^{-1}\dfrac{x}{3} + C.$$

c. An algebra step is needed to put this integral in a form that matches Table 5.2. We first write

$$\int \dfrac{dx}{16x^2 + 1} = \dfrac{1}{16}\int \dfrac{dx}{x^2 + \left(\frac{1}{16}\right)} = \dfrac{1}{16}\int \dfrac{dx}{x^2 + \left(\frac{1}{4}\right)^2}.$$

Setting $a = \frac{1}{4}$ in result (11) of Table 5.2 gives

$$\int \dfrac{dx}{16x^2 + 1} = \dfrac{1}{16}\int \dfrac{dx}{x^2 + \left(\frac{1}{4}\right)^2} = \dfrac{1}{16}\cdot 4\tan^{-1}4x + C = \dfrac{1}{4}\tan^{-1}4x + C.$$

Related Exercises 47–58 ◄

Introduction to Differential Equations

An equation involving an unknown function and it derivatives is called a **differential equation.** Here is an example to introduce you to this important subject.

Suppose you know that the derivative of a function f satisfies the equation

$$f'(x) = 2x + 10.$$

QUICK CHECK 4 Explain why an antiderivative of f' is f. ◄

To find a function f that satisfies this equation, we note that the solutions are antiderivatives of $2x + 10$, which are $x^2 + 10x + C$, where C is an arbitrary constant. So we have found an infinite number of solutions, all of the form $f(x) = x^2 + 10x + C$.

Now consider a more general differential equation of the form $f'(x) = g(x)$, where g is given and f is unknown. The solution f consists of antiderivatives of g, which involve an arbitrary constant. In most practical cases, the differential equation is accompanied by an **initial condition** that allows us to determine the arbitrary constant. Therefore, we consider problems of the form

$$f'(x) = g(x), \quad \text{where } g \text{ is given, and} \qquad \text{Differential equation}$$

$$f(a) = b, \qquad \text{where } a \text{ and } b \text{ are given.} \quad \text{Initial condition}$$

A differential equation coupled with an initial condition is called an **initial value problem**.

EXAMPLE 7 An initial value problem Solve the initial value problem $f'(x) = x^2 - 2x$ with $f(1) = \frac{1}{3}$.

SOLUTION The solution f is an antiderivative of $x^2 - 2x$. Therefore,

$$f(x) = \frac{x^3}{3} - x^2 + C,$$

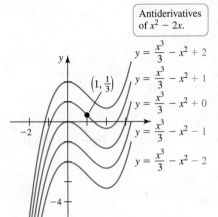

Antiderivatives of $x^2 - 2x$.

$y = \dfrac{x^3}{3} - x^2 + 2$

$y = \dfrac{x^3}{3} - x^2 + 1$

$y = \dfrac{x^3}{3} - x^2 + 0$

$y = \dfrac{x^3}{3} - x^2 - 1$

$y = \dfrac{x^3}{3} - x^2 - 2$

FIGURE 5.2

where C is an arbitrary constant. We have determined that the solution is a member of a family of functions, all of which differ by a constant. This family of functions is shown in Figure 5.2, where we see curves for various choices of C.

Using the initial condition $f(1) = \frac{1}{3}$, we choose C to single out the particular function in this family whose graph passes through the point $\left(1, \frac{1}{3}\right)$. Imposing the condition $f(1) = \frac{1}{3}$, we reason as follows:

$$f(x) = \frac{x^3}{3} - x^2 + C \quad \text{Family of solutions}$$

$$f(1) = \frac{1}{3} - 1 + C \quad \text{Substitute } x = 1.$$

$$\frac{1}{3} = \frac{1}{3} - 1 + C \quad f(1) = \frac{1}{3}$$

$$C = 1. \qquad \text{Solve for } C.$$

Therefore, the solution to the initial value problem is

$$f(x) = \frac{x^3}{3} - x^2 + 1,$$

which is the red curve in the family shown in Figure 5.2.

Related Exercises 59–82 ◀

> It is advisable to check that the solution satisfies the original problem: $f'(x) = x^2 - 2x$ and $f(1) = \frac{1}{3} - 1 + 1 = \frac{1}{3}$.

Motion Problems Revisited

QUICK CHECK 5 Position is an antiderivative of velocity. But there are infinitely many antiderivatives that differ by a constant. Explain how two objects can have the same velocity function but two different position functions. ◀

> The convention with motion problems is to assume that motion begins at $t = 0$. This means that initial conditions are specified at $t = 0$.

Antiderivatives allow us to revisit the topic of one-dimensional motion introduced in Section 3.6. Suppose the position of an object that moves along a line relative to an origin is $s(t)$, where $t \geq 0$ measures elapsed time. The velocity of the object is $v(t) = s'(t)$, which may now be read in terms of antiderivatives: *The position function is an antiderivative of the velocity*. If we are given the velocity function of an object and its position at a particular time, we can determine its position at all future times by solving an initial value problem.

We also know that the acceleration $a(t)$ of an object moving in one dimension is the rate of change of the velocity, which means $a(t) = v'(t)$. In antiderivative terms, this says that the velocity is an antiderivative of the acceleration. Thus, if we are given the acceleration of an object and its velocity at a particular time, we can determine its velocity at all times. These ideas lie at the heart of modeling the motion of objects.

Initial Value Problems for Velocity and Position

Suppose an object moves along a line with a (known) velocity $v(t)$, for $t \geq 0$. Then its position is found by solving the initial value problem

$$s'(t) = v(t), \ s(0) = s_0, \ \text{where } s_0 \text{ is the initial position.}$$

If the acceleration of the object $a(t)$ is given, then its velocity is found by solving the initial value problem

$$v'(t) = a(t), \ v(0) = v_0, \ \text{where } v_0 \text{ is the initial velocity.}$$

EXAMPLE 8   **A race** Runner A begins at the point $s(0) = 0$ and runs with velocity $v(t) = 2t$. Runner B begins with a head start at the point $S(0) = 8$ and runs with velocity $V(t) = 2$. Find the positions of the runners for $t \geq 0$ and determine who is ahead at $t = 6$ time units.

SOLUTION Let the position of Runner A be $s(t)$, with an initial position $s(0) = 0$. Then the position function satisfies the initial value problem

$$s'(t) = 2t, \ s(0) = 0.$$

The solution is an antiderivative of $s'(t) = 2t$, which has the form $s(t) = t^2 + C$. Substituting $s(0) = 0$, we find that $C = 0$. Therefore, the position of Runner A is given by $s(t) = t^2$, for $t \geq 0$.

Let the position of Runner B be $S(t)$, with an initial position $S(0) = 8$. This position function satisfies the initial value problem

$$S'(t) = 2, \ S(0) = 8.$$

The antiderivatives of $S'(t) = 2$ are $S(t) = 2t + C$. Substituting $S(0) = 8$ implies that $C = 8$. Therefore, the position of Runner B is given by $S(t) = 2t + 8$, for $t \geq 0$.

The graphs of the position functions are shown in Figure 5.3. Runner B begins with a head start but is overtaken when $s(t) = S(t)$, or when $t^2 = 2t + 8$. The solutions of this equation are $t = 4$ and $t = -2$. Only the positive solution is relevant because the race takes place for $t \geq 0$, so Runner A overtakes Runner B at $t = 4$, when $s = S = 16$. When $t = 6$, Runner A has the lead.

Related Exercises 83–96 ◄

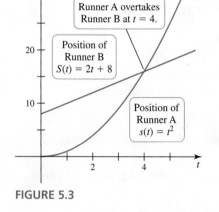

Runner A overtakes Runner B at $t = 4$.

Position of Runner B $S(t) = 2t + 8$

Position of Runner A $s(t) = t^2$

FIGURE 5.3

EXAMPLE 9   **Motion with gravity** Neglecting air resistance, the motion of an object moving vertically near Earth's surface is determined by the acceleration due to gravity, which is approximately 9.8 m/s^2. Suppose a stone is thrown vertically upward at $t = 0$ with a velocity of 40 m/s from the edge of a cliff that is 100 m above a river.

a. Find the velocity $v(t)$ of the object, for $t \geq 0$.

b. Find the position $s(t)$ of the object, for $t \geq 0$.

c. Find the maximum height of the object above the river.

d. With what speed does the object strike the river?

SOLUTION We establish a coordinate system in which the positive s-axis points vertically upward with $s = 0$ corresponding to the river (Figure 5.4). Let $s(t)$ be the position of the stone measured relative to the river, for $t \geq 0$. The initial velocity of the stone is $v(0) = 40 \text{ m/s}$ and the initial position of the stone is $s(0) = 100 \text{ m}$.

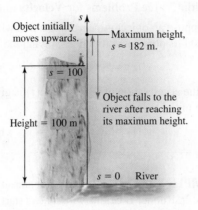

FIGURE 5.4

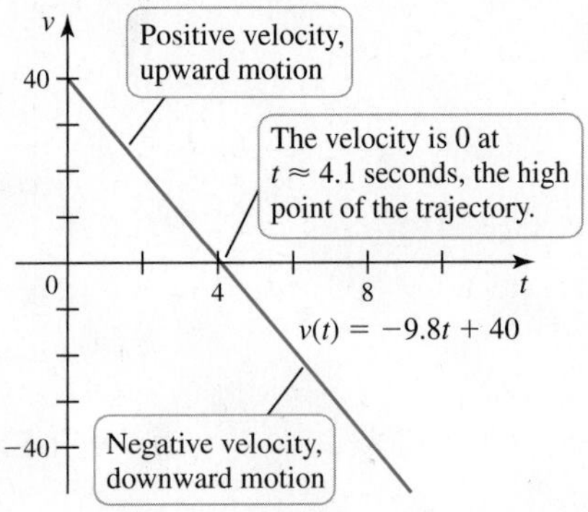

FIGURE 5.5

> The acceleration due to gravity at Earth's surface is approximately $g = 9.8 \text{ m/s}^2$, or $g = 32 \text{ ft/s}^2$. It varies even at sea level from about 9.8640 at the poles to 9.7982 at the equator. The equation $v'(t) = -g$ is an instance of Newton's Second Law of Motion and assumes that no other forces (such as air resistance) are present.

a. The acceleration due to gravity points in the *negative s*-direction. Therefore, the initial value problem governing the motion of the object is

$$\text{acceleration} = v'(t) = -9.8, \ v(0) = 40.$$

The antiderivatives of -9.8 are $v(t) = -9.8t + C$. The initial condition $v(0) = 40$ gives $C = 40$. Therefore, the velocity of the stone is

$$v(t) = -9.8t + 40.$$

As shown in Figure 5.5, the velocity decreases from its initial value $v(0) = 40$ until it reaches zero at the high point of the trajectory. This point is reached when

$$v(t) = -9.8t + 40 = 0$$

or when $t \approx 4.1$ s. For $t > 4.1$, the velocity becomes increasingly negative as the stone falls to Earth.

b. Knowing the velocity function of the stone, we can determine its position. The position function satisfies the initial value problem

$$v(t) = s'(t) = -9.8t + 40, \ s(0) = 100.$$

The antiderivatives of $-9.8t + 40$ are

$$s(t) = -4.9t^2 + 40t + C.$$

The initial condition $s(0) = 100$ implies $C = 100$, so the position function of the stone is

$$s(t) = -4.9t^2 + 40t + 100,$$

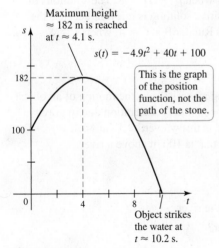

FIGURE 5.6

as shown in Figure 5.6. *Here is an important observation:* The parabolic graph of the position function is not the actual trajectory of the stone; the stone moves vertically along the s-axis.

c. The position function of the stone increases for $0 < t < 4.1$. At $t \approx 4.1$, the stone reaches a high point of $s(4.1) \approx 182$ m.

d. For $t > 4.1$, the position function decreases, and the stone strikes the river when $s(t) = 0$. The roots of this equation are $t \approx 10.2$ and $t \approx -2.0$. Only the first root is relevant because the motion starts at $t = 0$. Therefore, the stone strikes the ground at $t \approx 10.2$ s. Its speed (in m/s) at this instant is $|v(10.2)| \approx |-60| = 60$.

Related Exercises 97–100 ◄

SECTION 5.1 EXERCISES

Review Questions

1. Fill in the blanks with either of the words *the derivative* or *an antiderivative*: If $F'(x) = f(x)$, then f is _____ of F and F is _____ of f.

2. Describe the set of antiderivatives of $f(x) = 0$.

3. Describe the set of antiderivatives of $f(x) = 1$.

4. Why do two different antiderivatives of a function differ by a constant?

5. Give the antiderivatives of x^p. For what values of p does your answer apply?

6. Give the antiderivatives of e^{-x}.

7. Give the antiderivatives of $1/x$.

8. Evaluate $\int \cos ax \, dx$ and $\int \sin ax \, dx$, where a is a constant.

9. If $F(x) = x^2 - 3x + C$ and $F(-1) = 4$, what is the value of C?

10. For a given function f, explain the steps used to solve the initial value problem $F'(t) = f(t)$, $F(0) = 10$.

Basic Skills

11–22. Finding antiderivatives *Find the general antiderivative formula for the following functions. Check your work by taking derivatives.*

11. $f(x) = 5x^4$

12. $g(x) = 11x^{10}$

13. $f(x) = \sin 2x$

14. $g(x) = -4 \cos 4x$

15. $P(x) = 3 \sec^2 x$

16. $Q(s) = \csc^2 s$

17. $f(y) = -2/y^3$

18. $H(z) = -6z^{-7}$

19. $f(x) = e^x$

20. $h(y) = y^{-1}$

21. $G(s) = \dfrac{1}{s^2 + 1}$

22. $F(t) = \pi$

23–36. Indefinite integrals *Determine the following indefinite integrals. Check your work by differentiation.*

23. $\displaystyle\int (3x^5 - 5x^9) \, dx$

24. $\displaystyle\int (3u^{-2} - 4u^2 + 1) \, du$

25. $\displaystyle\int \left(4\sqrt{x} - \dfrac{4}{\sqrt{x}}\right) dx$

26. $\displaystyle\int \left(\dfrac{5}{t^2} + 4t^2\right) dt$

27. $\displaystyle\int (5s + 3)^2 \, ds$

28. $\displaystyle\int 5m(12m^3 - 10m) \, dm$

29. $\displaystyle\int (3x^{1/3} + 4x^{-1/3} + 6) \, dx$

30. $\displaystyle\int 6\sqrt[3]{x} \, dx$

31. $\displaystyle\int (3x + 1)(4 - x) \, dx$

32. $\displaystyle\int (4z^{1/3} - z^{-1/3}) \, dz$

33. $\displaystyle\int \left(\dfrac{3}{x^4} + 2 - \dfrac{3}{x^2}\right) dx$

34. $\displaystyle\int \sqrt[5]{r^2} \, dr$

35. $\displaystyle\int \dfrac{4x^4 - 6x^2}{x} \, dx$

36. $\displaystyle\int \dfrac{12t^8 - t}{t^3} \, dt$

37–46. Indefinite integrals involving trigonometric functions *Determine the following indefinite integrals. Check your work by differentiation.*

37. $\displaystyle\int (\sin 2y + \cos 3y) \, dy$

38. $\displaystyle\int \left(\sin 4t - \sin \dfrac{t}{4}\right) dt$

39. $\displaystyle\int (\sec^2 x - 1) \, dx$

40. $\displaystyle\int 2 \sec^2 2v \, dv$

41. $\displaystyle\int (\sec^2 \theta + \sec \theta \tan \theta) \, d\theta$

42. $\displaystyle\int \dfrac{\sin \theta - 1}{\cos^2 \theta} \, d\theta$

43. $\displaystyle\int (3t^2 + \sec^2 2t) \, dt$

44. $\displaystyle\int \csc 3\varphi \cot 3\varphi \, d\varphi$

45. $\displaystyle\int \sec 4\theta \tan 4\theta \, d\theta$

46. $\displaystyle\int \csc^2 6x \, dx$

47–58. Other indefinite integrals *Determine the following indefinite integrals. Check your work by differentiation.*

47. $\displaystyle\int \dfrac{1}{2y} \, dy$

48. $\displaystyle\int (e^{2t} + 2\sqrt{t}) \, dt$

49. $\displaystyle\int \dfrac{6}{\sqrt{25 - x^2}} \, dx$

50. $\displaystyle\int \dfrac{3}{4 + v^2} \, dv$

51. $\displaystyle\int \dfrac{dx}{x\sqrt{x^2 - 100}}$

52. $\displaystyle\int \dfrac{2}{16z^2 + 25} \, dz$

53. $\displaystyle\int \dfrac{1}{x\sqrt{x^2 - 25}} \, dx$

54. $\displaystyle\int (49 - x^2)^{-1/2} \, dx$

55. $\displaystyle\int \dfrac{t + 1}{t} \, dt$

56. $\displaystyle\int (22x^{10} - 24 e^{12x}) \, dx$

57. $\displaystyle\int e^{x+2} \, dx$

58. $\displaystyle\int \dfrac{10t^5 - 3}{t} \, dt$

59–66. Particular antiderivatives *For the following functions f, find the antiderivative F that satisfies the given condition.*

59. $f(x) = x^5 - 2x^{-2} + 1$; $F(1) = 0$

60. $f(t) = \sec^2 t$; $F(\pi/4) = 1$

61. $f(v) = \sec v \tan v$; $F(0) = 2$

62. $f(x) = (4\sqrt{x} + 6/\sqrt{x})/x^2$; $F(1) = 4$

63. $f(x) = 8x^3 - 2x^{-2}$; $F(1) = 5$

64. $f(u) = 2e^u + 3$; $F(0) = 8$

65. $f(y) = \dfrac{3y^3 + 5}{y}$; $F(1) = 3$

66. $f(\theta) = 2 \sin 2\theta - 4 \cos 4\theta$; $F\left(\dfrac{\pi}{4}\right) = 2$

67–76. Solving initial value problems *Find the solution of the following initial value problems.*

67. $f'(x) = 2x - 3$; $f(0) = 4$

68. $g'(x) = 7x^6 - 4x^3 + 12$; $g(1) = 24$

69. $g'(x) = 7x\left(x^6 - \dfrac{1}{7}\right)$; $g(1) = 2$

70. $h'(t) = 6 \sin 3t$; $h(\pi/6) = 6$

71. $f'(u) = 4(\cos u - \sin 2u)$; $f(\pi/6) = 0$

72. $p'(t) = 10e^{-t}$; $p(0) = 100$

73. $y'(t) = \dfrac{3}{t} + 6$; $y(1) = 8$

74. $u'(x) = \dfrac{e^{2x} + 4e^{-x}}{e^x}$; $u(\ln 2) = 2$

75. $y'(\theta) = \dfrac{\sqrt{2}\cos^3 \theta + 1}{\cos^2 \theta}$; $y\left(\dfrac{\pi}{4}\right) = 3$

76. $v'(x) = 4x^{1/3} + 2x^{-1/3}$; $v(8) = 40$

77–82. Graphing solutions *Graph several functions that satisfy the following differential equations. Then find and graph the particular function that satisfies the given initial condition.*

77. $f'(x) = 2x - 5$, $f(0) = 4$

78. $f'(x) = 3x^2 - 1$, $f(1) = 2$

79. $f'(x) = 3x + \sin \pi x$, $f(2) = 3$

80. $f'(s) = 4 \sec s \tan s$, $f(\pi/4) = 1$

81. $f'(t) = 1/t$, $f(1) = 4$

82. $f'(x) = 2 \cos 2x$, $f(0) = 1$

83–88. Velocity to position *Given the following velocity functions of an object moving along a line, find the position function with the given initial position. Then graph both the velocity and position functions.*

83. $v(t) = 2t + 4$; $s(0) = 0$

84. $v(t) = e^{-2t} + 4$; $s(0) = 2$

85. $v(t) = 2\sqrt{t}$; $s(0) = 1$

86. $v(t) = 2 \cos t$; $s(0) = 0$

87. $v(t) = 6t^2 + 4t - 10$; $s(0) = 0$

88. $v(t) = 2 \sin 2t$; $s(0) = 0$

89–94. Acceleration to position *Given the following acceleration functions of an object moving along a line, find the position function with the given initial velocity and position.*

89. $a(t) = -32$; $v(0) = 20, s(0) = 0$

90. $a(t) = 4$; $v(0) = -3, s(0) = 2$

91. $a(t) = 0.2 t$; $v(0) = 0, s(0) = 1$

92. $a(t) = 2 \cos t$; $v(0) = 1, s(0) = 0$

93. $a(t) = 3 \sin 2t$; $v(0) = 1, s(0) = 10$

94. $a(t) = 2e^{-t/6}$; $v(0) = 1, s(0) = 0$

95–96. Races *The velocity function and initial position of Runners A and B are given. Analyze the race that results by graphing the position functions of the runners and finding the time and positions (if any) at which they first pass each other.*

95. A: $v(t) = \sin t$, $s(0) = 0$; B: $V(t) = \cos t$, $S(0) = 0$

96. A: $v(t) = 2e^{-t}$, $s(0) = 0$; B: $V(t) = 4e^{-4t}$, $S(0) = 10$

97–100. Motion with gravity *Consider the following descriptions of the vertical motion of an object subject only to the acceleration due to gravity. Begin with the acceleration equation $a(t) = v'(t) = g$, where $g = -9.8 \, m/s^2$.*

a. Find the velocity of the object for all relevant times.
b. Find the position of the object for all relevant times.
c. Find the time when the object reaches its highest point. What is the height?
d. Find the time when the object strikes the ground.

97. A softball is popped up vertically (from the ground) with a velocity of 30 m/s.

98. A stone is thrown vertically upward with a velocity of 30 m/s from the edge of a cliff 200 m above a river.

99. A payload is released at an elevation of 400 m from a hot-air balloon that is rising at a rate of 10 m/s.

100. A payload is dropped at an elevation of 400 m from a hot-air balloon that is descending at a rate of 10 m/s.

Further Explorations

101. Explain why or why not Determine whether the following statements are true and give an explanation or counterexample.

a. $F(x) = x^3 - 4x + 100$ and $G(x) = x^3 - 4x - 100$ are antiderivatives of the same function.
b. If $F'(x) = f(x)$, then f is an antiderivative of F.
c. If $F'(x) = f(x)$, then $\int f(x)\, dx = F(x) + C$.
d. $f(x) = x^3 + 3$ and $g(x) = x^3 - 4$ are derivatives of the same function.
e. If $F'(x) = G'(x)$, then $F(x) = G(x)$.

102–109. Miscellaneous indefinite integrals *Determine the following indefinite integrals. Check your work by differentiation.*

102. $\displaystyle\int \left(\sqrt[3]{x^2} + \sqrt{x^3}\right) dx$

103. $\displaystyle\int \dfrac{e^{2x} - e^{-2x}}{2}\, dx$

104. $\displaystyle\int (4 \cos 4w - 3 \sin 3w)\, dw$

105. $\displaystyle\int (\csc^2 \theta + 2\theta^2 - 3\theta)\, d\theta$

106. $\displaystyle\int (\csc^2 \theta + 1)\, d\theta$

107. $\displaystyle\int \dfrac{1 + \sqrt{x}}{x}\, dx$

108. $\displaystyle\int \dfrac{2 + x^2}{1 + x^2}\, dx$

109. $\displaystyle\int \sqrt{x}\,(2x^6 - 4\sqrt[3]{x})\, dx$

110–113. Functions from higher derivatives *Find the function F that satisfies the following differential equations and initial conditions.*

110. $F''(x) = 1, F'(0) = 3, F(0) = 4$

111. $F''(x) = \cos x, F'(0) = 3, F(\pi) = 4$

112. $F'''(x) = 4x, F''(0) = 0, F'(0) = 1, F(0) = 3$

113. $F'''(x) = 672x^5 + 24x, F''(0) = 0, F'(0) = 2, F(0) = 1$

Applications

114. Mass on a spring A mass oscillates up and down on the end of a spring. Find its position s relative to the equilibrium position if its acceleration is $a(t) = \sin(\pi t)$ and its initial velocity and position are $v(0) = 3$ and $s(0) = 0$, respectively.

115. Flow rate A large tank is filled with water when an outflow valve is opened at $t = 0$. Water flows out at a rate, in gal/min, given by $Q'(t) = 0.1(100 - t^2)$, for $0 \le t \le 10$.

   a. Find the amount of water $Q(t)$ that has flowed out of the tank after t minutes, given the initial condition $Q(0) = 0$.
   b. Graph the flow function Q, for $0 \le t \le 10$.
   c. How much water flows out of the tank in 10 min?

116. General headstart problem Suppose that object A is located at $s = 0$ at time $t = 0$ and starts moving along the s-axis with a velocity given by $v(t) = 2at$, where $a > 0$. Object B is located at $s = c > 0$ at $t = 0$ and starts moving along the s-axis with a constant velocity given by $V(t) = b > 0$. Show that A overtakes B at time

$$t = \frac{b + \sqrt{b^2 + 4ac}}{2a}.$$

Additional Exercises

117. Using identities Use the identities $\sin^2 x = (1 - \cos 2x)/2$ and $\cos^2 x = (1 + \cos 2x)/2$ to find $\int \sin^2 x\, dx$ and $\int \cos^2 x\, dx$.

118–121. Verifying indefinite integrals *Verify the following indefinite integrals by differentiation. These integrals are derived in later chapters.*

118. $\displaystyle\int \frac{\cos \sqrt{x}}{\sqrt{x}}\, dx = 2 \sin \sqrt{x} + C$

119. $\displaystyle\int \frac{x}{\sqrt{x^2 + 1}}\, dx = \sqrt{x^2 + 1} + C$

120. $\displaystyle\int x^2 \cos x^3\, dx = \frac{1}{3} \sin x^3 + C$

121. $\displaystyle\int \frac{x}{(x^2 - 1)^2}\, dx = -\frac{1}{2(x^2 - 1)} + C$

QUICK CHECK **ANSWERS**

1. $\dfrac{d}{dx}(x^3) = 3x^2$ and $\dfrac{d}{dx}(-\cos x) = \sin x$ **2.** $e^x + C$,

$x^4 + C, \tan x + C$ **3.** $\dfrac{d}{dx}(-\cos (2x)/2 + C) = \sin 2x$

4. One function that can be differentiated to get f' is f. Therefore, f is an antiderivative of f'.   **5.** The two position functions involve two different initial positions; they differ by a constant. ◄

5.2 Approximating Areas under Curves

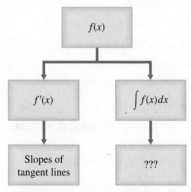

FIGURE 5.7

▷ Recall from Section 3.6 that the *displacement* of an object moving along a line is the difference between its initial and final position. If the velocity of an object is positive, its displacement equals the distance traveled.

The derivative of a function is associated with rates of change and slopes of tangent lines. We also know that antiderivatives (or indefinite integrals) reverse the derivative operation. Figure 5.7 summarizes our current understanding and raises the question: What is the geometric meaning of the integral? The following example reveals a clue.

Area under a Velocity Curve

Consider an object moving along a line with a known position function. You learned in previous chapters that the slope of the line tangent to the graph of the position function at a certain time gives the velocity v at that time. We now turn the situation around. If we know the velocity function of a moving object, what can we learn about its position function?

Imagine a car traveling at a constant velocity of 60 mi/hr along a straight highway over a two-hour period. The graph of the velocity function $v = 60$ on the interval $0 \le t \le 2$ is a horizontal line (Figure 5.8). The displacement of the car between $t = 0$ and $t = 2$ hr is found by a familiar formula:

$$\text{displacement} = \text{rate} \cdot \text{time}$$
$$= 60\ \text{mi/hr} \cdot 2\ \text{hr} = 120\ \text{mi}.$$

This product is the area of the rectangle formed by the velocity curve and the t-axis between $t = 0$ and $t = 2$ (Figure 5.9). In the case of constant positive velocity, we see that the area between the velocity curve and the t-axis is the displacement of the moving object.

> The side lengths of the rectangle in Figure 5.9 have units mi/hr and hr. Therefore, the units of the area are mi/hr · hr = mi, which is a unit of displacement.

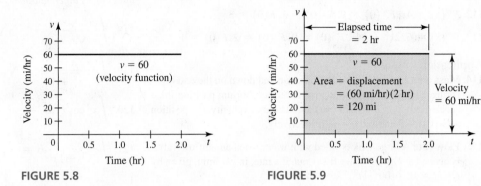

FIGURE 5.8   FIGURE 5.9

QUICK CHECK 1   What is the displacement of an object that travels at a constant velocity of 10 mi/hr for a half hour, 20 mi/hr for the next half hour, and 30 mi/hr for the next hour? ◄

Because objects do not necessarily move at a constant velocity, we first extend these ideas to positive velocities that *change* over an interval of time. One strategy is to divide the time interval into many subintervals and approximate the velocity on each subinterval by a constant velocity. Then the displacements on each subinterval are calculated and summed. This strategy produces only an approximation to the displacement; however, this approximation generally improves as the number of subintervals increases.

EXAMPLE 1   **Approximating the displacement** Suppose the velocity in m/s of an object moving along a line is given by the function $v = t^2$, where $0 \le t \le 8$. Approximate the displacement of the object by dividing the time interval $[\,0, 8\,]$ into n subintervals of equal length. On each subinterval, approximate the velocity by a constant equal to the value of v evaluated at the midpoint of the subinterval.

a. Begin by dividing $[\,0, 8\,]$ into $n = 2$ subintervals: $[\,0, 4\,]$ and $[\,4, 8\,]$.

b. Divide $[\,0, 8\,]$ into $n = 4$ subintervals: $[\,0, 2\,]$, $[\,2, 4\,]$, $[\,4, 6\,]$, and $[\,6, 8\,]$.

c. Divide $[\,0, 8\,]$ into $n = 8$ subintervals of equal length.

SOLUTION

a. We divide the interval $[\,0, 8\,]$ into $n = 2$ subintervals, $[\,0, 4\,]$ and $[\,4, 8\,]$, each with length 4. The velocity on each subinterval is approximated using the value of v evaluated at the midpoint of that subinterval (Figure 5.10a).

• We approximate the velocity on $[\,0, 4\,]$ by $v(2) = 2^2 = 4$ m/s. Traveling at 4 m/s for 4 s results in a displacement of 4 m/s · 4 s = 16 m.

• We approximate the velocity on $[\,4, 8\,]$ by $v(6) = 6^2 = 36$ m/s. Traveling at 36 m/s for 4 s results in a displacement of 36 m/s · 4 s = 144 m.

Therefore, an approximation to the displacement over the entire interval $[\,0, 8\,]$ is

$$(v(2) \cdot 4 \, \text{s}) + (v(6) \cdot 4 \, \text{s}) = (4 \, \text{m/s} \cdot 4 \, \text{s}) + (36 \, \text{m/s} \cdot 4 \, \text{s}) = 160 \, \text{m}.$$

b. With $n = 4$ (Figure 5.10b), each subinterval has length 2. The approximate displacement over the entire interval is

$$\underbrace{(1\,\text{m/s}\cdot 2\,\text{s})}_{v(1)} + \underbrace{(9\,\text{m/s}\cdot 2\,\text{s})}_{v(3)} + \underbrace{(25\,\text{m/s}\cdot 2\,\text{s})}_{v(5)} + \underbrace{(49\,\text{m/s}\cdot 2\,\text{s})}_{v(7)} = 168\,\text{m}.$$

c. With $n = 8$ subintervals (Figure 5.10c), the approximation to the displacement is 170 m. In each case, the approximate displacement is the sum of the areas of the rectangles under the velocity curve.

> The midpoint of each subinterval is used to approximate the velocity over that subinterval.

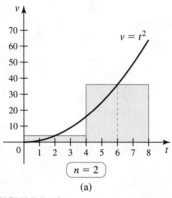
$n = 2$
(a)

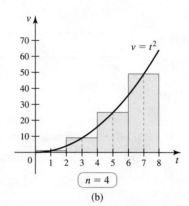
$n = 4$
(b)

$n = 8$
(c)

FIGURE 5.10

Related Exercises 9–16 ◄

QUICK CHECK 2 In Example 1, if we used $n = 32$ subintervals of equal length, what would be the length of each subinterval? Find the midpoint of the first and last subinterval. ◄

The progression in Example 1 may be continued. Larger values of n mean more rectangles; in general, more rectangles give a better fit to the region under the curve (Figure 5.11). With the help of a calculator, we can generate the approximations in Table 5.3 using $n = 1, 2, 4, 8, 16, 32,$ and 64 subintervals. Observe that as n increases, the approximations appear to approach a limit of approximately 170.7 m. The limit is the exact displacement, which is represented by the area of the region under the velocity curve. This strategy of taking limits of sums is developed fully in Section 5.3.

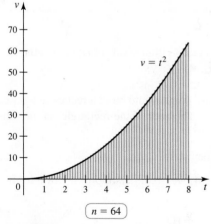
$n = 64$

FIGURE 5.11

Table 5.3 **Approximations to the area under the velocity curve $v = t^2$ on $[0, 8]$**

Number of subintervals	Length of each subinterval	Approximate displacement (area under curve)
1	8 s	128.0 m
2	4 s	160.0 m
4	2 s	168.0 m
8	1 s	170.0 m
16	0.5 s	170.5 m
32	0.25 s	170.625 m
64	0.125 s	170.65625 m

> The language "the area of the region bounded by the graph of a function" is often abbreviated as "the area under the curve."

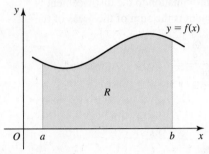

FIGURE 5.12

> Although the idea of integration was developed in the 17th century, it was almost 200 years later that the German mathematician Bernhard Riemann (1826–1866) worked on the mathematical theory underlying integration.

Approximating Areas by Riemann Sums

We now develop a method for approximating areas under curves. Consider a function f that is continuous and nonnegative on an interval $[a, b]$. The goal is to approximate the area of the region R bounded by the graph of f and the x-axis from $x = a$ to $x = b$ (Figure 5.12). We begin by dividing the interval $[a, b]$ into n subintervals of equal length,

$$[x_0, x_1], [x_1, x_2], \ldots, [x_{n-1}, x_n],$$

where $a = x_0$ and $b = x_n$ (Figure 5.13). The length of each subinterval, denoted Δx, is found by dividing the length of the interval by n:

$$\Delta x = \frac{b - a}{n}.$$

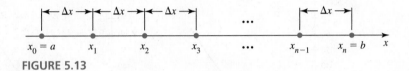

FIGURE 5.13

DEFINITION Regular Partition

Suppose $[a, b]$ is a closed interval containing n subintervals

$$[x_0, x_1], [x_1, x_2], \ldots, [x_{n-1}, x_n]$$

of equal length $\Delta x = \dfrac{b - a}{n}$ with $a = x_0$ and $b = x_n$. The endpoints $x_0, x_1, x_2, \ldots,$ x_{n-1}, x_n of the subintervals are called **grid points**, and they create a **regular partition** of the interval $[a, b]$. In general, the kth grid point is

$$x_k = a + k\Delta x, \text{ for } k = 0, 1, 2, \ldots, n.$$

QUICK CHECK 3 If the interval $[1, 9]$ is partitioned into 4 subintervals of equal length, what is Δx? List the grid points x_0, x_1, x_2, x_3, and x_4. ◄

In the kth subinterval $[x_{k-1}, x_k]$, we choose any point x_k^* and build a rectangle whose height is $f(x_k^*)$, the value of f at x_k^* (Figure 5.14). The area of the rectangle on the kth subinterval is

$$\text{height} \cdot \text{base} = f(x_k^*)\Delta x, \qquad \text{where } k = 1, 2, \ldots, n.$$

Summing the areas of the rectangles in Figure 5.14, we obtain an approximation to the area of R, which is called a **Riemann sum**:

$$f(x_1^*)\Delta x + f(x_2^*)\Delta x + \cdots + f(x_n^*)\Delta x.$$

Three notable Riemann sums are the *left*, *right*, and *midpoint Riemann sums*.

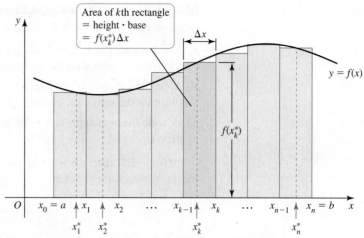

FIGURE 5.14

DEFINITION Riemann Sum

Suppose f is defined on a closed interval $[a, b]$, which is divided into n subintervals of equal length Δx. If x_k^* is any point in the kth subinterval $[x_{k-1}, x_k]$, for $k = 1, 2, \ldots, n$, then

$$f(x_1^*)\Delta x + f(x_2^*)\Delta x + \cdots + f(x_n^*)\Delta x$$

is called a **Riemann sum** for f on $[a, b]$. This sum is

- a **left Riemann sum** if x_k^* is the left endpoint of $[x_{k-1}, x_k]$ (Figure 5.15);
- a **right Riemann sum** if x_k^* is the right endpoint of $[x_{k-1}, x_k]$ (Figure 5.16); and
- a **midpoint Riemann sum** if x_k^* is the midpoint of $[x_{k-1}, x_k]$ (Figure 5.17), for $k = 1, 2, \ldots, n$.

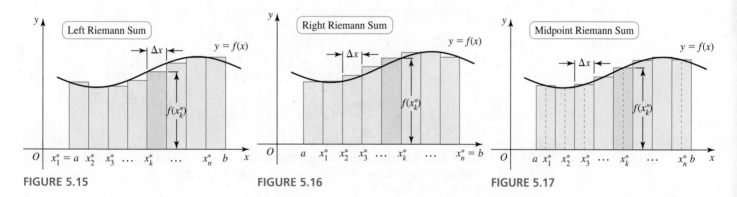

FIGURE 5.15

FIGURE 5.16

FIGURE 5.17

We now use this definition to approximate the area under the curve $y = \sin x$.

EXAMPLE 2 **Left and right Riemann sums** Let R be the region bounded by the graph of $f(x) = \sin x$ and the x-axis between $x = 0$ and $x = \pi/2$.

a. Approximate the area of R using a left Riemann sum with $n = 6$ subintervals. Illustrate the sum with the appropriate rectangles.

b. Approximate the area of R using a right Riemann sum with $n = 6$ subintervals. Illustrate the sum with the appropriate rectangles.

c. How do the area approximations in parts (a) and (b) compare to the actual area under the curve?

SOLUTION Dividing the interval $[a, b] = [0, \pi/2]$ into $n = 6$ subintervals means the length of each subinterval is

$$\Delta x = \frac{b - a}{n} = \frac{\pi/2 - 0}{6} = \frac{\pi}{12}.$$

a. To find the left Riemann sum, we set $x_1^*, x_2^*, \ldots, x_6^*$ equal to the left endpoints of the six subintervals. The heights of the rectangles are $f(x_k^*)$, for $k = 1, \ldots, 6$.

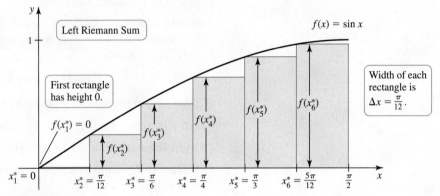

FIGURE 5.18

The resulting left Riemann sum (Figure 5.18) is

$$f(x_1^*)\Delta x + f(x_2^*)\Delta x + \cdots + f(x_6^*)\Delta x$$

$$= \left[\sin{(0)} \cdot \frac{\pi}{12} \right] + \left[\sin\left(\frac{\pi}{12}\right) \cdot \frac{\pi}{12} \right] + \left[\sin\left(\frac{\pi}{6}\right) \cdot \frac{\pi}{12} \right]$$

$$+ \left[\sin\left(\frac{\pi}{4}\right) \cdot \frac{\pi}{12} \right] + \left[\sin\left(\frac{\pi}{3}\right) \cdot \frac{\pi}{12} \right] + \left[\sin\left(\frac{5\pi}{12}\right) \cdot \frac{\pi}{12} \right]$$

$$\approx 0.863.$$

b. In a right Riemann sum, the right endpoints are used for $x_1^*, x_2^*, \ldots, x_6^*$, and the heights of the rectangles are $f(x_k^*)$, for $k = 1, \ldots, 6$.

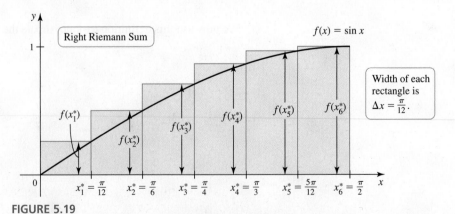

FIGURE 5.19

The resulting right Riemann sum (Figure 5.19) is

$$f(x_1^*)\Delta x + f(x_2^*)\Delta x + \cdots + f(x_6^*)\Delta x$$

$$= \left[\sin\left(\frac{\pi}{12}\right)\cdot\frac{\pi}{12}\right] + \left[\sin\left(\frac{\pi}{6}\right)\cdot\frac{\pi}{12}\right] + \left[\sin\left(\frac{\pi}{4}\right)\cdot\frac{\pi}{12}\right]$$

$$+ \left[\sin\left(\frac{\pi}{3}\right)\cdot\frac{\pi}{12}\right] + \left[\sin\left(\frac{5\pi}{12}\right)\cdot\frac{\pi}{12}\right] + \left[\sin\left(\frac{\pi}{2}\right)\cdot\frac{\pi}{12}\right]$$

$$\approx 1.125.$$

QUICK CHECK 4 If the function in Example 2 is replaced by $f(x) = \cos x$, does the left Riemann sum or the right Riemann sum overestimate the area under the curve? ◄

c. Looking at the graphs, we see that the left Riemann sum in part (a) underestimates the actual area of R, whereas the right Riemann sum in part (b) overestimates the area of R. Therefore, the area of R is between 0.863 and 1.125. As the number of rectangles increases, these approximations improve. *Related Exercises 17–26* ◄

EXAMPLE 3 **A midpoint Riemann sum** Let R be the region bounded by the graph of $f(x) = \sin x$ and the x-axis between $x = 0$ and $x = \pi/2$. Approximate the area of R using a midpoint Riemann sum with $n = 6$ subintervals. Illustrate the sum with the appropriate rectangles.

SOLUTION The grid points and the length of the subintervals $\Delta x = \pi/12$ are the same as in Example 2. To find the midpoint Riemann sum, we set $x_1^*, x_2^*, \ldots, x_6^*$ equal to the midpoints of the subintervals. The midpoint of the first subinterval is the average of x_0 and x_1, which is

$$x_1^* = \frac{x_1 + x_0}{2} = \frac{\pi/12 + 0}{2} = \frac{\pi}{24}.$$

The remaining midpoints are also computed by averaging the two nearest grid points.

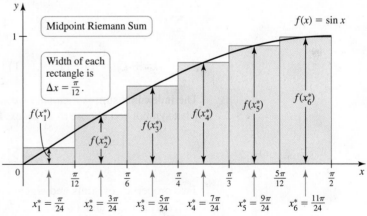

FIGURE 5.20

The resulting midpoint Riemann sum (Figure 5.20) is

$$f(x_1^*)\Delta x + f(x_2^*)\Delta x + \cdots + f(x_6^*)\Delta x$$

$$= \left[\sin\left(\frac{\pi}{24}\right)\cdot\frac{\pi}{12}\right] + \left[\sin\left(\frac{3\pi}{24}\right)\cdot\frac{\pi}{12}\right] + \left[\sin\left(\frac{5\pi}{24}\right)\cdot\frac{\pi}{12}\right]$$

$$+ \left[\sin\left(\frac{7\pi}{24}\right)\cdot\frac{\pi}{12}\right] + \left[\sin\left(\frac{9\pi}{24}\right)\cdot\frac{\pi}{12}\right] + \left[\sin\left(\frac{11\pi}{24}\right)\cdot\frac{\pi}{12}\right]$$

$$\approx 1.003.$$

Comparing the midpoint Riemann sum (Figure 5.20) with the left (Figure 5.18) and right (Figure 5.19) Riemann sums suggests that the midpoint sum is a more accurate estimate of the area under the curve. *Related Exercises 27–34* ◄

Table 5.4

x	$f(x)$
0	1
0.5	3
1.0	4.5
1.5	5.5
2.0	6.0

EXAMPLE 4   Riemann sums from tables Estimate the area A under the graph of f on the interval $[0, 2]$ using left and right Riemann sums with $n = 4$, where f is continuous but known only at the points in Table 5.4.

SOLUTION With $n = 4$ subintervals on the interval $[0, 2]$, $\Delta x = 2/4 = 0.5$. Using the left endpoint of each subinterval, the left Riemann sum is

$$A \approx (f(0) + f(0.5) + f(1.0) + f(1.5))\, \Delta x = (1 + 3 + 4.5 + 5.5)0.5 = 7.0.$$

Using the right endpoint of each subinterval, the right Riemann sum is

$$A \approx (f(0.5) + f(1.0) + f(1.5) + f(2.0))\Delta x = (3 + 4.5 + 5.5 + 6.0)0.5 = 9.5.$$

With only five function values, these estimates of the area are necessarily crude. Better estimates are obtained by using more subintervals and more function values.

Related Exercises 35–38 ◄

Sigma (Summation) Notation

Working with Riemann sums is cumbersome with large numbers of subintervals. Therefore, we pause for a moment to introduce some notation that simplifies our work.

Sigma (or **summation**) **notation** is used to express sums in a compact way. For example, the sum $1 + 2 + 3 + \cdots + 10$ is represented in sigma notation as $\sum_{k=1}^{10} k$. Here is how the notation works. The symbol Σ (*sigma*, the Greek capital S) stands for *sum*. The **index** k takes on all integer values from the lower limit ($k = 1$) to the upper limit ($k = 10$). The expression that immediately follows Σ (the **summand**) is evaluated for each value of k, and the resulting values are summed. Here are some examples.

$$\sum_{k=1}^{99} k = 1 + 2 + 3 + \cdots + 99 = 4950 \qquad \sum_{k=1}^{n} k = 1 + 2 + \cdots + n$$

$$\sum_{k=0}^{3} k^2 = 0^2 + 1^2 + 2^2 + 3^2 = 14 \qquad \sum_{k=1}^{4} (2k + 1) = 3 + 5 + 7 + 9 = 24$$

$$\sum_{k=-1}^{2} (k^2 + k) = [(-1)^2 + (-1)] + (0^2 + 0) + (1^2 + 1) + (2^2 + 2) = 8$$

The index in a sum is a *dummy variable*. It is internal to the sum, so it does not matter what symbol you choose as an index. For example,

$$\sum_{k=1}^{99} k = \sum_{n=1}^{99} n = \sum_{p=1}^{99} p.$$

Two properties of sums and sigma notation are useful in upcoming work. Suppose that $\{a_1, a_2, \ldots, a_n\}$ and $\{b_1, b_2, \ldots, b_n\}$ are two sets of real numbers, and suppose that c is a real number. Then we can factor multiplicative constants out of a sum:

Constant Multiple Rule $\qquad \sum_{k=1}^{n} ca_k = c \sum_{k=1}^{n} a_k.$

We can also split a sum into two sums:

Addition Rule $\qquad \sum_{k=1}^{n} (a_k + b_k) = \sum_{k=1}^{n} a_k + \sum_{k=1}^{n} b_k.$

In the coming examples and exercises, the following formulas for sums of powers of integers are essential.

> Formulas for $\sum_{k=1}^{n} k^p$, where p is a positive integer, have been known for centuries. The formulas for $p = 0, 1, 2,$ and 3 are relatively simple. The formulas become complicated as p increases.

THEOREM 5.4   Sums of Powers of Integers
Let n be a positive integer and c a real number.

$$\sum_{k=1}^{n} c = cn \qquad\qquad \sum_{k=1}^{n} k = \frac{n(n+1)}{2}$$

$$\sum_{k=1}^{n} k^2 = \frac{n(n+1)(2n+1)}{6} \qquad\qquad \sum_{k=1}^{n} k^3 = \frac{n^2(n+1)^2}{4}$$

Related Exercises 39–42 ◄

Riemann Sums Using Sigma Notation

With sigma notation, a Riemann sum has the convenient compact form

$$f(x_1^*)\Delta x + f(x_2^*)\Delta x + \cdots + f(x_n^*)\Delta x = \sum_{k=1}^{n} f(x_k^*)\Delta x.$$

To express left, right, and midpoint Riemann sums in sigma notation, we must identify the points x_k^*.

> For the left Riemann sum, note that $x_1^* = a + 0 \cdot \Delta x, x_2^* = a + 1 \cdot \Delta x,$ $x_3^* = a + 2 \cdot \Delta x,$ and in general, $x_k^* = a + (k-1)\Delta x.$

- For left Riemann sums, the left endpoints of the subintervals are
  $x_k^* = a + (k-1)\Delta x,$ for $k = 1, \ldots, n.$

> For the right Riemann sum, note that $x_1^* = a + 1 \cdot \Delta x, x_2^* = a + 2 \cdot \Delta x,$ $x_3^* = a + 3 \cdot \Delta x,$ and in general, $x_k^* = a + k\Delta x.$

- For right Riemann sums, the right endpoints of the subintervals are $x_k^* = a + k\Delta x,$ for $k = 1, \ldots, n.$

> For the midpoint Riemann sum, note that $x_1^* = a + \frac{1}{2} \cdot \Delta x, x_2^* = a + \frac{3}{2} \cdot \Delta x,$ $x_3^* = a + \frac{5}{2} \cdot \Delta x,$ and in general, $x_k^* = a + \left(k - \frac{1}{2}\right)\Delta x.$

- For midpoint Riemann sums, the midpoints of the subintervals are
  $x_k^* = a + \left(k - \frac{1}{2}\right)\Delta x,$ for $k = 1, \ldots, n.$

The three Riemann sums are written compactly as follows.

DEFINITION   Left, Right, and Midpoint Riemann Sums in Sigma Notation

Suppose f is defined on a closed interval $[a, b]$, which is divided into n subintervals of equal length Δx. If x_k^* is a point in the kth subinterval $[x_{k-1}, x_k]$, for $k = 1, 2, \ldots, n$, then the **Riemann sum** of f on $[a, b]$ is $\sum_{k=1}^{n} f(x_k^*)\Delta x.$ Three cases arise in practice.

- **left Riemann sum** if $x_k^* = a + (k-1)\Delta x$
- **right Riemann sum** if $x_k^* = a + k\Delta x$
- **midpoint Riemann sum** if $x_k^* = a + \left(k - \frac{1}{2}\right)\Delta x,$ for $k = 1, 2, \ldots, n$

EXAMPLE 5   Calculating Riemann sums Evaluate the left, right, and midpoint Riemann sums of $f(x) = x^3 + 1$ between $a = 0$ and $b = 2$ using $n = 50$ subintervals. Make a conjecture about the exact area of the region under the curve (Figure 5.21).

SOLUTION With $n = 50$, the length of each subinterval is

$$\Delta x = \frac{b-a}{n} = \frac{2-0}{50} = \frac{1}{25} = 0.04.$$

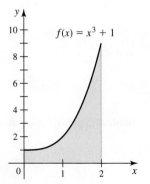

FIGURE 5.21

The value of x_k^* for the left Riemann sum is

$$x_k^* = a + (k-1)\Delta x = 0 + 0.04(k-1) = 0.04k - 0.04,$$

for $k = 1, 2, \ldots, 50$. Therefore, the left Riemann sum, evaluated with a calculator, is

$$\sum_{k=1}^{n} f(x_k^*)\Delta x = \sum_{k=1}^{50} f(0.04k - 0.04)0.04 = 5.842.$$

To evaluate the right Riemann sum, we let $x_k^* = a + k\Delta x = 0.04k$ and find that

$$\sum_{k=1}^{n} f(x_k^*)\Delta x = \sum_{k=1}^{50} f(0.04k)0.04 = 6.162.$$

For the midpoint Riemann sum, we let

$$x_k^* = a + \left(k - \frac{1}{2}\right)\Delta x = 0 + 0.04\left(k - \frac{1}{2}\right) = 0.04k - 0.02.$$

The value of the sum is

$$\sum_{k=1}^{n} f(x_k^*)\Delta x = \sum_{k=1}^{50} f(0.04k - 0.02)0.04 \approx 6.000.$$

Because f is increasing on $[0, 2]$, the left Riemann sum underestimates the area of the shaded region in Figure 5.21, while the right Riemann sum overestimates the area. Therefore, the exact area lies between 5.842 and 6.162. The midpoint Riemann sum usually gives the best estimate for increasing or decreasing functions.

Table 5.5 shows the left, right, and midpoint Riemann sum approximations for values of n up to 200. All three sets of approximations approach a value near 6, which is a reasonable estimate of the area under the curve. In Section 5.3, we show rigorously that the limit of all three Riemann sums as $n \to \infty$ is 6.

ALTERNATIVE SOLUTION It is worth examining another approach to Example 5. Consider the right Riemann sum given previously:

$$\sum_{k=1}^{n} f(x_k^*)\Delta x = \sum_{k=1}^{50} f(0.04k)0.04.$$

Rather than evaluating this sum with a calculator, we note that $f(0.04k) = (0.04k)^3 + 1$ and then use the properties of sums:

$$\sum_{k=1}^{n} f(x_k^*)\Delta x = \sum_{k=1}^{50} \underbrace{((0.04k)^3 + 1)}_{f(x_k^*)}\underbrace{0.04}_{\Delta x}$$

$$= \sum_{k=1}^{50} (0.04k)^3\, 0.04 + \sum_{k=1}^{50} 1 \cdot 0.04 \qquad \sum(a_k + b_k) = \sum a_k + \sum b_k$$

$$= (0.04)^4 \sum_{k=1}^{50} k^3 + 0.04 \sum_{k=1}^{50} 1. \qquad \sum ca_k = c\sum a_k$$

Using the summation formulas for powers of integers in Theorem 5.4, we find that

$$\sum_{k=1}^{50} 1 = 50 \quad \text{and} \quad \sum_{k=1}^{50} k^3 = \frac{50^2 \cdot 51^2}{4}.$$

Table 5.5 **Left, right, and midpoint Riemann sum approximations**

n	L_n	R_n	M_n
20	5.61	6.41	5.995
40	5.8025	6.2025	5.99875
60	5.86778	6.13444	5.99944
80	5.90063	6.10063	5.99969
100	5.9204	6.0804	5.9998
120	5.93361	6.06694	5.99986
140	5.94306	6.05735	5.9999
160	5.95016	6.05016	5.99992
180	5.95568	6.04457	5.99994
200	5.9601	6.0401	5.99995

Substituting the values of these sums into the right Riemann sum, its value is

$$\sum_{k=1}^{50} f(x_k^*)\Delta x = \frac{3851}{625} = 6.162,$$

confirming the result given by a calculator. The idea of evaluating Riemann sums for *arbitrary* values of n is used in Section 5.3, where we evaluate the limit of the Riemann sum as $n \to \infty$.

Related Exercises 43–46 ◄

SECTION 5.2 EXERCISES

Review Questions

1. Suppose an object moves along a line at 15 m/s for $0 \le t < 2$, and at 25 m/s for $2 \le t \le 5$, where t is measured in seconds. Sketch the graph of the velocity function and find the displacement of the object for $0 \le t \le 5$.

2. Given the graph of the positive velocity of an object moving along a line, what is the geometrical representation of its displacement over a time interval $[a, b]$?

3. Suppose you want to approximate the area of the region bounded by the graph of $f(x) = \cos x$ and the x-axis between $x = 0$ and $x = \pi/2$. Explain a possible strategy.

4. Explain how Riemann sum approximations to the area of a region under a curve change as the number of subintervals increases.

5. Suppose the interval $[1, 3]$ is partitioned into $n = 4$ subintervals. What is the subinterval length Δx? List the grid points x_0, x_1, x_2, x_3, and x_4. Which points are used for the left, right, and midpoint Riemann sums?

6. Suppose the interval $[2, 6]$ is partitioned into $n = 4$ subintervals with grid points $x_0 = 2, x_1 = 3, x_2 = 4, x_3 = 5$, and $x_4 = 6$. Write, but do not evaluate, the left, right, and midpoint Riemann sums for $f(x) = x^2$.

7. Does the right Riemann sum underestimate or overestimate the area of the region under the graph of a function that is positive and decreasing on an interval $[a, b]$? Explain.

8. Does the left Riemann sum underestimate or overestimate the area of the region under the graph of a function that is positive and increasing on an interval $[a, b]$? Explain.

Basic Skills

9. **Approximating displacement** The velocity in ft/s of an object moving along a line is given by $v = 3t^2 + 1$ on the interval $0 \le t \le 4$.

   a. Divide the interval $[0, 4]$ into $n = 4$ subintervals, $[0, 1]$, $[1, 2]$, $[2, 3]$, and $[3, 4]$. On each subinterval, assume the object moves at a constant velocity equal to v evaluated at the midpoint of the subinterval and use these approximations to estimate the displacement of the object on $[0, 4]$ (see part (a) of the figure).

   b. Repeat part (a) for $n = 8$ subintervals (see part (b) of the figure).

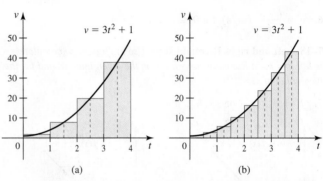

(a)   (b)

10. **Approximating displacement** The velocity in ft/s of an object moving along a line is given by $v = \sqrt{10t}$ on the interval $1 \le t \le 7$.

   a. Divide the time interval $[1, 7]$ into $n = 3$ subintervals, $[1, 3]$, $[3, 5]$, and $[5, 7]$. On each subinterval, assume the object moves at a constant velocity equal to v evaluated at the midpoint of the subinterval and use these approximations to estimate the displacement of the object on $[1, 7]$ (see part (a) of the figure).

   b. Repeat part (a) for $n = 6$ subintervals (see part (b) of the figure).

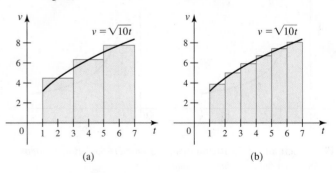

(a)   (b)

11–16. Approximating displacement *The velocity of an object is given by the following functions on a specified interval. Approximate the displacement of the object on this interval by subdividing the interval into the indicated number of subintervals. Use the left endpoint of each subinterval to compute the height of the rectangles.*

11. $v = 2t + 1$ (m/s), for $0 \le t \le 8$; $n = 2$

T 12. $v = e^t$ (m/s), for $0 \le t \le 3$; $n = 3$

13. $v = \dfrac{1}{2t + 1}$ (m/s), for $0 \le t \le 8$; $n = 4$

14. $v = t^2/2 + 4$ (ft/s), for $0 \le t \le 12$; $n = 6$

T 15. $v = 4\sqrt{t + 1}$ (mi/hr), for $0 \le t \le 15$; $n = 5$

16. $v = \dfrac{t + 3}{6}$ (m/s), for $0 \le t \le 4$; $n = 4$

17–18. Left and right Riemann sums *Use the figures to calculate the left and right Riemann sums for f on the given interval and for the given value of n.*

17. $f(x) = x + 1$ on $[1, 6]$; $n = 5$

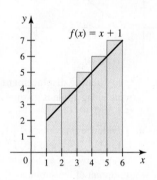

18. $f(x) = \dfrac{1}{x}$ on $[1, 5]$; $n = 4$

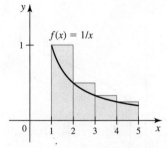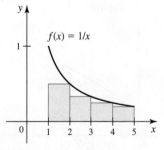

19–26. Left and right Riemann sums *Complete the following steps for the given function, interval, and value of n.*

a. *Sketch the graph of the function on the given interval.*
b. *Calculate Δx and the grid points $x_0, x_1, \ldots, x_n$.*
c. *Illustrate the left and right Riemann sums. Then determine which Riemann sum underestimates and which sum overestimates the area under the curve.*
d. *Calculate the left and right Riemann sums.*

19. $f(x) = x + 1$ on $[0, 4]$; $n = 4$

20. $f(x) = 9 - x$ on $[3, 8]$; $n = 5$

21. $f(x) = \cos x$ on $[0, \pi/2]$; $n = 4$

T 22. $f(x) = \sin^{-1}(x/3)$ on $[0, 3]$; $n = 6$

23. $f(x) = x^2 - 1$ on $[2, 4]$; $n = 4$

24. $f(x) = 2x^2$ on $[1, 6]$; $n = 5$

T 25. $f(x) = e^{x/2}$ on $[1, 4]$; $n = 6$

T 26. $f(x) = \ln 4x$ on $[1, 3]$; $n = 5$

27. **A midpoint Riemann sum** Approximate the area of the region bounded by the graph of $f(x) = 100 - x^2$ and the x-axis on $[0, 10]$ with $n = 5$ subintervals. Use the midpoint of each subinterval to determine the height of each rectangle (see figure).

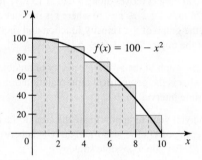

T 28. **A midpoint Riemann sum** Approximate the area of the region bounded by the graph of $f(t) = \cos(t/2)$ and the t-axis on $[0, \pi]$ with $n = 4$ subintervals. Use the midpoint of each subinterval to determine the height of each rectangle (see figure).

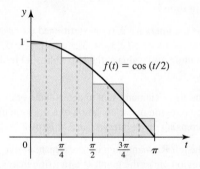

29–34. Midpoint Riemann sums *Complete the following steps for the given function, interval, and value of n.*

a. *Sketch the graph of the function on the given interval.*
b. *Calculate Δx and the grid points $x_0, x_1, \ldots, x_n$.*
c. *Illustrate the midpoint Riemann sum by sketching the appropriate rectangles.*
d. *Calculate the midpoint Riemann sum.*

29. $f(x) = 2x + 1$ on $[0, 4]$; $n = 4$

T 30. $f(x) = 2\cos^{-1} x$ on $[0, 1]$; $n = 5$

T 31. $f(x) = \sqrt{x}$ on $[1, 3]$; $n = 4$

32. $f(x) = x^2$ on $[0, 4]$; $n = 4$

33. $f(x) = \dfrac{1}{x}$ on $[1, 6]$; $n = 5$

34. $f(x) = 4 - x$ on $[-1, 4]$; $n = 5$

35–36. Riemann sums from tables *Use the tabulated values of f to evaluate the left and right Riemann sums for the given value of n.*

35. $n = 4$; $[0, 2]$

x	0	0.5	1	1.5	2
$f(x)$	5	3	2	1	1

36. $n = 8$; $[1, 5]$

x	1	1.5	2	2.5	3	3.5	4	4.5	5
$f(x)$	0	2	3	2	2	1	0	2	3

37. Displacement from a table of velocities The velocities (in miles/hour) of an automobile moving along a straight highway over a two-hr period are given in the following table.

t(hr)	0	0.25	0.5	0.75	1	1.25	1.5	1.75	2
v(mi/hr)	50	50	60	60	55	65	50	60	70

a. Sketch a smooth curve passing through the data points.
b. Find the midpoint Riemann sum approximation to the displacement on $[0, 2]$ with $n = 2$ and $n = 4$.

38. Displacement from a table of velocities The velocities (in meters/second) of an automobile moving along a straight freeway over a four-second period are given in the following table.

t(s)	0	0.5	1	1.5	2	2.5	3	3.5	4
v(m/s)	20	25	30	35	30	30	35	40	40

a. Sketch a smooth curve passing through the data points.
b. Find the midpoint Riemann sum approximation to the displacement on $[0, 4]$ with $n = 2$ and $n = 4$ subintervals.

39. Sigma notation Express the following sums using sigma notation. (Answers are not unique.)

a. $1 + 2 + 3 + 4 + 5$ b. $4 + 5 + 6 + 7 + 8 + 9$
c. $1^2 + 2^2 + 3^2 + 4^2$ d. $1 + \frac{1}{2} + \frac{1}{3} + \frac{1}{4}$

40. Sigma notation Express the following sums using sigma notation. (Answers are not unique.)

a. $1 + 3 + 5 + 7 + \cdots + 99$
b. $4 + 9 + 14 + \cdots + 44$
c. $3 + 8 + 13 + \cdots + 63$
d. $\frac{1}{1 \cdot 2} + \frac{1}{2 \cdot 3} + \frac{1}{3 \cdot 4} + \cdots + \frac{1}{49 \cdot 50}$

41. Sigma notation Evaluate the following expressions.

a. $\sum_{k=1}^{10} k$ b. $\sum_{k=1}^{6} (2k + 1)$

c. $\sum_{k=1}^{4} k^2$ d. $\sum_{n=1}^{5} (1 + n^2)$

e. $\sum_{m=1}^{3} \frac{2m + 2}{3}$ f. $\sum_{j=1}^{3} (3j - 4)$

g. $\sum_{p=1}^{5} (2p + p^2)$ h. $\sum_{n=0}^{4} \sin \frac{n\pi}{2}$

42. Evaluating sums Evaluate the following expressions by two methods.

(i) Use Theorem 5.4. (ii) Use a calculator.

a. $\sum_{k=1}^{45} k$ b. $\sum_{k=1}^{45} (5k - 1)$ c. $\sum_{k=1}^{75} 2k^2$

d. $\sum_{n=1}^{50} (1 + n^2)$ e. $\sum_{m=1}^{75} \frac{2m + 2}{3}$ f. $\sum_{j=1}^{20} (3j - 4)$

g. $\sum_{p=1}^{35} (2p + p^2)$ h. $\sum_{n=0}^{40} (n^2 + 3n - 1)$

43–46. Riemann sums for larger values of n *Complete the following steps for the given function f and interval.*

a. *For the given value of n, use sigma notation to write the left, right, and midpoint Riemann sums. Then evaluate each sum using a calculator.*
b. *Based on the approximations found in part (a), estimate the area of the region bounded by the graph of f and the x-axis on the interval.*

43. $f(x) = \sqrt{x}$, $[0, 4]$; $n = 40$

44. $f(x) = x^2 + 1$, $[-1, 1]$; $n = 50$

45. $f(x) = x^2 - 1$, $[2, 7]$; $n = 75$

46. $f(x) = \cos 2x$, $[0, \pi/4]$; $n = 60$

Further Explorations

47. Explain why or why not Determine whether the following statements are true and give an explanation or counterexample.

a. Consider the linear function $f(x) = 2x + 5$ and the region bounded by its graph and the x-axis on the interval $[3, 6]$. Suppose the area of this region is approximated using midpoint Riemann sums. Then the approximations give the exact area of the region for any number of subintervals.
b. A left Riemann sum always overestimates the area of a region bounded by a positive increasing function and the x-axis on an interval $[a, b]$.
c. For an increasing or decreasing nonconstant function on an interval $[a, b]$ and a given value of n, the value of the midpoint Riemann sum always lies between the values of the left and right Riemann sums.

48. Riemann sums for a semicircle Let $f(x) = \sqrt{1 - x^2}$.

a. Show that the graph of f is the upper half of a circle of radius 1 centered at the origin.
b. Estimate the area between the graph of f and the x-axis on the interval $[-1, 1]$ using a midpoint Riemann sum with $n = 25$.
c. Repeat part (b) using $n = 75$ rectangles.
d. What happens to the midpoint Riemann sums on $[-1, 1]$ as $n \to \infty$?

49–52. Identifying Riemann sums *Fill in the blanks with right or midpoint; an interval; and a value of n. In some cases, more than one answer works.*

49. $\sum_{k=1}^{4} f(1 + k) \cdot 1$ is a _____ Riemann sum for f on the interval $[\_\_, \_\_]$ with $n = $ _____.

50. $\sum_{k=1}^{4} f(2 + k) \cdot 1$ is a _____ Riemann sum for f on the interval

[___, ___] with $n = $ _____.

51. $\sum_{k=1}^{4} f(1.5 + k) \cdot 1$ is a _____ Riemann sum for f on the interval

[___, ___] with $n = $ _____.

52. $\sum_{k=1}^{8} f\left(1.5 + \frac{k}{2}\right) \cdot \frac{1}{2}$ is a _____ Riemann sum for f on the

interval [___, ___] with $n = $ _____.

53. Approximating areas Estimate the area of the region bounded by the graph of $f(x) = x^2 + 2$ and the x-axis on $[0, 2]$ in the following ways.

   a. Divide $[0, 2]$ into $n = 4$ subintervals and approximate the area of the region using a left Riemann sum. Illustrate the solution geometrically.

   b. Divide $[0, 2]$ into $n = 4$ subintervals and approximate the area of the region using a midpoint Riemann sum. Illustrate the solution geometrically.

   c. Divide $[0, 2]$ into $n = 4$ subintervals and approximate the area of the region using a right Riemann sum. Illustrate the solution geometrically.

54. Approximating area from a graph Approximate the area of the region bounded by the graph (see figure) and the x-axis by dividing the interval $[0, 6]$ into $n = 3$ subintervals. Use left and right Riemann sums to obtain two different approximations.

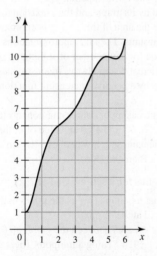

55. Approximating area from a graph Approximate the area of the region bounded by the graph (see figure) and the x-axis by divid-

ing the interval $[1, 7]$ into $n = 6$ subintervals. Use left and right Riemann sums to obtain two different approximations.

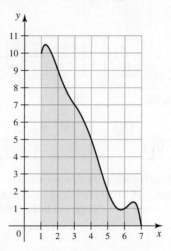

Applications

56. Displacement from a velocity graph Consider the velocity function for an object moving along a line (see figure).

   a. Describe the motion of the object over the interval $[0, 6]$.

   b. Use geometry to find the displacement of the object between $t = 0$ and $t = 3$.

   c. Use geometry to find the displacement of the object between $t = 3$ and $t = 5$.

   d. Assuming that the velocity remains 30 m/s, for $t \geq 4$, find the function that gives the displacement between $t = 0$ and any time $t \geq 4$.

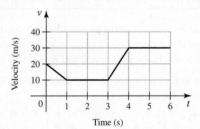

57. Displacement from a velocity graph Consider the velocity function for an object moving along a line (see figure).

   a. Describe the motion of the object over the interval $[0, 6]$.

   b. Use geometry to find the displacement of the object between $t = 0$ and $t = 2$.

   c. Use geometry to find the displacement of the object between $t = 2$ and $t = 5$.

   d. Assuming that the velocity remains 10 m/s, for $t \geq 5$, find the function that gives the displacement between $t = 0$ and any time $t \geq 5$.

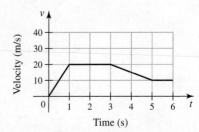

58. Flow rates Suppose a gauge at the outflow of a reservoir measures the flow rate of water in units of ft^3/hr. In Chapter 6, we show that the total amount of water that flows out of the reservoir is the area under the flow rate curve. Consider the flow-rate function shown in the figure.

  a. Find the amount of water (in units of ft^3) that flows out of the reservoir over the interval $[0, 4]$.

  b. Find the amount of water that flows out of the reservoir over the interval $[8, 10]$.

  c. Does more water flow out of the reservoir over the interval $[0, 4]$ or $[4, 6]$?

  d. Show that the units of your answer are consistent with the units of the variables on the axes.

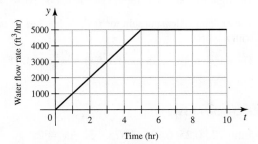

59. Mass from density A thin 10-cm rod is made of an alloy whose density varies along its length according to the function shown in the figure. Assume density is measured in units of g/cm. In Chapter 6, we show that the mass of the rod is the area under the density curve.

  a. Find the mass of the left half of the rod ($0 \leq x \leq 5$).

  b. Find the mass of the right half of the rod ($5 \leq x \leq 10$).

  c. Find the mass of the entire rod ($0 \leq x \leq 10$).

  d. Find the point along the rod at which it will balance (called the center of mass).

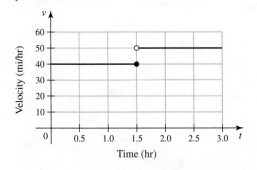

60–61. Displacement from velocity *The following functions describe the velocity of a car (in mi/hr) moving along a straight highway for a 3 hr interval. In each case, find the function that gives the displacement of the car over the interval $[0, t]$, where $0 \leq t \leq 3$.*

60. $v(t) = \begin{cases} 40 & \text{if } 0 \leq t \leq 1.5 \\ 50 & \text{if } 1.5 < t \leq 3 \end{cases}$

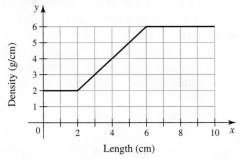

61. $v(t) = \begin{cases} 30 & \text{if } 0 \leq t \leq 2 \\ 50 & \text{if } 2 < t \leq 2.5 \\ 44 & \text{if } 2.5 < t \leq 3 \end{cases}$

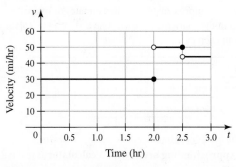

62–65. Functions with absolute value *Use a calculator and the method of your choice to approximate the area of the following regions. Present your calculations in a table, showing approximations using n = 16, 32, and 64 subintervals. Comment on whether your approximations appear to approach a limit.*

62. The region bounded by the graph of $f(x) = |25 - x^2|$ and the x-axis on the interval $[0, 10]$

63. The region bounded by the graph of $f(x) = |x(x^2 - 1)|$ and the x-axis on the interval $[-1, 1]$

64. The region bounded by the graph of $f(x) = |\cos 2x|$ and the x-axis on the interval $[0, \pi]$

65. The region bounded by the graph of $f(x) = |1 - x^3|$ and the x-axis on the interval $[-1, 2]$

Additional Exercises

66. Riemann sums for constant functions Let $f(x) = c$, where $c > 0$, be a constant function on $[a, b]$. Prove that any Riemann sum for any value of n gives the exact area of the region between the graph of f and the x-axis on $[a, b]$.

67. Riemann sums for linear functions Assume that the linear function $f(x) = mx + c$ is positive on the interval $[a, b]$. Prove that the midpoint Riemann sum with any value of n gives the exact area of the region between the graph of f and the x-axis on $[a, b]$.

68. Shape of the graph for left Riemann sums Suppose a left Riemann sum is used to approximate the area of the region bounded by the graph of a positive function and the x-axis on the interval $[a, b]$. Fill in the following table to indicate whether the resulting approximation underestimates or overestimates the exact area in the four cases shown. Use a sketch to explain your reasoning in each case.

	Increasing on $[a, b]$	Decreasing on $[a, b]$
Concave up on $[a, b]$		
Concave down on $[a, b]$		

69. Shape of the graph for right Riemann sums Suppose a right Riemann sum is used to approximate the area of the region bounded by the graph of a positive function and the x-axis on the interval $[a, b]$. Fill in the following table to indicate whether the resulting approximation underestimates or overestimates the exact area in the four cases shown. Use a sketch to explain your reasoning in each case.

	Increasing on $[a, b]$	Decreasing on $[a, b]$
Concave up on $[a, b]$		
Concave down on $[a, b]$		

Technology Exercises

70–75. Approximating areas with a calculator *Use a calculator and right Riemann sums to approximate the area of the region described. Present your calculations in a table showing the approximations for $n = 10, 30, 60,$ and 80 subintervals. Comment on whether your approximations appear to approach a limit.*

70. The region bounded by the graph of $f(x) = x^2 + 1$ and the x-axis on the interval $[0, 2]$

71. The region bounded by the graph of $f(x) = 4 - x^2$ and the x-axis on the interval $[-2, 2]$

72. The region bounded by the graph of $f(x) = 2^x$ and the x-axis on the interval $[1, 2]$

73. The region bounded by the graph of $f(x) = 2 - 2 \sin x$ and the x-axis on the interval $[-\pi/2, \pi/2]$

74. The region bounded by the graph of $f(x) = \sqrt{x + 1}$ and the x-axis on the interval $[0, 3]$

75. The region bounded by the graph of $f(x) = \ln x$ and the x-axis on the interval $[1, e]$

76–79. Sigma notation for Riemann sums *Use sigma notation to write the following Riemann sums. Then evaluate each Riemann sum using Theorem 5.4 or a calculator.*

76. The left Riemann sum for $f(x) = e^x$ on $[0, \ln 2]$ with $n = 40$

77. The right Riemann sum for $f(x) = x + 1$ on $[0, 4]$ with $n = 50$

78. The midpoint Riemann sum for $f(x) = 1 + \cos \pi x$ on $[0, 2]$ with $n = 50$

79. The midpoint Riemann sum for $f(x) = x^3$ on $[3, 11]$ with $n = 32$

QUICK CHECK ANSWERS

1. 45 mi   **2.** 0.25, 0.125, 7.875   **3.** $\Delta x = 2$; $\{1, 3, 5, 7, 9\}$ **4.** The left sum overestimates the area ◄

5.3   Definite Integrals

We introduced Riemann sums in Section 5.2 as a way to approximate the area of a region bounded by a curve $y = f(x)$ and the x-axis on an interval $[a, b]$. In that discussion, we assumed f to be nonnegative on the interval. Our next task is to discover the geometric meaning of Riemann sums when f is negative on some or all of $[a, b]$. Once this matter is settled, we can proceed to the main event of this section, which is to define the *definite integral*. With definite integrals, the approximations given by Riemann sums become exact.

Net Area

How do we interpret Riemann sums when f is negative at some or all points of $[a, b]$? The answer follows directly from the Riemann sum definition.

EXAMPLE 1   **Interpreting Riemann sums** Evaluate and interpret the following Riemann sums for $f(x) = 1 - x^2$ on the interval $[a, b]$ with n equally spaced subintervals.

a. A midpoint Riemann sum with $[a, b] = [1, 3]$ and $n = 4$

b. A left Riemann sum with $[a, b] = [0, 3]$ and $n = 6$

SOLUTION

a. The length of each subinterval is $\Delta x = \dfrac{b - a}{n} = \dfrac{3 - 1}{4} = 0.5$. So the grid points are

$$x_0 = 1, \quad x_1 = 1.5, \quad x_2 = 2, \quad x_3 = 2.5, \text{ and } x_4 = 3.$$

To compute the midpoint Riemann sum, we evaluate f at the midpoints of the subintervals, which are

$$x_1^* = 1.25, \quad x_2^* = 1.75, \quad x_3^* = 2.25, \text{ and } x_4^* = 2.75.$$

The resulting midpoint Riemann sum is

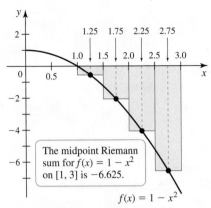

The midpoint Riemann sum for $f(x) = 1 - x^2$ on $[1, 3]$ is -6.625.

FIGURE 5.22

$$\sum_{k=1}^{n} f(x_k^*) \Delta x = \sum_{k=1}^{4} f(x_k^*)(0.5)$$
$$= f(1.25)(0.5) + f(1.75)(0.5) + f(2.25)(0.5) + f(2.75)(0.5)$$
$$= (-0.5625 - 2.0625 - 4.0625 - 6.5625)0.5$$
$$= -6.625.$$

All values of $f(x_k^*)$ are negative, so the Riemann sum is also negative. Because area is always a nonnegative quantity, this Riemann sum does not approximate an area. Notice, however, that the values of $f(x_k^*)$ are the *negative* of the heights of the corresponding rectangles (Figure 5.22). Therefore, the Riemann sum is an approximation to the *negative* of the area of the region bounded by the curve.

b. The length of each subinterval is $\Delta x = \dfrac{b - a}{n} = \dfrac{3 - 0}{6} = 0.5$, and the grid points are

$$x_0 = 0, \quad x_1 = 0.5, \quad x_2 = 1, \quad x_3 = 1.5, \quad x_4 = 2, \quad x_5 = 2.5, \text{ and } x_6 = 3.$$

To calculate the left Riemann sum, we set $x_1^*, x_2^*, \ldots, x_6^*$ equal to the left endpoints of the subintervals:

$$x_1^* = 0, \quad x_2^* = 0.5, \quad x_3^* = 1, \quad x_4^* = 1.5, \quad x_5^* = 2, \text{ and } x_6^* = 2.5.$$

The resulting left Riemann sum is

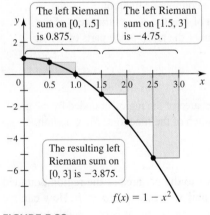

The left Riemann sum on $[0, 1.5]$ is 0.875.

The left Riemann sum on $[1.5, 3]$ is -4.75.

The resulting left Riemann sum on $[0, 3]$ is -3.875.

$f(x) = 1 - x^2$

FIGURE 5.23

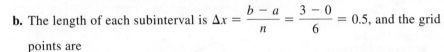

$$\sum_{k=1}^{n} f(x_k^*) \Delta x = \sum_{k=1}^{6} f(x_k^*)(0.5)$$
$$= \underbrace{(f(0) + f(0.5) + f(1)}_{\text{nonnegative contribution}} + \underbrace{f(1.5) + f(2) + f(2.5))}_{\text{negative contribution}} 0.5$$
$$= (1 + 0.75 + 0 - 1.25 - 3 - 5.25) 0.5$$
$$= -3.875.$$

In this case, the values of $f(x_k^*)$ are nonnegative for $k = 1, 2$, and 3 and negative for $k = 4, 5$, and 6 (Figure 5.23). Where f is positive, we get positive contributions to the Riemann sum, and where f is negative, we get negative contributions to the sum.

Related Exercises 11–20◄

Let's recap what was learned in Example 1. On intervals where $f(x) < 0$, Riemann sums approximate the *negative* of the area of the region bounded by the curve (Figure 5.24). In the more general case that f is positive on only part of $[a, b]$, we get positive contributions to the sum where f is positive and negative contributions to the sum where f is negative. In this case, Riemann sums approximate the area of the regions that lie above the x-axis *minus* the area of the regions that lie *below* the *x*-axis (Figure 5.25). This difference between the positive and negative contributions is called the *net area*; it can be positive, negative, or zero.

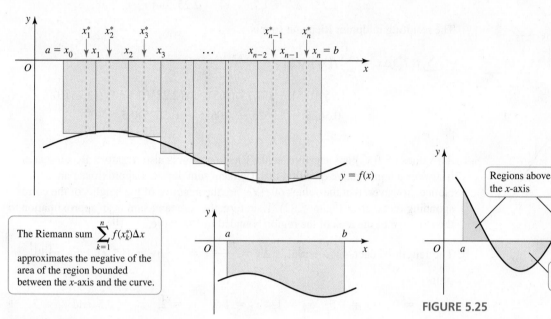

The Riemann sum $\sum_{k=1}^{n} f(x_k^*)\Delta x$ approximates the negative of the area of the region bounded between the *x*-axis and the curve.

FIGURE 5.24

FIGURE 5.25

> Net area suggests the difference between positive and negative contributions much like net change or net profit. Some texts use the term **signed area** for net area.

DEFINITION Net Area

Consider the region R bounded by the graph of a continuous function f and the *x*-axis between $x = a$ and $x = b$. The **net area** of R is the sum of the areas of the parts of R that lie above the *x*-axis *minus* the sum of the areas of the parts of R that lie below the *x*-axis on $[a, b]$.

QUICK CHECK 1 Suppose $f(x) = -5$. What is the net area of the region bounded by the graph of f and the *x*-axis on the interval $[1, 5]$? Make a sketch of the function and the region. ◄

The Definite Integral

Riemann sums for f on $[a, b]$ give *approximations* to the net area of the region bounded by the graph of f and the *x*-axis between $x = a$ and $x = b$, where $a < b$. How can we make these approximations exact? If f is continuous on $[a, b]$, it is reasonable to expect the Riemann sum approximations to approach the exact value of the net area as the number of subintervals $n \to \infty$ and as the length of the subintervals $\Delta x \to 0$ (Figure 5.26). In terms of limits, we write

$$\text{net area} = \lim_{n \to \infty} \sum_{k=1}^{n} f(x_k^*)\,\Delta x.$$

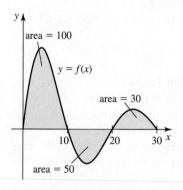

QUICK CHECK 2 Sketch a continuous function f that is positive over the interval $[0, 1)$ and negative over the interval $(1, 2]$, such that the net area of the region bounded by the graph of f and the *x*-axis on $[0, 2]$ is zero. ◄

The Riemann sums we have used so far involve regular partitions in which the subintervals have the same length Δx. We now introduce partitions of $[a, b]$ in which the lengths of the subintervals are not necessarily equal. A **general partition** of $[a, b]$ consists of the n subintervals

$$[x_0, x_1], [x_1, x_2], \ldots, [x_{n-1}, x_n],$$

where $x_0 = a$ and $x_n = b$. The length of the kth subinterval is $\Delta x_k = x_k - x_{k-1}$, for $k = 1, \ldots, n$. We let x_k^* be any point in the subinterval $[x_{k-1}, x_k]$. This general partition is used to define the *general Riemann sum*.

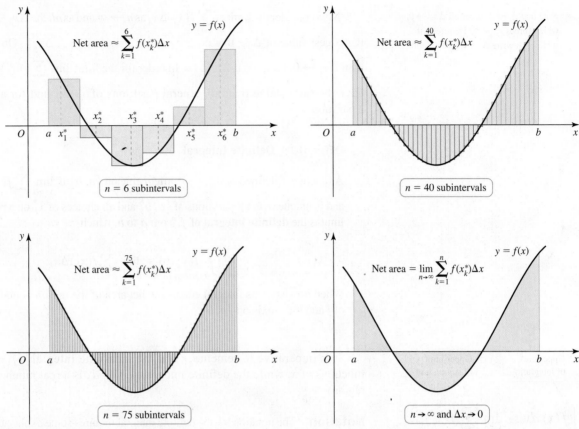

FIGURE 5.26 As the number of subintervals n increases, the Riemann sum approaches the net area of the region between the curve $y = f(x)$ and the x-axis on $[a, b]$.

> Examples of using general Riemann sums to approximate definite integrals are given in Exercises 84–85 of this section and in Section 5.7.

DEFINITION General Riemann Sum

Suppose $[x_0, x_1], [x_1, x_2], \ldots, [x_{n-1}, x_n]$ are subintervals of $[a, b]$ with

$$a = x_0 < x_1 < x_2 < \cdots < x_{n-1} < x_n = b.$$

Let Δx_k be the length of the subinterval $[x_{k-1}, x_k]$ and let x_k^* be any point in $[x_{k-1}, x_k]$, for $k = 1, 2, \ldots, n$.

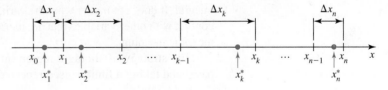

If f is defined on $[a, b]$, the sum

$$\sum_{k=1}^{n} f(x_k^*)\Delta x_k = f(x_1^*)\Delta x_1 + f(x_2^*)\Delta x_2 + \cdots + f(x_n^*)\Delta x_n$$

is called a **general Riemann sum for f on $[a, b]$**.

As was the case for regular Riemann sums, if we choose x_k^* to be the left endpoint of $[x_{k-1}, x_k]$, for $k = 1, 2, \ldots, n$, then the general Riemann sum is a left Riemann sum. Similarly, if we choose x_k^* to be the right endpoint of $[x_{k-1}, x_k]$, for $k = 1, 2, \ldots, n$, then the general Riemann sum is a right Riemann sum, and if we choose x_k^* to be the midpoint of then interval $[x_{k-1}, x_k]$, for $k = 1, 2, \ldots, n$, then the general Riemann sum is a midpoint Riemann sum.

> Note that $\Delta \to 0$ forces all $\Delta x_k \to 0$, which forces $n \to \infty$. Therefore, it suffices to write $\Delta \to 0$ in the limit.

Now consider the limit of $\sum_{k=1}^{n} f(x_k^*)\Delta x_k$ as $n \to \infty$ and as *all* the $\Delta x_k \to 0$. We let Δ denote the largest value of Δx_k; that is, $\Delta = \max\{\Delta x_1, \Delta x_2, \ldots, \Delta x_n\}$. Observe that if $\Delta \to 0$, then $\Delta x_k \to 0$, for $k = 1, 2, \ldots, n$. In order for the limit $\lim_{\Delta \to 0} \sum_{k=1}^{n} f(x_k^*)\Delta x_k$ to exist, it must have the same value over all general partitions of $[a, b]$ and for all choices of x_k^* on a partition.

DEFINITION Definite Integral

A function f defined on $[a, b]$ is **integrable** on $[a, b]$ if $\lim_{\Delta \to 0} \sum_{k=1}^{n} f(x_k^*)\Delta x_k$ exists and is unique over all partitions of $[a, b]$ and all choices of x_k^* on a partition. This limit is the **definite integral of f from a to b**, which we write

$$\int_a^b f(x)\, dx = \lim_{\Delta \to 0} \sum_{k=1}^{n} f(x_k^*)\Delta x_k.$$

When it exists, this integral equals the net area of the region bounded by the graph of f and the x-axis on $[a, b]$.

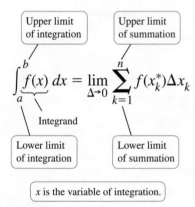

FIGURE 5.27

It is imperative to remember that the indefinite integral $\int f(x)\, dx$ is a family of functions of x, while the definite integral $\int_a^b f(x)\, dx$ is a real number (the net area of a region).

Notation　The notation for the definite integral requires some explanation. There is a direct match between the notation on either side of the equation in the definition (Figure 5.27). In the limit as $\Delta \to 0$, the finite sum, denoted $\sum$, becomes a sum with an infinite number of terms, denoted $\int$. The integral sign $\int$ is an elongated S for sum. In this limit, the lengths of the subintervals Δx_k are replaced with dx. The **limits of integration**, a and b, and the limits of summation also match: The lower limit in the sum, $k = 1$, corresponds to the left endpoint of the interval, $x = a$, and the upper limit in the sum, $k = n$, corresponds to the right endpoint of the interval, $x = b$. The function under the integral sign is called the **integrand**. Finally, the differential dx in the integral is an essential part of the notation; it tells us that the **variable of integration** is x.

The variable of integration is a dummy variable that is completely internal to the integral. It does not matter what the variable of integration is called, as long as it does not conflict with other variables that are in use. Therefore, the integrals in Figure 5.28 all have the same meaning.

The strategy of slicing a region into smaller parts, summing the results from the parts, and taking a limit is used repeatedly in calculus and its applications. We call this

> For Leibniz, who introduced this notation in 1675, dx represented the width of an infinitesimally thin rectangle and $f(x)\, dx$ represented the area of such a rectangle. He used $\int_a^b f(x)\, dx$ to denote the sum of all these areas from a to b.

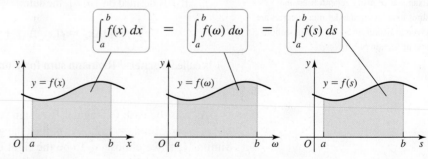

FIGURE 5.28

strategy the **slice-and-sum method**. It often results in a Riemann sum whose limit is a definite integral.

Evaluating Definite Integrals

Most of the functions encountered in this text are integrable (see Exercise 73 for an exception). In fact, if f is continuous on $[a, b]$ or if f is bounded on $[a, b]$ with a finite number of discontinuities, then f is integrable on $[a, b]$. The proof of this result goes beyond the scope of this text.

> A function f is bounded on an interval I if there is a number M such that $|f(x)| < M$ for all x in I.

THEOREM 5.5 Integrable Functions

If f is continuous on $[a, b]$ or bounded on $[a, b]$ with a finite number of discontinuities, then f is integrable on $[a, b]$.

When f is continuous on $[a, b]$, we have seen that the definite integral $\int_a^b f(x)\, dx$ is the net area bounded by the graph of f and the x-axis on $[a, b]$. Figure 5.29 illustrates how the idea of net area carries over to piecewise continuous functions.

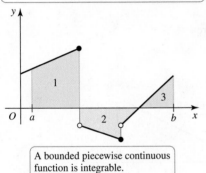

Net area $= \displaystyle\int_a^b f(x)\, dx$

$=$ area above x-axis (Regions 1 and 3) $-$ area below x-axis (Region 2)

A bounded piecewise continuous function is integrable.

FIGURE 5.29

QUICK CHECK 3 Graph $f(x) = x$ and use geometry to evaluate $\int_{-1}^1 x\, dx$. ◄

EXAMPLE 2 Identifying the limit of a sum Assume that

$$\lim_{\Delta \to 0} \sum_{k=1}^n (3x_k^{*2} + 2x_k^* + 1)\Delta x_k$$

is the limit of a Riemann sum for a function f on $[1, 3]$. Identify the function f and express the limit as a definite integral. What does the definite integral represent geometrically?

SOLUTION By comparing the sum $\displaystyle\sum_{k=1}^n (3x_k^{*2} + 2x_k^* + 1)\Delta x_k$ to the general Riemann sum $\displaystyle\sum_{k=1}^n f(x_k^*)\Delta x_k$, we see that $f(x) = 3x^2 + 2x + 1$. Because f is a polynomial, it is continuous on $[1, 3]$ and is, therefore, integrable on $[1, 3]$. It follows that

$$\lim_{\Delta \to 0} \sum_{k=1}^n (3x_k^{*2} + 2x_k^* + 1)\,\Delta x_k = \int_1^3 (3x^2 + 2x + 1)\, dx.$$

Because f is positive on $[1, 3]$, the definite integral $\int_1^3 (3x^2 + 2x + 1)\, dx$ is the area of the region bounded by the curve $y = 3x^2 + 2x + 1$ and the x-axis on $[1, 3]$ (Figure 5.30).

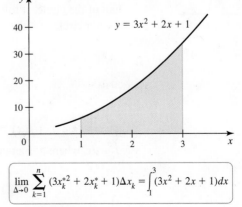

$$\lim_{\Delta \to 0} \sum_{k=1}^n (3x_k^{*2} + 2x_k^* + 1)\Delta x_k = \int_1^3 (3x^2 + 2x + 1)dx$$

FIGURE 5.30

Related Exercises 21–24 ◄

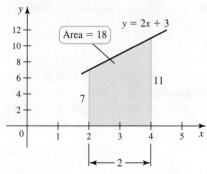

FIGURE 5.31

> **A trapezoid and its area** When $a = 0$,
> we get the area of a triangle. When
> $a = b$, we get the area of a rectangle.

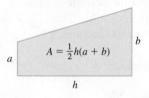

EXAMPLE 3   **Evaluating definite integrals using geometry** Use familiar area formulas to evaluate the following definite integrals.

a. $\int_2^4 (2x + 3)\, dx$ **b.** $\int_1^6 (2x - 6)\, dx$ **c.** $\int_3^4 \sqrt{1 - (x - 3)^2}\, dx$

SOLUTION To evaluate these definite integrals geometrically, a sketch of the corresponding region is essential.

a. The definite integral $\int_2^4 (2x + 3)\, dx$ is the area of the trapezoid bounded by the x-axis and the line $y = 2x + 3$ from $x = 2$ to $x = 4$ (Figure 5.31). The width of its base is 2, and the lengths of its two parallel sides are $f(2) = 7$ and $f(4) = 11$. Using the area formula for a trapezoid we have

$$\int_2^4 (2x + 3)\, dx = \frac{1}{2} \cdot 2(11 + 7) = 18.$$

b. A sketch shows that the regions bounded by the line $y = 2x - 6$ and the x-axis are triangles (Figure 5.32). The area of the triangle on the interval $[1, 3]$ is $\frac{1}{2} \cdot 2 \cdot 4 = 4$. Similarly, the area of the triangle on $[3, 6]$ is $\frac{1}{2} \cdot 3 \cdot 6 = 9$. The definite integral is the net area of the entire region, which is the area of the triangle above the x-axis minus the area of the triangle below the x-axis:

$$\int_1^6 (2x - 6)\, dx = \text{net area} = 9 - 4 = 5.$$

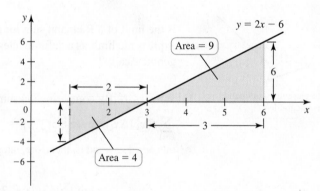

FIGURE 5.32

c. We first let $y = \sqrt{1 - (x - 3)^2}$ and observe that $y \geq 0$ when $2 \leq x \leq 4$. Squaring both sides leads to the equation $(x - 3)^2 + y^2 = 1$, whose graph is a circle of radius 1 centered at $(3, 0)$. Because $y \geq 0$, the graph of $y = \sqrt{1 - (x - 3)^2}$ is the upper half of the circle. It follows that the integral $\int_3^4 \sqrt{1 - (x - 3)^2}\, dx$ is the area of a quarter circle of radius 1 (Figure 5.33). Therefore,

$$\int_3^4 \sqrt{1 - (x - 3)^2}\, dx = \frac{1}{4}\pi(1)^2 = \frac{\pi}{4}.$$

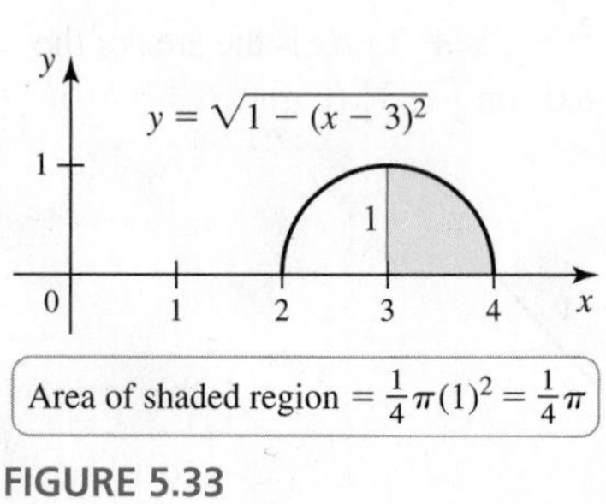

Related Exercises 25–32 ◄

Area of shaded region $= \frac{1}{4}\pi(1)^2 = \frac{1}{4}\pi$

FIGURE 5.33

QUICK CHECK 4 Let $f(x) = 5$ and use geometry to evaluate $\int_1^3 f(x)\, dx$. What is the value of $\int_a^b c\, dx$, where c is a real number? ◄

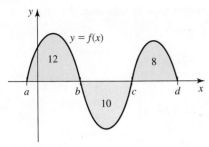

FIGURE 5.34

EXAMPLE 4   Definite integrals from graphs Figure 5.34 shows the graph of a function f with the areas of the regions bounded by its graph and the x-axis given. Find the values of the following definite integrals.

a. $\displaystyle\int_a^b f(x)\,dx$ **b.** $\displaystyle\int_b^c f(x)\,dx$

c. $\displaystyle\int_a^c f(x)\,dx$ **d.** $\displaystyle\int_b^d f(x)\,dx$

SOLUTION

a. Because f is positive on $[a, b]$, the value of the definite integral is the area of the region between the graph and the x-axis on $[a, b]$; that is, $\int_a^b f(x)\,dx = 12$.

b. Because f is negative on $[b, c]$, the value of the definite integral is the negative of the area of the corresponding region; that is, $\int_b^c f(x)\,dx = -10$.

c. The value of the definite integral is the area of the region on $[a, b]$ (where f is positive) minus the area of the region on $[b, c]$ (where f is negative). Therefore, $\int_a^c f(x)\,dx = 12 - 10 = 2$.

d. Reasoning as in part (c), we have $\int_b^d f(x)\,dx = -10 + 8 = -2$.

Related Exercises 33–40 ◄

Properties of Definite Integrals

Recall that the definite integral $\int_a^b f(x)\,dx$ was defined assuming that $a < b$. There are, however, occasions when it is necessary to allow the limits of integration to be reversed. If f is integrable on $[a, b]$, we define

$$\int_b^a f(x)\,dx = -\int_a^b f(x)\,dx.$$

In other words, reversing the limits of integration changes the sign of the integral.

Another fundamental property of integrals is that if we integrate from a point to itself, then the length of the interval of integration is zero, which means the definite integral is also zero.

QUICK CHECK 5 Evaluate $\int_a^b f(x)\,dx + \int_b^a f(x)\,dx$ assuming that f is integrable on $[a, b]$. ◄

DEFINITION   Reversing Limits and Identical Limits

Suppose f is integrable on $[a, b]$.

1. $\int_b^a f(x)\,dx = -\int_a^b f(x)\,dx$ **2.** $\int_a^a f(x)\,dx = 0$

Integral of a Sum Definite integrals possess other properties that often simplify their evaluation. Assume f and g are integrable on $[a, b]$. The first property states that their sum $f + g$ is integrable on $[a, b]$ and the integral of their sum is the sum of their integrals:

$$\int_a^b (f(x) + g(x))\,dx = \int_a^b f(x)\,dx + \int_a^b g(x)\,dx.$$

We prove this property, assuming that f and g are continuous. In this case, $f + g$ is continuous and, therefore, integrable. We then have

$$\int_a^b (f(x) + g(x))\, dx = \lim_{\Delta \to 0} \sum_{k=1}^n [f(x_k^*) + g(x_k^*)]\Delta x_k \qquad \text{Definition of definite integral}$$

$$= \lim_{\Delta \to 0} \left[\sum_{k=1}^n f(x_k^*)\Delta x_k + \sum_{k=1}^n g(x_k^*)\Delta x_k \right] \qquad \text{Split into two finite sums.}$$

$$= \lim_{\Delta \to 0} \sum_{k=1}^n f(x_k^*)\Delta x_k + \lim_{\Delta \to 0} \sum_{k=1}^n g(x_k^*)\Delta x_k \qquad \text{Split into two limits.}$$

$$= \int_a^b f(x)\, dx + \int_a^b g(x)\, dx. \qquad \text{Definition of definite integral}$$

Constants in Integrals Another property of definite integrals is that constants can be factored out of the integral. If f is integrable on $[a, b]$ and c is a constant, then cf is integrable on $[a, b]$ and

$$\int_a^b cf(x)\, dx = c \int_a^b f(x)\, dx.$$

The justification (Exercise 71) is based on the fact that for finite sums,

$$\sum_{k=1}^n cf(x_k^*)\Delta x_k = c\sum_{k=1}^n f(x_k^*)\Delta x_k.$$

Integrals over Subintervals If c lies between a and b, then the integral on $[a, b]$ may be split into two integrals. As shown in Figure 5.35, we have the property

$$\boxed{\int_a^b f(x)\, dx} = \boxed{\int_a^c f(x)\, dx} + \boxed{\int_c^b f(x)\, dx.}$$

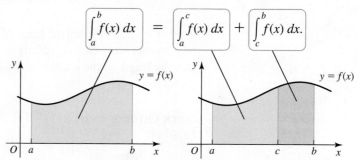

FIGURE 5.35

It is surprising that this same property also holds when c lies outside the interval $[a, b]$. For example, if $a < b < c$ and f is integrable on $[a, c]$, then it follows (Figure 5.36) that

$$\boxed{\int_a^b f(x)\, dx} = \boxed{\int_a^c f(x)\, dx} - \boxed{\int_b^c f(x)\, dx.}$$

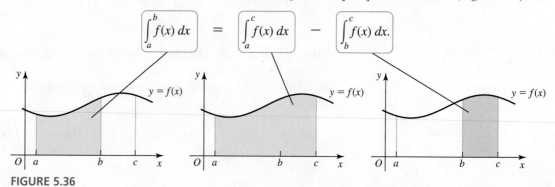

FIGURE 5.36

Because $\int_c^b f(x)\, dx = -\int_b^c f(x)\, dx$, we have the original property $\int_a^b f(x)\, dx = \int_a^c f(x)\, dx + \int_c^b f(x)\, dx$.

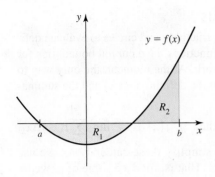

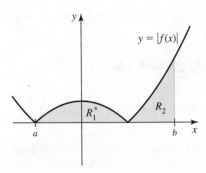

$$\int_a^b |f(x)| \, dx = \text{area of } R_1^* + \text{area of } R_2$$
$$= \text{area of } R_1 + \text{area of } R_2$$

FIGURE 5.37

Integrals of Absolute Values Finally, how do we interpret $\int_a^b |f(x)| \, dx$, the integral of the absolute value of a function? The graphs f and $|f|$ are shown in Figure 5.37. The integral $\int_a^b |f(x)| \, dx$ gives the area of regions R_1^* and R_2. But R_1 and R_1^* have the same area; therefore, $\int_a^b |f(x)| \, dx$ also gives the area of R_1 and R_2. The conclusion is that $\int_a^b |f(x)| \, dx$ is the area of the entire region (above and below the x-axis) that lies between the graph of f and the x-axis on $[a, b]$.

All these properties will be used frequently in upcoming work. It's worth collecting them in one table.

Table 5.6   Properties of definite integrals

Let f and g be integrable functions on an interval that contains a, b, and c.

1. $\displaystyle\int_a^a f(x) \, dx = 0$ Definition

2. $\displaystyle\int_b^a f(x) \, dx = -\int_a^b f(x) \, dx$ Definition

3. $\displaystyle\int_a^b (f(x) + g(x)) \, dx = \int_a^b f(x) \, dx + \int_a^b g(x) \, dx$

4. $\displaystyle\int_a^b cf(x) \, dx = c\int_a^b f(x) \, dx$ For any constant c

5. $\displaystyle\int_a^b f(x) \, dx = \int_a^c f(x) \, dx + \int_c^b f(x) \, dx$

6. The function $|f|$ is integrable on $[a, b]$, and $\int_a^b |f(x)| \, dx$ is the sum of the areas of the regions bounded by the graph of f and the x-axis on $[a, b]$.

EXAMPLE 5   Properties of integrals Assume that $\int_0^5 f(x) \, dx = 3$ and $\int_0^7 f(x) \, dx = -10$. Evaluate the following integrals, if possible.

a. $\displaystyle\int_0^7 2f(x) \, dx$ **b.** $\displaystyle\int_5^7 f(x) \, dx$ **c.** $\displaystyle\int_5^0 f(x) \, dx$

d. $\displaystyle\int_7^0 6f(x) \, dx$ **e.** $\displaystyle\int_0^7 |f(x)| \, dx$

SOLUTION

a. By Property 4 of Table 5.6, $\int_0^7 2\,f(x) \, dx = 2\int_0^7 f(x) \, dx = 2 \cdot (-10) = -20$.

b. By Property 5 of Table 5.6, $\int_0^7 f(x) \, dx = \int_0^5 f(x) \, dx + \int_5^7 f(x) \, dx$. Therefore, $\int_5^7 f(x) \, dx = \int_0^7 f(x) \, dx - \int_0^5 f(x) \, dx = -10 - 3 = -13$.

c. By Property 2 of Table 5.6,

$$\int_5^0 f(x) \, dx = -\int_0^5 f(x) \, dx = -3.$$

d. Using Properties 2 and 4 of Table 5.6, we have

$$\int_7^0 6f(x) \, dx = -\int_0^7 6f(x) \, dx = -6\int_0^7 f(x) \, dx = (-6)(-10) = 60.$$

e. This integral cannot be evaluated without knowing the intervals on which f is positive and negative. It could have any value greater than or equal to 10.

Related Exercises 41–46 ◀

QUICK CHECK 6 Evaluate $\int_{-1}^2 x \, dx$ and $\int_{-1}^2 |x| \, dx$ using geometry. ◀

Evaluating Definite Integrals Using Limits

In Example 3, we used area formulas for trapezoids, triangles, and circles to evaluate definite integrals. Regions bounded by more general functions have curved boundaries for which conventional geometrical methods do not work. At the moment, the only way to handle such integrals is to appeal to the definition of the definite integral and the summation formulas given in Theorem 5.4.

We know that if f is integrable on $[a, b]$, then $\int_a^b f(x)\, dx = \lim_{\Delta \to 0} \sum_{k=1}^n f(x_k^*)\Delta x_k$, for any partition of $[a, b]$ and any points x_k^*. To simplify these calculations, we use equally spaced grid points and right Riemann sums. That is, for each value of n, we let

$$\Delta x_k = \Delta x = \frac{b-a}{n} \text{ and } x_k^* = a + k\,\Delta x, \text{ for } k = 1, 2, \ldots, n. \text{ Then, as } n \to \infty \text{ and } \Delta \to 0,$$

$$\int_a^b f(x)\, dx = \lim_{\Delta \to 0} \sum_{k=1}^n f(x_k^*)\Delta x_k = \lim_{n \to \infty} \sum_{k=1}^n f(a + k\Delta x)\Delta x.$$

EXAMPLE 6 **Evaluating definite integrals** Find the value of $\int_0^2 (x^3 + 1)\, dx$ by evaluating a right Riemann sum and letting $n \to \infty$.

SOLUTION Based on approximations found in Example 5, Section 5.2, we conjectured that the value of this integral is 6. To verify this conjecture, we now evaluate the integral exactly. The interval $[a, b] = [0, 2]$ is divided into n subintervals of length $\Delta x = \frac{b-a}{n} = \frac{2}{n}$. The values of x_k^* for the right Riemann sum are

$$x_k^* = a + k\Delta x = 0 + k \cdot \frac{2}{n} = \frac{2k}{n}, \qquad \text{for } k = 1, 2, \ldots, n.$$

Letting $f(x) = x^3 + 1$, the right Riemann sum is

$$\sum_{k=1}^n f(x_k^*)\Delta x = \sum_{k=1}^n \left[\left(\frac{2k}{n} \right)^3 + 1 \right] \frac{2}{n}$$

$$= \frac{2}{n} \sum_{k=1}^n \left(\frac{8k^3}{n^3} + 1 \right) \qquad \sum_{k=1}^n ca_k = c \sum_{k=1}^n a_k$$

$$= \frac{2}{n} \left(\frac{8}{n^3} \sum_{k=1}^n k^3 + \sum_{k=1}^n 1 \right) \qquad \sum_{k=1}^n (a_k + b_k) = \sum_{k=1}^n a_k + \sum_{k=1}^n b_k$$

$$= \frac{2}{n} \left[\frac{8}{n^3} \left(\frac{n^2(n+1)^2}{4} \right) + n \right] \qquad \sum_{k=1}^n k^3 = \frac{n^2(n+1)^2}{4} \text{ and } \sum_{k=1}^n 1 = n; \text{ Theorem 5.4}$$

$$= \frac{4(n^2 + 2n + 1)}{n^2} + 2. \qquad \text{Simplify.}$$

Now we evaluate $\int_0^2 (x^3 + 1)\, dx$ by letting $n \to \infty$ in the Riemann sum:

$$\int_0^2 (x^3 + 1)\, dx = \lim_{n \to \infty} \sum_{k=1}^n f(x_k^*)\Delta x$$

$$= \lim_{n \to \infty} \left[\frac{4(n^2 + 2n + 1)}{n^2} + 2 \right]$$

$$= 4 \lim_{n \to \infty} \left(\frac{n^2 + 2n + 1}{n^2} \right) + \lim_{n \to \infty} 2$$

$$= 4(1) + 2 = 6.$$

Therefore, $\int_0^2 (x^3 + 1)\, dx = 6$, confirming our conjecture in Example 5, Section 5.2.

Related Exercises 47–52 ◄

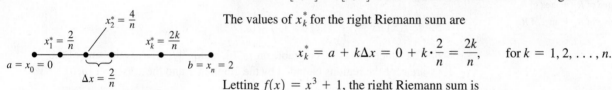

$$x_k^* = a + k\Delta x = \frac{2k}{n}$$
$$k = 1, \ldots, n$$

➤ An analogous calculation could be done using left Riemann sums or midpoint Riemann sums.

The Riemann sum calculations in Example 6 are tedious even if f is a simple function. For polynomials of degree 4 and higher, the calculations are much more challenging, and for rational and transcendental functions, advanced mathematical results are needed. The next section introduces more efficient methods for evaluating definite integrals.

SECTION 5.3 EXERCISES

Review Questions

1. Explain what net area means.

2. How do you interpret geometrically the definite integral of a function that changes sign on the interval of integration?

3. Under what conditions does the net area of a region equal the area of a region? When does the net area of a region differ from the area of a region?

4. Suppose that $f(x) < 0$ on the interval $[a, b]$. Using Riemann sums, explain why the definite integral $\int_a^b f(x)\, dx$ is negative.

5. Use graphs to evaluate $\int_0^{2\pi} \sin x\, dx$ and $\int_0^{2\pi} \cos x\, dx$.

6. Explain how the notation for Riemann sums, $\sum_{k=1}^{n} f(x_k^*)\Delta x$, corresponds to the notation for the definite integral, $\int_a^b f(x)\, dx$.

7. Give a geometrical explanation of why $\int_a^a f(x)\, dx = 0$.

8. Use Table 5.6 to rewrite $\int_1^6 (2x^3 - 4x)\, dx$ as the difference of two integrals.

9. Use geometry to find a formula for $\int_0^a x\, dx$, in terms of a.

10. If f is continuous on $[a, b]$ and $\int_a^b |f(x)|\, dx = 0$, what can you conclude about f?

Basic Skills

11–14. Approximating net area *The following functions are negative on the given interval.*

a. *Sketch the function on the given interval.*
b. *Approximate the net area bounded by the graph of f and the x-axis on the interval using a left, right, and midpoint Riemann sum with n = 4.*

11. $f(x) = -2x - 1;\ [0, 4]$

12. $f(x) = -4 - x^3;\ [3, 7]$

13. $f(x) = \sin 2x;\ [\pi/2, \pi]$

14. $f(x) = x^3 - 1;\ [-2, 0]$

15–20. Approximating net area *The following functions are positive and negative on the given interval.*

a. *Sketch the function on the given interval.*
b. *Approximate the net area bounded by the graph of f and the x-axis on the interval using a left, right, and midpoint Riemann sum with n = 4.*
c. *Use the sketch in part (a) to show which intervals of $[a, b]$ make positive and negative contributions to the net area.*

15. $f(x) = 4 - 2x;\ [0, 4]$

16. $f(x) = 8 - 2x^2;\ [0, 4]$

17. $f(x) = \sin 2x;\ [0, 3\pi/4]$

18. $f(x) = x^3;\ [-1, 2]$

19. $f(x) = \tan^{-1}(3x - 1);\ [0, 1]$

20. $f(x) = xe^{-x};\ [-1, 1]$

21–24. Identifying definite integrals as limits of sums *Consider the following limits of Riemann sums of a function f on $[a, b]$. Identify f and express the limit as a definite integral.*

21. $\displaystyle \lim_{\Delta \to 0} \sum_{k=1}^{n} (x_k^{*2} + 1)\Delta x_k;\ [0, 2]$

22. $\displaystyle \lim_{\Delta \to 0} \sum_{k=1}^{n} (4 - x_k^{*2})\Delta x_k;\ [-2, 2]$

23. $\displaystyle \lim_{\Delta \to 0} \sum_{k=1}^{n} x_k^* \ln x_k^* \Delta x_k;\ [1, 2]$

24. $\displaystyle \lim_{\Delta \to 0} \sum_{k=1}^{n} |x_k^{*2} - 1|\Delta x_k;\ [-2, 2]$

25–32. Net area and definite integrals *Use geometry (not Riemann sums) to evaluate the following definite integrals. Sketch a graph of the integrand, show the region in question, and interpret your result.*

25. $\displaystyle \int_0^4 (8 - 2x)\, dx$

26. $\displaystyle \int_{-4}^2 (2x + 4)\, dx$

27. $\displaystyle \int_{-1}^2 (-|x|)\, dx$

28. $\displaystyle \int_0^2 (1 - x)\, dx$

29. $\displaystyle \int_0^4 \sqrt{16 - x^2}\, dx$

30. $\displaystyle \int_{-1}^3 \sqrt{4 - (x - 1)^2}\, dx$

31. $\displaystyle \int_0^4 f(x)\, dx,$ where $f(x) = \begin{cases} 5 & \text{if } x \le 2 \\ 3x - 1 & \text{if } x > 2 \end{cases}$

32. $\displaystyle \int_1^{10} g(x)\, dx,$ where $g(x) = \begin{cases} 4x & \text{if } 0 \le x \le 2 \\ -8x + 16 & \text{if } 2 < x \le 3 \\ -8 & \text{if } x > 3 \end{cases}$

33–36. Net area from graphs *The figure shows the areas of regions bounded by the graph of f and the x-axis. Evaluate the following integrals.*

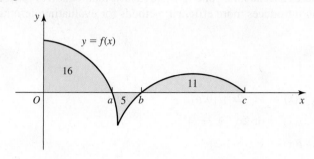

33. $\displaystyle\int_0^a f(x)\,dx$

34. $\displaystyle\int_0^b f(x)\,dx$

35. $\displaystyle\int_a^c f(x)\,dx$

36. $\displaystyle\int_0^c f(x)\,dx$

37–40. Net area from graphs *The accompanying figure shows four regions bounded by the graph of $y = x\sin x$: $R_1, R_2, R_3,$ and R_4, whose areas are $1, \pi - 1, \pi + 1,$ and $2\pi - 1$, respectively. (We verify these results later in the text.) Use this information to evaluate the following integrals.*

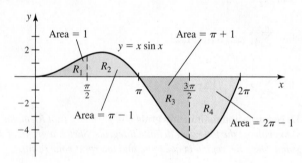

37. $\displaystyle\int_0^{\pi} x\sin x\,dx$

38. $\displaystyle\int_0^{3\pi/2} x\sin x\,dx$

39. $\displaystyle\int_0^{2\pi} x\sin x\,dx$

40. $\displaystyle\int_{\pi/2}^{2\pi} x\sin x\,dx$

41. Properties of integrals Use only the fact that $\int_0^4 3x(4 - x)\,dx = 32$ and the definitions and properties of integrals to evaluate the following integrals, if possible.

a. $\displaystyle\int_4^0 3x(4 - x)\,dx$

b. $\displaystyle\int_0^4 x(x - 4)\,dx$

c. $\displaystyle\int_4^0 6x(4 - x)\,dx$

d. $\displaystyle\int_0^8 3x(4 - x)\,dx$

42. Properties of integrals Suppose $\int_1^4 f(x)\,dx = 8$ and $\int_1^6 f(x)\,dx = 5$. Evaluate the following integrals.

a. $\displaystyle\int_1^4 (-3f(x))\,dx$

b. $\displaystyle\int_1^4 3f(x)\,dx$

c. $\displaystyle\int_6^4 12f(x)\,dx$

d. $\displaystyle\int_4^6 3f(x)\,dx$

43. Properties of integrals Suppose $\int_0^3 f(x)\,dx = 2$, $\int_3^6 f(x)\,dx = -5$, and $\int_3^6 g(x)\,dx = 1$. Evaluate the following integrals.

a. $\displaystyle\int_0^3 5f(x)\,dx$

b. $\displaystyle\int_3^6 (-3g(x))\,dx$

c. $\displaystyle\int_3^6 (3f(x) - g(x))\,dx$

d. $\displaystyle\int_6^3 (f(x) + 2g(x))\,dx$

44. Properties of integrals Suppose that $f(x) \geq 0$ on $[0, 2]$, $f(x) \leq 0$ on $[2, 5]$, $\int_0^2 f(x)\,dx = 6$, and $\int_2^5 f(x)\,dx = -8$. Evaluate the following integrals.

a. $\displaystyle\int_0^5 f(x)\,dx$

b. $\displaystyle\int_0^5 |f(x)|\,dx$

c. $\displaystyle\int_2^5 4|f(x)|\,dx$

d. $\displaystyle\int_0^5 (f(x) + |f(x)|)\,dx$

45–46. Using properties of integrals *Use the value of the first integral I to evaluate the two given integrals.*

45. $I = \displaystyle\int_0^1 (x^3 - 2x)\,dx = -\frac{3}{4}$

a. $\displaystyle\int_0^1 (4x - 2x^3)\,dx$

b. $\displaystyle\int_1^0 (2x - x^3)\,dx$

46. $I = \displaystyle\int_0^{\pi/2} (\cos\theta - 2\sin\theta)\,d\theta = -1$

a. $\displaystyle\int_0^{\pi/2} (2\sin\theta - \cos\theta)\,d\theta$

b. $\displaystyle\int_{\pi/2}^0 (4\cos\theta - 8\sin\theta)\,d\theta$

47–52. Limits of sums *Use the definition of the definite integral to evaluate the following definite integrals. Use right Riemann sums and Theorem 5.4.*

47. $\displaystyle\int_0^2 (2x + 1)\,dx$

48. $\displaystyle\int_1^5 (1 - x)\,dx$

49. $\displaystyle\int_3^7 (4x + 6)\, dx$

50. $\displaystyle\int_0^2 (x^2 - 1)\, dx$

51. $\displaystyle\int_1^4 (x^2 - 1)\, dx$

52. $\displaystyle\int_0^2 4x^3\, dx$

Further Explorations

53. Explain why or why not Determine whether the following statements are true and give an explanation or counterexample.

a. If f is a constant function on the interval $[a, b]$, then the right and left Riemann sums give the exact value of $\int_a^b f(x)\, dx$, for any positive integer n.

b. If f is a linear function on the interval $[a, b]$, then a midpoint Riemann sum gives the exact value of $\int_a^b f(x)\, dx$, for any positive integer n.

c. $\int_0^{2\pi/a} \sin ax\, dx = \int_0^{2\pi/a} \cos ax\, dx = 0$ (*Hint:* Graph the functions and use properties of trigonometric functions).

d. If $\int_a^b f(x)\, dx = \int_b^a f(x)\, dx$, then f is a constant function.

e. Property 4 of Table 5.6 implies that $\int_a^b x f(x)\, dx = x \int_a^b f(x)\, dx$.

54–57. Approximating definite integrals *Complete the following steps for the given integral and the given value of n.*

a. *Sketch the graph of the integrand on the interval of integration.*

b. *Calculate Δx and the grid points $x_0, x_1, \ldots, x_n$, assuming a regular partition.*

c. *Calculate the left and right Riemann sums for the given value of n.*

d. *Determine which Riemann sum (left or right) underestimates the value of the definite integral and which overestimates the value of the definite integral.*

54. $\displaystyle\int_0^2 (x^2 - 2)\, dx;\ n = 4$

55. $\displaystyle\int_3^6 (1 - 2x)\, dx;\ n = 6$

56. $\displaystyle\int_0^{\pi/2} \cos x\, dx;\ n = 4$

57. $\displaystyle\int_1^7 \frac{1}{x}\, dx;\ n = 6$

58–59. More properties of integrals Consider two functions f and g on $[1, 6]$ such that $\int_1^6 f(x)\, dx = 10$, $\int_1^6 g(x)\, dx = 5$, $\int_4^6 f(x)\, dx = 5$, and $\int_1^4 g(x)\, dx = 2$. Evaluate the following integrals.

58. a. $\displaystyle\int_1^4 3 f(x)\, dx$ **b.** $\displaystyle\int_1^6 (f(x) - g(x))\, dx$

c. $\displaystyle\int_1^4 (f(x) - g(x))\, dx$

59. a. $\displaystyle\int_4^6 (g(x) - f(x))\, dx$ **b.** $\displaystyle\int_4^6 8g(x)\, dx$

c. $\displaystyle\int_4^1 2 f(x)\, dx$

60–63. Area versus net area *Graph the following functions. Then use geometry (not Riemann sums) to find the area and the net area of the region described.*

60. The region between the graph of $y = 4x - 8$ and the x-axis, for $-4 \le x \le 8$

61. The region between the graph of $y = -3x$ and the x-axis, for $-2 \le x \le 2$

62. The region between the graph of $y = 3x - 6$ and the x-axis, for $0 \le x \le 6$

63. The region between the graph of $y = 1 - |x|$ and the x-axis, for $-2 \le x \le 2$

64–67. Area by geometry *Use geometry to evaluate the following integrals.*

64. $\displaystyle\int_{-2}^3 |x + 1|\, dx$

65. $\displaystyle\int_1^6 |2x - 4|\, dx$

66. $\displaystyle\int_1^6 (3x - 6)\, dx$

67. $\displaystyle\int_{-6}^4 \sqrt{24 - 2x - x^2}\, dx$

Additional Exercises

68. Integrating piecewise continuous functions Suppose f is continuous on the interval $[a, c]$ and on the interval $(c, b]$, where $a < c < b$, with a finite jump at c. Form a uniform partition on the interval $[a, c]$ with n grid points and another uniform partition on the interval $[c, b]$ with m grid points, where c is a grid point of both partitions. Write a Riemann sum for $\int_a^b f(x)\, dx$, and separate it into two pieces for $[a, c]$ and $[c, b]$. Explain why $\int_a^b f(x)\, dx = \int_a^c f(x)\, dx + \int_c^b f(x)\, dx$.

69–70. Piecewise continuous functions *Use geometry and the result of Exercise 68 to evaluate the following integrals.*

69. $\displaystyle\int_0^{10} f(x)\, dx$, where $f(x) = \begin{cases} 2 & \text{if } 0 \le x \le 5 \\ 3 & \text{if } 5 < x \le 10 \end{cases}$

70. $\displaystyle\int_1^6 f(x)\, dx$, where $f(x) = \begin{cases} 2x & \text{if } 1 \le x < 4 \\ 10 - 2x & \text{if } 4 \le x \le 6 \end{cases}$

71. Constants in integrals Use the definition of the definite integral to justify the property $\int_a^b c f(x)\, dx = c \int_a^b f(x)\, dx$, where f is continuous and c is a real number.

72. Zero net area If $0 < c < d$, then find the value of b (in terms of c and d) for which $\int_c^d (x + b)\, dx = 0$.

73. A nonintegrable function Consider the function defined on $[0, 1]$ such that $f(x) = 1$ if x is a rational number and $f(x) = 0$ if x is irrational. This function has an infinite number of discontinuities, and the integral $\int_0^1 f(x)\, dx$ does not exist. Show that the right, left, and midpoint Riemann sums on *regular* partitions with n subintervals equal 1 for all n. (*Hint:* Between any two real numbers lies a rational and an irrational number.)

74. Powers of x by Riemann sums Consider the integral $I(p) = \int_0^1 x^p\, dx$ where p is a positive integer.

  a. Write the left Riemann sum for the integral with n subintervals.

  b. It is a fact (proved by the 17th-century mathematicians Fermat and Pascal) that $\lim\limits_{n\to\infty} \dfrac{1}{n} \sum\limits_{k=0}^{n-1} \left(\dfrac{k}{n}\right)^p = \dfrac{1}{p+1}$. Use this fact to evaluate $I(p)$.

Technology Exercises

75–79. Approximating definite integrals with a calculator *Consider the following definite integrals.*

  a. *Write the left and right Riemann sums in sigma notation, for $n = 20, 50,$ and 100. Then evaluate the sums using a calculator.*

  b. *Based on your answers to part (a), make a conjecture about the value of the definite integral.*

75. $\displaystyle \int_0^1 (x^2 + 1)\, dx$

76. $\displaystyle \int_4^9 3\sqrt{x}\, dx$

77. $\displaystyle \int_0^1 \cos^{-1} x\, dx$

78. $\displaystyle \int_1^e \ln x\, dx$

79. $\displaystyle \int_{-1}^1 \pi \cos\left(\frac{\pi x}{2}\right) dx$

80–83. Midpoint Riemann sums with a calculator *Consider the following definite integrals.*

  a. *Write the midpoint Riemann sum in sigma notation for an arbitrary value of n.*

  b. *Evaluate each sum using a calculator with $n = 20, 50,$ and 100. Use these values to estimate the value of the integral.*

80. $\displaystyle \int_{-1}^2 \sin\left(\frac{\pi x}{4}\right) dx$

81. $\displaystyle \int_1^4 2\sqrt{x}\, dx$

82. $\displaystyle \int_0^{1/2} \sin^{-1} x\, dx$

83. $\displaystyle \int_0^4 (4x - x^2)\, dx$

84–85. General partitions *A Riemann sum for $\int_a^b f(x)\,dx$ may be formed using a general partition of the interval $[a, b]$ with non-uniform grid points. For the following integrals, carry out the following steps with the given general partition.*

  a. *Compute the left Riemann sum.*

  b. *Compute the midpoint Riemann sum.*

  c. *Compute the right Riemann sum.*

  d. *Compute the errors in the approximations in parts (a)–(c) given that $\int_a^b f(x)\,dx = 0$.*

  e. *Discuss the results of part (d).*

84. $\int_1^7 (19 - x^2)\,dx$; $n = 6$; non-uniform grid points $\{1, 2.5, 3, 4, 5.5, 6, 7\}$

85. $\int_1^5 x(x^2 - 13)\,dx$; $n = 7$; non-uniform grid points $\{1, 1.5, 2.5, 3, 3.25, 3.75, 4.5, 5\}$

QUICK CHECK ANSWERS

1. -20 **2.** $f(x) = 1 - x$ is one possibility.   **3.** 0
4. $10; c(b - a)$ **5.** 0 **6.** $\frac{3}{2}; \frac{5}{2}$ ◄

5.4 Fundamental Theorem of Calculus

Evaluating definite integrals using limits of Riemann sums, as described in Section 5.3, is usually not possible or practical. Fortunately, there is a powerful and practical method for evaluating definite integrals, which is developed in this section. Along the way, we discover the inverse relationship between differentiation and integration, expressed in the most important result of calculus, the Fundamental Theorem of Calculus. The first step in this process is to introduce *area functions* (first presented in Section 1.2).

Area Functions

The concept of an area function is crucial to the discussion about the connection between derivatives and integrals. We start with a continuous function $y = f(t)$ defined for $t \geq a$, where a is a fixed number. The *area function* for f with left endpoint a is denoted $A(x)$; it gives the net area of the region bounded by the graph of f and the

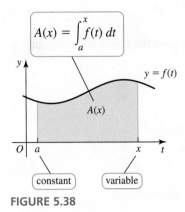

FIGURE 5.38

t-axis between $t = a$ and $t = x$ (Figure 5.38). The net area of this region is also given by the definite integral

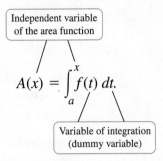

$$A(x) = \int_a^x f(t)\, dt.$$

Notice that x is the upper limit of the integral *and* the independent variable of the area function: As x changes, so does the net area under the curve. Because the symbol x is already in use as the independent variable for A, we must choose another symbol for the variable of integration. Any symbol—except x—can be used because it is a *dummy variable*; we have chosen t as the integration variable.

Figure 5.39 gives a general view of how an area function is generated. Suppose that f is a continuous function and a is a fixed number. Now choose a point $b > a$. The net area of the region between the graph of f and the t-axis on the interval $[a, b]$ is $A(b)$. Moving the right endpoint to $(c, 0)$ or $(d, 0)$ produces different regions with net areas $A(c)$ and $A(d)$, respectively. In general, if $x > a$ is a variable point, then $A(x) = \int_a^x f(t)\, dt$ is the net area of the region between the graph of f and the t-axis on the interval $[a, x]$.

> A dummy variable is a placeholder; its role can be played by any symbol that does not conflict with other variables in the problem.

> Notice that t is the independent variable when we plot f and x is the independent variable when we plot A.

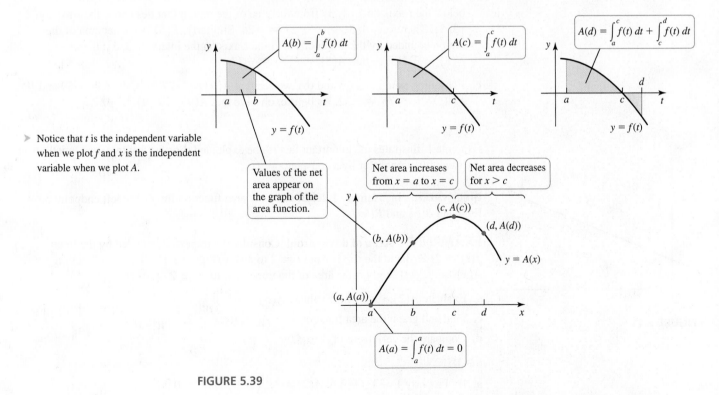

FIGURE 5.39

Figure 5.39 shows how $A(x)$ varies with respect to x. Notice that $A(a) = \int_a^a f(t)\, dt = 0$. Then, for $x > a$, the net area increases for $x < c$ at which point $f(c) = 0$. For $x > c$, the function f is negative, which produces a negative contribution to the area function. As a result, the area function decreases for $x > c$.

> **DEFINITION Area Function**
>
> Let f be a continuous function, for $t \geq a$. The **area function for f with left endpoint a** is
>
> $$A(x) = \int_a^x f(t)\, dt,$$
>
> where $x \geq a$. The area function gives the net area of the region bounded by the graph of f and the t-axis on the interval $[a, x]$.

The following two examples illustrate the idea of area functions.

EXAMPLE 1 Area of regions The graph of f is shown in Figure 5.40 with areas of various regions marked. Let $A(x) = \int_{-1}^x f(t)\, dt$ and $F(x) = \int_3^x f(t)\, dt$ be two area functions for f (note the different left endpoints). Evaluate the following area functions.

a. $A(3)$ and $F(3)$ **b.** $A(5)$ and $F(5)$ **c.** $A(9)$ and $F(9)$

SOLUTION

a. The value of $A(3) = \int_{-1}^3 f(t)\, dt$ is the net area of the region bounded by the graph of f and the t-axis on the interval $[-1, 3]$. Using the graph of f, we see that $A(3) = -27$ (because this region has an area of 27 and lies below the t-axis). On the other hand, $F(3) = \int_3^3 f(t)\, dt = 0$ by Property 1 of Table 5.6. Notice that $A(3) - F(3) = -27$.

b. The value of $A(5) = \int_{-1}^5 f(t)\, dt$ is found by subtracting the area of the region that lies below the t-axis on $[-1, 3]$ from the area of the region that lies above the t-axis on $[3, 5]$. Therefore, $A(5) = 3 - 27 = -24$. Similarly, $F(5)$ is the net area of the region bounded by the graph of f and the t-axis on the interval $[3, 5]$; therefore, $F(5) = 3$. Notice that $A(5) - F(5) = -27$.

c. Reasoning as in parts (a) and (b), we see that $A(9) = -27 + 3 - 35 = -59$ and $F(9) = 3 - 35 = -32$. As before, observe that $A(9) - F(9) = -27$.

Related Exercises 11–12 ◀

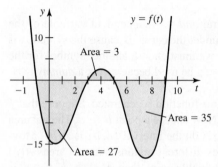

FIGURE 5.40

Example 1 illustrates the important fact (to be explained shortly) that two area functions of the same function differ by a constant.

QUICK CHECK 1 In Example 1, let $B(x)$ be the area function for f with left endpoint 5. Evaluate $B(5)$ and $B(9)$. ◀

EXAMPLE 2 Area of a trapezoid Consider the trapezoid bounded by the line $f(t) = 2t + 3$ and the t-axis from $t = 2$ to $t = x$ (Figure 5.41). The area function $A(x) = \int_2^x f(t)\, dt$ gives the area of the trapezoid, for $x \geq 2$.

a. Evaluate $A(2)$.   **b.** Evaluate $A(5)$.

c. Find and graph the area function $y = A(x)$, for $x \geq 2$.

d. Compare the derivative of A to f.

SOLUTION

a. By Property 1 of Table 5.6, $A(2) = \int_2^2 (2t + 3)\, dt = 0$.

b. Notice that $A(5)$ is the area of the trapezoid (Figure 5.41) bounded by the line $y = 2t + 3$ and the t-axis on the interval $[2, 5]$. Using the area formula for a trapezoid (Figure 5.42), we find that

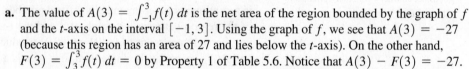

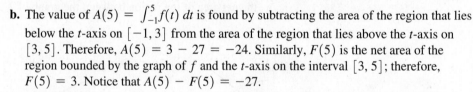

$$A(5) = \int_2^5 (2t + 3)\, dt = \frac{1}{2}\underbrace{(5 - 2)}_{\substack{\text{distance between}\\ \text{parallel sides}}} \cdot \underbrace{(f(2) + f(5))}_{\substack{\text{sum of parallel}\\ \text{side lengths}}} = \frac{1}{2} \cdot 3(7 + 13) = 30.$$

FIGURE 5.41

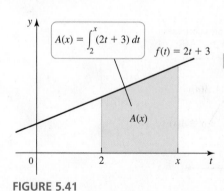

FIGURE 5.42

c. Now the right endpoint of the base is a variable $x \geq 2$ (Figure 5.43). The distance between the parallel sides of the trapezoid is $x - 2$. By the area formula for a trapezoid, the area of this trapezoid for any $x \geq 2$ is

$$A(x) = \frac{1}{2} \underbrace{(x - 2)}_{\substack{\text{distance between} \\ \text{parallel sides}}} \cdot \underbrace{(f(2) + f(x))}_{\substack{\text{sum of parallel} \\ \text{side lengths}}}$$

$$= \frac{1}{2}(x - 2)(7 + 2x + 3)$$

$$= (x - 2)(x + 5)$$

$$= x^2 + 3x - 10.$$

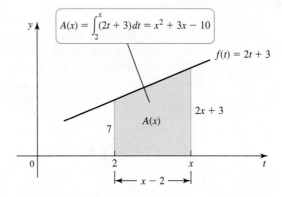

FIGURE 5.43

Expressing the area function in terms of an integral with a variable upper limit, we have

$$A(x) = \int_2^x (2t + 3) \, dt = x^2 + 3x - 10.$$

Because the line $f(t) = 2t + 3$ is above the t-axis, for $t \geq 2$, the area function $A(x) = x^2 + 3x - 10$ is an increasing function of x with $A(2) = 0$ (Figure 5.44).

d. Differentiating the area function, we find that

$$A'(x) = \frac{d}{dx}(x^2 + 3x - 10) = 2x + 3 = f(x).$$

Therefore, $A'(x) = f(x)$, or equivalently, the area function A is an antiderivative of f. We soon show that this relationship is not an accident; it is one part of the Fundamental Theorem of Calculus.

Related Exercises 13–22 ◄

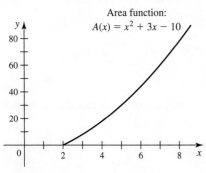

Area function:
$A(x) = x^2 + 3x - 10$

FIGURE 5.44

➤ Recall that if $A'(x) = f(x)$, then f is the derivative of A; equivalently, A is an antiderivative of f.

QUICK CHECK 2 Verify that the area function in Example 2c gives the correct area when $x = 6$ and $x = 10$. ◄

Fundamental Theorem of Calculus

Example 2 suggests that the area function A for a linear function f is an antiderivative of f; that is, $A'(x) = f(x)$. Our goal is to show that this conjecture holds for more general functions. Let's start with an intuitive argument.

Assume that f is a continuous function defined on an interval $[a, b]$. As before, $A(x) = \int_a^x f(t) \, dt$ is the area function for f with a left endpoint a: It gives the net area of the region bounded by the graph of f and the t-axis on the interval $[a, x]$, for $x \geq a$. Figure 5.45 is the key to the argument.

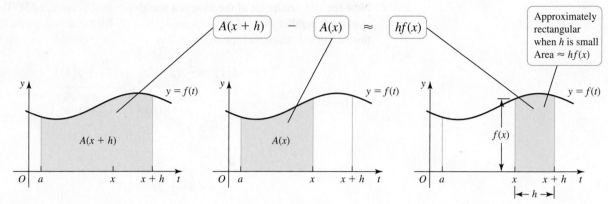

FIGURE 5.45

Note that with $h > 0$, $A(x + h)$ is the net area of the region whose base is the interval $[a, x + h]$, while $A(x)$ is the net area of the region whose base is the interval $[a, x]$. So the difference $A(x + h) - A(x)$ is the net area of the region whose base is the interval $[x, x + h]$. If h is small, the region in question is nearly rectangular with a base of length h and a height $f(x)$. Therefore, the net area of this region is

$$A(x + h) - A(x) \approx h f(x).$$

Dividing by h, we have

$$\frac{A(x + h) - A(x)}{h} \approx f(x).$$

> Recall that
>
> $$f'(x) = \lim_{h \to 0} \frac{f(x + h) - f(x)}{h}.$$
>
> If the function f is replaced with A, then
>
> $$A'(x) = \lim_{h \to 0} \frac{A(x + h) - A(x)}{h}.$$

An analogous argument can be made with $h < 0$. Now observe that as h tends to zero, this approximation improves. In the limit as $h \to 0$, we have

$$\underbrace{\lim_{h \to 0} \frac{A(x + h) - A(x)}{h}}_{A'(x)} = \underbrace{\lim_{h \to 0} f(x)}_{f(x)}.$$

We see that indeed $A'(x) = f(x)$. Because $A(x) = \int_a^x f(t)\, dt$, the result can also be written

$$A'(x) = \frac{d}{dx} \underbrace{\int_a^x f(t)\, dt}_{A(x)} = f(x),$$

which says that the derivative of the integral of f is f. A formal proof that $A'(x) = f(x)$ is given at the end of the section; but for the moment, we have a plausible argument. This conclusion is the first part of the Fundamental Theorem of Calculus.

THEOREM 5.6 (PART 1) Fundamental Theorem of Calculus
If f is continuous on $[a, b]$, then the area function

$$A(x) = \int_a^x f(t)\, dt, \quad \text{for} \quad a \le x \le b,$$

is continuous on $[a, b]$ and differentiable on (a, b). The area function satisfies $A'(x) = f(x)$; or, equivalently,

$$A'(x) = \frac{d}{dx} \int_a^x f(t)\, dt = f(x),$$

which means that the area function of f is an antiderivative of f on $[a, b]$.

Given that A is an antiderivative of f on $[a, b]$, it is one short step to a powerful method for evaluating definite integrals. Remember (Section 5.1) that any two antiderivatives of f differ by a constant. Assuming that F is any other antiderivative of f on $[a, b]$, we have

$$F(x) = A(x) + C, \text{ for } a \leq x \leq b.$$

Noting that $A(a) = 0$, it follows that

$$F(b) - F(a) = (A(b) + C) - (A(a) + C) = A(b).$$

Writing $A(b)$ in terms of a definite integral leads to the remarkable result

$$A(b) = \int_a^b f(x)\,dx = F(b) - F(a).$$

We have shown that to evaluate a definite integral of f, we

• find any antiderivative of f, which we call F; and

• compute $F(b) - F(a)$, the difference in the values of F between the upper and lower limits of integration.

This process is the essence of the second part of the Fundamental Theorem of Calculus.

THEOREM 5.6 (PART 2)   Fundamental Theorem of Calculus
If f is continuous on $[a, b]$ and F is any antiderivative of f on $[a, b]$, then

$$\int_a^b f(x)\,dx = F(b) - F(a).$$

It is customary and convenient to denote the difference $F(b) - F(a)$ by $F(x)\big|_a^b$. Using this shorthand, the Fundamental Theorem is summarized in Figure 5.46.

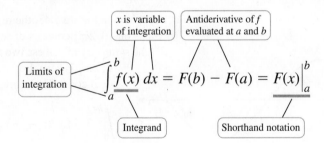

FIGURE 5.46

QUICK CHECK 3 Evaluate $\left(\dfrac{x}{x+1}\right)\Big|_1^2$. ◄

The Inverse Relationship between Differentiation and Integration

It is worth pausing to observe that the two parts of the Fundamental Theorem express the inverse relationship between differentiation and integration. Part 1 of the Fundamental Theorem says

$$\frac{d}{dx}\int_a^x f(t)\,dt = f(x),$$

or the derivative of the integral of f is f itself.

Noting that f is an antiderivative of f', Part 2 of the Fundamental Theorem says

$$\int_a^b f'(x)\,dx = f(b) - f(a),$$

or the definite integral of the derivative of f is given in terms of f evaluated at two points. In other words, the integral "undoes" the derivative.

This last relationship is important because it expresses the integral as an *accumulation* operation. Suppose we know the rate of change of f (which is f') on an interval $[a, b]$. The Fundamental Theorem says that we can integrate (that is, sum or accumulate) the rate of change over that interval and the result is simply the difference in f evaluated at the endpoints. You will see this accumulation property used in many ways in the next chapter. Now let's use the Fundamental Theorem to evaluate definite integrals.

EXAMPLE 3 Evaluating definite integrals Evaluate the following definite integrals using the Fundamental Theorem of Calculus, Part 2. Interpret each result geometrically.

a. $\displaystyle\int_0^{10} (60x - 6x^2)\,dx$ **b.** $\displaystyle\int_0^{2\pi} 3\sin x\,dx$ **c.** $\displaystyle\int_{1/16}^{1/4} \frac{\sqrt{t} - 1}{t}\,dt$

SOLUTION

a. Using the antiderivative rules of Section 5.1, an antiderivative of $60x - 6x^2$ is $30x^2 - 2x^3$. By the Fundamental Theorem, the value of the definite integral is

$$\int_0^{10} (60x - 6x^2)\,dx = (30x^2 - 2x^3)\Big|_0^{10} \qquad \text{Fundamental Theorem}$$

$$= (30 \cdot 10^2 - 2 \cdot 10^3) - (30 \cdot 0^2 - 2 \cdot 0^3) \qquad \begin{array}{l}\text{Evaluate at } x = 10 \\ \text{and } x = 0.\end{array}$$

$$= (3000 - 2000) - 0$$

$$= 1000. \qquad \text{Simplify.}$$

Because f is positive on $[0, 10]$, the definite integral $\int_0^{10}(60x - 6x^2)\,dx$ is the area of the region between the graph of f and the x-axis on the interval $[0, 10]$ (Figure 5.47).

b. As shown in Figure 5.48, the region bounded by the graph of $f(x) = 3\sin x$ and the x-axis on $[0, 2\pi]$ consists of two parts, one above the x-axis and one below the x-axis. By the symmetry of f, these two regions have the same area, so the definite integral over $[0, 2\pi]$ is zero. Let's confirm this fact. An antiderivative of $f(x) = 3\sin x$ is $-3\cos x$. Therefore, the value of the definite integral is

$$\int_0^{2\pi} 3\sin x\,dx = -3\cos x\Big|_0^{2\pi} \qquad \text{Fundamental Theorem}$$

$$= (-3\cos(2\pi)) - (-3\cos(0)) \qquad \text{Substitute.}$$

$$= -3 - (-3) = 0. \qquad \text{Simplify.}$$

c. Although the variable of integration is t, rather than x, we proceed as in parts (a) and (b) after simplifying the integrand:

$$\frac{\sqrt{t} - 1}{t} = \frac{1}{\sqrt{t}} - \frac{1}{t}.$$

Finding antiderivatives with respect to t and applying the Fundamental Theorem, we have

$$\int_{1/16}^{1/4} \frac{\sqrt{t} - 1}{t}\,dt = \int_{1/16}^{1/4} \left(t^{-1/2} - \frac{1}{t}\right)dt \qquad \begin{array}{l}\text{Simplify the} \\ \text{integrand.}\end{array}$$

$$= \left(2t^{1/2} - \ln|t|\right)\Big|_{1/16}^{1/4} \qquad \begin{array}{l}\text{Fundamental} \\ \text{Theorem}\end{array}$$

QUICK CHECK 4 Explain why f is an antiderivative of f'. ◄

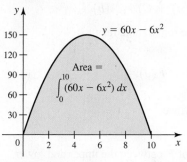

$y = 60x - 6x^2$

Area $=$
$\displaystyle\int_0^{10} (60x - 6x^2)\,dx$

FIGURE 5.47

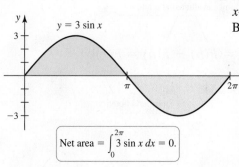

$y = 3\sin x$

Net area $= \displaystyle\int_0^{2\pi} 3\sin x\,dx = 0.$

FIGURE 5.48

➤ We know that
$$\frac{d}{dt}(t^{1/2}) = \frac{1}{2}t^{-1/2}.$$

Therefore,
$$\int \frac{1}{2}t^{-1/2}\,dt = t^{1/2} + C$$

and
$$\int \frac{dt}{\sqrt{t}} = \int t^{-1/2}\,dt = 2t^{1/2} + C.$$

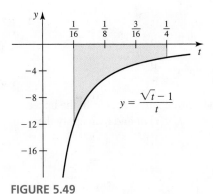

FIGURE 5.49

$$= \left(2\left(\frac{1}{4}\right)^{1/2} - \ln\frac{1}{4}\right) - \left(2\left(\frac{1}{16}\right)^{1/2} - \ln\frac{1}{16}\right) \quad \text{Evaluate.}$$

$$= 1 - \ln\frac{1}{4} - \frac{1}{2} + \ln\frac{1}{16} \quad \text{Simplify.}$$

$$= \frac{1}{2} - \ln 4 \approx -0.886.$$

The definite integral is negative because the graph of f lies below the t-axis (Figure 5.49). *Related Exercises 23–50◄*

EXAMPLE 4 Net areas and definite integrals The graph of $f(x) = 6x(x+1)(x-2)$ is shown in Figure 5.50. The region R_1 is bounded by the curve and the x-axis on the interval $[-1, 0]$, and R_2 is bounded by the curve and the x-axis on the interval $[0, 2]$.

a. Find the *net area* of the region between the curve and the x-axis on $[-1, 2]$.

b. Find the *area* of the region between the curve and the x-axis on $[-1, 2]$.

SOLUTION

a. The net area of the region is given by a definite integral. The integrand f is first expanded in order to find an antiderivative:

$$\int_{-1}^{2} f(x)\,dx = \int_{-1}^{2} (6x^3 - 6x^2 - 12x)\,dx. \quad \text{Expanding } f$$

$$= \left(\frac{3}{2}x^4 - 2x^3 - 6x^2\right)\Big|_{-1}^{2} \quad \text{Fundamental Theorem}$$

$$= -\frac{27}{2}. \quad \text{Simplify.}$$

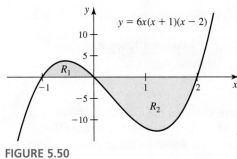

FIGURE 5.50

The net area of the region between the curve and the x-axis on $[-1, 2]$ is $-\frac{27}{2}$, which is the area of R_1 *minus* the area of R_2 (Figure 5.50). Because R_2 has a larger area than R_1, the net area is negative.

b. The region R_1 lies above the x-axis, so its area is

$$\int_{-1}^{0} (6x^3 - 6x^2 - 12x)\,dx = \left(\frac{3}{2}x^4 - 2x^3 - 6x^2\right)\Big|_{-1}^{0} = \frac{5}{2}.$$

The region R_2 lies below the x-axis, so its net area is negative:

$$\int_{0}^{2} (6x^3 - 6x^2 - 12x)\,dx = \left(\frac{3}{2}x^4 - 2x^3 - 6x^2\right)\Big|_{0}^{2} = -16.$$

Therefore, the *area* of R_2 is $-(-16) = 16$. The combined area of R_1 and R_2 is $\frac{5}{2} + 16 = \frac{37}{2}$. We could also find the area of this region directly by evaluating $\int_{-1}^{2} |f(x)|\,dx$. *Related Exercises 51–60◄*

Examples 3 and 4 make use of Part 2 of the Fundamental Theorem, which is the most potent tool for evaluating definite integrals. The remaining examples illustrate the use of the equally important Part 1 of the Fundamental Theorem.

EXAMPLE 5 Derivatives of integrals Use Part 1 of the Fundamental Theorem to simplify the following expressions.

a. $\dfrac{d}{dx}\displaystyle\int_{1}^{x} \sin^2 t \, dt$ **b.** $\dfrac{d}{dx}\displaystyle\int_{x}^{5} \sqrt{t^2 + 1} \, dt$ **c.** $\dfrac{d}{dx}\displaystyle\int_{0}^{x^2} \cos t^2 \, dt$

SOLUTION

a. Using Part 1 of the Fundamental Theorem, we see that

$$\frac{d}{dx}\int_1^x \sin^2 t \, dt = \sin^2 x.$$

b. To apply Part 1 of the Fundamental Theorem, the variable must appear in the upper limit. Therefore, we use the fact that $\int_a^b f(t) \, dt = -\int_b^a f(t) \, dt$ and then apply the Fundamental Theorem:

$$\frac{d}{dx}\int_x^5 \sqrt{t^2 + 1} \, dt = -\frac{d}{dx}\int_5^x \sqrt{t^2 + 1} \, dt = -\sqrt{x^2 + 1}.$$

c. The upper limit of the integral is not x, but a function of x. Therefore, the function to be differentiated is a composite function, which requires the Chain Rule. We let $u = x^2$ to produce

$$y = g(u) = \int_0^u \cos t^2 \, dt.$$

By the Chain Rule,

$$\frac{d}{dx}\int_0^{x^2} \cos t^2 \, dt = \frac{dy}{dx} = \frac{dy}{du}\frac{du}{dx} \qquad \text{Chain Rule}$$

$$= \left[\frac{d}{du}\int_0^u \cos t^2 \, dt\right](2x) \qquad \text{Substitute for } g; \text{ note that } u'(x) = 2x.$$

$$= (\cos u^2)(2x) \qquad \text{Fundamental Theorem}$$

$$= 2x \cos x^4. \qquad \text{Substitute } u = x^2.$$

Related Exercises 61–68 ◄

> Example 5c illustrates one case of Leibniz's Rule:
>
> $$\frac{d}{dx}\int_a^{g(x)} f(t) \, dt = f(g(x))g'(x).$$

EXAMPLE 6   Working with area functions Consider the function f shown in Figure 5.51 and its area function $A(x) = \int_0^x f(t) \, dt$, for $0 \le x \le 17$. Assume that the four regions $R_1, R_2, R_3,$ and R_4 have the same area. Based on the graph of f, do the following.

a. Find the zeros of A on $[0, 17]$.

b. Find the points on $[0, 17]$ at which A has local maxima or minima.

c. Sketch a graph of A, for $0 \le x \le 17$.

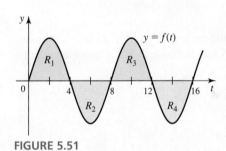

FIGURE 5.51

SOLUTION

a. The area function $A(x) = \int_0^x f(t) \, dt$ gives the net area bounded by the graph of f and the t-axis on the interval $[0, x]$ (Figure 5.52a). Therefore, $A(0) = \int_0^0 f(t) \, dt = 0$. Because R_1 and R_2 have the same area but lie on opposite sides of the t-axis, it follows that $A(8) = \int_0^8 f(t) \, dt = 0$. Similarly, $A(16) = \int_0^{16} f(t) \, dt = 0$. Therefore, the zeros of A are $x = 0, 8,$ and 16.

b. Observe that the function f is positive, for $0 < t < 4$, which implies that $A(x)$ increases as x increases from 0 to 4 (Figure 5.52b). Then, as x increases from 4 to 8, $A(x)$ decreases because f is negative, for $4 < t < 8$ (Figure 5.52c). Similarly, $A(x)$ increases as x increases from $x = 8$ to $x = 12$ (Figure 5.52d) and decreases from $x = 12$ to $x = 16$. By the First Derivative Test, A has local minima at $x = 8$ and $x = 16$ and local maxima at $x = 4$ and $x = 12$ (Figure 5.52e).

> Recall that local extrema occur only at interior points of the domain.

c. Combining the observations in parts (a) and (b) leads to a qualitative sketch of A (Figure 5.52e). Note that $A(x) \ge 0$, for all $x \ge 0$. It is not possible to determine function values (y-coordinates) on the graph of A.

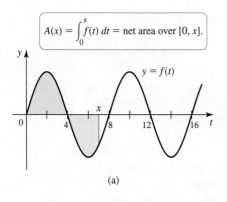

$A(x) = \int_0^x f(t)\, dt$ = net area over $[0, x]$.

(a)

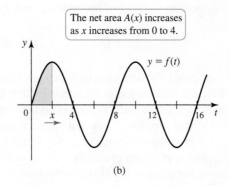

The net area $A(x)$ increases as x increases from 0 to 4.

(b)

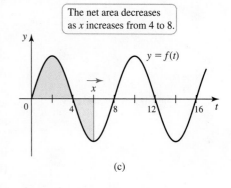

The net area decreases as x increases from 4 to 8.

(c)

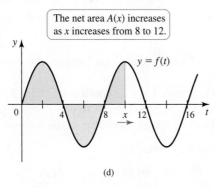

The net area $A(x)$ increases as x increases from 8 to 12.

(d)

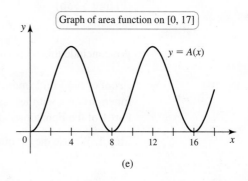

Graph of area function on $[0, 17]$

(e)

FIGURE 5.52

Related Exercises 69–80 ◄

EXAMPLE 7   The sine integral function Let

$$g(t) = \begin{cases} \dfrac{\sin t}{t} & \text{if } t > 0 \\ 1 & \text{if } t = 0. \end{cases}$$

Graph the *sine integral function* $S(x) = \int_0^x g(t)\, dt$, for $x \geq 0$.

SOLUTION Notice that S is an area function for g. The independent variable of S is x, while t has been chosen as the (dummy) variable of integration. A good way to start is by graphing the integrand g (Figure 5.53a). The function oscillates with a decreasing amplitude with $g(0) = 1$. Beginning with $S(0) = 0$, the area function S increases until $x = \pi$ because g is positive on $(0, \pi)$. However, on $(\pi, 2\pi)$, g is negative and the net area decreases. On $(2\pi, 3\pi)$, g is positive again, so S again increases. Therefore, the graph of S has alternating local maxima and minima. Because the amplitude of g decreases, each maximum of S is less than the previous maximum and each minimum of S is greater than the previous minimum (Figure 5.53b). Determining the exact value of S at these maxima and minima is difficult.

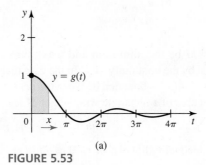

(a)

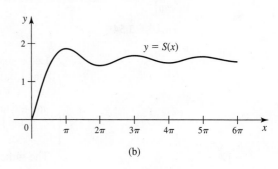

(b)

FIGURE 5.53

Appealing to Part 1 of the Fundamental Theorem, we find that

$$S'(x) = \frac{d}{dx}\int_0^x g(t)\,dt = \frac{\sin x}{x}, \text{ for } x > 0.$$

> Note that
>
> $$\lim_{x\to\infty} S'(x) = \lim_{x\to\infty} g(x) = 0.$$

As anticipated, the derivative of S changes sign at integer multiples of π. Specifically, S' is positive and S increases on the intervals $(0, \pi)$, $(2\pi, 3\pi)$, ..., $(2n\pi, (2n + 1)\pi)$, ..., while S' is negative and S decreases on the remaining intervals. Clearly, S has local maxima at $x = \pi, 3\pi, 5\pi, \ldots$, and it has local minima at $x = 2\pi, 4\pi, 6\pi, \ldots$.

One more observation is helpful. It can be shown that while S oscillates for increasing x, its graph gradually flattens out and approaches a horizontal asymptote. (Finding the exact value of this horizontal asymptote is challenging; see Exercise 109.) Assembling all these observations, the graph of the sine integral function emerges (Figure 5.53b).

Related Exercises 81–84 ◄

We conclude this section with a formal proof of the Fundamental Theorem of Calculus.

Proof of the Fundamental Theorem: Let f be continuous on $[a, b]$ and let A be the area function for f with left endpoint a. The first step is to prove that $A'(x) = f(x)$, which is Part 1 of the Fundamental Theorem. The proof of Part 2 then follows.

Step 1. We use the definition of the derivative,

$$A'(x) = \lim_{h\to 0}\frac{A(x + h) - A(x)}{h}.$$

First assume that $h > 0$. Using Figure 5.54 and Property 5 of Table 5.6, we have

$$A(x + h) - A(x) = \int_a^{x+h} f(t)\,dt - \int_a^x f(t)\,dt = \int_x^{x+h} f(t)\,dt.$$

That is, $A(x + h) - A(x)$ is the net area of the region bounded by the curve on the interval $[x, x + h]$.

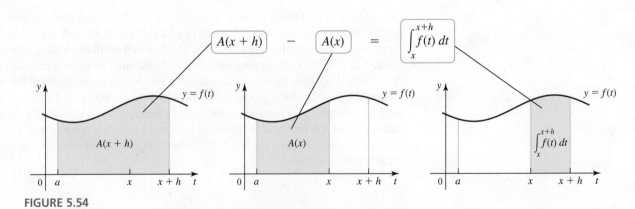

FIGURE 5.54

Let m and M be the minimum and maximum values of f on $[x, x + h]$, respectively, which exist by the continuity of f. In the case that $0 \le m \le M$ (illustrated in Figure 5.55), $A(x + h) - A(x)$ is bounded between the net area of a rectangle with height m and width h and the net area of a rectangle with height M and width h; that is,

$$mh \le A(x + h) - A(x) \le Mh.$$

The same inequality holds if $m \le 0 \le M$ or $m \le M \le 0$.

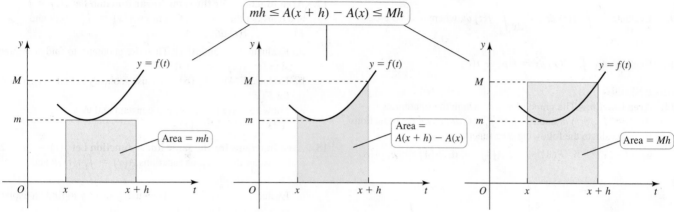

FIGURE 5.55

▷ The quantities m and M exist for any $h > 0$; however, their values depend on h.

Dividing these inequalities by h, we have

$$m \leq \frac{A(x+h) - A(x)}{h} \leq M.$$

The case $h < 0$ is handled similarly and leads to the same conclusion.

We now take the limit as $h \to 0$ across these inequalities. As $h \to 0$, m and M squeeze together toward the value of $f(x)$, because f is continuous at x. At the same time, as $h \to 0$, the quotient that is sandwiched between m and M approaches $A'(x)$:

$$\underbrace{\lim_{h \to 0} m}_{f(x)} = \underbrace{\lim_{h \to 0} \frac{A(x+h) - A(x)}{h}}_{A'(x)} = \underbrace{\lim_{h \to 0} M}_{f(x)}.$$

▷ Using right- and left-sided derivatives (Exercises 25–26 in Section 3.2) and Theorem 3.1, it can be shown that A is continuous at the endpoints of the interval $[a, b]$.

By the Squeeze Theorem (Theorem 2.5), we conclude that $A'(x) = f(x)$. Because A is differentiable on (a, b), A is continuous on (a, b) by Theorem 3.1.

Step 2. Having established that the area function A is an antiderivative of f, we know that $F(x) = A(x) + C$, where F is any antiderivative of f and C is a constant. Noting that $A(a) = 0$, it follows that

▷ Once again we use an important fact: Two antiderivatives of the same function differ by a constant.

$$F(b) - F(a) = (A(b) + C) - (A(a) + C) = A(b).$$

Writing $A(b)$ in terms of a definite integral, we have

$$A(b) = \int_a^b f(x)\, dx = F(b) - F(a),$$

which is Part 2 of the Fundamental Theorem. ◀

SECTION 5.4 EXERCISES

Review Questions

1. Suppose A is an area function of f. What is the relationship between f and A?

2. Suppose F is an antiderivative of f and A is an area function of f. What is the relationship between F and A?

3. Explain in words and write mathematically how the Fundamental Theorem of Calculus is used to evaluate definite integrals.

4. Let $f(x) = c$, where c is a positive constant. Explain why an area function of f is an increasing function.

5. The linear function $f(x) = 3 - x$ is decreasing on the interval $[0, 3]$. Is the area function for f increasing or decreasing on the interval $[0, 3]$? Draw a picture and explain.

6. Evaluate $\int_0^2 3x^2\, dx$ and $\int_{-2}^2 3x^2\, dx$.

7. Explain in words and express mathematically the inverse relationship between differentiation and integration as given by Part 1 of the Fundamental Theorem of Calculus.

8. Why can the constant of integration be omitted from the antiderivative when evaluating a definite integral?

9. Evaluate $\dfrac{d}{dx}\displaystyle\int_a^x f(t)\,dt$ and $\dfrac{d}{dx}\displaystyle\int_a^b f(t)\,dt$, where a and b are constants.

10. Explain why $\displaystyle\int_a^b f'(x)\,dx = f(b) - f(a)$.

Basic Skills

11. **Area functions** The graph of f is shown in the figure. Let $A(x) = \displaystyle\int_{-2}^x f(t)\,dt$ and $F(x) = \displaystyle\int_4^x f(t)\,dt$ be two area functions for f. Evaluate the following area functions.

   a. $A(-2)$ **b.** $F(8)$ **c.** $A(4)$ **d.** $F(4)$ **e.** $A(8)$

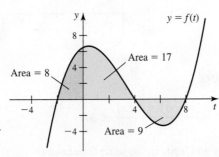

12. **Area functions** The graph of f is shown in the figure. Let $A(x) = \displaystyle\int_0^x f(t)\,dt$ and $F(x) = \displaystyle\int_2^x f(t)\,dt$ be two area functions for f. Evaluate the following area functions.

   a. $A(2)$ **b.** $F(5)$ **c.** $A(0)$ **d.** $F(8)$ **e.** $A(8)$
   f. $A(5)$ **g.** $F(2)$

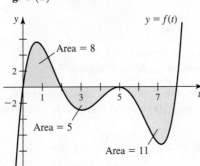

13–16. Area functions for constant functions *Consider the following functions f and real numbers a (see figure).*

a. *Find and graph the area function $A(x) = \displaystyle\int_a^x f(t)\,dt$ for f.*
b. *Verify that $A'(x) = f(x)$.*

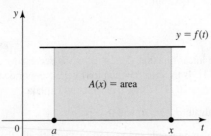

13. $f(t) = 5,\; a = 0$ 14. $f(t) = 10,\; a = 4$

15. $f(t) = 5,\; a = -5$ 16. $f(t) = 2,\; a = -3$

17. **Area functions for the same linear function** Let $f(t) = t$ and consider the two area functions $A(x) = \displaystyle\int_0^x f(t)\,dt$ and $F(x) = \displaystyle\int_2^x f(t)\,dt$.

   a. Evaluate $A(2)$ and $A(4)$. Then use geometry to find an expression for $A(x)$, for $x \geq 0$.
   b. Evaluate $F(4)$ and $F(6)$. Then use geometry to find an expression for $F(x)$, for $x \geq 2$.
   c. Show that $A(x) - F(x)$ is a constant and that $A'(x) = F'(x) = f(x)$.

18. **Area functions for the same linear function** Let $f(t) = 2t - 2$ and consider the two area functions $A(x) = \displaystyle\int_1^x f(t)\,dt$ and $F(x) = \displaystyle\int_4^x f(t)\,dt$.

   a. Evaluate $A(2)$ and $A(3)$. Then use geometry to find an expression for $A(x)$, for $x \geq 1$.
   b. Evaluate $F(5)$ and $F(6)$. Then use geometry to find an expression for $F(x)$, for $x \geq 4$.
   c. Show that $A(x) - F(x)$ is a constant and that $A'(x) = F'(x) = f(x)$.

19–22. Area functions for linear functions *Consider the following functions f and real numbers a (see figure).*

a. *Find and graph the area function $A(x) = \displaystyle\int_a^x f(t)\,dt$.*
b. *Verify that $A'(x) = f(x)$.*

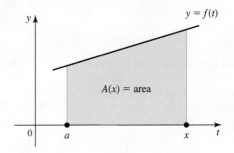

19. $f(t) = t + 5,\; a = -5$ 20. $f(t) = 2t + 5,\; a = 0$

21. $f(t) = 3t + 1,\; a = 2$ 22. $f(t) = 4t + 2,\; a = 0$

23–24. Definite integrals *Evaluate the following integrals using the Fundamental Theorem of Calculus. Discuss whether your result is consistent with the figure.*

23. $\displaystyle\int_0^1 (x^2 - 2x + 3)\,dx$ 24. $\displaystyle\int_{-\pi/4}^{7\pi/4} (\sin x + \cos x)\,dx$

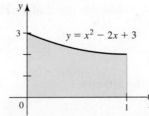
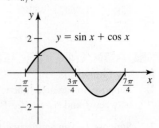

25–28. Definite integrals *Evaluate the following integrals using the Fundamental Theorem of Calculus. Sketch the graph of the integrand and shade the region whose net area you have found.*

25. $\displaystyle\int_{-2}^3 (x^2 - x - 6)\,dx$ 26. $\displaystyle\int_0^1 (x - \sqrt{x})\,dx$

27. $\displaystyle\int_0^5 (x^2 - 9)\, dx$

28. $\displaystyle\int_{1/2}^2 \left(1 - \frac{1}{x^2}\right) dx$

29–50. Definite integrals *Evaluate the following integrals using the Fundamental Theorem of Calculus.*

29. $\displaystyle\int_0^2 4x^3\, dx$

30. $\displaystyle\int_0^2 (3x^2 + 2x)\, dx$

31. $\displaystyle\int_0^1 (x + \sqrt{x})\, dx$

32. $\displaystyle\int_0^{\pi/4} 2\cos x\, dx$

33. $\displaystyle\int_1^9 \frac{2}{\sqrt{x}}\, dx$

34. $\displaystyle\int_4^9 \frac{2 + \sqrt{t}}{t}\, dt$

35. $\displaystyle\int_{-2}^2 (x^2 - 4)\, dx$

36. $\displaystyle\int_0^{\ln 8} e^x\, dx$

37. $\displaystyle\int_{1/2}^1 (x^{-3} - 8)\, dx$

38. $\displaystyle\int_0^4 x(x - 2)(x - 4)\, dx$

39. $\displaystyle\int_0^{\pi/4} \sec^2 \theta\, d\theta$

40. $\displaystyle\int_0^{1/2} \frac{dx}{\sqrt{1 - x^2}}$

41. $\displaystyle\int_{-2}^{-1} x^{-3}\, dx$

42. $\displaystyle\int_0^{\pi} (1 - \sin x)\, dx$

43. $\displaystyle\int_1^4 (1 - x)(x - 4)\, dx$

44. $\displaystyle\int_{-\pi/2}^{\pi/2} (\cos x - 1)\, dx$

45. $\displaystyle\int_1^2 \frac{3}{t}\, dt$

46. $\displaystyle\int_4^9 \frac{x - \sqrt{x}}{x^3}\, dx$

47. $\displaystyle\int_0^{\pi/8} \cos 2x\, dx$

48. $\displaystyle\int_0^1 10e^{2x}\, dx$

49. $\displaystyle\int_1^{\sqrt{3}} \frac{dx}{1 + x^2}$

50. $\displaystyle\int_{\pi/16}^{\pi/8} 8\csc^2 4x\, dx$

51–54. Areas *Find (i) the net area and (ii) the area of the following regions. Graph the function and indicate the region in question.*

51. The region bounded by $y = x^{1/2}$ and the x-axis between $x = 1$ and $x = 4$

52. The region above the x-axis bounded by $y = 4 - x^2$

53. The region below the x-axis bounded by $y = x^4 - 16$

54. The region bounded by $y = 6\cos x$ and the x-axis between $x = -\pi/2$ and $x = \pi$

55–60. Areas of regions *Find the area of the regions bounded by the graph of f and the x-axis on the given interval.*

55. $f(x) = x^2 - 25;\ [2, 4]$

56. $f(x) = x^3 - 1;\ [-1, 2]$

57. $f(x) = \dfrac{1}{x};\ [-2, -1]$

58. $f(x) = x(x + 1)(x - 2);\ [-1, 2]$

59. $f(x) = \sin x;\ [-\pi/4, 3\pi/4]$

60. $f(x) = \cos x;\ [\pi/2, \pi]$

61–68. Derivatives of integrals *Simplify the following expressions.*

61. $\displaystyle\frac{d}{dx}\int_3^x (t^2 + t + 1)\, dt$

62. $\displaystyle\frac{d}{dx}\int_0^x e^t\, dt$

63. $\displaystyle\frac{d}{dx}\int_2^{x^3} \frac{dp}{p^2}$

64. $\displaystyle\frac{d}{dx}\int_{x^2}^{10} \frac{dz}{z^2 + 1}$

65. $\displaystyle\frac{d}{dx}\int_x^1 \sqrt{t^4 + 1}\, dt$

66. $\displaystyle\frac{d}{dx}\int_x^0 \frac{dp}{p^2 + 1}$

67. $\displaystyle\frac{d}{dx}\int_{-x}^x \sqrt{1 + t^2}\, dt$

68. $\displaystyle\frac{d}{dx}\int_{e^x}^{e^{2x}} \ln t^2\, dt$

69. Matching functions with area functions Match the functions f, whose graphs are given in a–d, with the area functions $A(x) = \int_0^x f(t)\, dt$, whose graphs are given in A–D.

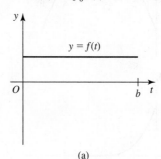

(a)

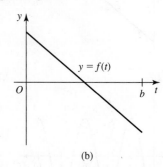

(b)

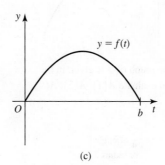

(c)

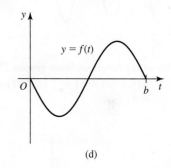

(d)

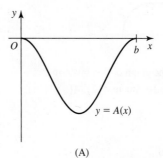

(A)

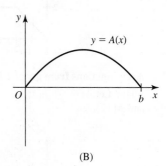

(B)

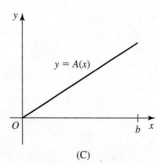

(C)

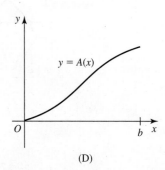

(D)

70–73. Working with area functions *Consider the function f and its graph.*

a. *Estimate the zeros of the area function $A(x) = \int_0^x f(t)\,dt$, for $0 \le x \le 10$.*

b. *Estimate the points (if any) at which A has a local maximum or minimum.*

c. *Sketch a graph of A, for $0 \le x \le 10$, without a scale on the y-axis.*

70.

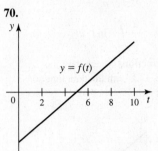

71.

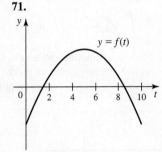

72.

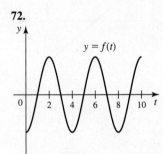

73.

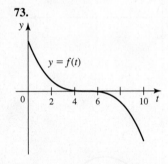

74. **Area functions from graphs** The graph of f is given in the figure. Let $A(x) = \int_0^x f(t)\,dt$ and evaluate $A(1)$, $A(2)$, $A(4)$, and $A(6)$.

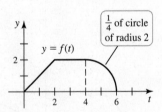

75. **Area functions from graphs** The graph of f is given in the figure. Let $A(x) = \int_0^x f(t)\,dt$ and evaluate $A(2)$, $A(5)$, $A(8)$, and $A(12)$.

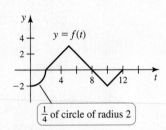

76–80. Working with area functions *Consider the function f and the points a, b, and c.*

a. *Find the area function $A(x) = \int_a^x f(t)\,dt$ using the Fundamental Theorem.*

b. *Graph f and A.*

c. *Evaluate $A(b)$ and $A(c)$. Interpret the results using the graphs of part (b).*

76. $f(x) = \sin x;\ a = 0, b = \pi/2, c = \pi$

77. $f(x) = e^x;\ a = 0, b = \ln 2, c = \ln 4$

78. $f(x) = -12x(x-1)(x-2);\ a = 0, b = 1, c = 2$

79. $f(x) = \cos \pi x;\ a = 0, b = \frac{1}{2}, c = 1$

80. $f(x) = \dfrac{1}{x};\ a = 1, b = 4, c = 6$

81–84. Functions defined by integrals *Consider the function g, which is given in terms of a definite integral with a variable upper limit.*

a. *Graph the integrand.*

b. *Calculate $g'(x)$.*

c. *Graph g, showing all your work and reasoning.*

81. $g(x) = \displaystyle\int_0^x \sin^2 t\,dt$ **82.** $g(x) = \displaystyle\int_0^x (t^2 + 1)\,dt$

83. $g(x) = \displaystyle\int_0^x \sin(\pi t^2)\,dt$ (a Fresnel integral)

84. $g(x) = \displaystyle\int_0^x \cos(\pi\sqrt{t})\,dt$

Further Explorations

85. **Explain why or why not** Determine whether the following statements are true and give an explanation or counterexample.

a. Suppose that f is a positive decreasing function, for $x > 0$. Then the area function $A(x) = \int_0^x f(t)\,dt$ is an increasing function of x.

b. Suppose that f is a negative increasing function, for $x > 0$. Then the area function $A(x) = \int_0^x f(t)\,dt$ is a decreasing function of x.

c. The functions $p(x) = \sin 3x$ and $q(x) = 4\sin 3x$ are antiderivatives of the same function.

d. If $A(x) = 3x^2 - x - 3$ is an area function for f, then $B(x) = 3x^2 - x$ is also an area function for f.

e. $\dfrac{d}{dx}\displaystyle\int_a^b f(t)\,dt = 0$

86–94. Definite integrals *Evaluate the following definite integrals using the Fundamental Theorem of Calculus.*

86. $\dfrac{1}{2}\displaystyle\int_0^{\ln 2} e^x\,dx$ **87.** $\displaystyle\int_1^4 \dfrac{x-2}{\sqrt{x}}\,dx$ **88.** $\displaystyle\int_1^2 \left(\dfrac{2}{s} - \dfrac{4}{s^3}\right)ds$

89. $\displaystyle\int_0^{\pi/3} \sec x \tan x\,dx$ **90.** $\displaystyle\int_{\pi/4}^{\pi/2} \csc^2\theta\,d\theta$ **91.** $\displaystyle\int_1^8 \sqrt[3]{y}\,dy$

92. $\displaystyle\int_{\sqrt{2}}^2 \dfrac{dx}{x\sqrt{x^2 - 1}}$ **93.** $\displaystyle\int_1^2 \dfrac{z^2 + 4}{z}\,dz$ **94.** $\displaystyle\int_0^{\sqrt{3}} \dfrac{3\,dx}{9 + x^2}$

95–98. Areas of regions *Find the area of the region R bounded by the graph of f and the x-axis on the given interval. Graph f and show the region R.*

95. $f(x) = 2 - |x|$; $[-2, 4]$

96. $f(x) = (1 - x^2)^{-1/2}$; $[-1/2, \sqrt{3}/2]$

97. $f(x) = x^4 - 4$; $[1, 4]$ **98.** $f(x) = x^2(x - 2)$; $[-1, 3]$

99–102. Derivatives and integrals *Simplify the given expressions.*

99. $\displaystyle\int_3^8 f'(t)\, dt$, where f' is continuous on $[3, 8]$

100. $\displaystyle\frac{d}{dx}\int_0^{x^2} \frac{dt}{t^2 + 4}$

101. $\displaystyle\frac{d}{dx}\int_0^{\cos x} (t^4 + 6)\, dt$

102. $\displaystyle\frac{d}{dx}\int_x^1 e^{t^2}\, dt$

103. $\displaystyle\frac{d}{dt}\left(\int_1^t \frac{3}{x}\, dx - \int_{t^2}^1 \frac{3}{x}\, dx\right)$

104. $\displaystyle\frac{d}{dt}\left(\int_0^t \frac{dx}{1 + x^2} + \int_0^{1/t} \frac{dx}{1 + x^2}\right)$

Additional Exercises

105. Zero net area Consider the function $f(x) = x^2 - 4x$.

  a. Graph f on the interval $x \geq 0$.
  b. For what value of $b > 0$ is $\int_0^b f(x)\, dx = 0$?
  c. In general, for the function $f(x) = x^2 - ax$, where $a > 0$, for what value of $b > 0$ (as a function of a) is $\int_0^b f(x)\, dx = 0$?

106. Cubic zero net area Consider the graph of the cubic $y = x(x - a)(x - b)$, where $0 < a < b$. Verify that the graph bounds a region above the x-axis, for $0 < x < a$, and bounds a region below the x-axis, for $a < x < b$. What is the relationship between a and b if the areas of these two regions are equal?

107. Maximum net area What value of $b > -1$ maximizes the integral
$$\int_{-1}^b x^2 (3 - x)\, dx?$$

108. Maximum net area Graph the function $f(x) = 8 + 2x - x^2$ and determine the values of a and b that maximize the value of the integral
$$\int_a^b (8 + 2x - x^2)\, dx.$$

109. An integral equation Use the Fundamental Theorem of Calculus, Part 1, to find the function f that satisfies the equation
$$\int_0^x f(t)\, dt = 2\cos x + 3x - 2.$$
Verify the result by substitution into the equation.

110. Max/min of area functions Suppose f is continuous on $[0, \infty)$ and $A(x)$ is the net area of the region bounded by the graph of f and the t-axis on $[0, x]$. Show that the local maxima and minima of A occur at the zeros of f. Verify this fact with the function $f(x) = x^2 - 10x$.

111. Asymptote of sine integral Use a calculator to approximate
$$\lim_{x\to\infty} S(x) = \lim_{x\to\infty} \int_0^x \frac{\sin t}{t}\, dt,$$
where S is the sine integral function (see Example 7). Explain your reasoning.

112. Sine integral Show that the sine integral $S(x) = \displaystyle\int_0^x \frac{\sin t}{t}\, dt$ satisfies the (differential) equation $xS'(x) + 2S''(x) + xS'''(x) = 0$.

113. Fresnel integral Show that the Fresnel integral $S(x) = \int_0^x \sin(t^2)\, dt$ satisfies the (differential) equation
$$(S'(x))^2 + \left(\frac{S''(x)}{2x}\right)^2 = 1.$$

114. Variable integration limits Evaluate $\displaystyle\frac{d}{dx}\int_{-x}^x (t^2 + t)\, dt$. (*Hint:* Separate the integral into two pieces.)

115. Discrete version of the Fundamental Theorem In this exercise, we work with a discrete problem and show why the relationship $\int_a^b f'(x)\, dx = f(b) - f(a)$ makes sense. Suppose we have a set of equally spaced grid points
$$\{a = x_0 < x_1 < x_2 < \cdots < x_{n-1} < x_n = b\},$$
where the distance between any two grid points is Δx. Suppose also that at each grid point x_k, a function value $f(x_k)$ is defined, for $k = 0, \ldots, n$.

  a. We now replace the integral with a sum and replace the derivative with a difference quotient. Explain why $\int_a^b f'(x)\, dx$ is analogous to $\displaystyle\sum_{k=1}^n \underbrace{\frac{f(x_k) - f(x_{k-1})}{\Delta x}}_{\approx f'(x_k)} \Delta x$.

  b. Simplify the sum in part (*a*) and show that it is equal to $f(b) - f(a)$.
  c. Explain the correspondence between the integral relationship and the summation relationship.

QUICK CHECK ANSWERS

1. $0, -35$ **2.** $A(6) = 44$; $A(10) = 120$ **3.** $\frac{2}{3} - \frac{1}{2} = \frac{1}{6}$
4. If f is differentiated, we get f'. Thus, f is an antiderivative of f'. ◄

5.5 Properties of Integrals and Average Value

With the Fundamental Theorem of Calculus in hand, we may begin an investigation of integration and its applications. In this section, we discuss the role of symmetry in integrals, we use the slice-and-sum strategy to define the average value of a function, and then we explore a theoretical result called the Mean Value Theorem for integrals.

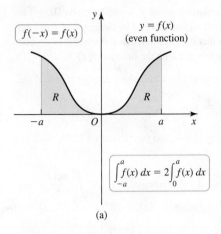

$$f(-x) = f(x)$$

$y = f(x)$
(even function)

$$\int_{-a}^{a} f(x)\,dx = 2\int_{0}^{a} f(x)\,dx$$

(a)

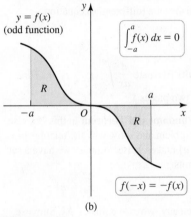

$y = f(x)$
(odd function)

$$\int_{-a}^{a} f(x)\,dx = 0$$

$$f(-x) = -f(x)$$

(b)

FIGURE 5.56

QUICK CHECK 1 If f and g are both even functions, is the product fg even or odd? Use the facts that $f(-x) = f(x)$ and $g(-x) = g(x)$. ◄

Integrating Even and Odd Functions

Symmetry appears throughout mathematics in many different forms, and its use often leads to insights and efficiencies. Here we use the symmetry of a function to simplify integral calculations.

Section 1.1 introduced the symmetry of even and odd functions. An **even function** satisfies the property $f(-x) = f(x)$, which means that its graph is symmetric about the y-axis (Figure 5.56a). Examples of even functions are $f(x) = \cos x$ and $f(x) = x^n$, where n is an even integer. An **odd function** satisfies the property $f(-x) = -f(x)$, which means that its graph is symmetric about the origin (Figure 5.56b). Examples of odd functions are $f(x) = \sin x$ and $f(x) = x^n$, where n is an odd integer.

Special things happen when we integrate even and odd functions on intervals centered at the origin. First, suppose f is an even function and consider $\int_{-a}^{a} f(x)\,dx$. From Figure 5.56a, we see that the integral of f on $[-a, 0]$ equals the integral of f on $[0, a]$. Therefore, the integral on $[-a, a]$ is twice the integral on $[0, a]$, or

$$\int_{-a}^{a} f(x)\,dx = 2\int_{0}^{a} f(x)\,dx.$$

On the other hand, suppose f is an odd function and consider $\int_{-a}^{a} f(x)\,dx$. As shown in Figure 5.56b, the integral on the interval $[-a, 0]$ is the negative of the integral on $[0, a]$. Therefore, the integral on $[-a, a]$ is zero, or

$$\int_{-a}^{a} f(x)\,dx = 0.$$

We summarize these results in the following theorem.

THEOREM 5.7 Integrals of Even and Odd Functions

Let a be a positive real number and let f be an integrable function on the interval $[-a, a]$.

• If f is even, $\int_{-a}^{a} f(x)\,dx = 2\int_{0}^{a} f(x)\,dx$.

• If f is odd, $\int_{-a}^{a} f(x)\,dx = 0$.

The following example shows how symmetry can simplify integration.

EXAMPLE 1 Integrating symmetric functions Evaluate the following integrals using symmetry arguments.

a. $\displaystyle\int_{-2}^{2} (x^4 - 3x^3)\,dx$ **b.** $\displaystyle\int_{-\pi/2}^{\pi/2} (\cos x - 4\sin^3 x)\,dx$

SOLUTION

a. Note that $x^4 - 3x^3$ is neither odd nor even, so Theorem 5.7 cannot be applied directly. However, we can split the integral and then use symmetry:

$$\int_{-2}^{2} (x^4 - 3x^3)\,dx = \int_{-2}^{2} x^4\,dx - 3\underbrace{\int_{-2}^{2} x^3\,dx}_{0} \qquad \text{Properties 3 and 4 of Table 5.6}$$

$$= 2\int_{0}^{2} x^4\,dx - 0 \qquad x^4 \text{ is even; } x^3 \text{ is odd.}$$

$$= 2\left(\frac{x^5}{5}\right)\Big|_{0}^{2} \qquad \text{Fundamental Theorem}$$

$$= 2\left(\frac{32}{5}\right) = \frac{64}{5}. \qquad \text{Simplify.}$$

Notice how the odd-powered term of the integrand is eliminated by symmetry. Integration of the even-powered term is simplified because the lower limit is zero.

b. The $\cos x$ term is an even function, so it can be integrated on the interval $[0, \pi/2]$. What about $\sin^3 x$? It is an odd function raised to an odd power, which results in an odd function; its integral on $[-\pi/2, \pi/2]$ is zero. Therefore,

$$\int_{-\pi/2}^{\pi/2} (\cos x - 4\sin^3 x)\, dx = 2\int_0^{\pi/2} \cos x\, dx - 0 \qquad \text{Symmetry}$$

$$= 2\sin x \Big|_0^{\pi/2} \qquad\qquad \text{Fundamental Theorem}$$

$$= 2(1 - 0) = 2. \qquad\quad \text{Simplify.}$$

Related Exercises 7–20 ◄

> There are a couple of ways to see that $\sin^3 x$ is an odd function. Its graph is symmetric about the origin, indicating that $\sin^3(-x) = -\sin^3 x$. Or by analogy, take an odd power of x and raise it to an odd power. For example, $(x^5)^3 = x^{15}$, which is odd. See Exercises 53–56 for direct proofs of symmetry in composite functions.

Average Value of a Function

If five people weigh 155, 143, 180, 105, and 123 lb, their average (mean) weight is

$$\frac{155 + 143 + 180 + 105 + 123}{5} = 141.2 \text{ lb}.$$

This idea generalizes quite naturally to functions. Consider a function f that is continuous on $[a, b]$. Let the grid points $x_0 = a, x_1, x_2, \ldots, x_n = b$ form a regular partition of $[a, b]$ with $\Delta x = \dfrac{b - a}{n}$. We now select a point x_k^* in each subinterval and compute $f(x_k^*)$, for $k = 1, \ldots, n$. The values of $f(x_k^*)$ may be viewed as a sampling of f on $[a, b]$. The average of these function values is

$$\frac{f(x_1^*) + f(x_2^*) + \cdots + f(x_n^*)}{n}.$$

Noting that $n = \dfrac{b - a}{\Delta x}$, we write the average of the n sample values as the Riemann sum

$$\frac{f(x_1^*) + f(x_2^*) + \cdots + f(x_n^*)}{(b - a)/\Delta x} = \frac{1}{b - a}\sum_{k=1}^{n} f(x_k^*)\Delta x.$$

Now suppose we increase n, taking more and more samples of f, while Δx decreases to zero. The limit of this sum is a definite integral that gives the average value $\bar{f}$ on $[a, b]$:

$$\bar{f} = \frac{1}{b - a}\lim_{n \to \infty}\sum_{k=1}^{n} f(x_k^*)\Delta x$$

$$= \frac{1}{b - a}\int_a^b f(x)\, dx.$$

This definition of the average value of a function is analogous to the definition of the average of a finite set of numbers.

DEFINITION   **Average Value of a Function**

The average value of an integrable function f on the interval $[a, b]$ is

$$\bar{f} = \frac{1}{b - a}\int_a^b f(x)\, dx.$$

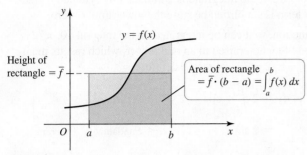

FIGURE 5.57

The average value of a function f on an interval $[a, b]$ has a clear geometrical interpretation. Multiplying both sides of the definition of average value by $(b - a)$, we have

$$\underbrace{(b - a)\bar{f}}_{\substack{\text{net area of} \\ \text{rectangle}}} = \underbrace{\int_a^b f(x)\, dx.}_{\substack{\text{net area of region} \\ \text{bounded by curve}}}$$

We see that the average value is the height of the rectangle with base $[a, b]$ that has the same net area as the region bounded by the graph of f on the interval $[a, b]$ (Figure 5.57). (We need to use net area in case f is negative on part of $[a, b]$, which could make $\bar{f}$ negative.)

QUICK CHECK 2 What is the average value of a constant function on an interval? What is the average value of an odd function on an interval $[-a, a]$? ◄

EXAMPLE 2 **Average elevation** A hiking trail has an elevation given by

$$f(x) = 60x^3 - 650x^2 + 1200x + 4500,$$

where f is measured in feet above sea level and x represents horizontal distance along the trail in miles, with $0 \le x \le 5$. What is the average elevation of the trail?

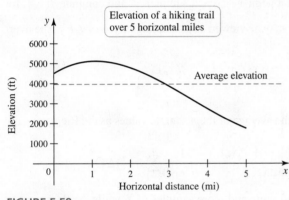

FIGURE 5.58

SOLUTION The trail ranges between elevations of about 2000 and 5000 ft (Figure 5.58). If we let the endpoints of the trail correspond to the horizontal distances $a = 0$ and $b = 5$, the average elevation of the trail in feet is

$$\bar{f} = \frac{1}{5}\int_0^5 (60x^3 - 650x^2 + 1200x + 4500)\, dx$$

$$= \frac{1}{5}\left(60\frac{x^4}{4} - 650\frac{x^3}{3} + 1200\frac{x^2}{2} + 4500x\right)\Bigg|_0^5 \quad \text{Fundamental Theorem}$$

$$= 3958\tfrac{1}{3}. \qquad\qquad\qquad\qquad\qquad\qquad \text{Simplify.}$$

The average elevation of the trail is slightly less than 3960 ft.

Related Exercises 21–34 ◄

Mean Value Theorem for Integrals

> Compare this statement to that of the Mean Value Theorem for Derivatives: There is at least one point c in (a, b) such that $f'(c)$ equals the average slope of f.

The average value of a function brings us close to an important theoretical result. The Mean Value Theorem for Integrals says that if f is continuous on $[a, b]$, then there is at least one point c in the interval (a, b) such that $f(c)$ equals the average value of f on (a, b). In other words, the horizontal line $y = \bar{f}$ intersects the graph of f for some point c in (a, b) (Figure 5.59). If f were not continuous, such a point might not exist.

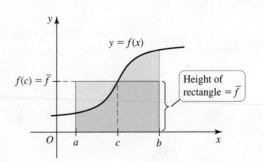

FIGURE 5.59

THEOREM 5.8   Mean Value Theorem for Integrals
Let f be continuous on the interval $[a, b]$. There exists a point c in (a, b) such that

$$f(c) = \bar{f} = \frac{1}{b - a} \int_a^b f(t)\, dt.$$

Proof: We begin by letting $F(x) = \int_a^x f(t)\, dt$ and noting that F is continuous on $[a, b]$ and differentiable on (a, b) (by Theorem 5.6, Part 1). We now apply the Mean Value Theorem for derivatives (Theorem 4.9) to F and conclude that there exists at least one point c in (a, b) such that

$$\underbrace{F'(c)}_{f(c)} = \frac{F(b) - F(a)}{b - a}.$$

By Theorem 5.6, Part 1, we know that $F'(c) = f(c)$, and by Theorem 5.6, Part 2, we know that

$$F(b) - F(a) = \int_a^b f(t)\,dt.$$

Combining these observations, we have

$$f(c) = \frac{1}{b - a} \int_a^b f(t)\,dt,$$

where c is a point in (a, b). ◄

> A more general form of the Mean Value Theorem states that if f and g are continuous on $[a, b]$ with $g(x) \geq 0$ on $[a, b]$, then there exists a number c in (a, b) such that
> $$\int_a^b f(x)g(x)\, dx = f(c) \int_a^b g(x)\, dx.$$

QUICK CHECK 3 Explain why $f(x) = 0$ for at least one point of (a, b) if f is continuous and $\int_a^b f(x)\, dx = 0$. ◄

The next example illustrates the relationship between the average value and the Mean Value Theorem for Integrals.

EXAMPLE 3   Average value equals function value Find the point(s) on the interval $[0, 1]$ at which $f(x) = 2x(1 - x)$ equals its average value on $[0, 1]$.

SOLUTION The average value of f on $[0, 1]$ is

$$\bar{f} = \frac{1}{1 - 0} \int_0^1 2x(1 - x)\, dx = \left(x^2 - \frac{2}{3}x^3 \right)\Big|_0^1 = \frac{1}{3}.$$

We must find the points on $(0, 1)$ at which $f(x) = \frac{1}{3}$ (Figure 5.60). Using the quadratic formula, the two solutions of $f(x) = 2x(1 - x) = \frac{1}{3}$ are

$$\frac{1 - \sqrt{1/3}}{2} \approx 0.211 \quad \text{and} \quad \frac{1 + \sqrt{1/3}}{2} \approx 0.789.$$

These two points are located symmetrically on either side of $x = \frac{1}{2}$. The two solutions, 0.211 and 0.789, are the same for $f(x) = ax(1 - x)$ for any nonzero value of a (Exercise 57).

Related Exercises 35–40◄

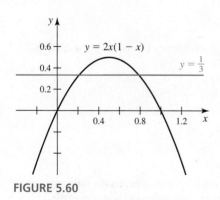

FIGURE 5.60

SECTION 5.5 EXERCISES

Review Questions

1. If f is an odd function, why is $\int_{-a}^{a} f(x)\, dx = 0$?

2. If f is an even function, why is $\int_{-a}^{a} f(x)\, dx = 2\int_{0}^{a} f(x)\, dx$?

3. Is x^{12} an even or odd function? Is $\sin x^2$ an even or odd function?

4. Explain how to find the average value of a function on an interval $[a, b]$ and why this definition is analogous to the definition of the average of a set of numbers.

5. Explain the statement that a continuous function on an interval $[a, b]$ equals its average value at some point on $[a, b]$.

6. Sketch the function $y = x$ on the interval $[0, 2]$, and let R be the region bounded by $y = x$ and the x-axis on $[0, 2]$. Now sketch a rectangle in the first quadrant whose base is $[0, 2]$ and whose area equals the area of R.

Basic Skills

7–16. Symmetry in integrals *Use symmetry to evaluate the following integrals.*

7. $\displaystyle\int_{-2}^{2} x^9\, dx$

8. $\displaystyle\int_{-200}^{200} 2x^5\, dx$

9. $\displaystyle\int_{-2}^{2} (3x^8 - 2)\, dx$

10. $\displaystyle\int_{-\pi/4}^{\pi/4} \cos x\, dx$

11. $\displaystyle\int_{-2}^{2} (x^9 - 3x^5 + 2x^2 - 10)\, dx$

12. $\displaystyle\int_{-\pi/2}^{\pi/2} 5 \sin x\, dx$

13. $\displaystyle\int_{-10}^{10} \frac{x}{\sqrt{200 - x^2}}\, dx$

14. $\displaystyle\int_{-\pi/2}^{\pi/2} (\cos 2x + \cos x \sin x - 3 \sin x^5)\, dx$

15. $\displaystyle\int_{-\pi/4}^{\pi/4} \sin^5 x\, dx$

16. $\displaystyle\int_{-1}^{1} (1 - |x|)\, dx$

17–20. Symmetry and definite integrals *Use symmetry to evaluate the following integrals. Draw a figure to interpret your result.*

17. $\displaystyle\int_{-\pi}^{\pi} \sin x\, dx$

18. $\displaystyle\int_{0}^{2\pi} \cos x\, dx$

19. $\displaystyle\int_{0}^{\pi} \cos x\, dx$

20. $\displaystyle\int_{0}^{2\pi} \sin x\, dx$

21–30. Average values *Find the average value of the following functions on the given interval. Draw a graph of the function and indicate the average value.*

21. $f(x) = x^3$; $[-1, 1]$

22. $f(x) = x^2 + 1$; $[-2, 2]$

23. $f(x) = \dfrac{1}{x^2 + 1}$; $[-1, 1]$

24. $f(x) = \cos 2x$; $\left[-\frac{\pi}{4}, \frac{\pi}{4}\right]$

25. $f(x) = 1/x$; $[1, e]$

26. $f(x) = e^{2x}$; $[0, \ln 2]$

27. $f(x) = \cos x$; $\left[-\frac{\pi}{2}, \frac{\pi}{2}\right]$

28. $f(x) = x(1 - x)$; $[0, 1]$

29. $f(x) = x^n$; $[0, 1]$, for any positive integer n

30. $f(x) = x^{1/n}$; $[0, 1]$, for any positive integer n

31. **Average distance on a parabola** What is the average distance between the parabola $y = 30x(20 - x)$ and the x-axis on the interval $[0, 20]$?

32. **Average elevation** The elevation of a path is given by $f(x) = x^3 - 5x^2 + 30$, where x measures horizontal distances. Draw a graph of the elevation function and find its average value, for $0 \le x \le 4$.

33. **Average height of an arch** The height of an arch above the ground is given by the function $y = 10 \sin x$, for $0 \le x \le \pi$. What is the average height of the arch above the ground?

34. **Average height of a wave** The surface of a water wave is described by $y = 5(1 + \cos x)$, for $-\pi \le x \le \pi$, where $y = 0$ corresponds to a trough of the wave (see figure). Find the average height of the wave above the trough on $[-\pi, \pi]$.

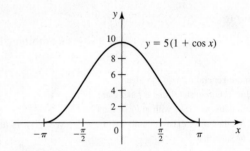

35–40. Mean Value Theorem for Integrals *Find or approximate the point(s) at which the given function equals its average value on the given interval.*

35. $f(x) = 8 - 2x$; $(0, 4)$

36. $f(x) = e^x$; $(0, 2)$

37. $f(x) = 1 - x^2/a^2$; $(0, a)$, where a is a positive real number

38. $f(x) = \dfrac{\pi}{4} \sin x$; $(0, \pi)$

39. $f(x) = 1 - |x|$; $(-1, 1)$

40. $f(x) = 1/x$; $(1, 4)$

Further Explorations

41. **Explain why or why not** Determine whether the following statements are true and give an explanation or counterexample.

   a. If f is symmetric about the line $x = 2$, then $\int_{0}^{4} f(x)\, dx = 2\int_{0}^{2} f(x)\, dx$.

   b. If f has the property $f(a + x) = -f(a - x)$, for all x, where a is a constant, then $\int_{a-2}^{a+2} f(x)\, dx = 0$.

   c. The average value of a linear function on an interval $[a, b]$ is the function value at the midpoint of $[a, b]$.

   d. Consider the function $f(x) = x(a - x)$ on the interval $[0, a]$, for $a > 0$. Its average value on $[0, a]$ is $\frac{1}{2}$ of its maximum value.

42–45. Symmetry in integrals *Use symmetry to evaluate the following integrals.*

42. $\displaystyle\int_{-\pi/4}^{\pi/4} \tan x \, dx$

43. $\displaystyle\int_{-\pi/4}^{\pi/4} \sec^2 x \, dx$

44. $\displaystyle\int_{-2}^{2} (1 - |x|^3) \, dx$

45. $\displaystyle\int_{-2}^{2} \frac{x^3 - 4x}{x^2 + 1} \, dx$

Applications

46. **Root mean square** The root mean square (or RMS) is used to measure the average value of oscillating functions (for example, sine and cosine functions that describe the current, voltage, or power in an alternating circuit). The RMS of a function f on the interval $[0, T]$ is

$$\bar{f}_{RMS} = \sqrt{\frac{1}{T} \int_0^T f(t)^2 \, dt}.$$

Compute the RMS of $f(t) = A \sin(\omega t)$, where A and ω are positive constants and T is any integer multiple of the period of f, which is $2\pi/\omega$.

47. **Gateway Arch** The Gateway Arch in St. Louis is 630 ft high and has a 630-ft base. Its shape can be modeled by the parabola

$$y = 630 \left[1 - \left(\frac{x}{315} \right)^2 \right].$$

Find the average height of the arch above the ground.

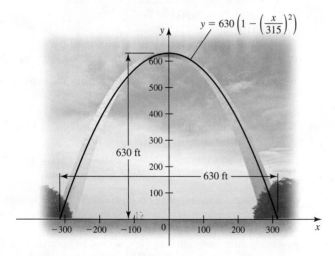

48. **Another Gateway Arch** Another description of the Gateway Arch is

$$y = 1260 - 315(e^{0.00418x} + e^{-0.00418x}),$$

where the base of the arch is $[-315, 315]$ and x and y are measured in feet. Find the average height of the arch above the ground.

49. **Planetary orbits** The planets orbit the Sun in elliptical orbits with the Sun at one focus. The equation of an ellipse whose dimensions are $2a$ in the x-direction and $2b$ in the y-direction is $\dfrac{x^2}{a^2} + \dfrac{y^2}{b^2} = 1.$

a. Let d^2 denote the square of the distance from a planet to the center of the ellipse at $(0, 0)$. Integrate over the interval $[-a, a]$ to show that the average value of d^2 is $(a^2 + 2b^2)/3$.

b. Show that in the case of a circle ($a = b = R$), the average value in part (a) is R^2.

c. Assuming $0 < b < a$, the coordinates of the Sun are $(\sqrt{a^2 - b^2}, 0)$. Let D^2 denote the square of the distance from the planet to the Sun. Integrate over the interval $[-a, a]$ to show that the average value of D^2 is $(4a^2 - b^2)/3$.

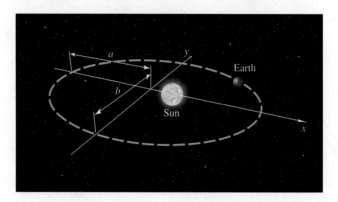

Additional Exercises

50. **Comparing a sine and a quadratic function** Consider the functions $f(x) = \sin x$ and $g(x) = \dfrac{4}{\pi^2} x(\pi - x)$.

a. Carefully graph f and g on the same set of axes. Verify that both functions have a single local maximum on the interval $[0, \pi]$ and they have the same maximum value on $[0, \pi]$.

b. On the interval $[0, \pi]$, which is true: $f(x) \geq g(x)$, $g(x) \geq f(x)$, or neither?

c. Compute and compare the average values of f and g on $[0, \pi]$.

51. **Using symmetry** Suppose f is an even function and
$$\int_{-8}^{8} f(x) \, dx = 18.$$

a. Evaluate $\displaystyle\int_{0}^{8} f(x) \, dx$ **b.** Evaluate $\displaystyle\int_{-8}^{8} x f(x) \, dx$

52. **Using symmetry** Suppose f is an odd function, $\displaystyle\int_{0}^{4} f(x) \, dx = 3$, and $\displaystyle\int_{0}^{8} f(x) \, dx = 9$.

a. Evaluate $\displaystyle\int_{-4}^{8} f(x) \, dx$ **b.** Evaluate $\displaystyle\int_{-8}^{4} f(x) \, dx$

53–56. Symmetry of composite functions *Prove that the integrand is either even or odd. Then give the value of the integral or show how it can be simplified. Assume that f and g are even functions and p and q are odd functions.*

53. $\int_{-a}^{a} f(g(x)) \, dx$ **54.** $\int_{-a}^{a} f(p(x)) \, dx$

55. $\int_{-a}^{a} p(g(x)) \, dx$ **56.** $\int_{-a}^{a} p(q(x)) \, dx$

57. Average value with a parameter Consider the function $f(x) = ax(1 - x)$ on the interval $[0, 1]$, where a is a positive real number.

    a. Find the average value of f as a function of a.

    b. Find the points at which the value of f equals its average value and prove that they are independent of a.

58. Square of the average For what polynomials f is it true that the square of the average value of f equals the average value of the square of f over all intervals $[a, b]$?

59. Problems of antiquity Several calculus problems were solved by Greek mathematicians long before the discovery of calculus. The following problems were solved by Archimedes using methods that predated calculus by 2000 years.

    a. Show that the area of a segment of a parabola is $\frac{4}{3}$ that of its inscribed triangle of greatest area. In other words, the area bounded by the parabola $y = a^2 - x^2$ and the x-axis is $\frac{4}{3}$ the area of the triangle with vertices $(\pm a, 0)$ and $(0, a^2)$. Assume that $a > 0$, but is unspecified.

    b. Show that the area bounded by the parabola $y = a^2 - x^2$ and the x-axis is $\frac{2}{3}$ the area of the rectangle with vertices $(\pm a, 0)$ and $(\pm a, a^2)$. Assume that $a > 0$, but is unspecified.

60. Unit area sine curve Find the value of c such that the region bounded by $y = c \sin x$ and the x-axis on the interval $[0, \pi]$ has area 1.

61. Unit area cubic Find the value of $c > 0$ such that the region bounded by the cubic $y = x(x - c)^2$ and the x-axis on the interval $[0, c]$ has area 1.

62. Unit area

    a. Consider the curve $y = 1/x$, for $x \geq 1$. For what value of $b > 0$ does the region bounded by this curve and the x-axis on the interval $[1, b]$ have an area of 1?

    b. Consider the curve $y = 1/x^p$, where $x \geq 1$, and $p < 2$ and $p \neq 1$ is a rational number. For what value of b (as a function of p) does the region bounded by this curve and the x-axis on the interval $[1, b]$ have unit area?

    c. Is $b(p)$ in part (b) an increasing or decreasing function of p? Explain.

63. A sine integral by Riemann sums Consider the integral $I = \int_{0}^{\pi/2} \sin x \, dx$.

    a. Write the left Riemann sum for I with n subintervals.

    b. Show that $\lim_{\theta \to 0} \left(\dfrac{\cos \theta + \sin \theta - 1}{2(1 - \cos \theta)} \right) = 1$.

    c. It is a fact that $\displaystyle\sum_{k=0}^{n-1} \sin\left(\dfrac{\pi k}{2n}\right) = \dfrac{\cos\left(\dfrac{\pi}{2n}\right) + \sin\left(\dfrac{\pi}{2n}\right) - 1}{2\left[1 - \cos\left(\dfrac{\pi}{2n}\right)\right]}$.

    Use this fact and part (b) to evaluate I by taking the limit of the Riemann sum as $n \to \infty$.

64. Alternate definitions of means Consider the function

$$f(t) = \frac{\int_a^b x^{t+1} \, dx}{\int_a^b x^t \, dx}.$$

Show that the following means can be defined in terms of f.

    a. Arithmetic mean: $f(0) = \dfrac{a + b}{2}$

    b. Geometric mean: $f\left(-\dfrac{3}{2}\right) = \sqrt{ab}$

    c. Harmonic mean: $f(-3) = \dfrac{2ab}{a + b}$

    d. Logarithmic mean: $f(-1) = \dfrac{b - a}{\ln b - \ln a}$

    (*Source: Mathematics Magazine* **78**, 5 (Dec 2005))

65. Symmetry of powers Fill in the following table with either **even** or **odd**, and prove each result. Assume n is a nonnegative integer and f^n means the nth power of f.

	f is even	f is odd
n is even	f^n is ____	f^n is ____
n is odd	f^n is ____	f^n is ____

66. Average value of the derivative Suppose that f' is a continuous function for all real numbers. Show that the average value of the derivative on an interval $[a, b]$ is $\bar{f}' = \dfrac{f(b) - f(a)}{b - a}$. Interpret this result in terms of secant lines.

67. Symmetry about a point A function f is symmetric about a point (c, d) if whenever $(c - x, d - y)$ is on the graph, then so is $(c + x, d + y)$. Functions that are symmetric about a point (c, d) are easily integrated on an interval with midpoint c.

    a. Show that if f is symmetric about (c, d) and $a > 0$, then $\int_{c-a}^{c+a} f(x) \, dx = 2af(c) = 2ad$.

    b. Graph the function $f(x) = \sin^2 x$ on the interval $[0, \pi/2]$ and show that the function is symmetric about the point $\left(\frac{\pi}{4}, \frac{1}{2}\right)$.

    c. Using only the graph of f (and no integration), show that $\int_{0}^{\pi/2} \sin^2 x \, dx = \dfrac{\pi}{4}$. (See the Guided Project *Symmetry in Integrals*.)

68. Bounds on an integral Suppose f is continuous on $[a, b]$ with $f''(x) > 0$ on the interval. It can be shown that

$$(b - a) f\left(\frac{a + b}{2}\right) \leq \int_a^b f(x) \, dx \leq (b - a) \frac{f(a) + f(b)}{2}.$$

    a. Assuming f is nonnegative on $[a, b]$, draw a figure to illustrate the geometric meaning of these inequalities. Discuss your conclusions.

    b. Divide these inequalities by $(b - a)$ and interpret the resulting inequalities in terms of the average value of f on $[a, b]$.

QUICK CHECK ANSWERS

1. $f(-x)g(-x) = f(x)g(x)$; therefore, fg is even.
2. The average value is the constant; the average value is 0.
3. The average value is zero on the interval; by the Mean Value Theorem for Integrals, $f(x) = 0$ at some point on the interval. ◄

5.6 Substitution Rule

Given just about any differentiable function, with enough know-how and persistence, you can compute its derivative. But the same cannot be said of antiderivatives. Many functions, even relatively simple ones, do not have antiderivatives that can be expressed in terms of familiar functions. Examples are $\sin x^2$, $(\sin x)/x$, and x^x. The immediate goal of this section is to enlarge the family of functions for which we can find antiderivatives. This campaign resumes in Chapter 7, where additional integration methods are developed.

Indefinite Integrals

One way to find new antiderivative rules is to start with familiar derivative rules and work backward. When applied to the Chain Rule, this strategy leads to the Substitution Rule. A few examples illustrate the technique.

EXAMPLE 1 **Antiderivatives by trial and error** Find $\int \cos 2x \, dx$.

SOLUTION The closest familiar indefinite integral related to this problem is

$$\int \cos x \, dx = \sin x + C,$$

> We assume C is an arbitrary constant without stating so each time it appears.

which is true because

$$\frac{d}{dx}(\sin x + C) = \cos x.$$

> The integral in Example 1 and all the integrals in Tables 5.1 and 5.2 (Section 5.1) are most easily evaluated using the Substitution Rule.

Therefore, we might *incorrectly* conclude that the indefinite integral of $\cos 2x$ is $\sin 2x + C$. However, by the Chain Rule,

$$\frac{d}{dx}(\sin 2x + C) = 2 \cos 2x \neq \cos 2x.$$

Note that $\sin 2x$ fails to be an antiderivative of $\cos 2x$ by a multiplicative factor of 2. A small adjustment corrects this problem. Let's try $\frac{1}{2} \sin 2x$:

$$\frac{d}{dx}\left(\frac{1}{2} \sin 2x\right) = \frac{1}{2} \cdot 2 \cos 2x = \cos 2x.$$

It works! So we have

$$\int \cos 2x \, dx = \frac{1}{2} \sin 2x + C.$$

Related Exercises 9–12 ◄

The trial-and-error approach of Example 1 does not work for complicated integrals. To develop a systematic method, consider a composite function $F(g(x))$, where F is an antiderivative of f; that is, $F' = f$. Using the Chain Rule to differentiate the composite function $F(g(x))$, we find that

$$\frac{d}{dx}[F(g(x))] = \underbrace{F'(g(x))}_{f(g(x))}g'(x) = f(g(x))g'(x)$$

This equation says that $F(g(x))$ is an antiderivative of $f(g(x))g'(x)$, which is written

$$\int f(g(x))g'(x) \, dx = F(g(x)) + C, \tag{1}$$

where F is any antiderivative of f.

▷ You can call the new variable anything
you want because it is just another
variable of integration. Typically, u is a
standard choice for the new variable.

Why is this approach called the *Substitution Rule* (or *Change of Variables Rule*)? In the composite function $f(g(x))$ in equation (1), we identify the "inner function" as $u = g(x)$, which implies that $du = g'(x) \, dx$. Making this identification, the integral in equation (1) is written

$$\int \underbrace{f(g(x))}_{f(u)} \underbrace{g'(x)dx}_{du} = \int f(u) \, du = F(u) + C.$$

We see that the integral $\int f(g(x))g'(x) \, dx$ with respect to x is replaced with a new integral $\int f(u)du$ with respect to the new variable u. In other words, we have substituted the new variable u for the old variable x. Of course, if the new integral with respect to u is no easier to find than the original integral, then the change of variables has not helped. The Substitution Rule requires some practice until certain patterns become familiar.

THEOREM 5.9   Substitution Rule for Indefinite Integrals

Let $u = g(x)$, where g' is continuous on an interval, and let f be continuous on the corresponding range of g. On that interval,

$$\int f(g(x))g'(x) \, dx = \int f(u) \, du.$$

In practice, Theorem 5.9 is used with following procedure.

PROCEDURE   Substitution Rule (Change of Variables)

1. Given an indefinite integral involving a composite function $f(g(x))$, identify an inner function $u = g(x)$ such that a constant multiple of $g'(x)$ appears in the integrand.

2. Substitute $u = g(x)$ and $du = g'(x) \, dx$ in the integral.

3. Evaluate the new indefinite integral with respect to u.

4. Write the result in terms of x using $u = g(x)$.

Disclaimer: Not all integrals yield to the Substitution Rule.

Mastery of the Substitution Rule comes only with practice. You should work through the following examples carefully.

EXAMPLE 2   Perfect substitutions Use the Substitution Rule to find the following indefinite integrals. Check your work by differentiating.

a. $\displaystyle\int 2(2x + 1)^3 \, dx$ **b.** $\displaystyle\int 10e^{10x} \, dx$

SOLUTION

a. We identify $u = 2x + 1$ as the inner function of the composite function $(2x + 1)^3$. Therefore, we choose the new variable $u = 2x + 1$, which implies that $\dfrac{du}{dx} = 2$, or $du = 2 \, dx$. Notice that $du = 2 \, dx$ appears as a factor in the integrand. The change of variables looks like this:

$$\int \underbrace{(2x+1)^3}_{u^3} \cdot \underbrace{2\, dx}_{du} = \int u^3\, du \qquad \text{Substitute } u = 2x+1, du = 2\, dx.$$

> It is a good idea to check the result. By the Chain Rule, we have
>
> $$\frac{d}{dx}\left[\frac{(2x+1)^4}{4} + C\right] = 2(2x+1)^3.$$

$$= \frac{u^4}{4} + C \qquad \text{Antiderivative}$$

$$= \frac{(2x+1)^4}{4} + C. \qquad \text{Replace } u \text{ with } 2x+1.$$

Notice that the final step uses $u = 2x + 1$ to return to the original variable.

b. The composite function e^{10x} has the inner function $u = 10x$, which implies that $du = 10\, dx$. The change of variables appears as

$$\int \underbrace{e^{10x}}_{e^u} \underbrace{10\, dx}_{du} = \int e^u\, du \qquad \text{Substitute } u = 10x, du = 10\, dx.$$

$$= e^u + C \qquad \text{Antiderivative}$$

$$= e^{10x} + C. \qquad \text{Replace } u \text{ with } 10x.$$

QUICK CHECK 1 Find a new variable u so that $\int 4x^3(x^4+5)^{10}\, dx = \int u^{10}\, du.$ ◄

In checking, we see that $\dfrac{d}{dx}(e^{10x} + C) = e^{10x} \cdot 10 = 10e^{10x}.$

Related Exercises 13–16 ◄

Most substitutions are not perfect. Example 3 shows a more typical situation.

EXAMPLE 3 Introducing a constant Find the following indefinite integrals.

a. $\displaystyle\int x^4(x^5 + 6)^9\, dx$ **b.** $\displaystyle\int \cos^3 x \sin x\, dx$

SOLUTION

a. The inner function of the composite function $(x^5 + 6)^9$ is $x^5 + 6$ and its derivative $5x^4$ also appears in the integrand (up to a multiplicative factor). Therefore, we use the substitution $u = x^5 + 6$, which implies that $du = 5x^4\, dx$ or $x^4\, dx = 1/5\, du$. By the Substitution Rule,

$$\int \underbrace{(x^5+6)^9}_{u^9} \underbrace{x^4\, dx}_{\frac{1}{5}du} = \int u^9 \cdot \frac{1}{5}\, du \qquad \begin{array}{l}\text{Substitute } u = x^5 + 6,\\[4pt] du = 5x^4\, dx \Rightarrow x^4\, dx = \dfrac{1}{5}\, du\end{array}$$

$$= \frac{1}{5}\int u^9\, du \qquad \int c\, f(x)\, dx = c\int f(x)\, dx$$

$$= \frac{1}{5} \cdot \frac{u^{10}}{10} + C \qquad \text{Antiderivative}$$

$$= \frac{1}{50}(x^5+6)^{10} + C. \qquad \text{Replace } u \text{ with } x^5 + 6.$$

b. The integrand can be written as $(\cos x)^3 \sin x$. The inner function in the composition is $\cos x$, which suggests the substitution $u = \cos x$. Note that $du = -\sin x\, dx$ or $\sin x\, dx = -du$. The change of variables appears as

$$\int \underbrace{\cos^3 x}_{u^3}\, \underbrace{\sin x\, dx}_{-du} = -\int u^3\, du \qquad \text{Substitute } u = \cos x, du = -\sin x\, dx.$$

$$= -\frac{u^4}{4} + C \qquad \text{Antiderivative}$$

$$= -\frac{\cos^4 x}{4} + C. \qquad \text{Replace } u \text{ with } \cos x.$$

Related Exercises 17–32 ◄

QUICK CHECK 2 In Example 3a, explain why the same substitution would not work as well for the integral $\int x^3(x^5 + 6)^9 \, dx$. ◄

Sometimes the choice for a u-substitution is not so obvious *or* more than one u-substitution works. The following example illustrates both of these points.

EXAMPLE 4   Variations on the substitution method Find $\int \dfrac{x}{\sqrt{x + 1}} \, dx$.

SOLUTION

Substitution 1 The composite function $\sqrt{x + 1}$ suggests the new variable $u = x + 1$. You might doubt whether this choice will work because $du = dx$, which leaves the x in the numerator of the integrand unaccounted for. But let's proceed. Letting $u = x + 1$, we have $x = u - 1$, $du = dx$, and

$$\int \frac{x}{\sqrt{x + 1}} \, dx = \int \frac{u - 1}{\sqrt{u}} \, du \qquad \text{Substitute } u = x + 1, \, du = dx.$$

$$= \int \left(\sqrt{u} - \frac{1}{\sqrt{u}} \right) du \qquad \text{Rewrite integrand.}$$

$$= \int \left(u^{1/2} - u^{-1/2} \right) du. \qquad \text{Fractional powers}$$

We integrate each term individually and then return to the original variable x:

$$\int \left(u^{1/2} - u^{-1/2} \right) du = \frac{2}{3} u^{3/2} - 2u^{1/2} + C \qquad \text{Antiderivatives}$$

$$= \frac{2}{3}(x + 1)^{3/2} - 2(x + 1)^{1/2} + C \qquad \text{Replace } u \text{ with } x + 1.$$

$$= \frac{2}{3}(x + 1)^{1/2}(x - 2) + C. \qquad \begin{array}{l} \text{Factor out } (x + 1)^{1/2} \text{ and} \\ \text{simplify.} \end{array}$$

▶ In Substitution 2, you could also use the fact that
$$u'(x) = \frac{1}{2\sqrt{x + 1}},$$
which implies
$$du = \frac{1}{2\sqrt{x + 1}} \, dx.$$

Substitution 2 Another possible substitution is $u = \sqrt{x + 1}$. Now $u^2 = x + 1$, $x = u^2 - 1$, and $dx = 2u \, du$. Making these substitutions leads to

$$\int \frac{x}{\sqrt{x + 1}} \, dx = \int \frac{u^2 - 1}{u} 2u \, du \qquad \text{Substitute } u = \sqrt{x + 1}, \, x = u^2 - 1.$$

$$= 2 \int (u^2 - 1) \, du \qquad \text{Simplify the integrand.}$$

$$= 2 \left(\frac{u^3}{3} - u \right) + C \qquad \text{Antiderivatives}$$

$$= \frac{2}{3}(x + 1)^{3/2} - 2(x + 1)^{1/2} + C \qquad \text{Replace } u \text{ with } \sqrt{x + 1}.$$

$$= \frac{2}{3}(x + 1)^{1/2}(x - 2) + C. \qquad \text{Factor out } (x + 1)^{1/2} \text{ and simplify.}$$

The same indefinite integral is found using either substitution.

Related Exercises 33–38 ◄

The substitution Rule allows to evaluate two important trigonometric integrals

EXAMPLE 5   New trigonometric integrals

a. Find $\int \tan x \, dx$.   **b.** Find $\int \sec x \, dx$.

SOLUTION

a. Recalling that $\tan x = \dfrac{\sin x}{\cos x}$, we make the substitution $u = \cos x$, which implies that $du = -\sin x \, dx$. The integral may then be evaluated:

$$\int \tan x \, dx = \int \frac{\sin x}{\cos x} \, dx = -\int \frac{du}{u} = -\ln |u| + C = -\ln |\cos x| + C.$$

Because $-\ln a = \ln \dfrac{1}{a}$, the integral may also be expressed in the form

$$\int \tan x \, dx = -\ln|\cos x| + C = \ln \left| \frac{1}{\cos x} \right| + C = \ln|\sec x| + C.$$

b. The indefinite integral of $\sec x$ requires more ingenuity. We multiply the integrand by $1 = \dfrac{\sec x + \tan x}{\sec x + \tan x}$ and then make a substitution:

$$\int \sec x \, dx = \int \sec x \frac{\sec x + \tan x}{\sec x + \tan x} \, dx \qquad \text{Multiply integrand by 1.}$$

$$= \int \frac{\sec^2 x + \sec x \tan x}{\sec x + \tan x} \, dx \qquad \text{Expand integrand.}$$

$$= \int \frac{du}{u} \qquad \begin{array}{l} \text{Let } u = \sec x + \tan x; \\ du = (\sec x \tan x + \sec^2 x)dx \end{array}$$

$$= \ln|u| + C \qquad \text{Integrate.}$$

$$= \ln|\sec x + \tan x| + C \qquad \text{Let } u = \sec x + \tan x.$$

The integrals of $\cot x$ and $\csc x$ are found in similar ways (Exercise 104).

Related Exercises 39–46 ◄

THEOREM 5.10   Trigonometric Integrals

$$\int \tan x \, dx = -\ln|\cos x| + C = \ln|\sec x| + C$$

$$\int \sec x \, dx = \ln|\sec x + \tan x| + C$$

$$\int \cot x \, dx = \ln|\sin x| + C$$

$$\int \csc x \, dx = -\ln|\csc x + \cot x| + C$$

We give these results in a more general form in Exercise 105.

Definite Integrals

The Substitution Rule is also used for definite integrals; in fact, there are two ways to proceed.

- You may use the Substitution Rule to find an antiderivative F and then use the Fundamental Theorem to evaluate $F(b) - F(a)$.

- Alternatively, once you have changed variables from x to u, you may change the limits of integration and complete the integration with respect to u. Specifically, if $u = g(x)$, the lower limit $x = a$ is replaced with $u = g(a)$ and the upper limit $x = b$ is replaced with $u = g(b)$.

The second option tends to be more efficient, and we use it whenever possible. This approach is summarized in the following theorem, which we then apply to several definite integrals.

> **THEOREM 5.11   Substitution Rule for Definite Integrals**
> Let $u = g(x)$, where g' is continuous on $[a, b]$ and let f be continuous on the range of g. Then
> $$\int_a^b f(g(x))g'(x)\,dx = \int_{g(a)}^{g(b)} f(u)\,du.$$

EXAMPLE 6   Definite integrals Evaluate the following integrals.

a. $\displaystyle\int_0^2 \frac{dx}{(x+3)^3}$ **b.** $\displaystyle\int_0^4 \frac{x}{x^2+1}\,dx$ **c.** $\displaystyle\int_0^{\pi/2} \sin^4 x \cos x\,dx$

SOLUTION

> When the integrand has the form $f(ax + b)$, the substitution $u = ax + b$ is often effective.

a. Let the new variable be $u = x + 3$ and then $du = dx$. Because we have changed the variable of integration from x to u, the limits of integration must also be expressed in terms of u. In this case,

$$x = 0 \text{ implies } u = 0 + 3 = 3, \quad \text{Lower limit}$$
$$x = 2 \text{ implies } u = 2 + 3 = 5. \quad \text{Upper limit}$$

The entire integration is carried out as follows:

$$\int_0^2 \frac{dx}{(x+3)^3} = \int_3^5 u^{-3}\,du \qquad\qquad \text{Substitute } u = x + 3, du = dx.$$

$$= -\frac{u^{-2}}{2}\Big|_3^5 \qquad\qquad\qquad \text{Fundamental Theorem}$$

$$= -\frac{1}{2}(5^{-2} - 3^{-2}) = \frac{8}{225}. \quad \text{Simplify.}$$

b. Notice that a multiple of the derivative of the denominator appears in the numerator; therefore, we let $u = x^2 + 1$, which implies that $du = 2x\,dx$, or $x\,dx = \frac{1}{2}\,du$. Changing limits of integration,

$$x = 0 \text{ implies } u = 0 + 1 = 1, \quad \text{Lower limit}$$
$$x = 4 \text{ implies } u = 4^2 + 1 = 17. \quad \text{Upper limit}$$

Changing variables, we have

$$\int_0^4 \frac{x}{x^2+1}\,dx = \frac{1}{2}\int_1^{17} u^{-1}\,du \qquad \text{Substitute } u = x^2 + 1, du = 2x\,dx.$$

$$= \frac{1}{2}\ln|u|\,\Big|_1^{17} \qquad\qquad \text{Fundamental Theorem}$$

$$= \frac{1}{2}(\ln 17 - \ln 1) \quad \text{Simplify.}$$

$$= \frac{1}{2}\ln 17 \approx 1.417. \quad \ln 1 = 0$$

c. Let $u = \sin x$, which implies that $du = \cos x\, dx$. The lower limit of integration becomes $u = 0$ and the upper limit becomes $u = 1$. Changing variables, we have

$$\int_0^{\pi/2} \sin^4 x \cos x\, dx = \int_0^1 u^4\, du \qquad u = \sin x,\, du = \cos x\, dx$$

$$= \left(\frac{u^5}{5}\right)\Big|_0^1 = \frac{1}{5}. \qquad \text{Fundamental Theorem}$$

Related Exercises 47–66 ◄

The Substitution Rule enables us to find two standard integrals that appear frequently in practice, $\int \sin^2 x\, dx$ and $\int \cos^2 x\, dx$. These integrals are handled using the identities

$$\sin^2 x = \frac{1 - \cos 2x}{2} \quad \text{and} \quad \cos^2 x = \frac{1 + \cos 2x}{2}.$$

EXAMPLE 7 **Integral of $\cos^2 \theta$** Evaluate $\int_0^{\pi/2} \cos^2 \theta\, d\theta$.

SOLUTION Working with the indefinite integral first, we use the identity for $\cos^2 \theta$:

$$\int \cos^2 \theta\, d\theta = \int \frac{1 + \cos 2\theta}{2}\, d\theta = \frac{1}{2}\int d\theta + \frac{1}{2}\int \cos 2\theta\, d\theta.$$

> See Exercise 116 for a generalization of Example 7.

The change of variables $u = 2\theta$ is now used for the second integral, and we have

$$\int \cos^2 \theta\, d\theta = \frac{1}{2}\int d\theta + \frac{1}{2}\int \cos 2\theta\, d\theta$$

$$= \frac{1}{2}\int d\theta + \frac{1}{2}\cdot\frac{1}{2}\int \cos u\, du \quad u = 2\theta,\, du = 2\, d\theta$$

$$= \frac{\theta}{2} + \frac{1}{4}\sin 2\theta + C. \qquad \text{Evaluate integrals; } u = 2\theta.$$

Using the Fundamental Theorem of Calculus, the value of the definite integral is

$$\int_0^{\pi/2} \cos^2 \theta\, d\theta = \left(\frac{\theta}{2} + \frac{1}{4}\sin 2\theta\right)\Big|_0^{\pi/2}$$

$$= \left(\frac{\pi}{4} + \frac{1}{4}\sin \pi\right) - \left(0 + \frac{1}{4}\sin 0\right) = \frac{\pi}{4}.$$

Related Exercises 67–74 ◄

Geometry of Substitution

The Substitution Rule may be interpreted graphically. To keep matters simple, consider the integral $\int_0^2 2(2x + 1)\, dx$. The graph of the integrand $y = 2(2x + 1)$ on the interval $[0, 2]$ is shown in Figure 5.61a, along with the region R whose area is given by the integral. The change of variables $u = 2x + 1$, $du = 2\, dx$, $u(0) = 1$, and $u(2) = 5$ leads to the new integral

$$\int_0^2 2(2x + 1)\, dx = \int_1^5 u\, du.$$

Figure 5.61b shows the graph of the new integrand $y = u$ on the interval $[1, 5]$ and the region R' whose area is given by the new integral. You can check that the areas of R and R' are equal. An analogous interpretation may be given to more complicated integrands and substitutions.

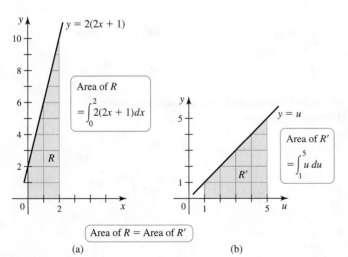

FIGURE 5.61

QUICK CHECK 3 Changes of variables occur frequently in mathematics. For example, suppose you want to solve the equation $x^4 - 13x^2 + 36 = 0$. If you use the substitution $u = x^2$, what is the new equation that must be solved for u? What are the roots of the original equation? ◄

SECTION 5.6 EXERCISES

Review Questions

1. On which derivative rule is the Substitution Rule based?

2. Why is the Substitution Rule is referred to as a change of variables.

3. The composite function $f(g(x))$ consists of an inner function g and an outer function f. If an integrand includes $f(g(x))$, which function is often a likely choice for a new variable u?

4. Find a suitable substitution for evaluating $\int \tan x \sec^2 x \, dx$, and explain your choice.

5. When using a change of variables $u = g(x)$ to evaluate the definite integral $\int_a^b f(g(x))g'(x) \, dx$, how are the limits of integration transformed?

6. If the change of variables $u = x^2 - 4$ is used to evaluate the definite integral $\int_2^4 f(x) \, dx$, what are the new limits of integration?

7. Find $\int \sin^2 x \, dx$.

8. What identity is needed to find $\int \tan x \, dx$?

Basic Skills

9–12. Trial and error *Find an antiderivative of the following functions by trial and error. Check your answer by differentiation.*

9. $f(x) = (x + 1)^{12}$ 10. $f(x) = e^{3x+1}$

11. $f(x) = \sqrt{2x + 1}$ 12. $f(x) = \cos(2x + 5)$

13–16. Substitution given *Use the given substitution to find the following indefinite integrals. Check your answer by differentiation.*

13. $\int 2x(x^2 + 1)^4 \, dx, \ u = x^2 + 1$

14. $\int 8x \cos(4x^2 + 3) \, dx, \ u = 4x^2 + 3$

15. $\int \sin^3 x \cos x \, dx, \ u = \sin x$

16. $\int (6x + 1)\sqrt{3x^2 + x} \, dx, \ u = 3x^2 + x$

17–32. Indefinite integrals *Use a change of variables to find the following indefinite integrals. Check your work by differentiation.*

17. $\int 2x(x^2 - 1)^{99} \, dx$ 18. $\int xe^{x^2} \, dx$

19. $\int \dfrac{2x^2}{\sqrt{1 - 4x^3}} \, dx$ 20. $\int \dfrac{(\sqrt{x} + 1)^4}{2\sqrt{x}} \, dx$

21. $\int (x^2 + x)^{10} (2x + 1) \, dx$ 22. $\int \dfrac{1}{10x - 3} \, dx$

23. $\int x^3(x^4 + 16)^6 \, dx$ 24. $\int \sin^{10} \theta \cos \theta \, d\theta$

25. $\int \dfrac{dx}{\sqrt{1 - 9x^2}}$ 26. $\int x^9 \sin x^{10} \, dx$

27. $\int (x^6 - 3x^2)^4 (x^5 - x) \, dx$

28. $\int \dfrac{x}{x - 2} \, dx$ (*Hint:* Let $u = x - 2$.)

29. $\int \dfrac{dx}{1 + 4x^2}$ 30. $\int \dfrac{3}{1 + 25x^2} \, dx$

31. $\int \dfrac{2}{x\sqrt{4x^2 - 1}} \, dx, x > \dfrac{1}{2}$ 32. $\int \dfrac{8x + 6}{2x^2 + 3x} \, dx$

33–38. Variations on the substitution method *Find the following integrals.*

33. $\int \dfrac{x}{\sqrt{x - 4}} \, dx$ 34. $\int \dfrac{y^2}{(y + 1)^4} \, dy$

35. $\int \dfrac{x}{\sqrt[3]{x + 4}} \, dx$ 36. $\int \dfrac{e^x - e^{-x}}{e^x + e^{-x}} \, dx$

37. $\int x\sqrt[3]{2x + 1} \, dx$ 38. $\int (x + 1)\sqrt{3x + 2} \, dx$

39–46. Trigonometric integrals *Evaluate the following integrals.*

39. $\int \tan 6x \, dx$ 40. $\int \sec 2x \, dx$

41. $\int (1 + \cot 4x) \, dx$ 42. $\int (x + \csc 3x) \, dx$

43. $\int x \tan x^2 \, dx$ 44. $\int e^x \sec e^x \, dx$

45. $\int \cot(1 + t) \, dt$ 46. $\int \dfrac{\tan \ln x}{x} \, dx$

47–60. Definite integrals *Use a change of variables to evaluate the following definite integrals.*

47. $\int_0^1 2x(4 - x^2) \, dx$ 48. $\int_0^2 \dfrac{2x}{(x^2 + 1)^2} \, dx$

49. $\int_0^{\pi/2} \sin^2 \theta \cos \theta \, d\theta$ 50. $\int_0^{\pi/4} \dfrac{\sin x}{\cos^2 x} \, dx$

51. $\int_{-1}^2 x^2 e^{x^3 + 1} \, dx$ 52. $\int_0^4 \dfrac{p}{\sqrt{9 + p^2}} \, dp$

53. $\int_{\pi/4}^{\pi/2} \dfrac{\cos x}{\sin^2 x}\, dx$

54. $\int_0^{\pi/4} \dfrac{\sin x}{\cos^3 x}\, dx$

55. $\int_{2/(5\sqrt{3})}^{2/5} \dfrac{dx}{x\sqrt{25x^2 - 1}}$

56. $\int_0^3 \dfrac{v^2 + 1}{\sqrt{v^3 + 3v + 4}}\, dv$

57. $\int_0^4 \dfrac{x}{x^2 + 1}\, dx$

58. $\int_0^{1/8} \dfrac{x}{\sqrt{1 - 16x^2}}\, dx$

59. $\int_{1/3}^{1/\sqrt{3}} \dfrac{4}{9x^2 + 1}\, dx$

60. $\int_0^{\ln 4} \dfrac{e^x}{3 + 2e^x}\, dx$

61. $\int_0^{\pi/2} \tan \dfrac{x}{2}\, dx$

62. $\int_{-\pi}^{\pi} 2 \sec \dfrac{x}{4}\, dx$

63. $\int_0^{\pi/3} \sec^2 x\, dx$

64. $\int_{\pi/12}^{\pi/6} 3 \cot 2\theta\, d\theta$

65. $\int_{\sqrt{\pi/2}}^{\sqrt{\pi/4}} y \csc y^2\, dy$

66. $\int_0^{\pi/4} \sec^2 x \tan^2 x\, dx$

67–74. Integrals with $\sin^2 x$ and $\cos^2 x$ *Evaluate the following integrals.*

67. $\int_{-\pi}^{\pi} \cos^2 x\, dx$

68. $\int \sin^2 x\, dx$

69. $\int \sin^2\!\left(\theta + \dfrac{\pi}{6}\right) d\theta$

70. $\int_0^{\pi/4} \cos^2 8\theta\, d\theta$

71. $\int_{-\pi/4}^{\pi/4} \sin^2 2\theta\, d\theta$

72. $\int x \cos^2 (x^2)\, dx$

73. $\int_0^{\pi/6} \dfrac{\sin 2y}{\sin^2 y + 2}\, dy$ (*Hint:* $\sin 2y = 2 \sin y \cos y$.)

74. $\int_0^{\pi/2} \sin^4 \theta\, d\theta$

Further Explorations

75. Explain why or why not Determine whether the following statements are true and give an explanation or counterexample. Assume that f, f', and f'' are continuous functions for all real numbers.

a. $\displaystyle\int f(x) f'(x)\, dx = \dfrac{1}{2}\,(f(x))^2 + C$

b. $\displaystyle\int (f(x))^n f'(x)\, dx = \dfrac{1}{n+1}\,(f(x))^{n+1} + C,\ n \neq -1$

c. $\displaystyle\int \sin 2x\, dx = 2 \int \sin x\, dx$

d. $\displaystyle\int (x^2 + 1)^9 dx = \dfrac{(x^2 + 1)^{10}}{10} + C$

e. $\displaystyle\int_a^b f'(x) f''(x)\, dx = f'(b) - f'(a)$

76–92. Additional integrals *Use a change of variables to evaluate the following integrals.*

76. $\int \sec 4w \tan 4w\, dw$

77. $\int \sec^2 10x\, dx$

78. $\int (\sin^5 x + 3 \sin^3 x - \sin x) \cos x\, dx$

79. $\int \dfrac{\csc^2 x}{\cot^3 x}\, dx$

80. $\int (x^{3/2} + 8)^5 \sqrt{x}\, dx$

81. $\int \sin x \sec^8 x\, dx$

82. $\int \dfrac{e^{2x}}{e^{2x} + 1}\, dx$

83. $\int_0^1 x\sqrt{1 - x^2}\, dx$

84. $\int_1^{e^2} \dfrac{\ln x}{x}\, dx$

85. $\int_2^3 \dfrac{x}{\sqrt[3]{x^2 - 1}}\, dx$

86. $\int_0^{6/5} \dfrac{dx}{25x^2 + 36}$

87. $\int_0^2 x^3 \sqrt{16 - x^4}\, dx$

88. $\int_{-1}^1 (x - 1)(x^2 - 2x)^7\, dx$

89. $\int_{-\pi}^0 \dfrac{\sin x}{2 + \cos x}\, dx$

90. $\int_0^1 \dfrac{(x + 1)(x + 2)}{2x^3 + 9x^2 + 12x + 36}\, dx$

91. $\int_1^2 \dfrac{4}{9x^2 + 6x + 1}\, dx$

92. $\int_0^{\pi/4} e^{\sin^2 x} \sin 2x\, dx$

93–96. Areas of regions *Find the area of the following regions.*

93. The region bounded by the graph of $f(x) = x \sin x^2$ and the x-axis between $x = 0$ and $x = \sqrt{\pi}$

94. The region bounded by the graph of $f(\theta) = \cos \theta \sin \theta$ and the θ-axis between $\theta = 0$ and $\theta = \pi/2$

95. The region bounded by the graph of $f(x) = (x - 4)^4$ and the x-axis between $x = 2$ and $x = 6$

96. The region bounded by the graph of $f(x) = \dfrac{x}{\sqrt{x^2 - 9}}$ and the x-axis between $x = 4$ and $x = 5$

97. Morphing parabolas The family of parabolas $y = (1/a) - x^2/a^3$, where $a > 0$, has the property that for $x \geq 0$, the x-intercept is $(a, 0)$ and the y-intercept is $(0, 1/a)$. Let $A(a)$ be the area of the region in the first quadrant bounded by the parabola and the x-axis. Find $A(a)$ and determine whether it is an increasing, decreasing, or constant function of a.

98. Substitutions Suppose that f is an even integrable function with $\int_0^8 f(x)\, dx = 9$.

a. Evaluate $\int_{-1}^1 x f(x^2)\, dx$.

b. Evaluate $\int_{-2}^2 x^2 f(x^3)\, dx$.

99. Substitutions Suppose that p is a nonzero real number and f is an odd function with $\int_0^1 f(x)\,dx = \pi$.

a. Evaluate $\int_0^{\pi/(2p)} \cos px\, f(\sin px)\,dx.$

b. Evaluate $\int_{-\pi/2}^{\pi/2} \cos x f(\sin x)\,dx.$

Applications

100. Periodic motion An object moves along a line with a velocity in m/s given by $v(t) = 8\cos(\pi t/6)$. Its initial position is $s(0) = 0$.

a. Graph the velocity function.

b. As discussed in Chapter 6, the position of the object is given by $s(t) = \int_0^t v(y)\,dy$, for $t \geq 0$. Find the position function, for $t \geq 0$.

c. What is the period of the motion—that is, starting at any point, how long does it take the object to return to that position?

101. Population models The population of a culture of bacteria has a growth rate given by $p'(t) = \dfrac{200}{(t+1)^r}$ bacteria per hour, for $t \geq 0$, where $r > 1$ is a real number. In Chapter 6 it is shown that the increase in the population over the time interval $[0, t]$ is given by $\int_0^t p'(s)\,ds$. (Note that the growth rate decreases in time, reflecting competition for space and food.)

a. Using the population model with $r = 2$, what is the increase in the population over the time interval $0 \leq t \leq 4$?

b. Using the population model with $r = 3$, what is the increase in the population over the time interval $0 \leq t \leq 6$?

c. Let ΔP be the increase in the population over a fixed time interval $[0, T]$. For fixed T, does ΔP increase or decrease with the parameter r? Explain.

d. A lab technician measures an increase in the population of 350 bacteria over the 10 hr period $[0, 10]$ Estimate the value of r that best fits this data point.

e. Looking ahead: Work with the population model using $r = 3$ in part (b) and find the increase in population over the time interval $[0, T]$, for any $T > 0$. If the culture is allowed to grow indefinitely $(T \to \infty)$, does the bacteria population increase without bound? Or does it approach a finite limit?

102. Average distance in a triangle Consider the right triangle with vertices $(0, 0)$, $(0, b)$, and $(a, 0)$, where $a > 0$ and $b > 0$. Show that the average vertical distance from points on the x-axis to the hypotenuse is $b/2$, for all $a > 0$.

103. Average value of sine functions Use a graphing utility to verify that the functions $f(x) = \sin kx$ have a period of $2\pi/k$, where $k = 1, 2, 3, \ldots$. Equivalently, the first "hump" of $f(x) = \sin kx$ occurs on the interval $[0, \pi/k]$. Verify that the average value of the first hump of $f(x) = \sin kx$ is independent of k. What is the average value?

Additional Exercises

104. Integrals of $\cot x$ and $\csc x$

a. Show that $\int \cot x\,dx = \ln|\sin x| + C.$

b. Show that $\int \csc x\,dx = -\ln|\csc x + \cot x| + C.$

105. General trigonometric integrals Let $a \neq 0$ be a real number.

a. Show that $\displaystyle\int \tan ax\,dx = \frac{1}{a}\ln|\sec ax| + C.$

b. Show that $\displaystyle\int \sec ax\,dx = \frac{1}{a}\ln|\sec ax + \tan ax| + C.$

106. Equal areas The area of the shaded region under the curve $y = 2\sin 2x$ in (a) equals the area of the shaded region under the curve $y = \sin x$ in (b). Explain why this is true without computing areas.

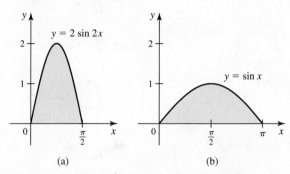

(a)   (b)

107. Equal areas The area of the shaded region under the curve $y = \dfrac{(\sqrt{x} - 1)^2}{2\sqrt{x}}$ on the interval $[4, 9]$ in (a) equals the area of the shaded region under the curve $y = x^2$ on the interval $[1, 2]$ in (b). Without computing areas, explain why.

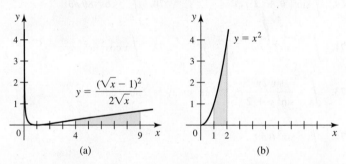

(a)   (b)

108–112. General results *Evaluate the following integrals in which the function f is unspecified. Note that $f^{(p)}$ is the pth derivative of f and f^p is the pth power of f. Assume f and its derivatives are continuous for all real numbers.*

108. $\displaystyle\int \left(5f^3(x) + 7f^2(x) + f(x)\right)f'(x)\,dx$

109. $\displaystyle\int_1^2 \left(5f^3(x) + 7f^2(x) + f(x)\right)f'(x)\,dx$, where $f(1) = 4$, $f(2) = 5$

110. $\displaystyle\int_0^1 f'(x)f''(x)\,dx$, where $f'(0) = 3$ and $f'(1) = 2$

111. $\displaystyle\int \left(f^{(p)}(x)\right)^n f^{(p+1)}(x)\,dx$, where p is a positive integer, $n \neq -1$

112. $\displaystyle\int 2\left(f^2(x) + 2f(x)\right)f(x)f'(x)\,dx$

113–115. More than one way *Occasionally, two different substitutions do the job. Use both of the given substitutions to evaluate the following integrals.*

113. $\displaystyle\int_0^1 x\sqrt{x + a}\, dx;\ a > 0$ $(u = \sqrt{x + a}\text{ and } u = x + a)$

114. $\displaystyle\int_0^1 x\sqrt[p]{x + a}\, dx;\ a > 0$ $(u = \sqrt[p]{x + a}\text{ and } u = x + a)$

115. $\displaystyle\int \sec^3 \theta \tan \theta\, d\theta$ $(u = \cos \theta\text{ and } u = \sec \theta)$

116. $\sin^2 ax$ and $\cos^2 ax$ integrals Use the Substitution Rule to prove that

$$\int \sin^2 ax\, dx = \frac{x}{2} - \frac{\sin (2ax)}{4a} + C \quad\text{and}$$

$$\int \cos^2 ax\, dx = \frac{x}{2} + \frac{\sin (2ax)}{4a} + C.$$

117. Integral of $\sin^2 x \cos^2 x$ Consider the integral
$I = \int \sin^2 x \cos^2 x\, dx$.

a. Find I using the identity $\sin 2x = 2 \sin x \cos x$.
b. Find I using the identity $\cos^2 x = 1 - \sin^2 x$.
c. Confirm that the results in parts (a) and (b) are consistent and compare the work involved in each method.

118. Substitution: shift Perhaps the simplest change of variables is the shift or translation given by $u = x + c$, where c is a real number.

a. Prove that shifting a function does not change the net area under the curve, in the sense that

$$\int_a^b f(x + c)\, dx = \int_{a+c}^{b+c} f(u)\, du.$$

b. Draw a picture to illustrate this change of variables in the case that $f(x) = \sin x$, $a = 0$, $b = \pi$, and $c = \pi/2$.

119. Substitution: scaling Another change of variables that can be interpreted geometrically is the scaling $u = cx$, where c is a real number. Prove and interpret the fact that

$$\int_a^b f(cx)\, dx = \frac{1}{c}\int_{ac}^{bc} f(u)\, du.$$

Draw a picture to illustrate this change of variables in the case that $f(x) = \sin x$, $a = 0$, $b = \pi$, and $c = \frac{1}{2}$.

120–123. Multiple substitutions *Use two or more substitutions to find the following integrals.*

120. $\displaystyle\int x \sin^4 x^2 \cos x^2\, dx$ (*Hint:* Begin with $u = x^2$; then use $v = \sin u$.)

121. $\displaystyle\int \frac{dx}{\sqrt{1 + \sqrt{1 + x}}}$ (*Hint:* Begin with $u = \sqrt{1 + x}$.)

122. $\displaystyle\int \tan^{10} 4x \sec^2 4x\, dx$ (*Hint:* Begin with $u = 4x$.)

123. $\displaystyle\int_0^{\pi/2} \frac{\cos \theta \sin \theta}{\sqrt{\cos^2 \theta + 16}}\, d\theta$ (*Hint:* Begin with $u = \cos \theta$.)

QUICK CHECK ANSWERS

1. $u = x^4 + 5$ **2.** With $u = x^5 + 6$, we have $du = 5x^4$, and x^4 does not appear in the integrand. **3.** New equation: $u^2 - 13u + 36 = 0$; roots: $x = \pm 2, \pm 3$ ◄

5.7 Numerical Integration

Situations arise in which the analytical methods we have developed so far cannot be used to evaluate a definite integral. For example, an integrand may not have an obvious antiderivative (such as $\cos x^2$ and $1/\ln x$), or perhaps the integrand is represented by individual data points, which makes finding an antiderivative impossible.

When analytical methods fail, we often turn to *numerical methods*, which are typically done on a calculator or computer. These methods do not produce exact values of definite integrals, but they provide approximations that are generally quite accurate. Many calculators, software packages, and computer algebra systems have built-in numerical integration methods. In this section, we explore some of these methods.

Absolute and Relative Error

Because numerical methods do not typically produce exact results, we should be concerned about the accuracy of approximations, which leads to the ideas of *absolute* and *relative error.*

> **DEFINITIONS Absolute and Relative Error**
>
> Suppose c is a computed numerical solution to a problem having an exact solution x. There are two common measures of the error in c as an approximation to x:
>
> $$\text{absolute error} = |c - x|$$
>
> and
>
> $$\text{relative error} = \frac{|c - x|}{|x|} \quad (\text{if } x \neq 0).$$

EXAMPLE 1   Absolute and relative error

The ancient Greeks used $\frac{22}{7}$ to approximate the value of π. Determine the absolute and relative error in this approximation to π.

SOLUTION Letting $c = \frac{22}{7}$ be the approximate value of $x = \pi$, we find that

$$\text{absolute error} = \left| \frac{22}{7} - \pi \right| \approx 1.3 \times 10^{-3}$$

and

$$\text{relative error} = \frac{|22/7 - \pi|}{|\pi|} \approx 4.0 \times 10^{-4} \approx 0.04\%.$$

Related Exercises 7–10 ◄

Midpoint Rule

Many numerical integration methods are based on the ideas that underlie Riemann sums; these methods approximate the net area of regions bounded by curves. A typical problem is shown in Figure 5.62, where we see a function f defined on an interval $[a, b]$. The goal is to approximate the value of $\int_a^b f(x)\, dx$. As with Riemann sums, we first partition the interval $[a, b]$ into n subintervals of equal length $\Delta x = (b - a)/n$. This partition establishes $n + 1$ grid points

$$x_0 = a, \quad x_1 = a + \Delta x, \quad x_2 = a + 2\Delta x, \ldots, \quad x_k = a + k\Delta x, \ldots, \quad x_n = b.$$

The kth subinterval is $[x_{k-1}, x_k]$, for $k = 1, 2, \ldots, n$.

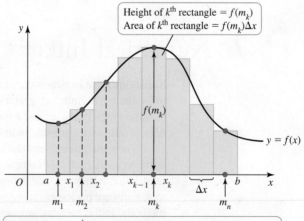

Midpoint Rule: $\displaystyle\int_a^b f(x)\, dx \approx f(m_1)\Delta x + f(m_2)\Delta x + \cdots + f(m_n)\Delta x$

FIGURE 5.62

The Midpoint Rule approximates the region under the curve using rectangles. The bases of the rectangles have width Δx. The height of the kth rectangle is $f(m_k)$, where $m_k = (x_{k-1} + x_k)/2$ is the midpoint of the kth subinterval (Figure 5.62). Therefore, the net area of the kth rectangle is $f(m_k)\Delta x$.

Let $M(n)$ be the Midpoint Rule approximation to the integral using n rectangles. Summing the net areas of the rectangles, we have

$$\int_a^b f(x)\,dx \approx M(n)$$

$$= f(m_1)\Delta x + f(m_2)\Delta x + \cdots + f(m_n)\Delta x$$

$$= \sum_{k=1}^n f\left(\frac{x_{k-1} + x_k}{2}\right)\Delta x.$$

> Recall that if $f(m_k) < 0$ for some k, then the net area of that rectangle is negative, which makes a negative contribution to the approximation (Section 5.3).

Just as with Riemann sums, the Midpoint Rule approximations to $\int_a^b f(x)\,dx$ generally improve as n increases.

> The Midpoint Rule is a midpoint Riemann sum, introduced in Section 5.2.

DEFINITION Midpoint Rule

Suppose f is defined and integrable on $[a, b]$. The **Midpoint Rule approximation** to $\int_a^b f(x)\,dx$ using n equally spaced subintervals on $[a, b]$ is

$$M(n) = f(m_1)\Delta x + f(m_2)\Delta x + \cdots + f(m_n)\Delta x$$

$$= \sum_{k=1}^n f\left(\frac{x_{k-1} + x_k}{2}\right)\Delta x,$$

where $\Delta x = (b - a)/n$, $x_k = a + k\Delta x$, and m_k is the midpoint of $[x_{k-1}, x_k]$, for $k = 1, \ldots, n$.

QUICK CHECK 1 To apply the Midpoint Rule on the interval $[3, 11]$ with $n = 4$, at what points must the integrand be evaluated? ◄

EXAMPLE 2 Applying the Midpoint Rule Approximate $\int_2^4 x^2\,dx$ using the Midpoint Rule with $n = 4$ and $n = 8$ subintervals.

SOLUTION With $a = 2, b = 4$, and $n = 4$ subintervals, the length of each subinterval is $\Delta x = (b - a)/n = 2/4 = 0.5$. The grid points are

$$x_0 = 2, \quad x_1 = 2.5, \quad x_2 = 3, \quad x_3 = 3.5, \quad \text{and} \quad x_4 = 4.$$

The integrand must be evaluated at the midpoints (Figure 5.63)

$$m_1 = 2.25, \quad m_2 = 2.75, \quad m_3 = 3.25, \quad \text{and} \quad m_4 = 3.75.$$

With $f(x) = x^2$ and $n = 4$, the Midpoint Rule approximation is

$$M(4) = f(m_1)\Delta x + f(m_2)\Delta x + f(m_3)\Delta x + f(m_4)\Delta x$$

$$= (m_1^2 + m_2^2 + m_3^2 + m_4^2)\Delta x$$

$$= (2.25^2 + 2.75^2 + 3.25^2 + 3.75^2) \cdot 0.5$$

$$= 18.625.$$

The exact area of the region is $\frac{56}{3}$, so this Midpoint Rule approximation has an absolute error of

$$|18.625 - 56/3| \approx 0.042$$

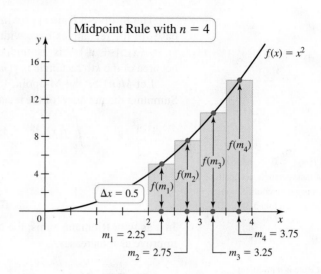

Midpoint Rule with $n = 4$

$f(x) = x^2$

$\Delta x = 0.5$

$f(m_1)$ $f(m_2)$ $f(m_3)$ $f(m_4)$

$m_1 = 2.25$ $m_4 = 3.75$
$m_2 = 2.75$ $m_3 = 3.25$

FIGURE 5.63

and a relative error of

$$\left| \frac{18.625 - 56/3}{56/3} \right| \approx 2.2 \times 10^{-3} = 0.223\%.$$

Using $n = 8$ subintervals, the midpoint approximation is

$$M(8) = \sum_{k=1}^{8} f(m_k) \Delta x = 18.65625,$$

which has an absolute error of about 0.0104 and a relative error of about 0.0558%. We see that increasing n and using more rectangles decreases the error in the approximations.

Related Exercises 11–14 ◄

The Trapezoid Rule

Area of a trapezoid

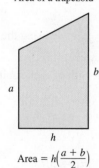

$$\text{Area} = h\left(\frac{a + b}{2}\right)$$

Another numerical method for estimating $\int_a^b f(x)\, dx$ is the Trapezoid Rule, which uses the same partition of the interval $[a, b]$ described for the Midpoint Rule. Instead of approximating the region under the curve by rectangles, the Trapezoid Rule uses (what else?) trapezoids. The bases of the trapezoids have length Δx. The sides of the kth trapezoid have lengths $f(x_{k-1})$ and $f(x_k)$, for $k = 1, 2, \ldots, n$ (Figure 5.64). Therefore, the net area of the kth trapezoid is $\left(\dfrac{f(x_{k-1}) + f(x_k)}{2}\right)\Delta x$.

Letting $T(n)$ be the Trapezoid Rule approximation to the integral using n subintervals, we have

> This derivation of the Trapezoid Rule assumes that f is nonnegative on $[a, b]$. However, the same argument can be used if f is negative on all or part of $[a, b]$. In fact, the argument illustrates how negative contributions to the net area arise when f is negative.

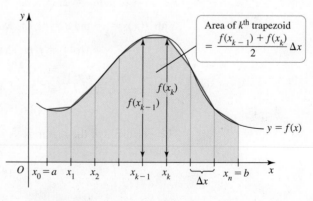

Area of kth trapezoid
$$= \frac{f(x_{k-1}) + f(x_k)}{2}\Delta x$$

$f(x_k)$

$f(x_{k-1})$

$y = f(x)$

$x_0 = a$ x_1 x_2 x_{k-1} x_k Δx $x_n = b$

Trapezoid Rule: $\int_a^b f(x)\,dx \approx \left(\frac{1}{2}f(x_0) + f(x_1) + \cdots + f(x_{n-1}) + \frac{1}{2}f(x_n)\right)\Delta x$

FIGURE 5.64

$$\int_a^b f(x)\, dx \approx T(n)$$

$$= \underbrace{\left(\frac{f(x_0) + f(x_1)}{2}\right)\Delta x}_{\text{area of first trapezoid}} + \underbrace{\left(\frac{f(x_1) + f(x_2)}{2}\right)\Delta x}_{\text{area of second trapezoid}} + \cdots + \underbrace{\left(\frac{f(x_{n-1}) + f(x_n)}{2}\right)\Delta x}_{\text{area of nth trapezoid}}$$

$$= \left(\frac{f(x_0)}{2} + \underbrace{\frac{f(x_1)}{2} + \frac{f(x_1)}{2}}_{f(x_1)} + \cdots + \underbrace{\frac{f(x_{n-1})}{2} + \frac{f(x_{n-1})}{2}}_{f(x_{n-1})} + \frac{f(x_n)}{2}\right)\Delta x$$

$$= \left(\frac{f(x_0)}{2} + \underbrace{f(x_1) + \cdots + f(x_{n-1})}_{\sum_{k=1}^{n-1} f(x_k)} + \frac{f(x_n)}{2}\right)\Delta x.$$

As with the Midpoint Rule, the Trapezoid Rule approximations generally improve as n increases.

DEFINITION Trapezoid Rule

Suppose f is defined and integrable on $[a, b]$. The **Trapezoid Rule approximation** to $\int_a^b f(x)\, dx$ using n equally spaced subintervals on $[a, b]$ is

$$T(n) = \left(\frac{1}{2}f(x_0) + \sum_{k=1}^{n-1} f(x_k) + \frac{1}{2}f(x_n)\right)\Delta x,$$

where $\Delta x = (b - a)/n$ and $x_k = a + k\Delta x$, for $k = 0, 1, \ldots, n$.

QUICK CHECK 2 Does the Trapezoid Rule underestimate or overestimate the value of $\int_0^4 x^2\, dx$? ◄

EXAMPLE 3 Applying the Trapezoid Rule Approximate $\int_2^4 x^2\, dx$ using the Trapezoid Rule with $n = 4$ subintervals.

SOLUTION As in Example 2, the grid points are

$$x_0 = 2, \quad x_1 = 2.5, \quad x_2 = 3, \quad x_3 = 3.5, \quad \text{and} \quad x_4 = 4.$$

With $f(x) = x^2$ and $n = 4$, the Trapezoid Rule approximation is

$$\begin{aligned} T(4) &= \tfrac{1}{2}f(x_0)\Delta x + f(x_1)\Delta x + f(x_2)\Delta x + f(x_3)\Delta x + \tfrac{1}{2}f(x_4)\Delta x \\ &= \left(\tfrac{1}{2}x_0^2 + x_1^2 + x_2^2 + x_3^2 + \tfrac{1}{2}x_4^2\right)\Delta x \\ &= \left(\tfrac{1}{2}\cdot 2^2 + 2.5^2 + 3^2 + 3.5^2 + \tfrac{1}{2}\cdot 4^2\right)\cdot 0.5 \\ &= 18.75. \end{aligned}$$

Figure 5.65 shows the approximation with $n = 4$ trapezoids. The exact area of the region is $56/3$, so the Trapezoid Rule approximation has an absolute error of about 0.0833 and a relative error of approximately 0.45%. Increasing n decreases this error.

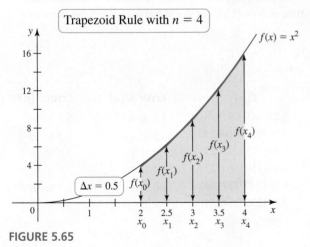

Trapezoid Rule with $n = 4$

$f(x) = x^2$

Related Exercises 15–18 ◄

FIGURE 5.65

EXAMPLE 4   Errors in the Midpoint and Trapezoid Rules Given that

$$\int_0^1 xe^{-x}\,dx = 1 - 2e^{-1},$$

find the absolute errors in the Midpoint Rule and Trapezoid Rule approximations to the integral with $n = 4, 8, 16, 32, 64$, and 128 subintervals.

SOLUTION Because the exact value of the integral is known (which often does *not* happen in practice), we can compute the error in various approximations. For example, if $n = 16$, then

$$\Delta x = \frac{1}{16} \quad \text{and} \quad x_k = \frac{k}{16}, \quad \text{for } k = 0, 1, \ldots, n.$$

Using sigma notation and a calculator, we have

$$M(16) = \sum_{k=1}^{16} f\left(\overbrace{\frac{(k-1)/16}{}}^{x_{k-1}} + \overbrace{\frac{k/16}{}}^{x_k} \middle/ 2 \right) \overbrace{\frac{1}{16}}^{\Delta x} = \sum_{k=1}^{16} f\left(\frac{2k-1}{32} \right) \frac{1}{16} \approx 0.26440383609318$$

and

$$T(16) = \left(\frac{1}{2}\underbrace{f(0)}_{x_0 = a} + \sum_{k=1}^{15} \underbrace{f(k/16)}_{x_k} + \frac{1}{2}\underbrace{f(1)}_{x_{16} = b} \right) \frac{1}{16} \approx 0.26391564480235.$$

The absolute error in the Midpoint Rule approximation with $n = 16$ is $|M(16) - (1 - 2e^{-1})| \approx 1.6 \times 10^{-4}$. The absolute error in the Trapezoid Rule approximation with $n = 16$ is $|T(16) - (1 - 2e^{-1})| \approx 3.3 \times 10^{-3}$.

The Midpoint Rule and Trapezoid Rule approximations to the integral, together with the associated absolute errors, are shown in Table 5.7 for various values of n. Notice that as n increases, the errors in both methods decrease, as expected. With $n = 128$ subintervals, the approximations $M(128)$ and $T(128)$ agree to four decimal places. Based on these approximations, a good approximation to the integral is 0.2642. The way in which the errors decrease is also worth noting. If you look carefully at both error columns in Table 5.7, you will see that each time n is doubled (or Δx is halved), the error decreases by a factor of approximately 4.

Table 5.7

n	$M(n)$	$T(n)$	Error $M(n)$	Error $T(n)$
4	0.26683456310319	0.25904504019141	2.6×10^{-3}	5.2×10^{-3}
8	0.26489148795740	0.26293980164730	6.5×10^{-4}	1.3×10^{-3}
16	0.26440383609318	0.26391564480235	1.6×10^{-4}	3.3×10^{-4}
32	0.26428180513718	0.26415974044777	4.1×10^{-5}	8.1×10^{-5}
64	0.26425129001915	0.26422077279247	1.0×10^{-5}	2.0×10^{-5}
128	0.26424366077837	0.26423603140581	2.5×10^{-6}	5.1×10^{-6}

Related Exercises 19–26 ◄

QUICK CHECK 3 Compute the approximate factor by which the error decreases in Table 7.5 between $T(16)$ and $T(32)$; between $T(32)$ and $T(64)$. ◄

We now apply the Midpoint and Trapezoid Rules to a problem with actual data.

EXAMPLE 5   World oil production Table 5.8 and Figure 5.66 show data for the rate of world crude oil production (in billions of barrels/yr) over a 16-year period. If the rate of oil production is given by the function R, then the total amount of oil produced in

Table 5.8

Year	World Crude Oil Production (billions barrels/yr)
1995	21.9
1996	22.3
1997	23.0
1998	23.7
1999	24.5
2000	23.7
2001	25.2
2002	24.8
2003	24.5
2004	25.2
2005	25.9
2006	26.3
2007	27.0
2008	26.9
2009	26.4
2010	27.0
2011	27.0

(*Source:* U.S. Energy Information Administration.)

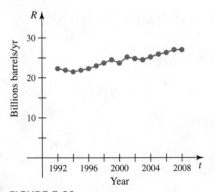

FIGURE 5.66
(*Source:* U.S. Energy Information Administration)

billions of barrels over the time period $a \leq t \leq b$ is $Q = \int_a^b R(t)\, dt$ (Section 6.1). Use the Midpoint and Trapezoid Rules to approximate the total oil produced between 1995 and 2011.

SOLUTION For convenience, let $t = 0$ represent 1995 and $t = 16$ represent 2011. We let $R(t)$ be the rate of oil production in the year corresponding to t (for example, $R(6) = 25.2$ is the rate in 2001). The goal is to approximate $Q = \int_0^{16} R(t)\, dt$. If we use $n = 4$ subintervals, then $\Delta t = 4$ yr. The resulting Midpoint and Trapezoid Rule approximations (in billions of barrels) are

$$Q \approx M(4) = (R(2) + R(6) + R(10) + R(14))\Delta t$$
$$= (23.0 + 25.2 + 25.9 + 26.4)4$$
$$= 402.0$$

and

$$Q \approx T(4) = \left[\frac{1}{2}R(0) + R(4) + R(8) + R(12) + \frac{1}{2}R(16) \right]\Delta t$$
$$= \left(\frac{1}{2} \cdot 21.9 + 24.5 + 24.5 + 27.0 + \frac{1}{2} \cdot 27.0 \right)4$$
$$= 401.8.$$

The two methods give reasonable agreement. Using $n = 8$ subintervals, with $\Delta t = 2$ yr, similar calculations give the approximations

$$Q \approx M(8) = 399.8 \quad \text{and} \quad Q \approx T(8) = 401.9.$$

The given data do not allow us to compute the next Midpoint Rule approximation $M(16)$. However, we can compute the next Trapezoid Rule approximation $T(16)$, and here is a good way to do it. If $T(n)$ and $M(n)$ are known, then the next Trapezoid Rule approximation is

$$T(2n) = \frac{T(n) + M(n)}{2}.$$

Using this trick, we find that

$$T(16) = \frac{T(8) + M(8)}{2} = \frac{401.9 + 399.8}{2} \approx 400.9.$$

Based on these calculations, the best approximation to the total oil produced between 1995 and 2011 is 400.9 billion barrels.

Related Exercises 27–28 ◄

General Partitions

The Trapezoid Rule, and left and right Riemann sums can be used to approximate integrals when the integrand is given at non-uniformly spaced grid points. Suppose $\int_a^b f(x)\, dx$ is to be approximated using the grid points

$$x_0 = a < x_1 < x_2 < \cdots < x_{n-1} < x_n = b.$$

As noted in Section 5.3, each subinterval in a general partition may have a different length, which we denote $\Delta x_k = x_k - x_{k-1}$, for $k = 1, 2, \ldots, n$. With this change, the formulas for the left and right Riemann sums still apply. To obtain the formula for the Trapezoid Rule, we sum the areas of the individual trapezoids. The result with n subintervals is

$$\int_a^b f(x)\,dx \approx T(n) = \underbrace{\frac{1}{2}(f(x_0) + f(x_1))\Delta x_1}_{\text{area of first trapezoid}} + \cdots + \underbrace{\frac{1}{2}(f(x_{n-1}) + f(x_n))\Delta x_n}_{\text{area of }n\text{th trapezoid}}$$

$$= \frac{1}{2}\sum_{k=1}^{n}(f(x_{k-1}) + f(x_k))\Delta x_k.$$

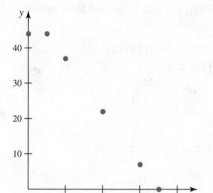

FIGURE 5.67

EXAMPLE 6 Estimating distance with a general partition A car is traveling 44 ft/s (30 mi/hr) when a deer leaps onto the road in front of the car. The alert driver applies the brakes and decelerates. The velocity of the car t seconds after the driver sees the deer is $v(t)$, values of which are given in the following table. If the car stops just before reaching the deer, how far did it travel on the time interval $[0, 3.5]$? Assume that the velocity function is constant on the interval $[0, 0.5]$ (due to the reaction time of the driver) and decreases on the interval $[0.5, 3.5]$ (Figure 5.67).

t (seconds)	0	0.5	1	2	3	3.5
$v(t)$ (ft/sec)	44	44	37	22	7	0

SOLUTION The distance traveled is $\int_0^{3.5} v(t)\,dt$, which we approximate using three methods with $n = 5$ subintervals. First notice that the lengths of the subintervals are

$$\Delta t_1 = 0.5,\ \Delta t_2 = 0.5,\ \Delta t_3 = 1,\ \Delta t_4 = 1,\ \text{and}\ \Delta t_5 = 0.5.$$

The estimate of the distance traveled given by the Trapezoid Rule is

$$\int_0^{3.5} v(t)\,dt \approx \frac{1}{2}(v(0) + v(0.5))\Delta t_1 + \frac{1}{2}(v(0.5) + v(1))\Delta t_2 + \frac{1}{2}(v(1) + v(2))\Delta t_3$$

$$+ \frac{1}{2}(v(2) + v(3))\Delta t_4 + \frac{1}{2}(v(3) + v(3.5))\Delta t_5$$

$$= \frac{1}{2}(44 + 44)\cdot 0.5 + \frac{1}{2}(44 + 37)\cdot 0.5 + \frac{1}{2}(37 + 22)\cdot 1$$

$$+ \frac{1}{2}(22 + 7)\cdot 1 + \frac{1}{2}(7 + 0)\cdot 0.5$$

$$= 88.$$

The approximation given by the left Riemann sum is

$$\int_0^{3.5} v(t)\,dt \approx v(0)\Delta t_1 + v(0.5)\Delta t_2 + v(1)\Delta t_3 + v(2)\Delta t_4 + v(3)\Delta t_5$$

$$= 44\cdot 0.5 + 44\cdot 0.5 + 37\cdot 1 + 22\cdot 1 + 7\cdot 0.5$$

$$= 106.5.$$

The approximation given by the right Riemann sum is

$$\int_0^{3.5} v(t)\,dt \approx v(0.5)\Delta t_1 + v(1)\Delta t_2 + v(2)\Delta t_3 + v(3)\Delta t_4 + v(3.5)\Delta t_5$$

$$= 44\cdot 0.5 + 37\cdot 0.5 + 22\cdot 1 + 7\cdot 1 + 0\cdot 0.5$$

$$= 69.5.$$

We see considerable discrepancies in these estimates. The fact that the velocity values decrease in time explains why the left Riemann sum overestimates the distance traveled and the right Riemann sum underestimates the distance. For the velocity function shown in Figure 5.67, the trapezoids (used by the Trapezoid Rule) provide a better approximation to the area under the velocity curve. A reasonable estimate of the distance traveled by the car is 88 ft.

Related Exercises 29–30

Errors in Numerical Integration

A detailed analysis of the errors in the methods we have discussed goes beyond the scope of the book. We state without proof the standard error theorems for these methods and note that Examples 2, 3, and 4 are consistent with these results.

THEOREM 5.12   Errors in Numerical Integration

Assume that f'' is continuous on the interval $[a, b]$ and that k is a real number such that $|f''(x)| < k$, for all x in $[a, b]$. The absolute errors in approximating the integral $\int_a^b f(x)\, dx$ by the Midpoint Rule and Trapezoid Rule with n subintervals satisfy the inequalities

$$E_M \le \frac{k(b-a)}{24}(\Delta x)^2 \quad \text{and} \quad E_T \le \frac{k(b-a)}{12}(\Delta x)^2,$$

respectively, where $\Delta x = (b-a)/n$.

The absolute errors associated with the Midpoint Rule and Trapezoid Rule are proportional to $(\Delta x)^2$. So if Δx is reduced by a factor of 2, the errors decrease roughly by a factor of 4, as shown in Example 4.

SECTION 5.7 EXERCISES

Review Questions

1. If the interval $[4, 18]$ is partitioned into $n = 28$ subintervals of equal length, what is Δx?

2. Explain geometrically how the Midpoint Rule is used to approximate a definite integral.

3. Explain geometrically how the Trapezoid Rule is used to approximate a definite integral.

4. If the Midpoint Rule is used on the interval $[-1, 11]$ with $n = 3$ subintervals, at what x-coordinates is the integrand evaluated?

5. If the Trapezoid Rule is used on the interval $[-1, 9]$ with $n = 5$ subintervals, at what x-coordinates is the integrand evaluated?

6. Describe how the errors in Trapezoid Rule approximations decrease as Δx decreases.

Basic Skills

7–10. Absolute and relative error *Compute the absolute and relative errors in using c to approximate x.*

7. $x = \pi;\ c = 3.14$

8. $x = \sqrt{2};\ c = 1.414$

9. $x = e;\ c = 2.72$

10. $x = e;\ c = 2.718$

11–14. Midpoint Rule approximations *Find the indicated Midpoint Rule approximations to the following integrals.*

11. $\int_2^{10} 2x^2\, dx$ using $n = 1, 2,$ and 4 subintervals

12. $\int_1^9 x^3\, dx$ using $n = 1, 2,$ and 4 subintervals

13. $\int_0^1 \sin \pi x\, dx$ using $n = 6$ subintervals

14. $\int_0^1 e^{-x}\, dx$ using $n = 8$ subintervals

15–18. Trapezoid Rule approximations *Find the indicated Trapezoid Rule approximations to the following integrals.*

15. $\int_2^{10} 2x^2\, dx$ using $n = 2, 4,$ and 8 subintervals

16. $\int_1^9 x^3\, dx$ using $n = 2, 4,$ and 8 subintervals

17. $\int_0^1 \sin \pi x\, dx$ using $n = 6$ subintervals

18. $\int_0^1 e^{-x}\, dx$ using $n = 8$ subintervals

19. Midpoint Rule, Trapezoid Rule, and relative error Find the Midpoint and Trapezoid Rule approximations to $\int_0^1 \sin \pi x \, dx$ using $n = 25$ subintervals. Compute the relative error of each approximation.

20. Midpoint Rule, Trapezoid Rule, and relative error Find the Midpoint and Trapezoid Rule approximations to $\int_0^1 e^{-x} \, dx$ using $n = 50$ subintervals. Compute the relative error of each approximation.

21–26. Comparing the Midpoint and Trapezoid Rules *Apply the Midpoint and Trapezoid Rules to the following integrals. Make a table similar to Table 5.7 showing the approximations and errors for $n = 4, 8, 16,$ and 32. The exact values of the integrals are given for computing the error.*

21. $\int_1^5 (3x^2 - 2x) \, dx = 100$ **22.** $\int_{-2}^6 \left(\dfrac{x^3}{16} - x\right) dx = 4$

23. $\int_0^{\pi/4} 3 \sin 2x \, dx = \frac{3}{2}$ **24.** $\int_1^e \ln x \, dx = 1$

25. $\int_0^\pi \sin x \cos 3x \, dx = 0$

26. $\int_0^8 e^{-2x} \, dx = \dfrac{1 - e^{-16}}{2} \approx 0.4999999$

27–28. Temperature data *Hourly temperature data for Boulder, CO, and San Francisco, CA over a 12-hr period on the same day of January are shown in the figure. Assume that these data are taken from a continuous temperature function $T(t)$. The average temperature over the 12-hr period is $\overline{T} = \dfrac{1}{12} \int_0^{12} T(t) \, dt$.*

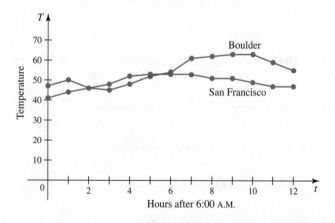

t	0	1	2	3	4	5	6	7	8	9	10	11	12
B	47	50	46	45	48	52	54	61	62	63	63	59	55
SF	41	44	46	48	52	53	53	53	51	51	49	47	47

27. Find an accurate approximation to the average temperature over the 12-hr period for Boulder. State your method.

28. Find an accurate approximation to the average temperature over the 12-hr period for San Francisco. State your method.

29. Approximating integrals A curling iron is plugged into an outlet at time $t = 0$. Its temperature T in degrees Fahrenheit, assumed to be a continuous function that is strictly increasing and concave down on $0 \le t \le 120$, is given at various times (in seconds) in the table.

t (seconds)	0	20	45	60	90	110	120
$T(t)$ (°F)	70	130	200	239	311	355	375

a. Approximate $\dfrac{1}{120} \int_0^{120} T(t) \, dt$ in three ways: using a left Riemann sum, a right Riemann sum, and the Trapezoid Rule. Interpret the value of $\dfrac{1}{120} \int_0^{120} T(t) \, dt$ in the context of this problem.

b. Which of the estimates in part (a) overestimate the value of $\dfrac{1}{120} \int_0^{120} T(t) \, dt$? Underestimate? Justify your answers with a simple sketch of the sums you computed.

c. Evaluate and interpret $\int_0^{120} T'(t) \, dt$ in the context of this problem.

30. Approximating integrals The function f is twice differentiable on $(-\infty, \infty)$. Values of f at various points on $[0, 20]$ are given in the table.

x	0	4	7	12	14	18	20
$f(x)$	3	0	-2	-1	2	4	7

a. Approximate $\int_0^{20} f(x) \, dx$ in three ways: using a left Riemann sum, a right Riemann sum, and the Trapezoid Rule.

b. A scatterplot of the data in the table is provided in the figure. Use the scatterplot to illustrate each of the approximations in part (a) by sketching appropriate rectangles for the Riemann sums and by sketching trapezoids for the Trapezoid Rule approximation.

c. Evaluate $\int_4^{12} (3f'(x) + 2) \, dx$.

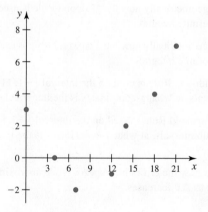

Further Explorations

31. Explain why or why not Determine whether the following statements are true and give an explanation or counterexample.

    a. The Trapezoid Rule is exact when used to approximate the definite integral of a linear function.

    b. If the number of subintervals used in the Midpoint Rule is increased by a factor of 3, the error is expected to decrease by a factor of 8.

    c. If the number of subintervals used in the Trapezoid Rule is increased by a factor of 4, the error is expected to decrease by a factor of 16.

32–35. Comparing the Midpoint and Trapezoid Rules *Compare the errors in the Midpoint and Trapezoid Rules with n = 4, 8, 16, and 32 subintervals when they are applied to the following integrals (with their exact values given).*

32. $\displaystyle\int_0^{\pi/2} \sin^6 x \, dx = \frac{5\pi}{32}$ **33.** $\displaystyle\int_0^{\pi/2} \cos^9 x \, dx = \frac{128}{315}$

34. $\displaystyle\int_0^1 (8x^7 - 7x^8) \, dx = \frac{2}{9}$ **35.** $\displaystyle\int_0^\pi \ln(5 + 3\cos x) \, dx = \pi \ln \frac{9}{2}$

Applications and Technology Exercises

36. Period of a pendulum A standard pendulum of length L swinging under only the influence of gravity (no resistance) has a period of

$$T = \frac{4}{\omega} \int_0^{\pi/2} \frac{d\varphi}{\sqrt{1 - k^2 \sin^2 \varphi}},$$

where $\omega^2 = g/L$, $k^2 = \sin^2(\theta_0/2)$, $g \approx 9.8 \text{ m/s}^2$ is the acceleration due to gravity, and θ_0 is the initial angle from which the pendulum is released (in radians). Use numerical integration to approximate the period of a pendulum with $L = 1$ m that is released from an angle of $\theta_0 = \pi/4$ rad.

37. Arc length of an ellipse The length of an ellipse with axes of length $2a$ and $2b$ is

$$\int_0^{2\pi} \sqrt{a^2 \cos^2 t + b^2 \sin^2 t} \, dt.$$

Use numerical integration and experiment with different values of n to approximate the length of an ellipse with $a = 4$ and $b = 8$.

38. Sine integral The theory of diffraction produces the sine integral function $\text{Si}(x) = \displaystyle\int_0^x \frac{\sin t}{t} \, dt$. Use the Midpoint Rule to approximate $\text{Si}(1)$ and $\text{Si}(10)$. (Recall that $\lim_{x\to 0} (\sin x)/x = 1$.) Experiment with the number of subintervals until you obtain approximations that have an error less than 10^{-3}. A rule of thumb is that if two successive approximations differ by less than 10^{-3}, then the error is usually less than 10^{-3}.

39. Normal distribution of heights The heights of U.S. men are normally distributed with a mean of 69 inches and a standard deviation of 3 inches. This means that the fraction of men with a height between a and b (with $a < b$) inches is given by the integral

$$\frac{1}{3\sqrt{2\pi}} \int_a^b e^{-((x-69)/3)^2/2} \, dx.$$

What percentage of American men are between 66 and 72 inches tall? Use the method of your choice, and experiment with the number of subintervals until you obtain successive approximations that differ by less than 10^{-3}.

40. Normal distribution of movie lengths A recent study revealed that the lengths of U.S. movies are normally distributed with a mean of 110 minutes and a standard deviation of 22 minutes. This means that the fraction of movies with lengths between a and b minutes (with $a < b$) is given by the integral

$$\frac{1}{22\sqrt{2\pi}} \int_a^b e^{-((x-110)/22)^2/2} \, dx.$$

What percentage of U.S. movies are between 1 hr and 1.5 hr long (60–90 min)?

41. U.S. oil produced and imported The figure shows the rate at which U.S. oil was produced and imported between 1920 and 2005 in units of millions of barrels per day. The total amount of oil produced or imported is given by the area of the region under the corresponding curve. Be careful with units because both days and years are used in this data set.

    a. Use numerical integration to estimate the amount of U.S. oil produced between 1940 and 2000. Use the method of your choice and experiment with values of n.

    b. Use numerical integration to estimate the amount of oil imported between 1940 and 2000. Use the method of your choice and experiment with values of n.

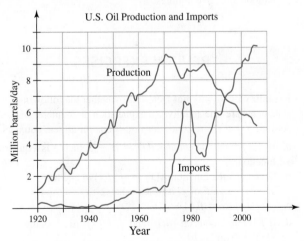

(*Source:* U.S. Energy Information Administration)

42. Estimating area with non-uniform data A piece of wood paneling must be cut in the shape shown in the figure. The coordinates of several points on its curved surface are also shown (with units of inches).

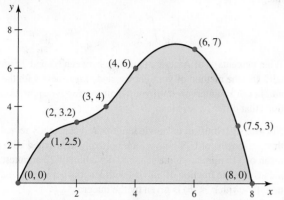

a. Estimate the surface area of the paneling using the Trapezoid Rule.
b. Estimate the surface area of the paneling using a left Riemann sum.
c. Could two identical pieces be cut from a 9-in by 9-in piece of wood? Answer carefully.

43. Estimating elevation with non-uniform data A hot-air balloon is launched from an elevation of 5400 ft above sea level. As it rises, the vertical velocity is computed using a device (called a variometer) that measures the change in atmospheric pressure. The vertical velocities at selected times are shown in the table (with units of ft/min).

t (min)	0	1	1.5	3	3.5	4	5
Velocity (ft/min)	0	100	120	150	110	90	80

a. Use the Trapezoid Rule to estimate the elevation of the balloon after five minutes. Remember that the balloon starts at an elevation of 5400 ft.
b. Use a right Riemann sum to estimate the elevation of the balloon after five minutes.

c. A polynomial that fits the data reasonably well is

$$g(t) = 3.49t^3 - 43.21t^2 + 142.43t - 1.75.$$

Estimate the elevation of the balloon after five minutes using this polynomial.

Additional Exercises

⊤ **44. Estimating error** Refer to Theorem 5.12 and let $f(x) = e^{x^2}$.
   a. Find a Trapezoid Rule approximation to $\int_0^1 e^{x^2}\,dx$ using $n = 50$ subintervals.
   b. Calculate $f''(x)$.
   c. Explain why $|f''(x)| < 18$ on $[0, 1]$, given that $e < 3$.
   d. Use Theorem 5.12 to find an upper bound on the absolute error in the estimate found in part (a).

⊤ **45. Estimating error** Refer to Theorem 5.12 and let $f(x) = \sin e^x$.
   a. Find a Trapezoid Rule approximation to $\int_0^1 \sin e^x\,dx$ using $n = 40$ subintervals.
   b. Calculate $f''(x)$.
   c. Explain why $|f''(x)| < 6$ on $[0, 1]$, given that $e < 3$. (*Hint:* Graph f''.)
   d. Find an upper bound on the absolute error in the estimate found in part (a) using Theorem 5.12.

46. Exact Trapezoid Rule Prove that the Trapezoid Rule is exact (no error) when approximating the definite integral of a linear function.

47. Trapezoid Rule and concavity Suppose f is positive and its first two derivatives are continuous on $[a, b]$. If f'' is positive on $[a, b]$, then is a Trapezoid Rule estimate of $\int_a^b f(x)\,dx$ an underestimate or overestimate of the integral? Justify your answer using Theorem 5.12 and an illustration.

QUICK CHECK ANSWERS

1. 4, 6, 8, 10   **2.** Overestimates   **3.** 4 and 4 ◄

CHAPTER 5   REVIEW EXERCISES

1. Explain why or why not Determine whether the following statements are true and give an explanation or counterexample. Assume f and f' are continuous functions for all real numbers.

a. If $A(x) = \int_a^x f(t)\,dt$ and $f(t) = 2t - 3$, then A is a quadratic function.
b. Given an area function $A(x) = \int_a^x f(t)\,dt$ and an antiderivative F of f, it follows that $A'(x) = F(x)$.
c. $\int_a^b f'(x)\,dx = f(b) - f(a)$.
d. If f is continuous on $[a, b]$ and $\int_a^b |f(x)|\,dx = 0$, then $f(x) = 0$ on $[a, b]$.
e. If the average value of f on $[a, b]$ is zero, then $f(x) = 0$ on $[a, b]$.
f. $\int_a^b (2f(x) - 3g(x))\,dx = 2\int_a^b f(x)\,dx + 3\int_b^a g(x)\,dx$.
g. $\int f'(g(x))g'(x)\,dx = f(g(x)) + C$.

2–15. Indefinite integrals *Determine the following indefinite integrals.*

2. $\displaystyle \int (x^8 - 3x^3 + 1)\,dx$

3. $\displaystyle \int (2x + 1)^2\,dx$

4. $\displaystyle \int \frac{x + 1}{x}\,dx$

5. $\displaystyle \int \left(\frac{1}{x^2} - \frac{2}{x^{5/2}} \right)\,dx$

6. $\displaystyle \int \frac{x^4 - 2\sqrt{x} + 2}{x^2}\,dx$

7. $\displaystyle \int (1 + \cos 3\theta)\,d\theta$

8. $\displaystyle \int 2\sec^2 \theta\,d\theta$

9. $\displaystyle \int \sec 2x \tan 2x\,dx$

10. $\displaystyle \int 2e^{2x}\,dx$

11. $\displaystyle \int \frac{12}{x}\,dx$

12. $\displaystyle \int \frac{dx}{\sqrt{1 - x^2}}$

13. $\displaystyle \int \frac{dx}{x^2 + 1}$

14. $\displaystyle \int \frac{1 + \tan \theta}{\sec \theta}\,d\theta$

15. $\displaystyle \int (\sqrt[4]{x^3} + \sqrt{x^5})\,dx$

16–19. Functions from derivatives *Find the function with the following properties.*

16. $f'(x) = 3x^2 - 1$ and $f(0) = 10$

17. $f'(t) = \sin t + 2t$ and $f(0) = 5$

18. $g'(t) = t^2 + t^{-2}$ and $g(1) = 1$

19. $h'(x) = \sin^2 x$ and $h(1) = 1$ (*Hint:* $\sin^2 x = (1 - \cos 2x)/2$.)

20. Motion along a line Two objects move along the x-axis with position functions $x_1(t) = 2 \sin t$ and $x_2(t) = \sin(t - \pi/2)$. At what times on the interval $[0, 2\pi]$ are the objects closest to each other and farthest from each other?

21. Vertical motion with gravity A rocket is launched vertically upward with an initial velocity of 120 m/s from a platform that is 125 m above the ground. Assume that the only force at work is gravity. Determine and graph the velocity and position functions of the rocket, for $t \geq 0$. Then describe the motion in words.

22. Velocity to displacement An object travels on the x-axis with a velocity given by $v(t) = 2t + 5$, for $0 \leq t \leq 4$.

  a. How far does the object travel, for $0 \leq t \leq 4$?
  b. What is the average value of v on the interval $[0, 4]$?
  c. True or false: The object would travel as far as in part (a) if it traveled at its average velocity (a constant), for $0 \leq t \leq 4$.

23. Area by geometry Use geometry to evaluate the following definite integrals, where the graph of f is given in the figure.

  a. $\displaystyle\int_0^4 f(x)\, dx$ **b.** $\displaystyle\int_6^4 f(x)\, dx$

  c. $\displaystyle\int_5^7 f(x)\, dx$ **d.** $\displaystyle\int_0^7 f(x)\, dx$

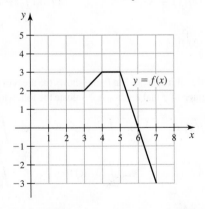

24. Displacement by geometry Use geometry to find the displacement of an object moving along a line for the time intervals (i) $0 \leq t \leq 5$, (ii) $3 \leq t \leq 7$, and (iii) $0 \leq t \leq 8$, where the graph of its velocity $v = g(t)$ is given in the figure.

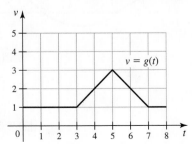

25. Ascent rate of a scuba diver Divers who ascend too quickly in the water risk *decompression illness*. A common recommendation for a maximum rate of ascent is 30 feet/minute with a 5-minute safety stop 15 feet below the surface of the water. Suppose a diver ascends to the surface in eight minutes according to the velocity function

$$v(t) = \begin{cases} 30 & \text{if } 0 \leq t \leq 2 \\ 0 & \text{if } 2 < t \leq 7 \\ 15 & \text{if } 7 < t \leq 8. \end{cases}$$

  a. Plot a graph of v.
  b. Compute the area under the velocity curve.
  c. Interpret the physical meaning of the area under the velocity curve.

26. Area functions Consider the graph of the function f in the figure, and let $F(x) = \int_0^x f(t)\, dt$ and $G(x) = \int_1^x f(t)\, dt$. Assume the graph consists of a line segment from $(0, -2)$ to $(2, 2)$ and two quarter circles of radius 2.

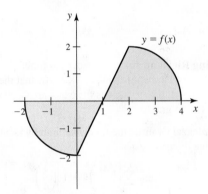

  a. Evaluate $F(2)$, $F(-2)$, and $F(4)$.
  b. Evaluate $G(-2)$, $G(0)$, and $G(4)$.
  c. Explain why there is a constant C such that $F(x) = G(x) + C$, for $-2 \leq x \leq 4$. Fill in the blank with a number:
    $F(x) = G(x) + \underline{\hspace{2cm}}$, for $-2 \leq x \leq 4$.

27. Area by geometry Use geometry to evaluate $\int_0^4 \sqrt{8x - x^2}\, dx$. (*Hint:* Complete the square of $8x - x^2$.)

28. Bagel output The manager of a bagel bakery collects the following production rate data (in bagels per minute) at six different times during the morning. Estimate the total number of bagels produced between 6:00 and 7:30 A.M. using the Trapezoid Rule, and a left and a right Riemann sum. Discuss how you would choose the best estimate of the number of bagels produced.

Time of day (A.M.)	Production rate (bagels/min)
6:00	45
6:30	75
6:45	60
7:00	50
7:30	40

29. Integration by Riemann sums Consider the integral
$\int_1^4 (3x - 2)\, dx$.

   a. Evaluate the right Riemann sum for the integral with $n = 3$.

   b. Use summation notation to write the right Riemann sum for an arbitrary positive integer n.

   c. Evaluate the definite integral by taking the limit as $n \to \infty$ of the Riemann sum in part (b).

   d. Confirm the result of part (c) by graphing $y = 3x - 2$ and using geometry to evaluate the integral, and also by evaluating $\int_1^4 (3x - 2)\, dx$ with the Fundamental Theorem of Calculus.

30–33. Limit definition of the definite integral *Use the limit definition of the definite integral with right Riemann sums and a regular partition* $\left(\int_a^b f(x)\, dx = \lim_{n \to \infty} \sum_{k=1}^{n} f(x_k^*)\Delta x \right)$ *to evaluate the following definite integrals. Use the Fundamental Theorem of Calculus to check your answer.*

30. $\int_0^1 (4x - 2)\, dx$ **31.** $\int_0^2 (x^2 - 4)\, dx$

32. $\int_1^2 (3x^2 + x)\, dx$ **33.** $\int_0^4 (x^3 - x)\, dx$

34. Evaluating Riemann sums Consider the function $f(x) = 3x + 4$ on the interval $[3, 7]$. Show that the midpoint Riemann sum with $n = 4$ gives the exact area of the region bounded by the graph.

35. Sum to integral Evaluate the following limit by identifying the integral that it represents:

$$\lim_{n \to \infty} \sum_{k=1}^{n} \left[\left(\frac{4k}{n} \right)^5 + 1 \right]\left(\frac{4}{n} \right).$$

36. Area function by geometry Use geometry to find the area $A(x)$ that is bounded by the graph of $f(t) = 2t - 4$ and the t-axis between the point $(2, 0)$ and the variable point $(x, 0)$, where $x \geq 2$. Verify that $A'(x) = f(x)$.

37–56. Evaluating integrals *Evaluate the following integrals.*

37. $\int_{-2}^2 (3x^4 - 2x + 1)\, dx$ **38.** $\int_0^{\pi/3} \cos 3x\, dx$

39. $\int_0^2 (x + 1)^3\, dx$ **40.** $\int_0^1 (4x^{21} - 2x^{16} + 1)\, dx$

41. $\int_{-1}^1 (9x^8 - 7x^6)\, dx$ **42.** $\int_{-2}^2 e^{4x+8}\, dx$

43. $\int_0^1 \sqrt{x}(\sqrt{x} + 1)\, dx$ **44.** $\int_1^2 \frac{x^2}{x^3 + 27}\, dx$

45. $\int_0^1 \frac{dx}{\sqrt{4 - x^2}}$ **46.** $\int_0^2 y^2 (3y^3 + 1)^{-1}\, dy$

47. $\int_0^3 \frac{x}{\sqrt{25 - x^2}}\, dx$ **48.** $\int_0^{\sqrt{\pi}} x \sin x^2 \cos^8 x^2\, dx$

49. $\int_0^{\pi} \sin^2 5\theta\, d\theta$ **50.** $\int_0^{\pi} (1 - \cos^2 3\theta)\, d\theta$

51. $\int_2^3 \frac{x^2 + 2x - 2}{x^3 + 3x^2 - 6x}\, dx$ **52.** $\int_0^{\ln 2} \frac{e^x}{1 + e^{2x}}\, dx$

53. $\int_{-\pi/3}^{\pi/6} \tan\left(x + \frac{\pi}{6} \right)\, dx$ **54.** $\int_0^{\pi/4} \sec^4 x \tan x\, dx$

55. $\int_{\sqrt{\pi/6}}^{\sqrt{\pi/2}} x \cot x^2\, dx$ **56.** $\int_0^{\pi/4} \frac{e^{\tan x}}{\cos^2 x}\, dx$

57–60. Area of regions *Compute the area of the region bounded by the graph of f and the x-axis on the given interval. You may find it useful to sketch the region.*

57. $f(x) = 16 - x^2$; $[-4, 4]$

58. $f(x) = x^3 - x$; $[-1, 0]$

59. $f(x) = 2 \sin(x/4)$; $[0, 2\pi]$

60. $f(x) = 1/(x^2 + 1)$; $[-1, \sqrt{3}]$

61–62. Area versus net area *Find (i) the net area and (ii) the area of the region bounded by the graph of f and the x-axis on the given interval. You may find it useful to sketch the region.*

61. $f(x) = x^4 - x^2$; $[-1, 1]$

62. $f(x) = x^2 - x$; $[0, 3]$

63. Symmetry properties Suppose that $\int_0^4 f(x)\, dx = 10$ and $\int_0^4 g(x)\, dx = 20$. Furthermore, suppose that f is an even function and g is an odd function. Evaluate the following integrals.

   a. $\int_{-4}^4 f(x)\, dx$ **b.** $\int_{-4}^4 3g(x)\, dx$

   c. $\int_{-4}^4 (4f(x) - 3g(x))\, dx$ **d.** $\int_0^1 8x f(4x^2)\, dx$

   e. $\int_{-2}^2 3x f(x)\, dx$

64. Properties of integrals The figure shows the areas of regions bounded by the graph of f and the x-axis. Evaluate the following integrals.

   a. $\int_a^c f(x)\, dx$ **b.** $\int_b^d f(x)\, dx$ **c.** $\int_c^b 2 f(x)\, dx$

   d. $\int_a^d 4 f(x)\, dx$ **e.** $\int_a^b 3 f(x)\, dx$ **f.** $\int_b^d 2 f(x)\, dx$

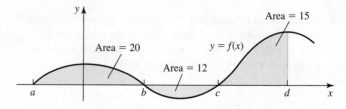

65–70. Properties of integrals *Suppose that* $\int_1^4 f(x)\,dx = 6,$ $\int_1^4 g(x)\,dx = 4,$ *and* $\int_3^4 f(x)\,dx = 2.$ *Evaluate the following integrals or state that there is not enough information.*

65. $\displaystyle\int_1^4 3f(x)\,dx$

66. $\displaystyle -\int_4^1 2f(x)\,dx$

67. $\displaystyle\int_1^4 (3f(x) - 2g(x))\,dx$

68. $\displaystyle\int_1^4 f(x)g(x)\,dx$

69. $\displaystyle\int_1^3 \frac{f(x)}{g(x)}\,dx$

70. $\displaystyle\int_4^1 (f(x) - g(x))\,dx$

71. Displacement from velocity A particle moves along a line with a velocity given by $v(t) = 5\sin \pi t$ starting with an initial position $s(0) = 0$. Find the displacement of the particle between $t = 0$ and $t = 2$, which is given by $s(t) = \int_0^2 v(t)\,dt$. Find the distance traveled by the particle during this interval, which is $\int_0^2 |v(t)|\,dt$.

72. Average height A baseball is launched into the outfield on a parabolic trajectory given by $y = 0.01x(200 - x)$. Find the average height of the baseball over the horizontal extent of its flight.

73. Average values Integration is not needed.

a. Find the average value of f shown in the figure on the interval $[1, 6]$ and then find the point(s) c on $(1, 6)$ guaranteed to exist by the Mean Value Theorem for Integrals.

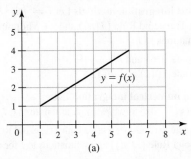
(a)

b. Find the average value of f shown in the figure on the interval $[2, 6]$, and then find the point(s) c on $(2, 6)$ guaranteed to exist by the Mean Value Theorem for Integrals.

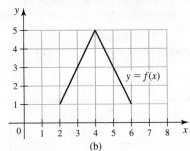
(b)

74. An unknown function The function f satisfies the equation $3x^4 - 48 = \int_2^x f(t)\,dt$. Find f and check your answer by substitution.

75. An unknown function Assume f' is continuous on $[2, 4]$, $\int_1^2 f'(2x)\,dx = 10$, and $f(2) = 4$. Evaluate $f(4)$.

76. Function defined by an integral Let $H(x) = \int_0^x \sqrt{4 - t^2}\,dt$, for $-2 \le x \le 2$.

a. Evaluate $H(0)$.
b. Evaluate $H'(1)$.
c. Evaluate $H'(2)$.
d. Use geometry to evaluate $H(2)$.
e. Find the value of s such that $H(x) = sH(-x)$.

77. Function defined by an integral Make a graph of the function

$$f(x) = \int_1^x \frac{dt}{t}, \text{ for } x \ge 1.$$ Be sure to include all of the evidence you used to arrive at the graph.

78–79 Area functions and the Fundamental Theorem Consider the function

$$f(x) = \begin{cases} x & \text{for } -2 \le x < 0 \\ \dfrac{x^2}{2} & \text{for } 0 \le x \le 2 \end{cases}$$

and its graph shown below.

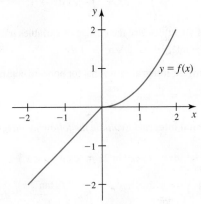

Let $F(x) = \int_{-1}^x f(t)\,dt$ and $G(x) = \int_{-2}^x f(t)\,dt$.

78. a. Evaluate $F(-2)$ and $F(2)$.
b. Use the Fundamental Theorem to find an expression for $F'(x)$, for $-2 \le x < 0$.
c. Use the Fundamental Theorem to find an expression for $F'(x)$, for $0 \le x \le 2$.
d. Evaluate $F'(-1)$ and $F'(1)$. Interpret these values.
e. Evaluate $F''(-1)$ and $F''(1)$.
f. Find a constant C such that $F(x) = G(x) + C$.

79. a. Evaluate $G(-1)$ and $G(1)$.
b. Use the Fundamental Theorem to find an expression for $G'(x)$, for $-2 \le x < 0$.
c. Use the Fundamental Theorem to find an expression for $G'(x)$, for $0 \le x \le 2$.
d. Evaluate $G'(0)$ and $G'(1)$. Interpret these values.
e. Find a constant C such that $F(x) = G(x) + C$.

80. Identifying functions Match the graphs A, B, and C in the figure with the functions $f(x), f'(x)$, and $\int_0^x f(t)\, dt$.

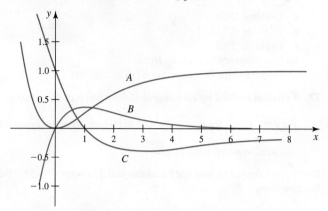

81. Geometry of integrals Without evaluating the integrals, explain why the following statement is true for positive integers n:

$$\int_0^1 x^n\, dx + \int_0^1 \sqrt[n]{x}\, dx = 1.$$

82. Change of variables Use the change of variables $u^3 = x^2 - 1$ to evaluate the integral $\int_1^3 x \sqrt[3]{x^2 - 1}\, dx$.

83. Inverse tangent integral Prove that for nonzero constants a and b,

$$\int \frac{dx}{a^2 x^2 + b^2} = \frac{1}{ab} \tan^{-1}\left(\frac{ax}{b}\right) + C.$$

84–89. Additional integrals *Evaluate the following integrals.*

84. $\displaystyle \int \frac{\sin 2x}{1 + \cos^2 x}\, dx$ (*Hint*: $\sin 2x = 2 \sin x \cos x$.)

85. $\displaystyle \int \frac{1}{x^2} \sin \frac{1}{x}\, dx$

86. $\displaystyle \int \frac{(\tan^{-1} x)^5}{1 + x^2}\, dx$

87. $\displaystyle \int \frac{dx}{(\tan^{-1} x)(1 + x^2)}$

88. $\displaystyle \int \frac{\sin^{-1} x}{\sqrt{1 - x^2}}\, dx$

89. $\displaystyle \int \frac{e^x - e^{-x}}{e^x + e^{-x}}\, dx$

90. Area with a parameter Let $a > 0$ be a real number and consider the family of functions $f(x) = \sin ax$ on the interval $[0, \pi/a]$.

a. Graph f, for $a = 1, 2, 3$.

b. Let $g(a)$ be the area of the region bounded by the graph of f and the x-axis on the interval $[0, \pi/a]$. Graph g for $0 < a < \infty$. Is g an increasing function, a decreasing function, or neither?

91. Equivalent equations Explain why if a function u satisfies the equation $u(x) + 2\int_0^x u(t)\, dt = 10$, then it also satisfies the equation $u'(x) + 2u(x) = 0$. Is it true that if u satisfies the second equation, then it satisfies the first equation?

📱 92. Area function properties Consider the function $f(x) = x^2 - 5x + 4$ and the area function $A(x) = \int_0^x f(t)\, dt$.

a. Graph f on the interval $[0, 6]$.

b. Compute and graph A on the interval $[0, 6]$.

c. Show that the local extrema of A occur at the zeros of f.

d. Give a geometrical and analytical explanation for the observation in part (c).

e. Find the approximate zeros of A, other than 0, and call them x_1 and x_2, where $x_1 < x_2$.

f. Find b such that the area bounded by the graph of f and the x-axis on the interval $[0, x_1]$ equals the area bounded by the graph of f and the x-axis on the interval $[x_1, b]$.

g. If f is an integrable function and $A(x) = \int_a^x f(t)\, dt$, is it always true that the local extrema of A occur at the zeros of f? Explain.

93. Function defined by an integral Let $f(x) = \int_0^x (t - 1)^{15}(t - 2)^9\, dt$.

a. Find the intervals on which f is increasing and the intervals on which f is decreasing.

b. Find the intervals on which f is concave up and the intervals on which f is concave down.

c. For what values of x does f have local minima? Local maxima?

d. Where are the inflection points of f?

94. Exponential inequalities Sketch a graph of $f(t) = e^t$ on an arbitrary interval $[a, b]$. Use the graph and compare areas of regions to prove that

$$e^{(a+b)/2} < \frac{e^b - e^a}{b - a} < \frac{e^a + e^b}{2}.$$

(*Source: Mathematics Magazine* **81**, 5 (Dec 2008))

📱 95. Numerical integration methods Let $I = \int_0^3 x^2\, dx = 9$ and consider the Trapezoid Rule $(T(n))$ and the Midpoint Rule $(M(n))$ approximations to I.

a. Compute $T(6)$ and $M(6)$.

b. Compute $T(12)$ and $M(12)$.

📱 96. Errors in numerical integration Let $I = \int_{-1}^2 (x^7 - 3x^5 - x^2 + \frac{7}{8})\, dx$ and note that $I = 0$.

a. Complete the following table with Trapezoid Rule $(T(n))$ and Midpoint Rule $(M(n))$ approximations to I for various values of n.

b. Fill in the error columns with the absolute errors in the approximations in part (a).

c. How do the errors in $T(n)$ decrease as n doubles in size?

d. How do the errors in $M(n)$ decrease as n doubles in size?

n	$T(n)$	Abs error in $T(n)$	$M(n)$	Abs error in $M(n)$
4				
8				
16				
32				
64				

97. Evaluate $\displaystyle \lim_{x \to 2} \frac{\int_2^x e^{t^2}\, dt}{x - 2}$.

98. Evaluate $\displaystyle \lim_{x \to 1} \frac{\int_1^{x^2} e^{t^3}\, dt}{x - 1}$.

AP® PRACTICE QUESTIONS

The following questions are intended to help you prepare for the AP exam.
They are not questions from actual AP exams.

Section 1 Part A, Multiple Choice, No Technology

1. $\int (5x - 1)\sqrt{x}\, dx$ equals

    (A) $2x^{5/2} - \dfrac{2}{3}x^{3/2} + C$

    (B) $2x^{3/2} - x^{1/2} + C$

    (C) $\dfrac{2}{5}x^{5/2} - \dfrac{2}{3}x^{3/2} + C$

    (D) $\dfrac{5}{3}x^{7/2} - \dfrac{2}{3}x^{5/2} + C$

    (E) $2x^{5/2} + \dfrac{2}{3}x^{3/2} + C$

2. The velocity (in m/s) of an object moving along a line is shown in the figure. How far does the object travel over the interval $0 \le t \le 5$, where t is measured in seconds?

    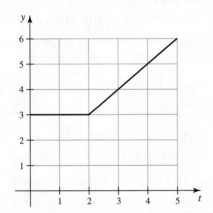

    (A) 5 m **(B)** 15 m **(C)** 19.5 m **(D)** 24 m **(E)** 13.5 m

3. The graph of a function f is shown in the figure. Compute the left Riemann sum for f on the interval $[0, 2]$ with $n = 4$ subintervals and a regular partition.

    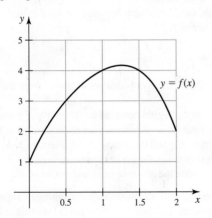

    (A) $\dfrac{13}{2}$ **(B)** $\dfrac{13}{4}$ **(C)** 13 **(D)** 6 **(E)** 12

4. The areas of the regions bounded by the graph of f and the x-axis on the interval $[-2, 3]$ are A and B, as shown in the figure. What is the value of $\int_{-2}^{0} 2f(x)\, dx - \int_{0}^{3} 3|f(x)|\, dx$?

    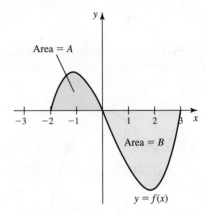

    (A) $2A - B$ **(B)** $2A + 3B$ **(C)** $2A - 3B$

    (D) $3A - 2B$ **(E)** $A - 3B$

5. Evaluate $\displaystyle\int_{1}^{2} \dfrac{4x^3 - 3}{x^4}\, dx$.

    (A) $\ln 16 - \dfrac{31}{32}$ **(B)** $4\ln 2 - \dfrac{3}{4}$ **(C)** $4\ln 2 + \dfrac{7}{8}$

    (D) $4\ln 2 + \dfrac{3}{4}$ **(E)** $\ln 16 - \dfrac{7}{8}$

6. Evaluate $\displaystyle\int_{-1}^{\sqrt{3}} \dfrac{3}{1 + x^2}\, dx$.

    (A) $\dfrac{\pi}{4}$ **(B)** $\dfrac{7\pi}{4}$ **(C)** $\dfrac{\pi}{12}$

    (D) $\dfrac{7\pi}{12}$ **(E)** $\dfrac{5\pi}{4}$

7. Evaluate $\displaystyle\int_{1}^{3} x\sqrt[3]{x^2 - 1}\, dx$.

    (A) 6   **(B)** $\dfrac{32}{3}$ **(C)** $\dfrac{3}{4}$

    (D) $\dfrac{3 \cdot 9^{4/3}}{8}$ **(E)** $\dfrac{3}{8}$

8. Evaluate $\dfrac{d}{dx}\displaystyle\int_{1}^{x^2} \cos t^2\, dt$.

    (A) 0   **(B)** $2x\cos x^4$ **(C)** $\cos x^4$

    (D) $-\sin x^2$ **(E)** $\displaystyle\int_{1}^{x^2} \sin t^2\, dt$

9. What is the average value of the function $y = \sin x$ on the interval $[0, \pi]$?

    (A) 0 **(B)** 1 **(C)** $\dfrac{2}{\pi}$ **(D)** π **(E)** $\dfrac{\pi}{2}$

10. Find the function f that satisfies $f'(t) = e^t - 2t + 3$ and $f(0) = 4$.

(A) $f(t) = e^t - t^2 + 3$

(B) $f(t) = 2e^t - t^2 + 3t + 2$

(C) $f(t) = 3e^t - t^2 + 3t + 1$

(D) $f(t) = e^t - t^2 + 3t + 3$

(E) $f(t) = e^t - \dfrac{1}{2}t^2 + 3t + 3$

11. Find the Trapezoid Rule approximation to $\int_0^5 f(x)\,dx$ using $n = 4$ subintervals and the points on the graph of f shown in the figure.

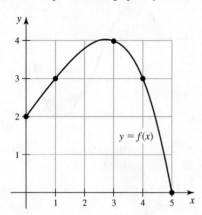

(A) 15   (B) 11   (C) $\dfrac{11}{2}$ (D) $\dfrac{23}{2}$ (E) $\dfrac{29}{2}$

12. Suppose $\int_0^4 f(x)\,dx = 12$, $\int_2^4 g(x)\,dx = -8$, and $\int_0^2 f(x)\,dx = 5$. What is the value of $\int_2^4 (3f(x) - 2g(x))\,dx$?

(A) 5   (B) 26   (C) 31   (D) 37   (E) 1

13. Consider the graph of f shown below.

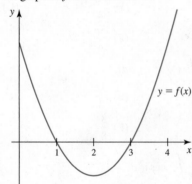

Which curve in the following figure is the graph of $\int_0^x f(t)\,dt$?

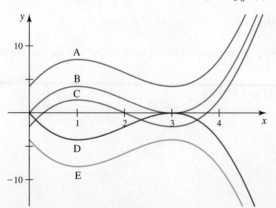

14. Suppose $f(x) = \int_1^x e^{-t^2}\,dt$. Then $\displaystyle\lim_{x \to 1} \frac{f(x)}{x - 1}$ equals

(A) 0   (B) 1   (C) e (D) $\dfrac{1}{e}$ (E) None of the above

15. Suppose f is an even integrable function with $\int_0^{27} f(x)\,dx = 12$. Find the value of $\int_{-3}^3 x^2 f(x^3)\,dx$.

(A) 8   (B) 0   (C) 24   (D) 12   (E) 2

Section 1 Part B, Multiple Choice, Technology Allowed

16. The graph of the function $f(x) = 12x^3 + 24x^2 - 60x - 72$ and the x-axis form the boundary of two regions. Find the combined area of those regions.

(A) 253   (B) 125   (C) -125 (D) 175   (E) 0

17. Find the value of the midpoint Riemann sum (with three decimal place accuracy) for $f(x) = \dfrac{1}{4x}$ on the interval $[1, 5]$ with $n = 8$ subintervals of equal length.

(A) 0.423   (B) 0.800   (C) 0.400   (D) 0.200   (E) 0.304

18. Suppose f is twice differentiable on $(-\infty, \infty)$. Values of f at various points on the interval $[-1, 10]$ are given in the table below.

x	-1	3	5	8	10
$f(x)$	4	2	4	6	8

Evaluate $\int_{-1}^{10} (2x + 0.5f'(x))\,dx$.

(A) 2   (B) 105   (C) 0   (D) 26   (E) 101

Section 2 Part A, Free Response, Technology Allowed

1. Let $f(x) = \sin x - \cos x$ and let $A(x) = \int_0^x f(t)\,dt$ be an area function for f.

a. Evaluate the integral to determine the area function A.

b. Graph A on the interval $[0, 2\pi]$.

c. Find the local maxima and minima of A on the interval $[0, 2\pi]$.

d. Explain the relationship between the local extrema of A and the zeros of f.

2. Let $g(x) = \dfrac{3x^2 + 3}{\sqrt[3]{x^3 + 3x + 1}}$.

a. Approximate the points that are excluded from the domain of g.

b. Let R_1 be the region bounded by the graph of g and the x-axis on the interval $[-4, -1]$ and let R_2 be the region bounded by the graph of g and the x-axis on the interval $[1, 4]$. Determine which region has the greater area.

c. Approximate the absolute minimum value of g on its domain.

3. The following table shows the daytime outdoor temperatures in °F on a summer day over a 12-hour period starting at 6 A.M. at a weather station, where t is measured in hours.

t (hours after 6 A.M.)	0	1	4	7	9	12
T (temperature at time t)	55	62	75	80	89	87

a. Estimate the value of $T'(8)$ with correct units of measurement. Interpret the meaning of your answer.

b. Evaluate $\int_0^{12} T'(t)\, dt$ and interpret the physical meaning of this result.

c. Use a left Riemann sum with five subintervals to approximate the value of $\frac{1}{12}\int_0^{12} T(t)\, dt$ and interpret the result.

d. Use a trapezoidal sum with five subintervals to approximate the value of $\frac{1}{12}\int_0^{12} T(t)\, dt$.

4. Suppose the function f is defined piecewise as

$$f(x) = \begin{cases} 1 - x^2 & \text{if } x < 0 \\ e^{-2x} & \text{if } x \geq 0 \end{cases} \quad \text{and define } g(x) = \int_{-1}^{x} f(t)\, dt.$$

a. Graph f on $[-1, 2]$.

b. Is f continuous at $x = 0$? Justify your answer.

c. Write f' as a piecewise-defined function and determine whether this function is continuous at $x = 0$.

d. Write g as a piecewise-defined function and determine whether this function is continuous at $x = 0$.

e. Find the average value of f on $[-1, 2]$.

5. Suppose $f(x) = \int_0^x e^{-t^2} dt$.

a. Find $f'(x)$ and $f''(x)$.

b. On what intervals is f increasing? On what intervals is f decreasing?

c. On what intervals is f concave up? On what intervals is f concave down?

d. What is the maximum slope of f? Where does it occur?

e. It can be shown that $\lim\limits_{x \to -\infty} f(x) = -\dfrac{\sqrt{\pi}}{2}$ and $\lim\limits_{x \to \infty} f(x) = \dfrac{\sqrt{\pi}}{2}$. Find the range of f and sketch a graph of f.

Section 2 Part B, Free Response, No Technology

6. At $t = 0$, a car moving on a long straight highway at 30 m/s begins decelerating at a rate of $a(t) = -0.5$ m/s^2.

a. Find the velocity $v(t)$ of the car, for $t \geq 0$.

b. After how many seconds does the velocity of the car reach zero?

c. How far does the car travel between $t = 0$ and the time its velocity reaches zero?

7. The function f is defined on $[-2, 6]$. Its graph, shown below, consists of a line segment, a quarter circle of radius 2, and a semicircle of radius 2, Let $g(x) = \int_0^x f(t)\, dt$.

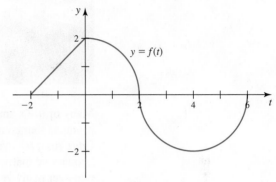

a. Find the values of $g(-2)$ and $g(4)$.

b. On what intervals is g increasing? On what intervals is g decreasing?

c. Find the value of $g'(0)$, or state that it does not exist.

d. Find the value of $g''(0)$, or state that it does not exist.

e. What value of x corresponds to the absolute maximum value of g on the interval $[-2, 6]$? What is the absolute maximum value of g?

Chapter 5 Guided Projects

Applications of the material in this chapter and related topics can be found in the following Guided Projects. For additional information, see the Preface.

- Limits of sums
- Distribution of wealth

- Symmetry in integrals
- Simpson's Rule

6 Applications of Integration

Many of life's amenities are obtained from resources extracted from the Earth. Think of products that come from oil, coal, natural gas, and minerals. Those resources occur in finite reserves that can be estimated. Suppose oil is extracted from an oil reservoir at a known rate that varies from day to day, or even hour to hour. If you know the extraction rate over many years, how do you estimate when the oil reserves will be exhausted? This problem and many analogous problems are ideally suited for calculus. The Fundamental Theorem of Calculus tells us that if we know the rate of change of a quantity over some period of time, then by integration (accumulation), we can compute the future value of the quantity or the net change in the quantity over that period of time. In this chapter, you will see this method applied to electrical power generation, drug dosing, ecological projects, traffic flow, and a variety of other problems in physics, engineering, biology, and ecology.

Chapter Preview
Now that we have some basic techniques for evaluating integrals, we turn our attention to the uses of integration, which are virtually endless. We first illustrate the general rule that if the rate of change of a quantity is known, then integration can be used to determine the net change or the future value of that quantity over a certain time interval. Next, we explore some rich geometric applications of integration: computing the area of regions bounded by several curves, the volume of three-dimensional solids, and the length of curves. A variety of physical applications of integration include finding the work done by a variable force and computing the total force exerted by water behind a dam. All these applications are unified by their use of the *slice-and-sum* strategy.

6.1 Velocity and Net Change

In previous chapters, we established the relationship between the position and velocity of an object moving along a line. With integration, we can now say much more about this relationship. Once we relate velocity and position through integration, we can make analogous observations about a variety of other practical problems, which include fluid flow, population growth, manufacturing costs, and production and consumption of natural resources. The ideas in this section come directly from the Fundamental Theorem of Calculus, and they are among the most powerful applications of calculus.

Velocity, Position, and Displacement

Suppose you are driving along a straight highway and your position relative to a reference point or origin is $s(t)$ for times $t \geq 0$. Your *displacement* over a time interval $[a, b]$ is the change in the position $s(b) - s(a)$ (Figure 6.1). If $s(b) > s(a)$, then your displacement is positive; when $s(b) < s(a)$, your displacement is negative.

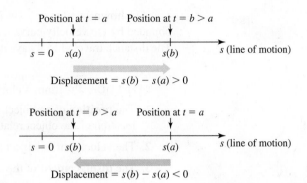

FIGURE 6.1

Now assume that $v(t)$ is the velocity of the object at a particular time t. Recall from Chapter 3 that $v(t) = s'(t)$, which means that s is an antiderivative of v. From the Fundamental Theorem of Calculus, it follows that

$$\int_a^b v(t)\, dt = \int_a^b s'(t)\, dt = s(b) - s(a) = \text{displacement}.$$

There is another instructive interpretation of this result. Suppose we replace the integral of the velocity by a right Riemann sum. The resulting approximation is

$$\text{displacement} \approx \sum_{k=1}^{n} v(t_k)\Delta t.$$

We now focus on one of the subintervals $[t_{k-1}, t_k]$, which corresponds to a time interval of length Δt. The displacement (or change in position) of a moving object over this time interval is approximately $v(t_k)\Delta t$. Notice that if $v(t_k) > 0$, the displacement is in the positive direction and if $v(t_k) < 0$, the displacement is in the negative direction. We see that the approximate displacement over the interval $[a, b]$ is obtained by summing the displacements over all the subintervals. As we take more subintervals of decreasing length, the exact displacement is given by a definite integral:

$$\text{displacement} = \lim_{n \to \infty} \sum_{k=1}^{n} \underbrace{v(t_k)\Delta t}_{\substack{\text{small} \\ \text{displacement}}} = \int_a^b v(t)\,dt.$$

Notice that the integral works as an *accumulator*. The product $v(t)\, dt$ corresponds to the displacement over a small time interval dt. When we integrate the velocity, we accumulate these displacements over the interval $[a, b]$. The outcome is the displacement (net change in position) between $t = a$ and $t = b$. Equivalently, the displacement over the time interval $[a, b]$ is the net area under the velocity curve over $[a, b]$ (Figure 6.2a).

Not to be confused with the displacement is the *distance traveled* over a time interval, which is the total distance traveled by the object, independent of the direction of motion. If the velocity is positive, the object moves in the positive direction and the displacement equals the distance traveled. However, if the velocity changes sign, then the displacement and the distance traveled are not generally equal.

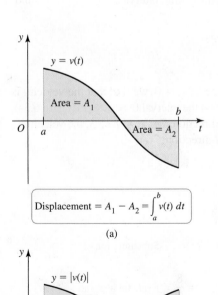

Displacement = $A_1 - A_2 = \displaystyle\int_a^b v(t)\, dt$

(a)

Distance traveled = $A_1 + A_2 = \displaystyle\int_a^b |v(t)|\, dt$

(b)

FIGURE 6.2

QUICK CHECK 1 A police officer leaves his station on a north-south freeway at 9 A.M., traveling north (the positive direction) for 40 mi between 9 A.M. and 10 A.M. From 10 A.M. to 11 A.M., he travels south to a point 20 mi south of the station. What are the distance traveled and the displacement between 9 A.M. and 11 A.M.? ◄

To compute the distance traveled, we need the magnitude, but not the sign, of the velocity. The magnitude of the velocity $|v(t)|$ is called the *speed*. The distance traveled over a small time interval dt is $|v(t)|\, dt$ (speed multiplied by elapsed time). Summing these distances, the distance traveled over the time interval $[a, b]$ is the integral of the speed; that is,

$$\text{distance traveled} = \int_a^b |v(t)|\, dt.$$

As shown in Figure 6.2b, integrating the speed produces the area (not net area) bounded by the velocity curve and the t-axis, which corresponds to the distance traveled. The distance traveled is always nonnegative.

DEFINITION   Position, Velocity, Displacement, and Distance

1. The **position** of an object moving along a line at time t, denoted $s(t)$, is the location of the object relative to the origin.

2. The **velocity** of an object at time t is $v(t) = s'(t)$.

3. The **displacement** of the object between $t = a$ and $t = b > a$ is

$$s(b) - s(a) = \int_a^b v(t)\, dt.$$

4. The **distance traveled** by the object between $t = a$ and $t = b > a$ is

$$\int_a^b |v(t)|\, dt,$$

where $|v(t)|$ is the **speed** of the object at time t.

QUICK CHECK 2   Describe a possible motion of an object along a line for $0 \le t \le 5$ for which the displacement and the distance traveled are different. ◄

EXAMPLE 1   Displacement from velocity   A jogger runs along a straight road with velocity(in mi/hr) $v(t) = 2t^2 - 8t + 6$, for $0 \le t \le 3$, where t is measured in hours.

a. Graph the velocity function over the interval $[0, 3]$. Determine when the jogger moves in the positive direction and when she moves in the negative direction.

b. Find the displacement of the jogger (in miles) on the time intervals $[0, 1]$, $[1, 3]$, and $[0, 3]$. Interpret these results.

c. Find the distance traveled over the interval $[0, 3]$.

SOLUTION

a. By solving $v(t) = 2t^2 - 8t + 6 = 2(t - 1)(t - 3) = 0$, we find that the velocity is zero at $t = 1$ and $t = 3$. The velocity is positive on the interval $0 \le t < 1$ (Figure 6.3a), which means the jogger moves in the positive s direction. For $1 < t < 3$, the velocity is negative and the jogger moves in the negative s direction.

b. The displacement (in miles) over the interval $[0, 1]$ is

$$
\begin{aligned}
s(1) - s(0) &= \int_0^1 v(t)\, dt \\[2mm]
&= \int_0^1 (2t^2 - 8t + 6)\, dt && \text{Substitute for } v. \\[2mm]
&= \left(\frac{2}{3}t^3 - 4t^2 + 6t \right)\Big|_0^1 = \frac{8}{3}. && \text{Evaluate integral.}
\end{aligned}
$$

A similar calculation shows that the displacement over the interval $[1, 3]$ is

$$s(3) - s(1) = \int_1^3 v(t)\, dt = -\frac{8}{3}.$$

Over the interval $[0, 3]$, the displacement is $\frac{8}{3} + \left(-\frac{8}{3}\right) = 0$, which means the jogger returns to the starting point after three hours.

c. From part (b), we can deduce the total distance traveled by the jogger. On the interval $[0, 1]$, the distance traveled is $\frac{8}{3}$ mi; on the interval $[1, 3]$, the distance traveled is also $\frac{8}{3}$ mi. Therefore, the distance traveled on $[0, 3]$ is $\frac{16}{3}$ mi. Alternatively (Figure 6.3b), we can integrate the speed and get the same result:

$$\int_0^3 |v(t)| \, dt = \int_0^1 (2t^2 - 8t + 6) \, dt + \int_1^3 (-(2t^2 - 8t + 6)) \, dt \quad \text{Definition of } |v(t)|$$

$$= \left(\frac{2}{3}t^3 - 4t^2 + 6t \right) \Big|_0^1 + \left(-\frac{2}{3}t^3 + 4t^2 - 6t \right) \Big|_1^3 \quad \text{Evaluate integrals.}$$

$$= \frac{16}{3}. \quad \text{Simplify.}$$

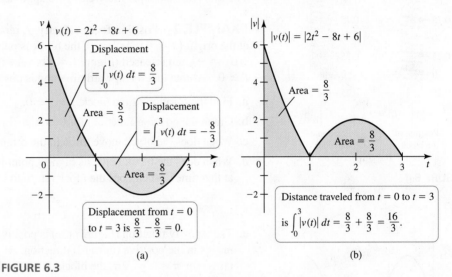

FIGURE 6.3

Related Exercises 7–12 ◄

Future Value of the Position Function

To find the displacement of an object, we do not need to know its initial position. For example, whether an object moves from $s = -20$ to $s = -10$ or from $s = 50$ to $s = 60$, its displacement is 10 units. What happens if we are interested in the actual *position* of the object at some future time?

Suppose we know the velocity of an object and its initial position $s(0)$. The goal is to find the position $s(t)$ at some future time $t \geq 0$. The Fundamental Theorem of Calculus gives us the answer directly. Because the position s is an antiderivative of the velocity v we have

> Note that t is the independent variable of the position function. Therefore, another (dummy) variable, in this case x, must be used as the variable of integration.

$$\int_0^t v(x) \, dx = \int_0^t s'(x) \, dx = s(x) \Big|_0^t = s(t) - s(0).$$

Rearranging this expression leads to the following result.

> Theorem 6.1 is a consequence (actually a statement) of the Fundamental Theorem of Calculus.

THEOREM 6.1 Position from Velocity

Given the velocity $v(t)$ of an object moving along a line and its initial position $s(0)$, the position function of the object for future times $t \geq 0$ is

$$\underbrace{s(t)}_{\substack{\text{position at} \\ \text{time } t}} = \underbrace{s(0)}_{\substack{\text{initial} \\ \text{position}}} + \underbrace{\int_0^t v(x) \, dx}_{\substack{\text{displacement} \\ \text{over } [0, t]}}.$$

Theorem 6.1 says that to find the position $s(t)$, we add the displacement over the interval $[0, t]$ to the initial position $s(0)$.

QUICK CHECK 3 Is the position $s(t)$ a number or a function? For fixed times $t = a$ and $t = b$, is the displacement $s(b) - s(a)$ a number or a function? ◄

There are two *equivalent* ways to determine the position function:

• Using antiderivatives (Section 5.1)

• Using Theorem 6.1

The latter method is usually more efficient, but either method produces the same result. The following example illustrates both approaches.

EXAMPLE 2 Position from velocity A block hangs at rest from a massless spring at the origin ($s = 0$). At $t = 0$, the block is pulled downward $\frac{1}{4}$ m to its initial position $s(0) = -\frac{1}{4}$ and released (Figure 6.4). Its velocity (in m/s) is given by $v(t) = \frac{1}{4}\sin t$, for $t \geq 0$. Assume that the upward direction is positive.

a. Find the position of the block, for $t \geq 0$.

b. Graph the position function, for $0 \leq t \leq 3\pi$.

c. When does the block move through the origin for the first time?

d. When does the block reach its highest point for the first time, and what is its position at that time? When does the block return to its lowest point?

SOLUTION

a. The velocity function (Figure 6.5a) is positive, for $0 < t < \pi$, which means the block moves in the positive (upward) direction. At $t = \pi$, the block comes to rest momentarily; for $\pi < t < 2\pi$, the block moves in the negative (downward) direction. We let $s(t)$ be the position at time $t \geq 0$ with the initial position $s(0) = -\frac{1}{4}$ m.

Method 1: Using antiderivatives Because the position is an antiderivative of the velocity, we have

$$s(t) = \int v(t)\, dt = \int \frac{1}{4}\sin t\, dt = -\frac{1}{4}\cos t + C.$$

To determine the arbitrary constant C, we substitute the initial condition $s(0) = -\frac{1}{4}$ into the expression for $s(t)$:

$$-\frac{1}{4} = -\frac{1}{4}\cos 0 + C.$$

Solving for C, we find that $C = 0$. Therefore, the position for any time $t \geq 0$ is

$$s(t) = -\frac{1}{4}\cos t.$$

Method 2: Using Theorem 6.1 Alternatively, we may use the relationship

$$s(t) = s(0) + \int_0^t v(x)\, dx.$$

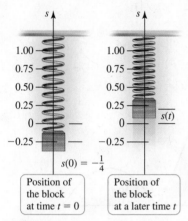

$s(0) = -\frac{1}{4}$

Position of the block at time $t = 0$

Position of the block at a later time t

FIGURE 6.4

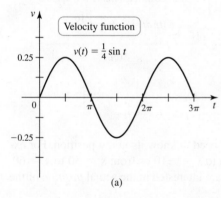

Velocity function

$v(t) = \frac{1}{4}\sin t$

(a)

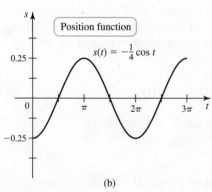

Position function

$s(t) = -\frac{1}{4}\cos t$

(b)

FIGURE 6.5

Substituting $v(x) = \frac{1}{4} \sin x$ and $s(0) = -\frac{1}{4}$, the position function is

$$s(t) = \underbrace{-\frac{1}{4}}_{s(0)} + \int_0^t \underbrace{\frac{1}{4} \sin x \, dx}_{v(x)}$$

$$= -\frac{1}{4} - \left(\frac{1}{4} \cos x \right) \Big|_0^t \qquad \text{Evaluate integral.}$$

$$= -\frac{1}{4} - \frac{1}{4}(\cos t - 1) \qquad \text{Simplify.}$$

$$= -\frac{1}{4} \cos t. \qquad \text{Simplify.}$$

> It is worth repeating that to find the displacement, we need to know only the velocity. To find the position, we must know both the velocity and the initial position $s(0)$.

b. The graph of the position function is shown in Figure 6.5b. We see that $s(0) = -\frac{1}{4}$ m, as prescribed.

c. The block initially moves in the positive s direction (upward), reaching the origin $(s = 0)$ when $s(t) = -\frac{1}{4} \cos t = 0$. So the block arrives at the origin for the first time when $t = \pi/2$.

d. The block moves in the positive direction and reaches its high point for the first time when $t = \pi$; the position at that moment is $s(\pi) = \frac{1}{4}$ m. The block then reverses direction and moves in the negative (downward) direction, reaching its low point at $t = 2\pi$. This motion repeats every 2π seconds.

Related Exercises 13–22 ◄

QUICK CHECK 4 Without doing further calculations, what are the displacement and distance traveled by the block in Example 2 over the interval $[0, 2\pi]$? ◄

> The terminal velocity of an object depends on its density, shape, size, and the medium through which it falls. Estimates for human beings in free fall in the lower atmosphere vary from 120 mi/hr (54 m/s) to 180 mi/hr (80 m/s).

EXAMPLE 3 Skydiving Suppose a skydiver leaps from a hovering helicopter and falls in a straight line. He reaches a terminal velocity of 80 m/s at $t = 0$ and falls for 19 seconds, at which time he opens his parachute. The velocity decreases linearly to 6 m/s over a 2-s period and then remains constant until he reaches the ground at $t = 40$ s. The motion is described by the velocity function

$$v(t) = \begin{cases} 80 & \text{if } 0 \le t < 19 \\ 783 - 37t & \text{if } 19 \le t < 21 \\ 6 & \text{if } 21 \le t \le 40. \end{cases}$$

Determine the altitude from which the skydiver jumped.

SOLUTION We let the position of the skydiver increase *downward* with the origin $(s = 0)$ corresponding to the position of the helicopter. The velocity is positive, so the distance traveled by the skydiver equals the displacement, which is

$$\int_0^{40} |v(t)| \, dt = \int_0^{19} 80 \, dt + \int_{19}^{21} (783 - 37t) \, dt + \int_{21}^{40} 6 \, dt$$

$$= 80t \Big|_0^{19} + \left(783t - \frac{37t^2}{2} \right) \Big|_{19}^{21} + 6t \Big|_{21}^{40} \qquad \text{Fundamental Theorem}$$

$$= 1720. \qquad \text{Evaluate and simplify.}$$

The skydiver jumped from 1720 m above the ground. Notice that the displacement of the skydiver is the area under the velocity curve (Figure 6.6).

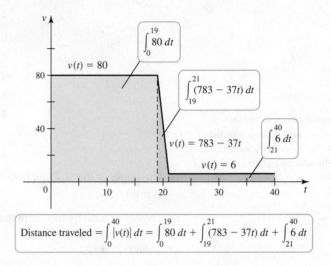

$$\text{Distance traveled} = \int_0^{40} |v(t)|\, dt = \int_0^{19} 80\, dt + \int_{19}^{21} (783 - 37t)\, dt + \int_{21}^{40} 6\, dt$$

FIGURE 6.6

Related Exercises 23–24◄

QUICK CHECK 5 Suppose (unrealistically) in Example 3 that the velocity of the skydiver is 80 m/s, for $0 \le t < 20$, and then it changes instantaneously to 6 m/s, for $20 \le t \le 40$. Sketch the velocity function, and without integrating, find the distance the skydiver falls in 40 s. ◄

Acceleration

Because the acceleration of an object moving along a line is given by $a(t) = v'(t)$, the relationship between velocity and acceleration is the same as the relationship between position and velocity. Given the acceleration of an object, the change in velocity over an interval $[a, b]$ is

$$\text{change in velocity} = v(b) - v(a) = \int_a^b v'(t)\, dt = \int_a^b a(t)\, dt.$$

Furthermore, if we know the acceleration and initial velocity $v(0)$, then the velocity at future times can also be found.

> Theorem 6.2 is a consequence of the Fundamental Theorem of Calculus.

THEOREM 6.2 Velocity from Acceleration
Given the acceleration $a(t)$ of an object moving along a line and its initial velocity $v(0)$, the velocity of the object for future times $t \ge 0$ is

$$v(t) = v(0) + \int_0^t a(x)\, dx.$$

EXAMPLE 4 Motion in a gravitational field An artillery shell is fired directly upward with an initial velocity of 300 m/s from a point 30 m above the ground (Figure 6.7). Assume that only the force of gravity acts on the shell and it produces an acceleration of 9.8 m/s². Find the velocity of the shell while the shell is in the air.

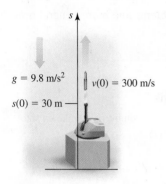

FIGURE 6.7

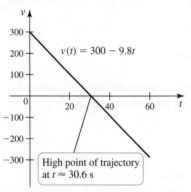

High point of trajectory at $t \approx 30.6$ s

FIGURE 6.8

▷ Note that the units in the integral are consistent. For example, if Q' has units of gallons/second and t and x have units of seconds, then $Q'(x)\,dx$ has units of (gallons/second)(seconds) = gallons, which are the units of Q.

▷ At the risk of being repetitious, Theorem 6.3 is also a consequence of the Fundamental Theorem of Calculus. We assume that Q' is an integrable function.

SOLUTION We let the positive direction be upward with the origin ($s = 0$) corresponding to the ground. The initial velocity of the shell is $v(0) = 300$ m/s. The acceleration due to gravity is downward; therefore, $a(t) = -9.8$ m/s². Integrating the acceleration, the velocity is

$$v(t) = \underbrace{v(0)}_{300\,\text{m/s}} + \int_0^t \underbrace{a(x)}_{-9.8\,\text{m/s}^2} dx = 300 + \int_0^t (-9.8)\,dx = 300 - 9.8t.$$

The velocity decreases from its initial value of 300 m/s, reaching zero at the high point of the trajectory when $v(t) = 300 - 9.8t = 0$, or at $t \approx 30.6$ s (Figure 6.8). At this point, the velocity becomes negative, and the shell begins its descent to Earth.

Knowing the velocity function, you could now find the position function using the methods of Example 3.

Related Exercises 25–35 ◀

Net Change and Future Value

Everything we have said about velocity, position, and displacement carries over to more general situations. Suppose you are interested in some quantity Q that changes over *time*; Q may represent the amount of water in a reservoir, the population of a cell culture, or the amount of a resource that is consumed or produced. If you are given the rate Q' at which Q changes, then integration allows you to calculate either the net change in the quantity Q or the future value of Q.

We argue just as we did for velocity and position: Because $Q(t)$ is an antiderivative of $Q'(t)$, the Fundamental Theorem of Calculus tells us that

$$\int_a^b Q'(t)\,dt = Q(b) - Q(a) = \text{net change in } Q \text{ over } [a, b].$$

Geometrically, the net change in Q over the time interval $[a, b]$ is the net area under the graph of Q' over $[a, b]$. In the language of accumulation, we interpret the product $Q'(t)\,dt$ as a change in Q over a small increment of time. Integrating $Q'(t)$ accumulates, or adds up, these small changes over the interval $[a, b]$. The result is the net change in Q between $t = a$ and $t = b$. Once again, we see that accumulating the rate of change of a quantity over an interval gives the net change in that quantity over the interval.

Alternatively, suppose we are given both the rate of change Q' and the initial value $Q(0)$. Integrating over the interval $[0, t]$, where $t \geq 0$, we have

$$\int_0^t Q'(x)\,dx = Q(t) - Q(0).$$

Rearranging this equation, we write the value of Q at any future time $t \geq 0$ as

$$\underbrace{Q(t)}_{\substack{\text{future}\\\text{value}}} = \underbrace{Q(0)}_{\substack{\text{initial}\\\text{value}}} + \underbrace{\int_0^t Q'(x)\,dx}_{\substack{\text{net change}\\\text{over } [0, t]}}.$$

THEOREM 6.3 Net Change and Future Value

Suppose a quantity Q changes over time at a known rate Q'. Then the **net change** in Q between $t = a$ and $t = b > a$ is

$$\underbrace{Q(b) - Q(a)}_{\text{net change in } Q} = \int_a^b Q'(t)\,dt.$$

Given the initial value $Q(0)$, the **future value** of Q at time $t \geq 0$ is

$$Q(t) = Q(0) + \int_0^t Q'(x)\,dx.$$

The correspondences between velocity–displacement problems and more general problems are shown in Table 6.1.

Table 6.1

Velocity–Displacement Problems	General Problems
Position $s(t)$	Quantity $Q(t)$ (such as volume or population size)
Velocity: $s'(t) = v(t)$	Rate of change: $Q'(t)$
Displacement: $s(b) - s(a) = \displaystyle\int_a^b v(t)\, dt$	Net change: $Q(b) - Q(a) = \displaystyle\int_a^b Q'(t)\, dt$
Future position: $s(t) = s(0) + \displaystyle\int_0^t v(x)\, dx$	Future value of Q: $Q(t) = Q(0) + \displaystyle\int_0^t Q'(x)\, dx$

Let's put Theorem 6.3 to use on some practical problems.

EXAMPLE 5   Cell growth A culture of cells in a lab has a population of 100 cells when nutrients are added at time $t = 0$. Suppose the population $N(t)$ increases at a rate given by

$$N'(t) = 90e^{-0.1t} \quad \text{cells/hr.}$$

Find $N(t)$, for $t \geq 0$.

> Although N is a positive integer (the number of cells), we treat it as a continuous variable in this example.

SOLUTION As shown in Figure 6.9, the growth rate is large when t is small (plenty of food and space) and decreases as t increases. Knowing that the initial population is $N(0) = 100$ cells, we can find the population $N(t)$ at any future time $t \geq 0$ using Theorem 6.3:

$$N(t) = N(0) + \int_0^t N'(x)\, dx$$

$$= \underbrace{100}_{N(0)} + \int_0^t \underbrace{90e^{-0.1x}}_{N'(x)}\, dx$$

$$= 100 + \left[\left(\frac{90}{-0.1} \right) e^{-0.1x} \right] \Bigg|_0^t \quad \text{Fundamental Theorem}$$

$$= 1000 - 900e^{-0.1t}. \quad \text{Simplify.}$$

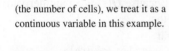
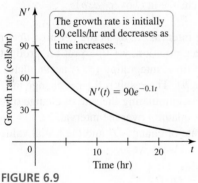

The growth rate is initially 90 cells/hr and decreases as time increases.

$N'(t) = 90e^{-0.1t}$

FIGURE 6.9

The graph of the population function (Figure 6.10) shows that the population increases, but at a decreasing rate. Note that the initial condition $N(0) = 100$ cells is satisfied and that the population size approaches 1000 cells as $t \to \infty$.

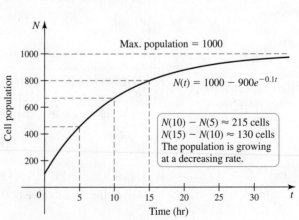

$N(t) = 1000 - 900e^{-0.1t}$

Max. population $= 1000$

$N(10) - N(5) \approx 215$ cells
$N(15) - N(10) \approx 130$ cells
The population is growing at a decreasing rate.

FIGURE 6.10

Related Exercises 36–42 ◄

EXAMPLE 6 **Net change in sea level** Table 6.2 lists rates of change $s'(t)$ in global sea level $s(t)$ at various years from 1995$(t = 0)$ to 2011$(t = 16)$, with rates of change reported in mm/yr.

Table 6.2

t (years from 1995)	0 (1995)	3 (1998)	5 (2000)	7 (2002)	8 (2003)	12 (2007)	14 (2009)	16 (2011)
s'(t) (mm/yr)	0.51	5.19	4.39	2.21	5.24	0.63	4.19	2.38

Source: Collecte Localisation Satellites/Centre national d'études spatiales

> The rate of change in sea level varies from one location on Earth to the next; sea level also varies seasonally and is influenced by ocean currents. The data in Table 6.2 reflect approximate rates of change at the beginning of each year listed, averaged over the entire globe.

a. Assuming s' is continuous on $[0, 16]$, explain how a definite integral can be used to find the net change in sea level from 1995 to 2011; then write the definite integral.

b. Use the data in Table 6.2 and generalize the Trapezoid Rule to estimate the value of the integral from part (a).

SOLUTION

a. The net change in any quantity Q over the interval $[a, b]$ is $Q(b) - Q(a)$. When the rate of change Q' is known, the net change in Q is found by integrating Q' over the same interval; that is,

$$\text{net change in } Q = Q(b) - Q(a) = \int_a^b Q'(t)\, dt. \quad \text{Fundamental Theorem}$$

Therefore, the net change in sea level from 1995 to 2011 is $\int_0^{16} s'(t)\, dt$.

b. The values from Table 6.2 are plotted in Figure 6.11, accompanied by seven trapezoids whose combined area approximates the net area $\int_0^{16} s'(t)\, dt$. Notice that the grid points (the t-values in Table 6.2) do not form a regular partition of the interval $[0, 16]$. Therefore, we must generalize the standard Trapezoid Rule and compute the area of each trapezoid separately.

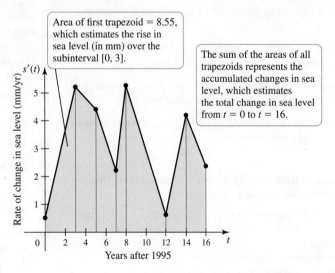

Area of first trapezoid = 8.55, which estimates the rise in sea level (in mm) over the subinterval [0, 3].

The sum of the areas of all trapezoids represents the accumulated changes in sea level, which estimates the total change in sea level from $t = 0$ to $t = 16$.

FIGURE 6.11

Area of a trapezoid

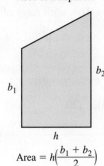

$$A = \frac{1}{2}(b_1 + b_2)h$$

$$\text{Area} = h\left(\frac{b_1 + b_2}{2}\right)$$

Focusing on the first trapezoid over the subinterval $[0, 3]$, we find that its area is

$$\underbrace{\text{area of first trapezoid}}_{A = \frac{1}{2}(b_1 + b_2)h} = \frac{1}{2} \cdot \underbrace{(s'(0) + s'(3)) \cdot 3}_{\text{measured in mm/yr yr}} = \frac{1}{2} \cdot (0.51 + 5.19) \cdot 3 = 8.55.$$

Because s' is measured in mm/yr and t is measured in yr, the area of this trapezoid (8.55) is interpreted as the net change in sea level from 1995 to 1998, measured in mm. As we add additional trapezoids to the ongoing sum that approximates $\int_0^{16} s'(t)\, dt$, the changes in sea level accumulate, resulting in the total change in sea level on $[0, 16]$. The sum of the areas of all seven trapezoids is

$$\underbrace{\frac{1}{2}(s'(0) + s'(3)) \cdot 3}_{\text{first trapezoid}} + \underbrace{\frac{1}{2}(s'(3) + s'(5)) \cdot 2}_{\text{second trapezoid...}} + \frac{1}{2}(s'(5) + s'(7)) \cdot 2 + \frac{1}{2}(s'(7) + s'(8)) \cdot 1$$

$$+ \frac{1}{2}(s'(8) + s'(12)) \cdot 4 + \frac{1}{2}(s'(12) + s'(14)) \cdot 2 + \underbrace{\frac{1}{2}(s'(14) + s'(16)) \cdot 2}_{\text{...last trapezoid}} = 51.585$$

An estimate of the rise in sea level from 1995 to 2011 is 51.585 mm.

Related Exercises 43–46 ◄

SECTION 6.1 EXERCISES

Review Questions

1. Explain the meaning of position, displacement, and distance traveled as they apply to an object moving along a line.

2. Suppose the velocity of an object moving along a line is positive. Are displacement and distance traveled equal? Explain.

3. Given the velocity function v of an object moving along a line, explain how definite integrals can be used to find the displacement of the object.

4. Explain how to use definite integrals to find the net change in a quantity, given the rate of change of that quantity.

5. Given the rate of change of a quantity Q and its initial value $Q(0)$, explain how to find the value of Q at a future time $t \geq 0$.

6. What is the result of integrating a population growth rate between times $t = a$ and $t = b$, where $b > a$?

Basic Skills

7–12. Displacement from velocity *Assume t is time measured in seconds and velocities have units of m/s.*

a. *Graph the velocity function over the given interval. Then determine when the motion is in the positive direction and when it is in the negative direction.*
b. *Find the displacement over the given interval.*
c. *Find the distance traveled over the given interval.*

7. $v(t) = 6 - 2t;\ 0 \leq t \leq 6$

8. $v(t) = 10 \sin 2t;\ 0 \leq t \leq 2\pi$

9. $v(t) = t^2 - 6t + 8;\ 0 \leq t \leq 5$

10. $v(t) = -t^2 + 5t - 4;\ 0 \leq t \leq 5$

11. $v(t) = t^3 - 5t^2 + 6t;\ 0 \leq t \leq 5$

12. $v(t) = 50e^{-2t};\ 0 \leq t \leq 4$

13–18. Position from velocity *Consider an object moving along a line with the following velocities and initial positions.*

a. *Graph the velocity function on the given interval and determine when the object is moving in the positive direction and when it is moving in the negative direction.*
b. *Determine the position function, for $t \geq 0$, using both the antiderivative method and the Fundamental Theorem of Calculus (Theorem 6.1). Check for agreement between the two methods.*
c. *Graph the position function on the given interval.*

13. $v(t) = \sin t$ on $[0, 2\pi];\ s(0) = 1$

14. $v(t) = -t^3 + 3t^2 - 2t$ on $[0, 3];\ s(0) = 4$

15. $v(t) = 6 - 2t$ on $[0, 5];\ s(0) = 0$

16. $v(t) = 3 \sin \pi t$ on $[0, 4];\ s(0) = 1$

17. $v(t) = 9 - t^2$ on $[0, 4];\ s(0) = -2$

18. $v(t) = 1/(t + 1)$ on $[0, 8];\ s(0) = -4$

19. **Oscillating motion** A mass hanging from a spring is set in motion, and its ensuing velocity is given by $v(t) = 2\pi \cos \pi t$, for $t \geq 0$. Assume that the positive direction is upward and that $s(0) = 0$.

a. Determine the position function, for $t \geq 0$.
b. Graph the position function on the interval $[0, 4]$.
c. At what times does the mass reach its low point the first three times?
d. At what times does the mass reach its high point the first three times?

20. Cycling distance A cyclist rides down a long straight road at a velocity (in m/min) given by $v(t) = 400 - 20t$, for $0 \le t \le 10$, where t is measured in minutes.

   a. How far does the cyclist travel in the first 5 min?
   b. How far does the cyclist travel in the first 10 min?
   c. How far has the cyclist traveled when her velocity is 250 m/min?

21. Flying into a headwind The velocity (in mi/hr) of an airplane flying into a headwind is given by $v(t) = 30(16 - t^2)$, for $0 \le t \le 3$. Assume that $s(0) = 0$ and t is measured in hours.

   a. Determine and graph the position function, for $0 \le t \le 3$.
   b. How far does the airplane travel in the first 2 hr?
   c. How far has the airplane traveled at the instant its velocity reaches 400 mi/hr?

22. Day hike The velocity (in mi/hr) of a hiker walking along a straight trail is given by $v(t) = 3 \sin^2(\pi t/2)$, for $0 \le t \le 4$. Assume that $s(0) = 0$ and t is measured in hours.

   a. Determine and graph the position function, for $0 \le t \le 4$. (*Hint:* $\sin^2 t = \frac{1}{2}(1 - \cos 2t)$)
   b. What is the distance traveled by the hiker in the first 15 min of the hike?
   c. What is the hiker's position at $t = 3$?

23. Piecewise velocity The velocity of a (fast) automobile on a straight highway is given by the function

$$v(t) = \begin{cases} 3t & \text{if } 0 \le t < 20 \\ 60 & \text{if } 20 \le t < 45 \\ 240 - 4t & \text{if } t \ge 45, \end{cases}$$

where t is measured in seconds and v has units of m/s.

   a. Graph the velocity function, for $0 \le t \le 70$. When is the velocity a maximum? When is the velocity zero?
   b. What is the distance traveled by the automobile in the first 30 s?
   c. What is the distance traveled by the automobile in the first 60 s?
   d. What is the position of the automobile when $t = 75$?

24. Probe speed A data collection probe is dropped from a stationary balloon, and it falls with a velocity (in m/s) given by $v(t) = 9.8t$, neglecting air resistance. After 10 s, a chute deploys and the probe immediately slows to a constant speed of 10 m/s, which it maintains until it enters the ocean.

   a. Graph the velocity function.
   b. How far does the probe fall in the first 30 s after it is released?
   c. If the probe was released from an altitude of 3 km, when does it enter the ocean?

25–32. Position and velocity from acceleration *Find the position and velocity of an object moving along a straight line with the given acceleration, initial velocity, and initial position.*

25. $a(t) = -32, v(0) = 70, s(0) = 10$

26. $a(t) = -32, v(0) = 50, s(0) = 0$

27. $a(t) = -9.8, v(0) = 20, s(0) = 0$

28. $a(t) = e^{-t}, v(0) = 60, s(0) = 40$

29. $a(t) = -0.01t, v(0) = 10, s(0) = 0$

30. $a(t) = \dfrac{20}{(t + 2)^2}, v(0) = 20, s(0) = 10$

31. $a(t) = \cos 2t, v(0) = 5, s(0) = 7$

32. $a(t) = \dfrac{2t}{(t^2 + 1)^2}, v(0) = 0, s(0) = 0$

33. Acceleration A drag racer accelerates at $a(t) = 88$ ft/s^2. Assume that $v(0) = 0$, $s(0) = 0$, and t is measured in seconds.

   a. Determine and graph the position function, for $t \ge 0$.
   b. How far does the racer travel in the first 4 s?
   c. At this rate, how long will it take the racer to travel $\frac{1}{4}$ mi?
   d. How long does it take the racer to travel 300 ft?
   e. How far has the racer traveled when it reaches a speed of 178 ft/s?

34. Deceleration A car slows down with an acceleration of $a(t) = -15$ ft/s^2. Assume that $v(0) = 60$ ft/s, $s(0) = 0$, and t is measured in seconds.

   a. Determine and graph the position function, for $t \ge 0$.
   b. How far does the car travel in the time it takes to come to rest?

35. Approaching a station At $t = 0$, a train approaching a station begins decelerating from a speed of 80 mi/hr according to the acceleration function $a(t) = -1280(1 + 8t)^{-3}$, where $t \ge 0$ is measured in hours. How far does the train travel between $t = 0$ and $t = 0.2$? Between $t = 0.2$ and $t = 0.4$? The units of acceleration are mi/hr^2.

36. Peak oil extraction The owners of an oil reserve begin extracting oil at time $t = 0$. Based on estimates of the reserves, suppose the projected extraction rate is given by $Q'(t) = 3t^2(40 - t)^2$, where $0 \le t \le 40$, Q is measured in millions of barrels, and t is measured in years.

   a. When does the peak extraction rate occur?
   b. How much oil is extracted in the first 10, 20, and 30 yr?
   c. What is the total amount of oil extracted in 40 yr?
   d. Is one-fourth of the total oil extracted in the first one-fourth of the extraction period? Explain.

37. Oil production An oil refinery produces oil at a variable rate given by

$$Q'(t) = \begin{cases} 800 & \text{if } 0 \le t < 30 \\ 2600 - 60t & \text{if } 30 \le t < 40 \\ 200 & \text{if } t \ge 40, \end{cases}$$

where t is measured in days and Q is measured in barrels.

   a. How many barrels are produced in the first 35 days?
   b. How many barrels are produced in the first 50 days?
   c. Without using integration, determine the number of barrels produced over the interval $[60, 80]$.

38–41. Population growth

38. Starting with an initial value of $P(0) = 55$, the population of a prairie dog community grows at a rate of $P'(t) = 20 - t/5$ (prairie dogs/month), for $0 \le t \le 200$, where t is measured in months.

   a. What is the population 6 months later?
   b. Find the population $P(t)$, for $0 \le t \le 200$.

39. When records were first kept $(t = 0)$, the population of a rural town was 250 people. During the following years, the population grew at a rate of $P'(t) = 30(1 + \sqrt{t})$, where t is measured in years.

   a. What is the population after 20 years?
   b. Find the population $P(t)$ at any time $t \ge 0$.

40. The population of a community of foxes is observed to fluctuate on a 10-year cycle due to variations in the availability of prey. When population measurements began $(t = 0)$, the population was 35 foxes. The growth rate in units of foxes/year was observed to be

$$P'(t) = 5 + 10 \sin\left(\frac{\pi t}{5}\right).$$

   a. What is the population 15 years later? 35 years later?
   b. Find the population $P(t)$ at any time $t \ge 0$.

41. A culture of bacteria in a Petri dish has an initial population of 1500 cells and grows at a rate (in cells/day) of $N'(t) = 100e^{-0.25t}$. Assume t is measured in days.

   a. What is the population after 20 days? After 40 days?
   b. Find the population $N(t)$ at any time $t \ge 0$.

42. Endangered species The population of an endangered species changes at a rate given by $P'(t) = 30 - 20t$ (individuals/year). Assume the initial population of the species is 300 individuals, and t is measured in years.

   a. What is the population after 5 years?
   b. When will the species become extinct?
   c. How does the extinction time change if the initial population is 100 individuals? 400 individuals?

43. Arctic sea ice Data for the area of sea ice in the Arctic is obtained from satellite images. The rate of change of the area of Arctic sea ice (in millions of km^2/yr) is shown in the table for the period 2003–2011. Use the Trapezoid Rule to estimate the net change in Arctic sea ice over this period. Interpret your answer.

Year	2003	2004	2006	2007	2009	2010	2011
Rate of change	0	-0.25	-0.65	-0.60	0.1	-0.40	-0.30

Source: National Snow and Ice Data Center

44. Atmospheric CO$_2$ Levels of carbon dioxide in the Earth's atmosphere are measured regularly at many stations around the world. The table shows the global rate of change in CO_2 levels (in parts per million year) for 2008 $(t = 0)$ to 2012 $(t = 4)$. Use the Trapezoid Rule to estimate the net change in atmospheric CO_2 over this time period. Interpret your answer.

t	0 (2008)	0.5	1	1.5	2	3	3.5	4
Rate of change	1.9	2.0	1.4	1.6	2.3	2.3	3.0	2.6

Source: National Oceanic and Atmospheric Administration

45. Vertical ascent At selected points along its length, the average rate of ascent of a mountain trail is measured (in vertical meters/ horizontal kilometer). The data over 4 km of trail are shown in the table. Use the Trapezoid Rule to approximate the total vertical ascent of the trail. Interpret your answer.

Horizontal distance (km)	0	0.5	1	2	2.5	3	4
Rate of change	80	120	150	100	100	120	160

46. Cycling energy A cyclist rides a bicycle equipped with pedals that measure his power output $P(t)$ (in watts) at time t. The energy output of the cyclist over a time interval $[a, b]$ is $\int_a^b P(t)\, dt$. The following power data are collected during a 2-hr bike ride. Use the Trapezoid Rule to approximate energy output for the ride, measured in watt-hours.

t (hr)	0	0.25	0.5	1	1.25	1.75	2
P (watts)	150	210	130	250	260	200	140

Further Explorations

47. Explain why or why not Determine whether the following statements are true and give an explanation or counterexample.

   a. The distance traveled by an object moving along a line is the same as the displacement of the object.
   b. When the velocity is positive on an interval, the displacement and the distance traveled on that interval are equal.
   c. Consider a tank that is filled and drained at a flow rate of $V'(t) = 1 - t^2/100$ (gal/min), for $t \ge 0$, where t is meaured in minutes. It follows that the volume of water in the tank increases for 10 min and then decreases until the tank is empty.
   d. The accumulated change in the quantity Q over the interval $[a, b]$ is $\int_a^b Q(t)\, dt$.

48–49. Velocity graphs *The figures show velocity functions for motion along a straight line. Assume the motion begins with an initial position of $s(0) = 0$. Determine the following:*

   a. *The displacement between $t = 0$ and $t = 5$*
   b. *The distance traveled between $t = 0$ and $t = 5$*
   c. *The position at $t = 5$*
   d. *A piecewise function for $s(t)$*

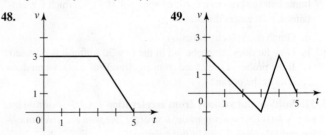

50–53. Equivalent constant velocity *Consider the following velocity functions. In each case, complete the sentence: The same distance could have been traveled over the given time period at a constant velocity of _____.*

50. $v(t) = 2t + 6$; for $0 \le t \le 8$

51. $v(t) = 1 - t^2/16$; for $0 \le t \le 4$

52. $v(t) = 2 \sin t$; for $0 \le t \le \pi$

53. $v(t) = t(25 - t^2)^{1/2}$; for $0 \le t \le 5$

54. Where do they meet? Kelly started at noon ($t = 0$) riding a bike from Niwot to Berthoud, a distance of 20 km, with velocity $v(t) = 15/(t + 1)^2$ (decreasing because of fatigue). Sandy started at noon ($t = 0$) riding a bike in the opposite direction from Berthoud to Niwot with velocity $u(t) = 20/(t + 1)^2$ (also decreasing because of fatigue). Assume distance is measured in kilometers and time is measured in hours.

   a. Make a graph of Kelly's distance from Niwot as a function of time.

   b. Make a graph of Sandy's distance from Berthoud as a function of time.

   c. When do they meet? How far has each person traveled when they meet?

   d. More generally, if the riders' speeds are $v(t) = A/(t + 1)^2$ and $u(t) = B/(t + 1)^2$ and the distance between the towns is D, what conditions on A, B, and D must be met to ensure that the riders will pass each other?

   e. Looking ahead: With the velocity functions given in part (d), make a conjecture about the maximum distance each person can ride (given unlimited time).

55. Bike race Theo and Sasha start at the same place on a straight road riding bikes with the following velocities (measured in mi/hr). Assume t is measured in miles.

      Theo: $v_T(t) = 10$, for $t \ge 0$,
      Sasha: $v_S(t) = 15t$, for $0 \le t \le 1$ and $v_S(t) = 15$, for $t > 1$.

   a. Graph the velocity functions for both riders.

   b. If the riders ride for 1 hr, who rides farther? Interpret your answer geometrically using the graphs of part (a).

   c. If the riders ride for 2 hr, who rides farther? Interpret your answer geometrically using the graphs of part (a).

   d. Which rider arrives first at the 10-, 15-, and 20-mi markers of the race? Interpret your answer geometrically using the graphs of part (a).

   e. Suppose Sasha gives Theo a head start of 0.2 mi and the riders ride for 20 mi. Who wins the race?

   f. Suppose Sasha gives Theo a head start of 0.2 hr and the riders ride for 20 mi. Who wins the race?

56. Two runners At noon ($t = 0$), Alicia starts running along a long straight road at 4 mi/hr. Her velocity decreases according to the function $v(t) = 4/(t + 1)$, for $t \ge 0$. At noon, Boris also starts running along the same road with a 2-mi head start on Alicia; his velocity is given by $u(t) = 2/(t + 1)$, for $t \ge 0$. Assume t is measured in hours.

   a. Find the position functions for Alicia and Boris, where $s = 0$ corresponds to Alicia's starting point.

   b. When, if ever, does Alicia overtake Boris?

57. Running in a wind A strong west wind blows across a circular running track. Abe and Bess start running at the south end of the track, and at the same time, Abe starts running clockwise and Bess

starts running counterclockwise. Abe runs with a speed (in mi/hr) given by $u(\varphi) = 3 - 2 \cos \varphi$ and Bess runs with a speed given by $v(\theta) = 3 + 2 \cos \theta$, where φ and θ are the central angles of the runners.

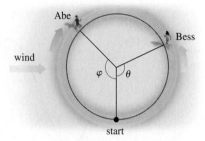

   a. Graph the speed functions u and v, and explain why they describe the runners' speeds (in light of the wind).

   b. Compute the average value of u and v (over one lap) with respect to the central angle.

   c. Challenge: If the track has a radius of $\frac{1}{10}$ mi, how long does it take each runner to complete one lap and who wins the race?

Applications

58. Filling a tank A 2000-liter cistern is empty when water begins flowing into it (at $t = 0$) at a rate (in L/min) given by $Q'(t) = 3\sqrt{t}$, where t is measured in minutes.

   a. How much water flows into the cistern in 1 hr?

   b. Find and graph the function that gives the amount of water in the tank at any time $t \ge 0$.

   c. When will the tank be full?

59. Depletion of natural resources Suppose that $r(t) = r_0 e^{-kt}$, with $k > 0$, is the rate at which a nation extracts oil, where $r_0 = 10^7$ barrels/yr is the current rate of extraction. Suppose also that the estimate of the total oil reserve is 2×10^9 barrels.

   a. Find $Q(t)$, the total amount of oil extracted by the nation after t years.

   b. Evaluate $\lim_{t \to \infty} Q(t)$ and explain the meaning of this limit.

   c. Find the minimum decay constant k for which the total oil reserves will last forever.

   d. Suppose $r_0 = 2 \times 10^7$ barrels/yr and the decay constant k is the minimum value found in part (c). How long will the total oil reserves last?

60. Snowplow problem With snow on the ground and falling at a constant rate, a snowplow began plowing down a long straight road at noon. The plow traveled twice as far in the first hour as it did in the second hour. At what time did the snow start falling? Assume the plowing rate is inversely proportional to the depth of the snow.

📖 61. Filling a reservoir A reservoir with a capacity of 2500 m³ is filled with a single inflow pipe. The reservoir is empty when the inflow pipe is opened at $t = 0$. Letting $Q(t)$ be the amount of water in the reservoir at time t, the flow rate of water into the reservoir (in m³/hr) oscillates on a 24-hr cycle (see figure) and is given by

$$Q'(t) = 20\left[1 + \cos\left(\frac{\pi t}{12}\right)\right].$$

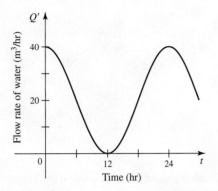

a. How much water flows into the reservoir in the first 2 hr?
b. Find and graph the function that gives the amount of water in the reservoir over the interval $[0, t]$, where $t \geq 0$.
c. When is the reservoir full?

62. **Blood flow** A typical human heart pumps 70 mL of blood with each stroke (stroke volume). Assuming a heart rate of 60 beats/min (1 beat/s), a reasonable model for the outflow rate of the heart is $V'(t) = 70(1 + \sin 2\pi t)$, where $V(t)$ is the amount of blood (in milliliters) pumped over the interval $[0, t]$, $V(0) = 0$, and t is measured in seconds.

a. Graph the outflow rate function.
b. Verify that the amount of blood pumped over a one-second interval is 70 mL.
c. Find the function that gives the total blood pumped between $t = 0$ and a future time $t > 0$.
d. What is the cardiac output over a period of 1 min? (Use calculus; then check your answer with algebra.)

63. **Air flow in the lungs** A simple model (with different parameters for different people) for the flow of air in and out of the lungs is

$$V'(t) = -\frac{\pi}{2}\sin\frac{\pi t}{2},$$

where $V(t)$ is the volume of air in the lungs at time $t \geq 0$, measured in liters, t is measured in seconds, and $t = 0$ corresponds to a time at which the lungs are full and exhalation begins. Only a fraction of the air in the lungs is exchanged with each breath. The amount that is exchanged is called the *tidal volume*.

a. Find and graph the volume function V assuming that $V(0) = 6$ L.
b. What is the breathing rate in breaths/min?
c. What is the tidal volume and what is the total capacity of the lungs?

64. **Oscillating growth rates** Some species have growth rates that oscillate with an (approximately) constant period P. Consider the growth rate function

$$N'(t) = A\sin\left(\frac{2\pi t}{P}\right) + r,$$

where A and r are constants with units of individuals/yr, and t is measured years. A species becomes extinct if its population ever reaches 0 after $t = 0$.

a. Suppose $P = 10$, $A = 20$, and $r = 0$. If the initial population is $N(0) = 10$, does the population ever become extinct? Explain.
b. Suppose $P = 10$, $A = 20$, and $r = 0$. If the initial population is $N(0) = 100$, does the population ever become extinct? Explain.
c. Suppose $P = 10$, $A = 50$, and $r = 5$. If the initial population is $N(0) = 10$, does the population ever become extinct? Explain.
d. Suppose $P = 10$, $A = 50$, and $r = -5$. Find the initial population $N(0)$ needed to ensure that the population never becomes extinct.

65. **Power and energy** Power and energy are often used interchangeably, but they are quite different. **Energy** is what makes matter move or heat up and is measured in units of **joules** (J) or **Calories** (Cal), where 1 Cal = 4184 J. One hour of walking consumes roughly 10^6 J, or 250 Cal. On the other hand, **power** is the rate at which energy is used and is measured in **watts** (W; 1 W = 1 J/s). Other useful units of power are **kilowatts** (1 kW = 10^3 W) and **megawatts** (1 MW = 10^6 W). If energy is used at a rate of 1 kW for 1 hr, the total amount of energy used is 1 **kilowatt-hour** (kWh), which is 3.6×10^6 J.

Suppose the power function of a large city over a 24-hr period is given by

$$P(t) = E'(t) = 300 - 200\sin\left(\frac{\pi t}{12}\right),$$

where P is measured in megawatts and $t = 0$ corresponds to 6 P.M. (see figure).

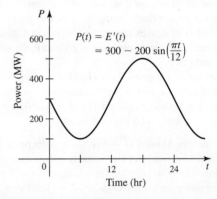

a. How much energy is consumed by this city in a typical 24-hr period? Express the answer in megawatt-hours and in joules.
b. Burning 1 kg of coal produces about 450 kWh of energy. How many kg of coal are required to meet the energy needs of the city for 1 day? For 1 year?
c. Fission of 1 g of uranium-235 (U-235) produces about 16,000 kWh of energy. How many grams of uranium are needed to meet the energy needs of the city for 1 day? For 1 year?
d. A typical wind turbine can generate electrical power at a rate of about 200 kW. Approximately how many wind turbines are needed to meet the average energy needs of the city?

66. **Variable gravity** At Earth's surface, the acceleration due to gravity is approximately $g = 9.8$ m/s² (with local variations). However, the acceleration decreases with distance from the

surface according to Newton's law of gravitation. At a distance of y meters from Earth's surface, the acceleration is given by

$$a(y) = -\frac{g}{(1 + y/R)^2},$$

where $R = 6.4 \times 10^6$ m is the radius of Earth.

a. Suppose a projectile is launched upward with an initial velocity of v_0 m/s. Let $v(t)$ be its velocity and $y(t)$ its height (in meters) above the surface t seconds after the launch. Neglecting forces such as air resistance, explain why $\dfrac{dv}{dt} = a(y)$ and $\dfrac{dy}{dt} = v(t)$.

b. Use the Chain Rule to show that $\dfrac{dv}{dt} = \dfrac{1}{2}\dfrac{d}{dy}(v^2)$.

c. Show that the equation of motion for the projectile is $\dfrac{1}{2}\dfrac{d}{dy}(v^2) = a(y)$, where $a(y)$ is given previously.

d. Integrate both sides of the equation in part (c) with respect to y using the fact that when $y = 0$, $v = v_0$. Show that

$$\frac{1}{2}(v^2 - v_0^2) = g\,R\left(\frac{1}{1 + y/R} - 1\right).$$

e. When the projectile reaches its maximum height, $v = 0$. Use this fact to determine that the maximum height is

$$y_{max} = \frac{Rv_0^2}{2gR - v_0^2}.$$

f. Graph y_{max} as a function of v_0. What is the maximum height when $v_0 = 500$ m/s, 1500 m/s, and 5 km/s?

g. Show that the value of v_0 needed to put the projectile into orbit (called the escape velocity) is $\sqrt{2gR}$.

67–68. Marginal cost *Economists use the cost function $C(x)$ to describe the cost of manufacturing x items. Also useful is the marginal cost function. If x items of a product have already been manufactured, the marginal cost $C'(x)$ is interpreted as the cost of manufacturing the $(x + 1)$st item. (Although x is an integer, it is treated as a continuous*

variable.) The marginal cost is typically a decreasing function because once the fixed setup costs have been paid, the price per additional item decreases. It follows that the cost of manufacturing items a through b, where $0 < a < b$, is $\int_a^b C'(x)\,dx$.

67. When $C'(x) = 200 - 0.05x$, compare the cost of manufacturing items 300–400 to the cost of manufacturing items 500–600. Interpret your result by graphing the marginal cost function.

68. When $C'(x) = 3000 - x - 0.001x^2$, compare the cost of manufacturing items 100–300 to the cost of manufacturing items 700–900. Interpret your result by graphing the marginal cost function.

Additional Exercises

69–72. Another look at the Fundamental Theorem

69. Suppose that f and g have continuous derivatives on an interval $[a, b]$. Prove that if $f(a) = g(a)$ and $f(b) = g(b)$, then $\int_a^b f'(x)\,dx = \int_a^b g'(x)\,dx$.

70. Use Exercise 69 to prove that if two runners start at the same time and place and finish at the same time and place, then *regardless of the velocities at which they run,* their displacements are equal.

71. Use Exercise 69 to prove that if two trails start at the same place and finish at the same place, then *regardless of the ups and downs of the trails,* they have the same net change in elevation.

72. Without evaluating integrals, prove that

$$\int_0^2 \frac{d}{dx}(12\sin(\pi x^2))\,dx = \int_0^2 \frac{d}{dx}(x^{10}(2 - x)^3)\,dx.$$

QUICK CHECK **ANSWERS**

1. Displacement $= -20$ mi (20 mi south); distance traveled $= 100$ mi   **2.** Suppose the object moves in the positive direction, for $0 \le t \le 3$, and then moves in the negative direction, for $3 < t \le 5$.   **3.** A function; a number   **4.** Displacement $= 0$; distance traveled $= 1$ **5.** 1720 m ◄

6.2 Regions Between Curves

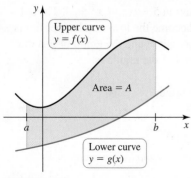

FIGURE 6.12

In this section, the method for finding the area of a region bounded by a single curve is generalized to regions bounded by two or more curves. Consider two functions f and g continuous on an interval $[a, b]$ on which $f(x) \ge g(x)$ (Figure 6.12). The goal is to find the area A of the region bounded by the two curves and the vertical lines $x = a$ and $x = b$.

Once again, we rely on the *slice-and-sum* strategy (Section 5.3) for finding areas by Riemann sums. The interval $[a, b]$ is partitioned into n subintervals using uniformly spaced grid points separated by a distance $\Delta x = (b - a)/n$ (Figure 6.13). On each subinterval, we build a rectangle extending from the lower curve to the upper curve. On the kth subinterval, a point x_k^* is chosen, and the height of the corresponding rectangle is taken to be $f(x_k^*) - g(x_k^*)$. Therefore, the area of the kth rectangle is $(f(x_k^*) - g(x_k^*))\,\Delta x$ (Figure 6.14). Summing the areas of the n rectangles gives an approximation to the area of the region between the curves:

$$A \approx \sum_{k=1}^{n}(f(x_k^*) - g(x_k^*))\,\Delta x.$$

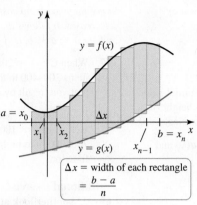

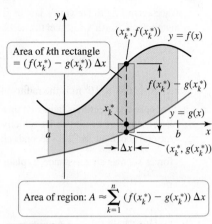

Δx = width of each rectangle
$= \dfrac{b - a}{n}$

FIGURE 6.13

Area of region: $A \approx \displaystyle\sum_{k=1}^{n} (f(x_k^*) - g(x_k^*)) \, \Delta x$

FIGURE 6.14

As the number of grid points increases, Δx approaches zero and these sums approach the area of the region between the curves; that is,

$$A = \lim_{n \to \infty} \sum_{k=1}^{n} (f(x_k^*) - g(x_k^*)) \Delta x.$$

The limit of these Riemann sums is a definite integral of the function $f - g$.

DEFINITION Area of a Region Between Two Curves

Suppose that f and g are continuous functions with $f(x) \geq g(x)$ on the interval $[a, b]$. The area of the region bounded by the graphs of f and g on $[a, b]$ is

$$A = \int_a^b (f(x) - g(x)) \, dx.$$

> It is helpful to interpret the area formula: $f(x) - g(x)$ is the length of a rectangle and dx represents its width. We sum (integrate) the areas of the rectangles $(f(x) - g(x)) \, dx$ to obtain the area of the region.

QUICK CHECK 1 In the area formula for a region between two curves, verify that if the lower curve is $g(x) = 0$, the formula becomes the usual formula for the area of the region bounded by $y = f(x)$ and the x-axis. ◄

EXAMPLE 1 Area between curves Find the area of the region bounded by the graphs of $f(x) = 5 - x^2$ and $g(x) = x^2 - 3$ (Figure 6.15).

SOLUTION A key step in the solution of many area problems is finding the intersection points of the boundary curves, which often determine the limits of integration. The intersection points of these two curves satisfy the equation $5 - x^2 = x^2 - 3$. The solutions to this equation are $x = -2$ and $x = 2$, which become the lower and upper limits of integration, respectively. The graph of f is the upper curve and the graph of g is the lower curve on the interval $[-2, 2]$. Therefore, the area of the region is

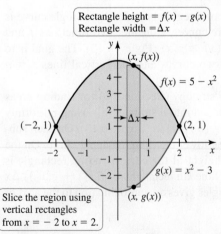

Slice the region using vertical rectangles from $x = -2$ to $x = 2$.

FIGURE 6.15

$$A = \int_{-2}^{2} (\underbrace{(5 - x^2)}_{f(x)} - \underbrace{(x^2 - 3)}_{g(x)})dx \qquad \text{Substitute for } f \text{ and } g.$$

$$= 2 \int_0^2 (8 - 2x^2)dx \qquad \text{Simplify and use symmetry.}$$

$$= 2\left(8x - \frac{2}{3}x^3 \right)\Big|_0^2 \qquad \text{Fundamental Theorem}$$

$$= \frac{64}{3}. \qquad \text{Simplify.}$$

Notice how the symmetry of the problem simplifies the integration. Also note that the area formula $A = \int_a^b (f(x) - g(x))\, dx$ is valid even if one or both curves lie below the x-axis. However, you must be sure that $f(x) \geq g(x)$ on $[a, b]$.

Related Exercise 5–14 ◄

QUICK CHECK 2 Interpret the area formula when written in the form $A = \int_a^b f(x)\, dx - \int_a^b g(x)\, dx$, where $f(x) \geq g(x) \geq 0$ on $[a, b]$. ◄

EXAMPLE 2   Compound region Find the area of the region bounded by the graphs of $f(x) = x + 3$ and $g(x) = |2x|$ (Figure 6.16a).

SOLUTION The lower boundary of the region is bounded by two different branches of the absolute value function. In situations like this, the region is divided into two (or more) subregions, whose areas are found independently and then summed; these regions are labeled R_1 and R_2 (Figure 6.16b). By the definition of absolute value,

$$g(x) = |2x| = \begin{cases} 2x & \text{if } x \geq 0 \\ -2x & \text{if } x < 0. \end{cases}$$

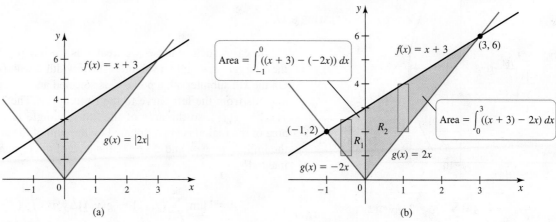

(a)

(b)

FIGURE 6.16

The left intersection point of f and g satisfies $-2x = x + 3$, or $x = -1$. The right intersection point satisfies $2x = x + 3$, or $x = 3$. We see that the region R_1 is bounded by the lines $y = x + 3$ and $y = -2x$ on the interval $[-1, 0]$. Similarly, region R_2 is bounded by the lines $y = x + 3$ and $y = 2x$ on $[0, 3]$ (Figure 6.16b). Therefore,

$$A = \underbrace{\int_{-1}^0 ((x + 3) - (-2x))\, dx}_{\text{area of region } R_1} + \underbrace{\int_0^3 ((x + 3) - 2x)\, dx}_{\text{area of region } R_2}$$

$$= \int_{-1}^0 (3x + 3)\, dx + \int_0^3 (-x + 3)\, dx \qquad \text{Simplify.}$$

$$= \left(\frac{3}{2}x^2 + 3x\right)\Big|_{-1}^0 + \left(-\frac{x^2}{2} + 3x\right)\Big|_0^3 \qquad \text{Fundamental Theorem}$$

$$= 0 - \left(\frac{3}{2} - 3\right) + \left(-\frac{9}{2} + 9\right) - 0 = 6. \qquad \text{Simplify.}$$

Related Exercises 15–22 ◄

Integrating With Respect To y

There are occasions when it is convenient to reverse the roles of x and y. Consider the regions shown in Figure 6.17 that are bounded by the graphs of $x = f(y)$ and $x = g(y)$, where $f(y) \geq g(y)$, for $c \leq y \leq d$ (which implies that the graph of f lies to the right of the graph of g). The lower and upper boundaries of the regions are $y = c$ and $y = d$, respectively.

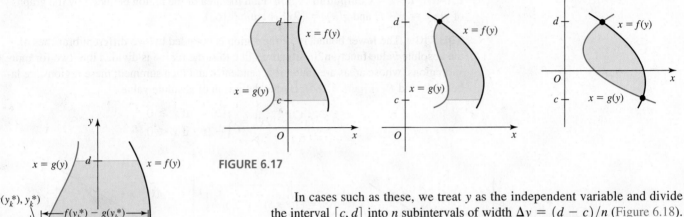

FIGURE 6.17

Area of region: $A \approx \displaystyle\sum_{k=1}^{n} (f(y_k^*) - g(y_k^*)) \, \Delta y$

FIGURE 6.18

▷ This area formula is identical to the one given on page 446; it is now expressed with respect to the y-axis. In this case, $f(y) - g(y)$ is the length of a rectangle and dy represents its width. We sum (integrate) the areas of the rectangles $(f(y) - g(y)) \, dy$ to obtain the area of the region.

In cases such as these, we treat y as the independent variable and divide the interval $[c, d]$ into n subintervals of width $\Delta y = (d - c)/n$ (Figure 6.18). On the kth subinterval, a point y_k^* is selected and we construct a rectangle that extends from the left curve to the right curve. The kth rectangle has length $f(y_k^*) - g(y_k^*)$, so the area of the kth rectangle is $(f(y_k^*) - g(y_k^*))\Delta y$. The area of the region is approximated by the sum of the areas of the rectangles. In the limit as $n \to \infty$ and $\Delta y \to 0$, the area of the region is given as the definite integral

$$A = \lim_{n \to \infty} \sum_{k=1}^{n} (f(y_k^*) - g(y_k^*))\Delta y = \int_c^d (f(y) - g(y)) \, dy.$$

DEFINITION Area of a Region Between Two Curves With Respect To y

Suppose that f and g are continuous functions with $f(y) \geq g(y)$ on the interval $[c, d]$. The area of the region bounded by the graphs $x = f(y)$ and $x = g(y)$ on $[c, d]$ is

$$A = \int_c^d (f(y) - g(y)) \, dy.$$

EXAMPLE 3   Integrating with respect to y Find the area of the region R bounded by the graphs of $y = x^3$, $y = x + 6$, and the x-axis.

SOLUTION The area of this region could be found by integrating with respect to x. But this approach requires splitting the region into two pieces (Figure 6.19). Alternatively, we can view y as the independent variable, express the bounding curves as functions of y, and make horizontal slices parallel to the x-axis (Figure 6.20).

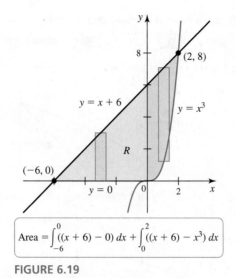

$$\text{Area} = \int_{-6}^{0}((x+6)-0)\,dx + \int_{0}^{2}((x+6)-x^3)\,dx$$

FIGURE 6.19

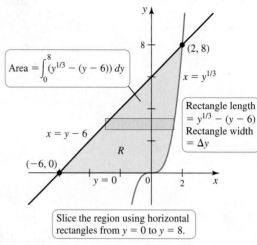

$$\text{Area} = \int_{0}^{8}(y^{1/3}-(y-6))\,dy$$

Rectangle length
$= y^{1/3}-(y-6)$
Rectangle width
$=\Delta y$

Slice the region using horizontal
rectangles from $y = 0$ to $y = 8$.

FIGURE 6.20

> You may use synthetic division or a root finder to factor the cubic polynomial in Example 3. Then the quadratic formula shows that the equation
>
> $$y^2 - 10y + 27 = 0$$
>
> has no real roots.

Solving for x in terms of y, the right curve $y = x^3$ becomes $x = f(y) = y^{1/3}$. The left curve $y = x + 6$ becomes $x = g(y) = y - 6$. The intersection point of the curves satisfies the equation $y^{1/3} = y - 6$, or $y = (y - 6)^3$. Expanding this equation gives the cubic equation

$$y^3 - 18y^2 + 107y - 216 = (y-8)(y^2 - 10y + 27) = 0,$$

whose only real root is $y = 8$. As shown in Figure 6.20, the areas of the slices through the region are summed from $y = 0$ to $y = 8$. Therefore, the area of the region is given by

QUICK CHECK 3 The region R is bounded by the curve $y = \sqrt{x}$, the line $y = x - 2$, and the x-axis. Express the area of R in terms of (a) integral(s) with respect to x and (b) integral(s) with respect to y. ◄

$$\int_{0}^{8}(y^{1/3}-(y-6))\,dy = \left(\frac{3}{4}y^{4/3} - \frac{y^2}{2} + 6y\right)\Bigg|_{0}^{8} \qquad \text{Fundamental Theorem}$$

$$= \left(\frac{3}{4}\cdot 16 - 32 + 48\right) - 0 = 28. \qquad \text{Simplify.}$$

Related Exercises 23–32 ◄

EXAMPLE 4   Calculus and geometry Find the area of the region R in the first quadrant bounded by the curves $y = x^{2/3}$ and $y = x - 4$ (Figure 6.21).

SOLUTION Slicing the region vertically and integrating with respect to x requires two integrals. Slicing the region horizontally requires a single integral with respect to y. The second approach appears to involve less work.

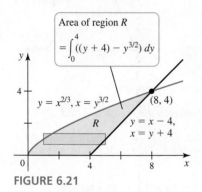

Area of region R
$= \int_{0}^{4}((y+4)-y^{3/2})\,dy$

FIGURE 6.21

Slicing horizontally, the right bounding curve is $x = y + 4$ and the left bounding curve is $x = y^{3/2}$. The two curves intersect at $(8, 4)$, so the limits of integration are $y = 0$ and $y = 4$. The area of R is

$$\int_{0}^{4}(\underbrace{(y+4)}_{\text{right curve}} - \underbrace{y^{3/2}}_{\text{left curve}})\,dy = \left(\frac{y^2}{2} + 4y - \frac{2}{5}y^{5/2}\right)\Bigg|_{0}^{4} = \frac{56}{5}.$$

Can this area be found using a different approach? Sometimes it helps to use geometry. Notice that the region R can be formed by taking the entire region under the curve $y = x^{2/3}$ on the interval $[0, 8]$ and then removing a triangle whose base is the interval $[4, 8]$ (Figure 6.22). The area of the region R_1 under the curve $y = x^{2/3}$ is

$$\int_{0}^{8}x^{2/3}\,dx = \frac{3}{5}x^{5/3}\Bigg|_{0}^{8} = \frac{96}{5}.$$

The triangle R_2 has a base of length 4 and a height of 4, so its area is $\frac{1}{2} \cdot 4 \cdot 4 = 8$. Therefore, the area of R is $\frac{96}{5} - 8 = \frac{56}{5}$, which agrees with the first calculation.

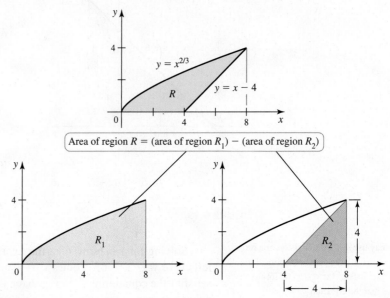

Area of region R = (area of region R_1) − (area of region R_2)

FIGURE 6.22

Related Exercises 33–38◄

QUICK CHECK 4 An alternative way to determine the area of the region in Example 3 (Figure 6.19) is to compute $18 + \int_0^2 (x + 6 - x^3)\, dx$. Why? ◄

SECTION 6.2 EXERCISES

Review Questions

1. Draw the graphs of two functions f and g that are continuous and intersect exactly twice on $(-\infty, \infty)$. Explain how to use integration to find the area of the region bounded by the two curves.

2. Draw the graphs of two functions f and g that are continuous and intersect exactly three times on $(-\infty, \infty)$. Explain how to use integration to find the area of the region bounded by the two curves.

3. Make a sketch to show a case in which the area bounded by two curves is most easily found by integrating with respect to x.

4. Make a sketch to show a case in which the area bounded by two curves is most easily found by integrating with respect to y.

Basic Skills

5–8. Finding area *Determine the area of the shaded region in the following figures.*

5.

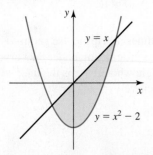

$y = x$

$y = x^2 - 2$

6.

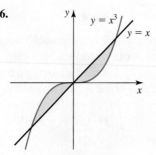

$y = x^3$

$y = x$

7.

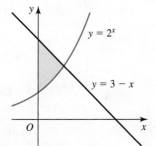

$y = 2^x$

$y = 3 - x$

8.

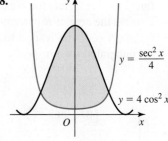

$y = \dfrac{\sec^2 x}{4}$

$y = 4\cos^2 x$

(*Hint:* Find the intersection point by inspection.)

9–14. Regions between curves *Sketch the region and find its area.*

9. The region bounded by $y = 2(x + 1)$, $y = 3(x + 1)$, and $x = 4$

10. The region bounded by $y = \cos x$ and $y = \sin x$ between $x = \pi/4$ and $x = 5\pi/4$

11. The region bounded by $y = e^x$, $y = e^{-2x}$, and $x = \ln 4$

12. The region bounded by $y = 2x$ and $y = x^2 + 3x - 6$

13. The region bounded by $y = \dfrac{2}{1 + x^2}$ and $y = 1$

14. The region bounded by $y = 24\sqrt{x}$ and $y = 3x^2$

15–22. Compound regions *Sketch the following regions (if a figure is not given) and then find the total area.*

15. The region bounded by $y = \sin x$, $y = \cos x$, and the x-axis between $x = 0$ and $x = \pi/2$

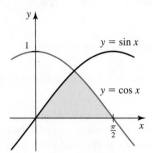

16. The regions between $y = \sin x$ and $y = \sin 2x$, for $0 \le x \le \pi$

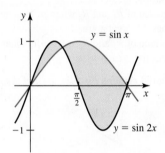

17. The region bounded by $y = x$, $y = 1/x$, $y = 0$, and $x = 2$

18. The region in the first quadrant on the interval $[0, 2]$ bounded by $y = 4x - x^2$ and $y = 4x - 4$

19. The region bounded by $y = 2 - |x|$ and $y = x^2$

20. The regions bounded by $y = x^3$ and $y = 9x$

21. The region bounded by $y = |x - 3|$ and $y = x/2$

22. The regions bounded by $y = x^2(3 - x)$ and $y = 12 - 4x$

23–26. Integrating with respect to y *Sketch the following regions (if a figure is not given) and find the total area by integrating with respect to y.*

23. The region bounded by $y = \sqrt{\dfrac{x}{2} + 1}$, $y = \sqrt{1 - x}$, and $y = 0$

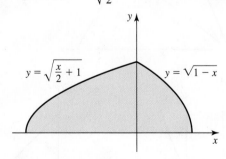

24. The region bounded by $x = \cos y$ and $x = -\sin 2y$ shown in the figure.

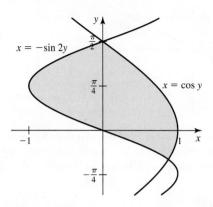

25. The region bounded by $x = y^2 - 3y + 12$ and $x = -2y^2 - 6y + 30$

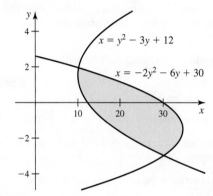

26. Both regions bounded by $x = y^3 - 4y^2 + 3y$ and $x = y^2 - y$

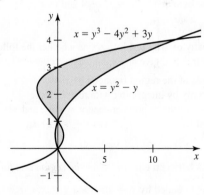

27–30. Two approaches *Express the area of the following shaded regions in terms of (a) one or more integrals with respect to x and (b) one or more integrals with respect to y. You do not need to evaluate the integrals.*

27.

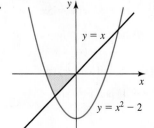

28.

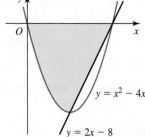

29.

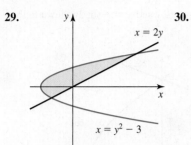

30.

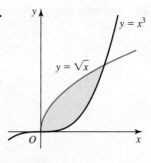

31–32. Two approaches *Find the area of the following regions by (a) integrating with respect to x and (b) integrating with respect to y. Be sure your results agree. Sketch the bounding curves and the region in question.*

31. The region bounded by $y = 2 - \dfrac{x}{2}$ and $x = 2y^2$

32. The region bounded by $x = 2 - y^2$ and $x = |y|$

33–38. Any method *Use any method (including geometry) to find the area of the following regions. In each case, sketch the bounding curves and the region in question.*

33. The region in the first quadrant bounded by $y = x^{2/3}$ and $y = 4$

34. The region in the first quadrant bounded by $y = 2$ and $y = 2 \sin x$ on the interval $[0, \pi/2]$

35. The region bounded by $y = e^x$, $y = 2e^{-x} + 1$, and $x = 0$

36. The region below the line $y = 2$ and above the curve $y = \sec^2 x$ on the interval $[0, \pi/4]$

37. The region between the line $y = x$ and the curve $y = 2x\sqrt{1 - x^2}$ in the first quadrant

38. The region bounded by $x = y^2 - 4$ and $y = x/3$

Further Explorations

39. Explain why or why not Determine whether the following statements are true and give an explanation or counterexample.

 a. The area of the region bounded by $y = x$ and $x = y^2$ can be found only by integrating with respect to x.

 b. The area of the region between $y = \sin x$ and $y = \cos x$ on the interval $[0, \pi/2]$ is $\int_0^{\pi/2}(\cos x - \sin x)\, dx$.

 c. $\int_0^1 (x - x^2)\, dx = \int_0^1 (\sqrt{y} - y)\, dy$

40–43. Regions between curves *Sketch the region and find its area.*

40. The region bounded by $y = \sin x$ and $y = x(x - \pi)$, for $0 \le x \le \pi$

41. The region bounded by $y = (x - 1)^2$ and $y = 7x - 19$

42. The region bounded by $y = 2$ and $y = \dfrac{1}{\sqrt{1 - x^2}}$

43. The region bounded by $y = x^2 - 2x + 1$ and $y = 5x - 9$

44–50. Either method *Use the most efficient strategy for computing the area of the following regions.*

44. The region bounded by $x = y(y - 1)$ and $x = -y(y - 1)$

45. The region bounded by $x = y(y - 1)$ and $y = x/3$

46. The region bounded by $y = x^3$, $y = -x^3$, and $3y - 7x - 10 = 0$

47. The region bounded by $y = \sqrt{x}$, $y = 2x - 15$, and $y = 0$

48. The region bounded by $y = x^2 - 4$, $4y - 5x - 5 = 0$, and $y = 0$, for $y \ge 0$

49. The region in the first quadrant bounded by $y = \dfrac{5}{2} - \dfrac{1}{x}$ and $y = x$

50. The region in the first quadrant bounded by $y = x^{-1}$, $y = 4x$, and $y = x/4$

51. Comparing areas Let $f(x) = x^p$ and $g(x) = x^{1/q}$, where $p > 1$ and $q > 1$ are positive integers. Let R_1 be the region in the first quadrant between $y = f(x)$ and $y = x$, and let R_2 be the region in the first quadrant between $y = g(x)$ and $y = x$.

 a. Find the area of R_1 and R_2 when $p = q$, and determine which region has the greater area.

 b. Find the area of R_1 and R_2 when $p > q$, and determine which region has the greater area.

 c. Find the area of R_1 and R_2 when $p < q$, and determine which region has the greater area.

52–55. Complicated regions *Find the area of the regions shown in the following figures.*

52.

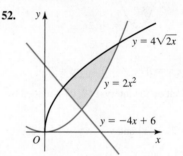

53.

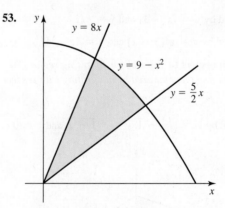

54.

55.

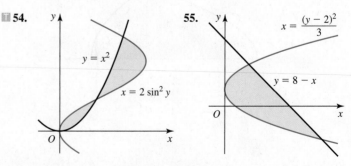

56–59. Roots and powers *Find the area of the following regions, expressing your results in terms of the positive integer $n \geq 2$.*

56. The region bounded by $f(x) = x$ and $g(x) = x^n$, for $x \geq 0$

57. The region bounded by $f(x) = x$ and $g(x) = x^{1/n}$, for $x \geq 0$

58. The region bounded by $f(x) = x^{1/n}$ and $g(x) = x^n$, for $x \geq 0$

59. Let A_n be the area of the region bounded by $f(x) = x^{1/n}$ and $g(x) = x^n$ on the interval $[0, 1]$, where n is a positive integer. Evaluate $\lim_{n \to \infty} A_n$ and interpret the result.

60–63. Bisecting regions *Given the following regions R, find the horizontal line $y = k$ that divides R into two subregions of equal area.*

60. R is the region bounded by $y = 1 - x$, the x-axis, and the y-axis.

61. R is the region bounded by $y = 1 - |x - 1|$ and the x-axis.

62. R *is* the region bounded by $y = 4 - x^2$ and the x-axis.

63. R is the region bounded by $y = \sqrt{x}$ and $y = x$.

Applications

64. Geometric probability Suppose a dartboard occupies the square $\{(x, y): 0 \leq |x| \leq 1, 0 \leq |y| \leq 1\}$. A dart is thrown randomly at the board many times (meaning it is equally likely to land at any point in the square). What fraction of the dart throws land closer to the edge of the board than the center? Equivalently, what is the probability that the dart lands closer to the edge of the board than the center? Proceed as follows.

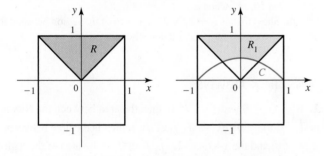

a. Argue that by symmetry, it is necessary to consider only one quarter of the board, say the region R: $\{(x, y): |x| \leq y \leq 1\}$.

b. Find the curve C in this region that is equidistant from the center of the board and the top edge of the board (see figure).

c. The probability that the dart lands closer to the edge of the board than the center is the ratio of the area of the region R_1 above C to the area of the entire region R. Compute this probability.

65. Lorenz curves and the Gini index A **Lorenz curve** is given by $y = L(x)$, where $0 \leq x \leq 1$ represents the lowest fraction of the population of a society in terms of wealth and $0 \leq y \leq 1$ represents the fraction of the total wealth that is owned by that fraction of the society. For example, the Lorenz curve in the

figure shows that $L(0.5) = 0.2$, which means that the lowest 0.5 (50%) of the society owns 0.2 (20%) of the wealth. (See the Guided Project *Distribution of Wealth* for more on Lorenz curves.)

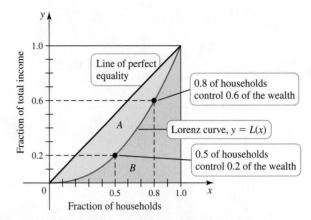

a. A Lorenz curve $y = L(x)$ is accompanied by the line $y = x$, called the **line of perfect equality**. Explain why this line is given this name.

b. Explain why a Lorenz curve satisfies the conditions $L(0) = 0, L(1) = 1, L(x) \leq x$, and $L'(x) \geq 0$ on $[0, 1]$.

c. Graph the Lorenz curves $L(x) = x^p$ corresponding to $p = 1.1, 1.5, 2, 3, 4$. Which value of p corresponds to the *most* equitable distribution of wealth (closest to the line of perfect equality)? Which value of p corresponds to the *least* equitable distribution of wealth? Explain.

d. The information in the Lorenz curve is often summarized in a single measure called the **Gini index**, which is defined as follows. Let A be the area of the region between $y = x$ and $y = L(x)$ (see figure) and let B be the area of the region between $y = L(x)$ and the x-axis. Then the Gini index is

$$G = \frac{A}{A + B}.$$ Show that $G = 2A = 1 - 2\int_0^1 L(x)\, dx.$

e. Compute the Gini index for the cases $L(x) = x^p$ and $p = 1.1, 1.5, 2, 3, 4$.

f. What is the smallest interval $[a, b]$ on which values of the Gini index lie for $L(x) = x^p$ with $p \geq 1$? Which endpoints of $[a, b]$ correspond to the least and most equitable distribution of wealth?

g. Consider the Lorenz curve described by $L(x) = 5x^2/6 + x/6$. Show that it satisfies the conditions $L(0) = 0, L(1) = 1$, and $L'(x) \geq 0$ on $[0, 1]$. Find the Gini index for this function.

Additional Exercises

66. Equal area properties for parabolas Consider the parabola $y = x^2$. Let P, Q, and R be points on the parabola with R between P and Q on the curve. Let ℓ_P, ℓ_Q, and ℓ_R be the lines tangent to the parabola at P, Q, and R, respectively (see figure). Let P' be the intersection point of ℓ_Q and ℓ_R, let Q' be the intersection point of ℓ_P and ℓ_R, and let R' be the intersection point of ℓ_P and ℓ_Q. Prove that Area $\triangle PQR = 2 \cdot$ Area $\triangle P'Q'R'$ in the following cases. (In fact, the property holds for any three points on any parabola.) (*Source: Mathematics Magazine* **81**, 2, Apr 2008)

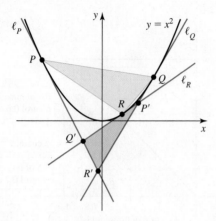

a. $P(-a, a^2)$, $Q(a, a^2)$, and $R(0, 0)$, where a is a positive real number

b. $P(-a, a^2)$, $Q(b, b^2)$, and $R(0, 0)$, where a and b are positive real numbers

c. $P(-a, a^2)$, $Q(b, b^2)$, and R is any point between P and Q on the curve

67. Minimum area Graph the curves $y = (x + 1)(x - 2)$ and $y = ax + 1$ for various values of a. For what value of a is the area of the region between the two curves a minimum?

68. An area function Graph the curves $y = a^2x^3$ and $y = \sqrt{x}$ for various values of $a > 0$. Note how the area $A(a)$ between the curves varies with a. Find and graph the area function $A(a)$. For what value of a is $A(a) = 16$?

69. Area of a curve defined implicitly Determine the area of the shaded region bounded by the curve $x^2 = y^4(1 - y^3)$ (see figure).

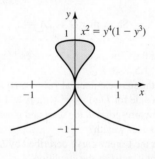

70. Rewrite first Find the area of the region bounded by the curve $x = \dfrac{1}{2y} - \sqrt{\dfrac{1}{4y^2} - 1}$ and the line $x = 1$ in the first quadrant. (*Hint:* Express y in terms of x.)

71. Area function for a cubic Consider the cubic polynomial $f(x) = x(x - a)(x - b)$, where $0 \le a \le b$.

a. For a fixed value of b, find the function $F(a) = \int_0^b f(x)\, dx$. For what value of a (which depends on b) is $F(a) = 0$?

b. For a fixed value of b, find the function $A(a)$ that gives the area of the region bounded by the graph of f and the x-axis between $x = 0$ and $x = b$. Graph this function and show that it has a minimum at $a = b/2$. What is the maximum value of $A(a)$, and where does it occur (in terms of b)?

72. Differences of even functions Assume f and g are even, integrable functions on $[-a, a]$, where $a > 1$. Suppose $f(x) > g(x) > 0$ on $[-a, a]$ and that the area bounded by the graphs of f and g on $[-a, a]$ is 10. What is the value of $\int_0^{\sqrt{a}} x[f(x^2) - g(x^2)]\, dx$?

73. Roots and powers Consider the functions $f(x) = x^n$ and $g(x) = x^{1/n}$, where $n \ge 2$ is a positive integer.

a. Graph f and g for $n = 2, 3$, and 4, for $x \ge 0$.

b. Give a geometric interpretation of the area function $A_n(x) = \int_0^x (f(s) - g(s))\, ds$, for $n = 2, 3, 4, \ldots$ and $x > 0$.

c. Find the positive root of $A_n(x) = 0$ in terms of n. Does the root increase or decrease with n?

74 Shifting sines Consider the functions $f(x) = a \sin 2x$ and $g(x) = (\sin x)/a$, where $a > 0$ is a real number.

a. Graph the two functions on the interval $[0, \pi/2]$, for $a = \frac{1}{2}, 1$, and 2.

b. Show that the curves have an intersection point x^* (other than $x = 0$) on $[0, \pi/2]$ that satisfies $\cos x^* = 1/(2a^2)$, provided $a > 1/\sqrt{2}$.

c. Find the area of the region between the two curves on $[0, x^*]$ when $a = 1$.

d. Show that as $a \to 1/\sqrt{2}^+$, the area of the region between the two curves on $[0, x^*]$ approaches zero.

QUICK CHECK ANSWERS

1. If $g(x) = 0$ and $f(x) \ge 0$, then the area between the curves is $\int_a^b (f(x) - 0)\, dx = \int_a^b f(x)\, dx$, which is the area between $y = f(x)$ and the x-axis.   **2.** $\int_a^b f(x)\, dx$ is the area of the region between the graph of f and the x-axis. $\int_a^b g(x)\, dx$ is the area of the region between the graph of g and the x-axis. The difference of the two integrals is the area of the region between the graphs of f and g.   **3. a.** $\int_0^2 \sqrt{x}\, dx + \int_2^4 (\sqrt{x} - x + 2)\, dx$ **b.** $\int_0^2 (y + 2 - y^2)\, dy$.   **4.** The area of the triangle to the left of the y-axis is 18. The area of the region to the right of the y-axis is given by the integral. ◄

6.3 Volume by Slicing

We have seen that integration is used to compute the area of two-dimensional regions bounded by curves. Integrals are also used to find the volume of three-dimensional regions (or solids). Once again, the slice-and-sum method is the key to solving these problems.

General Slicing Method

Consider a solid object that extends in the x-direction from $x = a$ to $x = b$. Imagine cutting through the solid, perpendicular to the x-axis at a particular point x, and suppose the area of the cross section created by the cut is given by a known integrable function A (Figure 6.23).

To find the volume of this solid, we first divide $[a, b]$ into n subintervals of length $\Delta x = (b - a)/n$. The endpoints of the subintervals are the grid points $x_0 = a, x_1$, $x_2, \ldots, x_n = b$. We now make cuts through the solid perpendicular to the x-axis at each grid point, which produces n slices of thickness Δx. (Imagine cutting a loaf of bread to create n slices of equal width.) On each subinterval, an arbitrary point x_k^* is identified. The kth slice through the solid has a thickness Δx, and we take $A(x_k^*)$ as a representative cross-sectional area of the slice. Therefore, the volume of the kth slice is approximately $A(x_k^*)\Delta x$ (Figure 6.24). Summing the volumes of the slices, the approximate volume of the solid is

$$V \approx \sum_{k=1}^{n} A(x_k^*)\Delta x.$$

As the number of slices increases ($n \to \infty$) and the thickness of each slice goes to zero ($\Delta x \to 0$), the exact volume V is obtained in terms of a definite integral (Figure 6.25):

$$V = \lim_{n \to \infty} \sum_{k=1}^{n} A(x_k^*)\Delta x = \int_a^b A(x)\, dx.$$

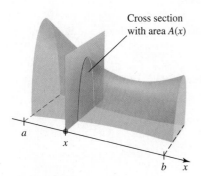

Cross section with area $A(x)$

FIGURE 6.23

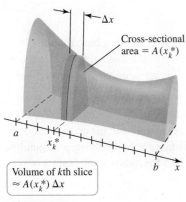

Δx

Cross-sectional area $= A(x_k^*)$

Volume of kth slice $\approx A(x_k^*)\,\Delta x$

FIGURE 6.24

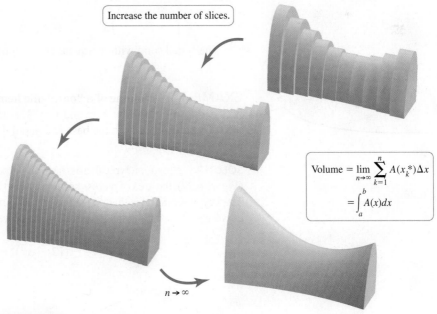

Increase the number of slices.

Volume $= \lim_{n \to \infty} \sum_{k=1}^{n} A(x_k^*)\Delta x$

$= \int_a^b A(x)dx$

$n \to \infty$

FIGURE 6.25

We summarize the important general slicing method, which will also be the basis of other volume formulas.

> The factors in this volume integral have meaning: $A(x)$ is the cross-sectional area of a slice and dx represents its thickness. Summing (integrating) the volumes of the slices $A(x)\,dx$ gives the volume of the solid.

General Slicing Method

Suppose a solid object extends from $x = a$ to $x = b$ and the cross section of the solid perpendicular to the x-axis has an area given by a function A that is integrable on $[a, b]$. The volume of the solid is

$$V = \int_a^b A(x)\,dx.$$

QUICK CHECK 1 Explain why the volume, as given by the general slicing method, is equal to the average value of $A(x)$ on $[a, b]$ multiplied by $b - a$. ◄

EXAMPLE 1 **Volume of a "parabolic cube"** Let R be the region in the first quadrant bounded by the coordinate axes and the curve $y = 1 - x^2$. A solid has a base formed by R, and cross sections through the solid perpendicular to the base and parallel to the y-axis are squares (Figure 6.26a). Find the volume of the solid.

SOLUTION Focus on a cross section through the solid at a point x, where $0 \le x \le 1$. That cross section is a square with sides of length $1 - x^2$. Therefore, the area of a typical cross section is $A(x) = (1 - x^2)^2$. Using the general slicing method, the volume of the solid is

$$
\begin{aligned}
V &= \int_0^1 A(x)\,dx & \text{General slicing method} \\[2mm]
&= \int_0^1 (1-x^2)^2\,dx & \text{Substitute for } A(x). \\[2mm]
&= \int_0^1 (1 - 2x^2 - x^4)\,dx & \text{Expand integrand.} \\[2mm]
&= \frac{8}{15}. & \text{Evaluate.}
\end{aligned}
$$

The actual solid with its square cross sections is shown in Figure 6.26b.

Related Exercise 7–16 ◄

EXAMPLE 2 **Volume of a "parabolic hemisphere"** A solid has a base that is bounded by the curves $y = x^2$ and $y = 2 - x^2$ in the xy-plane. Cross sections through the solid perpendicular to the base and parallel to the y-axis are semicircular disks. Find the volume of the solid.

SOLUTION Because a typical cross section perpendicular to the x-axis is a semicircular disk (Figure 6.27), the area of a cross section is $\frac{1}{2}\pi r^2$, where r is the radius of the cross section. The key observation is that this radius is one-half of the distance between the upper bounding curve $y = 2 - x^2$ and the lower bounding curve $y = x^2$. So the radius at the point x is

$$r = \frac{1}{2}\big((2 - x^2) - x^2\big) = 1 - x^2.$$

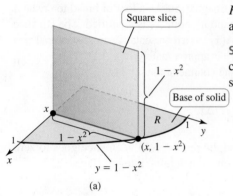

(a)

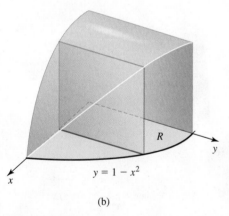

(b)

FIGURE 6.26

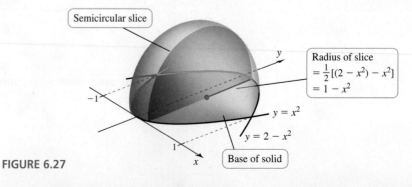

FIGURE 6.27

This means that the area of the semicircular cross section at the point x is

$$A(x) = \frac{1}{2}\pi r^2 = \frac{\pi}{2}(1-x^2)^2.$$

The intersection points of the two bounding curves satisfy $2 - x^2 = x^2$, which has solutions $x = \pm 1$. Therefore, the cross sections lie between $x = -1$ and $x = 1$. Integrating the cross-sectional areas, the volume of the solid is

$$V = \int_{-1}^{1} A(x)\,dx \qquad \text{General slicing method}$$

$$= \int_{-1}^{1} \frac{\pi}{2}(1-x^2)^2\,dx \qquad \text{Substitute for } A(x).$$

$$= \frac{\pi}{2}\int_{-1}^{1}(1 - 2x^2 + x^4)\,dx \qquad \text{Expand integand.}$$

$$= \frac{8\pi}{15}. \qquad \text{Evaluate.}$$

Related Exercises 7–16◄

QUICK CHECK 2 In Example 1, what is the cross-sectional area function $A(x)$ if cross sections perpendicular to the base are squares rather than semicircles? ◄

The Disk Method

We now consider a specific type of solid known as a **solid of revolution**. Suppose f is a continuous function with $f(x) \geq 0$ on an interval $[a, b]$. Let R be the region bounded by the graph of f, the x-axis, and the lines $x = a$ and $x = b$ (Figure 6.28). Now revolve R about the x-axis. As R revolves once about the x-axis, it sweeps out a three-dimensional solid of revolution (Figure 6.29). The goal is to find the volume of this solid, and it may be done using the general slicing method.

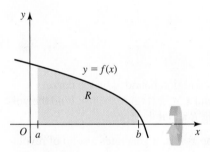

FIGURE 6.28

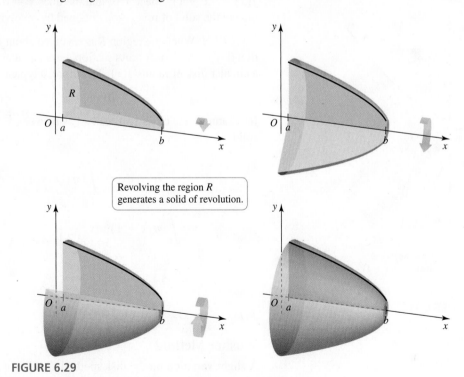

Revolving the region R generates a solid of revolution.

FIGURE 6.29

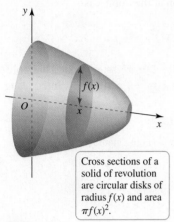

Cross sections of a solid of revolution are circular disks of radius $f(x)$ and area $\pi f(x)^2$.

FIGURE 6.30

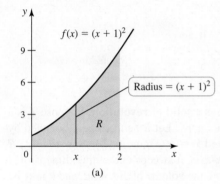

(a)

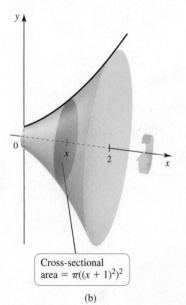

Cross-sectional area = $\pi((x + 1)^2)^2$

(b)

FIGURE 6.31

QUICK CHECK 3 What solid results when the region R is revolved about the x-axis if (a) R is a square with vertices $(0, 0)$, $(0, 2)$, $(2, 0)$, and $(2, 2)$ and (b) R is a triangle with vertices $(0, 0)$, $(0, 2)$, and $(2, 0)$? ◄

With a solid of revolution, the cross-sectional area function has a special form because all cross sections perpendicular to the x-axis are *circular disks* with radius $f(x)$ (Figure 6.30). Therefore, the cross section at the point x, where $a \le x \le b$, has area

$$A(x) = \pi(\text{radius})^2 = \pi f(x)^2.$$

By the general slicing method, the volume of the solid is

$$V = \int_a^b A(x) \, dx = \int_a^b \pi f(x)^2 \, dx.$$

Because each slice through the solid is a circular disk, the resulting method is called the *disk method*.

Disk Method About the x-Axis

Let f be continuous with $f(x) \ge 0$ on the interval $[a, b]$. If the region R bounded by the graph of f, the x-axis, and the lines $x = a$ and $x = b$ is revolved about the x-axis, the volume of the resulting solid of revolution is

$$V = \int_a^b \pi f(x)^2 \, dx.$$

EXAMPLE 3   Disk method at work Let R be the region bounded by the curve $f(x) = (x + 1)^2$, the x-axis, and the lines $x = 0$ and $x = 2$ (Figure 6.31a). Find the volume of the solid of revolution obtained by revolving R about the x-axis.

SOLUTION When the region R is revolved about the x-axis, it generates a solid of revolution (Figure 6.31b). A cross section perpendicular to the x-axis at the point $0 \le x \le 2$ is a circular disk of radius $f(x)$. Therefore, a typical cross section has area

$$A(x) = \pi f(x)^2 = \pi((x + 1)^2)^2.$$

Integrating these cross-sectional areas between $x = 0$ and $x = 2$ gives the volume of the solid:

$$V = \int_0^2 A(x) \, dx = \int_0^2 \pi((x + 1)^2)^2 \, dx \quad \text{Substitute for } A(x).$$

$$= \int_0^2 \pi(x + 1)^4 \, dx \qquad\qquad\qquad \text{Simplify.}$$

$$= \pi \left. \frac{u^5}{5} \right|_1^3 = \frac{242\pi}{5}. \qquad\qquad \text{Let } u = x + 1 \text{ and evaluate.}$$

Related Exercises 17–26 ◄

Washer Method

A slight variation on the disk method enables us to compute the volume of more exotic solids of revolution. Suppose that R is the region bounded by the graphs of f and g between $x = a$ and $x = b$, where $f(x) \ge g(x) \ge 0$ (Figure 6.32). If R is revolved about the x-axis to generate a solid of revolution, the resulting solid generally has a hole through it.

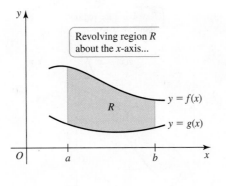

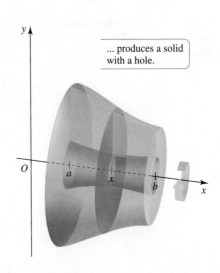

FIGURE 6.32

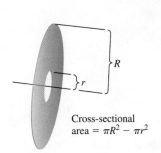

Cross-sectional
area $= \pi R^2 - \pi r^2$

Once again, we apply the general slicing method. In this case, a cross section through the solid perpendicular to the x-axis is a circular *washer* with an outer radius of $R = f(x)$ and an inner radius of $r = g(x)$, where $a \le x \le b$. The area of the cross section is the area of the entire disk minus the area of the hole, or

$$A(x) = \pi R^2 - \pi r^2 = \pi(f(x)^2 - g(x)^2).$$

(Figure 6.33). The general slicing method gives the area of the solid.

Washer Method About the x-Axis

Let f and g be continuous functions with $f(x) \ge g(x) \ge 0$ on $[a, b]$. Let R be the region bounded by $y = f(x)$, $y = g(x)$, and the lines $x = a$ and $x = b$. When R is revolved about the x-axis, the volume of the resulting solid of revolution is

$$V = \int_a^b \pi(f(x)^2 - g(x)^2)\, dx.$$

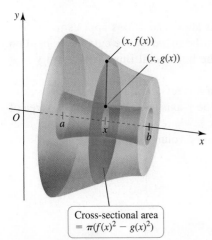

Cross-sectional area
$= \pi(f(x)^2 - g(x)^2)$

FIGURE 6.33

▸ The washer method is really two applications of the disk method. We compute the volume of the entire solid without the hole (by the disk method) and then subtract the volume of the hole (also computed by the disk method).

QUICK CHECK 4 Show that when $g(x) = 0$ in the washer method, the result is the disk method. ◂

EXAMPLE 4   Volume by the washer method The region R is bounded by the graphs of $f(x) = \sqrt{x}$ and $g(x) = x^2$ between $x = 0$ and $x = 1$. What is the volume of the solid that results when R is revolved about the x-axis?

SOLUTION The region R is bounded by the graphs of f and g with $f(x) \ge g(x)$ on $[0, 1]$, so the washer method is applicable (Figure 6.34). The area of a typical cross section at the point x is

$$A(x) = \pi(f(x)^2 - g(x)^2) = \pi((\sqrt{x})^2 - (x^2)^2) = \pi(x - x^4).$$

Therefore, the volume of the solid is

$$V = \int_0^1 \pi(x - x^4)\, dx \qquad \text{Washer method}$$

$$= \pi\left(\frac{x^2}{2} - \frac{x^5}{5}\right)\Bigg|_0^1 = \frac{3\pi}{10}. \qquad \text{Fundamental Theorem}$$

▷ The integrand in the washer method integral is $f(x)^2 - g(x)^2$, which is not equal to $(f(x) - g(x))^2$!

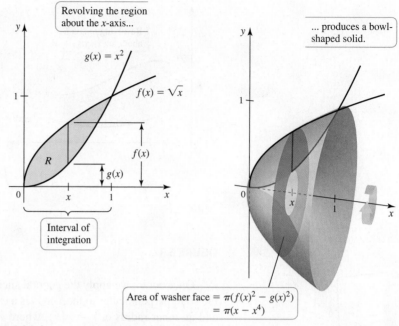

Revolving the region about the x-axis...

$g(x) = x^2$

$f(x) = \sqrt{x}$

R

$f(x)$

$g(x)$

Interval of integration

... produces a bowl-shaped solid.

Area of washer face $= \pi(f(x)^2 - g(x)^2)$
$= \pi(x - x^4)$

FIGURE 6.34

Related Exercises 27–34 ◀

QUICK CHECK 5 Suppose the region in Example 3 is revolved about the line $y = -1$ instead of the x-axis. (a) What is the inner radius of a typical washer? (b) What is the outer radius of a typical washer? ◀

Revolving About the y-Axis

Everything you learned about revolving regions about the x-axis applies to revolving regions about the y-axis. Consider a region R bounded by the curve $x = p(y)$ on the right, the curve $x = q(y)$ on the left, and the horizontal lines $y = c$ and $y = d$ (Figure 6.35a).

To find the volume of the solid generated when R is revolved about the y-axis, we use the general slicing method—now with respect to the y-axis (Figure 6.35b). The area of a typical cross section is $A(y) = \pi(p(y)^2 - q(y)^2)$, where $c \leq y \leq d$. As before, integrating these cross-sectional areas of the solid gives the volume.

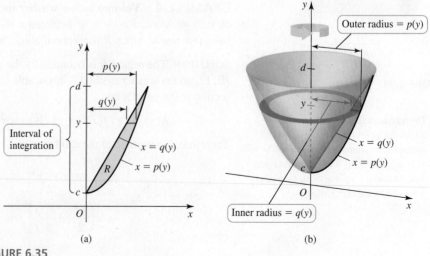

$p(y)$

$q(y)$

Interval of integration

$x = q(y)$

R $x = p(y)$

(a)

Outer radius $= p(y)$

$x = q(y)$

$x = p(y)$

Inner radius $= q(y)$

(b)

FIGURE 6.35

▶ The disk/washer method about the
y-axis is the disk/washer method about
the x-axis with x replaced with y.

Disk and Washer Methods About the y-Axis

Let p and q be continuous functions with $p(y) \geq q(y) \geq 0$ on $[c, d]$. Let R be the region bounded by $x = p(y)$, $x = q(y)$, and the lines $y = c$ and $y = d$. When R is revolved about the y-axis, the volume of the resulting solid of revolution is given by

$$V = \int_c^d \pi (p(y)^2 - q(y)^2) \, dy.$$

If $q(y) = 0$, the disk method results:

$$V = \int_c^d \pi p(y)^2 \, dy.$$

EXAMPLE 5   **Which solid has greater volume?** Let R be the region in the first quadrant bounded by the graphs of $x = y^3$ and $x = 4y$. Which is greater, the volume of the solid generated when R is revolved about the x-axis or the y-axis?

SOLUTION Solving $y^3 = 4y$, or equivalently, $y(y^2 - 4) = 0$, we find that the bounding curves of R intersect at the points $(0, 0)$ and $(8, 2)$. When the region R is revolved about the y-axis, it generates a funnel with a curved inner surface (Figure 6.36). Washer-shaped cross sections perpendicular to the y-axis extend from $y = 0$ to $y = 2$. The outer radius of the cross section at the point y is determined by the line $x = p(y) = 4y$. The inner radius of the cross section at the point y is determined by the curve $x = q(y) = y^3$. Applying the washer method, the volume of this solid is

$$V = \int_0^2 \pi (p(y)^2 - q(y)^2) \, dy \qquad \text{Washer method}$$

$$= \int_0^2 \pi (16y^2 - y^6) \, dy \qquad \text{Substitute for } p \text{ and } q.$$

$$= \pi \left(\frac{16}{3} y^3 - \frac{y^7}{7} \right) \Bigg|_0^2 \qquad \text{Fundamental Theorem}$$

$$= \frac{512\pi}{21}. \qquad \text{Evaluate.}$$

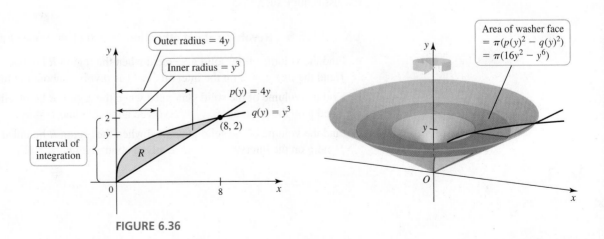

FIGURE 6.36

When the region R is revolved about the x-axis, it generates a different funnel (Figure 6.37). Vertical slices through the solid between $x = 0$ and $x = 8$ produce washers. The outer radius of the washer at the point x is determined by the curve $x = y^3$, or $y = f(x) = x^{1/3}$. The inner radius is determined by $x = 4y$, or $y = g(x) = x/4$. The volume of the resulting solid is

$$V = \int_0^8 \pi(f(x)^2 - g(x)^2)\, dx \quad \text{Washer method}$$

$$= \int_0^8 \pi\left(x^{2/3} - \frac{x^2}{16}\right) dx \quad \text{Substitute for } f \text{ and } g.$$

$$= \pi\left(\frac{3}{5}x^{5/3} - \frac{x^3}{48}\right)\Bigg|_0^8 \quad \text{Fundamental Theorem}$$

$$= \frac{128\pi}{15}. \quad \text{Evaluate.}$$

We see that revolving the region about the y-axis produces a solid of greater volume.

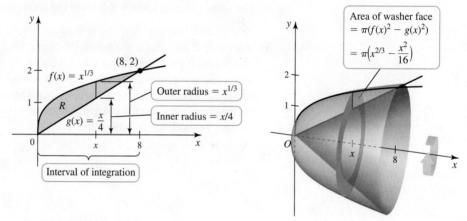

FIGURE 6.37

Related Exercises 35–44 ◀

QUICK CHECK 6 The region in the first quadrant bounded by $y = x$ and $y = x^3$ is revolved about the y-axis. Give the integral for the volume of the solid that is generated. ◀

The disk and washer methods may be generalized to handle situations where a region R is revolved about a line parallel to one of the coordinate axes. The next example discusses three such cases.

EXAMPLE 6   Revolving about other lines Let $f(x) = \sqrt{x} + 1$ and $g(x) = x^2 + 1$.

a. Find the volume of the solid generated when the region R bounded by the graph of f and the line $y = 2$ on the interval $[0, 1]$ is revolved about the line $y = 2$.

b. Find the volume of the solid generated when the region R bounded by the graphs of f and g on the interval $[0, 1]$ is revolved about the line $y = -1$.

c. Find the volume of the solid generated when the region R bounded by the graphs of f and g on the interval $[0, 1]$ is revolved about the line $x = 2$.

SOLUTION

a. Figure 6.38a shows the region R and the axis of revolution. Applying the disk method, we see that a disk located at a point x has a radius of $2 - f(x) = 2 - (\sqrt{x} + 1) = 1 - \sqrt{x}$. Therefore, the volume of the solid generated when R is revolved about $y = 2$ is

$$\int_0^1 \pi(1 - \sqrt{x})^2 \, dx = \pi \int_0^1 (1 - 2\sqrt{x} + x) \, dx = \frac{\pi}{6}.$$

b. When the graph of f is revolved about $y = -1$, it sweeps out a solid of revolution whose radius at a point x is $f(x) + 1 = \sqrt{x} + 2$. Similarly, when the graph of g is revolved about $y = -1$, it sweeps out a solid of revolution whose radius at a point x is $g(x) + 1 = x^2 + 2$ (Figure 6.38b). Using the washer method, the volume of the solid generated when R is revolved about $y = -1$ is

$$\int_0^1 \pi((\sqrt{x} + 2)^2 - (x^2 + 2)^2) \, dx$$

$$= \pi \int_0^1 (-x^4 - 4x^2 + x + 4\sqrt{x}) \, dx$$

$$= \frac{49\pi}{30}.$$

c. When the region R is revolved about the line $x = 2$, we use the washer method and integrate in the y-direction. First note that the graph of f is described by $y = \sqrt{x} + 1$, or equivalently, $x = (y - 1)^2$, for $y \geq 1$. Also, the graph of g is described by $y = x^2 + 1$, or equivalently, $x = \sqrt{y - 1}$, for $y \geq 1$ (Figure 6.38c). When the graph of f is revolved about the line $x = 2$, the radius of a typical disk at a point y is $2 - (y - 1)^2$. Similarly, when the graph of g is revolved about $x = 2$, the radius of a typical disk at a point y is $2 - \sqrt{y - 1}$. Finally, observe that the extent of the region R in the y-direction is the interval $1 \leq y \leq 2$.

Applying the washer method, simplifying the integrand, and integrating powers of y, the volume of the solid of revolution is

$$\int_1^2 \pi\left[(2 - (y - 1)^2)^2 - (2 - \sqrt{y - 1})^2\right] dy = \frac{31\pi}{30}.$$

Related Exercises 45–52 ◄

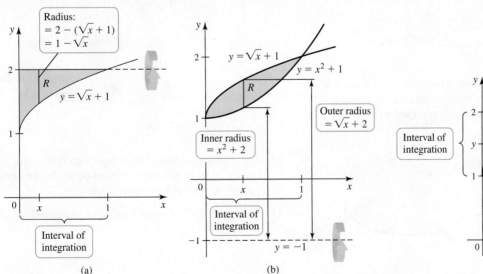

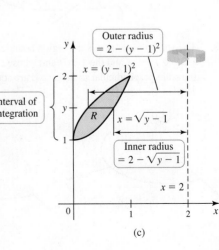

(a)   (b)   (c)

FIGURE 6.38

SECTION 6.3 EXERCISES

Review Questions

1. Suppose a cut is made through a solid object perpendicular to the x-axis at a particular point x. Explain the meaning of $A(x)$.

2. Describe how a solid of revolution is generated.

3. The region bounded by the curves $y = 2x$ and $y = x^2$ is revolved about the x-axis. Give an integral for the volume of the solid that is generated.

4. The region bounded by the curves $y = 2x$ and $y = x^2$ is revolved about the y-axis. Give an integral for the volume of the solid that is generated.

5. Why is the disk method a special case of the general slicing method?

6. A solid has a circular base and cross sections perpendicular to the base are squares. What method should be used to find the volume of the solid?

Basic Skills

7–16. General slicing method *Use the general slicing method to find the volume of the following solids.*

7. The solid whose base is the region bounded by the curves $y = x^2$ and $y = 2 - x^2$ and whose cross sections through the solid perpendicular to the x-axis are squares

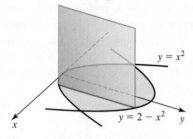

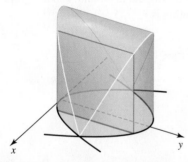

8. The solid whose base is the region bounded by the semicircle $y = \sqrt{1 - x^2}$ and the x-axis and whose cross sections through the solid perpendicular to the x-axis are squares

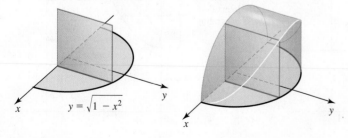

9. The solid whose base is the region bounded by the curve $y = \sqrt{\cos x}$ and the x-axis and whose cross sections through the solid perpendicular to the x-axis are isosceles right triangles with a horizontal leg in the xy-plane and a vertical leg above the x-axis

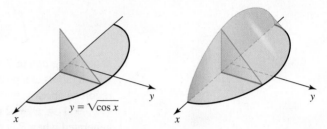

10. The solid with a circular base of radius 5 whose cross sections perpendicular to the base and parallel to the x-axis are equilateral triangles

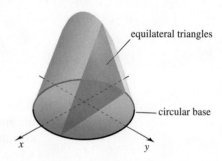

11. The solid with a semicircular base of radius 5 whose cross sections perpendicular to the base and parallel to the diameter are squares

12. The solid whose base is the region bounded by $y = x^2$ and the line $y = 1$ and whose cross sections perpendicular to the base and parallel to the x-axis are squares

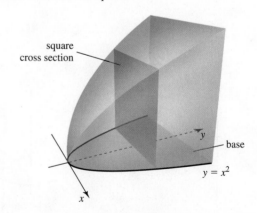

13. The solid whose base is the triangle with vertices $(0, 0)$, $(2, 0)$, and $(0, 2)$ and whose cross sections perpendicular to the base and parallel to the y-axis are semicircles

14. The pyramid with a square base 4 m on a side and a height of 2 m (Use calculus.)

15. The tetrahedron (pyramid with four triangular faces), all of whose edges have length 4

16. A circular cylinder of radius r and height h whose axis is at an angle of $\pi/4$ to the base

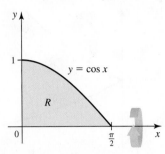

17–26. Disk method *Let R be the region bounded by the following curves. Use the disk method to find the volume of the solid generated when R is revolved about the x-axis.*

17. $y = 2x, y = 0, x = 3$ (Verify that your answer agrees with the volume formula for a cone.)

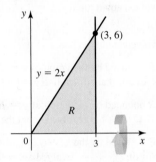

18. $y = 2 - 2x, y = 0, x = 0$ (Verify that your answer agrees with the volume formula for a cone.)

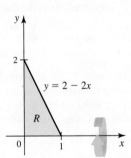

19. $y = e^{-x}, y = 0, x = 0, x = \ln 4$

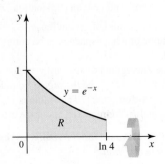

20. $y = \cos x, y = 0, x = 0$ (Recall that $\cos^2 x = \frac{1}{2}(1 + \cos 2x)$.)

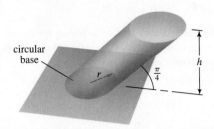

21. $y = \sin x, y = 0$, for $0 \le x \le \pi$ (Recall that $\sin^2 x = \frac{1}{2}(1 - \cos 2x)$.)

22. $y = \sqrt{25 - x^2}, y = 0$ (Verify that your answer agrees with the volume formula for a sphere.)

23. $y = \dfrac{1}{\sqrt[4]{1 - x^2}}, y = 0, x = 0$, and $x = \frac{1}{2}$

24. $y = \sec x, y = 0, x = 0$, and $x = \frac{\pi}{4}$

25. $y = \dfrac{1}{\sqrt{1 + x^2}}, y = 0, x = -1$, and $x = 1$

26. $y = \dfrac{1}{\sqrt[4]{1 - x^2}}, y = 0, x = -\frac{1}{2}$, and $x = \frac{1}{2}$

27–34. Washer method *Let R be the region bounded by the following curves. Use the washer method to find the volume of the solid generated when R is revolved about the x-axis.*

27. $y = x, y = 2\sqrt{x}$

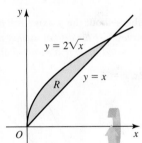

28. $y = x, y = \sqrt[4]{x}$

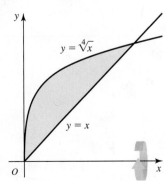

29. $y = e^{x/2}, y = e^{-x/2}, x = \ln 2, x = \ln 3$

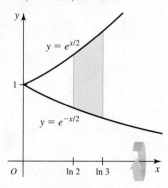

30. $y = x, y = x + 2, x = 0, x = 4$

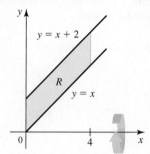

31. $y = x + 3, y = x^2 + 1$

32. $y = \sqrt{\sin x}, y = 1, x = 0$

33. $y = \sin x, y = \sqrt{\sin x}$, for $0 \le x \le \pi/2$

34. $y = |x|, y = 2 - x^2$

35–40. Disks/washers about the y-axis *Let R be the region bounded by the following curves. Use the disk or washer method to find the volume of the solid generated when R is revolved about the y-axis.*

35. $y = x, y = 2x, y = 6$

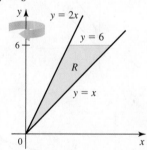

36. $y = 0, y = \ln x, y = 2, x = 0$

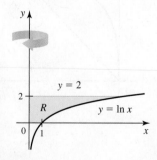

37. $y = x^3, y = 0, x = 2$

38. $y = \sqrt{x}, y = 0, x = 4$

39. $x = \sqrt{4 - y^2}, x = 0$

40. $y = \sin^{-1} x, x = 0, y = \pi/4$

41–44. Which is greater? *For the following regions R, determine which is greater—the volume of the solid generated when R is revolved about the x-axis or about the y-axis.*

41. R is bounded by $y = 2x$, the x-axis, and $x = 5$.

42. R is bounded by $y = 4 - 2x$, the x-axis, and the y-axis.

43. R is bounded by $y = 1 - x^3$, the x-axis, and the y-axis.

44. R is bounded by $y = x^2$ and $y = \sqrt{8x}$.

45–52. Revolution about other axes *Find the volume of the solid generated in the following situations.*

45. The region R bounded by the graphs of $x = 0$, $y = \sqrt{x}$, and $y = 1$ is revolved about the line $y = 1$.

46. The region R bounded by the graphs of $x = 0$, $y = \sqrt{x}$, and $y = 2$ is revolved about the line $x = 4$.

47. The region R bounded by the graph of $y = 2 \sin x$ and the x-axis on $[0, \pi]$ is revolved about the line $y = -2$.

48. The region R bounded by the graph of $y = \ln x$ and the y-axis on the interval $0 \le y \le 1$ is revolved about the line $x = -1$.

49. The region R bounded by the graphs of $y = \sin x$ and $y = 1 - \sin x$ on $[\frac{\pi}{6}, \frac{5\pi}{6}]$ is revolved about the line $y = -1$.

50. The region R in the first quadrant bounded by the graphs of $y = x$ and $y = 1 + \dfrac{x}{2}$ is revolved about the line $y = 3$.

51. The region R in the first quadrant bounded by the graphs of $y = 2 - x$ and $y = 2 - 2x$ is revolved about the line $x = 3$.

52. The region R is bounded by the graph of $f(x) = 2x(2 - x)$ and the x-axis. Which is greater—the volume of the solid generated when R is revolved about the line $y = 2$ or the volume of the solid generated when R is revolved about the line $y = 0$? Confirm your result by integration.

Further Explorations

53. **Explain why or why not** Determine whether the following statements are true and give an explanation or counterexample.

   a. A pyramid is a solid of revolution.

   b. The volume of a hemisphere can be computed using the disk method.

   c. Let R_1 be the region bounded by $y = \cos x$ and the x-axis on $[-\pi/2, \pi/2]$. Let R_2 be the region bounded by $y = \sin x$ and the x-axis on $[0, \pi]$. The volumes of the solids generated when R_1 and R_2 are revolved about the x-axis are equal.

54–60. Solids of revolution *Find the volume of the solid of revolution. Sketch the region in question.*

54. The region bounded by $y = (\ln x)/\sqrt{x}, y = 0$, and $x = 2$ revolved about the x-axis

55. The region bounded by $y = 1/\sqrt{x}$, $y = 0$, $x = 2$, and $x = 6$ revolved about the x-axis

56. The region bounded by $y = \dfrac{1}{\sqrt{x^2 + 1}}$ and $y = \dfrac{1}{\sqrt{2}}$ revolved about the x-axis

57. The region bounded by $y = e^x$, $y = 0$, $x = 0$, and $x = 2$ revolved about the x-axis

58. The region bounded by $y = e^{-x}$, $y = e^x$, $x = 0$, and $x = \ln 4$ revolved about the x-axis

59. The region bounded by $y = \ln x$, $y = \ln x^2$, and $y = \ln 8$ revolved about the y-axis

60. The region bounded by $y = e^{-x}$, $y = 0$, $x = 0$, and $x = p > 0$ revolved about the x-axis (Is the volume bounded as $p \to \infty$?)

61. Fermat's volume calculation (1636) Let R be the region bounded by the curve $y = \sqrt{x + a}$ (with $a > 0$), the y-axis, and the x-axis. Let S be the solid generated by rotating R about the y-axis. Let T be the inscribed cone that has the same circular base as S and height $\sqrt{a}$. Show that volume(S)/volume$(T) = \frac{8}{5}$.

62. Solid from a piecewise function Let

$$f(x) = \begin{cases} x & \text{if } 0 \le x \le 2 \\ 2x - 2 & \text{if } 2 < x \le 5 \\ -2x + 18 & \text{if } 5 < x \le 6. \end{cases}$$

Find the volume of the solid formed when the region bounded by the graph of f, the x-axis, and the line $x = 6$ is revolved about the x-axis.

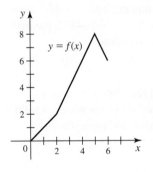
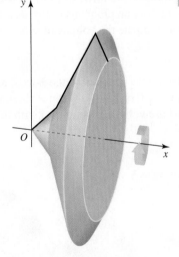

63. Solids from integrals Sketch a solid of revolution whose volume by the disk method is given by the following integrals. Indicate the function that generates the solid. Solutions are not unique.

a. $\displaystyle\int_0^{\pi} \pi \sin^2 x \, dx$

b. $\displaystyle\int_0^2 \pi (x^2 + 2x + 1) \, dx$

Applications

64. Volume of a wooden object A solid wooden object turned on a lathe has a length of 50 cm and diameters (measured in cm) shown in the figure. (A lathe is a tool that spins and cuts a block of wood so that it has circular cross sections.) Use left Riemann sums with evenly spaced grid points to estimate the volume of the object.

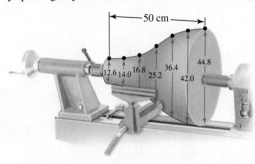

65. Cylinder, cone, hemisphere A right circular cylinder with height R and radius R has a volume of $V_C = \pi R^3$ (height = radius).

a. Find the volume of the cone that is inscribed in the cylinder with the same base as the cylinder and height R. Express the volume in terms of V_C.

b. Find the volume of the hemisphere that is inscribed in the cylinder with the same base as the cylinder. Express the volume in terms of V_C.

66. Water in a bowl A hemispherical bowl of radius 8 inches is filled to a depth of h inches, where $0 \le h \le 8$. Find the volume of water in the bowl as a function of h. (Check the special cases $h = 0$ and $h = 8$.)

67. A torus (doughnut) Find the volume of the torus formed when the circle of radius 2 centered at $(3, 0)$ is revolved about the y-axis. Use geometry to evaluate the integral.

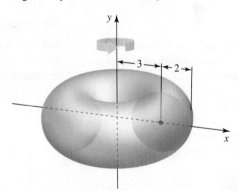

68. Which is greater? Let R be the region bounded by $y = x^2$ and $y = \sqrt{x}$. Use integration to determine which is greater—the volume of the solid generated when R is revolved about the x-axis or about the line $y = 1$.

Additional Exercises

69. Cavalieri's principle *Cavalieri's principle* states that if two solids of equal altitudes have the same cross-sectional areas at every height, then they have equal volumes (see figure).

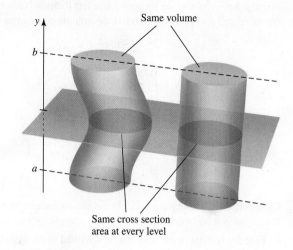

Same volume

Same cross section area at every level

a. Use the theory of this section to justify Cavalieri's principle.

b. Find the radius of a circular cylinder of height 10 m that has the same volume as a box whose dimensions in meters are $2 \times 2 \times 10$.

70. Limiting volume Consider the region R in the first quadrant bounded by $y = x^{1/n}$ and $y = x^n$, where $n > 1$ is a positive number.

   a. Find the volume $V(n)$ of the solid generated when R is revolved about the x-axis. Express your answer in terms of n.

   b. Evaluate $\lim_{n \to \infty} V(n)$. Interpret this limit geometrically.

QUICK CHECK ANSWERS

1. The average value of A on $[a, b]$ is $\overline{A} = \dfrac{1}{b - a} \displaystyle\int_a^b A(x)\, dx$.

Therefore, $V = (b - a)\overline{A}$.   **2.** $A(x) = (2 - 2x^2)^2$
3. (a) A cylinder with height 2 and radius 2; (b) a cone with height 2 and base radius 2   **4.** When $g(x) = 0$, the washer method $V = \int_a^b \pi (f(x)^2 - g(x)^2)\, dx$ reduces to the disk method $V = \int_a^b \pi (f(x)^2)\, dx$.   **5.** (a) Inner radius $= \sqrt{x} + 1$; (b) outer radius $= x^2 + 1$ **6.** $\int_0^1 \pi (y^{2/3} - y^2)\, dy$ ◄

6.4 Volume by Shells

You can solve many challenging volume problems using the disk/washer method. However, some volume problems are difficult to solve with this method. For this reason, we extend our discussion of volume problems to the *shell method*, which—like the disk/washer method—is used to compute the volume of solids of revolution.

Cylindrical Shells

> Why another method? Suppose R is the region in the first quadrant bounded by the graph of $y = x^2 - x^3$ and the x-axis (Figure 6.39). When R is revolved about the y-axis, the resulting solid has a volume that is difficult to compute using the washer method. The volume is much easier to compute using the shell method.

Let R be a region bounded by the graph of f, the x-axis, and the lines $x = a$ and $x = b$, where $0 \le a < b$ and $f(x) \ge 0$ on $[a, b]$. When R is revolved about the y-axis, a solid is generated (Figure 6.40) whose volume is computed with the slice-and-sum strategy.

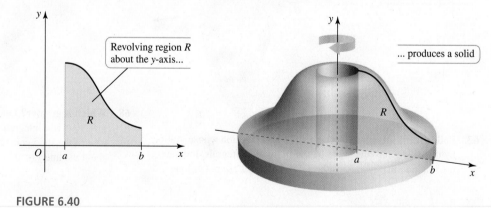

Revolving region R about the y-axis...

... produces a solid

FIGURE 6.40

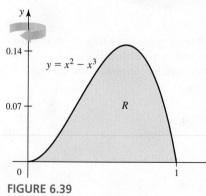

$y = x^2 - x^3$

R

FIGURE 6.39

We divide $[a, b]$ into n subintervals of length $\Delta x = (b - a)/n$ and identify an arbitrary point x_k^* on the kth subinterval, for $k = 1, \ldots, n$. Now observe the rectangle built on the kth subinterval with a height of $f(x_k^*)$ and a width Δx (Figure 6.41). As it revolves about the y-axis, this rectangle sweeps out a thin *cylindrical shell.*

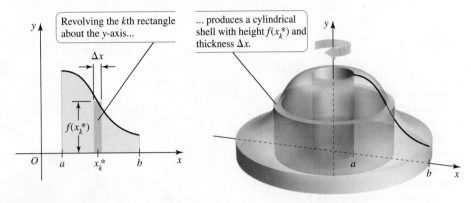

FIGURE 6.41

When the kth cylindrical shell is unwrapped (Figure 6.42), it approximates a thin rectangular slab. The approximate length of the slab is the circumference of a circle with radius x_k^*, which is $2\pi x_k^*$. The height of the slab is the height of the original rectangle $f(x_k^*)$, and its thickness is Δx; therefore, the volume of the kth shell is approximately

$$\underbrace{2\pi x_k^*}_{\text{length}} \cdot \underbrace{f(x_k^*)}_{\text{height}} \cdot \underbrace{\Delta x}_{\text{thickness}} = 2\pi x_k^* f(x_k^*) \Delta x.$$

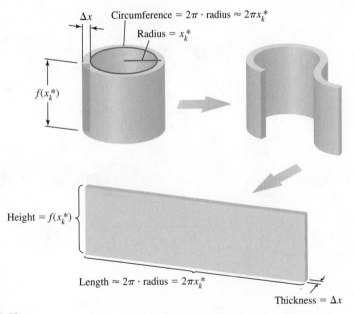

FIGURE 6.42

Summing the volumes of the n cylindrical shells gives an approximation to the volume of the entire solid:

$$V \approx \sum_{k=1}^{n} 2\pi x_k^* f(x_k^*) \Delta x.$$

As n increases and as Δx approaches 0 (Figure 6.43), we obtain the exact volume of the solid as a definite integral:

$$V = \lim_{n \to \infty} \sum_{k=1}^{n} 2\pi \underbrace{x_k^*}_{\substack{\text{shell} \\ \text{circumference}}} \overbrace{f(x_k^*)}^{\substack{\text{shell} \\ \text{height}}} \underbrace{\Delta x}_{\substack{\text{shell} \\ \text{thickness}}} = \int_a^b 2\pi x f(x)\, dx.$$

> Rather than memorizing, think of the meaning of the factors in this formula: $f(x)$ is the height of a single cylindrical shell, $2\pi x$ is the circumference of the shell, and dx corresponds to the thickness of a shell. Therefore, $2\pi x f(x)\, dx$ represents the volume of a single shell, and we sum the volumes from $x = a$ to $x = b$. Notice that the integrand for the shell method is the function $A(x)$ that gives the surface area of the shell of radius x, for $a \le x \le b$.

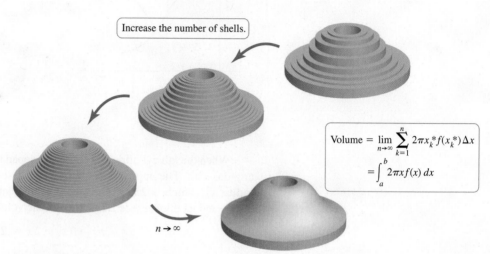

Increase the number of shells.

Volume $= \lim\limits_{n \to \infty} \sum\limits_{k=1}^{n} 2\pi x_k^* f(x_k^*) \Delta x$

$\qquad = \int_a^b 2\pi x f(x)\, dx$

$n \to \infty$

FIGURE 6.43

Before doing examples, we generalize this method as we did for the disk method. Suppose that the region R is bounded by two curves, $y = f(x)$ and $y = g(x)$, where $f(x) \ge g(x)$ on $[a, b]$ (Figure 6.44). What is the volume of the solid generated when R is revolved about the y-axis?

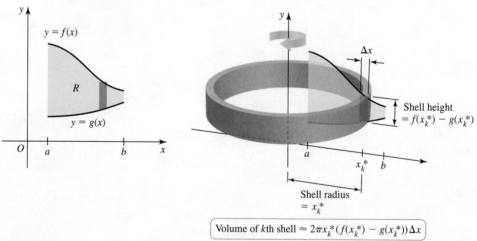

Shell height $= f(x_k^*) - g(x_k^*)$

Shell radius $= x_k^*$

Volume of kth shell $\approx 2\pi x_k^* (f(x_k^*) - g(x_k^*)) \Delta x$

FIGURE 6.44

The situation is similar to the case we just considered. A typical rectangle in R sweeps out a cylindrical shell, but now the height of the kth shell is $f(x_k^*) - g(x_k^*)$, for $k = 1, \dots, n$. As before, we take the radius of the kth shell to be x_k^*, which means the volume of the kth shell is approximated by $2\pi x_k^* (f(x_k^*) - g(x_k^*)) \Delta x$ (Figure 6.44). Summing the volumes of all the shells gives an approximation to the volume of the entire solid:

$$V \approx \sum_{k=1}^{n} \underbrace{2\pi x_k^*}_{\substack{\text{circumference} \\ \text{of shell}}} \underbrace{(f(x_k^*) - g(x_k^*))}_{\text{height of shell}} \Delta x.$$

Taking the limit as $n \to \infty$ (which implies that $\Delta x \to 0$), the exact volume is the definite integral

$$V = \lim_{n \to \infty} \sum_{k=1}^{n} 2\pi x_k^* (f(x_k^*) - g(x_k^*)) \Delta x = \int_a^b 2\pi x \, (f(x) - g(x)) \, dx.$$

We now have the formula for the Shell Method.

Volume by the Shell Method

Let f and g be continuous functions with $f(x) \geq g(x)$ on $[a, b]$. If R is the region bounded by the curves $y = f(x)$ and $y = g(x)$ between the lines $x = a$ and $x = b$, the volume of the solid generated when R is revolved about the y-axis is

$$V = \int_a^b 2\pi x (f(x) - g(x)) \, dx.$$

> An analogous formula for the shell method when R is revolved about the x-axis is obtained by reversing the roles of x and y:

$$V = \int_c^d 2\pi y (p(y) - q(y)) \, dy.$$

We assume R is bounded by the curves $x = p(y)$ and $x = q(y)$, where $p(y) \geq q(y)$ on $[c, d]$.

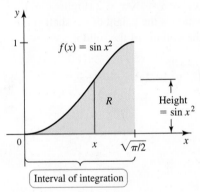

FIGURE 6.45

> When computing volumes using the shell method, it is best to sketch the region R in the xy-plane and draw a slice through the region that generates a typical shell.

EXAMPLE 1   A sine bowl Let R be the region bounded by the graph of $f(x) = \sin x^2$, the x-axis, and the vertical line $x = \sqrt{\pi/2}$ (Figure 6.45). Find the volume of the solid generated when R is revolved about the y-axis.

SOLUTION Revolving R about the y-axis produces a bowl-shaped region (Figure 6.46). The radius of a typical cylindrical shell is x, and its height is $f(x) = \sin x^2$. Therefore, the volume by the shell method is

$$V = \int_a^b \underbrace{2\pi x}_{\substack{\text{shell} \\ \text{circumference}}} \underbrace{f(x)}_{\substack{\text{shell} \\ \text{height}}} dx = \int_0^{\sqrt{\pi/2}} 2\pi x \sin x^2 \, dx.$$

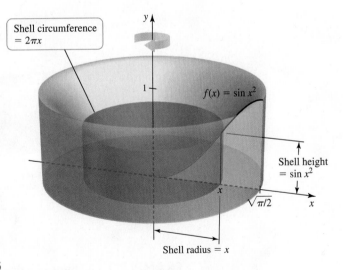

FIGURE 6.46

Now we make the change of variables $u = x^2$, which means that $du = 2x\,dx$. The lower limit $x = 0$ becomes $u = 0$, and the upper limit $x = \sqrt{\pi/2}$ becomes $u = \pi/2$. The volume of the solid is

$$V = \int_0^{\sqrt{\pi/2}} 2\pi x \sin x^2 \, dx = \pi \int_0^{\pi/2} \sin u \, du \qquad u = x^2, du = 2x\,dx$$

$$= \pi(-\cos u)\Big|_0^{\pi/2} \qquad \text{Fundamental Theorem}$$

$$= \pi[0 - (-1)] = \pi. \quad \text{Simplify.}$$

Related Exercises 5–14 ◄

> In Example 2, we could use the disk/washer method to compute the volume, but notice that this approach requires splitting the region into two subregions. A better approach is to use the shell method and integrate along the y-axis.

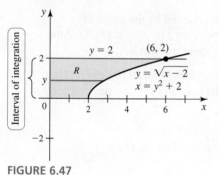

FIGURE 6.47

QUICK CHECK 1 The triangle bounded by the x-axis, the line $y = 2x$, and the line $x = 1$ is revolved about the y-axis. Give an integral that equals the volume of the resulting solid using the shell method. ◄

EXAMPLE 2   Shells about the x-axis Let R be the region in the first quadrant bounded by the graph of $y = \sqrt{x - 2}$ and the line $y = 2$. Find the volume of the solid generated when R is revolved about the x-axis.

SOLUTION The revolution is about the x-axis, so the integration in the shell method is with respect to y. A typical shell runs parallel to the x-axis and has radius y, where $0 \le y \le 2$; the shells extend from the y-axis to the curve $y = \sqrt{x - 2}$ (Figure 6.47). Solving $y = \sqrt{x - 2}$ for x, we have $x = y^2 + 2$, which is the height of the shell at the point y (Figure 6.48). Integrating with respect to y, the volume of the solid is

$$V = \int_0^2 \underbrace{2\pi y}_{\substack{\text{shell} \\ \text{circumference}}} \underbrace{(y^2 + 2)}_{\substack{\text{shell} \\ \text{height}}} dy = 2\pi \int_0^2 (y^3 + 2y) \, dy = 16\pi.$$

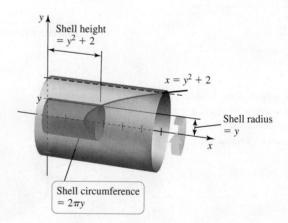

FIGURE 6.48

Related Exercises 15–26 ◄

EXAMPLE 3   Volume of a drilled sphere A cylindrical hole with radius r is drilled symmetrically through the center of a sphere with radius R, where $r \le R$. What is the volume of the remaining material?

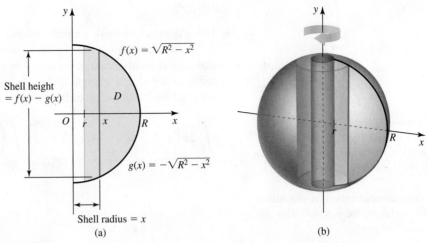

FIGURE 6.49

SOLUTION The y-axis is chosen to coincide with the axis of the cylindrical hole. We let D be the region in the xy-plane bounded above by $f(x) = \sqrt{R^2 - x^2}$, the upper half of a circle of radius R, and bounded below by $g(x) = -\sqrt{R^2 - x^2}$, the lower half of a circle of radius R, for $r \le x \le R$ (Figure 6.49a). Slices are taken perpendicular to the x-axis from $x = r$ to $x = R$. When a slice is revolved about the y-axis, it sweeps out a cylindrical shell that is concentric with the hole through the sphere (Figure 6.49b). The radius of a typical shell is x and its height is $f(x) - g(x) = 2\sqrt{R^2 - x^2}$. Therefore, the volume of the material that remains in the sphere is

$$V = \int_r^R 2\pi x \left(2\sqrt{R^2 - x^2}\right) dx$$

$$= -2\pi \int_{R^2 - r^2}^0 \sqrt{u}\, du \qquad u = R^2 - x^2, du = -2x\, dx$$

$$= 2\pi \left(\frac{2}{3} u^{3/2}\right)\Big|_0^{R^2 - r^2} \qquad \text{Fundamental Theorem}$$

$$= \frac{4\pi}{3}(R^2 - r^2)^{3/2}. \qquad \text{Simplify.}$$

It is important to check the result by examining special cases. In the case that $r = R$ (the radius of the hole equals the radius of the sphere), our calculation gives a volume of 0, which is correct. In the case that $r = 0$ (no hole in the sphere), our calculation gives the correct volume of a sphere, $\frac{4}{3}\pi R^3$.

Related Exercises 27–32 ◄

EXAMPLE 4 **Revolving about other lines** Let R be the region bounded by the curve $y = \sqrt{x}$, the line $y = 1$, and the y-axis (Figure 6.50a).

a. Use the shell method to find the volume of the solid generated when R is revolved about the line $x = -\frac{1}{2}$ (Figure 6.50b).

b. Use the disk/washer method to find the volume of the solid generated when R is revolved about the line $y = 1$ (Figure 6.50c).

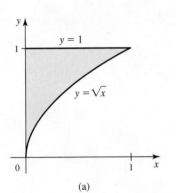

(a)

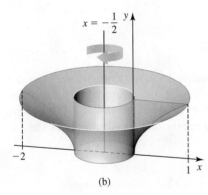

(b)

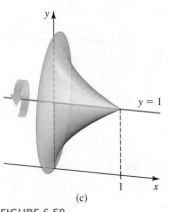

(c)

FIGURE 6.50

SOLUTION

a. Using the shell method, we must imagine taking slices through R parallel to the y-axis. A typical slice through R at a point x, where $0 \le x \le 1$, has length $1 - \sqrt{x}$. When that slice is revolved about the line $x = -\frac{1}{2}$, it sweeps out a cylindrical shell with a radius of $x + \frac{1}{2}$ and a height of $1 - \sqrt{x}$ (Figure 6.51). A slight modification of the standard shell method gives the volume of the solid:

▷ If we instead revolved about the y-axis ($x = 0$), the radius of the shell would be x. Because we are revolving about the line $x = -\frac{1}{2}$, the radius of the shell is $x + \frac{1}{2}$.

$$\int_0^1 2\pi \underbrace{\left(x + \frac{1}{2}\right)}_{\substack{\text{shell} \\ \text{radius}}} \underbrace{(1 - \sqrt{x})}_{\substack{\text{shell} \\ \text{height}}} dx = 2\pi \int_0^1 \left(x - x^{3/2} + \frac{1}{2} - \frac{x^{1/2}}{2}\right) dx \quad \text{Expand integrand.}$$

▷ The disk/washer method can also be used for part (a), and the shell method can also be used for part (b).

$$= \frac{8\pi}{15}. \quad \text{Evaluate integral.}$$

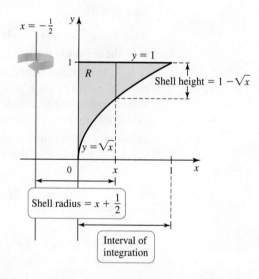

FIGURE 6.51

b. Using the disk/washer method, we take slices through R parallel to the y-axis. Consider a typical slice at a point x, where $0 \le x \le 1$. Its length, now measured with respect to the line $y = 1$, is $1 - \sqrt{x}$. When that slice is revolved about the line $y = 1$, it sweeps out a disk of radius $1 - \sqrt{x}$ (Figure 6.52). Applying the disk/washer formula, the volume of the solid is

$$\int_0^1 \pi \underbrace{(1 - \sqrt{x})^2}_{\substack{\text{radius of} \\ \text{disk}}} dx = \pi \int_0^1 (1 - 2\sqrt{x} + x)\, dx \quad \text{Expand integrand.}$$

$$= \frac{\pi}{6}. \quad \text{Evaluate integral.}$$

Related Exercises 33–40 ◄

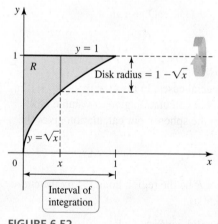

FIGURE 6.52

QUICK CHECK 2 Write the volume integral in Example 4b in the case that R is revolved about the line $y = -5$. ◄

Restoring Order

After working with slices, disks, washers, and shells, you may feel somewhat overwhelmed. How do you choose a method, and which method is best?

Notice that the disk method is just a special case of the washer method. So for solids of revolution, the choice is between the washer method and the shell method. In *principle*, either method can be used. In *practice*, one method usually produces an integral that is easier to evaluate than the other method. The following table summarizes these methods.

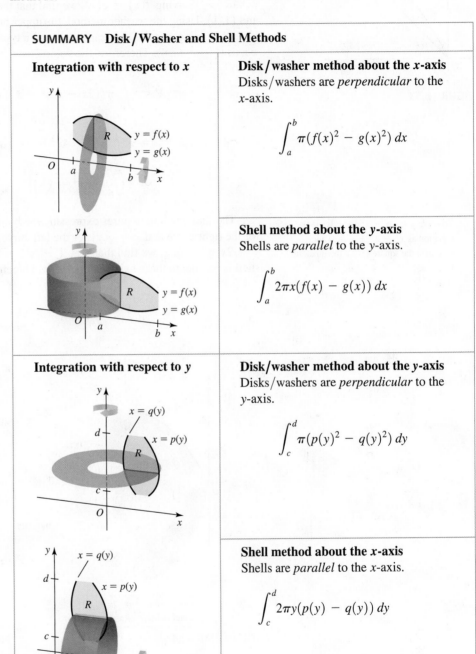

SUMMARY Disk/Washer and Shell Methods

Integration with respect to *x*	Disk/washer method about the *x*-axis
	Disks/washers are *perpendicular* to the *x*-axis. $$\int_a^b \pi(f(x)^2 - g(x)^2)\, dx$$
	Shell method about the *y*-axis Shells are *parallel* to the *y*-axis. $$\int_a^b 2\pi x(f(x) - g(x))\, dx$$
Integration with respect to *y*	**Disk/washer method about the *y*-axis** Disks/washers are *perpendicular* to the *y*-axis. $$\int_c^d \pi(p(y)^2 - q(y)^2)\, dy$$
	Shell method about the *x*-axis Shells are *parallel* to the *x*-axis. $$\int_c^d 2\pi y(p(y) - q(y))\, dy$$

The following example shows that while two methods may be used on a volume problem, one of them may be preferable.

y
$f(x) = 2x - x^2$
(1, 1)
R
$g(x) = x$
O
x

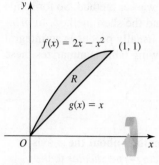

FIGURE 6.53

EXAMPLE 5 Volume by which method? The region R is bounded by the graphs of $f(x) = 2x - x^2$ and $g(x) = x$ on the interval $[0, 1]$ (Figure 6.53). Use the washer method and the shell method to find the volume of the solid formed when R is revolved about the x-axis.

SOLUTION Solving $f(x) = g(x)$, we find that the curves intersect at the points $(0, 0)$ and $(1, 1)$. Using the washer method, the upper bounding curve is the graph of f, the lower bounding curve is the graph of g, and a typical washer is perpendicular to the x-axis (Figure 6.54). Therefore, the volume is

$$V = \int_0^1 \pi((2x - x^2)^2 - x^2)\,dx \quad \text{Washer method}$$

$$= \pi \int_0^1 (x^4 - 4x^3 + 3x^2)\,dx \quad \text{Expand integrand.}$$

$$= \pi\left(\frac{x^5}{5} - x^4 + x^3\right)\Bigg|_0^1 = \frac{\pi}{5}. \quad \text{Evaluate integral.}$$

➤ To solve $y = 2x - x^2$ for x, write the equation as $x^2 - 2x + y = 0$ and complete the square or use the quadratic formula.

The shell method requires expressing the bounding curves in the form $x = p(y)$ for the right curve and $x = q(y)$ for the left curve. The right curve is $x = y$. Solving $y = 2x - x^2$ for x, we find that $x = 1 - \sqrt{1 - y}$ describes the left curve. A typical shell is parallel to the x-axis (Figure 6.55). Therefore, the volume is

$$V = \int_0^1 2\pi y\,(\underbrace{y}_{p(y)} - \underbrace{(1 - \sqrt{1 - y})}_{q(y)})\,dy.$$

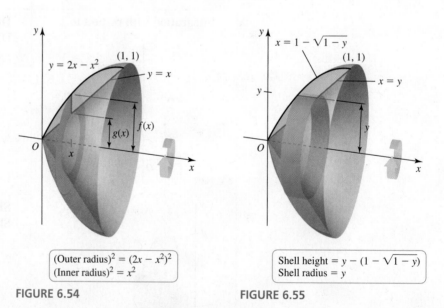

y
(1, 1)
$y = 2x - x^2$
$y = x$
$g(x)$
$f(x)$
O
x
x
(Outer radius)^2 = $(2x - x^2)^2$
(Inner radius)^2 = x^2

FIGURE 6.54

y
$x = 1 - \sqrt{1 - y}$
(1, 1)
$x = y$
y
y
O
x
Shell height = $y - (1 - \sqrt{1 - y})$
Shell radius = y

FIGURE 6.55

Although this integral can be evaluated (and equals $\frac{\pi}{5}$), it is decidedly more difficult than the integral required by the washer method. In this case, the washer method is preferable. Of course, the shell method may be preferable for other problems.

Related Exercises 41–48 ◀

QUICK CHECK 3 Suppose the region in Example 5 is revolved about the y-axis. Which method (washer or shell) leads to an easier integral? ◀

SECTION 6.4 EXERCISES

Review Questions

1. Assume f and g are continuous with $f(x) \geq g(x) \geq 0$ on $[a, b]$, where $0 \leq a < b$. The region bounded by the graphs of f and g and the lines $x = a$ and $x = b$ is revolved about the y-axis. Write the integral given by the shell method that equals the volume of the resulting solid.

2. Fill in the blanks: A region R is revolved about the y-axis. The volume of the resulting solid could (in principle) be found using the disk/washer method and integrating with respect to _____ or using the shell method and integrating with respect to _____.

3. Fill in the blanks: A region R is revolved about the x-axis. The volume of the resulting solid could (in principle) be found using the disk/washer method and integrating with respect to _____ or using the shell method and integrating with respect to _____.

4. Are shell method integrals easier to evaluate than washer method integrals? Explain.

Basic Skills

5–14. Shell method *Let R be the region bounded by the following curves. Use the shell method to find the volume of the solid generated when R is revolved about the y-axis.*

5. $y = x - x^2, y = 0$

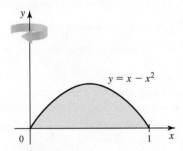

6. $y = -x^2 + 4x + 2, y = x^2 - 6x + 10$

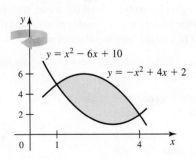

7. $y = (1 + x^2)^{-1}, y = 0, x = 0,$ and $x = 2$

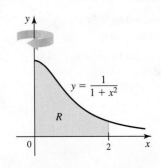

8. $y = 6 - x, y = 0, x = 2,$ and $x = 4$

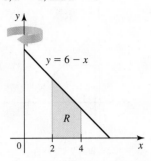

9. $y = 3x, y = 3,$ and $x = 0$ (Use integration and check your answer using the volume formula for a cone.)

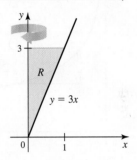

10. $y = 1 - x^2, x = 0,$ and $y = 0,$ in the first quadrant

11. $y = x^3 - x^8 + 1, y = 1$

12. $y = \sqrt{x}, y = 0,$ and $x = 1$

13. $y = \cos x^2, y = 0,$ for $0 \leq x \leq \sqrt{\pi/2}$

14. $y = \sqrt{4 - 2x^2}, y = 0,$ and $x = 0,$ in the first quadrant

15–26. Shell method *Let R be the region bounded by the following curves. Use the shell method to find the volume of the solid generated when R is revolved about the x-axis.*

15. $y = \sqrt{x}, y = 0,$ and $x = 4$

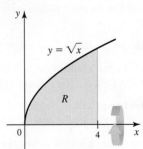

16. $y = 8, y = 2x + 2, x = 0,$ and $x = 2$

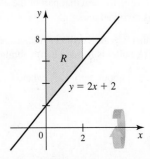

17. $y = 4 - x, y = 2,$ and $x = 0$

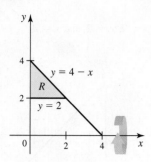

18. $x = \dfrac{4}{y + y^3}, x = \dfrac{1}{\sqrt{3}},$ and $y = 1$

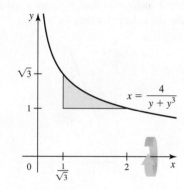

19. $y = x, y = 2 - x,$ and $y = 0$

20. $x = y^2, x = 4,$ and $y = 0$

21. $x = y^2, x = 0,$ and $y = 3$

22. $y = x^3, y = 1,$ and $x = 0$

23. $y = 2x^{-3/2}, y = 2, y = 16,$ and $x = 0$

24. $y = \sqrt{\sin^{-1} x}, y = \sqrt{\pi/2},$ and $x = 0$

25. $y = \sqrt{\cos^{-1} x},$ in the first quadrant

26. $y = \sqrt{50 - 2x^2},$ in the first quadrant

27–32. Shell method *Use the shell method to find the volume of the following solids.*

27. A right circular cone of radius 3 and height 8

28. The solid formed when a hole of radius 2 is drilled symmetrically along the axis of a right circular cylinder of height 6 and radius 4

29. The solid formed when a hole of radius 3 is drilled symmetrically along the axis of a right circular cone of radius 6 and height 9

30. The solid formed when a hole of radius 3 is drilled symmetrically through the center of a sphere of radius 6

31. The *ellipsoid* formed when that part of the ellipse $x^2 + 2y^2 = 4$ with $x \geq 0$ is revolved about the y-axis

32. A hole of radius $r \leq R$ is drilled symmetrically along the axis of a bullet. The bullet is formed by revolving the parabola
$$y = 6\left(1 - \frac{x^2}{R^2}\right)$$ about the y-axis, where $0 \leq x \leq R.$

33–36. Shell method about other lines *Let R be the region bounded by $y = x^2, x = 1,$ and $y = 0.$ Use the shell method to find the volume of the solid generated when R is revolved about the following lines.*

33. $x = -2$ **34.** $x = 1$ **35.** $y = -2$ **36.** $y = 2$

37–40. Different axes of revolution *Use either the washer or shell method to find the volume of the solid that is generated when the region in the first quadrant bounded by $y = x^2, y = 1,$ and $x = 0$ is revolved about the following lines.*

37. $y = -2$ **38.** $x = -1$ **39.** $y = 6$ **40.** $x = 2$

41–48. Washers vs. shells *Let R be the region bounded by the following curves. Let S be the solid generated when R is revolved about the given axis. If possible, find the volume of S by both the disk/washer and shell methods. Check that your results agree and state which method is easiest to apply.*

41. $y = x, y = x^{1/3};$ in the first quadrant; revolved about the x-axis

42. $y = x^2, y = 2 - x,$ and $x = 0;$ in the first quadrant; revolved about the y-axis

43. $y = 1/(x + 1), y = 1 - x/3;$ revolved about the x-axis

44. $y = (x - 2)^3 - 2, x = 0,$ and $y = 25;$ revolved about the y-axis

45. $y = \sqrt{\ln x}, y = \sqrt{\ln x^2},$ and $y = 1;$ revolved about the x-axis

46. $y = 6/(x + 3), y = 2 - x;$ revolved about the x-axis

47. $y = x - x^4, y = 0;$ revolved about the x-axis

48. $y = x - x^4, y = 0;$ revolved about the y-axis

Further Explorations

49. Explain why or why not Determine whether the following statements are true and give an explanation or counterexample.

   a. When using the shell method, the axis of the cylindrical shells is parallel to the axis of revolution.

   b. If a region is revolved about the y-axis, then the shell method must be used.

   c. If a region is revolved about the x-axis, then in principle, it is possible to use the disk/washer method and integrate with respect to x or the shell method and integrate with respect to y.

50–54. Solids of revolution *Find the volume of the following solids of revolution. Sketch the region in question.*

50. The region bounded by $y = (\ln x)/x^2, y = 0,$ and $x = 3$ revolved about the y-axis

51. The region bounded by $y = 1/x^2, y = 0, x = 2,$ and $x = 8$ revolved about the y-axis

52. The region bounded by $y = 1/(x^2 + 1), y = 0, x = 1,$ and $x = 4$ revolved about the y-axis

53. The region bounded by $y = e^x/x, y = 0, x = 1,$ and $x = 2$ revolved about the y-axis

54. The region bounded by $y^2 = \ln x, y^2 = \ln x^3,$ and $y = 2$ revolved about the x-axis

55–62. Choose your method *Find the volume of the following solids using the method of your choice.*

55. The solid formed when the region bounded by $y = x^2$ and $y = 2 - x^2$ is revolved about the x-axis

56. The solid formed when the region bounded by $y = \sin x$ and $y = 1 - \sin x$ between $x = \pi/6$ and $x = 5\pi/6$ is revolved about the x-axis

57. The solid formed when the region bounded by $y = x$, $y = 2x + 2$, $x = 2$, and $x = 6$ is revolved about the y-axis

58. The solid formed when the region bounded by $y = x^3$, the x-axis, and $x = 2$ is revolved about the x-axis

59. The solid whose base is the region bounded by $y = x^2$ and the line $y = 1$ and whose cross sections perpendicular to the base and parallel to the x-axis are semicircles

60. The solid formed when the region bounded by $y = 2$, $y = 2x + 2$, and $x = 6$ is revolved about the y-axis

61. The solid whose base is the square with vertices $(1, 0)$, $(0, 1)$, $(-1, 0)$, and $(0, -1)$ and whose cross sections perpendicular to the base and perpendicular to the x-axis are semicircles

62. The solid formed when the region bounded by $y = \sqrt{x}$, the x-axis, and $x = 4$ is revolved about the x-axis

63. **Equal volumes** Consider the region R bounded by the curves $y = ax^2 + 1$, $y = 0$, $x = 0$, and $x = 1$, for $a \geq -1$. Let S_1 and S_2 be solids generated when R is revolved about the x- and y-axes, respectively.

   a. Find V_1 and V_2, the volumes of S_1 and S_2, as functions of a.
   b. What are the values of $a \geq -1$ for which $V_1(a) = V_2(a)$?

64. **A hemisphere by several methods** Let R be the region in the first quadrant bounded by the circle $x^2 + y^2 = r^2$ and the coordinate axes. Find the volume of a hemisphere of radius r in the following ways.

   a. Revolve R about the x-axis and use the disk method.
   b. Revolve R about the x-axis and use the shell method.
   c. Assume the base of the hemisphere is in the xy-plane and use the general slicing method with slices perpendicular to the xy-plane and parallel to the x-axis.

65. **A cone by two methods** Verify that the volume of a right circular cone with a base radius of r and a height of h is $\pi r^2 h/3$. Use the region bounded by the line $y = rx/h$, the x-axis, and the line $x = h$, where the region is rotated about the x-axis. Then (a) use the disk method and integrate with respect to x, and (b) use the shell method and integrate with respect to y.

66. **A spherical cap** Consider the cap of thickness h that has been sliced from a sphere of radius r (see figure). Verify that the volume of the cap is $\pi h^2 (3r - h)/3$ using (a) the washer method, (b) the shell method, and (c) the general slicing method. Check for

consistency among the three methods and check the special cases $h = r$ and $h = 0$.

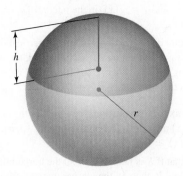

Applications

67. **Water in a bowl** A hemispherical bowl of radius 8 inches is filled to a depth of h inches, where $0 \leq h \leq 8$ ($h = 0$ corresponds to an empty bowl). Use the shell method to find the volume of water in the bowl as a function of h. (Check the special cases $h = 0$ and $h = 8$.)

68. **Wedge from a tree** Imagine a cylindrical tree of radius a. A wedge is cut from the tree by making two cuts: one in a horizontal plane P perpendicular to the axis of the cylinder and one that makes an angle θ with P, intersecting P along a diameter of the tree (see figure). What is the volume of the wedge?

69. **A torus (doughnut)** Find the volume of the torus formed when a circle of radius 2 centered at $(3, 0)$ is revolved about the y-axis. Use the shell method. You may need a computer algebra system or table of integrals to evaluate the integral.

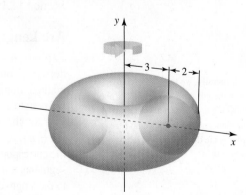

Additional Exercises

70. Different axes of revolution Suppose R is the region bounded by $y = f(x)$ and $y = g(x)$ on the interval $[a, b]$, where $f(x) \geq g(x)$.

  a. Show that if R is revolved about the vertical line $x = x_0$, where $x_0 < a$, then by the shell method, the volume of the resulting solid is $V = \int_a^b 2\pi(x - x_0)(f(x) - g(x))\,dx$.

  b. How is this formula changed if $x_0 > b$?

71. Different axes of revolution Suppose R is the region bounded by $y = f(x)$ and $y = g(x)$ on the interval $[a, b]$, where $f(x) \geq g(x) \geq 0$.

  a. Show that if R is revolved about the horizontal line $y = y_0$ that lies below R, then by the washer method, the volume of the resulting solid is

  $$V = \int_a^b \pi\left[(f(x) - y_0)^2 - (g(x) - y_0)^2\right] dx.$$

  b. How is this formula changed if the line $y = y_0$ lies above R?

72. Ellipsoids An ellipse centered at the origin is described by the equation $x^2/a^2 + y^2/b^2 = 1$. If an ellipse R is revolved about either axis, the resulting solid is an *ellipsoid*.

  a. Find the volume of the ellipsoid generated when R is revolved about the x-axis (in terms of a and b).

  b. Find the volume of the ellipsoid generated when R is revolved about the y-axis (in terms of a and b).

  c. Should the results of parts (a) and (b) agree? Explain.

73. Change of variables Suppose $f(x) > 0$ for all x and $\int_0^4 f(x)\,dx = 10$. Let R be the region in the first quadrant bounded by the coordinate axes, $y = f(x^2)$, and $x = 2$. Find the volume of the solid generated by revolving R about the y-axis.

74. Equal integrals Without evaluating integrals, explain why the following equalities are true. (*Hint:* Draw pictures.)

  a. $\displaystyle \pi\int_0^4 (8 - 2x)^2\,dx = 2\pi\int_0^8 y\left(4 - \frac{y}{2}\right) dy$

  b. $\displaystyle \int_0^2 (25 - (x^2 + 1)^2)\,dx = 2\int_1^5 y\sqrt{y - 1}\,dy$

75. Volumes without calculus Solve the following problems with *and* without calculus. A good picture helps.

  a. A cube with side length r is inscribed in a sphere, which is inscribed in a right circular cone, which is inscribed in a right circular cylinder. The side length (slant height) of the cone is equal to its diameter. What is the volume of the cylinder?

  b. A cube is inscribed in a right circular cone with a radius of 1 and a height of 3. What is the volume of the cube?

  c. A cylindrical hole 10 in long is drilled symmetrically through the center of a sphere. How much material is left in the sphere? (Enough information *is* given.)

QUICK CHECK ANSWERS

1. $\int_0^1 2\pi x(2x)\,dx$ **2.** $V = \int_0^1 \pi(36 - (\sqrt{x} + 5)^2)\,dx$
3. The shell method is easier. ◄

6.5 Length of Curves

The space station orbits Earth in an elliptical path. How far does it travel in one orbit? A baseball slugger launches a home run into the upper deck, and the sportscaster claims it landed 480 ft from home plate. But how far did the ball actually travel along its flight path? These questions deal with the length of trajectories or, more generally, with *arc length*. As you will see, their answers can be found by integration.

There are two common ways to formulate problems about arc length: The curve may be given explicitly in the form $y = f(x)$, or it may be defined *parametrically*. In this section, we deal with the first case. Parametric curves are introduced in Section 11.1.

Arc Length for $y = f(x)$

Suppose a curve is given by $y = f(x)$, where f is a function with a continuous first derivative on the interval $[a, b]$. The goal is to determine how far you would travel if you walked along the curve from $(a, f(a))$ to $(b, f(b))$. This distance is the arc length, which we denote L.

> More generally, we may choose any point in the kth subinterval and Δx may vary from one subinterval to the next. Using right endpoints, as we do here, simplifies the discussion and leads to the same result.

As shown in Figure 6.56, we divide $[a, b]$ into n subintervals of length $\Delta x = (b - a)/n$, where x_k is the right endpoint of the kth subinterval, for $k = 1, \ldots, n$. Joining the corresponding points on the curve by line segments, we obtain a polygonal line with n line segments. If n is large and Δx is small, the length of the polygonal line is a good approximation to the length of the actual curve. The strategy is to find the length of the polygonal line and then let n increase, while Δx goes to zero, to get the exact length of the curve.

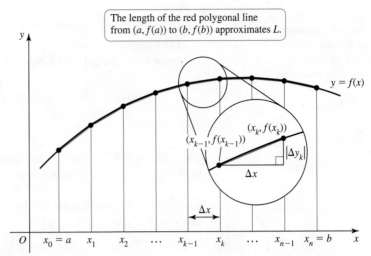

FIGURE 6.56

Consider the kth subinterval $[x_{k-1}, x_k]$ and the line segment between the points $(x_{k-1}, f(x_{k-1}))$ and $(x_k, f(x_k))$. We let the change in the y-coordinate between these points be

$$\Delta y_k = f(x_k) - f(x_{k-1}).$$

The kth line segment is the hypotenuse of a right triangle with sides of length Δx and $|\Delta y_k| = |f(x_k) - f(x_{k-1})|$. The length of each line segment is

$$\sqrt{(\Delta x)^2 + |\Delta y_k|^2}, \quad \text{for} \quad k = 1, 2, \ldots, n.$$

Summing these lengths, we obtain the length of the polygonal line, which approximates the length L of the curve:

$$L \approx \sum_{k=1}^{n} \sqrt{(\Delta x)^2 + |\Delta y_k|^2}.$$

> Notice that Δx is the same for each subinterval, but Δy_k depends on the subinterval.

In previous applications of the integral, we would, at this point, take the limit as $n \to \infty$ and $\Delta x \to 0$ to obtain a definite integral. However, because of the presence of the Δy_k term, we must complete one additional step before taking a limit. Notice that the slope of the line segment on the kth subinterval is $\Delta y_k / \Delta x$ (rise over run). By the Mean Value Theorem (see the margin figure and Section 4.6), this slope equals $f'(x_k^*)$ for some point x_k^* on the kth subinterval. Therefore,

$$L \approx \sum_{k=1}^{n} \sqrt{(\Delta x)^2 + |\Delta y_k|^2}$$

$$= \sum_{k=1}^{n} \sqrt{(\Delta x)^2 \left[1 + \left(\frac{\Delta y_k}{\Delta x} \right)^2 \right]} \quad \text{Factor out } (\Delta x)^2.$$

$$= \sum_{k=1}^{n} \sqrt{1 + \left(\frac{\Delta y_k}{\Delta x} \right)^2} \, \Delta x \quad \text{Bring } \Delta x \text{ out of the square root.}$$

$$= \sum_{k=1}^{n} \sqrt{1 + f'(x_k^*)^2} \, \Delta x. \quad \text{Mean Value Theorem}$$

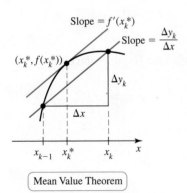

Now we have a Riemann sum. As n increases and as Δx approaches zero, the sum approaches a definite integral, which is also the exact length of the curve. We have

$$L = \lim_{n \to \infty} \sum_{k=1}^{n} \sqrt{1 + f'(x_k^*)^2} \, \Delta x = \int_a^b \sqrt{1 + f'(x)^2} \, dx.$$

> ▷ Note that $1 + f'(x)^2$ is positive, so the square root in the integrand is defined whenever f' exists. To ensure that $\sqrt{1 + f'(x)^2}$ is integrable on $[a, b]$, we require that f' be continuous.

> **DEFINITION Arc Length for $y = f(x)$**
>
> Let f have a continuous first derivative on the interval $[a, b]$. The length of the curve from $(a, f(a))$ to $(b, f(b))$ is
>
> $$L = \int_a^b \sqrt{1 + f'(x)^2}\, dx.$$

QUICK CHECK 1 What does the arc length formula give for the length of the line $y = x$ between $x = 0$ and $x = a$, where $a \geq 0$? ◀

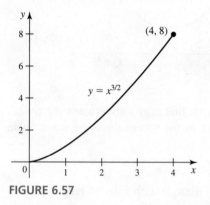

FIGURE 6.57

EXAMPLE 1   Arc length Find the length of the curve $f(x) = x^{3/2}$ between $x = 0$ and $x = 4$ (Figure 6.57).

SOLUTION Notice that $f'(x) = \frac{3}{2}x^{1/2}$, which is continuous on the interval $[0, 4]$. Using the arc length formula, we have

$$L = \int_a^b \sqrt{1 + f'(x)^2}\, dx = \int_0^4 \sqrt{1 + \left(\frac{3}{2}x^{1/2}\right)^2}\, dx \qquad \text{Substitute for } f'(x).$$

$$= \int_0^4 \sqrt{1 + \frac{9}{4}x}\, dx \qquad\qquad \text{Simplify.}$$

$$= \frac{4}{9}\int_1^{10} \sqrt{u}\, du \qquad\qquad u = 1 + \frac{9x}{4}, du = \frac{9}{4}dx$$

$$= \frac{4}{9}\left(\frac{2}{3}u^{3/2}\right)\Big|_1^{10} \qquad\qquad \text{Fundamental Theorem}$$

$$= \frac{8}{27}\left(10^{3/2} - 1\right). \qquad\qquad \text{Simplify.}$$

The length of the curve is $\frac{8}{27}(10^{3/2} - 1) \approx 9.1$ units.

Related Exercises 3–16 ◀

EXAMPLE 2   Arc length of an exponential curve Find the length of the curve $f(x) = 2e^x + \frac{1}{8}e^{-x}$ on the interval $[0, \ln 2]$.

SOLUTION We first calculate $f'(x) = 2e^x - \frac{1}{8}e^{-x}$ and $f'(x)^2 = 4e^{2x} - \frac{1}{2} + \frac{1}{64}e^{-2x}$. The length of the curve on the interval $[0, \ln 2]$ is

$$L = \int_0^{\ln 2} \sqrt{1 + f'(x)^2}\, dx = \int_0^{\ln 2} \sqrt{1 + \left(4e^{2x} - \frac{1}{2} + \frac{1}{64}e^{-2x}\right)}\, dx$$

$$= \int_0^{\ln 2} \sqrt{4e^{2x} + \frac{1}{2} + \frac{1}{64}e^{-2x}}\, dx \qquad \text{Simplify.}$$

$$= \int_0^{\ln 2} \sqrt{\left(2e^x + \frac{1}{8}e^{-x}\right)^2}\, dx \qquad \text{Factor.}$$

$$= \int_0^{\ln 2} \left(2e^x + \frac{1}{8}e^{-x}\right) dx \qquad \text{Simplify.}$$

$$= \left(2e^x - \frac{1}{8}e^{-x}\right)\Big|_0^{\ln 2} = \frac{33}{16}. \qquad \text{Evaluate the integral.}$$

Related Exercises 3–16 ◀

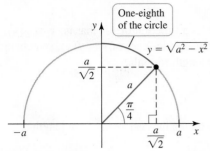

FIGURE 6.58

EXAMPLE 3   Circumference of a circle Confirm that the circumference of a circle of radius a is $2\pi a$.

SOLUTION The upper half of a circle of radius a centered at $(0, 0)$ is given by the function $f(x) = \sqrt{a^2 - x^2}$ for $|x| \leq a$ (Figure 6.58). So we might consider using the arc length formula on the interval $[-a, a]$ to find the length of a semicircle. However, the circle has vertical tangent lines at $x = \pm a$ and $f'(\pm a)$ is undefined, which prevents us from using the arc length formula. An alternative approach is to use symmetry and avoid the points $x = \pm a$. For example, let's compute the length of one-eighth of the circle on the interval $[0, a/\sqrt{2}]$ (Figure 6.58).

We first determine that $f'(x) = -\dfrac{x}{\sqrt{a^2 - x^2}}$, which is continuous on $[0, a/\sqrt{2}]$.

The length of one-eighth of the circle is

$$\int_0^{a/\sqrt{2}} \sqrt{1 + f'(x)^2}\, dx = \int_0^{a/\sqrt{2}} \sqrt{1 + \left(-\frac{x}{\sqrt{a^2 - x^2}}\right)^2}\, dx$$

$$= \int_0^{a/\sqrt{2}} \sqrt{\frac{a^2}{a^2 - x^2}}\, dx \qquad \text{Simplify.}$$

$$= a \int_0^{a/\sqrt{2}} \frac{dx}{\sqrt{a^2 - x^2}} \qquad \text{Simplify; } a > 0.$$

$$= a \left.\sin^{-1}\frac{x}{a}\right|_0^{a/\sqrt{2}} \qquad \text{Integrate.}$$

$$= a\left(\sin^{-1}\frac{1}{\sqrt{2}} - 0\right) \qquad \text{Evaluate.}$$

$$= \frac{\pi a}{4}. \qquad \text{Simplify.}$$

> The arc length integral for the semicircle on $[-a, a]$ is an example of an *improper integral*, a topic considered in Section 7.4.

It follows that the circumference of the full circle is $8(\pi a/4) = 2\pi a$ units.

Related Exercises 3–16 ◄

EXAMPLE 4   Looking ahead Consider the segment of the parabola $f(x) = x^2$ on the interval $[0, 2]$.

a. Write the integral for the length of the curve.

b. Use a calculator to evaluate the integral.

SOLUTION

a. Noting that $f'(x) = 2x$, the arc length integral is

$$\int_0^2 \sqrt{1 + f'(x)^2}\, dx = \int_0^2 \sqrt{1 + 4x^2}\, dx.$$

> When relying on technology, it is a good idea to check whether an answer is plausible. In Example 4, we found that the arc length of $y = x^2$ on $[0, 2]$ is approximately 4.647. The straight-line distance between $(0, 0)$ and $(2, 4)$ is $\sqrt{20} \approx 4.472$, so our answer is reasonable.

b. Even simple functions can lead to arc length integrals that are difficult, if not impossible, to evaluate analytically. Using integration techniques presented so far, this integral cannot be evaluated. Without an analytical method, we may use numerical integration to *approximate* the value of a definite integral (Section 5.7). Many calculators have built-in functions for this purpose. For this integral, the approximate arc length is

$$\int_0^2 \sqrt{1 + 4x^2}\, dx \approx 4.647.$$

Related Exercises 17–26 ◄

Arc Length for $x = g(y)$

Sometimes it is advantageous to describe a curve as a function of y—that is, $x = g(y)$. The arc length formula in this case is derived exactly as in the case of $y = f(x)$, switching the roles of x and y. The result is the following arc length formula.

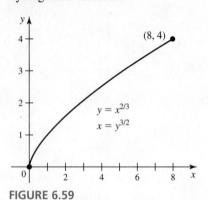

QUICK CHECK 2 What does the arc length formula give for the length of the line $x = y$ between $y = c$ and $y = d$, where $d \geq c$? Is the result consistent with the result given by the Pythagorean theorem? ◄

FIGURE 6.59

DEFINITION Arc Length for $x = g(y)$

Let $x = g(y)$ have a continuous first derivative on the interval $[c, d]$. The length of the curve from $(g(c), c)$ to $(g(d), d)$ is

$$L = \int_c^d \sqrt{1 + g'(y)^2}\, dy.$$

EXAMPLE 5   Arc length Find the length of the curve $y = f(x) = x^{2/3}$ between $x = 0$ and $x = 8$ (Figure 6.59).

SOLUTION The derivative of $f(x) = x^{2/3}$ is $f'(x) = \frac{2}{3}x^{-1/3}$, which is undefined at $x = 0$. Therefore, the arc length formula with respect to x cannot be used; yet the curve certainly appears to have a well-defined length.

The key is to describe the curve with y as the independent variable. Solving $y = x^{2/3}$ for x, we have $x = g(y) = \pm y^{3/2}$. Notice that when $x = 8$, $y = 8^{2/3} = 4$, which says that we should use the positive branch of $\pm y^{3/2}$. Therefore, finding the length of the curve $y = f(x) = x^{2/3}$ from $x = 0$ to $x = 8$ is equivalent to finding the length of the curve $x = g(y) = y^{3/2}$ from $y = 0$ to $y = 4$. This is precisely the problem solved in Example 1. The arc length is $\frac{8}{27}(10^{3/2} - 1) \approx 9.1$ units.

Related Exercises 27–30 ◄

QUICK CHECK 3 Write the integral for the length of the curve $x = \sin y$ on the interval $0 \leq y \leq \pi$. ◄

EXAMPLE 6   Ingenuity required Find the length of the curve $y = f(x) = \ln(x + \sqrt{x^2 - 1})$ on the interval $[1, \sqrt{2}]$ (Figure 6.60).

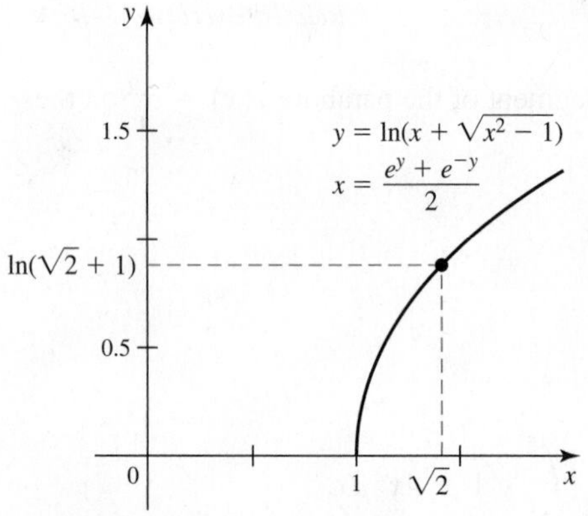

SOLUTION Calculating f' shows that the graph of f has a vertical tangent line at $x = 1$. Therefore, the integrand in the arc length integral is undefined at $x = 1$. An alternative strategy is to express the function in the form $x = g(y)$ and evaluate the arc length integral with respect to y. Noting that $x \geq 1$ and $y \geq 0$, we solve $y = \ln(x + \sqrt{x^2 - 1})$ for x in the following steps:

$$e^y = x + \sqrt{x^2 - 1} \qquad \text{Exponentiate both sides.}$$

$$e^y - x = \sqrt{x^2 - 1} \qquad \text{Subtract } x \text{ from both sides.}$$

$$e^{2y} - 2e^y x = -1 \qquad \text{Square both sides and cancel } x^2.$$

$$x = \frac{e^{2y} + 1}{2e^y} = \frac{e^y + e^{-y}}{2}. \qquad \text{Solve for } x.$$

We conclude that the given curve is also described by the function

$$x = g(y) = \frac{e^y + e^{-y}}{2}. \text{ The interval } 1 \leq x \leq \sqrt{2} \text{ corresponds to the interval}$$

FIGURE 6.60

➤ The function $\frac{1}{2}(e^y + e^{-y})$ is the **hyperbolic cosine**, denoted cosh y. The function $\frac{1}{2}(e^y - e^{-y})$ is the **hyperbolic sine**, denoted sinh y.

$0 \le y \le \ln(\sqrt{2} + 1)$ (Figure 6.60). Note that $g'(y) = \dfrac{e^y - e^{-y}}{2}$ is continuous on $[0, \ln(\sqrt{2} + 1)]$. The arc length is

$$\int_0^{\ln(\sqrt{2}+1)} \sqrt{1 + g'(y)^2}\, dy = \int_0^{\ln(\sqrt{2}+1)} \sqrt{1 + \left(\frac{e^y - e^{-y}}{2}\right)^2}\, dy \qquad \text{Substitute for } g'(y).$$

$$= \frac{1}{2}\int_0^{\ln(\sqrt{2}+1)} (e^y + e^{-y})\, dy \qquad \text{Simplify.}$$

$$= \frac{1}{2}(e^y - e^{-y})\Big|_0^{\ln(\sqrt{2}+1)} = 1. \qquad \begin{array}{l}\text{Fundamental}\\ \text{Theorem}\end{array}$$

Related Exercises 27–30 ◄

SECTION 6.5 EXERCISES

Review Questions

1. Explain the steps required to find the length of a curve $y = f(x)$ between $x = a$ and $x = b$.

2. Explain the steps required to find the length of a curve $x = g(y)$ between $y = c$ and $y = d$.

Basic Skills

3–6. Setting up arc length integrals *Write, simplify, but do not evaluate, an integral with respect to x that gives the length of the following curves on the given interval.*

3. $y = x^3 + 2;\ [-2, 5]$

4. $y = 2\cos 3x;\ [-\pi, \pi]$

5. $y = e^{-2x};\ [0, 2]$

6. $y = \ln x;\ [1, 10]$

7–16. Arc length calculations *Find the arc length of the following curves on the given interval by integrating with respect to x.*

7. $y = 2x + 1;\ [1, 5]$ (Use calculus.)

8. $y = 4 - 3x;\ [-3, 2]$ (Use calculus.)

9. $y = -8x - 3;\ [-2, 6]$ (Use calculus.)

10. $y = \dfrac{1}{2}(e^x + e^{-x});\ [-\ln 2, \ln 2]$

11. $y = \dfrac{1}{3}x^{3/2};\ [0, 60]$

12. $y = 3\ln x - \dfrac{x^2}{24};\ [1, 6]$

13. $y = \dfrac{(x^2 + 2)^{3/2}}{3};\ [0, 1]$

14. $y = \dfrac{x^{3/2}}{3} - x^{1/2};\ [4, 16]$

15. $y = \dfrac{x^4}{4} + \dfrac{1}{8x^2};\ [1, 2]$

16. $y = \dfrac{2}{3}x^{3/2} - \dfrac{1}{2}x^{1/2};\ [1, 9]$

▦ 17–26. Arc length by calculator

a. *Write and simplify the integral that gives the arc length of the following curves on the given interval.*

b. *If necessary, use technology to evaluate or approximate the integral.*

17. $y = x^2;\ [-1, 1]$

18. $y = \sin x;\ [0, \pi]$

19. $y = \ln x;\ [1, 4]$

20. $y = \dfrac{x^3}{3};\ [-1, 1]$

21. $y = \sqrt{x - 2};\ [3, 4]$

22. $y = \dfrac{8}{x^2};\ [1, 4]$

23. $y = \cos 2x;\ [0, \pi]$

24. $y = 4x - x^2;\ [0, 4]$

25. $y = \dfrac{1}{x};\ [1, 10]$

26. $y = \dfrac{1}{x^2 + 1};\ [-5, 5]$

27–30. Arc length calculations with respect to y *Find the arc length of the following curves by integrating with respect to y.*

27. $x = 2y - 4$, for $-3 \le y \le 4$ (Use calculus.)

28. $y = \ln(x - \sqrt{x^2 - 1})$, for $1 \le x \le \sqrt{2}$

29. $x = \dfrac{y^4}{4} + \dfrac{1}{8y^2}$, for $1 \le y \le 2$

30. $x = 2e^{\sqrt{2}y} + \dfrac{1}{16}e^{-\sqrt{2}y}$, for $0 \le y \le \dfrac{\ln 2}{\sqrt{2}}$

Further Explorations

31. **Explain why or why not** Determine whether the following statements are true and give an explanation or counterexample.

a. $\displaystyle\int_a^b \sqrt{1 + f'(x)^2}\, dx = \int_a^b (1 + f'(x))\, dx$

b. Assuming f' is continuous on the interval $[a, b]$, the length of the curve $y = f(x)$ on $[a, b]$ is the area under the curve $y = \sqrt{1 + f'(x)^2}$ on $[a, b]$.

c. Arc length may be negative if $f(x) < 0$ on part of the interval in question.

32. **Arc length for a line** Consider the segment of the line $y = mx + c$ on the interval $[a, b]$. Use the arc length formula to show that the length of the line segment is $(b - a)\sqrt{1 + m^2}$. Verify this result by computing the length of the line segment using the distance formula.

33. **Functions from arc length** What differentiable functions have an arc length on the interval $[a, b]$ given by the following integrals? Note that the answers are not unique. Give a family of functions that satisfy the conditions.

a. $\displaystyle\int_a^b \sqrt{1 + 16x^4}\, dx$

b. $\displaystyle\int_a^b \sqrt{1 + 36\cos^2 2x}\, dx$

34. Function from arc length Find a curve that passes through the point $(1, 5)$ and has an arc length on the interval $[2, 6]$ given by $\int_2^6 \sqrt{1 + 16x^{-6}}\, dx$.

35. Cosine vs. parabola Which curve has the greater length on the interval $[-1, 1]$, $y = 1 - x^2$ or $y = \cos(\pi x/2)$?

36. Function defined as an integral Write the integral that gives the length of the curve $y = f(x) = \int_0^x \sin t\, dt$ on the interval $[0, \pi]$.

Applications

37. Golden Gate cables The profile of the cables on a suspension bridge may be modeled by a parabola. The central span of the Golden Gate Bridge (see figure) is 1280 m long and 152 m high. The parabola $y = 0.00037x^2$ gives a good fit to the shape of the cables, where $|x| \le 640$, and x and y are measured in meters. Approximate the length of the cables that stretch between the tops of the two towers.

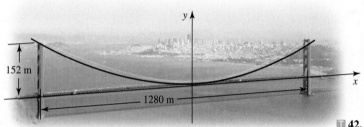

38. Gateway Arch The shape of the Gateway Arch in St. Louis (with a height and a base length of 630 ft) is modeled by the function $y = -630 \cosh(x/239.2) + 1260$, where $|x| \le 315$, and x and y are measured in feet (see figure). The function $\cosh x$ is the **hyperbolic cosine**, defined by $\cosh x = \dfrac{e^x + e^{-x}}{2}$. Estimate the length of the Gateway Arch.

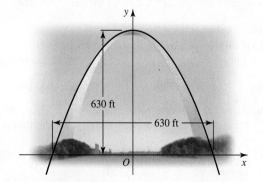

Additional Exercises

39. Lengths of related curves Suppose the graph of f on the interval $[a, b]$ has length L, where f' is continuous on $[a, b]$. Evaluate the following integrals in terms of L.

a. $\displaystyle\int_{a/2}^{b/2} \sqrt{1 + f'(2x)^2}\, dx$ **b.** $\displaystyle\int_{a/c}^{b/c} \sqrt{1 + f'(cx)^2}\, dx$ if $c \ne 0$

40. Lengths of symmetric curves Suppose a curve is described by $y = f(x)$ on the interval $[-b, b]$, where f' is continuous on $[-b, b]$. Show that if f is symmetric about the origin (f is odd) *or* f is symmetric about the y-axis (f is even), then the length of the curve $y = f(x)$ from $x = -b$ to $x = b$ is twice the length of the curve from $x = 0$ to $x = b$. Use a geometric argument and prove it using integration.

41. A family of exponential functions

a. Show that the arc length integral for the function
$$f(x) = Ae^{ax} + \frac{1}{4Aa^2}e^{-ax}, \text{ where } a > 0 \text{ and } A > 0,$$
may be integrated using methods you already know.

b. Verify that the arc length of the curve $y = f(x)$ on the interval $[0, \ln 2]$ is
$$A(2^a - 1) - \frac{1}{4a^2 A}(2^{-a} - 1).$$

42. Bernoulli's "parabolas" Johann Bernoulli (1667–1748) evaluated the arc length of curves of the form $y = x^{(2n+1)/2n}$, where n is a positive integer, on the interval $[0, a]$.

a. Write the arc length integral.

b. Make the change of variables $u^2 = 1 + \left(\dfrac{2n + 1}{2n}\right)^2 x^{1/n}$ to obtain a new integral with respect to u.

c. Use the Binomial Theorem to expand this integrand and evaluate the integral.

d. The case $n = 1$ ($y = x^{3/2}$) was done in Example 1. With $a = 1$, compute the arc length in the cases $n = 2$ and $n = 3$. Does the arc length increase or decrease with n?

e. Graph the arc length of the curves for $a = 1$ as a function of n.

QUICK CHECK ANSWERS

1. $\sqrt{2}a$ (The length of the line segment joining the points)
2. $\sqrt{2}(d - c)$ (The length of the line segment joining the points) **3.** $L = \int_0^\pi \sqrt{1 + \cos^2 y}\, dy$ ◄

6.6 Physical Applications

We continue this chapter on applications of integration with several problems from physics and engineering. The physical themes in these problems are mass, work, force, and pressure. The common mathematical theme is the use of the slice-and-sum strategy, which always leads to a definite integral.

Density and Mass

Density is the concentration of mass in an object and is usually measured in units of mass per volume (for example, g/cm^3). An object with *uniform* density satisfies the basic relationship

$$\text{mass} = \text{density} \cdot \text{volume}.$$

When the density of an object *varies*, this formula no longer holds, and we must appeal to calculus.

In this section, we introduce mass calculations for thin objects that can be viewed as line segments (such as wires or thin bars). The bar shown in Figure 6.61 has a density ρ that varies along its length. For one-dimensional objects, we use *linear density* with units of mass per length (for example, g/cm). What is the mass of such an object?

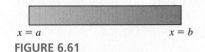

$x = a$ $\qquad\qquad\qquad\qquad$ $x = b$

FIGURE 6.61

QUICK CHECK 1 In Figure 6.61, suppose $a = 0$, $b = 3$, and the density of the rod in g/cm is $\rho(x) = (4 - x)$. (a) Where is the rod lightest and heaviest? (b) What is the density at the middle of the bar? ◄

We begin by dividing the bar, represented by the interval $a \le x \le b$, into n sub-intervals of equal length $\Delta x = (b - a)/n$ (Figure 6.62). Let x_k^* be any point in the kth subinterval, for $k = 1, \ldots, n$. The mass of the kth segment of the bar m_k is approximately the density at x_k^* multiplied by the length of the interval, or $m_k \approx \rho(x_k^*)\Delta x$. So the approximate mass of the entire bar is

$$\sum_{k=1}^{n} m_k \approx \sum_{k=1}^{n} \underbrace{\rho(x_k^*)\Delta x}_{m_k}.$$

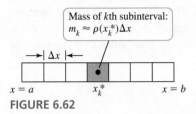

Mass of kth subinterval:
$m_k \approx \rho(x_k^*)\Delta x$

Δx

$x = a$ $\qquad$ x_k^* $\qquad$ $x = b$

FIGURE 6.62

The exact mass is obtained by taking the limit as $n \to \infty$ and as $\Delta x \to 0$, which produces a definite integral.

> Note that the units of the integral work out as they should: ρ has units of mass per length and dx has units of length; so $\rho(x)\, dx$ has units of mass.

DEFINITION Mass of a One-Dimensional Object

Suppose a thin bar or wire is represented by the interval $a \le x \le b$ with a density function ρ (with units of mass per length). The **mass** of the object is

$$m = \int_a^b \rho(x)\, dx.$$

> Another interpretation of the mass integral is that mass equals the average value of the density multiplied by the length of the bar $b - a$.

EXAMPLE 1   Mass from variable density A thin 2-m bar, represented by the interval $0 \le x \le 2$, is made of an alloy whose density in units of kg/m is given by $\rho(x) = (1 + x^2)$. What is the mass of the bar?

SOLUTION The mass of the bar in kilograms is

$$m = \int_a^b \rho(x)\, dx = \int_0^2 (1 + x^2)\, dx = \left(x + \frac{x^3}{3}\right)\Bigg|_0^2 = \frac{14}{3}.$$

Related Exercises 9–16 ◄

QUICK CHECK 2 A thin bar occupies the interval $0 \le x \le 2$ and has a density in kg/m of $\rho(x) = (1 + x^2)$. Using the minimum value of the density, what is a lower bound for the mass of the object? Using the maximum value of the density, what is an upper bound for the mass of the object? ◄

Work

Work can be described as the change in energy when a force causes a displacement of an object. When you carry a refrigerator up a flight of stairs or push a stalled car, you apply a force that results in the displacement of an object, and work is done. If a *constant* force F displaces an object a distance d in the direction of the force, the work done is the force multiplied by the distance:

$$\text{work} = \text{force} \cdot \text{distance}.$$

It is easiest to use metric units for force and work. A newton (N) is the force required to give a 1-kg mass an acceleration of 1 m/s^2. A joule (J) is 1 newton-meter (N-m), the work done by a 1-N force over a distance of 1 m.

Calculus enters the picture with *variable* forces. Suppose an object is moved along the x-axis by a variable force F that is directed along the x-axis (Figure 6.63). How much work is done in moving the object between $x = a$ and $x = b$? Once again, we use the slice-and-sum strategy.

The interval $[a, b]$ is divided into n subintervals of equal length $\Delta x = (b - a)/n$. We let x_k^* be any point in the kth subinterval, for $k = 1, \ldots, n$. On that subinterval, the force is approximately constant with a value of $F(x_k^*)$. Therefore, the work done in moving the object across the kth subinterval is approximately $F(x_k^*)\Delta x$ (force $\cdot$ distance). Summing the work done over each of the n subintervals, the total work over the interval $[a, b]$ is approximately

$$W \approx \sum_{k=1}^{n} F(x_k^*)\Delta x.$$

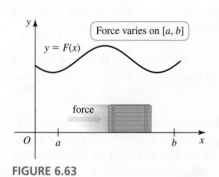

FIGURE 6.63

QUICK CHECK 3 Explain why the sum of the work over n subintervals is only an approximation to the total work. ◄

This approximation becomes exact when we take the limit as $n \to \infty$ and $\Delta x \to 0$. The total work done is the integral of the force over the interval $[a, b]$ (or, equivalently, the net area under the force curve in Figure 6.63).

> **DEFINITION Work**
>
> The work done by a variable force F moving an object along a line from $x = a$ to $x = b$ in the direction of the force is
>
> $$W = \int_a^b F(x)\, dx.$$

An application of force and work that is easy to visualize is the stretching and compression of a spring. Suppose an object is attached to a spring on a frictionless horizontal surface; the object slides back and forth under the influence of the spring. We say that the spring is at *equilibrium* when it is neither compressed nor stretched. It is convenient to let x be the position of the object, where $x = 0$ is the equilibrium position (Figure 6.64).

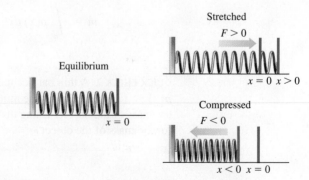

FIGURE 6.64

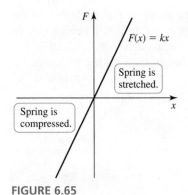

FIGURE 6.65

> Hooke's law was proposed by the English scientist Robert Hooke (1635–1703), who also coined the biological term *cell*. Hooke's law works well for springs made of many common materials. However, some springs obey more complicated spring laws (see Exercise 51).

> Notice again that the units in the integral are consistent. If F has units of N and x has units of m, then W has units of $F\,dx$, or N-m, which are the units of work $(1\text{ N-m} = 1\text{ J})$.

QUICK CHECK 4 In Example 2, explain why more work is needed in part (d) than in part (c), even though the displacement is the same. ◄

According to **Hooke's law**, the force required to keep the spring in a compressed or stretched position x units from the equilibrium position is $F(x) = kx$, where the positive spring constant k measures the stiffness of the spring. Note that to stretch the spring to a position $x > 0$, a force $F > 0$ (in the positive direction) is required. To compress the spring to a position $x < 0$, a force $F < 0$ (in the negative direction) is required (Figure 6.65). In other words, the force required to displace the spring is always in the direction of the displacement.

EXAMPLE 2   Compressing a spring Suppose a force of 10 N is required to stretch a spring 0.1 m from its equilibrium position and hold it in that position.

a. Assuming that the spring obeys Hooke's law, find the spring constant k.

b. How much work is needed to *compress* the spring 0.5 m from its equilibrium position?

c. How much work is needed to *stretch* the spring 0.25 m from its equilibrium position?

d. How much additional work is required to stretch the spring 0.25 m if it has already been stretched 0.1 m from its equilibrium position?

SOLUTION

a. The fact that a force of 10 N is required to keep the spring stretched at $x = 0.1$ m means (by Hooke's law) that $F(0.1) = k(0.1\text{ m}) = 10\text{ N}$. Solving for the spring constant, we find that $k = 100\text{ N/m}$. Therefore, Hooke's law for this spring is $F(x) = 100x$.

b. The work in joules required to compress the spring from $x = 0$ to $x = -0.5$ is

$$W = \int_a^b F(x)\,dx = \int_0^{-0.5} 100x\,dx = 50x^2\Big|_0^{-0.5} = 12.5.$$

c. The work in joules required to stretch the spring from $x = 0$ to $x = 0.25$ is

$$W = \int_a^b F(x)\,dx = \int_0^{0.25} 100x\,dx = 50x^2\Big|_0^{0.25} = 3.125.$$

d. The work in joules required to stretch the spring from $x = 0.1$ to $x = 0.35$ is

$$W = \int_a^b F(x)\,dx = \int_{0.1}^{0.35} 100x\,dx = 50x^2\Big|_{0.1}^{0.35} = 5.625.$$

Comparing parts (c) and (d), we see that more work is required to stretch the spring 0.25 m starting at $x = 0.1$ than starting at $x = 0$.   *Related Exercises 17–26* ◄

Lifting Problems   Another common work problem arises when the motion is vertical and the force is the gravitational force. The gravitational force exerted on an object with mass m is $F = mg$, where $g \approx 9.8\text{ m/s}^2$ is the acceleration due to gravity near the surface of Earth. The work in joules required to lift an object of mass m a vertical distance of y meters is

$$\text{work} = \text{force} \cdot \text{distance} = mgy.$$

This type of problem becomes interesting when the object being lifted is a body of water, a rope, or a chain. In these situations, different parts of the object are lifted different distances—so integration is necessary. Here is a typical situation and the strategy used.

Suppose a fluid such as water is pumped out of a tank to a height h above the bottom of the tank. How much work is required, assuming the tank is full of water? Three key observations lead to the solution.

• Water from different levels of the tank is lifted different vertical distances, requiring different amounts of work.

• Two equal volumes of water from the same horizontal plane are lifted the same distance and require the same amount of work.

• A volume V of water has mass ρV, where $\rho = 1\text{ g/cm}^3 = 1000\text{ kg/m}^3$ is the density of water.

> The choice of a coordinate system is somewhat arbitrary and may depend on the geometry of the problem. You can let the y-axis point upward or downward, and there are usually several logical choices for the location of $y = 0$. You should experiment with different coordinate systems.

To solve this problem, we let the y-axis point upward with $y = 0$ at the bottom of the tank. The body of water that must be lifted extends from $y = 0$ to $y = b$ (which *may* be the top of the tank). The level to which the water must be raised is $y = h$, where $h \geq b$ (Figure 6.66). We now slice the water into n horizontal layers, each having thickness Δy. The kth layer occupying the interval $[y_{k-1}, y_k]$, for $k = 1, \ldots, n$, is approximately y_k^* units above the bottom of the tank, where y_k^* is any point in $[y_{k-1}, y_k]$.

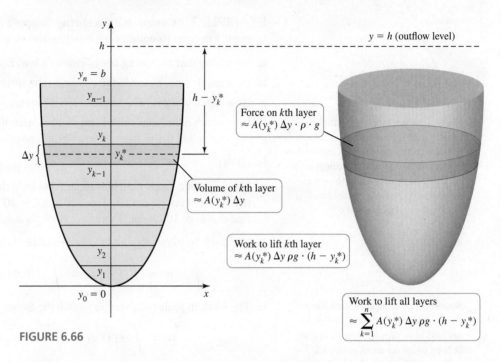

Force on kth layer $\approx A(y_k^*)\,\Delta y \cdot \rho \cdot g$

Volume of kth layer $\approx A(y_k^*)\,\Delta y$

Work to lift kth layer $\approx A(y_k^*)\,\Delta y\,\rho g \cdot (h - y_k^*)$

Work to lift all layers $\approx \displaystyle\sum_{k=1}^{n} A(y_k^*)\,\Delta y\,\rho g \cdot (h - y_k^*)$

FIGURE 6.66

The cross-sectional area of the kth layer at y_k^*, denoted $A(y_k^*)$, is determined by the shape of the tank; the solution depends on being able to find A for all values of y. Because the volume of the kth layer is approximately $A(y_k^*)\Delta y$, the force on the kth layer (its weight) is

$$F_k = mg \approx \underbrace{\overbrace{A(y_k^*)\Delta y}^{\text{volume}} \cdot \rho}_{\text{mass}} \cdot g.$$

To reach the level $y = h$, the kth layer is lifted an approximate distance of $(h - y_k^*)$ (Figure 6.66). So the work in lifting the kth layer to a height h is approximately

$$W_k = \underbrace{A(y_k^*)\Delta y \rho g}_{\text{force}} \cdot \underbrace{(h - y_k^*)}_{\text{distance}}.$$

Summing the work required to lift all the layers to a height h, the total work is

$$W \approx \sum_{k=1}^{n} W_k = \sum_{k=1}^{n} A(y_k^*)\rho g(h - y_k^*)\Delta y.$$

This approximation becomes more accurate as the width of the layers Δy tends to zero and the number of layers tends to infinity. In this limit, we obtain a definite integral from $y = 0$ to $y = b$. The total work required to empty the tank is

$$W = \lim_{n \to \infty} \sum_{k=1}^{n} A(y_k^*)\rho g(h - y_k^*)\Delta y = \int_0^b \rho g A(y)(h - y)\,dy.$$

This derivation assumes that the *bottom* of the tank is at $y = 0$, in which case the distance that the slice at level y must be lifted is $D(y) = h - y$. If you choose a different location for the origin, the function D will be different. Here is a general procedure for any choice of origin.

PROCEDURE **Solving Lifting Problems**

1. Draw a y-axis in the vertical direction (parallel to gravity) and choose a convenient origin. Assume the interval $[a, b]$ corresponds to the vertical extent of the fluid.

2. For $a \leq y \leq b$, find the cross-sectional area $A(y)$ of the horizontal slices and the distance $D(y)$ the slices must be lifted.

3. The work required to lift the water is

$$W = \int_a^b \rho g A(y) D(y) \, dy.$$

We now use this procedure in the next two examples.

EXAMPLE 3 **Pumping water** How much work is needed to pump all the water out of a cylindrical tank with a height of 10 m and a radius of 5 m? The water is pumped to an outflow pipe 15 m above the bottom of the tank.

SOLUTION Figure 6.67 shows the cylindrical tank filled to capacity and the outflow 15 m above the bottom of the tank. We let $y = 0$ represent the bottom of the tank and $y = 10$ represent the top of the tank. In this case, all horizontal slices are circular disks of radius $r = 5$ m. Therefore, for $0 \leq y \leq 10$, the cross-sectional area is

$$A(y) = \pi r^2 = \pi 5^2 = 25\pi.$$

Note that the water is pumped to a level $h = 15$ m above the bottom of the tank, so the lifting distance is $D(y) = 15 - y$. The resulting work integral is

$$W = \int_0^{10} \rho g \underbrace{A(y)}_{25\pi} \underbrace{D(y)}_{15-y} \, dy = 25\pi\rho g \int_0^{10} (15 - y) \, dy.$$

Substituting $\rho = 1000 \text{ kg/m}^3$ and $g = 9.8 \text{ m/s}^2$, the total work in joules is

$$W = 25\pi\rho g \int_0^{10} (15 - y) \, dy$$

$$= 25\pi \underbrace{(1000)}_{\rho} \underbrace{(9.8)}_{g} \left(15y - \frac{1}{2}y^2 \right) \Big|_0^{10}$$

$$\approx 7.700 \times 10^7.$$

The work required to pump the water out of the tank is approximately 77 million joules.
Related Exercises 27–37 ◄

QUICK CHECK 5 In the previous example, how would the integral change if the outflow pipe were at the top of the tank? ◄

EXAMPLE 4 **Pumping gasoline** A cylindrical tank with a length of 10 m and a radius of 5 m is on its side and half full of gasoline (Figure 6.68). How much work is required to empty the tank through an outlet pipe at the top of the tank? (The density of gasoline is $\rho \approx 737 \text{ kg/m}^3$.)

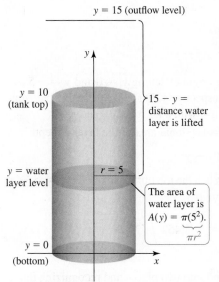

$y = 15$ (outflow level)

$y = 10$
(tank top)

$15 - y =$
distance water layer is lifted

$y =$ water layer level

$r = 5$

The area of water layer is $A(y) = \pi(5^2)$.

πr^2

$y = 0$
(bottom)

x

FIGURE 6.67

> Recall that $g \approx 9.8 \text{ m/s}^2$. You should verify that the units are consistent in this calculation: The units of $\rho, g, A(y), D(y)$, and dy are $\text{kg/m}^3, \text{m/s}^2, \text{m}^2, \text{m}$, and m, respectively. The resulting units of W are $\text{kg m}^2/\text{s}^2$, or J. A more convenient unit for large amounts of work and energy is the kilowatt-hour, which is 3.6 million joules.

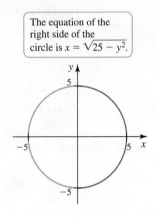

The equation of the right side of the circle is $x = \sqrt{25 - y^2}$.

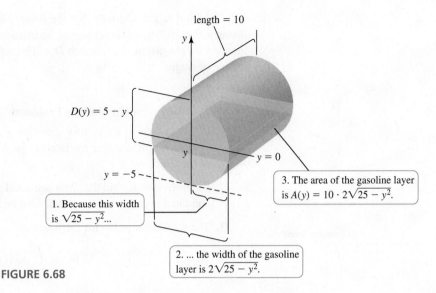

length = 10

$D(y) = 5 - y$

$y = 0$

$y = -5$

1. Because this width is $\sqrt{25 - y^2}$...

2. ... the width of the gasoline layer is $2\sqrt{25 - y^2}$.

3. The area of the gasoline layer is $A(y) = 10 \cdot 2\sqrt{25 - y^2}$.

FIGURE 6.68

▶ Again, there are several choices for the location of the origin. The location in this example makes $A(y)$ easy to compute.

SOLUTION In this problem, we choose a different origin by letting $y = 0$ and $y = -5$ correspond to the center and the bottom of the tank, respectively. For $-5 \le y \le 0$, a horizontal layer of gasoline located at a depth y is a rectangle with a length of 10 and width of $2\sqrt{25 - y^2}$ (Figure 6.68). Therefore, the cross-sectional area of the layer at depth y is

$$A(y) = 20\sqrt{25 - y^2}.$$

The distance the layer at level y must be lifted to reach the top of the tank is $D(y) = 5 - y$, where $5 \le D(y) \le 10$. The resulting work integral is

$$W = \underbrace{737}_{\rho}\underbrace{(9.8)}_{g} \int_{-5}^{0} \underbrace{20\sqrt{25 - y^2}}_{A(y)} \underbrace{(5 - y)}_{D(y)}\, dy = 144{,}452 \int_{-5}^{0} \sqrt{25 - y^2}\,(5 - y)\, dy.$$

This integral is evaluated by splitting the integrand into two pieces and recognizing that one piece is the area of a quarter circle of radius 5:

$$\int_{-5}^{0} \sqrt{25 - y^2}\,(5 - y)\, dy = 5 \underbrace{\int_{-5}^{0} \sqrt{25 - y^2}\, dy}_{\text{area of quarter circle}} - \underbrace{\int_{-5}^{0} y\sqrt{25 - y^2}\, dy}_{\text{let } u = 25 - y^2;\; du = -2y\, dy}$$

$$= 5 \cdot \frac{25\pi}{4} + \frac{1}{2}\int_{0}^{25} \sqrt{u}\, du$$

$$= \frac{125\pi}{4} + \frac{1}{3}u^{3/2}\Big|_{0}^{25} = \frac{375\pi + 500}{12}.$$

Multiplying this result by 144,452, we find that the work required is approximately 20.2 million joules.   *Related Exercises 27–37* ◀

Force and Pressure

Another application of integration deals with the force exerted on a surface by a body of water. Again, we need a few physical principles.

Pressure is a force per unit area, measured in units such as newtons per square meter (N/m^2). For example, the pressure of the atmosphere on the surface of Earth is about $14\ lb/in^2$ (approximately 100 kilopascals, or $10^5\ N/m^2$). As another example, if you stood on the bottom of a swimming pool, you would feel pressure due to the weight (force) of the column of water above your head. If your head is flat and has surface area $A\ m^2$ and it is h meters below the surface, then the column of water above your head has volume Ah m^3. That column of water exerts a force (its weight)

$$F = \text{mass} \cdot \text{acceleration} = \underbrace{\text{volume} \cdot \text{density}}_{\text{mass}} \cdot g = Ah\rho g,$$

where ρ is the density of water and g is the acceleration due to gravity. Therefore, the pressure on your head is the force divided by the surface area of your head:

$$\text{pressure} = \frac{\text{force}}{A} = \frac{Ah\rho g}{A} = \rho gh.$$

This pressure is called **hydrostatic pressure** (meaning the pressure of *water at rest*), and it has the following important property: *It has the same magnitude in all directions.* Specifically, the hydrostatic pressure on a vertical wall of the swimming pool at a depth h is also ρgh. This is the only fact needed to find the total force on vertical walls such as dams. We assume that the water completely covers the face of the dam.

The first step in finding the force on the face of the dam is to introduce a coordinate system. We choose a y-axis pointing upward with $y = 0$ corresponding to the base of the dam and $y = a$ corresponding to the top of the dam (Figure 6.69). Because the pressure varies with depth (y-direction), the dam is sliced horizontally into n strips of equal thickness Δy. The kth strip corresponds to the interval $[y_{k-1}, y_k]$, and we let y_k^* be any point in that interval. The depth of that strip is approximately $h = a - y_k^*$, so the hydrostatic pressure on that strip is approximately $\rho g(a - y_k^*)$.

The crux of any dam problem is finding the width of the strips as a function of y, which we denote $w(y)$. Each dam has its own width function; however, once the width function is known, the solution follows directly. The approximate area of the kth strip is its width multiplied by its thickness, or $w(y_k^*)\Delta y$. The force on the kth strip (which is the area of the strip multiplied by the pressure) is approximately

$$F_k = \underbrace{\rho g(a - y_k^*)}_{\text{pressure}} \underbrace{w(y_k^*)\Delta y}_{\text{area of strip}}.$$

Summing the forces over the n strips, the total force is

$$F \approx \sum_{k=1}^{n} F_k = \sum_{k=1}^{n} \rho g(a - y_k^*)w(y_k^*)\Delta y.$$

To find the exact force, we let the thickness of the strips tend to zero and the number of strips tend to infinity, which produces a definite integral. The limits of integration correspond to the base ($y = 0$) and top ($y = a$) of the dam. Therefore, the total force on the dam is

$$F = \lim_{n \to \infty} \sum_{k=1}^{n} \rho g(a - y_k^*)w(y_k^*)\Delta y = \int_0^a \rho g(a - y)w(y)\, dy.$$

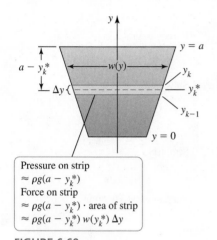

Pressure on strip
$\approx \rho g(a - y_k^*)$
Force on strip
$\approx \rho g(a - y_k^*) \cdot$ area of strip
$\approx \rho g(a - y_k^*)\, w(y_k^*)\, \Delta y$

FIGURE 6.69

▶ We have chosen $y = 0$ to be the base of the dam. Depending on the geometry of the problem, it may be more convenient (less computation) to let $y = 0$ be at the top of the dam. Experiment with different choices.

PROCEDURE   Solving Force/Pressure Problems

1. Draw a y-axis on the face of the dam in the vertical direction and choose a convenient origin (often taken to be the base of the dam).

2. Find the width function $w(y)$ for each value of y on the face of the dam.

3. If the base of the dam is at $y = 0$ and the top of the dam is at $y = a$, then the total force on the dam is

$$F = \int_0^a \rho g\underbrace{(a - y)}_{\text{depth}}\underbrace{w(y)}_{\text{width}}\, dy.$$

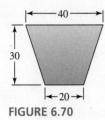

FIGURE 6.70

EXAMPLE 5   Force on a dam   A large vertical dam in the shape of a symmetric trapezoid has a height of 30 m, a width of 20 m at its base, and a width of 40 m at the top (Figure 6.70). What is the total force on the face of the dam when the reservoir is full?

SOLUTION   We place the origin at the center of the base of the dam (Figure 6.71). The right slanted edge of the dam is a segment of the line that passes through the points $(10, 0)$ and $(20, 30)$. An equation of that line is

$$y - 0 = \frac{30}{10}(x - 10) \quad \text{or} \quad y = 3x - 30 \quad \text{or} \quad x = \frac{1}{3}(y + 30).$$

▷ You should check the width function: $w(0) = 20$ (the width of the dam at its base) and $w(30) = 40$ (the width of the dam at its top).

Notice that at a depth of y, where $0 \le y \le 30$, the width of the dam is

$$w(y) = 2x = \frac{2}{3}(y + 30).$$

Using $\rho = 1000 \text{ kg/m}^3$ and $g = 9.8 \text{ m/s}^2$, the total force on the dam (in newtons) is

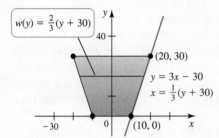

FIGURE 6.71

$$F = \int_0^a \rho g(a - y)w(y) \, dy \qquad \text{Force integral}$$

$$= \rho g \int_0^{30} \underbrace{(30 - y)}_{a - y} \underbrace{\frac{2}{3}(y + 30)}_{w(y)} \, dy \qquad \text{Substitute.}$$

$$= \frac{2}{3}\rho g \int_0^{30} (900 - y^2) \, dy \qquad \text{Simplify.}$$

$$= \frac{2}{3}\rho g \left(900y - \frac{y^3}{3} \right) \Big|_0^{30} \qquad \text{Fundamental Theorem}$$

$$\approx 1.176 \times 10^8.$$

The force of 1.176×10^8 N on the dam amounts to about 26 million pounds, or 13,000 tons.

Related Exercises 38–48 ◀

SECTION 6.6 EXERCISES

Review Questions

1. Suppose a 1-m cylindrical bar has a constant density of 1 g/cm for its left half and a constant density 2 g/cm for its right half. What is its mass?

2. Explain how to find the mass of a one-dimensional object with a variable density ρ.

3. How much work is required to move an object from $x = 0$ to $x = 5$ (measured in meters) in the presence of a constant force of 5 N acting along the x-axis?

4. Why must integration be used to find the work done by a variable force?

5. Why must integration be used to find the work required to pump water out of a tank?

6. Why must integration be used to find the total force on the face of a dam?

7. What is the pressure on a horizontal surface with an area of 2 m² that is 4 m underwater?

8. Explain why you integrate in the vertical direction (parallel to the acceleration due to gravity) rather than the horizontal direction to find the force on the face of a dam.

Basic Skills

9–16. Mass of one-dimensional objects *Find the mass of the following thin bars with the given density function.*

9. $\rho(x) = 1 + \sin x$; for $0 \le x \le \pi$

10. $\rho(x) = 1 + x^3$; for $0 \le x \le 1$

11. $\rho(x) = 2 - x/2$; for $0 \le x \le 2$

12. $\rho(x) = 5e^{-2x}$; for $0 \le x \le 4$

13. $\rho(x) = x\sqrt{2 - x^2}$; for $0 \le x \le 1$

14. $\rho(x) = \begin{cases} 1 & \text{if } 0 \le x \le 2 \\ 2 & \text{if } 2 < x \le 3 \end{cases}$

15. $\rho(x) = \begin{cases} 1 & \text{if } 0 \le x \le 2 \\ 1 + x & \text{if } 2 < x \le 4 \end{cases}$

16. $\rho(x) = \begin{cases} x^2 & \text{if } 0 \le x \le 1 \\ x(2-x) & \text{if } 1 < x \le 2 \end{cases}$

17. **Work from force** How much work is required to move an object from $x = 0$ to $x = 3$ (measured in meters) in the presence of a force (in N) given by $F(x) = 2x$ acting along the x-axis?

18. **Work from force** How much work is required to move an object from $x = 1$ to $x = 3$ (measured in meters) in the presence of a force (in N) given by $F(x) = 2/x^2$ acting along the x-axis?

19. **Compressing and stretching a spring** Suppose a force of 30 N is required to stretch and hold a spring 0.2 m from its equilibrium position.

    a. Assuming the spring obeys Hooke's law, find the spring constant k.
    b. How much work is required to compress the spring 0.4 m from its equilibrium position?
    c. How much work is required to stretch the spring 0.3 m from its equilibrium position?
    d. How much additional work is required to stretch the spring 0.2 m if it has already been stretched 0.2 m from its equilibrium position?

20. **Compressing and stretching a spring** Suppose a force of 15 N is required to stretch and hold a spring 0.25 m from its equilibrium position.

    a. Assuming the spring obeys Hooke's law, find the spring constant k.
    b. How much work is required to compress the spring 0.2 m from its equilibrium position?
    c. How much additional work is required to stretch the spring 0.3 m if it has already been stretched 0.25 m from its equilibrium position?

21. **Work done by a spring** A spring on a horizontal surface can be stretched and held 0.5 m from its equilibrium position with a force of 50 N.

    a. How much work is done in stretching the spring 1.5 m from its equilibrium position?
    b. How much work is done in compressing the spring 0.5 m from its equilibrium position?

22. **Shock absorber** A heavy-duty shock absorber is compressed 2 cm from its equilibrium position by a mass of 500 kg. How much work is required to compress the shock absorber 4 cm from its equilibrium position? (A mass of 500 kg exerts a force (in newtons) of 500 g, where $g \approx 9.8 \text{ m/s}^2$.)

23. **Calculating work for different springs** Calculate the work required to stretch the following springs 0.5 m from their equilibrium positions. Assume Hooke's law is obeyed.

    a. A spring that requires a force of 50 N to be stretched 0.2 m from its equilibrium position
    b. A spring that requires 50 J of work to be stretched 0.2 m from its equilibrium position

24. **Calculating work for different springs** Calculate the work required to stretch the following springs 0.4 m from their equilibrium positions. Assume Hooke's law is obeyed.

    a. A spring that requires a force of 50 N to be stretched 0.1 m from its equilibrium position
    b. A spring that requires 2 J of work to be stretched 0.1 m from its equilibrium position

25. **Calculating work** Calculate the work required to stretch the following springs 1.25 m from their equilibrium positions. Assume Hooke's law is obeyed.

    a. A spring that requires 100 J of work to be stretched 0.5 m from its equilibrium position
    b. A spring that requires a force of 250 N to be stretched 0.5 m from its equilibrium position

26. **Work function** A spring has a restoring force given by $F(x) = 25x$. Let $W(x)$ be the work required to stretch the spring from its equilibrium position ($x = 0$) to a variable distance x. Find and graph the work function. Compare the work required to stretch the spring x units from equilibrium to the work required to compress the spring x units from equilibrium.

27. **Emptying a swimming pool** A swimming pool has the shape of a box with a base that measures 25 m by 15 m and a uniform depth of 2.5 m. How much work is required to pump the water out of the pool when it is full?

28. **Emptying a cylindrical tank** A cylindrical water tank has height 8 m and radius 2 m (see figure).

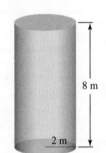

    a. If the tank is full of water, how much work is required to pump the water to the level of the top of the tank and out of the tank?
    b. Is it true that it takes half as much work to pump the water out of the tank when it is half full as when it is full? Explain.

29. **Emptying a half-full cylindrical tank** Suppose the water tank in Exercise 28 is half full of water. Determine the work required to empty the tank by pumping the water to a level 2 m above the top of the tank.

30. **Emptying a partially filled swimming pool** If the water in the swimming pool in Exercise 27 is 2 m deep, then how much work is required to pump all the water to a level 3 m above the bottom of the pool?

31. **Emptying a conical tank** A water tank is shaped like an inverted cone with height 6 m and base radius 1.5 m (see figure).

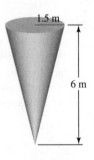

    a. If the tank is full, how much work is required to pump the water to the level of the top of the tank and out of the tank?
    b. Is it true that it takes half as much work to pump the water out of the tank when it is filled to half its depth as when it is full? Explain.

32. **Emptying a real swimming pool** A swimming pool is 20 m long and 10 m wide, with a bottom that slopes uniformly from a depth of 1 m at one end to a depth of 2 m at the other end (see figure). Assuming the pool is full, how much work is required to pump the water to a level 0.2 m above the top of the pool?

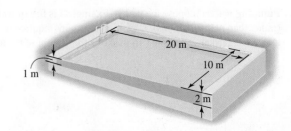

33. Filling a spherical tank A spherical water tank with an inner radius of 8 m has its lowest point 2 m above the ground. It is filled by a pipe that feeds the tank at its lowest point (see figure).

  a. Neglecting the volume of the inflow pipe, how much work is required to fill the tank if it is initially empty?
  b. Now assume that the inflow pipe feeds the tank at the top of the tank. Neglecting the volume of the inflow pipe, how much work is required to fill the tank if it is initially empty?

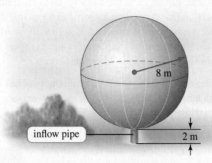

34. Emptying a water trough A water trough has a semicircular cross section with a radius of 0.25 m and a length of 3 m (see figure).

  a. How much work is required to pump the water out of the trough when it is full?
  b. If the length is doubled, is the required work doubled? Explain.
  c. If the radius is doubled, is the required work doubled? Explain.

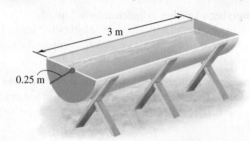

35. Emptying a water trough A cattle trough has a trapezoidal cross section with a height of 1 m and horizontal sides of length $\frac{1}{2}$ m and 1 m. Assume the length of the trough is 10 m (see figure).

  a. How much work is required to pump the water out of the trough (to the level of the top of the trough) when it is full?
  b. If the length is doubled, is the required work doubled? Explain.

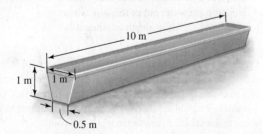

36. Pumping water Suppose the tank in Example 4 is full of water (rather than half full of gas). Determine the work required to pump all the water to an outlet pipe 15 m above the bottom of the tank.

37. Emptying a conical tank An inverted cone is 2 m high and has a base radius of $\frac{1}{2}$ m. If the tank is full, how much work is required to pump the water to a level 1 m above the top of the tank?

38–41. Force on dams *The following figures show the shape and dimensions of small dams. Assuming the water level is at the top of the dam, find the total force on the face of the dam.*

38.

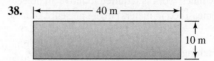

39.

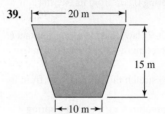

40.

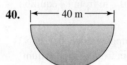

41.

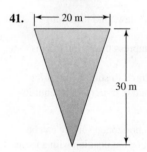

42. Parabolic dam The lower edge of a dam is defined by the parabola $y = x^2/16$ (see figure). Use a coordinate system with $y = 0$ at the bottom of the dam to determine the total force on the dam. Lengths are measured in meters. Assume the water level is at the top of the dam.

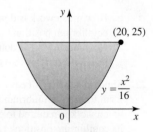

43. Orientation and force A plate shaped like an isosceles triangle with a height of 1m is placed on a vertical wall 1 m below the surface of a pool filled with water (see figure). Compute the force on the plate.

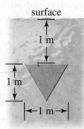

44. Force on the end of a tank Determine the force on a circular end of the tank in Figure 6.68 if the tank is full of gasoline. The density of gasoline is $\rho \approx 737 \text{ kg/m}^3$.

45. Force on a building A large building shaped like a box is 50 m high with a face that is 80 m wide. A strong wind blows directly at the face of the building, exerting a pressure of 150 N/m^2 at the ground and increasing with height according to $P(y) = 150 + 2y$, where y is the height above the ground. Calculate the total force on the building, which is a measure of the resistance that must be included in the design of the building.

46–48. Force on a window *A diving pool that is 4 m deep and full of water has a viewing window on one of its vertical walls. Find the force on the following windows.*

46. The window is a square, 0.5 m on a side, with the lower edge of the window on the bottom of the pool.

47. The window is a square, 0.5 m on a side, with the lower edge of the window 1 m from the bottom of the pool.

48. The window is a circle, with a radius of 0.5 m, tangent to the bottom of the pool.

Further Explorations

49. Explain why or why not Determine whether the following statements are true and give an explanation or counterexample.

  a. The mass of a thin wire is the length of the wire times its average density over its length.

  b. The work required to stretch a linear spring (that obeys Hooke's law) 100 cm from equilibrium is the same as the work required to compress it 100 cm from equilibrium.

  c. The work required to lift a 10-kg object vertically 10 m is the same as the work required to lift a 20-kg object vertically 5 m.

  d. The total force on a 10-ft^2 region on the (horizontal) floor of a pool is the same as the total force on a 10-ft^2 region on a (vertical) wall of the pool.

50. Mass of two bars Two bars of length L have densities $\rho_1(x) = 4e^{-x}$ and $\rho_2(x) = 6e^{-2x}$, for $0 \le x \le L$.

  a. For what values of L is bar 1 heavier than bar 2?

  b. As the lengths of the bars increase, do their masses increase without bound? Explain.

51. A nonlinear spring Hooke's law is applicable to idealized (linear) springs that are not stretched or compressed too far. Consider a nonlinear spring whose restoring force is given by $F(x) = 16x - 0.1x^3$, for $|x| \le 7$.

  a. Graph the restoring force and interpret it.

  b. How much work is done in stretching the spring from its equilibrium position ($x = 0$) to $x = 1.5$?

  c. How much work is done in compressing the spring from its equilibrium position ($x = 0$) to $x = -2$?

52. A vertical spring A 10-kg mass is attached to a spring that hangs vertically and is stretched 2 m from the equilibrium position of the spring. Assume a linear spring with $F(x) = kx$.

  a. How much work is required to compress the spring and lift the mass 0.5 m?

  b. How much work is required to stretch the spring and lower the mass 0.5 m?

53. Drinking juice A glass has circular cross sections that taper (linearly) from a radius of 5 cm at the top of the glass to a radius of 4 cm at the bottom. The glass is 15 cm high and full of orange juice. How much work is required to drink all the juice through a straw if your mouth is 5 cm above the top of the glass? Assume the density of orange juice equals the density of water.

54. Upper and lower half A cylinder with height 8 m and radius 3 m is filled with water and must be emptied through an outlet pipe 2 m above the top of the cylinder.

  a. Compute the work required to empty the water in the top half of the tank.

  b. Compute the work required to empty the (equal amount of) water in the lower half of the tank.

  c. Interpret the results of parts (a) and (b).

Applications

55. Work in a gravitational field For large distances from the surface of Earth, the gravitational force is given by $F(x) = GMm/(x + R)^2$, where $G = 6.7 \times 10^{-11} \text{ N·m}^2/\text{kg}^2$ is the gravitational constant, $M = 6 \times 10^{24}$ kg is the mass of Earth, m is the mass of the object in the gravitational field, $R = 6.378 \times 10^6$ m is the radius of Earth, and $x \ge 0$ is the distance above the surface of Earth (in meters).

  a. How much work is required to launch a rocket with a mass of 500 kg in a vertical flight path to a height of 2500 km (from Earth's surface)?

  b. Find the work required to launch the rocket to a height of x kilometers, for $x > 0$.

  c. How much work is required to reach outer space ($x \to \infty$)?

  d. Equate the work in part (c) to the initial kinetic energy of the rocket, $\frac{1}{2}mv^2$, to compute the escape velocity of the rocket.

56. Work by two different integrals A rigid body with a mass of 2 kg moves along a line due to a force that produces a position function $x(t) = 4t^2$, where x is measured in meters and t is measured in seconds. Find the work done during the first 5 s in two ways.

  a. Note that $x''(t) = 8$; then use Newton's second law ($F = ma = mx''(t)$) to evaluate the work integral $W = \int_{x_0}^{x_f} F(x)\, dx$, where x_0 and x_f are the initial and final positions, respectively.

  b. Change variables in the work integral and integrate with respect to t. Be sure your answer agrees with part (a).

57. Winding a chain A 30-m-long chain hangs vertically from a cylinder attached to a winch. Assume there is no friction in the system and that the chain has a density of 5 kg/m.

  a. How much work is required to wind the entire chain onto the cylinder using the winch?

  b. How much work is required to wind the chain onto the cylinder if a 50-kg block is attached to the end of the chain?

58. Coiling a rope A 60-m-long, 9.4-mm-diameter rope hangs free from a ledge. The density of the rope is 55 g/m. How much work is needed to pull the entire rope to the ledge?

59. Lifting a pendulum A body of mass m is suspended by a rod of length L that pivots without friction (see figure). The mass is slowly lifted along a circular arc to a height h.

  a. Assuming that the only force acting on the mass is the gravitational force, show that the component of this force acting along the arc of motion is $F = mg \sin \theta$.

  b. Noting that an element of length along the path of the pendulum is $ds = L \, d\theta$, evaluate an integral in θ to show that the work done in lifting the mass to a height h is mgh.

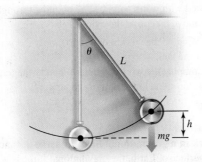

60. Orientation and force A plate shaped like an equilateral triangle 1 m on a side is placed on a vertical wall 1 m below the surface of a pool filled with water. On which plate in the figure is the force greater? Try to anticipate the answer and then compute the force on each plate.

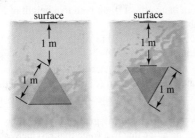

61. Orientation and force A square plate 1 m on a side is placed on a vertical wall 1 m below the surface of a pool filled with water. On which plate in the figure is the force greater? Try to anticipate the answer and then compute the force on each plate.

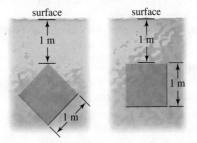

62. A calorie-free milkshake? Suppose a cylindrical glass with a diameter of $\frac{1}{12}$ m and a height of $\frac{1}{10}$ m is filled to the brim with a 400-Cal milkshake. If you have a straw that is 1.1 m long (so the top of the straw is 1 m above the top of the glass), do you burn off all the calories in the milkshake in drinking it? Assume that the density of the milkshake is 1 g/cm^3 (1 Cal = 4184 J).

63. Critical depth A large tank has a plastic window on one wall that is designed to withstand a force of 90,000 N. The square window is 2 m on a side, and its lower edge is 1 m from the bottom of the tank.

  a. If the tank is filled to a depth of 4 m, will the window withstand the resulting force?

  b. What is the maximum depth to which the tank can be filled without the window failing?

64. Buoyancy Archimedes' principle says that the buoyant force exerted on an object that is (partially or totally) submerged in water is equal to the weight of the water displaced by the object (see figure). Let $\rho_w = 1$ g/cm^3 = 1000 kg/m^3 be the density of water and let ρ be the density of an object in water. Let $f = \rho / \rho_w$. If $0 < f \le 1$, then the object floats with a fraction f of its volume submerged; if $f > 1$, then the object sinks.

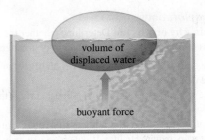

Consider a cubical box with sides 2 m long floating in water with one-half of its volume submerged ($\rho = \rho_w/2$). Find the force required to fully submerge the box (so its top surface is at the water level).

(See the Guided Project *Buoyancy and Archimedes' Principle* for further explorations of buoyancy problems.)

QUICK CHECK   ANSWERS

1. a. The bar is heaviest at the left end and lightest at the right end. **b.** $\rho = 2.5$ g/cm **2.** Minimum mass = 2 kg; maximum mass = 10 kg **3.** We assume that the force is constant over each subinterval, when, in fact, it varies over each subinterval. **4.** The restoring force of the spring increases as the spring is stretched ($F(x) = 100x$). Greater restoring forces are encountered on the interval $[0.1, 0.35]$ than on the interval $[0, 0.25]$. **5.** The factor $(15 - y)$ in the integral is replaced with $(10 - y)$ ◄

CHAPTER 6   REVIEW EXERCISES

1. **Explain why or why not** Determine whether the following statements are true and give an explanation or counterexample.

   a. A region R is revolved about the y-axis to generate a solid S. To find the volume of S, you could use either the disk/washer method and integrate with respect to y or the shell method and integrate with respect to x.

   b. Given only the velocity of an object moving on a line, it is possible to find its displacement, but not its position.

   c. If water flows into a tank at a constant rate (for example 6 gal/min), the volume of water in the tank increases according to a linear function of time.

2. **Displacement from velocity** The velocity of an object moving along a line is given by $v(t) = 20 \cos \pi t$ (in ft/s). What is the displacement of the object after 1.5 s?

3. **Position, displacement, and distance** A projectile is launched vertically from the ground at $t = 0$, and its velocity in flight (in m/s) is given by $v(t) = 20 - 10t$. Find the position, displacement, and distance traveled after t seconds, for $0 \le t \le 4$.

4. **Deceleration** At $t = 0$, a car begins decelerating from a velocity of 80 ft/s at a constant rate of 5 ft/s². Find its position function assuming $s(0) = 0$.

5. **An oscillator** The acceleration of an object moving along a line is given by $a(t) = 2 \sin\left(\dfrac{\pi t}{4}\right)$. The initial velocity and position are $v(0) = -\dfrac{8}{\pi}$ and $s(0) = 0$.

   a. Find the velocity and position for $t \ge 0$.

   b. What are the minimum and maximum values of s?

   c. Find the average velocity and average position over the interval $[0, 8]$.

6. **A race** Starting at the same point on a straight road, Anna and Benny begin running with velocities (in miles/hour) given by $v_A(t) = 2t + 1$ and $v_B(t) = 4 - t$, respectively.

   a. Graph the velocity functions, for $0 \le t \le 4$.

   b. If the runners run for 1 hr, who runs farther? Interpret your conclusion geometrically using the graph in part (a).

   c. If the runners run for 6 mi, who wins the race? Interpret your conclusion geometrically using the graph in part (a).

7. **Fuel consumption** A small plane in flight consumes fuel at a rate (in gal/min) given by

$$R'(t) = \begin{cases} 4t^{1/3} & \text{if } 0 \le t \le 8 \text{ (take-off)} \\ 2 & \text{if } t > 8 \text{ (cruising)}. \end{cases}$$

   a. Find a function R that gives the total fuel consumed, for $0 \le t \le 8$.

   b. Find a function R that gives the total fuel consumed, for $t \ge 0$.

   c. If the fuel tank capacity is 150 gal, when does the fuel run out?

8. **Variable flow rate** Water flows out of a tank at a rate (in m³/hr) given by $V'(t) = 15/(t + 1)$. If the tank initially holds 75 m³ of water, when will the tank be empty?

9. **Decreasing velocity** A projectile is fired upward, and its velocity in m/s is given by $v(t) = 200e^{-t/10}$, for $t \ge 0$.

   a. Graph the velocity function for $t \ge 0$.

   b. When does the velocity reach 50 m/s?

   c. Find and graph the position function for the projectile for $t \ge 0$ assuming $s(0) = 0$.

   d. Given unlimited time, can the projectile travel 2500 m? If so, at what time does the distance traveled equal 2500 m?

10. **Decreasing velocity** A projectile is fired upward, and its velocity (in m/s) is given by $v(t) = \dfrac{200}{\sqrt{t + 1}}$, for $t \ge 0$.

    a. Graph the velocity function for $t \ge 0$.

    b. Find and graph the position function for the projectile, for $t \ge 0$, assuming $s(0) = 0$.

    c. Given unlimited time, can the projectile travel 2500 m? If so, at what time does the distance traveled equal 2500 m?

11. **An exponential bike ride** Tom and Sue took a bike ride, both starting at the same time and position. Tom started riding at 20 mi/hr, and his velocity decreased according to the function $v(t) = 20e^{-2t}$ for $t \ge 0$. Sue started riding at 15 mi/hr, and her velocity decreased according to the function $u(t) = 15e^{-t}$ for $t \ge 0$.

    a. Find and graph the position functions of Tom and Sue.

    b. Find the times at which the riders had the same position at the same time.

    c. Who ultimately took the lead and remained in the lead?

12–19. **Areas of regions** *Use any method to find the area of the region described.*

12. The region in the first quadrant bounded by $y = x^p$ and $y = \sqrt[p]{x}$, where $p = 100$ and $p = 1000$

13. The region in the first quadrant bounded by $y = 4x$ and $y = x\sqrt{25 - x^2}$

14. The regions R_1 and R_2 (separately) shown in the figure, which are formed by the graphs of $y = 16 - x^2$ and $y = 5x - 8$

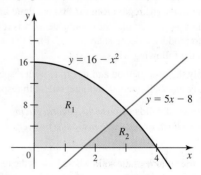

15. The regions $R_1, R_2,$ and R_3 (separately) shown in the figure, which are formed by the graphs of $y = 2\sqrt{x}, y = 3 - x,$ and $y = x(x - 3)$ (First find the intersection points by inspection.)

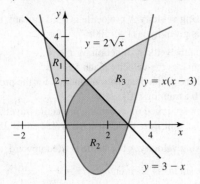

16. The region between $y = \sin x$ and $y = x$ over the interval $[0, 2\pi]$

17. The region bounded by $y = x^2, y = 2x^2 - 4x,$ and $y = 0$

18. The region in the first quadrant bounded by the curve $\sqrt{x} + \sqrt{y} = 1$

19. The region in the first quadrant bounded by $y = x/6$ and $y = 1 - |x/2 - 1|$

20. **An area function** Let $R(x)$ be the area of the shaded region between the graphs of $y = f(t)$ and $y = g(t)$ in the figure.

    a. Sketch a plausible graph of R, for $a \le x \le c$.
    b. Give expressions for $R(x)$ and $R'(x)$, for $a \le x \le c$.

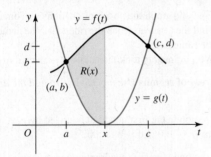

21. **An area function** Consider the functions $y = \dfrac{x^2}{a}$ and $y = \sqrt{\dfrac{x}{a}}$, where $a > 0$. Find $A(a)$, the area of the region between the curves.

22. **Two methods** The region R in the first quadrant bounded by the parabola $y = 4 - x^2$ and the coordinate axes is revolved about the y-axis to produce a dome-shaped solid. Find the volume of the solid in the following ways.

    a. Apply the disk method and integrate with respect to y.
    b. Apply the shell method and integrate with respect to x.

23–35. Volumes of solids *Choose the general slicing method, the disk/washer method, or the shell method to answer the following questions.*

23. What is the volume of the solid whose base is the region in the first quadrant bounded between $y = \sqrt{x}, y = 2 - x,$ and the x-axis, and whose cross sections perpendicular to the base and parallel to the y-axis are squares?

24. What is the volume of the solid whose base is the region in the first quadrant bounded between $y = \sqrt{x}, y = 2 - x,$ and the x-axis, and whose cross sections perpendicular to the base and parallel to the y-axis are semicircles?

25. What is the volume of the solid whose base is the region in the first quadrant bounded between $y = \sqrt{x}, y = 2 - x,$ and the y-axis and whose cross sections perpendicular to the base and parallel to the x-axis are squares?

26. The region bounded by the curves $y = -x^2 + 2x + 2$ and $y = 2x^2 - 4x + 2$ is revolved about the x-axis. What is the volume of the solid that is generated?

27. The region bounded by the curves $y = 1 + \sqrt{x}, y = 1 - \sqrt{x},$ and the line $x = 1$ is revolved about the y-axis. Find the volume of the resulting solid by (a) integrating with respect to x and (b) integrating with respect to y. Be sure your answers agree.

28. The region bounded by the curves $y = 2e^{-x}, y = e^x,$ and the y-axis is revolved about the x-axis. What is the volume of the solid that is generated?

29. The region bounded by the graphs of $x = 0, x = \sqrt{\ln y},$ and $x = \sqrt{2 - \ln y}$ in the first quadrant is revolved about the y-axis. What is the volume of the resulting solid?

30. The region bounded by the curves $y = \sec x$ and $y = 2$, for $0 \le x \le \frac{\pi}{3}$, is revolved about the x-axis. What is the volume of the solid that is generated?

31. The region bounded by $y = (1 - x^2)^{-1/2}$ and the x-axis over the interval $[0, \sqrt{3}/2]$ is revolved about the y-axis. What is the volume of the solid that is generated?

32. The region bounded by the graph of $y = 4 - x^2$ and the x-axis on the interval $[-2, 2]$ is revolved about the line $x = -2$. What is the volume of the solid that is generated?

33. The region bounded by the graphs of $y = (x - 2)^2$ and $y = 4$ is revolved about the line $y = 4$. What is the volume of the resulting solid?

34. The region bounded by the graphs of $y = 6x$ and $y = x^2 + 5$ is revolved about the line $y = -1$ and the line $x = -1$. Which of the resulting solids has the greater volume?

35. The region bounded by the graphs of $y = 2x, y = 6 - x,$ and $y = 0$ is revolved about the line $y = -2$ and the line $x = -2$. Which of the resulting solids has the greater volume?

36. **Area and volume** The region R is bounded by the curves $x = y^2 + 2, y = x - 4,$ and $y = 0$ (see figure).

    a. Write a single integral that gives the area of R.
    b. Write a single integral that gives the volume of the solid generated when R is revolved about the x-axis.
    c. Write a single integral that gives the volume of the solid generated when R is revolved about the y-axis.
    d. Suppose S is a solid whose base is R and whose cross sections perpendicular to R and parallel to the x-axis are semicircles. Write a single integral that gives the volume of S.

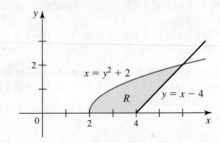

37. Comparing volumes Let R be the region bounded by $y = 1/x^p$ and the x-axis on the interval $[1, a]$, where $p > 0$ and $a > 1$ (see figure). Let V_x and V_y be the volumes of the solids generated when R is revolved about the x- and y-axes, respectively.

  a. With $a = 2$ and $p = 1$, which is greater, V_x or V_y?
  b. With $a = 4$ and $p = 3$, which is greater, V_x or V_y?
  c. Find a general expression for V_x in terms of a and p. Note that $p = \frac{1}{2}$ is a special case. What is V_x when $p = \frac{1}{2}$?
  d. Find a general expression for V_y in terms of a and p. Note that $p = 2$ is a special case. What is V_y when $p = 2$?
  e. Explain how parts (c) and (d) demonstrate that
$$\lim_{h \to 0} \frac{a^h - 1}{h} = \ln a.$$
  f. Find any values of a and p for which $V_x > V_y$.

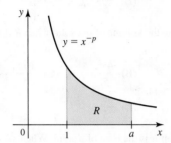

38–43. Arc length *Find the length of the following curves.*

38. $y = 2x + 4$ on the interval $[-2, 2]$ (Use calculus.)

39. $y = \ln(x + \sqrt{x^2 - 1})$ on the interval $[\sqrt{2}, \sqrt{5}]$

40. $y = x^3/6 + 1/(2x)$ on the interval $[1, 2]$

41. $y = x^{1/2} - x^{3/2}/3$ on the interval $[1, 3]$

42. $y = x^3/3 + x^2 + x + 1/(4x + 4)$ on the interval $[0, 4]$

43. $y = \ln x$ between $x = 1$ and $x = b > 1$ given that
$$\int \frac{\sqrt{x^2 + a^2}}{x} \, dx = \sqrt{x^2 + a^2} - a \ln\left(\frac{a + \sqrt{x^2 + a^2}}{x}\right) + C.$$

Use any means to approximate the value of b for which the curve has length 2.

44–46. Variable density in one dimension *Find the mass of the following thin bars.*

44. A bar on the interval $0 \le x \le 9$ with a density (in g/cm) given by $\rho(x) = 3 + 2\sqrt{x}$

45. A 3 m bar with a density (in g/m) of $\rho(x) = 150e^{-x/3}$, for $0 \le x \le 3$

46. A bar on the interval $0 \le x \le 6$ with a density
$$\rho(x) = \begin{cases} 1 & \text{if } 0 \le x < 2 \\ 2 & \text{if } 2 \le x < 4 \\ 4 & \text{if } 4 \le x \le 6. \end{cases}$$

47. Spring work

  a. It takes 50 N of force to stretch a spring 0.2 m from its equilibrium position. How much work is needed to stretch it an additional 0.5 m?
  b. It takes 50 J of work to stretch a spring 0.2 m from its equilibrium position. How much work is needed to stretch it an additional 0.5 m?

48. Pumping water A cylindrical water tank has a height of 6 m and a radius of 4 m. How much work is required to empty the full tank by pumping the water to an outflow pipe at the top of the tank?

49. Force on a dam Find the total force on the face of a semicircular dam with a radius of 20 m when its reservoir is full of water. The diameter of the semicircle is the top of the dam.

50. Equal area property for parabolas Let $f(x) = ax^2 + bx + c$ be an arbitrary quadratic function and choose two points $x = p$ and $x = q$. Let L_1 be the line tangent to the graph of f at the point $(p, f(p))$, and let L_2 be the line tangent to the graph at the point $(q, f(q))$. Let $x = s$ be the vertical line through the intersection point of L_1 and L_2. Finally, let R_1 be the region bounded by $y = f(x)$, L_1, and the vertical line $x = s$, and let R_2 be the region bounded by $y = f(x)$, L_2, and the vertical line $x = s$. Prove that the area of R_1 equals the area of R_2.

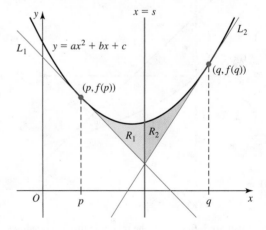

AP® PRACTICE QUESTIONS   *The following questions are intended to help you prepare for the AP exam. They are not questions from actual AP exams.*

Section 1 Part A, Multiple Choice, No Technology

1. Find the area of the shaded region bounded by the graphs of $y = 2x - 3$ and $y = 5 - x^2$ in the figure.

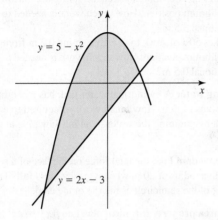

(A) 18   (B) 54   (C) 36
(D) 28   (E) 24

2. Find the area of the shaded region bounded by the graphs of $y = 1 - x$ and $x = y^2 - y$ in the figure.

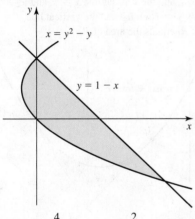

(A) 3   (B) $\dfrac{4}{3}$ (C) $\dfrac{2}{3}$
(D) 2   (E) 4

For Questions 3–6, let R be the region in the first quadrant bounded by the graphs of $y = 2x^2$ and $y = 2$.

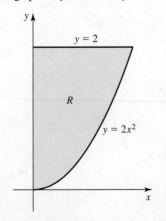

3. Determine the volume of the solid generated when R is revolved about the y-axis.

(A) π (B) $\dfrac{\pi}{2}$ (C) $\dfrac{2\pi}{3}$
(D) 2π (E) 4π

4. Find the volume of the solid generated when R is revolved about the x-axis.

(A) $\dfrac{32\pi}{5}$ (B) $\dfrac{4\pi}{5}$ (C) $\dfrac{16\pi}{5}$
(D) 5π (E) $\dfrac{8\pi}{5}$

5. Determine the volume of the solid when R is revolved about the line $y = 2$.

(A) $\dfrac{32\pi}{15}$ (B) $\dfrac{4\pi}{5}$ (C) $\dfrac{16\pi}{5}$
(D) 5π (E) $\dfrac{8\pi}{5}$

6. The region R is the base of a solid. When sliced perpendicular to the xy-plane and parallel to the x-axis, the cross sections of the solid are squares. What is the volume of the solid?

(A) 1   (B) 2   (C) $\dfrac{1}{2}$
(D) $\dfrac{3}{2}$ (E) 3

7. The region in the first quadrant bounded by $y = 1 - x$ and the two coordinate axes is the base of a solid. When sliced perpendicular to the xy-plane and parallel to the y-axis, the solid has semicircular cross sections. What is the volume of the solid?

(A) $\dfrac{\pi}{2}$ (B) $\dfrac{13\pi}{3}$ (C) $\dfrac{\pi}{4}$
(D) $\dfrac{\pi}{3}$ (E) $\dfrac{\pi}{24}$

8. At time $t = 0$, an object with an initial position $s(0) = 2$ begins moving in a straight line with a velocity $v(t) = 20e^{-t}$. What is its position when $t = \ln 6$?

(A) $\dfrac{50}{3}$ (B) $-\dfrac{44}{3}$ (C) $-\dfrac{50}{3}$
(D) $\dfrac{56}{3}$ (E) $\dfrac{17}{6}$

9. A block suspended on a spring bounces up and down with a velocity given by $v(t) = 3\sin\dfrac{\pi t}{6}$. How far does the block travel in 6 time units?

(A) $\dfrac{12}{\pi}$ (B) $\dfrac{36}{\pi}$ (C) $\dfrac{4}{\pi}$
(D) $\dfrac{3}{\pi}$ (E) 12

10. Runners A and B start at the same point and race along a straight road with the velocity functions shown in the figure. Which of the following statements is not true?

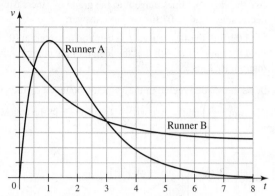

I. Over the time interval $3 \le t \le 8$, Runner B runs farther than Runner A.
II. Runners A and B are at the same position at $t = 1/2$.
III. Only Runner A increases her speed during some part of the race.

(A) I only
(B) II only
(C) III only
(D) I and II only
(E) II and III only

Section 1 Part B, Multiple Choice, Technology Allowed

11. The curves $f(x) = 4 - x$ and $g(x) = 4 - x^2$ intersect at two points. Find the arc length of the curve $y = g(x)$ between these points of intersection.

(A) 0.167
(B) 2.333
(C) 1.414
(D) 0.899
(E) 1.479

12. The line $y = 2x + 1$ and the curve $y = \sec^2 x$ form the boundaries of an infinite number of regions in the first quadrant. Find the approximate area of the leftmost of these regions.

(A) 0.633
(B) 0.125
(C) 0.582
(D) 0.454
(E) 0.239

13. Region R is bounded by the lines $y = 8x$, $y = 10 - 2x$, and the y-axis. Find the approximate value of c such that the vertical line $x = c$ divides R into two subregions of equal area.

(A) 0.293
(B) 0.350
(C) 0.244
(D) 0.451
(E) 0.397

14. The outflow rate of a large water reservoir varies periodically on a daily basis according to the function $R(t) = 20 + 10\cos\left(\frac{\pi t}{12}\right)$, where t is measured in hours and R is measured in thousands of gallons per hour. How many thousands of gallons of water flow out of the reservoir over the time interval $0 \le t \le 10$?

(A) $200 - \dfrac{60}{\pi}$
(B) 200
(C) $200 + \dfrac{60}{\pi}$
(D) 260
(E) 100

Section 2 Part A, Free Response, Technology Allowed

1. As a balloon is inflated, it maintains a spherical shape with radius r and volume $V = \dfrac{4}{3}\pi r^3$. The rate of change of the radius is given at selected times in the table.

t (min)	0	1	2	3	4
$r'(t)$ (in/min)	1	1/2	1/3	1/4	1/5

a. Use the Trapezoid Rule to approximate the radius of the balloon at $t = 1, 2, 3$, and 4 min.
b. Use the approximations to the radius in part (a) and the Trapezoid Rule to approximate the volume of the balloon at $t = 4$.
c. If you knew that, in fact, $r'(t) = \dfrac{1}{t+1}$, what would the exact volume of the balloon be at $t = 4$?

2. A pilot car escorts traffic through a construction zone on a straight north/south freeway. Starting at time $t = 0$, the pilot starts moving north. The velocity of the car (in mi/hr) at time t (measured in hours) is modeled by the following piecewise function.

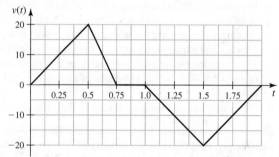

a. Determine the acceleration of the car 15 min into the trip.
b. When is the car moving south?
c. Evaluate $\int_0^2 v(t)\,dt$ and interpret the meaning of this integral.
d. What is the average velocity of the car during the first hour of the trip?
e. Evaluate $\int_0^2 |v(t)|\,dt$ and interpret the meaning of this integral.

3. Consider the region R in the first quadrant bounded by the graphs of $y = \sqrt{x-1}$ and $y = 7 - x$ (see figure).

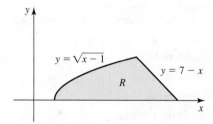

a. Find the area of R.
b. Determine the volume of the solid obtained by revolving R about the y-axis.
c. Determine the volume of the solid obtained by revolving R about the x-axis.

d. Find the volume of the solid whose base is R and whose cross sections through the solid perpendicular to the xy-plane and parallel to the x-axis are isosceles right triangles with one leg on the base of the solid.

4. An object is moving along the x-axis. The object starts at the origin at time $t = 0$, and its velocity is $v(t) = \sin(\pi e^t)$, for $0 \le t \le 20$.

a. Is the speed of the object increasing or decreasing when $t = 10$?

b. Determine the average velocity of the object on the interval $0 \le t \le 20$.

c. Find the total distance traveled by the object over the interval $0 \le t \le 20$.

d. How far is the object away from the origin when it first changes direction on the interval $0 \le t \le 20$?

5. At 9 A.M., it starts raining at a rate (in in/hr) given by the function

$$r(t) = \begin{cases} 0.5 & \text{if } 0 \le t \le 3 \\ 0.75 & \text{if } 3 < t \le 4.5 \\ 0.25 & \text{if } 4.5 < t \le 9. \end{cases}$$

a. How many inches of rain have fallen by 6 P.M.?

b. Determine a piecewise function $a(t)$ for the number of inches of rain that have fallen t hours after 9 A.M., for $0 \le t \le 9$.

c. An empty cylindrical glass with a circular base of radius of 2 inches and a height of 6 inches is placed outside at 9 A.M. Determine the rate of change of the volume of the water in the cup at 4 P.M. Recall that the volume of a circular cylinder with base radius r and height h is $\pi r^2 h$.

d. Determine the total volume of water in the glass at 6 P.M.

6. Tank A initially contains 1 liter of water and Tank B is initially empty; both tanks have a capacity of 20 liters. At $t = 0$, inflow valves are opened on both tanks. Tank A is filled at a rate of $r(t) = 5e^{-3t/2}$ L/min, while Tank B is filled at a rate of $R(t) = 4e^{-t/3}$ L/min. Assume t is measured in minutes.

a. How much water does each tank hold after 1 min?

b. Suppose water is allowed to flow into each tank indefinitely at the given rates. Find the amount of water in each tank as $t \to \infty$. Which tank ultimately holds more water?

Section 2 Part B, Free Response, No Technology

7. Consider the function $f(x) = \dfrac{1}{3}x^{3/2}$ where $x \ge 0$.

a. Are the slopes of lines tangent to the graph of f increasing or decreasing for $x \ge 0$? Justify your answer.

b. Find the length of the curve $y = f(x)$ on the interval $[0, 5]$.

c. Find the value of a such that the length of the curve on the interval $[0, a]$ is 39.

8. Let R be the shaded region in the xy-plane bounded by the graphs of $y = \sin\left(\dfrac{\pi x}{2}\right)$ and $y = \cos\left(\dfrac{\pi x}{2}\right)$, as shown in the following figure.

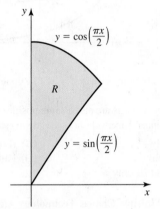

a. Find the slope of the line tangent to the graph of $y = \sin(\pi x/2)$ at $x = 1/3$.

b. Find the area of R.

c. Write, but do not evaluate, an integral that gives the volume of the solid when R is rotated about the line $y = 1$.

d. Write, but do not evaluate, an integral that gives the volume of a solid whose base is R and whose cross sections through the solid perpendicular to the xy-plane and parallel to the y-axis are rectangles. Assume the height of each rectangle is twice the length of its base through R.

Chapter 6 Guided Projects

Applications of the material in this chapter and related topics can be found in the following Guided Projects. For additional information, see the Preface.

- Means and tangent lines
- Landing an airliner
- Geometric probability
- Mathematics of the CD player
- Designing a water clock

- Buoyancy and Archimedes' principle
- Dipstick problems
- Hyperbolic functions
- Optimizing fuel use
- Inverse sine from geometry

7 Integration Techniques

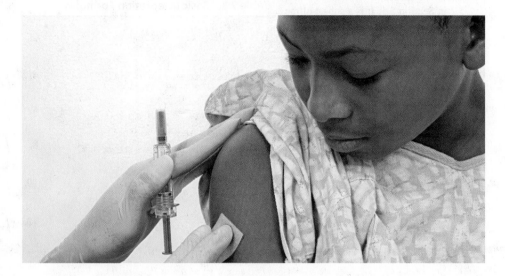

Concentration

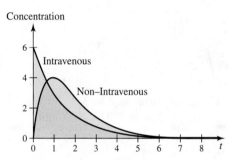

The most efficient way to administer a drug, such as an antibiotic, is with an intravenous system, which places the drug directly into the blood stream. If a drug is administered in other ways (injection, pill, nasal inhalant, or patch), the delivery is less efficient because some of the drug is absorbed before it reaches the bloodstream. The *bioavailability* of a drug measures the efficiency of a non-intravenous method compared to intravenous delivery. It provides important dosing information for physicians and pharmacologists, and analogous ideas appear in nutritional and environmental sciences. The bioavailability is computed by finding areas under the drug concentration curves. However, the areas must be computed, not over a finite time interval, but over the infinite interval $0 \le t < \infty$. In this chapter, we explore this sort of integral, which plays an important role in many applications.

Chapter Preview   In this chapter, we return to integration methods and present several new strategies that supplement the substitution (or change of variables) method. The new techniques are integration by parts, partial fractions, and trigonometric substitution. These *analytical* (pencil-and-paper) methods greatly enlarge the collection integrals that we can evaluate. The discussion also includes *improper integrals,* which have either infinite integrands or infinite intervals of integration. Such integrals have many practical applications and offer some surprising results.

7.1 Basic Approaches

Before plunging into new integration techniques, we devote this section to two practical goals. The first is to review what you learned about the substitution method in Section 5.6. The other is to introduce several basic simplifying procedures that are worth keeping in mind for any integral that you might be working on. After providing a table of some frequently used indefinite integrals (Table 7.1), we proceed by example.

> Table 7.1 is similar to Tables 5.1 and 5.2 in Section 5.1. It is a subset of the table of integrals at the back of the book.

Table 7.1   Basic Integration Formulas

1. $\displaystyle\int k\,dx = kx + C, k$ real

2. $\displaystyle\int x^p\,dx = \frac{x^{p+1}}{p+1} + C,\; p \neq -1$ real

3. $\displaystyle\int \cos ax\,dx = \frac{1}{a}\sin ax + C$

4. $\displaystyle\int \sin ax\,dx = -\frac{1}{a}\cos ax + C$

5. $\displaystyle\int \sec^2 ax\,dx = \frac{1}{a}\tan ax + C$

6. $\displaystyle\int \csc^2 ax\,dx = -\frac{1}{a}\cot ax + C$

7. $\displaystyle\int \sec ax \tan ax\,dx = \frac{1}{a}\sec ax + C$

8. $\displaystyle\int \csc ax \cot ax\,dx = -\frac{1}{a}\csc ax + C$

9. $\displaystyle\int e^{ax}\,dx = \frac{1}{a}e^{ax} + C$

10. $\displaystyle\int \frac{dx}{x} = \ln|x| + C$

11. $\displaystyle\int \frac{dx}{\sqrt{a^2 - x^2}} = \sin^{-1}\frac{x}{a} + C$

12. $\displaystyle\int \frac{dx}{a^2 + x^2} = \frac{1}{a}\tan^{-1}\frac{x}{a} + C$

13. $\displaystyle\int \frac{dx}{x\sqrt{x^2 - a^2}} = \frac{1}{a}\sec^{-1}\left|\frac{x}{a}\right| + C$

> A common choice for a change of variables is a linear term of the form $ax + b$.

EXAMPLE 1   Substitution review   Evaluate $\displaystyle\int_{-1}^{2} \frac{dx}{3 + 2x}$.

SOLUTION The expression $3 + 2x$ suggests the change of variables $u = 3 + 2x$. We find that $du = 2\,dx$; when $x = -1$, $u = 1$, and when $x = 2$, $u = 7$. The substitution may now be done:

$$\int_{-1}^{2} \frac{dx}{3 + 2x} = \int_{1}^{7} \frac{1}{u}\underbrace{\frac{du}{2}}_{dx} = \frac{1}{2}\ln|u|\Big|_{1}^{7} = \frac{1}{2}\ln 7.$$

Related Exercises 7–14 ◄

QUICK CHECK 1 What change of variable would you use for the integral $\int (6 + 5x)^8\,dx$? ◄

EXAMPLE 2   Subtle substitution   Evaluate $\displaystyle\int \frac{dx}{e^x + e^{-x}}$.

SOLUTION In this case, we see nothing in Table 7.1 that resembles the given integral. In a spirit of trial and error, we multiply numerator and denominator of the integrand by e^x:

$$\int \frac{dx}{e^x + e^{-x}} = \int \frac{e^x}{e^{2x} + 1}\,dx.$$

> Example 2 shows the useful technique of multiplying the integrand by 1. In this case, $1 = \dfrac{e^x}{e^x}$. The idea is used again in Example 6 of this section.

This form of the integrand suggests the substitution $u = e^x$, which implies that $du = e^x\,dx$. Making these substitutions, the integral becomes

$$\int \frac{e^x}{e^{2x} + 1}\,dx = \int \frac{du}{u^2 + 1} \qquad \text{Substitute } u = e^x, du = e^x\,dx.$$

$$= \tan^{-1} u + C \qquad \text{Table 7.1}$$

$$= \tan^{-1} e^x + C. \qquad u = e^x$$

Related Exercises 15–22 ◄

EXAMPLE 3   **Split up fractions**   Evaluate $\displaystyle\int \frac{\cos x + \sin^3 x}{\sec x}\, dx$.

SOLUTION   Don't overlook the opportunity to split a fraction into two or more fractions. In this case, the integrand is simplified in a useful way:

$$\int \frac{\cos x + \sin^3 x}{\sec x}\, dx = \int \frac{\cos x}{\sec x}\, dx + \int \frac{\sin^3 x}{\sec x}\, dx \qquad \text{Split fraction.}$$

$$= \int \cos^2 x\, dx + \int \sin^3 x \cos x\, dx. \qquad \sec x = \frac{1}{\cos x}$$

The first of the resulting integrals is evaluated using a half-angle formula (Example 6 of Section 5.6). In the second integral, the substitution $u = \sin x$ is used:

> **Half-angle formulas**
>
> $\cos^2 x = \dfrac{1 + \cos 2x}{2}$
>
> $\sin^2 x = \dfrac{1 - \cos 2x}{2}$

$$\int \frac{\cos x + \sin^3 x}{\sec x}\, dx = \int \cos^2 x\, dx + \int \sin^3 x \cos x\, dx$$

$$= \int \frac{1 + \cos 2x}{2}\, dx + \int \sin^3 x \cos x\, dx \qquad \text{Half-angle formula}$$

$$= \frac{1}{2}\int dx + \frac{1}{2}\int \cos 2x\, dx + \int u^3\, du \qquad u = \sin x,\, du = \cos x\, dx$$

$$= \frac{x}{2} + \frac{1}{4}\sin 2x + \frac{1}{4}\sin^4 x + C. \qquad \text{Evaluate integrals.}$$

Related Exercises 23–28 ◄

QUICK CHECK 2   Explain how to simplify the integrand of $\displaystyle\int \frac{x^3 + \sqrt{x}}{x^{3/2}}\, dx$ before integrating. ◄

EXAMPLE 4   **Division with rational functions**   Evaluate $\displaystyle\int \frac{x^2 + 2x - 1}{x + 4}\, dx$.

SOLUTION   When integrating rational functions (polynomials in the numerator and denominator), check to see if the function is *improper* (the degree of the numerator is greater than or equal to the degree of the denominator). In this example, we have an improper rational function, and long division is used to simplify it. The integration is done as follows:

> $$\begin{array}{r} x - 2 \\ x + 4 \overline{\smash{)}\, x^2 + 2x - 1} \\ \underline{x^2 + 4x} \\ -2x - 1 \\ \underline{-2x - 8} \\ 7 \end{array}$$

$$\int \frac{x^2 + 2x - 1}{x + 4}\, dx = \int (x - 2)\, dx + \int \frac{7}{x + 4}\, dx \qquad \text{Long division}$$

$$= \frac{x^2}{2} - 2x + 7 \ln |x + 4| + C. \qquad \text{Evaluate integrals.}$$

Related Exercises 29–32 ◄

EXAMPLE 5   **Complete the square**   Evaluate $\displaystyle\int \frac{dx}{\sqrt{-7 - 8x - x^2}}$.

QUICK CHECK 3   Explain how to simplify the integrand of $\displaystyle\int \frac{x + 1}{x - 1}\, dx$ before integrating. ◄

SOLUTION   We don't see an integral in Table 7.1 that looks like the given integral, so some preliminary work is needed. In this case, the key is to complete the square on the polynomial in the denominator. We find that

$$-7 - 8x - x^2 = -(x^2 + 8x + 7)$$

$$= -(x^2 + 8x + \underbrace{16 - 16}_{\text{add and subtract 16}} + 7) \qquad \text{Complete the square.}$$

$$= -((x + 4)^2 - 9) \qquad \text{Factor and combine terms.}$$

$$= 9 - (x + 4)^2. \qquad \text{Rearrange terms.}$$

After a change of variables, the integral is recognizable:

$$\int \frac{dx}{\sqrt{-7 - 8x - x^2}} = \int \frac{dx}{\sqrt{9 - (x + 4)^2}} \qquad \text{Complete the square.}$$

$$= \int \frac{du}{\sqrt{9 - u^2}} \qquad u = x + 4, \, du = dx$$

$$= \sin^{-1} \frac{u}{3} + C \qquad \text{Table 7.1}$$

$$= \sin^{-1} \left(\frac{x + 4}{3} \right) + C. \qquad \text{Replace } u \text{ with } x + 4.$$

Related Exercises 33–36 ◄

QUICK CHECK 4 Express $x^2 + 6x + 16$ in terms of a perfect square. ◄

EXAMPLE 6   Multiply by 1 Evaluate $\displaystyle\int \frac{dx}{1 + \cos x}$.

SOLUTION The key to evaluating this integral is admittedly not obvious, and the trick works only on special integrals. We multiply the integrand by 1 in the form

$$1 = \frac{1 - \cos x}{1 - \cos x}.$$

The integral is evaluated as follows:

$$\int \frac{dx}{1 + \cos x} = \int \frac{1}{1 + \cos x} \cdot \frac{1 - \cos x}{1 - \cos x} dx \qquad \text{Multiply by 1.}$$

$$= \int \frac{1 - \cos x}{1 - \cos^2 x} dx \qquad \text{Simplify.}$$

$$= \int \frac{1 - \cos x}{\sin^2 x} dx \qquad 1 - \cos^2 x = \sin^2 x$$

$$= \int \frac{1}{\sin^2 x} dx - \int \frac{\cos x}{\sin^2 x} dx \qquad \text{Split up the fraction.}$$

$$= \int \csc^2 x \, dx - \int \csc x \cot x \, dx \qquad \csc x = \frac{1}{\sin x}, \cot x = \frac{\cos x}{\sin x}$$

$$= -\cot x + \csc x + C. \qquad \text{Integrate using Table 7.1.}$$

Related Exercises 37–40 ◄

The techniques illustrated in this section are designed to transform or simplify an integrand before you apply a specific method. In fact, these ideas may help you recognize the best method to use. Keep them in mind as you learn new integration methods and improve your integration skills.

SECTION 7.1 EXERCISES

Review Questions

1. What change of variables would you use for the integral $\int (4 - 7x)^{-6} dx$?

2. Before integrating, how would you rewrite the integrand of $\int (x^4 + 2)^2 dx$?

3. What trigonometric identity is useful in evaluating $\int \sin^2 x \, dx$?

4. Describe a first step in integrating $\displaystyle\int \frac{x^3 - 2x + 4}{x - 1} dx$.

5. Describe a first step in integrating $\displaystyle\int \frac{10}{x^2 - 4x + 5} dx$.

6. Describe a first step in integrating $\displaystyle\int \frac{x^{10} - 2x^4 + 10x^2 + 1}{3x^3} dx$.

Basic Skills

7–14. Substitution Review *Evaluate the following integrals.*

7. $\displaystyle\int \frac{dx}{(3 - 5x)^4}$

8. $\displaystyle\int (9x - 2)^{-3} dx$

9. $\displaystyle\int_0^{3\pi/8} \sin\left(2x - \frac{\pi}{4} \right) dx$

10. $\displaystyle\int e^{3 - 4x} dx$

11. $\displaystyle\int \frac{\ln 2x}{x}\, dx$

12. $\displaystyle\int_{-5}^{0} \frac{dx}{\sqrt{4-x}}$

13. $\displaystyle\int \frac{e^x}{e^x + 1}\, dx$

14. $\displaystyle\int \frac{e^{2\sqrt{x}+1}}{\sqrt{x}}\, dx$

15–22. Subtle substitutions *Evaluate the following integrals.*

15. $\displaystyle\int \frac{e^x}{e^x - 2e^{-x}}\, dx$

16. $\displaystyle\int \frac{e^{2x}}{e^{2x} - 4e^{-x}}\, dx$

17. $\displaystyle\int_{1}^{e^2} \frac{\ln^2(x^2)}{x}\, dx$

18. $\displaystyle\int \frac{\sin^3 x}{\cos^5 x}\, dx$

19. $\displaystyle\int \frac{\cos^4 x}{\sin^6 x}\, dx$

20. $\displaystyle\int_{0}^{2} \frac{x(3x+2)}{\sqrt{x^3 + x^2 + 4}}\, dx$

21. $\displaystyle\int \frac{dx}{x^{-1} + 1}$

22. $\displaystyle\int \frac{dx}{x^{-1} + x^{-3}}$

23–28. Splitting fractions *Evaluate the following integrals.*

23. $\displaystyle\int \frac{x+2}{x^2 + 4}\, dx$

24. $\displaystyle\int_{4}^{9} \frac{x^{5/2} - x^{1/2}}{x^{3/2}}\, dx$

25. $\displaystyle\int \frac{\sin t + \tan t}{\cos^2 t}\, dt$

26. $\displaystyle\int \frac{4 + e^{-2x}}{e^{3x}}\, dx$

27. $\displaystyle\int \frac{2 - 3x}{\sqrt{1 - x^2}}\, dx$

28. $\displaystyle\int \frac{3x + 1}{\sqrt{4 - x^2}}\, dx$

29–32. Division with rational functions *Evaluate the following integrals.*

29. $\displaystyle\int \frac{x+2}{x+4}\, dx$

30. $\displaystyle\int_{2}^{4} \frac{x^2 + 2}{x - 1}\, dx$

31. $\displaystyle\int \frac{t^3 - 2}{t + 1}\, dt$

32. $\displaystyle\int \frac{6 - x^4}{x^2 + 4}\, dx$

33–36. Completing the square *Evaluate the following integrals.*

33. $\displaystyle\int \frac{dx}{x^2 - 2x + 10}$

34. $\displaystyle\int_{0}^{2} \frac{x}{x^2 + 4x + 8}\, dx$

35. $\displaystyle\int \frac{d\theta}{\sqrt{27 - 6\theta - \theta^2}}$

36. $\displaystyle\int \frac{x}{x^4 + 2x^2 + 1}\, dx$

37–40. Multiply by 1 *Evaluate the following integrals.*

37. $\displaystyle\int \frac{d\theta}{1 + \sin\theta}$

38. $\displaystyle\int \frac{1 - x}{1 - \sqrt{x}}\, dx$

39. $\displaystyle\int \frac{dx}{\sec x - 1}$

40. $\displaystyle\int \frac{d\theta}{1 - \csc\theta}$

Further Explorations

41. Explain why or why not Determine whether the following statements are true and give an explanation or counterexample.

    a. $\displaystyle\int \frac{3}{x^2 + 4}\, dx = \int \frac{3}{x^2}\, dx + \int \frac{3}{4}\, dx.$

    b. Long division simplifies the evaluation of the integral

    $\displaystyle\int \frac{x^3 + 2}{3x^4 + x}\, dx.$

    c. $\displaystyle\int \frac{1}{\sin x + 1}\, dx = \ln|\sin x + 1| + C$

    d. $\displaystyle\int \frac{1}{e^x}\, dx = \ln e^x + C$

42–54. Miscellaneous integrals *Use the approaches discussed in this section to evaluate the following integrals.*

42. $\displaystyle\int_{4}^{9} \frac{dx}{1 - \sqrt{x}}$

43. $\displaystyle\int_{-1}^{0} \frac{x}{x^2 + 2x + 2}\, dx$

44. $\displaystyle\int_{0}^{1} \sqrt{1 + \sqrt{x}}\, dx$

45. $\displaystyle\int \sin x \sin 2x\, dx$

46. $\displaystyle\int_{0}^{\pi/2} \sqrt{1 + \cos 2x}\, dx$

47. $\displaystyle\int \frac{dx}{x^{1/2} + x^{3/2}}$

48. $\displaystyle\int_{0}^{1} \frac{dx}{4 - \sqrt{x}}$

49. $\displaystyle\int \frac{x - 2}{x^2 + 6x + 13}\, dx$

50. $\displaystyle\int_{0}^{\pi/4} 3\sqrt{1 + \sin 2x}\, dx$

51. $\displaystyle\int \frac{e^x}{e^{2x} + 2e^x + 1}\, dx$

52. $\displaystyle\int_{0}^{\pi/8} \sqrt{1 - \cos 4x}\, dx$

53. $\displaystyle\int_{1}^{3} \frac{2}{x^2 + 2x + 1}\, dx$

54. $\displaystyle\int_{0}^{2} \frac{2}{x^3 + 3x^2 + 3x + 1}\, dx$

55. Different methods

    a. Evaluate $\int \tan x \sec^2 x\, dx$ using the substitution $u = \tan x$.

    b. Evaluate $\int \tan x \sec^2 x\, dx$ using the substitution $u = \sec x$.

    c. Reconcile the results in parts (a) and (b).

56. Different methods

    a. Evaluate $\int \cot x \csc^2 x\, dx$ using the substitution $u = \cot x$.

    b. Evaluate $\int \cot x \csc^2 x\, dx$ using the substitution $u = \csc x$.

    c. Reconcile the results in parts (a) and (b).

57. Different methods

    a. Evaluate $\displaystyle\int \frac{x^2}{x+1}\, dx$ using the substitution $u = x + 1$.

    b. Evaluate $\displaystyle\int \frac{x^2}{x+1}\, dx$ after first performing long division on $\dfrac{x^2}{x+1}$.

    c. Reconcile the results in parts (a) and (b).

58. Different methods

    a. Show that $\displaystyle\int \frac{dx}{\sqrt{x - x^2}} = \sin^{-1}(2x - 1) + C$ using the substitution $u = 2x - 1$ or $u = x - \dfrac{1}{2}$.

    b. Show that $\displaystyle\int \frac{dx}{\sqrt{x - x^2}} = 2\sin^{-1}\sqrt{x} + C$ using the substitution $u = \sqrt{x}$.

    c. Prove the identity $2\sin^{-1}\sqrt{x} - \sin^{-1}(2x - 1) = \dfrac{\pi}{2}$.

    (*Source: The College Mathematics Journal* **32**, 5 (Nov. 2001))

Applications

59. Area of a region between curves Find the area of the region bounded by the curves $y = \dfrac{x^2}{x^3 - 3x}$ and $y = \dfrac{1}{x^3 - 3x}$ on the interval $[2, 4]$.

60. Area of a region between curves Find the area of the entire region bounded by the curves $y = \dfrac{x^3}{x^2 + 1}$ and $y = \dfrac{8x}{x^2 + 1}$.

61. Volumes of solids Consider the region R bounded by the graph of $f(x) = \sqrt{x^2 + 1}$ and the x-axis on the interval $[0, 2]$.

    a. Find the volume of the solid formed when R is revolved about the x-axis.

    b. Find the volume of the solid formed when R is revolved about the y-axis.

62. Volumes of solids Consider the region R bounded by the graph of $f(x) = \dfrac{1}{x + 2}$ and the x-axis on the interval $[0, 3]$.

    a. Find the volume of the solid formed when R is revolved about the x-axis.

    b. Find the volume of the solid formed when R is revolved about the y-axis.

63. Arc length Find the length of the curve $y = x^{5/4}$ on the interval $[0, 1]$. (*Hint:* Write the arc length integral and let $u^2 = 1 + \left(\frac{5}{4}\right)^2 \sqrt{x}$.)

QUICK CHECK ANSWERS

1. Let $u = 6 + 5x$. **2.** Write the integrand as $x^{3/2} + x^{-1}$.

3. Use long division to write the integrand as $1 + \dfrac{2}{x - 1}$.

4. $(x + 3)^2 + 7$ ◄

7.2 Integration by Parts

The Substitution Rule (Section 5.6) arises when we reverse the Chain Rule for derivatives. In this section, we employ a similar strategy and reverse the Product Rule for derivatives. The result is an integration technique called *integration by parts*. To illustrate the importance of integration by parts, consider the indefinite integrals

$$\int e^x \, dx = e^x + C \quad \text{and} \quad \int x e^x \, dx = ?$$

The first integral is an elementary integral that we have already encountered. The second integral is only slightly different—and yet, the appearance of the product $x e^x$ in the integrand makes this integral (at the moment) impossible to evaluate. Integration by parts is ideally suited for evaluating integrals of *products* of functions.

Integration by Parts for Indefinite Integrals

Given two differentiable functions u and v, the Product Rule states that

$$\frac{d}{dx}\big(u(x)v(x)\big) = u'(x)v(x) + u(x)v'(x).$$

By integrating both sides, we can write this rule in terms of an indefinite integral:

$$u(x)v(x) = \int \big(u'(x)v(x) + u(x)v'(x)\big) \, dx.$$

Rearranging this expression in the form

$$\int u(x)\underbrace{v'(x) \, dx}_{dv} = u(x)v(x) - \int v(x)\underbrace{u'(x) \, dx}_{du}$$

leads to the basic relationship for *integration by parts*. It is expressed more compactly by noting that $du = u'(x) \, dx$ and $dv = v'(x) \, dx$. Suppressing the independent variable x, we have

$$\int u \, dv = uv - \int v \, du.$$

The integral $\int u \, dv$ is viewed as the given integral, and we use integration by parts to express it in terms of a new integral $\int v \, du$. The technique is successful if the new integral can be evaluated.

> | Integration by Parts
> |
> | Suppose that u and v are differentiable functions. Then
> |
> | $$\int u\, dv = uv - \int v\, du.$$

▶ The integration by parts calculation may be done without including the constant of integration—as long as it is included in the final result.

EXAMPLE 1 Integration by parts Evaluate $\int xe^x\, dx$.

SOLUTION The presence of *products* in the integrand often suggests integration by parts. We split the product xe^x into two factors, one of which must be identified as u and the other as dv (the latter always includes the differential dx). Powers of x are *often* good choices for u. The choice for dv should be easy to integrate. In this case, the choices $u = x$ and $dv = e^x\, dx$ are advisable. It follows that $du = dx$. The relationship $dv = e^x\, dx$ means that v is an antiderivative of e^x, which implies $v = e^x$. A table is helpful for organizing these calculations.

▶ The arrows show how to combine factors in the integration by parts formula. The first arrow indicates the product uv; the second arrow indicates the integrand $v\, du$.

Functions in original integral	$u = x$	$dv = e^x\, dx$
Functions in new integral	$du = dx$	$v = e^x$

The integration by parts rule is now applied:

$$\int \underbrace{x}_{u}\ \underbrace{e^x\, dx}_{dv} = \underbrace{x}_{u}\ \underbrace{e^x}_{v} - \int \underbrace{e^x}_{v}\ \underbrace{dx}_{du}.$$

The original integral $\int xe^x\, dx$ has been replaced with the integral of e^x, which is easier to evaluate: $\int e^x\, dx = e^x + C$. The entire procedure looks like this:

$$\int xe^x\, dx = xe^x - \int e^x\, dx \quad \text{Integration by parts}$$
$$= xe^x - e^x + C. \quad \text{Evaluate the new integral.}$$

Related Exercises 7–22 ◀

EXAMPLE 2 Integration by parts Evaluate $\int x \sin x\, dx$.

SOLUTION Remembering that powers of x are often a good choice for u, we form the following table.

▶ To make the table, first write the functions in the original integral:

$u = \underline{\hspace{1cm}}, dv = \underline{\hspace{1cm}}.$

Then find the functions in the new integral by differentiating u and integrating dv:

$du = \underline{\hspace{1cm}}, v = \underline{\hspace{1cm}}.$

$u = x$	$dv = \sin x\, dx$
$du = dx$	$v = -\cos x$

Applying integration by parts, we have

$$\int \underbrace{x}_{u}\ \underbrace{\sin x\, dx}_{dv} = \underbrace{x}_{u}\ \underbrace{(-\cos x)}_{v} - \int \underbrace{(-\cos x)}_{v}\ \underbrace{dx}_{du} \quad \text{Integration by parts}$$
$$= -x \cos x + \sin x + C. \quad \text{Evaluate } \int \cos x\, dx = \sin x.$$

Related Exercises 7–22 ◀

QUICK CHECK 1 What is the best choice for u and dv in evaluating $\int x \cos x\, dx$? ◀

In general, integration by parts works when we can easily integrate the choice for dv and when the new integral is easier to evaluate than the original. Integration by parts is often used for integrals of the form $\int x^n f(x)\, dx$, where n is a positive integer. Such integrals generally require the repeated use of integration by parts, as shown in the following example.

EXAMPLE 3 Repeated use of integration by parts

a. Evaluate $\int x^2 e^x \, dx$.

b. How would you evaluate $\int x^n e^x \, dx$, where n is a positive integer?

SOLUTION

a. The factor x^2 is a good choice for u, leaving $dv = e^x \, dx$. We then have

$$\int \underbrace{x^2}_{u} \underbrace{e^x \, dx}_{dv} = \underbrace{x^2}_{u} \underbrace{e^x}_{v} - \int \underbrace{e^x}_{v} \underbrace{2x \, dx}_{du}.$$

$u = x^2$	$dv = e^x \, dx$
$du = 2x \, dx$	$v = e^x$

Notice that the new integral on the right side is simpler than the original integral because the power of x has been reduced by one. In fact, the new integral was evaluated in Example 1. Therefore, after using integration by parts twice, we have

$$\int x^2 e^x \, dx = x^2 e^x - 2 \int x e^x \, dx \qquad \text{Integration by parts}$$

$$= x^2 e^x - 2(x e^x - e^x) + C \quad \text{Result of Example 1}$$

$$= e^x (x^2 - 2x + 2) + C. \qquad \text{Simplify.}$$

b. We now let $u = x^n$ and $dv = e^x \, dx$. The integration takes the form

$u = x^n$	$dv = e^x \, dx$
$du = nx^{n-1} \, dx$	$v = e^x$

$$\int x^n e^x \, dx = x^n e^x - n \int x^{n-1} e^x \, dx.$$

> An integral identity in which the power of a variable is reduced is called a **reduction formula**. Other examples of reduction formulas are explored in Exercises 44–51.

We see that integration by parts reduces the power of the variable in the integrand. The integral in part (a) with $n = 2$ requires two uses of integration by parts. You can probably anticipate that evaluating the integral $\int x^n e^x \, dx$ requires n applications of integration by parts to reach the integral $\int e^x \, dx$, which is easily evaluated.

Related Exercises 23–30 ◄

EXAMPLE 4 Repeated use of integration by parts Evaluate $\int e^{2x} \sin x \, dx$.

SOLUTION The integrand consists of a product, which suggests integration by parts. In this case, there is no obvious choice for u and dv, so let's try the following choices.

$u = e^{2x}$	$dv = \sin x \, dx$
$du = 2e^{2x} \, dx$	$v = -\cos x$

> In Example 4, we could also use $u = \sin x$ and $dv = e^{2x} \, dx$. In general, some trial and error may be required when using integration by parts.

The integral then becomes

$$\int e^{2x} \sin x \, dx = -e^{2x} \cos x + 2 \int e^{2x} \cos x \, dx. \qquad (1)$$

The original integral has been expressed in terms of a new integral, $\int e^{2x} \cos x \, dx$, which appears no easier to evaluate than the original integral. It is tempting to start over with a new choice of u and dv, but a little persistence pays off. Suppose we evaluate $\int e^{2x} \cos x \, dx$ using integration by parts with the following choices.

> When using integration by parts, the acronym LIPET *often* helps choose u. If the integrand has two or more functions, choose u to be the first function type that appears in the list
>
> **L**ogarithmic, **I**nverse trigonometric, **P**olynomial, **E**xponential, **T**rigonometric.

$u = e^{2x}$	$dv = \cos x \, dx$
$du = 2e^{2x} \, dx$	$v = \sin x$

Integrating by parts, we have

$$\int e^{2x} \cos x \, dx = e^{2x} \sin x - 2 \int e^{2x} \sin x \, dx. \qquad (2)$$

Now observe that equation (2) contains the original integral, $\int e^{2x} \sin x \, dx$. Substituting the result of equation (2) into equation (1), we find that

$$\int e^{2x} \sin x \, dx = -e^{2x} \cos x + 2 \int e^{2x} \cos x \, dx$$

$$= -e^{2x} \cos x + 2\left(e^{2x} \sin x - 2 \int e^{2x} \sin x \, dx\right) \quad \text{Substitute for } \int e^{2x} \cos x \, dx.$$

$$= -e^{2x} \cos x + 2e^{2x} \sin x - 4 \int e^{2x} \sin x \, dx. \quad \text{Simplify.}$$

Now it is a matter of solving for $\int e^{2x} \sin x \, dx$ and including the constant of integration:

$$\int e^{2x} \sin x \, dx = \frac{1}{5} e^{2x} (2 \sin x - \cos x) + C.$$

Related Exercises 23–30 ◄

Integration by Parts for Definite Integrals

Integration by parts with definite integrals presents two options. You can use the method outlined in Examples 1–4 to find an antiderivative and then evaluate it at the upper and lower limits of integration. Alternatively, the limits of integration can be incorporated directly into the integration by parts process. With the second approach, integration by parts for definite integrals has the following form.

> Integration by parts for definite integrals still has the form
> $$\int u \, dv = uv - \int v \, du.$$
> However, both definite integrals must be written with respect to x.

> **Integration by Parts for Definite Integrals**
>
> Let u and v be differentiable. Then
> $$\int_a^b u(x)v'(x) \, dx = u(x)v(x) \Big|_a^b - \int_a^b v(x)u'(x) \, dx.$$

EXAMPLE 5   A definite integral Evaluate $\int_1^2 \ln x \, dx$.

SOLUTION This example is instructive because the integrand does not appear to be a product. The key is to view the integrand as the product $(\ln x)(1 \, dx)$. Then the following choices are plausible.

$u = \ln x$	$dv = dx$
$du = \dfrac{1}{x} \, dx$	$v = x$

Using integration by parts, we have

$$\int_1^2 \underbrace{\ln x}_{u} \underbrace{dx}_{dv} = \left((\underbrace{\ln x}_{u})\underbrace{x}_{v}\right)\Big|_1^2 - \int_1^2 \underbrace{x}_{v} \underbrace{\frac{1}{x} \, dx}_{du} \quad \text{Integration by parts}$$

$$= (x \ln x - x)\Big|_1^2 \quad \text{Integrate and simplify.}$$

$$= (2 \ln 2 - 0) - (2 - 1) \quad \text{Evaluate.}$$

$$= 2 \ln 2 - 1 \approx 0.386. \quad \text{Simplify.}$$

Related Exercises 31–38 ◄

In Example 5, we evaluated a definite integral of $\ln x$. The corresponding indefinite integral can be added to our list of integration formulas.

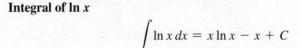

Integral of ln x

$$\int \ln x \, dx = x \ln x - x + C$$

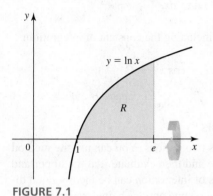

$y = \ln x$

R

0   1 e x

FIGURE 7.1

We now apply integration by parts to a familiar geometry problem.

EXAMPLE 6   Solids of revolution Let R be the region bounded by $y = \ln x$, the x-axis, and the line $x = e$ (Figure 7.1). Find the volume of the solid that is generated when the region R is revolved about the x-axis.

SOLUTION Revolving R about the x-axis generates a solid whose volume is computed with the disk method (Section 6.3). Its volume is

$$V = \int_1^e \pi (\ln x)^2 \, dx.$$

We integrate by parts with the following assignments.

$u = (\ln x)^2$	$dv = dx$
$du = \dfrac{2 \ln x}{x} dx$	$v = x$

> Recall that if $f(x) \geq 0$ on $[a, b]$ and the region bounded by the graph of f and the x-axis on $[a, b]$ is revolved about the x-axis, then the volume of the solid generated is
>
> $$V = \int_a^b \pi f(x)^2 \, dx.$$

The integration is carried out as follows, using the indefinite integral of $\ln x$ just given:

$$V = \int_1^e \pi (\ln x)^2 \, dx \qquad \text{Disk method}$$

$$= \pi \left(\underbrace{(\ln x)^2}_{u} \underbrace{x}_{v} \Big|_1^e - \int_1^e \underbrace{x}_{v} \underbrace{\frac{2 \ln x}{x} \, dx}_{du} \right) \qquad \text{Integration by parts}$$

$$= \pi \left(x(\ln x)^2 \Big|_1^e - 2 \int_1^e \ln x \, dx \right) \qquad \text{Simplify.}$$

$$= \pi \left(x(\ln x)^2 \Big|_1^e - 2(x \ln x - x) \Big|_1^e \right) \qquad \int \ln x \, dx = x \ln x - x + C$$

$$= \pi (e(\ln e)^2 - 2e \ln e + 2e - 2) \qquad \text{Evaluate.}$$

$$= \pi (e - 2) \approx 2.257. \qquad \text{Simplify.}$$

Related Exercises 39–42 ◄

SECTION 7.2 EXERCISES

Review Questions

1. On which derivative rule is integration by parts based?

2. How would you choose dv when evaluating $\int x^n e^{ax} \, dx$ using integration by parts?

3. How would you choose u when evaluating $\int x^n \cos ax \, dx$ using integration by parts?

4. Explain how integration by parts is used to evaluate a definite integral.

5. What type of integrand is a good candidate for integration by parts?

6. How would you choose u and dv to simplify $\int x^4 e^{-2x} \, dx$?

Basic Skills

7–22. Integration by parts *Evaluate the following integrals.*

7. $\displaystyle\int x \cos x \, dx$

8. $\displaystyle\int x \sin 2x \, dx$

9. $\displaystyle\int t e^t \, dt$

10. $\displaystyle\int 2x e^{3x} \, dx$

11. $\displaystyle\int \frac{x}{\sqrt{x+1}} \, dx$

12. $\displaystyle\int s e^{-2s} \, ds$

13. $\displaystyle\int x^2 \ln x^3 \, dx$

14. $\displaystyle\int \theta \sec^2 \theta \, d\theta$

15. $\displaystyle\int x^2 \ln x \, dx$

16. $\displaystyle\int x \ln x \, dx$

17. $\displaystyle\int \frac{\ln x}{x^{10}} \, dx$

18. $\displaystyle\int \sin^{-1} x \, dx$

19. $\displaystyle\int \tan^{-1} x \, dx$

20. $\displaystyle\int x \sec^{-1} x \, dx, \; x \geq 1$

21. $\displaystyle\int x \sin x \cos x \, dx$

22. $\displaystyle\int x \tan^{-1} x^2 \, dx$

23–30. Repeated integration by parts *Evaluate the following integrals.*

23. $\displaystyle\int t^2 e^{-t} \, dt$

24. $\displaystyle\int e^{3x} \cos 2x \, dx$

25. $\displaystyle\int e^{-x} \sin 4x \, dx$

26. $\displaystyle\int x^2 \ln^2 x \, dx$

27. $\displaystyle\int e^x \cos x \, dx$

28. $\displaystyle\int e^{-2\theta} \sin 6\theta \, d\theta$

29. $\displaystyle\int x^2 \sin 2x \, dx$

30. $\displaystyle\int x^2 e^{4x} \, dx$

31–38. Definite integrals *Evaluate the following definite integrals.*

31. $\displaystyle\int_0^\pi x \sin x \, dx$

32. $\displaystyle\int_1^e \ln 2x \, dx$

33. $\displaystyle\int_0^{\pi/2} x \cos 2x \, dx$

34. $\displaystyle\int_0^{\ln 2} x e^x \, dx$

35. $\displaystyle\int_1^{e^2} x^2 \ln x \, dx$

36. $\displaystyle\int_0^{1/\sqrt{2}} y \tan^{-1} y^2 \, dy$

37. $\displaystyle\int_{1/2}^{\sqrt{3}/2} \sin^{-1} y \, dy$

38. $\displaystyle\int_{2/\sqrt{3}}^2 z \sec^{-1} z \, dz$

39–42. Volumes of solids *Find the volume of the solid that is generated when the given region is revolved as described.*

39. The region bounded by $f(x) = e^{-x}$, $x = \ln 2$, and the coordinate axes is revolved about the y-axis.

40. The region bounded by $f(x) = \sin x$ and the x-axis on $[0, \pi]$ is revolved about the y-axis.

41. The region bounded by $f(x) = x \ln x$ and the x-axis on $[1, e^2]$ is revolved about the x-axis.

42. The region bounded by $f(x) = e^{-x}$ and the x-axis on $[0, \ln 2]$ is revolved about the line $x = \ln 2$.

Further Explorations

43. Explain why or why not Determine whether the following statements are true and give an explanation or counterexample.

  a. $\displaystyle\int uv' \, dx = \left(\int u \, dx\right)\left(\int v' \, dx\right)$

  b. $\displaystyle\int uv' \, dx = uv - \int vu' \, dx$

  c. $\displaystyle\int v \, du = uv - \int u \, dv$

44–47. Reduction formulas *Use integration by parts to derive the following reduction formulas.*

44. $\displaystyle\int x^n e^{ax} \, dx = \frac{x^n e^{ax}}{a} - \frac{n}{a} \int x^{n-1} e^{ax} \, dx, \quad \text{for } a \neq 0$

45. $\displaystyle\int x^n \cos ax \, dx = \frac{x^n \sin ax}{a} - \frac{n}{a} \int x^{n-1} \sin ax \, dx, \quad \text{for } a \neq 0$

46. $\displaystyle\int x^n \sin ax \, dx = -\frac{x^n \cos ax}{a} + \frac{n}{a} \int x^{n-1} \cos ax \, dx, \quad \text{for } a \neq 0$

47. $\displaystyle\int \ln^n x \, dx = x \ln^n x - n \int \ln^{n-1} x \, dx$

48–51. Applying reduction formulas *Use the reduction formulas in Exercises 44–47 to evaluate the following integrals.*

48. $\displaystyle\int x^2 e^{3x} \, dx$

49. $\displaystyle\int x^2 \cos 5x \, dx$

50. $\displaystyle\int x^3 \sin x \, dx$

51. $\displaystyle\int \ln^4 x \, dx$

52–53. Integrals involving $\int \ln x \, dx$ *Use a substitution to reduce the following integrals to $\int \ln u \, du$. Then evaluate the resulting integral.*

52. $\displaystyle\int \cos x \ln (\sin x) \, dx$

53. $\displaystyle\int \sec^2 x \ln (\tan x + 2) \, dx$

54. Two methods

  a. Evaluate $\int x \ln x^2 \, dx$ using the substitution $u = x^2$ and evaluating $\int \ln u \, du$.

  b. Evaluate $\int x \ln x^2 \, dx$ using integration by parts.

  c. Verify that your answers to parts (a) and (b) are consistent.

55. Logarithm base b Prove that

$$\int \log_b x \, dx = \frac{1}{\ln b} (x \ln x - x) + C.$$

56. Two integration methods Evaluate $\int \sin x \cos x \, dx$ using integration by parts. Then evaluate the integral using a substitution. Reconcile your answers.

57. Combining two integration methods Evaluate $\int \cos \sqrt{x} \, dx$ using a substitution followed by integration by parts.

58. Combining two integration methods Evaluate $\int_0^{\pi^2/4} \sin \sqrt{x} \, dx$ using a substitution followed by integration by parts.

59. Function defined as an integral Find the arc length of the function $f(x) = \int_e^x \sqrt{\ln^2 t - 1} \, dt$ on $[e, e^3]$.

60. A family of exponentials The curves $y = xe^{-ax}$ are shown in the figure for $a = 1, 2,$ and 3.

   a. Find the area of the region bounded by $y = xe^{-x}$ and the x-axis on the interval $[0, 4]$.

   b. Find the area of the region bounded by $y = xe^{-ax}$ and the x-axis on the interval $[0, 4]$, where $a > 0$.

   c. Find the area of the region bounded by $y = xe^{-ax}$ and the x-axis on the interval $[0, b]$. Because this area depends on a and b, we call it $A(a, b)$, where $a > 0$ and $b > 0$.

   d. Use part (c) to show that $A(1, \ln b) = 4A(2, (\ln b)/2)$.

   e. Does this pattern continue? Is it true that $A(1, \ln b) = a^2 A(a, (\ln b)/a)$?

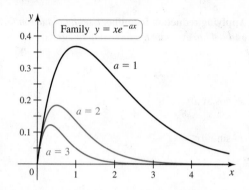

61. Solid of revolution Find the volume of the solid generated when the region bounded by $y = \cos x$ and the x-axis on the interval $[0, \pi/2]$ is revolved about the y-axis.

62. Between the sine and inverse sine Find the area of the region bounded by the curves $y = \sin x$ and $y = \sin^{-1} x$ on the interval $[0, \frac{1}{2}]$.

63. Comparing volumes Let R be the region bounded by $y = \sin x$ and the x-axis on the interval $[0, \pi]$. Which is greater, the volume of the solid generated when R is revolved about the x-axis or the volume of the solid generated when R is revolved about the y-axis?

64. Log integrals Use integration by parts to show that for $m \neq -1$,

$$\int x^m \ln x \, dx = \frac{x^{m+1}}{m + 1}\left(\ln x - \frac{1}{m + 1}\right) + C$$

and for $m = -1$,

$$\int \frac{\ln x}{x} dx = \frac{1}{2} \ln^2 x + C.$$

65. A useful integral

   a. Use integration by parts to show that if f' is continuous,

$$\int x f'(x) \, dx = x f(x) - \int f(x) \, dx.$$

   b. Use part (a) to evaluate $\int x e^{3x} \, dx$.

66. Integrating inverse functions Assume that f has an inverse on its domain.

   a. Let $y = f^{-1}(x)$ and show that

$$\int f^{-1}(x) \, dx = \int y f'(y) \, dy.$$

   b. Use part (a) and the result of Exercise 65 to show that

$$\int f^{-1}(x) \, dx = y f(y) - \int f(y) \, dy.$$

   c. Use the result of part (b) to evaluate $\int \ln x \, dx$ (express the result in terms of x).

   d. Use the result of part (b) to evaluate $\int \sin^{-1} x \, dx$.

   e. Use the result of part (b) to evaluate $\int \tan^{-1} x \, dx$.

67. Integral of $\sec^3 x$ Use integration by parts to show that

$$\int \sec^3 x \, dx = \frac{1}{2} \sec x \tan x + \frac{1}{2} \int \sec x \, dx.$$

68. Two useful exponential integrals Use integration by parts to derive the following formulas for real numbers a and b.

$$\int e^{ax} \sin bx \, dx = \frac{e^{ax}(a \sin bx - b \cos bx)}{a^2 + b^2} + C$$

$$\int e^{ax} \cos bx \, dx = \frac{e^{ax}(a \cos bx + b \sin bx)}{a^2 + b^2} + C$$

Applications

69. Oscillator displacements Suppose a mass on a spring that is slowed by friction has the position function $s(t) = e^{-t} \sin t$.

   a. Graph the position function. At what times does the oscillator pass through the position $s = 0$?

   b. Find the average value of the position on the interval $[0, \pi]$.

   c. Generalize part (b) and find the average value of the position on the interval $[n\pi, (n + 1)\pi]$, for $n = 0, 1, 2, \ldots$.

   d. Let a_n be the absolute value of the average position on the intervals $[n\pi, (n + 1)\pi]$, for $n = 0, 1, 2, \ldots$. Describe the pattern in the numbers $a_0, a_1, a_2, \ldots$.

Additional Exercises

70. Find the error Suppose you evaluate $\int \dfrac{dx}{x}$ using integration by parts. With $u = 1/x$ and $dv = dx$, you find that $du = -1/x^2 \, dx$, $v = x$, and

$$\int \frac{dx}{x} = \left(\frac{1}{x}\right)x - \int x\left(-\frac{1}{x^2}\right) dx = 1 + \int \frac{dx}{x}.$$

You conclude that $0 = 1$. Explain the problem with the calculation.

71. The idea of tabular integration Consider the integral $\int p_n(x) f(x) \, dx$, where p_n is an nth degree polynomial and f is a function that can be integrated at least $n + 1$ times. Let F_k represent the result of performing k indefinite integrals of f, for $k = 0, \ldots, n + 1$, where the constants of integration are omitted.

   a. With $n = 1$, show that

$$\int p_1(x) f(x) \, dx = p_1 F_1 - \int p_1'(x) F_1(x) \, dx = p_1 F_1 - p_1' F_2.$$

   Explain why only one integration by parts is required.

   b. With $n = 2$, show that

$$\int p_2(x) f(x) \, dx = p_2 F_1 - \int p_2'(x) F_1(x) \, dx$$

$$= p_2 F_1 - p_2' F_2 + \int p_2''(x) F_2(x) \, dx$$

$$= p_2 F_1 - p_2' F_2 + p_2'' F_3$$

   Explain why only two integrations by parts are required.

c. Use the result of part (b) to evaluate $\int (2x^2 - 3x + 1)e^{2x} dx$.

The work is simplified if you make a table with columns whose entries are $p_2^{(k)}$ and F_{k+1}, for $k = 0, 1, 2,$ and 3.

d. Show that in general,

$$\int p_n(x)f(x)dx = p_nF_1 - p_n'F_2 + p_n''F_3 - \cdots + (-1)^np_n^{(n)}F_{n+1}.$$

72. Integrating derivatives Use integration by parts to show that if f' is continuous on $[a, b]$, then

$$\int_a^b f(x)f'(x)\, dx = \frac{1}{2}\left(f(b)^2 - f(a)^2\right).$$

73. An identity Show that if f has a continuous second derivative on $[a, b]$ and $f'(a) = f'(b) = 0$, then

$$\int_a^b xf''(x)\, dx = f(a) - f(b).$$

74. An identity Show that if f and g have continuous second derivatives and $f(0) = f(1) = g(0) = g(1) = 0$, then

$$\int_0^1 f''(x)g(x)\, dx = \int_0^1 f(x)g''(x)\, dx.$$

75. Possible and impossible integrals Let $I_n = \int x^n e^{-x^2}\, dx$, where n is a nonnegative integer.

a. $I_0 = \int e^{-x^2}\, dx$ cannot be expressed in terms of elementary functions. Evaluate I_1.

b. Use integration by parts to evaluate I_3.

c. Use integration by parts and the result of part (b) to evaluate I_5.

d. Show that in general, if n is odd, then $I_n = -\frac{1}{2}e^{-x^2}p_{n-1}(x)$, where p_{n-1} is a polynomial of degree $n - 1$.

e. Argue that if n is even, then I_n cannot be expressed in terms of elementary functions.

76. Looking ahead (to Chapter 10) Suppose that a function f has derivatives of all orders near $x = 0$. By the Fundamental Theorem of Calculus,

$$f(x) - f(0) = \int_0^x f'(t)\, dt.$$

a. Evaluate the integral using integration by parts to show that

$$f(x) = f(0) + xf'(0) + \int_0^x f''(t)(x - t)\, dt.$$

b. Show that integrating by parts n times gives

$$f(x) = f(0) + xf'(0) + \frac{1}{2!}x^2f''(0) + \cdots + \frac{1}{n!}x^nf^{(n)}(0)$$
$$+ \frac{1}{n!}\int_0^x f^{(n+1)}(t)(x - t)^n\, dt + \cdots.$$

This expression, called the *Taylor series* for f at $x = 0$, is revisited in Chapter 10.

QUICK CHECK **ANSWERS**

1. Let $u = x$ and $dv = \cos x\, dx$.

2. $\dfrac{d}{dx}(x \ln x - x + C) = \ln x$

3. Integration by parts must be applied five times. ◄

7.3 Partial Fractions

In the next chapter, we will see that finding the velocity of a skydiver requires evaluating an integral of the form $\int \dfrac{dv}{a - bv^2}$, where a and b are constants. Similarly, finding the population of a species that is limited in size involves an integral of the form $\int \dfrac{dP}{aP(1 - bP)}$, where a and b are constants. These integrals have the common feature that their integrands are rational functions. Similar integrals result from modeling mechanical and electrical networks. The goal of this section is to introduce the *method of partial fractions* for integrating rational functions. When combined with standard and trigonometric substitutions (Section 7.5), this method allows us (in principle) to integrate any rational function.

> ➤ Recall that a rational function has the form p/q, where p and q are polynomials.

Method of Partial Fractions

Given a function such as

$$f(x) = \frac{1}{x - 2} + \frac{2}{x + 4},$$

it is a straightforward task to find a common denominator and write the equivalent expression

$$f(x) = \frac{(x + 4) + 2(x - 2)}{(x - 2)(x + 4)} = \frac{3x}{(x - 2)(x + 4)} = \frac{3x}{x^2 + 2x - 8}.$$

The purpose of partial fractions is to reverse this process. Given a rational function that is difficult to integrate, the method of partial fractions produces an equivalent function that is much easier to integrate.

QUICK CHECK 1 Find an antiderivative of $f(x) = \dfrac{1}{x - 2} + \dfrac{2}{x + 4}$. ◀

The Key Idea   Working with the same function, $f(x) = \dfrac{3x}{(x - 2)(x + 4)}$, our objective is to write it in the form

$$\frac{A}{x - 2} + \frac{B}{x + 4},$$

▷ Notice that the numerator of the original rational function does not affect the form of the partial fraction decomposition. The constants A and B are called *undetermined coefficients*.

where A and B are constants to be determined. This expression is called the **partial fraction decomposition** of the original function; in this case, it has two terms, one for each factor in the denominator of the original function.

The constants A and B are determined using the condition that the original function f and its partial fraction decomposition must be equal for all values of x in the domain of f; that is,

$$\frac{3x}{(x - 2)(x + 4)} = \frac{A}{x - 2} + \frac{B}{x + 4}. \tag{1}$$

▷ This step requires that $x \neq 2$ and $x \neq -4$; both values are outside the domain of f.

Multiplying both sides of equation (1) by $(x - 2)(x + 4)$ gives

$$3x = A(x + 4) + B(x - 2).$$

Collecting like powers of x results in

$$3x = (A + B)x + (4A - 2B). \tag{2}$$

If equation (2) is to hold for all values of x, then

• the coefficients of x^1 on both sides of the equation must be equal;

• the coefficients of x^0 (that is, the constants) on both sides of the equation must be equal.

$$3x + 0 = \overbrace{(A + B)}x + \overbrace{(4A - 2B)}$$

These observations leads to two equations for A and B.

$$\text{Equate coefficients of } x^1: \quad 3 = A + B$$
$$\text{Equate coefficients of } x^0: \quad 0 = 4A - 2B$$

The first equation says that $A = 3 - B$. Substituting $A = 3 - B$ into the second equation gives the equation $0 = 4(3 - B) - 2B$. Solving for B, we find that $6B = 12$, or $B = 2$. The value of A now follows; we have $A = 3 - B = 1$.

Substituting these values of A and B into equation (1), the partial fraction decomposition is

$$\frac{3x}{(x - 2)(x + 4)} = \frac{1}{x - 2} + \frac{2}{x + 4}.$$

Simple Linear Factors

The previous calculation illustrates the case of **simple linear factors**, meaning the denominator of the original function consists only of linear factors of the form $(x - r)$, which appear to the first power and no higher power. Here is the general procedure for this case.

> Like a fraction, a rational function is said to be in **reduced form** if the numerator and denominator have no common factors and it is said to be **proper** if the degree of the numerator is less than the degree of the denominator.

PROCEDURE **Partial Fractions with Simple Linear Factors**

Suppose $f(x) = p(x)/q(x)$, where p and q are polynomials with no common factors and with the degree of p less than the degree of q. Assume that q is the product of simple linear factors. The partial fraction decomposition is obtained as follows.

Step 1. **Factor the denominator q** in the form $(x - r_1)(x - r_2) \cdots (x - r_n)$, where $r_1, \ldots, r_n$ are real numbers.

Step 2. **Partial fraction decomposition** Form the partial fraction decomposition by writing

$$\frac{p(x)}{q(x)} = \frac{A_1}{(x - r_1)} + \frac{A_2}{(x - r_2)} + \cdots + \frac{A_n}{(x - r_n)}.$$

Step 3. **Clear denominators** Multiply both sides of the equation in Step 2 by $q(x) = (x - r_1)(x - r_2) \cdots (x - r_n)$, which produces conditions for $A_1, \ldots, A_n$.

Step 4. **Solve for coefficients** Equate like powers of x in Step 3 to solve for the undetermined coefficients $A_1, \ldots, A_n$.

QUICK CHECK 2 If the denominator of a reduced proper rational function is $(x - 1)(x + 5)(x - 10)$, what is the general form of its partial fraction decomposition? ◄

EXAMPLE 1 Integrating with partial fractions

a. Find the partial fraction decomposition for $f(x) = \dfrac{3x^2 + 7x - 2}{x^3 - x^2 - 2x}$.

b. Evaluate $\int f(x)\, dx$.

SOLUTION

a. The partial fraction decomposition is done in four steps.

Step 1: Factoring the denominator, we find that

$$x^3 - x^2 - 2x = x(x + 1)(x - 2),$$

in which only simple linear factors appear.

Step 2: The partial fraction decomposition has one term for each factor in the denominator:

> You can call the undetermined coefficients $A_1, A_2, A_3, \ldots$ or $A, B, C, \ldots$. The latter may be preferable because it avoids subscripts.

$$\frac{3x^2 + 7x - 2}{x(x + 1)(x - 2)} = \frac{A}{x} + \frac{B}{x + 1} + \frac{C}{x - 2}. \qquad (3)$$

The goal is to find the undetermined coefficients A, B, and C.

Step 3: We multiply both sides of equation (3) by $x(x + 1)(x - 2)$:

$$3x^2 + 7x - 2 = A(x + 1)(x - 2) + Bx(x - 2) + Cx(x + 1)$$
$$= (A + B + C)x^2 + (-A - 2B + C)x - 2A.$$

Step 4: We now equate coefficients of x^2, x^1, and x^0 on both sides of the equation in Step 3.

Equate coefficients of x^2: $A + B + C = 3$

Equate coefficients of x^1: $-A - 2B + C = 7$

Equate coefficients of x^0: $-2A = -2$

The third equation implies that $A = 1$, which is substituted into the first two equations to give

$$B + C = 2 \quad \text{and} \quad -2B + C = 8.$$

Solving for B and C, we conclude that $A = 1, B = -2$, and $C = 4$. Substituting the values of A, B, and C into equation (3), the partial fraction decomposition is

$$f(x) = \frac{1}{x} - \frac{2}{x+1} + \frac{4}{x-2}.$$

b. Integration is now straightforward:

$$\int \frac{3x^2 + 7x - 2}{x^3 - x^2 - 2x}\, dx = \int \left(\frac{1}{x} - \frac{2}{x+1} + \frac{4}{x-2} \right) dx \qquad \text{Partial fractions}$$

$$= \ln|x| - 2\ln|x+1| + 4\ln|x-2| + K \qquad \text{Integrate; arbitrary constant } K.$$

$$= \ln \frac{|x|(x-2)^4}{(x+1)^2} + K. \qquad \text{Properties of logarithms}$$

Related Exercises 5–26 ◄

A Shortcut (Convenient Values)

Solving for more than three unknown coefficients in a partial fraction decomposition may be difficult. In the case of simple linear factors, a shortcut saves work. In Example 1, Step 3 led to the equation

$$3x^2 + 7x - 2 = A(x+1)(x-2) + Bx(x-2) + Cx(x+1).$$

Because this equation holds for *all* values of x, it must hold for any particular value of x. By choosing values of x judiciously, it is easy to solve for A, B, and C. For example, setting $x = 0$ in this equation results in $-2 = -2A$, or $A = 1$. Setting $x = -1$ results in $-6 = 3B$, or $B = -2$, and setting $x = 2$ results in $24 = 6C$, or $C = 4$. In each case, we choose a value of x that eliminates all but one term on the right side of the equation.

EXAMPLE 2 Using the shortcut

a. Find the partial fraction decomposition for $f(x) = \dfrac{3x^2 + 2x + 5}{(x-1)(x^2 - x - 20)}$.

b. Evaluate $\displaystyle\int_2^4 f(x)\,dx$.

SOLUTION

a. We use four steps to obtain the partial fraction decomposition.

Step 1: The denominator of f can be factored as $(x-1)(x-5)(x+4)$, so the integrand has simple linear factors.

Step 2: We form the partial fraction decomposition with one term for each factor in the denominator:

$$\frac{3x^2 + 2x + 5}{(x - 1)(x - 5)(x + 4)} = \frac{A}{x - 1} + \frac{B}{x - 5} + \frac{C}{x + 4}. \tag{4}$$

The goal is to find the undetermined coefficients A, B, and C.

Step 3: We now multiply both sides of equation (4) by $(x - 1)(x - 5)(x + 4)$:

$$3x^2 + 2x + 5 = A(x - 5)(x + 4) + B(x - 1)(x + 4) + C(x - 1)(x - 5). \tag{5}$$

Step 4: The shortcut is now used to determine A, B, and C. Substituting $x = 1, 5$, and -4 in equation (5) allows us to solve directly for the coefficients:

$$\text{Letting } x = 1 \Rightarrow 10 = -20A + 0 \cdot B + 0 \cdot C \Rightarrow A = -\frac{1}{2};$$

$$\text{Letting } x = 5 \Rightarrow 90 = 0 \cdot A + 36B + 0 \cdot C \Rightarrow B = \frac{5}{2};$$

$$\text{Letting } x = -4 \Rightarrow 45 = 0 \cdot A + 0 \cdot B + 45C \Rightarrow C = 1.$$

Substituting the values of A, B, and C into equation (4) gives the partial fraction decomposition

$$f(x) = -\frac{1}{2}\frac{1}{x - 1} + \frac{5}{2}\frac{1}{x - 5} + \frac{1}{x + 4}.$$

b. We now carry out the integration.

$$\int_2^4 f(x)\,dx = \int_2^4 \left(-\frac{1}{2}\frac{1}{x - 1} + \frac{5}{2}\frac{1}{x - 5} + \frac{1}{x + 4} \right) dx \qquad \text{Partial fractions}$$

$$= \left(-\frac{1}{2}\ln|x - 1| + \frac{5}{2}\ln|x - 5| + \ln|x + 4| \right)\Big|_2^4 \qquad \text{Integrate.}$$

$$= -\frac{1}{2}\ln 3 + \frac{5}{2}\underbrace{\ln 1}_{0} + \ln 8 - \left(-\frac{1}{2}\underbrace{\ln 1}_{0} + \frac{5}{2}\ln 3 + \ln 6 \right) \qquad \text{Evaluate.}$$

$$= -3\ln 3 + \ln 8 - \ln 6 \qquad \text{Simplify.}$$

$$= \ln\frac{4}{81} \approx -3.008 \qquad \text{Log properties}$$

Related Exercises 5–26 ◀

Long Division The preceding discussion of partial fraction decomposition assumes that $f(x) = p(x)/q(x)$ is a proper rational function. If this is not the case and we are faced with an improper rational function f, we divide the denominator into the numerator and express f in two parts. One part will be a polynomial, and the other will be a proper rational function. For example, given the function

$$f(x) = \frac{2x^3 + 11x^2 + 28x + 33}{x^2 - x - 6},$$

we perform long division.

QUICK CHECK 3 What is the result of doing long division on $\dfrac{x}{x + 1}$? ◀

$$
\begin{array}{r}
2x\ +\ 13 \\
x^2 - x - 6\,\overline{)\,2x^3 + 11x^2 + 28x + 33} \\
\underline{2x^3 -\ 2x^2 - 12x} \\
13x^2 + 40x + 33 \\
\underline{13x^2 - 13x - 78} \\
53x + 111
\end{array}
$$

It follows that

$$f(x) = \underbrace{2x + 13}_{\substack{\text{polynomial;} \\ \text{easy to} \\ \text{integrate}}} + \underbrace{\frac{53x + 111}{x^2 - x - 6}}_{\substack{\text{apply partial fraction} \\ \text{decomposition}}}.$$

The first piece is easily integrated, and the second piece now qualifies for the methods described in this section.

EXAMPLE 3   Long division first Evaluate $\displaystyle\int \frac{2x^2 + 8x + 3}{x + 3}\, dx$.

SOLUTION   Notice the integrand is an improper rational function; that is, the degree of the numerator is greater than or equal to the degree of the denominator. The first step is to use long division to produce a proper rational function:

$$
\begin{array}{r}
2x + 2 \\
x + 3 \overline{)\, 2x^2 + 8x + 3} \\
\underline{2x^2 + 6x} \\
2x + 3 \\
\underline{2x + 6} \\
-3
\end{array}
$$

Therefore, the integrand may be written

$$\frac{2x^2 + 8x + 3}{x + 3} = 2x + 2 - \frac{3}{x + 3}.$$

The integration is now done (without partial fractions):

$$\int \frac{2x^2 + 8x + 3}{x + 3}\, dx = \int \left(2x + 2 - \frac{3}{x + 3} \right) dx \qquad \text{Long division}$$

$$= x^2 + 2x - 3 \ln|x + 3| + C. \quad \text{Evaluate integrals.}$$

Related Exercises 27–32 ◄

In closing, we mention that *in principle,* any rational function can be integrated. The partial fraction idea extends to cases in which the denominator of the integrand has repeated linear factors (such as $(x - 3)^2$) or quadratic factors that cannot be further factored (such as $x^2 + 1$ and $(x^2 + 4)^2$).

SECTION 7.3 EXERCISES

Review Questions

1. What kinds of functions can be integrated using partial fraction decomposition?

2. Give the form of the partial fraction decomposition of $\dfrac{x - 2}{x^2 - 3x - 18}$.

3. What terms should appear in the partial fraction decomposition of a proper rational function with a denominator of $x^3 + 5x^2 + 6x$?

4. What is the first step in integrating $\dfrac{x^2 + 2x - 3}{x + 1}$?

Basic Skills

5–12. Setting up partial fraction decomposition *Give the partial fraction decomposition for the following functions.*

5. $\dfrac{2}{x^2 - 2x - 8}$

6. $\dfrac{x - 9}{x^2 - 3x - 18}$

7. $\dfrac{5x - 7}{x^2 - 3x + 2}$

8. $\dfrac{11x - 10}{x^2 - x}$

9. $\dfrac{x^2}{x^3 - 16x}, x \neq 0$

10. $\dfrac{x^2 - 3x}{x^3 - 3x^2 - 4x}, x \neq 0$

11. $\dfrac{x + 2}{x^3 - 3x^2 + 2x}$

12. $\dfrac{x^2 - 4x + 11}{(x - 3)(x - 1)(x + 1)}$

13–26. Simple linear factors *Evaluate the following integrals.*

13. $\displaystyle\int \dfrac{3}{(x - 1)(x + 2)} \, dx$

14. $\displaystyle\int \dfrac{8}{(x - 2)(x + 6)} \, dx$

15. $\displaystyle\int \dfrac{6}{x^2 - 1} \, dx$

16. $\displaystyle\int \dfrac{dt}{t^2 - 9}$

17. $\displaystyle\int \dfrac{5x}{x^2 - x - 6} \, dx$

18. $\displaystyle\int \dfrac{21x^2}{x^3 - x^2 - 12x} \, dx$

19. $\displaystyle\int \dfrac{10x}{x^2 - 2x - 24} \, dx$

20. $\displaystyle\int \dfrac{y + 1}{y^3 + 3y^2 - 18y} \, dy$

21. $\displaystyle\int \dfrac{6x^2}{x^4 - 5x^2 + 4} \, dx$

22. $\displaystyle\int \dfrac{4x - 2}{x^3 - x} \, dx$

23. $\displaystyle\int \dfrac{x^2 + 12x - 4}{x^3 - 4x} \, dx$

24. $\displaystyle\int \dfrac{x^2 + 20x - 15}{x^3 + 4x^2 - 5x} \, dx$

25. $\displaystyle\int \dfrac{dx}{x^4 - 10x^2 + 9}$

26. $\displaystyle\int \dfrac{2}{x^2 - 4x - 32} \, dx$

27–32. Long division first Evaluate the following integrals.

27. $\displaystyle\int \dfrac{x^2 - 5x + 10}{x - 2} \, dx$

28. $\displaystyle\int \dfrac{4x^2 + 13x - 3}{x + 3}$

29. $\displaystyle\int \dfrac{4x^3 + 3x^2 - 25x + 7}{x^2 + x - 6} \, dx$

30. $\displaystyle\int \dfrac{x^3 - 8x^2 + 11x + 21}{x^2 - 3x - 4} \, dx$

31. $\displaystyle\int \dfrac{x^3 - 2x^2 - x + 3}{x - 2} \, dx$

32. $\displaystyle\int \dfrac{x^4 - x^3 - 2x^2 + 1}{x^3 - x^2 - 2x} \, dx$

Further Explorations

33. **Explain why or why not** Determine whether the following statements are true and give an explanation or counterexample.

   a. To evaluate $\displaystyle\int \dfrac{4x^6}{4 - x^2} \, dx$, the first step is to find the partial fraction decomposition of the integrand.

   b. The easiest way to evaluate $\displaystyle\int \dfrac{6x + 1}{3x^2 + x} \, dx$ is with a partial fraction decomposition of the integrand.

   c. The rational function $f(x) = \dfrac{1}{x^2 - 13x + 42}$ has simple linear factors in the denominator.

▦ **34–37. Areas of regions** *Find the area of the following regions. A graph of the relevant curves will help you find the limits of integration.*

34. The region bounded by the curve $y = x/(1 + x)$, the x-axis, and the line $x = 4$

35. The region bounded by the curve $y = 10/(x^2 - 2x - 24)$, the x-axis, and the lines $x = -2$ and $x = 2$

36. The region bounded by the curves $y = 1/x, y = x/(3x + 4)$, and the line $x = 10$

37. The region bounded by the curve $y = \dfrac{x^2 - 4x - 4}{x^2 - 4x - 5}$ and the x-axis

38–43. Volumes of solids *Find the volume of the following solids.*

38. The region bounded by $y = 1/(x + 1), y = 0, x = 0$, and $x = 2$ is revolved about the y-axis. (Use the shell method, Section 6.4.)

39. The region bounded by $y = \dfrac{1}{\sqrt{x^2 - 1}}$ and the x-axis between $x = 2$ and $x = 4$ is revolved about the x-axis.

40. The region bounded by $y = (1 - x^2)^{-1/2}$ and $y = 4$ is revolved about the x-axis.

41. The region bounded by $y = \dfrac{1}{\sqrt{x(3 - x)}}, y = 0, x = 1$, and $x = 2$ is revolved about the x-axis.

42. The region bounded by $y = \dfrac{1}{\sqrt{4 - x^2}}, y = 0, x = -1$, and $x = 1$ is revolved about the x-axis.

43. The region bounded by $y = 1/(x + 2), y = 0, x = 0$, and $x = 3$ is revolved about the line $x = -1$.

44. **What's wrong?** Why are there no constants A and B satisfying

$$\dfrac{x^2}{(x - 4)(x + 5)} = \dfrac{A}{x - 4} + \dfrac{B}{x + 5}?$$

45–56. Preliminary steps *The following integrals require a preliminary step such as long division or a change of variables before using partial fractions. Evaluate these integrals.*

45. $\displaystyle\int \dfrac{dx}{1 + e^x}$

46. $\displaystyle\int \dfrac{x^4 + 1}{x^3 - 9x} \, dx$

47. $\displaystyle\int \dfrac{3x^2 + 4x - 6}{x^2 - 3x + 2} \, dx$

48. $\displaystyle\int \dfrac{2x^3 + x^2 - 6x + 7}{x^2 + x - 6} \, dx$

49. $\displaystyle\int \dfrac{dt}{2 + e^{-t}}$

50. $\displaystyle\int \dfrac{dx}{1 - e^{2x}}$

51. $\displaystyle\int \dfrac{8 \cos \theta}{4 - \sin^2 \theta} \, d\theta$

52. $\displaystyle\int \sqrt{e^x + 1} \, dx$ (*Hint:* Let $u = \sqrt{e^x + 1}$.)

53. $\displaystyle\int \dfrac{e^x}{(e^x - 1)(e^x + 2)} \, dx$

54. $\displaystyle\int \dfrac{\cos x}{(\sin^3 x - 4 \sin x)} \, dx$

55. $\displaystyle\int \dfrac{dx}{(e^x + e^{-x})}$

56. $\displaystyle\int \dfrac{dy}{y(\sqrt{a} - \sqrt{y})}$, for $a > 0$. (*Hint:* Let $u = \sqrt{y}$)

57. **Another form of** $\displaystyle\int \sec x \, dx$.

   a. Verify the identity $\sec x = \dfrac{\cos x}{1 - \sin^2 x}$.

   b. Use the identity in part (a) to verify that

$$\int \sec x \, dx = \dfrac{1}{2} \ln \left| \dfrac{1 + \sin x}{1 - \sin x} \right| + C.$$

   (*Source: The College Mathematics Journal* **32**, 5 (Nov 2001))

58–63. Fractional powers *Use the indicated substitution to convert the given integral to an integral of a rational function. Evaluate the resulting integral.*

58. $\displaystyle\int \frac{dx}{x - \sqrt[3]{x}}$; $x = u^3$

59. $\displaystyle\int \frac{dx}{\sqrt[4]{x + 2} + 1}$; $x + 2 = u^4$

60. $\displaystyle\int \frac{dx}{x\sqrt{1 + 2x}}$; $1 + 2x = u^2$

61. $\displaystyle\int \frac{dx}{1 - \sqrt[3]{x}}$; $x = u^3$

62. $\displaystyle\int \frac{dx}{\sqrt{x} - \sqrt[4]{x}}$; $x = u^4$

63. $\displaystyle\int \frac{dx}{\sqrt{1 + \sqrt{x}}}$; $x = (u^2 - 1)^2$

■ 64. Arc length of the natural logarithm Consider the curve $y = \ln x$.

  a. Find the length of the curve from $x = 1$ to $x = a$, and call it $L(a)$. (*Hint:* The change of variables $u = \sqrt{x^2 + 1}$ allows evaluation by partial fractions.)

  b. Graph $L(a)$.

  c. As a increases, $L(a)$ increases as what power of a?

65–68. Rational functions of trigonometric functions *An integrand with trigonometric functions in the numerator and denominator can often be converted to a rational integrand using the substitution* $u = \tan(x/2)$ *or* $x = 2\tan^{-1} u$. *The following relations are used in making this change of variables.*

$$A: dx = \frac{2}{1 + u^2}\, du \quad B: \sin x = \frac{2u}{1 + u^2} \quad C: \cos x = \frac{1 - u^2}{1 + u^2}$$

You can verify relation A by differentiating $x = 2\tan^{-1} u$, *and you can verify relations B and C using a right-triangle diagram and the double-angle formulas*

$$\sin x = 2 \sin\left(\frac{x}{2}\right) \cos\left(\frac{x}{2}\right) \text{ and } \cos x = 2\cos^2\left(\frac{x}{2}\right) - 1.$$

65. Evaluate $\displaystyle\int \frac{dx}{1 - \cos x}$.

66. Evaluate $\displaystyle\int \frac{dx}{1 + \sin x + \cos x}$.

67. Evaluate $\displaystyle\int \frac{d\theta}{\cos \theta - \sin \theta}$.

68. Evaluate $\displaystyle\int \sec t\, dt$.

Applications

69. Three start-ups Three cars, A, B, and C, start from rest and accelerate along a line according to the following velocity functions:

$$v_A(t) = \frac{88t}{t + 1}, \quad v_B(t) = 88(1 - e^{-t/2}), \quad \text{and} \quad v_C(t) = \frac{88t^2}{t^2 + 3t + 2}.$$

  a. Which car has traveled farthest on the interval $0 \le t \le 5$?

  b. Which car has traveled farthest on the interval $0 \le t \le 10$?

  c. Find the position functions for the three cars assuming that all cars start at the origin.

  d. Which car ultimately gains the lead and remains in front?

■ 70. Skydiving A skydiver has a downward velocity given by

$$v(t) = V_T\left(\frac{1 - e^{-2gt/V_T}}{1 + e^{-2gt/V_T}}\right),$$

where $t = 0$ is the instant the skydiver starts falling, $g \approx 9.8 \text{ m/s}^2$ is the acceleration due to gravity, and V_T is the terminal velocity of the skydiver.

  a. Evaluate $v(0)$ and $\lim\limits_{t \to \infty} v(t)$, and interpret these results.

  b. Graph the velocity function.

  c. Verify by integration that the position function is given by

$$s(t) = V_T t + \frac{V_T^2}{g}\ln\left(\frac{1 + e^{-2gt/V_T}}{2}\right),$$

  where $s'(t) = v(t)$ and $s(0) = 0$.

  d. Graph the position function.

  (See the Guided Project *Terminal Velocity* for more details on free fall and terminal velocity.)

Additional Exercises

71. $\pi < \dfrac{22}{7}$ One of the earliest approximations to π is $\dfrac{22}{7}$. Verify that $0 < \displaystyle\int_0^1 \frac{x^4(1 - x)^4}{1 + x^2}\, dx = \frac{22}{7} - \pi$. Why can you conclude that $\pi < \dfrac{22}{7}$?

QUICK CHECK ANSWERS

1. $\ln|x - 2| + 2\ln|x + 4| = \ln|(x - 2)(x + 4)^2|$
2. $A/(x - 1) + B/(x + 5) + C/(x - 10)$
3. $1 - \dfrac{1}{x + 1}$ ◄

7.4 Improper Integrals

The definite integrals we have encountered so far involve finite-valued functions and finite intervals of integration. In this section, you will see that definite integrals can sometimes be evaluated when these conditions are not met. Here is an example. The energy required to launch a rocket from the surface of Earth ($R = 6370$ km from the center of Earth) to an altitude H is given by an integral of the form $\int_R^{R+H} k/x^2 \, dx$, where k is a constant that includes the mass of the rocket, the mass of Earth, and the gravitational constant. This integral may be evaluated for any finite altitude $H > 0$. Now suppose that the aim is to launch the rocket to an arbitrarily large altitude H so that it escapes Earth's gravitational field. The energy required is given by the preceding integral as $H \to \infty$, which we write $\int_R^{\infty} k/x^2 \, dx$. This integral is an example of an *improper integral*, and it has a finite value (which explains why it is possible to launch rockets to outer space). For historical reasons, the term *improper integral* is used for cases in which

- the interval of integration is infinite, or
- the integrand is unbounded on the interval of integration.

In this section, we explore improper integrals and their many uses.

Infinite Intervals

A simple example illustrates what can happen when integrating a function over an infinite interval. Consider the integral $\displaystyle\int_1^b \frac{1}{x^2} \, dx$, for any real number $b > 1$. As shown in Figure 7.2, this integral gives the area of the region bounded by the curve $y = x^{-2}$ and the x-axis between $x = 1$ and $x = b$. In fact, the value of the integral is

$$\int_1^b \frac{1}{x^2} \, dx = -\frac{1}{x} \Big|_1^b = 1 - \frac{1}{b}.$$

For example, if $b = 2$, the area under the curve is $\frac{1}{2}$; if $b = 3$, the area under the curve is $\frac{2}{3}$. In general, as b increases, the area under the curve increases.

Now let's ask what happens to the area as b becomes arbitrarily large. Letting $b \to \infty$, the area of the region under the curve is

$$\lim_{b \to \infty} \left(1 - \frac{1}{b} \right) = 1.$$

We have discovered, surprising as it may seem, a curve of *infinite* length that bounds a region with *finite* area (1 square unit).

We express this result as

$$\int_1^{\infty} \frac{1}{x^2} \, dx = 1,$$

which is an improper integral because ∞ appears in the upper limit. In general, to evaluate $\int_a^{\infty} f(x) \, dx$, we first integrate over a finite interval $[a, b]$ and then let $b \to \infty$. Similar procedures are used to evaluate $\int_{-\infty}^b f(x) \, dx$ and $\int_{-\infty}^{\infty} f(x) \, dx$.

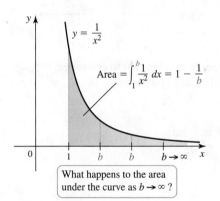

$y = \dfrac{1}{x^2}$

Area $= \displaystyle\int_1^b \frac{1}{x^2} \, dx = 1 - \frac{1}{b}$

What happens to the area under the curve as $b \to \infty$?

FIGURE 7.2

DEFINITIONS   Improper Integrals over Infinite Intervals

1. If f is continuous on $[a, \infty)$, then

$$\int_a^\infty f(x)\, dx = \lim_{b \to \infty} \int_a^b f(x)\, dx.$$

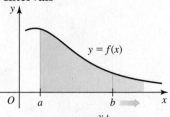

2. If f is continuous on $(-\infty, b]$, then

$$\int_{-\infty}^b f(x)\, dx = \lim_{a \to -\infty} \int_a^b f(x)\, dx.$$

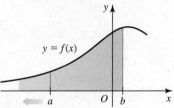

3. If f is continuous on $(-\infty, \infty)$, then

$$\int_{-\infty}^\infty f(x)\, dx = \lim_{a \to -\infty} \int_a^c f(x)\, dx$$

$$+ \lim_{b \to \infty} \int_c^b f(x)\, dx,$$

where c is any real number.

In each case, if the limit exists, the improper integral is said to **converge**; if the limit does not exist, the improper integral is said to **diverge**.

> Doubly infinite integrals (Case 3 in the definition) must be evaluated as two independent limits and not as
>
> $$\int_{-\infty}^\infty f(x)\, dx = \lim_{b \to \infty} \int_{-b}^b f(x)\, dx.$$

EXAMPLE 1   Infinite intervals Evaluate each integral.

a. $\displaystyle\int_0^\infty e^{-3x}\, dx$ **b.** $\displaystyle\int_{-\infty}^\infty \frac{dx}{1 + x^2}$

SOLUTION

a. Using the definition of the improper integral, we have

$$\int_0^\infty e^{-3x}\, dx = \lim_{b \to \infty} \int_0^b e^{-3x}\, dx \qquad \text{Definition of improper integral}$$

$$= \lim_{b \to \infty} \left(-\frac{1}{3} e^{-3x} \right) \Big|_0^b \qquad \text{Evaluate the integral.}$$

$$= \lim_{b \to \infty} \frac{1}{3} (1 - e^{-3b}) \qquad \text{Simplify.}$$

$$= \frac{1}{3} \left(1 - \underbrace{\lim_{b \to \infty} \frac{1}{e^{3b}}}_{\text{equals } 0} \right) = \frac{1}{3}. \qquad e^{-3b} = \frac{1}{e^{3b}}$$

In this case, the limit exists, so the integral converges and the region under the curve has a finite area of $\frac{1}{3}$ (Figure 7.3).

> Recall that
>
> $$\int \frac{dx}{a^2 + x^2} = \frac{1}{a}\tan^{-1}\frac{x}{a} + C.$$
>
> The graph of $y = \tan^{-1} x$ shows that
>
> $$\lim_{x \to \infty} \tan^{-1} x = \frac{\pi}{2}, \text{ and } \lim_{x \to -\infty} \tan^{-1} x = -\frac{\pi}{2}.$$

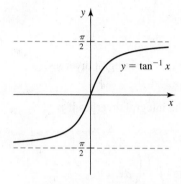

b. Using the definition of the improper integral, we choose $c = 0$ and write

$$\int_{-\infty}^{\infty} \frac{dx}{1 + x^2} = \lim_{a \to -\infty} \int_a^c \frac{dx}{1 + x^2} + \lim_{b \to \infty} \int_c^b \frac{dx}{1 + x^2} \qquad \text{Definition of improper integral}$$

$$= \lim_{a \to -\infty} \tan^{-1} x \Big|_a^0 + \lim_{b \to \infty} \tan^{-1} x \Big|_0^b \qquad \text{Evaluate integral; } c = 0$$

$$= \lim_{a \to -\infty} (0 - \tan^{-1} a) + \lim_{b \to \infty} (\tan^{-1} b - 0) \qquad \text{Simplify.}$$

$$= \frac{\pi}{2} + \frac{\pi}{2} = \pi. \qquad \text{Evaluate limits.}$$

Furthermore, the same result is obtained with any value of the intermediate point c. Therefore, the value of the integral is π (Figure 7.4).

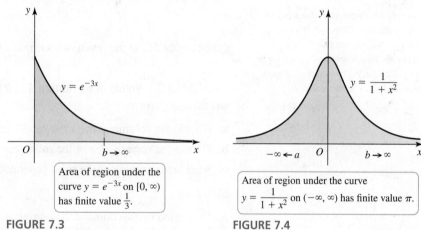

FIGURE 7.3

Area of region under the curve $y = e^{-3x}$ on $[0, \infty)$ has finite value $\frac{1}{3}$.

FIGURE 7.4

Area of region under the curve $y = \frac{1}{1 + x^2}$ on $(-\infty, \infty)$ has finite value π.

Related Exercises 5–28 ◄

QUICK CHECK 1 The function $f(x) = 1 + x^{-1}$ decreases to 1 as $x \to \infty$. Does $\int_1^\infty f(x)\,dx$ exist? ◄

EXAMPLE 2 **The family $f(x) = 1/x^p$** Consider the family of functions $f(x) = 1/x^p$, where p is a real number. For what values of p does $\int_1^\infty f(x)\,dx$ converge?

SOLUTION For $p > 0$, the functions $f(x) = 1/x^p$ approach zero as $x \to \infty$, with larger values of p giving greater rates of decrease (Figure 7.5). Assuming $p \neq 1$, the integral is evaluated as follows:

> Recall that for $p \neq 1$,
>
> $$\int \frac{1}{x^p}\,dx = \int x^{-p}\,dx$$
>
> $$= \frac{x^{-p+1}}{-p + 1} + C$$
>
> $$= \frac{x^{1-p}}{1 - p} + C.$$

$$\int_1^\infty \frac{1}{x^p}\,dx = \lim_{b \to \infty} \int_1^b x^{-p}\,dx \qquad \text{Definition of improper integral}$$

$$= \frac{1}{1 - p} \lim_{b \to \infty} \left(x^{1-p} \Big|_1^b \right) \qquad \text{Evaluate the integral on a finite interval.}$$

$$= \frac{1}{1 - p} \lim_{b \to \infty} (b^{1-p} - 1). \qquad \text{Simplify.}$$

It is easiest to consider three cases.

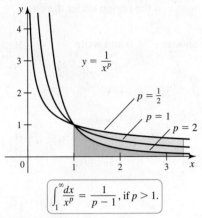

$$\int_1^\infty \frac{dx}{x^p} = \frac{1}{p-1}, \text{ if } p > 1.$$

FIGURE 7.5

Case 1:   If $p > 1$, then $p - 1 > 0$, and $b^{1-p} = 1/b^{p-1}$ approaches 0 as $b \to \infty$. Therefore, the interval converges and its value is

$$\int_1^\infty \frac{1}{x^p}\,dx = \frac{1}{1-p}\lim_{b\to\infty}\underbrace{(b^{1-p}-1)}_{\substack{\text{approaches}\\0}} = \frac{1}{p-1}.$$

Case 2:   If $p < 1$, then $1 - p > 0$, and the integral diverges:

$$\int_1^\infty \frac{1}{x^p}\,dx = \frac{1}{1-p}\lim_{b\to\infty}\underbrace{(b^{1-p}-1)}_{\substack{\text{arbitrarily}\\\text{large}}} = \infty.$$

Case 3:   If $p = 1$, then $\int_1^\infty \frac{1}{x}\,dx = \lim_{b\to\infty}(\ln b) = \infty$; so the integral diverges.

In summary, $\int_1^\infty \frac{1}{x^p}\,dx = \frac{1}{p-1}$ if $p > 1$, and the integral diverges if $p \le 1$.

Related Exercises 5–28 ◄

> Example 2 is important in the study of infinite series in Chapter 9. It shows that a continuous function f must do more than simply decrease to zero for its integral on $[a, \infty)$ to converge; it must decrease to zero *sufficiently fast*.

QUICK CHECK 2 Use the result of Example 2 to evaluate $\int_1^\infty \frac{1}{x^4}\,dx$. ◄

EXAMPLE 3   **Solids of revolution** Let R be the region bounded by the graph of $y = x^{-1}$ and the x-axis, for $x \ge 1$.

a. What is the volume of the solid generated when R is revolved about the x-axis?

b. What is the surface area of the solid generated when R is revolved about the x-axis?

c. What is the volume of the solid generated when R is revolved about the y-axis?

SOLUTION

a. The region in question and the corresponding solid of revolution are shown in Figure 7.6. We use the disk method (Section 6.3) over the interval $[1, b]$ and then let $b \to \infty$:

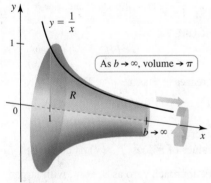

FIGURE 7.6

$$\text{Volume} = \int_1^\infty \pi(f(x))^2\,dx \qquad \text{Disk method}$$

$$= \pi \lim_{b\to\infty}\int_1^b \frac{1}{x^2}\,dx \qquad \text{Definition of improper integral}$$

$$= \pi \lim_{b\to\infty}\left(1 - \frac{1}{b}\right) = \pi. \qquad \text{Evaluate the integral.}$$

The improper integral exists, and the solid has a volume of π cubic units.

b. It can be shown that the area of the surface generated when the curve $y = f(x)$ is revolved about the x-axis on the interval $[1, b]$, where $b > 1$, is

$$\int_1^b 2\pi f(x)\sqrt{1 + f'(x)^2}\,dx.$$

The area of the surface generated on the interval $[1, \infty)$ is found by letting $b \to \infty$:

$$\text{Surface area} = 2\pi \lim_{b\to\infty}\int_1^b f(x)\sqrt{1 + f'(x)^2}\,dx \quad \text{Surface area formula; let } b \to \infty.$$

$$= 2\pi \lim_{b\to\infty}\int_1^b \frac{1}{x}\sqrt{1 + \left(-\frac{1}{x^2}\right)^2}\,dx \quad \text{Substitute } f \text{ and } f'.$$

$$= 2\pi \lim_{b\to\infty}\int_1^b \frac{1}{x^3}\sqrt{1 + x^4}\,dx. \quad \text{Simplify.}$$

Notice that on the interval of integration $x \geq 1$, $\sqrt{1 + x^4} > \sqrt{x^4} = x^2$, which means that

$$\frac{1}{x^3}\sqrt{1 + x^4} > \frac{x^2}{x^3} = \frac{1}{x}.$$

Therefore, for all b with $1 < b < \infty$, we have

$$\text{Surface area} = 2\pi \int_1^b \frac{1}{x^3}\sqrt{1 + x^4}\, dx > 2\pi \int_1^b \frac{1}{x}\, dx.$$

> The solid in Examples 3a and 3b is called *Gabriel's horn* or *Torricelli's trumpet*. We have shown—quite remarkably—that it has finite volume and infinite surface area.

Because $2\pi \lim\limits_{b\to\infty} \int_1^b \frac{1}{x}\, dx = \infty$ (by Example 2), the preceding inequality implies that $2\pi \lim\limits_{b\to\infty} \int_1^b \frac{1}{x^3}\sqrt{1 + x^4}\, dx = \infty$. Therefore, the integral diverges and the surface area of the solid is infinite.

> Recall that if $f(x) > 0$ on $[a, b]$ and the region bounded by the graph of f and the x-axis on $[a, b]$ is revolved about the y-axis, the volume of the solid generated is
> $$V = \int_a^b 2\pi x f(x)\, dx.$$

c. The region in question and the corresponding solid of revolution are shown in Figure 7.7. Using the shell method (Section 6.4) on the interval $[1, b)$ and letting $b \to \infty$, the volume is given by

$$\begin{aligned}
\text{Volume} &= \int_1^\infty 2\pi x f(x)\, dx && \text{Shell method} \\
&= 2\pi \int_1^\infty 1\, dx && f(x) = x^{-1} \\
&= 2\pi \lim_{b\to\infty} \int_1^b 1\, dx && \text{Definition of improper integral} \\
&= 2\pi \lim_{b\to\infty} (b - 1) && \text{Evaluate the integral over a finite interval.} \\
&= \infty. && \text{The improper integral diverges.}
\end{aligned}$$

Revolving the region R about the y-axis, the volume of the resulting solid is infinite.

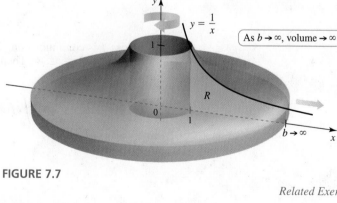

As $b \to \infty$, volume $\to \infty$

$y = \dfrac{1}{x}$

FIGURE 7.7

Related Exercises 29–34 ◀

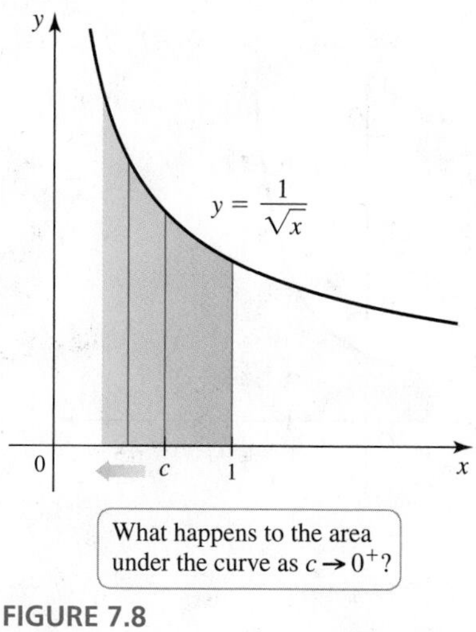

Unbounded Integrands

Improper integrals also occur when the integrand becomes infinite somewhere on the interval of integration. Consider the function $f(x) = 1/\sqrt{x}$ (Figure 7.8). Let's examine the area of the region bounded by the graph of f between $x = 0$ and $x = 1$. Notice that f is not even defined at $x = 0$, and it increases without bound as $x \to 0^+$.

$y = \dfrac{1}{\sqrt{x}}$

What happens to the area under the curve as $c \to 0^+$?

FIGURE 7.8

The idea here is to replace the lower limit 0 with a nearby positive number c and then consider the integral $\int_c^1 \frac{1}{\sqrt{x}}\, dx$, where $0 < c < 1$. We find that

$$\int_c^1 \frac{1}{\sqrt{x}}\, dx = 2\sqrt{x}\,\Big|_c^1 = 2(1 - \sqrt{c}).$$

To find the area of the region under the curve over the interval $(0, 1]$, we let $c \to 0^+$. The resulting area, which we denote $\int_0^1 \frac{dx}{\sqrt{x}}$, is

$$\lim_{c\to 0^+} \int_c^1 \frac{1}{\sqrt{x}}\, dx = \lim_{c\to 0^+} 2(1 - \sqrt{c}) = 2.$$

Once again we have a surprising result: Although the region in question has a boundary curve with infinite length, the area of the region is finite.

> The functions $f(x) = 1/x^p$ are unbounded at $x = 0$, for $p > 0$. It can be shown (Exercise 74) that
> $$\int_0^1 \frac{dx}{x^p} = \frac{1}{1 - p},$$
> provided $p < 1$. Otherwise, the integral diverges.

QUICK CHECK 3 Explain why the one-sided limit $c \to 0^+$ (instead of a two-sided limit) must be used in the previous calculation. ◄

The preceding example shows that if a function is unbounded at a point c, it may be possible to integrate that function over an interval that contains c. The point c may occur at either endpoint or at an interior point of the interval of integration.

DEFINITIONS Improper Integrals with an Unbounded Integrand

1. Suppose f is continuous on $(a, b]$ with $\lim_{x\to a^+} f(x) = \pm\infty$. Then

$$\int_a^b f(x)\, dx = \lim_{c\to a^+} \int_c^b f(x)\, dx.$$

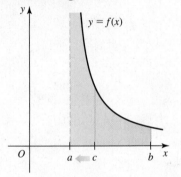

2. Suppose f is continuous on $[a, b)$ with $\lim_{x\to b^-} f(x) = \pm\infty$. Then

$$\int_a^b f(x)\, dx = \lim_{c\to b^-} \int_a^c f(x)\, dx.$$

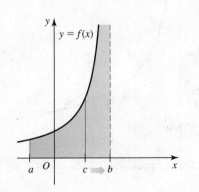

3. Suppose f is continuous on $[a, b]$ except at the interior point p where f is unbounded. Then

$$\int_a^b f(x)\,dx = \int_a^p f(x)\,dx + \int_p^b f(x)\,dx,$$

where the integrals on the right side are evaluated as improper integrals.

If the limits in cases 1–3 exist, the improper integrals **converge**; otherwise, they **diverge**.

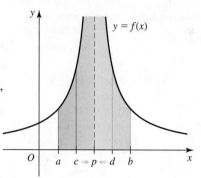

EXAMPLE 4   Infinite integrand Find the area of the region R between the graph of $f(x) = \dfrac{1}{\sqrt{9 - x^2}}$ and the x-axis on the interval $(-3, 3)$ (if it exists).

SOLUTION The integrand is even and has vertical asymptotes at $x = \pm 3$ (Figure 7.9). By symmetry, the area of R is given by

$$\int_{-3}^3 \frac{1}{\sqrt{9 - x^2}}\,dx = 2\int_0^3 \frac{1}{\sqrt{9 - x^2}}\,dx,$$

assuming these improper integrals exist. Because the integrand is unbounded at $x = 3$, we replace the upper limit with c, evaluate the resulting integral, and then let $c \to 3^-$:

$$2\int_0^3 \frac{dx}{\sqrt{9 - x^2}} = 2\lim_{c \to 3^-} \int_0^c \frac{dx}{\sqrt{9 - x^2}} \qquad \text{Definition of improper integral}$$

$$= 2\lim_{c \to 3^-} \sin^{-1}\frac{x}{3}\Big|_0^c \qquad \text{Evaluate the integral.}$$

$$= 2\lim_{c \to 3^-} \left(\underbrace{\sin^{-1}\frac{c}{3}}_{\text{approaches } \pi/2} - \underbrace{\sin^{-1} 0}_{\text{equals } 0}\right). \qquad \text{Simplify.}$$

Note that as $c \to 3^-$, $\sin^{-1}(c/3) \to \sin^{-1} 1 = \pi/2$. Therefore, the area of R is

$$2\int_0^3 \frac{1}{\sqrt{9 - x^2}}\,dx = 2\left(\frac{\pi}{2} - 0\right) = \pi.$$

Related Exercises 35–54 ◀

> Recall that
> $$\int \frac{dx}{\sqrt{a^2 - x^2}} = \sin^{-1}\frac{x}{a} + C.$$

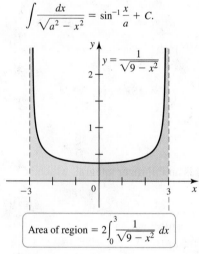

Area of region $= 2\displaystyle\int_0^3 \frac{1}{\sqrt{9 - x^2}}\,dx$

FIGURE 7.9

EXAMPLE 5   Infinite integrand at an interior point Evaluate $\displaystyle\int_1^{10} \frac{dx}{(x - 2)^{1/3}}$.

SOLUTION The integrand is unbounded at $x = 2$, which is an interior point of the interval of integration. We split the interval into two subintervals and evaluate an improper integral on each subinterval:

$$\int_1^{10} \frac{dx}{(x - 2)^{1/3}} = \lim_{a \to 2^-} \int_1^a \frac{dx}{(x - 2)^{1/3}} + \lim_{b \to 2^+} \int_b^{10} \frac{dx}{(x - 2)^{1/3}} \qquad \begin{array}{l}\text{Definition of}\\\text{improper integral}\end{array}$$

$$= \lim_{a \to 2^-} \frac{3}{2}(x - 2)^{2/3}\Big|_1^a + \lim_{b \to 2^+} \frac{3}{2}(x - 2)^{2/3}\Big|_b^{10} \qquad \begin{array}{l}\text{Evaluate}\\\text{integrals.}\end{array}$$

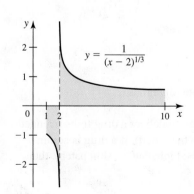

▶ We interpret the result of 9/2 from
Example 5 as the net area bounded by the
curve $y = 1/(x - 2)^{1/3}$ over the interval
[1, 10].

$$= \frac{3}{2}\left(\lim_{a \to 2^-}(a - 2)^{2/3} - (1 - 2)^{2/3}\right)$$

$$+ \frac{3}{2}\left((10 - 2)^{2/3} - \lim_{b \to 2^+}(b - 2)^{2/3}\right) \quad \text{Simplify.}$$

$$= \frac{3}{2}\left(0 - (-1)^{2/3} + 8^{2/3} - 0\right) = \frac{9}{2}. \quad \text{Evaluate limits.}$$

Related Exercises 35–54 ◀

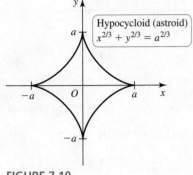

Hypocycloid (astroid)
$x^{2/3} + y^{2/3} = a^{2/3}$

FIGURE 7.10

EXAMPLE 6   **Length of a hypocycloid** Find the length L of the complete hypo-cycloid (or astroid; Figure 7.10) given by $x^{2/3} + y^{2/3} = a^{2/3}$, where $a > 0$.

SOLUTION Solving the equation $x^{2/3} + y^{2/3} = a^{2/3}$ for y, we find that the curve is described by the functions $f(x) = \pm(a^{2/3} - x^{2/3})^{3/2}$ (corresponding to the upper and lower halves of the curve). By symmetry, the length of the entire curve is four times the length of the curve in the first quadrant, which is given by $f(x) = (a^{2/3} - x^{2/3})^{3/2}$, for $0 \le x \le a$. We need the derivative f' for the arc length integral:

$$f'(x) = \frac{3}{2}(a^{2/3} - x^{2/3})^{1/2}\left(-\frac{2}{3}x^{-1/3}\right) = -x^{-1/3}(a^{2/3} - x^{2/3})^{1/2}.$$

Now the arc length can be computed:

$$L = 4\int_0^a \sqrt{1 + f'(x)^2}\, dx$$

$$= 4\int_0^a \sqrt{1 + (-x^{-1/3}(a^{2/3} - x^{2/3})^{1/2})^2}\, dx \quad \text{Substitute for } f'.$$

$$= 4\int_0^a \sqrt{a^{2/3}x^{-2/3}}\, dx \quad \text{Simplify.}$$

$$= 4a^{1/3}\int_0^a x^{-1/3}\, dx. \quad \text{Simplify.}$$

Because $x^{-1/3} \to \infty$ as $x \to 0^+$, the resulting integral is an improper integral, which is handled in the usual manner:

$$L = 4a^{1/3}\lim_{c \to 0^+}\int_c^a x^{-1/3}\, dx \quad \text{Improper integral}$$

$$= 4a^{1/3}\lim_{c \to 0^+}\left(\frac{3}{2}x^{2/3}\right)\Big|_c^a \quad \text{Integrate.}$$

$$= 6a^{1/3}\lim_{c \to 0^+}(a^{2/3} - \underbrace{c^{2/3}}_{\to 0}) \quad \text{Simplify.}$$

$$= 6a. \quad \text{Evaluate limit.}$$

The length of the entire hypocycloid is $6a$ units.

Related Exercises 55–56 ◀

We close with one of many practical uses of improper integrals.

EXAMPLE 7   **Bioavailability** The most efficient way to deliver a drug to its intended target site is to administer it intravenously (directly into the blood). If a drug is admin-istered any other way (for example, injection, orally, nasal inhalant, or skin patch), then

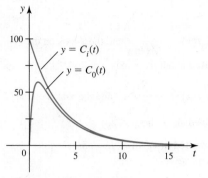

FIGURE 7.11

some of the drug is typically lost due to absorption before it gets to the blood. By definition, the bioavailability of a drug measures the effectiveness of a nonintravenous method compared to the intravenous method. The bioavailability of intravenous dosing is 100%.

Let the functions $C_i(t)$ and $C_o(t)$ give the concentration of a drug in the blood, for times $t \geq 0$, using intravenous and oral dosing, respectively. (These functions can be determined through clinical experiments.) Assuming the same amount of drug is initially administered by both methods, the bioavailability for an oral dose is defined to be

$$F = \frac{\text{AUC}_o}{\text{AUC}_i} = \frac{\displaystyle\int_0^\infty C_o(t)\, dt}{\displaystyle\int_0^\infty C_i(t)\, dt},$$

where AUC is used in the pharmacology literature to mean *area under the curve*.

Suppose the concentration of a certain drug in the blood in mg/L when given intravenously is $C_i(t) = 100e^{-0.3t}$, where $t \geq 0$ is measured in hours. Suppose also that the concentration of the same drug when delivered orally is $C_o(t) = 90(e^{-0.3t} - e^{-2.5t})$ (Figure 7.11). Find the bioavailability of the drug.

SOLUTION Evaluating the integrals of the concentration functions, we find that

$$\text{AUC}_i = \int_0^\infty C_i(t)\, dt = \int_0^\infty 100e^{-0.3t}\, dt$$

$$= \lim_{b \to \infty} \int_0^b 100e^{-0.3t}\, dt \qquad \text{Improper integral}$$

$$= \lim_{b \to \infty} \frac{1000}{3}\big(1 - \underbrace{e^{-0.3b}}_{\substack{\text{approaches} \\ \text{zero}}}\big) \qquad \text{Evaluate the integral.}$$

$$= \frac{1000}{3}. \qquad \text{Evaluate the limit.}$$

Similarly,

$$\text{AUC}_o = \int_0^\infty C_o(t)\, dt = \int_0^\infty 90(e^{-0.3t} - e^{-2.5t})\, dt$$

$$= \lim_{b \to \infty} \int_0^b 90(e^{-0.3t} - e^{-2.5t})\, dt \qquad \text{Improper integral}$$

$$= \lim_{b \to \infty} \big[300(1 - \underbrace{e^{-0.3b}}_{\substack{\text{approaches} \\ \text{zero}}}) - 36(1 - \underbrace{e^{-2.5b}}_{\substack{\text{approaches} \\ \text{zero}}})\big] \qquad \text{Evaluate the integral.}$$

$$= 264. \qquad \text{Evaluate the limit.}$$

Therefore, the bioavailability is $F = 264/(1000/3) = 0.792$, which means oral administration of the drug is roughly 80% as effective as intravenous dosing. Notice that F is the ratio of the areas under the two curves on the interval $[0, \infty)$.

Related Exercises 57–60◄

SECTION 7.4 EXERCISES

Review Questions

1. What are the two general ways in which an improper integral may occur?

2. Explain how to evaluate $\int_a^\infty f(x)\, dx$.

3. Explain how to evaluate $\int_0^1 x^{-1/2}\, dx$.

4. For what values of p does $\int_1^\infty x^{-p}\, dx$ converge?

Basic Skills

5–28. Infinite intervals of integration *Evaluate the following integrals or state that they diverge.*

5. $\displaystyle \int_1^\infty x^{-2}\, dx$

6. $\displaystyle \int_0^\infty \frac{dx}{(x+1)^3}$

7. $\displaystyle \int_{-\infty}^0 e^x\, dx$

8. $\displaystyle \int_1^\infty 2^{-x}\, dx$

9. $\displaystyle \int_2^\infty \frac{dx}{\sqrt{x}}$

10. $\displaystyle \int_{-\infty}^0 \frac{dx}{\sqrt[3]{2-x}}$

11. $\displaystyle \int_0^\infty e^{-2x}\, dx$

12. $\displaystyle \int_{4/\pi}^\infty \frac{1}{x^2}\sec^2\left(\frac{1}{x}\right) dx$

13. $\displaystyle \int_0^\infty e^{-ax}\, dx,\, a>0$

14. $\displaystyle \int_2^\infty \frac{dx}{x\ln x}$

15. $\displaystyle \int_{e^2}^\infty \frac{dx}{x\ln^p x},\, p>1$

16. $\displaystyle \int_0^\infty \frac{x}{\sqrt[5]{x^2+1}}\, dx$

17. $\displaystyle \int_{-\infty}^\infty xe^{-x^2}\, dx$

18. $\displaystyle \int_0^\infty \cos x\, dx$

19. $\displaystyle \int_2^\infty \frac{\cos(\pi/x)}{x^2}\, dx$

20. $\displaystyle \int_{-\infty}^\infty \frac{dx}{1+x^2}$

21. $\displaystyle \int_0^\infty \frac{e^x}{e^{2x}+1}\, dx$

22. $\displaystyle \int_{-\infty}^a \sqrt{e^x}\, dx,\, a\text{ real}$

23. $\displaystyle \int_1^\infty \frac{dx}{x(x+1)}$

24. $\displaystyle \int_1^\infty \frac{dx}{x^2+3x+2}$

25. $\displaystyle \int_1^\infty \frac{3x^2+1}{x^3+x}\, dx$

26. $\displaystyle \int_1^\infty \frac{1}{x^2}\sin\frac{\pi}{x}\, dx$

27. $\displaystyle \int_2^\infty \frac{dx}{(x+2)^2}$

28. $\displaystyle \int_1^\infty \frac{\tan^{-1} x}{x^2+1}\, dx$

29–34. Volumes on infinite intervals *Find the volume of the described solid of revolution or state that it does not exist.*

29. The region bounded by $f(x)=x^{-2}$ and the x-axis on the interval $[1,\infty)$ is revolved about the x-axis.

30. The region bounded by $f(x)=(x^2+1)^{-1/2}$ and the x-axis on the interval $[2,\infty)$ is revolved about the x-axis.

31. The region bounded by $f(x)=\sqrt{\dfrac{x+1}{x^3}}$ and the x-axis on the interval $[1,\infty)$ is revolved about the x-axis.

32. The region bounded by $f(x)=(x+1)^{-3}$ and the x-axis on the interval $[0,\infty)$ is revolved about the y-axis.

33. The region bounded by $f(x)=\dfrac{1}{\sqrt{x}\ln x}$ and the x-axis on the interval $[2,\infty)$ is revolved about the x-axis.

34. The region bounded by $f(x)=\dfrac{\sqrt{x}}{\sqrt[3]{x^2+1}}$ and the x-axis on the interval $[0,\infty)$ is revolved about the x-axis.

35–50. Integrals with unbounded integrands *Evaluate the following integrals or state that they diverge.*

35. $\displaystyle \int_0^8 \frac{dx}{\sqrt[3]{x}}$

36. $\displaystyle \int_0^{\pi/2} \tan\theta\, d\theta$

37. $\displaystyle \int_1^2 \frac{dx}{\sqrt{x-1}}$

38. $\displaystyle \int_{-3}^1 \frac{dx}{(2x+6)^{2/3}}$

39. $\displaystyle \int_0^{\pi/2} \sec x\tan x\, dx$

40. $\displaystyle \int_3^4 \frac{dx}{(x-3)^{3/2}}$

41. $\displaystyle \int_0^1 \frac{e^{\sqrt{x}}}{\sqrt{x}}\, dx$

42. $\displaystyle \int_0^{\ln 3} \frac{e^x}{(e^x-1)^{2/3}}\, dx$

43. $\displaystyle \int_0^1 \frac{x^3}{x^4-1}\, dx$

44. $\displaystyle \int_1^\infty \frac{dx}{\sqrt[3]{x-1}}$

45. $\displaystyle \int_0^{10} \frac{dx}{\sqrt[4]{10-x}}$

46. $\displaystyle \int_1^{11} \frac{dx}{(x-3)^{2/3}}$

47. $\displaystyle \int_0^1 \ln x^2\, dx$

48. $\displaystyle \int_{-2}^6 \frac{dx}{\sqrt{|x-2|}}$

49. $\displaystyle \int_{-2}^2 \frac{x\, dx}{\sqrt{4-x^2}}$

50. $\displaystyle \int_0^9 \frac{dx}{(x-1)^{1/3}}$

51–54. Volumes with infinite integrands *Find the volume of the described solid of revolution or state that it does not exist.*

51. The region bounded by $f(x)=(x-1)^{-1/4}$ and the x-axis on the interval $(1,2]$ is revolved about the x-axis.

52. The region bounded by $f(x)=(x^2-1)^{-1/4}$ and the x-axis on the interval $(1,2]$ is revolved about the y-axis.

53. The region bounded by $f(x)=(4-x)^{-1/3}$ and the x-axis on the interval $[0,4)$ is revolved about the y-axis.

54. The region bounded by $f(x)=(x+1)^{-3/2}$ and the x-axis on the interval $(-1,1]$ is revolved about the line $y=-1$.

55. **Arc length** Find the length of the hypocycloid (or astroid) $x^{2/3}+y^{2/3}=4$.

56. **Circumference of a circle** Use calculus to find the circumference of a circle with radius a.

57. **Bioavailability** When a drug is given intravenously, the concentration of the drug in the blood is $C_i(t)=250e^{-0.08t}$, for $t\ge 0$. When the same drug is given orally, the concentration of the drug in the blood is $C_o(t)=200(e^{-0.08t}-e^{-1.8t})$, for $t\ge 0$. Compute the bioavailability of the drug.

58. Draining a pool Water is drained from a swimming pool at a rate given by $R(t) = 100 \, e^{-0.05t}$ gal/hr. If the drain is left open indefinitely, how much water is drained from the pool?

59. Maximum distance An object moves on a line with velocity $v(t) = 10/(t + 1)^2$ mi/hr, for $t \geq 0$. What is the maximum distance the object can travel?

60. Depletion of oil reserves Suppose that the rate at which a company extracts oil is given by $r(t) = r_0 e^{-kt}$, where $r_0 = 10^7$ barrels/yr and $k = 0.005$ yr^{-1}. Suppose also that the estimate of the total oil reserve is 2×10^9 barrels. If the extraction continues indefinitely, will the reserve be exhausted?

Further Explorations

61. Explain why or why not Determine whether the following statements are true and give an explanation or counterexample.

   a. If f is continuous and $0 < f(x) < g(x)$ on the interval $[0, \infty)$, and $\int_0^\infty g(x) \, dx = M < \infty$, then $\int_0^\infty f(x) \, dx$ exists.

   b. If $\lim_{x \to \infty} f(x) = 1$, then $\int_0^\infty f(x) \, dx$ exists.

   c. If $\int_0^1 x^{-p} \, dx$ exists, then $\int_0^1 x^{-q} \, dx$ exists, where $q > p$.

   d. If $\int_1^\infty x^{-p} \, dx$ exists, then $\int_1^\infty x^{-q} \, dx$ exists, where $q > p$.

   e. $\displaystyle\int_1^\infty \frac{dx}{x^{3p+2}}$ exists, for $p > -\frac{1}{3}$.

62. Incorrect calculation What is wrong with this calculation?

$$\int_{-1}^1 \frac{dx}{x} = \ln |x| \, \bigg|_{-1}^1 = \ln 1 - \ln 1 = 0$$

63. Using symmetry Use symmetry to evaluate the following integrals.

   a. $\displaystyle\int_{-\infty}^\infty e^{|x|} \, dx$ **b.** $\displaystyle\int_{-\infty}^\infty \frac{x^3}{1 + x^8} \, dx$

64. Integral with a parameter For what values of p does the integral $\displaystyle\int_2^\infty \frac{dx}{x \ln^p x}$ exist, and what is its value (in terms of p)?

65. Improper integrals by numerical methods Use the Trapezoid Rule (Section 5.7) to approximate $\int_0^R e^{-x^2} \, dx$ with $R = 2, 4$, and 8. For each value of R, take $n = 4, 8, 16$, and 32, and compare approximations with successive values of n. Use these approximations to approximate $I = \int_0^\infty e^{-x^2} \, dx$.

66–68. Integration by parts Use integration by parts to evaluate the following integrals.

66. $\displaystyle\int_0^\infty xe^{-x} \, dx$ **67.** $\displaystyle\int_0^1 x \ln x \, dx$ **68.** $\displaystyle\int_1^\infty \frac{\ln x}{x^2} \, dx$

69. A close comparison Graph the integrands and then evaluate and compare the values of $\int_0^\infty xe^{-x^2} \, dx$ and $\int_0^\infty x^2 e^{-x^2} \, dx$.

70. Area between curves Let R be the region bounded by the graphs of $y = x^{-p}$ and $y = x^{-q}$, for $x \geq 1$, where $q > p > 1$. Find the area of R.

71. Area between curves Let R be the region bounded by the graphs of $y = e^{-ax}$ and $y = e^{-bx}$, for $x \geq 0$, where $a > b > 0$. Find the area of R.

72. An area function Let $A(a)$ denote the area of the region bounded by $y = e^{-ax}$ and the x-axis on the interval $[0, \infty)$. Graph the function $A(a)$, for $0 < a < \infty$. Describe how the area of the region decreases as the parameter a increases.

73. Regions bounded by exponentials Let $a > 0$ and let R be the region bounded by the graph of $y = e^{-ax}$ and the x-axis on the interval $[b, \infty)$.

   a. Find $A(a, b)$, the area of R as a function of a and b.

   b. Find the relationship $b = g(a)$ such that $A(a, b) = 2$.

   c. What is the minimum value of b (call it b^*) such that when $b > b^*$, $A(a, b) = 2$ for some value of $a > 0$?

74. The family $f(x) = 1/x^p$ revisited Consider the family of functions $f(x) = 1/x^p$, where p is a real number. For what values of p does the integral $\int_0^1 f(x) \, dx$ exist? What is its value?

75. When is the volume finite? Let R be the region bounded by the graph of $f(x) = x^{-p}$ and the x-axis, for $0 < x \leq 1$.

   a. Let S be the solid generated when R is revolved about the x-axis. For what values of p is the volume of S finite?

   b. Let S be the solid generated when R is revolved about the y-axis. For what values of p is the volume of S finite?

76. When is the volume finite? Let R be the region bounded by the graph of $f(x) = x^{-p}$ and the x-axis, for $x \geq 1$.

   a. Let S be the solid generated when R is revolved about the x-axis. For what values of p is the volume of S finite?

   b. Let S be the solid generated when R is revolved about the y-axis. For what values of p is the volume of S finite?

77–80. Numerical methods *Use numerical methods or a calculator to approximate the following integrals as closely as possible. The exact value of each integral is given.*

77. $\displaystyle\int_0^{\pi/2} \ln (\sin x) \, dx = \int_0^{\pi/2} \ln (\cos x) \, dx = -\frac{\pi \ln 2}{2}$

78. $\displaystyle\int_0^\infty \frac{\sin^2 x}{x^2} \, dx = \frac{\pi}{2}$

79. $\displaystyle\int_0^\infty \ln \left(\frac{e^x + 1}{e^x - 1} \right) dx = \frac{\pi^2}{4}$

80. $\displaystyle\int_0^1 \frac{\ln x}{1 + x} \, dx = -\frac{\pi^2}{12}$

Applications

81. Perpetual annuity Imagine that today you deposit \$$B$ in a savings account that earns interest at a rate of $p\%$ per year compounded continuously (Section 6.9). The goal is to draw an income of \$$I$ per year from the account forever. The amount of money that must be deposited is $B = I \int_0^\infty e^{-rt} \, dt$, where $r = p/100$. Suppose you find an account that earns 12% interest annually and you wish to have an income from the account of \$5000 per year. How much must you deposit today?

82. Draining a tank Water is drained from a 3000-gal tank at a rate that starts at 100 gal/hr and decreases continuously by 5%/hr. If the drain is left open indefinitely, how much water is drained from the tank? Can a full tank be emptied at this rate?

83. Decaying oscillations Let $a > 0$ and b be real numbers. Use integration to confirm the following identities. (See Exercise 68 of Section 7.2.)

a. $\displaystyle\int_0^\infty e^{-ax} \cos bx \, dx = \frac{a}{a^2 + b^2}$

b. $\displaystyle\int_0^\infty e^{-ax} \sin bx \, dx = \frac{b}{a^2 + b^2}$

84. Electronic chips Suppose the probability that a particular computer chip fails after a hours of operation is $0.00005 \int_a^\infty e^{-0.00005t} \, dt$.

a. Find the probability that the computer chip fails after 15,000 hr of operation.

b. Of the chips that are still operating after 15,000 hr, what fraction of these will operate for at least another 15,000 hr?

c. Evaluate $0.00005 \int_0^\infty e^{-0.00005t} \, dt$ and interpret its meaning.

85. Average lifetime The average time until a computer chip fails (see Exercise 84) is $0.00005 \int_0^\infty te^{-0.00005t} \, dt$. Find this value.

86. The Eiffel Tower property Let R be the region between the curves $y = e^{-cx}$ and $y = -e^{-cx}$ on the interval $[a, \infty)$, where $a \geq 0$ and $c > 0$. The center of mass of R is located at $(\bar{x}, 0)$, where $\bar{x} = \dfrac{\int_a^\infty xe^{-cx} \, dx}{\int_a^\infty e^{-cx} \, dx}$. (The profile of the Eiffel Tower is modeled by the two exponential curves.)

a. For $a = 0$ and $c = 2$, sketch the curves that define R and find the center of mass of R. Indicate the location of the center of mass.

b. With $a = 0$ and $c = 2$, find equations of the lines tangent to the curves at the points corresponding to $x = 0$.

c. Show that the tangent lines intersect at the center of mass.

d. Show that this same property holds for any $a \geq 0$ and any $c > 0$; that is, the tangent lines to the curves $y = \pm e^{-cx}$ at $x = a$ intersect at the center of mass of R.
(*Source:* P. Weidman and I. Pinelis, *Comptes Rendu, Mechanique* **332** (2004): 571–584. Also see the Guided Project *The Exponential Eiffel Tower*.)

87. Escape velocity and black holes The work required to launch an object from the surface of Earth to outer space is given by $W = \int_R^\infty F(x) \, dx$, where $R = 6370$ km is the approximate radius of Earth, $F(x) = GMm/x^2$ is the gravitational force between Earth and the object, G is the gravitational constant, M is the mass of Earth, m is the mass of the object, and $GM = 4 \times 10^{14} \text{ m}^3/\text{s}^2$.

a. Find the work required to launch an object in terms of m.

b. What escape velocity v_e is required to give the object a kinetic energy $\frac{1}{2}mv_e^2$ equal to W?

c. The French scientist Laplace anticipated the existence of black holes in the 18th century with the following argument: If a body has an escape velocity that equals or exceeds the speed of light, $c = 300{,}000$ km/s, then light cannot escape the body and it cannot be seen. Show that such a body has a radius $R \leq 2GM/c^2$. For Earth to be a black hole, what would its radius need to be?

88. Adding a proton to a nucleus The nucleus of an atom is positively charged because it consists of positively charged protons and uncharged neutrons. To bring a free proton toward a nucleus, a repulsive force $F(r) = kqQ/r^2$ must be overcome, where $q = 1.6 \times 10^{-19}$ C is the charge on the proton, $k = 9 \times 10^9$ N-m²/C², Q is the charge on the nucleus, and r is the distance between the center of the nucleus and the

proton. Find the work required to bring a free proton (assumed to be a point mass) from a large distance $(r \to \infty)$ to the edge of a nucleus that has a charge $Q = 50q$ and a radius of 6×10^{-11} m.

T 89. Gaussians An important function in statistics is the Gaussian (or normal distribution, or bell-shaped curve), $f(x) = e^{-ax^2}$.

a. Graph the Gaussian for $a = 0.5, 1$, and 2.

b. Given that $\displaystyle\int_{-\infty}^\infty e^{-ax^2} \, dx = \sqrt{\dfrac{\pi}{a}}$, compute the area under the curves in part (a).

c. Complete the square to evaluate $\int_{-\infty}^\infty e^{-(ax^2 + bx + c)} \, dx$, where $a > 0, b$, and c are real numbers.

90–94. Laplace transforms *A powerful tool in solving problems in engineering and physics is the Laplace transform. Given a function* $f(t)$*, the Laplace transform is a new function* $F(s)$ *defined by*

$$F(s) = \int_0^\infty e^{-st} f(t) \, dt,$$

where we assume that s *is a positive real number. For example, to find the Laplace transform of* $f(t) = e^{-t}$*, the following improper integral is evaluated:*

$$F(s) = \int_0^\infty e^{-st} e^{-t} \, dt = \int_0^\infty e^{-(s+1)t} \, dt = \frac{1}{s+1}.$$

Verify the following Laplace transforms, where a *is a real number.*

90. $f(t) = 1 \longrightarrow F(s) = \dfrac{1}{s}$ **91.** $f(t) = e^{at} \longrightarrow F(s) = \dfrac{1}{s-a}$

92. $f(t) = t \longrightarrow F(s) = \dfrac{1}{s^2}$

93. $f(t) = \sin at \longrightarrow F(s) = \dfrac{a}{s^2 + a^2}$

94. $f(t) = \cos at \longrightarrow F(s) = \dfrac{s}{s^2 + a^2}$

Additional Exercises

95. Improper integrals Evaluate the following improper integrals (Putnam Exam, 1939).

a. $\displaystyle\int_1^3 \frac{dx}{\sqrt{(x-1)(3-x)}}$ **b.** $\displaystyle\int_1^\infty \frac{dx}{e^{x+1} + e^{3-x}}$

96. A better way Compute $\int_0^1 \ln x \, dx$ using integration by parts. Then explain why $-\int_0^\infty e^{-x} \, dx$ (an easier integral) gives the same result.

97. Competing powers For what values of $p > 0$ is

$$\int_0^\infty \frac{dx}{x^p + x^{-p}} < \infty?$$

98. Gamma function The gamma function is defined by $\Gamma(p) = \int_0^\infty x^{p-1} e^{-x} \, dx$, for p not equal to zero or a negative integer.

a. Use the reduction formula

$$\int_0^\infty x^p e^{-x} \, dx = p \int_0^\infty x^{p-1} e^{-x} \, dx, \text{ for } p = 1, 2, 3, \ldots$$

to show that $\Gamma(p + 1) = p!$ (p factorial).

b. Use the substitution $x = u^2$ and the fact that

$$\int_0^\infty e^{-u^2}\, du = \frac{\sqrt{\pi}}{2} \text{ to show that } \Gamma\!\left(\frac{1}{2}\right) = \sqrt{\pi}.$$

99. Many methods needed Show that $\int_0^\infty \dfrac{\sqrt{x}\,\ln x}{(1 + x)^2}\, dx = \pi$ in the

following steps.

a. Integrate by parts with $u = \sqrt{x}\,\ln x$.
b. Change variables by letting $y = 1/x$.
c. Show that $\displaystyle\int_0^1 \frac{\ln x}{\sqrt{x}\,(1 + x)}\, dx = -\int_1^\infty \frac{\ln x}{\sqrt{x}\,(1 + x)}\, dx$ (and

both integrals converge). Conclude that $\displaystyle\int_0^\infty \frac{\ln x}{\sqrt{x}\,(1 + x)}\, dx = 0.$

d. Evaluate the remaining integral using the change of variables $z = \sqrt{x}$.
   (*Source: Mathematics Magazine* **59**, 1 (Feb 1986))

100. Riemann sums to integrals Show that

$$L = \lim_{n\to\infty}\!\left(\frac{1}{n}\ln n! - \ln n\right) = -1 \text{ in the following steps.}$$

a. Note that $n! = n(n - 1)(n - 2)\cdots 1$ and use $\ln(ab) = \ln a + \ln b$ to show that

$$L = \lim_{n\to\infty}\!\left[\left(\frac{1}{n}\sum_{k=1}^{n}\ln k\right) - \ln n\right]$$

$$= \lim_{n\to\infty}\frac{1}{n}\sum_{k=1}^{n}\ln\!\left(\frac{k}{n}\right).$$

b. Identify the limit of this sum as a Riemann sum for $\int_0^1 \ln x\, dx$. Integrate this improper integral by parts and reach the desired conclusion.

QUICK CHECK ANSWERS

1. The integral diverges. $\displaystyle\lim_{b\to\infty}\int_1^b (1 + x^{-1})\, dx = \lim_{b\to\infty}(x + \ln x)\big|_1^b$ does not exist. **2.** $\frac{1}{3}$ **3.** c must approach 0 through values in the interval of integration $(0, 1)$. Therefore, $c \to 0^+$. ◀

7.5 Trigonometric Substitutions

In this section, we consider three special changes of variable called *trigonometric substitutions*. These substitutions are used to evaluate integrals whose integrands have terms of the form $a^2 - x^2$, $x^2 - a^2$, or $x^2 + a^2$, where we assume that a is a positive real number. In all these cases, the substitution leads to a new integral that involves powers of trigonometric functions. Some of these integrals can be evaluated directly, while some may require advanced methods or a table of integrals.

The Substitution $x = a \sin \theta$

The first of the three trigonometric substitutions uses the sine function. We proceed by example.

EXAMPLE 1   The sine substitution Evaluate $\displaystyle\int \frac{dx}{(16 - x^2)^{3/2}}.$

SOLUTION While it is not an obvious choice, let's change the variable of integration x to a new variable θ using the substitution $x = 4 \sin \theta$. In making this substitution, we restrict θ to the interval $-\dfrac{\pi}{2} \le \theta \le \dfrac{\pi}{2}$, on which $\sin \theta$ is one-to-one. As θ varies over this interval, x varies over the interval $-4 \le x \le 4$. This change of variable implies that $dx = 4 \cos \theta\, d\theta$. We now simplify $(16 - x^2)^{3/2}$ with a calculation that is typical of trigonometric substitutions:

$$
\begin{aligned}
(16 - x^2)^{3/2} &= (16 - (4\sin\theta)^2)^{3/2} &&\text{Substitute } x = 4\sin\theta.\\
&= (16(1 - \sin^2\theta))^{3/2} &&\text{Factor.}\\
&= (16\cos^2\theta)^{3/2} &&1 - \sin^2\theta = \cos^2\theta\\
&= 64\cos^3\theta. &&\text{Simplify; note } \cos\theta \ge 0 \text{ on } -\tfrac{\pi}{2} \le \theta \le \tfrac{\pi}{2}.
\end{aligned}
$$

The next step is to replace the factors $(16 - x^2)^{3/2}$ and dx of the original integral and evaluate the new integral with respect to θ:

$$\int \underbrace{\frac{\overbrace{dx}^{4\cos\theta\,d\theta}}{(16 - x^2)^{3/2}}}_{64\cos^3\theta} = \int \frac{4\cos\theta}{64\cos^3\theta}\,d\theta$$

$$= \frac{1}{16}\int \frac{d\theta}{\cos^2\theta}$$

$$= \frac{1}{16}\int \sec^2\theta\,d\theta \quad \text{Simplify.}$$

$$= \frac{1}{16}\tan\theta + C. \quad \text{Evaluate integral.}$$

We must now express this result in terms of the original variable x. In many integrals, this step is most easily done using a reference triangle showing the relationship between x and θ. Figure 7.12 shows a right triangle with an angle θ and the sides labeled such that $x = 4\sin\theta$ (or $\sin\theta = x/4$). Using this triangle, we see that $\tan\theta = \dfrac{x}{\sqrt{16 - x^2}}$, which implies that

$$\int \frac{dx}{(16 - x^2)^{3/2}} = \frac{1}{16}\tan\theta + C = \frac{x}{16\sqrt{16 - x^2}} + C.$$

Related Exercises 7–16 ◄

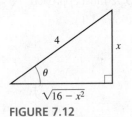

FIGURE 7.12

QUICK CHECK 1 Use a substitution of the form $x = a\sin\theta$ to transform $9 - x^2$ into an expression involving trigonometric functions. ◄

EXAMPLE 2   **Area of a circle** Verify that the area of a circle of radius $a > 0$ is πa^2.

SOLUTION The function $f(x) = \sqrt{a^2 - x^2}$ describes the upper half of a circle centered at the origin with radius a (Figure 7.13). The area of the region under this curve on the interval $[0, a]$ is the area of a quarter-circle. Therefore, the area of the full circle is $4\int_0^a \sqrt{a^2 - x^2}\,dx$.

We use the change of variables $x = a\sin\theta$, where $-\pi/2 \le \theta \le \pi/2$. Substituting $x = a\sin\theta$ into the integrand $\sqrt{a^2 - x^2}$, we find that

$$\sqrt{a^2 - x^2} = \sqrt{a^2 - a^2\sin^2\theta} \quad \text{Substitute } x = a\sin\theta.$$

$$= \sqrt{a^2(1 - \sin^2\theta)} \quad \text{Simplify.}$$

$$= \sqrt{a^2\cos^2\theta} \quad 1 - \sin^2\theta = \cos\theta$$

$$= |a\cos\theta| \quad \sqrt{x^2} = |x|$$

$$= a\cos\theta. \quad a > 0, \cos\theta > 0$$

The absolute value can be removed in the last step because $\cos\theta \ge 0$ on $-\pi/2 \le \theta \le \pi/2$ and a is assumed to be positive. Because this is a definite integral, we also change the limits of integration: When $x = 0$, $\sin\theta = 0$, or $\theta = 0$, and when

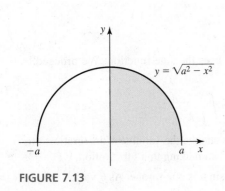

FIGURE 7.13

$x = a$, $\sin \theta = 1$, or $\theta = \dfrac{\pi}{2}$. Making these substitutions, the integral is evaluated as follows:

> The key identities for integrating $\sin^2 \theta$ and $\cos^2 \theta$ are
>
> $$\sin^2 \theta = \frac{1 - \cos 2\theta}{2} \quad \text{and}$$
>
> $$\cos^2 \theta = \frac{1 + \cos 2\theta}{2}.$$

$$4 \int_0^a \sqrt{a^2 - x^2}\, dx = 4 \int_0^{\pi/2} \underbrace{a \cos \theta}_{\substack{\text{integrand} \\ \text{simplified}}} \cdot \underbrace{a \cos \theta\, d\theta}_{dx} \qquad x = a \sin \theta,\, dx = a \cos \theta\, d\theta$$

$$= 4a^2 \int_0^{\pi/2} \cos^2 \theta\, du \qquad \text{Simplify.}$$

$$= 4a^2 \left(\frac{\theta}{2} + \frac{\sin 2\theta}{4} \right) \Big|_0^{\pi/2} \qquad \cos^2 \theta = \frac{1 + \cos 2\theta}{2}$$

$$= 4a^2 \left(\left(\frac{\pi}{4} + 0 \right) - (0 + 0) \right) = \pi a^2. \quad \text{Simplify.}$$

A similar calculation (Exercise 48) gives the area of an ellipse.

Related Exercises 17–38 ◄

The Substitutions $x = a \tan \theta$ and $x = a \sec \theta$

You have now seen examples of the sine substitution. The two additional trigonometric substitutions involve the tangent and secant functions. Figure 7.14 and Table 7.2 summarize all three substitutions for real numbers $a > 0$.

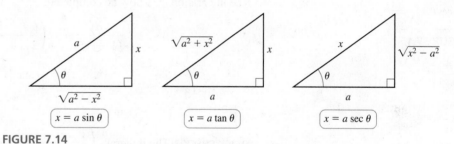

FIGURE 7.14

Table 7.2

The integral contains...	Corresponding substitution	Useful identity
$a^2 - x^2$	$x = a \sin \theta,\ -\dfrac{\pi}{2} \le \theta \le \dfrac{\pi}{2}$	$a^2 - a^2 \sin^2 \theta = a^2 \cos^2 \theta$
$a^2 + x^2$	$x = a \tan \theta,\ -\dfrac{\pi}{2} < \theta < \dfrac{\pi}{2}$	$a^2 + a^2 \tan^2 \theta = a^2 \sec^2 \theta$
$x^2 - a^2$	$x = a \sec \theta,\ 0 \le \theta < \dfrac{\pi}{2}$	$a^2 \sec^2 \theta - a^2 = a^2 \tan^2 \theta$

> To keep matters simple, we have assumed $0 \le \theta < \dfrac{\pi}{2}$ for the secant substitution $x = a \sec \theta$, which implies $x \ge a$.

QUICK CHECK 2 What change of variable would you try on the integrals

(a) $\displaystyle \int \frac{x^2}{\sqrt{x^2 + 9}}\, dx$ and (b) $\displaystyle \int \frac{3}{x\sqrt{16 - x^2}}\, dx$? ◄

EXAMPLE 3   A tangent substitution Evaluate $\displaystyle\int \frac{dx}{(1 + x^2)^2}$.

SOLUTION The factor $1 + x^2$ suggests the substitution $x = \tan\theta$. It follows that $\theta = \tan^{-1}x$, $dx = \sec^2\theta\,d\theta$, and

$$(1 + x^2)^2 = (1 + \tan^2\theta)^2 = \sec^4\theta.$$

Substituting these factors into the integral leads to

$$\int \frac{dx}{(1 + x^2)^2} = \int \frac{\sec^2\theta}{\sec^4\theta}\,d\theta \qquad x = \tan\theta, dx = \sec^2\theta\,d\theta$$

$$= \int \cos^2\theta\,d\theta \qquad \text{Simplify.}$$

$$= \left(\frac{\theta}{2} + \frac{\sin 2\theta}{4}\right) + C. \quad \text{Integrate } \cos^2\theta = \frac{1 + \cos 2\theta}{2}.$$

The final step is to return to the original variable x. The first term $\theta/2$ is replaced with $\frac{1}{2}\tan^{-1}x$. The second term involving $\sin 2\theta$ requires the identity $\sin 2\theta = 2\sin\theta\cos\theta$. The reference triangle in Figure 7.15 tells us that

$$\frac{1}{4}\sin 2\theta = \frac{1}{2}\sin\theta\cos\theta = \frac{1}{2}\frac{x}{\sqrt{1 + x^2}}\cdot\frac{1}{\sqrt{1 + x^2}} = \frac{x}{2(1 + x^2)}.$$

The integration may now be completed:

$$\int \frac{dx}{(1 + x^2)^2} = \left(\frac{\theta}{2} + \frac{\sin 2\theta}{4}\right) + C$$

$$= \frac{1}{2}\tan^{-1}x + \frac{x}{2(1 + x^2)} + C.$$

Related Exercises 17–38 ◄

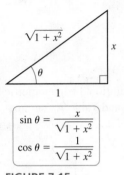

$\sin\theta = \dfrac{x}{\sqrt{1 + x^2}}$

$\cos\theta = \dfrac{1}{\sqrt{1 + x^2}}$

FIGURE 7.15

QUICK CHECK 3 The integral $\displaystyle\int \frac{dx}{a^2 + x^2} = \frac{1}{a}\tan^{-1}\frac{x}{a} + C$ was given in Section 5.1. Verify this result with the appropriate trigonometric substitution. ◄

EXAMPLE 4   A preliminary step Evaluate $\displaystyle\int \frac{dx}{(9 + 4x^2)^{3/2}}$.

SOLUTION This example illustrates that occasionally a preliminary step is needed to put an integral in one of the standard forms listed in Table 7.2. In this case, notice that $4x^2 = (2x)^2$, which suggests the substitution $u = 2x$. Therefore, we write

$$\int \frac{dx}{(9 + 4x^2)^{3/2}} = \int \frac{dx}{(9 + (2x)^2)^{3/2}} \qquad 4x^2 = (2x)^2$$

$$= \frac{1}{2}\int \frac{du}{(9 + u^2)^{3/2}}. \qquad u = 2x, du = 2dx$$

The integrand now has a term of the form $a^2 + u^2$, which calls for the substitution $u = 3\tan\theta$. It follows that $du = 3\sec^2\theta\,d\theta$ and

$$9 + u^2 = 9 + (3\tan\theta)^2 = 9(1 + \tan^2\theta) = 9\sec^2\theta.$$

Therefore, the integral may be written

$$\int \frac{dx}{(9 + 4x^2)^{3/2}} = \frac{1}{2}\int \frac{du}{(9 + u^2)^{3/2}} \qquad \text{Preliminary step}$$

$$= \frac{1}{2}\int \frac{3\sec^2\theta}{(9\sec^2\theta)^{3/2}}\,d\theta \quad u = 3\sec\theta$$

$$= \frac{1}{2}\cdot\frac{1}{9}\int \frac{d\theta}{\sec\theta} \qquad \text{Simplify.}$$

$$= \frac{1}{18}\int \cos\theta\,d\theta \qquad \text{Simplify.}$$

$$= \frac{1}{18}\sin\theta + C. \qquad \text{Integrate.}$$

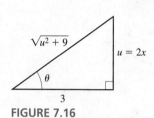

FIGURE 7.16

To express this result in terms of the original variable x, we use the reference triangle in Figure 7.16 and recall that $u = 2x$. This triangle has the property $u = 3\tan\theta$, or equivalently, $\tan\theta = \dfrac{u}{3} = \dfrac{2x}{3}$. Using the triangle, we find that $\sin\theta = \dfrac{u}{\sqrt{9 + u^2}} = \dfrac{2x}{\sqrt{9 + 4x^2}}$.

Making this substitution, we have

$$\int \frac{dx}{(9 + 4x^2)^{3/2}} = \frac{1}{18}\sin\theta + C = \frac{1}{18}\frac{2x}{\sqrt{9 + 4x^2}} + C = \frac{x}{9\sqrt{9 + 4x^2}} + C.$$

Related Exercises 17–38 ◄

EXAMPLE 5 **A definite integral** Evaluate $\displaystyle\int_3^6 \frac{\sqrt{x^2 - 9}}{x}\,dx$.

SOLUTION This integral calls for the secant substitution $x = 3\sec\theta$, which implies that $dx = 3\sec\theta\tan\theta\,d\theta$. We also change the limits of integration: when $x = 3, \theta = 0$ and when $x = 6, \theta = \dfrac{\pi}{3}$. The complete integration can now be done:

$$\int_3^6 \frac{\sqrt{x^2 - 9}}{x}\,dx = \int_0^{\pi/3} \frac{3\tan\theta}{3\sec\theta}\,3\sec\theta\tan\theta\,d\theta \quad x = 3\sec\theta,\, dx = 3\sec\theta\tan\theta\,d\theta$$

$$= 3\int_0^{\pi/3} \tan^2\theta\,d\theta \qquad \text{Simplify.}$$

$$= 3\int_0^{\pi/3} (\sec^2\theta - 1)\,d\theta \qquad \tan^2\theta = \sec^2\theta - 1$$

$$= 3(\tan\theta - \theta)\Big|_0^{\pi/3} \qquad \text{Evaluate integrals.}$$

$$= 3\sqrt{3} - \pi. \qquad \text{Simplify.}$$

Related Exercises 39–46 ◄

SECTION 7.5 EXERCISES

Review Questions

1. What change of variables is suggested by an integral containing $\sqrt{x^2 - 9}$?

2. What change of variables is suggested by an integral containing $\sqrt{x^2 + 36}$?

3. What change of variables is suggested by an integral containing $\sqrt{100 - x^2}$?

4. If $x = 4\tan\theta$, express $\sin\theta$ in terms of x.

5. If $x = 2\sin\theta$, express $\cot\theta$ in terms of x.

6. If $x = 8\sec\theta$, express $\tan\theta$ in terms of x, for $x \geq 8$.

Basic Skills

7–16. Sine substitution *Evaluate the following integrals.*

7. $\displaystyle\int_0^{5/2} \frac{dx}{\sqrt{25 - x^2}}$

8. $\displaystyle\int_0^{3/2} \frac{dx}{(9 - x^2)^{3/2}}$

9. $\displaystyle\int_5^{10} \sqrt{100 - x^2}\, dx$

10. $\displaystyle\int_0^{\sqrt{2}} \frac{x^2}{\sqrt{4 - x^2}}\, dx$

11. $\displaystyle\int_0^{1/2} \frac{x^2}{\sqrt{1 - x^2}}\, dx$

12. $\displaystyle\int_0^{1/2} \frac{dx}{(1 - x^2)^{3/2}}$

13. $\displaystyle\int \frac{dx}{(16 - x^2)^{1/2}}$

14. $\displaystyle\int \sqrt{36 - x^2}\, dx$

15. $\displaystyle\int \sqrt{9 - x^2}\, dx$

16. $\displaystyle\int (36 - x^2)^{-3/2}\, dx$

17–38. Trigonometric substitutions *Evaluate the following integrals.*

17. $\displaystyle\int \sqrt{64 - x^2}\, dx$

18. $\displaystyle\int \frac{dx}{\sqrt{x^2 - 49}}, \; x > 7$

19. $\displaystyle\int \frac{1}{(1 - x^2)^{3/2}}\, dx$

20. $\displaystyle\int \frac{1}{(1 + x^2)^{3/2}}\, dx$

21. $\displaystyle\int \frac{1}{x^2\sqrt{x^2 + 9}}\, dx$

22. $\displaystyle\int \frac{1}{x^2\sqrt{9 - x^2}}\, dx$

23. $\displaystyle\int \frac{dx}{\sqrt{36 - x^2}}$

24. $\displaystyle\int \frac{dx}{\sqrt{16 + 4x^2}}$

25. $\displaystyle\int \frac{dx}{\sqrt{x^2 - 81}}, \; x > 9$

26. $\displaystyle\int \frac{dx}{\sqrt{1 - 2x^2}}$

27. $\displaystyle\int \frac{dx}{(1 + 4x^2)^{3/2}}$

28. $\displaystyle\int \frac{dx}{(x^2 - 36)^{3/2}}, \; x > 6$

29. $\displaystyle\int \frac{x^2}{\sqrt{16 - x^2}}\, dx$

30. $\displaystyle\int \frac{dx}{(81 + x^2)^2}$

31. $\displaystyle\int \frac{dx}{x^2\sqrt{x^2 - 1}}, \; x > 1$

32. $\displaystyle\int \sqrt{9 - 4x^2}\, dx$

33. $\displaystyle\int \frac{dx}{x\sqrt{x^2 - 25}}, \; x > 5$

34. $\displaystyle\int \frac{dx}{x^2\sqrt{9x^2 - 1}}, \; x > \frac{1}{3}$

35. $\displaystyle\int \frac{x^2}{(100 - x^2)^{1/2}}\, dx$

36. $\displaystyle\int \frac{dx}{x^3\sqrt{x^2 - 100}}, \; x > 10$

37. $\displaystyle\int \frac{x^3}{(1 + x^2)^3}\, dx$

38. $\displaystyle\int \frac{dx}{x^3\sqrt{x^2 - 1}}, \; x > 1$

39–46. Evaluating definite integrals *Evaluate the following definite integrals.*

39. $\displaystyle\int_0^1 \frac{dx}{\sqrt{x^2 + 16}}$

40. $\displaystyle\int_{8\sqrt{2}}^{16} \frac{dx}{\sqrt{x^2 - 64}}$

41. $\displaystyle\int_{1/\sqrt{3}}^1 \frac{1}{x^2\sqrt{1 + x^2}}\, dx$

42. $\displaystyle\int_1^2 \frac{1}{x^2\sqrt{4 - x^2}}\, dx$

43. $\displaystyle\int_0^{1/\sqrt{3}} (x^2 + 1)^{-3/2}\, dx$

44. $\displaystyle\int_4^5 \frac{dx}{x^2\sqrt{x^2 - 9}}$

45. $\displaystyle\int_0^{1/3} \frac{dx}{(9x^2 + 1)^{3/2}}$

46. $\displaystyle\int_{10/\sqrt{3}}^{10} \frac{dx}{\sqrt{x^2 - 25}}$

Further Explorations

47. Explain why or why not Determine whether the following statements are true and give an explanation or counterexample.

a. If $x = 4 \tan \theta$, then $\csc \theta = 4/x$.

b. The integral $\int_1^2 \sqrt{1 - x^2}\, dx$ does not have a finite real value.

c. The integral $\int_1^2 \sqrt{x^2 - 1}\, dx$ does not have a finite real value.

48. Area of an ellipse The upper half of the ellipse centered at the origin with axes of length $2a$ and $2b$ is described by $y = \dfrac{b}{a}\sqrt{a^2 - x^2}$ (see figure). Find the area of the ellipse in terms of a and b.

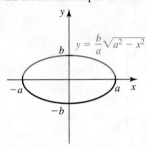

49. Area of a segment of a circle Use two approaches to show that the area of a cap (or segment) of a circle of radius r subtended by an angle θ (see figure) is given by

$$A_{\text{seg}} = \frac{1}{2}r^2\,(\theta - \sin \theta).$$

a. Find the area using geometry (no calculus).

b. Find the area using calculus.

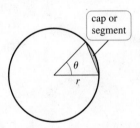

50. Area of a lune A lune is a crescent-shaped region bounded by the arcs of two circles. Let C_1 be a circle of radius 4 centered at the origin. Let C_2 be a circle of radius 3 centered at the point $(2, 0)$. Find the area of the lune (shaded in the figure) that lies inside C_1 and outside C_2.

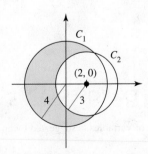

51. Area and volume Consider the function $f(x) = (9 + x^2)^{-1/2}$ and the region R on the interval $[0, 4]$ (see figure).

a. Find the area of R.

b. Find the volume of the solid generated when R is revolved about the x-axis.

c. Find the volume of the solid generated when R is revolved about the y-axis.

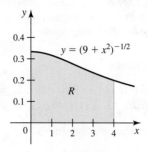

T 52. Area of a region Graph the function $f(x) = (16 + x^2)^{-3/2}$ and find the area of the region bounded by the curve and the x-axis on the interval $[0, 3]$.

T 53–55. Using the integral of $\sec^3 u$ *Graph the following functions and find the area under the curve on the given interval. Use the formula*

$$\int \sec^3 u \, du = \frac{1}{2}(\sec u \tan u + \ln|\sec u + \tan u|) + C.$$

53. $f(x) = (9 - x^2)^{-2}, \left[0, \frac{3}{2}\right]$

54. $f(x) = \sqrt{4 + x^2}, [0, 2]$

55. $f(x) = \sqrt{x^2 - 25}, [5, 10]$

56. Clever substitution Evaluate $\displaystyle\int \frac{dx}{1 + \sin x + \cos x}$ using the substitution $x = 2 \tan^{-1}\theta$. The identities $\sin x = 2\sin\dfrac{x}{2}\cos\dfrac{x}{2}$ and $\cos x = \cos^2\dfrac{x}{2} - \sin^2\dfrac{x}{2}$ are helpful.

Applications

57. A torus (doughnut) Find the volume of the solid torus formed when the circle of radius 4 centered at $(0, 6)$ is revolved about the x-axis.

58. Bagel wars Bob and Bruce bake bagels (shaped like tori). They both make standard bagels that have an inner radius of 0.5 in and an outer radius of 2.5 in. Bob plans to increase the volume of his bagels by decreasing the inner radius by 20% (leaving the outer radius unchanged). Bruce plans to increase the volume of his bagels by increasing the outer radius by 20% (leaving the inner radius unchanged). Whose new bagels will have the greater volume? Does this result depend on the size of the original bagels? Explain.

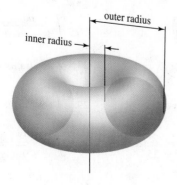

59. Electric field due to a line of charge A total charge of Q is distributed uniformly on a line segment of length $2L$ along the y-axis (see figure). The x-component of the electric field at a point $(a, 0)$ on the x-axis is given by

$$E_x(a) = \frac{kQa}{2L}\int_{-L}^{L}\frac{dy}{(a^2 + y^2)^{3/2}},$$

where k is a physical constant and $a > 0$.

a. Confirm that $E_x(a) = \dfrac{kQ}{a\sqrt{a^2 + L^2}}$.

b. Letting $\rho = Q/2L$ be the charge density on the line segment, show that if $L \to \infty$, then $E_x(a) = 2k\rho/a$.

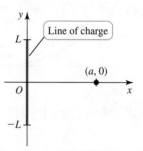

60. Magnetic field due to current in a straight wire A long, straight wire of length $2L$ on the y-axis carries a current I. According to the Biot-Savart Law, the magnitude of the magnetic field due to the current at a point $(a, 0)$ is given by

$$B(a) = \frac{\mu_0 I}{4\pi}\int_{-L}^{L}\frac{\sin\theta}{r^2}\,dy,$$

where μ_0 is a physical constant, $a > 0$, and θ, r, and y are related as shown in the figure.

a. Show that the magnitude of the magnetic field at $(a, 0)$ is

$$B(a) = \frac{\mu_0 IL}{2\pi a\sqrt{a^2 + L^2}}.$$

b. What is the magnitude of the magnetic field at $(a, 0)$ due to an infinitely long wire $(L \to \infty)$?

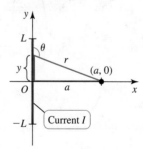

61. Fastest descent time The cycloid is the curve traced by a point on the rim of a rolling wheel. Imagine a wire shaped like an inverted cycloid (see figure). A bead sliding down this wire without friction has some remarkable properties. Among all wire shapes, the cycloid is the shape that produces the fastest descent time (see the Guided Project *The Amazing Cycloid* for more about this *brachistochrone property*). It can be shown that the descent time between any two points $0 \leq a < b \leq \pi$ on the curve is

$$\text{descent time} = \int_a^b \sqrt{\frac{1 - \cos t}{g(\cos a - \cos t)}}\, dt,$$

where g is the acceleration due to gravity, $t = 0$ corresponds to the top of the wire, and $t = \pi$ corresponds to the lowest point on the wire.

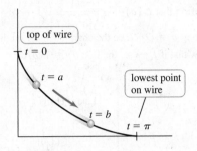

a. Find the descent time on the interval $[a, b]$ by making the substitution $u = \cos t$.

b. Show that when $b = \pi$, the descent time is the same for all values of a; that is, the descent time to the bottom of the wire is the same for all starting points.

QUICK CHECK ANSWERS

1. Use $x = 3 \sin \theta$ to obtain $9 \cos^2 \theta$.   **2.** (a) Use $x = 3 \tan \theta$. (b) Use $x = 4 \sin \theta$.   **3.** Let $x = a \tan \theta$, so that $dx = a \sec^2 \theta\, d\theta$. The new integral is $\int \dfrac{a \sec^2 \theta}{a^2(1 + \tan^2 \theta)}\, d\theta = \dfrac{1}{a} \int d\theta = \dfrac{1}{a} \theta + C = \dfrac{1}{a} \tan^{-1} \dfrac{x}{a} + C.$ ◄

CHAPTER 7   REVIEW EXERCISES

1. **Explain why or why not** Determine whether the following statements are true and give an explanation or counterexample.

a. The integral $\int x^2 e^{2x}\, dx$ can be evaluated analytically using integration by parts.

b. To evaluate the integral $\int \dfrac{dx}{\sqrt{x^2 - 100}}$ analytically, it is best to use partial fractions.

c. $\int 2 \sin x \cos x\, dx = -\dfrac{1}{2} \cos 2x + C.$

d. The best approach to evaluating $\int \dfrac{x^3 + 1}{3x^2}\, dx$ is to use the change of variables $u = x^3 + 1$.

2–7. Basic integration techniques *Use the methods introduced in Section 7.1 to evaluate the following integrals.*

2. $\displaystyle\int \cos\left(\frac{x}{2} + \frac{\pi}{3}\right) dx$

3. $\displaystyle\int \frac{3x}{\sqrt{x + 4}}\, dx$

4. $\displaystyle\int \frac{2 - \sin 2\theta}{\cos^2 2\theta}\, d\theta$

5. $\displaystyle\int_{-2}^{1} \frac{3}{x^2 + 4x + 13}\, dx$

6. $\displaystyle\int \frac{x^3 + 3x^2 + 1}{x^3 + 1}\, dx$

7. $\displaystyle\int \frac{\sqrt{t - 1}}{2t}\, dt$ (*Hint: Let $u = \sqrt{t - 1}$.*)

8–11. Integration by parts *Use integration by parts to evaluate the following integrals.*

8. $\displaystyle\int_{-1}^{\ln 2} \frac{3t}{e^t}\, dt$

9. $\displaystyle\int \frac{x}{2\sqrt{x + 2}}\, dx$

10. $\displaystyle\int x \tan^{-1} x\, dx$

11. $\displaystyle\int x \sin 2x\, dx$

12–15. Partial fractions *Use partial fractions to evaluate the following integrals.*

12. $\displaystyle\int \frac{8x + 5}{2x^2 + 3x + 1}\, dx$

13. $\displaystyle\int \frac{2x^2 + 7x + 4}{x^3 + 3x^2 + 2x}\, dx$

14. $\displaystyle\int_{-1/2}^{1/2} \frac{x^2 + 1}{x^2 - 1}\, dx$

15. $\displaystyle\int \frac{2x^3 + x^2 + x}{(1 - x^2)}\, dx$

16–19. Trigonometric substitutions *Evaluate the following integrals using a trigonometric substitution.*

16. $\displaystyle\int \frac{\sqrt{1 - x^2}}{x}\, dx$

17. $\displaystyle\int_{\sqrt{2}}^{2} \frac{\sqrt{x^2 - 1}}{x}\, dx$

18. $\displaystyle\int \frac{x^3}{\sqrt{4 - x^2}}\, dx$

19. $\displaystyle\int \frac{x^3}{\sqrt{x^2 + 4}}\, dx$

20–23. Improper integrals *Evaluate the following integrals.*

20. $\displaystyle\int_{-\infty}^{-1} \frac{dx}{(x - 1)^4}$

21. $\displaystyle\int_0^{\infty} x e^{-x}\, dx$

22. $\displaystyle\int_0^{8} \frac{dx}{\sqrt{2x}}$

23. $\displaystyle\int_0^{3} \frac{dx}{\sqrt{9 - x^2}}$

24–37. Miscellaneous Integrals *Evaluate the following integrals analytically.*

24. $\displaystyle\int \frac{x^2 - 4}{x + 4}\, dx$

25. $\displaystyle\int \frac{d\theta}{1 - \cos \theta}$

26. $\displaystyle\int x^2 \cos x\, dx$

27. $\displaystyle\int e^x \sin x\, dx$

28. $\displaystyle\int_1^{e} x^2 \ln x\, dx$

29. $\displaystyle\int \cos^2 4\theta\, d\theta$

30. $\displaystyle\int \frac{dx}{\sqrt{9x^2 - 25}}, x > \frac{5}{3}$

31. $\displaystyle\int \frac{dy}{y^2 \sqrt{9 - y^2}}$

32. $\displaystyle\int_0^{\sqrt{3}/2} \frac{x^2}{(1-x^2)^{3/2}}\,dx$

33. $\displaystyle\int_0^{\sqrt{3}/2} \frac{4}{9+4x^2}\,dx$

34. $\displaystyle\int_0^1 \sin^{-1} x\,dx$

35. $\displaystyle\int \frac{dx}{x^2 - 2x - 15}$

36. $\displaystyle\int \frac{2}{x^2 - 2x}\,dx$

37. $\displaystyle\int_0^1 \frac{dy}{(y+1)(y+2)}$

38–44. Preliminary work *Make a change of variables or use an algebra step before evaluating the following integrals.*

38. $\displaystyle\int_{-1}^1 \frac{dx}{x^2 + 2x + 5}$

39. $\displaystyle\int \frac{dx}{x^2 - x - 2}$

40. $\displaystyle\int \frac{3x^2 + x - 3}{x^2 - 1}\,dx$

41. $\displaystyle\int \frac{2x^2 - 4x}{x^2 - 4}\,dx$

42. $\displaystyle\int_{1/9}^{1/4} \frac{dx}{\sqrt{x}(1 + 8\sqrt{x})}$

43. $\displaystyle\int \frac{e^{2t}}{1 + e^{4t}}\,dt$

44. $\displaystyle\int_1^{16} \frac{dx}{x^{1/2} + x^{1/4}}$

45–48. Volumes *The region R is bounded by the curve $y = \ln x$ and the x-axis on the interval $[1, e]$. Find the volume of the solid that is generated when R is revolved in the following ways.*

45. About the x-axis

46. About the y-axis

47. About the line $x = 1$

48. About the line $y = 1$

49. Comparing volumes Let R be the region bounded by the graph of $y = \sin x$ and the x-axis on the interval $[0, \pi]$. Which is greater, the volume of the solid generated when R is revolved about the x-axis or the y-axis?

50. Comparing areas Show that the area of the region bounded by the graph of $y = ae^{-ax}$ and the x-axis on the interval $[0, \infty)$ is the same for all values of $a > 0$.

51. Zero log integral It is evident from the graph of $y = \ln x$ that for every real number a with $0 < a < 1$, there is a unique real number $b = g(a)$ with $b > 1$, such that $\int_a^b \ln x\,dx = 0$ (the net area bounded by the graph of $y = \ln x$ on $[a, b]$ is 0).

  a. Approximate $b = g\left(\frac{1}{2}\right)$.
  b. Approximate $b = g\left(\frac{1}{3}\right)$.
  c. Find the equation satisfied by all pairs of numbers (a, b) such that $b = g(a)$.
  d. Is g an increasing or decreasing function of a? Explain.

52. Arc length Find the length of the curve $y = \ln x$ on the interval $[1, e^2]$.

53. Average velocity Find the average velocity of a projectile whose velocity over the interval $0 \le t \le \pi$ is given by $v(t) = 10\sin 3t$.

54. Comparing distances Starting at the same time and place $(t = 0$ and $s = 0)$, the velocity of car A (in mi/hr) is given by $u(t) = 40/(t+1)$ and the velocity of car B (in mi/hr) is given by $v(t) = 40e^{-t/2}$.

  a. After $t = 2$ hr, which car has traveled the greater distance?
  b. After $t = 3$ hr, which car has traveled the greater distance?
  c. If allowed to travel indefinitely $(t \to \infty)$, which car will travel a finite distance?

55. Traffic flow When data from a traffic study are fitted to a curve, the flow rate of cars past a point on a highway is approximated by $R(t) = 800te^{-t/2}$ cars/hr. How many cars pass the measuring site during the time interval $0 \le t \le 4$?

56. Comparing integrals Graph the functions $f(x) = 1/x^2$, $g(x) = (\cos x)/x^2$, and $h(x) = (\cos^2 x)/x^2$. Without evaluating integrals and knowing that $\int_1^\infty f(x)\,dx$ has a finite value, determine whether $\int_1^\infty g(x)\,dx$ and $\int_1^\infty h(x)\,dx$ have finite values.

57. A family of logarithm integrals Let $I(p) = \displaystyle\int_1^e \frac{\ln x}{x^p}\,dx$, where p is a real number.

  a. Find an expression for $I(p)$, for all real values of p.
  b. Evaluate $\displaystyle\lim_{p\to\infty} I(p)$ and $\displaystyle\lim_{p\to-\infty} I(p)$.
  c. For what value of p is $I(p) = 1$?

58. Arc length Find the length of the curve
$$y = \frac{x}{2}\sqrt{3 - x^2} + \frac{3}{2}\sin^{-1}\frac{x}{\sqrt{3}} \text{ from } x = 0 \text{ to } x = 1.$$

59. Best approximation Let $I = \displaystyle\int_0^1 \frac{x^2 - x}{\ln x}\,dx$. Use any method you choose to find a good approximation to I. You may use the facts that $\displaystyle\lim_{x\to 0^+} \frac{x^2 - x}{\ln x} = 0$ and $\displaystyle\lim_{x\to 1} \frac{x^2 - x}{\ln x} = 1$.

60. Equal volumes

  a. Let R be the region bounded by the graph of $f(x) = x^{-p}$ and the x-axis, for $x \ge 1$. Let V_1 and V_2 be the volumes of the solids generated when R is revolved about the x-axis and the y-axis, respectively, if they exist. For what values of p (if any) is $V_1 = V_2$?
  b. Repeat part (a) on the interval $(0, 1]$.

61. Equal volumes Let R_1 be the region bounded by the graph of $y = e^{-ax}$ and the x-axis on the interval $[0, b]$ where $a > 0$ and $b > 0$. Let R_2 be the region bounded by the graph of $y = e^{-ax}$ and the x-axis on the interval $[b, \infty)$. Let V_1 and V_2 be the volumes of the solids generated when R_1 and R_2 are revolved about the x-axis. Find and graph the relationship between a and b for which $V_1 = V_2$.

AP® PRACTICE QUESTIONS

The following questions are intended to help you prepare for the AP exam. They are not questions from actual AP exams.

Section 1 Part A, Multiple Choice, No Technology

1. $\int \dfrac{\cos \sqrt{x}}{\sqrt{x}} dx =$

(A) $\sin \sqrt{x} + C.$ (B) $\dfrac{1}{2} \sin \sqrt{x} + C.$ (C) $2 \sin \sqrt{x} + C.$

(D) $\sqrt{x} \sin x + C.$ (E) $\dfrac{\sqrt{x}}{2} \sin x + C.$

2. $\int_1^e x \ln x \, dx =$

(A) $4e - 1.$ (B) $\dfrac{1}{4} e^2 + 1.$ (C) $\dfrac{1}{4} e^2.$

(D) $4e^2 + 1.$ (E) $\dfrac{1}{4}(e^2 + 1).$

3. $\int_1^4 \dfrac{6}{x(x - 6)} =$

(A) $\ln 10.$ (B) $6(\ln 2)(\ln 6).$ (C) $-6(\ln 2)(\ln 6).$

(D) $-\ln 10.$ (E) $\ln \dfrac{5}{2}.$

4. Suppose f' is a continuous function on $[0, 2], f(2) = 6,$ and $\int_0^2 f(x) \, dx = 4.$ Then the integral $\int_0^2 x f'(x) \, dx$

(A) equals 4.   (B) equals 6.

(C) equals 8.   (D) equals 10.

(E) cannot be determined from the given information.

5. Give the correct form of the partial fraction decomposition for $\dfrac{3}{x(4 - x^2)}.$

(A) $\dfrac{A}{x} + \dfrac{B}{2 - x} + \dfrac{C}{2 + x}$ (B) $\dfrac{A}{2 - x} + \dfrac{B}{2 + x}$

(C) $\dfrac{A}{x} + \dfrac{B}{4 - x^2}$ (D) $\dfrac{A}{x} + \dfrac{B}{4 - x} + \dfrac{C}{4 + x}$

(E) $\dfrac{3}{x} + \dfrac{B}{2 - x} + \dfrac{C}{2 + x}$

6. The area bounded between the graph of $y = x \sin x$ and the x-axis on the interval $[0, \pi]$ is

(A) 1.   (B) $2\pi.$ (C) $\pi.$ (D) $\dfrac{\pi^2}{2}.$ (E) $\pi^2.$

7. Evaluate $\int_3^4 \dfrac{dx}{\sqrt{2x - 6}}.$

(A) 2   (B) 4   (C) $2\sqrt{2}$

(D) $\sqrt{2}$ (E) The value of the integral is undefined.

8. The volume of the solid obtained by rotating the region bounded by the graph of $y = \sqrt{x}\, e^{x/2}$ and the x-axis on the interval $[0, 1]$ about the x-axis is

(A) $\pi.$ (B) $\dfrac{\pi}{2}.$ (C) $2\pi.$ (D) $\dfrac{\pi}{4}.$ (E) 1.

9. Evaluate $\int_1^\infty \dfrac{dx}{x^{3/2}}.$

(A) 1   (B) 2   (C) Does not exist.

(D) $\dfrac{2}{5}$ (E) $\dfrac{2}{3}$

10. Evaluate $\int_0^1 \dfrac{dx}{x^{1/3}}.$

(A) $\dfrac{2}{3}$ (B) $\dfrac{4}{3}$ (C) Does not exist.

(D) $\dfrac{3}{2}$ (E) 1

11. $\int \dfrac{6}{x^2 + 2x - 8} dx =$

(A) $\ln|x^2 + 2x - 8| + C.$ (B) $6 \ln|x^2 + 2x - 8| + C.$

(C) $\ln|x + 4| - \ln|x - 2| + C.$

(D) $\dfrac{1}{6} \ln\left|\dfrac{x - 2}{x + 4}\right| + C.$

(E) $\ln|x - 2| - \ln|x + 4| + C.$

12. What is the best first step in evaluating $\int_0^4 \dfrac{x^2 + x + 3}{2x + 1} dx?$

(A) Form a partial fraction decomposition.

(B) Let $u = 2x + 1.$

(C) Let $u = x^2 + x + 3.$

(D) Use integration by parts.

(E) Use long division.

Section 1 Part B, Multiple Choice, Technology Allowed

13. Let $f(x) = 1 - \dfrac{\sqrt{3}}{\sqrt{4 - x^2}}.$ Find the area of the region bounded by the curve $y = f(x)$ and the x-axis.

(A) 0.814   (B) 0.186   (C) 1.286

(D) 0.423   (E) 0.093

14. Let $F(x)$ be an antiderivative of $f(x) = \ln x,$ where $F(1) = -1.$ The value of $\int_1^e F(x) \, dx$ is

(A) 2.097.   (B) -1.097.

(C) 1.000.   (D) -2.437.

(E) -1.552.

Section 2 Part A, Free Response, Technology Allowed

1. Let $f(x) = \sin x^2.$

a. The function f has infinitely many local maxima with a positive x-coordinate; one of these has the smallest x-coordinate. Find the value of the x-coordinate of that point.

b. Find the area of the region bounded by the graph of f and the x-axis on the interval $[0, a]$, where a is the smallest positive zero of $f.$

c. Suppose $\rho(x)$, measured in units of kilograms per meter, represents the linear density function for a thin metal rod on the interval $[a, b]$, where x is measured in meters. The *total moment* for the rod, used to compute its center of mass, is given by

$$M = \int_a^b x\rho(x)\, dx.$$

Find the total moment M for a rod whose density function is $\rho(x) = \sin x^2$ on the interval $[0, 1]$. Report your answer with correct units.

d. Write, but do not evaluate, a definite integral for the arc length of f on the interval $[0, \pi]$.

2. Consider the function $f(x) = \dfrac{1}{\sqrt{1 + x^2}}$.

a. The finite region R is bounded by the curve $y = f(x)$ and the line $y = \dfrac{1}{\sqrt{2}}$. Find the volume of the solid generated when R is revolved about the x-axis.

b. Given the fact that $\displaystyle\int \dfrac{dx}{\sqrt{1 + x^2}} = \ln\left|\sqrt{1 + x^2} + x\right| + C$, find the value of a such that the area bounded by $y = f(x)$ and the x-axis on the interval $[0, a]$ is equal to 1.

Section 2 Part B, Free Response, No Technology

3. Let $f(x) = e^{x^2 - 9}$.

a. Find $f'(x)$.

b. Determine the equation of the line tangent to the graph of f at $x = 3$.

c. Define the function $g(x) = \begin{cases} f(x) & \text{if } x \le 3 \\ 2x - 5 & \text{if } x > 3. \end{cases}$
Use the definition of continuity to determine whether g is continuous at $x = 3$.

d. Evaluate $\int_0^3 x e^{x^2 - 9}\, dx$.

4. Let $f(x) = x^2 e^{-x}$.

a. For what value(s) of x does f have a local minimum?

b. On what interval(s) is f increasing?

c. Evaluate $\int_0^\infty f(x)\, dx$.

d. For what constant k is the function $g(x) = \begin{cases} f(x) & \text{if } x \le 1 \\ e^{kx} & \text{if } x > 1 \end{cases}$ continuous at $x = 1$?

5. Suppose $f'(x) = (x - 6)e^x$ and $f(0) = 1$.

a. Find the equation of the line tangent to the graph of f at $x = 0$.

b. Determine where the graph of f is both increasing and concave up.

c. Determine the absolute minimum value of f. Justify your answer.

Chapter 7 Guided Projects

Applications of the material in this chapter and related topics can be found in the following Guided Projects. For additional information, see the Preface.

- How long will your iPod last?

- Mercator projections

Differential Equations

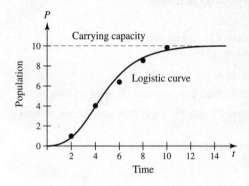

The first mathematical models of population growth predicted unbounded (exponential) growth. However, the English minister, biologist, and economist Thomas Malthus realized in the 19th century that no population grows without bound forever. Eventually, factors such as lack of resources or shortage of space limit growth. A population model that features self-regulating or limited growth is the *logistic model*. Its many variations are used to describe and make predictions about everything from cell cultures to human populations to the spread of rumors. In the early stages of logistic growth, populations grow exponentially as if there were no limiting factors. However, the growth rate steadily decreases and the population approaches a steady state called the *carrying capacity*. Often the model can be "tuned" by fitting it to actual data. The important fact for our purposes is that the logistic model takes the form of a differential equation—the topic of this chapter.

Chapter Preview
If you wanted to demonstrate the utility of mathematics to a skeptic a good topic would be *differential equations*. This vast subject lies at the heart of mathematical modeling and is used in engineering, physics, chemistry, biology, geophysics, economics and finance, and health sciences. Its many applications include analyzing the stability of buildings and bridges, simulating planet and satellite orbits, describing chemical reactions, modeling populations and epidemics, predicting weather, locating oil reserves, forecasting financial markets, producing medical images, and simulating drug kinetics. Differential equations rely heavily on calculus and are usually studied in advanced courses that follow calculus. Nevertheless, you have now seen enough calculus to take a brief tour of this rich and powerful subject.

8.1 Basic Ideas

If you studied Section 5.1 or 6.1, then you saw a preview of differential equations. Given the derivative of a function (for example, a velocity or some other rate of change), these two sections showed how to find the function itself by integration. This process amounts to solving a differential equation.

More generally, a differential equation involves an unknown function y and its derivatives. The unknown in a differential equation is not a number (as in an algebraic equation), but rather a *function*. Examples of differential equations are

> Common choices for the independent variable in a differential equation are x and t, with t being used for time-dependent problems.

$$\text{(A) } \frac{d^2y}{dx^2} + 16y = 0, \quad \text{(B) } \frac{dy}{dx} + 4y = \cos x, \quad \text{and} \quad \text{(C) } y'(t) = 0.1y(100 - y).$$

In each case, the goal is to find functions y that satisfy the equation. To be clear about what we mean by a solution, consider equation (A). If we substitute $y = \cos 4x$ and $y'' = -16 \cos 4x$ into this equation, we find that

$$\underbrace{-16 \cos 4x}_{y''} + \underbrace{16 \cos 4x}_{16y} = 0,$$

which implies that $y = \cos 4x$ is a solution of the equation. You should verify that $y = C \cos 4x$ is also a solution, for any real number C (as is $y = C \sin 4x$).

EXAMPLE 1 **Verifying solutions** Exponential growth processes (for example, cell populations and bank accounts) involve functions of the form $y = Ce^{kt}$, where $C > 0$ and $k > 0$ are real numbers.

a. Show by substitution that the exponential function $y = 10e^{2.5t}$ is a solution of the differential equation $y'(t) = 2.5y$.

b. Show by substitution that the function $y = Ce^{2.5t}$ is a solution of the same differential equation, for *any* constant C.

SOLUTION

a. We differentiate $y = 10e^{2.5t}$ to obtain $y'(t) = 2.5 \cdot 10e^{2.5t}$. Now observe that

$$y'(t) = \underbrace{2.5 \cdot 10e^{2.5t}}_{y'(t)} = 2.5 \cdot \underbrace{10e^{2.5t}}_{y} = 2.5y.$$

Therefore, the function $y = 10e^{2.5t}$ satisfies the equation $y'(t) = 2.5y$.

b. In the calculation of part (a), if 10 is replaced with an arbitrary constant C, we find that

$$y'(t) = \underbrace{2.5 \cdot Ce^{2.5t}}_{y'(t)} = 2.5 \cdot \underbrace{Ce^{2.5t}}_{y} = 2.5y.$$

The functions $y = Ce^{2.5t}$ also satisfy the equation, where C is an arbitrary constant.

Related Exercises 7–10◄

Let's discuss the terminology associated with differential equations. The **order** of a differential equation is the highest order that appears on a derivative in the equation. For example, the equations $y' + 4y = \cos x$ and $y' = 0.1y(100 - y)$ (equations B and C on p. 548) are first-order, and $y'' + 16y = 0$ (equation A on p. 548) is second-order.

    Linear differential equations (first- and second-order) have the form

> A *linear* differential equation cannot have terms such as y^2, yy', or $\sin y$, where y is the unknown function.

$$\underbrace{y'(x) + p(x)y(x) = f(x)}_{\text{First-order}} \quad \text{and} \quad \underbrace{y''(x) + p(x)y'(x) + q(x)y(x) = f(x),}_{\text{Second-order}}$$

where p, q, and f are given functions that depend only on the independent variable x. Of the equations on p. 548, (A) and (B) are linear, but (C) is **nonlinear** (because the right side contains y^2).

    A differential equation is often accompanied by **initial conditions** that specify the values of y, and possibly its derivatives, at a particular point. In general, an nth-order equation requires n initial conditions. A differential equation, together with the appropriate number of initial conditions, is called an **initial value problem**. The typical first-order initial value problem that we study in this chapter has the form

> The term *initial condition* originates with equations in which the independent variable is *time*. In such problems, the initial state of the system (for example, position and velocity) is specified at some initial time (often $t = 0$).

$$y'(t) = f(t, y) \quad \text{Differential equation}$$
$$y(0) = A, \quad \quad \text{Initial condition}$$

where A is given and f is a given expression that involves t and/or y.

EXAMPLE 2   Solution of an initial value problem Consider the differential equation in Example 1. Find the solution of the initial value problem

$$y'(t) = 2.5y \qquad \text{Differential equation}$$

$$y(0) = 3.2. \qquad \text{Initial condition}$$

SOLUTION By Example 1b, functions of the form $y = Ce^{2.5t}$ satisfy the differential equation $y'(t) = 2.5y$, where C is an arbitrary constant. We now use the initial condition $y(0) = 3.2$ to determine the constant C. Noting that $y(0) = Ce^{2.5 \cdot 0} = C$, the condition $y(0) = 3.2$ implies that $C = 3.2$.

Therefore, $y = 3.2e^{2.5t}$ is a solution of the initial value problem. Figure 8.1 shows the family of curves $y = Ce^{2.5t}$ for several different values of the constant C. It also shows the function $y = 3.2e^{2.5t}$ highlighted in red, which is the solution of the initial value problem.

Related Exercises 11–14 ◄

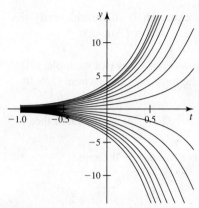

FIGURE 8.1

> ➤ A technicality: To keep matters simple, we use *general solution* to refer to the largest family of solutions of a differential equation. Some nonlinear equations may have isolated solutions that are not included in this family of solutions. For example, you can check that for real numbers C, the functions $y = 1/(C - t)$ satisfy the equation $y'(t) = y^2$. Therefore, we call $y = 1/(C - t)$ the general solution, even though it does not include $y = 0$, which is also a solution.

Solving a first-order differential equation requires integration—you must "undo" the derivative $y'(t)$ to find $y(t)$. One integration introduces one arbitrary constant, which generates an entire family of solutions. Solving an nth-order differential equation typically requires n integrations, which introduce n arbitrary constants; again, the result is a family of solutions. For any differential equation, the largest family of solutions generated by the arbitrary constants is called the **general solution**. For instance in Example 1, we found the general solution $y = Ce^{2.5t}$.

EXAMPLE 3   General solutions Find the general solution of the following differential equations. Notice that in these equations, the unknown function y does not appear on the right side of the equation.

a. $y'(t) = 5 \cos t + 6 \sin 3t$ \qquad\qquad **b.** $y''(t) = 10t^3 - 144t^7 + 12t$

SOLUTION

a. The solution of the equation consists of the antiderivatives of $5 \cos t + 6 \sin 3t$. Taking the indefinite integral of both sides of the equation, we have

$$\int y'(t)\, dt = \int (5 \cos t + 6 \sin 3t)\, dt \qquad \text{Integrate both sides with respect to } t.$$

$$y = 5 \sin t - 2 \cos 3t + C, \qquad \text{Evaluate integrals.}$$

where C is an arbitrary constant. The function $y = 5 \sin t - 2 \cos 3t + C$ is the general solution of the differential equation.

> ➤ When integrating both sides of an equation, a constant of integration needs to be included only once.

b. In this second-order equation, we are given $y''(t)$ in terms of the independent variable t. Taking the indefinite integral of both sides of the equation yields

$$\int y''(t)\, dt = \int (10t^3 - 144t^7 + 12t)\, dt \qquad \text{Integrate both sides with respect to } t.$$

$$y'(t) = \frac{5}{2}t^4 - 18t^8 + 6t^2 + C_1. \qquad \text{Evaluate integrals.}$$

Integrating once gives $y'(t)$ and introduces an arbitrary constant that we call C_1. We now integrate again:

$$\int y'(t)\, dt = \int \left(\frac{5}{2}t^4 - 18t^8 + 6t^2 + C_1\right) dt \qquad \text{Integrate both sides with respect to } t.$$

$$y = \frac{1}{2}t^5 - 2t^9 + 2t^3 + C_1 t + C_2. \qquad \text{Evaluate integrals.}$$

QUICK CHECK 1 What are the orders of the equations in Example 3? Are they linear or nonlinear?◄

This function, which involves two arbitrary constants, is the general solution of the differential equation.

Related Exercises 15–22◄

We now consider an initial value problem in which we first find the general solution and then satisfy an initial condition.

EXAMPLE 4   **An initial value problem** Solve the initial value problem

$$y'(t) = 10e^{-t/2}, \quad y(0) = 4, \text{ for } t \ge 0.$$

SOLUTION The general solution is found by taking the indefinite integral of both sides of the differential equation with respect to t:

$$\int y'(t)\, dt = \int 10e^{-t/2}\, dt \qquad \text{Integrate both sides with respect to } t.$$

$$y = -20e^{-t/2} + C. \qquad \text{Evaluate integrals.}$$

We have found the general solution, which involves one arbitrary constant. To determine its value, we use the initial condition by substituting $t = 0$ and $y = 4$ into the general solution:

$$\underbrace{y(0)}_{4} = -20e^{-0/2} + C = -20 + C,$$

> If an initial value problem represents a system that evolves in time (for example, a population or a trajectory), then the initial condition $y(0) = A$ gives the initial state of the system. In such cases, the solution is usually graphed only for $t \ge 0$. More generally, if a specific interval of interest is not specified, the solution is customarily represented on the domain of the solution; that is, the initial condition may not appear at an endpoint of the solution curve.

which implies that $4 = -20 + C$ or $C = 24$. Therefore, the solution of the initial value problem is $y = -20e^{-t/2} + 24$ (Figure 8.2). You should check that this function satisfies both the differential equation and the initial condition.

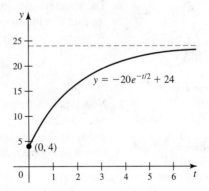

QUICK CHECK 2 What is the solution of the initial value problem in Example 4 with the initial condition $y(0) = 16$?◄

FIGURE 8.2

Related Exercises 23–28◄

Differential Equations in Action

We close this section with two examples of differential equations that are used to model particular physical systems. In Example 7 of Section 5.1, we investigated one-dimensional motion in a gravitational field. It is useful to revisit this problem using the language of differential equations.

EXAMPLE 5 **Motion in a gravitational field** A stone is launched vertically upward with a velocity of v_0 from a point s_0 meters above the ground, where $v_0 > 0$ and $s_0 \geq 0$. Assume that the stone is launched at time $t = 0$ and that $s(t)$ is the position of the stone at time $t \geq 0$ (the positive s-axis points in the upward direction). By Newton's Second Law of Motion, assuming no air resistance, the position of the stone is governed by the differential equation $s''(t) = -g$, where $g = 9.8 \text{ m/s}^2$ is the acceleration due to gravity (in the downward direction).

> According to Newton's Second Law, the mass of an object multiplied by its acceleration equals the sum of the external forces acting on the object at all times: $ma = F$.

a. Find the position $s(t)$ of the stone for all times at which the stone is above the ground.

b. At what time does the stone reach its highest point and what is its height above the ground?

c. Does the stone go higher if it is launched at $v(0) = v_0 = 39.2 \text{ m/s}$ from the ground ($s_0 = 0$) or at $v_0 = 19.6 \text{ m/s}$ from a height of $s_0 = 50$ m?

SOLUTION

> To find the time at which the stone reaches its highest point, we could also locate the local maximum of the position function, which requires solving $s'(t) = v(t) = 0$.

a. Integrating both sides of the differential equation $s''(t) = -9.8$ gives the velocity $v(t)$:

$$\int s''(t)\, dt = -\int 9.8\, dt \qquad \text{Integrate both sides.}$$

$$s'(t) = v(t) = -9.8t + C_1. \quad \text{Evaluate integrals.}$$

To evaluate the constant C_1, we use the initial condition $v(0) = v_0$, finding that $v(0) = -9.8 \cdot 0 + C_1 = C_1 = v_0$. Therefore, $C_1 = v_0$ and the velocity is $v = s'(t) = -9.8t + v_0$.

Integrating both sides of this velocity equation gives the position function:

$$\int s'(t)\, dt = \int (-9.8t + v_0)\, dt \quad \text{Integrate both sides.}$$

$$s = -4.9t^2 + v_0 t + C_2. \quad \text{Evaluate integrals.}$$

We now use the initial condition $s(0) = s_0$ to evaluate C_2, finding that

$$s(0) = -4.9 \cdot 0^2 + v_0 \cdot 0 + C_2 = C_2 = s_0.$$

Therefore, $C_2 = s_0$ and the position function is $s = -4.9t^2 + v_0 t + s_0$, where v_0 and s_0 are given. This function is valid while the stone is in flight. Notice that we have solved an initial value problem for the position of the stone.

b. The stone reaches its highest point when $v(t) = 0$. Solving $v(t) = -9.8t + v_0 = 0$, we find that the stone reaches its highest point when $t = v_0/9.8$, measured in seconds. So the position at the highest point is

$$s_{\max} = s\left(\frac{v_0}{9.8}\right) = -4.9\left(\frac{v_0}{9.8}\right)^2 + v_0\left(\frac{v_0}{9.8}\right) + s_0 = \frac{v_0^2}{19.6} + s_0.$$

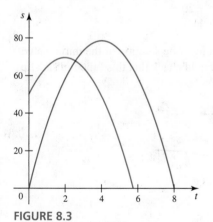

FIGURE 8.3

> The curves in Figure 8.3 are not the trajectories of the stones. The motion is one-dimensional because the stones travel along a vertical line.

c. Now it is a matter of substituting the given values of s_0 and v_0. In the first case, with $v_0 = 39.2$ and $s_0 = 0$, we have $s_{\max} = 78.4$ m. In the second case, with $v_0 = 19.6$ and $s_0 = 50$, we have $s_{\max} = 69.6$ m. The position functions in the two cases are shown in Figure 8.3. We see that the stone goes higher with $v_0 = 39.2$ and $s_0 = 0$.

Related Exercises 29–30 ◄

QUICK CHECK 3 In Example 5, find the highest point of the stone if it is launched upward at 9.8 m/s from an initial height of 100 m. ◄

> Evangelista Torricelli was an Italian mathematician and physicist who lived from 1608 to 1647. He is credited with inventing the barometer.

EXAMPLE 6 **Flow from a tank** Imagine a large cylindrical tank with cross-sectional area A. The bottom of the tank has a circular drain with cross-sectional area a. Assume the tank is initially filled with water to a height $h(0) = H$ (Figure 8.4). According to Torricelli's law, the height of the water as it flows out of the tank is described by the differential equation

$$h'(t) = -k\sqrt{h}, \quad \text{where } t \geq 0, k = \frac{a}{A}\sqrt{2g},$$

and $g = 9.8 \text{ m/s}^2$ is the acceleration due to gravity.

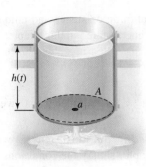

FIGURE 8.4

a. According to the differential equation, is h an increasing or decreasing function of t, for $t \geq 0$?

b. Verify by substitution that the solution of the initial value problem is

$$h = \left(\sqrt{H} - \frac{kt}{2} \right)^2.$$

c. Graph the solution for $H = 1.44$ m, $A = 1$ m^2, and $a = 0.05$ m^2.

d. After how many seconds is the tank in part (c) empty?

SOLUTION

a. Because $k > 0$, the differential equation implies that $h'(t) < 0$, for $t \geq 0$. Therefore, the height of the water decreases in time, consistent with the fact that the tank is being drained.

b. We first check the initial condition. Substituting $t = 0$ into the proposed solution, we see that

$$h(0) = \left(\sqrt{H} - \frac{k \cdot 0}{2} \right)^2 = (\sqrt{H})^2 = H.$$

Differentiating the proposed solution, we have

$$h'(t) = 2 \underbrace{\left(\sqrt{H} - \frac{kt}{2} \right)}_{\sqrt{h}} \left(-\frac{k}{2} \right) = -k\sqrt{h}.$$

Therefore, h satisfies the initial condition and the differential equation.

c. With the given values of the parameters,

$$k = \frac{a}{A} \sqrt{2g} = \frac{0.05 \text{ m}^2}{1 \text{ m}^2} \sqrt{2 \cdot 9.8 \text{ m/s}^2} \approx 0.22 \text{ m}^{1/2}/\text{s},$$

and the solution becomes

$$h = \left(\sqrt{H} - \frac{kt}{2} \right)^2 \approx (\sqrt{1.44} - 0.11t)^2 = (1.2 - 0.11t)^2.$$

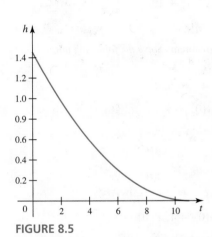

FIGURE 8.5

The graph of the solution (Figure 8.5) shows the height of the water decreasing from $h(0) = 1.44$ to zero at $t \approx 11$ s.

d. Solving the equation

$$h = (1.2 - 0.11t)^2 = 0,$$

we find that the tank is empty at $t \approx 10.9$ s.

Related Exercises 31–32 ◄

QUICK CHECK 4 In Example 6, if the height function were given by $h = (4.2 - 0.14t)^2$, at what time would the tank be empty? ◄

Final Note   In this section, we found solutions to initial value problems without worrying about whether there might be other solutions. Once we find a solution to an initial value problem, how can we be sure there aren't other solutions? More generally, given a particular initial value problem, how do we know whether a solution exists and whether it is unique?

These theoretical questions have answers, and they are provided by powerful *existence and uniqueness theorems*. These theorems and their proofs are quite technical and are handled in advanced courses. Here is an informal statement of an existence and unique-ness theorem for a particular class of initial value problems encountered in this chapter:

The solution of the general first-order initial value problem

$$y'(t) = f(t, y), y(a) = A$$

exists and is unique in some region that contains the point (a, A) provided f is a "well-behaved" function in that region.

The technical challenges arise in defining *well-behaved* in the most general way possible. The initial value problems we consider in this chapter satisfy the conditions of this theorem and can be assumed to have unique solutions.

SECTION 8.1 EXERCISES

Review Questions

1. What is the order of $y''(t) + 9y(t) = 10$?

2. Is $y''(t) + 9y(t) = 10$ linear or nonlinear?

3. How many arbitrary constants appear in the general solution of $y''(t) + 9y(t) = 10$?

4. If the general solution of a differential equation is $y = Ce^{-3t} + 10$, then what function satisfies the initial condition $y(0) = 5$?

5. Does the function $y = 2t$ satisfy the differential equation $y'''(t) + y'(t) = 2$?

6. Does the function $y = 6e^{-3t}$ satisfy the initial value problem $y'(t) - 3y(t) = 0, y(0) = 6$?

Basic Skills

7–10. Verifying solutions *Verify that the given function y is a solution of the differential equation that follows it. Assume that C is an arbitrary constant.*

7. $y = Ce^{-5t}$; $y'(t) + 5y = 0$

8. $y = Ct^{-3}$; $ty'(t) + 3y = 0$

9. $y = C_1 \sin 4t + C_2 \cos 4t$; $y''(t) + 16y = 0$

10. $y = C_1 e^{-x} + C_2 e^x$; $y''(x) - y = 0$

11–14. Verifying solutions of initial value problems *Verify that the given function y is a solution of the initial value problem that follows it.*

11. $y = 16e^{2t} - 10$; $y'(t) - 2y = 20, y(0) = 6$

12. $y = 8t^6 - 3$; $ty'(t) - 6y = 18, y(1) = 5$

13. $y = -3 \cos 3t$; $y''(t) + 9y = 0, y(0) = -3, y'(0) = 0$

14. $y = \frac{1}{4}(e^{2x} - e^{-2x})$; $y''(x) - 4y = 0, y(0) = 0, y'(0) = 1$

15–22. Finding general solutions *Find the general solution of each differential equation. Use $C, C_1, C_2, \ldots$ to denote arbitrary constants.*

15. $y'(t) = 3 + e^{-2t}$

16. $y'(t) = 12t^5 - 20t^4 + 2 - 6t^{-2}$

17. $\dfrac{dy}{dx} = 4 \tan 2x - 3 \cos x$

18. $p'(x) = \dfrac{e^x}{1 + e^x}$

19. $y''(t) = 60t^4 - 4 + 12t^{-3}$

20. $y''(t) = 15e^{3t} + \sin 4t$

21. $u''(x) = 55x^9 + 36x^7 - 21x^5 + 10x^{-3}$

22. $v''(x) = xe^x$

23–28. Solving initial value problems *Solve the following initial value problems.*

23. $y'(t) = 1 + e^t; y(0) = 4$

24. $y'(t) = \sin t + \cos 2t; y(0) = 4$

25. $\dfrac{dy}{dx} = 3x^2 - 3x^{-4}; y(1) = 0$

26. $y'(x) = 4 \sec^2 2x; y(0) = 8$

27. $y''(t) = 12t - 20t^3; y(0) = 1, y'(0) = 0$

28. $u''(x) = 4e^{2x} - 8e^{-2x}; u(0) = 1, u'(0) = 3$

29–30. Motion in a gravitational field *An object is fired vertically upward with an initial velocity $v(0) = v_0$ from an initial position $s(0) = s_0$.*

a. *For the following values of v_0 and s_0, find the position and velocity functions for all times at which the object is above the ground.*

b. *Find the time at which the highest point of the trajectory is reached and the height of the object at that time.*

29. $v_0 = 29.4 \text{ m/s}, s_0 = 30 \text{ m}$

30. $v_0 = 49 \text{ m/s}, s_0 = 60 \text{ m}$

31–32. Draining tanks *Consider the tank problem in Example 6. For the following parameter values, find the water height function. Then determine the approximate time at which the tank is first empty and graph the solution.*

31. $H = 1.96 \text{ m}, A = 1.5 \text{ m}^2, a = 0.3 \text{ m}^2$

32. $H = 2.25 \text{ m}, A = 2 \text{ m}^2, a = 0.5 \text{ m}^2$

Further Explorations

33. Explain why or why not Determine whether the following statements are true and give an explanation or counterexample.

    a. The general solution of the differential equation $y'(t) = 1$ is $y = t$.

    b. The differential equation $y''(t) - y(t)y'(t) = 0$ is second-order and linear.

    c. To find the solution of an initial value problem, you usually begin by finding a general solution of the differential equation.

34–37. General solutions *Find the general solution of the following differential equations.*

34. $y'(t) = t \sin t^2 + 1$

35. $u'(x) = \dfrac{2(x-1)}{x^2 + 4}$

36. $\dfrac{dv}{dt} = \dfrac{4}{t^2 - 4}$

37. $y''(x) = \dfrac{x}{(1 - x^2)^{3/2}}$

38–41. Solving initial value problems *Find the solution of the following initial value problems.*

38. $y'(t) = te^t, y(0) = -1$

39. $\dfrac{du}{dx} = \dfrac{1}{x^2 + 16} - 4, u(0) = 2$

40. $p'(x) = \dfrac{2}{x^2 + x}, p(1) = 0$

41. $y''(t) = \sin 2t, y(0) = 0, y'(0) = 1$

42–47. Verifying general solutions *Verify that the given function is a solution of the differential equation that follows it.*

42. $u = Ce^{1/(4t^4)}; \ u'(t) + \dfrac{1}{t^5} u = 0$

43. $u = C_1 e^t + C_2 te^t; \ u''(t) - 2u'(t) + u = 0$

44. $g = C_1 e^{-2x} + C_2 xe^{-2x} + 2; \ g''(x) + 4g'(x) + 4g = 8$

45. $u = C_1 t^2 + C_2 t^3; \ t^2 u''(t) - 4tu'(t) + 6u = 0$

46. $u = C_1 t^5 + C_2 t^{-4} - t^3; \ t^2 u''(t) - 20u = 14t^3$

47. $z = C_1 e^{-t} + C_2 e^{2t} + C_3 e^{-3t} - e^t;$
    $z'''(t) + 2z''(t) - 5z'(t) - 6z = 8e^t$

48. A second-order equation Consider the differential equation $y'' - k^2 y = 0$, where $k > 0$ is a real number.

    a. Verify by substitution that when $k = 1$, a solution of the equation is $y = C_1 e^t + C_2 e^{-t}$. You may assume that this function is the general solution.

    b. Verify by substitution that when $k = 2$, the general solution of the equation is $y = C_1 e^{2t} + C_2 e^{-2t}$.

    c. Give the general solution of the equation for an arbitrary constant $k > 0$ and verify your conjecture.

49. Another second-order equation Consider the differential equation $y''(t) + k^2 y = 0$, where k is a positive real number.

    a. Verify by substitution that when $k = 1$, a solution of the equation is $y = C_1 \sin t + C_2 \cos t$. You may assume that this function is the general solution.

    b. Verify by substitution that when $k = 2$, the general solution of the equation is $y = C_1 \sin 2t + C_2 \cos 2t$.

    c. Give the general solution of the equation for arbitrary $k > 0$ and verify your conjecture.

Applications

In this section, several models are presented and the solution of the associated differential equation is given. Later in the chapter, we present methods for solving these differential equations.

50. Drug infusion The delivery of a drug (such as an antibiotic) through an intravenous line may be modeled by the differential equation $m'(t) + km = I$, where $m(t)$ is the mass of the drug in the blood at time $t \geq 0$, k is a constant that describes the rate at which the drug is absorbed, and I is the infusion rate.

    a. Show by substitution that if the initial mass of drug in the blood is zero $(m(0) = 0)$, then the solution of the initial value problem is $m = \dfrac{I}{k}(1 - e^{-kt})$.

    b. Graph the solution for $I = 10$ mg/hr and $k = 0.05$ hr^{-1}.

    c. Evaluate $\lim_{t \to \infty} m(t)$, the steady-state drug level, and verify the result using the graph in part (b).

51. Logistic population growth Widely used models for population growth involve the *logistic equation* $P'(t) = rP\left(1 - \dfrac{P}{K}\right)$, where $P(t)$ is the population, for $t \geq 0$, and $r > 0$ and $K > 0$ are given constants.

    a. Verify by substitution that the general solution of the equation is $P = \dfrac{K}{1 + Ce^{-rt}}$, where C is an arbitrary constant.

    b. Find the value of C that corresponds to the initial condition $P(0) = 50$.

    c. Graph the solution for $P(0) = 50$, $r = 0.1$, and $K = 300$.

    d. Find $\lim_{t \to \infty} P(t)$ and check that the result is consistent with the graph in part (c).

52. Free fall One possible model that describes the free fall of an object in a gravitational field subject to air resistance uses the equation $v'(t) = g - bv$, where $v(t)$ is the velocity of the object for $t \geq 0$, $g = 9.8$ m/s^2 is the acceleration due to gravity, and $b > 0$ is a constant that involves the mass of the object and the air resistance.

    a. Verify by substitution that a solution of the equation, subject to the initial condition $v(0) = 0$, is $v = \dfrac{g}{b}(1 - e^{-bt})$.

    b. Graph the solution with $b = 0.1$ s^{-1}.

    c. Using the graph in part (c), estimate the terminal velocity, which is given by $\lim_{t \to \infty} v(t)$.

53. Chemical rate equations The reaction of certain chemical compounds can be modeled using a differential equation of the form $y'(t) = -ky^n(t)$, where $y(t)$ is the concentration of the compound for $t \geq 0$, $k > 0$ is a constant that determines the speed of the reaction, and n is a positive integer called the *order* of the reaction. Assume that the initial concentration of the compound is $y(0) = y_0 > 0$.

a. Consider a first-order reaction ($n = 1$) and show that the solution of the initial value problem is $y = y_0 e^{-kt}$.

b. Consider a second-order reaction ($n = 2$) and show that the solution of the initial value problem is $y = \dfrac{y_0}{y_0 kt + 1}$.

c. Let $y_0 = 1$ and $k = 0.1$. Graph the first-order and second-order solutions found in parts (a) and (b). Compare the two reactions.

T 54. Tumor growth The growth of cancer tumors may be modeled by the Gompertz growth equation. Let $M(t)$ be the mass of a tumor, for $t \geq 0$. The relevant initial value problem is

$$\frac{dM}{dt} = -rM \ln\left(\frac{M}{K}\right), \quad M(0) = M_0,$$

where r and K are positive constants and $0 < M_0 < K$.

a. Show by substitution that the solution of the initial value problem is

$$M = K\left(\frac{M_0}{K}\right)^{\exp(-rt)}.$$

b. Graph the solution for $M_0 = 100$ and $r = 0.05$.

c. For the solution in part (b), compute $\lim\limits_{t \to \infty} M(t)$, the limiting size of the tumor, and check for consistency with the graph.

55–56. Discovering properties of solutions *The following exercises show how information about solutions can be obtained without solving the differential equation.*

55. Consider the differential equation $y'(t) = y/2$ with the initial condition $y(0) = A$.

a. Show that if $A > 0$, then the solution of the initial value problem is increasing and that if $A < 0$, then the solution of the initial value problem is decreasing, for $t > 0$.

b. Show that if $A > 0$, then the graph of the solution is concave up and that if $A < 0$, then the graph of the solution is concave down, for $t > 0$.

c. Sketch the solution of the initial value problem with $A = 2$ (without finding the solution).

56. Consider the differential equation $y'(t) = 4y - 8$ with the initial condition $y(0) = 3$. This equation could model harvesting, where the coefficient 4 represents the natural growth rate of the product and the coefficient 8 is the harvesting rate.

a. Is the solution of the initial value problem increasing or decreasing, for $t > 0$?

b. Is the graph of the solution concave up or concave down, for $t > 0$?

c. Sketch the solution of the initial value problem (without finding the solution).

d. If the initial condition is $y(0) = 1$, is the resulting solution increasing or decreasing? Is it concave up or concave down?

e. Sketch the solution in part (d).

f. Assume the initial condition is instead $y(0) = A$. For what values of A is the solution of the initial value problem increasing?

QUICK CHECK   ANSWERS

1. The first equation is first-order and linear. The second equation is second-order and linear.   2. $y = -20e^{-t/2} + 36$
3. $s_{\max} = 104.9$ m   4. The tank is empty at $t = 30$ s. ◀

8.2 Slope Fields and Euler's Method

One goal of this chapter is to present methods for solving various kinds of differential equations. However, before taking up that task, we spend a few pages investigating a remarkable fact: It is possible to visualize and draw approximate graphs of the solutions of a differential equation without ever solving the equation. You might wonder how one can graph a function without knowing a formula for it. It turns out that the differential equation itself contains enough information to draw accurate graphs of its solutions. The tool that makes this visualization possible and allows us to explore the geometry of a differential equation is called the *slope field*.

Slope Fields

We now focus on first-order differential equations of the form $\dfrac{dy}{dt} = f(t, y)$, where the notation $f(t, y)$ means an expression involving the independent variable t and/or the unknown function y. Recall that f is given and the goal is to find the unknown function y. A solution of this equation can be graphed in the ty-plane. The differential equation simply says that at a point (t, y) of a solution curve, the slope of the curve is $y'(t) = f(t, y)$. A **slope field** is a picture that shows the slope of the solution at selected points of the ty-plane. The following examples illustrate how to draw slope fields.

EXAMPLE 1   Graphing a slope field Draw a slope field for the differential equation $y'(t) = \dfrac{1}{t^2 + 1}$ using the points whose t- and y-coordinates are $t = -2, -1, 0, 1, 2$ and $y = -2, -1, 0, 1, 2$.

SOLUTION The differential equation says that at a point (t, y) of a solution curve, the slope of the curve is $y'(t) = \dfrac{1}{t^2 + 1}$. Notice that in this case, the slope at the point (t, y) is independent of the value of y. For example, with $t = 0$ and for all values of y, the slope of the solution curve is $y'(0) = \dfrac{1}{0 + 1} = 1$.

To construct the slope field, we plot a short line segment with slope 1 at the points $(0, -2), (0, -1), (0, 0), (0, 1)$, and $(0, 2)$ (Figure 8.6a). The length of the line segment is not critical; however, its slope should indicate the slope given by the differential equation. Table 8.1 shows the slopes at the other specified points.

We now insert line segments with these slopes at the corresponding points. The result is the slope field shown in Figure 8.6a. More points could be included for a more detailed picture (Figure 8.6b).

> If the function f in the differential equation is even slightly complicated, drawing the slope field by hand is tedious. In this case, it's best to use a calculator or software.

Table 8.1

Slope at (t, y)	$t = -2$	$t = -1$	$t = 0$	$t = 1$	$t = 2$
$y = -2$	0.2	0.5	1	0.5	0.2
$y = -1$	0.2	0.5	1	0.5	0.2
$y = 0$	0.2	0.5	1	0.5	0.2
$y = 1$	0.2	0.5	1	0.5	0.2
$y = 2$	0.2	0.5	1	0.5	0.2

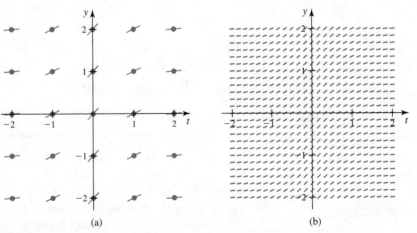

(a)   (b)

FIGURE 8.6

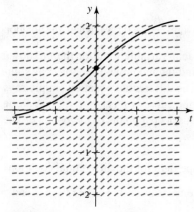

FIGURE 8.7

The beauty of a slope field, even when it is drawn without much detail, is that it allows us to visualize solutions. For example, the solution of the differential equation $y'(t) = \dfrac{1}{t^2 + 1}$ that passes through the point $(0, 1)$ is shown in Figure 8.7. We see that at every point of the solution curve, the slope of the curve matches the slope field.

Related Exercises 5–8◄

QUICK CHECK 1 In Example 1, do the slopes of the solution curves increase or decrease as t increases for $t \geq 0$? Explain. ◄

EXAMPLE 2   Another slope field

a. Draw a slope field for the differential equation $y'(t) = 2ty$ using the points whose t- and y-coordinates are $t = -1, -0.5, 0, 0.5, 1$ and $y = 0, 1, 2$.

b. Sketch the solution curve that passes through the point $(0, 1)$.

SOLUTION Notice that in this case, the slope field depends on both t and y.

a. Table 8.2 shows the slopes at the specified points. In each case, the slope is $f(t, y) = 2ty$.

Table 8.2

Slope at (t, y)	$t = -1$	$t = -0.5$	$t = 0$	$t = 0.5$	$t = 1$
$y = 0$	0	0	0	0	0
$y = 1$	-2	-1	0	1	2
$y = 2$	-4	-2	0	2	4

Notice that when $t < 0$ and $y > 0$, the solution curves have negative slopes. When $t > 0$ and $y > 0$, the solution curves have positive slopes. At points on the lines $t = 0$ and $y = 0$, the solution curves have slope 0. With $t > 0$ and $y > 0$, the slopes of a solution curve are positive and increase as t increases; we conclude that if y is a solution of the differential equation, then $\lim\limits_{t \to \infty} y(t) = \infty$. The slope field through the given points is shown in Figure 8.8a, with a more detailed version in Figure 8.8b.

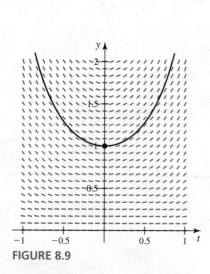

FIGURE 8.9

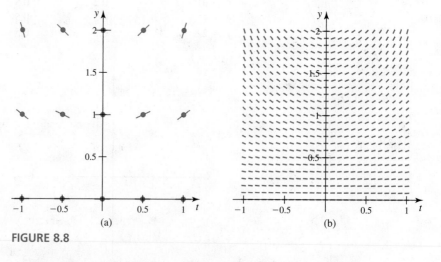

FIGURE 8.8

b. Using the slope field of Figure 8.8b, we can visualize the solution curve that passes through $(0, 1)$ and follows the slope field. The function corresponding to the curve decreases to the left of $(0, 1)$ (for $t < 0$) and increases without bound to the right of $(0, 1)$ (for $t > 0$) (Figure 8.9).

Related Exercises 9–12◄

QUICK CHECK 2 Describe the appearance of the slope field in Example 2 for $y < 0$ (compared to the slope field shown in Figure 8.8). ◄

Examples 1 and 2 suggest the following procedure for generating slope fields.

PROCEDURE **Sketching a Slope Field by Hand for $y'(t) = f(t, y)$**

A detailed slope field is not usually needed to obtain useful qualitative information about the solution curves.

1. Select a small number of points within the chosen window. Usually, a 4×4 or 5×5 grid of points suffices.

2. At each selected point (t, y), make a small line segment with slope $f(t, y)$. The length of the line segment is not important, but its slope should be reasonably accurate.

Examples 1 and 2 demonstrated how to construct a slope field and sketch a solution curve. The next three examples show how further analysis of the slope field provides detailed information about solutions.

EXAMPLE 3 **Slope field for a linear differential equation** Figure 8.10 shows the slope field for the equation $y'(t) = y - 2$, for $t \geq 0$ and $y \geq 0$. For what initial conditions at $t = 0$ are the solutions constant? Increasing? Decreasing?

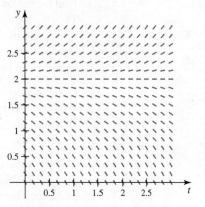

FIGURE 8.10

SOLUTION The slope field has horizontal line segments (slope zero) for $y = 2$. Therefore, $y'(t) = 0$ when $y = 2$, for all $t \geq 0$. These horizontal line segments correspond to a solution that is constant in time; that is, if the initial condition is $y(0) = 2$, then the solution is $y = 2$, for all $t \geq 0$.

We also see that the slope field has line segments with positive slopes above the line $y = 2$ (with increasing slopes as you move away from $y = 2$). Therefore, $y'(t) > 0$ when $y > 2$, and solutions are increasing in this region. Similarly, the slope field has line segments with negative slopes below the line $y = 2$ (with increasingly negative slopes as you move away from $y = 2$). Therefore, $y'(t) < 0$ when $y < 2$, and solutions are decreasing in this region.

Combining these observations, we see that if the initial condition satisfies $y(0) > 2$, the resulting solution is increasing, for $t \geq 0$. If the initial condition satisfies $y(0) < 2$, the resulting solution is decreasing, for $t \geq 0$. Figure 8.11 shows the solution curves with initial conditions $y(0) = 2.25$, $y(0) = 2$, and $y(0) = 1.75$.

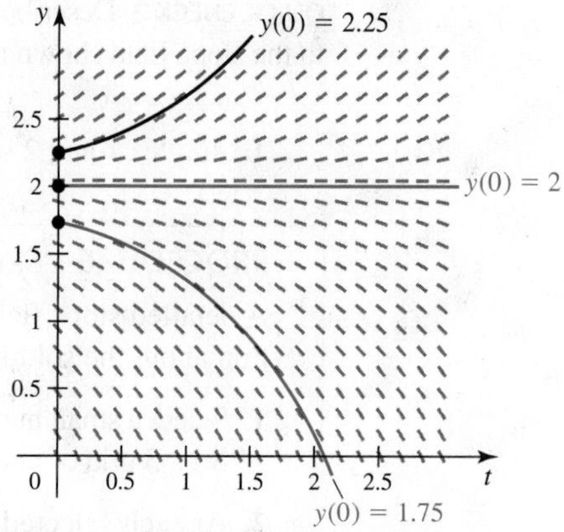

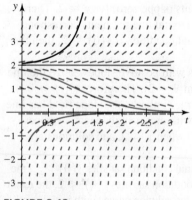

FIGURE 8.11

Related Exercises 13–24 ◄

QUICK CHECK 3 Assuming that solutions are unique (at most one solution curve passes through each point), explain why a solution curve cannot cross the line $y = 2$ in Example 3. ◄

> A differential equation in which the function f is independent of t is said to be **autonomous**.

For a differential equation of the form $y'(t) = f(y)$ (that is, the function f depends only on y), the following steps are useful in sketching the slope field. Notice that because the slope field depends only on y, it has the same slope on any given horizontal line. A detailed slope field is usually not required. You need to draw only a few line segments to indicate in which direction the solution is changing. Here is a procedure for analyzing a slope field in this special case.

PROCEDURE **Sketching a Slope Field by Hand for $y'(t) = f(y)$**

1. Find the values of y for which $f(y) = 0$. For example, suppose that $f(a) = 0$. Then we have $y'(t) = 0$ whenever $y = a$, and the slope field at all points (t, a) consists of horizontal line segments. If the initial condition is $y(0) = a$, then the solution is $y = a$, for all $t \geq 0$. Such a constant solution is called an **equilibrium solution**.

2. Find the values of y for which $f(y) > 0$. For example, suppose that $f(b) > 0$. Then $y'(t) > 0$ whenever $y = b$. The slope field at all points (t, b) has line segments with positive slopes and the solution is increasing at those points.

3. Find the values of y for which $f(y) < 0$. For example, suppose that $f(c) < 0$. Then $y'(t) < 0$ whenever $y = c$. The slope field at all points (t, c) has line segments with negative slopes and the solution is decreasing at those points.

EXAMPLE 4 **Slope field for a simple nonlinear equation** Consider the differential equation $y'(t) = y(y - 2)$, for $t \geq 0$.

a. For what initial conditions $y(0) = a$ is the resulting solution constant? Increasing? Decreasing?

b. Sketch the slope field for the equation.

SOLUTION

a. We follow the steps given in the procedure box.

1. Letting $f(y) = y(y - 2)$, we see that $f(y) = 0$ when $y = 0$ or $y = 2$. Therefore, the slope field has horizontal line segments when $y = 0$ and $y = 2$. As a result, the constant functions $y = 0$ and $y = 2$ are equilibrium solutions (Figure 8.12).

FIGURE 8.12

2. The solution of the inequality $f(y) = y(y - 2) > 0$ is $y < 0$ or $y > 2$. Therefore, below the line $y = 0$ and above the line $y = 2$, the slope field has positive slopes and the solutions are increasing in these regions.
3. The solution of the inequality $f(y) = y(y - 2) < 0$ is $0 < y < 2$. Therefore, between the lines $y = 0$ and $y = 2$, the slope field has negative slopes and the solutions are decreasing in this region.

b. The slope field is shown in Figure 8.12 with several representative solution curves.

Related Exercises 25–28◄

QUICK CHECK 4 In Example 4, is the solution to the equation increasing or decreasing for $t \geq 0$ if the initial condition is $y(0) = 2.01$? Is it increasing or decreasing for $t \geq 0$ if the initial condition is $y(1) = -1$?◄

EXAMPLE 5 **Slope field for the logistic equation** The logistic equation is commonly used to model populations with a *stable equilibrium* solution (called the *carrying capacity*). Consider the logistic equation

$$\frac{dP}{dt} = 0.1P\left(1 - \frac{P}{300}\right), \text{ for } t \geq 0.$$

a. Sketch the slope field of the equation.
b. Sketch solution curves corresponding to the initial conditions $P(0) = 50$, $P(0) = 150$, and $P(0) = 350$.
c. Find and interpret $\lim_{t \to \infty} P(t)$.
d. Show that the solution curve is concave down for $150 < P < 300$ and concave up for $0 < P < 150$ and $P > 300$.

SOLUTION

> The constant solutions $P = 0$ and $P = 300$ are equilibrium solutions. The solution $P = 0$ is an **unstable equilibrium** because nearby solution curves move away from $P = 0$. By contrast, the solution $P = 300$ is a **stable equilibrium** because nearby solution curves are attracted to $P = 300$.

a. We follow the steps in the procedure box for sketching the slope field. Because P represents a population, we assume that $P \geq 0$.

  1. Notice that $P'(t) = 0$ when $P = 0$ or $P = 300$. Therefore, if the initial population is either $P = 0$ or $P = 300$, then $P'(t) = 0$, for all $t \geq 0$, and the solution is constant. For this reason, we expect the slope field to have horizontal lines (with zero slope) at $P = 0$ and $P = 300$.
  2. The equation implies that $P'(t) > 0$ provided $0 < P < 300$. Therefore, the slope field has positive slopes and the solutions are increasing, for $t \geq 0$ and $0 < P < 300$.
  3. The equation also implies that $P'(t) < 0$ provided $P > 300$ (we assumed that $P \geq 0$). Therefore, the slope field has negative slopes and the solutions are decreasing, for $t \geq 0$ and $P > 300$.

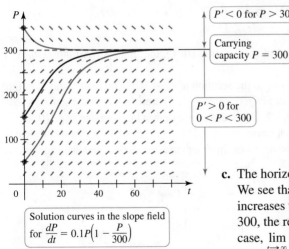

Solution curves in the slope field for $\frac{dP}{dt} = 0.1P\left(1 - \frac{P}{300}\right)$

FIGURE 8.13

$\boxed{P' < 0 \text{ for } P > 300}$

$\boxed{\text{Carrying capacity } P = 300}$

$\boxed{P' > 0 \text{ for } 0 < P < 300}$

b. Figure 8.13 shows the slope field with three solution curves corresponding to the three different initial conditions.

c. The horizontal line $P = 300$ corresponds to the carrying capacity of the population. We see that if the initial population is positive and less than 300, the resulting solution increases to the carrying capacity from below. If the initial population is greater than 300, the resulting solution decreases to the carrying capacity from above. In either case, $\lim_{t \to \infty} = P(t) = 300$.

d. We assume that the solution is differentiable at least twice. Differentiating both sides of the differential equation using the Chain Rule, we find that

$$P''(t) = \frac{d}{dt}\left(0.1P\left(1 - \frac{P}{300}\right)\right) = 0.1\frac{d}{dt}\left(P - \frac{1}{300}P^2\right), \text{ which implies that}$$

$$P''(t) = 0.1\left(P'(t) - \frac{1}{300} \cdot 2PP'(t)\right) = 0.1P'(t)\left(1 - \frac{P}{150}\right).$$

Three observations follow from this calculation.

- By part (a), $P'(t) > 0$ provided $0 < P < 300$. Therefore, if $0 < P < 150$, then $1 - \dfrac{P}{150} > 0$ and $P''(t) > 0$. It follows that the solution curve is concave up when $0 < P < 150$.

- If $150 < P < 300$, then again $P'(t) > 0$; but now $1 - \dfrac{P}{150} < 0$, which means that $P''(t) < 0$. Therefore, the solution curve is concave down when $150 < P < 300$.

- Finally, if $P > 300$, then $P'(t) < 0$ (by part (a)) and $1 - \dfrac{P}{150} < 0$, which implies that $P''(t) > 0$. In this case, the solution curve is concave up.

These conclusions are confirmed in Figure 8.13.

Related Exercises 29–32 ◄

QUICK CHECK 5 According to Figure 8.13, for what approximate value of P is the growth rate of the solution the greatest? ◄

Euler's Method

> Euler proposed his method for finding approximate solutions to differential equations 200 years before digital computers were invented.

As shown in previous examples, a slope field provides valuable qualitative information about the solutions of a differential equation *without solving the equation*. In addition, it turns out that slope fields are the basis for many computer-based methods for approximating solutions of a differential equation. The computer begins with the initial condition and advances the solution in small steps, always following the slope field at each time step. The simplest method that uses this idea is called *Euler's method*.

Consider the differential equation $y'(t) = f(t, y) = 2t - y$ subject to the initial condition $y(0) = 1$. Suppose we want to compute approximations to this solution at the equally spaced points

$$t_0 = 0, t_1 = 0.2, t_2 = 0.4, t_3 = 0.6, t_4 = 0.8, \text{ and } t_5 = 1.$$

The spacing between these points is called the **time step,** denoted Δt; in this case, we have chosen $\Delta t = 0.2$. Euler's method computes the approximations, which we denote $u_0, u_1, u_2, u_3, u_4,$ and u_5, where

$$u_0 = y(t_0) = y(0) = 1, \quad u_1 \approx y(t_1), \quad u_2 \approx y(t_2),$$
$$u_3 \approx y(t_3), \quad u_4 \approx y(t_4), \text{ and } u_5 \approx y(t_5).$$

Notice that because we are given the initial condition $(0, 1)$, the first approximation $u_0 = 1$ at $t_0 = 0$ is exact.

> If you look closely, you will see that Euler's method is an application of linear approximation. We assume that the solution is known at a point (t_k, u_k), and then find an approximate solution at the nearby point $(t_k + \Delta t, u_{k+1})$ using a tangent line with a known slope.

We now seek the approximation u_1 to the solution at $t_1 = 0.2$. The slope field says that the slope of the solution curve at $(0, u_0)$ is $f(0, 1) = -1$. Therefore, we take a step of length $\Delta t = 0.2$ in the t-direction with slope -1. Equivalently, we draw a line segment from $(0, u_0)$ to $(\Delta t, u_1)$ with slope -1, where u_1 must be determined. The geometry of the method is shown in Figure 8.14 for both positive and negative slopes. In either case, the slope of the line segment is

$$\text{slope} = f(0, u_0) = \frac{u_1 - u_0}{\Delta t}.$$

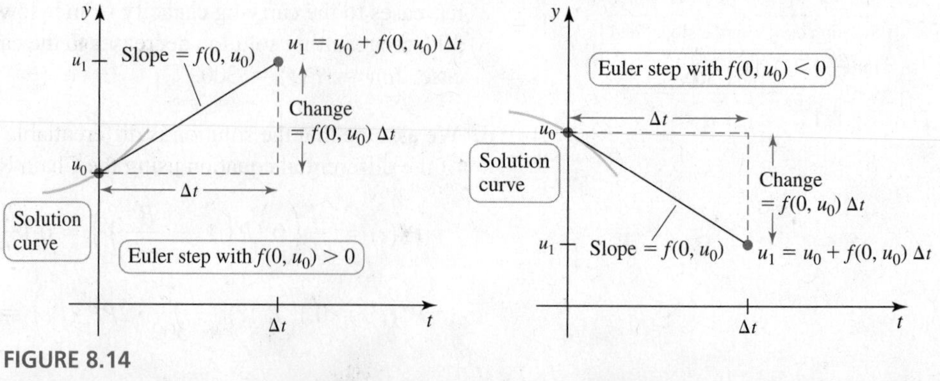

FIGURE 8.14

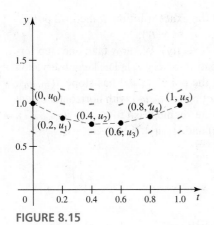

FIGURE 8.15

Solving this equation for u_1, we find that

$$u_1 = u_0 + \underbrace{f(0, u_0)\Delta t}_{\text{vertical change}}.$$

In other words, u_1 is found by starting at u_0 and adding the vertical change $f(0, u_0)\Delta t$. Therefore, the approximation to the solution at $t = t_1$ is

$$u_1 = u_0 + \underbrace{f(0, u_0)}_{} \underbrace{\Delta t}_{0.2} = 1 + \underbrace{f(0, 1)}_{-1} \cdot 0.2 = 0.8.$$

Euler's method consists of repeating this calculation, always using the current approximation to determine the next approximation (Figure 8.15). With $u_1 = 0.8$ as the approximation at $t_1 = 0.2$, we now compute the approximation u_2 at $t_2 = 0.4$. The slope field says that the slope of the solution curve at $(0.2, u_1)$ is $f(0.2, 0.8) = -0.4$. Therefore, we draw a line segment with slope -0.4 between $(0.2, u_1)$ and $(0.4, u_2)$, where u_2 must be determined. Arguing as before, we have

$$u_2 = u_1 + f(0.2, u_1) \underbrace{\Delta t}_{0.2} = 0.8 + \underbrace{f(0.2, 0.8)}_{-0.4} \cdot 0.2 = 0.72.$$

The next three Euler steps are also shown in Figure 8.15 and are computed as follows. The approximation to $y(0.6)$ is

$$u_3 = u_2 + f(0.4, u_2) \underbrace{\Delta t}_{0.2} = 0.72 + \underbrace{f(0.4, 0.72)}_{0.08} \cdot 0.2 = 0.736.$$

The approximation to $y(0.8)$ is

$$u_4 = u_3 + f(0.6, u_3) \underbrace{\Delta t}_{0.2} = 0.736 + \underbrace{f(0.6, 0.736)}_{0.464} \cdot 0.2 \approx 0.829.$$

Finally, the approximation to $y(1)$ is

$$u_5 = u_4 + f(0.8, u_4) \underbrace{\Delta t}_{0.2} = 0.829 + \underbrace{f(0.8, 0.829)}_{0.771} \cdot 0.2 \approx 0.983.$$

Table 8.3 shows the Euler approximations that we have computed. Before presenting more examples of Euler's method, let's give a general formulation of the method.

Table 8.3

k	t_k	u_k	Slope $= f(t_k, u_k)$
0	0	1	-1
1	0.2	0.8	-0.4
2	0.4	0.72	0.08
3	0.6	0.736	0.464
4	0.8	0.829	0.771
5	1	0.983	—

Related Exercises 33–36 ◀

Suppose we want to approximate the solution to the initial value problem $y'(t) = f(t, y)$, $y(0) = A$ on an interval $[0, T]$. We begin by dividing the interval $[0, T]$ into N time steps of equal length $\Delta t = \dfrac{T}{N}$. In so doing, we create a set of grid points (Figure 8.16)

$$t_0 = 0, t_1 = \Delta t, t_2 = 2\Delta t, \ldots, t_k = k\Delta t, \ldots, t_N = N\Delta t = T.$$

$$\Delta t = \frac{T}{N}$$

$t_0 = 0 \quad t_1 = \Delta t \qquad t_k = k\Delta t \qquad t_N = T$

FIGURE 8.16

▶ See Exercise 57 for setting up Euler's
method on a more general interval $[a, b]$.

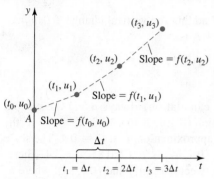

FIGURE 8.17

The goal is to compute a set of *approximations* to the exact solution at the grid points, which we denote u_k, for $k = 0, 1, 2, \ldots, N$; that is, $u_k \approx y(t_k)$.

The initial condition says that $u_0 = y(0) = A$ (exactly). We now take one step forward in time of length Δt and compute an approximation u_1 to $y(t_1)$. The key observation is that according to the slope field, the solution at the point (t_0, u_0) has slope $f(t_0, u_0)$. We obtain u_1 from u_0 by drawing a line segment starting at (t_0, u_0) with horizontal extent Δt and slope $f(t_0, u_0)$. The other endpoint of the line segment is (t_1, u_1) (Figure 8.17). Applying the slope formula to the two points (t_0, u_0) and (t_1, u_1), we have

$$f(t_0, u_0) = \frac{u_1 - u_0}{\Delta t}.$$

Solving for u_1, we find that

$$u_1 = u_0 + f(t_0, u_0)\Delta t.$$

This basic *Euler step* is now repeated for each time step until we reach $t = T$. That is, having computed u_1, we apply the same argument to obtain u_2. From u_2, we compute u_3. In general, u_{k+1} is computed from u_k, for $k = 0, 1, 2, \ldots, N - 1$. Hand calculations with Euler's method quickly become laborious. The method is usually carried out on a calculator, on a spreadsheet, or with a computer program. It is also included in many software packages.

PROCEDURE   Euler's Method for $y'(t) = f(t, y), y(0) = A$ on $[0, T]$

1. Choose either a time step Δt or a positive integer N such that $\Delta t = \dfrac{T}{N}$ and $t_k = k\Delta t$, for $k = 0, 1, 2, \ldots, N$.

2. Let $u_0 = y(0) = A$.

3. For $k = 0, 1, 2, \ldots, N - 1$, compute

$$u_{k+1} = u_k + f(t_k, u_k)\Delta t.$$

Each u_k is an approximation to the exact solution $y(t_k)$.

EXAMPLE 6   Using Euler's method Find an approximate solution to the initial value problem $y'(t) = t - \dfrac{y}{2}, y(0) = 1$, on the interval $[0, 2]$. Use the time steps $\Delta t = 0.2$ ($N = 10$) and $\Delta t = 0.1$ ($N = 20$). Which time step gives a better approximation to the exact solution, which is $y = 5e^{-t/2} + 2t - 4$?

SOLUTION With a time step of $\Delta t = 0.2$, the grid points on the interval $[0, 2]$ are

$$t_0 = 0.0, t_1 = 0.2, t_2 = 0.4, \ldots, t_{10} = 2.0.$$

We identify $f(t, y) = t - \dfrac{y}{2}$ and let u_k be the Euler approximation to $y(t_k)$. Euler's method takes the form

$$u_0 = y(0) = 1, \quad u_{k+1} = u_k + f(t_k, u_k)\Delta t = u_k + \left(t_k - \frac{u_k}{2}\right)\Delta t,$$

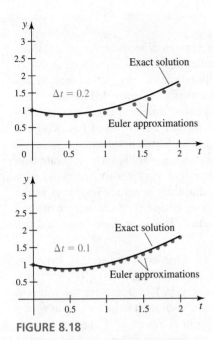

FIGURE 8.18

➤ Because Euler's method produces small errors at each time step, taking a large number of time steps may eventually lead to an unacceptable accumulation of errors. When more accuracy is needed, it may be best to use other methods that require more work per time step, but also give more accurate results.

where $k = 0, 1, 2, \ldots, 9$. For example, the value of the approximation u_1 is given by

$$u_1 = u_0 + f(t_0, u_0)\Delta t = u_0 + \left(t_0 - \frac{u_0}{2}\right)\Delta t = 1 + \left(0 - \frac{1}{2}\right) \cdot 0.2 = 0.900,$$

and the value of u_2 is given by

$$u_2 = u_1 + f(t_1, u_1)\Delta t = u_1 + \left(t_1 - \frac{u_1}{2}\right)\Delta t = 0.9 + \left(0.2 - \frac{0.9}{2}\right) \cdot 0.2 = 0.850.$$

A similar procedure is used with $\Delta t = 0.1$. In this case, $N = 20$ time steps are needed to cover the interval $[0, 2]$. The results of the two calculations are shown in Figure 8.18, where the exact solution appears as a solid curve and the Euler approximations are shown as points. From these graphs, it appears that the time step $\Delta t = 0.1$ gives better approximations to the solution.

A more detailed account of these calculations is given in Table 8.4, which shows the numerical values of the Euler approximations for $\Delta t = 0.2$ and $\Delta t = 0.1$. Notice that the approximations with $\Delta t = 0.1$ are tabulated at *every other* time step so that they may be compared to the $\Delta t = 0.2$ approximations.

Table 8.4

t_k	$u_k(\Delta t = 0.2)$	$u_k(\Delta t = 0.1)$	$e_k(\Delta t = 0.2)$	$e_k(\Delta t = 0.1)$
0.0	1.000	1.000	0.000	0.000
0.2	0.900	0.913	0.0242	0.0117
0.4	0.850	0.873	0.0437	0.0211
0.6	0.845	0.875	0.0591	0.0286
0.8	0.881	0.917	0.0711	0.0345
1.0	0.952	0.994	0.0802	0.0390
1.2	1.057	1.102	0.0869	0.0423
1.4	1.191	1.238	0.0914	0.0446
1.6	1.352	1.401	0.0943	0.0460
1.8	1.537	1.586	0.0957	0.0468
2.0	1.743	1.792	0.0960	0.0470

How accurate are these approximations? Although it does not generally happen in practice, we can solve this particular initial value problem exactly. (You can check that the solution is $y = 5e^{-t/2} + 2t - 4$.) We investigate the accuracy of the Euler approximations by computing the *error*, $e_k = |u_k - y(t_k)|$, at each grid point. The error simply measures the difference between the exact solution and the corresponding approximations. The last two columns of Table 8.4 show the errors associated with the approximations. We see that at every grid point, the approximations with $\Delta t = 0.1$ have errors with roughly half the magnitude of the errors with $\Delta t = 0.2$.

This pattern is typical of Euler's method. If we focus on one point in time, halving the time step roughly halves the error. However, nothing is free: Halving the time step also requires twice as many time steps and twice the amount of computational work to cover the same time interval.

Related Exercises 37–48◄

QUICK CHECK 6 Notice that the errors in Table 8.4 increase in time for both time steps. Give a possible explanation for this increase in the errors. ◄

Final Notes

1. Euler's method is the simplest of a collection of *numerical methods* for approximating solutions of differential equations (often studied in *numerical analysis* courses). As we have seen, Euler's method uses linear approximation; that is, the method follows the slope field using line segments. This idea works well provided the slope field varies smoothly and slowly. In less well-behaved cases, Euler's method may encounter difficulties. More robust and accurate methods do a better job of following the slope field (for example, by using parabolas or higher-degree polynomials instead of linear approximation). While these refined methods are generally more accurate than Euler's method, they often require more computational work per time step. As with Euler's method, all methods have the property that their accuracy improves as the time step decreases. The upshot is that there are often trade-offs in choosing a method to approximate the solution of a differential equation. However, Euler's method is a good place to start and may be adequate.

2. Additional insight into Euler's method is found by considering the second derivative of the solution. Suppose that y is a solution of the differential equation $y'(t) = f(t, y)$. Furthermore, assume that at a point t_0, we have $y'(t_0) > 0$ and on the interval $[t_0, t_0 + \Delta t]$, we have $y''(t) > 0$. In other words, the solution is increasing at t_0 and concave up on an interval to the right of t_0. As shown in Figure 8.19, the line tangent to the solution curve at t_0 lies below the curve itself. Because Euler's method uses the slope of the tangent line to compute the next approximation, the Euler approximation at $t_0 + \Delta t$ underestimates the value of the solution at $t_0 + \Delta t$. We leave it as an exercise (Exercise 62) to determine whether Euler's method overestimates or underestimates the solution in three other cases.

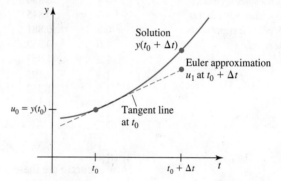

FIGURE 8.19

3. A useful connection can be made between Euler's method, Riemann sums, and the Fundamental Theorem of Calculus. Suppose we know the solution of the differential equation $y'(t) = f(t, y)$ at a point (t_0, y_0) and want to approximate the solution at $t = t_0 + \Delta t$. By the Fundamental Theorem, we know that

$$\int_{t_0}^{t_0 + \Delta t} y'(t)\,dt = y(t_0 + \Delta t) - y(t_0) \quad \text{or} \quad y(t_0 + \Delta t) = y(t_0) + \int_{t_0}^{t_0 + \Delta t} y'(t)\,dt.$$

Now we use the fact that $y'(t) = f(t, y)$ and approximate the integral with a left Riemann sum with $n = 1$ subinterval. The result is

$$\underbrace{y(t_0 + \Delta t)}_{\approx u_1} = \underbrace{y(t_0)}_{u_0} + \int_{t_0}^{t_0 + \Delta t} f(t, y(t))\, dt$$

$$\approx \underbrace{y(t_0)}_{u_0} + f(t_0, \underbrace{y(t_0)}_{u_0})\Delta t.$$

Letting $u_0 = y(t_0)$ and $u_1 \approx y(t_0 + \Delta t)$ be the approximation to the solution at $t = t_0 + \Delta t$, we obtain one step of Euler's method:

$$u_1 = u_0 + f(t_0, u_0)\Delta t.$$

SECTION 8.2 EXERCISES

Review Questions

1. Explain how to sketch the slope field of the equation $y'(t) = f(t, y)$, where f is given.

2. Consider the differential equation $y'(t) = t^2 - 3y^2$ and the solution curve that passes through the point $(3, 1)$. What is the slope of the curve at $(3, 1)$?

3. Consider the initial value problem $y'(t) = t^2 - 3y^2$, $y(3) = 1$. What is the approximation to $y(3.1)$ given by Euler's method with a time step of $\Delta t = 0.1$?

4. Give a geometric explanation of how Euler's method works.

Basic Skills

5–8. Slope fields *For the following differential equations, complete the table with values in the slope field. Then sketch the slope field using the computed slopes.*

5. $y'(t) = -2y$

	$t = 0$	$t = 1$	$t = 2$
$y = 0$			
$y = 1$			
$y = 2$			

6. $y'(t) = t - y$

	$t = 0$	$t = 1$	$t = 2$
$y = -2$			
$y = -1$			
$y = 0$			
$y = 1$			
$y = 2$			

7. $y'(t) = \dfrac{y}{t}$

	$t = 1$	$t = 2$	$t = 3$
$y = 0$			
$y = 1$			
$y = 2$			
$y = 3$			

8. $y'(t) = t(y - 1)$

	$t = -2$	$t = -1$	$t = 0$	$t = 1$	$t = 2$
$y = 0$					
$y = 1$					
$y = 2$					

9–12. Slope fields and solution curves *For the following differential equations, carry out these steps.*

a. *Complete the table with values in the slope field.*
b. *Sketch the slope field using the computed slopes.*
c. *Sketch the solution curve that passes through the given point using the window defined by the points in the table.*

9. $y'(t) = 2t - 4;\ (2, 1)$

	$t = 0$	$t = 1$	$t = 2$	$t = 3$
$y = 0$				
$y = 1$				
$y = 2$				

10. $y'(t) = -2y;\ (0, 2)$

	$t = 0$	$t = 1$	$t = 2$
$y = -1$			
$y = 0$			
$y = 1$			
$y = 2$			
$y = 3$			

11. $y'(t) = t - y;\ (0, -1)$

	$t = 0$	$t = 1$	$t = 2$	$t = 3$
$y = -1$				
$y = 0$				
$y = 1$				
$y = 2$				

12. $y'(t) = ty;\left(0, \dfrac{1}{2}\right)$

	$t = 0$	$t = 0.5$	$t = 1$	$t = 1.5$	$t = 2$
$y = 0$					
$y = 1$					
$y = 2$					

13–14. Slope fields *A differential equation and its slope field are shown in the following figures. Sketch a graph of the solution curve that passes through the given initial conditions.*

13. $y'(t) = \dfrac{t^2}{y^2 + 1}$, $y(0) = -2$
and $y(-2) = 0$

14. $y'(t) = \dfrac{\sin t}{y}$, $y(-2) = -2$
and $y(-2) = 2$

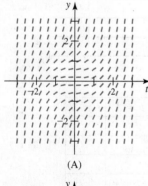
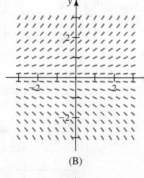

15. Matching slope fields Match equations a–d with slope fields A–D.

a. $y'(t) = \dfrac{t}{2}$

b. $y'(t) = \dfrac{y}{2}$

c. $y'(t) = \dfrac{t^2 + y^2}{2}$

d. $y'(t) = \dfrac{y}{t}$

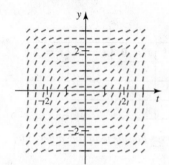

(A)

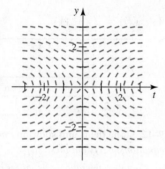

(B)

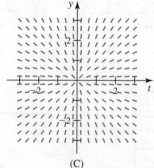

(C)

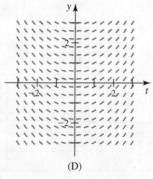

(D)

16. Identifying slope fields Which of the differential equations a–d corresponds to the following slope field? Explain your reasoning.

a. $y'(t) = 0.5(y + 1)(t - 1)$
b. $y'(t) = -0.5(y + 1)(t - 1)$
c. $y'(t) = 0.5(y - 1)(t + 1)$
d. $y'(t) = -0.5(y - 1)(t + 1)$

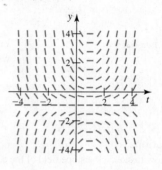

⊤ 17–19. Slope fields with technology

a. *Plot a slope field for the following differential equations. Use a graphing utility and the specified window.*

b. *Find the constant solutions.*

c. *Determine the initial conditions that produce solutions that are increasing, for $t \geq 0$.*

17. $y'(t) = 0.05(y + 1)^2(t - 1)^2$, $|t| \leq 3$ and $|y| \leq 3$

18. $y'(t) = (y - 1)\sin \pi t$, $0 \leq t \leq 2, 0 \leq y \leq 2$

19. $y'(t) = t(y - 1)$, $0 \leq t \leq 2, 0 \leq y \leq 2$

20–24. Sketching slope fields

a. *Sketch a slope field for the following differential equations using the window $[-2, 2] \times [-2, 2]$. A detailed slope field is not needed.*

b. *Sketch the solution curve that corresponds to the given initial condition.*

20. $y'(t) = y - 3, y(0) = 1$

21. $y'(t) = 4 - y, y(0) = -1$

22. $y'(t) = y(2 - y), y(0) = 1$

23. $y'(x) = \sin x, y(-2) = 2$

24. $y'(x) = \sin y, y(-2) = \dfrac{1}{2}$

25–28. Increasing and decreasing solutions *Consider the following differential equations.*

a. *Find the solutions that are constant, for $t \geq 0$ (the equilibrium solutions).*

b. *In what regions are solutions increasing? Decreasing?*

c. *Which initial conditions $y(0) = A$ lead to solutions that are increasing in time? Decreasing?*

d. *Sketch the slope field and verify that it is consistent with parts (a)–(c). A detailed slope field is not needed.*

25. $y'(t) = (y - 1)(1 + y)$

26. $y'(t) = (y - 2)(y + 1)$

27. $y'(t) = \cos y$, for $|y| \leq \pi$

28. $y'(t) = y(y + 3)(4 - y)$

29–32. Logistic equations *Consider the following logistic equations. In each case, sketch the slope field, draw the solution curve for each initial condition, and find the equilibrium solutions. A detailed slope field is not needed. Assume $t \geq 0$ and $P \geq 0$.*

29. $P'(t) = 0.05P\left(1 - \dfrac{P}{500}\right)$; $P(0) = 100, P(0) = 400,$
$P(0) = 700$

30. $P'(t) = 0.1P\left(1 - \dfrac{P}{1200}\right)$; $P(0) = 600, P(0) = 800,$
$P(0) = 1600$

31. $P'(t) = 0.02P\left(4 - \dfrac{P}{800}\right)$; $P(0) = 1600, P(0) = 2400,$
$P(0) = 4000$

32. $P'(t) = 0.05P - 0.001P^2$; $P(0) = 10, P(0) = 40,$
$P(0) = 80$

33–36. Euler's method tables *For each of the following initial value problems, complete the given table with Euler approximations.*

33. $y'(t) = f(t, y) = 1 - y, y(0) = 2$

k	t_k	u_k	Slope $= f(t_k, u_k)$
0	0		
1	0.5		
2	1		—

34. $y'(t) = f(t, y) = y - t, y(1) = -1$

k	t_k	u_k	Slope $= f(t_k, u_k)$
0	1		
1	1.25		
2	1.5		
3	1.75		—

35. $y'(t) = f(t, y) = ty, y(0) = 3$

k	t_k	u_k	Slope $= f(t_k, u_k)$
0	0		
1	0.2		
2	0.4		
3	0.6		—

36. $y'(t) = f(t, y) = \dfrac{2t}{y}, y(1) = 2$

k	t_k	u_k	Slope $= f(t_k, u_k)$
0	1		
1	1.2		
2	1.4		
3	1.6		
4	1.8		
5	2		—

37–40. Two steps of Euler's method *For the following initial value problems, compute the first two approximations u_1 and u_2 given by Euler's method using the given time step.*

37. $y'(t) = 2y, y(0) = 2$; $\Delta t = 0.5$

38. $y'(t) = -y, y(0) = -1$; $\Delta t = 0.2$

39. $y'(t) = 2 - y, y(0) = 1$; $\Delta t = 0.1$

40. $y'(t) = t + y, y(0) = 4$; $\Delta t = 0.5$

41–44. Errors in Euler's method *Consider the following initial value problems.*

a. *Find the approximations to $y(0.2)$ and $y(0.4)$ using Euler's method with time steps of $\Delta t = 0.2, 0.1, 0.05,$ and 0.025.*

b. *Using the exact solution given, compute the errors in the Euler approximations at $t = 0.2$ and $t = 0.4$.*

c. *Which time step results in the more accurate approximation? Explain your observations.*

d. *In general, how does halving the time step affect the error at $t = 0.2$ and $t = 0.4$?*

41. $y'(t) = -y, y(0) = 1$; $y = e^{-t}$

42. $y'(t) = \dfrac{y}{2}, y(0) = 2$; $y = 2e^{t/2}$

43. $y'(t) = 4 - y, y(0) = 3$; $y = 4 - e^{-t}$

44. $y'(t) = 2t + 1, y(0) = 0$; $y = t^2 + t$

45–48. Computing Euler approximations *Use a calculator or computer program to carry out the following steps.*

a. *Approximate the value of $y(T)$ using Euler's method with the given time step on the interval $[0, T]$.*

b. *Using the exact solution (also given), find the error in the approximation to $y(T)$ (only at the right endpoint of the time interval).*

c. *Repeating parts (a) and (b) using half the time step used in those calculations, again find an approximation to $y(T)$.*

d. *Compare the errors in the approximations to $y(T)$.*

45. $y'(t) = -2y, y(0) = 1$; $\Delta t = 0.2, T = 2$; $y = e^{-2t}$

46. $y'(t) = 6 - 2y, y(0) = -1$; $\Delta t = 0.2, T = 3$;
$y = 3 - 4e^{-2t}$

47. $y'(t) = t - y, y(0) = 4$; $\Delta t = 0.2, T = 4$;
$y = 5e^{-t} + t - 1$

48. $y'(t) = \dfrac{t}{y}, y(0) = 4$; $\Delta t = 0.1, T = 2$; $y = \sqrt{t^2 + 16}$

Further Explorations

49. Explain why or why not Determine whether the following statements are true and give an explanation or counterexample.

 a. A slope field allows you to visualize the solution of a differential equation, but it does not give exact values of the solution at particular points.

 b. Euler's method is used to compute exact values of the solution of an initial value problem.

50–55. Equilibrium solutions *A differential equation of the form $y'(t) = f(y)$ is said to be **autonomous** (the function f depends only on y). The constant function $y = y_0$ is an equilibrium solution of the equation provided $f(y_0) = 0$ (because then $y'(t) = 0$ and the solution remains constant for all t). Note that equilibrium solutions correspond to horizontal lines in the slope field. Note also that for autonomous equations, the slope field is independent of t. Carry out the following analysis on the given equations.*

 a. Find the equilibrium solutions.

 b. Sketch the slope field, for $t \geq 0$.

 c. Sketch the solution curve that corresponds to the initial condition $y(0) = 1$.

50. $y'(t) = 2y + 4$

51. $y'(t) = 6 - 2y$

52. $y'(t) = y(2 - y)$

53. $y'(t) = y(y - 3)$

54. $y'(t) = \sin y$

55. $y'(t) = y(y - 3)(y + 2)$

56. Slope field analysis Consider the first-order initial value problem $y'(t) = ay + b, y(0) = A$, for $t \geq 0$, where a, b, and A are real numbers.

 a. Explain why $y = -b/a$ is an equilibrium solution and corresponds to a horizontal line in the slope field.

 b. Draw a representative slope field in the case that $a > 0$. Show that if $A > -b/a$, then the solution increases for $t \geq 0$ and if $A < -b/a$, then the solution decreases for $t \geq 0$.

 c. Draw a representative slope field in the case that $a < 0$. Show that if $A > -b/a$, then the solution decreases for $t \geq 0$ and if $A < -b/a$, then the solution increases for $t \geq 0$.

57. Euler's method on more general grids Suppose the solution of the initial value problem $y'(t) = f(t, y), y(a) = A$ is to be approximated on the interval $[a, b]$.

 a. If $N + 1$ grid points are used (including the endpoints), what is the time step Δt?

 b. Write the first step of Euler's method to compute u_1.

 c. Write the general step of Euler's method that applies, for $k = 0, 1, \ldots, N - 1$.

Applications

58–60. Analyzing models *The following models were discussed in Section 8.1. In each case, carry out the indicated analysis using direction fields.*

58. Drug infusion The delivery of a drug (such as an antibiotic) through an intravenous line may be modeled by the differential equation $m'(t) + km = I$, where $m(t)$ is the mass of the drug in the blood at time $t \geq 0$, k is a constant that describes the rate at which the drug is absorbed, and I is the infusion rate. Let $I = 10 \text{ mg/hr}$ and $k = 0.05 \text{ hr}^{-1}$.

 a. Draw the slope field, for $0 \leq t \leq 100, 0 \leq y \leq 600$.

 b. What is the equilibrium solution?

 c. For what initial values $m(0) = A$ are solutions increasing? Decreasing?

59. Free fall A model that describes the free fall of an object in a gravitational field subject to air resistance uses the equation $v'(t) = g - bv$, where $v(t)$ is the velocity of the object, for $t \geq 0$, $g = 9.8 \text{ m/s}^2$ is the acceleration due to gravity, and $b > 0$ is a constant that involves the mass of the object and the air resistance. Let $b = 0.1 \text{ s}^{-1}$.

 a. Draw the slope field for $0 \leq t \leq 60, 0 \leq y \leq 150$.

 b. For what initial values $v(0) = A$ are solutions increasing? Decreasing?

 c. What is the equilibrium solution?

60. Chemical rate equations Consider the chemical rate equations $y'(t) = -ky$ (a first-order reaction) and $y'(t) = -ky^2$ (a second-order reaction), where $y(t)$ is the concentration of the compound for $t \geq 0$ and $k > 0$ is a constant that determines the speed of the reaction. Assume that the initial concentration of the compound is $y(0) = y_0 > 0$.

 a. Let $k = 0.3$ and make a sketch of the slope fields for both equations. What is the equilibrium solution in both cases?

 b. Suppose the initial concentration is $y(0) = 20$. Judging from the slope fields in part (a), which reaction reaches a concentration of $y = 5$ faster?

Additional Exercises

61. Convergence of Euler's method Suppose Euler's method is applied to the initial value problem $y'(t) = ay, y(0) = 1$, which has the exact solution $y = e^{at}$. For this exercise, let h denote the time step (rather than Δt). The grid points are then given by $t_k = kh$. We let u_k be the Euler approximation to the exact solution $y(t_k)$, for $k = 0, 1, 2, \ldots$.

 a. Show that Euler's method applied to this problem can be written $u_0 = 1, u_{k+1} = (1 + ah)u_k$, for $k = 0, 1, 2, \ldots$.

 b. Show by substitution that $u_k = (1 + ah)^k$ is a solution of the equations in part (a), for $k = 0, 1, 2, \ldots$.

 c. Recall from Section 4.7 that $\lim_{h \to 0} (1 + ah)^{1/h} = e^a$. Use this fact to show that as the time step goes to zero ($h \to 0$, with $t_k = kh$ fixed), the approximations given by Euler's method approach the exact solution of the initial value problem; that is, $\lim_{h \to 0} u_k = \lim_{h \to 0} (1 + ah)^k = y(t_k) = e^{at_k}$.

62. Concavity and Euler's method Suppose the solutions of the differential equation $y'(t) = f(t, y)$ are approximated using Euler's method. Suppose also that the solution is known at the point $t = t_0$. Does the Euler approximation to the solution at $t = t_0 + \Delta t$ overestimate or underestimate the solution in the following cases? Draw a figure to explain your answer.

 a. $y'(t_0) > 0$ and $y'' < 0$ on $[t_0, t_0 + \Delta t]$

 b. $y'(t_0) < 0$ and $y'' > 0$ on $[t_0, t_0 + \Delta t]$

 c. $y'(t_0) < 0$ and $y'' < 0$ on $[t_0, t_0 + \Delta t]$

63. Euler's method and linear approximation Consider the initial value problem $y'(t) = 2y - 4, y(0) = 3$.

    a. Suppose you want to approximate the solution at $t = 0.5$. What are the values of $y(0)$ and $y'(0)$?

    b. Use the linear approximation to y at $t = 0$ to estimate $y(0.5)$ given the values in part (a).

    c. Explain why the formula in part (b) is equivalent to one step of Euler's method using a time step of 0.5.

    d. More generally, consider the initial value problem $y'(t) = f(t, y), y(0) = A$, where f represents a formula involving t and y. Use linear approximation to estimate the solution $y(\Delta t)$ and explain why it is the same approximation given by Euler's method.

Technology Exercises

64–68. Creating slope fields *Carry out the following steps for each differential equation.*

    a. *Use a graphing utility or software to create the slope field with the window $[0, 4] \times [-4, 4]$.*

    b. *For each initial condition, describe the behavior of the solution as t increases. For example, does the solution increase without bound? Does it approach a constant value?*

64. $y' = y^2(2 - y); y(0) = 1, y(0) = -1$

65. $y' = (t - 1)(y - 1); y(0) = 2, y(0) = -3$

66. $y' = y^2(y^2 + y - 6); y(0) = 1, y(0) = -2, y(0) = 2.1$

67. $y' = (\sin 2t)(\sin y); y(0) = \pi, y(0) = 1, y(0) = -2$

68. $y' = 3t^2 e^{-y}; y(0) = 0, y(0) = 1, y(0) = -2$

69. Euler's method program Use software or write a program to approximate the solution to the initial value problem $y' = t - y, y(0) = 2$.

    a. Use time steps of $\Delta t = 0.1$ and $\Delta t = 0.05$ to compute approximate solutions on the interval $[0, 1]$.

    b. Use the exact solution of the problem $y = t + 3e^{-t} - 1$ to determine the error in the solutions of part (a) at $t = 1$.

    c. Comment on the relative accuracy of the two solutions.

    d. What would you do if you wanted to reduce the error in the approximations to $y(1)$ by a factor of 2? By a factor of 4?

QUICK CHECK ANSWERS

1. Decrease   **2.** A reflection across the horizontal axis   **3.** To cross the line $y = 2$, the solution must have a slope different than zero when $y = 2$. However, according to the slope field, a solution on the line $y = 2$ must have zero slope.   **4.** The solutions originating at both initial conditions are increasing.   **5.** The slope field is steepest when $P = 150$.   **6.** Each step of Euler's method introduces an error. With each successive step of the calculation, the errors could accumulate (or propagate). ◄

8.3 Separable Differential Equations

Sketching solutions of a differential equation using its slope field is a powerful technique, and it provides a wealth of information about the solutions. However, valuable as they are, slope fields do not produce the actual solutions of a differential equation. In this section, we examine methods that lead to the solutions of certain differential equations in terms of an algebraic expression (often called an *analytical solution*). The equations we consider are first-order and belong to a class called *separable equations*.

Method of Solution

The most general first-order differential equation has the form $y'(t) = f(t, y)$, where $f(t, y)$ is an expression that may involve both the independent variable t and the unknown function y. We have a *chance* of solving such an equation if it can be written in the form

$$g(y)\frac{dy}{dt} = h(t).$$

> If a differential equation has the form $y'(t) = f(t)$ (that is, the right side depends only on t), then solving the equation amounts to finding the antiderivatives of f, a problem discussed in Sections 5.1 and 8.1.

In this equation, the factor $g(y)$ involves only y, and $h(t)$ involves only t; that is, the variables have been separated. An equation that can be written in this form is said to be **separable**.

In general, we solve a separable differential equation by integrating both sides of the equation with respect to t:

$$\int g(y) \underbrace{\frac{dy}{dt} dt}_{dy} = \int h(t) \, dt \qquad \text{Integrate both sides with respect to } t.$$

$$\int g(y) \, dy = \int h(t) \, dt. \qquad \text{Change variables on left; } dy = \frac{dy}{dt} dt.$$

The change of variables on the left side of the equation leaves us with two integrals to evaluate, one with respect to y and one with respect to t. Finding a solution depends on evaluating these integrals (equivalently, finding antiderivatives).

QUICK CHECK 1 Which of the following equations are separable?

(A) $\dfrac{dy}{dt} = y + t$,   (B) $\dfrac{dy}{dt} = \dfrac{ty}{t+1}$,   and   (C) $\dfrac{dy}{dx} = e^{x+y}$ ◄

EXAMPLE 1   A separable equation Find a function that satisfies the following initial value problem.

$$\frac{dy}{dt} = y^2 e^{-t}, \quad y(0) = \frac{1}{2}, \quad \text{for } t \ge 0.$$

SOLUTION The equation is written in separable form by dividing both sides of the equation by y^2 to give $\dfrac{1}{y^2} \dfrac{dy}{dt} = e^{-t}$. We now integrate both sides of the equation with respect to t and evaluate the resulting integrals:

$$\int \underbrace{\frac{1}{y^2} \frac{dy}{dt} dt}_{dy} = \int e^{-t} \, dt$$

> In practice, the change of variable on the left side is often omitted, and we go directly to the second step, which is to integrate the left side with respect to y and the right side with respect to t.

> Notice that each integration produces a constant of integration. The two constants of integration may be combined in one constant.

$$\int \frac{dy}{y^2} = \int e^{-t} \, dt \qquad \text{Change variables on left side.}$$

$$-\frac{1}{y} = -e^{-t} + C. \qquad \text{Evaluate integrals.}$$

Solving for y gives the general solution

$$y = \frac{1}{e^{-t} - C}.$$

The initial condition $y(0) = \frac{1}{2}$ implies that

$$y(0) = \frac{1}{e^0 - C} = \frac{1}{1 - C} = \frac{1}{2}.$$

It follows that $C = -1$, so the solution to the initial value problem is

$$y = \frac{1}{e^{-t} + 1}.$$

The solution (Figure 8.20) passes through $(0, \frac{1}{2})$ and approaches the asymptote $y = 1$ because $\lim\limits_{t \to \infty} \dfrac{1}{e^{-t} + 1} = 1$. The solution curve is also consistent with the underlying slope field.

Related Exercises 5–26 ◄

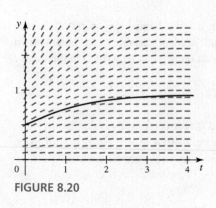

FIGURE 8.20

QUICK CHECK 2 Write $y'(t) = (t^2 + 1)/y^3$ in separated form. ◄

Example 1 illustrates the following procedure for solving separable equations.

PROCEDURE   Solving Separable Equations

In practice, the following steps are used to solve a first-order separable differential equation that has the form $g(y)\dfrac{dy}{dt} = h(t)$.

1. Separate variables and write $g(y)dy = h(t)dt$.

2. Integrate the left side with respect to y and the right side with respect to t; that is, find the antiderivatives of g and h:

$$\int g(y)dy = \int h(t)dt.$$

3. Both integrations produce an arbitrary constant of integration that may be combined in one arbitrary constant.

4. If an initial condition is given, use it to evaluate the arbitrary constant.

EXAMPLE 2   Another separable equation Find the solutions of the equation $\dfrac{dy}{dx} = e^{-y}\sin x$ subject to the three different initial conditions

$$y(0) = 1, \quad y\left(\frac{\pi}{2}\right) = \frac{1}{2}, \quad \text{and} \quad y(0) = -3.$$

SOLUTION Writing the equation in the form $e^y \dfrac{dy}{dx} = \sin x$, we see that it is separable. Integrating both sides, we have

$$\int e^y \, dy = \int \sin x \, dx \qquad \text{Integrate both sides.}$$

$$e^y = -\cos x + C. \quad \text{Evaluate integrals.}$$

The general solution y is found by taking logarithms of both sides of this equation:

$$y = \ln(C - \cos x).$$

The three initial conditions are now used to evaluate the constant C for the three solutions:

$$y(0) = 1 \Rightarrow 1 = \ln(C - \cos 0) = \ln(C - 1) \Rightarrow e = C - 1 \Rightarrow C = e + 1,$$

$$y\left(\frac{\pi}{2}\right) = \frac{1}{2} \Rightarrow \frac{1}{2} = \ln\left(C - \cos\frac{\pi}{2}\right) = \ln C \Rightarrow C = e^{1/2}, \text{ and}$$

$$y(0) = -3 \Rightarrow -3 = \ln(C - \cos 0) = \ln(C - 1) \Rightarrow e^{-3} = C - 1 \Rightarrow C = e^{-3} + 1.$$

Substituting these values of C into the general solution gives the solutions of the three initial value problems (Figure 8.21). The small dots on each curve indicate the initial condition for each solution.

Related Exercises 5–26 ◄

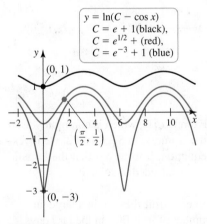

$$y = \ln(C - \cos x)$$
$$C = e + 1 \text{(black)},$$
$$C = e^{1/2} + \text{(red)},$$
$$C = e^{-3} + 1 \text{ (blue)}$$

FIGURE 8.21

QUICK CHECK 3 Find the value of the constant C in Example 2 with the initial condition $y(\pi) = 0$. ◄

Even if we can evaluate the integrals necessary to solve a separable equation, the solution may not be easily expressed in an explicit form. Here is an example of a solution that is best left in implicit form.

EXAMPLE 3   **An implicit solution** Find and graph the solution of the initial value problem

$$\cos y \frac{dy}{dt} = \sin^2 t \cos t, \quad y(0) = \frac{\pi}{6}.$$

SOLUTION Notice that the variables are already separated in this equation. Integrating both sides of the equation, we have

> For the integral on the right side, we use the substitution $u = \sin t$. The integral becomes $\int u^2\, du = \frac{1}{3}u^3 + C$.

$$\int \cos y\, dy = \int \sin^2 t \cos t\, dt \quad \text{Integrate both sides.}$$

$$\sin y = \frac{1}{3}\sin^3 t + C. \quad \text{Evaluate integrals.}$$

To impose the initial condition in this case, it is best to leave the general solution in implicit form. Substituting $t = 0$ and $y = \frac{\pi}{6}$ into the general solution, we find that

$$\sin\frac{\pi}{6} = \frac{1}{3}\sin^3 0 + C \quad \text{or} \quad C = \frac{1}{2}.$$

Therefore, the solution of the initial value problem is

$$\sin y = \frac{1}{3}\sin^3 t + \frac{1}{2}.$$

> Care must be used when graphing and interpreting implicit solutions. The graph of
>
> $$\sin y = \frac{1}{3}\sin^3 t + \frac{1}{2}$$
>
> is a family of an infinite number of curves.
>
>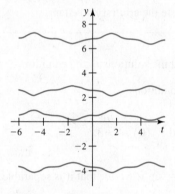
>
> You must choose the curve that satisfies the initial condition, as shown in Figure 8.22.

In order to graph the solution in this implicit form, it is easiest to use graphing software. The result is shown in Figure 8.22.

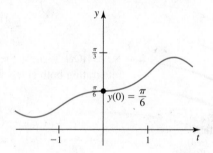

FIGURE 8.22

Related Exercises 27–32 ◄

QUICK CHECK 4 Find the value of the constant C in Example 3 with the initial condition $y\left(\frac{\pi}{6}\right) = 0.$ ◄

Logistic Equation Revisited

In Section 8.1, we introduced the logistic equation (Exercise 51), which is commonly used for modeling populations, epidemics, and the spread of rumors. In Section 8.2, we investigated the slope field associated with the logistic equation. It turns out that the logistic equation is a separable equation, so we now have the tools needed to solve it.

EXAMPLE 4   **Logistic population growth** Assume 50 fruit flies are in a large jar at the beginning of an experiment. Let $P(t)$ be the number of fruit flies in the jar t days later. At first, the population grows exponentially, but due to limited space and food supply, the growth rate decreases and the population is prevented from growing without bound. This experiment is modeled by the *logistic equation*

$$\frac{dP}{dt} = 0.1P\left(1 - \frac{P}{300}\right), \text{ for } t \ge 0,$$

together with the initial condition $P(0) = 50$. Solve this initial value problem.

SOLUTION We see that the equation is separable by writing it in the form

$$\frac{dP}{P\left(1 - \dfrac{P}{300}\right)} = 0.1\, dt.$$

Integrating both sides leads to the equation

$$\int \frac{dP}{P\left(1 - \dfrac{P}{300}\right)} = \int 0.1 \, dt. \tag{1}$$

The integral on the right side of equation (1) is $\int 0.1 \, dt = 0.1t + C$.

Because the integrand on the left side is a rational function of P, we use partial fractions. You should verify that

$$\frac{1}{P\left(1 - \dfrac{P}{300}\right)} = \frac{300}{P(300 - P)} = \frac{1}{P} + \frac{1}{300 - P}$$

and therefore,

$$\int \frac{dP}{P\left(1 - \dfrac{P}{300}\right)} = \int \left(\frac{1}{P} + \frac{1}{300 - P}\right) dP = \ln \left| \frac{P}{300 - P} \right| + C.$$

After integration, equation (1) becomes

$$\ln \left| \frac{P}{300 - P} \right| = 0.1t + C. \tag{2}$$

The next step is to solve for P, which is tangled up inside the logarithm. We first exponentiate both sides of equation (2) to obtain

$$\left| \frac{P}{300 - P} \right| = e^C \cdot e^{0.1t}.$$

We can remove the absolute value on the left side of equation (2) by writing

$$\frac{P}{300 - P} = \pm e^C \cdot e^{0.1t}.$$

> There are not many times in mathematics when we can redefine a constant in the middle of a calculation. When working with arbitrary constants, it may be possible, if it is done carefully.

> We could also use the initial condition in equation (3) to solve for C.

At this point, a useful trick simplifies matters. Because C is an arbitrary constant, $\pm e^C$ is also an arbitrary constant, so we rename $\pm e^C$ as C. We now have

$$\frac{P}{300 - P} = Ce^{0.1t}. \tag{3}$$

Solving equation (3) for P and replacing $1/C$ with C gives the general solution

$$P = \frac{300}{1 + Ce^{-0.1t}}.$$

Figure 8.23 shows the general solution, with curves corresponding to several different values of C. Using the initial condition $P(0) = 50$, we find the value of C for our specific problem is $C = 5$. It follows that the solution of the initial value problem is

$$P = \frac{300}{1 + 5e^{-0.1t}}.$$

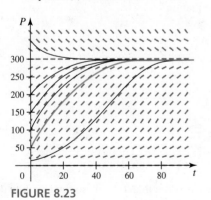

FIGURE 8.23

Figure 8.23 also shows this solution (in red) among the curves in the general solution. A significant feature of this model is that for $0 < P(0) < 300$, the population increases, but not without bound. Instead, it approaches an equilibrium, or steady-state, solution with a value of

$$\lim_{t \to \infty} P(t) = \lim_{t \to \infty} \frac{300}{1 + 5e^{-0.1t}} = 300,$$

which is the maximum population that the environment (space and food supply) can sustain. This equilibrium population is called the **carrying capacity**. Notice that all the curves in the general solution approach the carrying capacity as t increases.

Related Exercises 33–34 ◄

Newton's Law of Cooling

Imagine taking a fired bowl out of a hot pottery kiln and putting it on a rack to cool at room temperature. Your intuition tells you that because the temperature of the bowl is greater than the temperature of the room, the pot cools and its temperature approaches the temperature of the room. (We assume that the room is sufficiently large that the heating of the room by the bowl is negligible.)

This process is modeled using a first-order differential equation similar to those studied in this section. That equation is often called **Newton's Law of Cooling**, and it is based on the familiar observation that *heat flows from hot to cold*. The solution of the equation gives the temperature of the bowl at all times after it is removed from the kiln.

We let $t = 0$ be the time at which the bowl is removed from the kiln. The temperature of the bowl at any time $t \geq 0$ is $T(t)$, and $T(0) = T_0$ is the temperature of the bowl as it comes out of the kiln. We also let A be the ambient room temperature. Both T_0 and A are assumed to be known.

Newton's Law of Cooling states that the rate at which the temperature changes at any time is proportional to the temperature *difference* between the bowl and the room at that time; that is,

$$\frac{dT}{dt} = -k(T(t) - A),$$

where $k > 0$ is a constant determined by the thermal properties of the bowl. Notice that the equation makes sense.

• If $T(t) > A$ (the bowl is hotter than the room), then $\dfrac{dT}{dt} < 0$, and the temperature of the bowl decreases (cooling).

• If $T(t) < A$ (the bowl is colder than the room), then $\dfrac{dT}{dt} > 0$, and the temperature of the bowl increases (heating).

We see that Newton's Law of Cooling amounts to a separable first-order equation that we know how to solve. Separating variables in the equation

$$\frac{dT}{dt} = -k(T - A),$$

we have

$$\frac{dT}{T - A} = -k\,dt.$$

Integrating both sides of the equation gives

$$\ln|T - A| = -kt + C,$$

where C is an arbitrary constant. For the moment, we assume that $T > A$, so the absolute value may be removed. Exponentiating both sides of the equation, we have

$$T - A = e^{-kt+C} = e^{-kt} \cdot \underbrace{e^C}_{\text{redefine as } C} = Ce^{-kt}.$$

We have used the standard practice of redefining the arbitrary constant C: If C is arbitrary, then e^C is also arbitrary. We now solve for the general solution:

$$T(t) = Ce^{-kt} + A.$$

It may also be shown that the same solution is obtained in the case that $T < A$ (Exercise 58). When we use the initial condition $T(0) = T_0$ to determine C, we find that

$$T(0) = C + A = T_0 \Rightarrow C = T_0 - A.$$

Therefore, the solution of the initial value problem is

$$T(t) = (T_0 - A)^{-kt} + A.$$

QUICK CHECK 5 Verify that the solution of the initial value problem satisfies $T(0) = T_0$. What is the solution of the problem if $T_0 = A$? ◄

Newton's Law of Cooling models the cooling process well when the object is a good conductor of heat and when the temperature is fairly uniform throughout the object.

EXAMPLE 5   Cooling a bowl A bowl is removed from a pottery kiln at a temperature of 200°C and placed on a rack in a room with an ambient temperature of 20°C. Two minutes after the bowl is removed, its temperature is 160°C. Find the temperature of the bowl for all $t \geq 0$.

SOLUTION Letting $A = 20$, the general solution of the cooling equation is

$$T(t) = Ce^{-kt} + 20.$$

As always, the arbitrary constant is determined using the initial condition $T(0) = 200$. Substituting this condition, we find that

$$T(0) = C + 20 = 200 \quad \Rightarrow \quad C = 180.$$

> The value of the constant k is known for common materials. Example 5 illustrates one way to estimate the constant experimentally.

The solution at this point is $T(t) = 180e^{-kt} + 20$, but notice that the constant k is still unknown. It is determined using the additional fact that $T(2) = 160$. We substitute this condition into the solution and solve for k:

$$T(2) = 180e^{-2k} + 20 = 160 \qquad \text{Substitute } t = 2.$$
$$180e^{-2k} = 140 \qquad \text{Rearrange.}$$
$$e^{-2k} = \frac{140}{180} = \frac{7}{9} \qquad \text{Rearrange.}$$
$$k = -\frac{1}{2}\ln\frac{7}{9} \approx 0.126. \quad \text{Solve for } k.$$

Therefore, the solution for $t \geq 0$ is

$$T(t) = 180e^{-kt} + 20 \approx 180e^{-0.126t} + 20.$$

The graph of T (Figure 8.24) confirms that $T(0) = 200$ and that $T(2) = 160$. Notice also that $\lim_{t \to \infty} T(t) = 20$, meaning that the temperature of the bowl approaches the ambient temperature as $t \to \infty$. Equivalently, the solution $T = 20$ is a stable equilibrium of the system.   *Related Exercises 35–38* ◄

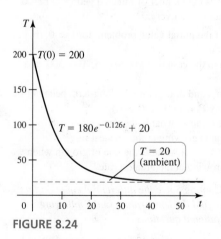

FIGURE 8.24

QUICK CHECK 6 In general, what is the equilibrium temperature for any Newton cooling problem? ◄

SECTION 8.3 EXERCISES

Review Questions

1. What is a separable first-order differential equation?

2. Is the equation $t^2 \dfrac{dy}{dt} = \dfrac{t+4}{y^2}$ separable?

3. Is the equation $\dfrac{dy}{dt} = 2y - t$ separable?

4. Explain how to solve a separable differential equation of the form
$$g(y)\frac{dy}{dt} = h(t).$$

Basic Skills

5–16. Solving separable equations *Find the general solution of the following equations. Express the solution explicitly as a function of the independent variable.*

5. $t^{-3}\dfrac{dy}{dt} = 1$

6. $e^{4t}\dfrac{dy}{dt} = 5$

7. $\dfrac{dy}{dt} = \dfrac{3t^2}{y}$

8. $\dfrac{dy}{dx} = y(x^2 + 1)$

9. $y'(t) = e^{y/2}\sin t$

10. $x^2\dfrac{dw}{dx} = \sqrt{w}(3x + 1), x > 0$

11. $x^2 y'(x) = y^2, x > 0$

12. $(t^2 + 1)^3 yy'(t) = t(y^2 + 4)$

13. $y'(t)\csc t = \dfrac{-y^3}{2}$

14. $y'(t)e^{t/2} = y^2 + 4$

15. $u'(x) = e^{2x - u}$

16. $xu'(x) = u^2 - 4, x > 0$

17–26. Solving initial value problems *Determine whether the following equations are separable. If so, solve the initial value problem.*

17. $t\dfrac{dy}{dt} = 1, \ y(1) = 2$

18. $\sec t\dfrac{dy}{dt} = 1, \ y(0) = 1$

19. $2y\dfrac{dy}{dt} = 3t^2, \ y(0) = 9$

20. $\dfrac{dy}{dt} = e^{ty}, \ y(0) = 1$

21. $\dfrac{dy}{dt} = ty + 2, \ y(1) = 2$

22. $y'(t) = y(4t^3 + 1), \ y(0) = 4$

23. $y'(t) = \dfrac{e^t}{2y}, \ y(\ln 2) = 1$

24. $(\sec x)y'(x) = y^3, \ y(0) = 3$

25. $\dfrac{dy}{dx} = e^{x-y}, \ y(0) = \ln 3$

26. $y'(t) = \cos^2 y, \ y(1) = \dfrac{\pi}{4}$

27–32. Solutions in implicit form *Solve the following initial value problems and leave the solution in implicit form. Use graphing software to plot the solution. If the implicit solution describes more than one curve, be sure to indicate which curve corresponds to the solution of the initial value problem.*

27. $y'(t) = \dfrac{t}{y}, \ y(1) = 2$

28. $y'(x) = \dfrac{1 + x}{2 - y}, \ y(1) = 1$

29. $u'(x) = \csc u\cos\dfrac{x}{2}, \ u(\pi) = \dfrac{\pi}{2}$

30. $yy'(x) = \dfrac{2x}{(2 + y^2)^2}, \ y(1) = -1$

31. $y'(x) = \sqrt{\dfrac{x+1}{y+4}}, \ y(3) = 5$

32. $z'(x) = \dfrac{z^2 + 4}{x^2 + 16}, \ z(4) = 2$

33. **Logistic equation for a population** A community of hares on an island has a population of 50 when observations begin (at $t = 0$). The population is modeled by the initial value problem
$$\frac{dP}{dt} = 0.08P\left(1 - \frac{P}{200}\right), P(0) = 50.$$

   a. Find and graph the solution of the initial value problem, for $t \geq 0$.
   b. What is the steady-state population?
   c. What is the population size when the population is growing at the greatest rate?
   d. What is the rate of growth when the population is growing at the greatest rate?

34. **Logistic equation for an epidemic** When an infected person is introduced into a closed and otherwise healthy community, the number of people who contract the disease (in the absence of any intervention) may be modeled by the logistic equation
$$\frac{dP}{dt} = kP\left(1 - \frac{P}{A}\right), P(0) = P_0,$$
where k is a positive infection rate, A is the number of people in the community, and P_0 is the number of infected people at $t = 0$. The model also assumes no recovery.

   a. Find the solution of the initial value problem, for $t \geq 0$, in terms of k, A, and P_0.
   b. Graph the solution in the case that $k = 0.025, A = 300$, and $P_0 = 1$.
   c. For a fixed value of k and A, describe the long-term behavior of the solutions, for any P_0 with $0 < P_0 < A$.
   d. For fixed values of k and A, what is the population size when the population is growing at the greatest rate?
   e. For fixed values of k and A, what is the rate of growth when the population is growing at the greatest rate?

35–38. Newton's Law of Cooling *Solve the differential equation for Newton's Law of Cooling to find the temperature in the following cases. Then answer any additional questions.*

35. A cup of coffee has a temperature of 90°C when it is poured and allowed to cool in a room with a temperature of 25°C. One minute after the coffee is poured, its temperature is 85°C. How long must you wait until the coffee is cool enough to drink, say 30°C?

36. An iron rod is removed from a blacksmith's forge at a temperature of 900°C. Assume that $k = 0.02$ and the rod cools in a room with a temperature of 30°C. When does the temperature of the rod reach 100°C?

37. A glass of milk is moved from a refrigerator with a temperature of 5°C to a room with a temperature of 20°C. One minute later the milk has warmed to a temperature of 7°C. After how many minutes does the milk have a temperature of 18°C?

38. A pot of boiling soup $(100°C)$ is put in a cellar with a temperature of 10°C. After 30 min, the soup has cooled to 80°C. When will the temperature of the soup reach 30°C?

Further Explorations

39. Explain why or why not Determine whether the following statements are true and give an explanation or counterexample.

   a. The equation $u'(x) = (x^2 u^7)^{-1}$ is separable.

   b. The general solution of the separable equation

   $$y'(t) = \frac{t}{y^7 + 10y^4}$$ can be expressed explicitly with y in terms of t.

   c. The general solution of the equation $yy'(x) = xe^{-y}$ can be found using integration by parts.

40–43. Solutions of separable equations *Solve the following initial value problems. When possible, give the solution as an explicit function of t.*

40. $e^y y'(t) = \dfrac{\ln^2 t}{t}$, $y(1) = \ln 2$ **41.** $y'(t) = \dfrac{3y(y+1)}{t}$, $y(1) = 1$

42. $y'(t) = \dfrac{\cos^2 t}{2y}$, $y(0) = -2$ **43.** $y'(t) = \dfrac{y+3}{5t+6}$, $y(2) = 0$

44–45. Implicit solutions for separable equations *For the following separable equations, carry out the indicated analysis.*

   a. *Find the general solution of the equation.*

   b. *Find the value of the arbitrary constant associated with each initial condition. (Each initial condition requires a different constant.)*

   c. *Use the graph of the general solution that is provided to sketch the solution curve for each initial condition.*

44. $y^2 y'(t) = t^2 + \dfrac{2}{3}t$; $y(-1) = 1, y(1) = 0, y(-1) = -1$

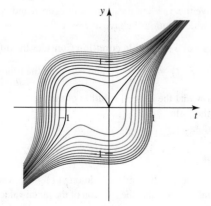

45. $e^{-y/2}y'(x) = 4x\sin x^2 - x$; $y(0) = 0,$
   $y(0) = \ln\left(\dfrac{1}{4}\right), y\left(\sqrt{\dfrac{\pi}{2}}\right) = 0$

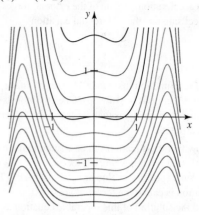

46. Orthogonal trajectories Two curves are orthogonal to each other if their tangent lines are perpendicular at each point of intersection. A family of curves forms **orthogonal trajectories** with another family of curves if each curve in one family is orthogonal to each curve in the other family. Use the following steps to find the orthogonal trajectories of the family of ellipses $2x^2 + y^2 = a^2$.

   a. Apply implicit differentiation to $2x^2 + y^2 = a^2$ to show that $\dfrac{dy}{dx} = \dfrac{-2x}{y}$.

   b. The family of trajectories orthogonal to $2x^2 + y^2 = a^2$ satisfies the differential equation $\dfrac{dy}{dx} = \dfrac{y}{2x}$. Why?

   c. Solve the differential equation in part (b) to verify that $y^2 = e^C|x|$, and then explain why it follows that $y^2 = kx$. Therefore, the family of parabolas $y^2 = kx$ forms the orthogonal trajectories of the family of ellipses $2x^2 + y^2 = a^2$.

47. Orthogonal trajectories Use the method in Exercise 46 to find the orthogonal trajectories for the family of circles $x^2 + y^2 = a^2$.

Applications

48. Logistic equation for spread of rumors Sociologists model the spread of rumors using logistic equations. The key assumption is that at any given time, a fraction y of the population, where $0 \le y \le 1$, knows the rumor, while the remaining fraction $1 - y$ does not. Furthermore, the rumor spreads by interactions between those who know the rumor and those who do not. The number of such interactions is proportional to $y(1 - y)$. Therefore, the equation that describes the spread of the rumor is $y'(t) = ky(1 - y)$, where k is a positive real number. The number of people who initially know the rumor is $y(0) = y_0$, where $0 \le y_0 \le 1$.

   a. Solve this initial value problem and give the solution in terms of k and y_0.

   b. Assume $k = 0.3$ weeks^{-1} and graph the solution for $y_0 = 0.1$ and $y_0 = 0.7$.

   c. Describe and interpret the long-term behavior of the rumor function, for any $0 < y_0 \le 1$.

49. Free fall An object in free fall may be modeled by assuming that the only forces at work are the gravitational force and air resistance. By Newton's Second Law of Motion (mass · acceleration = sum of the external forces), the velocity of the object satisfies the differential equation

$$\underbrace{m}_{\text{mass}} \cdot \underbrace{v'(t)}_{\text{acceleration}} = \underbrace{mg + f(v)}_{\text{external forces}},$$

where f is a function that models the air resistance (assuming the positive direction is downward). One common assumption (often used for motion in air) is that $f(v) = -kv^2$, where $k > 0$ is a drag coefficient.

a. Show that the equation can be written in the form $v'(t) = g - av^2$, where $a = k/m$.
b. For what (positive) value of v is $v'(t) = 0$? (This equilibrium solution is called the *terminal velocity*.)
c. Find the solution of this separable equation assuming $v(0) = 0$ and $0 < v^2 < g/a$.
d. Graph the solution found in part (c) with $g = 9.8 \text{ m/s}^2$, $m = 1$, and $k = 0.1$, and verify that the terminal velocity agrees with the value found in part (b).

50. Free fall Using the background given in Exercise 49, assume the resistance is given by $f(v) = -Rv$, where $R > 0$ is a drag coefficient (an assumption often made for a heavy medium such as water or oil).

a. Show that the equation can be written in the form $v'(t) = g - bv$, where $b = R/m$.
b. For what value of v is $v'(t) = 0$? (This equilibrium solution is called the terminal velocity.)
c. Find the solution of this separable equation assuming $v(0) = 0$ and $0 < v < g/b$.
d. Graph the solution found in part (c) with $g = 9.8 \text{ m/s}^2$, $m = 1$, and $R = 0.1$, and verify that the terminal velocity agrees with the value found in part (b).

51. Torricelli's law An open cylindrical tank initially filled with water drains through a hole in the bottom of the tank according to Torricelli's law (see figure). If $h(t)$ is the depth of water in the tank, for $t \geq 0$, then Torricelli's law implies $h'(t) = -2k\sqrt{h}$, where k is a constant that includes $g = 9.8 \text{ m/s}^2$, the radius of the tank, and the radius of the drain. Assume that the initial depth of the water is $h(0) = H$.

a. Find the solution of the initial value problem.
b. Find the solution in the case that $k = 0.1$ and $H = 0.5$ m.
c. In part (b), how long does it take for the tank to drain?
d. Graph the solution in part (b) and check that it is consistent with part (c).

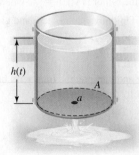

52. Chemical rate equations Let $y(t)$ be the concentration of a substance in a chemical reaction (typical units are moles/liter). The change in the concentration, under appropriate conditions, is modeled by the equation $\dfrac{dy}{dt} = -ky^n$, where $k > 0$ is a rate constant and the positive integer n is the order of the reaction.

a. Show that for a first-order reaction ($n = 1$), the concentration obeys an exponential decay law.
b. Solve the initial value problem for a second-order reaction ($n = 2$) assuming $y(0) = y_0$.
c. Graph the concentration for a first-order and second-order reaction with $k = 0.1$ and $y_0 = 1$.

53. Tumor growth The Gompertz growth equation is often used to model the growth of tumors. Let $M(t)$ be the mass of a tumor at time $t \geq 0$. The relevant initial value problem is

$$\frac{dM}{dt} = -rM \ln\left(\frac{M}{K}\right), M(0) = M_0,$$

where r and K are positive constants and $0 < M_0 < K$.

a. Graph the growth rate function $R(M) = -rM \ln\left(\dfrac{M}{K}\right)$ (which equals $M'(t)$) assuming $r = 1$ and $K = 4$. For what values of M is the growth rate positive? For what value of M is the growth rate a maximum?
b. Solve the initial value problem and graph the solution for $r = 1$, $K = 4$, and $M_0 = 1$. Describe the growth pattern of the tumor. Is the growth unbounded? If not, what is the limiting size of the tumor?
c. In the general solution, what is the meaning of K?

Additional Exercises

54. Technology for an initial value problem Solve $y'(t) = ye^t \cos^3 4t$, $y(0) = 1$, and plot the solution for $0 \leq t \leq \pi$.

55. Blowup in finite time Consider the initial value problem $y'(t) = y^{n+1}$, $y(0) = y_0$, where n is a positive integer.

a. Solve the initial value problem with $n = 1$ and $y_0 = 1$.
b. Solve the initial value problem with $n = 2$ and $y_0 = \dfrac{1}{\sqrt{2}}$.
c. Solve the problem for positive integers n and $y_0 = n^{-1/n}$. How do solutions behave as $t \to 1^-$?

56. Analysis of a separable equation Consider the differential equation $y'(t) = \dfrac{y(y + 1)}{t(t + 2)}$ and carry out the following analysis.

a. Show that the general solution of the equation can be written in the form

$$y = \frac{\sqrt{t}}{C\sqrt{t + 2} - \sqrt{t}}.$$

b. Now consider the initial condition $y(1) = A$, where A is a real number. Show that the solution of the initial value problem is

$$y = \frac{\sqrt{t}}{\left(\dfrac{1 + A}{\sqrt{3}A}\right)\sqrt{t + 2} - \sqrt{t}}.$$

c. Find and graph the solution that satisfies the initial condition $y(1) = 1$.

d. Describe the behavior of the solution in part (c) as t increases from $t = 1$.

e. Find and graph the solution that satisfies the initial condition $y(1) = 2$.

f. Describe the behavior of the solution in part (e) as t increases from $t = 1$.

g. In the cases in which the solution is bounded for $t > 0$, what is the value of $\lim_{t \to \infty} y(t)$?

57. Analysis of a separable equation Consider the differential equation $yy'(t) = \frac{1}{2}e^t + t$ and carry out the following analysis.

a. Find the general solution of the equation and express it explicitly as a function of t in two cases: $y > 0$ and $y < 0$.

b. Find the solutions that satisfy the initial conditions $y(-1) = 1$ and $y(-1) = 2$.

c. Graph the solutions in part (b) and describe their behavior as t increases.

d. Find the solutions that satisfy the initial conditions $y(-1) = -1$ and $y(-1) = -2$.

e. Graph the solutions in part (d) and describe their behavior as t increases.

58. Newton's Law of cooling—Case 2 Solve the equation $T'(t) = -k(T - A)$ in the case that $T < A$ and show that the general solution is $T = Ce^{-kt} + A$.

8.4 Exponential Models

In this final section, we explore one of the simplest and perhaps most important of all differential equations. It is the equation that describes exponential growth and decay. The solutions of this equation have wide-ranging applications in finance, medicine, ecology, biology, economics, pharmacokinetics, anthropology, and physics.

Exponential Growth

Many quantities in the world around us obey (approximately) a simple rule: The rate of change of the quantity is proportional to the amount of the quantity present at any particular time. Suppose $y(t)$ is such a quantity defined for times $t \geq 0$. If y represents a population, then $y'(t)$ is the **growth rate** (or **absolute growth rate)** with units such as people/month or cells/hour. Because the growth rate of y is proportional to y, it satisfies the differential equation $y'(t) = ky$, where $k > 0$ is a constant of proportionality, called the **rate constant**. The differential equation says that the more people or cells present, the faster the population grows.

The equation $\dfrac{dy}{dt} = ky$ is a separable differential equation. Following the method given in Section 8.3, its solution is found as follows:

$$\frac{dy}{y} = dt \qquad \text{Separate variables.}$$

$$\int \frac{dy}{y} = \int dt \qquad \text{Integrate both sides.}$$

$$\ln|y| = t + C \qquad \text{Evaluate integrals.}$$

$$|y| = e^t \, \underbrace{e^C}_{C} \qquad \text{Exponentiate both sides.}$$

In general, y may be positive or negative. So we rename the constant e^C as C, where C may be positive or negative. By doing so, the absolute value may be removed around y, and the general solution of the equation is $y = Ce^t$, where C is an arbitrary constant. Because $k > 0$, the solutions of this equation are exponential functions that increase with t (Figure 8.25).

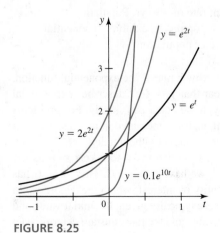

FIGURE 8.25

▶ A consumer price index that increases at a constant rate of 4%/yr increases exponentially. A currency that is devalued at a constant rate of 3%/mon decreases exponentially. By contrast, linear growth is characterized by constant absolute growth rates, such as 500 people/yr or $400/mon.

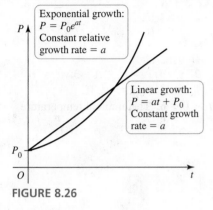

FIGURE 8.26

Another way to talk about growth rates is to use the **relative growth rate**, which is the growth rate divided by the current value of that quantity—that is, $y'(t)/y$. For example, if y is a population, the relative growth rate is the fraction or percentage by which the population grows each unit of time. Examples of relative growth rates are 5%/yr or *a factor of 1.2/mon*. Therefore, when the equation $y'(t) = ky$ is written in the form $y'(t)/y = k$, it has another interpretation. It says that *a quantity that grows exponentially has a constant relative growth rate.* Constant relative or percent change is the hallmark of exponential growth.

Figure 8.26 shows two population functions. The linear growth function has a constant (absolute) growth rate. The exponential growth function has a constant relative growth rate.

EXAMPLE 1 Linear vs. exponential growth Suppose the population P of the city of Pine has a growth rate given by $\dfrac{dP}{dt} = 125$, while the city of Spruce has a populations S with growth rate $\dfrac{dS}{dt} = 0.1S$, where t is measured in years. Compare the growth rates of Pine and Spruce when each city has 150 residents and again when each city has 15,000 residents.

SOLUTION For any population size, Pine grows at the rate of 125 people/yr. However, the growth rate of Spruce depends on the population size. When Spruce has 150 residents, the growth rate is

$$\frac{dS}{dt} = 0.1(150) = 15,$$

or 15 people/yr. When Spruce has a population of 15,000, the growth rate is

$$\frac{dS}{dt} = 0.1(15000) = 1500,$$

or 1500 people/yr. Table 8.5 shows that Pine's growth rate is constant, while Spruce's growth rate is small when its population is small and increases as the population increases. Pine has a constant (absolute) growth rate and Spruce has a constant relative growth. As a result, Pine's population increases linearly and Spruce's population increases exponentially, as shown in Figure 8.27, assuming both cities have an initial population of 1500.

Related Exercises 9–10

Table 8.5

P	$\dfrac{dP}{dt}$	S	$\dfrac{dS}{dt}$
150	125	150	15
1500	125	1500	150
15,000	125	15,000	1500
150,000	125	150,000	15,000

QUICK CHECK 1 Population A increases at a constant rate of 4%/yr. Population B increases at a constant rate of 500 people/yr. Which population exhibits exponential growth? What kind of growth is exhibited by the other population? ◀

The rate constant k in $y = Ce^{kt}$ determines the growth rate of the exponential function. We adopt the convention that $k > 0$; then it is clear that $y = Ce^{kt}$ describes exponential growth and $y = Ce^{-kt}$ describes exponential decay, to be discussed shortly. For problems that involve time, the units of k are time^{-1}; for example, if t is measured in months, the units of k are month^{-1}. In this way, the exponent kt is dimensionless (without units).

Unless there is good reason to do otherwise, it is customary to take $t = 0$ as the reference point for time. Notice that with $y = Ce^{kt}$, we have $y(0) = C$. Therefore, C has a simple meaning: It is the **initial value** of the quantity of interest, which we denote y_0. In the examples that follow, two pieces of information are typically given: the initial value and clues for determining the rate constant k. The initial value and the rate constant determine an exponential growth function completely.

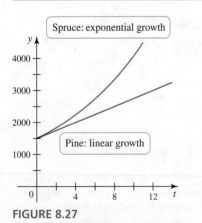

FIGURE 8.27

▶ The unit time^{-1} is read *per unit time*. For example, month^{-1} is read *per month*.

> ### Exponential Growth Functions
> Exponential growth is described by functions of the form $y = y_0e^{kt}$. The initial value of y at $t = 0$ is $y(0) = y_0$, and the **rate constant** $k > 0$ determines the rate of growth. Exponential growth is characterized by a constant relative growth rate.

Because exponential growth is characterized by a constant relative growth rate, the time required for a quantity to double (a 100% increase) is constant. Therefore, one way to describe an exponentially growing quantity is to give its *doubling time*. To compute the time it takes for the function $y = y_0e^{kt}$ to double in value, say from y_0 to $2y_0$, we find the value of t that satisfies

$$y = 2y_0 \quad \text{or} \quad y_0e^{kt} = 2y_0.$$

> Note that the initial value y_0 appears on both sides of this equation. It may be canceled, meaning that the doubling time is independent of the initial condition: *The doubling time is constant for all t.*

Canceling y_0 from the equation $y_0e^{kt} = 2y_0$ leaves the equation $e^{kt} = 2$. Taking logarithms of both sides, we have $\ln e^{kt} = \ln 2$, or $kt = \ln 2$, which has the solution $t = \dfrac{\ln 2}{k}$. We denote this doubling time T_2 so that $T_2 = \dfrac{\ln 2}{k}$. If y increases exponentially, the time it takes to double from 100 to 200 is the same as the time it takes to double from 1000 to 2000.

> **QUICK CHECK 2** Verify that the time needed for $y = y_0e^{kt}$ to double from y_0 to $2y_0$ is the same as the time needed to double from $2y_0$ to $4y_0$. ◄

> ### DEFINITION Doubling Time
> The quantity described by the function $y = y_0e^{kt}$, for $k > 0$, has a constant
> **doubling time** of $T_2 = \dfrac{\ln 2}{k}$, with the same units as t.

> It is a common mistake to assume that if the annual growth rate is 1.4%/yr, then $k = 1.4\% = 0.014 \text{ year}^{-1}$. The rate constant k must be calculated, as it is in Example 2, to give $k = 0.013976$. For larger growth rates, the difference between k and the growth rate is greater.

EXAMPLE 2 World population Human population growth rates vary geographically and fluctuate over time. The overall growth rate for world population peaked at an annual rate of 2.1%/yr in the 1960s. Assume a world population of 6.0 billion in 1999 $(t = 0)$ and 6.9 billion in 2009 $(t = 10)$.

a. Find an exponential growth function for the world population that fits the two data points.

b. Find the doubling time for the world population using the model in part (a).

c. Find the (absolute) growth rate $y'(t)$ and graph it, for $0 \le t \le 50$.

d. How fast was the population growing in 2014 $(t = 15)$?

SOLUTION

a. Let $y(t)$ be world population measured in billions of people t years after 1999. We use the growth function $y = y_0e^{kt}$, where y_0 and k must be determined. The initial value is $y_0 = 6$ (billion). To determine the rate constant k, we use the fact that $y(10) = 6.9$. Substituting $t = 10$ into the growth function with $y_0 = 6$ implies

$$y(10) = 6e^{10k} = 6.9.$$

Solving for k yields the rate constant $k = \dfrac{\ln(6.9/6)}{10} \approx 0.013976 \approx 0.014 \text{ year}^{-1}$.

Therefore, the growth function is

$$y = 6e^{0.014t}.$$

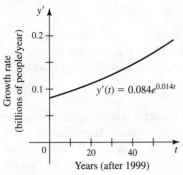

FIGURE 8.28

▷ Converted to a daily rate (dividing by 365), the world population in 2014 increased at a rate of roughly 284,000 people per day.

b. The doubling time of the population is

$$T_2 = \frac{\ln 2}{k} \approx \frac{\ln 2}{0.014} \approx 50 \text{ yr}.$$

c. Working with the growth function $y = 6e^{0.014t}$, we find that

$$y'(t) = 6\,(0.014)e^{0.014t} = 0.084e^{0.014t},$$

which has units of *billions of people/year*. As shown in Figure 8.28 the growth rate itself increases exponentially.

d. In 2014 $(t = 15)$, the growth rate was

$$y'(15) = 0.084e^{(0.014)(15)} \approx 0.104 \text{ billion people/yr},$$

or roughly 104 million people/yr.

Related Exercises 11–20◀

QUICK CHECK 3 Assume $y(t) = 100e^{0.05t}$. By what percentage does y increase when t increases by 1 unit?◀

A Financial Model   Exponential functions are used in many financial applications, several of which are explored in the exercises. For now, consider a simple savings account in which an initial deposit earns interest that is reinvested in the account. Interest payments are made on a regular basis (for example, annually, monthly, and daily), or interest may be compounded continuously. In all cases, the balance in the account increases exponentially at a rate that can be determined from the advertised **annual percentage yield** (or **APY**) of the account. Assuming that no additional deposits are made, the balance in the account is given by the exponential growth function $y = y_0 e^{kt}$, where y_0 is the initial deposit, t is measured in years, and k is determined by the annual percentage yield.

EXAMPLE 3   Compounding   The APY of a savings account is the percentage increase in the balance over the course of a year. Suppose you deposit $500 in a savings account that has an APY of 6.18%/yr. Assume that the interest rate remains constant and that no additional deposits or withdrawals are made. How long will it take for the balance to reach $2500?

▷ If the balance increases by 6.18% in 1 yr, it increases by a factor of 1.0618 in 1 yr.

SOLUTION   Because the balance grows by a fixed percentage every year, it grows exponentially. Letting $y(t)$ be the balance t years after the initial deposit of $y_0 = \$500$, we have $y = y_0 e^{kt}$, where the rate constant k must be determined. Note that if the initial balance is y_0, 1 yr later the balance is 6.18% more, or

$$y(1) = 1.0618\, y_0 = y_0 e^{k}.$$

Solving for k, we find that the rate constant is

$$k = \ln 1.0618 \approx 0.060 \text{ yr}^{-1}.$$

Therefore, the balance at any time $t \geq 0$ is $y(t) = 500e^{0.060t}$. To determine the time required for the balance to reach $2500, we solve the equation

$$y = 500e^{0.060t} = 2500.$$

Dividing by 500 and taking the natural logarithm of both sides yields

$$0.060t = \ln 5.$$

The balance reaches $2500 in $t = (\ln 5)/0.060 \approx 26.824 \text{ yr}.$

Related Exercises 11–20◀

Resource Consumption   Among the many resources that people use, energy is certainly one of the most important. The basic unit of energy is the **joule** (J), roughly the energy needed to lift a 0.1-kg object (say an orange) 1 m. The *rate* at which energy is consumed is called **power**. The basic unit of power is the **watt** (W), where 1 W = 1 J/s. If you turn on a 100-W lightbulb for 1 min, the bulb consumes energy at a rate of 100 J/s, and it uses a total of 100 J/s · 60 s = 6000 J of energy.

A more useful measure of energy for large quantities is the **kilowatt-hour** (kWh). A kilowatt is 1000 W or 1000 J/s. So if you consume energy at the rate of 1 kW for 1 hr (3600 s), you use a total of 1000 J/s · 3600 s = 3.6×10^6 J, which is 1 kWh. A person running for one hour consumes roughly 1 kWh of energy. A typical house uses on the order of 1000 kWh of energy in a month.

Assume that the total energy used (by a person, machine, or city) is given by the function $E(t)$. Because the power $P(t)$ is the rate at which energy is used, we have $P(t) = E'(t)$. Using the ideas of Section 6.1, the total amount of energy used between the times $t = a$ and $t = b$ is

$$\text{total energy used} = \int_a^b E'(t)\, dt = \int_a^b P(t)\, dt.$$

We see that energy is the area under the power curve. With this background, we can investigate a situation in which the rate of energy consumption increases exponentially.

EXAMPLE 4   Energy consumption   At the beginning of 2010, the rate of energy consumption for the city of Denver was 7000 megawatts (MW), where 1 MW = 10^6 W. That rate was expected to increase at an annual growth rate of 2%/yr.

a. Find the function that gives the power or rate of energy consumption for all times after the beginning of 2010.

b. Find the total amount of energy used during 2014.

c. Find the function that gives the total (cumulative) amount of energy used by the city between 2010 and any time $t \geq 0$.

SOLUTION

> In 1 yr, the power function increases by 2% or by a factor of 1.02.

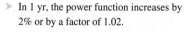

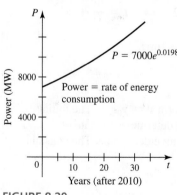

FIGURE 8.29

a. Let $t \geq 0$ be the number of years after the beginning of 2010, and let $P(t)$ be the power function that gives the rate of energy consumption at time t. Because P increases at a constant rate of 2%/yr, it increases exponentially. Therefore, $P = P_0 e^{kt}$, where $P_0 = 7000$ MW. We determine k as before by setting $t = 1$; after one year, the power is

$$P(1) = P_0 e^k = 1.02 P_0.$$

Canceling P_0 and solving for k, we find that $k = \ln 1.02 \approx 0.0198$. Therefore, the power function (Figure 8.29) is

$$P = 7000 e^{0.0198t}, \quad \text{for } t \geq 0.$$

b. The entire year 2014 corresponds to the interval $4 \leq t \leq 5$. Substituting $P(t) = 7000 e^{0.0198t}$, the total energy used in 2014 was

$$\int_4^5 P(t)\, dt = \int_4^5 7000 e^{0.0198t}\, dt \quad \text{Substitute for } P(t).$$

$$= \frac{7000}{0.0198} e^{0.0198t} \Big|_4^5 \quad \text{Fundamental Theorem}$$

$$\approx 7652. \quad \text{Evaluate.}$$

Because the units of P are MW and t is measured in years, the units of energy are MW-yr. To convert to MWh, we multiply by 8760 hr/yr to get the total energy of about 6.7×10^7 MWh (or 6.7×10^{10} kWh).

c. The total energy used between $t = 0$ and any future time t is given by the future value formula (Section 6.1):

$$E(t) = E(0) + \int_0^t E'(s)\,ds = E(0) + \int_0^t P(s)\,ds.$$

Assuming $t = 0$ corresponds to the beginning of 2010, we take $E(0) = 0$. Substituting again for the power function P, the total energy (in MW-yr) at time t is

$$
\begin{aligned}
E(t) &= E(0) + \int_0^t P(s)\,ds \\[2mm]
&= 0 + \int_0^t 7000 e^{0.0198s}\,ds && \text{Substitute for } P(s) \text{ and } E(0). \\[2mm]
&= \frac{7000}{0.0198} e^{0.0198s} \Big|_0^t && \text{Fundamental Theorem} \\[2mm]
&\approx 353{,}535(e^{0.0198t} - 1). && \text{Evaluate.}
\end{aligned}
$$

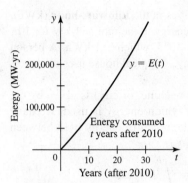

FIGURE 8.30

As shown in Figure 8.30, when the rate of energy consumption increases exponentially, the total amount of energy consumed also increases exponentially.

Related Exercises 11–20 ◄

Exponential Decay

Everything you have learned about exponential growth carries over directly to exponential decay. A function that decreases exponentially has the form $y = y_0 e^{-kt}$, where $y_0 = y(0)$ is the initial value and $k > 0$ is the rate constant. Such functions satisfy the differential equation $y'(t) = -ky$.

Exponential decay is characterized by a constant relative decay rate and by a constant *half-life*. For example, radioactive plutonium has a half-life of 24,000 yr. An initial sample of 1 mg decays to 0.5 mg after 24,000 yr and to 0.25 mg after 48,000 yr. To compute the half-life, we determine the time required for the quantity $y = y_0 e^{-kt}$ to reach one half of its current value; that is, we solve $y_0 e^{-kt} = y_0/2$ for t. Canceling y_0 and taking logarithms of both sides, we find that

> **QUICK CHECK 4** If a quantity decreases by a factor of 8 every 30 yr, what is its half-life? ◄

$$e^{-kt} = \frac{1}{2} \quad \Rightarrow \quad -kt = \ln\left(\frac{1}{2}\right) = -\ln 2 \quad \Rightarrow \quad t = \frac{\ln 2}{k}.$$

The half-life is given by the same formula as the doubling time.

Exponential Decay Functions

Exponential decay is described by functions of the form $y = y_0 e^{-kt}$. The initial value of y is $y(0) = y_0$, and the rate constant $k > 0$ determines the rate of decay. Exponential decay is characterized by a constant relative decay rate. The constant **half-life** is $T_{1/2} = \dfrac{\ln 2}{k}$, with the same units as t.

Radiometric Dating   A powerful method for estimating the age of ancient objects (for example, fossils, bones, meteorites, and cave paintings) relies on the radioactive decay of certain elements. A common version of radiometric dating uses the carbon isotope C-14, which is present in all living matter. When a living organism dies, it ceases to replace C-14, and the C-14 that is present decays with a half-life of about $T_{1/2} = 5730$ yr. Comparing the C-14 in a living organism to the amount in a dead sample provides an estimate of its age.

EXAMPLE 5 **Radiometric dating** Researchers determine that a fossilized bone has 30% of the C-14 of a live bone. Estimate the age of the bone. Assume a half-life for C-14 of 5730 yr.

SOLUTION The exponential decay function $y = y_0 e^{-kt}$ represents the amount of C-14 in the bone t years after its owner died. By the half-life formula, $T_{1/2} = (\ln 2)/k$. Substituting $T_{1/2} = 5730$ yr, the rate constant is

$$k = \frac{\ln 2}{T_{1/2}} = \frac{\ln 2}{5730 \text{ yr}} \approx 0.000121 \text{ yr}^{-1}.$$

Assume that the amount of C-14 in a living bone is y_0. Over t years, the amount of C-14 in the fossilized bone decays to 30% of its initial value, or $0.3y_0$. Using the decay function, we have

$$0.3y_0 = y_0 e^{-0.000121t}.$$

Solving for t, the age of the bone (in years) is

$$t = \frac{\ln 0.3}{-0.000121} \approx 9950.$$

Related Exercises 21–26 ◀

Pharmacokinetics Pharmacokinetics describes the processes by which drugs are assimilated by the body. The elimination of most drugs from the body may be modeled by an exponential decay function with a known half-life (alcohol is a notable exception). The simplest models assume that an entire drug dose is immediately absorbed into the blood. This assumption is a bit of an idealization; more refined mathematical models can account for the absorption process.

▶ **Half-lives of common drugs**

Penicillin	1 hr
Amoxicillin	1 hr
Nicotine	2 hr
Morphine	3 hr
Tetracycline	9 hr
Digitalis	33 hr
Phenobarbital	2–6 days

EXAMPLE 6 **Pharmacokinetics** An exponential decay function $y = y_0 e^{-kt}$ models the amount of drug in the blood t hr after an initial dose of $y_0 = 100$ mg is administered. Assume the half-life of the drug is 16 hr.

a. Find the exponential decay function that governs the amount of drug in the blood.

b. How much time is required for the drug to reach 1% of the initial dose (1 mg)?

c. If a second 100-mg dose is given 12 hr after the first dose, how much time is required for the drug level to reach 1 mg?

SOLUTION

a. Knowing that the half-life is 16 hr, the rate constant is

$$k = \frac{\ln 2}{T_{1/2}} = \frac{\ln 2}{16 \text{ hr}} \approx 0.0433 \text{ hr}^{-1}.$$

Therefore, the decay function is $y = 100e^{-0.0433t}$.

b. The time required for the drug to reach 1 mg is the solution of

$$100e^{-0.0433t} = 1.$$

Solving for t, we have

$$t = \frac{\ln 0.01}{-0.0433 \text{ hr}^{-1}} \approx 106 \text{ hr}.$$

It takes more than 4 days for the drug to be reduced to 1% of the initial dose.

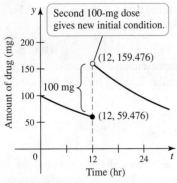

FIGURE 8.31

c. Using the exponential decay function of part (a), the amount of drug in the blood after 12 hr is

$$y(12) = 100e^{-0.0433 \cdot 12} \approx 59.476 \text{ mg}.$$

The second 100-mg dose given after 12 hr increases the amount of drug (assuming instantaneous absorption) to 159.5 mg. This amount becomes the new initial value for another exponential decay process (Figure 8.31). Measuring t from the time of the second dose, the amount of drug in the blood is

$$y = 159.476e^{-0.0433t}.$$

The amount of drug reaches 1 mg when

$$y = 159.476e^{-0.0433t} = 1,$$

which implies that

$$t = \frac{-\ln 159.5}{-0.0433 \text{ hr}^{-1}} = 117.134 \text{ hr}.$$

Approximately 117 hr after the second dose (or 129 hr after the first dose), the amount of drug reaches 1 mg.

Related Exercises 27–30 ◄

SECTION 8.4 EXERCISES

Review Questions

1. In terms of relative growth rate, what is the defining property of exponential growth?

2. Give two pieces of information that may be used to formulate an exponential growth or decay function.

3. Explain the meaning of doubling time.

4. Explain the meaning of half-life.

5. How are the rate constant and the doubling time related?

6. How are the rate constant and the half-life related?

7. Give two examples of processes that are modeled by exponential growth.

8. Give two examples of processes that are modeled by exponential decay.

Basic Skills

9–10. Absolute and relative growth rates *Two functions f and g are given. Show that the growth rate of the linear function is constant and the relative growth rate of the exponential function is constant.*

9. $f(t) = 100 + 10.5t, \ g(t) = 100e^{t/10}$

10. $f(t) = 2200 + 400t, \ g(t) = 400 \cdot 2^{t/20}$

11–16. Designing exponential growth functions *Devise the exponential growth function that fits the given data; then answer the accompanying questions. Be sure to identify the reference point $(t = 0)$ and units of time.*

11. **Population** The population of a town with a 2010 population of 90,000 grows at a rate of 2.4%/yr. In what year will the population double its initial value (to 180,000)?

12. **Population** The population of Clark County, Nevada, was 2 million in 2013. Assuming an annual growth rate of 4.5%/yr, what will the county population be in 2020?

13. **Population** The current population of a town is 50,000 and is growing exponentially. If the population is projected to be 55,000 in 10 yr, then what will be the population 20 yr from now?

14. **Savings account** How long will it take an initial deposit of $1500 to increase in value to $2500 in a saving account with an APY of 3.1%? Assume the interest rate remains constant and no additional deposits or withdrawals are made.

15. **Rising costs** Between 2005 and 2010, the average rate of inflation was about 3%/yr (as measured by the Consumer Price Index). If a cart of groceries cost $100 in 2005, what will it cost in 2015 assuming the rate of inflation remains constant?

16. **Cell growth** The number of cells in a tumor doubles every 6 weeks starting with 8 cells. After how many weeks does the tumor have 1500 cells?

17. **Projection sensitivity** According to the 2010 census, the U.S. population was 309 million with an estimated growth rate of 0.8%/yr.

   a. Based on these figures, find the doubling time and project the population in 2050.

   b. Suppose the actual growth rates are just 0.2 percentage points lower and higher than 0.8%/yr (0.6% and 1.0%). What are the resulting doubling times and projected 2050 populations?

   c. Comment on the sensitivity of these projections to the growth rate.

18. Energy consumption On the first day of the year ($t = 0$), a city uses electricity at a rate of 2000 MW. That rate is projected to increase at a rate of 1.3%/yr.

    a. Based on these figures, find an exponential growth function for the power (rate of electricity use) for the city.

    b. Find the total energy (in MW-yr) used by the city over four full years beginning at $t = 0$.

    c. Find a function that gives the total energy used (in MW-yr) between $t = 0$ and any future time $t > 0$.

19. Population of Texas Texas had the largest increase in population of any state in the United States from 2000 to 2010. During that decade, Texas grew from 20.9 million in 2000 to 25.1 million in 2010. Use an exponential growth model to predict the population of Texas in 2025.

20. Oil consumption Starting in 2010 ($t = 0$), the rate at which oil is consumed by a small country increases at a rate of 1.5%/yr, starting with an initial rate of 1.2 million barrels/yr.

    a. How much oil is consumed over the course of the year 2010 (between $t = 0$ and $t = 1$)?

    b. Find the function that gives the amount of oil consumed between $t = 0$ and any future time t.

    c. How many years after 2010 will the amount of oil consumed since 2010 reach 10 million barrels?

21–25. Designing exponential decay functions *Devise an exponential decay function that fits the following data; then answer the accompanying questions. Be sure to identify the reference point ($t = 0$) and units of time.*

21. Crime rate The homicide rate decreases at a rate of 3%/yr in a city that had 800 homicides/yr in 2010. At this rate, when will the homicide rate reach 600 homicides/yr?

22. Drug metabolism A drug is eliminated from the body at a rate of 15%/hr. After how many hours does the amount of drug reach 10% of the initial dose?

23. Atmospheric pressure The pressure of Earth's atmosphere at sea level is approximately 1000 millibars and decreases exponentially with elevation. At an elevation of 30,000 ft (approximately the altitude of Mt. Everest), the pressure is one-third of the sea-level pressure. At what elevation is the pressure half of the sea-level pressure? At what elevation is it 1% of the sea-level pressure?

24. China's population China's one-child policy was implemented with a goal of reducing China's population to 700 million by 2050 (from 1.2 billion in 2000). Suppose China's population declines at a rate of 0.5%/yr. Will this rate of decline be sufficient to meet the goal?

25. Population of Michigan The population of Michigan decreased from 9.94 million in 2000 to 9.88 million in 2010. Use an exponential model to predict the population in 2020. Explain why an exponential (decay) model might not be an appropriate long-term model of the population of Michigan.

26. Depreciation of equipment A large die-casting machine used to make automobile engine blocks is purchased for $2.5 million. For tax purposes, the value of the machine can be depreciated by 6.8% of its current value each year.

    a. What is the value of the machine after 10 yr?

    b. After how many years is the value of the machine 10% of its original value?

27. Valium metabolism The drug Valium is eliminated from the bloodstream with a half-life of 36 hr. Suppose that a patient receives an initial dose of 20 mg of Valium at midnight.

    a. How much Valium is in the patient's blood at noon the next day?

    b. When will the Valium concentration reach 10% of its initial level?

28. Carbon dating The half-life of C-14 is about 5730 yr.

    a. Archaeologists find a piece of cloth painted with organic dyes. Analysis of the dye in the cloth shows that only 77% of the C-14 originally in the dye remains. When was the cloth painted?

    b. A well-preserved piece of wood found at an archaeological site has 6.2% of the C-14 that it had when it was alive. Estimate when the wood was cut.

29. Uranium dating Uranium-238 (U-238) has a half-life of 4.5 billion yr. Geologists find a rock containing a mixture of U-238 and lead, and determine that 85% of the original U-238 remains; the other 15% has decayed into lead. How old is the rock?

30. Radioiodine treatment Roughly 12,000 Americans are diagnosed with thyroid cancer every year, which accounts for 1% of all cancer cases. It occurs in women three times as frequently as in men. Fortunately, thyroid cancer can be treated successfully in many cases with radioactive iodine, or I-131. This unstable form of iodine has a half-life of 8 days and is given in small doses measured in millicuries.

    a. Suppose a patient is given an initial dose of 100 millicuries. Find the function that gives the amount of I-131 in the body after $t \geq 0$ days.

    b. How long does it take for the amount of I-131 to reach 10% of the initial dose?

    c. Finding the initial dose to give a particular patient is a critical calculation. How does the time to reach 10% of the initial dose change if the initial dose is increased by 5%?

Further Explorations

31. Explain why or why not Determine whether the following statements are true and give an explanation or counterexample.

    a. A quantity that increases at 6%/yr obeys the growth function $y = y_0 e^{0.06t}$.

    b. If a quantity increases by 10%/yr, it increases by 30% over 3 yr.

    c. A quantity decreases by one-third every month. Therefore, it decreases exponentially.

    d. If the rate constant of an exponential growth function is increased, its doubling time is decreased.

    e. If a quantity increases exponentially, the time required to increase by a factor of 10 remains constant for all time.

32. Tripling time A quantity increases according to the exponential function $y = y_0 e^{kt}$. What is the tripling time for the quantity? What is the time required for the quantity to increase p-fold?

33. Constant doubling time Prove that the doubling time for an exponentially increasing quantity is constant for all time.

34. Overtaking City A has a current population of 500,000 people and grows at a rate of 3%/yr. City B has a current population of 300,000 and grows at a rate of 5%/yr.

  a. When will the cities have the same population?
  b. Suppose City C has a current population of $y_0 < 500,000$ and a growth rate of $p > 3\%/\text{yr}$. What is the relationship between y_0 and p such that the Cities A and C have the same population in 10 yr?

35. A slowing race Starting at the same time and place, Abe and Bob race, running at velocities $u = 4/(t + 1)$ mi/hr and $v = 4e^{-t/2}$ mi/hr, respectively, for $t \geq 0$.

  a. Who is ahead after $t = 5$ hr? After $t = 10$ hr?
  b. Find and graph the position functions of both runners. Which runner can run only a finite distance in an unlimited amount of time?

Applications

36. Law of 70 Bankers use the law of 70, which says that if an account increases at a fixed rate of $p\%/\text{yr}$, its doubling time is approximately $70/p$. Explain why and when this statement is true.

37. Compounded inflation The U.S. government reports the rate of inflation (as measured by the Consumer Price Index) both monthly and annually. Suppose that for a particular month, the *monthly* rate of inflation is reported as 0.8%. Assuming that this rate remains constant, what is the corresponding *annual* rate of inflation? Is the annual rate 12 times the monthly rate? Explain.

38. Acceleration, velocity, position Suppose the acceleration of an object moving along a line is given by $a(t) = -kv(t)$, where k is a positive constant and v is the object's velocity. Assume that the initial velocity and position are given by $v(0) = 10$ and $s(0) = 0$, respectively.

  a. Use $a(t) = v'(t)$ to find the velocity of the object as a function of time.
  b. Use $v(t) = s'(t)$ to find the position of the object as a function of time.
  c. Use the fact that $dv/dt = (dv/ds)(ds/dt)$ (by the Chain Rule) to find the velocity as a function of position.

39. Free fall (adapted from Putnam Exam, 1939) An object moves freely in a straight line except for air resistance, which is proportional to its speed; this means its acceleration is $a(t) = -kv(t)$. The speed of the object decreases from 1000 ft/s to 900 ft/s over a distance of 1200 ft. Approximate the time required for this deceleration to occur. (Exercise 38 may be useful.)

40. A running model A model for the startup of a runner in a short race results in the velocity function $v = a(1 - e^{-t/c})$, where a and c are positive constants and v has units of m/s. (*Source: A Theory of Competitive Running, Joe Keller, Physics Today* **26** (Sep 1973))

  a. Graph the velocity function for $a = 12$ and $c = 2$. What is the runner's maximum velocity?
  b. Using the velocity in part (a) and assuming $s(0) = 0$, find the position function $s(t)$, for $t \geq 0$.
  c. Graph the position function and estimate the time required to run 100 m.

41. Tumor growth Suppose the cells of a tumor are idealized as spheres, each with a radius of 5 μm (micrometers). The number of cells has a doubling time of 35 days. Approximately how long

will it take a single cell to grow into a multi-celled spherical tumor with a volume of 0.5 cm^3 (1 cm = 10,000 μm)? Assume that the tumor spheres are tightly packed.

42. Carbon emissions from China and the United States The burning of fossil fuels releases greenhouse gases (roughly 60% carbon dioxide) into the atmosphere. In 2010, the United States released approximately 5.8 billion metric tons of carbon dioxide (Environmental Protection Agency estimate), while China released approximately 8.2 billion metric tons (U. S. Department of Energy estimate). Reasonable estimates of the growth rate in carbon dioxide emissions are 4% per year for the United States and 9% per year for China. In 2010, the U.S. population was 309 million, growing at a rate of 0.7% per year, and the population of China was 1.3 billion, growing at a rate of 0.5% per year.

  a. Find exponential growth functions for the amount of carbon dioxide released by the United States and China. Let $t = 0$ correspond to 2010.
  b. According to the models in part (a), when will Chinese emissions double that of the United States?
  c. What was the amount of carbon dioxide released by the United States and China *per capita* in 2010?
  d. Find exponential growth functions for the per capita amount of carbon dioxide released by the United States and China in the years after 2010. Let $t = 0$ correspond to 2010.
  e. Use the models of part (d) to determine the year in which per capita emissions in the two countries are equal.

43. A revenue model The owner of a clothing store understands that the demand for shirts decreases with the price. In fact, she has developed a model that predicts that at a price of $\$x$ per shirt, she can sell $D(x) = 40e^{-x/50}$ shirts in a day. It follows that the revenue (total money taken in) in a day is $R(x) = xD(x)$ ($\$x/\text{shirt} \cdot D(x)$ shirts). What price should the owner charge to maximize revenue?

Additional Exercises

44. Geometric means A quantity grows exponentially according to $y = y_0e^{kt}$. What is the relationship between m, n, and p such that $y(p) = \sqrt{y(m)y(n)}$?

45. Equivalent growth functions The same exponential growth function can be written in the forms $y = y_0e^{kt}$, $y = y_0(1 + r)^t$, and $y = y_02^{t/T_2}$. Write k as a function of r, r as a function of T_2, and T_2 as a function of k.

46. General relative growth rates Define the relative growth rate of the function f over the time interval T to be the relative change in f over an interval of length T:

$$R_T = \frac{f(t + T) - f(t)}{f(t)}.$$

Show that for the exponential function $y(t) = y_0e^{kt}$, the relative growth rate R_T is constant for any T; that is, choose any T and show that R_T is constant for all t.

QUICK CHECK ANSWERS

1. Population A grows exponentially; population B grows linearly. **3.** The function $100e^{0.05t}$ increases by a factor of 1.0513, or by 5.13%, in 1 unit of time. **4.** 10 yr ◄

CHAPTER 8   REVIEW EXERCISES

1. Explain why or why not Determine whether the following statements are true and give an explanation or counterexample.

  a. The differential equation $y' + 2y = t$ is first-order, linear, and separable.

  b. The differential equation $y'y = 2t^2$ is first-order, linear, and separable.

  c. The function $y = t + 1/t$ satisfies the initial value problem $ty' + y = 2t, y(1) = 2$.

  d. The slope field for the differential equation $y'(t) = t + y(t)$ is plotted in the ty-plane.

  e. Euler's method gives the exact solution to the initial value problem $y' = ty^2, y(0) = 3$ on the interval $[0, a]$ provided a is not too large.

2–10. General solutions *Use the method of your choice to find the general solution of the following differential equations.*

2. $\dfrac{dy}{dt} + 3y = 0$

3. $\dfrac{dy}{dt} + 2y = 6$

4. $p'(x) = 4p + 8$

5. $\dfrac{dy}{dt} = 2ty$

6. $\dfrac{dy}{dt} = \sqrt{\dfrac{y}{t}}$

7. $\dfrac{dy}{dt} = \dfrac{y}{t^2 + 1}$

8. $y'(x) = \dfrac{\sin x}{2y}$

9. $\dfrac{dy}{dt} = (2t + 1)(y^2 + 1)$

10. $z'(t) = \dfrac{tz}{t^2 + 1}$

11–18. Solving initial value problems *Use the method of your choice to find the solution of the following initial value problems.*

11. $\dfrac{dy}{dt} = 2t + \cos t, y(0) = 1$

12. $\dfrac{dy}{dt} = -3y + 9, y(0) = 4$

13. $Q'(t) = Q - 8, Q(1) = 0$

14. $y'(x) = \dfrac{x}{y}, y(2) = 4$

15. $u'(t) = \left(\dfrac{u}{t}\right)^{1/3}, u(1) = 8$

16. $y'(x) = 4x \csc y, y(0) = \pi/2$

17. $s'(t) = \dfrac{1}{2s(t + 2)}, s(-1) = 4, t \geq -1$

18. $\theta'(x) = 4x \cos^2 \theta, \theta(0) = \pi/4$

19. Slope fields Consider the slope field for the equation $y' = y(2 - y)$ shown in the figure and initial conditions of the form $y(0) = A$.

  a. Sketch a solution on the slope field with the initial condition $y(0) = 1$.

  b. Sketch a solution on the slope field with the initial condition $y(0) = 3$.

  c. For what values of A are the corresponding solutions increasing, for $t \geq 0$?

  d. For what values of A are the corresponding solutions decreasing, for $t \geq 0$?

  e. Identify the equilibrium solutions for the differential equation.

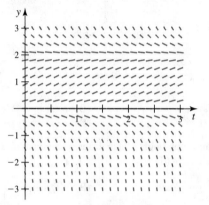

20. Slope fields The slope field for the equation $y'(t) = t - y$, for $|t| \leq 4$ and $|y| \leq 4$, is shown in the figure.

  a. Use the slope field to sketch the solution curve that passes through the point $\left(0, \dfrac{1}{2}\right)$.

  b. Use the slope field to sketch the solution curve that passes through the point $\left(0, -\dfrac{1}{2}\right)$.

  c. In what region of the ty-plane are solutions increasing? Decreasing?

  d. Complete the following sentence. The solution of the differential equation with the initial condition $y(0) = A$, where A is a real number, approaches the line _____ as $t \to \infty$.

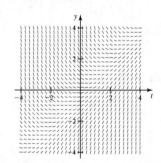

21. Identifying a slope field Which differential equation has the following slope field?

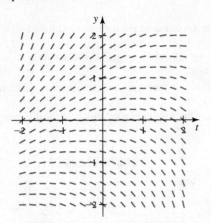

(A) $y'(t) = y + t$ (B) $y'(t) = y - t$
(C) $y'(t) = t - y$ (D) $y'(t) = 3y + t$

22. Matching slope fields Match differential equations (A)–(D) with slope fields (a)–(d).

(A) $y'(t) = \sin ty$ (B) $y'(t) = \dfrac{y}{t + 1}$

(C) $y'(t) = y - 2t$ (D) $y'(t) = y^2(2 - y)$

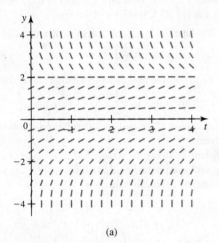

(a)

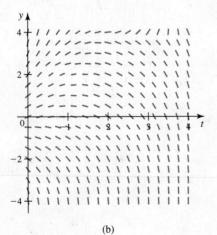

(b)

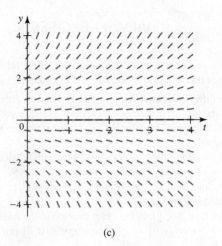

(c)

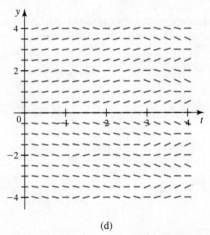

(d)

23–24. Euler's method tables For each of the following initial value problems, complete the given table with Euler approximations.

23. $y'(t) = y - 2, y(0) = 1$

k	t_k	u_k	Slope $= f(t_k, u_k)$
0	0		
1	0.25		
2	0.5		
3	0.75		—

24. $y'(t) = y + t, y(-1) = 2$

k	t_k	u_k	Slope $= f(t_k, u_k)$
0	−1		
1	−0.75		
2	−0.5		
3	−0.25		
4	0		—

25. Euler's method Consider the initial value problem

$$y'(t) = \frac{1}{2y}, y(0) = 1.$$

a. Use Euler's method with $\Delta t = 0.1$ to compute approximations to $y(0.1)$ and $y(0.2)$.

b. Use Euler's method with $\Delta t = 0.05$ to compute approximations to $y(0.1)$ and $y(0.2)$.

c. The exact solution of this initial value problem is $y = \sqrt{t + 1}$. Compute the errors in the approximations to $y(0.2)$ found in parts (a) and (b). Which approximation gives the smaller error?

26–29. Equilibrium solutions *For what initial conditions* $y(0) = A$ *do the following equations have solutions that are constant for all* $t \geq 0$?

26. $y'(t) = y(2 - y)$ **27.** $y'(t) = y(3 + y)(y - 5)$

28. $y'(t) = \sin 2y$, for $|y| < \pi$ **29.** $y'(t) = y^3 - y^2 - 2y$

30. Logistic growth The population of a rabbit community is governed by the initial value problem

$$P'(t) = 0.2 P\left(1 - \frac{P}{1200}\right), P(0) = 50.$$

a. Find the equilibrium solutions.

b. Find the population, for all times $t \geq 0$.

c. What is the carrying capacity of the population?

d. What is the population when the growth rate is a maximum?

e. For what positive values of P is the solution curve concave up? Concave down?

31. Newton's Law of Cooling A cup of coffee is removed from a microwave oven with a temperature of 80°C and allowed to cool in a room with a temperature of 25°C. Five minutes later, the temperature of the coffee is 60°C.

a. Find the rate constant k for the cooling process.

b. Find the temperature of the coffee, for $t \geq 0$.

c. When does the temperature of the coffee reach 50°C?

32. Newton's Law of Cooling An iron bar is removed from a forge with a temperature of 300° and allowed to cool in a room with a temperature of 60°. According to Newton's Law of Cooling, the temperature of the bar is governed by the equation $T'(t) = -k(T - 60)$, with $T(0) = 300$ and $k > 0$.

a. Find the solution to this equation for arbitrary k.

b. Ten minutes after the bar is removed from the forge, it has cooled to 240°. Use this fact to determine the constant k.

c. Graph the solution, and check that the initial condition is satisfied.

d. Evaluate $\lim_{t \to \infty} T(t)$ and interpret this result.

33. Radioactive decay The mass of radioactive material in a sample has decreased by 30% since the decay began. Assuming a half-life of 1500 yr, how long ago did the decay begin?

34. Population growth Growing from an initial population of 150,000 at a constant annual growth rate of 4%/yr, how long will it take a city to reach a population of 1 million?

35. Savings account A savings account advertises an annual percentage yield (APY) of 5.4%, which means that the balance in the account increases at an annual growth rate of 5.4%/yr.

a. Find the balance in the account for $t \geq 0$ with an initial deposit of $1500, assuming the APY remains fixed and no additional deposits or withdrawals are made.

b. What is the doubling time of the balance?

c. After how many years does the balance reach $5000?

AP® PRACTICE QUESTIONS   *The following questions are intended to help you prepare for the AP exam. They are not questions from actual AP exams.*

Section 1 Part A, Multiple Choice, No Technology

1. Which of the following differential equations are separable?

(I) $y' + ty = 9$
(II) $y' + 3y = 4$
(III) $y' + y^2 = 0$

(A) I and II only   (B) II and III only
(C) I only   (D) II only
(E) III only

2. Which differential equation has the following slope field?

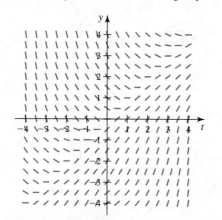

(A) $y' + y(1 - y)$ (B) $y' = 2y$
(C) $y' = t + y$ (D) $y' = t^2 - 1$
(E) $y' = t - y$

3. Make a sketch of the slope field for the equation $\dfrac{dy}{dt} = y - y^2$, and then sketch the solution curve with the initial condition $y(0) = 0.5$, for $t \geq 0$. On which interval do the solution values lie?

(A) $(0, 0.5]$ (B) $[0.5, 1)$
(C) $(0.5, \infty)$ (D) $(-\infty, 0.5]$
(E) $(0, 1)$

4. Which of the following slope fields is generated by the equation
$y' = y^2(2 - y)$?

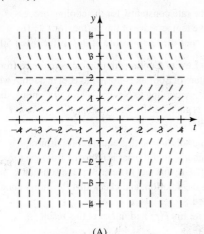

(A)

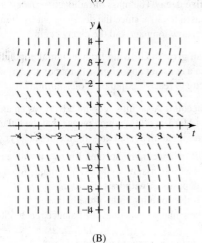

(B)

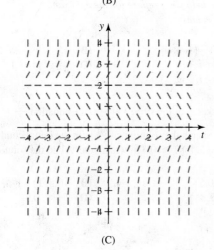

(C)

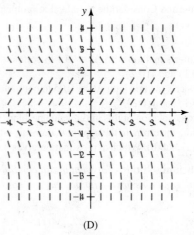

(D)

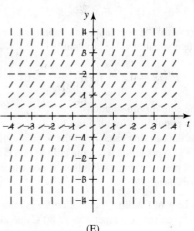

(E)

5. Find the function that satisfies the equation $y' + 3t^2 = \sin \pi t$, where $y(1) = -1$.

(A) $y = -t^3 - \cos \pi t - 1$

(B) $y = -t^3 - \dfrac{1}{\pi} \cos \pi t - \dfrac{1}{\pi}$

(C) $y = -t^3 + \dfrac{1}{\pi} \cos \pi t + \dfrac{1}{\pi}$

(D) $y = t^3 + \dfrac{1}{\pi} \cos \pi t - 2 + \dfrac{1}{\pi}$

(E) $y = t^3 - \cos \pi t - 3$

6. Find the solution of $\dfrac{dy}{dt} = \left(\dfrac{2}{3}t + 1\right)y^{-2}$, where $y(0) = 2$.

(A) $y = (t^2 + 3t + \sqrt{2})^{1/2}$

(B) $y = -t^2 - 3t + 2$

(C) $y = \left(\dfrac{t^2}{3} - 3t + 8\right)^{1/3}$

(D) $y = (t^2 + 3t + 8)^{1/3}$

(E) $y = \left(\dfrac{t^2}{3} + 3t + 8\right)^{1/3}$

7. The population of fish in a hatchery with regular harvesting is modeled by $\frac{dp}{dt} = 0.5p - 100$. Which of the following statements describes the population when the initial fish population is $p(0) = 100$?

   (A) The population increases without bound.
   (B) The population increases and approaches a steady-state value of 200.
   (C) The population decreases and reaches zero in a finite amount of time.
   (D) The population initially decreases, but then increases and approaches a steady-state value of 200.
   (E) Harvesting balances natural growth and the population remains 100 for all time.

8. Euler's method is applied to the initial value problem $y' = y + 10t$, $y(0) = 1$ with a time step of $\Delta t = 0.1$. Find the resulting approximation to $y(0.2)$.

   (A) 1.641   (B) 2.304
   (C) 1.425   (D) 1.213
   (E) 1.310

9. The slope field of a differential equation is shown below. Which function could be a solution of the equation?

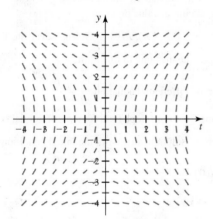

   (A) $y = \sqrt{t^2 - 4}$ (B) $y = 2e^t$

   (C) $y = 2\cos t$ (D) $y = \frac{2}{t + 1}$

   (E) $y = 4 - t^2$

10. The solution of an initial value problem has the following graph.

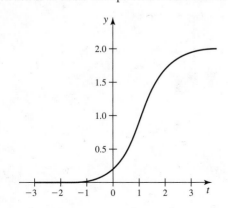

Which initial value problem could produce this solution?

   (A) $y' = y(y - 2)$, $y(0) = 0.2$
   (B) $y' = y(2 - y)$, $y(0) = 0.2$
   (C) $y' = \cos y$, $y(0) = 0.2$
   (D) $y' = -ty$, $y(0) = 0.2$
   (E) $y' = 3y$, $y(0) = 0.2$

11. The solution curve for the initial value problem $\frac{dy}{dt} = \frac{y}{10}(10 - y)$, $y(0) = 2$ has which of the following properties?

   (I)   It is concave up for values of t near $t = 0$.
   (II) It is increasing for all $t \geq 0$.
   (III) The line tangent to the curve at the point where $y = 5$ has slope $m = 2.5$.

   (A) III only   (B) I and II only
   (C) I and III only   (D) II and III only
   (E) I, II, and III

12. The solution to the differential equation $\frac{dy}{dt} = -2y$, with the initial condition $y(0) = 2$, is

   (A) $y = t^2 + 2$.   (B) $y = -t^2 + 2$.
   (C) $y = -2e^{-2t} + 4$.   (D) $y = 2e^{-2t}$.
   (E) $y = -2e^{2t} + 4$.

13. Assume that $y(t)$ is a solution to the differential equation $\frac{dy}{dt} = -6y(y - 4)$ with $y(0) = 2$. As $t \to \infty$,

   (A) $y(t) \to \infty$.   (B) $y(t) \to -\infty$.
   (C) $y(t) \to 4$.   (D) $y(t) \to 0$.
   (E) $y(t) \to 2$.

Section 1 Part B, Multiple Choice, Technology Allowed

14. Consider the initial value problem $y' = t + y$, $y(0) = 1$. Make a sketch of the slope field and determine which of the following values is closest to the value of $y(2)$.

   (A) 1   (B) 8
   (C) 2   (D) 0
   (E) −1

15. Consider the initial value problem $y' = y^2 - t$, $y(0) = 0$. Use Euler's method with a time step of $\Delta t = \frac{1}{3}$ to approximate the value of $y(1)$.

   (A) −0.329   (B) 0.173
   (C) 0   (D) −0.626
   (E) 0.449

16. Consider the initial value problem $y' = ty$, $y(3) = 2$. Use the linear approximation to y at $t = 3$ to approximate the value of $y(\pi)$.

   (A) 2.708   (B) 9.849
   (C) 2.850   (D) 1.150
   (E) 18.849

Section 2 Part A, Free Response, Technology Allowed

1. Assume f and f' are continuous on $(-\infty, \infty)$ and $f(0) = 1$. Use the table of values for f' to complete parts (a)–(e).

x	0	0.1	0.2	0.3	0.4
$f'(x)$	1.0	1.2	1.4	1.6	1.8

 a. Use a midpoint Riemann sum with two subintervals of equal length to estimate the value of $\displaystyle\int_0^{0.4} f'(x)\,dx$.

 b. Use your answer to part (a) to estimate the value of $f(0.4)$.

 c. Determine the equation of the line tangent to the graph of f at $x = 0$.

 d. Use the line tangent to the graph of f at $x = 0$ to estimate the value of $f(0.4)$.

 e. Use Euler's method, starting at $x = 0$, with two steps of equal length, to estimate the value of $f(0.4)$.

2. Suppose that Euler's method is used to approximate the solution of the initial value problem $y' = \dfrac{t}{y}$, $y(0) = 4$.

 a. Find an approximation to $y(0.4)$ using a time step of $\Delta t = 0.2$.

 b. Reduce the time step to $\Delta t = 0.1$ and find an approximation to $y(0.4)$.

 c. Given that the solution to the equation is $y = \sqrt{t^2 + 16}$, find the errors in the approximations in parts (a) and (b).

 d. By approximately what factor is the error reduced when the time step is reduced by a factor of 2?

Section 2 Part B, Free Response, No Technology

3. Consider the differential equation $y' = -\dfrac{y^2}{(x+1)^2}$, where $x > -1$.

 a. Plot the slope field at the four points in the figure below.

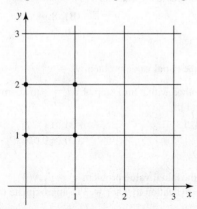

 b. Find the general solution of the equation (in terms of an arbitrary constant C).

 c. Find the solution with the initial condition $y(0) = 2$.

 d. For the solution in part (c), evaluate $\lim\limits_{x \to \infty} y(x)$.

4. Consider the initial value problem $\dfrac{dy}{dt} = \dfrac{y}{2} - 4$, $y(0) = A$, for $t \geq 0$.

 a. Find the solution in terms of A.

 b. Find the solution with $A = 2$ and evaluate $\lim\limits_{t \to \infty} y(t)$.

 c. Find the solution with $A = 12$ and evaluate $\lim\limits_{t \to \infty} y(t)$.

 d. Find the value of B that makes the following sentence true: If $A > B$, then y increases for $t \geq 0$, and if $A < B$, then y decreases for $t \geq 0$.

5. The number of wild rabbits in a rural county is 500 when observations begin in 2013. Biologists estimate that the rabbit population P will satisfy the differential equation $\dfrac{dP}{dt} = \dfrac{1}{2}(1000 - P)$, where t is measured in years.

 a. Is the rabbit population growing faster when there are 600 rabbits or 800 rabbits in the county?

 b. Use the line tangent to the graph of P at $t = 0$ to approximate the number of rabbits in 2014 when $t = 1$.

 c. Write $\dfrac{d^2P}{dt^2}$ in terms of P. Use the second derivative to determine whether the estimate in part (b) is an underestimate or overestimate of the population when $t = 1$.

 d. Solve the initial value problem $\dfrac{dP}{dt} = \dfrac{1}{2}(1000 - P)$, $P(0) = 500$ and evaluate $\lim\limits_{t \to \infty} P(t)$. Interpret the meaning of this limit.

6. Consider the differential equation $\dfrac{dy}{dt} = \dfrac{ty}{5}$.

 a. Use the following slope field for the differential equation to sketch the solution curve with the initial conditions $y(0) = \dfrac{1}{2}$ and $y(0) = -\dfrac{1}{2}$.

b. Write an equation of the line tangent to the solution curve at the point $(2, 1)$.

c. Solve the initial value problem $\dfrac{dy}{dt} = \dfrac{ty}{5}$, $y(0) = 1$.

d. Compute $\dfrac{d^2y}{dt^2}$ as a function of t and y and show that

$\dfrac{d^2y}{dt^2} = \dfrac{y}{25}(t^2 + 5)$. Then explain why solution curves are concave up for all t when $y(0) > 0$ and concave down for all t when $y(0) < 0$.

Chapter 8 Guided Projects

Applications of the material in this chapter and related topics can be found in the following Guided Projects. For additional information, see the Preface.

- Cooling coffee
- Euler's method for differential equations
- Predator-prey models
- Period of the pendulum

- Terminal velocity
- Logistic growth
- A pursuit problem

9 Sequences and Infinite Series

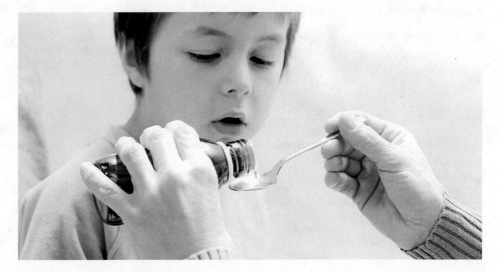

Most of us have taken medication in periodic doses—perhaps an antibiotic every 8 hr or an aspirin every day. Under such a regimen, the concentration of the medication in the blood varies: After a dose, the concentration spikes and then decays with a half-life characteristic of the drug. Following the next dose, the concentration spikes and decays again, and this pattern continues after each dose. The red dots on the graph below represent the concentrations immediately following a dose and they form a *sequence*—a list of numbers. As we go farther and farther out in that list, how do these numbers behave? Do they increase without bound? Or do they level off and reach a steady-state concentration? Clearly these are important questions for physicians and patients. Whether or not a sequence approaches a *limit* is determined by the *convergence* of the sequence. In this chapter, we study sequences and their applications, not only to periodic dosing, but also to mathematically similar problems such as harvesting and financial loans.

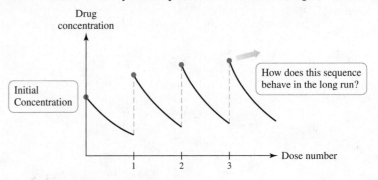

Chapter Preview
This chapter covers topics that lie at the foundation of calculus—indeed, at the foundation of mathematics. The first task is to make a clear distinction between a *sequence* and an *infinite series*. A sequence is an ordered *list* of numbers, $a_1, a_2, \ldots,$ while an infinite series is a *sum* of numbers, $a_1 + a_2 + \cdots$. The idea of convergence to a limit is important for both sequences and series, but convergence is analyzed differently in the two cases. To determine limits of sequences, we use the same tools used for limits of functions at infinity. Convergence of infinite series is a different matter, and we develop the required methods in this chapter. The study of infinite series begins with *geometric series*, which have theoretical importance and are used to answer many practical questions (When is your auto loan paid off? How much antibiotic is in your blood if you take three pills per day?). We then present several tests to determine whether series with positive terms converge. Finally, alternating series, whose terms alternate in sign, are discussed in anticipation of power series in the next chapter.

9.1 An Overview

> Keeping with common practice, the terms *series* and *infinite series* are used interchangeably throughout this chapter.

To understand sequences and series, you must understand how they differ and how they are related. The purposes of this opening section are to introduce sequences and series in concrete terms, and to illustrate their differences and their relationships with each other.

Examples of Sequences

Consider the following *list* of numbers:

$$\{1, 4, 7, 10, 13, 16, \ldots\}.$$

Each number in the list is obtained by adding 3 to the previous number in the list. With this rule, we could extend the list indefinitely.

> The dots (. . . , an *ellipsis*) after the last number of a sequence mean that the list goes on indefinitely.

This list is an example of a *sequence*, where each number in the sequence is called a **term** of the sequence. We denote sequences in any of the following forms:

$$\{a_1, a_2, a_3, \ldots, a_n, \ldots\}, \qquad \{a_n\}_{n=1}^{\infty}, \quad \text{or} \quad \{a_n\}.$$

The subscript n that appears in a_n is called an **index**, and it indicates the order of terms in the sequence. The choice of a starting index is arbitrary, but sequences usually begin with $n = 0$ or $n = 1$.

The sequence $\{1, 4, 7, 10, \ldots\}$ can be defined in two ways. First, we have the rule that each term of the sequence is 3 more than the previous term; that is, $a_2 = a_1 + 3$, $a_3 = a_2 + 3, a_4 = a_3 + 3$, and so forth. In general, we see that

$$a_1 = 1 \quad \text{and} \quad a_{n+1} = a_n + 3, \qquad \text{for } n = 1, 2, 3, \ldots.$$

This way of defining a sequence is called a *recurrence relation* (or an *implicit formula*). It specifies the initial term of the sequence (in this case, $a_1 = 1$) and gives a general rule for computing the next term of the sequence from previous terms. For example, if you know a_{100}, the recurrence relation can be used to find a_{101}.

Suppose instead you want to find a_{147} directly without computing the first 146 terms of the sequence. The first four terms of the sequence can be written

$$a_1 = 1 + (3 \cdot 0), \qquad a_2 = 1 + (3 \cdot 1), \qquad a_3 = 1 + (3 \cdot 2), \qquad a_4 = 1 + (3 \cdot 3).$$

Observe the pattern: The nth term of the sequence is 1 plus 3 multiplied by $n - 1$, or

$$a_n = 1 + 3(n - 1) = 3n - 2, \qquad \text{for } n = 1, 2, 3, \ldots.$$

QUICK CHECK 1 Find a_{10} for the sequence $\{1, 4, 7, 10, \ldots\}$ using the recurrence relation and then again using the explicit formula for the nth term. ◄

With this *explicit formula*, the nth term of the sequence is determined directly from the value of n. For example, with $n = 147$,

$$a_{147} = 3 \cdot \underbrace{147}_{n} - 2 = 439.$$

DEFINITION Sequence

A **sequence** $\{a_n\}$ is an ordered list of numbers of the form

$$\{a_1, a_2, a_3, \ldots, a_n, \ldots\}.$$

A sequence may be generated by a **recurrence relation** of the form $a_{n+1} = f(a_n)$, for $n = 1, 2, 3, \ldots$, where a_1 is given. A sequence may also be defined with an **explicit formula** of the form $a_n = f(n)$, for $n = 1, 2, 3, \ldots$.

> When defined by an explicit formula $a_n = f(n)$, it is evident that sequences are functions. The domain is generally a subset of the nonnegative integers, and one real number a_n is assigned to each integer in the domain.

EXAMPLE 1   Explicit formulas Use the explicit formula for $\{a_n\}_{n=1}^{\infty}$ to write the first four terms of each sequence. Sketch a graph of the sequence.

a. $a_n = \dfrac{1}{2^n}$ **b.** $a_n = \dfrac{(-1)^n n}{n^2 + 1}$

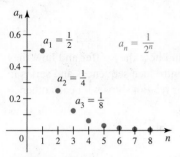

FIGURE 9.1

> The "switch" $(-1)^n$ is used frequently to alternate the signs of the terms of sequences and series.

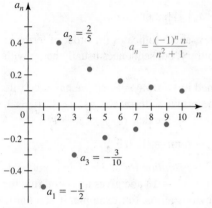

FIGURE 9.2

QUICK CHECK 2 Find an explicit formula for the sequence $\{1, 3, 7, 15, \ldots\}$ (Example 2). ◄

> In Example 3, the starting index is $n = 0$. Other choices are possible.

SOLUTION

a. Substituting $n = 1, 2, 3, 4, \ldots$ into the explicit formula $a_n = \dfrac{1}{2^n}$, we find that the terms of the sequence are

$$\left\{\frac{1}{2}, \frac{1}{2^2}, \frac{1}{2^3}, \frac{1}{2^4}, \ldots\right\} = \left\{\frac{1}{2}, \frac{1}{4}, \frac{1}{8}, \frac{1}{16}, \ldots\right\}.$$

The graph of a sequence is the graph of a function that is defined only on a set of integers. In this case, we plot the coordinate pairs (n, a_n), for $n = 1, 2, 3, \ldots$, resulting in a graph consisting of individual points. The graph of the sequence $a_n = \dfrac{1}{2^n}$ suggests that the terms of this sequence approach 0 as n increases (Figure 9.1).

b. Substituting $n = 1, 2, 3, 4, \ldots$ into the explicit formula, the terms of the sequence are

$$\left\{\frac{(-1)^1(1)}{1^2 + 1}, \frac{(-1)^2 2}{2^2 + 1}, \frac{(-1)^3 3}{3^2 + 1}, \frac{(-1)^4 4}{4^2 + 1}, \ldots\right\} = \left\{-\frac{1}{2}, \frac{2}{5}, -\frac{3}{10}, \frac{4}{17}, \ldots\right\}.$$

From the graph (Figure 9.2), we see that the terms of the sequence alternate in sign and appear to approach 0 as n increases.   *Related Exercises 9–16* ◄

EXAMPLE 2 **Recurrence relations** Use the recurrence relation for $\{a_n\}_{n=1}^{\infty}$ to write the first four terms of the sequences

$$a_{n+1} = 2a_n + 1, a_1 = 1 \quad \text{and} \quad a_{n+1} = 2a_n + 1, a_1 = -1.$$

SOLUTION Notice that the recurrence relation is the same for the two sequences; only the first term differs. The first four terms of the two sequences are as follows.

n	a_n with $a_1 = 1$	a_n with $a_1 = -1$
1	$a_1 = 1$ (given)	$a_1 = -1$ (given)
2	$a_2 = 2a_1 + 1 = 2 \cdot 1 + 1 = 3$	$a_2 = 2a_1 + 1 = 2(-1) + 1 = -1$
3	$a_3 = 2a_2 + 1 = 2 \cdot 3 + 1 = 7$	$a_3 = 2a_2 + 1 = 2(-1) + 1 = -1$
4	$a_4 = 2a_3 + 1 = 2 \cdot 7 + 1 = 15$	$a_4 = 2a_3 + 1 = 2(-1) + 1 = -1$

We see that the terms of the first sequence increase without bound, while all terms of the second sequence are -1. Clearly, the initial term of the sequence may determine the behavior of the entire sequence.   *Related Exercises 17–22* ◄

EXAMPLE 3 **Working with sequences** Consider the following sequences.

a. $\{a_n\} = \{-2, 5, 12, 19, \ldots\}$ **b.** $\{b_n\} = \{3, 6, 12, 24, 48, \ldots\}$

(i) Find the next two terms of the sequence.

(ii) Find a recurrence relation that generates the sequence.

(iii) Find an explicit formula for the nth term of the sequence.

SOLUTION

a. (i) Each term is obtained by adding 7 to its predecessor. The next two terms are $19 + 7 = 26$ and $26 + 7 = 33$.

(ii) Because each term is seven more than its predecessor, a recurrence relation is

$$a_{n+1} = a_n + 7, a_0 = -2, \quad \text{for } n = 0, 1, 2, \ldots.$$

(iii) Notice that $a_0 = -2$, $a_1 = -2 + (1 \cdot 7)$, and $a_2 = -2 + (2 \cdot 7)$, so an explicit formula is

$$a_n = 7n - 2, \quad \text{for } n = 0, 1, 2, \ldots.$$

b. (i) Each term is obtained by multiplying its predecessor by 2. The next two terms are $48 \cdot 2 = 96$ and $96 \cdot 2 = 192$.

(ii) Because each term is two times its predecessor, a recurrence relation is

$$a_{n+1} = 2a_n, a_0 = 3, \quad \text{for } n = 0, 1, 2, \ldots.$$

(iii) To obtain an explicit formula, note that $a_0 = 3$, $a_1 = 3(2^1)$, and $a_2 = 3(2^2)$. In general,

$$a_n = 3(2^n), \quad \text{for } n = 0, 1, 2, \ldots.$$

Related Exercises 23–30 ◄

Limit of a Sequence

Perhaps the most important question about a sequence is this: If you go farther and farther out in the sequence, $a_{100}, \ldots, a_{10,000}, \ldots, a_{100,000}, \ldots$, how do the terms of the sequence behave? Do they approach a specific number, and if so, what is that number? Or do they grow in magnitude without bound? Or do they wander around with or without a pattern?

The long-term behavior of a sequence is described by its **limit**. We work with the following informal definition.

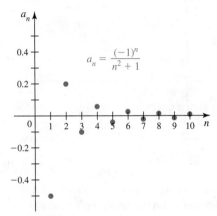

FIGURE 9.3

> **DEFINITION Limit of a Sequence**
>
> If the terms of a sequence $\{a_n\}$ approach a unique number L as n increases—that is, if a_n can be made arbitrarily close to L by taking n sufficiently large—then we say $\lim_{n \to \infty} a_n = L$ exists, and the sequence **converges** to L. If the terms of the sequence do not approach a single number as n increases, the sequence has no limit, and the sequence **diverges**.

EXAMPLE 4 Limit of a sequence Write the first four terms of each sequence. If you believe the sequence converges, make a conjecture about its limit. If the sequence appears to diverge, explain why.

a. $\left\{ \dfrac{(-1)^n}{n^2 + 1} \right\}_{n=1}^{\infty}$ Explicit formula

b. $\{\cos n\pi\}_{n=1}^{\infty}$ Explicit formula

c. $\{a_n\}_{n=1}^{\infty}$, where $a_{n+1} = -2a_n$, $a_1 = 1$ Recurrence relation

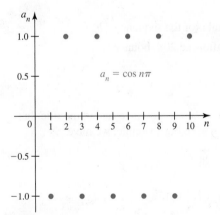

FIGURE 9.4

SOLUTION

a. Beginning with $n = 1$, the first four terms of the sequence are

$$\left\{ \frac{(-1)^1}{1^2 + 1}, \frac{(-1)^2}{2^2 + 1}, \frac{(-1)^3}{3^2 + 1}, \frac{(-1)^4}{4^2 + 1}, \ldots \right\} = \left\{ -\frac{1}{2}, \frac{1}{5}, -\frac{1}{10}, \frac{1}{17}, \ldots \right\}.$$

The terms decrease in magnitude and approach zero with alternating signs. The limit appears to be 0 (Figure 9.3).

b. The first four terms of the sequence are

$$\{\cos \pi, \cos 2\pi, \cos 3\pi, \cos 4\pi, \ldots\} = \{-1, 1, -1, 1, \ldots\}.$$

In this case, the terms of the sequence alternate between -1 and $+1$, and never approach a single value. Therefore, the sequence diverges (Figure 9.4).

c. The first four terms of the sequence are

$$\{1, -2a_1, -2a_2, -2a_3, \ldots\} = \{1, -2, 4, -8, \ldots\}.$$

Because the magnitudes of the terms increase without bound, the sequence diverges (Figure 9.5).

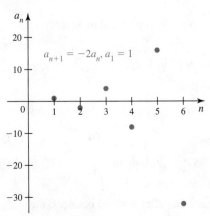

FIGURE 9.5

Related Exercises 31–40 ◄

EXAMPLE 5   Limit of a sequence Enumerate and graph the terms of the following sequence and make a conjecture about its limit.

$$a_n = \frac{4n^3}{n^3 + 1}, \qquad \text{for } n = 1, 2, 3, \ldots. \quad \text{Explicit formula}$$

SOLUTION The first 14 terms of the sequence $\{a_n\}$ are tabulated in Table 9.1 and graphed in Figure 9.6. The terms appear to approach 4.

Table 9.1

n	a_n	n	a_n
1	2.000	8	3.992
2	3.556	9	3.995
3	3.857	10	3.996
4	3.938	11	3.997
5	3.968	12	3.998
6	3.982	13	3.998
7	3.988	14	3.999

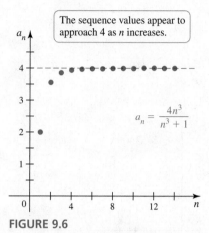

The sequence values appear to approach 4 as n increases.

$$a_n = \frac{4n^3}{n^3 + 1}$$

FIGURE 9.6

Related Exercises 41–54 ◄

Let's apply these ideas to a practical example.

EXAMPLE 6   A bouncing ball A basketball tossed straight up in the air reaches a high point and falls to the floor. Each time the ball bounces on the floor, it rebounds to 0.8 of its previous height. Let h_n be the high point after the nth bounce, with the initial height being $h_0 = 20$ ft.

a. Find a recurrence relation and an explicit formula for the sequence $\{h_n\}$.

b. What is the high point after the 10th bounce? after the 20th bounce?

c. Speculate on the limit of the sequence $\{h_n\}$.

SOLUTION

a. We first write and graph the heights of the ball for several bounces using the rule that each height is 0.8 of the previous height (Figure 9.7). For example, we have

$$h_0 = 20 \text{ ft},$$
$$h_1 = 0.8\, h_0 = 16 \text{ ft},$$
$$h_2 = 0.8\, h_1 = 0.8^2\, h_0 = 12.8 \text{ ft},$$
$$h_3 = 0.8\, h_2 = 0.8^3\, h_0 = 10.24 \text{ ft, and}$$
$$h_4 = 0.8\, h_3 = 0.8^4\, h_0 \approx 8.192 \text{ ft}.$$

Each number in the list is 0.8 of the previous number. Therefore, the recurrence relation for the sequence of heights is

$$h_{n+1} = 0.8\, h_n, h_0 = 20, \qquad \text{for } n = 0, 1, 2, 3, \ldots.$$

To find an explicit formula for the nth term, note that

$$h_1 = h_0 \cdot 0.8, \qquad h_2 = h_0 \cdot 0.8^2, \qquad h_3 = h_0 \cdot 0.8^3, \qquad \text{and} \qquad h_4 = h_0 \cdot 0.8^4.$$

In general, we have

$$h_n = h_0 \cdot 0.8^n = 20 \cdot 0.8^n, \qquad \text{for } n = 0, 1, 2, 3, \ldots,$$

which is an explicit formula for the terms of the sequence.

b. Using the explicit formula for the sequence, we see that after $n = 10$ bounces, the next height is

$$h_{10} = 20 \cdot 0.8^{10} \approx 2.147 \text{ ft}.$$

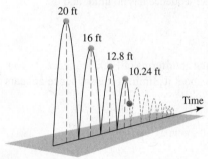

The height of each bounce of the basketball is 0.8 of the height of the previous bounce.

20 ft

16 ft

12.8 ft

10.24 ft

Time

FIGURE 9.7

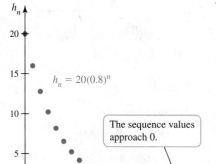

$h_n = 20(0.8)^n$

The sequence values approach 0.

FIGURE 9.8

After $n = 20$ bounces, the next height is

$$h_{20} = 20 \cdot 0.8^{20} \approx 0.231 \text{ ft.}$$

c. The terms of the sequence (Figure 9.8) appear to decrease and approach 0. A reasonable conjecture is that $\lim_{n \to \infty} h_n = 0$.   *Related Exercises 55–58* ◄

Infinite Series and the Sequence of Partial Sums

An infinite series can be viewed as a *sum* of an infinite set of numbers; it has the form

$$a_1 + a_2 + \cdots + a_n + \cdots,$$

where the terms of the series, $a_1, a_2, \ldots,$ are real numbers. How is it possible to sum an infinite set of numbers and produce a finite number? Here is an informative example.

Consider a unit square (sides of length 1) that is subdivided as shown in Figure 9.9. We let S_n be the area of the colored region in the nth figure of the progression. The area of the colored region in the first figure is

$$S_1 = \frac{1}{2} \cdot 1 = \frac{1}{2}. \qquad \frac{1}{2} = \frac{2^1 - 1}{2^1}$$

The area of the colored region in the second figure is S_1 plus the area of the smaller blue square, which is $\frac{1}{2} \cdot \frac{1}{2} = \frac{1}{4}$. Therefore,

$$S_2 = \frac{1}{2} + \frac{1}{4} = \frac{3}{4}. \qquad \frac{3}{4} = \frac{2^2 - 1}{2^2}$$

The area of the colored region in the third figure is S_2 plus the area of the smaller green rectangle, which is $\frac{1}{2} \cdot \frac{1}{4} = \frac{1}{8}$. Therefore,

$$S_3 = \frac{1}{2} + \frac{1}{4} + \frac{1}{8} = \frac{7}{8}. \qquad \frac{7}{8} = \frac{2^3 - 1}{2^3}$$

Continuing in this manner, we find that

$$S_n = \frac{1}{2} + \frac{1}{4} + \frac{1}{8} + \cdots + \frac{1}{2^n} = \frac{2^n - 1}{2^n}.$$

If this process is continued indefinitely, the area of the colored region S_n approaches the area of the unit square, which is 1. So it is plausible that

$$\lim_{n \to \infty} S_n = \underbrace{\frac{1}{2} + \frac{1}{4} + \frac{1}{8} + \cdots}_{\text{sum continues indefinitely}} = 1.$$

This example shows that it is possible to sum an infinite set of numbers and obtain a finite number—in this case, the sum is 1. The sequence $\{S_n\}$ generated in this example is extremely important. It is called a *sequence of partial sums*, and its limit is the value of the infinite series $\frac{1}{2} + \frac{1}{4} + \frac{1}{8} + \cdots$.

The idea of a sequence of partial sums is nicely illustrated by the decimal expansion of 1.

EXAMPLE 7 **Working with series** Consider the infinite series

$$0.9 + 0.09 + 0.009 + 0.0009 + \cdots,$$

where each term of the sum is $\frac{1}{10}$ of the previous term.

a. Find the sum of the first one, two, three, four, and five terms of the series.

b. What value would you assign to the infinite series $0.9 + 0.09 + 0.009 + \cdots$?

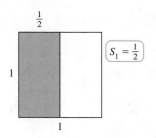

$S_1 = \frac{1}{2}$

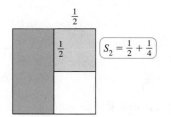

$S_2 = \frac{1}{2} + \frac{1}{4}$

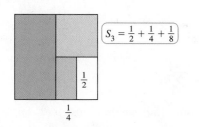

$S_3 = \frac{1}{2} + \frac{1}{4} + \frac{1}{8}$

$S_4 = \frac{1}{2} + \frac{1}{4} + \frac{1}{8} + \frac{1}{16}$

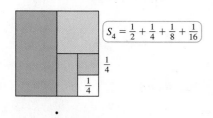

$S_n = \frac{1}{2} + \frac{1}{4} + \cdots + \frac{1}{2^n}$

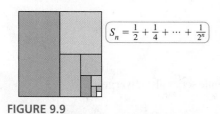

FIGURE 9.9

SOLUTION

a. Let S_n denote the sum of the first n terms of the given series. Then

$$S_1 = 0.9,$$
$$S_2 = 0.9 + 0.09 = 0.99,$$
$$S_3 = 0.9 + 0.09 + 0.009 = 0.999,$$
$$S_4 = 0.9 + 0.09 + 0.009 + 0.0009 = 0.9999, \text{ and}$$
$$S_5 = 0.9 + 0.09 + 0.009 + 0.0009 + 0.00009 = 0.99999.$$

b. Notice that the sums $S_1, S_2, \ldots, S_n$ form a sequence $\{S_n\}$, which is a sequence of partial sums. As more and more terms are included, the values of S_n approach 1. Therefore, a reasonable conjecture for the value of the series is 1:

$$\underbrace{\underbrace{\underbrace{0.9}_{S_1 = 0.9} + 0.09}_{S_2 = 0.99} + 0.009}_{S_3 = 0.999} + 0.0009 + \cdots = 1.$$

> **QUICK CHECK 3** Reasoning as in Example 7, what is the value of $0.3 + 0.03 + 0.003 + \cdots$?◄

Related Exercises 59–62 ◄

> Recall the summation notation introduced in Chapter 5: $\sum_{k=1}^{n} a_k$ means $a_1 + a_2 + \cdots + a_n$.

The general nth term of the sequence in Example 7 can be written as

$$S_n = \underbrace{0.9 + 0.09 + 0.009 + \cdots + 0.0\ldots9}_{n \text{ terms}} = \sum_{k=1}^{n} 9 \cdot 0.1^k.$$

We observed that $\lim_{n \to \infty} S_n = 1$. For this reason, we write

$$\lim_{n \to \infty} S_n = \lim_{n \to \infty} \underbrace{\sum_{k=1}^{n} 9 \cdot 0.1^k}_{S_n} = \underbrace{\sum_{k=1}^{\infty} 9 \cdot 0.1^k}_{\text{new object}} = 1.$$

By letting $n \to \infty$, a new mathematical object $\sum_{k=1}^{\infty} 9 \cdot 0.1^k$ is created. It is an infinite series, and its value is the *limit* of the sequence of partial sums.

> The term *series* is used for historical reasons. When you see *series*, you should think *sum*.

DEFINITION Infinite Series

Given a set of numbers $\{a_1, a_2, a_3, \ldots\}$, the sum

$$a_1 + a_2 + a_3 + \cdots = \sum_{k=1}^{\infty} a_k$$

is called an **infinite series**. Its **sequence of partial sums** $\{S_n\}$ has the terms

$$S_1 = a_1$$
$$S_2 = a_1 + a_2$$
$$S_3 = a_1 + a_2 + a_3$$
$$\vdots$$
$$S_n = a_1 + a_2 + a_3 + \cdots + a_n = \sum_{k=1}^{n} a_k, \quad \text{for } n = 1, 2, 3, \ldots.$$

> **QUICK CHECK 4** Do the series $\sum_{k=1}^{\infty} 1$ and $\sum_{k=1}^{\infty} k$ converge or diverge? ◄

If the sequence of partial sums $\{S_n\}$ has a limit L, the infinite series **converges** to that limit, and we write

$$\sum_{k=1}^{\infty} a_k = \lim_{n \to \infty} \underbrace{\sum_{k=1}^{n} a_k}_{S_n} = \lim_{n \to \infty} S_n = L.$$

If the sequence of partial sums diverges, the infinite series also **diverges**.

EXAMPLE 8 **Sequence of partial sums** Consider the infinite series

$$\sum_{k=1}^{\infty} \frac{1}{k(k+1)}.$$

a. Find the first four terms of the sequence of partial sums.

b. Find an expression for S_n and make a conjecture about the value of the series.

SOLUTION

a. The sequence of partial sums can be evaluated explicitly:

$$S_1 = \sum_{k=1}^{1} \frac{1}{k(k+1)} = \frac{1}{2},$$

$$S_2 = \sum_{k=1}^{2} \frac{1}{k(k+1)} = \frac{1}{2} + \frac{1}{6} = \frac{2}{3},$$

$$S_3 = \sum_{k=1}^{3} \frac{1}{k(k+1)} = \frac{1}{2} + \frac{1}{6} + \frac{1}{12} = \frac{3}{4}, \text{ and}$$

$$S_4 = \sum_{k=1}^{4} \frac{1}{k(k+1)} = \frac{1}{2} + \frac{1}{6} + \frac{1}{12} + \frac{1}{20} = \frac{4}{5}.$$

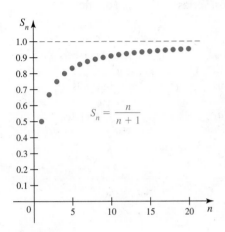

FIGURE 9.10

b. Based on the pattern in the sequence of partial sums, a reasonable conjecture is that $S_n = \dfrac{n}{n+1}$, for $n = 1, 2, 3, \ldots$, which produces the sequence $\left\{ \dfrac{1}{2}, \dfrac{2}{3}, \dfrac{3}{4}, \dfrac{4}{5}, \dfrac{5}{6}, \ldots \right\}$ (Figure 9.10). Because $\lim\limits_{n \to \infty} \dfrac{n}{n+1} = 1$, we conclude that

$$\lim_{n \to \infty} S_n = \sum_{k=1}^{\infty} \frac{1}{k(k+1)} = 1,$$

Related Exercises 63–66 ◀

which means the series converges to 1.

QUICK CHECK 5 Find the first four terms of the sequence of partial sums for the series $\sum_{k=1}^{\infty} (-1)^k k$. Does the series converge or diverge? ◀

Summary

This section features three key ideas to keep in mind.

• A *sequence* $\{a_1, a_2, \ldots, a_n, \ldots\}$ is an ordered *list* of numbers.

• An *infinite series* $\sum_{k=1}^{\infty} a_k = a_1 + a_2 + a_3 + \cdots$ is a *sum* of numbers.

• The *sequence of partial sums* $S_n = a_1 + a_2 + \cdots + a_n$ is a sequence that is used to evaluate the series $\sum_{k=1}^{\infty} a_k$.

For sequences, we ask about the behavior of the individual terms as we go out farther and farther in the list; that is, we ask about $\lim\limits_{n \to \infty} a_n$. For infinite series, we examine the sequence of partial sums related to the series. If the sequence of partial sums $\{S_n\}$ has a limit, then the infinite series $\sum_{k=1}^{\infty} a_k$ converges to that limit. If the sequence of partial sums does not have a limit, the infinite series diverges.

Table 9.2 shows the correspondences between sequences/series and functions, and between summation and integration. For a sequence, the index n plays the role of the independent variable and takes on integer values; the terms of the sequence $\{a_n\}$ correspond to the dependent variable.

With sequences $\{a_n\}$, the idea of accumulation corresponds to summation, whereas with functions, accumulation corresponds to integration. A finite sum is analogous to integrating a function over a finite interval. An infinite series is analogous to integrating a function over an infinite interval.

Table 9.2

	Sequences/Series	Functions
Independent variable	n	x
Dependent variable	a_n	$f(x)$
Domain	Integers	Real numbers
	e.g., $n = 1, 2, 3, \ldots$	e.g., $\{x: x \geq 1\}$
Accumulation	Sums	Integrals
Accumulation over a finite interval	$\displaystyle\sum_{k=1}^{n} a_k$	$\displaystyle\int_{1}^{n} f(x)\, dx$
Accumulation over an infinite interval	$\displaystyle\sum_{k=1}^{\infty} a_k$	$\displaystyle\int_{1}^{\infty} f(x)\, dx$

SECTION 9.1 EXERCISES

Review Questions

1. Define *sequence* and give an example.

2. Suppose the sequence $\{a_n\}$ is defined by the explicit formula $a_n = 1/n$, for $n = 1, 2, 3, \ldots$. Write out the first five terms of the sequence.

3. Suppose the sequence $\{a_n\}$ is defined by the recurrence relation $a_{n+1} = na_n$, for $n = 1, 2, 3, \ldots$, where $a_1 = 1$. Write out the first five terms of the sequence.

4. Define *finite sum* and give an example.

5. Define *infinite series* and give an example.

6. Given the series $\displaystyle\sum_{k=1}^{\infty} k$, evaluate the first four terms of its sequence of partial sums $S_n = \displaystyle\sum_{k=1}^{n} k$.

7. The terms of a sequence of partial sums are defined by $S_n = \displaystyle\sum_{k=1}^{n} k^2$, for $n = 1, 2, 3, \ldots$. Evaluate the first four terms of the sequence.

8. Consider the infinite series $\displaystyle\sum_{k=1}^{\infty} \frac{1}{k}$. Evaluate the first four terms of the sequence of partial sums.

Basic Skills

9–16. Explicit formulas *Write the first four terms of the sequence* $\{a_n\}_{n=1}^{\infty}$.

9. $a_n = 1/10^n$

10. $a_n = 3n + 1$

11. $a_n = \dfrac{(-1)^n}{2^n}$

12. $a_n = 2 + (-1)^n$

13. $a_n = \dfrac{2^{n+1}}{2^n + 1}$

14. $a_n = n + 1/n$

15. $a_n = 1 + \sin(\pi n/2)$

16. $a_n = 2n^2 - 3n + 1$

17–22. Recurrence relations *Write the first four terms of the sequence* $\{a_n\}$ *defined by the following recurrence relations.*

17. $a_{n+1} = 2a_n; \quad a_1 = 2$

18. $a_{n+1} = a_n/2; \quad a_1 = 32$

19. $a_{n+1} = 3a_n - 12; \quad a_1 = 10$

20. $a_{n+1} = a_n^2 - 1; \quad a_1 = 1$

21. $a_{n+1} = 3a_n^2 + n + 1; \quad a_1 = 0$

22. $a_{n+1} = a_n + a_{n-1}; \quad a_1 = 1, a_0 = 1$

23–30. Working with sequences *Several terms of a sequence* $\{a_n\}_{n=1}^{\infty}$ *are given.*

a. *Find the next two terms of the sequence.*
b. *Find a recurrence relation that generates the sequence (supply the initial value of the index and the first term of the sequence).*
c. *Find an explicit formula for the general nth term of the sequence.*

23. $\left\{1, \dfrac{1}{2}, \dfrac{1}{4}, \dfrac{1}{8}, \dfrac{1}{16}, \ldots\right\}$

24. $\{1, -2, 3, -4, 5, \ldots\}$

25. $\{-5, 5, -5, 5, \ldots\}$

26. $\{2, 5, 8, 11, \ldots\}$

27. $\{1, 2, 4, 8, 16, \ldots\}$

28. $\{1, 4, 9, 16, 25, \ldots\}$

29. $\{1, 3, 9, 27, 81, \ldots\}$

30. $\{64, 32, 16, 8, 4, \ldots\}$

31–40. Limits of sequences *Write the terms a_1, a_2, a_3, and a_4 of the following sequences. If the sequence appears to converge, make a conjecture about its limit. If the sequence diverges, explain why.*

31. $a_n = 10^n - 1; \ n = 1, 2, 3, \ldots$

32. $a_n = n^4 + 1; \ n = 1, 2, 3, \ldots$

33. $a_n = \dfrac{1}{10^n}; \ n = 1, 2, 3, \ldots$

34. $a_{n+1} = a_n/10; \ a_0 = 1$

35. $a_n = \dfrac{(-1)^n}{2^n}; \ n = 1, 2, 3, \ldots$

36. $a_n = 1 - 10^{-n}; \ n = 1, 2, 3, \ldots$

37. $a_{n+1} = 1 + \dfrac{a_n}{2}; \ a_0 = 2$

38. $a_{n+1} = 9 + a_n/10; \ a_0 = 9$

39. $a_{n+1} = a_n/11 + 50; \ a_0 = 50$

40. $a_{n+1} = 10a_n - 1; \ a_0 = 0$

41–46. Explicit formulas for sequences *Consider the formulas for the following sequences. Using a calculator, make a table with at least 10 terms and determine a plausible value for the limit of the sequence or state that the sequence diverges.*

41. $\cot^{-1} 2^n; \ n = 1, 2, 3, \ldots$

42. $a_n = 2 \tan^{-1} (1000n); \ n = 1, 2, 3, \ldots$

43. $a_n = n^2 - n; \ n = 1, 2, 3, \ldots$

44. $a_n = \dfrac{100n - 1}{10n}; \ n = 1, 2, 3, \ldots$

45. $a_n = \dfrac{5^n}{5^n + 1}; \ n = 1, 2, 3, \ldots$

46. $a_n = 2^n \sin (2^{-n}); \ n = 1, 2, 3, \ldots$

47–48. Limits from graphs *Consider the following sequences.*
a. *Find the first four terms of the sequence.*
b. *Based on part (a) and the figure, determine a plausible limit of the sequence.*

47. $a_n = 2 + 2^{-n}; \ n = 1, 2, 3, \ldots$

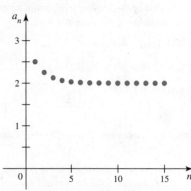

48. $a_n = \dfrac{n^2}{n^2 - 1}; \ n = 2, 3, 4, \ldots$

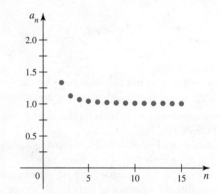

49–54. Recurrence relations *Consider the following recurrence relations. Using a calculator, make a table with at least 10 terms and determine a plausible value for the limit of the sequence or state that the sequence diverges.*

49. $a_{n+1} = \dfrac{1}{2}a_n + 2; \ a_0 = 3$

50. $a_n = \dfrac{1}{4}a_{n-1} - 3; \ a_0 = 1$

51. $a_{n+1} = 2a_n + 1; \ a_0 = 0$

52. $a_{n+1} = a_n/10 + 3; \ a_0 = 10$

53. $a_{n+1} = \dfrac{1}{2}\sqrt{a_n} + 3; \ a_0 = 1000$

54. $a_{n+1} = \sqrt{1 + a_n}; \ a_0 = 1$

55–58. Heights of bouncing balls *Suppose a ball is thrown upward to a height of h_0 meters. Each time the ball bounces, it rebounds to a fraction r of its previous height. Let h_n be the height after the nth bounce. Consider the following values of h_0 and r.*

a. *Find the first four terms of the sequence of heights $\{h_n\}$.*
b. *Find an explicit formula for the nth term of the sequence $\{h_n\}$.*

55. $h_0 = 20, \ r = 0.5$

56. $h_0 = 10, \ r = 0.9$

57. $h_0 = 30, \ r = 0.25$

58. $h_0 = 20, \ r = 0.75$

59–62. Sequences of partial sums *For the following infinite series, find the first four terms of the sequence of partial sums. Then make a conjecture about the value of the infinite series.*

59. $0.3 + 0.03 + 0.003 + \cdots$

60. $0.6 + 0.06 + 0.006 + \cdots$

61. $4 + 0.9 + 0.09 + 0.009 + \cdots$

62. $1 + \frac{1}{2} + \frac{1}{4} + \frac{1}{8} + \cdots$

63–66. Formulas for sequences of partial sums *Consider the following infinite series.*

a. *Find the first four terms of the sequence of partial sums.*
b. *Use the results of part (a) to find a formula for S_n.*
c. *Find the value of the series.*

63. $\displaystyle\sum_{k=1}^{\infty} \frac{2}{(2k-1)(2k+1)}$ **64.** $\displaystyle\sum_{k=1}^{\infty} \frac{1}{2^k}$

65. $\displaystyle\sum_{k=1}^{\infty} \frac{1}{4k^2 - 1}$ **66.** $\displaystyle\sum_{k=1}^{\infty} \frac{2}{3^k}$

Further Explorations

67. **Explain why or why not** Determine whether the following statements are true and give an explanation or counterexample.

a. The sequence of partial sums for the series $1 + 2 + 3 + \cdots$ is $\{1, 3, 6, 10, \ldots\}$.
b. If a sequence of positive numbers converges, then the terms of the sequence must decrease in size.
c. If the terms of the sequence $\{a_n\}$ are positive and increase in size, then the sequence of partial sums for the series
$$\sum_{k=1}^{\infty} a_k \text{ diverges.}$$

68–69. Distance traveled by bouncing balls *Suppose a ball is thrown upward to a height of h_0 meters. Each time the ball bounces, it rebounds to a fraction r of its previous height. Let h_n be the height after the nth bounce and let S_n be the total distance the ball has traveled at the moment of the nth bounce.*

a. *Find the first four terms of the sequence $\{S_n\}$.*
b. *Make a table of 20 terms of the sequence $\{S_n\}$ and determine a plausible value for the limit of $\{S_n\}$.*

68. $h_0 = 20, \ r = 0.5$

69. $h_0 = 20, \ r = 0.75$

70–77. Sequences of partial sums *Consider the following infinite series.*

a. *Write out the first four terms of the sequence of partial sums.*
b. *Estimate the limit of $\{S_n\}$ or state that it does not exist.*

70. $\displaystyle\sum_{k=1}^{\infty} \cos(\pi k)$ **71.** $\displaystyle\sum_{k=1}^{\infty} 9(0.1)^k$

72. $\displaystyle\sum_{k=1}^{\infty} 1.5^k$ **73.** $\displaystyle\sum_{k=1}^{\infty} 3^{-k}$

74. $\displaystyle\sum_{k=1}^{\infty} k$ **75.** $\displaystyle\sum_{k=1}^{\infty} (-1)^k$

76. $\displaystyle\sum_{k=1}^{\infty} (-1)^k k$ **77.** $\displaystyle\sum_{k=1}^{\infty} \frac{3}{10^k}$

Applications

78–81. Practical sequences *Consider the following situations that generate a sequence.*

a. *Write out the first five terms of the sequence.*
b. *Find an explicit formula for the terms of the sequence.*
c. *Find a recurrence relation that generates the sequence.*
d. *Using a calculator or a graphing utility, estimate the limit of the sequence or state that it does not exist.*

78. **Population growth** When a biologist begins a study, a colony of prairie dogs has a population of 250. Regular measurements reveal that each month the prairie dog population increases by 3%. Let p_n be the population (rounded to whole numbers) at the end of the nth month, where the initial population is $p_0 = 250$.

79. **Radioactive decay** A material transmutes 50% of its mass to another element every 10 yr due to radioactive decay. Let M_n be the mass of the radioactive material at the end of the nth decade, where the initial mass of the material is $M_0 = 20$ g.

80. **Consumer Price Index** The Consumer Price Index (the CPI is a measure of the U.S. cost of living) is given a base value of 100 in the year 1984. Assume the CPI has increased by an average of 3%/yr since 1984. Let c_n be the CPI n years after 1984, where $c_0 = 100$.

81. **Drug elimination** Jack took a 200-mg dose of a strong painkiller at midnight. Every hour, 5% of the drug is washed out of his bloodstream. Let d_n be the amount of drug in Jack's blood n hours after the drug was taken, where $d_0 = 200$ mg.

82. **A square root finder** A well-known method for approximating $\sqrt{c}$ for a positive real number c consists of the following recurrence relation (based on Newton's method; see Section 4.8). Let $a_0 = c$ and
$$a_{n+1} = \frac{1}{2}\left(a_n + \frac{c}{a_n}\right), \quad \text{for } n = 0, 1, 2, 3, \ldots.$$

a. Use this recurrence relation to approximate $\sqrt{10}$. How many terms of the sequence are needed to approximate $\sqrt{10}$ with an error less than 0.01? How many terms of the sequence are needed to approximate $\sqrt{10}$ with an error less than 0.0001? (To compute the error, assume a calculator gives the exact value.)
b. Use this recurrence relation to approximate $\sqrt{c}$, for $c = 2, 3, \ldots, 10$. Make a table showing how many terms of the sequence are needed to approximate $\sqrt{c}$ with an error less than 0.01.

QUICK CHECK ANSWERS

1. $a_{10} = 28$ **2.** $a_n = 2^n - 1, \ n = 1, 2, 3, \ldots$
3. $0.33333\ldots = \frac{1}{3}$ **4.** Both diverge.   **5.** $S_1 = -1, S_2 = 1,$
$S_3 = -2, S_4 = 2$; the series diverges. ◄

9.2 Sequences

The previous section sets the stage for an in-depth investigation of sequences and infinite series. This section is devoted to sequences, and the remainder of the chapter deals with series.

Limit of a Sequence and Limit Laws

A fundamental question about sequences concerns the behavior of the terms as we go out farther and farther in the sequence. For example, in the sequence

$$\{a_n\}_{n=0}^{\infty} = \left\{\frac{1}{n^2 + 1}\right\}_{n=0}^{\infty} = \left\{1, \frac{1}{2}, \frac{1}{5}, \frac{1}{10}, \ldots\right\},$$

the terms remain positive and decrease to 0. We say that this sequence converges and its limit is 0, written $\lim_{n\to\infty} a_n = 0$. Similarly, the terms of the sequence

$$\{b_n\}_{n=1}^{\infty} = \left\{(-1)^n \frac{n(n + 1)}{2}\right\}_{n=1}^{\infty} = \{-1, 3, -6, 10, \ldots\}$$

increase in magnitude and do not approach a unique value as n increases. In this case, we say that the sequence diverges.

Limits of sequences are really no different from limits at infinity of functions except that the variable n assumes only integer values as $n \to \infty$. This idea works as follows.

Given a sequence $\{a_n\}$, we define a function f such that $f(n) = a_n$ for all indices n. For example, if $a_n = n/(n + 1)$, then we let $f(x) = x/(x + 1)$. By the methods of Section 2.5, we know that $\lim_{x\to\infty} f(x) = 1$; because the terms of the sequence lie on the graph of f, it follows that $\lim_{n\to\infty} a_n = 1$ (Figure 9.11). This reasoning is the basis of the following theorem.

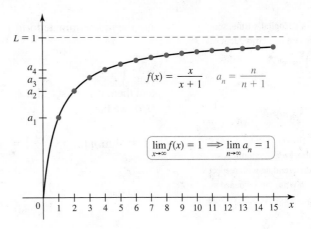

FIGURE 9.11

> The converse of Theorem 9.1 is not true. For example, if $a_n = \cos 2\pi n$, then $\lim_{n\to\infty} a_n = 1$, but $\lim_{x\to\infty} \cos 2\pi x$ does not exist.

THEOREM 9.1   Limits of Sequences from Limits of Functions
Suppose f is a function such that $f(n) = a_n$ for all positive integers n. If $\lim_{x\to\infty} f(x) = L$, then the limit of the sequence $\{a_n\}$ is also L.

Because of the correspondence between limits of sequences and limits of functions at infinity, we have the following properties that are analogous to those for functions given in Theorem 2.3.

> The limit of a sequence $\{a_n\}$ is determined by the terms in the *tail* of the sequence—the terms with large values of n. If the sequences $\{a_n\}$ and $\{b_n\}$ differ in their first 100 terms but have identical terms for $n > 100$, then they have the same limit. For this reason, the initial index of a sequence (for example, $n = 0$ or $n = 1$) is often not specified.

THEOREM 9.2   Limit Laws for Sequences

Assume that the sequences $\{a_n\}$ and $\{b_n\}$ have limits A and B, respectively. Then,

1. $\lim\limits_{n \to \infty} (a_n \pm b_n) = A \pm B$

2. $\lim\limits_{n \to \infty} ca_n = cA$, where c is a real number

3. $\lim\limits_{n \to \infty} a_n b_n = AB$

4. $\lim\limits_{n \to \infty} \dfrac{a_n}{b_n} = \dfrac{A}{B}$, provided $B \neq 0$.

EXAMPLE 1   Limits of sequences Determine the limits of the following sequences.

a. $a_n = \dfrac{3n^3}{n^3 + 1}$ **b.** $b_n = \left(\dfrac{5 + n}{n}\right)^n$ **c.** $c_n = n^{1/n}$

SOLUTION

a. A function with the property that $f(n) = a_n$ is $f(x) = \dfrac{3x^3}{x^3 + 1}$. Dividing numerator and denominator by x^3 (or appealing to Theorem 2.7), we find that $\lim\limits_{x \to \infty} f(x) = 3$. (Alternatively, we can apply l'Hôpital's Rule and obtain the same result.) Either way, we conclude that $\lim\limits_{n \to \infty} a_n = 3$.

b. The limit

$$\lim_{n \to \infty} b_n = \lim_{n \to \infty} \left(\frac{5 + n}{n}\right)^n = \lim_{n \to \infty} \left(1 + \frac{5}{n}\right)^n$$

> For a review of l'Hôpital's Rule, see Section 4.7, where we showed that
> $$\lim_{x \to \infty} \left(1 + \frac{a}{x}\right)^x = e^a.$$

has the indeterminate form 1^∞. Recall that for this limit (Section 4.7), we first evaluate

$$L = \lim_{n \to \infty} \ln\left(1 + \frac{5}{n}\right)^n = \lim_{n \to \infty} n \ln\left(1 + \frac{5}{n}\right),$$

and then, if L exists, $\lim\limits_{n \to \infty} b_n = e^L$. Using l'Hôpital's Rule for the indeterminate form $0/0$, we have

> When using l'Hôpital's Rule, it is customary to treat n as a continuous variable and differentiate with respect to n, rather than write the sequence as a function of x, as was done in Example 1a.

$$L = \lim_{n \to \infty} n \ln\left(1 + \frac{5}{n}\right) = \lim_{n \to \infty} \frac{\ln\left(1 + (5/n)\right)}{1/n} \qquad \text{Indeterminate form } 0/0$$

$$= \lim_{n \to \infty} \frac{\dfrac{1}{1 + (5/n)}\left(-\dfrac{5}{n^2}\right)}{-1/n^2} \qquad \text{L'Hôpital's Rule}$$

$$= \lim_{n \to \infty} \frac{5}{1 + (5/n)} = 5. \qquad \text{Simplify; } 5/n \to 0 \text{ as } n \to \infty.$$

Because $\lim\limits_{n \to \infty} b_n = e^L = e^5$, we have $\lim\limits_{n \to \infty}\left(\dfrac{5 + n}{n}\right)^n = e^5$.

c. The limit has the form ∞^0, so we first evaluate $L = \lim\limits_{n \to \infty} \ln n^{1/n} = \lim\limits_{n \to \infty} \dfrac{\ln n}{n}$; if L exists, then $\lim\limits_{n \to \infty} c_n = e^L$. Using either l'Hôpital's Rule or the relative growth rates in Section 4.7, we find that $L = 0$. Therefore, $\lim\limits_{n \to \infty} c_n = e^0 = 1$.

Related Exercises 9–34 ◄

Terminology for Sequences

We now introduce some terminology for sequences that is similar to that used for functions. The following terms are used to describe sequences $\{a_n\}$.

DEFINITIONS   Terminology for Sequences

$\{a_n\}$ is **increasing** if $a_{n+1} > a_n$; for example, $\{0, 1, 2, 3, \ldots\}$.

$\{a_n\}$ is **nondecreasing** if $a_{n+1} \geq a_n$; for example, $\{1, 1, 2, 2, 3, 3, \ldots\}$.

$\{a_n\}$ is **decreasing** if $a_{n+1} < a_n$; for example, $\{2, 1, 0, -1, \ldots\}$.

$\{a_n\}$ is **nonincreasing** if $a_{n+1} \leq a_n$; for example, $\{0, -1, -1, -2, -2, -3, -4, \ldots\}$.

$\{a_n\}$ is **monotonic** if it is either nonincreasing or nondecreasing (it moves in one direction).

$\{a_n\}$ is **bounded** if there is number M such that $|a_n| \leq M$, for all relevant values of n.

For example, the sequence

$$\{a_n\} = \left\{1 - \frac{1}{n}\right\}_{n=1}^{\infty} = \left\{0, \frac{1}{2}, \frac{2}{3}, \frac{3}{4}, \ldots\right\}$$

satisfies $|a_n| \leq 1$, for $n \geq 1$, and its terms are increasing in size. Therefore, the sequence is bounded and increasing; it is also monotonic (Figure 9.12). The sequence

$$\{a_n\} = \left\{1 + \frac{1}{n}\right\}_{n=1}^{\infty} = \left\{2, \frac{3}{2}, \frac{4}{3}, \frac{5}{4}, \ldots\right\}$$

satisfies $|a_n| \leq 2$, for $n \geq 1$, and its terms are decreasing in size. Therefore, the sequence is bounded and decreasing; it is also monotonic (Figure 9.12).

QUICK CHECK 1 Classify the following sequences as bounded, monotonic, or neither.

a. $\left\{\frac{1}{2}, \frac{3}{4}, \frac{7}{8}, \frac{15}{16}, \ldots\right\}$

b. $\left\{1, -\frac{1}{2}, \frac{1}{4}, -\frac{1}{8}, \frac{1}{16}, \ldots\right\}$

c. $\{1, -2, 3, -4, 5, \ldots\}$

d. $\{1, 1, 1, 1, \ldots\}$ ◄

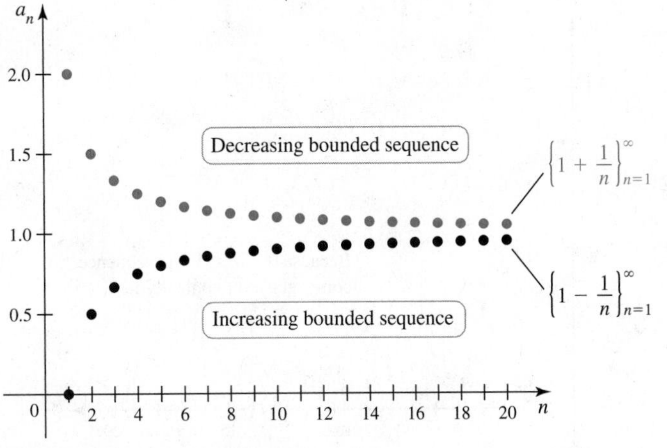

FIGURE 9.12

EXAMPLE 2   Limits of sequences and graphing Compare and contrast the behavior of $\{a_n\}$ and $\{b_n\}$ as $n \to \infty$.

a. $a_n = \dfrac{n^{3/2}}{n^{3/2} + 1}$ **b.** $b_n = \dfrac{(-1)^n n^{3/2}}{n^{3/2} + 1}$

SOLUTION

a. The sequence $\{a_n\}$ consists of positive terms. Dividing the numerator and denominator of a_n by $n^{3/2}$, we see that

$$\lim_{n \to \infty} a_n = \lim_{n \to \infty} \frac{n^{3/2}}{n^{3/2} + 1} = \lim_{n \to \infty} \frac{1}{1 + \underbrace{\frac{1}{n^{3/2}}}_{\text{approaches 0 as } n \to \infty}} = 1.$$

The terms of this sequence are increasing and bounded (Figure 9.13).

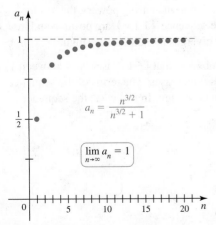

FIGURE 9.13

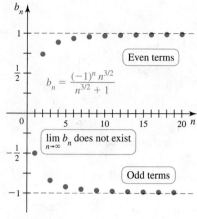

$$b_n = \frac{(-1)^n n^{3/2}}{n^{3/2} + 1}$$

Even terms

$\lim_{n \to \infty} b_n$ does not exist

Odd terms

FIGURE 9.14

b. The terms of the bounded sequence $\{b_n\}$ alternate in sign. Using the result of part (a), it follows that the even terms form an increasing sequence that approaches 1 and the odd terms form a decreasing sequence that approaches -1 (Figure 9.14). Therefore, the sequence diverges, illustrating the fact that the presence of $(-1)^n$ may significantly alter the behavior of a sequence.

Related Exercises 35–44 ◄

Among the most important sequences for our upcoming work are geometric sequences.

Geometric Sequences

Geometric sequences have the property that each term is obtained by multiplying the previous term by a fixed constant, called the **ratio**. They have the form $\{r^n\}$ or $\{ar^n\}$, where the ratio r and $a \neq 0$ are real numbers.

EXAMPLE 3   **Geometric sequences**   Graph the following sequences and discuss their behavior.

a. $\{0.75^n\}$ **b.** $\{(-0.75)^n\}$ **c.** $\{1.15^n\}$ **d.** $\{(-1.15)^n\}$

SOLUTION

a. When a number less than 1 in magnitude is raised to increasing powers, the resulting numbers decrease to zero. The sequence $\{0.75^n\}$ converges monotonically to zero (Figure 9.15).

b. Note that $\{(-0.75)^n\} = \{(-1)^n 0.75^n\}$. Observe also that $(-1)^n$ oscillates between 1 and -1, while 0.75^n decreases to zero as n increases. Therefore, the sequence oscillates and converges to zero (Figure 9.16).

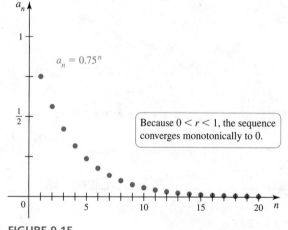

FIGURE 9.15   **FIGURE 9.16**

$a_n = 0.75^n$

Because $0 < r < 1$, the sequence converges monotonically to 0.

Because $(-r)^n = (-1)^n r^n$ and $0 < r < 1$, the sequence oscillates *and* converges to 0.

$a_n = (-0.75)^n$

c. When a number greater than 1 in magnitude is raised to increasing powers, the resulting numbers increase in magnitude. The terms of the sequence $\{1.15^n\}$ are positive and increase without bound. In this case, the sequence diverges monotonically (Figure 9.17).

d. We write $\{(-1.15)^n\} = \{(-1)^n 1.15^n\}$ and observe that $(-1)^n$ oscillates between 1 and -1, while 1.15^n increases without bound as n increases. The terms of the sequence increase in magnitude without bound and alternate in sign. In this case, the sequence oscillates and diverges (Figure 9.18).

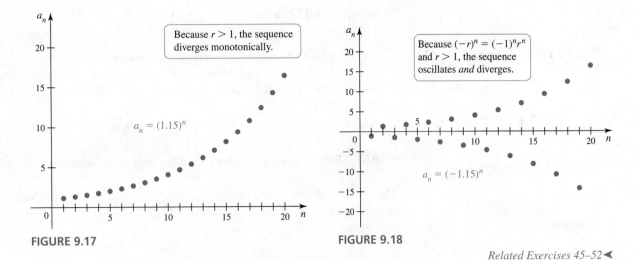

FIGURE 9.17

FIGURE 9.18

Related Exercises 45–52 ◄

QUICK CHECK 2 Describe the behavior of $\{r^n\}$ in the cases $r = -1$ and $r = 1$. ◄

The results of Example 3 and Quick Check 2 are summarized in the following theorem.

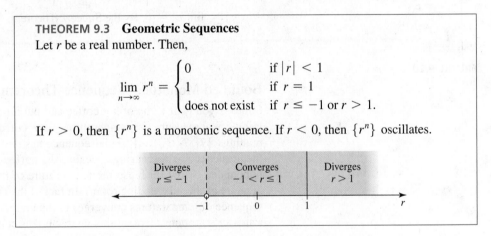

THEOREM 9.3   Geometric Sequences

Let r be a real number. Then,

$$\lim_{n \to \infty} r^n = \begin{cases} 0 & \text{if } |r| < 1 \\ 1 & \text{if } r = 1 \\ \text{does not exist} & \text{if } r \le -1 \text{ or } r > 1. \end{cases}$$

If $r > 0$, then $\{r^n\}$ is a monotonic sequence. If $r < 0$, then $\{r^n\}$ oscillates.

The previous examples show that a sequence may display any of the following behaviors:

• It may converge to a single value, which is the limit of the sequence.

• Its terms may increase in magnitude without bound (either with one sign or with mixed signs), in which case the sequence diverges.

• Its terms may remain bounded but settle into an oscillating pattern in which the terms approach two or more values; in this case, the sequence diverges.

Not illustrated in the preceding examples is one other type of behavior: The terms of a sequence may remain bounded, but wander chaotically forever without a pattern. In this case, the sequence also diverges.

We cite two theorems that are used either to establish that a sequence has a limit or to find limits. The first theorem is a direct analog of the Squeeze Theorem from Section 2.3.

The Squeeze Theorem

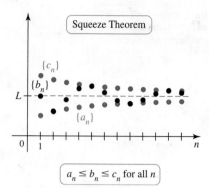

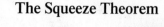

$a_n \le b_n \le c_n$ for all n

FIGURE 9.19

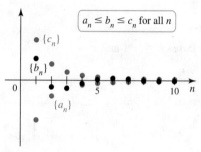

$a_n \le b_n \le c_n$ for all n

FIGURE 9.20

> **THEOREM 9.4   Squeeze Theorem for Sequences**
> Let $\{a_n\}$, $\{b_n\}$, and $\{c_n\}$ be sequences with $a_n \le b_n \le c_n$ for all integers n greater than some index N. If $\lim\limits_{n \to \infty} a_n = \lim\limits_{n \to \infty} c_n = L$, then $\lim\limits_{n \to \infty} b_n = L$ (Figure 9.19).

EXAMPLE 4   Squeeze Theorem Find the limit of the sequence $b_n = \dfrac{\cos n}{n^2 + 1}$.

SOLUTION The goal is to find two sequences $\{a_n\}$ and $\{c_n\}$ whose terms lie below and above the terms of the given sequence $\{b_n\}$. Note that $-1 \le \cos n \le 1$, for all n. Therefore,

$$\underbrace{-\frac{1}{n^2 + 1}}_{a_n} \le \underbrace{\frac{\cos n}{n^2 + 1}}_{b_n} \le \underbrace{\frac{1}{n^2 + 1}}_{c_n}.$$

Letting $a_n = -\dfrac{1}{n^2 + 1}$ and $c_n = \dfrac{1}{n^2 + 1}$, we have $a_n \le b_n \le c_n$, for $n \ge 1$. Furthermore, $\lim\limits_{n \to \infty} a_n = \lim\limits_{n \to \infty} c_n = 0$. By the Squeeze Theorem, $\lim\limits_{n \to \infty} b_n = 0$ (Figure 9.20).

Related Exercises 53–58 ◄

Bounded Monotonic Sequence Theorem

Suppose you pour a cup of hot coffee and put it on your desk to cool. Assume that every minute you measure the temperature of the coffee to create a sequence of temperature readings $\{T_1, T_2, T_3, \ldots\}$. This sequence has two notable properties: First, the terms of the sequence are decreasing (because the coffee is cooling), and second, the sequence is bounded below (because the temperature of the coffee cannot be less than the temperature of the surrounding room). In fact, if the measurements continue indefinitely, the sequence of temperatures converges to the temperature of the room. This example illustrates an important theorem that characterizes convergent sequences in terms of boundedness and monotonicity. The theorem is easy to believe, but its proof is beyond the scope of this text.

> **THEOREM 9.5   Bounded Monotonic Sequences**
> A bounded monotonic sequence converges.

Figure 9.21 shows the two cases of this theorem. In the first case, we see a nondecreasing sequence, all of whose terms are less than M. It must converge to a limit less than or equal to M. Similarly, a nonincreasing sequence, all of whose terms are greater than N, must converge to a limit greater than or equal to N.

> **Some optional terminology** M is called an *upper bound* of the first sequence in Figure 9.21, and N is a *lower bound* of the second sequence. A number M^* is the *least upper bound* of a sequence (or a set) if it is the smallest of all the upper bounds. It is a fundamental property of the real numbers that if a sequence (or a nonempty set) is bounded above, then it has a least upper bound. It can be shown that an increasing sequence that is bounded above converges to its least upper bound. Similarly, a decreasing sequence that is bounded below converges to its greatest lower bound.

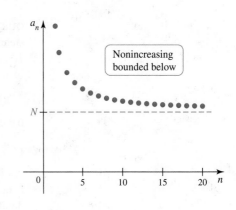

FIGURE 9.21

We now turn to the question raised in the chapter opening: If you take a medication on a regular basis, does the amount of medication in your blood increase without bound or does it eventually level off? We can answer the question by analyzing a sequence.

An Application: Recurrence Relations

> Most drugs decay exponentially in the bloodstream and have a characteristic half-life assuming that the drug is absorbed quickly into the blood.

EXAMPLE 5   Sequences for drug doses Suppose your doctor prescribes a 100-mg dose of an antibiotic to be taken every 12 hr. Furthermore, the drug is known to have a half-life of 12 hr; that is, every 12 hr half of the drug in your blood is eliminated.

a. Find the sequence that gives the amount of drug in your blood immediately after each dose.

b. Use a graph to propose the limit of this sequence; that is, in the long run, how much drug do you have in your blood?

c. Find the limit of the sequence directly.

SOLUTION

a. Let d_n be the amount of drug in the blood immediately following the nth dose, where $n = 1, 2, 3, \ldots$ and $d_1 = 100$ mg. We want to write a recurrence relation that gives the amount of drug in the blood after the $(n + 1)$th dose (d_{n+1}) in terms of the amount of drug after the nth dose (d_n). In the 12 hr between the nth dose and the $(n + 1)$th dose, half of the drug in the blood is eliminated, *and* another 100 mg of drug is added. So we have

$$d_{n+1} = 0.5\, d_n + 100, \qquad \text{for } n = 1, 2, 3, \ldots, \text{ with } d_1 = 100,$$

which is the recurrence relation for the sequence $\{d_n\}$.

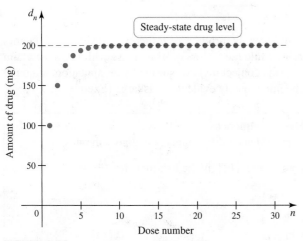

FIGURE 9.22

b. We see from Figure 9.22 that after about 10 doses (5 days) the amount of antibiotic in the blood is close to 200 mg, and—importantly for your body—it never exceeds 200 mg.

c. The graph of part (b) gives evidence that the terms of the sequence are increasing and bounded (Exercise 90). By the Bounded Monotonic Sequence Theorem, the sequence has a limit; therefore, $\lim\limits_{n \to \infty} d_n = L$ and $\lim\limits_{n \to \infty} d_{n+1} = L$. We now take the limit of both sides of the recurrence relation:

$$
\begin{aligned}
d_{n+1} &= 0.5\, d_n + 100 && \text{Recurrence relation} \\
\lim_{n \to \infty} d_{n+1} &= 0.5 \lim_{n \to \infty} d_n + \lim_{n \to \infty} 100 && \text{Limits of both sides} \\
\underbrace{\phantom{\lim_{n \to \infty} d_{n+1}}}_{L} &\quad \underbrace{\phantom{0.5 \lim_{n \to \infty} d_n}}_{L} \\
L &= 0.5L + 100 && \text{Substitute } L.
\end{aligned}
$$

Solving for L, the steady-state drug level is $L = 200$.

Related Exercises 59–62 ◄

QUICK CHECK 3 If a drug had the same half-life as in Example 5, (i) how would the steady-state level of drug in the blood change if the regular dose were 150 mg instead of 100 mg? (ii) How would the steady-state level change if the dosing interval were 6 hr instead of 12 hr?◄

In Section 4.7, we investigated the growth rates of functions. We close this section by developing the analogous results for sequences.

Growth Rates of Sequences

All the hard work we did in Section 4.7 to establish the relative growth rates of functions is now applied to sequences. Here is the question: Given two nondecreasing sequences of positive terms $\{a_n\}$ and $\{b_n\}$, which sequence grows faster as $n \to \infty$? As with functions, to compare growth rates, we evaluate $\lim\limits_{n \to \infty} a_n/b_n$. If $\lim\limits_{n \to \infty} a_n/b_n = 0$, then $\{b_n\}$ grows faster than $\{a_n\}$. If $\lim\limits_{n \to \infty} a_n/b_n = \infty$, then $\{a_n\}$ grows faster than $\{b_n\}$.

Using the results of Section 4.7, we immediately arrive at the following ranking of growth rates of sequences as $n \to \infty$, with positive real numbers $p, q, r, s,$ and $b > 1$:

$$\{\ln^q n\} \ll \{n^p\} \ll \{n^p \ln^r n\} \ll \{n^{p+s}\} \ll \{b^n\} \ll \{n^n\}.$$

As before, the notation $\{a_n\} \ll \{b_n\}$ means $\{b_n\}$ *grows faster than* $\{a_n\}$ as $n \to \infty$. Another important sequence that should be added to the list is the **factorial sequence** $\{n!\}$, where $n! = n(n - 1)(n - 2) \cdots 2 \cdot 1$.

Where does the factorial sequence $\{n!\}$ appear in the list? The following argument provides some intuition. Notice that

$$n^n = \underbrace{n \cdot n \cdot n \cdots n}_{n \text{ factors}}, \qquad \text{whereas}$$

$$n! = \underbrace{n \cdot (n - 1) \cdot (n - 2) \cdots 2 \cdot 1}_{n \text{ factors}}.$$

The nth term of both sequences involves the product of n factors; however, the factors of $n!$ decrease, while the factors of n^n are the same. Based on this observation, we conclude that $\{n^n\}$ grows faster than $\{n!\}$, and we have the ordering $\{n!\} \ll \{n^n\}$. But where does $\{n!\}$ appear in the list relative to $\{b^n\}$? Again, some intuition is gained by noting that

$$b^n = \underbrace{b \cdot b \cdot b \cdots b}_{n \text{ factors}}, \qquad \text{whereas}$$

$$n! = \underbrace{n \cdot (n - 1) \cdot (n - 2) \cdots 2 \cdot 1}_{n \text{ factors}}.$$

The nth term of both sequences involves the product of n factors; however, the factors of b^n remain constant as n increases, while the factors of $n!$ increase with n. So we claim that $\{n!\}$ grows faster than $\{b^n\}$. This conjecture is supported by computation, although the outcome of the race may not be immediately evident if b is large (Exercise 85).

▶ $0! = 1$ (by definition)
$1! = 1$
$2! = 2 \cdot 1! = 2$
$3! = 3 \cdot 2! = 6$
$4! = 4 \cdot 3! = 24$
$5! = 5 \cdot 4! = 120$
$6! = 6 \cdot 5! = 720$

THEOREM 9.6 Growth Rates of Sequences
The following sequences are ordered according to increasing growth rates as

$n \to \infty$; that is, if $\{a_n\}$ appears before $\{b_n\}$ in the list, then $\lim\limits_{n \to \infty} \dfrac{a_n}{b_n} = 0$

and $\lim\limits_{n \to \infty} \dfrac{b_n}{a_n} = \infty$:

$$\{\ln^q n\} \ll \{n^p\} \ll \{n^p \ln^r n\} \ll \{n^{p+s}\} \ll \{b^n\} \ll \{n!\} \ll \{n^n\}.$$

The ordering applies for positive real numbers $p, q, r, s,$ and $b > 1$.

QUICK CHECK 4 Which sequence grows faster: $\{\ln n\}$ or $\{n^{1.1}\}$? What is

$$\lim_{n\to\infty} \frac{n^{1,000,000}}{e^n}?$$◄

It is worth noting that the rankings in Theorem 9.6 do not change if a sequence is multiplied by a positive constant (Exercise 98).

EXAMPLE 6 Convergence and growth rates Compare growth rates of sequences to determine whether the following sequences converge.

a. $\left\{\dfrac{\ln n^{10}}{0.00001n}\right\}$ **b.** $\left\{\dfrac{n^8 \ln n}{n^{8.001}}\right\}$ **c.** $\left\{\dfrac{n!}{10^n}\right\}$

SOLUTION

a. Because $\ln n^{10} = 10 \ln n$, the sequence in the numerator is a constant multiple of the sequence $\{\ln n\}$. Similarly, the sequence in the denominator is a constant multiple of the sequence $\{n\}$. By Theorem 9.6, $\{n\}$ grows faster than $\{\ln n\}$ as $n \to \infty$; therefore, the sequence $\left\{\dfrac{\ln n^{10}}{0.00001n}\right\}$ converges to zero.

b. The sequence in the numerator is $\{n^p \ln^r n\}$ of Theorem 9.6 with $p = 8$ and $r = 1$. The sequence in the denominator is $\{n^{p+s}\}$ of Theorem 9.6 with $p = 8$ and $s = 0.001$. Because $\{n^{p+s}\}$ grows faster than $\{n^p \ln^r n\}$ as $n \to \infty$, we conclude that $\left\{\dfrac{n^8 \ln n}{n^{8.001}}\right\}$ converges to zero.

c. Using Theorem 9.6, we see that $n!$ grows faster than any exponential function as $n \to \infty$. Therefore, $\lim\limits_{n\to\infty} \dfrac{n!}{10^n} = \infty$, and the sequence diverges. Figure 9.23 gives a visual comparison of the growth rates of $\{n!\}$ and $\{10^n\}$. Because these sequences grow so quickly, we plot the logarithm of the terms. The exponential sequence $\{10^n\}$ dominates the factorial sequence $\{n!\}$ until $n = 25$ terms. At that point, the factorial sequence overtakes the exponential sequence.

Related Exercises 63–68◄

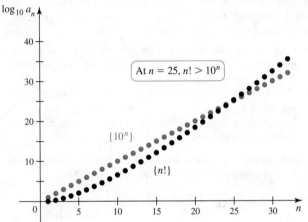

At $n = 25$, $n! > 10^n$

$\{10^n\}$

$\{n!\}$

FIGURE 9.23

SECTION 9.2 EXERCISES

Review Questions

1. Give an example of a nonincreasing sequence with a limit.

2. Give an example of a nondecreasing sequence without a limit.

3. Give an example of a bounded sequence that has a limit.

4. Give an example of a bounded sequence without a limit.

5. For what values of r does the sequence $\{r^n\}$ converge? Diverge?

6. Explain how the methods used to find the limit of a function as $x \to \infty$ are used to find the limit of a sequence.

7. Compare the growth rates of $\{n^{100}\}$ and $\{e^{n/100}\}$ as $n \to \infty$.

8. Explain how two sequences that differ only in their first 10 terms can have the same limit.

Basic Skills

9–34. Limits of sequences *Find the limits of the following sequences or determine that the limit does not exist.*

9. $\left\{\dfrac{n^3}{n^4 + 1}\right\}$ 10. $\left\{\dfrac{n^{12}}{3n^{12} + 4}\right\}$ 11. $\left\{\dfrac{3n^3 - 1}{2n^3 + 1}\right\}$

12. $\left\{\dfrac{2e^n + 1}{e^n}\right\}$ 13. $\left\{\dfrac{3^{n+1} + 3}{3^n}\right\}$ 14. $\left\{\dfrac{k}{\sqrt{9k^2 + 1}}\right\}$

15. $\{\tan^{-1} n\}$ 16. $\sqrt{n^2 + 1} - n$ 17. $\left\{\dfrac{\tan^{-1} n}{n}\right\}$

18. $\{n^{2/n}\}$ 19. $\left\{\left(1 + \dfrac{2}{n}\right)^n\right\}$ 20. $\left\{\left(\dfrac{n}{n + 5}\right)^n\right\}$

21. $\left\{\sqrt{\left(1 + \dfrac{1}{2n}\right)^n}\right\}$ 22. $\left\{\left(1 + \dfrac{4}{n}\right)^{3n}\right\}$ 23. $\left\{\dfrac{n}{e^n + 3n}\right\}$

24. $\left\{\dfrac{\ln(1/n)}{n}\right\}$ 25. $\left\{\left(\dfrac{1}{n}\right)^{1/n}\right\}$ 26. $\left\{\left(1 - \dfrac{4}{n}\right)^n\right\}$

27. $\{b_n\}$ where $b_n = \begin{cases} n/(n + 1) & \text{if } n \le 5000 \\ ne^{-n} & \text{if } n > 5000 \end{cases}$

28. $\{\ln(n^3 + 1) - \ln(3n^3 + 10n)\}$

29. $\{\ln \sin(1/n) + \ln n\}$

30. $\{n(1 - \cos(1/n))\}$

31. $\{n \sin (6/n)\}$

32. $\left\{ \dfrac{(-1)^n}{n} \right\}$

33. $\left\{ \dfrac{(-1)^n n}{n+1} \right\}$

34. $\left\{ \dfrac{(-1)^{n+1} n^2}{2n^3 + n} \right\}$

35–44. Limits of sequences and graphing *Find the limits of the following sequences or determine that the limit does not exist. Verify your result with a graphing utility.*

35. $a_n = \sin\left(\dfrac{n\pi}{2} \right)$

36. $a_n = \dfrac{(-1)^n n}{n+1}$

37. $a_n = \dfrac{\sin (n\pi/3)}{\sqrt{n}}$

38. $a_n = \dfrac{3^n}{3^n + 4^n}$

39. $a_n = 1 + \cos\left(\dfrac{1}{n} \right)$

40. $a_n = \dfrac{e^{-n}}{2 \sin (e^{-n})}$

41. $a_n = e^{-n} \cos n$

42. $a_n = \dfrac{\ln n}{n^{1.1}}$

43. $a_n = (-1)^n \sqrt[n]{n}$

44. $a_n = \cot\left(\dfrac{n\pi}{2n+2} \right)$

45–52. Geometric sequences *Determine whether the following sequences converge or diverge, and state whether they are monotonic or whether they oscillate. Give the limit when the sequence converges.*

45. $\{0.2^n\}$

46. $\{1.2^n\}$

47. $\{(-0.7)^n\}$

48. $\{(-1.01)^n\}$

49. $\{1.00001^n\}$

50. $\{2^{n+1} 3^{-n}\}$

51. $\{(-2.5)^n\}$

52. $\{(-0.003)^n\}$

53–58. Squeeze Theorem *Find the limits of the following sequences or state that they diverge.*

53. $\left\{ \dfrac{\cos n}{n} \right\}$

54. $\left\{ \dfrac{\sin 6n}{5n} \right\}$

55. $\left\{ \dfrac{\sin n}{2^n} \right\}$

56. $\left\{ \dfrac{\cos (n\pi/2)}{\sqrt{n}} \right\}$

57. $\left\{ \dfrac{2 \tan^{-1} n}{n^3 + 4} \right\}$

58. $\left\{ \dfrac{n \sin^3 (n\pi/2)}{n+1} \right\}$

59. Periodic dosing Many people take aspirin on a regular basis as a preventive measure for heart disease. Suppose a person takes 80 mg of aspirin every 24 hr. Assume also that aspirin has a half-life of 24 hr; that is, every 24 hr, half of the drug in the blood is eliminated.

a. Find a recurrence relation for the sequence $\{d_n\}$ that gives the amount of drug in the blood after the nth dose, where $d_1 = 80$.

b. Using a calculator, determine the limit of the sequence. In the long run, how much drug is in the person's blood?

c. Confirm the result of part (b) by finding the limit of $\{d_n\}$ directly.

60. A car loan Marie takes out a $20,000 loan for a new car. The loan has an annual interest rate of 6% or, equivalently, a monthly interest rate of 0.5%. Each month, the bank adds interest to the loan balance (the interest is always 0.5% of the current balance), and then Marie makes a $200 payment to reduce the loan balance. Let B_n be the loan balance immediately after the nth payment, where $B_0 = \$20,000$.

a. Write the first five terms of the sequence $\{B_n\}$.

b. Find a recurrence relation that generates the sequence $\{B_n\}$.

c. Determine how many months are needed to reduce the loan balance to zero.

61. A savings plan James begins a savings plan in which he deposits $100 at the beginning of each month into an account that earns 9% interest annually or, equivalently, 0.75%/month. To be clear, on the first day of each month, the bank adds 0.75% of the current balance as interest, and then James deposits $100. Let B_n be the balance in the account after the nth deposit, where $B_0 = \$0$.

a. Write the first five terms of the sequence $\{B_n\}$.

b. Find a recurrence relation that generates the sequence $\{B_n\}$.

c. Determine how many months are needed to reach a balance of $5000.

62. Diluting a solution Suppose a tank is filled with 100 L of a 40% alcohol solution (by volume). You repeatedly perform the following operation: Remove 2 L of the solution from the tank and replace them with 2 L of 10% alcohol solution.

a. Let C_n be the concentration of the solution in the tank after the nth replacement, where $C_0 = 40\%$. Write the first five terms of the sequence $\{C_n\}$.

b. After how many replacements does the alcohol concentration reach 15%?

c. Determine the limiting (steady-state) concentration of the solution that is approached after many replacements.

63–68. Growth rates of sequences *Use Theorem 9.6 to find the limits of the following sequences or state that they diverge.*

63. $\left\{ \dfrac{n!}{n^n} \right\}$

64. $\left\{ \dfrac{3^n}{n!} \right\}$

65. $\left\{ \dfrac{n^{10}}{\ln^{20} n} \right\}$

66. $\left\{ \dfrac{n^{10}}{\ln^{1000} n} \right\}$

67. $\left\{ \dfrac{n^{1000}}{2^n} \right\}$

68. $\left\{ \dfrac{e^{n/10}}{2^n} \right\}$

Further Explorations

69. Explain why or why not Determine whether the following statements are true and give an explanation or counterexample.

a. If $\lim\limits_{n \to \infty} a_n = 1$ and $\lim\limits_{n \to \infty} b_n = 3$, then $\lim\limits_{n \to \infty} \dfrac{b_n}{a_n} = 3$.

b. If $\lim\limits_{n \to \infty} a_n = 0$ and $\lim\limits_{n \to \infty} b_n = \infty$, then $\lim\limits_{n \to \infty} a_n b_n = 0$.

c. The convergent sequences $\{a_n\}$ and $\{b_n\}$ differ in their first 100 terms, but $a_n = b_n$, for $n > 100$. It follows that $\lim\limits_{n \to \infty} a_n = \lim\limits_{n \to \infty} b_n$.

d. If $\{a_n\} = \left\{ 1, \frac{1}{2}, \frac{1}{3}, \frac{1}{4}, \frac{1}{5}, \ldots \right\}$ and $\{b_n\} = \left\{ 1, 0, \frac{1}{2}, 0, \frac{1}{3}, 0, \frac{1}{4}, 0, \ldots \right\}$, then $\lim\limits_{n \to \infty} a_n = \lim\limits_{n \to \infty} b_n$.

e. If the sequence $\{a_n\}$ converges, then the sequence $\{(-1)^n a_n\}$ converges.

f. If the sequence $\{a_n\}$ diverges, then the sequence $\{0.000001 a_n\}$ diverges.

70–71. Reindexing *Express each sequence $\{a_n\}_{n=1}^{\infty}$ as an equivalent sequence of the form $\{b_n\}_{n=3}^{\infty}$.*

70. $\{2n + 1\}_{n=1}^{\infty}$

71. $\{n^2 + 6n - 9\}_{n=1}^{\infty}$

72–79. More sequences *Evaluate the limits of the following sequences.*

72. $a_n = \int_1^n x^{-2}\,dx$

73. $a_n = \dfrac{75^{n-1}}{99^n} + \dfrac{5^n \sin n}{8^n}$

74. $a_n = \tan^{-1}\left(\dfrac{10n}{10n + 4}\right)$

75. $a_n = \cos(0.99^n) + \dfrac{7^n + 9^n}{63^n}$

76. $a_n = \dfrac{4^n + 5n!}{n! + 2^n}$ **77.** $a_n = \dfrac{6^n + 3^n}{6^n + n^{100}}$

78. $a_n = \dfrac{n^8 + n^7}{n^7 + n^8 \ln n}$ **79.** $a_n = \dfrac{7^n}{n^7 5^n}$

80. Recurrence to explicit formula Find an explicit formula that defines the sequence generated by the recurrence relation
$$a_{n+1} = \frac{2a_n}{a_n + 1}, \; a_0 = 2.$$

81–84. Sequences by recurrence relations *Consider the following sequences defined by a recurrence relation. Use a calculator, analytical methods, and/or graphing to make a conjecture about the value of the limit or determine that the limit does not exist.*

81. $a_{n+1} = 2a_n(1 - a_n);\; a_0 = 0.3,\; n = 0, 1, 2, \ldots$

82. $a_{n+1} = \frac{1}{2}(a_n + 2/a_n);\; a_0 = 2,\; n = 0, 1, 2, \ldots$

83. $a_{n+1} = 4a_n(1 - a_n);\; a_0 = 0.5,\; n = 0, 1, 2, \ldots$

84. $a_{n+1} = \sqrt{2 + a_n};\; a_0 = 1,\; n = 0, 1, 2, \ldots$

85. Crossover point The sequence $\{n!\}$ ultimately grows faster than the sequence $\{b^n\}$, for any $b > 1$, as $n \to \infty$. However, b^n is generally greater than $n!$ for small values of n. Use a calculator to determine the smallest value of n such that $n! > b^n$ for each of the cases $b = 2$, $b = e$, and $b = 10$.

Applications

86. Fish harvesting A fishery manager knows that her fish population naturally increases at a rate of 1.5%/month, while 80 fish are harvested each month. Let F_n be the fish population after the nth month, where $F_0 = 4000$ fish.

   a. Write out the first five terms of the sequence $\{F_n\}$.
   b. Find a recurrence relation that generates the sequence $\{F_n\}$.
   c. Does the fish population decrease or increase in the long run?
   d. Determine whether the fish population decreases or increases in the long run if the initial population is 5500 fish.
   e. Determine the initial fish population F_0 below which the population decreases.

87. The hungry hippo problem A pet hippopotamus weighing 200 lb today gains 5 lb/day with a food cost of 45¢/day. The price for hippos is 65¢/lb today but is falling 1¢/day.

   a. Let h_n be the profit in selling the hippo on the nth day, where $h_0 = (200\,\text{lb}) \cdot (\$0.65/\text{lb}) = \$130$. Write out the first 10 terms of the sequence $\{h_n\}$.
   b. How many days after today should the hippo be sold to maximize the profit?

88. Sleep model After many nights of observation, you notice that if you oversleep one night, you tend to undersleep the following night, and vice versa. This pattern of compensation is described by the relationship
$$x_{n+1} = \frac{1}{2}(x_n + x_{n-1}), \quad \text{for } n = 1, 2, 3, \ldots,$$
where x_n is the number of hours of sleep you get on the nth night and $x_0 = 7$ and $x_1 = 6$ are the number of hours of sleep on the first two nights, respectively.

   a. Write out the first six terms of the sequence $\{x_n\}$ and confirm that the terms alternately increase and decrease.
   b. Show that the explicit formula
$$x_n = \frac{19}{3} + \frac{2}{3}\left(-\frac{1}{2}\right)^n, \text{ for } n \geq 0,$$
   generates the terms of the sequence in part (a).
   c. What is the limit of the sequence?

89. Calculator algorithm The CORDIC (<u>CO</u>ordinate <u>R</u>otation <u>DI</u>gital <u>C</u>alculation) algorithm is used by most calculators to evaluate trigonometric and logarithmic functions. An important number in the CORDIC algorithm, called the *aggregate constant*, is
$$\prod_{n=0}^{\infty} \frac{2^n}{\sqrt{1 + 2^{2n}}}, \text{ where } \prod_{n=0}^{N} a_n \text{ represents the product } a_0 \cdot a_1 \cdots a_N.$$
This infinite product is the limit of the sequence
$$\left\{ \prod_{n=0}^{0} \frac{2^n}{\sqrt{1 + 2^{2n}}}, \prod_{n=0}^{1} \frac{2^n}{\sqrt{1 + 2^{2n}}}, \prod_{n=0}^{2} \frac{2^n}{\sqrt{1 + 2^{2n}}}, \ldots \right\}.$$
Estimate the value of the aggregate constant.

Additional Exercises

90. Bounded monotonic proof Use mathematical induction to prove that the drug dose sequence in Example 5,
$$d_{n+1} = 0.5d_n + 100, d_1 = 100, \quad \text{for } n = 1, 2, 3, \ldots,$$
is bounded and monotonic.

91. Repeated square roots Consider the expression
$$\sqrt{1 + \sqrt{1 + \sqrt{1 + \sqrt{1 + \cdots}}}}, \text{ where the process continues indefinitely.}$$

   a. Show that this expression can be built in steps using the recurrence relation $a_0 = 1, a_{n+1} = \sqrt{1 + a_n}$, for $n = 0, 1, 2, 3, \ldots$. Explain why the value of the expression can be interpreted as $\lim_{n \to \infty} a_n$, provided the limit exists.
   b. Evaluate the first five terms of the sequence $\{a_n\}$.
   c. Estimate the limit of the sequence. Compare your estimate with $(1 + \sqrt{5})/2$, a number known as the *golden mean*.
   d. Assuming the limit exists, use the method of Example 5 to determine the limit exactly.
   e. Repeat the preceding analysis for the expression
$$\sqrt{p + \sqrt{p + \sqrt{p + \sqrt{p + \cdots}}}}, \text{ where } p > 0. \text{ Make a}$$
   table showing the approximate value of this expression for various values of p. Does the expression seem to have a limit for all positive values of p?

92. A sequence of products Find the limit of the sequence

$$\{a_n\}_{n=2}^\infty = \left\{ \left(1 - \frac{1}{2}\right)\left(1 - \frac{1}{3}\right) \cdots \left(1 - \frac{1}{n}\right) \right\}_{n=2}^\infty.$$

93. Continued fractions The expression

$$1 + \cfrac{1}{1 + \cfrac{1}{1 + \cfrac{1}{1 + \cfrac{1}{1 + \cdots}}}},$$

where the process continues indefinitely, is called a *continued fraction*.

a. Show that this expression can be built in steps using the recurrence relation $a_0 = 1, a_{n+1} = 1 + 1/a_n$, for $n = 0, 1, 2, 3, \ldots$. Explain why the value of the expression can be interpreted as $\lim_{n \to \infty} a_n$, provided the limit exists.

b. Evaluate the first five terms of the sequence $\{a_n\}$.

c. Using computation and/or graphing, estimate the limit of the sequence.

d. Assuming the limit exists, use the method of Example 5 to determine the limit exactly. Compare your estimate with $(1 + \sqrt{5})/2$, a number known as the *golden mean*.

e. Assuming the limit exists, use the same ideas to determine the value of

$$a + \cfrac{b}{a + \cfrac{b}{a + \cfrac{b}{a + \cfrac{b}{a + \cdots}}}},$$

where a and b are positive real numbers.

94. Towers of powers For a positive real number p, the tower of exponents $p^{p^{p^{\cdot^{\cdot^{\cdot}}}}}$ continues indefinitely and the expression is ambiguous. The tower could be built from the top as the limit of the sequence $\{p^p, (p^p)^p, ((p^p)^p)^p, \ldots\}$, in which case $a_1 = p^p, a_2 = (p^p)^p, a_3 = ((p^p)^p)^p, \ldots$. This sequence is defined recursively as

$$a_{n+1} = a_n^p \quad \text{(building from the top)}, \tag{1}$$

where $a_1 = p^p$. The tower could also be built from the bottom as the limit of the sequence $\{p^p, p^{(p^p)}, p^{(p^{(p^p)})}, \ldots\}$, in which case the sequence is defined to be

$$a_{n+1} = p^{a_n} \quad \text{(building from the bottom)}, \tag{2}$$

where again $a_1 = p^p$.

a. Estimate the value of the tower with $p = 0.5$ by building from the top. That is, use tables to estimate the limit of the sequence defined recursively by (1) with $p = 0.5$. Estimate the maximum value of $p > 0$ for which the sequence has a limit.

b. Estimate the value of the tower with $p = 1.2$ by building from the bottom. That is, use tables to estimate the limit of the sequence defined recursively by (2) with $p = 1.2$. Estimate the maximum value of $p > 1$ for which the sequence has a limit.

95. Fibonacci sequence The famous Fibonacci sequence was proposed by Leonardo Pisano, also known as Fibonacci, in about A.D. 1200 as a model for the growth of rabbit populations. It is given by the recurrence relation $f_{n+1} = f_n + f_{n-1}$, for $n = 1, 2, 3, \ldots$, where $f_0 = 1, f_1 = 1$. Each term of the sequence is the sum of its two predecessors.

a. Write out the first 10 terms of the sequence.

b. Is the sequence bounded?

c. Estimate or determine $\varphi = \lim_{n \to \infty} \dfrac{f_{n+1}}{f_n}$, the ratio of the successive terms of the sequence. Provide evidence that $\varphi = (1 + \sqrt{5})/2$, a number known as the *golden mean*.

d. Use mathematical induction to verify the remarkable result that

$$f_n = \frac{1}{\sqrt{5}}(\varphi^n - (-1)^n \varphi^{-n}).$$

96. Arithmetic-geometric mean Pick two positive numbers a_0 and b_0 with $a_0 > b_0$, and write out the first few terms of the two sequences $\{a_n\}$ and $\{b_n\}$:

$$a_{n+1} = \frac{a_n + b_n}{2}, \quad b_{n+1} = \sqrt{a_n b_n}, \quad \text{for } n = 0, 1, 2, \ldots$$

(Recall that the arithmetic mean $A = (p + q)/2$ and the geometric mean $G = \sqrt{pq}$ of two positive numbers p and q satisfy $A \geq G$.)

a. Show that $a_n > b_n$ for all n.

b. Show that $\{a_n\}$ is a decreasing sequence and $\{b_n\}$ is an increasing sequence.

c. Conclude that $\{a_n\}$ and $\{b_n\}$ converge.

d. Show that $a_{n+1} - b_{n+1} < (a_n - b_n)/2$, and conclude that $\lim_{n \to \infty} a_n = \lim_{n \to \infty} b_n$. The common value of these limits is called the arithmetic-geometric mean of a_0 and b_0, denoted $\text{AGM}(a_0, b_0)$.

e. Estimate $\text{AGM}(12, 20)$. Estimate Gauss' constant $1/\text{AGM}(1, \sqrt{2})$.

97. The hailstone sequence Here is a fascinating (unsolved) problem known as the hailstone problem (or the Ulam Conjecture or the Collatz Conjecture). It involves sequences in two different ways. First, choose a positive integer N and call it a_0. This is the *seed* of a sequence. The rest of the sequence is generated as follows: For $n = 0, 1, 2, \ldots$

$$a_{n+1} = \begin{cases} a_n/2 & \text{if } a_n \text{ is even} \\ 3a_n + 1 & \text{if } a_n \text{ is odd.} \end{cases}$$

However, if $a_n = 1$ for any n, then the sequence terminates.

a. Compute the sequence that results from the seeds $N = 2, 3, 4, \ldots, 10$. You should verify that in all these cases, the sequence eventually terminates. The hailstone conjecture (still unproved) states that for all positive integers N, the sequence terminates after a finite number of terms.

b. Now define the hailstone sequence $\{H_k\}$, which is the number of terms needed for the sequence $\{a_n\}$ to terminate starting with a seed of k. Verify that $H_2 = 1, H_3 = 7$, and $H_4 = 2$.

c. Plot as many terms of the hailstone sequence as is feasible. How did the sequence get its name? Does the conjecture appear to be true?

98. Prove that if $\{a_n\} \ll \{b_n\}$ (as used in Theorem 9.6), then $\{ca_n\} \ll \{db_n\}$, where c and d are positive real numbers.

99. Convergence proof Consider the sequence defined by $a_{n+1} = \sqrt{3a_n}$, for $n \geq 1, a_1 = \sqrt{3}$.

   a. Show that $\{a_n\}$ is increasing.
   b. Show that $\{a_n\}$ is bounded between 0 and 3.
   c. Explain why $\lim_{n \to \infty} a_n$ exists.
   d. Find $\lim_{n \to \infty} a_n$.

100–104. Comparing sequences *In the following exercises, two sequences are given, one of which initially has smaller values, but eventually "overtakes" the other sequence. Find the sequence with the larger growth rate and the value of n at which it overtakes the other sequence.*

100. $a_n = \sqrt{n}$ and $b_n = 2 \ln n, n \geq 3$

101. $a_n = e^{n/2}$ and $b_n = n^5, n \geq 2$

102. $a_n = n^{1.001}$ and $b_n = \ln n^{10}, n \geq 1$

103. $a_n = n!$ and $b_n = n^{0.7n}, n \geq 2$

104. $a_n = n^{10}$ and $b_n = n^9 \ln^3 n, n \geq 7$

105. Comparing sequences with a parameter For what values of a does the sequence $\{n!\}$ grow faster than the sequence $\{n^{an}\}$? (*Hint*: Stirling's formula may be helpful: $n! \approx (\sqrt{2\pi n}) n^n e^{-n}$, for large values of n).

QUICK CHECK **ANSWERS**

1. a. Bounded, monotonic **b.** Bounded, not monotonic **c.** Not bounded, not monotonic **d.** Bounded, monotonic (both nonincreasing and nondecreasing) **2.** If $r = -1$, the sequence is $\{-1, 1, -1, 1, \ldots\}$, the terms alternate in sign, and the sequence diverges. If $r = 1$, the sequence is $\{1, 1, 1, 1, \ldots\}$, the terms are constant, and the sequence converges. **3.** Both changes would increase the steady-state level of drug. **4.** $\{n^{1.1}\}$ grows faster; the limit is 0. ◄

9.3 Infinite Series

▶ The sequence of partial sums may be visualized nicely as follows:

$$\underbrace{\underbrace{\underbrace{a_1 + a_2 + a_3 + a_4 + \cdots}_{S_1}}_{S_2}}_{S_3} {}_{\cdots}$$

We begin our discussion of infinite series with *geometric series*. These series arise more frequently than any other infinite series, they are used in many practical problems, and they illustrate all the essential features of infinite series in general. First let's summarize some important ideas from Section 9.1.

Recall that every infinite series $\sum_{k=1}^{\infty} a_k$ has a sequence of partial sums:

$$S_1 = a_1, \qquad S_2 = a_1 + a_2, \qquad S_3 = a_1 + a_2 + a_3,$$

and in general $S_n = \sum_{k=1}^{n} a_k$, for $n = 1, 2, 3, \ldots$.

If the sequence of partial sums $\{S_n\}$ converges—that is, if $\lim_{n \to \infty} S_n = L$—then the value of the infinite series is also L. If the sequence of partial sums diverges, then the infinite series also diverges.

In summary, to evaluate an infinite series, it is necessary to determine a formula for the sequence of partial sums $\{S_n\}$ and then find its limit. This procedure can be carried out with the series that we discuss in this section: geometric series and telescoping series.

Geometric Sums and Series

▶ Geometric *sequences* have the form $\{r^k\}$ or $\{ar^k\}$. Geometric *sums* and *series* have the form $\sum r^k$ or $\sum ar^k$.

As a preliminary step to geometric series, we study **geometric sums**, which are *finite sums* in which each term is a constant multiple of the previous term. A geometric sum with n terms has the form

$$S_n = a + ar + ar^2 + \cdots + ar^{n-1} = \sum_{k=0}^{n-1} ar^k,$$

a. $\displaystyle\sum_{k=0}^{10} \left(\tfrac{1}{2}\right)^k$ **b.** $\displaystyle\sum_{k=0}^{20} \frac{1}{k}$

c. $\displaystyle\sum_{k=0}^{30} (2k + 1)$ ◄

> The notation $\displaystyle\sum_{k=0}^{\infty} ar^k$ appears to have an undefined first term when $r = 0$. The notation is understood to mean $a + ar + ar^2 + \cdots$ and therefore, the series has a value of a when $r = 0$.

QUICK CHECK 2 Verify that the geometric sum formula gives the correct result for the sums $1 + \tfrac{1}{2}$ and $\tfrac{1}{2} + \tfrac{1}{4} + \tfrac{1}{8}$. ◄

where $a \neq 0$ and r are real numbers; r is called the **ratio** of the sum and a is its first term. For example, the geometric sum with $r = 0.1$, $a = 0.9$, and $n = 4$ is

$$0.9 + 0.09 + 0.009 + 0.0009 = 0.9(1 + 0.1 + 0.01 + 0.001)$$

$$= \sum_{k=0}^{3} 0.9(0.1^k).$$

Our goal is to find a formula for the value of the geometric sum

$$S_n = a + ar + ar^2 + \cdots + ar^{n-1}, \tag{1}$$

for any values of a, r, and the positive integer n. Doing so requires a clever maneuver. The first step is to multiply both sides of equation (1) by the ratio r:

$$rS_n = r(a + ar + ar^2 + ar^3 + \cdots + ar^{n-1})$$

$$= ar + ar^2 + ar^3 + \cdots + ar^{n-1} + ar^n. \tag{2}$$

We now subtract equation (2) from equation (1). Notice how most of the terms on the right sides of these equations cancel, leaving

$$S_n - rS_n = a - ar^n.$$

Assuming $r \neq 1$ and solving for S_n results in a general formula for the value of a geometric sum:

$$S_n = a\,\frac{1 - r^n}{1 - r}. \tag{3}$$

Having dealt with geometric *sums*, it is a short step to geometric *series*. We simply note that the geometric sums $S_n = \displaystyle\sum_{k=0}^{n-1} ar^k$ form the sequence of partial sums for the geometric series $\displaystyle\sum_{k=0}^{\infty} ar^k$. The value of the geometric series is the limit of its sequence of partial sums (provided it exists). Using equation (3), we have

$$\underbrace{\sum_{k=0}^{\infty} ar^k}_{\text{geometric series}} = \lim_{n\to\infty} \underbrace{\sum_{k=0}^{n-1} ar^k}_{\text{geometric sum } S_n} = \lim_{n\to\infty} a\,\frac{1 - r^n}{1 - r}.$$

To compute this limit we must examine the behavior of r^n as $n \to \infty$. Recall from our work with geometric sequences (Section 9.2) that

$$\lim_{n\to\infty} r^n = \begin{cases} 0 & \text{if } |r| < 1 \\ 1 & \text{if } r = 1 \\ \text{does not exist} & \text{if } r \leq -1 \text{ or } r > 1. \end{cases}$$

Case 1: $|r| < 1$ Because $\displaystyle\lim_{n\to\infty} r^n = 0$, we have

$$\lim_{n\to\infty} S_n = \lim_{n\to\infty} a\,\frac{1 - r^n}{1 - r} = a\,\frac{1 - \overbrace{\lim_{n\to\infty} r^n}^{0}}{1 - r} = \frac{a}{1 - r}.$$

In the case that $|r| < 1$, the geometric series *converges* to $\dfrac{a}{1 - r}$.

Case 2: $|r| > 1$ In this case, $\lim\limits_{n \to \infty} r^n$ does not exist, so $\lim\limits_{n \to \infty} S_n$ does not exist and the series *diverges.*

Case 3: $|r| = 1$ If $r = 1$, then the geometric series is $\sum\limits_{k=0}^{\infty} a = a + a + a + \cdots$, which diverges. If $r = -1$, the geometric series is $a \sum\limits_{k=0}^{\infty} (-1)^k = a - a + a - \cdots$, which also diverges (because the sequence of partial sums oscillates between 0 and a).

We summarize these results in Theorem 9.7.

QUICK CHECK 3 Evaluate $\frac{1}{2} + \frac{1}{4} + \frac{1}{8} + \frac{1}{16} + \cdots$. ◄

THEOREM 9.7   Behavior of Geometric Series

Let $a \neq 0$ and r be real numbers. If $|r| < 1$, then $\sum\limits_{k=0}^{\infty} ar^k = \dfrac{a}{1 - r}$. If $|r| \geq 1$, then the series diverges.

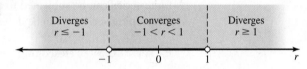

| Diverges $r \leq -1$ | Converges $-1 < r < 1$ | Diverges $r \geq 1$ |

QUICK CHECK 4 Explain why $\sum\limits_{k=0}^{\infty} 0.2^k$ converges and why $\sum\limits_{k=0}^{\infty} 2^k$ diverges. ◄

EXAMPLE 1   Geometric series Evaluate the following geometric series or state that the series diverges.

a. $\sum\limits_{k=0}^{\infty} 1.1^k$ **b.** $\sum\limits_{k=0}^{\infty} e^{-k}$ **c.** $\sum\limits_{k=2}^{\infty} 3(-0.75)^k$

SOLUTION

a. The ratio of this geometric series is $r = 1.1$. Because $|r| \geq 1$, the series diverges.

b. Note that $e^{-k} = \dfrac{1}{e^k} = \left(\dfrac{1}{e}\right)^k$. Therefore, the ratio of the series is $r = \dfrac{1}{e}$, and its first term is $a = 1$. Because $|r| < 1$, the series converges and its value is

$$\sum\limits_{k=0}^{\infty} e^{-k} = \sum\limits_{k=0}^{\infty} \left(\frac{1}{e}\right)^k = \frac{1}{1 - (1/e)} = \frac{e}{e - 1} \approx 1.582.$$

c. Writing out the first few terms of the series is helpful:

$$\sum\limits_{k=2}^{\infty} 3(-0.75)^k = \underbrace{3(-0.75)^2}_{a} + \underbrace{3(-0.75)^3}_{ar} + \underbrace{3(-0.75)^4}_{ar^2} + \cdots.$$

> The series in Example 1c is called an *alternating series* because the terms alternate in sign. Such series are discussed in detail in Section 9.6.

We see that the first term of the series is $a = 3(-0.75)^2$, and the ratio of the series is $r = -0.75$. Because $|r| < 1$, the series converges, and its value is

$$\sum\limits_{k=2}^{\infty} 3(-0.75)^k = \frac{3(-0.75)^2}{1 - (-0.75)} = \frac{27}{28}.$$

Related Exercises 7–40 ◄

EXAMPLE 2 **Decimal expansions as geometric series** Write $1.0\overline{35} = 1.0353535\ldots$ as a geometric series and express its value as a fraction.

SOLUTION Notice that the decimal part of this number is a convergent geometric series with $a = 0.035$ and $r = 0.01$:

$$1.0353535\ldots = 1 + \underbrace{0.035 + 0.00035 + 0.0000035 + \cdots}_{\text{geometric series with } a = 0.035 \text{ and } r = 0.01}.$$

Evaluating the series, we have

$$1.0353535\ldots = 1 + \frac{a}{1 - r} = 1 + \frac{0.035}{1 - 0.01} = 1 + \frac{35}{990} = \frac{205}{198}.$$

Related Exercises 41–54 ◀

Telescoping Series

With geometric series, we carried out the entire evaluation process by finding a formula for the sequence of partial sums and evaluating the limit of the sequence. Not many infinite series can be subjected to this sort of analysis. With another class of series, called **telescoping series**, it can be done. Here is an example.

EXAMPLE 3 **Telescoping series** Evaluate the following series.

a. $\displaystyle\sum_{k=1}^{\infty}\left(\frac{1}{3^k} - \frac{1}{3^{k+1}}\right)$ **b.** $\displaystyle\sum_{k=1}^{\infty}\frac{1}{k(k+1)}$

SOLUTION

a. The nth term of the sequence of partial sums is

$$S_n = \sum_{k=1}^{n}\left(\frac{1}{3^k} - \frac{1}{3^{k+1}}\right) = \left(\frac{1}{3} - \frac{1}{3^2}\right) + \left(\frac{1}{3^2} - \frac{1}{3^3}\right) + \cdots + \left(\frac{1}{3^n} - \frac{1}{3^{n+1}}\right)$$

$$= \frac{1}{3} + \underbrace{\left(-\frac{1}{3^2} + \frac{1}{3^2}\right)}_{0} + \cdots + \underbrace{\left(-\frac{1}{3^n} + \frac{1}{3^n}\right)}_{0} - \frac{1}{3^{n+1}} \quad \text{Regroup terms.}$$

$$= \frac{1}{3} - \frac{1}{3^{n+1}}. \qquad\qquad\qquad\qquad\qquad \text{Simplify.}$$

> The series in Example 3a is also a difference of geometric series and its value can be found using Theorem 9.7.

Observe that the interior terms of the sum cancel (or telescope), leaving a simple expression for S_n. Taking the limit, we find that

$$\sum_{k=1}^{\infty}\left(\frac{1}{3^k} - \frac{1}{3^{k+1}}\right) = \lim_{n\to\infty} S_n = \lim_{n\to\infty}\left(\frac{1}{3} - \underbrace{\frac{1}{3^{n+1}}}_{\to\, 0}\right) = \frac{1}{3}.$$

> See Section 7.3 for a review of partial fractions.

b. Using the method of partial fractions, the sequence of partial sums is

$$S_n = \sum_{k=1}^{n}\frac{1}{k(k+1)} = \sum_{k=1}^{n}\left(\frac{1}{k} - \frac{1}{k+1}\right).$$

Writing out this sum, we see that

$$S_n = \left(1 - \frac{1}{2}\right) + \left(\frac{1}{2} - \frac{1}{3}\right) + \left(\frac{1}{3} - \frac{1}{4}\right) + \cdots + \left(\frac{1}{n} - \frac{1}{n+1}\right)$$

$$= 1 + \underbrace{\left(-\frac{1}{2} + \frac{1}{2}\right)}_{0} + \underbrace{\left(-\frac{1}{3} + \frac{1}{3}\right)}_{0} + \cdots + \underbrace{\left(-\frac{1}{n} + \frac{1}{n}\right)}_{0} - \frac{1}{n+1}$$

$$= 1 - \frac{1}{n+1}.$$

Again, the sum telescopes and all the interior terms cancel. The result is a simple formula for the nth term of the sequence of partial sums. The value of the series is

$$\sum_{k=1}^{\infty} \frac{1}{k(k+1)} = \lim_{n \to \infty} S_n = \lim_{n \to \infty}\left(1 - \frac{1}{n+1}\right) = 1.$$

Related Exercises 55–68 ◄

SECTION 9.3 EXERCISES

Review Questions

1. What is the defining characteristic of a geometric series? Give an example.

2. What is the difference between a geometric sum and a geometric series?

3. What is meant by the *ratio* of a geometric series?

4. Does a geometric sum always have a finite value?

5. Does a geometric series always have a finite value?

6. What is the condition for convergence of the geometric series $\sum_{k=0}^{\infty} ar^k$?

Basic Skills

7–18. Geometric sums *Evaluate the following geometric sums.*

7. $\sum_{k=0}^{8} 3^k$

T 8. $\sum_{k=0}^{10}\left(\frac{1}{4}\right)^k$

T 9. $\sum_{k=0}^{20}\left(\frac{2}{5}\right)^{2k}$

10. $\sum_{k=4}^{12} 2^k$

T 11. $\sum_{k=0}^{9}\left(-\frac{3}{4}\right)^k$

T 12. $\sum_{k=1}^{5}(-2.5)^k$

13. $\sum_{k=0}^{6} \pi^k$

T 14. $\sum_{k=1}^{10}\left(\frac{4}{7}\right)^k$

15. $\sum_{k=0}^{20}(-1)^k$

16. $1 + \frac{2}{3} + \frac{4}{9} + \frac{8}{27}$

T 17. $\frac{1}{4} + \frac{1}{12} + \frac{1}{36} + \frac{1}{108} + \cdots + \frac{1}{2916}$

T 18. $\frac{1}{5} + \frac{3}{25} + \frac{9}{125} + \cdots + \frac{243}{15,625}$

19–34. Geometric series *Evaluate the geometric series or state that it diverges.*

19. $\sum_{k=0}^{\infty}\left(\frac{1}{4}\right)^k$

20. $\sum_{k=0}^{\infty}\left(\frac{3}{5}\right)^k$

21. $\sum_{k=0}^{\infty} 0.9^k$

22. $1 + \frac{2}{7} + \frac{2^2}{7^2} + \frac{2^3}{7^3} + \cdots$

23. $1 + 1.01 + 1.01^2 + 1.01^3 + \cdots$

24. $1 + \frac{1}{\pi} + \frac{1}{\pi^2} + \frac{1}{\pi^3} + \cdots$

25. $\sum_{k=1}^{\infty} e^{-2k}$

26. $\sum_{m=2}^{\infty} \frac{5}{2^m}$

27. $\sum_{k=1}^{\infty} 2^{-3k}$

28. $\sum_{k=3}^{\infty} \frac{3 \cdot 4^k}{7^k}$

29. $\sum_{k=4}^{\infty} \frac{1}{5^k}$

30. $\sum_{k=0}^{\infty}\left(\frac{4}{3}\right)^{-k}$

31. $1 + \frac{e}{\pi} + \frac{e^2}{\pi^2} + \frac{e^3}{\pi^3} + \cdots$

32. $\frac{1}{16} + \frac{3}{64} + \frac{9}{256} + \frac{27}{1024} + \cdots$

T 33. $\sum_{k=0}^{\infty}\left(\frac{1}{4}\right)^k 5^{6-k}$

T 34. $\sum_{k=2}^{\infty}\left(\frac{3}{8}\right)^{3k}$

35–40. Geometric series with alternating signs *Evaluate the geometric series or state that it diverges.*

35. $\sum_{k=0}^{\infty}\left(-\frac{9}{10}\right)^k$

36. $\sum_{k=1}^{\infty}\left(-\frac{2}{3}\right)^k$

37. $3\sum_{k=0}^{\infty} \frac{(-1)^k}{\pi^k}$

38. $\sum_{k=1}^{\infty}(-e)^{-k}$

39. $\sum_{k=2}^{\infty}(-0.15)^k$

40. $\sum_{k=1}^{\infty} 3\left(-\frac{1}{8}\right)^{3k}$

41–54. Decimal expansions *Write each repeating decimal first as a geometric series and then as a fraction (a ratio of two integers).*

41. $0.\overline{3} = 0.333\ldots$

42. $0.\overline{6} = 0.666\ldots$

43. $0.\overline{1} = 0.111\ldots$

44. $0.\overline{5} = 0.555\ldots$

45. $0.\overline{09} = 0.090909\ldots$

46. $0.\overline{27} = 0.272727\ldots$

47. $0.\overline{037} = 0.037037\ldots$

48. $0.\overline{027} = 0.027027\ldots$

49. $0.\overline{12} = 0.121212\ldots$

50. $1.\overline{25} = 1.252525\ldots$

51. $0.\overline{456} = 0.456456456\ldots$

52. $1.00\overline{39} = 1.00393939\ldots$

53. $0.00\overline{952} = 0.00952952\ldots$

54. $5.12\overline{83} = 5.12838383\ldots$

55–68. Telescoping series *For the following telescoping series, find a formula for the nth term of the sequence of partial sums $\{S_n\}$. Then evaluate $\lim_{n \to \infty} S_n$ to obtain the value of the series or state that the series diverges.*

55. $\sum_{k=1}^{\infty}\left(\frac{1}{k+1} - \frac{1}{k+2}\right)$

56. $\sum_{k=1}^{\infty}\left(\frac{1}{k+2} - \frac{1}{k+3}\right)$

57. $\sum_{k=1}^{\infty} \frac{1}{(k+6)(k+7)}$

58. $\sum_{k=0}^{\infty} \frac{1}{(3k+1)(3k+4)}$

59. $\sum_{k=3}^{\infty} \frac{4}{(4k-3)(4k+1)}$

60. $\sum_{k=3}^{\infty} \frac{2}{(2k-1)(2k+1)}$

61. $\sum_{k=1}^{\infty} \ln\left(\frac{k+1}{k}\right)$

62. $\sum_{k=1}^{\infty}(\sqrt{k+1} - \sqrt{k})$

63. $\sum_{k=1}^{\infty} \frac{1}{(k+p)(k+p+1)}$, where p is a positive integer

64. $\displaystyle\sum_{k=1}^{\infty} \frac{1}{(ak + 1)(ak + a + 1)}$, where a is a positive integer

65. $\displaystyle\sum_{k=1}^{\infty}\left(\frac{1}{\sqrt{k + 1}} - \frac{1}{\sqrt{k + 3}} \right)$

66. $\displaystyle\sum_{k=0}^{\infty}\left[\sin\left(\frac{(k + 1)\pi}{2k + 1} \right) - \sin\left(\frac{k\pi}{2k - 1} \right) \right]$

67. $\displaystyle\sum_{k=0}^{\infty} \frac{1}{16k^2 + 8k - 3}$

68. $\displaystyle\sum_{k=1}^{\infty} (\tan^{-1}(k + 1) - \tan^{-1} k)$

Further Explorations

69. **Explain why or why not** Determine whether the following statements are true and give an explanation or counterexample.

a. $\displaystyle\sum_{k=1}^{\infty}\left(\frac{\pi}{e} \right)^{-k}$ is a convergent geometric series.

b. If a is a real number and $\displaystyle\sum_{k=12}^{\infty} a^k$ converges, then $\displaystyle\sum_{k=1}^{\infty} a^k$ converges.

c. If the series $\displaystyle\sum_{k=1}^{\infty} a^k$ converges and $|a| < |b|$, then the series $\displaystyle\sum_{k=1}^{\infty} b^k$ converges.

d. Viewed as a function of r, the geometric series $1 + r + r^2 + r^3 + \cdots$ takes on all values in the interval $\left(\frac{1}{2}, \infty \right)$.

e. Viewed as a function of r, the geometric series $\displaystyle\sum_{k=1}^{\infty} r^k$ takes on all values in the interval $\left(-\frac{1}{2}, \infty \right)$.

70–73. Evaluating series *Evaluate the series or state that it diverges.*

70. $\displaystyle\sum_{k=1}^{\infty} \left[\sin^{-1}(1/k) - \sin^{-1}(1/(k + 1)) \right]$

71. $\displaystyle\sum_{k=1}^{\infty} \frac{(-2)^k}{3^{k+1}}$ **72.** $\displaystyle\sum_{k=1}^{\infty} \frac{\pi^k}{e^{k+1}}$

73. $\displaystyle\sum_{k=2}^{\infty} \frac{\ln((k + 1)k^{-1})}{(\ln k) \ln (k + 1)}$

74. **Evaluating an infinite series two ways** Evaluate the series $\displaystyle\sum_{k=1}^{\infty}\left(\frac{1}{2^k} - \frac{1}{2^{k+1}} \right)$ two ways as outlined in parts (a) and (b).

a. Evaluate $\displaystyle\sum_{k=1}^{\infty}\left(\frac{1}{2^k} - \frac{1}{2^{k+1}} \right)$ using a telescoping series argument.

b. Evaluate $\displaystyle\sum_{k=1}^{\infty}\left(\frac{1}{2^k} - \frac{1}{2^{k+1}} \right)$ using a geometric series argument after first simplifying $\frac{1}{2^k} - \frac{1}{2^{k+1}}$ by obtaining a common denominator.

75. **Evaluating an infinite series two ways** Evaluate the series $\displaystyle\sum_{k=1}^{\infty}\left(\frac{4}{3^k} - \frac{4}{3^{k+1}} \right)$ two ways as outlined in parts (a) and (b).

a. Evaluate $\displaystyle\sum_{k=1}^{\infty}\left(\frac{4}{3^k} - \frac{4}{3^{k+1}} \right)$ using a telescoping series argument.

b. Evaluate $\displaystyle\sum_{k=1}^{\infty}\left(\frac{4}{3^k} - \frac{4}{3^{k+1}} \right)$ using a geometric series argument after first simplifying $\frac{4}{3^k} - \frac{4}{3^{k+1}}$ by obtaining a common denominator.

76. **Zeno's paradox** The Greek philosopher Zeno of Elea (who lived about 450 B.C.) invented many paradoxes, the most famous of which tells of a race between the swift warrior Achilles and a tortoise. Zeno argued

> *The slower when running will never be overtaken by the quicker; for that which is pursuing must first reach the point from which that which is fleeing started, so that the slower must necessarily always be some distance ahead.*

In other words, by giving the tortoise a head start, Achilles will never overtake the tortoise because every time Achilles reaches the point where the tortoise was, the tortoise has moved ahead. Resolve this paradox by assuming that Achilles gives the tortoise a 1-mi head start and runs 5 mi/hr to the tortoise's 1 mi/hr. How far does Achilles run before he overtakes the tortoise, and how long does it take?

77. **Archimedes' quadrature of the parabola** The Greeks solved several calculus problems almost 2000 yr before the discovery of calculus. One example is Archimedes' calculation of the area of the region R bounded by a segment of a parabola, which he did using the "method of exhaustion." As shown in the figure, the idea was to fill R with an infinite sequence of triangles. Archimedes began with an isosceles triangle inscribed in the parabola, with area A_1, and proceeded in stages, with the number of new triangles doubling at each stage. He was able to show (the key to the solution) that at each stage, the area of a new triangle is $\frac{1}{8}$ of the area of a triangle at the previous stage; for example, $A_2 = \frac{1}{8}A_1$, and so forth. Show, as Archimedes did, that the area of R is $\frac{4}{3}$ times the area of A_1.

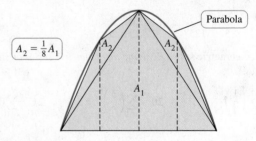

78. **Value of a series**

a. Find the value of the series

$$\sum_{k=1}^{\infty} \frac{3^k}{(3^{k+1} - 1)(3^k - 1)}.$$

b. For what values of a does the series

$$\sum_{k=1}^{\infty} \frac{a^k}{(a^{k+1} - 1)(a^k - 1)}$$

converge, and in those cases, what is its value?

Applications

79. House loan Suppose you take out a home mortgage for $180,000 at a monthly interest rate of 0.5%. If you make payments of $1000/month, after how many months will the loan balance be zero? Estimate the answer by graphing the sequence of loan balances and then obtain an exact answer using infinite series.

80. Car loan Suppose you borrow $20,000 for a new car at a monthly interest rate of 0.75%. If you make payments of $600/month, after how many months will the loan balance be zero? Estimate the answer by graphing the sequence of loan balances and then obtain an exact answer using infinite series.

81. Fish harvesting A fishery manager knows that her fish population naturally increases at a rate of 1.5%/month. At the end of each month, 120 fish are harvested. Let F_n be the fish population after the nth month, where $F_0 = 4000$ fish. Assume that this process continues indefinitely. Use infinite series to find the long-term (steady-state) population of the fish exactly.

82. Periodic doses Suppose that you take 200 mg of an antibiotic every 6 hr. The half-life of the drug is 6 hr (the time it takes for half of the drug to be eliminated from your blood). Use infinite series to find the long-term (steady-state) amount of antibiotic in your blood.

83. China's one-son policy In 1978, in an effort to reduce population growth, China instituted a policy that allows only one child per family. One unintended consequence has been that, because of a cultural bias toward sons, China now has many more young boys than girls. To solve this problem, some people have suggested replacing the one-child policy with a one-son policy: A family may have children until a boy is born. Suppose that the one-son policy were implemented and that natural birth rates remained the same (half boys and half girls). Using geometric series, compare the total number of children under the two policies.

84. Double glass An insulated window consists of two parallel panes of glass with a small spacing between them. Suppose that each pane reflects a fraction p of the incoming light and transmits the remaining light. Considering all reflections of light between the panes, what fraction of the incoming light is ultimately transmitted by the window? Assume the amount of incoming light is 1.

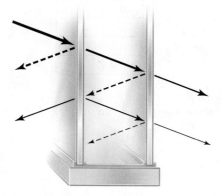

85. Bouncing ball for time Suppose a rubber ball, when dropped from a given height, returns to a fraction p of that height. In the absence of air resistance, a ball dropped from a height h requires $\sqrt{2h/g}$ seconds to fall to the ground, where $g \approx 9.8$ m/s² is the acceleration due to gravity. The time taken to bounce *up* to a given height equals the time to fall from that height to the ground. How long does it take for a ball dropped from 10 m to come to rest?

86. Multiplier effect Imagine that the government of a small community decides to give a total of W, distributed equally, to all its citizens. Suppose that each month each citizen saves a fraction p of his or her new wealth and spends the remaining $1 - p$ in the community. Assume no money leaves or enters the community and all the spent money is redistributed throughout the community.

  a. If this cycle of saving and spending continues for many months, how much money is ultimately spent? Specifically, by what factor is the initial investment of W increased? (Economists refer to this increase in the investment as the *multiplier effect*.)

  b. Evaluate the limits $p \to 0$ and $p \to 1$ and interpret their meanings.

(See the Guided Project *Economic stimulus packages* for more on stimulus packages.)

87. Snowflake island fractal The fractal called the *snowflake island* (or *Koch island*) is constructed as follows: Let I_0 be an equilateral triangle with sides of length 1. The figure I_1 is obtained by replacing the middle third of each side of I_0 with a new outward equilateral triangle with sides of length $1/3$ (see figure). The process is repeated where I_{n+1} is obtained by replacing the middle third of each side of I_n with a new outward equilateral triangle with sides of length $1/3^{n+1}$. The limiting figure as $n \to \infty$ is called the snowflake island.

  a. Let L_n be the perimeter of I_n. Show that $\lim\limits_{n\to\infty} L_n = \infty$.

  b. Let A_n be the area of I_n. Find $\lim\limits_{n\to\infty} A_n$. It exists!

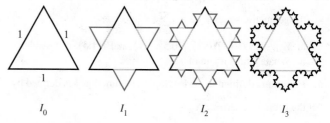

I_0 I_1 I_2 I_3

Additional Exercises

88. Decimal expansions

  a. Consider the number 0.555555..., which can be viewed as the series $5\sum\limits_{k=1}^{\infty} 10^{-k}$. Evaluate the geometric series to obtain a rational value of 0.555555....

  b. Consider the number 0.54545454..., which can be represented by the series $54\sum\limits_{k=1}^{\infty} 10^{-2k}$. Evaluate the geometric series to obtain a rational value of the number.

  c. Now generalize parts (a) and (b). Suppose you are given a number with a decimal expansion that repeats in cycles of length p, say, $n_1, n_2, \ldots, n_p$, where $n_1, \ldots, n_p$ are integers between 0 and 9. Explain how to use geometric series to obtain a rational form of the number.

  d. Try the method of part (c) on the number 0.123456789123456789....

  e. Prove that $0.\overline{9} = 1$.

89. Remainder term Consider the geometric series $S = \sum_{k=0}^{\infty} r^k$,

which has the value $1/(1 - r)$ provided $|r| < 1$. Let

$$S_n = \sum_{k=0}^{n-1} r^k = \frac{1 - r^n}{1 - r}$$ be the sum of the first n terms. The

remainder R_n is the error in approximating S by S_n. Show that

$$R_n = S - S_n = \frac{r^n}{1 - r}.$$

90–93. Comparing remainder terms *Use Exercise 89 to determine how many terms of each series are needed so that the partial sum is within 10^{-6} of the value of the series (that is, to ensure $|R_n| < 10^{-6}$).*

90. a. $\sum_{k=0}^{\infty} 0.6^k$ **b.** $\sum_{k=0}^{\infty} 0.15^k$

91. a. $\sum_{k=0}^{\infty} (-0.8)^k$ **b.** $\sum_{k=0}^{\infty} 0.2^k$

92. a. $\sum_{k=0}^{\infty} 0.72^k$ **b.** $\sum_{k=0}^{\infty} (-0.25)^k$

93. a. $\sum_{k=0}^{\infty} \left(\frac{1}{\pi}\right)^k$ **b.** $\sum_{k=0}^{\infty} \left(\frac{1}{e}\right)^k$

94. Functions defined as series Suppose a function f is defined by

the geometric series $f(x) = \sum_{k=0}^{\infty} x^k$.

a. Evaluate $f(0), f(0.2), f(0.5), f(1)$, and $f(1.5)$, if possible.
b. What is the domain of f?

95. Functions defined as series Suppose a function f is defined by

the geometric series $f(x) = \sum_{k=0}^{\infty} (-1)^k x^k$.

a. Evaluate $f(0), f(0.2), f(0.5), f(1)$, and $f(1.5)$, if possible.
b. What is the domain of f?

96. Functions defined as series Suppose a function f is defined by

the geometric series $f(x) = \sum_{k=0}^{\infty} x^{2k}$.

a. Evaluate $f(0), f(0.2), f(0.5), f(1)$, and $f(1.5)$, if possible.
b. What is the domain of f?

97. Series in an equation For what values of x does the geometric series

$$f(x) = \sum_{k=0}^{\infty} \left(\frac{1}{1 + x}\right)^k$$

converge? Solve $f(x) = 3$.

98. Bubbles Imagine a stack of hemispherical soap bubbles with decreasing radii $r_1 = 1, r_2, r_3, \ldots$ (see figure). Let h_n be the distance between the diameters of bubble n and bubble $n + 1$, and let H_n be the total height of the stack with n bubbles.

a. Use the Pythagorean theorem to show that in a stack with n bubbles, $h_1^2 = r_1^2 - r_2^2, h_2^2 = r_2^2 - r_3^2$, and so forth. Note that for the last bubble $h_n = r_n$.

b. Use part (a) to show that the height of a stack with n bubbles is

$$H_n = \sqrt{r_1^2 - r_2^2} + \sqrt{r_2^2 - r_3^2} + \cdots + \sqrt{r_{n-1}^2 - r_n^2} + r_n.$$

c. The height of a stack of bubbles depends on how the radii decrease. Suppose that $r_1 = 1, r_2 = a, r_3 = a^2, \ldots, r_n = a^{n-1}$, where $0 < a < 1$ is a fixed real number. In terms of a, find the height H_n of a stack with n bubbles.

d. Suppose the stack in part (c) is extended indefinitely ($n \to \infty$). In terms of a, how high would the stack be?

e. Challenge problem: Fix n and determine the sequence of radii $r_1, r_2, r_3, \ldots, r_n$ that maximizes H_n, the height of the stack with n bubbles.

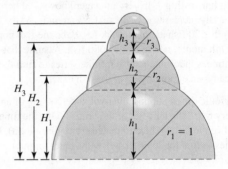

Technology Exercises

99. Values of the geometric series Consider the geometric series

$$f(r) = \sum_{k=0}^{\infty} r^k, \text{ where } |r| < 1.$$

a. Fill in the following table that shows the value of the series $f(r)$ for various values of r.

r	$f(r)$
-0.9	
-0.7	
-0.5	
-0.2	
0	
0.2	
0.5	
0.7	
0.9	

b. Graph f, for $|r| < 1$.
c. Evaluate $\lim_{r \to 1^-} f(r)$ and $\lim_{r \to -1^+} f(r)$.

100. Convergence rates Consider series $S = \sum_{k=0}^{\infty} r^k$, where $|r| < 1$,

and its sequence of partial sums $S_n = \sum_{k=0}^{n} r^k$.

a. Complete the following table showing the smallest value of n, call it $N(r)$, such that $|S - S_n| < 10^{-4}$, for various values of r. For example, with $r = 0.5$ and $S = 2$, we find that $|S - S_{13}| = 1.2 \times 10^{-4}$ and $|S - S_{14}| = 6.1 \times 10^{-5}$. Therefore, $N(0.5) = 14$.

r	$N(r)$
-0.9	
-0.7	
-0.5	
-0.2	
0	
0.2	
0.5	
0.7	
0.9	

b. Make a graph of $N(r)$ for the values of r in part (a).

c. How does the rate of convergence of the geometric series depend on r?

QUICK CHECK ANSWERS

1. b and c   2. Using the formula, the values are $\frac{3}{2}$ and $\frac{7}{8}$.   3. 1   4. The first converges because $|r| = 0.2 < 1$; the second diverges because $|r| = 2 > 1$. ◄

9.4 The Divergence and Integral Tests

With geometric series and telescoping series, the sequence of partial sums can be found and its limit can be evaluated (when it exists). Unfortunately, it is difficult or impossible to find an explicit formula for the sequence of partial sums for most infinite series. Therefore, it is difficult to obtain the exact value of most convergent series.

In light of these observations, we now shift our focus and ask a simple *yes* or *no* question: Given an infinite series, does it converge? If the answer is *no*, the series diverges and there are no more questions to ask. If the answer is *yes*, the series converges and it may be possible to estimate its value.

The Divergence Test

One of the simplest and most useful tests determines whether an infinite series *diverges*. Though our focus in this section and the next is on series with positive terms, the Divergence Test applies to series with arbitrary terms.

THEOREM 9.8 Divergence Test

If $\sum a_k$ converges, then $\lim_{k \to \infty} a_k = 0$. Equivalently, if $\lim_{k \to \infty} a_k \neq 0$, then the series diverges.

Important note: Theorem 9.8 cannot be used to conclude that a series converges.

Proof: Let $\{S_k\}$ be the sequence of partial sums for the series $\sum a_k$. Assuming the series converges, it has a finite value, call it S, where

$$S = \lim_{k \to \infty} S_k = \lim_{k \to \infty} S_{k-1}.$$

Note that $S_k - S_{k-1} = a_k$. Therefore,

$$\lim_{k \to \infty} a_k = \lim_{k \to \infty} (S_k - S_{k-1}) = S - S = 0;$$

> If the statement *if p, then q* is true, then its contrapositive, *if (not q), then (not p)*, is also true. However its converse, *if q, then p*, is not necessarily true. Try it out on the true statement *if I live in Paris, then I live in France.*

that is, $\lim\limits_{k\to\infty} a_k = 0$ (Figure 9.24). The second part of the test follows immediately because it is the *contrapositive* of the first part (see margin note). ◄

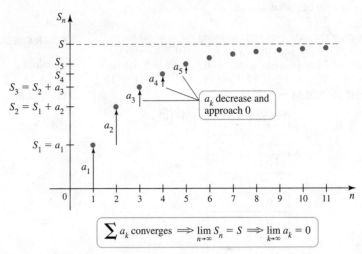

$$\sum a_k \text{ converges} \implies \lim_{n\to\infty} S_n = S \implies \lim_{k\to\infty} a_k = 0$$

FIGURE 9.24

EXAMPLE 1   Using the Divergence Test Determine whether the following series diverge or state that the Divergence Test is inconclusive.

a. $\displaystyle\sum_{k=0}^{\infty} \frac{k}{k+1}$ **b.** $\displaystyle\sum_{k=1}^{\infty} \frac{1+3^k}{2^k}$ **c.** $\displaystyle\sum_{k=1}^{\infty} \frac{1}{k}$ **d.** $\displaystyle\sum_{k=1}^{\infty} \frac{1}{k^2}$

SOLUTION Recall that if $\lim\limits_{k\to\infty} a_k \neq 0$, then the series $\sum a_k$ diverges.

a. $\lim\limits_{k\to\infty} a_k = \lim\limits_{k\to\infty} \dfrac{k}{k+1} = 1 \neq 0$

The terms of the series do not tend to zero, so the series diverges by the Divergence Test.

b. $\lim\limits_{k\to\infty} a_k = \lim\limits_{k\to\infty} \dfrac{1+3^k}{2^k}$

$\qquad = \lim\limits_{k\to\infty} \left[\underbrace{2^{-k}}_{\to 0} + \underbrace{\left(\frac{3}{2}\right)^k}_{\to\infty} \right]$ Simplify.

$\qquad = \infty$

In this case, $\lim\limits_{k\to\infty} a_k \neq 0$, so the corresponding series $\displaystyle\sum_{k=1}^{\infty} \dfrac{1+3^k}{2^k}$ diverges by the Divergence Test.

c. $\lim\limits_{k\to\infty} a_k = \lim\limits_{k\to\infty} \dfrac{1}{k} = 0$

In this case, the terms of the series approach zero, so the Divergence Test is inconclusive. Remember, the Divergence Test cannot be used to prove that a series converges.

QUICK CHECK 1 Apply the Divergence Test to the geometric series $\sum r^k$. For what values of r does the series diverge? ◄

d. $\lim\limits_{k\to\infty} a_k = \lim\limits_{k\to\infty} \dfrac{1}{k^2} = 0$

As in part (c), the terms of the series approach 0, so the Divergence Test is inconclusive.

Related Exercises 9–18 ◄

To summarize: If the terms a_k of a given series do *not* tend to zero as $k \to \infty$, then the series diverges. Unfortunately, the test is easy to misuse. It's tempting to conclude that if the terms of the series tend to zero, then the series converges. However, look again at the series in Example 1c and 1d. Although it is true that $\lim\limits_{k \to \infty} a_k = 0$ for both series, we will soon discover that one of them converges while the other diverges. We cannot tell which behavior to expect based only on the observation that $\lim\limits_{k \to \infty} a_k = 0$.

The Harmonic Series

We now look at an example that has a surprising result. Consider the infinite series

$$\sum_{k=1}^{\infty} \frac{1}{k} = 1 + \frac{1}{2} + \frac{1}{3} + \frac{1}{4} + \frac{1}{5} + \cdots,$$

a famous series known as the **harmonic series**. Does it converge? As explained in Example 1(c), this question cannot be answered by the Divergence Test, despite the fact that $\lim\limits_{k \to \infty} \frac{1}{k} = 0$. Suppose instead you try to answer the convergence question by writing out the terms of the sequence of partial sums:

$$S_1 = 1, \qquad\qquad S_2 = 1 + \frac{1}{2} = \frac{3}{2},$$

$$S_3 = 1 + \frac{1}{2} + \frac{1}{3} = \frac{11}{6}, \qquad S_4 = 1 + \frac{1}{2} + \frac{1}{3} + \frac{1}{4} = \frac{25}{12},$$

and in general,

$$S_n = \sum_{k=1}^{n} \frac{1}{k} = 1 + \frac{1}{2} + \frac{1}{3} + \frac{1}{4} + \cdots + \frac{1}{n}.$$

There is no obvious pattern in this sequence, and in fact, no explicit formula for S_n exists, so we analyze the sequence numerically. Have a look at the first 200 terms of the sequence of partial sums shown in Figure 9.25. What do you think—does the series converge? The terms of the sequence of partial sums increase, but at a decreasing rate. They could approach a limit or they could increase without bound.

Computing additional terms of the sequence of partial sums does not provide conclusive evidence. Table 9.3 shows that the sum of the first million terms is less than 15; the sum of the first 10^{40} terms—an unimaginably large number of terms—is less than 100. This is a case in which computation alone is not sufficient to determine whether a series converges. We need another way to determine whether the series converges.

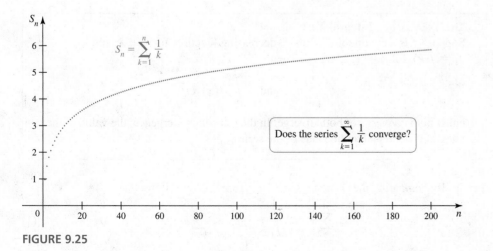

Does the series $\sum\limits_{k=1}^{\infty} \frac{1}{k}$ converge?

FIGURE 9.25

Table 9.3

n	S_n	n	S_n
10^3	≈ 7.485	10^{10}	≈ 23.603
10^4	≈ 9.788	10^{20}	≈ 46.629
10^5	≈ 12.090	10^{30}	≈ 69.655
10^6	≈ 14.393	10^{40}	≈ 92.681

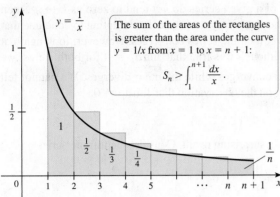

FIGURE 9.26

> Recall that $\int \dfrac{dx}{x} = \ln|x| + C$. In Section 7.4, we showed that $\int_1^\infty \dfrac{dx}{x^p}$ diverges for $p \le 1$. Therefore, $\int_1^\infty \dfrac{dx}{x}$ diverges.

Observe that the nth term of the sequence of partial sums,

$$S_n = \sum_{k=1}^n \frac{1}{k} = 1 + \frac{1}{2} + \frac{1}{3} + \frac{1}{4} + \cdots + \frac{1}{n},$$

is represented geometrically by a left Riemann sum of the function $y = \dfrac{1}{x}$ on the interval $[1, n + 1]$ (Figure 9.26). This fact follows by noticing that the areas of the rectangles, from left to right, are $1, \dfrac{1}{2}, \ldots,$ and $\dfrac{1}{n}$. Comparing the sum of the areas of these n rectangles with the area the curve, which is $\displaystyle\int_1^{n+1} \dfrac{dx}{x}$, we see that $S_n > \displaystyle\int_1^{n+1} \dfrac{dx}{x}$.

We know that $\displaystyle\int_1^{n+1} \dfrac{dx}{x} = \ln(n + 1)$ increases without bound as n increases. Because S_n exceeds $\displaystyle\int_1^{n+1} \dfrac{dx}{x}$, S_n also increases without bound; therefore, $\displaystyle\lim_{n \to \infty} S_n = \infty$ and the harmonic series $\displaystyle\sum_{k=1}^\infty \dfrac{1}{k}$ diverges. This argument justifies the following theorem.

THEOREM 9.9 Harmonic Series

The harmonic series $\displaystyle\sum_{k=1}^\infty \dfrac{1}{k} = 1 + \dfrac{1}{2} + \dfrac{1}{3} + \dfrac{1}{4} + \dfrac{1}{5} + \cdots$ diverges—even though the terms of the series approach zero.

We worked hard to prove that the harmonic series diverges. The ideas used in that argument are now used to prove a new and powerful convergence test. This test and the tests presented in Section 9.5 apply only to series with positive terms.

The Integral Test

The method used to prove that the harmonic series diverges leads to an alternative approach to the question of convergence called the Integral Test. The fact that infinite series are sums and that integrals are limits of sums suggests a connection between series and integrals. The Integral Test exploits this connection.

THEOREM 9.10 Integral Test

Suppose f is a continuous, positive, decreasing function, for $x \ge 1$, and let $a_k = f(k)$, for $k = 1, 2, 3, \ldots$ Then

$$\sum_{k=1}^\infty a_k \quad \text{and} \quad \int_1^\infty f(x)\, dx$$

either both converge or both diverge. In the case of convergence, the value of the integral is *not* equal to the value of the series.

> The Integral Test also applies if the terms of the series a_k are decreasing for $k > N$ for some finite $N > 1$. The proof can be modified to account for this situation.

Proof: By comparing the shaded regions in Figure 9.27, it follows that

$$\sum_{k=2}^n a_k < \int_1^n f(x)\, dx < \sum_{k=1}^{n-1} a_k. \tag{1}$$

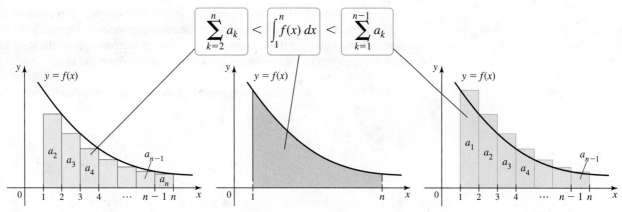

FIGURE 9.27

The proof must demonstrate two results: If the improper integral $\int_1^\infty f(x)\,dx$ has a finite value, then the infinite series converges, *and* if the infinite series converges, then the improper integral has a finite value. First suppose that the improper integral $\int_1^\infty f(x)\,dx$ has a finite value, say I. We have

$$\sum_{k=1}^{n} a_k = a_1 + \sum_{k=2}^{n} a_k \qquad \text{Separate the first term of the series.}$$

$$< a_1 + \int_1^n f(x)\,dx \qquad \text{Left inequality in expression (1)}$$

$$< a_1 + \int_1^\infty f(x)\,dx \qquad f \text{ is positive, so } \int_1^n f(x)\,dx < \int_1^\infty f(x)\,dx.$$

$$= a_1 + I.$$

> In this proof, we rely twice on the Bounded Monotonic Sequence Theorem of Section 9.2: A bounded monotonic sequence converges.

This argument implies that the terms of the sequence of partial sums $S_n = \sum_{k=1}^{n} a_k$ are bounded above by $a_1 + I$. Because $\{S_n\}$ is also increasing (the series consists of positive terms), the sequence of partial sums converges, which means the series $\sum_{k=1}^{\infty} a_k$ converges (to a value less than or equal to $a_1 + I$).

Now suppose the infinite series $\sum_{k=1}^{\infty} a_k$ converges and has a value S. We have

$$\int_1^n f(x)\,dx < \sum_{k=1}^{n-1} a_k \qquad \text{Right inequality in expression (1)}$$

> The proof of Theorem 9.10 can be strengthened to show that, in fact, the value of the integral is always strictly less than the value of the series.

$$< \sum_{k=1}^{\infty} a_k \qquad \text{Terms } a_k \text{ are positive.}$$

$$= S. \qquad \text{Value of infinite series}$$

We see that the sequence $\left\{\int_1^n f(x)\,dx\right\}$ is increasing (because $f(x) > 0$) and bounded above by a fixed number S. Therefore, the improper integral $\int_1^\infty f(x)\,dx = \lim_{n\to\infty} \int_1^n f(x)\,dx$ has a finite value (less than or equal to S).

We have shown that if $\int_1^\infty f(x)\,dx$ is finite, then $\sum a_k$ converges and vice versa. The same inequalities imply that $\int_1^\infty f(x)\,dx$ and $\sum a_k$ also diverge together. ◄

The Integral Test is used to determine *whether* a series converges or diverges. For this reason, adding or subtracting a few terms in the series *or* changing the lower limit of integration to another finite point does not change the outcome of the test. Therefore, the test depends neither on the lower index in the series nor on the lower limit of the integral.

EXAMPLE 2   Applying the Integral Test Determine whether the following series converge.

a. $\displaystyle\sum_{k=1}^{\infty} \frac{k}{k^2 + 1}$ **b.** $\displaystyle\sum_{k=3}^{\infty} \frac{1}{\sqrt{2k - 5}}$ **c.** $\displaystyle\sum_{k=0}^{\infty} \frac{1}{k^2 + 4}$

SOLUTION

a. The function associated with this series is $f(x) = x/(x^2 + 1)$, which is positive, for $x \geq 1$. We must also show that the terms of the series are decreasing beyond some fixed term of the series. The first few terms of the series are $\left\{ \frac{1}{2}, \frac{2}{5}, \frac{3}{10}, \frac{4}{17}, \ldots \right\}$, and it appears that the terms are decreasing. When the decreasing property is difficult to confirm, one approach is to use derivatives to show that the associated function is decreasing. In this case, we have

$$f'(x) = \underbrace{\frac{d}{dx}\left(\frac{x}{x^2 + 1}\right) = \frac{x^2 + 1 - 2x^2}{(x^2 + 1)^2}}_{\text{Quotient Rule}} = \frac{1 - x^2}{(x^2 + 1)^2}.$$

For $x > 1, f'(x) < 0$, which implies that the function and the terms of the series are decreasing. The integral that determines convergence is

$$\int_1^{\infty} \frac{x}{x^2 + 1}\, dx = \lim_{b \to \infty} \int_1^b \frac{x}{x^2 + 1}\, dx \qquad \text{Definition of improper integral}$$

$$= \lim_{b \to \infty} \frac{1}{2} \ln{(x^2 + 1)} \Big|_1^b \qquad \text{Evaluate integral.}$$

$$= \frac{1}{2} \lim_{b \to \infty} \left(\ln{(b^2 + 1)} - \ln 2 \right) \quad \text{Simplify.}$$

$$= \infty. \qquad\qquad \lim_{b \to \infty} \ln{(b^2 + 1)} = \infty$$

Because the integral diverges, the series diverges.

b. The Integral Test may be modified to accommodate initial indices other than $k = 1$. The terms of this series decrease, for $k \geq 3$. In this case, the relevant integral is

$$\int_3^{\infty} \frac{dx}{\sqrt{2x - 5}} = \lim_{b \to \infty} \int_3^b \frac{dx}{\sqrt{2x - 5}} \qquad \text{Definition of improper integral}$$

$$= \lim_{b \to \infty} \sqrt{2x - 5} \Big|_3^b \qquad\qquad \text{Evaluate integral.}$$

$$= \infty. \qquad\qquad\qquad \lim_{b \to \infty} \sqrt{2b - 5} = \infty$$

Because the integral diverges, the series also diverges.

c. The terms of the series are positive and decrease, for $k \geq 0$. The relevant integral is

$$\int_0^\infty \frac{dx}{x^2 + 4} = \lim_{b \to \infty} \int_0^b \frac{dx}{x^2 + 4} \qquad \text{Definition of improper integral}$$

$$= \lim_{b \to \infty} \frac{1}{2} \tan^{-1} \frac{x}{2} \Big|_0^b \qquad \text{Evaluate integral.}$$

$$= \frac{1}{2} \underbrace{\lim_{b \to \infty} \tan^{-1} \frac{b}{2}}_{\frac{\pi}{2}} - \tan^{-1} 0 \quad \text{Simplify.}$$

$$= \frac{\pi}{4}. \qquad \tan^{-1} x \to \frac{\pi}{2}, \text{ as } x \to \infty.$$

Because the integral is finite (equivalently, it converges), the infinite series also converges $\left(\text{but not to } \dfrac{\pi}{4}\right)$.

Related Exercises 19–28 ◄

The *p*-Series

The Integral Test is used to analyze the convergence of an entire family of infinite series, $\displaystyle\sum_{k=1}^\infty \frac{1}{k^p}$, known as the *p-series*.

EXAMPLE 3   **The *p*-series** For what values of p does the *p*-series $\displaystyle\sum_{k=1}^\infty \frac{1}{k^p}$ converge?

SOLUTION Notice that $p = 1$ corresponds to the harmonic series, which diverges. To apply the Integral Test, observe that the terms of the given series are positive and decreasing, for $p > 0$. The function associated with the series is $f(x) = \dfrac{1}{x^p}$. The relevant integral is $\displaystyle\int_1^\infty x^{-p} \, dx = \int_1^\infty \frac{dx}{x^p}$. Appealing to Example 2 in Section 7.4, recall that this integral converges for $p > 1$ and diverges for $p \leq 1$. Therefore, by the Integral Test, the *p*-series $\displaystyle\sum_{k=1}^\infty \frac{1}{k^p}$ converges for $p > 1$ and diverges for $0 < p \leq 1$. For example, the series

$$\sum_{k=1}^\infty \frac{1}{k^3} \quad \text{and} \quad \sum_{k=1}^\infty \frac{1}{\sqrt{k}}$$

converge and diverge, respectively. For $p < 0$, the series diverges by the Divergence Test. This argument justifies the following theorem.

Related Exercises 29–34 ◄

QUICK CHECK 2 Which of the following series are *p*-series, and which series converge?

a. $\displaystyle\sum_{k=1}^\infty k^{-0.8}$ **b.** $\displaystyle\sum_{k=1}^\infty 2^{-k}$ **c.** $\displaystyle\sum_{k=10}^\infty k^{-4}$ ◄

THEOREM 9.11   Convergence of the *p*-Series

The *p*-series $\displaystyle\sum_{k=1}^\infty \frac{1}{k^p}$ converges for $p > 1$ and diverges for $p \leq 1$.

EXAMPLE 4   **Using the *p*-series test** Determine whether the following series converge or diverge.

a. $\sum_{k=1}^{\infty} \dfrac{1}{\sqrt[4]{k^3}}$ **b.** $\sum_{k=4}^{\infty} \dfrac{1}{(k-1)^2}$

SOLUTION

a. This series is a *p*-series with $p = \frac{3}{4}$. By Theorem 9.11, it diverges.

b. The series

$$\sum_{k=4}^{\infty} \frac{1}{(k-1)^2} = \sum_{k=3}^{\infty} \frac{1}{k^2} = \frac{1}{3^2} + \frac{1}{4^2} + \frac{1}{5^2} + \cdots$$

is a convergent *p*-series $(p = 2)$ without the first two terms. As we prove shortly, adding or removing a finite number of terms does not affect the convergence of a series. Therefore, the given series converges.

Related Exercises 29–34 ◄

Estimating the Value of Infinite Series

The Integral Test is powerful in its own right, but it comes with an added bonus. It can be used to estimate the value of a series. We define the **remainder** to be the error in approximating a convergent infinite series by the sum of its first *n* terms; that is,

$$R_n = \underbrace{\sum_{k=1}^{\infty} a_k}_{\substack{\text{value of} \\ \text{series}}} - \underbrace{\sum_{k=1}^{n} a_k}_{\substack{\text{approximation based} \\ \text{on first } n \text{ terms}}} = a_{n+1} + a_{n+2} + a_{n+3} + \cdots.$$

QUICK CHECK 3 If Σa_k is a convergent series of positive terms, why is $R_n \geq 0$? ◄

The remainder consists of the *tail* of the series—those terms beyond a_n.

We now argue much as we did in the proof of the Integral Test. Let *f* be a continuous, positive, decreasing function such that $f(k) = a_k$, for all relevant *k*. From Figure 9.28, we see that $\int_{n+1}^{\infty} f(x)\, dx < R_n$.

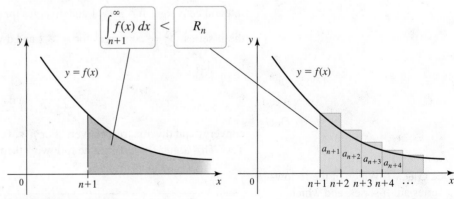

FIGURE 9.28

Similarly, Figure 9.29 shows that $R_n < \int_n^\infty f(x)\, dx$.

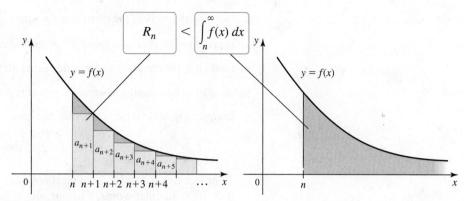

FIGURE 9.29

Combining these two inequalities, the remainder is squeezed between two integrals:

$$\int_{n+1}^\infty f(x)\, dx < R_n < \int_n^\infty f(x)\, dx. \qquad (2)$$

If the integrals can be evaluated, this result provides an estimate of the remainder.

There is, however, another equally useful way to express this result. Notice that the value of the series is

$$S = \sum_{k=1}^\infty a_k = \underbrace{\sum_{k=1}^n a_k}_{S_n} + R_n,$$

which is the sum of the first n terms S_n and the remainder R_n. Adding S_n to each term of (2), we have

$$\underbrace{S_n + \int_{n+1}^\infty f(x)\, dx}_{L_n} < \underbrace{\sum_{k=1}^\infty a_k}_{S_n + R_n = S} < \underbrace{S_n + \int_n^\infty f(x)\, dx}_{U_n}.$$

These inequalities can be abbreviated as $L_n < S < U_n$, where S is the exact value of the series, and L_n and U_n are lower and upper bounds for S, respectively. If the integrals can be evaluated, it is straightforward to compute S_n (by summing the first n terms of the series) and to compute both L_n and U_n.

THEOREM 9.12   Estimating Series with Positive Terms

Let f be a continuous, positive, decreasing function, for $x \geq 1$, and let $a_k = f(k)$, for $k = 1, 2, 3, \ldots$. Let $S = \sum_{k=1}^\infty a_k$ be a convergent series and let $S_n = \sum_{k=1}^n a_k$ be the sum of the first n terms of the series. The remainder $R_n = S - S_n$ satisfies

$$R_n < \int_n^\infty f(x)\, dx.$$

Furthermore, the exact value of the series is bounded as follows:

$$S_n + \int_{n+1}^\infty f(x)\, dx < \sum_{k=1}^\infty a_k < S_n + \int_n^\infty f(x)\, dx.$$

EXAMPLE 5   Approximating a *p*-series

a. How many terms of the convergent *p*-series $\displaystyle\sum_{k=1}^{\infty} \frac{1}{k^2}$ must be summed to obtain an approximation that is within 10^{-3} of the exact value of the series?

b. Find an approximation to the series using 50 terms of the series.

SOLUTION The function associated with this series is $f(x) = 1/x^2$.

a. Using the bound on the remainder, we have

$$R_n < \int_n^\infty f(x)\,dx = \int_n^\infty \frac{dx}{x^2} = \frac{1}{n}.$$

To ensure that $R_n < 10^{-3}$, we must choose n so that $1/n < 10^{-3}$, which implies that $n > 1000$. In other words, we must sum at least 1001 terms of the series to be sure that the remainder is less than 10^{-3}.

b. Using the bounds on the series itself, we have $L_n < S < U_n$, where S is the exact value of the series, and

$$L_n = S_n + \int_{n+1}^\infty \frac{dx}{x^2} = S_n + \frac{1}{n+1} \quad \text{and} \quad U_n = S_n + \int_n^\infty \frac{dx}{x^2} = S_n + \frac{1}{n}.$$

> The values of *p*-series with even values of *p* are generally known. For example, with $p = 2$ the series converges to $\pi^2/6$ (a proof is outlined in Exercise 66); with $p = 4$, the series converges to $\pi^4/90$. The values of *p*-series with odd values of *p* are not known.

Therefore, the series is bounded as follows:

$$S_n + \frac{1}{n+1} < S < S_n + \frac{1}{n},$$

where S_n is the sum of the first n terms. Using a calculator to sum the first 50 terms of the series, we find that $S_{50} \approx 1.625133$. The exact value of the series is in the interval

$$S_{50} + \frac{1}{50+1} < S < S_{50} + \frac{1}{50},$$

or $1.644741 < S < 1.645133$. Taking the average of these two bounds as our approximation of S, we find that $S \approx 1.644937$. This estimate is better than simply using S_{50}. Figure 9.30a shows the lower and upper bounds, L_n and U_n, respectively, for $n = 1, 2, \ldots, 50$. Figure 9.30b shows these bounds on an enlarged scale for $n = 50, 51, \ldots, 100$. These figures illustrate how the exact value of the series is squeezed into a narrowing interval as n increases.

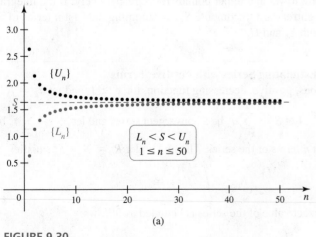

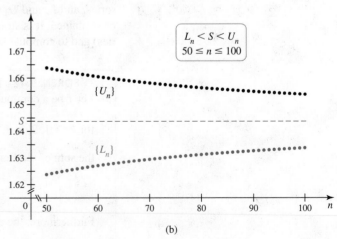

(a)

(b)

FIGURE 9.30

Related Exercises 35–42 ◄

Properties of Convergent Series

We close this section with several properties that will be useful in upcoming work. The notation $\sum a_k$, without initial and final values of k, is used to refer to a general infinite series whose terms may be positive or negative (or both).

> The **leading terms** of an infinite series are those at the beginning with a small index. The **tail** of an infinite series consists of the terms at the "end" of the series with a large and increasing index. The convergence or divergence of an infinite series depends on the tail of the series, while the value of a convergent series is determined primarily by the leading terms.

THEOREM 9.13 Properties of Convergent Series

1. Suppose $\sum a_k$ converges to A, and let c be a real number. The series $\sum ca_k$ converges, and $\sum ca_k = c\sum a_k = cA$.

2. Suppose $\sum a_k$ converges to A and $\sum b_k$ converges to B. The series $\sum(a_k \pm b_k)$ converges, and $\sum(a_k \pm b_k) = \sum a_k \pm \sum b_k = A \pm B$.

3. *Whether* a series converges does not depend on a finite number of terms added to or removed from the series. Specifically, if M is a positive integer, then $\sum_{k=1}^{\infty} a_k$ and $\sum_{k=M}^{\infty} a_k$ both converge or both diverge. However, the *value* of a convergent series does change if nonzero terms are added or deleted.

Proof: These properties are proved using properties of finite sums and limits of sequences. To prove Property 1, assume that $\sum_{k=1}^{\infty} a_k$ converges to A and note that

$$\sum_{k=1}^{\infty} ca_k = \lim_{n \to \infty} \sum_{k=1}^{n} ca_k \qquad \text{Definition of infinite series}$$

$$= \lim_{n \to \infty} c \sum_{k=1}^{n} a_k \qquad \text{Property of finite sums}$$

$$= c \lim_{n \to \infty} \sum_{k=1}^{n} a_k \qquad \text{Property of limits}$$

$$= c \sum_{k=1}^{\infty} a_k \qquad \text{Definition of infinite series}$$

$$= cA. \qquad \text{Value of the series}$$

Property 2 is proved in a similar way (Exercise 62).

Property 3 follows by noting that for finite sums with $1 < M < n$,

$$\sum_{k=M}^{n} a_k = \sum_{k=1}^{n} a_k - \sum_{k=1}^{M-1} a_k.$$

Letting $n \to \infty$ in this equation and assuming that $\sum_{k=1}^{\infty} a_k = A$, it follows that

$$\sum_{k=M}^{\infty} a_k = \underbrace{\sum_{k=1}^{\infty} a_k}_{A} - \underbrace{\sum_{k=1}^{M-1} a_k}_{\text{finite number}}.$$

QUICK CHECK 4 Explain why if $\sum_{k=1}^{\infty} a_k$ converges, then the series $\sum_{k=5}^{\infty} a_k$ (with a different starting index) also converges. Do the two series have the same value? ◄

Because the right side has a finite value, $\sum_{k=M}^{\infty} a_k$ converges. Similarly, if $\sum_{k=M}^{\infty} a_k$ converges, then $\sum_{k=1}^{\infty} a_k$ converges. By an analogous argument, if one of these series diverges, then the other series diverges.

◄

Use caution when applying Theorem 9.13. For example, you can write

$$\sum_{k=2}^{\infty} \frac{1}{k(k-1)} = \sum_{k=2}^{\infty}\left(\frac{1}{k-1} - \frac{1}{k}\right)$$

and then recognize a telescoping series (that converges to 1). An *incorrect* application of Theorem 9.13 would be to write

$$\sum_{k=2}^{\infty}\left(\frac{1}{k-1} - \frac{1}{k}\right) = \underbrace{\sum_{k=2}^{\infty} \frac{1}{k-1}}_{\text{diverges}} - \underbrace{\sum_{k=2}^{\infty} \frac{1}{k}}_{\text{diverges}} \qquad \text{This is } \textit{incorrect!}$$

and then conclude that the original series diverges. Neither $\displaystyle\sum_{k=2}^{\infty} \frac{1}{k-1}$ nor $\displaystyle\sum_{k=2}^{\infty} \frac{1}{k}$ converges; therefore, Property 2 of Theorem 9.13 does not apply.

EXAMPLE 6   Using properties of series Evaluate the infinite series

$$S = \sum_{k=1}^{\infty}\left[5\left(\frac{2}{3}\right)^k - \frac{2^{k-1}}{7^k}\right].$$

SOLUTION We examine the two series $\displaystyle\sum_{k=1}^{\infty} 5\left(\frac{2}{3}\right)^k$ and $\displaystyle\sum_{k=1}^{\infty} \frac{2^{k-1}}{7^k}$ individually. The first series is a geometric series and is evaluated using the methods of Section 9.3. Its first few terms are

$$\sum_{k=1}^{\infty} 5\left(\frac{2}{3}\right)^k = 5\left(\frac{2}{3}\right) + 5\left(\frac{2}{3}\right)^2 + 5\left(\frac{2}{3}\right)^3 + \cdots.$$

The first term of the series is $a = 5\left(\frac{2}{3}\right)$ and the ratio is $r = \frac{2}{3} < 1$; therefore,

$$\sum_{k=1}^{\infty} 5\left(\frac{2}{3}\right)^k = \frac{a}{1-r} = \left[\frac{5\left(\frac{2}{3}\right)}{1-\frac{2}{3}}\right] = 10.$$

Writing out the first few terms of the second series, we see that it, too, is geometric:

$$\sum_{k=1}^{\infty} \frac{2^{k-1}}{7^k} = \frac{1}{7} + \frac{2}{7^2} + \frac{2^2}{7^3} + \cdots.$$

The first term is $a = \frac{1}{7}$ and the ratio is $r = \frac{2}{7} < 1$; therefore,

$$\sum_{k=1}^{\infty} \frac{2^{k-1}}{7^k} = \frac{a}{1-r} = \frac{\frac{1}{7}}{1-\frac{2}{7}} = \frac{1}{5}.$$

Both series converge. By Property 2 of Theorem 9.13, we combine the two series and have $S = 10 - \frac{1}{5} = \frac{49}{5}$. *Related Exercises 43–50* ◄

QUICK CHECK 5 For a series with positive terms, explain why the sequence of partial sums $\{S_n\}$ is an increasing sequence. ◄

SECTION 9.4 EXERCISES

Review Questions

1. If we know that $\lim_{k\to\infty} a_k = 1$, then what can we say about $\displaystyle\sum_{k=1}^{\infty} a_k$?

2. Is it true that if the terms of a series of positive terms decrease to zero, then the series converges? Explain using an example.

3. Can the Integral Test be used to determine whether a series diverges?

4. For what values of p does the series $\displaystyle\sum_{k=1}^{\infty} \frac{1}{k^p}$ converge? For what values of p does it diverge?

5. For what values of p does the series $\displaystyle\sum_{k=10}^{\infty} \frac{1}{k^p}$ converge (initial index is 10)? For what values of p does it diverge?

6. Explain why the sequence of partial sums for a series with positive terms is an increasing sequence.

7. Define the remainder of an infinite series.

8. If a series of positive terms converges, does it follow that the remainder R_n must decrease to zero as $n \to \infty$? Explain.

Basic Skills

9–18. Divergence Test *Use the Divergence Test to determine whether the following series diverge or state that the test is inconclusive.*

9. $\displaystyle\sum_{k=0}^{\infty} \frac{k}{2k+1}$

10. $\displaystyle\sum_{k=1}^{\infty} \frac{k}{k^2+1}$

11. $\displaystyle\sum_{k=2}^{\infty} \frac{k}{\ln k}$

12. $\displaystyle\sum_{k=1}^{\infty} \frac{k^2}{2^k}$

13. $\displaystyle\sum_{k=0}^{\infty} \frac{1}{1000+k}$

14. $\displaystyle\sum_{k=1}^{\infty} \frac{k^3}{k^3+1}$

15. $\displaystyle\sum_{k=2}^{\infty} \frac{\sqrt{k}}{\ln^{10} k}$

16. $\displaystyle\sum_{k=1}^{\infty} \frac{\sqrt{k^2+1}}{k}$

17. $\displaystyle\sum_{k=1}^{\infty} k^{1/k}$

18. $\displaystyle\sum_{k=1}^{\infty} \frac{k^3}{k!}$

19–28. Integral Test *Use the Integral Test to determine the convergence or divergence of the following series, or state that the conditions of the test are not satisfied and, therefore, the test does not apply.*

19. $\displaystyle\sum_{k=2}^{\infty} \frac{1}{e^k}$

20. $\displaystyle\sum_{k=1}^{\infty} \frac{k}{\sqrt{k^2+4}}$

21. $\displaystyle\sum_{k=1}^{\infty} ke^{-2k^2}$

22. $\displaystyle\sum_{k=1}^{\infty} \frac{1}{\sqrt[3]{k+10}}$

23. $\displaystyle\sum_{k=0}^{\infty} \frac{1}{\sqrt{k+8}}$

24. $\displaystyle\sum_{k=2}^{\infty} \frac{1}{k(\ln k)^2}$

25. $\displaystyle\sum_{k=1}^{\infty} \frac{k}{e^k}$

26. $\displaystyle\sum_{k=3}^{\infty} \frac{1}{k \ln k \ln (\ln k)}$

27. $\displaystyle\sum_{k=1}^{\infty} \frac{|\sin k|}{k^2}$

28. $\displaystyle\sum_{k=1}^{\infty} \frac{k}{(k^2+1)^3}$

29–34. p-series *Determine the convergence or divergence of the following series.*

29. $\displaystyle\sum_{k=1}^{\infty} \frac{1}{k^{10}}$

30. $\displaystyle\sum_{k=2}^{\infty} \frac{k^e}{k^\pi}$

31. $\displaystyle\sum_{k=3}^{\infty} \frac{1}{(k-2)^4}$

32. $\displaystyle\sum_{k=1}^{\infty} 2k^{-3/2}$

33. $\displaystyle\sum_{k=1}^{\infty} \frac{1}{\sqrt[3]{k}}$

34. $\displaystyle\sum_{k=1}^{\infty} \frac{1}{\sqrt[3]{27k^2}}$

■ 35–42. Remainders and estimates *Consider the following convergent series.*

a. *Find an upper bound for the remainder in terms of n.*

b. *Find how many terms are needed to ensure that the remainder is less than 10^{-3}.*

c. *Find lower and upper bounds (L_n and U_n, respectively) on the exact value of the series.*

d. *Find an interval in which the value of the series must lie if you approximate it using ten terms of the series.*

35. $\displaystyle\sum_{k=1}^{\infty} \frac{1}{k^6}$

36. $\displaystyle\sum_{k=1}^{\infty} \frac{1}{k^8}$

37. $\displaystyle\sum_{k=1}^{\infty} \frac{1}{3^k}$

38. $\displaystyle\sum_{k=2}^{\infty} \frac{1}{k(\ln k)^2}$

39. $\displaystyle\sum_{k=1}^{\infty} \frac{1}{k^{3/2}}$

40. $\displaystyle\sum_{k=1}^{\infty} e^{-k}$

41. $\displaystyle\sum_{k=1}^{\infty} \frac{1}{k^3}$

42. $\displaystyle\sum_{k=1}^{\infty} ke^{-k^2}$

43–50. Properties of series *Use the properties of infinite series to evaluate the following series.*

43. $\displaystyle\sum_{k=1}^{\infty} \frac{4}{12^k}$

44. $\displaystyle\sum_{k=2}^{\infty} 3e^{-k}$

45. $\displaystyle\sum_{k=0}^{\infty} \left(3\left(\frac{2}{5}\right)^k - 2\left(\frac{5}{7}\right)^k\right)$

46. $\displaystyle\sum_{k=1}^{\infty} \left(2\left(\frac{3}{5}\right)^k + 3\left(\frac{4}{9}\right)^k\right)$

47. $\displaystyle\sum_{k=1}^{\infty} \left(\frac{1}{3}\left(\frac{5}{6}\right)^k + \frac{3}{5}\left(\frac{7}{9}\right)^k\right)$

48. $\displaystyle\sum_{k=0}^{\infty} \left(\frac{1}{2}(0.2)^k + \frac{3}{2}(0.8)^k\right)$

49. $\displaystyle\sum_{k=1}^{\infty} \left(\left(\frac{1}{6}\right)^k + \left(\frac{1}{3}\right)^{k-1}\right)$

50. $\displaystyle\sum_{k=0}^{\infty} \frac{2-3^k}{6^k}$

Further Explorations

51. Explain why or why not Determine whether the following statements are true and give an explanation or counterexample.

a. If $\displaystyle\sum_{k=1}^{\infty} a_k$ converges, then $\displaystyle\sum_{k=10}^{\infty} a_k$ converges.

b. If $\displaystyle\sum_{k=1}^{\infty} a_k$ diverges, then $\displaystyle\sum_{k=10}^{\infty} a_k$ diverges.

c. If Σa_k converges, then $\Sigma (a_k + 0.0001)$ also converges.

d. If Σp^k diverges, then $\Sigma (p + 0.001)^k$ diverges, for a fixed real number p.

e. If Σk^{-p} converges, then $\Sigma k^{-p+0.001}$ converges.

f. If $\displaystyle\lim_{k \to \infty} a_k = 0$, then Σa_k converges.

52–57. Choose your test *Determine whether the following series converge or diverge.*

52. $\displaystyle\sum_{k=1}^{\infty} \sqrt{\frac{k+1}{k}}$

53. $\displaystyle\sum_{k=1}^{\infty} \frac{1}{(3k+1)(3k+4)}$

54. $\displaystyle\sum_{k=0}^{\infty} \frac{10}{k^2+9}$

55. $\displaystyle\sum_{k=0}^{\infty} \frac{k}{\sqrt{k^2+1}}$

56. $\displaystyle\sum_{k=1}^{\infty} \frac{2^k+3^k}{4^k}$

57. $\displaystyle\sum_{k=2}^{\infty} \frac{4}{k \ln^2 k}$

58. Log p-series Consider the series $\displaystyle\sum_{k=2}^{\infty} \frac{1}{k(\ln k)^p}$, where p is a real number.

a. Use the Integral Test to determine the values of p for which this series converges.

b. Does this series converge faster for $p = 2$ or $p = 3$? Explain.

59. Loglog p-series Consider the series $\displaystyle\sum_{k=3}^{\infty} \frac{1}{k \ln k(\ln \ln k)^p}$, where p is a real number.

a. For what values of p does this series converge?

b. Which of the following series converges faster? Explain.

$$\sum_{k=2}^{\infty} \frac{1}{k(\ln k)^2} \quad \text{or} \quad \sum_{k=3}^{\infty} \frac{1}{k \ln k(\ln \ln k)^2}?$$

60. Find a series Find a series that

a. converges faster than $\sum \dfrac{1}{k^2}$ but slower than $\sum \dfrac{1}{k^3}$.

b. diverges faster than $\sum \dfrac{1}{k}$ but slower than $\sum \dfrac{1}{\sqrt{k}}$.

c. converges faster than $\sum \dfrac{1}{k \ln^2 k}$ but slower than $\sum \dfrac{1}{k^2}$.

Additional Exercises

61. A divergence proof Give an argument similar to that given in the text for the harmonic series to show that $\sum\limits_{k=1}^{\infty} \dfrac{1}{\sqrt{k}}$ diverges.

62. Properties proof Use the ideas in the proof of Property 1 of Theorem 9.13 to prove Property 2 of Theorem 9.13.

63. Property of divergent series Prove that if $\sum a_k$ diverges, then $\sum c a_k$ also diverges, where $c \neq 0$ is a constant.

64. Prime numbers The prime numbers are those positive integers that are divisible by only 1 and themselves (2, 3, 5, 7, 11, 13, ...). A celebrated theorem states that the sequence of prime numbers $\{p_k\}$ satisfies $\lim\limits_{k \to \infty} p_k/(k \ln k) = 1$. Show that $\sum\limits_{k=2}^{\infty} \dfrac{1}{k \ln k}$ diverges, which implies that the series $\sum\limits_{k=1}^{\infty} \dfrac{1}{p_k}$ diverges.

65. The zeta function The Riemann zeta function is the subject of extensive research and is associated with several renowned unsolved problems. It is defined by $\zeta(x) = \sum\limits_{k=1}^{\infty} \dfrac{1}{k^x}$. When x is a real number, the zeta function becomes a p-series. For even positive integers p, the value of $\zeta(p)$ is known exactly. For example,

$$\sum_{k=1}^{\infty} \frac{1}{k^2} = \frac{\pi^2}{6}, \quad \sum_{k=1}^{\infty} \frac{1}{k^4} = \frac{\pi^4}{90}, \quad \text{and} \quad \sum_{k=1}^{\infty} \frac{1}{k^6} = \frac{\pi^6}{945}, \ldots.$$

Use the estimation techniques described in the text to approximate $\zeta(3)$ and $\zeta(5)$ (whose values are not known exactly) with a remainder less than 10^{-3}.

66. Showing that $\sum\limits_{k=1}^{\infty} \dfrac{1}{k^2} = \dfrac{\pi^2}{6}$ In 1734, Leonhard Euler informally proved that $\sum\limits_{k=1}^{\infty} \dfrac{1}{k^2} = \dfrac{\pi^2}{6}$. An elegant proof is outlined here that uses the inequality

$$\cot^2 x < \frac{1}{x^2} < 1 + \cot^2 x \quad \left(\text{provided that } 0 < x < \frac{\pi}{2} \right)$$

and the identity

$$\sum_{k=1}^{n} \cot^2(k\theta) = \frac{n(2n-1)}{3}, \quad \text{for } n = 1, 2, 3, \ldots, \text{ where } \theta = \frac{\pi}{2n+1}.$$

a. Show that $\sum\limits_{k=1}^{n} \cot^2(k\theta) < \dfrac{1}{\theta^2} \sum\limits_{k=1}^{n} \dfrac{1}{k^2} < n + \sum\limits_{k=1}^{n} \cot^2(k\theta)$.

b. Use the inequality in part (a) to show that

$$\frac{n(2n-1)\pi^2}{3(2n+1)^2} < \sum_{k=1}^{n} \frac{1}{k^2} < \frac{n(2n+2)\pi^2}{3(2n+1)^2}.$$

c. Use the Squeeze Theorem to conclude that $\sum\limits_{k=1}^{\infty} \dfrac{1}{k^2} = \dfrac{\pi^2}{6}$.

(*Source: The College Mathematics Journal* 24, 5, Nov 1993)

67. Reciprocals of odd squares Assume that $\sum\limits_{k=1}^{\infty} \dfrac{1}{k^2} = \dfrac{\pi^2}{6}$ (Exercises 65 and 66) and that the terms of this series may be rearranged without changing the value of the series. Determine the sum of the reciprocals of the squares of the odd positive integers.

68. Shifted p-series Consider the sequence $\{F_n\}$ defined by

$$F_n = \sum_{k=1}^{\infty} \frac{1}{k(k+n)},$$

for $n = 0, 1, 2, \ldots$. When $n = 0$, the series is a p-series, and we have $F_0 = \pi^2/6$ (Exercises 65 and 66).

a. Explain why $\{F_n\}$ is a decreasing sequence.

b. Plot $\{F_n\}$, for $n = 1, 2, \ldots, 20$.

c. Based on your experiments, make a conjecture about $\lim\limits_{n \to \infty} F_n$.

69. A sequence of sums Consider the sequence $\{x_n\}$ defined for $n = 1, 2, 3, \ldots$ by

$$x_n = \sum_{k=n+1}^{2n} \frac{1}{k} = \frac{1}{n+1} + \frac{1}{n+2} + \cdots + \frac{1}{2n}.$$

a. Write out the terms x_1, x_2, x_3.

b. Show that $\dfrac{1}{2} \leq x_n < 1$, for $n = 1, 2, 3, \ldots$.

c. Show that x_n is the right Riemann sum for $\displaystyle\int_1^2 \dfrac{dx}{x}$ using n subintervals.

d. Conclude that $\lim\limits_{n \to \infty} x_n = \ln 2$.

70. The harmonic series and Euler's constant

a. Sketch the function $f(x) = 1/x$ on the interval $[1, n+1]$, where n is a positive integer. Use this graph to verify that

$$\ln(n+1) < 1 + \frac{1}{2} + \frac{1}{3} + \cdots + \frac{1}{n} < 1 + \ln n.$$

b. Let S_n be the sum of the first n terms of the harmonic series, so part (a) says $\ln(n+1) < S_n < 1 + \ln n$. Define the new sequence $\{E_n\}$ by

$$E_n = S_n - \ln(n+1), \quad \text{for } n = 1, 2, 3, \ldots.$$

Show that $E_n > 0$, for $n = 1, 2, 3, \ldots$.

c. Using a figure similar to that used in part (a), show that

$$\frac{1}{n+1} > \ln(n+2) - \ln(n+1).$$

d. Use parts (a) and (c) to show that $\{E_n\}$ is an increasing sequence ($E_{n+1} > E_n$).

e. Use part (a) to show that $\{E_n\}$ is bounded above by 1.

f. Conclude from parts (d) and (e) that $\{E_n\}$ has a limit less than or equal to 1. This limit is known as **Euler's constant** and is denoted γ (the Greek lowercase gamma).

g. By computing terms of $\{E_n\}$, estimate the value of γ and compare it to the value $\gamma \approx 0.5772$. (It has been conjectured, but not proved, that γ is irrational.)

h. The preceding arguments show that the sum of the first n terms of the harmonic series satisfy $S_n \approx 0.5772 + \ln(n+1)$. How many terms must be summed for the sum to exceed 10?

71. Stacking dominoes Consider a set of identical dominoes that are 2 inches long. The dominoes are stacked on top of each other with their long edges aligned so that each domino overhangs the one beneath it *as far as possible* (see figure).

  a. If there are n dominoes in the stack, what is the *greatest* distance that the top domino can be made to overhang the bottom domino? (*Hint:* Put the nth domino beneath the previous $n-1$ dominoes.)

  b. If we allow for infinitely many dominoes in the stack, what is the greatest distance that the top domino can be made to overhang the bottom domino?

72. Gabriel's wedding cake Consider a wedding cake of infinite height, each layer of which is a right circular cylinder of height 1. The bottom layer of the cake has a radius of 1, the second layer has a radius of $1/2$, the third layer has a radius of $1/3$, and the nth layer has a radius of $1/n$.

  a. To determine how much frosting is needed to cover the cake, find the surface area of the lateral (vertical) sides of the wedding cake. What is the area of the horizontal surfaces of the cake?

b. Determine the volume of the cake. (*Hint:* Use the result of Exercise 66.)

c. Comment on your answers to parts (a) and (b).

(*Source: The College Mathematics Journal* 30, 1, Jan 1999)

QUICK CHECK ANSWERS

1. The series diverges for $|r| \geq 1$.   **2. a.** Divergent p-series
b. Convergent geometric series   **c.** Convergent p-series
3. The remainder is $R_n = a_{n+1} + a_{n+2} + \cdots$, which consists of positive numbers.   **4.** Removing a finite number of terms does not change whether the series converges. It generally changes the value of the series.   **5.** Given the nth term of the sequence of partial sums S_n, the next term is obtained by adding a positive number. So $S_{n+1} > S_n$, which means the sequence is increasing. ◄

9.5 The Ratio, Root, and Comparison Tests

We now consider several additional convergence tests for series with positive terms: the Ratio Test, the Root Test, and two comparison tests. The Ratio Test will be used frequently throughout the next chapter, and comparison tests are valuable when no other test works. As in Section 9.4, these tests determine *whether* an infinite series converges, but they do not establish the value of the series.

The Ratio Test

The Integral Test is powerful, but limited, because it requires evaluating integrals. For example, the series $\sum 1/k!$, with a factorial term, cannot be handled by the Integral Test. The next test significantly enlarges the set of infinite series that we can analyze.

> In words, the Ratio Test says the limit of the ratio of successive terms of the series must be less than 1 for convergence of the series.

THEOREM 9.14   The Ratio Test

Let $\sum a_k$ be an infinite series with positive terms and let $r = \lim\limits_{k \to \infty} \dfrac{a_{k+1}}{a_k}$.

1. If $0 \leq r < 1$, the series converges.
2. If $r > 1$ (including $r = \infty$), the series diverges.
3. If $r = 1$, the test is inconclusive.

Proof (outline): We omit the details of the proof, but the idea behind the proof provides insight. Let's assume that the limit r exists. Then, as k gets large and the ratio a_{k+1}/a_k approaches r, we have $a_{k+1} \approx ra_k$. Therefore, as one goes farther and farther out in the series, it behaves like

$$a_k + a_{k+1} + a_{k+2} + \cdots \approx a_k + ra_k + r^2 a_k + r^3 a_k + \cdots$$
$$= a_k(1 + r + r^2 + r^3 + \cdots).$$

The tail of the series, which determines whether the series converges, behaves like a geometric series with ratio r. We know that if $0 \leq r < 1$, the geometric series converges, and if $r > 1$, the series diverges, which is the conclusion of the Ratio Test.   ◄

EXAMPLE 1   Using the Ratio Test Use the Ratio Test to determine whether the following series converge.

a. $\displaystyle\sum_{k=1}^{\infty} \frac{10^k}{k!}$ **b.** $\displaystyle\sum_{k=1}^{\infty} \frac{k^k}{k!}$ **c.** $\displaystyle\sum_{k=1}^{\infty} e^{-k}(k^2 + 4)$

SOLUTION In each case, the limit of the ratio of successive terms is determined.

> Recall that
> $$k! = k \cdot (k-1) \cdots 2 \cdot 1.$$
> Therefore,
> $$(k+1)! = (k+1)k!.$$

a. $r = \lim\limits_{k\to\infty} \dfrac{a_{k+1}}{a_k} = \lim\limits_{k\to\infty} \dfrac{10^{k+1}/(k+1)!}{10^k/k!}$ Substitute a_{k+1} and a_k.

$\qquad = \lim\limits_{k\to\infty} \dfrac{10^{k+1}}{10^k} \cdot \dfrac{k!}{(k+1)k!}$ Invert and multiply.

$\qquad = \lim\limits_{k\to\infty} \dfrac{10}{k+1} = 0.$ Simplify and evaluate the limit.

Because $r = 0$, the series converges by the Ratio Test.

b. $r = \lim\limits_{k\to\infty} \dfrac{a_{k+1}}{a_k} = \lim\limits_{k\to\infty} \dfrac{(k+1)^{k+1}/(k+1)!}{k^k/k!}$ Substitute a_{k+1} and a_k.

$\qquad = \lim\limits_{k\to\infty} \left(\dfrac{k+1}{k}\right)^k$ Simplify.

> Recall from Section 4.7 that
> $$\lim_{k\to\infty}\left(1+\frac{1}{k}\right)^k = e \approx 2.718.$$

$\qquad = \lim\limits_{k\to\infty} \left(1 + \dfrac{1}{k}\right)^k = e.$ Simplify and evaluate the limit.

Because $r = e > 1$, the series diverges by the Ratio Test. Alternatively, we could have noted that $\lim\limits_{k\to\infty} k^k/k! = \infty$ (Section 9.2) and used the Divergence Test to reach the same conclusion.

c. $r = \lim_{k \to \infty} \dfrac{a_{k+1}}{a_k} = \lim_{k \to \infty} \dfrac{e^{-(k+1)}\left((k+1)^2 + 4\right)}{e^{-k}(k^2 + 4)}$ Substitute a_{k+1} and a_k.

$\qquad\qquad = \lim_{k \to \infty} \dfrac{e^{-k}e^{-1}(k^2 + 2k + 5)}{e^{-k}(k^2 + 4)}$ Simplify.

$\qquad\qquad = e^{-1}\underbrace{\lim_{k \to \infty} \dfrac{k^2 + 2k + 5}{k^2 + 1}}_{1}$ Simplify.

$\qquad\qquad = e^{-1}.$

Because $e^{-1} = \dfrac{1}{e} < 1$, the series converges by the Ratio Test.

Related Exercises 9–18 ◄

QUICK CHECK 1 Evaluate $10!/9!$, $(k+2)!/k!$, and $k!/(k+1)!$ ◄

The Ratio Test is conclusive for many series. Nevertheless, observe what happens when the Ratio Test is applied to the harmonic series $\sum_{k=1}^{\infty} \dfrac{1}{k}$:

$$r = \lim_{k \to \infty} \frac{a_{k+1}}{a_k} = \lim_{k \to \infty} \frac{1/(k+1)}{1/k} = \lim_{k \to \infty} \frac{k}{k+1} = 1,$$

> At the end of this section, we offer guidelines that help you to decide which convergence test is best suited for a given series.

which means the test is inconclusive. We know the harmonic series diverges, yet the Ratio Test cannot be used to establish this fact. Like all the convergence tests presented so far, the Ratio Test works only for certain classes of series. For this reason, it is useful to present a few additional convergence tests.

QUICK CHECK 2 Verify that the Ratio Test is inconclusive for $\sum_{k=1}^{\infty} \dfrac{1}{k^2}$. What test could be applied to show that $\sum_{k=1}^{\infty} \dfrac{1}{k^2}$ converges? ◄

The Root Test

Occasionally, a series arises for which the preceding tests are difficult to apply. In these situations, the Root Test may be the tool that is needed.

THEOREM 9.15   The Root Test
Let $\sum a_k$ be an infinite series with nonnegative terms and let $\rho = \lim_{k \to \infty} \sqrt[k]{a_k}$.

1. If $0 \le \rho < 1$, the series converges.
2. If $\rho > 1$ (including $\rho = \infty$), the series diverges.
3. If $\rho = 1$, the test is inconclusive.

Proof (outline): Assume that the limit ρ exists. If k is large, we have $\rho \approx \sqrt[k]{a_k}$ or $a_k \approx \rho^k$. For large values of k, the tail of the series, which determines whether a series converges, behaves like

$$a_k + a_{k+1} + a_{k+2} + \cdots \approx \rho^k + \rho^{k+1} + \rho^{k+2} + \cdots.$$

Therefore, the tail of the series is approximately a geometric series with ratio ρ. If $0 \le \rho < 1$, the geometric series converges, and if $\rho > 1$, the series diverges, which is the conclusion of the Root Test.   ◄

EXAMPLE 2   Using the Root Test   Use the Root Test to determine whether the following series converge.

a. $\displaystyle\sum_{k=1}^{\infty}\left(\frac{4k^2-3}{7k^2+6}\right)^k$ **b.** $\displaystyle\sum_{k=1}^{\infty}\frac{2^k}{k^{10}}$

SOLUTION

a. The required limit is

$$\rho = \lim_{k\to\infty}\sqrt[k]{\left(\frac{4k^2-3}{7k^2+6}\right)^k} = \lim_{k\to\infty}\frac{4k^2-3}{7k^2+6} = \frac{4}{7}.$$

Because $0 \le \rho < 1$, the series converges by the Root Test.

b. In this case,

$$\rho = \lim_{k\to\infty}\sqrt[k]{\frac{2^k}{k^{10}}} = \lim_{k\to\infty}\frac{2}{k^{10/k}} = \lim_{k\to\infty}\frac{2}{(k^{1/k})^{10}} = 2. \quad \lim_{k\to\infty}k^{1/k} = 1$$

Because $\rho > 1$, the series diverges by the Root Test.

     We could have used the Ratio Test for both series in this example, but the Root Test is easier to apply in each case. In part (b), the Divergence Test leads to the same conclusion.

Related Exercises 19–26◀

The Comparison Test

Tests that use known series to test unknown series are called *comparison tests*. The first test is the Basic Comparison Test or simply the Comparison Test.

> **THEOREM 9.16   Comparison Test**
> Let $\sum a_k$ and $\sum b_k$ be series with positive terms.
> **1.** If $0 < a_k \le b_k$ and $\sum b_k$ converges, then $\sum a_k$ converges.
> **2.** If $0 < b_k \le a_k$ and $\sum b_k$ diverges, then $\sum a_k$ diverges.

> ▷ Whether a series converges depends on the behavior of terms in the tail (large values of the index). So the inequalities $0 < a_k \le b_k$ and $0 < b_k \le a_k$ need not hold for all terms of the series. They must hold for all $k > N$ for some positive integer N.

Proof: Assume that $\sum b_k$ converges, which means that $\sum b_k$ has a finite value B. The sequence of partial sums for $\sum a_k$ satisfies

$$S_n = \sum_{k=1}^{n}a_k \le \sum_{k=1}^{n}b_k \quad a_k \le b_k$$

$$< \sum_{k=1}^{\infty}b_k \qquad \text{Positive terms are added to a finite sum.}$$

$$= B. \qquad \text{Value of series}$$

Therefore, the sequence of partial sums for $\sum a_k$ is increasing and bounded above by B. By the Bounded Monotonic Sequence Theorem (Theorem 9.5), the sequence of partial sums of $\sum a_k$ has a limit, which implies that $\sum a_k$ converges. The second case of the theorem is proved in a similar way. ◀

     The Comparison Test can be illustrated with graphs of sequences of partial sums. Consider the series

$$\sum_{k=1}^{\infty}a_k = \sum_{k=1}^{\infty}\frac{1}{k^2+10} \quad \text{and} \quad \sum_{k=1}^{\infty}b_k = \sum_{k=1}^{\infty}\frac{1}{k^2}.$$

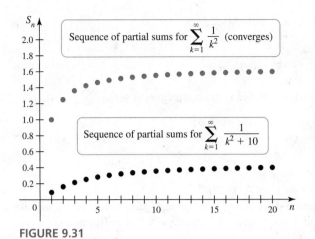

FIGURE 9.31

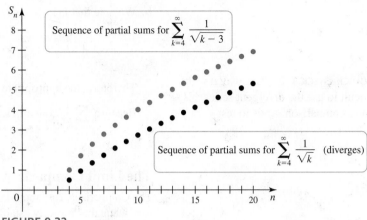

FIGURE 9.32

Because $\dfrac{1}{k^2 + 10} < \dfrac{1}{k^2}$, it follows that $a_k < b_k$, for $k \geq 1$. Furthermore, $\sum b_k$ is a convergent p-series. By the Comparison Test, we conclude that $\sum a_k$ also converges (Figure 9.31). The second case of the Comparison Test is illustrated with the series

$$\sum_{k=4}^{\infty} a_k = \sum_{k=4}^{\infty} \frac{1}{\sqrt{k-3}} \quad \text{and} \quad \sum_{k=4}^{\infty} b_k = \sum_{k=4}^{\infty} \frac{1}{\sqrt{k}}.$$

Now $\dfrac{1}{\sqrt{k}} < \dfrac{1}{\sqrt{k-3}}$, for $k \geq 4$. Therefore, $b_k < a_k$, for $k \geq 4$. Because $\sum b_k$ is a divergent p-series, by the Comparison Test, $\sum a_k$ also diverges. Figure 9.32 shows that the sequence of partial sums for $\sum a_k$ lies above the sequence of partial sums for $\sum b_k$. Because the sequence of partial sums for $\sum b_k$ diverges, the sequence of partial sums for $\sum a_k$ also diverges.

The key in using the Comparison Test is finding an appropriate comparison series. Plenty of practice will enable you to spot patterns and choose good comparison series.

EXAMPLE 3 Using the Comparison Test Determine whether the following series converge.

a. $\displaystyle\sum_{k=1}^{\infty} \frac{k^3}{2k^4 - 1}$ **b.** $\displaystyle\sum_{k=2}^{\infty} \frac{\ln k}{k^3}$

SOLUTION In using comparison tests, it's helpful to get a feel for how the terms of the given series are decreasing. If they are not decreasing, the series diverges.

a. As we go farther and farther out in this series $(k \to \infty)$, the terms behave like

$$\frac{k^3}{2k^4 - 1} \approx \frac{k^3}{2k^4} = \frac{1}{2k}.$$

> If $\sum a_k$ diverges, then $\sum c a_k$ also diverges for any constant $c \neq 0$ (Exercise 63 of Section 9.4).

So a reasonable choice for a comparison series is the divergent series $\sum \dfrac{1}{2k}$. We must now show that the terms of the given series are *greater* than the terms of the comparison series. It is done by noting that $2k^4 - 1 < 2k^4$. Inverting both sides, we have

$$\frac{1}{2k^4 - 1} > \frac{1}{2k^4}, \quad \text{which implies that} \quad \frac{k^3}{2k^4 - 1} > \frac{k^3}{2k^4} = \frac{1}{2k}.$$

Because $\sum \dfrac{1}{2k}$ diverges, case (2) of the Comparison Test implies that the given series also diverges.

b. We note that $\ln k < k$, for $k \geq 2$, and then divide by k^3:

$$\frac{\ln k}{k^3} < \frac{k}{k^3} = \frac{1}{k^2}.$$

QUICK CHECK 3 Explain why it is difficult to use the divergent series $\sum 1/k$ as a comparison series to test $\sum 1/(k + 1)$. ◄

Therefore, the appropriate comparison series is the convergent p-series $\sum \dfrac{1}{k^2}$. Because $\sum \dfrac{1}{k^2}$ converges, the given series converges.

Related Exercises 27–38 ◄

The Limit Comparison Test

The Comparison Test should be tried if there is an obvious comparison series and the necessary inequality is easily established. Notice, however, that if the series in Example 3a were

$$\sum_{k=1}^{\infty} \frac{k^3}{2k^4 + 10} \quad \text{instead of} \quad \sum_{k=1}^{\infty} \frac{k^3}{2k^4 - 1}, \text{ then the comparison to the series } \sum \frac{1}{2k} \text{ would}$$

not work. Rather than fiddling with inequalities, it is often easier to use a more refined test called the *Limit Comparison Test*, which we state without proof.

QUICK CHECK 4 For case (1) of the Limit Comparison Test, we must have $0 < L < \infty$. Why can either a_k or b_k be chosen as the known comparison series? That is, why can L be the limit of a_k/b_k or b_k/a_k? ◄

> **THEOREM 9.17   The Limit Comparison Test**
> Let $\sum a_k$ and $\sum b_k$ be series with positive terms and let
>
> $$\lim_{k \to \infty} \frac{a_k}{b_k} = L.$$
>
> **1.** If $0 < L < \infty$ (that is, L is a finite positive number), then $\sum a_k$ and $\sum b_k$ either both converge or both diverge.
>
> **2.** If $L = 0$ and $\sum b_k$ converges, then $\sum a_k$ converges.
>
> **3.** If $L = \infty$ and $\sum b_k$ diverges, then $\sum a_k$ diverges.

EXAMPLE 4   Using the Limit Comparison Test Determine whether the following series converge.

a. $\displaystyle\sum_{k=1}^{\infty} \frac{5k^4 - 2k^2 + 3}{2k^6 - k + 5}$ **b.** $\displaystyle\sum_{k=1}^{\infty} \frac{\ln k}{k^2}$

SOLUTION In both cases, we must find a comparison series whose terms behave like the terms of the given series as $k \to \infty$.

a. As $k \to \infty$, a rational function behaves like the ratio of the leading (highest-power) terms. In this case, as $k \to \infty$,

$$\frac{5k^4 - 2k^2 + 3}{2k^6 - k + 5} \approx \frac{5k^4}{2k^6} = \frac{5}{2k^2}.$$

Therefore, a reasonable comparison series is the convergent p-series $\displaystyle\sum_{k=1}^{\infty} \frac{1}{k^2}$ (the factor of $5/2$ does not affect whether the given series converges). Having chosen a comparison series, we compute the limit L:

$$
\begin{aligned}
L &= \lim_{k \to \infty} \frac{(5k^4 - 2k^2 + 3)/(2k^6 - k + 5)}{1/k^2} && \text{Ratio of terms of series} \\
&= \lim_{k \to \infty} \frac{k^2(5k^4 - 2k^2 + 3)}{2k^6 - k + 5} && \text{Simplify.} \\
&= \lim_{k \to \infty} \frac{5k^6 - 2k^4 + 3k^2}{2k^6 - k + 5} = \frac{5}{2}. && \text{Simplify and evaluate the limit.}
\end{aligned}
$$

We see that $0 < L < \infty$; therefore, the given series converges.

b. Why is this series interesting? We know that $\displaystyle\sum_{k=1}^{\infty} \frac{1}{k^2}$ converges and that $\displaystyle\sum_{k=1}^{\infty} \frac{1}{k}$ diverges.

The given series $\displaystyle\sum_{k=1}^{\infty} \frac{\ln k}{k^2}$ is "between" these two series. This observation suggests

that we use either $\displaystyle\sum_{k=1}^{\infty} \frac{1}{k^2}$ or $\displaystyle\sum_{k=1}^{\infty} \frac{1}{k}$ as a comparison series. In the first case, letting

$a_k = \ln k/k^2$ and $b_k = 1/k^2$, we find that

$$L = \lim_{k \to \infty} \frac{a_k}{b_k} = \lim_{k \to \infty} \frac{\ln k/k^2}{1/k^2} = \lim_{k \to \infty} \ln k = \infty.$$

Case (3) of the Limit Comparison Test does not apply here because the comparison

series $\displaystyle\sum_{k=1}^{\infty} \frac{1}{k^2}$ converges; we can reach the conclusion of case (3) only when the

comparison series diverges.

If, instead, we use the comparison series $\displaystyle\sum b_k = \sum \frac{1}{k}$, then

$$L = \lim_{k \to \infty} \frac{a_k}{b_k} = \lim_{k \to \infty} \frac{\ln k/k^2}{1/k} = \lim_{k \to \infty} \frac{\ln k}{k} = 0.$$

Case (2) of the Limit Comparison Test does not apply here because the comparison

series $\displaystyle\sum_{k=1}^{\infty} \frac{1}{k}$ diverges. Notice that case (2) is relevant only when the comparison series

converges.

With a bit more cunning, the Limit Comparison Test becomes conclusive. A series

that lies "between" $\displaystyle\sum_{k=1}^{\infty} \frac{1}{k^2}$ and $\displaystyle\sum_{k=1}^{\infty} \frac{1}{k}$ is the convergent p-series $\displaystyle\sum_{k=1}^{\infty} \frac{1}{k^{3/2}}$; we try it as a

comparison series. Letting $a_k = \ln k/k^2$ and $b_k = 1/k^{3/2}$, we find that

$$L = \lim_{k \to \infty} \frac{a_k}{b_k} = \lim_{k \to \infty} \frac{\ln k/k^2}{1/k^{3/2}} = \lim_{k \to \infty} \frac{\ln k}{\sqrt{k}} = 0.$$

(This limit is evaluated using l'Hôpital's Rule or by recalling that $\ln k$ grows more

slowly than any positive power of k.) Now case (2) of the Limit Comparison Test

applies; the comparison series $\displaystyle\sum \frac{1}{k^{3/2}}$ converges, so the given series converges.

Related Exercises 27–38 ◄

Guidelines for Choosing a Test

We close by outlining a procedure that puts the various convergence tests in perspective. Here is a reasonable course of action when testing a series of positive terms $\sum a_k$ for convergence.

1. Begin with the Divergence Test. If you show that $\displaystyle\lim_{k \to \infty} a_k \neq 0$, then the series diverges and your work is finished. The order of growth rates of sequences given in Section 9.2 is useful for evaluating $\displaystyle\lim_{k \to \infty} a_k$. (Recall that the Divergence Test also applies to series with arbitrary terms.)

2. Is the series a special series? Recall the convergence properties for the following series.
   - Geometric series: $\sum ar^k$ converges for $|r| < 1$ and diverges for $|r| \geq 1$ $(a \neq 0)$.
   - p-series: $\displaystyle\sum \frac{1}{k^p}$ converges for $p > 1$ and diverges for $p \leq 1$.
   - Check also for a telescoping series.

3. If the general kth term of the series looks like a function you can integrate, then try the Integral Test.

4. If the general kth term of the series involves $k!$, k^k, or a^k, where a is a constant, the Ratio Test is advisable. Series with k in an exponent may yield to the Root Test.

5. If the general kth term of the series is a rational function of k (or a root of a rational function), use the Comparison or the Limit Comparison Test with the families of series given in Step 2 as comparison series.

These guidelines will help, but in the end, convergence tests are mastered through practice. It's your turn.

SECTION 9.5 EXERCISES

Review Questions

1. Explain how the Ratio Test works.

2. Explain how the Root Test works.

3. Explain how the Limit Comparison Test works.

4. What is the first test you should use in analyzing the convergence of a series?

5. What tests are advisable if a series of positive terms involves a factorial term?

6. What tests are best for the series $\sum a_k$ when a_k is a rational function of k?

7. Explain why, with a series of positive terms, the sequence of partial sums is an increasing sequence.

8. Do the tests discussed in this section tell you the value of the series? Explain.

Basic Skills

9–18. The Ratio Test *Use the Ratio Test to determine whether the following series converge.*

9. $\displaystyle\sum_{k=1}^{\infty} \frac{1}{k!}$ **10.** $\displaystyle\sum_{k=1}^{\infty} \frac{2^k}{k!}$ **11.** $\displaystyle\sum_{k=1}^{\infty} \frac{k^2}{4^k}$ **12.** $\displaystyle\sum_{k=1}^{\infty} \frac{2^k}{k^k}$

13. $\displaystyle\sum_{k=1}^{\infty} ke^{-k}$ **14.** $\displaystyle\sum_{k=1}^{\infty} \frac{k!}{k^k}$ **15.** $\displaystyle\sum_{k=1}^{\infty} \frac{2^k}{k^{99}}$ **16.** $\displaystyle\sum_{k=1}^{\infty} \frac{k^6}{k!}$

17. $\displaystyle\sum_{k=1}^{\infty} \frac{(k!)^2}{(2k)!}$ **18.** $\displaystyle \frac{1}{2} + \frac{16}{4} + \frac{81}{8} + \frac{256}{16} + \cdots$

19–26. The Root Test *Use the Root Test to determine whether the following series converge.*

19. $\displaystyle\sum_{k=1}^{\infty} \left(\frac{4k^3 + k}{9k^3 + k + 1} \right)^k$ **20.** $\displaystyle\sum_{k=1}^{\infty} \left(\frac{k+1}{2k} \right)^k$

21. $\displaystyle\sum_{k=1}^{\infty} \frac{k^2}{2^k}$ **22.** $\displaystyle\sum_{k=1}^{\infty} \left(1 + \frac{3}{k} \right)^{k^2}$

23. $\displaystyle\sum_{k=1}^{\infty} \left(\frac{k}{k+1} \right)^{2k^2}$ **24.** $\displaystyle\sum_{k=1}^{\infty} \left(\frac{1}{\ln (k+1)} \right)^k$

25. $\displaystyle 1 + \left(\frac{1}{2} \right)^2 + \left(\frac{1}{3} \right)^3 + \left(\frac{1}{4} \right)^4 + \cdots$

26. $\displaystyle\sum_{k=1}^{\infty} \frac{k}{e^k}$

27–38. Comparison tests *Use the Comparison Test or Limit Comparison Test to determine whether the following series converge.*

27. $\displaystyle\sum_{k=1}^{\infty} \frac{1}{k^2 + 4}$ **28.** $\displaystyle\sum_{k=1}^{\infty} \frac{k^2 + k - 1}{k^4 + 4k^2 - 3}$

29. $\displaystyle\sum_{k=1}^{\infty} \frac{k^2 - 1}{k^3 + 4}$ **30.** $\displaystyle\sum_{k=1}^{\infty} \frac{0.0001}{k + 4}$

31. $\displaystyle\sum_{k=1}^{\infty} \frac{1}{k^{3/2} + 1}$ **32.** $\displaystyle\sum_{k=1}^{\infty} \sqrt{\frac{k}{k^3 + 1}}$

33. $\displaystyle\sum_{k=1}^{\infty} \frac{\sin (1/k)}{k^2}$ **34.** $\displaystyle\sum_{k=1}^{\infty} \frac{1}{3^k - 2^k}$

35. $\displaystyle\sum_{k=1}^{\infty} \frac{1}{2k - \sqrt{k}}$ **36.** $\displaystyle\sum_{k=1}^{\infty} \frac{1}{k\sqrt{k} + 2}$

37. $\displaystyle\sum_{k=1}^{\infty} \frac{\sqrt[3]{k^2 + 1}}{\sqrt{k^3 + 2}}$ **38.** $\displaystyle\sum_{k=2}^{\infty} \frac{1}{(k \ln k)^2}$

Further Explorations

39. Explain why or why not Determine whether the following statements are true and give an explanation or counterexample.

a. Suppose that $0 < a_k < b_k$. If $\sum a_k$ converges, then $\sum b_k$ converges.

b. Suppose that $0 < a_k < b_k$. If $\sum a_k$ diverges, then $\sum b_k$ diverges.

c. Suppose $0 < b_k < c_k < a_k$. If $\sum a_k$ converges, then $\sum b_k$ and $\sum c_k$ converge.

d. The Ratio Test is always inconclusive when applied to $\sum a_k$, where a_k is a rational function of k.

40–69. Choose your test *Use the test of your choice to determine whether the following series converge.*

40. $\displaystyle \left(\frac{1}{2} \right)^2 + \left(\frac{2}{3} \right)^3 + \left(\frac{3}{4} \right)^4 + \cdots$

41. $\displaystyle\sum_{k=1}^{\infty} \left(1 + \frac{2}{k} \right)^k$ **42.** $\displaystyle\sum_{k=1}^{\infty} \left(\frac{k^2}{2k^2 + 1} \right)^k$ **43.** $\displaystyle\sum_{k=1}^{\infty} \frac{k^{100}}{(k+1)!}$

44. $\displaystyle\sum_{k=1}^{\infty} \frac{\sin^2 k}{k^2}$ **45.** $\displaystyle\sum_{k=1}^{\infty} (\sqrt[k]{k} - 1)^{2k}$ **46.** $\displaystyle\sum_{k=1}^{\infty} \frac{2^k}{e^k - 1}$

47. $\displaystyle\sum_{k=1}^{\infty} \frac{k^2 + 2k + 1}{3k^2 + 1}$ **48.** $\displaystyle\sum_{k=1}^{\infty} \frac{1}{5^k - 1}$

49. $\displaystyle\sum_{k=3}^{\infty} \frac{1}{\ln k}$ **50.** $\displaystyle\sum_{k=3}^{\infty} \frac{1}{5^k - 3^k}$ **51.** $\displaystyle\sum_{k=1}^{\infty} \frac{1}{\sqrt{k^3 - k + 1}}$

52. $\displaystyle\sum_{k=1}^{\infty} \frac{(k!)^3}{(3k)!}$

53. $\displaystyle\sum_{k=1}^{\infty} \left(\frac{1}{k} + 2^{-k}\right)$

54. $\displaystyle\sum_{k=2}^{\infty} \frac{5\ln k}{k}$

55. $\displaystyle\sum_{k=1}^{\infty} \frac{2^k k!}{k^k}$

56. $\displaystyle\sum_{k=1}^{\infty} \left(1 - \frac{1}{k}\right)^{k^2}$

57. $\displaystyle\sum_{k=1}^{\infty} \frac{k^8}{k^{11} + 3}$

58. $\displaystyle\sum_{k=1}^{\infty} \frac{1}{(1 + p)^k}, \; p > 0$

59. $\displaystyle\sum_{k=1}^{\infty} \frac{1}{k^{1+p}}, \; p > 0$

60. $\displaystyle\sum_{k=2}^{\infty} \frac{1}{k^2 \ln k}$

61. $\displaystyle\sum_{k=1}^{\infty} \ln\left(\frac{k+2}{k+1}\right)$

62. $\displaystyle\sum_{k=1}^{\infty} k^{-1/k}$

63. $\displaystyle\sum_{k=2}^{\infty} \frac{1}{k^{\ln k}}$

64. $\displaystyle\sum_{k=1}^{\infty} \sin^2\left(\frac{1}{k}\right)$

65. $\displaystyle\sum_{k=1}^{\infty} \tan\frac{1}{k}$

66. $\displaystyle\sum_{k=2}^{\infty} 100k^{-k}$

67. $\dfrac{1}{1\cdot 3} + \dfrac{1}{3\cdot 5} + \dfrac{1}{5\cdot 7} + \cdots$

68. $\dfrac{1}{2^2} + \dfrac{2}{3^2} + \dfrac{3}{4^2} + \cdots$

69. $\dfrac{1}{1!} + \dfrac{4}{2!} + \dfrac{9}{3!} + \dfrac{16}{4!} + \cdots$

70–77. Convergence parameter *Find the values of the parameter $p \geq 0$ for which the following series converge.*

70. $\displaystyle\sum_{k=2}^{\infty} \frac{1}{(\ln k)^p}$

71. $\displaystyle\sum_{k=2}^{\infty} \frac{\ln k}{k^p}$

72. $\displaystyle\sum_{k=2}^{\infty} \frac{1}{k \ln k \, (\ln \ln k)^p}$

73. $\displaystyle\sum_{k=2}^{\infty} \left(\frac{\ln k}{k}\right)^p$

74. $\displaystyle\sum_{k=0}^{\infty} \frac{k! \, p^k}{(k+1)^k}$ (*Hint:* Stirling's formula is useful: $k! \approx (\sqrt{2\pi k})k^k e^{-k}$ for large k.)

75. $\displaystyle\sum_{k=1}^{\infty} \frac{k\,p^k}{k+1}$

76. $\displaystyle\sum_{k=1}^{\infty} \ln\left(\frac{k}{k+1}\right)^p$

77. $\displaystyle\sum_{k=1}^{\infty} \left(1 - \frac{p}{k}\right)^k$

78. Series of squares Prove that if Σa_k is a convergent series of positive terms, then the series Σa_k^2 also converges.

79. Geometric series revisited We know from Section 9.3 that the geometric series $\Sigma ar^k \; (a \neq 0)$ converges if $0 < r < 1$ and diverges if $r > 1$. Prove these facts using the Integral Test, the Ratio Test, and the Root Test. Now consider all values of r—what can be determined about the geometric series using the Divergence Test?

80. Two sine series Determine whether the following series converge.

a. $\displaystyle\sum_{k=1}^{\infty} \sin\frac{1}{k}$

b. $\displaystyle\sum_{k=1}^{\infty} \frac{1}{k} \sin\frac{1}{k}$

Additional Exercises

81. Using the Limit Comparison Test Show that if $\displaystyle\lim_{k\to\infty} \frac{a_k}{b_k} = L$, where $0 < L < \infty$, then $0 < \displaystyle\lim_{k\to\infty} \frac{b_k}{a_k} < \infty$. Explain why, in using the Limit Comparison Test, either a_k or b_k can be chosen as the known comparison series.

82–87. A glimpse ahead to power series *Use the Ratio Test to determine the values of $x \geq 0$ for which each series converges.*

82. $\displaystyle\sum_{k=1}^{\infty} \frac{x^k}{k!}$

83. $\displaystyle\sum_{k=1}^{\infty} x^k$

84. $\displaystyle\sum_{k=1}^{\infty} \frac{x^k}{k}$

85. $\displaystyle\sum_{k=1}^{\infty} \frac{x^k}{k^2}$

86. $\displaystyle\sum_{k=1}^{\infty} \frac{x^{2k}}{k^2}$

87. $\displaystyle\sum_{k=1}^{\infty} \frac{x^k}{2^k}$

88. Infinite products An infinite product $P = a_1 a_2 a_3 \ldots$, which is denoted $\displaystyle\prod_{k=1}^{\infty} a_k$, is the limit of the *sequence of partial products* $\{a_1, a_1 a_2, a_1 a_2 a_3, \ldots\}$.

a. Show that the infinite product converges (which means its sequence of partial products converges) provided the series $\displaystyle\sum_{k=1}^{\infty} \ln a_k$ converges. Assume that $a_k \neq 0$ for all k.

b. Consider the infinite product

$$P = \prod_{k=2}^{\infty}\left(1 - \frac{1}{k^2}\right) = \frac{3}{4}\cdot\frac{8}{9}\cdot\frac{15}{16}\cdot\frac{24}{25}\cdots.$$

Write out the first few terms of the sequence of partial products,

$$P_n = \prod_{k=2}^{n}\left(1 - \frac{1}{k^2}\right)$$

(for example, $P_2 = \frac{3}{4}, P_3 = \frac{2}{3}$). Write out enough terms to determine the value of the product, which is $\displaystyle\lim_{n\to\infty} P_n$.

c. Use the results of parts (a) and (b) to evaluate the series

$$\sum_{k=2}^{\infty} \ln\left(1 - \frac{1}{k^2}\right).$$

89. Infinite products *Use the ideas of Exercise 88 to evaluate the following infinite products.*

a. $\displaystyle\prod_{k=0}^{\infty} e^{1/2^k} = e \cdot e^{1/2} \cdot e^{1/4} \cdot e^{1/8} \cdots$

b. $\displaystyle\prod_{k=2}^{\infty}\left(1 - \frac{1}{k}\right) = \frac{1}{2}\cdot\frac{2}{3}\cdot\frac{3}{4}\cdot\frac{4}{5}\cdots$

90. An early limit Working in the early 1600s, the mathematicians Wallis, Pascal, and Fermat were attempting to determine the area of the region under the curve $y = x^p$ between $x = 0$ and $x = 1$, where p is a positive integer. Using arguments that predated the Fundamental Theorem of Calculus, they were able to prove that

$$\lim_{n\to\infty} \frac{1}{n}\sum_{k=0}^{n-1}\left(\frac{k}{n}\right)^p = \frac{1}{p+1}.$$

Use what you know about Riemann sums and integrals to verify this limit.

QUICK CHECK ANSWERS

1. 10; $(k+2)(k+1)$; $1/(k+1)$ **2.** The Integral Test or p-series with $p = 2$ **3.** To use the Comparison Test, we would need to show that $1/(k+1) > 1/k$, which is not true.

4. If $\displaystyle\lim_{k\to\infty} \frac{a_k}{b_k} = L$ for $0 < L < \infty$, then $\displaystyle\lim_{k\to\infty} \frac{b_k}{a_k} = \frac{1}{L}$, where $0 < 1/L < \infty$. ◄

9.6 Alternating Series

Our previous discussion focused on infinite series with positive terms, which is certainly an important part of the entire subject. But there are many interesting series with terms of mixed sign. For example, the series

$$1 + \frac{1}{2} - \frac{1}{3} - \frac{1}{4} + \frac{1}{5} + \frac{1}{6} - \frac{1}{7} - \frac{1}{8} + \cdots$$

has the pattern that two positive terms are followed by two negative terms and vice versa. Clearly, infinite series could have a variety of sign patterns, so we need to restrict our attention.

Fortunately, the simplest sign pattern is also the most important. We consider **alternating series** in which the signs strictly alternate, as in the series

$$\sum_{k=1}^{\infty} \frac{(-1)^{k+1}}{k} = 1 - \frac{1}{2} + \frac{1}{3} - \frac{1}{4} + \frac{1}{5} - \frac{1}{6} + \frac{1}{7} - \frac{1}{8} + \cdots.$$

The factor $(-1)^{k+1}$ (or $(-1)^k$) has the pattern $\{\ldots, 1, -1, 1, -1, \ldots\}$ and provides the alternating signs.

Alternating Harmonic Series

Let's see what is different about alternating series by working with the series $\sum_{k=1}^{\infty} \frac{(-1)^{k+1}}{k}$, which is called the **alternating harmonic series**. Recall that this series *without* the alternating signs, $\sum_{k=1}^{\infty} \frac{1}{k}$, is the *divergent* harmonic series. So an immediate question is whether the presence of alternating signs affects the convergence of a series.

We investigate this question by looking at the sequence of partial sums for the series. In this case, the first four terms of the sequence of partial sums are

$$S_1 = 1$$

$$S_2 = 1 - \frac{1}{2} = \frac{1}{2}$$

$$S_3 = 1 - \frac{1}{2} + \frac{1}{3} = \frac{5}{6}$$

$$S_4 = 1 - \frac{1}{2} + \frac{1}{3} - \frac{1}{4} = \frac{7}{12}.$$

Plotting the first 30 terms of the sequence of partial sums results in Figure 9.33, which has several noteworthy features.

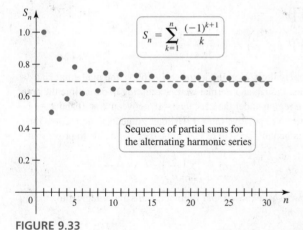

$$S_n = \sum_{k=1}^{n} \frac{(-1)^{k+1}}{k}$$

Sequence of partial sums for the alternating harmonic series

FIGURE 9.33

- The terms of the sequence of partial sums appear to converge to a limit; if they do, it means that, while the harmonic series diverges, the *alternating* harmonic series converges. We will soon learn that taking a divergent series with positive terms and making it an alternating series *may* turn it into a convergent series.

- For series with *positive* terms, the sequence of partial sums is necessarily an increasing sequence. Because the terms of an alternating series alternate in sign, the sequence of partial sums is not increasing (Figure 9.33).

- For the alternating harmonic series, the odd terms of the sequence of partial sums form a decreasing sequence and the even terms form an increasing sequence. As a result, the limit of the sequence of partial sums lies between any two consecutive terms of the sequence.

QUICK CHECK 1 Write out the first few terms of the sequence of partial sums for the alternating series $1 - 2 + 3 - 4 + 5 - 6 + \cdots$. Does this series appear to converge or diverge? ◄

Alternating Series Test

▷ Depending on the sign of the first term of the series, an alternating series may be written with $(-1)^k$ or $(-1)^{k+1}$.

▷ Recall that the Divergence Test of Section 9.4 applies to all series: If the terms of *any* series (including an alternating series) do not tend to zero, then the series diverges.

We now consider alternating series in general, which are written $\sum(-1)^{k+1}a_k$, where $a_k > 0$. With the exception of the Divergence Test, none of the convergence tests for series with positive terms applies to alternating series. The fortunate news is that one test works for most alternating series—and it is easy to use.

THEOREM 9.18   The Alternating Series Test

The alternating series $\sum(-1)^{k+1}a_k$ converges provided

1. the terms of the series are nonincreasing in magnitude ($0 < a_{k+1} \le a_k$, for k greater than some index N) and

2. $\lim\limits_{k\to\infty} a_k = 0$.

There is potential for confusion here. *For series of positive terms,* $\lim\limits_{k\to\infty} a_k = 0$ *does not imply convergence. For alternating series with nonincreasing terms,* $\lim\limits_{k\to\infty} a_k = 0$ *does imply convergence.*

Proof: The proof is short and instructive; it relies on Figure 9.34. We consider an alternating series in the form

$$\sum_{k=1}^{\infty}(-1)^{k+1}a_k = a_1 - a_2 + a_3 - a_4 + \cdots.$$

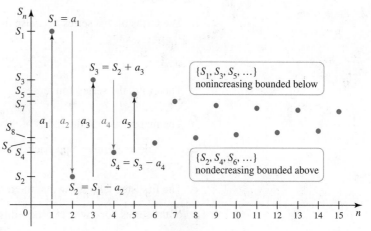

FIGURE 9.34

Because the terms of the series are nonincreasing in magnitude, the even terms of the sequence of partial sums $\{S_{2k}\} = \{S_2, S_4, \ldots\}$ form a nondecreasing sequence that is bounded above by S_1. By the Bounded Monotonic Sequence Theorem (Section 9.2), this sequence must have a limit; call it L. Similarly, the odd terms of the sequence of partial sums $\{S_{2k-1}\} = \{S_1, S_3, \ldots\}$ form a nonincreasing sequence that is bounded below by S_2. By the Bounded Monotonic Sequence Theorem, this sequence also has a limit; call it L'. At the moment, we cannot conclude that $L = L'$. However, notice that $S_{2k} = S_{2k-1} - a_{2k}$. By the condition that $\lim\limits_{k\to\infty} a_k = 0$, it follows that

$$\underbrace{\lim_{k\to\infty}S_{2k}}_{L} = \underbrace{\lim_{k\to\infty}S_{2k-1}}_{L'} - \underbrace{\lim_{k\to\infty}a_{2k}}_{0},$$

or $L = L'$. Therefore, the sequence of partial sums converges to a (unique) limit and the corresponding alternating series converges to that limit.   ◄

Now we can confirm that the alternating harmonic series $\sum_{k=1}^{\infty} \frac{(-1)^{k+1}}{k}$ converges.

This fact follows immediately from the Alternating Series Test because the terms $a_k = \frac{1}{k}$ decrease and $\lim_{k \to \infty} a_k = 0$.

$\sum_{k=1}^{\infty} \frac{1}{k}$

• Diverges
• Partial sums increase

$\sum_{k=1}^{\infty} \frac{(-1)^{k+1}}{k}$

• Converges
• Partial sums oscillate

THEOREM 9.19   Alternating Harmonic Series

The alternating harmonic series $\sum_{k=1}^{\infty} \frac{(-1)^{k+1}}{k} = 1 - \frac{1}{2} + \frac{1}{3} - \frac{1}{4} + \frac{1}{5} - \cdots$

converges (even though the harmonic series $\sum_{k=1}^{\infty} \frac{1}{k} = 1 + \frac{1}{2} + \frac{1}{3} + \frac{1}{4} + \frac{1}{5} + \cdots$

diverges).

QUICK CHECK 2 Explain why the value of a convergent alternating series, with terms that are nonincreasing in magnitude, is trapped between successive terms of the sequence of partial sums. ◄

EXAMPLE 1   Alternating Series Test Determine whether the following series converge or diverge.

a. $\sum_{k=1}^{\infty} \frac{(-1)^{k+1}}{k^2}$ **b.** $2 - \frac{3}{2} + \frac{4}{3} - \frac{5}{4} + \cdots$ **c.** $\sum_{k=2}^{\infty} \frac{(-1)^k \ln k}{k}$

SOLUTION

a. The terms of this series decrease in magnitude, for $k \geq 1$. Furthermore,

$$\lim_{k \to \infty} a_k = \lim_{k \to \infty} \frac{1}{k^2} = 0.$$

Therefore, the series converges.

b. The magnitudes of the terms of this series are $a_k = \frac{k+1}{k} = 1 + \frac{1}{k}$. While these terms decrease, they approach 1, not 0, as $k \to \infty$. By the Divergence Test, the series diverges.

c. The first step is to show that the terms decrease in magnitude after some fixed term of the series. One way to proceed is to look at the function $f(x) = \frac{\ln x}{x}$, which generates the terms of the series. By the Quotient Rule, $f'(x) = \frac{1 - \ln x}{x^2}$. The fact that $f'(x) < 0$, for $x > e$, implies that the terms $\frac{\ln k}{k}$ decrease, for $k \geq 3$. As long as the terms of the series decrease for all k greater than some fixed integer, the first condition of the test is met. Furthermore, using l'Hôpital's Rule or the fact that $\{\ln k\}$ increases more slowly than $\{k\}$ (Section 9.2), we see that

$$\lim_{k \to \infty} a_k = \lim_{k \to \infty} \frac{\ln k}{k} = 0.$$

The conditions of the Alternating Series Test are met and the series converges.

Related Exercises 11–28 ◄

Remainders in Alternating Series

Recall that if a series converges to a value S, then the remainder is $R_n = S - S_n$, where S_n is the sum of the first n terms of the series. The magnitude of the remainder is the *absolute error* in approximating S by S_n.

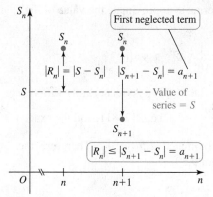

FIGURE 9.35

An upper bound on the magnitude of the remainder in an alternating series is found by observing that when the terms are nonincreasing in magnitude, the value of the series is always trapped between successive terms of the sequence of partial sums. Therefore, as shown in Figure 9.35,

$$|R_n| = |S - S_n| \le |S_{n+1} - S_n| = a_{n+1}.$$

This argument is a proof of the following theorem.

THEOREM 9.20   Remainder in Alternating Series

Let $\sum_{k=1}^{\infty} (-1)^{k+1} a_k$ be a convergent alternating series with terms that are nonincreasing in magnitude. Let $R_n = S - S_n$ be the remainder in approximating the value of that series by the sum of its first n terms. Then $|R_n| \le a_{n+1}$. In other words, the magnitude of the remainder is less than or equal to the magnitude of the first neglected term.

EXAMPLE 2   Remainder in an alternating series

a. It turns out that $\ln 2 = 1 - \dfrac{1}{2} + \dfrac{1}{3} - \dfrac{1}{4} + \cdots = \sum_{k=1}^{\infty} \dfrac{(-1)^{k+1}}{k}$. How many terms of the series are required to approximate $\ln 2$ with a maximum error less than 10^{-6}? The exact value of the series is given but is not needed to answer the question.

b. If $n = 9$ terms of the series $-1 + \dfrac{1}{2!} - \dfrac{1}{3!} + \dfrac{1}{4!} - \cdots = \sum_{k=1}^{\infty} \dfrac{(-1)^k}{k!}$

are summed, what is the maximum error committed in approximating the value of the series (which is $e^{-1} - 1$)?

SOLUTION

Notice that both series meet the conditions of Theorem 9.20.

a. The series is expressed as the sum of the first n terms plus the remainder:

$$\sum_{k=1}^{\infty} \frac{(-1)^{k+1}}{k} = \underbrace{1 - \frac{1}{2} + \frac{1}{3} - \frac{1}{4} + \cdots + \frac{(-1)^{n+1}}{n}}_{S_n \;=\; \text{the sum of the first } n \text{ terms}} + \underbrace{\frac{(-1)^{n+2}}{n+1}}_{\substack{|R_n| \;=\; |S - S_n| \text{ is less} \\ \text{than the magnitude} \\ \text{of this term}}} + \cdots.$$

In magnitude, the remainder is less than or equal to the magnitude of the $(n + 1)$st term:

$$|R_n| = |S - S_n| \le a_{n+1} = \frac{1}{n+1}.$$

To ensure that the error is less than 10^{-6}, we require that

$$a_{n+1} = \frac{1}{n+1} < 10^{-6}, \quad \text{or} \quad n + 1 > 10^6.$$

Therefore, it takes 1 million terms of the series to approximate $\ln 2$ with an error less than 10^{-6}.

b. The series may be expressed as the sum of the first nine terms plus the remainder:

$$\sum_{k=1}^{\infty} \frac{(-1)^k}{k!} = \underbrace{-1 + \frac{1}{2!} - \frac{1}{3!} + \cdots - \frac{1}{9!}}_{S_9 \;=\; \text{sum of first 9 terms}} + \underbrace{\frac{1}{10!}}_{\substack{|R_9| \;=\; |S - S_9| \\ \text{is less than} \\ \text{this term}}} - \cdots.$$

The error committed when using the first nine terms to approximate the value of the series satisfies

$$|R_9| = |S - S_9| \le a_{10} = \frac{1}{10!} \approx 2.8 \times 10^{-7}.$$

Therefore, the maximum error is no greater than 2.8×10^{-7}. As a check, the difference between the sum of the first nine terms, $\sum_{k=1}^{9} \frac{(-1)^k}{k!} \approx -0.632120811$, and the exact value, $S = e^{-1} - 1 \approx -0.632120559$, is approximately 2.5×10^{-7}. Therefore, the actual error satisfies the bound given by Theorem 9.20.

Related Exercises 29–44◄

QUICK CHECK 3 Compare and comment on the speed of convergence of the two series in the previous example. Why does one series converge more rapidly than the other? ◄

Absolute and Conditional Convergence

In this final segment, some terminology about series is introduced that is needed in Chapter 10. We now let the notation $\sum a_k$ denote any series—a series of positive terms, an alternating series, or even a more general infinite series.

Look again at the alternating harmonic series $\sum (-1)^{k+1}/k$, which converges. The corresponding series of positive terms, $\sum 1/k$, is the harmonic series, which diverges. We saw in Example 1a that the alternating series $\sum (-1)^{k+1}/k^2$ converges, and the corresponding *p*-series of positive terms $\sum 1/k^2$ also converges. These examples illustrate that removing the alternating signs in a convergent series *may* or *may not* result in a convergent series. The terminology that we now introduce distinguishes these cases.

> **DEFINITION Absolute and Conditional Convergence**
>
> If $\sum |a_k|$ converges, then $\sum a_k$ **converges absolutely**. If $\sum |a_k|$ diverges and $\sum a_k$ converges, then $\sum a_k$ **converges conditionally**.

The series $\sum (-1)^{k+1}/k^2$ is an example of an absolutely convergent series because the series of absolute values,

$$\sum_{k=1}^{\infty} \left| \frac{(-1)^{k+1}}{k^2} \right| = \sum_{k=1}^{\infty} \frac{1}{k^2},$$

is a convergent *p*-series. In this case, removing the alternating signs in the series does *not* affect its convergence.

On the other hand, the convergent alternating harmonic series $\sum (-1)^{k+1}/k$ has the property that the corresponding series of absolute values,

$$\sum_{k=1}^{\infty} \left| \frac{(-1)^{k+1}}{k} \right| = \sum_{k=1}^{\infty} \frac{1}{k},$$

does *not* converge. In this case, removing the alternating signs in the series *does* affect convergence, so this series does not converge absolutely. Instead, we say it converges conditionally. A convergent series (such as $\sum (-1)^{k+1}/k$) may not converge absolutely. However, if a series converges absolutely, then it converges.

> **THEOREM 9.21   Absolute Convergence Implies Convergence**
> If $\sum |a_k|$ converges, then $\sum a_k$ converges (absolute convergence implies convergence).
> If $\sum a_k$ diverges, then $\sum |a_k|$ diverges.

Proof: Because $|a_k| = a_k$ or $|a_k| = -a_k$, it follows that $0 \le a_k + |a_k| \le 2|a_k|$. By assumption $\sum |a_k|$ converges, which, in turn, implies that $2\sum |a_k|$ converges. Using the Comparison Test and the inequality $0 \le a_k + |a_k| \le 2|a_k|$, it follows that $\sum (a_k + |a_k|)$ converges. Now note that

$$\sum a_k = \sum (a_k + |a_k| - |a_k|) = \underbrace{\sum (a_k + |a_k|)}_{\text{converges}} - \underbrace{\sum |a_k|}_{\text{converges}}.$$

We see that $\sum a_k$ is the sum of two convergent series, so it also converges. The second statement of the theorem is logically equivalent to the first statement. ◄

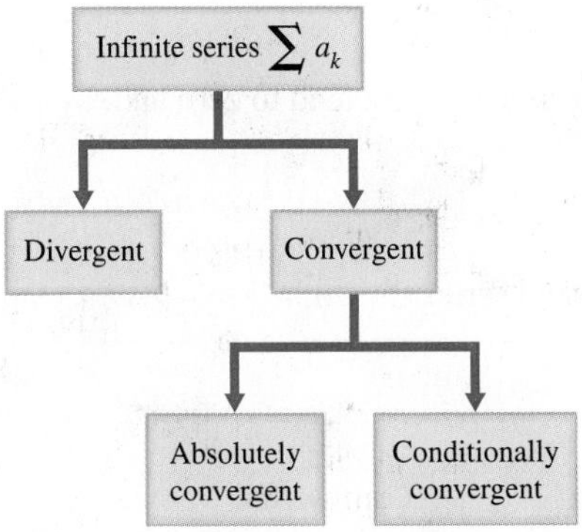

Figure 9.36 gives an overview of absolute and conditional convergence. It shows the universe of all infinite series, split first according to whether they converge or diverge. Convergent series are further divided between absolutely and conditionally convergent series.

Here are a few more consequences of these definitions.

- The distinction between absolute and conditional convergence is relevant only for series of mixed sign, which includes alternating series. If a series of positive terms converges, it converges absolutely; conditional convergence does not apply.

- To test for absolute convergence, we test the series $\sum |a_k|$, which is a series of positive terms. Therefore, the convergence tests of Sections 9.4 and 9.5 (for positive-term series) are used to determine absolute convergence.

Infinite series $\sum a_k$

Divergent

Convergent

Absolutely convergent

Conditionally convergent

FIGURE 9.36

QUICK CHECK 4 Explain why a convergent series of positive terms converges absolutely. ◄

EXAMPLE 3   Absolute and conditional convergence Determine whether the following series diverge, converge absolutely, or converge conditionally.

a. $\displaystyle\sum_{k=1}^{\infty} \frac{(-1)^{k+1}}{\sqrt{k}}$ **b.** $\displaystyle\sum_{k=1}^{\infty} \frac{(-1)^{k+1}}{\sqrt{k^3}}$ **c.** $\displaystyle\sum_{k=1}^{\infty} \frac{\sin k}{k^2}$ **d.** $\displaystyle\sum_{k=1}^{\infty} \frac{(-1)^k k}{k+1}$

SOLUTION

a. We examine the series of absolute values,

$$\sum_{k=1}^{\infty} \left| \frac{(-1)^{k+1}}{\sqrt{k}} \right| = \sum_{k=1}^{\infty} \frac{1}{\sqrt{k}},$$

which is a divergent p-series (with $p = \frac{1}{2} < 1$). Therefore, the given alternating series does not converge absolutely. To determine whether the series converges conditionally, we look at the original series—with alternating signs. The magnitude of the terms of this series decrease with $\lim_{k\to\infty} 1/\sqrt{k} = 0$, so by the Alternating Series Test, the series converges. Because this series converges, but not absolutely, it converges conditionally.

b. To assess absolute convergence, we look at the series of absolute values,

$$\sum_{k=1}^{\infty} \left| \frac{(-1)^{k+1}}{\sqrt{k^3}} \right| = \sum_{k=1}^{\infty} \frac{1}{k^{3/2}},$$

which is a convergent p-series (with $p = \frac{3}{2} > 1$). Therefore, the original alternating series converges absolutely (and by Theorem 9.21 it converges).

c. The terms of this series do not strictly alternate sign (the first few signs are $+++---$), so the Alternating Series Test does not apply. Because $|\sin k| \le 1$, the terms of the series of absolute values satisfy

$$\left| \frac{\sin k}{k^2} \right| = \frac{|\sin k|}{k^2} \le \frac{1}{k^2}.$$

The series $\sum \dfrac{1}{k^2}$ is a convergent p-series. Therefore, by the Comparison Test, the series $\sum \left| \dfrac{\sin k}{k^2} \right|$ converges, which implies that the series $\sum \dfrac{\sin k}{k^2}$ converges absolutely (and by Theorem 9.21 it converges).

d. Notice that $\lim\limits_{k \to \infty} k/(k+1) = 1$. The terms of the series do not tend to zero and, by the Divergence Test, the series diverges.

Related Exercises 45–56 ◄

We close the chapter with the summary of tests and series shown in Table 9.4.

Table 9.4 Special Series and Convergence Tests

Series or Test	Form of Series	Condition for Convergence	Condition for Divergence	Comments
Geometric series	$\displaystyle\sum_{k=0}^{\infty} ar^k,\, a \ne 0$	$\lvert r \rvert < 1$	$\lvert r \rvert \ge 1$	If $\lvert r \rvert < 1$, then $\displaystyle\sum_{k=0}^{\infty} ar^k = \frac{a}{1-r}.$
Divergence Test	$\displaystyle\sum_{k=1}^{\infty} a_k$	Does not apply	$\lim\limits_{k \to \infty} a_k \ne 0$	Cannot be used to prove convergence
Integral Test	$\displaystyle\sum_{k=1}^{\infty} a_k$, where $a_k = f(k)$ and f is continuous, positive, and decreasing	$\displaystyle\int_1^{\infty} f(x)\,dx < \infty$	$\displaystyle\int_1^{\infty} f(x)\,dx$ does not exist	The value of the integral is not the value of the series.
p-Series	$\displaystyle\sum_{k=1}^{\infty} \frac{1}{k^p}$	$p > 1$	$p \le 1$	Useful for comparison tests
Ratio Test	$\displaystyle\sum_{k=1}^{\infty} a_k$, where $a_k > 0$	$\lim\limits_{k \to \infty} \dfrac{a_{k+1}}{a_k} < 1$	$\lim\limits_{k \to \infty} \dfrac{a_{k+1}}{a_k} > 1$	Inconclusive if $\lim\limits_{k \to \infty} \dfrac{a_{k+1}}{a_k} = 1$
Root Test	$\displaystyle\sum_{k=1}^{\infty} a_k$, where $a_k \ge 0$	$\lim\limits_{k \to \infty} \sqrt[k]{a_k} < 1$	$\lim\limits_{k \to \infty} \sqrt[k]{a_k} > 1$	Inconclusive if $\lim\limits_{k \to \infty} \sqrt[k]{a_k} = 1$
Comparison Test	$\displaystyle\sum_{k=1}^{\infty} a_k$, where $a_k > 0$	$0 < a_k \le b_k$ and $\displaystyle\sum_{k=1}^{\infty} b_k$ converges	$0 < b_k \le a_k$ and $\displaystyle\sum_{k=1}^{\infty} b_k$ diverges	$\displaystyle\sum_{k=1}^{\infty} a_k$ is given; you supply $\displaystyle\sum_{k=1}^{\infty} b_k$.
Limit Comparison Test	$\displaystyle\sum_{k=1}^{\infty} a_k$, where $a_k > 0, b_k > 0$	$0 \le \lim\limits_{k \to \infty} \dfrac{a_k}{b_k} < \infty$ and $\displaystyle\sum_{k=1}^{\infty} b_k$ converges	$\lim\limits_{k \to \infty} \dfrac{a_k}{b_k} > 0$ and $\displaystyle\sum_{k=1}^{\infty} b_k$ diverges	$\displaystyle\sum_{k=1}^{\infty} a_k$ is given; you supply $\displaystyle\sum_{k=1}^{\infty} b_k$.
Alternating Series Test	$\displaystyle\sum_{k=1}^{\infty} (-1)^k a_k$, where $a_k > 0$, $0 < a_{k+1} \le a_k$	$\lim\limits_{k \to \infty} a_k = 0$	$\lim\limits_{k \to \infty} a_k \ne 0$	Remainder R_n satisfies $\lvert R_n \rvert \le a_{n+1}$
Absolute Convergence	$\displaystyle\sum_{k=1}^{\infty} a_k,\, a_k$ arbitrary	$\displaystyle\sum_{k=1}^{\infty} \lvert a_k \rvert$ converges		Applies to arbitrary series

SECTION 9.6 EXERCISES

Review Questions

1. Explain why the sequence of partial sums for an alternating series is not an increasing sequence.

2. Describe how to apply the Alternating Series Test.

3. Why does the value of a converging alternating series with terms that are nonincreasing in magnitude lie between any two consecutive terms of its sequence of partial sums?

4. Suppose an alternating series with terms that are nonincreasing in magnitude converges to a value L. Explain how to estimate the remainder that occurs when the series is terminated after n terms.

5. Explain why the magnitude of the remainder in an alternating series with terms that are nonincreasing in magnitude is less than or equal to the magnitude of the first neglected term.

6. Give an example of a convergent alternating series that fails to converge absolutely.

7. Is it possible for a series of positive terms to converge conditionally? Explain.

8. Why does absolute convergence imply convergence?

9. Is it possible for an alternating series to converge absolutely but not conditionally?

10. Give an example of a series that converges conditionally but not absolutely.

Basic Skills

11–28. Alternating Series Test *Determine whether the following series converge.*

11. $\displaystyle\sum_{k=0}^{\infty} \frac{(-1)^k}{2k+1}$

12. $\displaystyle\sum_{k=1}^{\infty} \frac{(-1)^k}{\sqrt{k}}$

13. $\displaystyle\sum_{k=1}^{\infty} \frac{(-1)^k k}{3k+2}$

14. $\displaystyle\sum_{k=1}^{\infty} (-1)^k \left(1 + \frac{1}{k}\right)^k$

15. $\displaystyle\sum_{k=1}^{\infty} \frac{(-1)^{k+1}}{k^3}$

16. $\displaystyle\sum_{k=0}^{\infty} \frac{(-1)^k}{k^2+10}$

17. $\displaystyle\sum_{k=1}^{\infty} (-1)^{k+1} \frac{k^2}{k^3+1}$

18. $\displaystyle\sum_{k=2}^{\infty} (-1)^k \frac{\ln k}{k^2}$

19. $\displaystyle\sum_{k=2}^{\infty} (-1)^k \frac{k^2-1}{k^2+3}$

20. $\displaystyle\sum_{k=0}^{\infty} \left(-\frac{1}{5}\right)^k$

21. $\displaystyle\sum_{k=2}^{\infty} (-1)^k \left(1 + \frac{1}{k}\right)$

22. $\displaystyle\sum_{k=1}^{\infty} \frac{\cos \pi k}{k^2}$

23. $\displaystyle\sum_{k=1}^{\infty} (-1)^{k+1} \frac{k^{10}+2k^5+1}{k(k^{10}+1)}$

24. $\displaystyle\sum_{k=2}^{\infty} \frac{(-1)^k}{k \ln^2 k}$

25. $\displaystyle\sum_{k=1}^{\infty} (-1)^{k+1} k^{1/k}$

26. $\displaystyle\sum_{k=1}^{\infty} (-1)^{k+1} \frac{k!}{k^k}$

27. $\displaystyle\sum_{k=0}^{\infty} \frac{(-1)^k}{\sqrt{k^2+4}}$

28. $\displaystyle\sum_{k=1}^{\infty} (-1)^k k \sin \frac{1}{k}$

29–38. Remainders in alternating series *Determine how many terms of the following convergent series must be summed to be sure that the remainder is less than 10^{-4} in magnitude. Although you do not need it, the exact value of the series is given in each case.*

29. $\ln 2 = \displaystyle\sum_{k=1}^{\infty} \frac{(-1)^{k+1}}{k}$

30. $\dfrac{1}{e} = \displaystyle\sum_{k=0}^{\infty} \frac{(-1)^k}{k!}$

31. $\dfrac{\pi}{4} = \displaystyle\sum_{k=0}^{\infty} \frac{(-1)^k}{2k+1}$

32. $\dfrac{\pi^2}{12} = \displaystyle\sum_{k=1}^{\infty} \frac{(-1)^{k+1}}{k^2}$

33. $\dfrac{7\pi^4}{720} = \displaystyle\sum_{k=1}^{\infty} \frac{(-1)^{k+1}}{k^4}$

34. $\dfrac{\pi^3}{32} = \displaystyle\sum_{k=0}^{\infty} \frac{(-1)^k}{(2k+1)^3}$

35. $\dfrac{\pi\sqrt{3}}{9} + \dfrac{\ln 2}{3} = \displaystyle\sum_{k=0}^{\infty} \frac{(-1)^k}{3k+1}$

36. $\dfrac{31\pi^6}{30{,}240} = \displaystyle\sum_{k=1}^{\infty} \frac{(-1)^{k+1}}{k^6}$

37. $\pi = \displaystyle\sum_{k=0}^{\infty} \frac{(-1)^k}{4^k} \left(\frac{2}{4k+1} + \frac{2}{4k+2} + \frac{1}{4k+3}\right)$

38. $\dfrac{\pi\sqrt{3}}{9} - \dfrac{\ln 2}{3} = \displaystyle\sum_{k=0}^{\infty} \frac{(-1)^k}{3k+2}$

39–44. Estimating infinite series *Estimate the value of the following convergent series with an absolute error less than 10^{-3}.*

39. $\displaystyle\sum_{k=1}^{\infty} \frac{(-1)^k}{k^5}$

40. $\displaystyle\sum_{k=1}^{\infty} \frac{(-1)^k}{(2k+1)^3}$

41. $\displaystyle\sum_{k=1}^{\infty} \frac{(-1)^k k}{k^2+1}$

42. $\displaystyle\sum_{k=1}^{\infty} \frac{(-1)^k k}{k^4+1}$

43. $\displaystyle\sum_{k=1}^{\infty} \frac{(-1)^k}{k^k}$

44. $\displaystyle\sum_{k=1}^{\infty} \frac{(-1)^{k+1}}{(2k+1)!}$

45–56. Absolute and conditional convergence *Determine whether the following series converge absolutely, converge conditionally, or diverge.*

45. $\displaystyle\sum_{k=1}^{\infty} \frac{(-1)^k}{k^{2/3}}$

46. $\displaystyle\sum_{k=1}^{\infty} \frac{(-1)^k}{\sqrt{k}}$

47. $\displaystyle\sum_{k=1}^{\infty} \frac{(-1)^{k+1}}{k^{3/2}}$

48. $\displaystyle\sum_{k=1}^{\infty} \left(-\frac{1}{3}\right)^k$

49. $\displaystyle\sum_{k=1}^{\infty} \frac{\cos k}{k^3}$

50. $\displaystyle\sum_{k=1}^{\infty} \frac{(-1)^k k^2}{\sqrt{k^6+1}}$

51. $\displaystyle\sum_{k=1}^{\infty} (-1)^k \tan^{-1} k$

52. $\displaystyle\sum_{k=1}^{\infty} (-1)^k e^{-k}$

53. $\displaystyle\sum_{k=1}^{\infty} \frac{(-1)^k k}{2k+1}$

54. $\displaystyle\sum_{k=2}^{\infty} \frac{(-1)^k}{\ln k}$

55. $\displaystyle\sum_{k=1}^{\infty} \frac{(-1)^k \tan^{-1} k}{k^3}$

56. $\displaystyle\sum_{k=1}^{\infty} \frac{(-1)^{k+1} e^k}{(k+1)!}$

Further Explorations

57. **Explain why or why not** Determine whether the following statements are true and give an explanation or counterexample.

   a. A series that converges must converge absolutely.
   b. A series that converges absolutely must converge.
   c. A series that converges conditionally must converge.
   d. If Σa_k diverges, then $\Sigma |a_k|$ diverges.
   e. If Σa_k^2 converges, then Σa_k converges.
   f. If $a_k > 0$ and Σa_k converges, then Σa_k^2 converges.
   g. If Σa_k converges conditionally, then $\Sigma |a_k|$ diverges.

58. Alternating Series Test Show that the series

$$\frac{1}{3} - \frac{2}{5} + \frac{3}{7} - \frac{4}{9} + \cdots = \sum_{k=1}^{\infty} (-1)^{k+1} \frac{k}{2k+1}$$

diverges. Which condition of the Alternating Series Test is not satisfied?

59. Alternating *p*-series Given that $\sum_{k=1}^{\infty} \frac{1}{k^2} = \frac{\pi^2}{6}$, show that

$\sum_{k=1}^{\infty} \frac{(-1)^{k+1}}{k^2} = \frac{\pi^2}{12}$. (Assume the result of Exercise 63.)

60. Alternating *p*-series Given that $\sum_{k=1}^{\infty} \frac{1}{k^4} = \frac{\pi^4}{90}$, show that

$\sum_{k=1}^{\infty} \frac{(-1)^{k+1}}{k^4} = \frac{7\pi^4}{720}$. (Assume the result of Exercise 63.)

61. Geometric series In Section 9.3, we established that the geometric series $\sum r^k$ converges provided $|r| < 1$. Notice that if $-1 < r < 0$, the geometric series is also an alternating series. Use the Alternating Series Test to show that for $-1 < r < 0$, the series $\sum r^k$ converges.

62. Even and odd terms Prove that if an alternating series converges absolutely, then its positive terms form a convergent series and its negative terms form a convergent series.

Additional Exercises

63. Rearranging series It can be proved that if a series converges absolutely, then its terms may be summed in any order without changing the value of the series. However, if a series converges conditionally, then the value of the series depends on the order of summation. For example, the (conditionally convergent) alternating harmonic series has the value

$$1 - \frac{1}{2} + \frac{1}{3} - \frac{1}{4} + \cdots = \ln 2.$$

Show that by rearranging the terms (so the sign pattern is $++-$),

$$1 + \frac{1}{3} - \frac{1}{2} + \frac{1}{5} + \frac{1}{7} - \frac{1}{4} + \cdots = \frac{3}{2} \ln 2.$$

64. A better remainder Suppose an alternating series $\sum (-1)^k a_k$, with terms that are nonincreasing in magnitude, converges to S and the sum of the first n terms of the series is S_n. Suppose also that the difference between the magnitudes of consecutive terms decreases with k. It can be shown that for $n \geq 1$,

$$\left| S - \left(S_n + \frac{(-1)^{n+1} a_{n+1}}{2} \right) \right| \leq \frac{1}{2} |a_{n+1} - a_{n+2}|.$$

a. Interpret this inequality and explain why it gives a better approximation to S than simply using S_n to approximate S.

b. For the following series, determine how many terms of the series are needed to approximate its exact value with an error less than 10^{-6} using both S_n and the method explained in part (a).

(i) $\sum_{k=1}^{\infty} \frac{(-1)^k}{k}$ **(ii)** $\sum_{k=2}^{\infty} \frac{(-1)^k}{k \ln k}$ **(iii)** $\sum_{k=2}^{\infty} \frac{(-1)^k}{\sqrt{k}}$

65. A fallacy Explain the fallacy in the following argument.

Let $x = \frac{1}{1} + \frac{1}{3} + \frac{1}{5} + \frac{1}{7} + \cdots$ and

$y = \frac{1}{2} + \frac{1}{4} + \frac{1}{6} + \frac{1}{8} + \cdots$. It follows that $2y = x + y$, which implies that $x = y$. On the other hand,

$$x - y = \left(1 - \frac{1}{2}\right) + \left(\frac{1}{3} - \frac{1}{4}\right) + \left(\frac{1}{5} - \frac{1}{6}\right) + \cdots > 0$$

$$\underbrace{\phantom{\left(1 - \frac{1}{2}\right)}}_{>0} \quad \underbrace{\phantom{\left(\frac{1}{3} - \frac{1}{4}\right)}}_{>0} \quad \underbrace{\phantom{\left(\frac{1}{5} - \frac{1}{6}\right)}}_{>0}$$

is a sum of positive terms, so $x > y$. Therefore, we have shown that $x = y$ and $x > y$.

Technology Exercises

66. Remainders in alternating series Given any convergent infinite series $\sum a_k$, let $N(r)$ be the number of terms of the series that must be summed to guarantee that the remainder is less than 10^{-r} in magnitude, where r is a positive integer.

a. Graph the function $N(r)$ for the three alternating *p*-series

$$\sum_{k=1}^{\infty} \frac{(-1)^{k+1}}{k^p}, \text{ for } p = 1, 2, \text{ and } 3. \text{ Compare the three graphs}$$

and discuss what they mean about the rates of convergence of the three series.

b. Carry out the procedure of part (a) for the series $\sum_{k=1}^{\infty} \frac{(-1)^{k+1}}{k!}$

and compare the rates of convergence of all four series.

QUICK CHECK ANSWERS

1. $1, -1, 2, -2, 3, -3, \ldots$; series diverges. **2.** The even terms of the sequence of partial sums approach the value of the series from one side; the odd terms of the sequence of partial sums approach the value of the series from the other side. **3.** The second series with $k!$ in the denominators converges much more quickly than the first series because $k!$ increases much faster than k as $k \to \infty$. **4.** If a series has positive terms, the series of absolute values is the same as the series itself. ◀

CHAPTER 9   REVIEW EXERCISES

1. **Explain why or why not** Determine whether the following statements are true and give an explanation or counterexample.

   a. The terms of the sequence $\{a_n\}$ increase in magnitude, so the limit of the sequence does not exist.

   b. The terms of the series $\sum 1/\sqrt{k}$ approach zero, so the series converges.

   c. The terms of the sequence of partial sums of the series $\sum a_k$ approach $\frac{5}{2}$, so the infinite series converges to $\frac{5}{2}$.

   d. An alternating series that converges absolutely must converge conditionally.

   e. The sequence $a_n = \dfrac{n^2}{n^2 + 1}$ converges.

   f. The sequence $a_n = \dfrac{(-1)^n n^2}{n^2 + 1}$ converges.

   g. The series $\displaystyle\sum_{k=1}^{\infty} \dfrac{k^2}{k^2 + 1}$ converges.

   h. The sequence of partial sums associated with the series $\displaystyle\sum_{k=1}^{\infty} \dfrac{1}{k^2 + 1}$ converges.

2–10. Limits of sequences *Evaluate the limit of the sequence, or state that it does not exist.*

2. $a_n = \dfrac{n^2 + 4}{\sqrt{4n^4 + 1}}$

3. $a_n = \dfrac{8^n}{n!}$

4. $a_n = \left(1 + \dfrac{3}{n}\right)^{2n}$

5. $a_n = \sqrt[n]{n}$

6. $a_n = n - \sqrt{n^2 - 1}$

7. $a_n = \left(\dfrac{1}{n}\right)^{1/\ln n}$

8. $a_n = \sin\left(\dfrac{\pi n}{6}\right)$

9. $a_n = \dfrac{(-1)^n}{0.9^n}$

10. $a_n = \tan^{-1} n$

11. **Sequence of partial sums** Consider the series

$$\sum_{k=1}^{\infty} \frac{1}{k(k+2)} = \frac{1}{2}\sum_{k=1}^{\infty}\left(\frac{1}{k} - \frac{1}{k+2}\right).$$

   a. Write the first four terms of the sequence of partial sums $S_1, \ldots, S_4$.

   b. Write the nth term of the sequence of partial sums S_n.

   c. Find $\lim\limits_{n\to\infty} S_n$ and evaluate the series.

12–20. Evaluating series *Evaluate the following infinite series or state that the series diverges.*

12. $\displaystyle\sum_{k=1}^{\infty}\left(\frac{9}{10}\right)^k$

13. $\displaystyle\sum_{k=1}^{\infty} 3(1.001)^k$

14. $\displaystyle\sum_{k=0}^{\infty}\left(-\frac{1}{5}\right)^k$

15. $\displaystyle\sum_{k=1}^{\infty} \frac{1}{k(k+1)}$

16. $\displaystyle\sum_{k=2}^{\infty}\left(\frac{1}{\sqrt{k}} - \frac{1}{\sqrt{k-1}}\right)$

17. $\displaystyle\sum_{k=1}^{\infty}\left(\frac{3}{3k-2} - \frac{3}{3k+1}\right)$

18. $\displaystyle\sum_{k=1}^{\infty} 4^{-3k}$

19. $\displaystyle\sum_{k=1}^{\infty} \frac{2^k}{3^{k+2}}$

20. $\displaystyle\sum_{k=0}^{\infty}\left(\left(\frac{1}{3}\right)^k - \left(\frac{2}{3}\right)^{k+1}\right)$

21. **Sequences of partial sums** The sequences of partial sums for three series are shown in the figures. Assume that the pattern in the sequences continues as $n \to \infty$.

   a. Does it appear that series A converges? If so, what is its (approximate) value?

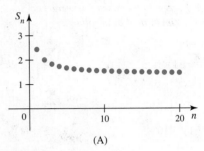

(A)

   b. What can you conclude about the convergence or divergence of series B?

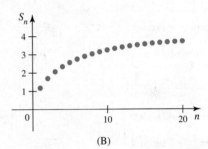

(B)

   c. Does it appear that series C converges? If so, what is its (approximate) value?

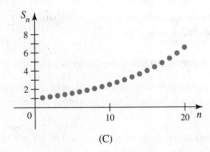

(C)

22–42. Convergence or divergence *Use a convergence test of your choice to determine whether the following series converge or diverge.*

22. $\displaystyle\sum_{k=1}^{\infty} \frac{2}{k^{3/2}}$

23. $\displaystyle\sum_{k=1}^{\infty} k^{-2/3}$

24. $\displaystyle\sum_{k=1}^{\infty} \frac{2k^2 + 1}{\sqrt{k^3 + 2}}$

25. $\displaystyle\sum_{k=1}^{\infty} \frac{2^k}{e^k}$

26. $\displaystyle\sum_{k=1}^{\infty}\left(\frac{k}{k+3}\right)^{2k}$

27. $\displaystyle\sum_{k=1}^{\infty} \frac{2^k k!}{k^k}$

28. $\displaystyle\sum_{k=1}^{\infty} \frac{1}{\sqrt{k}\sqrt{k+1}}$

29. $\displaystyle\sum_{k=1}^{\infty} \frac{3}{2 + e^k}$

30. $\displaystyle\sum_{k=1}^{\infty} k \sin\frac{1}{k}$

31. $\displaystyle\sum_{k=1}^{\infty} \frac{\sqrt[k]{k}}{k^3}$

32. $\displaystyle\sum_{k=1}^{\infty} \frac{1}{1 + \ln k}$

33. $\displaystyle\sum_{k=1}^{\infty} k^5 e^{-k}$

34. $\displaystyle\sum_{k=4}^{\infty} \frac{2}{k^2 - 10}$

35. $\displaystyle\sum_{k=1}^{\infty} \frac{\ln k^2}{k^2}$

36. $\displaystyle\sum_{k=1}^{\infty} ke^{-k}$

37. $\displaystyle\sum_{k=0}^{\infty} \frac{2 \cdot 4^k}{(2k + 1)!}$

38. $\displaystyle\sum_{k=0}^{\infty} \frac{9^k}{(2k)!}$

39. $\displaystyle\sum_{k=1}^{\infty} \left(\frac{k^3 + k + 1}{2k^3 - 1}\right)^k$

40. $\displaystyle\sum_{k=1}^{\infty} \frac{e^k + 2}{3e^k - 2}$

41. $\displaystyle\sum_{k=1}^{\infty} \left(1 + \frac{3}{k}\right)^{k/2}$

42. $\displaystyle\sum_{k=2}^{\infty} k^{-\ln k}$

43–50. Alternating series *Determine whether the following series converge or diverge. In the case of convergence, state whether the convergence is conditional or absolute.*

43. $\displaystyle\sum_{k=2}^{\infty} \frac{(-1)^k}{k^2 - 1}$

44. $\displaystyle\sum_{k=1}^{\infty} \frac{(-1)^{k+1}(k^2 + 4)}{2k^2 + 1}$

45. $\displaystyle\sum_{k=1}^{\infty} (-1)^k ke^{-k}$

46. $\displaystyle\sum_{k=1}^{\infty} \frac{(-1)^k}{\sqrt{k^2 + 1}}$

47. $\displaystyle\sum_{k=1}^{\infty} \frac{(-1)^{k+1}10^k}{k!}$

48. $\displaystyle\sum_{k=2}^{\infty} \frac{(-1)^k}{k \ln k}$

49. $\displaystyle\sum_{k=1}^{\infty} \frac{(-2)^{k+1}}{k^2}$

50. $\displaystyle\sum_{k=0}^{\infty} \frac{(-1)^k}{e^k + e^{-k}}$

51. Sequences vs. series

a. Find the limit of $\left\{\left(-\dfrac{4}{5}\right)^k\right\}$.

b. Evaluate $\displaystyle\sum_{k=0}^{\infty} \left(-\frac{4}{5}\right)^k$.

52. Sequences vs. series

a. Find the limit of $\left\{\dfrac{1}{k} - \dfrac{1}{k + 1}\right\}$.

b. Evaluate $\displaystyle\sum_{k=1}^{\infty} \left(\frac{1}{k} - \frac{1}{k + 1}\right)$.

53. Partial sums Let S_n be the nth partial sum of $\displaystyle\sum_{k=1}^{\infty} a_k = 8$. Find $\displaystyle\lim_{k \to \infty} a_k$ and $\displaystyle\lim_{n \to \infty} S_n$.

54. Remainder term Let R_n be the remainder associated with $\displaystyle\sum_{k=1}^{\infty} \frac{1}{k^5}$.

Find an upper bound for R_n (in terms of n). How many terms of the series must be summed to approximate the series with an error less than 10^{-4}?

55. Conditional p-series Find the values of p for which $\displaystyle\sum_{k=1}^{\infty} \frac{(-1)^k}{k^p}$ converges conditionally.

56. Logarithmic p-series Show that the series $\displaystyle\sum_{k=2}^{\infty} \frac{1}{k(\ln k)^p}$ converges provided $p > 1$.

57. Error in a finite sum Approximate the series $\displaystyle\sum_{k=1}^{\infty} \frac{1}{5^k}$ by evaluating the first 20 terms. Compute the maximum error in the approximation.

58. Error in a finite sum Approximate the series $\displaystyle\sum_{k=1}^{\infty} \frac{1}{k^5}$ by evaluating the first 20 terms. Compute the maximum error in the approximation.

59. Error in a finite alternating sum How many terms of the series $\displaystyle\sum_{k=1}^{\infty} \frac{(-1)^{k+1}}{k^4}$ must be summed to ensure that the maximum error is less than 10^{-8}?

60. Equations involving series Solve the following equations for x.

a. $\displaystyle\sum_{k=0}^{\infty} e^{kx} = 2$

b. $\displaystyle\sum_{k=0}^{\infty} (3x)^k = 4$

c. $\displaystyle\sum_{k=1}^{\infty} \left(\frac{x}{kx - \frac{x}{2}} - \frac{x}{kx + \frac{x}{2}}\right) = 6$

61. Building a tunnel—first scenario A crew of workers is constructing a tunnel through a mountain. Understandably, the rate of construction decreases because rocks and earth must be removed a greater distance as the tunnel gets longer. Suppose that each week the crew digs 0.95 of the distance it dug the previous week. In the first week, the crew constructed 100 m of tunnel.

a. How far does the crew dig in 10 weeks? 20 weeks? N weeks?
b. What is the longest tunnel the crew can build at this rate?

62. Building a tunnel—second scenario As in Exercise 61, a crew of workers is constructing a tunnel. The time required to dig 100 m increases by 10% each week, starting with 1 week to dig the first 100 m. Can the crew complete a 1.5-km (1500-m) tunnel in 30 weeks? Explain.

63. Pages of circles On page 1 of a book, there is one circle of radius 1. On page 2, there are two circles of radius $\frac{1}{2}$. On page n there are 2^{n-1} circles of radius 2^{-n+1}.

a. What is the sum of the areas of the circles on page n of the book?
b. Assuming the book continues indefinitely ($n \to \infty$), what is the sum of the areas of all the circles in the book?

64. Sequence on a calculator Let $\{x_n\}$ be generated by the recurrence relation $x_0 = 1$ and $x_{n+1} = x_n + \cos x_n$, for $n = 0, 1, 2, \ldots$. Use a calculator (in radian mode) to generate as many terms of the sequence $\{x_n\}$ needed to find the integer p such that $\displaystyle\lim_{n \to \infty} x_n = \pi/p$.

65. A savings plan Suppose that you open a savings account by depositing $100. The account earns interest at an annual rate of 3%/yr (0.25%/month). At the end of each month, you earn interest on the current balance, and then you deposit $100. Let B_n be the balance at the beginning of the nth month, where $B_0 = \$100$.

a. Find a recurrence relation for the sequence $\{B_n\}$.
b. Find an explicit formula that gives B_n, for $n = 0, 1, 2, 3, \ldots$.

66. Sequences of integrals Find the limits of the sequences $\{a_n\}$ and $\{b_n\}$.

a. $a_n = \displaystyle\int_0^1 x^n \, dx, \ n \geq 1$

b. $b_n = \displaystyle\int_1^n \frac{dx}{x^p}, \ p > 1, n \geq 1$

67. Sierpinski triangle The fractal called the *Sierpinski triangle* is the limit of a sequence of figures. Starting with the equilateral triangle with sides of length 1, an inverted equilateral triangle with sides of length $\frac{1}{2}$ is removed. Then, three inverted equilateral triangles with sides of length $\frac{1}{4}$ are removed from this figure (see figure). The process continues in this way. Let T_n be the total area of the removed triangles after stage n of the process. The area of an equilateral triangle with side length L is $A = \sqrt{3}L^2/4$.

a. Find T_1 and T_2, the total area of the removed triangles after stages 1 and 2, respectively.

b. Find T_n, for $n = 1, 2, 3, \ldots$.

c. Find $\lim_{n \to \infty} T_n$.

d. What is the area of the original triangle that remains as $n \to \infty$?

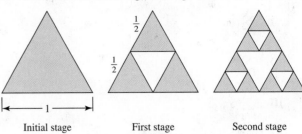

Initial stage   First stage   Second stage

68. Max sine sequence Let $a_n = \max\{\sin 1, \sin 2, \ldots, \sin n\}$, for $n = 1, 2, 3, \ldots$, where max $\{\ldots\}$ denotes the maximum element of the set. Does $\{a_n\}$ converge? If so, make a conjecture about the limit.

AP® **PRACTICE QUESTIONS**   *The following questions are intended to help you prepare for the AP exam. They are not questions from actual AP exams.*

Section 1 Part A, Multiple Choice, No Technology

1. The number $0.009009009\ldots$, which can also be expressed as $0.\overline{009}$, is equal to which of the following quantities?

I. $\dfrac{1}{110}$

II. $\displaystyle\sum_{k=1}^{\infty} \dfrac{9}{1000^k}$

III. $\dfrac{1}{111}$

(A) I only   (B) II only
(C) III only   (D) I and II only
(E) II and III only

2. Evaluate $\displaystyle\lim_{n \to \infty} \dfrac{3n^2 - n + 1}{\sqrt{4n^4 + 1}}$.

(A) $\dfrac{3}{4}$ (B) $\dfrac{1}{2}$

(C) 0 (D) $\dfrac{3}{2}$

(E) The limit does not exist.

3. The infinite series $\displaystyle\sum_{k=1}^{\infty} \dfrac{(-e)^k}{\pi^{k-1}}$

(A) Diverges.
(B) Converges, but the exact value of this series cannot be determined.
(C) Equals 0.
(D) Equals $\dfrac{e}{e + \pi}$.
(E) Equals $-\dfrac{e\pi}{e + \pi}$.

4. Which of the following series converge to 3?

I. $\displaystyle\sum_{k=1}^{\infty} \dfrac{3k^2}{k^2 + 4}$

II. $\displaystyle\sum_{k=0}^{\infty} \dfrac{2}{3^k}$

III. $\displaystyle\sum_{k=1}^{\infty} \dfrac{(-1)^{k+1}4}{3^{k-1}}$

(A) I only   (B) II only
(C) III only   (D) I and II only
(E) II and III only

5. Which of the following sequences converge to 2?

I. $a_n = 2n^{1/n}$

II. $b_n = 2\left(\dfrac{1}{n}\right)^n$

III. $c_n = \dfrac{\sqrt{4n^2 + 12}}{n}$

(A) I and II only   (B) I and III only
(C) I only   (D) II only
(E) III only

6. Assume $\displaystyle\sum_{k=1}^{\infty} a_k$ is a series with positive terms that converges to S. Let $S_n = \displaystyle\sum_{k=1}^{n} a_k$. Which of the following statements is *not* true?

(A) $S_n < S$
(B) $S_n < S_{n+1}$, for all $n \geq 1$
(C) $\displaystyle\lim_{n \to \infty} S_n < S$
(D) $\{S_n\}$ is a sequence of partial sums.
(E) $\displaystyle\lim_{k \to \infty} a_k = 0$

7. Which of the following series diverge?

    I. $\displaystyle\sum_{k=1}^{\infty} (\ln 2)^k$

    II. $\displaystyle\sum_{k=1}^{\infty} \frac{(-1)^k}{k}$

    III. $\displaystyle\sum_{k=1}^{\infty} \frac{3}{k^{3/2}}$

    (A) I only
    (B) II only
    (C) III only
    (D) None of the series diverges.
    (E) All the series diverge.

8. For what values of p does the series $\displaystyle\sum_{k=0}^{\infty} \frac{2}{(k+1)^p}$ converge?

    (A) For all real numbers p
    (B) For real numbers $p > 1$
    (C) For real numbers $p < 0$
    (D) For real numbers $p > 0$
    (E) For real numbers $p \geq 1$

9. Which of the following statements is true of the series $\displaystyle\sum_{k=1}^{\infty} \frac{(-1)^{k+1}}{k^2}$?

    (A) It converges conditionally.
    (B) Its sequence of partial sums is increasing.
    (C) It diverges.
    (D) Its value is zero.
    (E) It converges absolutely.

10. The sum of the geometric series $\dfrac{2}{5} + \dfrac{3}{10} + \dfrac{9}{40} + \dfrac{27}{160} + \cdots$ is

    (A) $\dfrac{1}{10}$.
    (B) $\dfrac{8}{5}$.
    (C) $\dfrac{3}{2}$.
    (D) $\dfrac{7}{6}$.
    (E) $\dfrac{5}{4}$.

11. Suppose f is continuous, positive, and decreasing for $x \geq 1$ with $0 < \displaystyle\int_1^{\infty} f(x)\,dx = A < \infty$. Which of the following statements is true in general?

    (A) $\displaystyle\sum_{k=1}^{\infty} f(k)$ converges.

    (B) $\displaystyle\sum_{k=1}^{\infty} f(k) = A$

    (C) $\displaystyle\sum_{k=1}^{\infty} f(k)$ could converge or diverge.

    (D) $\displaystyle\sum_{k=1}^{\infty} f(k)$ diverges

    (E) $\displaystyle\sum_{k=1}^{\infty} f(k) < A$

Section 1 Part B, Multiple Choice, Technology Allowed

12. How many terms of the convergent series $\displaystyle\sum_{k=1}^{\infty} \frac{(-1)^{k+1}}{k^4}$ must be summed (at a minimum) to ensure that the remainder is less than 2×10^{-4} in magnitude?

    (A) 99
    (B) 11
    (C) 8
    (D) 101
    (E) 21

13. Which of the following series converge?

    I. $\displaystyle\sum_{k=1}^{\infty} \frac{3^k + 4}{5^k}$

    II. $\displaystyle\sum_{k=1}^{\infty} \frac{k!k!}{(2k)!}$

    III. $\displaystyle\sum_{k=1}^{\infty} \frac{2^k}{k!}$

    (A) I only
    (B) I and II only
    (C) III only
    (D) None of the series converges.
    (E) All these series converge.

14. How many terms of the convergent series $\displaystyle\sum_{k=2}^{\infty} \frac{(-1)^{k+1}}{k^{3/2}\ln k}$ must be summed (at a minimum) to ensure that the remainder is less than 10^{-2} in magnitude?

    (A) Up to and including the $k = 11$ term
    (B) Up to and including the $k = 13$ term
    (C) Up to and including the $k = 9$ term
    (D) Up to and including the $k = 21$ term
    (E) Up to and including the $k = 5$ term

Section 2 Part A, Free Response, Technology Allowed

1. Suppose you want to approximate the value of the convergent series $\displaystyle\sum_{k=0}^{\infty} \frac{(-1)^k}{(2k+1)^3} = 1 - \frac{1}{3^3} + \frac{1}{5^3} - \cdots$.

    a. What is the fewest number of terms of the series you should use to ensure that the remainder is less than 5×10^{-4} in magnitude? Justify your answer.
    b. Find the approximation that results if you use the terms in part (a).
    c. Does the approximation in part (b) underestimate or overestimate the value of the series? Explain your answer.

Section 2 Part B, Free Response, No Technology

2. A ball is dropped, and on each bounce, it returns to 80% of its previous height.

    a. Determine the total distance the ball travels in the upward direction if it is dropped from a height of 10 ft.
    b. Determine the total distance the ball travels in the downward direction if it is dropped from a height of 10 ft.

c. Determine the height from which a ball must be dropped so that its total distance traveled in the downward direction is 150 ft.

d. Another ball is dropped from a height of 50 ft, and each time it bounces, it rebounds to a fraction r of its previous height, where $0 < r < 1$. Determine the fraction r if the total distance traveled by the ball in the downward direction is 300 ft.

3. Consider the series $\sum_{k=1}^{\infty} \frac{k+1}{k^2 + 2k}$.

   a. Apply the Divergence Test to this series. What do you conclude?

   b. Apply the Ratio Test to the series. What do you conclude?

   c. Apply the Integral Test to the series. What do you conclude?

4. Consider the series $S = \sum_{k=0}^{\infty} \left(-\frac{2}{3}\right)^k$.

   a. Find a formula that gives the value of $S_n = \sum_{k=0}^{n} \left(-\frac{2}{3}\right)^k$, for $n \geq 1$.

   b. Evaluate $\lim_{n \to \infty} S_n$, where S_n is given in part (a).

   c. Explain the relationship between S and $\lim_{n \to \infty} S_n$.

5. Let $S = \sum_{k=1}^{\infty} \frac{2}{k^2 + 1}$.

   a. Evaluate the integral $I = \int_1^{\infty} \frac{2}{x^2 + 1}\, dx$.

   b. Use a comparison test to determine whether the series that defines S converges.

   c. Use the Integral Test to determine whether the series that defines S converges.

6. **a.** Evaluate $\lim_{n \to \infty} n^2 e^{-n}$.

   b. Determine whether the series $\sum_{k=1}^{\infty} (-1)^{k+1} k^2 e^{-k}$ converges.

   c. Determine whether the series $\sum_{k=1}^{\infty} k^2 e^{-k}$ converges.

   d. Does the series in part (b) converge conditionally or absolutely?

Chapter 9 Guided Projects

Applications of the material in this chapter and related topics can be found in the following Guided Projects. For additional information, see the Preface.

- Chaos!
- Financial matters
- Periodic drug dosing
- Economic stimulus packages

- The mathematics of loans
- Archimedes' approximation to π
- Exact values of infinite series
- Conditional convergence in a crystal lattice

10 Power Series

Imagine throwing a stone into a calm lake or striking the head of a large bass drum. Both these actions excite circular waves on the surface that propagate outward from the point of contact. These circular waves—as well as propagating waves in other geometries—are described by differential equations (Chapter 8). Sometimes these wave equations have solutions that consist of familiar functions, such as sines and cosines. However, more typically, the solutions of wave equations cannot be written in nice compact formulas. Instead, the simplest way to write these solutions is in terms of *power series*, which is the subject of this chapter.

Power series provide an entirely new way to represent both familiar functions and new functions that you have not yet encountered. For example, the graph below shows three solutions to a circular wave equation. These solutions are from the family of *Bessel functions* and all three functions are defined in terms of a power series. This chapter provides just a glimpse of a new branch of mathematics that has immense theoretical and practical importance.

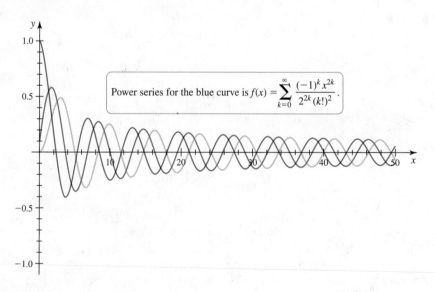

Power series for the blue curve is $f(x) = \sum\limits_{k=0}^{\infty} \dfrac{(-1)^k x^{2k}}{2^{2k}(k!)^2}$.

Chapter Preview   Until now, you have worked with infinite series consisting of real numbers. In this chapter, we make a seemingly small but significant change by considering infinite series whose terms include powers of a variable. With this change, an infinite series becomes a *power series*. One of the most fundamental ideas in all of calculus is that functions can be represented by power series. As a first step toward this result, we look at approximating functions using polynomials. The transition from polynomials to power series is then straightforward, and we learn how to represent the familiar functions of mathematics in terms of power series called *Taylor series*. The remainder of the chapter is devoted to the properties and many uses of Taylor series.

10.1 Approximating Functions with Polynomials

Power series provide a way to represent familiar functions and to define new functions. For this reason, power series—like sets and functions—are among the most fundamental entities in mathematics.

What Is a Power Series?

A *power series* is an infinite series of the form

$$\sum_{k=0}^{\infty} c_k x^k = \underbrace{c_0 + c_1 x + c_2 x^2 + \cdots + c_n x^n}_{n\text{th-degree polynomial}} + \underbrace{c_{n+1} x^{n+1} + \cdots}_{\text{terms continue}},$$

or, more generally,

$$\sum_{k=0}^{\infty} c_k (x - a)^k = \underbrace{c_0 + c_1 (x - a) + \cdots + c_n (x - a)^n}_{n\text{th-degree polynomial}} + \underbrace{c_{n+1}(x - a)^{n+1} + \cdots}_{\text{terms continue}},$$

where the *center* of the series a and the coefficients c_k are constants. This type of series is called a power series because it consists of powers of x or $(x - a)$.

Viewed another way, a power series is built up from polynomials of increasing degree, as shown in the following progression.

$$
\left.
\begin{aligned}
&\text{Degree 0: } c_0 \\
&\text{Degree 1: } c_0 + c_1 x \\
&\text{Degree 2: } c_0 + c_1 x + c_2 x^2 \\
&\qquad \vdots \qquad \vdots \qquad \vdots \\
&\text{Degree } n: c_0 + c_1 x + c_2 x^2 + \cdots + c_n x^n = \sum_{k=0}^{n} c_k x^k
\end{aligned}
\right\} \text{Polynomials}
$$

$$\qquad \vdots \qquad \vdots \qquad \vdots$$

$$c_0 + c_1 x + c_2 x^2 + \cdots + c_n x^n + \cdots = \sum_{k=0}^{\infty} c_k x^k \Big\} \text{Power series}$$

According to this perspective, a power series is a "super-polynomial." For this reason, we begin our exploration of power series by using polynomials to approximate functions.

Polynomial Approximation

An important observation motivates our work. To evaluate a polynomial $\left(\text{say, } f(x) = x^8 - 4x^5 + \frac{1}{2}\right)$, all we need is arithmetic—addition, subtraction, multiplication, and division. However, algebraic functions $\left(\text{say, } f(x) = \sqrt[3]{x^4 - 1}\right)$ and the trigonometric, logarithmic, and exponential functions usually cannot be evaluated exactly using arithmetic. Therefore, it makes practical sense to use the simplest of functions, polynomials, to approximate more complicated functions.

Linear and Quadratic Approximation

In Section 4.5, you learned that if a function f is differentiable at a point a, then it can be approximated near a by its tangent line, which is the linear approximation to f at the point a. Recall that the linear approximation at a is

$$y - f(a) = f'(a)(x - a) \quad \text{or} \quad y = f(a) + f'(a)(x - a).$$

Because the linear approximation is a first-degree polynomial, we name it p_1:

$$p_1(x) = f(a) + f'(a)(x - a).$$

This polynomial has some important properties: It matches f in *value* and in *slope* at a. In other words (Figure 10.1),

$$p_1(a) = f(a) \quad \text{and} \quad p_1{}'(a) = f'(a).$$

Linear approximation works well if f has a fairly constant slope near a. However, if f has a lot of curvature near a, then the tangent line may not provide an accurate approximation. To remedy this situation, we create a quadratic approximating polynomial by adding one new term to the linear polynomial. Denoting this new polynomial p_2, we let

$$p_2(x) = \underbrace{f(a) + f'(a)(x - a)}_{p_1(x)} + \underbrace{c_2(x - a)^2}_{\text{quadratic term}}.$$

The new term consists of a coefficient c_2 that must be determined and a quadratic factor $(x - a)^2$.

To determine c_2 and to ensure that p_2 is a good approximation to f near the point a, we require that p_2 agree with f in value, slope, and concavity at a; that is, p_2 must satisfy the matching conditions

$$p_2(a) = f(a), p_2{}'(a) = f'(a), \quad \text{and} \quad p_2{}''(a) = f''(a),$$

where we assume that f and its first and second derivatives exist at a (Figure 10.2).

> ▶ Matching concavity (second derivatives) ensures that the graph of p_2 bends in the same direction as the graph of f at a.

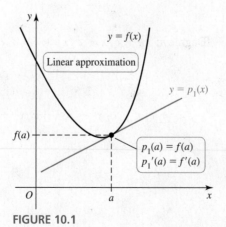

FIGURE 10.1

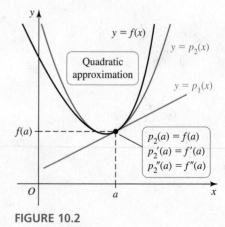

FIGURE 10.2

Substituting $x = a$ into p_2, we see immediately that $p_2(a) = f(a)$, so the first matching condition is met. Differentiating p_2 once, we have

$$p_2'(x) = f'(a) + 2c_2(x - a).$$

So $p_2'(a) = f'(a)$, and the second matching condition is also met. Because $p_2''(a) = 2c_2$, the third matching condition is

$$p_2''(a) = 2c_2 = f''(a).$$

It follows that $c_2 = \frac{1}{2}f''(a)$; therefore, the quadratic approximating polynomial is

$$p_2(x) = \underbrace{f(a) + f'(a)(x - a)}_{p_1(x)} + \frac{f''(a)}{2}(x - a)^2.$$

EXAMPLE 1   Linear and quadratic approximations for $\ln x$

a. Find the linear approximation to $f(x) = \ln x$ at $x = 1$.

b. Find the quadratic approximation to $f(x) = \ln x$ at $x = 1$.

c. Use these approximations to estimate the value of $\ln 1.05$.

SOLUTION

a. Note that $f(1) = 0$, $f'(x) = 1/x$, and $f'(1) = 1$. Therefore, the linear approximation to $f(x) = \ln x$ at $x = 1$ is

$$p_1(x) = f(1) + f'(1)(x - 1) = 0 + 1(x - 1) = x - 1.$$

As shown in Figure 10.3, p_1 matches f in value $(p_1(1) = f(1))$ and in slope $(p_1'(1) = f'(1))$ at $x = 1$.

b. We first compute $f''(x) = -1/x^2$ and $f''(1) = -1$. Building on the linear approximation found in part (a), the quadratic approximation is

$$p_2(x) = \underbrace{x - 1}_{p_1(x)} + \underbrace{\frac{1}{2}f''(1)(x - 1)^2}_{c_2}$$

$$= (x - 1) - \frac{1}{2}(x - 1)^2.$$

Because p_2 matches f in value, slope, and concavity at $x = 1$, it provides a better approximation to f near $x = 1$ (Figure 10.3).

c. To approximate $\ln 1.05$, we substitute $x = 1.05$ into each polynomial approximation:

$$p_1(1.05) = 1.05 - 1 = 0.05 \text{ and} \qquad \text{Linear approximation}$$

$$p_2(1.05) = (1.05 - 1) - \frac{1}{2}(1.05 - 1)^2 \approx 0.0488. \quad \text{Quadratic approximation}$$

The value of $\ln 1.05$ given by a calculator, rounded to five decimal places, is 0.04879, showing the improvement in quadratic approximation over linear approximation.

Related Exercises 7–14 ◄

We now extend the idea of linear and quadratic approximating polynomials to obtain higher degree polynomials that generally provide better approximations.

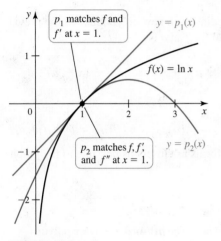

p_1 matches f and f' at $x = 1$.

$y = p_1(x)$

$f(x) = \ln x$

p_2 matches f, f', and f'' at $x = 1$.

$y = p_2(x)$

FIGURE 10.3

Taylor Polynomials

Assume that f and its first n derivatives exist at a; our goal is to find an nth-degree polynomial that approximates the values of f near a. The first step is to use p_2 to obtain a cubic polynomial p_3 of the form

$$p_3(x) = p_2(x) + c_3(x - a)^3$$

that satisfies the four matching conditions

$$p_3(a) = f(a), \quad p_3'(a) = f'(a), \quad p_3''(a) = f''(a), \quad \text{and} \quad p_3'''(a) = f'''(a).$$

Because p_3 is built "on top of" p_2, the first three matching conditions are met. The last condition, $p_3'''(a) = f'''(a)$, is used to determine c_3. A short calculation shows that $p_3'''(x) = 3 \cdot 2c_3 = 3!c_3$, so the last matching condition is $p_3'''(a) = 3!c_3 = f'''(a)$. Solving for c_3, we have $c_3 = \dfrac{f'''(a)}{3!}$. Therefore, the cubic approximating polynomial is

$$p_3(x) = \underbrace{f(a) + f'(a)(x - a) + \frac{f''(a)}{2!}(x - a)^2}_{p_2(x)} + \frac{f'''(a)}{3!}(x - a)^3.$$

QUICK CHECK 1 Verify that p_3 satisfies $p_3^{(k)}(a) = f^{(k)}(a)$, for $k = 0, 1, 2$, and 3. ◄

Continuing in this fashion (Exercise 74), building each new polynomial on the previous polynomial, the nth approximating polynomial for f at a is

$$p_n(x) = f(a) + f'(a)(x - a) + \frac{f''(a)}{2!}(x - a)^2 + \cdots + \frac{f^{(n)}(a)}{n!}(x - a)^n.$$

It satisfies the $n + 1$ matching conditions

$$p_n(a) = f(a), \quad p_n'(a) = f'(a), \quad p_n''(a) = f''(a), \ldots, p_n^{(n)}(a) = f^{(n)}(a).$$

These conditions ensure that the graph of p_n conforms as closely as possible to the graph of f near a (Figure 10.4).

▶ Building on ideas that were already circulating in the early 18th century, Brook Taylor (1685–1731) published Taylor's Theorem in 1715. He is also credited with discovering integration by parts.

▶ Recall that $2! = 2 \cdot 1$, $3! = 3 \cdot 2 \cdot 1$, $k! = k \cdot (k - 1)!$, and by definition $0! = 1$.

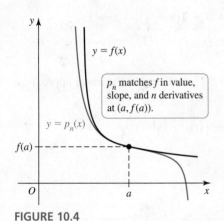

p_n matches f in value, slope, and n derivatives at $(a, f(a))$.

FIGURE 10.4

▶ Recall that $f^{(n)}$ denotes the nth derivative of f. By convention, the zeroth derivative $f^{(0)}$ is f itself.

DEFINITION Taylor Polynomials

Let f be a function with f', f'', ..., $f^{(n)}$ defined at a. The **nth-order Taylor polynomial** for f with its **center** at a, denoted p_n, has the property that it matches f in value, slope, and all derivatives up to the nth derivative at a; that is,

$$p_n(a) = f(a), p_n'(a) = f'(a), \ldots, p_n^{(n)}(a) = f^{(n)}(a).$$

The nth-order Taylor polynomial centered at a is

$$p_n(x) = f(a) + f'(a)(x - a) + \frac{f''(a)}{2!}(x - a)^2 + \cdots + \frac{f^{(n)}(a)}{n!}(x - a)^n.$$

More compactly, $p_n(x) = \displaystyle\sum_{k=0}^{n} c_k(x - a)^k$, where the **coefficients** are

$$c_k = \frac{f^{(k)}(a)}{k!}, \qquad \text{for } k = 0, 1, 2, \ldots, n.$$

EXAMPLE 2 **Taylor polynomials for $\sin x$** Find the Taylor polynomials $p_1, \ldots, p_7$ centered at $x = 0$ for $f(x) = \sin x$.

SOLUTION We begin by differentiating f repeatedly and evaluating the derivatives at 0; these calculations allow us to compute the coefficients c_k, for $k = 0, 1, \ldots, 7$. Notice that a pattern emerges:

$$f(x) = \sin x \Rightarrow f(0) = 0$$
$$f'(x) = \cos x \Rightarrow f'(0) = 1$$
$$f''(x) = -\sin x \Rightarrow f''(0) = 0$$
$$f'''(x) = -\cos x \Rightarrow f'''(0) = -1$$
$$f^{(4)}(x) = \sin x \Rightarrow f^{(4)}(0) = 0.$$

The derivatives of $\sin x$ at 0 cycle through the values $\{0, 1, 0, -1\}$. Therefore, $f^{(5)}(0) = 1$, $f^{(6)}(0) = 0$, and $f^{(7)}(0) = -1$.

We now construct the Taylor polynomials that approximate $f(x) = \sin x$ near 0, beginning with the linear polynomial. The polynomial of order $n = 1$ is

$$p_1(x) = f(0) + f'(0)(x - 0) = x,$$

whose graph is the line through the origin with slope 1 (Figure 10.5). Notice that f and p_1 agree in value ($f(0) = p_1(0) = 0$) and in slope ($f'(0) = p_1'(0) = 1$) at 0. We see that p_1 provides a good fit to f near 0, but the graphs diverge visibly for $|x| > 0.5$.

The polynomial of order $n = 2$ is

$$p_2(x) = \underbrace{f(0)}_{0} + \underbrace{f'(0)x}_{1} + \underbrace{\frac{f''(0)}{2!}x^2}_{0} = x,$$

so p_2 is the same as p_1.

The polynomial of order $n = 3$ is

$$p_3(x) = \underbrace{f(0) + f'(0)x + \frac{f''(0)}{2!}x^2}_{p_2(x) = x} + \underbrace{\frac{f'''(0)}{3!}x^3}_{-1/3!} = x - \frac{x^3}{6}.$$

We have designed p_3 to agree with f in value, slope, concavity, and third derivative at 0 (Figure 10.6). Consequently, p_3 provides a better approximation to f over a larger interval than p_1.

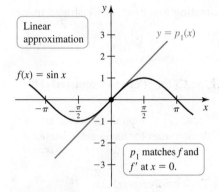

FIGURE 10.5

➤ It is worth repeating that the next polynomial in the sequence is obtained by adding one new term to the previous polynomial. For example,

$$p_3(x) = p_2(x) + \frac{f'''(a)}{3!}(x - a)^3.$$

QUICK CHECK 2 Verify each of the following properties for $f(x) = \sin x$: $p_3(x) = x - x^3/6$, $f(0) = p_3(0), f'(0) = p_3'(0)$, $f''(0) = p_3''(0)$, and $f'''(0) = p_3'''(0)$. ◄

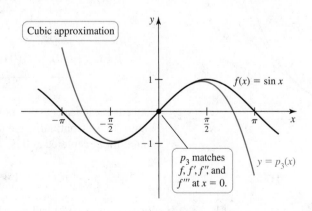

FIGURE 10.6

The procedure for finding Taylor polynomials may be extended to polynomials of any order. Because the even derivatives of $f(x) = \sin x$ are zero at 0, $p_4(x) = p_3(x)$. For the same reason, $p_6(x) = p_5(x)$:

$$p_6(x) = p_5(x) = x - \frac{x^3}{3!} + \frac{x^5}{5!}. \qquad \frac{f^{(5)}(0)}{5!} = \frac{1}{5!}$$

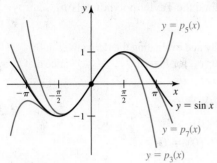

FIGURE 10.7

Finally, the Taylor polynomial of order $n = 7$ is

$$p_7(x) = x - \frac{x^3}{3!} + \frac{x^5}{5!} - \frac{x^7}{7!}. \qquad \frac{f^{(7)}(0)}{7!} = -\frac{1}{7!}$$

From Figure 10.7 we see that as the order of the Taylor polynomials increases, more accurate approximations to $f(x) = \sin x$ are obtained over larger intervals centered at 0. For example, p_7 is a good fit to $f(x) = \sin x$ over the interval $[-\pi, \pi]$. Notice that $\sin x$ and its Taylor polynomials (centered at 0) are all odd functions.

Related Exercises 15–22◄

QUICK CHECK 3 Why do the Taylor polynomials for $\sin x$ centered at 0 consist only of odd powers of x? ◄

Approximations with Taylor Polynomials

Taylor polynomials find widespread use in approximating functions, as illustrated in the following examples.

EXAMPLE 3 Taylor polynomials for e^x

a. Find the Taylor polynomials of order $n = 0, 1, 2$, and 3 for $f(x) = e^x$ centered at 0. Graph f and the polynomials.

b. Use the polynomials in part (a) to approximate $e^{0.1}$ and $e^{-0.25}$. Find the absolute errors, $|f(x) - p_n(x)|$, in the approximations. Use calculator values for the exact values of f.

> Recall that if c is an approximation to x, the absolute error in c is $|x - c|$ and the relative error in c is $|x - c|/|x|$. We use *error* to refer to *absolute error*.

SOLUTION

a. Recall that the formula for the coefficients in the Taylor polynomials is

$$c_k = \frac{f^{(k)}(0)}{k!}, \qquad \text{for } k = 0, 1, 2, \ldots, n.$$

With $f(x) = e^x$, we have $f^{(k)}(x) = e^x$. Therefore, $f^{(k)}(0) = 1$ and $c_k = 1/k!$, for $k = 0, 1, 2, 3 \ldots$. The first four polynomials are

$$p_0(x) = f(0) = 1,$$
$$p_1(x) = \underbrace{f(0)}_{p_0(x) = 1} + \underbrace{f'(0)}_{1}x = 1 + x,$$

$$p_2(x) = \underbrace{f(0) + f'(0)x}_{p_1(x) = 1 + x} + \underbrace{\frac{f''(0)}{2!}}_{1/2}x^2 = 1 + x + \frac{x^2}{2}, \quad \text{and}$$

$$p_3(x) = \underbrace{f(0) + f'(0)x + \frac{f''(0)}{2!}x^2}_{p_2(x) = 1 + x + x^2/2} + \underbrace{\frac{f^{(3)}(0)}{3!}}_{1/6}x^3 = 1 + x + \frac{x^2}{2} + \frac{x^3}{6}.$$

Notice that each successive polynomial provides a better fit to $f(x) = e^x$ near 0 (Figure 10.8). Continuing the pattern in these polynomials, the nth-order Taylor polynomial for e^x centered at 0 is

> Taylor polynomials for $f(x) = e^x$ centered at 0. Approximations improve as n increases.

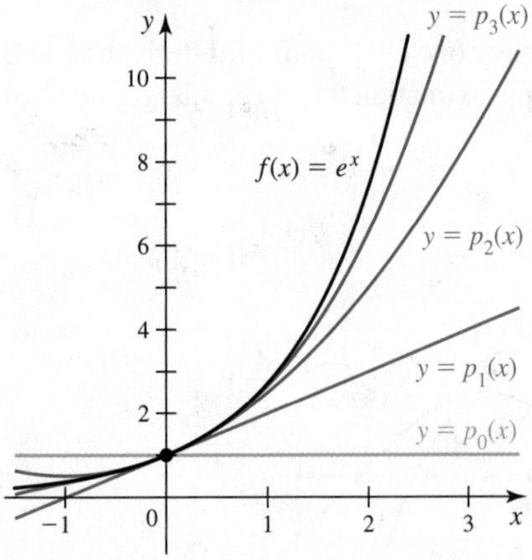

FIGURE 10.8

$$p_n(x) = 1 + x + \frac{x^2}{2!} + \frac{x^3}{3!} + \cdots + \frac{x^n}{n!} = \sum_{k=0}^{n} \frac{x^k}{k!}.$$

b. We evaluate $p_n(0.1)$ and $p_n(-0.25)$, for $n = 0, 1, 2, 3$, and compare these values to the calculator values of $e^{0.1} \approx 1.1051709$ and $e^{-0.25} \approx 0.77880078$. The results are shown in Table 10.1. Observe that the errors in the approximations decrease as n increases. In addition, the errors in approximating $e^{0.1}$ are smaller in magnitude than the errors in approximating $e^{-0.25}$ because $x = 0.1$ is closer to the center of the polynomials than $x = -0.25$. Reasonable approximations based on these calculations are $e^{0.1} \approx 1.105$ and $e^{-0.25} \approx 0.78$.

> A rule of thumb in finding estimates based on several approximations: Keep all the digits that are common to the last two approximations after rounding.

QUICK CHECK 4 Write out the next two Taylor polynomials p_4 and p_5 for $f(x) = e^x$ in Example 3. ◄

Table 10.1

n	Approximation $p_n(0.1)$	Absolute Error $\lvert e^{0.1} - p_n(0.1) \rvert$	Approximation $p_n(-0.25)$	Absolute Error $\lvert e^{-0.25} - p_n(-0.25) \rvert$
0	1	1.1×10^{-1}	1	2.2×10^{-1}
1	1.1	5.2×10^{-3}	0.75	2.9×10^{-2}
2	1.105	1.7×10^{-4}	0.78125	2.4×10^{-3}
3	1.105167	4.3×10^{-6}	0.778646	1.5×10^{-4}

Related Exercises 23–28 ◄

EXAMPLE 4   Approximating a real number using Taylor polynomials Use polynomials of order $n = 0, 1, 2,$ and 3 to approximate $\sqrt{18}$.

SOLUTION Letting $f(x) = \sqrt{x}$, we choose the center $a = 16$ because it is near 18, and f and its derivatives are easy to evaluate at 16. The Taylor polynomials have the form

$$p_n(x) = f(16) + f'(16)(x - 16) + \frac{f''(16)}{2!}(x - 16)^2 + \cdots + \frac{f^{(n)}(16)}{n!}(x - 16)^n.$$

We now evaluate the required derivatives:

$$f(x) = \sqrt{x} \Rightarrow f(16) = 4$$

$$f'(x) = \frac{1}{2}x^{-1/2} \Rightarrow f'(16) = \frac{1}{8}$$

$$f''(x) = -\frac{1}{4}x^{-3/2} \Rightarrow f''(16) = -\frac{1}{256}$$

$$f'''(x) = \frac{3}{8}x^{-5/2} \Rightarrow f'''(16) = \frac{3}{8192}.$$

Therefore, the polynomial p_3 (which includes p_0, p_1, and p_2) is

$$p_3(x) = \underbrace{4}_{p_0(x)} + \frac{1}{8}(x - 16) - \frac{1}{512}(x - 16)^2 + \frac{1}{16{,}384}(x - 16)^3.$$

The Taylor polynomials (Figure 10.9) give better approximations to f as the order of the polynomial increases.

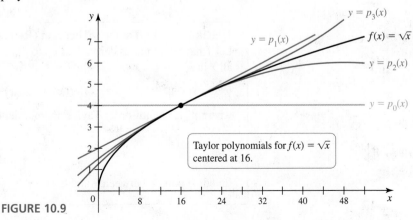

Taylor polynomials for $f(x) = \sqrt{x}$ centered at 16.

FIGURE 10.9

Letting $x = 18$, we obtain the approximations to $\sqrt{18}$ and the associated absolute errors shown in Table 10.2. (A calculator is used for the value of $\sqrt{18}$.) As expected, the errors decrease as n increases. Based on these calculations, a reasonable approximation is $\sqrt{18} \approx 4.24$.

Table 10.2

n	Approximation $p_n(18)$	Absolute Error $\lvert\sqrt{18} - p_n(18)\rvert$
0	4	2.4×10^{-1}
1	4.25	7.4×10^{-3}
2	4.242188	4.5×10^{-4}
3	4.242676	3.5×10^{-5}

Related Exercises 29–48 ◀

QUICK CHECK 5 At what point would you center the Taylor polynomials for $\sqrt{x}$ and $\sqrt[4]{x}$ to approximate $\sqrt{51}$ and $\sqrt[4]{15}$, respectively? ◀

Remainder in a Taylor Polynomial

Taylor polynomials provide good approximations to functions near a specific point. But how accurate are the approximations? To answer this question we define the *remainder* in a Taylor polynomial. If p_n is the Taylor polynomial for f of order n, then the remainder at the point x is

$$R_n(x) = f(x) - p_n(x).$$

The absolute value of the remainder is the error made in approximating $f(x)$ by $p_n(x)$. Equivalently, we have $f(x) = p_n(x) + R_n(x)$, which says that f consists of two components: the polynomial approximation and the associated remainder.

> **DEFINITION Remainder in a Taylor Polynomial**
>
> Let p_n be the Taylor polynomial of order n for f. The **remainder** in using p_n to approximate f at the point x is
>
> $$R_n(x) = f(x) - p_n(x).$$

The idea of a remainder is illustrated in Figure 10.10, where we see the remainders associated with various Taylor polynomials for $f(x) = e^x$ centered at 0 (Example 3). For fixed order n, the remainders tend to increase in magnitude as x moves farther from the center of the polynomials (in this case 0). And for fixed x, remainders decrease in magnitude to zero with increasing n.

The remainder for a Taylor polynomial may be written quite concisely, which enables us to estimate remainders. The following result is known as *Taylor's Theorem* (or the *Remainder Theorem*).

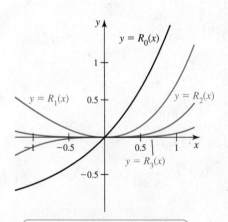

Remainders increase in magnitude as $\lvert x \rvert$ increases. Remainders decrease in magnitude to zero as n increases.

FIGURE 10.10

> **THEOREM 10.1 Taylor's Theorem (Remainder Theorem)**
>
> Let f have continuous derivatives up to $f^{(n+1)}$ on an open interval I containing a. For all x in I,
>
> $$f(x) = p_n(x) + R_n(x),$$
>
> where p_n is the nth-order Taylor polynomial for f centered at a, and the remainder is
>
> $$R_n(x) = \frac{f^{(n+1)}(c)}{(n+1)!} (x - a)^{n+1},$$
>
> for some point c between x and a.

Discussion: The remainder for a Taylor polynomial can be expressed in several different forms; the form in Theorem 10.1 is called the *Lagrange form* of the remainder. We make two observations about Theorem 10.1 and outline a proof in Exercise 92. First, the case $n = 0$ is the Mean Value Theorem (Section 4.6), which states that

$$\frac{f(x) - f(a)}{x - a} = f'(c),$$

where c is a point between x and a. Rearranging this expression we have

$$f(x) = \underbrace{f(a)}_{p_0(x)} + \underbrace{f'(c)(x - a)}_{R_0(x)},$$

$$= p_0(x) + R_0(x),$$

which is Taylor's Theorem with $n = 0$. Not surprisingly, the term $f^{(n+1)}(c)$ in Taylor's Theorem comes from a Mean Value Theorem argument.

The second observation makes the remainder easier to remember. If you write the $(n + 1)$st Taylor polynomial p_{n+1}, the highest-degree term is $\dfrac{f^{(n+1)}(a)}{(n + 1)!}(x - a)^{n+1}$. Replacing $f^{(n+1)}(a)$ with $f^{(n+1)}(c)$ results in the remainder for p_n.

Estimating the Remainder

The remainder has both practical and theoretical importance. We deal with practical matters now and theoretical matters in Section 10.3. The remainder is used to estimate errors in approximations and to determine the number of terms of a Taylor polynomial needed to achieve a prescribed accuracy.

Because c is generally unknown, the difficulty in estimating the remainder is finding a bound for $|f^{(n+1)}(c)|$. Assuming this can be done, the following theorem gives a standard estimate for the remainder term; it is called the *Lagrange error bound*.

THEOREM 10.2   Estimate of the Remainder (Lagrange Error Bound)
Let n be a fixed positive integer. Suppose there exists a number M such that $|f^{(n+1)}(c)| \le M$, for all c between a and x inclusive. The remainder in the nth-order Taylor polynomial for f centered at a satisfies

$$|R_n(x)| = |f(x) - p_n(x)| \le M \frac{|x - a|^{n+1}}{(n + 1)!}.$$

Proof: The proof requires taking the absolute value of the remainder in Theorem 10.1, replacing $|f^{(n+1)}(c)|$ with a larger quantity M, and forming an inequality.   ◀

EXAMPLE 5   Estimating the remainder for cos x Find a bound for the magnitude of the remainder for the Taylor polynomials of $f(x) = \cos x$ centered at 0.

SOLUTION According to Theorem 10.1 with $a = 0$, we have

$$R_n(x) = \frac{f^{(n+1)}(c)}{(n + 1)!}x^{n+1},$$

where c is a point between 0 and x. Notice that $f^{(n+1)}(c) = \pm\sin c$ or $f^{(n+1)}(c) = \pm\cos c$, depending on the value of n. In all cases, $|f^{(n+1)}(c)| \le 1$. Therefore, we take $M = 1$ in Theorem 10.2, and the absolute value of the remainder can be bounded as

$$|R_n(x)| = \left|\frac{f^{(n+1)}(c)}{(n + 1)!}x^{n+1}\right| \le \frac{|x|^{n+1}}{(n + 1)!}.$$

For example, if we approximate cos 0.1 using the Taylor polynomial p_{10}, the maximum error satisfies

$$|R_{10}(0.1)| \le \frac{0.1^{11}}{11!} \approx 2.5 \times 10^{-19}.$$

Related Exercises 49–54◄

EXAMPLE 6   Estimating the remainder for e^x Find a Lagrange error bound in approximating $e^{0.45}$ using the Taylor polynomial of order $n = 6$ for $f(x) = e^x$ centered at 0.

SOLUTION Using Theorem 10.2, the Lagrange error bound is given by

$$|R_n(x)| \le M\frac{|x - a|^{n+1}}{(n + 1)!},$$

where M is chosen such that $|f^{(n+1)}(c)| \le M$, for all c between a and x inclusive. Notice that $f(x) = e^x$ implies that $f^{(k)}(x) = e^x$, for $k = 0, 1, 2, \ldots$. In this particular problem, we have $n = 6$, $a = 0$, and $x = 0.45$, so the bound on the remainder takes the form

$$|R_6(0.45)| \le M\frac{|0.45 - 0|^7}{7!} \approx 7.4 \times 10^{-7}M,$$

where M is chosen such that $|f^{(7)}(c)| = e^c \le M$, for all c in the interval $[0, 0.45]$. Because e^c is an increasing function of c, its maximum value on the interval $[0, 0.45]$ occurs at $c = 0.45$, and is $e^{0.45}$. However, $e^{0.45}$ cannot be evaluated exactly (it is the number we are approximating), so we must find a number M such that $e^{0.45} \le M$. Here is one of many ways to obtain a bound: Observe that $e^{0.45} < e^{1/2} < 4^{1/2} = 2$ and take $M = 2$. Therefore, a bound on the remainder is

$$|R_6(0.45)| \le 7.4 \times 10^{-7}M \approx 1.5 \times 10^{-6}.$$

> Recall that if $f(x) = e^x$, then
> $$p_n(x) = \sum_{k=0}^{n} \frac{x^k}{k!}.$$

QUICK CHECK 6 In Example 6, find an approximate upper bound for $R_7(0.45)$. ◄

Using the Taylor polynomial derived in Example 3 with $n = 6$, the resulting approximation to $e^{0.45}$ is

$$p_6(0.45) = \sum_{k=0}^{6} \frac{0.45^k}{k!} \approx 1.568311;$$

it has an error that does not exceed 1.5×10^{-6}. *Related Exercises 55–60◄*

EXAMPLE 7   Error bound The nth-order Taylor polynomial for $f(x) = \ln(1 - x)$ centered at 0 is

$$p_n(x) = -\sum_{k=1}^{n} \frac{x^k}{k} = -x - \frac{x^2}{2} - \frac{x^3}{3} - \cdots - \frac{x^n}{n}.$$

a. Find a bound on the error in approximating $\ln(1 - x)$ by $p_3(x)$ for values of x in the interval $\left[-\frac{1}{2}, \frac{1}{2}\right]$.

b. How many terms of the Taylor polynomial are needed to approximate values of $f(x) = \ln(1 - x)$ with an error less than 10^{-3} on the interval $\left[-\frac{1}{2}, \frac{1}{2}\right]$?

SOLUTION

a. The remainder for the Taylor polynomial p_3 is $R_3(x) = \dfrac{f^{(4)}(c)}{4!}x^4$, where c is

between 0 and x. Computing four derivatives of f, we find that $f^{(4)}(x) = -\dfrac{6}{(1 - x)^4}$.

On the interval $\left[-\frac{1}{2}, \frac{1}{2}\right]$, the maximum magnitude of this derivative occurs at $x = \frac{1}{2}$ $\left(\text{because the denominator is smallest at } x = \frac{1}{2}\right)$ and is $6/\left(\frac{1}{2}\right)^4 = 96$. Similarly, the factor x^4 has its maximum magnitude at $x = \pm\frac{1}{2}$ and it is $\left(\frac{1}{2}\right)^4 = \frac{1}{16}$. Therefore,

$$|R_3(x)| \le \frac{96}{4!} \cdot \left(\frac{1}{16}\right) = 0.25 \text{ on the interval } \left[-\frac{1}{2}, \frac{1}{2}\right]. \text{ The error in approximating } f(x)$$

by $p_3(x)$, for $-\frac{1}{2} \le x \le \frac{1}{2}$, does not exceed 0.25.

b. For any positive integer n, the remainder is $R_n(x) = \dfrac{f^{(n+1)}(c)}{(n+1)!}x^{n+1}$. Differentiating f several times reveals that

$$f^{(n+1)}(x) = -\frac{n!}{(1-x)^{n+1}}.$$

On the interval $\left[-\frac{1}{2}, \frac{1}{2}\right]$, the maximum magnitude of this derivative occurs at $x = \frac{1}{2}$ and is $n!/\left(\frac{1}{2}\right)^{n+1}$. Similarly, x^{n+1} has its maximum magnitude at $x = \pm\frac{1}{2}$, and it is $\left(\frac{1}{2}\right)^{n+1}$. Therefore, a bound on the remainder is

$$|R_n(x)| \le \frac{n!\,2^{n+1}}{(n+1)!}\frac{1}{2^{n+1}} = \frac{1}{n+1}.$$

To ensure that the error is less than 10^{-3} on the entire interval $\left[-\frac{1}{2}, \frac{1}{2}\right]$, n must satisfy $|R_n| \le \dfrac{1}{n+1} < 10^{-3}$ or $n > 999$. The error is likely to be significantly less than 10^{-3} if x is near 0.

Related Exercises 61–72 ◀

SECTION 10.1 EXERCISES

Review Questions

1. Suppose you use a second-order Taylor polynomial centered at 0 to approximate a function f. What matching conditions are satisfied by the polynomial?

2. Does the accuracy of an approximation given by a Taylor polynomial generally increase or decrease with the order of the approximation? Explain.

3. The first three Taylor polynomials for $f(x) = \sqrt{1+x}$ centered at 0 are $p_0(x) = 1$, $p_1(x) = 1 + \dfrac{x}{2}$, and $p_2(x) = 1 + \dfrac{x}{2} - \dfrac{x^2}{8}$. Find three approximations to $\sqrt{1.1}$.

4. In general, how many terms do the Taylor polynomials p_2 and p_3 have in common?

5. How is the remainder $R_n(x)$ in a Taylor polynomial defined?

6. Explain how to estimate the remainder (or find the Lagrange error bound) in an approximation given by a Taylor polynomial.

Basic Skills

7–14. Linear and quadratic approximation

a. Find the linear approximating polynomial for the following functions centered at the given point a.

b. Find the quadratic approximating polynomial for the following functions centered at the given point a.

c. Use the polynomials obtained in parts (a) and (b) to approximate the given quantity.

7. $f(x) = 8x^{3/2}, a = 1$; approximate $8(1.1^{3/2})$.

8. $f(x) = \dfrac{1}{x}, a = 1$; approximate $\dfrac{1}{1.05}$.

9. $f(x) = e^{-x}, a = 0$; approximate $e^{-0.2}$.

10. $f(x) = \sqrt{x}, a = 4$; approximate $\sqrt{3.9}$.

11. $f(x) = (1 + x)^{-1}, a = 0$; approximate $1/1.05$.

12. $f(x) = \cos x, a = \pi/4$; approximate $\cos(0.24\pi)$.

13. $f(x) = x^{1/3}, a = 8$; approximate $7.5^{1/3}$.

14. $f(x) = \tan^{-1} x, a = 0$; approximate $\tan^{-1} 0.1$.

15–22. Taylor polynomials

a. Find the nth-order Taylor polynomials of the given function centered at 0, for $n = 0, 1$, and 2.

b. Graph the Taylor polynomials and the function.

15. $f(x) = \cos x$

16. $f(x) = e^{-x}$

17. $f(x) = \ln(1 - x)$

18. $f(x) = (1 + x)^{-1/2}$

19. $f(x) = \tan x$

20. $f(x) = (1 + x)^{-2}$

21. $f(x) = (1 + x)^{-3}$

22. $f(x) = \sin^{-1} x$

23–28. Approximations with Taylor polynomials

a. Use the given Taylor polynomial p_2 to approximate the given quantity.

b. Compute the absolute error in the approximation assuming the exact value is given by a calculator.

23. Approximate $\sqrt{1.05}$ using $f(x) = \sqrt{1+x}$ and $p_2(x) = 1 + x/2 - x^2/8$.

24. Approximate $\sqrt[3]{1.1}$ using $f(x) = \sqrt[3]{1+x}$ and $p_2(x) = 1 + x/3 - x^2/9$.

25. Approximate $\dfrac{1}{\sqrt{1.08}}$ using $f(x) = \dfrac{1}{\sqrt{1+x}}$ and $p_2(x) = 1 - x/2 + 3x^2/8$.

26. Approximate $\ln 1.06$ using $f(x) = \ln(1 + x)$ and $p_2(x) = x - x^2/2$.

27. Approximate $e^{-0.15}$ using $f(x) = e^{-x}$ and $p_2(x) = 1 - x + x^2/2$.

28. Approximate $\dfrac{1}{1.12^3}$ using $f(x) = \dfrac{1}{(1+x)^3}$ and $p_2(x) = 1 - 3x + 6x^2$.

29–38. Taylor polynomials centered at $a \neq 0$

a. Find the nth-order Taylor polynomials for the given function f centered at the given point a, for $n = 0, 1,$ and 2.

b. Graph the Taylor polynomials and the function.

29. $f(x) = x^3, a = 1$

30. $f(x) = 8\sqrt{x}, a = 1$

31. $f(x) = \sin x, a = \pi/4$

32. $f(x) = \cos x, a = \pi/6$

33. $f(x) = \sqrt{x}, a = 9$

34. $f(x) = \sqrt[3]{x}, a = 8$

35. $f(x) = \ln x, a = e$

36. $f(x) = \sqrt[4]{x}, a = 16$

37. $f(x) = \tan^{-1} x + x^2 + 1, a = 1$

38. $f(x) = e^x, a = \ln 2$

39–48. Approximations with Taylor polynomials

a. Approximate the given quantities using Taylor polynomials with $n = 3$.

b. Compute the absolute error in the approximation assuming the exact value is given by a calculator.

39. $e^{0.12}$

40. $\cos(-0.2)$

41. $\tan(-0.1)$

42. $\ln(1.05)$

43. $\sqrt{1.06}$

44. $\sqrt[4]{79}$

45. $\sqrt{101}$

46. $\sqrt[3]{126}$

47. $\sin 3$

48. $(1.03)^{-2}$

49–54. Remainders *Find the remainder R_n for the nth-order Taylor polynomial centered at a for the given functions. Express the result for a general value of n.*

49. $f(x) = \sin x; \ a = 0$

50. $f(x) = \cos 2x; \ a = 0$

51. $f(x) = e^{-x}; \ a = 0$

52. $f(x) = \cos x; \ a = \pi/2$

53. $f(x) = \sin x; \ a = \pi/2$

54. $f(x) = 1/(1 - x); \ a = 0$

55–60. Estimating errors *Find the Lagrange error bound in approximating the following quantities with the nth-order Taylor polynomial centered at 0. Estimates are not unique.*

55. $\sin 0.3; \ n = 4$

56. $\cos 0.45; \ n = 3$

57. $e^{0.25}; \ n = 4$

58. $\tan 0.3; \ n = 2$

59. $e^{-0.5}; \ n = 4$

60. $\ln 1.04; \ n = 3$

61–66. Maximum error *Use the Lagrange error bound to estimate the maximum error in the following approximations on the given interval. Error bounds are not unique.*

61. $\sin x \approx x - x^3/6; \ [-\pi/4, \pi/4]$

62. $\cos x \approx 1 - x^2/2; \ [-\pi/4, \pi/4]$

63. $e^x \approx 1 + x + x^2/2; \ \left[-\frac{1}{2}, \frac{1}{2}\right]$

64. $\tan x \approx x; \ [-\pi/6, \pi/6]$

65. $\ln(1 + x) \approx x - x^2/2; \ [-0.2, 0.2]$

66. $\sqrt{1 + x} \approx 1 + x/2; \ [-0.1, 0.1]$

67–72. Number of terms *What is the minimum order of the Taylor polynomial required to approximate the following quantities with an absolute error no greater than 10^{-3}? (The answer depends on your choice of a center.)*

67. $e^{-0.5}$

68. $\sin 0.2$

69. $\cos(-0.25)$

70. $\ln 0.85$

71. $\sqrt{1.06}$

72. $1/\sqrt{0.85}$

Further Explorations

73. Explain why or why not Determine whether the following statements are true and give an explanation or counterexample.

a. The Taylor polynomials for $f(x) = e^{-2x}$ centered at 0 consist of even powers only.

b. Let $f(x) = x^5 - 1$. The Taylor polynomial for f of order 10 centered at 0 is f itself.

c. The nth-order Taylor polynomial for $f(x) = \sqrt{1 + x^2}$ centered at 0 consists only of even powers of x.

d. Suppose f'' is continuous on an interval that contains the point a, where f has an inflection point at a. Then the second-order Taylor polynomial for f at a is linear.

74. Taylor coefficients for $x = a$ Follow the procedure in the text to show that the nth-order Taylor polynomial that matches f and its derivatives up to order n at a has coefficients

$$c_k = \frac{f^{(k)}(a)}{k!}, \text{ for } k = 0, 1, 2, \ldots, n.$$

75. Matching functions with polynomials Match functions a–f with Taylor polynomials A–F (all centered at 0). Give reasons for your choices.

a. $\sqrt{1 + 2x}$ **A.** $p_2(x) = 1 + 2x + 2x^2$

b. $\dfrac{1}{\sqrt{1 + 2x}}$ **B.** $p_2(x) = 1 - 6x + 24x^2$

c. e^{2x} **C.** $p_2(x) = 1 + x - \dfrac{x^2}{2}$

d. $\dfrac{1}{1 + 2x}$ **D.** $p_2(x) = 1 - 2x + 4x^2$

e. $\dfrac{1}{(1 + 2x)^3}$ **E.** $p_2(x) = 1 - x + \dfrac{3}{2}x^2$

f. e^{-2x} **F.** $p_2(x) = 1 - 2x + 2x^2$

76. Dependence of errors on x Consider $f(x) = \ln(1 - x)$ and its Taylor polynomials given in Example 7.

a. Graph $y = |f(x) - p_2(x)|$ and $y = |f(x) - p_3(x)|$ on the interval $\left[-\frac{1}{2}, \frac{1}{2}\right]$ (two curves).

b. At what points of $\left[-\frac{1}{2}, \frac{1}{2}\right]$ is the error largest? Smallest?

c. Are these results consistent with the theoretical error bounds obtained in Example 7?

Applications

77–84. Small argument approximations *Consider the following common approximations when x is near zero.*

a. Estimate $f(0.1)$ and give a bound on the error in the approximation.

b. Estimate $f(0.2)$ and give a bound on the error in the approximation.

77. $f(x) = \sin x \approx x$

78. $f(x) = \tan x \approx x$

79. $f(x) = \cos x \approx 1 - x^2/2$

80. $f(x) = \tan^{-1} x \approx x$

81. $f(x) = \sqrt{1 + x} \approx 1 + x/2$

82. $f(x) = \ln(1 + x) \approx x - x^2/2$

83. $f(x) = e^x \approx 1 + x$

84. $f(x) = \sin^{-1} x \approx x$

85. Errors in approximations Suppose you approximate $f(x) = \sin x$ at the points $x = -0.2, -0.1, 0.0, 0.1$, and 0.2 using the Taylor polynomials $p_3 = x - x^3/6$ and $p_5 = x - x^3/6 + x^5/120$. Assume that the exact value of $\sin x$ is given by a calculator.

   a. Complete the table showing the absolute errors in the approximations at each point. Show two significant digits.

x	$\lvert \sin x - p_3(x) \rvert$	$\lvert \sin x - p_5(x) \rvert$
-0.2		
-0.1		
0.0		
0.1		
0.2		

   b. In each error column, how do the errors vary with x? For what values of x are the errors the largest and smallest in magnitude?

86–89. Errors in approximations *Carry out the procedure described in Exercise 85 with the following functions and Taylor polynomials.*

86. $f(x) = \cos x, \ p_2(x) = 1 - \dfrac{x^2}{2}, \ p_4(x) = 1 - \dfrac{x^2}{2} + \dfrac{x^4}{24}$

87. $f(x) = e^{-x}, \ p_1(x) = 1 - x, \ p_2(x) = 1 - x + \dfrac{x^2}{2}$

88. $f(x) = \ln(1 + x), \ p_1(x) = x, \ p_2(x) = x - \dfrac{x^2}{2}$

89. $f(x) = \tan x, \ p_1(x) = x, \ p_3(x) = x + \dfrac{x^3}{3}$

90. Best expansion point Suppose you wish to approximate $\cos(\pi/12)$ using Taylor polynomials. Is the approximation more accurate if you use Taylor polynomials centered at 0 or $\pi/6$? Use a calculator for numerical experiments and check for consistency with Theorem 10.2. Does the answer depend on the order of the polynomial?

91. Best expansion point Suppose you wish to approximate $e^{0.35}$ using Taylor polynomials. Is the approximation more accurate if you use Taylor polynomials centered at 0 or $\ln 2$? Use a calculator for numerical experiments and check for consistency with Theorem 10.2. Does the answer depend on the order of the polynomial?

Additional Exercises

92. Proof of Taylor's Theorem There are several proofs of Taylor's Theorem, which lead to various forms of the remainder. The following proof is instructive because it leads to two different forms of the remainder and it relies on the Fundamental Theorem of Calculus, integration by parts, and the Mean Value Theorem for Integrals. Assume that f has at least $n + 1$ continuous derivatives on an interval containing a.

   a. Show that the Fundamental Theorem of Calculus can be written in the form

   $$f(x) = f(a) + \int_a^x f'(t) \, dt.$$

   b. Use integration by parts ($u = f'(t), \ dv = dt$) to show that

   $$f(x) = f(a) + (x - a)f'(a) + \int_a^x (x - t)f''(t) \, dt.$$

   c. Show that n integrations by parts gives

   $$f(x) = f(a) + \frac{f'(a)}{1!}(x - a) + \frac{f''(a)}{2!}(x - a)^2 + \cdots$$
   $$+ \frac{f^{(n)}(a)}{n!}(x - a)^n + \int_a^x \frac{f^{(n+1)}(t)}{n!}(x - t)^n \, dt.$$

   d. *Challenge:* The result in part (c) looks like $f(x) = p_n(x) + R_n(x)$, where p_n is the nth-order Taylor polynomial and R_n is a new form of the remainder term, known as the integral form of the remainder term. Use the Mean Value Theorem for Integrals (Section 5.5) to show that R_n can be expressed in the form

   $$R_n(x) = \frac{f^{(n+1)}(c)}{(n + 1)!}(x - a)^{n+1},$$

   where c is between a and x.

93. Tangent line is p_1 Let f be differentiable at $x = a$.

   a. Find the equation of the line tangent to the curve $y = f(x)$ at $(a, f(a))$.

   b. Verify that the Taylor polynomial p_1 centered at a describes the tangent line found in part (a).

94. Local extreme points and inflection points Suppose f has continuous first and second derivatives at a.

   a. Show that if f has a local maximum at a, then the Taylor polynomial p_2 centered at a also has a local maximum at a.

   b. Show that if f has a local minimum at a, then the Taylor polynomial p_2 centered at a also has a local minimum at a.

   c. Is it true that if f has an inflection point at a, then the Taylor polynomial p_2 centered at a also has an inflection point at a?

   d. Are the converses to parts (a) and (b) true? If p_2 has a local extreme point at a, does f have the same type of point at a?

Technology Exercises

95. Approximating sin x Let $f(x) = \sin x$, and let p_n and q_n be nth-order Taylor polynomials for f centered at 0 and π, respectively.

a. Find p_5 and q_5.

b. Graph f, p_5, and q_5 on the interval $[-\pi, 2\pi]$. On what interval is p_5 a better approximation to f than q_5? On what interval is q_5 a better approximation to f than p_5?

c. Complete the following table by showing the errors in the approximations given by p_5 and q_5 at selected points.

x	$|\sin x - p_5(x)|$	$|\sin x - q_5(x)|$
$\pi/4$		
$\pi/2$		
$3\pi/4$		
$5\pi/4$		
$7\pi/4$		

d. At which points in the table is p_5 a better approximation to f than q_5? At which points do p_5 and q_5 give equal approximations to f? Explain your observations.

96. Approximating ln x Let $f(x) = \ln x$, and let p_n and q_n be the nth-order Taylor polynomials for f centered at 1 and e, respectively.

a. Find p_3 and q_3.

b. Graph f, p_3, and q_3 on the interval $(0, 4]$.

c. Complete the following table by showing the errors in the approximations given by p_3 and q_3 at selected points.

x	$|\ln x - p_3(x)|$	$|\ln x - q_3(x)|$
0.5		
1.0		
1.5		
2		
2.5		
3		
3.5		

d. At which points in the table is p_3 a better approximation to $\ln x$ than q_3? Explain your observations.

97. Approximating square roots Let p_1 and q_1 be the first-order Taylor polynomials for $f(x) = \sqrt{x}$, centered at 36 and 49, respectively.

a. Find p_1 and q_1.

b. Complete the following table showing the errors when using p_1 and q_1 to approximate to $f(x)$ at $x = 37, 39, 41, 43, 45,$ and 47. Use a calculator to obtain an exact value of $f(x)$.

x	$|\sqrt{x} - p_1(x)|$	$|\sqrt{x} - q_1(x)|$
37		
39		
41		
43		
45		
47		

c. At which points in the table is p_1 a better approximation to f than q_1? Explain this result.

98. A different kind of approximation When approximating a function f using a Taylor polynomial, we use information about f and its derivatives at one point. An alternative approach (called *interpolation*) uses information about f at several different points. Suppose we wish to approximate $f(x) = \sin x$ on the interval $[0, \pi]$.

a. Write the (quadratic) Taylor polynomial p_2 for f centered at $\dfrac{\pi}{2}$.

b. Now consider a quadratic interpolating polynomial $q(x) = ax^2 + bx + c$. The coefficients a, b, and c are chosen such that the following conditions are satisfied:

$$q(0) = f(0), q\left(\frac{\pi}{2}\right) = f\left(\frac{\pi}{2}\right), \text{ and } q(\pi) = f(\pi).$$

Show that $q(x) = -\dfrac{4}{\pi^2}x^2 + \dfrac{4}{\pi}x$.

c. Graph f, p_2, and q on $[0, \pi]$.

d. Find the error in approximating $f(x) = \sin x$ at the points $\dfrac{\pi}{4}, \dfrac{\pi}{2}, \dfrac{3\pi}{4}$, and π using p_2 and q.

e. Which function, p_2 or q, is a better approximation to f on $[0, \pi]$? Explain.

QUICK CHECK ANSWERS

3. $f(x) = \sin x$ is an odd function, and its even-ordered derivatives are zero at 0, so its Taylor polynomials are also odd functions. **4.** $p_4(x) = p_3(x) + \dfrac{x^4}{4!}$; $p_5(x) = p_4(x) + \dfrac{x^5}{5!}$

5. $x = 49$ and $x = 16$ are good choices. **6.** Because $e^{0.45} < 2$, $|R_7(0.45)| < 2\dfrac{0.45^8}{8!} \approx 8.3 \times 10^{-8}$. ◄

10.2 Properties of Power Series

The preceding section demonstrated that Taylor polynomials provide accurate approximations to many functions and that, in general, the approximations improve as the degree of the polynomials increases. In this section, we take the next step and let the degree of the Taylor polynomials increase without bound to produce a *power series*.

Geometric Series as Power Series

A good way to become familiar with power series is to return to *geometric series*, first encountered in Section 9.3. Recall that for a fixed number r,

$$\sum_{k=0}^{\infty} r^k = 1 + r + r^2 + \cdots = \frac{1}{1 - r}, \quad \text{provided } |r| < 1.$$

It's a small change to replace the real number r with the variable x. In doing so, the geometric series becomes a new representation of a familiar function:

$$\sum_{k=0}^{\infty} x^k = 1 + x + x^2 + \cdots = \frac{1}{1 - x}, \quad \text{provided } |x| < 1.$$

This infinite series is a power series and it is a representation of the function $1/(1 - x)$ that is valid on the interval $|x| < 1$.

In general, power series are used to represent familiar functions such as trigonometric, exponential, and logarithmic functions. They are also used to define new functions. For example, consider the function defined by

$$g(x) = \sum_{k=1}^{\infty} \frac{(-1)^k k}{4^k} x^{2k}.$$

The term *function* is used advisedly because it's not yet clear whether g really is a function. If so, is it a continuous function? Does it have a derivative? Judging by its graph (Figure 10.11), g appears to be a rather ordinary continuous function (which is identified at the end of the chapter).

In fact, power series satisfy the defining property of all functions: For each admissible value of x, a power series has at most one value. For this reason, we refer to a power series as a function, although the domain, properties, and identity of the function may need to be discovered.

> Figure 10.11 shows an approximation to the graph of g made by summing the first 500 terms of the power series at selected values of x on the interval $(-2, 2)$.

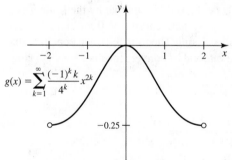

$$g(x) = \sum_{k=1}^{\infty} \frac{(-1)^k k}{4^k} x^{2k}$$

FIGURE 10.11

QUICK CHECK 1 By substituting $x = 0$ in the power series for g, evaluate $g(0)$ for the function in Figure 10.11. ◄

Convergence of Power Series

First, let's establish some terminology associated with power series.

DEFINITION Power Series

A **power series** has the general form

$$\sum_{k=0}^{\infty} c_k (x - a)^k,$$

where a and c_k are real numbers, and x is a variable. The c_k's are the **coefficients** of the power series and a is the **center** of the power series. The set of values of x for which the series converges is its **interval of convergence**. The **radius of convergence** of the power series, denoted R, is the distance from the center of the series to the boundary of the interval of convergence (Figure 10.12).

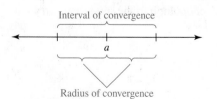

FIGURE 10.12

▶ Suppose we test $\sum a_k$ for absolute convergence using the Ratio Test. If

$$r = \lim_{k \to \infty} \left| \frac{a_{k+1}}{a_k} \right| < 1,$$

it follows that $\sum |a_k|$ converges, which in turn implies that $\sum a_k$ converges (Theorem 9.21). On the other hand, if $r > 1$, then for large k we have $|a_{k+1}| > |a_k|$, which means the terms of the sequence $\{a_k\}$ grow in magnitude as $k \to \infty$. Therefore, $\lim_{k \to \infty} a_k \neq 0$, and $\sum a_k$ diverges by the Divergence Test. If $r = 1$, the Ratio Test is inconclusive. A similar argument can be made when using the Root Test to determine the interval of convergence. If $\rho < 1$, $\sum a_k$ converges; if $\rho > 1$, the series diverges; and if $\rho = 1$, the test is inconclusive.

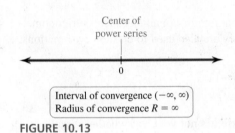

Center of power series

0

| Interval of convergence $(-\infty, \infty)$ |
| Radius of convergence $R = \infty$ |

FIGURE 10.13

How do we determine the interval of convergence? The presence of the terms x^k or $(x - a)^k$ in a power series suggests using the Ratio Test or the Root Test. Furthermore, because these terms could be positive or negative, we test a power series for absolute convergence. By Theorem 9.21, if we determine the values of x for which the series converges absolutely, we have a set of values for which the series converges. The following examples illustrate how the Ratio and Root Tests are used to determine the interval and radius of convergence.

EXAMPLE 1   Interval and radius of convergence Find the interval and radius of convergence for each power series.

a. $\sum_{k=0}^{\infty} \dfrac{x^k}{k!}$ **b.** $\sum_{k=0}^{\infty} \dfrac{(-1)^k (x - 2)^k}{4^k}$ **c.** $\sum_{k=1}^{\infty} k! \, x^k$

SOLUTION

a. The center of the power series is 0 and the terms of the series are $x^k / k!$. Due to the presence of the factor $k!$ we test the series for absolute convergence using the Ratio Test:

$$r = \lim_{k \to \infty} \frac{|x^{k+1}/(k + 1)!|}{|x^k / k!|} \qquad \text{Ratio Test for absolute convergence}$$

$$= \lim_{k \to \infty} \frac{|x|^{k+1}}{|x|^k} \cdot \frac{k!}{(k + 1)!} \qquad \text{Invert and multiply.}$$

$$= |x| \lim_{k \to \infty} \frac{1}{k + 1} = 0. \qquad \text{Simplify and take the limit with } x \text{ fixed.}$$

Notice that in taking the limit as $k \to \infty$, x is held fixed. Recall that by the Ratio Test, the series converges absolutely provided $0 \le r < 1$. Because $r = 0$ for all real numbers x, the series converges absolutely for all x. Using Theorem 9.21, we conclude that the series converges for all x. Therefore, the interval of convergence is $(-\infty, \infty)$ (Figure 10.13) and the radius of convergence is $R = \infty$.

b. We test for absolute convergence using the Root Test:

$$\rho = \lim_{k \to \infty} \sqrt[k]{\left| \frac{(-1)^k (x - 2)^k}{4^k} \right|} = \frac{|x - 2|}{4}.$$

In this case, ρ depends on the value of x. For absolute convergence, x must satisfy

$$\rho = \frac{|x - 2|}{4} < 1,$$

▶ Either the Root Test or the Ratio Test works for the power series in Example 1b.

which implies that $|x - 2| < 4$. Using standard techniques for solving inequalities, the solution set is $-4 < x - 2 < 4$, or $-2 < x < 6$, and we conclude that the series converges absolutely on $(-2, 6)$. By Theorem 9.21, the series converges on $(-2, 6)$. When $x < -2$ or $x > 6$, we have $\rho > 1$, so the series diverges on these intervals (the terms of the series do not approach 0 as $k \to \infty$ and the Divergence Test applies).

The Root Test does not give information about convergence at the endpoints, $x = -2$ and $x = 6$, because at these points, the Root Test results in $\rho = 1$. To test for convergence at the endpoints, we substitute each endpoint into the series and carry out separate tests. At $x = -2$, the power series becomes

$$\sum_{k=0}^{\infty} \frac{(-1)^k (x - 2)^k}{4^k} = \sum_{k=0}^{\infty} \frac{4^k}{4^k} \qquad \text{Substitute } x = -2 \text{ and simplify.}$$

$$= \sum_{k=0}^{\infty} 1. \qquad \text{Diverges by Divergence Test}$$

> The Ratio and Root Tests determine the radius of convergence conclusively. However, the interval of convergence is not determined until the endpoints are tested.

The series clearly diverges at the left endpoint. At $x = 6$, the power series is

$$\sum_{k=0}^{\infty} \frac{(-1)^k(x-2)^k}{4^k} = \sum_{k=0}^{\infty} (-1)^k \frac{4^k}{4^k} \quad \text{Substitute } x = 6 \text{ and simplify.}$$

$$= \sum_{k=0}^{\infty} (-1)^k. \quad \text{Diverges by Divergence Test}$$

This series also diverges at the right endpoint. Therefore, the interval of convergence is $(-2, 6)$ (Figure 10.14) and the radius of convergence is $R = 4$.

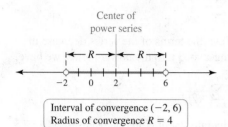

Center of power series

Interval of convergence $(-2, 6)$
Radius of convergence $R = 4$

FIGURE 10.14

c. To test for absolute convergence, the Ratio Test is preferable:

$$r = \lim_{k \to \infty} \frac{|(k+1)! \, x^{k+1}|}{|k! \, x^k|} \quad \text{Ratio Test}$$

$$= |x| \lim_{k \to \infty} \frac{(k+1)!}{k!} \quad \text{Simplify.}$$

$$= |x| \lim_{k \to \infty} (k+1) \quad \text{Simplify.}$$

$$= \infty. \quad \text{If } x \neq 0$$

We see that $r > 1$ for all $x \neq 0$, so the series diverges on $(-\infty, 0)$ and $(0, \infty)$. The only way to satisfy $r < 1$ is to take $x = 0$, in which case the power series has a value of 0. The interval of convergence of the power series consists of the single point $x = 0$ (Figure 10.15) and the radius of convergence is $R = 0$.

Related Exercises 9–28 ◄

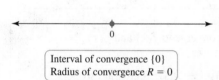

Interval of convergence {0}
Radius of convergence $R = 0$

FIGURE 10.15

> Theorem 10.3 implies that the interval of convergence is symmetric about the center of the series. The theorem says nothing about convergence at the endpoints. For example, the radius of convergence is $R = 2$ for the intervals of convergence $(2, 6)$, $(2, 6]$, $[2, 6)$, and $[2, 6]$.

Example 1 illustrates the three common types of intervals of convergence, which are summarized in the following theorem (see Appendix C for a proof).

THEOREM 10.3 Convergence of Power Series

A power series $\sum_{k=0}^{\infty} c_k(x-a)^k$ centered at a converges in one of three ways:

1. The series converges for all x, in which case the interval of convergence is $(-\infty, \infty)$ and the radius of convergence is $R = \infty$.
2. There is a real number $R > 0$ such that the series converges for $|x - a| < R$ and diverges for $|x - a| > R$, in which case the radius of convergence is R.
3. The series converges only at a, in which case the radius of convergence is $R = 0$.

EXAMPLE 2 Interval and radius of convergence Use the Ratio Test to find the radius and interval of convergence of $\sum_{k=1}^{\infty} \frac{(x-2)^k}{\sqrt{k}}$.

QUICK CHECK 2 What are the interval and radius of convergence of the geometric series $\sum x^k$? ◄

> The power series in Example 2 could also be analyzed using the Root Test.

SOLUTION

$$r = \lim_{k \to \infty} \frac{|(x-2)^{k+1}/\sqrt{k+1}|}{|(x-2)^k/\sqrt{k}|} \quad \text{Ratio Test for absolute convergence}$$

$$= |x-2| \lim_{k \to \infty} \sqrt{\frac{k}{k+1}} \quad \text{Simplify.}$$

$$= |x-2| \sqrt{\underbrace{\lim_{k \to \infty} \frac{k}{k+1}}_{1}} \quad \text{Limit Law}$$

$$= |x-2| \quad \text{Limit equals 1.}$$

The series converges absolutely (and therefore converges) for all x such that $r < 1$, which implies $|x - 2| < 1$, or $1 < x < 3$. On the intervals $x < 1$ and $x > 3$, we have $r > 1$ and the series diverges.

We now test the endpoints. Substituting $x = 1$ into the power series, we have

$$\sum_{k=1}^{\infty} \frac{(x-2)^k}{\sqrt{k}} = \sum_{k=1}^{\infty} \frac{(-1)^k}{\sqrt{k}}.$$

This series converges by the Alternating Series Test (the terms of the series decrease in magnitude and approach 0 as $k \to \infty$). Substituting $x = 3$ into the power series, we have

$$\sum_{k=1}^{\infty} \frac{(x-2)^k}{\sqrt{k}} = \sum_{k=1}^{\infty} \frac{1}{\sqrt{k}},$$

which is a divergent p-series. We conclude that the interval of convergence is $1 \leq x < 3$ and the radius of convergence is $R = 1$ (Figure 10.16).   *Related Exercises 9–28* ◄

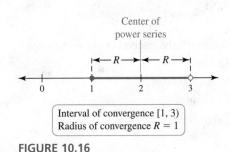

Center of
power series

Interval of convergence $[1, 3)$
Radius of convergence $R = 1$

FIGURE 10.16

Combining Power Series

A power series defines a function on its interval of convergence. When power series are combined algebraically, new functions are defined. The following theorem, stated without proof, gives three common ways to combine power series.

> ▶ New power series can also be defined as the product and quotient of power series. The calculation of the coefficients of such series is more challenging (Exercise 75).

> ▶ Theorem 10.4 also applies to power series centered at points other than $x = 0$. Property 1 applies directly; Properties 2 and 3 apply with slight modifications.

THEOREM 10.4   Combining Power Series
Suppose the power series $\sum c_k x^k$ and $\sum d_k x^k$ converge to $f(x)$ and $g(x)$, respectively, on an interval I.

1. **Sum and difference:** The power series $\sum (c_k \pm d_k)x^k$ converges to $f(x) \pm g(x)$ on I.

2. **Multiplication by a power:** Suppose m is an integer such that $k + m \geq 0$ for all terms of the power series $x^m \sum c_k x^k = \sum c_k x^{k+m}$. This series converges to $x^m f(x)$ for all $x \neq 0$ in I. When $x = 0$, the series converges to $\lim_{x \to 0} x^m f(x)$.

3. **Composition:** If $h(x) = bx^m$, where m is a positive integer and b is a nonzero real number, the power series $\sum c_k (h(x))^k$ converges to the composite function $f(h(x))$, for all x such that $h(x)$ is in I.

EXAMPLE 3   Combining power series Given the geometric series

$$\frac{1}{1-x} = \sum_{k=0}^{\infty} x^k = 1 + x + x^2 + x^3 + \cdots, \qquad \text{for } |x| < 1,$$

find the power series and interval of convergence for the following functions.

a. $\dfrac{x^5}{1-x}$ **b.** $\dfrac{1}{1-2x}$ **c.** $\dfrac{1}{1+x^2}$

SOLUTION

a.
$$\frac{x^5}{1-x} = x^5 \left(1 + x + x^2 + \cdots\right) \quad \text{Theorem 10.4, Property 2}$$

$$= x^5 + x^6 + x^7 + \cdots$$

$$= \sum_{k=0}^{\infty} x^{k+5}$$

This geometric series has a ratio $r = x$ and converges when $|r| = |x| < 1$. The interval of convergence is $|x| < 1$.

b. We substitute $2x$ for x in the power series for $\dfrac{1}{1-x}$:

$$\frac{1}{1-2x} = 1 + (2x) + (2x)^2 + \cdots \qquad \text{Theorem 10.4, Property 3}$$

$$= \sum_{k=0}^{\infty} (2x)^k.$$

This geometric series has a ratio $r = 2x$ and converges provided $|r| = |2x| < 1$ or $|x| < \frac{1}{2}$. The interval of convergence is $|x| < \frac{1}{2}$.

c. We substitute $-x^2$ for x in the power series for $\dfrac{1}{1-x}$:

$$\frac{1}{1+x^2} = 1 + (-x^2) + (-x^2)^2 + \cdots \qquad \text{Theorem 10.4, Property 3}$$

$$= 1 - x^2 + x^4 - \cdots$$

$$= \sum_{k=0}^{\infty} (-1)^k x^{2k}.$$

This geometric series has a ratio of $r = -x^2$ and converges provided $|r| = |-x^2| = |x^2| < 1$ or $|x| < 1$.

Related Exercises 29–40 ◄

Differentiating and Integrating Power Series

Some properties of polynomials carry over to power series, but others do not. For example, a polynomial is defined for all values of x, whereas a power series is defined only on its interval of convergence. In general, the properties of polynomials carry over to power series when the power series is restricted to its interval of convergence. The following result illustrates this principle.

> ▶ Theorem 10.5 makes no claim about the convergence of the differentiated or integrated series at the endpoints of the interval of convergence.

THEOREM 10.5   Differentiating and Integrating Power Series
Suppose the power series $\sum c_k (x - a)^k$ converges for $|x - a| < R$ and defines a function f on that interval.

1. Then f is differentiable (which implies continuous) for $|x - a| < R$, and f' is found by differentiating the power series for f term by term; that is,

$$f'(x) = \sum k c_k (x - a)^{k-1},$$

for $|x - a| < R$.

2. The indefinite integral of f is found by integrating the power series for f term by term; that is,

$$\int f(x)\,dx = \sum c_k \frac{(x - a)^{k+1}}{k + 1} + C,$$

for $|x - a| < R$, where C is an arbitrary constant.

The proof of this theorem requires advanced ideas and is omitted. However, some discussion is in order before turning to examples. The statements in Theorem 10.5 about term-by-term differentiation and integration say two things. First, the differentiated and integrated power series converge, provided x belongs to the interior of the interval of convergence. But the theorem claims more than convergence. According to the theorem, the differentiated and integrated power series converge to the derivative and indefinite integral of f, respectively, on the interior of the interval of convergence. Let's use this theorem to develop new power series.

EXAMPLE 4   Differentiating and integrating power series Consider the geometric series

$$f(x) = \frac{1}{1-x} = \sum_{k=0}^{\infty} x^k = 1 + x + x^2 + x^3 + \cdots, \quad \text{for } |x| < 1.$$

a. Differentiate this series term by term to find the power series for f' and identify the function it represents.

b. Integrate this series term by term and identify the function it represents.

SOLUTION

a. We know that $f'(x) = (1-x)^{-2}$. Differentiating the series, we find that

$$f'(x) = \frac{d}{dx}(1 + x + x^2 + x^3 + \cdots) \quad \text{Differentiate the power series for } f.$$

$$= 1 + 2x + 3x^2 + \cdots \quad \text{Differentiate term by term.}$$

$$= \sum_{k=0}^{\infty} (k+1)x^k. \quad \text{Summation notation}$$

Therefore, on the interval $|x| < 1$,

$$f'(x) = (1-x)^{-2} = \sum_{k=0}^{\infty}(k+1)x^k.$$

Theorem 10.5 does not make any claims about the convergence of the differential series to f' at the endpoints. In this case, substituting $x = \pm 1$ into the power series for f' reveals that the series diverges at both endpoints.

b. Integrating f and integrating the power series term by term, we have

$$\int \frac{dx}{1-x} = \int (1 + x + x^2 + x^3 + \cdots)\, dx,$$

which implies that

$$-\ln|1-x| = x + \frac{x^2}{2} + \frac{x^3}{3} + \frac{x^4}{4} + \cdots + C,$$

where C is an arbitrary constant. Notice that the left side is 0 when $x = 0$. The right side is 0 when $x = 0$ provided we choose $C = 0$. Because $|x| < 1$, the absolute value sign on the left side may be removed. Multiplying both sides by -1, we have a series representation for $\ln(1-x)$:

$$\ln(1-x) = -x - \frac{x^2}{2} - \frac{x^3}{3} - \frac{x^4}{4} - \cdots = -\sum_{k=1}^{\infty}\frac{x^k}{k}.$$

It is interesting to test the endpoints of the interval $|x| < 1$. When $x = 1$, the series is (a multiple of) the divergent harmonic series, and when $x = -1$, the series is the convergent alternating harmonic series (Section 9.6). So the interval of convergence is $-1 \leq x < 1$. Although we know the series converges at $x = -1$, Theorem 10.5 guarantees convergence to $\ln(1 - x)$ only at the interior points. We cannot use Theorem 10.5 to claim that the series converges to $\ln 2$ at $x = -1$. In fact, it does, as shown in Section 10.3.

Related Exercises 41–46 ◄

QUICK CHECK 3 Use the result of Example 4 to write a series representation for $\ln \frac{1}{2} = -\ln 2$. ◄

EXAMPLE 5 Functions to power series Find power series representations centered at 0 for the following functions and give their intervals of convergence.

a. $\tan^{-1} x$ **b.** $\ln\left(\dfrac{1 + x}{1 - x}\right)$

SOLUTION In both cases, we work with known power series and use differentiation, integration, and other combinations.

a. The key is to recall that

$$\int \frac{dx}{1 + x^2} = \tan^{-1} x + C$$

and that, by Example 3c,

$$\frac{1}{1 + x^2} = 1 - x^2 + x^4 - \cdots, \qquad \text{provided } |x| < 1.$$

We now integrate both sides of this last expression:

$$\int \frac{dx}{1 + x^2} = \int (1 - x^2 + x^4 - \cdots)\, dx,$$

which implies that

$$\tan^{-1} x = x - \frac{x^3}{3} + \frac{x^5}{5} - \cdots + C.$$

Substituting $x = 0$ and noting that $\tan^{-1} 0 = 0$, the two sides of this equation agree provided we choose $C = 0$. Therefore,

$$\tan^{-1} x = x - \frac{x^3}{3} + \frac{x^5}{5} - \cdots = \sum_{k=0}^{\infty} \frac{(-1)^k x^{2k+1}}{2k + 1}.$$

> Again, Theorem 10.5 does not guarantee that the power series in Example 5a converges to $\tan^{-1} x$ at $x = \pm 1$. In fact, it does.

By Theorem 10.5, this power series converges to $\tan^{-1} x$ for $|x| < 1$. Testing the endpoints separately, we find that it also converges at $x = \pm 1$. Therefore, the interval of convergence is $[-1, 1]$.

b. We have already seen (Example 4) that

$$\ln(1 - x) = -x - \frac{x^2}{2} - \frac{x^3}{3} - \cdots.$$

> Nicolaus Mercator (1620–1687) and Sir Isaac Newton (1642–1727) independently derived the power series for $\ln(1 + x)$, which is called the *Mercator series*.

Replacing x with $-x$, we have

$$\ln(1 - (-x)) = \ln(1 + x) = x - \frac{x^2}{2} + \frac{x^3}{3} - \cdots.$$

Subtracting these two power series gives

$$\ln\left(\frac{1+x}{1-x}\right) = \ln(1+x) - \ln(1-x) \quad \text{Properties of logarithms}$$

$$= \underbrace{\left(x - \frac{x^2}{2} + \frac{x^3}{3} - \cdots\right)}_{\ln(1+x)} - \underbrace{\left(-x - \frac{x^2}{2} - \frac{x^3}{3} - \cdots\right)}_{\ln(1-x)}, \quad \text{for } |x| < 1$$

$$= 2\left(x + \frac{x^3}{3} + \frac{x^5}{5} + \cdots\right) \quad \text{Combine, Theorem 10.4.}$$

$$= 2\sum_{k=0}^{\infty} \frac{x^{2k+1}}{2k+1}. \quad \text{Summation notation}$$

QUICK CHECK 4 Verify that the power series in Example 5b does not converge at the endpoints $x = \pm 1$. ◄

This power series is the difference of two power series, both of which converge on the interval $|x| < 1$. Therefore, by Theorem 10.4, the new series also converges on $|x| < 1$.

Related Exercises 47–52 ◄

If you look carefully, every example in this section is ultimately based on the geometric series. Using this single series, we were able to develop power series for many other functions. Imagine what we could do with a few more basic power series. The following section accomplishes precisely that end. There, we discover power series for many of the standard functions of calculus.

SECTION 10.2 EXERCISES

Review Questions

1. Write the first four terms of a power series with coefficients $c_0, c_1, c_2,$ and c_3 centered at 0.

2. Write the first four terms of a power series with coefficients $c_0, c_1, c_2,$ and c_3 centered at 3.

3. What tests are used to determine the radius of convergence of a power series?

4. Explain why a power series is tested for *absolute* convergence.

5. Do the interval and radius of convergence of a power series change when the series is differentiated or integrated? Explain.

6. What is the radius of convergence of the power series $\sum c_k (x/2)^k$ if the radius of convergence of $\sum c_k x^k$ is R?

7. What is the interval of convergence of the power series $\sum (4x)^k$?

8. How are the radii of convergence of the power series $\sum c_k x^k$ and $\sum (-1)^k c_k x^k$ related?

Basic Skills

9–28. Interval and radius of convergence *Determine the radius of convergence of the following power series. Then test the endpoints to determine the interval of convergence.*

9. $\sum (2x)^k$

10. $\sum \frac{(2x)^k}{k!}$

11. $\sum \frac{(x-1)^k}{k}$

12. $\sum \frac{(x-1)^k}{k!}$

13. $\sum (kx)^k$

14. $\sum k!(x-10)^k$

15. $\sum \sin^k\left(\frac{1}{k}\right)x^k$

16. $\sum \frac{2^k(x-3)^k}{k}$

17. $\sum \left(\frac{x}{3}\right)^k$

18. $\sum (-1)^k \frac{x^k}{5^k}$

19. $\sum \frac{x^k}{k^k}$

20. $\sum (-1)^k \frac{k(x-4)^k}{2^k}$

21. $\sum \frac{k^2 x^{2k}}{k!}$

22. $\sum k(x-1)^k$

23. $\sum \frac{x^{2k+1}}{3^{k-1}}$

24. $\sum \left(-\frac{x}{10}\right)^{2k}$

25. $\sum \frac{(x-1)^k k^k}{(k+1)^k}$

26. $\sum \frac{(-2)^k (x+3)^k}{3^{k+1}}$

27. $\sum \frac{k^{20} x^k}{(2k+1)!}$

28. $\sum (-1)^k \frac{x^{3k}}{27^k}$

29–34. Combining power series *Use the geometric series*

$$f(x) = \frac{1}{1-x} = \sum_{k=0}^{\infty} x^k, \quad \text{for } |x| < 1,$$

to find the power series representation for the following functions (centered at 0). Give the interval of convergence of the new series.

29. $f(3x) = \dfrac{1}{1-3x}$

30. $g(x) = \dfrac{x^3}{1-x}$

31. $h(x) = \dfrac{2x^3}{1-x}$

32. $f(x^3) = \dfrac{1}{1-x^3}$

33. $p(x) = \dfrac{4x^{12}}{1-x}$

34. $f(-4x) = \dfrac{1}{1+4x}$

35–40. Combining power series *Use the power series representation*

$$f(x) = \ln(1-x) = -\sum_{k=1}^{\infty} \frac{x^k}{k}, \quad \text{for } -1 \le x < 1,$$

to find the power series for the following functions (centered at 0). Give the interval of convergence of the new series.

35. $f(3x) = \ln(1-3x)$ **36.** $g(x) = x^3 \ln(1-x)$

37. $h(x) = x \ln(1-x)$ **38.** $f(x^3) = \ln(1-x^3)$

39. $p(x) = 2x^6 \ln(1-x)$ **40.** $f(-4x) = \ln(1+4x)$

41–46. Differentiating and integrating power series *Find the power series representation for g centered at 0 by differentiating or integrating the power series for f (perhaps more than once). Give the interval of convergence for the resulting series.*

41. $g(x) = \dfrac{1}{(1-x)^2}$ using $f(x) = \dfrac{1}{1-x}$

42. $g(x) = \dfrac{1}{(1-x)^3}$ using $f(x) = \dfrac{1}{1-x}$

43. $g(x) = \dfrac{1}{(1-x)^4}$ using $f(x) = \dfrac{1}{1-x}$

44. $g(x) = \dfrac{x}{(1+x^2)^2}$ using $f(x) = \dfrac{1}{1+x^2}$

45. $g(x) = \ln(1-3x)$ using $f(x) = \dfrac{1}{1-3x}$

46. $g(x) = \ln(1+x^2)$ using $f(x) = \dfrac{x}{1+x^2}$

47–52. Functions to power series *Find power series representations centered at 0 for the following functions using known power series. Give the interval of convergence for the resulting series.*

47. $f(x) = \dfrac{1}{1+x^2}$ **48.** $f(x) = \dfrac{1}{1-x^4}$

49. $f(x) = \dfrac{3}{3+x}$ **50.** $f(x) = \ln\sqrt{1-x^2}$

51. $f(x) = \ln\sqrt{4-x^2}$ **52.** $f(x) = \tan^{-1}(4x^2)$

Further Explorations

53. Explain why or why not Determine whether the following statements are true and give an explanation or counterexample.

  a. The interval of convergence of the power series $\sum c_k (x-3)^k$ could be $(-2, 8)$.
  b. $\sum(-2x)^k$ converges, for $-\frac{1}{2} < x < \frac{1}{2}$.
  c. If $f(x) = \sum c_k x^k$ on the interval $|x| < 1$, then $f(x^2) = \sum c_k x^{2k}$ on the interval $|x| < 1$.
  d. If $f(x) = \sum c_k x^k = 0$, for all x on an interval $(-a, a)$, then $c_k = 0$, for all k.

54. Radius of convergence Find the radius of convergence of

$$\sum \left(1 + \frac{1}{k}\right)^{k^2} x^k.$$

55. Radius of convergence Find the radius of convergence of $\sum \dfrac{k! x^k}{k^k}$.

56–59. Summation notation *Write the following power series in summation (sigma) notation.*

56. $1 + \dfrac{x}{2} + \dfrac{x^2}{4} + \dfrac{x^3}{6} + \cdots$ **57.** $1 - \dfrac{x}{2} + \dfrac{x^2}{3} - \dfrac{x^3}{4} + \cdots$

58. $x - \dfrac{x^3}{4} + \dfrac{x^5}{9} - \dfrac{x^7}{16} + \cdots$ **59.** $-\dfrac{x^2}{1!} + \dfrac{x^4}{2!} - \dfrac{x^6}{3!} + \dfrac{x^8}{4!} - \cdots$

60. Scaling power series If the power series $f(x) = \sum c_k x^k$ has an interval of convergence of $|x| < R$, what is the interval of convergence of the power series for $f(ax)$, where $a \ne 0$ is a real number?

61. Shifting power series If the power series $f(x) = \sum c_k x^k$ has an interval of convergence of $|x| < R$, what is the interval of convergence of the power series for $f(x - a)$, where $a \ne 0$ is a real number?

62–67. Series to functions *Find the function represented by the following series and find the interval of convergence of the series. (Not all these series are power series.)*

62. $\displaystyle\sum_{k=0}^{\infty} (x^2 + 1)^{2k}$ **63.** $\displaystyle\sum_{k=0}^{\infty} (\sqrt{x} - 2)^k$

64. $\displaystyle\sum_{k=1}^{\infty} \dfrac{x^{2k}}{4k}$ **65.** $\displaystyle\sum_{k=0}^{\infty} e^{-kx}$

66. $\displaystyle\sum_{k=1}^{\infty} \dfrac{(x-2)^k}{3^{2k}}$ **67.** $\displaystyle\sum_{k=0}^{\infty} \left(\dfrac{x^2 - 1}{3}\right)^k$

68. A useful substitution Replace x with $x - 1$ in the series

$$\ln(1+x) = \sum_{k=1}^{\infty} \frac{(-1)^{k+1} x^k}{k} \quad \text{to obtain a power series for } \ln x$$

centered at $x = 1$. What is the interval of convergence for the new power series?

69–72. Exponential function *In Section 10.3, we show that the power series for the exponential function centered at 0 is*

$$e^x = \sum_{k=0}^{\infty} \frac{x^k}{k!}, \quad \text{for } -\infty < x < \infty.$$

Use the methods of this section to find the power series for the following functions. Give the interval of convergence for the resulting series.

69. $f(x) = e^{-x}$ **70.** $f(x) = e^{2x}$

71. $f(x) = e^{-3x}$ **72.** $f(x) = x^2 e^x$

Additional Exercises

73. Powers of x multiplied by a power series Prove that if

$$f(x) = \sum_{k=0}^{\infty} c_k x^k \text{ converges with radius of convergence } R, \text{ then the}$$

power series for $x^m f(x)$ also converges with radius of convergence R, for positive integers m.

T 74. Remainders Let

$$f(x) = \sum_{k=0}^{\infty} x^k = \frac{1}{1-x} \quad \text{and} \quad S_n(x) = \sum_{k=0}^{n-1} x^k.$$

The remainder in truncating the power series after n terms is $R_n = f(x) - S_n(x)$, which now depends on x.

a. Show that $R_n(x) = x^n / (1 - x)$.

b. Graph the remainder function on the interval $|x| < 1$ for $n = 1, 2, 3$. Discuss and interpret the graph. Where on the interval is $|R_n(x)|$ largest? Smallest?

c. For fixed n, minimize $|R_n(x)|$ with respect to x. Does the result agree with the observations in part (b)?

d. Let $N(x)$ be the number of terms required to reduce $|R_n(x)|$ to less than 10^{-6}. Graph the function $N(x)$ on the interval $|x| < 1$. Discuss and interpret the graph.

75. Product of power series Let

$$f(x) = \sum_{k=0}^{\infty} c_k x^k \quad \text{and} \quad g(x) = \sum_{k=0}^{\infty} d_k x^k.$$

a. Multiply the power series together as if they were polynomials, collecting all terms that are multiples of 1, x, and x^2. Write the first three terms of the product $f(x)g(x)$.

b. Find a general expression for the coefficient of x^n in the product series, for $n = 0, 1, 2, \ldots$.

76. Inverse sine Given the power series

$$\frac{1}{\sqrt{1 - x^2}} = 1 + \frac{1}{2}x^2 + \frac{1 \cdot 3}{2 \cdot 4}x^4 + \frac{1 \cdot 3 \cdot 5}{2 \cdot 4 \cdot 6}x^6 + \cdots,$$

for $-1 < x < 1$, find the power series for $f(x) = \sin^{-1} x$ centered at 0.

77. Computing with power series Consider the following function and its power series:

$$f(x) = \frac{1}{(1 - x)^2} = \sum_{k=1}^{\infty} k x^{k-1}, \quad \text{for } -1 < x < 1.$$

a. Let $S_n(x)$ be the sum of the first n terms of the series. With $n = 5$ and $n = 10$, graph $f(x)$ and $S_n(x)$ at the sample points $x = -0.9, -0.8, \ldots, -0.1, 0, 0.1, \ldots, 0.8, 0.9$ (two graphs). Where is the difference in the graphs the greatest?

b. What value of n is needed to guarantee that $|f(x) - S_n(x)| < 0.01$ at all of the sample points?

QUICK CHECK ANSWERS

1. $g(0) = 0$ **2.** $|x| < 1, R = 1$

3. Substituting $x = 1/2, \ln(1/2) = -\ln 2 = -\sum_{k=1}^{\infty} \frac{1}{2^k k}$.

10.3 Taylor Series

In the preceding section, we saw that a power series represents a function on its interval of convergence. This section explores the opposite question: Given a function, what is its power series representation? We have already made significant progress in answering this question because we know how Taylor polynomials are used to approximate functions. We now extend Taylor polynomials to produce power series—called *Taylor series*—that provide series representations of functions.

Taylor Series for a Function

Suppose a function f has derivatives $f^{(k)}(a)$ of *all* orders at the point a. If we write the nth-order Taylor polynomial for f centered at a and allow n to increase indefinitely, a power series is obtained:

$$\underbrace{c_0 + c_1(x - a) + c_2(x - a)^2 + \cdots + c_n(x - a)^n}_{\text{Taylor polynomial of order } n} + \underbrace{\cdots}_{n \to \infty} = \sum_{k=0}^{\infty} c_k(x - a)^k.$$

The coefficients of the Taylor polynomial are given by

$$c_k = \frac{f^{(k)}(a)}{k!}, \quad \text{for } k = 0, 1, 2, \ldots.$$

▷ Maclaurin series are named after the
Scottish mathematician Colin Maclaurin
(1698–1746), who described them (with
credit to Taylor) in a textbook in 1742.

These coefficients are also the coefficients of the power series, which is called the *Taylor series for f centered at a*. It is the natural extension of the set of Taylor polynomials for f at a. The special case of a Taylor series centered at 0 is called a *Maclaurin series*.

DEFINITION Taylor / Maclaurin Series for a Function

Suppose the function f has derivatives of all orders on an interval centered at the point a. The **Taylor series for f centered at a** is

$$f(a) + f'(a)\,(x - a) + \frac{f''(a)}{2!}\,(x - a)^2 + \frac{f^{(3)}(a)}{3!}\,(x - a)^3 + \cdots$$

$$= \sum_{k=0}^{\infty} \frac{f^{(k)}(a)}{k!}\,(x - a)^k.$$

A Taylor series centered at 0 is called a **Maclaurin series**.

For the Taylor series to be useful, we need to know two things:

• the values of x for which the power series converges; that is, the interval of convergence, and

▷ There are unusual cases in which the
Taylor series for a function converges to
a different function (Exercise 90).

• the values of x for which the power series for f equals f.

The second question is more subtle and is postponed for a few pages. For now, we find the Taylor series for f centered at a point, but we refrain from saying $f(x)$ equals the power series.

QUICK CHECK 1 Verify that if the Taylor series for f centered at a is evaluated at $x = a$, then the Taylor series equals $f(a)$. ◄

EXAMPLE 1   Maclaurin series and convergence Find the Maclaurin series (which is the Taylor series centered at 0) for the following functions. Find the interval of convergence.

a. $f(x) = \cos x$ **b.** $f(x) = \dfrac{1}{1 - x}$

SOLUTION The procedure for finding the coefficients of a Taylor series is the same as for Taylor polynomials; most of the work is computing the derivatives of f.

a. The Maclaurin series has the form

$$\sum_{k=0}^{\infty} c_k x^k, \qquad \text{where } c_k = \frac{f^{(k)}(0)}{k!}, \quad \text{for } k = 0, 1, 2, \ldots.$$

We evaluate derivatives of $f(x) = \cos x$ at $x = 0$.

$$f(x) = \cos x \implies f(0) = 1$$
$$f'(x) = -\sin x \implies f'(0) = 0$$
$$f''(x) = -\cos x \implies f''(0) = -1$$
$$f'''(x) = \sin x \implies f'''(0) = 0$$
$$f^{(4)}(x) = \cos x \implies f^{(4)}(0) = 1$$
$$\vdots \qquad\qquad \vdots$$

Because the odd-order derivatives are zero, $c_k = \dfrac{f^{(k)}(0)}{k!} = 0$ when k is odd. Using the even-order derivatives, we have

$$c_0 = f(0) = 1, \qquad\qquad c_2 = \frac{f^{(2)}(0)}{2!} = -\frac{1}{2!},$$

$$c_4 = \frac{f^{(4)}(0)}{4!} = \frac{1}{4!}, \qquad c_6 = \frac{f^{(6)}(0)}{6!} = -\frac{1}{6!},$$

and in general, $c_{2k} = \dfrac{(-1)^k}{(2k)!}$. Therefore, the Maclaurin series for f is

$$1 - \frac{x^2}{2!} + \frac{x^4}{4!} - \frac{x^6}{6!} + \cdots = \sum_{k=0}^{\infty} \frac{(-1)^k}{(2k)!} x^{2k}.$$

Notice that this series contains all the Taylor polynomials. In this case, it consists only of even powers of x, reflecting the fact that $\cos x$ is an even function.

For what values of x does the series converge? As discussed in Section 10.2, we apply the Ratio Test to $\displaystyle\sum_{k=0}^{\infty} \left| \frac{(-1)^k}{(2k)!} x^{2k} \right|$ to test for absolute convergence:

$$r = \lim_{k \to \infty} \left| \frac{(-1)^{k+1} x^{2(k+1)}/(2(k+1))!}{(-1)^k x^{2k}/(2k)!} \right| \qquad r = \lim_{k \to \infty} \left| \frac{a_{k+1}}{a_k} \right|$$

$$= \lim_{k \to \infty} \left| \frac{x^2}{(2k+2)(2k+1)} \right| = 0. \qquad \text{Simplify and take the limit with } x \text{ fixed.}$$

In this case, $r < 1$ for all x, so the Maclaurin series converges absolutely for all x, which implies (by Theorem 9.21) that the series converges for all x. We conclude the interval of convergence is $-\infty < x < \infty$.

b. We proceed in a similar way with $f(x) = 1/(1-x)$ by evaluating the derivatives of f at 0:

$$f(x) = \frac{1}{1-x} \;\Rightarrow\; f(0) = 1,$$

$$f'(x) = \frac{1}{(1-x)^2} \;\Rightarrow\; f'(0) = 1,$$

$$f''(x) = \frac{2}{(1-x)^3} \;\Rightarrow\; f''(0) = 2!,$$

$$f'''(x) = \frac{3 \cdot 2}{(1-x)^4} \;\Rightarrow\; f'''(0) = 3!,$$

$$f^{(4)}(x) = \frac{4 \cdot 3 \cdot 2}{(1-x)^5} \;\Rightarrow\; f^{(4)}(0) = 4!,$$

and in general, $f^{(k)}(0) = k!$. Therefore, the Maclaurin series coefficients are $c_k = \dfrac{f^{(k)}(0)}{k!} = \dfrac{k!}{k!} = 1$, for $k = 0, 1, 2, \ldots$. The series for f centered at 0 is

$$1 + x + x^2 + x^3 + \cdots = \sum_{k=0}^{\infty} x^k.$$

This power series is familiar! The Maclaurin series for $f(x) = 1/(1-x)$ is a geometric series. We could apply the Ratio Test, but we have already demonstrated that this series converges for $|x| < 1$.

Related Exercises 9–20 ◄

➤ In Example 1a, we note that both $\cos x$ and its Maclaurin series are even functions. Be cautious with this observation: A Taylor series for an even function centered at a point different from 0 may be even, odd, or neither. A similar behavior occurs with odd functions.

➤ Recall that

$$(2k+2)! = (2k+2)(2k+1)(2k)!.$$

Therefore, $\dfrac{(2k)!}{(2k+2)!} = \dfrac{1}{(2k+2)(2k+1)}.$

The preceding example has an important lesson. *There is only one power series representation for a given function about a given point; however, there may be several ways to find it.*

QUICK CHECK 2 Based on Example 1b, what is the Taylor series for $f(x) = (1 + x)^{-1}$? ◄

EXAMPLE 2   Center other than 0 Find the first four nonzero terms of the Taylor series for $f(x) = \sqrt[3]{x}$ centered at 8.

SOLUTION Notice that f has derivatives of all orders at $x = 8$. The Taylor series centered at 8 has the form

$$\sum_{k=0}^{\infty} c_k(x - 8)^k, \quad \text{where } c_k = \frac{f^{(k)}(8)}{k!}.$$

Next, we evaluate derivatives:

$$f(x) = x^{1/3} \Rightarrow f(8) = 2,$$

$$f'(x) = \frac{1}{3}x^{-2/3} \Rightarrow f'(8) = \frac{1}{12},$$

$$f''(x) = -\frac{2}{9}x^{-5/3} \Rightarrow f''(8) = -\frac{1}{144}, \quad \text{and}$$

$$f'''(x) = \frac{10}{27}x^{-8/3} \Rightarrow f'''(8) = \frac{5}{3456}.$$

We now assemble the power series:

$$2 + \frac{1}{12}(x - 8) + \frac{1}{2!}\left(-\frac{1}{144}\right)(x - 8)^2 + \frac{1}{3!}\left(\frac{5}{3456}\right)(x - 8)^3 + \cdots$$

$$= 2 + \frac{1}{12}(x - 8) - \frac{1}{288}(x - 8)^2 + \frac{5}{20,736}(x - 8)^3 + \cdots.$$

Related Exercises 21–28 ◄

EXAMPLE 3   Manipulating Maclaurin series Let $f(x) = e^x$.

a. Find the Maclaurin series for f.

b. Find its interval of convergence.

c. Use the Maclaurin series for e^x to find the Maclaurin series for the functions $x^4 e^x$, e^{-2x}, and e^{-x^2}.

SOLUTION

a. The coefficients of the Taylor polynomials for $f(x) = e^x$ centered at 0 are $c_k = 1/k!$ (Example 3, Section 10.1). They are also the coefficients of the Maclaurin series. Therefore, the Maclaurin series for e^x is

$$1 + \frac{x}{1!} + \frac{x^2}{2!} + \cdots + \frac{x^n}{n!} + \cdots = \sum_{k=0}^{\infty} \frac{x^k}{k!}.$$

b. By the Ratio Test,

$$r = \lim_{k \to \infty} \left| \frac{x^{k+1}/(k + 1)!}{x^k/k!} \right| \qquad \text{Substitute } (k + 1)\text{st and } k\text{th terms.}$$

$$= \lim_{k \to \infty} \left| \frac{x}{k + 1} \right| = 0. \qquad \text{Simplify; take the limit with } x \text{ fixed.}$$

Because $r < 1$ for all x, the interval of convergence is $-\infty < x < \infty$.

c. As stated in Theorem 10.4, power series may be added, multiplied by powers of x, or composed with functions on their intervals of convergence. Therefore, the Maclaurin series for $x^4 e^x$ is

$$x^4 \sum_{k=0}^{\infty} \frac{x^k}{k!} = \sum_{k=0}^{\infty} \frac{x^{k+4}}{k!} = x^4 + \frac{x^5}{1!} + \frac{x^6}{2!} + \cdots + \frac{x^{k+4}}{k!} + \cdots.$$

Similarly, e^{-2x} is the composition $f(-2x)$. Replacing x with $-2x$ in the Maclaurin series for f, the series representation for e^{-2x} is

$$\sum_{k=0}^{\infty} \frac{(-2x)^k}{k!} = \sum_{k=0}^{\infty} \frac{(-1)^k (2x)^k}{k!} = 1 - 2x + 2x^2 - \frac{4}{3}x^3 + \cdots.$$

The Maclaurin series for e^{-x^2} is obtained by replacing x with $-x^2$ in the power series for f. The resulting series is

$$\sum_{k=0}^{\infty} \frac{(-x^2)^k}{k!} = \sum_{k=0}^{\infty} \frac{(-1)^k x^{2k}}{k!} = 1 - x^2 + \frac{x^4}{2!} - \frac{x^6}{3!} + \cdots.$$

QUICK CHECK 3 Find the first three terms of the Maclaurin series for $2xe^x$ and e^{-x}. ◄

Because the interval of convergence of $f(x) = e^x$ is $-\infty < x < \infty$, the manipulations used to obtain the series for $x^4 e^x$, e^{-2x}, or e^{-x^2} do not change the interval of convergence. If in doubt about the interval of convergence of a new series, apply the Ratio Test.

Related Exercises 29–38 ◄

EXAMPLE 4   Another power series Consider the function $f(x) = \sqrt{1 + x}$.

a. Find the first four terms of the Maclaurin series for f (centered at 0).

b. Approximate $\sqrt{1.15}$ to three decimal places. Assume the series for f converges to f on its interval of convergence, which is $[-1, 1]$

SOLUTION

a. We first compute the derivatives needed for the coefficients of the power series:

$$f(x) = (1 + x)^{1/2} \Rightarrow f(0) = 1,$$

$$f'(x) = \frac{1}{2}(1 + x)^{-1/2} \Rightarrow f'(0) = \frac{1}{2},$$

$$f''(x) = -\frac{1}{4}(1 + x)^{-3/2} \Rightarrow f''(0) = -\frac{1}{4}, \quad \text{and}$$

$$f'''(x) = \frac{3}{8}(1 + x)^{-5/2} \Rightarrow f'''(0) = \frac{3}{8}.$$

The leading terms of the Maclaurin series are

$$1 + \frac{1}{2}x - \frac{1}{4}\frac{1}{2!}x^2 + \frac{3}{8}\frac{1}{3!}x^3 - \cdots$$

$$= 1 + \frac{1}{2}x - \frac{1}{8}x^2 + \frac{1}{16}x^3 - \cdots.$$

> The remainder theorem for alternating series (Section 9.6) could be used in Example 4 to estimate the number of terms of the Maclaurin series needed to achieve a desired accuracy.

Table 10.3

n	Approximations $p_n(0.15)$
0	1.0
1	1.075
2	1.0721875
3	1.072398438

b. Truncating the series in part (a) produces Taylor polynomials p_n that may be used to approximate $f(0.15) = \sqrt{1.15}$. With $x = 0.15$, we find the polynomial approximations shown in Table 10.3. Four terms of the power series ($n = 3$) give $\sqrt{1.15} \approx 1.072$. Because the approximations with $n = 2$ and $n = 3$ agree to three decimal places, when rounded, the approximation 1.072 is accurate to three decimal places.

Related Exercises 39–44 ◄

QUICK CHECK 4 Use two and three terms of the series in Example 4 to approximate $\sqrt{1.1}$. ◄

EXAMPLE 5 A useful technique Consider the functions

$$f(x) = \sqrt[3]{1 + x} \quad \text{and} \quad g(x) = \sqrt[3]{c + x}, \quad \text{where } c > 0 \text{ is a constant}.$$

a. Find the first four terms of the Maclaurin series for f.

b. Use part (a) to find the first four terms of the Maclaurin series for g.

c. Use part (b) to approximate $\sqrt[3]{23}, \sqrt[3]{24}, \ldots, \sqrt[3]{31}$. Assume the series for g converges to g on its interval of convergence.

SOLUTION

a. The derivatives needed for the coefficients of the power series are

$$f(x) = (1 + x)^{1/3} \Rightarrow f(0) = 1,$$

$$f'(x) = \frac{1}{3}(1 + x)^{-2/3} \Rightarrow f'(0) = \frac{1}{3},$$

$$f''(x) = -\frac{2}{9}(1 + x)^{-5/3} \Rightarrow f''(0) = -\frac{2}{9}, \quad \text{and}$$

$$f'''(x) = \frac{10}{27}(1 + x)^{-8/3} \Rightarrow f'''(0) = \frac{10}{27}.$$

The leading terms of the Maclaurin series are

$$1 + \frac{1}{3}x - \frac{2}{9}\frac{1}{2!}x^2 + \frac{10}{27}\frac{1}{3!}x^3 - \cdots$$

$$= 1 + \frac{1}{3}x - \frac{1}{9}x^2 + \frac{5}{81}x^3 - \cdots.$$

b. To avoid deriving a new series for $g(x) = \sqrt[3]{c + x}$, a few steps of algebra allow us to use part (a). Note that

$$g(x) = \sqrt[3]{c + x} = \sqrt[3]{c\left(1 + \frac{x}{c}\right)} = \sqrt[3]{c} \cdot \sqrt[3]{1 + \frac{x}{c}} = \sqrt[3]{c} \cdot f\left(\frac{x}{c}\right).$$

In other words, g can be expressed in terms of f, for which we already have a power series. The power series for g is obtained by substituting x/c into the power series for f and multiplying by $\sqrt[3]{c}$:

$$g(x) = \sqrt[3]{c}\underbrace{\left(1 + \frac{1}{3}\left(\frac{x}{c}\right) - \frac{1}{9}\left(\frac{x}{c}\right)^2 + \frac{5}{81}\left(\frac{x}{c}\right)^3 - \cdots\right)}_{f(x/c)}.$$

It can be shown that the series for f in part (a) converges to f for $|x| \leq 1$. Therefore, the series for $f(x/c)$ converges to $f(x/c)$, provided $|x/c| \leq 1$, or, equivalently, for $|x| \leq c$.

c. The series of part (b) may be truncated after four terms to approximate cube roots. For example, note that $\sqrt[3]{29} = \sqrt[3]{\underbrace{27}_{c} + \underbrace{2}_{x}}$, so we take $c = 27$ and $x = 2$.

The choice $c = 27$ is made because 29 is near 27 and $\sqrt[3]{c} = \sqrt[3]{27} = 3$ is easy to evaluate. Substituting $c = 27$ and $x = 2$, we find that

$$\sqrt[3]{29} \approx \sqrt[3]{27}\left(1 + \frac{1}{3}\left(\frac{2}{27}\right) - \frac{1}{9}\left(\frac{2}{27}\right)^2 + \frac{5}{81}\left(\frac{2}{27}\right)^3\right) \approx 3.072.$$

The same method is used to approximate the cube roots of 23, 24, . . . , 30, 31 (Table 10.4). The absolute error is the difference between the approximation and the value given by a calculator. Notice that the errors increase as we move away from 27.

Table 10.4

	Approximation	Absolute Error
$\sqrt[3]{23}$	2.844	6.7×10^{-5}
$\sqrt[3]{24}$	2.885	2.0×10^{-5}
$\sqrt[3]{25}$	2.924	3.9×10^{-6}
$\sqrt[3]{26}$	2.962	2.4×10^{-7}
$\sqrt[3]{27}$	3	0
$\sqrt[3]{28}$	3.037	2.3×10^{-7}
$\sqrt[3]{29}$	3.072	3.5×10^{-6}
$\sqrt[3]{30}$	3.107	1.7×10^{-5}
$\sqrt[3]{31}$	3.141	5.4×10^{-5}

Related Exercises 45–56 ◄

The functions $(1 + x)^{1/2}$ and $(1 + x)^{1/3}$ in Examples 4 and 5, respectively, have the form $f(x) = (1 + x)^p$, where p is a real number. The Maclaurin series for functions of this form are called **binomial series**, and they can be written in one general form for all real numbers p. The coefficients of the binomial series are shown in Table 10.5 (Exercise 91).

Convergence of Taylor Series

It may seem that the story of Taylor series is over. But there is a technical point that is easily overlooked. Given a function f, we know how to write its Taylor series centered at a point a, and we know how to find its interval of convergence. We still do not know that the series actually converges to f. The remaining task is to determine when the Taylor series for f actually converges to f on its interval of convergence. Fortunately, the necessary tools have already been presented in Taylor's Theorem (Theorem 10.1), which gives the remainder for Taylor polynomials.

Assume f has derivatives of *all* orders on an open interval containing the point a. Taylor's Theorem tells us that

$$f(x) = p_n(x) + R_n(x),$$

where p_n is the nth-order Taylor polynomial for f centered at a,

$$R_n(x) = \frac{f^{(n+1)}(c)}{(n + 1)!}(x - a)^{n+1}$$

is the remainder, and c is a point between x and a. We see that the remainder, $R_n(x) = f(x) - p_n(x)$, measures the difference between f and the approximating polynomial p_n. When we say the Taylor series converges to f at a point x, we mean the value of the Taylor series at x equals $f(x)$; that is, $\lim_{n\to\infty} p_n(x) = f(x)$. The following theorem makes these ideas precise.

> **THEOREM 10.6   Convergence of Taylor Series**
> Let f have derivatives of all orders on an open interval I containing a. The Taylor series for f centered at a converges to f, for all x in I, if and only if $\lim_{n \to \infty} R_n(x) = 0$, for all x in I, where
>
> $$R_n(x) = \frac{f^{(n+1)}(c)}{(n+1)!}(x-a)^{n+1}$$
>
> is the remainder at x (with c between x and a).

Proof: The theorem requires derivatives of *all* orders. Therefore, by Taylor's Theorem (Theorem 10.1), the remainder exists in the given form for all n. Let p_n denote the nth-order Taylor polynomial and note that $\lim_{n \to \infty} p_n(x)$ is the Taylor series for f centered at a, evaluated at a point x in I.

First, assume that $\lim_{n \to \infty} R_n(x) = 0$ on the interval I and recall that $p_n(x) = f(x) - R_n(x)$. Taking limits of both sides, we have

$$\underbrace{\lim_{n \to \infty} p_n(x)}_{\text{Taylor series}} = \lim_{n \to \infty}\left(f(x) - R_n(x)\right) = \underbrace{\lim_{n \to \infty} f(x)}_{f(x)} - \underbrace{\lim_{n \to \infty} R_n(x)}_{0} = f(x).$$

We conclude that the Taylor series $\lim_{n \to \infty} p_n(x)$ equals $f(x)$, for all x in I.

Conversely, if the Taylor series converges to f, then $f(x) = \lim_{n \to \infty} p_n(x)$ and

$$0 = f(x) - \lim_{n \to \infty} p_n(x) = \lim_{n \to \infty}\underbrace{\left(f(x) - p_n(x)\right)}_{R_n(x)} = \lim_{n \to \infty} R_n(x).$$

It follows that $\lim_{n \to \infty} R_n(x) = 0$, for all x in I. ◀

Even with an expression for the remainder, it may be difficult to show that $\lim_{n \to \infty} R_n(x) = 0$. The following examples illustrate cases in which it is possible.

EXAMPLE 6   Remainder in the Maclaurin series for e^x Show that the Maclaurin series for $f(x) = e^x$ converges to $f(x)$, for $-\infty < x < \infty$.

SOLUTION As shown in Example 3, the Maclaurin series for $f(x) = e^x$ is

$$\sum_{k=0}^{\infty} \frac{x^k}{k!} = 1 + x + \frac{x^2}{2!} + \cdots + \frac{x^n}{n!} + \cdots,$$

which converges for $-\infty < x < \infty$. In Example 6 of Section 10.1 it was shown that the remainder is

$$R_n(x) = \frac{e^c}{(n+1)!}x^{n+1},$$

where c is between 0 and x. Notice that the intermediate point c varies with n, but it is always between 0 and x. Therefore, e^c is between $e^0 = 1$ and e^x; in fact, $e^c \le e^{|x|}$, for all n. It follows that

$$|R_n(x)| \le \frac{e^{|x|}}{(n+1)!}|x|^{n+1}.$$

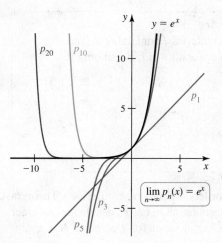

FIGURE 10.17

Holding x fixed, we have

$$\lim_{n \to \infty} |R_n(x)| = \lim_{n \to \infty} \frac{e^{|x|}}{(n+1)!} |x|^{n+1} = e^{|x|} \lim_{n \to \infty} \frac{|x|^{n+1}}{(n+1)!} = 0,$$

where we used the fact that $\lim_{n \to \infty} x^n/n! = 0$, for $-\infty < x < \infty$ (Section 9.2). Because $\lim_{n \to \infty} |R_n(x)| = 0$, it follows that for all real numbers x, the Taylor series converges to e^x, or

$$e^x = \sum_{k=0}^{\infty} \frac{x^k}{k!} = 1 + x + \frac{x^2}{2!} + \cdots + \frac{x^n}{n!} + \cdots.$$

The convergence of the Taylor series to e^x is illustrated in Figure 10.17, where Taylor polynomials of increasing degree are graphed together with e^x.

Related Exercises 57–60◄

EXAMPLE 7 **Maclaurin series convergence for $\cos x$** Show that the Maclaurin series for $\cos x$,

$$1 - \frac{x^2}{2!} + \frac{x^4}{4!} - \frac{x^6}{6!} + \cdots = \sum_{k=0}^{\infty} (-1)^k \frac{x^{2k}}{(2k)!},$$

converges to $f(x) = \cos x$, for $-\infty < x < \infty$.

SOLUTION To show that the power series converges to f, we must show that $\lim_{n \to \infty} |R_n(x)| = 0$, for $-\infty < x < \infty$. According to Taylor's Theorem with $a = 0$,

$$R_n(x) = \frac{f^{(n+1)}(c)}{(n+1)!} x^{n+1},$$

where c is between 0 and x. Notice that $f^{(n+1)}(c) = \pm \sin c$ or $f^{(n+1)}(c) = \pm \cos c$. In all cases, $|f^{(n+1)}(c)| \leq 1$. Therefore, the absolute value of the remainder term is bounded as

$$|R_n(x)| = \left| \frac{f^{(n+1)}(c)}{(n+1)!} x^{n+1} \right| \leq \frac{|x|^{n+1}}{(n+1)!}.$$

Holding x fixed and using $\lim_{n \to \infty} x^n/n! = 0$, we see that $\lim_{n \to \infty} R_n(x) = 0$ for all x. Therefore, the given power series converges to $f(x) = \cos x$, for all x; that is, $\cos x = \sum_{k=0}^{\infty} \frac{(-1)^k x^{2k}}{(2k)!}$. The convergence of the Taylor series to $\cos x$ is illustrated in Figure 10.18.

Related Exercises 57–60◄

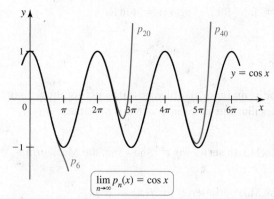

FIGURE 10.18

The procedure used in Examples 6 and 7 can be carried out for all the Taylor series we have worked with so far (with varying degrees of difficulty). In each case, the Taylor series converges to the function it represents on the interval of convergence. Table 10.5 summarizes commonly used Taylor series centered at 0 and the functions to which they converge.

▷ Table 10.5 asserts, without proof, that in several cases, the Taylor series for f converges to f at the endpoints of the interval of convergence. Proving convergence at the endpoints generally requires advanced techniques. It may also be done using the following theorem:

   Suppose the Taylor series for f centered at 0 converges to f on the interval $(-R, R)$. If the series converges at $x = R$, then it converges to $\lim\limits_{x \to R^-} f(x)$. If the series converges at $x = -R$, then it converges to $\lim\limits_{x \to -R^+} f(x)$.

   For example, this theorem would allow us to conclude that the series for $\ln(1 + x)$ converges to $\ln 2$ at $x = 1$.

Table 10.5

$$\frac{1}{1-x} = 1 + x + x^2 + \cdots + x^k + \cdots = \sum_{k=0}^{\infty} x^k, \quad \text{for } |x| < 1$$

$$\frac{1}{1+x} = 1 - x + x^2 - \cdots + (-1)^k x^k + \cdots = \sum_{k=0}^{\infty} (-1)^k x^k, \quad \text{for } |x| < 1$$

$$e^x = 1 + x + \frac{x^2}{2!} + \cdots + \frac{x^k}{k!} + \cdots = \sum_{k=0}^{\infty} \frac{x^k}{k!}, \quad \text{for } |x| < \infty$$

$$\sin x = x - \frac{x^3}{3!} + \frac{x^5}{5!} - \cdots + \frac{(-1)^k x^{2k+1}}{(2k+1)!} + \cdots = \sum_{k=0}^{\infty} \frac{(-1)^k x^{2k+1}}{(2k+1)!}, \quad \text{for } |x| < \infty$$

$$\cos x = 1 - \frac{x^2}{2!} + \frac{x^4}{4!} - \cdots + \frac{(-1)^k x^{2k}}{(2k)!} + \cdots = \sum_{k=0}^{\infty} \frac{(-1)^k x^{2k}}{(2k)!}, \quad \text{for } |x| < \infty$$

$$\ln(1+x) = x - \frac{x^2}{2} + \frac{x^3}{3} - \cdots + \frac{(-1)^{k+1} x^k}{k} + \cdots = \sum_{k=1}^{\infty} \frac{(-1)^{k+1} x^k}{k}, \quad \text{for } -1 < x \le 1$$

$$-\ln(1-x) = x + \frac{x^2}{2} + \frac{x^3}{3} + \cdots + \frac{x^k}{k} + \cdots = \sum_{k=1}^{\infty} \frac{x^k}{k}, \quad \text{for } -1 \le x < 1$$

$$\tan^{-1} x = x - \frac{x^3}{3} + \frac{x^5}{5} - \cdots + \frac{(-1)^k x^{2k+1}}{2k+1} + \cdots = \sum_{k=0}^{\infty} \frac{(-1)^k x^{2k+1}}{2k+1}, \quad \text{for } |x| \le 1$$

▷ The final series listed in Table 10.5 is known as the binomial series.

$$(1+x)^p = \sum_{k=0}^{\infty} \binom{p}{k} x^k, \quad \text{for } |x| < 1 \text{ and } \binom{p}{k} = \frac{p(p-1)(p-2)\cdots(p-k+1)}{k!}, \binom{p}{0} = 1$$

SECTION 10.3 EXERCISES

Review Questions

1. How are the Taylor polynomials for a function f centered at a related to the Taylor series for the function f centered at a?

2. What conditions must be satisfied by a function f to have a Taylor series centered at a?

3. How do you find the coefficients of the Taylor series for f centered at a?

4. How do you find the interval of convergence of a Taylor series?

5. Suppose you know the Maclaurin series for f and it converges for $|x| < 1$. How do you find the Maclaurin series for $f(x^2)$ and where does it converge?

6. For what values of p does the Taylor series for $f(x) = (1 + x)^p$ centered at 0 terminate?

7. In terms of the remainder, what does it mean for a Taylor series for a function f to converge to f?

8. Write the Maclaurin series for e^{2x}.

Basic Skills

9–20. Maclaurin series

a. Find the first four nonzero terms of the Maclaurin series for the given function.
b. Write the power series using summation notation.
c. Determine the interval of convergence of the series.

9. $f(x) = e^{-x}$

10. $f(x) = \cos 2x$

11. $f(x) = (1 + x^2)^{-1}$

12. $f(x) = \ln(1 + x)$

13. $f(x) = e^{2x}$

14. $f(x) = (1 + 2x)^{-1}$

15. $f(x) = \tan^{-1} x$

16. $f(x) = \sin 3x$

17. $f(x) = 3^x$

18. $f(x) = \log_3(x + 1)$

19. $f(x) = (1 + 3x)^{-1}$

20. $f(x) = (2 + x)^{-1}$

21–28. Taylor series centered at $a \ne 0$

a. Find the first four nonzero terms of the Taylor series for the given function centered at a.
b. Write the power series using summation notation.

21. $f(x) = \sin x, a = \pi/2$

22. $f(x) = \cos x, a = \pi$

23. $f(x) = 1/x, a = 1$

24. $f(x) = 1/x, a = 2$

25. $f(x) = \ln x, a = 3$

26. $f(x) = e^x, a = \ln 2$

27. $f(x) = 2^x, a = 1$

28. $f(x) = 10^x, a = 2$

29–38. Manipulating Taylor series *Use the Taylor series in Table 10.5 to find the first four nonzero terms of the Taylor series for the following functions centered at 0.*

29. $\ln(1 + x^2)$

30. $\sin x^2$

31. $\dfrac{1}{1 - 2x}$

32. $\ln(1 + 2x)$

33. $\begin{cases} e^x - 1/x & \text{if } x \neq 0 \\ 1 & \text{if } x = 0 \end{cases}$

34. $\cos 3x^2$

35. $(1 + x^4)^{-1}$

36. $x \tan^{-1} x^2$

37. $(9 + x^2)^{-1}$

38. $x \ln(1 - x^2)$

39–44. More Maclaurin series

a. Find the first four nonzero terms of the Maclaurin series for the given function.

b. Use the first four terms of the series to approximate the given quantity.

39. $f(x) = (1 + x)^{-2}$; approximate $1/1.21 = 1/1.1^2$.

40. $f(x) = \sqrt{1 + x}$; approximate $\sqrt{1.06}$.

41. $f(x) = \sqrt[4]{1 + x}$; approximate $\sqrt[4]{1.12}$.

42. $f(x) = (1 + x)^{-3}$; approximate $1/1.331 = 1/1.1^3$.

43. $f(x) = (1 + x)^{-2/3}$; approximate $1.18^{-2/3}$.

44. $f(x) = (1 + x)^{2/3}$; approximate $1.02^{2/3}$.

45–50. Working with Maclaurin series *Use properties of power series, substitution, and factoring to find the first four nonzero terms of the Maclaurin series for the following functions. Use part (3) of Theorem 10.4 (p. 684) to find the interval of convergence for the new series. Use the Maclaurin series*

$$\sqrt{1 + x} = 1 + \frac{x}{2} - \frac{x^2}{8} + \frac{x^3}{16} - \cdots, \quad \text{for } -1 \leq x \leq 1.$$

45. $\sqrt{1 + x^2}$

46. $\sqrt{4 + x}$

47. $\sqrt{9 - 9x}$

48. $\sqrt{1 - 4x}$

49. $\sqrt{a^2 + x^2}$, $a > 0$

50. $\sqrt{4 - 16x^2}$

51–56. Working with Maclaurin series *Use properties of power series, substitution, and factoring of constants to find the first four nonzero terms of the Maclaurin series for the following functions. Use the Maclaurin series*

$$(1 + x)^{-2} = 1 - 2x + 3x^2 - 4x^3 + \cdots, \quad \text{for } -1 \leq x < 1.$$

51. $(1 + 4x)^{-2}$

52. $\dfrac{1}{(1 - 4x)^2}$

53. $\dfrac{1}{(4 + x^2)^2}$

54. $(x^2 - 4x + 5)^{-2}$

55. $\dfrac{1}{(3 + 4x)^2}$

56. $\dfrac{1}{(1 + 4x^2)^2}$

57–60. Remainders *Find the remainder in the Taylor series centered at the point a for the following functions. Then show that* $\lim\limits_{n \to \infty} R_n(x) = 0$ *for all x in the interval of convergence.*

57. $f(x) = \sin x, a = 0$

58. $f(x) = \cos 2x, a = 0$

59. $f(x) = e^{-x}, a = 0$

60. $f(x) = \cos x, a = \pi/2$

Further Explorations

61. Explain why or why not Determine whether the following statements are true and give an explanation or counterexample.

   a. The function $f(x) = \sqrt{x}$ has a Taylor series centered at 0.

   b. The function $f(x) = \csc x$ has a Taylor series centered at $\pi/2$.

   c. If f has a Taylor series that converges only on $(-2, 2)$, then $f(x^2)$ has a Taylor series that also converges only on $(-2, 2)$.

   d. If $p(x)$ is the Taylor series for f centered at 0, then $p(x - 1)$ is the Taylor series for f centered at 1.

   e. The Taylor series for an even function about 0 has only even powers of x.

62–69. Any method *Use any analytical method to find the first three nonzero terms of the Taylor series centered at 0 for the following functions.*

62. $f(x) = \cos 2x + 2 \sin x$

63. $f(x) = \dfrac{e^x + e^{-x}}{2}$

64. $f(x) = \sec x$

65. $f(x) = (1 + x^2)^{-2/3}$

66. $f(x) = \tan x$

67. $f(x) = \sqrt{1 - x^2}$

68. $f(x) = b^x$, for $b > 0, b \neq 1$

69. $f(x) = \dfrac{1}{x^4 + 2x^2 + 1}$

70–73. Approximating powers *Compute the coefficients for the Taylor series for the following functions about the given point a and then use the first four terms of the series to approximate the given number.*

70. $f(x) = \sqrt{x}$ with $a = 36$; approximate $\sqrt{39}$.

71. $f(x) = \sqrt[3]{x}$ with $a = 64$; approximate $\sqrt[3]{60}$.

72. $f(x) = 1/\sqrt{x}$ with $a = 4$; approximate $1/\sqrt{3}$.

73. $f(x) = \sqrt[4]{x}$ with $a = 16$; approximate $\sqrt[4]{13}$.

74. Geometric series Recall that the Taylor series for $f(x) = 1/(1 - x)$ about 0 is the geometric series $\sum\limits_{k=0}^{\infty} x^k$. Show that this series can also be found by computing the coefficients using the definition of the Taylor series.

75. Integer coefficients Show that the first five nonzero coefficients of the Taylor series for $f(x) = \sqrt{1 + 4x}$ about 0 are integers.

76. Choosing a good center Suppose you want to approximate $\sqrt{72}$ using four terms of a Taylor series. Compare the accuracy of the approximations obtained using Taylor series for $\sqrt{x}$ centered at 64 and 81.

77. Alternative means By comparing the first four terms, show that the Maclaurin series for $\sin^2 x$ can be found (a) by squaring the Maclaurin series for $\sin x$, (b) by using the identity $\sin^2 x = (1 - \cos 2x)/2$, or (c) by computing the coefficients using the definition.

78. Alternative means By comparing the first four terms, show that the Maclaurin series for $\cos^2 x$ can be found (a) by squaring the Maclaurin series for $\cos x$, (b) by using the identity $\cos^2 x = (1 + \cos 2x)/2$, or (c) by computing the coefficients using the definition.

79. Designer series Find a power series that has $(2, 6)$ as an interval of convergence.

80–81. Patterns in coefficients *Find the next two terms of the following Taylor series.*

80. $\sqrt{1 + x}$: $1 + \dfrac{1}{2}x - \dfrac{1}{2 \cdot 4}x^2 + \dfrac{1 \cdot 3}{2 \cdot 4 \cdot 6}x^3 - \cdots$.

81. $\dfrac{1}{\sqrt{1 + x}}$: $1 - \dfrac{1}{2}x + \dfrac{1 \cdot 3}{2 \cdot 4}x^2 - \dfrac{1 \cdot 3 \cdot 5}{2 \cdot 4 \cdot 6}x^3 + \cdots$.

82. Composition of series Use composition of series to find the first three terms of the Maclaurin series for the following functions.

    a. $e^{\sin x}$ **b.** $e^{\tan x}$ **c.** $\sqrt{1 + \sin^2 x}$

Applications

83–86. Approximations *Choose a Taylor series and center point to approximate the following quantities with an error of 10^{-4} or less.*

83. $\cos 40°$

84. $\sin(0.98\pi)$

85. $\sqrt[3]{83}$

86. $1/\sqrt[4]{17}$

87. Different approximation strategies Suppose you want to approximate $\sqrt[3]{128}$ to within 10^{-4} of the exact value.

    a. Use a Taylor polynomial for $f(x) = (125 + x)^{1/3}$ centered at 0.

    b. Use a Taylor polynomial for $f(x) = x^{1/3}$ centered at 125.

    c. Compare the two approaches. Are they equivalent?

Additional Exercises

88. Mean Value Theorem Explain why the Mean Value Theorem (Theorem 4.9 of Section 4.6) is a special case of Taylor's Theorem.

89. Version of the Second Derivative Test Assume that f has at least two continuous derivatives on an interval containing a with

$f'(a) = 0$. Use Taylor's Theorem to prove the following version of the Second Derivative Test:

    a. If $f''(x) > 0$ on some interval containing a, then f has a local minimum at a.

    b. If $f''(x) < 0$ on some interval containing a, then f has a local maximum at a.

90. Nonconvergence to f Consider the function

$$f(x) = \begin{cases} e^{-1/x^2} & \text{if } x \neq 0 \\ 0 & \text{if } x = 0. \end{cases}$$

    a. Use the definition of the derivative to show that $f'(0) = 0$.

    b. Assume the fact that $f^{(k)}(0) = 0$, for $k = 1, 2, 3, \ldots$. (You can write a proof using the definition of the derivative.) Write the Taylor series for f centered at 0.

    c. Explain why the Taylor series for f does not converge to f for $x \neq 0$.

91. Binomial Series Derive the coefficients of the binomial series shown in Table 10.5.

Technology Exercises

92. Taylor series convergence Let $f(x) = \ln(1 + x)$ and let p_n be the nth-order Taylor polynomial for f centered at 0.

    a. Write out the polynomials $p_1, \ldots, p_5$.

    b. Graph f and $p_1, \ldots, p_5$ on the interval $[-1, 1]$.

    c. On what parts of the interval $[-1, 1]$ is the convergence to f the slowest?

    d. What is the error in $p_1, \ldots, p_5$ when they are used to approximate $f(1)$?

    e. How large must n be to ensure that $|f(0.5) - p_n(0.5)| < 0.01$?

    f. How large must n be to ensure that $|f(1) - p_n(1)| < 0.01$?

93. Taylor series convergence Let $f(x) = \dfrac{1}{1 - x}$ and let p_n be the nth-order Taylor polynomial for f centered at 0.

    a. Write out the polynomials $p_1, \ldots, p_5$.

    b. Graph f and $p_1, \ldots, p_5$ on the interval $[-1, 1]$.

    c. On what parts of the interval $[-1, 1]$ is the convergence to f the slowest?

    d. At what point is the error zero when $p_1, \ldots, p_5$ are used to approximate $f(0)$?

    e. What is the error in $p_1, \ldots, p_5$ when they are used to approximate $f(0.9)$?

    f. How large must n be to ensure that $|f(0.9) - p_n(0.9)| < 0.01$?

QUICK CHECK ANSWERS

1. When evaluated at $x = a$, all terms of the series are zero except the first term, which is $f(a)$. Therefore, the series equals $f(a)$ at this point.
2. $1 - x + x^2 - x^3 + x^4 - \cdots$ **3.** $2x + 2x^2 + x^3$; $1 - x + x^2/2$ **4.** 1.05, 1.04875 ◄

10.4 Working with Taylor Series

We now know the Taylor series for many familiar functions, and we have tools for working with power series. The goal of this final section is to illustrate additional techniques associated with power series. As you will see, power series cover the entire landscape of calculus from limits and derivatives to integrals and approximation. We present five different topics, which you can explore selectively.

Limits by Taylor Series

An important use of Taylor series is evaluating limits. Two examples illustrate the essential ideas.

EXAMPLE 1   A limit by Taylor series Evaluate $\lim\limits_{x \to 0} \dfrac{x^2 + 2\cos x - 2}{3x^4}$.

> L'Hôpital's Rule may be impractical when it must be used more than once on the same limit or when derivatives are difficult to compute.

SOLUTION Because the limit has the indeterminate form $0/0$, l'Hôpital's Rule can be used, which requires four applications of the rule. Alternatively, because the limit involves values of x near 0, we substitute the Maclaurin series for $\cos x$. Recalling that

$$\cos x = 1 - \frac{x^2}{2} + \frac{x^4}{24} - \frac{x^6}{720} + \cdots, \quad \text{Table 10.5, page 699}$$

we have

> In using series to evaluate limits, it is often not obvious how many terms of the Taylor series to use. When in doubt, include extra (higher-power) terms. The dots in the calculation stand for powers of x greater than the last power that appears.

$$\lim_{x \to 0} \frac{x^2 + 2\cos x - 2}{3x^4} = \lim_{x \to 0} \frac{x^2 + 2\left(1 - \dfrac{x^2}{2} + \dfrac{x^4}{24} - \dfrac{x^6}{720} + \cdots\right) - 2}{3x^4} \quad \text{Substitute for } \cos x.$$

$$= \lim_{x \to 0} \frac{x^2 + \left(2 - x^2 + \dfrac{x^4}{12} - \dfrac{x^6}{360} + \cdots\right) - 2}{3x^4} \quad \text{Simplify.}$$

$$= \lim_{x \to 0} \frac{\dfrac{x^4}{12} - \dfrac{x^6}{360} + \cdots}{3x^4} \quad \text{Simplify.}$$

> **QUICK CHECK 1** Use the Taylor series $\sin x = x - x^3/6 + \cdots$ to verify that $\lim\limits_{x \to 0} (\sin x)/x = 1$. ◄

$$= \lim_{x \to 0} \left(\frac{1}{36} - \frac{x^2}{1080} + \cdots\right) = \frac{1}{36}. \quad \begin{array}{l}\text{Use Theorem 10.4,} \\ \text{Property 2;} \\ \text{evaluate limit.}\end{array}$$

Related Exercises 7–24 ◄

EXAMPLE 2   A limit by Taylor series Evaluate

$$\lim_{x \to \infty} \left(6x^5 \sin \frac{1}{x} - 6x^4 + x^2\right).$$

SOLUTION A Taylor series may be centered at any finite point in the domain of the function, but we don't have the tools needed to expand a function about $x = \infty$. Using a technique introduced earlier, we replace x with $1/t$ and note that as $x \to \infty$, $t \to 0^+$. The new limit becomes

$$\lim_{x \to \infty} \left(6x^5 \sin \frac{1}{x} - 6x^4 + x^2\right) = \lim_{t \to 0^+} \left(\frac{6\sin t}{t^5} - \frac{6}{t^4} + \frac{1}{t^2}\right) \quad \text{Replace } x \text{ with } 1/t.$$

$$= \lim_{t \to 0^+} \left(\frac{6\sin t - 6t + t^3}{t^5}\right). \quad \text{Common denominator}$$

This limit has the indeterminate form $0/0$. We now expand $\sin t$ in a Taylor series centered at $t = 0$. Because

$$\sin t = t - \frac{t^3}{6} + \frac{t^5}{120} - \frac{t^7}{5040} + \cdots, \quad \text{Table 10.5, page 699}$$

the value of the original limit is

$$\lim_{t \to 0^+} \left(\frac{6 \sin t - 6t + t^3}{t^5} \right)$$

$$= \lim_{t \to 0^+} \left(\frac{6\left(t - \dfrac{t^3}{6} + \dfrac{t^5}{120} - \dfrac{t^7}{5040} + \cdots \right) - 6t + t^3}{t^5} \right) \quad \text{Substitute for } \sin t.$$

$$= \lim_{t \to 0^+} \left(\frac{\dfrac{t^5}{20} - \dfrac{t^7}{840} + \cdots}{t^5} \right) \quad \text{Simplify.}$$

$$= \lim_{t \to 0^+} \left(\frac{1}{20} - \frac{t^2}{840} + \cdots \right) = \frac{1}{20}. \quad \begin{array}{l}\text{Use Theorem 10.4,} \\ \text{Property 2; evaluate limit.}\end{array}$$

Related Exercises 7–24 ◄

Differentiating Power Series

The following examples illustrate ways in which term-by-term differentiation (Theorem 10.5) may be used.

EXAMPLE 3 **Power series for derivatives** Differentiate the Maclaurin series for $f(x) = \sin x$ to verify that $\dfrac{d}{dx}(\sin x) = \cos x$.

SOLUTION The Maclaurin series for $f(x) = \sin x$ is

$$\sin x = x - \frac{x^3}{3!} + \frac{x^5}{5!} - \frac{x^7}{7!} + \cdots,$$

and it converges for $-\infty < x < \infty$. By Theorem 10.5, the differentiated series also converges for $-\infty < x < \infty$ and it converges to $f'(x)$. Differentiating, we have

$$\frac{d}{dx} \left(x - \frac{x^3}{3!} + \frac{x^5}{5!} - \frac{x^7}{7!} + \cdots \right) = 1 - \frac{x^2}{2!} + \frac{x^4}{4!} - \frac{x^6}{6!} + \cdots = \cos x.$$

QUICK CHECK 2 Differentiate the power series for $\cos x$ (given in Example 3) and identify the result. ◄

The differentiated series is the Maclaurin series for $\cos x$, confirming that $f'(x) = \cos x$.

Related Exercises 25–32 ◄

EXAMPLE 4 **A differential equation** Find a power series solution of the differential equation $y'(t) = y(t) + 2$, subject to the initial condition $y(0) = 6$. Identify the function represented by the power series.

SOLUTION Because the initial condition is given at $t = 0$, we assume the solution has a Taylor series centered at 0 of the form $y(t) = \displaystyle\sum_{k=0}^{\infty} c_k t^k$, where the coefficients c_k must be determined. Recall that the coefficients of the Taylor series are given by

$$c_k = \frac{y^{(k)}(0)}{k!}, \quad \text{for } k = 0, 1, 2, \ldots.$$

If we can determine $y^{(k)}(0)$, for $k = 0, 1, 2, \ldots$, the coefficients of the series are also determined.

Substituting the initial condition $t = 0$ and $y = 6$ into the power series

$$y(t) = c_0 + c_1 t + c_2 t^2 + \cdots,$$

we find that

$$6 = c_0 + c_1(0) + c_2(0)^2 + \cdots.$$

It follows that $c_0 = 6$. To determine $y'(0)$, we substitute $t = 0$ into the differential equation; the result is $y'(0) = y(0) + 2 = 6 + 2 = 8$. Therefore, $c_1 = y'(0)/1! = 8$.

The remaining derivatives are obtained by successively differentiating the differential equation and substituting $t = 0$. We find that $y''(0) = y'(0) = 8$, $y'''(0) = y''(0) = 8$, and in general, $y^{(k)}(0) = 8$, for $k = 2, 3, 4, \ldots$. Therefore,

$$c_k = \frac{y^{(k)}(0)}{k!} = \frac{8}{k!}, \text{ for } k = 1, 2, 3, \ldots,$$

and the Taylor series for the solution is

$$
\begin{aligned}
y(t) &= c_0 + c_1 t + c_2 t^2 + \cdots \\
&= 6 + \frac{8}{1!}t + \frac{8}{2!}t^2 + \frac{8}{3!}t^3 + \cdots.
\end{aligned}
$$

To identify the function represented by this series, we write

$$
\begin{aligned}
y(t) &= \underbrace{-2 + 8}_{6} + \frac{8}{1!}t + \frac{8}{2!}t^2 + \frac{8}{3!}t^3 + \cdots \\
&= -2 + 8\underbrace{\left(1 + t + \frac{t^2}{2!} + \frac{t^3}{3!} + \cdots\right)}_{e^t}.
\end{aligned}
$$

> You should check that $y(t) = -2 + 8e^t$ satisfies $y'(t) = y(t) + 2$ and $y(0) = 6$.

The power series that appears is the Taylor series for e^t. Therefore, the solution is $y(t) = -2 + 8e^t$.

Related Exercises 33–36 ◀

Integrating Power Series

The following example illustrates the use of power series in approximating integrals that cannot be evaluated by analytical methods.

EXAMPLE 5 **Approximating a definite integral** Approximate the value of the integral $\int_0^1 e^{-x^2}\,dx$ with an error no greater than 5×10^{-4}.

SOLUTION The antiderivative of e^{-x^2} cannot be expressed in terms of familiar functions. The strategy is to write the Maclaurin series for e^{-x^2} and integrate it term by term. Recall that integration of a power series is valid within its interval of convergence (Theorem 10.5). Beginning with the Maclaurin series

$$e^x = 1 + x + \frac{x^2}{2!} + \frac{x^3}{3!} + \cdots + \frac{x^n}{n!} + \cdots,$$

which converges for $-\infty < x < \infty$, we replace x with $-x^2$ to obtain

$$e^{-x^2} = 1 - x^2 + \frac{x^4}{2!} - \frac{x^6}{3!} + \cdots + \frac{(-1)^n x^{2n}}{n!} + \cdots,$$

which also converges for $-\infty < x < \infty$. By the Fundamental Theorem of Calculus,

$$
\begin{aligned}
\int_0^1 e^{-x^2}\,dx &= \left(x - \frac{x^3}{3} + \frac{x^5}{5 \cdot 2!} - \frac{x^7}{7 \cdot 3!} + \cdots + \frac{(-1)^n x^{2n+1}}{(2n+1)n!} + \cdots\right)\Bigg|_0^1 \\
&= 1 - \frac{1}{3} + \frac{1}{5 \cdot 2!} - \frac{1}{7 \cdot 3!} + \cdots + \frac{(-1)^n}{(2n+1)n!} + \cdots.
\end{aligned}
$$

Because the definite integral is expressed as an alternating series, the magnitude of the remainder in truncating the series is less than the magnitude of the first neglected term, which is $\left| \dfrac{(-1)^{n+1}}{(2n+3)(n+1)!} \right|$. By trial and error, we find that the magnitude of this term is less than 5×10^{-4} if $n \geq 5$ (with $n = 5$, we have $\dfrac{1}{13 \cdot 6!} \approx 1.07 \times 10^{-4}$). The sum of the terms of the series up to $n = 5$ gives the approximation

$$\int_0^1 e^{-x^2}\, dx \approx 1 - \frac{1}{3} + \frac{1}{5 \cdot 2!} - \frac{1}{7 \cdot 3!} + \frac{1}{9 \cdot 4!} - \frac{1}{11 \cdot 5!} \approx 0.747.$$

Related Exercises 37–44 ◄

> The integral in Example 5 is important in statistics and probability theory because of its relationship to the *normal distribution*.

Representing Real Numbers

When values of x are substituted into a convergent power series, the result may be a series representation of a familiar real number. The following example illustrates some techniques.

EXAMPLE 6   Evaluating infinite series

a. Use the Maclaurin series for $f(x) = \tan^{-1} x$ to evaluate

$$1 - \frac{1}{3} + \frac{1}{5} - \cdots = \sum_{k=0}^{\infty} \frac{(-1)^k}{2k+1}.$$

b. Let $f(x) = (e^x - 1)/x$, for $x \neq 0$, and $f(0) = 1$. Use the Maclaurin series for f to evaluate $f'(1)$ and $\displaystyle\sum_{k=1}^{\infty} \frac{k}{(k+1)!}$.

SOLUTION

a. From Table 10.5 (page 699) we see that for $|x| \leq 1$,

$$\tan^{-1} x = x - \frac{x^3}{3} + \frac{x^5}{5} - \cdots + \frac{(-1)^k x^{2k+1}}{2k+1} + \cdots = \sum_{k=0}^{\infty} \frac{(-1)^k x^{2k+1}}{2k+1}.$$

Substituting $x = 1$, we have

$$\tan^{-1} 1 = 1 - \frac{1^3}{3} + \frac{1^5}{5} - \cdots = \sum_{k=0}^{\infty} \frac{(-1)^k}{2k+1}.$$

> The series in Example 6a (known as the *Gregory series*) is one of a multitude of series representations of π. Because this series converges slowly, it does not provide an efficient way to approximate π.

Because $\tan^{-1} 1 = \pi/4$, the value of the series is $\pi/4$.

b. Using the Maclaurin series for e^x, the series for $f(x) = (e^x - 1)/x$ is

$$f(x) = \frac{e^x - 1}{x} = \frac{1}{x}\left(\left(1 + x + \frac{x^2}{2!} + \frac{x^3}{3!} + \cdots \right) - 1 \right) \qquad \text{Substitute series for } e^x.$$

$$= 1 + \frac{x}{2!} + \frac{x^2}{3!} + \frac{x^3}{4!} + \cdots = \sum_{k=1}^{\infty} \frac{x^{k-1}}{k!}, \qquad \text{Theorem 10.4, Property 2.}$$

which converges for $-\infty < x < \infty$. By the Quotient Rule,

$$f'(x) = \frac{xe^x - (e^x - 1)}{x^2}.$$

Differentiating the series for f term by term (Theorem 10.5), we find that

$$f'(x) = \frac{d}{dx}\left(1 + \frac{x}{2!} + \frac{x^2}{3!} + \frac{x^3}{4!} + \cdots\right)$$

$$= \frac{1}{2!} + \frac{2x}{3!} + \frac{3x^2}{4!} + \cdots = \sum_{k=1}^{\infty} \frac{kx^{k-1}}{(k+1)!}.$$

We now have two expressions for f'; they are evaluated at $x = 1$ to show that

$$f'(1) = 1 = \sum_{k=1}^{\infty} \frac{k}{(k+1)!}.$$

Related Exercises 45–54 ◄

QUICK CHECK 3 What value of x would you substitute into the Maclaurin series for $\tan^{-1} x$ to obtain a series representation for $\pi/6$? ◄

Representing Functions as Power Series

Power series have a fundamental role in mathematics in defining functions and providing alternative representations of familiar functions. As an overall review, we close this chapter with two examples that use many techniques for working with power series.

EXAMPLE 7   Identify the series Identify the function represented by the power series $\sum_{k=0}^{\infty} \frac{(1-2x)^k}{k!}$ and give its interval of convergence.

SOLUTION The Maclaurin series for the exponential function,

$$e^x = \sum_{k=0}^{\infty} \frac{x^k}{k!},$$

converges for $-\infty < x < \infty$. Replacing x with $1 - 2x$ produces the given series:

$$\sum_{k=0}^{\infty} \frac{(1-2x)^k}{k!} = e^{1-2x}.$$

This replacement is allowed because $1 - 2x$ is within the interval of convergence of the series for e^x; that is, $-\infty < 1 - 2x < \infty$, for all x. Therefore, the given series represents e^{1-2x}, for $-\infty < x < \infty$.

Related Exercises 55–64 ◄

EXAMPLE 8   Mystery series The power series $\sum_{k=1}^{\infty} \frac{(-1)^k k}{4^k} x^{2k}$ appeared in the opening of Section 10.2. Determine the interval of convergence of the power series and find the function it represents on this interval.

SOLUTION Applying the Ratio Test to the series, we determine that it converges when $|x^2/4| < 1$, which implies that $|x| < 2$. A quick check of the endpoints of the original series confirms that it diverges at $x = \pm 2$. Therefore, the interval of convergence is $|x| < 2$.

To find the function represented by the series, we apply several maneuvers until we obtain a geometric series. First note that

$$\sum_{k=1}^{\infty} \frac{(-1)^k k}{4^k} x^{2k} = \sum_{k=1}^{\infty} k\left(-\frac{1}{4}\right)^k x^{2k}.$$

The series on the right is not a geometric series because of the presence of the factor k. The key is to realize that k could appear in this way through differentiation; specifically, something like $\frac{d}{dx}(x^{2k}) = 2kx^{2k-1}$. To achieve terms of this form, we write

$$\underbrace{\sum_{k=1}^{\infty} \frac{(-1)^k k}{4^k} x^{2k}}_{\text{original series}} = \sum_{k=1}^{\infty} k\left(-\frac{1}{4}\right)^k x^{2k}$$

$$= \frac{1}{2}\sum_{k=1}^{\infty} 2k\left(-\frac{1}{4}\right)^k x^{2k} \qquad \text{Multiply and divide by 2.}$$

$$= \frac{x}{2}\sum_{k=1}^{\infty} 2k\left(-\frac{1}{4}\right)^k x^{2k-1}. \qquad \text{Remove } x \text{ from the series.}$$

Now we identify the last series as the derivative of another series:

$$\underbrace{\sum_{k=1}^{\infty} \frac{(-1)^k k}{4^k} x^{2k}}_{\text{original series}} = \frac{x}{2}\sum_{k=1}^{\infty}\left(-\frac{1}{4}\right)^k \underbrace{2kx^{2k-1}}_{\frac{d}{dx}(x^{2k})}$$

$$= \frac{x}{2}\sum_{k=1}^{\infty}\left(-\frac{1}{4}\right)^k \frac{d}{dx}(x^{2k}) \qquad \text{Identify a derivative.}$$

$$= \frac{x}{2}\frac{d}{dx}\left(\sum_{k=1}^{\infty}\left(-\frac{x^2}{4}\right)^k\right). \qquad \text{Combine factors; term-by-term differentiation}$$

This last series is a geometric series with a ratio $r = -x^2/4$ and first term $-x^2/4$; therefore, its value is $\dfrac{-x^2/4}{1+(x^2/4)}$, provided $\left|\dfrac{x^2}{4}\right| < 1$, or $|x| < 2$. We now have

$$\underbrace{\sum_{k=1}^{\infty} \frac{(-1)^k k}{4^k} x^{2k}}_{\text{original series}} = \frac{x}{2}\frac{d}{dx}\left(\sum_{k=1}^{\infty}\left(-\frac{x^2}{4}\right)^k\right)$$

$$= \frac{x}{2}\frac{d}{dx}\left(\frac{-x^2/4}{1+(x^2/4)}\right) \qquad \text{Sum of geometric series}$$

$$= \frac{x}{2}\frac{d}{dx}\left(\frac{-x^2}{4+x^2}\right) \qquad \text{Simplify.}$$

$$= -\frac{4x^2}{(4+x^2)^2}. \qquad \text{Differentiate and simplify.}$$

Therefore, the function represented by the power series on $(-2, 2)$ has been uncovered; it is

$$f(x) = -\frac{4x^2}{(4+x^2)^2}.$$

Notice that f is defined for $-\infty < x < \infty$ (Figure 10.19), but its power series centered at 0 converges to f only on $(-2, 2)$.

Related Exercises 55–64 ◄

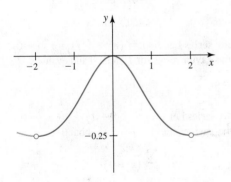

$$\sum_{k=1}^{\infty} \frac{(-1)^k k}{4^k} x^{2k} = -\frac{4x^2}{(4+x^2)^2} \text{ on } (-2, 2)$$

FIGURE 10.19

SECTION 10.4 EXERCISES

Review Questions

1. Explain the strategy presented in this section for evaluating a limit of the form $\lim_{x \to a} f(x)/g(x)$, where f and g have Taylor series centered at a.

2. Explain the method presented in this section for approximating $\int_a^b f(x)\,dx$, where f has a Taylor series with an interval of convergence centered at a that includes b.

3. How would you approximate $e^{-0.6}$ using the Taylor series for e^x?

4. Suggest a Taylor series and a method for approximating π.

5. If $f(x) = \sum_{k=0}^{\infty} c_k x^k$ and the series converges for $|x| < b$, what is the power series for $f'(x)$?

6. What condition must be met by a function f for it to have a Taylor series centered at a?

Basic Skills

7–24. Limits *Evaluate the following limits using Taylor series.*

7. $\displaystyle\lim_{x \to 0} \frac{e^x - 1}{x}$

8. $\displaystyle\lim_{x \to 0} \frac{\tan^{-1} x - x}{x^3}$

9. $\displaystyle\lim_{x \to 0} \frac{-x - \ln(1 - x)}{x^2}$

10. $\displaystyle\lim_{x \to 0} \frac{\sin 2x}{x}$

11. $\displaystyle\lim_{x \to 0} \frac{e^x - e^{-x}}{x}$

12. $\displaystyle\lim_{x \to 0} \frac{1 + x - e^x}{4x^2}$

13. $\displaystyle\lim_{x \to 0} \frac{2\cos 2x - 2 + 4x^2}{2x^4}$

14. $\displaystyle\lim_{x \to \infty} x \sin \frac{1}{x}$

15. $\displaystyle\lim_{x \to 0} \frac{\ln(1 + x) - x + x^2/2}{x^3}$

16. $\displaystyle\lim_{x \to 4} \frac{x^2 - 16}{\ln(x - 3)}$

17. $\displaystyle\lim_{x \to 0} \frac{3\tan^{-1} x - 3x + x^3}{x^5}$

18. $\displaystyle\lim_{x \to 0} \frac{\sqrt{1 + x} - 1 - (x/2)}{4x^2}$

19. $\displaystyle\lim_{x \to 0} \frac{12x - 8x^3 - 6\sin 2x}{x^5}$

20. $\displaystyle\lim_{x \to 1} \frac{x - 1}{\ln x}$

21. $\displaystyle\lim_{x \to 2} \frac{x - 2}{\ln(x - 1)}$

22. $\displaystyle\lim_{x \to \infty} x(e^{1/x} - 1)$

23. $\displaystyle\lim_{x \to 0} \frac{e^{-2x} - 4e^{-x/2} + 3}{2x^2}$

24. $\displaystyle\lim_{x \to 0} \frac{(1 - 2x)^{-1/2} - e^x}{8x^2}$

25–32. Power series for derivatives

a. *Differentiate the Taylor series about 0 for the following functions.*
b. *Identify the function represented by the differentiated series.*
c. *Give the interval of convergence of the power series for the derivative.*

25. $f(x) = e^x$

26. $f(x) = \cos x$

27. $f(x) = \ln(1 + x)$

28. $f(x) = \sin x^2$

29. $f(x) = e^{-2x}$

30. $f(x) = (1 - x)^{-1}$

31. $f(x) = \tan^{-1} x$

32. $f(x) = -\ln(1 - x)$

33–36. Differential equations

a. *Find a power series for the solution of the following differential equations, subject to the given initial conditions.*
b. *Identify the function represented by the power series.*

33. $y'(t) - y(t) = 0,\ y(0) = 2$

34. $y'(t) + 4y(t) = 8,\ y(0) = 0$

35. $y'(t) - 3y(t) = 10,\ y(0) = 2$

36. $y'(t) = 6y(t) + 9,\ y(0) = 2$

37–44. Approximating definite integrals *Use a Taylor series to approximate the following definite integrals. Retain as many terms as needed to ensure the error is less than 10^{-4}.*

37. $\displaystyle\int_0^{0.25} e^{-x^2}\,dx$

38. $\displaystyle\int_0^{0.2} \sin x^2\,dx$

39. $\displaystyle\int_{-0.35}^{0.35} \cos 2x^2\,dx$

40. $\displaystyle\int_0^{0.2} \sqrt{1 + x^4}\,dx$

41. $\displaystyle\int_0^{0.35} \tan^{-1} x\,dx$

42. $\displaystyle\int_0^{0.4} \ln(1 + x^2)\,dx$

43. $\displaystyle\int_0^{0.5} \frac{dx}{\sqrt{1 + x^6}}$

44. $\displaystyle\int_0^{0.2} \frac{\ln(1 + t)}{t}\,dt$

45–50. Approximating real numbers *Use an appropriate Taylor series to find the first four nonzero terms of an infinite series that is equal to the following numbers.*

45. e^2

46. $\sqrt{e}$

47. $\cos 2$

48. $\sin 1$

49. $\ln \frac{3}{2}$

50. $\tan^{-1} \frac{1}{2}$

51. **Evaluating an infinite series** Let $f(x) = (e^x - 1)/x$, for $x \neq 0$, and $f(0) = 1$. Use the Taylor series for f about 0 and evaluate $f(1)$ to find the value of $\displaystyle\sum_{k=0}^{\infty} \frac{1}{(k + 1)!}$.

52. **Evaluating an infinite series** Let $f(x) = (e^x - 1)/x$, for $x \neq 0$, and $f(0) = 1$. Use the Taylor series for f and f' about 0 to evaluate $f'(2)$ to find the value of $\displaystyle\sum_{k=1}^{\infty} \frac{k \, 2^{k-1}}{(k + 1)!}$.

53. **Evaluating an infinite series** Write the Taylor series for $f(x) = \ln(1 + x)$ about 0 and find its interval of convergence. Assume the Taylor series converges to f on the interval of convergence. Evaluate $f(1)$ to find the value of $\displaystyle\sum_{k=1}^{\infty} \frac{(-1)^{k+1}}{k}$ (the alternating harmonic series).

54. Evaluating an infinite series Write the Maclaurin series for $f(x) = \ln(1 + x)$ and find the interval of convergence.

Evaluate $f\left(-\frac{1}{2}\right)$ to find the value of $\displaystyle\sum_{k=1}^{\infty} \frac{1}{k \cdot 2^k}$.

55–64. Representing functions by power series *Identify the functions represented by the following power series.*

55. $\displaystyle\sum_{k=0}^{\infty} \frac{x^k}{2^k}$

56. $\displaystyle\sum_{k=0}^{\infty} (-1)^k \frac{x^k}{3^k}$

57. $\displaystyle\sum_{k=0}^{\infty} (-1)^k \frac{x^{2k}}{4^k}$

58. $\displaystyle\sum_{k=0}^{\infty} 2^k x^{2k+1}$

59. $\displaystyle\sum_{k=1}^{\infty} \frac{x^k}{k}$

60. $\displaystyle\sum_{k=0}^{\infty} \frac{(-1)^k x^{k+1}}{4^k}$

61. $\displaystyle\sum_{k=1}^{\infty} (-1)^k \frac{kx^{k+1}}{3^k}$

62. $\displaystyle\sum_{k=1}^{\infty} \frac{x^{2k}}{k}$

63. $\displaystyle\sum_{k=2}^{\infty} \frac{k(k-1)x^k}{3^k}$

64. $\displaystyle\sum_{k=2}^{\infty} \frac{x^k}{k(k-1)}$

Further Explorations

65. Explain why or why not Determine whether the following statements are true and give an explanation or counterexample.

a. To evaluate $\displaystyle\int_0^2 \frac{dx}{1-x}$, one could expand the integrand in a Taylor series and integrate term by term.

b. To approximate $\pi/3$, one could substitute $x = \sqrt{3}$ into the Taylor series for $\tan^{-1} x$.

c. $\displaystyle\sum_{k=0}^{\infty} \frac{(\ln 2)^k}{k!} = 2$.

66–68. Limits with a parameter *Use Taylor series to evaluate the following limits. Express the result in terms of the parameter(s).*

66. $\displaystyle\lim_{x \to 0} \frac{e^{ax} - 1}{x}$

67. $\displaystyle\lim_{x \to 0} \frac{\sin ax}{\sin bx}$

68. $\displaystyle\lim_{x \to 0} \frac{\sin ax - \tan^{-1} ax}{bx^3}$

69. A limit by Taylor series Use Taylor series to evaluate

$$\lim_{x \to 0} \left(\frac{\sin x}{x}\right)^{1/x^2}.$$

70. Inverse hyperbolic sine A function known as the *inverse hyperbolic sine* is defined in several ways; among them are

$$\sinh^{-1} x = \ln\left(x + \sqrt{x^2 + 1}\right) = \int_0^x \frac{dt}{\sqrt{1 + t^2}}.$$

Find the first four terms of the Taylor series for $\sinh^{-1} x$ using these two definitions (and be sure they agree).

71–74. Derivative trick *Here is an alternative way to evaluate higher derivatives of a function f that may save time. Suppose you can find the Taylor series for f centered at the point a without evaluating derivatives (for example, from a known series). Explain why $f^{(k)}(a) = k!$*

multiplied by the coefficient of $(x - a)^k$. Use this idea to evaluate $f^{(3)}(0)$ and $f^{(4)}(0)$ for the following functions. Use known series and do not evaluate derivatives.

71. $f(x) = e^{\cos x}$

72. $f(x) = \dfrac{x^2 + 1}{\sqrt[3]{1 + x}}$

73. $f(x) = \displaystyle\int_0^x \sin t^2 \, dt$

74. $f(x) = \displaystyle\int_0^x \frac{1}{1 + t^4} \, dt$

Applications

75. Probability: tossing for a head The expected (average) number of tosses of a fair coin required to obtain the first head is $\displaystyle\sum_{k=1}^{\infty} k\left(\frac{1}{2}\right)^k$. Evaluate this series and determine the expected number of tosses. (*Hint:* Differentiate a geometric series.)

76. Probability: sudden death playoff Teams A and B go into sudden death overtime after playing to a tie. The teams alternate possession of the ball, and the first team to score wins. Each team has a $\frac{1}{6}$ chance of scoring when it has the ball, with Team A having the ball first.

a. The probability that Team A ultimately wins is $\displaystyle\sum_{k=0}^{\infty} \frac{1}{6}\left(\frac{5}{6}\right)^{2k}$. Evaluate this series.

b. The expected number of rounds (possessions by either team) required for the overtime to end is $\dfrac{1}{6}\displaystyle\sum_{k=1}^{\infty} k\left(\frac{5}{6}\right)^{k-1}$. Evaluate this series.

⊤ 77. Elliptic integrals The period of a pendulum is given by

$$T = 4\sqrt{\frac{\ell}{g}} \int_0^{\pi/2} \frac{d\theta}{\sqrt{1 - k^2 \sin^2 \theta}} = 4\sqrt{\frac{\ell}{g}} F(k),$$

where ℓ is the length of the pendulum, $g \approx 9.8 \text{ m/s}^2$ is the acceleration due to gravity, $k = \sin(\theta_0/2)$, and θ_0 is the initial angular displacement of the pendulum (in radians). The integral in this formula $F(k)$ is called an **elliptic integral**, and it cannot be evaluated analytically.

a. Approximate $F(0.1)$ by expanding the integrand in a Taylor series and integrating term by term.

b. How many terms of the Taylor series do you suggest using to obtain an approximation to $F(0.1)$ with an error less than 10^{-3}?

c. Would you expect to use fewer or more terms (than in part (b)) to approximate $F(0.2)$ to the same accuracy? Explain.

78. Sine integral function The function $\text{Si}(x) = \displaystyle\int_0^x \frac{\sin t}{t} \, dt$ is called the *sine integral function*.

a. Expand the integrand in a Taylor series about 0.

b. Integrate the series to find a Taylor series for Si.

c. Approximate $\text{Si}(0.5)$ and $\text{Si}(1)$. Use enough terms of the series so the error in the approximation does not exceed 10^{-3}.

79. Fresnel integrals The theory of optics gives rise to the two *Fresnel integrals*

$$S(x) = \int_0^x \sin t^2 \, dt \quad \text{and} \quad C(x) = \int_0^x \cos t^2 \, dt.$$

a. Compute $S'(x)$ and $C'(x)$.

b. Expand $\sin t^2$ and $\cos t^2$ in a Maclaurin series and then integrate to find the first four nonzero terms of the Maclaurin series for S and C.

c. Use the polynomials in part (b) to approximate $S(0.05)$ and $C(-0.25)$.

d. How many terms of the Maclaurin series are required to approximate $S(0.05)$ with an error no greater than 10^{-4}?

e. How many terms of the Maclaurin series are required to approximate $C(-0.25)$ with an error no greater than 10^{-6}?

80. Error function An essential function in statistics and the study of the normal distribution is the *error function*

$$\text{erf}(x) = \frac{2}{\sqrt{\pi}} \int_0^x e^{-t^2} \, dt.$$

a. Compute the derivative of $\text{erf}(x)$.

b. Expand e^{-t^2} in a Maclaurin series; then integrate to find the first four nonzero terms of the Maclaurin series for erf.

c. Use the polynomial in part (b) to approximate $\text{erf}(0.15)$ and $\text{erf}(-0.09)$.

d. Estimate the error in the approximations of part (c).

81. Bessel functions Bessel functions arise in the study of wave propagation in circular geometries (for example, waves on a circular drum head). They are conveniently defined as power series. One of an infinite family of Bessel functions is

$$J_0(x) = \sum_{k=0}^{\infty} \frac{(-1)^k}{2^{2k}(k!)^2} x^{2k}.$$

a. Write out the first four terms of J_0.

b. Find the radius and interval of convergence of the power series for J_0.

c. Differentiate J_0 twice and show (by keeping terms through x^6) that J_0 satisfies the equation $x^2 y''(x) + x y'(x) + x^2 y(x) = 0$.

Additional Exercises

82. Power series for $\sec x$ Use the identity $\sec x = \dfrac{1}{\cos x}$ and long division to find the first four terms of the Maclaurin series for $\sec x$.

83. Symmetry

a. Use infinite series to show that $\cos x$ is an even function. That is, show $\cos(-x) = \cos x$.

b. Use infinite series to show that $\sin x$ is an odd function. That is, show $\sin(-x) = -\sin x$.

84. Behavior of $\csc x$ We know that $\lim_{x \to 0^+} \csc x = \infty$. Use long division to determine exactly how $\csc x$ grows as $x \to 0^+$. Specifically, find a, b, and c (all positive) in the following sentence: As $x \to 0^+$, $\csc x \approx \dfrac{a}{x^b} + cx$.

85. L'Hôpital's Rule by Taylor series Suppose f and g have Taylor series about the point a.

a. If $f(a) = g(a) = 0$ and $g'(a) \neq 0$, evaluate $\lim_{x \to a} f(x)/g(x)$ by expanding f and g in their Taylor series. Show that the result is consistent with l'Hôpital's Rule.

b. If $f(a) = g(a) = f'(a) = g'(a) = 0$ and $g''(a) \neq 0$, evaluate $\lim_{x \to a} \dfrac{f(x)}{g(x)}$ by expanding f and g in their Taylor series. Show that the result is consistent with two applications of l'Hôpital's Rule.

86. Newton's derivation of the sine and arcsine series Newton discovered the binomial series (see Table 10.5) and then used it ingeniously to obtain many more results. Here is a case in point.

a. Referring to the figure, show that $x = \sin s$ or $s = \sin^{-1} x$.

b. The area of a circular sector of radius r subtended by an angle θ is $\frac{1}{2} r^2 \theta$. Show that the area of the circular sector APE is $s/2$, which implies that

$$s = 2 \int_0^x \sqrt{1 - t^2} \, dt - x\sqrt{1 - x^2}.$$

c. Use the power series for $f(x) = \sqrt{1 - x^2}$ to obtain the first few terms of the Taylor series for $s = \sin^{-1} x$.

d. Newton next inverted the series in part (c) to obtain the Taylor series for $x = \sin s$. He did this by assuming that $\sin s = \sum a_k s^k$ and solving $x = \sin(\sin^{-1} x)$ for the coefficients a_k. Find the first few terms of the Taylor series for $\sin s$ using this idea (a computer algebra system might be helpful as well).

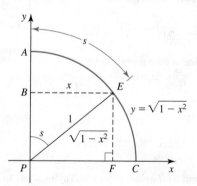

Technology Exercises

87. Approximating π The challenge of producing accurate approximations of π has a long and colorful history; one approach uses series that converge to π (or to multiples of π). Consider the identity

$$\frac{\pi}{4} = \tan^{-1}\frac{1}{2} + \tan^{-1}\frac{1}{3}.$$

a. Use the identity to write a series representation for $\pi/4$. Express your answer as a single series in summation notation.

b. Estimate $\pi/4$ using five terms of the series in part (a).

c. Use the Alternating Series Remainder Theorem to find a bound on the error in the estimate obtained in part (b).

d. Use part (a) to obtain a series representation for π. How many terms of the series are needed to estimate π with an error of less than 10^{-6}?

88. A more efficient approximation of π In 1706, John Machin improved the method of Exercise 87 using the identity

$$\frac{\pi}{4} = 4 \tan^{-1}\frac{1}{5} - \tan^{-1}\frac{1}{239}.$$

    a. Use the identity to write a series representation for $\pi/4$. Express your answer as a single series in summation notation. Then use the Alternating Series Remainder Theorem to estimate the error introduced when this series is terminated after 5 terms.

    b. Modify the series in part (a) to obtain a series for π. How many terms of this modified series are needed to approximate π with an error of less than 10^{-6}? Compare your results with Exercise 87, part (d).

CHAPTER 10   REVIEW EXERCISES

1. Explain why or why not Determine whether the following statements are true and give an explanation or counterexample.

    a. Let p_n be the nth-order Taylor polynomial for f centered at 2. The approximation $p_3(2.1) \approx f(2.1)$ is likely to be more accurate than the approximation $p_2(2.2) \approx f(2.2)$.

    b. If the Taylor series for f centered at 3 has a radius of convergence of 6, then the interval of convergence is $[-3, 9]$.

    c. The interval of convergence of the power series $\sum c_k x^k$ could be $\left(-\frac{7}{3}, \frac{7}{3}\right)$.

    d. The Maclaurin series for $f(x) = (1 + x)^{12}$ has a finite number of nonzero terms.

2–9. Taylor polynomials Find the nth-order Taylor polynomial for the following functions centered at the given point a.

2. $f(x) = \sin 2x$, $n = 3$, $a = 0$

3. $f(x) = \cos x^2$, $n = 2$, $a = 0$

4. $f(x) = e^{-x}$, $n = 2$, $a = 0$

5. $f(x) = \ln(1 + x)$, $n = 3$, $a = 0$

6. $f(x) = \cos x$, $n = 2$, $a = \pi/4$

7. $f(x) = \ln x$, $n = 2$, $a = 1$

8. $f(x) = (1 + x)^{-1}$, $n = 4$, $a = 0$

9. $f(x) = \tan^{-1} x$, $n = 3$, $a = 1$

10–13. Approximations

a. Find the Taylor polynomials of order $n = 0, 1,$ and 2 for the given functions centered at the given point a.

b. Make a table showing the approximations and the absolute error in these approximations using a calculator for the exact function value.

10. $f(x) = \cos x$, $a = 0$; approximate $\cos(-0.08)$.

11. $f(x) = e^x$, $a = 0$; approximate $e^{-0.08}$.

12. $f(x) = \sqrt{1 + x}$, $a = 0$; approximate $\sqrt{1.08}$.

13. $f(x) = \sin x$, $a = \pi/4$; approximate $\sin(\pi/5)$.

14–16. Estimating remainders Find the remainder term $R_n(x)$ for the Taylor series centered at 0 for the following functions. Find an upper bound for the magnitude of the remainder on the given interval for the given value of n. (The bound is not unique.)

14. $f(x) = e^x$; bound $R_3(x)$, for $|x| < 1$.

15. $f(x) = \sin x$; bound $R_3(x)$, for $|x| < \pi$.

16. $f(x) = \ln(1 - x)$; bound $R_3(x)$, for $|x| < 1/2$.

17–24. Radius and interval of convergence Use the Ratio or Root Test to determine the radius of convergence of the following power series. Test the endpoints to determine the interval of convergence, when appropriate.

17. $\sum \dfrac{k^2 x^k}{k!}$

18. $\sum \dfrac{x^{4k}}{k^2}$

19. $\sum (-1)^k \dfrac{(x + 1)^{2k}}{k!}$

20. $\sum \dfrac{(x - 1)^k}{k \cdot 5^k}$

21. $\sum \left(\dfrac{x}{9}\right)^{3k}$

22. $\sum \dfrac{(x + 2)^k}{\sqrt{k}}$

23. $\sum \dfrac{(x + 2)^k}{2^k \ln k}$

24. $x + \dfrac{x^3}{3} + \dfrac{x^5}{5} + \dfrac{x^7}{7} + \cdots$

25–30. Power series from the geometric series Use the geometric series $\displaystyle\sum_{k=0}^{\infty} x^k = \dfrac{1}{1 - x}$, for $|x| < 1$, to determine the Maclaurin series and the interval of convergence for the following functions.

25. $f(x) = \dfrac{1}{1 - x^2}$

26. $f(x) = \dfrac{1}{1 + x^3}$

27. $f(x) = \dfrac{1}{1 - 3x}$

28. $f(x) = \dfrac{10x}{1 + x}$

29. $f(x) = \dfrac{1}{(1 - x)^2}$

30. $f(x) = \ln(1 + x^2)$

31–38. Taylor series *Write out the first three nonzero terms of the Taylor series for the following functions centered at the given point a. Then write the series using summation notation.*

31. $f(x) = e^{3x}, a = 0$

32. $f(x) = 1/x, a = 1$

33. $f(x) = \cos x, a = \pi/2$

34. $f(x) = -\ln(1 - x), a = 0$

35. $f(x) = \tan^{-1} x, a = 0$

36. $f(x) = \sin 2x, a = -\pi/2$

37. $f(x) = (1 + 4x^2)^{-1}, a = 0$

38. $f(x) = \dfrac{1}{4 + x^2}, a = 0$

39–42. More Maclaurin series *Write out the first three terms of the Maclaurin series for the following functions.*

39. $f(x) = (1 + x)^{1/3}$ **40.** $f(x) = (1 + x)^{-1/2}$

41. $f(x) = (1 + x/2)^{-3}$ **42.** $f(x) = (1 + 2x)^{-5}$

43–46. Convergence *Write the remainder term $R_n(x)$ for the Taylor series for the following functions centered at the given point a. Then show that $\lim\limits_{n \to \infty} |R_n(x)| = 0$, for all x in the given interval.*

43. $f(x) = e^{-x}, a = 0, -\infty < x < \infty$

44. $f(x) = \sin x, a = 0, -\infty < x < \infty$

45. $f(x) = \ln(1 + x), a = 0, -\frac{1}{2} \leq x \leq \frac{1}{2}$

46. $f(x) = \sqrt{1 + x}, a = 0, -\frac{1}{2} \leq x \leq \frac{1}{2}$

47–52. Limits by power series *Use Taylor series to evaluate the following limits.*

47. $\lim\limits_{x \to 0} \dfrac{x^2/2 - 1 + \cos x}{x^4}$

48. $\lim\limits_{x \to 0} \dfrac{2 \sin x - \tan^{-1} x - x}{2x^5}$

49. $\lim\limits_{x \to 4} \dfrac{\ln(x - 3)}{x^2 - 16}$

50. $\lim\limits_{x \to 0} \dfrac{\sqrt{1 + 2x} - 1 - x}{x^2}$

51. $\lim\limits_{x \to 0} \dfrac{\sec x - \cos x - x^2}{x^4}$

52. $\lim\limits_{x \to 0} \dfrac{(1 + x)^{-2} - \sqrt[3]{1 - 6x}}{2x^2}$

53–56. Definite integrals by power series *Use a Taylor series to approximate the following definite integrals. Retain as many terms as necessary to ensure the error is less than 10^{-3}.*

53. $\displaystyle\int_0^{1/2} e^{-x^2}\, dx$ **54.** $\displaystyle\int_0^{1/2} \tan^{-1} x\, dx$

55. $\displaystyle\int_0^1 x \cos x\, dx$ **56.** $\displaystyle\int_0^{1/2} x^2 \tan^{-1} x\, dx$

57–60. Approximating real numbers *Use an appropriate Taylor series to find the first four nonzero terms of an infinite series that is equal to the following numbers. There is more than one way to choose the center of the series.*

57. $\sqrt{119}$ **58.** $\sin 20°$

59. $\tan^{-1}\left(-\frac{1}{3}\right)$ **60.** $\sqrt[3]{69}$

61. **A differential equation** Find a power series solution of the differential equation $y'(x) - 4y + 12 = 0$, subject to the condition $y(0) = 4$. Identify the solution in terms of known functions.

62. **Rejected quarters** The probability that a random quarter is *not* rejected by a vending machine is given by the integral $11.4 \int_0^{0.14} e^{-102x^2}\, dx$ (assuming that the weights of quarters are normally distributed with a mean of 5.670 g and a standard deviation of 0.07 g). Expand the integrand in $n = 2$ and $n = 3$ terms of a Taylor series and integrate to find two estimates of the probability. Check for agreement between the two estimates.

63. **Approximating ln 2** Consider the following three ways to approximate ln 2.

   a. Use the Taylor series for $\ln(1 + x)$ centered at 0 and evaluate it at $x = 1$ (convergence was asserted in Table 10.5). Write the resulting infinite series.

   b. Use the Taylor series for $\ln(1 - x)$ centered at 0 and the identity $\ln 2 = -\ln\left(\dfrac{1}{2}\right)$. Write the resulting infinite series.

   c. Use the property $\ln(a/b) = \ln a - \ln b$ and the series of parts (a) and (b) to find the Taylor series for $f(x) = \ln\left(\dfrac{1 + x}{1 - x}\right)$ centered at 0.

   d. At what value of x should the series in part (c) be evaluated to approximate ln 2? Write the resulting infinite series for ln 2.

   e. Using four terms of the series, which of the three series derived in parts (a), (b), and (d) gives the best approximation to ln 2? Can you explain why?

64. **Graphing Taylor polynomials** Consider the function $f(x) = (1 + x)^{-4}$.

   a. Find the Taylor polynomials p_0, p_1, p_2, and p_3 centered at 0.

   b. Use a graphing utility to plot the Taylor polynomials and f, for $-1 < x < 1$.

   c. For each Taylor polynomial, give the interval on which its graph appears indistinguishable from the graph of f.

The following questions are intended to help you prepare for the AP exam. They are not questions from actual AP exams.

Section 1 Part A, Multiple Choice, No Technology

1. The function f satisfies $f(2) = 0, f'(2) = 1, f''(2) = -2$, and $f'''(2) = 4$. The third-order Taylor polynomial for f centered at 2 is

   (A) $p_3(x) = x - 2x^2 + 4x^3$.

   (B) $p_3(x) = x - x^2 + \dfrac{2}{3}x^3$.

   (C) $p_3(x) = (x + 2) - 2(x + 2)^2 + 4(x + 2)^3$.

   (D) $p_3(x) = (x - 2) - 2(x - 2)^2 + 4(x - 2)^3$.

   (E) $p_3(x) = (x - 2) - (x - 2)^2 + \dfrac{2}{3}(x - 2)^3$.

2. Given that the nth-order Taylor polynomial for $f(x) = (1 - x)^{-1}$ is $p_n(x) = \displaystyle\sum_{k=0}^{n} x^k$, what is the nth-order Taylor polynomial centered at 0 for $f(x) = (1 + 3x)^{-1}$?

   (A) $\displaystyle\sum_{k=0}^{n} (3x)^k$

   (B) $-\displaystyle\sum_{k=0}^{n} 9^k x^k$

   (C) $\displaystyle\sum_{k=0}^{n} (-1)^k (3x)^{2k}$

   (D) $\displaystyle\sum_{k=0}^{n} (-3x)^k$

   (E) $\displaystyle\sum_{k=0}^{n} (-1)^k \left(\dfrac{x}{3}\right)^k$

3. The Taylor polynomial of order 5 for $f(x) = \sin x$ centered at π is

   (A) $(x - \pi) - \dfrac{1}{6}(x - \pi)^3 + \dfrac{1}{120}(x - \pi)^5$.

   (B) $(x - \pi) - (x - \pi)^3 + (x - \pi)^5$.

   (C) $-(x - \pi) + \dfrac{1}{6}(x - \pi)^3 - \dfrac{1}{120}(x - \pi)^5$.

   (D) $-(x - \pi) + (x - \pi)^3 - (x - \pi)^5$.

   (E) $-(x - \pi) + \dfrac{1}{3}(x - \pi)^3 - \dfrac{1}{5}(x - \pi)^5$.

4. On what interval does the series $\displaystyle\sum_{k=1}^{\infty} \dfrac{(3x)^{2k}}{k!}$ converge?

   (A) $-\infty < x < \infty$

   (B) $-\dfrac{1}{3} < x < \dfrac{1}{3}$

   (C) $-\dfrac{1}{3} \leq x \leq \dfrac{1}{3}$

   (D) $-\dfrac{1}{3} < x \leq \dfrac{1}{3}$

   (E) $-\dfrac{1}{3} \leq x < \dfrac{1}{3}$

5. On what interval does the series $\displaystyle\sum_{k=1}^{\infty} \dfrac{(3x)^{2k}}{k + 1}$ converge?

   (A) $-\infty < x < \infty$

   (B) $-\dfrac{1}{3} < x < \dfrac{1}{3}$

   (C) $-\dfrac{1}{3} \leq x \leq \dfrac{1}{3}$

   (D) $-\dfrac{1}{3} < x \leq \dfrac{1}{3}$

   (E) $-\dfrac{1}{3} \leq x < \dfrac{1}{3}$

6. The third nonzero term of the Maclaurin series (Taylor series centered at 0) for $f(x) = \cos(2x^3)$ is

   (A) $16x^{12}$.

   (B) $\dfrac{2}{3}x^{12}$.

   (C) $\dfrac{2}{3}x^4$.

   (D) $\dfrac{1}{24}x^4$.

   (E) $\dfrac{1}{12}x^{12}$.

7. Given that $f^{(n)}(0) = (-2)^n$, for $n = 0, 1, 2, \ldots$, find the Maclaurin series for f.

   (A) $1 - 2x + 4x^2 - 8x^3 + \cdots$

   (B) $1 + 2x + 4x^2 + 8x^3 + \cdots$

   (C) $1 - 2x + 2x^2 - \dfrac{8}{3}x^3 + \cdots$

   (D) $1 - 2x + 2x^2 - \dfrac{4}{3}x^3 + \cdots$

   (E) $1 + 2x + 2x^2 + \dfrac{4}{3}x^3 + \cdots$

8. Find $f^{(3)}(0)$ if the Maclaurin series for f is $1 - 2x + 4x^2 - 8x^3 + 16x^4 - \cdots$.

   (A) 48

   (B) -48

   (C) 8

   (D) -8

   (E) 384

9. Let f be twice differentiable on an open interval that contains the point a, and suppose f has an inflection point at a. Let p_1 and p_2 be the linear and quadratic approximations to f at a, respectively. Which of the following are true?

   (I) $f''(a) = 0$ (II) p_2 is linear   (III) $p_1 = p_2$

   (A) I only

   (B) I and II only

   (C) I, II, and III

   (D) II and III only

   (E) III only

Section 1 Part B, Multiple Choice, Technology Allowed

10. Let $f(x) = e^{-x}$ and consider its Taylor series centered at 0. How many terms of the series are needed to approximate $f(0.3)$ with an error no greater than $1/1000$?

    (A) 1
    (B) 2
    (C) 3
    (D) 4
    (E) 5

11. Which approximation to $\sqrt{e}$ is given by the first three nonzero terms of the Taylor series for e^x centered at 0?

    (A) 1.625
    (B) 1.648
    (C) 1.649
    (D) 1.650
    (E) 1.655

Section 2 Part A, Free Response, Technology Allowed

1. Let $f(x) = \cos\dfrac{x}{2}$, and let p_4 and q_4 be the fourth-order Taylor polynomials for f centered at 0 and π, respectively.

    a. Write out the terms of p_4 and q_4.

    b. Which polynomial gives the better approximation to $f\left(\dfrac{\pi}{2}\right)$? Explain.

    c. Write the remainder $R_n(x)$ for the series centered at 0 with $x = 2$, expressing your result for arbitrary values of n.

    d. Show that with $x = 2$ and $n = 4$, the remainder in part (c) is no greater than $\dfrac{1}{120}$.

2. Recall that $\dfrac{1}{1-x} = \sum_{k=0}^{\infty} x^k$, for $|x| < 1$.

    a. Write the Maclaurin series for $g(x) = \dfrac{1}{1-x^2}$.

    b. Find the interval of convergence for the Maclaurin series for g. Show your reasoning.

    c. Let $h(x) = \displaystyle\int_0^x g(t)\,dt$. Find the first three nonzero terms of the Maclaurin series for h.

Section 2 Part B, Free Response, No Technology

3. Consider the function $f(x) = \ln(1 + 2x)$.

    a. Write the first three nonzero terms of the Maclaurin series for f.

    b. Find a formula for the nth term of the Taylor series in part (a).

    c. Complete the following sentence: In order to approximate $f(0.2)$ with an error no greater than $\dfrac{1}{200}$, you should use at least n terms of the series, where n satisfies the inequality _____ .

4. Consider the power series $g(x) = \sum_{k=1}^{\infty} \dfrac{(-1)^k (x+2)^k}{k^2}$.

    a. Find the interval of convergence of the series. Show all your work.

    b. Show that if at least 10 terms of the series are used, then $g(-1)$ is approximated with an error less than $\dfrac{1}{100}$.

    c. Write $g(-3)$, $g(-2)$, and $g(-1)$ in numerical order, from smallest to largest. Show the work that leads to your answer.

5. Let $f(x) = \sin x^2$.

    a. Write the first three nonzero terms of the Maclaurin series for f.

    b. Find a formula for the nth term of the series in part (a).

    c. Use the first two terms of your answer to part (a) to estimate $\int_0^1 \sin x^2\,dx$. Explain why the error in this estimate is less than $\dfrac{1}{1000}$.

    d. Evaluate $\displaystyle\lim_{x\to 0} \dfrac{x^6}{x^2 - \sin x^2}$.

6. The function f is defined by the Maclaurin series $f(x) = \sum_{k=1}^{\infty} \dfrac{kx^k}{k!}$, for all real x.

    a. Does f have a local maximum, local minimum, or neither at $x = 0$? Justify your answer.

    b. Evaluate $f^{(10)}(0)$; show your work.

    c. Show that f is increasing on $[0, \infty)$.

    d. Suppose $f(1)$ is approximated by using the first four terms of the series that defines it. Use the Lagrange error bound and the fact that $f^{(5)}(x) = e^x(x + 5)$ to determine whether this approximation differs from the actual value of $f(1)$ by less than $1/100$.

Chapter 10 Guided Projects

Applications of the material in this chapter and related topics can be found in the following Guided Projects.
For additional information, see the Preface.

- Series approximations to π
- Euler's formula (Taylor series with complex numbers)
- Stirling's formula and $n!$

- Three-sigma quality control
- Fourier series

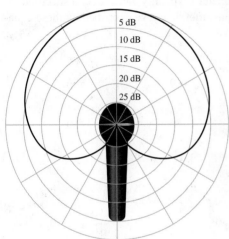

5 dB
10 dB
15 dB
20 dB
25 dB

Microphones are everywhere. They are used by rock stars playing to a stadium full of fans, by newscasters interviewing famous mathematicians, by scientists recording the songs of whales, and by you when chatting with a friend on your smartphone. One distinguishing feature of a particular microphone is its *pick-up pattern,* which describes the way the microphone receives sound. For example, omnidirectional microphones pick up sounds coming from all directions, while bidirectional microphones are sensitive to sounds from two directions. One kind of unidirectional microphone (sound coming from one direction) has a pick-up pattern shaped like a curve called a *cardioid.* The cardioid shows the strength of the signal received by the microphone from various directions. Because a microphone and the sound waves it receives involve three dimensions, the figure shows only a cross section of the pick-up pattern, which is a solid of revolution generated by revolving the cardioid about the axis of the microphone. A cardioid is one of many curves that are most easily described using *polar coordinates.* In this chapter, we study new ways to generate curves, including those that involve polar coordinates.

Chapter Preview
Until now, all our work has involved the Cartesian coordinate system with functions of the form $y = f(x)$. There are, however, alternative ways to generate curves and represent functions. We begin by introducing parametric equations, which are used to represent curves in two and three dimensions, particularly trajectories of moving objects. The calculus of parametric curves allows us to compute slopes of tangent lines and lengths of curves. The next important topic of the chapter is the polar coordinate system, which is useful for working in circular geometries. Once the algebra of polar coordinates is established, we turn to calculus in this setting, investigating tangent lines, areas bounded by curves, and arc length. While the connection is not immediately obvious, there is a close relationship between parametric curves and *vectors.* Specifically, parametric equations are another way to view what are called *vector-valued functions.* Therefore, we explore vector-valued functions in two dimensions. Finally, all this work is put to good use as we investigate the motion of objects in two dimensions.

11.1 Parametric Equations

So far, we have used functions of the form $y = F(x)$ to describe curves in the xy-plane. In this section, we look at another way to define curves, known as *parametric equations.* As you will see, parametric curves enable us to describe both common and exotic curves; they are also indispensable for modeling the trajectories of moving objects.

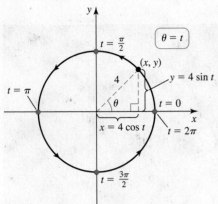

FIGURE 11.1

Basic Ideas

A motor boat travels counterclockwise around a circular course with a radius of 4 miles, completing one lap every 2π hours at a constant speed. Suppose we wish to describe the points on the path of the boat $(x(t), y(t))$ at any time $t \geq 0$, where t is measured in hours. We assume that the boat starts on the positive x-axis at the point $(4, 0)$ (Figure 11.1). Note that the angle θ corresponding to the position of the boat increases by 2π radians every 2π hours beginning with $\theta = 0$ when $t = 0$; therefore, $\theta = t$, for $t \geq 0$. It follows that the x- and y-coordinates of the boat are

$$x = 4\cos\theta = 4\cos t \quad \text{and} \quad y = 4\sin\theta = 4\sin t,$$

where $t \geq 0$. You can confirm that when $t = 0$, the boat is at the starting point $(4, 0)$ and when $t = 2\pi$, it returns to the starting point. The equations $x = 4\cos t$ and $y = 4\sin t$ are examples of **parametric equations**. They specify x and y in terms of a third variable t called a **parameter**, which often represents time.

In general, parametric equations have the form

$$x = f(t), \quad y = g(t),$$

where f and g are given functions and the parameter t typically varies over a specified interval, such as $a \leq t \leq b$ (Figure 11.2). The **parametric curve** described by these equations consists of the points in the plane that satisfy

$$(x, y) = (f(t), g(t)), \quad \text{for } a \leq t \leq b.$$

▷ With parametric equations, the parameter t is the independent variable. There are two dependent variables, x and y.

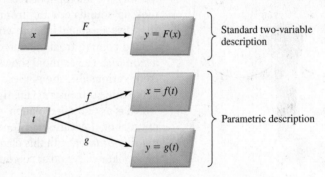

FIGURE 11.2

The first step is to learn how to graph parametric equations.

EXAMPLE 1   Parametric parabola Graph and analyze the parametric equations

$$x = f(t) = 2t, \quad y = g(t) = \frac{1}{2}t^2 - 4, \quad \text{for } 0 \leq t \leq 8.$$

SOLUTION Plotting individual points often helps in visualizing a parametric curve. Table 11.1 shows the values of x and y corresponding to several values of t on the interval $[0, 8]$. By plotting the (x, y) pairs in Table 11.1 and connecting them with a smooth curve, we obtain the graph shown in Figure 11.3. As t increases from its initial value of $t = 0$ to its final value of $t = 8$, the curve is generated from the initial point $(0, -4)$ to the final point $(16, 28)$. Notice that the values of the parameter do not appear in the graph. The only signature of the parameter is the direction in which the curve is generated: In this case, it unfolds upward and to the right.

Table 11.1

t	x	y	(x, y)
0	0	-4	$(0, -4)$
1	2	$-\frac{7}{2}$	$(2, -\frac{7}{2})$
2	4	-2	$(4, -2)$
3	6	$\frac{1}{2}$	$(6, \frac{1}{2})$
4	8	4	$(8, 4)$
5	10	$\frac{17}{2}$	$(10, \frac{17}{2})$
6	12	14	$(12, 14)$
7	14	$\frac{41}{2}$	$(14, \frac{41}{2})$
8	16	28	$(16, 28)$

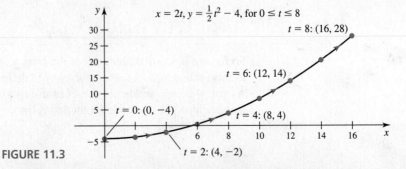

FIGURE 11.3

Sometimes it is possible to eliminate the parameter from a set of parametric equations and obtain a description of the curve in terms of x and y. In this case, from the x-equation, we have $t = \dfrac{x}{2}$, which may be substituted into the y-equation to give

$$y = \frac{1}{2}t^2 - 4 = \frac{1}{2}\left(\frac{x}{2}\right)^2 - 4 = \frac{x^2}{8} - 4.$$

QUICK CHECK 1 Identify the graph generated by the parametric equations $x = t^2, y = t$, for $-10 \le t \le 10$. ◄

Expressed in this form, we identify the graph as part of a parabola. Because t lies in the interval $0 \le t \le 8$ and $x = 2t$, it follows that x lies in the interval $0 \le x \le 16$. Therefore, the parametric equations generate the segment of the parabola for $0 \le x \le 16$.

Related Exercises 9–18 ◄

Given a pair of parametric equations, the preceding example shows that as the parameter increases, the corresponding curve unfolds in a particular direction. The following definition captures this fact and is important in upcoming work.

> **DEFINITION Positive Orientation**
>
> The direction in which a parametric curve is generated as the parameter increases is called the **positive orientation** of the curve.

The question of orientation is particularly important for closed curves such as circles.

EXAMPLE 2 Parametric circle Graph and analyze the parametric equations

$$x = 4 \cos 2\pi t, \quad y = 4 \sin 2\pi t, \quad \text{for } 0 \le t \le 1.$$

SOLUTION For each value of t in Table 11.2, the corresponding ordered pairs (x, y) are recorded. Plotting these points as t increases from $t = 0$ to $t = 1$ results in a graph that appears to be a circle of radius 4; it is generated with positive orientation in the counterclockwise direction, beginning and ending at $(4, 0)$ (Figure 11.4). Letting t increase beyond $t = 1$ would simply retrace the same curve.

Table 11.2

t	(x, y)
0	$(4, 0)$
$\frac{1}{8}$	$(2\sqrt{2}, 2\sqrt{2})$
$\frac{1}{4}$	$(0, 4)$
$\frac{3}{8}$	$(-2\sqrt{2}, 2\sqrt{2})$
$\frac{1}{2}$	$(-4, 0)$
$\frac{3}{4}$	$(0, -4)$
1	$(4, 0)$

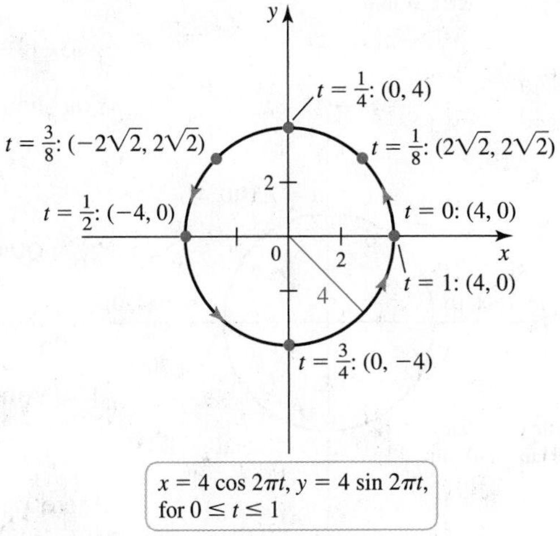

$x = 4 \cos 2\pi t, y = 4 \sin 2\pi t,$
for $0 \le t \le 1$

FIGURE 11.4

> Recall that $\cos^2 \theta + \sin^2 \theta = 1$ for any angle θ. Letting $\theta = 2\pi t$, we have $\cos^2 2\pi t + \sin^2 2\pi t = 1$.

To identify the curve conclusively, the parameter t is eliminated by writing

$$x^2 + y^2 = (4 \cos 2\pi t)^2 + (4 \sin 2\pi t)^2$$
$$= 16\underbrace{(\cos^2 2\pi t + \sin^2 2\pi t)}_{1} = 16.$$

We see that the graph of the parametric equations is the circle $x^2 + y^2 = 16$, whose positive orientation is in the counterclockwise direction.

Related Exercises 19–30 ◄

Generalizing Example 2 for nonzero real numbers a and b in the parametric equations $x = a \cos bt$, $y = a \sin bt$, notice that

$$x^2 + y^2 = (a \cos bt)^2 + (a \sin bt)^2$$
$$= a^2 \underbrace{(\cos^2 bt + \sin^2 bt)}_{1} = a^2.$$

Therefore, the parametric equations $x = a \cos bt$, $y = a \sin bt$ describe all or part of the circle $x^2 + y^2 = a^2$, centered at the origin with radius $|a|$, for any nonzero value of b. The circle is traversed once as t varies over any interval of length $2\pi/|b|$. If t represents time, the circle is traversed in $2\pi/|b|$ time units, which means we can vary the speed at which the curve unfolds by varying b. If $b > 0$, the positive orientation is in the counterclockwise direction. If $b < 0$, the curve is generated in the clockwise direction.

More generally, the parametric equations

$$x = x_0 + a \cos bt, \quad y = y_0 + a \sin bt$$

> Recall that the functions $\sin bt$ and $\cos bt$ have period $2\pi/|b|$. The equations $x = a \cos bt$, $y = -a \sin bt$ also describe a circle of radius $|a|$, as do the equations $x = \pm a \sin bt$, $y = \pm a \cos bt$, as t varies over an interval of length $2\pi/|b|$.

describe all or part of the circle $(x - x_0)^2 + (y - y_0)^2 = a^2$, centered at (x_0, y_0) with radius $|a|$. If $b > 0$, then the circle is generated in the counterclockwise direction. Example 3 shows that a single curve—for example, a circle of radius 4—may be parameterized in many different ways.

EXAMPLE 3   Circular path

A turtle walks with constant speed in the counterclockwise direction on a circular track of radius 4 ft centered at the origin. Starting from the point $(4, 0)$, the turtle completes one lap in 30 minutes. Find a parametric description of the path of the turtle at any time $t \geq 0$, where t is measured in minutes.

SOLUTION Example 2 showed that a circle of radius of 4, generated in the counterclockwise direction, may be described by the parametric equations

$$x = 4 \cos bt, \quad y = 4 \sin bt, \text{ where } b > 0.$$

> In Example 3, the constant $|b|$ is called the *angular frequency* because it is the number of radians the object moves per unit time. The turtle travels 2π rad every 30 min, so the angular frequency is $2\pi/30 = \pi/15$ rad/min. Because radians have no units, the angular frequency in this case has units *per minute*, written min^{-1}.

The *angular frequency* b must be chosen so that, as t varies from 0 to 30, the product bt varies from 0 to 2π. Specifically, when $t = 30$, we must have $30b = 2\pi$, or $b = \pi/15$ rad/min. Therefore, the parametric equations for the turtle's motion are

$$x = 4 \cos\left(\frac{\pi t}{15}\right), \quad y = 4 \sin\left(\frac{\pi t}{15}\right), \quad \text{for } 0 \leq t \leq 30.$$

You should check that as t varies from 0 to 30, the points (x, y) make one complete circuit of a circle of radius 4 (Figure 11.5).

Related Exercises 31–34 ◄

QUICK CHECK 2 Give the center and radius of the circle generated by the equations $x = 3 \sin t$, $y = -3 \cos t$, for $0 \leq t \leq 2\pi$. Specify the direction of positive orientation. ◄

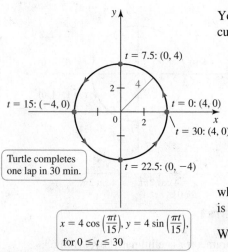

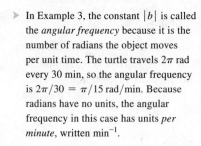

$x = 4 \cos\left(\frac{\pi t}{15}\right)$, $y = 4 \sin\left(\frac{\pi t}{15}\right)$,
for $0 \leq t \leq 30$

FIGURE 11.5

Among the most important of all parametric equations are

$$x = x_0 + at, \, y = y_0 + bt, \quad \text{for} \quad -\infty < t < \infty,$$

where x_0, y_0, a, and b are constants with $a \neq 0$. The curve described by these equations is easily found by eliminating the parameter. The first step is to solve the x-equation for t. When $t = \dfrac{x - x_0}{a}$ is substituted into the y-equation, the result is an equation for y in terms of x:

$$y = y_0 + bt = y_0 + b\left(\frac{x - x_0}{a}\right) \quad \text{or} \quad y - y_0 = \frac{b}{a}(x - x_0).$$

This equation describes a line with slope $\dfrac{b}{a}$ passing through the point (x_0, y_0).

> **SUMMARY** **Parametric Equation of a Line**
>
> The equations
>
> $$x = x_0 + at, \ y = y_0 + bt, \ \text{for} -\infty < t < \infty,$$
>
> where x_0, y_0, a, and b are constants with $a \neq 0$, describe a line with slope $\dfrac{b}{a}$ passing through the point (x_0, y_0). If $a = 0$ and $b \neq 0$, the line is vertical.

Notice that the parametric description of a given line is not unique: If k is any nonzero constant, the numbers a and b may be replaced with ka and kb, respectively, and the resulting equations describe the same line (although it may be generated in the opposite direction and at a different speed).

EXAMPLE 4 **Parametric equations of lines**

a. Consider the parametric equations $x = -2 + 3t, y = 4 - 6t$, for $-\infty < t < \infty$, which describe a line. Find the slope-intercept form of the line.

b. Find two sets of parametric equations for the line with slope $\dfrac{1}{3}$ that passes through the point $(2, 1)$.

c. Find parametric equations for the line segment starting at $P(4, 7)$ and ending at $Q(2, -3)$.

SOLUTION

a. To eliminate the parameter, first solve the x-equation for t to find that $t = \dfrac{x + 2}{3}$. Replacing t in the y-equation yields

$$y = 4 - 6\left(\frac{x + 2}{3}\right) = 4 - 2x - 4 = -2x.$$

The line passes through the origin with slope -2.

b. We use the general parametric equations of a line given in the Summary box. Because the slope of the line is $\dfrac{1}{3}$, we let $a = 3$ and $b = 1$. Letting $x_0 = 2$ and $y_0 = 1$, parametric equations for the line are $x = 2 + 3t, y = 1 + t$, for $-\infty < t < \infty$. The line passes through $(2, 1)$ when $t = 0$ and rises to the right as t increases (Figure 11.6). Notice that other choices for a and b also work. For example, with $a = -6$ and $b = -2$, the equations are $x = 2 - 6t, y = 1 - 2t$, for $-\infty < t < \infty$. These equations describe the same line, but now, as t increases, the line is generated in the opposite direction (descending to the left).

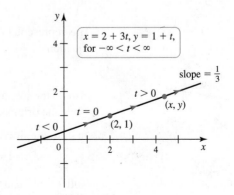

FIGURE 11.6

▶ The choices $a = -1$ and $b = -5$ result in a slope of $b/a = 5$. These choices also imply that as we move from P to Q, a decrease in x corresponds to a decrease in y.

▶ Realize that lines and line segments may have unexpected parametric representations. For example, the equations $x = \sin t, y = 2 \sin t$ represent the line segment $y = 2x$, where $-1 \le x \le 1$.

c. The slope of this line is $\dfrac{7 - (-3)}{4 - 2} = 5$. However, notice that when the line segment is traversed from P to Q, both x and y are decreasing (Figure 11.7). To account for the direction in which the line segment is generated, we let $a = -1$ and $b = -5$. Because $P(4, 7)$ is the starting point of the line segment, we choose $x_0 = 4$ and $y_0 = 7$. The resulting equations are $x = 4 - t, y = 7 - 5t$. Notice that $t = 0$ corresponds to the starting point $(4, 7)$. Because the equations describe a line *segment,* the interval for t must be restricted. What value of t corresponds to the endpoint of the line segment $Q(2, -3)$? Setting $x = 4 - t = 2$, we find that $t = 2$. As a check, we set $y = 7 - 5t = -3$, which also implies that $t = 2$. (If these two calculations do not give the same value of t, it probably means the slope was not computed correctly.) Therefore, the equations for the line segment are $x = 4 - t, y = 7 - 5t$, for $0 \le t \le 2$.

QUICK CHECK 3 Describe the curve generated by $x = 3 + 2t$, $y = -12 - 6t$, for $-\infty < t < \infty$. ◀

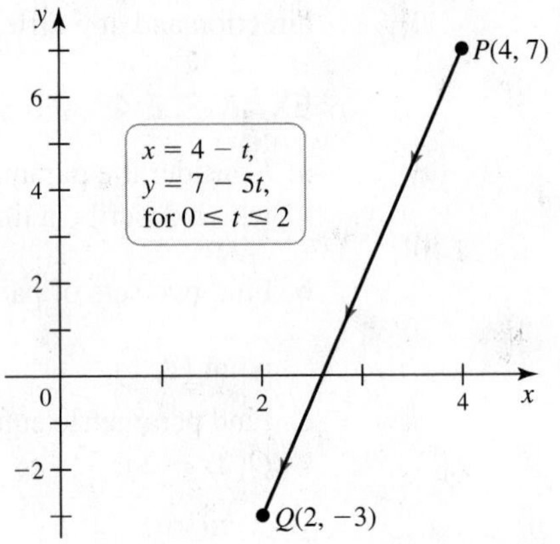

FIGURE 11.7

Related Exercises 35–42 ◀

EXAMPLE 5   Parametric equations of curves   A common task is to parameterize curves given either by Cartesian equations or by graphs. Find a parametric representation of the following curves.

a. The segment of the parabola $y = 9 - x^2$, for $-1 \le x \le 3$
b. The complete curve $x = (y - 5)^2 + \sqrt{y}$
c. The piecewise linear path connecting $P(-2, 0)$ to $Q(0, 3)$ to $R(4, 0)$ (in that order), where the parameter varies over the interval $0 \le t \le 2$

SOLUTION

a. The simplest way to represent a curve $y = f(x)$ parametrically is to let $x = t$ and $y = f(t)$, where t is the parameter. We must then find the appropriate interval for the parameter. Using this approach, the curve $y = 9 - x^2$ has the parametric representation

$$x = t, \quad y = 9 - t^2, \quad \text{for} \quad -1 \le t \le 3.$$

This representation is not unique. For example, you can verify that the parametric equations

$$x = 1 - t, \quad y = 9 - (1 - t)^2, \quad \text{for} \quad -2 \le t \le 2$$

also do the job, although these equations trace the parabola from right to left, while the original equations trace the curve from left to right (Figure 11.8).

b. In this case, it is easier to let $y = t$. Then a parametric description of the curve is

$$x = (t - 5)^2 + \sqrt{t}, \quad y = t.$$

Notice that t can take values only in the interval $[0, \infty)$. As $t \to \infty$, we see that $x \to \infty$ and $y \to \infty$ (Figure 11.9).

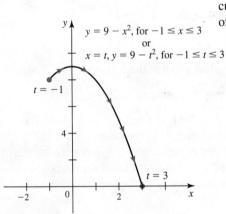

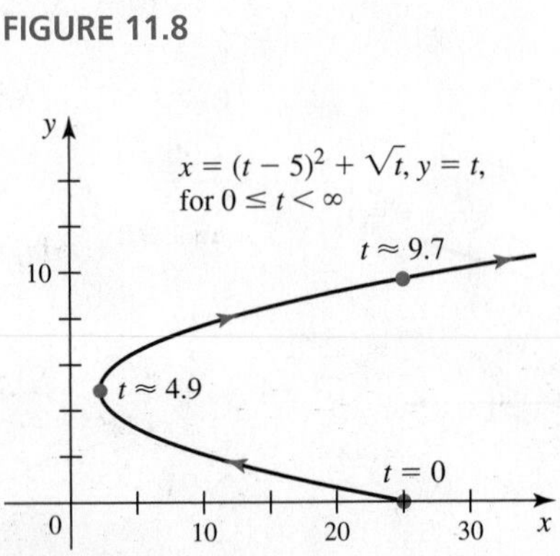

FIGURE 11.8

FIGURE 11.9

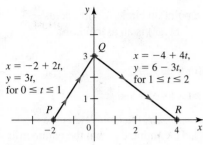

$x = -2 + 2t,$
$y = 3t,$
for $0 \le t \le 1$

$x = -4 + 4t,$
$y = 6 - 3t,$
for $1 \le t \le 2$

FIGURE 11.10

c. The path consists of two line segments (Figure 11.10) that can be parameterized separately in the form $x = x_0 + at$ and $y = y_0 + bt$. The line segment PQ originates at $P(-2, 0)$ and unfolds in the positive x-direction with slope $\frac{3}{2}$. It can be represented as

$$x = -2 + 2t, \quad y = 3t, \quad \text{for } 0 \le t \le 1.$$

Finding the parametric equations for the line segment QR requires some ingenuity. We want the line segment to originate at $Q(0, 3)$ when $t = 1$ and end at $R(4, 0)$ when $t = 2$. Observe that when $t = 1, x = 0$ and when $t = 2, x = 4$. Substituting these pairs of values into the general x-equation $x = x_0 + at$, we obtain the equations

$$x_0 + a = 0 \quad x = 0 \text{ when } t = 1$$
$$x_0 + 2a = 4. \quad x = 4 \text{ when } t = 2$$

Solving for x_0 and a, we find that $x_0 = -4$ and $a = 4$. Applying a similar procedure to the general y-equation $y = y_0 + bt$, the relevant conditions are

$$y_0 + b = 3 \quad y = 3 \text{ when } t = 1$$
$$y_0 + 2b = 0. \quad y = 0 \text{ when } t = 2$$

Solving for y_0 and b, we find that $y_0 = 6$ and $b = -3$. Putting it all together, the equations for the line segment QR are

$$x = -4 + 4t, y = 6 - 3t, \text{ for } 1 \le t \le 2.$$

You can verify that the points $Q(0, 3)$ and $R(4, 0)$ correspond to $t = 1$ and $t = 2$, respectively. Furthermore, the slope of the line is $\dfrac{b}{a} = -\dfrac{3}{4}$, which is correct.

Related Exercises 43–46 ◄

QUICK CHECK 4 Find parametric equations for the line segment that goes from $Q(0, 3)$ to $P(-2, 0)$. ◄

We close this section with two geometric applications of parametric equations.

EXAMPLE 6   Rolling wheels Many fascinating curves are generated by points on rolling wheels. The path of a light on the rim of a wheel rolling on a flat surface (Figure 11.11a) is a **cycloid**, which has the parametric equations

$$x = a(t - \sin t), \quad y = a(1 - \cos t), \quad \text{for } t \ge 0,$$

where $a > 0$. Use a graphing utility to graph the cycloid with $a = 1$. On what interval does the parameter generate the first arch of the cycloid?

SOLUTION The graph of the cycloid, for $0 \le t \le 3\pi$, is shown in Figure 11.11b. The wheel completes one full revolution on the interval $0 \le t \le 2\pi$, which gives one arch of the cycloid.

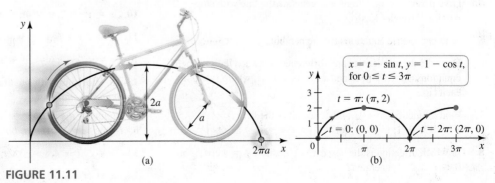

(a)

$x = t - \sin t, y = 1 - \cos t,$
for $0 \le t \le 3\pi$

$t = \pi: (\pi, 2)$

$t = 0: (0, 0)$ $t = 2\pi: (2\pi, 0)$

(b)

FIGURE 11.11

Related Exercises 47–56 ◄

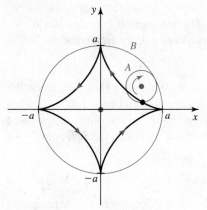

FIGURE 11.12

EXAMPLE 7   More rolling wheels The path of a point on circle A with radius $\dfrac{a}{4}$ that rolls on the inside of circle B with radius a (Figure 11.12) is an **astroid** or a **hypocycloid**. Its parametric equations are

$$x = a \cos^3 t, \quad y = a \sin^3 t, \quad \text{for } 0 \le t \le 2\pi.$$

Graph the astroid with $a = 1$ and find its equation in terms of x and y.

SOLUTION Because both $\cos^3 t$ and $\sin^3 t$ have a period of 2π, the complete curve is generated on the interval $0 \le t \le 2\pi$ (Figure 11.13). To eliminate t from the parametric equations, note that $x^{2/3} = \cos^2 t$ and $y^{2/3} = \sin^2 t$. Therefore,

$$x^{2/3} + y^{2/3} = \cos^2 t + \sin^2 t = 1,$$

where the Pythagorean identity has been used. We see that an alternative description of the astroid is $x^{2/3} + y^{2/3} = 1$.   *Related Exercises 47–56* ◄

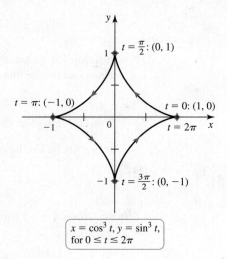

$$x = \cos^3 t, \; y = \sin^3 t,$$
$$\text{for } 0 \le t \le 2\pi$$

FIGURE 11.13

SECTION 11.1 EXERCISES

Review Questions

1. Explain how a pair of parametric equations generates a curve in the xy-plane.

2. Give two pairs of parametric equations that generate a circle centered at the origin with radius 6.

3. Give parametric equations that describe a full circle of radius R, centered at the origin, with clockwise orientation, where the parameter varies over the interval $[0, 10]$.

4. Give parametric equations that generate the line with slope -2 passing through $(1, 3)$.

5. Find parametric equations for the parabola $y = x^2$.

6. Describe the similarities and differences between the parametric equations $x = t, y = t^2$ and $x = -t, y = t^2$, where $t \ge 0$ in each case.

7. Find a function $y = f(x)$ that describes the curve $x = -2t + 1, y = 3t^2$, for $-\infty < t < \infty$.

8. In which direction is the curve $x = -2 \sin t, y = 4 \cos t$, for $0 \le t \le 2\pi$, generated?

Basic Skills

9–12. Working with parametric equations *Consider the following parametric equations.*

a. *Make a brief table of values of t, x, and y.*
b. *Plot the (x, y) pairs in the table and the complete parametric curve, indicating the positive orientation (the direction of increasing t).*
c. *Eliminate the parameter to obtain an equation in x and y.*
d. *Describe the curve.*

9. $x = 2t, y = 3t - 4; \; -10 \le t \le 10$

10. $x = t^2 + 2, y = 4t; \; -4 \le t \le 4$

11. $x = -t + 6, y = 3t - 3; \; -5 \le t \le 5$

12. $x = t^3 - 1, y = 5t + 1; \; -3 \le t \le 3$

13–18. Working with parametric equations *Consider the following parametric equations.*

a. *Eliminate the parameter to obtain an equation in x and y.*
b. *Describe the curve and indicate the positive orientation.*

13. $x = \sqrt{t} + 4, y = 3\sqrt{t}; \; 0 \le t \le 16$

14. $x = (t + 1)^2, y = t + 2; \; -10 \le t \le 10$

15. $x = \cos t, y = \sin^2 t; \; 0 \le t \le \pi$

16. $x = 1 - \sin^2 s, y = \cos s$; $\pi \le s \le 2\pi$

17. $x = r - 1, y = r^3$; $-4 \le r \le 4$

18. $x = e^{2t}, y = e^t + 1$; $0 \le t \le 25$

19–24. Circles and arcs *Eliminate the parameter to find a description of the following circles or circular arcs in terms of x and y. Give the center and radius, and indicate the positive orientation.*

19. $x = 3 \cos t, y = 3 \sin t$; $\pi \le t \le 2\pi$

20. $x = 3 \cos t, y = 3 \sin t$; $0 \le t \le \pi/2$

21. $x = \cos t, y = 1 + \sin t$; $0 \le t \le 2\pi$

22. $x = 2 \sin t - 3, y = 2 \cos t + 5$; $0 \le t \le 2\pi$

23. $x = -7 \cos 2t, y = -7 \sin 2t$; $0 \le t \le \pi$

24. $x = 1 - 3 \sin 4\pi t, y = 2 + 3 \cos 4\pi t$; $0 \le t \le \frac{1}{2}$

25–30. Parametric equations of circles *Find parametric equations for the following circles and give an interval for the parameter values. Graph the circle and find a description in terms of x and y. Answers are not unique.*

25. A circle centered at the origin with radius 4, generated counterclockwise

26. A circle centered at the origin with radius 12, generated clockwise with initial point $(0, 12)$

27. A circle centered at $(2, 3)$ with radius 1, generated counterclockwise

28. A circle centered at $(2, 0)$ with radius 3, generated clockwise

29. A circle centered at $(-2, -3)$ with radius 8, generated clockwise

30. A circle centered at $(2, -4)$ with radius $\frac{3}{2}$, generated counterclockwise with initial point $\left(\frac{7}{2}, -4\right)$

31–34. Circular motion *Find parametric equations that describe the circular path of the following objects. Assume (x, y) denotes the position of the object relative to the origin at the center of the circle. Use the units of time specified in the problem. There is more than one way to describe any circle.*

31. A go-cart moves counterclockwise with constant speed around a circular track of radius 400 m, completing a lap in 1.5 min.

32. The tip of the 15-inch second hand of a clock completes one revolution in 60 seconds.

33. A bicyclist rides counterclockwise with constant speed around a circular velodrome track with a radius of 50 m, completing one lap in 24 s.

34. A Ferris wheel has a radius of 20 m and completes a revolution in the clockwise direction at constant speed in 3 min. Assume that x and y measure the horizontal and vertical positions of a seat on the Ferris wheel relative to a coordinate system whose origin is at the low point of the wheel. Assume the seat begins moving at the origin.

35–38. Parametric lines *Find the slope of each line and a point on the line. Then graph the line.*

35. $x = 3 + t, y = 1 - t$

36. $x = 4 - 3t, y = -2 + 6t$

37. $x = 8 + 2t, y = 1$

38. $x = 1 + 2t/3, y = -4 - 5t/2$

39–42. Line segments *Find a parametric description of the line segment from the point P to the point Q. Solutions are not unique.*

39. $P(0, 0), Q(2, 8)$ **40.** $P(1, 3), Q(-2, 6)$

41. $P(-1, -3), Q(6, -16)$ **42.** $P(8, 2), Q(-2, -3)$

43–46. Curves to parametric equations *Give a pair of parametric equations that describes the following curves. Graph the curve and indicate the positive orientation. If not given, specify the interval over which the parameter varies.*

43. The segment of the parabola $y = 2x^2 - 4$, where $-1 \le x \le 5$

44. The complete curve $x = y^3 - 3y$

45. The piecewise linear path from $P(-2, 3)$ to $Q(2, -3)$ to $R(3, 5)$, using parameter values $0 \le t \le 2$

46. The path consisting of the line segment from $(-4, 4)$ to $(0, 8)$, followed by the segment of the parabola $y = 8 - 2x^2$ from $(0, 8)$ to $(2, 0)$, using parameter values $0 \le t \le 3$

47–52. More parametric curves *Use a graphing utility to graph the following curves. Be sure to choose an interval for the parameter that generates all features of interest.*

47. Spiral $x = t \cos t, y = t \sin t$; $t \ge 0$

48. Witch of Agnesi $x = 2 \cot t, y = 1 - \cos 2t$

49. Folium of Descartes $x = \dfrac{3t}{1 + t^3}, y = \dfrac{3t^2}{1 + t^3}$

50. Involute of a circle $x = \cos t + t \sin t, y = \sin t - t \cos t$

51. Evolute of an ellipse $x = \dfrac{a^2 - b^2}{a} \cos^3 t, y = \dfrac{a^2 - b^2}{b} \sin^3 t$; $a = 4$ and $b = 3$

52. Cissoid of Diocles $x = 2 \sin 2t, y = \dfrac{2 \sin^3 t}{\cos t}$

53–56. Beautiful curves *Consider the family of curves*

$$x = \left(2 + \frac{1}{2} \sin at\right) \cos\left(t + \frac{\sin bt}{c}\right),$$

$$y = \left(2 + \frac{1}{2} \sin at\right) \sin\left(t + \frac{\sin bt}{c}\right).$$

Plot the curve for the given values of a, b, and c with $0 \le t \le 2\pi$. (Source: Mathematica in Action, Stan Wagon, Springer, 2010; created by Norton Starr, Amherst College.)

53. $a = b = 5, c = 2$ **54.** $a = 6, b = 12, c = 3$

55. $a = 18, b = 18, c = 7$ **56.** $a = 7, b = 4, c = 1$

Further Explorations

57. Explain why or why not Determine whether the following statements are true and give an explanation or counterexample.

    a. The equations $x = -\cos t, y = -\sin t$, for $0 \le t \le 2\pi$, generate a circle in the clockwise direction.

    b. An object following the parametric curve $x = 2 \cos 2\pi t$, $y = 2 \sin 2\pi t$ circles the origin once every 1 time unit.

    c. The parametric equations $x = t, y = t^2$, for $t \ge 0$, describe the complete parabola $y = x^2$.

    d. The parametric equations $x = \cos t, y = \sin t$, for $-\pi/2 \le t \le \pi/2$, describe a semicircle.

58–61. Words to curves *Find parametric equations for the following curves. Include an interval for the parameter values. Answers are not unique.*

58. The left half of the parabola $y = x^2 + 1$, originating at $(0, 1)$

59. The line that passes through the points $(1, 1)$ and $(3, 5)$, oriented in the direction of increasing x

60. The lower half of the circle centered at $(-2, 2)$ with radius 6, oriented in the counterclockwise direction

61. The upper half of the parabola $x = y^2$, originating at $(0, 0)$

62. Matching curves and equations Match equations a–d with graphs A–D. Explain your reasoning.

  a. $x = t^2 - 2, y = t^3 - t$
  b. $x = \cos(t + \sin 50t), y = \sin(t + \cos 50t)$
  c. $x = t + \cos 2t, y = t - \sin 4t$
  d. $x = 2\cos t + \cos 20t, y = 2\sin t + \sin 20t$

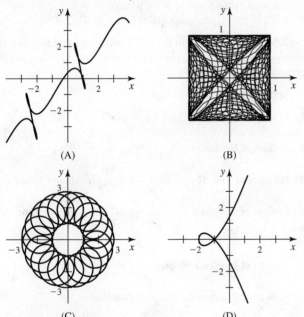

(A) (B)

(C) (D)

63–64. Ellipses *An **ellipse** (discussed in detail in Appendix B) is generated by the parametric equations $x = a\cos t, y = b\sin t$. If $0 < a < b$, then the long axis (or **major axis**) lies on the y-axis and the short axis (or **minor axis**) lies on the x-axis. If $0 < b < a$, the axes are reversed. The lengths of the axes in the x- and y-directions are 2a and 2b, respectively.*

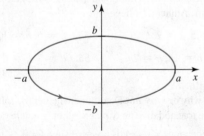

Sketch the graph of the following ellipses. Specify an interval in t over which the entire curve is generated.

63. $x = 4\cos t, y = 9\sin t$ **64.** $x = 12\sin 2t, y = 3\cos 2t$

65–68. Parametric equations of ellipses *Find parametric equations (not unique) of the following ellipses (see Exercises 63–64). Graph the ellipse and find a description in terms of x and y.*

65. An ellipse centered at the origin with major axis of length 6 on the x-axis and minor axis of length 3 on the y-axis, generated counterclockwise

66. An ellipse centered at the origin with major and minor axes of lengths 12 and 2, on the x- and y-axes, respectively, generated clockwise

67. An ellipse centered at $(-2, -3)$ with major and minor axes of lengths 30 and 20, parallel to the x- and y-axes, respectively, generated counterclockwise (*Hint:* Shift the parametric equations.)

68. An ellipse centered at $(0, -4)$ with major and minor axes of lengths 10 and 3, parallel to the x- and y-axes, respectively, generated clockwise (*Hint:* Shift the parametric equations.)

69. Intersecting lines Consider the following pairs of lines. Determine whether the lines are parallel or intersecting. If the lines intersect at a single point, then determine that point.

  a. $x = 1 + s, y = 2s$ and $x = 1 + 2t, y = 3t$
  b. $x = 2 + 5s, y = 1 + s$ and $x = 4 + 10t, y = 3 + 2t$
  c. $x = 1 + 3s, y = 4 + 2s$ and $x = 4 - 3t, y = 6 + 4t$

70. Multiple descriptions Which of the following parametric equations describe the same curve?

  a. $x = 2t^2, y = 4 + t; -4 \le t \le 4$
  b. $x = 2t^4, y = 4 + t^2; -2 \le t \le 2$
  c. $x = 2t^{2/3}, y = 4 + t^{1/3}; -64 \le t \le 64$

71–74. Eliminating the parameter *Eliminate the parameter to express the following parametric equations as a single equation in x and y.*

71. $x = 2\sin 8t, y = 2\cos 8t$ **72.** $x = \sin 8t, y = 2\cos 8t$

73. $x = t, y = \sqrt{4 - t^2}$ **74.** $x = \sqrt{t + 1}, y = \dfrac{1}{t + 1}$

75–76. Equivalent descriptions *Find real numbers a and b such that equations A and B describe the same curve.*

75. A: $x = 10\sin t, y = 10\cos t; 0 \le t \le 2\pi$
    B: $x = 10\sin 3t, y = 10\cos 3t; a \le t \le b$

76. A: $x = t + t^3, y = 3 + t^2; -2 \le t \le 2$
    B: $x = t^{1/3} + t, y = 3 + t^{2/3}; a \le t \le b$

77–78. Lissajous curves *Consider the following Lissajous curves. Graph the curve and estimate the coordinates of the points on the curve at which there is (a) a horizontal tangent line and (b) a vertical tangent line. (See the Guided Project Parametric Art for more on Lissajous curves.)*

77. $x = \sin 2t, y = 2\sin t$;   **78.** $x = \sin 4t, y = \sin 3t$;
    $0 \le t \le 2\pi$ $0 \le t \le 2\pi$

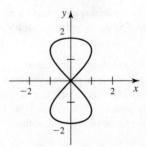 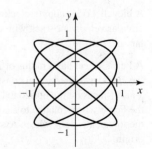

79. Lamé curves The *Lamé curve* described by $\left|\dfrac{x}{a}\right|^n + \left|\dfrac{y}{b}\right|^n = 1$, where a, b, and n are positive real numbers, is a generalization of an ellipse.

  a. Express this equation in parametric form (four sets of equations are needed).
  b. Graph the curve for $a = 4$ and $b = 2$, for various values of n.
  c. Describe how the curves change as n increases.

Applications

80. Paths of moons An idealized model of the path of a moon (relative to the Sun) moving with constant speed in a circular orbit around a planet, where the planet in turn revolves around the Sun, is given by the parametric equations

$$x(\theta) = a \cos \theta + \cos n\theta, \quad y(\theta) = a \sin \theta + \sin n\theta.$$

The distance from the moon to the planet is taken to be 1, the distance from the planet to the Sun is a, and n is the number of times the moon orbits the planet for every 1 revolution of the planet around the Sun. Plot the graph of the path of a moon for the given constants; then conjecture which values of n produce loops for a fixed value of a.

a. $a = 4, n = 3$ **b.** $a = 4, n = 4$ **c.** $a = 4, n = 5$

81. Paths of the moons of Earth and Jupiter Use the equations in Exercise 80 to plot the paths of the following moons in our solar system.

a. Each year our moon revolves around Earth about $n = 13.4$ times, and the distance from the Sun to Earth is approximately $a = 389.2$ times the distance from Earth to our moon.

b. Plot a graph of the path of Callisto (one of Jupiter's moons) that corresponds to values of $a = 727.5$ and $n = 259.6$. Plot a small portion of the graph to see the detailed behavior of the orbit.

c. Plot a graph of the path of Io (another of Jupiter's moons) that corresponds to values of $a = 1846.2$ and $n = 2448.8$. Plot a small portion of the path of Io to see the loops in its orbit.

(*Source for Exercises 80–81: The Sun, the Moon, and Convexity, The College Mathematics Journal*, 32, Sep 2001)

82. Air drop A plane traveling horizontally at 80 m/s over flat ground at an elevation of 3000 m releases an emergency packet. The trajectory of the packet is given by

$$x = 80t, \quad y = -4.9t^2 + 3000, \quad \text{for } t \geq 0,$$

where the origin is the point on the ground directly beneath the plane at the moment of the release. Graph the trajectory of the packet and find the coordinates of the point where the packet lands.

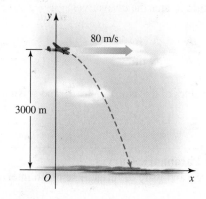

83. Air drop—inverse problem A plane traveling horizontally at 100 m/s over flat ground at an elevation of 4000 m must drop an emergency packet on a target on the ground. The trajectory of the packet is given by

$$x = 100t, \quad y = -4.9t^2 + 4000, \quad \text{for } t \geq 0,$$

where the origin is the point on the ground directly beneath the plane at the moment of the release. How many horizontal meters before the target should the packet be released in order to hit the target?

84. Projectile explorations A projectile launched from the ground with an initial speed of 20 m/s and a launch angle θ follows a trajectory approximated by

$$x = (20 \cos \theta)t, \quad y = -4.9t^2 + (20 \sin \theta)t,$$

where x and y are the horizontal and vertical positions of the projectile relative to the launch point $(0, 0)$.

a. Graph the trajectory for various values of θ in the range $0 < \theta < \pi/2$.

b. Based on your observations, what value of θ gives the greatest range (the horizontal distance between the launch and landing points)?

Additional Exercises

85. General equations for a circle Prove that the equations

$$x = a \cos t + b \sin t, \quad y = c \cos t + d \sin t,$$

where a, b, c, and d are real numbers, describe a circle of radius R provided $a^2 + c^2 = b^2 + d^2 = R^2$ and $ab + cd = 0$.

Technology Exercises

86–88. More Lissajous curves *Lissajous curves are generated by the parametric equations*

$$x = A \cos at \qquad y = B \sin bt,$$

where varying the amplitudes A and B, and the frequencies a and b, gives a large variety of figures. Note that the only effect of A and B is to stretch or compress the figure in the x- and y-directions, respectively. Therefore, we take A = B = 1 and focus on the roles of a and b, which we take to be integers.

86. Consider the equations $x = \cos 3t$, $y = \sin 2t$. Before using a graphing utility, it's advisable to find an interval for the parameter values that generates the complete curve. What is the period of the $\cos 3t$? What is the period of $\sin 2t$? Explain why an interval that generates the complete curve is $[0, 2\pi]$, but not $[0, \pi]$. Does the interval $[-\pi, \pi]$, which also has length 2π, generate the complete curve as well? Experiment with different intervals for the parameter and graph the complete Lissajous curve $x = \cos 3t$, $y = \sin 2t$.

87. A nice family of Lissajous curves is generated by letting a be an odd integer and $b = a \pm 1$. Graph the following beautiful curves.

a. $x = \cos 5t, y = \sin 4t$ **b.** $x = \cos 3t, y = \sin 4t$
c. $x = \cos 5t, y = \sin 6t$ **d.** $x = \cos 9t, y = \sin 8t$

88. What is the effect of introducing a *phase angle* in the equations? For example, plot and describe the curve $x = \cos (5t + \theta_0)$, $y = \sin 4t$, for various values of θ_0. (Suggestion: choose several multiples of $\pi/32$ for θ_0.) As another example, plot and describe the curve $x = \cos(2t + \theta_0)$, $y = \sin t$, for various values of θ_0. In all cases, you should notice that the graphs stay within a rectangle $\{(x, y): a \leq x \leq b, c \leq y \leq d\}$. Find the values of a, b, c, and d, and explain why the graphs do not extend beyond the rectangle.

■ 89–90. Hypocycloids *Imagine a circle of radius r rolling on the inside of a larger circle of radius R, where R = kr with k > 1. The path traced out by a point on the circumference of the smaller circle is a* **hypocycloid,** *described by the parametric equations*

$$x = r(k - 1) \cos t + r \cos (k - 1)t,$$
$$y = r(k - 1) \sin t - r \sin (k - 1)t.$$

89. Plot the *asteroid*, which is the hypocycloid that results with $r = 1$ and $k = 4$. How many cusps does the curve have?

90. Graph several hypocycloids with varying values of k and provide evidence for the fact that if k is an integer, then the resulting curve closes on itself and has k cusps. Assume $r = 1$.

11.2 Calculus with Parametric Equations

Having gained an understanding of parametric equations, we now ask some familiar calculus questions. For example, at all points of a smooth parametric curve, it is possible to draw a tangent line. How do we find the slope of that tangent line? As another example, consider the trajectory of a moving object, which can be represented by a parametric curve. Determining the distance traveled by the object as it moves along the curve requires computing the arc length of the curve. How do we find the arc length of a parametric curve? We now answer these questions.

Derivatives and Parametric Equations

Parametric equations express a relationship between the variables x and y. Therefore, it makes sense to ask about $\dfrac{dy}{dx}$, the rate of change of y with respect to x at a point on a parametric curve.

Once we know how to compute $\dfrac{dy}{dx}$, the derivative can be used to determine slopes of lines tangent to parametric curves.

Consider the parametric equations $x = f(t), y = g(t)$ on an interval on which both f and g are differentiable. The Chain Rule relates the derivatives $\dfrac{dy}{dt}, \dfrac{dx}{dt}$, and $\dfrac{dy}{dx}$:

$$\frac{dy}{dt} = \frac{dy}{dx} \frac{dx}{dt}.$$

Provided that $\dfrac{dx}{dt} \ne 0$, we divide both sides of this equation by $\dfrac{dx}{dt}$ and solve for $\dfrac{dy}{dx}$ to obtain the following result.

> The derivative $\dfrac{dy}{dx}$ in Theorem 11.1 is a function of t and it represents the slope of the parametric curve $x = f(t), y = g(t)$ at a point corresponding to t.

THEOREM 11.1   Derivative for Parametric Curves

Let $x = f(t)$ and $y = g(t)$, where f and g are differentiable on an interval $[a, b]$. Then

$$\frac{dy}{dx} = \frac{dy/dt}{dx/dt} = \frac{g'(t)}{f'(t)},$$

provided $f'(t) \ne 0$.

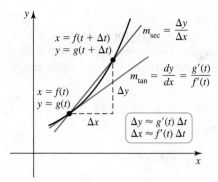

FIGURE 11.14

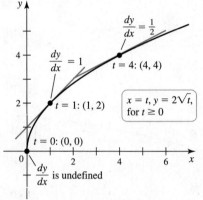

FIGURE 11.15

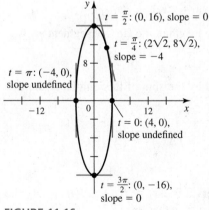

FIGURE 11.16

▷ In general, the equations $x = a \cos t$, $y = b \sin t$, for $0 \le t \le 2\pi$, describe an ellipse. The constants a and b can be seen as horizontal and vertical scalings of the unit circle $x = \cos t$, $y = \sin t$.

Figure 11.14 gives a geometric explanation of Theorem 11.1. The slope of the line tangent to a curve at a point is $\dfrac{dy}{dx} = \lim\limits_{\Delta x \to 0} \dfrac{\Delta y}{\Delta x}$. Using linear approximation (Section 4.5), we have $\Delta x \approx f'(t)\Delta t$ and $\Delta y \approx g'(t)\Delta t$, with these approximations improving as $\Delta t \to 0$. Notice also that $\Delta t \to 0$ as $\Delta x \to 0$. Therefore, the slope of the tangent line is

$$\frac{dy}{dx} = \lim_{\Delta x \to 0} \frac{\Delta y}{\Delta x} = \lim_{\Delta t \to 0} \frac{g'(t)\Delta t}{f'(t)\Delta t} = \frac{g'(t)}{f'(t)}.$$

QUICK CHECK 1 Find the slope of the line $x = 4t$, $y = 2t$, for $-\infty < t < \infty$. ◀

EXAMPLE 1 **Slopes of tangent lines** Find $\dfrac{dy}{dx}$ for the following curves. Interpret the result and determine the points (if any) at which the curve has a horizontal or a vertical tangent line.

a. $x = f(t) = t$, $y = g(t) = 2\sqrt{t}$, for $t \ge 0$
b. $x = f(t) = 4 \cos t$, $y = g(t) = 16 \sin t$, for $0 \le t \le 2\pi$

SOLUTION

a. We find that $f'(t) = 1$ and $g'(t) = 1/\sqrt{t}$. Therefore,

$$\frac{dy}{dx} = \frac{g'(t)}{f'(t)} = \frac{1/\sqrt{t}}{1} = \frac{1}{\sqrt{t}},$$

provided $t \ne 0$. Notice that $\dfrac{dy}{dx} \ne 0$ for $t > 0$, so the curve has no horizontal tangent lines.

On the other hand, as $t \to 0^+$, we see that $\dfrac{dy}{dx} \to \infty$. Therefore, the curve has a vertical tangent line at the point $(0, 0)$. To eliminate t from the parametric equations, we substitute $t = x$ into the y-equation to find that $y = 2\sqrt{x}$. Because $y \ge 0$, the curve is the upper half of a parabola (Figure 11.15). Slopes of tangent lines at other points on the curve are found by substituting the corresponding values of t. For example, the point $(4, 4)$ corresponds to $t = 4$ and the slope of the tangent line at that point is $1/\sqrt{4} = \frac{1}{2}$.

b. These parametric equations describe an **ellipse** (Section 11.1, Exercises 63–64) with a major axis of length 32 on the y-axis and a minor axis of length 8 on the x-axis (Figure 11.16). In this case, $f'(t) = -4 \sin t$ and $g'(t) = 16 \cos t$. Therefore,

$$\frac{dy}{dx} = \frac{g'(t)}{f'(t)} = \frac{16 \cos t}{-4 \sin t} = -4 \cot t.$$

At $t = 0$ and $t = \pi$, $\cot t$ is undefined. Notice that

$$\lim_{t \to 0^+} \frac{dy}{dx} = \lim_{t \to 0^+} (-4 \cot t) = -\infty \quad \text{and} \quad \lim_{t \to 0^-} \frac{dy}{dx} = \lim_{t \to 0^-} (-4 \cot t) = \infty.$$

Consequently, a vertical tangent line occurs at the point corresponding to $t = 0$, which is $(4, 0)$ (Figure 11.16). A similar argument shows that a vertical tangent line occurs at the point corresponding to $t = \pi$, which is $(-4, 0)$.

At $t = \pi/2$ and $t = 3\pi/2$, $\cot t = 0$ and the curve has horizontal tangent lines at the corresponding points $(0, \pm 16)$. Slopes of tangent lines at other points on the curve may be found. For example, the point $(2\sqrt{2}, 8\sqrt{2})$ corresponds to $t = \pi/4$; the slope of the tangent line at that point is $-4 \cot \pi/4 = -4$.

Related Exercises 5–10◀

▸ Arc length for curves of the form $y = f(x)$ was discussed in Section 6.5. Look for the parallels between that discussion and the one in this section.

Arc Length of Parametric Curves

Consider the parametric curve C given by $x = f(t)$, $y = g(t)$, for $a \leq t \leq b$, where f' and g' are continuous on $[a, b]$. To find the length of the curve between the points $(f(a), g(a))$ and $(f(b), g(b))$, we first subdivide the interval $[a, b]$ into n subintervals using the grid points

$$a = t_0 < t_1 < t_2 < \cdots < t_n = b.$$

The next step is to connect consecutive points on the curve,

$$(f(t_0), g(t_0)), \ldots, (f(t_k), g(t_k)), \ldots, (f(t_n), g(t_n)),$$

with line segments (Figure 11.17a).

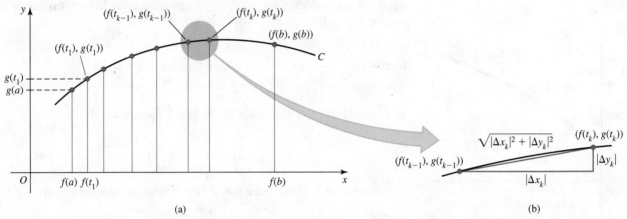

(a)

(b)

FIGURE 11.17

The kth line segment is the hypotenuse of a right triangle, whose legs have lengths $|\Delta x_k|$ and $|\Delta y_k|$, where

$$\Delta x_k = f(t_k) - f(t_{k-1}) \quad \text{and} \quad \Delta y_k = g(t_k) - g(t_{k-1}),$$

for $k = 1, 2, \ldots, n$ (Figure 11.17b). Therefore, the length of the kth line segment is

$$\sqrt{|\Delta x_k|^2 + |\Delta y_k|^2}.$$

The length of the entire curve L is approximated by the sum of the lengths of the line segments:

$$L \approx \sum_{k=1}^{n} \sqrt{|\Delta x_k|^2 + |\Delta y_k|^2} = \sum_{k=1}^{n} \sqrt{(\Delta x_k)^2 + (\Delta y_k)^2}. \tag{1}$$

The goal is to express this sum as a Riemann sum.

The change in $x = f(t)$ over the kth subinterval is $\Delta x_k = f(t_k) - f(t_{k-1})$. By the Mean Value Theorem, there is a point t_k^* in (t_{k-1}, t_k) such that

$$\underbrace{\overbrace{\frac{f(t_k) - f(t_{k-1})}{\underbrace{t_k - t_{k-1}}_{\Delta t_k}}}^{\Delta x_k}} = f'(t_k^*).$$

So the change in x as t changes by $\Delta t_k = t_k - t_{k-1}$ is

$$\Delta x_k = f(t_k) - f(t_{k-1}) = f'(t_k^*)\Delta t_k.$$

Similarly, the change in y over the kth subinterval is

$$\Delta y_k = g(t_k) - g(t_{k-1}) = g'(\hat{t}_k)\Delta t_k,$$

where $\hat{t}_k$ is also a point in (t_{k-1}, t_k). We now substitute these expressions for Δx_k and Δy_k into equation (1):

$$L \approx \sum_{k=1}^{n} \sqrt{(\Delta x_k)^2 + (\Delta y_k)^2}$$

$$= \sum_{k=1}^{n} \sqrt{(f'(t_k^*)\Delta t_k)^2 + (g'(\hat{t}_k)\Delta t_k)^2} \qquad \text{Substitute for } \Delta x_k \text{ and } \Delta y_k.$$

$$= \sum_{k=1}^{n} \sqrt{f'(t_k^*)^2 + g'(\hat{t}_k)^2}\,\Delta t_k. \qquad \text{Factor } \Delta t_k \text{ out of square root.}$$

The intermediate points t_k^* and $\hat{t}_k$ both approach t_k as n increases and as Δt_k approaches zero. Therefore, given the conditions on f' and g', the limit of this sum as $n \to \infty$ and $\Delta t_k \to 0$, for all k, exists and equals a definite integral:

$$L = \lim_{n \to \infty} \sum_{k=1}^{n} \sqrt{f'(t_k^*)^2 + g'(\hat{t}_k)^2}\,\Delta t_k = \int_a^b \sqrt{f'(t)^2 + g'(t)^2}\,dt.$$

> Arc length integrals are usually difficult to evaluate exactly. The few easily evaluated integrals appear in the examples and exercises. Often numerical methods must be used to approximate the more challenging integrals (see Example 4).

DEFINITION Arc Length of Parametric Curves

Consider the parametric curve $x = f(t)$, $y = g(t)$ where f' and g' are continuous, and the curve is traversed once for $a \le t \le b$. The **arc length** of the curve between $(f(a), g(a))$ and $(f(b), g(b))$ is

$$L = \int_a^b \sqrt{f'(t)^2 + g'(t)^2}\,dt = \int_a^b \sqrt{\left(\frac{dx}{dt}\right)^2 + \left(\frac{dy}{dt}\right)^2}\,dt$$

QUICK CHECK 2 Use the arc length formula to find the length of the line $x = t$, $y = t$, for $0 \le t \le 1$. ◄

Let's use the arc length integral to derive the formula for the circumference of a circle.

EXAMPLE 2   Circumference of a circle Prove that the circumference of a circle of radius $a > 0$ is $2\pi a$.

SOLUTION A circle of radius a is described by

$$x = f(t) = a\cos t, \ y = g(t) = a\sin t, \text{ for } 0 \le t \le 2\pi.$$

Note that $f'(t) = -a \sin t$ and $g'(t) = a \cos t$. The circumference is

$$L = \int_0^{2\pi} \sqrt{f'(t)^2 + g'(t)^2}\, dt \qquad \text{Arc length formula}$$

$$= \int_0^{2\pi} \sqrt{(-a \sin t)^2 + (a \cos t)^2}\, dt \qquad \text{Substitute for } f' \text{ and } g'.$$

$$= a \int_0^{2\pi} \sqrt{\sin^2 t + \cos^2 t}\, dt \qquad \text{Factor } a > 0 \text{ out of square root.}$$

$$= a \int_0^{2\pi} 1\, dt \qquad \sin^2 t + \cos^2 t = 1$$

$$= 2\pi a. \qquad \text{Integrate a constant.}$$

Related Exercises 11–20 ◄

EXAMPLE 3   Length of a hypocycloid (or astroid) Find the length of the complete hypocycloid given by $x = \cos^3 t$, $y = \sin^3 t$, where $0 \le t \le 2\pi$ (Figure 11.18).

SOLUTION The length of the entire curve is four times the length of the curve in the first quadrant. You should verify that the curve in the first quadrant is generated as the parameter varies from $t = 0$ (corresponding to $(1, 0)$) to $t = \pi/2$ (corresponding to $(0, 1)$). Letting $f(t) = \cos^3 t$ and $g(t) = \sin^3 t$, we have

$$f'(t) = -3 \cos^2 t \sin t \quad \text{and} \quad g'(t) = 3 \sin^2 t \cos t.$$

The arc length of the full curve is

$$L = 4 \int_0^{\pi/2} \sqrt{f'(t)^2 + g'(t)^2}\, dt \qquad \text{Factor of 4 by symmetry}$$

$$= 4 \int_0^{\pi/2} \sqrt{(-3 \cos^2 t \sin t)^2 + (3 \sin^2 t \cos t)^2}\, dt \qquad \text{Substitute for } f' \text{ and } g'.$$

$$= 4 \int_0^{\pi/2} \sqrt{9 \cos^4 t \sin^2 t + 9 \cos^2 t \sin^4 t}\, dt \qquad \text{Simplify terms.}$$

$$= 4 \int_0^{\pi/2} 3 \sqrt{\cos^2 t \sin^2 t \underbrace{(\cos^2 t + \sin^2 t)}_{1}}\, dt \qquad \text{Factor.}$$

$$= 12 \int_0^{\pi/2} \cos t \sin t\, dt. \qquad \cos t \sin t \ge 0, \text{ for } 0 \le t \le \frac{\pi}{2}$$

Letting $u = \sin t$ with $du = \cos t\, dt$, we have

$$L = 12 \int_0^{\pi/2} \cos t \sin t\, dt = 12 \int_0^1 u\, du = 6.$$

The length of the entire hypocycloid is 6 units.

Related Exercises 11–20 ◄

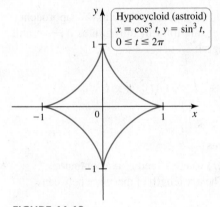

Hypocycloid (astroid)
$x = \cos^3 t, y = \sin^3 t,$
$0 \le t \le 2\pi$

FIGURE 11.18

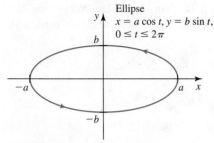

Ellipse
$x = a \cos t, y = b \sin t,$
$0 \le t \le 2\pi$

FIGURE 11.19

> The German astronomer and mathematician Johannes Kepler (1571–1630) worked with the meticulously gathered data of Tycho Brahe to formulate three empirical laws obeyed by planets and comets orbiting the sun. The work of Kepler formed the foundation for Newton's laws of gravitation developed 50 years later.

> In September 2006, Pluto joined the ranks of Ceres, Haumea, Makemake, and Eris as one of five dwarf planets in our solar system.

The next example gives a practical application of an arc length integral that is difficult to evaluate exactly.

EXAMPLE 4   Lengths of planetary orbits According to Kepler's first law, the planets revolve about the sun in elliptical orbits. The parametric equations for an ellipse in the xy-plane are

$$x = f(t) = a \cos t, y = g(t) = b \sin t, \quad \text{for } 0 \le t \le 2\pi.$$

If $a > b > 0$, then $2a$ is the length of the major axis and $2b$ is the length of the minor axis (Figure 11.19). Verify the lengths of the planetary orbits given in Table 11.3. Distances are given in terms of the astronomical unit (AU), which is the length of the semimajor axis of Earth's orbit, or about 93 million miles.

Table 11.3

Planet	Semimajor axis, a (AU)	Semiminor axis, b (AU)	$\alpha = \dfrac{b}{a}$	Orbit length (AU)
Mercury	0.387	0.379	0.979	2.407
Venus	0.723	0.723	1.000	4.543
Earth	1.000	0.999	0.999	6.280
Mars	1.524	1.517	0.995	9.554
Jupiter	5.203	5.179	0.995	32.616
Saturn	9.539	9.524	0.998	59.888
Uranus	19.182	19.161	0.999	120.458
Neptune	30.058	30.057	1.000	188.857

SOLUTION Using the arc length formula, the length of a general elliptical orbit is

$$L = \int_0^{2\pi} \sqrt{f'(t)^2 + g'(t)^2}\, dt$$

$$= \int_0^{2\pi} \sqrt{(-a \sin t)^2 + (b \cos t)^2}\, dt \quad \text{Substitute for } f'(t) \text{ and } g'(t).$$

$$= \int_0^{2\pi} \sqrt{a^2 \sin^2 t + b^2 \cos^2 t}\, dt. \quad \text{Simplify.}$$

Factoring a^2 out of the square root and letting $\alpha = \dfrac{b}{a}$, we have

$$L = \int_0^{2\pi} \sqrt{a^2 \left(\sin^2 t + (b/a)^2 \cos^2 t\right)}\, dt \quad \text{Factor out } a^2.$$

$$= a \int_0^{2\pi} \sqrt{\sin^2 t + \alpha^2 \cos^2 t}\, dt \quad \text{Let } \alpha = \dfrac{b}{a}.$$

$$= 4a \int_0^{\pi/2} \sqrt{\sin^2 t + \alpha^2 \cos^2 t}\, dt. \quad \text{Use symmetry; quarter orbit on } [0, \pi/2].$$

> The integral that gives the length of an ellipse is a *complete elliptic integral of the second kind*. Many reference books and software packages provide approximate values of this integral.

Unfortunately, an antiderivative for this integrand cannot be found in terms of elementary functions, so we have two options: This integral is well known, and values have been tabulated for various values of α. Alternatively, we may use a calculator to

> Though rounded values for α appear in Table 11.3, the calculations in Example 4 were done in full precision, and rounded to three decimal places only in the final step.

approximate the integral numerically (see Section 5.7). Using numerical integration, the orbit lengths in Table 11.3 are obtained. For example, the length of Mercury's orbit with $a = 0.387$ and $\alpha = 0.979$ is

$$L = 4a \int_0^{\pi/2} \sqrt{\sin^2 t + \alpha^2 \cos^2 t}\, dt$$

$$= 1.548 \int_0^{\pi/2} \sqrt{\sin^2 t + 0.959 \cos^2 t}\, dt \quad \text{Simplify.}$$

$$\approx 2.407. \qquad\qquad\qquad \text{Approximate using calculator.}$$

The fact that α is close to 1 for all the planets means that their orbits are nearly circular. For this reason, the lengths of the orbits shown in the table are nearly equal to $2\pi a$, which is the length of a circular orbit with radius a.

Related Exercises 21–24 ◀

SECTION 11.2 EXERCISES

Review Questions

1. Explain how to find the slope of the line tangent to the curve $x = f(t), y = g(t)$ at the point $(f(a), g(a))$.

2. Explain how to find points on the curve $x = f(t), y = g(t)$ at which there is a horizontal tangent line.

3. Find the length of the line $x = t, y = 2t$, for $3 \leq t \leq 4$.

4. Explain how to find the length of the curve $x = f(t), y = g(t)$, for $a \leq t \leq b$.

Basic Skills

5–10. Derivatives *Consider the following parametric curves.*

a. *Determine* $\dfrac{dy}{dx}$ *in terms of t and evaluate it at the given value of t.*

b. *Make a sketch of the curve showing the tangent line at the point corresponding to the given value of t.*

5. $x = 2 + 4t, y = 4 - 8t; \ t = 2$

6. $x = 3 \sin t, y = 3 \cos t; \ t = \pi/2$

7. $x = \cos t, y = 8 \sin t; \ t = \pi/2$

8. $x = 2t, y = t^3; \ t = -1$

9. $x = t + 1/t, y = t - 1/t; \ t = 1$

10. $x = \sqrt{t}, y = 2t; \ t = 4$

11–20. Arc length calculations *Find the length of the following curves.*

11. $x = 3t^2 - 1, y = 4t^2 + 5$, for $0 \leq t \leq 1$

12. $x = 3t - 1, y = 4t + 5$, for $-1 \leq t \leq 2$

13. $x = 3 \cos t, y = 3 \sin t$, for $0 \leq t \leq \pi$

14. $x = 4 \cos 3t, y = 4 \sin 3t$, for $0 \leq t \leq 2\pi/3$

15. $x = \cos t + t \sin t, y = \sin t - t \cos t$, for $0 \leq t \leq \pi/2$

16. $x = \cos t + \sin t, y = \cos t - \sin t$, for $0 \leq t \leq 2\pi$

17. $x = t^2/2, y = 2/3(t + 1/4)^{3/2}$, for $0 \leq t \leq 3$

18. $x = t^2/2, y = (2t + 1)^{3/2}/3$, for $0 \leq t \leq 2$

19. $x = \cos^3 t, y = \sin^3 t$, for $0 \leq t \leq \pi/2$

20. $x = 2t^2, y = t^3$, for $0 \leq t \leq 1$

21–24. Arc length approximations *Use a calculator to approximate the length of the following curves. In each case, simplify the arc length integral as much as possible before finding an approximation.*

21. $x = 2 \cos t, y = 2 \sin 2t$, for $0 \leq t \leq 2\pi$

22. $x = \sin 3t, y = \cos t$, for $0 \leq t \leq 2\pi$

23. $x = t^2/2, y = t$, for $-2 \leq t \leq 2$

24. $x = e^{-t}, y = t$, for $0 \leq t \leq \ln 3$

Further Explorations

25. **Explain why or why not** Determine whether the following statements are true and give an explanation or counterexample.

    a. There are two points on the curve $x = -4 \cos t, y = 4 \sin t$, for $0 \leq t \leq 2\pi$, at which there is a vertical tangent line.

    b. The curves $x = f(t), y = g(t)$ and $x = g(t), y = f(t)$ have the same length over the interval $[a, b]$.

    c. The curve $x = f(t), y = g(t)$, for $0 \leq a \leq t \leq b$, and the curve $x = f(t^2), y = g(t^2)$, for $\sqrt{a} \leq t \leq \sqrt{b}$, have the same length.

    d. The equations $x = t^{2/3}, y = t^{2/3}$, for $-\infty < t < \infty$, describe a complete line (with no endpoints).

26–29. Tangent lines *Find an equation of the line tangent to the curve at the point corresponding to the given value of t.*

26. $x = \sin t, y = \cos t; \ t = \pi/4$

27. $x = t^2 - 1, y = t^3 + t; \ t = 2$

28. $x = e^t, y = \ln(t + 1); \ t = 0$

29. $x = \cos t + t \sin t, y = \sin t - t \cos t; \ t = \pi/4$

30–35. Slopes of tangent lines *Find all points at which the following curves have the given slope.*

30. $x = 2t, y = 3t^2 + 1$; slope $= -\frac{3}{2}$

31. $x = 4 \cos t, y = 4 \sin t$; slope $= \frac{1}{2}$

32. $x = 2 \cos t, y = 8 \sin t$; slope $= -1$

33. $x = t + 1/t, y = t - 1/t$; slope $= 1$

34. $x = 2 + \sqrt{t}, y = 2 - 4t$; slope $= -8$

35. $x = e^{2t}/2, y = e^{-t}$; slope $= -e$

36. Length of a line segment Consider the line segment joining the points $P(x_0, y_0)$ and $Q(x_1, y_1)$.

    a. Find a parametric description of the line segment PQ.

    b. Use the arc length formula to find the length of PQ.

    c. Use geometry (distance formula) to verify the result of part (b).

37. A special case Suppose a curve is described by $x = A\,h(t), y = B\,h(t)$, for $a \le t \le b$, where A and B are constants and h has a continuous derivative.

    a. Show that the length of the curve is

$$\sqrt{A^2 + B^2} \int_a^b |h'(t)|\, dt.$$

    b. Use part (a) to find the length of the curve $x = 2t^3, y = 5t^3$, for $0 \le t \le 4$.

    c. Use part (a) to find the length of the curve $x = 4/t, y = 10/t$, for $1 \le t \le 8$.

Applications

38. A cycloid A cycloid is the path traced by a point on a circle rolling on a flat surface (think of a light on the rim of a moving bicycle wheel). The cycloid generated by a circle of radius a is given by the parametric equations

$$x = a(t - \sin t), \quad y = a(1 - \cos t);$$

the parameter range $0 \le t \le 2\pi$ produces one arch of the cycloid (see figure). Show that the length of one arch of a cycloid is $8a$.

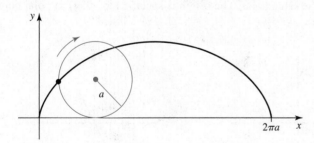

39. Projectile trajectories A projectile (such as a baseball or a cannonball) launched from the origin with an initial horizontal velocity u_0 and an initial vertical velocity v_0 moves in a parabolic trajectory given by

$$x = u_0 t, \quad y = -\tfrac{1}{2}gt^2 + v_0 t, \quad \text{for } t \ge 0,$$

where air resistance is neglected and $g \approx 9.8 \text{ m/s}^2$ is the acceleration due to gravity.

    a. Let $u_0 = 20 \text{ m/s}$ and $v_0 = 25 \text{ m/s}$. Assuming the projectile is launched over horizontal ground, at what time does it return to Earth?

    b. Find the integral that gives the length of the trajectory from launch to landing.

    c. Evaluate the integral in part (b) by first making the change of variables $u = -gt + v_0$. The resulting integral is evaluated either by making a second change of variables or by using a calculator. What is the length of the trajectory?

    d. How far does the projectile land from its launch site?

Additional Exercises

40. Second derivative Assume a curve is given by the parametric equations $x = f(t)$ and $y = g(t)$, where f and g are twice differentiable. Use the Chain Rule to show that

$$y''(x) = \frac{f'(t)g''(t) - g'(t)f''(t)}{(f'(t))^3}.$$

41. Arc length for $y = f(x)$ The arc length formula for functions of the form $y = f(x)$ on $[a, b]$ found in Section 6.5 is

$$L = \int_a^b \sqrt{1 + f'(x)^2}\, dx.$$

Derive this formula from the arc length formula for parametric curves. (*Hint:* Let $x = t$ be the parameter.)

QUICK CHECK **ANSWERS**

1. $\dfrac{1}{2}$ **2.** $\sqrt{2}$ ◄

11.3 Polar Coordinates

Suppose you work for a company that designs heat shields for space vehicles. The shields are thin plates that are either rectangular or circular in shape. To solve the heat transfer equations for these two shields, you must choose a coordinate system that best fits the geometry of the problem. A Cartesian (rectangular) coordinate system is a natural choice for the rectangular shields (Figure 11.20a). However, it does not provide a good fit for the circular shields (Figure 11.20b). On the other hand, a **polar coordinate** system, in which the coordinates are constant on circles and rays, is much better suited for the circular shields (Figure 11.20c).

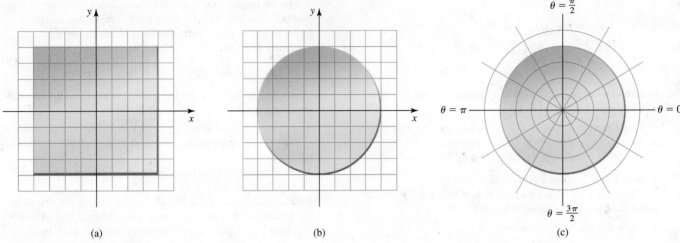

FIGURE 11.20

Defining Polar Coordinates

> Polar points and curves are plotted on a rectangular coordinate system, with standard "*x*" and "*y*" labels attached to the axes. However, plotting polar points and curves is often easier using polar graph paper, which has concentric circles centered at the origin and rays emanating from the origin (Figure 11.20c).

Like Cartesian coordinates, polar coordinates are used to locate points in the plane. When working in polar coordinates, the origin of the coordinate system is also called the **pole**, and the positive *x*-axis is called the **polar axis**. The polar coordinates for a point *P* have the form (r, θ). **The radial coordinate** *r* describes the *signed*, or *directed*, distance from the origin to *P*. The **angular coordinate** θ describes an angle whose initial side is the positive *x*-axis and whose terminal side lies on the ray passing through the origin and *P* (Figure 11.21a). Positive angles are measured counterclockwise from the positive *x*-axis.

QUICK CHECK 1 Which of the following coordinates represent the same point: $\left(3, \dfrac{\pi}{2}\right), \left(3, \dfrac{3\pi}{2}\right), \left(3, \dfrac{5\pi}{2}\right),$ $\left(-3, -\dfrac{\pi}{2}\right),$ and $\left(-3, \dfrac{3\pi}{2}\right)$? ◄

With polar coordinates, points have more than one representation for two reasons. First, angles are determined up to multiples of 2π radians, so the coordinates (r, θ) and $(r, \theta \pm 2\pi)$ refer to the same point (Figure 11.21b). Second, the radial coordinate may be negative, which is interpreted as follows: The points (r, θ) and $(-r, \theta)$ are reflections of each other through the origin (Figure 11.21c). This means that (r, θ), $(-r, \theta + \pi)$, and $(-r, \theta - \pi)$ all refer to the same point. The origin is specified as $(0, \theta)$ in polar coordinates, where θ is any angle.

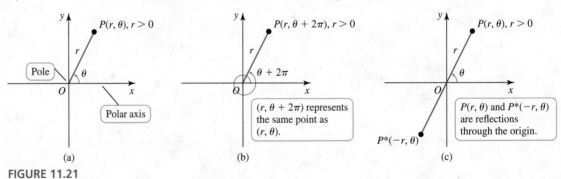

FIGURE 11.21

EXAMPLE 1   Points in polar coordinates Graph the following points in polar coordinates: $Q\left(1, \frac{5\pi}{4}\right), R\left(-1, \frac{7\pi}{4}\right),$ and $S\left(2, -\frac{3\pi}{2}\right)$. Give two alternative representations for each point.

SOLUTION The point $Q\left(1, \frac{5\pi}{4}\right)$ is one unit from the origin *O* on a line *OQ* that makes an angle of $\frac{5\pi}{4}$ with the positive *x*-axis (Figure 11.22a). Subtracting 2π from the angle, the point *Q* can be represented as $\left(1, -\frac{3\pi}{4}\right)$. Subtracting π from the angle and negating the radial coordinate implies *Q* also has the coordinates $\left(-1, \frac{\pi}{4}\right)$.

To locate the point $R\left(-1, \frac{7\pi}{4}\right)$, it is easiest first to find the point $R^*\left(1, \frac{7\pi}{4}\right)$ in the fourth quadrant. Then $R\left(-1, \frac{7\pi}{4}\right)$ is the reflection of R^* through the origin (Figure 11.22b). Other representations of R include $\left(-1, -\frac{\pi}{4}\right)$ and $\left(1, \frac{3\pi}{4}\right)$.

The point $S\left(2, -\frac{3\pi}{2}\right)$ is two units from the origin, found by rotating *clockwise* through an angle of $\frac{3\pi}{2}$ (Figure 11.22c). The point S can also be represented as $\left(2, \frac{\pi}{2}\right)$ or $\left(-2, -\frac{\pi}{2}\right)$.

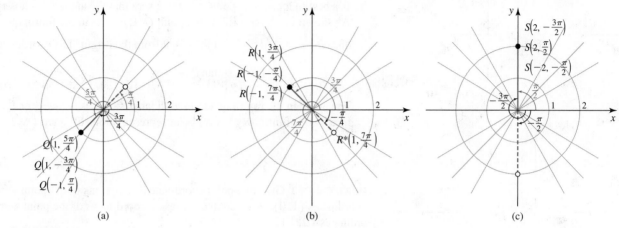

(a)　　　　　　(b)　　　　　　(c)

FIGURE 11.22

Related Exercises 9–14 ◄

Converting Between Cartesian and Polar Coordinates

We often need to convert between Cartesian and polar coordinates. The conversion equations emerge when we look at a right triangle (Figure 11.23) in which

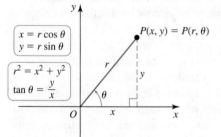

FIGURE 11.23

$$\cos \theta = \frac{x}{r} \quad \text{and} \quad \sin \theta = \frac{y}{r}.$$

Given a point with polar coordinates (r, θ), we see that its Cartesian coordinates are $x = r \cos \theta$ and $y = r \sin \theta$. Conversely, given a point with Cartesian coordinates (x, y), its radial polar coordinate satisfies $r^2 = x^2 + y^2$. The coordinate θ is determined using the relation $\tan \theta = y/x$, where the quadrant in which θ lies is determined by the signs of x and y. Figure 11.23 illustrates the conversion formulas for a point P in the first quadrant. The same relationships hold if P is in any of the other three quadrants.

QUICK CHECK 2 Draw versions of Figure 11.23 with P in the second, third, and fourth quadrants. Verify that the same conversion formulas hold in all cases. ◄

> To determine θ, you may also use the relationships $\cos \theta = x/r$ and $\sin \theta = y/r$. Either method requires checking the signs of x and y to be sure that θ is in the correct quadrant.

PROCEDURE　**Converting Coordinates**

A point with polar coordinates (r, θ) has Cartesian coordinates (x, y), where

$$x = r \cos \theta \quad \text{and} \quad y = r \sin \theta.$$

A point with Cartesian coordinates (x, y) has polar coordinates (r, θ), where

$$r^2 = x^2 + y^2 \quad \text{and} \quad \tan \theta = \frac{y}{x}.$$

EXAMPLE 2　Converting coordinates

a. Express the point with polar coordinates $P\left(2, \frac{3\pi}{4}\right)$ in Cartesian coordinates.

b. Express the point with Cartesian coordinates $Q(1, -1)$ in polar coordinates.

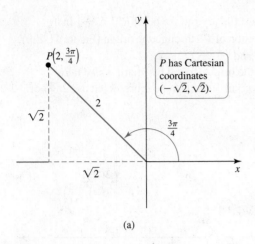

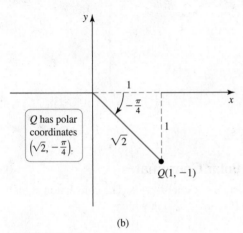

FIGURE 11.24

SOLUTION

a. The point $P\left(2, \frac{3\pi}{4}\right)$ has Cartesian coordinates

$$x = r \cos \theta = 2 \cos \left(\tfrac{3\pi}{4}\right) = -\sqrt{2} \quad \text{and}$$
$$y = r \sin \theta = 2 \sin \left(\tfrac{3\pi}{4}\right) = \sqrt{2}.$$

As shown in Figure 11.24a, P is in the second quadrant.

b. It's best to locate this point first to be sure that the angle θ is chosen correctly. As shown in Figure 11.24b, the point $Q(1, -1)$ is in the fourth quadrant at a distance $r = \sqrt{1^2 + (-1)^2} = \sqrt{2}$ from the origin. The coordinate θ satisfies

$$\tan \theta = \frac{y}{x} = \frac{-1}{1} = -1.$$

The angle in the fourth quadrant with $\tan \theta = -1$ is $\theta = -\frac{\pi}{4}$ or $\frac{7\pi}{4}$. Therefore, two (of infinitely many) polar representations of Q are $\left(\sqrt{2}, -\frac{\pi}{4}\right)$ and $\left(\sqrt{2}, \frac{7\pi}{4}\right)$.

Related Exercises 15–26 ◄

QUICK CHECK 3 Give two polar coordinate descriptions of the point with Cartesian coordinates $(1, 0)$. What are the Cartesian coordinates of the point with polar coordinates $\left(2, \frac{\pi}{2}\right)$? ◄

Basic Curves in Polar Coordinates

A curve in polar coordinates is the set of points that satisfy an equation in r and θ. Some sets of points are easier to describe in polar coordinates than in Cartesian coordinates. Let's begin by examining polar equations of circles, lines, and spirals.

The polar equation $r = 3$ is satisfied by the set of points whose distance from the origin is 3. The angle θ is arbitrary because it is not specified by the equation, so the graph of $r = 3$ is the circle of radius 3 centered at the origin. In general, the equation $r = a$ describes a circle of radius $|a|$ centered at the origin (Figure 11.25a).

The equation $\theta = \pi/3$ is satisfied by the points whose angle with respect to the positive x-axis is $\pi/3$. Because r is unspecified, it is arbitrary (and can be positive or negative). Therefore, $\theta = \pi/3$ describes the line through the origin making an angle of $\pi/3$ with the positive x-axis. More generally, $\theta = \theta_0$ describes the line through the origin making an angle of θ_0 with the positive x-axis (Figure 11.25b).

➤ If the equation $\theta = \theta_0$ is accompanied by the condition $r \geq 0$, the resulting set of points is a *ray* emanating from the origin.

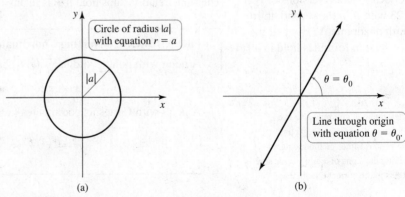

FIGURE 11.25

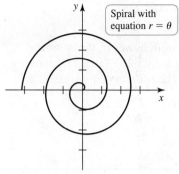

FIGURE 11.26

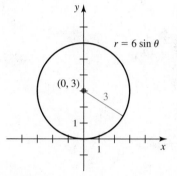

FIGURE 11.27

The simplest polar equation that involves both r and θ is $r = \theta$. Restricting θ to the interval $\theta \geq 0$, we see that as θ increases, r increases. Therefore, as θ increases, the points on the curve move away from the origin as they circle the origin in a counterclockwise direction, generating a spiral (Figure 11.26).

QUICK CHECK 4 Describe the polar curves $r = 12$, $r = 6\theta$, and $r \sin \theta = 10$. ◄

EXAMPLE 3 **Polar to Cartesian coordinates** Convert the polar equation $r = 6 \sin \theta$ to Cartesian coordinates and describe the corresponding graph.

SOLUTION Multiplying both sides of the equation by r produces the equation $r^2 = 6r \sin \theta$. Using the conversion relations $r^2 = x^2 + y^2$ and $y = r \sin \theta$, the equation

$$\underbrace{r^2}_{x^2 + y^2} = \underbrace{6r \sin \theta}_{6y}$$

becomes $x^2 + y^2 - 6y = 0$. Completing the square gives the equation

$$x^2 + \underbrace{y^2 - 6y + 9}_{(y-3)^2} - 9 = x^2 + (y - 3)^2 - 9 = 0.$$

We recognize $x^2 + (y - 3)^2 = 9$ as the equation of a circle of radius 3 centered at $(0, 3)$ (Figure 11.27).

Related Exercises 27–36 ◄

Calculations similar to those in Example 3 lead to the following equations of circles in polar coordinates.

SUMMARY **Circles in Polar Coordinates**

The equation $r = a$ describes a circle of radius $|a|$ centered at $(0, 0)$.

The equation $r = 2a \sin \theta$ describes a circle of radius $|a|$ centered at $(0, a)$.

The equation $r = 2a \cos \theta$ describes a circle of radius $|a|$ centered at $(a, 0)$.

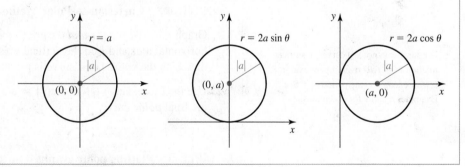

Graphing in Polar Coordinates

Equations in polar coordinates often describe curves that are difficult to represent in Cartesian coordinates. Partly for this reason, curve-sketching methods for polar coordinates differ from those used for curves in Cartesian coordinates. Conceptually, the easiest graphing method is to choose several values of θ, calculate the corresponding r-values, and tabulate the coordinates. The points are then plotted and connected with a smooth curve.

> When a curve is described as $r = f(\theta)$, it is natural to tabulate points in θ-r format, just as we list points in x-y format for $y = f(x)$. Despite this fact, the standard form for writing an ordered pair in polar coordinates is (r, θ).

Table 11.4

θ	$r = 1 + \sin\theta$
0	1
$\pi/6$	$3/2$
$\pi/2$	2
$5\pi/6$	$3/2$
π	1
$7\pi/6$	$1/2$
$3\pi/2$	0
$11\pi/6$	$1/2$
2π	1

EXAMPLE 4   Plotting a polar curve Graph the polar equation $r = f(\theta) = 1 + \sin\theta$.

SOLUTION The domain of f consists of all real values of θ; however, the complete curve is generated by letting θ vary over any interval of length 2π. Table 11.4 shows several (r, θ) pairs, which are plotted in Figure 11.28. The resulting curve, called a **cardioid**, is symmetric about the y-axis.

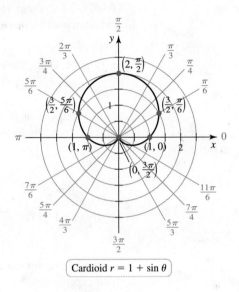

Cardioid $r = 1 + \sin\theta$

FIGURE 11.28

Related Exercises 37–48 ◄

Cartesian-to-Polar Method   Plotting polar curves point by point is time consuming, and important details may not be revealed. Here is an alternative procedure for graphing polar curves that is usually quicker and more reliable.

> For some (but not all) curves, it suffices to graph $r = f(\theta)$ over any interval in θ whose length is the period of f. See Examples 6 and 9 for exceptions.

PROCEDURE   Cartesian-to-Polar Method for Graphing $r = f(\theta)$

1. Graph $r = f(\theta)$ *as if r and θ were Cartesian coordinates* with θ on the horizontal axis and r on the vertical axis. Be sure to choose an interval for θ on which the entire polar curve is produced.

2. Use the Cartesian graph in Step 1 as a guide to sketch the points (r, θ) on the final *polar* curve.

EXAMPLE 5   Plotting polar graphs Use the Cartesian-to-polar method to graph the polar equation $r = 1 + \sin\theta$ (Example 4).

SOLUTION Viewing r and θ as Cartesian coordinates, the graph of $r = 1 + \sin\theta$ on the interval $[0, 2\pi]$ is a standard sine curve with amplitude 1 shifted up 1 unit (Figure 11.29). Notice that the graph begins with $r = 1$ at $\theta = 0$, increases to $r = 2$ at $\theta = \pi/2$, decreases to $r = 0$ at $\theta = 3\pi/2$ (which indicates an intersection with the origin on the polar graph), and increases to $r = 1$ at $\theta = 2\pi$. The second row of Figure 11.29 shows the final polar curve (a cardioid) as it is transferred from the Cartesian curve.

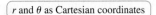

r and *θ* as Cartesian coordinates

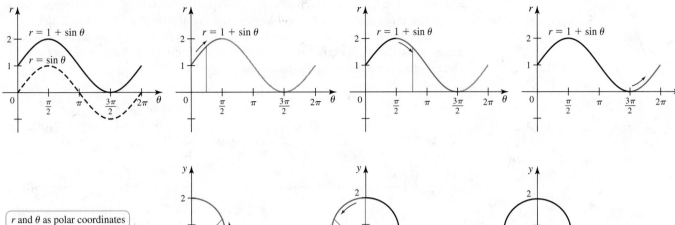

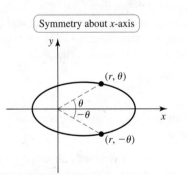

r and *θ* as polar coordinates

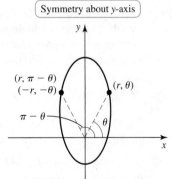

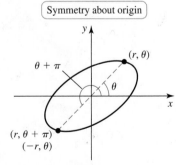

FIGURE 11.29

Related Exercises 37–48 ◄

Symmetry   Given a polar equation in r and θ, three types of symmetry are easy to spot (Figure 11.30).

SUMMARY   **Symmetry in Polar Equations**

Symmetry about the *x*-axis occurs if the point (r, θ) is on the graph whenever $(r, -\theta)$ is on the graph.

Symmetry about the *y*-axis occurs if the point (r, θ) is on the graph whenever $(r, \pi - \theta) = (-r, -\theta)$ is on the graph.

Symmetry about the origin occurs if the point (r, θ) is on the graph whenever $(-r, \theta) = (r, \theta + \pi)$ is on the graph.

> ➤ Any two of these three symmetries implies the third. For example, if a graph is symmetric about both the *x*- and *y*-axes, then it must be symmetric about the origin.

Symmetry about *x*-axis

(r, θ)

θ

$-\theta$

$(r, -\theta)$

Symmetry about *y*-axis

$(r, \pi - \theta)$
$(-r, -\theta)$

(r, θ)

$\pi - \theta$

θ

Symmetry about origin

(r, θ)

$\theta + \pi$

θ

$(r, \theta + \pi)$
$(-r, \theta)$

FIGURE 11.30

QUICK CHECK 5 Identify the symmetry in the graph of (a) $r = 4 + 4 \cos \theta$ and (b) $r = 4 \sin \theta$. ◄

For instance, consider the polar equation $r = 1 + \sin \theta$ in Example 5. If (r, θ) satisfies the equation, then $(r, \pi - \theta)$ also satisfies the equation because $\sin \theta = \sin (\pi - \theta)$. Therefore, the graph is symmetric about the *y*-axis, as shown in Figure 11.30. Testing for symmetry produces a more accurate graph and often simplifies the task of graphing polar equations.

EXAMPLE 6   Plotting polar graphs   Graph the polar equation $r = 3 \sin 2\theta$.

SOLUTION   The Cartesian graph of $r = 3 \sin 2\theta$ on the interval $[0, 2\pi]$ has amplitude 3 and period π (Figure 11.31a). The θ-intercepts occur at $\theta = 0, \pi/2, \pi, 3\pi/2$, and 2π, which correspond to the intersections with the origin on the polar graph. Furthermore, the arches of the Cartesian curve between θ-intercepts correspond to loops in the polar curve. The resulting polar curve is a **four-leaf rose** (Figure 11.31b).

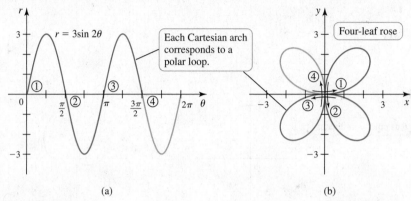

FIGURE 11.31

The graph is symmetric about the x-axis, the y-axis, and the origin. It is instructive to see how these symmetries are justified. To prove symmetry about the y-axis, notice that

$$(r, \theta) \text{ on the graph} \Rightarrow r = 3 \sin 2\theta$$
$$\Rightarrow r = -3 \sin 2(-\theta) \qquad \sin(-\theta) = -\sin\theta$$
$$\Rightarrow -r = 3 \sin 2(-\theta) \qquad \text{Simplify.}$$
$$\Rightarrow (-r, -\theta) \text{ on the graph.}$$

We see that if (r, θ) is on the graph, then $(-r, -\theta)$ is also on the graph, which implies symmetry about the y-axis. Similarly, to prove symmetry about the origin, notice that

$$(r, \theta) \text{ on the graph} \Rightarrow r = 3 \sin 2\theta$$
$$\Rightarrow r = 3 \sin(2\theta + 2\pi) \qquad \sin(\theta + 2\pi) = \sin\theta$$
$$\Rightarrow r = 3 \sin(2(\theta + \pi)) \qquad \text{Simplify.}$$
$$\Rightarrow (r, \theta + \pi) \text{ on the graph.}$$

We have shown that if (r, θ) is on the graph, then $(r, \theta + \pi)$ is also on the graph, which implies symmetry about the origin. Symmetry about the y-axis and the origin imply symmetry about the x-axis. Had we proved these symmetries in advance, we could have graphed the curve only in the first quadrant—reflections about the x- and y-axes would produce the full curve.

Related Exercises 37–48◄

> **Subtle Point**
>
> The fact that one point has infinitely many representations in polar coordinates presents potential pitfalls. In Example 6, you can show that $(-r, \theta)$ does *not* satisfy the equation $r = 3 \sin 2\theta$ when (r, θ) satisfies the equation. And yet, as shown, the graph is symmetric about the origin because $(r, \theta + \pi)$ satisfies the equation whenever (r, θ) satisfies the equation. Note that $(-r, \theta)$ and $(r, \theta + \pi)$ are the same point.

EXAMPLE 7   Plotting polar graphs   Graph the polar equation $r^2 = 9 \cos \theta$. Use a graphing utility to check your work.

SOLUTION   The graph of this equation has symmetry about the origin (because of the r^2) and about the x-axis (because of $\cos \theta$). These two symmetries imply symmetry about the y-axis.

A preliminary step is required before using the Cartesian-to-polar method for graphing the curve. Solving the given equation for r, we find that $r = \pm 3\sqrt{\cos \theta}$. Notice that $\cos \theta < 0$, for $\pi/2 < \theta < 3\pi/2$, so the curve does not exist on that interval. Therefore, we plot the curve on the intervals $0 \le \theta \le \pi/2$ and $3\pi/2 \le \theta \le 2\pi$ (the interval

$\left[-\frac{\pi}{2}, \frac{\pi}{2}\right]$ would also work). Both the positive and negative values of r are included in the Cartesian graph (Figure 11.32a).

Now we are ready to transfer points from the Cartesian graph to the final polar graph (Figure 11.32b). The resulting curve is called a **lemniscate**.

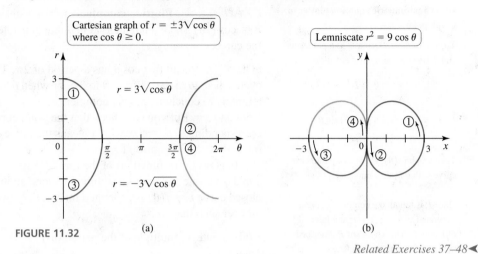

Cartesian graph of $r = \pm 3\sqrt{\cos \theta}$ where $\cos \theta \geq 0$.

$r = 3\sqrt{\cos \theta}$

$r = -3\sqrt{\cos \theta}$

Lemniscate $r^2 = 9 \cos \theta$

FIGURE 11.32   (a)   (b)

Related Exercises 37–48◄

EXAMPLE 8 Matching polar and Cartesian graphs The butterfly curve is described by the equation

$$r = e^{\sin \theta} - 2 \cos 4\theta, \quad \text{for } 0 \leq \theta \leq 2\pi,$$

which is plotted in Cartesian and polar coordinates in Figure 11.33. Follow the Cartesian graph through the points $A, B, C, \ldots, N, O$ and mark the corresponding points on the polar curve.

SOLUTION Point A in Figure 11.33a has the Cartesian coordinates $(\theta = 0, r = -1)$. The corresponding point in the polar plot (Figure 11.33b) with polar coordinates $(-1, 0)$ is marked A. Point B in the Cartesian plot is on the θ-axis; therefore, $r = 0$. The corresponding point in the polar plot is the origin. The same argument used to locate B applies to $F, H, J, L,$ and N, all of which appear at the origin in the polar plot. In general, the local and endpoint maxima and minima in the Cartesian graph ($A, C, D, E, G, I, K, M,$ and O) correspond to the extreme points of the loops of the polar plot and are marked accordingly in Figure 11.33b.

> See Exercise 113 for a spectacular enhancement of the butterfly curve.

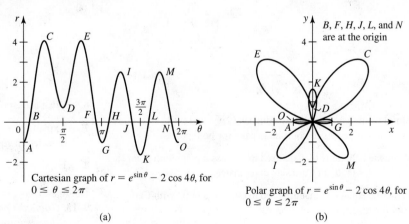

Cartesian graph of $r = e^{\sin \theta} - 2 \cos 4\theta$, for $0 \leq \theta \leq 2\pi$

Polar graph of $r = e^{\sin \theta} - 2 \cos 4\theta$, for $0 \leq \theta \leq 2\pi$

$B, F, H, J, L,$ and N are at the origin

(a)   (b)

FIGURE 11.33

(*Source:* T. H. Fay, *Amer. Math. Monthly* 96, 1989; revived in S. Wagon and E. Packel, *Animating Calculus*, Freeman, 1994.)

Related Exercises 49–52◄

Using Graphing Utilities

When graphing polar curves that eventually close on themselves, it is necessary to specify an interval in θ that generates the entire curve. In some cases, this problem is a challenge in itself.

EXAMPLE 9 **Plotting complete curves** Consider the closed curve described by $r = \cos(2\theta/5)$. Give an interval in θ that generates the entire curve and then graph the curve.

SOLUTION Recall that $\cos\theta$ has a period of 2π. Therefore, $\cos(2\theta/5)$ completes one cycle when $2\theta/5$ varies from 0 to 2π, or when θ varies from 0 to 5π. Therefore, it is tempting to conclude that the complete curve $r = \cos(2\theta/5)$ is generated as θ varies from 0 to 5π. But you can check that the point corresponding to $\theta = 0$ is *not* the point corresponding to $\theta = 5\pi$, which means the curve does not close on itself over the interval $[0, 5\pi]$ (Figure 11.34a).

In general, for functions of the form $f(\theta) = \sin(p\theta/q)$ or $f(\theta) = \cos(p\theta/q)$, where p and q are integers with no common factors, an interval $[0, P]$ over which the complete closed curve $r = f(\theta)$ is generated must satisfy two conditions: P is the smallest positive number such that

- P is an integer multiple of the period of f (so that $f(0) = f(P)$), and
- P is an integer multiple of 2π (so that the points $(0, f(0))$ and $(P, f(P))$ are the same).

To graph the *complete* curve $r = \cos(2\theta/5)$, we must find an interval $[0, P]$, where P is a multiple of 5π and a multiple of 2π. The smallest number satisfying these conditions is 10π. Graphing $r = \cos(2\theta/5)$ over the interval $[0, 10\pi]$ produces the complete curve (Figure 11.34b).

> **Using a parametric equation plotter to graph polar curves**
>
> To graph $r = f(\theta)$, treat θ as a parameter and define the parametric equations
> $$x = r\cos\theta = \underbrace{f(\theta)}_{r}\cos\theta$$
> $$y = r\sin\theta = \underbrace{f(\theta)}_{r}\sin\theta$$
> Then graph $(x(\theta), y(\theta))$ as a parametric curve with θ as the parameter.

> ➤ Once P is found, the complete curve is generated as θ varies over any interval of length P. This choice of P described here ensures that the complete curve is generated. Smaller values of P work in some cases.

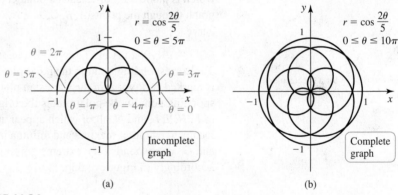

FIGURE 11.34

Related Exercises 53–60 ◄

SECTION 11.3 EXERCISES

Review Questions

1. Plot the points with polar coordinates $\left(2, \frac{\pi}{6}\right)$ and $\left(-3, -\frac{\pi}{2}\right)$. Give two alternative sets of coordinate pairs for both points.

2. Write the equations that are used to express a point with polar coordinates (r, θ) in Cartesian coordinates.

3. Write the equations that are used to express a point with Cartesian coordinates (x, y) in polar coordinates.

4. What is the polar equation of a circle of radius $|a|$ centered at the origin?

5. What is the polar equation of the vertical line $x = 5$?

6. What is the polar equation of the horizontal line $y = 5$?

7. Explain three symmetries in polar graphs and how they are detected in equations.

8. Explain the Cartesian-to-polar method for graphing polar curves.

Basic Skills

9–13. *Graph the points with the following polar coordinates. Give two alternative representations of the points in polar coordinates.*

9. $\left(2, \frac{\pi}{4}\right)$

10. $\left(3, \frac{2\pi}{3}\right)$

11. $\left(-1, -\frac{\pi}{3}\right)$

12. $\left(2, \frac{7\pi}{4}\right)$

13. $\left(-4, \frac{3\pi}{2}\right)$

14. Points in polar coordinates *Give two sets of polar coordinates for each of the points A–F in the figure.*

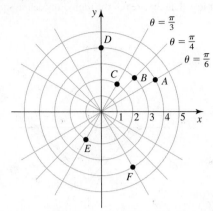

15–20. Converting coordinates *Express the following polar coordinates in Cartesian coordinates.*

15. $\left(3, \frac{\pi}{4}\right)$ **16.** $\left(1, \frac{2\pi}{3}\right)$ **17.** $\left(1, -\frac{\pi}{3}\right)$

18. $\left(2, \frac{7\pi}{4}\right)$ **19.** $\left(-4, \frac{3\pi}{4}\right)$ **20.** $\left(4, 5\pi\right)$

21–26. Converting coordinates *Express the following Cartesian coordinates in polar coordinates in at least two different ways.*

21. $(2, 2)$ **22.** $(-1, 0)$

23. $(1, \sqrt{3})$ **24.** $(-9, 0)$

25. $(-4, 4\sqrt{3})$ **26.** $(4, 4\sqrt{3})$

27–36. Polar-to-Cartesian coordinates *Convert the following equations to Cartesian coordinates. Describe the resulting curve.*

27. $r \cos \theta = -4$ **28.** $r = \cot \theta \csc \theta$

29. $r = 2$ **30.** $r = 3 \csc \theta$

31. $r = 2 \sin \theta + 2 \cos \theta$ **32.** $\sin \theta = |\cos \theta|$

33. $r \cos \theta = \sin 2\theta$ **34.** $r = \sin \theta \sec^2 \theta$

35. $r = 8 \sin \theta$ **36.** $r = \dfrac{1}{2 \cos \theta + 3 \sin \theta}$

37–40. Simple curves *Tabulate and plot enough points to sketch a graph of the following equations.*

37. $r = 8 \cos \theta$ **38.** $r = 4 + 4 \cos \theta$

39. $r(\sin \theta - 2 \cos \theta) = 0$ **40.** $r = 1 - \cos \theta$

41–48. Graphing polar curves *Graph the following equations. Use a graphing utility to check your work and produce a final graph.*

41. $r = 1 - \sin \theta$ **42.** $r = 2 - 2 \sin \theta$

43. $r = \sin^2(\theta/2)$ **44.** $r^2 = 4 \sin \theta$

45. $r^2 = 16 \cos \theta$ **46.** $r^2 = 16 \sin 2\theta$

47. $r = \sin 3\theta$ **48.** $r = 2 \sin 5\theta$

49–52. Matching polar and Cartesian curves *A Cartesian and a polar graph of $r = f(\theta)$ are given in the figures. Mark the points on the polar graph that correspond to the points shown on the Cartesian graph.*

49. $r = 1 - 2 \sin 3\theta$

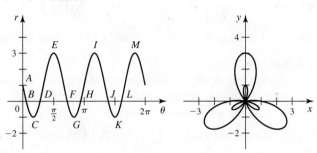

50. $r = \sin(1 + 3 \cos \theta)$

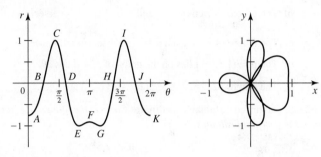

51. $r = \dfrac{1}{4} - \cos 4\theta$

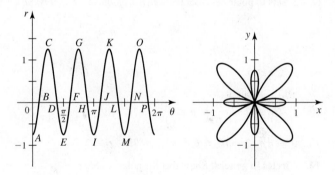

52. $r = \cos \theta + \sin 2\theta$

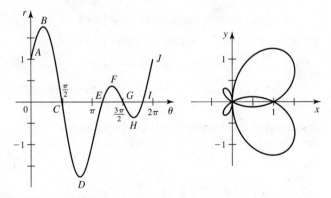

53–60. Using a graphing utility *Use a graphing utility to graph the following equations. In each case, give the smallest interval $[0, P]$ that generates the entire curve (if possible).*

53. $r = \theta \sin \theta$ **54.** $r = 2 - 4 \cos 5\theta$

55. $r = \cos 3\theta + \cos^2 2\theta$ **56.** $r = \sin^2 2\theta + 2 \sin 2\theta$

57. $r = \cos\left(\dfrac{3\theta}{5}\right)$

58. $r = \sin\left(\dfrac{3\theta}{7}\right)$

59. $r = 1 - 3\cos 2\theta$

60. $r = 1 - 2\sin 5\theta$

Further Explorations

61. Explain why or why not Determine whether the following statements are true and give an explanation or counterexample.

a. The point with Cartesian coordinates $(-2, 2)$ has polar coordinates $\left(2\sqrt{2}, \dfrac{3\pi}{4}\right), \left(2\sqrt{2}, \dfrac{11\pi}{4}\right), \left(2\sqrt{2}, -\dfrac{5\pi}{4}\right)$, and $\left(-2\sqrt{2}, -\dfrac{\pi}{4}\right)$.

b. The graphs of $r\cos\theta = 4$ and $r\sin\theta = -2$ intersect exactly once.

c. The graphs of $r = 2$ and $\theta = \dfrac{\pi}{4}$ intersect exactly once.

d. The point $\left(3, \dfrac{\pi}{2}\right)$ lies on the graph of $r = 3\cos 2\theta$.

e. The graphs of $r = 2\sec\theta$ and $r = 3\csc\theta$ are lines.

62–65. Cartesian-to-polar coordinates *Convert the following equations to polar coordinates.*

62. $y = 3$

63. $y = x^2$

64. $(x - 1)^2 + y^2 = 1$

65. $y = \dfrac{1}{x}$

66–73. Sets in polar coordinates *Sketch the following sets of points (r, θ).*

66. $r = 3$

67. $\theta = \dfrac{2\pi}{3}$

68. $2 \le r \le 8$

69. $\dfrac{\pi}{2} \le \theta \le \dfrac{3\pi}{4}$

70. $1 < r < 2$ and $\dfrac{\pi}{6} \le \theta \le \dfrac{\pi}{3}$

71. $|\theta| \le \dfrac{\pi}{3}$

72. $0 \le r < 3$ and $0 \le \theta \le \pi$

73. $r \ge 2$

74. Circles in general Show that the polar equation

$$r^2 - 2r\left(a\cos\theta + b\sin\theta\right) = R^2 - a^2 - b^2$$

describes a circle of radius R centered at (a, b).

75. Circles in general Show that the polar equation

$$r^2 - 2rr_0\cos\left(\theta - \theta_0\right) = R^2 - r_0^2$$

describes a circle of radius R whose center has polar coordinates (r_0, θ_0).

76–81. Equations of circles *Use the results of Exercises 74–75 to describe and graph the following circles.*

76. $r^2 - 6r\cos\theta = 16$

77. $r^2 - 4r\cos\left(\theta - \dfrac{\pi}{3}\right) = 12$

78. $r^2 - 8r\cos\left(\theta - \dfrac{\pi}{2}\right) = 9$

79. $r^2 - 2r(2\cos\theta + 3\sin\theta) = 3$

80. $r^2 + 2r(\cos\theta - 3\sin\theta) = 4$

81. $r^2 - 2r(-\cos\theta + 2\sin\theta) = 4$

82. Equations of circles Find equations of the circles in the figure. Determine whether the combined area of the circles is greater than or less than the area of the region inside the square but outside the circles.

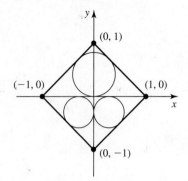

83. Vertical lines Consider the polar curve $r = 2\sec\theta$.

a. Graph the curve on the intervals $\left(\dfrac{\pi}{2}, \dfrac{3\pi}{2}\right), \left(\dfrac{3\pi}{2}, \dfrac{5\pi}{2}\right)$, and $\left(\dfrac{5\pi}{2}, \dfrac{7\pi}{2}\right)$, In each case, state the direction in which the curve is generated as θ increases.

b. Show that on any interval $\left(\dfrac{n\pi}{2}, \dfrac{(n + 2)\pi}{2}\right)$, where n is an odd integer, the graph is the vertical line $x = 2$.

84. Lines in polar coordinates

a. Show that an equation of the line $y = mx + b$ in polar coordinates is $r = \dfrac{b}{\sin\theta - m\cos\theta}$.

b. Use the figure to find an alternative polar equation of a line, $r\cos(\theta_0 - \theta) = r_0$. Note that $Q(r_0, \theta_0)$ is a fixed point on the line such that OQ is perpendicular to the line and $r_0 \ge 0$; $P(r, \theta)$ is an arbitrary point on the line.

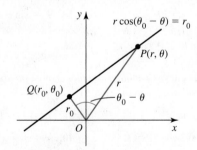

85–88. Equations of lines *Use the result of Exercise 84 to describe and graph the following lines.*

85. $r\cos\left(\dfrac{\pi}{3} - \theta\right) = 3$

86. $r\cos\left(\theta + \dfrac{\pi}{6}\right) = 4$

87. $r(\sin\theta - 4\cos\theta) - 3 = 0$

88. $r(4\sin\theta - 3\cos\theta) = 6$

89. The limaçon family The equations $r = a + b\cos\theta$ and $r = a + b\sin\theta$ describe curves known as *limaçons* (from Latin for *snail*). We have already encountered cardioids, which occur when $|a| = |b|$. The limaçon has an inner loop if $|a| < |b|$. The limaçon has a dent or dimple if $|b| < |a| < 2|b|$. And the limaçon is oval-shaped if $|a| > 2|b|$. Match the limaçons in the figures A–F with equations a–f.

a. $r = -1 + \sin \theta$ b. $r = -1 + 2 \cos \theta$
c. $r = 2 + \sin \theta$ d. $r = 1 - 2 \cos \theta$
e. $r = 1 + 2 \sin \theta$ f. $r = 1 + \frac{2}{3} \sin \theta$

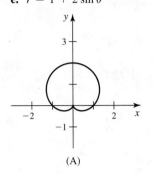

(A)

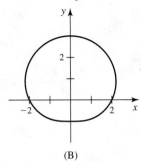

(B)

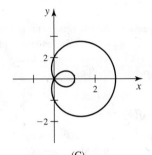

(C)

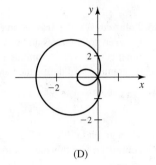

(D)

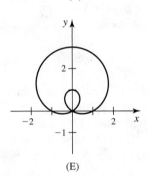

(E)

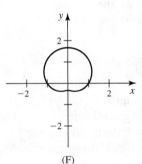

(F)

90. Limiting limaçon Consider the family of limaçons
$r = 1 + b \cos \theta$. Describe how the curves change as $b \to \infty$.

91–94. The lemniscate family *Equations of the form $r^2 = a \sin 2\theta$ and $r^2 = a \cos 2\theta$ describe lemniscates (see Example 7). Graph the following lemniscates.*

91. $r^2 = \cos 2\theta$ **92.** $r^2 = 4 \sin 2\theta$

93. $r^2 = -2 \sin 2\theta$ **94.** $r^2 = -8 \cos 2\theta$

95–98. The rose family *Equations of the form $r = a \sin m\theta$ or $r = a \cos m\theta$, where a is a real number and m is a positive integer, have graphs known as roses (see Example 6). Graph the following roses.*

95. $r = \sin 2\theta$ **96.** $r = 4 \cos 3\theta$

97. $r = 2 \sin 4\theta$ **98.** $r = 6 \sin 5\theta$

99. Number of rose petals Show that the graph of $r = a \sin m\theta$ or $r = a \cos m\theta$ is a rose with m leaves if m is an odd integer and a rose with $2m$ leaves if m is an even integer.

100–102. Spirals *Graph the following spirals. Indicate the direction in which the spiral is generated as θ increases, where $\theta > 0$. Let $a = 1$ and $a = -1$.*

100. Spiral of Archimedes: $r = a\theta$ **101.** Logarithmic spiral: $r = e^{a\theta}$

102. Hyperbolic spiral: $r = \dfrac{a}{\theta}$

103–106. Intersection points *Points at which the graphs of $r = f(\theta)$ and $r = g(\theta)$ intersect must be determined carefully. Solving $f(\theta) = g(\theta)$ identifies some—but perhaps not all—intersection points. The reason is that the curves may pass through the same point for different values of θ. Use analytical methods and a graphing utility to find all the intersection points of the following curves.*

103. $r = 2 \cos \theta$ and $r = 1 + \cos \theta$

104. $r^2 = 4 \cos \theta$ and $r = 1 + \cos \theta$

105. $r = 1 - \sin \theta$ and $r = 1 + \cos \theta$

106. $r^2 = \cos 2\theta$ and $r^2 = \sin 2\theta$

Applications

107. Earth–Mars system A simplified model assumes that the orbits of Earth and Mars are circular with radii of 2 and 3, respectively, and that Earth completes one orbit in one year while Mars takes two years. When $t = 0$, Earth is at $(2, 0)$ and Mars is at $(3, 0)$; both orbit the Sun (at $(0, 0)$) in a counterclockwise direction. The position of Mars relative to Earth is given by the parametric equations

$$x = (3 - 4 \cos \pi t) \cos \pi t + 2, \quad y = (3 - 4 \cos \pi t) \sin \pi t.$$

a. Graph the parametric equations, for $0 \le t \le 2$.
b. Letting $r = (3 - 4 \cos \pi t)$, explain why the path of Mars relative to Earth is a limaçon (Exercise 89).

108. Channel flow Water flows in a shallow semicircular channel with inner and outer radii of 1 m and 2 m (see figure). At a point $P(r, \theta)$ in the channel, the flow is in the tangential direction (counterclockwise along circles), and it depends only on r, the distance from the center of the semicircles.

a. Express the region formed by the channel as a set in polar coordinates.
b. Express the inflow and outflow regions of the channel as sets in polar coordinates.
c. Suppose the tangential velocity of the water in m/s is given by $v(r) = 10r$, for $1 \le r \le 2$. Is the velocity greater at $\left(1.5, \frac{\pi}{4}\right)$ or $\left(1.2, \frac{3\pi}{4}\right)$? Explain.
d. Suppose the tangential velocity of the water is given by $v(r) = \dfrac{20}{r}$, for $1 \le r \le 2$. Is the velocity greater at $\left(1.8, \frac{\pi}{6}\right)$ or $\left(1.3, \frac{2\pi}{3}\right)$? Explain.
e. The total amount of water that flows through the channel (across a cross section of the channel $\theta = \theta_0$) is proportional to $\int_1^2 v(r) \, dr$. Is the total flow through the channel greater for the flow in part (c) or (d)?

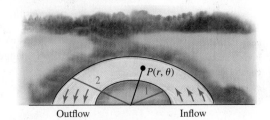

Additional Exercises

109. Special circles Show that the equation $r = a \cos \theta + b \sin \theta$, where a and b are real numbers, describes a circle. Find the center and radius of the circle.

110. Cartesian lemniscate Find the equation in Cartesian coordinates of the lemniscate $r^2 = a^2 \cos 2\theta$, where a is a real number.

111. Subtle symmetry Without using a graphing utility, determine the symmetries (if any) of the curve $r = 4 - \sin (\theta/2)$.

112. Complete curves Consider the polar curve $r = \cos (n\theta/m)$, where n and m are integers.

   a. Graph the complete curve when $n = 2$ and $m = 3$.
   b. Graph the complete curve when $n = 3$ and $m = 7$.
   c. Find a general rule in terms of m and n (where m and n have no common factors) for determining the least positive number P such that the complete curve is generated over the interval $[0, P]$.

Technology Exercises

113. Enhanced butterfly curve The butterfly curve of Example 8 is enhanced by adding a term:

$$r = e^{\sin \theta} - 2 \cos 4\theta + \sin^5 (\theta/12), \quad \text{for } 0 \le \theta \le 24\pi.$$

   a. Graph the curve.
   b. Explain why the new term produces the observed effect.

   (*Source:* S. Wagon and E. Packel, *Animating Calculus*, Freeman, 1994.)

114. Finger curves Consider the curve $r = f(\theta) = \cos (a^\theta) - 1.5$, where $a = (1 + 12\pi)^{1/(2\pi)} \approx 1.789$ (see figure).

   a. Show that $f(0) = f(2\pi)$ and find the point on the curve that corresponds to $\theta = 0$ and $\theta = 2\pi$.
   b. Is the same curve produced over the intervals $[-\pi, \pi]$ and $[0, 2\pi]$?
   c. Let $f(\theta) = \cos (a^\theta) - b$, where $a = (1 + 2k\pi)^{1/(2\pi)}$, k is an integer, and b is a real number. Show that $f(0) = f(2\pi)$ and that the curve closes on itself.

   d. Plot the curve with various values of k. How many fingers can you produce?

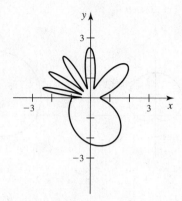

115. Polar curves as parametric equations An important connection between polar curves and parametric equations enables you to plot polar curves with a graphing utility. To graph $r = f(\theta)$, treat θ as a parameter and define the parametric equations

$$x = r \cos \theta = f(\theta) \cos \theta \text{ and}$$
$$y = r \sin \theta = f(\theta) \sin \theta.$$

Then graph $(x(\theta), y(\theta))$ as a parametric curve with θ as the parameter. Use this method to graph the following curves.

   a. The m-leaf roses $r = 2 \sin m\theta$, for $m = 3, 5,$ and 7.
   b. The $2m$-leaf roses $r = 2 \cos m\theta$, for $m = 2, 4,$ and 6.

QUICK CHECK ANSWERS

1. All the points are the same except $(3, 3\pi/2)$.   **3.** Polar coordinates: $(1, 0)$, $(1, 2\pi)$; Cartesian coordinates: $(0, 2)$
4. A circle centered at the origin with radius 12; a double spiral; the horizontal line $y = 10$ **5.** (a) Symmetric about the x-axis; (b) symmetric about the y-axis ◄

11.4 Calculus in Polar Coordinates

Having learned about the *geometry* of polar coordinates, we now have the groundwork needed to explore *calculus* in polar coordinates. Familiar topics, such as slopes of tangent lines and areas bounded by curves, are now revisited in a different setting.

Slopes of Tangent Lines

Given a function $y = f(x)$, the slope of the line tangent to the graph at a given point is $\dfrac{dy}{dx}$ or $f'(x)$. So it may be tempting to conclude that the slope of a curve described by the polar equation $r = f(\theta)$ is $\dfrac{dr}{d\theta} = f'(\theta)$. Unfortunately, it's not that simple.

> ▶ The slope is the change in the vertical coordinate divided by the change in the horizontal coordinate, independent of the coordinate system. In polar coordinates, neither r nor θ corresponds to a vertical or horizontal coordinate.

The key observation is that the slope of a tangent line—in any coordinate system—is the rate of change of the vertical coordinate y with respect to the horizontal coordinate x, which is $\dfrac{dy}{dx}$. We begin by writing the polar equation $r = f(\theta)$ in parametric form with θ as a parameter:

$$x = r \cos \theta = f(\theta) \cos \theta \quad \text{and} \quad y = r \sin \theta = f(\theta) \sin \theta. \tag{1}$$

From Section 11.2, when x and y are defined parametrically as differentiable functions of θ, the derivative is $\dfrac{dy}{dx} = \dfrac{dy/d\theta}{dx/d\theta}$. Using the Product Rule to compute $dy/d\theta$ and $dx/d\theta$ in equation (1), we have

$$\frac{dy}{dx} = \overbrace{\underbrace{\frac{f'(\theta)\sin\theta + f(\theta)\cos\theta}{f'(\theta)\cos\theta - f(\theta)\sin\theta}}_{dx/d\theta}}^{dy/d\theta}. \qquad (2)$$

If the graph passes through the origin for some angle θ_0, then $f(\theta_0) = 0$, and equation (2) simplifies to

$$\frac{dy}{dx} = \frac{\sin\theta_0}{\cos\theta_0} = \tan\theta_0,$$

provided $f'(\theta_0) \neq 0$. Assuming $\cos\theta_0 \neq 0$, $\tan\theta_0$ is the slope of the line $\theta = \theta_0$, which also passes through the origin. We conclude that if $f(\theta_0) = 0$, then the tangent line at $(0, \theta_0)$ is simply $\theta = \theta_0$ (Figure 11.35). If $f(\theta_0) = 0$, $f'(\theta_0) \neq 0$, and $\cos\theta_0 = 0$, the graph has a vertical tangent line at the origin.

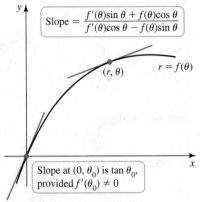

$$\text{Slope} = \frac{f'(\theta)\sin\theta + f(\theta)\cos\theta}{f'(\theta)\cos\theta - f(\theta)\sin\theta}$$

(r, θ)

$r = f(\theta)$

Slope at $(0, \theta_0)$ is $\tan\theta_0$, provided $f'(\theta_0) \neq 0$

FIGURE 11.35

QUICK CHECK 1 Verify that if $y = f(\theta)\sin\theta$, then $y'(\theta) = f'(\theta)\sin\theta + f(\theta)\cos\theta$ (which was used earlier to find dy/dx). ◄

> **THEOREM 11.2 Slope of a Tangent Line**
> Let f be a differentiable function at θ_0. The slope of the line tangent to the curve $r = f(\theta)$ at the point $(f(\theta_0), \theta_0)$ is
>
> $$\frac{dy}{dx} = \frac{f'(\theta_0)\sin\theta_0 + f(\theta_0)\cos\theta_0}{f'(\theta_0)\cos\theta_0 - f(\theta_0)\sin\theta_0},$$
>
> provided the denominator is nonzero at the point. At angles θ_0 for which $f(\theta_0) = 0$, $f'(\theta_0) \neq 0$, and $\cos\theta_0 \neq 0$, the tangent line is $\theta = \theta_0$ with slope $\tan\theta_0$.

EXAMPLE 1 Slopes on a circle Find the slopes of the lines tangent to the circle $r = f(\theta) = 10$.

SOLUTION In this case, $f(\theta)$ is constant (independent of θ). Therefore, $f'(\theta) = 0$, $f(\theta) \neq 0$, and the slope formula becomes

$$\frac{dy}{dx} = \frac{f'(\theta)\sin\theta + f(\theta)\cos\theta}{f'(\theta)\cos\theta - f(\theta)\sin\theta} = -\frac{\cos\theta}{\sin\theta} = -\cot\theta.$$

We can check a few points to see that this result makes sense. With $\theta = 0$ and $\theta = \pi$, the slope $\dfrac{dy}{dx} = -\cot\theta$ is undefined, which is correct because the tangent lines are vertical at these points (Figure 11.36). With $\theta = \pi/2$ and $\theta = 3\pi/2$, the slope is zero; with $\theta = 3\pi/4$ and $\theta = 7\pi/4$, the slope is 1; and with $\theta = \pi/4$ and $\theta = 5\pi/4$, the slope is -1. At all points $P(r, \theta)$ on the circle, the slope of the line OP from the origin to P is $\tan\theta$, which is the negative reciprocal of $-\cot\theta$. Therefore, OP is perpendicular to the tangent line at all points P on the circle.

Related Exercises 5–14 ◄

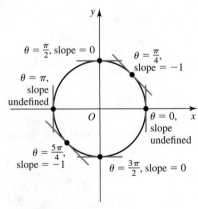

$\theta = \frac{\pi}{2}$, slope $= 0$

$\theta = \frac{\pi}{4}$, slope $= -1$

$\theta = \pi$, slope undefined

O

$\theta = 0$, slope undefined

$\theta = \frac{5\pi}{4}$, slope $= -1$

$\theta = \frac{3\pi}{2}$, slope $= 0$

FIGURE 11.36

EXAMPLE 2 Vertical and horizontal tangent lines Find the points on the interval $-\pi \leq \theta \leq \pi$ at which the cardioid $r = f(\theta) = 1 - \cos\theta$ has a vertical or horizontal tangent line.

SOLUTION Applying Theorem 11.2, we find that

$$\frac{dy}{dx} = \frac{f'(\theta)\sin\theta + f(\theta)\cos\theta}{f'(\theta)\cos\theta - f(\theta)\sin\theta}$$

$$\overbrace{}^{\sin^2\theta = 1 - \cos^2\theta}$$

$$= \frac{\sin\theta\sin\theta + (1 - \cos\theta)\cos\theta}{\underbrace{\sin\theta\cos\theta - (1 - \cos\theta)\sin\theta}_{\sin\theta\,(2\cos\theta - 1)}} \qquad \text{Substitute for } f(\theta) \text{ and } f'(\theta).$$

$$= -\frac{(2\cos^2\theta - \cos\theta - 1)}{\sin\theta\,(2\cos\theta - 1)} \qquad \text{Simplify.}$$

$$= -\frac{(2\cos\theta + 1)(\cos\theta - 1)}{\sin\theta\,(2\cos\theta - 1)}. \qquad \text{Factor the numerator.}$$

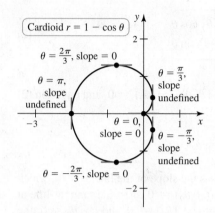

Cardioid $r = 1 - \cos\theta$

$\theta = \frac{2\pi}{3}$, slope = 0

$\theta = \pi$, slope undefined

$\theta = \frac{\pi}{3}$, slope undefined

$\theta = 0$, slope = 0

$\theta = -\frac{\pi}{3}$, slope undefined

$\theta = -\frac{2\pi}{3}$, slope = 0

FIGURE 11.37

The points with a horizontal tangent line satisfy $\dfrac{dy}{dx} = 0$ and occur where the numerator is zero and the denominator is nonzero. The numerator is zero when $\theta = 0$ and $\pm 2\pi/3$. Because the denominator is *not* zero when $\theta = \pm 2\pi/3$, horizontal tangent lines occur at $\theta = \pm 2\pi/3$ (Figure 11.37).

Vertical tangent lines occur where the numerator of $\dfrac{dy}{dx}$ is nonzero and the denominator is zero. The denominator is zero when $\theta = 0$, $\pm\pi$, and $\pm\pi/3$, and the numerator is not zero at $\theta = \pm\pi$ and $\pm\pi/3$. Therefore, vertical tangent lines occur at $\theta = \pm\pi$ and $\pm\pi/3$.

The point $(0, 0)$ on the curve must be handled carefully because both the numerator and denominator of $\dfrac{dy}{dx}$ equal 0 at $\theta = 0$. Notice that with $f(\theta) = 1 - \cos\theta$, we have $f(0) = f'(0) = 0$. Therefore, $\dfrac{dy}{dx}$ may be computed as a limit using l'Hôpital's Rule. As $\theta \to 0^+$, we find that

$$\frac{dy}{dx} = \lim_{\theta \to 0^+}\left[-\frac{(2\cos\theta + 1)(\cos\theta - 1)}{\sin\theta\,(2\cos\theta - 1)}\right]$$

$$= \lim_{\theta \to 0^+} \frac{4\cos\theta\sin\theta - \sin\theta}{-2\sin^2\theta + 2\cos^2\theta - \cos\theta} \qquad \text{L'Hôpital's Rule}$$

$$= \frac{0}{1} = 0. \qquad \text{Evaluate the limit.}$$

A similar calculation using l'Hôpital's Rule shows that as $\theta \to 0^-$, $\dfrac{dy}{dx} \to 0$. Therefore, the curve has a slope of 0 at $(0, 0)$.

Related Exercises 15–20 ◄

QUICK CHECK 2 What is the slope of the line tangent to the cardioid in Example 2 at the point corresponding to $\theta = \pi/4$? ◄

Area of Regions Bounded by Polar Curves

The problem of finding the area of a region bounded by polar curves brings us back to the slice-and-sum strategy used extensively in Chapters 5 and 6. The objective is to find the area of the region R bounded by the graph of $r = f(\theta)$ between the two rays $\theta = \alpha$ and $\theta = \beta$ (Figure 11.38a). We assume that f is continuous and nonnegative on $[\alpha, \beta]$.

The area of R is found by slicing the region in the radial direction creating wedge-shaped slices. The interval $[\alpha, \beta]$ is partitioned into n subintervals by choosing the grid points

$$\alpha = \theta_0 < \theta_1 < \theta_2 < \cdots < \theta_k < \cdots < \theta_n = \beta.$$

We let $\Delta\theta_k = \theta_k - \theta_{k-1}$, for $k = 1, 2, \ldots, n$, and we let θ_k^* be any point of the interval $[\theta_{k-1}, \theta_k]$. The kth slice is approximated by the sector of a circle swept out by an

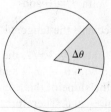

Area of circle $= \pi r^2$

Area of $\Delta\theta/(2\pi)$ of a circle

$$= \left(\frac{\Delta\theta}{2\pi}\right)\pi r^2 = \frac{1}{2}r^2\Delta\theta$$

angle $\Delta\theta_k$ with radius $f(\theta_k^*)$ (Figure 11.38b). Therefore, the area of the kth slice is approximately $\frac{1}{2}f(\theta_k^*)^2\Delta\theta_k$, for $k = 1, 2, \ldots, n$ (Figure 11.38c). To find the approximate area of R, we sum the areas of these slices:

$$\text{area} \approx \sum_{k=1}^{n}\frac{1}{2}f(\theta_k^*)^2\,\Delta\theta_k.$$

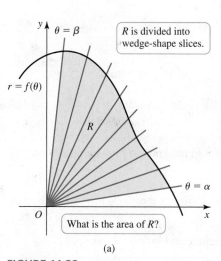

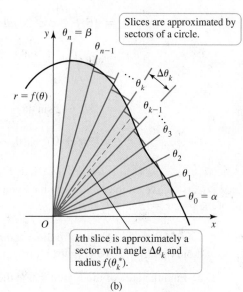

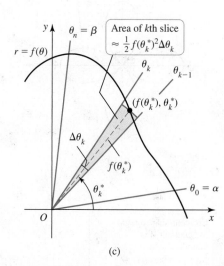

FIGURE 11.38

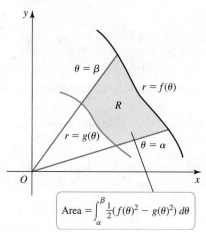

FIGURE 11.39

▷ If R is bounded by the graph of $r = f(\theta)$ between $\theta = \alpha$ and $\theta = \beta$, then $g(\theta) = 0$ and the area of R is
$$\int_{\alpha}^{\beta}\frac{1}{2}f(\theta)^2\,d\theta.$$

▷ Though we assume $r = f(\theta) \geq 0$ when deriving the formula for the area of a region bounded by a polar curve, the formula is valid when $r < 0$ (see, for example, Exercise 58).

This approximation is a Riemann sum, and the approximation improves as we take more sectors ($n \to \infty$) and let $\Delta\theta_k \to 0$, for all k. The exact area is given by $\lim_{n\to\infty}\sum_{k=1}^{n}\frac{1}{2}f(\theta_k^*)^2\,\Delta\theta_k$, which we identify as the definite integral $\int_{\alpha}^{\beta}\frac{1}{2}f(\theta)^2\,d\theta$.

With a slight modification, a more general result is obtained for the area of a region R bounded by two curves, $r = f(\theta)$ and $r = g(\theta)$, between the rays $\theta = \alpha$ and $\theta = \beta$ (Figure 11.39). We assume that f and g are continuous and $f(\theta) \geq g(\theta) \geq 0$ on $[\alpha, \beta]$. To find the area of R, we subtract the area of the region bounded by $r = g(\theta)$ from the area of the entire region bounded by $r = f(\theta)$ (all between $\theta = \alpha$ and $\theta = \beta$); that is,

$$\text{area} = \int_{\alpha}^{\beta}\frac{1}{2}f(\theta)^2\,d\theta - \int_{\alpha}^{\beta}\frac{1}{2}g(\theta)^2\,d\theta = \int_{\alpha}^{\beta}\frac{1}{2}(f(\theta)^2 - g(\theta)^2)\,d\theta.$$

DEFINITION Area of Regions in Polar Coordinates

Let R be the region bounded by the graphs of $r = f(\theta)$ and $r = g(\theta)$, between $\theta = \alpha$ and $\theta = \beta$, where f and g are continuous and $f(\theta) \geq g(\theta) \geq 0$ on $[\alpha, \beta]$. The area of R is

$$\int_{\alpha}^{\beta}\frac{1}{2}(f(\theta)^2 - g(\theta)^2)\,d\theta.$$

QUICK CHECK 3 Use integration to find the area of the circle $r = f(\theta) = 8$, for $0 \leq \theta \leq 2\pi$. ◁

EXAMPLE 3 Area of a polar region Find the area of the four-leaf rose $r = f(\theta) = 2\cos 2\theta$.

SOLUTION The graph of the rose (Figure 11.40) *appears* to be symmetric about the x- and y-axes; in fact, these symmetries can be proved. Appealing to this symmetry, we

> The equation $r = 2\cos 2\theta$ is unchanged when θ is replaced with $-\theta$ (symmetry about the x-axis) and when θ is replaced with $\pi - \theta$ (symmetry about the y-axis).

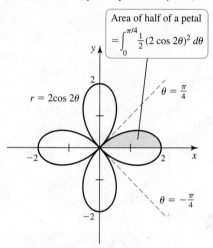

Area of half of a petal
$= \int_0^{\pi/4} \frac{1}{2}(2\cos 2\theta)^2 \, d\theta$

$r = 2\cos 2\theta$

$\theta = \frac{\pi}{4}$

$\theta = -\frac{\pi}{4}$

FIGURE 11.40

find the area of one-half of a leaf and then multiply the result by 8 to obtain the area of the full rose. The upper half of the rightmost leaf is generated as θ increases from $\theta = 0$ (when $r = 2$) to $\theta = \pi/4$ (when $r = 0$). Therefore, the area of the entire rose is

$$8 \int_0^{\pi/4} \frac{1}{2} f(\theta)^2 \, d\theta = 4 \int_0^{\pi/4} (2\cos 2\theta)^2 \, d\theta \qquad f(\theta) = 2\cos 2\theta$$

$$= 16 \int_0^{\pi/4} \cos^2 2\theta \, d\theta \qquad \text{Simplify.}$$

$$= 16 \int_0^{\pi/4} \frac{1 + \cos 4\theta}{2} \, d\theta \qquad \text{Half-angle formula}$$

$$= (8\theta + 2\sin 4\theta)\Big|_0^{\pi/4} \qquad \text{Fundamental Theorem}$$

$$= (2\pi + 0) - (0 + 0) = 2\pi. \qquad \text{Simplify.}$$

Related Exercises 21–36 ◄

QUICK CHECK 4 Give an interval over which you could integrate to find the area of one leaf of the rose $r = 2\sin 3\theta$. ◄

EXAMPLE 4   Areas of polar regions Consider the circle $r = 1$ and the cardioid $r = 1 + \cos\theta$ (Figure 11.41).

a. Find the area of the region inside the circle and inside the cardioid.

b. Find the area of the region inside the circle and outside the cardioid.

SOLUTION

a. The points of intersection of the two curves can be found by solving $1 + \cos\theta = 1$, or $\cos\theta = 0$. The solutions are $\theta = \pm\pi/2$. The region inside the circle and inside the cardioid consists of two subregions:

- a semicircle with radius 1 in the first and fourth quadrants bounded by the circle $r = 1$, and

- two crescent-shaped regions in the second and third quadrants bounded by the cardioid $r = 1 + \cos\theta$ and the y-axis.

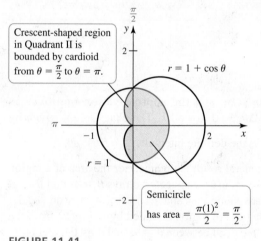

Crescent-shaped region in Quadrant II is bounded by cardioid from $\theta = \frac{\pi}{2}$ to $\theta = \pi$.

$r = 1 + \cos\theta$

$r = 1$

Semicircle has area $= \frac{\pi(1)^2}{2} = \frac{\pi}{2}$.

FIGURE 11.41

The area of the semicircle is $\pi/2$. To find the area of the upper crescent-shaped region in the second quadrant, notice that it is bounded by $r = 1 + \cos\theta$, as θ varies from $\pi/2$ to π. Therefore, its area is

$$\int_{\pi/2}^{\pi} \frac{1}{2}(1 + \cos\theta)^2 \, d\theta = \int_{\pi/2}^{\pi} \frac{1}{2}(1 + 2\cos\theta + \cos^2\theta) \, d\theta \qquad \text{Expand.}$$

$$= \frac{1}{2} \int_{\pi/2}^{\pi} \left(1 + 2\cos\theta + \frac{1 + \cos 2\theta}{2}\right) d\theta \qquad \begin{array}{l}\text{Half-angle}\\ \text{formula}\end{array}$$

$$= \frac{1}{2}\left(\theta + 2\sin\theta + \frac{\theta}{2} + \frac{\sin 2\theta}{4}\right)\Big|_{\pi/2}^{\pi} \qquad \begin{array}{l}\text{Fundamental}\\ \text{Theorem}\end{array}$$

$$= \frac{3\pi}{8} - 1. \qquad \text{Simplify.}$$

The area of the entire region (two crescents and a semicircle) is

$$2\left(\frac{3\pi}{8} - 1\right) + \frac{\pi}{2} = \frac{5\pi}{4} - 2.$$

b. The region inside the circle and outside the cardioid is bounded by the outer curve $r = 1$ and the inner curve $r = 1 + \cos\theta$ on the interval $\left[\dfrac{\pi}{2}, \dfrac{3\pi}{2}\right]$ (Figure 11.41).

Using the symmetry about the x-axis, the area of the region is

$$2\int_{\pi/2}^{\pi} \frac{1}{2}\left(1^2 - (1 + \cos\theta)^2\right)d\theta = \int_{\pi/2}^{\pi}\left(-2\cos\theta - \cos^2\theta\right)d\theta \quad \text{Simplify the integrand.}$$

$$= 2 - \frac{\pi}{4}. \quad \text{Evaluate the integral.}$$

Note that the regions in parts (a) and (b) comprise the interior of a circle of radius 1; indeed, their areas have a sum of π.

Related Exercises 21–36 ◄

Part of the challenge in setting up area integrals in polar coordinates is finding the points of intersection of two polar curves. The following example shows some of the subtleties of this process.

EXAMPLE 5   Points of intersection   Find the points of intersection of the circle $r = 3\cos\theta$ and the cardioid $r = 1 + \cos\theta$ (Figure 11.42).

SOLUTION   The fact that a point has multiple representations in polar coordinates may lead to subtle difficulties in finding intersection points. We first proceed algebraically. Equating the two expressions for r and solving for θ, we have

$$3\cos\theta = 1 + \cos\theta \quad \text{or} \quad \cos\theta = \frac{1}{2},$$

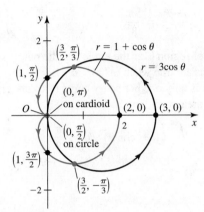

$r = 1 + \cos\theta$

$r = 3\cos\theta$

$\left(\frac{3}{2}, \frac{\pi}{3}\right)$

$\left(1, \frac{\pi}{2}\right)$

$(0, \pi)$
on cardioid

$(2, 0)$ $(3, 0)$

$\left(0, \frac{\pi}{2}\right)$
on circle

$\left(1, \frac{3\pi}{2}\right)$

$\left(\frac{3}{2}, -\frac{\pi}{3}\right)$

FIGURE 11.42

which has roots $\theta = \pm\pi/3$. Therefore, two intersection points are $(3/2, \pi/3)$ and $(3/2, -\pi/3)$ (Figure 11.42). Without examining graphs of the curves, we might be tempted to stop here. Yet, the figure shows another intersection point at the origin O that has not been detected. To find the third intersection point, we must investigate the way in which the two curves are generated. As θ increases from 0 to 2π, the cardioid is generated counterclockwise, beginning at $(2, 0)$. The cardioid passes through O when $\theta = \pi$. As θ increases from 0 to π, the circle is generated counterclockwise, beginning at $(3, 0)$. The circle passes through O when $\theta = \pi/2$. Therefore, the intersection point O is $(0, \pi)$ on the cardioid (and these coordinates do not satisfy the equation of the circle), while O is $(0, \pi/2)$ on the circle (and these coordinates do not satisfy the equation of the cardioid). There is no foolproof rule for detecting such "hidden" intersection points. Care must be used.

Related Exercises 37–40 ◄

EXAMPLE 6   Computing areas   Example 5 discussed the points of intersection of the curves $r = 3\cos\theta$ (a circle) and $r = 1 + \cos\theta$ (a cardioid). Use those results to compute the areas of the following non-overlapping regions in Figure 11.43.

a. region A   **b.** region B   **c.** region C

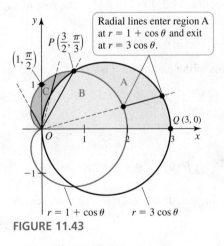

Radial lines enter region A
at $r = 1 + \cos\theta$ and exit
at $r = 3\cos\theta$.

$P\left(\frac{3}{2}, \frac{\pi}{3}\right)$

$\left(1, \frac{\pi}{2}\right)$

$Q(3, 0)$

$r = 1 + \cos\theta$ $r = 3\cos\theta$

FIGURE 11.43

SOLUTION

a. It is evident that region A is bounded on the inside by the cardioid and on the outside by the circle between the points $Q(\theta = 0)$ and $P(\theta = \pi/3)$. Therefore, the area of region A is

$$\frac{1}{2}\int_0^{\pi/3}\left((3\cos\theta)^2 - (1 + \cos\theta)^2\right)d\theta$$

$$= \frac{1}{2}\int_0^{\pi/3}\left(8\cos^2\theta - 1 - 2\cos\theta\right)d\theta \quad \text{Simplify.}$$

$$= \frac{1}{2}\int_0^{\pi/3}\left(3 + 4\cos 2\theta - 2\cos\theta\right)d\theta \quad \cos^2\theta = \frac{1 + \cos 2\theta}{2}$$

$$= \frac{1}{2}\left(3\theta + 2\sin 2\theta - 2\sin\theta\right)\Big|_0^{\pi/3} = \frac{\pi}{2}. \quad \text{Evaluate integral.}$$

➤ One way to verify that the inner and outer boundaries of a region have been correctly identified is to draw a ray from the origin through the region—the ray should enter the region at the inner boundary and exit the region at the outer boundary. In Example 6a, this is the case for every ray through region A, for $0 \le \theta \le \pi/3$.

b. Examining region B, notice that a ray drawn from the origin enters the region immediately. There is no inner boundary, and the outer boundary is $r = 1 + \cos\theta$ on $0 \le \theta \le \pi/3$ and $r = 3\cos\theta$ on $\pi/3 \le \theta \le \pi/2$ (recall from Example 5 that $\theta = \pi/2$ is the angle at which the circle intersects the origin). Therefore, we slice the region into two parts at $\theta = \pi/3$ and write two integrals for its area:

$$\text{area of region B} = \frac{1}{2}\int_0^{\pi/3}(1 + \cos\theta)^2\,d\theta + \frac{1}{2}\int_{\pi/3}^{\pi/2}(3\cos\theta)^2\,d\theta.$$

While these integrals may be evaluated directly, it's easier to notice that

$$\text{area of region B} = \text{area of semicircle } OPQ - \text{area of region A}.$$

Because $r = 3\cos\theta$ is a circle with a radius of $3/2$, we have

$$\text{area of region B} = \frac{1}{2}\cdot\pi\left(\frac{3}{2}\right)^2 - \frac{\pi}{2} = \frac{5\pi}{8}.$$

c. It's easy to *incorrectly* identify the inner boundary of region C as the circle and the outer boundary as the cardioid. While these identifications are true when $\pi/3 \le \theta \le \pi/2$ (notice again the radial lines in Figure 11.43), there is only one boundary curve (the cardioid) when $\pi/2 \le \theta \le \pi$. We conclude that the area of region C is

$$\frac{1}{2}\int_{\pi/3}^{\pi/2}\left((1 + \cos\theta)^2 - (3\cos\theta)^2\right)d\theta + \frac{1}{2}\int_{\pi/2}^{\pi}(1 + \cos\theta)^2\,d\theta = \frac{\pi}{8}.$$

Related Exercises 41–44 ◄

Arc Length of a Polar Curve

> Recall from Section 11.3 that to convert from polar to Cartesian coordinates we use the relations
>
> $x = r\cos\theta$ and $y = r\sin\theta$.

We now answer the arc length question for polar curves: Given the polar equation $r = f(\theta)$, what is the length of the corresponding curve for $\alpha \le \theta \le \beta$? The key idea is to express the polar equation as a set of parametric equations in Cartesian coordinates and then use the arc length formula derived in Section 11.2. Letting θ play the role of a parameter and using $r = f(\theta)$, the parametric equations for the polar curve are

$$x = r\cos\theta = f(\theta)\cos\theta \quad\text{and}\quad y = r\sin\theta = f(\theta)\sin\theta,$$

where $\alpha \le \theta \le \beta$. The arc length formula in terms of the parameter θ is

$$L = \int_\alpha^\beta \sqrt{\left(\frac{dx}{d\theta}\right)^2 + \left(\frac{dy}{d\theta}\right)^2}\,d\theta,$$

where

$$\frac{dx}{d\theta} = f'(\theta)\cos\theta - f(\theta)\sin\theta \quad\text{and}\quad \frac{dy}{d\theta} = f'(\theta)\sin\theta + f(\theta)\cos\theta.$$

When substituted into the arc length formula and simplified, the result is a new arc length integral.

Arc Length of a Polar Curve

Let f have a continuous derivative on the interval $[\alpha, \beta]$. The **arc length** of the polar curve $r = f(\theta)$ on $[\alpha, \beta]$ is

$$L = \int_\alpha^\beta \sqrt{f(\theta)^2 + f'(\theta)^2}\,d\theta.$$

QUICK CHECK 5 Use the arc length formula to verify that the circumference of the circle $r = f(\theta) = 1$, for $0 \le \theta \le 2\pi$, is 2π. ◄

EXAMPLE 7   Arc length of polar curves

a. Find the arc length of the cardioid $r = 1 + \cos\theta$ (Figure 11.44).

b. Find the arc length of the spiral $r = f(\theta) = \theta$, for $0 \le \theta \le 2\pi$ (Figure 11.45).

SOLUTION

a. The cardioid is symmetric about the x-axis and its upper half is generated for $0 \le \theta \le \pi$. The length of the full curve is twice the length of its upper half:

$$L = 2\int_0^\pi \sqrt{(1 + \cos\theta)^2 + (-\sin\theta)^2}\, d\theta \qquad f(\theta) = 1 + \cos\theta; f'(\theta) = -\sin\theta$$

$$= 2\int_0^\pi \sqrt{2 + 2\cos\theta}\, d\theta \qquad\qquad \text{Simplify.}$$

$$= 2\int_0^\pi \sqrt{4\cos^2(\theta/2)}\, d\theta \qquad\qquad 1 + \cos\theta = 2\cos^2(\theta/2)$$

$$= 4\int_0^\pi \cos(\theta/2)\, d\theta \qquad\qquad \cos(\theta/2) \ge 0, \text{ for } 0 \le \theta \le \pi$$

$$= 8\sin(\theta/2)\Big|_0^\pi = 8. \qquad\qquad \text{Integrate and simplify.}$$

b. We set up the arc length integral and then evaluate it using numerical integration on a calculator:

$$L = \int_0^{2\pi} \sqrt{\theta^2 + 1}\, d\theta \approx 21.256. \qquad f(\theta) = \theta \text{ and } f'(\theta) = 1$$

Another strategy is to evaluate the integral analytically using a trigonometric substitution and a result given in Exercises 53–55 of Section 7.5.

Related Exercises 45–54 ◄

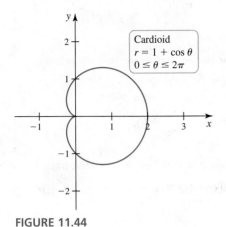

FIGURE 11.44

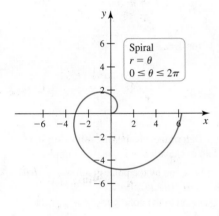

FIGURE 11.45

SECTION 11.4 EXERCISES

Review Questions

1. Express the polar equation $r = f(\theta)$ in parametric form in Cartesian coordinates, where θ is the parameter.

2. How do you find the slope of the line tangent to the polar graph of $r = f(\theta)$ at a point?

3. Explain why the slope of the line tangent to the polar graph of $r = f(\theta)$ is not $\dfrac{dr}{d\theta}$.

4. What integral must be evaluated to find the area of the region bounded by the polar graphs of $r = f(\theta)$ and $r = g(\theta)$ on the interval $\alpha \le \theta \le \beta$, where $f(\theta) \ge g(\theta) \ge 0$?

5. Consider the polar graphs of $r = f(\theta)$ and $r = g(\theta)$. Explain why the solutions of the equation $f(\theta) = g(\theta)$ may not reveal all the intersection points of the curves.

6. How do you find the arc length of the polar curve $r = f(\theta)$, for $\alpha \le \theta \le \beta$, assuming f' is continuous on $[\alpha, \beta]$?

Basic Skills

7–14. Slopes of tangent lines *Find the slope of the line tangent to the following polar curves at the given points. At the points where the curve intersects the origin (when this occurs), find the equation of the tangent line in polar coordinates.*

7. $r = 1 - \sin\theta$; $\left(\frac{1}{2}, \frac{\pi}{6}\right)$

8. $r = 4\cos\theta$; $\left(2, \frac{\pi}{3}\right)$

9. $r = 8\sin\theta$; $\left(4, \frac{5\pi}{6}\right)$

10. $r = 4 + \sin\theta$; $(4, 0)$ and $\left(3, \frac{3\pi}{2}\right)$

11. $r = 6 + 3\cos\theta$; $(3, \pi)$ and $(9, 0)$

12. $r = 2\sin 3\theta$; at the tips of the leaves

13. $r = 4\cos 2\theta$; at the tips of the leaves

14. $r = 1 + 2\sin 2\theta$; $\left(3, \frac{\pi}{4}\right)$

15–20. Horizontal and vertical tangents *Find the points at which the following polar curves have a horizontal or a vertical tangent line.*

15. $r = 4 \cos \theta$

16. $r = 2 + 2 \sin \theta$

17. $r = \sin 2\theta$

18. $r = 3 + 6 \sin \theta$

19. $r = 1 - \sin \theta$

20. $r = \sec \theta$

21–36. Areas of regions *Make a sketch of the region and its bounding curves. Find the area of the region.*

21. The region inside the curve $r = \sqrt{\cos \theta}$

22. The region inside the right lobe of $r = \sqrt{\cos 2\theta}$

23. The region inside the circle $r = 8 \sin \theta$

24. The region inside the cardioid $r = 4 + 4 \sin \theta$

25. The region inside the limaçon $r = 2 + \cos \theta$

26. The region inside all the leaves of the rose $r = 3 \sin 2\theta$

27. The region inside one leaf of $r = \cos 3\theta$

28. The region inside the inner loop of $r = \cos \theta - \frac{1}{2}$

29. The region outside the circle $r = \frac{1}{2}$ and inside the circle $r = \cos \theta$

30. The region inside the curve $r = \sqrt{\cos \theta}$ and outside the circle $r = \dfrac{1}{\sqrt{2}}$

31. The region inside the curve $r = \sqrt{\cos \theta}$ and inside the circle $r = \dfrac{1}{\sqrt{2}}$ in the first quadrant

32. The region inside the right lobe of $r = \sqrt{\cos 2\theta}$ and inside the circle $r = \dfrac{1}{\sqrt{2}}$ in the first quadrant

33. The region inside one leaf of the rose $r = \cos 5\theta$

34. The region inside the rose $r = 4 \cos 2\theta$ and outside the circle $r = 2$

35. The region inside the rose $r = 4 \sin 2\theta$ and inside the circle $r = 2$

36. The region inside the lemniscate $r^2 = 2 \sin 2\theta$ and outside the circle $r = 1$

37–40. Intersection points *Use algebraic methods to find as many intersection points of the following curves as possible. Use graphical methods to identify the remaining intersection points.*

37. $r = 3 \sin \theta$ and $r = 3 \cos \theta$

38. $r = 2 + 2 \sin \theta$ and $r = 2 - 2 \sin \theta$

39. $r = 1 + \sin \theta$ and $r = 1 + \cos \theta$

40. $r = 1$ and $r = \sqrt{2} \cos 2\theta$

41–44. Finding areas *In Exercises 37–40, you found the intersection points of pairs of curves. Find the area of the entire region that lies within both of the following pairs of curves.*

41. $r = 3 \sin \theta$ and $r = 3 \cos \theta$

42. $r = 2 + 2 \sin \theta$ and $r = 2 - 2 \sin \theta$

43. $r = 1 + \sin \theta$ and $r = 1 + \cos \theta$

44. $r = 1$ and $r = \sqrt{2} \cos 2\theta$

45–54. Arc length of polar curves *Find the length of the following polar curves.*

45. The complete circle $r = a \sin \theta$, where $a > 0$

46. The complete cardioid $r = 2 - 2 \sin \theta$

47. The spiral $r = \theta^2$, where $0 \le \theta \le 2\pi$

48. The spiral $r = e^\theta$, where $0 \le \theta \le 2\pi n$, for a positive integer n

49. The complete cardioid $r = 4 + 4 \sin \theta$

50. The spiral $r = 4\theta^2$, for $0 \le \theta \le 6$

51. The spiral $r = 2e^{2\theta}$, for $0 \le \theta \le \ln 8$

52. The curve $r = \sin^2\left(\dfrac{\theta}{2}\right)$, for $0 \le \theta \le \pi$

53. The curve $r = \sin^3\left(\dfrac{\theta}{3}\right)$, for $0 \le \theta \le \dfrac{\pi}{2}$

54. The parabola $r = \dfrac{\sqrt{2}}{1 + \cos \theta}$, for $0 \le \theta \le \dfrac{\pi}{2}$

Further Explorations

55. Explain why or why not Determine whether the following statements are true, and give an explanation or a counterexample.

  a. The area of the region bounded by the polar graph of $r = f(\theta)$ on the interval $[\alpha, \beta]$ is $\int_\alpha^\beta f(\theta) \, d\theta$.

  b. The slope of the line tangent to the polar curve $r = f(\theta)$ at a point (r, θ) is $f'(\theta)$.

56. Multiple identities Explain why the point $\left(-1, \dfrac{3\pi}{2}\right)$ is on the polar graph of $r = 1 + \cos \theta$ even though it does not satisfy the equation $r = 1 + \cos \theta$.

57–60. Area of plane regions *Find the areas of the following regions.*

57. The region common to the circles $r = 2 \sin \theta$ and $r = 1$

58. The region inside the inner loop of the limaçon $r = 2 + 4 \cos \theta$

59. The region inside the outer loop but outside the inner loop of the limaçon $r = 3 - 6 \sin \theta$

60. The region common to the circle $r = 3 \cos \theta$ and the cardioid $r = 1 + \cos \theta$

61. Spiral tangent lines Use a graphing utility to determine the first three points with $\theta \ge 0$ at which the spiral $r = 2\theta$ has a horizontal tangent line. Find the first three points with $\theta \ge 0$ at which the spiral $r = 2\theta$ has a vertical tangent line.

62. Area of roses Assume m is a positive integer.

  a. *Even number of leaves*: What is the relationship between the total area enclosed by the $4m$-leaf rose $r = \cos(2m\theta)$ and m?

  b. *Odd number of leaves*: What is the relationship between the total area enclosed by the $(2m + 1)$-leaf rose $r = \cos((2m + 1)\theta)$ and m?

63. Regions bounded by a spiral Let R_n be the region bounded by the nth turn and the $(n + 1)$st turn of the spiral $r = e^{-\theta}$ in the first and second quadrants, for $\theta \geq 0$ (see figure).

   a. Find the area A_n of R_n.

   b. Evaluate $\lim\limits_{n\to\infty} A_n$.

   c. Evaluate $\lim\limits_{n\to\infty} A_{n+1}/A_n$.

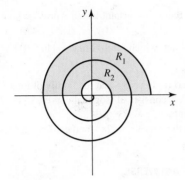

64–67. Area of polar regions *Find the area of the regions bounded by the following curves.*

64. The complete three-leaf rose $r = 2 \cos 3\theta$

65. The lemniscate $r^2 = 6 \sin 2\theta$

66. The limaçon $r = 2 - 4 \sin \theta$

67. The limaçon $r = 4 - 2 \cos \theta$

68. Spiral arc length Consider the spiral $r = \theta^2$, for $\theta \geq 0$.

   a. Find the arc length of the spiral, for $0 \leq \theta \leq \sqrt{12}$.

   b. Find $L(\theta)$, the arc length of the spiral on the interval $[0, \theta]$, for any $\theta \geq 0$.

   c. Show that $L'(\theta) > 0$. Is $L''(\theta)$ positive or negative? Interpret your answers.

69. Spiral arc length Find the length of the entire spiral $r = e^{-a\theta}$, for $\theta \geq 0$ and $a > 0$.

Applications

70. Blood vessel flow A blood vessel with a circular cross section of constant radius R carries blood that flows parallel to the axis of the vessel with a velocity of $v(r) = V\left(1 - \dfrac{r^2}{R^2}\right)$, where V is a constant and r is the distance from the axis of the vessel.

   a. Where is the velocity a maximum? A minimum?

   b. Find the average velocity of the blood over a cross section of the vessel.

   c. Suppose the velocity in the vessel is given by
$$v(r) = V\left(1 - \frac{r^2}{R^2}\right)^{1/p},$$
   where $p \geq 1$. Graph the velocity profiles for $p = 1, 2,$ and 6 on the interval $0 \leq r \leq R$. Find the average velocity in the vessel as a function of p. How does the average velocity behave as $p \to \infty$?

71–73. Grazing goat problems *Consider the following sequence of problems related to grazing goats tied to a rope. (See the Guided Project Grazing Goat Problems.)*

71. A circular corral of unit radius is enclosed by a fence. A goat inside the corral is tied to the fence with a rope of length $0 \leq a \leq 2$ (see figure). What is the area of the region (inside the corral) that the goat can graze? Check your answer with the special cases $a = 0$ and $a = 2$.

72. A circular concrete slab of unit radius is surrounded by grass. A goat is tied to the edge of the slab with a rope of length $0 \leq a \leq 2$ (see figure). What is the area of the grassy region that the goat can graze? Note that the rope can extend over the concrete slab. Check your answer with the special cases $a = 0$ and $a = 2$.

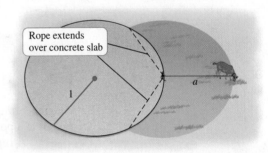

Rope extends over concrete slab

73. A circular corral of unit radius is enclosed by a fence. A goat is outside the corral and tied to the fence with a rope of length $0 \leq a \leq \pi$ (see figure). What is the area of the region (outside the corral) that the goat can reach?

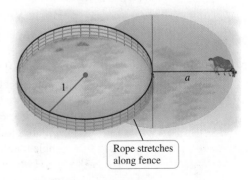

Rope stretches along fence

Additional Exercises

74. Tangents and normals Let a polar curve be described by $r = f(\theta)$ and let ℓ be the line tangent to the curve at the point $P(x, y) = P(r, \theta)$ (see figure).

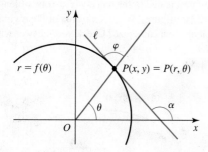

a. Explain why $\tan \alpha = \dfrac{dy}{dx}$.

b. Explain why $\tan \theta = \dfrac{y}{x}$.

c. Let φ be the angle between ℓ and the line through O and P. Prove that $\tan \varphi = \dfrac{f(\theta)}{f'(\theta)}$.

d. Prove that the values of θ for which ℓ is parallel to the x-axis satisfy $\tan \theta = -\dfrac{f(\theta)}{f'(\theta)}$.

e. Prove that the values of θ for which ℓ is parallel to the y-axis satisfy $\tan \theta = \dfrac{f(\theta)}{f'(\theta)}$.

75. Isogonal curves Let a curve be described by $r = f(\theta)$, where $f(\theta) > 0$ on its domain. Referring to the figure of Exercise 74, a curve is **isogonal** provided the angle φ is constant for all θ.

a. Prove that φ is constant for all θ provided $\cot \varphi = \dfrac{f'(\theta)}{f(\theta)}$ is constant, which implies that $\dfrac{d}{d\theta}(\ln f(\theta)) = k$, where k is a constant.

b. Use part (a) to prove that the family of logarithmic spirals $r = Ce^{k\theta}$ consists of isogonal curves, where C and k are constants.

c. Graph the curve $r = 2e^{2\theta}$ and confirm the result of part (b).

QUICK CHECK ANSWERS

1. Apply the Product Rule.   2. $\sqrt{2} + 1$

3. Area $= \displaystyle\int_{0}^{2\pi} \tfrac{1}{2}(8)^2 \, d\theta = 64\pi$

4. $\left[0, \frac{\pi}{3}\right]$ or $\left[\frac{\pi}{3}, \frac{2\pi}{3}\right]$ (among others)   5. 2π ◂

11.5 Vectors in the Plane

FIGURE 11.46

Imagine a raft drifting down a river, carried by the current. The speed and direction of the raft at a point may be represented by an arrow (Figure 11.46). The length of the arrow represents the speed of the raft at that point; longer arrows correspond to greater speeds. The orientation of the arrow gives the direction in which the raft is headed at that point. The arrows at points A and C in Figure 11.46 have the same length and direction, indicating that the raft has the same speed and heading at these locations. The arrow at B is shorter and points to the left of the rock, indicating that the raft slows down as it nears the rock.

Basic Vector Operations

The arrows that describe the raft's motion are examples of *vectors*—quantities that have both *length* (or *magnitude*) and *direction*. Vectors arise naturally in many situations. For example, electric and magnetic fields, the flow of air over an airplane wing, and the velocity and acceleration of elementary particles are described by vectors (Figure 11.47). In this section, we examine vectors in the xy-plane.

The vector whose *tail* is at the point P and whose *head* is at the point Q is denoted $\overrightarrow{PQ}$ (Figure 11.48). The vector $\overrightarrow{QP}$ has its tail at Q and its head at P. We also label vectors with single boldfaced characters such as $\mathbf{u}$ and $\mathbf{v}$.

Two vectors $\mathbf{u}$ and $\mathbf{v}$ are **equal**, written $\mathbf{u} = \mathbf{v}$, if they have equal length and point in the same direction (Figure 11.49). An important fact is that equal vectors do not necessarily have the same location. *Any* two vectors with the same length and direction are equal.

> ▶ The vector $\mathbf{v}$ is commonly handwritten as $\vec{v}$.

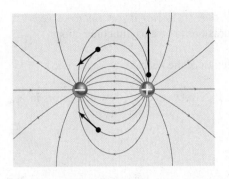

Electric field vectors due to two charges

FIGURE 11.47

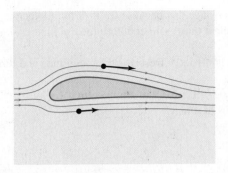

Velocity vectors of air flowing over an airplane wing

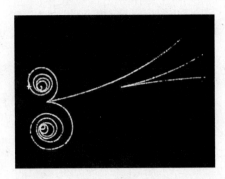

Tracks of elementary particles in a cloud chamber are aligned with the velocity vectors of the particles.

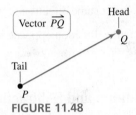

Vector $\overrightarrow{PQ}$

Head

Tail

P

Q

FIGURE 11.48

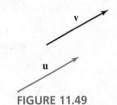

v

u

Vectors **u** and **v** are *equal* if they have the same length and direction.

FIGURE 11.49

Not all quantities are represented by vectors. For example, mass, temperature, and price have magnitude, but no direction. Such quantities are described by real numbers and are called *scalars*.

> In this book, *scalar* is another word for *real number*.

Vectors, Equal Vectors, Scalars, Zero Vector

Vectors are quantities that have both length (or magnitude) and direction. Two vectors are **equal** if they have the same magnitude and direction. Quantities having magnitude but no direction are called **scalars**. One exception is the **zero vector**, denoted **0**: It has length 0 and no direction.

Scalar Multiplication

A scalar c and a vector **v** can be combined using scalar-vector multiplication, or simply *scalar multiplication*. The resulting vector, denoted $c\mathbf{v}$, is called a *scalar multiple* of **v**. The magnitude of $c\mathbf{v}$ is $|c|$ multiplied by the magnitude of **v**. The vector $c\mathbf{v}$ has the same direction as **v** if $c > 0$. If $c < 0$, then $c\mathbf{v}$ and **v** point in opposite directions. If $c = 0$, then the product $0\mathbf{v} = \mathbf{0}$ (the zero vector).

For example, the vector $3\mathbf{v}$ is three times as long as **v** and has the same direction as **v**. The vector $-2\mathbf{v}$ is twice as long as **v**, but it points in the opposite direction. The vector $\frac{1}{2}\mathbf{v}$ points in the same direction as **v** and has half the length of **v** (Figure 11.50). The vectors **v**, $3\mathbf{v}$, $-2\mathbf{v}$, and $\frac{1}{2}\mathbf{v}$ are examples of *parallel vectors*: Each one is a scalar multiple of the others.

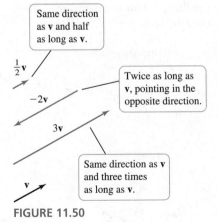

$\frac{1}{2}\mathbf{v}$ — Same direction as **v** and half as long as **v**.

$-2\mathbf{v}$ — Twice as long as **v**, pointing in the opposite direction.

$3\mathbf{v}$ — Same direction as **v** and three times as long as **v**.

v

FIGURE 11.50

DEFINITION Scalar Multiples and Parallel Vectors

Given a scalar c and a vector **v**, the **scalar multiple** $c\mathbf{v}$ is a vector whose magnitude is $|c|$ multiplied by the magnitude of **v**. If $c > 0$, then $c\mathbf{v}$ has the same direction as **v**. If $c < 0$, then $c\mathbf{v}$ and **v** point in opposite directions. Two vectors are **parallel** if they are scalar multiples of each other.

> For convenience, we write $-\mathbf{u}$ for $(-1)\mathbf{u}$, $-c\mathbf{u}$ for $(-c)\mathbf{u}$, and $\mathbf{u}/c$ for $\left(\dfrac{1}{c}\right)\mathbf{u}$.

Notice that because $0\mathbf{v} = \mathbf{0}$ for all vectors $\mathbf{v}$, *the zero vector is parallel to all vectors.* While it may seem counterintuitive, this result turns out to be a useful convention.

QUICK CHECK 1 Describe the magnitude and direction of the vector $-5\mathbf{v}$ relative to $\mathbf{v}$. ◄

EXAMPLE 1 Parallel vectors Using Figure 11.51a, write the following vectors in terms of $\mathbf{u}$ or $\mathbf{v}$.

a. $\overrightarrow{PQ}$ **b.** $\overrightarrow{QP}$ **c.** $\overrightarrow{QR}$ **d.** $\overrightarrow{RS}$

SOLUTION

a. The vector $\overrightarrow{PQ}$ has the same direction and length as $\mathbf{u}$; therefore, $\overrightarrow{PQ} = \mathbf{u}$. These two vectors are equal even though they have different locations (Figure 11.51b).

b. Because $\overrightarrow{QP}$ and $\mathbf{u}$ have equal length, but opposite directions, $\overrightarrow{QP} = (-1)\mathbf{u} = -\mathbf{u}$.

c. $\overrightarrow{QR}$ points in the same direction as $\mathbf{v}$ and is twice as long as $\mathbf{v}$, so $\overrightarrow{QR} = 2\mathbf{v}$.

d. $\overrightarrow{RS}$ points in the direction opposite to that of $\mathbf{u}$ with three times the length of $\mathbf{u}$. Consequently, $\overrightarrow{RS} = -3\mathbf{u}$.

Related Exercises 17–20 ◄

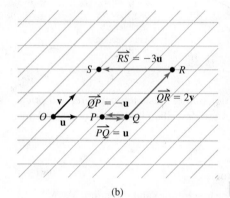

(a)

(b)

FIGURE 11.51

Vector Addition and Subtraction

To illustrate the idea of vector addition, consider a plane flying horizontally at a constant speed in a crosswind (Figure 11.52). The length of vector $\mathbf{v}_a$ represents the plane's *airspeed,* which is the speed the plane would have in still air; $\mathbf{v}_a$ points in the direction of the nose of the plane. The wind vector $\mathbf{w}$ points in the direction of the crosswind and has a length equal to the speed of the crosswind. The combined effect of the motion of the plane and the wind is the *vector sum* $\mathbf{v}_g = \mathbf{v}_a + \mathbf{w}$, which is the velocity of the plane relative to the ground.

QUICK CHECK 2 Sketch the sum $\mathbf{v}_a + \mathbf{w}$ in Figure 11.52 if the direction of $\mathbf{w}$ is reversed. ◄

Figure 11.53 illustrates two ways to form the vector sum of two nonzero vectors $\mathbf{u}$ and $\mathbf{v}$ geometrically. The first method, called the **Triangle Rule**, places the tail of $\mathbf{v}$ at the head of $\mathbf{u}$. The sum $\mathbf{u} + \mathbf{v}$ is the vector that extends from the tail of $\mathbf{u}$ to the head of $\mathbf{v}$ (Figure 11.53b).

When $\mathbf{u}$ and $\mathbf{v}$ are not parallel, another way to form $\mathbf{u} + \mathbf{v}$ is to use the **Parallelogram Rule**. The *tails* of $\mathbf{u}$ and $\mathbf{v}$ are connected to form adjacent sides of a parallelogram; then the remaining two sides of the parallelogram are sketched. The sum $\mathbf{u} + \mathbf{v}$ is the vector that coincides with the diagonal of the parallelogram, beginning at the tails of $\mathbf{u}$ and $\mathbf{v}$ (Figure 11.53c). The Triangle Rule and Parallelogram Rule each produce the same vector sum $\mathbf{u} + \mathbf{v}$.

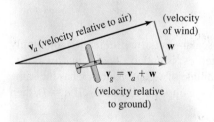

FIGURE 11.52

QUICK CHECK 3 Use the Triangle Rule to show that the vectors in Figure 11.53 satisfy $\mathbf{u} + \mathbf{v} = \mathbf{v} + \mathbf{u}$. ◄

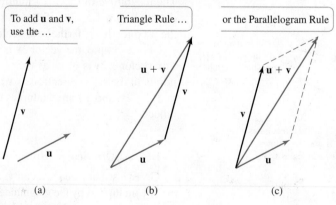

(a)   (b)   (c)

FIGURE 11.53

The difference $\mathbf{u} - \mathbf{v}$ is defined to be the sum $\mathbf{u} + (-\mathbf{v})$. By the Triangle Rule, the tail of $-\mathbf{v}$ is placed at the head of $\mathbf{u}$; then $\mathbf{u} - \mathbf{v}$ extends from the tail of $\mathbf{u}$ to the head of $-\mathbf{v}$ (Figure 11.54a). Equivalently, when the tails of $\mathbf{u}$ and $\mathbf{v}$ coincide, $\mathbf{u} - \mathbf{v}$ has its tail at the head of $\mathbf{v}$ and its head at the head of $\mathbf{u}$ (Figure 11.54b).

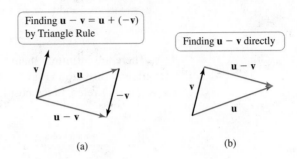

FIGURE 11.54   (a)   (b)

EXAMPLE 2   Vector operations Use Figure 11.55 to write the following vectors as sums of scalar multiples of $\mathbf{v}$ and $\mathbf{w}$.

a. $\overrightarrow{OP}$ **b.** $\overrightarrow{OQ}$ **c.** $\overrightarrow{QR}$

SOLUTION

a. Using the Triangle Rule, we start at O, move three lengths of $\mathbf{v}$ in the direction of $\mathbf{v}$ and then two lengths of $\mathbf{w}$ in the direction of $\mathbf{w}$ to reach P. Therefore, $\overrightarrow{OP} = 3\mathbf{v} + 2\mathbf{w}$ (Figure 11.56a).

b. The vector $\overrightarrow{OQ}$ coincides with the diagonal of a parallelogram having adjacent sides equal to $3\mathbf{v}$ and $-\mathbf{w}$. By the Parallelogram Rule, $\overrightarrow{OQ} = 3\mathbf{v} - \mathbf{w}$ (Figure 11.56b).

c. The vector $\overrightarrow{QR}$ lies on the diagonal of a parallelogram having adjacent sides equal to $\mathbf{v}$ and $2\mathbf{w}$. Therefore, $\overrightarrow{QR} = \mathbf{v} + 2\mathbf{w}$ (Figure 11.56c).

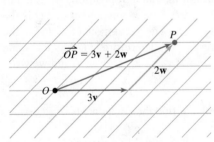

FIGURE 11.55

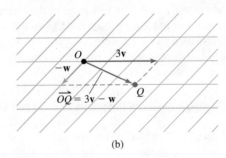

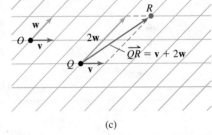

(a)   (b)   (c)

FIGURE 11.56

Related Exercises 21–22 ◄

Vector Components

So far, vectors have been examined from a geometric point of view. To do calculations with vectors, it is necessary to introduce a coordinate system. We begin by considering a vector $\mathbf{v}$ whose tail is at the origin in the Cartesian plane and whose head is at the point (v_1, v_2) (Figure 11.57a).

> Round brackets (a, b) enclose the *coordinates* of a point, while angle brackets $\langle a, b \rangle$ enclose the *components* of a vector. Note that in component form, the zero vector is $\mathbf{0} = \langle 0, 0 \rangle$.

DEFINITION Position Vectors and Vector Components

A vector $\mathbf{v}$ with its tail at the origin and head at the point (v_1, v_2) is called a **position vector** (or is said to be in **standard position**) and is written $\langle v_1, v_2 \rangle$. The real numbers v_1 and v_2 are the x- and y-**components** of $\mathbf{v}$, respectively. The position vectors $\mathbf{u} = \langle u_1, u_2 \rangle$ and $\mathbf{v} = \langle v_1, v_2 \rangle$ are **equal** if and only if $u_1 = v_1$ and $u_2 = v_2$.

There are infinitely many vectors equal to the position vector $\mathbf{v}$, all with the same length and direction (Figure 11.57b). It is important to abide by the convention that $\mathbf{v} = \langle v_1, v_2 \rangle$ refers to the position vector $\mathbf{v}$ *or to any other vector equal to* $\mathbf{v}$.

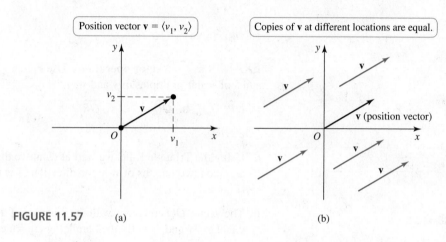

FIGURE 11.57   (a)   (b)

Now consider the vector $\overrightarrow{PQ}$, equal to $\mathbf{v}$, but not in standard position, with its tail at the point $P(x_1, y_1)$ and its head at the point $Q(x_2, y_2)$. The x-component of $\overrightarrow{PQ}$ is the difference in the x-coordinates of Q and P, or $x_2 - x_1$. The y-component of $\overrightarrow{PQ}$ is the difference in the y-coordinates, $y_2 - y_1$ (Figure 11.58). Therefore, $\overrightarrow{PQ}$ has the same length and direction as the position vector $\langle v_1, v_2 \rangle = \langle x_2 - x_1, y_2 - y_1 \rangle$, and we write $\overrightarrow{PQ} = \langle x_2 - x_1, y_2 - y_1 \rangle$.

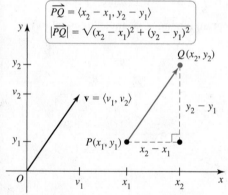

$$\overrightarrow{PQ} = \langle x_2 - x_1, y_2 - y_1 \rangle$$
$$|\overrightarrow{PQ}| = \sqrt{(x_2 - x_1)^2 + (y_2 - y_1)^2}$$

FIGURE 11.58

QUICK CHECK 4 Given the points $P(2, 3)$ and $Q(-4, 1)$, find the components of $\overrightarrow{PQ}$. ◄

As already noted, there are infinitely many vectors equal to a given position vector. All these vectors have the same length and direction; therefore, they are all equal. In other words, two arbitrary vectors are **equal** if they are equal to the same position vector. For example, the vector $\overrightarrow{PQ}$ from $P(2, 5)$ to $Q(6, 3)$ and the vector $\overrightarrow{AB}$ from $A(7, 12)$ to $B(11, 10)$ are equal because they are both equal to the position vector $\langle 4, -2 \rangle$.

Magnitude

The magnitude of a vector is simply its length. By the Pythagorean Theorem and Figure 11.58, we have the following definition.

> Just as the absolute value $|p - q|$ gives the distance between two points on the number line, the magnitude $|\overrightarrow{PQ}|$ is the distance between the points P and Q in the xy-plane. The magnitude of a vector is also called its **norm**.

DEFINITION Magnitude of a Vector

Given the points $P(x_1, y_1)$ and $Q(x_2, y_2)$, the **magnitude**, or **length**, of $\overrightarrow{PQ} = \langle x_2 - x_1, y_2 - y_1 \rangle$, denoted $|\overrightarrow{PQ}|$, is the distance between P and Q:

$$|\overrightarrow{PQ}| = \sqrt{(x_2 - x_1)^2 + (y_2 - y_1)^2}.$$

The magnitude of the position vector $\mathbf{v} = \langle v_1, v_2 \rangle$ is $|\mathbf{v}| = \sqrt{v_1^2 + v_2^2}$.

EXAMPLE 3 **Calculating components and magnitude** Given the points $O(0, 0)$, $P(-3, 4)$, and $Q(6, 5)$, find the components and magnitude of the following vectors.

a. $\overrightarrow{OP}$ **b.** $\overrightarrow{PQ}$

SOLUTION

a. The vector $\overrightarrow{OP}$ is the position vector whose head is located at $P(-3, 4)$. Therefore, $\overrightarrow{OP} = \langle -3, 4 \rangle$ and the magnitude is $|\overrightarrow{OP}| = \sqrt{(-3)^2 + 4^2} = 5$.

b. $\overrightarrow{PQ} = \langle 6 - (-3), 5 - 4 \rangle = \langle 9, 1 \rangle$ and $|\overrightarrow{PQ}| = \sqrt{9^2 + 1^2} = \sqrt{82}$.

Related Exercises 23–27 ◄

Vector Operations in Terms of Components

We now show how vector addition, vector subtraction, and scalar multiplication are performed using components. Suppose $\mathbf{u} = \langle u_1, u_2 \rangle$ and $\mathbf{v} = \langle v_1, v_2 \rangle$. The vector sum of $\mathbf{u}$ and $\mathbf{v}$ is $\mathbf{u} + \mathbf{v} = \langle u_1 + v_1, u_2 + v_2 \rangle$. This definition of a vector sum is consistent with the Parallelogram Rule given earlier (Figure 11.59).

For a scalar c and a vector $\mathbf{u}$, the scalar multiple $c\mathbf{u}$ is $c\mathbf{u} = \langle cu_1, cu_2 \rangle$; that is, the scalar c multiplies each component of $\mathbf{u}$. If $c > 0$, $\mathbf{u}$ and $c\mathbf{u}$ have the same direction (Figure 11.60a). If $c < 0$, $\mathbf{u}$ and $c\mathbf{u}$ have opposite directions (Figure 11.60b). In either case, $|c\mathbf{u}| = |c||\mathbf{u}|$ (Exercise 87).

Notice that $\mathbf{u} - \mathbf{v} = \mathbf{u} + (-\mathbf{v})$, where $-\mathbf{v} = \langle -v_1, -v_2 \rangle$ Therefore, the vector difference of $\mathbf{u}$ and $\mathbf{v}$ is $\mathbf{u} - \mathbf{v} = \langle u_1 - v_1, u_2 - v_2 \rangle$.

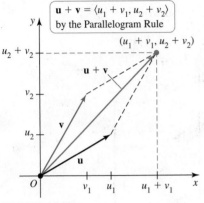

$$\mathbf{u} + \mathbf{v} = \langle u_1 + v_1, u_2 + v_2 \rangle$$ by the Parallelogram Rule

FIGURE 11.59

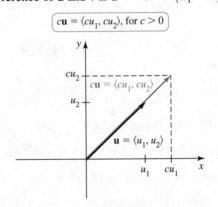

$c\mathbf{u} = \langle cu_1, cu_2 \rangle$, for $c > 0$

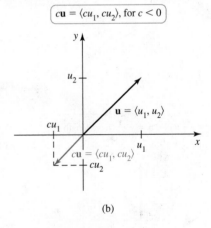

$c\mathbf{u} = \langle cu_1, cu_2 \rangle$, for $c < 0$

FIGURE 11.60   (a)   (b)

DEFINITION Vector Operations

Suppose c is a scalar, $\mathbf{u} = \langle u_1, u_2 \rangle$, and $\mathbf{v} = \langle v_1, v_2 \rangle$.

$$\mathbf{u} + \mathbf{v} = \langle u_1 + v_1, u_2 + v_2 \rangle \quad \text{Vector addition}$$

$$\mathbf{u} - \mathbf{v} = \langle u_1 - v_1, u_2 - v_2 \rangle \quad \text{Vector subtraction}$$

$$c\mathbf{u} = \langle cu_1, cu_2 \rangle \quad \text{Scalar multiplication}$$

EXAMPLE 4 **Vector operations** Let $\mathbf{u} = \langle -1, 2 \rangle$ and $\mathbf{v} = \langle 2, 3 \rangle$.

a. Evaluate $|\mathbf{u} + \mathbf{v}|$ **b.** Simplify $2\mathbf{u} - 3\mathbf{v}$.

c. Find two vectors half as long as $\mathbf{u}$ and parallel to $\mathbf{u}$.

SOLUTION

a. Because $\mathbf{u} + \mathbf{v} = \langle -1, 2 \rangle + \langle 2, 3 \rangle = \langle 1, 5 \rangle$, we have $|\mathbf{u} + \mathbf{v}| = \sqrt{1^2 + 5^2} = \sqrt{26}$.

b. $2\mathbf{u} - 3\mathbf{v} = 2\langle -1, 2 \rangle - 3\langle 2, 3 \rangle = \langle -2, 4 \rangle - \langle 6, 9 \rangle = \langle -8, -5 \rangle$

c. The vectors $\frac{1}{2}\mathbf{u} = \frac{1}{2}\langle -1, 2 \rangle = \langle -\frac{1}{2}, 1 \rangle$ and $-\frac{1}{2}\mathbf{u} = -\frac{1}{2}\langle -1, 2 \rangle = \langle \frac{1}{2}, -1 \rangle$ have half the length of $\mathbf{u}$ and are parallel to $\mathbf{u}$.

Related Exercises 28–41 ◄

Unit Vectors

A **unit vector** is any vector with length 1. Two useful unit vectors are the **coordinate unit vectors** $\mathbf{i} = \langle 1, 0 \rangle$ and $\mathbf{j} = \langle 0, 1 \rangle$ (Figure 11.61). These vectors are directed along the coordinate axes and allow us to express all vectors in an alternative form. For example, by the Triangle Rule (Figure 11.62a),

$$\langle 3, 4 \rangle = 3\langle 1, 0 \rangle + 4\langle 0, 1 \rangle = 3\mathbf{i} + 4\mathbf{j}.$$

In general, the vector $\mathbf{v} = \langle v_1, v_2 \rangle$ (Figure 11.62b) is also written

$$\mathbf{v} = v_1 \langle 1, 0 \rangle + v_2 \langle 0, 1 \rangle = v_1 \mathbf{i} + v_2 \mathbf{j}.$$

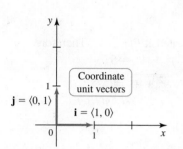

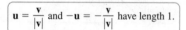
$\mathbf{j} = \langle 0, 1 \rangle$

$\mathbf{i} = \langle 1, 0 \rangle$

FIGURE 11.61

> Coordinate unit vectors are also called **standard basis vectors**.

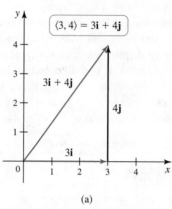

$\langle 3, 4 \rangle = 3\mathbf{i} + 4\mathbf{j}$

$3\mathbf{i} + 4\mathbf{j}$

$3\mathbf{i}$ $4\mathbf{j}$

(a)

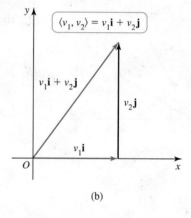

$\langle v_1, v_2 \rangle = v_1\mathbf{i} + v_2\mathbf{j}$

$v_1\mathbf{i} + v_2\mathbf{j}$

$v_2\mathbf{j}$

$v_1\mathbf{i}$

(b)

FIGURE 11.62

Given a nonzero vector $\mathbf{v}$, we sometimes need to construct a new vector parallel to $\mathbf{v}$ of a specified length. Dividing $\mathbf{v}$ by its length, we obtain the vector $\mathbf{u} = \dfrac{\mathbf{v}}{|\mathbf{v}|}$. Because $\mathbf{u}$ is a positive scalar multiple of $\mathbf{v}$, it follows that $\mathbf{u}$ has the same direction as $\mathbf{v}$. Furthermore, $\mathbf{u}$ is a unit vector because $|\mathbf{u}| = \dfrac{|\mathbf{v}|}{|\mathbf{v}|} = 1$. The vector $-\mathbf{u} = -\dfrac{\mathbf{v}}{|\mathbf{v}|}$ is also a unit vector (Figure 11.63). Therefore, $\pm\dfrac{\mathbf{v}}{|\mathbf{v}|}$ are unit vectors parallel to $\mathbf{v}$ that point in opposite directions.

To construct a vector that points in the direction of $\mathbf{v}$ and has a specified length $c > 0$, we form the vector $\dfrac{c\mathbf{v}}{|\mathbf{v}|}$. It is a positive scalar multiple of $\mathbf{v}$, so it points in the direction of $\mathbf{v}$, and its length is $\left|\dfrac{c\mathbf{v}}{|\mathbf{v}|}\right| = |c|\dfrac{|\mathbf{v}|}{|\mathbf{v}|} = c$. The vector $-\dfrac{c\mathbf{v}}{|\mathbf{v}|}$ points in the opposite direction and also has length c.

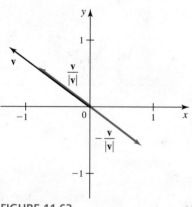

$\mathbf{u} = \dfrac{\mathbf{v}}{|\mathbf{v}|}$ and $-\mathbf{u} = -\dfrac{\mathbf{v}}{|\mathbf{v}|}$ have length 1.

$\mathbf{v}$

$\dfrac{\mathbf{v}}{|\mathbf{v}|}$

$-\dfrac{\mathbf{v}}{|\mathbf{v}|}$

FIGURE 11.63

QUICK CHECK 5 Find vectors of length 10 parallel to the unit vector $\mathbf{u} = \left\langle \dfrac{3}{5}, \dfrac{4}{5} \right\rangle$. ◄

EXAMPLE 5 **Magnitude and unit vectors** Consider the points $P(1, -2)$ and $Q(6, 10)$.

a. Find $\overrightarrow{PQ}$ and two unit vectors parallel to $\overrightarrow{PQ}$.

b. Find two vectors of length 2 parallel to $\overrightarrow{PQ}$.

SOLUTION

a. $\overrightarrow{PQ} = \langle 6 - 1, 10 - (-2) \rangle = \langle 5, 12 \rangle$, or $5\mathbf{i} + 12\mathbf{j}$. Because $|\overrightarrow{PQ}| = \sqrt{5^2 + 12^2} = \sqrt{169} = 13$, a unit vector parallel to $\overrightarrow{PQ}$ is

$$\frac{\overrightarrow{PQ}}{|\overrightarrow{PQ}|} = \frac{\langle 5, 12 \rangle}{13} = \left\langle \frac{5}{13}, \frac{12}{13} \right\rangle = \frac{5}{13}\mathbf{i} + \frac{12}{13}\mathbf{j}.$$

The unit vector parallel to $\overrightarrow{PQ}$ in the opposite direction is $\left\langle -\frac{5}{13}, -\frac{12}{13} \right\rangle$.

b. To obtain two vectors of length 2 that are parallel to $\overrightarrow{PQ}$, we multiply the unit vector $\frac{5}{13}\mathbf{i} + \frac{12}{13}\mathbf{j}$ by ± 2:

$$2\left(\frac{5}{13}\mathbf{i} + \frac{12}{13}\mathbf{j}\right) = \frac{10}{13}\mathbf{i} + \frac{24}{13}\mathbf{j} \quad \text{and} \quad -2\left(\frac{5}{13}\mathbf{i} + \frac{12}{13}\mathbf{j}\right) = -\frac{10}{13}\mathbf{i} - \frac{24}{13}\mathbf{j}.$$

Related Exercises 42–47 ◄

QUICK CHECK 6 Verify that the vector $\left\langle \frac{5}{13}, \frac{12}{13} \right\rangle$ has length 1. ◄

Properties of Vector Operations

> The Parallelogram Rule illustrates the commutative property $\mathbf{u} + \mathbf{v} = \mathbf{v} + \mathbf{u}$.

When we stand back and look at vector operations, ten general properties emerge. For example, the first property says that vector addition is commutative, which means $\mathbf{u} + \mathbf{v} = \mathbf{v} + \mathbf{u}$. This property is proved by letting $\mathbf{u} = \langle u_1, u_2 \rangle$ and $\mathbf{v} = \langle v_1, v_2 \rangle$. By the commutative property of addition for real numbers,

$$\mathbf{u} + \mathbf{v} = \langle u_1 + v_1, u_2 + v_2 \rangle = \langle v_1 + u_1, v_2 + u_2 \rangle = \mathbf{v} + \mathbf{u}.$$

The proofs of other properties are outlined in Exercises 82–85.

SUMMARY **Properties of Vector Operations**

Suppose $\mathbf{u}$, $\mathbf{v}$, and $\mathbf{w}$ are vectors and a and c are scalars. Then the following properties hold.

1. $\mathbf{u} + \mathbf{v} = \mathbf{v} + \mathbf{u}$	Commutative property of addition
2. $(\mathbf{u} + \mathbf{v}) + \mathbf{w} = \mathbf{u} + (\mathbf{v} + \mathbf{w})$	Associative property of addition
3. $\mathbf{v} + \mathbf{0} = \mathbf{v}$	Additive identity
4. $\mathbf{v} + (-\mathbf{v}) = \mathbf{0}$	Additive inverse
5. $c(\mathbf{u} + \mathbf{v}) = c\mathbf{u} + c\mathbf{v}$	Distributive property 1
6. $(a + c)\mathbf{v} = a\mathbf{v} + c\mathbf{v}$	Distributive property 2
7. $0\mathbf{v} = \mathbf{0}$	Multiplication by zero scalar
8. $c\mathbf{0} = \mathbf{0}$	Multiplication by zero vector
9. $1\mathbf{v} = \mathbf{v}$	Multiplicative identity
10. $a(c\mathbf{v}) = (ac)\mathbf{v}$	Associative property of scalar multiplication

These properties allow us to solve vector equations. For example, to solve the equation $\mathbf{u} + \mathbf{v} = \mathbf{w}$ for $\mathbf{u}$, we proceed as follows:

$$(\mathbf{u} + \mathbf{v}) + (-\mathbf{v}) = \mathbf{w} + (-\mathbf{v}) \quad \text{Add } -\mathbf{v} \text{ to both sides.}$$

$$\mathbf{u} + \underbrace{(\mathbf{v} + (-\mathbf{v}))}_{0} = \mathbf{w} + (-\mathbf{v}) \quad \text{Property 2}$$

$$\mathbf{u} + \mathbf{0} = \mathbf{w} - \mathbf{v} \quad \text{Property 4}$$

$$\mathbf{u} = \mathbf{w} - \mathbf{v}. \quad \text{Property 3}$$

> **QUICK CHECK 7** Solve $3\mathbf{u} + 4\mathbf{v} = 12\mathbf{w}$ for $\mathbf{u}$. ◄

Applications of Vectors

Vectors have countless practical applications, particularly in the physical sciences and engineering. These applications are explored throughout the remainder of the book. For now, we present two common uses of vectors: to describe velocities and forces.

Velocity Vectors   Consider a motorboat crossing a river whose current is everywhere represented by the constant vector $\mathbf{w}$ (Figure 11.64); this means that $|\mathbf{w}|$ is the speed of the moving water and $\mathbf{w}$ points in the direction of the moving water. Assume that the vector $\mathbf{v}_w$ gives the direction and speed of the boat relative to the water. The combined effect of $\mathbf{w}$ and $\mathbf{v}_w$ is the sum $\mathbf{v}_g = \mathbf{v}_w + \mathbf{w}$, which gives the speed and direction of the boat that would be observed by someone on the shore (or on the ground).

> ► *Speed of the boat relative to the water* means the speed the boat would have in still water (or relative to someone traveling with the current).

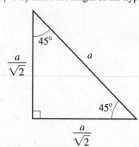

FIGURE 11.64

EXAMPLE 6   Speed of a boat in a current Assume the water in a river moves southwest (45° west of south) at 4 mi/hr. If a motorboat is traveling due east at 15 mi/hr relative to the shore, determine the speed of the boat and its heading relative to the moving water (Figure 11.64).

SOLUTION To solve this problem, the vectors are placed in a coordinate system (Figure 11.65). Because the boat is moving east at 15 mi/hr, the velocity relative to the shore is $\mathbf{v}_g = \langle 15, 0 \rangle$. To obtain the components of $\mathbf{w} = \langle w_x, w_y \rangle$, observe that $|\mathbf{w}| = 4$ and the lengths of the sides of the 45–45–90 triangle in Figure 11.65 are

$$|w_x| = |w_y| = |\mathbf{w}| \cos 45° = \frac{4}{\sqrt{2}} = 2\sqrt{2}.$$

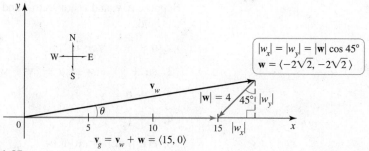

FIGURE 11.65

> ► Recall that the lengths of the legs of a 45–45–90 triangle are equal and are $(1/\sqrt{2})$ times the length of the hypotenuse.

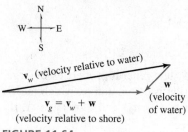

Given the orientation of $\mathbf{w}$ (southwest), $\mathbf{w} = \langle -2\sqrt{2}, -2\sqrt{2} \rangle$. Because $\mathbf{v}_g = \mathbf{v}_w + \mathbf{w}$ (Figure 11.65),

$$\mathbf{v}_w = \mathbf{v}_g - \mathbf{w} = \langle 15, 0 \rangle - \langle -2\sqrt{2}, -2\sqrt{2} \rangle$$
$$= \langle 15 + 2\sqrt{2}, 2\sqrt{2} \rangle.$$

The magnitude of $\mathbf{v}_w$ is

$$|\mathbf{v}_w| = \sqrt{(15 + 2\sqrt{2})^2 + (2\sqrt{2})^2} \approx 18.$$

Therefore, the speed of the boat relative to the water is approximately 18 mi/hr.

The heading of the boat is given by the angle θ between $\mathbf{v}_w$ and the positive x-axis. The x-component of $\mathbf{v}_w$ is $15 + 2\sqrt{2}$ and the y-component is $2\sqrt{2}$. Therefore,

$$\theta = \tan^{-1}\left(\frac{2\sqrt{2}}{15 + 2\sqrt{2}}\right) \approx 9°.$$

The heading of the boat is approximately 9° north of east, and its speed relative to the water is approximately 18 mi/hr.

Related Exercises 48–53 ◄

> The magnitude of $\mathbf{F}$ is typically measured in pounds (lb) or newtons (N), where $1\,\mathrm{N} = 1\,\mathrm{kg}\text{-}\mathrm{m}/\mathrm{s}^2$.

> The vector $\langle \cos\theta, \sin\theta \rangle$ is a unit vector. Therefore, any position vector $\mathbf{v}$ may be written $\mathbf{v} = \langle |\mathbf{v}|\cos\theta, |\mathbf{v}|\sin\theta \rangle$, where θ is the angle that $\mathbf{v}$ makes with the positive x-axis.

Force Vectors Suppose a child pulls on the handle of a wagon at an angle of θ with the horizontal (Figure 11.66a). The vector $\mathbf{F}$ represents the force exerted on the wagon; it has a magnitude $|\mathbf{F}|$ and a direction given by θ. We denote the horizontal and vertical components of $\mathbf{F}$ by F_x and F_y, respectively. Then, $F_x = |\mathbf{F}|\cos\theta$, $F_y = |\mathbf{F}|\sin\theta$, and the force vector is $\mathbf{F} = \langle |\mathbf{F}|\cos\theta, |\mathbf{F}|\sin\theta \rangle$ (Figure 11.66b).

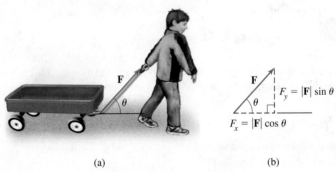

(a)   (b)

FIGURE 11.66

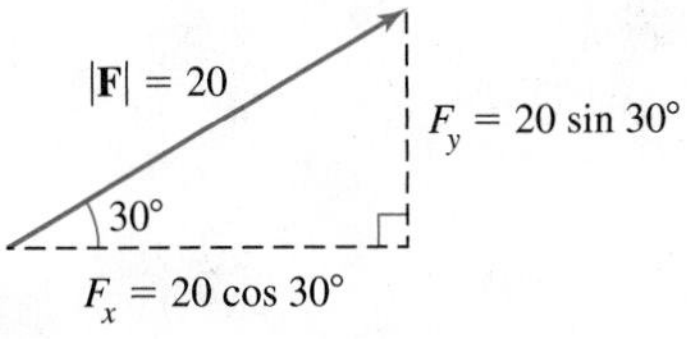

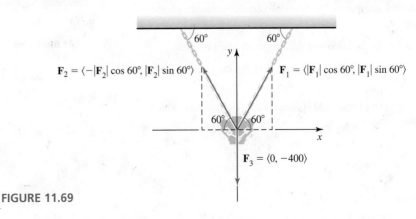

FIGURE 11.67

EXAMPLE 7 **Finding force vectors** A child pulls a wagon (Figure 11.66) with a force of $|\mathbf{F}| = 20$ lb at an angle of $\theta = 30°$ to the horizontal. Find the force vector $\mathbf{F}$.

SOLUTION The force vector (Figure 11.67) is

$$\mathbf{F} = \langle |\mathbf{F}|\cos\theta, |\mathbf{F}|\sin\theta \rangle = \langle 20\cos 30°, 20\sin 30° \rangle = \langle 10\sqrt{3}, 10 \rangle.$$

Related Exercises 54–58 ◄

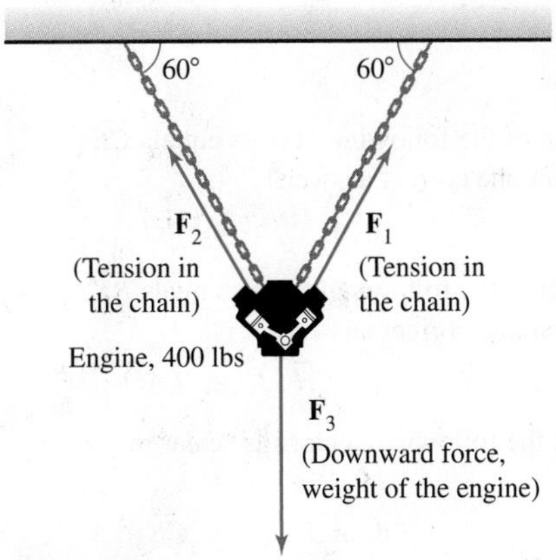

EXAMPLE 8 **Balancing forces** A 400-lb engine is suspended from two chains that form 60° angles with a horizontal ceiling (Figure 11.68). How much weight does each chain support?

SOLUTION Let $\mathbf{F}_1$ and $\mathbf{F}_2$ denote the forces exerted by the chains on the engine and let $\mathbf{F}_3$ be the downward force due to the weight of the engine (Figure 11.68). Placing the vectors in a standard coordinate system (Figure 11.69), we find that $\mathbf{F}_1 = \langle |\mathbf{F}_1|\cos 60°, |\mathbf{F}_1|\sin 60° \rangle$, $\mathbf{F}_2 = \langle -|\mathbf{F}_2|\cos 60°, |\mathbf{F}_2|\sin 60° \rangle$, and $\mathbf{F}_3 = \langle 0, -400 \rangle$.

FIGURE 11.68

> The components of $\mathbf{F}_2$ in Example 8 can also be computed using an angle of 120°. That is,
> $$\mathbf{F}_2 = \langle |\mathbf{F}_2|\cos 120°, |\mathbf{F}_2|\sin 120° \rangle.$$

FIGURE 11.69

If the engine is in equilibrium (so the chains and engine are stationary), the sum of the forces is zero; that is, $\mathbf{F}_1 + \mathbf{F}_2 + \mathbf{F}_3 = \mathbf{0}$ or $\mathbf{F}_1 + \mathbf{F}_2 = -\mathbf{F}_3$. Therefore,

$$\langle\, |\mathbf{F}_1|\cos 60° - |\mathbf{F}_2|\cos 60°, |\mathbf{F}_1|\sin 60° + |\mathbf{F}_2|\sin 60° \,\rangle = \langle 0, 400 \rangle.$$

Equating corresponding components, we obtain two equations to be solved for $|\mathbf{F}_1|$ and $|\mathbf{F}_2|$:

$$|\mathbf{F}_1|\cos 60° - |\mathbf{F}_2|\cos 60° = 0 \text{ and}$$
$$|\mathbf{F}_1|\sin 60° + |\mathbf{F}_2|\sin 60° = 400.$$

Factoring the first equation, we find that $(|\mathbf{F}_1| - |\mathbf{F}_2|)\cos 60° = 0$, which implies that $|\mathbf{F}_1| = |\mathbf{F}_2|$. Replacing $|\mathbf{F}_2|$ with $|\mathbf{F}_1|$ in the second equation gives $2|\mathbf{F}_1|\sin 60° = 400$. Noting that $\sin 60° = \sqrt{3}/2$ and solving for $|\mathbf{F}_1|$, we find that $|\mathbf{F}_1| = 400/\sqrt{3} \approx 231$. Each chain must be able to support a weight of approximately 231 lb.

Related Exercises 54–58 ◀

SECTION 11.5 EXERCISES

Review Questions

1. Interpret the following statement: Points have a location, but no size or direction; nonzero vectors have a size and direction, but no location.

2. What is a position vector?

3. Draw x- and y-axes on a page and mark two points P and Q. Then draw $\vec{PQ}$ and $\vec{QP}$.

4. On the diagram of Exercise 3, draw the position vector that is equal to $\vec{PQ}$.

5. Given a position vector $\mathbf{v}$, why are there infinitely many vectors equal to $\mathbf{v}$?

6. Explain how to add two vectors geometrically.

7. Explain how to find a scalar multiple of a vector geometrically.

8. Given two points P and Q, how are the components of $\vec{PQ}$ determined?

9. If $\mathbf{u} = \langle u_1, u_2 \rangle$ and $\mathbf{v} = \langle v_1, v_2 \rangle$, how do you find $\mathbf{u} + \mathbf{v}$?

10. If $\mathbf{v} = \langle v_1, v_2 \rangle$ and c is a scalar, how do you find $c\mathbf{v}$?

11. How do you compute the magnitude of $\mathbf{v} = \langle v_1, v_2 \rangle$?

12. Express the vector $\mathbf{v} = \langle v_1, v_2 \rangle$ in terms of the unit vectors $\mathbf{i}$ and $\mathbf{j}$.

13. How do you compute $|\vec{PQ}|$ from the coordinates of the points P and Q?

14. Explain how to find two unit vectors parallel to a vector $\mathbf{v}$.

15. How do you find a vector of length 10 in the direction of $\mathbf{v} = \langle 3, -2 \rangle$?

16. If a force of magnitude 100 is directed 45° south of east, what are its components?

Basic Skills

17–22. Vector operations *Refer to the figure and carry out the following vector operations.*

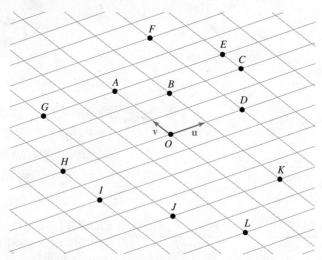

17. **Scalar multiples** Which of the following vectors equals $\vec{CE}$? (There may be more than one correct answer.)

   a. $\mathbf{v}$ b. $\frac{1}{2}\vec{HI}$ c. $\frac{1}{3}\vec{OA}$ d. $\mathbf{u}$ e. $\frac{1}{2}\vec{IH}$

18. **Scalar multiples** Which of the following vectors equals $\vec{BK}$? (There may be more than one correct answer.)

   a. $6\mathbf{v}$ b. $-6\mathbf{v}$ c. $3\vec{HI}$ d. $3\vec{IH}$ e. $2\vec{AO}$

19. **Scalar multiples** Write the following vectors as scalar multiples of $\mathbf{u}$ or $\mathbf{v}$.

   a. $\vec{OA}$ b. $\vec{OD}$ c. $\vec{OH}$ d. $\vec{AG}$ e. $\vec{CE}$

20. **Scalar multiples** Write the following vectors as scalar multiples of $\mathbf{u}$ or $\mathbf{v}$.

   a. $\vec{IH}$ b. $\vec{HI}$ c. $\vec{JK}$ d. $\vec{FD}$ e. $\vec{EA}$

21. Vector addition Write the following vectors as sums of scalar multiples of **u** and **v**.

a. $\overrightarrow{OE}$ b. $\overrightarrow{OB}$ c. $\overrightarrow{OF}$ d. $\overrightarrow{OG}$ e. $\overrightarrow{OC}$
f. $\overrightarrow{OI}$ g. $\overrightarrow{OJ}$ h. $\overrightarrow{OK}$ i. $\overrightarrow{OL}$

22. Vector addition Write the following vectors as sums of scalar multiples of **u** and **v**.

a. $\overrightarrow{BF}$ b. $\overrightarrow{DE}$ c. $\overrightarrow{AF}$ d. $\overrightarrow{AD}$ e. $\overrightarrow{CD}$
f. $\overrightarrow{JD}$ g. $\overrightarrow{JI}$ h. $\overrightarrow{DB}$ i. $\overrightarrow{IL}$

23. Components and magnitudes Define the points $O(0, 0)$, $P(3, 2)$, $Q(4, 2)$, and $R(-6, -1)$. For each vector, do the following.

(i) Sketch the vector in an *xy*-coordinate system.
(ii) Compute the magnitude of the vector.

a. $\overrightarrow{OP}$ b. $\overrightarrow{QP}$ c. $\overrightarrow{RQ}$

24–27. Components and equality *Define the points* $P(-3, -1)$ $Q(-1, 2)$, $R(1, 2)$, $S(3, 5)$, $T(4, 2)$, *and* $U(6, 4)$.

24. Sketch $\overrightarrow{PU}$, $\overrightarrow{TR}$, and $\overrightarrow{SQ}$ and the corresponding position vectors.

25. Sketch $\overrightarrow{QU}$, $\overrightarrow{PT}$, and $\overrightarrow{RS}$ and the corresponding position vectors.

26. Find the equal vectors among $\overrightarrow{PQ}$, $\overrightarrow{RS}$, and $\overrightarrow{TU}$.

27. Which of the vectors $\overrightarrow{QT}$ or $\overrightarrow{SU}$ is equal to $\langle 5, 0 \rangle$?

28–33. Vector operations *Let* $\mathbf{u} = \langle 4, -2 \rangle$, $\mathbf{v} = \langle -4, 6 \rangle$ *and* $\mathbf{w} = \langle 0, 8 \rangle$. *Express the following vectors in the form* $\langle a, b \rangle$.

28. $\mathbf{u} + \mathbf{v}$ **29.** $\mathbf{w} - \mathbf{u}$ **30.** $2\mathbf{u} + 3\mathbf{v}$

31. $\mathbf{w} - 3\mathbf{v}$ **32.** $10\mathbf{u} - 3\mathbf{v} + \mathbf{w}$ **33.** $8\mathbf{w} + \mathbf{v} - 6\mathbf{u}$

34–41. Vector operations *Let* $\mathbf{u} = \langle 3, -4 \rangle$, $\mathbf{v} = \langle 1, 1 \rangle$, *and* $\mathbf{w} = \langle -1, 0 \rangle$. *Carry out the following computations.*

34. Find $|\mathbf{u} + \mathbf{v}|$.   **35.** Find $|-2\mathbf{v}|$.

36. Find $|\mathbf{u} + \mathbf{v} + \mathbf{w}|$.   **37.** Find $|2\mathbf{u} + 3\mathbf{v} - 4\mathbf{w}|$.

38. Find two vectors parallel to **u** with four times the magnitude of **u**.

39. Find two vectors parallel to **v** with three times the magnitude of **v**.

40. Which has the greater magnitude, $2\mathbf{u}$ or $7\mathbf{v}$?

41. Which has the greater magnitude, $\mathbf{u} - \mathbf{v}$ or $\mathbf{w} - \mathbf{u}$?

42–47. Unit vectors *Define the points* $P(-4, 1)$, $Q(3, -4)$, *and* $R(2, 6)$. *Carry out the following calculations.*

42. Express $\overrightarrow{PQ}$ in the form $a\mathbf{i} + b\mathbf{j}$.

43. Express $\overrightarrow{QR}$ in the form $a\mathbf{i} + b\mathbf{j}$.

44. Find the unit vector with the same direction as $\overrightarrow{QR}$.

45. Find two unit vectors parallel to $\overrightarrow{PR}$.

46. Find two vectors parallel to $\overrightarrow{RP}$ with length 4.

47. Find two vectors parallel to $\overrightarrow{QP}$ with length 4.

48. A boat in a current The water in a river moves south at 10 mi/hr. If a motorboat is traveling due east at a speed of 20 mi/hr relative

to the shore, determine the speed and direction of the boat relative to the moving water.

49. Another boat in a current The water in a river moves south at 5 km/hr. If a motorboat is traveling due east at a speed of 40 km/hr relative to the water, determine the speed of the boat relative to the shore.

50. Parachute in the wind In still air, a parachute with a payload falls vertically at a terminal speed of 4 m/s. Find the direction and magnitude of its terminal velocity relative to the ground if it falls in a steady wind blowing horizontally from west to east at 10 m/s.

51. Airplane in a wind An airplane flies horizontally from east to west at 320 mi/hr relative to the air. If it flies in a steady 40 mi/hr wind that blows horizontally toward the southwest (45° south of west), find the speed and direction of the airplane relative to the ground.

52. Canoe in a current A woman in a canoe paddles due west at 4 mi/hr relative to the water in a current that flows northwest at 2 mi/hr. Find the speed and direction of the canoe relative to the shore.

53. Boat in a wind A sailboat floats in a current that flows due east at 1 m/s. Due to a wind, the boat's actual speed relative to the shore is $\sqrt{3}$ m/s in a direction 30° north of east. Find the speed and direction of the wind.

54. Towing a boat A boat is towed with a force of 150 lb with a rope that makes an angle of 30° to the horizontal. Find the horizontal and vertical components of the force.

55. Pulling a suitcase Suppose you pull a suitcase with a strap that makes a 60° angle with the horizontal. The magnitude of the force you exert on the suitcase is 40 lb.

a. Find the horizontal and vertical components of the force.
b. Is the horizontal component of the force greater if the angle of the strap is 45° instead of 60°?
c. Is the vertical component of the force greater if the angle of the strap is 45° instead of 60°?

56. Which is greater? Which has a greater horizontal component, a 100-N force directed at an angle of 60° above the horizontal or a 60-N force directed at an angle of 30° above the horizontal?

57. Suspended load If a 500-lb load is suspended by two chains (see figure), what is the magnitude of the force each chain must be able to support?

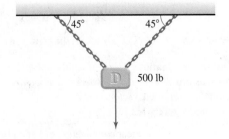

58. Net force Three forces are applied to an object, as shown in the figure. Find the magnitude and direction of the sum of the forces.

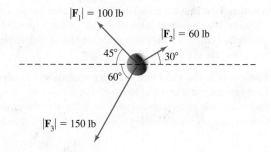

Further Explorations

59. Explain why or why not Determine whether the following statements are true and give an explanation or counterexample.

   a. José travels from point A to point B in the plane by following vector $\mathbf{u}$, then vector $\mathbf{v}$, and then vector $\mathbf{w}$. If he starts at A and follows $\mathbf{w}$, then $\mathbf{v}$, and then $\mathbf{u}$, he still arrives at B.

   b. Maria travels from A to B in the plane by following the vector $\mathbf{u}$. By following $-\mathbf{u}$, she returns from B to A.

   c. The magnitude of $\mathbf{u} + \mathbf{v}$ is at least the magnitude of $\mathbf{u}$.

   d. The magnitude of $\mathbf{u} + \mathbf{v}$ is at least the magnitude of $\mathbf{u}$ plus the magnitude of $\mathbf{v}$.

   e. Parallel vectors have the same length.

   f. If $\overrightarrow{AB} = \overrightarrow{CD}$, then $A = C$ and $B = D$.

   g. If $\mathbf{u}$ and $\mathbf{v}$ are perpendicular, then $|\mathbf{u} + \mathbf{v}| = |\mathbf{u}| + |\mathbf{v}|$.

   h. If $\mathbf{u}$ and $\mathbf{v}$ are parallel and have the same direction, then $|\mathbf{u} + \mathbf{v}| = |\mathbf{u}| + |\mathbf{v}|$.

60. Finding vectors from two points Given the points $A(-2, 0)$, $B(6, 16)$, $C(1, 4)$, $D(5, 4)$, $E(\sqrt{2}, \sqrt{2})$, and $F(3\sqrt{2}, -4\sqrt{2})$, find the position vector equal to the following vectors.

   a. $\overrightarrow{AB}$ **b.** $\overrightarrow{AC}$ **c.** $\overrightarrow{EF}$ **d.** $\overrightarrow{CD}$

61. Unit vectors

   a. Find two unit vectors parallel to $\mathbf{v} = 6\mathbf{i} - 8\mathbf{j}$.

   b. Find b if $\mathbf{v} = \langle \frac{1}{3}, b \rangle$ is a unit vector.

   c. Find all values of a such that $\mathbf{w} = a\mathbf{i} - \dfrac{a}{3}\mathbf{j}$ is a unit vector.

62. Equal vectors For the points $A(3, 4)$, $B(6, 10)$, $C(a + 2, b + 5)$, and $D(b + 4, 2 - a)$, find the values of a and b such that $\overrightarrow{AB} = \overrightarrow{CD}$.

63–66. Vector equations *Use the properties of vectors to solve the following equations for the unknown vector* $\mathbf{x} = \langle a, b \rangle$. *Let* $\mathbf{u} = \langle 2, -3 \rangle$ *and* $\mathbf{v} = \langle -4, 1 \rangle$.

63. $10\mathbf{x} = \mathbf{u}$ **64.** $2\mathbf{x} + \mathbf{u} = \mathbf{v}$

65. $3\mathbf{x} - 4\mathbf{u} = \mathbf{v}$ **66.** $-4\mathbf{x} = \mathbf{u} - 8\mathbf{v}$

67–69. Linear combinations *A sum of scalar multiples of two or more vectors (such as* $c_1\mathbf{u} + c_2\mathbf{v} + c_3\mathbf{w}$, *where* c_i *are scalars) is called a* **linear combination** *of the vectors. Let* $\mathbf{i} = \langle 1, 0 \rangle$, $\mathbf{j} = \langle 0, 1 \rangle$, $\mathbf{u} = \langle 1, 1 \rangle$, *and* $\mathbf{v} = \langle -1, 1 \rangle$.

67. Express $\langle 4, -8 \rangle$ as a linear combination of $\mathbf{i}$ and $\mathbf{j}$ (that is, find scalars c_1 and c_2 such that $\langle 4, -8 \rangle = c_1\mathbf{i} + c_2\mathbf{j}$).

68. Express $\langle 4, -8 \rangle$ as a linear combination of $\mathbf{u}$ and $\mathbf{v}$.

69. For arbitrary real numbers a and b, express $\langle a, b \rangle$ as a linear combination of $\mathbf{u}$ and $\mathbf{v}$.

70–71. Solving vector equations *Solve the following pairs of equations for the vectors* $\mathbf{u}$ *and* $\mathbf{v}$. *Assume* $\mathbf{i} = \langle 1, 0 \rangle$ *and* $\mathbf{j} = \langle 0, 1 \rangle$.

70. $2\mathbf{u} = \mathbf{i}, \mathbf{u} - 4\mathbf{v} = \mathbf{j}$

71. $2\mathbf{u} + 3\mathbf{v} = \mathbf{i}, \mathbf{u} - \mathbf{v} = \mathbf{j}$

72–75. Designer vectors *Find the following vectors.*

72. The vector that is 3 times $\langle 3, -5 \rangle$ plus -9 times $\langle 6, 0 \rangle$

73. The vector in the direction of $\langle 5, -12 \rangle$ with length 3

74. The vector in the direction opposite that of $\langle 6, -8 \rangle$ with length 10

75. The position vector for your final location if you start at the origin and walk along $\langle 4, -6 \rangle$ followed by $\langle 5, 9 \rangle$

Applications

76. Ant on a page An ant walks due east at a constant speed of 2 mi/hr on a sheet of paper that rests on a table. Suddenly the sheet of paper starts moving southeast at $\sqrt{2}$ mi/hr. Describe the motion of the ant relative to the table.

77. Clock vectors Consider the 12 vectors that have their tails at the center of a (circular) clock and their heads at the numbers on the edge of the clock.

   a. What is the sum of these 12 vectors?

   b. If the 12:00 vector is removed, what is the sum of the remaining 11 vectors?

   c. By removing one or more of these 12 clock vectors, explain how to make the sum of the remaining vectors as large as possible in magnitude.

   d. If the clock vectors originate at 12:00 and point to the other 11 numbers, what is the sum of the vectors?
      (*Source: Calculus,* by Gilbert Strang. Wellesley-Cambridge Press, 1991.)

78. Three-way tug-of-war Three people located at A, B, and C pull on ropes tied to a ring. Find the magnitude and direction of the force with which C must pull so that no one moves (the system is in equilibrium).

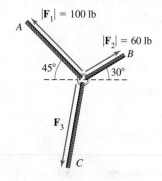

79. Net force Jack pulls east on a rope attached to a camel with a force of 40 lb. Jill pulls north on a rope attached to the same camel with a force of 30 lb. What is the magnitude and direction of the force on the camel? Assume the vectors lie in a horizontal plane.

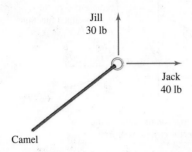

80. Mass on a plane A 100-kg object rests on an inclined plane at an angle of 30° to the floor. Find the components of the force perpendicular to and parallel to the plane. (The vertical component of the force exerted by an object of mass m is its weight, which is mg, where $g = 9.8 \text{ m/s}^2$ is the acceleration due to gravity.)

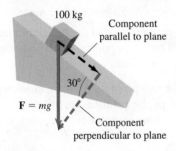

Additional Exercises

81–85. Vector properties *Prove the following vector properties using components. Then make a sketch to illustrate the property geometrically. Suppose* **u**, **v**, *and* **w** *are vectors in the xy-plane and a and c are scalars.*

81. $\mathbf{u} + \mathbf{v} = \mathbf{v} + \mathbf{u}$ Commutative property

82. $(\mathbf{u} + \mathbf{v}) + \mathbf{w} = \mathbf{u} + (\mathbf{v} + \mathbf{w})$ Associative property

83. $a(c\mathbf{v}) = (ac)\mathbf{v}$ Associative property

84. $a(\mathbf{u} + \mathbf{v}) = a\mathbf{u} + a\mathbf{v}$ Distributive property 1

85. $(a + c)\mathbf{v} = a\mathbf{v} + c\mathbf{v}$ Distributive property 2

86. Midpoint of a line segment Use vectors to show that the midpoint of the line segment joining $P(x_1, y_1)$ and $Q(x_2, y_2)$ is the point $\left(\dfrac{x_1 + x_2}{2}, \dfrac{y_1 + y_2}{2}\right)$. (*Hint:* Let O be the origin and

let M be the midpoint of PQ. Draw a picture and show that $\overrightarrow{OM} = \overrightarrow{OP} + \frac{1}{2}\overrightarrow{PQ} = \overrightarrow{OP} + \frac{1}{2}(\overrightarrow{OQ} - \overrightarrow{OP})$.)

87. Magnitude of scalar multiple Prove that $|c\mathbf{v}| = |c||\mathbf{v}|$, where c is a scalar and **v** is a vector.

88. Equality of vectors Assume $\overrightarrow{PQ}$ equals $\overrightarrow{RS}$. Does it follow that $\overrightarrow{PR}$ is equal to $\overrightarrow{QS}$? Explain your answer.

89. Linear independence A pair of nonzero vectors in the plane is *linearly dependent* if one vector is a scalar multiple of the other. Otherwise, the pair is *linearly independent*.

  a. Which pairs of the following vectors are linearly dependent and which are linearly independent: $\mathbf{u} = \langle 2, -3 \rangle$, $\mathbf{v} = \langle -12, 18 \rangle$, and $\mathbf{w} = \langle 4, 6 \rangle$?
  b. Geometrically, what does it mean for a pair of nonzero vectors in the plane to be linearly dependent? Linearly independent?
  c. Prove that if a pair of vectors **u** and **v** is linearly independent, then given any vector **w**, there are constants c_1 and c_2 such that $\mathbf{w} = c_1\mathbf{u} + c_2\mathbf{v}$.

90. Perpendicular vectors Show that two nonzero vectors $\mathbf{u} = \langle u_1, u_2 \rangle$ and $\mathbf{v} = \langle v_1, v_2 \rangle$ are perpendicular to each other if $u_1 v_1 + u_2 v_2 = 0$.

91. Parallel and perpendicular vectors Let $\mathbf{u} = \langle a, 5 \rangle$ and $\mathbf{v} = \langle 2, 6 \rangle$.

  a. Find the value of a such that **u** is parallel to **v**.
  b. Find the value of a such that **u** is perpendicular to **v**.

92. The Triangle Inequality Suppose **u** and **v** are vectors in the plane.

  a. Use the Triangle Rule for adding vectors to explain why $|\mathbf{u} + \mathbf{v}| \leq |\mathbf{u}| + |\mathbf{v}|$. This result is known as the *Triangle Inequality*.
  b. Under what conditions is $|\mathbf{u} + \mathbf{v}| = |\mathbf{u}| + |\mathbf{v}|$?

QUICK CHECK ANSWERS

1. The vector $-5\mathbf{v}$ is five times as long as **v** and points in the opposite direction.   **2.** $\mathbf{v}_a + \mathbf{w}$ points in a northeasterly direction.
3. Constructing $\mathbf{u} + \mathbf{v}$ and $\mathbf{v} + \mathbf{u}$ using the Triangle Rule produces vectors having the same direction and magnitude.
4. $\overrightarrow{PQ} = \langle -6, -2 \rangle$ **5.** $10\mathbf{u} = \langle 6, 8 \rangle$ and $-10\mathbf{u} = \langle -6, -8 \rangle$
6. $\left|\left\langle \dfrac{5}{13}, \dfrac{12}{13} \right\rangle\right| = \sqrt{\dfrac{25 + 144}{169}} = \sqrt{\dfrac{169}{169}} = 1$
7. $\mathbf{u} = -\frac{4}{3}\mathbf{v} + 4\mathbf{w}$ ◄

11.6 Calculus of Vector-Valued Functions

Imagine a projectile moving along a path in a plane; it could be an electron or a comet, a soccer ball or a rocket. If you take a snapshot of the object, its position is described by a static position vector $\mathbf{r} = \langle x, y \rangle$. However, if you want to describe the full trajectory of the object as it unfolds in time, you must represent the object's position with a *vector-valued function* such as $\mathbf{r}(t) = \langle x(t), y(t) \rangle$ whose components change in time (Figure 11.70). The goal of this section is to describe continuous motion by using vector-valued functions.

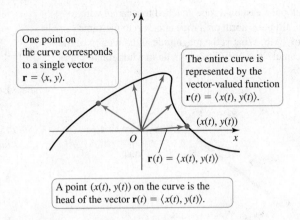

One point on the curve corresponds to a single vector $\mathbf{r} = \langle x, y \rangle$.

The entire curve is represented by the vector-valued function $\mathbf{r}(t) = \langle x(t), y(t) \rangle$.

$(x(t), y(t))$

$\mathbf{r}(t) = \langle x(t), y(t) \rangle$

A point $(x(t), y(t))$ on the curve is the head of the vector $\mathbf{r}(t) = \langle x(t), y(t) \rangle$.

FIGURE 11.70

Vector-Valued Functions

A function of the form $\mathbf{r}(t) = \langle x(t), y(t) \rangle$ may be viewed in two ways.

- It is a pair of parametric equations that describe a curve in the plane.
- It is also a **vector-valued function**, which means that the two dependent variables (x and y) are the components of $\mathbf{r}$, and each component varies with respect to a single independent variable t (that often represents time).

Here is the connection between these two perspectives: As t varies, a point $(x(t), y(t))$ on a parametric curve is also the head of the position vector $\mathbf{r}(t) = \langle x(t), y(t) \rangle$. It is useful to keep both of these interpretations in mind as you work with vector-valued functions.

Lines in the Plane

Two distinct points in the xy-plane determine a unique line. Alternatively, one point and a direction also determine a unique line. We use both these properties to derive parametric equations for lines in the plane. The result is an example of a vector-valued function in the xy-plane.

Let ℓ be the line passing through the point $P_0(x_0, y_0)$ parallel to the nonzero vector $\mathbf{v} = \langle a, b \rangle$, where P_0 and $\mathbf{v}$ are given. The fixed point P_0 is associated with the position vector $\mathbf{r}_0 = \overrightarrow{OP_0} = \langle x_0, y_0 \rangle$. We let $P(x, y)$ be a variable point on ℓ and let $\mathbf{r} = \overrightarrow{OP} = \langle x, y \rangle$ be the position vector associated with P (Figure 11.71). Because ℓ is parallel to $\mathbf{v}$, the vector $\overrightarrow{P_0P}$ is also parallel to $\mathbf{v}$; therefore, $\overrightarrow{P_0P} = t\mathbf{v}$, where t is a real number. By vector addition, we see that $\overrightarrow{OP} = \overrightarrow{OP_0} + \overrightarrow{P_0P}$, or $\overrightarrow{OP} = \overrightarrow{OP_0} + t\mathbf{v}$. It follows that

$$\underbrace{\langle x, y \rangle}_{\mathbf{r} \, = \, \overrightarrow{OP}} = \underbrace{\langle x_0, y_0 \rangle}_{\mathbf{r}_0 \, = \, \overrightarrow{OP_0}} + t\underbrace{\langle a, b \rangle}_{\mathbf{v}} \quad \text{or} \quad \mathbf{r} = \mathbf{r}_0 + t\mathbf{v}.$$

Equating the components, the line is described by the parametric equations (also derived in Section 11.1)

$$x = x_0 + at, \qquad y = y_0 + bt, \qquad \text{for } -\infty < t < \infty.$$

The parameter t determines the location of points on the line, where $t = 0$ corresponds to P_0. If t increases from 0, we move along the line in the direction of $\mathbf{v}$, and if t decreases from 0, we move along the line in the direction of $-\mathbf{v}$. As t varies over all real numbers ($-\infty < t < \infty$), the vector $\mathbf{r}$ sweeps out the entire line ℓ. If, instead of knowing the direction $\mathbf{v}$ of the line, we are

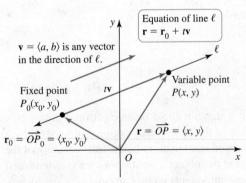

Equation of line ℓ
$\mathbf{r} = \mathbf{r}_0 + t\mathbf{v}$

$\mathbf{v} = \langle a, b \rangle$ is any vector in the direction of ℓ.

Fixed point $P_0(x_0, y_0)$

$t\mathbf{v}$

Variable point $P(x, y)$

$\mathbf{r}_0 = \overrightarrow{OP_0} = \langle x_0, y_0 \rangle$

$\mathbf{r} = \overrightarrow{OP} = \langle x, y \rangle$

FIGURE 11.71

given two points $P_0(x_0, y_0)$ and $P_1(x_1, y_1)$, then the direction of the line is $\mathbf{v} = \overrightarrow{P_0 P_1} = \langle x_1 - x_0, y_1 - y_0 \rangle$.

QUICK CHECK 1 Describe the line $\mathbf{r}(t) = t\mathbf{j}$, for $-\infty < t < \infty$. Describe the line $\mathbf{r}(t) = t(\mathbf{i} + \mathbf{j})$, for $-\infty < t < \infty$. ◀

> Although we often refer to *the* equation of a line, there are infinitely many equations for the same line. The direction vector is determined only up to a scalar multiple.

Equation of a Line

An **equation of the line** passing through the point $P_0(x_0, y_0)$ in the direction of the vector $\mathbf{v} = \langle a, b \rangle$ is $\mathbf{r} = \mathbf{r}_0 + t\mathbf{v}$, or

$$\langle x, y \rangle = \langle x_0, y_0 \rangle + t\langle a, b \rangle, \quad \text{for} \quad -\infty < t < \infty.$$

Equivalently, the parametric equations of the line are

$$x = x_0 + at, \quad y = y_0 + bt, \quad \text{for} \quad -\infty < t < \infty.$$

EXAMPLE 1 Equation of a line Find an equation of the line ℓ that passes through the point $P_0(1, 2)$ in the direction of $\mathbf{v} = \langle 5, -3 \rangle$.

SOLUTION We are given $\mathbf{r}_0 = \langle 1, 2 \rangle$. Therefore, an equation of the line is

$$\mathbf{r}(t) = \mathbf{r}_0 + t\mathbf{v} = \langle 1, 2 \rangle + t\langle 5, -3 \rangle = \langle 1 + 5t, 2 - 3t \rangle,$$

for $-\infty < t < \infty$ (Figure 11.72). The corresponding parametric equations are

$$x = 1 + 5t, \quad y = 2 - 3t, \quad \text{for} \quad -\infty < t < \infty.$$

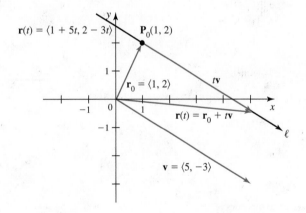

FIGURE 11.72

Related Exercises 13–24 ◀

EXAMPLE 2 Equation of a line Let ℓ be the line that passes through the points $P_0(-3, 5)$ and $P_1(4, 2)$. Find an equation of ℓ.

SOLUTION The direction of the line is

$$\mathbf{v} = \overrightarrow{P_0 P_1} = \langle 4 - (-3), 2 - 5 \rangle = \langle 7, -3 \rangle.$$

Therefore, with $\mathbf{r}_0 = \langle -3, 5 \rangle$, the equation of ℓ is

$$\begin{aligned} \mathbf{r}(t) &= \mathbf{r}_0 + t\mathbf{v} \\ &= \langle -3, 5 \rangle + t\langle 7, -3 \rangle \\ &= \langle -3 + 7t, 5 - 3t \rangle. \end{aligned}$$

Related Exercises 13–24 ◀

QUICK CHECK 2 In the equation of the line

$$\mathbf{r}(t) = \langle x_0, y_0 \rangle + t \langle x_1 - x_0, y_1 - y_0 \rangle,$$

what value of t corresponds to the point $P_0(x_0, y_0)$? What value of t corresponds to the point $P_1(x_1, y_1)$? ◄

EXAMPLE 3 Equation of a line segment Find an equation of the line segment from $P_0(-1, 3)$ to $P_1(2, -1)$.

SOLUTION The same ideas used to find an equation of an entire line work here. We just restrict the values of the parameter t so that only the given line segment is generated. The direction of the line segment is

$$\mathbf{v} = \overrightarrow{P_0P_1} = \langle 2 - (-1), -1 - 3 \rangle = \langle 3, -4 \rangle.$$

Letting $\mathbf{r}_0 = \langle -1, 3 \rangle$, the equation of the line through P_0 and P_1 is

$$\mathbf{r}(t) = \mathbf{r}_0 + t\mathbf{v} = \langle -1 + 3t, 3 - 4t \rangle.$$

Notice that if $t = 0$, then $\mathbf{r}(0) = \langle -1, 3 \rangle$, which is a vector with endpoint P_0. If $t = 1$, then $\mathbf{r}(1) = \langle 2, -1 \rangle$, which is a vector with endpoint P_1. Letting t vary from 0 to 1 generates the line segment from P_0 to P_1 (Figure 11.73). Therefore, an equation of the line segment is

$$\mathbf{r}(t) = \langle -1 + 3t, 3 - 4t \rangle, \text{ for } 0 \le t \le 1.$$

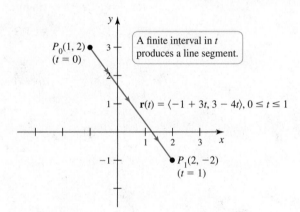

FIGURE 11.73

Related Exercises 25–28 ◄

▷ When x and y are linear functions of t, the resulting curve is a line or line segment.

QUICK CHECK 3 Find two other vector equations that describe the line segment in Example 3. ◄

Curves in the Plane

We now explore general vector-valued functions of the form

$$\mathbf{r}(t) = \langle x(t), y(t) \rangle = x(t)\mathbf{i} + y(t)\mathbf{j},$$

where x and y are defined on an interval $a \le t \le b$. The **domain** of $\mathbf{r}$ is the largest set of values of t on which both x and y are defined.

Figure 11.74 illustrates how a parameterized curve is generated by such a function. As the parameter t varies over the interval $a \le t \le b$, each value of t produces a position vector that corresponds to a point on the curve, starting at the initial vector $\mathbf{r}(a)$ and ending at the terminal vector $\mathbf{r}(b)$. The resulting parameterized curve can either have finite length or extend indefinitely. The curve may also

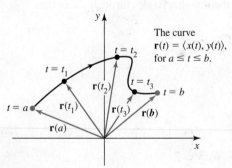

FIGURE 11.74

cross itself or close and retrace itself. The concept of the orientation of a curve, introduced in Section 11.1, also carries over to vector-valued functions: The positive orientation of $\mathbf{r}(t)$ is the direction in which its graph is generated as t increases.

EXAMPLE 4   A circle and spiral

a. Describe the curve defined by the function

$$\mathbf{r}(t) = \langle a \cos t, a \sin t \rangle, \quad \text{for } 0 \le t \le 2\pi \text{ and } a > 0.$$

b. Sketch the curve described by the function

$$\mathbf{r}(t) = \langle e^{-t/10} \cos t, e^{-t/10} \sin t \rangle, \quad \text{for } 0 \le t < \infty.$$

SOLUTION

a. Notice that the components of this equation are $x = a \cos t$, $y = a \sin t$, which are the parametric equations of the circle of radius a centered at the origin oriented in the counterclockwise direction.

b. From part (a), the graph of the circle $\mathbf{r}(t) = \langle a \cos t, a \sin t \rangle$ can be viewed as the path of a point orbiting the origin at a constant distance of a. By replacing a with $e^{-t/10}$, we obtain the function $\mathbf{r}(t) = \langle e^{-t/10} \cos t, e^{-t/10} \sin t \rangle$; it describes the path of a point orbiting the origin at a distance of $e^{-t/10}$, which decreases as t increases. For every increase in t of 2π units (one circuit about the origin), the distance from the curve to the origin decreases by a factor of $e^{-2\pi/10} \approx 0.533$. Therefore, this equation describes an inward counterclockwise spiral (Figure 11.75). Because the parameter $t \to \infty$, the spiral gets arbitrarily close to the origin.

Related Exercises 29–36 ◄

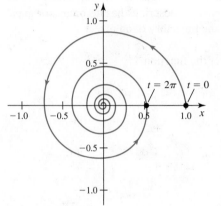

FIGURE 11.75

Limits and Continuity for Vector-Valued Functions

We have now presented vector-valued functions and established their relationship to parametric equations. Quite naturally, the next step is to investigate the calculus of vector-valued functions. The concepts of limits, derivatives, and integrals are direct extensions of what you have already learned.

The limit of a vector-valued function $\mathbf{r}(t) = x(t)\mathbf{i} + y(t)\mathbf{j}$ is defined much as it is for scalar-valued functions. If there is a vector $\mathbf{L}$ such that the scalar function $|\mathbf{r}(t) - \mathbf{L}|$ can be made arbitrarily small by taking t sufficiently close to a, then we write $\lim_{t \to a} \mathbf{r}(t) = \mathbf{L}$ and say the limit of $\mathbf{r}$ as t approaches a is $\mathbf{L}$. Therefore, we make the following definition.

DEFINITION Limit of a Vector-Valued Function

A vector-valued function $\mathbf{r}$ approaches the limit $\mathbf{L}$ as t approaches a, written $\lim_{t \to a} \mathbf{r}(t) = \mathbf{L}$, provided $\lim_{t \to a} |\mathbf{r}(t) - \mathbf{L}| = 0$.

This definition and a short calculation lead to a straightforward method for computing limits of the vector-valued function $\mathbf{r} = \langle x, y \rangle$. Suppose that

$$\lim_{t \to a} x(t) = L_1 \quad \text{and} \quad \lim_{t \to a} y(t) = L_2.$$

Then

$$\lim_{t \to a} \mathbf{r}(t) = \left\langle \lim_{t \to a} x(t), \lim_{t \to a} y(t) \right\rangle = \langle L_1, L_2 \rangle.$$

In other words, the limit of $\mathbf{r}$ is determined by computing the limits of its components.

The limits laws in Chapter 2 have analogs for vector-valued functions. For example, if $\lim\limits_{t\to a} \mathbf{r}(t)$ and $\lim\limits_{t\to a} \mathbf{s}(t)$ exist and c is a scalar, then

$$\lim_{t\to a} (\mathbf{r}(t) + \mathbf{s}(t)) = \lim_{t\to a} \mathbf{r}(t) + \lim_{t\to a} \mathbf{s}(t) \quad \text{and} \quad \lim_{t\to a} c\mathbf{r}(t) = c \lim_{t\to a} \mathbf{r}(t).$$

The idea of continuity also extends directly to vector-valued functions. A function $\mathbf{r}(t) = x(t)\mathbf{i} + y(t)\mathbf{j}$ is continuous at a provided $\lim\limits_{t\to a} \mathbf{r}(t) = \mathbf{r}(a)$. Specifically, if the component functions x and y are continuous at a, then $\mathbf{r}$ is also continuous at a and vice versa. The function $\mathbf{r}$ is continuous on an interval I if it is continuous for all t in I.

Continuity has the same intuitive meaning in this setting as it does for scalar-valued functions. If $\mathbf{r}$ is continuous on an interval, the curve it describes has no breaks or gaps, which is an important property when $\mathbf{r}$ describes the trajectory of an object.

EXAMPLE 5 Limits and continuity Consider the function

$$\mathbf{r}(t) = \left\langle 3e^{-t/2}, \frac{t}{t + 1} \right\rangle, \quad \text{for } -\infty < t < \infty.$$

a. Evaluate $\lim\limits_{t\to 2} \mathbf{r}(t)$.

b. Evaluate $\lim\limits_{t\to\infty} \mathbf{r}(t)$.

c. At what points is $\mathbf{r}$ continuous?

SOLUTION

a. We evaluate the limit of each component of $\mathbf{r}$:

$$\lim_{t\to 2} \mathbf{r}(t) = \lim_{t\to 2} \left\langle 3e^{-t/2}, \frac{t}{t + 1} \right\rangle = \left\langle \lim_{t\to 2} 3e^{-t/2}, \lim_{t\to 2} \frac{t}{t + 1} \right\rangle = \left\langle 3e^{-1}, \frac{2}{3} \right\rangle.$$

b. Again, we evaluate the limit component-wise:

$$\lim_{t\to\infty} \mathbf{r}(t) = \lim_{t\to\infty} \left\langle 3e^{-t/2}, \frac{t}{t + 1} \right\rangle = \left\langle \lim_{t\to\infty} 3e^{-t/2}, \lim_{t\to\infty} \frac{t}{t + 1} \right\rangle = \langle 0, 1 \rangle.$$

c. The x-component of $\mathbf{r}$ is continuous for all t. The y-component is continuous except at $t = -1$. Therefore, $\mathbf{r}$ is continuous for all t provided $t \neq -1$.

Related Exercises 37–42 ◄

The Derivative and Tangent Vector

Just as with ordinary functions of one variable, the idea of a limit allows us to define the derivative. Consider the function $\mathbf{r}(t) = x(t)\mathbf{i} + y(t)\mathbf{j}$, where x and y are differentiable functions on an interval $a < t < b$. The first task is to explain the meaning of the *derivative* of a vector-valued function and to show how to compute it. We begin with the definition of the derivative—now with a vector perspective:

$$\mathbf{r}'(t) = \lim_{\Delta t\to 0} \frac{\Delta \mathbf{r}}{\Delta t} = \lim_{\Delta t\to 0} \frac{\mathbf{r}(t + \Delta t) - \mathbf{r}(t)}{\Delta t}.$$

Substituting $\mathbf{r}(t) = \langle x(t), y(t) \rangle$ into this definition and working with individual components, a short calculation shows that

$$\mathbf{r}'(t) = \langle x'(t), y'(t) \rangle.$$

In other words, to differentiate a vector-valued function, we simply differentiate each of its components with respect to t. This means that all the familiar derivative rules can be used for vector-valued functions.

The geometry of this limit is important. The function $\mathbf{r}(t) = \langle x(t), y(t) \rangle$ describes a curve in the plane. Let P be a point on that curve associated with the position vector $\mathbf{r}(t)$ and let Q be a nearby point associated with the position vector $\mathbf{r}(t + \Delta t)$, where $\Delta t > 0$ is a small increment in t (Figure 11.76a). The difference $\Delta \mathbf{r} = \mathbf{r}(t + \Delta t) - \mathbf{r}(t)$ is the vector $\overrightarrow{PQ}$, where we assume $\Delta \mathbf{r} \neq 0$. Because Δt is a scalar, the direction of $\Delta \mathbf{r}/\Delta t$ is the same as the direction of $\overrightarrow{PQ}$.

As Δt approaches 0, Q approaches P and the vector $\Delta \mathbf{r}/\Delta t$ approaches a limiting vector that we denote $\mathbf{r}'(t)$ (Figure 11.76b). This new vector $\mathbf{r}'(t)$ has two important interpretations.

> An analogous argument can be given for the case $\Delta t < 0$, with the same result. Figure 11.76 illustrates the tangent vector $\mathbf{r}'(t)$ for $\Delta t > 0$.

> The condition $\mathbf{r}'(t) \neq \mathbf{0}$ ensures that the curve is smooth and has a tangent vector at every point.

- The vector $\mathbf{r}'$ points in the direction of the curve at each point of the curve. For this reason, $\mathbf{r}'$ is a *tangent vector* at each point (provided it is not the zero vector).

- The vector $\mathbf{r}'(t)$ is the derivative of $\mathbf{r}$ with respect to t; it gives the rate of change of the function $\mathbf{r}$ at each point of the curve. In fact, if $\mathbf{r}$ is the position vector of a moving object, then $\mathbf{r}'$ is the velocity vector of the object, which always points in the direction of motion, and $|\mathbf{r}'|$ is the speed of the object.

We summarize these observations in the following definition.

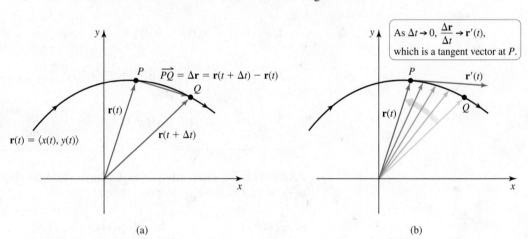

FIGURE 11.76

DEFINITION **Derivative and Tangent Vector**

Let $\mathbf{r}(t) = x(t)\mathbf{i} + y(t)\mathbf{j}$, where x and y are differentiable functions on (a, b). Then $\mathbf{r}$ has a **derivative** (or is **differentiable**) on (a, b) and

$$\mathbf{r}'(t) = x'(t)\mathbf{i} + y'(t)\mathbf{j}.$$

Provided $\mathbf{r}'(t) \neq \mathbf{0}$, $\mathbf{r}'(t)$ is a **tangent vector** (or velocity vector) at the point corresponding to $\mathbf{r}(t)$.

EXAMPLE 6 **Derivative of vector functions** Compute the derivative of the following functions.

a. $\mathbf{r}(t) = \langle t^3, 3t^2 \rangle$ **b.** $\mathbf{r}(t) = e^{-t}\mathbf{i} + 10\sqrt{t}\,\mathbf{j}$

SOLUTION

a. $\mathbf{r}'(t) = \langle 3t^2, 6t \rangle$; note that $\mathbf{r}$ is differentiable for all t.

b. $\mathbf{r}'(t) = -e^{-t}\mathbf{i} + \dfrac{5}{\sqrt{t}}\mathbf{j}$; the function $\mathbf{r}$ is differentiable for $t > 0$.

Related Exercises 43–56 ◄

> **QUICK CHECK 4** Let $\mathbf{r}(t) = \langle t, t \rangle$. Compute $\mathbf{r}'(t)$ and interpret the result. ◄

Derivative Rules   The familiar rules for derivatives carry over directly to vector-valued functions. These rules are generally proved by working on the individual components of the vector function.

THEOREM 11.3   Derivative Rules

Let $\mathbf{u}$ and $\mathbf{v}$ be differentiable vector-valued functions and let f be a differentiable scalar-valued function, all at a point t. Let $\mathbf{c}$ be a constant vector. The following rules apply.

1. $\dfrac{d}{dt}(\mathbf{c}) = \mathbf{0}$ Constant Rule

2. $\dfrac{d}{dt}(\mathbf{u}(t) + \mathbf{v}(t)) = \mathbf{u}'(t) + \mathbf{v}'(t)$ Sum Rule

3. $\dfrac{d}{dt}(f(t)\mathbf{u}(t)) = f'(t)\mathbf{u}(t) + f(t)\mathbf{u}'(t)$ Product Rule

4. $\dfrac{d}{dt}(\mathbf{u}(f(t))) = \mathbf{u}'(f(t))f'(t)$ Chain Rule

---

EXAMPLE 7   Derivative rules   Compute the following derivatives, where $\mathbf{u}(t) = \langle t, t^2 \rangle$ and $\mathbf{v}(t) = \langle \sin t, 2\cos t \rangle$.

a. $\dfrac{d}{dt}(\mathbf{u}(t^2))$ **b.** $\dfrac{d}{dt}(t^2\mathbf{v}(t))$

SOLUTION

a. Note that $\mathbf{u}'(t) = \langle 1, 2t \rangle$. Using the Chain Rule, we have

$$\frac{d}{dt}(\mathbf{u}(t^2)) = \mathbf{u}'(t^2)\frac{d}{dt}(t^2) = \underbrace{\langle 1, 2t^2 \rangle}_{u'(t^2)}(2t) = \langle 2t, 4t^3 \rangle.$$

b. $\dfrac{d}{dt}(t^2\mathbf{v}(t)) = \dfrac{d}{dt}(t^2)\mathbf{v}(t) + t^2\dfrac{d}{dt}(\mathbf{v}(t))$ Product Rule

$= 2t\,\mathbf{v}(t) + t^2\mathbf{v}'(t)$

$= 2t\underbrace{\langle \sin t, 2\cos t \rangle}_{\mathbf{v}(t)} + t^2\underbrace{\langle \cos t, -2\sin t \rangle}_{\mathbf{v}'(t)}$ Differentiate.

$= \langle 2t\sin t + t^2\cos t, 4t\cos t - 2t^2\sin t \rangle$ Collect terms.

Related Exercises 57–60 ◄

Higher-Order Derivatives Higher-order derivatives of vector-valued functions are computed in the expected way: We simply differentiate each component multiple times. Second derivatives feature prominently in the next section, playing the role of acceleration.

EXAMPLE 8 **Higher-order derivatives** Compute the first, second, and third derivative of $\mathbf{r}(t) = \langle t^2, 8 \ln t \rangle$.

SOLUTION Differentiating once, we have $\mathbf{r}'(t) = \langle 2t, 8/t \rangle$. Differentiating again produces $\mathbf{r}''(t) = \langle 2, -8/t^2 \rangle$. Differentiating once more, we have $\mathbf{r}'''(t) = \langle 0, 16/t^3 \rangle$.

Related Exercises 61–66 ◀

Integrals of Vector-Valued Functions

An **antiderivative** of the vector function $\mathbf{r}$ is a function $\mathbf{R}$ such that $\mathbf{R}' = \mathbf{r}$. If

$$\mathbf{r}(t) = f(t)\mathbf{i} + g(t)\mathbf{j}$$

then an antiderivative of $\mathbf{r}$ is

$$\mathbf{R}(t) = F(t)\mathbf{i} + G(t)\mathbf{j}$$

where F and G are antiderivatives of f and g respectively. This fact follows by differentiating the components of $\mathbf{R}$ and verifying that $\mathbf{R}' = \mathbf{r}$. The collection of all antiderivatives of $\mathbf{r}$ is the *indefinite integral* of $\mathbf{r}$.

DEFINITION **Indefinite Integral of a Vector-Valued Function**

Let $\mathbf{r}(t) = f(t)\mathbf{i} + g(t)\mathbf{j}$ be a vector function and let $\mathbf{R}(t) = F(t)\mathbf{i} + G(t)\mathbf{j}$, where F and G are antiderivatives of f and g respectively. The **indefinite integral** of $\mathbf{r}$ is

$$\int \mathbf{r}(t) \, dt = \mathbf{R}(t) + \mathbf{C},$$

where $\mathbf{C}$ is an arbitrary constant vector. Alternatively, in component form,

$$\int \langle f(t), g(t) \rangle \, dt = \langle F(t), G(t) \rangle + \langle C_1, C_2 \rangle.$$

EXAMPLE 9 **Indefinite integrals** Compute

$$\int \left(\frac{t}{\sqrt{t^2 + 2}} \mathbf{i} + e^{-3t} \mathbf{j} \right) dt.$$

> The substitution $u = t^2 + 2$ is used to evaluate the first component of the integral.

SOLUTION We compute the indefinite integral of each component:

$$\int \left(\frac{t}{\sqrt{t^2 + 2}} \mathbf{i} + e^{-3t} \mathbf{j} \right) dt$$

$$= \left(\sqrt{t^2 + 2} + C_1 \right) \mathbf{i} + \left(-\frac{1}{3} e^{-3t} + C_2 \right) \mathbf{j}$$

$$= \sqrt{t^2 + 2} \, \mathbf{i} - \frac{1}{3} e^{-3t} \mathbf{j} + \mathbf{C}. \quad \text{Let } \mathbf{C} = C_1 \mathbf{i} + C_2 \mathbf{j}.$$

QUICK CHECK 5 Let $\mathbf{r}(t) = \langle 1, 2t \rangle$. Compute $\int \mathbf{r}(t) \, dt$. ◀

The constants C_1 and C_2 are combined to form one vector constant $\mathbf{C}$ at the end of the calculation.

Related Exercises 67–72 ◀

EXAMPLE 10   Finding one antiderivative Find $\mathbf{r}(t)$ such that $\mathbf{r}'(t) = \langle 10, \sin t \rangle$ and $\mathbf{r}(0) = \langle 0, 1 \rangle$.

SOLUTION The required function $\mathbf{r}$ is an antiderivative of $\langle 10, \sin t \rangle$:

$$\mathbf{r}(t) = \int \langle 10, \sin t \rangle \, dt = \langle 10t, -\cos t \rangle + \mathbf{C},$$

where $\mathbf{C}$ is an arbitrary constant vector. The condition $\mathbf{r}(0) = \langle 0, 1 \rangle$ allows us to determine $\mathbf{C}$; substituting $t = 0$ implies that $\mathbf{r}(0) = \langle 0, -1 \rangle + \mathbf{C} = \langle 0, 1 \rangle$. Solving for $\mathbf{C}$, we have $\mathbf{C} = \langle 0, 1 \rangle - \langle 0, -1 \rangle = \langle 0, 2 \rangle$. Therefore,

$$\mathbf{r}(t) = \langle 10t, 2 - \cos t \rangle.$$

Related Exercises 73–78◄

Definite integrals are evaluated by applying the Fundamental Theorem of Calculus to each component of a vector-valued function.

DEFINITION Definite Integral of a Vector-Valued Function

Let $\mathbf{r}(t) = f(t)\,\mathbf{i} + g(t)\,\mathbf{j}$, where f and g are integrable on the interval $[a, b]$. The **definite integral** of $\mathbf{r}$ on $[a, b]$ is

$$\int_a^b \mathbf{r}(t) \, dt = \left(\int_a^b f(t) \, dt \right)\mathbf{i} + \left(\int_a^b g(t) \, dt \right)\mathbf{j}.$$

EXAMPLE 11   Definite integrals Evaluate

$$\int_0^\pi \left(\mathbf{i} + 3 \cos \frac{t}{2}\mathbf{j} \right) dt.$$

SOLUTION

$$\int_0^\pi \left(\mathbf{i} + 3 \cos \frac{t}{2}\mathbf{j} \right) dt = t\mathbf{i} \Big|_0^\pi + 6 \sin \frac{t}{2}\mathbf{j} \Big|_0^\pi \qquad \text{Evaluate integrals for each component.}$$

$$= \pi\mathbf{i} + 6\mathbf{j} \qquad \text{Simplify.}$$

Related Exercises 79–86◄

With the tools of differentiation and integration in hand, we are prepared to tackle some practical problems, notably the motion of objects in the plane.

SECTION 11.6 EXERCISES

Review Questions

1. How many independent variables does the function $\mathbf{r}(t) = \langle x(t), y(t) \rangle$ have?

2. How many dependent scalar variables does the function $\mathbf{r}(t) = \langle x(t), y(t) \rangle$ have?

3. Why is $\mathbf{r}(t) = \langle x(t), y(t) \rangle$ called a vector-valued function?

4. Find a vector in the direction of the line segment from $P_0(x_0, y_0)$ to $P_1(x_1, y_1)$.

5. What is the equation for the line through the points $P_0(x_0, y_0)$ and $P_1(x_1, y_1)$?

6. How do you determine whether $\mathbf{r}(t) = x(t)\mathbf{i} + y(t)\mathbf{j}$ is continuous at $t = a$?

7. How do you evaluate $\lim_{t \to a} \mathbf{r}(t)$, where $\mathbf{r}(t) = \langle x(t), y(t) \rangle$?

8. What is the derivative of $\mathbf{r}(t) = \langle x(t), y(t) \rangle$?

9. Explain the geometric meaning of $\mathbf{r}'(t)$.

10. Compute $\mathbf{r}''(t)$ when $\mathbf{r}(t) = \langle t^{10}, 8t \rangle$.

11. How do you find the indefinite integral of $\mathbf{r}(t) = \langle f(t), g(t) \rangle$?

12. How do you evaluate $\int_a^b \mathbf{r}(t) \, dt$?

Basic Skills

13–24. Equations of lines *Find parametric equations of the following lines.*

13. The line through $(0, 0)$ in the direction of the vector $\mathbf{v} = \langle 4, 7 \rangle$

14. The line through $(-3, 2)$ in the direction of the vector $\mathbf{v} = \langle 1, -2 \rangle$

15. The line through $(0, 1)$ parallel to the y-axis

16. The line through $(0, 1)$ parallel to the x-axis

17. The line through $(0, 0)$ and $(1, 2)$

18. The line through $(1, 0)$ and $(3, -3)$

19. The line through $(-3, 4)$ and $(5, -1)$

20. The line through $(0, 4)$ and $(10, -5)$

21. The line through $(0, 0)$ that is parallel to the line $\mathbf{r}(t) = \langle 3 - 2t, 5 + 8t \rangle$

22. The line through $(1, -3)$ that is parallel to the line $\mathbf{r}(t) = \langle 3 + 4t, 5 - t \rangle$

23. The line through $(0, 0)$ that is perpendicular to $\mathbf{u} = \langle 1, 0 \rangle$

24. The line through $(-3, 4)$ that is perpendicular to $\mathbf{u} = \langle 1, 1 \rangle$

25–28. Line segments *Find an equation of the line segment from the first point to the second point.*

25. $(0, 0)$ and $(1, 2)$

26. $(1, 0)$ and $(0, -2)$

27. $(2, 4)$ and $(7, 5)$

28. $(-1, -8)$ and $(-9, 5)$

29–36. Curves in the plane *Graph the curves described by the following functions, indicating the direction of positive orientation.*

29. $\mathbf{r}(t) = \cos t\,\mathbf{i} + \sin t\,\mathbf{j}$, for $0 \le t \le 2\pi$

30. $\mathbf{r}(t) = \langle 4 \cos t, 16 \sin t \rangle$, for $0 \le t \le 2\pi$

31. $\mathbf{r}(t) = 3 \cos t\,\mathbf{i} + t\,\mathbf{j}$, for $0 \le t \le 2\pi$

32. $\mathbf{r}(t) = 2 \cos t\,\mathbf{i} + 4 \sin t\,\mathbf{j}$, for $0 \le t \le 2\pi$

33. $\mathbf{r}(t) = \langle t \cos t, t \sin t \rangle$, for $0 \le t \le 6\pi$

34. $\mathbf{r}(t) = 4 \sin t\,\mathbf{i} + 6 \cos t\,\mathbf{j}$, for $0 \le t \le 2\pi$

35. $\mathbf{r}(t) = e^{-t/20} \sin t\,\mathbf{i} + e^{-t/20} \cos t\,\mathbf{j}$, for $0 \le t < \infty$

36. $\mathbf{r}(t) = e^{-t}\mathbf{i} + 3 \cos t\,\mathbf{j}$, for $0 \le t \le 6$

37–42. Limits *Evaluate the following limits.*

37. $\lim\limits_{t \to \pi/2} \left(\cos 2t\,\mathbf{i} - 4 \sin t\,\mathbf{j} \right)$

38. $\lim\limits_{t \to \ln 2} (2e^t\mathbf{i} + 6e^{-t}\mathbf{j})$

39. $\lim\limits_{t \to \infty} \left(\tan^{-1} t\,\mathbf{i} - \dfrac{2t}{t+1}\,\mathbf{j} \right)$

40. $\lim\limits_{t \to 2} \left(\dfrac{t}{t^2 + 1}\,\mathbf{i} - 4e^{-t} \sin \pi t\,\mathbf{j} \right)$

41. $\lim\limits_{t \to 0} \left(\dfrac{\sin t}{t}\,\mathbf{i} - \dfrac{e^t - t - 1}{t}\,\mathbf{j} \right)$

42. $\lim\limits_{t \to 0} \left(\dfrac{\tan t}{t}\,\mathbf{i} - \dfrac{3t}{\sin t}\,\mathbf{j} \right)$

43–50. Derivatives of vector-valued functions *Differentiate the following functions.*

43. $\mathbf{r}(t) = \langle \cos t, t^2 \rangle$

44. $\mathbf{r}(t) = 4e^t\mathbf{i} + 5\mathbf{j}$

45. $\mathbf{r}(t) = \langle 2t^3, 6\sqrt{t} \rangle$

46. $\mathbf{r}(t) = \langle 4, 3 \cos 2t \rangle$

47. $\mathbf{r}(t) = e^t\mathbf{i} + 2e^{-t}\mathbf{j}$

48. $\mathbf{r}(t) = \tan t\,\mathbf{i} + \sec t\,\mathbf{j}$

49. $\mathbf{r}(t) = \langle te^{-t}, t \ln t \rangle$

50. $\mathbf{r}(t) = \langle (t + 1)^{-1}, \tan^{-1} t \rangle$

51–56. Tangent vectors *Find $\mathbf{r}'(t)$ at the given value of t for the following parametric curves.*

51. $\mathbf{r}(t) = \langle t, 3t^2 \rangle, t = 1$

52. $\mathbf{r}(t) = e^t\mathbf{i} + e^{3t}\mathbf{j}, t = 0$

53. $\mathbf{r}(t) = \langle t, \cos 2t \rangle, t = \dfrac{\pi}{2}$

54. $\mathbf{r}(t) = 2 \sin t\,\mathbf{i} + 3 \cos t\,\mathbf{j}, t = \pi$

55. $\mathbf{r}(t) = \langle 2t^4, 6t^{3/2} \rangle, t = 1$

56. $\mathbf{r}(t) = \langle 2e^t, e^{-2t} \rangle, t = \ln 3$

57–60. Derivative rules *Let*

$$\mathbf{u}(t) = 2t^3\mathbf{i} + (t^2 - 1)\mathbf{j} \text{ and } \mathbf{v}(t) = e^t\mathbf{i} + 2e^{-t}\mathbf{j}.$$

Compute the derivative of the following functions.

57. $(t^{12} + 3t)\mathbf{u}(t)$

58. $(4t^8 - 6t^3)\mathbf{v}(t)$

59. $\mathbf{u}(t^4 - 2t)$

60. $\mathbf{v}(\sqrt{t})$

61–66. Higher-order derivatives *Compute $\mathbf{r}''(t)$ and $\mathbf{r}'''(t)$ for the following functions.*

61. $\mathbf{r}(t) = \langle t^2 + 1, t + 1 \rangle$

62. $\mathbf{r}(t) = \langle 3t^{12} - t^2, t^8 + t^3 \rangle$

63. $\mathbf{r}(t) = \langle \cos 3t, \sin 4t \rangle$

64. $\mathbf{r}(t) = \langle e^{4t}, 2e^{-4t} + 1 \rangle$

65. $\mathbf{r}(t) = \sqrt{t + 4}\,\mathbf{i} + \dfrac{t}{t + 1}\,\mathbf{j}$

66. $\mathbf{r}(t) = \tan t\,\mathbf{i} + \left(t + \dfrac{1}{t} \right)\mathbf{j}$

67–72. Indefinite integrals *Compute the indefinite integral of the following functions.*

67. $\mathbf{r}(t) = \langle t^4 - 3t, 2t - 1 \rangle$

68. $\mathbf{r}(t) = \langle 5t^{-4} - t^2, t^6 - 4t^3 \rangle$

69. $\mathbf{r}(t) = \langle 2 \cos t, 2 \sin 3t \rangle$

70. $\mathbf{r}(t) = te^t \mathbf{i} + t \sin t^2 \mathbf{j}$

71. $\mathbf{r}(t) = e^{3t}\mathbf{i} + \dfrac{1}{1 + t^2}\mathbf{j}$

72. $\mathbf{r}(t) = 2^t\mathbf{i} + \dfrac{1}{1 + 2t}\mathbf{j}$

73–78. Finding r from r′ *Find the function* **r** *that satisfies the given conditions.*

73. $\mathbf{r}'(t) = \langle e^t, \sin t \rangle;\ \mathbf{r}(0) = \langle 2, 2 \rangle$

74. $\mathbf{r}'(t) = \langle 0, 2 \rangle;\ \mathbf{r}(1) = \langle 4, 3 \rangle$

75. $\mathbf{r}'(t) = \langle 1, 2t \rangle;\ \mathbf{r}(1) = \langle 4, 3 \rangle$

76. $\mathbf{r}'(t) = \langle \sqrt{t}, \cos \pi t \rangle;\ \mathbf{r}(1) = \langle 2, 3 \rangle$

77. $\mathbf{r}'(t) = \langle e^{2t}, 1 - 2e^{-t} \rangle;\ \mathbf{r}(0) = \langle 1, 1 \rangle$

78. $\mathbf{r}'(t) = \dfrac{t}{t^2 + 1}\mathbf{i} + te^{-t^2}\mathbf{j};\ \mathbf{r}(0) = \mathbf{i} + \dfrac{3}{2}\mathbf{j}$

79–86. Definite integrals *Evaluate the following definite integrals.*

79. $\displaystyle\int_{-1}^{1} (\mathbf{i} + t\mathbf{j})\, dt$

80. $\displaystyle\int_{1}^{4} (6t^2\mathbf{i} + 8t^3\mathbf{j})\, dt$

81. $\displaystyle\int_{0}^{\ln 2} (e^t\mathbf{i} + e^t \cos(\pi e^t)\mathbf{j})\, dt$

82. $\displaystyle\int_{1/2}^{1} \left(\dfrac{3}{1 + 2t}\mathbf{i} - \pi \csc^2\left(\dfrac{\pi}{2}t\right)\mathbf{j} \right) dt$

83. $\displaystyle\int_{-\pi}^{\pi} (\sin t\mathbf{i} + \cos t\mathbf{j})\, dt$

84. $\displaystyle\int_{0}^{\ln 2} (e^{-t}\mathbf{i} + 2e^{2t}\mathbf{j})\, dt$

85. $\displaystyle\int_{0}^{2} te^t(\mathbf{i} + 2\mathbf{j})\, dt$

86. $\displaystyle\int_{0}^{\pi/4} (\sec^2 t\mathbf{i} - 2\cos t\mathbf{j})\, dt$

Further Explorations

87. Explain why or why not Determine whether the following statements are true and give an explanation or counterexample.

a. The line $\mathbf{r}(t) = \langle 3, -1 \rangle + t\langle 6, -2 \rangle$ passes through the origin.

b. Any two nonparallel lines in the plane intersect.

c. The curve $\mathbf{r}(t) = \langle e^{-t}\sin t, e^{-t}\cos t \rangle$ approaches a point as $t \to \infty$.

d. If $\mathbf{r}(t) = e^{-t^2}\langle 1, 1 \rangle$ then $\displaystyle\lim_{t \to \infty}\mathbf{r}(t) = \lim_{t \to -\infty}\mathbf{r}(t)$.

e. The vectors $\mathbf{r}(t)$ and $\mathbf{r}'(t)$ are parallel for all values of t in the domain.

f. If f and g are odd integrable functions and a is a real number, then

$$\int_{-a}^{a} (f(t)\mathbf{i} + g(t)\mathbf{j})\, dt = \mathbf{0}.$$

88–91. Domains *Find the domain of the following vector-valued functions.*

88. $\mathbf{r}(t) = \dfrac{2}{t - 1}\mathbf{i} + \dfrac{3}{t + 2}\mathbf{j}$

89. $\mathbf{r}(t) = \sqrt{t + 2}\,\mathbf{i} + \sqrt{2 - t}\,\mathbf{j}$

90. $\mathbf{r}(t) = \cos 2t\,\mathbf{i} + e^{\sqrt{t}}\mathbf{j}$

91. $\mathbf{r}(t) = \sqrt{4 - t^2}\,\mathbf{i} + \sqrt{t}\,\mathbf{j}$

92–95. Tangent lines *Suppose the vector-valued function* $\mathbf{r}(t) = \langle x(t), y(t) \rangle$ *is differentiable on an interval containing the point* t_0. *The line tangent to* $\mathbf{r}(t)$ *at* $t = t_0$ *is the line parallel to the tangent vector* $\mathbf{r}'(t_0)$ *that passes through* $(x(t_0), y(t_0))$. *For each of the following functions, find the line tangent to the curve at* $t = t_0$. *Choose an orientation for the line that is the same as the direction of* $\mathbf{r}'$.

92. $\mathbf{r}(t) = \langle e^t, e^{2t} \rangle;\ t_0 = 0$

93. $\mathbf{r}(t) = \langle 2 + \cos t, 3 + \sin 2t \rangle;\ t_0 = \dfrac{\pi}{2}$

94. $\mathbf{r}(t) = \langle \sqrt{2t + 1}, \sin \pi t \rangle;\ t_0 = 4$

95. $\mathbf{r}(t) = \langle 3t - 1, 7t + 2 \rangle;\ t_0 = 1$

96–99. Derivative rules *Let* $\mathbf{u}(t) = \langle 1, t \rangle, \mathbf{v}(t) = \langle t^2, -2t \rangle$, *and* $g(t) = 2\sqrt{t}$. *Compute the derivative of the following functions.*

96. $\mathbf{u}(t^3)$ **97.** $\mathbf{v}(e^t)$

98. $g(t)\mathbf{v}(t)$ **99.** $\mathbf{v}(g(t))$

QUICK CHECK ANSWERS

1. The y-axis; the line $y = x$ in the xy-plane   **2.** When $t = 0$, the point on the line is P_0; when $t = 1$, the point on the line is P_1.   **3.** $\mathbf{r}(t) = \langle -1 - 2t, 3 + 4t \rangle$, $\mathbf{r}(t) = \langle 1 + 2t, -1 - 4t \rangle$ **4.** $\mathbf{r}(t)$ describes a line, so its tangent vector $\mathbf{r}'(t) = \langle 1, 1 \rangle$ has constant direction and magnitude.   **5.** $\langle t, t^2 \rangle + \mathbf{C}$, where $\mathbf{C} = \langle a, b \rangle$, and a and b are real numbers ◄

11.7 Two-Dimensional Motion

It is a remarkable fact that given the forces acting on an object, and its initial position and velocity, the motion of the object can be modeled for all future times. To be sure, the accuracy of the results depends on how well the various forces on the object are described. For example, it may be more difficult to predict the trajectory of a spinning soccer ball than the path of a space station orbiting Earth. Nevertheless, as shown in this section, by combining Newton's Second Law of Motion with everything we have learned about vectors, it is possible to solve a variety of moving body problems.

Position, Velocity, Speed, Acceleration

Until now, we have studied objects that move in one dimension (along a line). The next step is to consider the motion of objects in two dimensions (in a plane). We work in the xy-plane and let the vector-valued function $\mathbf{r}(t) = \langle x(t), y(t) \rangle$ describe the *position* of a moving object at times $t \geq 0$. The curve described by $\mathbf{r}$ is the *path* or *trajectory* of the object (Figure 11.77). Just as with one-dimensional motion, the rate of change of the position function with respect to time is the *instantaneous velocity* of the object—a vector with two components corresponding to the velocity in the x- and y-directions:

$$\mathbf{v}(t) = \mathbf{r}'(t) = \langle x'(t), y'(t) \rangle.$$

This expression should look familiar. The velocity vectors of a moving object are simply tangent vectors; that is, at any point, the velocity vector is tangent to the trajectory (Figure 11.77).

As with one-dimensional motion, the *speed* of an object moving in two-dimensions is the magnitude of its velocity vector:

$$|\mathbf{v}(t)| = |\langle x'(t), y'(t) \rangle| = \sqrt{x'(t)^2 + y'(t)^2}.$$

The speed is a nonnegative scalar-valued function.

Finally, the *acceleration* of a moving object is the rate of change of the velocity:

$$\mathbf{a}(t) = \mathbf{v}'(t) = \mathbf{r}''(t).$$

While the position vector gives the path of a moving object and the velocity vector is always tangent to the path, the acceleration vector is more difficult to visualize. Figure 11.78 shows one particular instance of two-dimensional motion. The trajectory is a segment of a parabola and is traced out by the position vectors (shown at $t = 0$ and 1). As expected, the velocity vectors are tangent to the trajectory. In this case, the acceleration is $\mathbf{a} = \langle -2, 0 \rangle$; it is constant in magnitude and direction for all times. The relationships among $\mathbf{r}$, $\mathbf{v}$, and $\mathbf{a}$ are explored in the coming examples.

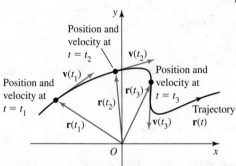

FIGURE 11.77

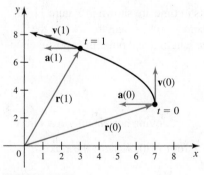

FIGURE 11.78

> **DEFINITION Position, Velocity, Speed, Acceleration**
>
> Let the **position** of an object moving in the xy-plane be given by $\mathbf{r}(t) = \langle x(t), y(t) \rangle$, for $t \geq 0$. The **velocity** of the object is
>
> $$\mathbf{v}(t) = \mathbf{r}'(t) = \langle x'(t), y'(t) \rangle.$$
>
> The **speed** of the object is the scalar function
>
> $$|\mathbf{v}(t)| = \sqrt{x'(t)^2 + y'(t)^2}.$$
>
> The **acceleration** of the object is $\mathbf{a}(t) = \mathbf{v}'(t) = \mathbf{r}''(t)$.

QUICK CHECK 1 Given $\mathbf{r}(t) = \langle t, t^2 \rangle$, find $\mathbf{v}(t)$ and $\mathbf{a}(t)$. ◄

EXAMPLE 1 **Velocity and acceleration from position** Consider the two-dimensional motion given by the position vector

$$\mathbf{r}(t) = \langle x(t), y(t) \rangle = \langle 3\cos t, 3\sin t \rangle, \quad \text{for } 0 \le t \le 2\pi.$$

a. Sketch the trajectory of the object.

b. Find the velocity and speed of the object.

c. Find the acceleration of the object.

d. Sketch the position, velocity, and acceleration vectors, for $t = 0, \pi/2, \pi$, and $3\pi/2$.

SOLUTION

a. Notice that

$$x(t)^2 + y(t)^2 = 9(\cos^2 t + \sin^2 t) = 9,$$

which is the equation of a circle centered at the origin with radius 3. The object moves on this circle in the counterclockwise direction (Figure 11.79).

b. $\mathbf{v}(t) = \langle x'(t), y'(t) \rangle = \langle -3\sin t, 3\cos t \rangle$ Velocity vector

$$|\mathbf{v}(t)| = \sqrt{x'(t)^2 + y'(t)^2}$$ Definition of speed

$$= \sqrt{(-3\sin t)^2 + (3\cos t)^2}$$

$$= \sqrt{9\underbrace{(\sin^2 t + \cos^2 t)}_{1}} = 3$$

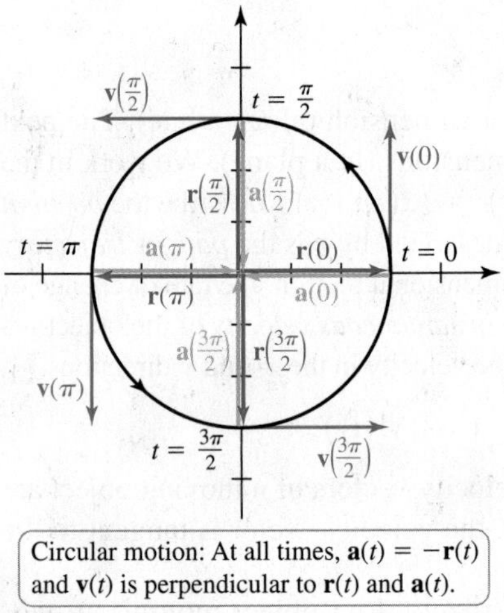

The velocity vector has a constant magnitude and a continuously changing direction.

c. Differentiating the velocity, we find that $\mathbf{a}(t) = \mathbf{v}'(t) = \langle -3\cos t, -3\sin t \rangle = -\mathbf{r}(t)$. In this case, the acceleration vector is the negative of the position vector at all times.

d. The relationships among $\mathbf{r}$, $\mathbf{v}$, and $\mathbf{a}$ at four points in time are shown in Figure 11.79. The velocity vector is always tangent to the trajectory and has length 3, while the acceleration vector and position vector each have length 3 and point in opposite directions. At all times, $\mathbf{v}$ is perpendicular to $\mathbf{r}$ and $\mathbf{a}$.

Related Exercises 7–20 ◄

Circular motion: At all times, $\mathbf{a}(t) = -\mathbf{r}(t)$ and $\mathbf{v}(t)$ is perpendicular to $\mathbf{r}(t)$ and $\mathbf{a}(t)$.

FIGURE 11.79

EXAMPLE 2 **Motion in the plane** An object begins moving horizontally from the origin with a velocity $\mathbf{v}(t) = \left\langle 2e^{-t/10}, 1 - \dfrac{4}{t+1} \right\rangle$, for $t \ge 0$. Assume the x-axis points east and the y-axis points north.

a. At what times is the object moving eastward?

b. At what times is the object moving northward?

c. Find the acceleration of the object and determine when the object accelerates or decelerates in the x- and y-directions.

d. Find the position vector for the object when $t \ge 0$.

e. Describe the path of the object and verify your result using a graphing calculator.

SOLUTION

a. The x-component of the object's velocity is $2e^{-t/10}$, which is positive for all times. Therefore, the object moves eastward for $t \ge 0$.

b. The object moves in the positive y-direction (north) when the y-component of the velocity is positive, or when $1 - \dfrac{4}{t+1} > 0$. Noting that $t + 1 > 0$, this inequality implies that $t > 3$. You can also verify that $1 - \dfrac{4}{t + 1} < 0$ when $0 \le t < 3$.

Therefore, the object moves north when $t > 3$ and south when $0 \le t < 3$.

c. The acceleration vector of the object is

$$\mathbf{a}(t) = \mathbf{v}'(t) = \left\langle -\frac{1}{5}e^{-t/10}, \frac{4}{(t + 1)^2} \right\rangle.$$

The x-component of the acceleration is negative for all times, so the object decelerates in the x-direction. The y-component of the acceleration is positive for all times, so the object accelerates in the y-direction.

d. The position vector is found by integrating the velocity vector and using the initial condition $\mathbf{r}(0) = \langle 0, 0 \rangle$. We find that

$$\mathbf{r}(t) = \langle x(t), y(t) \rangle = \int \left\langle 2e^{-t/10}, 1 - \frac{4}{t + 1} \right\rangle dt = \left\langle -20e^{-t/10}, t - 4 \ln (t + 1) \right\rangle + \mathbf{C}.$$

The initial condition $\mathbf{r}(0) = \langle 0, 0 \rangle$ implies that $\langle 0, 0 \rangle = \langle -20, 0 \rangle + \mathbf{C}$, or $\mathbf{C} = \langle 20, 0 \rangle$. Therefore, the position vector is

$$\mathbf{r}(t) = \langle 20 - 20e^{-t/10}, t - 4 \ln (t + 1) \rangle.$$

e. The x-coordinate of the position is $20 - 20e^{-t/10}$, which is positive for $t > 0$. However, notice that $\lim\limits_{t \to \infty} (20 - 20e^{-t/10}) = 20$. Therefore, the object moves eastward at all times but never crosses the line $x = 20$. The object moves southward for $0 \le t < 3$, and reaches its southernmost point at $t = 3$, with coordinates

$$\mathbf{r}(3) = \langle 20 - 20e^{-3/10}, 3 - 4 \ln 4 \rangle \approx \langle 5.184, -2.545 \rangle.$$

For $t > 3$, the object moves northward and its y-coordinate increases without bound because $\lim\limits_{t \to \infty} (t - 4 \ln(t + 1)) = \infty$. The path of the object is shown in Figure 11.80, for $0 \le t \le 33$. Notice that the path has a vertical asymptote at $x = 20$.

Related Exercises 21–22 ◄

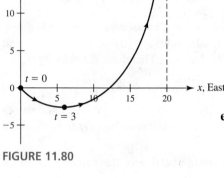

FIGURE 11.80

Two-Dimensional Motion in a Gravitational Field

Newton's Second Law of Motion, which is used to model the motion of most objects, states that

$$\underbrace{\text{Mass}}_{m} \cdot \underbrace{\text{acceleration}}_{\mathbf{a}(t) = \mathbf{r}''(t)} = \underbrace{\text{sum of all forces.}}_{\sum \mathbf{F}_k}$$

In other words, the governing law says something about the *acceleration* of an object, and in order to describe the motion fully, we must find the velocity and position from the acceleration.

Finding Velocity and Position from Acceleration   We begin with the case of two-dimensional projectile motion in which the only force acting on the object is the gravitational force; for the moment, air resistance and other possible external forces are neglected.

A convenient coordinate system uses a y-axis that points vertically upward and an x-axis that points in the direction of horizontal motion. The gravitational force is in the negative y-direction and is given by $\mathbf{F} = \langle 0, -mg \rangle$, where m is the mass of the object and $g \approx 9.8 \text{ m/s}^2 \approx 32 \text{ ft/s}^2$ is the acceleration due to gravity (Figure 11.81).

With these observations, Newton's Second Law takes the form

$$m\, \mathbf{a}(t) = \mathbf{F} = \langle 0, -mg \rangle.$$

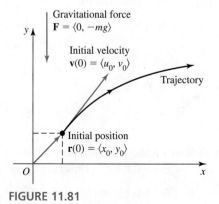

FIGURE 11.81

Significantly, the mass of the object cancels, leaving the vector equation

$$\mathbf{a}(t) = \langle 0, -g \rangle. \qquad (1)$$

In order to find the velocity $\mathbf{v}(t) = \langle x'(t), y'(t) \rangle$ and the position $\mathbf{r}(t) = \langle x(t), y(t) \rangle$ from this equation, we must be given the following **initial conditions**:

Initial velocity at $t = 0$: $\mathbf{v}(0) = \langle u_0, v_0 \rangle$ and

Initial position at $t = 0$: $\mathbf{r}(0) = \langle x_0, y_0 \rangle$.

We now proceed in two steps.

> Recall that an antiderivative of 0 is a constant C and an antiderivative of $-g$ is $-gt + C$.

1. **Solve for the velocity** The velocity is an antiderivative of the acceleration in equation (1). Integrating the acceleration, we have

$$\mathbf{v}(t) = \int \mathbf{a}(t)\, dt = \int \langle 0, -g \rangle\, dt = \langle C_1, -gt + C_2 \rangle = \langle 0, -gt \rangle + \mathbf{C},$$

> You have a choice. You may do these calculations in vector notation, as we have done here, or you may work with individual components.

where $\mathbf{C} = \langle C_1, C_2 \rangle$ is an arbitrary constant vector. The arbitrary constant is determined by substituting $t = 0$ and using the initial condition $\mathbf{v}(0) = \langle u_0, v_0 \rangle$. We find that $\mathbf{v}(0) = \langle 0, 0 \rangle + \mathbf{C} = \langle u_0, v_0 \rangle$, or $\mathbf{C} = \langle u_0, v_0 \rangle$. Therefore, the velocity is

$$\mathbf{v}(t) = \langle 0, -gt \rangle + \langle u_0, v_0 \rangle = \langle u_0, -gt + v_0 \rangle. \qquad (2)$$

Notice that the horizontal component of velocity is simply the initial horizontal velocity u_0 for all time. The vertical component of velocity decreases linearly from its initial value of v_0.

2. **Solve for the position** The position is an antiderivative of the velocity given by equation (2):

$$\mathbf{r}(t) = \int \mathbf{v}(t)\, dt = \int \langle u_0, -gt + v_0 \rangle\, dt = \left\langle u_0 t, -\frac{1}{2} gt^2 + v_0 t \right\rangle + \mathbf{C},$$

where $\mathbf{C}$ is an arbitrary constant vector. Substituting $t = 0$, we have $\mathbf{r}(0) = \langle 0, 0 \rangle + \mathbf{C} = \langle x_0, y_0 \rangle$, which implies that $\mathbf{C} = \langle x_0, y_0 \rangle$. Therefore, the position of the object, for $t \geq 0$, is

$$\mathbf{r}(t) = \left\langle u_0 t, -\frac{1}{2} gt^2 + v_0 t \right\rangle + \langle x_0, y_0 \rangle = \left\langle \underbrace{u_0 t + x_0}_{x(t)}, \underbrace{-\frac{1}{2} gt^2 + v_0 t + y_0}_{y(t)} \right\rangle.$$

SUMMARY   Two-Dimensional Motion in a Gravitational Field

Consider an object moving in a plane with a horizontal x-axis and a vertical y-axis, subject only to the force of gravity. Given the initial velocity $\mathbf{v}(0) = \langle u_0, v_0 \rangle$ and the initial position $\mathbf{r}(0) = \langle x_0, y_0 \rangle$, the velocity of the object, for $t \geq 0$, is

$$\mathbf{v}(t) = \langle x'(t), y'(t) \rangle = \langle u_0, -gt + v_0 \rangle$$

and the position is

$$\mathbf{r}(t) = \langle x(t), y(t) \rangle = \left\langle u_0 t + x_0, -\frac{1}{2} gt^2 + v_0 t + y_0 \right\rangle.$$

EXAMPLE 3   Flight of a baseball A baseball is hit from 3 ft above home plate with an initial velocity in ft/s of $\mathbf{v}(0) = \langle u_0, v_0 \rangle = \langle 80, 80 \rangle$. Neglect all forces other than gravity.

a. Find the position and velocity of the ball between the time it is hit and the time it first hits the ground.

b. Show that the trajectory of the ball is a segment of a parabola.

c. Assuming a flat playing field, how far does the ball travel horizontally? Plot the trajectory of the ball.

d. What is the maximum height of the ball?

e. Does the ball clear a 20-ft fence that is 380 ft from home plate (directly under the path of the ball)?

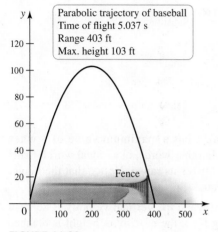

FIGURE 11.82

▷ The equation in part (c) can be solved using the quadratic formula or a root-finder on a calculator.

SOLUTION Assume the origin is located at home plate. Because distances are measured in feet, we use $g = 32 \text{ ft/s}^2$.

a. Substituting $x_0 = 0$ and $y_0 = 3$ into the equation for **r**, the position of the ball is

$$\mathbf{r}(t) = \langle x(t), y(t) \rangle = \langle 80t, -16t^2 + 80t + 3 \rangle, \quad \text{for } t \geq 0. \tag{3}$$

We then compute $\mathbf{v}(t) = \mathbf{r}'(t) = \langle 80, -32t + 80 \rangle$.

b. Equation (3) says that the horizontal position is $x = 80t$ and the vertical position is $y = -16t^2 + 80t + 3$. Substituting $t = x/80$ into the equation for y gives

$$y = -16\left(\frac{x}{80}\right)^2 + x + 3 = -\frac{x^2}{400} + x + 3,$$

which is the equation of a parabola.

c. The ball lands on the ground at the value of $t > 0$ for which $y = 0$. Solving $y(t) = -16t^2 + 80t + 3 = 0$, we find that $t \approx -0.037$ and $t \approx 5.037$ s. The first root is not relevant for the problem at hand, so we conclude that the ball lands when $t \approx 5.037$ s. The horizontal distance traveled by the ball is $x(5.037) \approx 403$ ft. The path of the ball in the xy-coordinate system is shown in Figure 11.82.

d. The ball reaches its maximum height at the time its vertical velocity is zero. Solving $y'(t) = -32t + 80 = 0$, we find that $t = 2.5$ s. The height at that time is $y(2.5) = 103$ ft.

e. The ball reaches a horizontal distance of 380 ft (the distance to the fence) when $x(t) = 80t = 380$. Solving for t, we find that $t = 4.75$ s. The height of the ball at that time is $y(4.75) = 22$ ft. So, indeed, the ball clears a 20-ft fence.

Related Exercises 23–28◄

QUICK CHECK 2 Write the functions $x(t)$ and $y(t)$ in Example 3 in the case that $x_0 = 0$, $y_0 = 2$, $u_0 = 100$, and $v_0 = 60$. ◄

Range, Time of Flight, Maximum Height   Having solved one specific motion problem, we can now make some general observations about two-dimensional projectile motion in a gravitational field. Assume that the motion of an object begins at the origin; that is, $x_0 = y_0 = 0$. Assume also that the object is launched at an angle of α ($0 \leq \alpha \leq \pi/2$) above the horizontal with an initial speed $|\mathbf{v}_0|$ (Figure 11.83). This means that the initial velocity is

$$\langle u_0, v_0 \rangle = \langle |\mathbf{v}_0| \cos \alpha, |\mathbf{v}_0| \sin \alpha \rangle.$$

Substituting these values into the general expressions for the velocity and position, we find that the velocity of the object is

$$\mathbf{v}(t) = \langle u_0, -gt + v_0 \rangle = \langle |\mathbf{v}_0| \cos \alpha, -gt + |\mathbf{v}_0| \sin \alpha \rangle.$$

The position of the object (with $x_0 = y_0 = 0$) is

$$\mathbf{r}(t) = \langle x(t), y(t) \rangle = \langle (|\mathbf{v}_0| \cos \alpha)t, -gt^2/2 + (|\mathbf{v}_0| \sin \alpha)t \rangle.$$

Notice that the motion is determined entirely by the parameters $|\mathbf{v}_0|$ and α. Several general conclusions now follow.

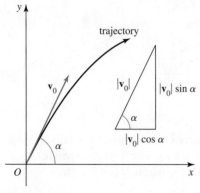

FIGURE 11.83

▶ The other root of the equation $y(t) = 0$ is $t = 0$, the time the object leaves the ground.

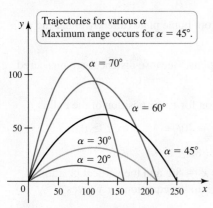

FIGURE 11.84

QUICK CHECK 3 Show that the range attained with an angle α equals the range attained with the angle $\pi/2 - \alpha$. ◄

1. Assuming the object is launched from the origin over horizontal ground, it returns to the ground when $y(t) = -gt^2/2 + (|\mathbf{v}_0| \sin \alpha)t = 0$. Solving for t, the **time of flight** is $T = 2|\mathbf{v}_0|(\sin \alpha)/g$.

2. The **range** of the object, which is the horizontal distance it travels, is the x-coordinate of the trajectory when $t = T$:

$$x(T) = (|\mathbf{v}_0| \cos \alpha)T$$

$$= (|\mathbf{v}_0| \cos \alpha)\frac{2|\mathbf{v}_0| \sin \alpha}{g} \qquad \text{Substitute for } T.$$

$$= \frac{2|\mathbf{v}_0|^2 \sin \alpha \cos \alpha}{g} \qquad \text{Simplify.}$$

$$= \frac{|\mathbf{v}_0|^2 \sin 2\alpha}{g}. \qquad 2 \sin \alpha \cos \alpha = \sin 2\alpha$$

Note that on the interval $0 \le \alpha \le \pi/2$, $\sin 2\alpha$ has a maximum value of 1 when $\alpha = \pi/4$, so the maximum range is $|\mathbf{v}_0|^2/g$. In other words, in an ideal world, firing an object from the ground at a 45° angle maximizes its range. Notice that the ranges obtained with the angles α and $\pi/2 - \alpha$ are equal (Figure 11.84).

3. The maximum height of the object is reached when the vertical velocity is zero, or when $y'(t) = -gt + |\mathbf{v}_0| \sin \alpha = 0$. Solving for t, the maximum height is reached at $t = |\mathbf{v}_0|(\sin \alpha)/g = T/2$, which is half the time of flight. The object spends equal amounts of time ascending and descending. The maximum height is

$$y\left(\frac{T}{2}\right) = \frac{(|\mathbf{v}_0| \sin \alpha)^2}{2g}.$$

4. Finally, by eliminating t from the equations for $x(t)$ and $y(t)$, it can be shown (Exercise 55) that the trajectory of the object is a segment of a parabola.

SUMMARY   Two-Dimensional Motion

Assume an object traveling over horizontal ground, acted on only by the gravitational force, has an initial position $\langle x_0, y_0 \rangle = \langle 0, 0 \rangle$ and initial velocity $\langle u_0, v_0 \rangle = \langle |\mathbf{v}_0| \cos \alpha, |\mathbf{v}_0| \sin \alpha \rangle$. The trajectory, which is a segment of a parabola, has the following properties.

$$\text{time of flight} = T = \frac{2|\mathbf{v}_0| \sin \alpha}{g}$$

$$\text{range} = \frac{|\mathbf{v}_0|^2 \sin 2\alpha}{g}$$

$$\text{maximum height} = y\left(\frac{T}{2}\right) = \frac{(|\mathbf{v}_0| \sin \alpha)^2}{2g}$$

EXAMPLE 4   Flight of a golf ball A golf ball is driven down a horizontal fairway with an initial speed of 55 m/s at an initial angle of 25° (from a tee with negligible height). Neglect all forces except gravity and assume that the ball's trajectory lies in a plane.

a. How far does the ball travel horizontally and when does it land?

b. What is the maximum height of the ball?

c. At what angles should the ball be hit to reach a green that is 300 m from the tee?

SOLUTION

a. Using the range formula with $\alpha = 25°$ and $|\mathbf{v}_0| = 55$ m/s, the ball travels

$$\frac{|\mathbf{v}_0|^2 \sin 2\alpha}{g} = \frac{(55 \text{ m/s})^2 \sin (50°)}{9.8 \text{ m/s}^2} \approx 236 \text{ m}.$$

The time of the flight is

$$T = \frac{2|\mathbf{v}_0| \sin \alpha}{g} = \frac{2(55 \text{ m/s}) \sin 25°}{9.8 \text{ m/s}^2} \approx 4.744 \text{ s}.$$

b. The maximum height of the ball is

$$\frac{(|\mathbf{v}_0| \sin \alpha)^2}{2g} = \frac{((55 \text{ m/s}) (\sin 25°))^2}{2(9.8 \text{ m/s}^2)} \approx 27.566 \text{ m}.$$

c. Letting R denote the range and solving the range formula for $\sin 2\alpha$, we find that $\sin 2\alpha = Rg/|\mathbf{v}_0|^2$. For a range of $R = 300$ m and an initial speed of $|\mathbf{v}_0| = 55$ m/s, the required angle satisfies

$$\sin 2\alpha = \frac{Rg}{|\mathbf{v}_0|^2} = \frac{(300 \text{ m}) (9.8 \text{ m/s}^2)}{(55 \text{ m/s})^2} \approx 0.972.$$

To travel a horizontal distance of exactly 300 m, the required angles are $\alpha = \frac{1}{2} \sin^{-1} (0.972) \approx 38.205°$ or $51.795°$.

Related Exercises 29–34 ◄

SECTION 11.7 EXERCISES

Review Questions

1. Given the position function **r** of a moving object, explain how to find the velocity, speed, and acceleration of the object.

2. What is the relationship between the position and velocity vectors for motion on a circle?

3. State Newton's Second Law of Motion in vector form.

4. Write Newton's Second Law of Motion for two-dimensional motion with only the gravitational force (acting in the y-direction).

5. Given the acceleration of an object and its initial velocity, how do you find the velocity of the object, for $t \geq 0$?

6. Given the velocity of an object and its initial position, how do you find the position of the object, for $t \geq 0$?

Basic Skills

7–18. Velocity and acceleration from position *Consider the following position functions.*

a. Find the velocity and speed of the object.
b. Find the acceleration of the object.

7. $\mathbf{r}(t) = \langle 3t^2 + 1, 4t^2 + 3 \rangle$, for $t \geq 0$

8. $\mathbf{r}(t) = \left\langle \frac{5}{2}t^2 + 3, 6t^2 + 10 \right\rangle$, for $t \geq 0$

9. $\mathbf{r}(t) = \langle 2 + 2t, 1 - 4t \rangle$, for $t \geq 0$

10. $\mathbf{r}(t) = \langle 1 - t^2, 3 + 2t^3 \rangle$, for $t \geq 0$

11. $\mathbf{r}(t) = \langle 8 \sin t, 8 \cos t \rangle$, for $0 \leq t \leq 2\pi$

12. $\mathbf{r}(t) = \langle 3 \cos t, 4 \sin t \rangle$, for $0 \leq t \leq 2\pi$

13. $\mathbf{r}(t) = \langle e^t \cos t, e^t \sin t \rangle$, for $t \geq 0$

14. $\mathbf{r}(t) = \langle 5e^{2t}, 12e^{2t} \rangle$, for $t \geq 0$

15. $\mathbf{r}(t) = \langle 3 + t, 2 - 4t \rangle$, for $t \geq 0$

16. $\mathbf{r}(t) = \langle \cos e^t, \sin e^t \rangle$, for $0 \leq t \leq \pi/2$

▯ 17–20. Comparing trajectories *Consider the following position functions* **r** *and* **R** *for two objects.*

a. Find the interval $[c, d]$ over which the **R** *trajectory is the same as the* **r** *trajectory over $[a, b]$.*
b. Find the velocity for both objects.
c. Graph the speed of the two objects over the intervals $[a, b]$ and $[c, d]$ respectively.

17. $\mathbf{r}(t) = \langle t, t^2 \rangle$, $[a, b] = [0, 2]$,
    $\mathbf{R}(t) = \langle 2t, 4t^2 \rangle$ on $[c, d]$

18. $\mathbf{r}(t) = \langle 1 + 3t, 2 + 4t \rangle$, $[a, b] = [0, 6]$,
    $\mathbf{R}(t) = \langle 1 + 9t, 2 + 12t \rangle$ on $[c, d]$

19. $\mathbf{r}(t) = \langle \cos t, 4 \sin t \rangle$, $[a, b] = [0, 2\pi]$,
    $\mathbf{R}(t) = \langle \cos 3t, 4 \sin 3t \rangle$ on $[c, d]$

20. $\mathbf{r}(t) = \langle 2 - e^t, 4 - e^{-t} \rangle$, $[a, b] = [0, \ln 10]$,
    $\mathbf{R}(t) = \langle 2 - t, 4 - 1/t \rangle$ on $[c, d]$

21–22. Motion in the plane *For each velocity function, carry out the following steps. Assume the object begins moving from the origin at $t = 0$. Assume also that the x-axis points east and the y-axis points north.*

a. At what times is the object moving eastward? Northward?
b. Find the position vector for the object.
▯ *c. Describe the path of the object and plot your result with a graphing calculator.*

21. $\mathbf{v}(t) = \left\langle \frac{1}{t + 1}, e^{-t} \right\rangle$, for $t \geq 0$

22. $\mathbf{v}(t) = \langle e^{-t}(1 - t), \sin t \rangle$, for $0 \leq t \leq 2\pi$

23–28. Solving equations of motion *Given an acceleration vector, initial velocity* $\langle u_0, v_0 \rangle$, *and initial position* $\langle x_0, y_0 \rangle$, *find the velocity and position vectors, for $t \geq 0$.*

23. $\mathbf{a}(t) = \langle 0, 1 \rangle$, $\langle u_0, v_0 \rangle = \langle 2, 3 \rangle$, $\langle x_0, y_0 \rangle = \langle 0, 0 \rangle$

24. $\mathbf{a}(t) = \langle 1, 2 \rangle$, $\langle u_0, v_0 \rangle = \langle 1, 1 \rangle$, $\langle x_0, y_0 \rangle = \langle 2, 3 \rangle$

25. $\mathbf{a}(t) = \langle 0, 10 \rangle$, $\langle u_0, v_0 \rangle = \langle 0, 5 \rangle$, $\langle x_0, y_0 \rangle = \langle 1, -1 \rangle$

26. $\mathbf{a}(t) = \langle 1, t \rangle$, $\langle u_0, v_0 \rangle = \langle 2, -1 \rangle$, $\langle x_0, y_0 \rangle = \langle 0, 8 \rangle$

27. $\mathbf{a}(t) = \langle \cos t, 2 \sin t \rangle$, $\langle u_0, v_0 \rangle = \langle 0, 1 \rangle$, $\langle x_0, y_0 \rangle = \langle 1, 0 \rangle$

28. $\mathbf{a}(t) = \langle e^{-t}, 1 \rangle$, $\langle u_0, v_0 \rangle = \langle 1, 0 \rangle$, $\langle x_0, y_0 \rangle = \langle 0, 0 \rangle$

29–34. Two-dimensional motion *Consider the motion of the following objects. Assume the x-axis is horizontal, the positive y-axis is vertical, the ground is horizontal, and only the gravitational force acts on the object.*

a. *Find the velocity and position vectors, for $t \geq 0$.*
b. *Graph the trajectory.*
c. *Determine the time of flight and range of the object.*
d. *Determine the maximum height of the object.*

29. A soccer ball has an initial position $\langle x_0, y_0 \rangle = \langle 0, 0 \rangle$ when it is kicked with an initial velocity of $\langle u_0, v_0 \rangle = \langle 30, 6 \rangle$ m/s.

30. A golf ball has an initial position $\langle x_0, y_0 \rangle = \langle 0, 0 \rangle$ when it is hit at an angle of $30°$ with an initial speed of 150 ft/s.

31. A baseball has an initial position (in feet) of $\langle x_0, y_0 \rangle = \langle 0, 6 \rangle$ when it is thrown with an initial velocity of $\langle u_0, v_0 \rangle = \langle 80, 10 \rangle$ ft/s.

32. A baseball is thrown horizontally from a height of 10 ft above the ground with a speed of 132 ft/s.

33. A projectile is launched from a platform 20 ft above the ground at an angle of $60°$ with a speed of 250 ft/s. Assume the origin is at the base of the platform.

34. A rock is thrown from the edge of a vertical cliff 40 m above the ground at an angle of $45°$ with a speed of $10\sqrt{2}$ m/s. Assume the origin is at the foot of the cliff.

Further Explorations

35. Explain why or why not Determine whether the following statements are true and give an explanation or counterexample.

a. If the speed of an object is constant, then its velocity components are constant.
b. The functions $\mathbf{r}(t) = \langle \cos t, \sin t \rangle$ and $\mathbf{R}(t) = \langle \sin t^2, \cos t^2 \rangle$ generate the same set of points, for $t \geq 0$.
c. A velocity vector of variable magnitude cannot have a constant direction.
d. If the acceleration of an object is zero, for all $t \geq 0$ ($\mathbf{a}(t) = \mathbf{0}$), then the velocity of the object is constant.
e. If you double the initial speed of a projectile, its range also doubles (assume no forces other than gravity act on the projectile).
f. If you double the initial speed of a projectile, its time of flight also doubles (assume no forces other than gravity).
g. A trajectory with $\mathbf{v}(t) = \mathbf{a}(t) \neq \mathbf{0}$, for all t, is possible.

36–39. Trajectory properties *Find the time of flight, range, and maximum height of the following two-dimensional trajectories, assuming no forces other than gravity. In each case, the initial position is $\langle 0, 0 \rangle$ and the initial velocity is $\mathbf{v}_0 = \langle u_0, v_0 \rangle$.*

36. $\langle u_0, v_0 \rangle = \langle 10, 20 \rangle$ ft/s

37. Initial speed $|\mathbf{v}_0| = 150$ m/s, launch angle $\alpha = 30°$

38. $\langle u_0, v_0 \rangle = \langle 40, 80 \rangle$ m/s

39. Initial speed $|\mathbf{v}_0| = 400$ ft/s, launch angle $\alpha = 60°$

40. Motion on the moon The acceleration due to gravity on the moon is approximately $g/6$ (one-sixth its value on Earth). Compare the time of flight, range, and maximum height of a projectile on the moon with the corresponding values on Earth.

41. Firing angles A projectile is fired over horizontal ground from the origin with an initial speed of 60 m/s. What firing angles will produce a range of 300 m?

42. Firing strategies Suppose you wish to fire a projectile over horizontal ground from the origin and attain a range of 1000 m.

a. Make a graph of the initial speed required for all firing angles $0 < \alpha < \pi/2$.
b. What firing angle requires the least initial speed?

43. Nonuniform straight-line motion Consider the motion of an object given by the position function

$$\mathbf{r}(t) = f(t) \langle a, b \rangle + \langle x_0, y_0 \rangle, \quad \text{for } t \geq 0,$$

where a, b, x_0 and y_0 are constants, and f is a differentiable scalar function, for $t \geq 0$.

a. Explain why this function describes motion along a line.
b. Find the velocity function. In general, is the velocity constant in magnitude or direction along the path?

44. A race Two people travel from $P(4, 0)$ to $Q(-4, 0)$ along the paths given by

$$\mathbf{r}(t) = \langle 4 \cos (\pi t/8), 4 \sin (\pi t/8) \rangle \quad \text{and}$$
$$\mathbf{R}(t) = \langle 4 - t, (4 - t)^2 - 16 \rangle.$$

a. Graph both paths between P and Q.
b. Graph the speeds of both people between P and Q.
c. Who arrives at Q first?

45. Circular motion Consider an object moving along the circular trajectory $\mathbf{r}(t) = \langle A \cos \omega t, A \sin \omega t \rangle$, where A and ω are constants.

a. Over what time interval $[0, T]$ does the object traverse the circle once?
b. Find the velocity and speed of the object. Is the velocity constant in either direction or magnitude? Is the speed constant?
c. Find the acceleration of the object.
d. How are the position and velocity related? How are the position and acceleration related?
e. Sketch the position, velocity, and acceleration vectors at four different points on the trajectory with $A = \omega = 1$.

46. A linear trajectory An object moves along a straight line from the point $P(1, 2)$ to the point $Q(-6, 8)$.

a. Find a position function $\mathbf{r}$ that describes the motion if it occurs with a constant speed over the time interval $[0, 5]$.

b. Find a position function $\mathbf{r}$ that describes the motion if it occurs with speed e^t.

47. A circular trajectory An object moves clockwise around a circle centered at the origin with radius 5 m beginning at the point $(0, 5)$.

a. Find a position function $\mathbf{r}$ that describes the motion if the object moves with a constant speed, completing 1 lap every 12 s.

b. Find a position function $\mathbf{r}$ that describes the motion if it occurs with speed e^{-t}.

Applications

48. Golf shot A golfer stands 390 ft (130 yd) horizontally from the hole and 40 ft below the hole (see figure). Assuming the ball is hit with an initial speed of 150 ft/s, at what angle(s) should it be hit to land in the hole? Assume that the path of the ball lies in a plane.

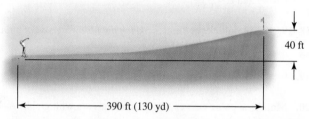

390 ft (130 yd)

40 ft

49. Another golf shot A golfer stands 420 ft (140 yd) horizontally from the hole and 50 ft above the hole (see figure). Assuming the ball is hit with an initial speed of 120 ft/s, at what angle(s) should it be hit to land in the hole? Assume that the path of the ball lies in a plane.

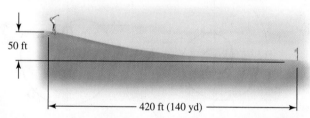

50 ft

420 ft (140 yd)

50. Initial velocity of a golf shot A golfer stands 390 ft horizontally from the hole and 40 ft below the hole (see figure for Exercise 48). If the ball is struck and leaves the ground at an initial angle of 45° with the horizontal, then with what initial velocity should it be hit to land in the hole?

51. Initial velocity of a golf shot A golfer stands 420 ft horizontally from the hole and 50 ft above the hole (see figure for Exercise 49). If the ball is struck and leaves the ground at an initial angle of 30° with the horizontal, then with what initial velocity should it be hit to land in the hole?

52. Ski jump The lip of a ski jump is 8 m above the outrun that is sloped at an angle of 30° to the horizontal (see figure).

a. If the initial velocity of a ski jumper at the lip of the jump is $\langle 40, 0 \rangle$ m/s, what is the length of the jump (distance from the origin to the landing point)? Assume only gravity affects the motion.

b. Assume that air resistance produces a constant horizontal acceleration of 0.15 m/s² opposing the motion. What is the length of the jump?

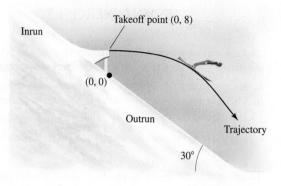

Inrun

Takeoff point (0, 8)

(0, 0)

Outrun

Trajectory

30°

53. Time of flight, range, height Derive the formulas for time of flight, range, and maximum height in the case that an object is launched from the initial position $\langle 0, y_0 \rangle$ with initial velocity $|\mathbf{v}_0| \langle \cos \alpha, \sin \alpha \rangle$.

54. Trajectory with a sloped landing Assume an object is launched from the origin with an initial speed $|\mathbf{v}_0|$ at an angle α to the horizontal, where $0 < \alpha < \dfrac{\pi}{2}$.

a. Find the time of flight, range, and maximum height (relative to the launch point) of the trajectory if the ground slopes *downward* at a constant angle of θ from the launch site, where $0 < \theta < \dfrac{\pi}{2}$.

b. Find the time of flight, range, and maximum height of the trajectory if the ground slopes *upward* at a constant angle of θ from the launch site. Assume $\tan \theta < \dfrac{1}{2} \tan \alpha$.

Additional Exercises

55. Parabolic trajectories Show that the two-dimensional trajectory

$$x(t) = u_0 t + x_0 \quad \text{and} \quad y(t) = -\frac{gt^2}{2} + v_0 t + y_0, \quad \text{for } 0 \le t \le T,$$

of an object moving in a gravitational field is a segment of a parabola for some value of $T > 0$. Find T such that $y(T) = 0$.

56. Equal area property Consider the ellipse $\mathbf{r}(t) = \langle a \cos t, b \sin t \rangle$, for $0 \le t \le 2\pi$, where a and b are real numbers. Let θ be the angle between the position vector and the x-axis.

a. Show that $\tan \theta = (b/a) \tan t$.

b. Find $\theta'(t)$.

c. Recall that the area bounded by the polar curve $r = f(\theta)$ on the interval $[0, \theta]$ is $A(\theta) = \dfrac{1}{2} \displaystyle\int_0^\theta (f(u))^2 \, du$.

Letting $f(\theta(t)) = |\mathbf{r}(\theta(t))|$, show that $A'(t) = \dfrac{1}{2} ab$.

d. Conclude that as an object moves around the ellipse, it sweeps out equal areas in equal times.

QUICK CHECK ANSWERS

1. $\mathbf{v}(t) = \langle 1, 2t \rangle, \mathbf{a}(t) = \langle 0, 2 \rangle$

2. $x(t) = 100t, y(t) = -16t^2 + 60t + 2$

3. $\sin \left(2 \left(\dfrac{\pi}{2} - \alpha \right) \right) = \sin (\pi - 2\alpha) = \sin 2\alpha$ ◄

1. Explain why or why not Determine whether the following statements are true and give an explanation or counterexample.

a. A set of parametric equations for a given curve is always unique.

b. The equations $x = e^t, y = 2e^t$, for $-\infty < t < \infty$, describe a line passing through the origin with slope 2.

c. The polar coordinates $\left(3, -\dfrac{3\pi}{4}\right)$ and $\left(-3, \dfrac{\pi}{4}\right)$ describe the same point in the plane.

d. The area of the region between the inner and outer loops of the limaçon $r = f(\theta) = 1 - 4\cos\theta$ is $\dfrac{1}{2}\displaystyle\int_0^{2\pi} (f(\theta))^2 \, d\theta$.

e. Given two vectors $\mathbf{u}$ and $\mathbf{v}$, it is always true that $2\mathbf{u} + \mathbf{v} = \mathbf{v} + 2\mathbf{u}$.

f. The vector in the direction of $\mathbf{u}$ with the length of $\mathbf{v}$ equals the vector in the direction of $\mathbf{v}$ with the length of $\mathbf{u}$.

g. If $\mathbf{u} \neq \mathbf{0}$ and $\mathbf{u} + \mathbf{v} = \mathbf{0}$, then $\mathbf{u}$ and $\mathbf{v}$ are parallel.

2–5. Parametric curves

a. *Plot the following curves, indicating the positive orientation.*

b. *Eliminate the parameter to obtain an equation in x and y.*

c. *Identify or briefly describe the curve.*

d. *Evaluate $\dfrac{dy}{dx}$ at the specified point.*

2. $x = t^2 + 4, y = 6 - t$, for $-\infty < t < \infty$; $(5, 5)$

3. $x = e^t, y = 3e^{-2t}$, for $-\infty < t < \infty$; $(1, 3)$

4. $x = 10\sin 2t, y = 16\cos 2t$, for $0 \le t \le \pi$; $(5\sqrt{3}, 8)$

5. $x = \ln t, y = 8\ln t^2$, for $1 \le t \le e^2$; $(1, 16)$

6. Circles Which of the following functions describe one complete circuit of circle centered at the origin? In those cases, give the orientation of the circle.

a. $\mathbf{r}(t) = \langle \cos 5t, \sin 5t \rangle$, for $-\dfrac{2\pi}{5} \le t \le \dfrac{3\pi}{5}$

b. $\mathbf{r}(t) = \langle \cos^2 t, \sin^2 t \rangle$, for $0 \le t \le 2\pi$

c. $\mathbf{r}(t) = \langle \sin e^t, \cos e^t \rangle$, for $0 \le t \le \ln 2\pi$

d. $\mathbf{r}(t) = \langle \sin t^3, \cos t^3 \rangle$, for $-\sqrt[3]{\pi} \le t \le \sqrt[3]{\pi}$

e. $\mathbf{r}(t) = \langle \cos \ln t, \sin \ln t \rangle$, for $1 \le t \le e^{2\pi}$

7–9. Eliminating the parameter *Eliminate the parameter to find a description of the following curves in terms of x and y. Give a geometric description and the positive orientation of the curve.*

7. $x = 4\cos t, y = 3\sin t;\ 0 \le t \le 2\pi$

8. $x = 4\cos t - 1, y = 4\sin t + 2;\ 0 \le t \le 2\pi$

9. $x = \sin t - 3, y = \cos t + 6;\ 0 \le t \le \pi$

10. Parametric to polar equations Find a description of the following curve in polar coordinates and describe the curve.

$x = (1 + \cos t)\cos t,\ y = (1 + \cos t)\sin t + 6;\ 0 \le t \le 2\pi$

11–16. Parametric description *Write parametric equations for the following curves. Solutions are not unique.*

11. The circle $x^2 + y^2 = 9$, oriented clockwise

12. The upper half of the ellipse $\dfrac{x^2}{9} + \dfrac{y^2}{4} = 1$, oriented counterclockwise

13. The right side of the ellipse $\dfrac{x^2}{9} + \dfrac{y^2}{4} = 1$, oriented counterclockwise

14. The line $y - 3 = 4(x + 2)$

15. The line segment from $P(-1, 0)$ to $Q(1, 1)$ and the line segment from Q to P

16. The segment of the curve $f(x) = x^3 + 2x$ from $(0, 0)$ to $(2, 12)$

17. Tangent lines Find an equation of the line tangent to the cycloid $x = t - \sin t, y = 1 - \cos t$ at the points corresponding to $t = \dfrac{\pi}{6}$ and $t = \dfrac{2\pi}{3}$.

18–19. Sets in polar coordinates *Sketch the following sets of points.*

18. $4 \le r^2 \le 9$

19. $0 \le r \le 4, -\dfrac{\pi}{2} \le \theta \le -\dfrac{\pi}{3}$

20. Matching polar curves Match equations a–f with graphs A–F.

a. $r = 3\sin 4\theta$ b. $r^2 = 4\cos\theta$

c. $r = 2 - 3\sin\theta$ d. $r = 1 + 2\cos\theta$

e. $r = 3\cos 3\theta$ f. $r = e^{-\theta/6}$

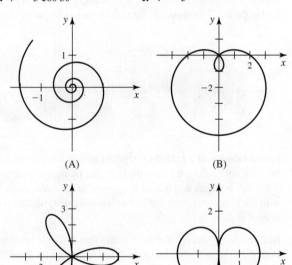

(A)   (B)

(C)   (D)

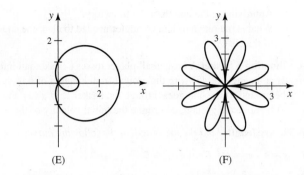

(E)   (F)

21. **Polar valentine** Liz wants to show her love for Jake by passing him a valentine on her graphing calculator. Sketch each of the following curves and determine which one Liz should use to get a heart-shaped curve.

    a. $r = 5 \cos \theta$ b. $r = 1 - \sin \theta$ c. $r = \cos 3\theta$

22. **Jake's response** Jake responds to Liz (Exercise 21) with a graph that shows that his love for her is infinite. Sketch each of the following curves. Which one should Jake send to Liz to get a sideways figure-8 curve (infinity symbol)?

    a. $r = \theta$, for $\theta \geq 0$ b. $r = \frac{1}{2} + \sin \theta$ c. $r^2 = \cos 2\theta$

23. **Polar conversion** Write the equation

    $$r^2 + r(2 \sin \theta - 6 \cos \theta) = 0$$

    in Cartesian coordinates and identify the corresponding curve.

24. **Polar conversion** Consider the equation $r = 4/(\sin \theta + \cos \theta)$.

    a. Convert the equation to Cartesian coordinates and identify the curve it describes.
    b. Graph the curve and indicate the points that correspond to $\theta = 0$, and $\pi/2$.
    c. Give an interval in θ on which the entire curve is generated.

25. **Cartesian conversion** Write the circle $(x - 4)^2 + y^2 = 16$ in polar coordinates and state values of θ that produce the entire graph of the circle.

26. **Cartesian conversion** Write the parabola $x = y^2$ in polar coordinates and state values of θ that produce the entire graph of the parabola.

27. **Intersection points** Consider the polar equations $r = 1$ and $r = 2 - 4 \cos \theta$.

    a. Graph the curves. How many intersection points do you observe?
    b. Give the approximate polar coordinates of the intersection points.

28–31. Slopes of tangent lines

a. *Find all points where the following curves have vertical and horizontal tangent lines.*
b. *Find the slope of the lines tangent to the curve at the origin (when relevant).*
c. *Sketch the curve and all the tangent lines identified in parts (a) and (b).*

28. $r = 2 \cos 2\theta$ 29. $r = 4 + 2 \sin \theta$

30. $r = 3 - 6 \cos \theta$ 31. $r^2 = 2 \cos 2\theta$

32–37. Areas of regions *Find the area of the following regions. In each case, graph the curve(s) and shade the region in question.*

32. The region enclosed by all the leaves of the rose $r = 3 \sin 4\theta$

33. The region enclosed by the limaçon $r = 3 - \cos \theta$

34. The region inside the limaçon $r = 2 + \cos \theta$ and outside the circle $r = 2$

35. The region inside the lemniscate $r^2 = 4 \cos 2\theta$ and outside the circle $r = \frac{1}{2}$

36. The area that is inside both the cardioids $r = 1 - \cos \theta$ and $r = 1 + \cos \theta$

37. The area that is inside the cardioid $r = 1 + \cos \theta$ and outside the cardioid $r = 1 - \cos \theta$

38–41. Drawing vectors *Let $\mathbf{u} = \langle 3, -4 \rangle$ and $\mathbf{v} = \langle -1, 2 \rangle$. Use geometry to sketch the following vectors.*

38. $\mathbf{u} - \mathbf{v}$ 39. $-3\mathbf{v}$

40. $\mathbf{u} + 2\mathbf{v}$ 41. $2\mathbf{v} - \mathbf{u}$

42–45. Working with vectors *Let $\mathbf{u} = \langle 2, 4 \rangle$ and $\mathbf{v} = \langle -6, 10 \rangle$.*

42. Compute $\mathbf{u} - 3\mathbf{v}$.   43. Compute $|\mathbf{u} + \mathbf{v}|$.

44. Find the unit vector with the same direction as $\mathbf{u}$.

45. Find a vector parallel to $\mathbf{v}$ with length 2.

46. **Scalar multiples** Find scalars a and b such that

    $$\langle -2, 6 \rangle = a\langle 1, 2 \rangle + b\langle 3, 1 \rangle.$$

47. **Velocity vectors** Assume the positive x-axis points east and the positive y-axis points north.

    a. An airliner flies northwest at a constant altitude at 550 mi/hr in calm air. Find a and b such that its velocity may be expressed in the form $\mathbf{v} = a\mathbf{i} + b\mathbf{j}$.
    b. An airliner flies northwest at a constant altitude at 550 mi/hr relative to the air in a southerly crosswind $\mathbf{w} = \langle 0, 40 \rangle$. Find the velocity of the airliner relative to the ground.

48. **Combined force** An object at the origin is acted on by the forces $\mathbf{F}_1 = -10\mathbf{i}$, $\mathbf{F}_2 = 40\mathbf{j}$, and $\mathbf{F}_3 = -50\mathbf{i} + 20\mathbf{j}$. Find the magnitude of the combined force and describe with a sketch the direction of the force.

49. **Falling probe** A remote sensing probe falls vertically with a terminal velocity of 60 m/s when it encounters a horizontal crosswind blowing north at 4 m/s and an updraft blowing vertically at 10 m/s. Find the magnitude and direction of the resulting velocity relative to the ground.

50. **Work** A 180-lb man stands on a hillside that makes an angle of 30° with the horizontal, producing a force of $\mathbf{W} = \langle 0, -180 \rangle$. Find the component of his weight in the downward direction perpendicular to the hillside and in the downward direction parallel to the hillside (see figure).

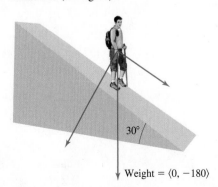

30°

Weight = $\langle 0, -180 \rangle$

51–53. Curves in the plane *Sketch the curves described by the following functions, indicating the orientation of the curve. Use analysis and describe the shape of the curve before using a graphing utility.*

51. $\mathbf{r}(t) = 4\cos t\,\mathbf{i} + 4\sin t\,\mathbf{j}$, for $0 \le t \le 2\pi$

52. $\mathbf{r}(t) = e^t\,\mathbf{i} + 2e^t\,\mathbf{j}$, for $t \ge 0$

53. $\mathbf{r}(t) = \sin t\,\mathbf{i} + \sqrt{2}\cos t\,\mathbf{j}$, for $0 \le t \le 2\pi$

54. Baseball motion A toddler on level ground throws a baseball into the air at an angle of 30° with the ground from a height of 2 ft. Assuming the ball lands 10 ft from the child, determine the initial speed of the ball.

55. Projectile motion A projectile is launched from the origin, which is a point 50 ft from a 30-ft vertical cliff (see figure). It is launched at a speed of $50\sqrt{2}$ ft/s at an angle of 45° to the horizontal. Assume that the ground is horizontal on top of the cliff and that only the gravitational force affects the motion of the object.

a. Give the coordinates of the landing spot of the projectile on the top of the cliff.

b. What is the maximum height reached by the projectile?

c. What is the time of flight?

d. Write an integral that gives the length of the trajectory.

e. Approximate the length of the trajectory.

f. What is the range of launch angles needed to clear the edge of the cliff?

56. Shooting a basket A basketball player tosses a basketball into the air at an angle of 45° with the ground from a height of 6 ft above the ground. If the ball goes through the basket 15 ft away and 10 ft above the ground, determine the initial velocity of the ball.

57–59. Arc length *Find the arc length of the following curves.*

57. $x = t^3, y = 4t^2$, for $0 \le t \le 2$

58. $x = \dfrac{2}{9}t^{9/2}, y = \dfrac{1}{3}t^3$, for $0 \le t \le 2$

59. $x = t, y = \ln(\sec t)$, for $0 \le t \le \pi/6$

60–61. Arc length of polar curves *Approximate the length of the following curves.*

60. The limaçon $r = 3 + 2\cos\theta$

61. The limaçon $r = 3 - 6\cos\theta$

62-65. Working with vector-valued functions *For each vector-valued function* **r**, *carry out the following steps.*

a. Evaluate $\lim\limits_{t\to 0}\mathbf{r}(t)$ and $\lim\limits_{t\to\infty}\mathbf{r}(t)$, if each exists.

b. Find $\mathbf{r}'(t)$ and evaluate $\mathbf{r}'(0)$.

c. Find $\mathbf{r}''(t)$.

d. Evaluate $\int \mathbf{r}(t)\,dt$.

62. $\mathbf{r}(t) = \langle t+1, t^2 - 3\rangle$

63. $\mathbf{r}(t) = \left\langle \dfrac{1}{2t+1}, \dfrac{t}{t+1}\right\rangle$

64. $\mathbf{r}(t) = \langle e^{-2t}, te^{-t}\rangle$

65. $\mathbf{r}(t) = \langle \sin 2t, 3\cos 4t\rangle$

AP® PRACTICE QUESTIONS   *The following questions are intended to help you prepare for the AP exam. They are not questions from actual AP exams.*

Section 1 Part A, Multiple Choice, No Technology

1. Which equation describes the line defined by the parametric equations $x = 2t, y = -3t + 3, -\infty < t < \infty$?

(A) $3x + 2y = 5$ (B) $3x + 2y = 6$

(C) $2x + y = 5$ (D) $6x + y = 6$

(E) $6x + y = 3$

2. The trajectory of an object moving in the plane is given by
$$x = \frac{1}{1+t^2}, y = \frac{1}{t+6}, \text{ for } -5 \le t \le 5.$$
Over what time interval is the object moving in the negative x-direction?

I $(-5, 0)$ **II** $(0, 5)$ **III** $(-\sqrt{6}, \sqrt{6})$

(A) I only   (B) II only   (C) III only

(D) I and II only   (E) I and III only

3. The curve given by the equations $x = 2t^2, y = t^3$, for $0 \le t \le 1$, has length

(A) 3.   (B) $\dfrac{4}{3}$.   (C) $\dfrac{72}{27}$.   (D) $\dfrac{43}{18}$.   (E) $\dfrac{61}{27}$.

4. The integral $\dfrac{1}{2}\displaystyle\int_0^{\pi/4} \sin^2 4\theta\, d\theta$ equals the area of which shaded region?

(A)

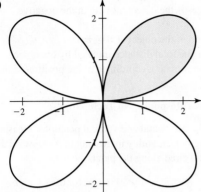

(B)

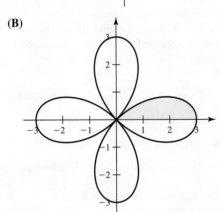

(C)

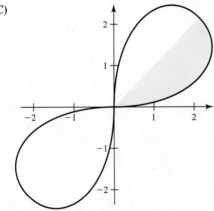

(D)

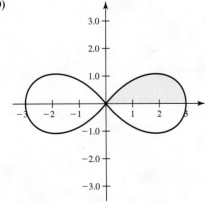

(E)

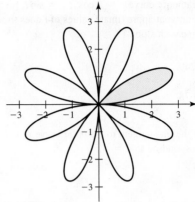

5. Find the area of the region bounded by the cardioid $r = 1 - \cos\theta$.

(A) π (B) 2π (C) 2 (D) $\dfrac{3\pi}{2}$ (E) $\dfrac{\pi}{2}$

6. An object moves along the path $\mathbf{r}(t) = \langle t, 1 - 2t + t^2 \rangle$, for $0 \le t \le 3$. At what time is its speed a minimum?

(A) 2.5   (B) 3   (C) 2   (D) 0   (E) 1

7. Find the position vector of an object whose velocity is $\mathbf{v}(t) = \langle -16t + 40, 0 \rangle$ and whose initial position is $\mathbf{r}(0) = \langle 0, 10 \rangle$.

(A) $\mathbf{r}(t) = \langle -8t^2 + 40t, 10t \rangle$

(B) $\mathbf{r}(t) = \langle -8t^2 + 40t, 10 \rangle$

(C) $\mathbf{r}(t) = \langle -16t + 40, 10 \rangle$

(D) $\mathbf{r}(t) = \langle -8t^2 + 40t + 10, 0 \rangle$

(E) $\mathbf{r}(t) = \langle -16t^2 + 40t, 10 \rangle$

8. What is the length of the spiral $r = \theta^2$, for $0 \le \theta \le \sqrt{5}$?

(A) $\dfrac{17}{3}$ (B) $\dfrac{23}{3}$ (C) 7 (D) $\dfrac{19}{3}$ (E) $\dfrac{26}{5}$

9. The equation of the line tangent to the curve $x = \sin(3t - 6), y = e^{t-2}$ at $(0, 1)$ is

(A) $y = x + \dfrac{1}{3}$.

(B) $y = -\dfrac{1}{3}x + 1$.

(C) $y = \dfrac{1}{3}x + 1$.

(D) $y = 1$.

(E) $y = \dfrac{2}{3}x + 1$.

Section 1 Part B, Multiple Choice, Technology Allowed

10. Find the area of the region outside the circle $r = 1$ and inside the curve $r = 1 + \sin\theta$.

(A) $2 + \dfrac{\pi}{2} \approx 3.571$ (B) 1

(C) $2 + \dfrac{\pi}{4} \approx 2.785$ (D) $1 + \dfrac{\pi}{2} \approx 2.571$

(E) $2 + \pi \approx 5.142$

11. Consider the parametric curve $x = 2 \cos t$, $y = \sin t$, for $-\pi \leq t \leq \pi$. For what approximate values of t does the curve have a tangent line with slope 1?

(A) ± 0.464

(B) $-1.107, 4.249$

(C) ± 0.107

(D) $-0.464, 2.678$

(E) $-0.785, 2.356$

12. What is slope of the line tangent to the polar curve $r = 1 - \sin \theta$ at the point corresponding to $\theta = 0$?

(A) $\dfrac{1}{2}$

(B) 1

(C) $-\dfrac{1}{2}$

(D) -1

(E) The tangent line is vertical.

Section 2 Part A, Free Response, Technology Allowed

1. A small rocket is fired upward from a platform 10 m above the ground with an initial velocity in m/s of $\langle 10, 30 \rangle$. Assume the origin is at the base of the platform, the y-axis points upward, the launch occurs at $t = 0$, and the acceleration due to gravity is 9.8 m/s^2.

   a. Find the velocity vector of the rocket for all times at which the rocket is in the air.

   b. Find the position vector of the rocket for all times at which the rocket is in the air.

   c. At approximately what time does the rocket return to the ground?

   d. Assuming horizontal ground, approximately how far does the rocket travel horizontally before it returns to the ground?

2. At time $t \geq 0$, the velocity of an object in m/s is

   $$\mathbf{v}(t) = \left\langle 2(1 - e^{-t}), -\frac{4}{2t + 1} \right\rangle.$$ Its initial position is $\mathbf{r}(0) = \langle 8, 6 \rangle$.

   a. For what times is the object moving in the positive x-direction?

   b. For what times is the object moving in the positive y-direction?

   c. Find the approximate speed of the object at $t = 2$.

   d. Find the exact acceleration of the object at $t = 2$.

   e. Find the approximate position of the object at $t = 2$.

3. The velocity of an object in ft/s is $\mathbf{v}(t) = \langle \sin t, e^{\cos t} - 1 \rangle$, for $0 \leq t \leq 2\pi$. Its initial position is $\mathbf{r}(0) = \langle 0, 0 \rangle$.

   a. For what times is the object moving in the negative x-direction?

   b. For what times is the object moving in the negative y-direction?

   c. Find the speed of the object at $t = \pi$.

   d. Approximate the total distance traveled by the object.

   e. Find the approximate y-coordinate of the position of the object at $t = 1$.

Section 2 Part B, Free Response, No Technology

4. Let x and y be the horizontal and vertical positions, measured in feet, of a moving object, with y increasing in the upward direction. The object is fired along the parabolic path

   $$\mathbf{r} = \langle x, y \rangle = \langle 8t, -16t^2 + 64t \rangle, \text{ for } 0 \leq t \leq T.$$

   a. Find the velocity vector for the projectile.

   b. At what time T does the projectile strike the ground?

   c. Assuming a horizontal ground, how far does the projectile travel horizontally before it strikes the ground?

   d. What is the maximum height reached by the projectile?

5. Consider the curve C described by the parametric equations

   $$x = 3 \cos t, y = 4 \sin t, \text{ for } 0 \leq t \leq 2\pi.$$

   a. At what points on C does the tangent line have slope $\dfrac{4}{3}$?

   b. Does the curve have any vertical tangent lines? If so, at what points?

   c. Write an integral that gives the length of C.

   d. If C is the path of a moving object, at what times is the object moving entirely in the x-direction?

Chapter 11 Guided Projects

Applications of the material in this chapter and related topics can be found in the following Guided Projects. For additional information, see the Preface.

- The amazing cycloid
- Parametric art
- Polar art
- Grazing goat problems
- Designing a trajectory
- Bezier curves for graphic design

A Appendix

The goal of this appendix is to establish the essential notation, terminology, and algebraic skills that are used throughout the book.

Algebra

EXAMPLE 1 Algebra review

a. Evaluate $(-32)^{2/5}$.

b. Simplify $\dfrac{1}{x-2} - \dfrac{1}{x+2}$.

c. Solve the equation $\dfrac{x^4 - 5x^2 + 4}{x - 1} = 0$.

SOLUTION

a. Recall that $(-32)^{2/5} = ((-32)^{1/5})^2$. Because $(-32)^{1/5} = \sqrt[5]{-32} = -2$, we have $(-32)^{2/5} = (-2)^2 = 4$.
Another option is to write $(-32)^{2/5} = ((-32)^2)^{1/5} = 1024^{1/5} = 4$.

b. Finding a common denominator and simplifying leads to

$$\frac{1}{x-2} - \frac{1}{x+2} = \frac{(x+2) - (x-2)}{(x-2)(x+2)} = \frac{4}{x^2 - 4}.$$

c. Notice that $x = 1$ cannot be a solution of the equation because the left side of the equation is undefined at $x = 1$. Because $x - 1 \neq 0$, both sides of the equation can be multiplied by $x - 1$ to produce $x^4 - 5x^2 + 4 = 0$. After factoring, this equation becomes $(x^2 - 4)(x^2 - 1) = 0$, which implies $x^2 - 4 = (x - 2)(x + 2) = 0$ or $x^2 - 1 = (x - 1)(x + 1) = 0$. The roots of $x^2 - 4 = 0$ are $x = \pm 2$ and the roots of $x^2 - 1 = 0$ are $x = \pm 1$. Excluding $x = 1$, the roots of the original equation are $x = -1$ and $x = \pm 2$.

Related Exercises 15–26 ◀

Sets of Real Numbers

The set of real numbers is denoted $(-\infty, \infty)$. Figure A.1 shows the notation for **open intervals**, **closed intervals**, and various **bounded** and **unbounded intervals**. Notice that either interval notation or set notation may be used.

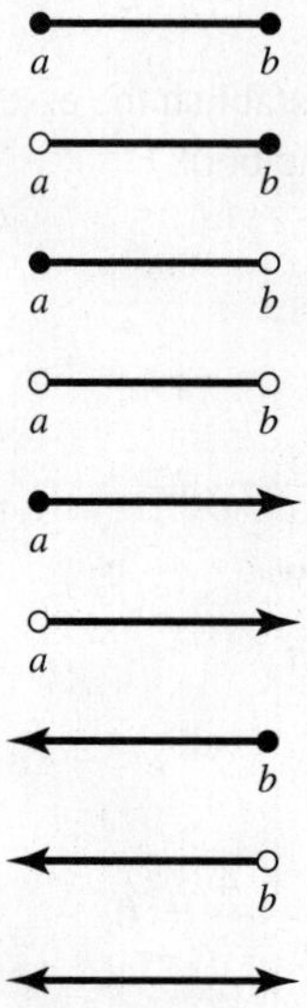

$[a, b] = \{x: a \leq x \leq b\}$		Closed, bounded interval
$(a, b] = \{x: a < x \leq b\}$		Bounded interval
$[a, b) = \{x: a \leq x < b\}$		Bounded interval
$(a, b) = \{x: a < x < b\}$		Open, bounded interval
$[a, \infty) = \{x: x \geq a\}$		Unbounded interval
$(a, \infty) = \{x: x > a\}$		Unbounded interval
$(-\infty, b] = \{x: x \leq b\}$		Unbounded interval
$(-\infty, b) = \{x: x < b\}$		Unbounded interval
$(-\infty, \infty) = \{x: -\infty < x < \infty\}$		Unbounded interval

FIGURE A.1

EXAMPLE 2   Solving inequalities Solve the following inequalities.

a. $-x^2 + 5x - 6 < 0$ **b.** $\dfrac{x^2 - x - 2}{x - 3} \leq 0$

SOLUTION

a. We multiply by -1, reverse the inequality, and then factor:

$$x^2 - 5x + 6 > 0 \quad \text{Multiply by } -1.$$
$$(x - 2)(x - 3) > 0. \quad \text{Factor.}$$

The roots of the corresponding equation $(x - 2)(x - 3) = 0$ are $x = 2$ and $x = 3$. These roots partition the number line (Figure A.2) into three intervals: $(-\infty, 2)$, $(2, 3)$, and $(3, \infty)$. On each interval, the product $(x - 2)(x - 3)$ does not change sign. To determine the sign of the product on a given interval, a **test value** x is selected and the sign of $(x - 2)(x - 3)$ is determined at x.

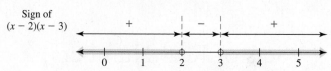

Sign of $(x - 2)(x - 3)$

FIGURE A.2

A convenient choice for x in $(-\infty, 2)$ is $x = 0$. At this test value,

$$(x - 2)(x - 3) = (-2)(-3) > 0.$$

Using a test value of $x = 2.5$ in the interval $(2, 3)$, we have

$$(x - 2)(x - 3) = (0.5)(-0.5) < 0.$$

A test value of $x = 4$ in $(3, \infty)$ gives

$$(x - 2)(x - 3) = (2)(1) > 0.$$

Therefore, $(x - 2)(x - 3) > 0$ on $(-\infty, 2)$ and $(3, \infty)$. We conclude that the inequality $-x^2 + 5x - 6 < 0$ is satisfied for all x in either $(-\infty, 2)$ or $(3, \infty)$ (Figure A.2).

➤ The set of numbers $\{x: x \text{ is in } (-\infty, 2)$ or $(3, \infty)\}$ may also be expressed using the union symbol:

$$(-\infty, 2) \cup (3, \infty).$$

b. The expression $\dfrac{x^2 - x - 2}{x - 3}$ can change sign only at points where the numerator or denominator of $\dfrac{x^2 - x - 2}{x - 3}$ equals 0. Because

$$\frac{x^2 - x - 2}{x - 3} = \frac{(x + 1)(x - 2)}{x - 3},$$

the numerator is 0 when $x = -1$ or $x = 2$, and the denominator is 0 at $x = 3$. Therefore, we examine the sign of $\dfrac{(x + 1)(x - 2)}{x - 3}$ on the intervals $(-\infty, -1)$, $(-1, 2)$, $(2, 3)$, and $(3, \infty)$.

Using test values on these intervals, we see that $\dfrac{(x + 1)(x - 2)}{x - 3} < 0$ on $(-\infty, -1)$ and $(2, 3)$. Furthermore, the expression is 0 when $x = -1$ and $x = 2$. Therefore, $\dfrac{x^2 - x - 2}{x - 3} \leq 0$ for all values of x in either $(-\infty, -1]$ or $[2, 3)$ (Figure A.3).

Test Value	$x + 1$	$x - 2$	$x - 3$	Result
-2	$-$	$-$	$-$	$-$
0	$+$	$-$	$-$	$+$
2.5	$+$	$+$	$-$	$-$
4	$+$	$+$	$+$	$+$

Sign of
$\dfrac{(x + 1)(x - 2)}{x - 3}$

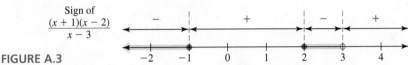

FIGURE A.3

Related Exercises 27–30 ◀

Absolute Value

The **absolute value** of a real number x, denoted $|x|$, is the distance between x and the origin on the number line (Figure A.4). More generally, $|x - y|$ is the distance between the points x and y on the number line. The absolute value has the following definition and properties.

> The absolute value is useful in simplifying square roots. Because $\sqrt{a}$ is nonnegative, we have $\sqrt{a^2} = |a|$. For example, $\sqrt{3^2} = 3$ and $\sqrt{(-3)^2} = \sqrt{9} = 3$. Note that the solutions of $x^2 = 9$ are $|x| = 3$ or $x = \pm 3$.

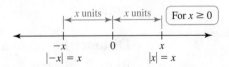

FIGURE A.4

Definition and Properties of the Absolute Value

The absolute value of a real number x is defined as

$$|x| = \begin{cases} x & \text{if } x \geq 0 \\ -x & \text{if } x < 0. \end{cases}$$

Let a be a positive real number.

1. $|x| = a \Leftrightarrow x = \pm a$ **2.** $|x| < a \Leftrightarrow -a < x < a$

3. $|x| > a \Leftrightarrow x > a$ or $x < -a$ **4.** $|x| \leq a \Leftrightarrow -a \leq x \leq a$

5. $|x| \geq a \Leftrightarrow x \geq a$ or $x \leq -a$ **6.** $|x + y| \leq |x| + |y|$

> Property 6 is called the **triangle inequality**.

EXAMPLE 3   Inequalities with absolute values Solve the following inequalities. Then sketch the solution on the number line and express it in interval notation.

a. $|x - 2| < 3$ **b.** $|2x - 6| \geq 10$

SOLUTION

a. Using Property 2 of the absolute value, $|x - 2| < 3$ is written as

$$-3 < x - 2 < 3.$$

Adding 2 to each term of these inequalities results in $-1 < x < 5$ (Figure A.5). This set of numbers is written as $(-1, 5)$ in interval notation.

b. Using Property 5, the inequality $|2x - 6| \geq 10$ implies that

$$2x - 6 \geq 10 \quad \text{or} \quad 2x - 6 \leq -10.$$

We add 6 to both sides of the first inequality to obtain $2x \geq 16$, which implies $x \geq 8$. Similarly, the second inequality yields $x \leq -2$ (Figure A.6). In interval notation, the solution is $(-\infty, -2]$ or $[8, \infty)$.

Related Exercises 31–34 ◄

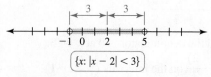

$\{x: |x - 2| < 3\}$

FIGURE A.5

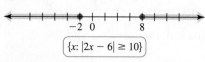

$\{x: |2x - 6| \geq 10\}$

FIGURE A.6

Cartesian Coordinate System

The conventions of the **Cartesian coordinate system** or **xy-coordinate system** are illustrated in Figure A.7.

> The familiar (x, y) coordinate system is named after René Descartes (1596–1650). However, it was introduced independently and simultaneously by Pierre de Fermat (1601–1665).

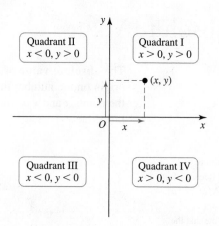

FIGURE A.7

Distance Formula and Circles

By the Pythagorean theorem (Figure A.8), we have the following formula for the distance between two points $P_1(x_1, y_1)$ and $P_2(x_2, y_2)$.

Distance Formula

The distance between the points $P_1(x_1, y_1)$ and $P_2(x_2, y_2)$ is

$$|P_1 P_2| = \sqrt{(x_2 - x_1)^2 + (y_2 - y_1)^2}.$$

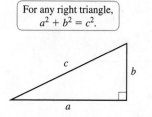

FIGURE A.8

A **circle** is the set of points in the plane whose distance from a fixed point (the **center**) is constant (the **radius**). This definition leads to the following equations that describe a circle.

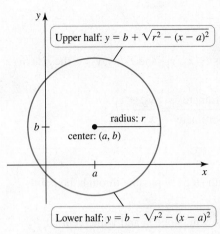

Upper half: $y = b + \sqrt{r^2 - (x - a)^2}$

radius: r

center: (a, b)

Lower half: $y = b - \sqrt{r^2 - (x - a)^2}$

FIGURE A.9

Equation of a Circle

The equation of a circle centered at (a, b) with radius r is

$$(x - a)^2 + (y - b)^2 = r^2.$$

Solving for y, the equations of the upper and lower halves of the circle (Figure A.9) are

$$y = b + \sqrt{r^2 - (x - a)^2} \qquad \text{Upper half of the circle}$$
$$y = b - \sqrt{r^2 - (x - a)^2}. \qquad \text{Lower half of the circle}$$

EXAMPLE 4   Sets involving circles

a. Find the equation of the circle with center $(2, 4)$ passing through $(-2, 1)$.

b. Describe the set of points satisfying $x^2 + y^2 - 4x - 6y < 12$.

SOLUTION

a. The radius of the circle equals the length of the line segment between the center $(2, 4)$ and the point on the circle $(-2, 1)$, which is

$$\sqrt{(2 - (-2))^2 + (4 - 1)^2} = 5.$$

Therefore, the equation of the circle is

$$(x - 2)^2 + (y - 4)^2 = 25.$$

b. To put this inequality in a recognizable form, we complete the square on the left side of the inequality:

$$x^2 + y^2 - 4x - 6y = x^2 - 4x \underbrace{+ 4 - 4}_{} + y^2 - 6y \underbrace{+ 9 - 9}_{}$$

Add and subtract the square of half the coefficient of x.   Add and subtract the square of half the coefficient of y.

$$= \underbrace{x^2 - 4x + 4}_{(x - 2)^2} + \underbrace{y^2 - 6y + 9}_{(y - 3)^2} - 4 - 9$$

$$= (x - 2)^2 + (y - 3)^2 - 13.$$

Therefore, the original inequality becomes

$$(x - 2)^2 + (y - 3)^2 - 13 < 12, \quad \text{or} \quad (x - 2)^2 + (y - 3)^2 < 25.$$

This inequality describes those points that lie within the circle centered at $(2, 3)$ with radius 5 (Figure A.10). Note that a dashed curve is used to indicate that the circle itself is not part of the solution.

> Recall that the procedure shown here for completing the square works when the coefficient on the quadratic term is 1. When the coefficient is not 1, it must be factored out before completing the square.

> A **circle** is the set of all points whose distance from a fixed point is a constant. A **disk** is the set of all points within and possibly on a circle.

The solution to
$(x - 2)^2 + (y - 3)^2 < 25$
is the interior of a circle.

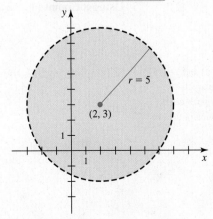

$r = 5$

$(2, 3)$

FIGURE A.10

Related Exercises 35–36 ◄

Equations of Lines

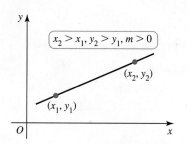

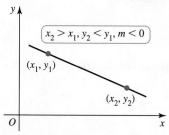

FIGURE A.11

The **slope** m of the line passing through the points $P_1(x_1, y_1)$ and $P_2(x_2, y_2)$ is the *rise over run* (Figure A.11), computed as

$$m = \frac{\text{change in vertical coordinate}}{\text{change in horizontal coordinate}} = \frac{y_2 - y_1}{x_2 - x_1}.$$

Equations of a Line

Point-slope form The equation of the line with slope m passing through the point (x_1, y_1) is $y - y_1 = m(x - x_1)$.

Slope-intercept form The equation of the line with slope m and y-intercept $(0, b)$ is $y = mx + b$ (Figure A.12a).

General linear equation The equation $Ax + By + C = 0$ describes a line in the plane, provided A and B are not both zero.

Vertical and horizontal lines The vertical line that passes through $(a, 0)$ has an equation $x = a$; its slope is undefined. The horizontal line through $(0, b)$ has an equation $y = b$, with slope equal to 0 (Figure A.12b).

> Given a particular line, we often talk about *the* equation of a line. But the equation of a specific line is not unique. Having found one equation, we can multiply it by any nonzero constant to produce another equation of the same line.

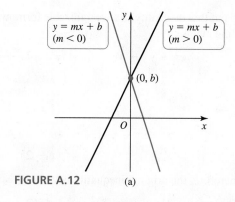

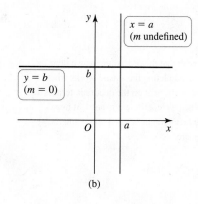

FIGURE A.12   (a)   (b)

EXAMPLE 5 Working with linear equations Find an equation of the line passing through the points $(1, -2)$ and $(-4, 5)$.

SOLUTION The slope of the line through the points $(1, -2)$ and $(-4, 5)$ is

$$m = \frac{5 - (-2)}{-4 - 1} = \frac{7}{-5} = -\frac{7}{5}.$$

Using the point $(1, -2)$, the point-slope form of the equation is

$$y - (-2) = -\frac{7}{5}(x - 1).$$

> Because both points $(1, -2)$ and $(-4, 5)$ lie on the line and must satisfy the equation of the line, either point can be used to determine an equation of the line.

Solving for y yields the slope-intercept form of the equation:

$$y = -\frac{7}{5}x - \frac{3}{5}.$$

Related Exercises 37–40 ◄

Parallel and Perpendicular Lines

Two lines in the plane may have either of two special relationships to each other: They may be parallel or perpendicular.

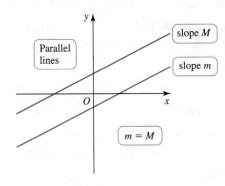

> **Parallel Lines**
>
> Two distinct nonvertical lines are **parallel** if they have the same slope; that is, the lines with equations $y = mx + b$ and $y = Mx + B$ are parallel if and only if $m = M$. Two distinct vertical lines are parallel.

EXAMPLE 6   Parallel lines Find an equation of the line parallel to $3x - 6y + 12 = 0$ that intersects the x-axis at $(4, 0)$.

SOLUTION Solving the equation $3x - 6y + 12 = 0$ for y, we have

$$y = \frac{1}{2}x + 2.$$

This line has a slope of $\frac{1}{2}$ and any line parallel to it has a slope of $\frac{1}{2}$. Therefore, the line that passes through $(4, 0)$ with slope $\frac{1}{2}$ has the point-slope equation $y - 0 = \frac{1}{2}(x - 4)$. After simplifying, an equation of the line is

$$y = \frac{1}{2}x - 2.$$

Notice that the slopes of the two lines are the same; only the y-intercepts differ.

Related Exercises 41–42 ◄

> The slopes of perpendicular lines are *negative reciprocals* of each other.

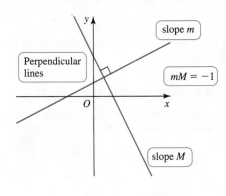

> **Perpendicular Lines**
>
> Two lines with slopes $m \neq 0$ and $M \neq 0$ are **perpendicular** if and only if $mM = -1$, or equivalently, $m = -1/M$.

EXAMPLE 7   Perpendicular lines Find an equation of the line passing through the point $(-2, 5)$ perpendicular to the line $\ell: 4x - 2y + 7 = 0$.

SOLUTION The equation of ℓ can be written $y = 2x + \frac{7}{2}$, which reveals that its slope is 2. Therefore, the slope of any line perpendicular to ℓ is $-\frac{1}{2}$. The line with slope $-\frac{1}{2}$ passing through the point $(-2, 5)$ is

$$y - 5 = -\frac{1}{2}(x + 2), \quad \text{or} \quad y = -\frac{x}{2} + 4.$$

Related Exercises 43–44 ◄

APPENDIX A EXERCISES

Review Questions

1. State the meaning of $\{x : -4 < x \leq 10\}$. Express the set $\{x : -4 < x \leq 10\}$ using interval notation and draw it on a number line.

2. Write the interval $(-\infty, 2)$ in set notation and draw it on a number line.

3. Give the definition of $|x|$.

4. Write the inequality $|x - 2| \leq 3$ without absolute value symbols.

5. Write the inequality $|2x - 4| \geq 3$ without absolute value symbols.

6. Write an equation of the set of all points that are a distance 5 units from the point $(2, 3)$.

7. Explain how to find the distance between two points whose coordinates are known.

8. Sketch the set of points $\{(x, y): x^2 + (y - 2)^2 > 16\}$.

9. Give an equation of the upper half of the circle centered at the origin with radius 6.

10. What are the possible solution sets of the equation $x^2 + y^2 + Cx + Dy + E = 0$?

11. Give an equation of the line with slope m that passes through the point $(4, -2)$.

12. Give an equation of the line with slope m and y-intercept $(0, 6)$.

13. What is the relationship between the slopes of two parallel lines?

14. What is the relationship between the slopes of two perpendicular lines?

Basic Skills

15–20. Algebra review *Simplify or evaluate the following expressions without a calculator.*

15. $(1/8)^{-2/3}$

16. $\sqrt[3]{-125} + \sqrt{1/25}$

17. $(u + v)^2 - (u - v)^2$

18. $\dfrac{(a + h)^2 - a^2}{h}$

19. $\dfrac{1}{x + h} - \dfrac{1}{x}$

20. $\dfrac{2}{x + 3} - \dfrac{2}{x - 3}$

21–26. Algebra review

21. Factor $y^2 - y^{-2}$.

22. Solve $x^3 - 9x = 0$.

23. Solve $u^4 - 11u^2 + 18 = 0$.

24. Solve $4^x - 6(2^x) = -8$.

25. Simplify $\dfrac{(x + h)^3 - x^3}{h}$, for $h \neq 0$.

26. Rewrite $\dfrac{\sqrt{x + h} - \sqrt{x}}{h}$, where $h \neq 0$, without square roots in the numerator.

27–30. Solving inequalities *Solve the following inequalities and draw the solution on a number line.*

27. $x^2 - 6x + 5 < 0$

28. $\dfrac{x + 1}{x + 2} < 6$

29. $\dfrac{x^2 - 9x + 20}{x - 6} \leq 0$

30. $x\sqrt{x - 1} > 0$

31–34. Inequalities with absolute values *Solve the following inequalities. Then draw the solution on a number line and express it using interval notation.*

31. $|3x - 4| > 8$

32. $1 \leq |x| \leq 10$

33. $3 < |2x - 1| < 5$

34. $2 < |\frac{x}{2} - 5| < 6$

35–36. Circle calculations *Solve the following problems.*

35. Find the equation of the lower half of the circle with center $(-1, 2)$ and radius 3.

36. Describe the set of points that satisfy $x^2 + y^2 + 6x + 8y \geq 25$.

37–40. Working with linear equations *Find an equation of the line ℓ that satisfies the given condition. Then draw the graph of ℓ.*

37. ℓ has slope $5/3$ and y-intercept $(0, 4)$.

38. ℓ has undefined slope and passes through $(0, 5)$.

39. ℓ has y-intercept $(0, -4)$ and x-intercept $(5, 0)$.

40. ℓ is parallel to the x-axis and passes through the point $(2, 3)$.

41–42. Parallel lines *Find an equation of the following lines and draw their graphs.*

41. the line with y-intercept $(0, 12)$ parallel to the line $x + 2y = 8$

42. the line with x-intercept $(-6, 0)$ parallel to the line $2x - 5 = 0$

43–44. Perpendicular lines *Find an equation of the following lines.*

43. the line passing through $(3, -6)$ perpendicular to the line $y = -3x + 2$

44. the perpendicular bisector of the line joining the points $(-9, 2)$ and $(3, -5)$

Further Explorations

45. **Explain why or why not** State whether the following statements are true and give an explanation or counterexample.

   a. $\sqrt{16} = \pm 4$.

   b. $\sqrt{4^2} = \sqrt{(-4)^2}$.

   c. There are two real numbers that satisfy the condition $|x| = -2$.

   d. $|\pi^2 - 9| < 0$.

   e. The point $(1, 1)$ is inside the circle of radius 1 centered at the origin.

   f. $\sqrt{x^4} = x^2$ for all real numbers x.

   g. $\sqrt{a^2} < \sqrt{b^2}$ implies $a < b$ for all real numbers a and b.

46–48. Intervals to sets *Express the following intervals in set notation. Use absolute value notation when possible.*

46. $(-\infty, 12)$

47. $(-\infty, -2]$ or $[4, \infty)$

48. $(2, 3]$ or $[4, 5)$

49–50. Sets in the plane *Graph each set in the xy-plane.*

49. $\{(x, y): |x - y| = 0\}$

50. $\{(x, y): |x| = |y|\}$

Conic Sections

Conic sections are best visualized as the Greeks did over 2000 years ago by slicing a double cone with a plane (Figure B.1). Three of the seven different sets of points that arise in this way are *ellipses*, *parabolas*, and *hyperbolas*. These curves have practical applications and broad theoretical importance. For example, celestial bodies travel in orbits that are modeled by ellipses and hyperbolas. Mirrors for telescopes are designed using the properties of conic sections. And architectural structures, such as domes and arches, are sometimes based on these curves.

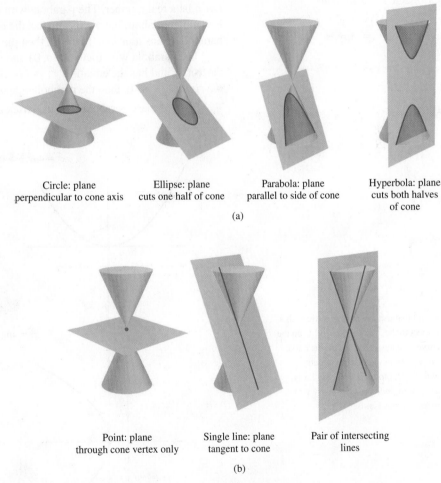

Circle: plane
perpendicular to cone axis

Ellipse: plane
cuts one half of cone

Parabola: plane
parallel to side of cone

Hyperbola: plane
cuts both halves
of cone

(a)

Point: plane
through cone vertex only

Single line: plane
tangent to cone

Pair of intersecting
lines

(b)

FIGURE B.1 The standard conic sections (a) are the intersection sets of a double cone and a plane that does not pass through the vertex of the cone. Degenerate conic sections (lines and points) are produced when a plane passes through the vertex of the cone (b).

Parabolas

A **parabola** is the set of points in a plane that are equidistant from a fixed point F (called the **focus**) and a fixed line (called the **directrix**). In the four standard orientations, a parabola may open upward, downward, to the right, or to the left. We derive the equation of the parabola that opens upward.

Suppose the focus F is on the y-axis at $(0, p)$ and the directrix is the horizontal line $y = -p$, where $p > 0$. The parabola is the set of points P that satisfy the defining property $|PF| = |PL|$, where $L(x, -p)$ is the point on the directrix closest to P

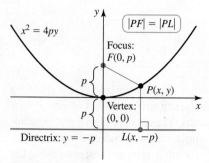

$x^2 = 4py$

$|PF| = |PL|$

Focus:
$F(0, p)$

p

$P(x, y)$

Vertex:
$(0, 0)$

p

Directrix: $y = -p$ $L(x, -p)$

FIGURE B.2

QUICK CHECK 1 Verify that
$\sqrt{x^2 + (y - p)^2} = y + p$ is
equivalent to $x^2 = 4py$. ◄

(Figure B.2). Consider an arbitrary point $P(x, y)$ that satisfies this condition. Applying the distance formula, we have

$$\underbrace{\sqrt{x^2 + (y - p)^2}}_{|PF|} = \underbrace{y + p}_{|PL|}.$$

Squaring both sides of this equation and simplifying gives the equation $x^2 = 4py$. This is the equation of a parabola that is symmetric about the y-axis and opens upward. The **vertex** of the parabola is the point closest to the directrix; in this case it is $(0, 0)$ (which satisfies $|PF| = |PL| = p$).

The equations of the other three standard parabolas are derived in a similar way.

Equations of Four Standard Parabolas

Let p be a real number. The parabola with focus at $(0, p)$ and directrix $y = -p$ is symmetric about the y-axis and has the equation $x^2 = 4py$. If $p > 0$, then the parabola opens *upward*; if $p < 0$, then the parabola opens *downward*.

The parabola with focus at $(p, 0)$ and directrix $x = -p$ is symmetric about the x-axis and has the equation $y^2 = 4px$. If $p > 0$, then the parabola opens *to the right*; if $p < 0$, then the parabola opens *to the left*.

Each of these parabolas has its vertex at the origin (Figure B.3).

> Recall that a curve is symmetric with respect to the x-axis if $(x, -y)$ is on the curve whenever (x, y) is on the curve. So, a y^2-term indicates symmetry with respect to the x-axis. Similarly, an x^2-term indicates symmetry with respect to the y-axis.

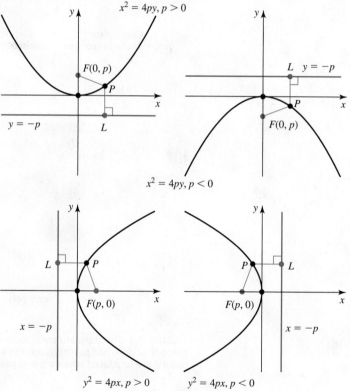

FIGURE B.3

QUICK CHECK 2 In which direction do the following parabolas open?
a. $y^2 = -4x$ **b.** $x^2 = 4y$ ◄

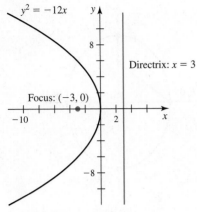

$$y^2 = -12x$$

FIGURE B.4

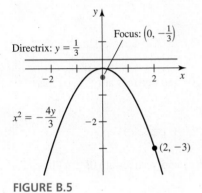

$$x^2 = -\frac{4y}{3}$$

FIGURE B.5

EXAMPLE 1 **Graphing parabolas** Find the focus and directrix of the parabola $y^2 = -12x$. Sketch its graph.

SOLUTION The y^2-term indicates that the parabola is symmetric with respect to the x-axis. Rewriting the equation as $x = -y^2/12$, we see that $x \le 0$ for all y, implying that the parabola opens to the left. Comparing $y^2 = -12x$ to the standard form $y^2 = 4px$, we see that $p = -3$; therefore, the focus is $(-3, 0)$, and the directrix is $x = 3$ (Figure B.4).

Related Exercises 13–18◄

EXAMPLE 2 **Equations of parabolas** Find the equation of the parabola with vertex $(0, 0)$ that opens downward and passes through the point $(2, -3)$.

SOLUTION The standard parabola that opens downward has the equation $x^2 = 4py$. The point $(2, -3)$ must satisfy this equation. Substituting $x = 2$ and $y = -3$ into $x^2 = 4py$, we find that $p = -\frac{1}{3}$. Therefore, the focus is at $(0, -\frac{1}{3})$, the directrix is $y = \frac{1}{3}$, and the equation of the parabola is $x^2 = -4y/3$, or $y = -3x^2/4$ (Figure B.5).

Related Exercises 19–26◄

Reflection Property Parabolas have a property that makes them useful in the design of reflectors and transmitters. A particle approaching a parabola on any line parallel to the axis of the parabola is reflected on a line that passes through the focus (Figure B.6); this property is used to focus incoming light by a parabolic mirror on a telescope. Alternatively, signals emanating from the focus are reflected on lines parallel to the axis, a property used to design radio transmitters and headlights (Exercise 83).

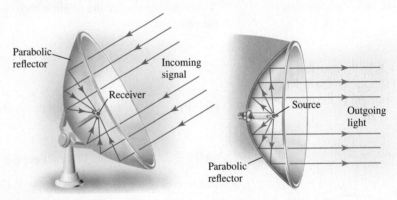

FIGURE B.6

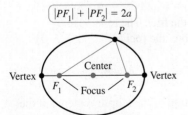

$$\boxed{|PF_1| + |PF_2| = 2a}$$

FIGURE B.7

Ellipses

An **ellipse** is the set of points in a plane whose distances from two fixed points have a constant sum that we denote $2a$ (Figure B.7). Each of the two fixed points is a **focus** (plural **foci**). The equation of an ellipse is simplest if the foci are on the x-axis at $(\pm c, 0)$ or on the y-axis at $(0, \pm c)$. In either case, the **center** of the ellipse is $(0, 0)$. If the foci are on the x-axis, the points $(\pm a, 0)$ lie on the ellipse and are called **vertices**. If the foci are on the y-axis, the vertices are $(0, \pm a)$ (Figure B.8). A short calculation (Exercise 85) using the definition of the ellipse results in the following equations for an ellipse.

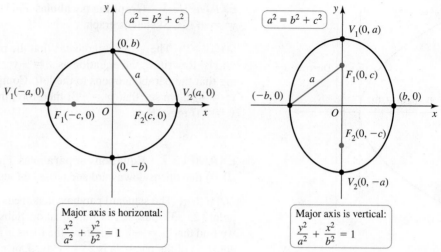

FIGURE B.8

> When necessary, we may distinguish between the *major-axis vertices* $(\pm a, 0)$ or $(0, \pm a)$, and the *minor-axis vertices* $(\pm b, 0)$ or $(0, \pm b)$. The word *vertices* (without further description) is understood to mean *major-axis vertices*.

QUICK CHECK 3 In the case that the vertices and foci are on the *x*-axis, show that the length of the minor axis of an ellipse is $2b$. ◄

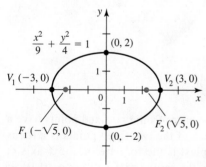

FIGURE B.9

Equations of Standard Ellipses

An ellipse centered at the origin with foci at $(\pm c, 0)$ and vertices at $(\pm a, 0)$ has the equation

$$\frac{x^2}{a^2} + \frac{y^2}{b^2} = 1, \quad \text{where } a^2 = b^2 + c^2.$$

An ellipse centered at the origin with foci at $(0, \pm c)$ and vertices at $(0, \pm a)$ has the equation

$$\frac{y^2}{a^2} + \frac{x^2}{b^2} = 1, \quad \text{where } a^2 = b^2 + c^2.$$

In both cases, $a > b > 0$ and $a > c > 0$, the length of the long axis (called the **major axis**) is $2a$, and the length of the short axis (called the **minor axis**) is $2b$.

EXAMPLE 3   Graphing ellipses Find the vertices, foci, and the length of the major and minor axes of the ellipse $\dfrac{x^2}{9} + \dfrac{y^2}{4} = 1$. Graph the ellipse.

SOLUTION Because $9 > 4$, we identify $a^2 = 9$ and $b^2 = 4$. Therefore, $a = 3$ and $b = 2$. The lengths of the major and minor axes are $2a = 6$ and $2b = 4$, respectively. The vertices are at $(\pm 3, 0)$ and lie on the *x*-axis, as do the foci. The relationship $c^2 = a^2 - b^2$ implies that $c^2 = 5$, or $c = \sqrt{5}$. Therefore, the foci are at $(\pm \sqrt{5}, 0)$. The graph of the ellipse is shown in Figure B.9.

Related Exercises 27–32 ◄

EXAMPLE 4   Equation of an ellipse Find the equation of the ellipse centered at the origin with its foci on the *y*-axis, a major axis of length 8, and a minor axis of length 4. Graph the ellipse.

SOLUTION Because the length of the major axis is 8, the vertices are located at $(0, \pm 4)$, and $a = 4$. Because the length of the minor axis is 4, we have $b = 2$. Therefore, the equation of the ellipse is

$$\frac{y^2}{16} + \frac{x^2}{4} = 1.$$

$\dfrac{y^2}{16} + \dfrac{x^2}{4} = 1$

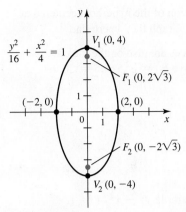

FIGURE B.10

> Asymptotes that are not parallel to one of the coordinate axes, as in the case of the standard hyperbolas, are called **oblique**, or **slant**, **asymptotes**.

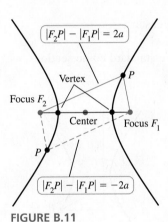

FIGURE B.11

> Notice that the asymptotes for hyperbolas are $y = \pm bx/a$ when the vertices are on the x-axis and $y = \pm ax/b$ when the vertices are on the y-axis (the roles of a and b are reversed).

Using the relation $c^2 = a^2 - b^2$, we find that $c = 2\sqrt{3}$ and the foci are at $(0, \pm 2\sqrt{3})$. The ellipse is shown in Figure B.10.

Related Exercises 33–38 ◄

Hyperbolas

A **hyperbola** is the set of points in a plane whose distances from two fixed points have a constant difference, either $2a$ or $-2a$ (Figure B.11). As with ellipses, the two fixed points are called **foci**. The equation of a hyperbola is simplest if the foci are on either the x-axis at $(\pm c, 0)$ or on the y-axis at $(0, \pm c)$. If the foci are on the x-axis, the points $(\pm a, 0)$ on the hyperbola are called the **vertices**. In this case, the hyperbola has no y-intercepts, but it has the **asymptotes** $y = \pm bx/a$, where $b^2 = c^2 - a^2$. Similarly, if the foci are on the y-axis, the vertices are $(0, \pm a)$, the hyperbola has no x-intercepts, and it has the asymptotes $y = \pm ax/b$ (Figure B.12). A short calculation (Exercise 86) using the definition of the hyperbola results in the following equations for standard hyperbolas.

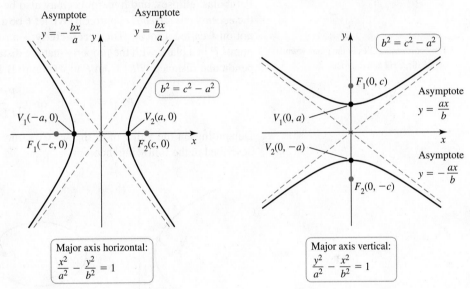

FIGURE B.12

Equations of Standard Hyperbolas

A hyperbola centered at the origin with foci at $(\pm c, 0)$ and vertices at $(\pm a, 0)$ has the equation

$$\frac{x^2}{a^2} - \frac{y^2}{b^2} = 1, \quad \text{where} \quad b^2 = c^2 - a^2.$$

The hyperbola has **asymptotes** $y = \pm bx/a$.

A hyperbola centered at the origin with foci at $(0, \pm c)$ and vertices at $(0, \pm a)$ has the equation

$$\frac{y^2}{a^2} - \frac{x^2}{b^2} = 1, \quad \text{where} \quad b^2 = c^2 - a^2.$$

The hyperbola has **asymptotes** $y = \pm ax/b$.
In both cases, $c > a > 0$ and $c > b > 0$.

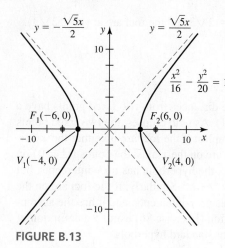

$y = -\dfrac{\sqrt{5}x}{2}$ $y = \dfrac{\sqrt{5}x}{2}$

$\dfrac{x^2}{16} - \dfrac{y^2}{20} = 1$

$F_1(-6, 0)$ $F_2(6, 0)$

$V_1(-4, 0)$ $V_2(4, 0)$

FIGURE B.13

> The conic section lies in the plane formed by the directrix and the focus.

EXAMPLE 5   Graphing hyperbolas Find the equation of the hyperbola centered at the origin with vertices at $(\pm 4, 0)$ and foci at $(\pm 6, 0)$. Graph the hyperbola.

SOLUTION Because the foci are on the x-axis, the vertices are also on the x-axis, and there are no y-intercepts. With $a = 4$ and $c = 6$, we have $b^2 = c^2 - a^2 = 20$, or $b = 2\sqrt{5}$. Therefore, the equation of the hyperbola is

$$\frac{x^2}{16} - \frac{y^2}{20} = 1.$$

The asymptotes are $y = \pm bx/a = \pm\sqrt{5}x/2$ (Figure B.13).

Related Exercises 39–50 ◄

QUICK CHECK 4 Identify the vertices and foci of the hyperbola $y^2 - x^2/4 = 1$. ◄

Eccentricity and Directrix

Parabolas, ellipses, and hyperbolas may also be developed in a single unified way called the *eccentricity-directrix* approach. We let ℓ be a line called the **directrix** and F be a point not on ℓ called a **focus**. The **eccentricity** is a real number $e > 0$. Consider the set C of points P in a plane with the property that the distance $|PF|$ equals e multiplied by the perpendicular distance $|PL|$ from P to ℓ (Figure B.14); that is,

$$|PF| = e|PL| \quad \text{or} \quad \frac{|PF|}{|PL|} = e = \text{constant}.$$

Depending on the value of e, the set C is one of the three standard conic sections, as described in the following theorem.

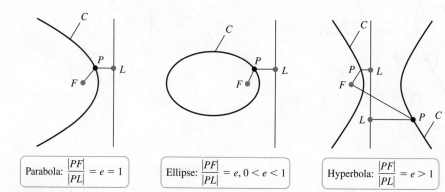

Parabola: $\dfrac{|PF|}{|PL|} = e = 1$ Ellipse: $\dfrac{|PF|}{|PL|} = e, 0 < e < 1$ Hyperbola: $\dfrac{|PF|}{|PL|} = e > 1$

FIGURE B.14

> Theorem B.1 for ellipses and hyperbolas describes how the entire curve is generated using just one focus and one directrix. Nevertheless, every ellipse or hyperbola has two foci and two directrices.

THEOREM B.1   Eccentricity-Directrix Theorem

Let ℓ be a line, F a point not on ℓ, and $e > 0$ a real number. Let C be the set of points P in a plane with the property that $\dfrac{|PF|}{|PL|} = e$, where $|PL|$ is the perpendicular distance from P to ℓ.

1. If $e = 1$, C is a **parabola**.

2. If $0 < e < 1$, C is an **ellipse**.

3. If $e > 1$, C is a **hyperbola**.

The proof of the theorem is straightforward; it establishes relationships between five parameters a, b, c, d, and e that are characteristic of any ellipse or hyperbola. The relationships are given in the following summary.

QUICK CHECK 5 Given an ellipse with $a = 3$ and $e = \frac{1}{2}$, what are the values of b, c, and d? ◄

EXAMPLE 6   Equations of ellipses Find the equation of the ellipse centered at the origin with foci at $(0, \pm 4)$ and eccentricity $e = \frac{1}{2}$. Give the length of the major and minor axes, the location of the vertices, and the directrices. Graph the ellipse.

SOLUTION An ellipse with its major axis along the y-axis has the equation

$$\frac{y^2}{a^2} + \frac{x^2}{b^2} = 1,$$

where a and b must be determined (with $a > b$). Because the foci are at $(0, \pm 4)$, we have $c = 4$. Using $e = \frac{1}{2}$ and the relation $c = ae$, it follows that $a = c/e = 8$. So, the length of the major axis is $2a = 16$, and the major-axis vertices are $(0, \pm 8)$. Also $d = a/e = 16$, so the directrices are $y = \pm 16$. Finally, $b^2 = a^2 - c^2 = 48$, or $b = 4\sqrt{3}$. So, the length of the minor axis is $2b = 8\sqrt{3}$, and the minor-axis vertices are $(\pm 4\sqrt{3}, 0)$ (Figure B.15). The equation of the ellipse is

$$\frac{y^2}{64} + \frac{x^2}{48} = 1.$$

Related Exercises 51–54 ◄

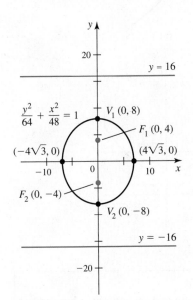

FIGURE B.15

Polar Equations of Conic Sections

It turns out that conic sections have a natural representation in polar coordinates, provided we use the eccentricity-directrix approach given in Theorem B.3. Furthermore, a single polar equation covers parabolas, ellipses, and hyperbolas.

When working in polar equations, the key is to place a focus of the conic section at the origin of the coordinate system. We begin by placing one focus F at the origin and taking a directrix perpendicular to the x-axis through $(d, 0)$, where $d > 0$ (Figure B.16).

We now use the definition $\dfrac{|PF|}{|PL|} = e$, where $P(r, \theta)$ is an arbitrary point on the conic. As shown in Figure B.16, $|PF| = r$ and $|PL| = d - r\cos\theta$. The condition $\dfrac{|PF|}{|PL|} = e$ implies that $r = e(d - r\cos\theta)$. Solving for r, we have

$$r = \frac{ed}{1 + e\cos\theta}.$$

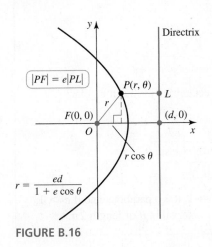

FIGURE B.16

A similar derivation (Exercise 74) with the directrix at $x = -d$, where $d > 0$, results in the equation

$$r = \frac{ed}{1 - e \cos \theta}.$$

For horizontal directrices at $y = \pm d$ (Figure B.17), a similar argument (Exercise 74) leads to the equations

$$r = \frac{ed}{1 \pm e \sin \theta}.$$

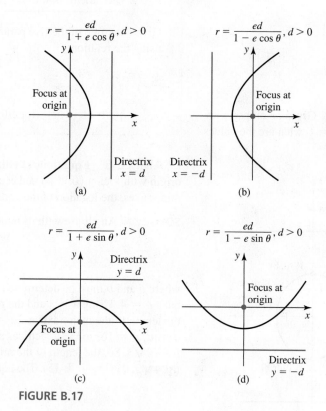

FIGURE B.17

THEOREM B.2   Polar Equations of Conic Sections

Let $d > 0$. The conic section with a focus at the origin and eccentricity e has the polar equation

$$r = \frac{ed}{1 + e \cos \theta} \quad \text{or} \quad r = \frac{ed}{1 - e \cos \theta}.$$

if one directrix is $x = d$ if one directrix is $x = -d$

The conic section with a focus at the origin and eccentricity e has the polar equation

$$r = \frac{ed}{1 + e \sin \theta} \quad \text{or} \quad r = \frac{ed}{1 - e \sin \theta}.$$

if one directrix is $y = d$ if one directrix is $y = -d$

If $0 < e < 1$, the conic section is an ellipse; if $e = 1$, it is a parabola; and if $e > 1$, it is a hyperbola. The curves are defined over any interval in θ of length 2π.

QUICK CHECK 6 On which axis do the vertices and foci of the conic section $r = 2/(1 - 2 \sin \theta)$ lie? ◄

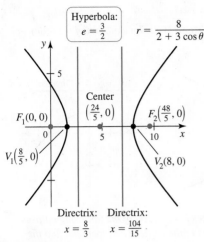

Hyperbola:
$e = \frac{3}{2}$ $r = \dfrac{8}{2 + 3\cos\theta}$

Center $\left(\frac{24}{5}, 0\right)$

$F_1(0, 0)$ $F_2\left(\frac{48}{5}, 0\right)$

$V_1\left(\frac{8}{5}, 0\right)$ $V_2(8, 0)$

Directrix: Directrix:
$x = \frac{8}{3}$ $x = \frac{104}{15}$

FIGURE B.18

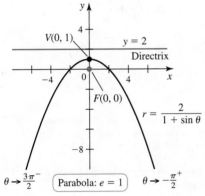

$V(0, 1)$ $y = 2$
Directrix

$F(0, 0)$

$r = \dfrac{2}{1 + \sin\theta}$

$\theta \to \frac{3\pi}{2}^-$ Parabola: $e = 1$ $\theta \to -\frac{\pi}{2}^+$

FIGURE B.19

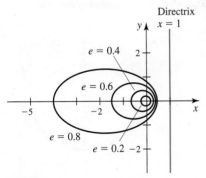

Directrix
$x = 1$

$e = 0.4$

$e = 0.6$

$e = 0.8$

$e = 0.2$

FIGURE B.20

EXAMPLE 7   Conic sections in polar coordinates Find the vertices, foci, and directrices of the following conic sections. Graph each curve and check your work with a graphing utility.

a. $r = \dfrac{8}{2 + 3\cos\theta}$ **b.** $r = \dfrac{2}{1 + \sin\theta}$

SOLUTION

a. The equation must be expressed in standard polar form for a conic section. Dividing numerator and denominator by 2, we have

$$r = \frac{4}{1 + \frac{3}{2}\cos\theta},$$

which allows us to identify $e = \frac{3}{2}$. Therefore, the equation describes a hyperbola (because $e > 1$) with one focus at the origin.

The directrices are vertical (because $\cos\theta$ appears in the equation). Knowing that $ed = 4$, we have $d = \frac{4}{e} = \frac{8}{3}$, and one directrix is $x = \frac{8}{3}$. Letting $\theta = 0$ and $\theta = \pi$, the polar coordinates of the vertices are $\left(\frac{8}{5}, 0\right)$ and $(-8, \pi)$; equivalently, the vertices are $\left(\frac{8}{5}, 0\right)$ and $(8, 0)$ in Cartesian coordinates (Figure B.18). The center of the hyperbola is halfway between the vertices; therefore, its Cartesian coordinates are $\left(\frac{24}{5}, 0\right)$. The distance between the focus at $(0, 0)$ and the nearest vertex $\left(\frac{8}{5}, 0\right)$ is $\frac{8}{5}$. Therefore, the other focus is $\frac{8}{5}$ units to the right of the vertex $(8, 0)$. So, the Cartesian coordinates of the foci are $\left(\frac{48}{5}, 0\right)$ and $(0, 0)$. Because the directrices are symmetric about the center and the left directrix is $x = \frac{8}{3}$, the right directrix is $x = \frac{104}{15} \approx 6.9$. The graph of the hyperbola (Figure B.18) is generated as θ varies from 0 to 2π $\left(\text{with } \theta \neq \pm\cos^{-1}\left(-\frac{2}{3}\right)\right)$.

b. The equation is in standard form, and it describes a parabola because $e = 1$. The sole focus is at the origin. The directrix is horizontal (because of the $\sin\theta$ term); $ed = 2$ implies that $d = 2$, and the directrix is $y = 2$. The parabola opens downward because of the plus sign in the denominator. The vertex corresponds to $\theta = \frac{\pi}{2}$ and has polar coordinates $\left(1, \frac{\pi}{2}\right)$, or Cartesian coordinates $(0, 1)$. Setting $\theta = 0$ and $\theta = \pi$, the parabola crosses the x-axis at $(2, 0)$ and $(2, \pi)$ in polar coordinates, or $(\pm 2, 0)$ in Cartesian coordinates. As θ increases from $-\frac{\pi}{2}$ to $\frac{\pi}{2}$, the right branch of the parabola is generated and as θ increases from $\frac{\pi}{2}$ to $\frac{3\pi}{2}$, the left branch of the parabola is generated (Figure B.19).

Related Exercises 55–64 ◀

EXAMPLE 8   Conics in polar coordinates Use a graphing utility to plot the curves $r = \dfrac{e}{1 + e\cos\theta}$, with $e = 0.2, 0.4, 0.6,$ and 0.8. Comment on the effect of varying the eccentricity, e.

SOLUTION Because $0 < e < 1$, all the curves are ellipses. Notice that the equation is in standard form with $d = 1$; therefore, the curves have the same directrix, $x = d = 1$. As the eccentricity increases, the ellipses becomes more elongated. Small values of e correspond to more circular ellipses (Figure B.20).

Related Exercises 65–66 ◀

APPENDIX B EXERCISES

Review Questions

1. Give the property that defines all parabolas.

2. Give the property that defines all ellipses.

3. Give the property that defines all hyperbolas.

4. Sketch the three basic conic sections in standard position with vertices and foci on the x-axis.

5. Sketch the three basic conic sections in standard position with vertices and foci on the y-axis.

6. What is the equation of the standard parabola with its vertex at the origin that opens downward?

7. What is the equation of the standard ellipse with vertices at $(\pm a, 0)$ and foci at $(\pm c, 0)$?

8. What is the equation of the standard hyperbola with vertices at $(0, \pm a)$ and foci at $(0, \pm c)$?

9. Given vertices $(\pm a, 0)$ and eccentricity e, what are the coordinates of the foci of an ellipse and a hyperbola?

10. Give the equation in polar coordinates of a conic section with a focus at the origin, eccentricity e, and a directrix $x = d$, where $d > 0$.

11. What are the equations of the asymptotes of a standard hyperbola with vertices on the x-axis?

12. How does the eccentricity determine the type of conic section?

Basic Skills

13–18. Graphing parabolas *Sketch the graph of the following parabolas. Specify the location of the focus and the equation of the directrix. Use a graphing utility to check your work.*

13. $x^2 = 12y$ 14. $y^2 = 20x$ 15. $x = -y^2/16$

16. $4x = -y^2$ 17. $8y = -3x^2$ 18. $12x = 5y^2$

19–24. Equations of parabolas *Find an equation of the following parabolas, assuming the vertex is at the origin.*

19. A parabola that opens to the right with directrix $x = -4$

20. A parabola that opens downward with directrix $y = 6$

21. A parabola with focus at $(3, 0)$

22. A parabola with focus at $(-4, 0)$

23. A parabola symmetric about the y-axis that passes through the point $(2, -6)$

24. A parabola symmetric about the x-axis that passes through the point $(1, -4)$

25–26. From graphs to equations *Write an equation of the following parabolas.*

25.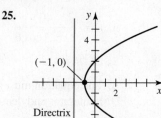

26.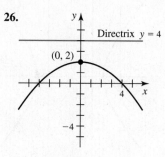

27–32. Graphing ellipses *Sketch the graph of the following ellipses. Plot and label the coordinates of the vertices and foci, and find the lengths of the major and minor axes. Use a graphing utility to check your work.*

27. $\dfrac{x^2}{4} + y^2 = 1$ 28. $\dfrac{x^2}{9} + \dfrac{y^2}{4} = 1$

29. $\dfrac{x^2}{4} + \dfrac{y^2}{16} = 1$ 30. $x^2 + \dfrac{y^2}{9} = 1$

31. $\dfrac{x^2}{5} + \dfrac{y^2}{7} = 1$ 32. $12x^2 + 5y^2 = 60$

33–36. Equations of ellipses *Find an equation of the following ellipses, assuming the center is at the origin. Sketch a graph labeling the vertices and foci.*

33. An ellipse whose major axis is on the x-axis with length 8 and whose minor axis has length 6

34. An ellipse with vertices $(\pm 6, 0)$ and foci $(\pm 4, 0)$

35. An ellipse with vertices $(\pm 5, 0)$, passing through the point $\left(4, \frac{3}{5}\right)$

36. An ellipse with vertices $(0, \pm 10)$, passing through the point $(\sqrt{3}/2, 5)$

37–38. From graphs to equations *Write an equation of the following ellipses.*

37.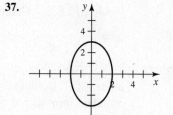

38.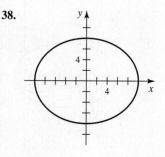

39–44. Graphing hyperbolas *Sketch the graph of the following hyperbolas. Specify the coordinates of the vertices and foci, and find the equations of the asymptotes. Use a graphing utility to check your work.*

39. $\dfrac{x^2}{4} - y^2 = 1$

40. $\dfrac{y^2}{16} - \dfrac{x^2}{9} = 1$

41. $4x^2 - y^2 = 16$

42. $25y^2 - 4x^2 = 100$

43. $\dfrac{x^2}{3} - \dfrac{y^2}{5} = 1$

44. $10x^2 - 7y^2 = 140$

45–48. Equations of hyperbolas *Find an equation of the following hyperbolas, assuming the center is at the origin. Sketch a graph labeling the vertices, foci, and asymptotes. Use a graphing utility to check your work.*

45. A hyperbola with vertices $(\pm 4, 0)$ and foci $(\pm 6, 0)$

46. A hyperbola with vertices $(\pm 1, 0)$ that passes through $\left(\frac{5}{3}, 8\right)$

47. A hyperbola with vertices $(\pm 2, 0)$ and asymptotes $y = \pm 3x/2$

48. A hyperbola with vertices $(0, \pm 4)$ and asymptotes $y = \pm 2x$

49–50. From graphs to equations *Write an equation of the following hyperbolas.*

49.

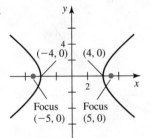

50.

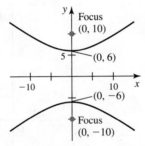

51–54. Eccentricity-directrix approach *Find an equation of the following curves, assuming the center is at the origin. Sketch a graph labeling the vertices, foci, asymptotes, and directrices. Use a graphing utility to check your work.*

51. An ellipse with vertices $(\pm 9, 0)$ and eccentricity $\frac{1}{3}$

52. An ellipse with vertices $(0, \pm 9)$ and eccentricity $\frac{1}{4}$

53. A hyperbola with vertices $(\pm 1, 0)$ and eccentricity 3

54. A hyperbola with vertices $(0, \pm 4)$ and eccentricity 2

55–60. Polar equations for conic sections *Graph the following conic sections, labeling the vertices, foci, directrices, and asymptotes (if they exist). Use a graphing utility to check your work.*

55. $r = \dfrac{4}{1 + \cos \theta}$

56. $r = \dfrac{4}{2 + \cos \theta}$

57. $r = \dfrac{1}{2 - \cos \theta}$

58. $r = \dfrac{6}{3 + 2 \sin \theta}$

59. $r = \dfrac{1}{2 - 2 \sin \theta}$

60. $r = \dfrac{12}{3 - \cos \theta}$

61–64. Tracing hyperbolas and parabolas *Graph the following equations. Then use arrows and labeled points to indicate how the curve is generated as θ increases from 0 to 2π.*

61. $r = \dfrac{1}{1 + \sin \theta}$

62. $r = \dfrac{1}{1 + 2 \cos \theta}$

63. $r = \dfrac{3}{1 - \cos \theta}$

64. $r = \dfrac{1}{1 - 2 \cos \theta}$

65. Parabolas with a graphing utility Use a graphing utility to graph the parabolas $y^2 = 4px$, for $p = -5, -2, -1, 1, 2,$ and 5 on the same set of axes. Explain how the shapes of the curves vary as p changes.

66. Hyperbolas with a graphing utility Use a graphing utility to graph the hyperbolas $r = \dfrac{e}{1 + e \cos \theta}$, for $e = 1.1, 1.3, 1.5, 1.7,$ and 2 on the same set of axes. Explain how the shapes of the curves vary as e changes.

Further Explorations

67. Explain why or why not Determine whether the following statements are true and give an explanation or counterexample.

  a. The hyperbola $x^2/4 - y^2/9 = 1$ has no y-intercepts.

  b. On every ellipse, there are exactly two points at which the curve has slope s, where s is any real number.

  c. Given the directrices and foci of a standard hyperbola, it is possible to find its vertices, eccentricity, and asymptotes.

  d. The point on a parabola closest to the focus is the vertex.

68–71. Tangent lines *Find an equation of the line tangent to the following curves at the given point.*

68. $y^2 = 8x; \ (8, -8)$

69. $x^2 = -6y; \ (-6, -6)$

70. $r = \dfrac{1}{1 + \sin \theta}; \ \left(\dfrac{2}{3}, \dfrac{\pi}{6}\right)$

71. $y^2 - \dfrac{x^2}{64} = 1; \ \left(6, -\dfrac{5}{4}\right)$

72–73. Graphs to polar equations *Find a polar equation for each conic section. Assume one focus is at the origin.*

72.

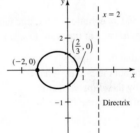

73.

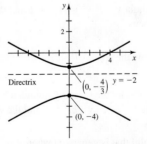

74. Deriving polar equations for conics Modify Figure B.16 to derive the polar equation of a conic section with a focus at the origin in the following three cases.

  a. Vertical directrix at $x = -d$, where $d > 0$

  b. Horizontal directrix at $y = d$, where $d > 0$

  c. Horizontal directrix at $y = -d$, where $d > 0$

75. Another construction for a hyperbola Suppose two circles, whose centers are at least $2a$ units apart (see figure), are centered at F_1 and F_2, respectively. The radius of one circle is $2a + r$ and the radius of the other circle is r, where $r \geq 0$. Show that as r increases, the intersection point P of the two circles describes one branch of a hyperbola with foci at F_1 and F_2.

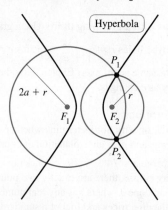

76. The ellipse and the parabola Let R be the region bounded by the upper half of the ellipse $x^2/2 + y^2 = 1$ and the parabola $y = x^2/\sqrt{2}$.

a. Find the area of R.
b. Which is greater, the volume of the solid generated when R is revolved about the x-axis or the volume of the solid generated when R is revolved about the y-axis?

77. Tangent lines for an ellipse Show that an equation of the line tangent to the ellipse $x^2/a^2 + y^2/b^2 = 1$ at the point (x_0, y_0) is

$$\frac{xx_0}{a^2} + \frac{yy_0}{b^2} = 1.$$

78. Tangent lines for a hyperbola Find an equation of the line tangent to the hyperbola $x^2/a^2 - y^2/b^2 = 1$ at the point (x_0, y_0).

79. Volume of an ellipsoid Suppose that the ellipse $x^2/a^2 + y^2/b^2 = 1$ is revolved about the x-axis. What is the volume of the solid enclosed by the *ellipsoid* that is generated? Is the volume different if the same ellipse is revolved about the y-axis?

80. Area of a sector of a hyperbola Consider the region R bounded by the right branch of the hyperbola $x^2/a^2 - y^2/b^2 = 1$ and the vertical line through the right focus.

a. What is the area of R?
b. Sketch a graph that shows how the area of R varies with the eccentricity e, for $e > 1$.

81. Volume of a hyperbolic cap Consider the region R bounded by the right branch of the hyperbola $x^2/a^2 - y^2/b^2 = 1$ and the vertical line through the right focus.

a. What is the volume of the solid that is generated when R is revolved about the x-axis?
b. What is the volume of the solid that is generated when R is revolved about the y-axis?

82. Volume of a paraboloid (Archimedes) The region bounded by the parabola $y = ax^2$ and the horizontal line $y = h$ is revolved about the y-axis to generate a solid bounded by a surface called

a *paraboloid* (where $a > 0$ and $h > 0$). Show that the volume of the solid is $\frac{3}{2}$ the volume of the cone with the same base and vertex.

Applications
(See the Guided Project Properties of Conic Sections for additional applications of conic sections.)

83. Reflection property of parabolas Consider the parabola $y = x^2/4p$ with its focus at $F(0, p)$ (see figure). The goal is to show that the angle of incidence between the ray ℓ and the tangent line L (α in the figure) equals the angle of reflection between the line PF and L (β in the figure). If these two angles are equal, then the reflection property is proved because ℓ is reflected through F.

a. Let $P(x_0, y_0)$ be a point on the parabola. Show that the slope of the line tangent to the curve at P is $\tan \theta = x_0/(2p)$.
b. Show that $\tan \varphi = (p - y_0)/x_0$.
c. Show that $\alpha = \pi/2 - \theta$; therefore, $\tan \alpha = \cot \theta$.
d. Note that $\beta = \theta + \varphi$. Use the tangent addition formula

$$\tan (\theta + \varphi) = \frac{\tan \theta + \tan \varphi}{1 - \tan \theta \tan \varphi}$$ to show that

$\tan \alpha = \tan \beta = 2p/x_0$.
e. Conclude that because α and β are acute angles, $\alpha = \beta$.

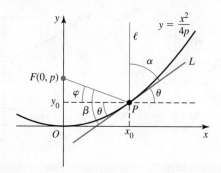

84. Golden Gate Bridge Completed in 1937, San Francisco's Golden Gate Bridge is 2.7 km long and weighs about 890,000 tons. The length of the span between the two central towers is 1280 m; the towers themselves extend 152 m above the roadway. The cables that support the deck of the bridge between the two towers hang in a parabola (see figure). Assuming the origin is midway between the towers on the deck of the bridge, find an equation that describes the cables. How long is a guy wire that hangs vertically from the cables to the roadway 500 m from the center of the bridge?

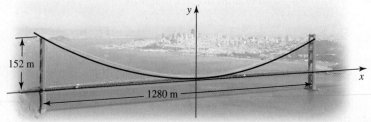

Additional Exercises

85. Equation of an ellipse Consider an ellipse to be the set of points in a plane whose distances from two fixed points have a constant sum $2a$. Derive the equation of an ellipse. Assume the two fixed points are on the x-axis equidistant from the origin.

86. Equation of a hyperbola Consider a hyperbola to be the set of points in a plane whose distances from two fixed points have a constant difference of $2a$ or $-2a$. Derive the equation of a hyperbola. Assume the two fixed points are on the x-axis equidistant from the origin.

87. Equidistant set Show that the set of points equidistant from a circle and a line not passing through the circle is a parabola. Assume the circle, line, and parabola lie in the same plane.

88. Polar equation of a conic Show that the polar equation of an ellipse or hyperbola with one focus at the origin, major axis of length $2a$ on the x-axis, and eccentricity e is

$$r = \frac{a(1 - e^2)}{1 + e \cos \theta}.$$

89. Shared asymptotes Suppose that two hyperbolas with eccentricities e and E have perpendicular major axes and share a set of asymptotes. Show that $e^{-2} + E^{-2} = 1$.

90–94. Focal chords *A* **focal chord** *of a conic section is a line through a focus joining two points of the curve. The* **latus rectum** *is the focal chord perpendicular to the major axis of the conic. Prove the following properties.*

90. The lines tangent to the endpoints of any focal chord of a parabola $y^2 = 4px$ intersect on the directrix and are perpendicular.

91. Let L be the latus rectum of the parabola $y^2 = 4px$, for $p > 0$. Let F be the focus of the parabola, P be any point on the parabola to the left of L, and D be the (shortest) distance between P and L. Show that for all P, $D + |FP|$ is a constant. Find the constant.

92. The length of the latus rectum of the parabola $y^2 = 4px$ or $x^2 = 4py$ is $4|p|$.

93. The length of the latus rectum of an ellipse centered at the origin is $2b^2/a = 2b\sqrt{1 - e^2}$.

94. The length of the latus rectum of a hyperbola centered at the origin is $2b^2/a = 2b\sqrt{e^2 - 1}$.

95. Confocal ellipse and hyperbola Show that an ellipse and a hyperbola that have the same two foci intersect at right angles.

96. Approach to asymptotes Show that the vertical distance between a hyperbola $x^2/a^2 - y^2/b^2 = 1$ and its asymptote $y = bx/a$ approaches zero as $x \to \infty$, where $0 < b < a$.

97. Sector of a hyperbola Let H be the right branch of the hyperbola $x^2 - y^2 = 1$ and let ℓ be the line $y = m(x - 2)$ that passes through the point $(2, 0)$ with slope m, where $-\infty < m < \infty$. Let R be the region in the first quadrant bounded by H and ℓ (see figure). Let $A(m)$ be the area of R. Note that for some values of m, $A(m)$ is not defined.

a. Find the x-coordinates of the intersection points between H and ℓ as functions of m; call them $u(m)$ and $v(m)$, where $v(m) > u(m) > 1$. For what values of m are there two intersection points?

b. Evaluate $\lim_{m \to 1^+} u(m)$ and $\lim_{m \to 1^+} v(m)$.

c. Evaluate $\lim_{m \to \infty} u(m)$ and $\lim_{m \to \infty} v(m)$.

d. Evaluate and interpret $\lim_{m \to \infty} A(m)$.

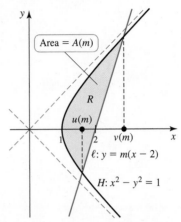

98. The anvil of a hyperbola Let H be the hyperbola $x^2 - y^2 = 1$ and let S be the 2-by-2 square bisected by the asymptotes of H. Let R be the anvil-shaped region bounded by the hyperbola and the horizontal lines $y = \pm p$ (see figure).

a. For what value of p is the area of R equal to the area of S?

b. For what value of p is the area of R twice the area of S?

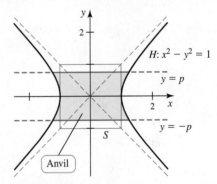

99. Parametric equations for an ellipse Consider the parametric equations

$$x = a \cos t + b \sin t, \quad y = c \cos t + d \sin t,$$

where $a, b, c,$ and d are real numbers.

a. Show that (apart from a set of special cases) the equations describe an ellipse of the form $Ax^2 + Bxy + Cy^2 = K$, where $A, B, C,$ and K are constants.

b. Show that (apart from a set of special cases), the equations describe an ellipse with its axes aligned with the x- and y-axes provided $ab + cd = 0$.

c. Show that the equations describe a circle provided $ab + cd = 0$ and $c^2 + d^2 = a^2 + b^2 \neq 0$.

C Appendix

Proofs of Selected Theorems

THEOREM 2.3 Limit Laws

Assume $\lim\limits_{x \to a} f(x)$ and $\lim\limits_{x \to a} g(x)$ exist. The following properties hold, where c is a real number, and $m > 0$ and $n > 0$ are integers.

1. **Sum** $\lim\limits_{x \to a} [f(x) + g(x)] = \lim\limits_{x \to a} f(x) + \lim\limits_{x \to a} g(x)$

2. **Difference** $\lim\limits_{x \to a} [f(x) - g(x)] = \lim\limits_{x \to a} f(x) - \lim\limits_{x \to a} g(x)$

3. **Constant multiple** $\lim\limits_{x \to a} [cf(x)] = c \lim\limits_{x \to a} f(x)$

4. **Product** $\lim\limits_{x \to a} [f(x)g(x)] = \left[\lim\limits_{x \to a} f(x)\right]\left[\lim\limits_{x \to a} g(x)\right]$

5. **Quotient** $\lim\limits_{x \to a} \left[\dfrac{f(x)}{g(x)}\right] = \dfrac{\lim\limits_{x \to a} f(x)}{\lim\limits_{x \to a} g(x)}$, provided $\lim\limits_{x \to a} g(x) \neq 0$

6. **Power** $\lim\limits_{x \to a} [f(x)]^n = \left[\lim\limits_{x \to a} f(x)\right]^n$

7. **Fractional power** $\lim\limits_{x \to a} [f(x)]^{n/m} = \left[\lim\limits_{x \to a} f(x)\right]^{n/m}$, provided $f(x) \geq 0$, for x near a, if m is even and n/m is reduced to lowest terms

---

Proof: The proof of Law 1 is given in Example 5 of Section 2.7. The proof of Law 2 is analogous to that of Law 1; the triangle inequality in the form $|x - y| \leq |x| + |y|$ is used. The proof of Law 3 is outlined in Exercise 26 of Section 2.7. The proofs of Laws 4 and 5 are given below. The proof of Law 6 involves the repeated use of Law 4. The proof of Law 7 is given in advanced texts. ◄

Proof of Product Law: Let $L = \lim\limits_{x \to a} f(x)$ and $M = \lim\limits_{x \to a} g(x)$. Using the definition of a limit, the goal is to show that given any $\varepsilon > 0$, it is possible to specify a $\delta > 0$ such that $|f(x)g(x) - LM| < \varepsilon$ whenever $0 < |x - a| < \delta$. Notice that

$$
\begin{aligned}
|f(x)g(x) - LM| &= |f(x)g(x) - Lg(x) + Lg(x) - LM| &&\text{Add and subtract } Lg(x).\\
&= |(f(x) - L)g(x) + (g(x) - M)L| &&\text{Group terms.}\\
&\leq |(f(x) - L)g(x)| + |(g(x) - M)L| &&\text{Triangle inequality}\\
&= |f(x) - L||g(x)| + |g(x) - M||L|. &&|xy| = |x||y|
\end{aligned}
$$

We now use the definition of the limits of f and g, and note that L and M are fixed real numbers. Given $\varepsilon > 0$, there exist $\delta_1 > 0$ and $\delta_2 > 0$ such that

$$
|f(x) - L| < \frac{\varepsilon}{2(|M| + 1)} \quad \text{and} \quad |g(x) - M| < \frac{\varepsilon}{2(|L| + 1)}
$$

> ► Real numbers x and y obey the triangle inequality $|x + y| \leq |x| + |y|$.

▶ $|g(x) - M| < 1$ implies that $g(x)$ is less than 1 unit from M. Therefore, whether $g(x)$ and M are positive or negative, $|g(x)| < |M| + 1$.

whenever $0 < |x - a| < \delta_1$ and $0 < |x - a| < \delta_2$, respectively. Furthermore, by the definition of the limit of g, there exits a $\delta_3 > 0$ such that $|g(x) - M| < 1$ whenever $0 < |x - a| < \delta_3$. It follows that $|g(x)| < |M| + 1$ whenever $0 < |x - a| < \delta_3$. Now take δ to be the minimum of δ_1, δ_2, and δ_3. Then for $0 < |x - a| < \delta$, we have

$$|f(x)g(x) - LM| \le \underbrace{|f(x) - L|}_{<\frac{\varepsilon}{2(|M| + 1)}}\underbrace{|g(x)|}_{<(|M| + 1)} + \underbrace{|g(x) - M|}_{<\frac{\varepsilon}{2(|L| + 1)}}|L|$$

$$< \frac{\varepsilon}{2} + \frac{\varepsilon}{2}\underbrace{\frac{|L|}{|L| + 1}}_{<1} < \frac{\varepsilon}{2} + \frac{\varepsilon}{2} = \varepsilon.$$

It follows that $\lim\limits_{x \to a} [f(x)g(x)] = LM$.   ◀

Proof of Quotient Law: We first prove that if $\lim\limits_{x \to a} g(x) = M$ exists, where $M \ne 0$, then $\lim\limits_{x \to a} \dfrac{1}{g(x)} = \dfrac{1}{M}$. The Quotient Law then follows by replacing g by $1/g$ in the Product Law. Therefore, the goal is to show that given any $\varepsilon > 0$, it is possible to specify a $\delta > 0$ such that $\left| \dfrac{1}{g(x)} - \dfrac{1}{M} \right| < \varepsilon$ whenever $0 < |x - a| < \delta$. First note that $M \ne 0$ and $g(x)$ can be made arbitrarily close to M. For this reason, there exists a $\delta_1 > 0$ such that $|g(x)| > |M|/2$ whenever $0 < |x - a| < \delta_1$. Furthermore, using the definition of the limit of g, given any $\varepsilon > 0$, there exists a $\delta_2 > 0$ such that $|g(x) - M| < \dfrac{\varepsilon |M|^2}{2}$ whenever $0 < |x - a| < \delta_2$. Now take δ to be the minimum of δ_1 and δ_2. Then for $0 < |x - a| < \delta$, we have

▶ Note that if $|g(x)| > |M|/2$, then $1/|g(x)| < 2/|M|$.

$$\left| \frac{1}{g(x)} - \frac{1}{M} \right| = \left| \frac{M - g(x)}{Mg(x)} \right| \qquad \text{Common denominator}$$

$$= \frac{1}{|M|} \underbrace{\frac{1}{|g(x)|}}_{<\frac{2}{|M|}} \underbrace{|g(x) - M|}_{<\frac{\varepsilon |M|^2}{2}} \qquad \text{Rewrite.}$$

$$< \frac{1}{|M|} \cdot \frac{2}{|M|} \cdot \frac{\varepsilon |M|^2}{2} = \varepsilon. \qquad \text{Simplify.}$$

By the definition of a limit, we have $\lim\limits_{x \to a} \dfrac{1}{g(x)} = \dfrac{1}{M}$. The proof can be completed by applying the Product Law with g replaced by $1/g$.   ◀

THEOREM 10.3   Convergence of Power Series

A power series $\sum\limits_{k=0}^{\infty} c_k(x - a)^k$ centered at a converges in one of three ways.

1. The series converges for all x, in which case the interval of convergence is $(-\infty, \infty)$ and the radius of convergence is $R = \infty$.

2. There is a real number $R > 0$ such that the series converges for $|x - a| < R$ and diverges for $|x - a| > R$, in which case the radius of convergence is R.

3. The series converges only at a, in which case the radius of convergence is $R = 0$.

Proof: Without loss of generality, we take $a = 0$. (If $a \neq 0$, the following argument may be shifted so it is centered at $x = a$.) The proof hinges on a preliminary result:

If $\sum_{k=0}^{\infty} c_k x^k$ converges for $x = b \neq 0$, then it converges absolutely, for

$|x| < |b|$. If $\sum_{k=0}^{\infty} c_k x^k$ diverges for $x = d$, then it diverges, for $|x| > |d|$.

To prove these facts, assume that $\sum_{k=0}^{\infty} c_k b^k$ converges, which implies that $\lim_{k \to \infty} c_k b^k = 0$. Then there exists a real number $M > 0$ such that $|c_k b^k| < M$, for $k = 0, 1, 2, 3, \ldots$. It follows that

$$\sum_{k=0}^{\infty} |c_k x^k| = \sum_{k=0}^{\infty} \underbrace{|c_k b^k|}_{<M} \left| \frac{x}{b} \right|^k < M \sum_{k=0}^{\infty} \left| \frac{x}{b} \right|^k.$$

If $|x| < |b|$, then $|x/b| < 1$ and $\sum_{k=0}^{\infty} \left| \frac{x}{b} \right|^k$ is a convergent geometric series. Therefore,

$\sum_{k=0}^{\infty} |c_k x^k|$ converges by the comparison test, which implies that $\sum_{k=0}^{\infty} c_k x^k$ converges absolutely for $|x| < |b|$. The second half of the preliminary result is proved by supposing the series diverges at $x = d$. The series cannot converge at a point x_0 with $|x_0| > |d|$ because by the preceding argument, it would converge for $|x| < |x_0|$, which includes $x = d$. Therefore, the series diverges for $|x| > |d|$.

Now we may deal with the three cases in the theorem. Let S be the set of real numbers for which the series converges, which always includes 0. If $S = \{0\}$, then we have Case 3. If S consists of all real numbers, then we have Case 1. For Case 2, assume that $d \neq 0$ is a point at which the series diverges. By the preliminary result, the series diverges for $|x| > |d|$. Therefore, if x is in S, then $|x| < |d|$, which implies that S is bounded. By the Least Upper Bound Property for real numbers, S has a least upper bound R, such that $x \leq R$, for all x in S. If $|x| > R$, then x is not in S and the series diverges. If $|x| < R$, then x is not the least upper bound of S and there exists a number b in S with $|x| < b \leq R$.

Because the series converges at $x = b$, by the preliminary result, $\sum_{k=0}^{\infty} |c_k x^k|$ converges for

$|x| < |b|$. Therefore, the series $\sum_{k=0}^{\infty} c_k x^k$ converges absolutely (hence converges) for $|x| < R$ and diverges for $|x| > R$.   ◀

> The Least Upper Bound Property for real numbers states that if a nonempty set S is bounded (that is, there exists a number M, called an *upper bound*, such that $x \leq M$ for all x in S), then S has a *least upper bound L*, which is the smallest of the upper bounds.

Selected Answers

CHAPTER 1

Section 1.1 Exercises, pp. 10–13

1. A function is a rule that assigns to each value of the independent variable in the domain a unique value of the dependent variable in the range. **3.** A graph represents a function if and only if every vertical line intersects the graph at most once. **5.** The first statement is true of a function, by definition. **7.** $2; -2$
9. $f(-x) = f(x)$

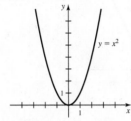

11. B **13.** $D = $ all real numbers, $R = [-10, \infty)$
15. $D = [-2, 2], R = [0, 2]$
17. $D = $ all real numbers, $R = $ all real numbers
19. $D = [-3, 3]; R = [0, 27]$ **21.** The independent variable is t; the dependent variable is d; $D = [0, 8]$. **23.** The independent variable is h; the dependent variable is V. $D = [0, 50]$.
25. 96 **27.** $1/z^3$ **29.** $1/(y^3 - 3)$ **31.** $(u^2 - 4)^3$ **33.** $\dfrac{x-3}{10-3x}$
35. x **37.** $g(x) = x^3 - 5; f(x) = x^{10}; D = $ all real numbers
39. $g(x) = x^4 + 2, f(x) = \sqrt{x}; D = $ all real numbers
41. $(f \circ g)(x) = |x^2 - 4|; D = $ all real numbers
43. $(f \circ G)(x) = \dfrac{1}{|x-2|}; D = \{x : x \neq 2\}$
45. $(G \circ g \circ f)(x) = \dfrac{1}{x^2 - 6}; D = \{x : x \neq \sqrt{6}, -\sqrt{6}\}$
47. $x^4 - 8x^2 + 12$ **49.** $f(x) = x - 3$ **51.** $f(x) = x^2$
53. $f(x) = x^2$ **55. a.** 4 **b.** 1 **c.** 3 **d.** 3 **e.** 7 **f.** 8
57. $2x + h; x + a$ **59.** $-\dfrac{2}{x(x+h)}; -\dfrac{2}{ax}$
61. $\dfrac{1}{(x+h+1)(x+1)}; \dfrac{1}{(a+1)(x+1)}$
63. $3x^2 + 3xh + h^2 - 2; x^2 + ax + a^2 - 2$
65. $\dfrac{4(2x+h)}{x^2(x+h)^2}; \dfrac{4(x+a)}{a^2x^2}$
67. a.

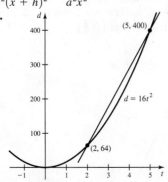

b. $m_{\text{sec}} = 112$ ft/s; the object falls at an average rate of 112 ft/s.

69. a.

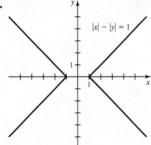

b. $m_{\text{sec}} = -2 \text{ cm}^3/\text{atmosphere}$; the volume decreases at an average rate of $2 \text{ cm}^3/\text{atmosphere}$ over the interval $0.5 \leq p \leq 2$.
71. y-axis **73.** No symmetry **75.** x-axis, y-axis, origin **77.** Origin
79. A is even, B is odd, C is even **81. a.** True **b.** False **c.** True
d. False **e.** False **f.** True **g.** True **h.** False **i.** True

83.

85. $f(x) = 3x - 2, f(x) = -3x + 4$ **87.** $f(x) = x^2 - 6$
89. $\dfrac{1}{\sqrt{x+h} + \sqrt{x}}; \dfrac{1}{\sqrt{x} + \sqrt{a}}$
91. $\dfrac{3}{\sqrt{x}(x+h) + x\sqrt{x+h}}; \dfrac{3}{x\sqrt{a} + a\sqrt{x}}$
93. a. $[0, 3 + \sqrt{14}]$

b. At time $t = 3$, the maximum height is 224 ft.

95. None **97.** Origin **99.** y-axis **101.** y-axis
103. a. 4 **b.** 1 **c.** 3 **d.** -2 **e.** -1 **f.** 7

Section 1.2 Exercises, pp. 22–28

1. A formula, a graph, a table, words **3.** Set of all real numbers except points at which the denominator is zero

5.

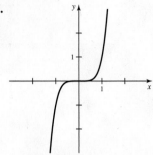

7. Shift the graph to the left 2 units.   **9.** Compress the graph horizontally by a factor of 3.   **11.** $y = -\frac{2}{3}x - 1$
13. $y = 2x + 1$

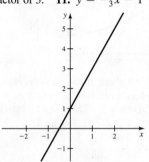

15. $d = -3p/50 + 27; D = [0, 450]$

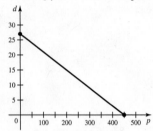

17. $p(t) = 24t + 500; 860$

19. $y = \begin{cases} x + 3 & \text{if } x < 0 \\ -\frac{1}{2}x + 3 & \text{if } x \geq 0 \end{cases}$

21. $c(t) = \begin{cases} 0.05t & \text{if } 0 \leq t \leq 60 \\ 1.2 + 0.03t & \text{if } 60 < t \leq 120 \end{cases}$

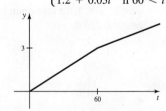

23.

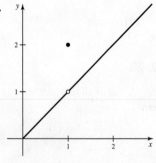

25.

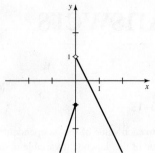

27.

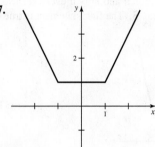

29. a.

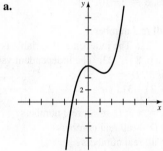

b. D = all real numbers   **c.** Peak near $x = 0$; valley near $x = 1.3$; x-intercept approx $(-1.3, 0)$; y-intercept $(0, 6)$
31. a.

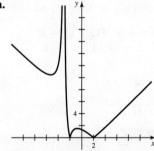

b. $D = \{x : x \neq -3\}$ **c.** Undefined at $x = -3$; peak near $x = -0.8$; valleys near $x = -5.2$, and at $x = -2$ and $x = 2$; x-intercepts $(0, -2)$ and $(0, 2)$; y-intercept $\left(0, \frac{4}{3}\right)$
33. a.

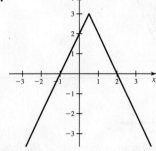

b. $D = (-\infty, \infty)$.   **c.** One peak at $x = \frac{1}{2}$; y-intercept at $(0, 2)$; x-intercepts $(-1, 0)$ and $(2, 0)$

35. $s(x) = 2$ **37.** $s(x) = \begin{cases} 1 & \text{if } x < 0 \\ -\frac{1}{2} & \text{if } x > 0 \end{cases}$

39. a. 12   **b.** 36   **c.** $A(x) = 6x$

41. a. 12   **b.** 21   **c.** $A(x) = \begin{cases} 8x - x^2 & \text{if } 0 \le x \le 3 \\ 2x + 9 & \text{if } x > 3 \end{cases}$

43. $f(x) = |x - 2| + 3$; $g(x) = -|x + 2| - 1$
45. a. Shift 3 units to the right.

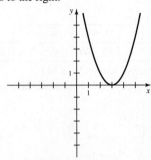

b. Scale horizontally by a factor of 2 and shift 2 units to the right.

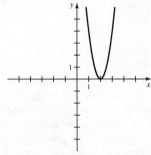

c. Shift to the right 2 units, scale vertically by a factor of 3, reflect across the x-axis, and shift up 4 units.

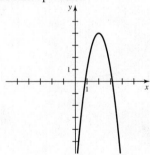

d. Scale horizontally by a factor of $\frac{1}{3}$, shift right 2 units, scale vertically by a factor of 6, and shift up 1 unit

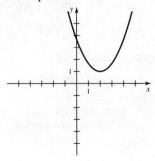

47. Shift the graph of $y = x^2$ right 2 units and up 1 unit.

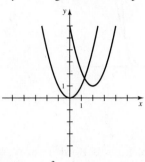

49. Stretch the graph of $y = x^2$ vertically by a factor of 3 and reflect across the x-axis.   **51.** Shift the graph of $y = x^2$ left 3 units and stretch vertically by a factor of 2.   **53.** Shift the graph of $y = x^2$ to the left $\frac{1}{2}$ unit, stretch vertically by a factor of 4, reflect across the x-axis, and then shift up 13 units to obtain the graph of h.
55. a. True   **b.** False   **c.** True   **d.** False
57. $(0, 0)$ and $(4, 16)$ **59.** $y = \sqrt{x} - 1$
61. $y = 5x$; $D = [0, h]$, where h is the maximum numbers of hours you can run

63. $y = 3200/x$; $D = (0, p]$, where p is the maximum gas price of interest

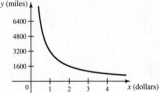

65.

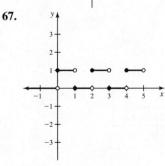

67.

69.

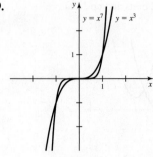

71. a. A, D, F, I   **b.** E   **c.** B, H   **d.** I   **e.** A
73. a.

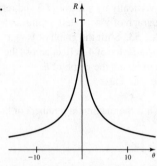

b. $\theta = 0$; vision is sharpest when we look straight ahead.
c. $|\theta| \leq 0.19°$ (less than $\frac{1}{5}$ of a degree).
75. a. $p(t) = 328.3t + 1875$ **b.** 4830
77. a. $f(m) = 350m + 1200$ **b.** Buy
79. $0 \leq h \leq 2$

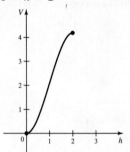

81. a. $S(x) = x^2 + \dfrac{500}{x}$ **b.** ≈ 6.30 ft

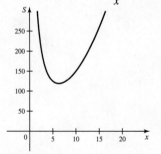

85. a.

n	1	2	3	4	5
$f(n)$	1	2	6	24	120

b.   **c.** 10

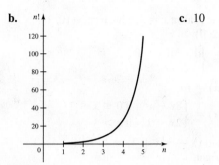

87. a.

n	1	2	3	4	5	6	7	8	9	10
$T(n)$	1	5	14	30	55	91	140	204	285	385

b. $D = \{n: n \text{ is a positive integer}\}$ **c.** 14
89. a. $\{x: x \neq \pm 3\}$ **b.** Symmetric about the origin (odd function)
c.

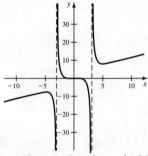

d. $-1, 0, 1$ **e.** Local max $(-5.2, -7.8)$; local min $(5.2, 7.8)$
f. As x approaches 3 from the left, $f(x)$ is negative and increases in magnitude without bound; as x approaches 3 from the right, $f(x)$ increases without bound.   **g.** As x becomes large and positive, $f(x)$ increases without bound; as x becomes large and negative, $f(x)$ increases in magnitude without bound.   **91. a.** $D =$ all real numbers   **b.** Symmetric about the origin (odd function)
c.

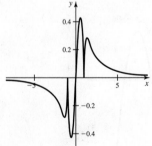

d. $x = -1, 0, 1$ **e.** $(0, 0)$ **f.** $x = -1$ and $x = 1$;
g. Local max $(-1, 0), (0.6, 0.4), (1.4, 0.3)$; local min $(1, 0), (-0.6, -0.4), (-1.4, -0.3)$ **h.** $f(x)$ approaches 0 in both cases.

Section 1.3 Exercises, pp. 37–40

1. $D =$ all real numbers; $R = (0, \infty)$ **3.** If a function f is not one-to-one, there are domain values, x_1 and x_2, such that $x_1 \neq x_2$ but $f(x_1) = f(x_2)$. If f^{-1} exists, by definition $f^{-1}(f(x_1)) = x_1$ and $f^{-1}(f(x_2)) = x_2$ so that f^{-1} assigns two different range values to the single domain value of $f(x_1)$.

5.

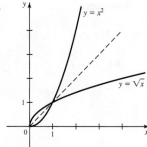

7. The expression $\log_b x$ represents the power to which b must be raised to obtain x. **9.** $D = (0, \infty)$; $R =$ all real numbers
11. $(-\infty, -1]$, $[-1, 1]$, $[1, \infty)$
13.

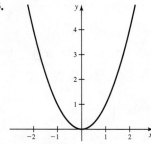

15. $(-\infty, \infty)$ **17.** $(-\infty, 5) \cup (5, \infty)$ **19.** $(-\infty, 0), (0, \infty)$
21. a. $f^{-1}(x) = \frac{1}{2}x$ **23. a.** $f^{-1}(x) = (6 - x)/4$
25. a. $f^{-1}(x) = (x - 5)/3$ **27. a.** $f^{-1}(x) = x^2 - 2, x \geq 0$
29. a. $f_1(x) = \sqrt{1 - x^2};\ \ 0 \leq x \leq 1$
$\quad\quad f_2(x) = \sqrt{1 - x^2};\ \ -1 \leq x \leq 0$
$\quad\quad f_3(x) = -\sqrt{1 - x^2};\ \ -1 \leq x \leq 0$
$\quad\quad f_4(x) = -\sqrt{1 - x^2};\ \ 0 \leq x \leq 1$
b. $f_1^{-1}(x) = \sqrt{1 - x^2};\ \ 0 \leq x \leq 1$
$\quad\ f_2^{-1}(x) = -\sqrt{1 - x^2};\ \ 0 \leq x \leq 1$
$\quad\ f_3^{-1}(x) = -\sqrt{1 - x^2};\ \ -1 \leq x \leq 0$
$\quad\ f_4^{-1}(x) = \sqrt{1 - x^2};\ \ -1 \leq x \leq 0$
31. $f^{-1}(x) = \dfrac{8 - x}{4}$

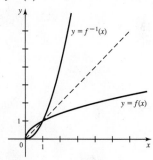

33. $f^{-1}(x) = x^2, x \geq 0$

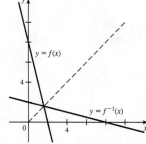

35. $f^{-1}(x) = \sqrt[4]{x - 4}, x \geq 4$

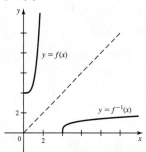

37. $f^{-1}(x) = \sqrt{x - 5} + 1, x \geq 5$

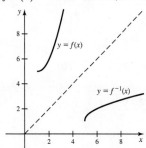

39.

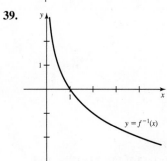

41. 1000 **43.** 2 **45.** $1/e$ **47.** -0.2 **49.** 1.19 **51.** $-0.09\overline{6}$
53. $\ln 21/\ln 7$ **55.** $\ln 5/(3 \ln 3) + 4/3$ **57.** $650 \ln 2 \approx 451$ years
59. $\ln 15/\ln 2 \approx 3.907$ **61.** $\ln 40/\ln 4 \approx 2.661$ **63.** $e^{x \ln 2}$
65. $\log_5 |x|/\log_5 e$ **67.** e **69. a.** False **b.** False **c.** False
d. True **e.** False **f.** False **g.** True
71. A is $y = \log_2 x$. B is $y = \log_4 x$. C is $y = \log_{10} x$.
73.

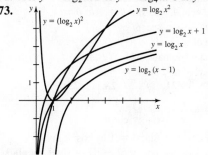

75. $f^{-1}(x) = \sqrt[3]{x} - 1, D =$ all real numbers
77. $f_1^{-1}(x) = \sqrt{2/x - 2}, D_1 = (0, 1]$; $f_2^{-1}(x) = -\sqrt{2/x - 2}$,
$D_2 = (0, 1]$ **79. b.** $\dfrac{p(t + 12)}{p(t)} = 2$ **c.** 38,400
d. $12 \ln 3/\ln 2 \approx 19.020$ hr **e.** 72.707 hr

81. a. No   **b.** $f^{-1}(h) = 2 - \sqrt{\dfrac{64 - h}{16}}$

c. $f^{-1}(h) = 2 + \sqrt{\dfrac{64 - h}{16}}$ **d.** 0.542 s   **e.** 3.837 s

83. Let $y = \log_b x$. Then $b^y = x$ and $(1/b)^y = 1/x$. Hence, $y = -\log_{1/b} x$. Thus, $\log_{1/b} x = -y = -\log_b x$.

87. a.

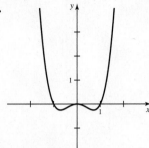

f is one-to-one on the intervals $(-\infty, -0.7]$, $[-0.7, 0]$, $[0, 0.7]$, and $[0.7, \infty)$.

b. $x = \sqrt{\dfrac{1 \pm \sqrt{4y + 1}}{2}}, \ -\sqrt{\dfrac{1 \pm \sqrt{4y + 1}}{2}}$

93. a. $(1.631, 0.489), (5.938, 1.781)$

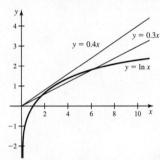

b. No intersection points   **c.** $a = 0.4, (2.7, 1)$ **95.** $A \approx 10.3$

Section 1.4 Exercises, pp. 49–53

1. $\sin \theta = $ opp/hyp; $\cos \theta = $ adj/hyp; $\tan \theta = $ opp/adj; $\cot \theta = $ adj/opp; $\sec \theta = $ hyp/adj; $\csc \theta = $ hyp/opp
3. The radian measure of an angle θ is the length of an arc s on the unit circle associated with θ.   **5.** $\sin^2 \theta + \cos^2 \theta = 1$, $1 + \cot^2 \theta = \csc^2 \theta$, $\tan^2 \theta + 1 = \sec^2 \theta$
7. $\{x : x \text{ is an odd multiple of } \pi/2\}$
9. Sine is not one-to-one on its domain.   **11.** Yes; no
13. Vertical asymptotes at $x = \pi/2$ and $x = -\pi/2$
15. $-\frac{1}{2}$ **17.** 1   **19.** $-1/\sqrt{3}$ **21.** $1/\sqrt{3}$ **23.** 1   **25.** -1

27. Undefined   **29.** $\sec \theta = \dfrac{r}{x} = \dfrac{1}{x/r} = \dfrac{1}{\cos \theta}$

31. Dividing both sides of $\cos^2 \theta + \sin^2 \theta = 1$ by $\cos^2 \theta$ gives $1 + \tan^2 \theta = \sec^2 \theta$.   **33.** Because $\cos(\pi/2 - \theta) = \sin \theta$, for all θ, $1/\cos(\pi/2 - \theta) = 1/\sin \theta$, excluding integer multiples of π,

and $\sec(\pi/2 - \theta) = \csc \theta$.   **35.** $\dfrac{\sqrt{2 + \sqrt{3}}}{2} = \dfrac{\sqrt{6} + \sqrt{2}}{4}$

37. $\pi/4 + n\pi, n = 0, \pm 1, \pm 2, \ldots$ **39.** $\pi/6, 5\pi/6, 7\pi/6, 11\pi/6$

41. $\pi/4 + 2n\pi, 3\pi/4 + 2n\pi$, where n is an integer
43. $\pi/12, 5\pi/12, 3\pi/4, 13\pi/12, 17\pi/12, 7\pi/4$
45. $0, \pi/2, \pi, 3\pi/2$ **47.** $\pi/2$ **49.** $\pi/4$ **51.** $\pi/3$ **53.** $2\pi/3$

55. -1 **57.** $\sqrt{1 - x^2}$ **59.** $\dfrac{\sqrt{4 - x^2}}{2}$ **61.** $2x\sqrt{1 - x^2}$

63. $\cos^{-1} x + \cos^{-1}(-x) = \theta + (\pi - \theta) = \pi$

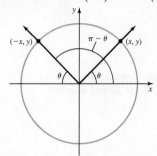

65. The functions are equal.   **67.** $\pi/3$ **69.** $\pi/3$ **71.** $\pi/4$
73. $\pi/2 - 2$ **75.** $\dfrac{1}{\sqrt{x^2 + 1}}$ **77.** $1/x$ **79.** $|x|/\sqrt{x^2 + 16}$

81. $\sin^{-1} \dfrac{x}{6} = \tan^{-1}\left(\dfrac{x}{\sqrt{36 - x^2}}\right) = \sec^{-1}\left(\dfrac{6}{\sqrt{36 - x^2}}\right)$

83. a. False   **b.** False   **c.** False   **d.** False   **e.** True   **f.** False
g. True   **h.** False   **85.** $\sin \theta = \frac{12}{13}$; $\tan \theta = \frac{12}{5}$; $\sec \theta = \frac{13}{5}$;

$\csc \theta = \frac{13}{12}$; $\cot \theta = \frac{5}{12}$ **87.** $\sin \theta = \dfrac{12}{13}$; $\cos \theta = \dfrac{5}{13}$; $\tan \theta = \dfrac{12}{5}$;

$\sec \theta = \dfrac{13}{5}$; $\cot \theta = \dfrac{5}{12}$ **89.** Amp = 3; period = 6π

91. Amp = 3.6; period = 48   **93.** Stretch the graph of $y = \cos x$ horizontally by a factor of 3; stretch vertically by a factor of 2; and reflect across the x-axis.

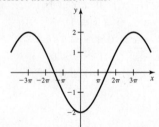

95. Stretch the graph of $y = \cos x$ horizontally by a factor of $24/\pi$; then stretch it vertically by a factor of 3.6 and shift it up 2 units.

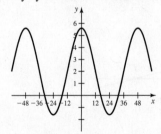

97. $y = 3 \sin(\pi x/12 - 3\pi/4) + 13$ **99.** About 6 ft
101. $y = -2 \cos 2x$ **103.** $y = \sin(x - \pi/4)$
105. $d(t) = 10 \cos(4\pi t/3)$ **107.** h

109. $s(t) = 117.5 - 87.5 \sin\left(\dfrac{\pi}{182.5}(t - 95)\right)$

$S(t) = 843.5 + 87.5 \sin\left(\dfrac{\pi}{182.5}(t - 67)\right)$

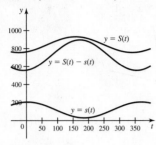

111. Area of circle is πr^2; $\theta/(2\pi)$ represents the proportion of area swept out by a central angle θ. Thus, the area of such a sector is $(\theta/2\pi)\pi r^2 = r^2\theta/2$.

115. a. $\{x\colon x \neq 0\}$ **b.**

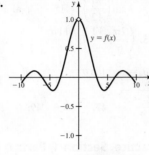

c. $x = 0$ is not in the domain of f **d.** Approximately $\{y\colon -0.22 \leq y \leq 1\}$ **e.** $\{x\colon x = n\pi, n \neq 0 \text{ an integer}\}$
f. sinc x approaches zero as $|x|$ increases.
117. a. Two terms

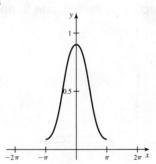

b. Three terms

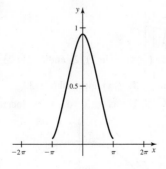

Four terms

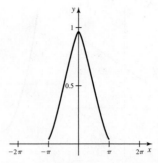

c. Seven terms; the graphs approach the function $f(x) = 1 - \left|\frac{x}{\pi}\right|$, on $[-\pi, \pi]$.

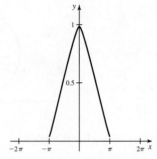

Chapter 1 Review Exercises, pp. 54–56

1. a. True   **b.** False   **c.** False   **d.** True   **e.** False   **f.** False
g. True
3. a.

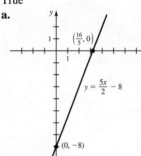

b.

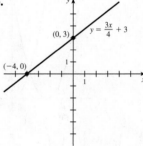

c.

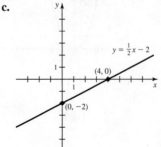

5. $f(x) = \begin{cases} 4x & \text{if } x < 0 \\ 0 & \text{if } x \geq 0 \end{cases}$

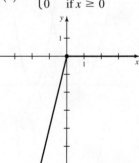

7. a.

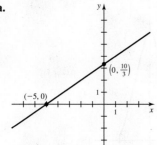

b.

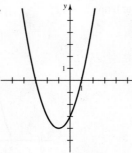

c.

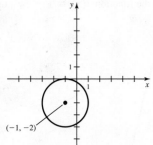

d.

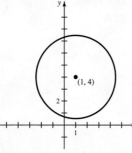

9. D_f = all real numbers, R_f = all real numbers; $D_g = [0, \infty), R_g = [0, \infty)$

11. $B = -\dfrac{1}{500}a + 212$

13. a.

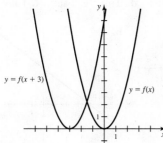

b.

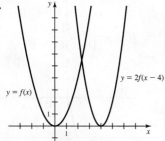

c.

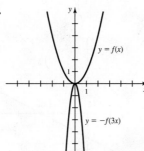

d.

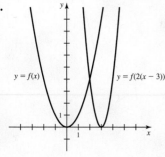

15. a. 1   **b.** $\sqrt{x^3}$ **c.** $\sin^3 \sqrt{x}$ **d.** All real numbers   **e.** $[-1, 1]$
17. $2x + h - 2; x + a - 2$ **19.** $3x^2 + 3xh + h^2; x^2 + ax + a^2$
21. a. y-axis   **b.** y-axis   **c.** x-axis, y-axis, origin   **23.** $x = 2$;
base does not matter   **25.** $(-\infty, 0], [0, 2]$, and $[2, \infty)$
27. $f^{-1}(x) = 2 + \sqrt{x - 1}$

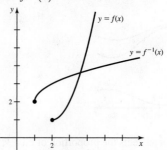

29. a. $3\pi/4$ **b.** $144°$ **c.** $40\pi/3$ **31. a.** $f(t) = -2 \cos\left(\dfrac{\pi t}{3}\right)$
b. $f(t) = 5 \sin\left(\dfrac{\pi t}{12}\right) + 15$ **33. a.** F   **b.** E   **c.** D   **d.** B   **e.** C
f. A   **35.** $\left(\dfrac{7\pi}{6}, -\dfrac{1}{2}\right); \left(\dfrac{11\pi}{6}, -\dfrac{1}{2}\right)$ **37.** $\dfrac{\pi}{6}$ **39.** $-\dfrac{\pi}{2}$ **41.** x

43. $\cos \theta = \dfrac{5}{13}; \tan \theta = \dfrac{12}{5}; \cot \theta = \dfrac{5}{12}; \sec \theta = \dfrac{13}{5}; \csc \theta = \dfrac{13}{12}$

45. $\dfrac{\sqrt{4 - x^2}}{2}$ **47.** $\dfrac{\pi}{2} - \theta$ **49.** 0   **51.** $1 - 2x^2$

AP® Practice, Section 1, Parts A and B, pp. 57–58

1. D   **2.** A   **3.** B   **4.** C   **5.** E   **6.** A   **7.** D   **8.** C   **9.** D
10. A   **11.** C   **12.** C   **13.** B   **14.** A

AP® Practice, Section 2, Parts A and B, pp. 58–59

1. a. $\left\{x: x \neq -\dfrac{\ln 2}{2}\right\}$
b.

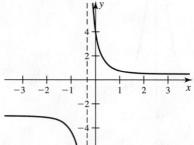

c. No intervals   **d.** $(-\infty, -(\ln 2)/2)$ and $(-(\ln 2)/2, \infty)$

e. $f(x)$ approaches $\dfrac{1}{2}$.   **f.** $f(x)$ approaches -3.
2. a. $[-3, 3]$ **b.** $[0, 3]$ **c.** ± 3 **d.** 3   **e.** Increase
f. Decrease   **g.**

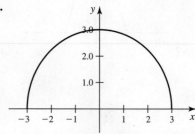

3. a. $f(x) = 2 \sin\left(2\left(x - \dfrac{\pi}{4}\right)\right); a = 2, b = \dfrac{\pi}{4}, c = 2$

b.

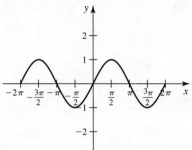

c.

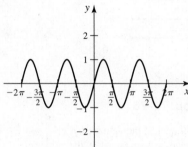

d.

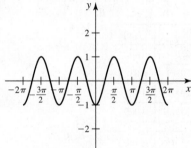

e.

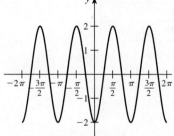

4. Distance, measured in feet; time, measured in seconds

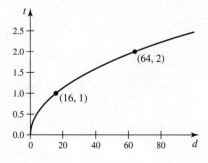

b. $t = \dfrac{d}{48} + \dfrac{2}{3}$; units: seconds per foot.

c. $\dfrac{1}{4} \dfrac{1}{\sqrt{d} + \sqrt{a}}$; measures average rate of change in the fall time with respect to the fall distance over the interval $[a, d]$.

CHAPTER 2

Section 2.1 Exercises, pp. 66–67

1. $\dfrac{s(b) - s(a)}{b - a}$ **3.** $\dfrac{f(b) - f(a)}{b - a}$ **5.** The instantaneous velocity at $t = a$ is the slope of the line tangent to the position curve at $t = a$. **7.** 20 **9. a.** 48 **b.** 64 **c.** 80 **d.** $16(6 - h)$ **11. a.** 36 **b.** 44 **c.** 52 **d.** 60 **13.** $m_{sec} = 60$; the slope is the average velocity of the object over the interval $[0.5, 2]$.

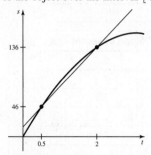

15.

Time interval	Average velocity
$[1, 2]$	80
$[1, 1.5]$	88
$[1, 1.1]$	94.4
$[1, 1.01]$	95.84
$[1, 1.001]$	95.984
$v_{inst} = 96$	

17. 47.84, 47.984, 47.9984; instantaneous velocity appears to be 48.

19.

Time interval	Average velocity
$[2, 3]$	20
$[2.9, 3]$	5.60
$[2.99, 3]$	4.16
$[2.999, 3]$	4.016
$[2.9999, 3]$	4.002
$v_{inst} = 4$	

21.

Time interval	Average velocity
$[3, 3.5]$	-24
$[3, 3.1]$	-17.6
$[3, 3.01]$	-16.16
$[3, 3.001]$	-16.016
$[3, 3.0001]$	-16.002
$v_{inst} = -16$	

23.

Time interval	Average velocity
$[0, 1]$	36.372
$[0, 0.5]$	67.318
$[0, 0.1]$	79.468
$[0, 0.01]$	79.995
$[0, 0.001]$	80.000
$v_{inst} = 80$	

25.

Interval	Slope of secant line
$[1, 2]$	6
$[1.5, 2]$	7
$[1.9, 2]$	7.8
$[1.99, 2]$	7.98
$[1.999, 2]$	7.998
$m_{tan} = 8$	

27.

Interval	Slope of secant line
$[0, 1]$	1.718
$[0, 0.5]$	1.297
$[0, 0.1]$	1.052
$[0, 0.01]$	1.005
$[0, 0.001]$	1.001
$m_{tan} = 1$	

29. a.

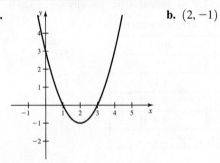

b. $(2, -1)$

c.

Interval	Slope of secant line
$[2, 2.5]$	0.5
$[2, 2.1]$	0.1
$[2, 2.01]$	0.01
$[2, 2.001]$	0.001
$[2, 2.0001]$	0.0001
$m_{tan} = 0$	

31. a.

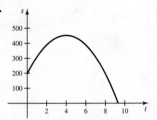

b. $t = 4$

c.

Interval	Slope of secant line
$[4, 4.5]$	-8
$[4, 4.1]$	-1.6
$[4, 4.01]$	-0.16
$[4, 4.001]$	-0.016
$[4, 4.0001]$	-0.0016
$v_{inst} = 0$	

d. $0 \le t < 4$
e. $4 < t \le 9$

33. $0.637, 0.959, 1, 1$

Section 2.2 Exercises, pp. 72–76

1. As x approaches a from either side, the values of $f(x)$ approach L.   **3.** As x approaches a from the right, the values of $f(x)$ approach L.   **5.** $L = M$.   **7. a.** 5   **b.** 3   **c.** Does not exist   **d.** 1   **e.** 2   **9. a.** -1 **b.** 1   **c.** 2   **d.** 2

11. a.

x	$f(x)$	x	$f(x)$
1.9	3.9	2.1	4.1
1.99	3.99	2.01	4.01
1.999	3.999	2.001	4.001
1.9999	4.000	2.0001	4.000

b. 4

13. a.

t	$g(t)$	t	$g(t)$
8.9	5.983	9.1	6.0166
8.99	5.998	9.01	6.00167
8.999	6.000	9.001	6.000

b. 6

15. From the graph and table, the limit appears to be 0.

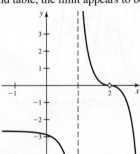

x	1.99	1.999	1.9999	2.0001	2.001	2.01
$f(x)$	0.00217	0.000145	0.0000109	-0.0000109	-0.000145	-0.00217

17. From the graph and table, the limit appears to be 2.

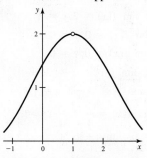

x	0.9	0.99	0.999	1.001	1.01	1.1
$f(x)$	1.993342	1.999933	1.999999	1.999999	1.999933	1.993342

19. $\lim_{x \to 5^+} f(x) = 10$; $\lim_{x \to 5^-} f(x) = 10$; $\lim_{x \to 5} f(x) = 10$

21. a. 0 **b.** 1 **c.** 0 **d.** Does not exist; $\lim_{x \to 1^-} f(x) \neq \lim_{x \to 1^+} f(x)$

23. a. 3 **b.** 2 **c.** 2 **d.** 2 **e.** 2 **f.** 4 **g.** 1 **h.** Does not exist
i. 3 **j.** 3 **k.** 3 **l.** 3

25. a.

x	$\sin\left(1/x\right)$
$2/\pi$	1
$2/(3\pi)$	-1
$2/(5\pi)$	1
$2/(7\pi)$	-1
$2/(9\pi)$	1
$2/(11\pi)$	-1

The value alternates between 1 and -1.
b. The function alternates between 1 and -1 infinitely many times on the interval $(0, h)$ no matter how small $h > 0$ becomes.
c. Does not exist.

27. a. False **b.** False **c.** False **d.** False **e.** True

29.

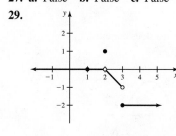

31.

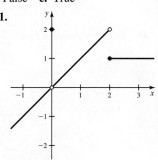

33. Approximately 403.4 **35.** 1 **37. a.** $-2, -1, 1, 2$
b. 2, 2, 2 **c.** $\lim_{x \to a^-} \lfloor x \rfloor = a - 1$ and $\lim_{x \to a^+} \lfloor x \rfloor = a$, if a is an integer **d.** $\lim_{x \to a^-} \lfloor x \rfloor = \lfloor a \rfloor$ and $\lim_{x \to a^+} \lfloor x \rfloor = \lfloor a \rfloor$, if a is not an integer **e.** $\lim_{x \to a} \lfloor x \rfloor = \lfloor a \rfloor$ provided a is not an integer.

39. a.

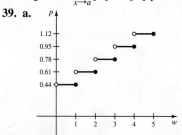

b. \$0.95

c. $\lim_{x \to 1^+} f(w) = 0.61$ is the cost of a letter that weighs just over 1 oz; $\lim_{x \to 1^-} f(w) = 0.44$ is the cost of a letter that weighs just under 1 oz. **d.** No; $\lim_{x \to 4^+} f(w) \neq \lim_{x \to 4^-} f(w)$

41. a. 8 **b.** 5 **43.** 0 **45.** 16 **47. a.** 2; 3; 4 **b.** p **49.** $\dfrac{p}{q}$

Section 2.3 Exercises, pp. 84–87

1. $\lim_{x \to a} f(x) = f(a)$ **3.** Those values of a for which the denominator is not zero. **5.** $\dfrac{x^2 - 7x + 12}{x - 3} = x - 4$ for $x \neq 3$. **7.** 20 **9.** 4 **11.** 5 **13.** -45 **15.** 4 **17.** 32; Constant Multiple Law **19.** 5; Difference Law **21.** 12; Quotient and Product Laws **23.** 32; Power Law **25.** 8
27. 3 **29.** 3 **31.** -5 **33. a.** 2 **b.** 0 **c.** Does not exist

35. a. 0 **b.** $\sqrt{x - 2}$ is undefined for $x < 2$.

37. $\lim_{x \to 0^-} |x| = \lim_{x \to 0^-} (-x) = 0$ and $\lim_{x \to 0^+} |x| = \lim_{x \to 0^+} x = 0$

39. 2 **41.** -8 **43.** -1 **45.** -12 **47.** $\frac{1}{6}$ **49.** $2\sqrt{a}$ **51.** $\frac{1}{8}$

53. a.

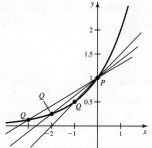

b. $\dfrac{2^x - 1}{x}$

c.

x	$\dfrac{2^x - 1}{x}$
-1	0.5
-0.1	0.670
-0.01	0.691
-0.001	0.693
-0.0001	0.693
-0.00001	0.693
Limit $\approx$ 0.693	

55. a. Because $\left| \sin \dfrac{1}{x} \right| \leq 1$ for all $x \neq 0$, we have that

$$|x| \left| \sin \dfrac{1}{x} \right| \leq |x|.$$

That is, $\left| x \sin \dfrac{1}{x} \right| \leq |x|$, so that $-|x| \leq x \sin \dfrac{1}{x} \leq |x|$ for all $x \neq 0$.

b.

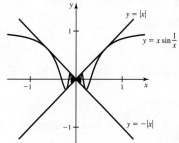

c. $\lim_{x \to 0} -|x| = 0$ and $\lim_{x \to 0} |x| = 0$; by part (a) and the Squeeze Theorem, $\lim_{x \to 0} x \sin \dfrac{1}{x} = 0$

57. a.

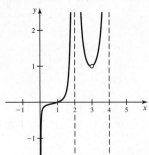

b. $\lim\limits_{x \to 0} \dfrac{\sin x}{x} = 1$

59. a. False **b.** False **c.** False **d.** False **e.** False
61. 8 **63.** 5 **65.** 10 **67.** -3 **69.** $a = -13$;

$\lim\limits_{x \to -1} g(x) = 6$ **71.** 6 **73.** $5a^4$ **75.** $\dfrac{1}{3}$ **77.** 2 **79.** -54

81. $f(x) = x - 1, g(x) = \dfrac{5}{x - 1}$ **83.** $b = 2$ and $c = -8$; Yes

85. $\lim\limits_{S \to 0^+} r(S) = 0$; the radius of the cylinder approaches 0 as the
surface area of the cylinder approaches 0. **87.** 0.0435 N/C **89.** 6; 4

Section 2.4 Exercises, pp. 93–96

1. $\lim\limits_{x \to a^+} f(x) = -\infty$ means that as x approaches a from the right, the
values of $f(x)$ are negative and become arbitrarily large. **3.** A verti-
cal line $x = a$ that the graph of a function approaches as x approaches
a **5.** $-\infty$ **7.** ∞ **9. a.** ∞ **b.** ∞ **c.** ∞ **d.** ∞ **e.** $-\infty$
f. Does not exist **11. a.** $-\infty$ **b.** $-\infty$ **c.** $-\infty$ **d.** ∞ **e.** $-\infty$
f. Does not exist **13. a.** ∞ **b.** $-\infty$ **c.** $-\infty$ **d.** ∞
15.

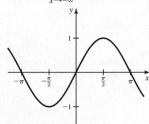

17. a. ∞ **b.** $-\infty$ **c.** Does not exist **19. a.** $-\infty$ **b.** $-\infty$
c. $-\infty$ **21. a.** ∞ **b.** $-\infty$ **c.** Does not exist **23.** -5 **25.** ∞
27. a. $-\infty$ **b.** $-\infty$ **c.** $-\infty$ **29. a.** $\dfrac{1}{10}$ **b.** $-\infty$ **c.** ∞; vertical
asymptote: $x = -5$ **31.** $x = 3$; $\lim\limits_{x \to 3^-} f(x) = -\infty$; $\lim\limits_{x \to 3^+} f(x) = \infty$;
$\lim\limits_{x \to 3} f(x)$ does not exist. **33.** $x = 0$ and $x = 2$; $\lim\limits_{x \to 0^+} f(x) = \infty$;
$\lim\limits_{x \to 0^-} f(x) = -\infty$; $\lim\limits_{x \to 0} f(x)$ does not exist; $\lim\limits_{x \to 2^+} f(x) = \infty$;
$\lim\limits_{x \to 2^-} f(x) = \infty$; $\lim\limits_{x \to 2} f(x) = \infty$ **35.** ∞ **37.** $-\infty$ **39. a.** $-\infty$
b. ∞ **c.** $-\infty$ **d.** ∞ **41. a.** False **b.** True **c.** False

43. $f(x) = \dfrac{1}{x - 6}$ **45. a.** $a = 4$ or $a = 3$

b. Either $a > 4$ or $a < 3$ **c.** $3 < a < 4$

47. a. $\dfrac{1}{\sqrt[3]{h}}$, regardless of the sign of h **b.** $\lim\limits_{h \to 0^+} \dfrac{1}{\sqrt[3]{h}} = \infty$;

$\lim\limits_{h \to 0^-} \dfrac{1}{\sqrt[3]{h}} = -\infty$; the tangent line at $(0, 0)$ is vertical.
49. $x = 0$ **51.** $x = -1$ **53.** $\theta = 10k + 5$, for any integer $kx = 0$

Section 2.5 Exercises, pp. 104–106

1. The values of $f(x)$ approach 10 as x increases without bound
negatively. **3.** 0 **5.** $\lim\limits_{x \to \infty} f(x) = -\infty$; $\lim\limits_{x \to -\infty} f(x) = \infty$
7. ∞; 0; 0 **9.** 3 **11.** 0 **13.** 0 **15.** ∞ **17.** 0 **19.** ∞

21. $-\infty$ **23.** 0 **25.** $\lim\limits_{x \to \infty} f(x) = \lim\limits_{x \to -\infty} f(x) = \dfrac{1}{5}$; $y = \dfrac{1}{5}$
27. $\lim\limits_{x \to \infty} f(x) = 2$; $\lim\limits_{x \to -\infty} f(x) = 2$; $y = 2$
29. $\lim\limits_{x \to \infty} f(x) = \lim\limits_{x \to -\infty} f(x) = 0$; $y = 0$
31. $\lim\limits_{x \to \infty} f(x) = \lim\limits_{x \to -\infty} f(x) = 0$; $y = 0$
33. $\lim\limits_{x \to \infty} f(x) = \infty$; $\lim\limits_{x \to -\infty} f(x) = -\infty$; none
35. $\lim\limits_{x \to \infty} f(x) = \dfrac{2}{3}$; $\lim\limits_{x \to -\infty} f(x) = -2$; $y = \dfrac{2}{3}$; $y = -2$
37. $\lim\limits_{x \to \infty} f(x) = \lim\limits_{x \to -\infty} f(x) = \dfrac{1}{4 + \sqrt{3}}$; $y = \dfrac{1}{4 + \sqrt{3}}$
39. $\lim\limits_{x \to \infty} (-3e^{-x}) = 0$; $\lim\limits_{x \to -\infty} (-3e^{-x}) = -\infty$

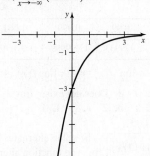

41. $\lim\limits_{x \to \infty} (1 - \ln x) = -\infty$; $\lim\limits_{x \to 0^+} (1 - \ln x) = \infty$

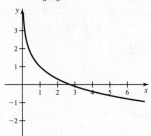

43. $\lim\limits_{x \to \infty} \sin x$ does not exist; $\lim\limits_{x \to -\infty} \sin x$ does not exist

45. a. False **b.** False **c.** True
47. a. $\lim\limits_{x \to \infty} f(x) = 2$; $\lim\limits_{x \to -\infty} f(x) = 2$; $y = 2$
b. $x = 0$; $\lim\limits_{x \to 0^+} f(x) = \infty$; $\lim\limits_{x \to 0^-} f(x) = -\infty$
49. a. $\lim\limits_{x \to \infty} f(x) = 3$; $\lim\limits_{x \to -\infty} f(x) = 3$; $y = 3$
b. $x = -3$ and $x = 4$; $\lim\limits_{x \to -3^-} f(x) = \infty$; $\lim\limits_{x \to -3^+} f(x) = -\infty$;
$\lim\limits_{x \to 4^-} f(x) = -\infty$; $\lim\limits_{x \to 4^+} f(x) = \infty$
51. a. $\lim\limits_{x \to \infty} f(x) = 1$; $\lim\limits_{x \to -\infty} f(x) = 1$; $y = 1$
b. $x = 0$; $\lim\limits_{x \to 0^+} f(x) = \infty$; $\lim\limits_{x \to 0^-} f(x) = -\infty$
53. a. $\lim\limits_{x \to \infty} f(x) = 1$; $\lim\limits_{x \to -\infty} f(x) = -1$; $y = 1$ and $y = -1$
b. No vertical asymptotes **55. a.** $\lim\limits_{x \to \infty} f(x) = 0$; $\lim\limits_{x \to -\infty} f(x) = 0$;
$y = 0$ **b.** No vertical asymptotes **57. a.** $\dfrac{\pi}{2}$ **b.** $\dfrac{\pi}{2}$

59. a. $\lim\limits_{x \to \infty} \sinh x = \infty$; $\lim\limits_{x \to -\infty} \sinh x = -\infty$

b. $\sinh 0 = 0$

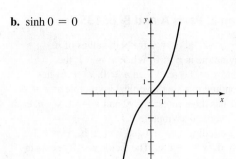

61.

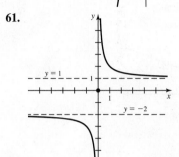

63. $x = 0; y = 2$ **65.** 3500 **67.** No steady state
69. 2 **71.** 1 **73.** 0 **75.** $\lim\limits_{x \to \infty} f(x) = 0; \lim\limits_{x \to -\infty} f(x) = \infty; y = 0$

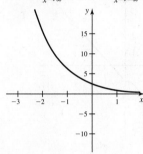

77. $x = \pm 3, x = -\frac{1}{2} \ln 2 \approx -0.347$

Section 2.6 Exercises, pp. 116–119

1. a, c **3.** A function is continuous on an interval if it is
continuous at each point of the interval. If the interval contains
endpoints, then the function must be right or left continuous at the
endpoints. **5. a.** $\lim\limits_{x \to a^-} f(x) = f(a)$ **b.** $\lim\limits_{x \to a^+} f(x) = f(a)$
7. $\{x : x \neq 0\}, \{x : x \neq 0\}$ **9.** $a = 2$, item 3; $a = 3$,
item 2; $a = 1$, item 1 **11.** $a = 1$, item 1; $a = 2$, item 2; $a = 3$,
item 1 **13.** Yes; $\lim\limits_{x \to 5} f(x) = f(5)$ **15.** No; $f(1)$ is undefined.
17. No; $\lim\limits_{x \to 1} f(x) = 2$ but $f(1) = 3$. **19.** No; $f(4)$ is undefined.
21. $(-\infty, \infty)$ **23.** $(-\infty, -3), (-3, 3), (3, \infty)$
25. $(-\infty, -2), (-2, 2), (2, \infty)$ **27.** 1 **29.** 16
31. $2\sqrt{6}$ **33.** $\ln 2$ **35.** $[0, 1), (1, 2), (2, 3], (3, 4]$
37. $[0, 1), (1, 2), [2, 3), (3, 5]$ **39. a.** $\lim\limits_{x \to 1} f(x)$ does not exist.
b. Continuous from the right **c.** $(-\infty, 1), [1, \infty)$
41. $(-\infty, -2\sqrt{2}]; [2\sqrt{2}, \infty)$ **43.** $(-\infty, \infty)$ **45.** $(-\infty, \infty)$
47. 3 **49.** 4 **51.** $(n\pi, (n + 1)\pi)$, where n is an integer; $\sqrt{2}, -\infty$
53. $\left(\frac{\pi}{2} + n\pi, \frac{\pi}{2} + (n + 1)\pi\right)$ where n is an integer;
$\infty, \sqrt{3} - 2$ **55.** $(-\infty, 0), (0, \infty); \infty; -\infty$
57. a. A is continuous on $[0, 0.08]$ and 7000 is between $A(0) = 5000$
and $A(0.08) = 11,098.20$. So by the Intermediate Value Theorem, there
is at least one c in $(0, 0.08)$ such that $A(c) = 7000$.

b.

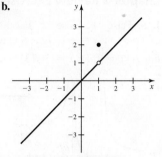

$c \approx 0.034$ or 3.4%

59. b. $x \approx 0.835$ **61. b.** $x \approx -0.285$;
$x \approx 0.778; x \approx 4.507$ **63. b.** $x \approx -0.567$
65. a. True **b.** True **c.** False **d.** False **67.** $(-\infty, \infty)$
69. $[0, 16), (16, \infty)$ **71.** 1 **73.** 2 **75.** $-\frac{1}{2}$ **77.** 0 **79.** $-\infty$
81. The vertical line
segments should not appear.

83. a, b.

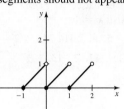

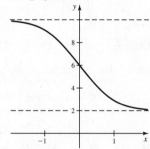

85. a. 2 **b.** 8 **c.** No; $\lim\limits_{x \to 1^-} g(x) = 2$ and $\lim\limits_{x \to 1^+} g(x) = 8$
87. $\lim\limits_{x \to 0} f(x) = 6$, $\lim\limits_{x \to -\infty} f(x) = 10$,
and $\lim\limits_{x \to \infty} f(x) = 2$; no vertical
asymptotes; and $y = 2$ and
$y = 10$ are the horizontal
asymptotes.

89. $x_1 = \frac{1}{7}; x_2 = \frac{1}{2}; x_3 = \frac{3}{5}$ **91. a.** $A(r)$ is continuous on
$[0.01, 0.10]$ and $A(0.01) = 2615.55$, while $A(0.10) = 3984.36$.
Thus, $A(0.01) < 3500 < A(0.10)$. So by the Intermediate Value
Theorem, there exists c in $(0.01, 0.10)$ such that $A(c) = 3500$.
Therefore, c is the desired interest rate. **b.** $r \approx 7.28\%$ **93.** Yes.
Imagine there is a clone of the monk who walks down the path at the
same time the monk walks up the path. The monk and his clone
must cross paths at some time between dawn and dusk. **95.** No; f
cannot be made continuous at $x = a$ by redefining $f(a)$.
97. $\lim\limits_{x \to 2} f(x) = -3$; define $f(2)$ to be -3. **99. a.** Yes **b.** No
101. $a = 0$ removable discontinuity; $a = 1$ infinite discontinuity.
103. a. For example, $f(x) = \dfrac{1}{x - 1}, g(x) = x+1$. **b.** For continuity,
g must be continuous at 0 and f must be continuous at $g(0)$.

Section 2.7 Exercises, pp. 128–131

1. 1 **3.** c **5.** Given any $\varepsilon > 0$, there exists a $\delta > 0$ such that
$|f(x) - L| < \varepsilon$ whenever $0 < |x - a| < \delta$. **7.** $0 < \delta \le 2$
9. a. $\delta = 1$ **b.** $\delta = \frac{1}{2}$ **11. a.** $\delta = 2$ **b.** $\delta = \frac{1}{2}$
13. a. $\delta = 1$ **b.** $\delta = 0.79$ **15. a.** $\delta \approx 1$ **b.** $\delta \approx \frac{1}{2}$ **c.** $\delta = \varepsilon$
17. a. $\delta = 1$ **b.** $\delta = \frac{1}{2}$ **c.** $\delta = \frac{\varepsilon}{2}$ **19.** $\delta = \frac{\varepsilon}{8}$ **21.** $\delta = \varepsilon$
23. $\delta = \sqrt{\varepsilon}$ **27. a.** Use any $\delta > 0$. **b.** $\delta = \varepsilon$ **29.** $\delta = 1/\sqrt{N}$
31. $\delta = 1/\sqrt{N - 1}$ **33. a.** False **b.** False **c.** True **d.** True

35. $\delta = \min\{1, 6\varepsilon\}$ **37.** $\delta = \min\left\{\dfrac{1}{20}, \dfrac{\varepsilon}{200}\right\}$ **39.** For $x > a$,

$|x - a| = x - a$.   **41. a.** $\delta = \dfrac{\varepsilon}{2}$ **b.** $\delta = \dfrac{\varepsilon}{3}$ **c.** Since

$\lim\limits_{x\to 0^+} f(x) = \lim\limits_{x\to 0^-} f(x) = -4, \lim\limits_{x\to 0} f(x) = -4.$ **43.** $\delta = \varepsilon^2$

45. a. For each $N > 0$, there is a corresponding $\delta > 0$
such that $f(x) > N$ whenever $a < x < a + \delta$.   **b.** For each $N < 0$,
there is a corresponding $\delta > 0$ such that $f(x) < N$ whenever
$a - \delta < x < a$.   **c.** For each $N > 0$, there is a corresponding $\delta > 0$
such that $f(x) > N$ whenever $a - \delta < x < a$.   **47.** $\delta = 1/N$
49. $\delta = (-10/M)^{1/4}$ **51.** $N = \dfrac{1}{\varepsilon}$ **53.** $N = M - 1$

Chapter 2 Review Exercises, pp. 131–133

1. a. False   **b.** False   **c.** False   **d.** True   **e.** False   **f.** False
g. True   **3.** $x = -1$; $\lim\limits_{x\to -1} f(x)$ does not exist; $x = 1$;
$\lim\limits_{x\to 1} f(x) \neq f(1)$; $x = 3$; $f(3)$ is undefined.   **5. a.** 1.414   **b.** $\sqrt{2}$
7.

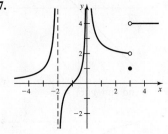

9. $\sqrt{11}$ **11.** 2   **13.** $\dfrac{1}{3}$

15. $-\dfrac{1}{16}$ **17.** 108   **19.** $\dfrac{1}{108}$ **21.** 0

23. b. $\lim\limits_{x\to 0} -x^2 \leq \lim\limits_{x\to 0} x^2 \sin\dfrac{1}{x} \leq \lim\limits_{x\to 0} x^2$;

$0 \leq \lim\limits_{x\to 0} x^2 \sin\dfrac{1}{x} \leq 0$;

$\lim\limits_{x\to 0} x^2 \sin\dfrac{1}{x} = 0$

25. $-\infty$ **27.** ∞ **29.** $-\infty$ **31.** $\dfrac{1}{2}$ **33.** ∞ **35.** $\dfrac{3\pi}{2} + 2$

37. $\lim\limits_{x\to\infty} f(x) = -4$; $\lim\limits_{x\to -\infty} f(x) = -4$

39. $\lim\limits_{x\to\infty} f(x) = 1$; $\lim\limits_{x\to -\infty} f(x) = -\infty$ **41.** Horizontal asymptotes

at $y = \dfrac{2}{\pi}$ and $y = -\dfrac{2}{\pi}$; vertical asymptote at $x = 0$ **43.** No; $f(5)$

does not exist.   **45.** Right continuous; $\lim\limits_{x\to 3^+} h(x) = h(3)$

47. $(-\infty, -\sqrt{5}]$ and $[\sqrt{5}, \infty)$; left-continuous at $-\sqrt{5}$ and right-
continuous at $\sqrt{5}$ **49.** $(-\infty, -5)$, $(-5, 0)$, $(0, 5)$, and $(5, \infty)$
51. $a = 3, b = 0$ **53.**

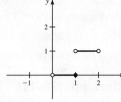

55. a. $m(0) < 30 < m(5)$ and $m(5) > 30 > m(15)$.   **b.** $m = 30$
when $t \approx 2.4$ and $t \approx 10.8$.   **c.** No; the maximum amount is
approximately $m(5.5) \approx 38.5$.   **57.** $\delta = \varepsilon$ **59.** $\delta = 1/\sqrt[4]{N}$.

AP® Practice, Section 1, Parts A and B, pp. 134–135

1. D   **2.** A   **3.** C   **4.** A   **5.** D   **6.** B   **7.** C   **8.** C   **9.** A
10. B   **11.** B   **12.** C   **13.** A   **14.** A   **15.** B   **16.** C   **17.** C
18. D   **19.** E

AP® Practice, Section 2, Parts A and B, p. 135

1. a. 1   **b.** 2   **c.** $p - q$ **2. a.** $y = 0$ for both values of n.
b. When $n = 1$, the asymptote is $x = 0$. When $n = -1$, the
asymptotes are $x = 0$ and $x = 1$.   **c.** When $n \geq 0$, $x^3 + nx$ has
one (real) root, corresponding to a single vertical asymptote at $x = 0$.
When $n \leq -2$, $x^3 + nx$ has three roots: $x = 0$ and $x = \pm\sqrt{-n}$, each
of which correspond to a vertical asymptote.
3. a. All real numbers excluding $x = -4$ and $x = 2$ **b.** $x = -2$
c. $\lim\limits_{x\to\infty} f(x) = 5$; $y = 5$ **d.** $x = -4$ **e.** The factor $x - 2$ occurs in
both the denominator and the numerator.
4. a.

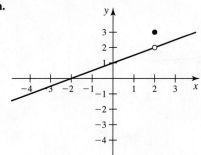

b.

c.

d.

CHAPTER 3

Section 3.1 Exercises, pp. 143–145

1. Given the point $(a, f(a))$ and any point $(x, f(x))$ near $(a, f(a))$, the slope of the secant line joining these points is $\dfrac{f(x) - f(a)}{x - a}$. The limit of this quotient as x approaches a is the slope of the tangent line at the point. **3.** The average rate of change over the interval $[a, x]$ is $\dfrac{f(x) - f(a)}{x - a}$. The limit $\lim\limits_{x \to a} \dfrac{f(x) - f(a)}{x - a}$ is the slope of the tangent line; it is also the limit of average rates of change, which is the instantaneous rate of change at $x = a$. **5.** $f'(a)$ is the slope of the tangent line at $(a, f(a))$ or the instantaneous rate of change of f at a. **7.** $\dfrac{dy}{dx}$ is the limit of $\dfrac{\Delta y}{\Delta x}$ and is the rate of change of y with respect to x.

9. a. 6 **b.** $y = 6x - 14$ **c.**

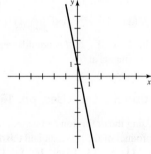

11. a. -5 **b.** $y = -5x + 1$ **c.**

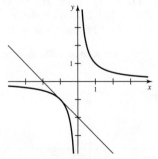

13. a. -1 **b.** $y = -x - 2$ **c.**

15. a. 8.667, 13.333 11 **b.** 15, 15, 15 **c.** Millions of daily users per month **d.** Decreasing **17. a.** 2 **b.** $y = 2x + 1$ **19. a.** 4 **b.** $y = 4x - 8$ **21. a.** 3 **b.** $y = 3x - 2$ **23. a.** $\dfrac{2}{25}$ **b.** $y = \dfrac{2}{25}x + \dfrac{7}{25}$ **25. a.** $\dfrac{1}{4}$ **b.** $y = \dfrac{1}{4}x + \dfrac{7}{4}$

27. a. $f'(-3) = 8$ **b.** $y = 8x$ **29. a.** $f'(-2) = -14$ **b.** $y = -14x - 16$ **31. a.** $f'\left(\dfrac{1}{4}\right) = -4$ **b.** $y = -4x + 3$ **33. a.** $\dfrac{1}{3}$ **b.** $y = \dfrac{1}{3}x + \dfrac{5}{3}$ **35. a.** $-\dfrac{1}{100}$ **b.** $y = -\dfrac{x}{100} + \dfrac{3}{20}$ **37. a.** $f'(x) = 6x + 2$ **b.** $y = 8x - 13$ **c.**

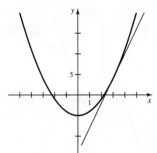

39. a. $f'(x) = 10x - 6$ **b.** $y = 14x - 19$ **c.**

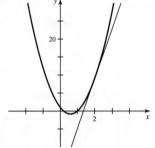

41. a. $2ax + b$ **b.** $8x - 3$ **c.** 5 **43.** $-\dfrac{1}{4}$ **45.** $\dfrac{1}{5}$ **47. a.** True **b.** False **c.** True **49. a.** $f'(x) = \dfrac{3}{2\sqrt{3x + 1}}$ **b.** $y = \dfrac{3x}{10} + \dfrac{13}{5}$ **51. a.** $f'(x) = \dfrac{-6}{(3x + 1)^2}$ **b.** $y = -\dfrac{3x}{2} - \dfrac{5}{2}$ **53. a.** C, D **b.** A, B, E **c.** A, B, E, D, C **55. a.** Approximately 10 kW; approximately -5 kW **b.** $t = 6$ and $t = 18$ **c.** $t = 12$ **57.** $f(x) = \dfrac{1}{x + 1}$; $a = 2$; $-\dfrac{1}{9}$ **59.** $f(x) = x^4$; $a = 2$; 32 **61.** No; f is not continuous at $x = 2$. **63.** $a = 4$

Section 3.2 Exercises, pp. 150–153

1. The slope of a curve at a point is independent of the function value at that point. **3.** Yes

5.

7. a–C; b–C; c–A; d–B

9. a–D; b–C; c–B; d–A　**11.**

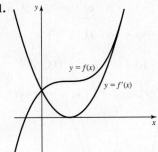

13.

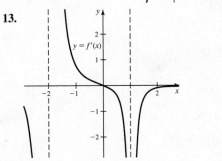

15. a. $x = 1$　**b.** $x = 1, x = 2$　**c.**

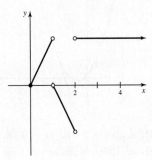

17. a. True　**b.** True　**c.** False

19. Yes.

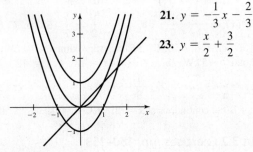

21. $y = -\dfrac{1}{3}x - \dfrac{2}{3}$

23. $y = \dfrac{x}{2} + \dfrac{3}{2}$

25. b. $f'_+(2) = 1, f'_-(2) = -1$　**c.** f is continuous but not differentiable at $x = 2$.

27. a.　　　　Vertical tangent line $x = 2$

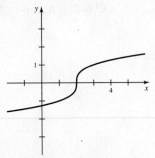

b.　　　　Vertical tangent line $x = -1$

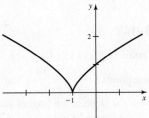

c.　　　　Vertical tangent line $x = 4$

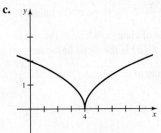

d.　　　　Vertical tangent line $x = 0$

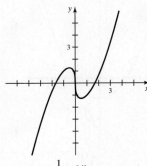

29. $f'(x) = \dfrac{1}{3}x^{-2/3}$ and $\displaystyle\lim_{x\to0^-} |f'(x)| = \lim_{x\to0^+} |f'(x)| = \infty$

31. b. 1　**c.** 1　**d.** f is not differentiable at 0 because it is not continuous at 0.

Section 3.3 Exercises, pp. 160–163

1. Using the definition can be tedious.　**3.** $f(x) = e^x$　**5.** Compute the product of the constant and the derivative of the function.　**7.** $5x^4$
9. 0　**11.** 1　**13.** $15x^2$　**15.** 8　**17.** $200t$　**19.** $12x^3 + 7$
21. $40x^3 - 32$　**23.** $6w^2 + 6w + 10$　**25.** $18x^2 + 6x + 4$
27. $4x^3 + 4x$　**29.** $2w$, for $w \neq 0$　**31.** 1, for $x \neq 1$

33. $\dfrac{1}{2\sqrt{x}}$,　for $x \neq a$　**35. a.** $y = -6x + 5$

b.

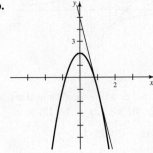

37. a. $y = 3x + 3 - 3 \ln 3$ **b.**

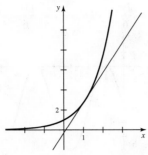

39. a. $x = 3$ **b.** $x = 4$ **41. a.** $(-1, 11), (2, -16)$ **b.** $(-3, -41)$, $(4, 36)$ **43. a.** $(4, 4)$ **b.** $(16, 0)$ **45.** $f'(x) = 20x^3 + 30x^2 + 3$; $f''(x) = 60x^2 + 60x$; $f^{(3)}(x) = 120x + 60$
47. $f'(x) = 1; f''(x) = f^{(3)}(x) = 0$ for $x \neq -1$
49. a. False **b.** True **c.** False **d.** False **e.** False
51. a. $y = 7x - 1$ **b.** $y = -2x + 5$ **c.** $y = 16x + 4$ **53.** -10
55. 4 **57.** 7.5 **59. a.** $f(x) = \sqrt{x}; a = 9$ **b.** $f'(9) = \dfrac{1}{6}$
61. a. $f(x) = x^{100}; a = 1$ **b.** $f'(1) = 100$ **63.** 3 **65.** 1
67. $f(x) = e^x; a = 0; f'(0) = 1$ **69. a.** $d'(t) = 32 t$; ft/s; the velocity of the stone **b.** 576 ft; approx. 131 mi/hr

71. a. $\dfrac{dD}{dg} = 0.10g + 35$; mi/gal; the rate of change of the range of the car with respect to the capacity of the tank.
b. 35 mi/gal 35.5 mi/gal 36 mi/gal; the gas mileage improves when driving longer distances. **c.** Approx. 427 mi
79. b.

c. Changing 0.01 to 0.001 does not change the graph. We see the graph of the derivative of f.

81. b.

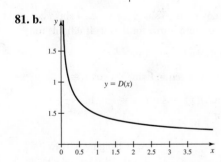

c. Changing 0.01 to 0.001 does not change the graph visibly. We see the graph of the derivative of f.

Section 3.4 Exercises, pp. 170–172

1. $\dfrac{d}{dx}[f(x) \cdot g(x)] = f'(x) g(x) + f(x) g'(x)$ **3.** $\dfrac{d}{dx}(x^n) = nx^{n-1}$, for any integer n **5.** $y' = ke^{kx}$, for any real number k **7.** $36x^5 - 12x^3$
9. $e^t t^4(t + 5)$ **11.** $4x^3$ **13.** $e^w(w^3 + 3w^2 - 1)$ **15. a.** $6x + 1$
17. a. $18y^5 - 52y^3 + 8y$ **19.** $\dfrac{1}{(x + 1)^2}$ **21.** $\dfrac{e^x}{(e^x + 1)^2}$
23. $e^{-x}(1 - x)$ **25.** $-\dfrac{1}{(t - 1)^2}$ **27.** $\dfrac{e^x(x^2 - 2x - 1)}{(x^2 - 1)^2}$

29. a. $2w$, for $w \neq 0$ **31.** 1 **33. a.** $y = -\dfrac{3x}{2} + \dfrac{17}{2}$
b.

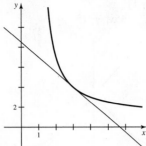

35. a. $y = 3x + 1$ **b.**

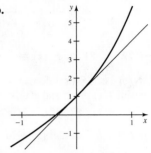

37. $-27x^{-10}$ **39.** $6t - \dfrac{42}{t^8}$ **41.** $-\dfrac{3}{t^2} - \dfrac{2}{t^3}$ **43.** $e^{7x}(7x + 1)$
45. $45e^{3x}$ **47.** $e^{-3x}(1 - 3x)$ **49.** $\dfrac{2}{3}e^x - e^{-x}$
51. a. $p'(t) = \left(\dfrac{20}{t + 2}\right)^2$ **b.** $p'(5) \approx 8.163$ **c.** $t = 0$
d. $\displaystyle\lim_{t \to \infty} p'(t) = 0$; the population approaches a steady state.
e.

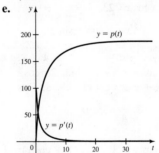

53. a. $Q'(t) = -1.386e^{-0.0693t}$ **b.** -1.386 mg/hr; -1.207 mg/hr
c. $\displaystyle\lim_{t \to \infty} Q(t) = 0$—eventually none of the drug remains in the bloodstream; $\displaystyle\lim_{t \to \infty} Q'(t) = 0$—the rate at which the body excretes the drug goes to zero over time. **55. a.** $x = -\dfrac{1}{2}$ **b.** The line tangent to the graph of f at $x = -\dfrac{1}{2}$ is horizontal. **57.** $\dfrac{e^x(x^2 - x - 5)}{(x - 2)^2}$
59. $\dfrac{e^x(x^2 + x + 1)}{(x + 1)^2}$ **61. a.** False **b.** False **c.** False **d.** True
63. $f'(x) = x e^{3x}(3x + 2)$
$f''(x) = e^{3x}(9x^2 + 12x + 2)$
$f'''(x) = 9e^{3x}(3x^2 + 6x + 2)$
65. $f'(x) = \dfrac{x^2 + 2x - 7}{(x + 1)^2}$
$f''(x) = \dfrac{16}{(x + 1)^3}$

67. $8x - \dfrac{2}{(5x+1)^2}$ **69.** $\dfrac{r - 6\sqrt{r} - 1}{2\sqrt{r}(r+1)^2}$

71. $300x^9 + 135x^8 + 105x^6 + 120x^3 + 45x^2 + 15$

73. a. $y = -\dfrac{108}{169}x + \dfrac{567}{169}$ **b.**

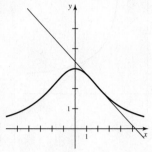

75. $-\dfrac{3}{2}$ **77.** $\dfrac{1}{9}$ **79.** $\dfrac{7}{8}$ **81. a.** $F'(x) = -\dfrac{1.8 \times 10^{10}\, Qq}{x^3}\,\text{N/m}$

b. $-1.8 \times 10^{19}\,\text{N/m}$ **c.** $|F'(x)|$ decreases as x increases.
83. One possible pair: $f(x) = e^{ax}$ and $g(x) = e^{bx}$,
where $b = \dfrac{a}{a-1}$, $a \neq 1$.   **87.** $f''g + 2f'g' + fg''$
91. a. $f'gh + fg'h + fgh'$ **b.** $2e^{2x}(x^2 + 3x - 2)$

Section 3.5 Exercises, pp. 179–181

1. $\dfrac{\sin x}{x}$ is undefined at $x = 0$.   **3.** The tangent and cotangent functions
are defined as ratios of the sine and cosine functions.   **5.** -1

7. 3   **9.** $\dfrac{7}{3}$ **11.** 5   **13.** 7   **15.** $\dfrac{1}{4}$ **17.** $\cos x - \sin x$

19. $e^{-x}(\cos x - \sin x)$ **21.** $\sin x + x \cos x$ **23.** $-\dfrac{1}{1 + \sin x}$

25. $\cos^2 x - \sin^2 x = \cos 2x$ **27.** $-2 \sin x \cos x = -\sin 2x$

33. $\sec x \tan x - \csc x \cot x$ **35.** $e^{5x} \csc x(5 - \cot x)$ **37.** $-\dfrac{\csc x}{1 + \csc x}$

39. $\cos^2 z - \sin^2 z = \cos 2z$ **41.** $2 \cos x - x \sin x$ **43.** $2e^x \cos x$
45. $2 \csc^2 x \cot x$ **47.** $2\left(\sec^2 x \tan x + \csc^2 x \cot x\right)$ **49. a.** False

b. False   **c.** True   **d.** True   **51.** $\dfrac{a}{b}$ **53.** $\dfrac{3}{4}$ **55.** 0

57. $x \cos 2x + \dfrac{1}{2} \sin 2x$ **59.** $\dfrac{1}{2 \sin x \cos x - 1}$ **61.** $\dfrac{2 \sin x}{(1 + \cos x)^2}$

63. a. $y = \sqrt{3}x + 2 - \dfrac{\pi\sqrt{3}}{6}$ **b.**

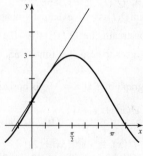

65. a. $y = -2\sqrt{3}x + \dfrac{2\sqrt{3}\pi}{3} + 1$ **b.**

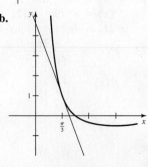

67. $x = \dfrac{7\pi}{6} + 2k\pi$ and $x = \dfrac{11\pi}{6} + 2k\pi$, where k is any integer

69. a.

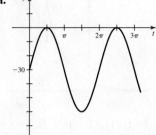

b. $v(t) = 30 \cos t$

c.

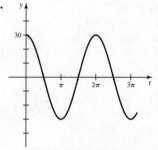

d. $v(t) = 0$ for $t = (2k + 1)\dfrac{\pi}{2}$, where k is any nonnegative
integer. The position is $y = 0$ if k is even or $y = -60$ if k is odd.
e. $v(t)$ is at a maximum at $t = 2k\pi$, where k is a nonnegative
integer; the position is $y = -30$
f. $a(t) = -30 \sin t$

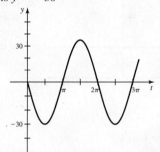

77. $a = 0$ **79. a.** $2 \sin x \cos x$ **b.** $3 \sin^2 x \cos x$ **c.** $4 \sin^3 x \cos x$
d. $n \sin^{n-1} x \cos x$ The conjecture is true for $n = 1$. If it holds for
$n = k$, then when $n = k + 1$, we have $\dfrac{d}{dx}(\sin^{k+1} x) = $
$\dfrac{d}{dx}(\sin^k x \cdot \sin x) = \sin^k x \cos x + \sin x \cdot k \sin^{k-1} x \cos x = $
$(k + 1) \sin^k x \cos x$.   **81. a.** $f(x) = \sin x; a = \dfrac{\pi}{6}$ **b.** $\dfrac{\sqrt{3}}{2}$
83. a. $f(x) = \cot x; a = \dfrac{\pi}{4}$ **b.** -2

85. b.

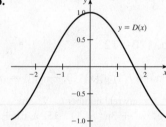

c. Changing 0.01 to
0.001 does not change
the graph visibly. We
see the graph of the
derivative of f.

87. b.

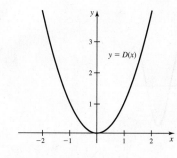

c. Changing 0.01 to 0.001 does not change the graph visibly. We see the graph of the derivative of *f*.

Section 3.6 Exercises, pp. 186–191

1. The average rate of change is $\dfrac{f(x + \Delta x) - f(x)}{\Delta x}$, whereas the instantaneous rate of change is the limit as Δx goes to zero in this quotient.   **3.** Small   **5.** If the position of the object at time t is $s(t)$, then the acceleration at time t is $a(t) = \dfrac{d^2 s}{dt^2}$.   **7. a.** 40 mi/hr
b. 40 mi/hr; yes   **c.** −60 mi/hr; −60 mi/hr; south   **d.** The police car drives away from the police station going north until about 10:08, when it turns around and heads south, toward the police station. It continues south until it passes the police station at about 11:02 and keeps going south until about 11:40, when it turns around and heads north until 12:00.
9. a.

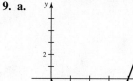

b. $v(t) = 2t - 4$; stationary at $t = 2$, to the right on $(2, 5]$, to the left on $[0, 2)$

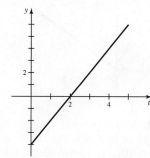

c. $v(1) = -2$ ft/s; $a(1) = 2$ ft/s²   **d.** $a(2) = 2$ ft/s²   **e.** $(2, 5]$
11. a.

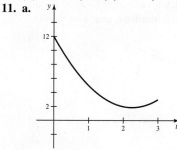

b. $v(t) = 4t - 9$; stationary at $t = \dfrac{9}{4}$, to the right on $\left(\dfrac{9}{4}, 3\right]$, to the left on $\left[0, \dfrac{9}{4}\right)$

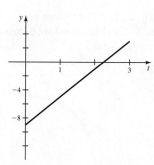

c. $v(1) = -5$ ft/s; $a(1) = 4$ ft/s²   **d.** $a\left(\dfrac{9}{4}\right) = 4$ ft/s²   **e.** $\left(\dfrac{9}{4}, 3\right]$
13. a.

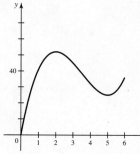

b. $v(t) = 6t^2 - 42t + 60$; stationary at $t = 2$ and $t = 5$, to the right on $[0, 2)$ and $(5, 6]$, to the left on $(2, 5)$

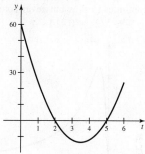

c. $v(1) = 24$ ft/s; $a(1) = -30$ ft/s²   **d.** $a(2) = -18$ ft/s;
$a(5) = 18$ ft/s²   **e.** $\left(2, \dfrac{7}{2}\right)$, $(5, 6]$ **15. a.** $v(t) = -32t + 64$
b. At $t = 2$ **c.** 96 ft   **d.** At $t = 2 + \sqrt{6}$ **e.** $-32\sqrt{6}$ ft/s
f. $(2, 2 + \sqrt{6})$ **17. a.** 98,300 people/yr
b. 99,920 people/yr in 1997; 95,600 people/yr in 2005
c. $p'(t) = -0.54t + 101$; population increased, growth rate is positive but decreasing.   **19. a.** False   **b.** True   **c.** False
d. True   **21.** 240 ft   **23.** 64 ft/s   **25. a.** $t = 1, 2, 3$
b. It is moving in the positive direction for t in $(0, 1)$ and $(2, 3)$; it is moving in the negative direction for t in $(1, 2)$ and $t > 3$.
c.

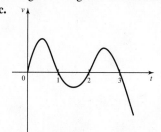

d. $(0, 0.5)$, $(1, 1.5)$, $(2, 2.5)$, and $(3, \infty)$

27. a. 1930, 1.1 million people/yr　**b.** 1960, 2.9 million people/yr
c. The population did not decrease.　**d.** (1905, 1915), (1930, 1960),
(1980, 1990)

29. a.

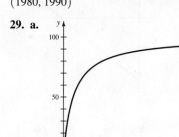

b. $v = \dfrac{100}{(t + 1)^2}$

c.

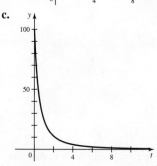

The marble moves fastest at the beginning and slows considerably
over the first 5 s. It continues to slow but never actually stops.
d. $t = 4\,s$　**e.** $t = -1 + \sqrt{2} \approx 0.414$ s

31. a. $R(p) = \dfrac{100p}{p^2 + 1}$

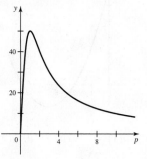

b. $R'(p) = \dfrac{100(1 - p^2)}{(p^2 + 1)^2}$　**c.** $p = 1$

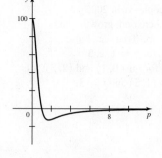

33. a.

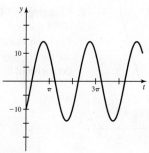

b. $\dfrac{dx}{dt} = 10 \cos t + 10 \sin t$　**c.** $t = \dfrac{3\pi}{4} + k\pi$, where k is any
positive integer.　**d.** The graph implies that the spring never stops
oscillating. In reality, the weight would eventually come to rest.
35. a. Juan starts faster than Jean and opens up a big lead. Then,
Juan slows down while Jean speeds up. Jean catches up, and the race
finishes in a tie.　**b.** Same average velocity　**c.** Tie　**d.** At $t = 2$,
$\theta'(2) = \dfrac{\pi}{2}$ rad/min; $\theta'(4) = \pi =$ Jean's greatest velocity　**e.** At

$t = 2$, $\varphi'(2) = \dfrac{\pi}{2}$ rad/min; $\varphi'(0) = \pi =$ Juan's greatest velocity

37. a.　　　　　　　　　　　　　　　　$V(0) = 4{,}000{,}000$ m^3

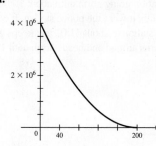

b. 200 hr

c.

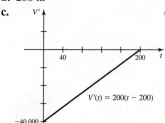

d. The magnitude of the flow rate
is greatest (most negative) at
$t = 0$ and least (zero) at $t = 200$.

39. a. $v(t) = -15e^{-t}(\sin t + \cos t)$; $v(1) \approx -7.6$ m/s,
$v(3) \approx 0.63$ m/s　**b.** Down $(0, 2.4)$ and $(5.5, 8.6)$; up $(2.4, 5.5)$ and
$(8.6, 10)$　**c.** Approximately 0.65 m/s　**41. a.** $-T'(1) = -80$,
$-T'(3) = 80$　**b.** $-T'(x) < 0$　for $0 \le x < 2$; $-T'(x) > 0$
for　$2 < x \le 4$　**c.** Near $x = 0$, with $x > 0$, $-T'(x) < 0$, so
heat flows toward the end of the rod. Similarly, near $x = 4$, with
$x < 4$, $-T'(x) > 0$.
43. a.

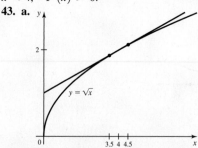

b.

h	Approximation	Error
0.1	0.25002	2.0×10^{-5}
0.01	0.25	2.0×10^{-7}
0.001	0.25	2.0×10^{-9}

c. Values of x on both sides of 4 are used regardless of whether h is positive or negative. **d.** The centered difference approximations are more accurate than the forward and backward difference formulas.
45. a. $0.395, 0.415$ **b.** $0.0204, 0.000343$

Section 3.7 Exercises, pp. 198–202

1. $\dfrac{dy}{dx} = \dfrac{dy}{du} \cdot \dfrac{du}{dx}; \dfrac{d}{dx}(f(g(x))) = f'(g(x)) \cdot g'(x)$ **3.** $g(x), x$

5. The inner function is $x^2 + 10$ and the outer function is u^{-5}

7. $30(3x + 7)^9$ **9.** $5\sin^4 x \cos x$ **11.** $5e^{5x-7}$ **13.** $\dfrac{x}{\sqrt{x^2 + 1}}$

15. $10x \sec^2(5x^2)$ **17.** $e^x \sec e^x \tan e^x$

19. $10(6x + 7)(3x^2 + 7x)^9$ **21.** $\dfrac{5}{\sqrt{10x + 1}}$

23. $-\dfrac{315x^2}{(7x^3 + 1)^4}$ **25.** $3\sec(3x + 1)\tan(3x + 1)$ **27.** $e^x \sec^2 e^x$

29. $(12x^2 + 3)\cos(4x^3 + 3x + 1)$ **31.** $\dfrac{\cos(2\sqrt{x})}{\sqrt{x}}$

33. $5\sec x (\sec x + \tan x)^5$ **35. a.** $u = \cos x, y = u^3$;

$\dfrac{dy}{dx} = -3\cos^2 x \sin x$ **b.** $u = x^3, y = \cos u; \dfrac{dy}{dx} = -3x^2 \sin x^3$

37. a. 100 **b.** -100 **c.** -16 **d.** 40 **e.** 40
39. -1.004 hPa/min **41.** $y' = 25(12x^5 - 9x^2)(2x^6 - 3x^3 + 3)^{24}$

43. $y' = 30(1 + 2\tan x)^{14}\sec^2 x$ **45.** $y' = -\dfrac{\cot x \csc^2 x}{\sqrt{1 + \cot^2 x}}$

47. $e^x \cos(\sin(e^x))\cos(e^x)$
49. $y' = -15\sin^4(\cos 3x)(\sin 3x)[\cos(\cos 3x)]$

51. $y' = \dfrac{3e^{\sqrt{3x}}}{2\sqrt{3x}}\sec^2(e^{\sqrt{3x}})$ **53.** $y' = \dfrac{1}{2\sqrt{x + \sqrt{x}}}\left(1 + \dfrac{1}{2\sqrt{x}}\right)$

55. $y' = f'(g(x^2))g'(x^2)\,2x$ **57.** $\dfrac{5x^4}{(x + 1)^6}$

59. $x e^{x^2+1}(2\sin x^3 + 3x\cos x^3)$ **61.** $5\theta^2 \sec 5\theta \tan 5\theta + 2\theta \sec 5\theta$

63. $4(x + 2)^3(x^2 + 1)^3(3x^2 + 4x + 1)$ **65.** $\dfrac{2x^3 - \sin 2x}{\sqrt{x^4 + \cos 2x}}$

67. $2(p + \pi)(\sin p^2 + p(p + \pi)\cos p^2)$ **69. a.** True **b.** True

c. True **d.** False **71.** $2\cos x^2 - 4x^2 \sin x^2$

73. $4e^{-2x^2}(4x^2 - 1)$ **75.** $y' = \dfrac{f'(x)}{2\sqrt{f(x)}}$

77. $y = -9x + 35$

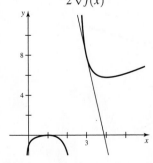

79. a. $h(4) = 9, h'(4) = -6$ **b.** $y = -6x + 33$
81. $y = 6x + 3 - 3\ln 3$

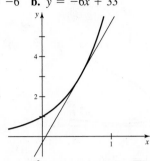

83. a. -3π **b.** -5π **85. a.** $\dfrac{d^2 y}{dt^2} = -\dfrac{y_0 k}{m}\cos\left(t\sqrt{\dfrac{k}{m}}\right)$

87. a.

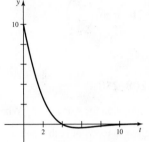

b. $v(t) = -5e^{-t/2}\left[\dfrac{\pi}{4}\sin\left(\dfrac{\pi t}{8}\right) + \cos\left(\dfrac{\pi t}{8}\right)\right]$

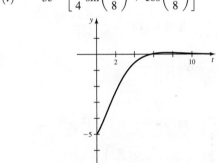

89. a. 10.88 hr **b.** $D'(t) = \dfrac{6\pi}{365}\sin\left(\dfrac{2\pi(t + 10)}{365}\right)$

c. 2.87 min/day; on March 1, the length of day is increasing at a rate of about 2.87 min/day.
d.

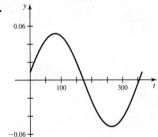

e. Most rapidly, approximately March 22 and September 22; least rapidly, approximately December 21 and June 21

91. a. $E'(t) = 400 + 200\cos\left(\dfrac{\pi t}{12}\right) \text{ MW}$ **b.** At noon;

$E'(0) = 600 \text{ MW}$ **c.** At midnight; $E'(12) = 200 \text{ MW}$

d.

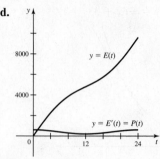

93. a. $f'(x) = -2\cos x \sin x + 2\sin x \cos x = 0$
b. $f(0) = \cos^2 0 + \sin^2 0 = 1; f(x) = 1$ for all x; that is,
$\cos^2 x + \sin^2 x = 1$ **97. a.** $h(x) = (x^2 - 3)^5; a = 2$ **b.** 20

99. a. $h(x) = \sin(x^2); a = \dfrac{\pi}{2}$ **b.** $\pi \cos\left(\dfrac{\pi^2}{4}\right)$

101. $10f'(25)$

Section 3.8 Exercises, pp. 208–210

1. There may be more than one expression for y or y'.   **3.** When derived implicitly, $\dfrac{dy}{dx}$ is usually given in terms of both x and y.

5. a. $-\dfrac{x^3}{y^3}$ **b.** 1   **7. a.** $\dfrac{2}{y}$ **b.** 1   **9. a.** $\dfrac{20x^3}{\cos y}$

b. -20 **11. a.** $-\dfrac{1}{\sin y}$ **b.** -1 **13.** $\dfrac{1 - y\cos(xy)}{x\cos(xy) - 1}$

15. $-\dfrac{1}{1 + \sin y}$ **17.** $\dfrac{1}{2y\sin(y^2) + e^y}$

19. $\dfrac{3x^2(x - y)^2 + 2y}{2x}$ **21.** $\dfrac{13y - 18x^2}{21y^2 - 13x}$

23. $\dfrac{5\sqrt{x^4 + y^2} - 2x^3}{y - 6y^2\sqrt{x^4 + y^2}}$ **25. a.** $2^2 + 2 \cdot 1 + 1^2 = 7$

b. $y = -\dfrac{5}{4}x + \dfrac{7}{2}$ **27. a.** $\sin\pi + 5\left(\dfrac{\pi^2}{5}\right) = \pi^2$

b. $y = \dfrac{\pi(1 + \pi)}{1 + 2\pi} + \dfrac{5}{1 + 2\pi}x$

29. a. $\cos\left(\dfrac{\pi}{2} - \dfrac{\pi}{4}\right) + \sin\dfrac{\pi}{4} = \sqrt{2}$ **b.** $y = \dfrac{x}{2}$

31. $-\dfrac{1}{4y^3}$ **33.** $\dfrac{\sin y}{(\cos y - 1)^3}$ **35.** $\dfrac{4e^{2y}}{(1 - 2e^{2y})^3}$

37. $\dfrac{5}{4}x^{1/4}$ **39.** $\dfrac{10}{3(5x + 1)^{1/3}}$

41. $-\dfrac{3}{2^{7/4}x^{3/4}(4x - 3)^{5/4}}$ **43.** $\dfrac{2}{9x^{2/3}\sqrt[3]{1 + \sqrt[3]{x}}}$

45. $-\dfrac{1}{4}$ **47.** $-\dfrac{24}{13}$ **49.** -5 **51. a.** False   **b.** True   **c.** False
d. False   **53. a.** $y = x - 1$ and $y = -x + 2$
b.

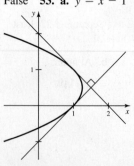

55. a. $y' = -\dfrac{2xy}{x^2 + 4}$ **b.** $y = \dfrac{1}{2}x + 2, y = -\dfrac{1}{2}x + 2$

c. $-\dfrac{16x}{(x^2 + 4)^2}$ **57. a.** $\left(\dfrac{5}{4}, \dfrac{1}{2}\right)$ **b.** No

59. a. $\dfrac{dy}{dx} = 0$ on the $y = 1$ branch; $\dfrac{dy}{dx} = \dfrac{1}{2y + 1}$ on the other two branches.

b. $f_1(x) = 1, f_2(x) = \dfrac{-1 + \sqrt{4x - 3}}{2}, f_3(x) = \dfrac{-1 - \sqrt{4x - 3}}{2}$

c.

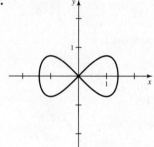

61. a. $\dfrac{dy}{dx} = \dfrac{x - x^3}{y}$ **b.** $f_1(x) = \sqrt{x^2 - \dfrac{x^4}{2}}; f_2(x) = -\sqrt{x^2 - \dfrac{x^4}{2}}$

c.

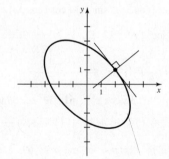

63. $y = \dfrac{4x}{5} - \dfrac{3}{5}$

65. $y = -\dfrac{1 + 2\pi}{5}x + \pi\left(\dfrac{25 + \pi + 2\pi^2}{25}\right)$

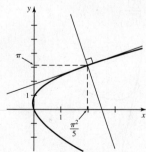

67. $y = -2x + \dfrac{5\pi}{4}$

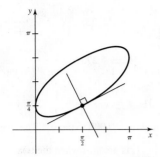

69. a. Tangent line $y = -\dfrac{9x}{11} + \dfrac{20}{11}$; normal line $y = \dfrac{11x}{9} - \dfrac{2}{9}$

b.

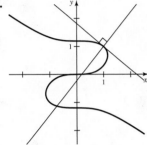

71. a. Tangent line $y = -\dfrac{x}{3} + \dfrac{8}{3}$; normal line $y = 3x - 4$

b.

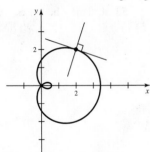

73. a. $\dfrac{dK}{dL} = -\dfrac{K}{2L}$ **b.** -4 **75.** $\dfrac{dr}{dh} = \dfrac{h - 2r}{h}$; -3

77. Note that for $y = mx$, $\dfrac{dy}{dx} = m = \dfrac{y}{x}$; for $x^2 + y^2 = a^2$, $\dfrac{dy}{dx} = -\dfrac{x}{y}$.

79. For $xy = a$, $\dfrac{dy}{dx} = -\dfrac{y}{x}$. For $x^2 - y^2 = b$, $\dfrac{dy}{dx} = \dfrac{x}{y}$. Since

$\left(-\dfrac{y}{x}\right)\cdot\left(\dfrac{x}{y}\right) = -1$, the families of curves are orthogonal trajectories.

81. $\dfrac{7y^2 - 3x^2 - 4xy^2 - 4x^3}{2y(2x^2 + 2y^2 - 7x)}$ **83.** $\dfrac{2y^2(5 + 8x\sqrt{y})}{(1 + 2x\sqrt{y})^3}$

85. No horizontal tangent line; vertical tangent lines at $(2, 1)$ and $(-2, 1)$ **87.** No horizontal tangent line;

vertical tangent lines at $(0, 0), \left(\dfrac{3\sqrt{3}}{2}, \sqrt{3}\right), \left(-\dfrac{3\sqrt{3}}{2}, -\sqrt{3}\right)$

Section 3.9 Exercises, pp. 218–221

1. $x = e^y \Rightarrow 1 = e^y y'(x) \Rightarrow y'(x) = \dfrac{1}{e^y} = \dfrac{1}{x}$.

3. $\dfrac{d}{dx}(\ln kx) = \dfrac{d}{dx}(\ln k + \ln x) = \dfrac{d}{dx}(\ln x)$

5. $f'(x) = \dfrac{1}{x \ln b}$. If $b = e$, then $f'(x) = \dfrac{1}{x}$.   **7.** $f(x) = e^{h(x)\ln g(x)}$

9. $\dfrac{1}{x}$ **11.** $\dfrac{2}{x}$ **13.** $\cot x$ **15.** $-\dfrac{2}{(x^2 - 1)}$

17. $\dfrac{x^2 + 1}{x} + 2x \ln x$.   **19.** $\dfrac{1}{x \ln x}$

21. $\dfrac{1}{x(\ln x + 1)^2}$ **23.** $8^x \ln 8$ **25.** $5 \cdot 4^x \ln 4$

27. $3^x \cdot x^2 (x \ln 3 + 3)$ **29.** $A' = 1000(1.045)^{4t} \ln(1.045)$

31. a. About 28.7 s   **b.** $-\dfrac{46.512 \text{ s}}{1000 \text{ ft}}$ **c.** $\dfrac{dT}{da} = -2.74 \cdot 2^{-0.274a} \ln 2$

At $t = 8$, $\dfrac{dT}{da} = -\dfrac{0.4156 \text{ min}}{1000 \text{ ft}}$

$= -\dfrac{24.938 \text{ s}}{1000 \text{ ft}}$.

If a plane is traveling at 30,000 feet and it increases its altitude by 1,000 feet, the time of useful consciousness would decrease by about 25 seconds.

33. a. About 67.19 hr

b. $Q'(12) = -9.815 \ \mu\text{Ci/hr}$
$Q'(24) = -5.201 \ \mu\text{Ci/hr}$
$Q'(48) = -1.461 \ \mu\text{Ci/hr}$

The rate at which iodine-123 leaves the body decreases with time.

35. $2^x \ln 2$ **37.** $e^y y^{e-1}(y + e)$ **39.** $2e^{2\theta}$

41. $\dfrac{\sqrt{x}}{2}(10x - 9)$ **43.** $\dfrac{2^x \ln 2}{(2^x + 1)^2}$

45. $x^{\cos x - 1}(\cos x - x \ln x \sin x)$; $-\ln\left(\dfrac{\pi}{2}\right)$

47. $x^{\sqrt{x}}\left(\dfrac{2 + \ln x}{2\sqrt{x}}\right)$; $4(2 + \ln 4)$

49. $\dfrac{(\sin x)^{\ln x}(\ln(\sin x) + x(\ln x)\cot x)}{x}$; 0

51. $y = x \sin 1 + 1 - \sin 1$ **53.** $y = e^{2/e}$ and $y = e^{-2/e}$

55. $y' = \dfrac{8x}{(x^2 - 1)\ln 3}$ **57.** $-\sin x (\ln(\cos^2 x) + 2)$

59. $-\dfrac{\ln 4}{x \ln^2 x}$ **61.** $\dfrac{(x + 1)^{10}}{(2x - 4)^8}\left[\dfrac{10}{x + 1} - \dfrac{8}{x - 2}\right]$

63. $2x^{(\ln x) - 1} \ln x$

65. $\dfrac{(x + 1)^{3/2}(x - 4)^{5/2}}{(5x + 3)^{2/3}} \cdot$

$\left[\dfrac{3}{2(x + 1)} + \dfrac{5}{2(x - 4)} - \dfrac{10}{3(5x + 3)}\right]$

67. $(\sin x)^{\tan x}(1 + \sec^2 x \ln(\sin x))$

69. a. False   **b.** False   **c.** False   **d.** False   **e.** True

71. $-\dfrac{1}{x^2 \ln 10}$ **73.** $\dfrac{2}{x}$ **75.** $3^x \ln 3$ **77.** $\dfrac{12}{3x + 1}$

79. $\dfrac{1}{2x}$ **81.** $\dfrac{2}{2x - 1} + \dfrac{3}{x + 2} + \dfrac{8}{1 - 4x}$

83. $y = 2$

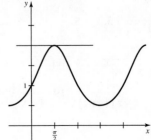

85. $10x^{10x}(1 + \ln x)$

87. $x^{\cos x}\left(\dfrac{\cos x}{x} - \ln x \sin x\right)$

89. $\left(1 + \dfrac{1}{x}\right)^x\left[\ln\left(1 + \dfrac{1}{x}\right) - \dfrac{1}{x + 1}\right]$

91. $x^{9+x^{10}}(1 + 10 \ln x)$

93. a.

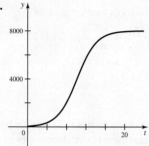

b. $t = 2 \ln (265) \approx 11.2$ years; about 14.5 years

c. $P'(0) \approx 25$ fish/yr; $P'(5) \approx 264$ fish/yr

d.

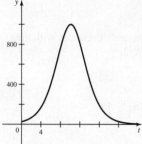

The population is growing fastest after about 10 years.

95. b. $r(11) \approx 0.0133$; $r(21) \approx 0.0118$; the relative growth rate is decreasing.   **c.** $\lim\limits_{t\to\infty} r(t) = 0$; as the population gets close to carrying capacity, the growth rate approaches zero.

97. a. $A(5) = \$17,443$
$A(15) = \$72,705$
$A(25) = \$173,248$
$A(35) = \$356,178$
$\$5526.20$/year, $\$10,054.30$/year, $\$18,293$/year

b. $A(40) = \$497,873$

c. $\dfrac{dA}{dt} = 600,000 \ln (1.005)[(1.005)^{12t}]$
$\approx (2992.5)(1.005)^{12t}$
A increases at an increasing rate.

99. $p = e^{1/e}; (e, e)$ **101.** $\dfrac{1}{e}$ **103.** $27(1 + \ln 3)$

Section 3.10 Exercises, pp. 229–231

1. $\dfrac{d}{dx}(\sin^{-1} x) = \dfrac{1}{\sqrt{1 - x^2}}$; $\dfrac{d}{dx}(\tan^{-1} x) = \dfrac{1}{1 + x^2}$

$\dfrac{d}{dx}(\sec^{-1} x) = \dfrac{1}{|x| \sqrt{x^2 - 1}}$ **3.** $\dfrac{1}{5}$ **5.** $\dfrac{1}{4}$ **7.** $\dfrac{2}{\sqrt{1 - 4x^2}}$

9. $-\dfrac{4w}{\sqrt{1 - 4w^2}}$ **11.** $-\dfrac{2e^{-2x}}{\sqrt{1 - e^{-4x}}}$ **13.** $\dfrac{10}{100x^2 + 1}$

15. $\dfrac{4y}{1 + (2y^2 - 4)^2}$ **17.** $-\dfrac{1}{2\sqrt{z}(1 + z)}$ **19.** $\dfrac{1}{|x| \sqrt{x^2 - 1}}$

21. $-\dfrac{1}{|2u + 1| \sqrt{u^2 + u}}$ **23.** $\dfrac{2y}{(y^2 + 1)^2 + 1}$

25. $\dfrac{1}{x|\ln x| \sqrt{(\ln x)^2 - 1}}$ **27.** $-\dfrac{e^x \sec^2 (e^x)}{|\tan e^x| \sqrt{\tan^2 e^x - 1}}$

29. $-\dfrac{e^s}{1 + e^{2s}}$ **31.** $y = x + \dfrac{\pi}{4} - \dfrac{1}{2}$ **33.** $y = -\dfrac{4}{\sqrt{6}}x + \dfrac{\pi}{3} + \dfrac{2}{\sqrt{3}}$

35. a. Approximately -0.00055 rad/m. The magnitude of the change in angular size, $\left|\dfrac{d\theta}{dx}\right|$, is greatest when the boat is at the skyscraper (i.e., at $x = 0$).

b.

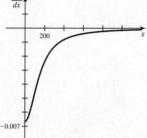

37. $\dfrac{1}{3}$ **39.** $-\dfrac{1}{5}$ **41.** $\dfrac{1}{2}$ **43.** 4   **45.** $\dfrac{1}{12}$ **47.** $\dfrac{1}{4}$ **49.** $\dfrac{5}{4}$ **51. a.** $\dfrac{1}{2}$

b. $\dfrac{2}{3}$ **c.** Cannot be determined   **d.** $\dfrac{3}{2}$ **53. a.** True   **b.** False

c. True   **d.** True   **e.** True

55. a.

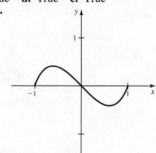

b. $f'(x) = 2x \sin^{-1} x + \dfrac{x^2 - 1}{\sqrt{1 - x^2}}$

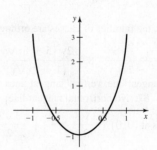

57. a.

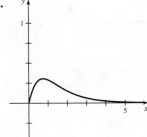

b. $f'(x) = \dfrac{e^{-x}}{1 + x^2} - e^{-x}\tan^{-1}(x)$

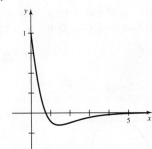

59. $(f^{-1})'(x) = \dfrac{1}{3}$ **61.** $(f^{-1})'(x) = \dfrac{1}{2\sqrt{x+4}}$

63. $(f^{-1})'(x) = 2x$ **65.** $(f^{-1})'(x) = -\dfrac{2}{x^3}$

67. a. $\sin\theta = \dfrac{10}{\ell}$ implies $\theta = \sin^{-1}\dfrac{10}{\ell}$.

Thus, $\dfrac{d\theta}{d\ell} = \dfrac{1}{\sqrt{1 - \left(\dfrac{10}{\ell}\right)^2}} \cdot (-10\ell^{-2}) = -\dfrac{10}{\ell\sqrt{\ell^2 - 100}}$.

b. $d\theta/d\ell = -0.00408, -0.0289,$ and -0.198

c. $\displaystyle\lim_{\ell\to 10^+}\dfrac{d\theta}{d\ell} = -\infty$ **d.** The length ℓ is decreasing.

69. a. $\dfrac{d\theta}{dc} = \dfrac{1}{\sqrt{D^2 - c^2}}$ **b.** $\dfrac{1}{D}$

73. Use the identity $\cot^{-1}x + \tan^{-1}x = \dfrac{\pi}{2}$.

Section 3.11 Exercises, pp. 235–240

1. As the side length s of a cube changes, the surface area $6s^2$ changes as well. **3.** The other two opposite sides decrease in length.
5. a. $40\ \text{m}^2/\text{s}$ **b.** $80\ \text{m}^2/\text{s}$

c.

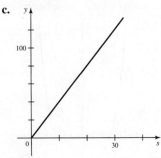

7. a. $4\ \text{m}^2/\text{s}$ **b.** $\sqrt{2}\ \text{m}^2/\text{s}$ **c.** $2\sqrt{2}\ \text{m}/\text{s}$ **9. a.** $\dfrac{1}{4\pi}\ \text{cm}/\text{s}$

b. $\dfrac{1}{2}\ \text{cm}/\text{s}$ **11.** $-40\pi\ \text{ft}^2/\text{min}$ **13.** $\dfrac{3}{80\pi}\ \text{in}./\text{min}$

17. At the point $\left(\dfrac{1}{2}, \dfrac{1}{4}\right)$ **19.** $\dfrac{1}{500}\ \text{m}/\text{min}$; 2000 min

21. $10\tan 20°\ \text{km}/\text{hr} \approx 3.6\ \text{km}/\text{hr}$ **23.** $\dfrac{5}{24}\ \text{ft}/\text{s}$

25. $-\dfrac{8}{3}\ \text{ft}/\text{s}, -\dfrac{32}{3}\ \text{ft}/\text{s}$ **27.** $2592\pi\ \text{cm}^3/\text{s}$ **29.** $-\dfrac{8}{9\pi}\ \text{ft}/\text{s}$

31. $9\pi\ \text{ft}^3/\text{min}$ **33.** $\dfrac{2}{5}\ \text{m}^2/\text{min}$ **35.** $57.89\ \text{ft}/\text{s}$ **37.** $4.66\ \text{in}/\text{s}$

39. $\dfrac{3\sqrt{5}}{2}\ \text{ft}/\text{s}$ **41.** $720.3\ \text{mi}/\text{hr}$ **43.** $11.06\ \text{m}/\text{hr}$

45. a. $187.5\ \text{ft}/\text{s}$ **b.** $0.938\ \text{rad}/\text{s}$ **47.** $\dfrac{d\theta}{dt} = 0.543\ \text{rad}/\text{hr}$

49. $\dfrac{1}{5}\ \text{rad}/\text{s}, \dfrac{1}{8}\ \text{rad}/\text{s}$ **51.** $\dfrac{d\theta}{dt} = 0\ \text{rad}/\text{s}$, for all $t \geq 0$

53. $-0.0201\ \text{rad}/\text{s}$ **55. a.** $-\dfrac{\sqrt{3}}{10}\ \text{m}/\text{hr}$ **b.** $-1\ \text{m}^2/\text{hr}$

Chapter 3 Review Exercises, pp. 240–243

1. a. False **b.** False **c.** False **d.** False **e.** True
3. a. 16 **b.** $y = 16x - 10$

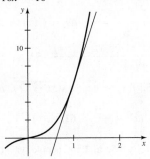

5. a. $-\dfrac{3}{4}$ **b.** $y = -\dfrac{3x}{4} + \dfrac{1}{2}$

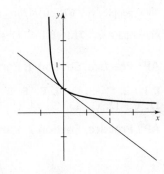

7. a. 2.70 million people/yr **b.** The slope of the secant line through the two points is approximately equal to the slope of that tangent line at $t = 55$. **c.** 2.217 million people/yr **9. a.** $40\ \text{m}/\text{s}$
b. $20/3\ \text{m}/\text{s}$ **c.** $15\ \text{m}/\text{s}$

d.

e. The skydiver deployed the parachute.

13.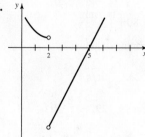

15. $2x^2 + 2\pi x + 7$ **17.** $5t^2 \cos t + 10t \sin t$

19. $(8\theta + 12) \sec^2 (\theta^2 + 3\theta + 2)$ **21.** $\dfrac{32u^2 + 8u + 1}{(8u + 1)^2}$

23. $\sec^2 (\sin \theta) \cdot \cos \theta$ **25.** $\dfrac{9x \sin x - 2 \sin x + 6x^2 \cos x - 2x \cos x}{\sqrt{3x - 1}}$

27. $(2 + \ln x) \ln x$ **29.** $(2x - 1) 2^{x^2 - x} \ln 2$ **31.** $-\dfrac{1}{|x| \sqrt{x^2 - 1}}$

33. 1   **35.** $\sqrt{3} + \dfrac{\pi}{6}$ **37.** $\dfrac{dy}{dx} = \dfrac{y \cos x}{(y - 1)(1 + \sin x)}$

39. $-\dfrac{xy}{x^2 + 2y^2}$ **41.** $y = x$ **43.** $y = -\dfrac{4x}{5} + \dfrac{24}{5}$

45. $x = 4; x = 6$ **47.** $\dfrac{\cos \sqrt{x}}{2 \sqrt{x}}, -\dfrac{\sqrt{x} \sin \sqrt{x} + \cos \sqrt{x}}{4x^{3/2}},$

$\dfrac{3\sqrt{x} \sin \sqrt{x} + (3 - x) \cos \sqrt{x}}{8x^{5/2}}$ **49.** $x^2 f'(x) + 2xf(x)$

51. $\dfrac{g(x)(xf'(x) + f(x)) - xf(x)g'(x)}{g^2(x)}$ **53. a.** 27   **b.** $\dfrac{25}{27}$ **c.** 294

d. 1215   **e.** $\dfrac{1}{9}$ **55.** $f(x) = \tan (\pi\sqrt{3x - 11})$, $a = 5; f'(5) = \dfrac{3\pi}{4}$

57. $\dfrac{6}{13}$ **59.** $(f^{-1})'(x) = -\dfrac{3}{x^4}$ **61. a.** $(f^{-1})'\left(\dfrac{1}{\sqrt{2}}\right) = \sqrt{2}$

63. a. $\dfrac{1}{4}$ **b.** 1   **c.** $\dfrac{1}{3}$ **65. a.** 6550 people/yr   **b.** $p'(40) =$ 4800 people/yr   **67.** 50 mi/hr   **69.** $-5 \sin (65°)$ ft/s or -4.53 ft/s   **71.** -0.166 rad/s

AP® Practice, Section 1, Parts A and B, pp. 243–244

1. B   **2.** C   **3.** C   **4.** E   **5.** E   **6.** A   **7.** B   **8.** D   **9.** C   **10.** A
11. C   **12.** C   **13.** C   **14.** C   **15.** D   **16.** C   **17.** B

AP® Practice, Section 2, Parts A and B, p. 245

1. a.

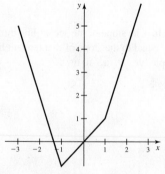

b. $-\dfrac{4}{3}, 0$ **c.**

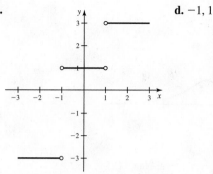

d. $-1, 1$

2. a. 0   **b.** $(0, 0.087)$ **c.** $(0.087, 0.405)$ **d.** $t \approx 0.405$
e. $t \approx 0.405$ **3. a.** A–c; B–d; C–a; D–b   **b.** f–C; f'–B; f''–A
4.

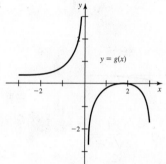

5. The length of the hypotenuse is increasing at 3/5 m/s.
6. a. Note that $\lim\limits_{x \to 0^-} f(x) = \lim\limits_{x \to 0^+} f(x) = 1$ which implies that $\lim\limits_{x \to 0} f(x) = 1$. Because $f(0)$ is also equal to 1, f is continuous at 1.
b. The slope of the line tangent to $e^{-\pi x}$ at 0 is the same as the slope of the line tangent to $1 - \sin \pi x$ at 0 (both slopes are $-\pi$).

c. $f'(x) = \begin{cases} -\pi e^{-\pi x} & \text{if } x \le 0 \\ -\pi \cos \pi x & \text{if } x > 0 \end{cases}; x = 0.5$ **d.** $y = -\pi x + 1$

7. a. $-\dfrac{x + y}{x + 4y}$ **b.** Horizontal tangents at $(2, -2)$ and $(-2, 2)$
c. Vertical tangents at $(4, -1)$ and $(-4, 1)$

CHAPTER 4

Section 4.1 Exercise, pp. 253–256

1. f has an absolute maximum at c in $[a, b]$ if $f(x) \le f(c)$ for all x in $[a, b]$. f has an absolute minimum at c in $[a, b]$ if $f(x) \ge f(c)$ for all x in $[a, b]$.   **3.** The function must be continuous on a closed interval.   **5.**

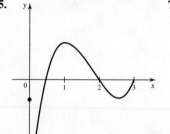

7.

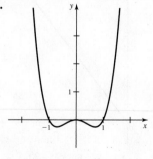

9. Evaluate the function at the critical points and at the endpoints of the interval.   **11.** Abs. min at $x = c_2$; abs. max at $x = b$ **13.** Abs. min at $x = a$; no abs. max   **15.** Local min at $x = q, s$; local max at $x = p, r$; abs. min at $x = a$; abs. max at $x = b$ **17.** Local max at $x = p$ and $x = r$; local min at $x = q$; abs. max at $x = p$; abs. min at $x = b$

19.

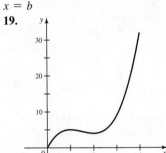

21.

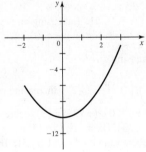

23. a. $x = \dfrac{2}{3}$ **b.** Local min   **25. a.** $x = \pm 3$ **b.** $x = -3$ local max; $x = 3$ local min.   **27. a.** $x = -\dfrac{2}{3}, \dfrac{1}{3}$ **b.** $x = -\dfrac{2}{3}$ local max; $x = \dfrac{1}{3}$ local min.   **29. a.** $x = \pm 1$ **b.** $x = -1$ local min; $x = 1$ local max   **31. a.** $x = 0$ **b.** Local min   **33. a.** $x = 1$ **b.** $x = 1$ local min   **35. a.** $x = -\dfrac{4}{5}, 0$ **b.** $x = -\dfrac{4}{5}$ local max; $x = 0$ local min.   **37. a.** $x = 0$ **b.** Abs. max: -1 at $x = 3$; abs. min: -10 at $x = 0$ **c.**

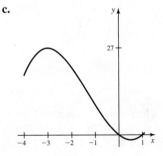

39. a. $x = \dfrac{\pi}{2}$ **b.** Abs. max: 1 at $x = 0, \pi$; abs. min: 0 at $x = \dfrac{\pi}{2}$ **c.**

41. a. $x = \pm\dfrac{\pi}{6}$ **b.** Abs. max: 1 at $x = \dfrac{\pi}{6}$; abs. min: -1 at $x = -\dfrac{\pi}{6}$ **c.**

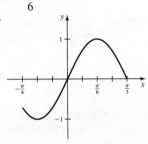

43. a. $x = \dfrac{1}{2e}$ **b.** Abs. min: $(\sqrt{1/e})^{1/e}$ at $x = \dfrac{1}{2e}$; abs. max: 2 at $x = 1$ **c.**

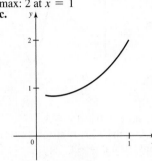

45. a. $x = \dfrac{1}{\sqrt{2}}$ **b.** Abs. max: $1 + \pi$ at $x = -1$; abs. min: 1 at $x = 1$ **c.**

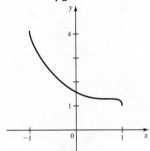

47. a. $-1, 1$ **b.** Abs. max: 5 at $x = -2$; abs. min: -2 at $x = 1$ **c.**

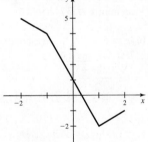

49. a. $x = -3, \tfrac{1}{2}$ **b.** Abs. max: 27 at $x = -3$; abs. min: $-\tfrac{19}{12}$ at $x = \tfrac{1}{2}$ **c.**

51. $t = 2\,$s   **53. a.** 50   **b.** 45   **55. a.** False   **b.** False   **c.** False   **d.** True   **57. a.** $x = -0.96, 2.18, 5.32$ **b.** Abs. max: 3.716 at $x = 2.177$; abs. min: -32.797 at $x = 5.319$

c.

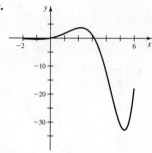

59. a. $x = 0$ **b.** Abs. max: $\sqrt{2}$ at $x = \pm\pi/4$; abs. min: 1 at $x = 0$ **c.**

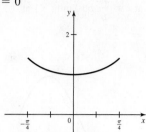

61. a. $x = 0$ and $x = 3$ **b.** Abs. max: $27/e^3$ at $x = 3$; abs. min: $-e$ at $x = -1$ **c.**

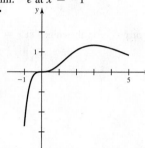

63. a. $x = 8$ **b.** Abs. max: $3\sqrt{2}$ at $x = 6$ and $x = 12$; abs. min: 4 at $x = 8$ **c.**

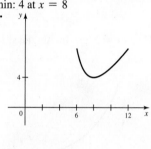

65. If $a \geq 0$, there is no critical point. If $a < 0$, $x = 2a/3$ is the only critical point. **67.** $x = \pm a$ **69. a.** $x = \tan^{-1}2 + k\pi$, for $k = -2, -1, 0, 1$ **b.** $x = \tan^{-1}2 + k\pi$, for $k = -2, 0$ correspond to local max; $x = \tan^{-1}2 + k\pi$, for $k = -1, 1$ correspond to local min. **c.** Abs. max: 2.24; abs. min: -2.24 **71. a.** $x = -\frac{1}{8}$ and $x = 3$ **b.** $x = -\frac{1}{8}$ corresponds to a local min; $x = 3$ is neither **c.** Abs. max: 51.23; abs. min: -12.352
73. a. $x = 5 - 4\sqrt{2} \approx -0.658$ **b.** $x = 5 - 4\sqrt{2}$ corresponds to a local max. **c.** No abs. max or min **75.** Abs. max: 4 at $x = -1$; abs. min: -8 at $x = 3$ **77. a.** $T(x) = \dfrac{\sqrt{2500 + x^2}}{2} + \dfrac{50 - x}{4}$
b. $x = 50/\sqrt{3} \approx 28.868$ **c.** $T(50/\sqrt{3}) = 34.151, T(0) = 37.50, T(50) = 35.355$
d.

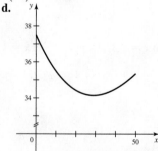

79. a. 1, 3, 0, 1 **b.** h does not have a local extremum at $x = 2$ but it is possible that g has a local extremum at $x = 2$. **81. a.** Local min at $x = -c$ **b.** Local max at $x = -c$ **83. a.** $f(x) - f(c) \leq 0$ for all x near c **b.** $\displaystyle\lim_{x \to c^+} \frac{f(x) - f(c)}{x - c} \leq 0$
c. $\displaystyle\lim_{x \to c^-} \frac{f(x) - f(c)}{x - c} \geq 0$ **d.** Because $f'(c)$ exists,
$\displaystyle\lim_{x \to c^+} \frac{f(x) - f(c)}{x - c} = \lim_{x \to c^-} \frac{f(x) - f(c)}{x - c}$. By parts (b) and (c), we must have that $f'(c) = 0$.

Section 4.2 Exercise, pp. 267–271

1. f is increasing on I if $f'(x) > 0$ for all x in I; f is decreasing on I if $f'(x) < 0$ for all x in I. **3.**

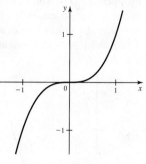

5. The tangent lines lie below the graph of f. **7.** A point in the domain at which f changes concavity **9.** Yes. Consider the graph of $y = \sqrt{x}$ on $(0, \infty)$.
11. 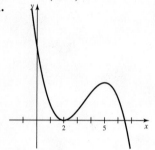 **13.**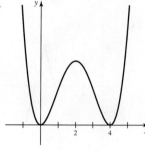

15.

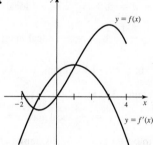

17. Increasing on $(-\infty, 0)$; decreasing on $(0, \infty)$ **19.** Decreasing on $(-\infty, 1)$; increasing on $(1, \infty)$ **21.** Increasing on $(-\infty, 1/2)$; decreasing on $(1/2, \infty)$ **23.** Increasing on $(-\infty, 0), (1, 2)$; decreasing on $(0, 1), (2, \infty)$ **25.** Increasing on $\left(-\dfrac{1}{\sqrt{e}}, 0\right), \left(\dfrac{1}{\sqrt{e}}, \infty\right)$; decreasing on $\left(-\infty, -\dfrac{1}{\sqrt{e}}\right), \left(0, \dfrac{1}{\sqrt{e}}\right)$ **27.** Increasing on the intervals $(-\pi, -2\pi/3), (-\pi/3, 0), (\pi/3, 2\pi/3)$; decreasing on the intervals $(-2\pi/3, -\pi/3), (0, \pi/3), (2\pi/3, \pi)$
29. Increasing on $(0, \infty)$; decreasing on $(-\infty, 0)$ **31.** Increasing on $(-\infty, \infty)$ **33.** Decreasing on $(-\infty, 1), (4, \infty)$; increasing on $(1, 4)$
35. Increasing on $\left(-\infty, -\frac{1}{2}\right), \left(0, \frac{1}{2}\right)$; decreasing on $\left(-\frac{1}{2}, 0\right), \left(\frac{1}{2}, \infty\right)$
37. Increasing on $(-1, 1)$; decreasing on $(-\infty, -1), (1, \infty)$
39. a. $x = 0$ **b.** Local min at $x = 0$ **c.** Abs. min: 3 at $x = 0$; abs. max: 12 at $x = -3$ **41. a.** $x = \pm 3/\sqrt{2}$ **b.** Local min at $x = -3/\sqrt{2}$; local max at $x = 3/\sqrt{2}$ **c.** Abs. max: 9/2 at $x = 3/\sqrt{2}$; abs. min: $-9/2$ at $x = -3/\sqrt{2}$ **43. a.** $x = \pm\sqrt{3}$
b. Local min at $x = -\sqrt{3}$; local max at $x = \sqrt{3}$ **c.** Abs. max: 28 at $x = -4$; abs. min: $-6\sqrt{3}$ at $x = -\sqrt{3}$ **45. a.** $x = 0$ and $x = 2$
b. Local max at $x = 0$; local min at $x = 2$ **c.** Abs. min: -29.24 at $x = -5$; abs. max: 0 at $x = 0$ and $x = 5$ **47. a.** $x = e^{-2}$
b. Local min at $x = e^{-2}$ **c.** Abs. min: $-2/e$ at $x = e^{-2}$; no abs. max

49. Abs. max: $1/e$ at $x = 1$ **51.** Abs. min: $36\sqrt[3]{\pi/6}$ at $x = \sqrt[3]{6/\pi}$.

53.   **55.**

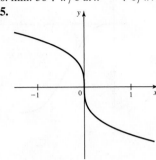

57. Concave up on $(-\infty, 0)$ and $(1, \infty)$; concave down on $(0, 1)$; (inflection points at $x = 0$ and $x = 1$ **59.** Concave up on $(-\infty, 0)$ and $(2, \infty)$; concave down on $(0, 2)$; inflection points at $x = 0$ and $x = 2$ **61.** Concave down on $(-\infty, 1)$, concave up on $(1, \infty)$; inflection point at $x = 1$.   **63.** Concave up on $(-1/\sqrt{3}, 1/\sqrt{3})$; concave down on $(-\infty, -1/\sqrt{3})$; $(1/\sqrt{3}, \infty)$; inflection points at $t = \pm 1/\sqrt{3}$ **65.** Concave up on $(-\infty, -1)$ and $(1, \infty)$; concave down on $(-1, 1)$; inflection points at $x = \pm 1$ **67.** Concave up on $(0, 1)$; concave down on $(1, \infty)$; inflection point at $x = 1$
69. Concave up on $(0, 2)$ and $(4, \infty)$; concave down on $(-\infty, 0)$ and $(2, 4)$; inflection points at $x = 0, 2, 4$ **71.** Critical pt. $x = 0, 2$; local max at $x = 0$, local min at $x = 2$ **73.** Critical pt. at $x = 0$; local max at $x = 0$ **75.** Critical pt. at $x = 6$; local min at $x = 6$
77. Critical pts. at $x = 0$ and $x = 1$; local max at $x = 0$; local min at $x = 1$ **79.** Critical pts. at $x = 0$ and $x = 2$; local min at $x = 0$; local max at $x = 2$ **81.** Critical pt. $x = e^5$; local min at $x = e^5$
83. a. True   **b.** False   **c.** True   **d.** False   **e.** False
85.   **87.** a–f–g, b–e–i, c–d–h

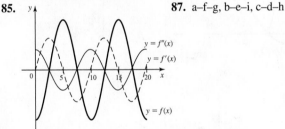

89.

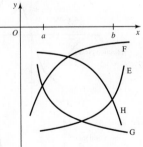

91.   **93.**

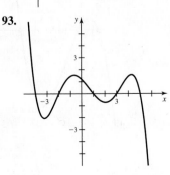

95. a. Increasing on $(-2, 2)$; decreasing on $(-3, -2)$ **b.** Critical pts. at $x = -2$ and $x = 0$; local min at $x = -2$; neither a local max or min at $x = 0$ **c.** Inflection pts. at $x = -1$ and $x = 0$ **d.** Concave up on $(-3, -1)$ and $(0, 2)$; concave down on $(-1, 0)$
e.   **f.**

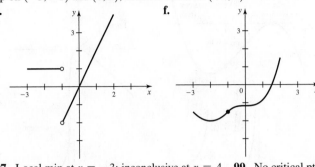

97. Local min at $x = -3$; inconclusive at $x = 4$ **99.** No critical pts.
101. a. $E = \dfrac{p}{p - 50}$ **b.** -1.4% **c.** $E'(p) = -\dfrac{ab}{(a - bp)^2} < 0$, for $p \geq 0, p \neq a/b$ **d.** $E(p) = -b$, for $p \geq 0$ **103. a.** 300
b. $t = \sqrt{10}$ **c.** $t = \sqrt{b/3}$ **105. a.** $f''(x) = 6x + 2a = 0$ when $x = -a/3$ **b.** $f(-a/3) - f(-a/3 + x) = (a^2/3)x - bx - x^3$; also, $f(-a/3 - x) - f(-a/3) = (a^2/3)x - bx - x^3$

Section 4.3 Exercise, pp. 278–281

1. We need to know on which interval(s) to graph f.
3. No; the domain of any polynomial is $(-\infty, \infty)$; there are no vertical asymptotes. Also, $\lim\limits_{x \to \pm\infty} p(x) = \pm\infty$ where p is any polynomial; there are no horizontal asymptotes.   **5.** Evaluate the function at the critical points and at the endpoints. Then find the largest and smallest values among those candidates.

7.   **9.**

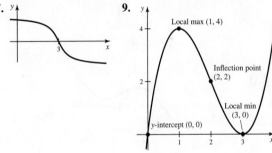

11.

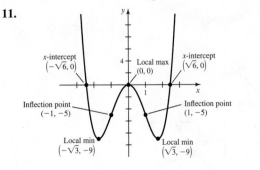

13.

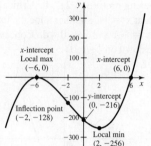

x-intercept
Local max
$(-6, 0)$

x-intercept
$(6, 0)$

Inflection point
$(-2, -128)$

y-intercept
$(0, -216)$

Local min
$(2, -256)$

15.

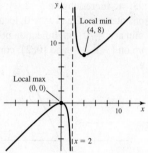

Local min
$(4, 8)$

Local max
$(0, 0)$

y-intercept
$(0, -216)$

$x = 2$

27.

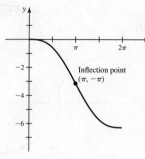

Inflection point
$(\pi, -\pi)$

29.

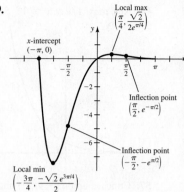

Local max
$\left(\dfrac{\pi}{4}, \dfrac{\sqrt{2}}{2e^{\pi/4}}\right)$

x-intercept
$(-\pi, 0)$

Inflection point
$\left(\dfrac{\pi}{2}, e^{-\pi/2}\right)$

Inflection point
$\left(-\dfrac{\pi}{2}, -e^{\pi/2}\right)$

Local min
$\left(-\dfrac{3\pi}{4}, \dfrac{-\sqrt{2}\,e^{3\pi/4}}{2}\right)$

17.

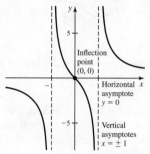

Inflection
point
$(0, 0)$

Horizontal
asymptote
$y = 0$

Vertical
asymptotes
$x = \pm 1$

19.

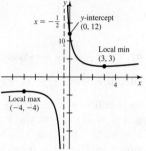

$x = -\dfrac{1}{2}$

y-intercept
$(0, 12)$

Local min
$(3, 3)$

Local max
$(-4, -4)$

31.

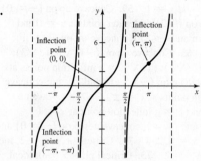

Inflection
point
$(0, 0)$

Inflection
point
(π, π)

Inflection
point
$(-\pi, -\pi)$

21.

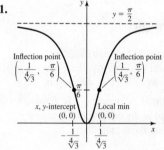

$y = \dfrac{\pi}{2}$

Inflection point
$\left(-\dfrac{1}{\sqrt[4]{3}}, -\dfrac{\pi}{6}\right)$

Inflection point
$\left(\dfrac{1}{\sqrt[4]{3}}, \dfrac{\pi}{6}\right)$

$\dfrac{\pi}{6}$

x, y-intercept
$(0, 0)$

Local min
$(0, 0)$

$-\dfrac{1}{\sqrt[4]{3}}$ $\dfrac{1}{\sqrt[4]{3}}$

33.

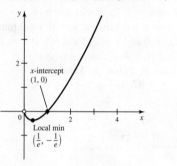

x-intercept
$(1, 0)$

Local min
$\left(\dfrac{1}{e}, -\dfrac{1}{e}\right)$

23.

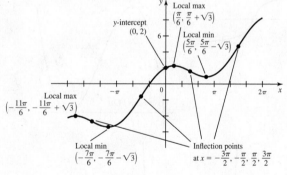

Local max
$\left(\dfrac{\pi}{6}, \dfrac{\pi}{6} + \sqrt{3}\right)$

y-intercept
$(0, 2)$

Local min
$\left(\dfrac{5\pi}{6}, \dfrac{5\pi}{6} - \sqrt{3}\right)$

Local max
$\left(-\dfrac{11\pi}{6}, -\dfrac{11\pi}{6} + \sqrt{3}\right)$

Local min
$\left(-\dfrac{7\pi}{6}, -\dfrac{7\pi}{6} - \sqrt{3}\right)$

Inflection points
at $x = -\dfrac{3\pi}{2}, -\dfrac{\pi}{2}, \dfrac{\pi}{2}, \dfrac{3\pi}{2}$

35.

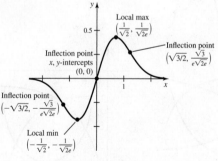

Local max
$\left(\dfrac{1}{\sqrt{2}}, \dfrac{1}{\sqrt{2e}}\right)$

Inflection point
$\left(\sqrt{3/2}, \dfrac{\sqrt{3}}{e\sqrt{2e}}\right)$

Inflection point
x, y-intercepts
$(0, 0)$

Inflection point
$\left(-\sqrt{3/2}, -\dfrac{\sqrt{3}}{e\sqrt{2e}}\right)$

Local min
$\left(-\dfrac{1}{\sqrt{2}}, -\dfrac{1}{\sqrt{2e}}\right)$

25.

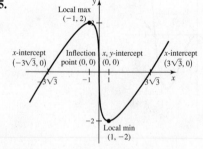

Local max
$(-1, 2)$

x-intercept
$(-3\sqrt{3}, 0)$

Inflection
point $(0, 0)$

x, y-intercept
$(0, 0)$

x-intercept
$(3\sqrt{3}, 0)$

$-3\sqrt{3}$ -1 1 $3\sqrt{3}$

Local min
$(1, -2)$

37.

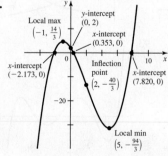

Local max
$\left(-1, \dfrac{14}{3}\right)$

y-intercept
$(0, 2)$

x-intercept
$(0.353, 0)$

x-intercept
$(-2.173, 0)$

x-intercept
$(-2.173, 0)$

Inflection
point
$\left(2, -\dfrac{40}{3}\right)$

x-intercept
$(7.820, 0)$

Local min
$\left(5, -\dfrac{94}{3}\right)$

39.

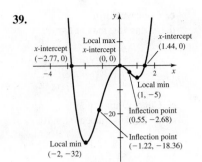

41.

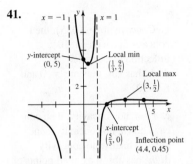

43. a. False **b.** False **c.** False **d.** True

45.

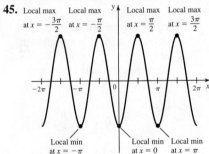

47.

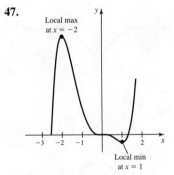

49. Critical pts. at $x = 1, 3$; local max at $x = 1$; local min at $x = 3$; inflection pt. at $x = 2$; increasing on $(0, 1)$, $(3, 4)$; decreasing on $(1, 3)$; concave up on $(2, 4)$; concave down on $(0, 2)$

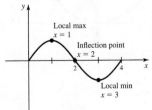

51.

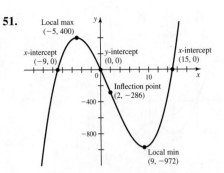

53.

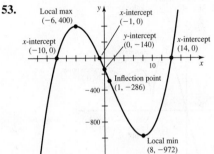

55. Local max of $e^{1/e}$ at $x = e$

57.

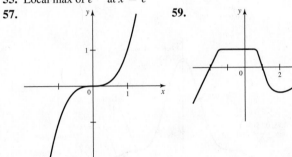

59.

61.

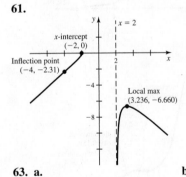

63. a.

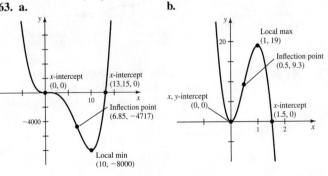

b.

65.

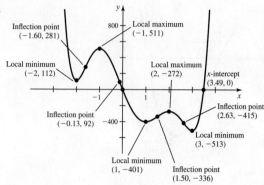

Inflection point (−1.60, 281)
Local maximum (−1, 511)
800
Local minimum (−2, 112)
Local maximum (2, −272)
x-intercept (3.49, 0)
−1
1
Inflection point (−0.13, 92)
−400
Inflection point (2.63, −415)
Local minimum (3, −513)
Local minimum (1, −401)
Inflection point (1.50, −336)

67.

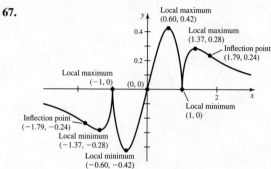

Local maximum (0.60, 0.42)
Local maximum (1.37, 0.28)
0.4
Inflection point (1.79, 0.24)
0.2
Local maximum (−1, 0)
(0, 0)
2
x
Local minimum (1, 0)
Inflection point (−1.79, −0.24)
Local minimum (−1.37, −0.28)
Local minimum (−0.60, −0.42)

69. a.

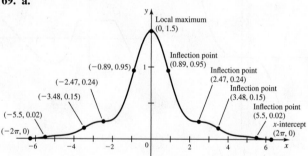

Local maximum (0, 1.5)
Inflection point (0.89, 0.95)
(−0.89, 0.95)
Inflection point (2.47, 0.24)
(−2.47, 0.24)
Inflection point (3.48, 0.15)
(−3.48, 0.15)
Inflection point (5.5, 0.02)
(−5.5, 0.02)
x-intercept (2π, 0)
(−2π, 0)
−6   −4   −2   0   2   4   6   x

b.

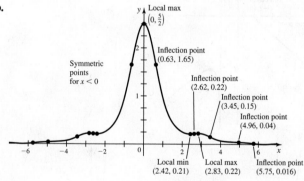

Local max (0, 5/2)
2
Inflection point (0.63, 1.65)
Symmetric points for x < 0
Inflection point (2.62, 0.22)
1
Inflection point (3.45, 0.15)
Inflection point (4.96, 0.04)
−6   −4   −2   0   2   4   6   x
Local min (2.42, 0.21)
Local max (2.83, 0.22)
Inflection point (5.75, 0.016)

71. (A) a.

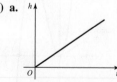

b. Water is being added at all times   **c.** No concavity
d. h' has an abs. max at all points of $[0, 10]$.

(B) a.

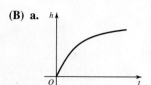

c. Concave down
d. h' has abs. max at $t = 0$.

(C) a.

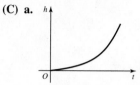

c. Concave up
d. h' has abs. max at $t = 10$.

(D) a.

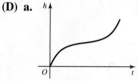

c. Concave up on $(0, 5)$, then concave down on $(5, 10)$; inflection pt. at $t = 5$
d. h' has abs. max at $t = 0$ and $t = 10$.

(E) a.

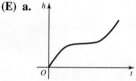

c. First, no concavity; then concave down, no concavity, concave up; and finally, no concavity
d. h' has abs. max at all points of an interval $[0, a]$ and $[b, 10]$.

(F) a.

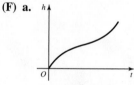

c. Concave down on $(0, 5)$; concave up on $(5, 10)$; inflection pt. at $t = 5$
d. h' has abs. max at $t = 0$ and $t = 10$.

73. $f'(0)$ does not exist.

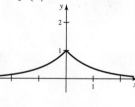

75.

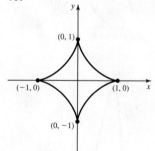

(0, 1)
(−1, 0)   (1, 0)   x
(0, −1)

77.

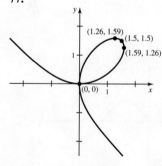

(1.26, 1.59)
(1.5, 1.5)
(1.59, 1.26)
1
(0, 0)   1   x

79.

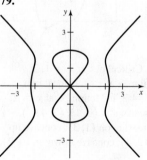

3
−3   3   x
−3

81.

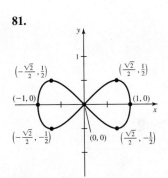

$\left(-\frac{\sqrt{2}}{2}, \frac{1}{2}\right)$ $\left(\frac{\sqrt{2}}{2}, \frac{1}{2}\right)$

$(-1, 0)$ $(1, 0)$

$\left(-\frac{\sqrt{2}}{2}, -\frac{1}{2}\right)$ $(0, 0)$ $\left(\frac{\sqrt{2}}{2}, -\frac{1}{2}\right)$

83.

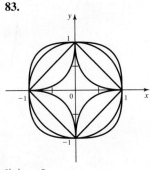

85. a. $x < a$ **b.** $f(a) = 0$, $\lim\limits_{x \to -\infty} f(x) = 0$
c. $f'(x) = (a - x)^{x-1}((a - x)\ln(a - x) - x)$
d. See part (c). **e.** z and $f(z)$ increase as a increases.

87.

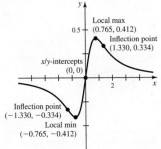

Local max
(0.765, 0.412)
Inflection point
(1.330, 0.334)
x/y-intercepts
(0, 0)
Inflection point
(−1.330, −0.334)
Local min
(−0.765, −0.412)

89.

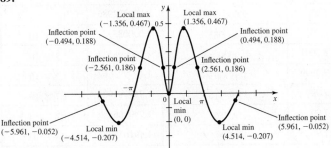

Local max
(−1.356, 0.467)
Local max
(1.356, 0.467)
Inflection point
(−0.494, 0.188)
Inflection point
(0.494, 0.188)
Inflection point
(−2.561, 0.186)
Inflection point
(2.561, 0.186)
Local min
(0, 0)
Inflection point
(−5.961, −0.052)
Inflection point
(5.961, −0.052)
Local min
(−5.961, −0.052)
Local min
(−4.514, −0.207)
Local min
(4.514, −0.207)

Section 4.4 Exercise, pp. 285–291

1. Objective function, constraints **3.** $Q = x^2(10 - x)$;
$Q = (10 - y)^2 y$ **5.** Width $=$ length $= \frac{5}{2}$ m
7. Width $=$ length $= 10$ **9.** $\frac{23}{2}$ and $\frac{23}{2}$ **11.** $5\sqrt{2}$ and $5\sqrt{2}$
13. $x = \sqrt{6}, y = 2\sqrt{6}$ **15.** Length $=$ width $=$ height $= \sqrt[3]{100}$
17. $\dfrac{4}{\sqrt[3]{5}}$ ft by $\dfrac{4}{\sqrt[3]{5}}$ ft by $5^{2/3}$ ft **19.** $(5, 15)$, distance ≈ 47.4
21. a. A point $8/\sqrt{5}$ mi from the point on the shore nearest the woman
in the direction of the restaurant **b.** $9/\sqrt{13}$ mi/hr **23.** 18.22 ft
25. $\dfrac{10}{\sqrt{2}}$ cm by $\dfrac{5}{\sqrt{2}}$ cm **27.** $h = \dfrac{20}{\sqrt{3}}; r = 20\sqrt{\dfrac{2}{3}}$ **29.** $\sqrt{15}$ m
by $2\sqrt{15}$ m **31.** $r/h = \sqrt{2}$ **33.** $r = h = \sqrt[3]{450/\pi}$ m
35. The point $12/(\sqrt[3]{2} + 1) \approx 5.31$ m from the weaker source
37. A point $7\sqrt{3}/6$ mi from the point on shore nearest the island, in
the direction of the power station **39. a.** $P = 2/\sqrt{3}$ units from the
midpoint of the base **41.** $r = \sqrt{6}, h = \sqrt{3}$ **43.** For $L \leq 4r$,
max at $\theta = 0$ and $\theta = 2\pi$; min at $\theta = \cos^{-1}(-L/(4r))$
and $\theta = 2\pi - \cos^{-1}(-L/(4r))$. For $L > 4r$, max at $\theta = 0$
and $\theta = 2\pi$; min at $\theta = \pi$.

45. a. $r = \sqrt[3]{177/\pi} \approx 3.83$ cm; $h = 2\sqrt[3]{177/\pi} \approx 7.67$ cm
b. $r = \sqrt[3]{177/2\pi} \approx 3.04$ cm; $h = 2\sqrt[3]{708/\pi} \approx 12.17$ cm
part (b) is closer to the real can. **47.** $\sqrt{30} \approx 5.5$ ft **49.** When the
seat is at its lowest point **51.** $r = \sqrt{2}R/\sqrt{3}; h = 2R/\sqrt{3}$
53. a. $r = 2R/3; h = \frac{1}{3}H$ **b.** $r = R/2; h = H/2$ **55.** 3:1
57. $(1 + \sqrt{3})$ mi ≈ 2.732 mi **59.** You can run 12 mi/hr if you
run toward the point $3/16$ mi ahead of the locomotive (when it
passes the point nearest you). **61. a.** $(-6/5, 2/5)$ **b.** Approx
$(0.59, 0.65)$ **c. (i)** $(p - \frac{1}{2}, \sqrt{p - \frac{1}{2}})$ **(ii)** $(0, 0)$ **63. a.** 0, 30, 25
b. 42.5 mi/hr **c.** The units of $p/g(v)$ are $\$/$mi and so are the units
of w/v. Thus, $L\left(\dfrac{p}{g(v)} + \dfrac{w}{v}\right)$ gives the total cost of a trip of L miles.
d. Approximately 62.883 mi/hr **e.** Neither; the zeros of $C'(v)$ are
independent of L. **f.** Decreased slightly, to 62.532 mi/hr
g. Decreased to 60.8 mi/hr **65. b.** Because the speed of
light is constant, travel time is minimized when distance is
minimized. **67.** Let the angle of the cuts be ϕ_1 and ϕ_2, where
$\phi_1 + \phi_2 = \theta$. The volume of the notch is proportional to
$\tan \phi_1 + \tan \phi_2 = \tan \phi_1 + \tan(\theta - \phi_1)$, which is minimized
when $\phi_1 = \phi_2 = \dfrac{\theta}{2}$. **69.** $x \approx 38.81, y \approx 55.03$

Section 4.5 Exercise, pp. 300–301

1.

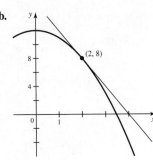

$(1, f(1))$

3. $f(x) \approx f(a) + f'(a)(x - a)$
5. $dy = f'(x)\, dx$ **7.** 61 mi/hr; 61.017 mi/hr
9. $L(x) = T(0) + T'(0)(x - 0) = D - (D/60)x = D(1 - x/60)$
11. 84 min; 84.210 min
13. a. $L(x) = -4x + 16$ **b.**

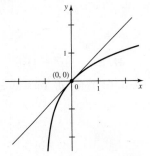

$(2, 8)$

c. 7.6 **d.** 0.13% error
15. a. $L(x) = x$ **b.**

$(0, 0)$

c. 0.9   **d.** 40% error   **17. a.** $L(x) = 1$
b.

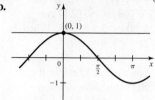

c. 1   **d.** 0.005% error   **19. a.** $y = \dfrac{1}{2} - \dfrac{x}{48}$
b.

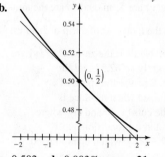

c. 0.502   **d.** 0.003% error   **21.** $a = 200; \frac{1}{203} \approx 0.00493$
23. $a = 144; \sqrt{146} \approx 12\frac{1}{12}$ **25.** $a = 1; \ln 1.05 \approx 0.05$
27. $a = 0; e^{0.06} \approx 1.06$ **29.** $a = 512; \dfrac{1}{\sqrt[3]{510}} \approx \dfrac{769}{6144} \approx 0.125$
31. $\Delta V \approx 10\pi \text{ ft}^3$ **33.** $\Delta V \approx -40\pi \text{ cm}^3$
35. $\Delta S \approx -\dfrac{59\pi}{5\sqrt{34}} \text{ m}^2$ **37. a.** $L(x) = -2x + 4$
b.

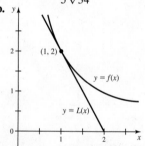

c. Underestimates   **d.** $f''(1) = 4 > 0$

39. a. $L(x) = -\dfrac{1}{2}x + \dfrac{1}{2}(1 + \ln 2)$ **b.**

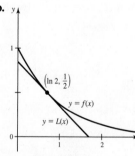

c. Underestimates   **d.** $f''(\ln 2) = \dfrac{1}{2} > 0$

41. $dy = 2\, dx$ **43.** $dy = -\dfrac{3}{x^4}\, dx$

45. $dy = a \sin x\, dx$ **47.** $dy = (9x^2 - 4)\, dx$ **49.** $dy = \sec^2 x\, dx$

51. a. True   **b.** False   **c.** True   **d.** True   **53.** 2.7

55. $L(x) = 1 - x$;   **a.**

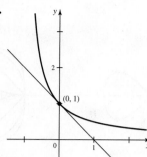

b. $1/1.1 \approx 0.9$ **c.** 1% error
57. $L(x) = 1 - x$ **a.**

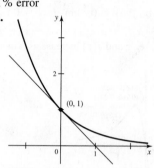

b. $e^{-0.03} \approx 0.97$ **c.** 0.046% error
61. $L(x) = 2 + (x - 8)/12$

x	Linear Approx.	Exact Value	Percent Error
8.1	$2.008\overline{3}$	2.00829885	1.7×10^{-3}
8.01	$2.0008\overline{3}$	2.000832986	1.7×10^{-5}
8.001	$2.00008\overline{3}$	2.00008333	1.7×10^{-7}
8.0001	$2.000008\overline{3}$	2.000008333	1.7×10^{-9}
7.9999	$1.999991\overline{6}$	1.999991667	1.7×10^{-9}
7.999	$1.99991\overline{6}$	1.999916663	1.7×10^{-7}
7.99	$1.9991\overline{6}$	1.999166319	1.7×10^{-5}
7.9	$1.991\overline{6}$	1.991631701	1.8×10^{-3}

63. a. f; the rate at which f' is changing at 1 is smaller than the rate at which g' is changing at 1. The graph of f bends away from the linear function more slowly than the graph of g.   **b.** The larger the value of $|f''(a)|$, the greater the deviation of the curve $y = f(x)$ from the tangent line at points near $x = a$.

Section 4.6 Exercise, pp. 306–308

1. If f is a continuous function on the closed interval $[a, b]$ and is differentiable on (a, b) and the slope of the secant line that joins $(a, f(a))$ to $(b, f(b))$ is zero, then there is at least one value c in (a, b) at which the slope of the line tangent to f at $(c, f(c))$ is also zero.

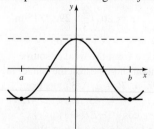

3. $f(x) = |x|$ is not differentiable at 0.

5.

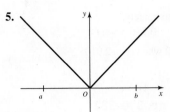

7. $x = \frac{1}{3}$ **9.** $x = \pi/4$ **11.** Does not apply   **13.** $x = \frac{5}{3}$
15. Average lapse rate $= -6.3°/\text{km}$. You cannot conclude that the lapse rate at a point exceeds the threshold value.
17. a. Yes   **b.** $c = \frac{1}{2}$
c.

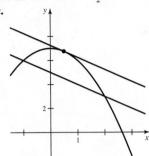

19. a. Yes   **b.** $c = \ln\left(\dfrac{3}{\ln 4}\right)$
c.

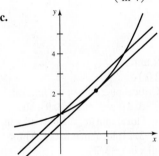

21. a. Yes   **b.** $c = \sqrt{1 - 9/\pi^2}$
c.

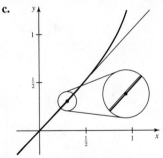

23. a. Does not apply
25. a. False   **b.** True   **c.** False   **27.** h and p
29.

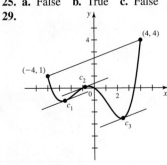

31. There are no points because f is not differentiable at $x = 2$.
33. The car's average velocity is $(30 - 0)/(28/60) = 64.3 \text{ mi/hr}$. By the MVT, the car's instantaneous velocity was 64.3 mi/hr at some time.   **35.** Average speed $= 11.6 \text{ mi/hr}$. By the MVT, the speed was exactly 11.6 mi/hr at least once. By the Intermediate Value Theorem, all speeds between 0 and 11.6 mi/hr were reached. Because the initial and final speed was 0 mi/hr, the speed of 11 mi/hr was reached at least twice.
37. $\dfrac{f(b) - f(a)}{b - a} = A(a + b) + B$ and $f'(x) = 2Ax + B$;

$2Ax + B = A(a + b) + B$ implies that $x = \dfrac{a + b}{2}$, the midpoint

of $[a, b]$.   **39.** $\tan^2 x$ and $\sec^2 x$ differ by a constant; in fact, $\tan^2 x - \sec^2 x = -1$.   **41.** Bolt's average speed was 37.58 km/hr, so he exceeded 37 km/hr during the race.   **43. b.** $c = \frac{1}{2}$

Section 4.7 Exercise, pp. 319–321

1. If $\lim_{x \to a} f(x) = 0$ and $\lim_{x \to a} g(x) = 0$, then we say $\lim_{x \to a} f(x)/g(x)$ is an indeterminate form $0/0$.   **3.** Take the limit of the quotient of the derivatives of the functions.   **5.** If $\lim_{x \to a} f(x)g(x)$ has the indeterminate form $0 \cdot \infty$, then $\lim_{x \to a}\left(\dfrac{f(x)}{1/g(x)}\right)$ has the indeterminate form $0/0$ or ∞/∞.   **7.** If $\lim_{x \to a} f(x) = 1$ and $\lim_{x \to a} g(x) = \infty$, then

$f(x)^{g(x)} \to 1^\infty$ as $x \to a$, which is meaningless; so direct substitution

does not work.   **9.** $\lim_{x \to \infty} \dfrac{g(x)}{f(x)} = 0$

11. $\ln x, x^3, 2^x, x^x$ **13.** -1 **15.** $1/2$ **17.** $1/e$ **19.** $\frac{12}{5}$ **21.** 4
23. $\frac{9}{16}$ **25.** $\frac{1}{2}$ **27.** $1/24$ **29.** 1 **31.** 4 **33.** $-\frac{1}{2}$ **35.** $1/\pi^2$
37. $\frac{1}{2}$ **39.** $-\frac{2}{3}$ **41.** 1 **43.** $\frac{1}{3}$ **45.** 1 **47.** $\frac{7}{6}$ **49.** 1 **51.** 0
53. 0 **55.** 1 **57.** 1 **59.** e **61.** e^a **63.** e^{a+1} **65.** 1
67. e **69.** $e^{0.01x}$ **71.** Comparable growth rates   **73.** x^x
75. 1.00001^x **77.** x^x **79.** e^{x^2} **81. a.** False   **b.** False
c. False   **d.** False   **e.** True   **f.** True   **83.** $\frac{2}{5}$ **85.** $-\frac{9}{4}$
87. 0 **89.** $\frac{1}{6}$ **91.** ∞ **93.** $(\ln 3)/(\ln 2)$ **95.** $\frac{1}{2}$
97. a. Approx. 3.43×10^{15} **b.** Approx. 3536 **c.** e^{100}
d. Approx. 163 **99.** 1 **101.** $\ln a - \ln b$
103. b. $\lim_{m \to \infty}(1 + r/m)^m = \lim_{m \to \infty}\left(1 + \dfrac{1}{(m/r)}\right)^{(m/r)r} = e^r$

105. $\sqrt{a/c}$ **107.** $\lim_{x \to \infty} \dfrac{x^p}{b^x} = \lim_{t \to \infty} \dfrac{\ln^p t}{t \ln^p b} = 0$

109. Show $\lim_{x \to \infty} \dfrac{\log_a x}{\log_b x} = \dfrac{\ln b}{\ln a} \ne 0$.

111. $1/3$ **115. a.** $b > e$ **b.** e^{ax} grows faster than e^x as $x \to \infty$, for $a > 1$; e^{ax} grows slower than e^x as $x \to \infty$, for $0 < a < 1$.

Section 4.8 Exercise, pp. 328–330

1. Newton's method generates a sequence of x-intercepts of lines tangent to the graph of f to approximate the roots of f.   **3.** Generally, if two successive Newton approximations agree in their first p digits, then those approximations have p digits of accuracy. The method is terminated when the desired accuracy is reached.

5. $x_{n+1} = x_n - \dfrac{x_n^2 - 6}{2x_n} = \dfrac{x_n^2 + 6}{2x_n}$; $x_1 = 2.5, x_2 = 2.45$

7. $x_{n+1} = x_n - \dfrac{e^{-x_n} - x_n}{e^{-x_n} - 1}$; $x_1 = 0.564$, $x_2 = 0.567$

9.

k	x_k
0	4.000000
1	3.250000
2	3.163462
3	3.162278
4	3.162278
5	3.162278
6	3.162278
7	3.162278
8	3.162278
9	3.162278
10	3.162278

11.

k	x_k
0	1.500000
1	0.101436
2	0.501114
3	0.510961
4	0.510973
5	0.510973
6	0.510973
7	0.510973
8	0.510973
9	0.510973
10	0.510973

13.

n	x_n
0	1.500000
1	1.443890
2	1.361976
3	1.268175
4	1.196179
5	1.168571
6	1.165592
7	1.165561
8	1.165561
9	1.165561
10	1.165561

15. $x \approx 0, 1.895, -1.895$ **17.** $x \approx -2.115, 0.254, 1.861$
19. $x \approx 0.0630, 2.230$ **21.** $x \approx 2.798$ **23.** $x \approx -0.667, 1.5, 1.667$ **25.** The method converges more slowly for f, because of the double root at $x = 1$.

n	x_n for f	x_n for g
0	2	2
1	1.5	1.25
2	1.25	1.025
3	1.125	1.0003
4	1.0625	1
5	1.03125	1
6	1.01563	1
7	1.00781	1
8	1.00391	1
9	1.00195	1
10	1.00098	1

27. a. True. **b.** False. **c.** False   **29.** $x \approx 1.153, 2.424, -3.577$
31. $x = 0$ and $x \approx 1.047$ **33.** $x \approx -0.335, 1.333$ **35.** $x \approx 0.179$
37. $x \approx 0.621, 3.0365$
39.

k	x_k	Error	Residual
0	0.5	0.5	0.000976563
1	0.45	0.45	0.000340506
2	0.405	0.405	0.000118727
3	0.3645	0.3645	0.0000413976
4	0.32805	0.32805	0.0000144345
5	0.295245	0.295245	5.03298×10^{-6}
6	0.265721	0.265721	1.75489×10^{-6}
7	0.239148	0.239148	6.11893×10^{-7}
8	0.215234	0.215234	2.13354×10^{-7}
9	0.193710	0.193710	7.43919×10^{-8}
10	0.174339	0.174339	2.59389×10^{-8}

41. $a = e$ **43.** $x \approx 0.143$ is approximately $\frac{1}{7}$.
45. a. $t = \pi/4 \approx 0.785$ **b.** $y = -0.586$ when $t \approx 1.339$
c. $t = \dfrac{3\pi}{4} \approx 2.356$ **d.** $y = 0.122$ when $t \approx 2.910$
47. $\lambda = 1.290, 2.373, 3.409$

Chapter 4 Review Exercises, pp. 330–332

1. a. False **b.** False **c.** True **d.** True **e.** False
3.

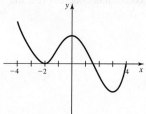

5.

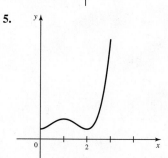

7. $x = 3$ and $x = -2$; no abs. max or min
9. $x = 1/e$; abs. min at $(1/e, 10 - 2/e)$
11.

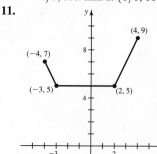

Critical pts.: all x in the interval $[-3, 2]$; abs. max: $(4, 9)$; abs. and local min at $(x, 5)$ for all x in $[-3, 2]$; local max. at $(x, 5)$ for all x in $(-3, 2)$

13.

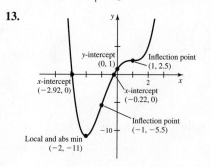

15.

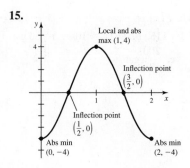

17.

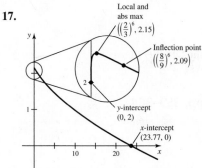

19.

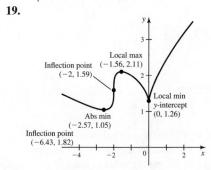

21. $r = 4\sqrt{6}/3;\ h = 4\sqrt{3}/3$ **23.** $x = 14, y = 7$
25. $p = q = 5\sqrt{2}$ **27. a.** $L(x) = \frac{2}{9}x + 3$ **b.** $\frac{85}{9} \approx 9.444$
29. $f(x) = 1/x^2;\ a = 4;\ 1/4.2^2 \approx 9/160 = 0.0563$
31. $\Delta h \approx -112$ ft   **33. a.** $\frac{100}{9}$ cells/week   **b.** $t = 2$ weeks
35. $-0.434259, 0.767592, 1$ **37.** $0, \pm 0.949$
39. 0   **41.** 12   **43.** $\frac{2}{3}$ **45.** ∞ **47.** 0   **49.** 1   **51.** 0   **53.** 1
55. 1   **57.** $1/e^3$ **59.** 1   **61.** $x^{1/2}$ **63.** $\sqrt{x}$ **65.** 3^x
67. Comparable growth rates   **69.** 1; 1
71. 0   **73.** $\lim\limits_{x\to 0^+} f(x) = 1;\ \lim\limits_{x\to 0^+} g(x) = 0$

AP® Practice, Section 1, Parts A and B, pp. 333–334

1. C   **2.** A   **3.** C   **4.** C   **5.** E   **6.** D   **7.** B   **8.** A   **9.** E
10. A   **11.** C   **12.** B   **13.** E   **14.** B   **15.** D   **16.** B   **17.** D
18. B   **19.** D

AP® Practice, Section 2, Parts A and B, pp. 334–335

1. a. $y = -\frac{3}{2}x + \frac{5}{2}$ **b.** Horizontal tangents at $(1.414, \pm 0.586)$ and
at $(-1.414, \pm 3.414)$; vertical tangent at $x \approx -2.847$ **c.** The curve
and line intersect once at $(-2.778, -1.111)$; substituting
$y = 2x/5$ into the equation for C results in the cubic equation
$x^3 - 4x^2/25 - 6x + 6 = 0$, whose only real root is $x \approx -2.778$.
2. a. relative minimum of 1.627 at $x \approx 1.404$; relative

maximum of 2 at $x = 0$ **b.** $L(x) = \frac{\pi^3}{6} + \frac{\pi^2}{2}(x - \pi)$

c. $\frac{3\pi^2}{2} - \frac{\pi^3}{3} \approx 4.469$ **d.** The approximation is an underestimate.
The graph of f is concave up on $(0.739, \infty)$ ($f''(x) = x - \cos x > 0$
on that interval), which includes the points at which the approximation

is being made.   **3. a.** All real numbers except 0   **b.** $\frac{1}{2}$

c. $f(0) = \frac{1}{2}$ **d.** $\frac{a - b}{c}$ **4. a.** All real numbers except 0

b. Local minimum at $x = 2$ and local maximum at $x = -2$
c. Concave up for $0 < x < \infty$; concave down for $-\infty < x < 0$

d. $x = 0$ **e.** $\infty; -\infty$ **5. a.** $f'(x) = \frac{2k - 3x}{2\sqrt{k - x}};$

$f''(x) = \frac{3x - 4k}{4(k - x)^{3/2}}$ **b.** $k = 3$ **c.** $-\infty$ **d.** There is no absolute

minimum because $\lim\limits_{x\to -\infty} f(x) = -\infty$.   **6. a.** Local maximum
of 1 at $x = 1$ **b.** $x > 2$ **c.** $x < 1$ **d.** $0; -\infty$
e.

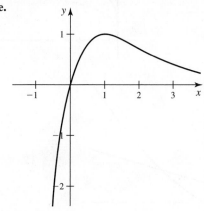

CHAPTER 5

Section 5.1 Exercises, pp. 347–349

1. The derivative, an antiderivative   **3.** $x + C$, where C is an arbitrary

constant   **5.** $\frac{x^{p+1}}{p+1} + C$, where $p \neq -1$ **7.** $\ln|x| + C$

9. 0   **11.** $x^5 + C$ **13.** $-\frac{1}{2}\cos 2x + C$ **15.** $3\tan x + C$
17. $y^{-2} + C$ **19.** $e^x + C$ **21.** $\tan^{-1}s + C$ **23.** $\frac{1}{2}x^6 - \frac{1}{2}x^{10} + C$
25. $\frac{8}{3}x^{3/2} - 8x^{1/2} + C$ **27.** $\frac{25}{3}s^3 + 15s^2 + 9s + C$
29. $\frac{9}{4}x^{4/3} + 6x^{2/3} + 6x + C$ **31.** $-x^3 + \frac{11}{2}x^2 + 4x + C$
33. $-x^{-3} + 2x + 3x^{-1} + C$ **35.** $x^4 - 3x^2 + C$
37. $-\frac{1}{2}\cos 2y + \frac{1}{3}\sin 3y + C$ **39.** $\tan x - x + C$
41. $\tan\theta + \sec\theta + C$ **43.** $t^3 + \frac{1}{2}\tan 2t + C$ **45.** $\frac{1}{4}\sec 4\theta + C$
47. $\frac{1}{2}\ln|y| + C$ **49.** $6\sin^{-1}(x/5) + C$ **51.** $\frac{1}{10}\sec^{-1}|x/10| + C$
53. $\frac{1}{5}\sec^{-1}\left|\frac{x}{5}\right| + C$ **55.** $t + \ln|t| + C$ **57.** $e^{x+2} + C$
59. $x^6/6 + 2/x + x - 19/6$ **61.** $\sec v + 1$ **63.** $2x^4 + 2x^{-1} + 1$
65. $y^3 + 5\ln|y| + 2$ **67.** $f(x) = x^2 - 3x + 4$
69. $g(x) = \frac{7}{8}x^8 - \frac{x^2}{2} + \frac{13}{8}$ **71.** $f(u) = 4\sin u + 2\cos 2u - 3$
73. $y(t) = 3\ln|t| + 6t + 2$ **75.** $y(\theta) = \sqrt{2}\sin\theta + \tan\theta + 1$

77. $f(x) = x^2 - 5x + 4$

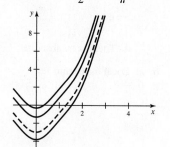

79. $f(x) = \dfrac{3x^2}{2} - \dfrac{\cos \pi x}{\pi} + \dfrac{1 - 3\pi}{\pi}$ **81.** $f(t) = \ln t + 4$

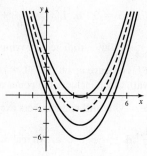

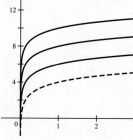

83. $s(t) = t^2 + 4t$

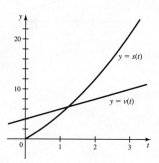

85. $s(t) = \frac{4}{3}t^{3/2} + 1$ **87.** $s(t) = 2t^3 + 2t^2 - 10t$

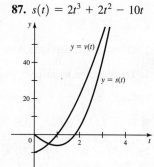

89. $-16t^2 + 20t$ **91.** $\frac{1}{30}t^3 + 1$ **93.** $-\frac{3}{4}\sin 2t + \frac{5}{2}t + 10$
95. Runner A overtakes runner B at $t = \pi/2$.
97. a. $v(t) = -9.8t + 30$ **b.** $s(t) = -4.9t^2 + 30t$
c. 45.918 m at time $t = 3.061$ **d.** $t = 6.122$
99. a. $v(t) = -9.8t + 10$ **b.** $s(t) = -4.9t^2 + 10t + 400$
c. 405.102 m at time $t = 1.020$ **d.** $t = 10.113$ **101. a.** True
b. False   **c.** True   **d.** False   **e.** False   **103.** $(e^{2x} + e^{-2x})/4 + C$
105. $-\cot \theta + 2\theta^3/3 - 3\theta^2/2 + C$ **107.** $\ln|x| + 2\sqrt{x} + C$

109. $\frac{4}{15}x^{15/2} - \frac{24}{11}x^{11/6} + C$ **111.** $F(x) = -\cos x + 3x + 3 - 3\pi$
113. $F(x) = 2x^8 + x^4 + 2x + 1$ **115. a.** $Q(t) = 10t - t^3/30$ gal
b.   **c.** $\dfrac{200}{3}$ gal

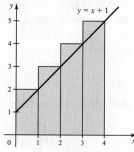

117. $\int \sin^2 x\, dx = x/2 - (\sin 2x)/4 + C;$
$\int \cos^2 x\, dx = x/2 + (\sin 2x)/4 + C$

Section 5.2 Exercises, pp. 359–364

1.

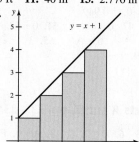

Displacement $= 105$ m
3. Subdivide the interval $[0, \pi/2]$ into several subintervals, which
will be the bases of rectangles that fit under the curve. The heights
of the rectangles are computed by taking the value of $\cos x$ at the
right-hand endpoint of each base. We calculate the area of each
rectangle and add them to get a lower bound on the area.
5. $\frac{1}{2}$; 1, 1.5, 2, 2.5, 3; 1, 1.5, 2, 2.5; 1.5, 2, 2.5, 3; 1.25, 1.75, 2.25, 2.75
7. Underestimate; the rectangles all fit under the curve.   **9. a.** 67 ft
b. 67.75 ft   **11.** 40 m   **13.** 2.776 m   **15.** 148.963 mi   **17.** 20; 25
19. a. c.

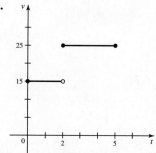

Left Riemann sum underestimates area.   Right Riemann sum overestimates area.

b. $\Delta x = 1; x_0 = 0, x_1 = 1, x_2 = 2, x_3 = 3, x_4 = 4$ **d.** 10, 14

21. a. c.

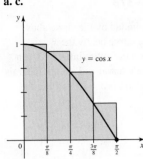
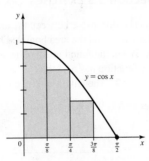

Left Riemann sum overestimates area.   Right Riemann sum underestimates area.

b. $\Delta x = \pi/8; 0, \pi/8, \pi/4, 3\pi/8, \pi/2$ **d.** 1.185; 0.791

23. a, c.

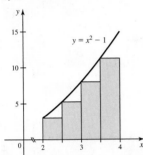
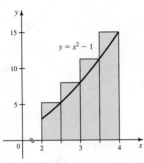

Left Riemann sum underestimates area.   Right Riemann sum overestimates area.

b. $\Delta x = \frac{1}{2}; 2, 2.5, 3, 3.5, 4$ **d.** 13.75; 19.75

25. a. c.

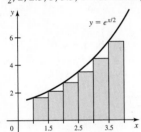
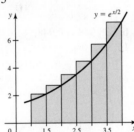

Left Riemann sum underestimates area.   Right Riemann sum overestimates area.

b. $\Delta x = 0.5; x_0 = 1, x_1 = 1.5, x_2 = 2, x_3 = 2.5, x_4 = 3, x_5 = 3.5,$
$x_6 = 4$ **d.** 10.105, 12.975   **27.** 670

29. a. c.

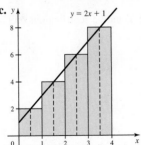

b. $\Delta x = 1; 0, 1, 2, 3, 4$ **d.** 20

31. a. c.

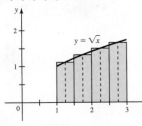

b. $\Delta x = \frac{1}{2}; 1, \frac{3}{2}, 2, \frac{5}{2}, 3$
d. 2.800

33. a. c.

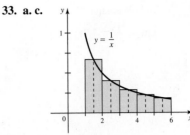

b. $\Delta x = 1; 1, 2, 3, 4, 5, 6$
d. 1.756

35. 5.5, 3.5   **37. b.** 110, 117.5

39. a. $\sum\limits_{k=1}^{5} k$ **b.** $\sum\limits_{k=1}^{6} (k + 3)$ **c.** $\sum\limits_{k=1}^{4} k^2$ **d.** $\sum\limits_{k=1}^{4} \frac{1}{k}$

41. a. 55   **b.** 48   **c.** 30   **d.** 60   **e.** 6   **f.** 6   **g.** 85   **h.** 0

43. a. Left: $\dfrac{1}{10} \sum\limits_{k=1}^{40} \sqrt{\dfrac{k - 1}{10}} \approx 5.227$; right: $\dfrac{1}{10} \sum\limits_{k=1}^{40} \sqrt{\dfrac{k}{10}} \approx 5.427$;

midpoint: $\dfrac{1}{10} \sum\limits_{k=1}^{40} \sqrt{\dfrac{2k - 1}{20}} \approx 5.335$ **b.** $\frac{16}{3}$

45. a. Left: $\dfrac{1}{15} \sum\limits_{k=1}^{75} \left[\left(\dfrac{k + 29}{15}\right)^2 - 1\right] \approx 105.170$;

right: $\dfrac{1}{15} \sum\limits_{k=1}^{75} \left[\left(\dfrac{k + 30}{15}\right)^2 - 1\right] \approx 108.170$;

midpoint: $\dfrac{1}{15} \sum\limits_{k=1}^{75} \left[\left(\dfrac{2k + 59}{30}\right)^2 - 1\right] \approx 106.665$ **b.** 106.7

47. a. True   **b.** False   **c.** True.   **49.** Right; $[1, 5]$; 4
51. Midpoint; $[2, 6]$; 4
53. a.

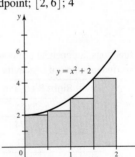

Left Riemann sum is
$\dfrac{23}{4} = 5.75$.

b.

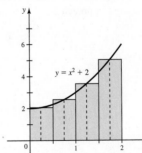

Midpoint Riemann
sum is $\dfrac{53}{8} = 6.625$.

c.

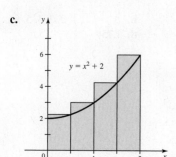

Right Riemann sum is $\dfrac{31}{4} = 7.75$.

55. Left sum: 34; right sum: 24 **57. a.** The object is speeding up on the interval $[0, 1]$, moving at a constant rate on $[1, 3]$, slowing down on $[3, 5]$, and maintaining a constant velocity on $[5, 6]$. **b.** 30 m **c.** 50 m **d.** $s(t) = 30 + 10t$ **59. a.** 14.5 g **b.** 29.5 g **c.** 44 g **d.** $\dfrac{19}{3}$ cm **61.** $s(t) = \begin{cases} 30t & \text{if } 0 \le t \le 2 \\ 50t - 40 & \text{if } 2 < t \le 2.5 \\ 44t - 25 & \text{if } 2.5 < t \le 3 \end{cases}$

63.

n	Midpoint Riemann sum
16	0.504
32	0.501
64	0.500

The sums approach 0.5.

65.

n	Midpoint Riemann sum
16	4.726
32	4.744
64	4.749

The sums approach 4.75.

69. Underestimates for decreasing functions, independent of concavity; overestimates for increasing functions, independent of concavity.

71.

n	Right Riemann sum
10	10.56
30	10.655
60	10.664
80	10.665

The sums approach $\dfrac{32}{3}$.

73.

n	Right Riemann sum
10	5.655
30	6.074
60	6.178
80	6.205

The sums approach 2π.

75.

n	Right Riemann sum
10	1.0844
30	1.0285
60	1.0143
80	1.0107

The sums approach 1.

77. $\displaystyle\sum_{k=1}^{50} \left(\dfrac{4k}{50} + 1\right) \cdot \dfrac{4}{50} = 12.160$

79. $\displaystyle\sum_{k=1}^{32} \left(3 + \dfrac{2k - 1}{8}\right)^3 \cdot \dfrac{1}{4} \approx 3639.125$

Section 5.3 Exercises, pp. 375–378

1. The difference between the area bounded by the curve above the x-axis and the area bounded by the curve below the x-axis **3.** When the function is nonnegative on the entire interval; when the function has negative values on the interval. **5.** Both integrals $= 0$. **7.** The length of the interval $[a, a]$ is $a - a = 0$, so the net area is 0. **9.** $\dfrac{a^2}{2}$

11. a.

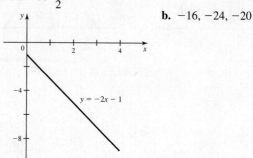

b. $-16, -24, -20$

13. a.

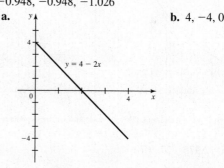

b. $-0.948, -0.948, -1.026$

15. a.

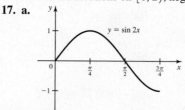

b. $4, -4, 0$

c. Positive contributions on $[0, 2)$; negative contributions on $(2, 4]$

17. a.

$y = \sin 2x$

b. $\approx 0.735, \approx 0.146, \approx 0.530$ **c.** Positive contribution on $(0, \pi/2)$; negative contribution on $(\pi/2, 3\pi/4]$

19. a. 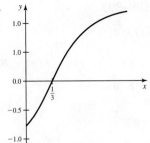   **b.** 0.0823; 0.555; 0.326

c. Positive contributions on $\left(\frac{1}{3}, 1\right]$; negative contributions on $\left[0, \frac{1}{3}\right)$

21. $\displaystyle\int_0^2 (x^2 + 1)\, dx$ **23.** $\displaystyle\int_1^2 x \ln x \, dx$

25. 16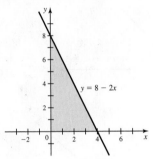

27. $-\frac{5}{2}$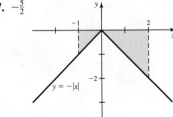

29. 4π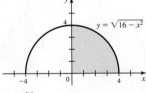

31. 26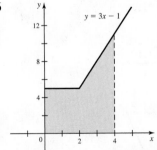

33. 16   **35.** 6   **37.** π **39.** -2π **41. a.** -32 **b.** $-\frac{32}{3}$
c. -64 **d.** Not possible   **43. a.** 10   **b.** -3 **c.** -16
d. 3   **45. a.** $\frac{3}{2}$ **b.** $-\frac{3}{4}$ **47.** 6   **49.** 104   **51.** 18
53. a. True   **b.** True   **c.** True   **d.** False   **e.** False

55. a.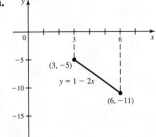

b. $\Delta x = \frac{1}{2}$; 3, 3.5, 4, 4.5, 5, 5.5, 6   **c.** -22.5; -25.5
d. The left Riemann sum overestimates the integral; the right Riemann sum underestimates the integral.

57. a.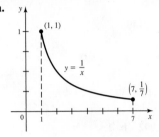

b. $\Delta x = 1$; 1, 2, 3, 4, 5, 6, 7   **c.** 2.450, 1.593   **d.** The left Riemann sum overestimates the integral; the right Riemann sum underestimates the integral.   **59. a.** -2 **b.** 24   **c.** -10

61. 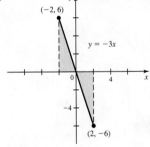   The area is 12; the net area is 0.

63. 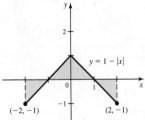   The area is 2; the net area is 0.

65. 17   **67.** $25\pi/2$ **69.** 25   **73.** For any such partition on the interval $[0, 1]$, the grid points are $x_k = k/n$, for $k = 0, 1, \ldots, n$. That is, x_k is rational for each k so that $f(x_k) = 1$, for $k = 0, 1, \ldots, n$. Therefore, the left, right, and midpoint Riemann sums are $\displaystyle\sum_{k=1}^{n} 1 \cdot (1/n) = 1$.

75. a. Left: $\displaystyle\sum_{k=1}^{20} \left[\left(\frac{k-1}{20}\right)^2 + 1\right] \cdot \frac{1}{20} = 1.309$;

right: $\displaystyle\sum_{k=1}^{20} \left[\left(\frac{k}{20}\right)^2 + 1\right] \cdot \frac{1}{20} = 1.359$;

left: $\displaystyle\sum_{k=1}^{50}\left[\left(\frac{k-1}{50}\right)^2+1\right]\cdot\frac{1}{50}=1.323;$

right: $\displaystyle\sum_{k=1}^{50}\left[\left(\frac{k}{50}\right)^2+1\right]\cdot\frac{1}{50}=1.343;$

left: $\displaystyle\sum_{k=1}^{100}\left[\left(\frac{k-1}{100}\right)^2+1\right]\cdot\frac{1}{100}=1.328;$

right: $\displaystyle\sum_{k=1}^{100}\left[\left(\frac{k}{100}\right)^2+1\right]\cdot\frac{1}{100}=1.338$ **b.** $\dfrac{4}{3}$

77. a. Left: $\displaystyle\sum_{k=1}^{20}\cos^{-1}\left(\frac{k-1}{20}\right)\frac{1}{20}=1.0362;$

right: $\displaystyle\sum_{k=1}^{20}\cos^{-1}\left(\frac{k}{20}\right)\frac{1}{20}=0.958;$

left: $\displaystyle\sum_{k=1}^{50}\cos^{-1}\left(\frac{k-1}{50}\right)\frac{1}{50}=1.0149;$

right: $\displaystyle\sum_{k=1}^{50}\cos^{-1}\left(\frac{k}{50}\right)\frac{1}{50}=0.983;$

left: $\displaystyle\sum_{k=1}^{100}\cos^{-1}\left(\frac{k-1}{100}\right)\frac{1}{100}=1.00757;$

right: $\displaystyle\sum_{k=1}^{100}\cos^{-1}\left(\frac{k}{100}\right)\frac{1}{100}=0.992$ **b.** 1.

79. a. Left: $\displaystyle\sum_{k=1}^{20}\pi\cos\left(\frac{\pi}{2}\left(-1+\frac{2(k-1)}{20}\right)\right)\cdot\frac{2}{20}\approx3.992;$

right: $\displaystyle\sum_{k=1}^{20}\pi\cos\left(\frac{\pi}{2}\left(-1+\frac{2k}{20}\right)\right)\cdot\frac{2}{20}\approx3.992;$

left: $\displaystyle\sum_{k=1}^{50}\pi\cos\left(\frac{\pi}{2}\left(-1+\frac{2(k-1)}{50}\right)\right)\cdot\frac{2}{50}\approx3.999;$

right: $\displaystyle\sum_{k=1}^{50}\pi\cos\left(\frac{\pi}{2}\left(-1+\frac{2k}{50}\right)\right)\cdot\frac{2}{50}\approx3.999;$

left: $\displaystyle\sum_{k=1}^{100}\pi\cos\left(\frac{\pi}{2}\left(-1+\frac{2(k-1)}{100}\right)\right)\cdot\frac{2}{100}\approx4.000;$

right: $\displaystyle\sum_{k=1}^{100}\pi\cos\left(\frac{\pi}{2}\left(-1+\frac{2k}{100}\right)\right)\cdot\frac{2}{100}\approx4.000$ **b.** 4

81. a. $\displaystyle\sum_{k=1}^{n}\sqrt{2\left(1+\left(k-\frac{1}{2}\right)\frac{3}{n}\right)}\cdot\frac{3}{n}$

b.

n	Midpoint Riemann sum
20	9.334
50	9.333
100	9.333

Estimate: 9.33

83. a. $\displaystyle\sum_{k=1}^{n}\left[4\left(k-\frac{1}{2}\right)\frac{4}{n}-\left(\left(k-\frac{1}{2}\right)\frac{4}{n}\right)^2\right]\cdot\frac{4}{n}$

b.

n	Midpoint Riemann sum
20	10.680
50	10.669
100	10.667

Estimate: 10.67

85. a. -18.223 **b.** -1.330 **c.** 23.543 **d.** $18.223, 1.330, 23.543$
e. The midpoint Riemann sum is most accurate.

Section 5.4 Exercises, pp. 389–393

1. A is an antiderivative of f; $A'(x)=f(x)$

3. Let f be continuous on $[a,b]$. Then $\displaystyle\int_a^b f(x)\,dx=F(b)-F(a)$, where F is any antiderivative of f.   **5.** Increasing
7. The derivative of the integral of f is f, or
$$\frac{d}{dx}\left(\int_a^x f(t)\,dt\right)=f(x).$$ **9.** $f(x), 0$
11. a. 0   **b.** -9 **c.** 25   **d.** 0   **e.** 16
13. a. $A(x)=5x$

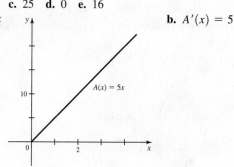

b. $A'(x)=5$

15. a. $A(x)=5x+25$

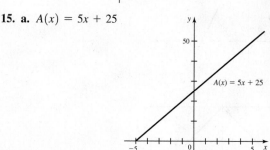

b. $A'(x)=5$

17. a. $A(2)=2, A(4)=8; A(x)=\frac{1}{2}x^2$
b. $F(4)=6, F(6)=16; F(x)=\frac{1}{2}x^2-2$
c. $A(x)-F(x)=\frac{1}{2}x^2-\left(\frac{1}{2}x^2-2\right)=2$
19. a.

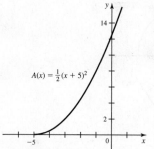

b. $A'(x)=\left[\frac{1}{2}(x+5)^2\right]'=x+5=f(x)$
21. a.

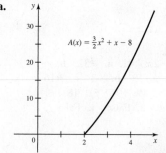

b. $A'(x) = (\frac{3}{2}x^2 + x - 8)' = 3x + 1 = f(x)$ **23.** $\frac{7}{3}$

25. $-\frac{125}{6}$

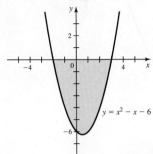

$y = x^2 - x - 6$

27. $-\frac{10}{3}$

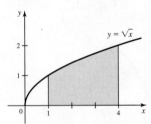

$y = x^2 - 9$

29. 16   **31.** $\frac{7}{6}$ **33.** 8   **35.** $-\frac{32}{3}$ **37.** $-\frac{5}{2}$ **39.** 1   **41.** $-\frac{3}{8}$

43. $\frac{9}{2}$ **45.** $3 \ln 2$ **47.** $\sqrt{2}/4$ **49.** $\frac{\pi}{12}$ **51.** (i) $\frac{14}{3}$ (ii) $\frac{14}{3}$

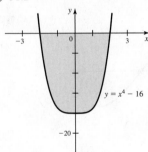

$y = \sqrt{x}$

53. (i) -51.2 (ii) 51.2

$y = x^4 - 16$

55. Area $= \frac{94}{3}$ **57.** Area $= \ln 2$ **59.** Area $= 2$ **61.** $x^2 + x + 1$

63. $3/x^4$ **65.** $-\sqrt{x^4 + 1}$ **67.** $2\sqrt{1 + x^2}$

69. a–C, b–B, c–D, d–A

71. a. $x = 0, x \approx 3$ **b.** Local min at $x \approx 1.5$; local max at $x \approx 8.5$ **c.**

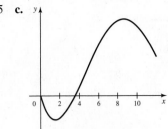

73. a. $x = 0, 10$ **b.** Local max at $x = 5$

c.

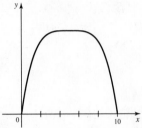

75. $-\pi, -\pi + \frac{9}{2}, -\pi + 9, 5 - \pi$

77. a. $A(x) = e^x - 1$ **b.**

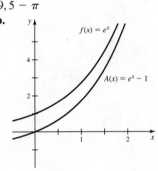

$f(x) = e^x$

$A(x) = e^x - 1$

c. $A(\ln 2) = 1$; $A(\ln 4) = 3$

79. a. $A(x) = \frac{1}{\pi} \sin \pi x$

b.

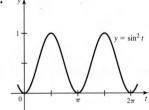

$f(x) = \cos \pi x$

$A(x) = \frac{1}{\pi} \sin \pi x$

c. $A\left(\frac{1}{2}\right) = \frac{1}{\pi}$; $A(1) = 0$

81. a.

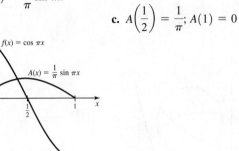

$y = \sin^2 t$

b. $g'(x) = \sin^2 x$

c.

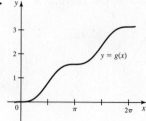

83. a.

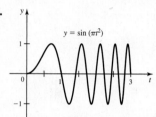

b. $g'(x) = \sin(\pi x^2)$

c.

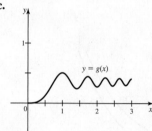

85. a. True **b.** True **c.** False **d.** True **e.** True
87. $\frac{2}{3}$ **89.** 1 **91.** $\frac{45}{4}$ **93.** $\frac{3}{2} + 4\ln 2$
95.

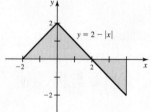

Area $= 6$
97.

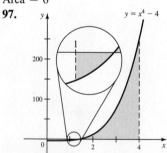

Area ≈ 194.051
99. $f(8) - f(3)$ **101.** $-(\cos^4 x + 6)\sin x$ **103.** $\frac{9}{t}$

105. a.

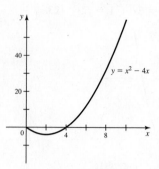

b. $b = 6$ **c.** $b = \dfrac{3a}{2}$

107. 3 **109.** $f(x) = -2\sin x + 3$ **111.** $\pi/2 \approx 1.571$
113. $(S'(x))^2 + \left(\dfrac{S''(x)}{2x}\right)^2 = (\sin x^2)^2 + \left(\dfrac{2x\cos x^2}{2x}\right)^2 =$

$\sin^2 x^2 + \cos^2 x^2 = 1$ **115.** The summation relationship is a discrete analog of the Fundamental Theorem. Summing the difference quotient and integrating the derivative over the relevant interval both give the difference of the function values at the endpoints.

Section 5.5 Exercises, pp. 398–400

1. If f is odd, the region between f and the positive x-axis and between f and the negative x-axis are reflections of each other through the origin. Thus, on $[-a, a]$, the areas cancel each other out.
3. Even; even **5.** If f is continuous on $[a, b]$, then there is a c
in (a, b) such that $f(c) = \dfrac{1}{b-a}\displaystyle\int_a^b f(x)\,dx$. **7.** 0 **9.** $\frac{1000}{3}$
11. $-\frac{88}{3}$ **13.** 0 **15.** 0
17. 0

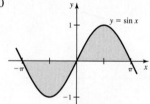

19. 0

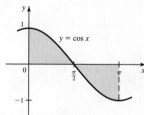

21. 0

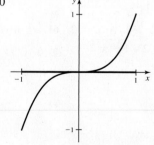

23. $\dfrac{\pi}{4}$

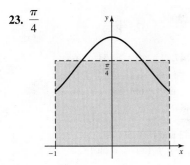

25. $\dfrac{1}{(e-1)}$

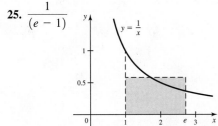

27. $\dfrac{2}{\pi}$ **29.** $1/(n+1)$

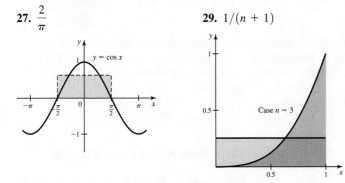

31. 2000   **33.** $20/\pi$ **35.** 2   **37.** $a/\sqrt{3}$ **39.** $\pm\frac{1}{2}$
41. a. True   **b.** True   **c.** True   **d.** False
43. 2   **45.** 0   **47.** 420 ft   **51. a.** 9   **b.** 0
53. $f(g(-x)) = f(g(x)) \Rightarrow$ the integrand is even;
$$\int_{-a}^{a} f(g(x))\, dx = 2\int_{0}^{a} f(g(x))\, dx$$
55. $p(g(-x)) = p(g(x)) \Rightarrow$ the integrand is even;
$$\int_{-a}^{a} p(g(x))\, dx = 2\int_{0}^{2} p(g(x))\, dx$$
57. a. $a/6$ **b.** $(3 \pm \sqrt{3})/6$, independent of a **61.** $c = \sqrt[4]{12}$
65.

Even	Even
Even	Odd

Section 5.6 Exercises, pp. 408–411

1. The Chain Rule   **3.** $u = g(x)$ **5.** We let a become $g(a)$ and b
become $g(b)$.   **7.** $\dfrac{x}{2} - \dfrac{\sin 2x}{4} + C$ **9.** $\dfrac{(x+1)^{13}}{13} + C$
11. $\dfrac{(2x+1)^{3/2}}{3} + C$ **13.** $\dfrac{(x^2+1)^5}{5} + C$ **15.** $\frac{1}{4}\sin^4 x + C$
17. $\dfrac{(x^2-1)^{100}}{100} + C$ **19.** $-\dfrac{(1-4x^3)^{1/2}}{3} + C$
21. $\dfrac{(x^2+x)^{11}}{11} + C$ **23.** $\dfrac{(x^4+16)^7}{28} + C$ **25.** $\dfrac{\sin^{-1} 3x}{3} + C$

27. $\dfrac{(x^6-3x^2)^5}{30} + C$ **29.** $\frac{1}{2}\tan^{-1} 2x + C$ **31.** $2\sec^{-1} 2x + C$
33. $\frac{2}{3}(x-4)^{1/2}(x+8) + C$ **35.** $\frac{3}{5}(x+4)^{2/3}(x-6) + C$
37. $\frac{3}{112}(2x+1)^{4/3}(8x-3) + C$ **39.** $-\frac{1}{6}\ln|\cos 6x| + C$
41. $x + \dfrac{1}{4}\ln|\sin 4x| + C$ **43.** $-\dfrac{1}{2}\ln|\cos x^2| + C$
45. $\ln|\sin(1+t)| + C$ **47.** $\frac{7}{2}$ **49.** $\frac{1}{3}$ **51.** $(e^9 - 1)/3$
53. $\sqrt{2} - 1$ **55.** $\dfrac{\pi}{6}$ **57.** $\frac{1}{2}\ln 17$ **59.** $\dfrac{\pi}{9}$ **61.** $\ln 2$ **63.** $\sqrt{3}$
65. $-\dfrac{1}{2}\ln(1+\sqrt{2})$ **67.** π **69.** $\dfrac{\theta}{2} - \dfrac{1}{4}\sin\left(\dfrac{6\theta+\pi}{3}\right) + C$
71. $\dfrac{\pi}{4}$ **73.** $\ln\dfrac{9}{8}$ **75. a.** True   **b.** True   **c.** False
d. False   **e.** False   **77.** $\frac{1}{10}\tan 10x + C$ **79.** $\frac{1}{2}\tan^2 x + C$
81. $\frac{1}{7}\sec^7 x + C$ **83.** $\frac{1}{3}$ **85.** $\frac{3}{4}(4 - 3^{2/3})$ **87.** $\frac{32}{3}$ **89.** $-\ln 3$
91. $\frac{1}{7}$ **93.** 1   **95.** $\frac{64}{5}$ **97.** $\frac{2}{3}$; constant   **99. a.** π/p **b.** 0
101. a. 160   **b.** $\dfrac{4800}{49} \approx 98$ **c.** $\Delta p = \displaystyle\int_{0}^{T} \dfrac{200}{(t+1)^r}\, dt$; decreases
as r increases   **d.** $r \approx 1.278$ **e.** As $t \to \infty$, the population
approaches 100.   **103.** $2/\pi$ **107.** One area is $\displaystyle\int_{4}^{9} \dfrac{(\sqrt{x}-1)^2}{2\sqrt{x}}\, dx$.
Changing variables by letting $u = \sqrt{x} - 1$ yields $\int_{1}^{2} u^2\, du$, which is the
other area.   **109.** $7297/12$ **111.** $\dfrac{(f^{(p)}(x))^{n+1}}{n+1} + C$
113. $\frac{2}{15}(3 - 2a)(1+a)^{3/2} + \frac{4}{15}a^{5/2}$ **115.** $\frac{1}{3}\sec^3\theta + C$
117. a. $I = \frac{1}{8}x - \frac{1}{32}\sin 4x + C$ **b.** $I = \frac{1}{8}x - \frac{1}{32}\sin 4x + C$
121. $\dfrac{4}{3}(-2 + \sqrt{1+x})\sqrt{1 + \sqrt{1+x}} + C$ **123.** $-4 + \sqrt{17}$

Section 5.7 Exercises, pp. 419–422

1. $\frac{1}{2}$ **3.** The Trapezoid Rule approximates areas under curves using
trapezoids.   **5.** $-1, 1, 3, 5, 7, 9$ **7.** $1.6 \times 10^{-3}; 5.1 \times 10^{-4}$
9. $1.7 \times 10^{-3}; 6.3 \times 10^{-4}$ **11.** 576; 640; 656   **13.** 0.644
15. 704; 672; 664   **17.** 0.622   **19.** $M(25) = 0.637$,
$T(25) = 0.636; 6.6 \times 10^{-4}, 1.3 \times 10^{-3}$
21.

n	$M(n)$	Abs. Error $M(n)$	$T(n)$	Abs. Error $T(n)$
4	99	1.0	102	2.0
8	99.75	2.5×10^{-1}	100.5	5×10^{-1}
16	99.9375	6.3×10^{-2}	100.125	1.3×10^{-1}
32	99.984375	1.6×10^{-2}	100.03125	3.1×10^{-2}

23.

n	$M(n)$	Abs. Error $M(n)$	$T(n)$	Abs. Error $T(n)$
4	1.50968181	9.7×10^{-3}	1.48067370	1.9×10^{-2}
8	1.50241228	2.4×10^{-3}	1.49517776	4.8×10^{-3}
16	1.50060256	6.0×10^{-4}	1.49879502	1.2×10^{-3}
32	1.50015061	1.5×10^{-4}	1.49969879	3.0×10^{-4}

25. Because the integrand has odd symmetry about the midpoint of
the interval of integration, the Trapezoid Rule and the Midpoint Rule
give zero with even values of n.

27. 54.5 using Trapezoid Rule
29. a. Left sum: 204.917; right sum: 261.375; Trapezoid Rule: 233.146; the approximations measure the average temperature of the curling iron on $[0, 120]$. **b.** Left sum: underestimate; right sum: overestimate; Trapezoid Rule: underestimate **c.** 305 °F is the change in temperature over $[0, 120]$. **31. a.** True **b.** False **c.** True
33.

n	$M(n)$	Abs. Error $M(n)$	$T(n)$	Abs. Error $T(n)$
4	0.40635058	1.4×10^{-6}	0.40634782	1.4×10^{-6}
8	0.40634921	7.6×10^{-10}	0.40634921	7.6×10^{-10}
16	0.40634921	6.6×10^{-13}	0.40634921	6.6×10^{-13}
32	0.40634921	8.9×10^{-16}	0.40634921	7.8×10^{-16}

35.

n	$M(n)$	Abs. Error $M(n)$	$T(n)$	Abs. Error $T(n)$
4	4.72531819	1.2×10^{-4}	4.72507878	1.2×10^{-4}
8	4.72519851	9.1×10^{-9}	4.72519849	9.1×10^{-9}
16	4.72519850	0.	4.72519850	8.9×10^{-16}
32	4.72519850	0.	4.72519850	8.9×10^{-16}

37. Approximations will vary; exact value is $38.754\ldots$.
39. Approximations will vary; approximately 68.269%
41. a. Approximately 1.6×10^{11} barrels
b. Approximately 7.3×10^{10} barrels **43. a.** 5907.5 **b.** 5965
c. 5917 **45. a.** $T(40) = 0.875$ **b.** $f''(x) = e^x \cos e^x - e^{2x} \sin e^x$
d. $E_T \le \dfrac{1}{3200}$ **47.** Overestimate

Chapter 5 Review Exercises, pp. 422–426

1. a. True **b.** False **c.** True **d.** True **e.** False **f.** True
g. True **3.** $\frac{4}{3}x^3 + 2x^2 + x + C$ **5.** $-\dfrac{1}{x} + \dfrac{4}{3}x^{-3/2} + C$
7. $\theta + \frac{1}{3}\sin 3\theta + C$ **9.** $\frac{1}{2}\sec 2x + C$ **11.** $12 \ln |x| + C$
13. $\tan^{-1}x + C$ **15.** $\frac{4}{7}x^{7/4} + \frac{2}{7}x^{7/2} + C$
17. $f(t) = -\cos t + t^2 + 6$
19. $h(x) = \dfrac{x}{2} - \dfrac{1}{4}\sin 2x + \left(\dfrac{1}{2} + \dfrac{\sin 2}{4}\right)$
21. $v(t) = -9.8t + 120$; $s(t) = -4.9t^2 + 120t + 125$; the rocket reaches a maximum height of 859.694 m at time $t = 12.245$ s and then falls to the ground, hitting at time $t = 25.491$ s. **23. a.** 8.5 **b.** -4.5 **c.** 0 **d.** 11.5
25. a.   **b.** 75

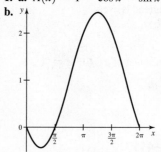

c. The area is the distance the diver ascends. **27.** 4π
29. a. $1[(3 \cdot 2 - 2) + (3 \cdot 3 - 2) + (3 \cdot 4 - 2)] \approx 21$
b. $\displaystyle\sum_{k=1}^{n} \dfrac{3}{n}\left[3\left(1 + \dfrac{3k}{n}\right) - 2\right]$ **c.** $\dfrac{33}{2}$ **31.** $-\dfrac{16}{3}$

33. 56 **35.** $\displaystyle\int_0^4 (1 + x^5)\, dx = \dfrac{2060}{3}$ **37.** $\frac{212}{5}$

39. 20 **41.** 0 **43.** $\frac{7}{6}$ **45.** $\frac{\pi}{6}$ **47.** 1 **49.** $\frac{\pi}{2}$ **51.** $\frac{1}{3}\ln\frac{9}{2}$
53. $\frac{1}{2}\ln 3$ **55.** $\frac{1}{2}\ln 2$ **57.** $\frac{256}{3}$ **59.** 8 **61.** $-\frac{4}{15}; \frac{4}{15}$
63. a. 20 **b.** 0 **c.** 80 **d.** 10 **e.** 0 **65.** 18
67. 10 **69.** Not enough information
71. Displacement $= 0$; distance $= 20/\pi$
73. a. $5/2, c = 3.5$ **b.** $3, c = 3$ and $c = 5$ **75.** 24
77. $f(1) = 0$; $f'(x) > 0$ on $[1, \infty)$; $f''(x) < 0$ on $[1, \infty)$

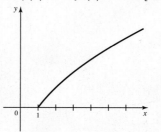

79. a. $-\frac{3}{2}, -\frac{11}{6}$ **b.** x **c.** $\frac{x^2}{2}$ **d.** $0, \frac{1}{2}$ **e.** $\frac{3}{2}$
85. $\cos\dfrac{1}{x} + C$ **87.** $\ln |\tan^{-1} x| + C$ **89.** $\ln (e^x + e^{-x}) + C$
91. Differentiating the first equation gives the second equation; no
93. a. Increasing on $(-\infty, 1)$ and $(2, \infty)$; decreasing on $(1, 2)$
b. Concave up on $(\frac{13}{8}, \infty)$; concave down on $(-\infty, \frac{13}{8})$
c. Local max at $x = 1$; local min at $x = 2$
d. Inflection point at $x = \frac{13}{8}$ **95. a.** $T(6) = 9.125, M(6) = 8.938$
b. $T(12) = 9.031$ $M(12) = 8.984$ **97.** e^4

AP® Practice, Section 1, Parts A and B, pp. 427–428

1. A **2.** C **3.** D **4.** C **5.** E **6.** B **7.** A **8.** B **9.** C
10. D **11.** E **12.** D **13.** B **14.** D **15.** A **16.** A
17. C **18.** E

AP® Practice, Section 2, Parts A and B, pp. 428–429

1. a. $A(x) = 1 - \cos x - \sin x$
b.

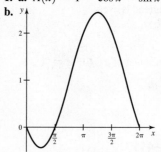

c. A local minimum of $1 - \sqrt{2}$ occurs at $x = \pi/4$; a local maximum of $1 + \sqrt{2}$ occurs at $x = 5\pi/4$. **d.** The roots of f correspond to the values of x where A has a local extreme value.
2. a. $x = -0.322$ is excluded. **b.** The area of R_1 is approximately 23.557 and the area of R_2 is 22.763. Therefore, R_1 has the greater area.
c. 2.628 **3. a.** The temperature at $t = 8$ is changing at approximately 4.5°F/hr. **b.** 32°F; the change in temperature from 6 A.M. to 6 P.M. **c.** 74.417°F; the approximate average temperature between 6 A.M. and 6 P.M. **d.** 77.458°F

4. a.

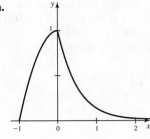

b. Yes; $f(0) = \lim_{x \to 0} f(x) = 1$

c. $f'(x) = \begin{cases} -2x & \text{if } x < 0 \\ -2e^{-2x} & \text{if } x \geq 0 \end{cases}$

$\lim_{x \to 0^-} f'(x)$ does not exist because $\lim_{x \to 0^-} f'(x) = 0$ and

$\lim_{x \to 0^+} f'(x) = -2$. Therefore, $f'(x)$ is not continuous at $x = 0$.

d. $g(x) = \begin{cases} \dfrac{2}{3} + x - \dfrac{x^3}{3} & \text{if } x < 0 \\ \dfrac{7}{6} - \dfrac{1}{2}e^{-2x} & \text{if } x \geq 0 \end{cases}$;

g is continuous at $x = 0$ because $g(0) = \lim_{x \to 0} g(x) = \dfrac{2}{3}$.

e. $\dfrac{7e^4 - 3}{18e^4} \approx 0.386$

5. a. $f'(x) = e^{-x^2}$ and $f''(x) = -2xe^{-x^2}$
b. f is increasing on $(-\infty, \infty)$; f is never decreasing.
c. f is concave up on $(-\infty, 0)$; f is concave down on $(0, \infty)$.
d. The maximum slope of f is 1 and it occurs at $x = 0$.
e. The range of f is $\left(-\dfrac{\sqrt{\pi}}{2}, \dfrac{\sqrt{\pi}}{2} \right)$.

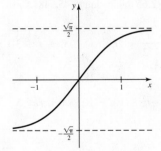

6. a. $v(t) = -0.5t + 30$, for $t \geq 0$ **b.** 60 s   **c.** 900 m
7. a. $g(-2) = -2$; $g(4) = 0$ **b.** Increasing on $(-2, 2)$;
decreasing on $(2, 6)$ **c.** $g'(0) = 2$ **d.** $g''(0) = f'(0)$, which does
not exist   **e.** $x = 2$; the absolute maximum value is π.

CHAPTER 6

Section 6.1 Exercises, pp. 440–445

1. The position $s(t)$ is the location of the object relative to the origin. The
displacement is the change in position between time $t = a$ and $t = b$. The
distance traveled between $t = a$ and $t = b$ is $\int_a^b |v(t)| \, dt$, where $v(t)$
is the velocity at time t.   **3.** The displacement between $t = a$ and
$t = b$ is $\int_a^b v(t) \, dt$.   **5.** $Q(t) = Q(0) + \int_0^t Q'(x) \, dx$

7. a.

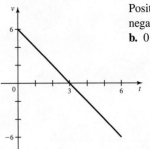

Positive direction for $0 \leq t < 3$;
negative direction for $3 < t \leq 6$
b. 0   **c.** 18 m

9. a.

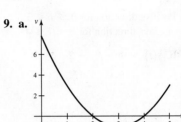

Positive direction for
$0 \leq t < 2$ and $4 < t \leq 5$;
negative direction for
$2 < t < 4$ **b.** $\dfrac{20}{3}$ m

c. $\dfrac{28}{3}$ m

11. a.

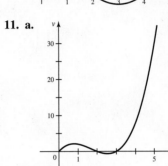

Positive direction for
$0 < t < 2$ and $3 < t \leq 5$;
negative direction for $2 < t < 3$
b. $\dfrac{275}{12}$ m   **c.** $\dfrac{95}{4}$ m

13. a.

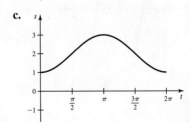

Positive direction for
$0 < t < \pi$; negative
direction for $\pi < t < 2\pi$
b. $s(t) = -\cos t + 2$

c.

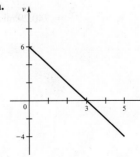

15. a.

Positive direction for
$0 \leq t < 3$; negative direction
for $3 < t \leq 5$

b. $s(t) = 6t - t^2$ **c.**

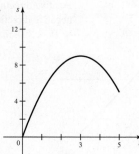

17. a.

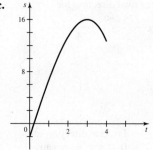

Positive direction for $0 \le t < 3$; negative direction for $3 < t \le 4$

b. $s(t) = 9t - \dfrac{t^3}{3} - 2$

c.

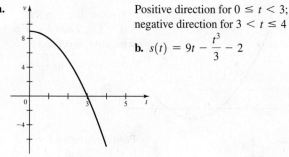

19. a. $s(t) = 2 \sin \pi t$ **b.**

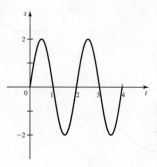

c. $\dfrac{3}{2}, \dfrac{7}{2}, \dfrac{11}{2}$ **d.** $\dfrac{1}{2}, \dfrac{5}{2}, \dfrac{9}{2}$

21. a. $s(t) = 10t(48 - t^2)$

b. 880 mi

c. $\dfrac{2720\sqrt{6}}{9} \approx 740.29$ mi

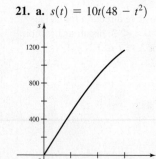

23.

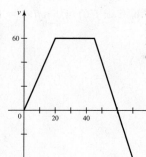

a. Velocity is a maximum for $20 \le t \le 45$; $v = 0$ at $t = 0$ and $t = 60$ **b.** 1200 m
c. 2550 m **d.** 2100 m

25. $v(t) = -32t + 70; s(t) = -16t^2 + 70t + 10$
27. $v(t) = -9.8t + 20; s(t) = -4.9t^2 + 20t$
29. $v(t) = -\dfrac{1}{200}t^2 + 10; s(t) = -\dfrac{1}{600}t^3 + 10t$
31. $v(t) = \dfrac{1}{2}\sin 2t + 5; s(t) = -\dfrac{1}{4}\cos 2t + 5t + \dfrac{29}{4}$

33.

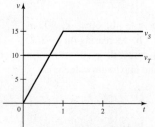

a. $s(t) = 44t^2$
b. 704 ft
c. $\sqrt{30} \approx 5.477$ s
d. $\dfrac{5\sqrt{33}}{11} \approx 2.611$ s
e. Approx. 180.023 ft

35. 6.154 mi; 1.465 mi **37. a.** 27,250 barrels **b.** 31,000 barrels **c.** 4000 barrels **39. a.** 2639 people
b. $P(t) = 250 + 20t^{3/2} + 30t$ **41. a.** 1897 cells; 1900 cells
b. $N(t) = -400e^{-0.25t} + 1900$ **43.** -2.65 million km^2 **45.** 487.5 m
47. a. False **b.** True **c.** True **d.** False

49. a. 3 **b.** $\dfrac{13}{3}$ **c.** 3 **d.** $s(t) = \begin{cases} -\dfrac{t^2}{2} + 2t, & 0 \le t \le 3 \\[2mm] \dfrac{3t^2}{2} - 10t + 18, & 3 < t \le 4 \\[2mm] -t^2 + 10t - 22, & 4 < t \le 5 \end{cases}$

51. $\dfrac{2}{3}$ **53.** $\dfrac{25}{3}$

55. a.

b. Theo **c.** Sasha **d.** Theo hits the 10-mi mark before Sasha; Sasha and Theo hit the 15-mi mark at the same time; Sasha hits the 20-mi mark before Theo. **e.** Sasha **f.** Theo

57. a. Abe initially runs into a headwind; Bess initially runs with a tailwind.

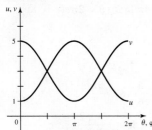

b. 3 mi/hr for both runners   **c.** $\pi\sqrt{5}/25$ hr for both runners

59. a. $\dfrac{10^7(1 - e^{-kt})}{k}$ **b.** $\dfrac{10^7}{k}$ = total number of barrels of oil

extracted if the nation extracts the oil indefinitely where it is

assumed that the nation has at least $\dfrac{10^7}{k}$ barrels of oil in reserve

c. $k = \dfrac{1}{200} = 0.005$ **d.** Approximately 138.6 yr

61. a. $\dfrac{120}{\pi} + 40 \approx 78.20 \text{ m}^3$

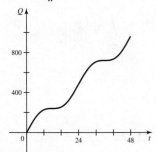

b. $Q(t) = 20\left[t + \dfrac{12}{\pi} \sin\left(\dfrac{\pi}{12}t\right)\right]$ **c.** Approximately 122.6 hr

63. a. $V(t) = 5 + \cos\dfrac{\pi t}{2}$ **b.** 15 breaths/min   **c.** 2 L, 6 L

65. a. 7200 MWh or 2.592×10^{13} J   **b.** 16,000 kg; 5,840,000 kg
c. 450 g; 164,250 g   **d.** About 1500 turbines   **67.** It costs more
to manufacture items 300–400 ($18,250) than to manufacture items
500–600 ($17,250).

69. $\displaystyle\int_a^b f'(x)dx = f(b) - f(a) = g(b) - g(a) = \int_a^b g'(x)dx$

Section 6.2 Exercises, pp. 450–454

1.

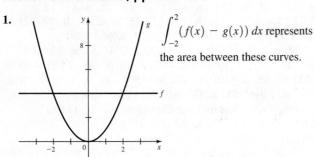

$\displaystyle\int_{-2}^2 (f(x) - g(x))\, dx$ represents
the area between these curves.

3. See solution to Exercise 1.

5. $\dfrac{9}{2}$ **7.** $\dfrac{5}{2} - \dfrac{1}{\ln 2}$ **9.** $\dfrac{25}{2}$ **11.** $\dfrac{81}{32}$ **13.** $\pi - 2$ **15.** $2 - \sqrt{2}$

17. $\dfrac{1}{2} + \ln 2$ **19.** $\dfrac{7}{3}$ **21.** 3   **23.** 2   **25.** $\dfrac{125}{2}$

27. a. $\displaystyle\int_{-\sqrt{2}}^{-1}(2 - x^2)\, dx + \int_{-1}^0 (-x)\, dx$ **b.** $\displaystyle\int_{-1}^0 (y + \sqrt{y + 2})\, dy$

29. a. $\displaystyle 2\int_{-3}^{-2}\sqrt{x + 3}\, dx + \int_{-2}^6 \left(\sqrt{x + 3} - \dfrac{x}{2}\right) dx$

b. $\displaystyle\int_{-1}^3 (2y - (y^2 - 3))\, dy$

31. 9

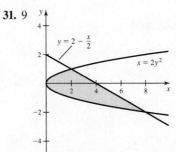

33. $\dfrac{64}{5}$ **35.** $\ln 2$ **37.** $\dfrac{5}{24}$ **39. a.** False   **b.** False   **c.** True

41. $\dfrac{1}{6}$ **43.** $\dfrac{9}{2}$ **45.** $\dfrac{32}{3}$ **47.** $\dfrac{63}{4}$ **49.** $\dfrac{15}{8} - 2\ln 2$

51. a. Area $(R_1) = \dfrac{p - 1}{2(p + 1)}$ for all positive integers p;

area $(R_2) = \dfrac{q - 1}{2(q + 1)}$ for all positive integers q; they are equal.

b. R_1 has greater area.   **c.** R_2 has greater area.

53. $\dfrac{17}{3}$ **55.** $\dfrac{81}{2}$ **57.** $\dfrac{n - 1}{2(n + 1)}$ **59.** $A_n = \dfrac{n - 1}{n + 1}$; $\displaystyle\lim_{n\to\infty} A_n = 1$;

the region approximates a square with side length of 1.

61. $k = 1 - \dfrac{1}{\sqrt{2}}$ **63.** $k = \dfrac{1}{2}$ **65. a.** The lowest $p\%$

of households owns exactly $p\%$ of the wealth for $0 \le p \le 100$.
b. The function must be one-to-one and its graph must lie below
$y = x$ because the poorest $p\%$ cannot own more than $p\%$ of the
wealth.   **c.** $p = 1.1$ is most equitable; $p = 4$ is least equitable.

e. $G(p) = \dfrac{p - 1}{p + 1}$ **f.** $0 \le G \le 1$ for $p \ge 1$ **g.** $\dfrac{5}{18}$ **67.** -1

69. $\dfrac{4}{9}$ **71. a.** $F(a) = \dfrac{ab^3}{6} - \dfrac{b^4}{12}$; $F(a) = 0$ if $a = \dfrac{b}{2}$

b. Because $A'\left(\dfrac{b}{2}\right) = 0$ and $A''\left(\dfrac{b}{2}\right) > 0$, A has a minimum

at $a = \dfrac{b}{2}$. The maximum value of $\dfrac{b^4}{12}$ occurs if $a = 0$ or $a = b$.

73. a.

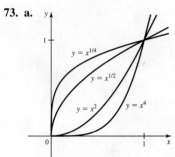

b. $A_n(x)$ is the net area of the region between the graphs of f and g from 0 to x.   **c.** $x = n^{n/(n^2-1)}$; the root decreases with n.

Section 6.3 Exercises, pp. 464–468

1. $A(x)$ is the area of the cross section through the solid at the point x.

3. $\displaystyle\int_0^2 \pi(4x^2 - x^4)\,dx$ **5.** The cross sections are disks and $A(x)$ is the area of a disk.   **7.** $\dfrac{64}{15}$ **9.** 1   **11.** $\dfrac{1000}{3}$ **13.** $\dfrac{\pi}{3}$ **15.** $\dfrac{16\sqrt{2}}{3}$

17. 36π **19.** $\dfrac{15\pi}{32}$ **21.** $\dfrac{\pi^2}{2}$ **23.** $\dfrac{\pi^2}{6}$ **25.** $\dfrac{\pi^2}{2}$ **27.** $\dfrac{32\pi}{3}$

29. $\dfrac{5\pi}{6}$ **31.** $\dfrac{117\pi}{5}$ **33.** $\dfrac{4\pi - \pi^2}{4}$ **35.** 54π **37.** $\dfrac{64\pi}{5}$ **39.** $\dfrac{32\pi}{3}$

41. Volumes are equal.   **43.** x-axis   **45.** $\dfrac{\pi}{6}$ **47.** $2\pi(8 + \pi)$

49. $(6\sqrt{3} - 2\pi)\pi$ **51.** 4π **53. a.** False   **b.** True   **c.** True

55. $\pi \ln 3$ **57.** $\dfrac{\pi}{2}(e^4 - 1)$ **59.** $\dfrac{49\pi}{2}$

61. Volume $(S) = 8\pi a^{5/2}/15$; volume $(T) = \pi a^{5/2}/3$

63. a.

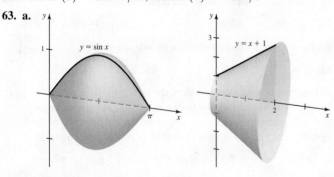

65. a. $\frac{1}{3}V_C$ **b.** $\frac{2}{3}V_C$ **67.** $24\pi^2$ **69. b.** $\dfrac{2}{\sqrt{\pi}}$ m

Section 6.4 Exercises, pp. 477–480

1. $\displaystyle\int_a^b 2\pi x(f(x) - g(x))\,dx$ **3.** $x; y$ **5.** $\dfrac{\pi}{6}$ **7.** $\pi \ln 5$ **9.** π **11.** $\dfrac{\pi}{5}$

13. π **15.** 8π **17.** $\dfrac{32\pi}{3}$ **19.** $\dfrac{2\pi}{3}$ **21.** $\dfrac{81\pi}{2}$ **23.** 90π **25.** π

27. 24π **29.** 54π **31.** $16\sqrt{2}\,\pi/3$ **33.** $\dfrac{11\pi}{6}$ **35.** $\dfrac{23\pi}{15}$

37. $\dfrac{52\pi}{15}$ **39.** $\dfrac{36\pi}{5}$ **41.** $\dfrac{4\pi}{15}$; either method   **43.** $\dfrac{8\pi}{27}$; shell method

45. $\pi(\sqrt{e} - 1)^2$; shell method   **47.** $\dfrac{\pi}{9}$; washer method

49. a. True   **b.** False   **c.** True   **51.** $4\pi \ln 2$ **53.** $2\pi e(e - 1)$

55. $\dfrac{16\pi}{3}$ **57.** $608\pi/3$ **59.** $\dfrac{\pi}{4}$ **61.** $\dfrac{\pi}{3}$

63. a. $V_1 = \dfrac{\pi}{15}(3a^2 + 10a + 15)$ $V_2 = \dfrac{\pi}{2}(a + 2)$

b. $V(S_1) = V(S_2)$ for $a = 0$ and $a = -\dfrac{5}{6}$ **67.** $\dfrac{\pi h^2}{3}(24 - h)$

69. $24\pi^2$ **73.** 10π **75. a.** $\dfrac{27\sqrt{3}\pi r^3}{8}$ **b.** $\dfrac{54\sqrt{2}}{(3 + \sqrt{2})^3}$ **c.** $\dfrac{500\pi}{3}$

Section 6.5 Exercises, pp. 485–486

1. Determine whether f has a continuous derivative on $[a, b]$. If so, calculate $f'(x)$ and evaluate the integral

$$\int_a^b \sqrt{1 + f'(x)^2}\,dx. \quad \textbf{3.} \int_{-2}^5 \sqrt{1 + 9x^4}\,dx \quad \textbf{5.} \int_0^2 \sqrt{1 + 4e^{-4x}}\,dx$$

7. $4\sqrt{5}$ **9.** $8\sqrt{65}$ **11.** 168   **13.** $\dfrac{4}{3}$ **15.** $\dfrac{123}{32}$

17. a. $\displaystyle\int_{-1}^1 \sqrt{1 + 4x^2}\,dx$ **b.** 2.958   **19. a.** $\displaystyle\int_1^4 \sqrt{1 + \dfrac{1}{x^2}}\,dx$

b. 3.343   **21. a.** $\displaystyle\int_3^4 \sqrt{\dfrac{4x - 7}{4x - 8}}\,dx$ **b.** 1.083

23. a. $\displaystyle\int_0^\pi \sqrt{1 + 4\sin^2 2x}\,dx$ **b.** 5.270

25. a. $\displaystyle\int_1^{10} \sqrt{1 + 1/x^4}\,dx$ **b.** 9.153   **27.** $7\sqrt{5}$

29. $\dfrac{123}{32}$ **31. a.** False   **b.** True   **c.** False

33. a. $f(x) = \pm\dfrac{4x^3}{3} + C$ **b.** $f(x) = \pm 3\sin 2x + C$

35. $y = 1 - x^2$ **37.** Approximately 1326 m   **39. a.** $L/2$ **b.** L/c

Section 6.6 Exercises, pp. 494–498

1. 150 g   **3.** 25 J   **5.** Different volumes of water are moved different distances.   **7.** 39,200 N/m²

9. $\pi + 2$ **11.** 3   **13.** $\dfrac{2\sqrt{2} - 1}{3}$ **15.** 10   **17.** 9 J

19. a. $k = 150$ **b.** 12 J   **c.** 6.75 J   **d.** 9 J   **21. a.** 112.5 J
b. 12.5 J   **23. a.** 31.25 J   **b.** 312.5 J   **25. a.** 625 J   **b.** 390.625 J
27. 1.148×10^7 J   **29.** 3.941×10^6 J   **31. a.** $66{,}150\pi$ J
b. No   **33. a.** 2.102×10^8 J   **b.** 3.783×10^8 J   **35. a.** 32,667 J
b. Yes   **37.** 7.697×10^3 J   **39.** 1.470×10^7 N   **41.** 2.940×10^7 N
43. 6533 N   **45.** 8×10^5 N   **47.** 6737.5 N   **49. a.** True   **b.** True
c. True   **d.** False   **51. a.** Compared to a linear spring $F(x) = 16x$, the restoring force is less for large displacements.   **b.** 17.87 J
c. 31.6 J   **53.** 0.28 J   **55. a.** 8.874×10^9 J
b. $\dfrac{500\,GMx}{R(x + R)} = \dfrac{(2 \times 10^{17})x}{R(x + R)}$ J   **c.** $\dfrac{GMm}{R}$ **d.** $v = \sqrt{2GM/R}$

57. a. $2250g$ J   **b.** $3750g$ J   **61.** Left plate, $F = 16,730$ N; right plate, $F = 14,700$ N   **63. a.** Yes   **b.** 4.296 m

Chapter 6 Review Exercises, pp. 499–501

1. a. True   **b.** True   **c.** True   **3.** $s(t) = 20t - 5t^2$;

displacement $= 20t - 5t^2$; $D(t) = \begin{cases} 20t - 5t^2 & \text{if } 0 \le t < 2 \\ 5t^2 - 20t + 40 & \text{if } 2 \le t \le 4 \end{cases}$

5. a. $v(t) = -\dfrac{8}{\pi}\cos\dfrac{\pi t}{4}$ $s(t) = -\dfrac{32}{\pi^2}\sin\dfrac{\pi t}{4}$

b. Min value $= -\dfrac{32}{\pi^2}$; max value $= \dfrac{32}{\pi^2}$ **c.** 0; 0

7. a. $R(t) = 3t^{4/3}$ **b.** $R(t) = \begin{cases} 3t^{4/3} & \text{if } 0 \le t \le 8 \\ 2t + 32 & \text{if } t > 8 \end{cases}$

c. $t = 59$ min

9. a.

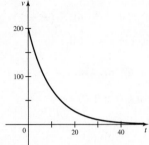

b. $10\ln 4 \approx 13.86$ s

c. $s(t) = 2000(1 - e^{-t/10})$ **d.** No

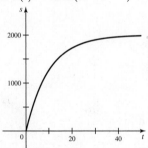

11. a. $s_{\text{Tom}}(t) = -10e^{-2t} + 10$
$s_{\text{Sue}}(t) = -15e^{-t} + 15$

b. $t = 0$ and $t = \ln 2$
c. Sue

13. $\dfrac{7}{3}$ **15.** $R_1: \dfrac{17}{6}$; $R_2: \dfrac{47}{6}$; $R_3: \dfrac{11}{2}$ **17.** 8   **19.** 1

21. $\dfrac{1}{3}$ **23.** $\dfrac{5}{6}$ **25.** $\dfrac{8}{15}$ **27.** $\dfrac{8\pi}{5}$ **29.** $\pi(e-1)^2$ **31.** π

33. $\dfrac{512\pi}{15}$ **35.** Revolving about $y = -2$, the volume is 80π; revolving about $x = -2$, the volume is 112π.

39. 1   **41.** $2\sqrt{3} - \dfrac{4}{3}$

43. $\sqrt{b^2 + 1} - \sqrt{2} + \ln\left(\dfrac{(\sqrt{b^2+1}-1)(1+\sqrt{2})}{b}\right)$;

$b \approx 2.715$ **45.** $\left(450 - \dfrac{450}{e}\right)$ g

47. a. 56.25 J   **b.** 562.5 J   **49.** 5.2×10^7 J

AP® Practice, Section 1, Parts A and B, pp. 502–503

1. C   **2.** B   **3.** A   **4.** C   **5.** A   **6.** A   **7.** E   **8.** D   **9.** B
10. B   **11.** E   **12.** D   **13.** A   **14.** C

AP® Practice, Section 2, Parts A and B, pp. 503–504

1. a. $r(1) \approx 0.750, r(2) \approx 1.167, r(3) \approx 1.458, r(4) \approx 1.683$

b. $V \approx 19.477$ **c.** $V = \dfrac{4\pi}{3}\ln^3 5 \approx 17.463$ **2. a.** 40 mi/hr^2

b. $1 < t < 2$ **c.** -2.5; the pilot car is 2.5 mi south of its starting position after 2 hr   **d.** 7.5 mi/hr   **e.** 17.5 mi; the total distance traveled by the pilot car in 2 hr.   **3. a.** $\dfrac{22}{3}$ **b.** $\dfrac{884\pi}{15}$

c. $\dfrac{32\pi}{3}$ **d.** $\dfrac{248}{15}$ **4. a.** Increasing   **b.** -0.219 **c.** 12.978

d. 8.676   **5. a.** 3.75 inches

b. $a(t) = \begin{cases} 0.5t & \text{if } 0 \le t \le 3 \\ 1.5 + 0.75(t-3) & \text{if } 3 < t \le 4.5 \\ 2.625 + 0.25(t-4.5) & \text{if } 4.5 < t \le 9 \end{cases}$ **c.** π in^3/hr

d. 47.124 in^3 **6. a.** A 3.590 L; B 3.402 L   **b.** A 4.333 L; B 12 L

7. a. $f''(x) = \dfrac{1}{4\sqrt{x}} > 0$, so the slopes of tangent lines are

increasing.   **b.** $\dfrac{19}{3}$ **c.** $a = 21$ **8. a.** $\dfrac{\pi\sqrt{3}}{4}$ **b.** $\dfrac{2(\sqrt{2}-1)}{\pi}$

c. $\displaystyle\int_0^{1/2} \pi\left(\left(1 - \sin\left(\dfrac{\pi x}{2}\right)\right)^2 - \left(1 - \cos\left(\dfrac{\pi x}{2}\right)\right)^2\right) dx$

d. $\displaystyle\int_0^{1/2} 2\left(\cos\left(\dfrac{\pi x}{2}\right) - \sin\left(\dfrac{\pi x}{2}\right)\right)^2 dx$

CHAPTER 7

Section 7.1 Exercises, pp. 508–510

1. $u = 4 - 7x$ **3.** $\sin^2 x = \dfrac{1 - \cos 2x}{2}$

5. Complete the square in $x^2 - 4x + 5$.

7. $\dfrac{1}{15(3 - 5x)^3} + C$ **9.** $\dfrac{\sqrt{2}}{4}$ **11.** $\dfrac{1}{2}\ln^2 2x + C$

13. $\ln(e^x + 1) + C$ **15.** $\dfrac{1}{2}\ln|e^{2x} - 2| + C$ **17.** $\dfrac{32}{3}$

19. $-\dfrac{1}{5}\cot^5 x + C$ **21.** $x - \ln|x + 1| + C$

23. $\dfrac{1}{2}\ln(x^2 + 4) + \tan^{-1}\dfrac{x}{2} + C$

25. $\dfrac{\sec^2 t}{2} + \sec t + C$ or $\dfrac{\tan^2 t}{2} + \sec t + C$

27. $3\sqrt{1 - x^2} + 2\sin^{-1} x + C$ **29.** $x - 2\ln|x + 4| + C$

31. $\dfrac{t^3}{3} - \dfrac{t^2}{2} + t - 3\ln|t + 1| + C$

33. $\dfrac{1}{3}\tan^{-1}\left(\dfrac{x - 1}{3}\right) + C$ **35.** $\sin^{-1}\left(\dfrac{\theta + 3}{6}\right) + C$

37. $\tan\theta - \sec\theta + C$ **39.** $-x - \cot x - \csc x + C$

41. a. False   **b.** False   **c.** False   **d.** False   **43.** $\dfrac{\ln 4 - \pi}{4}$

45. $\dfrac{2\sin^3 x}{3} + C$ **47.** $2\tan^{-1}\sqrt{x} + C$

49. $\dfrac{1}{2}\ln(x^2 + 6x + 13) - \dfrac{5}{2}\tan^{-1}\left(\dfrac{x + 3}{2}\right) + C$

51. $-\dfrac{1}{e^x + 1} + C$ **53.** $\dfrac{1}{2}$ **55. a.** $\dfrac{\tan^2 x}{2} + C$ **b.** $\dfrac{\sec^2 x}{2} + C$

c. The antiderivatives differ by a constant.

57. a. $\dfrac{1}{2}(x + 1)^2 - 2(x + 1) + \ln|x + 1| + C$

b. $\dfrac{x^2}{2} - x + \ln|x + 1| + C$ **c.** The antiderivatives differ

by a constant.   **59.** $\dfrac{\ln 26}{3}$ **61. a.** $\dfrac{14\pi}{3}$

b. $\dfrac{2}{3}(5\sqrt{5} - 1)\pi$ **63.** $\dfrac{2048 + 1763\sqrt{41}}{9375}$

Section 7.2 Exercises, pp. 514–517

1. Product Rule   **3.** $u = x^n$ **5.** Products for which the choice for dv is easily integrated and when the resulting new integral is no more difficult than the original   **7.** $x\sin x + \cos x + C$

9. $te^t - e^t + C$ **11.** $\dfrac{2}{3}(x - 2)\sqrt{x + 1} + C$

13. $\dfrac{x^3}{3}(\ln x^3 - 1) + C$ **15.** $\dfrac{x^3}{9}(3\ln x - 1) + C$

17. $-\dfrac{1}{9x^9}\left(\ln x + \dfrac{1}{9}\right) + C$ **19.** $x\tan^{-1} x - \dfrac{1}{2}\ln(x^2 + 1) + C$

21. $\dfrac{1}{8}\sin 2x - \dfrac{x}{4}\cos 2x + C$ **23.** $-e^{-t}(t^2 + 2t + 2) + C$

25. $-\dfrac{e^{-x}}{17}(\sin 4x + 4\cos 4x) + C$ **27.** $\dfrac{e^x}{2}(\sin x + \cos x) + C$

29. $\dfrac{1}{4}(1 - 2x^2)\cos 2x + \dfrac{1}{2}x\sin 2x + C$ **31.** π

33. $-\dfrac{1}{2}$ **35.** $\dfrac{1}{9}(5e^6 + 1)$ **37.** $\left(\dfrac{2\sqrt{3} - 1}{12}\right)\pi + \dfrac{1 - \sqrt{3}}{2}$

39. $\pi(1 - \ln 2)$ **41.** $\dfrac{2\pi}{27}(13e^6 - 1)$ **43. a.** False   **b.** True

c. True   **45.** Let $u = x^n$ and $dv = \cos ax\, dx$.

47. Let $u = \ln^n x$ and $dv = dx$.

49. $\dfrac{x^2\sin 5x}{5} + \dfrac{2x\cos 5x}{25} - \dfrac{2\sin 5x}{125} + C$

51. $x\ln^4 x - 4x\ln^3 x + 12x\ln^2 x - 24x\ln x + 24x + C$

53. $(\tan x + 2)\ln(\tan x + 2) - \tan x + C$

55. $\displaystyle\int \log_b x\, dx = \int \dfrac{\ln x}{\ln b}\, dx = \dfrac{1}{\ln b}(x\ln x - x) + C$

57. $2\sqrt{x}\sin\sqrt{x} + 2\cos\sqrt{x} + C$ **59.** $2e^3$ **61.** $\pi(\pi - 2)$

63. x-axis: $\dfrac{\pi^2}{2}$; y-axis: $2\pi^2$ **65. a.** Let $u = x$ and

$dv = f'(x)\, dx$.   **b.** $\dfrac{e^{3x}}{9}(3x - 1) + C$ **67.** Use $u = \sec x$ and

$dv = \sec^2 x\, dx$.   **69. a.** $t = k\pi$ for $k = 0, 1, 2, \ldots$

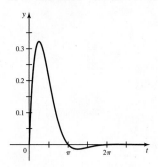

b. $\dfrac{e^{-\pi} + 1}{2\pi}$ **c.** $(-1)^n\left(\dfrac{e^\pi + 1}{2\pi e^{(n+1)\pi}}\right)$ **d.** $a_n = a_{n-1}\cdot\dfrac{1}{e^\pi}$

71. c. $e^{2x}\left(x^2 - \dfrac{5}{2}x + \dfrac{7}{4}\right) + C$ **73.** Let $u = x$ and $dv = f''(x)$.

75. a. $I_1 = -\dfrac{1}{2}e^{-x^2} + C$ **b.** $I_3 = -\dfrac{1}{2}e^{-x^2}(x^2 + 1) + C$

c. $I_5 = -\dfrac{1}{2}e^{-x^2}(x^4 + 2x^2 + 2) + C$

Section 7.3 Exercises, pp. 522–524

1. Rational functions   **3.** $\dfrac{A}{x}, \dfrac{B}{x + 2}, \dfrac{C}{x + 3}$ **5.** $\dfrac{1/3}{x - 4} - \dfrac{1/3}{x + 2}$

7. $\dfrac{2}{x - 1} + \dfrac{3}{x - 2}$ **9.** $\dfrac{1/2}{x - 4} + \dfrac{1/2}{x + 4}$ **11.** $-\dfrac{3}{x - 1} + \dfrac{1}{x} + \dfrac{2}{x - 2}$

13. $\ln\left|\dfrac{x - 1}{x + 2}\right| + C$ **15.** $3\ln\left|\dfrac{x - 1}{x + 1}\right| + C$

17. $\ln|(x - 3)^3(x + 2)^2| + C$ **19.** $\ln|(x - 6)^6(x + 4)^4| + C$

21. $\ln\left|\dfrac{(x - 2)^2(x + 1)}{(x + 2)^2(x - 1)}\right| + C$ **23.** $\ln\left|\dfrac{x(x - 2)^3}{(x + 2)^3}\right| + C$

25. $\ln\left|\dfrac{(x - 3)^{1/3}(x + 1)}{(x + 3)^{1/3}(x - 1)}\right|^{1/16} + C$

27. $\dfrac{1}{2}x^2 - 3x + 4\ln|x - 2| + C$

29. $2x^2 - x + \dfrac{1}{5} \ln \left| \dfrac{x-2}{x+3} \right| + C$

31. $\dfrac{1}{3}x^3 - x + \ln|x-2| + C$ **33. a.** False   **b.** False

c. True   **35.** $\ln 6$ **37.** $4\sqrt{2} + \frac{1}{3}\ln\left(\frac{3 - 2\sqrt{2}}{3 + 2\sqrt{2}}\right)$

39. $\dfrac{\pi}{2}\ln\dfrac{9}{5}$ **41.** $\frac{2}{3}\pi\ln 2$ **43.** $2\pi\left(3 + \ln\frac{2}{5}\right)$

45. $x - \ln(1 + e^x) + C$ **47.** $3x + \ln\dfrac{(x-2)^{14}}{|x-1|} + C$

49. $\ln\sqrt{2e^t + 1} + C$ **51.** $2\ln\left(\dfrac{2 + \sin\theta}{2 - \sin\theta}\right) + C$

53. $\ln\left|\dfrac{e^x - 1}{e^x + 2}\right|^{1/3} + C$ **55.** $\tan^{-1} e^x + C$

59. $\frac{4}{3}(x+2)^{3/4} - 2(x+2)^{1/2} + 4(x+2)^{1/4} - $
$\ln\left((x+2)^{1/4} + 1\right)^4 + C$

61. $-3x^{1/3} - \dfrac{3}{2}x^{2/3} - 3\ln|1 - x^{1/3}| + C$

63. $\frac{4}{3}\sqrt{1 + \sqrt{x}}(\sqrt{x} - 2) + C$

65. $-\cot x - \csc x + C$ or $-\cot(x/2) + C$

67. $\dfrac{\sqrt{2}}{2}\ln\left|\dfrac{\sqrt{2} + 1 + \tan(\theta/2)}{\sqrt{2} - 1 - \tan(\theta/2)}\right| + C$

69. a. Car A **b.** Car B

c. $S_A(t) = 88t - 88\ln|t + 1|$;
$S_B(t) = 88(t - 2 + 2e^{-t/2})$
$S_C(t) = 88\left(t + \ln\dfrac{16(t+1)}{(t+2)^4}\right)$

d. Car B

71. Because $\dfrac{x^4(1-x)^4}{1 + x^2} > 0$ on $(0, 1)$, $\displaystyle\int_0^1 \dfrac{x^4(1 - x^4)}{1 + x^2}\,dx > 0$;

thus, $\dfrac{22}{7} > \pi$.

Section 7.4 Exercises, pp. 534–537

1. The interval of integration is infinite or the integrand is unbounded on the interval of integration.

3. $\displaystyle\int_0^1 \dfrac{1}{\sqrt{x}}\,dx = \lim_{b\to 0^+}\int_b^1 \dfrac{1}{\sqrt{x}}\,dx$ **5.** 1   **7.** 1

9. Diverges   **11.** $\frac{1}{2}$ **13.** $\dfrac{1}{a}$ **15.** $\dfrac{1}{(p-1)2^{p-1}}$ **17.** 0   **19.** $\dfrac{1}{\pi}$

21. $\dfrac{\pi}{4}$ **23.** $\ln 2$ **25.** Diverges   **27.** $\dfrac{1}{4}$ **29.** $\dfrac{\pi}{3}$ **31.** $3\pi/2$

33. $\pi/\ln 2$ **35.** 6   **37.** 2   **39.** Diverges   **41.** $2(e - 1)$

43. Diverges   **45.** $4 \cdot 10^{3/4}/3$ **47.** -2 **49.** 0   **51.** 2π

53. $\dfrac{72 \cdot 2^{1/3}\pi}{5}$ **55.** 48   **57.** 0.764   **59.** 10 mi   **61. a.** True

b. False   **c.** False   **d.** True   **e.** True   **63. a.** 2   **b.** 0

65. Approximately 0.886227   **67.** $-\frac{1}{4}$ **69.** $\dfrac{1}{2}$; $\sqrt{\pi}/4 \approx 0.443$

71. $1/b - 1/a$ **73. a.** $A(a, b) = \dfrac{e^{-ab}}{a}$, for $a > 0$

b. $b = g(a) = -\dfrac{1}{a}\ln 2a$ **c.** $b^* = -2/e$ **75. a.** $p < \frac{1}{2}$ **b.** $p < 2$

81. \$41,666.67   **85.** 20,000 hr

87. a. $6.279 \times 10^7 m$ J   **b.** 11.207 km/s   **c.** ≤ 9 mm

89. a.

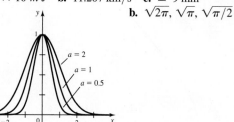

b. $\sqrt{2\pi}$, $\sqrt{\pi}$, $\sqrt{\pi/2}$

c. $e^{(b^2 - 4ac)/(4a)}\sqrt{\pi/a}$ **95. a.** π **b.** $\pi/(4e^2)$ **97.** $p > 1$

Section 7.5 Exercises, pp. 541–544

1. $x = 3\sec\theta$ **3.** $x = 10\sin\theta$ **5.** $\dfrac{\sqrt{4 - x^2}}{x}$ **7.** $\dfrac{\pi}{6}$

9. $25\left(\dfrac{2\pi}{3} - \dfrac{\sqrt{3}}{2}\right)$ **11.** $\dfrac{\pi}{12} - \dfrac{\sqrt{3}}{8}$ **13.** $\sin^{-1}\dfrac{x}{4} + C$

15. $\dfrac{x}{2}\sqrt{9 - x^2} + \dfrac{9}{2}\sin^{-1}\dfrac{x}{3} + C$

17. $\dfrac{x}{2}\sqrt{64 - x^2} + 32\sin^{-1}\dfrac{x}{8} + C$

19. $\dfrac{x}{\sqrt{1 - x^2}} + C$ **21.** $-\dfrac{\sqrt{x^2 + 9}}{9x} + C$

23. $\sin^{-1}\dfrac{x}{6} + C$ **25.** $\ln(x + \sqrt{x^2 - 81}) + C$

27. $\dfrac{x}{\sqrt{1 + 4x^2}} + C$ **29.** $8\sin^{-1}\dfrac{x}{4} - \dfrac{x\sqrt{16 - x^2}}{2} + C$

31. $\dfrac{\sqrt{x^2 - 1}}{x} + C$ **33.** $\dfrac{1}{5}\sec^{-1}\dfrac{x}{5} + C$

35. $-\dfrac{x}{2}\sqrt{100 - x^2} + 50\sin^{-1}\dfrac{x}{10} + C$

37. $\dfrac{x^4}{4(x^2 + 1)^2} + C$ **39.** $\ln\left(\dfrac{1 + \sqrt{17}}{4}\right)$ **41.** $2 - \sqrt{2}$

43. $\dfrac{1}{2}$ **45.** $\dfrac{\sqrt{2}}{6}$ **47. a.** False   **b.** True   **c.** False

49. a. b. $\dfrac{r^2}{2}(\theta - \sin\theta)$ **51. a.** $\ln 3$ **b.** $\dfrac{\pi}{3}\tan^{-1}\dfrac{4}{3}$ **c.** 4π

53. $\dfrac{1}{81} + \dfrac{\ln 3}{108}$

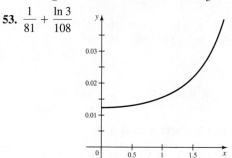

55. $25(\sqrt{3} - \ln\sqrt{2 + \sqrt{3}})$ **57.** $192\pi^2$

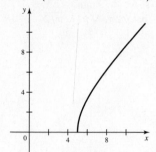

59. b. $\lim\limits_{L\to\infty} \dfrac{kQ}{a\sqrt{a^2 + L^2}} = \lim\limits_{L\to\infty} 2\rho k \dfrac{1}{a\sqrt{\left(\dfrac{a}{L}\right)^2 + 1}} = \dfrac{2\rho k}{a}$

61. a. $\dfrac{1}{\sqrt{g}}\left[\dfrac{\pi}{2} - \sin^{-1}\left(\dfrac{2\cos b - \cos a + 1}{\cos a + 1}\right)\right]$

b. For $b = \pi$, the descent time is $\dfrac{\pi}{\sqrt{g}}$, a constant.

Chapter 7 Review Exercises, pp. 544–545

1. a. True   **b.** False   **c.** True   **d.** False
3. $2(x - 8)\sqrt{x + 4} + C$ **5.** $\pi/4$
7. $\sqrt{t - 1} - \tan^{-1}\sqrt{t - 1} + C$
9. $\dfrac{1}{3}\sqrt{x + 2}(x - 4) + C$ **11.** $\dfrac{1}{4}\sin 2x - \dfrac{1}{2}x\cos 2x + C$
13. $\ln\left|\dfrac{x^2(x + 1)}{x + 2}\right| + C$ **15.** $-x^2 - x - \ln|(1 - x)^2(1 + x)| + C$
17. $\sqrt{3} - 1 - \dfrac{\pi}{12}$ **19.** $\dfrac{1}{3}\sqrt{x^2 + 4}(x^2 - 8) + C$
21. 1   **23.** $\dfrac{\pi}{2}$ **25.** $-\cot\theta - \csc\theta + C$ **27.** $\dfrac{e^x}{2}(\sin x - \cos x) + C$
29. $\dfrac{\theta}{2} + \dfrac{1}{16}\sin 8\theta + C$ **31.** $-\dfrac{1}{9y}\sqrt{9 - y^2} + C$ **33.** $\pi/9$
35. $\dfrac{1}{8}\ln\left|\dfrac{x - 5}{x + 3}\right| + C$ **37.** $\ln\dfrac{4}{3}$ **39.** $\dfrac{1}{3}\ln\left|\dfrac{x - 2}{x + 1}\right| + C$
41. $2(x - 2\ln|x + 2|) + C$ **43.** $\dfrac{1}{2}\tan^{-1}e^{2t} + C$
45. $\pi(e - 2)$ **47.** $\dfrac{\pi}{2}(e^2 - 3)$ **49.** y-axis
51. a. 1.603   **b.** 1.870   **c.** $b\ln b - b = a\ln a - a$
d. Decreasing   **53.** $20/(3\pi)$ **55.** 1901 cars
57. a. $I(p) = \dfrac{1}{(p - 1)^2}(1 - pe^{1-p})$ if $p \neq 1, I(1) = \dfrac{1}{2}$
b. $0, \infty$ **c.** $I(0) = 1$ **59.** 0.4054651   **61.** $a = \ln 2/(2b)$

AP® Practice, Section 1, Parts A and B, p. 546

1. C   **2.** E   **3.** D   **4.** C   **5.** A   **6.** C   **7.** D   **8.** A   **9.** B
10. D   **11.** E   **12.** E   **13.** B   **14.** B

AP® Practice, Section 2, Parts A and B, pp. 546–547

1. a. $x = \sqrt{\pi/2} \approx 1.253$ **b.** $\displaystyle\int_0^{\sqrt{\pi}} \sin x^2\,dx \approx 0.895$
c. $\frac{1}{2}(1 - \cos 1) \approx 0.230$ kg-m   **d.** $\displaystyle\int_0^{\pi} \sqrt{1 + 4x^2\cos^2 x^2}\,dx$
2. a. $\dfrac{\pi^2}{2} - \pi \approx 1.793$ **b.** $a = \dfrac{e^2 - 1}{2e} \approx 1.175$
3. a. $f'(x) = 2xe^{x^2-9}$ **b.** $y = 6x - 17$ **c.** $\lim\limits_{x\to 3^-}g(x) =$
$1 = \lim\limits_{x\to 3^+}g(x) \Rightarrow \lim\limits_{x\to 3}g(x) = 1 = g(3) \Rightarrow g$ is continuous at $x = 3$.
d. $\dfrac{1}{2}\left(1 - \dfrac{1}{e^9}\right)$ **4. a.** $x = 0$ **b.** $(0, 2)$ **c.** 2   **d.** $k = -1$
5. a. $y = -6x + 1$ **b.** $(6, \infty)$ **c.** $f(6) = 8 - e^6$

CHAPTER 8

Section 8.1 Exercises, pp. 554–556

1. Second-order   **3.** 2   **5.** Yes   **15.** $y = 3t - \dfrac{e^{-2t}}{2} + C$
17. $y = 2\ln|\sec 2x| - 3\sin x + C$
19. $y = 2t^6 - 2t^2 + 6t^{-1} + C_1t + C_2$
21. $u = \dfrac{x^{11}}{2} + \dfrac{x^9}{2} - \dfrac{x^7}{2} + \dfrac{5}{x} + C_1x + C_2$
23. $y = e^t + t + 3$ **25.** $y = x^3 + x^{-3} - 2$
27. $y = -t^5 + 2t^3 + 1$
29. a. $s = -4.9t^2 + 29.4t + 30, v = -9.8t + 29.4$
b. Highest point of 74.1 m is reached at $t = 3$ s.
31. $h = (1.4 - 0.2t\sqrt{2g})^2 \approx (1.4 - 0.44t)^2$; tank is empty
when $t \approx 3.162$ s.

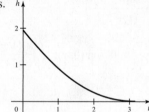

33. a. False   **b.** False   **c.** True
35. $u = \ln(x^2 + 4) - \tan^{-1}\dfrac{x}{2} + C$ **37.** $y = \sin^{-1} x + C_1 x + C_2$
39. $u = \dfrac{1}{4}\tan^{-1}\dfrac{x}{4} - 4x + 2$ **41.** $y = -\dfrac{1}{4}\sin 2t + \dfrac{3}{2}t$
49. c. $y = C_1\sin kt + C_2\cos kt$ **51. b.** $C = \dfrac{K - 50}{50}$
c.   **d.** 300

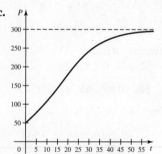

53. c. The decay rate is greater for the $n = 1$ model.

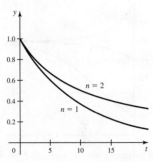

55. a. Because $y' = \dfrac{y}{2}$, y' has the same sign as y. Therefore, if $y(0) = A > 0$, then $y' > 0$ and y is increasing, for $t > 0$. By a similar argument, if $A < 0$, then y is decreasing, for $t > 0$.

b. Using part (a), $y'' = \dfrac{y'}{2} > 0$ if $A > 0$. Therefore, the graph of the solution is concave up, for $t > 0$. By a similar argument, if $A < 0$, then the graph is concave down, for $t > 0$.

c.

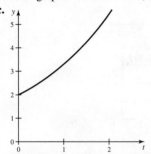

Section 8.2 Exercises, pp. 567–571

1. At selected points (t_0, y_0) in the region of interest, draw a short line segment with slope $f(t_0, y_0)$.   **3.** $y(3.1) \approx 1.6$

5.

	$t = 0$	$t = 1$	$t = 2$
$y = 0$	0	0	0
$y = 1$	−2	−2	−2
$y = 2$	−4	−4	−4

7.

	$t = 1$	$t = 2$	$t = 3$
$y = 0$	0	0	0
$y = 1$	1	1/2	1/3
$y = 2$	2	1	2/3
$y = 3$	3	3/2	1

9. a.

	$t = 0$	$t = 1$	$t = 2$	$t = 3$
$y = 0$	−4	−2	0	2
$y = 1$	−4	−2	0	2
$y = 2$	−4	−2	0	2

b. c.

11. a.

	$t = 0$	$t = 1$	$t = 2$	$t = 3$
$y = -1$	1	2	3	4
$y = 0$	0	1	2	3
$y = 1$	−1	0	1	2
$y = 2$	−2	−1	0	1

b. c.

13.

15. a. D   **b.** B   **c.** A   **d.** C

17. a.

b. An initial condition of $y(0) = -1$ leads to a constant solution.
c. For any other initial condition, the solutions are increasing over time.

19. a.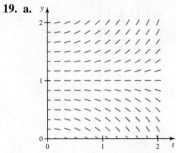

b. An initial condition of $y(0) = 1$ leads to a constant solution.
c. Initial conditions $y(0) = A$ lead to solutions that are increasing if $A > 1$.

21. a. b. 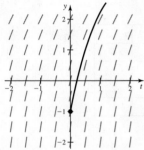   **23. a. b.**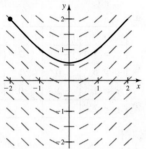

25. a. $y = 1, y = -1$
b. Solutions are increasing for $|y| > 1$, decreasing for $|y| < 1$.   **c.** Initial conditions $y(0) = A$ lead to increasing solutions if $|A| > 1$ and decreasing solutions if $|A| < 1$.
d.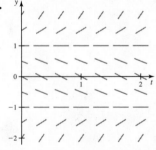

27. a. $y = \dfrac{\pi}{2}, y = -\dfrac{\pi}{2}$ **b.** Solutions are increasing for $|y| < \dfrac{\pi}{2}$, decreasing for $\dfrac{\pi}{2} < |y| < \pi$.   **c.** Initial conditions $y(0) = A$ lead to increasing solutions if $|A| < \dfrac{\pi}{2}$ and decreasing solutions if $\dfrac{\pi}{2} < |A| < \pi$.

d.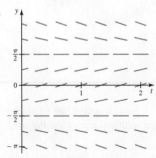

29. The equilibrium solutions are $P = 0$ and $P = 500$.

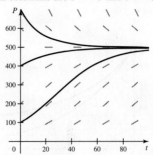

31. The equilibrium solutions are $P = 0$ and $P = 3200$.

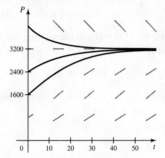

33.

k	t_k	u_k	Slope $= f(t_k, u_k)$
0	0	2	-1
1	0.5	1.5	-0.5
2	1	1.25	—

35.

k	t_k	u_k	Slope $= f(t_k, u_k)$
0	0	3	0
1	0.2	3	0.6
2	0.4	3.12	1.248
3	0.6	3.370	—

37. $y(0.5) \approx u_1 = 4; y(1) \approx u_2 = 8$
39. $y(0.1) \approx u_1 = 1.1; y(0.2) \approx u_2 = 1.19$
41. a.

Δt	Approximation to $y(0.2)$	Approximation to $y(0.4)$
0.2	0.800	0.640
0.1	0.810	0.656
0.05	0.815	0.663
0.025	0.817	0.667

b.

Δt	Errors for $y(0.2)$	Errors for $y(0.4)$
0.2	1.9×10^{-2}	3.0×10^{-2}
0.1	8.7×10^{-3}	1.4×10^{-2}
0.05	4.2×10^{-3}	6.9×10^{-3}
0.025	2.0×10^{-3}	3.4×10^{-3}

c. Time step $\Delta t = 0.025$; smaller time steps generally produce more accurate results.   **d.** Halving the time steps results in approximately halving the error.

43. a.

Δt	Approximation to $y(0.2)$	Approximation to $y(0.4)$
0.2	3.200	3.360
0.1	3.190	3.344
0.05	3.185	3.337
0.025	3.183	3.333

b.

Δt	Errors for $y(0.2)$	Errors for $y(0.4)$
0.2	1.9×10^{-2}	3.0×10^{-2}
0.1	8.7×10^{-3}	1.4×10^{-2}
0.05	4.2×10^{-3}	6.9×10^{-3}
0.025	2.0×10^{-3}	3.4×10^{-3}

c. Time step $\Delta t = 0.025$; smaller time steps generally produce more accurate results.   **d.** Halving the time step results in approximately halving the error.   **45. a.** $y(2) \approx 0.00604662$
b. 1.2×10^{-2} **c.** $y(2) \approx 0.0115292$ **d.** Error in part (c) this is approximately half of the error in part (b).
47. a. $y(4) \approx 3.05765$ **b.** 3.4×10^{-2} **c.** $y(4) \approx 3.0739$
d. Error in part (c) this is approximately half of the error in part (b).
49. a. True   **b.** False
51. a. $y = 3$ **b. c.**

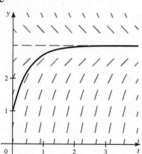

53. a. $y = 0$ and $y = 3$ **b. c.**

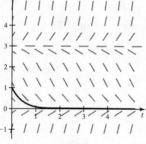

55. a. $y = -2$, $y = 0$, and $y = 3$ **b. c.**

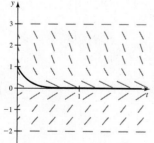

57. a. $\Delta t = \dfrac{b - a}{N}$ **b.** $u_1 = A + f(a, A)\dfrac{b - a}{N}$

c. $u_{k+1} = u_k + f(t_k, u_k)\dfrac{b - a}{N}$, where $u_0 = A$ and

$t_k = a + \dfrac{k(b - a)}{N}$, for $k = 0, 1, 2, \ldots, N - 1$

59. a.

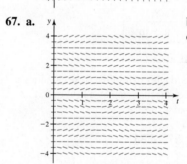

b. Increasing for $A < 98$ and decreasing for $A > 98$ **c.** $v = 98$
63. a. $y(0) = 3, y'(0) = 2$ **b.** 4   **c.** Both linear approximation and Euler's methods state that $y(0.5) \approx y(0) + y'(0) \cdot 0.5$.
d. Both linear approximation and Euler's method state that
$y(\Delta t) \approx y(0) + f(0, A) \cdot \Delta t = A + f(0, A)\,\Delta t$.

65. a.

b. For $y(0) = 2$, the solution initially decreases, then increases without bound. For $y(0) = -3$, the solution initially increases, then decreases without bound.

67. a.

b. In most cases, the solution oscillates as t increases.

69. a–b. $\Delta t = 0.1$

k	t_k	u_k	$y(t_k)$	e_k
0	0	2	2	0
1	0.1	1.8	1.81451	1.5×10^{-2}
2	0.2	1.63	1.65619	2.6×10^{-2}
3	0.3	1.487	1.52245	3.5×10^{-2}
4	0.4	1.3683	1.41096	4.3×10^{-2}
5	0.5	1.27147	1.31959	4.8×10^{-2}
6	0.6	1.19432	1.24643	5.2×10^{-2}
7	0.7	1.13489	1.18976	5.5×10^{-2}
8	0.8	1.09140	1.14799	5.7×10^{-2}
9	0.9	1.06226	1.11971	5.7×10^{-2}
10	1	1.04604	1.10364	5.8×10^{-2}

$\Delta t = 0.05$

k	t_k	u_k	$y(t_k)$	e_k
0	0	2	2	0
1	0.05	1.9	1.90369	3.7×10^{-3}
2	0.1	1.8075	1.81451	7.0×10^{-3}
3	0.15	1.72213	1.73212	1.0×10^{-2}
4	0.2	1.64352	1.65619	1.3×10^{-2}
5	0.25	1.57134	1.58640	1.5×10^{-2}
6	0.3	1.50528	1.52245	1.7×10^{-2}
7	0.35	1.44501	1.46406	1.9×10^{-2}
8	0.4	1.39026	1.41096	2.1×10^{-2}
9	0.45	1.34075	1.36288	2.2×10^{-2}
10	0.5	1.29621	1.31959	2.3×10^{-2}
11	0.55	1.25640	1.28085	2.4×10^{-2}
12	0.6	1.22108	1.24643	2.5×10^{-2}
13	0.65	1.19003	1.21614	2.6×10^{-2}
14	0.7	1.16302	1.18976	2.7×10^{-2}
15	0.75	1.13987	1.16710	2.7×10^{-2}
16	0.8	1.12038	1.14799	2.8×10^{-2}
17	0.85	1.10436	1.13224	2.8×10^{-2}
18	0.9	1.09164	1.11971	2.8×10^{-2}
19	0.95	1.08206	1.11022	2.8×10^{-2}
20	1	1.07546	1.10364	2.8×10^{-2}

c. With $\Delta t = 0.05$, the error are roughly half of the corresponding errors with $\Delta t = 0.1$.   **d.** Reduce the time step by a factor of 2. Reduce the time step by a factor of 4.

Section 8.3 Exercises, pp. 578–581

1. A first-order separable differential equation has the form $g(y)\dfrac{dy}{dt} = h(t)$, where the factor $g(y)$ is a function of y and $h(t)$ is a function of t.   **3.** No   **5.** $y = \dfrac{t^4}{4} + C$

7. $y = \pm\sqrt{2t^3 + C}$ **9.** $y = -2\ln\left(\dfrac{1}{2}\cos t + C\right)$

11. $y = \dfrac{x}{1 + Cx}$ **13.** $y = \pm\dfrac{1}{\sqrt{C - \cos t}}$

15. $u = \ln\left(\dfrac{e^{2x}}{2} + C\right)$ **17.** $y = \ln t + 2$ **19.** $y = \sqrt{t^3 + 81}$

21. Not separable   **23.** $y = \sqrt{e^t - 1}$ **25.** $y = \ln(e^x + 2)$

27. $y^2 - t^2 = 3$

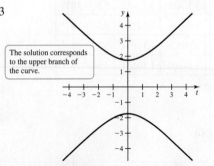

The solution corresponds to the upper branch of the curve.

29. $\cos u = 2 - 2\sin\dfrac{x}{2}$

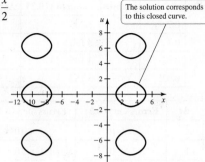

The solution corresponds to this closed curve.

31. $(y + 4)^{3/2} = (x + 1)^{3/2} + 19$

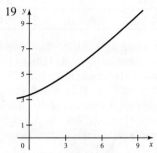

33. a. $P = \dfrac{200}{1 + 3e^{-0.08t}}$ **b.** 200   **c.** $P = 100$ **d.** $P' = 4$

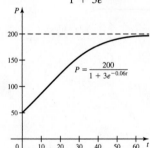

$P = \dfrac{200}{1 + 3e^{-0.06t}}$

35. Approx. 32 min   **37.** Approx. 14 min   **39. a.** True
b. False   **c.** True   **41.** $y = \dfrac{t^3}{2 - t^3}$

43. $y = \dfrac{3}{2}(-2 + 2^{1/5}(6 + 5t)^{1/5})$

45. a. $y = -2\ln\left(\dfrac{x^2}{4} + \cos x^2 + C\right)$ **b.** $C = 0, 1, 1 - \dfrac{\pi}{8}$

c.

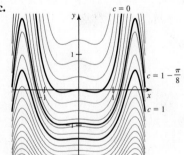

47. $y = kx$ **49. b.** $V = \sqrt{\dfrac{gm}{k}}$ **c.** $v = \sqrt{\dfrac{g}{a}}\dfrac{Ce^{2\sqrt{ag}\,t} - 1}{Ce^{2\sqrt{ag}t} + 1}$,

where $a = \dfrac{k}{m}$

d. $V = 9.90$ m/s

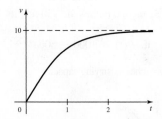

51. a. $h = (\sqrt{H} - kt)^2$ **b.** $h = (\sqrt{0.5} - 0.1t)^2$ **c.** Approximately 7.071 s **d.**

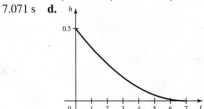

53. a.

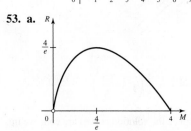

R is positive if $0 < M < 4$; R has a maximum value when

$M = \dfrac{4}{e}$; $\lim\limits_{M \to 0} R(M) = 0$. **b.** $M(t) = 4^{1-e^{-t}}$; the tumor grows quickly at first and then the rate of growth slows down; the limiting size of the tumor is 4.

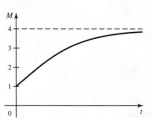

c. K is the limiting size of the tumor.

55. a. $y = \dfrac{1}{1 - t}$ **b.** $y = \dfrac{1}{\sqrt{2}\sqrt{1 - t}}$

c. $y = \dfrac{1}{(n(1 - t))^{1/n}}$; as $t \to 1^-$, $y \to \infty$

57. a. $y = \pm\sqrt{t^2 + e^t + C}$

b. $y = \sqrt{t^2 + e^t - \dfrac{1}{e}}$; $y = \sqrt{t^2 + e^t + 3 - \dfrac{1}{e}}$

c. As t increases, y increases without bound.

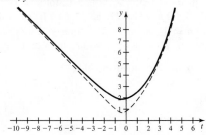

d. $y = -\sqrt{t^2 + e^t - \dfrac{1}{e}}$; $y = -\sqrt{t^2 + e^t + 3 - \dfrac{1}{e}}$

e. As t increases, y decreases without bound.

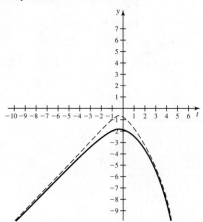

Section 8.4 Exercises, pp. 588–590

1. The relative growth rate is constant. **3.** The time it takes for a function to double in value **5.** $T_2 = \dfrac{\ln 2}{k}$ **7.** Compound interest, world population **9.** $\dfrac{df}{dt} = 10.5$; $\dfrac{dg}{dt} \cdot \dfrac{1}{g} = \dfrac{10e^{t/10}}{100e^{t/10}} = \dfrac{1}{10}$

11. $P(t) = 90{,}000\, e^{t \ln 1.024}$ people with $t = 0$ in 2010; in 2039

13. $P = 50{,}000\, e^{t(\ln 1.1)/10}$; 60,500 **15.** $y = 100\, e^{t \ln 1.03}$ with $t = 0$ in 2005; $134.39 **17. a.** $T_2 \approx 87$ yr; 2050 pop ≈ 425 million

b. $T_2 \approx 116$ yr; 2050 pop ≈ 393 million

$T_2 \approx 70$ yr; 2050 pop ≈ 460 million **19.** About 33 million

21. $y = 800\, e^{t \ln 0.97}$ with $t = 0$ in 2010; 2019

23. $p = 1000\, e^{-z(\ln 3)/30{,}000}$ with $z = 0$ sea level; 18,928 ft; 125,754 ft

25. $P = 9.94\, e^{t(\ln 0.994)/10}$ in millions with $t = 0$ in 2000; about 9.82 million; the population decline may stop if the economy improves. **27. a.** 15.87 mg **b.** 119.589 hr ≈ 5 days

29. Approximately 1.055 billion yr **31. a.** False **b.** False

c. True **d.** True **e.** True **33.** If $A(t) = A_0 e^{kt}$ and $A(T) = 2A_0$, then $e^{kT} = 2$ and $T = \dfrac{\ln 2}{k}$. The doubling time is constant.

35. a. Bob; Abe **b.** $y = 4 \ln(t + 1)$ and $y = 8 - 8e^{-t/2}$; Bob

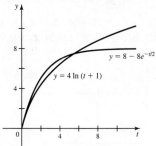

37. 10.034%; no **39.** Approximately 1.264 s

41. Approximately 1044 days **43.** $50

45. $k = \ln(1 + r)$; $r = 2^{(1/T_2)} - 1$; $T_2 = \dfrac{(\ln 2)}{k}$

Chapter 8 Review Exercises, pp. 591–593

1. a. False **b.** False **c.** True **d.** True **e.** False
3. $y = Ce^{-2t} + 3$ **5.** $y = Ce^{t^2}$ **7.** $y = Ce^{\tan^{-1}t}$
9. $y = \tan(t^2 + t + C)$ **11.** $y = \sin t + t^2 + 1$
13. $Q = 8(1 - e^{t-1})$ **15.** $u = (3 + t^{2/3})^{3/2}$
17. $s = \sqrt{16 + \ln(t + 2)}$
19. a, b.

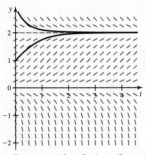

c. $0 < A < 2$ **d.** $A > 2$ or $A < 0$ **e.** $y = 0$ and $y = 2$
21. B
23.

k	t_k	u_k	Slope $= f(t_k, u_k)$
0	0	1	-1
1	0.25	0.75	-1.25
2	0.5	0.438	-1.563
3	0.75	0.0469	—

25. a. 1.05, 1.09762 **b.** 1.04939, 1.09651
c. 2.2×10^{-3}; 1.1×10^{-3}; the error in part (b) is smaller.
27. $A = -3, A = 0, A = 5$ **29.** $A = -1, A = 0, A = 2$
31. a. $k = -\dfrac{1}{5}\ln\left(\dfrac{7}{11}\right) \approx 0.0904$ **b.** $T = 55\,e^{-kt} + 25$
c. Approximately 8.7 min **33.** 771.86 yr
35. a. $1500\,(1.054)^t$ **b.** 13.18 yr **c.** 22.89 yr

AP® Practice, Section 1, Parts A and B, pp. 593–595

1. B **2.** E **3.** B **4.** A **5.** B **6.** D **7.** C **8.** E **9.** A
10. B **11.** E **12.** D **13.** C **14.** B **15.** A **16.** C

AP® Practice, Section 2, Parts A and B, pp. 596–597

1. a. 0.56 **b.** 1.56 **c.** $y = 1 + x$ **d.** 1.4 **e.** 1.48
2. a. $y(0.4) \approx 4.01$ **b.** $y(0.4) \approx 4.015$ **c.** 0.00995; 0.00497
d. Reduced by a factor of 2
3. a.

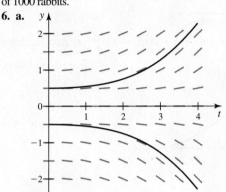

b. $y = \dfrac{x + 1}{C(x + 1) - 1}$
c. $y = \dfrac{2(x + 1)}{3x + 1}$ **d.** $\dfrac{2}{3}$

4. a. $y = (A - 8)e^{t/2} + 8$ **b.** $y = -6e^{t/2} + 8$; $-\infty$
c. $y = 4e^{t/2} + 8$; ∞ **d.** $B = 8$ **5. a.** 600 rabbits **b.** 750 rabbits
c. $\dfrac{d^2P}{dt^2} = \dfrac{1}{4}P - 250$; overestimate **d.** $P(t) = 1000 - 500e^{-t/2}$;
$\lim\limits_{t\to\infty} P(t) = 1000$; the population approaches a carrying capacity
of 1000 rabbits.
6. a.

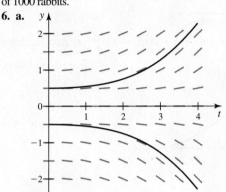

b. $y = \dfrac{2}{5}t + \dfrac{1}{5}$ **c.** $y = e^{t^2/10}$
d. $\dfrac{d^2y}{dt^2} = \dfrac{d}{dt}\left(\dfrac{ty}{5}\right) = \dfrac{1}{5}\left(y + t\dfrac{dy}{dt}\right) = \dfrac{1}{5}\left(y + \dfrac{t^2y}{5}\right) = \dfrac{y}{25}(t^2 + 5)$.
$\dfrac{d^2y}{dt^2} > 0$ when $y > 0$, which implies the solution curves are concave up.
$\dfrac{d^2y}{dt^2} < 0$ when $y < 0$, which implies the solution curves are concave
down.

CHAPTER 9

Section 9.1 Exercises, pp. 606–608

1. A sequence is an ordered list of numbers. Example: $1, \dfrac{1}{3}, \dfrac{1}{9}, \dfrac{1}{27}, \ldots$
3. 1, 1, 2, 6, 24 **5.** Given a sequence $\{a_1, a_2, \ldots\}$, an infinite
series is the sum $a_1 + a_2 + a_3 + \cdots$. Example: $\displaystyle\sum_{k=1}^{\infty} \dfrac{1}{k^2}$
7. 1, 5, 14, 30 **9.** $\dfrac{1}{10}, \dfrac{1}{100}, \dfrac{1}{1000}, \dfrac{1}{10,000}$ **11.** $-\dfrac{1}{2}, \dfrac{1}{4}, -\dfrac{1}{8}, \dfrac{1}{16}$
13. $\dfrac{4}{3}, \dfrac{8}{5}, \dfrac{16}{9}, \dfrac{32}{17}$ **15.** 2, 1, 0, 1 **17.** 2, 4, 8, 16
19. 10, 18, 42, 114 **21.** 0, 2, 15, 679 **23. a.** $\dfrac{1}{32}, \dfrac{1}{64}$
b. $a_1 = 1$, $a_{n+1} = \dfrac{1}{2}a_n$, for $n \geq 1$ **c.** $a_n = \dfrac{1}{2^{n-1}}$, for $n \geq 1$
25. a. $-5, 5$ **b.** $a_1 = -5$, $a_{n+1} = -a_n$, for $n \geq 1$
c. $a_n = (-1)^n \cdot 5$, for $n \geq 1$ **27. a.** 32, 64 **b.** $a_1 = 1$,
$a_{n+1} = 2a_n$, for $n \geq 1$ **c.** $a_n = 2^{n-1}$, for $n \geq 1$
29. a. 243, 729 **b.** $a_1 = 1$, $a_{n+1} = 3a_n$, for $n \geq 1$ **c.** $a_n = 3^{n-1}$,
for $n \geq 1$ **31.** 9, 99, 999, 9999; diverges

33. $\dfrac{1}{10}, \dfrac{1}{100}, \dfrac{1}{1000}, \dfrac{1}{10,000}$; converges to 0   **35.** $-\dfrac{1}{2}, \dfrac{1}{4}, -\dfrac{1}{8}, \dfrac{1}{16}$; converges to 0   **37.** 2, 2, 2, 2; converges to 2   **39.** 54.545, 54.959, 54.996, 55.000; converges to 55   **41.** 0   **43.** Diverges

45. 1   **47. a.** $\dfrac{5}{2}, \dfrac{9}{4}, \dfrac{17}{8}, \dfrac{33}{16}$ **b.** 2   **49.** 4   **51.** Diverges

53. 4   **55. a.** $20, 10, 5, \dfrac{5}{2}$ **b.** $h_n = 20\left(\dfrac{1}{2}\right)^n$, $n \ge 0$

57. a. $30, \dfrac{15}{2}, \dfrac{15}{8}, \dfrac{15}{32}$ **b.** $h_n = 30\left(\dfrac{1}{4}\right)^n$, $n \ge 0$

59. $S_1 = 0.3, S_2 = 0.33, S_3 = 0.333, S_4 = 0.3333$; $\dfrac{1}{3}$

61. $S_1 = 4, S_2 = 4.9, S_3 = 4.99, S_4 = 4.999$; 5

63. a. $\dfrac{2}{3}, \dfrac{4}{5}, \dfrac{6}{7}, \dfrac{8}{9}$ **b.** $S_n = \dfrac{2n}{2n+1}$ **c.** $\lim\limits_{n\to\infty} S_n = 1$

65. a. $\dfrac{1}{3}, \dfrac{2}{5}, \dfrac{3}{7}, \dfrac{4}{9}$ **b.** $S_n = \dfrac{n}{2n+1}$ **c.** $\lim\limits_{n\to\infty} S_n = \dfrac{1}{2}$

67. a. True   **b.** False   **c.** True   **69. a.** 40, 70, 92.5, 109.375   **b.** 160   **71. a.** 0.9, 0.99, 0.999, 0.9999   **b.** 1   **73. a.** $\dfrac{1}{3}, \dfrac{4}{9}, \dfrac{13}{27}, \dfrac{40}{81}$ **b.** $\dfrac{1}{2}$ **75. a.** $-1, 0, -1, 0$ **b.** Does not exist

77. a. 0.3, 0.33, 0.333, 0.3333   **b.** $\dfrac{1}{3}$ **79. a.** $20, 10, 5, \dfrac{5}{2}, \dfrac{5}{4}$
b. $M_n = 20\left(\dfrac{1}{2}\right)^n$, for $n \ge 0$ **c.** $M_0 = 20, M_{n+1} = \dfrac{1}{2}M_n$, for $n \ge 0$ **d.** $\lim\limits_{n\to\infty} a_n = 0$
81. a. 200, 190, 180.5, 171.475, 162.901   **b.** $d_n = 200(0.95)^n$, for $n \ge 0$ **c.** $d_0 = 200, d_{n+1} = (0.95)d_n$, for $n \ge 0$ **d.** $\lim\limits_{n\to\infty} d_n = 0$

Section 9.2 Exercises, pp. 617–621

1. $a_n = \dfrac{1}{n}$, $n \ge 1$ **3.** $a_n = \dfrac{n}{n+1}$, $n \ge 1$
5. Converges for $-1 < r \le 1$, diverges otherwise   **7.** $\{e^{n/100}\}$ grows faster as $n \to \infty$.   **9.** 0   **11.** $\dfrac{3}{2}$ **13.** 3   **15.** $\dfrac{\pi}{2}$ **17.** 0
19. e^2 **21.** $e^{1/4}$ **23.** 0   **25.** 1   **27.** 0   **29.** 0
31. 6   **33.** Does not exist   **35.** Does not exist   **37.** 0   **39.** 2
41. 0   **43.** Does not exist   **45.** Converges monotonically; 0
47. Converges, oscillates; 0   **49.** Diverges monotonically
51. Diverges, oscillates   **53.** 0   **55.** 0   **57.** 0
59. a. $d_{n+1} = \dfrac{1}{2}d_n + 80$, for $n \ge 1$ **b.** 160 mg
61. a. $0, $100, $200.75, $302.26, $404.53
b. $B_{n+1} = 1.0075B_n + 100$, for $n \ge 0$ **c.** During the 43rd month
63. 0   **65.** Diverges   **67.** 0   **69. a.** True   **b.** False
c. True   **d.** True   **e.** False   **f.** True   **71.** $\{n^2 + 2n - 17\}_{n=3}^{\infty}$
73. 0   **75.** 1   **77.** 1   **79.** Diverges   **81.** 1/2   **83.** 0
85. $n = 4, n = 6, n = 25$
87. a. $h_n = (200 + 5n)(0.65 - 0.01n) - 0.45n$, for $n \ge 0$
b. The profit is maximized after 8 days.   **89.** 0.607   **91. b.** 1, 1.414, 1.554, 1.598, 1.612   **c.** Approximately 1.618   **e.** $\dfrac{1 + \sqrt{1 + 4p}}{2}$
93. b. 1, 2, 1.5, 1.667, 1.6   **c.** Approximately 1.618

e. $\dfrac{a + \sqrt{a^2 + 4b}}{2}$ **95. a.** 1, 1, 2, 3, 5, 8, 13, 21, 34, 55   **b.** No
99. d. 3   **101.** $\{a_n\}$; $n = 36$ **103.** $\{a_n\}$; $n = 19$ **105.** $a < 1$

Section 9.3 Exercises, pp. 625–629

1. The next term in the series is generated by multiplying the previous term by the constant r (the ratio of the series).
Example: $2 + 1 + \dfrac{1}{2} + \dfrac{1}{4} + \cdots$ **3.** The constant r in the series $\sum\limits_{k=0}^{\infty} ar^k$ **5.** No   **7.** 9841   **9.** Approx. 1.190

11. Approx. 0.539   **13.** $\dfrac{1 - \pi^7}{1 - \pi}$ **15.** 1   **17.** $\dfrac{1093}{2916}$ **19.** $\dfrac{4}{3}$

21. 10   **23.** Diverges   **25.** $\dfrac{1}{e^2 - 1}$ **27.** $\dfrac{1}{7}$ **29.** $\dfrac{1}{500}$ **31.** $\dfrac{\pi}{\pi - e}$

33. Approx. 16,447.368   **35.** $\dfrac{10}{19}$ **37.** $\dfrac{3\pi}{\pi + 1}$ **39.** $\dfrac{9}{460}$

41. $0.\overline{3} = \sum\limits_{k=1}^{\infty} 3(0.1)^k = \dfrac{1}{3}$ **43.** $0.\overline{1} = \sum\limits_{k=1}^{\infty} (0.1)^k = \dfrac{1}{9}$

45. $0.\overline{09} = \sum\limits_{k=1}^{\infty} 9(0.01)^k = \dfrac{1}{11}$

47. $0.\overline{037} = \sum\limits_{k=1}^{\infty} 37(0.001)^k = \dfrac{1}{27}$

49. $0.\overline{12} = \sum\limits_{k=0}^{\infty} 0.12(0.01)^k = \dfrac{4}{33}$

51. $0.\overline{456} = \sum\limits_{k=0}^{\infty} 0.456(0.001)^k = \dfrac{152}{333}$

53. $0.00\overline{952} = \sum\limits_{k=0}^{\infty} 0.00952(0.001)^k = \dfrac{238}{24,975}$

55. $S_n = \dfrac{n}{2n + 4}; \dfrac{1}{2}$ **57.** $S_n = \dfrac{1}{7} - \dfrac{1}{n + 7}; \dfrac{1}{7}$

59. $S_n = \dfrac{1}{9} - \dfrac{1}{4n + 1}; \dfrac{1}{9}$ **61.** $S_n = \ln(n + 1)$; diverges

63. $S_n = \dfrac{1}{p + 1} - \dfrac{1}{n + p + 1}; \dfrac{1}{p + 1}$

65. $S_n = \left(\dfrac{1}{\sqrt{2}} + \dfrac{1}{\sqrt{3}}\right) - \left(\dfrac{1}{\sqrt{n + 2}} + \dfrac{1}{\sqrt{n + 3}}\right); \dfrac{1}{\sqrt{2}} + \dfrac{1}{\sqrt{3}}$

67. $S_n = -\dfrac{n + 1}{4n + 3}; -\dfrac{1}{4}$ **69. a.** True   **b.** True   **c.** False

d. True   **e.** True   **71.** $-\dfrac{2}{15}$ **73.** $\dfrac{1}{\ln 2}$ **75. a, b.** $\dfrac{4}{3}$

77. $\sum\limits_{k=0}^{\infty} \left(\dfrac{1}{4}\right)^k A_1 = \dfrac{A_1}{1 - 1/4} = \dfrac{4}{3}A_1$ **79.** 462 months   **81.** 0

83. There will be twice as many children.   **85.** $\sqrt{\dfrac{20}{g}} \dfrac{1 + \sqrt{p}}{1 - \sqrt{p}} s$

87. a. $L_n = 3\left(\dfrac{4}{3}\right)^n$, so $\lim\limits_{n\to\infty} L_n = \infty$ **b.** $\lim\limits_{n\to\infty} A_n = \dfrac{2\sqrt{3}}{5}$

89. $R_n = S - S_n = \dfrac{1}{1 - r} - \left(\dfrac{1 - r^n}{1 - r}\right) = \dfrac{r^n}{1 - r}$

91. a. 60   **b.** 9   **93. a.** 13   **b.** 15   **95. a.** $1, \dfrac{5}{6}, \dfrac{2}{3}$, undefined, undefined   **b.** $|x| < 1$ **97.** Converges for x in $(-\infty, -2)$ or $(0, \infty)$; $x = \dfrac{1}{2}$

99. a.

r	$f(r)$
-0.9	0.526
-0.7	0.588
-0.5	0.667
-0.2	0.833
0	1
0.2	1.250
0.5	2
0.7	3.333
0.9	10

b.

c. $\lim_{r \to 1^-} f(r) = \lim_{r \to 1^-} \dfrac{1}{1 - r} = \infty$; $\lim_{r \to -1^+} f(r) = \lim_{r \to -1^+} \dfrac{1}{1 - r} = \dfrac{1}{2}$

Section 9.4 Exercises, pp. 640–643

1. The series diverges.   **3.** Yes, if the terms are positive and decreasing.
5. Converges for $p > 1$ and diverges otherwise   **7.** $R_n = S - S_n$
9. Diverges   **11.** Diverges   **13.** Inconclusive
15. Diverges   **17.** Diverges   **19.** Converges   **21.** Converges
23. Diverges   **25.** Converges   **27.** Test does not apply
29. Converges   **31.** Converges   **33.** Diverges

35. a. $\dfrac{1}{5n^5}$ **b.** 3 **c.** $L_n = S_n + \dfrac{1}{5(n + 1)^5}$; $U_n = S_n + \dfrac{1}{5n^5}$

d. $(1.017342754, 1.017343512)$ **37. a.** $\dfrac{3^{-n}}{\ln 3}$ **b.** 7

c. $L_n = S_n + \dfrac{3^{-n-1}}{\ln 3}$; $U_n = S_n + \dfrac{3^{-n}}{\ln 3}$

d. $(0.499996671, 0.500006947)$ **39. a.** $\dfrac{2}{\sqrt{n}}$ **b.** $4 \times 10^6 + 1$

c. $L_n = S_n + \dfrac{2}{\sqrt{n + 1}}$; $U_n = S_n + \dfrac{2}{\sqrt{n}}$

d. $(2.598359182, 2.627792025)$ **41. a.** $\dfrac{1}{2n^2}$ **b.** 23

c. $L_n = S_n + \dfrac{1}{2(n + 1)^2}$; $U_n = S_n + \dfrac{1}{2n^2}$

d. $(1.201664217, 1.202531986)$ **43.** $\dfrac{4}{11}$ **45.** -2 **47.** $\dfrac{113}{30}$

49. $\dfrac{17}{10}$ **51. a.** True   **b.** True   **c.** False   **d.** False   **e.** False

f. False   **53.** Converges   **55.** Diverges   **57.** Converges

59. a. $p > 1$ **b.** $\displaystyle\sum_{k=2}^{\infty} \dfrac{1}{k(\ln k)^2}$ converges faster.

65. $\zeta(3) \approx 1.202$, $\zeta(5) \approx 1.037$ **67.** $\dfrac{\pi^2}{8}$ **69. a.** $\dfrac{1}{2}, \dfrac{7}{12}, \dfrac{37}{60}$

71. a. $\displaystyle\sum_{k=2}^{n} \dfrac{1}{k}$ **b.** The distance can be made arbitrarily large.

Section 9.5 Exercises, pp. 650–651

1. Take the limit of the ratio of consecutive terms of the series as $n \to \infty$
The value of the limit determines whether the series converges.   **3.** Find
an appropriate comparison series. Then take the limit of the ratio of the

terms of the given series and the comparison series as $n \to 1 \infty$.
The value of the limit determines whether the series converges.
5. Ratio Test   **7.** $S_{n+1} - S_n = a_{n+1} > 0$; therefore,
$S_{n+1} > S_n$ **9.** Converges   **11.** Converges   **13.** Converges
15. Diverges   **17.** Converges   **19.** Converges   **21.** Converges
23. Converges   **25.** Converges   **27.** Converges   **29.** Diverges
31. Converges   **33.** Converges   **35.** Diverges   **37.** Diverges
39. a. False   **b.** True   **c.** True   **d.** True   **41.** Diverges
43. Converges   **45.** Converges   **47.** Diverges   **49.** Diverges
51. Converges   **53.** Diverges   **55.** Converges   **57.** Converges
59. Converges   **61.** Diverges   **63.** Converges   **65.** Diverges
67. Converges   **69.** Converges   **71.** $p > 1$ **73.** $p > 1$
75. $p < 1$ **77.** Diverges for all p **79.** Diverges if $|r| \geq 1$
83. $0 \leq x < 1$ **85.** $0 \leq x \leq 1$ **87.** $0 \leq x < 2$ **89. a.** e^2 **b.** 0

Section 9.6 Exercises, pp. 659–660

1. Because $S_{n+1} - S_n = (-1)^n a_{n+1}$ alternates sign
3. Because $\lim_{k \to \infty} a_k = 0$ and the terms $(-1)^k a_k$ alternate in sign
5. $|R_n| = |S - S_n| \leq |S_{n+1} - S_n| = a_{n+1}$ **7.** No; if a
series of positive terms converges, if does so absolutely and
not conditionally.   **9.** Yes, $\displaystyle\sum_{k=1}^{\infty} \dfrac{(-1)^k}{k^2}$ has this property.
11. Converges   **13.** Diverges   **15.** Converges   **17.** Converges
19. Diverges   **21.** Diverges   **23.** Converges   **25.** Diverges
27. Converges   **29.** $10{,}000$ **31.** 5000 **33.** 10 **35.** 3334
37. 6 **39.** -0.973 **41.** -0.269 (the sum of the first 999 terms)
43. -0.783 **45.** Converges conditionally   **47.** Converges absolutely
49. Converges absolutely   **51.** Diverges   **53.** Diverges
55. Converges absolutely   **57. a.** False   **b.** True   **c.** True
d. True   **e.** False   **f.** True   **g.** True   **61.** The conditions of
the Alternating Series Test are met; therefore, $\displaystyle\sum_{k=1}^{\infty} r^k$ converges for
$-1 < r < 0$.   **65.** x and y are divergent series.

Chapter 9 Review Exercises, pp. 661–663

1. a. False   **b.** False   **c.** True   **d.** False   **e.** True
f. False   **g.** False   **h.** True   **3.** 0 **5.** 1 **7.** $\dfrac{1}{e}$

9. Diverges   **11. a.** $\dfrac{1}{3}, \dfrac{11}{24}, \dfrac{21}{40}, \dfrac{17}{30}$

b. $S_1 = \dfrac{1}{3}, S_n = \dfrac{1}{2}\left(\dfrac{3}{2} - \dfrac{1}{n + 1} - \dfrac{1}{n + 2}\right), n \geq 1$ **c.** $\dfrac{3}{4}$

13. Diverges   **15.** 1 **17.** 3 **19.** $\dfrac{2}{9}$ **21. a.** Yes; 1.5

b. Convergence uncertain   **c.** Appears to diverge
23. Diverges   **25.** Converges   **27.** Converges   **29.** Converges
31. Converges   **33.** Converges   **35.** Converges   **37.** Converges
39. Converges   **41.** Diverges   **43.** Converges absolutely
45. Converges absolutely   **47.** Converges absolutely

49. Diverges   **51. a.** 0 **b.** $\dfrac{5}{9}$ **53.** $\lim_{k \to \infty} a_k = 0$, $\lim_{n \to \infty} S_n = 8$
55. $0 < p \leq 1$ **57.** 0.25 (to 14 digits); 6.5×10^{-15} **59.** 100

61. a. 803 m, 1283 m, $2000(1 - 0.95^N)$ m
b. 2000 m   **63. a.** $\dfrac{\pi}{2^{n-1}}$ **b.** 2π

65. a. $B_{n+1} = 1.0025B_n + 100, B_0 = 100$
b. $B_n = 40{,}000(1.0025^{n+1} - 1)$

67. a. $T_1 = \dfrac{\sqrt{3}}{16}, T_2 = \dfrac{7\sqrt{3}}{64}$ **b.** $T_n = \dfrac{\sqrt{3}}{4}\left(1 - \left(\dfrac{3}{4}\right)^n\right)$

c. $\lim\limits_{n\to\infty} T_n = \dfrac{\sqrt{3}}{4}$ **d.** 0

AP® Practice, Section 1, Parts A and B, pp. 663–664

1. E   **2.** D   **3.** E   **4.** E   **5.** B   **6.** C   **7.** D   **8.** B   **9.** E
10. B   **11.** A   **12.** C   **13.** E   **14.** A

AP® Practice, Section 2, Parts A and B, pp. 664–665

1. a. 6 terms (up to and including the $k = 5$ term)   **b.** 0.969

c. Underestimates   **2. a.** 40 ft   **b.** 50 ft   **c.** 30 ft   **d.** $r = \dfrac{5}{6}$

3. a. Inconclusive   **b.** Inconclusive   **c.** Diverges

4. a. $S_n = \dfrac{3}{5}\left(1 - \left(-\dfrac{2}{3}\right)^{n+1}\right)$ **b.** $\dfrac{3}{5}$ **c.** $\lim\limits_{n\to\infty} S_n = \dfrac{3}{5}$

5. a. $\dfrac{\pi}{2}$ **b.** Converges   **c.** Converges

6. a. 0   **b.** Converges   **c.** Converges   **d.** Absolutely

CHAPTER 10

Section 10.1 Exercises, pp. 677–680

1. $f(0) = p_2(0), f'(0) = p_2'(0)$, and $f''(0) = p_2''(0)$
3. $1, 1.05, 1.049$ **5.** $R_n(x) = f(x) - p_n(x)$
7. a. $p_1(x) = 8 + 12(x - 1)$ **b.** $p_2(x) = 8 + 12(x - 1) + 3(x - 1)^2$ **c.** $9.2; 9.23$ **9. a.** $p_1(x) = 1 - x$

b. $p_2(x) = 1 - x + \dfrac{x^2}{2}$ **c.** $0.8, 0.82$ **11. a.** $p_1(x) = 1 - x$
b. $p_2(x) = 1 - x + x^2$ **c.** $0.95, 0.953$

13. a. $p_1(x) = 2 + \dfrac{1}{12}(x - 8)$ **b.** $p_2(x) = 2 + \dfrac{1}{12}(x - 8) - \dfrac{1}{288}(x - 8)^2$ **c.** $1.958, 1.957$

15. a. $p_0(x) = 1, p_1(x) = 1, p_2(x) = 1 - \dfrac{x^2}{2}$

b.

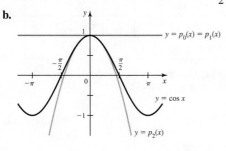

17. a. $p_0(x) = 0, p_1(x) = -x, p_2(x) = -x - \dfrac{x^2}{2}$

b.

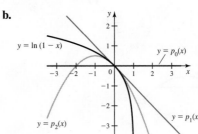

19. a. $p_0(x) = 0, p_1(x) = x, p_2(x) = x$

b.

21. a. $p_0(x) = 1, p_1(x) = 1 - 3x, p_2(x) = 1 - 3x + 6x^2$

b.

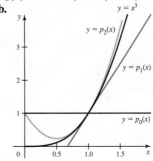

23. a. 1.025 **b.** 7.6×10^{-6} **25. a.** 0.962 **b.** 1.5×10^{-4}
27. a. 0.861 **b.** 5.4×10^{-4}
29. a. $p_0(x) = 1, p_1(x) = 1 + 3(x - 1),$
$p_2(x) = 1 + 3(x - 1) + 3(x - 1)^2$
b.

31. a. $p_0(x) = \dfrac{\sqrt{2}}{2}, p_1(x) = \dfrac{\sqrt{2}}{2} + \dfrac{\sqrt{2}}{2}\left(x - \dfrac{\pi}{4}\right),$

$p_2(x) = \dfrac{\sqrt{2}}{2} + \dfrac{\sqrt{2}}{2}\left(x - \dfrac{\pi}{4}\right) - \dfrac{\sqrt{2}}{4}\left(x - \dfrac{\pi}{4}\right)^2$

b.

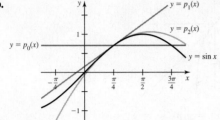

33. a. $p_0(x) = 3, p_1(x) = 3 + \dfrac{(x-9)}{6},$

$p_2(x) = 3 + \dfrac{(x-9)}{6} - \dfrac{(x-9)^2}{216}$

b.

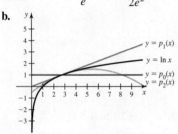

35. a. $p_0(x) = 1, p_1(x) = 1 + \dfrac{x-e}{e},$

$p_2(x) = 1 + \dfrac{x-e}{e} - \dfrac{(x-e)^2}{2e^2}$

b.

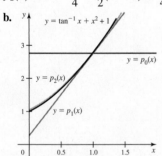

37. a. $p_0(x) = 2 + \dfrac{\pi}{4}, p_1(x) = 2 + \dfrac{\pi}{4} + \dfrac{5}{2}(x-1),$

$p_2(x) = 2 + \dfrac{\pi}{4} + \dfrac{5}{2}(x-1) + \dfrac{3}{4}(x-1)^2$

b.

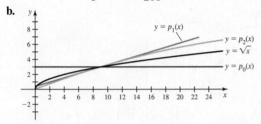

39. a. 1.127   **b.** 8.9×10^{-6} **41. a.** -0.100 **b.** 1.3×10^{-6}
43. a. 1.030   **b.** 4.9×10^{-7} **45. a.** 10.050   **b.** 3.9×10^{-9}
47. a. 0.141   **b.** 4.7×10^{-7}

49. $R_n(x) = \dfrac{\sin^{(n+1)}(c)}{(n+1)!} x^{n+1}$, for c between x and 0.

51. $R_n(x) = \dfrac{(-1)^{n+1} e^{-c}}{(n+1)!} x^{n+1}$, for c between x and 0.

53. $R_n(x) = \dfrac{\sin^{(n+1)}(c)}{(n+1)!} \left(x - \dfrac{\pi}{2}\right)^{n+1}$, for c between x and $\dfrac{\pi}{2}$.

55. 2.0×10^{-5} **57.** 1.6×10^{-5} ($e^{0.25} < 2$)   **59.** 2.6×10^{-4}
61. With $n = 4$, max error $= 2.5 \times 10^{-3}$ **63.** With $n = 2$, max
error $= 4.2 \times 10^{-2}$ ($e^{0.5} < 2$)   **65.** With $n = 2$, max
error $= 5.4 \times 10^{-3}$ **67.** 4   **69.** 3   **71.** 1   **73. a.** False   **b.** True
c. True   **d.** True   **75. a.** C   **b.** E   **c.** A   **d.** D   **e.** B   **f.** F
77. a. 0.1; 1.7×10^{-4} **b.** 0.2; 1.3×10^{-3}
79. a. 0.995; 4.2×10^{-6} **b.** 0.98; 6.7×10^{-5}
81. a. 1.05; 1.3×10^{-3} **b.** 1.1; 5×10^{-3}
83. a. 1.1; 10^{-2} **b.** 1.2; 4×10^{-2}
85. a.

x	$|\sin x - p_3(x)|$	$|\sin x - p_5(x)|$
-0.2	2.7×10^{-6}	2.5×10^{-9}
-0.1	8.3×10^{-8}	2.0×10^{-11}
0.0	0	0
0.1	8.3×10^{-8}	2.0×10^{-11}
0.2	2.7×10^{-6}	2.5×10^{-9}

b. The error increases as $|x|$ increases.
87. a.

x	$|e^{-x} - p_1(x)|$	$|e^{-x} - p_2(x)|$
-0.2	2.1×10^{-2}	1.4×10^{-3}
-0.1	5.2×10^{-3}	1.7×10^{-4}
0.0	0	0
0.1	4.8×10^{-3}	1.6×10^{-4}
0.2	1.9×10^{-2}	1.3×10^{-3}

b. The error increases as $|x|$ increases.
89. a.

x	$|\tan x - p_1(x)|$	$|\tan x - p_3(x)|$
-0.2	2.7×10^{-3}	4.3×10^{-5}
-0.1	3.3×10^{-4}	1.3×10^{-6}
0.0	0	0
0.1	3.3×10^{-4}	1.3×10^{-6}
0.2	2.7×10^{-3}	4.3×10^{-5}

b. The error increases as $|x|$ increases.   **91.** Centered at $x = 0$
for all n **93. a.** $y = f(a) + f'(a)(x - a)$

95. a. $p_5(x) = x - \dfrac{x^3}{6} + \dfrac{x^5}{120};$

$q_5(x) = -(x - \pi) + \dfrac{1}{6}(x - \pi)^3 - \dfrac{1}{120}(x - \pi)^5$

b.

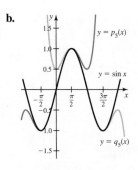

p_5 is a better approximation on $[-\pi, \pi/2]$; q_5 is a better approximation on $(\pi/2, 2\pi]$.

c.

x	$\lvert\sin x - p_5(x)\rvert$	$\lvert\sin x - q_5(x)\rvert$
$\pi/4$	3.6×10^{-5}	7.4×10^{-2}
$\pi/2$	4.5×10^{-3}	4.5×10^{-3}
$3\pi/4$	7.4×10^{-2}	3.6×10^{-5}
$5\pi/4$	2.3	3.6×10^{-5}
$7\pi/4$	20	7.4×10^{-2}

d. p_5 is a better approximation at $x = \pi/4$; at $x = \pi/2$ the approximations are equal.

97. a. $p_1(x) = 6 + \dfrac{1}{12}(x - 36)$; $q_1(x) = 7 + \dfrac{1}{14}(x - 49)$

b.

x	$\lvert\sqrt{x} - p_1(x)\rvert$	$\lvert\sqrt{x} - q_1(x)\rvert$
37	5.7×10^{-4}	6.0×10^{-2}
39	5.0×10^{-3}	4.1×10^{-2}
41	1.4×10^{-2}	2.5×10^{-2}
43	2.6×10^{-2}	1.4×10^{-2}
45	4.2×10^{-2}	6.1×10^{-3}
47	6.1×10^{-2}	1.5×10^{-3}

c. p_1 is a better approximation at $x = 37, 39, 41$.

Section 10.2 Exercises, pp. 688–690

1. $c_0 + c_1 x + c_2 x^2 + c_3 x^3$ **3.** Ratio and Root Tests   **5.** The radius of convergence does not change. The interval of convergence may change.   **7.** $\lvert x\rvert < \dfrac{1}{4}$ **9.** $R = \frac{1}{2}$; $(-\frac{1}{2}, \frac{1}{2})$ **11.** $R = 1$; $[0, 2)$
13. $R = 0$; $\{x : x = 0\}$ **15.** $R = \infty$; $(-\infty, \infty)$
17. $R = 3$; $(-3, 3)$ **19.** $R = \infty$; $(-\infty, \infty)$
21. $R = \infty$; $(-\infty, \infty)$ **23.** $R = \sqrt{3}$; $(-\sqrt{3}, \sqrt{3})$
25. $R = 1$; $(0, 2)$ **27.** $R = \infty$; $(-\infty, \infty)$
29. $\displaystyle\sum_{k=0}^{\infty}(3x)^k$; $(-\frac{1}{3}, \frac{1}{3})$ **31.** $2\displaystyle\sum_{k=0}^{\infty}x^{k+3}$; $(-1, 1)$
33. $4\displaystyle\sum_{k=0}^{\infty}x^{k+12}$; $(-1, 1)$ **35.** $-\displaystyle\sum_{k=1}^{\infty}\dfrac{(3x)^k}{k}$; $[-\frac{1}{3}, \frac{1}{3})$
37. $-\displaystyle\sum_{k=1}^{\infty}\dfrac{x^{k+1}}{k}$; $[-1, 1)$ **39.** $-2\displaystyle\sum_{k=1}^{\infty}\dfrac{x^{k+6}}{k}$; $[-1, 1)$
41. $\displaystyle\sum_{k=1}^{\infty}kx^{k-1}$; $(-1, 1)$

43. $\displaystyle\sum_{k=3}^{\infty}\dfrac{k(k-1)(k-2)}{6}x^{k-3}$; $(-1, 1)$

45. $-\displaystyle\sum_{k=1}^{\infty}\dfrac{3^k x^k}{k}$; $[-\frac{1}{3}, \frac{1}{3})$ **47.** $\displaystyle\sum_{k=0}^{\infty}(-x^2)^k$; $(-1, 1)$

49. $\displaystyle\sum_{k=0}^{\infty}\left(-\dfrac{x}{3}\right)^k$; $(-3, 3)$ **51.** $\ln 2 - \dfrac{1}{2}\displaystyle\sum_{k=1}^{\infty}\dfrac{x^{2k}}{k4^k}$; $(-2, 2)$

53. a. True   **b.** True   **c.** True   **d.** True   **55.** e

57. $\displaystyle\sum_{k=0}^{\infty}\dfrac{(-1)^k x^k}{k+1}$ **59.** $\displaystyle\sum_{k=1}^{\infty}\dfrac{(-x^2)^k}{k!}$ **61.** $\lvert x - a\rvert < R$

63. $\dfrac{1}{3 - \sqrt{x}}$; $1 < x < 9$ **65.** $\dfrac{e^x}{e^x - 1}$; $0 < x < \infty$

67. $\dfrac{3}{4 - x^2}$; $-2 < x < 2$ **69.** $\displaystyle\sum_{k=0}^{\infty}\dfrac{(-x)^k}{k!}$; $-\infty < x < \infty$

71. $\displaystyle\sum_{k=0}^{\infty}\dfrac{(-3x)^k}{k!}$; $-\infty < x < \infty$

73. $\displaystyle\lim_{k\to\infty}\left\lvert\dfrac{c_{k+1}x^{k+1}}{c_k x^k}\right\rvert = \lim_{k\to\infty}\left\lvert\dfrac{c_{k+1}x^{k+m+1}}{c_k x^{k+m}}\right\rvert$;

so by the Ratio Test, the two series have the same radius of convergence.
75. a. $f(x)\,g(x) = c_0 d_0 + (c_0 d_1 + c_1 d_0)x$
$\qquad\qquad\qquad + (c_0 d_2 + c_1 d_1 + c_2 d_0)x^2 + \cdots.$

b. $\displaystyle\sum_{k=0}^{n}c_k d_{n-k}$ **77. b.** $n = 112$

Section 10.3 Exercises, pp. 699–701

1. The nth Taylor polynomial is the nth partial sum of the corresponding Taylor series.   **3.** Calculate $c_k = \dfrac{f^{(k)}(a)}{k!}$, for $k = 0, 1, 2, \ldots$.   **5.** Replace x with x^2 in the Taylor series for $f(x)$; $\lvert x\rvert < 1$.   **7.** The Taylor series for a function f converges to f on an interval if, for all x in the interval, $\lim_{n\to\infty} R_n(x) = 0$, where $R_n(x)$ is the remainder at x.   **9. a.** $1 - x + \dfrac{x^2}{2!} - \dfrac{x^3}{3!}$ **b.** $\displaystyle\sum_{k=0}^{\infty}\dfrac{(-1)^k x^k}{k!}$

c. $(-\infty, \infty)$ **11. a.** $1 - x^2 + x^4 - x^6$ **b.** $\displaystyle\sum_{k=0}^{n}(-1)^k x^{2k}$

c. $(-1, 1)$ **13. a.** $1 + 2x + \dfrac{(2x)^2}{2!} + \dfrac{(2x)^3}{3!}$ **b.** $\displaystyle\sum_{k=0}^{\infty}\dfrac{(2x)^k}{k!}$

c. $(-\infty, \infty)$ **15. a.** $x - \dfrac{x^3}{3} + \dfrac{x^5}{5} - \dfrac{x^7}{7}$ **b.** $\displaystyle\sum_{k=0}^{\infty}\dfrac{(-1)^k x^{2k+1}}{2k+1}$

c. $[-1, 1]$ **17. a.** $1 + (\ln 3)x + \dfrac{\ln^2 3}{2}x^2 + \dfrac{\ln^3 3}{6}x^3$

b. $\displaystyle\sum_{k=0}^{\infty}\dfrac{\ln^k 3}{k!}x^k$ **c.** $(-\infty, \infty)$ **19. a.** $1 - 3x + 9x^2 - 27x^3$

b. $\displaystyle\sum_{k=0}^{\infty}(-3x)^k$ **c.** $\left(-\dfrac{1}{3}, \dfrac{1}{3}\right)$

21. a. $1 - \dfrac{(x - \pi/2)^2}{2!} + \dfrac{(x - \pi/2)^4}{4!} - \dfrac{(x - \pi/2)^6}{6!}$

b. $\displaystyle\sum_{k=0}^{\infty}\dfrac{(-1)^k}{(2k)!}(x - \pi/2)^{2k}$ **23. a.** $1 - (x - 1) + (x - 1)^2 - (x - 1)^3$

b. $\displaystyle\sum_{k=0}^{\infty}(-1)^k(x - 1)^k$ **25. a.** $\ln 3 + \dfrac{x - 3}{3} - \dfrac{(x - 3)^2}{3^2 \cdot 2} +$

$\dfrac{(x - 3)^3}{3^3 \cdot 3}$ **b.** $\ln 3 + \displaystyle\sum_{k=1}^{\infty}\dfrac{(-1)^{k+1}(x - 3)^k}{k3^k}$

27. a. $2 + 2(\ln 2)(x - 1) + (\ln^2 2)(x - 1)^2 + \dfrac{\ln^3 2}{3}(x - 1)^3$

b. $\displaystyle\sum_{k=0}^{\infty} \dfrac{2(x - 1)^k \ln^k 2}{k!}$　**29.** $x^2 - \dfrac{x^4}{2} + \dfrac{x^6}{3} - \dfrac{x^8}{4}$

31. $1 + 2x + 4x^2 + 8x^3$　**33.** $1 + \dfrac{x}{2} + \dfrac{x^2}{6} + \dfrac{x^3}{24}$

35. $1 - x^4 + x^8 - x^{12}$　**37.** $\dfrac{1}{9} - \dfrac{x^2}{81} + \dfrac{x^4}{729} - \dfrac{x^6}{6561}$

39. a. $1 - 2x + 3x^2 - 4x^3$　**b.** 0.826

41. a. $1 + \dfrac{1}{4}x - \dfrac{3}{32}x^2 + \dfrac{7}{128}x^3$　**b.** 1.029

43. a. $1 - \dfrac{2}{3}x + \dfrac{5}{9}x^2 - \dfrac{40}{81}x^3$　**b.** 0.895

45. $1 + \dfrac{x^2}{2} - \dfrac{x^4}{8} + \dfrac{x^6}{16}; \, [-1, 1]$

47. $3 - \dfrac{3x}{2} - \dfrac{3x^2}{8} - \dfrac{3x^3}{16}; \, [-1, 1)$

49. $a + \dfrac{x^2}{2a} - \dfrac{x^4}{8a^3} + \dfrac{x^6}{16a^5}; \, [-a, a]$

51. $1 + 8x + 48x^2 + 256x^3$

53. $\dfrac{1}{16} - \dfrac{x^2}{32} + \dfrac{3x^4}{256} - \dfrac{x^6}{256}$

55. $\dfrac{1}{9} - \dfrac{2}{9}\left(\dfrac{4x}{3}\right) + \dfrac{3}{9}\left(\dfrac{4x}{3}\right)^2 - \dfrac{4}{9}\left(\dfrac{4x}{3}\right)^3$

57. $R_n(x) = \dfrac{f^{(n+1)}(c)}{(n+1)!} x^{n+1}$, where c is between 0 and x, and $f^{(n+1)}(c) = \pm\sin c$ or $\pm\cos c$. Therefore, $|R_n(x)| \le \dfrac{|x|^{n+1}}{(n+1)!} \to 0$ as $n \to \infty$, for $-\infty < x < \infty$.

59. $R_n(x) = \dfrac{f^{(n+1)}(c)}{(n+1)!} x^{n+1}$, where c is between 0 and x, and $f^{(n+1)}(c) = (-1)^n e^{-c}$. Therefore, $|R_n(x)| \le \dfrac{|x|^{n+1}}{e^c (n+1)!} \to 0$ as $n \to \infty$, for $-\infty < x < \infty$.　**61. a.** False　**b.** True　**c.** False　**d.** False

e. True　**63.** $1 + \dfrac{x^2}{2!} + \dfrac{x^4}{4!}$　**65.** $1 - \dfrac{2}{3}x^2 + \dfrac{5}{9}x^4$

67. $1 - \dfrac{1}{2}x^2 - \dfrac{1}{8}x^4$　**69.** $1 - 2x^2 + 3x^4$

71. 3.915　**73.** 1.899　**79.** $\displaystyle\sum_{k=0}^{\infty} \left(\dfrac{x - 4}{2}\right)^k$

81. $\dfrac{1 \cdot 3 \cdot 5 \cdot 7}{2 \cdot 4 \cdot 6 \cdot 8} x^4, -\dfrac{1 \cdot 3 \cdot 5 \cdot 7 \cdot 9}{2 \cdot 4 \cdot 6 \cdot 8 \cdot 10} x^5$　**83.** $a = \dfrac{\pi}{4}; 0.766$

85. $a = 64; 4.362$　**87. a.** Use three terms of the Taylor series for $\sqrt[3]{125 + x}$ centered at $a = 0$; 5.03968　**b.** Use three terms of the Taylor series for $\sqrt[3]{x}$ centered at $a = 125$; 5.03968　**c.** Yes

93. a. $p_5(x) = 1 + x + x^2 + x^3 + x^4 + x^5$

b.

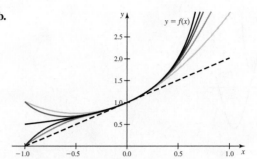

c. Convergence is slowest near $x = \pm 1$.　**d.** At $x = 0$

e.

n	$\|f(0.9) - p_n(0.9)\|$
1	8.1
2	7.3
3	6.6
4	5.9
5	5.3

f. 65

Section 10.4 Exercises, pp. 708–711

1. Replace f and g with their Taylor series centered at a and evaluate the limit.　**3.** Substitute $x = -0.6$ into the Taylor series for e^x centered at 0. Because the resulting series is an alternating series, the error can be estimated.　**5.** $f'(x) = \displaystyle\sum_{k=1}^{\infty} kc_k x^{k-1}$　**7.** 1

9. $\dfrac{1}{2}$　**11.** 2　**13.** $\dfrac{2}{3}$　**15.** $\dfrac{1}{3}$　**17.** $\dfrac{3}{5}$　**19.** $-\dfrac{8}{5}$

21. 1　**23.** $\dfrac{3}{4}$　**25. a.** $1 + x + \dfrac{x^2}{2!} + \cdots + \dfrac{x^n}{n!} + \cdots$

b. e^x　**c.** $-\infty < x < \infty$　**27. a.** $1 - x + x^2 - \cdots$

$(-1)^{n-1}x^{n-1} + \cdots$　**b.** $\dfrac{1}{1 + x}$　**c.** $|x| < 1$

29. a. $-2 + 4x - 8 \cdot \dfrac{x^2}{2!} + \cdots + (-2)^n \dfrac{x^{n-1}}{(n-1)!} + \cdots$

b. $-2e^{-2x}$　**c.** $-\infty < x < \infty$　**31. a.** $1 - x^2 + x^4 - \cdots$

b. $\dfrac{1}{1 + x^2}$　**c.** $-1 < x < 1$　**33. a.** $2 + 2t + \dfrac{2t^2}{2!} + \cdots + \dfrac{2t^n}{n!} + \cdots$　**b.** $y = 2e^t$　**35. a.** $2 + 16t + 24t^2 + 24t^3 + \cdots + \dfrac{3^{n-1} \cdot 16}{n!} t^n + \cdots$　**b.** $y = \dfrac{16}{3}e^{3t} - \dfrac{10}{3}$

37. 0.245　**39.** 0.696　**41.** $\left(\dfrac{0.35^2}{2} - \dfrac{0.35^4}{12}\right) \approx 0.060$

43. 0.499　**45.** $1 + 2 + \dfrac{2^2}{2!} + \dfrac{2^3}{3!}$

47. $1 - 2 + \dfrac{2}{3} - \dfrac{4}{45}$　**49.** $\dfrac{1}{2} - \dfrac{1}{8} + \dfrac{1}{24} - \dfrac{1}{64}$

51. $e - 1$　**53.** $\displaystyle\sum_{k=1}^{\infty} \dfrac{(-1)^{k+1}x^k}{k}; (-1, 1]; \ln 2$　**55.** $\dfrac{2}{2 - x}$

57. $\dfrac{4}{4 + x^2}$　**59.** $-\ln(1 - x)$　**61.** $-\dfrac{3x^2}{(3 + x)^2}$

63. $\dfrac{6x^2}{(3 - x)^3}$　**65. a.** False　**b.** False　**c.** True　**67.** $\dfrac{a}{b}$

69. $e^{-1/6}$ **71.** $f^{(3)}(0) = 0; f^{(4)}(0) = 4e$
73. $f^{(3)}(0) = 2; f^{(4)}(0) = 0$ **75.** 2
77. a. 1.575 using four terms   **b.** At least three
c. More terms would be needed.   **79. a.** $S'(x) =$

$\sin x^2; C'(x) = \cos x^2$ **b.** $\dfrac{x^3}{3} - \dfrac{x^7}{7 \cdot 3!} + \dfrac{x^{11}}{11 \cdot 5!} - \dfrac{x^{15}}{15 \cdot 7!};$

$x - \dfrac{x^5}{5 \cdot 2!} + \dfrac{x^9}{9 \cdot 4!} - \dfrac{x^{13}}{13 \cdot 6!}$ **c.** $S(0.05) \approx 4.167 \times 10^{-5}$

$C(-0.25) \approx -0.250$ **d.** 1   **e.** 2

81. a. $1 - \dfrac{x^2}{4} + \dfrac{x^4}{64} - \dfrac{x^6}{2304}$ **b.** $-\infty < x < \infty, R = \infty$

83. a. The Maclaurin series for $\cos x$ consists of even powers of x, which are even functions.   **b.** The Maclaurin series for $\sin x$ consists of odd powers of x, which are

odd functions.   **87. a.** $\dfrac{\pi}{4} = \sum\limits_{k=0}^{\infty} \dfrac{(-1)^k}{2k+1}\left(\dfrac{1}{2^{2k+1}} + \dfrac{1}{3^{2k+1}}\right)$

b. 0.785   **c.** Error $< 4.5 \times 10^{-5}$ **d.** 9 terms

Chapter 10 Review Exercises, pp. 711–712

1. a. True   **b.** False   **c.** True   **d.** True   **3.** $p_2(x) = 1$

5. $p_3(x) = x - \dfrac{x^2}{2} + \dfrac{x^3}{3}$ **7.** $p_2(x) = (x - 1) - \dfrac{(x-1)^2}{2}$

9. $p_3(x) = \dfrac{\pi}{4} + \dfrac{1}{2}(x - 1) - \dfrac{1}{4}(x - 1)^2 + \dfrac{1}{12}(x - 1)^3$

11. a. $p_2(x) = 1 + x + \dfrac{x^2}{2}$

b.

n	$p_n(x)$	Error
0	1	7.7×10^{-2}
1	0.92	3.1×10^{-3}
2	0.9232	8.4×10^{-5}

13. a. $p_2(x) = \dfrac{\sqrt{2}}{2} + \dfrac{\sqrt{2}}{2}\left(x - \dfrac{\pi}{4}\right) - \dfrac{\sqrt{2}}{4}\left(x - \dfrac{\pi}{4}\right)^2$

b.

n	$p_n(x)$	Error
0	0.7071	1.2×10^{-1}
1	0.5960	8.2×10^{-3}
2	0.5873	4.7×10^{-4}

15. $|R_3(x)| < \dfrac{\pi^4}{4!}$ **17.** $(-\infty, \infty), R = \infty$ **19.** $(-\infty, \infty); R = \infty$

21. $(-9, 9); R = 9$ **23.** $[-4, 0); R = 2$ **25.** $\sum\limits_{k=0}^{\infty} x^{2k}; (-1, 1)$

27. $\sum\limits_{k=0}^{\infty} 3^k x^k; \left(-\dfrac{1}{3}, \dfrac{1}{3}\right)$ **29.** $\sum\limits_{k=1}^{\infty} k x^{k-1}; (-1, 1)$

31. $1 + 3x + \dfrac{9x^2}{2!}; \sum\limits_{k=0}^{\infty} \dfrac{(3x)^k}{k!}$ **33.** $-(x - \pi/2) +$

$\dfrac{(x - \pi/2)^3}{3!} - \dfrac{(x - \pi/2)^5}{5!}; \sum\limits_{k=0}^{\infty} (-1)^{k+1} \dfrac{(x - \pi/2)^{2k+1}}{(2k+1)!}$

35. $x - \dfrac{x^3}{3} + \dfrac{x^5}{5}; \sum\limits_{k=0}^{\infty} \dfrac{(-1)^k x^{2k+1}}{2k+1}$ **37.** $1 - 4x^2 + 16x^4; \sum\limits_{k=0}^{\infty} (-4x^2)^k$

39. $1 + \dfrac{x}{3} - \dfrac{x^2}{9}$ **41.** $1 - \dfrac{3}{2}x + \dfrac{3}{2}x^2$

43. $R_n(x) = \dfrac{(-1)^{n+1} e^{-c}}{(n+1)!} x^{n+1}$, where c is between 0 and

$x. \lim\limits_{n \to \infty} |R_n(x)| = \lim\limits_{n \to \infty}\left(\dfrac{|x^{n+1}|}{e^{|c|}} \cdot \dfrac{1}{(n+1)!}\right) = 0$ for $-\infty < x < \infty$.

45. $R_n(x) = \dfrac{(-1)^n (1 + c)^{-(n+1)}}{n+1} x^{n+1}$ where c is between 0 and x.

$|R_n(x)| = \left(\dfrac{|x|}{1+c}\right)^{n+1} \cdot \dfrac{1}{n+1} < 1^{n+1} \cdot \dfrac{1}{n+1} \to 0$ as $n \to \infty$ for

$|x| \le \dfrac{1}{2}$.   **47.** $\dfrac{1}{24}$ **49.** $\dfrac{1}{8}$ **51.** $\dfrac{1}{6}$ **53.** 0.461   **55.** 0.382

57. $11 - \dfrac{1}{11} - \dfrac{1}{2 \cdot 11^3} - \dfrac{1}{2 \cdot 11^5}$ **59.** $-\dfrac{1}{3} + \dfrac{1}{3 \cdot 3^3} - \dfrac{1}{5 \cdot 3^5} + \dfrac{1}{7 \cdot 3^7}$

61. $y = 4 + 4x + \dfrac{4^2}{2!}x^2 + \dfrac{4^3}{3!}x^3 + \cdots + \dfrac{4^n}{n!}x^n + \cdots = 3 + e^{4x}$

63. a. $\sum\limits_{k=1}^{\infty} \dfrac{(-1)^{k+1}}{k}$ **b.** $\sum\limits_{k=1}^{\infty} \dfrac{1}{k2^k}$ **c.** $2\sum\limits_{k=0}^{\infty} \dfrac{x^{2k+1}}{2k+1}$

d. $x = \dfrac{1}{3}; 2\sum\limits_{k=0}^{\infty} \dfrac{1}{3^{2k+1}(2k+1)}$ **e.** Series in part (d)

AP® Practice, Section 1, Parts A and B, pp. 713–714

1. E   **2.** D   **3.** C   **4.** A   **5.** B   **6.** B   **7.** D   **8.** B
9. C   **10.** D   **11.** A

AP® Practice, Section 2, Parts A and B, p. 714

1. a. $p_4(x) = 1 - \dfrac{x^2}{8} + \dfrac{x^4}{384}; q_4(x) = -\dfrac{1}{2}(x - \pi) + \dfrac{1}{48}(x - \pi)^3$
b. The error with p_4 is 3.2×10^{-4}; the error with q_4 is 2.5×10^{-3}.
Therefore, p_4 gives a better approximation.

c. $R_n(2) = \dfrac{f^{(n+1)}(c)}{(n+1)!} 2^{n+1}$, where $0 < c < 2$, and where

$f^{(n+1)}(c) = \begin{cases} \dfrac{(-1)^{1+n/2}}{2^{n+1}} \sin \dfrac{c}{2} & \text{if } n \text{ is even} \\ \dfrac{(-1)^{(n+1)/2}}{2^{n+1}} \cos \dfrac{c}{2} & \text{if } n \text{ is odd} \end{cases}$ **d.** Note that

$|f^{(n+1)}(c)| \le \dfrac{1}{2^{n+1}}$. Therefore, $|R_4(2)| \le \dfrac{1}{5!} = \dfrac{1}{120}$.   **2. a.** $\sum\limits_{k=0}^{\infty} x^{2k}$

b. $-1 < x < 1$ **c.** $x + \dfrac{x^3}{3} + \dfrac{x^5}{5}$ **3. a.** $2x - 2x^2 + \dfrac{8}{3}x^3$

b. $\dfrac{(-1)^{n+1}(2x)^n}{n}$ **c.** $\dfrac{0.4^{n+1}}{n+1} \le \dfrac{1}{200}$ **4. a.** $-3 \le x \le -1$

b. The magnitude of the first neglected term is $\dfrac{1}{(k+1)^2}$, which is less than 1/100 provided $k \ge 10$.   **c.** Note that $g(-3) > 0, g(-2) = 0$, and $g(-1) < 0$. Therefore, $g(-1) < g(-2) < g(-3)$.

5. a. $x^2 - \dfrac{x^6}{3!} + \dfrac{x^{10}}{5!}$ **b.** $\dfrac{(-1)^{n+1} x^{4n-2}}{(2n-1)!}$ **c.** $\dfrac{13}{42} \approx 0.310$; the first

neglected term in the integrated series is $\dfrac{1}{1320}$, which is less than $\dfrac{1}{1000}$.

d. 6   **6. a.** Neither; $f'(0) = 1$ **b.** 10   **c.** $f'(x) > 0$, for $x > 0$

d. $|R_4| \le \dfrac{e}{20}$. Therefore, we cannot conclude that the error is less than $1/100$.

CHAPTER 11

Section 11.1 Exercises, pp. 722–726

1. Plotting the points $\{(f(t), g(t)): a \le t \le b\}$ generates a curve in the xy-plane.   **3.** $x = R \cos (\pi t/5), y = -R \sin (\pi t/5)$

5. $x = t, y = t^2, -\infty < t < \infty$ **7.** $y = \dfrac{3}{4}(x - 1)^2$

9. a.

t	-10	-4	0	4	10
x	-20	-8	0	8	20
y	-34	-16	-4	8	26

b.

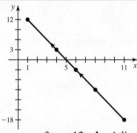

c. $y = \frac{3}{2}x - 4$

d. A line segment rising to the right as t increases

11. a.

t	-5	-2	0	2	5
x	11	8	6	4	1
y	-18	-9	-3	3	12

b.

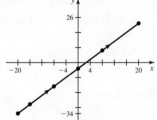

c. $y = -3x + 15$ **d.** A line segment to the left as t increases

13. a. $y = 3x - 12$ **b.** A line starting at $(4, 0)$ and ending at $(8, 12)$
15. a. $y = 1 - x^2, -1 \le x \le 1$ **b.** A parabola opening downward with a vertex at $(0, 1)$ starting at $(1, 0)$ and ending at $(-1, 0)$ **17. a.** $y = (x + 1)^3$ **b.** A cubic function rising to the right as r increases   **19.** $x^2 + y^2 = 9$, center $(0, 0)$; radius 3; lower half of circle generated counterclockwise
21. $x^2 + (y - 1)^2 = 1$; center $(0, 1)$; radius 1; circle generated counterclockwise starting at $(1, 1)$ **23.** $x^2 + y^2 = 49$; center $(0, 0)$; radius 7; circle generated counterclockwise   **25.** $x = 4 \cos t$, $y = 4 \sin t, 0 \le t \le 2\pi$; $x^2 + y^2 = 16$

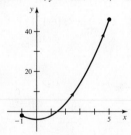

27. $x = \cos t + 2, y = \sin t + 3, 0 \le t \le 2\pi$; $(x - 2)^2 + (y - 3)^2 = 1$

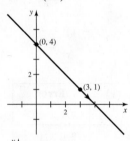

29. $x = 8 \sin t - 2, y = 8 \cos t - 3, 0 \le t \le 2\pi$; $(x + 2)^2 + (y + 3)^2 = 64$

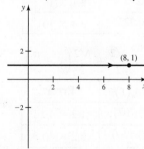

31. $x = 400 \cos \left(\dfrac{4\pi t}{3}\right), y = 400 \sin \left(\dfrac{4\pi t}{3}\right), 0 \le t \le 1.5$

33. $x = 50 \cos \left(\dfrac{\pi t}{12}\right), y(t) = 50 \sin \left(\dfrac{\pi t}{12}\right), 0 \le t \le 24$

35. Slope: -1; point: $(3, 1)$

37. Slope: 0; point: $(8, 1)$

39. $x = 2t, y = 8t, 0 \le t \le 1$
41. $x = -1 + 7t, y = -3 - 13t, 0 \le t \le 1$
43. $x = t, y = 2t^2 - 4, -1 \le t \le 5$ (not unique)

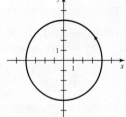

45. $x = 4t - 2, y = -6t + 3, 0 \le t \le 1$;
$x = t + 1, y = 8t - 11, 1 \le t \le 2$ (not unique)

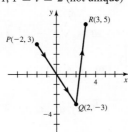

47.

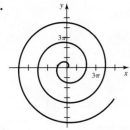

49.

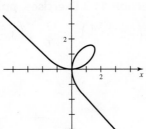

51.

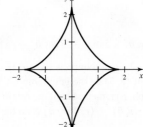

53.

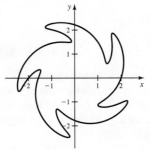

55.

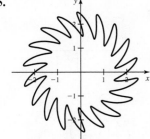

57. a. False **b.** True **c.** False **d.** True
59. $x = 1 + 2t, y = 1 + 4t, -\infty < t < \infty$ **61.** $x = t^2, y = t, t \ge 0$
63. $0 \le t \le 2\pi$

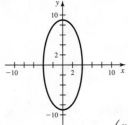

65. $x = 3 \cos t, y = \frac{3}{2} \sin t, 0 \le t \le 2\pi; \left(\dfrac{x}{3}\right)^2 + \left(\dfrac{2y}{3}\right)^2 = 1$

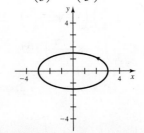

67. $x = 15 \cos t - 2, y = 10 \sin t - 3, 0 \le t \le 2\pi$;
$\left(\dfrac{x+2}{15}\right)^2 + \left(\dfrac{y+3}{10}\right)^2 = 1$

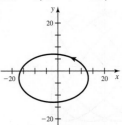

69. a. Lines intersect at $(1, 0)$. **b.** Lines are parallel.
c. Lines intersect at $(4, 6)$. **71.** $x^2 + y^2 = 4$ **73.** $y = \sqrt{4 - x^2}$

75. $a = p, b = p + \dfrac{2\pi}{3}$, for all real p **77. a.** $(0, 2)$ and $(0, -2)$

b. $(1, \sqrt{2}), (1, -\sqrt{2}), (-1, \sqrt{2}), (-1, -\sqrt{2})$
79. a. $x = \pm a \cos^{2/n} t, y = \pm b \sin^{2/n} t$ **c.** The curves become more rectangular as n increases.
81. a.

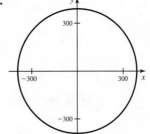

b.

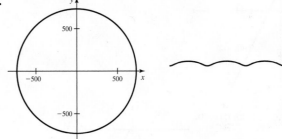

c.

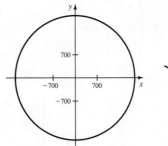

83. Approx. 2857 m
87. a.

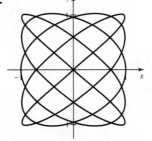

b.

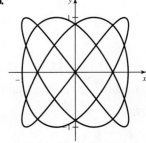

c. 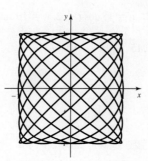   **d.**

89. Four cusps

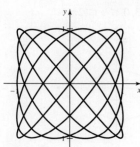

Section 11.2 Exercises, pp. 732–733

1. Compute $\dfrac{g'(a)}{f'(a)}$.   **3.** $\sqrt{5}$ **5. a.** $\dfrac{dy}{dx} = -2; -2$

b.

7. a. $\dfrac{dy}{dx} = -8 \cot t; 0$ **b.**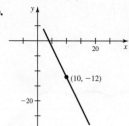

9. a. $\dfrac{dy}{dx} = \dfrac{t^2 + 1}{t^2 - 1}, t \neq 0$; undefined   **b.**

11. 5   **13.** 3π **15.** $\dfrac{\pi^2}{8}$ **17.** 6   **19.** $\dfrac{3}{2}$ **21.** 18.859

23. 5.916   **25. a.** True   **b.** True   **c.** True   **d.** False

27. $y = \dfrac{13}{4}x + \dfrac{1}{4}$ **29.** $y = x - \dfrac{\pi\sqrt{2}}{4}$ **31.** $\left(-\dfrac{4}{\sqrt{5}}, \dfrac{8}{\sqrt{5}}\right)$ and

$\left(\dfrac{4}{\sqrt{5}}, -\dfrac{8}{\sqrt{5}}\right)$ **33.** There is no such point.   **35.** $\left(\dfrac{1}{2}e^{-2/3}, e^{1/3}\right)$

37. a. $\displaystyle\int_a^b \sqrt{(Ah'(t))^2 + (Bh'(t))^2}\, dt =$

$\displaystyle\int_a^b \sqrt{(A^2 + B^2)(h'(t))^2}\, dt = \sqrt{A^2 + B^2}\int_a^b |h'(t)|\, dt$

b. $64\sqrt{29}$ **c.** $\dfrac{7\sqrt{29}}{4}$ **39. a.** 5.102 s

b. $\displaystyle\int_0^{5.102} \sqrt{400 + (25 - 9.8t)^2}\, dt$ **c.** 124.431 m   **d.** 102.041 m

Section 11.3 Exercises, pp. 742–746

1. $\left(-2, -\dfrac{5\pi}{6}\right), \left(2, \dfrac{13\pi}{6}\right); \left(3, \dfrac{\pi}{2}\right), \left(3, \dfrac{5\pi}{2}\right)$

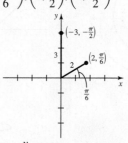

3. $r^2 = x^2 + y^2, \tan\theta = \dfrac{y}{x}$ **5.** $r\cos\theta = 5$ or $r = 5\sec\theta$

7. x-axis symmetry occurs if (r, θ) on the graph implies $(r, -\theta)$ is on the graph. y-axis symmetry occurs if (r, θ) on the graph implies $(r, \pi - \theta) = (-r, -\theta)$ is on the graph. Symmetry about the origin occurs if (r, θ) on the graph implies $(-r, \theta) = (r, \theta + \pi)$ is on the graph.

9.   **11.**

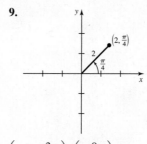   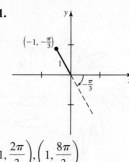

$\left(-2, -\dfrac{3\pi}{4}\right), \left(2, \dfrac{9\pi}{4}\right)$ $\left(1, \dfrac{2\pi}{3}\right), \left(1, \dfrac{8\pi}{3}\right)$

13. $\left(4, \dfrac{\pi}{2}\right), \left(4, \dfrac{5\pi}{2}\right)$

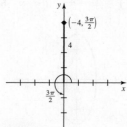

15. $\left(\dfrac{3\sqrt{2}}{2}, \dfrac{3\sqrt{2}}{2}\right)$ **17.** $\left(\dfrac{1}{2}, -\dfrac{\sqrt{3}}{2}\right)$ **19.** $(2\sqrt{2}, -2\sqrt{2})$

21. $\left(2\sqrt{2}, \dfrac{\pi}{4}\right), \left(-2\sqrt{2}, \dfrac{5\pi}{4}\right)$ **23.** $\left(2, \dfrac{\pi}{3}\right), \left(-2, \dfrac{4\pi}{3}\right)$

25. $\left(8, \dfrac{2\pi}{3}\right), \left(-8, -\dfrac{\pi}{3}\right)$ **27.** $x = -4$; vertical line passing through

$(-4, 0)$ **29.** $x^2 + y^2 = 4$; circle centered at $(0, 0)$ of radius 2

31. $(x - 1)^2 + (y - 1)^2 = 2$; circle of radius $\sqrt{2}$ centered at $(1, 1)$

33. $x^2 + (y - 1)^2 = 1$; circle of radius 1 centered at $(0, 1)$ and $x = 0$; *y*-axis   **35.** $x^2 + (y - 4)^2 = 16$; circle of radius 4 centered at $(0, 4)$

37.

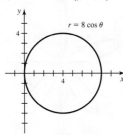

$r = 8 \cos \theta$

39.

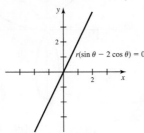

$r(\sin \theta - 2 \cos \theta) = 0$

59. $[0, 2\pi]$

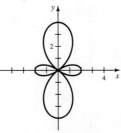

61. a. True   **b.** True   **c.** False   **d.** True   **e.** True
63. $r = \tan \theta \sec \theta$ **65.** $r^2 = \sec \theta \csc \theta$ or $r^2 = 2 \csc 2\theta$
67.

69.

41.

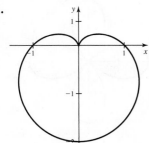

43.

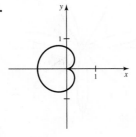

71.

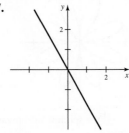

73.

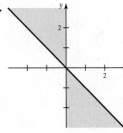

45.

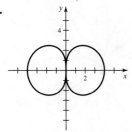

47.

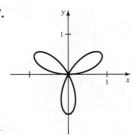

71.

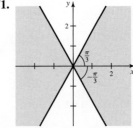

$\frac{\pi}{3}$
$-\frac{\pi}{3}$

73.

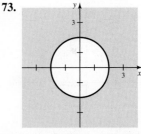

49.

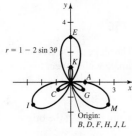

$r = 1 - 2 \sin 3\theta$
Origin:
B, D, F, H, J, L

51.

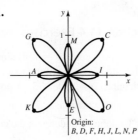

Origin:
B, D, F, H, J, L, N, P

77. A circle of radius 4 and center $\left(2, \frac{\pi}{3}\right)$ (polar coordinates)

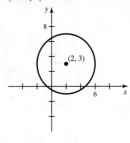

$\bullet \left(2, \frac{\pi}{3}\right)$

79. A circle of radius 4 centered at $(2, 3)$ (Cartesian coordinates)

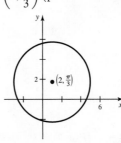

$(2, 3)$

53.

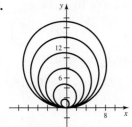

No finite interval $[0, P]$ generates the entire curve.

55. $[0, 2\pi]$

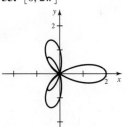

57. $[0, 5\pi]$

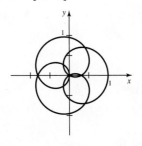

81. A circle of radius 3 centered at $(-1, 2)$ (Cartesian coordinates)

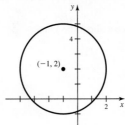

$(-1, 2) \bullet$

83. a. Same graph on all three intervals

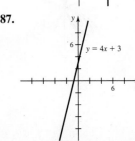

85.

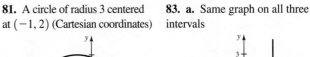

$y = -\frac{x}{\sqrt{3}} + 2\sqrt{3}$

87.

$y = 4x + 3$

89. a. A **b.** C **c.** B **d.** D **e.** E **f.** F

91.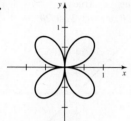

93.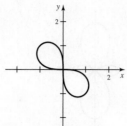

95.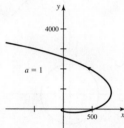

97.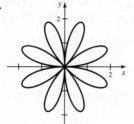

101.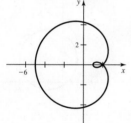

For $a = -1$, the spiral winds inward toward the origin.

103. $(2, 0)$ and $(0, 0)$

105. $(0, 0), \left(\dfrac{2 - \sqrt{2}}{2}, \dfrac{3\pi}{4}\right), \left(\dfrac{2 + \sqrt{2}}{2}, \dfrac{7\pi}{4}\right)$

107. a.

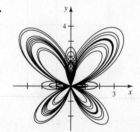

109. $r = a \cos\theta + b \sin\theta = \dfrac{a}{r}(r\cos\theta) + \dfrac{b}{r}(r\sin\theta) = \dfrac{a}{r}x + \dfrac{b}{r}y$; therefore, $\left(x - \dfrac{a}{2}\right)^2 + \left(y - \dfrac{b}{2}\right)^2 = \dfrac{a^2 + b^2}{4}$. Center: $\left(\dfrac{a}{2}, \dfrac{b}{2}\right)$; radius: $\dfrac{\sqrt{a^2 + b^2}}{2}$ **111.** Symmetry about the x-axis

113. a.

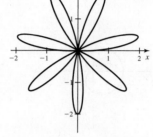

115. a.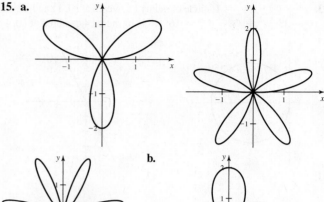

b.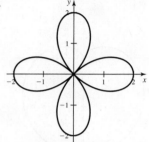

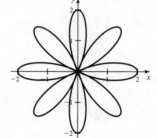

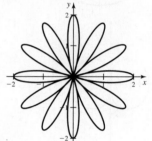

Section 11.4 Exercises, pp. 753–756

1. $x = f(\theta)\cos\theta, y = f(\theta)\sin\theta$ **3.** The slope of the tangent line is the rate of change of the vertical coordinate with respect to the horizontal coordinate. **5.** A point on both curves may have different polar representations. **7.** $0; \theta = \dfrac{\pi}{2}$ **9.** $-\sqrt{3}; \theta = 0$

11. Undefined, undefined; the curve does not intersect the origin.

13. 0 at $\left(-4, \dfrac{\pi}{2}\right)$ and $\left(-4, \dfrac{3\pi}{2}\right)$, undefined at $(4, 0)$ and $(4, \pi)$; $\theta = \pi/4, \theta = 3\pi/4$ **15.** Horizontal: $\left(2\sqrt{2}, \dfrac{\pi}{4}\right), \left(-2\sqrt{2}, \dfrac{3\pi}{4}\right)$; vertical: $\left(0, \dfrac{\pi}{2}\right), (4, 0)$ **17.** Horizontal: $(0, 0)$ $(0.943, 0.955)$, $(-0.943, 2.186), (0.943, 4.097), (-0.943, 5.328)$; vertical: $(0, 0)$, $(0.943, 0.615), (-0.943, 2.526), (0.943, 3.757), (-0.943, 5.668)$

19. Horizontal: $\left(\dfrac{1}{2}, \dfrac{\pi}{6}\right), \left(\dfrac{1}{2}, \dfrac{5\pi}{6}\right), \left(2, \dfrac{3\pi}{2}\right)$; vertical: $\left(\dfrac{3}{2}, \dfrac{7\pi}{6}\right), \left(\dfrac{3}{2}, \dfrac{11\pi}{6}\right), \left(0, \dfrac{\pi}{2}\right)$

21. 1

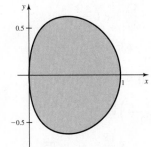

23. 16π

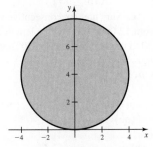

25. $\dfrac{9\pi}{2}$

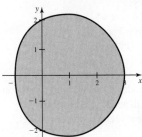

27. $\dfrac{\pi}{12}$

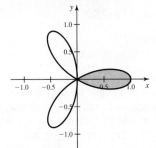

29. $\dfrac{1}{24}(3\sqrt{3} + 2\pi)$ **31.** $\dfrac{1}{4}(2 - \sqrt{3}) + \dfrac{\pi}{12}$

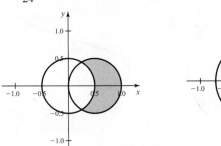

33. $\dfrac{\pi}{20}$

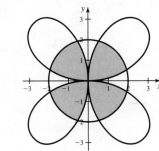

35. $4\left(\dfrac{4\pi}{3} - \sqrt{3}\right)$

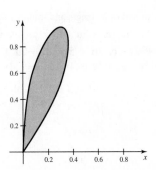

37. $(0, 0), \left(\dfrac{3}{\sqrt{2}}, \dfrac{\pi}{4}\right)$ **39.** $\left(1 + \dfrac{1}{\sqrt{2}}, \dfrac{\pi}{4}\right), \left(1 - \dfrac{1}{\sqrt{2}}, \dfrac{5\pi}{4}\right), (0, 0)$

41. $\dfrac{9}{8}(\pi - 2)$ **43.** $\dfrac{3\pi}{2} - 2\sqrt{2}$

45. πa **47.** $\dfrac{8}{3}\left((1 + \pi^2)^{3/2} - 1\right)$ **49.** 32   **51.** $63\sqrt{5}$

53. $\dfrac{2\pi - 3\sqrt{3}}{8}$ **55. a.** False   **b.** False   **57.** $\dfrac{2\pi}{3} - \dfrac{\sqrt{3}}{2}$

59. $9\pi + 27\sqrt{3}$ **61.** Horizontal: $(0, 0), (4.058, 2.029)$, $(9.826, 4.913)$; vertical: $(1.721, 0.860), (6.851, 3.426), (12.875, 6.437)$

63. a. $A_n = \dfrac{1}{4e^{(4n+2)\pi}} - \dfrac{1}{4e^{4n\pi}} - \dfrac{1}{4e^{(4n-2)\pi}} + \dfrac{1}{4e^{(4n-4)\pi}}$ **b.** 0

c. $e^{-4\pi}$ **65.** 6   **67.** 18π **69.** $\dfrac{\sqrt{1 + a^2}}{a}, a > 0$

71. $(a^2 - 2)\theta^* + \pi - \sin 2\theta^*$, where $\theta^* = \cos^{-1}(a/2)$

73. $a^2\left(\dfrac{\pi}{2} + \dfrac{a}{3}\right)$

Section 11.5 Exercises, pp. 766–769

1. All vectors with the same direction and magnitude are equal, regardless of their location.

3.

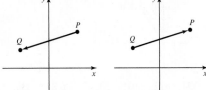

5. There are infinitely many vectors with the same direction and length as **v**.   **7.** If the scalar c is positive, extend the given vector by a factor of c in the same direction. If $c < 0$, reverse the direction of the vector and extend it by a factor of $|c|$.

9. $\mathbf{u} + \mathbf{v} = \langle u_1 + v_1, u_2 + v_2 \rangle$ **11.** $|\langle v_1, v_2 \rangle| = \sqrt{v_1^2 + v_2^2}$

13. If P has coordinates (p_1, p_2) and Q has coordinates (q_1, q_2), then the magnitude of $\overrightarrow{PQ}$ is $\sqrt{(q_1 - p_1)^2 + (q_2 - p_2)^2}$.

15. Multiply **v** by the reciprocal of its length and multiply the result by 10.
17. a, c, e   **19. a.** 3**v**   **b.** 2**u**   **c.** −3**u**   **d.** −2**u**   **e.** **v**
21. a. 3**u** + 3**v**   **b.** **u** + 2**v**   **c.** 2**u** + 5**v**   **d.** −2**u** + 3**v**
e. 3**u** + 2**v**   **f.** −3**u** − 2**v**   **g.** −2**u** − 4**v**   **h.** **u** − 4**v**   **i.** −**u** − 6**v**
23. a.

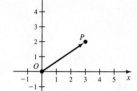

$$\vec{OP} = \langle 3, 2 \rangle = 3\mathbf{i} + 2\mathbf{j}$$
$$|\vec{OP}| = \sqrt{13}$$

b.

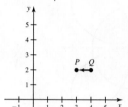

$$\vec{QP} = \langle -1, 0 \rangle = -\mathbf{i}$$
$$|\vec{QP}| = 1$$

c.

$$\vec{RQ} = \langle 10, 3 \rangle = 10\mathbf{i} + 3\mathbf{j}$$
$$|\vec{RQ}| = \sqrt{109}$$

25. $\vec{QU} = \langle 7, 2 \rangle, \vec{PT} = \langle 7, 3 \rangle, \vec{RS} = \langle 2, 3 \rangle$

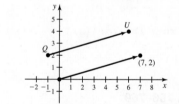

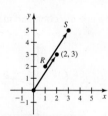

27. $\vec{QT}$ **29.** $\langle -4, 10 \rangle$ **31.** $\langle 12, -10 \rangle$ **33.** $\langle -28, 82 \rangle$ **35.** $2\sqrt{2}$
37. $\sqrt{194}$ **39.** $\langle 3, 3 \rangle, \langle -3, -3 \rangle$ **41.** **w** − **u**   **43.** −**i** + 10**j**
45. $\pm \dfrac{1}{\sqrt{61}} \langle 6, 5 \rangle$ **47.** $\left\langle -\dfrac{28}{\sqrt{74}}, \dfrac{20}{\sqrt{74}} \right\rangle, \left\langle \dfrac{28}{\sqrt{74}}, -\dfrac{20}{\sqrt{74}} \right\rangle$
49. $5\sqrt{65}$ km/hr ≈ 40.311 km/hr   **51.** 349.431 mi/hr in the direction 4.643° south of west   **53.** 1 m/s in the direction 30° east of north
55. a. $\langle 20, 20\sqrt{3} \rangle$ **b.** Yes   **c.** No   **57.** $250\sqrt{2}$ lb
59. a. True   **b.** True   **c.** False   **d.** False   **e.** False   **f.** False

g. False   **h.** True   **61. a.** $\left\langle \dfrac{3}{5}, -\dfrac{4}{5} \right\rangle$ and $\left\langle -\dfrac{3}{5}, \dfrac{4}{5} \right\rangle$
b. $b = \pm \dfrac{2\sqrt{2}}{3}$ **c.** $a = \pm \dfrac{3}{\sqrt{10}}$ **63.** $\mathbf{x} = \left\langle \dfrac{1}{5}, -\dfrac{3}{10} \right\rangle$
65. $\mathbf{x} = \left\langle \dfrac{4}{3}, -\dfrac{11}{3} \right\rangle$ **67.** 4**i** − 8**j**
69. $\langle a, b \rangle = \left(\dfrac{a + b}{2} \right) \mathbf{u} + \left(\dfrac{b - a}{2} \right) \mathbf{v}$
71. $\mathbf{u} = \tfrac{1}{5}\mathbf{i} + \tfrac{3}{5}\mathbf{j}, \mathbf{v} = \tfrac{1}{5}\mathbf{i} - \tfrac{2}{5}\mathbf{j}$ **73.** $\left\langle \dfrac{15}{13}, -\dfrac{36}{13} \right\rangle$ **75.** $\langle 9, 3 \rangle$
77. a. 0   **b.** The 6:00 vector   **c.** Sum any six consecutive vectors.   **d.** A vector pointing from 12:00 to 6:00 with a length 12 times the radius of the clock   **79.** 50 lb in the direction 36.870° north of east
81. $\mathbf{u} + \mathbf{v} = \langle u_1, u_2 \rangle + \langle v_1, v_2 \rangle = \langle u_1 + v_1, u_2 + v_2 \rangle$
$\qquad = \langle v_1 + u_1, v_2 + u_2 \rangle = \langle v_1, v_2 \rangle + \langle u_1, u_2 \rangle$
$\qquad = \mathbf{v} + \mathbf{u}$
83. $a(c\mathbf{v}) = a(c\langle v_1, v_2 \rangle) = a\langle cv_1, cv_2 \rangle$
$\qquad = \langle acv_1, acv_2 \rangle = \langle (ac)v_1, (ac)v_2 \rangle$
$\qquad = ac\langle v_1, v_2 \rangle = (ac)\mathbf{v}$
85. $(a + c)\mathbf{v} = (a + c)\langle v_1, v_2 \rangle$
$\qquad = \langle (a + c)v_1, (a + c)v_2 \rangle$
$\qquad = \langle av_1 + cv_1, av_2 + cv_2 \rangle$
$\qquad = \langle av_1, av_2 \rangle + \langle cv_1, cv_2 \rangle$
$\qquad = a\langle v_1, v_2 \rangle + c\langle v_1, v_2 \rangle$
$\qquad = a\mathbf{v} + c\mathbf{v}$
89. a. $\{\mathbf{u}, \mathbf{v}\}$ are linearly dependent. $\{\mathbf{u}, \mathbf{w}\}$ and $\{\mathbf{v}, \mathbf{w}\}$ are linearly independent.   **b.** Two linearly dependent vectors are parallel. Two linearly independent vectors are not parallel.
91. a. $\tfrac{5}{3}$ **b.** −15

Section 11.6 Exercises, pp. 778–780

1. One   **3.** Its output is a vector.
5. $\langle x, y \rangle = \langle x_0, y_0 \rangle + t\langle x_1 - x_0, y_1 - y_0 \rangle$
7. $\lim\limits_{t \to a} \mathbf{r}(t) = \langle \lim\limits_{t \to a} x(t), \lim\limits_{t \to a} y(t) \rangle$
9. $\mathbf{r}'(t)$ is a vector tangent to and pointing in the direction of the curve $\mathbf{r}(t)$.   **11.** Find the indefinite integral of each component of $\mathbf{r}(t)$.
13. $\mathbf{r}(t) = t\langle 4, 7 \rangle$ **15.** $\mathbf{r}(t) = t\langle 0, 1 \rangle$ **17.** $\mathbf{r}(t) = t\langle 1, 2 \rangle$
19. $\mathbf{r}(t) = \langle -3, 4 \rangle + t\langle 8, -5 \rangle$ **21.** $\mathbf{r}(t) = t\langle -2, 8 \rangle$
23. $\mathbf{r}(t) = t\langle 0, 1 \rangle$ **25.** $\mathbf{r}(t) = t\langle 1, 2 \rangle, 0 \leq t \leq 1$
27. $\mathbf{r}(t) = \langle 2, 4 \rangle + t\langle 5, 1 \rangle, 0 \leq t \leq 1$
29.   **31.**

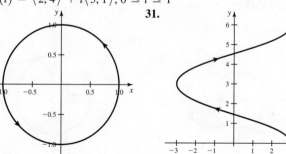

33.   **35.**

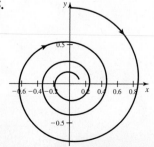

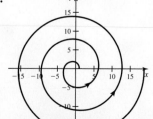

37. $-\mathbf{i} - 4\mathbf{j}$ **39.** $\dfrac{\pi}{2}\mathbf{i} - 2\mathbf{j}$ **41. i**   **43.** $\langle -\sin t, 2t \rangle$

45. $\left\langle 6t^2, \dfrac{3}{\sqrt{t}} \right\rangle$ **47.** $\langle e^t, -2e^{-t} \rangle$ **49.** $\langle e^{-t}(1 - t), 1 + \ln t \rangle$

51. $\langle 1, 6 \rangle$ **53.** $\langle 1, 0 \rangle$ **55.** $\langle 8, 9 \rangle$

57. $\langle 30t^{14} + 24t^3, 14t^{13} - 12t^{11} + 9t^2 - 3 \rangle$

59. $4t(2t^3 - 1)(t^3 - 2)\langle 3t(t^3 - 2), 1 \rangle$ **61.** $\langle 2, 0 \rangle, \langle 0, 0 \rangle$

63. $\langle -9\cos 3t, -16\sin 4t \rangle, \langle 27\sin 3t, -64\cos 4t \rangle$

65. $\left\langle -\dfrac{1}{4}(t + 4)^{-3/2}, -2(t + 1)^{-3} \right\rangle, \left\langle \dfrac{3}{8}(t + 4)^{-5/2}, 6(t + 1)^{-4} \right\rangle$

67. $\left\langle \dfrac{t^5}{5} - \dfrac{3t^2}{2}, t^2 - t \right\rangle + \mathbf{C}$ **69.** $\left\langle 2\sin t, -\dfrac{2}{3}\cos 3t \right\rangle + \mathbf{C}$

71. $\frac{1}{3}e^{3t}\mathbf{i} + \tan^{-1}t\,\mathbf{j} + \mathbf{C}$ **73.** $\mathbf{r}(t) = \langle e^t + 1, 3 - \cos t \rangle$

75. $\mathbf{r}(t) = \langle t + 3, t^2 + 2 \rangle$ **77.** $\mathbf{r}(t) = \langle \frac{1}{2}e^{2t} + \frac{1}{2}, 2e^{-t} + t - 1 \rangle$

79. $\langle 2, 0 \rangle$ **81. i**   **83.** $\langle 0, 0 \rangle$ **85.** $(e^2 + 1)\langle 1, 2 \rangle$ **87. a.** True
b. True   **c.** True   **d.** True   **e.** False   **f.** True   **89.** $|t| \le 2$
91. $0 \le t \le 2$ **93.** $\langle 2 - t, 3 - 2t \rangle$ **95.** $\langle 2 + 3t, 9 + 7t \rangle$

97. $\langle 2e^{2t}, -2e^t \rangle$ **99.** $\left\langle 4, -\dfrac{2}{\sqrt{t}} \right\rangle$

Section 11.7 Exercises, pp. 787–789

1. $\mathbf{v}(t) = \mathbf{r}'(t)$, speed $= |\mathbf{r}'(t)|, \mathbf{a}(t) = \mathbf{r}''(t)$ **3.** $m\mathbf{a}(t) = \mathbf{F}$

5. $\mathbf{v}(t) = \displaystyle\int \mathbf{a}(t)\,dt = \langle v_1(t), v_2(t) \rangle + \mathbf{C}$. Use initial conditions to

find **C**.   **7. a.** $\langle 6t, 8t \rangle, 10t$ **b.** $\langle 6, 8 \rangle$ **9. a.** $\langle 2, -4 \rangle, 2\sqrt{5}$
b. $\langle 0, 0 \rangle$ **11. a.** $\langle 8\cos t, -8\sin t \rangle, 8$ **b.** $\langle -8\sin t, -8\cos t \rangle$
13. a. $e^t \langle \cos t - \sin t, \cos t + \sin t \rangle, \sqrt{2}et$ **b.** $2e^t \langle -\sin t, \cos t \rangle$
15. a. $\langle 1, -4 \rangle, \sqrt{17}$ **b.** $\langle 0, 0 \rangle$ **17. a.** $[c, d] = [0, 1]$
b. $\mathbf{r}'(t) = \langle 1, 2t \rangle, \mathbf{R}'(t) = \langle 2, 8t \rangle$
c.

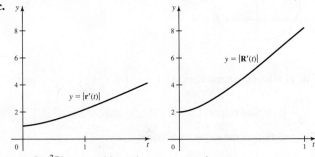

19. a. $[0, \frac{2\pi}{3}]$ **b.** $\mathbf{r}'(t) = \langle -\sin t, 4\cos t \rangle$,
$\mathbf{R}'(t) = \langle -3\sin 3t, 12\cos 3t \rangle$
c.

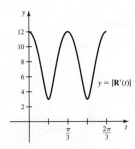

21. a. East, $t \ge 0$; north, $t \ge 0$ **b.** $\langle \ln(t + 1), 1 - e^{-t} \rangle$
c.

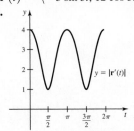

23. $\mathbf{v}(t) = \langle 2, t + 3 \rangle; \mathbf{r}(t) = \left\langle 2t, \dfrac{t^2}{2} + 3t \right\rangle$

25. $\mathbf{v}(t) = \langle 0, 10t + 5 \rangle, \mathbf{r}(t) = \langle 1, 5t^2 + 5t - 1 \rangle$
27. $\mathbf{v}(t) = \langle \sin t, -2\cos t + 3 \rangle$,
  $\mathbf{r}(t) = \langle -\cos t + 2, -2\sin t + 3t \rangle$
29. a. $\mathbf{v}(t) = \langle 30, -9.8t + 6 \rangle, \mathbf{r}(t) = \langle 30t, -4.9t^2 + 6t \rangle$
b.

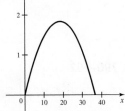

c $T \approx 1.224$ s, range ≈ 36.735 m
d. 1.835 m

31. a. $\mathbf{v}(t) = \langle 80, 10 - 32t \rangle, \mathbf{r}(t) = \langle 80t, -16t^2 + 10t + 6 \rangle$
b.

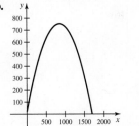

c. 1 s, 80 ft
d. 7.563 ft

33. a. $\mathbf{v}(t) = \langle 125, -32t + 125\sqrt{3} \rangle$,
$\mathbf{r}(t) = \langle 125t, -16t^2 + 125\sqrt{3}t + 20 \rangle$
b.

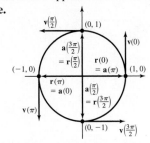

c. 13.623 s; 1702.880 ft
d. 752.422 ft

35. a. False   **b.** True   **c.** False   **d.** True   **e.** False   **f.** True
g. True   **37.** 15.306 s, 1988.324 m, 286.990 m   **39.** 21.651 s,
4330.127 ft, 1875 ft   **41.** Approximately 27.376° and 62.624°
43. a. The direction of $\mathbf{r}$ does not change.   **b.** Constant in direction, not
in magnitude   **45. a.** $\left[0, \dfrac{2\pi}{\omega}\right]$ **b.** $\mathbf{v}(t) = \langle -A\omega\sin \omega t, A\omega\cos \omega t \rangle$
is not constant; $|\mathbf{v}(t)| = |A\omega|$ is constant.
c. $\mathbf{a}(t) = \langle -A\omega^2\cos \omega t, -A\omega^2\sin \omega t \rangle$ **d.** $\mathbf{r}$ and $\mathbf{v}$ are orthogonal; $\mathbf{r}$
and $\mathbf{a}$ have opposite directions.
e.

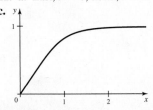

47. a. $r(t) = \left\langle 5 \sin\left(\dfrac{\pi t}{6}\right), 5 \cos\left(\dfrac{\pi t}{6}\right) \right\rangle$

b. $r(t) = \left\langle 5 \sin\left(\dfrac{1 - e^{-t}}{5}\right), 5 \cos\left(\dfrac{1 - e^{-t}}{5}\right) \right\rangle$

49. $23.584°$ or $59.627°$ **51.** 113.429 ft/s

53. $T = \dfrac{|v_0| \sin \alpha + \sqrt{|v_0|^2 \sin^2 \alpha + 2gy_0}}{g}$, range $= |v_0| (\cos \alpha) T$,

max. height $= y_0 + \dfrac{|v_0|^2 \sin^2 \alpha}{2g}$

Chapter 11 Review Exercises, pp. 790–792

1. a. False   **b.** False   **c.** True   **d.** False   **e.** True   **f.** False
g. True

3. a.

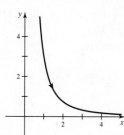

b. $y = \dfrac{3}{x^2}$

c. The right branch of the function $y = \dfrac{3}{x^2}$ **d.** -6

5. a.

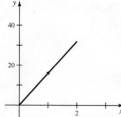

b. $y = 16x$

c. A line segment from $(0, 0)$ to $(2, 32)$ **d.** 16 **7.** $\dfrac{x^2}{16} + \dfrac{y^2}{9} = 1$;
ellipse oriented counterclockwise   **9.** $(x + 3)^2 + (y - 6)^2 = 1$;
right half of a circle centered at $(-3, 6)$ of radius 1 oriented
clockwise   **11.** $x = 3 \sin t, y = 3 \cos t, 0 \le t \le 2\pi$
13. $x = 3 \cos t, y = 2 \sin t, -\dfrac{\pi}{2} \le t \le \dfrac{\pi}{2}$
15. $x = -1 + 2t, y = t, 0 \le t \le 1; x = 1 - 2t, y = 1 - t,$
$0 \le t \le 1$ **17.** At $t = \dfrac{\pi}{6}: y = (2 + \sqrt{3})x +$
$\left(2 - \dfrac{\pi}{3} - \dfrac{\pi\sqrt{3}}{6}\right)$; at $t = \dfrac{2\pi}{3}: y = \dfrac{x}{\sqrt{3}} + 2 - \dfrac{2\pi}{3\sqrt{3}}$
19.

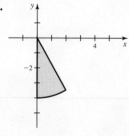

21. Liz should choose $r = 1 - \sin \theta$.

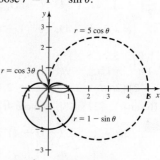

23. $(x - 3)^2 + (y + 1)^2 = 10$; a circle of radius $\sqrt{10}$ centered at
$(3, -1)$ **25.** $r = 8 \cos \theta, 0 \le \theta \le \pi$
27. a. 4 intersection points

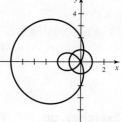

b. $(1, \pm 1.318), (-1, \pm 0.723)$

29. a. Horizontal tangents at $\left(6, \dfrac{\pi}{2}\right), \left(2, \dfrac{3\pi}{2}\right)$; vertical tangents at
$(4.732, 2.767), (4.732, 0.374)$ **b.** There is no point at the origin.
c.

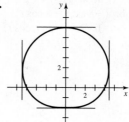

31. a. Horizontal tangent lines at $\left(1, \dfrac{\pi}{6}\right), \left(1, \dfrac{5\pi}{6}\right), \left(1, \dfrac{7\pi}{6}\right)$, and
$\left(1, \dfrac{11\pi}{6}\right)$; vertical tangent lines at $(\sqrt{2}, 0)$ and $(\sqrt{2}, \pi)$
b. Tangent lines at the origin have slopes ± 1.
c.

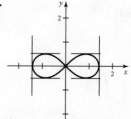

33. $\dfrac{19\pi}{2}$

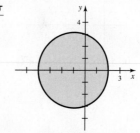

35. $\dfrac{1}{4}\left(\sqrt{255} - \cos^{-1}\dfrac{1}{16}\right)$

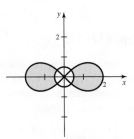

37. 41

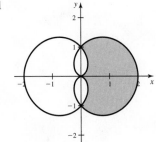

39.

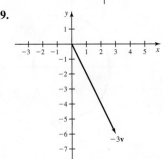

41.

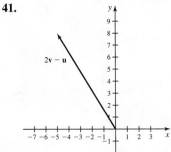

43. $\sqrt[2]{53}$ **45.** $\pm\dfrac{\langle -6, 10\rangle}{\sqrt{34}}$ **47. a.** $\mathbf{v} = -275\sqrt{2}\mathbf{i} + 275\sqrt{2}\mathbf{j}$
b. $-275\sqrt{2}\mathbf{i} + (275\sqrt{2} + 40)\mathbf{j}$
49. 50.160 m/s; 85.426° below the horizontal in the northerly horizontal direction

51.

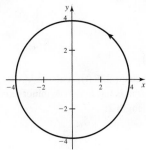

53.

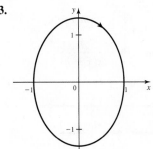

55. a. $(116, 30)$ **b.** 39.063 ft   **c.** 2.315 s

d. $\displaystyle\int_0^{2.315}\sqrt{50^2 + (-32t + 50)^2}\,dt$ **e.** 128.704 ft

f. 41.523° to 79.441°   **57.** $\dfrac{488}{27}$ **59.** $\dfrac{1}{2}\ln 3$

61. 40.095   **63. a.** $\langle 1, 0\rangle; \langle 0, 1\rangle$

b. $\left\langle -\dfrac{2}{(2t+1)^2}, \dfrac{1}{(t+1)^2}\right\rangle; \langle -2, 1\rangle$ **c.** $\left\langle \dfrac{8}{(2t+1)^3}, -\dfrac{2}{(t+1)^3}\right\rangle$

d. $\left\langle \dfrac{1}{2}\ln|2t+1|, t - \ln|t+1|\right\rangle + \mathbf{C}$

65. a. $\langle 0, 3\rangle$; does not exist

b. $\langle 2\cos 2t, -12\sin 4t\rangle; \langle 2, 0\rangle$ **c.** $\langle -4\sin 2t, -48\cos 4t\rangle$

d. $\left\langle -\dfrac{1}{2}\cos 2t, \dfrac{3}{4}\sin 4t\right\rangle + \mathbf{C}$

AP® Practice, Section 1, Parts A and B, pp. 792–794

1. B   **2.** B   **3.** E   **4.** E   **5.** D   **6.** E   **7.** B   **8.** D   **9.** C
10. C   **11.** D   **12.** D

AP® Practice, Section 2, Parts A and B, p. 792–794

1. a. $\mathbf{v} = \langle 10, -9.8t + 30\rangle$ **b.** $\mathbf{r}(t) = \langle 10t, -4.9t^2 + 30t + 10\rangle$
c. $t \approx 6.439$ s   **d.** 64.394 m   **2. a.** $t > 0$ **b.** Never

c. 1.905 m/s   **d.** $\left\langle \dfrac{2}{e^2}, \dfrac{8}{25}\right\rangle$ m/s²   **e.** $\langle 10.271, 2.781\rangle$ m

3. a. $\pi < t < 2\pi$ **b.** $\dfrac{\pi}{2} < t < \dfrac{3\pi}{2}$ **c.** $1 - e^{-1}$ ft/s
d. 6.743 ft   **e.** 1.342 ft   **4. a.** $\mathbf{v} = \langle 8, -32t + 64\rangle$
b. $t = 4$ s   **c.** 32 ft   **d.** 64 ft

5. a. $\left(-\dfrac{3}{\sqrt{2}}, \dfrac{4}{\sqrt{2}}\right), \left(\dfrac{3}{\sqrt{2}}, -\dfrac{4}{\sqrt{2}}\right)$ **b.** $(3, 0), (-3, 0)$

c. $\displaystyle\int_0^{2\pi}\sqrt{9\sin^2 t + 16\cos^2 t}\,dt = \int_0^{2\pi}\sqrt{9 + 7\cos^2 t}\,dt$

d. $t = \dfrac{\pi}{2}, \dfrac{3\pi}{2}$

APPENDIX A

Exercises, pp. 801–802

1. The set of real numbers greater than -4 and less than or equal to 10; $(-4, 10]$;

3. $|x| = \begin{cases} x & \text{if } x \geq 0 \\ -x & \text{if } x < 0 \end{cases}$ **5.** $2x - 4 \geq 3$ or $2x - 4 \leq -3$

7. Take the square root of the sum of the squares of the differences of the x- and y-coordinates.

9. $y = \sqrt{36 - x^2}$ **11.** $m = \dfrac{y + 2}{x - 4}$ or $y = m(x - 4) - 2$

13. They are equal.   **15.** 4   **17.** $4uv$ **19.** $-\dfrac{h}{x(x + h)}$

21. $(y - y^{-1})(y + y^{-1})$ **23.** $u = \pm\sqrt{2}, \pm 3$

25. $3x^2 + 3xh + h^2$ **27.** $(1, 5)$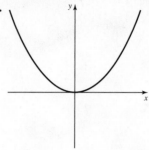

29. $(-\infty, 4] \cup [5, 6)$

31. $\{x: x < -4/3 \text{ or } x > 4\}; \left(-\infty, -\frac{4}{3}\right) \cup (4, \infty)$

33. $\{x: -2 < x < -1 \text{ or } 2 < x < 3\}; (-2, -1) \cup (2, 3)$

35. $y = 2 - \sqrt{9 - (x + 1)^2}$

37. $y = \dfrac{5}{3}x + 4$

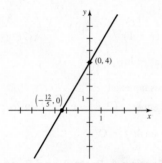

39. $y = \dfrac{4}{5}x - 4$

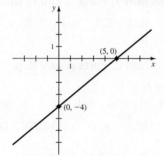

41. $x + 2y = 24$

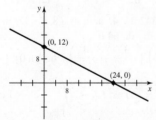

43. $y = \dfrac{1}{3}x - 7$ **45. a.** False   **b.** True   **c.** False   **d.** False
e. False   **f.** True   **g.** False   **47.** $\{x: |x - 1| \geq 3\}$
49.

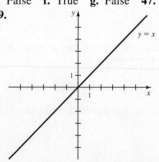

APPENDIX B

Exercises, pp. 812–815

1. A parabola is the set of all points in a plane equidistant from a fixed point and a fixed line.   **3.** A hyperbola is the set of all points in a plane with the property that the difference of the distances from the point to two fixed points is constant.

5.

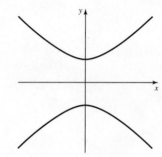

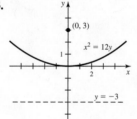

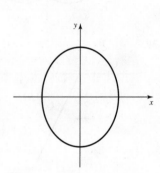

7. $\left(\dfrac{x}{a}\right)^2 + \dfrac{y^2}{a^2 - c^2} = 1$ **9.** $(\pm ae, 0)$ **11.** $y = \pm\dfrac{b}{a}x$

13.   **15.**

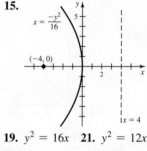

17.

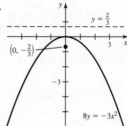

19. $y^2 = 16x$ **21.** $y^2 = 12x$

23. $x^2 = -\dfrac{2}{3}y$ **25.** $y^2 = 4(x + 1)$

27.

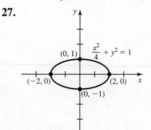

Vertices: $(\pm 2, 0)$; foci: $(\pm\sqrt{3}, 0)$; major axis has length 4; minor axis has length 2.

29.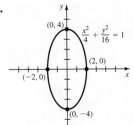

Vertices: $(0, \pm 4)$; foci: $(0, \pm 2\sqrt{3})$; major axis has length 8; minor axis has length 4.

31.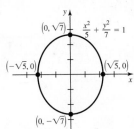

Vertices: $(0, \pm\sqrt{7})$; foci: $(0, \pm\sqrt{2})$; major axis has length $2\sqrt{7}$; minor axis has length $2\sqrt{5}$.

33.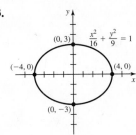

35.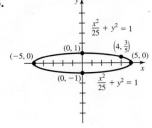

37. $\dfrac{x^2}{4} + \dfrac{y^2}{9} = 1$

39.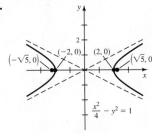

Vertices: $(\pm 2, 0)$; foci: $(\pm\sqrt{5}, 0)$; asymptotes: $y = \pm\dfrac{1}{2}x$

41.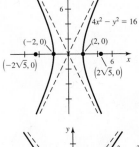

Vertices: $(\pm 2, 0)$; foci: $(\pm 2\sqrt{5}, 0)$; asymptotes: $y = \pm 2x$

43.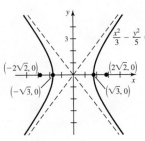

Vertices: $(\pm\sqrt{3}, 0)$; foci: $(\pm 2\sqrt{2}, 0)$; asymptotes: $y = \pm\sqrt{\dfrac{5}{3}}x$

45.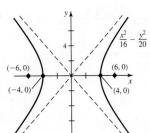

Vertices: $(\pm 4, 0)$; foci: $(\pm 6, 0)$; asymptotes: $y = \pm\dfrac{\sqrt{5}}{2}x$

47.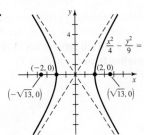

Vertices: $(\pm 2, 0)$; foci: $(\pm\sqrt{13}, 0)$; asymptotes: $y = \pm\dfrac{3}{2}x$

49. $\dfrac{x^2}{16} - \dfrac{y^2}{9} = 1$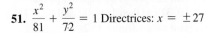

51. $\dfrac{x^2}{81} + \dfrac{y^2}{72} = 1$ Directrices: $x = \pm 27$

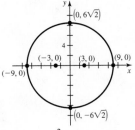

53. $x^2 - \dfrac{y^2}{8} = 1$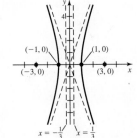

55.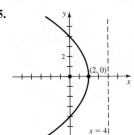

Vertex: $(2, 0)$; focus: $(0, 0)$; directrix: $x = 4$

57.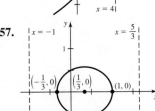

Vertices: $(1, 0)$, $\left(-\dfrac{1}{3}, 0\right)$; center: $\left(\dfrac{1}{3}, 0\right)$; foci: $(0, 0)$, $\left(\dfrac{2}{3}, 0\right)$; directrices: $x = -1$, $x = \dfrac{5}{3}$

59.

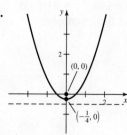

Vertex: $\left(0, -\dfrac{1}{4}\right)$; focus: $(0, 0)$;

directrix: $y = -\dfrac{1}{2}$

61.

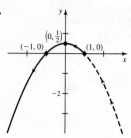

The parabola starts at $(1, 0)$ and goes through quadrants I, II, and III for θ in $[0, 3\pi/2]$; then it approaches $(1, 0)$ by traveling through quadrant IV on $(3\pi/2, 2\pi)$.

63.

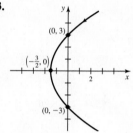

The parabola begins in the first quadrant and passes through the points $(0, 3)$ and then $\left(-\frac{3}{2}, 0\right)$ and $(0, -3)$ as θ ranges from 0 to 2π.

65. The parabolas open to the right if $p > 0$, open to the left if $p < 0$, and are more vertically compressed as $|p|$ decreases.

67. a. True **b.** True **c.** True **d.** True **69.** $y = 2x + 6$

71. $y = -\frac{3}{40}x - \frac{4}{5}$ **73.** $r = \dfrac{4}{1 - 2\sin\theta}$

77. $\dfrac{dy}{dx} = \left(-\dfrac{b^2}{a^2}\right)\left(\dfrac{x}{y}\right)$, so $\dfrac{y - y_0}{x - x_0} = \left(-\dfrac{b^2}{a^2}\right)\left(\dfrac{x_0}{y_0}\right)$, which is

equivalent to the given equation.   **79.** $\dfrac{4\pi b^2 a}{3}$; $\dfrac{4\pi a^2 b}{3}$; yes, if $a \neq b$

81. a. $\dfrac{\pi b^2}{3a^2}(a - c)^2(2a + c)$ **b.** $\dfrac{4\pi b^4}{3a}$ **91.** $2p$

97. a. $u(m) = \dfrac{2m^2 - \sqrt{3m^2 + 1}}{m^2 - 1}$; $v(m) = \dfrac{2m^2 + \sqrt{3m^2 + 1}}{m^2 - 1}$;

2 intersection points for $|m| > 1$ **b.** $\frac{5}{4}, \infty$ **c.** $2, 2$
d. $2\sqrt{3} - \ln(\sqrt{3} + 2)$

Index

TABLE OF INTEGRALS

Substitution Rule	Integration by Parts
$\displaystyle \int f(g(x))g'(x)\, dx = \int f(u)\, du \quad (u = g(x))$	$\displaystyle \int u\, dv = uv - \int v\, du$
$\displaystyle \int_a^b f(g(x))g'(x)\, dx = \int_{g(a)}^{g(b)} f(u)\, du$	$\displaystyle \int_a^b uv'\, dx = uv \Big|_a^b - \int_a^b vu'\, dx$

Basic Integrals

1. $\displaystyle \int x^n\, dx = \frac{1}{n+1}x^{n+1} + C;\ n \neq -1$

2. $\displaystyle \int \frac{dx}{x} = \ln|x| + C$

3. $\displaystyle \int \cos ax\, dx = \frac{1}{a}\sin ax + C$

4. $\displaystyle \int \sin ax\, dx = -\frac{1}{a}\cos ax + C$

5. $\displaystyle \int \tan x\, dx = \ln|\sec x| + C$

6. $\displaystyle \int \cot x\, dx = \ln|\sin x| + C$

7. $\displaystyle \int \sec x\, dx = \ln|\sec x + \tan x| + C$

8. $\displaystyle \int \csc x\, dx = -\ln|\csc x + \cot x| + C$

9. $\displaystyle \int e^{ax}\, dx = \frac{1}{a}e^{ax} + C$

10. $\displaystyle \int b^{ax}\, dx = \frac{1}{a \ln b}b^{ax} + C;\ b > 0, b \neq 1$

11. $\displaystyle \int \ln x\, dx = x\ln x - x + C$

12. $\displaystyle \int \log_b x\, dx = \frac{1}{\ln b}(x\ln x - x) + C$

13. $\displaystyle \int \frac{dx}{\sqrt{a^2 - x^2}} = \sin^{-1}\frac{x}{a} + C$

14. $\displaystyle \int \frac{dx}{x^2 + a^2} = \frac{1}{a}\tan^{-1}\frac{x}{a} + C$

15. $\displaystyle \int \frac{dx}{x\sqrt{x^2 - a^2}} = \frac{1}{a}\sec^{-1}\left|\frac{x}{a}\right| + C$

16. $\displaystyle \int \sin^{-1} x\, dx = x\sin^{-1}x + \sqrt{1 - x^2} + C$

17. $\displaystyle \int \cos^{-1} x\, dx = x\cos^{-1}x - \sqrt{1 - x^2} + C$

18. $\displaystyle \int \tan^{-1} x\, dx = x\tan^{-1}x - \frac{1}{2}\ln(1 + x^2) + C$

19. $\displaystyle \int \sec^{-1} x\, dx = x\sec^{-1}x - \ln(x + \sqrt{x^2 - 1}) + C$

20. $\displaystyle \int \sinh x\, dx = \cosh x + C$

21. $\displaystyle \int \cosh x\, dx = \sinh x + C$

22. $\displaystyle \int \text{sech}^2 x\, dx = \tanh x + C$

23. $\displaystyle \int \text{csch}^2 x\, dx = -\coth x + C$

24. $\displaystyle \int \text{sech}\, x \tanh x\, dx = -\text{sech}\, x + C$

25. $\displaystyle \int \text{csch}\, x \coth x\, dx = -\text{csch}\, x + C$

26. $\displaystyle \int \tanh x\, dx = \ln \cosh x + C$

27. $\displaystyle \int \coth x\, dx = \ln|\sinh x| + C$

28. $\displaystyle \int \text{sech}\, x\, dx = \tan^{-1} \sinh x + C$

29. $\displaystyle \int \text{csch}\, x\, dx = \ln|\tanh(x/2)| + C$

Trigonometric Integrals

30. $\displaystyle \int \cos^2 x\, dx = \frac{x}{2} + \frac{\sin 2x}{4} + C$

31. $\displaystyle \int \sin^2 x\, dx = \frac{x}{2} - \frac{\sin 2x}{4} + C$

32. $\displaystyle \int \sec^2 ax\, dx = \frac{1}{a}\tan ax + C$

33. $\displaystyle \int \csc^2 ax\, dx = -\frac{1}{a}\cot ax + C$

34. $\displaystyle \int \tan^2 x\, dx = \tan x - x + C$

35. $\displaystyle \int \cot^2 x\, dx = -\cot x - x + C$

36. $\displaystyle \int \cos^3 x\, dx = -\frac{1}{3}\sin^3 x + \sin x + C$

37. $\displaystyle \int \sin^3 x\, dx = \frac{1}{3}\cos^3 x - \cos x + C$

38. $\int \sec^3 x\, dx = \dfrac{1}{2}\sec x \tan x + \dfrac{1}{2}\ln|\sec x + \tan x| + C$

39. $\int \csc^3 x\, dx = -\dfrac{1}{2}\csc x \cot x - \dfrac{1}{2}\ln|\csc x + \cot x| + C$

40. $\int \tan^3 x\, dx = \dfrac{1}{2}\tan^2 x - \ln|\sec x| + C$

41. $\int \cot^3 x\, dx = -\dfrac{1}{2}\cot^2 x - \ln|\sin x| + C$

42. $\int \sec^n ax \tan ax\, dx = \dfrac{1}{na}\sec^n ax + C;\ n \neq 0$

43. $\int \csc^n ax \cot ax\, dx = -\dfrac{1}{na}\csc^n ax + C;\ n \neq 0$

44. $\int \dfrac{dx}{1 + \sin ax} = -\dfrac{1}{a}\tan\left(\dfrac{\pi}{4} - \dfrac{ax}{2}\right) + C$

45. $\int \dfrac{dx}{1 - \sin ax} = \dfrac{1}{a}\tan\left(\dfrac{\pi}{4} + \dfrac{ax}{2}\right) + C$

46. $\int \dfrac{dx}{1 + \cos ax} = \dfrac{1}{a}\tan\dfrac{ax}{2} + C$

47. $\int \dfrac{dx}{1 - \cos ax} = -\dfrac{1}{a}\cot\dfrac{ax}{2} + C$

48. $\int \sin mx \cos nx\, dx = -\dfrac{\cos(m+n)x}{2(m+n)} - \dfrac{\cos(m-n)x}{2(m-n)} + C;\ m^2 \neq n^2$

49. $\int \sin mx \sin nx\, dx = \dfrac{\sin(m-n)x}{2(m-n)} - \dfrac{\sin(m+n)x}{2(m+n)} + C;\ m^2 \neq n^2$

50. $\int \cos mx \cos nx\, dx = \dfrac{\sin(m-n)x}{2(m-n)} + \dfrac{\sin(m+n)x}{2(m+n)} + C;\ m^2 \neq n^2$

Reduction Formulas for Trigonometric Functions

51. $\int \cos^n x\, dx = \dfrac{1}{n}\cos^{n-1} x \sin x + \dfrac{n-1}{n}\int \cos^{n-2} x\, dx$

52. $\int \sin^n x\, dx = -\dfrac{1}{n}\sin^{n-1} x \cos x + \dfrac{n-1}{n}\int \sin^{n-2} x\, dx$

53. $\int \tan^n x\, dx = \dfrac{\tan^{n-1} x}{n-1} - \int \tan^{n-2} x\, dx;\ n \neq 1$

54. $\int \cot^n x\, dx = -\dfrac{\cot^{n-1} x}{n-1} - \int \cot^{n-2} x\, dx;\ n \neq 1$

55. $\int \sec^n x\, dx = \dfrac{\sec^{n-2} x \tan x}{n-1} + \dfrac{n-2}{n-1}\int \sec^{n-2} x\, dx;\ n \neq 1$

56. $\int \csc^n x\, dx = -\dfrac{\csc^{n-2} x \cot x}{n-1} + \dfrac{n-2}{n-1}\int \csc^{n-2} x\, dx;\ n \neq 1$

57. $\int \sin^m x \cos^n x\, dx = -\dfrac{\sin^{m-1} x \cos^{n+1} x}{m+n} + \dfrac{m-1}{m+n}\int \sin^{m-2} x \cos^n x\, dx;\ m \neq -n$

58. $\int \sin^m x \cos^n x\, dx = \dfrac{\sin^{m+1} x \cos^{n-1} x}{m+n} + \dfrac{n-1}{m+n}\int \sin^m x \cos^{n-2} x\, dx;\ m \neq -n$

59. $\int x^n \sin ax\, dx = -\dfrac{x^n \cos ax}{a} + \dfrac{n}{a}\int x^{n-1} \cos ax\, dx;\ a \neq 0$

60. $\int x^n \cos ax\, dx = \dfrac{x^n \sin ax}{a} - \dfrac{n}{a}\int x^{n-1} \sin ax\, dx;\ a \neq 0$

Integrals Involving $a^2 - x^2$; $a > 0$

61. $\int \sqrt{a^2 - x^2}\, dx = \dfrac{x}{2}\sqrt{a^2 - x^2} + \dfrac{a^2}{2}\sin^{-1}\dfrac{x}{a} + C$

62. $\int \dfrac{dx}{x\sqrt{a^2 - x^2}} = -\dfrac{1}{a}\ln\left|\dfrac{a + \sqrt{a^2 - x^2}}{x}\right| + C$

63. $\int \dfrac{dx}{x^2\sqrt{a^2 - x^2}} = -\dfrac{\sqrt{a^2 - x^2}}{a^2 x} + C$

64. $\int x^2\sqrt{a^2 - x^2}\, dx = \dfrac{x}{8}(2x^2 - a^2)\sqrt{a^2 - x^2} + \dfrac{a^4}{8}\sin^{-1}\dfrac{x}{a} + C$

65. $\int \dfrac{\sqrt{a^2 - x^2}}{x^2}\, dx = -\dfrac{1}{x}\sqrt{a^2 - x^2} - \sin^{-1}\dfrac{x}{a} + C$

66. $\int \dfrac{x^2}{\sqrt{a^2 - x^2}}\, dx = -\dfrac{x}{2}\sqrt{a^2 - x^2} + \dfrac{a^2}{2}\sin^{-1}\dfrac{x}{a} + C$

67. $\int \dfrac{dx}{a^2 - x^2} = \dfrac{1}{2a}\ln\left|\dfrac{x + a}{x - a}\right| + C$

Integrals Involving $x^2 - a^2$; $a > 0$

68. $\int \sqrt{x^2 - a^2}\, dx = \dfrac{x}{2}\sqrt{x^2 - a^2} - \dfrac{a^2}{2}\ln|x + \sqrt{x^2 - a^2}| + C$

69. $\int \dfrac{dx}{\sqrt{x^2 - a^2}} = \ln|x + \sqrt{x^2 - a^2}| + C$

70. $\int \dfrac{dx}{x^2\sqrt{x^2 - a^2}} = \dfrac{\sqrt{x^2 - a^2}}{a^2 x} + C$

71. $\int x^2\sqrt{x^2 - a^2}\, dx = \dfrac{x}{8}(2x^2 - a^2)\sqrt{x^2 - a^2} - \dfrac{a^4}{8}\ln|x + \sqrt{x^2 - a^2}| + C$

72. $\int \dfrac{\sqrt{x^2 - a^2}}{x^2}\, dx = \ln|x + \sqrt{x^2 - a^2}| - \dfrac{\sqrt{x^2 - a^2}}{x} + C$

73. $\int \dfrac{x^2}{\sqrt{x^2 - a^2}}\, dx = \dfrac{a^2}{2}\ln|x + \sqrt{x^2 - a^2}| + \dfrac{x}{2}\sqrt{x^2 - a^2} + C$

74. $\int \dfrac{dx}{x^2 - a^2} = \dfrac{1}{2a}\ln\left|\dfrac{x - a}{x + a}\right| + C$

75. $\int \dfrac{dx}{x(x^2 - a^2)} = \dfrac{1}{2a^2}\ln\left|\dfrac{x^2 - a^2}{x^2}\right| + C$

Integrals Involving $a^2 + x^2$; $a > 0$

76. $\displaystyle\int \sqrt{a^2 + x^2}\, dx = \frac{x}{2}\sqrt{a^2 + x^2} + \frac{a^2}{2}\ln\left(x + \sqrt{a^2 + x^2}\right) + C$

77. $\displaystyle\int \frac{dx}{\sqrt{a^2 + x^2}} = \ln\left(x + \sqrt{a^2 + x^2}\right) + C$

78. $\displaystyle\int \frac{dx}{x\sqrt{a^2 + x^2}} = \frac{1}{a}\ln\left|\frac{a - \sqrt{a^2 + x^2}}{x}\right| + C$

79. $\displaystyle\int \frac{dx}{x^2\sqrt{a^2 + x^2}} = -\frac{\sqrt{a^2 + x^2}}{a^2 x} + C$

80. $\displaystyle\int x^2\sqrt{a^2 + x^2}\, dx = \frac{x}{8}(a^2 + 2x^2)\sqrt{a^2 + x^2} - \frac{a^4}{8}\ln\left(x + \sqrt{a^2 + x^2}\right) + C$

81. $\displaystyle\int \frac{\sqrt{a^2 + x^2}}{x^2}\, dx = \ln\left|x + \sqrt{a^2 + x^2}\right| - \frac{\sqrt{a^2 + x^2}}{x} + C$

82. $\displaystyle\int \frac{x^2}{\sqrt{a^2 + x^2}}\, dx = -\frac{a^2}{2}\ln\left(x + \sqrt{a^2 + x^2}\right) + \frac{x\sqrt{a^2 + x^2}}{2} + C$

83. $\displaystyle\int \frac{\sqrt{a^2 + x^2}}{x}\, dx = \sqrt{a^2 + x^2} - a\ln\left|\frac{a + \sqrt{a^2 + x^2}}{x}\right| + C$

84. $\displaystyle\int \frac{dx}{(a^2 + x^2)^{3/2}} = \frac{x}{a^2\sqrt{a^2 + x^2}} + C$

85. $\displaystyle\int \frac{dx}{x(a^2 + x^2)} = \frac{1}{2a^2}\ln\left(\frac{x^2}{a^2 + x^2}\right) + C$

Integrals Involving $ax \pm b$; $a \neq 0, b > 0$

86. $\displaystyle\int (ax + b)^n\, dx = \frac{(ax + b)^{n+1}}{a(n + 1)} + C;\ n \neq -1$

87. $\displaystyle\int \left(\sqrt{ax + b}\right)^n dx = \frac{2}{a}\frac{\left(\sqrt{ax + b}\right)^{n+2}}{n + 2} + C;\ n \neq -2$

88. $\displaystyle\int \frac{dx}{x\sqrt{ax - b}} = \frac{2}{\sqrt{b}}\tan^{-1}\sqrt{\frac{ax - b}{b}} + C;\ b > 0$

89. $\displaystyle\int \frac{dx}{x\sqrt{ax + b}} = \frac{1}{\sqrt{b}}\ln\left|\frac{\sqrt{ax + b} - \sqrt{b}}{\sqrt{ax + b} + \sqrt{b}}\right| + C;\ b > 0$

90. $\displaystyle\int \frac{x}{ax + b}\, dx = \frac{x}{a} - \frac{b}{a^2}\ln|ax + b| + C$

91. $\displaystyle\int \frac{x^2}{ax + b}\, dx = \frac{1}{2a^3}\left((ax + b)^2 - 4b(ax + b) + 2b^2\ln|ax + b|\right) + C$

92. $\displaystyle\int \frac{dx}{x^2(ax + b)} = -\frac{1}{bx} + \frac{a}{b^2}\ln\left|\frac{ax + b}{x}\right| + C$

93. $\displaystyle\int x\sqrt{ax + b}\, dx = \frac{2}{15a^2}(3ax - 2b)(ax + b)^{3/2} + C$

94. $\displaystyle\int \frac{x}{\sqrt{ax + b}}\, dx = \frac{2}{3a^2}(ax - 2b)\sqrt{ax + b} + C$

95. $\displaystyle\int x(ax + b)^n\, dx = \frac{(ax + b)^{n+1}}{a^2}\left(\frac{ax + b}{n + 2} - \frac{b}{n + 1}\right) + C;\ n \neq -1, -2$

96. $\displaystyle\int \frac{dx}{x(ax + b)} = \frac{1}{b}\ln\left|\frac{x}{ax + b}\right| + C$

Integrals with Exponential and Trigonometric Functions

97. $\displaystyle\int e^{ax}\sin bx\, dx = \frac{e^{ax}(a\sin bx - b\cos bx)}{a^2 + b^2} + C$

98. $\displaystyle\int e^{ax}\cos bx\, dx = \frac{e^{ax}(a\cos bx + b\sin bx)}{a^2 + b^2} + C$

Integrals with Exponential and Logarithmic Functions

99. $\displaystyle\int \frac{dx}{x\ln x} = \ln|\ln x| + C$

100. $\displaystyle\int x^n \ln x\, dx = \frac{x^{n+1}}{n + 1}\left(\ln x - \frac{1}{n + 1}\right) + C;\ n \neq -1$

101. $\displaystyle\int xe^x\, dx = xe^x - e^x + C$

102. $\displaystyle\int x^n e^{ax}\, dx = \frac{1}{a}x^n e^{ax} - \frac{n}{a}\int x^{n-1}e^{ax}\, dx;\ a \neq 0$

103. $\displaystyle\int \ln^n x\, dx = x\ln^n x - n\int \ln^{n-1} x\, dx$

Miscellaneous Formulas

104. $\displaystyle\int x^n \cos^{-1} x\, dx = \frac{1}{n + 1}\left(x^{n+1}\cos^{-1}x + \int \frac{x^{n+1}dx}{\sqrt{1 - x^2}}\right);\ n \neq -1$

105. $\displaystyle\int x^n \sin^{-1} x\, dx = \frac{1}{n + 1}\left(x^{n+1}\sin^{-1}x - \int \frac{x^{n+1}dx}{\sqrt{1 - x^2}}\right);\ n \neq -1$

106. $\displaystyle\int x^n \tan^{-1} x\, dx = \frac{1}{n + 1}\left(x^{n+1}\tan^{-1}x - \int \frac{x^{n+1}dx}{x^2 + 1}\right);\ n \neq -1$

107. $\displaystyle\int \sqrt{2ax - x^2}\, dx = \frac{x - a}{2}\sqrt{2ax - x^2} + \frac{a^2}{2}\sin^{-1}\left(\frac{x - a}{a}\right) + C;\ a > 0$

108. $\displaystyle\int \frac{dx}{\sqrt{2ax - x^2}} = \sin^{-1}\left(\frac{x - a}{a}\right) + C;\ a > 0$

GRAPHS OF ELEMENTARY FUNCTIONS

Linear functions

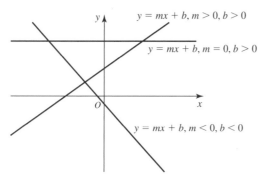

$y = mx + b, m > 0, b > 0$

$y = mx + b, m = 0, b > 0$

$y = mx + b, m < 0, b < 0$

Quadratic functions

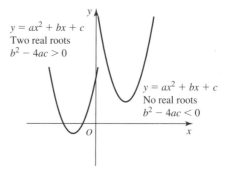

$y = ax^2 + bx + c$
Two real roots
$b^2 - 4ac > 0$

$y = ax^2 + bx + c$
No real roots
$b^2 - 4ac < 0$

Positive even powers

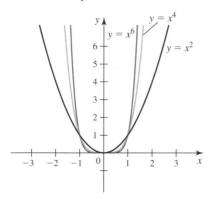

$y = x^6$
$y = x^4$
$y = x^2$

Positive odd powers

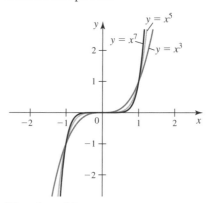

$y = x^5$
$y = x^7$
$y = x^3$

Negative even powers

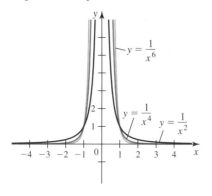

$y = \dfrac{1}{x^6}$
$y = \dfrac{1}{x^4}$
$y = \dfrac{1}{x^2}$

Negative odd powers

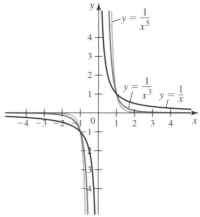

$y = \dfrac{1}{x^5}$
$y = \dfrac{1}{x^3}$
$y = \dfrac{1}{x}$

Exponential functions

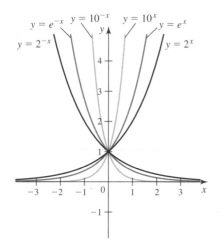

$y = e^{-x}$ $y = 10^{-x}$ $y = 10^x$ $y = e^x$
$y = 2^{-x}$ $y = 2^x$

Natural logarithmic and exponential functions

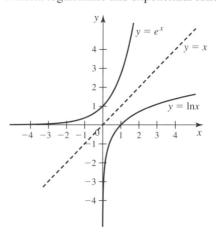

$y = e^x$
$y = x$
$y = \ln x$